American Sports History Series

edited by
David B. Biesel

1. *Effa Manley and the Newark Eagles* by James Overmyer, 1993.
2. *The United States and World Cup Competition: An Encyclopedic History of the United States in International Competition* by Colin Jose, 1994.
3. *Slide, Kelly, Slide: The Wild Life and Times of Mike "King" Kelly, Baseball's First Superstar* by Marty Appel, 1996.
4. *Baseball by the Numbers* by Mark Stang and Linda Harkness, 1997.
5. *Roller Skating for Gold* by David H. Lewis, 1997.
6. *Baseball's Biggest Blunder: The Bonus Rule of 1953–1957* by Brent Kelley, 1997.
7. *Lights On! The Wild Century-Long Saga of Night Baseball* by David Pietrusza, 1997.
8. *Windy City Wars: Labor, Leisure, and Sport in the Making of Chicago* by Gerald R. Gems, 1997.
9. *The American Soccer League 1921–1931: The Golden Years of American Soccer* by Colin Jose, 1998.
10. *The League That Failed,* by David Quentin Voigt, 1998.
11. *Jimmie Foxx: The Pride of Sudlersville* by Mark R. Millikin, 1998.
12. *Baseball's Radical for All Seasons: A Biography of John Montgomery Ward* by David Stevens, 1998.
13. *College Basketball's National Championships: The Complete Record of Every Tournament Ever Played* by Morgan G. Brenner, 1998.
14. *Chris Von der Ahe and the St. Louis Browns* by J. Thomas Hetrick, 1999.
15. *Before the Glory: The Best Players in the Pre-NBA Days of Pro Basketball* by William F. Himmelman and Karel de Veer, 1999.

A related title by the series editor:

Can You Name That Team? A Guide to Professional Baseball, Football, Soccer, Hockey, and Basketball Teams and Leagues by David B. Biesel, 1991

COLLEGE BASKETBALL'S NATIONAL CHAMPIONSHIPS

The Complete Record
of Every Tournament Ever Played

Morgan G. Brenner

American Sports History Series, No. 13

The Scarecrow Press, Inc.
Lanham, Maryland, and London
1999

SCARECROW PRESS, INC.

Published in the United States of America
by Scarecrow Press, Inc.
4720 Boston Way
Lanham, Maryland 20706

4 Pleydell Gardens, Folkestone
Kent CT20 2DN, England

Copyright © 1999 by Morgan G. Brenner

Book design and composition by Margaret S. Brenner
Cover design by Timothy M. La Palme

British Library Cataloguing in Publication Information Available

Library of Congress Cataloging-in-Publication Data

Brenner, Morgan B.
    College basketball's national championships : the complete record of
every tournament ever played / Morgan G. Brenner.
        p.   cm. -- (American sports history series : no. 13)
    Includes bibliographical references
    ISBN 0-8108-3474-X (alk. paper)
    1. Basketball--Tournaments--United States. 2. Basketball--Records--
United States. 3. College sports--Records--United States.
I. Title.   II. Series.
GV885.45.B74   1999
793.323'63'0973--DC 21   98-41568
                                                              CIP

⊖™ The paper used in this publication meets the minimum requirements of
American National Standard for Information Sciences—Permanence of
Paper for Printed Library Materials, ANSI/NISO Z39.48–1992.
Manufactured in the United States of America.

CONTENTS

Section 1 Association National Championship Tournaments

PREFACE

During the late 1980s when the NCAA Final Four was becoming known (in some circles) as the Duke Invitational Tournament, I began, as a fan, to develop for my own use some information about the Blue Devils and the tournaments. In the process, I discovered that there have been other national championship tournaments and that they have not been chronicled—and, well, . . .

In compiling the data for this book, there were two main challenges. The first was to learn of all of the national championship tournaments that ever have been held— particularly difficult since some were not exactly front page news. As a result of digging through every conceivable reference and from conversations with veteran basketball people, I believe that all have been uncovered. The second was that for many of the tournaments, complete results do not exist in the various basketball publications, at association offices, or at colleges; and some associations and colleges no longer exist.

For some tournaments, I started with only the name of the winner, but I was able to reconstruct quite a few by "working backward." I called the winning college, asked whom it played, called the opponents and asked whom they played and with what result, called those colleges, etc., etc. However, there were times that when I called a college, the athletics director or sports information director knew nothing about the school's participation in the event.

One association, which has a game-by-game, round-by-round record of some of its tournaments, made available several boxes of unsorted files and papers—its archives! Therein, I discovered copies of old newsletters which provided the results of most of the missing tournaments.

In a number of situations, I was able to determine where the tournament was held and obtain the results through microfilm of the local newspaper. However, to make life interesting, some of the tournaments were held in cities that have no Sunday paper—and the finals were held on Saturday!

Along the way, I decided that it would be worthwhile to include the season won-lost record and the name of the coach of all of the participating teams. While most of the won- lost records and coaches' names were found in the several annual guides and directories, some were not. And, frequently, the college could not provide the information.

There was also a challenge with school names. Some colleges have changed their names, and there have been mergers. There are many schools with the same or similar name—sometimes in the same state—and the various publications and association records did not bother to differentiate.

Nevertheless, in this book, for the first time anywhere are the final standings and other pertinent data for 493 association national championship tournaments and for 105 nonassociation national championship tournaments. But, there is some missing information. Somewhere, someone has it! Perhaps you played for or coached "that team" or participated in "that tournament," or you remember that a parent or grandparent did, and you will send a photocopy of a news clipping or such from the family scrapbook. Please submit it (with some kind of authentication) through the publisher so that it can be included in the next edition.

There may be use for this book by athletic associations and colleges, and certainly, the media should find it valuable. As a piece of historical research, it may have its place in the archives. Most importantly, I hope that Joe and Jane Fan will have a blast with it.

It's been great fun!

Morgan G. Brenner
Havertown, PA

Acknowledgements

This book could not have resulted without the help of many, many people who graciously provided information or directed me to it. To acknowledge everyone who assisted would produce a list as long as the book itself—and we would forget someone.

Among those who helped are athletics directors, coaches, sports information directors, secretaries, administrative assistants, and some extremely conscientious and helpful people at the several athletic associations. Many of these people went the "extra mile" to uncover obscure information which quite often required research into dusty archives.

A big thank you to Gregory A. Ciskowski of the Amarillo (TX) *Globe News* for many hours of wading through microfilm to obtain the results of the pre-1998 National Women's Invitational Tournaments and related information.

And, an equally big thank you to Ronald D. Bush of the Chattanooga (TN) *Free Press* for many hours of wading through microfilm to obtain the results of most of the NCCAA Men's Division I tournaments and related information.

And an extra special thank you to Wayne R. Patterson, former research specialist at the Naismith Memorial Basketball Hall of Fame and to Douglas A. Stark, current librarian and archivist. During my several, several-day sojourns there, they gave me access to their entire facility and graciously found information that, I think, even they didn't know they had. The endless shelves of various annual guides were indispensable.

Jim W. Classen, athletics director and men's basketball coach at Grace University, Omaha, Nebraska, provided much of the information on the NBCAA tournaments.

William J. Miller, Jr., commissioner of the NSCAA, loaned all of the association's files from which most of the tournaments were reconstructed.

A very special thank you to the staff of the research department of The Haverford Township Free Library, Delaware County, Pennsylvania, for tracking down and obtaining microfilm and books that provided much information and direction.

Joseph A. Kozak of Larko Printing Co., Havertown, Pennsylvania, somehow managed to make photocopies from ungainly originals and in the early days provided welcome fax service.

To all who contributed—directly and indirectly—thank you.

INTRODUCTION

Probably no other sports event has captured public interest as has "March Madness." The NCAA men's division I basketball tournament begins with 64 teams at eight sites and climaxes three-and-a-half weeks later with its national championship game before perhaps fifty thousand spectators and a television audience of millions.

But it's not the only kid on the block. In 1998, there were 19 senior college national championship tournaments in as many as three divisions in five collegiate athletic associations—plus the men's and women's National Invitation Tournaments. Since the game began, there have been 493 senior college association national championship tournaments plus another 105 nonassociation senior college so-called national championship tournaments. 12,507 teams, from 1,316 schools, have participated in these 598 tournaments.

The first national championship basketball tournament was held, according to the records of its sponsor, the Amateur Athletic Union, in New York City in 1897. (Our research indicates that it was in 1898.) After a sporadic beginning, it settled in following World War I to become basketball's oldest and longest running post-season event. Until the early 1950s, it was unquestionably *the* Tournament with as many as 64 teams from all over the country playing before packed houses in a week-long hoop-lovers paradise.

In the early years of the game, the AAU event was the only opportunity for post-season play for college teams. In 1901, Nebraska and Minnesota were the first to participate. Beginning in 1915, colleges teams participated in every AAU tournament through 1955—as many as 15-20 of them each year through the 1930s—even winning several of them. Thereafter, there were sporadic appearances by one or two NAIA teams through 1972. Several NAIA colleges also participated in the USA Basketball Tournament in the 1980s and 1990s with LIFE (GA) the last school in 1994.

Women's post-season college basketball also began with the AAU tournaments with East Central (OK) and Memphis the first to participate in 1928. From the 1950s through the 1970s, five and six women's teams played each year in the (usually) 32-team event with Wayland Baptist College (The Flying Queens) under the legendary Harley Redin becoming a dynasty-to-end-all-dynasties with ten championships and 8 second place finishes.

The first all-college post-season tournament was held in conjunction with the 1904 Olympic games in St. Louis when teams from Hiram, Wheaton, and Latter Day Saints Business College participated in a round-robin tournament billed as a "demonstration."

The year 1935 marked the beginning of the transition of basketball dominance from the AAU to the colleges. After 15 years in Kansas City, the AAU tournament moved to Denver. Seeking a replacement event, local business and civic leaders asked Dr. Naismith, then at Kansas, legendary Kansas coach Phog Allen, and others to put together a tournament of college teams. In 1937, eight midwestern small-college teams participated in what would become the NAIA national championship tournament. The following year, the first NIT tournament was held in New York, matching eight of the "big schools," and in 1939, the NCAA tournament began.

Soon virtually every college had a team—all aiming for the NCAA, NAIA, or NIT tournament—or for what was left of the AAU tournament. By the 1960s, television and the glamour of the big-name schools took hold, and the NCAA became dominant. The NAIA was for the smaller schools—most of them in the South, Midwest, and Southwest. In the late 1960s other national associations began—NSCAA, NCCAA, NBCAA— involving schools that by size and philosophy could not participate in the NCAA or NAIA. Women's tournaments began in 1969 with what would become the AIAW event. By 1975 the NCAA had added divisions II and III for its smaller schools, and in 1992 the NAIA added division II.

To think that Dr. Naismith simply wanted to come up with something to keep the students active between football and baseball seasons!

Key to Abbreviations

ASSN: The National Athletic Association which conducted the tournament. When an association has changed its name, only the current or last name is used. **AIAW:** Association for Intercollegiate Athletics for Women, **LCC:** League of Christian Colleges, **NAIA:** National Association of Intercollegiate Athletics, **NASC:** National Athletic Steering Committee, **NBCAA:** National Bible College Athletic Association, **NCAA:** National Collegiate Athletic Association, **NCCAA:** National Christian College Athletic Association, **NSCAA:** National Small College Athletic Association.

BD: Type of bid. **A:** Automatic, qualifying for the tournament by having won a conference regular season or tournament championship or by having won a district, region, or such championship; **L:** At-large, qualifying for the tournament, not having won a conference regular season or tournament championship or not having won a district, region or such championship, by being selected by the tournament committee; **H:** Host, qualifying for the tournament by serving as the "host" institution; **I:** Invitation, qualifying for the tournament as a result of a specific invitation from the tournament committee (normally the entire tournament field is by invitation and the tournament is called the "... Invitational", or such); **P:** Play-in, qualifying for the tournament by winning a "play-off" game against another contending team.

BYE: Bye awarded to a team in the tournament pairings. Byes normally are given to higher seeded teams from the first round to the second round when the number of participating teams is not a multiple of or divisor of 16. For example, "To R 16" indicates that a team received a bye to the round in which 16 teams played. The round from which the bye was awarded can be determined from the listing of the number of teams in the tournament (**#T**). There are instances when the bye "skipped" a round; e.g., from the round of 16 to the round of four (R16>R4)—often when a scheduled opponent did not appear or because of a quirk in the number of teams and the resultant pairings.

COACH: Name of the coach who is "credited" by the school with the season. Every attempt has been made to use full names, including middle initials and nicknames, so as to avoid confusion with other coaches of similar name—and there are many! Unfortunately, athletics department records frequently do not include the full name of the coach—in fact, even the "personnel" office does not always have it. Coaches seem to have a propensity for being known as "Just Plain Bill". Thus, in cases of coaches with similar names, they may or may not be the same person.

Nicknames are indicated within quotation marks when they are obvious nicknames; e.g., "Swish", or when they are a nonstandard shortened version of the first name and the given first name is known; e.g., "Willie." "Bill," as the standard shortened version, is not indicated as a nickname.

Occasionally, coaches were replaced during the season. In such cases, the coach who is "credited" with the season by the school or who coached for the majority of the season is listed.

An entry of "Unknown" indicates that the school has no record of the name of the coach for the particular season.

No entry; i.e., a blank, indicates that the name of the coach has not been located.

DIV: Division of the association. Divisions normally are a function of the enrollment of a school; e.g., under 500 full-time students, division II; above 500 full-time students, division I. **I:** Division I, **II:** Division II, **III:** Division III, **L:** Large School Division, **S:** Small School Division.

No entry indicates that the association did not conduct divisional competition in the year.

F: Finish. A numeral that indicates a team's final finish or place/standing in the tournament.

Numbers 1 and 2 indicate first and second place; i.e., the winner and loser of the championship (final) game.

Numbers 3 and 4 indicate third and fourth places; i.e., the winner and loser of a consolation game played between the two losers in first round (semi-finals) of the final four. When no consolation game is played between the losers in the first round of the final four, a 3 is awarded to both teams.

Numbers above 4, in multiples of 4, indicate the final finish or place/standing of a team in a standard single elimination tournament as a representation of the number of teams playing in the tournament when the team lost and was eliminated. Thus, 16 indicates that the team lost and was eliminated in the "sweet sixteen" round—and, thus, finished 16th; 64 indicates that the team lost in the first round of a 64 team tournament and, thus, finished 64th.

When consecutive numbers such as 5, 6, 7, 8 are used, they indicate the actual final place/standing of a team as a result of some type of consolation bracket play when the teams that lose in the first round continue play.

L: Games lost, complete season—including tournament play.

Won-Lost records are as accurate as available data allows. In many cases, different numbers can be found in different sources. In some situations, a school counted a win or loss against a team not recognized by an association; thus, in records provided by the association, such game is not counted.

When possible, the record provided by the school is used. When apparent typographical errors produced discrepancies, various sources were used to determine the correct numbers, and the author's judgement was the final determiner.

Forfeits are not necessarily reflected in the W-L record unless such create the school's "official record."

An "X" indicates that the school has no record of the W-L record for the particular year. No entry; i.e., a blank, indicates that the W-L record has not been located.

Nonassociation Tournaments. ARC: American Red Cross Benefit; **CCA:** Collegiate Commissioners Tournament; **NCI:** National Catholic College/Invitational Tournament; **NCT:** National Campus Tournament; **NIT:** National (Women's) Invitation(al) Tournament; **OLY:** Olympic Trials/Demonstration Tournament.

REG: Region (grouping) within the tournament field in which a team is placed for tournament play.

The indicated regions (or such) are only those made for tournament play—normally for competitive balance and/or seeding purposes. They may or may not reflect the geographical region of the country in which the school is located, and they may or may not reflect a region or such in which a team played during the regular season or in some type of tournament qualification play.

In most cases, when a tournament is seeded and "regioned," seedings are within the region. **DS:** Deep South; **E:** East(ern); **E(A):** East(ern), Section A, to create four "groups" without having four specific regions; **E(B):** East(ern), Section B, to create four "groups" without having four specific regions; **FW:** Far West(ern); **GL:** Great Lakes; **MA:** Mid-Atlantic; **ME:** Mid-East(ern); **MV:** Missouri Valley; **MW:** Mid-West(ern); **NC:** North Central; **NE:** North East(ern); **NENG:** New England; **PC:** Pacific Coast; **S:** South(ern); **SA:** South Atlantic; **SC:** South Central; **SP:** South Pacific; **SW:** South West(ern); **W:** West(ern); **W(A):** West(ern), Section A, to create four "groups" without having four specific regions; **W(B):** West(ern), Section B, to create four "groups" without having four specific regions.

SCHOOL NAME: See Appendix A for references.

The "official" name of the school as listed in *The College Handbook*, published by The College Board, Princeton, NJ, is used, but the word "University" or "College" is not included with the school name unless necessary to differentiate between two schools that have the same name except that one is a university and one is a college.

Where a school is not included in *The College Handbook* but is included in *The National Directory of College Athletics* or in *The Blue Book of College Athletics*, the name as listed therein is used.

When two or more schools have the same or similar names, the USPS state abbreviation for the state in which the school is located is included in parentheses.

When there is what is often called a "directional" school without the state name, e.g., Northern State, the state code; e.g., (SD), is used to provide specific identification.

When a school has changed its name, the current or last name is used.

Schools that merged and lost their original identity are listed by their original name for years before the merger and by the merged name for years after the merger.

State schools with a city name are indicated by "Name of State": City; e.g., California: Los Angeles.

For schools that no longer exist, the name is the last known name.

Junior and community/city colleges are indicated by either JC or CC (JC: Junior College; CC: City or Community College). Note that many junior and community/city colleges do not use the JC or CC indication. Community/city technical colleges are listed as CTC or TCC. Junior/community colleges are included only if they participated in a tournament conducted by a senior college association. A separate book will be devoted to junior/community college national championship tournaments.

SD: Seed. A numeral indicating the seed awarded to a team in the tournament.

1 is the highest or best seed. A No. 1 seed normally would play the lowest seed; e.g., a No. 16 seed, in the first round.

For some tournaments, seeds were not specifically indicated although there is evidence that teams were seeded. In such cases, the seeds were assumed by the placement of the teams in the pairings brackets—under the assumption that the tournament committee followed standard procedure in placing the teams on the pairings chart.

In most cases, when a tournament is seeded and "regioned," seedings are within the region.

#T: Number of teams. A numeral that indicates the number of teams that played in the tournament. When teams did not appear, the tournament is treated as if the team was not scheduled to be in the tournament.

W: Games won, complete season—including tournament play.

Won-Lost records are as accurate as available data allows. In many cases, different numbers can be found in different sources. In some situations, a school counted a win or loss against a team not recognized by an association; thus in records provided by the association, such game is not counted.

When possible, the record provided by the school is used. When apparent typographical errors produced discrepancies, various sources were used to determine the correct numbers, and the author's judgement was the final determiner.

Forfeits are not necessarily reflected in the W-L record unless such create the school's "official record".

An "X" indicates that the school has no record of the W-L record for the particular year.

No entry; i.e., a blank, indicates that the W-L record has not been located.

YEAR: The year the season ended; i.e., 1967 is the season of 1966-67.

Section 1

ASSOCIATION NATIONAL CHAMPIONSHIP TOURNAMENTS

Since 1937, when Kansas City civic leaders began what now is the NAIA tournament as a replacement for the departed AAU tourney, 493 national collegiate championship tournaments have been conducted by eight national collegiate athletic associations—five of which still operate. In those tournaments, 11,053 teams have competed.

For some schools, there has been but one tournament appearance; for others, tournament appearances (and championships) probably seem like a birth-right. And for many very fine educational institutions, many of which have a long basketball heritage, there have been no tournament appearances.

This section details each of those tournaments in two formats. First is a listing for each association in alphabetical order, first for men and then for women (if applicable), by year, by division, by order of finish (the standings) of each participating team. Thus, one can see who all of the participants were and where they finished in a given tournament. Second is a listing for each association of every school that ever participated in that association's tournament. The information is presented for each school, first for men and then for women (if applicable) in order of finish. Thus, one can see how many times the men's and women's teams from a given school participated in a particular association's tournament and how they finished in each appearance.

A brief history of each association and its tournament is provided as an introduction to each tournament.

Association for Intercollegiate Athletics for Women

NAMES: 1969-1971: CIAW (Committee for Intercollegiate Athletics for Women); 1972: C/AIAW; 1973-1982: AIAW

HISTORY: In its brief history, the AIAW laid the groundwork for women's collegiate sports. The excitement with which it was received by the fans and the enthusiasm of its members paved the way for the women's sports to be incorporated into the NCAA, NAIA, and other associations. Founded in 1971 by women athletics administrators, the AIAW was the first self-governing organization for women's collegiate sports. Goals, policies, and regulations were established by the institutional representatives. Previously, schools that conducted women's sports programs were members of the Amateur Athletic Union (AAU)—if they belonged to any organization.

With fewer than 300 members, the AIAW was created as the Committee for Intercollegiate Athletics for Women (CIAW), a substructure of the National Association for Girls and Women in Sports (NAGWS) of the American Alliance for Health, Physical Education, and Recreation (AAHPER). It established its own legal identity in 1979, but still retained close ties with NAGWS.

In its first year, the AIAW offered seven national championships, but by the early 1980s, it offered as many as 40 in some 18 different sports. From 1973 through 1977, the AIAW conducted a junior college basketball tournament—discontinuing it after the National Junior College Athletic Association (NJCAA) began its own women's event in 1975. The AIAW was dissolved in July 1983, after conducting its last basketball tournament in 1982, virtually all schools having aligned either with the NAIA or the NCAA after those two organizations adopted women's sports.

TOURNAMENT DIVISIONS: Open: 1969-1974; Large: 1975-1979; Small: 1975-1979; I: 1980-1982; II: 1980-1982; III: 1980-1982

DEFINITION OF DIVISIONS: Large: More than 3,000 full-time female undergraduate students; Small: Fewer than 3,000 full-time female undergraduate students; I: Financial Aid of 100% of AIAW limits; II: Financial Aid of 50% of AIAW limits; III: Financial Aid of 10% of AIAW limits. With the institution of the three-division arrangement, schools were permitted to designate a division by sport.

TOURNAMENT OPERATION: The first three tournaments, 1969-1971, were invitational events that led to the creation of the AIAW. For the sake of simplicity, these tournaments are included in this book as if they were AIAW events, and participating teams are listed as if they were AIAW members.

The first official AIAW tournament was held in 1972, the organization's first year of existence. There was only one division for the first three years; but from 1975 through 1979, there were two divisions, and from 1980-1982, there were three divisions.

All of the invitational, open, large, and small division tournaments were 16 team events—except for the first small division event in 1975 which had 12 teams. When the three-division arrangement was adopted in 1980, 24 teams played in all three divisions for the first year. In 1981, divisions II and III dropped to 16 teams, and in the last year of the organization, all three divisions had 16 teams.

Through the years of the open tournament, a consolation bracket was played among the eight teams that lost in the first-round. The AIAW designated the winner of that bracket as 5th place. For the purposes of this book, the loser is designated as 6th place. The two semifinal teams, which did not play, are designated as 12th place. The four teams that lost in the first-round (again) are designated as 16th place.

In 1975, the two divisions expanded the consolation bracket into a complete double-elimination format which lasted through 1977 in the large division and through 1979 in the small division. The AIAW designated the winner of that bracket as 5th place. For the purposes of this book, the loser is designated as 6th place. The two semifinal teams are designated as 8th place while the winners in the first-round are designated as 12th place. The four teams that lost in the first-round (again) are designated as 16th place. In 1978 and 1979, the large division played consolation games in each of the four regions; the winners are designated as 12th place, the losers as 16th place.

With the institution of three divisions in 1980, all tournaments went to a conventional single-elimination format with a 3rd/4th place game but with no regional consolation games.

NOTES ON DATA COLLECTION: It is believed that all official AIAW tournaments were seeded. However, seeding information is unavailable except for scattered years and, therefore, is not included for any tournament.

It is also believed that, at least after the mid-1970's, tournament qualification was the result of winning a regional or district tournament. However, information on the type of bid is generally unavailable and, therefore, is not included for any tournament.

There are missing won-lost records and coaches names, particularly in the early years. Most are the result of incomplete records at the schools, for many schools did not maintain women's data until the late 1970s or even the early 1980s. Further, women's information was not included in the several annual directories until the early 1980s.

The AIAW's junior college tournaments are not included.

Tournament Results

F	School	o	Bye	W	L	Coach
1969						
1	West Chester			12	0	Eckman, Carol
2	Western Carolina			14	3	Westmoreland, Betty
3	Iowa Wesleyan			X	X	Sammons, Betty
4	Iowa			6	2	Barnes, Dr. Mildred
5	Towson			10	1	Verkruzen, Margo
6	Purdue			X	X	Unknown

F	School	Bye	W	L	Coach
8	Lynchburg		9	5	Asbury, Jackie
	Southern Connecticut State		8	2	O'Neal, Louise
	Southern Illinois		11	2	West, Charlotte
	Ursinus		4	2	Snell, Eleanor
12	Central Michigan		4	3	Tate, Kathy Edwards
	Northeastern (MA)		8	1	Rowlands, Dr. Jeanne
16	Ball State		X	X	Unknown
	Dayton		4	7	Bowman, Judith
	Kentucky		X	X	Unknown
	Ohio State		8	2	Bailey, Phyllis J.

1970

F	School	Bye	W	L	Coach
1	California State: Fullerton		17	1	Moore, Billie Jean
2	West Chester		12	2	Eckman, Carol
3	Ursinus		7	1	Snell, Eleanor
4	Western Carolina		16	3	Westmoreland, Betty
5	Southern Illinois		13	2	West, Charlotte
6	Cortland State		X	X	Erbaugh, Sally
8	East Stroudsburg		8	4	Murphy, Betty Lou
	Iowa Wesleyan		X	X	Sammons, Betty
	Kansas State		10	7	Akers, Judy
	Southern Connecticut State		8	3	O'Neal, Louise
12	Illinois State		X	X	Mabry, Laurie
	Towson		9	3	Kelly, Darlene
16	Bridgewater State (MA)		X	X	Schneider, Judy
	Cedarville		8	5	Jeremiah, Dr. Maryalyce
	Northeastern (MA)		5	6	Rowlands, Dr. Jeanne
	Springfield (MA)		7	5	Bush, Jone

1971

F	School	Bye	W	L	Coach
1	Mississippi Women		21	3	Upton, Jill
2	West Chester		15	4	Eckman, Carol
3	Southern Connecticut State		12	5	O'Neal, Louise
4	North Carolina: Greensboro		12	8	Galloway, Dr. June
5	California State: Fullerton		20	1	Moore, Billie Jean
6	Kansas		7	8	Mawson, Marlene
8	California: Davis		X	X	Unknown
	East Stroudsburg		13	3	Murphy, Betty Lou
	Indiana		X	X	Unknown
	Kansas State		12	12	Akers, Judy
12	Queens (NY)		23	4	Kyvallos, Lucille
	Winthrop		18	7	Kancevitch, Mary
16	Illinois State		13	9	Hutchison, Dr. Jill
	Louisville		7	2	Hudson, Becky
	Marshall		13	4	Lawson, Donna
	Western Carolina		13	4	Westmoreland, Betty

F	School	Bye	W	L	Coach
1972					
1	Immaculata (PA)		24	1	Rush, Cathy
2	West Chester		16	1	Eckman, Carol
3	California State: Fullerton		19	1	Moore, Billie Jean
4	Mississippi Women		20	5	Upton, Jill
5	Queens (NY)		27	2	Kyvallos, Lucille
6	California State: Long Beach		13	6	Schaafsma, Dr. Frances
8	Indiana		17	2	Gorton, Bea
	Northern Illinois		15	3	Bell, Dr. Mary
	Phillips (OK)				Amaya, Lou
	Tennessee: Martin		20	8	Gearn, Nadine
12	Southern Connecticut State		7	2	O'Neal, Louise
	Utah State		X	X	Gardner, Fern
16	Illinois State		11	6	Hutchison, Dr. Jill
	South Dakota State		17	2	Marske, Ruth
	Tennessee Tech		26	6	Meadors, Marynell Hutsell
	Washington State		11	4	Durrant, Sue
1973					
1	Immaculata (PA)		20	0	Rush, Cathy
2	Queens (NY)		22	5	Kyvallos, Lucille
3	Southern Connecticut State		12	2	O'Neal, Louise
4	Indiana		17	3	Gorton, Bea
5	Kansas State		20	6	Akers, Judy
6	California: Riverside		X	X	Knox, Donna J.
8	East Stroudsburg		11	4	Murphy, Betty Lou
	Mercer		19	4	Collins, Peggy E.
	Stephen F Austin State		21	6	Gunter, Sue
	Western Washington		24	2	Goodrich, Lynda
12	East Carolina		18	12	Bolton, Catherine
	South Carolina		X	X	Meade, Violet M.
16	California State: Long Beach		13	5	Schaafsma, Dr. Frances
	Indiana State		16	7	Godleski, Edith
	Lehman		X	X	McBride, Ethel
	Utah State		13	5	Gardner, Fern
1974					
1	Immaculata (PA)		20	1	Rush, Cathy
2	Mississippi College		26	4	Nixon, Ed
3	Southern Connecticut State		19	5	O'Neal, Louise
4	William Penn		21	8	Spencer, Robert L.
5	Wayland Baptist		37	5	Weese, Dean
6	Tennessee Tech		26	5	Meadors, Marynell Hutsell
8	Indiana		16	5	Gorton, Bea
	Queens (NY)		22	4	Kyvallos, Lucille
12	California State: Fullerton		19	2	Moore, Billie Jean
	Illinois State		21	4	Foster, Dr. Gooch
	Stephen F Austin State		27	7	Gunter, Sue
	Western Washington		22	5	Goodrich, Lynda

F	School	Bye	W	L	Coach
16	California State: Fresno		10	11	Pickel, Donna
	East Stroudsburg		13	6	Jenkins, Jan
	Kansas State		21	9	Akers, Judy
	Utah State		13	5	Gardner, Fern

1975 Division L

F	School	Bye	W	L	Coach
1	Delta State		28	0	Wade, L. Margaret
2	Immaculata (PA)		23	3	Rush, Cathy
3	California State: Fullerton		19	4	Moore, Billie Jean
4	Southern Connecticut State		15	5	O'Neal, Louise
5	Wayland Baptist		34	1	Weese, Dean
6	Kansas State		24	9	Akers, Judy
8	Federal City		20	4	Stockard, Bessie A.
	William Penn		33	3	Spencer, Robert L.
12	Ohio State		18	5	Wilson, Debbie
	Queens (NY)		19	8	Kyvallos, Lucille
	Stephen F Austin State		32	7	Gunter, Sue
	Tennessee Tech		26	5	Meadors, Marynell Hutsell
16	Boise State		22	3	Thorngren, Connie
	James Madison		17	8	Jaynes, Betty F.
	Utah State		12	4	Gardner, Fern
	West Georgia		10	9	McNabb, Dorothy

1975 Division S

F	School	Bye	W	L	Coach
1	Phillips (OK)				Amaya, Lou
2	Talladega		20	5	Laster, Jr. "Tiny"
3	Ashland		19	3	Jones, Dr. Ruth
4	Emporia State		13	8	Caruthers, Linda
5	California Polytechnic: Pomona		16	6	May, Darlene
6	Midland Lutheran		18	8	Bracker, Joanne
8	Biola		16	2	Norman, Betty
	Northern Kentucky	To R8	19	8	Moore, Marilyn
9	Seton Hall	To R8	13	5	Dilley, Sue
10	Montana State: Billings	To R8	9	6	Ponikuar, Linda
12	Southern Colorado	To R8	10	5	Banks, Jessie
	Southern Utah		X	X	Bryant, Sandy

1976 Division L

F	School	Bye	W	L	Coach
1	Delta State		33	1	Wade, L. Margaret
2	Immaculata (PA)		25	3	Rush, Cathy
3	Wayland Baptist		34	5	Weese, Dean
4	William Penn		30	5	Spencer, Robert L.
5	Tennessee Tech		28	2	Meadors, Marynell Hutsell
6	Montclair State		20	5	Wendelken, Maureen
8	Mississippi College		33	10	Nixon, Ed
	Southern Connecticut State		17	6	O'Neal, Louise
12	Baylor		31	6	Fallen, Olga
	California State: Fullerton		14	5	Moore, Billie Jean
	California State: Long Beach		18	7	Schaafsma, Dr. Frances
	Queens (NY)		20	5	Kyvallos, Lucille

F	School	Bye	W	L	Coach
16	Pennsylvania State		10	10	Meiser-McKnett, Patricia
	Portland State		19	13	Nelson, Loyal D. "Sharkey"
	Utah		19	5	Gardner, Fern
	Wisconsin: La Crosse		19	4	Connolly, Mary

1976 DIVISION S

F	School	Bye	W	L	Coach
1	Berry		20	3	James, Kay
2	West Georgia		15	4	McNabb, Dorothy
3	Phillips (OK)		28	7	Blakely, Tom
4	Ashland		20	6	Jones, Dr. Ruth
5	Southeastern Louisiana		30	2	Puckett, Linda
6	Francis Marion		23	9	Hatchell, Sylvia Rhyne
8	California Polytechnic: Pomona		20	6	May, Darlene
	Princeton		17	8	Walsh, Patricia
12	Biola		18	6	Norman, Betty
	Seton Hall		14	8	Dilley, Sue
	Tarkio		20	6	Bussard, Gary
	Union (TN)		26	3	Birmingham, Peggy
16	Fort Lewis		13	2	Spickard, Karen
	George Williams		17	2	Langbein, Mary
	Grand View		X	X	Boson, Karen.
	Montana State: Billings		16	4	Ponikuar, Linda

1977 DIVISION L

F	School	Bye	W	L	Coach
1	Delta State		32	3	Wade, L. Margaret
2	Louisiana State		29	8	Coleman, "Jinks"
3	Tennessee		28	5	Summitt, Patricia Head
4	Immaculata (PA)		28	5	Rush, Cathy
5	Baylor		34	10	Fallen, Olga
6	Southern Connecticut State		20	6	Perrelli, Donald
8	Tennessee Tech		28	8	Meadors, Marynell Hutsell
	Utah		26	3	Gardner, Fern
12	Kansas State		23	12	Akers, Judy
	Mississippi College		22	14	Nixon, Ed
	Missouri		28	12	Rutherford, Dr. Joann
	Saint Joseph's (PA)		23	5	Portland, Rene Muth
16	California State: Fullerton		19	2	Moore, Billie Jean
	Michigan State		23	6	Langeland, Karen
	Minnesota		15	14	Wells, Linda
	Western Washington		21	7	Goodrich, Lynda

1977 DIVISION S

F	School	Bye	W	L	Coach
1	Southeastern Louisiana		30	2	Puckett, Linda
2	Phillips (OK)		31	2	Blakely, Tom
3	Berry		23	4	James, Kay
4	Biola		22	7	Norman, Betty
5	California Polytechnic: Pomona		28	6	May, Darlene
6	Tarkio		32	6	Bussard, Gary
8	Francis Marion		21	11	Hatchell, Sylvia Rhyne
	High Point		29	2	Alley, Jennifer

F	School	Bye	W	L	Coach
12	Ashland		15	7	Wetters, Barbara
	Dayton		21	8	Dreidame, R. Elaine
	Eastern Connecticut State		22	6	Miller, Dr. C. Robert
	West Georgia		15	5	McNabb, Dorothy
16	Colorado College		20	5	Golden, Laura L.
	Montana State: Billings		15	4	Caneff, Marcia
	Salisbury State		14	11	Morrison, Mariuna
	Ursinus		4	10	Stahl, Sue

1978 Division L

F	School	Bye	W	L	Coach
1	California: Los Angeles		27	3	Moore, Billie Jean
2	Maryland		27	4	Weller, Christine J.
3	Montclair State		25	7	Wendelken, Maureen
4	Wayland Baptist		33	5	Weese, Dean
8	North Carolina State		29	5	Yow, Sandra Kay
	Queens (NY)		24	3	Kyvallos, Lucille
	Southern Connecticut State		19	11	Perrelli, Donald
	Stephen F Austin State		25	14	Gunter, Sue
12	Brigham Young		22	6	Leishman, Dr. Courtney M.
	Mississippi		25	15	Dunn, Lin
	Missouri		26	6	Rutherford, Dr. Joann
	Valdosta State		27	4	Worth, Lyndal
16	Ohio State		23	8	Wilson, Debbie
	Tennessee		27	4	Summitt, Patricia Head
	Utah		21	9	Gardner, Fern
	Washington		26	5	Neir, Kathie

1978 Division S

F	School	Bye	W	L	Coach
1	High Point		30	8	Briley, Wanda
2	South Carolina State		30	5	Simon, Willie J.
3	Berry		23	6	Cronic, Ann
4	Biola		26	8	Norman, Betty
5	Southeastern Louisiana		30	4	Puckett, Linda
6	Shorter (GA)		31	5	Evans, Ellen
8	Arkansas: Monticello		19	7	Lavender, Mary Jane
	Francis Marion		22	11	Hatchell, Sylvia Rhyne
12	Dayton		24	6	Dreidame, R. Elaine
	Midland Lutheran		29	4	Bracker, Joanne
	Pepperdine		29	6	Meyers, Patty
	William Penn		30	7	Spencer, Robert L.
16	Eastern New Mexico		17	8	Barras, Bernie
	Eastern Washington		24	9	Smithpeters, Bill
	Fordham		25	8	Mosolino, Kathy
	Seton Hall		21	8	Dilley, Sue

1979 Division L

F	School	Bye	W	L	Coach
1	Old Dominion		35	1	Stanley, Marianne Crawford
2	Louisiana Tech		34	4	Hogg, Sonja
3	Tennessee		30	9	Summitt, Patricia Head
4	California: Los Angeles		24	10	Moore, Billie Jean

F	School	Bye	W	L	Coach
8	Fordham		27	7	Mosolino, Kathy
	Maryland		22	7	Weller, Christine J.
	Northwestern (IL)		25	4	DiStanislao, Mary
	Wayland Baptist		24	10	Weese, Dean
12	Brigham Young		21	7	Leishman, Dr. Courtney M.
	Kansas		29	8	Washington, Marian
	Rutgers		28	4	Grentz, Theresa Shank
	Valdosta State		27	8	Worth, Lyndal
16	California State: Long Beach		24	8	Schaafsma, Dr. Frances
	Kansas State		20	11	Akers, Judy
	Oregon State		15	7	Hill, Aki
	Southern Connecticut State		18	11	Perrelli, Donald

1979 DIVISION S

F	School	Bye	W	L	Coach
1	South Carolina State		33	2	Simon, Willie J.
2	Dayton		33	3	Jeremiah, Dr. Maryalyce
3	Niagara		30	6	Roickle, Mary
4	Tuskegee		34	5	Laster, Jr. "Tiny"
5	Tougaloo		47	11	Pennington, Andrew
6	High Point		33	4	Briley, Wanda
8	Charleston (WV)		30	7	Francis, Robert A. "Bud"
	Southeastern Louisiana		27	8	Puckett, Linda
12	Air Force		19	5	Schichtle, Dave
	Emporia State		19	10	Jones, Debbie
	Pepperdine		27	13	Meyers, Patty
	Seton Hall		26	8	Dilley, Sue
16	Eastern Washington		28	7	Smithpeters, Bill
	North Dakota State		12	19	McKinnon, Paul
	San Francisco		18	10	Bugler, Walt
	Texas Wesleyan		32	5	Satern, Miriam

1980 DIVISION I

F	School	Bye	W	L	Coach
1	Old Dominion	To R16	37	1	Stanley, Marianne Crawford
2	Tennessee	To R16	33	5	Summitt, Patricia Head
3	South Carolina		30	6	Parsons, Pam
4	Louisiana Tech	To R16	40	5	Hogg, Sonja
8	California State: Long Beach	To R16	28	6	Bonvicini, Joan
	Maryland	To R16	21	9	Weller, Christine J.
	Rutgers		28	5	Grentz, Theresa Shank
	Stephen F Austin State	To R16	27	6	Gunter, Sue
16	Brigham Young		24	9	Leishman, Dr. Courtney M.
	Kansas		29	7	Washington, Marian
	Kansas State		26	9	Hickey, Lynn
	North Carolina State		28	8	Yow, Sandra Kay
	Northwestern (IL)	To R16	24	5	DiStanislao, Mary
	Oregon		24	5	Heiny, Elwin
	Providence	To R16	22	7	Gilbride, Timothy J.
	Texas		33	4	Conradt, Jody
24	Boston University		18	9	O'Callaghan, Jo Ann
	Central Missouri State		26	5	Barnes, Dr. Mildred
	Cheyney		26	7	Stringer, C. Vivian
	Detroit		25	8	Kruszewski, Sue

F	School	Bye	W	L	Coach
	Kentucky		24	5	Yow, Deborah Ann
	Mercer		29	6	Fontaine, Jane
	San Francisco		28	5	Bugler, Walt
	Southern California		22	12	Sharp, Linda

1980 Division II

F	School	Bye	W	L	Coach
1	Dayton	To R16	36	2	Jeremiah, Dr. Maryalyce
2	Charleston (SC)	To R16	32	8	Wilson, Nancy R.
3	William Penn		37	5	Spencer, Robert L.
4	Louisiana		24	11	Schneider, Frank
8	California Polytechnic: Pomona		27	13	May, Darlene
	Charleston (WV)	To R16	27	8	Francis, Robert A. "Bud"
	Lenoir-Rhyne		28	4	Smith, Pat
	Morgan State		22	5	Fields, LaRue
16	Arkansas Tech	To R16	29	2	Yeager, Jim
	Berry	To R16	25	4	Cronic, Ann
	California State: Los Angeles		19	13	Marquis, Dick
	Langston		26	11	Colon, Bob
	Saint John Fisher	To R16	31	4	Kahler, Phillip I.
	Saint Peter's		27	4	Granelli, Mike
	South Carolina State	To R16	30	5	Simon, Willie J.
	West Alabama	To R16	24	12	Bridges, Avie
24	Air Force		17	10	Holt, "Chuck"
	Carson-Newman		28	8	Bivens, Lewis
	Hofstra		20	11	Pyser, Harvey
	Idaho		25	6	VanDerveer, Tara
	Nebraska: Omaha		23	13	Mankenberg, Cherri
	Niagara		24	6	Roickle, Mary
	Southeastern Oklahoma State		23	8	Hudson, Vicki
	West Georgia		17	12	Mosley, Nancy

1980 Division III

F	School	Bye	W	L	Coach
1	Worcester State	To R16	24	2	Devlin, Donna
2	Wisconsin: La Crosse	To R16	24	4	Toburan, Karen
3	Scranton	To R16	20	4	Strong, Michael J.
4	Mount Mercy	To R16	29	8	Ranson, Dr. Leonard
8	Biola		15	14	Norman, Betty
	Juniata		24	4	Latimore, Nancy Harden
	Lee (TN)	To R16	23	8	Walston, Ken
	San Francisco State	To R16	20	12	Manwaring, Emily
16	Adrian		22	6	Walsh, Nancy
	Eastern Connecticut State		16	10	Miller, Dr. C. Robert
	Mcmurry	To R16	17	11	Hicks, Renee
	Minnesota: Morris		17	9	Michaelson, Maren
	Notre Dame (IN)		20	10	Petro, Sharon
	Pittsburgh: Johnstown		21	7	Horner, Clyde L.
	Tarleton State		27	10	Lowrey, Jan
	Western Oregon	To R16	25	4	Carey, Jon
24	Bridgewater (VA)		22	7	Mapp, Laura
	Christopher Newport		18	13	Lee, Phil
	Columbia (SC)		15	13	Patenaude, Donald P.
	Elizabethtown		22	5	Kauffman, Yvonne E.

F	School	Bye	W	L	Coach
	Linfield		17	9	Vealey, Robin
	Pacific Lutheran		16	14	Hemion, Kathy
	Spring Arbor		21	5	Dunckel, Darrell
	Willamette		17	7	Howard, Fran

1981 DIVISION I

F	School	Bye	W	L	Coach
1	Louisiana Tech	To R16	34	0	Hogg, Sonja
2	Tennessee	To R16	25	6	Summitt, Patricia Head
3	Old Dominion	To R16	28	7	Stanley, Marianne Crawford
4	Southern California	To R16	26	8	Sharp, Linda
8	California State: Long Beach	To R16	27	7	Bonvicini, Joan
	California: Los Angeles		29	7	Moore, Billie Jean
	Cheyney	To R16	26	3	Stringer, C. Vivian
	Maryland	To R16	19	9	Weller, Christine J.
16	Illinois State		22	8	Hutchison, Dr. Jill
	Jackson State (MS)		32	9	Magee, Sadie E.
	Kansas	To R16	27	5	Washington, Marian
	Kentucky		25	6	Hall, Terry
	North Carolina State		21	10	Yow, Sandra Kay
	Oregon		25	7	Heiny, Elwin
	Rutgers		27	6	Grentz, Theresa Shank
	Stephen F Austin State		24	11	Otwell, Mary Ann
24	Clemson		23	8	Tribble, Annie S.
	Colorado		28	5	Walseth, Russell M. "Sox"
	Georgia State		28	5	Jarrett, Jim
	Minnesota		28	7	Hanson, Ellen Mosher
	Northwestern (IL)		22	12	Lynch, Annette
	Oregon State		22	6	Hill, Aki
	Syracuse		26	8	Jacobs, Barbara
	Texas		28	8	Conradt, Jody

1981 DIVISION II

F	School	Bye	W	L	Coach
1	William Penn		43	3	Spencer, Robert L.
2	Charleston (SC)		25	9	Wilson, Nancy R.
3	California Polytechnic: Pomona		30	9	May, Darlene
4	Lenoir-Rhyne		27	8	Smith, Pat
8	Abilene Christian		31	7	McCoy, Burl
	Eastern Illinois		25	8	Hilke, Barbara
	Louisiana		15	16	Schneider, Frank
	Tuskegee		27	11	Laster, Jr. "Tiny"
16	Biola		26	5	Norman, Betty
	Colorado College		20	8	Golden, Laura L.
	Dayton		27	7	Makowski, Linda
	Idaho		22	8	Dobratz, Patty Jo
	Morgan State		24	4	Fields, LaRue
	Southwest Missouri State		25	10	Gasser, Martha "Marti"
	Springfield (MA)		18	7	Shapiro, Harvey P.
	William Carey (MS)		19	8	Halford, Bobby

F	School	Bye	W	L	Coach
1981 Division III					
1	Wisconsin: La Crosse		27	5	Hansen, Mary
2	Mount Mercy		31	7	Ranson, Dr. Leonard
3	Worcester State		28	2	Devlin, Donna
4	Pittsburgh: Johnstown		26	4	Horner, Clyde L.
8	California: Davis		23	8	Gill, Pam
	Elizabethtown		18	6	Kauffman, Yvonne E.
	Knoxville		23	10	Robinson, Edward
	San Francisco State		17	18	Manwaring, Emily
16	Bethany (KS)		20	8	Wood, Nancy
	Columbia (SC)		X	X	Patenaude, Donald P.
	Concordia (OR)		28	1	Kunert, Charles J. "Chuck"
	Rhode Island College		14	11	Conley, Joseph
	Roanoke		21	6	Agee, Lynne
	Spring Arbor		24	6	Dunckel, Darrell
	Tarleton State		26	9	Lowrey, Jan
	Wisconsin: Whitewater		19	9	Jones, Dianne
1982 Division I					
1	Rutgers		25	7	Grentz, Theresa Shank
2	Texas		35	4	Conradt, Jody
3	Villanova		29	4	Perretta, Harry
4	Wayland Baptist		19	15	Wilson, Cathy
8	California		23	10	Foster, Dr. Gooch
	Delta State		24	15	Garmon, Frances
	Minnesota		18	10	Hanson, Ellen Mosher
	Wisconsin		21	13	Qualls, Edwina
16	Arkansas		26	10	Mossman, Matilda Willis
	Central Missouri State		20	9	Hoehn, Jorja E.
	Colorado		28	8	Walseth, Russell M. "Sox"
	Georgia Southern		26	5	Evans, Ellen
	Miami (OH)		24	9	Wettig, Pamela
	Montana		22	5	Selvig, Robin
	Saint John's (NY)		25	7	Perrelli, Donald
	Vanderbilt		20	14	Lee, Phil
1982 Division II					
1	Francis Marion		27	7	Hatchell, Sylvia Rhyne
2	Charleston (SC)		33	7	Wilson, Nancy R.
3	William Penn		27	10	Spencer, Robert L.
4	North Dakota State		21	11	Ruley, Amy J.
8	Biola		19	12	Norman, Betty
	Butler (IN)		23	3	Mason, Linda
	Central Oklahoma		25	10	Kelly, John
	West Alabama		29	7	Izard, Jim
16	Canisius		26	5	Pares, Sr. Maria
	Centenary (LA)		22	10	Saint Andre, Joe
	Central Florida		24	15	Sanchez, Joe
	Colorado College		16	12	Puckett, Linda

F	School	Bye	W	L	Coach
	Florida International		20	8	Russo, Cindy
	Hofstra		27	9	Pyser, Harvey
	Idaho		27	5	Dobratz, Patty Jo
	Wisconsin: Green Bay		28	9	Hammerle, Carol

1982 DIVISION III

F	School	Bye	W	L	Coach
1	Concordia: Moorhead		31	3	Langseth, Marc
2	Mount Mercy		24	11	Ranson, Dr. Leonard
3	Wisconsin: Whitewater		25	6	Jones, Dianne
4	Millersville		14	7	Schlegel, Debra
8	Knoxville		26	5	Robinson, Edward
	Malone		25	6	Long, Dr. Patricia L. "Patty"
	McMurry		22	10	Hicks, Renee
	North Central (IL)		28	9	Morgan, R. Wayne
16	Aquinas (MI)		20	8	Tibaldi, Patti
	Baker (KS)		20	9	Currie, Cindy
	Bridgewater (VA)		16	11	Mapp, Laura
	Columbia (SC)		15	15	Patenaude, Donald P.
	Kean		18	12	Hannisch, Patricia
	New Rochelle		X	X	Kern, Louis
	Puget Sound		18	16	Hovde, Chet
	Western Oregon		24	6	Carey, Jon

School Participation History

Year	Div	F	Bye	#T	W	L	Coach
ABILENE CHRISTIAN							
1981	II	8		16	31	7	McCoy, Burl
ADRIAN							
1980	III	16		24	22	6	Walsh, Nancy
AIR FORCE							
1979	S	12		16	19	5	Schichtle, Dave
1980	II	24		24	17	10	Holt, "Chuck"
AQUINAS (MI)							
1982	III	16		16	20	8	Tibaldi, Patti
ARKANSAS							
1982	I	16		16	26	10	Mossman, Matilda Willis
ARKANSAS TECH							
1980	II	16	To R16	24	29	2	Yeager, Jim
ARKANSAS: MONTICELLO							
1978	S	8		16	19	7	Lavender, Mary Jane
ASHLAND							
1975	S	3		12	19	3	Jones, Dr. Ruth
1976	S	4		16	20	6	Jones, Dr. Ruth
1977	S	12		16	15	7	Wetters, Barbara

Year	Div	F	Bye	#T	W	L	Coach
BAKER (KS)							
1982	III	16		16	20	9	Currie, Cindy
BALL STATE							
1969		16		16	X	X	Unknown
BAYLOR							
1977	L	5		16	34	10	Fallen, Olga
1976	L	12		16	31	6	Fallen, Olga
BERRY							
1976	S	1		16	20	3	James, Kay
1977	S	3		16	23	4	James, Kay
1978	S	3		16	23	6	Cronic, Ann
1980	II	16	To R16	24	25	4	Cronic, Ann
BETHANY (KS)							
1981	III	16		16	20	8	Wood, Nancy
BIOLA							
1977	S	4		16	22	7	Norman, Betty
1978	S	4		16	26	8	Norman, Betty
1975	S	8		12	16	2	Norman, Betty
1980	III	8		24	15	14	Norman, Betty
1982	II	8		16	19	12	Norman, Betty
1976	S	12		16	18	6	Norman, Betty
1981	II	16		16	26	5	Norman, Betty
BOISE STATE							
1975	L	16		16	22	3	Thorngren, Connie
BOSTON UNIVERSITY							
1980	I	24		24	18	9	O'Callaghan, Jo Ann
BRIDGEWATER (VA)							
1982	III	16		16	16	11	Mapp, Laura
1980	III	24		24	22	7	Mapp, Laura
BRIDGEWATER STATE (MA)							
1970		16		16	X	X	Schneider, Judy
BRIGHAM YOUNG							
1978	L	12		16	22	6	Leishman, Dr. Courtney M.
1979	L	12		16	21	7	Leishman, Dr. Courtney M.
1980	I	16		24	24	9	Leishman, Dr. Courtney M.
BUTLER (IN)							
1982	II	8		16	23	3	Mason, Linda
CALIFORNIA							
1982	I	8		16	23	10	Foster, Dr. Gooch

Year	Div	F	Bye	#T	W	L	Coach
CALIFORNIA POLYTECHNIC: POMONA							
1981	II	3		16	30	9	May, Darlene
1975	S	5		12	16	6	May, Darlene
1977	S	5		16	28	6	May, Darlene
1976	S	8		16	20	6	May, Darlene
1980	II	8		24	27	13	May, Darlene
CALIFORNIA STATE: FRESNO							
1974		16		16	10	11	Pickel, Donna
CALIFORNIA STATE: FULLERTON							
1970		1		16	17	1	Moore, Billie Jean
1972		3		16	19	1	Moore, Billie Jean
1975	L	3		16	19	4	Moore, Billie Jean
1971		5		16	20	1	Moore, Billie Jean
1974		12		16	19	2	Moore, Billie Jean
1976	L	12		16	14	5	Moore, Billie Jean
1977	L	16		16	19	2	Moore, Billie Jean
CALIFORNIA STATE: LONG BEACH							
1972		6		16	13	6	Schaafsma, Dr. Frances
1980	I	8	To R16	24	28	6	Bonvicini, Joan
1981	I	8	To R16	24	27	7	Bonvicini, Joan
1976	L	12		16	18	7	Schaafsma, Dr. Frances
1973		16		16	13	5	Schaafsma, Dr. Frances
1979	L	16		16	24	8	Schaafsma, Dr. Frances
CALIFORNIA STATE: LOS ANGELES							
1980	II	16		24	19	13	Marquis, Dick
CALIFORNIA: DAVIS							
1971		8		16	X	X	Unknown
1981	III	8		16	23	8	Gill, Pam
CALIFORNIA: LOS ANGELES							
1978	L	1		16	27	3	Moore, Billie Jean
1979	L	4		16	24	10	Moore, Billie Jean
1981	I	8		24	29	7	Moore, Billie Jean
CALIFORNIA: RIVERSIDE							
1973		6		16	X	X	Knox, Donna J.
CANISIUS							
1982	II	16		16	26	5	Pares, Sr. Maria
CARSON-NEWMAN							
1980	II	24		24	28	8	Bivens, Lewis
CEDARVILLE							
1970		16		16	8	5	Jeremiah, Dr. Maryalyce
CENTENARY (LA)							
1982	II	16		16	22	10	Saint Andre, Joe

Year	Div	F	Bye	#T	W	L	Coach
CENTRAL FLORIDA							
1982	II	16		16	24	15	Sanchez, Joe
CENTRAL MICHIGAN							
1969		12		16	4	3	Tate, Kathy Edwards
CENTRAL MISSOURI STATE							
1982	I	16		16	20	9	Hoehn, Jorja E.
1980	I	24		24	26	5	Barnes, Dr. Mildred
CENTRAL OKLAHOMA							
1982	II	8		16	25	10	Kelly, John
CHARLESTON (SC)							
1980	II	2	To R16	24	32	8	Wilson, Nancy R.
1981	II	2		16	25	9	Wilson, Nancy R.
1982	II	2		16	33	7	Wilson, Nancy R.
CHARLESTON (WV)							
1979	S	8		16	30	7	Francis, Robert A. "Bud"
1980	II	8	To R16	24	27	8	Francis, Robert A. "Bud"
CHEYNEY							
1981	I	8	To R16	24	X	X	Stringer, C. Vivian
1980	I	24		24	26	7	Stringer, C. Vivian
CHRISTOPHER NEWPORT							
1980	III	24		24	18	13	Lee, Phil
CLEMSON							
1981	I	24		24	23	8	Tribble, Annie S.
COLORADO							
1982	I	16		16	28	8	Walseth, Russell M. "Sox"
1981	I	24		24	28	5	Walseth, Russell M. "Sox"
COLORADO COLLEGE							
1977	S	16		16	20	5	Golden, Laura L.
1981	II	16		16	20	8	Golden, Laura L.
1982	II	16		16	16	12	Puckett, Linda
COLUMBIA (SC)							
1981	III	16		16	X	X	Patenaude, Donald P.
1982	III	16		16	15	15	Patenaude, Donald P.
1980	III	24		24	15	13	Patenaude, Donald P.
CONCORDIA (OR)							
1981	III	16		16	28	1	Kunert, Charles J. "Chuck"
CONCORDIA: MOORHEAD							
1982	III	1		16	31	3	Langseth, Marc
CORTLAND STATE							
1970		6		16	X	X	Erbaugh, Sally

Year	Div	F	Bye	#T	W	L	Coach
DAYTON							
1980	II	1	To R16	24	36	2	Jeremiah, Dr. Maryalyce
1979	S	2		16	33	3	Jeremiah, Dr. Maryalyce
1977	S	12		16	21	8	Dreidame, R. Elaine
1978	S	12		16	24	6	Dreidame, R. Elaine
1969		16		16	4	7	Bowman, Judith
1981	II	16		16	27	7	Makowski, Linda
DELTA STATE							
1975	L	1		16	28	0	Wade, L. Margaret
1976	L	1		16	33	1	Wade, L. Margaret
1977	L	1		16	32	3	Wade, L. Margaret
1982	I	8		16	24	15	Garmon, Frances
DETROIT							
1980	I	24		24	25	8	Kruszewski, Sue
EAST CAROLINA							
1973		12		16	18	12	Bolton, Catherine
EAST STROUDSBURG							
1970		8		16	8	4	Murphy, Betty Lou
1971		8		16	13	3	Murphy, Betty Lou
1973		8		16	11	4	Murphy, Betty Lou
1974		16		16	13	6	Jenkins, Jan
EASTERN CONNECTICUT STATE							
1977	S	12		16	22	6	Miller, Dr. C. Robert
1980	III	16		24	16	10	Miller, Dr. C. Robert
EASTERN ILLINOIS							
1981	II	8		16	25	8	Hilke, Barbara
EASTERN NEW MEXICO							
1978	S	16		16	17	8	Barras, Bernie
EASTERN WASHINGTON							
1978	S	16		16	24	9	Smithpeters, Bill
1979	S	16		16	28	7	Smithpeters, Bill
ELIZABETHTOWN							
1981	III	8		16	18	6	Kauffman, Yvonne E.
1980	III	24		24	22	5	Kauffman, Yvonne E.
EMPORIA STATE							
1975	S	4		12	13	8	Caruthers, Linda
1979	S	12		16	19	10	Jones, Debbie
FEDERAL CITY							
1975	L	8		16	20	4	Stockard, Bessie A.
FLORIDA INTERNATIONAL							
1982	II	16		16	20	8	Russo, Cindy

Year	Div	F	Bye	#T	W	L	Coach
FORDHAM							
1979	L	8		16	27	7	Mosolino, Kathy
1978	S	16		16	25	8	Mosolino, Kathy
FORT LEWIS							
1976	S	16		16	13	2	Spickard, Karen
FRANCIS MARION							
1982	II	1		16	27	7	Hatchell, Sylvia Rhyne
1976	S	6		16	23	9	Hatchell, Sylvia Rhyne
1977	S	8		16	21	11	Hatchell, Sylvia Rhyne
1978	S	8		16	22	11	Hatchell, Sylvia Rhyne
GEORGE WILLIAMS							
1976	S	16		16	17	2	Langbein, Mary
GEORGIA SOUTHERN							
1982	I	16		16	26	5	Evans, Ellen
GEORGIA STATE							
1981	I	24		24	28	5	Jarrett, Jim
GRAND VIEW							
1976	S	16		16	X	X	Boson, Karen
HIGH POINT							
1978	S	1		16	30	8	Briley, Wanda
1979	S	6		16	33	4	Briley, Wanda
1977	S	8		16	29	2	Alley, Jennifer
HOFSTRA							
1982	II	16		16	27	9	Pyser, Harvey
1980	II	24		24	20	11	Pyser, Harvey
IDAHO							
1981	II	16		16	22	8	Dobratz, Patty Jo
1982	II	16		16	27	5	Dobratz, Patty Jo
1980	II	24		24	25	6	VanDerveer, Tara
ILLINOIS STATE							
1970		12		16	X	X	Mabry, Laurie
1974		12		16	21	4	Foster, Dr. Gooch
1971		16		16	13	9	Hutchison, Dr. Jill
1972		16		16	11	6	Hutchison, Dr. Jill
1981	I	16		24	22	8	Hutchison, Dr. Jill
IMMACULATA (PA)							
1972		1		16	24	1	Rush, Cathy
1973		1		16	20	0	Rush, Cathy
1974		1		16	20	1	Rush, Cathy
1975	L	2		16	23	3	Rush, Cathy
1976	L	2		16	25	3	Rush, Cathy
1977	L	4		16	28	5	Rush, Cathy

Year	Div	F	Bye	#T	W	L	Coach
INDIANA							
1973		4		16	17	3	Gorton, Bea
1971		8		16	X	X	Unknown
1972		8		16	17	2	Gorton, Bea
1974		8		16	16	5	Gorton, Bea
INDIANA STATE							
1973		16		16	16	7	Godleski, Edith
IOWA							
1969		4		16	6	2	Barnes, Dr. Mildred
IOWA WESLEYAN							
1969		3		16	X	X	Sammons, Betty
1970		8		16	X	X	Sammons, Betty
JACKSON STATE (MS)							
1981	I	16		24	32	9	Magee, Sadie E.
JAMES MADISON							
1975	L	16		16	17	8	Jaynes, Betty F.
JUNIATA							
1980	III	8		24	24	4	Latimore, Nancy Harden
KANSAS							
1971		6		16	7	8	Mawson, Marlene
1979	L	12		16	29	8	Washington, Marian
1980	I	16		24	29	7	Washington, Marian
1981	I	16	To R16	24	27	5	Washington, Marian
KANSAS STATE							
1973		5		16	20	6	Akers, Judy
1975	L	6		16	24	9	Akers, Judy
1970		8		16	10	7	Akers, Judy
1971		8		16	12	12	Akers, Judy
1977	L	12		16	23	12	Akers, Judy
1974		16		16	21	9	Akers, Judy
1979	L	16		16	20	11	Akers, Judy
1980	I	16		24	26	9	Hickey, Lynn
KEAN							
1982	III	16		16	18	12	Hannisch, Patricia
KENTUCKY							
1969		16		16	X	X	Unknown
1981	I	16		24	25	6	Hall, Terry
1980	I	24		24	24	5	Yow, Deborah Ann
KNOXVILLE							
1981	III	8		16	23	10	Robinson, Edward
1982	III	8		16	26	5	Robinson, Edward
LANGSTON							
1980	II	16		24	26	11	Colon, Bob

Year	Div	F	Bye	#T	W	L	Coach
LEE (TN)							
1980	III	8	To R16	24	23	8	Walston, Ken
LEHMAN							
1973		16		16	X	X	McBride, Ethel
LENOIR-RHYNE							
1981	II	4		16	27	8	Smith, Pat
1980	II	8		24	28	4	Smith, Pat
LINFIELD							
1980	III	24		24	17	9	Vealey, Robin
LOUISIANA							
1980	II	4		24	24	11	Schneider, Frank
1981	II	8		16	15	16	Schneider, Frank
LOUISIANA STATE							
1977	L	2		16	29	8	Coleman, "Jinks"
LOUISIANA TECH							
1981	I	1	To R16	24	34	0	Hogg, Sonja
1979	L	2		16	34	4	Hogg, Sonja
1980	I	4	To R16	24	40	5	Hogg, Sonja
LOUISVILLE							
1971		16		16	7	2	Hudson, Becky
LYNCHBURG							
1969		8		16	9	5	Asbury, Jackie
MALONE							
1982	III	8		16	25	6	Long, Dr. Patricia L. "Patty"
MARSHALL							
1971		16		16	13	4	Lawson, Donna
MARYLAND							
1978	L	2		16	27	4	Weller, Christine J.
1979	L	8		16	22	7	Weller, Christine J.
1980	I	8	To R16	24	21	9	Weller, Christine J.
1981	I	8	To R16	24	19	9	Weller, Christine J.
MCMURRY							
1982	III	8		16	22	10	Hicks, Renee
1980	III	16	To R16	24	17	11	Hicks, Renee
MERCER							
1973		8		16	19	4	Collins, Peggy E.
1980	I	24		24	29	6	Fontaine, Jane
MIAMI (OH)							
1982	I	16		16	24	9	Wettig, Pamela

Year	Div	F	Bye	#T	W	L	Coach
MICHIGAN STATE							
1977	L	16		16	23	6	Langeland, Karen
MIDLAND LUTHERAN							
1975	S	6		12	18	8	Bracker, Joanne
1978	S	12		16	29	4	Bracker, Joanne
MILLERSVILLE							
1982	III	4		16	14	7	Schlegel, Debra
MINNESOTA							
1982	I	8		16	18	10	Hanson, Ellen Mosher
1977	L	16		16	15	14	Wells, Linda
1981	I	24		24	28	7	Hanson, Ellen Mosher
MINNESOTA: MORRIS							
1980	III	16		24	17	9	Michaelson, Maren
MISSISSIPPI							
1978	L	12		16	25	15	Dunn, Lin
MISSISSIPPI COLLEGE							
1974		2		16	26	4	Nixon, Ed
1976	L	8		16	33	10	Nixon, Ed
1977	L	12		16	22	14	Nixon, Ed
MISSISSIPPI WOMEN							
1971		1		16	21	3	Upton, Jill
1972		4		16	20	5	Upton, Jill
MISSOURI							
1977	L	12		16	28	12	Rutherford, Dr. Joann
1978	L	12		16	26	6	Rutherford, Dr. Joann
MONTANA							
1982	I	16		16	22	5	Selvig, Robin
MONTANA STATE: BILLINGS							
1975	S	10	To R8	12	9	6	Ponikvar, Linda
1976	S	16		16	16	4	Ponikvar, Linda
1977	S	16		16	15	4	Caneff, Marcia
MONTCLAIR STATE							
1978	L	3		16	25	7	Wendelken, Maureen
1976	L	6		16	20	5	Wendelken, Maureen
MORGAN STATE							
1980	II	8		24	22	5	Fields, LaRue
1981	II	16		16	24	4	Fields, LaRue
MOUNT MERCY							
1981	III	2		16	31	7	Ranson, Dr. Leonard
1982	III	2		16	24	11	Ranson, Dr. Leonard
1980	III	4	To R16	24	29	8	Ranson, Dr. Leonard

Year	Div	F	Bye	#T	W	L	Coach
NEBRASKA: OMAHA							
1980	II	24		24	23	13	Mankenberg, Cherri
NEW ROCHELLE							
1982	III	16		16	X	X	Kern, Louis
NIAGARA							
1979	S	3		16	30	6	Roickle, Mary
1980	II	24		24	24	6	Roickle, Mary
NORTH CAROLINA STATE							
1978	L	8		16	29	5	Yow, Sandra Kay
1980	I	16		24	28	8	Yow, Sandra Kay
1981	I	16		24	21	10	Yow, Sandra Kay
NORTH CAROLINA: GREENSBORO							
1971		4		16	12	8	Galloway, Dr. June
NORTH CENTRAL (IL)							
1982	III	8		16	28	9	Morgan, R. Wayne
NORTH DAKOTA STATE							
1982	II	4		16	21	11	Ruley, Amy J.
1979	S	16		16	12	19	McKinnon, Paul
NORTHEASTERN (MA)							
1969		12		16	8	1	Rowlands, Dr. Jeanne
1970		16		16	5	6	Rowlands, Dr. Jeanne
NORTHERN ILLINOIS							
1972		8		16	15	3	Bell, Dr. Mary
NORTHERN KENTUCKY							
1975	S	8	To R8	12	19	8	Moore, Marilyn
NORTHWESTERN (IL)							
1979	L	8		16	25	4	DiStanislao, Mary
1980	I	16	To R16	24	24	5	DiStanislao, Mary
1981	I	24		24	22	12	Lynch, Annette
NOTRE DAME (IN)							
1980	III	16		24	20	10	Petro, Sharon
OHIO STATE							
1975	L	12		16	18	5	Wilson, Debbie
1969		16		16	8	2	Bailey, Phyllis J.
1978	L	16		16	23	8	Wilson, Debbie
OLD DOMINION							
1979	L	1		16	35	1	Stanley, Marianne Crawford
1980	I	1	To R16	24	37	1	Stanley, Marianne Crawford
1981	I	3	To R16	24	28	7	Stanley, Marianne Crawford

Year	Div	F	Bye	#T	W	L	Coach
OREGON							
1980	I	16		24	24	5	Heiny, Elwin
1981	I	16		24	25	7	Heiny, Elwin
OREGON STATE							
1979	L	16		16	15	7	Hill, Aki
1981	I	24		24	22	6	Hill, Aki
PACIFIC LUTHERAN							
1980	III	24		24	16	14	Hemion, Kathy
PENNSYLVANIA STATE							
1976	L	16		16	10	10	Meiser-McKnett, Patricia
PEPPERDINE							
1978	S	12		16	29	6	Meyers, Patty
1979	S	12		16	27	13	Meyers, Patty
PHILLIPS (OK)							
1975	S	1		12			Amaya, Lou
1977	S	2		16	31	2	Blakely, Tom
1976	S	3		16	28	7	Blakely, Tom
1972		8		16			Amaya, Lou
PITTSBURGH: JOHNSTOWN							
1981	III	4		16	26	4	Horner, Clyde L.
1980	III	16		24	21	7	Horner, Clyde L.
PORTLAND STATE							
1976	L	16		16	19	13	Nelson, Loyal D. "Sharkey"
PRINCETON							
1976	S	8		16	17	8	Walsh, Patricia
PROVIDENCE							
1980	I	16	To R16	24	22	7	Gilbride, Timothy J.
PUGET SOUND							
1982	III	16		16	18	16	Hovde, Chet
PURDUE							
1969		6		16	X	X	Unknown
QUEENS (NY)							
1973		2		16	22	5	Kyvallos, Lucille
1972		5		16	27	2	Kyvallos, Lucille
1974		8		16	22	4	Kyvallos, Lucille
1978	L	8		16	24	3	Kyvallos, Lucille
1971		12		16	23	4	Kyvallos, Lucille
1975	L	12		16	19	8	Kyvallos, Lucille
1976	L	12		16	20	5	Kyvallos, Lucille
RHODE ISLAND COLLEGE							
1981	III	16		16	14	11	Conley, Joseph

Year	Div	F	Bye	#T	W	L	Coach
ROANOKE							
1981	III	16		16	21	6	Agee, Lynne
RUTGERS							
1982	I	1		16	25	7	Grentz, Theresa Shank
1980	I	8		24	28	5	Grentz, Theresa Shank
1979	L	12		16	28	4	Grentz, Theresa Shank
1981	I	16		24	27	6	Grentz, Theresa Shank
SAINT JOHN FISHER							
1980	II	16	To R16	24	31	4	Kahler, Phillip I.
SAINT JOHN'S (NY)							
1982	I	16		16	25	7	Perrelli, Donald
SAINT JOSEPH'S (PA)							
1977	L	12		16	23	5	Portland, Rene Muth
SAINT PETER'S							
1980	II	16		24	27	4	Granelli, Mike
SALISBURY STATE							
1977	S	16		16	14	11	Morrison, Mariuna
SAN FRANCISCO							
1979	S	16		16	18	10	Bugler, Walter
1980	I	24		24	28	5	Bugler, Walter
SAN FRANCISCO STATE							
1980	III	8	To R16	24	20	12	Manwaring, Emily
1981	III	8		16	17	18	Manwaring, Emily
SCRANTON							
1980	III	3	To R16	24	20	4	Strong, Michael J.
SETON HALL							
1975	S	9	To R8	12	13	5	Dilley, Sue
1976	S	12		16	14	8	Dilley, Sue
1979	S	12		16	26	8	Dilley, Sue
1978	S	16		16	21	8	Dilley, Sue
SHORTER (GA)							
1978	S	6		16	31	5	Evans, Ellen
SOUTH CAROLINA							
1980	I	3		24	30	6	Parsons, Pam
1973		12		16	X	X	Meade, Violet M.
SOUTH CAROLINA STATE							
1979	S	1		16	33	2	Simon, Willie J.
1978	S	2		16	30	5	Simon, Willie J.
1980	II	16	To R16	24	30	5	Simon, Willie J.
SOUTH DAKOTA STATE							
1972		16		16	17	2	Marske, Ruth

Year	Div	F	Bye	#T	W	L	Coach
SOUTHEASTERN LOUISIANA							
1977	S	1		16	30	2	Puckett, Linda
1976	S	5		16	30	2	Puckett, Linda
1978	S	5		16	30	4	Puckett, Linda
1979	S	8		16	27	8	Puckett, Linda
SOUTHEASTERN OKLAHOMA STATE							
1980	II	24		24	23	8	Hudson, Vicki
SOUTHERN CALIFORNIA							
1981	I	4	To R16	24	26	8	Sharp, Linda
1980	I	24		24	22	12	Sharp, Linda
SOUTHERN COLORADO							
1975	S	12	To R8	12	10	5	Banks, Jessie
SOUTHERN CONNECTICUT STATE							
1971		3		16	12	5	O'Neal, Louise
1973		3		16	12	2	O'Neal, Louise
1974		3		16	19	5	O'Neal, Louise
1975	L	4		16	15	5	O'Neal, Louise
1977	L	6		16	20	6	Perrelli, Donald
1969		8		16	8	2	O'Neal, Louise
1970		8		16	8	3	O'Neal, Louise
1976	L	8		16	17	6	O'Neal, Louise
1978	L	8		16	19	11	Perrelli, Donald
1972		12		16	7	2	O'Neal, Louise
1979	L	16		16	18	11	Perrelli, Donald
SOUTHERN ILLINOIS							
1970		5		16	13	2	West, Charlotte
1969		8		16	11	2	West, Charlotte
SOUTHERN UTAH							
1975	S	12		12	X	X	Bryant, Sandy
SOUTHWEST MISSOURI STATE							
1981	II	16		16	25	10	Gasser, Martha "Marti"
SPRING ARBOR							
1981	III	16		16	24	6	Dunckel, Darrell
1980	III	24		24	21	5	Dunckel, Darrell
SPRINGFIELD (MA)							
1970		16		16	7	5	Bush, Jone
1981	II	16		16	18	7	Shapiro, Harvey P.
STEPHEN F AUSTIN STATE							
1973		8		16	21	6	Gunter, Sue
1978	L	8		16	25	14	Gunter, Sue
1980	I	8	To R16	24	27	6	Gunter, Sue
1974		12		16	27	7	Gunter, Sue
1975	L	12		16	32	7	Gunter, Sue
1981	I	16		24	24	11	Otwell, Mary Ann

Year	Div	F	Bye	#T	W	L	Coach
SYRACUSE							
1981	I	24		24	26	8	Jacobs,.Barbara
TALLADEGA							
1975	S	2		12	20	5	Laster, Jr. "Tiny"
TARKIO							
1977	S	6		16	32	6	Bussard, Gary
1976	S	12		16	20	6	Bussard, Gary
TARLETON STATE							
1980	III	16		24	27	10	Lowrey, Jan
1981	III	16		16	26	9	Lowrey, Jan
TENNESSEE							
1980	I	2	To R16	24	33	5	Summitt, Patricia Head
1981	I	2	To R16	24	25	6	Summitt, Patricia Head
1977	L	3		16	·28	5	Summitt, Patricia Head
1979	L	3		16	30	9	Summitt, Patricia Head
1978	L	16		16	27	4	Summitt, Patricia Head
TENNESSEE TECH							
1976	L	5		16	28	2	Meadors, Marynell Hutsell
1974		6		16	26	5	Meadors, Marynell Hutsell
1977	L	8		16	28	8	Meadors, Marynell Hutsell
1975	L	12		16	26	5	Meadors, Marynell Hutsell
1972		16		16	26	6	Meadors, Marynell Hutsell
TENNESSEE: MARTIN							
1972		8		16	20	8	Gearn, Nadine
TEXAS							
1982	I	2		16	35	4	Conradt, Jody
1980	I	16		24	33	4	Conradt, Jody
1981	I	24		24	28	8	Conradt, Jody
TEXAS WESLEYAN							
1979	S	16		16	32	5	Satern, Miriam
TOUGALOO							
1979	S	5		16	47	11	Pennington, Andrew
TOWSON							
1969		5		16	10	1	Verkruzen, Margo
1970		12		16	9	3	Verkruzen, Margo
TUSKEGEE							
1979	S	4		16	34	5	Laster, Jr. "Tiny"
1981	II	8		16	27	11	Laster, Jr. "Tiny"
UNION (TN)							
1976	S	12		16	26	3	Birmingham, Peggy

Year	Div	F	Bye	#T	W	L	Coach
URSINUS							
1970		3		16	7	1	Snell, Eleanor
1969		8		16	4	2	Snell, Eleanor
1977	S	16		16	4	10	Stahl, Sue
UTAH							
1977	L	8		16	26	3	Gardner, Fern
1976	L	16		16	19	5	Gardner, Fern
1978	L	16		16	21	9	Gardner, Fern
UTAH STATE							
1972		12		16	X	X	Gardner, Fern
1973		16		16	13	5	Gardner, Fern
1974		16		16	13	5	Gardner, Fern
1975	L	16		16	12	4	Gardner, Fern
VALDOSTA STATE							
1978	L	12		16	27	4	Worth, Lyndal
1979	L	12		16	27	8	Worth, Lyndal
VANDERBILT							
1982	I	16		16	20	14	Lee, Phil
VILLANOVA							
1982	I	3		16	29	4	Perretta, Harry
WASHINGTON							
1978	L	16		16	26	5	Neir, Kathie
WASHINGTON STATE							
1972		16		16	11	4	Durrant, Sue
WAYLAND BAPTIST							
1976	L	3		16	34	5	Weese, Dean
1978	L	4		16	33	5	Weese, Dean
1982	I	4		16	19	15	Wilson, Cathy
1974		5		16	37	5	Weese, Dean
1975	L	5		16	34	1	Weese, Dean
1979	L	8		16	24	10	Weese, Dean
WEST ALABAMA							
1982	II	8		16	29	7	Izard, Jim
1980	II	16	To R16	24	24	12	Bridges, Avie
WEST CHESTER							
1969		1		16	12	0	Eckman, Carol
1970		2		16	12	2	Eckman, Carol
1971		2		16	15	4	Eckman, Carol
1972		2		16	16	1	Eckman, Carol
WEST GEORGIA							
1976	S	2		16	15	4	McNabb, Dorothy
1977	S	12		16	15	5	McNabb, Dorothy
1975	L	16		16	10	9	McNabb, Dorothy
1980	II	24		24	17	12	Mosley, Nancy

Year	Div	F	Bye	#T	W	L	Coach
WESTERN CAROLINA							
1969		2		16	14	3	Westmoreland, Betty
1970		4		16	16	3	Westmoreland, Betty
1971		16		16	13	4	Westmoreland, Betty
WESTERN OREGON							
1980	III	16	To R16	24	25	4	Carey, Jon
1982	III	16		16	24	6	Carey, Jon
WESTERN WASHINGTON							
1973		8		16	24	2	Goodrich, Lynda
1974		12		16	22	5	Goodrich, Lynda
1977	L	16		16	21	7	Goodrich, Lynda
WILLAMETTE							
1980	III	24		24	17	7	Howard, Fran
WILLIAM CAREY (MS)							
1981	II	16		16	19	8	Halford, Bobby
WILLIAM PENN							
1981	II	1		16	43	3	Spencer, Robert L.
1980	II	3		24	37	5	Spencer, Robert L.
1982	II	3		16	27	10	Spencer, Robert L.
1974		4		16	21	8	Spencer, Robert L.
1976	L	4		16	30	5	Spencer, Robert L.
1975	L	8		16	33	3	Spencer, Robert L.
1978	S	12		16	30	7	Spencer, Robert L.
WINTHROP							
1971		12		16	18	7	Kancevitch, Mary
WISCONSIN							
1982	I	8		16	21	13	Qualls, Edwina
WISCONSIN: GREEN BAY							
1982	II	16		16	28	9	Hammerle, Carol
WISCONSIN: LA CROSSE							
1981	III	1		16	27	5	Hansen, Mary
1980	III	2	To R16	24	24	4	Toburan, Karen
1976	L	16		16	19	4	Connolly, Mary
WISCONSIN: WHITEWATER							
1982	III	3		16	25	6	Jones, Dianne
1981	III	16		16	19	9	Jones, Dianne
WORCESTER STATE							
1980	III	1	To R16	24	24	2	Devlin, Donna
1981	III	3		16	28	2	Devlin, Donna

League of Christian Colleges

HISTORY: The League of Christian Colleges was the creation of Dr. Charles Wilkerson and his son, Keith, both then at Gulf Coast Christian (Faith Baptist) College, Plaquemine, Louisiana, as an inexpensive, simply structured, inter- denominational alternative for post-season play for small biblically based colleges. Many of the schools were also members of NCCAA division IIA or NBCAA division II but chose to participate in the LCC tournaments.

TOURNAMENT DIVISIONS: Open: 1996-1997

TOURNAMENT OPERATION: Both tournaments, with seven teams in 1996 and five in 1997, were seeded with all places determined. There apparently was no specific qualification method, and it seems that participation was the result of a decision by a school. The 1996 tournament was scheduled to have eight teams. As a result of the withdrawal of the No. 8 seed, the No. 1 seed was given a bye, and the tournament then played the original schedule.

The 1997 event was scheduled to have six teams with the top two seeds receiving byes into the round of four. The withdrawal of the No. 4 seed caused the No. 5 seed to become the No. 4 and receive a bye. The No. 6 seed became the No. 5 seed and played the No. 3 seed in the only first-round game with the winner advancing to the round of four with the three byes.

NOTES ON DATA COLLECTION: Since there apparently was no specific qualification method for the tournaments, information on the type of bid is not included.

Tournament Results

F	School	SD	Bye	W	L	Coach
1996						
1	Gulf Coast Christian	2		23	17	Wilkerson, Keith
2	Wesley (MS)	5		10	13	Devore, William, Jr.
3	Taylor: Fort Wayne	1	To R4	19	10	Hamilton, Marvin E. "Bud"
4	East Coast Bible	3		5	19	Ayres, "Rusty"
5	American Baptist	6		16	7	Robinson, Rev. Norman
6	California Christian	4		8	17	McAllister, Jim
7	Bay Ridge Christian	7		7	14	Zamora, Edward
1997						
1	Wesley (MS)	5		13	16	Devore, William, Jr.
2	Gulf Coast Christian	1	To R4	29	6	Wilkerson, Dr. Charles
3	Dallas Christian	3		19	13	Wilkerson, Keith
4	East Coast Bible	2	To R4	12	17	Smith, Phillip D.
5	Bay Ridge Christian	4	To R4	0	17	Lewis, Percy

School Participation History

Year	F	SD	Bye	#T	W	L	Coach
AMERICAN BAPTIST							
1996	5	6		7	16	7	Robinson, Rev. Norman
BAY RIDGE CHRISTIAN							
1997	5	4	To R4	5	0	17	Lewis, Percy
1996	7	7		7	7	14	Zamora, Edward

Year	F	SD	Bye	#T	W	L	Coach
CALIFORNIA CHRISTIAN							
1996	6	4		7	8	17	McAllister, Jim
DALLAS CHRISTIAN							
1997	3	3		5	19	13	Wilkerson, Keith
EAST COAST BIBLE							
1996	4	3		7	5	19	Ayres, "Rusty"
1997	4	2	To R4	5	12	17	Smith, Phillip D.
GULF COAST CHRISTIAN							
1996	1	2		7	23	17	Wilkerson, Keith
1997	2	1	To R4	5	29	6	Wilkerson, Dr. Charles
TAYLOR: FORT WAYNE							
1996	3	1	To R4	7	19	10	Hamilton, Marvin E. "Bud"
WESLEY (MS)							
1997	1	5		5	13	16	Devore, William, Jr.
1996	2	5		7	10	13	Devore, William, Jr.

National Association of Intercollegiate Athletics

NAMES: 1937-1940: National Small College Basketball Association (NSCBA); 1941-1952: National Association of Intercollegiate Basketball (NAIB); 1953- : National Association of Intercollegiate Athletics (NAIA)

HISTORY: Following the AAU decision to move its 1935 national championship tournament to Denver, Kansas City would be without post-season basketball for the first time in 15 years. To fill the void, local business leaders asked Emil S. Liston, then athletics director at nearby Baker University; Dr. James A. Naismith, the game's inventor, then at the University of Kansas; J. A. Reilly, who would manage the tournament; and George Goldman, then manager of Municipal Auditorium, to come up with a replacement event.

It took two years, but in 1937, the National Small College Basketball Association (NSCBA) tournament brought together, on an invitational basis, eight small college teams, champions and runners-up from four Midwest conferences. It was won by Central Missouri State whose prize was a trophy designed by Naismith.

Thus began post-season college basketball. The NIT followed in 1938, and the NCAA tournament started in 1939; but the NSCBA tournament, which became the NAIA in 1953, is the longest-running national collegiate tournament in any sport.

After the inaugural effort, except for a World War II hiatus in 1944, 32 men's open or division I teams (16 in 1945) have traveled to Kansas City—first to storied Municipal Auditorium, then, after 1975, to newly built Kemper Arena—and beginning in 1994, to Mabee Arena in Tulsa, Oklahoma, for a five-day survival-of-the-fittest tournament. If you win, you keep playing—every day! If you lose, you go home! Women's and division II tournaments, which began in 1992, have been held at various sites, but with the same grueling format.

In 1940, largely through the efforts of Liston, the NSCBA became the National Association of Intercollegiate Basketball (NAIB), and in 1952, when the first all- encompassing rules and standards were adopted, it became the National Association of Intercollegiate Athletics (NAIA).

In 1948, the NAIB became the first national athletics organization to offer intercollegiate post-season opportunities to black student-athletes, and in 1953, historically black institutions were voted into membership.

Beginning in 1952 and continuing into the early 1980s, national championships were added for men in 14 additional sports. Women's championships began in 1981.

TOURNAMENT DIVISIONS: **Men** Open: 1937-1991; I: 1992- ; II: 1992- . **Women** Open: 1981-1991; I: 1992- ; II: 1992- .

DEFINITION OF DIVISIONS: I: 15 scholarship maximum; II: 8 scholarship maximum.

TOURNAMENT OPERATION: Although the 1937 tournament was an invitational event that led to the creation of the NAIA, for the sake of simplicity, it is included in this book as if it were an NAIA event, and participating teams are listed as if they were NAIA members.

The NAIA men's tournaments have been a bracket-maker's dream and a tribute to consistency. Except for the first one, the eight-team invitational, and the 1945 edition which followed the one-year hiatus for World War II and had 16 teams, every open and division I tournament has been a conventional single-elimination 32-team event. Through 1988, a 3rd/4th place game was played. Division II began in 1992 with 20 teams in its first two years and grew to 24 in 1994 and to 32 in 1995—all as conventional single-elimination events with no 3rd/4th place game.

The women's tournaments have also been a bracket-maker's dream and a tribute to consistency. Beginning in 1981 as an eight-team event, it went to 16 teams in 1984 and to 32 in 1991—all in a single-elimination format. Through 1988, 3rd/4th place games were played. Division II began in 1992 with 20 teams in its first two years, grew to 24 in 1994, and to 32 in 1995—all as conventional single-elimination events with no 3rd/4th place game.

It is believed that beginning in 1951, tournament teams qualified by winning one of 32 geographic district tournaments. The qualification method prior to 1951 is unknown. District champions, and thus automatic qualification, are unknown prior to 1958. Beginning in 1994, regular season or tournament winners of affiliated conferences, plus regional tournaments for the independent teams, replaced the district tournaments as the method of qualifying for the national championship tournament.

Seedings apparently began in 1957. In men's division I, the top eight teams were seeded for the first two years. Thereafter all tournaments have had the top 16 seeded. Division II used eight seeds for the first two years, trying a one-year experiment with all 24 in 1994, and then going with 16 thereafter. For the women's tournaments, division I had eight seeds through 1990 and 16 thereafter. Division II used eight seeds for the first two years, trying a one-year experiment with all 24 in 1994, and then going with 16 thereafter.

Tournament Results—Men

F	School	SD	BD	Bye	W	L	Coach
1937							
1	Central Missouri State		I		17	3	Reid, Tad C.
2	Morningside		I		16	4	Rogers, R. Glenn "Honie"
3	Southwestern (KS)		I		14	11	Monypeny, William W.
4	Central Arkansas		I		21	8	Woodson, Warren B.
8	Baker (KS)		I		14	3	Liston, Emil S.
	Benedictine (KS)		I		17	3	Mullins, Larry
	Dakota Wesleyan		I		12	5	Belding, Lester C.
	Luther		I		12	8	Peterson, Hamlet E., Sr.

F	School	SD	BD	Bye	W	L	Coach
1938							
1	Central Missouri State				24	3	Reid, Tad C.
2	Roanoke				19	2	White, Gordon C. 'Pap'
3	Murray State (KY)				27	4	Cutchin, Carlisle C.
4	Washburn				10	13	Errickson, Charles D. 'Dee'
8	Delta State				15	6	Dickson, A. D.
	Jordan College & Seminary						
	New Mexico State				22	3	Hines, Gerald H. 'Jerry'
	Saint Ambrose				15	5	Duford, Wilford J. 'Dukes'
16	Central Oklahoma				17	6	Hamilton, Dale E.
	Idaho State				19	7	Wicks, Guy P.
	Marshall				28	4	Henderson, Eli Camden 'Cam'
	North Texas				15	8	Shands, Harry G. 'Pete'
	Northwest Missouri State				15	6	Stalcup, Wilbur N. 'Sparky'
	Simpson (IA)				16	5	Casey, Francis L. 'Frank'
	Valparaiso				13	6	Christiansen, J. M. 'Jake'
	West Texas A&M				27	6	Baggett, Al
32	Central Arkansas				12	9	Woodson, Warren B.
	Dakota Wesleyan				11	10	Belding, Lester C.
	Drake (IA)				14	6	Williams, Evan O. 'Bill'
	Drury				18	3	Weiser, Albert L.
	Kansas Wesleyan				9	7	Unknown
	Manchester				14	5	Stauffer, Robert
	McPherson				13	8	Astle, W. P. 'Buck'
	Morningside				14	5	Rogers, R. Glenn 'Honie'
	Nebraska Wesleyan				13	3	Thomas, Dwight P.
	Ottawa				11	8	Godlove, Richard M.
	Peru State				15	3	Baller, Stewart 'Stu'
	Sioux Falls				14	5	Olsen, Francis R.
	Western Kentucky				30	3	Diddle, Edgar A., Sr.
	Western Oregon				16	6	Cox, J. Alfred 'Al'
	Westminster (MO)				12	9	Kimbrell, Eugene F.
	Winona State				14	4	Fisk, Charles
1939							
1	Southwestern (KS)				21	2	Gardner, George
2	San Diego State				24	7	Gross, Morris H.
3	Glenville State				25	3	Rohrbaugh, A. F. 'Nate'
4	Peru State				18	7	Wheeler, A. G. 'Al'
8	Central Missouri State				21	7	Scott, Tom
	Manchester				16	5	Stauffer, Robert
	Northwest Missouri State				14	7	Stalcup, Wilbur N. 'Sparky'
	Saint Ambrose				20	2	Duford, Wilford J. 'Dukes'
16	Augustana (IL)				17	6	Almquist, H. V.
	Culver-Stockton				16	8	Herington, William A.
	Dakota Wesleyan				11	2	Belding, Lester C.
	Murray State (KY)				13	8	Cutchin, Carlisle C.
	Texas A&M: Commerce				15	6	Vinzant, Dennis
	Trinity (TX)				12	3	Wilkins, Leland J.
	Wayne State (MI)				14	5	Ertell, Newman H.
	Westminster (MO)				15	8	Kimbrell, Eugene F.

F	School	SD	BD	Bye	W	L	Coach
32	Alfred Holbrook				15	5	Beattie, Mendell E.
	Anderson (IN)				15	6	Nay, Edgar
	Central Oklahoma				16	5	Hamilton, Dale E.
	Delta State				16	7	Dickson, A. D.
	High Point				22	4	Yow, C. Virgil
	Jordan College & Seminary						
	Loras				14	6	Coyne, Fr. Daniel B.
	New Mexico Tech				21	5	Butler, Dr. Louis C. "Pete"
	Northern State (SD)				18	2	Robertson, Harley R.
	Northwestern State (LA)				16	4	Prather, H. Lee
	Simpson (IA)				14	7	Casey, Francis L. "Frank"
	Southwest Missouri State				15	4	McDonald, A. C. "Andy"
	Wayne State (NE)				12	9	Hickman, W. Ray
	West Texas A&M				21	9	Baggett, Al
	Winona State				10	8	Fisk, Charles
	Wisconsin: Eau Claire				15	2	Zorn, Willis R., Sr. "Bill"

1940

F	School	SD	BD	Bye	W	L	Coach
1	Tarkio				20	4	Kyle, Newton P.
2	San Diego State				22	6	Gross, Morris H.
3	Delta State				24	6	Dickson, A. D.
4	Hamline				12	5	Hutton, Joseph W., Sr.
8	Northwest Missouri State				22	1	Stalcup, Wilbur N. "Sparky"
	Pittsburg State				16	11	Lance, John F.
	Southwestern (KS)				14	9	Monypeny, William W.
	Texas Wesleyan				22	2	Miller, W. A. "Gus"
16	Appalachian State				18	3	Stewart, A. L. "Flucie"
	Glenville State				22	3	Rohrbaugh, A. F. "Nate"
	Kansas Wesleyan				23	8	Johnson, Eugene
	Peru State				19	6	Wheeler, A. G. "Al"
	Southeastern Oklahoma State				X	X	Sullivan, Bloomer
	Texas A&M: Commerce				23	7	Vinzant, Dennis
	West Texas A&M				26	8	Baggett, Al
	Wisconsin: Superior				15	3	Whereatt, Ted
32	Alfred Holbrook				16	4	Beattie, Mendell E.
	Augustana (IL)				10	9	Almquist, H. V.
	Bemidji State				13	3	Frost, Reuben B. "Jack"
	Central Arkansas				18	8	Woodson, Warren B.
	Central Missouri State				17	8	Scott, Tom
	Dakota Wesleyan				12	5	Belding, Lester C.
	East Central (OK)				25	5	McBride, Floyd H. "Mickey"
	Loras				14	6	Coyne, Fr. Daniel B.
	Northern State (SD)				17	5	Robertson, Harley R.
	Northwestern State (LA)				19	2	Prather, H. Lee
	Pacific (OR)				17	12	Miller, Pete
	Ripon				14	6	Lamphear, George
	Saint Joseph's (IN)				16	7	Dienhart, Joseph S.
	Simpson (IA)				20	4	Casey, Francis L. "Frank"
	Upper Iowa				8	6	Dorman, Dr. John E.
	Wayne State (NE)				12	6	Morrison, James H.

F	School	SD	BD	Bye	W	L	Coach
1941							
1	San Diego State				24	7	Gross, Morris H.
2	Murray State (KY)				25	5	Cutchin, Carlisle C.
3	West Texas A&M				29	6	Baggett, Al
4	California: Santa Barbara				22	10	Wilton, Wilton M. "Willie"
8	Appalachian State				17	3	Canipe, Clyde
	Delta State				16	7	Dickson, A. D.
	Northwest Missouri State				19	4	Stalcup, Wilbur N. "Sparky"
	Texas Wesleyan				25	2	Miller, W. A. "Gus"
16	Alma				23	3	MacDonald, Gordon D.
	Baltimore				17	3	Unknown
	Bemidji State				14	3	Frost, Reuben B. "Jack"
	Culver-Stockton				16	5	Herington, William A.
	Northwestern State (LA)				17	2	Prather, H. Lee
	Saint Mary's (MN)						
	Stephen F Austin State				21	6	Shelton, Robert H.
	Wisconsin: Superior				17	2	Whereatt, Ted
32	Baker (KS)				14	8	Liston, Emil S.
	Central Missouri State				17	9	Scott, Tom
	Dakota Wesleyan				16	5	Belding, Lester C.
	Dubuque				15	3	Mercer, Kenneth E. "Moco"
	Evansville				12	4	Slyker, William V.
	Morningside				9	7	Rogers, R. Glenn "Honie"
	Nebraska: Omaha				12	13	Johnk, Harold
	Oklahoma Panhandle State				19	8	Iba, Clarence V.
	Pittsburg State				18	6	Lance, John F.
	Simpson (IA)				19	3	Casey, Francis L. "Frank"
	Sioux Falls				12	4	Olsen, Francis R.
	Tarkio				14	4	Kyle, Newton P.
	Texas: El Paso				17	6	Pennington, Marshall
	Wayne State (NE)				13	7	Morrison, James H.
	Western Montana				16	4	Straugh, William T.
	Western Oregon				14	10	Cox, J. Alfred "Al"
1942							
1	Hamline				20	2	Hutton, Joseph W., Sr.
2	Southeastern Oklahoma State				X	X	Sullivan, Bloomer
3	Pittsburg State				23	5	Lance, John F.
4	Central Missouri State				19	7	Scott, Tom
8	Bemidji State				14	6	Frost, Reuben B. "Jack"
	East Central (OK)				20	10	McBride, Floyd H. "Mickey"
	Indiana State				17	4	Curtis, Glenn M.
	Missouri Valley				17	8	Ashford, Volney C.
16	Evansville				12	6	Slyker, William V.
	High Point				24	1	Yow, C. Virgil
	Luther				15	4	Peterson, Hamlet E., Sr.
	San Diego State				13	9	Gross, Morris H.
	Simpson (IA)				17	6	Casey, Francis L. "Frank"
	Southwestern (KS)				16	5	Monypeny, William W.
	Texas Tech				16	11	Hoffman, Burl
	Wisconsin: Stout				9	6	Johnson, Ray

F	School	SD	BD	Bye	W	L	Coach
32	Central Arkansas				25	3	Roberts, Lloyd
	Chadron State				17	4	Armstrong, Ross O.
	Delta State				15	10	Dickson, A. D.
	Eastern Washington				18	7	Reese, William B. "Red"
	Louisiana Tech				13	8	Crowley, Cecil C.
	Morehead State (KY)				12	10	Johnson, Ellis T.
	Murray State (KY)				18	4	Mountjoy, L. Rice
	Panzer				14	5	Gorton, Albert J.
	Pepperdine				18	7	Duer, Alva O. "Al"
	Peru State				13	9	Wheeler, A. G. "Al"
	Portland				14	7	Fitzpatrick, Edwin J.
	Texas A&M: Commerce				10	13	Vinzant, Dennis
	Texas Wesleyan				15	5	Unknown
	Western New Mexico				17	4	Wooden, Maurice
	Wisconsin: Stevens Point				9	3	Kobal, Eddie
	Yankton				13	3	Arnold, Lorne S.

1943

F	School	SD	BD	Bye	W	L	Coach
1	Southeast Missouri State				19	6	Harris, Charles P.
2	Northwest Missouri State				18	7	Stalcup, Wilbur N. "Sparky"
3	North Texas				15	15	Russell, Lloyd
4	Murray State (KY)				21	5	Miller, John
8	Appalachian State				15	3	Smawley, Belus
	Eastern Washington				27	5	Brumblay, Robert C.
	Hamline				21	2	Hutton, Joseph W., Sr.
	Pepperdine				23	8	Duer, Alva O. "Al"
16	East Central (OK)				18	6	Powell, C. J.
	Eastern Oregon				18	5	Quinn, E. Robert
	Kansas Wesleyan				18	4	Johnson, Eugene
	Luther				12	3	Peterson, Hamlet E., Sr.
	Saint Cloud State				12	3	Kasch, Warren
	Southwestern (KS)				17	5	Monypeny, William W.
	Westminster (MO)				11	7	Kimbrell, Eugene F.
	York (NE)				16	4	Tonkin, R. E.
32	Akron				17	4	Beichly, Russell J.
	Central Methodist				11	4	Vanatta, Robert
	Dakota Wesleyan				21	2	Belding, Lester C.
	Illinois Wesleyan				7	14	Horenberger, Jack
	Indiana State				13	4	Curtis, Glenn M.
	Lawrence Tech				18	13	Ridler, Don
	Loyola (IL)				12	10	Connelly, John J.
	Nebraska: Kearney				12	6	White, Dr. Clifford W.
	Ouachita Baptist				12	7	Bradshaw, Wesley W.
	Simpson (IA)				14	5	Casey, Francis L. "Frank"
	South Dakota State				15	6	McCrady, Thurlo E.
	Southeastern Oklahoma State				X	X	Sullivan, Bloomer
	Southwest Missouri State				12	13	McDonald, A. C. "Andy"
	Texas Wesleyan				26	4	Unknown
	Valparaiso				17	4	Ellis, Loren E.
	Wisconsin: Stout				10	2	Johnson, Ray

F	School	SD	BD	Bye	W	L	Coach
1945							
1	Loyola New Orleans				22	11	Orsley, Jack C.
2	Pepperdine				25	11	Duer, Alva O. "Al"
3	Eastern Kentucky				20	5	Rankin, Dr. Rome
4	Southern Illinois				15	7	Martin, Glenn "Abe"
8	Canterbury				14	12	Johnson, Glenn A.
	Central Methodist				12	1	Vanatta, Robert
	Doane				6	12	Dutcher, Jim
	West Texas A&M				16	10	Miller, W. A. "Gus"
16	Catawba				16	5	Kirkland, Gordon A.
	Eastern Washington				27	5	Brumblay, Robert C.
	Peru State				6	8	Wheeler, A. G. "Al"
	Phillips (OK)						
	Simpson (IA)				16	4	Casey, Francis L. "Frank"
	Washburn				12	9	Errickson, Charles D. "Dee"
	Wichita State				14	4	Binford, Melvin J.
	Wisconsin: Eau Claire				10	8	Zorn, Willis R., Sr. "Bill"
1946							
1	Southern Illinois				20	6	Martin, Glenn "Abe"
2	Indiana State				21	7	Curtis, Glenn M.
3	Pepperdine				27	8	Duer, Alva O. "Al"
4	Loyola New Orleans				22	11	Orsley, Jack C.
8	Dakota Wesleyan				16	6	Green, Ray
	Drury				12	9	Weiser, Albert L.
	Eastern Washington				31	4	Reese, William B. "Red"
	Nevada				24	9	Lawlor, Glenn J. "Jake"
16	Augsburg				19	2	Carlson, Robert
	Culver-Stockton				18	4	Herington, William A.
	Houston				10	4	Pasche, Alden
	Loras				18	9	Dowd, Vincent J.
	Northern Arizona				11	7	Brickey, Frank
	Northern Iowa				13	7	Nordley, Oliver M.
	Southeastern Oklahoma State				26	4	Sullivan, Bloomer
	West Texas A&M				19	8	Miller, W. A. "Gus"
32	Central Arkansas				16	12	McGibbony, Charles
	Central Missouri State				13	7	Scott, Tom
	Eastern Kentucky				20	5	Rankin, Dr. Rome
	Hastings				16	5	Douglas, Louis H.
	High Point				10	8	James, Ralph
	Louisiana Tech				16	8	Crowley, Cecil C.
	Montana State				17	10	Breeden, John W. "Brick"
	Morningside				15	4	Buckingham, Albert W.
	New Mexico Tech				20	9	Finley, Charles L. "Chuck"
	Panzer				18	3	Gorton, Albert J.
	Peru State				16	6	Wheeler, A. G. "Al"
	Rockhurst				15	8	Powell, Bill
	Saint Cloud State				12	2	Lynch, George H.
	Washburn				13	7	Errickson, Charles D. "Dee"
	Wichita State				14	9	Binford, Melvin J.
	Wisconsin: Eau Claire				18	4	Zorn, Willis R., Sr. "Bill"

F	School	SD	BD	Bye	W	L	Coach
1947							
1	Marshall				32	5	Henderson, Eli Camden "Cam"
2	Mankato State				24	4	Witham, James A.
3	Northern Arizona				20	7	Brickey, Frank
4	Emporia State				18	9	Fish, Everett D. "Gus"
8	Beloit				22	5	Stanley, Dolph
	Eastern Washington				22	9	Reese, William B. "Red"
	Southeastern Oklahoma State				13	7	Sullivan, Bloomer
	Truman State (MO)				30	2	King, W. Boyd
16	Canterbury				13	9	Johnson, Glenn A.
	Dakota Wesleyan				25	3	Gorby, Dave
	DePauw				16	3	Hickman, Harold E. "Hal"
	Hamline				22	5	Hutton, Joseph W., Sr.
	Hastings				20	6	Owens, Larry
	Houston				15	7	Pasche, Alden
	Texas Wesleyan				32	4	Edwards, Johnnie O.
	Whittier				30	2	Bonham, Aubrey R.
32	Arkansas State				17	16	Tomlinson, J. A. "Ike"
	Culver-Stockton				18	2	Herington, William A.
	Delta State				23	5	Marlar, Luther W. "Luke"
	Eastern Illinois				13	7	Healey, Dr. William A.
	Lawrence Tech				26	4	Ridler, Don
	Linfield				20	8	Lever, Henry W.
	Loras				24	5	Dowd, Vincent J.
	Loyola (MD)				21	12	Reitz, Emil G., Jr. "Lefty"
	Montana State				25	11	Breeden, John W. "Brick"
	New Mexico				11	8	Clements, Woodrow W.
	Northwestern State (LA)				15	5	Prather, H. Lee
	Oglethorpe				22	6	Phillips, "Swede"
	Southern Illinois				19	10	Holder, Lynn C.
	Western Carolina				15	11	McDonald, Marion G.
	Wisconsin: River Falls				18	7	Schlagenhauf, George K.
	Youngstown State				12	10	Rosselli, Dominic L. "Dom"
1948							
1	Louisville				29	6	Hickman, Bernard L. "Peck"
2	Indiana State				27	7	Wooden, John R.
3	Hamline				28	3	Hutton, Joseph W., Sr.
4	Xavier (OH)				24	8	Hirt, Lewis R.
8	Beloit				24	3	Stanley, Dolph
	Manhattan				23	6	Norton, Kenneth A.
	Mankato State				16	11	Witham, James A.
	San Jose State				23	9	McPherson, Walter J.
16	Arizona State				13	11	Lavik, Rudolph H.
	Brigham Young				16	11	Millet, W. Floyd
	Central Connecticut State				14	5	Merrick, Ross
	Emporia State				20	7	Fish, Everett D. "Gus"
	Gonzaga				24	11	McGrath, Claude F.
	Lawrence Tech				22	6	Ridler, Don
	Marshall				22	11	Henderson, Eli Camden "Cam"
	Southern Illinois				22	4	Holder, Lynn C.

F	School	SD	BD	Bye	W	L	Coach
32	Appalachian State				20	8	Hoover, Francis
	Central Arkansas				21	2	Smith, Glen M.
	Delta State				17	5	Ricks, John Ray
	Denver				18	11	Ketchum, Ellison E.
	East Central (OK)				17	5	McBride, Floyd H. "Mickey"
	Loyola (MD)				24	7	Reitz, Emil G., Jr. "Lefty"
	Mercer				18	4	Cowan, James M.
	Montana				21	11	Dahlberg, George P.
	Northern Iowa				14	6	Nordley, Oliver M.
	Northwestern State (LA)				19	6	Prather, H. Lee
	Peru State				20	3	Kyle, Newton P.
	Saint Francis (PA)				15	8	Hughes, Dr. William T. "Skip"
	South Dakota State				19	6	Frost, Reuben B. "Jack"
	Southern Oregon				24	3	Schopf, Dr. Theodore G.
	Texas Wesleyan				19	13	Edwards, Johnnie O.
	Truman State (MO)				29	2	King, W. Boyd

1949

F	School	SD	BD	Bye	W	L	Coach
1	Hamline				29	1	Hutton, Joseph W., Sr.
2	Regis (CO)				36	3	Varnell, Harry Lee
3	Beloit				29	4	Stanley, Dolph
4	Indiana State				24	8	Longfellow, John L.
8	Eastern Illinois				23	6	Healey, Dr. William A.
	Emporia State				20	10	Fish, Everett D. "Gus"
	Northwestern State (LA)				23	5	Prather, H. Lee
	Texas Tech				21	9	Robison, Polk F.
16	Brigham Young				22	14	Millet, W. Floyd
	Indianapolis				20	9	Nicoson, Angus J.
	Loyola (MD)				25	8	Reitz, Emil G., Jr. "Lefty"
	North Dakota				14	15	Cunningham, H. B.
	Northern Iowa				16	6	Nordley, Oliver M.
	Saint Thomas (MN)				22	7	Sokol, Paul
	San Jose State				22	13	McPherson, Walter J.
	Southwest Missouri State				25	2	McDonald, A. C. "Andy"
32	Arkansas State				14	12	Tomlinson, J. A. "Ike"
	Cedarville				17	12	Beattie, Mendell E.
	Central Connecticut State				21	4	Merrick, Ross
	Delta State				18	11	Ricks, John Ray
	Eastern New Mexico				19	8	Garten, Alvin D.
	Erskine				19	7	McMillan, John D. "Johnny"
	Hawaii				21	6	Gallon, Dr. Arthur J.
	Lawrence Tech				16	10	Ridler, Don
	Miami (FL)				19	8	Morris, Hart
	Northwestern Oklahoma State				18	9	Highfill, C. L. "Dick"
	Peru State				20	6	Kyle, Newton P.
	Portland				22	11	Torson, James M. "Mush"
	Puget Sound				21	6	Heinrick, John P.
	Waynesburg				17	11	Gustine, Frank
	Western Montana				16	17	Straugh, William T.
	Wisconsin: River Falls				10	2	Schlagenhauf, George K.

F	School	SD	BD	Bye	W	L	Coach
1950							
1	Indiana State				27	8	Longfellow, John L.
2	East Central (OK)				31	5	McBride, Floyd H. "Mickey"
3	Central Methodist				29	4	Vanatta, Robert
4	Tampa University				20	14	Gaddis, Mike
8	Baldwin-Wallace				12	16	Watts, Ray E.
	Brooklyn				24	5	Baggett, Al
	Central Washington				24	8	Nicholson, Leo S.
	Davis & Elkins				29	5	Brown, Robert N. "Red"
16	Arkansas Tech				26	2	Hindsman, Sam F., Jr.
	Hamline				29	3	Hutton, Joseph W., Sr.
	Pepperdine				21	12	Dowell, Robert L. "Duck"
	Portland				19	12	Torson, James M. "Mush"
	Puget Sound				19	12	Heinrick, John P.
	Texas A&M: Commerce				14	15	Tully, Darrell
	Westminster (PA)				25	5	Washabaugh, Grover C.
	Wisconsin: River Falls				26	5	Schlagenhauf, George K.
32	American				22	8	Cassell, Stafford H.
	Appalachian State				20	8	Hoover, Francis
	Central Connecticut State				16	6	Merrick, Ross
	Delta State				19	6	Ricks, John Ray
	Eastern Illinois				21	5	Healey, Dr. William A.
	Kalamazoo				13	8	Grow, Lloyd E.
	Kansas Wesleyan				22	2	Forsberg, Wallace A. "Wally"
	Montana				27	4	Dahlberg, George P.
	Morningside				13	14	Buckingham, Albert W.
	Murray State (KY)				18	13	Hodges, Harlan
	New Mexico State				15	13	McCarty, George C.
	Peru State				22	6	Kyle, Newton P.
	Regis (CO)				17	16	Varnell, Harry Lee
	Saint Thomas (MN)				18	7	Sokol, Paul
	South Dakota				11	11	Deklotz, George
	Southeastern Louisiana				13	11	Marlar, Luther W. "Luke"
1951							
1	Hamline				27	2	Hutton, Joseph W., Sr.
2	Millikin				24	7	Allan, Ralph W.
3	Baldwin-Wallace				19	7	Wagner, J. Larsen
4	Regis (CO)				19	8	Varnell, Harry Lee
8	Evansville				23	7	McCutchan, Arad A.
	Florida State				18	9	Kennedy, Jesse K. "Bud"
	Memphis				17	8	Tarry, McCoy
	New Mexico State				15	11	McCarty, George C.
16	Arkansas Tech				25	6	Hindsman, Sam F., Jr.
	Central Methodist				24	5	Pink, Ralph J.
	East Texas Baptist				15	5	Stephens, John O.
	Hastings				23	3	McLaughlin, Tom
	Morningside				18	7	Buckingham, Albert W.
	Ottawa				19	7	Meek, Donald
	Pepperdine				25	8	Dowell, Robert L. "Duck"
	Southwest Texas State				21	5	Jowers, Milton W.

F	School	SD	BD	Bye	W	L	Coach
32	American				18	10	Cassell, Stafford H.
	East Central (OK)				22	7	McBride, Floyd H. "Mickey"
	Eastern New Mexico				19	9	Garten, Alvin D.
	Glenville State				19	11	Ratliff, Carlos C.
	High Point				20	11	Davis, Dr. Robert M.
	Hillsdale				9	11	Wisniewski, Irvin C.
	Morehead State (KY)				13	11	Johnson, Ellis T.
	Pacific (CA)				19	11	Kjeldsen, Chris K.
	Pacific Lutheran				20	11	Harshman, Marvel K. "Marv"
	Portland				23	6	Torson, James M. "Mush"
	Providence				14	10	Cuddy, James V. "Viv"
	Rocky Mountain				17	14	Klindt, Herbert J.
	South Dakota State				16	12	Frost, Reuben B. "Jack"
	Southeastern Louisiana				13	10	Marlar, Luther W. "Luke"
	Westminster (PA)				22	6	Washabaugh, Grover C.
	Wisconsin: Eau Claire				17	6	Zorn, Willis R., Sr. "Bill"

1952

F	School	SD	BD	Bye	W	L	Coach
1	Southwest Missouri State				27	5	Vanatta, Robert
2	Murray State (KY)				24	10	Hodges, Harlan
3	Southwest Texas State				30	1	Jowers, Milton W.
4	Portland				24	11	Torson, James M. "Mush"
8	Hamline				24	5	Hutton, Joseph W., Sr.
	Lawrence Tech				23	2	Ridler, Don
	Morningside				20	10	Buckingham, Albert W.
	Whitworth (WA)				23	14	McGregor, James B.
16	Eastern Illinois				24	2	Healey, Dr. William A.
	Indiana State				19	10	Longfellow, John L.
	Memphis				25	10	Lambert, Dr. Eugene W.
	Millikin				21	6	Allan, Ralph W.
	Montana State				22	14	Breeden, John W. "Brick"
	New Mexico State				22	11	McCarty, George C.
	Utah State				19	14	Baker, H. Cecil
	West Texas A&M				19	9	Miller, W. A. "Gus"
32	American International				15	10	Rodis, Nicholas
	Arkansas Tech				26	4	Hindsman, Sam F., Jr.
	Baltimore				16	8	Bartheleme, Albert L.
	Centenary (LA)				17	17	Delaney, F. H. "Buss"
	Chadron State				18	7	Young, Loy
	Clarion				19	1	Kribbs, Benton A.
	Elon				25	11	Mathis, Graham L. "Doc"
	Fairleigh Dickinson: Rutherford/Teaneck				22	4	Holub, Richard
	Findlay				16	6	Renninger, Donald S.
	Huron				21	4	Lundeen, Ralph J.
	Pepperdine				20	4	Dowell, Robert L. "Duck"
	Southern Mississippi				29	8	Floyd, Lee P.
	Tampa University				11	15	Bailey, Sam
	Washburn				17	10	McDonald, Marion G.
	West Liberty State				22	6	Wehr, Richard W.
	Wisconsin: Whitewater				16	6	Weigandt, Robert

F	School	SD	BD	Bye	W	L	Coach
1953							
1	Southwest Missouri State				24	4	Vanatta, Robert
2	Hamline				23	9	Hutton, Joseph W., Sr.
3	Indiana State				23	8	Longfellow, John L.
4	Texas A&M: Commerce				25	5	Rogers, Bobby
8	Findlay				13	7	Renninger, Donald S.
	Nebraska Wesleyan				25	3	Peterson, Dr. Irvin L.
	Southern Mississippi				27	8	Floyd, Lee P.
	Tennessee State				18	4	Cash, Clarence B.
16	Arizona State				13	12	Kajikawa, William
	Arkansas Tech				20	1	Hindsman, Sam F., Jr.
	Benedictine (KS)				21	8	Nolan, Ralph
	Eastern Illinois				16	9	Healey, Dr. William A.
	Loyola (MD)				17	9	Reitz, Emil G., Jr. "Lefty"
	Point Loma Nazarene				34	2	Keoppel, Kenneth P.
	Saint Peter's				18	8	Kennedy, Don, Sr.
	Stetson				14	10	Morland, Richard B.
32	Adams State				19	8	Crawford, Ronald
	Adrian				18	7	Boyett, Theodore R.
	Arnold				17	11	Maroon, Tuffie
	Charleston (WV)				21	9	King, Carl E. "Eddie"
	East Carolina				15	7	Porter, Howard G.
	East Tennessee State				26	4	Brooks, John Madison
	Geneva				22	5	Aultman, Clifford J.
	Gonzaga				15	14	Anderson, Thor H. "Hank"
	Louisiana Tech				17	10	Crowley, Cecil C.
	Midwestern State (TX)				18	8	Clynch, Dallas C.
	North Dakota				14	10	Bogan, Louis
	Northern Iowa				14	11	Nordley, Oliver M.
	Portland				16	14	Torson, James M. "Mush"
	Ricks				16	15	Parkinson, Berkley H. "Brick"
	Southwestern Oklahoma State				24	6	Williams, Rankin
	Wisconsin: River Falls				13	8	Belfori, Phil
1954							
1	Benedictine (KS)				24	5	Nolan, Ralph
2	Western Illinois				19	9	Morley, Leroy "Stix"
3	Southwest Missouri State				20	6	Matthews, Edwin "Eddie"
4	Arkansas Tech				28	3	Hindsman, Sam F., Jr.
8	Point Loma Nazarene				29	5	Keoppel, Kenneth P.
	Saint Peter's				17	7	Kennedy, Don, Sr.
	Southeastern Louisiana				22	10	Marlar, Luther W. "Luke"
	Texas A&M: Commerce				23	5	Rogers, Bobby
16	Geneva				21	8	Aultman, Clifford J.
	Gustavus Adolphus				23	9	Young, Verl "Gus"
	Lawrence Tech				24	5	Maconochie, Walter "Scotty"
	Nebraska Wesleyan				19	5	Peterson, Dr. Irvin L.
	Regis (CO)				15	15	Moore, Harvey E.
	Rio Grande				20	7	Oliver, Newt
	Saint Ambrose				20	3	Duax, Robert J.
	Southeastern Oklahoma State				X	X	Sullivan, Bloomer

F	School	SD	BD	Bye	W	L	Coach
32	Bridgeport				12	9	Glines, Herbert E.
	Carroll (WI)				15	7	Huddleston, Don
	Charleston (WV)				16	13	King, Carl E. "Eddie"
	East Carolina				13	8	Porter, Howard G.
	East Tennessee State				23	4	Brooks, John Madison
	Georgetown (KY)				15	10	Davis, Dr. Robert M.
	Indiana State				12	15	Longfellow, John L.
	Mercer				19	9	Cowan, James M.
	Montana State				18	11	Breeden, John W. "Brick"
	North Dakota				13	11	Bogan, Louis
	Northern Arizona				19	7	Gregg, Herbert
	Portland				9	19	Torson, James M. "Mush"
	Southern Mississippi				23	8	Floyd, Lee P.
	Tennessee State				17	6	Cash, Clarence B.
	Wayland Baptist				21	4	Redin, Harley J.
	Whitworth (WA)				21	4	Smith, Art

1955

F	School	SD	BD	Bye	W	L	Coach
1	Texas A&M: Commerce				29	5	Rogers, Bobby
2	Southeastern Oklahoma State				37	5	Sullivan, Bloomer
3	Western Illinois				27	3	Morley, Leroy "Stix"
4	Arkansas Tech				31	5	Hindsman, Sam F., Jr.
8	Alderson-Broaddus				31	6	Pyles, Rex E. "Roxie"
	Beloit				22	4	Stanley, Dolph
	Franciscan				28	5	Kuzma, Harry
	Gustavus Adolphus				22	7	Young, Verl "Gus"
16	Barton				23	6	McComas, James E. "Jack"
	Florida State				22	4	Kennedy, Jesse K. "Bud"
	Louisiana Tech				20	10	Crowley, Cecil C.
	Nebraska Wesleyan				21	5	Peterson, Dr. Irvin L.
	Quincy (IL)				14	8	Forester, Harry
	Southwestern (KS)				20	8	Cotton, Dr. John J. "Jack"
	Texas Southern				28	3	Adams, Edward H.
	Truman State (MO)				19	6	King, W. Boyd
32	Adrian				21	4	Skala, Jim
	Coe				14	8	Thomsen, Theron "Tommy"
	Evansville				20	6	McCutchan, Arad A.
	Geneva				19	8	Aultman, Clifford J.
	Georgetown (KY)				22	5	Davis, Dr. Robert M.
	Loyola Marymount				16	9	Donovan, William J.
	Middle Tennessee State				11	16	Greer, Charles N., Jr.
	Minot State				20	5	Parker, Herb
	Montana State				11	16	Lemm, Walter H. "Wally"
	Portland State				30	9	Nelson, Loyal D. "Sharkey"
	Regis (CO)				14	14	Moore, Harvey E.
	Saint Francis (NY)				21	8	Lynch, Daniel J.
	Southern Connecticut State				18	5	McDowell, Owen W.
	Southern Mississippi				11	17	Finley, Charles L. "Chuck"
	Wayland Baptist				22	6	Redin, Harley J.
	Whitworth (WA)				21	8	Smith, Art

F	School	SD	BD	Bye	W	L	Coach
1956							
1	McNeese State				33	3	Ward, Ralph O.
2	Texas Southern				31	4	Adams, Edward H.
3	Pittsburg State				27	2	Lance, John F.
4	Wheaton (IL)				28	4	Pfund, Leroy H. "Lee"
8	Gustavus Adolphus				20	9	Young, Verl "Gus"
	Midwestern State (TX)				21	8	Clynch, Dallas C.
	Tennessee State				26	8	McLendon, John B., Jr.
	Western Illinois				28	3	Morley, Leroy "Stix"
16	Central State (OH)				18	7	Gibbs, George Edwin
	Geneva				24	3	Aultman, Clifford J.
	Georgia Southern				21	7	Scearce, J. B., Jr.
	Pacific Lutheran				25	6	Harshman, Marvel K. "Marv"
	Rockhurst				25	5	Brehmer, Joseph "Buddy"
	San Diego State				23	6	Ziegenfuss, Dr. George
	Stephen F Austin State				24	6	Stephens, John O.
	Wisconsin: Eau Claire				20	5	Zorn, Willis R., Sr. "Bill"
32	Alderson-Broaddus				23	12	Pyles, Rex E. "Roxie"
	American International				16	7	Callahan, William E.
	Arkansas Tech				15	6	Hindsman, Sam F., Jr.
	Coe				20	5	Levy, Marv
	East Tennessee State				20	7	Brooks, John Madison
	Eastern New Mexico				11	16	Garten, Alvin D.
	Elon				23	6	Mathis, Graham L. "Doc"
	Georgetown (KY)				17	8	Davis, Dr. Robert M.
	Hastings				18	6	Bogue, Russell
	Indianapolis				23	6	Nicoson, Angus J.
	Kalamazoo				14	9	Steffen, Raymond
	Montana State				15	14	Lambert, Keith "Dobbie"
	Portland State				21	8	Nelson, Loyal D. "Sharkey"
	Rider				16	7	Leyden, Thomas A.
	South Dakota State				17	7	Walseth, Russell M. "Sox"
	Southeastern Oklahoma State				20	10	Sullivan, Bloomer
1957							
1	Tennessee State				31	4	McLendon, John B., Jr.
2	Southeastern Oklahoma State	7			30	5	Sullivan, Bloomer
3	Pacific Lutheran	1			28	1	Harshman, Marvel K. "Marv"
4	Eastern Illinois				17	14	Carey, Robert A.
8	Hamline	6			22	4	Hutton, Joseph W., Sr.
	Texas Southern	8			32	2	Adams, Edward H.
	Western Illinois	4			22	3	Morley, Leroy "Stix"
	Youngstown State	2			23	4	Rosselli, Dominic L. "Dom"
16	Ball State				19	8	Hinga, John "Jim"
	Emporia State				20	9	Fish, Everett D. "Gus"
	Portland	5			18	12	Negratti, Dr. Albert E.
	Southwest Texas State				22	7	Jowers, Milton W.

F	School	SD	BD	Bye	W	L	Coach
	Stetson				17	8	Morland, Richard B.
	Thomas More (KY)	3			19	7	Wolf, Charles
	William Jewell				23	6	Nelson, James A.
	Wisconsin: Stevens Point				17	6	Quandt, Hale F.
32	Adelphi				13	12	Faherty, George E.
	Adrian				16	6	Albeck, Charles Stanley "Stan"
	Austin Peay State				24	9	Aaron, David B.
	Elon				24	6	Mathis, Graham L. "Doc"
	Millersville				18	6	DeHart, Richard C.
	New Mexico Highlands				18	4	Gibson, Don
	Northern State (SD)				22	5	Wachs, Bob
	Northwest Nazarene				24	9	Hills, Orrin E.
	Southern Arkansas				15	8	Waller, P. T. "Duddy"
	Southern Connecticut State				16	7	McDowell, Owen W.
	Troy State: Troy				19	8	Fraser, Morley
	Upper Iowa				17	6	Eischeid, Everett E. "Eb"
	Wayland Baptist				20	9	Redin, Harley J.
	Wayne State (NE)				15	9	Obye, Charles H. "Chuck"
	West Virginia Tech				26	3	Baisi, Neal D.
	Westmont				23	6	Siemens, John R.

1958

F	School	SD	BD	Bye	W	L	Coach
1	Tennessee State	3		A	31	3	McLendon, John B., Jr.
2	Western Illinois	1		A	27	1	Morley, Leroy "Stix"
3	Texas Southern			A	29	5	Adams, Edward H.
4	Georgetown (KY)			A	22	6	Davis, Dr. Robert M.
8	Coe	2		A	20	7	Schulz, Robert
	Texas A&M: Commerce	7		A	23	7	Rogers, Bobby
	West Virginia Wesleyan	5		A	29	5	Ellis, Franklin C. "Hank"
	Youngstown State	8		A	24	6	Rosselli, Dominic L. "Dom"
16	Anderson (IN)			A	23	6	Macholtz, Robert W.
	Drury	6		A	15	7	Weiser, Albert L.
	Indiana (PA)			A	25	3	McKnight, Regis "Peck"
	Northern State (SD)			A	25	3	Wachs, Bob
	Pacific Lutheran	4		A	21	6	Harshman, Marvel K. "Marv"
	Point Loma Nazarene			A	27	4	Cartwright, Chalmer A.
	Western Montana			A	22	7	Straugh, William T.
	Wisconsin: Platteville			A	21	3	Barth, John
32	Arkansas Tech			A	17	4	Hindsman, Sam F., Jr.
	Assumption (MA)			A	16	4	Laska, Andrew
	Austin			A	17	9	Gass, Floyd
	Benedictine (KS)			A	20	6	Nolan, Ralph
	Eastern New Mexico			A	17	10	Garten, Alvin D.
	Georgia Southern			A	12	15	Scearce, J. B., Jr.
	Hastings			A	18	10	Bogue, Russell
	Lenoir-Rhyne			A	24	4	Wells, Bill
	Minnesota: Duluth			A	20	3	Olson, Norman H.
	Northern Michigan			A	15	3	Albeck, Charles Stanley "Stan"
	Oklahoma Baptist University			A	19	8	Bass, Robert E.
	Portland			A	18	11	Negratti, Dr. Albert E.

F	School	SD	BD	Bye	W	L	Coach
	Quincy (IL)		A		17	11	Goff, James "Pim"
	Rider		A		17	8	Leyden, Thomas A.
	Troy State: Troy		A		16	6	Archer, John A.
	Union (TN)		A		17	14	Russell, Jack L.
1959							
1	Tennessee State	1	A		32	1	McLendon, John B., Jr.
2	Pacific Lutheran	3	A		26	3	Lundgaard, Gene C.
3	Southwest Texas State	5	A		25	6	Jowers, Milton W.
4	Fort Hays State	15	A		23	4	Suran, Cade
8	Georgia Southern		A		19	12	Scearce, J. B., Jr.
	Illinois State	8	A		24	5	Collie, Dr. James E., Sr.
	Lenoir-Rhyne	16	A		24	6	Wells, Bill
	West Virginia Wesleyan	2	A		34	2	Ellis, Franklin C. "Hank"
16	Central Arkansas		A		24	4	Harton, Cliff
	Central Oklahoma	14	A		21	10	Smith, John
	Fairleigh Dickinson: Rutherford/Teaneck		A		17	11	Holub, Richard
	Grambling State	4	A		28	1	Hobdy, Frederick C.
	Indiana State	6	A		18	9	Klueh, Duane M.
	Minnesota: Duluth	10	A		22	4	Olson, Norman H.
	Westminster (PA)	12	A		19	8	Ridl, Charles G. "Buzz"
	Youngstown State	9	A		19	9	Rosselli, Dominic L. "Dom"
32	Austin		A		29	14	Gass, Floyd
	Central Connecticut State		A		19	4	Moore, Dr. William M.
	Christian Brothers		A		19	7	Raymonds, Henry C. "Hank"
	Culver-Stockton	13	A		19	7	Herington, William A.
	Kentucky State		A		14	11	Brown, James B.
	Linfield		A		18	11	Helser, Roy
	Morningside		A		14	9	Obye, Charles H. "Chuck"
	Nebraska Wesleyan		A		23	5	Peterson, Dr. Irvin L.
	Northern Michigan		A		16	8	Albeck, Charles Stanley "Stan"
	Northern State (SD)		A		19	3	Wachs, Bob
	Pikeville	7	A		28	7	Daniels, William
	Troy State: Troy		A		19	11	Archer, John A.
	Western Montana		A		17	8	Straugh, William T.
	Westminster (UT)		A		16	7	Richardson, Howard D.
	Whittier		A		20	7	Bonham, Aubrey R.
	Wisconsin: Platteville	11	A		18	4	Barth, John
1960							
1	Southwest Texas State	2	A		28	3	Jowers, Milton W.
2	Westminster (PA)	4	A		24	3	Ridl, Charles G. "Buzz"
3	Tennessee State	1	A		28	5	Hunter, Harold
4	William Jewell		A		23	10	Nelson, James A.
8	Grambling State	6	A		26	5	Hobdy, Frederick C.
	Hamline	5	A		23	4	Hutton, Joseph W., Sr.
	New Mexico Highlands		A		18	7	Gibson, Don
	Wofford	8	A		25	6	Alexander, Eugene F.

F	School	SD	BD	Bye	W	L	Coach
16	Arkansas: Monticello		A		18	8	Beard, Leslie "Shorty"
	Findlay		A		14	9	Houdeshell, Dr. James D.
	Oklahoma Baptist University		A		23	6	Bass, Robert E.
	Parsons		A		17	12	Nelson, Oscar B.
	Savannah State		A		27	4	Wright, Theodore A., Sr.
	Thomas More (KY)	11	A		19	13	Wolf, Charles
	West Virginia Wesleyan	16	A		23	6	Ellis, Franklin C. "Hank"
	Whittier	13	A		23	9	Bonham, Aubrey R.
32	Albertson		A		16	13	Brown, James A. "Babe"
	Central Connecticut State		A		16	5	Detrick, William
	Christian Brothers	10	A		21	7	Raymonds, Henry C. "Hank"
	Ferris State		A		15	6	Wink, James M.
	Maryland: Eastern Shore		A		22	6	Taylor, Nathaniel C. "Nay"
	Midwestern State (TX)		A		17	13	Vinzant, Dennis
	Nebraska Wesleyan	14	A		21	7	Peterson, Dr. Irvin L.
	North Alabama		A		14	11	Billingham, Edmond E.
	Oakland City (IN)		A		17	6	Disler, Delbert C.
	Pittsburg State	9	A		18	4	Lance, John F.
	Southern Illinois	3	A		20	9	Gallatin, Harry J.
	Stetson	7	A		16	13	Wilkes, Dr. Glenn N., Sr.
	Valley City State		A		17	5	Osmon, William E.
	Western Washington	12	A		19	7	Hubbard, Jack
	Willamette	15	A		24	4	Lewis, John R.
	Wisconsin: Oshkosh		A		15	8	Kitzman, Eric

1961

1	Grambling State	13	A		32	4	Hobdy, Frederick C.
2	Georgetown (KY)	3	A		26	9	Davis, Dr. Robert M.
3	Northern Michigan	2	A		24	3	Albeck, Charles Stanley "Stan"
4	Westminster (PA)	1	A		23	5	Ridl, Charles G. "Buzz"
8	Anderson (IN)	5	A		26	4	Macholtz, Robert W.
	Central Oklahoma	7	A		21	7	Smith, John
	Southwest Texas State	11	A		21	8	Jowers, Milton W.
	Winston-Salem State	9	A		26	5	Gaines, Clarence E. "Big House"
16	East Texas Baptist		A		16	7	Kennedy, R. C.
	Emporia State	12	A		17	6	Fish, Everett D. "Gus"
	Illinois Wesleyan	10	A		17	11	Horenberger, Jack
	Missouri Valley		A		18	9	Redford, Grover C.
	Newberry	16	A		23	8	Quinn, Thomas R.
	Peru State		A		17	7	McIntire, John "Jack"
	Redlands	14	A		26	7	Fulmer, Lee
	West Virginia State		A		13	12	Cardwell, Mark H.
32	Carson-Newman		A		26	7	Campbell, Richard
	Central Arkansas		A		20	6	Harton, Cliff
	Central Connecticut State		A		17	4	Detrick, William
	Franciscan	6	A		16	11	Smith, Wayne
	Gustavus Adolphus		A		15	11	Skoog, Myer U. "Whitey"
	Linfield		A		18	11	Helser, Roy
	Maryland: Eastern Shore	15	A		17	6	Taylor, Nathaniel C. "Nay"
	Northern State (SD)		A		16	7	Wachs, Bob

F	School	SD	BD	Bye	W	L	Coach
	Oglethorpe	4	A		20	4	Pinholster, Garland F.
	Saint Bernard		A		17	16	Richard, Charles W.
	Saint Norbert		A		13	13	Kosnar, Romie R.
	Savannah State		A				Wright, Theodore A., Sr.
	Simpson (IA)		A		13	12	Deaton, Les H.
	Western Montana		A		21	7	Straugh, William T.
	Westminster (UT)		A		15	8	Richardson, Howard D.
	Whitworth (WA)	8	A		19	10	Kamm, Richard

1962

F	School	SD	BD	Bye	W	L	Coach
1	Prairie View A&M	2	A		20	3	Moore, Dr. Leroy G., Jr.
2	Westminster (PA)	1	A		26	3	Ridl, Charles G. "Buzz"
3	Southeastern Oklahoma State	13	A		28	9	Sullivan, Bloomer
4	Western Illinois	7	A		21	11	Morley, Leroy "Stix"
8	California State: Fullerton	9	A		24	7	Omalev, Alex
	Carson-Newman		A		29	7	Campbell, Richard
	Ferris State	12	A		23	3	Wink, James M.
	Northern Arizona		A		17	9	Gregg, Herbert
16	Charleston (WV)	15	A		27	6	Moran, Garland
	Lewis & Clark (OR)		A		20	11	Goddard, Jim
	Peru State	14	A		23	5	McIntire, John "Jack"
	Saint Cloud State	10	A		22	4	Severson, Marlowe "Red"
	Savannah State	6	A		28	3	Wright, Theodore A., Sr.
	Texas: Pan American	5	A		25	5	Williams, Samuel
	William Jewell	16	A		21	7	Nelson, James A.
	Winston-Salem State	4	A		24	5	Gaines, Clarence E. "Big House"
32	Albertson		A		18	10	Carrow, Dr. Richard W.
	Ashland		A		21	4	Stoker, Bob
	Belmont Abbey		A		16	9	McGuire, Alfred J.
	Buena Vista	11	A		25	3	Ewalt, Merritt A.
	Central Connecticut State		A		14	9	Detrick, William
	Fort Hays State	8	A		19	4	Suran, Cade
	Georgetown (KY)	3	A		23	7	Davis, Dr. Robert M.
	Indiana State		A		19	9	Klueh, Duane M.
	Mayville State		A		17	17	Meyer, Alvin H.
	McMurry		A		24	4	Kimbrell, Hershell
	North Alabama		A		17	9	Billingham, Edmond E.
	Ouachita Baptist		A		15	14	Vining, Bill C., Sr.
	Pacific Lutheran		A		17	9	Lundgaard, Gene C.
	Pratt		A		19	5	Picariello, Saverio J. "Pic"
	Saint Norbert		A		14	10	Kosnar, Romie R.
	Stetson		A		16	12	Wilkes, Dr. Glenn N., Sr.

1963

F	School	SD	BD	Bye	W	L	Coach
1	Texas: Pan American	12	A		22	6	Williams, Samuel
2	Western Carolina	10	A		28	7	Gudger, James F.
3	Grambling State	1	A		30	3	Hobdy, Frederick C.
4	Fort Hays State	15	A		21	7	Suran, Cade
8	Carson-Newman	9	A		25	4	Campbell, Richard
	Lewis & Clark (OR)	14	A		23	6	Goddard, Jim
	Northern Michigan	13	A		19	8	Albeck, Charles Stanley "Stan"
	Rockhurst	6	A		27	4	Brehmer, Joseph "Buddy"

F	School	SD	BD	Bye	W	L	Coach
16	Alliance	11	A		19	6	Haluch, Thaddeus F.
	Athens State		A		23	9	Belcher, Oba E.
	Augsburg	2	A		23	2	Anderson, Ernest W.
	Central State (OH)		A		18	11	Lucas, William C.
	Indiana State	8	A		10	11	Klueh, Duane M.
	Miles		A		20	5	Wilkins, Arthur "Pete"
	Stetson		A		15	13	Wilkes, Dr. Glenn N., Sr.
	Transylvania		A		20	9	Newton, Charles M. "Cm"
32	Arkansas Tech		A		19	9	Hindsman, Sam F., Jr.
	Central Connecticut State	16	A		22	1	Detrick, William
	Eastern New Mexico		A		14	8	Garten, Alvin D.
	Howard Payne	5	A		22	7	Whitis, Glen
	Montana State: Billings		A		19	6	Harkins, Mike L.
	Oklahoma Baptist University	4	A		21	7	Bass, Robert E.
	Pacific Lutheran		A		18	10	Lundgaard, Gene C.
	Parsons		A		21	8	Nelson, Oscar B.
	Peru State		A		14	11	McIntire, John "Jack"
	Rider		A		20	8	Greenwood, Robert
	United States International		A		17	15	Kloppenburg, Bob
	West Virginia State		A		17	9	Cardwell, Mark H.
	Western Illinois	7	A		19	8	Morley, Leroy "Stix"
	Winston-Salem State	3	A		23	7	Gaines, Clarence E. "Big House"
	Wisconsin: Oshkosh		A		15	10	Young, Russ
	Yankton		A		18	7	Cowman, Douglas

1964

F	School	SD	BD	Bye	W	L	Coach
1	Rockhurst	10	A		27	6	Brehmer, Joseph "Buddy"
2	Texas: Pan American	1	A		28	6	Williams, Samuel
3	Carson-Newman	4	A		31	4	Campbell, Richard
4	Emporia State	6	A		22	9	Fish, Everett D. "Gus"
8	Central Oklahoma	5	A		23	4	Winters, Mark
	High Point	2	A		25	4	Quinn, Thomas R.
	Mansfield	8	A		20	4	Clark, William J.
	Saint Mary's (TX)		A		15	13	Messbarger, Ed
16	Georgetown (KY)	9	A		21	10	Davis, Dr. Robert M.
	Georgia Southern	15	A		20	11	Scearce, J. B., Jr.
	Grambling State	3	A		26	4	Hobdy, Frederick C.
	Huntingdon		A		25	6	Posey, Neal N.
	Indianapolis	7	A		26	3	Nicoson, Angus J.
	Kentucky State	11	A		18	7	McLendon, John B., Jr.
	Pacific Lutheran	12	A		20	7	Lundgaard, Gene C.
	Saint Cloud State	16	A		19	5	Severson, Marlowe "Red"
32	Albuquerque		A		17	8	
	Buena Vista		A		18	7	Ewalt, Merritt A.
	Cedarville		A		19	6	Callan, Dr. Donald
	Central Connecticut State	14	A		25	1	Detrick, William
	Charleston (WV)		A		20	11	Moran, Garland
	Dakota Wesleyan		A		21	3	Fosness, Gordon
	Ferris State		A		19	4	Wink, James M.
	Hastings	13	A		23	4	Farrell, Dr. Lynn

F	School	SD	BD	Bye	W	L	Coach
	Jersey City State		A		20	6	Gelston, Oliver S. "Ollie"
	Lewis & Clark (OR)		A		20	8	Sempert, Dean
	Miles		A		13	7	Wilkins, Arthur "Pete"
	Montana State: Billings		A		16	8	Harkins, Mike L.
	Ouachita Baptist		A		22	5	Vining, Bill C., Sr.
	Quincy (IL)		A		13	13	Ortwerth, John G.
	Redlands		A		19	11	Fulmer, Lee
	Wisconsin: La Crosse		A		20	2	De Voll, Clifton

1965

F	School	SD	BD	Bye	W	L	Coach
1	Central State (OH)	1	A		30	0	Lucas, William C.
2	Oklahoma Baptist University	15	A		25	7	Bass, Robert E.
3	Ouachita Baptist		A		27	10	Vining, Bill C., Sr.
4	Fairmont State		A		32	4	Retton, Joe
8	Augsburg	9	A		26	4	Anderson, Ernest W.
	Benedictine (KS)	5	A		26	3	Nolan, Ralph
	Southern: Baton Rouge	3	A		25	5	Mack, Richard
	Winston-Salem State	11	A		25	8	Gaines, Clarence E. "Big House"
16	Albany State (GA)		A		27	6	Rainey, Robert C.
	Alliance	13	A		18	8	Haluch, Thaddeus F.
	Hastings	8	A		24	4	Farrell, Dr. Lynn
	High Point	6	A		29	4	Quinn, Thomas R.
	Lewis (IL)		A		21	6	Gillespie, Gordon A.
	Midwestern State (TX)	16	A		28	6	Vinzant, Dennis
	Montana State: Billings		A		12	17	Harkins, Mike L.
	Southwestern Louisiana	2	A		20	10	Shipley, Beryl C.
32	Central Connecticut State		A		19	5	Detrick, William
	Central Washington	14	A		20	6	Nicholson, Dean
	Indiana Tech		A		24	3	Macy, Robert
	Jacksonville (FL)		A		15	11	Williams, Joe L.
	Lincoln (MO)	10	A		13	12	Staggers, Jonathan L.
	Linfield		A		21	7	Wilson, Ted
	Mansfield	7	A		16	6	Clark, William J.
	Maryland: Eastern Shore		A		16	6	Taylor, Nathaniel C. "Nay"
	Northern Michigan		A		19	6	Albeck, Charles Stanley "Stan"
	Saint Norbert		A		17	9	Kosnar, Romie R.
	Southern Colorado		A		21	7	Simmons, Harry H.
	Stephen F Austin State		A		19	7	Brown, Marshall
	Transylvania	12	A		21	10	Rose, Lee
	United States International		A		21	13	Kloppenburg, Bob
	Upper Iowa	4	A		21	5	Jack, Stanley
	Valley City State		A		15	7	Osmon, William E.

1966

F	School	SD	BD	Bye	W	L	Coach
1	Oklahoma Baptist University	11	A		26	7	Bass, Robert E.
2	Georgia Southern	4	A		26	6	Scearce, J. B., Jr.
3	Grambling State	3	A		28	6	Hobdy, Frederick C.
4	Norfolk State	9	A		26	6	Fears, Ernest D., Jr.

F	School	SD	BD	Bye	W	L	Coach
8	Carson-Newman	2	A		25	6	Hamilton, Larry
	Central State (OH)	1	A		24	6	Lucas, William C.
	Illinois Wesleyan	12	A		21	10	Bridges, Dennis L.
	Rockhurst	10	A		20	8	Brehmer, Joseph "Buddy"
16	Albuquerque	7	A		25	5	Smith, Ernie
	Athens State		A		20	10	Belcher, Oba E.
	Carroll (MT)		A		20	12	Askew, Presley
	Central Michigan	6	A		23	6	Kjolhede, Theodore
	Charleston (WV)	15	A		26	6	Meckfessel, Richard
	Lakeland (WI)		A		21	8	Woltzen, Duane A.
	Midwestern State (TX)	5	A		26	6	Vinzant, Dennis
	Southern Arkansas		A		23	5	Watson, W. T.
32	Bethune-Cookman	14	A		20	8	McClairen, Jack "Cy"
	Central Washington		A		21	8	Nicholson, Dean
	Dickinson State (ND)		A		21	4	Jessen, Laverne
	Edinboro		A		18	5	McDonald, James
	Guilford	13	A		18	8	Steele, Jerry
	Howard Payne		A		20	10	Whitis, Glen
	Indianapolis		A		17	8	Nicoson, Angus J.
	Linfield	16	A		23	6	Wilson, Ted
	Millersville		A		19	7	DeHart, Richard C.
	Monmouth (NJ)		A		26	4	Boylan, William T.
	New Haven		A		29	2	Ormrod, Donald R.
	Peru State		A		15	10	McIntire, John "Jack"
	Pittsburg State	8	A		18	10	Lambert, Paul M.
	Saint Thomas (MN)		A		24	4	Feely, Thomas J.
	United States International		A		21	9	Kloppenburg, Bob
	Upper Iowa		A		20	4	Jack, Stanley

1967

F	School	SD	BD	Bye	W	L	Coach
1	Benedictine (KS)	1	A		27	2	Nolan, Ralph
2	Oklahoma Baptist University	3	A		25	7	Bass, Robert E.
3	Central Washington	6	A		27	4	Nicholson, Dean
4	Charleston (WV)	4	A		28	5	Meckfessel, Richard
8	Eastern New Mexico	2	A		24	7	Miller, Harry E.
	Saint Mary's (TX)	8	A		22	9	Messbarger, Ed
	Southwestern Louisiana	7	A		20	11	Shipley, Beryl C.
	Tennessee Wesleyan	5	A		30	5	Farmer, Dwain
16	Central Michigan	10	A		22	3	Kjolhede, Throdore
	Chadron State		A		22	6	Payton, Mack
	Guilford	11	A		20	6	Steele, Jerry
	Midwestern State (TX)	12	A		21	11	Vinzant, Dennis
	Saint Thomas (MN)	15	A		22	7	Feely, Thomas J.
	Southern Arkansas	16	A		25	4	Watson, W. T.
	Valdosta State	14	A		27	8	Colson, Gary W.
	Westminster (PA)	9	A		22	6	Ridl, Charles G. "Buzz"
32	Albany State (GA)		A		25	6	Rainey, Robert C.
	Alcorn State		A		20	8	Hopkins, Robert M.
	Claremont McKenna		A		23	7	Ducey, Ted
	Dickinson State (ND)		A		21	5	Jessen, Laverne

F	School	SD	BD	Bye	W	L	Coach
	Findlay		A		15	10	Houdeshell, Dr. James D.
	Howard Payne		A		22	7	Whitis, Glen
	Indianapolis		A		18	10	Nicoson, Angus J.
	Linfield		A		20	10	Wilson, Ted
	Massachusetts: Boston		A		18	7	Loscutoff, James, Jr.
	Millersville	13	A		21	6	DeHart, Richard C.
	Montana State: Billings		A		14	18	Harkins, Mike L.
	New Jersey		A		18	9	Wissel, Dr. Harold R. "Hal"
	Quincy (IL)		A		17	14	Ortwerth, John G.
	Rockhurst		A		18	11	Rehm, J. Dolor
	Wartburg		A		19	7	Levick, Lewis J. "Buzz"
	Wisconsin: Oshkosh		A		17	6	White, Dr. Robert

1968

F	School	SD	BD	Bye	W	L	Coach
1	Central State (OH)	3	A		29	4	Lucas, William C.
2	Fairmont State		A		24	6	Retton, Joe
3	Wisconsin: Oshkosh		A		23	6	White, Dr. Robert
4	Westminster (PA)	6	A		22	8	Ridl, Charles G. "Buzz"
8	Central Washington	10	A		22	8	Nicholson, Dean
	Dickinson State (ND)		A		23	6	Limke, Denis
	Drury		A		24	5	Harding, Bill
	Eastern Michigan		A		18	9	Dutcher, James D.
16	Alcorn State	7	A		24	3	Hopkins, Robert M.
	Hanover	15	A		22	11	Collier, John R.
	Monmouth (NJ)	11	A		27	2	Boylan, William T.
	Montana State: Billings		A		20	9	Harkins, Mike L.
	New Haven		A		17	12	Ormrod, Donald R.
	Northeastern State (OK)	8	A		26	4	Dobbins, Dr. Jack
	Saint Cloud State	5	A		25	4	Severson, Marlowe "Red"
	Valdosta State	14	A		23	10	Colson, Gary W.
32	Albany State (GA)	13	A		32	8	Rainey, Robert C.
	Albuquerque		A		13	4	Smith, Ernie
	Athens State		A		16	14	Belcher, Oba E.
	Bishop		A		23	6	Jones, Dr. Emanuel M.
	Guilford	1	A		25	5	Steele, Jerry
	Henderson State		A		23	10	Dyer, Don
	Millersville		A		17	8	DeHart, Richard C.
	Millikin		A		21	4	Williams, Don E.
	Oklahoma Christian	4	A		18	4	Davis, Frank
	Point Loma Nazarene		A		26	5	Cartwright, Chalmer A.
	Southern Oregon		A		23	6	Holmes, William J.
	Stephen F Austin State	2	A		27	3	Brown, Marshall
	Union (KY)	9	A		27	6	Moore, Pete
	Washburn	12	A		18	8	Cafer, Glenn
	Wayne State (NE)	16	A		24	3	Svenningson, Allen
	Westmar		A		21	7	Knudtson, Paul O.

1969

F	School	SD	BD	Bye	W	L	Coach
1	Eastern New Mexico	12	A		24	7	Miller, Harry E.
2	Maryland: Eastern Shore		A		24	7	Robinson, Joe
3	Central Washington	15	A		24	9	Nicholson, Dean
4	Elizabeth City State	9	A		21	2	Vaughan, Robert L. "Bobby"

F	School	SD	BD	Bye	W	L	Coach
8	Henderson State	11	A		26	5	Dyer, Don
	High Point	4	A		28	3	Vaughn, Robert F. "Bobby"
	Monmouth (NJ)		A		24	6	Boylan, William T.
	Washburn	16	A		20	10	Cafer, Glenn
16	Eastern Michigan	5	A		20	9	Dutcher, James D.
	Fairmont State	1	A		26	2	Retton, Joe
	Gannon	6	A		23	6	Bayer, John D. "Denny"
	Howard Payne	2	A		27	4	Whitis, Glen
	North Carolina: Asheville		A		19	9	Hartman, Robert L.
	Southwestern Oklahoma State	8	A		23	8	Jobe, Jerry
	Whittier	13	A		23	5	Guevara, Ivan T.
	Wisconsin: Stout		A		21	4	Mintz, Dwain P.
32	Central State (OH)	3	A		21	7	Lucas, William C.
	Georgetown (KY)		A		24	11	Davis, Dr. Robert M.
	Grambling State	14	A		21	9	Hobdy, Frederick C.
	Indianapolis		A		20	10	Nicoson, Angus J.
	Jackson State (MS)		A		19	18	Covington, Paul E.
	Linfield	10	A		24	4	Wilson, Ted
	Millikin		A		16	9	Williams, Don E.
	Missouri: Saint Louis		A		19	7	Smith, Charles G. "Chuck"
	New Haven		A		20	3	Burns, Donald E.
	Saint John's (MN)		A		20	9	Smith, James E.
	Texas A&M: Corpus Christi		A		13	17	Smith, Ray
	Valdosta State		A		18	11	Melvin, James
	Wartburg	7	A		25	1	Levick, Lewis J. "Buzz"
	Wayne State (NE)		A		23	4	Gunther, David
	Western Montana		A		22	7	Keltz, Donald "Casey"
	Yankton		A		22	4	Holwerda, Jim

1970

F	School	SD	BD	Bye	W	L	Coach
1	Kentucky State	4	A		29	3	Mitchell, Lucias
2	Central Washington	3	A		31	2	Nicholson, Dean
3	Eastern New Mexico	6	A		26	6	Miller, Harry E.
4	Guilford	8	A		32	5	Steele, Jerry
8	Central State (OH)	5	A		24	5	Lucas, William C.
	Jackson State (MS)	7	A		22	4	Covington, Paul E.
	Maryland: Eastern Shore	2	A		23	1	Robinson, Joe
	Stephen F Austin State	1	A		29	1	Brown, Marshall
16	Arkansas Tech		A		22	10	Dopson, Dewaard
	Augusta State	16	A		23	2	Vanover, Marvin
	Charleston (WV)	15	A		25	8	Meckfessel, Richard
	Eastern Michigan	9	A		22	7	Dutcher, James D.
	Northeast Louisiana	10	A		16	9	Fant, Leonard "Lenny"
	Wartburg	14	A		26	3	Levick, Lewis J. "Buzz"
	Wiley		A		20	10	White, Calvin
	Wisconsin: Eau Claire	13	A		23	2	Anderson, Kenneth A.
32	Benedictine (KS)		A		17	9	Nolan, Ralph
	California (PA)		A		20	5	Witchery, Myles B.
	Campbell		A		24	5	Roberts, Danny
	Drury	12	A		22	7	Harding, Bill

F	School	SD	BD	Bye	W	L	Coach
	East Central (OK)		A		17	8	Anderson, Jerry
	Hanover	11	A		22	6	Collier, John R.
	Illinois Wesleyan		A		21	4	Bridges, Dennis L.
	Linfield		A		23	7	Wilson, Ted
	Monmouth (NJ)		A		17	11	Boylan, William T.
	Montana State: Billings		A		20	9	Harkins, Mike L.
	Northern State (SD)		A		20	7	Wachs, Bob
	Saint Thomas (MN)		A		26	3	Feely, Thomas J.
	South Carolina State		A		21	7	Jobe, Ben
	Wayne State (NE)		A		23	6	Gunther, David
	Western New England		A		14	6	Geldart, Eric, Jr.
	Whittier		A		21	8	Guevara, Ivan T.

1971

F	School	SD	BD	Bye	W	L	Coach
1	Kentucky State	1	A		31	2	Mitchell, Lucias
2	Eastern Michigan	6	A		22	11	Dutcher, James D.
3	Elizabeth City State	12	A		25	9	Vaughan, Robert L. "Bobby"
4	Fairmont State	2	A		32	3	Retton, Joe
8	Grambling State	9	A		16	8	Hobdy, Frederick C.
	North Carolina A&T	7	A		24	8	Irvin, Calvin C.
	Stephen F Austin State	4	A		20	6	Brown, Marshall
	Wisconsin: Eau Claire	3	A		27	2	Anderson, Kenneth A.
16	Central Washington	16	A		24	9	Nicholson, Dean
	Earlham	14	A		24	5	Harris, Delmer W.
	Great Falls		A		24	6	Dods, Ray
	Indiana (PA)	5	A		24	4	Sledzik, Herman L.
	Jackson State (MS)	10	A		23	7	Covington, Paul E.
	Northern State (SD)		A		22	8	Wachs, Bob
	Rowan		A		21	6	Collins, Jack
	Whittier	11	A		23	7	Guevara, Ivan T.
32	Augusta State	15	A		20	4	Vanover, Marvin
	Doane		A		18	10	Erickson, Robert
	Drury		A		18	9	Harding, Bill
	East Central (OK)	8	A		24	5	Anderson, Jerry
	Eastern New Mexico		A		19	10	Ball, "Buddy"
	Illinois Wesleyan	13	A		19	8	Bridges, Dennis L.
	Kansas Newman		A		16	5	Rineberg, Rick
	Lewis & Clark (OR)		A		19	10	Sempert, Dean
	Mansfield		A		18	8	Wilson, Edward W.
	North Carolina: Asheville		A		20	10	Hartman, Robert L.
	Northwestern (IA)		A		23	5	Jacobsen, Dr. Don
	Ohio Dominican		A		17	6	Nangle, Gene
	Saint Thomas (MN)		A		24	5	Feely, Thomas J.
	Southern Arkansas		A		23	5	Watson, W. T.
	Texas Southern		A		17	2	Gordon, Lavalius C.
	Western New England		A		19	7	Geldart, Eric, Jr.

1972

F	School	SD	BD	Bye	W	L	Coach
1	Kentucky State	3	A		28	5	Mitchell, Lucias
2	Wisconsin: Eau Claire	1	A		29	2	Anderson, Kenneth A.
3	Stephen F Austin State	2	A		25	2	Brown, Marshall
4	Gardner-Webb	4	A		20	3	Holbrook, Edwin "Eddie"

F	School	SD	BD	Bye	W	L	Coach
8	Augustana (IL)	9	A		25	4	Borcherding, James
	Saint Thomas (MN)	11	A		24	8	Feely, Thomas J.
	Western Washington	5	A		26	4	Randall, Charles R. "Chuck"
	Westmont	10	A		21	9	Byron, Thomas C.
16	Adams State		A		18	11	Lutz, Dr. Loren
	Belhaven	16	A		22	6	Rugg, Charles R.
	Glenville State	8	A		26	7	Lilly, Jesse
	Northeastern State (OK)	12	A		23	8	Dobbins, Dr. Jack
	Ouachita Baptist	6	A		26	5	Vining, Bill C., Sr.
	Pittsburg State	13	A		22	8	Johnson, Robert A.
	West Georgia	14	A		28	6	Kaiser, Roger A.
	Xavier (LA)	7	A		22	5	Hopkins, Robert M.
32	Bishop		A		23	11	Alexander, Charles
	Edinboro		A		17	9	McDonald, James
	Elizabeth City State		A		17	12	Vaughan, Robert L. "Bobby"
	Findlay		A		16	11	Houdeshell, Dr. James D.
	Hillsdale		A		25	8	Ekker, Ronald
	Maryland: Eastern Shore		A		14	6	Bates, John H.
	Minot State		A		22	3	Luther, Wes
	Missouri Southern State		A		22	9	Davis, Frank
	Montana State: Billings		A		19	6	Harkins, Mike L.
	Nebraska: Kearney		A		18	7	Hueser, Jerry
	Northwestern (IA)		A		21	7	Jacobsen, Dr. Don
	Quinnipiac		A		21	9	Kahn, Burt
	Rowan		A		16	9	Collins, Jack
	Tri-State		A		19	11	Peterman, Mark
	Western Carolina		A		20	16	Hartbarger, James
	Willamette	15	A		23	6	Boutin, Dr. James

1973

F	School	SD	BD	Bye	W	L	Coach
1	Guilford		A		29	5	Jensen, Jack
2	Maryland: Eastern Shore	8	A		26	5	Bates, John H.
3	Augustana (IL)	2	A		29	2	Borcherding, James
4	Slippery Rock		A		23	7	Hankinson, Mel
8	Oklahoma Baptist University		A		20	11	Wallace, H. Eugene
	Westmont		A		25	6	Mulder, Ronald
	Wisconsin: Green Bay	4	A		28	4	Buss, David R.
	Xavier (LA)		A		21	6	Hopkins, Robert M.
16	Defiance		A		25	5	Hohenberger, D. Marvin
	Ferris State		A		26	4	Wink, James M.
	Missouri Southern State		A		17	11	Davis, Frank
	Quinnipiac		A		22	7	Kahn, Burt
	Sam Houston State	1	A		28	1	Porter, Archie
	South Carolina State		A		17	14	Jobe, Ben
	Valdosta State		A		17	8	Dominey, James
	Winona State		A		23	4	Wothke, Les

F	School	SD	BD	Bye	W	L	Coach
32	Alcorn State	7	A		25	4	Whitney, David L., Sr. "Davey"
	Dallas Baptist		A		24	11	Sheiron, Steve
	Fairmont State	6	A		23	5	Retton, Joe
	George Fox		A		16	15	Miller, Lorin
	Grand Canyon		A		19	10	Lindsey, Ben
	Hanover		A		18	8	Collier, John R.
	Hastings		A		25	5	Farrell, Dr. Lynn
	Keene State		A		19	8	Theulen, Glenn H.
	Kentucky State	3	A		25	5	Mitchell, Lucias
	Marist		A		15	12	Petro, Ronald
	Marymount (KS)	5	A		25	3	Cochran, Ken
	Montana State: Billings		A		22	10	Harkins, Mike L.
	North Carolina: Pembroke		A		20	8	Gani, Lancey E.
	Ouachita Baptist		A		22	6	Vining, Bill C., Sr.
	South Dakota Tech		A		19	8	Riley, Michael L.
	Wartburg		A		21	8	Levick, Lewis J. "Buzz"

1974

F	School	SD	BD	Bye	W	L	Coach
1	West Georgia	14	A		29	4	Kaiser, Roger A.
2	Alcorn State	4	A		29	6	Whitney, David L., Sr. "Davey"
3	Kentucky State	2	A		28	5	Mitchell, Lucias
4	Saint Mary's (TX)	16	A		24	9	Messbarger, Ed
8	Augustana (IL)	8	A		25	4	Borcherding, James
	Hanover	5	A		29	4	Collier, John R.
	Indiana (PA)		A		21	8	Davis, Carl D.
	Midwestern State (TX)	7	A		30	7	Stockton, Dr. Gerald E.
16	Fairmont State	1	A		28	3	Retton, Joe
	Gardner-Webb	3	A		25	3	Holbrook, Edwin "Eddie"
	Grand Canyon	6	A		28	2	Lindsey, Ben
	Hastings	15	A		27	4	Farrell, Dr. Lynn
	Missouri Western State	13	A		25	6	Filbert, Gary
	Northwestern State (LA)	12	A		21	9	Hildebrand, Tynes
	Saint Thomas (MN)	10	A		26	4	Feely, Thomas J.
	Washburn		A		17	12	Cafer, Glenn
32	Azusa Pacific	11	A		28	5	Hamlow, Dr. Clifford
	Cameron		A		24	6	Miller, Raymond H. "Red"
	Central Arkansas		A		22	9	Nixon, Don
	Central Washington		A		17	10	Nicholson, Dean
	Defiance		A		22	6	Hohenberger, D. Marvin
	Erskine		A		25	6	Myers, W. C. "Red"
	Grand Valley State		A		23	6	Villemure, Thomas
	Huron		A		21	7	Swanhorst, Robert
	Keene State		A		16	9	Theulen, Glenn H.
	Millersville		A		21	5	DeHart, Richard C.
	Monmouth (NJ)		A		19	9	Boylan, William T.
	Oregon Tech		A		24	5	Miles, Daniel J.
	Roger Williams		A		20	4	Drennan, Thomas A.
	Virginia State		A		22	8	Deane, Harold A., Sr.
	Wartburg		A		23	5	Levick, Lewis J. "Buzz"
	Wisconsin: Eau Claire	9	A		24	5	Anderson, Kenneth A.

F	School	SD	BD	Bye	W	L	Coach
1975							
1	Grand Canyon	5	A		30	3	Lindsey, Ben
2	Midwestern State (TX)	7	A		31	6	Stockton, Dr. Gerald E.
3	Alcorn State	8	A		25	10	Whitney, David L., Sr. "Davey"
4	Saint Mary's (TX)	3	A		24	7	Messbarger, Ed
8	Fairmont State	2	A		30	16	Retton, Joe
	Malone		A		27	6	Bowerman, Jay
	Winston-Salem State	11	A		23	7	Gaines, Clarence E. "Big House"
	Wisconsin: Parkside	13	A		24	9	Stephens, Steve
16	Central Washington	6	A		21	6	Nicholson, Dean
	Edinboro	9	A		17	3	McDonald, James
	Illinois Wesleyan	12	A		23	7	Bridges, Dennis L.
	Marymount (KS)	4	A		29	4	Cochran, Ken
	Millersville		A		17	10	DeHart, Richard C.
	Norfolk State	10	A		23	5	Christian, Charles O.
	Tri-State	16	A		25	7	Peterman, Mark
	Winona State	15	A		22	7	Wothke, Les
32	Bryant		A		21	8	Folliard, Thomas J.
	Central Arkansas		A		19	11	Nixon, Don
	East Central (OK)		A		16	11	Anderson, Jerry
	Ferris State	14	A		22	5	Wink, James M.
	Husson		A		23	5	MacGregor, Dr. D. Bruce
	Kentucky State	1	A		26	3	Mitchell, Lucias
	Monmouth (NJ)		A		22	7	Boylan, William T.
	Montana State: Billings		A		20	8	Harkins, Mike L.
	Montevallo		A		23	9	Jones, Bill L.
	Morningside		A		17	12	Callahan, Dan
	Nebraska: Kearney		A		21	7	Hueser, Jerry
	Newberry		A		24	9	Gordon, Nield
	Palm Beach Atlantic		A		22	4	Perides, George L.
	United States International		A		20	9	Kloppenburg, Bob
	Willamette		A		24	5	Boutin, Dr. James
	William Jewell		A		22	9	Hickman, John A.
1976							
1	Coppin State	9	A		39	2	Bates, John H.
2	Henderson State	6	A		28	3	Dyer, Don
3	Marymount (KS)	4	A		31	3	Cochran, Ken
4	Lincoln Memorial		A		28	9	Jackson, Wilford "Jack"
8	Alabama: Huntsville		A		26	9	Willis, A. L. "Kayo"
	Lake Superior State		A		24	4	Douma, Edward
	Newberry	15	A		30	5	Gordon, Nield
	Texas Southern	16	A		23	10	Moreland, Robert E.
16	California Baptist	10	A		28	4	Evans, Floyd C.
	Central Washington	13	A		23	7	Nicholson, Dean
	Doane		A		21	9	Erickson, Robert
	Edinboro	14	A		24	5	Conti, Guy
	Fairmont State	1	A		28	1	Retton, Joe
	Grand Canyon	2	A		27	3	Lindsey, Ben
	Illinois Wesleyan	11	A		23	7	Bridges, Dennis L.
	Wisconsin: Parkside	8	A		24	7	Stephens, Steve

F	School	SD	BD	Bye	W	L	Coach
32	Alcorn State	3	A		27	4	Whitney, David L., Sr. "Davey"
	Briar Cliff		A		19	8	Nacke, Ray
	Central State (OH)		A		20	10	Wims, Dr. Lu D.
	Dowling		A		31	4	Berg, Richard C.
	Franklin (IN)		A		16	10	Thompson, Ed
	Guilford	7	A		21	6	Jensen, Jack
	Gustavus Adolphus		A		19	10	Skoog, Myer U. "Whitey"
	Howard Payne		A		22	12	Derryberry, Bob
	Husson		A		25	1	MacGregor, Dr. D. Bruce
	Linfield		A		20	9	Wilson, Ted
	Montana State: Billings		A		20	10	Harkins, Mike L.
	Norfolk State	12	A		23	7	Christian, Charles O.
	Pikeville	5	A		26	5	Martin, Wayne M.
	Southern Nazarene		A		26	10	Poteet, Jim
	Southwest Baptist		A		19	10	Garrett, Howard V.
	West Florida		A		19	12	Beck, Marvin G.

1977

F	School	SD	BD	Bye	W	L	Coach
1	Texas Southern	5	A		31	5	Moreland, Robert E.
2	Campbell		A		23	10	Roberts, Danny
3	Henderson State	7	A		29	4	Dyer, Don
4	Grand Valley State	8	A		30	4	Villemure, Thomas
8	Alcorn State	14	A		26	9	Whitney, David L., Sr. "Davey"
	Central Washington	16	A		24	8	Nicholson, Dean
	Illinois Wesleyan	2	A		25	6	Bridges, Dennis L.
	Texas A&M: Commerce	13	A		25	9	Gudger, James F.
16	Alabama: Huntsville		A		19	10	Willis, A. L. "Kayo"
	Clarion	9	A		27	3	DeGregorio, Joseph
	Dowling		A		29	7	Berg, Richard C.
	Emporia State		A		24	6	Slaymaker, Dr. Ron
	Hawaii: Hilo	15	A		21	5	Yagi, James "Jimmy"
	Newberry	1	A		36	1	Gordon, Nield
	Southwestern Oklahoma State	11	A		24	5	Hauser, George
	Wisconsin: Parkside	12	A		20	10	Stephens, Steve
32	Augsburg		A		23	7	Inniger, Ervin L., Jr.
	Briar Cliff		A		19	9	Nacke, Ray
	Central State (OH)		A		18	11	Wims, Dr. Lu D.
	Fairmont State	4	A		21	5	Retton, Joe
	Hastings		A		25	5	Farrell, Dr. Lynn
	Keene State		A		22	7	Theulen, Glenn H.
	Kentucky State	3	A		27	3	Oliver, James V.
	Lincoln Memorial	6	A		30	5	Jackson, Wilford "Jack"
	Missouri: Kansas City		A		21	9	Corwin, Darrell
	Mount Marty		A		23	9	Evans, Frank
	Paine		A		18	13	Tulberi, Ernest
	Saint Augustine's		A		24	8	Heartley, Harvey D.
	Southern Utah		A		21	7	Jack, Stanley
	Spring Garden		A		16	10	Burke, Les
	Tri-State		A		28	5	Peterman, Mark
	Whittier	10	A		24	5	Jacobs, Dave

F	School	SD	BD	Bye	W	L	Coach
1978							
1	Grand Canyon	2	A		30	3	Lindsey, Ben
2	Nebraska: Kearney		A		19	8	Hueser, Jerry
3	Quincy (IL)	5	A		30	5	Hanks, Sherrill
4	Texas A&M: Commerce	6	A		26	10	Gudger, James F.
8	Central State (OH)		A		19	11	Wims, Dr. Lu D.
	Drury	3	L		29	4	Matthews, Dr. Edsel
	Missouri Southern State	13	A		27	9	Williams, "Chuck"
	Winston-Salem State	1	A		28	4	Gaines, Clarence E. "Big House"
16	Birmingham-Southern	11	A		29	5	Walcavich, Greg
	Briar Cliff	16	A		25	4	Nacke, Ray
	Erskine		A		21	12	Myers, W. C. "Red"
	Hawaii: Hilo	15	A		25	5	Yagi, James "Jimmy"
	Ouachita Baptist	4	A		25	5	Vining, Bill C., Sr.
	Saint John's (MN)		A		23	8	Smith, James E.
	Westmont		A		23	9	Kammerer, Glen "Chet"
	Wisconsin: Parkside	9	A		19	11	Stephens, Steve
32	Central Washington	14	A		21	8	Nicholson, Dean
	Cumberland (KY)		A		27	10	Trivette, Ken
	Dowling		A		21	6	Berg, Richard C.
	Fairmont State	7	A		27	6	Retton, Joe
	Franklin (IN)		A		19	6	Lovell, Robert
	Hampton	10	A		24	7	Ford, Henry "Hank"
	Kansas Newman		A		21	11	Skinner, David N.
	Lake Superior State	12	A		23	4	Douma, Edward
	Lemoyne-Owen		A		20	10	Johnson, Jerry C.
	Mercyhurst	8	A		24	2	Fox, Richard A.
	Midwestern State (TX)		A		21	13	Stockton, Dr. Gerald E.
	Mississippi Valley State		A		15	20	Gaines, William "Pop"
	Montana State: Billings		A		22	10	Chidester, Ted H.
	Southern Maine		A		21	7	Bouchard, Joey A.
	Southern Nazarene		A		24	12	Poteet, Jim
	Southern Tech (GA)		A		26	6	Florian, Fran
1979							
1	Drury	3	A		33	2	Kirksey, Jerry L.
2	Henderson State	5	A		29	4	Riese, Bobby
3	Southwest Texas State	8	A		29	7	Wall, Daniel P.
4	Midwestern State (TX)		A		24	17	Stockton, Dr. Gerald E.
8	Briar Cliff	6	A		28	3	Nacke, Ray
	Cameron	1	A		34	2	Nichols, Lonnie
	Marymount (KS)		A		26	6	Cochran, Ken
	Quincy (IL)		A		23	10	Hanks, Sherrill
16	Central Washington	7	A		25	6	Nicholson, Dean
	High Point	11	A		20	5	Steele, Jerry
	Nebraska: Kearney	14	A		25	8	Hueser, Jerry
	Norfolk State	15	A		23	8	Mitchell, Lucias
	Saint John's (MN)	9	A		27	3	Smith, James E.
	Southern Tech (GA)	13	A		24	4	Florian, Fran
	Tri-State	16	L		31	4	Peterman, Mark
	Wisconsin: Eau Claire	12	A		24	7	Anderson, Kenneth A.

F	School	SD	BD	Bye	W	L	Coach
32	Birmingham-Southern	4	A		29	4	Walcavich, Greg
	California State:		A		21	9	Yanai, David
	Dominguez Hills						
	Central State (OH)		A		22	7	Wims, Dr. Lu D.
	Dakota Wesleyan		A		26	3	Fosness, Gordon
	Grand Canyon	2	A		24	4	Lindsey, Ben
	Grand Valley State	10	A		22	4	Villemure, Thomas
	Hanover		A		22	5	Collier, John R.
	Kentucky State		A		18	11	Theard, Floyd M.
	Lemoyne-Owen		A		22	12	Johnson, Jerry C.
	Louisiana		A		22	6	Allgood, Billy
	Oregon Tech		A		23	5	Miles, Daniel J.
	Point Park		A		26	5	Conboy, Gerald "Jerry"
	Saint John Fisher		A		21	7	Wanzer, Robert F. "Bobby"
	Southern Maine		A		21	7	Bouchard, Joey A.
	Southern Wesleyan		A		25	10	Drennon, Craig
	West Virginia Wesleyan		A		24	8	Hess, Gary

1980

F	School	SD	BD	Bye	W	L	Coach
1	Cameron	3	A		28	3	Nichols, Lonnie
2	Alabama State	1	A		32	2	Oliver, James V.
3	Huron		A		32	4	Carrier, Bruce
4	Wisconsin: Eau Claire	2	A		30	4	Anderson, Kenneth A.
8	Central Arkansas		A		19	14	Dyer, Don
	Central Washington	7	A		27	6	Nicholson, Dean
	Clarion		A		23	9	DeGregorio, Joseph
	Lemoyne-Owen		A		26	8	Johnson, Jerry C.
16	Abilene Christian	6	A		24	4	Tate, Willard N.
	Biola	10	A		26	4	Lyon, Howard
	Franklin (IN)		A		22	6	Lovell, Robert
	Loras		A		23	12	Mullen, Robert
	Marymount (KS)	15	A		19	14	Cochran, Ken
	Rockhurst	9	A		20	5	Reynolds, Jerry
	Saint Augustine's	14	A		24	7	Heartley, Harvey D.
	South Carolina: Aiken		A		21	18	Wall, Larry
32	Augsburg	8	L		25	1	Johnson, Rees
	Cumberland (KY)		A		25	10	Vernon, Randy
	Defiance		A		23	8	Hohenberger, D. Marvin
	Dillard		A		19	12	Brown, John D.
	Dowling		A		24	5	Berg, Richard C.
	Fairmont State	11	A		23	4	Retton, Joe
	Franklin Pierce		A		29	2	Kirsh, Bruce
	Grand Canyon	4	A		21	4	Lindsey, Ben
	Hampton	16	A		21	10	Ford, Henry "Hank"
	Hawaii: Hilo	13	L		26	6	Yagi, James "Jimmy"
	Illinois Wesleyan		A		17	11	Bridges, Dennis L.
	Moorhead State (MN)		A		21	9	Schellhase, David G., Jr.
	Nebraska: Kearney	5	A		24	3	Hueser, Jerry
	Paul Quinn	12	A		32	10	Boyd, Wesley
	Saginaw Valley State		A		24	7	Pratt, Dr. Robert L.
	Southern Tech (GA)		A		25	10	Perides, George L.

F	School	SD	BD	Bye	W	L	Coach
1981							
1	Southern Nazarene	6	A		36	6	Gresham, Dr. Loren
2	Alabama: Huntsville	5	A		30	7	Willis, A. L. "Kayo"
3	Wisconsin: Eau Claire	2	A		29	5	Anderson, Kenneth A.
4	Hillsdale	16	A		28	7	Morse, Bill
8	Augsburg	3	A		29	2	Johnson, Rees
	Hanover		A		26	8	Collier, John R.
	Huron	7	A		30	4	Carrier, Bruce
	Midwestern State (TX)		A		25	18	Stockton, Dr. Gerald E.
16	Biola	10	A		25	7	Lyon, Howard
	Briar Cliff	1	A		23	2	Nacke, Ray
	Lincoln Memorial		A		24	8	Kilby, L. J.
	Nebraska: Kearney	14	A		25	7	Hueser, Jerry
	South Carolina: Spartanburg		A		22	12	Waters, Jerry O.
	Southern Tech (GA)	11	A		28	5	Perides, George L.
	Waynesburg		A		24	6	Marisa, Rudy
	Western Oregon	12	L		22	3	Boutin, Dr. James
32	Campbellsville		A		21	8	Cunningham, Lou
	Cedarville	15	A		25	4	Callan, Dr. Donald
	Central Washington		A		21	12	Nicholson, Dean
	Chicago State		A		23	9	Hallberg, Robert J.
	Dominican (NY)		A		17	14	Kelly, Steve
	Drury		A		19	12	Walker, Marvin
	Fairmont State		A		26	5	Retton, Joe
	Fort Hays State	4	A		30	4	Rosado, Joe
	Franklin Pierce		A		31	4	Kirsh, Bruce
	Gardner-Webb		A		25	11	Wiles, Jim R.
	Henderson State	13	A		25	8	Kirksey, Jerry L.
	Norfolk State		A		19	10	Mitchell, Lucias
	Rockhurst	8	L		22	3	Reynolds, Jerry
	Saint Mary's (TX)		A		19	9	Meyer, Herbert "Buddy"
	Western New Mexico	9	A		26	4	Drangmeister, Richard
	Xavier (LA)		A		21	8	Alexander, Denny
1982							
1	South Carolina: Spartanburg	14	A		27	5	Waters, Jerry O.
2	Biola	1	A		39	1	Lyon, Howard
3	Hampton		A		28	8	Ford, Henry "Hank"
4	Nebraska: Kearney		A		26	10	Hueser, Jerry
8	Henderson State	10	A		23	6	Kirksey, Jerry L.
	Saginaw Valley State		A		24	8	Pratt, Dr. Robert L.
	Western Oregon	4	A		25	1	Boutin, Dr. James
	Wisconsin: Eau Claire	6	A		26	6	Anderson, Kenneth A.
16	Briar Cliff		A		21	10	Nacke, Ray
	Central Washington	15	A		22	7	Nicholson, Dean
	Hanover	12	A		26	6	Collier, John R.
	Moorhead State (MN)		A		24	7	Schellhase, David G., Jr.

F	School	SD	BD	Bye	W	L	Coach
	Quincy (IL)	16	A		25	12	Hanks, Sherrill
	Saint Mary's (TX)		A		19	9	Meyer, Herbert "Buddy"
	Saint Thomas Aquinas	11	A		34	4	Possinger, David F.
	Southern Tech (GA)	9	A		27	5	Perides, George L.
32	Birmingham-Southern		A		18	15	Walcavich, Greg
	Catawba	7	A		26	7	Moir, Sam A.
	Cedarville		A		17	11	Callan, Dr. Donald
	Cumberland (KY)		A		20	16	Vernon, Randy
	Franklin Pierce		A		27	8	Kirsh, Bruce
	Lipscomb	5	A		33	4	Meyer, Dr. Don W.
	Mary		A		30	3	Bortke, Al
	Missouri Western State		A		25	7	Filbert, Gary
	Oklahoma Christian	2	A		33	3	Jobe, Jerry
	Paul Quinn		A		25	13	Boyd, Wesley
	Stephen F Austin State	8	L		24	6	Miller, Harry E.
	Washburn		A		22	9	Chipman, Bob
	West Virginia Tech		A		24	10	Sutherland, Tom
	Western New Mexico	13	A		20	5	Drangmeister, Richard
	Westminster (PA)		A		21	7	Galbreath, Dr. C. Ronald
	Xavier (LA)	3	A		29	2	Alexander, Denny

1983

F	School	SD	BD	Bye	W	L	Coach
1	Charleston (SC)	12	A		24	5	Kresse, John
2	West Virginia Wesleyan	14	L		32	6	Stewart, Bruce
3	Fort Hays State	10	A		32	4	Morse, Bill
4	Chaminade	1	A		27	3	Lopes, Merv
8	Carson-Newman	11	A		31	5	Jones, Dr. Chris
	Liberty		A		23	9	Meyer, Jeff
	Loras	15	A		25	5	Smith, Doug
	Santa Fe (NM)		A		25	9	Roybal, Leonard "Lennie"
16	Chicago State	3	A		23	4	Hallberg, Robert J.
	Oklahoma Panhandle State	5	A		31	4	Layton, Terry
	Saginaw Valley State	16	A		24	8	Pratt, Dr. Robert L.
	Saint Mary's (TX)	6	A		26	7	Meyer, Herbert "Buddy"
	Saint Thomas Aquinas	7	A		35	3	Possinger, David F.
	Salem-Teikyo		A		22	9	Barnhart, Ray
	Texas Wesleyan	13	A		22	6	Newman, Tommy
	Wisconsin: Stevens Point	9	A		26	4	Bennett, Richard
32	Alabama: Huntsville		A		25	11	Willis, A. L. "Kayo"
	Catawba	8	A		29	4	Moir, Sam A.
	Cumberland (KY)	4	A		33	3	Vernon, Randy
	Drury		A		22	12	Walker, Marvin
	Husson		A		22	7	MacGregor, Dr. D. Bruce
	Lincoln (PA)		A		11	16	Jones, Melvin L.
	Nebraska: Kearney		A		25	11	Hueser, Jerry
	North Georgia		A		23	9	Ensley, William E.
	Northern State (SD)		A		22	10	Wachs, Bob
	Point Loma Nazarene		A		22	13	Foster, Ben
	Point Park		A		20	12	Conboy, Gerald "Jerry"
	Saint John's (MN)		A		18	12	Smith, James E.

F	School	SD	BD	Bye	W	L	Coach
	Southern Arkansas		A		18	11	Ingram, Monroe
	Tri-State		A		26	7	Peterman, Mark
	Walsh	2	A		34	1	Huggins, Robert
	William Carey (MS)		A		20	9	Knight, Steve
1984							
1	Fort Hays State	2	A		26	2	Morse, Bill
2	Wisconsin: Stevens Point	9	A		28	4	Bennett, Richard
3	Chicago State	3	A		24	4	Hallberg, Robert J.
4	Westmont	4	A		25	2	Kammerer, Glen "Chet"
8	Chaminade	6	A		23	6	Lopes, Merv
	Saint Thomas Aquinas	5	A		38	3	Possinger, David F.
	Waynesburg		A		25	6	Marisa, Rudy
	West Virginia Wesleyan	1	A		31	3	Stewart, Bruce
16	Central Washington		A		23	10	Nicholson, Dean
	Cumberland (KY)	11	A		27	4	Vernon, Randy
	Lyon		A		22	11	Garner, Terry
	Nebraska: Kearney		A		28	9	Hueser, Jerry
	North Carolina: Pembroke		A		26	7	Lee, Billy
	Saint Mary's (TX)	10	A		25	8	Meyer, Herbert "Buddy"
	Southern Wesleyan		A		22	10	Shaver, Tom
	William Carey (MS)	16	A		26	7	Knight, Steve
32	Albertson		A		22	7	Holly, Martin W. "Marty"
	Birmingham-Southern	15	A		23	8	Dean, Joe
	Cabrini		A		22	12	Dzik, John L.
	Carson-Newman	12	A		31	8	Jones, Dr. Chris
	Denver	7	A		28	4	Theard, Floyd
	Franklin Pierce		A		27	10	Kirsh, Bruce
	Hillsdale		A		23	9	Halstead, Ron
	Marycrest International	13	A		31	7	O'Neill, Kevin
	Midwestern State (TX)		A		25	16	Stockton, Dr. Gerald E.
	Missouri Western State		A		21	10	Shear, Lawrence "Skip"
	North Georgia		A		17	15	Ensley, William E.
	Northern State (SD)	14	A		28	4	Wachs, Bob
	Phillips (OK)		A		25	13	Wilson, Robert H.
	Saint John's (MN)		A		20	8	Smith, James E.
	Taylor		A		21	10	Patterson, Paul
	Walsh	8	A		26	3	Peters, Dan
1985							
1	Fort Hays State	1	A		35	3	Morse, Bill
2	Wayland Baptist	11	A		30	10	Adams, Mark L.
3	Marycrest International	7	A		34	6	Merchant, Jim
4	Central Washington		A		25	11	Nicholson, Dean
8	Athens State		A		20	7	Murrell, Harold
	Charleston (SC)	3	A		25	3	Kresse, John
	Drury		A		26	10	Walker, Marvin
	West Virginia Wesleyan	4	A		28	4	Cameron, Rich

F	School	SD	BD	Bye	W	L	Coach
16	Georgia Southwestern	8	A		28	5	Duhon, Glenn D.
	Hillsdale		A		20	13	Halstead, Ron
	Lipscomb		A		25	9	Meyer, Dr. Don W.
	Minnesota: Duluth		A		23	8	Race, Dale M.
	Pfeiffer		A		23	9	Lentz, John
	Rio Grande	13	A		31	5	Lawhorn, John
	Southeastern Oklahoma State	14	A		24	8	Hedden, Jack E.
	Wisconsin: Stevens Point	2	A		25	5	Bennett, Richard
32	Albertson	9	A		20	3	Holly, Martin W. "Marty"
	Berea		A		20	10	Wierwille, Roland R.
	Biola	5	A		29	4	Lyon, Howard
	Cabrini		A		22	12	Dzik, John L.
	Castleton State		A		23	7	Van Gundy, Stan A.
	Hawaii Pacific	12	A		27	11	Smith, Paul
	Hendrix		A		21	11	Garrison, Cliff
	Indiana-Purdue: Indianapolis		A		21	15	Lovell, Robert
	Mesa State		A		23	8	Schakel, Doug
	Nebraska: Kearney		A		21	11	Hueser, Jerry
	Quincy (IL)		A		15	17	Hanks, Sherrill
	Rocky Mountain		A		23	10	Adams, Mark E. "Bucky"
	Saint Thomas Aquinas	6	A		36	6	Possinger, David F.
	Southwestern (TX)	10	A		24	9	Peak, Paul
	Waynesburg	15	A		23	5	Marisa, Rudy
	William Carey (MS)	16	A		20	7	Knight, Steve

1986

F	School	SD	BD	Bye	W	L	Coach
1	Lipscomb	11	A		35	4	Meyer, Dr. Don W.
2	Arkansas: Monticello		A		26	10	Sharpe, Gary A.
3	Southeastern Oklahoma State	4	A		30	4	Hedden, Jack E.
4	Saint Thomas Aquinas	7	A		37	6	Possinger, David F.
8	Central Washington	14	A		27	6	Nicholson, Dean
	Charleston (SC)	16	A		26	9	Kresse, John
	Charleston (WV)	2	A		30	5	Williams, "Tex"
	Southwestern (TX)		A		20	12	Peak, Paul
16	Barton		A		25	10	Edwards, Gary
	Birmingham-Southern	3	A		28	4	Dean, Joe
	Cumberland (KY)	1	A		32	3	Vernon, Randy
	Drury	15	A		25	10	Walker, Marvin
	Emporia State	6	A		31	5	Slaymaker, Dr. Ron
	Huron	13	A		28	3	Paulsen, Fred
	Wayland Baptist	9	A		23	5	Adams, Mark L.
	Wisconsin: Eau Claire	12	A		24	7	Anderson, Kenneth A.
32	Albertson		A		23	7	Holly, Martin W. "Marty"
	Briar Cliff	8	A		23	4	Nacke, Ray
	Brigham Young: Hawaii		A		17	13	Chidester, Ted H.
	Cabrini		A		24	7	Dzik, John L.

F	School	SD	BD	Bye	W	L	Coach
	Findlay		A		25	6	Niekamp, Ron
	Franklin Pierce		A		24	7	Kirsh, Bruce
	Minnesota: Duluth		A		23	8	Race, Dale M.
	Nebraska: Kearney		A		17	15	Hueser, Jerry
	Quincy (IL)		A		21	11	Hanks, Sherrill
	Saginaw Valley State		A		20	11	Pratt, Dr. Robert L.
	Southern Colorado		A		20	12	Drangmeister, Richard
	Taylor		A		26	7	Patterson, Paul
	Waynesburg	10	A		24	1	Marisa, Rudy
	Webber	5	A		25	1	Creola, Nick J.
	Westmont		A		23	8	Kammerer, Glen "Chet"
	William Carey (MS)		A		20	15	Knight, Steve

1987

F	School	SD	BD	Bye	W	L	Coach
1	Washburn	6	A		35	4	Chipman, Bob
2	West Virginia State	4	A		31	4	Carse, Craig
3	Central Washington	10	A		32	9	Nicholson, Dean
4	Georgetown (KY)	16	A		30	8	Reid, James B.
8	Auburn: Montgomery	14	A		25	8	Chapman, Larry F.
	Hawaii: Hilo	15	A		25	10	Wilson, Robert H.
	Trevecca Nazarene	9	A		30	4	Wilson, Frank
	Waynesburg		A		23	6	Marisa, Rudy
16	Charleston (SC)	2	A		25	1	Kresse, John
	Oklahoma City	1	A		34	1	Lemons, A. E. "Abe"
	Oregon Tech	13	A		33	5	Miles, Daniel J.
	Saint Joseph's (ME)		A		26	6	Simonds, Rick
	Saint Mary's (TX)	8	A		27	5	Meyer, Herbert "Buddy"
	Saint Thomas Aquinas	7	A		32	5	Possinger, David F.
	Taylor		A		25	8	Patterson, Paul
	Valley City State		A		21	6	Parker, Bob
32	Barton		A		25	9	Edwards, Gary
	Biola	3	A		29	2	Lyon, Howard
	Cabrini		A		24	8	Dzik, John L.
	Eureka		A		26	3	Darnall, David
	Harding		A		18	14	Bucy, Jess
	Minnesota: Duluth		A		24	7	Race, Dale M.
	Missouri Southern State		A		20	13	Williams, "Chuck"
	Nebraska: Kearney	12	A		26	8	Hueser, Jerry
	Northwestern (IA)		A		27	5	Douma, Les
	Northwood (MI)		A		16	15	Miller, Pat
	Rio Grande		A		28	8	Lawhorn, John
	Southern Tech (GA)	11	A		27	7	Perides, George L.
	Wayland Baptist		A		22	11	Adams, Mark L.
	Western State (CO)		A		19	13	Gibbons, Terry
	William Carey (MS)		A		23	13	Knight, Steve
	Wisconsin: Eau Claire	5	A		26	4	Anderson, Kenneth A.

F	School	SD	BD	Bye	W	L	Coach
1988							
1	Grand Canyon	11	A		37	6	Westphal, Paul D.
2	Auburn: Montgomery	4	A		26	2	Chapman, Larry F.
3	Charleston (SC)	9	A		30	5	Kresse, John
4	Waynesburg	2	A		32	3	Marisa, Rudy
8	Albertson	14	A		28	6	Holly, Martin W. "Marty"
	Dordt		A		25	5	Vander Berg, Rick
	Saint Thomas Aquinas	1	A		39	2	Possinger, David F.
	William Jewell	5	A		32	2	Holley, Larry R.
16	Fort Hays State	6	A		28	5	Morse, Bill
	Grace (IN)		A		31	5	Kessler, James C.
	Lipscomb	3	A		33	3	Meyer, Dr. Don W.
	McKendree	7	A		35	1	Statham, Harry M.
	Minnesota: Duluth	15	A		25	6	Race, Dale M.
	Ozarks (AR)		A		25	9	Allen, Jimmy W.
	Western Washington	12	A		28	8	Jackson, Brad
	Wisconsin: Eau Claire	16	A		23	8	Anderson, Kenneth A.
32	Belmont Abbey		A		22	9	Eastman, Kevin
	Defiance		A		24	7	Hohenberger, D. Marvin
	East Texas Baptist		A		19	13	Webb, Dr. Jimmy Ray
	Eastern (PA)		A		30	6	Ware, Nate
	Franklin Pierce		A		16	15	Kirsh, Bruce
	Georgia College		A		25	9	Hodges, Bill
	Hastings		A		27	6	Trader, Mike
	Hawaii Pacific		A		19	13	Smith, Paul
	Hillsdale		A		13	18	Halstead, Ron
	Huron		A		24	8	Paulsen, Fred
	Mobile	10	A		31	3	Elder, Dr. Bill
	Paul Quinn	13	A		29	5	Summers, James "Zip"
	Southern Nazarene		A		26	11	Martin, Bobby
	Transylvania	8	A		24	3	Lane, Don
	West Virginia Tech		A		21	10	Sutherland, Tom
	Westmont		A		23	9	Kammerer, Glen "Chet"
1989							
1	Saint Mary's (TX)	8	A		28	5	Meyer, Herbert "Buddy"
2	East Central (OK)	14	A		25	7	Cobb, K. Wayne
3	Central Washington	13	A		32	10	Nicholson, Dean
	Wisconsin: Eau Claire	2	A		29	4	Anderson, Kenneth A.
8	Albertson	16	A		24	9	Holly, Martin W. "Marty"
	Hastings		A		26	9	Trader, Mike
	Siena Heights		A		31	7	Smith, Fred
	Wheeling Jesuit	5	A		31	4	DeFruscio, Jay
16	Auburn: Montgomery	7	A		24	7	Chapman, Larry F.
	Charleston (SC)	4	A		21	5	Kresse, John
	Cumberland (KY)	9	A		26	7	Vernon, Randy
	Drury	12	A		24	9	Walker, Marvin
	Saint Ambrose		A		26	8	Shovlain, Ray
	Washburn	15	A		24	9	Chipman, Bob
	Wayland Baptist	3	A		30	6	Cooper, Rick
	Western Montana		A		19	9	Keltz, Donald "Casey"

F	School	SD	BD	Bye	W	L	Coach
32	Belmont	10	A		25	10	Byrd, Rick
	Biola		A		29	8	Holmquist, Dr. David G.
	Brigham Young: Hawaii		A		24	9	Hess, Dr. Charles "Chic"
	Georgia College		A		22	10	Hodges, Bill
	Grand Canyon	1	A		26	5	Westphal, Bill
	Guilford		A		16	10	Jensen, Jack
	Holy Family (PA)		A		30	9	Williams, Dan
	Husson	6	A		35	3	MacGregor, Dr. D. Bruce
	Minnesota: Duluth		A		25	6	Race, Dale M.
	Olivet Nazarene		A		22	9	Hodge, Ralph
	Saint Rose		A		28	5	Beaury, Brian
	Southern Arkansas	11	A		24	6	Ingram, Monroe
	Taylor		A		27	8	Patterson, Paul
	Tiffin		A		21	12	Hammond, Jim
	Waynesburg		A		19	7	Marisa, Rudy
	William Carey (MS)		A		21	13	Knight, Steve

1990

F	School	SD	BD	Bye	W	L	Coach
1	Birmingham-Southern	4	A		31	3	Reboul, Duane
2	Wisconsin: Eau Claire	2	A		30	4	Anderson, Kenneth A.
3	Georgetown (KY)	11	A		29	7	Reid, James B.
	Lipscomb	1	A		41	5	Meyer, Dr. Don W.
8	Central Washington	7	A		31	5	Nicholson, Dean
	Oral Roberts	3	A		36	6	Trickey, Ken
	Pfeiffer		A		22	11	Lutz, Bob
	South Carolina: Spartanburg	5	A		29	3	Waters, Jerry O.
16	Alderson-Broaddus	10	A		28	7	Dodd, Steve
	Central Arkansas		A		24	11	Dyer, Don
	Columbia (MO)		A		30	8	Burchard, Bob
	Grand Canyon	12	A		25	10	Westphal, Bill
	Indiana-Purdue: Indianapolis		A		23	14	Lovell, Robert
	Minnesota: Duluth	6	A		26	6	Race, Dale M.
	Southern California College	15	A		26	9	Reynolds, Bill
	Southwestern (TX)		A		19	9	Peak, Paul
32	Briar Cliff		A		24	7	Nacke, Ray
	Geneva		A		22	9	Slocum, Jerry
	George Fox	9	A		29	5	Vernon, Mark
	Georgia College	13	A		24	8	Hodges, Bill
	Hawaii Pacific		A		19	15	Sellitto, Anthony, Jr.
	Husson		A		26	13	MacGregor, Dr. D. Bruce
	King's (NY)		A		27	6	Harris, William R.
	Louisiana		A		21	8	Rushing, Gene
	Malone	14	A		25	9	Smith, Harold T.
	Midland Lutheran		A		17	15	McGill, Richard "Rich"
	Northern State (SD)		A		23	9	Olson, Robert
	Olivet Nazarene		A		26	10	Hodge, Ralph

F	School	SD	BD	Bye	W	L	Coach
	Paul Quinn	16	A		31	7	Summers, James 'Zip'
	Philadelphia Pharmacy		A		25	6	Morgan, Robert C.
	Siena Heights	8	A		29	7	Smith, Fred
	Washburn		A		20	12	Chipman, Bob

1991

F	School	SD	BD	Bye	W	L	Coach
1	Oklahoma City	2	A		27	3	Johnson, Darrel
2	Central Arkansas	5	A		29	5	Dyer, Don
3	Pfeiffer	6	A		29	4	Lutz, Bob
	Taylor	9	A		34	4	Patterson, Paul
8	Athens State	13	A		20	9	Murrell, Harold
	Lipscomb	3	A		35	4	Meyer, Dr. Don W.
	Saint Mary's (MI)		A		6	19	Donahue, Glen
	Wisconsin: Eau Claire	1	A		29	3	Anderson, Kenneth A.
16	Albertson	10	A		24	5	Holly, Martin W. 'Marty'
	Briar Cliff	14	A		27	6	Nacke, Ray
	Concord	15	A		28	8	Cox, Steve
	Minnesota: Duluth	4	A		27	5	Race, Dale M.
	Northern State (SD)		A		26	8	Olson, Robert
	Rio Grande	12	A		32	5	Lawhorn, John
	Saint Mary's (TX)	11	A		24	7	Meyer, Herbert 'Buddy'
	Westmont	16	A		22	10	Kammerer, Glen 'Chet'
32	Campbellsville		A		19	12	Cunningham, Lou
	Concordia (NE)		A		23	11	Schmidt, Grant
	Emporia State		A		18	13	Slaymaker, Dr. Ron
	Francis Marion		A		22	10	Hill, Lewis
	Georgia Southwestern	8	A		27	6	Duhon, Glenn D.
	Hawaii Pacific: Loa		A		21	12	Tucker, Steve
	Holy Family (PA)		A		27	7	Williams, Dan
	Maine: Machias		A		22	5	Casey, Sean
	Olivet Nazarene		A		22	13	Hodge, Ralph
	Park (MO)		A		26	7	Francis, David
	Saint Rose		A		20	9	Beaury, Brian
	Saint Vincent		A		20	7	Matthews, Bernie
	Southern Colorado		A		25	8	Folda, Joe
	Wayland Baptist	7	A		26	3	Cooper, Rick
	Whitworth (WA)		A		22	9	Friedrichs, Dr. Warren
	Xavier (LA)		A		21	12	Valdery, Dale

1992 DIVISION I

F	School	SD	BD	Bye	W	L	Coach
1	Oklahoma City	1	A		38	0	Johnson, Darrel
2	Central Arkansas	7	A		28	5	Dyer, Don
3	Brigham Young: Hawaii	6	A		28	7	Wagner, A. Kenyon 'Ken'
	Pfeiffer	5	A		30	5	Lutz, Bob
8	Biola	4	A		33	4	Holmquist, Dr. David G.
	Cumberland (KY)		A		25	8	Vernon, Randy
	Erskine	15	A		27	7	Hicklin, Robbie
	Georgetown (KY)	3	L		34	2	Reid, James B.

F	School	SD	BD	Bye	W	L	Coach
16	Birmingham-Southern	14	L		28	7	Reboul, Duane
	Lipscomb	11	L		31	5	Meyer, Dr. Don W.
	Minnesota: Duluth		A		23	9	Race, Dale M.
	Northwestern Oklahoma State	13	L		25	7	Battisti, Bob
	Olivet Nazarene		A		25	11	Hodge, Ralph
	Spring Hill		A		24	11	Nash, Carl
	Urbana	16	A		26	9	Ronai, Robert G.
	Wisconsin: Stevens Point	2	A		27	2	Parker, Bob
32	Berry		A		27	8	Smyly, Todd
	Briar Cliff	10	A		25	4	Nacke, Ray
	Charleston (WV)		A		21	9	White, Greg
	Columbia Union		A		18	16	Murray, Rick
	Emporia State		A		26	8	Slaymaker, Dr. Ron
	Faulkner	12	A		27	6	Kelsey, Tom
	Findlay		L		23	8	Niekamp, Ron
	Lewis-Clark State (ID)		A		24	11	Pfeifer, George
	Malone		L		26	9	Smith, Harold T.
	McKendree		L		31	6	Statham, Harry M.
	Saint Mary's (MI)		A		26	6	Donahue, Glen
	Taylor	9	A		29	5	Patterson, Paul
	Union (TN)		A		19	15	McCormick, Rick
	Wayland Baptist	8	A		28	6	Cooper, Rick
	Western State (CO)		A		19	10	Helman, Dr. Jay W.
	Wisconsin: Eau Claire		L		20	9	Anderson, Kenneth A.

1992 Division II

F	School	SD	BD	Bye	W	L	Coach
1	Grace (IN)	6	A	To R16	32	5	Kessler, James C.
2	Northwestern (IA)		A	To R16	25	8	Barry, Todd
3	Concordia (NE)		A	To R16	26	10	Schmidt, Grant
	Dakota State		A		19	16	McDermott, Brian
8	Franklin (IN)	3	L	To R16	25	4	Prather, Kerry
	George Fox		L		24	11	Vernon, Mark
	MidAmerica Nazarene	2	A	To R16	27	10	Lamar, Jon "Rocky"
	William Jewell		A	To R16	23	13	Holley, Larry R.
16	Eureka	4	A	To R16	25	4	Darnall, David
	Florida Memorial		A		17	12	Parker, Alfred
	Husson		L		27	10	MacGregor, Dr. D. Bruce
	King (TN)	1	A	To R16	28	3	Street, Marty
	Northwest Nazarene	7	A	To R16	26	9	Weidenbach, Ed
	Saint Joseph's (ME)	8	A	To R16	24	6	Simonds, Rick
	Tarleton State	5	A	To R16	26	10	Reisman, Lonn
	Tiffin		A	To R16	23	10	Hammomd, Jim
20	Edgewood		A		21	10	Larson, G. Steven
	King's (NY)		A		20	13	Showers, Ken
	Missouri Valley		L		23	11	Fifer, Tom
	Philadelphia Pharmacy		A		26	7	Morgan, Robert C.

F	School	SD	BD	Bye	W	L	Coach
1993 Division I							
1	Hawaii Pacific	3	A		30	4	Sellitto, Anthony, Jr.
2	Oklahoma Baptist University	1	A		34	4	Hoffman, Bob
3	Georgetown (KY)		L		29	8	Reid, James B.
3	Midwestern State (TX)		A		25	12	Stockton, Dr. Gerald E.
8	Lenoir-Rhyne		A		25	7	Lentz, John
	Lipscomb	4	A		34	4	Meyer, Dr. Don W.
	Minnesota: Morris		A		22	10	Ford, Perry
	Urbana		L		26	8	Ronai, Robert G.
16	Belmont		L		30	6	Byrd, Rick
	Birmingham-Southern	5	A		29	7	Reboul, Duane
	Briar Cliff	14	A		27	6	Nacke, Ray
	Central Washington	10	A		29	7	Coleman, Gil
	Life (GA)	13	L		30	5	Kaiser, Roger A.
	Oklahoma City	6	L		25	7	Case, Win
	Ozarks (AR)		A		23	9	Johnson, John K. "Johnny"
	Salem-Teikyo	16	A		24	7	Carey, Michael A.
32	Azusa Pacific	2	A		30	4	Odell, William M.
	Benedict		A		23	4	Washington, Willie
	Central Arkansas		L		20	8	Dyer, Don
	Cumberland (KY)		A		28	7	Vernon, Randy
	Drury		A		19	12	Stanfield, Gary
	Findlay	15	A		26	6	Niekamp, Ron
	Geneva	7	A		28	3	Slocum, Jerry
	Incarnate Word	8	A		28	4	Kaspar, Danny
	Kennesaw State		A		19	12	Zenoni, Phil
	McKendree		A		27	9	Statham, Harry M.
	Pfeiffer	9	L		23	6	Lutz, Bob
	Presbyterian	12	L		27	5	Nibert, Gregg
	Spring Hill		A		22	9	Nash, Carl
	Taylor		A		27	7	Patterson, Paul
	Tri-State		A		20	11	Hack, Dick
	Wisconsin: Stevens Point	11	A		23	5	Parker, Bob
1993 Division II							
1	Willamette	3	L	To R16	29	4	James, Gordon "Gordie"
2	Northern State (SD)	1	A	To R16	34	2	Olson, Robert
3	Northwest Nazarene		L		20	13	Weidenbach, Ed
	William Jewell	4	A	To R16	27	10	Holley, Larry R.
8	Albertson		L	To R16	22	8	Holly, Martin W. "Marty"
	Eureka		A	To R16	24	5	Darnall, David
	Peru State	5	A	To R16	27	6	Gibbs, John
	Walsh	6	A	To R16	29	5	Loy, Steve
16	Alice Lloyd		A	To R16	27	6	Stepp, Jim
	Embry-Riddle (FL)		L		28	8	Ridder, Steven
	Grace (IN)	2	A	To R16	27	6	Kessler, James C.
	Northwestern (IA)		A		19	11	Barry, Todd

F	School	SD	BD	Bye	W	L	Coach
	Tarleton State	7	A	To R16	22	11	Reisman, Lonn
	Tiffin		L	To R16	21	12	Hammond, Jim
	Webber	8	A	To R16	27	7	Dunlap, John H.
	Wilmington (DE)		A		19	13	Newsome, Kevin
20	Caldwell		A		21	8	Corino, Mark A.
	Concordia (WI)		A		18	9	Stelmachowicz, Dr. Cary
	Ottawa		A		18	12	Carrier, Andy
	Saint Joseph's (ME)		A		22	7	Scheinman, John

1994 Division I

F	School	SD	BD	Bye	W	L	Coach
1	Oklahoma City	5	A		28	7	Case, Win
2	Life (GA)		A		27	10	Kaiser, Roger A.
3	Midwestern State (TX)		A		23	12	Stockton, Dr. Gerald E.
	Oklahoma Baptist University	16	L		29	8	Hoffman, Bob
8	Belmont	8	A		30	7	Byrd, Rick
	Benedict	15	A		29	3	Washington, Willie
	Drury	4	A		27	4	Stanfield, Gary
	Hawaii Pacific	6	A		27	8	Sellitto, Anthony, Jr.
16	Azusa Pacific	11	L		29	5	Odell, William M.
	Georgetown (KY)	1	A		33	2	Reid, James B.
	Georgia Southwestern		A		24	10	Duhon, Glenn D.
	Northwestern Oklahoma State	2	A		29	2	Battisti, Bob
	Pfeiffer	9	A		24	6	Lutz, Bob
	Saint Mary's (TX)		A		21	10	Meyer, Herbert "Buddy"
	Westminster (PA)	13	A		25	3	Galbreath, Dr. C. Ronald
	Westmont		A		19	13	Moore, John
32	Auburn: Montgomery		A		20	12	Chapman, Larry F.
	Hawaii: Hilo		L		17	12	Wilson, Robert H.
	Incarnate Word		L		25	6	Kaspar, Danny
	Lipscomb	12	L		29	6	Meyer, Dr. Don W.
	Master's	10	A		28	5	Oates, Bill
	Missouri Baptist		A		25	10	Pitzer, Lowell S.
	Mobile	7	L		32	3	Elder, Dr. Bill
	Oklahoma Christian	14	L		23	11	Hays, Dan
	Ozarks (AR)		A		22	13	Johnson, John K. "Johnny"
	Rocky Mountain		A		17	14	Matlock, Gary
	Saint Francis (IL)		A		16	15	Sullivan, Pat
	Salem-Teikyo	3	A		24	4	Carey, Michael A.
	Siena Heights		A		27	8	Smith, Fred
	Spring Hill		A		22	10	Niland, Joseph P., Jr.
	Transylvania		A		25	8	Lane, Don
	Western Washington		A		24	7	Jackson, Brad

1994 Division II

F	School	SD	BD	Bye	W	L	Coach
1	Eureka	6	A	To R16	27	4	Darnell, David
2	Northern State (SD)	4	A	To R16	25	9	Olson, Robert
3	Lewis & Clark (OR)	8	L	To R16	23	9	Gaillard, Bob
	Northwest Nazarene	11	A		26	8	Weidenbach, Ed

F	School	SD	BD	Bye	W	L	Coach
8	Huron	16	A		21	10	Paulsen, Fred
	Northwestern (IA)	2	A	To R16	27	4	Barry, Todd
	Taylor	1	A	To R16	29	5	Patterson, Paul
	Willamette	3	A	To R16	24	6	James, Gordon "Gordie"
16	Alice Lloyd	7	A	To R16	27	7	Stepp, Jim
	Bethel (IN)	5	A	To R16	30	5	Lightfoot, Mike
	Central Methodist	9	A		30	7	Sherman, Jeff
	Jamestown	24	A		13	14	Meyer, Jerry
	McMurry	21	A		21	8	Holmes, Ron
	Ohio Dominican	14	A		23	9	Digenova, Ed
	Saint Ambrose	18	A		24	10	Shovlain, Ray
	Tabor	20	A		21	10	Brubacher, Don
24	Black Hills State	19	L		19	11	Olson, Mike
	Husson	12	A		28	4	MacGregor, Dr. D. Bruce
	Lakeland (WI)	22	A		25	11	Jonas, Craig
	Lynn	10	A		23	7	Price, Jeff
	Saint Thomas (FL)	23	A		17	18	Tuell, Gary
	Saint Thomas Aquinas	17	A		24	8	O'Donnell, Dennis
	Tarleton State	15	A		16	12	Reisman, Lonn
	Westbrook	13	A		30	5	Graffam, Jim

1995 DIVISION I

F	School	SD	BD	Bye	W	L	Coach
1	Birmingham-Southern	5	A		35	2	Reboul, Duane
2	Pfeiffer	11	A		25	8	Lutz, Bob
3	Arkansas Tech	7	A		29	6	Barnes, Marty
	Belmont	1	A		37	2	Byrd, Rick
8	Georgia Southwestern	4	A		30	5	Duhon, Glenn D.
	Master's	8	A		31	5	Oates, Bill
	Montana State: Northern		A		17	19	Baker, Loren
	Oklahoma City	3	A		30	3	Case, Win
16	Central Washington		A		20	14	Sparling, Greg
	Fresno Pacific		A		24	8	Sargent, Jim
	Geneva		A		26	6	Slocum, Jerry
	Hawaii Pacific	13	A		25	9	Sellitto, Anthony, Jr.
	Lipscomb		L		30	7	Meyer, Dr. Don W.
	Oklahoma Christian	12	L		28	9	Hays, Dan
	Transylvania	14	L		26	8	Lane, Don
	Voorhees		A		25	12	Bernstein, Jeff
32	Columbia (MO)	10	L		29	6	Burchard, Bob
	Concord		A		20	11	Cox, Steve
	Georgetown (KY)	6	A		32	4	Reid, James B.
	Incarnate Word		A		26	8	Kaspar, Danny
	Iowa Wesleyan		A		21	15	Woolton, Joel
	Life (GA)	2	A		31	3	Kaiser, Roger A.
	Mary Hardin-Baylor		L		23	8	Herbst, Richard
	Midwestern State (TX)		A		19	11	Ray, Jeff
	Minnesota: Morris	16	A		20	9	Ford, Perry
	Oklahoma Baptist University	15	L		28	6	Hoffman, Bob
	Olivet Nazarene		A		21	15	Hodge, Ralph
	Rio Grande		A		26	10	Lawhorn, John

F	School	SD	BD	Bye	W	L	Coach
	Saint Mary's (TX)	9	L		24	6	Meyer, Herbert "Buddy"
	Southern: New Orleans		A		21	11	Hill, Earl R.
	Southwestern Oklahoma State		A		20	12	Hauser, George
	Spring Arbor		A		19	17	Noll, Doug

1995 DIVISION II

F	School	SD	BD	Bye	W	L	Coach
1	Bethel (IN)	3	A		38	2	Lightfoot, Mike
2	Northwest Nazarene	5	A		27	7	Weidenbach, Ed
3	Northern State (SD)	1	A		28	5	Olson, Robert
	William Jewell	10	A		29	10	Holley, Larry R.
8	Concordia (NE)	2	A		30	4	Schmidt, Grant
	Hastings	8	L		21	7	Trader, Mike
	Ozarks (MO)	6	A		29	5	Waller, Allan J.
	Willamette		L		20	12	James, Gordon "Gordie"
16	Alice Lloyd	16	A		26	10	Stepp, Jim
	Indiana Tech	4	A		24	6	Kline, Dan
	Lewis & Clark (OR)		A		17	14	Gaillard, Bob
	Nova Southeastern	11	L		22	12	Michaels, Jim
	Ohio Dominican		A		19	16	DiGenova, Ed
	Saint Ambrose		L		24	12	Shovlain, Ray
	Saint Thomas Aquinas	12	A		25	9	O'Donnell, Dennis
	Viterbo	9	A		27	7	Murphy, Michael
32	Albertson	7	L		21	8	Holly, Martin W. "Marty"
	Dakota Wesleyan	15	A		19	11	Martin, Doug
	Edgewood	14	A		20	8	Larson, G. Steven
	Howard Payne		A		12	13	Pattillo, Charles
	Husson		A		23	9	Caruso, Warren
	Loyola New Orleans		A		15	13	Hernandez, Jerry
	MidAmerica Nazarene		L		21	15	Lamar, Jon "Rocky"
	Milligan		L		24	12	Scruggs, Rick
	Minot State		A		14	13	Limke, Dick
	Mount Vernon Nazarene	13	L		22	10	Fleming, Scott
	Nyack		L		26	8	Bailey, Dan
	Ottawa		A		21	9	Carrier, Andy
	Trinity International (IL)		A		24	8	Bruehl, Alan
	Webber		A		21	15	Dunlap, John H.
	Westbrook		A		24	10	Graffam, Jim
	Wilmington (DE)		A		20	11	Newsome, Kevin

1996 DIVISION I

F	School	SD	BD	Bye	W	L	Coach
1	Oklahoma City	14	L		33	5	Case, Win
2	Georgetown (KY)	1	A		36	3	Reid, James B.
3	Belmont		L		28	11	Byrd, Rick
	Lipscomb	4	A		33	6	Meyer, Dr. Don W.
8	Birmingham-Southern	6	L		25	5	Reboul, Duane
	Cumberland (TN)	10	L		28	6	Petrone, Mike
	East Central (OK)		L		22	7	Cobb, K. Wayne
	Geneva		L		24	7	Slocum, Jerry

F	School	SD	BD	Bye	W	L	Coach
16	Arkansas Tech		A		19	10	Barnes, Marty
	Brigham Young: Hawaii	5	A		24	7	Wagner, Kenyon "Ken"
	Findlay		A		25	10	Niekamp, Ron
	Hawaii Pacific	7	L		27	6	Sellitto, Anthony, Jr.
	Life (GA)	2	A		31	6	Kaiser, Roger A.
	Master's	3	A		28	7	Oates, Bill
	McKendree		A		25	9	Statham, Harry M.
	Oklahoma Baptist University	8	A		29	6	Hoffman, Bob
32	Azusa Pacific	12	L		26	8	Odell, William M.
	Claflin		A		18	13	Guyden, James "Gus"
	Columbia (MO)		L		27	8	Burchard, Bob
	East Texas Baptist	13	A		28	5	West, Bert
	Harding	11	A		24	6	Morgan, Jeff
	Lewis-Clark State (ID)	16	A		19	9	Pfeifer, George
	Montana State: Northern	9	A		24	9	Baker, Loren
	North Georgia		A		21	16	Dunn, Randy
	Saint Francis (IL)		A		19	10	Sullivan, Pat
	Saint Mary's (TX)		A		19	11	Meyer, Herbert "Buddy"
	Saint Xavier		L		28	6	Keasler, Mike
	Southeastern Oklahoma State		A		24	10	Robinson, Tony
	Talladega		A		18	16	Tucker, Wylie N.
	Westminster (PA)	15	A		21	8	Galbreath, Dr. C. Ronald
	Westmont		A		19	13	Moore, John
	Xavier (LA)		A		22	11	Valdery, Dale

1996 DIVISION II

F	School	SD	BD	Bye	W	L	Coach
1	Albertson	3	A		31	3	Holly, Martin W. "Marty"
2	Whitworth (WA)	4	A		26	5	Friedrichs, Dr. Warren
3	Walsh	2	A		30	3	Loy, Steve
	William Jewell	9	L		30	9	Holley, Larry R.
8	Doane		A		21	16	Erickson, Robert
	Northwest Nazarene		H		19	13	Weidenbach, Ed
	Tabor	16	A		25	7	Zimmerman, Don
	Wisconsin Lutheran		A		22	7	Noon, Ed
16	Alice Lloyd	15	L		27	8	Stepp, Jim
	Bethel (IN)	1	A		35	2	Lightfoot, Mike
	Embry-Riddle (FL)	8	A		25	11	Ridder, Steven
	Huron		A		18	14	Paulsen, Fred
	Lewis & Clark (OR)		L		17	10	Gaillard, Bob
	MidAmerica Nazarene	13	A		20	17	Lamar, Jon "Rocky"
	Mount Mercy	11	A		29	6	Gavin, Paul
	Trinity International (IL)	12	L		25	6	Bruehl, Alan
32	Baker (KS)		L		25	10	Weaver, Rick
	Berea		A		18	9	Wierwille, Roland R.
	Bluefield (VA)		A		22	12	Ayers, Walter
	Caldwell		A		21	9	Corino, Mark A.

F	School	SD	BD	Bye	W	L	Coach
	Concordia (NE)	5	L		25	6	Schmidt, Grant
	Green Mountain		A		21	9	Dempsey, Matthew J.
	Holy Family (PA)		A		24	11	Williams, Dan
	Howard Payne		A		14	14	Pattillo, Charles
	Mayville State		A		17	11	Miles, Tim
	Northland		A		19	11	Swan, David
	Ozarks (MO)	10	A		25	7	Waller, Allan J.
	Philadelphia Pharmacy		L		23	6	Morgan, Robert C.
	Saint Joseph's (ME)	6	A		24	4	Simonds, Rick
	Siena Heights		A		21	10	Smith, Fred
	Taylor	14	L		23	13	Patterson, Paul
	Western Oregon	7	L		22	8	Kelly, Tom

1997 Division I

F	School	SD	BD	Bye	W	L	Coach
1	Life (GA)	1	A		37	1	Kaiser, Roger A.
2	Oklahoma Baptist University	3	A		36	4	Hoffman, Bob
3	Cumberland (KY)	13	L		31	7	Vernon, Randy
	Point Park		A		23	8	Rager, Robert
8	Birmingham-Southern	8	A		28	6	Reboul, Duane
	Central Washington		A		18	13	Sparling, Greg
	Hawaii Pacific	2	A		26	4	Sellitto, Anthony, Jr.
	McKendree		L		28	9	Statham, Harry M.
16	Azusa Pacific	12	A		29	8	Odell, William M.
	Biola	14	L		28	6	Holmquist, Dr. David G.
	Brigham Young: Hawaii		L		21	8	Wagner, A. Kenyon "Ken"
	Claflin		A		25	8	Guydon, James "Gus"
	Dillard		A		20	13	Loyd, Gerry
	Findlay	6	A		27	5	Niekamp, Ron
	Georgetown (KY)	15	A		26	9	Osborne, "Happy"
	Southeastern Oklahoma State	9	L		27	4	Robinson, Tony
32	Benedict	4	L		30	3	Washington, Willie
	Carroll (MT)		A		22	11	Turcott, Gary
	Columbia (MO)		A		27	8	Burchard, Bob
	East Central (OK)	10	A		22	6	Cobb, K. Wayne
	Georgia Southwestern		A		23	9	Barksdale, Randolph
	Huston-Tillotson		A		20	9	Littlefield, Terrence
	Incarnate Word	5	A		25	4	Kaspar, Danny
	Lindsey Wilson		A		23	13	Dodd, Steve
	Lipscomb	7	A		30	6	Meyer, Dr. Don W.
	Master's		A		21	11	Oates, Bill
	Olivet Nazarene		A		21	13	Hodge, Ralph
	Phillips (OK)		L		23	9	Chappell, Rand
	Saint Mary's (TX)	11	L		22	7	Meyer, Herbert "Buddy"
	Southern Nazarene		L		25	9	Martin, Bobby
	Transylvania	16	L		23	8	Lane, Don
	William Carey (MS)		A		22	14	Knight, Steve

F	School	SD	BD	Bye	W	L	Coach
1997 DIVISION II							
1	Bethel (IN)	2	L		34	5	Lightfoot, Mike
2	Siena Heights	5	A		30	7	Smith, Fred
3	Tabor	16	A		24	9	Brubacher, Don
	William Jewell	14	A		29	10	Holley, Larry R.
8	Black Hills State	11	L		24	6	Olson, Mike
	Northwest Nazarene	9	L		26	8	Weidenbach, Ed
	Ozarks (MO)		A		23	11	Waller, Allan J.
	Spring Arbor	7	L		29	6	Noll, Doug
16	Embry-Riddle (FL)	12	L		25	8	Ridder, Steven
	Evangel	8	A		28	8	Jenkins, Stephen M.
	Lewis & Clark (OR)	10	L		22	5	Gaillard, Bob
	Oregon Tech	3	L		29	6	Miles, Daniel J.
	Pacific (OR)	4	A		22	6	Schumann, Ken
	Saint Thomas Aquinas	1	A		34	2	O'Donnell, Dennis G.
	Urbana	6	A		26	8	Ronai, Robert G.
	Western Baptist	15	A		27	10	Hills, Tim
32	Concordia (NE)		A		18	14	Schmidt, Grant
	Green Mountain		A		21	8	Dempsey, Matthew J.
	Holy Names (CA)		A		20	15	Whitworth, Steve
	Howard Payne		A		16	10	Pattillo, Charles
	Husson		A		20	12	Caruso, Warren
	Indiana: Southeast		A		19	13	Morris, Jim
	Mayville State		A		18	11	Miles, Tim
	Peru State	13	A		25	9	Gibbs, John
	Philadelphia Pharmacy		A		20	6	Morgan, Robert C.
	Saint Ambrose		A		27	7	Shovlain, Ray
	Saint Thomas (FL)		A		17	17	Tuell, Gary
	South Dakota Tech		A		17	13	Welsh, Hugh
	Taylor		A		22	13	Patterson, Paul
	Tennessee Wesleyan		A		23	12	Adams, Steve
	Virginia Intermont		A		20	14	Worrell, Phil
	Wisconsin Lutheran		A		19	10	Noon, Ed
1998 DIVISION I							
1	Georgetown (KY)	4	L		36	3	Osborne, "Happy"
2	Southern Nazarene	14	A		29	9	Martin, Bobby
3	Azusa Pacific	1	A		35	5	Odell, William M.
	Park (MO)	15	L		27	8	English, Claude
8	Central Washington		A		20	11	Sparling, Greg
	East Central (OK)		A		21	9	Cobb, K. Wayne
	Incarnate Word	9	A		27	5	Kaspar, Daniel J. "Danny"
	Saint Vincent	10	A		29	5	Matthews, Bernie
16	Benedict		A		22	9	Washington, Willie
	Biola	11	L		30	7	Holmquist, Dr. David G.
	Life (GA)	3	A		32	4	Kaiser, Roger A.
	Montana State: Northern		L		26	9	Walker, Tim
	Oklahoma City	8	L		26	5	Case, Win
	Olivet Nazarene		A		28	9	Hodge, Ralph
	Phillips (OK)	2	L		31	3	Chappell, Rand
	Transylvania		A		24	9	Lane, Don

F	School	SD	BD	Bye	W	L	Coach
32	Birmingham-Southern	7	A		28	5	Reboul, Duane
	Brigham Young: Hawaii	12	L		19	8	Wagner, A. Kenyon "Ken"
	Cumberland (KY)		A		16	17	Vernon, Randy
	Freed-Hardeman		L		24	11	McCutchen, Mike
	Georgia Southwestern		A		25	11	Barksdale, Randolph
	Hannibal-LaGrange		A		20	12	Thomas, Kent
	Hawaii Pacific	6	A		22	5	Sellitto, Anthony, Jr.
	Houston Baptist	13	L		26	6	Cottrell, Ron
	Huston-Tillotson		A		16	12	Littlefield, Terrence
	Lindsey Wilson		A		23	12	Dodd, Steve
	Master's		A		23	12	Oates, Bill
	Mobile	16	A		27	9	Sanderson, Scott
	Montana Tech		A		22	11	Dessing, Rick
	Saint Mary's (TX)		L		20	7	Meyer, Herbert "Buddy"
	Southern: New Orleans		A		20	15	Hill, Earl R.
	Union (TN)	5	A		30	5	Turner, Ralph

1998 Division II

F	School	SD	BD	Bye	W	L	Coach
1	Bethel (IN)	1	L		37	3	Lightfoot, Mike
2	Oregon Tech	15	L		26	11	Miles, Daniel J. "Danny"
3	Mount Marty	13	L		23	9	Thorson, Jim
	Northwest Nazarene	11	A		27	10	Sanders, Rich
8	Lewis & Clark (OR)	10	A		22	7	Gaillard, Dr. Bob
	Mayville State	3	A		23	7	Grove, Paul
	Mount Vernon Nazarene	5	L		27	7	Flemming, Scott
	Whitworth (WA)	8	A		20	8	Friedrichs, Dr. Warren
16	Black Hills State		A		21	8	Olson, Mike
	Briar Cliff	16	A		23	12	Beard, Michael
	Cardinal Stritch (WI)		A		24	9	Fox, Denny
	Holy Names (CA)		A		26	11	Whitworth, Steve
	Siena Heights	4	A		28	9	Smith, Fred
	Warner Southern	6	L		26	8	Bays, Gary R.
	Western Baptist	12	A		25	11	Hills, Tim
	William Jewell	2	A		28	9	Holley, Larry R.
32	Bellevue (NE)		A		17	14	Richards, Brett
	Berea		A		20	10	Wierwille, Roland R.
	Caldwell		A		23	7	Corino, Mark A.
	Castleton State		A		19	8	Blake, Dave
	Central Methodist	9	A		26	8	Sherman, Jeff
	Concordia (NE)	7	A		26	7	Schmidt, Grant
	Embry-Riddle (FL)		A		23	12	Ridder, Steven
	Indiana Tech		A		21	9	Kline, Dan
	King (TN)		A		20	14	Polsgrove, Scott
	Marian (IN)	14	A		22	7	Grimes, John
	Mary Hardin-Baylor		A		14	12	Herbst, Richard
	Saint Ambrose		A		20	16	Shovlain, Ray
	Saint Joseph's (ME)		A		24	5	Simonds, Rick
	Southwestern (KS)		A		14	16	Horstmann, Brad
	Virginia Intermont		A		21	13	Worrell, Phil
	Walsh		A		25	10	Loy, Steve

Tournament Results—Women

F	School	SD	BD	Bye	W	L	Coach
1981							
1	Kentucky State	7	A		21	7	Mitchell, Ron
2	Texas Southern	1	A		23	9	Gillespie, Nathaniel A.
3	Northern State (SD)	5	A		28	4	Fredrickson, Curt
4	Azusa Pacific	3	A		18	15	Hebel, Dr. Susan L.
8	Berry	2	A		16	9	Paul, Brenda
	Missouri Western State	4	A		24	7	Bumpus, Debbie
	Saginaw Valley State	6	A		14	13	Reall, Marsha
	Virginia State	8	A		18	15	Bey, Leon Wright
1982							
1	Southwestern Oklahoma State	1	A		34	0	Loftin, John D.
2	Missouri Southern State	6	A		23	12	Phillips, James
3	Saginaw Valley State	4	A		27	5	Reall, Marsha
4	Berry	2	A		29	4	Paul, Brenda
8	California Baptist	7	A		25	6	King, David F.
	Charleston (WV)	3	A		27	7	Francis, Robert A. "Bud"
	Spring Garden	8	A		29	4	Soroka, Michael
	Texas Southern	5	A		23	8	Gillespie, Nathaniel A.
1983							
1	Southwestern Oklahoma State	1	A		30	4	Loftin, John D.
2	Alabama: Huntsville	6	A		27	8	Dunaway, Donna Caldwell
3	Missouri: Kansas City	4	A		30	5	Norman, Nancy
4	Portland	7	A		27	6	Olmstead, David
8	Campbellsville	3	A		24	5	Wise, Donna H.
	Nazareth (NY)	8	A		19	11	Gomez, Marguerite "Margie"
	Saginaw Valley State	5	A		25	6	Reall, Marsha
	Wayland Baptist	2	A		22	10	Wilson, Cathy
1984							
1	North Carolina: Asheville		A		32	5	Carroll, Helen
2	Portland	3	A		30	6	Olmstead, David
3	Dillard	4	A		26	3	Teamer, Mary D.
4	Berry	7	L		32	5	Paul, Brenda
8	Charleston (WV)		A		24	9	Francis, Robert A. "Bud"
	Francis Marion	6	A		28	5	Hatchell, Sylvia Rhyne
	Saginaw Valley State	2	A		30	1	Reall, Marsha
	Southwestern Oklahoma State	1	A		31	1	Loftin, John D.
16	Biola		A		22	11	Norman, Betty
	Carson-Newman	5	A		26	6	Bivens, Lewis
	Central Arkansas	8	A		24	4	Marvel, Ronnie
	Georgian Court		A		18	4	Sonday, Bob
	Jamestown		A		15	7	Kohler, Robert
	Saint Ambrose		A		28	4	Buckles, Ken
	Tarleton State		A		26	6	Lowrey, Jan
	Wisconsin: Milwaukee		A		25	8	Kelling, Mary Ann

F	School	SD	BD	Bye	W	L	Coach
1985							
1	Southwestern Oklahoma State	1	A		34	0	Loftin, John D.
2	Saginaw Valley State	3	A		32	1	Reall, Marsha
3	Wayland Baptist	4	A		31	5	Ketterman, Dave
4	Midland Lutheran		A		26	5	Bracker, Joanne
8	Carson-Newman	5	L		32	3	Bivens, Lewis
	Missouri: Kansas City	8	A		29	6	Norman, Nancy
	Northeastern Illinois		A		29	13	Margaritis, John
	Portland	2	A		26	8	Olmstead, David
16	Bluefield State (WV)		A		24	4	Mandeville, Kenneth A. "Kenny"
	Claflin	7	A		27	5	Brownlee, Nelson C.
	Indiana Tech		A		20	9	Hewlet, Kathy
	Louisiana	6	A		27	4	Schneider, Frank
	North Carolina: Pembroke		A		26	5	Lee, Billy
	Saint Mary's (CA)		A		21	9	Rubenstein, Terri
	Southern Maine		A		23	6	Costello, Dr. Richard A.
	Wisconsin: Milwaukee		A		25	7	Kelling, Mary Ann
1986							
1	Francis Marion	1	A		36	2	Hatchell, Sylvia Rhyne
2	Wayland Baptist	3	A		31	5	Evans, Floyd C.
3	Louisiana	2	A		24	2	Johnson, Shelia Thompson
4	Georgia Southwestern	5	L		25	4	Hawver, Dr. Greg
8	Oklahoma Christian	4	A		27	8	Findley, Stephanie
	Saginaw Valley State	6	A		24	3	Charney, Claudette
	Western Washington	7	A		25	8	Goodrich, Lynda
	Wingate		A		26	6	Jacumin, Johnny
16	Azusa Pacific	8	A		30	5	Hebel, Dr. Susan L.
	Charleston (WV)		A		19	12	Francis, Robert A. "Bud"
	Cumberland (KY)		A		24	6	Morgan, Henry
	Dominican (NY)		A		20	15	Baxter, Stephen
	Morningside		A		20	11	Arnold, John
	Mount Marty		A		24	8	Anderson, Warren
	Ouachita Baptist		A		18	13	Honnell, Virginia
	Wisconsin: Green Bay		A		21	9	Hammerle, Carol
1987							
1	Southwestern Oklahoma State	2	A		30	2	Loftin, John D.
2	North Georgia	4	A		27	4	Jarrett, Lynn
3	Wisconsin: Green Bay	8	A		24	6	Hammerle, Carol
4	Arkansas Tech	6	A		29	6	Dickerson, Jim
8	Saginaw Valley State	3	A		30	2	Charney, Claudette
	Saint Ambrose		A		29	3	Bluder, Lisa
	Wayland Baptist	1	A		31	1	Evans, Floyd C.
	Wingate	5	A		29	4	Jacumin, Johnny
16	Auburn: Montgomery		A		20	11	Tilley, Colby
	Bemidji State		L		25	2	Mathison, Sherri
	Bluefield State (WV)		A		20	8	Mandeville, Kenneth A. "Kenny"
	Fresno Pacific		A		28	3	Janzen, Dennis

F	School	SD	BD	Bye	W	L	Coach
	Indiana-Purdue: Indianapolis		A		22	8	Price, Jim
	Nebraska: Kearney		A		21	9	Wurtz, Dan
	Saint Joseph's (ME)		A		21	9	Stead, Bob
	Western Oregon	7	A		26	6	Carey, Jon
1988							
1	Oklahoma City	4	A		28	6	Colon, Bob
2	Claflin	2	A		37	2	Brownlee, Nelson C.
3	Arkansas Tech	3	A		29	5	Foley, Joe M.
4	Wingate	1	A		33	2	Jacumin, Johnny
8	Dillard		A		28	5	Teamer, Mary D.
	Minnesota: Duluth		A		18	12	Stromme, Karen
	Saint Ambrose	5	A		32	5	Bluder, Lisa
	Union (TN)	8	L		29	3	Blackstock, Dr. David
16	Central Washington		A		31	5	Frederick, Dr. Gary C.
	Charleston (WV)		A		21	13	Bennett-Travinski, Linda
	Cumberland (KY)		A		25	10	Morgan, Henry
	Rocky Mountain		A		20	11	Malby, Jeff
	Saginaw Valley State	7	A		25	7	Charney, Claudette
	Saint Joseph's (ME)		A		21	9	McDevitt, Michael
	Southern Utah		A		18	8	Adams, Boyd
	Wayland Baptist	6	A		28	7	Evans, Floyd C.
1989							
1	Southern Nazarene	3	A		36	2	Hoffman, Bob
2	Claflin	1	A		35	1	Brownlee, Nelson C.
3	Arkansas Tech	2	A		35	2	Foley, Joe M.
	Saint Ambrose	4	A		36	2	Bluder, Lisa
8	Central State (OH)	8	A		29	2	Check, Theresa
	Doane		A		27	7	Steinmeyer, Gene
	Wayland Baptist	7	A		30	8	Evans, Floyd C.
	Western Washington		A		30	5	Goodrich, Lynda
16	Fresno Pacific		A		24	8	Stanley, Kent
	Glenville State		A		19	7	Shepherd, Dr. Russell M.
	Minnesota: Duluth	6	A		26	6	Stromme, Karen
	Saint Thomas Aquinas		A		25	2	McManus, Michael
	Tri-State		A		25	8	DeRocher, Cindy
	Union (TN)		A		26	6	Blackstock, Dr. David
	Washburn		L		29	3	Dick, Patricia D.
	Wingate	5	A		26	3	Jacumin, Johnny
1990							
1	Southwestern Oklahoma State	4	A		30	4	Loftin, John D.
2	Arkansas: Monticello	2	A		34	3	Early, Alvy
3	Claflin	3	A		33	3	Brownlee, Nelson C.
	Saint Ambrose	1	A		34	1	Bluder, Lisa
8	Central State (OH)		A		25	5	Check, Theresa
	Simon Fraser	6	A		29	7	McNeill, Allison
	Wayland Baptist		A		31	11	Estes, Sheryl
	Western New Mexico		A		25	6	Irvin, Dexter

F	School	SD	BD	Bye	W	L	Coach
16	Aquinas (MI)		L		26	6	Tibaldi, Patti
	Campbellsville		A		21	11	Wise, Donna H.
	Charleston (WV)		A		25	8	Bennett-Travinski, Linda
	Georgian Court		A		27	3	Emery, Debra
	Lipscomb	7	A		30	8	Bennett, Frank
	Minnesota: Duluth		A		24	7	Stromme, Karen
	Montana State: Northern	5	A		28	3	Baker, Loren
	Wingate	8	A		27	6	Jacumin, Johnny

1991 Division I

F	School	SD	BD	Bye	W	L	Coach
1	Fort Hays State	4	A		34	2	Klein, John
2	Southwestern Oklahoma State	2	A		31	3	Loftin, John D.
3	Claflin	1	A		31	2	Brownlee, Nelson C.
	Indiana-Purdue: Indianapolis		A		20	12	Wilhoit, Julie A.
8	Belmont	10	A		32	5	Cross, Tony
	Saint Edward's	9	A		31	2	McKey, David
	Wayland Baptist	5	A		27	8	Estes, Sheryl
	Wingate	6	L		28	3	Jacumin, Johnny
16	Central Arkansas	16	A		22	8	Marvel, Ronnie
	Central State (OH)	11	A		27	5	Check, Theresa
	Dominican (IL)	8	A		32	2	Trefilek, Thomas J.
	Midland Lutheran	14	A		22	8	Bracker, Joanne
	Minnesota: Duluth	12	A		26	6	Stromme, Karen
	Montana State: Northern	13	A		26	5	Baker, Loren
	Mount Mercy	7	A		28	4	Slifer, David
	Western Oregon		A		26	11	Carey, Jon
32	Auburn: Montgomery		A		24	9	Tilley, Colby
	Belmont Abbey	15	A		23	6	Kebbe, Elaine
	Berry		A		26	8	Guinn, Connie
	Campbellsville		A		22	8	Wise, Donna H.
	Charleston (WV)		A		21	8	Bennett-Travinski, Linda
	Georgian Court		A		25	5	Emery, Debra
	Holy Family (PA)		A		24	5	Soroka, Michael
	Mobile		A		22	8	Berger, Curt
	Northwood (MI)		A		20	12	Vielbig, Mary
	Point Loma Nazarene		A		24	8	Olin, Dr. Bill
	Rockhurst		A		25	8	Rietzke, Tracy
	Saint Joseph's (ME)		A		24	5	McDevitt, Michael
	Seton Hill		A		14	12	Shrader, Robert
	Simon Fraser	3	A		28	3	McNeill, Allison
	Western New Mexico		A		18	8	Irvin, Dexter
	Wisconsin: Stout		A		19	11	Thomas, Mark

1992 Division I

F	School	SD	BD	Bye	W	L	Coach
1	Arkansas Tech	2	A		35	1	Foley, Joe M.
2	Wayland Baptist	4	A		29	6	Estes, Sheryl
3	Saint Edward's	8	L		30	3	McKey, David
	Southwestern Oklahoma State	3	A		30	4	Loftin, John D.

F	School	SD	BD	Bye	W	L	Coach
8	Belmont	10	A		31	5	Cross, Tony
	Claflin	6	A		28	2	Brownlee, Nelson C.
	Simon Fraser	1	A		31	2	McNeill, Allison
	Union (TN)	12	L		31	5	Blackstock, Dr. David
16	Berry	15	A		26	8	Guinn, Connie
	Doane	14	L		26	9	Steinmeyer, Gene
	Fresno Pacific		L		25	6	Stanley, Kent
	Kennesaw State		L		22	9	Walker, Ron
	Louisiana		A		18	13	Brooks, Billy C.
	Northwestern Oklahoma State		L		24	7	Barton, Milburn
	Saint Ambrose	7	A		29	4	Osborn, Rhonda
	Southern Nazarene	5	L		31	3	Finkbeiner, Jerry
32	Auburn: Montgomery	11	A		25	8	Tilley, Colby
	Campbellsville		A		24	6	Wise, Donna H.
	Carson-Newman		L		22	11	Carter, Eddie
	Central State (OH)		A		24	8	Check, Theresa
	Charleston (WV)		A		20	6	Bennett-Travinski, Linda
	Concordia (CA)		A		25	5	Schlichtemeier, Kent
	Dominican (IL)	16	A		28	4	Trefilek, Thomas J.
	Emporia State		L		14	17	Schierling, Val
	Midland Lutheran	9	A		25	5	Bracker, Joanne
	Minnesota: Duluth		A		16	14	Stromme, Karen
	Montevallo	13	L		23	7	Van Atta, Gary
	New Mexico Highlands		A		21	9	Roybal, Cindy
	North Carolina: Pembroke		L		24	7	Pitts, Linda
	Saint Vincent		A		20	9	Zawacki, Kristen
	William Woods		A		25	3	Ternes, Roger
	Wingate		A		22	11	Jacumin, Johnny

1992 Division II

F	School	SD	BD	Bye	W	L	Coach
1	Northern State (SD)	6	L	To R16	30	4	Fredrickson, Curt
2	Tarleton State	4	A	To R16	30	8	Lowrey, Jan
3	Mount Saint Joseph	8	A	To R16	20	8	Dowell, T. Jean
	Western Oregon	7	A	To R16	26	9	Carey, Jon
8	Indiana Tech	3	A	To R16	28	3	Cobb, Gary
	Montana State: Northern	1	A	To R16	30	2	Winn, Sherry
	Mount Mercy	2	A	To R16	30	5	Slifer, David
	Pacific (OR)		L	To R16	23	6	Olmstead, David
16	Aquinas (MI)		A		22	12	Tibaldi, Patti
	Cardinal Stritch (WI)		L	To R16	25	5	Panella, Richard "Rich"
	Concordia (WI)		A	To R16	22	4	Surridge, Dr. Jack
	Culver-Stockton		A		22	11	Turpin, Kathy
	Saint Joseph's (ME)		A		23	8	McDevitt, Michael
	Tabor	5	A	To R16	26	3	Kliewer, Karl
	Tusculum		A	To R16	24	9	Botta, Angelo
	Wilmington (DE)		A		25	11	Rogers, "Rusty"
20	Bloomfield		A		22	8	Manfria, Donald
	Concordia (NE)		A		23	13	Everts, Dr. Carl
	Florida Memorial		A		12	7	Marshall, Kenneth
	Olivet Nazarene		A		18	10	Glass, Robyn

F	School	SD	BD	Bye	W	L	Coach
1993 DIVISION I							
1	Arkansas Tech	4	A		31	5	Foley, Joe M.
2	Union (TN)	2	A		33	5	Blackstock, Dr. David
3	Southern Nazarene	1	A		30	5	Finkbeiner, Jerry
	Southwestern Oklahoma State	3	L		29	4	Loftin, John D.
8	Lipscomb	6	L		28	6	Bennett, Frank
	Montevallo	7	A		26	5	Van Atta, Gary
	Saint Edward's	5	A		28	3	McKey, David
	Wayland Baptist	8	A		25	9	Estes, Sheryl
16	Auburn: Montgomery	14	L		27	6	Tilley, Colby
	Campbellsville	11	A		27	5	Wise, Donna H.
	Central State (OH)	12	A		25	5	Check, Theresa
	Hastings	10	A		31	2	Rhodus, Dr. Ken
	Midwestern State (TX)	13	L		22	8	Ray, Jeff
	Minnesota: Duluth	16	A		22	8	Stromme, Karen
	Oklahoma Christian		L		20	12	Findley, Stephanie
	Oklahoma City		L		23	9	Colon, Bob
32	Arkansas: Monticello	9	L		25	11	Early, Alvy
	Bluefield State (WV)		A		26	3	Jessee, Thomas
	Carson-Newman		L		22	8	Carter, Eddie
	Catawba		A		24	9	Peters, Gary
	Claflin		A		24	10	Brownlee, Nelson C.
	Concordia (CA)		L		26	5	Schlichtemeier, Kent
	Dominican (IL)		A		30	4	Trefilek, Thomas J.
	Fresno Pacific		A		21	8	Stanley, Kent
	Kennesaw State		A		19	11	Walker, Ron
	Mobile		A		22	9	Berger, Curt
	Rockhurst		A		30	2	Rietzke, Tracy
	Saint Vincent		A		23	10	Zawacki, Kristen
	Seattle		L		20	7	Cox, Dave
	Simon Fraser		A		26	8	McNeill, Allison
	William Carey (MS)	15	L		28	4	English, Tracy
	Wingate		L		23	8	Jacumin, Johnny
1993 DIVISION II							
1	Montana State: Northern	1	A	To R16	35	3	Winn, Sherry
2	Northern State (SD)	3	L	To R16	28	7	Fredrickson, Curt
3	Husson	5	A	To R16	28	3	Walker, Mary "Kissy"
	Tarleton State		A	To R16	21	13	Lowrey, Jan
8	Georgetown (KY)	8	A	To R16	27	5	Johnson, Susan
	Indiana Tech	4	A	To R16	25	5	Cobb, Gary
	Mount Mercy	2	A	To R16	28	5	Slifer, David
	Western Oregon	6	A	To R16	26	10	Carey, Jon
16	Aquinas (MI)		A		23	8	Tibaldi, Patti
	Concordia (WI)		A	To R16	23	4	Surridge, Dr. Jack
	Findlay		L	To R16	26	5	Neff, Sheryl
	King (TN)	7	A	To R16	23	4	Nida, Al

F	School	SD	BD	Bye	W	L	Coach
	Ozarks (MO)		A		19	13	Franks, Joe
	Peru State		A		21	10	Davidson, Dr. E. Wayne
	Saint Thomas Aquinas		A		24	9	McManus, Michael
	Sterling (KS)		A	To R16	25	4	Kruse, Lonnie
20	Florida Memorial		A		13	13	Marshall, Kenneth
	Saint Joseph's (ME)		L		24	5	McDevitt, Michael
	Trinity International (IL)		A		24	6	Seils, David S.
	Wilmington (DE)		A		26	6	Rogers, "Rusty"

1994 Division I

F	School	SD	BD	Bye	W	L	Coach
1	Southern Nazarene	1	A		34	0	Finkbeiner, Jerry
2	Lipscomb	7	L		31	7	Bennett, Frank
3	Auburn: Montgomery	4	A		24	4	Tilley, Colby
	Montevallo	6	L		28	7	Van Atta, Gary
8	Arkansas Tech	2	A		30	3	Foley, Joe M.
	Belmont	3	A		32	3	Cross, Tony
	Southwestern Oklahoma State	5	A		25	7	Loftin, John D.
	Union (TN)	8	L		27	6	Blackstock, Dr. David
16	Campbellsville	10	A		26	6	Wise, Donna H.
	Central State (OH)	13	A		25	6	Check, Theresa
	Midwestern State (TX)	12	A		28	6	Ray, Jeff
	Minnesota: Duluth		A		20	11	Stromme, Karen
	Phillips (OK)	14	L		24	7	Carter, Carole
	Saint Ambrose		L		27	6	Becker, Robin
	Simon Fraser	9	A		26	5	McNeill, Allison
	Southeastern Oklahoma State	6 1	L		21	7	Keith, Nick
32	Berry		A		23	9	Guinn, Connie
	Claflin	11	A		26	5	Brownlee, Nelson C.
	Dominican (IL)		A		22	12	Schaefer, Bill
	East Texas Baptist		L		27	6	Reeves, Kent
	Fresno Pacific		A		23	7	Stanley, Kent
	Lees-McRae		A		19	10	Dixon, Janet
	Lindenwood		A		24	7	Crotz, Stephen
	Mary Hardin-Baylor		A		19	16	Foster, Cliffa
	Montana State: Northern		A		26	6	Winn, Sherry
	Oklahoma City		L		22	10	Colon, Bob
	Rio Grande		L		27	7	Smalley, David
	Rockhurst		L		28	4	Rietzke, Tracy
	Saint Vincent		A		21	9	Zawacki, Kristen
	Western New Mexico		A		9	15	Reid, Jason
	Wheeling Jesuit		A		23	5	Hustead, Don
	Xavier (LA)	15	A		28	4	Joseph, Janice

1994 Division II

F	School	SD	BD	Bye	W	L	Coach
1	Northern State (SD)	1	A	To R16	32	1	Fredrickson, Curt
2	Western Oregon	3	A	To R16	31	6	Carey, Jon
3	Concordia (WI)	4	A	To R16	25	4	Surridge, Dr. Jack
	Mount Mercy	2	A	To R16	31	4	Slifer, David

F	School	SD	BD	Bye	W	L	Coach
8	Findlay	7	L	To R16	25	5	Neff, Sheryl
	Lewis & Clark (OR)	6	A	To R16	26	5	Petrie, Paula
	Oklahoma Panhandle State	10	A		19	12	Olson, Jerry
	Shawnee State (OH)	16	A		20	12	Hagen-Smith, Robin
16	Evangel	14	A		26	10	Bowen, Lynn
	Hardin-Simmons	5	A	To R16	24	4	Roewe-Goodenough, Julie
	Huntington	17	A		19	8	Culler, Lori
	Indiana Tech	8	A	To R16	20	7	Cobb, Gary
	Mary	11	A		21	6	Haug, Roger
	South Dakota Tech	20	A		18	11	Felderman, Barbara
	Tennessee Wesleyan	24	A		20	15	Harrison, Stan
	Wilmington (DE)	22	A		21	8	Rogers, "Rusty"
24	Caldwell	18	A		21	6	Costello, Bob
	Friends	19	A		23	7	Carter, Jeff
	Georgetown (KY)	23	A		19	11	Johnson, Susan
	Hastings	13	A		20	11	Rhodus, Dr. Ken
	Lynn	12	A		24	5	Olson, Dan
	Saint Joseph's (ME)	9	A		23	5	McDevitt, Michael
	Spring Arbor	21	A		22	10	Britsch, Tom
	Westbrook	15	A		24	4	Brooks-Ewald, Caroline

1995 Division I

F	School	SD	BD	Bye	W	L	Coach
1	Southern Nazarene	1	A		30	2	Finkbeiner, Jerry
2	Southeastern Oklahoma State	7	L		29	5	Keith, Nick
3	Lipscomb	3	A		34	5	Bennett, Frank
	Southwestern Oklahoma State	5	A		30	5	Loftin, John D.
8	Arkansas: Monticello	6	A		27	6	Early, Alvy
	Auburn: Montgomery	2	A		34	3	Tilley, Colby
	Campbellsville	9	A		28	7	Wise, Donna H.
	Simon Fraser	13	A		23	8	McNeill, Allison
16	Arkansas Tech	8	L		28	6	Foley, Joe M.
	Midwestern State (TX)		L		20	10	Williams, Wayne
	Montevallo	16	L		22	10	Van Atta, Gary
	Oklahoma Christian	14	L		24	9	Findley, Stephanie
	Saint Martin's	15	L		31	5	Peters, Ray
	Union (TN)	4	L		31	3	Blackstock, Dr. David
	Wayland Baptist	10	L		27	8	Estes, Sheryl
	Xavier (LA)	12	A		25	5	Joseph, Janice
32	Belmont Abbey		L		24	6	Kebbe, Elaine
	Central State (OH)		A		20	9	Check, Theresa
	Clayton State		A		19	13	Nestopoulos, Chris
	Dominican (IL)		A		12	16	Smith, Dennis
	East Texas Baptist		L		23	9	Reeves, Kent
	Fresno Pacific		A		21	10	Stanley, Kent
	High Point		A		22	7	Ellenberg, Dr. Joe
	Lindenwood		A		21	12	Crotz, Stephen

F	School	SD	BD	Bye	W	L	Coach
	Mary Hardin-Baylor		L		24	8	Foster, Cliffa
	Montana State: Northern	11	A		25	4	Winn, Sherry
	Rockhurst		A		24	7	Rietzke, Tracy
	Saint Mary's (TX)		A		25	7	Weeaks, Thomas
	Saint Vincent		A		26	7	Zawacki, Kristen
	Salem-Teikyo		A		26	3	Biesenthal, Tammy
	Voorhees		A		21	13	Baker, Cedric W.
	Western New Mexico		A		21	8	Reid, Jason

1995 Division II

F	School	SD	BD	Bye	W	L	Coach
1	Western Oregon	8	A		23	9	Rogers, "Rusty"
2	Northwest Nazarene	10	L		23	7	Schmidt, Roger
3	Concordia (WI)	6	A		20	4	Surridge, Dr. Jack
	Shawnee State (OH)	5	L		31	5	Hagen-Smith, Robin
8	Bethany (KS)		A		21	10	Wiles, Annette
	Findlay	2	A		32	2	Kleinfelter, Eileen
	Mount Mercy	3	A		31	6	Slifer, David
	Northern State (SD)	1	A		28	3	Fredrickson, Curt
16	Brescia		A		23	8	Buchanan, Lee
	Doane	4	A		30	6	Steinmeyer, Gene
	Huron	7	A		26	5	Warwick, Shane
	Indiana Tech	15	A		19	7	Cobb, Gary
	Midland Lutheran	11	L		22	7	Bracker, Joanne
	Sterling (KS)		L		24	6	Kruse, Lonnie
	Tri-State	12	A		23	8	DeRocher, Cindy
	Whitworth (WA)		A		19	12	Higgs, Helen
32	Bloomfield		A		21	8	Manfria, Donald
	Culver-Stockton	14	L		29	6	Clampitt, Randy
	Friends		L		23	6	Carter, Jeff
	Hardin-Simmons		A		19	8	Roewe-Goodenough, Julie
	Houghton		A		21	6	Lord, Harold "Skip"
	Husson		A		23	6	Walker, Mary "Kissy"
	Mary	13	A		18	8	Haug, Roger
	Missouri Valley	9	A		27	9	Piha, Elaine
	Ozarks (MO)		A		18	13	Franks, Joe
	Saint Francis (IN)		A		20	12	Westendorf, Larry
	Saint Thomas Aquinas		L		26	4	McManus, Michael
	Tennessee Wesleyan		A		23	12	Harrison, Stan
	Trinity International (IL)		L		22	4	Seils, David S.
	Tusculum	16	L		27	7	Botta, Angelo
	Webber		A		18	12	Bronaugh, Thurman
	Westbrook		A		19	10	Brooks-Ewald, Caroline

1996 Division I

F	School	SD	BD	Bye	W	L	Coach
1	Southern Nazarene	2	A		34	2	Finkbeiner, Jerry
2	Southeastern Oklahoma State	1	A		30	2	Keith, Nick
3	Lipscomb	5	L		31	6	Bennett, Frank
	Union (TN)	3	A		34	4	Blackstock, Dr. David

F	School	SD	BD	Bye	W	L	Coach
8	Auburn: Montgomery	4	A		31	6	Skinner, Paula
	Central State (OH)	8	A		30	4	Check, Theresa
	Simon Fraser	10	L		31	6	McNeill, Allison
	Western Washington	6	A		26	7	Dollo, Carmen
16	Arkansas Tech	16	L		23	8	Foley, Joe M.
	Campbellsville		A		21	8	Wise, Donna H.
	East Central (OK)	7	L		30	5	Franz, Kent
	Mary Hardin-Baylor		A		22	8	Foster, Cliffa
	Montana State: Northern	12	A		24	5	Winn, Sherry
	Montevallo	11	L		24	5	Van Atta, Gary
	Western New Mexico	13	A		25	6	Reid, Jason
	Xavier (LA)	9	A		28	6	Joseph, Janice
32	Belmont	15	L		26	8	Cross, Tony
	Biola		A		19	12	Andressen, Amber
	Claflin		A		21	9	Brownlee, Nelson C.
	Daemen		A		27	5	Skolen, David
	Georgia Southwestern		A		22	10	Drown, Kip
	Harding		L		24	5	Harnden, Greg
	LeTourneau		A		19	10	Otwell, Mary Ann
	Lewis-Clark State (ID)		L		25	7	Divilbiss, Mike
	Lindenwood		A		21	11	Crotz, Stephen
	Northwestern Oklahoma State		L		19	13	Barton, Milburn
	Oklahoma Baptist University		L		21	12	Norris, Scott
	Purdue: Calumet		A		27	5	Hayes, Gary
	Rockhurst		L		26	3	Rietzke, Tracy
	Saint Mary's (TX)		L		20	11	Weeaks, Thomas
	Southwestern Oklahoma State		L		20	9	Loftin, John D.
	Wayland Baptist	14	L		25	9	Estes, Sheryl

1996 DIVISION II

F	School	SD	BD	Bye	W	L	Coach
1	Western Oregon	1	A		31	4	Rogers, "Rusty"
2	Huron	3	A		30	5	Warwick, Shane
3	Doane	2	A		31	7	Steinmeyer, Gene
	Evangel	4	A		31	5	Bowen, Lynn
8	Black Hills State	12	L		24	7	Schamber, Robin
	Briar Cliff		A		23	11	Powell, Michael
	Saint Ambrose	7	A		30	6	Becker, Robin
	Tri-State		H		20	12	DeRocher, Cindy
16	Bethany (KS)	13	L		26	5	Wiles, Annette
	Cardinal Stritch (WI)		L		20	8	Panella, Richard "Rich"
	Findlay	14	L		25	8	Kleinfelter, Eileen
	Georgetown (KY)		L		21	10	Johnson, Susan
	Midland Lutheran	9	L		26	6	Bracker, Joanne
	Saint Francis (IN)		A		20	12	Westendorf, Larry
	Shawnee State (OH)	5	A		31	4	Hagen-Smith, Robin
	Tusculum	11	A		30	5	Curtis, Merry Beth

F	School	SD	BD	Bye	W	L	Coach
32	Brescia	6	A		27	4	Buchanan, Lee
	Holy Family (PA)		A		25	8	McLaughlin, Michael
	Husson		A		21	8	Walker, Mary "Kissy"
	Judson (IL)		A		21	9	Gum, Tory
	Minot State		A		17	11	Green, Shelia L.
	Mount Saint Joseph		A		25	16	McKee, Rebecca
	Northwest Nazarene	10	L		17	10	Schmidt, Roger
	Ozarks (MO)		A		18	10	Franks, Joe
	Pacific (OR)		A		17	10	Olmstead, David
	Saint Thomas Aquinas	16	A		25	6	McManus, Michael
	South Dakota Tech		L		19	11	Felderman, Barbara
	Spring Arbor		A		26	9	Britsch, Tom
	Sterling (KS)	8	A		28	1	Kruse, Lonnie
	Sul Ross State		A		13	8	Sample, Dr. Chet
	Westbrook		A		21	12	Martin, John
	Willamette	15	L		19	8	Petrie, Paula

1997 DIVISION I

F	School	SD	BD	Bye	W	L	Coach
1	Southern Nazarene	4	A		32	4	Finkbeiner, Jerry
2	Union (TN)	3	A		35	5	Blackstock, Dr. David
3	Arkansas Tech	1	A		29	4	Foley, Joe M.
	Southwestern Oklahoma State	7	L		28	5	Loftin, John D.
8	Central State (OH)	5	L		29	3	Check, Theresa
	Oklahoma Baptist University	6	L		28	9	Norris, Scott
	Simon Fraser	2	A		31	4	McNeill, Allison
	Wayland Baptist	9	L		25	8	Pointer, Johnna
16	Campbellsville	15	A		24	9	Wise, Donna H.
	Freed-Hardeman		A		26	11	Neal, Dale
	Harding	10	L		26	4	Harnden, Greg
	Lewis-Clark State (ID)	8	L		25	7	Divilbiss, Mike
	Lipscomb	16	L		26	10	Bennett, Frank
	Mary Hardin-Baylor		A		22	8	Foster, Cliffa
	Southeastern Oklahoma State	14	L		24	6	Keith, Nick
	Xavier (LA)		A		29	7	Joseph, Janice
32	Auburn: Montgomery		A		19	11	Crotz, Stephen
	Claflin		L		22	10	Brownlee, Nelson C.
	Concordia (CA)		A		28	6	Wolter, Dave
	Daemen		A		27	6	Skolen, David
	East Central (OK)	13	A		19	9	Franz, Kent
	Hannibal-Lagrange		A		25	8	Barnes, Daren
	Indiana: South Bend		A		24	10	Wisnewski, Mary
	LeTourneau		A		26	4	Otwell, Mary Ann
	Montana State: Northern	12	A		25	7	Winn, Sherry
	North Georgia		A		26	7	Burson, Buffie
	Oklahoma Christian		L		22	11	Findley, Stephanie
	Rio Grande		A		23	12	Smalley, David

F	School	SD	BD	Bye	W	L	Coach
	Saint Mary's (TX)		L		23	8	Weeaks, Thomas
	Tougaloo		A		19	16	Brown, Yolanda
	Transylvania		A		27	7	Turner, Mark
	Voorhees		A		19	12	Baker, Cedric W.

1997 Division II

F	School	SD	BD	Bye	W	L	Coach
1	Northwest Nazarene	3	A		27	7	Schmidt, Roger
2	Black Hills State	8	A		27	7	Schamber, Robin
3	Doane	10	A		28	9	Steinmeyer, Gene
	Southern Oregon	12	L		25	9	Huyett, Shirley
8	Brescia	4	A		30	6	Buchanan, Lee
	Briar Cliff	2	A		37	1	Powell, Michael
	Concordia (NE)	16	L		26	6	Lemke, Dr. Mark
	Saint Francis (IN)	11	A		28	8	Westendorf, Larry
16	Austin		A		24	4	Potera, Robin
	Central Methodist		A		28	8	Davis, Mike
	Holy Family (PA)		A		28	5	McLaughlin, Michael
	Milligan		A		30	5	Aubrey, Richard
	Ozarks (MO)	6	A		29	3	Franks, Joe
	Shawnee State (OH)	1	A		29	2	Hagen-Smith, Robin
	Sterling (KS)	7	A		28	2	Kruse, Lonnie
	Tri-State	5	A		23	6	DeRocher, Cindy
32	Benedictine (KS)		A		26	6	Huber, Steve
	Cardinal Stritch (WI)		L		22	6	Panella, Richard "Rich"
	Castleton State		A		21	6	Conover, Richard
	Concordia (WI)		A		18	9	Witte, Ken
	Covenant		A		21	7	Smialek, Tami
	Dominican (CA)		A		23	8	Powell, Roneil
	Grand View	9	A		28	7	Sharer, Missy
	Madonna		A		14	15	Jansen, Marylou
	Maine: Farmington		A		20	5	MacPhee, Leonard R.
	Mary	13	A		20	7	Haug, Roger
	Puget Sound		A		22	5	Bricker, Dr. Beth
	Saint Ambrose	14	L		28	6	Becker, Robin
	Saint Thomas Aquinas		A		21	8	McManus, Michael
	South Dakota Tech	15	L		21	9	Felderman, Barbara
	Taylor		L		28	8	Krause, Tina
	Tusculum		A		20	10	Curtis, Merry Beth

1998 Division I

F	School	SD	BD	Bye	W	L	Coach
1	Union (TN)	1	A		35	3	Blackstock, Dr. David
2	Southern Nazarene	3	L		31	6	Wiginton, Craig
3	Findlay		A		26	7	Kleinfelter, Eileen
	Simon Fraser	2	A		31	6	McNeill, Allison
8	Campbellsville	6	A		25	8	Wise, Donna H.
	Lewis-Clark State (ID)	12	L		22	8	Divilbiss, Mike
	Oklahoma Baptist University	8	L		28	7	Norris, Scott
	Wayland Baptist	7	A		25	11	Pointer, Johnna

F	School	SD	BD	Bye	W	L	Coach
16	Auburn: Montgomery	10	A		23	10	Crotz, Stephen
	East Central (OK)		A		20	11	Franz, Kent
	Montana State: Northern	16	A		25	9	Peters, Ray
	Oklahoma City		L		19	13	Stanley, Kent
	Phillips (OK)	5	L		25	7	Price, Denny
	Rockhurst	9	A		23	6	Mitts, Maryann
	Southeastern Oklahoma State	14	L		22	6	Keith, Nick
	Xavier (LA)	4	A		27	4	Joseph, Janice
32	Central State (OH)	11	L		25	7	Check, Theresa A.
	Claflin		A		23	10	Brownlee, Nelson C.
	Freed-Hardeman		A		24	11	Neal, Dale
	Georgia Southwestern		A		22	12	Drown, Kip
	Incarnate Word		A		19	10	Walling, Sally
	Indiana: South Bend		A		23	6	Wisnewski, Mary
	LeTourneau		A		24	10	Otwell, Mary Ann
	Lipscomb	15	L		23	12	Bennett, Frank
	Louisiana		A		23	7	Brooks, Billy C.
	McKendree		A		20	15	Miller, Melissa
	Northwestern Oklahoma State		L		25	8	Barton, Milburn
	Pikeville		A		21	14	Watson, Bill
	Saint Vincent		A		26	5	Zawacki, Kristen
	Southern California College		A		29	6	Davis, Russ
	Southwestern Oklahoma State		L		21	8	Loftin, John D.
	Western Washington	13	L		21	9	Dollo, Carmen

1998 DIVISION II

F	School	SD	BD	Bye	W	L	Coach
1	Walsh			L	29	5	Smesco, Carl
2	Mary Hardin-Baylor			A	24	6	Van Auken, Jeff
3	Doane	10		L	29	9	Steinmeyer, Gene
	South Dakota Tech	4		A	28	4	Felderman, Barbara
8	Central Methodist	15	A		25	8	Davis, Mike
	Holy Family (PA)	11	A		33	5	McLaughlin, Michael
	Saint Francis (IN)	12	L		31	6	Westendorf, Larry
	Spring Arbor		A		23	11	Britsch, Tom
16	Benedictine (KS)	8	A		28	7	Huber, Steve
	Briar Cliff	1	A		31	4	Powell, Michael
	Grand View	3	A		32	4	Sharer, Missy
	Holy Names (CA)		A		23	8	DeLuca, Mark
	Shawnee State (OH)	5	A		25	5	Hagen-Smith, Robin
	Southern Oregon	2	A		28	4	Huyett, Shirley
	Sterling (KS)		A		26	7	Kruse, Lonnie
	Taylor		A		20	15	Krause, Tina
32	Albertson	16	L		22	9	Corman, Todd
	Black Hills State	7	L		25	5	Dobbs, Kevin
	Cardinal Stritch (WI)		A		27	5	Panella, Richard 'Rich'
	Castleton State		A		21	7	Conover, Richard

F	School	SD	BD	Bye	W	L	Coach
	Concordia (NE)	9	A		24	8	Lemke, Dr. Mark
	Illinois: Springfield		A		23	8	Stiles-Krone, Juli
	Maine: Farmington		A		20	5	MacPhee, Leonard R.
	Milligan		A		27	8	Aubrey, Richard "Rich"
	Minot State		A		20	8	Green, Sheila L.
	Ozarks (MO)	14	A		24	7	Wilson, George
	Pacific Lutheran		A		21	7	Rigell, Gil
	Puget Sound		A		15	13	Bricker, Dr. Beth
	Saint Thomas Aquinas	13	A		25	4	McManus, Michael
	Tennessee Wesleyan		A		19	12	Harrison, Stan
	Webber		A		14	18	Saxon, Michelle
	Western Oregon	6	L		24	11	Rogers, "Rusty"

School Participation History

Year	M/W	Div	F	SD	BD	Bye	#T	W	L	Coach
ABILENE CHRISTIAN										
1980	M	16	6		A		32	24	4	Tate, Willard N.
ADAMS STATE										
1972	M	16			A		32	18	11	Lutz, Dr. Loren
1953		32					32	19	8	Crawford, Ronald
ADELPHI										
1957	M	32					32	13	12	Faherty, George E.
ADRIAN										
1953	M	32					32	18	7	Boyett, Theodore R.
1955		32					32	21	4	Skala, Jim
1957		32					32	16	6	Albeck, Charles Stanley "Stan"
AKRON										
1943	M	32					32	17	4	Beichly, Russell J.
ALABAMA STATE										
1980	M	2	1		A		32	32	2	Oliver, James V.
ALABAMA: HUNTSVILLE										
1981	M	2	5		A		32	30	7	Willis, A. L. "Kayo"
1976		8			A		32	26	9	Willis, A. L. "Kayo"
1977		16			A		32	19	10	Willis, A. L. "Kayo"
1983		32			A		32	25	11	Willis, A. L. "Kayo"
1983	W	2	6		A		8	27	8	Dunaway, Donna Caldwell
ALBANY STATE (GA)										
1965	M	16			A		32	27	6	Rainey, Robert C.
1967		32			A		32	25	6	Rainey, Robert C.
1968		32	13		A		32	32	8	Rainey, Robert C.

Year	M/W	Div	F	SD	BD	Bye	#T	W	L	Coach
ALBERTSON										
1996	M	II	1	3	A		32	31	3	Holly, Martin W. "Marty"
1988			8	14	A		32	28	6	Holly, Martin W. "Marty"
1989			8	16	A		32	24	9	Holly, Martin W. "Marty"
1993		II	8		L	To R16	20	22	8	Holly, Martin W. "Marty"
1991			16	10	A		32	24	5	Holly, Martin W. "Marty"
1960			32		A		32	16	13	Brown, James A. "Babe"
1962			32		A		32	18	10	Carrow, Dr. Richard W.
1984			32		A		32	22	7	Holly, Martin W. "Marty"
1985			32	9	A		32	20	3	Holly, Martin W. "Marty"
1986			32		A		32	23	7	Holly, Martin W. "Marty"
1995		II	32	7	L		32	21	8	Holly, Martin W. "Marty"
1998	W	II	32	16	L		32	22	9	Corman, Todd
ALBUQUERQUE										
1966	M		16	7	A		32	25	5	Smith, Ernie
1964			32		A		32	17	8	
1968			32		A		32	13	4	Smith, Ernie
ALCORN STATE										
1974	M		2	4	A		32	29	6	Whitney, David L., Sr. "Davey"
1975			3	8	A		32	25	10	Whitney, David L., Sr. "Davey"
1977			8	14	A		32	26	9	Whitney, David L., Sr. "Davey"
1968			16	7	A		32	24	3	Hopkins, Robert M.
1967			32		A		32	20	8	Hopkins, Robert M.
1973			32	7	A		32	25	4	Whitney, David L., Sr. "Davey"
1976			32	3	A		32	27	4	Whitney, David L., Sr. "Davey"
ALDERSON-BROADDUS										
1955	M		8				32	31	6	Pyles, Rex E. "Roxie"
1990			16	10	A		32	28	7	Dodd, Steve
1956			32				32	23	12	Pyles, Rex E. "Roxie"
ALFRED HOLBROOK										
1939	M		32				32	15	5	Beattie, Mendell E.
1940			32				32	16	4	Beattie, Mendell E.
ALICE LLOYD										
1993	M	II	16		A	To R16	20	27	6	Stepp, Jim
1996		II	16	15	L		32	27	8	Stepp, Jim
ALLIANCE										
1963	M		16	11	A		32	19	6	Haluch, Thaddeus F.
1965			16	13	A		32	18	8	Haluch, Thaddeus F.
ALMA										
1941	M		16				32	23	3	MacDonald, Gordon D.
AMERICAN										
1950	M		32				32	22	8	Cassell, Stafford H.
1951			32				32	18	10	Cassell, Stafford H.

Year	M/W	Div	F	SD	BD	Bye	#T	W	L	Coach
AMERICAN INTERNATIONAL										
1952	M		32				32	15	10	Rodis, Nicholas
1956			32				32	16	7	Callahan, William E.
ANDERSON (IN)										
1961	M		8	5	A		32	26	4	Macholtz, Robert W.
1958			16		A		32	23	6	Macholtz, Robert W.
1939			32				32	15	6	Nay, Edgar
APPALACHIAN STATE										
1941	M		8				32	17	3	Canipe, Clyde
1943			8				32	15	3	Smawley, Belus
1940			16				32	18	3	Stewart, A. L. "Flucie"
1948			32				32	20	8	Hoover, Francis
1950			32				32	20	8	Hoover, Francis
AQUINAS (MI)										
1990	W		16		L		16	26	6	Tibaldi, Patti
1992		II	16		A		20	22	12	Tibaldi, Patti
1993		II	16		A		20	23	8	Tibaldi, Patti
ARIZONA STATE										
1948	M		16				32	13	11	Lavik, Rudolph H.
1953			16				32	13	12	Kajikawa, William
ARKANSAS STATE										
1947	M		32				32	17	16	Tomlinson, J. A. "Ike"
1949			32				32	14	12	Tomlinson, J. A. "Ike"
ARKANSAS TECH										
1995	M	I	3	7	A		32	29	6	Barnes, Marty
1954			4				32	28	3	Hindsman, Sam F., Jr.
1955			4				32	31	5	Hindsman, Sam F., Jr.
1950			16				32	26	2	Hindsman, Sam F., Jr.
1951			16				32	25	6	Hindsman, Sam F., Jr.
1953			16				32	20	1	Hindsman, Sam F., Jr.
1970			16		A		32	22	10	Dopson, Dewaard
1996		I	16		A		32	19	10	Barnes, Marty
1952			32				32	26	4	Hindsman, Sam F., Jr.
1956			32				32	15	6	Hindsman, Sam F., Jr.
1958			32		A		32	17	4	Hindsman, Sam F., Jr.
1963			32		A		32	19	9	Hindsman, Sam F., Jr.
1992	W	I	1	2	A		32	35	1	Foley, Joe M.
1993		I	1	4	A		32	31	5	Foley, Joe M.
1988			3	3	A		16	29	5	Foley, Joe M.
1989			3	2	A		16	35	2	Foley, Joe M.
1997		I	3	1	A		32	29	4	Foley, Joe M.
1987			4	6	A		16	29	6	Dickerson, Jim
1994		I	8	2	A		32	30	3	Foley, Joe M.
1995		I	16	8	L		32	28	6	Foley, Joe M.
1996		I	16	16	L		32	23	8	Foley, Joe M.
ARKANSAS: MONTICELLO										
1986	M		2		A		32	26	10	Sharpe, Gary A.
1960			16		A		32	18	8	Beard, Leslie "Shorty"

Year	M/W	Div	F	SD	BD	Bye	#T	W	L	Coach
1990	W		2	2	A		16	34	3	Early, Alvy
1995		I	8	6	A		32	27	6	Early, Alvy
1993		I	32	9	L		32	25	11	Early, Alvy

ARNOLD

Year	M/W	Div	F	SD	BD	Bye	#T	W	L	Coach
1953	M		32				32	17	11	Maroon, Tuffie

ASHLAND

Year	M/W	Div	F	SD	BD	Bye	#T	W	L	Coach
1962	M		32		A		32	21	4	Stoker, Bob

ASSUMPTION (MA)

Year	M/W	Div	F	SD	BD	Bye	#T	W	L	Coach
1958	M		32		A		32	16	4	Laska, Andrew

ATHENS STATE

Year	M/W	Div	F	SD	BD	Bye	#T	W	L	Coach
1985	M		8		A		32	20	7	Murrell, Harold
1991			8	13	A		32	20	9	Murrell, Harold
1963			16		A		32	23	9	Belcher, Oba E.
1966			16		A		32	20	10	Belcher, Oba E.
1968			32		A		32	16	14	Belcher, Oba E.

AUBURN: MONTGOMERY

Year	M/W	Div	F	SD	BD	Bye	#T	W	L	Coach
1988	M		2	4	A		32	26	2	Chapman, Larry F.
1987			8	14	A		32	25	8	Chapman, Larry F.
1989			16	7	A		32	24	7	Chapman, Larry F.
1994		I	32		A		32	20	12	Chapman, Larry F.
1994	W	I	3	4	A		32	24	4	Tilley, Colby
1995		I	8	2	A		32	34	3	Tilley, Colby
1996		I	8	4	A		32	31	6	Skinner, Paula
1987			16		A		16	20	11	Tilley, Colby
1993		I	16	14	L		32	27	6	Tilley, Colby
1998		I	16	10	A		32	23	10	Crotz, Stephen
1991			32		A		32	24	9	Tilley, Colby
1992		I	32	11	A		32	25	8	Tilley, Colby
1997		I	32		A		32	19	11	Crotz, Stephen

AUGSBURG

Year	M/W	Div	F	SD	BD	Bye	#T	W	L	Coach
1965	M		8	9	A		32	26	4	Anderson, Ernest W.
1981			8	3	A		32	29	2	Johnson, Rees
1946			16				32	19	2	Carlson, Robert
1963			16	2	A		32	23	2	Anderson, Ernest W.
1977			32		A		32	23	7	Inniger, Ervin L., Jr.
1980			32	8	L		32	25	1	Johnson, Rees

AUGUSTA STATE

Year	M/W	Div	F	SD	BD	Bye	#T	W	L	Coach
1970	M		16	16	A		32	23	2	Vanover, Marvin
1971			32	15	A		32	20	4	Vanover, Marvin

AUGUSTANA (IL)

Year	M/W	Div	F	SD	BD	Bye	#T	W	L	Coach
1973	M		3	2	A		32	29	2	Borcherding, James
1972			8	9	A		32	25	4	Borcherding, James
1974			8	8	A		32	25	4	Borcherding, James
1939			16				32	17	6	Almquist, H. V.
1940			32				32	10	9	Almquist, H. V.

Year	M/W	Div	F	SD	BD	Bye	#T	W	L	Coach
AUSTIN										
1958	M		32		A		32	17	9	Gass, Floyd
1959			32		A		32	29	14	Gass, Floyd
1997	W	II	16		A		32	24	4	Potera, Robin
AUSTIN PEAY STATE										
1957	M		32				32	24	9	Aaron, David B.
AZUSA PACIFIC										
1998	M	I	3	1	A		32	35	5	Odell, William M.
1994		I	16	11	L		32	29	5	Odell, William M.
1997		I	16	12	A		32	29	8	Odell, William M.
1974			32	11	A		32	28	5	Hamlow, Dr. Clifford
1993		I	32	2	A		32	30	4	Odell, William M.
1996		I	32	12	L		32	26	8	Odell, William M.
1981	W		4	3	A		8	18	15	Hebel, Dr. Susan L.
1986			16	8	A		16	30	5	Hebel, Dr. Susan L.
BAKER (KS)										
1937	M		8		I		8	14	3	Liston, Emil S.
1941			32				32	14	8	Liston, Emil S.
1996		II	32		L		32	25	10	Weaver, Rick
BALDWIN-WALLACE										
1951	M		3				32	19	7	Wagner, J. Larsen
1950			8				32	12	16	Watts, Ray E.
BALL STATE										
1957	M		16				32	19	8	Hinga, John "Jim"
BALTIMORE										
1941	M		16				32	17	3	Unknown
1952			32				32	16	8	Bartheleme, Albert L.
BARTON										
1955	M		16				32	23	6	McComas, James E. "Jack"
1986			16		A		32	25	10	Edwards, Gary
1987			32		A		32	25	9	Edwards, Gary
BELHAVEN										
1972	M		16	16	A		32	22	6	Rugg, Charles R.
BELLEVUE (NE)										
1998	M	II	32		A		32	17	14	Richards, Brett
BELMONT										
1995	M	I	3	1	A		32	37	2	Byrd, Rick
1996		I	3		L		32	28	11	Byrd, Rick
1994		I	8	8	A		32	30	7	Byrd, Rick
1993		I	16		L		32	30	6	Byrd, Rick
1989			32	10	A		32	25	10	Byrd, Rick

Year	M/W	Div	F	SD	BD	Bye	#T	W	L	Coach
1991	W		8	10	A		32	32	5	Cross, Tony
1992		I	8	10	A		32	31	5	Cross, Tony
1994		I	8	3	A		32	32	3	Cross, Tony
1996		I	32	15	L		32	26	8	Cross, Tony

BELMONT ABBEY

1962	M		32		A		32	16	9	McGuire, Alfred J.
1988			32		A		32	22	9	Eastman, Kevin
1991	W		32	15	A		32	23	6	Kebbe, Elaine
1995		I	32		L		32	24	6	Kebbe, Elaine

BELOIT

1949	M		3				32	29	4	Stanley, Dolph
1947			8				32	22	5	Stanley, Dolph
1948			8				32	24	3	Stanley, Dolph
1955			8				32	22	4	Stanley, Dolph

BEMIDJI STATE

1942	M		8				32	14	6	Frost, Reuben B. `Jack`
1941			16				32	14	3	Frost, Reuben B. `Jack`
1940			32				32	13	3	Frost, Reuben B. `Jack`
1987	W		16		L		16	25	2	Mathison, Sherri

BENEDICT

1994	M	I	8	15	A		32	29	3	Washington, Willie
1998		I	16		A		32	22	9	Washington, Willie
1993		I	32		A		32	23	4	Washington, Willie
1997		I	32	4	L		32	30	3	Washington, Willie

BENEDICTINE (KS)

1954	M		1				32	24	5	Nolan, Ralph
1967			1	1	A		32	27	2	Nolan, Ralph
1937			8		I		8	17	3	Mullins, Larry
1965			8	5	A		32	26	3	Nolan, Ralph
1953			16				32	21	8	Nolan, Ralph
1958			32		A		32	20	6	Nolan, Ralph
1970			32		A		32	17	9	Nolan, Ralph
1998	W	II	16	8	A		32	28	7	Huber, Steve
1997		II	32		A		32	26	6	Huber, Steve

BEREA

1985	M		32		A		32	20	10	Wierwille, Roland R.
1996		II	32		A		32	18	9	Wierwille, Roland R.
1998		II	32		A		32	20	10	Wierwille, Roland R.

BERRY

1992	M	I	32		A		32	27	8	Smyly, Todd
1982	W		4	2	A		8	29	4	Paul, Brenda
1984			4	7	L		16	32	5	Paul, Brenda
1981			8	2	A		8	16	9	Paul, Brenda
1992		I	16	15	A		32	26	8	Guinn, Connie
1991			32		A		32	26	8	Guinn, Connie
1994		I	32		A		32	23	9	Guinn, Connie

Year	M/W	Div	F	SD	BD	Bye	#T	W	L	Coach
BETHANY (KS)										
1995	W	II	8		A		32	21	10	Wiles, Annette
1996		II	16	13	L		32	26	5	Wiles, Annette
BETHEL (IN)										
1995	M	II	1	3	A		32	38	2	Lightfoot, Mike
1997		II	1	2	L		32	34	5	Lightfoot, Mike
1998		II	1	1	L		32	37	3	Lightfoot, Mike
1994		II	16	5	A	To R16	24	30	5	Lightfoot, Mike
1996		II	16	1	A		32	35	2	Lightfoot, Mike
BETHUNE-COOKMAN										
1966	M		32	14	A		32	20	8	McClairen, Jack "Cy"
BIOLA										
1982	M		2	1	A		32	39	1	Lyon, Howard
1992		I	8	4	A		32	33	4	Holmquist, Dr. David G.
1980			16	10	A		32	26	4	Lyon, Howard
1981			16	10	A		32	25	7	Lyon, Howard
1997		I	16	14	L		32	28	6	Holmquist, Dr. David G.
1998		I	16	11	L		32	30	7	Holmquist, Dr. David G.
1985			32	5	A		32	29	4	Lyon, Howard
1987			32	3	A		32	29	2	Lyon, Howard
1989			32		A		32	29	8	Holmquist, Dr. David G.
1984	W		16		A		16	22	11	Norman, Betty
1996		I	32		A		32	19	12	Andressen, Amber
BIRMINGHAM-SOUTHERN										
1990	M		1	4	A		32	31	3	Reboul, Duane
1995		I	1	5	A		32	35	2	Reboul, Duane
1996		I	8	6	L		32	25	5	Reboul, Duane
1997		I	8	8	A		32	28	6	Reboul, Duane
1978			16	11	A		32	29	5	Walcavich, Greg
1986			16	3	A		32	28	4	Dean, Joe, Jr.
1992		I	16	14	L		32	28	7	Reboul, Duane
1993		I	16	5	A		32	29	7	Reboul, Duane
1979			32	4	A		32	29	4	Walcavich, Greg
1982			32		A		32	18	15	Walcavich, Greg
1984			32	15	A		32	23	8	Dean, Joe, Jr.
1998		I	32	7	A		32	28	5	Reboul, Duane
BISHOP										
1968	M		32		A		32	23	6	Jones, Dr. Emanuel M.
1972			32		A		32	23	11	Alexander, Charles
BLACK HILLS STATE										
1997	M	II	8	11	L		32	24	6	Olson, Mike
1998		II	16		A		32	21	8	Olson, Mike
1994		II	24	19	L		24	19	11	Olson, Mike
1997	W	II	2	8	A		32	27	7	Schamber, Robin
1996		II	8	12	L		32	24	7	Schamber, Robin
1998		II	32	7	L		32	25	5	Dobbs, Kevin

Year	M/W	Div	F	SD	BD	Bye	#T	W	L	Coach
BLOOMFIELD										
1992	W	II	20		A		20	22	8	Manfria, Donald
1995		II	32		A		32	21	8	Manfria, Donald
BLUEFIELD (VA)										
1996	M	II	32		A		32	22	12	Ayers, Walter
BLUEFIELD STATE (WV)										
1985	W		16		A		16	24	4	Mandeville, Kenneth A. "Kenny"
1987			16		A		16	20	8	Mandeville, Kenneth A. "Kenny"
1993		I	32		A		32	26	3	Jessee, Thomas
BRESCIA										
1997	W	II	8	4	A		32	30	6	Buchanan, Lee
1995		II	16		A		32	23	8	Buchanan, Lee
1996		II	32	6	A		32	27	4	Buchanan, Lee
BRIAR CLIFF										
1979	M		8	6	A		32	28	3	Nacke, Ray
1978			16	16	A		32	25	4	Nacke, Ray
1981			16	1	A		32	23	2	Nacke, Ray
1982			16		A		32	21	10	Nacke, Ray
1991			16	14	A		32	27	6	Nacke, Ray
1993		I	16	14	A		32	27	6	Nacke, Ray
1998		II	16	16	A		32	23	12	Beard, Michael
1976			32		A		32	19	8	Nacke, Ray
1977			32		A		32	19	9	Nacke, Ray
1986			32	8	A		32	23	4	Nacke, Ray
1990			32		A		32	24	7	Nacke, Ray
1992		I	32	10	A		32	25	4	Nacke, Ray
1996	W	II	8		A		32	23	11	Powell, Michael
1997		II	8	2	A		32	37	1	Powell, Michael
1998		II	16	1	A		32	31	4	Powell, Michael
BRIDGEPORT										
1954	M		32				32	12	9	Glines, Herbert E.
BRIGHAM YOUNG										
1948	M		16				32	16	11	Millet, W. Floyd
1949			16				32	22	14	Millet, W. Floyd
BRIGHAM YOUNG: HAWAII										
1992	M	I	3	6	A		32	28	7	Wagner, A. Kenyon "Ken"
1996		I	16	5	A		32	24	7	Wagner, A. Kenyon "Ken"
1997		I	16		L		32	21	8	Wagner, A. Kenyon "Ken"
1986			32		A		32	17	13	Chidester, Ted H.
1989			32		A		32	24	9	Hess, Dr. Charles "Chic"
1998		I	32	12	L		32	19	8	Wagner, A. Kenyon "Ken"
BROOKLYN										
1950	M		8				32	24	5	Baggett, Al

Year	M/W	Div	F	SD	BD	Bye	#T	W	L	Coach
BRYANT										.
1975	M		32		A		32	21	8	Folliard, Thomas J.
BUENA VISTA										
1962	M		32	11	A		32	25	3	Ewalt, Merritt A.
1964			32		A		32	18	7	Ewalt, Merritt A.
CABRINI										
1984	M		32		A		32	22	12	Dzik, John L.
1985			32		A		32	22	12	Dzik, John L.
1986			32		A		32	24	7	Dzik, John L.
1987			32		A		32	24	8	Dzik, John L.
CALDWELL										
1993	M	II	20		A		20	21	8	Corino, Mark A.
1996		II	32		A		32	21	9	Corino, Mark A.
1998		II	32		A		32	· 23	7	Corino, Mark A.
1994	W	II	24	18	A		24	21	6	Costello, Bob
CALIFORNIA (PA)										
1970	M		32		A		32	20	5	Witchery, Myles B.
CALIFORNIA BAPTIST										
1976	M		16	10	A		32	28	4	Evans, Floyd C.
1982	W		8	7	A		8	25	6	King, David F.
CALIFORNIA STATE: DOMINGUEZ HILLS										
1979	M		32		A		32	21	9	Yanai, David
CALIFORNIA STATE: FULLERTON										
1962	M		8	9	A		32	24	7	Omalev, Alex
CALIFORNIA: SANTA BARBARA										
1941	M		4				32	22	10	Wilton, Wilton M. "Willie"
CAMERON										
1980	M		1	3	A		32	28	3	Nichols, Lonnie
1979			8	1	A		32	34	2	Nichols, Lonnie
1974			32		A		32	24	6	Miller, Raymond H. "Red"
CAMPBELL										
1977	M		2		A		32	23	10	Roberts, Danny
1970			32		A		32	24	5	Roberts, Danny
CAMPBELLSVILLE										
1981	M		32		A		32	21	8	Cunningham, Lou
1991			32		A		32	19	12	Cunningham, Lou
1983	W		8	3	A		8	24	5	Wise, Donna H.
1995		I	8	9	A		32	28	7	Wise, Donna H.
1998		I	8	6	A		32	25	8	Wise, Donna H.
1990			16		A		16	21	11	Wise, Donna H.

Year	M/W	Div	F	SD	BD	Bye	#T	W	L	Coach
1993	I		16	11	A		32	27	5	Wise, Donna H.
1994	I		16	10	A		32	26	6	Wise, Donna H.
1996	I		16		A		32	21	8	Wise, Donna H.
1997	I		16	15	A		32	24	9	Wise, Donna H.
1991			32		A		32	22	8	Wise, Donna H.
1992	I		32		A		32	24	6	Wise, Donna H.

CANTERBURY

Year	M/W	Div	F	SD	BD	Bye	#T	W	L	Coach
1945	M		8				16	14	12	Johnson, Glenn A.
1947			16				32	13	9	Johnson, Glenn A.

CARDINAL STRITCH (WI)

Year	M/W	Div	F	SD	BD	Bye	#T	W	L	Coach
1998	M	II	16		A		32	24	9	Fox, Denny
1992	W	II	16		L	To R16	20	25	5	Panella, Richard "Rich"
1996		II	16		L		32	20	8	Panella, Richard "Rich"
1997		II	32		L		32	22	6	Panella, Richard "Rich"
1998		II	32		A		32	27	5	Panella, Richard "Rich"

CARROLL (MT)

Year	M/W	Div	F	SD	BD	Bye	#T	W	L	Coach
1966	M		16		A		32	20	12	Askew, Presley
1997	I		32		A		32	22	11	Turcott, Gary

CARROLL (WI)

Year	M/W	Div	F	SD	BD	Bye	#T	W	L	Coach
1954	M		32				32	15	7	Huddleston, Don

CARSON-NEWMAN

Year	M/W	Div	F	SD	BD	Bye	#T	W	L	Coach
1964	M		3	4	A		32	31	4	Campbell, Richard
1962			8		A		32	29	7	Campbell, Richard
1963			8	9	A		32	25	4	Campbell, Richard
1966			8	2	A		32	25	6	Hamilton, Larry
1983			8	11	A		32	31	5	Jones, Dr. Chris
1961			32		A		32	26	7	Campbell, Richard
1984			32	12	A		32	31	8	Jones, Dr. Chris
1985	W		8	5	L		16	32	3	Bivens, Lewis
1984			16	5	A		16	26	6	Bivens, Lewis
1992	I		32		L		32	22	11	Carter, Eddie
1993	I		32		L		32	22	8	Carter, Eddie

CASTLETON STATE

Year	M/W	Div	F	SD	BD	Bye	#T	W	L	Coach
1985	M		32		A		32	23	7	Van Gundy, Stan A.
1998		II	32		A		32	19	8	Blake, Dave
1997	W	II	32		A		32	21	6	Conover, Richard
1998		II	32		A		32	21	7	Conover, Richard

CATAWBA

Year	M/W	Div	F	SD	BD	Bye	#T	W	L	Coach
1945	M		16				16	16	5	Kirkland, Gordon A.
1982			32	7	A		32	26	7	Moir, Sam A.
1983			32	8	A		32	29	4	Moir, Sam A.
1993	W	I	32		A		32	24	9	Peters, Gary

Year	M/W	Div	F	SD	BD	Bye	#T	W	L	Coach
CEDARVILLE										
1949	M		32				32	17	12	Beattie, Mendell E.
1964			32		A		32	19	6	Callan, Dr. Donald
1981			32	15	A		32	25	4	Callan, Dr. Donald
1982			32		A		32	17	11	Callan, Dr. Donald
CENTENARY (LA)										
1952	M		32				32	17	17	Delaney, F. H. "Buss"
CENTRAL ARKANSAS										
1991	M		2	5	A		32	29	5	Dyer, Don
1992		I	2	7	A		32	28	5	Dyer, Don
1937			4		I		8	21	8	Woodson, Warren B.
1980			8		A		32	19	14	Dyer, Don
1959			16		A		32	24	4	Harton, Cliff
1990			16		A		32	24	11	Dyer, Don
1938			32				32	12	9	Woodson, Warren B.
1940			32				32	18	8	Woodson, Warren B.
1942			32				32	25	3	Roberts, Lloyd
1946			32				32	16	12	McGibbony, Charles
1948			32				32	21	2	Smith, Glen M.
1961			32		A		32	20	6	Harton, Cliff
1974			32		A		32	22	9	Nixon, Don
1975			32		A		32	19	11	Nixon, Don
1993		I	32		L		32	20	8	Dyer, Don
1984	W		16	8	A		16	24	4	Marvel, Ronnie
1991			16	16	A		32	22	8	Marvel, Ronnie
CENTRAL CONNECTICUT STATE										
1948	M		16				32	14	5	Merrick, Ross
1949			32				32	21	4	Merrick, Ross
1950			32				32	16	6	Merrick, Ross
1959			32		A		32	19	4	Moore, Dr. William M.
1960			32		A		32	16	5	Detrick, William
1961			32		A		32	17	4	Detrick, William
1962			32		A		32	14	9	Detrick, William
1963			32	16	A		32	22	1	Detrick, William
1964			32	14	A		32	25	1	Detrick, William
1965			32		A		32	19	5	Detrick, William
CENTRAL METHODIST										
1950	M		3				32	29	4	Vanatta, Robert
1945			8				16	12	1	Vanatta, Robert
1951			16				32	24	5	Pink, Ralph J.
1994		II	16	9	A		24	30	7	Sherman, Jeff
1943			32				32	11	4	Vanatta, Robert
1998		II	32	9	A		32	26	8	Sherman, Jeff
1998	W	II	8	15	A		32	25	8	Davis, Mike
1997		II	16		A		32	28	8	Davis, Mike

Year	M/W	Div	F	SD	BD	Bye	#T	W	L	Coach
CENTRAL MICHIGAN										
1966	M		16	6	A		32	23	6	Kjolhede, Theodore
1967			16	10	A		32	22	3	Kjolhede, Throdore
CENTRAL MISSOURI STATE										
1937	M		1		I		8	17	3	Reid, Tad C.
1938			1				32	24	3	Reid, Tad C.
1942			4				32	19	7	Scott, Tom
1939			8				32	21	7	Scott, Tom
1940			32				32	17	8	Scott, Tom
1941			32				32	17	9	Scott, Tom
1946			32				32	13	7	Scott, Tom
CENTRAL OKLAHOMA										
1961	M		8	7	A		32	21	7	Smith, John
1964			8	5	A		32	23	4	Winters, Mark
1938			16				32	17	6	Hamilton, Dale E.
1959			16	14	A		32	21	10	Smith, John
1939			32				32	16	5	Hamilton, Dale E.
CENTRAL STATE (OH)										
1965	M		1	1	A		32	30	0	Lucas, William C.
1968			1	3	A		32	29	4	Lucas, William C.
1966			8	1	A		32	24	6	Lucas, William C.
1970			8	5	A		32	24	5	Lucas, William C.
1978			8		A		32	19	11	Wims, Dr. Lu D.
1956			16				32	18	7	Gibbs, George Edwin
1963			16		A		32	18	11	Lucas, William C.
1969			32	3	A		32	21	7	Lucas, William C.
1976			32		A		32	20	10	Wims, Dr. Lu D.
1977			32		A		32	18	11	Wims, Dr. Lu D.
1979			32		A		32	22	7	Wims, Dr. Lu D.
1989	W		8	8	A		16	29	2	Check, Theresa A.
1990			8		A		16	25	5	Check, Theresa A.
1996		I	8	8	A		32	30	4	Check, Theresa A.
1997		I	8	5	L		32	29	3	Check, Theresa A.
1991			16	11	A		32	27	5	Check, Theresa A.
1993		I	16	12	A		32	25	5	Check, Theresa A.
1994		I	16	13	A		32	25	6	Check, Theresa A.
1992		I	32		A		32	24	8	Check, Theresa A.
1995		I	32		A		32	20	9	Check, Theresa A.
1998		I	32	11	L		32	25	7	Check, Theresa A.
CENTRAL WASHINGTON										
1970	M		2	3	A		32	31	2	Nicholson, Dean
1967			3	6	A		32	27	4	Nicholson, Dean
1969			3	15	A		32	24	9	Nicholson, Dean
1987			3	10	A		32	32	9	Nicholson, Dean
1989			3	13	A		32	32	10	Nicholson, Dean
1985			4		A		32	25	11	Nicholson, Dean
1950			8				32	24	8	Nicholson, Leo S.
1968			8	10	A		32	22	8	Nicholson, Dean

Year	M/W	Div	F	SD	BD	Bye	#T	W	L	Coach
1977			8	16	A		32	24	8	Nicholson, Dean
1980			8	7	A		32	27	6	Nicholson, Dean
1986			8	14	A		32	27	6	Nicholson, Dean
1990			8	7	A		32	31	5	Nicholson, Dean
1997		I	8		A		32	18	13	Sparling, Greg
1998		I	8		A		32	20	11	Sparling, Greg
1971			16	16	A		32	24	9	Nicholson, Dean
1975			16	6	A		32	21	6	Nicholson, Dean
1976			16	13	A		32	23	7	Nicholson, Dean
1979			16	7	A		32	25	6	Nicholson, Dean
1982			16	15	A		32	22	7	Nicholson, Dean
1984			16		A		32	23	10	Nicholson, Dean
1993		I	16	10	A		32	29	7	Coleman, Gil
1995		I	16		A		32	20	14	Sparling, Greg
1965			32	14	A		32	20	6	Nicholson, Dean
1966			32		A		32	21	8	Nicholson, Dean
1974			32		A		32	17	10	Nicholson, Dean
1978			32	14	A		32	21	8	Nicholson, Dean
1981			32		A		32	21	12	Nicholson, Dean
1988	W		16		A		16	31	5	Frederick, Dr. Gary C.

CHADRON STATE

Year	M/W	Div	F	SD	BD	Bye	#T	W	L	Coach
1967	M		16		A		32	22	6	Payton, Mack
1942			32				32	17	4	Armstrong, Ross O.
1952			32				32	18	7	Young, Loy

CHAMINADE

Year	M/W	Div	F	SD	BD	Bye	#T	W	L	Coach
1983	M		4	1	A		32	27	3	Lopes, Merv
1984			8	6	A		32	23	6	Lopes, Merv

CHARLESTON (SC)

Year	M/W	Div	F	SD	BD	Bye	#T	W	L	Coach
1983	M		1	12	A		32	24	5	Kresse, John
1988			3	9	A		32	30	5	Kresse, John
1985			8	3	A		32	25	3	Kresse, John
1986			8	16	A		32	26	9	Kresse, John
1987			16	2	A		32	25	1	Kresse, John
1989			16	4	A		32	21	5	Kresse, John

CHARLESTON (WV)

Year	M/W	Div	F	SD	BD	Bye	#T	W	L	Coach
1967	M		4	4	A		32	28	5	Meckfessel, Richard
1986			8	2	A		32	30	5	Williams, "Tex"
1962			16	15	A		32	27	6	Moran, Garland
1966			16	15	A		32	26	6	Meckfessel, Richard
1970			16	15	A		32	25	8	Meckfessel, Richard
1953			32				32	21	9	King, Carl E. "Eddie"
1954			32				32	16	13	King, Carl E. "Eddie"
1964			32		A		32	20	11	Moran, Garland
1992		I	32		A		32	21	9	White, Greg
1982	W		8	3	A		8	27	7	Francis, Robert A. "Bud"
1984			8		A		16	24	9	Francis, Robert A. "Bud"
1986			16		A		16	19	12	Francis, Robert A. "Bud"
1988			16		A		16	21	13	Bennett-Travinski, Linda

Year	M/W	Div	F	SD	BD	Bye	#T	W	L	Coach
1990			16		A		16	25	8	Bennett-Travinski, Linda
1991			32		A		32	21	8	Bennett-Travinski, Linda
1992		I	32		A		32	20	6	Bennett-Travinski, Linda

CHICAGO STATE

1984	M		3	3	A		32	24	4	Hallberg, Robert J.
1983			16	3	A		32	23	4	Hallberg, Robert J.
1981			32		A		32	23	9	Hallberg, Robert J.

CHRISTIAN BROTHERS

1959	M		32		A		32	19	7	Raymonds, Henry C. "Hank"
1960			32	10	A		32	21	7	Raymonds, Henry C. "Hank"

CLAFLIN

1997	M	I	16		A		32	25	8	Guydon, James "Gus"
1996		I	32		A		32	18	13	Guyden, James "Gus"
1988	W		2	2	A		16	37	2	Brownlee, Nelson C.
1989			2	1	A		16	35	1	Brownlee, Nelson C.
1990			3	3	A		16	33	3	Brownlee, Nelson C.
1991			3	1	A		32	31	2	Brownlee, Nelson C.
1992		I	8	6	A		32	28	2	Brownlee, Nelson C.
1985			16	7	A		16	27	5	Brownlee, Nelson C.
1993		I	32		A		32	24	10	Brownlee, Nelson C.
1994		I	32	11	A		32	26	5	Brownlee, Nelson C.
1996		I	32		A		32	21	9	Brownlee, Nelson C.
1997		I	32		L		32	22	10	Brownlee, Nelson C.
1998		I	32		A		32	23	10	Brownlee, Nelson C.

CLAREMONT MCKENNA

1967	M		32		A		32	23	7	Ducey, Ted

CLARION

1980	M		8		A		32	23	9	DeGregorio, Joseph
1977			16	9	A		32	27	3	DeGregorio, Joseph
1952			32				32	19	1	Kribbs, Benton A.

CLAYTON STATE

1995	W	I	32		A		32	19	13	Nestopoulos, Chris

COE

1958	M		8	2	A		32	20	7	Schulz, Robert
1955			32				32	14	8	Thomsen, Theron "Tommy"
1956			32				32	20	5	Levy, Marv

COLUMBIA (MO)

1990	M		16		A		32	30	8	Burchard, Bob
1995		I	32	10	L		32	29	6	Burchard, Bob
1996		I	32		L		32	27	8	Burchard, Bob
1997		I	32		A		32	27	8	Burchard, Bob

COLUMBIA UNION

1992	M	I	32		A		32	18	16	Murray, Rick

Year	M/W	Div	F	SD	BD	Bye	#T	W	L	Coach
CONCORD										
1991	M		16	15	A		32	28	8	Cox, Steve
1995		I	32		A		32	20	11	Cox, Steve
CONCORDIA (CA)										
1992	W	I	32		A		32	25	5	Schlichtemeier, Kent
1993		I	32		L		32	26	5	Schlichtemeier, Kent
1997		I	32		A		32	28	6	Wolter, Dave
CONCORDIA (NE)										
1992	M	II	3		A	To R16	20	26	10	Schmidt, Grant
1995		II	8	2	A		32	30	4	Schmidt, Grant
1991			32		A		32	23	11	Schmidt, Grant
1996		II	32	5	L		32	25	6	Schmidt, Grant
1997		II	32		A		32	18	14	Schmidt, Grant
1998		II	32	7	A		32	26	7	Schmidt, Grant
1997	W	II	8	16	L		32	26	6	Lemke, Dr. Mark
1992		II	20		A		20	23	13	Everts, Dr. Carl
1998		II	32	9	A		32	24	8	Lemke, Dr. Mark
CONCORDIA (WI)										
1993	M	II	20		A		20	18	9	Stelmachowicz, Dr. Cary
1994	W	II	3	4	A	To R16	24	25	4	Surridge, Dr. Jack
1995		II	3	6	A		32	20	4	Surridge, Dr. Jack
1992		II	16		A	To R16	20	22	4	Surridge, Dr. Jack
1993		II	16		A	To R16	20	23	4	Surridge, Dr. Jack
1997		II	32		A		32	18	9	Witte, Ken
COPPIN STATE										
1976	M		1	9	A		32	39	2	Bates, John H.
COVENANT										
1997	W	II	32		A		32	21	7	Smialek, Tami
CULVER-STOCKTON										
1939	M		16				32	16	8	Herington, William A.
1941			16				32	16	5	Herington, William A.
1946			16				32	18	4	Herington, William A.
1947			32				32	18	2	Herington, William A.
1959			32	13	A		32	19	7	Herington, William A.
1992	W	II	16		A		20	22	11	Turpin, Kathy
1995		II	32	14	L		32	29	6	Clampitt, Randy
CUMBERLAND (KY)										
1997	M	I	3	13	L		32	31	7	Vernon, Randy
1992		I	8		A		32	25	8	Vernon, Randy
1984			16	11	A		32	27	4	Vernon, Randy
1986			16	1	A		32	32	3	Vernon, Randy
1989			16	9	A		32	26	7	Vernon, Randy
1978			32		A		32	27	10	Trivette, Ken
1980			32		A		32	25	10	Vernon, Randy
1982			32		A		32	20	16	Vernon, Randy

Year	M/W	Div	F	SD	BD	Bye	#T	W	L	Coach
1983			32	4	A		32	33	3	Vernon, Randy
1993		I	32		A		32	28	7	Vernon, Randy
1998		I	32		A		32	16	17	Vernon, Randy
1986	W		16		A		16	24	6	Morgan, Henry
1988			16		A		16	25	10	Morgan, Henry

CUMBERLAND (TN)

Year	M/W	Div	F	SD	BD	Bye	#T	W	L	Coach
1996	M	I	8	10	L		32	28	6	Petrone, Mike

DAEMEN

Year	M/W	Div	F	SD	BD	Bye	#T	W	L	Coach
1996	W	I	32		A		32	27	5	Skolen, David
1997		I	32		A		32	27	6	Skolen, David

DAKOTA STATE

Year	M/W	Div	F	SD	BD	Bye	#T	W	L	Coach
1992	M	II	3		A		20	19	16	McDermott, Brian

DAKOTA WESLEYAN

Year	M/W	Div	F	SD	BD	Bye	#T	W	L	Coach
1937	M		8			I	8	12	5	Belding, Lester C.
1946			8				32	16	6	Green, Ray
1939			16				32	11	2	Belding, Lester C.
1947			16				32	25	3	Gorby, Dave
1938			32				32	11	10	Belding, Lester C.
1940			32				32	12	5	Belding, Lester C.
1941			32				32	16	5	Belding, Lester C.
1943			32				32	21	2	Belding, Lester C.
1964			32		A		32	21	3	Fosness, Gordon
1979			32		A		32	26	3	Fosness, Gordon
1995		II	32	15	A		32	19	11	Martin, Doug

DALLAS BAPTIST

Year	M/W	Div	F	SD	BD	Bye	#T	W	L	Coach
1973	M		32		A		32	24	11	Sheiron, Steve

DAVIS & ELKINS

Year	M/W	Div	F	SD	BD	Bye	#T	W	L	Coach
1950	M		8				32	29	5	Brown, Robert N. 'Red

DEFIANCE

Year	M/W	Div	F	SD	BD	Bye	#T	W	L	Coach
1973	M		16		A		32	25	5	Hohenberger, D. Marvin
1974			32		A		32	22	6	Hohenberger, D. Marvin
1980			32		A		32	23	8	Hohenberger, D. Marvin
1988			32		A		32	24	7	Hohenberger, D. Marvin

DELTA STATE

Year	M/W	Div	F	SD	BD	Bye	#T	W	L	Coach
1940	M		3				32	24	6	Dickson, A. D.
1938			8				32	15	6	Dickson, A. D.
1941			8				32	16	7	Dickson, A. D.
1939			32				32	16	7	Dickson, A. D.
1942			32				32	15	10	Dickson, A. D.
1947			32				32	23	5	Marlar, Luther W. 'Luke'
1948			32				32	17	5	Ricks, John Ray
1949			32				32	18	11	Ricks, John Ray
1950			32				32	19	6	Ricks, John Ray

Year	M/W	Div	F	SD	BD	Bye	#T	W	L	Coach
DENVER										
1948	M		32				32	18	11	Ketchum, Ellison E.
1984			32	7	A		32	28	4	Theard, Floyd M.
DEPAUW										
1947	M		16				32	16	3	Hickman, Harold E. "Hal"
DICKINSON STATE (ND)										
1968	M		8		A		32	23	6	Limke, Denis
1966			32		A		32	21	4	Jessen, Laverne
1967			32		A		32	21	5	Jessen, Laverne
DILLARD										
1997	M	I	16		A		32	23	13	Lloyd, Jerry
1980			32		A		32	19	12	Brown, John D.
1984	W		3	4	A		16	26	3	Teamer, Mary D.
1988			8		A		16	28	5	Teamer, Mary D.
DOANE										
1945	M		8				16	6	12	Dutcher, Jim
1996		II	8		A		32	21	16	Erickson, Robert
1976			16		A		32	21	9	Erickson, Robert
1971			32		A		32	18	10	Erickson, Robert
1996	W	II	3	2	A		32	31	7	Steinmeyer, Gene
1997		II	3	10	A		32	28	9	Steinmeyer, Gene
1998		II	3	10	L		32	29	9	Steinmeyer, Gene
1989			8		A		16	27	7	Steinmeyer, Gene
1992		I	16	14	L		32	26	9	Steinmeyer, Gene
1995		II	16	4	A		32	30	6	Steinmeyer, Gene
DOMINICAN (CA)										
1997	W	II	32		A		32	23	7	Powell, Roneil
DOMINICAN (IL)										
1991	W		16	8	A		32	32	2	Trefilek, Thomas J.
1992		I	32	16	A		32	28	4	Trefilek, Thomas J.
1993		I	32		A		32	30	4	Trefilek, Thomas J.
1994		I	32		A		32	22	12	Schaefer, Bill
1995		I	32		A		32	12	16	Smith, Dennis
DOMINICAN (NY)										
1981	M		32		A		32	17	14	Kelly, Steve
1986	W		16		A		16	20	15	Baxter, Stephen
DORDT										
1988	M		8		A	·	32	25	5	Vander Berg, Rick
DOWLING										
1977	M		16		A		32	29	7	Berg, Richard C.
1976			32		A		32	31	4	Berg, Richard C.
1978			32		A		32	21	6	Berg, Richard C.
1980			32		A		32	24	5	Berg, Richard C.

Year	M/W	Div	F	SD	BD	Bye	#T	W	L	Coach
DRAKE (IA)										
1938	M		32				32	14	6	Williams, Evan O. "Bill"
DRURY										
1979	M		1	3	A		32	33	2	Kirksey, Jerry L.
1946			8				32	12	9	Weiser, Albert L.
1968			8		A		32	24	5	Harding, Bill
1978			8	3	L		32	29	4	Matthews, Dr. Edsel
1985			8		A		32	26	10	Walker, Marvin
1994		I	8	4	A		32	27	4	Stanfield, Gary
1958			16	6	A		32	15	7	Weiser, Albert L.
1986			16	15	A		32	25	10	Walker, Marvin
1989			16	12	A		32	24	9	Walker, Marvin
1938			32				32	18	3	Weiser, Albert L.
1970			32	12	A		32	22	7	Harding, Bill
1971			32		A		32	18	9	Harding, Bill
1981			32		A		32	19	12	Walker, Marvin
1983			32		A		32	22	12	Walker, Marvin
1993		I	32		A		32	19	12	Stanfield, Gary
DUBUQUE										
1941	M		32				32	15	3	Mercer, Kenneth E. "Moco"
EARLHAM										
1971	M		16	14	A		32	24	5	Harris, Delmer W.
EAST CAROLINA										
1953	M		32				32	15	7	Porter, Howard G.
1954			32				32	13	8	Porter, Howard G.
EAST CENTRAL (OK)										
1950	M		2				32	31	5	McBride, Floyd H. "Mickey"
1989			2	14	A		32	25	7	Cobb, K. Wayne
1942			8				32	20	10	McBride, Floyd H. "Mickey"
1996		I	8		L		32	22	7	Cobb, K. Wayne
1998		I	8		A		32	21	9	Cobb, K. Wayne
1943			16				32	18	6	Powell, C. J.
1940			32				32	25	5	McBride, Floyd H. "Mickey"
1948			32				32	17	5	McBride, Floyd H. "Mickey"
1951			32				32	22	7	McBride, Floyd H. "Mickey"
1970			32		A		32	17	8	Anderson, Jerry
1971			32	8	A		32	24	5	Anderson, Jerry
1975			32		A		32	16	11	Anderson, Jerry
1997		I	32	10	A		32	22	6	Cobb, K. Wayne
1996	W	I	16	7	L		32	30	5	Franz, Kent
1998		I	16		A		32	20	11	Franz, Kent
1997		I	32	13	A		32	19	9	Franz, Kent
EAST TENNESSEE STATE										
1953	M		32				32	26	4	Brooks, John Madison
1954			32				32	23	4	Brooks, John Madison
1956			32				32	20	7	Brooks, John Madison

Year	M/W	Div	F	SD	BD	Bye	#T	W	L	Coach
EAST TEXAS BAPTIST										
1951	M		16				32	15	5	Stephens, John O.
1961			16		A		32	16	7	Kennedy, R. C.
1988			32		A		32	19	13	Webb, Dr. Jimmy Ray
1996		I	32	13	A		32	28	5	West, Bert
1994	W	I	32		L		32	27	6	Reeves, Kent
1995		I	32		L		32	23	9	Reeves, Kent
EASTERN (PA)										
1988	M		32		A		32	30	6	Ware, Nate
EASTERN ILLINOIS										
1957	M		4				32	17	14	Carey, Robert A.
1949			8				32	23	6	Healey, Dr. William A.
1952			16				32	24	2	Healey, Dr. William A.
1953			16				32	16	9	Healey, Dr. William A.
1947			32				32	13	7	Healey, Dr. William A.
1950			32				32	21	5	Healey, Dr. William A.
EASTERN KENTUCKY										
1945	M		3				16	20	5	Rankin, Dr. Rome
1946			32				32	20	5	Rankin, Dr. Rome
EASTERN MICHIGAN										
1971	M		2	6	A		32	22	11	Dutcher, James D.
1968			8		A		32	18	9	Dutcher, James D.
1969			16	5	A		32	20	9	Dutcher, James D.
1970			16	9	A		32	22	7	Dutcher, James D.
EASTERN NEW MEXICO										
1969	M		1	12	A		32	24	7	Miller, Harry E.
1970			3	6	A		32	26	6	Miller, Harry E.
1967			8	2	A		32	24	7	Miller, Harry E.
1949			32				32	19	8	Garten, Alvin D.
1951			32				32	19	9	Garten, Alvin D.
1956			32				32	11	16	Garten, Alvin D.
1958			32		A		32	17	10	Garten, Alvin D.
1963			32		A		32	14	8	Garten, Alvin D.
1971			32		A		32	19	10	Ball, "Buddy"
EASTERN OREGON										
1943	M		16				32	18	5	Quinn, E. Robert
EASTERN WASHINGTON										
1943	M		8				32	27	5	Brumblay, Robert C.
1946			8				32	31	4	Reese, William B. "Red"
1947			8				32	22	9	Reese, William B. "Red"
1945			16				16	27	5	Brumblay, Robert C.
1942			32				32	18	7	Reese, William B. "Red"
EDGEWOOD										
1992	M	II	20		A		20	21	10	Larson, G. Steven
1995		II	32	14	A		32	20	8	Larson, G. Steven

Year	M/W	Div	F	SD	BD	Bye	#T	W	L	Coach
EDINBORO										
1975	M		16	9	A		32	17	3	McDonald, James
1976			16	14	A		32	24	5	Conti, Guy
1966			32		A		32	18	5	McDonald, James
1972			32		A		32	17	9	McDonald, James
ELIZABETH CITY STATE										
1971	M		3	12	A		32	25	9	Vaughan, Robert L. "Bobby"
1969			4	9	A		32	21	2	Vaughan, Robert L. "Bobby"
1972			32		A		32	17	12	Vaughan, Robert L. "Bobby"
ELON										
1952	M		32				32	25	11	Mathis, Graham L. "Doc"
1956			32				32	23	6	Mathis, Graham L. "Doc"
1957			32				32	24	6	Mathis, Graham L. "Doc"
EMBRY-RIDDLE (FL)										
1993	M	II	16			L	20	28	8	Ridder, Steven
1996		II	16	8	A		32	25	11	Ridder, Steven
1997		II	16	12	L		32	25	8	Ridder, Steven
1998		II	32		A		32	23	12	Ridder, Steven
EMPORIA STATE										
1947	M		4				32	18	9	Fish, Everett D. "Gus"
1964			4	6	A		32	22	9	Fish, Everett D. "Gus"
1949			8				32	20	10	Fish, Everett D. "Gus"
1948			16				32	20	7	Fish, Everett D. "Gus"
1957			16				32	20	9	Fish, Everett D. "Gus"
1961			16	12	A		32	17	6	Fish, Everett D. "Gus"
1977			16		A		32	24	6	Slaymaker, Dr. Ron
1986			16	6	A		32	31	5	Slaymaker, Dr. Ron
1991			32		A		32	18	13	Slaymaker, Dr. Ron
1992		I	32		A		32	26	8	Slaymaker, Dr. Ron
1992	W	I	32		L		32	14	17	Schierling, Val
ERSKINE										
1992	M	I	8	15	A		32	27	7	Hicklin, Robbie
1978			16		A		32	21	12	Myers, W. C. "Red"
1949			32				32	19	7	McMillan, John D. "Johnny"
1974			32		A		32	25	6	Myers, W. C. "Red"
EUREKA										
1994	M	II	1	6	A	To R16	24	27	4	Darnell, David
1993		II	8		A	To R16	20	24	5	Darnall, David
1992		II	16	4	A	To R16	20	25	4	Darnall, David
1987			32		A		32	26	3	Darnall, David
EVANGEL										
1997	M	II	16	8	A		32	29	8	Jenkins, Stephen M.
1996	W	II	3	4	A		32	31	5	Bowen, Lynn
1994		II	16	14	A		24	26	10	Bowen, Lynn

Year	M/W	Div	F	SD	BD	Bye	#T	W	L	Coach
EVANSVILLE										
1951	M		8				32	23	7	McCutchan, Arad A.
1942			16				32	12	6	Slyker, William V.
1941			32				32	12	4	Slyker, William V.
1955			32				32	20	6	McCutchan, Arad A.
FAIRLEIGH DICKINSON: RUTHERFORD/TEANECK										
1959	M		16			A	32	17	11	Holub, Richard
1952			32				32	22	4	Holub, Richard
FAIRMONT STATE										
1968	M		2			A	32	24	6	Retton, Joe
1965			4			A	32	32	4	Retton, Joe
1971			4	2		A	32	32	3	Retton, Joe
1975			8	2		A	32	30	16	Retton, Joe
1969			16	1		A	32	26	2	Retton, Joe
1974			16	1		A	32	28	3	Retton, Joe
1976			16	1		A	32	28	1	Retton, Joe
1973			32	6		A	32	23	5	Retton, Joe
1977			32	4		A	32	21	5	Retton, Joe
1978			32	7		A	32	27	6	Retton, Joe
1980			32	11		A	32	23	4	Retton, Joe
1981			32			A	32	26	5	Retton, Joe
FAULKNER										
1992	M	I	32	12		A	32	27	6	Kelsey, Tom
FERRIS STATE										
1962	M		8	12		A	32	23	3	Wink, James M.
1973			16			A	32	26	4	Wink, James M.
1960			32			A	32	15	6	Wink, James M.
1964			32			A	32	19	4	Wink, James M.
1975			32	14		A	32	22	5	Wink, James M.
FINDLAY										
1953	M		8				32	13	7	Renninger, Donald S.
1960			16			A	32	14	9	Houdeshell, Dr. James D.
1996		I	16			A	32	25	10	Niekamp, Ron
1997		I	16	6		A	32	27	5	Niekamp, Ron
1952			32				32	16	6	Renninger, Donald S.
1967			32			A	32	15	10	Houdeshell, Dr. James D.
1972			32			A	32	16	11	Houdeshell, Dr. James D.
1986			32			A	32	25	6	Niekamp, Ron
1992		I	32			L	32	23	8	Niekamp, Ron
1993		I	32	15		A	32	26	6	Niekamp, Ron
1998	W	I	3			A	32	26	7	Kleinfelter, Eileen
1994		II	8	7		L	To R16	24	25	5	Neff, Sheryl
1995		II	8	2		A	32	32	2	Kleinfelter, Eileen
1993		II	16			L	To R16	20	26	5	Neff, Sheryl
1996		II	16	14		L	32	25	8	Kleinfelter, Eileen

Year	M/W	Div	F	SD	BD	Bye	#T	W	L	Coach
FLORIDA MEMORIAL										
1992	M	II	16		A		20	17	12	Parker, Alfred
1992	W	II	20		A		20	12	7	Marshall, Kenneth
1993		II	20		A		20	13	13	Marshall, Kenneth
FLORIDA STATE										
1951	M		8				32	18	9	Kennedy, Jesse K. "Bud"
1955			16				32	22	4	Kennedy, Jesse K. "Bud"
FORT HAYS STATE										
1984	M		1	2	A		32	26	2	Morse, Bill
1985			1	1	A		32	35	3	Morse, Bill
1983			3	10	A		32	32	4	Morse, Bill
1959			4	15	A		32	23	4	Suran, Cade
1963			4	15	A		32	21	7	Suran, Cade
1988			16	6	A		32	28	5	Morse, Bill
1962			32	8	A		32	19	4	Suran, Cade
1981			32	4	A		32	30	4	Rosado, Joe
1991	W		1	4	A		32	34	2	Klein, John
FRANCIS MARION										
1991	M		32		A		32	22	10	Hill, Lewis
1986	W		1	1	A		16	36	2	Hatchell, Sylvia Rhyne
1984			8	6	A		16	28	5	Hatchell, Sylvia Rhyne
FRANCISCAN										
1955	M		8				32	28	5	Kuzma, Harry
1961			32	6	A		32	16	11	Smith, Wayne
FRANKLIN (IN)										
1992	M	II	8	3	L	To R16	20	25	4	Prather, Kerry
1980			16		A		32	22	6	Lovell, Robert
1976			32		A		32	16	10	Thompson, Ed
1978			32		A		32	19	6	Lovell, Robert
FRANKLIN PIERCE										
1980	M		32		A		32	29	2	Kirsh, Bruce
1981			32		A		32	31	4	Kirsh, Bruce
1982			32		A		32	27	8	Kirsh, Bruce
1984			32		A		32	27	10	Kirsh, Bruce
1986			32		A		32	24	7	Kirsh, Bruce
1988			32		A		32	16	15	Kirsh, Bruce
FREED-HARDEMAN										
1998	M	I	32		L		32	24	11	McCutchen, Mike
1997	W	I	16		A		32	26	11	Neal, Dale
1998		I	32		A		32	24	11	Neal, Dale
FRESNO PACIFIC										
1995	M	I	16		A		32	24	8	Sargent, Jim

Year	M/W	Div	F	SD	BD	Bye	#T	W	L	Coach
1987	W		16		A		16	28	3	Janzen, Dennis
1989			16		A		16	24	8	Stanley, Kent
1992		I	16		L		32	25	6	Stanley, Kent
1993		I	32		A		32	21	8	Stanley, Kent
1994		I	32		A		32	23	7	Stanley, Kent
1995		I	32		A		32	21	10	Stanley, Kent

FRIENDS

Year	M/W	Div	F	SD	BD	Bye	#T	W	L	Coach
1994	W	II	24	19	A		24	23	7	Carter, Jeff
1995		II	32		L		32	23	6	Carter, Jeff

GANNON

Year	M/W	Div	F	SD	BD	Bye	#T	W	L	Coach
1969	M		16	6	A		32	23	6	Bayer, John D. "Denny"

GARDNER-WEBB

Year	M/W	Div	F	SD	BD	Bye	#T	W	L	Coach
1972	M		4	4	A		32	20	3	Holbrook, Edwin "Eddie"
1974			16	3	A		32	25	3	Holbrook, Edwin "Eddie"
1981			32		A		32	25	11	Wiles, Jim R.

GENEVA

Year	M/W	Div	F	SD	BD	Bye	#T	W	L	Coach
1996	M	I	8		L		32	24	7	Slocum, Jerry
1954			16				32	21	8	Aultman, Clifford J.
1956			16				32	24	3	Aultman, Clifford J.
1995		I	16		A		32	26	6	Slocum, Jerry
1953			32				32	22	5	Aultman, Clifford J.
1955			32				32	19	8	Aultman, Clifford J.
1990			32		A		32	22	9	Slocum, Jerry
1993		I	32	7	A		32	28	3	Slocum, Jerry

GEORGE FOX

Year	M/W	Div	F	SD	BD	Bye	#T	W	L	Coach
1992	M	II	8		L		20	24	11	Vernon, Mark
1973			32		A		32	16	15	Miller, Lorin
1990			32	9	A		32	29	5	Vernon, Mark

GEORGETOWN (KY)

Year	M/W	Div	F	SD	BD	Bye	#T	W	L	Coach
1998	M	I	1	4	L		32	36	3	Osborne, "Happy"
1961			2	3	A		32	26	9	Davis, Dr. Robert M.
1996		I	2	1	A		32	36	3	Reid, James B.
1990			3	11	A		32	29	7	Reid, James B.
1993		I	3		L		32	29	8	Reid, James B.
1958			4		A		32	22	6	Davis, Dr. Robert M.
1987			4	16	A		32	30	8	Reid, James B.
1992		I	8	3	L		32	34	2	Reid, James B.
1964			16	9	A		32	21	10	Davis, Dr. Robert M.
1994		I	16	1	A		32	33	2	Reid, James B.
1997		I	16	15	A		32	27	9	Osborne, "Happy"
1954			32				32	15	10	Davis, Dr. Robert M.
1955			32				32	22	5	Davis, Dr. Robert M.
1956			32				32	17	8	Davis, Dr. Robert M.
1962			32	3	A		32	23	7	Davis, Dr. Robert M.
1969			32		A		32	24	11	Davis, Dr. Robert M.
1995		I	32	6	A		32	32	4	Reid, James B.

Year	M/W	Div	F	SD	BD	Bye	#T	W	L	Coach
1993	W	II	8	8	A	To R16	20	27	5	Johnson, Susan
1996		II	16		L		32	21	10	Johnson, Susan
1994		II	24	23	A		24	19	11	Johnson, Susan

GEORGIA COLLEGE

Year	M/W	Div	F	SD	BD	Bye	#T	W	L	Coach
1988	M		32		A		32	25	9	Hodges, Bill
1989			32		A		32	22	10	Hodges, Bill
1990			32	13	A		32	24	8	Hodges, Bill

GEORGIA SOUTHERN

Year	M/W	Div	F	SD	BD	Bye	#T	W	L	Coach
1966	M		2	4	A		32	26	6	Scearce, J. B., Jr.
1959			8		A		32	19	12	Scearce, J. B., Jr.
1956			16				32	21	7	Scearce, J. B., Jr.
1964			16	15	A		32	20	11	Scearce, J. B., Jr.
1958			32		A		32	12	15	Scearce, J. B., Jr.

GEORGIA SOUTHWESTERN

Year	M/W	Div	F	SD	BD	Bye	#T	W	L	Coach
1995	M	I	8	4	A		32	30	5	Duhon, Glenn D.
1985			16	8	A		32	28	5	Duhon, Glenn D.
1994		I	16		A		32	24	10	Duhon, Glenn D.
1991			32	8	A		32	27	6	Duhon, Glenn D.
1997		I	32		A		32	23	9	Barksdale, Randolph
1998		I	32		A		32	25	11	Barksdale, Randolph
1986	W		4	5	L		16	25	4	Hawver, Dr. Greg
1996		I	32		A		32	22	10	Drown, Kip
1998		I	32		A		32	22	12	Drown, Kip

GEORGIAN COURT

Year	M/W	Div	F	SD	BD	Bye	#T	W	L	Coach
1984	W		16		A		16	18	4	Sonday, Bob
1990			16		A		16	27	3	Emery, Debra
1991			32		A		32	25	5	Emery, Debra

GLENVILLE STATE

Year	M/W	Div	F	SD	BD	Bye	#T	W	L	Coach
1939	M		3				32	25	3	Rohrbaugh, A. F. "Nate"
1940			16				32	22	3	Rohrbaugh, A. F. "Nate"
1972			16	8	A		32	26	7	Lilly, Jesse
1951			32				32	19	11	Ratliff, Carlos C.
1989	W		16		A		16	19	7	Shepherd, Dr. Russell M.

GONZAGA

Year	M/W	Div	F	SD	BD	Bye	#T	W	L	Coach
1948	M		16				32	24	11	McGrath, Claude F.
1953			32				32	15	14	Anderson, Thor H. "Hank"

GRACE (IN)

Year	M/W	Div	F	SD	BD	Bye	#T	W	L	Coach
1992	M	II	1	6	A	To R16	20	32	5	Kessler, James C.
1988			16		A		32	31	5	Kessler, James C.
1993		II	16	2	A	To R16	20	27	6	Kessler, James C.

GRAMBLING STATE

Year	M/W	Div	F	SD	BD	Bye	#T	W	L	Coach
1961	M		1	13	A		32	32	4	Hobdy, Frederick C.
1963			3	1	A		32	30	3	Hobdy, Frederick C.
1966			3	3	A		32	28	6	Hobdy, Frederick C.
1960			8	6	A		32	26	5	Hobdy, Frederick C.

Year	M/W	Div	F	SD	BD	Bye	#T	W	L	Coach
1971			8	9	A		32	16	8	Hobdy, Frederick C.
1959			16	4	A		32	28	1	Hobdy, Frederick C.
1964			16	3	A		32	26	4	Hobdy, Frederick C.
1969			32	14	A		32	21	9	Hobdy, Frederick C.

GRAND CANYON

Year	M/W	Div	F	SD	BD	Bye	#T	W	L	Coach
1975	M		1	5	A		32	30	3	Lindsey, Ben
1978			1	2	A		32	30	3	Lindsey, Ben
1988			1	11	A		32	37	6	Westphal, Paul D.
1974			16	6	A		32	28	2	Lindsey, Ben
1976			16	2	A		32	27	3	Lindsey, Ben
1990			16	12	A		32	25	10	Westphal, Bill
1973			32		A		32	19	10	Lindsey, Ben
1979			32	2	A		32	24	4	Lindsey, Ben
1980			32	4	A		32	21	4	Lindsey, Ben
1989			32	1	A		32	26	5	Westphal, Bill

GRAND VALLEY STATE

Year	M/W	Div	F	SD	BD	Bye	#T	W	L	Coach
1977	M		4	8	A		32	30	4	Villemure, Thomas
1974			32		A		32	23	6	Villemure, Thomas
1979			32	10	A		32	22	4	Villemure, Thomas

GRAND VIEW

Year	M/W	Div	F	SD	BD	Bye	#T	W	L	Coach
1998	W	II	16	3	A		32	32	4	Sharer, Missy
1997		II	32	9	A		32	28	7	Sharer, Missy

GREAT FALLS

Year	M/W	Div	F	SD	BD	Bye	#T	W	L	Coach
1971	M		16		A		32	24	6	Dods, Ray

GREEN MOUNTAIN

Year	M/W	Div	F	SD	BD	Bye	#T	W	L	Coach
1996	M	II	32		A		32	21	9	Dempsey, Matthew J.
1997		II	32		A		32	21	8	Dempsey, Matthew J.

GUILFORD

Year	M/W	Div	F	SD	BD	Bye	#T	W	L	Coach
1973	M		1		A		32	29	5	Jensen, Jack
1970			4	8	A		32	32	5	Steele, Jerry
1967			16	11	A		32	20	6	Steele, Jerry
1966			32	13	A		32	18	8	Steele, Jerry
1968			32	1	A		32	25	5	Steele, Jerry
1976			32	7	A		32	21	6	Jensen, Jack
1989			32		A		32	16	10	Jensen, Jack

GUSTAVUS ADOLPHUS

Year	M/W	Div	F	SD	BD	Bye	#T	W	L	Coach
1955	M		8				32	22	7	Young, Verl "Gus"
1956			8				32	20	9	Young, Verl "Gus"
1954			16				32	23	9	Young, Verl "Gus"
1961			32		A		32	15	11	Skoog, Myer U. "Whitey"
1976			32		A		32	19	10	Skoog, Myer U. "Whitey"

HAMLINE

Year	M/W	Div	F	SD	BD	Bye	#T	W	L	Coach
1942	M		1				32	20	2	Hutton, Joseph W., Sr.
1949			1				32	29	1	Hutton, Joseph W., Sr.
1951			1				32	27	2	Hutton, Joseph W., Sr.
1953			2				32	23	9	Hutton, Joseph W., Sr.

Year	M/W	Div	F	SD	BD	Bye	#T	W	L	Coach
1948			3				32	28	3	Hutton, Joseph W., Sr.
1940			4				32	12	5	Hutton, Joseph W., Sr.
1943			8				32	21	2	Hutton, Joseph W., Sr.
1952			8				32	24	5	Hutton, Joseph W., Sr.
1957			8	6			32	22	4	Hutton, Joseph W., Sr.
1960			8	5		A	32	23	4	Hutton, Joseph W., Sr.
1947			16				32	22	5	Hutton, Joseph W., Sr.
1950			16				32	29	3	Hutton, Joseph W., Sr.

HAMPTON

Year	M/W	Div	F	SD	BD	Bye	#T	W	L	Coach
1982	M		3			A	32	28	8	Ford, Henry "Hank"
1978			32	10		A	32	24	7	Ford, Henry "Hank"
1980			32	16		A	32	21	10	Ford, Henry "Hank"

HANNIBAL-LAGRANGE

Year	M/W	Div	F	SD	BD	Bye	#T	W	L	Coach
1998	M	I	32			A	32	20	12	Thomas, Kent
1997	W	I	32			A	32	25	8	Barnes, Daren

HANOVER

Year	M/W	Div	F	SD	BD	Bye	#T	W	L	Coach
1974	M		8	5		A	32	29	4	Collier, John R.
1981			8			A	32	26	8	Collier, John R.
1968			16	15		A	32	22	11	Collier, John R.
1982			16	12		A	32	26	6	Collier, John R.
1970			32	11		A	32	22	6	Collier, John R.
1973			32			A	32	18	8	Collier, John R.
1979			32			A	32	22	5	Collier, John R.

HARDIN-SIMMONS

Year	M/W	Div	F	SD	BD	Bye	#T	W	L	Coach
1994	W	II	16	5		A	To R16	24	24	4	Roewe-Goodenough, Julie
1995		II	32			A		32	19	8	Roewe-Goodenough, Julie

HARDING

Year	M/W	Div	F	SD	BD	Bye	#T	W	L	Coach
1987	M		32			A	32	18	14	Bucy, Jess
1996		I	32	11		A	32	24	6	Morgan, Jeff
1997	W	I	16	10		L	32	26	4	Harnden, Greg
1996		I	32			L	32	24	5	Harnden, Greg

HASTINGS

Year	M/W	Div	F	SD	BD	Bye	#T	W	L	Coach
1989	M		8			A	32	26	9	Trader, Mike
1995		II	8	8		L	32	21	7	Trader, Mike
1947			16				32	20	6	Owens, Larry
1951			16				32	23	3	McLaughlin, Tom
1965			16	8		A	32	24	4	Farrell, Dr. Lynn
1974			16	15		A	32	27	4	Farrell, Dr. Lynn
1946			32				32	16	5	Douglas, Louis H.
1956			32				32	18	6	Bogue, Russell
1958			32			A	32	18	10	Bogue, Russell
1964			32	13		A	32	23	4	Farrell, Dr. Lynn
1973			32			A	32	25	5	Farrell, Dr. Lynn
1977			32			A	32	25	5	Farrell, Dr. Lynn
1988			32			A	32	27	6	Trader, Mike
1993	W	I	16	10		A	32	31	2	Rhodus, Dr. Ken
1994		II	24	13		A	24	20	11	Rhodus, Dr. Ken

Year	M/W	Div	F	SD	BD	Bye	#T	W	L	Coach
HAWAII										
1949	M		32				32	21	6	Gallon, Dr. Arthur J.
HAWAII PACIFIC										
1993	M	I	1	3	A		32	30	4	Sellitto, Anthony, Jr.
1994		I	8	6	A		32	27	8	Sellitto, Anthony, Jr.
1997		I	8	2	A		32	26	4	Sellitto, Anthony, Jr.
1995		I	16	13	A		32	25	9	Sellitto, Anthony, Jr.
1996		I	16	7	L		32	27	6	Sellitto, Anthony, Jr.
1985			32	12	A		32	27	11	Smith, Paul
1988			32		A		32	19	13	Smith, Paul
1990			32		A		32	19	15	Sellitto, Anthony, Jr.
1998		I	32	6	A		32	22	5	Sellitto, Anthony, Jr.
HAWAII PACIFIC: LOA										
1991	M		32		A		32	21	12	Tucker, Steve
HAWAII: HILO										
1987	M		8	15	A		32	25	10	Wilson, Robert H.
1977			16	15	A		32	21	5	Yagi, James "Jimmy"
1978			16	15	A		32	25	5	Yagi, James "Jimmy"
1980			32	13	L		32	26	6	Yagi, James "Jimmy"
1994		I	32		L		32	17	12	Wilson, Robert H.
HENDERSON STATE										
1976	M		2	6	A		32	28	3	Dyer, Don
1979			2	5	A		32	29	4	Riese, Bobby
1977			3	7	A		32	29	4	Dyer, Don
1969			8	11	A		32	26	5	Dyer, Don
1982			8	10	A		32	23	6	Kirksey, Jerry L.
1968			32		A		32	23	10	Dyer, Don
1981			32	13	A		32	25	8	Kirksey, Jerry L.
HENDRIX										
1985	M		32		A		32	21	11	Garrison, Cliff
HIGH POINT										
1964	M		8	2	A		32	25	4	Quinn, Thomas R.
1969			8	4	A		32	28	3	Vaughn, Robert F. "Bobby"
1942			16				32	24	1	Yow, C. Virgil
1965			16	6	A		32	29	4	Quinn, Thomas R.
1979			16	11	A		32	20	5	Steele, Jerry
1939			32				32	22	4	Yow, C. Virgil
1946			32				32	10	8	James, Ralph
1951			32				32	20	11	Davis, Dr. Robert M.
1995	W	I	32		A		32	22	7	Ellenberg, Dr. Joe
HILLSDALE										
1981	M		4	16	A		32	28	7	Morse, Bill
1985			16		A		32	20	13	Halstead, Ron
1951			32				32	9	11	Wisniewski, Irvin C.
1972			32		A		32	25	8	Ekker, Ronald
1984			32		A		32	23	9	Halstead, Ron
1988			32		A		32	13	18	Halstead, Ron

Year	M/W	Div	F	SD	BD	Bye	#T	W	L	Coach
HOLY FAMILY (PA)										
1989	M		32		A		32	30	9	Williams, Dan
1991			32		A		32	27	7	Williams, Dan
1996		II	32		A		32	24	11	Williams, Dan
1998	W	II	8	11	A		32	33	5	McLaughlin, Michael
1997		II	16		A		32	28	5	McLaughlin, Michael
1991			32		A		32	24	5	Soroka, Michael
1996		II	32		A		32	25	8	McLaughlin, Michael
HOLY NAMES (CA)										
1998	M	II	16		A		32	26	11	Whitworth, Steve
1997		II	32		A		32	20	15	Whitworth, Steve
1998	W	II	16		A		32	23	8	DeLuca, Mark
HOUGHTON										
1995	W	II	32		A		32	21	6	Lord, Harold "Skip"
HOUSTON										
1946	M		16				32	10	4	Pasche, Alden
1947			16				32	15	7	Pasche, Alden
HOUSTON BAPTIST										
1998	M	I	32	13	L		32	26	6	Cottrell, Ron
HOWARD PAYNE										
1969	M		16	2	A		32	27	4	Whitis, Glen
1963			32	5	A		32	22	7	Whitis, Glen
1966			32		A		32	20	10	Whitis, Glen
1967			32		A		32	22	7	Whitis, Glen
1976			32		A		32	22	12	Derryberry, Bob
1995		II	32		A		32	12	13	Pattillo, Charles
1996		II	32		A		32	14	14	Pattillo, Charles
1997		II	32		A		32	16	10	Pattillo, Charles
HUNTINGDON										
1964	M		16		A		32	25	6	Posey, Neal N.
HUNTINGTON										
1994	W	II	16	17	A		24	19	8	Culler, Lori
HURON										
1980	M		3		A		32	32	4	Carrier, Bruce
1981			8	7	A		32	30	4	Carrier, Bruce
1994		II	8	16	A		24	21	10	Paulsen, Fred
1986			16	13	A		32	28	3	Paulsen, Fred
1996		II	16		A		32	18	14	Paulsen, Fred
1952			32				32	21	4	Lundeen, Ralph J.
1974			32		A		32	21	7	Swanhorst, Robert
1988			32		A		32	24	8	Paulsen, Fred
1996	W	II	2	3	A		32	30	5	Warwick, Shane
1995		II	16	7	A		32	26	5	Warwick, Shane

Year	M/W	Div	F	SD	BD	Bye	#T	W	L	Coach
HUSSON										
1992	M	II	16		L		20	27	10	MacGregor, Dr. D. Bruce
1994		II	24	12	A		24	28	4	MacGregor, Dr. D. Bruce
1975			32		A		32	23	5	MacGregor, Dr. D. Bruce
1976			32		A		32	25	1	MacGregor, Dr. D. Bruce
1983			32		A		32	22	7	MacGregor, Dr. D. Bruce
1989			32	6	A		32	35	3	MacGregor, Dr. D. Bruce
1990			32		A		32	26	13	MacGregor, Dr. D. Bruce
1995		II	32		A		32	23	9	Caruso, Warren
1997		II	32		A		32	20	12	Caruso, Warren
1993	W	II	3	5	A	To R16	20	28	3	Walker, Mary "Kissy"
1995		II	32		A		32	23	6	Walker, Mary "Kissy"
1996		II	32		A		32	21	8	Walker, Mary "Kissy"
HUSTON-TILLOTSON										
1997	M	I	32		A		32	20	9	Littlefield, Terrence
1998		I	32		A		32	16	12	Littlefield, Terrence
IDAHO STATE										
1938	M		16				32	19	7	Wicks, Guy P.
ILLINOIS STATE										
1959	M		8	8	A		32	24	5	Collie, Dr. James E., Sr.
ILLINOIS WESLEYAN										
1966	M		8	12	A		32	21	10	Bridges, Dennis L.
1977			8	2	A		32	25	6	Bridges, Dennis L.
1961			16	10	A		32	17	11	Horenberger, Jack
1975			16	12	A		32	23	7	Bridges, Dennis L.
1976			16	11	A		32	23	7	Bridges, Dennis L.
1943			32				32	7	14	Horenberger, Jack
1970			32		A		32	21	4	Bridges, Dennis L.
1971			32	13	A		32	19	8	Bridges, Dennis L.
1980			32		A		32	17	11	Bridges, Dennis L.
ILLINOIS: SPRINGFIELD										
1998	W	II	32		A		32	23	8	Stiles-Krone, Juli
INCARNATE WORD										
1998	M	I	8	9	A		32	27	5	Kaspar, Daniel J. "Danny"
1993		I	32	8	A		32	28	4	Kaspar, Daniel J. "Danny"
1994		I	32		L		32	25	6	Kaspar, Daniel J. "Danny"
1995		I	32		A		32	26	8	Kaspar, Daniel J. "Danny"
1997		I	32	5	A		32	25	4	Kaspar, Daniel J. "Danny"
1998	W	I	32		A		32	19	10	Walling, Sally
INDIANA (PA)										
1974	M		8		A		32	21	8	Davis, Carl D.
1958			16		A		32	25	3	McKnight, Regis "Peck"
1971			16	5	A		32	24	4	Sledzik, Herman L.

Year	M/W	Div	F	SD	BD	Bye	#T	W	L	Coach
INDIANA STATE										
1950	M		1				32	27	8	Longfellow, John L.
1946			2				32	21	7	Curtis, Glenn M.
1948			2				32	27	7	Wooden, John R.
1953			3				32	23	8	Longfellow, John L.
1949			4				32	24	8	Longfellow, John L.
1942			8				32	17	4	Curtis, Glenn M.
1952			16				32	19	10	Longfellow, John L.
1959			16	6	A		32	18	9	Klueh, Duane M.
1963			16	8	A		32	10	11	Klueh, Duane M.
1943			32				32	13	4	Curtis, Glenn M.
1954			32				32	12	15	Longfellow, John L.
1962			32		A		32	19	9	Klueh, Duane M.
INDIANA TECH										
1995	M	II	16	4	A		32	24	6	Kline, Dan
1965			32		A		32	24	3	Macy, Robert
1998		II	32		A		32	21	9	Kline, Dan
1992	W	II	8	3	A	To R16	20	28	3	Cobb, Gary
1993		II	8	4	A	To R16	20	25	5	Cobb, Gary
1985			16		A		16	20	9	Hewlet, Kathy
1994		II	16	8	A	To R16	24	20	7	Cobb, Gary
1995		II	16	15	A		32	19	7	Cobb, Gary
INDIANA-PURDUE: INDIANAPOLIS										
1990	M		16		A		32	23	14	Lovell, Robert
1985			32		A		32	21	15	Lovell, Robert
1991	W		3		A		32	20	12	Wilhoit, Julie A.
1987			16		A		16	22	8	Price, Jim
INDIANA: SOUTH BEND										
1997	W	I	32		A		32	24	10	Wisnewski, Mary
1998		I	32		A		32	23	6	Wisnewski, Mary
INDIANA: SOUTHEAST										
1997	M	II	32		A		32	20	13	Morris, Jim
INDIANAPOLIS										
1949	M		16				32	20	9	Nicoson, Angus J.
1964			16	7	A		32	26	3	Nicoson, Angus J.
1956			32				32	23	6	Nicoson, Angus J.
1966			32		A		32	17	8	Nicoson, Angus J.
1967			32		A		32	18	10	Nicoson, Angus J.
1969			32		A		32	20	10	Nicoson, Angus J.
IOWA WESLEYAN										
1995	M	I	32		A		32	21	15	Woolton, Joel
JACKSON STATE (MS)										
1970	M		8	7	A		32	22	4	Covington, Paul E.
1971			16	10	A		32	23	7	Covington, Paul E.
1969			32		A		32	19	18	Covington, Paul E.

Year	M/W	Div	F	SD	BD	Bye	#T	W	L	Coach
JACKSONVILLE (FL)										
1965	M		32			A		32	15	11	Williams, Joe L.
JAMESTOWN										
1994	M	II	16	24		A		24	13	14	Meyer, Jerry
1984	W		16			A		16	15	7	Kohler, Robert
JERSEY CITY STATE										
1964	M		32			A		32	20	6	Gelston, Oliver S. "Ollie"
JORDAN COLLEGE & SEMINARY										
1938	M		8					32			
1939			32					32			
JUDSON (IL)										
1996	W	II	32			A		32	21	9	Gum, Tory
KALAMAZOO										
1950	M		32					32	13	8	Grow, Lloyd E.
1956			32					32	14	9	Steffen, Raymond
KANSAS NEWMAN										
1971	M		32			A		32	16	5	Rineberg, Rick
1978			32			A		32	21	11	Skinner, David N.
KANSAS WESLEYAN										
1940	M		16					32	23	8	Johnson, Eugene
1943			16					32	18	4	Johnson, Eugene
1938			32					32	9	7	Unknown
1950			32					32	22	2	Forsberg, Wallace A. "Wally"
KEENE STATE										
1973	M		32			A		32	19	8	Theulen, Glenn H.
1974			32			A		32	16	9	Theulen, Glenn H.
1977			32			A		32	22	7	Theulen, Glenn H.
KENNESAW STATE										
1993	M	I	32			A		32	19	12	Zenoni, Phil
1992	W	I	16			L		32	22	9	Walker, Ron
1993		I	32			A		32	19	11	Walker, Ron
KENTUCKY STATE										
1970	M		1	4		A		32	29	3	Mitchell, Lucias
1971			1	1		A		32	31	2	Mitchell, Lucias
1972			1	3		A		32	28	5	Mitchell, Lucias
1974			3	2		A		32	28	5	Mitchell, Lucias
1964			16	11		A		32	18	7	McLendon, John B., Jr.
1959			32			A		32	14	11	Brown, James B.
1973			32	3		A		32	25	5	Mitchell, Lucias
1975			32	1		A		32	26	3	Mitchell, Lucias
1977			32	3		A		32	27	3	Oliver, James V.
1979			32			A		32	18	11	Theard, Floyd M.
1981	W		1	7		A		8	21	7	Mitchell, Ron

Year	M/W	Div	F	SD	BD	Bye	#T	W	L	Coach
KING (TN)										
1992	M	II	16	1	A	To R16	32	28	3	Street, Marty
1998		II	32		A		32	20	14	Polsgrove, Scott
1993	W	II	16	7	A	To R16	20	23	4	Nida, Al
KING'S (NY)										
1992	M	II	20		A		20	20	13	Showers, Ken
1990			32		A		32	27	6	Harris, William R.
LAKE SUPERIOR STATE										
1976	M		8		A		32	24	4	Douma, Edward
1978			32	12	A		32	23	4	Douma, Edward
LAKELAND (WI)										
1966	M		16		A		32	21	8	Woltzen, Duane A.
1994		II	24	22	A		24	25	11	Jonas, Craig
LAWRENCE TECH										
1952	M		8				32	23	2	Ridler, Don
1948			16				32	22	6	Ridler, Don
1954			16				32	24	5	Maconochie, Walter "Scotty"
1943			32				32	18	13	Ridler, Don
1947			32				32	26	4	Ridler, Don
1949			32				32	16	10	Ridler, Don
LEES-MCRAE										
1994	W	I	32		A		32	19	10	Dixon, Janet
LEMOYNE-OWEN										
1980	M		8		A		32	26	8	Johnson, Jerry C.
1978			32		A		32	20	10	Johnson, Jerry C.
1979			32		A		32	22	12	Johnson, Jerry C.
LENOIR-RHYNE										
1959	M		8	16	A		32	24	6	Wells, Bill
1993		I	8		A		32	25	7	Lentz, John
1958			32		A		32	24	4	Wells, Bill
LETOURNEAU										
1996	W	I	32		A		32	19	10	Otwell, Mary Ann
1997		I	32		A		32	30	4	Otwell, Mary Ann
1998		I	32		A		32	24	10	Otwell, Mary Ann
LEWIS & CLARK (OR)										
1994	M	II	3	8	L	To R16	24	23	9	Gaillard, Dr. Bob
1963			8	14	A		32	23	6	Goddard, Jim
1998		II	8	10	A		32	22	7	Gaillard, Dr. Bob
1962			16		A		32	20	11	Goddard, Jim
1995		II	16		A		32	17	14	Gaillard, Dr. Bob
1996		II	16		L		32	17	10	Gaillard, Dr. Bob
1997		II	16	10	L		32	22	6	Gaillard, Dr. Bob
1964			32		A		32	20	8	Sempert, Dean
1971			32		A		32	19	10	Sempert, Dean
1994	W	II	8	6	A	To R16	24	26	5	Petrie, Paula

Year	M/W	Div	F	SD	BD	Bye	#T	W	L	Coach
LEWIS (IL)										
1965	M		16		A		32	21	6	Gillespie, Gordon A.
LEWIS-CLARK STATE (ID)										
1992	M	I	32		A		32	24	11	Pfeifer, George
1996		I	32	16	A		32	19	9	Pfeifer, George
1998	W	I	8	12	L		32	22	8	Divilbiss, Mike
1997		I	16	8	L		32	25	7	Divilbiss, Mike
1996		I	32		L		32	25	7	Divilbiss, Mike
LIBERTY										
1983	M		8		A		32	23	9	Meyer, Jeff
LIFE (GA)										
1997	M	I	1	1	A		32	37	1	Kaiser, Roger A.
1994		I	2		A		32	27	10	Kaiser, Roger A.
1993		I	16	13	L		32	30	5	Kaiser, Roger A.
1996		I	16	2	A		32	31	6	Kaiser, Roger A.
1998		I	16	3	A		32	32	4	Kaiser, Roger A.
1995		I	32	2	A		32	31	3	Kaiser, Roger A.
LINCOLN (MO)										
1965	M		32	10	A		32	13	12	Staggers, Jonathan L.
LINCOLN (PA)										
1983	M		32		A		32	11	16	Jones, Melvin L.
LINCOLN MEMORIAL										
1976	M		4		A		32	28	9	Jackson, Wilford "Jack"
1981			16		A		32	24	8	Kilby, L. J.
1977			32	6	A		32	30	5	Jackson, Wilford "Jack"
LINDENWOOD										
1994	W	I	32		A		32	24	7	Crotz, Stephen
1995		I	32		A		32	21	12	Crotz, Stephen
1996		I	32		A		32	21	11	Crotz, Stephen
LINDSEY WILSON										
1997	M	I	32		A		32	23	13	Dodd, Steve
1998		I	32		A		32	23	12	Dodd, Steve
LINFIELD										
1947	M		32				32	20	8	Lever, Henry W.
1959			32		A		32	18	11	Helser, Roy
1961			32		A		32	18	11	Helser, Roy
1965			32		A		32	21	7	Wilson, Ted
1966			32	16	A		32	23	6	Wilson, Ted
1967			32		A		32	20	10	Wilson, Ted
1969			32	10	A		32	24	4	Wilson, Ted
1970			32		A		32	23	7	Wilson, Ted
1976			32		A		32	20	9	Wilson, Ted

Year	M/W	Div	F	SD	BD	Bye	#T	W	L	Coach
LIPSCOMB										
1986	M		1	11		A	32	35	4	Meyer, Dr. Don W.
1990			3	1		A	32	41	5	Meyer, Dr. Don W.
1996		I	3	4		A	32	33	6	Meyer, Dr. Don W.
1991			8	3		A	32	35	4	Meyer, Dr. Don W.
1993		I	8	4		A	32	34	4	Meyer, Dr. Don W.
1985			16			A	32	25	9	Meyer, Dr. Don W.
1988			16	3		A	32	33	3	Meyer, Dr. Don W.
1992		I	16	11		L	32	31	5	Meyer, Dr. Don W.
1995		I	16			L	32	30	7	Meyer, Dr. Don W.
1982			32	5		A	32	33	4	Meyer, Dr. Don W.
1994		I	32	12		L	32	29	6	Meyer, Dr. Don W.
1997		I	32	7		A	32	30	6	Meyer, Dr. Don W.
1994	W	I	2	7		L	32	31	7	Bennett, Frank
1995		I	3	3		A	32	34	5	Bennett, Frank
1996		I	3	5		L	32	31	6	Bennett, Frank
1993		I	8	6		L	32	28	6	Bennett, Frank
1990			16	7		A	16	30	8	Bennett, Frank
1997		I	16	16		L	32	26	10	Bennett, Frank
1998		I	32	15		L	32	23	12	Bennett, Frank
LORAS										
1983	M		8	15		A	32	25	5	Smith, Doug
1946			16				32	18	9	Dowd, Vincent J.
1980			16			A	32	23	12	Mullen, Robert
1939			32				32	14	6	Coyne, Fr. Daniel B.
1940			32				32	14	6	Coyne, Fr. Daniel B.
1947			32				32	24	5	Dowd, Vincent J.
LOUISIANA										
1979	M		32			A	32	22	6	Allgood, Billy
1990			32			A	32	21	8	Rushing, Gene
1986	W		3	2		A	16	24	2	Johnson, Shelia Thompson
1985			16	6		A	16	27	4	Schneider, Frank
1992		I	16			A	32	18	13	Brooks, Billy C.
1998		I	32			A	32	23	7	Brooks, Billy C.
LOUISIANA TECH										
1955	M		16				32	20	10	Crowley, Cecil C.
1942			32				32	13	8	Crowley, Cecil C.
1946			32				32	16	8	Crowley, Cecil C.
1953			32				32	17	10	Crowley, Cecil C.
LOUISVILLE										
1948	M		1				32	29	6	Hickman, Bernard L. "Peck"
LOYOLA (IL)										
1943	M		32				32	12	10	Connelly, John J.

Year	M/W	Div	F	SD	BD	Bye	#T	W	L	Coach
Loyola (MD)										
1949	M		16				32	25	8	Reitz, Emil G., Jr. "Lefty"
1953			16				32	17	9	Reitz, Emil G., Jr. "Lefty"
1947			32				32	21	12	Reitz, Emil G., Jr. "Lefty"
1948			32				32	24	7	Reitz, Emil G., Jr. "Lefty"
Loyola Marymount										
1955	M		32				32	16	9	Donovan, William J.
Loyola New Orleans										
1945	M		1				16	22	11	Orsley, Jack C.
1946			4				32	22	11	Orsley, Jack C.
1995		II	32			A	32	15	13	Hernandez, Jerry
Luther										
1937	M		8			I	8	12	8	Peterson, Hamlet E., Sr.
1942			16				32	15	4	Peterson, Hamlet E., Sr.
1943			16				32	12	3	Peterson, Hamlet E., Sr.
Lynn										
1994	M	II	24	10		A	24	23	7	Price, Jeff
1994	W	II	24	12		A	24	24	5	Olson, Dan
Lyon										
1984	M		16			A	32	22	11	Garner, Terry
Madonna										
1997	W	II	32			A	32	14	15	Jansen, Marylou
Maine: Farmington										
1997	W	II	32			A	32	20	5	MacPhee, Leonard R.
1998		II	32			A	32	20	5	MacPhee, Leonard R.
Maine: Machias										
1991	M		32			A	32	22	5	Casey, Sean
Malone										
1975	M		8			A	32	27	6	Bowerman, Jay
1990			32	14		A	32	25	9	Smith, Harold T.
1992		I	32			L	32	26	9	Smith, Harold T.
Manchester										
1939	M		8				32	16	5	Stauffer, Robert
1938			32				32	14	5	Stauffer, Robert
Manhattan										
1948	M		8				32	23	6	Norton, Kenneth A.
Mankato State										
1947	M		2				32	24	4	Witham, James A.
1948			8				32	16	11	Witham, James A.

Year	M/W	Div	F	SD	BD	Bye	#T	W	L	Coach
MANSFIELD										
1964	M		8	8	A		32	20	4	Clark, William J.
1965			32	7	A		32	16	6	Clark, William J.
1971			32		A		32	18	8	Wilson, Edward W.
MARIAN (IN)										
1998	M	II	32	14	A		32	22	7	Grimes, John
MARIST										
1973	M		32		A		32	15	12	Petro, Ronald
MARSHALL										
1947	M		1				32	32	5	Henderson, Eli Camden "Cam"
1938			16				32	28	4	Henderson, Eli Camden "Cam"
1948			16				32	22	11	Henderson, Eli Camden "Cam"
MARY										
1982	M		32		A		32	30	3	Bortke, Al
1994	W	II	16	11	A		24	21	6	Haug, Roger
1995		II	32	13	A		32	18	8	Haug, Roger
1997		II	32	13	A		32	20	6	Haug, Roger
MARY HARDIN-BAYLOR										
1995	M	I	32		L		32	23	8	Herbst, Richard
1998		II	32		A		32	14	12	Herbst, Richard
1998	W	II	2		A		32	24	6	Van Auken, Jeff
1996		I	16		A		32	22	8	Foster, Cliffa
1997		I	16		A		32	22	8	Foster, Cliffa
1994		I	32		A		32	19	16	Foster, Cliffa
1995		I	32		L		32	24	8	Foster, Cliffa
MARYCREST INTERNATIONAL										
1985	M		3	7	A		32	34	6	Merchant, Jim
1984			32	13	A		32	31	7	O'Neill, Kevin
MARYLAND: EASTERN SHORE										
1969	M		2		A		32	24	7	Robinson, Joe
1973			2	8	A		32	26	5	Bates, John H.
1970			8	2	A		32	23	1	Robinson, Joe
1960			32		A		32	22	6	Taylor, Nathaniel C. "Nay"
1961			32	15	A		32	17	6	Taylor, Nathaniel C. "Nay"
1965			32		A		32	16	6	Taylor, Nathaniel C. "Nay"
1972			32		A		32	14	6	Bates, John H.
MARYMOUNT (KS)										
1976	M		3	4	A		32	31	3	Cochran, Ken
1979			8		A		32	26	6	Cochran, Ken
1975			16	4	A		32	29	4	Cochran, Ken
1980			16	15	A		32	19	14	Cochran, Ken
1973			32	5	A		32	25	3	Cochran, Ken
MASSACHUSETTS: BOSTON										
1967	M		32		A		32	18	7	Loscutoff, James, Jr.

Year	M/W	Div	F	SD	BD	Bye	#T	W	L	Coach
MASTER'S										
1995	M	I	8	8	A		32	31	5	Oates, Bill
1996		I	16	3	A		32	28	7	Oates, Bill
1994		I	32	10	A		32	28	5	Oates, Bill
1997		I	32		A		32	21	11	Oates, Bill
1998		I	32		A		32	23	12	Oates, Bill
MAYVILLE STATE										
1998	M	II	8	3	A		32	23	7	Grove, Paul
1962			32		A		32	17	17	Meyer, Alvin H.
1996		II	32		A		32	17	11	Miles, Tim
1997		II	32		A		32	18	11	Miles, Tim
MCKENDREE										
1997	M	I	8		L		32	28	9	Statham, Harry M.
1988			16	7	A		32	35	1	Statham, Harry M.
1996		I	16		A		32	25	9	Statham, Harry M.
1992		I	32		L		32	31	6	Statham, Harry M.
1993		I	32		A		32	27	9	Statham, Harry M.
1998	W	I	32		A		32	20	15	Miller, Melissa
MCMURRY										
1994	M	II	16	21	A		24	21	8	Holmes, Ron
1962			32		A		32	24	4	Kimbrell, Hershell
MCNEESE STATE										
1956	M		1				32	33	3	Ward, Ralph O.
MCPHERSON										
1938	M		32				32	13	8	Astle, W. P. "Buck"
MEMPHIS										
1951	M		8				32	17	8	Tarry, McCoy
1952			16				32	25	10	Lambert, Dr. Eugene W.
MERCER										
1948	M		32				32	18	4	Cowan, James M.
1954			32				32	19	9	Cowan, James M.
MERCYHURST										
1978	M		32	8	A		32	24	2	Fox, Richard A.
MESA STATE										
1985	M		32		A		32	23	8	Schakel, Doug
MIAMI (FL)										
1949	M		32				32	19	8	Morris, Hart
MIDAMERICA NAZARENE										
1992	M	II	8	2	A	To R16	20	27	10	Lamar, Jon "Rocky"
1996		II	16	13	A		32	20	17	Lamar, Jon "Rocky"
1995		II	32		L		32	21	15	Lamar, Jon "Rocky"

Year	M/W	Div	F	SD	BD	Bye	#T	W	L	Coach
MIDDLE TENNESSEE STATE										
1955	M		32				32	11	16	Greer, Charles N., Jr.
MIDLAND LUTHERAN										
1990	M		32		A		32	17	15	McGill, Richard "Rich"
1985	W		4		A		16	26	5	Bracker, Joanne
1991			16	14	A		32	22	8	Bracker, Joanne
1995		II	16	11	L		32	22	7	Bracker, Joanne
1996		II	16	9	L		32	26	6	Bracker, Joanne
1992		I	32	9	A		32	25	5	Bracker, Joanne
MIDWESTERN STATE (TX)										
1975	M		2	7	A		32	31	6	Stockton, Dr. Gerald E.
1993		I	3		A		32	25	12	Stockton, Dr. Gerald E.
1994		I	3		A		32	23	12	Stockton, Dr. Gerald E.
1979			4		A		32	24	17	Stockton, Dr. Gerald E.
1956			8				32	21	8	Clynch, Dallas C.
1974			8	7	A		32	30	7	Stockton, Dr. Gerald E.
1981			8		A		32	25	18	Stockton, Dr. Gerald E.
1965			16	16	A		32	28	6	Vinzant, Dennis
1966			16	5	A		32	26	6	Vinzant, Dennis
1967			16	12	A		32	21	11	Vinzant, Dennis
1953			32				32	18	8	Clynch, Dallas C.
1960			32		A		32	17	13	Vinzant, Dennis
1978			32		A		32	21	13	Stockton, Dr. Gerald E.
1984			32		A		32	25	16	Stockton, Dr. Gerald E.
1995		I	32		A		32	19	11	Ray, Jeff
1993	W	I	16	13	L		32	22	8	Ray, Jeff
1994		I	16	12	A		32	28	6	Ray, Jeff
1995		I	16		L		32	20	10	Williams, Wayne
MILES										
1963	M		16		A		32	20	5	Wilkins, Arthur "Pete"
1964			32		A		32	13	7	Wilkins, Arthur "Pete"
MILLERSVILLE										
1975	M		16		A		32	17	10	DeHart, Richard C.
1957			32				32	18	6	DeHart, Richard C.
1966			32		A		32	19	7	DeHart, Richard C.
1967			32	13	A		32	21	6	DeHart, Richard C.
1968			32		A		32	17	8	DeHart, Richard C.
1974			32		A		32	21	5	DeHart, Richard C.
MILLIGAN										
1995	M	II	32		L		32	24	12	Scruggs, Rick
1997	W	II	16		A		32	30	5	Aubrey, Richard "Rich"
1998		II	32		A		32	27	8	Aubrey, Richard "Rich"
MILLIKIN										
1951	M		2				32	24	7	Allan, Ralph W.
1952			16				32	21	6	Allan, Ralph W.
1968			32		A		32	21	4	Williams, Don E.
1969			32		A		32	16	9	Williams, Don E.

Year	M/W	Div	F	SD	BD	Bye	#T	W	L	Coach
MINNESOTA: DULUTH										
1959	M		16	10	A		32	22	4	Olson, Norman H.
1985			16		A		32	23	8	Race, Dale M.
1988			16	15	A		32	25	6	Race, Dale M.
1990			16	6	A		32	26	6	Race, Dale M.
1991			16	4	A		32	27	5	Race, Dale M.
1992		I	16		A		32	23	9	Race, Dale M.
1958			32		A		32	20	3	Olson, Norman H.
1986			32		A		32	23	8	Race, Dale M.
1987			32		A		32	24	7	Race, Dale M.
1989			32		A		32	25	6	Race, Dale M.
1988	W		8		A		16	18	12	Stromme, Karen
1989			16	6	A		16	26	6	Stromme, Karen
1990			16		A		16	24	7	Stromme, Karen
1991			16	12	A		32	26	6	Stromme, Karen
1993		I	16	16	A		32	22	8	Stromme, Karen
1994		I	16		A		32	20	11	Stromme, Karen
1992		I	32		A		32	16	14	Stromme, Karen
MINNESOTA: MORRIS										
1993	M	I	8		A		32	22	10	Ford, Perry
1995		I	32	16	A		32	20	9	Ford, Perry
MINOT STATE										
1955	M		32				32	20	5	Parker, Herb
1972			32		A		32	22	3	Luther, Wes
1995		II	32		A		32	14	13	Limke, Dick
1996	W	II	32		A		32	17	11	Green, Sheila L.
1998		II	32		A		32	20	8	Green, Sheila L.
MISSISSIPPI VALLEY STATE										
1978	M		32		A		32	15	20	Gaines, William "Pop"
MISSOURI BAPTIST										
1994	M	I	32		A		32	25	10	Pitzer, Lowell S.
MISSOURI SOUTHERN STATE										
1978	M		8	13	A		32	27	9	Williams, "Chuck"
1973			16		A		32	17	11	Davis, Frank
1972			32		A		32	22	9	Davis, Frank
1987			32		A		32	20	13	Williams, "Chuck"
1982	W		2	6	A		8	23	12	Phillips, James
MISSOURI VALLEY										
1942	M		8				32	17	8	Ashford, Volney C.
1961			16		A		32	18	9	Redford, Grover C.
1992		II	20		L		20	23	11	Fifer, Tom
1995	W	II	32	9	A		32	27	9	Piha, Elaine

Year	M/W	Div	F	°	SD	BD	Bye	#T	W	L	Coach
MISSOURI WESTERN STATE											
1974	M		16	13	A			32	25	6	Filbert, Gary
1982			32		A			32	25	7	Filbert, Gary
1984			32		A			32	21	10	Shear, Lawrence "Skip"
1981	W		8	4	A			8	24	7	Bumpus, Debbie
MISSOURI: KANSAS CITY											
1977	M		32		A			32	21	9	Corwin, Darrell
1983	W		3	4	A			8	30	5	Norman, Nancy
1985			8	8	A			16	29	6	Norman, Nancy
MISSOURI: SAINT LOUIS											
1969	M		32		A			32	19	7	Smith, Charles G. "Chuck"
MOBILE											
1988	M		32	10	A			32	31	3	Elder, Dr. Bill
1994		I	32	7	L			32	32	3	Elder, Dr. Bill
1998		I	32	16	A			32	27	9	Sanderson, Scott
1991	W		32		A			32	22	8	Berger, Curt
1993		I	32		A			32	22	9	Berger, Curt
MONMOUTH (NJ)											
1969	M		8		A			32	24	6	Boylan, William T.
1968			16	11	A			32	27	2	Boylan, William T.
1966			32		A			32	26	4	Boylan, William T.
1970			32		A			32	17	11	Boylan, William T.
1974			32		A			32	19	9	Boylan, William T.
1975			32		A			32	22	7	Boylan, William T.
MONTANA											
1948	M		32					32	21	11	Dahlberg, George P.
1950			32					32	27	4	Dahlberg, George P.
MONTANA STATE											
1952	M		16					32	22	14	Breeden, John W. "Brick"
1946			32					32	17	10	Breeden, John W. "Brick"
1947			32					32	25	11	Breeden, John W. "Brick"
1954			32					32	18	11	Breeden, John W. "Brick"
1955			32					32	11	16	Lemm, Walter H. "Wally"
1956			32					32	15	14	Lambert, Keith "Dobbie"
MONTANA STATE: BILLINGS											
1965	M		16		A			32	12	17	Harkins, Mike L.
1968			16		A			32	20	9	Harkins, Mike L.
1963			32		A			32	19	6	Harkins, Mike L.
1964			32		A			32	16	8	Harkins, Mike L.
1967			32		A			32	14	18	Harkins, Mike L.
1970			32		A			32	20	9	Harkins, Mike L.
1972			32		A			32	19	6	Harkins, Mike L.
1973			32		A			32	22	10	Harkins, Mike L.
1975			32		A			32	20	8	Harkins, Mike L.
1976			32		A			32	20	10	Harkins, Mike L.
1978			32		A			32	22	10	Chidester, Ted H.

Year	M/W	Div	F	SD	BD	Bye	#T	W	L	Coach
MONTANA STATE: NORTHERN										
1995	M	I	8		A		32	17	19	Baker, Loren
1998		I	16		L		32	26	9	Walker, Tim
1996		I	32	9	A		32	24	9	Baker, Loren
1993	W	II	1	1	A	To R16	20	35	3	Winn, Sherry
1992		II	8	1	A	To R16	20	30	2	Winn, Sherry
1990			16	5	A		16	28	3	Baker, Loren
1991			16	13	A		32	26	5	Baker, Loren
1996		I	16	12	A		32	24	5	Winn, Sherry
1998		I	16	16	A		32	25	9	Peters, Ray
1994		I	32		A		32	26	6	Winn, Sherry
1995		I	32	11	A		32	25	4	Winn, Sherry
1997		I	32	12	A		32	25	7	Winn, Sherry
MONTANA TECH										
1998	M	I	32		A		32	22	11	Dessing, Rick
MONTEVALLO										
1975	M		32		A		32	23	9	Jones, Bill L.
1994	W	I	3	6	L		32	28	7	Van Atta, Gary
1993		I	8	7	A		32	26	5	Van Atta, Gary
1995		I	16	16	L		32	22	10	Van Atta, Gary
1996		I	16	11	L		32	24	5	Van Atta, Gary
1992		I	32	13	L		32	23	7	Van Atta, Gary
MOORHEAD STATE (MN)										
1982	M		16		A		32	24	7	Schellhase, David G., Jr.
1980			32		A		32	21	9	Schellhase, David G., Jr.
MOREHEAD STATE (KY)										
1942	M		32				32	12	10	Johnson, Ellis T.
1951			32				32	13	11	Johnson, Ellis T.
MORNINGSIDE										
1937	M		2		I		8	16	4	Rogers, R. Glenn "Honie"
1952			8				32	20	10	Buckingham, Albert W.
1951			16				32	18	7	Buckingham, Albert W.
1938			32				32	14	5	Rogers, R. Glenn "Honie"
1941			32				32	9	7	Rogers, R. Glenn "Honie"
1946			32				32	15	4	Buckingham, Albert W.
1950			32				32	13	14	Buckingham, Albert W.
1959			32		A		32	14	9	Obye, Charles H. "Chuck"
1975			32		A		32	17	12	Callahan, Dan
1986	W		16		A		16	20	11	Arnold, John
MOUNT MARTY										
1998	M	II	3	13	L		32	23	9	Thorson, Jim
1977			32		A		32	23	9	Evans, Frank
1986	W		16		A		16	24	8	Anderson, Warren
MOUNT MERCY										
1996	M	II	16	11	A		32	29	6	Gavin, Paul

Year	M/W	Div	F	SD	BD	Bye	#T	W	L	Coach
1994	W	II	3	2	A	To R16	24	31	4	Slifer, David
1992		II	8	2	A	To R16	20	30	5	Slifer, David
1993		II	8	2	A	To R16	20	28	5	Slifer, David
1995		II	8	3	A		32	31	6	Slifer, David
1991			16	7	A		32	28	4	Slifer, David

MOUNT SAINT JOSEPH

Year	M/W	Div	F	SD	BD	Bye	#T	W	L	Coach
1992	W	II	3	8	A	To R16	20	20	8	Dowell, T. Jean
1996		II	32		A		32	25	16	McKee, Rebecca

MOUNT VERNON NAZARENE

Year	M/W	Div	F	SD	BD	Bye	#T	W	L	Coach
1998	M	II	8	5	L		32	27	7	Flemming, Scott
1995		II	32	13	L		32	22	10	Flemming, Scott

MURRAY STATE (KY)

Year	M/W	Div	F	SD	BD	Bye	#T	W	L	Coach
1941	M		2				32	25	5	Cutchin, Carlisle C.
1952			2				32	24	10	Hodges, Harlan
1938			3				32	27	4	Cutchin, Carlisle C.
1943			4				32	21	5	Miller, John
1939			16				32	13	8	Cutchin, Carlisle C.
1942			32				32	18	4	Mountjoy, L. Rice
1950			32				32	18	13	Hodges, Harlan

NAZARETH (NY)

Year	M/W	Div	F	SD	BD	Bye	#T	W	L	Coach
1983	W		8	8	A		8	19	11	Gomez, Marguerite "Margie"

NEBRASKA WESLEYAN

Year	M/W	Div	F	SD	BD	Bye	#T	W	L	Coach
1953	M		8				32	25	3	Peterson, Dr. Irvin L.
1954			16				32	19	5	Peterson, Dr. Irvin L.
1955			16				32	21	5	Peterson, Dr. Irvin L.
1938			32				32	13	3	Thomas, Dwight P.
1959			32		A		32	23	5	Peterson, Dr. Irvin L.
1960			32	14	A		32	21	7	Peterson, Dr. Irvin L.

NEBRASKA: KEARNEY

Year	M/W	Div	F	SD	BD	Bye	#T	W	L	Coach
1978	M		2		A		32	19	8	Hueser, Jerry
1982			4		A		32	26	10	Hueser, Jerry
1979			16	14	A		32	25	8	Hueser, Jerry
1981			16	14	A		32	25	7	Hueser, Jerry
1984			16		A		32	28	9	Hueser, Jerry
1943			32				32	12	6	White, Dr. Clifford W.
1972			32		A		32	18	7	Hueser, Jerry
1975			32		A		32	21	7	Hueser, Jerry
1980			32	5	A		32	24	3	Hueser, Jerry
1983			32		A		32	25	11	Hueser, Jerry
1985			32		A		32	21	11	Hueser, Jerry
1986			32		A		32	17	15	Hueser, Jerry
1987			32	12	A		32	26	8	Hueser, Jerry
1987	W		16		A		16	21	9	Wurtz, Dan

NEBRASKA: OMAHA

Year	M/W	Div	F	SD	BD	Bye	#T	W	L	Coach
1941	M		32				32	12	13	Johnk, Harold

Year	M/W	Div	F	SD	BD	Bye	#T	W	L	Coach
NEVADA										
1946	M		8				32	24	9	Lawlor, Glenn J. "Jake"
NEW HAVEN										
1968	M		16		A		32	17	12	Ormrod, Donald R.
1966			32		A		32	29	2	Ormrod, Donald R.
1969			32		A		32	20	3	Burns, Donald E.
NEW JERSEY										
1967	M		32		A		32	18	9	Wissel, Dr. Harold R. "Hal"
NEW MEXICO										
1947	M		32				32	11	8	Clements, Woodrow W.
NEW MEXICO HIGHLANDS										
1960	M		8		A		32	18	7	Gibson, Don
1957			32				32	18	4	Gibson, Don
1992	W	I	32		A		32	21	9	Roybal, Cindy
NEW MEXICO STATE										
1938	M		8				32	22	3	Hines, Gerald H. "Jerry"
1951			8				32	15	11	McCarty, George C.
1952			16				32	22	11	McCarty, George C.
1950			32				32	15	13	McCarty, George C.
NEW MEXICO TECH										
1939	M		32				32	21	5	Butler, Dr. Louis C. "Pete"
1946			32				32	20	9	Finley, Charles L. "Chuck"
NEWBERRY										
1976	M		8	15	A		32	30	5	Gordon, Nield
1961			16	16	A		32	23	8	Quinn, Thomas R.
1977			16	1	A		32	36	1	Gordon, Nield
1975			32		A		32	24	9	Gordon, Nield
NORFOLK STATE										
1966	M		4	9	A		32	26	6	Fears, Ernest D., Jr.
1975			16	10	A		32	23	5	Christian, Charles O.
1979			16	15	A		32	23	8	Mitchell, Lucias
1976			32	12	A		32	23	7	Christian, Charles O.
1981			32		A		32	19	10	Mitchell, Lucias
NORTH ALABAMA										
1960	M		32		A		32	14	11	Billingham, Edmond E.
1962			32		A		32	17	9	Billingham, Edmond E.
NORTH CAROLINA A&T										
1971	M		8	7	A		32	24	8	Irvin, Calvin C.
NORTH CAROLINA: ASHEVILLE										
1969	M		16		A		32	19	9	Hartman, Robert L.
1971			32		A		32	20	10	Hartman, Robert L.
1984	W		1		A		16	32	5	Carroll, Helen

Year	M/W	Div	F	SD	BD	Bye	#T	W	L	Coach
NORTH CAROLINA: PEMBROKE										
1984	M		16		A		32	26	7	Lee, Billy
1973			32		A		32	20	8	Gani, Lancey E.
1985	W		16		A		16	26	5	Lee, Billy
1992		I	32		L		32	24	7	Pitts, Linda
NORTH DAKOTA										
1949	M		16				32	14	15	Cunningham, H. B.
1953			32				32	14	10	Bogan, Louis
1954			32				32	13	11	Bogan, Louis
NORTH GEORGIA										
1983	M		32		A		32	23	9	Ensley, William E.
1984			32		A		32	17	15	Ensley, William E.
1996		I	32		A		32	21	16	Dunn, Randy
1987	W		2	4	A		16	27	4	Jarrett, Lynn
1997		I	32		A		32	26	7	Burson-Watson, Buffie
NORTH TEXAS										
1943	M		3				32	15	15	Russell, Lloyd
1938			16				32	15	8	Shands, Harry G. "Pete"
NORTHEAST LOUISIANA										
1970	M		16	10	A		32	16	9	Fant, Leonard "Lenny"
NORTHEASTERN ILLINOIS										
1985	W		8		A		16	29	13	Margaritis, John
NORTHEASTERN STATE (OK)										
1968	M		16	8	A		32	26	4	Dobbins, Dr. Jack
1972			16	12	A		32	23	8	Dobbins, Dr. Jack
NORTHERN ARIZONA										
1947	M		3				32	20	7	Brickey, Frank
1962			8		A		32	17	9	Gregg, Herbert
1946			16				32	11	7	Brickey, Frank
1954			32				32	19	7	Gregg, Herbert
NORTHERN IOWA										
1946	M		16				32	13	7	Nordley, Oliver M.
1949			16				32	16	6	Nordley, Oliver M.
1948			32				32	14	6	Nordley, Oliver M.
1953			32				32	14	11	Nordley, Oliver M.
NORTHERN MICHIGAN										
1961	M		3	2	A		32	24	3	Albeck, Charles Stanley "Stan"
1963			8	13	A		32	19	8	Albeck, Charles Stanley "Stan"
1958			32		A		32	15	3	Albeck, Charles Stanley "Stan"
1959			32		A		32	16	8	Albeck, Charles Stanley "Stan"
1965			32		A		32	19	6	Albeck, Charles Stanley "Stan"

Year	M/W	Div	F	SD	BD	Bye	#T	W	L	Coach
NORTHERN STATE (SD)										
1993	M	II	2	1	A	To R16	20	34	2	Olson, Robert
1994		II	2	4	A	To R16	24	25	9	Olson, Robert
1995		II	3	1	A		32	28	5	Olson, Robert
1958			16		A		32	25	3	Wachs, Bob
1971			16		A		32	22	8	Wachs, Bob
1991			16		A		32	26	8	Olson, Robert
1939			32				32	18	2	Robertson, Harley R.
1940			32				32	17	5	Robertson, Harley R.
1957			32				32	22	5	Wachs, Bob
1959			32		A		32	19	3	Wachs, Bob
1961			32		A		32	16	7	Wachs, Bob
1970			32		A		32	20	7	Wachs, Bob
1983			32		A		32	22	10	Wachs, Bob
1984			32	14	A		32	28	4	Wachs, Bob
1990			32		A		32	23	9	Olson, Robert
1992	W	II	1	6	L	To R16	20	30	4	Fredrickson, Curt
1994		II	1	1	A	To R16	24	32	1	Fredrickson, Curt
1993		II	2	3	L	To R16	20	28	7	Fredrickson, Curt
1981			3	5	A		8	28	4	Fredrickson, Curt
1995		II	8	1	A		32	28	3	Fredrickson, Curt
NORTHLAND										
1996	M	II	32		A		32	19	11	Swan, David
NORTHWEST MISSOURI STATE										
1943	M		2				32	18	7	Stalcup, Wilbur N. "Sparky"
1939			8				32	14	7	Stalcup, Wilbur N. "Sparky"
1940			8				32	22	1	Stalcup, Wilbur N. "Sparky"
1941			8				32	19	4	Stalcup, Wilbur N. "Sparky"
1938			16				32	15	6	Stalcup, Wilbur N. "Sparky"
NORTHWEST NAZARENE										
1995	M	II	2	5	A		32	27	7	Weidenbach, Ed
1993		II	3		L		20	20	13	Weidenbach, Ed
1994		II	3	11	A		24	26	8	Weidenbach, Ed
1998		II	3	11	A		32	27	10	Sanders, Rich
1996		II	8		H		32	19	13	Weidenbach, Ed
1997		II	8	9	L		32	26	8	Weidenbach, Ed
1992		II	16	7	A	To R16	20	26	9	Weidenbach, Ed
1957			32				32	24	9	Hills, Orrin E.
1997	W	II	1	3	A		32	27	7	Schmidt, Roger
1995		II	2	10	L		32	23	7	Schmidt, Roger
1996		II	32	10	L		32	17	10	Schmidt, Roger
NORTHWESTERN (IA)										
1992	M	II	2		A	To R16	20	25	8	Barry, Todd
1994		II	8	2	A	To R16	24	27	4	Barry, Todd
1993		II	16		A		20	19	11	Barry, Todd
1971			32		A		32	23	5	Jacobsen, Dr. Don
1972			32		A		32	21	7	Jacobsen, Dr. Don
1987			32		A		32	27	5	Douma, Les

Year	M/W	Div	F	SD	BD	Bye	#T	W	L	Coach
NORTHWESTERN OKLAHOMA STATE										
1992	M	I	16	13	L		32	25	7	Battisti, Bob
1994		I	16	2	A		32	29	2	Battisti, Bob
1949			32				32	18	9	Highfill, C. L. "Dick"
1992	W	I	16		L		32	24	7	Barton, Milburn
1996		I	32		L		32	19	13	Barton, Milburn
1998		I	32		L		32	25	8	Barton, Milburn
NORTHWESTERN STATE (LA)										
1949	M		8				32	23	5	Prather, H. Lee
1941			16				32	17	2	Prather, H. Lee
1974			16	12	A		32	21	9	Hildebrand, Tynes
1939			32				32	16	4	Prather, H. Lee
1940			32				32	19	2	Prather, H. Lee
1947			32				32	15	5	Prather, H. Lee
1948			32				32	19	6	Prather, H. Lee
NORTHWOOD (MI)										
1987	M		32		A		32	16	15	Miller, Pat
1991	W		32		A		32	20	12	Vielbig, Mary
NOVA SOUTHEASTERN										
1995	M	II	16	11	L		32	22	12	Michaels, Jim
NYACK										
1995	M	II	32		L		32	26	8	Bailey, Dan
OAKLAND CITY (IN)										
1960	M		32		A		32	17	6	Disler, Delbert C.
OGLETHORPE										
1947	M		32				32	22	6	Phillips, "Swede"
1961			32	4	A		32	20	4	Pinholster, Garland F.
OHIO DOMINICAN										
1994	M	II	16	14	A		24	23	9	DiGenova, Ed
1995		II	16		A		32	19	16	DiGenova, Ed
1971			32		A		32	17	6	Nangle, Gene
OKLAHOMA BAPTIST UNIVERSITY										
1966	M		1	11	A		32	26	7	Bass, Robert E.
1965			2	15	A		32	25	7	Bass, Robert E.
1967			2	3	A		32	25	7	Bass, Robert E.
1993		I	2	1	A		32	34	4	Hoffman, Bob
1997		I	2	3	A		32	36	4	Hoffman, Bob
1994		I	3	16	L		32	29	8	Hoffman, Bob
1973			8		A		32	20	11	Wallace, H. Eugene
1960			16		A		32	23	6	Bass, Robert E.
1996		I	16	8	A		32	29	6	Hoffman, Bob
1958			32		A		32	19	8	Bass, Robert E.
1963			32	4	A		32	21	7	Bass, Robert E.
1995		I	32	15	L		32	28	6	Hoffman, Bob

Year	M/W	Div	F	SD	BD	Bye	#T	W	L	Coach
1997	W	I	8	6	L		32	28	9	Norris, Scott
1998		I	8	8	L		32	28	7	Norris, Scott
1996		I	32		L		32	21	12	Norris, Scott

OKLAHOMA CHRISTIAN

Year	M/W	Div	F	SD	BD	Bye	#T	W	L	Coach
1995	M	I	16	12	L		32	28	9	Hays, Dan
1968			32	4	A		32	18	4	Davis, Frank
1982			32	2	A		32	33	3	Jobe, Jerry
1994		I	32	14	L		32	23	11	Hays, Dan
1986	W		8	4	A		16	27	8	Findley, Stephanie
1993		I	16		L		32	20	12	Findley, Stephanie
1995		I	16	14	L		32	24	9	Findley, Stephanie
1997		I	32		L		32	22	11	Findley, Stephanie

OKLAHOMA CITY

Year	M/W	Div	F	SD	BD	Bye	#T	W	L	Coach
1991	M		1	2	A		32	27	3	Johnson, Darrel
1992		I	1	1	A		32	38	0	Johnson, Darrel
1994		I	1	5	A		32	28	7	Case, Win
1996		I	1	14	L		32	33	5	Case, Win
1995		I	8	3	A		32	30	3	Case, Win
1987			16	1	A		32	34	1	Lemons, A. E. "Abe"
1993		I	16	6	L		32	25	7	Case, Win
1998		I	16	8	L		32	26	5	Case, Win
1988	W		1	4	A		16	28	6	Colon, Bob
1993		I	16		L		32	23	9	Colon, Bob
1998		I	16		L		32	19	13	Stanley, Kent
1994		I	32		L		32	22	10	Colon, Bob

OKLAHOMA PANHANDLE STATE

Year	M/W	Div	F	SD	BD	Bye	#T	W	L	Coach
1983	M		16	5	A		32	31	4	Layton, Terry
1941			32				32	19	8	Iba, Clarence V.
1994	W	II	8	10	A		24	19	12	Olson, Jerry

OLIVET NAZARENE

Year	M/W	Div	F	SD	BD	Bye	#T	W	L	Coach
1992	M	I	16		A		32	25	11	Hodge, Ralph
1998		I	16		A		32	28	9	Hodge, Ralph
1989			32		A		32	22	9	Hodge, Ralph
1990			32		A		32	26	10	Hodge, Ralph
1991			32		A		32	22	13	Hodge, Ralph
1995		I	32		A		32	21	15	Hodge, Ralph
1997		I	32		A		32	21	13	Hodge, Ralph
1992	W	II	20		A		20	18	10	Glass, Robyn

ORAL ROBERTS

Year	M/W	Div	F	SD	BD	Bye	#T	W	L	Coach
1990	M		8	3	A		32	36	6	Trickey, Ken

OREGON TECH

Year	M/W	Div	F	SD	BD	Bye	#T	W	L	Coach
1998	M	II	2	15	L		32	26	11	Miles, Daniel J. "Danny"
1987			16	13	A		32	33	5	Miles, Daniel J. "Danny"
1997		II	16	3	L		32	29	6	Miles, Daniel J. "Danny"
1974			32		A		32	24	5	Miles, Daniel J. "Danny"
1979			32		A		32	23	5	Miles, Daniel J. "Danny"

Year	M/W	Div	F	SD	BD	Bye	#T	W	L	Coach
OTTAWA										
1951	M		16				32	19	7	Meek, Donald
1993		II	20		A		20	18	12	Carrier, Andy
1938			32				32	11	8	Godlove, Richard M.
1995		II	32		A		32	21	9	Carrier, Andy
OUACHITA BAPTIST										
1965	M		3		A		32	27	10	Vining, Bill C., Sr.
1972			16	6	A		32	26	5	Vining, Bill C., Sr.
1978			16	4	A		32	25	5	Vining, Bill C., Sr.
1943			32				32	12	7	Bradshaw, Wesley W.
1962			32		A		32	15	14	Vining, Bill C., Sr.
1964			32		A		32	22	5	Vining, Bill C., Sr.
1973			32		A		32	22	6	Vining, Bill C., Sr.
1986	W		16		A		16	18	13	Honnell, Virginia
OZARKS (AR)										
1988	M		16		A		32	25	9	Allen, Jimmy W.
1993		I	16		A		32	23	9	Johnson, John K. "Johnny"
1994		I	32		A		32	22	13	Johnson, John K. "Johnny"
OZARKS (MO)										
1995	M	II	8	6	A		32	29	5	Waller, Allan J.
1997		II	8		A		32	23	11	Waller, Allan J.
1996		II	32	10	A		32	25	7	Waller, Allan J.
1993	W	II	16		A		20	19	13	Franks, Joe
1997		II	16	6	A		32	29	3	Franks, Joe
1995		II	32		A		32	18	13	Franks, Joe
1996		II	32		A		32	18	10	Franks, Joe
1998		II	32	14	A		32	24	7	Wilson, George
PACIFIC (CA)										
1951	M		32				32	19	11	Kjeldsen, Chris K.
PACIFIC (OR)										
1997	M	II	16	4	A		32	22	6	Schumann, Ken
1940			32				32	17	12	Miller, Pete
1992	W	II	8		L	To R16	20	23	6	Olmstead, David
1996		II	32		A		32	17	10	Olmstead, David
PACIFIC LUTHERAN										
1959	M		2	3	A		32	26	3	Lundgaard, Gene C.
1957			3	1			32	28	1	Harshman, Marvel K. "Marv"
1956			16				32	25	6	Harshman, Marvel K. "Marv"
1958			16	4	A		32	21	6	Harshman, Marvel K. "Marv"
1964			16	12	A		32	20	7	Lundgaard, Gene C.
1951			32				32	20	11	Harshman, Marvel K. "Marv"
1962			32		A		32	17	9	Lundgaard, Gene C.
1963			32		A		32	18	10	Lundgaard, Gene C.
1998	W	II	32		A		32	21	7	Rigell, Gil

Year	M/W	Div	F	SD	BD	Bye	#T	W	L	Coach
PAINE										
1977	M		32		A		32	18	13	Tulberi, Ernest
PALM BEACH ATLANTIC										
1975	M		32		A		32	22	4	Perides, George L.
PANZER										
1942	M		32				32	14	5	Gorton, Albert J.
1946			32				32	18	3	Gorton, Albert J.
PARK (MO)										
1998	M	I	3	15	L		32	27	8	English, Claude
1991			32		A		32	26	7	Francis, David
PARSONS										
1960	M		16		A		32	17	12	Nelson, Oscar B.
1963			32		A		32	21	8	Nelson, Oscar B.
PAUL QUINN										
1980	M		32	12	A		32	32	10	Boyd, Wesley
1982			32		A		32	25	13	Boyd, Wesley
1988			32	13	A		32	29	5	Summers, James 'Zip'
1990			32	16	A		32	31	7	Summers, James 'Zip'
PEPPERDINE										
1945	M		2				16	25	11	Duer, Alva O. 'Al'
1946			3				32	27	8	Duer, Alva O. 'Al'
1943			8				32	23	8	Duer, Alva O. 'Al'
1950			16				32	21	12	Dowell, Robert L. 'Duck'
1951			16				32	25	8	Dowell, Robert L. 'Duck'
1942			32				32	18	7	Duer, Alva O. 'Al'
1952			32				32	20	4	Dowell, Robert L. 'Duck'
PERU STATE										
1939	M		4				32	18	7	Wheeler, A. G. 'Al'
1993		II	8	5	A	To R16	20	27	6	Gibbs, John
1940			16				32	19	6	Wheeler, A. G. 'Al'
1945			16				16	6	8	Wheeler, A. G. 'Al'
1961			16		A		32	17	7	McIntire, John 'Jack'
1962			16	14	A		32	23	5	McIntire, John 'Jack'
1938			32				32	15	3	Baller, Stewart 'Stu'
1942			32				32	13	9	Wheeler, A. G. 'Al'
1946			32				32	16	6	Wheeler, A. G. 'Al'
1948			32				32	20	3	Kyle, Newton P.
1949			32				32	20	6	Kyle, Newton P.
1950			32				32	22	6	Kyle, Newton P.
1963			32		A		32	14	11	McIntire, John 'Jack'
1966			32		A		32	15	10	McIntire, John 'Jack'
1997		II	32	13	A		32	25	9	Gibbs, John
1993	W	II	16		A		20	21	10	Davidson, Dr. E. Wayne

Year	M/W	Div	F	SD	BD	Bye	#T	W	L	Coach
PFEIFFER										
1995	M	I	2	11	A		32	25	8	Lutz, Bob
1991			3	6	A		32	29	4	Lutz, Bob
1992		I	3	5	A		32	30	5	Lutz, Bob
1990			8		A		32	22	11	Lutz, Bob
1985			16		A		32	23	9	Lentz, John
1994		I	16	9	A		32	24	6	Lutz, Bob
1993		I	32	9	L		32	23	6	Lutz, Bob
PHILADELPHIA PHARMACY										
1992	M	II	20		A		20	26	7	Morgan, Robert C.
1990			32		A		32	25	6	Morgan, Robert C.
1996		II	32		L		32	23	6	Morgan, Robert C.
1997		II	32		A		32	20	6	Morgan, Robert C.
PHILLIPS (OK)										
1945	M		16				16			
1998		I	16	2	L		32	31	3	Chappell, Rand
1984			32		A		32	25	13	Wilson, Robert H.
1997		I	32		L		32	23	9	Chappell, Rand
1994	W	I	16	14	L		32	24	7	Carter, Carole
1998		I	16	5	L		32	25	7	Price, Denny
PIKEVILLE										
1959	M		32	7	A		32	28	7	Daniels, William
1976			32	5	A		32	26	5	Martin, Wayne M.
1998	W	I	32		A		32	21	14	Watson, Bill
PITTSBURG STATE										
1942	M		3				32	23	5	Lance, John F.
1956			3				32	27	2	Lance, John F.
1940			8				32	16	11	Lance, John F.
1972			16	13	A		32	22	8	Johnson, Robert A.
1941			32				32	18	6	Lance, John F.
1960			32	9	A		32	18	4	Lance, John F.
1966			32	8	A		32	18	10	Lambert, Paul M.
POINT LOMA NAZARENE										
1954	M		8				32	29	5	Keoppel, Kenneth P.
1953			16				32	34	2	Keoppel, Kenneth P.
1958			16		A		32	27	4	Cartwright, Chalmer A.
1968			32		A		32	26	5	Cartwright, Chalmer A.
1983			32		A		32	22	13	Foster, Ben
1991	W		32		A		32	24	8	Olin, Dr. Bill
POINT PARK										
1997	M	I	3		A		32	23	8	Rager, Robert
1979			32		A		32	26	5	Conboy, Gerald "Jerry"
1983			32		A		32	20	12	Conboy, Gerald "Jerry"

Year	M/W	Div	F	SD	BD	Bye	#T	W	L	Coach
PORTLAND										
1952	M		4				32	24	11	Torson, James M. "Mush"
1950			16				32	19	12	Torson, James M. "Mush"
1957			16	5			32	18	12	Negratti, Dr. Albert E.
1942			32				32	14	7	Fitzpatrick, Edwin J.
1949			32				32	22	11	Torson, James M. "Mush"
1951			32				32	23	6	Torson, James M. "Mush"
1953			32				32	16	14	Torson, James M. "Mush"
1954			32				32	9	19	Torson, James M. "Mush"
1958			32		A		32	18	11	Negratti, Dr. Albert E.
1984	W		2	3	A		16	30	6	Olmstead, David
1983			4	7	A		8	27	6	Olmstead, David
1985			8	2	A		16	26	8	Olmstead, David
PORTLAND STATE										
1955	M		32				32	30	9	Nelson, Loyal D. "Sharkey"
1956			32				32	21	8	Nelson, Loyal D. "Sharkey"
PRAIRIE VIEW A&M										
1962	M		1	2	A		32	20	3	Moore, Dr. Leroy G., Jr.
PRATT										
1962	M		32		A		32	19	5	Picariello, Saverio J. "Pic"
PRESBYTERIAN										
1993	M	I	32	12	L		32	27	5	Nibert, Gregg
PROVIDENCE										
1951	M		32				32	14	10	Cuddy, James V. "Viv"
PUGET SOUND										
1950	M		16				32	19	12	Heinrick, John P.
1949			32				32	21	6	Heinrick, John P.
1997	W	II	32		A		32	22	5	Bricker, Dr. Beth
1998		II	32		A		32	15	13	Bricker, Dr. Beth
PURDUE: CALUMET										
1996	W	I	32		A		32	27	5	Hayes, Gary
QUINCY (IL)										
1978	M		3	5	A		32	30	5	Hanks, Sherrill D.
1979			8		A		32	23	10	Hanks, Sherrill D.
1955			16				32	14	8	Forester, Harry
1982			16	16	A		32	25	12	Hanks, Sherrill D.
1958			32		A		32	17	11	Goff, James "Pim"
1964			32		A		32	13	13	Ortwerth, John G.
1967			32		A		32	17	14	Ortwerth, John G.
1985			32		A		32	15	17	Hanks, Sherrill D.
1986			32		A		32	21	11	Hanks, Sherrill D.
QUINNIPIAC										
1973	M		16		A		32	22	7	Kahn, Burt
1972			32		A		32	21	9	Kahn, Burt

Year	M/W	Div	F	SD	BD	Bye	#T	W	L	Coach
REDLANDS										
1961	M		16	14	A		32	26	7	Fulmer, Lee
1964			32		A		32	19	11	Fulmer, Lee
REGIS (CO)										
1949	M		2				32	36	3	Varnell, Harry Lee
1951			4				32	19	8	Varnell, Harry Lee
1954			16				32	15	15	Moore, Harvey E.
1950			32				32	17	16	Varnell, Harry Lee
1955			32				32	14	14	Moore, Harvey E.
RICKS										
1953	M		32				32	16	15	Parkinson, Berkley H. "Brick"
RIDER										
1956	M		32				32	16	7	Leyden, Thomas A.
1958			32		A		32	17	8	Leyden, Thomas A.
1963			32		A		32	20	8	Greenwood, Robert
RIO GRANDE										
1954	M		16				32	20	7	Oliver, Newt
1985			16	13	A		32	31	5	Lawhorn, John
1991			16	12	A		32	32	5	Lawhorn, John
1987			32		A		32	28	8	Lawhorn, John
1995		I	32		A		32	26	10	Lawhorn, John
1994	W	I	32		L		32	27	7	Smalley, David
1997		I	32		A		32	23	12	Smalley, David
RIPON										
1940	M		32				32	14	6	Lamphear, George
ROANOKE										
1938	M		2				32	19	2	White, Gordon C. "Pap"
ROCKHURST										
1964	M		1	10	A		32	27	6	Brehmer, Joseph "Buddy"
1963			8	6	A		32	27	4	Brehmer, Joseph "Buddy"
1966			8	10	A		32	20	8	Brehmer, Joseph "Buddy"
1956			16				32	25	5	Brehmer, Joseph "Buddy"
1980			16	9	A		32	20	5	Reynolds, Jerry
1946			32				32	15	8	Powell, Bill
1967			32		A		32	18	11	Rehm, J. Dolor
1981			32	8	L		32	22	3	Reynolds, Jerry
1998	W	I	16	9	A		32	23	6	Mitts, Maryann
1991			32		A		32	25	8	Rietzke, Tracy
1993		I	32		A		32	30	2	Rietzke, Tracy
1994		I	32		L		32	28	4	Rietzke, Tracy
1995		I	32		A		32	24	7	Rietzke, Tracy
1996		I	32		L		32	26	3	Rietzke, Tracy

Year	M/W	Div	F	SD	BD	Bye	#T	W	L	Coach
ROCKY MOUNTAIN										
1951	M		32				32	17	14	Klindt, Herbert J.
1985			32		A		32	23	10	Adams, Mark E. "Bucky"
1994		I	32		A		32	17	14	Matlock, Gary
1988	W		16		A		16	20	11	Malby, Jeff
ROGER WILLIAMS										
1974	M		32		A		32	20	4	Drennan, Thomas A.
ROWAN										
1971	M		16		A		32	21	6	Collins, Jack
1972			32		A		32	16	9	Collins, Jack
SAGINAW VALLEY STATE										
1982	M		8		A		32	24	8	Pratt, Dr. Robert L.
1983			16	16	A		32	24	8	Pratt, Dr. Robert L.
1980			32		A		32	24	7	Pratt, Dr. Robert L.
1986			32		A		32	20	11	Pratt, Dr. Robert L.
1985	W		2	3	A		16	32	1	Reall, Marsha
1982			3	4	A		8	27	5	Reall, Marsha
1981			8	6	A		8	14	13	Reall, Marsha
1983			8	5	A		8	25	6	Reall, Marsha
1984			8	2	A		16	30	1	Reall, Marsha
1986			8	6	A		16	24	3	Charney, Claudette
1987			8	3	A		16	30	2	Charney, Claudette
1988			16	7	A		16	25	7	Charney, Claudette
SAINT AMBROSE										
1938	M		8				32	15	5	Duford, Wilford J. "Dukes"
1939			8				32	20	2	Duford, Wilford J. "Dukes"
1954			16				32	20	3	Duax, Robert J.
1989			16		A		32	26	8	Shovlain, Ray
1994		II	16	18	A		24	24	10	Shovlain, Ray
1995		II	16		L		32	24	12	Shovlain, Ray
1997		II	32		A		32	24	12	Shovlain, Ray
1998		II	32		A		32	20	16	Shovlain, Ray
1989	W		3	4	A		16	36	2	Bluder, Lisa
1990			3	1	A		16	34	1	Bluder, Lisa
1987			8		A		16	29	3	Bluder, Lisa
1988			8	5	A		16	32	5	Bluder, Lisa
1996		II	8	7	A		32	30	6	Becker, Robin
1984			16		A		16	28	4	Buckles, Ken
1992		I	16	7	A		32	29	4	Osborn, Rhonda
1994		I	16		L		32	27	6	Becker, Robin
1997		II	32	14	L		32	28	6	Becker, Robin
SAINT AUGUSTINE'S										
1980	M		16	14	A		32	24	7	Heartley, Harvey D.
1977			32		A		32	24	8	Heartley, Harvey D.

Year	M/W	Div	F	SD	BD	Bye	#T	W	L	Coach
SAINT BERNARD										
1961	M		32		A		32	17	16	Richard, Charles W.
SAINT CLOUD STATE										
1943	M		16				32	12	3	Kasch, Warren
1962			16	10	A		32	22	4	Severson, Marlowe "Red"
1964			16	16	A		32	19	5	Severson, Marlowe "Red"
1968			16	5	A		32	25	4	Severson, Marlowe "Red"
1946			32				32	12	2	Lynch, George H.
SAINT EDWARD'S										
1992	W	I	3	8	L		32	30	3	McKey, David
1991			8	9	A		32	31	2	McKey, David
1993		I	8	5	A		32	28	3	McKey, David
SAINT FRANCIS (IL)										
1994	M	I	32		A		32	16	15	Sullivan, Pat
1996		I	32		A		32	19	10	Sullivan, Pat
SAINT FRANCIS (IN)										
1997	W	II	8	11	A		32	28	8	Westendorf, Larry
1998		II	8	12	L		32	31	6	Westendorf, Larry
1996		II	16		A		32	20	12	Westendorf, Larry
1995		II	32		A		32	20	12	Westendorf, Larry
SAINT FRANCIS (NY)										
1955	M		32				32	21	8	Lynch, Daniel J.
SAINT FRANCIS (PA)										
1948	M		32				32	15	8	Hughes, Dr. William T. "Skip"
SAINT JOHN FISHER										
1979	M		32		A		32	21	7	Wanzer, Robert F. "Bobby"
SAINT JOHN'S (MN)										
1978	M		16		A		32	23	8	Smith, James E.
1979			16	9	A		32	27	3	Smith, James E.
1969			32		A		32	20	9	Smith, James E.
1983			32		A		32	18	12	Smith, James E.
1984			32		A		32	20	8	Smith, James E.
SAINT JOSEPH'S (IN)										
1940	M		32				32	16	7	Dienhart, Joseph S.
SAINT JOSEPH'S (ME)										
1987	M		16		A		32	26	6	Simonds, Rick
1992		II	16	8	A	To R16	20	24	6	Simonds, Rick
1993		II	20		A		20	22	7	Scheinman, John
1996		II	32	6	A		32	24	4	Simonds, Rick
1998		II	32		A		32	24	5	Simonds, Rick
1987	W		16		A		16	21	9	Stead, Bob
1988			16		A		16	21	9	McDevitt, Michael
1992		II	16		A		20	23	8	McDevitt, Michael
1993		II	20		L		20	24	5	McDevitt, Michael
1994		II	24	9	A		24	23	5	McDevitt, Michael
1991			32		A		32	24	5	McDevitt, Michael

Year	M/W	Div	F	SD	BD	Bye	#T	W	L	Coach
SAINT MARTIN'S										
1995	W	I	16	15	L		32	31	5	Peters, Ray
SAINT MARY'S (CA)										
1985	W		16		A		16	21	9	Rubenstein, Terri
SAINT MARY'S (MI)										
1991	M		8		A		32	6	19	Donahue, Glen
1992		I	32		A		32	26	6	Donahue, Glen
SAINT MARY'S (MN)										
1941	M		16				32			
SAINT MARY'S (TX)										
1989	M		1	8	A		32	28	5	Meyer, Herbert "Buddy"
1974			4	16	A		32	24	9	Messbarger, Ed
1975			4	3	A		32	24	7	Messbarger, Ed
1964			8		A		32	15	13	Messbarger, Ed
1967			8	8	A		32	22	9	Messbarger, Ed
1982			16		A		32	19	9	Meyer, Herbert "Buddy"
1983			16	6	A		32	26	7	Meyer, Herbert "Buddy"
1984			16	10	A		32	25	8	Meyer, Herbert "Buddy"
1987			16	8	A		32	27	5	Meyer, Herbert "Buddy"
1991			16	11	A		32	24	7	Meyer, Herbert "Buddy"
1994		I	16		A		32	21	10	Meyer, Herbert "Buddy"
1981			32		A		32	19	9	Meyer, Herbert "Buddy"
1995		I	32	9	L		32	24	6	Meyer, Herbert "Buddy"
1996		I	32		A		32	19	11	Meyer, Herbert "Buddy"
1997		I	32	11	L		32	22	6	Meyer, Herbert "Buddy"
1998		I	32		L		32	20	7	Meyer, Herbert "Buddy"
1995	W	I	32		A		32	25	7	Weeaks, Thomas
1996		I	32		L		32	20	11	Weeaks, Thomas
1997		I	32		L		32	21	7	Weeaks, Thomas
SAINT NORBERT										
1961	M		32		A		32	13	13	Kosnar, Romie R.
1962			32		A		32	14	10	Kosnar, Romie R.
1965			32		A		32	17	9	Kosnar, Romie R.
SAINT PETER'S										
1954	M		8				32	17	7	Kennedy, Don, Sr.
1953			16				32	18	8	Kennedy, Don, Sr.
SAINT ROSE										
1989	M		32		A		32	28	5	Beaury, Brian
1991			32		A		32	20	9	Beaury, Brian
SAINT THOMAS (FL)										
1994	M	II	24	23	A		24	17	18	Tuell, Gary
1997		II	32		A		32	17	17	Tuell, Gary

Year	M/W	Div	F	SD	BD	Bye	#T	W	L	Coach
SAINT THOMAS (MN)										
1972	M		8	11	A		32	24	8	Feely, Thomas J.
1949			16				32	22	7	Sokol, Paul
1967			16	15	A		32	22	7	Feely, Thomas J.
1974			16	10	A		32	26	4	Feely, Thomas J.
1950			32				32	18	7	Sokol, Paul
1966			32		A		32	24	4	Feely, Thomas J.
1970			32		A		32	26	3	Feely, Thomas J.
1971			32		A		32	24	5	Feely, Thomas J.
SAINT THOMAS AQUINAS										
1986	M		4	7	A		32	37	6	Possinger, David F.
1984			8	5	A		32	38	3	Possinger, David F.
1988			8	1	A		32	39	2	Possinger, David F.
1982			16	11	A		32	34	4	Possinger, David F.
1983			16	7	A		32	35	3	Possinger, David F.
1987			16	7	A		32	32	5	Possinger, David F.
1995		II	16	12	A		32	25	9	O'Donnell, Dennis G.
1997		II	16	1	A		32	34	2	O'Donnell, Dennis G.
1994		II	24	17	A		24	24	8	O'Donnell, Dennis G.
1985			32	6	A		32	36	6	Possinger, David F.
1989	W		16		A		16	25	2	McManus, Michael
1993		II	16		A		20	24	9	McManus, Michael
1995		II	32		L		32	26	4	McManus, Michael
1996		II	32	16	A		32	25	6	McManus, Michael
1997		II	32		A		32	21	8	McManus, Michael
1998		II	32	13	A		32	25	4	McManus, Michael
SAINT VINCENT										
1998	M	I	8	10	A		32	29	5	Matthews, Bernie
1991			32		A		32	20	7	Matthews, Bernie
1992	W	I	32		A		32	20	9	Zawacki, Kristen
1993		I	32		A		32	23	10	Zawacki, Kristen
1994		I	32		A		32	21	9	Zawacki, Kristen
1995		I	32		A		32	26	7	Zawacki, Kristen
1998		I	32		A		32	26	5	Zawacki, Kristen
SAINT XAVIER										
1996	M	I	32		L		32	28	6	Keasler, Mike
SALEM-TEIKYO										
1983	M		16		A		32	22	9	Barnhart, Ray
1993		I	16	16	A		32	24	7	Carey, Michael A.
1994		I	32	3	A		32	24	4	Carey, Michael A.
1995	W	I	32		A		32	26	3	Biesenthal, Tammy
SAM HOUSTON STATE										
1973	M		16	1	A		32	28	1	Porter, Archie

Year	M/W	Div	F	SD	BD	Bye	#T	W	L	Coach
SAN DIEGO STATE										
1941	M		1				32	24	7	Gross, Morris H.
1939			2				32	24	7	Gross, Morris H.
1940			2				32	22	6	Gross, Morris H.
1942			16				32	13	9	Gross, Morris H.
1956			16				32	23	6	Ziegenfuss, Dr. George
SAN JOSE STATE										
1948	M		8				32	23	9	McPherson, Walter J.
1949			16				32	22	13	McPherson, Walter J.
SANTA FE (NM)										
1983	M		8		A		32	25	9	Roybal, Leonard "Lennie"
SAVANNAH STATE										
1960	M		16		A		32	27	4	Wright, Theodore A., Sr.
1962			16	6	A		32	28	3	Wright, Theodore A., Sr.
1961			32		A		32			Wright, Theodore A., Sr.
SEATTLE										
1993	W	I	32		L		32	20	7	Cox, Dave
SETON HILL										
1991	W		32		A		32	14	12	Shrader, Robert
SHAWNEE STATE (OH)										
1995	W	II	3	5	L		32	31	5	Hagen-Smith, Robin
1994		II	8	16	A		24	20	12	Hagen-Smith, Robin
1996		II	16	5	A		32	31	4	Hagen-Smith, Robin
1997		II	16	1	A		32	29	2	Hagen-Smith, Robin
1998		II	16	5	A		32	25	5	Hagen-Smith, Robin
SIENA HEIGHTS										
1997	M	II	2	5	A		32	30	7	Smith, Fred
1989			8		A		32	31	7	Smith, Fred
1998		II	16	4	A		32	28	9	Smith, Fred
1990			32	8	A		32	29	7	Smith, Fred
1994		I	32		A		32	27	8	Smith, Fred
1996		II	32		A		32	21	10	Smith, Fred
SIMON FRASER										
1998	W	I	3	2	A		32	31	6	McNeill, Allison
1990			8	6	A		16	29	7	McNeill, Allison
1992		I	8	1	A		32	31	2	McNeill, Allison
1995		I	8	13	A		32	23	8	McNeill, Allison
1996		I	8	10	L		32	31	6	McNeill, Allison
1997		I	8	2	A		32	31	4	McNeill, Allison
1994		I	16	9	A		32	26	5	McNeill, Allison
1991			32	3	A		32	28	3	McNeill, Allison
1993		I	32		A		32	26	8	McNeill, Allison
SIMPSON (IA)										
1938	M		16				32	16	5	Casey, Francis L. "Frank"
1942			16				32	17	6	Casey, Francis L. "Frank"
1945			16				16	16	4	Casey, Francis L. "Frank"
1939			32				32	14	7	Casey, Francis L. "Frank"

Year	M/W	Div	F	SD	BD	Bye	#T	W	L	Coach
1940			32				32	20	4	Casey, Francis L. "Frank"
1941			32				32	19	3	Casey, Francis L. "Frank"
1943			32				32	14	5	Casey, Francis L. "Frank"
1961			32			A	32	13	12	Deaton, Les H.

SIOUX FALLS

Year	M/W	Div	F	SD	BD	Bye	#T	W	L	Coach
1938	M		32				32	14	5	Olsen, Francis R.
1941			32				32	12	4	Olsen, Francis R.

SLIPPERY ROCK

Year	M/W	Div	F	SD	BD	Bye	#T	W	L	Coach
1973	M		4			A	32	23	7	Hankinson, Mel

SOUTH CAROLINA STATE

Year	M/W	Div	F	SD	BD	Bye	#T	W	L	Coach
1973	M		16			A	32	17	14	Jobe, Ben
1970			32			A	32	21	7	Jobe, Ben

SOUTH CAROLINA: AIKEN

Year	M/W	Div	F	SD	BD	Bye	#T	W	L	Coach
1980	M		16			A	32	21	18	Wall, Larry

SOUTH CAROLINA: SPARTANBURG

Year	M/W	Div	F	SD	BD	Bye	#T	W	L	Coach
1982	M		1	14		A	32	27	5	Waters, Jerry O.
1990			8	5		A	32	29	3	Waters, Jerry O.
1981			16			A	32	22	12	Waters, Jerry O.

SOUTH DAKOTA

Year	M/W	Div	F	SD	BD	Bye	#T	W	L	Coach
1950	M		32				32	11	11	Deklotz, George

SOUTH DAKOTA STATE

Year	M/W	Div	F	SD	BD	Bye	#T	W	L	Coach
1943	M		32				32	15	6	McCrady, Thurlo E.
1948			32				32	19	6	Frost, Reuben B. "Jack"
1951			32				32	16	12	Frost, Reuben B. "Jack"
1956			32				32	17	7	Walseth, Russell M. "Sox"

SOUTH DAKOTA TECH

Year	M/W	Div	F	SD	BD	Bye	#T	W	L	Coach
1973	M		32			A	32	19	8	Riley, Michael L.
1997		II	32			A	32	17	13	Welsh, Hugh
1998	W	II	3	4		A	32	28	4	Felderman, Barbara
1994		II	16	20		A	24	18	11	Felderman, Barbara
1996		II	32			L	32	19	11	Felderman, Barbara
1997		II	32	15		L	32	21	9	Felderman, Barbara

SOUTHEAST MISSOURI STATE

Year	M/W	Div	F	SD	BD	Bye	#T	W	L	Coach
1943	M		1				32	19	6	Harris, Charles P.

SOUTHEASTERN LOUISIANA

Year	M/W	Div	F	SD	BD	Bye	#T	W	L	Coach
1954	M		8				32	22	10	Marlar, Luther W. "Luke"
1950			32				32	13	11	Marlar, Luther W. "Luke"
1951			32				32	13	10	Marlar, Luther W. "Luke"

SOUTHEASTERN OKLAHOMA STATE

Year	M/W	Div	F	SD	BD	Bye	#T	W	L	Coach
1942	M		2				32	X	X	Sullivan, Bloomer
1955			2				32	37	5	Sullivan, Bloomer
1957			2	7			32	30	5	Sullivan, Bloomer
1962			3	13		A	32	28	9	Sullivan, Bloomer

Year	M/W	Div	F	SD	BD	Bye	#T	W	L	Coach
1986			3	4		A	32	30	4	Hedden, Jack E.
1947			8				32	13	7	Sullivan, Bloomer
1940			16				32	X	X	Sullivan, Bloomer
1946			16				32	26	4	Sullivan, Bloomer
1954			16				32	X	X	Sullivan, Bloomer
1985			16	14		A	32	24	8	Hedden, Jack E.
1997		I	16	9		L	32	27	4	Robinson, Tony
1943			32				32	X	X	Sullivan, Bloomer
1956			32				32	20	10	Sullivan, Bloomer
1996		I	32			A	32	24	10	Robinson, Tony
1995	W	I	2	7		L	32	29	5	Keith, Nick
1996		I	2	1		A	32	30	2	Keith, Nick
1994		I	16	16		L	32	21	7	Keith, Nick
1997		I	16	14		L	32	24	6	Keith, Nick
1998		I	16	14		L	32	22	6	Keith, Nick

SOUTHERN ARKANSAS

Year	M/W	Div	F	SD	BD	Bye	#T	W	L	Coach
1966	M		16			A	32	23	5	Watson, W. T.
1967			16	16		A	32	25	4	Watson, W. T.
1957			32				32	15	8	Waller, P. T. "Duddy"
1971			32			A	32	23	5	Watson, W. T.
1983			32			A	32	18	11	Ingram, Monroe
1989			32	11		A	32	24	6	Ingram, Monroe

SOUTHERN CALIFORNIA COLLEGE

Year	M/W	Div	F	SD	BD	Bye	#T	W	L	Coach
1990	M		16	15		A	32	26	9	Reynolds, Bill
1998	W	I	32			A	32	29	6	Davis, Russ

SOUTHERN COLORADO

Year	M/W	Div	F	SD	BD	Bye	#T	W	L	Coach
1965	M		32			A	32	21	7	Simmons, Harry H.
1986			32			A	32	20	12	Drangmeister, Richard
1991			32			A	32	25	8	Folda, Joe

SOUTHERN CONNECTICUT STATE

Year	M/W	Div	F	SD	BD	Bye	#T	W	L	Coach
1955	M		32				32	18	5	McDowell, Owen W.
1957			32				32	16	7	McDowell, Owen W.

SOUTHERN ILLINOIS

Year	M/W	Div	F	SD	BD	Bye	#T	W	L	Coach
1946	M		1				32	20	6	Martin, Glenn "Abe"
1945			4				16	15	7	Martin, Glenn "Abe"
1948			16				32	22	4	Holder, Lynn C.
1947			32				32	19	10	Holder, Lynn C.
1960			32	3		A	32	20	9	Gallatin, Harry J.

SOUTHERN MAINE

Year	M/W	Div	F	SD	BD	Bye	#T	W	L	Coach
1978	M		32			A	32	21	7	Bouchard, Joey A.
1979	M		32			A	32	21	7	Bouchard, Joey A.
1985	W		16			A	16	23	6	Costello, Dr. Richard A.

Year	M/W	Div	F	SD	BD	Bye	#T	W	L	Coach
SOUTHERN MISSISSIPPI										
1953	M		8				32	27	8	Floyd, Lee P.
1952			32				32	29	8	Floyd, Lee P.
1954			32				32	23	8	Floyd, Lee P.
1955			32				32	11	17	Finley, Charles L. "Chuck"
SOUTHERN NAZARENE										
1981	M		1	6	A		32	36	6	Gresham, Dr. Loren
1998		I	2	14	A		32	29	9	Martin, Bobby
1976			32		A		32	26	10	Poteet, Jim
1978			32		A		32	24	12	Poteet, Jim
1988			32		A		32	26	11	Martin, Bobby
1997		I	32		L		32	25	9	Martin, Bobby
1989	W		1	3	A		16	36	2	Hoffman, Bob
1994		I	1	1	A		32	34	0	Finkbeiner, Jerry
1995		I	1	1	A		32	30	2	Finkbeiner, Jerry
1996		I	1	2	A		32	34	2	Finkbeiner, Jerry
1997		I	1	4	A		32	32	4	Finkbeiner, Jerry
1998		I	2	3	L		32	31	6	Wiginton, Craig
1993		I	3	1	A		32	30	5	Finkbeiner, Jerry
1992		I	16	5	L		32	31	3	Finkbeiner, Jerry
SOUTHERN OREGON										
1948	M		32				32	24	3	Schopf, Dr. Theodore G.
1968			32		A		32	23	6	Holmes, William J.
1997	W	II	3	12	L		32	25	9	Huyett, Shirley
1998		II	16	2	A		32	28	4	Huyett, Shirley
SOUTHERN TECH (GA)										
1979	M		16	13	A		32	24	4	Florian, Fran
1981			16	11	A		32	28	5	Perides, George L.
1982			16	9	A		32	27	5	Perides, George L.
1978			32		A		32	26	6	Florian, Fran
1980			32		A		32	25	10	Perides, George L.
1987			32	11	A		32	27	7	Perides, George L.
SOUTHERN UTAH										
1977	M		32		A		32	21	7	Jack, Stanley
1988	W		16		A		16	18	8	Adams, Boyd
SOUTHERN WESLEYAN										
1984	M		16		A		32	22	10	Shaver, Tom
1979			32		A		32	25	10	Drennon, Craig
SOUTHERN: BATON ROUGE										
1965	M		8	3	A		32	25	5	Mack, Richard
SOUTHERN: NEW ORLEANS										
1995	M	I	32		A		32	21	11	Hill, Earl R.
1998		I	32		A		32	20	15	Hill, Earl R.
SOUTHWEST BAPTIST										
1976	M		32		A		32	19	10	Garrett, Howard V.

Year	M/W	Div	F	SD	BD	Bye	#T	W	L	Coach
SOUTHWEST MISSOURI STATE										
1952	M		1				32	27	5	Vanatta, Robert
1953			1				32	24	4	Vanatta, Robert
1954			3				32	20	6	Matthews, Edwin "Eddie"
1949			16				32	25	2	McDonald, A. C. "Andy"
1939			32				32	15	4	McDonald, A. C. "Andy"
1943			32				32	12	13	McDonald, A. C. "Andy"
SOUTHWEST TEXAS STATE										
1960	M		1	2	A		32	28	3	Jowers, Milton W.
1952			3				32	30	1	Jowers, Milton W.
1959			3	5	A		32	25	6	Jowers, Milton W.
1979			3	8	A		32	29	7	Wall, Daniel P.
1961			8	11	A		32	21	8	Jowers, Milton W.
1951			16				32	21	5	Jowers, Milton W.
1957			16				32	22	7	Jowers, Milton W.
SOUTHWESTERN (KS)										
1939	M		1				32	21	2	Gardner, George
1937			3			I	8	14	11	Monypeny, William W.
1940			8				32	14	9	Monypeny, William W.
1942			16				32	16	5	Monypeny, William W.
1943			16				32	17	5	Monypeny, William W.
1955			16				32	20	8	Cotton, Dr. John J. "Jack"
1998		II	32		A		32	14	16	Horstmann, Brad
SOUTHWESTERN (TX)										
1986	M		8		A		32	20	12	Peak, Paul
1990			16		A		32	19	9	Peak, Paul
1985			32	10	A		32	24	9	Peak, Paul
SOUTHWESTERN LOUISIANA										
1967	M		8	7	A		32	20	11	Shipley, Beryl C.
1965			16	2	A		32	20	10	Shipley, Beryl C.
SOUTHWESTERN OKLAHOMA STATE										
1969	M		16	8	A		32	23	8	Jobe, Jerry
1977			16	11	A		32	24	5	Hauser, George
1953			32				32	24	6	Williams, Rankin
1995		I	32		A		32	20	12	Hauser, George
1982	W		1	1	A		8	34	0	Loftin, John D.
1983			1	1	A		8	30	4	Loftin, John D.
1985			1	1	A		16	34	0	Loftin, John D.
1987			1	2	A		16	30	2	Loftin, John D.
1990			1	4	A		16	30	4	Loftin, John D.
1991			2	2	A		32	31	3	Loftin, John D.
1992		I	3	3	A		32	30	4	Loftin, John D.
1993		I	3	3	L		32	29	4	Loftin, John D.
1995		I	3	5	A		32	30	5	Loftin, John D.
1997		I	3	7	L		32	28	5	Loftin, John D.
1984			8	1	A		16	31	1	Loftin, John D.
1994		I	8	5	A		32	25	7	Loftin, John D.

Year	M/W	Div	F	SD	BD	Bye	#T	W	L	Coach
1996		I	32		L		32	20	9	Loftin, John D.
1998		I	32		L		32	21	8	Loftin, John D.

SPRING ARBOR

Year	M/W	Div	F	SD	BD	Bye	#T	W	L	Coach
1997	M	II	8	7	L		32	29	7	Noll, Doug
1995		I	32		A		32	19	17	Noll, Doug
1998	W	II	8		A		32	23	11	Britsch, Tom
1994		II	24	21	A		24	22	10	Britsch, Tom
1996		II	32		A		32	26	9	Britsch, Tom

SPRING GARDEN

Year	M/W	Div	F	SD	BD	Bye	#T	W	L	Coach
1977	M		32		A		32	16	10	Burke, Les
1982	W		8	8	A		8	29	4	Soroka, Michael

SPRING HILL

Year	M/W	Div	F	SD	BD	Bye	#T	W	L	Coach
1992	M	I	16		A		32	24	11	Nash, Carl
1993		I	32		A		32	22	9	Nash, Carl
1994		I	32		A		32	22	10	Niland, Joseph P., Jr.

STEPHEN F AUSTIN STATE

Year	M/W	Div	F	SD	BD	Bye	#T	W	L	Coach
1972	M		3	2	A		32	25	2	Brown, Marshall
1970			8	1	A		32	29	1	Brown, Marshall
1971			8	4	A		32	20	6	Brown, Marshall
1941			16				32	21	6	Shelton, Robert H.
1956			16				32	24	6	Stephens, John O.
1965			32		A		32	19	7	Brown, Marshall
1968			32	2	A		32	27	3	Brown, Marshall
1982			32	8	L		32	24	6	Miller, Harry E.

STERLING (KS)

Year	M/W	Div	F	SD	BD	Bye	#T	W	L	Coach
1993	W	II	16		A	To R16	20	25	4	Kruse, Lonnie
1995		II	16		L		32	24	6	Kruse, Lonnie
1997		II	16	7	A		32	28	2	Kruse, Lonnie
1998		II	16		A		32	26	7	Kruse, Lonnie
1996		II	32	8	A		32	28	1	Kruse, Lonnie

STETSON

Year	M/W	Div	F	SD	BD	Bye	#T	W	L	Coach
1953	M		16				32	14	10	Morland, Richard B.
1957			16				32	17	8	Morland, Richard B.
1963			16		A		32	15	13	Wilkes, Dr. Glenn N., Sr.
1960			32	7	A		32	16	13	Wilkes, Dr. Glenn N., Sr.
1962			32		A		32	16	12	Wilkes, Dr. Glenn N., Sr.

SUL ROSS STATE

Year	M/W	Div	F	SD	BD	Bye	#T	W	L	Coach
1996	W	II	32		A		32	13	8	Sample, Dr. Chet

TABOR

Year	M/W	Div	F	SD	BD	Bye	#T	W	L	Coach
1997	M	II	3	16	A		32	24	9	Brubacher, Don
1996		II	8	16	A		32	25	7	Zimmerman, Don
1994		II	16	20	A		24	21	10	Brubacher, Don
1992	W	II	16	5	A	To R16	20	26	3	Kliewer, Karl

TALLADEGA

Year	M/W	Div	F	SD	BD	Bye	#T	W	L	Coach
1996	M	I	32		A		32	18	16	Tucker, Wylie N.

Year	M/W	Div	F	SD	BD	Bye	#T	W	L	Coach
TAMPA UNIVERSITY										
1950	M		4				32	20	14	Gaddis, Mike
1952			32				32	11	15	Bailey, Sam
TARKIO										
1940	M		1				32	20	4	Kyle, Newton P.
1941			32				32	14	4	Kyle, Newton P.
TARLETON STATE										
1992	M	II	16	5	A	To R16	20	26	10	Reisman, Lonn
1993		II	16	7	A	To R16	20	22	11	Reisman, Lonn
1994		II	24	15	A		24	16	12	Reisman, Lonn
1992	W	II	2	4	A	To R16	20	30	8	Lowrey, Jan
1993		II	3		A	To R16	20	21	13	Lowrey, Jan
1984			16		A		16	26	6	Lowrey, Jan
TAYLOR										
1991	M		3	9	A		32	34	4	Patterson, Paul
1994		II	8	1	A	To R16	24	29	5	Patterson, Paul
1987			16		A		32	25	8	Patterson, Paul
1984			32		A		32	21	10	Patterson, Paul
1986			32		A		32	26	7	Patterson, Paul
1989			32		A		32	27	8	Patterson, Paul
1992		I	32	9	A		32	29	5	Patterson, Paul
1993		I	32		A		32	27	7	Patterson, Paul
1996		II	32	14	L		32	23	13	Patterson, Paul
1997		II	32		A		32	22	13	Patterson, Paul
1998	W	II	16		A		32	20	15	Krause, Tina
1997		II	32		L		32	28	8	Krause, Tina
TENNESSEE STATE										
1957	M		1				32	29	5	McLendon, John B., Jr.
1958			1	3	A		32	31	3	McLendon, John B., Jr.
1959			1	1	A		32	32	1	McLendon, John B., Jr.
1960			3	1	A		32	27	5	Hunter, Harold
1953			8				32	20	5	Cash, Clarence B.
1956			8				32	24	9	McLendon, John B., Jr.
1954			32				32	17	6	Cash, Clarence B.
TENNESSEE WESLEYAN										
1967	M		8	5	A		32	30	5	Farmer, Dwain
1997		II	32		A		32	23	12	Adams, Steve
1994	W	II	16	24	A		24	20	15	Harrison, Stan
1995		II	32		A		32	23	12	Harrison, Stan
1998		II	32		A		32	19	12	Harrison, Stan
TEXAS A&M: COMMERCE										
1955	M		1				32	29	5	Rogers, Bobby
1953			4				32	25	5	Rogers, Bobby
1978			4	6	A		32	26	10	Gudger, James F.
1954			8				32	23	5	Rogers, Bobby

Year	M/W	Div	F	SD	BD	Bye	#T	W	L	Coach
1958			8	7	A		32	23	7	Rogers, Bobby
1977			8	13	A		32	25	9	Gudger, James F.
1939			16				32	15	6	Vinzant, Dennis
1940			16				32	23	7	Vinzant, Dennis
1950			16				32	14	15	Tully, Darrell
1942			32				32	10	13	Vinzant, Dennis

TEXAS A&M: CORPUS CHRISTI

Year	M/W	Div	F	SD	BD	Bye	#T	W	L	Coach
1969	M		32		A		32	13	17	Smith, Ray

TEXAS SOUTHERN

Year	M/W	Div	F	SD	BD	Bye	#T	W	L	Coach
1977	M		1	5	A		32	31	5	Moreland, Robert E.
1956			2				32	31	4	Adams, Edward H.
1958			3		A		32	29	5	Adams, Edward H.
1957			8	8			32	32	2	Adams, Edward H.
1976			8	16	A		32	23	10	Moreland, Robert E.
1955			16				32	28	3	Adams, Edward H.
1971			32		A		32	17	2	Gordon, Lavalius C.
1981	W		2	1	A		8	23	9	Gillespie, Nathaniel A.
1982			8	5	A		8	23	8	Gillespie, Nathaniel A.

TEXAS TECH

Year	M/W	Div	F	SD	BD	Bye	#T	W	L	Coach
1949	M		8				32	21	9	Robison, Polk F.
1942			16				32	16	11	Hoffman, Burl

TEXAS WESLEYAN

Year	M/W	Div	F	SD	BD	Bye	#T	W	L	Coach
1940	M		8				32	22	2	Miller, W. A. "Gus"
1941			8				32	25	2	Miller, W. A. "Gus"
1947			16				32	32	4	Edwards, Johnnie O.
1983			16	13	A		32	22	6	Newman, Tommy
1942			32				32	15	5	Unknown
1943			32				32	26	4	Unknown
1948			32				32	19	13	Edwards, Johnnie O.

TEXAS: EL PASO

Year	M/W	Div	F	SD	BD	Bye	#T	W	L	Coach
1941	M		32				32	17	6	Pennington, Marshall

TEXAS: PAN AMERICAN

Year	M/W	Div	F	SD	BD	Bye	#T	W	L	Coach
1963	M		1	12	A		32	22	6	Williams, Samuel
1964			2	1	A		32	28	6	Williams, Samuel
1962			16	5	A		32	25	5	Williams, Samuel

THOMAS MORE (KY)

Year	M/W	Div	F	SD	BD	Bye	#T	W	L	Coach
1957	M		16	3			32	19	7	Wolf, Charles
1960			16	11	A		32	19	13	Wolf, Charles

TIFFIN

Year	M/W	Div	F	SD	BD	Bye	#T	W	L	Coach
1992	M	II	16		A	To R16	20	23	10	Hammomd, Jim
1993		II	16		L	To R16	20	21	12	Hammond, Jim
1989			32		A		32	21	12	Hammond, Jim

TOUGALOO

Year	M/W	Div	F	SD	BD	Bye	#T	W	L	Coach
1997	W	I	32		A		32	19	17	Brown, Yolanda

Year	M/W	Div	F	SD	BD	Bye	#T	W	L	Coach
TRANSYLVANIA										
1963	M		16		A		32	20	9	Newton, Charles M. "CM"
1995		I	16	14	L		32	26	8	Lane, Don
1998		I	16		A		32	24	9	Lane, Don
1965			32	12	A		32	21	10	Rose, Lee H.
1988			32	8	A		32	24	3	Lane, Don
1994		I	32		A		32	25	8	Lane, Don
1997		I	32	16	L		32	23	8	Lane, Don
1997	W	I	32		A		32	27	7	Turner, Mark
TREVECCA NAZARENE										
1987	M		8	9	A		32	30	4	Wilson, Frank
TRI-STATE										
1975	M		16	16	A		32	25	7	Peterman, Mark
1979			16	16	L		32	31	4	Peterman, Mark
1972			32		A		32	19	11	Peterman, Mark
1977			32		A		32	28	5	Peterman, Mark
1983			32		A		32	26	7	Peterman, Mark
1993		I	32		A		32	20	11	Hack, Dick
1996	W	II	8		H		32	20	12	DeRocher, Cindy
1989			16		A		16	25	8	DeRocher, Cindy
1995		II	16	12	A		32	23	8	DeRocher, Cindy
1997		II	16	5	A		32	23	6	DeRocher, Cindy
TRINITY (TX)										
1939	M		16				32	12	3	Wilkins, Leland J.
TRINITY INTERNATIONAL (IL)										
1996	M	II	16	12	L		32	25	6	Bruehl, Alan
1995		II	32		A		32	24	8	Bruehl, Alan
1993	W	II	20		A		20	24	6	Seils, David S.
1995		II	32		L		32	22	4	Seils, David S.
TROY STATE: TROY										
1957	M		32				32	19	8	Fraser, Morley
1958			32		A		32	16	6	Archer, John A.
1959			32		A		32	19	11	Archer, John A.
TRUMAN STATE (MO)										
1947	M		8				32	30	2	King, W. Boyd
1955			16				32	19	6	King, W. Boyd
1948			32				32	29	2	King, W. Boyd
TUSCULUM										
1992	W	II	16		A	To R16	20	24	9	Botta, Angelo
1996		II	16	11	A		32	30	5	Curtis, Merry Beth
1995		II	32	16	L		32	27	7	Botta, Angelo
1997		II	32		A		32	20	10	Curtis, Merry Beth
UNION (KY)										
1968	M		32	9	A		32	27	6	Moore, Pete

Year	M/W	Div	F	SD	BD	Bye	#T	W	L	Coach
UNION (TN)										
1958	M		32		A		32	17	14	Russell, Jack L.
1992		I	32		A		32	19	15	McCormick, Rick
1998		I	32	5	A		32	30	5	Turner, Ralph
1998	W	I	1	1	A		32	35	3	Blackstock, Dr. David
1993		I	2	2	A		32	33	5	Blackstock, Dr. David
1997		I	2	3	A		32	35	5	Blackstock, Dr. David
1996		I	3	3	A		32	34	4	Blackstock, Dr. David
1988			8	8	L		16	29	3	Blackstock, Dr. David
1992		I	8	12	L		32	31	5	Blackstock, Dr. David
1994		I	8	8	L		32	27	6	Blackstock, Dr. David
1989			16		A		16	26	6	Blackstock, Dr. David
1995		I	16	4	L		32	31	3	Blackstock, Dr. David
UNITED STATES INTERNATIONAL										
1963	M		32		A		32	17	15	Kloppenburg, Bob
1965			32		A		32	21	13	Kloppenburg, Bob
1966			32		A		32	21	9	Kloppenburg, Bob
1975			32		A		32	20	9	Kloppenburg, Bob
UPPER IOWA										
1940	M		32				32	8	6	Dorman, Dr. John E.
1957			32				32	17	6	Eischeid, Everett E. "Eb"
1965			32	4	A		32	21	5	Jack, Stanley
1966			32		A		32	20	4	Jack, Stanley
URBANA										
1993	M	I	8		L		32	26	8	Ronai, Robert G.
1992		I	16	16	A		32	26	9	Ronai, Robert G.
1997		II	16	6	A		32	26	8	Ronai, Robert G.
UTAH STATE										
1952	M		16				32	19	14	Baker, H. Cecil
VALDOSTA STATE										
1967	M		16	14	A		32	27	8	Colson, Gary W.
1968			16	14	A		32	23	10	Colson, Gary W.
1973			16		A		32	17	8	Dominey, James
1969			32		A		32	18	11	Melvin, James
VALLEY CITY STATE										
1987	M		16		A		32	21	6	Parker, Bob
1960			32		A		32	17	5	Osmon, William E.
1965			32		A		32	15	7	Osmon, William E.
VALPARAISO										
1938	M		16				32	13	6	Christiansen, J. M. "Jake"
1943			32				32	17	4	Ellis, Loren E.
VIRGINIA INTERMONT										
1997	M	II	32		A		32	21	13	Worrell, Phil
1998		II	32		A		32	21	13	Worrell, Phil
VIRGINIA STATE										
1974	M		32		A		32	22	8	Deane, Harold A., Sr.
1981	W		8	8	A		8	18	15	Bey, Leon Wright

Year	M/W	Div	F	SD	BD	Bye	#T	W	L	Coach
VITERBO										
1995	M	II	16	9	A		32	27	7	Murphy, Michael
VOORHEES										
1995	M	I	16		A		32	25	12	Bernstein, Jeff
1995	W	I	32		A		32	21	13	Baker, Cedric W.
1997		I	32		A		32	19	12	Baker, Cedric W.
WALSH										
1996	M	II	3	2	A		32	30	3	Loy, Steve
1993		II	8	6	A	To R16	20	29	5	Loy, Steve
1983			32	2	A		32	34	1	Huggins, Robert
1984			32	8	A		32	26	3	Peters, Dan
1998		II	32		A		32	25	10	Loy, Steve
1998	W	II	1		L		32	29	5	Smesco, Carl
WARNER SOUTHERN										
1998	M	II	16	6	L		32	26	8	Bays, Gary R.
WARTBURG										
1970	M		16	14	A		32	26	3	Levick, Lewis J. "Buzz"
1967			32		A		32	19	7	Levick, Lewis J. "Buzz"
1969			32	7	A		32	25	1	Levick, Lewis J. "Buzz"
1973			32		A		32	21	8	Levick, Lewis J. "Buzz"
1974			32		A		32	23	5	Levick, Lewis J. "Buzz"
WASHBURN										
1987	M		1	6	A		32	35	4	Chipman, Bob
1938			4				32	10	13	Errickson, Charles D. "Dee"
1969			8	16	A		32	20	10	Cafer, Glenn
1945			16				16	12	9	Errickson, Charles D. "Dee"
1974			16		A		32	17	12	Cafer, Glenn
1989			16	15	A		32	24	9	Chipman, Bob
1946			32				32	13	7	Errickson, Charles D. "Dee"
1952			32				32	17	10	McDonald, Marion G.
1968			32	12	A		32	18	8	Cafer, Glenn
1982			32		A		32	22	9	Chipman, Bob
1990			32		A		32	20	12	Chipman, Bob
1989	W		16		L		16	29	3	Dick, Patricia D.
WAYLAND BAPTIST										
1985	M		2	11	A		32	30	10	Adams, Mark L.
1986			16	9	A		32	23	5	Adams, Mark L.
1989			16	3	A		32	30	6	Cooper, Rick
1954			32				32	21	4	Redin, Harley J.
1955			32				32	22	6	Redin, Harley J.
1957			32				32	20	9	Redin, Harley J.
1987			32		A		32	22	11	Adams, Mark L.
1991			32	7	A		32	26	3	Cooper, Rick
1992		I	32	8	A		32	28	6	Cooper, Rick

158   College Basketball's National Championships

Year	M/W	Div	F	SD	BD	Bye	#T	W	L	Coach
1986	W		2	3	A		16	31	5	Evans, Floyd C.
1992		I	2	4	A		32	29	6	Estes, Sheryl
1985			3	4	A		16	31	5	Ketterman, Dave
1983			8	2	A		8	22	10	Wilson, Cathy
1987			8	1	A		16	31	1	Evans, Floyd C.
1989			8	7	A		16	30	8	Evans, Floyd C.
1990			8		A		16	31	11	Estes, Sheryl
1991			8	5	A		32	27	8	Estes, Sheryl
1993		I	8	8	A		32	25	9	Estes, Sheryl
1997		I	8	9	L		32	25	8	Pointer, Johnna
1998		I	8	7	A		32	25	11	Pointer, Johnna
1988			16	6	A		16	28	7	Evans, Floyd C.
1995		I	16	10	L		32	27	8	Estes, Sheryl
1996		I	32	14	L		32	25	9	Estes, Sheryl

WAYNE STATE (MI)

Year	M/W	Div	F	SD	BD	Bye	#T	W	L	Coach
1939	M		16				32	14	5	Ertell, Newman H.

WAYNE STATE (NE)

Year	M/W	Div	F	SD	BD	Bye	#T	W	L	Coach
1939	M		32				32	12	9	Hickman, W. Ray
1940			32				32	12	6	Morrison, James H.
1941			32				32	13	7	Morrison, James H.
1957			32				32	15	9	Obye, Charles H. "Chuck"
1968			32	16	A		32	24	3	Svenningson, Allen
1969			32		A		32	23	4	Gunther, David
1970			32		A		32	23	6	Gunther, David

WAYNESBURG

Year	M/W	Div	F	SD	BD	Bye	#T	W	L	Coach
1988	M		4	2	A		32	32	3	Marisa, Rudy
1984			8		A		32	25	6	Marisa, Rudy
1987			8		A		32	23	6	Marisa, Rudy
1981			16		A		32	24	6	Marisa, Rudy
1949			32				32	17	11	Gustine, Frank
1985			32	15	A		32	23	5	Marisa, Rudy
1986			32	10	A		32	24	1	Marisa, Rudy
1989			32		A		32	19	7	Marisa, Rudy

WEBBER

Year	M/W	Div	F	SD	BD	Bye	#T	W	L	Coach
1993	M	II	16	8	A	To R16	20	27	7	Dunlap, John H.
1986			32	5	A		32	25	1	Creola, Nick J.
1995		II	32		A		32	21	15	Dunlap, John H.
1995	W	II	32		A		32	18	12	Bronaugh, Thurman
1998		II	32		A		32	14	18	Saxon, Michelle

WEST FLORIDA

Year	M/W	Div	F	SD	BD	Bye	#T	W	L	Coach
1976	M		32		A		32	19	12	Beck, Marvin G.

WEST GEORGIA

Year	M/W	Div	F	SD	BD	Bye	#T	W	L	Coach
1974	M		1	14	A		32	29	4	Kaiser, Roger A.
1972			16	14	A		32	28	6	Kaiser, Roger A.

Year	M/W	Div	F	SD	BD	Bye	#T	W	L	Coach
WEST LIBERTY STATE										
1952	M		32				32	22	6	Wehr, Richard W.
WEST TEXAS A&M										
1941	M		3				32	29	6	Baggett, Al
1945			8				16	16	10	Miller, W. A. "Gus"
1938			16				32	27	6	Baggett, Al
1940			16				32	26	8	Baggett, Al
1946			16				32	19	8	Miller, W. A. "Gus"
1952			16				32	19	9	Miller, W. A. "Gus"
1939			32				32	21	9	Baggett, Al
WEST VIRGINIA STATE										
1987	M		2	4		A	32	31	4	Carse, Craig
1961			16			A	32	13	12	Cardwell, Mark H.
1963			32			A	32	17	9	Cardwell, Mark H.
WEST VIRGINIA TECH										
1957	M		32				32	26	3	Baisi, Neal D.
1982			32			A	32	24	10	Sutherland, Tom
1988			32			A	32	21	10	Sutherland, Tom
WEST VIRGINIA WESLEYAN										
1983	M		2	14		L	32	32	6	Stewart, Bruce
1958			8	5		A	32	29	5	Ellis, Franklin C. "Hank"
1959			8	2		A	32	34	2	Ellis, Franklin C. "Hank"
1984			8	1		A	32	31	3	Stewart, Bruce
1985			8	4		A	32	28	4	Cameron, Rich
1960			16	16		A	32	23	6	Ellis, Franklin C. "Hank"
1979			32			A	32	24	8	Hess, Gary
WESTBROOK										
1994	M	II	24	13		A	24	30	5	Graffam, Jim
1995		II	32			A	32	24	10	Graffam, Jim
1994	W	II	24	15		A	24	24	4	Brooks-Ewald, Caroline
1995		II	32			A	32	19	10	Brooks-Ewald, Caroline
1996		II	32			A	32	21	12	Martin, John
WESTERN BAPTIST										
1997	M	II	16	15		A	32	27	10	Hills, Tim
1998		II	16	12		A	32	25	11	Hills, Tim
WESTERN CAROLINA										
1963	M		2	10		A	32	28	7	Gudger, James F.
1947			32				32	15	11	McDonald, Marion G.
1972			32			A	32	20	16	Hartbarger, James
WESTERN ILLINOIS										
1954	M		2				32	19	9	Morley, Leroy "Stix"
1958			2	1		A	32	27	1	Morley, Leroy "Stix"
1955			3				32	27	3	Morley, Leroy "Stix"
1962			4	7		A	32	21	11	Morley, Leroy "Stix"

Year	M/W	Div	F	SD	BD	Bye	#T	W	L	Coach
1956			8				32	28	3	Morley, Leroy "Stix"
1957			8	4			32	22	3	Morley, Leroy "Stix"
1963			32	7	A		32	19	8	Morley, Leroy "Stix"

WESTERN KENTUCKY

Year	M/W	Div	F	SD	BD	Bye	#T	W	L	Coach
1938	M		32				32	30	3	Diddle, Edgar A., Sr.

WESTERN MONTANA

Year	M/W	Div	F	SD	BD	Bye	#T	W	L	Coach
1958	M		16		A		32	22	7	Straugh, William T.
1989	M		16		A		32	19	9	Keltz, Donald "Casey"
1941			32				32	16	4	Straugh, William T.
1949			32				32	16	17	Straugh, William T.
1959			32		A		32	17	8	Straugh, William T.
1961			32		A		32	21	7	Straugh, William T.
1969			32		A		32	22	7	Keltz, Donald "Casey"

WESTERN NEW ENGLAND

Year	M/W	Div	F	SD	BD	Bye	#T	W	L	Coach
1970	M		32		A		32	14	6	Geldart, Eric, Jr.
1971			32		A		32	19	7	Geldart, Eric, Jr.

WESTERN NEW MEXICO

Year	M/W	Div	F	SD	BD	Bye	#T	W	L	Coach
1942	M		32				32	17	4	Wooden, Maurice
1981			32	9	A		32	26	4	Drangmeister, Richard
1982			32	13	A		32	20	5	Drangmeister, Richard
1990	W		8		A		16	25	6	Irvin, Dexter
1996		I	16	13	A		32	25	6	Reid, Jason
1991			32		A		32	18	8	Irvin, Dexter
1994		I	32		A		32	9	15	Reid, Jason
1995		I	32		A		32	21	8	Reid, Jason

WESTERN OREGON

Year	M/W	Div	F	SD	BD	Bye	#T	W	L	Coach
1982	M		8	4	A		32	25	1	Boutin, Dr. James
1981			16	12	L		32	22	3	Boutin, Dr. James
1938			32				32	16	6	Cox, J. Alfred "Al"
1941			32				32	14	10	Cox, J. Alfred "Al"
1996		II	32	7	L		32	22	8	Kelly, Tom
1995	W	II	1	8	A		32	23	9	Rogers, "Rusty"
1996		II	1	1	A		32	31	4	Rogers, "Rusty"
1994		II	2	3	A	To R16	24	31	6	Carey, Jon
1992		II	3	7	A	To R16	20	26	9	Carey, Jon
1993		II	8	6	A	To R16	20	26	10	Carey, Jon
1987			16	7	A		16	26	6	Carey, Jon
1991			16		A		32	26	11	Carey, Jon
1998		II	32	6	L		32	24	11	Rogers, "Rusty"

WESTERN STATE (CO)

Year	M/W	Div	F	SD	BD	Bye	#T	W	L	Coach
1987	M		32		A		32	19	13	Gibbons, Terry
1992		I	32		A		32	19	10	Helman, Dr. Jay W.

WESTERN WASHINGTON

Year	M/W	Div	F	SD	BD	Bye	#T	W	L	Coach
1972	M		8	5	A		32	26	4	Randall, Charles R. "Chuck"
1988			16	12	A		32	28	8	Jackson, Brad
1960			32	12	A		32	19	7	Hubbard, Jack
1994		I	32		A		32	24	7	Jackson, Brad

Year	M/W	Div	F	SD	BD	Bye	#T	W	L	Coach
1986	W		8	7	A		16	25	8	Goodrich, Lynda
1989			8		A		16	30	5	Goodrich, Lynda
1996		I	8	6	A		32	26	7	Dollo, Carmen
1998		I	32	13	L		32	21	9	Dollo, Carmen

WESTMAR

Year	M/W	Div	F	SD	BD	Bye	#T	W	L	Coach
1968	M		32		A		32	21	7	Knudtson, Paul O.

WESTMINSTER (MO)

Year	M/W	Div	F	SD	BD	Bye	#T	W	L	Coach
1939	M		16				32	15	8	Kimbrell, Eugene F.
1943			16				32	11	7	Kimbrell, Eugene F.
1938			32				32	12	9	Kimbrell, Eugene F.

WESTMINSTER (PA)

Year	M/W	Div	F	SD	BD	Bye	#T	W	L	Coach
1960	M		2	4	A		32	24	3	Ridl, Charles G. "Buzz"
1962			2	1	A		32	26	3	Ridl, Charles G. "Buzz"
1961			4	1	A		32	23	5	Ridl, Charles G. "Buzz"
1968			4	6	A		32	22	8	Ridl, Charles G. "Buzz"
1950			16				32	25	5	Washabaugh, Grover C.
1959			16	12	A		32	19	8	Ridl, Charles G. "Buzz"
1967			16	9	A		32	22	6	Ridl, Charles G. "Buzz"
1994		I	16	13	A		32	25	3	Galbreath, Dr. C. Ronald
1951			32				32	22	6	Washabaugh, Grover C.
1982			32		A		32	21	7	Galbreath, Dr. C. Ronald
1996		I	32	15	A		32	21	8	Galbreath, Dr. C. Ronald

WESTMINSTER (UT)

Year	M/W	Div	F	SD	BD	Bye	#T	W	L	Coach
1959	M		32		A		32	16	7	Richardson, Howard D.
1961			32		A		32	15	8	Richardson, Howard D.

WESTMONT

Year	M/W	Div	F	SD	BD	Bye	#T	W	L	Coach
1984	M		4	4	A		32	25	2	Kammerer, Glen "Chet"
1972			8	10	A		32	21	9	Byron, Thomas C.
1973			8		A		32	25	6	Mulder, Ronald
1978			16		A		32	23	9	Kammerer, Glen "Chet"
1991			16	16	A		32	22	10	Kammerer, Glen "Chet"
1994		I	16		A		32	19	13	Moore, John
1957			32				32	23	6	Siemens, John R.
1986			32		A		32	23	8	Kammerer, Glen "Chet"
1988			32		A		32	23	9	Kammerer, Glen "Chet"
1996		I	32		A		32	19	13	Moore, John

WHEATON (IL)

Year	M/W	Div	F	SD	BD	Bye	#T	W	L	Coach
1956	M		4				32	28	4	Pfund, Leroy H. "Lee"

WHEELING JESUIT

Year	M/W	Div	F	SD	BD	Bye	#T	W	L	Coach
1989	M		8	5	A		32	31	4	DeFruscio, Jay
1994	W	I	32		A		32	23	5	Hustead, Don

Year	M/W	Div	F	SD	BD	Bye	#T	W	L	Coach
WHITTIER										
1947	M		16				32	30	2	Bonham, Aubrey R.
1960			16	13	A		32	23	9	Bonham, Aubrey R.
1969			16	13	A		32	23	5	Guevara, Ivan T.
1971			16	11	A		32	23	7	Guevara, Ivan T.
1959			32		A		32	20	7	Bonham, Aubrey R.
1970			32		A		32	21	8	Guevara, Ivan T.
1977			32	10	A		32	24	5	Jacobs, Dave
WHITWORTH (WA)										
1996	M	II	2	4	A		32	26	5	Friedrichs, Dr. Warren
1952			8				32	23	14	McGregor, James B.
1998		II	8	8	A		32	20	8	Friedrichs, Dr. Warren
1954			32				32	21	4	Smith, Art
1955			32				32	21	8	Smith, Art
1961			32	8	A		32	19	10	Kamm, Richard
1991			32		A		32	22	9	Friedrichs, Dr. Warren
1995	W	II	16		A		32	19	12	Higgs, Helen
WICHITA STATE										
1945	M		16				16	14	4	Binford, Melvin J.
1946			32				32	14	9	Binford, Melvin J.
WILEY										
1970	M		16		A		32	20	10	White, Calvin
WILLAMETTE										
1993	M	II	1	3	L	To R16	20	29	4	James, Gordon "Gordie"
1994		II	8	3	A	To R16	24	24	6	James, Gordon "Gordie"
1995		II	8		L		32	20	12	James, Gordon "Gordie"
1960			32	15	A		32	24	4	Lewis, John R.
1972			32	15	A		32	23	6	Boutin, Dr. James
1975			32		A		32	24	5	Boutin, Dr. James
1996	W	II	32	15	L		32	19	8	Petrie, Paula
WILLIAM CAREY (MS)										
1984	M		16	16	A		32	26	7	Knight, Steve
1983			32		A		32	20	9	Knight, Steve
1985			32	16	A		32	20	7	Knight, Steve
1986			32		A		32	20	15	Knight, Steve
1987			32		A		32	23	13	Knight, Steve
1989			32		A		32	21	13	Knight, Steve
1997		I	32		A		32	22	14	Knight, Steve
1993	W	I	32	15	L		32	28	4	English, Tracy
WILLIAM JEWELL										
1993	M	II	3	4	A	To R16	20	27	10	Holley, Larry R.
1995		II	3	10	A		32	29	10	Holley, Larry R.
1996		II	3	9	L		32	30	9	Holley, Larry R.
1997		II	3	14	A		32	29	10	Holley, Larry R.

Year	M/W	Div	F	SD	BD	Bye	#T	W	L	Coach
1960			4		A		32	23	10	Nelson, James A.
1988			8	5	A		32	32	2	Holley, Larry R.
1992		II	8		A	To R16	20	23	13	Holley, Larry R.
1957			16				32	23	6	Nelson, James A.
1962			16	16	A		32	21	7	Nelson, James A.
1998		II	16	2	A		32	28	9	Holley, Larry R.
1975			32		A		32	22	9	Hickman, John A.

WILLIAM WOODS

Year	M/W	Div	F	SD	BD	Bye	#T	W	L	Coach
1992	W	I	32		A		32	25	3	Ternes, Roger

WILMINGTON (DE)

Year	M/W	Div	F	SD	BD	Bye	#T	W	L	Coach
1993	M	II	16		A		20	19	13	Newsome, Kevin
1995		II	32		A		32	20	11	Newsome, Kevin
1992	W	II	16		A		20	25	11	Rogers, "Rusty"
1994		II	16	22	A		24	21	8	Rogers, "Rusty"
1993		II	20		A		20	26	6	Rogers, "Rusty"

WINGATE

Year	M/W	Div	F	SD	BD	Bye	#T	W	L	Coach
1988	W		4	1	A		16	33	2	Jacumin, Johnny
1986			8		A		16	26	6	Jacumin, Johnny
1987			8	5	A		16	29	4	Jacumin, Johnny
1991			8	6	L		32	28	3	Jacumin, Johnny
1989			16	5	A		16	26	3	Jacumin, Johnny
1990			16	8	A		16	27	6	Jacumin, Johnny
1992		I	32		A		32	22	11	Jacumin, Johnny
1993		I	32		L		32	23	8	Jacumin, Johnny

WINONA STATE

Year	M/W	Div	F	SD	BD	Bye	#T	W	L	Coach
1973	M		16		A		32	23	4	Wothke, Les
1975			16	15	A		32	22	7	Wothke, Les
1938			32				32	14	4	Fisk, Charles
1939			32				32	10	8	Fisk, Charles

WINSTON-SALEM STATE

Year	M/W	Div	F	SD	BD	Bye	#T	W	L	Coach
1961	M		8	9	A		32	26	5	Gaines, Clarence E. "Big House"
1965			8	11	A		32	25	8	Gaines, Clarence E. "Big House"
1975			8	11	A		32	23	7	Gaines, Clarence E. "Big House"
1978			8	1	A		32	28	4	Gaines, Clarence E. "Big House"
1962			16	4	A		32	24	5	Gaines, Clarence E. "Big House"
1963			32	3	A		32	23	7	Gaines, Clarence E. "Big House"

WISCONSIN LUTHERAN

Year	M/W	Div	F	SD	BD	Bye	#T	W	L	Coach
1996	M	II	8		A		32	22	7	Noon, Ed
1997		II	32		A		32	19	10	Noon, Ed

WISCONSIN: EAU CLAIRE

Year	M/W	Div	F	SD	BD	Bye	#T	W	L	Coach
1972	M		2	1	A		32	29	2	Anderson, Kenneth A.
1990			2	2	A		32	30	4	Anderson, Kenneth A.
1981			3	2	A		32	29	5	Anderson, Kenneth A.
1989			3	2	A		32	29	4	Anderson, Kenneth A.

Year	M/W	Div	F	SD	BD	Bye	#T	W	L	Coach
1980			4	2	A		32	30	4	Anderson, Kenneth A.
1971			8	3	A		32	27	2	Anderson, Kenneth A.
1982			8	6	A		32	26	6	Anderson, Kenneth A.
1991			8	1	A		32	29	3	Anderson, Kenneth A.
1945			16				16	10	8	Zorn, Willis R., Sr. "Bill"
1956			16				32	20	5	Zorn, Willis R., Sr. "Bill"
1970			16	13	A		32	23	2	Anderson, Kenneth A.
1979			16	12	A		32	24	7	Anderson, Kenneth A.
1986			16	12	A		32	24	7	Anderson, Kenneth A.
1988			16	16	A		32	23	8	Anderson, Kenneth A.
1939			32				32	15	2	Zorn, Willis R., Sr. "Bill"
1946			32				32	18	4	Zorn, Willis R., Sr. "Bill"
1951			32				32	17	6	Zorn, Willis R., Sr. "Bill"
1974			32	9	A		32	24	5	Anderson, Kenneth A.
1987			32	5	A		32	26	4	Anderson, Kenneth A.
1992		I	32		L		32	20	9	Anderson, Kenneth A.

WISCONSIN: GREEN BAY

Year	M/W	Div	F	SD	BD	Bye	#T	W	L	Coach
1973	M		8	4	A		32	28	4	Buss, David R.
1987	W		3	8	A		16	24	6	Hammerle, Carol
1986			16		A		16	21	9	Hammerle, Carol

WISCONSIN: LA CROSSE

Year	M/W	Div	F	SD	BD	Bye	#T	W	L	Coach
1964	M		32		A		32	20	2	De Voll, Clifton

WISCONSIN: MILWAUKEE

Year	M/W	Div	F	SD	BD	Bye	#T	W	L	Coach
1984	W		16		A		16	25	8	Kelling, Mary Ann
1985			16		A		16	25	7	Kelling, Mary Ann

WISCONSIN: OSHKOSH

Year	M/W	Div	F	SD	BD	Bye	#T	W	L	Coach
1968	M		3		A		32	23	6	White, Dr. Robert
1960			32		A		32	15	8	Kitzman, Eric
1963			32		A		32	15	10	Young, Russ
1967			32		A		32	17	6	White, Dr. Robert

WISCONSIN: PARKSIDE

Year	M/W	Div	F	SD	BD	Bye	#T	W	L	Coach
1975	M		8	13	A		32	24	9	Stephens, Steve
1976			16	8	A		32	24	7	Stephens, Steve
1977			16	12	A		32	20	10	Stephens, Steve
1978			16	9	A		32	19	11	Stephens, Steve

WISCONSIN: PLATTEVILLE

Year	M/W	Div	F	SD	BD	Bye	#T	W	L	Coach
1958	M		16		A		32	21	3	Barth, John
1959			32	11	A		32	18	4	Barth, John

WISCONSIN: RIVER FALLS

Year	M/W	Div	F	SD	BD	Bye	#T	W	L	Coach
1950	M		16				32	26	5	Schlagenhauf, George K.
1947			32				32	18	7	Schlagenhauf, George K.
1949			32				32	10	2	Schlagenhauf, George K.
1953			32				32	13	8	Belfori, Phil
1992		I	16	2	A		32	27	2	Parker, Bob
1942			32				32	9	3	Kobal, Eddie
1993		I	32	11	A		32	23	5	Parker, Bob

Year	M/W	Div	F	SD	BD	Bye	#T	W	L	Coach
WISCONSIN: STEVENS POINT										
1984	M		2	9	A		32	28	4	Bennett, Richard
1957			16				32	17	6	Quandt, Hale F.
1983			16	9	A		32	26	4	Bennett, Richard
1985			16	2	A		32	25	5	Bennett, Richard
WISCONSIN: STOUT										
1942	M		16				32	9	6	Johnson, Ray
1969			16		A		32	21	4	Mintz, Dwain P.
1943			32				32	10	2	Johnson, Ray
1991	W		32		A		32	19	11	Thomas, Mark
WISCONSIN: SUPERIOR										
1940	M		16				32	15	3	Whereatt, Ted
1941			16				32	17	2	Whereatt, Ted
WISCONSIN: WHITEWATER										
1952	M		32				32	16	6	Weigandt, Robert
WOFFORD										
1960	M		8	8	A		32	25	6	Alexander, Eugene F.
XAVIER (LA)										
1973	M		8		A		32	21	6	Hopkins, Robert M.
1972			16	7	A		32	22	5	Hopkins, Robert M.
1981			32		A		32	21	8	Alexander, Denny
1982			32	3	A		32	29	2	Alexander, Denny
1991			32		A		32	21	12	Valdery, Dale
1996		I	32		A		32	22	11	Valdery, Dale
1995	W	I	16	12	A		32	25	5	Joseph, Janice
1996		I	16	9	A		32	28	6	Joseph, Janice
1997		I	16		A		32	29	7	Joseph, Janice
1998		I	16	4	A		32	27	4	Joseph, Janice
1994		I	32	15	A		32	28	4	Joseph, Janice
XAVIER (OH)										
1948	M		4				32	24	8	Hirt, Lewis R.
YANKTON										
1942	M		32				32	13	3	Arnold, Lorne S.
1963			32		A		32	18	7	Cowman, Douglas
1969			32		A		32	22	4	Holwerda, Jim
YORK (NE)										
1943	M		16				32	16	4	Tonkin, R. E.
YOUNGSTOWN STATE										
1957	M		8	2			32	23	4	Rosselli, Dominic L. "Dom"
1958			8	8	A		32	24	6	Rosselli, Dominic L. "Dom"
1959			16	9	A		32	19	9	Rosselli, Dominic L. "Dom"
1947			32				32	12	10	Rosselli, Dominic L. "Dom"

National Athletic Steering Committee

HISTORY: Prior to the late 1950s, the so-called historically black colleges—some 90, generally state-supported and mostly south of the Mason-Dixon Line—were not part of the mainstream of college basketball. They were not members of the NCAA or the NAIA and, thus, could not participate in the national championship tournaments of those two associations, the only two then in operation. Segregation not withstanding, they were not "big" enough for the NIT.

They did, however, compete among themselves in five well-established conferences: the Southern Intercollegiate Athletic Conference (SIAC), which began play in 1915-16; the Central Intercollegiate Athletic Association (CIAA), 1923-24; the Southwestern Athletic Conference (SWAC), 1938-39; the Midwest Athletic Association (MWAA), 1923-24 through 1966-67; and the South Central Athletic Conference (SCAC), 1953-54 through 1961-62.

In 1953, Tennessee State, then Tennessee A&I, of Nashville, under coach Clarence Cash, became the first historically black college to participate in a national collegiate association championship tournament, the 32- team NAIA annual event in Kansas City, Missouri. Just four years later, in 1957, the legendary John McLendon led the Tigers to the first of three consecutive NAIA titles.

The road to Tennessee State's achievements began in 1946. Until then, the issue of historically black colleges or even black players in the NAIA tournament had not arisen. Although the NAIA bylaws did not prohibit tournament participation by black players, the operating committee, nevertheless, imposed its own ban—citing assumed racial philosophies in Kansas City. Thus, in 1946, Rosamond Wilson, a reserve on the Morningside College (IA) team and the first black member of a participating team, was relegated to sitting on the bench as "team manager" while his team played.

At the 1947 tournament, Alvin O. Duer, president of the NAIA with the support of executive director Emil Liston, met with association leaders from the southern schools to discuss the subject of black player participation—to no avail.

Then, prior to the 1948 tournament, Lou Wilke, chairman of the Olympic Basketball Committee, wrote to Liston, protesting the exclusion of black players in the tournament and suggesting that it could jeopardize the NAIA's participation in the Olympic trials. Liston immediately polled the executive committee, and by a 7-2 vote the ban was lifted. Several days later, Clarence Walker of John Wooden's Indiana State team became the first black to play in a collegiate national championship tournament.

The following year, the CIAA petitioned the National Association of Basketball Coaches to allow historically black colleges to participate in both the NCAA and NAIA tournaments. Since the petition was favorably received by the NABC, the next step was a formal presentation to the two associations. However, because the NCAA convention was held in Dallas in 1951, and the hotel advised that its segregation policy would be followed, the black members boycotted the meeting.

As a result, on August 15, 1951, The National Athletic Steering Committee (NASC) was formed with an specific goal: a black college in a tournament. Consequently, in the same year, Central State (OH) applied, and was accepted, for NAIA membership. Shortly thereafter, embarrassed NAIA officials claimed ignorance of the school's heritage and rescinded the approval—again citing the assumed possible difficulties in Kansas City. Undaunted, Mark Greene, athletics director of the school, and Duer began a campaign to allow historically black colleges into the tournament.

For 1952, agreement was reached that the top historically black colleges, under the sponsorship of the NASC, would play a post-season tournament with the winner going into the NAIA tournament. The NAIA later reconsidered, but the NASC event was held. It was won by Tennessee State, thus claiming the first Black College National Championship.

Subsequently, after Duer achieved agreement among NAIA officials, district 29, comprised of all of the historically black colleges, was created for 1953 with the district champion going to Kansas City. Tennessee State's victory in that district tournament enabled it to become the first historically black college to participate in a national championship tournament, advancing to the Elite Eight.

In 1954 and 1955, the district 29 tournament continued. Tennessee State won in 1954 but was eliminated in the first round at Kansas City. In 1955, Texas Southern broke the Tiger's district streak and then advanced to the Sweet Sixteen in Kansas City.

In 1956, because of the large number of historically black colleges, district 29 was divided into two districts, 29 and 6, thus ending the Black College National Championship Tournament. In the first two-district season, Tennessee State won district 29 and Texas Southern won district 6, and both went to Kansas City—along with Central State (OH) which qualified as a wild-card. Texas Southern was runner-up to McNeese State while John McLendon's first Tennessee State team advanced to the Elite Eight, and Central State advanced to the Sweet Sixteen.

In 1957, while Tennessee State (district 29) won its historic first national title, Texas Southern (district 6) advanced to the Elite Eight. In 1958, while Tennessee State (district 29) won its second crown, Texas Southern (district 6) finished third.

The NAIA began to redistrict in 1959 so that the historically black colleges would participate in the district in which they were geographically located. The process was completed for the 1968-1969 season.

In the 16 years (1953-1968) during which historically black colleges participated in the NAIA tournament before total district integration, these colleges produced seven national champions, five Final Four teams, and seven Elite Eight teams.

While the NAIA broke the "color barrier", the NCAA was quick to follow. In 1957, five historically black colleges qualified for the first-ever division II tournament. In succeeding years, as many as six historically black colleges qualified. Winston-Salem State, 1967, became the first historically black college to win an NCAA title, followed by Morgan State in 1974. Alcorn State, 1980, was the first historically black college to participate in an NCAA division I tournament, and Maryland: Eastern Shore, 1974, was the first one in the NIT.

In the NSCAA, Friendship JC (SC) was the first historically black college to participate, finishing 6th in 1967. Kittrell (NC) won in 1970.

According to John McLendon, until complete integration of the NAIA districts was accomplished in 1968-1969, the historically black college with the highest finish in the NAIA tournament was declared the Black College National Champion.

TOURNAMENT OPERATION: Technically, the first two tournaments are the only NASC sponsored events. In the latter two years, the tournaments were for the NAIA district 29 championship. For the sake of simplicity, all of the tournaments are included in this book as if they were NASC events, and participating teams are listed as if they were NASC members.

Little is known about the selection of the participants or the determination of the pairings; i.e., seedings, if any. It is believed that one criterion for participation was a championship of one of the four or five black college conferences than in operation. Probably the steering committee itself, in the first two years, and in conjunction with NAIA officials in the last two years, selected the at-large entries and determined the pairings. All four tournaments were conventional single-elimination formats with a 3rd/4th place game.

NOTES ON DATA COLLECTION: Since the tournaments apparently were unseeded and since the method of qualification is unknown, information on seeds and type of bid is not included.

Tournament Results

F	School	W	L	Coach
1952				
1	Tennessee State	19	4	Cash, Clarence B.
2	Central State (OH)	18	3	Gibbs, George Edwin
3	Texas Southern	29	10	Adams, Edward H.
4	Southern: Baton Rouge	23	5	Lee, Robert Henry

F	School	W	L	Coach
8	Clark Atlanta	19	3	Epps, Leonidas S. II "Sonny"
	Fayetteville State	30	7	Gaines, William A. "Gus"
	Florida A&M	26	2	Oglesby, Edward E. "Rock"
	West Virginia State	14	7	Cardwell, Mark H.

1953

F	School	W	L	Coach
1	Tennessee State	20	5	Cash, Clarence B.
2	Bethune-Cookman	24	2	Matthews, Rudolph "Bunky"
3	Southern: Baton Rouge	22	9	Lee, Robert Henry
4	Philander Smith	27	5	Hearnton, William C., Sr.
8	Florida A&M	17	5	Oglesby, Edward E. "Rock"
	Lincoln (MO)	X	X	Unknown
	North Carolina Central	17	7	Brown, Floyd H.
	Virginia State	14	8	Matthews, Shelton M.

1954

F	School	W	L	Coach
1	Tennessee State	17	6	Cash, Clarence B.
2	North Carolina Central	23	7	Brown, Floyd H.
3	Texas Southern	30	5	Adams, Edward H.
4	Southern: Baton Rouge	27	7	Lee, Robert Henry
8	Florida A&M	19	7	Oglesby, Edward E. "Rock"
	Savannah State	23	10	Wright, Theodore A., Sr.
	Virginia Union	14	4	Harris, Thomas H.
	Xavier (LA)	15	5	Hawkins, James E. "Red"

1955

F	School	W	L	Coach
1	Texas Southern	28	3	Adams, Edward H.
2	Tennessee State	28	5	McLendon, John B., Jr.
3	Philander Smith	20	8	Hearnton, William C., Sr.
4	Grambling State	24	8	Robinson, Eddie G.
8	Bethune-Cookman	19	5	Unknown
	Florida A&M	20	2	Oglesby, Edward E. "Rock"
	North Carolina Central	21	6	Brown, Floyd H.
	Virginia Union	21	6	Harris, Thomas H.

School Participation History

Year	F	#T	W	L	Coach
BETHUNE-COOKMAN					
1953	2	8	24	2	Matthews, Rudolph "Bunky"
1955	8	8	19	5	Unknown
CENTRAL STATE (OH)					
1952	2	8	18	3	Gibbs, George Edwin
CLARK ATLANTA					
1952	8	8	19	3	Epps, Leonidas S. II "Sonny"
FAYETTEVILLE STATE					
1952	8	8	30	7	Gaines, William A. "Gus"

Year	F	#T	W	L	Coach
FLORIDA A&M					
1952	8	8	26	2	Oglesby, Edward E. "Rock"
1953	8	8	17	5	Oglesby, Edward E. "Rock"
1954	8	8	19	7	Oglesby, Edward E. "Rock"
1955	8	8	20	2	Oglesby, Edward E. "Rock"
GRAMBLING STATE					
1955	4	8	24	8	Robinson, Eddie G.
LINCOLN (MO)					
1953	8	8	X	X	Unknown
NORTH CAROLINA CENTRAL					
1954	2	8	23	7	Brown, Floyd H.
1953	8	8	17	7	Brown, Floyd H.
1955	8	8	21	6	Brown, Floyd H.
PHILANDER SMITH					
1955	3	8	20	8	Hearnton, William C., Sr.
1953	4	8	27	5	Hearnton, William C., Sr.
SAVANNAH STATE					
1954	8	8	23	10	Wright, Theodore A., Sr.
SOUTHERN: BATON ROUGE					
1953	3	8	22	9	Lee, Robert Henry
1952	4	8	23	5	Lee, Robert Henry
1954	4	8	27	7	Lee, Robert Henry
TENNESSEE STATE					
1952	1	8	19	4	Cash, Clarence B.
1953	1	8	20	5	Cash, Clarence B.
1954	1	8	17	6	Cash, Clarence B.
1955	2	8	28	5	McLendon, John B., Jr.
TEXAS SOUTHERN					
1955	1	8	28	3	Adams, Edward H.
1952	3	8	29	10	Adams, Edward H.
1954	3	8	30	5	Adams, Edward H.
VIRGINIA STATE					
1953	8	8	14	8	Matthews, Shelton M.
VIRGINIA UNION					
1954	8	8	14	4	Harris, Thomas H.
1955	8	8	21	6	Harris, Thomas H.
WEST VIRGINIA STATE					
1952	8	8	14	7	Cardwell, Mark H.
XAVIER (LA)					
1954	8	8	15	5	Hawkins, James E. "Red"

National Bible College Athletic Association

HISTORY: In 1981, at the suggestion of Fred Pierce, then athletics director at Saint Paul Bible College (now Crown College), the 1st and 2nd place teams from the Northern Intercollegiate Christian and the Midwest Christian College Conferences met at Faith Baptist Bible College, Ankeny, Iowa, in the Mid-America Bible College Basketball Tournament.

This tournament led to the formation of the National Bible College Athletic Association. At the time, the National Christian College Athletic Association had been in operation since 1968 and had added a division II for Bible colleges in 1976. However, a number of the Bible schools felt that the NCCAA did not meet their needs and chose to institute their own organization.

The first official NBCAA basketball tournament was held in 1982. In 1983, a women's division was added, and in 1984 a men's division II was added. Other sports were added beginning in 1985.

A prerequisite for membership in the NBCAA is that a school must require a minimum of 20 semester hours of Bible study for graduation.

TOURNAMENT DIVISIONS: Men Open: 1981-1983, 1998; I: 1984-1997; II: 1984-1997. **Women** Open: 1983- .

DEFINITION OF DIVISIONS: I: in the top 40% of schools based on the association's "power rating" system; II: not in the top 40% of schools based on the association's "power rating" system. Note: Until recently, the definition was based on enrollment: I: more than 150 students; II: less than 150 students

TOURNAMENT OPERATION: The first tournament in 1981 was not an official NBCAA tournament. However, for the sake of simplicity, it is included in this book as if it were an NBCAA event, and participating teams are listed as if they were NBCAA members.

All tournaments, men and women—all divisions, have played a conventional consolation bracket format with all places determined—although in some years the game for the two last-place spots was not played. In no tournament have there been more than eight teams, although several men's division II events had as few as three teams and used a round-robin format. It is believed that seedings began for both men and women in 1989.

Apparently, qualification for the tournaments resulted, for the most part, from a region or district championship. However, information is generally unavailable.

NOTES ON DATA COLLECTION: Some conflicting information has been found with the seedings. The seeds provided in the data have been taken from pairings charts in tournament programs. For most years, the actual seed was indicated and used in the data. For years when the seeding was not specifically indicated, it is believed that the conventional arrangement was used by the committee. For those years, the seedings in the data reflect that assumption.

Since information on the tournament qualification is generally unavailable, information on the type of bid is not included.

There are missing won-lost records and coaches names. Most are the result of incomplete records at the schools. In other cases, the schools did not provide information to the several annual directories.

Tournament Results—Men

F	School	SD	Bye	W	L	Coach
1981						
1	Calvary Bible			22	4	Schneeberger, Robert W.
2	Barclay			14	8	Bryan, Dewayne
3	Trinity Bible			13	15	Carlin, Scott B.
4	North Central Bible			X	X	Lockwood, Glen
1982						
1	Calvary Bible			26	1	Schneeberger, Robert W.
2	Grace (NE)			22	5	Classen, Jim W.
3	Central Christian (MO)			17	10	Smith, Larry R.
4	North Central Bible			15	9	Lowenberg, Doug
5	Pillsbury Baptist Bible			18	8	Wahlberg, Tom
6	Maranatha Baptist Bible (WI)			7	17	Terrill, Jerry
7	Minnesota Bible			6	10	Comeaux, R. Mark
8	Southeastern Assemblies			19	10	Campbell, Dale
1983						
1	Northwest Christian			24	5	Buckley, Jim
2	Crown (MN)			24	9	Pierce, Bud
3	Maranatha Baptist Bible (WI)			11	13	Terrill, Jerry
4	North Central Bible			16	13	Lowenberg, Doug
5	Pillsbury Baptist Bible			18	15	Wahlberg, Tom
6	Landmark Baptist (FL)			X	X	Quinlan, Keith
7	Calvary Bible			15	11	Schneeberger, Robert W.
	Grace (NE)			20	5	Classen, Jim W.
1984 DIVISION I						
1	Northwest Christian			24	4	Lipp, David
2	North Central Bible			31	1	Myers, Dennis
3	Pillsbury Baptist Bible			14	13	Leeman, Gordon
4	Faith Baptist Bible (IA)			18	12	Thompson, David G.
5	Baptist University (GA)					Rapson,
6	Southeastern Assemblies			18	9	Campbell, Dale
7	Grace (NE)			18	8	Classen, Jim W.
8	Maranatha Baptist Bible (WI)			4	19	Terrill, Jerry
1984 DIVISION II						
1	Minnesota Bible		To R2	19	8	Comeaux, R. Mark
2	Vennard			10	16	Engbrecht, Dr. Dennis D.
3	Emmaus Bible			X	X	Suriano, Louis
1985 DIVISION I						
1	Northwest Christian			25	4	Lipp, David
2	Trinity Bible			6	19	Tatum, Bob
3	North Central Bible			18	11	Myers, Dennis
4	Grace (NE)			23	4	Classen, Jim W.

F	School	SD	Bye	W	L	Coach
5	Calvary Bible			20	12	Schneeberger, Robert W.
6	Pillsbury Baptist Bible			16	11	Deckert, Wayne
7	Southwestern Assemblies			X	X	Bryan, Terry
8	Crown (MN)			X	X	Pierce, Bud

1985 DIVISION II

1	Midwest Christian			X	X	Williams, Charles R.
2	Northwest Bible			X	X	Carter, Ron
3	Nebraska Christian			10	14	Boelton, Allen
4	Vennard			15	16	Engbrecht, Dr. Dennis D.

1986 DIVISION I

1	Northwest Christian			19	11	Kennedy, Don
2	North Central Bible			22	12	Myers, Dennis
3	Pillsbury Baptist Bible			16	10	Deckert, Wayne
4	Crown (MN)			X	X	Pierce, Bud
5	Ozark Christian			X	X	Berlin, Terry
6	Southwestern Assemblies			X	X	Bryan, Terry
7	Grace (NE)			16	11	Classen, Jim W.
8	Calvary Bible			19	8	Schneeberger, Robert W.

1986 DIVISION II

1	Nebraska Christian			12	14	Lahm, Chris
2	Association Free Lutheran Bible			11	7	Palke, Mike
3	Vennard			13	12	Engbrecht, Dr. Dennis D.

1987 DIVISION I

1	Northwest Christian			21	8	Halupa, Paul
2	Simpson (CA)			X	X	Kress, Paul
3	North Central Bible			X	X	Myers, Dennis
4	Pillsbury Baptist Bible					Deckert, Wayne
5	Calvary Bible			19	9	Schneeberger, Robert W.
6	Southwestern Assemblies			15	17	Bryan, Terry
7	Nebraska Christian			16	13	Lahm, Chris
8	Free Will Baptist Bible			1	5	Deel, Byron

1987 DIVISION II

1	Arizona Bible			X	X	Steele, Kevin
2	Vennard			11	14	Owens, Dennis
3	Minnesota Bible			X	X	Comeaux, R. Mark
4	Emmaus Bible			X	X	Elifritz, Bill

1988 DIVISION I

1	LIFE Bible (CA)			19	6	Updike, Blake
2	North Central Bible			22	13	Myers, Dennis
3	Pillsbury Baptist Bible			15	9	Deckert, Wayne
4	Southwestern Assemblies			X	X	Bryan, Terry
5	Crown (MN)			X	X	Pierce, Bud
6	Calvary Bible			21	7	Miller, Steve
7	Hillsdale Free Will Baptist			15	10	Lawrence, Aaron
8	Nebraska Christian			19	10	Lahm, Chris

F	School	SD	Bye	W	L	Coach
1988 Division II						
1	Arlington Baptist			X	X	Jones, Dr. Griffin
2	American Indian			X	X	Cupp, Larry
3	Association			2	12	Quanbeck, Keith
	Free Lutheran Bible					
4	Central Indian Bible			X	X	Grant, Timothy L.
1989 Division I						
1	Northwest Christian	1	To R4	19	12	Rodenburg, Jeff
2	North Central Bible	7		X	X	Myers, Dennis
3	Southwestern Assemblies	4		X	X	Bryan, Terry
4	Calvary Bible	3		23	5	Miller, Steve
5	Trinity Bible	6		15	18	Tatum, Bob
6	Grace (NE)	2		12	14	Classen, Jim W.
	Ozark Christian	5		X	X	Williams, Charles R.
1989 Division II						
1	Hillsdale Free Will Baptist	1	To R4	23	12	Lawrence, Aaron
2	Nebraska Christian	2	To R4	19	8	Lahm, Chris
3	Association	4		6	15	Johnson, Mark
	Free Lutheran Bible					
4	Oklahoma Baptist College	3		3	19	Keiser, Keith
5	Arizona Bible	6		X	X	Gremler, Dwayne
6	Arlington Baptist	5		X	X	Cash, Durwood M. "Woody"
1990 Division I						
1	Ozark Christian	4		X	X	Williams, Charles R.
2	Calvary Bible	3		25	3	Miller, Steve
3	Northwest Christian	1		22	11	Rodenburg, Jeff
4	Manhattan Christian	2		19	9	Rupe, Marvin
5	San Jose Christian	7		21	9	Miller, Glen
6	Grace (NE)	5		17	11	Classen, Jim W.
7	Crown (MN)	6		12	20	Newman, Joe
8	Trinity Bible	8		18	13	Wagler, Keith
1990 Division II						
1	Nebraska Christian	1		19	10	Lahm, Chris
2	Hillsdale Free Will Baptist	3		20	15	Lawrence, Aaron
3	Pacific West Coast	2		X	X	Thomas, Mike
	Baptist Bible					
4	West Coast Christian	4		12	14	Crank, Frank
5	Baptist Christian (LA)	8				
6	Vennard	6		8	16	Penn, Brad
7	Minnesota Bible	5		4	10	Kester, John
8	Arlington Baptist	7		X	X	Cash, Durwood M. "Woody"
1991 Division I						
1	San Jose Christian	5		27	7	Miller, Glen
2	Ozark Christian	3		26	9	Williams, Charles R.
3	Pacific Christian	1		32	18	Erickson, Lee W.
4	Manhattan Christian	2		19	9	Rupe, Marvin

F	School	SD	Bye	W	L	Coach
5	Grace (NE)	4		20	7	Classen, Jim W.
6	Multnomah Bible	6		18	17	Aldrich, Dr. Joseph
7	Calvary Bible	8		17	11	Miller, Steve
8	Crown (MN)	7		17	17	Newman, Joe

1991 DIVISION II

F	School	SD	Bye	W	L	Coach
1	Hillsdale Free Will Baptist	4		23	11	Lisenbee, Tim
2	West Coast Christian	2		24	12	McGough, Michael
3	Pacific West Coast Baptist Bible	1	To R4	20	7	Thomas, Mike
4	California Christian	3		23	8	Crank, Frank
5	Nebraska Christian	5		15	13	Lahm, Chris
6	Association Free Lutheran Bible	6		5	9	Berntson, Tim
7	Oklahoma Baptist College	7		9	14	Sisson, Doug

1992 DIVISION I

F	School	SD	Bye	W	L	Coach
1	Ozark Christian	2		28	13	Williams, Charles R.
2	Grace (NE)	1		22	5	Classen, Jim W.
3	Pacific Christian	5		X	X	Erickson, Lee W.
4	San Jose Christian	3		23	17	Miller, Glen
5	Manhattan Christian	4		21	7	Johnson, Stuart
6	LIFE Bible (CA)	7		18	12	Updike, Mike
7	Calvary Bible	6		17	11	Miller, Steve
8	Trinity Bible	8		8	21	Wagler, Keith

1992 DIVISION II

F	School	SD	Bye	W	L	Coach
1	Latin American Bible (CA)	1		30	2	Elisaldez, Ken
2	Hillsdale Free Will Baptist	2		10	8	Lisenbee, Tim
3	Pacific West Coast Baptist Bible	3		X	X	Thomas, Mike
4	Nebraska Christian	4		17	12	Lahm, Chris
5	Florida Christian	8		12	17	Chambers, Aaron
6	Vennard	7		9	12	Christiansen, Les
7	Tomlinson	5		20	15	Smith, Phillip D.
8	Association Free Lutheran Bible	6		10	9	Unverzagt, Joel

1993 DIVISION I

F	School	SD	Bye	W	L	Coach
1	San Jose Christian	2		22	14	Miller, Glen
2	Multnomah Bible	4		19	13	Skagen, James C.
3	Grace (NE)	1	To R4	23	3	Classen, Jim W.
4	Manhattan Christian	3	To R4	21	5	Johnson, Stuart
5	Calvary Bible	5		15	12	Miller, Steve
6	Southwestern Assemblies	6		X	X	Pratt, Bruce

1993 DIVISION II

F	School	SD	Bye	W	L	Coach
1	Nebraska Christian	3		19	9	Lahm, Chris
2	Oklahoma Baptist College	4		13	12	Sisson, Doug
3	Arizona Bible	1		15	7	Kuyper, Tom
4	Vennard	7		10	15	Christiansen, Les

F	School	SD	Bye	W	L	Coach
5	Hillsdale Free Will Baptist	2		21	20	Lisenbee, Tim
6	Southwestern Christian Ministries	5		18	18	Arthur, Mark
7	Emmaus Bible	6		6	14	Reeves, John
8	Minnesota Bible	8		7	10	Addison, Don

1994 Division I

1	San Jose Christian	2		26	11	Miller, Glen
2	Grace (NE)	1	To R4	24	3	Classen, Jim W.
3	Southwestern Assemblies	6		X	X	Garippa, Steven P.
4	Manhattan Christian	4		14	13	Johnson, Stuart
5	Arlington Baptist	5		10	20	Bosher, Clark
6	Dallas Christian	3		10	15	Dickens, Charles "Chip"
7	Southeastern Bible	7		3	17	Brigham, Ben

1994 Division II

1	Nebraska Christian	1		20	8	Lahm, Chris
2	Hillsdale Free Will Baptist	6		22	14	Lisenbee, Tim
3	Southwestern Christian Ministries	5		18	16	Arthur, Mark
4	Oklahoma Baptist College	7		29	8	Sisson, Doug
5	Minnesota Bible	3		10	10	Comeaux, R. Mark
6	Association Free Lutheran Bible	8		X	X	Greven, John
7	Puget Sound Christian	2		15	10	McNichols, Troy
8	Arizona Bible	4		12	12	Kuyper, Tom

1995 Division I

1	San Jose Christian	3		28	11	Miller, Glen
2	Multnomah Bible	1		27	2	Reese, Chris
3	Southwestern Christian Ministries	5		26	4	Arthur, Mark
4	Grace (NE)	2		23	4	Classen, Jim W.
5	Manhattan Christian	7		20	8	Condra, Shawn
6	Rhema Bible	4		17	7	Ivey, Lance
7	Southwestern Assemblies	6		20	8	Garippa, Steven P.
8	Association Free Lutheran Bible	8		3	15	Greven, John

1995 Division II

1	Puget Sound Christian	2		17	11	McNichols, Troy
2	Gulf Coast Christian	5		12	19	Wilkerson, Dr. Charles
3	Nebraska Christian	1		22	11	Lahm, Chris
4	Messenger	3		21	17	Stallman, David S.
5	Arizona Bible	4		17	9	Kuyper, Tom
6	Vennard	6		9	19	Van Amburg, L. D.
7	Hillsdale Free Will Baptist	7		17	12	Lisenbee, Tim
8	Barclay	8		6	20	Anders, L. Lee

F	School	SD	Bye	W	L	Coach
1996 Division I						
1	Multnomah Bible	4		20	16	Reese, Chris
2	Rhema Bible	2		19	8	Ivey, Lance
3	Nebraska Christian	1		23	6	Lahm, Chris
4	Southwestern Christian Ministries	3		26	16	Arthur, Mark
5	Southwestern Assemblies	5		8	17	Garippa, Steven P.
6	Grace (NE)	6		12	15	Classen, Jim W.
7	LIFE Bible (CA)	7		11	23	Meyer, Rick
8	Columbia Bible (BC)	8		8	23	Schmidt, Robert "Rob"
1996 Division II						
1	Hillsdale Free Will Baptist	2		13	17	Archer, Kelly
2	Puget Sound Christian	1	To R4	17	13	McNichols, Troy
3	Gulf Coast Christian	3		23	17	Wilkerson, Keith
4	Wesley (MS)	5		10	13	Devore, William, Jr.
5	Central Christian (MO)	4		13	13	Cobb, Russell
6	Messenger	7		10	15	Stallman, David S.
7	Association Free Lutheran Bible	6		5	13	Greven, John
1997 Division I						
1	Gulf Coast Christian	1		29	6	Wilkerson, Dr. Charles
2	Rhema Bible	2		22	8	Ivey, Lance
3	Dallas Christian	3		19	13	Wilkerson, Keith
4	San Jose Christian	4		11	17	Miller, Glen
5	Southwestern Assemblies	7		19	19	Garippa, Steven P.
6	Grace (NE)	5		13	14	Classen, Jim W.
7	Columbia Bible (BC)	6		12	26	Schmidt, Robert "Rob"
8	Multnomah Bible	8		12	24	Reese, Chris
1997 Division II						
1	Southwestern Christian Ministries	2		26	15	Arthur, Mark
2	Hillsdale Free Will Baptist	5		16	20	Archer, Kelly
3	Nebraska Christian	1		21	8	Lahm, Chris
4	Arizona Bible	3		15	15	Kuyper, Tom
5	Wesley (MS)	6		13	16	Devore, William, Jr.
6	Association Free Lutheran Bible	4		11	19	Greven, John
7	Messenger	8		5	19	Stallman, David S.
8	Minnesota Bible	7		3	13	Wager, Al
1998						
1	Southwestern Assemblies	5		20	8	Garippa, Rev. Steven P.
2	Southwestern Christian Ministries	3		21	17	Arthur, Mark
3	California Christian	1		30	8	Wilkerson, Dr. Charles
4	Hillsdale Free Will Baptist	2		24	12	Archer, Kelly
5	Puget Sound Christian	4		18	13	McNichols, Troy
6	Messenger	7		4	25	Hall, Homer D.
7	Association Free Lutheran Bible	6		4	15	Monseth, Ben
8	Oklahoma Baptist College	8		2	15	Kelly, Guy

Tournament Results—Women

F	School	SD	Bye	W	L	Coach
1983						
1	Crown (MN)			X	X	Hardy, Don
2	Calvary Bible			9	7	Hensarling, Anne
3	Trinity Bible			11	8	Long, Rod P.
4	Maranatha Baptist Bible (WI)			4	13	Unknown
1984						
1	Crown (MN)			X	X	Hardy, Don
2	Calvary Bible			9	5	Hensarling, Anne
3	Canadian Bible					Moore, Timothy L.
4	Valley Forge Christian			X	X	Baker, William J.
1985						
1	Crown (MN)			X	X	Guavin, Julie
2	Trinity Bible			16	6	Long, Rod P.
3	North Central Bible			7	8	Goodrich, Dr. Larry
4	Calvary Bible			6	15	Hensarling, Anne
1986						
1	North Central Bible			15	16	Myers, Dennis
2	Faith Baptist Bible (IA)			9	5	Nihart, Lanny
3	Trinity Bible			11	10	Wagler, Keith
4	Calvary Bible			6	8	Hensarling, Anne
5	Pillsbury Baptist Bible			3	7	
6	Crown (MN)			X	X	Rogness, Tony
7	Vennard					
1987						
1	North Central Bible			X	X	Myers, Dennis
2	Crown (MN)			X	X	Rogness, Tony
3	Calvary Bible			16	7	Hensarling, Anne
4	Trinity Bible			7	14	Wagler, Keith
1988						
1	Ozark Christian			X	X	Williams, Charles R.
2	Crown (MN)			X	X	Moats, Candace
3	Calvary Bible			9	9	Hensarling, Anne
	Trinity Bible			16	12	Wagler, Keith
1989						
1	Calvary Bible	4		16	1	Hensarling, Anne
2	Ozark Christian	3		X	X	Williams, Charles R.
3	North Central Bible	2		X	X	Myers, Dennis
4	Hillsdale Free Will Baptist	1		5	12	Lawrence, Aaron
1990						
1	Calvary Bible	6		12	9	Shook, John
2	Faith Baptist Bible (IA)	1	To R4	11	2	Nihart, Lanny
3	Crown (MN)	2	To R4	9	9	Moats, Candace
4	Trinity Bible	4		4	17	Tatum, Bob
5	Grace (NE)	5		6	7	Krehbiel, Gary
6	Hillsdale Free Will Baptist	3		10	8	Lisenbee, Tim

F	School	SD	Bye	W	L	Coach
1991						
1	Crown (MN)	1	To R4	19	9	Rogness, Tony
2	Association Free Lutheran Bible	2	R4>R2	9	6	Jacobson, Wanda
3	Faith Baptist Bible (IA)	3		8	7	Nihart, Lanny
4	Calvary Bible	5		3	15	Rose, Brenda
5	Southeastern Bible	4				Green, Kimball
1992						
1	Hillsdale Free Will Baptist	3		9	13	Braisher, Kelly
2	Association Free Lutheran Bible	1		12	4	Jacobson, Wanda
3	Grace (NE)	2		7	1	Regier, Larry
4	Tomlinson	4		13	17	Smith, Phillip D.
1993						
1	Grace (NE)	1	To R4	19	0	Regier, Larry
2	Manhattan Christian	3	To R4	11	6	Cott, Wendy
3	Northland Baptist Bible	2		12	9	Bowman, Reba
4	Association Free Lutheran Bible	4		8	9	Jacobson, Wanda
5	Calvary Bible	5		5	7	Rose, Brenda
6	Hillsdale Free Will Baptist	6		12	12	Braisher, Kelly
1994						
1	Grace (NE)	1		15	0	Reiger, Larry
2	Association Free Lutheran Bible	3		X	X	Greven, Wendy Qualley
3	Manhattan Christian	2		10	8	Cott, Wendy
4	Southeastern Assemblies	4		18	10	Skinner, Dean B., Jr.
1995						
1	Grace (NE)	1	To R4	17	2	Johnson, Duwayne
2	Minnesota Bible	2		7	5	Nordrum, Joel
3	Messenger	4		4	13	Hall, Homer
4	Association Free Lutheran Bible	5		X	X	Greven, Wendy Qualley
5	Central Christian (MO)	3		4	15	Stohs, Randy
1996						
1	Grace (NE)	1	To R4	19	0	Johnson, Duwayne
2	Nebraska Christian	2	To R4	10	12	Kissack, Rick
3	Hillsdale Free Will Baptist	3		10	13	Hill, Roni
4	Association Free Lutheran Bible	6		2	12	Greven, Wendy Qualley
5	Central Christian (MO)	4		3	16	Stohs, Randy
6	Messenger	5		5	12	Hall, Homer
1997						
1	Hillsdale Free Will Baptist	3		12	10	Archer, Kelly
2	Grace (NE)	4		10	14	Johnson, Duwayne
3	Nebraska Christian	2		16	8	Kissack, Rick
4	Association Free Lutheran Bible	1		9	8	Greven, Wendy Qualley

F	School	SD	Bye	W	L	Coach
1998						
1	Nebraska Christian	1		21	8	Fuehrer, Mike
2	Hillsdale Free Will Baptist	3		14	8	Brisco, Tabia
3	Southwestern Assemblies	2		11	14	Goodrich, Dr. Larry
4	Association Free Lutheran Bible	4		2	15	Olson, Sarah

School Participation History

Year	M/W	Div	F	SD	Bye	#T	W	L	Coach
AMERICAN INDIAN									
1988	M	II	2	2		4	X	X	Cupp, Larry
ARIZONA BIBLE									
1987	M	II	1	1		4	X	X	Steele, Kevin
1993		II	3	1		8	15	7	Kuyper, Tom
1997		II	4	3		8	15	15	Kuyper, Tom
1989		II	5	6		6	X	X	Gremler, Dwayne
1995		II	5	4		8	17	9	Kuyper, Tom
1994		II	8	4		8	12	12	Kuyper, Tom
ARLINGTON BAPTIST									
1988	M	II	1	1		4	X	X	Jones, Dr. Griffin
1994		I	5	5		7	10	20	Bosher, Clark
1989		II	6	5		6	X	X	Cash, Durwood M. "Woody"
1990		II	8	6		8	X	X	Cash, Durwood M. "Woody"
ASSOCIATION FREE LUTHERAN BIBLE									
1986	M	II	2			3	11	7	Palke, Mike
1988		II	3	4		4	2	12	Quanbeck, Keith
1989		II	3	4		6	6	15	Johnson, Mark
1991		II	6	6		7	5	9	Berntson, Tim
1994		II	6	8		8	X	X	Greven, John
1997		II	6	4		8	11	19	Greven, John
1996		II	7	6		7	5	13	Greven, John
1998			7	6		8	4	15	Monseth, Ben
1992		II	8	3		8	10	9	Unverzagt, Joel
1995		I	8	8		8	3	15	Greven, John
1991	W		2	3	R4>R2	6	9	6	Jacobson, Wanda
1992			2	1		4	12	4	Jacobson, Wanda
1994			2	3		4	X	X	Greven, Wendy Qualley
1993			4	4		6	8	9	Jacobson, Wanda
1995			4	5		5	X	X	Greven, Wendy Qualley
1996			4	6		6	2	12	Greven, Wendy Qualley
1997			4	1		4	9	8	Greven, Wendy Qualley
1998			4	4		4	2	15	Olson, Sarah
BAPTIST CHRISTIAN (LA)									
1990	M	II	5	8		8			

Year	M/W	Div	F	SD	Bye	#T	W	L	Coach
BAPTIST UNIVERSITY (GA)									
1984	M	I	5	3		8			Rapson,
BARCLAY									
1981	M		2			4	14	8	Bryan, DeWayne
1995		II	8	8		8	6	20	Anders, L. Lee
CALIFORNIA CHRISTIAN									
1998	M		3	1		8	30	8	Wilkerson, Dr. Charles
1991		II	4	3		7	23	8	Crank, Frank
CALVARY BIBLE									
1981	M		1			4	22	4	Schneeberger, Robert W.
1982			1	2		8	26	1	Schneeberger, Robert W.
1990		I	2	3		8	25	3	Miller, Steve
1989		I	4	3		7	23	5	Miller, Steve
1985		I	5	1		8	20	12	Schneeberger, Robert W.
1987		I	5	4		8	19	9	Schneeberger, Robert W.
1993		I	5	5		6	15	12	Miller, Steve
1988		I	6	4		8	21	7	Miller, Steve
1983			7	7		8	15	11	Schneeberger, Robert W.
1991		I	7	8		8	17	11	Miller, Steve
1992		I	7	6		8	17	11	Miller, Steve
1986		I	8	2		8	19	8	Schneeberger, Robert W.
1989	W		1	4		4	16	1	Hensarling, Anne
1990			1	6		6	12	9	Shook, John
1983			2			4	9	7	Hensarling, Anne
1984			2			4	9	5	Hensarling, Anne
1987			3			4	16	7	Hensarling, Anne
1988			3			4	9	9	Hensarling, Anne
1985			4			4	6	15	Hensarling, Anne
1986			4			7	6	8	Hensarling, Anne
1991			4	6		6	3	15	Rose, Brenda
1993			5	5		6	5	7	Rose, Brenda
CANADIAN BIBLE									
1984	W		3			4			Moore, Timothy L.
CENTRAL CHRISTIAN (MO)									
1982	M		3	8		8	17	10	Smith, Larry R.
1996		II	5	4		7	13	13	Cobb, Russell
1995	W		5	3		5	4	15	Stohs, Randy
1996			5	4		6	3	16	Stohs, Randy
CENTRAL INDIAN BIBLE									
1988	M	II	4	3		4	X	X	Grant, Timothy L.
COLUMBIA BIBLE									
1997	M	I	7	6		8	12	26	Schmidt, Robert "Rob"
1996		I	8	8		8	8	23	Schmidt, Robert "Rob"

Year	M/W	Div	F	SD	Bye	#T	W	L	Coach
CROWN (MN)									
1983	M		2	4		8	24	9	Pierce, Bud
1986		I	4	7		8	X	X	Pierce, Bud
1988		I	5	6		8	X	X	Pierce, Bud
1990		I	7	6		8	12	20	Newman, Joe
1985		I	8	6		8	X	X	Pierce, Bud
1991		I	8	7		8	17	17	Newman, Joe
1983	W		1	1		4	X	X	Hardy, Don
1984			1	1		4	X	X	Hardy, Don
1985			1	1		4	X	X	Guavin, Julie
1991			1	1	To R4	6	19	9	Rogness, Tony
1987			2	2		4	X	X	Rogness, Tony
1988			2	2		4	X	X	Moats, Candace
1990			3	2	To R4	6	9	9	Moats, Candace
1986			6	6		7	X	X	Rogness, Tony
DALLAS CHRISTIAN									
1997	M	I	3	3		8	19	13	Wilkerson, Keith
1994		I	6	3		7	10	15	Dickens, Charles "Chip"
EMMAUS BIBLE									
1987	M	II	4	4		4	X	X	Elifritz, Bill
1984		II	3			3	X	X	Suriano, Louis
1993		II	7	6		8	6	14	Reeves, John
FAITH BAPTIST BIBLE (IA)									
1984	M	I	4	6		8	18	12	Thompson, David G.
1986	W		2			7	9	5	Nihart, Lanny
1990			2	1	To R4	6	11	2	Nihart, Lanny
1991			3	4		6	8	7	Nihart, Lanny
FLORIDA CHRISTIAN									
1992	M	II	5	8		8	12	17	Chambers, Aaron
FREE WILL BAPTIST BIBLE									
1987	M	I	8	8		8	1	5	Deel, Byron
GRACE (NE)									
1982	M		2	4		8	22	5	Classen, Jim W.
1992		I	2	1		8	22	5	Classen, Jim W.
1994		I	2	1	To R4	7	24	3	Classen, Jim W.
1993		I	3	1	To R4	6	23	3	Classen, Jim W.
1985		I	4	2		8	23	4	Classen, Jim W.
1995		I	4	2		8	23	4	Classen, Jim W.
1991		I	5	4		8	20	7	Classen, Jim W.
1990		I	6	5		8	17	11	Classen, Jim W.
1996		I	6	6		8	12	15	Classen, Jim W.
1997		I	6	5		8	13	14	Classen, Jim W.
1983			7	8		8	20	5	Classen, Jim W.
1984		I	7	8		8	18	8	Classen, Jim W.
1986		I	7	5		8	16	11	Classen, Jim W.
1989		I	7	2		7	12	14	Classen, Jim W.

Year	M/W	Div	F	SD	Bye	#T	W	L	Coach
1993	W		1	1	To R4	6	19	0	Regier, Larry
1994			1	1		4	15	0	Reiger, Larry
1995			1	1	To R4	5	17	2	Johnson, DuWayne
1996			1	1	To R4	6	19	0	Johnson, DuWayne
1997			2	4		4	10	14	Johnson, DuWayne
1992			3	2		4	7	1	Regier, Larry
1990			5	5		6	6	7	Krehbiel, Gary

GULF COAST CHRISTIAN

Year	M/W	Div	F	SD	Bye	#T	W	L	Coach
1997	M	I	1	1		8	29	6	Wilkerson, Dr. Charles
1995		II	2	5		8	12	19	Wilkerson, Dr. Charles
1996		II	3	3		7	23	17	Wilkerson, Keith

HILLSDALE FREE WILL BAPTIST

Year	M/W	Div	F	SD	Bye	#T	W	L	Coach
1989	M	II	1	1	To R4	6	23	12	Lawrence, Aaron
1991		II	1	4		7	23	11	Lisenbee, Tim
1996		II	1	2		7	13	17	Archer, Kelly
1990		II	2	7		8	20	15	Lawrence, Aaron
1992		II	2	2		8	10	8	Lisenbee, Tim
1994		II	2	6		8	22	14	Lisenbee, Tim
1997		II	2	5		8	16	20	Archer, Kelly
1998			4	2		8	24	12	Archer, Kelly
1993		II	5	2		8	21	20	Lisenbee, Tim
1988		I	7	7		8	15	10	Lawrence, Aaron
1995		II	7	7		8	17	12	Lisenbee, Tim
1992	W		1	3		4	9	13	Braisher, Kelly
1997			1	3		4	12	10	Archer, Kelly
1998			2	3		4	14	8	Brisco, Tabia
1996			3	3		6	10	13	Hill, Roni
1989			4	1		4	5	12	Lawrence, Aaron
1990			6	3		6	10	8	Lisenbee, Tim
1993			6	6		6	12	12	Braisher, Kelly

LANDMARK BAPTIST (FL)

Year	M/W	Div	F	SD	Bye	#T	W	L	Coach
1983	M		6	5		8	X	X	Quinlan, Keith

LATIN AMERICAN BIBLE (CA)

Year	M/W	Div	F	SD	Bye	#T	W	L	Coach
1992	M	II	1	1		8	30	2	Elisaldez, Ken

LIFE BIBLE (CA)

Year	M/W	Div	F	SD	Bye	#T	W	L	Coach
1988	M	I	1	3		8	19	6	Updike, Blake
1992		I	6	7		8	18	12	Updike, Mike
1996		I	7	7		8	11	23	Meyer, Rick

MANHATTAN CHRISTIAN

Year	M/W	Div	F	SD	Bye	#T	W	L	Coach
1990	M	I	4	2		8	19	9	Rupe, Marvin
1991		I	4	2		8	19	9	Rupe, Marvin
1993		I	4	2	To R4	6	21	5	Johnson, Stuart
1994		I	4	4		7	14	13	Johnson, Stuart
1992		I	5	4		8	21	7	Johnson, Stuart
1995		I	5	7		8	20	8	Condra, Shawn
1993	W		2	3	To R4	6	11	6	Cott, Wendy
1994			3	2		4	10	8	Cott, Wendy

Year	M/W	Div	F	SD	Bye	#T	W	L	Coach
MARANATHA BAPTIST BIBLE (WI)									
1983	M		3	1		8	11	13	Terrill, Jerry
1982			6	7		8	7	17	Terrill, Jerry
1984		I	8	7		8	4	19	Terrill, Jerry
1983	W		4			4	4	13	Unknown
MESSENGER									
1995	M	II	4	3		8	21	17	Stallman, David S.
1996		II	6	7		7	10	15	Stallman, David S.
1998			6	7		8	4	25	Hall, Homer D.
1997		II	7	8		8	5	19	Stallman, David S.
1995	W		3	4		5	4	13	Hall, Homer D.
1996			6	5		6	5	12	Hall, Homer D.
MIDWEST CHRISTIAN									
1985	M	II	1	1		4	X	X	Williams, Charles R.
MINNESOTA BIBLE									
1984	M	II	1			3	19	8	Comeaux, R. Mark
1987		II	3	2		4	X	X	Comeaux, R. Mark
1994		II	5	3		8	10	10	Comeaux, R. Mark
1982			7	5		8	6	10	Comeaux, R. Mark
1990		II	7	5		8	4	10	Kester, John
1993		II	8	8		8	7	10	Addison, Don
1997		II	8	7		8	3	13	Wager, Al
1995	W		2	2		5	7	5	Nordrum, Joel
MULTNOMAH BIBLE									
1996	M	I	1	4		8	20	16	Reese, Chris
1993		I	2	4		6	19	13	Skagen, James C.
1995		I	2	1		8	27	2	Reese, Chris
1991		I	6	6		8	18	17	Aldrich, Dr. Joseph
1997		I	8	8		8	12	24	Reese, Chris
NEBRASKA CHRISTIAN									
1986	M	II	1			3	12	14	Lahm, Chris
1990		II	1	1		8	19	10	Lahm, Chris
1993		II	1	3		8	19	9	Lahm, Chris
1994		II	1	1		8	20	8	Lahm, Chris
1989		II	2	2	To R4	6	19	8	Lahm, Chris
1985		II	3	4		4	10	14	Boelton, Allen
1995		II	3	1		8	22	11	Lahm, Chris
1996		I	3	1		8	23	6	Lahm, Chris
1997		II	3	1		8	21	8	Lahm, Chris
1992		II	4	4		8	17	12	Lahm, Chris
1991		II	5	5		7	15	13	Lahm, Chris
1987		I	7	2		8	16	13	Lahm, Chris
1988		I	8	8		8	19	10	Lahm, Chris
1998	W		1	1		4	21	8	Fuehrer, Mike
1996			2	2	To R4	6	10	12	Kissack, Rick
1997			3	2		4	16	8	Kissack, Rick

Year	M/W	Div	F	SD	Bye	#T	W	L	Coach
NORTH CENTRAL BIBLE									
1984	M	I	2	2		8	31	1	Myers, Dennis
1986		I	2	3		8	22	12	Myers, Dennis
1988		I	2	1		8	22	13	Myers, Dennis
1989		I	2	7		7	X	X	Myers, Dennis
1985		I	3	4		8	18	11	Myers, Dennis
1987		I	3	1		8	X	X	Myers, Dennis
1981			4			4	X	X	Lockwood, Glen
1982			4	6		8	15	9	Lowenberg, Doug
1983			4	2		8	16	13	Lowenberg, Doug
1986	W		1			7	15	16	Myers, Dennis
1987			1			4	X	X	Myers, Dennis
1985			3			4	7	8	Goodrich, Dr. Larry
1989			3	2		4	X	X	Myers, Dennis
NORTHLAND BAPTIST BIBLE									
1993	W		3	2		6	12	9	Bowman, Reba
NORTHWEST BIBLE									
1985	M	II	2	3		4	X	X	Carter, Ron
NORTHWEST CHRISTIAN									
1983	M		1	6		8	24	5	Buckley, Jim
1984		I	1	1		8	24	4	Lipp, David
1985		I	1	3		8	25	4	Lipp, David
1986		I	1	1		8	19	11	Kennedy, Don
1987		I	1	7		8	21	8	Halupa, Paul
1989		I	1	1	To R4	7	19	12	Rodenburg, Jeff
1990		I	3	1		8	22	11	Rodenburg, Jeff
OKLAHOMA BAPTIST COLLEGE									
1993	M	II	2	4		8	13	12	Sisson, Doug
1989		II	4	3		6	3	19	Keiser, Keith
1994		II	4	7		8	29	8	Sisson, Doug
1991		II	7	7		7	9	14	Sisson, Doug
1998			8	8		8	2	15	Kelly, Guy
OZARK CHRISTIAN									
1990	M	I	1	4		8	X	X	Williams, Charles R.
1992		I	1	2		8	28	13	Williams, Charles R.
1991		I	2	3		8	26	9	Williams, Charles R.
1986		I	5	6		8	X	X	Berlin, Terry
1989		I	6	5		7	X	X	Williams, Charles R.
1988	W		1			4	X	X	Williams, Charles R.
1989			2	3		4	X	X	Williams, Charles R.
PACIFIC CHRISTIAN									
1991	M	I	3	1		8	32	18	Erickson, Lee W.
1992		I	3	5		8	X	X	Erickson, Lee W.
PACIFIC WEST COAST BAPTIST BIBLE									
1990	M	II	3	3		8	X	X	Thomas, Mike
1991		II	3	1	To R4	7	20	7	Thomas, Mike
1992		II	3	6		8	X	X	Thomas, Mike

Year	M/W	Div	F	SD	Bye	#T	W	L	Coach
PILLSBURY BAPTIST BIBLE									
1984	M	I	3	4		8	14	13	Leeman, Gordon
1986		I	3	4		8	16	10	Deckert, Wayne
1988		I	3	2		8	15	9	Deckert, Wayne
1987		I	4	3		8			Deckert, Wayne
1982			5	1		8	18	8	Wahlberg, Tom
1983			5	3		8	18	15	Wahlberg, Tom
1985		I	6	7		8	16	11	Deckert, Wayne
1986	W		5			7	3	7	
PUGET SOUND CHRISTIAN									
1995	M	II	1	2		8	17	11	McNichols, Troy
1996		II	2	1	To R4	7	17	13	McNichols, Troy
1998			5	4		8	18	13	McNichols, Troy
1994		II	7	2		8	15	10	McNichols, Troy
RHEMA BIBLE									
1996	M	I	2	2		8	19	8	Ivey, Lance
1997		I	2	2		8	22	8	Ivey, Lance
1995		I	6	4		8	17	7	Ivey, Lance
SAN JOSE CHRISTIAN									
1991	M	I	1	5		8	27	7	Miller, Glen
1993		I	1	3		6	22	14	Miller, Glen
1994		I	1	2		7	26	11	Miller, Glen
1995		I	1	3		8	28	11	Miller, Glen
1992		I	4	3		8	23	17	Miller, Glen
1997		I	4	4		8	11	17	Miller, Glen
1990		I	5	7		8	21	9	Miller, Glen
SIMPSON (CA)									
1987	M	I	2	5		8	X	X	Kress, Paul
SOUTHEASTERN ASSEMBLIES									
1984	M	I	6	5		8	18	9	Campbell, Dale
1982			8	3		8	19	10	Campbell, Dale
1994	W		4	4		4	18	10	Skinner, Dean B., Jr.
SOUTHEASTERN BIBLE									
1994	M	I	7	7		7	3	17	Brigham, Benjamin E.
1991	W		5	5		6			Green, Kimball
SOUTHWESTERN ASSEMBLIES									
1998	M		1	5		8	20	8	Garippa, Rev. Steven P.
1989		I	3	4		7	X	X	Bryan, Terry
1994		I	3	6		7	X	X	Garippa, Rev. Steven P.
1988		I	4	5		8	X	X	Bryan, Terry
1996		I	5	5		8	8	17	Garippa, Rev. Steven P.
1997		I	5	7		8	19	19	Garippa, Rev. Steven P.
1986		I	6	8		8	X	X	Bryan, Terry
1987		I	6	6		8	15	17	Bryan, Terry

Year	M/W	Div	F	SD	Bye	#T	W	L	Coach
1993		I	6	6		6	X	X	Pratt, Bruce
1985		I	7	5		8	X	X	Bryan, Terry
1995		I	7	6		8	20	8	Garippa, Rev. Steven P.
1998	W		3	2		4	11	14	Goodrich, Dr. Larry

SOUTHWESTERN CHRISTIAN MINISTRIES

Year	M/W	Div	F	SD	Bye	#T	W	L	Coach
1997	M	II	1	2		8	26	15	Arthur, Mark
1998			2	3		8	21	17	Arthur, Mark
1994		II	3	5		8	18	16	Arthur, Mark
1995		I	3	5		8	26	4	Arthur, Mark
1996		I	4	3		8	26	16	Arthur, Mark
1993		II	6	5		8	18	18	Arthur, Mark

TOMLINSON

Year	M/W	Div	F	SD	Bye	#T	W	L	Coach
1992	M	II	7	5		8	20	15	Smith, Phillip D.
1992	W		4	4		4	13	17	Smith, Phillip D.

TRINITY BIBLE

Year	M/W	Div	F	SD	Bye	#T	W	L	Coach
1985	M	I	2	8		8	6	19	Tatum, Bob
1981			3			4	13	15	Carlin, Scott B.
1989		I	5	6		7	15	18	Tatum, Bob
1990		I	8	8		8	18	13	Wagler, Keith
1992		I	8	8		8	8	21	Wagler, Keith
1985	W		2			4	16	6	Long, Rod P.
1983			3			4	11	8	Long, Rod P.
1986			3			7	11	10	Wagler, Keith
1988			3			4	16	12	Wagler, Keith
1987			4			4	7	14	Wagler, Keith
1990			4	4		6	4	17	Tatum, Bob

VALLEY FORGE CHRISTIAN

Year	M/W	Div	F	SD	Bye	#T	W	L	Coach
1984	W		4			4	X	X	Baker, William J.

VENNARD

Year	M/W	Div	F	SD	Bye	#T	W	L	Coach
1984	M	II	2		To R2	3	10	16	Engbrecht, Dr. Dennis D.
1986		II	3			3	13	12	Engbrecht, Dr. Dennis D.
1985		II	4	2		4	15	16	Engbrecht, Dr. Dennis D.
1987		II	2	3		4	11	14	Owens, Dennis
1993		II	4	7		8	10	15	Christiansen, Les
1990		II	6	2		8	8	16	Penn, Brad
1992		II	6	7		8	9	12	Christiansen, Les
1995		II	6	6		8	9	19	Van Amburg, L. D.
1986	W		7			7			

WESLEY (MS)

Year	M/W	Div	F	SD	Bye	#T	W	L	Coach
1996	M	II	4	5		7	10	13	Devore, William, Jr.
1997		II	5	6		8	13	16	Devore, William, Jr.

WEST COAST CHRISTIAN

Year	M/W	Div	F	SD	Bye	#T	W	L	Coach
1991	M	II	2	2		7	24	12	McGough, Michael
1990		II	4	4		8	12	14	Crank, Frank

National Collegiate Athletic Association

NAMES: 1906-1910: IAAUS (Intercollegiate Athletic Association of The United States); 1911- : NCAA (National Collegiate Athletic Association)

HISTORY: In the early days of college football, the "flying wedge" was the major offense. Coupled with other mass formations, gang tackling, and the generally rugged nature of the game, it produced numerous injuries and even deaths. Campaigns began to either abolish or reform it. At the instigation of President Theodore Roosevelt, reform began late in 1905. In early December, 13 schools met to initiate changes in playing rules. On December 28, 62 schools met to form the IAAUS which was officially constituted on March 31, 1906, and then became the NCAA in 1910.

In the early years, the NCAA was primarily a rule-making and discussion group, but after its first national championship—track and field—in 1921, more rules committees were formed and more championships were added. Following World War II, a series of developments began to further transform the NCAA. The so-called "Sanity Code," which had been adopted to establish guidelines for recruiting and financial aid, had failed to curb abuses. The number of post-season football games was increasing, television was becoming an issue, membership was increasing, and even more championships were being conducted.

In 1951 Walter Byers became the first full-time executive director, and the following year the national headquarters was established in Kansas City. Shortly thereafter, a program to control live television of football was adopted, enforcement powers were given to the council, and legislation was adopted governing post-season football.

In 1973 membership was divided into three legislative and competitive divisions, and five years later subdivisions I-A and I-AA were created for football. Women's sports were added in 1980. In 1985, action was taken to strengthen the association's compliance and enforcement powers. Throughout the years, membership has continued to grow, and the NCAA now is the dominant organization in collegiate athletics.

TOURNAMENT DIVISIONS: Men Open: 1938-1956; I: 1957- (University); II: 1957- (College); III: 1975- (Small College). **Women** I: 1982- (University); II: 1982- (College); III: 1982- (Small College).

Note: Divisions I, II, and III were not the official designations until the 1975 tournament. Previously, the divisions were designated as university and college. However, for the sake of simplicity and consistency, I, II, III are used throughout this book.

DEFINITION OF DIVISIONS: Determination of the division in which its teams will compete is made by a school, based upon three primary criteria: a. strength of schedule (i.e., number of games against other schools in the same division); b. financial aid provided to student-athletes (basketball, currently—division I: 13 scholarships; division II: 10 scholarships; division III: no financial aid); c. number of sports sponsored.

TOURNAMENT OPERATION: Undergoing growth the likes of which no other association ever has experienced, the NCAA men's tournaments have been a bracket-makers nightmare. In many years, the number of participating teams was other than a multiple of or divisor of 16—creating some most interesting bracketing arrangements.

Through 1950, the tournament format was uncomplicated. There were eight teams, one from each district, selected by the district committee, with the East champion meeting the West champion for the title. In 1951 expansion began; and in 1957 division II was instituted, followed in 1975 by division III. The number of participating teams in each division for each year is listed below:

Year	I	II	III	Year	I	II	III	Year	I	II	III
MEN											
1951	16	—	—	1962-1964	25	32	—	1976	32	32	28
1952	16	—	—	1965	23	32	—	1977-1978	32	32	30
1953	22	—	—	1966	22	36	—	1979	40	32	32
1954-1955	24	—	—	1967-1968	23	36	—	1980-1982	48	32	32
1956	25	—	—	1969-1971	25	32	—	1983	52	32	32
1957	23	32	—	1972	25	36	—	1984	53	32	32
1958	24	32	—	1973	25	42	—	1985-1988	64	32	32
1959	23	32	—	1974	25	44	—	1989-1994	64	32	40
1960	25	32	—	1975	32	44	30	1995-1998	64	48	64
1961	24	32	—								
WOMEN											
1982	32	16	16	1986-1987	40	24	32	1994	64	32	40
1983	36	24	32	1988	40	32	32	1995-1997	64	48	64
1984-1985	32	24	32	1989-1993	48	32	32	1998	64	48	48

On the men's side, the 1951 expansion began the system of conference champions as automatic qualifiers. In the first year, ten conferences were so honored, and the balance of the field was filled with at-large selections. Over the years, the number of conferences has increased, as have the number of them that receive automatic bids—currently around 30.

In 1952, another break with tradition occurred when four regions were created and the four champions met in the first pure Final Four. From 1952 through 1955, the regions were merely an A and B section of the traditional East and West groupings. In 1956, they were renamed East, Mideast, Midwest, and Farwest; and although they have had different names over the years, the concept has remained the same.

As the number of teams increased, some rather innovative brackets were utilized—and there were not always an equal number of teams in each region. In the years between 1953 and 1974, when the number of teams was somewhere in the low to mid 20s, byes were used extensively (and apparently somewhat at random) in the first-round so that there were 16 teams in the second round. One of the more creative tools was the play-ins utilized in 1983 and 1984 to pare down the 52 and 53 teams, respectively, to a workable 48.

Seedings began in 1979 with a conventional single-elimination format in each region. 3rd/4th place games have had an on-again/off-again life, although they have not been played since 1981. Regional consolation games were held in the eight team events for 6th place—sometimes in one region, sometimes in both regions—and for 12th place from 1951 through 1975.

In Division II, which began as the college division in 1957, formats were somewhat more stable. The four-region format with automatic (conference champions) and at-large bids was used for the first year. Beginning in 1958, the still-used eight regions began—although there were not always an equal number of teams in each region. From 1968-1971 the use of automatic bids was halted. From 1958 through 1995, the first-round losers played for 24th place—although in some years not every region played the game. A 3rd/4th place game was held through 1982

In 1975, division III was added (and the official use of the present nomenclature began). It began with 30 teams and remained at approximately that number until 1989 when it expanded to 48 and then to 64 in 1995, with the eight (although sometimes only seven) region format. First-round losers played for 24th place through 1989, and a 3rd/4th place game has been played in all years.

The beginning of seedings in divisions II and III is uncertain. Apparently the seeding was left to the regional committees, and information for many years is not available.

The women's tournaments have been nice and consistent— even expanding in workable increments of participating teams. Seedings began in division I in 1987, but the onset of seedings in divisions II and III is uncertain. As with the men's tournaments, seedings were done by the regional committees, and much information is unavailable. All divisions have always used the four (division I) or eight (division II and II) region formats. Division III played a region consolation for 24th place from 1983 through 1989. Division I never played a 3rd/4th place game, but division II did in 1982 and then since 1989 while division III has played it since 1982.

NOTES ON DATA COLLECTION: As noted above, information on the seedings for both men's and women's divisions II and III tournaments for many years is unavailable. It is believed that seedings may have begun in the mid-1980's. Seedings are included for the years when known.

In men's division I, there are some missing entries in the "Bid" column. They are the result of a tie for the regular season championship in a conference that qualified for an automatic bid, there was no known play-off, no tournament, both teams received a bid, but neither the NCAA, the conference, or the involved teams know which team received the automatic bid and which received the at-large bid. Automatic bids for men's division II prior to 1975 are unavailable

Tournament Results—Men

F	School	SD	Reg	BD	Bye	W	L	Coach
1939								
1	Oregon		W	L		29	5	Hobson, Dr. Howard A. "Hobby"
2	Ohio State		E	L		16	7	Olsen, Harold G.
3	Oklahoma		W	L		12	9	Drake, Bruce
	Villanova		E	L		20	5	Severance, Alexander G.
6	Utah State		W	L		17	7	Romney, Ernest L. "Dick"
8	Brown		E	L		17	3	Allen, George E. "Eck"
	Texas		W	L		19	6	Gray, Jack S.
	Wake Forest		E	L		18	6	Greason, Murray
1940								
1	Indiana		E	L		20	3	McCracken, E. Branch
2	Kansas		W	L		19	6	Allen, Dr. Forrest C. "Phog"
3	Duquesne		E	L		20	3	Davies, Charles R. "Chick"
	Southern California		W	L		20	3	Barry, Justin M. "Sam"
6	Rice		W	L		22	3	Brannon, Byron A. "Buster"
8	Colorado		W	L		17	4	Cox, Forrest B. "Frosty"
	Springfield (MA)		E	L		16	3	Hickox, Edward J. "Eddie"
	Western Kentucky		E	L		24	6	Diddle, Edgar A., Sr.
1941								
1	Wisconsin		E	L		20	3	Foster, Harold E. "Bud"
2	Washington State		W	L		26	6	Friel, John B. "Jack"
3	Arkansas		W	L		20	3	Rose, Glen
	Pittsburgh		E	L		13	6	Carlson, Dr. H. Clifford "Doc"
6	Creighton		W	L		18	7	Hickey, Edgar S. "Eddie"
	Dartmouth		E	L		19	5	Cowles, Osborne "Ozzie"
8	North Carolina		E	L		15	8	Lange, William
	Wyoming		W	L		14	6	Shelton, Everett F.

F	School	SD	Reg	BD	Bye	W	L	Coach
1942								
1	Stanford		W	L		27	4	Dean, Everett S.
2	Dartmouth		E	L		22	4	Cowles, Osborne "Ozzie"
3	Colorado		W	L		16	2	Cox, Forrest B. "Frosty"
	Kentucky		E	L		19	6	Rupp, Adolph F.
6	Kansas		W	L		17	5	Allen, Dr. Forrest C. "Phog"
	Pennsylvania State		E	L		18	3	Lawther, John D.
8	Illinois		E	L		18	5	Mills, Douglas R.
	Rice		W	L		22	5	Brannon, Byron A. "Buster"
1943								
1	Wyoming		W	L		31	2	Shelton, Everett F.
2	Georgetown (DC)		E	L		22	5	Ripley, Elmer H.
3	De Paul		E	L		19	5	Meyer, Raymond J.
	Texas		W	L		19	7	Gilstrap, H. C. "Bully"
6	Dartmouth		E	L		20	3	Cowles, Osborne "Ozzie"
	Oklahoma		W	L		18	9	Drake, Bruce
8	New York		E	L		16	6	Cann, Howard G.
	Washington		W	L		24	7	Edmundson, Clarence S. "Hec"
1944								
1	Utah		W	L		21	4	Peterson, Vadal
2	Dartmouth		E	L		19	2	Brown, Earl M.
3	Iowa State		W	L		14	4	Menze, Louis E.
	Ohio State		E	L		14	7	Olsen, Harold G.
6	Missouri		W	L		10	9	Edwards, George R.
	Temple		E	L		14	9	Cody, Joshua C.
8	Catholic		E	L		17	7	Long, John J.
	Pepperdine		W	L		22	13	Duer, Alva O. "Al"
1945								
1	Oklahoma State		W	L		27	4	Iba, Henry P. "Hank"
2	New York		E	L		14	7	Cann, Howard G.
3	Arkansas		W	L		17	9	Lambert, Dr. Eugene W.
	Ohio State		E	L		15	5	Olsen, Harold G.
6	Kentucky		E	L		22	4	Rupp, Adolph F.
	Oregon		W	L		30	13	Hobson, Dr. Howard A. "Hobby"
8	Tufts		E	L		10	8	Cochran, Arthur M.
	Utah		W	L		17	4	Peterson, Vadal
1946								
1	Oklahoma State		W	L		31	2	Iba, Henry P. "Hank"
2	North Carolina		E	L		30	5	Carnevale, Bernard L. "Ben"
3	Ohio State		E	L		16	5	Olsen, Harold G.
4	California		W	L		30	6	Price, Clarence M. "Nibs"
6	Colorado		W	L		12	6	Cox, Forrest B. "Frosty"
	New York		E	L		19	3	Cann, Howard G.
8	Baylor		W	L		25	5	Henderson, R. E. "Bill"
	Harvard		E	L		20	3	Stahl, Floyd S.

F	School	SD	Reg	BD	Bye	W	L	Coach
1947								
1	Holy Cross (MA)		E	L		27	3	Julian, Alvin F. "Doggie"
2	Oklahoma		W	L		24	7	Drake, Bruce
3	Texas		W	L		26	2	Gray, Jack S.
4	City College		E	L		17	6	Holman, Nathan "Nat"
6	Oregon State		W	L		28	5	Gill, Amory T. "Slats"
	Wisconsin		E	L		16	6	Foster, Harold E. "Bud"
8	Navy		E	L		16	3	Carnevale, Bernard L. "Ben"
	Wyoming		W	L		22	6	Shelton, Everett F.
1948								
1	Kentucky		E	L		36	3	Rupp, Adolph F.
2	Baylor		W	L		24	8	Henderson, R. E. "Bill"
3	Holy Cross (MA)		E	L		26	4	Julian, Alvin F. "Doggie"
4	Kansas State		W	L		22	6	Gardner, James H. "Jack"
6	Michigan		E	L		16	6	McCoy, Ernest B.
	Washington		W	L		23	11	McLarney, Arthur
8	Columbia (NY)		E	L		21	3	Ridings, Gordon H.
	Wyoming		W	L		18	9	Shelton, Everett F.
1949								
1	Kentucky		E	L		32	2	Rupp, Adolph F.
2	Oklahoma State		W	L		23	5	Iba, Henry P. "Hank"
3	Illinois		E	L		21	4	Combes, Harry A.
4	Oregon State		W	L		24	12	Gill, Amory T. "Slats"
6	Arkansas		W	L		15	11	Lambert, Dr. Eugene W.
	Villanova		E	L		23	4	Severance, Alexander G.
8	Wyoming		W	L		25	10	Shelton, Everett F.
	Yale		E	L		22	8	Hobson, Dr. Howard A. "Hobby"
1950								
1	City College		E	L		24	5	Holman, Nathan "Nat"
2	Bradley		W	L		32	5	Anderson, Forrest A. "Forddy"
3	North Carolina State		E	L		27	6	Case, Everett N.
4	Baylor		W	L		14	13	Henderson, R. E. "Bill"
6	Brigham Young		W	L		22	12	Watts, Stanley H.
	Ohio State		E	L		22	4	Dye, William H. H. "Tippy"
8	California: Los Angeles		W	L		24	7	Wooden, John R.
	Holy Cross (MA)		E	L		27	4	Sheary, Lester H. "Buster"
1951								
1	Kentucky		E	A		32	2	Rupp, Adolph F.
2	Kansas State		W	A		25	4	Gardner, James H. "Jack"
3	Illinois		E	A		22	5	Combes, Harry A.
4	Oklahoma State		W	A		29	6	Iba, Henry P. "Hank"
6	Saint John's (NY)		E	L		26	5	McGuire, Frank J.
	Washington		W	A		24	6	Dye, William H. H. "Tippy"
8	Brigham Young		W	A		28	9	Watts, Stanley H.
	North Carolina State		E	A		30	7	Case, Everett N.
16	Arizona		W	A		24	6	Enke, Fred A.
	Columbia (NY)		E	A		21	1	Rossini, Lucio "Lou"
	Connecticut		E	L		22	4	Greer, Hugh S.
	Louisville		E	L		19	7	Hickman, Bernard L. "Peck"

F	School	SD	Reg	BD	Bye	W	L	Coach
	Montana State	W	L			24	12	Breeden, John W. "Brick"
	San Jose State	W	L			18	12	McPherson, Walter J.
	Texas A&M	W	A			17	12	Floyd, John L.
	Villanova	E	L			25	7	Severance, Alexander G.

1952

F	School	SD	Reg	BD	Bye	W	L	Coach
1	Kansas	W(A)	A			28	3	Allen, Dr. Forrest C. "Phog"
2	Saint John's (NY)	E(A)	L			25	5	McGuire, Frank J.
3	Illinois	E(B)	A			22	4	Combes, Harry A.
4	Santa Clara	W(B)	L			17	12	Feerick, Robert J.
8	Duquesne	E(B)	L			23	4	Moore, Donald W. "Dudey"
	Kentucky	E(A)	A			29	3	Rupp, Adolph F.
	Saint Louis	W(A)	A			23	8	Hickey, Edgar S. "Eddie"
	Wyoming	W(B)	A			28	7	Shelton, Everett F.
12	Dayton	E(B)	L			28	5	Blackburn, L. Thomas
	North Carolina State	E(A)	A			24	10	Case, Everett N.
	Oklahoma City	W(B)	L			19	8	Parrack, Doyle K.
	Texas Christian	W(A)	A			24	4	Brannon, Byron A. "Buster"
16	California: Los Angeles	W(B)	A			20	12	Wooden, John R.
	New Mexico State	W(A)	A			22	11	McCarty, George C.
	Pennsylvania State	E(A)	L			20	6	Gross, Elmer A.
	Princeton	E(B)	A			16	11	Cappon, Franklin C. "Cappy"

1953

F	School	SD	Reg	BD	Bye	W	L	Coach
1	Indiana	E(B)	A	To R16		23	3	McCracken, E. Branch
2	Kansas	W(B)	A	To R16		19	6	Allen, Dr. Forrest C. "Phog"
3	Washington	W(A)	A	To R16		28	3	Dye, William H. H. "Tippy"
4	Louisiana State	E(A)	A	To R16		22	3	Rabenhorst, Harry A.
8	Holy Cross (MA)	E(A)	L			20	6	Sheary, Lester H. "Buster"
	Notre Dame (IN)	E(B)	L			19	5	Jordan, John J.
	Oklahoma State	W(B)	A	To R16		23	7	Iba, Henry P. "Hank"
	Santa Clara	W(A)	L			20	7	Feerick, Robert J.
12	Pennsylvania	E(B)	A	To R16		22	5	Dallmar, Howard "Howie"
	Seattle	W(A)	L			28	4	Brightman, Horace Albert "Al"
	Texas Christian	W(B)	A	To R16		15	8	Brannon, Byron A. "Buster"
	Wake Forest	E(A)	A	To R16		22	7	Greason, Murray
16	De Paul	E(B)	L			19	9	Meyer, Raymond J.
	Lebanon Valley	E(A)	L			19	3	Marquette, George R. "Rinso"
	Oklahoma City	W(B)	L	To R16		18	6	Parrack, Doyle K.
	Wyoming	W(A)	A	To R16		20	10	Shelton, Everett F.
22	Eastern Kentucky	E(B)	L			16	9	McBrayer, Paul S.
	Fordham	E(A)	L			18	8	Bach, John W. "Johhny"
	Hardin-Simmons	W(A)	A			19	12	Scott, Bill
	Idaho State	W(A)	A			18	7	Belko, Steven
	Miami (OH)	E(B)	A			17	6	Rohr, William D.
	Navy	E(A)	L			16	5	Carnevale, Bernard L. "Ben"

1954

F	School	SD	Reg	BD	Bye	W	L	Coach
1	La Salle	E(B)	L			26	4	Loeffler, Kenneth D.
2	Bradley	W(A)	L			19	13	Anderson, Forrest A. "Forddy"
3	Pennsylvania State	E(A)	L			18	6	Gross, Elmer A.
4	Southern California	W(B)	A	To R16		19	14	Twogood, Forrest F.

F	School	SD	Reg	BD	Bye	W	L	Coach
8	Navy	W(B)	L			18	8	Carnevale, Bernard L. "Ben"
	Notre Dame (IN)	W(A)	L			22	3	Jordan, John J.
	Oklahoma State	E(A)	A	To R16		24	5	Iba, Henry P. "Hank"
	Santa Clara	E(B)	L			20	7	Feerick, Robert J.
12	Idaho State	W(B)	A			22	5	Belko, Steven
	Indiana	E(A)	A	To R16		20	4	McCracken, E. Branch
	North Carolina State	E(B)	A			26	7	Case, Everett N.
	Rice	W(A)	A	To R16		23	5	Suman, Donald W.
16	Colorado	W(A)	A	To R16		11	11	Lee, Horace B. "Bebe"
	Colorado State	W(B)	A	To R16		22	7	Strannigan, William M.
	Cornell (NY)	E(B)	A	To R16		17	7	Greene, Royner C.
	Louisiana State	E(A)	A	To R16		20	5	Rabenhorst, Harry A.
24	Connecticut	E(B)	A			23	3	Greer, Hugh S.
	Fordham	E(B)	L			18	6	Bach, John W. "Johnny"
	George Washington	E(B)	A			23	3	Reinhart, William J.
	Loyola New Orleans	E(A)	L			15	9	McCafferty, James J.
	Oklahoma City	W(A)	L			18	7	Parrack, Doyle K.
	Seattle	W(B)	L			26	2	Brightman, Horace Albert "Al"
	Texas Tech	W(B)	A			20	5	Robison, Polk F.
	Toledo	E(A)	A			13	10	Bush, Gerald "Jerry"

1955

F	School	SD	Reg	BD	Bye	W	L	Coach
1	San Francisco	W(B)	L			28	1	Woolpert, Philip D.
2	La Salle	E(B)	L			26	5	Loeffler, Kenneth D.
3	Colorado	W(A)	A	To R16		19	6	Lee, Horace B. "Bebe"
4	Iowa	E(A)	A	To R16		19	7	O'Connor, Frank "Bucky"
8	Bradley	W(A)	L			9	20	Vanatta, Robert
	Canisius	E(B)	A			18	7	Curran, J. Joseph
	Marquette	E(A)	L			24	3	Nagle, Joel "Jack"
	Oregon State	W(B)	A	To R16		22	8	Gill, Amory T. "Slats"
12	Kentucky	E(A)	A	To R16		23	3	Rupp, Adolph F.
	Tulsa	W(A)	A	To R16		21	7	Iba, Clarence V.
	Utah	W(B)	A	To R16		24	4	Gardner, James H. "Jack"
	Villanova	E(B)	L			18	10	Severance, Alexander G.
16	Pennsylvania State	E(A)	L			18	10	Egli, John S.
	Princeton	E(B)	A	To R16		13	12	Cappon, Franklin C. "Cappy"
	Seattle	W(B)	L			22	7	Brightman, Horace Albert "Al"
	Southern Methodist (TX)	W(A)	A	To R16		15	10	Hayes, Elmore O. "Doc"
24	Duke	E(B)	A			20	8	Bradley, Harold L.
	Idaho State	W(B)	A			18	8	Belko, Steven
	Memphis	E(A)	L			17	5	Lambert, Dr. Eugene W.
	Miami (OH)	E(A)	A			14	9	Rohr, William D.
	Oklahoma City	W(A)	L			9	18	Parrack, Doyle K.
	West Texas A&M	W(B)	A			15	7	Miller, W. A. "Gus"
	West Virginia	E(B)	A			19	11	Schaus, Frederick A.
	Williams	E(B)	L			14	4	Shaw, Alex J.

F	School	SD	Reg	BD	Bye	W	L	Coach
1956								
1	San Francisco	FW	A	To R16		29	0	Woolpert, Philip D.
2	Iowa	MW	A	To R16		20	6	O'Connor, Frank "Bucky"
3	Temple	E	L			27	4	Litwack, Harry
4	Southern Methodist (TX)	W	A			25	4	Hayes, Elmore O. "Doc"
8	Canisius	E	L			19	7	Curran, J. Joseph
	Kentucky	MW	A	To R16		20	6	Rupp, Adolph F.
	Oklahoma City	W	L			20	7	Lemons, A. E. "Abe"
	Utah	FW	A	To R16		22	6	Gardner, James H. "Jack"
12	California: Los Angeles	FW	A	To R16		22	6	Wooden, John R.
	Dartmouth	E	A			18	11	Julian, Alvin F. "Doggie"
	Kansas State	W	A	To R16		17	8	Winter, Fred "Tex"
	Morehead State (KY)	MW	A			19	10	Laughlin, Robert
16	Connecticut	E	A			17	11	Greer, Hugh S.
	Houston	W	A	To R16		19	7	Pasche, Alden
	Seattle	FW	L			18	11	Brightman, Horace Albert "Al"
	Wayne State (MI)	MW	L			18	3	Mason, Joel G.
25	De Paul	MW	L			16	8	Meyer, Raymond J.
	Holy Cross (MA)	E	L			22	5	Leenig, Roy H.
	Idaho State	FW	A			18	8	Belko, Steven
	Manhattan	E	L			16	8	Norton, Kenneth A.
	Marshall	MW	A			18	5	Rivlin, Jule
	Memphis	W	L			20	7	Lambert, Dr. Eugene W.
	North Carolina State	E	A			24	4	Case, Everett N.
	Texas Tech	W	A			13	12	Robison, Polk F.
	West Virginia	E	A			21	9	Schaus, Frederick A.
1957 DIVISION I								
1	North Carolina	E	A			32	0	McGuire, Frank J.
2	Kansas	W	A	To R16		24	3	Harp, Richard
3	San Francisco	W	A	To R16		21	7	Woolpert, Philip D.
4	Michigan State	ME	A	To R16		16	10	Anderson, Forrest A. "Forddy"
8	California	W	A	To R16		21	5	Newell, Peter F.
	Kentucky	ME	A	To R16		23	5	Rupp, Adolph F.
	Oklahoma City	MW	L			19	9	Lemons, A. E. "Abe"
	Syracuse	E	L			18	7	Guley, Marcel "Marc"
12	Brigham Young	W	A	To R16		19	9	Watts, Stanley H.
	Canisius	E	L			22	6	Curran, J. Joseph
	Notre Dame (IN)	ME	L			20	8	Jordan, John J.
	Southern Methodist (TX)	MW	A	To R16		22	4	Hayes, Elmore O. "Doc"
16	Idaho State	W	A			25	4	Grayson, John A.
	Lafayette (PA)	E	L	To R16		22	5	Davidson, George E.
	Pittsburgh	ME	L			16	11	Timmons, Robert W.
	Saint Louis	MW	A	To R16		19	9	Hickey, Edgar S. "Eddie"
23	Connecticut	E	A			17	8	Greer, Hugh S.
	Hardin-Simmons	W	A			17	9	Scott, Bill
	Loyola New Orleans	MW	L			14	12	McCafferty, James J.
	Miami (OH)	ME	A			17	8	Rohr, William D.
	Morehead State (KY)	ME	A			19	8	Laughlin, Robert
	West Virginia	E	A			25	5	Schaus, Frederick A.
	Yale	E	L			18	8	Vancisin, Joseph R.

F	School	SD	Reg	BD	Bye	W	L	Coach
1957 Division II								
1	Wheaton (IL)	MW	A			28	1	Pfund, Leroy H. "Lee"
2	Kentucky Wesleyan	ME	L			16	12	Wilson, Robert R. "Bullet"
3	Mount Saint Mary's (MD)	E	A			27	5	Phelan, James J.
4	California State: Los Angeles	FW	L			20	11	Elliott, Abe "Sax"
8	Buffalo State University	ME	L			18	7	Serfustini, Dr. Leonard T.
	Rider	E	L			20	7	Leyden, Thomas A.
	San Diego State	FW	A			17	10	Ziegenfuss, Dr. George
	South Dakota	MW	A			19	4	Clodfelter, Duane
16	Beloit	MW	L			17	6	Stanley, Dolph
	East Tennessee State	ME	L			18	10	Brooks, John Madison
	Evansville	ME	L			18	8	McCutchan, Arad A.
	Jackson State (MS)	MW	A			22	2	Wilson, Dr. Harrison B.
	Linfield	FW	L			17	11	Helser, Roy
	North Carolina Central	E	A			21	6	Brown, Floyd H.
	Regis (CO)	FW	L			15	10	Moore, Harvey E.
	Saint Michael's (VT)	E	L			17	6	Jacobs, George W. "Doc"
32	Amherst	E	L			17	4	Wilson, Richard E. "Rick"
	Capital	ME	A			14	6	Regan, Harold E.
	Centenary (LA)	ME	L			16	9	Mooty, Harold D.
	Chapman	FW	L			16	11	Perkins, Donald C.
	City College	E	L			11	8	Polansky, David
	DePauw	ME	L			12	9	Luther, Calvin C.
	Drexel	E	A			14	3	Cozen, Samuel D.
	Florida A&M	E	A			25	6	Oglesby, Edward E. "Rock"
	Illinois State	ME	A			14	13	Goff, James "Pim"
	Minnesota: Duluth	MW	L			15	7	Olson, Norman H.
	Monmouth (IL)	MW	A			18	5	Larson, Charles
	Nevada	FW	A			16	8	Lawlor, Glenn J. "Jake"
	Pacific (OR)	FW	L			12	12	Adams, Vic
	Philander Smith	MW	L			12	14	Hearnton, W. C., Sr.
	Wartburg	FW	L			19	8	Bundgaard, Dr. Alex C. "Ax"
	Wisconsin: Superior	MW	L			13	9	Vergamini, Carl
1958 Division I								
1	Kentucky	ME	A	To R16		23	6	Rupp, Adolph F.
2	Seattle	W	L			23	6	Castellani, John
3	Temple	E	L	To R16		27	3	Litwack, Harry
4	Kansas State	MW	A	To R16		22	5	Winter, Fred "Tex"
8	California	W	A	To R16		19	9	Newell, Peter F.
	Dartmouth	E	L			22	5	Julian, Alvin F. "Doggie"
	Notre Dame (IN)	ME	L			24	5	Jordan, John J.
	Oklahoma State	MW	L			21	8	Iba, Henry P. "Hank"
12	Cincinnati	MW	A	To R16		25	3	Smith, George D.
	Indiana	ME	A	To R16		13	11	McCracken, E. Branch
	Maryland	E	A			22	7	Millikan, Harry A. "Bud"
	San Francisco	W	A	To R16		25	2	Woolpert, Philip D.
16	Arkansas	MW	A	To R16		17	10	Rose, Glen
	Idaho State	W	A			22	6	Grayson, John A.
	Manhattan	E	A			16	10	Norton, Kenneth A.
	Miami (OH)	ME	A			18	9	Shrider, Richard G.

F	School	SD	Reg	BD	Bye	W	L	Coach
24	Arizona State		W	A		13	13	Wulk, Ned W.
	Boston College		E	L		15	6	Martin, Donald
	Connecticut		E	A		17	10	Greer, Hugh S.
	Loyola New Orleans		MW	L		16	9	Harding, James F.
	Pittsburgh		ME	L		18	7	Timmons, Robert W.
	Tennessee Tech		ME	A		17	9	Oldham, John O.
	West Virginia		E	A		26	2	Schaus, Frederick A.
	Wyoming		W	A		13	14	Shelton, Everett F.

1958 DIVISION II

F	School	SD	Reg	BD	Bye	W	L	Coach
1	South Dakota		MW			22	5	Clodfelter, Duane
2	Saint Michael's (VT)		NE			19	5	Jacobs, George W. "Doc"
3	Evansville		ME			23	4	McCutchan, Arad A.
4	Wheaton (IL)		GL			27	3	Pfund, Leroy H. "Lee"
8	American		E			22	6	Carrasco, David L.
	Chapman		PC	L		22	5	Perkins, Donald C.
	Grambling State		SC			27	4	Hobdy, Frederick C.
	Southwest Missouri State		SW			22	2	Matthews, Edwin "Eddie"
16	Adelphi		NE			18	8	Faherty, George E.
	Akron		ME			20	6	Beichly, Russell J.
	California State: Fresno		PC			19	8	Vandenburgh, William G.
	Hope		GL			19	3	DeVette, Russell B.
	Knox		MW			17	7	Adams, Frank E.
	North Carolina A&T		SC			21	4	Irvin, Calvin C.
	Regis (CO)		SW	L		14	9	Moore, Harvey E.
	Wagner		E			18	9	Sutter, Herbert E.
24	Arkansas State		SW	L		18	9	Rauth, John H.
	Brandeis		NE	L		18	4	Stein, Harvey
	Buffalo State University		E	L		17	8	Serfustini, Dr. Leonard T.
	California State: Chico		PC			10	17	Maxey, Gene
	Northern Illinois		GL	L		10	12	Healey, Dr. William A.
	South Carolina State		SC	L		18	9	Martin, Edward A.
	Wabash		ME	L		12	9	Brock, Bob L.
	Wartburg		MW	L		16	9	Bundgaard, Dr. Alex C. "Ax"
32	Austin Peay State		ME			17	9	Aaron, David B.
	Centenary (LA)		SW	L		13	10	Mooty, Harold D.
	Gustavus Adolphus		MW	L		15	11	Skoog, Myer U. "Whitey"
	Linfield		PC			18	9	Helser, Roy
	Philadelphia Textiles		E			17	7	Harris, Walter "Bucky"
	Philander Smith		SC	L		14	10	
	Rensselaer		NE	L		14	6	Kalbaugh, R. William, Sr.
	Saint Norbert		GL	L		14	11	Nicks, Mel J.

1959 DIVISION I

F	School	SD	Reg	BD	Bye	W	L	Coach
1	California		W	A	To R16	25	4	Newell, Peter F.
2	West Virginia		E	A		29	5	Schaus, Frederick A.
3	Cincinnati		MW	A	To R16	26	4	Smith, George D.
4	Louisville		ME	L		19	12	Hickman, Bernard L. "Peck"
8	Boston University		E	L		20	7	Zunic, Matthew
	Kansas State		MW	A	To R16	25	2	Winter, Fred "Tex"
	Michigan State		ME	A	To R16	19	4	Anderson, Forrest A. "Forddy"
	Saint Mary's (CA)		W	A	To R16	19	6	Weaver, James

F	School	SD	Reg	BD	Bye	W	L	Coach
12	Idaho State	W	A			21	7	Grayson, John A.
	Kentucky	ME	A	To R16		24	3	Rupp, Adolph F.
	Navy	E	L			18	6	Carnevale, Bernard L. "Ben"
	Texas Christian	MW	A	To R16		20	6	Brannon, Byron A. "Buster"
16	De Paul	MW	L			13	11	Meyer, Raymond J.
	Marquette	ME	L			23	6	Hickey, Edgar S. "Eddie"
	Saint Joseph's (PA)	E	A	To R16		22	5	Ramsay, Dr. John T. "Jack"
	Utah	W	A	To R16		21	7	Gardner, James H. "Jack"
23	Bowling Green State	ME	A			18	8	Anderson, W. Harold "Andy"
	Connecticut	E	A			17	7	Greer, Hugh S.
	Dartmouth	E	L			22	6	Julian, Alvin F. "Doggie"
	Eastern Kentucky	ME	A			16	6	McBrayer, Paul S.
	New Mexico State	W	A			17	11	Askew, Presley
	North Carolina	E	A			20	5	McGuire, Frank J.
	Portland	MW	L			19	8	Negratti, Dr. Albert E.

1959 Division II

F	School	SD	Reg	BD	Bye	W	L	Coach
1	Evansville	ME	L			21	6	McCutchan, Arad A.
2	Southwest Missouri State	SW				23	3	Matthews, Edwin "Eddie"
3	North Carolina A&T	SC				26	4	Irvin, Calvin C.
4	California State: Los Angeles	PC				20	8	Elliott, Abe "Sax"
8	American	E				22	7	Carrasco, David L.
	Hope	GL				20	3	DeVette, Russell B.
	Saint Michael's (VT)	NE				19	7	Jacobs, George W. "Doc"
	South Dakota State	MW				17	7	Iverson, James
16	Centenary (LA)	SW	L			14	14	Sigler, Orvis
	Chapman	PC	L			23	4	Perkins, Donald C.
	Florida A&M	SC				15	3	Oglesby, Edward E. "Rock"
	Hofstra	E				20	7	Van Breda Kolff, Willem "Butch"
	Knox	MW				20	3	Adams, Frank E.
	Le Moyne	NE				18	6	Niland, Thomas J., Jr.
	Wheaton (IL)	GL				23	4	Pfund, Leroy H. "Lee"
	Wittenberg	ME				19	3	Mears, Ramon "Ray"
24	Abilene Christian	SW	L			20	7	Nutt, Dee
	Adelphi	E				22	6	Faherty, George E.
	Belmont Abbey	ME	L			21	2	McGuire, Alfred J.
	Buffalo State University	NE	L			16	7	Serfustini, Dr. Leonard T.
	Lincoln (MO)	SC	L			14	9	Frank, James
	Wabash	GL	L			11	8	Brock, Bob L.
	Wartburg	MW				21	5	Bundgaard, Dr. Alex C. "Ax"
	Willamette	PC				18	9	Lewis, John R.
32	Augustana (IL)	MW	L			12	12	Kallis, Lenny
	California State: Sacramento	PC				12	12	Wolf, Harold
	Loras	GL	L			17	7	Dowd, Vincent J.
	Southern Illinois	ME	L			18	8	Gallatin, Harry J.
	Tuskegee	SC	L			13	9	Owen, Ross C.
	Wesleyan (CT)	E				13	5	Wood, John L.
	Western Illinois	SW	L			16	11	Morley, Leroy "Stix"
	Williams	NE	L			15	9	Shaw, Alex J.

F	School	SD	Reg	BD	Bye	W	L	Coach
1960 Division I								
1	Ohio State	ME	A	To R16		25	3	Taylor, Fred R.
2	California	W	L			28	2	Newell, Peter F.
3	Cincinnati	MW	A	To R16		28	2	Smith, George D.
4	New York	E	L			22	5	Rossini, Lucio 'Lou'
8	Duke	E	A			17	11	Bubas, Victor A.
	Georgia Tech	ME	A	To R16		22	6	Hyder, John C. 'Whack'
	Kansas	MW	A	To R16		19	9	Harp, Richard
	Oregon	W	L			19	10	Belko, Steven
12	De Paul	MW	L			17	7	Meyer, Raymond J.
	Utah	W	A			26	3	Gardner, James H. 'Jack'
	West Virginia	ME	A			26	5	Schaus, Frederick A.
	Western Kentucky	ME	A			21	7	Diddle, Edgar A., Sr.
16	Ohio University	ME	A			16	8	Snyder, James E.
	Saint Joseph's (PA)	E	A	To R16		20	7	Ramsay, Dr. John T. 'Jack'
	Santa Clara	W	A	To R16		21	10	Feerick, Robert J.
	Texas	MW	A	To R16		18	8	Bradley, Harold L.
25	Air Force	MW	L			12	10	Spear, Robert
	Connecticut	E	A			17	9	Greer, Hugh S.
	Idaho State	W	L			21	5	Evans, John P.
	Miami (FL)	ME	L			23	4	Hale, William Bruce
	Navy	E	L			16	6	Carnevale, Bernard L. 'Ben'
	New Mexico State	W	A			20	7	Askew, Presley
	Notre Dame (IN)	ME	L			17	9	Jordan, John J.
	Princeton	E	L			15	9	Cappon, Franklin C. 'Cappy'
	Southern California	W	L			16	11	Twogood, Forrest F.
1960 Division II								
1	Evansville	ME				25	4	McCutchan, Arad A.
2	Chapman	PC	L			24	6	Perkins, Donald C.
3	Kentucky Wesleyan	SC	L			18	11	Plain, T. L.
4	Cornell (IA)	MW				16	6	Maaske, Paul M.
8	American	E				22	7	Carrasco, David L.
	Saint Michael's (VT)	NE				13	10	Jacobs, George W. 'Doc'
	Truman State (MO)	SW				19	5	King, W. Boyd
	Wheaton (IL)	GL	L			16	10	Pfund, Leroy H. 'Lee'
16	Abilene Christian	SW	L			16	12	Nutt, Dee
	Austin Peay State	SC				22	5	Aaron, David B.
	California State: Fresno	PC				18	10	Vandenburgh, William G.
	Fairfield	E				17	9	Bisacca, George R.
	Lincoln (MO)	GL				14	9	Frank, James
	Prairie View A&M	MW	L			21	5	Moore, Dr. Leroy G., Jr.
	Saint Anselm	NE	L			15	4	Grenert, Albert F.
	Wabash	ME	L			13	7	Brock, Bob L.
24	Assumption (MA)	NE	L			14	6	Laska, Andrew
	Belmont Abbey	SC	L			19	6	McGuire, Alfred J.
	Buffalo State University	ME	L			16	7	Serfustini, Dr. Leonard T.
	Lamar	SW	L			18	9	Martin, Jack T.

F	School	SD	Reg	BD	Bye	W	L	Coach
	South Dakota State	MW				17	7	Iverson, James
	Trinity (TX)	PC	L			18	9	Robinson, Leslie W.
	Upsala	E	L			19	8	Wieboldt, Frederick W.
	Wisconsin: Milwaukee	GL				18	4	Rebholz, Russ
32	Arkansas State	ME	L			14	13	Rauth, John H.
	Augustana (IL)	GL	L			14	10	Kallis, Lenny
	Colorado College	SW	L			17	5	Eastlack, Leon C. "Red"
	Drexel	E				12	8	Cozen, Samuel D.
	Johnson C Smith	SC				18	7	McGirt, Edward C.
	Le Moyne	NE				13	5	Niland, Thomas J., Jr.
	San Francisco State	PC				12	14	Rundell, Paul
	Wartburg	MW				18	7	Bundgaard, Dr. Alex C. "Ax"

1961 Division I

F	School	SD	Reg	BD	Bye	W	L	Coach
1	Cincinnati	MW	A	To R16		27	3	Jucker, Edwin L.
2	Ohio State	ME	A	To R16		27	1	Taylor, Fred R.
3	Saint Joseph's (PA)	E	A	To R16		25	5	Ramsay, Dr. John T. "Jack"
4	Utah	W	A	To R16		23	8	Gardner, James H. "Jack"
8	Arizona State	W	A			23	6	Wulk, Ned W.
	Kansas State	MW	A	To R16		22	5	Winter, Fred "Tex"
	Kentucky	ME	A	To R16		19	9	Rupp, Adolph F.
	Wake Forest	E	A			19	11	McKinney, Horace A. "Bones"
12	Louisville	ME	L			21	8	Hickman, Bernard L. "Peck"
	Loyola Marymount	W	A	To R16		20	7	Arndt, John C.
	Saint Bonaventure	E	L			24	4	Donovan, Edward J. "Eddie"
	Texas Tech	MW	A	To R16		15	10	Robison, Polk F.
16	Houston	MW	L			17	11	Lewis, Guy V.
	Morehead State (KY)	ME	A			19	12	Laughlin, Robert
	Princeton	E	L			18	8	McCandles, J. L. "Jake"
	Southern California	W	A			21	8	Twogood, Forrest F.
24	George Washington	E	A			9	17	Reinhart, William J.
	Marquette	MW	L			16	11	Hickey, Edgar S. "Eddie"
	Ohio University	ME	A			17	7	Snyder, James E.
	Oregon	W	L			15	12	Belko, Steven
	Rhode Island	E	A			18	9	Calverley, Ernest A.
	Saint John's (NY)	E	L			20	5	Lapchick, Joseph B.
	Seattle	W	L			18	8	Cazzetta, Vincent C.
	Xavier (OH)	ME	L			17	10	McCafferty, James J.

1961 Division II

F	School	SD	Reg	BD	Bye	W	L	Coach
1	Wittenberg	ME				25	4	Mears, Ramon "Ray"
2	Southeast Missouri State	SW				25	3	Parsley, Charles H., Sr.
3	South Dakota State	MW				21	6	Iverson, James
4	Mount Saint Mary's (MD)	E				26	5	Phelan, James J.
8	Austin Peay State	SC	L			22	9	Aaron, David B.
	California: Santa Barbara	PC				20	8	Gallon, Dr. Arthur J.
	Chicago	GL	L			19	4	Stampf, Joseph M.
	Williams	NE				22	3	Shaw, Alex J.
16	Albright	E				19	9	Renken, Dr. Wilbur G.
	Bates	NE	L			15	9	Peck, Robert R.
	Belmont Abbey	SC	L			17	7	McGuire, Alfred J.
	California State: Long Beach	PC	L			15	11	Perry, Richard H.

F	School	SD	Reg	BD	Bye	W	L	Coach
	Lincoln (MO)		GL	L		20	8	Frank, James
	Prairie View A&M		MW			25	2	Moore, Dr. Leroy G., Jr.
	Southern Illinois		SW			21	6	Gallatin, Harry J.
	Wabash		ME	L		15	7	Brock, Bob L.
24	Chapman		PC	L		17	11	Perkins, Donald C.
	Cornell (IA)		MW			17	6	Maaske, Paul M.
	Evansville		GL	L		11	16	McCutchan, Arad A.
	Kentucky Wesleyan		SC	L		15	8	Plain, T. L.
	Rochester (NY)		NE	L		17	6	Brown, Lyle D.
	Trinity (TX)		SW	L		20	6	Robinson, Leslie W.
	Virginia Union		E	L		23	6	Harris, Thomas H.
	Youngstown State		ME	L		21	7	Rosselli, Dominic L. "Dom"
32	Colorado College		SW			18	9	Eastlack, Leon C. "Red"
	Fairfield		E			17	7	Bisacca, George R.
	MacMurray		GL	L		18	9	Wall, William L.
	Nevada		PC			13	7	Spencer, Jackson
	South Carolina State		ME			23	7	Martin, Edward A.
	Springfield (MA)		NE	L		16	10	Steitz, Dr. Edward S.
	Tennessee: Chattanooga		SC			17	8	Bartlett, Thomas G. "Tommy"
	Wisconsin: Superior		MW	L		15	8	Vergamini, Carl

1962 Division I

F	School	SD	Reg	BD	Bye	W	L	Coach
1	Cincinnati		MW	A	To R16	29	2	Jucker, Edwin L.
2	Ohio State		ME	A	To R16	26	2	Taylor, Fred R.
3	Wake Forest		E	A		22	9	McKinney, Horace A. "Bones"
4	California: Los Angeles		W	A	To R16	18	11	Wooden, John R.
8	Colorado		MW	A	To R16	19	7	Walseth, Russell M. "Sox"
	Kentucky		ME	A	To R16	23	3	Rupp, Adolph F.
	Oregon State		W	L		24	5	Gill, Amory T. "Slats"
	Villanova		E	L		21	7	Kraft, John J. "Jack"
12	Butler (IN)		ME	L		22	6	Hinkle, Paul D. "Tony"
	Creighton		MW	L		21	5	McManus, John J. "Red"
	New York		E	L		20	5	Rossini, Lucio "Lou"
	Pepperdine		W	A	To R16	20	7	Dowell, Robert L. "Duck"
16	Saint Joseph's (PA)		E	A	To R16	18	10	Ramsay, Dr. John T. "Jack"
	Texas Tech		MW	A		19	8	Gibson, Eugene F.
	Utah State		W	A		22	7	Anderson, Ladell
	Western Kentucky		ME	A		17	10	Diddle, Edgar A., Sr.
25	Air Force		MW	L		16	7	Spear, Robert
	Arizona State		W	A		23	4	Wulk, Ned W.
	Bowling Green State		ME	A		21	4	Anderson, W. Harold "Andy"
	Detroit		ME	L		15	12	Calihan, Robert J.
	Massachusetts		E	A		15	9	Zunic, Matthew
	Memphis		MW	L		15	7	Vanatta, Robert
	Seattle		W	L		18	9	Cazzetta, Vincent C.
	West Virginia		E	A		24	6	King, George S., Jr.
	Yale		E	L		18	6	Vancisin, Joseph R.

F	School	SD	Reg	BD	Bye	W	L	Coach
1962 DIVISION II								
1	Mount Saint Mary's (MD)	E				24	6	Phelan, James J.
2	California State: Sacramento	PC				21	10	Shelton, Everett F.
3	Southern Illinois	SC				21	10	Gallatin, Harry J.
4	Nebraska Wesleyan	MW	L			20	8	Peterson, Dr. Irvin L.
8	Northeastern (MA)	NE	L			17	8	Dukeshire, Richard E.
	Southeast Missouri State	SW				18	7	Parsley, Charles H., Sr.
	Valparaiso	GL	L			17	8	Meadows, Dr. Paul
	Wittenberg	ME				21	5	Mears, Ramon "Ray"
16	Arkansas State	SW	L			17	7	Rauth, John H.
	California Polytechnic: Pomona	PC	L			17	8	Stull, Robert B. "Lefty"
	Concordia (IL)	GL	L			20	4	Spitz, Donald A.
	Evansville	SC	L			14	11	McCutchan, Arad A.
	Fairfield	NE				20	5	Bisacca, George R.
	Florida A&M	ME				26	1	Oglesby, Edward E. "Rock"
	Hofstra	E				24	4	Van Breda Kolff, Willem "Butch"
	Northern Iowa	MW				19	5	Stewart, Norman E.
24	Albright	E	L			18	10	Renken, Dr. Wilbur G.
	Hamline	MW	L			18	4	Hutton, Joseph W., Sr.
	Kentucky State	GL				16	10	Brown, James B.
	Lamar	SW				20	8	Martin, Jack T.
	North Carolina A&T	SC				20	7	Irvin, Calvin C.
	Saint Anselm	NE	L			17	4	Grenert, Albert F.
	Seattle Pacific	PC	L			20	7	Habegger, Lester N. "Gus"
	Youngstown State	ME	L			16	12	Rosselli, Dominic L. "Dom"
32	Abilene Christian	SW	L			16	12	Nutt, Dee
	California State: Fresno	PC				19	7	Miller, Harry E.
	Gannon	ME	L			16	9	McCluskey, Edward J.
	Grinnell	MW				18	4	Pfitsch, John A.
	Illinois State	GL	L			16	11	Collie, Dr. James E., Sr.
	Long Island: C W Post	E	L			16	6	Kaftan, Dr. George A.
	Rochester (NY)	NE	L			17	5	Brown, Lyle D.
	Union (TN)	SC	L			16	13	Russell, Jack L.
1963 DIVISION I								
1	Loyola (IL)	ME	L			29	2	Ireland, George M.
2	Cincinnati	MW	A	To R16		26	2	Jucker, Edwin L.
3	Duke	E	A	To R16		27	3	Bubas, Victor A.
4	Oregon State	W	L			22	9	Gill, Amory T. "Slats"
8	Arizona State	W	A			26	3	Wulk, Ned W.
	Colorado	MW	A	To R16		19	7	Walseth, Russell M. "Sox"
	Illinois	ME	A	To R16		20	6	Combes, Harry A.
	Saint Joseph's (PA)	E	A			23	5	Ramsay, Dr. John T. "Jack"
12	Mississippi State	ME	A	To R16		22	6	McCarthy, James H. "Babe"
	San Francisco	W	A	To R16		18	9	Peletta, Peter P.
	Texas	MW	A			20	7	Bradley, Harold L.
	West Virginia	E	A			23	8	King, George S., Jr.
16	Bowling Green State	ME	A			19	8	Anderson, W. Harold "Andy"
	California: Los Angeles	W	A	To R16		20	9	Wooden, John R.
	New York	E	L			18	5	Rossini, Lucio "Lou"
	Oklahoma City	MW	L			19	10	Lemons, A. E. "Abe"

F	School	SD	Reg	BD	Bye	W	L	Coach
25	Colorado State	MW	L			18	5	Williams, James J.
	Connecticut	E	A			18	7	Shabel, Fred A.
	Notre Dame (IN)	ME	L			17	9	Jordan, John J.
	Pittsburgh	E	L			19	6	Timmons, Robert W.
	Princeton	E	A			19	6	Van Breda Kolff, Willem "Butch"
	Seattle	W	L			21	6	Cazzetta, Vincent C.
	Tennessee Tech	ME	A			16	8	Oldham, John O.
	Texas: El Paso	MW	L			19	7	Haskins, Donald L.
	Utah State	W	L			20	7	Anderson, Ladell

1963 DIVISION II

F	School	SD	Reg	BD	Bye	W	L	Coach
1	South Dakota State	MW				22	5	Iverson, James
2	Wittenberg	ME				26	2	Miller, Eldon
3	Oglethorpe	SC	L			21	7	Pinholster, Garland F.
4	Southern Illinois	SW	L			20	10	Hartman, Jack
8	California State: Fresno	PC				20	8	Miller, Harry E.
	Evansville	GL				21	6	McCutchan, Arad A.
	Northeastern (MA)	NE	L			21	6	Dukeshire, Richard E.
	Philadelphia Textiles	E	L			21	3	Harris, Walter "Bucky"
16	Bloomsburg	E	L			17	4	Foster, William E.
	Chapman	PC	L			20	7	Perkins, Donald C.
	Lamar	SW				22	5	Martin, Jack T.
	Nebraska Wesleyan	MW	L			23	4	Peterson, Dr. Irvin L.
	South Carolina State	ME				19	8	Martin, Edward A.
	Springfield (MA)	NE	L			20	6	Steitz, Dr. Edward S.
	Tennessee State	SC				22	6	Hunter, Harold
	Washington (MO)	GL				18	8	Smith, Charles G. "Chuck"
24	Arkansas State	SW	L			15	11	Rauth, John H.
	Assumption (MA)	NE	L			14	5	Laska, Andrew
	Bellarmine	SC				21	6	Groza, Alex J.
	California: Santa Barbara	PC	L			16	9	Gallon, Dr. Arthur J.
	Concordia (IL)	GL	L			19	5	Spitz, Donald A.
	Hofstra	E				23	7	Lynner, Paul K.
	Michigan Tech	MW				17	5	Cox, Verdie T.
	Youngstown State	ME	L			18	9	Rosselli, Dominic L. "Dom"
32	Augustana (IL)	GL				18	6	Kallis, Lenny
	Austin Peay State	SC	L			18	11	Fisher, George
	Buffalo State University	ME	L			16	7	Serfustini, Dr. Leonard T.
	Cornell (IA)	MW				16	7	Maaske, Paul M.
	Fairleigh Dickinson: Rutherford/Teaneck	NE				16	12	Holub, Richard
	Mount Saint Mary's (MD)	E				13	12	Phelan, James J.
	San Francisco State	PC				14	13	Rundell, Paul
	Southeast Missouri State	SW				21	4	Parsley, Charles H., Sr.

1964 DIVISION I

F	School	SD	Reg	BD	Bye	W	L	Coach
1	California: Los Angeles	W	A	To R16		30	0	Wooden, John R.
2	Duke	E	A	To R16		26	5	Bubas, Victor A.
3	Michigan	ME	A	To R16		23	5	Strack, David H.
4	Kansas State	MW	A	To R16		22	7	Winter, Fred "Tex"

F	School	SD	Reg	BD	Bye	W	L	Coach
8	Connecticut	E	A			16	11	Shabel, Fred A.
	Ohio University	ME	A			21	6	Snyder, James E.
	San Francisco	W	A	To R16		23	5	Peletta, Peter P.
	Wichita State	MW	A	To R16		23	6	Miller, Ralph H. "Cappy"
12	Loyola (IL)	ME	L			22	6	Ireland, George M.
	Seattle	W	L			22	6	Boyd, William R. "Bob"
	Texas: El Paso	MW	L			25	3	Haskins, Donald L.
	Villanova	E	L			24	4	Kraft, John J. "Jack"
16	Creighton	MW	L			22	7	McManus, John J. "Red"
	Kentucky	ME	A	To R16		21	6	Rupp, Adolph F.
	Princeton	E	A			20	9	Van Breda Kolff, Willem "Butch"
	Utah State	W	L			21	8	Anderson, Ladell
25	Arizona State	W	A			16	11	Wulk, Ned W.
	Louisville	ME	L			15	10	Hickman, Bernard L. "Peck"
	Murray State (KY)	ME	A			16	9	Luther, Calvin C.
	Oklahoma City	MW	L			15	11	Lemons, A. E. "Abe"
	Oregon State	W	L			25	4	Gill, Amory T. "Slats"
	Providence	E	L			20	6	Mullaney, Joseph A., Sr.
	Temple	E	A			17	8	Litwack, Harry
	Texas A&M	MW	A			18	7	Metcalf, Dr. Shelby R.
	Virginia Military	E	A			12	12	Miller, Louis F. "Weenie"

1964 DIVISION II

F	School	SD	Reg	BD	Bye	W	L	Coach
1	Evansville	GL				26	3	McCutchan, Arad A.
2	Akron	ME				24	7	Laterza, Anthony
3	North Carolina A&T	SC				23	7	Irvin, Calvin C.
4	Northern Iowa	MW				23	4	Stewart, Norman E.
8	Adelphi	NE				22	6	Faherty, George E.
	California Polytechnic: Pomona	PC	L			23	6	Stull, Robert B. "Lefty"
	Hofstra	E	L			23	6	Lynner, Paul K.
	Southeast Missouri State	SW				19	6	Parsley, Charles H., Sr.
16	Abilene Christian	SW	L			18	9	Nutt, Dee
	California State: Fresno	PC				20	5	Miller, Harry E.
	Elizabethtown	E				20	5	Smith, Donald P.
	Fisk	SC	L			18	6	Thompson, Herbert B. "Bus"
	Le Moyne	ME				18	6	Niland, Thomas J., Jr.
	Mankato State	MW	L			19	6	Morris, William
	Northeastern (MA)	NE	L			17	8	Dukeshire, Richard E.
	Southern Illinois	GL	L			14	8	Hartman, Jack
24	Assumption (MA)	NE	L			19	2	Laska, Andrew
	Jackson State (MS)	GL				21	6	Covington, Paul E.
	Kentucky Wesleyan	SC	L			15	8	Plain, T. L.
	Lamar	SW				19	6	Martin, Jack T.
	Philadelphia Textiles	E	L			18	6	Harris, Walter "Bucky"
	Seattle Pacific	PC	L			17	8	Habegger, Lester N. "Gus"
	Washington (MO)	MW	L			16	8	Smith, Charles G. "Chuck"
	Youngstown State	ME	L			24	3	Rosselli, Dominic L. "Dom"
32	Ball State	GL	L			19	8	Hinga, John "Jim"
	Catholic	E				16	12	Young, Thomas J.
	Centre	SC	L			14	8	Phillips, Lewis
	Ithaca	ME	L			16	5	Wood, Carlton

F	School	SD	Reg	BD	Bye	W	L	Coach
	Nebraska Wesleyan	MW	L			20	6	Peterson, Dr. Irvin L.
	Nevada	PC				14	13	Spencer, Jackson
	Northern Colorado	SW	L			18	8	Sage, Dr. George H.
	Springfield (MA)	NE	L			17	8	Steitz, Dr. Edward S.

1965 Division I

F	School	SD	Reg	BD	Bye	W	L	Coach
1	California: Los Angeles	FW	A	To R16		28	2	Wooden, John R.
2	Michigan	ME	A	To R16		24	4	Strack, David H.
3	Princeton	E	A			23	6	Van Breda Kolff, Willem "Butch"
4	Wichita State	MW	A	To R16		21	9	Thompson, Gary
8	Oklahoma State	MW	A	To R16		20	7	Iba, Henry P. "Hank"
	Providence	E	L			24	2	Mullaney, Joseph A., Sr.
	San Francisco	FW	A			24	5	Peletta, Peter P.
	Vanderbilt	ME	A	To R16		24	4	Skinner, Roy G.
12	Dayton	ME	L			22	7	Donoher, Donald J. "Mickey"
	North Carolina State	E	A	To R16		21	5	Maravich, Peter "Press"
	Oklahoma City	FW	L			21	10	Lemons, A. E. "Abe"
	Southern Methodist (TX)	MW	A	To R16		17	10	Hayes, Elmore O. "Doc"
16	Brigham Young	FW	A	To R16		21	7	Watts, Stanley H.
	De Paul	ME	L			17	10	Meyer, Raymond J.
	Houston	MW	L			19	10	Lewis, Guy V.
	Saint Joseph's (PA)	E	A			26	3	Ramsay, Dr. John T. "Jack"
23	Colorado State	FW	L			16	8	Williams, James J.
	Connecticut	E	A			23	3	Shabel, Fred A.
	Eastern Kentucky	ME	A			19	6	Baechtold, James E.
	Notre Dame (IN)	MW	L			15	12	Dee, John F., Jr.
	Ohio University	ME	A			19	7	Snyder, James E.
	Pennsylvania State	E	L			20	4	Egli, John S.
	West Virginia	E	A			14	15	King, George S., Jr.

1965 Division II

F	School	SD	Reg	BD	Bye	W	L	Coach
1	Evansville	SC				29	0	McCutchan, Arad A.
2	Southern Illinois	GL	L			20	6	Hartman, Jack
3	North Dakota	MW				26	5	Fitch, William C. "Billy"
4	Saint Michael's (VT)	NE				21	7	Markey, Edward P.
8	Akron	ME				21	7	Laterza, Anthony
	Philadelphia Textiles	E	L			22	4	Harris, Walter "Bucky"
	Seattle Pacific	PC	L			22	7	Habegger, Lester N. "Gus"
	Washington (MO)	SW				21	6	Smith, Charles G. "Chuck"
16	Abilene Christian	SW				17	9	Nutt, Dee
	Assumption (MA)	NE	L			16	6	Laska, Andrew
	Bellarmine	SC	L			15	8	Groza, Alex J.
	Buffalo State University	ME	L			19	3	Serfustini, Dr. Leonard T.
	California State: Fresno	PC				20	7	Miller, Harry E.
	Central Michigan	GL	L			19	7	Kjolhede, Theodore
	Long Island	E				16	7	Rubin, Roy
	Moorhead State (MN)	MW				21	4	MacLeod, Larry
24	Central Missouri State	SW				19	6	Hall, Joe B.
	Cheyney	E				24	1	Blitman, Howard
	Franciscan	ME	L			21	4	Bayer, John D. "Denny"
	Hartwick	NE	L			19	2	Coniam, Charles Jack

F	School	SD	Reg	BD	Bye	W	L	Coach
	Jackson State (MS)	GL	L			21	7	Wilson, Dr. Harrison B.
	Minnesota: Duluth	MW	L			20	8	Olson, Norman H.
	Norfolk State	SC				22	3	Fears, Ernest D., Jr.
	San Francisco State	PC				16	11	Rundell, Paul
32	Albright	E				20	8	Renken, Dr. Wilbur G.
	Bethune-Cookman	SC				18	6	McClairen, Jack "Cy"
	Concordia (IL)	GL	L			18	6	Faszholz, Thomas O.
	Doane	SW	L			16	9	Erickson, Robert
	Le Moyne	NE				18	5	Niland, Thomas J., Jr.
	Nevada: Las Vegas	PC	L			19	8	Gregory, Ed
	Northern Colorado	MW				19	8	Sage, Dr. George H.
	Randolph-Macon	ME				19	5	Webb, Paul E.

1966 DIVISION I

F	School	SD	Reg	BD	Bye	W	L	Coach
1	Texas: El Paso	MW	L			28	1	Haskins, Donald L.
2	Kentucky	ME	A	To R16		27	2	Rupp, Adolph F.
3	Duke	E	A	To R16		26	4	Bubas, Victor A.
4	Utah	W	A	To R16		23	8	Gardner, James H. "Jack"
8	Kansas	MW	A	To R16		23	4	Owens, Ted
	Michigan	ME	A	To R16		18	8	Strack, David H.
	Oregon State	W	A	To R16		21	7	Valenti, Paul B.
	Syracuse	E	L	To R16		22	6	Lewis, Frederick B., Jr.
12	Houston	W	L			23	6	Lewis, Guy V.
	Saint Joseph's (PA)	E	A			24	5	Ramsay, Dr. John T. "Jack"
	Southern Methodist (TX)	MW	A	To R16		17	9	Hayes, Elmore O. "Doc"
	Western Kentucky	ME	A			25	3	Oldham, John O.
16	Cincinnati	MW	A	To R16		21	7	Baker, Taylor "Tay"
	Davidson	E	A			21	7	Driesell, Charles G. "Lefty"
	Dayton	ME	L			23	6	Donoher, Donald J. "Mickey"
	Pacific (CA)	W	A	To R16		22	6	Edwards, Richard B.
22	Colorado State	W	L			14	8	Williams, James J.
	Loyola (IL)	ME	L			22	3	Ireland, George M.
	Miami (OH)	ME	A			18	7	Shrider, Richard G.
	Oklahoma City	MW	L			24	5	Lemons, A. E. "Abe"
	Providence	E	L			22	5	Mullaney, Joseph A., Sr.
	Rhode Island	E	A			20	8	Calverley, Ernest A.

1966 DIVISION II

F	School	SD	Reg	BD	Bye	W	L	Coach
1	Kentucky Wesleyan	SC	L	To R32		24	6	Strong, Guy Rowland
2	Southern Illinois	GL	L	To R32		22	7	Hartman, Jack
3	Akron	ME		To R32		24	4	Laterza, Anthony
4	North Dakota	MW		To R32		24	5	Fitch, William C. "Billy"
8	Abilene Christian	SW		To R32		21	7	Nutt, Dee
	California State: Fresno	PC		To R32		21	8	Gregory, Ed
	Central Connecticut State	NE	L			23	3	Detrick, William
	Long Island	E		To R32		22	4	Rubin, Roy
16	Assumption (MA)	NE	L			18	6	Laska, Andrew
	Cheyney	E		To R32		26	1	Blitman, Howard
	Evansville	GL		To R32		18	9	McCutchan, Arad A.
	Franciscan	ME	L	To R32		17	9	Bayer, John D. "Denny"

F	School	SD	Reg	BD	Bye	W	L	Coach
	Oglethorpe	SC	L		To R32	22	6	Pinholster, Garland F.
	Seattle Pacific	PC	L		To R32	23	5	Habegger, Lester N. "Gus"
	Southwest Missouri State	SW			To R32	19	6	Thomas, William J.
	Valparaiso	MW	L		To R32	19	9	Bartow, B. Gene
22	Albright	E			To R32	18	11	Renken, Dr. Wilbur G.
	Arkansas State	SW	L		To R32	17	9	Speight, Marvin
	Lamar	GL	L		To R32	17	9	Martin, Jack T.
	Nevada	PC			To R32	21	6	Spencer, Jackson
	Winston-Salem State	SC			To R32	21	5	Gaines, Clarence E. "Big House"
	Youngstown State	ME	L		To R32	19	7	Rosselli, Dominic L. "Dom"
32	Benedictine (IL)	MW	L		To R32	18	4	LaScala, Anthony
	Drexel	E	L		To R32	20	4	Cozen, Samuel D.
	Indiana State	GL			To R32	22	6	Klueh, Duane M.
	Jackson State (MS)	SW			To R32	24	7	Wilson, Dr. Harrison B.
	Northeastern (MA)	NE	L			18	8	Dukeshire, Richard E.
	Northern Colorado	MW			To R32	21	6	Sage, Dr. George H.
	Philadelphia Textiles	NE	L			20	6	McKinney, John P. "Jack"
	Randolph-Macon	ME			To R32	21	7	Webb, Paul E.
	San Diego	PC	L		To R32	17	11	Woolpert, Philip D.
	South Carolina State	SC			To R32	23	3	Martin, Edward A.
34	American International	NE	L			18	8	Callahan, William E.
	Le Moyne	NE	L			16	6	Niland, Thomas J., Jr.
36	Potsdam State	NE				16	5	LaGrand, Lou
	Springfield (MA)	NE	L			20	6	Steitz, Dr. Edward S.

1967 Division I

F	School	SD	Reg	BD	Bye	W	L	Coach
1	California: Los Angeles	W	A		To R16	30	0	Wooden, John R.
2	Dayton	ME	L			25	6	Donoher, Donald J. "Mickey"
3	Houston	MW	L			27	4	Lewis, Guy V.
4	North Carolina	E	A		To R16	26	6	Smith, Dean E.
8	Boston College	E	L			21	3	Cousy, Robert J.
	Pacific (CA)	W	A		To R16	24	4	Edwards, Richard B.
	Southern Methodist (TX)	MW	A		To R16	20	6	Hayes, Elmore O. "Doc"
	Virginia Polytechnic	ME	L			20	7	Shannon, Howard P. "Howie"
12	Indiana	ME	A		To R16	18	8	Watson, Lou
	Louisville	MW	A		To R16	23	5	Hickman, Bernard L. "Peck"
	Princeton	E	A			25	3	Van Breda Kolff, Willem "Butch"
	Texas: El Paso	W	L			22	6	Haskins, Donald L.
16	Kansas	MW	A		To R16	23	4	Owens, Ted
	Saint John's (NY)	E	L			23	5	Carnesecca, Louis P. "Lou"
	Tennessee	ME	A		To R16	21	7	Mears, Ramon "Ray"
	Wyoming	W	A		To R16	15	14	Strannigan, William M.
23	Connecticut	E	A			17	7	Shabel, Fred A.
	New Mexico State	MW	L			15	11	Henson, Louis R.
	Seattle	W	L			18	8	Purcell, Lionel
	Temple	E	A			20	8	Litwack, Harry
	Toledo	ME	A			23	2	Nichols, Robert J.
	West Virginia	E	A			19	9	Waters, Raymond C. "Bucky"
	Western Kentucky	ME	A			23	3	Oldham, John O.

F	School	SD	Reg	BD	Bye	W	L	Coach
1967 DIVISION II								
1	Winston-Salem State	ME			To R32	30	2	Gaines, Clarence E. "Big House"
2	Southwest Missouri State	SW			To R32	23	5	Thomas, William J.
3	Kentucky Wesleyan	SC		L	To R32	25	4	Strong, Guy Rowland
4	Illinois State	MW			To R32	18	13	Collie, Dr. James E., Sr.
8	Cheyney	E			To R32	23	7	Blitman, Howard
	Long Island	NE				22	7	Rubin, Roy
	San Diego State	PC			To R32	24	5	Ziegenfuss, Dr. George
	Valparaiso	GL		L	To R32	21	8	Bartow, B. Gene
16	Akron	ME		L	To R32	20	5	Laterza, Anthony
	Indiana State	GL			To R32	21	5	Klueh, Duane M.
	Lincoln (MO)	SW		L	To R32	24	3	Staggers, Jonathan L.
	Louisiana Tech	MW			To R32	20	8	Robertson, Robert "Scotty"
	Nevada: Las Vegas	PC		L	To R32	21	6	Todd, Rolland
	Philadelphia Textiles	E		L	To R32	20	7	McKinney, John P. "Jack"
	Saint Michael's (VT)	NE				23	4	Markey, Edward P.
	South Carolina State	SC			To R32	18	5	Martin, Edward A.
23	Arkansas State	SW			To R32	17	7	Speight, Marvin
	Baldwin-Wallace	ME			To R32	22	9	Thompson, Hugh
	California: Davis	PC			To R32	21	7	Carlson, Joe E.
	Luther	GL			To R32	16	8	Finanger, Kenton
	North Dakota	MW			To R32	20	6	Fitch, William C. "Billy"
	Tennessee State	SC			To R32	20	7	Hunter, Harold
	Wagner	E			To R32	19	9	Sellitto, Chester
32	Arkansas: Pine Bluff	SW			To R32	24	7	Clemmons, Hubert O.
	Assumption (MA)	NE	L			17	5	Laska, Andrew
	Central Connecticut State	NE	L			17	8	Detrick, William
	Drexel	E			To R32	13	10	Cozen, Samuel D.
	Mount Saint Mary's (MD)	ME			To R32	18	9	Phelan, James J.
	Parsons	MW	L		To R32	18	9	Nelson, Oscar B.
	Portland State	PC	L		To R32	16	9	Pericin, Marion J.
	Southern Colorado	GL	L		To R32	19	6	Simmons, Harry H.
	Stetson	SC			To R32	17	10	Wilkes, Dr. Glenn N., Sr.
34	Northeastern (MA)	NE	L			22	4	Dukeshire, Richard E.
	Rochester (NY)	NE	L			15	7	Brown, Lyle D.
36	American International	NE	L			19	6	Callahan, William E.
	Buffalo State College	NE				17	6	MacAdam, Howard B.
1968 DIVISION I								
1	California: Los Angeles	W	A		To R16	29	1	Wooden, John R.
2	North Carolina	E	A		To R16	28	4	Smith, Dean E.
3	Ohio State	ME	A		To R16	21	8	Taylor, Fred R.
4	Houston	MW	L			31	2	Lewis, Guy V.
8	Davidson	E	A			24	5	Driesell, Charles G. "Lefty"
	Kentucky	ME	A		To R16	22	5	Rupp, Adolph F.
	Santa Clara	W	A		To R16	22	4	Garibaldi, Richard A.
	Texas Christian	MW	A		To R16	15	11	Swaim, Johnny
12	Columbia (NY)	E	L			23	5	Rohan, John P. "Jack"
	Louisville	MW	A		To R16	21	7	Dromo, John
	Marquette	ME	L			23	6	McGuire, Alfred J.
	New Mexico State	W	L			23	6	Henson, Louis R.

F	School	SD	Reg	BD	Bye	W	L	Coach
16	East Tennessee State	ME	A			19	8	Brooks, John Madison
	Kansas State	MW	A		To R16	19	9	Winter, Fred "Tex"
	New Mexico	W	A		To R16	23	5	King, Bob
	Saint Bonaventure	E	L			23	2	Weise, Lawrence J.
23	Boston College	E	L			17	8	Cousy, Robert J.
	Bowling Green State	ME	A			18	7	Fitch, William C. "Billy"
	Florida State	ME	L			19	8	Durham, Hugh
	La Salle	E	A			20	8	Harding, James F.
	Loyola (IL)	MW	L			15	9	Ireland, George M.
	Saint John's (NY)	E	L			19	8	Carnesecca, Louis P. "Lou"
	Weber State	W	A			21	6	Motta, John R. "Dick"

1968 DIVISION II

F	School	SD	Reg	BD	Bye	W	L	Coach
1	Kentucky Wesleyan	SC	L		To R32	28	3	Daniels, Bob
2	Indiana State	GL			To R32	23	8	Stauffer, Gordon
3	Trinity (TX)	SW	L		To R32	23	7	Polk, James Robert "Bob"
4	Ashland	MW	L		To R32	24	6	Musselman, William
8	American International	NE	L			21	5	Callahan, William E.
	Cheyney	E	L		To R32	22	7	Blitman, Howard
	Evansville	MW	L		To R32	20	8	McCutchan, Arad A.
	Nevada: Las Vegas	PC	L		To R32	22	7	Todd, Rolland
16	Buffalo State College	NE				17	7	MacAdam, Howard B.
	California: Irvine	PC	L		To R32	20	8	Davis, Richard L.
	Illinois State	GL			To R32	25	3	Collie, Dr. James E., Sr.
	Norfolk State	ME			To R32	24	2	Fears, Ernest D., Jr.
	Southwest Missouri State	MW			To R32	19	6	Thomas, William J.
	Texas: Pan American	SW	L		To R32	21	6	Williams, Samuel
	Union (TN)	SC	L		To R32	22	3	Henry, Bill
	Wagner	E			To R32	21	8	Sellitto, Chester
23	Denison	ME			To R32	18	5	Scott, Richard S.
	Jackson State (MS)	SW			To R32	24	3	Covington, Paul E.
	Lincoln (MO)	MW	L		To R32	20	3	Staggers, Jonathan L.
	Oglethorpe	SC	L		To R32	21	6	Carter, Bill
	Philadelphia Textiles	E	L		To R32	21	6	Magee, Herbert
	San Diego State	PC			To R32	20	6	Ziegenfuss, Dr. George
	South Dakota State	GL			To R32	20	7	Marking, James
32	Bethune-Cookman	SC			To R32	24	7	McClairen, Jack "Cy"
	Bridgeport	NE	L			19	8	Webster, Bruce
	California: Davis	PC			To R32	16	11	Hamilton, Robert I.
	DePauw	GL			To R32	16	8	McCall, Elmer
	McNeese State	SW			To R32	20	5	Ward, Ralph O.
	Muhlenberg	E			To R32	14	11	Moyer, Kenneth T.
	Roanoke	ME			To R32	22	8	Moir, Charles
	Rochester (NY)	NE	L			13	8	Brown, Lyle D.
	Southern Colorado	MW	L		To R32	19	9	Simmons, Harry H.
34	Assumption (MA)	NE	L			15	7	O'Brien, Joseph M.
	Northeastern (MA)	NE	L			19	9	Dukeshire, Richard E.
36	Le Moyne	NE	L			14	8	Niland, Thomas J., Jr.
	Springfield (MA)	NE	L			17	9	Bilik, Dr. Edward R.

F	School	SD	Reg	BD	Bye	W	L	Coach
1969 Division I								
1	California: Los Angeles	W	A	To R16		29	1	Wooden, John R.
2	Purdue	ME	A	To R16		23	5	King, George S., Jr.
3	Drake (IA)	MW	A	To R16		26	5	John, Maurice E. 'Maury'
4	North Carolina	E	A	To R16		27	5	Smith, Dean E.
8	Colorado State	MW	L			17	7	Williams, James J.
	Davidson	E	A			27	3	Driesell, Charles G. 'Lefty'
	Marquette	ME	L			24	5	McGuire, Alfred J.
	Santa Clara	W	A	To R16		27	2	Garibaldi, Richard A.
12	Colorado	MW	A	To R16		21	7	Walseth, Russell M. 'Sox'
	Duquesne	E	L			21	5	Manning, John 'Red'
	Kentucky	ME	A	To R16		23	5	Rupp, Adolph F.
	Weber State	W	A			27	3	Johnson, Phil
16	Miami (OH)	ME	A			15	12	Locke, Taylor O. 'Tates'
	New Mexico State	W	L			24	5	Henson, Louis R.
	Saint John's (NY)	E	L			23	6	Carnesecca, Louis P. 'Lou'
	Texas A&M	MW	A			18	9	Metcalf, Dr. Shelby R.
25	Brigham Young	W	A			17	11	Watts, Stanley H.
	Dayton	MW	L			20	7	Donoher, Donald J. 'Mickey'
	Murray State (KY)	ME	A			22	6	Luther, Calvin C.
	Notre Dame (IN)	ME	L			20	7	Dee, John F., Jr.
	Princeton	E	A			19	7	Carril, Peter J.
	Saint Joseph's (PA)	E	A			17	11	McKinney, John P. 'Jack'
	Seattle	W	L			19	8	Buckwalter, Morris 'Bucky'
	Trinity (TX)	MW	L			19	5	Polk, James Robert 'Bob'
	Villanova	E	L			21	5	Kraft, John J. 'Jack'
1969 Division II								
1	Kentucky Wesleyan	S	L			25	5	Daniels, Bob
2	Southwest Missouri State	MW	L			24	5	Thomas, William J.
3	American International	NENG	L			21	4	Callahan, William E.
4	Ashland	MW	L			26	4	Musselman, William
8	Illinois State	GL	L			19	10	Collie, Dr. James E., Sr.
	Montclair State	E	L			24	3	Gelston, Oliver S. 'Ollie'
	Oglethorpe	SA	L			22	5	Carter, Bill
	San Francisco State	W	L			20	9	Rundell, Paul
16	Alcorn State	S	L			26	1	Hopkins, Robert M.
	Cheyney	MW	L			25	3	Coma, Dr. Anthony S. 'Doc'
	Mount Saint Mary's (MD)	SA	L			21	8	Phelan, James J.
	Nevada: Las Vegas	W	L			21	7	Todd, Rolland
	South Dakota State	MW	L			18	6	Marking, James
	Springfield (MA)	NENG	L			16	9	Bilik, Dr. Edward R.
	Valparaiso	GL	L			16	12	Bartow, B. Gene
	Wagner	E	L			18	10	Sellitto, Chester
24	Albany State (NY)	E	L			18	6	Sauers, Dr. Richard J.
	Assumption (MA)	NENG	L			17	7	O'Brien, Joseph M.
	California: Irvine	W	L			19	9	Davis, Richard L.
	Lincoln (MO)	MW	L			19	7	Staggers, Jonathan L.

F	School	SD	Reg	BD	Bye	W	L	Coach
	Norfolk State	SA	L			18	2	Fears, Ernest D., Jr.
	North Park	GL	L			21	5	McCarrell, Dan
	Philadelphia Textiles	MW	L			20	5	Magee, Herbert
	Transylvania	S	L			20	7	Rose, Lee H.
32	Bellarmine	S	L			19	9	Spalding, James R.
	California: Davis	W	L			18	10	Hamilton, Robert I.
	Central Connecticut State	NENG	L			20	8	Detrick, William
	Concordia (IL)	GL	L			20	4	Faszholz, Thomas O.
	Le Moyne	E	L			15	8	Niland, Thomas J., Jr.
	Old Dominion	SA	L			21	10	Allen, William "Sonny"
	Saint Olaf	MW	L			17	7	Gelle, Robert D.
	Wittenberg	MW	L			19	6	Miller, Eldon

1970 Division I

F	School	SD	Reg	BD	Bye	W	L	Coach
1	California: Los Angeles	W	A	To R16		28	2	Wooden, John R.
2	Jacksonville (FL)	ME	L			27	2	Williams, Joe L.
3	New Mexico State	MW	L			27	3	Henson, Louis R.
4	Saint Bonaventure	E	L			25	3	Weise, Lawrence J.
8	Drake (IA)	MW	A	To R16		22	7	John, Maurice E. "Maury"
	Kentucky	ME	A	To R16		26	2	Rupp, Adolph F.
	Utah State	W	L			22	7	Anderson, Ladell
	Villanova	E	L			22	7	Kraft, John J. "Jack"
12	Iowa	ME	A	To R16		20	5	Miller, Ralph H. "Cappy"
	Kansas State	MW	A	To R16		20	8	Fitzsimmons, Lowell "Cotton"
	North Carolina State	E	A	To R16		23	7	Sloan, Norman L., Jr.
	Santa Clara	W	A	To R16		23	6	Garibaldi, Richard A.
16	California State: Long Beach	W	L			24	5	Tarkanian, Jerry
	Houston	MW	L			25	5	Lewis, Guy V.
	Niagara	E	L			22	7	Layden, Frank P.
	Notre Dame (IN)	ME	L			21	8	Dee, John F., Jr.
25	Davidson	E	A			22	5	Holland, M. Terrance "Terry"
	Dayton	MW	L			19	8	Donoher, Donald J. "Mickey"
	Ohio University	ME	A			20	5	Snyder, James E.
	Pennsylvania	E	A			25	2	Harter, Dick
	Rice	MW	A			14	11	Knodel, Don
	Temple	E	A			15	13	Litwack, Harry
	Texas: El Paso	W	A			17	8	Haskins, Donald L.
	Weber State	W	A			20	7	Johnson, Phil
	Western Kentucky	ME	A			22	3	Oldham, John O.

1970 Division II

F	School	SD	Reg	BD	Bye	W	L	Coach
1	Philadelphia Textiles	ME	L			29	2	Magee, Herbert
2	Tennessee State	S	L			21	8	Martin, Edward A.
3	California: Riverside	W	L			19	10	Goss, Freddie
4	Buffalo State College	E	L			19	3	MacAdam, Howard B.
8	American International	NENG	L			17	8	Callahan, William E.
	Saint Joseph's (IN)	GL	L			15	11	Holstein, James H.
	South Dakota State	MW	L			22	4	Marking, James
	Stetson	SA	L			22	7	Wilkes, Dr. Glenn N., Sr.

F	School	SD	Reg	BD	Bye	W	L	Coach
16	Ashland	ME	L			23	4	Musselman, William
	Assumption (MA)	NENG	L			17	5	O'Brien, Joseph M.
	Central Michigan	GL	L			21	5	Kjolhede, Theodore
	Central Missouri State	MW	L			19	6	Short, Norman N.
	Georgia Southern	SA	L			17	6	Radovich, Frank
	Kentucky Wesleyan	S	L			18	10	Daniels, Bob
	Montclair State	E	L			23	3	Gelston, Oliver S. 'Ollie'
	Puget Sound	W	L			24	4	Zech, Don
24	Bellarmine	S	L			16	10	Spalding, James R.
	Boise State	W	L			20	8	Satterfield, Murray
	Capital	GL	L			20	4	Chickerella, Vincent
	Cheyney	ME	L			25	3	Coma, Dr. Anthony S. 'Doc'
	Hartwick	E	L			18	6	Chipman, Dr. Leroy
	Old Dominion	S	L			21	7	Allen, William 'Sonny'
	Southwest Missouri State	MW	L			17	11	Thomas, William J.
	Springfield (MA)	NENG	L			17	8	Bilik, Dr. Edward R.
32	California State: Sacramento	W	L			17	11	Heron, Jack
	Cornell (IA)	MW	L			16	8	Maaske, Paul M.
	Mount Saint Mary's (MD)	SA	L			20	6	Phelan, James J.
	Saint Anselm	NENG	L			14	11	Grenert, Albert F.
	Stony Brook State	E	L			19	6	Massimino, Roland V. 'Rollie'
	Transylvania	S	L			21	7	Rose, Lee H.
	Wayne State (MI)	GL	L			14	10	Gompert, Frank J.
	Youngstown State	ME	L			22	5	Rosselli, Dominic L. 'Dom'

1971 Division I

F	School	SD	Reg	BD	Bye	W	L	Coach
1	California: Los Angeles	W	A	To R16		29	1	Wooden, John R.
2	Villanova	E	L			22	7	Kraft, John J. 'Jack'
3	Western Kentucky	ME	A			24	6	Oldham, John O.
4	Kansas	MW	A	To R16		27	3	Owens, Ted
8	California State: Long Beach	W	L			24	5	Tarkanian, Jerry
	Drake (IA)	MW	A	To R16		21	8	John, Maurice E. 'Maury'
	Ohio State	ME	A	To R16		20	6	Taylor, Fred R.
	Pennsylvania	E	A			28	1	Harter, Dick
12	Fordham	E	L			26	3	Phelps, Richard F. 'Digger'
	Houston	MW	L			22	7	Lewis, Guy V.
	Marquette	ME	L			28	1	McGuire, Alfred J.
	Pacific (CA)	W	A	To R16		22	6	Edwards, Richard B.
16	Brigham Young	W	A			18	11	Watts, Stanley H.
	Kentucky	ME	A	To R16		22	6	Rupp, Adolph F.
	Notre Dame (IN)	MW	L			20	9	Dee, John F., Jr.
	South Carolina	E	A	To R16		23	6	McGuire, Frank J.
25	Duquesne	E	L			21	4	Manning, John 'Red'
	Furman	E	A			15	12	Williams, Joe L.
	Jacksonville (FL)	ME	L			22	4	Wasdin, Tom
	Miami (OH)	ME	A			20	5	Hedric, Darrell
	New Mexico State	MW	L			19	8	Henson, Louis R.
	Saint Joseph's (PA)	E	A			19	9	McKinney, John P. 'Jack'
	Texas Christian	MW	A			15	12	Swaim, Johnny
	Utah State	W	L			20	7	Anderson, Ladell
	Weber State	W	A			21	6	Johnson, Phil

F	School	SD	Reg	BD	Bye	W	L	Coach
1971 DIVISION II								
1	Evansville	GL	L			22	8	McCutchan, Arad A.
2	Old Dominion	SA	L			21	9	Allen, William "Sonny"
3	Southwestern Louisiana	S	L			25	4	Shipley, Beryl C.
4	Kentucky Wesleyan	MW	L			22	8	Daniels, Bob
8	Assumption (MA)	NENG	L			25	2	O'Brien, Joseph M.
	Cheyney	ME	L			23	6	Coma, Dr. Anthony S. "Doc"
	Hartwick	E	L			20	6	Chipman, Dr. Leroy
	Puget Sound	W	L			21	5	Zech, Don
16	Buffalo State College	E	L			18	4	MacAdam, Howard B.
	Central Connecticut State	NENG	L			20	7	Detrick, William
	Central Michigan	GL	L			18	9	Kjolhede, Theodore
	Norfolk State	SA	L			26	4	Smith, Robert L.
	Philadelphia Textiles	ME	L			22	6	Magee, Herbert
	Seattle Pacific	W	L			16	10	Habegger, Lester N. "Gus"
	Tennessee State	S	L			24	3	Martin, Edward A.
	Truman State (MO)	MW	L			18	9	King, W. Boyd
24	Akron	ME	L			20	6	Webb, Dr. Wyatt
	Ashland	GL	L			25	3	Musselman, William
	California Polytechnic: San Luis Obispo	W	L			17	11	Stoner, Neale R.
	Louisiana Tech	S	L			23	5	Robertson, Robert "Scotty"
	Montclair State	E	L			18	6	Gelston, Oliver S. "Ollie"
	North Dakota State	MW	L			18	9	Belk, Lyle V.
	Sacred Heart (CT)	NENG	L			22	6	Feeley, J. Donald
	Stetson	SA	L			19	9	Wilkes, Dr. Glenn N., Sr.
32	Augustana (IL)	GL	L			20	6	Borcherding, James
	Long Island: C W Post	E	L			20	6	Kaftan, Dr. George A.
	New Orleans	S	L			23	3	Greene, Ronald L.
	Roanoke	SA	L			23	8	Moir, Charles
	Saint Olaf	MW	L			20	4	Gelle, Robert D.
	San Francisco State	W	L			16	12	Waugh, Gerald R.
	Stonehill	NENG	L			20	6	Dougher, James D.
	Wooster	ME	L			23	3	Van Wie, Alvin J. "Al"
1972 DIVISION I								
1	California: Los Angeles	W	A	To R16		30	0	Wooden, John R.
2	Florida State	ME	L			27	6	Durham, Hugh
3	North Carolina	E	A	To R16		26	5	Smith, Dean E.
4	Louisville	MW	A	To R16		26	5	Crum, Denzil E. "Denny"
8	California State: Long Beach	W	A			25	4	Tarkanian, Jerry
	Kansas State	MW	A	To R16		19	9	Hartman, Jack
	Kentucky	ME	A	To R16		21	7	Rupp, Adolph F.
	Pennsylvania	E	A			25	3	Daly, Charles J. "Chuck"
12	Minnesota	ME	A	To R16		18	7	Musselman, William
	San Francisco	W	A	To R16		20	8	Gaillard, Bob
	South Carolina	E	L			24	5	McGuire, Frank J.
	Southwestern Louisiana	MW	L			25	4	Shipley, Beryl C.

F	School	SD	Reg	BD	Bye	W	L	Coach
16	Marquette		ME	L		25	4	McGuire, Alfred J.
	Texas		MW	A		19	9	Black, Leon
	Villanova		E	L		20	8	Kraft, John J. "Jack"
	Weber State		W	A		18	11	Visscher, Gene
25	Brigham Young		W	A		21	5	Watts, Stanley H.
	East Carolina		E	A		14	15	Quinn, Thomas R.
	Eastern Kentucky		ME	A		15	11	Strong, Guy Rowland
	Hawaii		W	L		24	3	Rocha, Ephraim J. "Red"
	Houston		MW	L		20	7	Lewis, Guy V.
	Marshall		MW	L		23	4	Tacy, Carl R.
	Ohio University		ME	A		15	11	Snyder, James E.
	Providence		E	L		21	6	Gavitt, David R.
	Temple		E	A		23	8	Litwack, Harry

1972 DIVISION II

F	School	SD	Reg	BD	Bye	W	L	Coach
1	Roanoke		SA		To R32	28	4	Moir, Charles
2	Akron		ME	L	To R32	26	5	Webb, Dr. Wyatt
3	Tennessee State		S	L	To R32	26	2	Martin, Edward A.
4	Eastern Michigan		GL	L	To R32	24	7	Dutcher, James D.
8	Assumption (MA)		NENG	L	To R32	21	6	O'Brien, Joseph M.
	Long Island: Southampton		E	L	To R32	22	5	Colclough, James
	Missouri: Saint Louis		MW	L	To R32	21	6	Smith, Charles G. "Chuck"
	Southern Colorado		W		To R32	19	9	Simmons, Harry H.
16	Bentley		NENG	L	To R32	26	2	Shields, Elwood N. "Al"
	Delta State		S		To R32	19	8	Waters, Jack
	Evansville		GL		To R32	22	6	McCutchan, Arad A.
	Hartford		E	L	To R32	18	6	McCullough, Gordon F.
	Lincoln (MO)		MW		To R32	22	6	Corbett, Donald
	Saint Thomas (FL)		SA	L	To R32	17	10	Stibler, Kenneth
	Seattle Pacific		W	L	To R32	17	11	Habegger, Lester N. "Gus"
	Youngstown State		ME	L		22	7	Rosselli, Dominic L. "Dom"
24	Bridgeport		NENG	L	To R32	17	9	Webster, Bruce
	California: Riverside		W		To R32	19	9	Goss, Freddie
	Florida Southern		SA	L	To R32	24	4	Jarrett, Jim
	Ithaca		E		To R32	15	8	Hurst, Hugh
	Kentucky Wesleyan		GL	L	To R32	17	10	Daniels, Bob
	New Orleans		S	L		16	10	Greene, Ronald L.
	Philadelphia Textiles		ME			22	7	Magee, Herbert
	South Dakota		MW		To R32	18	10	Mulcahy, Robert
32	Buffalo State College		E		To R32	13	14	MacAdam, Howard B.
	California: Irvine		W	L	To R32	16	12	Tift, Timothy
	Cheyney		ME		To R32	22	6	Coma, Dr. Anthony S. "Doc"
	Mercer		SA	L	To R32	17	7	Morrison, Dwane A.
	Sacred Heart (CT)		NENG		To R32	24	4	Feeley, J. Donald
	Saint Olaf		MW			18	7	Gelle, Robert D.
	Transylvania		S	L	To R32	21	6	Rose, Lee H.
	Wittenberg		GL		To R32	17	10	Hamilton, Robert D.
36	Alabama State		S			22	3	Boozer, Bernard
	Gannon		ME	L		19	7	Markey, David C.
	South Dakota State		MW	L		17	8	Marking, James
	Widener		ME			19	9	Rowe, C. Alan

F	School	SD	Reg	BD	Bye	W	L	Coach
1973 DIVISION I								
1	California: Los Angeles	W	A	To R16		30	0	Wooden, John R.
2	Memphis	MW	A	To R16		24	6	Bartow, B. Gene
3	Indiana	ME	A	To R16		22	6	Knight, Robert M.
4	Providence	E	L			27	4	Gavitt, David R.
8	Kansas State	MW	A	To R16		23	5	Hartman, Jack
	Kentucky	ME	A	To R16		20	8	Hall, Joe B.
	Maryland	E	A	To R16		23	7	Driesell, Charles G. "Lefty"
	San Francisco	W	A	To R16		23	5	Gaillard, Bob
12	California State: Long Beach	W	A			26	3	Tarkanian, Jerry
	Marquette	ME	L			25	4	McGuire, Alfred J.
	South Carolina	MW	L			22	7	McGuire, Frank J.
	Syracuse	E	L			24	5	Danforth, Roy
16	Arizona State	W	A			19	9	Wulk, Ned W.
	Austin Peay State	ME	A			22	7	Kelly, Lake
	Pennsylvania	E	A			21	7	Daly, Charles J. "Chuck"
	Southwestern Louisiana	MW	L			24	5	Shipley, Beryl C.
25	Furman	E	A			20	9	Williams, Joe L.
	Houston	MW	L			23	4	Lewis, Guy V.
	Jacksonville (FL)	ME	L			21	6	Wasdin, Tom
	Miami (OH)	ME	A			18	9	Hedric, Darrell
	Oklahoma City	W	L			21	6	Lemons, A. E. "Abe"
	Saint John's (NY)	E	L			19	7	Mulzoff, Frank
	Saint Joseph's (PA)	E	A			22	6	McKinney, John P. "Jack"
	Texas Tech	MW	A			19	8	Myers, Gerald
	Weber State	W	A			20	7	Visscher, Gene
1973 DIVISION II								
1	Kentucky Wesleyan	GL	L	To R32		24	6	Jones, Bob
2	Tennessee State	S	L	To R32		22	8	Martin, Edward A.
3	Assumption (MA)	NENG	L	To R32		25	3	O'Brien, Joseph M.
4	Brockport State	E				24	6	Panaggio, Mauro
8	Akron	ME	L	To R32		22	5	Webb, Dr. Wyatt
	California: Riverside	W				25	5	Goss, Freddie
	Coe	MW		To R32		24	1	Jackson, Marcus
	Roanoke	SA		To R32		23	6	Moir, Charles
16	Bentley	NENG	L	To R32		24	3	Shields, Elwood N. "Al"
	California State: Bakersfield	W		To R32		19	9	Larson, Jim
	Franciscan	ME	L			22	7	Sparling, Edward L.
	Hartwick	E	L	To R32		19	7	Chipman, Dr. Leroy
	Old Dominion	SA	L	To R32		19	9	Allen, William "Sonny"
	South Dakota State	MW		To R32		18	8	Marking, James
	Southeastern Louisiana	S		To R32		21	7	Foy, E. W.
	Valparaiso	GL		To R32		17	11	Purden, William
24	Bridgeport	NENG	L			20	9	Webster, Bruce
	Capital	GL		To R32		22	5	Chickerella, Vincent
	Cheyney	ME				23	5	Chaney, John
	Fayetteville State	SA				19	10	Reeves, Thomas

F	School	SD	Reg	BD	Bye	W	L	Coach
	Long Island: C W Post	E	L		To R32	20	5	Brown, Herbert M.
	San Diego	W	L		To R32	19	9	Bickerstaff, Bernard T.
	Southwest Missouri State	MW			To R32	19	8	Thomas, William J.
	Tennessee: Chattanooga	S	L		To R32	19	9	Shumate, Ron
32	Loyola (MD)	SA				16	13	Doherty, Edward C.
	Philadelphia Textiles	ME			To R32	25	4	Magee, Herbert
	Potsdam State	E	L			18	6	Welsh, John Gerald "Jerry"
	Puget Sound	W	L		To R32	19	9	Zech, Don
	Saint Michael's (VT)	NENG	L			18	9	Baumann, Walter E.
	Southern Colorado	MW			To R32	19	9	Simmons, Harry H.
	Transylvania	S	L			20	7	Rose, Lee H.
	Wooster	GL			To R32	19	10	Van Wie, Alvin J. "Al"
42	Albany State (GA)	S				23	6	Jones, Oliver
	Eckerd	SA	L			17	5	Harley, James R.
	Hartford	NENG	L			17	7	McCullough, Gordon F.
	Hiram	ME				19	4	Hollinger, William H.
	Jersey City State	E				16	10	Schiner, Lawrence R.
	Lebanon Valley	ME				24	3	Sorrentino, Louis A.
	Rensselaer	E				16	9	Kalbaugh, R. William, Sr.
	Saint Thomas (FL)	SA	L			18	6	Stibler, Kenneth
	Sonoma State	W				18	9	Trumbo, William R.
	Stonehill	NENG	L			19	7	Dougher, James D.

1974 Division I

F	School	SD	Reg	BD	Bye	W	L	Coach
1	North Carolina State	E	A		To R16	30	1	Sloan, Norman L., Jr.
2	Marquette	ME	L			26	5	McGuire, Alfred J.
3	California: Los Angeles	W	A		To R16	26	4	Wooden, John R.
4	Kansas	MW	A		To R16	23	7	Owens, Ted
8	Michigan	ME	A		To R16	22	5	Orr, John M. "Johnny"
	Oral Roberts	MW	L			23	6	Trickey, Ken
	Pittsburgh	E	L			25	4	Ridl, Charles G. "Buzz"
	San Francisco	W	A		To R16	19	9	Gaillard, Bob
12	Creighton	MW	L			23	7	Sutton, Eddie
	New Mexico	W	A			22	7	Ellenberger, Norman
	Notre Dame (IN)	ME	L			26	3	Phelps, Richard F. "Digger"
	Providence	E	L			28	4	Gavitt, David R.
16	Dayton	W	L			20	9	Donoher, Donald J. "Mickey"
	Furman	E	A			22	9	Williams, Joe L.
	Louisville	MW	A		To R16	21	7	Crum, Denzil E. "Denny"
	Vanderbilt	ME	A		To R16	23	5	Skinner, Roy G.
25	Austin Peay State	ME	A			17	10	Kelly, Lake
	California State: Los Angeles	W	A			17	10	Miller, Robert
	Idaho State	W	A			20	8	Killingsworth, James
	Ohio University	ME	A			16	11	Snyder, James E.
	Pennsylvania	E	A			21	6	Daly, Charles J. "Chuck"
	Saint Joseph's (PA)	E	A			19	11	McKinney, John P. "Jack"
	South Carolina	E	L			22	5	McGuire, Frank J.
	Syracuse	MW	L			19	7	Danforth, Roy
	Texas	MW	A			12	15	Black, Leon

F	School	SD	Reg	BD	Bye	W	L	Coach

1974 DIVISION II

F	School	SD	Reg	BD	Bye	W	L	Coach
1	Morgan State	E			To R32	28	5	Frazier, Nathaniel
2	Southwest Missouri State	MW			To R32	21	9	Thomas, William J.
3	Assumption (MA)	NENG	L		To R32	22	7	O'Brien, Joseph M.
4	New Orleans	S	L		To R32	21	9	Greene, Ronald L.
8	Bloomsburg	ME	L			22	6	Chronister, Charles W.
	California: Riverside	W	L		To R32	18	10	Goss, Freddie
	Norfolk State	SA				21	9	Christian, Charles O.
	Saint Joseph's (IN)	GL	L			20	6	Weinert, John P.
16	Albright	ME			To R32	19	9	Renken, Dr. Wilbur G.
	Fisk	S				25	4	Lawson, Ronald
	Hartford	NENG	L		To R32	20	4	McCullough, Gordon F.
	Hartwick	E	L		To R32	22	5	Chipman, Dr. Leroy
	Kentucky Wesleyan	MW	L		To R32	20	6	Jones, Bob
	Old Dominion	SA	L		To R32	20	7	Allen, William 'Sonny'
	Sonoma State	W				18	10	Trumbo, William R.
	Wittenberg	GL				22	4	Hamilton, Robert D.
24	California Polytechnic: San Luis Obispo	W			To R32	18	10	Wheeler, Ernie
	Evansville	GL			To R32	19	9	McCutchan, Arad A.
	King's (PA)	ME			To R32	20	7	Donohue, Ed
	North Dakota	MW				21	8	Gunther, Dave
	Roanoke	SA			To R32	24	6	Hankinson, Mel
	Saint Michael's (VT)	NENG	L		To R32	17	11	Baumann, Walter E.
	Siena (NY)	E	L			18	9	Kirsch, William
	Tennessee State	S	L		To R32	22	6	Martin, Edward A.
32	Bentley	NENG	L		To R32	18	7	Shields, Elwood N. 'Al'
	California State: Chico	W			To R32	20	10	Mathiesen, Peter
	Hiram	ME				20	4	Hollinger, William H.
	Potsdam State	E				18	9	Welsh, John Gerald 'Jerry'
	Rollins	SA	L			18	9	Jucker, Edwin L.
	Saint Cloud State	MW	L			17	12	Olson, Noel W.
	Southern: Baton Rouge	S	L		To R32	17	13	Stewart, Carl E.
	Wisconsin: Green Bay	GL	L		To R32	20	8	Buss, David R.
44	Chicago	GL	L			16	4	Stampf, Joseph M
	Coe	GL	L			18	5	Jackson, Marcus
	James Madison	S	L			20	6	Campanelli, Lou
	Jersey City State	E				20	6	Schiner, Lawrence R.
	Johns Hopkins	ME				17	9	Rupert, Gary
	Miles	SA				21	6	Wilkins, Arthur 'Pete'
	Monmouth (IL)	MW				18	5	Glasgow, Dr. Terry
	North Dakota State	MW	L			17	10	Skaar, Marv
	Ohio Northern	ME	L			18	7	Daugherty, Gale E.
	Randolph-Macon	SA				23	6	Webb, Paul E.
	Saint Lawrence	E				17	6	Evans, Paul
	San Diego	W	L			16	11	Bickerstaff, Bernard T.

F	School	SD	Reg	BD	Bye	W	L	Coach
1975 DIVISION I								
1	California: Los Angeles	W	A			28	3	Wooden, John R.
2	Kentucky	ME	A			26	5	Hall, Joe B.
3	Louisville	MW	A			28	3	Crum, Denzil E. "Denny"
4	Syracuse	E	L			23	9	Danforth, Roy
8	Arizona State	W	A			25	4	Wulk, Ned W.
	Indiana	ME	A			31	1	Knight, Robert M.
	Kansas State	E	L			20	9	Hartman, Jack
	Maryland	MW	L			24	5	Driesell, Charles G. "Lefty"
12	Central Michigan	ME	A			22	6	Parfitt, Richard
	Cincinnati	MW	L			23	6	Catlett, Gale
	Nevada: Las Vegas	W	A			24	5	Tarkanian, Jerry
	North Carolina	E	A			23	8	Smith, Dean E.
16	Boston College	E	L			21	9	Zuffelato, Bob
	Montana	W	A			21	8	Heathcote, George "Jud"
	Notre Dame (IN)	MW	L			19	10	Phelps, Richard F. "Digger"
	Oregon State	ME	L			19	12	Miller, Ralph H. "Cappy"
32	Alabama	W	L			22	5	Newton, Charles M. "CM"
	Creighton	MW	L			20	7	Apke, Tom
	Furman	E	A			22	7	Williams, Joe L.
	Georgetown (DC)	ME	L			18	10	Thompson, John R., Jr.
	Kansas	MW	A			19	8	Owens, Ted
	La Salle	E	A			22	7	Westhead, Paul W.
	Marquette	ME	L			23	4	McGuire, Alfred J.
	Michigan	W	L			19	8	Orr, John M. "Johnny"
	Middle Tennessee State	ME	A			23	5	Earle, James P. "Jimmy"
	New Mexico State	E	L			20	7	Henson, Louis R.
	Pennsylvania	E	A			23	5	Daly, Charles J. "Chuck"
	Rutgers	MW	L			22	7	Young, Thomas J.
	San Diego State	W	A			14	13	Vezie, Tim
	Texas A&M	MW	A			20	7	Metcalf, Dr. Shelby R.
	Texas: El Paso	ME	L			20	6	Haskins, Donald L.
	Utah State	W	L			21	6	Belnap, Gordon "Dutch"
1975 DIVISION II								
1	Old Dominion	SA	L			25	6	Allen, William "Sonny"
2	New Orleans	SC	L			23	7	Greene, Ronald L.
3	Assumption (MA)	NENG	L			22	8	O'Brien, Joseph M.
4	Tennessee State	S	L			19	9	Martin, Edward A.
8	Akron	GL	L			20	9	Webb, Dr. Wyatt
	California: Riverside	W				19	9	Goss, Freddie
	Gannon	E				25	4	Sparling, Edward L.
	North Dakota	NC				22	7	Gunther, Dave
16	Bentley	NENG	L			23	2	Shields, Elwood N. "Al"
	Lincoln (MO)	SC				19	9	Corbett, Donald
	Long Island: C W Post	E	L			24	4	Brown, Herbert M.
	Nebraska: Omaha	NC	L			17	11	Hanson, Bob
	Puget Sound	W	L			17	10	Zech, Don
	Randolph-Macon	SA				27	3	Webb, Paul E.
	Saint Joseph's (IN)	GL				21	7	Weinert, John P.
	Tennessee: Chattanooga	S	L			19	9	Shumate, Ron

F	School	SD	Reg	BD	Bye	W	L	Coach
24	Armstrong Atlantic State	S				19	7	Alexander, Bill
	Augustana (SD)	NC	L			20	8	Klein, Mel
	Baltimore	SA	L			19	11	Szymanski, Frank A.
	California: Davis	W				16	12	Hamilton, Robert I.
	Eastern Illinois	GL	L			20	8	Eddy, Donald R.
	Hartford	NENG	L			18	7	McCullough, Gordon F.
	Philadelphia Textiles	E	L			21	6	Magee, Herbert
	Southern: Baton Rouge	SC	L			19	8	Stewart, Carl E.
32	Alabama State	S	L			16	13	Laisure, W. Floyd
	California: Irvine	W	L			16	11	Tift, Timothy
	Hartwick	E	L			19	7	Chipman, Dr. Leroy
	Missouri: Rolla	NC	L			16	9	Key, Billy A.
	Morgan State	SA	L			19	10	Frazier, Nathaniel
	Sacred Heart (CT)	NENG	L			20	8	Feeley, J. Donald
	West Georgia	SC				18	8	Kaiser, Roger A.
	Youngstown State	GL	L			19	9	Rosselli, Dominic L. "Dom"

1975 DIVISION III

F	School	SD	Reg	BD	Bye	W	L	Coach
1	Lemoyne-Owen	S	L			27	5	Johnson, Jerry C.
2	Rowan	SA	L			21	10	Collins, Jack
3	Augustana (IL)	MW	L			22	8	Borcherding, James
4	Brockport State	E	L			23	5	Panaggio, Mauro
8	Brandeis	NE	L			20	7	Brannum, Robert W.
	Doane	W	L	To R16		16	9	Erickson, Robert
	Mansfield	MA	L			18	10	Wilson, Edward W.
	Wittenberg	GL	L			20	8	Hamilton, Robert D.
16	Hamline	W	L	To R16		19	11	Meyer, Dr. Don W.
	Marietta	GL	L			19	4	Roach, J. Philip
	Miles	S	L			21	8	Wilkins, Arthur "Pete"
	Saint Lawrence	E	L			20	6	Evans, Paul
	Scranton	MA	L			20	9	Bessoir, Robert M.
	Suffolk (MA)	NE	L			19	7	Law, Charles
	Wartburg	MW	L			22	6	Levick, Lewis J. "Buzz"
	William Patterson	SA	L			20	6	Adams, John K.
23	Coe	MW	L			18	6	Tune, Don
	Hiram	GL	L			15	7	Hollinger, William H.
	Massachusetts: Boston	NE	L			23	4	Loscutoff, James, Jr.
	Methodist	SA	L			21	5	Gallagher, Joe
	Rensselaer	E	L			13	9	Kalbaugh, R. William, Sr.
	Transylvania	S	L			20	7	Rose, Lee H.
	Widener	MA	L			19	8	Rowe, C. Alan
30	Albany State (NY)	E	L			15	10	Sauers, Dr. Richard J.
	Allegheny	GL	L			15	7	Sundstrom, Norman A.
	Franklin & Marshall	MA	L			16	11	Robinson, Glenn R.
	Knox	MW	L			16	7	Knosher, Harlan D.
	Rhode Island College	NE	L			16	9	Baird, William M.
	South University (TN)	S	L			19	7	Petty, Malcolm "Mac"
	Washington & Lee	SA	L			15	12	Canfield, Verne D.

F	School	SD	Reg	BD	Bye	W	L	Coach
1976 Division I								
1	Indiana	ME	A			32	0	Knight, Robert M.
2	Michigan	MW	L			25	7	Orr, John M. "Johnny"
3	California: Los Angeles	W	A			27	5	Bartow, B. Gene
4	Rutgers	E	L			31	2	Young, Thomas J.
8	Arizona	W	A			24	9	Snowden, Frederick
	Marquette	ME	L			27	2	McGuire, Alfred J.
	Missouri	MW	A			26	5	Stewart, Norman E.
	Virginia Military	E	A			22	10	Blair, William H., Jr.
16	Alabama	ME	A			23	5	Newton, Charles M. "CM"
	Connecticut	E	L			19	10	Rowe, Donald E. "Dee"
	De Paul	E	L			20	9	Meyer, Raymond J.
	Nevada: Las Vegas	W	L			29	2	Tarkanian, Jerry
	Notre Dame (IN)	MW	L			23	6	Phelps, Richard F. "Digger"
	Pepperdine	W	A			22	6	Colson, Gary W.
	Texas Tech	MW	A			25	6	Myers, Gerald
	Western Michigan	ME	A			25	3	Miller, Eldon
32	Boise State	W	A			18	11	Connor, Doran "Bus"
	Cincinnati	MW	L			25	6	Catlett, Gale
	Georgetown (DC)	W	L			21	7	Thompson, John R., Jr.
	Hofstra	E	A			18	12	Gaeckler, D. Roger
	Memphis	W	L			21	9	Yates, Wayne E.
	North Carolina	ME	L			25	4	Smith, Dean E.
	Princeton	E	A			22	5	Carril, Peter J.
	Saint John's (NY)	ME	L			23	6	Carnesecca, Louis P. "Lou"
	San Diego State	W	A			16	13	Vezie, Tim
	Syracuse	MW	L			20	9	Danforth, Roy
	Tennessee	E	L			21	6	Mears, Ramon "Ray"
	Virginia	E	A			18	12	Holland, M. Terrance "Terry"
	Virginia Polytechnic	ME	L			21	7	DeVoe, Donald E.
	Washington	MW	L			22	6	Harshman, Marvel K. "Marv"
	Western Kentucky	ME	A			20	9	Richards, Jim
	Wichita State	MW	A			18	10	Miller, Harry E.
1976 Division II								
1	Puget Sound	W	L			27	7	Zech, Don
2	Tennessee: Chattanooga	S	L			23	9	Shumate, Ron
3	Eastern Illinois	GL	L			23	8	Eddy, Donald R.
4	Old Dominion	SA	L			19	12	Webb, Paul E.
8	Bridgeport	NENG	L			24	5	Webster, Bruce
	Cheyney	E	L			24	5	Chaney, John
	Nicholls State	SC	L			22	4	Landry, Donald
	North Dakota	NC				22	7	Gunther, Dave
16	Assumption (MA)	NENG	L			16	12	O'Brien, Joseph M.
	Baltimore	SA	A			20	10	Szymanski, Frank A.
	California State: Bakersfield	W	A			23	5	Wenihan, Pat
	Evansville	GL	L			20	9	McCutchan, Arad A.
	Grambling State	SC	L			22	9	Hobdy, Frederick C.
	Philadelphia Textiles	E	L			25	3	Magee, Herbert
	Valdosta State	S	A			15	13	Dominey, James
	Wisconsin: Green Bay	NC	L			21	8	Buss, David R.

F	School	SD	Reg	BD	Bye	W	L	Coach
24	Bentley	NENG	L			17	12	Shields, Elwood N. 'Al'
	Buffalo State College	E	L			20	8	Borschel, Thomas
	California Polytechnic: Pomona	W	L			16	13	Hogan, Don
	Lincoln (MO)	SC	L			20	8	Corbett, Donald
	Mankato State	NC				18	10	Raymond, Lloyd E. 'Butch'
	Morgan State	SA	L			22	6	Frazier, Nathaniel
	Rollins	S	L			19	6	Jucker, Edwin L.
	Wright State (OH)	GL	L			20	8	Jackson, Marcus
32	California: Davis	W	L			18	10	Hamilton, Robert I.
	Central Florida	S	A			20	5	Clark, Eugene A. 'Torchy'
	Hartwick	E	L			21	5	Chipman, Dr. Leroy
	James Madison	SA	L			18	9	Campanelli, Lou
	Missouri: Rolla	SC	A			18	9	Key, Billy A.
	Nebraska: Omaha	NC	L			16	13	Hanson, Bob
	Quinnipiac	NENG	L			19	9	Kahn, Burt
	Saint Joseph's (IN)	GL	L			17	11	Weinert, John P.

1976 DIVISION III

F	School	SD	Reg	BD	Bye	W	L	Coach
1	Scranton	MA	A			27	5	Bessoir, Robert M.
2	Wittenberg	GL	L			24	5	Hamilton, Robert D.
3	Augustana (IL)	MW	L	R14>R4		21	7	Borcherding, James
4	Plattsburgh State	E	A			16	14	Law, Norman
7	Miles	S	A			23	8	Wilkins, Arthur 'Pete'
	Rhode Island College	NE	L			17	9	Baird, William M.
	Shepherd	SA	L			30	13	Starkey, Robert G.
14	Ashland	GL	L			20	7	Gottfried, Joe
	City College	E	L			16	14	Layne, Floyd
	Coe	MW	A			23	1	Tune, Don
	Massachusetts: Dartmouth	NE	L			17	9	Wheeler, Bruce E.
	Monmouth (NJ)	SA	L			22	5	Boylan, William T.
	Transylvania	S	L			19	8	Lane, Don
	Widener	MA	A			22	7	Rowe, C. Alan
21	Lemoyne-Owen	S	L			18	9	Johnson, Jerry C.
	Mansfield	MA	L			17	7	Wilson, Edward W.
	Massachusetts: Boston	NE	A			22	5	Loscutoff, James, Jr.
	Oberlin	GL	A			16	11	Penn, Patrick
	Rochester Tech (NY)	E	L			19	8	Catey, Bill
	Rowan	SA	L			18	10	Collins, Jack
	Simpson (IA)	MW	L			17	9	Starr, Richard
28	Cornell (IA)	MW	L			15	9	Maaske, Paul M.
	Grove City	MA	L			16	6	Barr, John F.
	Hiram	GL	A			16	6	Hollinger, William H.
	Lynchburg	SA	A			22	8	Proffitt, Wayne
	Rensselaer	E	A			17	9	Kalbaugh, R. William, Sr.
	South University (TN)	S	L			17	10	Petty, Malcolm 'Mac'
	Suffolk (MA)	NE	L			19	6	Law, Charles

F	School	SD	Reg	BD	Bye	W	L	Coach
1977 Division 1								
1	Marquette	MW	L			25	7	McGuire, Alfred J.
2	North Carolina	E	A			28	5	Smith, Dean E.
3	Nevada: Las Vegas	W	L			29	3	Tarkanian, Jerry
4	North Carolina: Charlotte	ME	L			28	5	Rose, Lee H.
8	Idaho State	W	A			25	5	Killingsworth, James
	Kentucky	E	L			26	4	Hall, Joe B.
	Michigan	ME	A			26	4	Orr, John M. "Johnny"
	Wake Forest	MW	L			22	8	Tacy, Carl R.
16	California: Los Angeles	W	A			24	5	Bartow, B. Gene
	Detroit	ME	L			25	4	Vitale, Dick
	Kansas State	MW	A			23	8	Hartman, Jack
	Notre Dame (IN)	E	L			22	7	Phelps, Richard F. "Digger"
	Southern Illinois	MW	A			22	7	Lambert, Paul M.
	Syracuse	ME	L			26	4	Boeheim, James A., Jr.
	Utah	W	A			22	7	Pimm, Jerry
	Virginia Military	E	A			26	4	Schmaus, Charlie
32	Arizona	MW	L			21	6	Snowden, Frederick
	Arkansas	MW	A			26	2	Sutton, Eddie
	California State: Long Beach	W	A			21	8	Jones, Dwight
	Central Michigan	ME	A			18	10	Parfitt, Richard
	Cincinnati	MW	A			25	5	Catlett, Gale
	Duquesne	E	A			15	15	Cinicola, John L.
	Hofstra	E	A			23	7	Gaeckler, D. Roger
	Holy Cross (MA)	ME	L			23	6	Blaney, George R.
	Louisville	W	L			21	7	Crum, Denzil E. "Denny"
	Middle Tennessee State	ME	A			20	9	Earle, James P. "Jimmy"
	Princeton	E	A			21	5	Carril, Peter J.
	Providence	MW	L			24	5	Gavitt, David R.
	Purdue	E	L			19	9	Schaus, Frederick A.
	Saint John's (NY)	W	L			22	9	Carnesecca, Louis P. "Lou"
	San Francisco	W	A			29	2	Gaillard, Bob
	Tennessee	ME	A			22	6	Mears, Ramon "Ray"
1977 Division II								
1	Tennessee: Chattanooga	S	L			27	5	Shumate, Ron
2	Randolph-Macon	GL	L			23	8	Nunnally, Hal
3	North Alabama	SC				24	7	Jones, Bill L.
4	Sacred Heart (CT)	NENG	L			28	4	Feeley, J. Donald
8	California Polytechnic: San Luis Obispo	W	A			19	11	Wheeler, Ernie
	Cheyney	E	L			20	8	Chaney, John
	North Dakota	NC	A			26	4	Gunther, Dave
	Towson State	SA	A			27	3	Angotti, Vincent
16	Baltimore	SA	L			24	4	Szymanski, Frank A.
	Central Florida	S	A			24	4	Clark, Eugene A. "Torchy"
	Eastern Illinois	GL	L			18	11	Eddy, Donald R.
	Hartwick	E	L			22	4	Chipman, Dr. Leroy

F	School	SD	Reg	BD	Bye	W	L	Coach
	Merrimack	NENG	L			19	9	Monahan, Frank T.
	Puget Sound	W	L			22	7	Zech, Don
	Troy State: Troy	SC				15	14	Bizilia, Wes
	Wisconsin: Green Bay	NC	L			26	3	Buss, David R.
24	Assumption (MA)	NENG	L			19	10	O'Brien, Joseph M.
	Gannon	E	L			20	8	Sparling, Edward L.
	Lincoln (MO)	SC	A			22	6	Corbett, Donald
	Nebraska: Omaha	NC	L			17	12	Hanson, Bob
	Seattle Pacific	W	L			20	9	Swagerty, Keith
	Valdosta State	S	L			23	6	Dominey, James
	Virginia Union	SA	L			25	5	Moore, Robert D.
	Youngstown State	GL	L			22	7	Rosselli, Dominic L. "Dom"
32	Armstrong Atlantic State	S	A			15	15	Alexander, Bill
	Augustana (SD)	NC	L			16	12	Klein, Mel
	Bellarmine	GL	L			17	11	Reibel, Joseph C.
	Bridgeport	NENG	L			19	10	Webster, Bruce
	California State: Hayward	W	L			16	13	Staggers, Jonathan L.
	Philadelphia Textiles	E	L			22	6	Magee, Herbert
	Southern: Baton Rouge	SC	L			19	11	Stewart, Carl E.
	Winston-Salem State	SA	A			17	11	Gaines, Clarence E. "Big House"

1977 DIVISION III

F	School	SD	Reg	BD	Bye	W	L	Coach
1	Wittenberg	GL	L			23	5	Hunter, Larry
2	Oneonta State	E	L			21	6	Flewelling, F. Don
3	Scranton	MA	L			24	8	Bessoir, Robert M.
4	Hamline	MW	L			22	8	Litzenberger, Fred L.
8	Massachusetts: Boston	NE	A			25	3	Loscutoff, James, Jr.
	Nebraska Wesleyan	W	L	To R16		16	11	Peterson, Dr. Irvin L.
	Rose-Hulman	S	L			24	4	Mutchner, John
	William Patterson	SA	L			21	5	Adams, John K.
16	Albany State (NY)	E	A			19	7	Sauers, Dr. Richard J.
	Albright	MA	A			20	9	Renken, Dr. Wilbur G.
	Ashland	GL	L			20	6	Gottfried, Joe
	Bishop	W	L	To R16		15	9	Lilly, Sylvester "Ben"
	Brandeis	NE	L			16	11	Brannum, Robert W.
	Central (IA)	MW	L			17	6	Walvoord, Jack
	Methodist	SA	A			18	8	Miller, Joe F.
	Transylvania	S	L			15	12	Lane, Don
23	Augustana (IL)	MW	L			20	7	Borcherding, James
	Franklin & Marshall	MA	L			22	5	Robinson, Glenn R.
	Knoxville	S	L			14	11	Arwood, Vic
	Muskingum	GL	A			22	6	Burson, Dr. James
	Rowan	SA	A			17	11	Collins, Jack
	Stony Brook State	E	L			21	6	Bash, Dr. M. Ronald
	Suffolk (MA)	NE	L			16	7	Law, Charles
30	Beloit	MW	A			15	7	Knapton, William B.
	Carnegie Mellon	GL	A			18	6	Maloney, Dave
	Clark Atlanta	S	A			20	7	Epps, Leonidas S. II "Sonny"
	Ithaca	E	A			15	10	Lehnus, Darryl

F	School	SD	Reg	BD	Bye	W	L	Coach
	Washington & Lee	SA	A			23	5	Canfield, Verne D.
	Widener	MA	A			20	9	Rowe, C. Alan
	Worcester State	NE	L			17	10	Hippert, Edward "Eddie"

1978 DIVISION I

F	School	SD	Reg	BD	Bye	W	L	Coach
1	Kentucky	ME	A			30	2	Hall, Joe B.
2	Duke	E	A			27	7	Foster, William E.
3	Arkansas	W	L			32	4	Sutton, Eddie
4	Notre Dame (IN)	MW	L			23	8	Phelps, Richard F. "Digger"
8	California State: Fullerton	W	A			23	9	Dye, Bobby
	De Paul	MW	L			27	3	Meyer, Raymond J.
	Michigan State	ME	A			25	5	Heathcote, George "Jud"
	Villanova	E	A			23	9	Massimino, Roland V. "Rollie"
16	California: Los Angeles	W	A			25	3	Cunningham, Dr. Gary A.
	Indiana	E	L			21	8	Knight, Robert M.
	Louisville	MW	A			23	7	Crum, Denzil E. "Denny"
	Miami (OH)	ME	A			19	9	Hedric, Darrell
	Pennsylvania	E	A			20	8	Weinhauer, Bob
	San Francisco	W	A			23	6	Gaillard, Bob
	Utah	MW	L			23	6	Pimm, Jerry
	Western Kentucky	ME	A			16	14	Richards, Jim
32	Creighton	MW	A			19	9	Apke, Tom
	Florida State	ME	L			23	6	Durham, Hugh
	Furman	E	A			19	11	Williams, Joe L.
	Houston	MW	A			25	8	Lewis, Guy V.
	Kansas	W	L			24	5	Owens, Ted
	La Salle	E	L			18	12	Westhead, Paul W.
	Marquette	ME	L			24	4	Raymonds, Henry C. "Hank"
	Missouri	MW	A			14	16	Stewart, Norman E.
	New Mexico	W	A			24	4	Ellenberger, Norman
	North Carolina	W	L			23	8	Smith, Dean E.
	Providence	ME	L			24	8	Gavitt, David R.
	Rhode Island	E	L			24	7	Kraft, John J. "Jack"
	Saint Bonaventure	E	L			21	8	Satalin, James D.
	Saint John's (NY)	MW	L			21	7	Carnesecca, Louis P. "Lou"
	Syracuse	ME	L			22	6	Boeheim, James A., Jr.
	Weber State	W	A			19	10	McCarthy, Neil N.

1978 DIVISION II

F	School	SD	Reg	BD	Bye	W	L	Coach
1	Cheyney	E	L			27	2	Chaney, John
2	Wisconsin: Green Bay	NC	L			30	2	Buss, David R.
3	Eastern Illinois	GL	L			21	10	Eddy, Donald R.
4	Central Florida	S	A			26	4	Clark, Eugene A. "Torchy"
8	Elizabeth City State	SA	L			18	6	Vaughan, Robert L. "Bobby"
	Lincoln (MO)	SC	L			22	6	Corbett, Donald
	Sacred Heart (CT)	NENG	L			21	9	Feeley, J. Donald
	San Diego	W	L			22	7	Brovelli, Jim
16	Augustana (SD)	NC	A			18	11	Klein, Mel
	California State: Northridge	W	A			22	7	Cassidy, Peter L.
	Florida A&M	S	A			23	6	Triplett, Ajac
	Merrimack	NENG	L			22	6	Monahan, Frank T.

F	School	SD	Reg	BD	Bye	W	L	Coach
	Philadelphia Textiles	E	L			18	10	Magee, Herbert
	Southern Indiana	GL	L			19	9	Boultinghouse, Wayne
	Southwest Missouri State	SC	A			21	7	Thomas, William J.
	Towson State	SA	A			26	4	Angotti, Vincent
24	Albany State (GA)	SA	L			20	9	Jones, Oliver
	Bridgeport	NENG	L			19	10	Webster, Bruce
	Hartwick	E	L			22	4	Lambros, Nicholas H.
	Mississippi College	SC	A			22	7	Hines, Dr. Douglas
	Puget Sound	W	L			20	10	Zech, Don
	Saint Joseph's (IN)	GL	L			19	8	Waggoner, George
	South Dakota State	NC	L			17	12	Zulk, Gene
	West Alabama	S	L			18	8	Brackett, Ken
32	Adelphi	E	L			18	8	Kessler, Marvin
	Augusta State	S	L			20	8	Vanover, Marvin
	Bryant	NENG	L			20	6	Folliard, Thomas J.
	California: Davis	W	L			19	10	Hamilton, Robert I.
	Chapman	NC	L			19	10	Rider, Dr. Rich
	Columbus State (GA)	SC	L			19	8	Clements, Frank M. "Sonny"
	New York Polytechnic	SA	L			20	5	Stern, Sam
	Northern Kentucky	GL	L			20	8	Hils, Martin

1978 DIVISION III

F	School	SD	Reg	BD	Bye	W	L	Coach
1	North Park	MW	L			29	2	McCarrell, Dan
2	Widener	MA	A			16	5	Rowe, C. Alan
3	Albion	GL	A			21	6	Turner, Michael
4	Stony Brook State	E	L			27	9	Bash, Dr. M. Ronald
8	Brandeis	NE	L			19	6	Brannum, Robert W.
	Humboldt State	W	L	To R16		17	10	Cosentino, Jim
	Kean	SA	A			23	5	Palermo, Joseph
	Knoxville	S	A			16	10	Simmons, Dwayne
16	Ashland	W	L	To R16		19	7	Gottfried, Joe
	Bethany (WV)	GL	A			18	5	Dafler, Jim
	Massachusetts: Boston	NE	A			21	4	Fitzpatrick, Paul
	Minnesota: Morris	MW	L			22	6	Glas, Richard "Rich"
	Saint Lawrence	E	A			19	6	Evans, Paul
	Slippery Rock	MA	L			17	10	Zimmerman, Doug
	Washington & Lee	SA	A			22	6	Canfield, Verne D.
	Wooster	S	L			21	6	Van Wie, Alvin J. "Al"
23	Central (IA)	MW	L			21	4	Walvoord, Jack
	Clark (MA)	NE	L			17	7	Halas, Wally
	Jersey City State	SA	L			20	7	Weinstein, Paul
	Otterbein	GL	A			20	9	Reynolds, Dick
	Potsdam State	E	A			15	9	Welsh, John Gerald "Jerry"
	Scranton	MA	A			22	7	Bessoir, Robert M.
	Transylvania	S	L			20	6	Lane, Don
30	DePauw	S	L			14	12	McCall, Elmer
	Manhattanville	E	L			17	11	Cohane, Tim
	Ripon	MW	A			15	10	Weiske, Kermit G. "Doc"
	Rose-Hulman	GL	L			20	7	Mutchner, John

F	School	SD	Reg	BD	Bye	W	L	Coach
	Suffolk (MA)		NE	L		15	10	Law, Charles
	Upsala		MA	L		19	9	Adubato, Richard
	Virginia Wesleyan		SA	A		17	13	Forsyth, Donald M.

1979 DIVISION I

F	School	SD	Reg	BD	Bye	W	L	Coach
1	Michigan State	2	ME	A	To R32	26	6	Heathcote, George "Jud"
2	Indiana State	1	MW	A	To R32	33	1	Hodges, Bill
3	De Paul	2	W	L	To R32	26	6	Meyer, Raymond J.
4	Pennsylvania	9	E	A		25	7	Weinhauer, Bob
8	Arkansas	2	MW	A	To R32	25	5	Sutton, Eddie
	California: Los Angeles	1	W	A	To R32	25	5	Cunningham, Dr. Gary A.
	Notre Dame (IN)	1	ME	L	To R32	24	6	Phelps, Richard F. "Digger"
	Saint John's (NY)	10	E	L		21	11	Carnesecca, Louis P. "Lou"
16	Louisiana State	3	ME	L	To R32	23	6	Brown, Dale
	Louisville	3	MW	L	To R32	24	8	Crum, Denzil E. "Denny"
	Marquette	3	W	L	To R32	22	7	Raymonds, Henry C. "Hank"
	Oklahoma	5	MW	A	To R32	21	10	Bliss, David
	Rutgers	6	E	A	To R32	22	9	Young, Thomas J.
	San Francisco	4	W	A	To R32	22	7	Belluomini, Dan
	Syracuse	4	E	L	To R32	26	4	Boeheim, James A., Jr.
	Toledo	5	ME	A	To R32	22	8	Nichols, Robert J.
32	Appalachian State	6	ME	A	To R32	23	6	Cremins, Bobby
	Brigham Young	5	W	A	To R32	20	8	Arnold, Frank H.
	Connecticut	5	E	L	To R32	21	8	Perno, Dominic P. "Dom"
	Duke	2	E	L	To R32	22	8	Foster, William E.
	Georgetown (DC)	3	E	L	To R32	24	5	Thompson, John R., Jr.
	Iowa	4	ME	L	To R32	20	8	Olson, Robert Luther "Lute"
	Lamar	10	ME	A		23	9	Tubbs, Billy
	North Carolina	1	E	A	To R32	23	6	Smith, Dean E.
	Pacific (CA)	6	W	A	To R32	18	12	Morrison, Stanley M.
	Pepperdine	9	W	L		22	10	Colson, Gary W.
	South Alabama	6	MW	L	To R32	20	7	Ellis, Cliff
	Southern California	7	W	L		20	9	Boyd, William R. "Bob"
	Tennessee	8	ME	A		21	12	DeVoe, Donald E.
	Texas	4	MW	L	To R32	21	8	Lemons, A. E. "Abe"
	Virginia Polytechnic	8	MW	A		22	9	Moir, Charles
	Weber State	7	MW	A		25	9	McCarthy, Neil N.
40	Detroit	7	ME	L		22	6	Gaines, David "Smokey"
	Eastern Kentucky	9	ME	A		21	8	Byhre, Ed
	Iona	8	E	L		23	6	Valvano, James T.
	Jacksonville (FL)	9	MW	A		19	11	Locke, Taylor O. "Tates"
	New Mexico State	10	MW	L		22	10	Hayes, Ken
	Temple	7	E	A		25	4	Casey, Don
	Utah	8	W	L		20	10	Pimm, Jerry
	Utah State	10	W	L		19	11	Belnap, Gordon "Dutch"

1979 DIVISION II

F	School	SD	Reg	BD	Bye	W	L	Coach
1	North Alabama		S	L		22	9	Jones, Bill L.
2	Wisconsin: Green Bay		NC	L		24	8	Buss, David R.
3	Cheyney		E	L		24	7	Chaney, John
4	Bridgeport		NENG	L		25	8	Webster, Bruce

F	School	SD	Reg	BD	Bye	W	L	Coach
8	Maryland: Baltimore County	SA	L			21	8	Jones, Billy
	Nicholls State	SC	A			21	7	Landry, Donald
	Puget Sound	W	L			23	6	Zech, Don
	Saint Joseph's (IN)	GL	L			20	10	Waggoner, George
16	Assumption (MA)	NENG	L			18	11	O'Brien, Joseph M.
	California: Riverside	W	L			21	5	Goss, Freddie
	Hartwick	E	L			22	5	Lambros, Nicholas H.
	Northern Iowa	NC	L			18	11	Berry, James
	Rollins	SC	L			17	11	Jucker, Edwin L.
	Valdosta State	S	L			20	8	Dominey, James
	Virginia Union	SA	L			18	8	Robbins, Charles David "Dave"
	Wright State (OH)	GL	L			20	8	Underhill, Ralph
24	Albany State (GA)	E	L			20	9	Jones, Oliver
	Bentley	NENG	L			22	6	Hammel, Brian
	Eastern Illinois	GL	L			19	10	Eddy, Donald R.
	Mount Saint Mary's (MD)	SA	L			18	10	Phelan, James J.
	Nebraska: Omaha	NC	A			20	9	Hanson, Bob
	San Diego	W	L			19	7	Brovelli, Jim
	Southeast Missouri State	SC	L			19	9	Williams, Carroll
	Tuskegee	S	A			18	11	Thompson, Charles
32	California State: Northridge	W	A			20	9	Cassidy, Peter L.
	Florida Southern	S	A			18	12	Wissel, Dr. Harold R. "Hal"
	North Dakota	NC	L			19	9	Gunther, Dave
	Northern Michigan	GL	L			18	11	Brown, Glenn C.
	Philadelphia Textiles	E	L			20	8	Magee, Herbert
	Quinnipiac	NENG	L			20	5	Kahn, Burt
	Roanoke	SA	L			25	3	Green, Ed
	Truman State (MO)	SC	A			20	8	Simms, Willard

1979 Division III

F	School	SD	Reg	BD	Bye	W	L	Coach
1	North Park	MW	L			26	5	McCarrell, Dan
2	Potsdam State	E	A			24	7	Welsh, John Gerald "Jerry"
3	Franklin & Marshall	MA	A			27	5	Robinson, Glenn R.
4	Centre	S	L			25	5	Bryant, Tom C.
8	Baldwin-Wallace	GL	L			21	7	Rupert, Bob
	Chaminade	W	L			24	5	Lopes, Merv
	Clark (MA)	NE	L			20	6	Halas, Wally
	Jersey City State	SA	A			24	5	Weinstein, Paul
16	Central (IA)	MW	A			20	5	Walvoord, Jack
	Elizabethtown	MA	A			17	9	Smith, Donald P.
	Framingham State	NE	A			22	6	Grealey, Bruce
	Saint Lawrence	E	A			18	7	Evans, Paul
	Savannah State	S	L			20	10	Ellington, Russell
	Upsala	SA	L			23	4	Chapman, Tom
	Whittier	W	L			16	12	Jacobs, Dave
	Wittenberg	GL	A			23	6	Hunter, Larry
24	Albany State (NY)	S	L			20	7	Sauers, Dr. Richard J.
	Albion	GL	A			20	4	Turner, Michael
	Beloit	MW	A			18	7	Knapton, William B.
	Coast Guard	NE	L			21	3	Broaca, Peter F.

F	School	SD	Reg	BD	Bye	W	L	Coach
	Grove City		MA	L		18	7	Barr, John F.
	Humboldt State		W	L		18	9	Conentino, Jim
	Stony Brook State		E	L		24	3	Kendall, Dick
	Virginia Wesleyan		SA	A		23	6	Forsyth, Donald M.
32	Albright		MA	L		18	10	Renken, Dr. Wilbur G.
	Allegheny		GL	A		17	8	Sundstrom, Norman A.
	Lane (TN)		S	A		18	11	Shaw, Dr. Willie G. "Hawk"
	Lynchburg		SA	A		17	12	Proffitt, Wayne
	Manhattanville		E	L		17	11	Cohane, Tim
	Minnesota: Morris		MW	L		19	9	Glas, Richard "Rich"
	Rhode Island College		NE	L		21	7	Possinger, David F.
	William Penn		W	L		20	7	Richardson, Leon

1980 Division I

F	School	SD	Reg	BD	Bye	W	L	Coach
1	Louisville	2	MW	A	To R32	33	3	Crum, Denzil E. "Denny"
2	California: Los Angeles	8	W	L		22	10	Brown, Lawrence H.
3	Purdue	6	ME	L		23	10	Rose, Lee
4	Iowa	5	E	L		23	10	Olson, Robert Luther "Lute"
8	Clemson	6	W	L		23	9	Foster, William C.
	Duke	4	ME	A	To R32	24	9	Foster, William E.
	Georgetown (DC)	3	E	L	To R32	26	6	Thompson, John R., Jr.
	Louisiana State	1	MW	A	To R32	26	6	Brown, Dale
16	Indiana	2	ME	A	To R32	21	8	Knight, Robert M.
	Kentucky	1	ME	L	To R32	29	6	Hall, Joe B.
	Lamar	10	W	A		22	11	Tubbs, Billy
	Maryland	2	E	L	To R32	24	7	Driesell, Charles G. "Lefty"
	Missouri	5	MW	L		25	6	Stewart, Norman E.
	Ohio State	4	W	L	To R32	21	8	Miller, Eldon
	Syracuse	1	E	L	To R32	26	4	Boeheim, James A., Jr.
	Texas A&M	6	MW	A		26	8	Metcalf, Dr. Shelby R.
32	Alcorn State	8	MW	A		28	2	Whitney, David L., Sr. "Davey"
	Arizona State	5	W	L		22	7	Wulk, Ned W.
	Brigham Young	3	W	A	To R32	24	5	Arnold, Frank H.
	De Paul	1	W	L	To R32	26	2	Meyer, Raymond J.
	Florida State	8	ME	L		22	9	Williams, Joe L.
	Iona	6	E	L		29	5	Valvano, James T.
	Kansas State	7	MW	A		22	9	Hartman, Jack
	North Carolina	3	MW	L	To R32	21	8	Smith, Dean E.
	North Carolina State	4	E	L	To R32	20	8	Sloan, Norman L., Jr.
	Notre Dame (IN)	4	MW	L	To R32	22	6	Phelps, Richard F. "Digger"
	Oregon State	2	W	A	To R32	26	4	Miller, Ralph H. "Cappy"
	Pennsylvania	12	ME	A		17	12	Weinhauer, Bob
	Saint John's (NY)	3	ME	L	To R32	24	5	Carnesecca, Louis P. "Lou"
	Tennessee	7	E	L		18	11	DeVoe, Donald E.
	Villanova	8	E	A		23	8	Massimino, Roland V. "Rollie"
	Virginia Polytechnic	7	ME	L		21	8	Moir, Charles
48	Arkansas	10	MW	L		21	8	Sutton, Eddie
	Bradley	11	MW	A		23	10	Versace, Dick
	Furman	10	E	A		23	7	Holbrook, Edwin "Eddie"
	Holy Cross (MA)	11	E	L		19	11	Blaney, George R.

F	School	SD	Reg	BD	Bye	W	L	Coach
	La Salle	11	ME	A		22	9	Ervin, David "Lefty"
	Loyola Marymount	12	W	A		14	14	Jacobs, Ron
	Marquette	9	E	L		18	9	Raymonds, Henry C. "Hank"
	Old Dominion	9	W	L		25	5	Webb, Paul E.
	San Jose State	12	MW	A		17	12	Berry, William
	South Alabama	9	MW	L		23	6	Ellis, Cliff
	Toledo	9	ME	A		23	6	Nichols, Robert J.
	Utah State	11	W	L		18	9	Tueller, Rod
	Virginia Commonwealth	12	E	A		18	12	Barnett, J. D.
	Washington State	5	ME	L		22	6	Raveling, George
	Weber State	7	W	A		26	3	McCarthy, Neil N.
	Western Kentucky	10	ME	A		21	8	Keady, Lloyd Eugene "Gene"

1980 DIVISION II

F	School	SD	Reg	BD	Bye	W	L	Coach
1	Virginia Union		SA	L		26	4	Robbins, Charles David "Dave"
2	New York Polytechnic		E	L		26	3	Stern, Sam
3	Florida Southern		S	A		28	5	Wissel, Dr. Harold R. "Hal"
4	North Alabama		SC	L		21	10	Jones, Bill L.
8	California: Riverside		W	L		22	6	Masi, John
	New Hampshire College		NENG	L		22	8	Sullivan, Thomas R.
	Northern Michigan		GL	L		24	6	Brown, Glenn C.
	South Dakota State		NC	A		23	7	Zulk, Gene
16	California Polytechnic: San Luis Obispo		W	A		22	7	Wheeler, Ernie
	Central Florida		S	L		25	4	Clark, Eugene A. "Torchy"
	Eastern Illinois		GL	L		22	7	Eddy, Donald R.
	Hartwick		E	L		21	5	Lambros, Nicholas H.
	Maryland: Baltimore County		SA	L		23	5	Jones, Billy
	Nicholls State		SC	L		18	8	Sanders, Jerry
	Springfield (MA)		NENG	L		20	7	Bilik, Dr. Edward R.
	Western Illinois		NC	L		19	10	Margenthaler, Jack
24	Central Missouri State		SC	A		26	2	Smith, Tom
	Cheyney		E	L		23	5	Chaney, John
	Mount Saint Mary's (MD)		SA	L		22	7	Phelan, James J.
	Puget Sound		W	L		21	8	Zech, Don
	Quinnipiac		NENG	L		22	7	Kahn, Burt
	Stonehill		NC	L		18	10	Folliard, Thomas J.
	West Georgia		S	L		24	6	Kaiser, Roger A.
	Wright State (OH)		GL	L		25	3	Underhill, Ralph
32	Benedict		SA	L		21	7	Holmes, Michael
	Bethune-Cookman		S	A		13	16	McClairen, Jack "Cy"
	Bryant		NENG	L		20	7	Drury, Leon A. "Lee"
	Gannon		E	L		20	9	Fox, Richard A.
	Jacksonville State (AL)		SC	A		20	7	Jones, Bill E.
	North Dakota		NC	L		18	12	Gunther, Dave
	San Francisco State		W	L		21	8	Damon, Dr. E. Lyle
	Southern Indiana		GL	L		20	9	Boultinghouse, Wayne

F	School	SD	Reg	BD	Bye	W	L	Coach
1980 DIVISION III								
1	North Park		MW	L		28	3	McCarrell, Dan
2	Upsala		SA	L		25	5	Chapman, Tom
3	Wittenberg		GL	L		29	3	Hunter, Larry
4	Longwood		NE	L		28	3	Bash, Dr. M. Ronald
8	Albright		MA	L		27	3	Renken, Dr. Wilbur G.
	Jersey City State		W	L		25	4	Weinstein, Paul
	Lane (TN)		S	L		19	9	Shaw, Dr. Willie G. "Hawk"
	Potsdam State		E	A		26	4	Welsh, John Gerald "Jerry"
16	Albany State (NY)		E	L		21	6	Sauers, Dr. Richard J.
	Augustana (IL)		MW	L		20	7	Borcherding, James
	Clark (MA)		NE	L		21	6	Halas, Wally
	Humboldt State		W	L		18	10	Cosentino, Jim
	Ohio Northern		GL	A		24	5	Daugherty, Gale E.
	Savannah State		S	A		24	5	Ellington, Russell
	Scranton		MA	A		18	11	Bessoir, Robert M.
	William Patterson		SA	A		20	7	Adams, John K.
24	Allegheny		SA	A		20	4	Reynders, John C.
	Beloit		W	L		19	5	Knapton, William B.
	Calvin		GL	A		18	6	Vroon, A. Donald
	Dickinson (PA)		MA	A		19	8	Evans, Gene
	Rhodes		S	L		22	6	Hilgeman, Herb
	Ripon		MW	A		20	5	Weiske, Kermit G. "Doc"
	Salem State		NE	A		19	9	Lavacchia, Joseph A.
	Stony Brook State		E	L		19	9	Kendall, Dick
32	Central (IA)		MW	A		18	8	Walvoord, Jack
	Framingham State		NE	L		20	8	Grealey, Bruce
	North Carolina: Greensboro		S	A		16	12	Hargett, Larry
	Occidental		W	L		15	13	Westphal, Bill
	Saint Lawrence		E	A		22	5	Evans, Paul
	Ursinus		MA	L		17	10	Werley, "Skip"
	Wabash		GL	L		20	6	Petty, Malcolm "Mac"
	Washington & Lee		SA	A		14	15	Canfield, Verne D.
1981 DIVISION I								
1	Indiana	3	ME	A	To R32	26	9	Knight, Robert M.
2	North Carolina	2	W	A	To R32	29	8	Smith, Dean E.
3	Virginia	1	E	L	To R32	29	4	Holland, M. Terrance "Terry"
4	Louisiana State	1	MW	L	To R32	31	5	Brown, Dale
8	Brigham Young	6	E	L		25	7	Arnold, Frank H.
	Kansas State	8	W	L		24	9	Hartman, Jack
	Saint Joseph's (PA)	9	ME	L		25	8	Lynam, James F.
	Wichita State	6	MW	L		26	7	Smithson, Eugene
16	Alabama: Birmingham	7	ME	L		23	9	Bartow, B. Gene
	Arkansas	5	MW	L		24	8	Sutton, Eddie
	Boston College	5	ME	L		23	7	Davis, Dr. Thomas
	Illinois	4	W	L	To R32	21	8	Henson, Louis R.
	Kansas	7	MW	A		24	8	Owens, Ted
	Notre Dame (IN)	2	E	L	To R32	23	6	Phelps, Richard F. "Digger"
	Tennessee	4	E	L	To R32	21	8	DeVoe, Donald E.
	Utah	3	W	L	To R32	25	5	Pimm, Jerry

F	School	SD	Reg	BD	Bye	W	L	Coach
32	Arizona State	2	MW	L	To R32	24	4	Wulk, Ned W.
	California: Los Angeles	3	E	L	To R32	20	7	Brown, Lawrence H.
	De Paul	1	ME	L	To R32	27	2	Meyer, Raymond J.
	Iowa	3	MW	L	To R32	21	7	Olson, Robert Luther "Lute"
	James Madison	10	E	L		21	9	Campanelli, Lou
	Kentucky	2	ME	L	To R32	22	6	Hall, Joe B.
	Lamar	8	MW	A		25	5	Foster, Pat
	Louisville	4	MW	A	To R32	21	9	Crum, Denzil E. "Denny"
	Maryland	6	ME	L		21	10	Driesell, Charles G. "Lefty"
	Northeastern (MA)	11	W	A		24	6	Calhoun, James A.
	Oregon State	1	W	A	To R32	26	2	Miller, Ralph H. "Cappy"
	Pittsburgh	10	W	A		19	12	Chipman, Dr. Leroy
	Villanova	9	E	L		20	11	Massimino, Roland V. "Rollie"
	Virginia Commonwealth	5	E	A		24	5	Barnett, J. D.
	Wake Forest	4	ME	L	To R32	22	7	Tacy, Carl R.
	Wyoming	5	W	A		24	6	Brandenburg, Jim
48	Ball State	12	ME	A		20	10	Yoder, Steve
	California State: Fresno	6	W	A		25	4	Grant, Boyd "Tiny"
	Creighton	8	ME	A		21	9	Apke, Tom
	Georgetown (DC)	7	E	L		20	12	Thompson, John R., Jr.
	Houston	8	E	L		21	9	Lewis, Guy V.
	Howard (DC)	12	W	A		17	12	Williamson, Altha B.
	Idaho	7	W	A		25	4	Monson, Don
	Long Island	12	E	L		18	11	Lizzo, Paul
	Mercer	12	MW	A		18	12	Bibb, Bill
	Mississippi	10	MW	A		16	14	Weltlich, Robert
	Missouri	9	MW	L		22	10	Stewart, Norman E.
	Princeton	11	E	A		18	10	Carril, Peter J.
	San Francisco	9	W	A		24	7	Barry, Peter
	Southern: Baton Rouge	11	MW	A		17	11	Stewart, Carl E.
	Tennessee: Chattanooga	11	ME	A		21	9	Arnold, Murray
	Western Kentucky	10	ME	A		21	8	Haskins, Clem S.

1981 DIVISION II

F	School	SD	Reg	BD	Bye	W	L	Coach
1	Florida Southern		S	A		24	8	Wissel, Dr. Harold R. "Hal"
2	Mount Saint Mary's (MD)		SA	L		28	3	Phelan, James J.
3	California Polytechnic: San Luis Obispo		E			24	8	Wheeler, Ernie
4	Wisconsin: Green Bay		NC	L		23	9	Buss, David R.
8	New Hampshire College		NENG	L		23	7	Sullivan, Thomas R.
	North Alabama		SC	A		22	9	Jones, Bill L.
	Northern Michigan		GL	L		21	9	Brown, Glenn C.
	Puget Sound		W	L		24	5	Zech, Don
16	California State: Dominguez Hills		W			20	5	Yanai, David
	Central Florida		S	L		23	5	Clark, Eugene A. "Torchy"
	Clarion		E	L		23	6	DeGregorio, Joseph
	Elizabeth City State		SA	L		22	9	Vaughan, Robert L. "Bobby"
	North Dakota		NC	L		23	8	Gunther, Dave
	Sacred Heart (CT)		NENG	L		20	9	Bike, Dave
	Truman State (MO)		SC	A		19	11	Simms, Willard
	Western Illinois		GL	L		21	8	Margenthaler, Jack

F	School	SD	Reg	BD	Bye	W	L	Coach
24	Cheyney	SA	L			21	8	Chaney, John
	Jacksonville State (AL)	SC	L			22	8	Jones, Bill E.
	Monmouth (NJ)	E	A			25	4	Kornegay, Ron
	Montana State: Billings	W	L			20	8	Edwards, Dick
	North Dakota State	NC	A			20	9	Inniger, Ervin L., Jr.
	Stonehill	NENG	L			21	9	Folliard, Thomas J.
	West Georgia	S	L			23	5	Kaiser, Roger A.
	Wright State (OH)	GL	L			25	4	Underhill, Ralph
32	Bloomsburg	E	A			23	7	Chronister, Charles W.
	California State: Chico	W	A			18	11	Mathiesen, Peter
	Central Missouri State	NC	L			20	9	Nance, Lynn
	Lincoln (MO)	SC	L			22	8	Coleman, Ronald E.
	Morehouse	S	A			17	12	McAfee, Arthur J., Jr.
	Randolph-Macon	SA	L			21	8	Nunnally, Hal
	Southern Indiana	GL	A			21	8	Boultinghouse, Wayne
	Springfield (MA)	NENG	L			20	9	Bilik, Dr. Edward R.

1981 DIVISION III

F	School	SD	Reg	BD	Bye	W	L	Coach
1	Potsdam State	E	L			30	2	Welsh, John Gerald 'Jerry'
2	Augustana (IL)	MW	L			25	6	Borcherding, James
3	Ursinus	MA	L			23	8	Werley, 'Skip'
4	Otterbein	GL	L			23	9	Reynoids, Dick
8	Clark (MA)	NE	L			24	3	Halas, Wally
	Savannah State	S	L			25	4	Ellington, Russell
	Upsala	SA	L			23	6	Chapman, Tom
	Whittier	W	L			19	10	Jacobs, Dave
16	Albany State (NY)	E	A			23	5	Sauers, Dr. Richard J.
	Beloit	MW	A			24	2	Knapton, William B.
	Montclair State	SA	A			15	12	Gelston, Oliver S. 'Ollie'
	Muskingum	W	L			19	8	Burson, Dr. James
	Rhodes	S	A			23	3	Hilgeman, Herb
	Rochester (NY)	NE	L			20	7	Neer, Mike
	William Patterson	MA	L			19	6	Adams, John K.
	Wittenberg	GL	A			28	3	Hunter, Larry
24	Dubuque	W	L			20	8	Davison, Jon L.
	Franklin & Marshall	MA	A			26	3	Robinson, Glenn R.
	Roanoke	SA	A			27	2	Green, Ed
	Saint Andrews Presbyterian	S	A			23	7	Riley, Doug
	Saint Lawrence	E	A			20	6	Talbot, Leon
	Salem State	NE	A			23	6	Lavacchia, Joseph A.
	Wabash	GL	L			19	6	Petty, Malcolm 'Mac'
	William Penn	MW	A			20	7	Richardson, Leon
32	Allegheny	SA	A			16	8	Reynders, John C.
	California State: Stanislaus	W	L			16	12	Sanderson, Douglas R.
	Calvin	GL	A			15	11	Vroon, A. Donald
	Massachusetts: Boston	NE	L			19	8	Dowd, Kevin
	North Park	MW	L			16	12	McCarrell, Dan
	Rose-Hulman	S	L			18	7	Mutchner, John
	Scranton	MA	A			18	11	Bessoir, Robert M.
	Staten Island	E	L			21	8	Pickman, Dr. Evan T.

F	School	SD	Reg	BD	Bye	W	L	Coach
1982 Division I								
1	North Carolina	1	E	A	To R32	32	2	Smith, Dean E.
2	Georgetown (DC)	1	W	A	To R32	30	7	Thompson, John R., Jr.
3	Houston	6	MW	L		25	8	Lewis, Guy V.
	Louisville	3	ME	L	To R32	23	10	Crum, Denzil E. "Denny"
8	Alabama: Birmingham	4	ME	A	To R16	25	6	Bartow, B. Gene
	Boston College	8	MW	L		22	10	Davis, Dr. Thomas
	Oregon State	2	W	A	To R32	25	5	Miller, Ralph H. "Cappy"
	Villanova	3	E	L	To R32	24	8	Massimino, Roland V. "Rollie"
16	Alabama	4	E	A	To R32	24	7	Sanderson, Winfrey "Wimp"
	California State: Fresno	4	W	A	To R32	27	3	Grant, Boyd "Tiny"
	Idaho	3	W	A	To R32	27	3	Monson, Don
	Kansas State	5	MW	L		23	8	Hartman, Jack
	Memphis	2	E	A	To R32	24	5	Kirk, Dana
	Minnesota	2	ME	A	To R32	23	6	Dutcher, James D.
	Missouri	2	MW	A	To R32	27	4	Stewart, Norman E.
	Virginia	1	ME	L	To R32	30	4	Holland, M. Terrance "Terry"
32	Arkansas	4	MW	A	To R32	23	6	Sutton, Eddie
	De Paul	1	MW	L	To R32	26	2	Meyer, Raymond J.
	Indiana	5	ME	L		19	10	Knight, Robert M.
	Iowa	6	W	L		21	8	Olson, Robert Luther "Lute"
	James Madison	9	E	L		24	6	Campanelli, Lou
	Marquette	7	MW	L		23	9	Raymonds, Henry C. "Hank"
	Middle Tennessee State	11	ME	A		22	8	Simpson, Stanley "Ramrod"
	Northeastern (MA)	11	E	A		23	7	Calhoun, James A.
	Pepperdine	7	W	A		22	7	Harrick, Jim
	Saint John's (NY)	5	E	L		21	9	Carnesecca, Louis P. "Lou"
	Tennessee	9	ME	L		20	10	DeVoe, Donald E.
	Tennessee: Chattanooga	10	ME	A		27	4	Arnold, Murray
	Tulsa	3	MW	A	To R32	24	6	Richardson, Nolan
	Wake Forest	7	E	L		21	9	Tacy, Carl R.
	West Virginia	5	W	L		27	4	Catlett, Gale
	Wyoming	8	W	A		23	7	Brandenburg, Jim
48	Alcorn State	11	MW	A		22	8	Whitney, David L., Sr. "Davey"
	Evansville	10	MW	A		23	6	Walters, Dick
	Kentucky	6	ME	L		22	8	Hall, Joe B.
	North Carolina A&T	12	W	L		19	9	Corbett, Donald
	North Carolina State	7	ME	L		22	10	Valvano, James T.
	Northeast Louisiana	11	W	A		19	11	Vining, Mike
	Northern Illinois	12	MW	A		16	14	McDougal, John
	Ohio State	8	E	L		21	10	Miller, Eldon
	Old Dominion	10	E	L		18	12	Webb, Paul E.
	Pennsylvania	12	E	A		17	10	Weinhauer, Bob
	Pittsburgh	10	W	L		20	10	Chipman, Dr. Leroy
	Robert Morris	12	ME	L		17	13	Furjanic, Matt, Jr.
	Saint Joseph's (PA)	6	E	A		25	5	Boyle, Jim
	San Francisco	9	MW	L		25	6	Barry, Peter
	Southern California	9	W	L		19	9	Morrison, Stanley M.
	Southwestern Louisiana	8	ME	A		24	8	Paschal, Bobby

F	School	SD	Reg	BD	Bye	W	L	Coach

1982 Division II

1	District of Columbia	SA	L			25	5	Jones, William S.
2	Florida Southern	S	L			22	10	Wissel, Dr. Harold R. "Hal"
3	Kentucky Wesleyan	GL	L			27	5	Pollio, Mike
4	California State: Bakersfield	W	A			25	6	Dye, Bobby
8	Cheyney	E	A			28	3	Chaney, John
	North Dakota	NC	A			27	5	Gunther, Dave
	Sacred Heart (CT)	NENG	L			26	6	Bike, Dave
	Southeast Missouri State	SC	A			21	10	Shumate, Ron
16	Bloomsburg	E	L			24	7	Chronister, Charles W.
	California Polytechnic: San Luis Obispo	W	L			23	6	Wheeler, Ernie
	Central State (OH)	GL	L			21	8	Wims, Dr. Lu D.
	Mount Saint Mary's (MD)	SA	L			20	8	Phelan, James J.
	Nebraska: Omaha	NC	L			22	7	Hanson, Bob
	Southern Connecticut State	NENG	L			22	8	Leary, Arthur
	Tennessee: Martin	SC	L			20	11	Tolis, Art
	West Alabama	S	A			20	10	Murphy, Ed
24	Alaska: Anchorage	W	L			21	1	Larrabee, Harry
	Central Missouri State	SC	L			20	9	Nance, Lynn
	Edinboro	E	L			22	8	Conti, Guy
	Lewis (IL)	NC	A			20	9	Schwarz, "Chuck"
	Saint Thomas (FL)	S	A			15	13	Stibler, Kenneth
	Springfield (MA)	NENG	L			21	8	Bilik, Dr. Edward R.
	Virginia State	SA	L			19	9	Laisure, W. Floyd
	Wright State (OH)	GL	L			22	7	Underhill, Ralph
32	Bellarmine	GL	L			20	9	Reibel, Joseph C.
	Central Florida	SC	L			21	8	Clark, Eugene A. "Torchy"
	Monmouth (NJ)	E	L			21	9	Kornegay, Ron
	Montana State: Billings	NC	L			19	10	Douglass, Pat
	Northwest Missouri State	S	L			20	10	Sinn, Dr. Lionel L.
	San Francisco State	W	A			20	10	Wilson, Kevin
	Stonehill	NENG	L			21	8	Folliard, Thomas J.
	Virginia Union	SA	L			18	7	Robbins, Charles David "Dave"

1982 Division III

1	Wabash	GL	L			24	4	Petty, Malcolm "Mac"
2	Potsdam State	NE	L			20	10	Welsh, John Gerald "Jerry"
3	Brooklyn	E	L			22	9	Reiner, Mark
4	California State: Stanislaus	W	L			18	13	Sanderson, Douglas R.
8	Augustana (IL)	MW	L			22	6	Borcherding, James
	Capital	S	L			20	9	Grube, David
	Roanoke	SA	A			27	4	Green, Ed
	Ursinus	MA	L			19	11	Werley, "Skip"
16	Bishop	W	L			16	7	Lilly, Sylvester "Ben"
	Hope	GL	A			19	5	Van Wieren, Dr. Glenn
	Luther	MW	A			23	4	Leix, Jim
	Saint Andrews Presbyterian	S	A			27	3	Riley, Doug

F	School	SD	Reg	BD	Bye	W	L	Coach
	Salem State		NE	A		20	8	Lavacchia, Joseph A.
	Staten Island		E	L		25	4	Pickman, Dr. Evan T.
	Upsala		SA	L		23	4	Chapman, Tom
	Widener		MA	A		23	6	Rowe, C. Alan
24	Clark (MA)		NE	L		17	9	Halas, Wally
	Ithaca		E	A		22	5	Baker, Tom
	Montclair State		SA	A		17	8	Gelston, Oliver S. "Ollie"
	North Park		W	L		18	10	McCarrell, Dan
	Ohio Northern		GL	L		22	7	Daugherty, Gale E.
	Rose-Hulman		S	A		18	10	Mutchner, John
	Scranton		MA	A		23	6	Bessoir, Robert M.
	Wisconsin: Milwaukee		MW	L		20	6	Voight, Bob
32	Beloit		MW	A		19	6	Knapton, William B.
	Bethany (WV)		SA	A		15	9	Dafler, Jim
	Buffalo State University		E	A		13	17	Hughes, Virgil William
	Dickinson (PA)		MA	L		16	11	Evans, Gene
	Virginia Wesleyan		S	L		20	10	Forsyth, Donald M.
	Whittier		W	L		14	14	Jacobs, Dave
	Wittenberg		GL	A		20	10	Hunter, Larry
	Worcester Polytechnic		NE	L		14	11	Kaufman, Kenneth J.

1983 Division I

F	School	SD	Reg	BD	Bye	W	L	Coach
1	North Carolina State	6	W	A		26	10	Valvano, James T.
2	Houston	1	MW	A	To R32	31	3	Lewis, Guy V.
3	Georgia	4	E	A	To R32	24	10	Durham, Hugh
	Louisville	1	ME	A	To R32	32	4	Crum, Denzil E. "Denny"
8	Kentucky	3	ME	L	To R32	23	8	Hall, Joe B.
	North Carolina	2	E	L	To R32	28	8	Smith, Dean E.
	Villanova	3	MW	L	To R32	24	8	Massimino, Roland V. "Rollie"
	Virginia	1	W	L	To R32	29	5	Holland, M. Terrance "Terry"
16	Arkansas	4	ME	L	To R32	26	4	Sutton, Eddie
	Boston College	4	W	L	To R32	25	7	Williams, Gary
	Indiana	2	ME	A	To R32	24	6	Knight, Robert M.
	Iowa	7	MW	L		21	10	Olson, Robert Luther "Lute"
	Memphis	4	MW	L	To R32	23	8	Kirk, Dana
	Ohio State	3	E	L	To R32	20	10	Miller, Eldon
	Saint John's (NY)	1	E	A	To R32	28	5	Carnesecca, Louis P. "Lou"
	Utah	10	W	A		18	14	Pimm, Jerry
32	California: Los Angeles	2	W	A	To R32	23	6	Farmer, Larry
	Georgetown (DC)	5	MW	L		22	10	Thompson, John R., Jr.
	James Madison	10	E	L		20	11	Campanelli, Lou
	Lamar	11	MW	A		23	8	Foster, Pat
	Maryland	8	MW	L		20	10	Driesell, Charles G. "Lefty"
	Missouri	2	MW	L	To R32	26	8	Stewart, Norman E.
	Nevada: Las Vegas	3	W	A	To R32	28	3	Tarkanian, Jerry
	Ohio University	11	ME	A		23	9	Nee, Danny
	Oklahoma	7	ME	L		24	9	Tubbs, Billy
	Princeton	12	W	A		20	9	Carril, Peter J.
	Purdue	5	ME	L		21	9	Keady, Lloyd Eugene "Gene"
	Rutgers	9	E	L		23	8	Young, Thomas J.

F	School	SD	Reg	BD	Bye	W	L	Coach
	Syracuse	6	E	L		21	10	Boeheim, James A., Jr.
	Tennessee	8	ME	L		20	12	DeVoe, Donald E.
	Virginia Commonwealth	5	E	L		24	7	Barnett, J. D.
	Washington State	8	W	L		23	7	Raveling, George
48	Alabama	6	MW	L		20	12	Sanderson, Winfrey "Wimp"
	Alabama: Birmingham	10	ME	A		19	14	Bartow, B. Gene
	Alcorn State	12	MW	A		22	10	Whitney, David L., Sr. "Davey"
	Illinois	7	W	L		21	11	Henson, Louis R.
	Illinois State	6	ME	A		24	7	Donewald, Bob
	La Salle	12	E	A		18	14	Ervin, David "Lefty"
	Marquette	9	ME	L		19	10	Raymonds, Henry C. "Hank"
	Morehead State (KY)	11	E	A		19	11	Martin, Wayne M.
	Oklahoma State	5	W	A		24	7	Hansen, Paul N.
	Pepperdine	11	W	A		20	9	Harrick, Jim
	Robert Morris	12	ME	A		23	8	Furjanic, Matt, Jr.
	Southwestern Louisiana	8	E	L		22	7	Paschal, Bobby
	Tennessee: Chattanooga	9	MW	A		26	4	Arnold, Murray
	Utah State	10	MW	L		20	9	Tueller, Rod
	Weber State	9	W	A		23	8	McCarthy, Neil N.
	West Virginia	7	E	A		23	8	Catlett, Gale
52	Boston University	13	E	L		21	10	Pitino, Richard A. "Rick"
	Georgia Southern	13	ME	A		18	12	Kerns, Frank
	North Carolina A&T	13	W	A		23	8	Corbett, Donald
	Xavier (OH)	13	MW	A		22	8	Staak, Bob

1983 Division II

1	Wright State (OH)		GL	L		28	4	Underhill, Ralph
2	District of Columbia		SA	L		29	3	Jones, William S.
3	California State: Bakersfield		W	L		25	5	Dye, Bobby
	Morningside		NC	A		26	6	Callahan, Dan
8	Bloomsburg		E	L		23	10	Chronister, Charles W.
	Jacksonville State (AL)		S	A		24	8	Jones, Bill E.
	Sacred Heart (CT)		NENG	A		27	5	Bike, Dave
	Southeast Missouri State		SC	A		25	6	Shumate, Ron
16	American International		NENG	L		23	9	Powell, Jim
	Central Missouri State		SC	L		23	7	Nance, Lynn
	Chapman		W	L		21	8	Hazzard, Walter R., Jr.
	Kentucky Wesleyan		GL	A		22	8	Pollio, Mike
	North Dakota State		NC	L		21	9	Inniger, Ervin L., Jr.
	Philadelphia Textiles		E	L		23	7	Magee, Herbert
	Saint Augustine's		SA	L		22	6	Heartley, Harvey D.
	West Georgia		S	L		22	7	Kaiser, Roger A.
24	Assumption (MA)		NENG	A		21	11	O'Brien, Joseph M.
	Ferris State		NC	L		20	9	Ludwig, H. Thomas
	Florida Southern		S	A		23	8	Scholz, George
	Hampton		SA	A		23	7	Ford, Henry "Hank"
	Lewis (IL)		GL	L		20	10	Schwarz, "Chuck"
	Long Island: C W Post		E	L		22	9	Galeazzi, Thomas J.
	San Francisco State		W	A		21	9	Damon, Dr. E. Lyle
	Stephen F Austin State		SC	L		21	10	Miller, Harry E.

F	School	SD	Reg	BD	Bye	W	L	Coach
32	Central Connecticut State		NENG	L		21	9	Detrick, William
	Cheyney		E	A		26	6	Songster, Charles
	Humboldt State		W	L		18	12	Wood, Tom
	Nebraska: Omaha		NC	L		19	11	Hanson, Bob
	Randolph-Macon		SA	L		20	10	Nunnally, Hal
	Southern Connecticut State		GL	L		23	9	Leary, Arthur
	Tennessee: Martin		SC	L		21	10	Hancock, Tom
	West Chester		S	L		19	9	Voss, Earl

1983 Division III

F	School	SD	Reg	BD	Bye	W	L	Coach
1	Scranton		MA	A		29	3	Bessoir, Robert M.
2	Wittenberg		GL	A		26	6	Hunter, Larry
3	Roanoke		SA	A		31	2	Green, Ed
4	Wisconsin: Whitewater		MW	L		25	6	Vander Meulen, David
8	California State: Stanislaus		W	L		16	13	Sanderson, Douglas R.
	Clark (MA)		NE	L		23	4	Halas, Wally
	Lemoyne-Owen		S	A		24	6	Johnson, Jerry C.
	Potsdam State		E	A		23	6	Welsh, John Gerald "Jerry"
16	Bridgewater State (MA)		NE	A		21	6	Byron, Paul
	Hartwick		E	L		17	9	Lambros, Nicholas H.
	Hope		GL	A		19	4	Van Wieren, Dr. Glenn
	Millikin		MW	L		21	7	Ramsey, Joe
	Saint Andrews Presbyterian		S	A		26	4	Riley, Doug
	Sonoma State		W	L		16	12	Walker, Dick
	Widener		MA	A		21	8	Rowe, C. Alan
	William Patterson		SA	A		19	9	Adams, John K.
24	Bishop		W	L		18	8	Lilly, Sylvester "Ben"
	Capital		GL	L		22	7	Grube, David
	Grove City		MA	L		21	4	Barr, John F.
	Massachusetts: Boston		NE	L		19	9	Titus, Charles
	Rust		S	L		24	6	Hayes, Naylond
	Union (NY)		E	L		21	5	Scanlon, William M.
	Upsala		SA	L		19	7	Chapman, Tom
	William Penn		MW	A		19	7	Richardson, Leon
32	Augustana (IL)		W	L		18	10	Borcherding, James
	Beloit		MW	A		18	7	Knapton, William B.
	Centre		S	A		16	11	Bryant, Tom C.
	Ithaca		E	A		19	8	Baker, Tom
	John Carroll		GL	A		17	7	Baab, Tim
	Moravian		MA	L		19	8	Walker, James R.
	Muskingum		NE	L		19	9	Burson, Dr. James
	North Carolina Wesleyan		SA	L		21	9	McCarthy, John

1984 Division I

F	School	SD	Reg	BD	Bye	W	L	Coach
1	Georgetown (DC)	1	W	A	To R32	34	3	Thompson, John R., Jr.
2	Houston	2	MW	A	To R32	32	5	Lewis, Guy V.
3	Kentucky	1	ME	A	To R32	29	5	Hall, Joe B.
	Virginia	7	E	L		21	12	Holland, M. Terrance "Terry"
8	Dayton	10	W	L		21	11	Donoher, Donald J. "Mickey"
	Illinois	2	ME	A	To R32	26	5	Henson, Louis R.
	Indiana	4	E	L	To R32	22	9	Knight, Robert M.
	Wake Forest	4	MW	L	To R32	23	9	Tacy, Carl R.

F	School	SD	Reg	BD	Bye	W	L	Coach
16	De Paul	1	MW	L	To R32	27	3	Meyer, Raymond J.
	Louisville	5	ME	L		24	11	Crum, Denzil E. "Denny"
	Maryland	3	ME	A	To R32	24	8	Driesell, Charles G. "Lefty"
	Memphis	6	MW	A		26	7	Kirk, Dana
	Nevada: Las Vegas	5	W	A		29	6	Tarkanian, Jerry
	North Carolina	1	E	L	To R32	28	3	Smith, Dean E.
	Syracuse	3	E	L	To R32	23	9	Boeheim, James A., Jr.
	Washington	6	W	A		24	7	Harshman, Marvel K. "Marv"
32	Arkansas	2	E	L	To R32	25	7	Sutton, Eddie
	Brigham Young	8	ME	L		20	11	Anderson, Ladell
	Duke	3	W	L	To R32	24	10	Krzyzewski, Michael W.
	Illinois State	8	MW	L		23	8	Donewald, Bob
	Kansas	5	MW	A		22	10	Brown, Lawrence H.
	Louisiana Tech	10	MW	A		26	7	Russo, Andy
	Oklahoma	2	W	L	To R32	29	5	Tubbs, Billy
	Purdue	3	MW	L	To R32	22	7	Keady, Lloyd Eugene "Gene"
	Richmond	12	E	L		22	10	Tarrant, Dick
	Southern Methodist (TX)	9	W	L		25	8	Bliss, David
	Temple	8	E	L		26	5	Chaney, John
	Texas: El Paso	4	W	A	To R32	27	4	Haskins, Donald L.
	Tulsa	4	ME	A	To R32	27	4	Richardson, Nolan
	Villanova	7	ME	L		19	12	Massimino, Roland V. "Rollie"
	Virginia Commonwealth	6	E	L		23	7	Barnett, J. D.
	West Virginia	11	ME	A		20	12	Catlett, Gale
48	Alabama	9	MW	L		18	12	Sanderson, Winfrey "Wimp"
	Alabama: Birmingham	9	ME	A		23	11	Bartow, B. Gene
	Alcorn State	12	MW	A		21	10	Whitney, David L., Sr. "Davey"
	Auburn	5	E	L		20	11	Smith, Charles H. "Sonny"
	California State: Fresno	7	MW	L		25	8	Grant, Boyd "Tiny"
	Iona	10	E	A		23	8	Kennedy, Patrick
	Louisiana State	7	W	L		18	11	Brown, Dale
	Marshall	10	ME	A		25	6	Huckabay, Rick
	Miami (OH)	8	W	A		24	6	Hedric, Darrell
	Morehead State (KY)	12	ME	A		25	6	Martin, Wayne M.
	Nevada	11	W	A		17	14	Allen, William "Sonny"
	Northeastern (MA)	11	E	A		27	5	Calhoun, James A.
	Oral Roberts	11	MW	A		21	10	Acres, Richard
	Oregon State	6	ME	L		22	7	Miller, Ralph H. "Cappy"
	Princeton	12	W	A		18	10	Carril, Peter J.
	Saint John's (NY)	9	E	L		18	12	Carnesecca, Louis P. "Lou"
53	Houston Baptist	13	MW	A		24	7	Iba, Clarence Eugene "Gene"
	Long Island	13	E	L		20	11	Lizzo, Paul
	North Carolina A&T	13	ME	A		22	7	Corbett, Donald
	Rider	13	E	A		20	11	Carpenter, John B.
	San Diego	13	W	A		18	10	Brovelli, Jim

1984 Division II

1	Central Missouri State		SC	A		29	3	Nance, Lynn
2	Saint Augustine's		E	L		23	7	Heartley, Harvey D.
3	Kentucky Wesleyan		GL	A		28	3	Pollio, Mike
	North Alabama		S	A		27	7	Jones, Bill L.

F	School	SD	Reg	BD	Bye	W	L	Coach
8	Morningside		NC	L		22	9	Callahan, Dan
	Sacred Heart (CT)		NENG	L		26	7	Bike, Dave
	San Francisco State		W	A		21	11	Wilson, Kevin
	Virginia Union		SA	L		27	6	Robbins, Charles David "Dave"
16	Jacksonville State (AL)		SC	L		23	8	Jones, Bill E.
	Lewis (IL)		GL	L		22	8	Schwarz, "Chuck"
	Long Island: C W Post		E	L		26	5	Galeazzi, Thomas J.
	Norfolk State		SA	A		29	2	Christian, Charles O.
	Puget Sound		W	L		22	8	Zech, Don
	South Dakota State		NENG	L		21	9	Zulk, Gene
	Wayne State (MI)		NC	L		21	9	Parker, Charles
	West Georgia		S	L		26	4	Kaiser, Roger A.
24	Bellarmine		GL	L		21	9	Reibel, Joseph C.
	Central Connecticut State		NENG	L		26	6	Detrick, William
	Chapman		W	L		22	6	Hazzard, Walter R., Jr.
	Columbus State (GA)		SC	L		22	7	Eidsness, John
	Mansfield		E	A		26	6	Wilson, Edward W.
	Nebraska: Omaha		NC	A		23	7	Hanson, Bob
	Randolph-Macon		SA	L		26	5	Nunnally, Hal
	Tampa University		S	A		20	11	Schmidt, Richard
32	Albany State (GA)		S	A		10	19	Jones, Oliver
	American International		NENG	A		23	8	Powell, Jim
	California State: Bakersfield		GL	L		21	8	Parks, Jim
	California: Riverside		W	A		22	6	Masi, John
	Gannon		E	L		20	11	Fox, Richard A.
	Northern Michigan		NC	L		21	9	Brown, Glenn C.
	Northwest Missouri State		SC	L		24	7	Sinn, Dr. Lionel L.
	Winston-Salem State		SA	L		20	10	Gaines, Clarence E. "Big House"

1984 DIVISION III

F	School	SD	Reg	BD	Bye	W	L	Coach
1	Wisconsin: Whitewater		MW	L		27	4	Vander Meulen, David
2	Clark (MA)		NE	L		21	7	Halas, Wally
3	DePauw		GL	L		25	5	Steele, Mike
4	Upsala		SA	L		25	5	Chapman, Tom
8	Lemoyne-Owen		S	A		24	5	Johnson, Jerry C.
	Montclair State		MA	L		22	6	Gelston, Oliver S. "Ollie"
	Nazareth (NY)		E	L		21	6	Nelson, William H.
	Nebraska Wesleyan		W	L		23	5	Schmutte, Jerry
16	Framingham State		NE	A		24	2	Grealey, Bruce
	Heidelberg		GL	L		24	7	Hill, John D.
	North Carolina Wesleyan		S	A		21	8	McCarthy, John
	Potsdam State		W	L		21	7	Welsh, John Gerald "Jerry"
	Roanoke		SA	A		27	2	Green, Ed
	Saint Norbert		MW	A		21	4	Heideman, Mike
	Staten Island		E	L		25	4	Pickman, Dr. Evan T.
	Susquehanna		MA	L		21	7	Harnum, Donald
24	Buffalo State College		E	A		23	5	Bihr, Richard J.
	Capital		GL	A		23	6	Grube, David
	Claremont McKenna		W	L		16	10	Wells, David
	Hiram		NE	L		15	9	Hollinger, William H.

F	School	SD	Reg	BD	Bye	W	L	Coach
	Millsaps		S	L		20	6	Holcomb, Don
	North Central (IL)		MW	L		18	10	Warden, Bill
	Scranton		MA	A		23	6	Bessoir, Robert M.
	William Patterson		SA	A		22	6	Adams, John K.
32	Centre		S	A		18	9	Bryant, Tom C.
	Franklin & Marshall		MA	A		21	8	Robinson, Glenn R.
	Hope		GL	A		22	2	Van Wieren, Dr. Glenn
	Illinois Wesleyan		MW	A		17	11	Bridges, Dennis L.
	Luther		W	A		20	7	Leix, Jim
	Norwich		NE	L		21	6	Hockenbury, Edward J.
	Saint Lawrence		E	A		14	13	Talbot, Leon
	Washington (MD)		SA	L		19	7	Finnegan, Tom

1985 Division I

F	School	SD	Reg	BD	Bye	W	L	Coach
1	Villanova	8	SE	L		25	10	Massimino, Roland V. "Rollie"
2	Georgetown (DC)	1	E	A		35	3	Thompson, John R., Jr.
3	Memphis	2	MW	A		31	4	Kirk, Dana
	Saint John's (NY)	1	W	L		31	4	Carnesecca, Louis P. "Lou"
8	Georgia Tech	2	E	A		27	8	Cremins, Bobby
	North Carolina	2	SE	L		27	9	Smith, Dean E.
	North Carolina State	3	W	L		23	10	Valvano, James T.
	Oklahoma	1	MW	A		31	6	Tubbs, Billy
16	Alabama	7	W	L		23	10	Sanderson, Winfrey "Wimp"
	Auburn	11	SE	A		22	12	Smith, Charles H. "Sonny"
	Boston College	11	MW	L		20	11	Williams, Gary
	Illinois	3	E	L		26	9	Henson, Louis R.
	Kentucky	12	W	L		18	13	Hall, Joe B.
	Louisiana Tech	5	MW	A		29	3	Russo, Andy
	Loyola (IL)	4	E	A		27	6	Sullivan, Gene
	Maryland	5	SE	L		25	12	Driesell, Charles G. "Lefty"
32	Alabama: Birmingham	7	MW	L		25	9	Bartow, B. Gene
	Arkansas	9	W	L		22	13	Sutton, Eddie
	Duke	3	MW	L		23	8	Krzyzewski, Michael W.
	Georgia	6	E	L		22	9	Durham, Hugh
	Illinois State	9	MW	L		22	8	Donewald, Bob
	Kansas	3	SE	L		26	8	Brown, Lawrence H.
	Michigan	1	SE	A		26	4	Frieder, Bill
	Navy	13	SE	A		26	6	Evans, Paul
	Nevada: Las Vegas	4	W	A		28	4	Tarkanian, Jerry
	Notre Dame (IN)	7	SE	L		21	9	Phelps, Richard F. "Digger"
	Ohio State	4	MW	L		20	10	Miller, Eldon
	Southern Methodist (TX)	5	E	L		23	10	Bliss, David
	Syracuse	7	E	L		22	9	Boeheim, James A., Jr.
	Temple	8	E	A		25	6	Chaney, John
	Texas: El Paso	11	W	L		22	10	Haskins, Donald L.
	Virginia Commonwealth	2	W	A		26	6	Barnett, J. D.
64	Arizona	10	W	L		21	10	Olson, Robert Luther "Lute"
	Dayton	9	SE	L		19	10	Donoher, Donald J. "Mickey"
	De Paul	10	E	L		19	10	Meyer, Joseph E. "Joey"
	Fairleigh Dickinson: Rutherford/Teaneck	16	SE	A		21	10	Green, Tom

F	School	SD	Reg	BD	Bye	W	L	Coach
	Iona	13	E	A		26	5	Kennedy, Patrick
	Iowa	8	W	L		21	11	Raveling, George
	Iowa State	13	MW	L		21	13	Orr, John M. "Johnny"
	Lehigh	16	E	A		12	19	Schneider, Thomas
	Louisiana State	4	SE	L		19	10	Brown, Dale
	Marshall	15	W	A		21	13	Huckabay, Rick
	Mercer	15	E	A		22	9	Bibb, Bill
	Miami (OH)	12	SE	L		20	11	Peirson, Jerry
	Michigan State	10	MW	L		19	10	Heathcote, George "Jud"
	Middle Tennessee State	15	SE	A		17	14	Stewart, Bruce
	Nevada	14	W	A		21	10	Allen, William "Sonny"
	North Carolina A&T	16	MW	A		19	10	Corbett, Donald
	Northeastern (MA)	14	E	A		22	9	Calhoun, James A.
	Ohio University	14	SE	A		22	8	Nee, Danny
	Old Dominion	12	E	L		19	12	Webb, Paul E.
	Oregon State	10	SE	L		22	9	Miller, Ralph H. "Cappy"
	Pennsylvania	15	MW	A		13	14	Littlepage, Craig K.
	Pepperdine	14	MW	A		23	9	Harrick, Jim
	Pittsburgh	12	MW	L		17	12	Chipman, Dr. Leroy
	Purdue	6	SE	L		20	9	Keady, Lloyd Eugene "Gene"
	San Diego State	13	W	A		23	8	Gaines, David "Smokey"
	Southern California	8	MW	L		19	10	Morrison, Stanley M.
	Southern: Baton Rouge	16	W	A		19	11	Hopkins, Robert M.
	Texas Tech	6	MW	A		23	8	Myers, Gerald
	Tulsa	6	W	L		23	8	Richardson, Nolan
	Virginia Polytechnic	9	E	L		20	9	Moir, Charles
	Washington	5	W	A		22	10	Harshman, Marvel K. "Marv"
	Wichita State	11	E	A		18	13	Smithson, Eugene

1985 DIVISION II

F	School	SD	Reg	BD	Bye	W	L	Coach
1	Jacksonville State (AL)		S	A		31	1	Jones, Bill E.
2	South Dakota State		NC	A		26	7	Zulk, Gene
3	Kentucky Wesleyan		GL	L		24	7	Pollio, Mike
	Mount Saint Mary's (MD)		SA	L		28	5	Phelan, James J.
8	American International		NENG	A		29	4	Powell, Jim
	California State: Hayward		W	A		21	8	Hulst, Gary
	Long Island: C W Post		E	L		24	7	Galeazzi, Thomas J.
	Southeast Missouri State		SC	A		24	8	Shumate, Ron
16	California State: Northridge		W	A		20	10	Cassidy, Peter L.
	Delta State		SC	L		20	11	Murphy, Ed
	Grand Valley State		NC	L		21	8	Villemure, Thomas
	Philadelphia Textiles		E	L		24	7	Magee, Herbert
	Sacred Heart (CT)		NENG	L		25	7	Bike, Dave
	Tampa University		S	A		23	8	Schmidt, Richard
	Winston-Salem State		SA	L		16	12	Gaines, Clarence E. "Big House"
	Wright State (OH)		GL	L		22	7	Underhill, Ralph
24	Bridgeport		NENG	A		26	6	Webster, Bruce
	Central Missouri State		SC	L		22	7	Nance, Lynn
	Florida Southern		S	L		24	7	Scholz, George
	Millersville		E	L		27	4	Kochan, John

F	School	SD	Reg	BD	Bye	W	L	Coach
	Norfolk State		W	L		23	7	Christian, Charles O.
	Northern Michigan		NC	L		23	6	Brown, Glenn C.
	Southern Indiana		GL	L		18	11	Burns, Creighton
	Virginia Union		SA	L		31	1	Robbins, Charles David "Dave"
32	Alabama A&M		SC	L		21	10	Jobe, Ben
	Albany State (GA)		S	A		15	15	Jones, Oliver
	Bentley		NENG	L		25	6	Sullivan, Frank
	California (PA)		E	A		17	13	Loomis, Tim
	Gannon		NC	L		22	9	Chapman, Tom
	Lewis (IL)		GL	L		22	8	Schwarz, "Chuck"
	Montana State: Billings		W	L		23	7	Douglass, Pat
	Randolph-Macon		SA	L		23	8	Nunnally, Hal

1985 Division III

F	School	SD	Reg	BD	Bye	W	L	Coach
1	North Park		MW	A		27	4	Djurickovic, Bosko
2	Potsdam State		E	L		27	4	Welsh, John Gerald "Jerry"
3	Nebraska Wesleyan		W	L		25	3	Schmutte, Jerry
4	Widener		MA	A		25	7	Rowe, C. Alan
8	Centre		S	A		19	8	Bryant, Tom C.
	William Patterson		SA	A		22	7	Adams, John K.
	Wittenberg		GL	A		27	4	Hunter, Larry
	Worcester Polytechnic		NE	L		20	8	Kaufman, Kenneth J.
16	Buffalo State College		E	A		22	5	Bihr, Richard J.
	Central (IA)		W	A		16	9	Walvoord, Jack
	Clark (MA)		NE	L		20	6	Halas, Wally
	Hope		GL	A		22	4	Van Wieren, Dr. Glenn
	Lemoyne-Owen		S	A		22	7	Johnson, Jerry C.
	New Jersey		SA	A		23	6	Bannon, Kevin
	Scranton		MA	A		18	11	Bessoir, Robert M.
	Wisconsin: Whitewater		MW	L		20	8	Vander Meulen, David
24	Albany State (NY)		NE	L		22	6	Sauers, Dr. Richard J.
	Greensboro		S	A		21	7	Mikels, Ron
	Hartwick		E	L		19	7	Lambros, Nicholas H.
	Lycoming		MA	L		19	7	Burch, Clarence W. "Dutch"
	Monmouth (IL)		MW	A		18	7	Glasgow, Dr. Terry
	Otterbein		GL	L		23	4	Reynolds, Dick
	Redlands		W	A		19	9	Smith, Gary H.
	Salisbury State		SA	L		23	6	Lambert, Edward W. "Ward"
32	Alfred		E	A		17	11	Frederes, Ronald
	Augsburg		S	A		21	7	Boots, David
	DePauw		GL	L		21	7	Steele, Mike
	North Central (IL)		MW	L		20	7	Warden, Bill
	Roanoke		SA	A		21	9	Green, Ed
	Saint John's (MN)		W	A		16	12	Smith, James E.
	Washington & Jefferson		MA	A		18	6	Unice, John
	Westfield State		NE	A		10	15	White, Hilton

1986 Division I

F	School	SD	Reg	BD	Bye	W	L	Coach
1	Louisville	2	W	A		32	7	Crum, Denzil E. "Denny"
2	Duke	1	E	A		37	3	Krzyzewski, Michael W.
3	Kansas	1	MW	A		35	4	Brown, Lawrence H.
	Louisiana State	11	SE	L		26	12	Brown, Dale

F	School	SD	Reg	BD	Bye	W	L	Coach
8	Auburn	8	W	L		22	11	Smith, Charles H. "Sonny"
	Kentucky	1	SE	A		32	4	Sutton, Eddie
	Navy	7	E	A		30	5	Evans, Paul
	North Carolina State	6	MW	L		21	13	Valvano, James T.
16	Alabama	5	SE	L		24	9	Sanderson, Winfrey "Wimp"
	Cleveland State (OH)	14	E	L		29	4	Mackey, Kevin
	De Paul	12	E	L		18	13	Meyer, Joseph E. "Joey"
	Georgia Tech	2	SE	L		27	7	Cremins, Bobby
	Iowa	11	MW	L		20	12	Raveling, George
	Michigan State	5	MW	L		23	8	Heathcote, George "Jud"
	Nevada: Las Vegas	4	W	A		33	5	Tarkanian, Jerry
	North Carolina	3	W	L		28	6	Smith, Dean E.
32	Alabama: Birmingham	6	W	L		25	11	Bartow, B. Gene
	Arkansas: Little Rock	14	MW	A		23	11	Newell, Mike
	Bradley	7	W	L		32	3	Versace, Dick
	Georgetown (DC)	4	MW	L		24	8	Thompson, John R., Jr.
	Illinois	4	SE	L		22	10	Henson, Louis R.
	Maryland	5	W	L		19	14	Driesell, Charles G. "Lefty"
	Memphis	3	SE	L		28	6	Kirk, Dana
	Michigan	2	MW	A		28	5	Frieder, Bill
	Oklahoma	4	E	L		26	9	Tubbs, Billy
	Old Dominion	8	E	L		23	8	Young, Thomas J.
	Saint John's (NY)	1	W	A		31	5	Carnesecca, Louis P. "Lou"
	Saint Joseph's (PA)	6	E	A		26	6	Boyle, Jim
	Syracuse	2	E	L		26	6	Boeheim, James A., Jr.
	Temple	9	MW	L		25	6	Chaney, John
	Villanova	10	SE	L		23	14	Massimino, Roland V. "Rollie"
	Western Kentucky	8	SE	L		23	8	Haskins, Clem S.
64	Akron	15	MW	A		22	8	Huggins, Robert
	Arizona	9	W	A		23	9	Olson, Robert Luther "Lute"
	Ball State	14	SE	A		21	10	Brown, Al
	Brown	15	E	A		16	11	Cingiser, Mike
	Davidson	16	SE	A		20	11	Hussey, Bobby W.
	Drexel	15	W	A		19	12	Burke, Edward J.
	Fairfield	13	SE	A		24	7	Buonaguro, Mitch
	Indiana	3	E	L		21	8	Knight, Robert M.
	Iowa State	7	MW	L		22	11	Orr, John M. "Johnny"
	Jacksonville (FL)	8	MW	A		21	10	Wenzel, Robert
	Marist	15	SE	A		19	12	Furjanic, Matt, Jr.
	Miami (OH)	10	MW	L		24	7	Peirson, Jerry
	Mississippi Valley State	16	E	A		20	11	Stribling, Lafayette
	Missouri	11	W	L		21	14	Stewart, Norman E.
	Montana State	16	W	A		14	17	Starner, Stu
	Nebraska	9	SE	L		19	11	Iba, Moe
	North Carolina A&T	16	MW	A		22	8	Corbett, Donald
	Northeast Louisiana	13	W	A		20	10	Vining, Mike
	Northeastern (MA)	13	E	A		26	5	Calhoun, James A.
	Notre Dame (IN)	3	MW	L		23	6	Phelps, Richard F. "Digger"

F	School	SD	Reg	BD	Bye	W	L	Coach
	Pepperdine	12	W	A		25	5	Harrick, Jim
	Purdue	6	SE	L		22	10	Keady, Lloyd Eugene "Gene"
	Richmond	11	E	L		23	7	Tarrant, Dick
	Texas Tech	13	MW	A		17	14	Myers, Gerald
	Texas: El Paso	10	W	A		27	6	Haskins, Donald L.
	Tulsa	10	E	A		23	9	Barnett, J. D.
	Utah	14	W	L		20	10	Archibald, Lynn
	Virginia	5	E	L		19	11	Holland, M. Terrance "Terry"
	Virginia Polytechnic	7	SE	L		22	9	Moir, Charles
	Washington	12	MW	L		19	12	Russo, Andy
	West Virginia	9	E	L		22	11	Catlett, Gale
	Xavier (OH)	12	SE	A		25	5	Gillen, Pete

1986 Division II

F	School	SD	Reg	BD	Bye	W	L	Coach
1	Sacred Heart (CT)		NENG	A		30	4	Bike, Dave
2	Southeast Missouri State		SC	A		27	7	Shumate, Ron
3	Cheyney		E	A		28	5	Songster, Charles
	Florida Southern		S	A		24	9	Scholz, George
8	California State: Hayward		W	A		24	8	Hulst, Gary
	Norfolk State		SA	L		26	5	Christian, Charles O.
	Wayne State (MI)		NC	L		23	8	Parker, Charles
	Wright State (OH)		GL	L		28	3	Underhill, Ralph
16	Alaska: Anchorage		W	L		22	10	Larrabee, Harry
	Delta State		SC	A		23	8	Murphy, Ed
	Gannon		E	A		25	6	Chapman, Tom
	Mount Saint Mary's (MD)		SA	A		26	4	Phelan, James J.
	New Hampshire College		NENG	L		24	7	Spirou, Stanley
	Saint Cloud State		NC	A		26	4	Raymond, Lloyd E. "Butch"
	Southern Illinois: Edwardsville		GL	L		23	7	Graham, Larry
	Tampa University		S	L		22	8	Schmidt, Richard
24	Abilene Christian		SC	A		23	7	Martin, Mike
	California: Riverside		W	A		24	7	Masi, John
	Kentucky Wesleyan		GL	L		22	8	Chapman, Wayne G.
	Millersville		E	L		24	6	Kochan, John
	Montana State: Billings		NC	L		22	8	Douglass, Pat
	Springfield (MA)		NENG	A		20	12	Bilik, Dr. Edward R.
	Virginia Union		SA	L		24	8	Robbins, Charles David "Dave"
	West Georgia		S	L		20	9	Kaiser, Roger A.
32	Alabama A&M		S	A		23	9	Jobe, Ben
	Augustana (SD)		NC	L		18	11	Gross, Bill
	California Polytechnic: San Luis Obispo		W	L		23	8	Wheeler, Ernie
	Edinboro		E	L		18	13	Sims, James
	Lewis (IL)		GL	A		24	6	Schwarz, "Chuck"
	Saint Anselm		NENG	L		21	9	Brown, Robert D.
	Sam Houston State		SC	L		27	6	McPherson, Robert
	Winston-Salem State		SA	L		15	12	Gaines, Clarence E. "Big House"

F	School	SD	Reg	BD	Bye	W	L	Coach
	1986 DIVISION III							
1	Potsdam State		E	A		32	0	Welsh, John Gerald "Jerry"
2	Lemoyne-Owen		S	A		29	3	Johnson, Jerry C.
3	Nebraska Wesleyan		W	L		26	5	Schmutte, Jerry
4	Jersey City State		SA	A		24	8	Brown, Charles H.
8	Illinois Wesleyan		MW	A		19	10	Bridges, Dennis L.
	Massachusetts: Dartmouth		NE	L		22	7	Baptiste, Brian
	Otterbein		GL	A		28	3	Reynolds, Dick
	Susquehanna		MA	A		22	8	Harnum, Donald
16	Alfred		E	A		23	3	Frederes, Ronald
	Centre		S	A		21	7	Bryant, Tom C.
	DePauw		GL	L		26	2	Steele, Mike
	Dubuque		W	A		21	7	Davison, Jon L.
	Franklin & Marshall		MA	A		19	10	Robinson, Glenn R.
	Ripon		MW	A		19	6	Gillespie, Robert
	Salem State		NE	A		22	6	Thibodeau, Thomas
	Upsala		SA	L		20	6	Thompson, Russ
24	Christopher Newport		S	A		19	11	Woollum, C. J.
	Clark (MA)		NE	L		21	6	Halas, Wally
	Nazareth (NY)		E	L		23	5	Nelson, William H.
	New Jersey		SA	L		22	7	Bannon, Kevin
	Saint John's (MN)		W	A		23	5	Smith, James E.
	Washington (MD)		MA	A		20	6	Finnegan, Tom
	Wisconsin: Whitewater		MW	L		24	4	Vander Meulen, David
	Wittenberg		GL	L		23	5	Hunter, Larry
32	Calvin		GL	A		20	6	Douma, Edward
	John Carroll		S	A		11	13	Baab, Tim
	New York		E	L		21	6	Layne, Floyd
	North Park		MW	L		21	7	Djurickovic, Bosko
	Pomona-Pitzer		W	A		16	12	Popovich, Gregg
	Roanoke		SA	A		16	14	Green, Ed
	Scranton		MA	L		20	9	Bessoir, Robert M.
	Western Connecticut State		NE	L		25	3	Campbell, Bob
	1987 DIVISION I							
1	Indiana	1	MW	A		30	4	Knight, Robert M.
2	Syracuse	2	E	L		31	7	Boeheim, James A., Jr.
3	Nevada: Las Vegas	1	W	A		37	2	Tarkanian, Jerry
	Providence	6	SE	L		25	9	Pitino, Richard A. "Rick"
8	Georgetown (DC)	1	SE	A		29	5	Thompson, John R., Jr.
	Iowa	2	W	L		30	5	Davis, Dr. Thomas
	Louisiana State	10	MW	L		24	15	Brown, Dale
	North Carolina	1	E	L		32	4	Smith, Dean E.
16	Alabama	2	SE	A		28	5	Sanderson, Winfrey "Wimp"
	De Paul	3	MW	L		28	3	Meyer, Joseph E. "Joey"
	Duke	5	MW	L		24	9	Krzyzewski, Michael W.
	Florida	6	E	L		23	11	Sloan, Norman L., Jr.
	Kansas	5	SE	L		25	11	Brown, Lawrence H.
	Notre Dame (IN)	5	E	L		24	8	Phelps, Richard F. "Digger"
	Oklahoma	6	W	L		24	10	Tubbs, Billy
	Wyoming	12	W	A		24	10	Brandenburg, Jim

F	School	SD	Reg	BD	Bye	W	L	Coach
32	Auburn	8	MW	L		18	13	Smith, Charles H. "Sonny"
	Austin Peay State	14	SE	A		20	12	Kelly, Lake
	California: Los Angeles	4	W	A		25	7	Hazzard, Walter R., Jr.
	Kansas State	9	W	L		20	11	Kruger, Lon
	Michigan	9	E	L		20	12	Frieder, Bill
	New Orleans	7	SE	L		26	4	Dees, Benny
	Ohio State	9	SE	L		20	13	Williams, Gary
	Pittsburgh	3	W	L		25	8	Evans, Paul
	Purdue	3	E	L		25	5	Keady, Lloyd Eugene "Gene"
	Saint John's (NY)	6	MW	L		21	9	Carnesecca, Louis P. "Lou"
	Southwest Missouri State	13	SE	L		28	6	Spoonhour, Charles
	Temple	2	MW	A		32	4	Chaney, John
	Texas Christian	4	E	L		24	7	Killingsworth, James
	Texas: El Paso	7	W	L		25	7	Haskins, Donald L.
	Western Kentucky	10	E	L		29	9	Arnold, Murray
	Xavier (OH)	13	MW	A		19	13	Gillen, Pete
64	Alabama: Birmingham	11	SE	A		21	11	Bartow, B. Gene
	Arizona	10	W	L		18	12	Olson, Robert Luther "Lute"
	Brigham Young	10	SE	L		21	11	Anderson, Ladell
	Bucknell	16	SE	A		22	9	Woollum, Charles R.
	Central Michigan	13	W	A		22	8	Coles, Charles "Charlie"
	Clemson	4	SE	L		25	6	Ellis, Cliff
	Fairfield	16	MW	A		15	16	Buonaguro, Mitch
	Georgia	8	W	L		18	12	Durham, Hugh
	Georgia Southern	15	E	A		20	11	Kerns, Frank
	Georgia Tech	7	MW	L		16	13	Cremins, Bobby
	Houston	12	SE	L		18	12	Foster, Pat
	Idaho State	16	W	A		15	16	Boutin, Dr. James
	Illinois	3	SE	L		23	8	Henson, Louis R.
	Kentucky	8	SE	L		18	11	Sutton, Eddie
	Louisiana Tech	14	MW	A		22	8	Eagles, Tommy Joe
	Marist	14	W	A		20	10	Magarity, David
	Marshall	13	E	A		25	6	Huckabay, Rick
	Middle Tennessee State	12	E	L		22	7	Stewart, Bruce
	Missouri	4	MW	A		24	10	Stewart, Norman E.
	Navy	8	E	A		26	6	Herrmann, Pete
	North Carolina A&T	15	SE	A		24	6	Corbett, Donald
	North Carolina State	11	E	A		20	15	Valvano, James T.
	Northeastern (MA)	14	E	A		27	7	Fogel, Karl
	Pennsylvania	16	E	A		13	14	Schneider, Thomas
	San Diego	9	MW	L		24	6	Egan, Henry "Hank"
	Santa Clara	15	W	A		18	14	Williams, Carroll M.
	Southern: Baton Rouge	15	MW	A		19	12	Jobe, Ben
	Texas A&M	12	MW	A		17	14	Metcalf, Dr. Shelby R.
	Tulsa	11	W	L		22	8	Barnett, J. D.
	Virginia	5	W	L		21	10	Holland, M. Terrance "Terry"
	West Virginia	7	E	L		23	8	Catlett, Gale
	Wichita State	11	MW	A		22	11	Fogler, Eddie

F	School	SD	Reg	BD	Bye	W	L	Coach
1987 DIVISION II								
1	Kentucky Wesleyan	GL				28	5	Chapman, Wayne G.
2	Gannon	E	L			28	6	Chapman, Tom
3	Delta State	SC	L			24	9	Rives, Steve
	Montana State: Billings	W	A			24	7	Douglass, Pat
8	Florida Southern	S	A			26	6	Scholz, George
	New Hampshire College	NENG	L			24	8	Spirou, Stanley
	Norfolk State	SA	L			28	3	Christian, Charles O.
	Saint Cloud State	NC	A			24	7	Raymond, Lloyd E. "Butch"
16	Alaska: Anchorage	W	L			23	7	Abegglen, Ron
	Ferris State	NC	L			20	9	Ludwig, H. Thomas
	Millersville	E	A			27	4	Kochan, John
	Mount Saint Mary's (MD)	SA	L			26	5	Phelan, James J.
	Sacred Heart (CT)	NENG	A			19	13	Bike, Dave
	Southeast Missouri State	SC	A			20	11	Shumate, Ron
	Southern Illinois: Edwardsville	GL	L			23	7	Graham, Larry
	West Georgia	S	A			26	5	Kaiser, Roger A.
24	California State: Hayward	W	A			12	19	Hulst, Gary
	Lock Haven	NC	L			22	9	Kanaskie, Kurt
	Long Island: C W Post	E	L			25	5	Galeazzi, Thomas J.
	Saint Anselm	NENG	A			25	5	Dickson, Keith
	Southern Indiana	GL				24	6	Bial, Mark
	Tampa University	S	L			26	6	Schmidt, Richard
	Virginia Union	SA	A			25	7	Robbins, Charles David "Dave"
	West Texas A&M	SC	L			24	7	Moss, Gary
32	Abilene Christian	SC	L			18	8	Martin, Mike
	Alabama A&M	S	A			23	7	Pettaway, L. Vann
	California State: Dominguez Hills	W	A			22	9	Yanai, David
	District of Columbia	SA	L			24	6	Jones, William S.
	Johnson C Smith	GL	L			21	9	Moore, Robert D.
	New Haven	NENG	L			23	9	Grove, Stuart
	Saint Michael's (VT)	E	A			20	11	Casciano, James Paul
	Wayne State (MI)	NC	L			20	10	Parker, Charles
1987 DIVISION III								
1	North Park	MW	A			28	3	Djurickovic, Bosko
2	Clark (MA)	NE	L			27	3	Halas, Wally
3	Wittenberg	GL	A			25	8	Hunter, Larry
4	Richard Stockton	SA	A			23	8	Matthews, Gerald
8	North Carolina Wesleyan	S	L			24	7	Chambers, Bill
	Potsdam State	E	A			28	1	Welsh, John Gerald "Jerry"
	Wartburg	W	A			19	8	Levick, Lewis J. "Buzz"
	Widener	MA	A			26	4	Rowe, C. Alan
16	California State: Stanislaus	SA	L			20	8	Thomason, Bob
	Franklin & Marshall	MA	L			22	7	Robinson, Glenn R.
	Gustavus Adolphus	W	A			15	13	Brock, Charles
	Illinois Wesleyan	MW	L			17	10	Bridges, Dennis L.

F	School	SD	Reg	BD	Bye	W	L	Coach
	Massachusetts: Dartmouth		NE	L		27	1	Baptiste, Brian
	Nazareth (NY)		E	L		22	6	Daley, Michael
	Otterbein		GL	L		23	6	Reynolds, Dick
	Washington (MO)		S	L		21	7	Edwards, Mark
24	Calvin		GL	L		21	5	Douma, Edward
	Claremont McKenna		W	A		21	7	Wells, David
	DePauw		MW	L		22	6	Steele, Mike
	Norwich		NE	L		21	5	Hockenbury, Edward J.
	Roanoke		SA	A		19	10	Green, Ed
	Rust		S	A		20	9	Hayes, Naylond
	Scranton		MA	A		22	7	Bessoir, Robert M.
	Stony Brook State		E	L		21	6	Castiglie, Joe
32	Allegheny		MA	L		21	8	Reynders, John C.
	Centre		S	A		20	8	Bryant, Tom C.
	Hope		GL	A		21	5	Van Wieren, Dr. Glenn
	Ithaca		E	A		16	12	Baker, Tom
	Jersey City State		SA	L		19	8	Brown, Charles H.
	Nebraska Wesleyan		W	L		21	7	Schmutte, Jerry
	North Adams State		NE	A		20	6	Quattrocchi, John
	Ripon		MW	A		17	8	Gillespie, Robert

1988 Division I

F	School	SD	Reg	BD	Bye	W	L	Coach
1	Kansas	6	MW	L		27	11	Brown, Lawrence H.
2	Oklahoma	1	SE	A		35	4	Tubbs, Billy
3	Arizona	1	W	A		35	3	Olson, Robert Luther `Lute`
	Duke	2	E	A		28	7	Krzyzewski, Michael W.
8	Kansas State	4	ME	L		25	9	Kruger, Lon
	North Carolina	2	W	L		27	7	Smith, Dean E.
	Temple	1	E	A		32	2	Chaney, John
	Villanova	6	SE	L		24	13	Massimino, Roland V. `Rollie`
16	Iowa	5	W	L		24	10	Davis, Dr. Thomas
	Kentucky	2	SE	A		27	6	Sutton, Eddie
	Louisville	5	SE	A		24	11	Crum, Denzil E. `Denny`
	Michigan	3	W	L		26	8	Frieder, Bill
	Purdue	1	MW	A		29	4	Keady, Lloyd Eugene `Gene`
	Rhode Island	11	E	L		28	7	Penders, Thomas V.
	Richmond	13	E	A		26	7	Tarrant, Dick
	Vanderbilt	7	MW	L		20	11	Newton, Charles M. `CM`
32	Auburn	8	SE	L		19	11	Smith, Charles H. `Sonny`
	Brigham Young	4	SE	L		26	6	Anderson, Ladell
	De Paul	5	MW	L		22	8	Meyer, Joseph E. `Joey`
	Florida	6	W	L		23	12	Sloan, Norman L., Jr.
	Georgetown (DC)	8	E	L		20	10	Thompson, John R., Jr.
	Georgia Tech	5	E	L		22	10	Cremins, Bobby
	Illinois	3	SE	L		23	10	Henson, Louis R.
	Loyola Marymount	10	W	A		28	4	Westhead, Paul W.
	Maryland	7	SE	L		18	13	Wade, Bob
	Memphis	9	MW	L		20	12	Finch, Larry O.
	Murray State (KY)	14	MW	A		22	9	Newton, Steve
	Nevada: Las Vegas	4	W	L		28	6	Tarkanian, Jerry

F	School	SD	Reg	BD	Bye	W	L	Coach
	Pittsburgh	2	MW	L		24	7	Evans, Paul
	Seton Hall	8	W	L		22	13	Carlesimo, Peter J. "PJ"
	Southern Methodist (TX)	7	E	A		28	7	Bliss, David
	Syracuse	3	E	A		26	9	Boeheim, James A., Jr.
64	Arkansas	11	SE	L		21	9	Richardson, Nolan
	Baylor	8	MW	L		23	11	Iba, Clarence Eugene "Gene"
	Boise State	14	W	A		24	6	Dye, Bobby
	Boston University	15	E	A		23	8	Jarvis, Mike
	Bradley	9	SE	A		26	5	Albeck, Charles Stanley "Stan"
	California: Santa Barbara	10	SE	L		22	8	Pimm, Jerry
	Cornell (NY)	16	W	A		17	10	Dement, Mike
	Eastern Michigan	15	MW	A		22	8	Braun, Ben
	Fairleigh Dickinson: Teaneck	16	MW	A		23	7	Green, Tom
	Florida State	12	W	L		19	11	Kennedy, Patrick
	Indiana	4	E	L		19	10	Knight, Robert M.
	Iowa State	12	E	L		20	12	Orr, John M. "Johnny"
	La Salle	13	MW	A		24	10	Morris, William T. "Speedy"
	Lehigh	16	E	A		21	10	McCaffrey, Fran
	Louisiana State	9	E	L		16	14	Brown, Dale
	Missouri	6	E	L		19	11	Stewart, Norman E.
	North Carolina A&T	14	E	A		26	3	Corbett, Donald
	North Carolina State	3	MW	L		24	8	Valvano, James T.
	North Carolina: Charlotte	13	SE	A		22	9	Mullins, Jeffrey V., Jr.
	North Texas	15	W	A		17	13	Gales, Jimmy
	Notre Dame (IN)	10	E	L		20	9	Phelps, Richard F. "Digger"
	Oregon State	12	SE	L		20	11	Miller, Ralph H. "Cappy"
	Saint John's (NY)	11	W	L		17	12	Carnesecca, Louis P. "Lou"
	Southern: Baton Rouge	15	SE	A		24	7	Jobe, Ben
	Southwest Missouri State	13	W	A		22	7	Spoonhour, Charles
	Tennessee: Chattanooga	16	SE	A		20	13	McCarthy, Mack
	Texas: El Paso	9	W	L		23	10	Haskins, Donald L.
	Texas: San Antonio	14	SE	A		22	9	Burmeister, Ken
	Utah State	10	MW	A		21	10	Tueller, Rod
	Wichita State	12	MW	L		20	10	Fogler, Eddie
	Wyoming	7	W	A		26	6	Dees, Benny
	Xavier (OH)	11	MW	A		26	4	Gillen, Pete

1988 DIVISION II

F	School		Reg	BD	Bye	W	L	Coach
1	Massachusetts: Lowell		NENG	A		27	7	Doucette, Don
2	Alaska: Anchorage		W	A		24	10	Abegglen, Ron
3	Florida Southern		S	A		31	3	Scholz, George
4	Troy State: Troy		SA	L		24	10	Maestri, Don
8	Alabama A&M		GL	A		29	3	Pettaway, L. Vann
	Ferris State		NC	L		25	5	Ludwig, H. Thomas
	Gannon		E	L		24	8	Chapman, Tom
	Southeast Missouri State		SC	A		28	4	Shumate, Ron
16	California (PA)		E	A		25	6	Boone, Jim
	California State: Hayward		W	A		18	13	Hulst, Gary
	California: Riverside		NC	L		22	8	Masi, John
	Kentucky Wesleyan		GL			23	7	Chapman, Wayne G.

F	School	SD	Reg	BD	Bye	W	L	Coach
	Missouri: Saint Louis	SC	A			22	9	Meckfessel, Richard
	New Haven	NENG	L			26	5	Grove, Stuart
	North Carolina Central	SA	L			26	3	Bernard, Michael J.
	Tampa University	S	L			24	8	Schmidt, Richard
24	California State: Bakersfield	W	A			21	10	Douglass, Pat
	Le Moyne	E	A			24	6	Beilein, John
	Lewis (IL)	GL				22	8	Davis, Al
	North Alabama	S	A			17	14	Jones, Bill L.
	Quinnipiac	NENG	A			18	13	Kahn, Burt
	Saint Cloud State	NC	A			26	4	Raymond, Lloyd E. "Butch"
	South Dakota State	SC	L			21	9	Thorson, Jim
	Virginia Union	SA	A			25	6	Robbins, Charles David "Dave"
32	Angelo State	SC	L			22	11	Messbarger, Ed
	Ashland	GL	L			18	10	Lyons, Roger
	Assumption (MA)	NENG	L			20	12	Renkens, Jack
	Augustana (SD)	NC	L			20	10	Gross, Bill
	California State: Sacramento	W	L			22	8	Anders, Joe
	Kutztown	E	L			21	10	Binder, Rick
	Norfolk State	S	L			23	8	Christian, Charles O.
	Virginia State	SA	L			21	12	Deane, Harold A., Sr.

1988 DIVISION III

F	School	SD	Reg	BD	Bye	W	L	Coach
1	Ohio Wesleyan	GL	L			27	5	Mehaffey, Dr. Eugene L.
2	Scranton	MA	A			29	3	Bessoir, Robert M.
3	Nebraska Wesleyan	W	L			24	6	Schmutte, Jerry
4	Hartwick	E	L			23	6	Lambros, Nicholas H.
8	Clark (MA)	NE	L			21	7	Clark, Kevin
	Illinois Wesleyan	MW	L			23	6	Bridges, Dennis L.
	New Jersey	SA	L			26	4	Bannon, Kevin
	Washington (MO)	S	L			22	7	Edwards, Mark
16	Buffalo State College	E	A			19	10	Bihr, Richard J.
	Centre	S	A			13	15	Bryant, Tom C.
	Dubuque	W	A			21	7	Davison, Jon L.
	Emory & Henry	SA	L			17	9	Johnson, Robert J.
	Franklin & Marshall	MA	A			24	5	Robinson, Glenn R.
	Hope	GL	A			19	8	Van Wieren, Dr. Glenn
	Massachusetts: Dartmouth	NE	L			24	4	Baptiste, Brian
	Millikin	MW	L			22	6	Ramsey, Joe
24	Allegheny	MA	L			24	6	Reynders, John C.
	Ohio Northern	GL	L			21	9	Daugherty, Gale E.
	Potsdam State	E	L			24	5	Welsh, John Gerald "Jerry"
	Richard Stockton	SA	A			22	5	Matthews, Gerald
	Rust	S	A			23	5	Hayes, Naylond
	Saint John's (MN)	W	A			19	10	Smith, James E.
	Southern Maine	NE	L			21	8	Brown, Robert D.
	Wisconsin: Whitewater	MW	L			22	6	Vander Meulen, David
32	Bridgewater (VA)	SA	A			24	5	Leatherman, Bill
	Cabrini	MA	L			23	7	Dzik, John L.
	Christopher Newport	S	A			15	15	Woollum, C. J.
	Claremont McKenna	W	A			19	8	Wells, David

F	School	SD	Reg	BD	Bye	W	L	Coach
	Monmouth (IL)		MW	A		14	11	Glasgow, Dr. Terry
	Muskingum		GL	A		21	9	Burson, Dr. James
	North Adams State		NE	A		18	9	Sokaitis, Al
	Staten Island		E	L		21	9	Ruppert, Howie

1989 DIVISION I

F	School	SD	Reg	BD	Bye	W	L	Coach
1	Michigan	3	SE	L		30	7	Fisher, Stephen L.
2	Seton Hall	3	W	L		31	7	Carlesimo, Peter J. "PJ"
3	Duke	2	E	L		28	8	Krzyzewski, Michael W.
	Illinois	1	MW	L		31	5	Henson, Louis R.
8	Georgetown (DC)	1	E	A		29	5	Thompson, John R., Jr.
	Nevada: Las Vegas	4	W	A		29	8	Tarkanian, Jerry
	Syracuse	2	MW	L		30	8	Boeheim, James A., Jr.
	Virginia	5	SE	L		22	11	Holland, M. Terrance "Terry"
16	Arizona	1	W	A		29	4	Olson, Robert Luther "Lute"
	Indiana	2	W	A		27	8	Knight, Robert M.
	Louisville	4	MW	A		24	9	Crum, Denzil E. "Denny"
	Minnesota	11	E	L		19	12	Haskins, Clem S.
	Missouri	3	MW	A		29	8	Stewart, Norman E.
	North Carolina	2	SE	A		29	8	Smith, Dean E.
	North Carolina State	5	E	L		22	9	Valvano, James T.
	Oklahoma	1	SE	L		30	6	Tubbs, Billy
32	Arkansas	5	MW	A		25	7	Richardson, Nolan
	Ball State	9	MW	A		29	3	Majerus, Rick
	California: Los Angeles	7	SE	L		21	10	Harrick, Jim
	Clemson	9	W	L		19	11	Ellis, Cliff
	Colorado State	10	MW	L		23	10	Grant, Boyd "Tiny"
	De Paul	12	W	L		21	12	Meyer, Joseph E. "Joey"
	Evansville	11	W	L		25	6	Crews, Jim
	Iowa	4	E	L		23	10	Davis, Dr. Thomas
	Louisiana Tech	9	SE	L		23	9	Eagles, Tommy Joe
	Middle Tennessee State	13	SE	A		23	8	Stewart, Bruce
	Notre Dame (IN)	9	E	L		21	9	Phelps, Richard F. "Digger"
	Siena (NY)	14	E	A		25	5	Deane, Mike
	South Alabama	11	SE	A		23	9	Arrow, Ronnie
	Texas	11	MW	L		25	9	Penders, Thomas V.
	Texas: El Paso	7	W	A		26	7	Haskins, Donald L.
	West Virginia	7	E	L		26	5	Catlett, Gale
64	Alabama	6	SE	A		23	8	Sanderson, Winfrey "Wimp"
	Arkansas: Little Rock	13	MW	A		23	8	Newell, Mike
	Bucknell	15	MW	A		23	8	Woollum, Charles R.
	Creighton	14	MW	A		20	11	Barone, Anthony A. "Tony"
	East Tennessee State	16	SE	A		20	11	Robinson, Leslie G.
	Florida	7	MW	L		21	13	Sloan, Norman L., Jr.
	Florida State	4	SE	L		22	8	Kennedy, Patrick
	George Mason	15	W	A		20	11	Nestor, Ernie
	Georgia Tech	6	MW	L		20	12	Cremins, Bobby
	Idaho	13	W	A		25	6	Davis, Kermit, Jr.
	Iowa State	10	SE	L		17	12	Orr, John M. "Johnny"
	Kansas State	6	E	L		19	11	Kruger, Lon

F	School	SD	Reg	BD	Bye	W	L	Coach
	La Salle	8	SE	A		26	6	Morris, William T. "Speedy"
	Louisiana State	10	W	L		20	12	Brown, Dale
	Loyola Marymount	12	MW	A		20	11	Westhead, Paul W.
	McNeese State	16	MW	A		16	14	Welch, Steve
	Memphis	5	W	L		21	11	Finch, Larry O.
	Oregon State	6	W	L		22	8	Miller, Ralph H. "Cappy"
	Pittsburgh	8	MW	L		17	13	Evans, Paul
	Princeton	16	E	A		19	8	Carril, Peter J.
	Providence	12	SE	L		18	11	Barnes, Richard D. "Rick"
	Robert Morris	16	W	A		21	9	Durham, Jarrett
	Rutgers	13	E	A		18	13	Wenzel, Robert
	Saint Mary's (CA)	8	W	L		25	5	Nance, Lynn
	South Carolina	12	E	L		19	11	Felton, George
	South Carolina State	15	E	A		25	8	Alexander, Cyrus "Cy"
	Southern: Baton Rouge	15	SE	A		20	11	Jobe, Ben
	Southwest Missouri State	14	W	A		21	10	Spoonhour, Charles
	Stanford	3	E	L		26	7	Montgomery, Mike
	Tennessee	10	E	L		19	11	DeVoe, Donald E.
	Vanderbilt	8	E	L		19	14	Newton, Charles M. "CM"
	Xavier (OH)	14	SE	A		21	12	Gillen, Pete

1989 Division II

F	School	SD	Reg	BD	Bye	W	L	Coach
1	North Carolina Central		SA	L		28	4	Bernard, Michael J.
2	Southeast Missouri State		SC	L		27	6	Shumate, Ron
3	California: Riverside		W	A		30	4	Masi, John
4	Jacksonville State (AL)		S	A		27	6	Jones, Bill E.
8	Kentucky Wesleyan		GL	A		24	7	Chapman, Wayne G.
	Millersville		E	A		26	7	Kochan, John
	Sacred Heart (CT)		NENG	L		22	10	Bike, Dave
	Wisconsin: Milwaukee		NC	L		24	7	Antrim, Steve
16	Bellarmine		GL	L		22	8	Reibel, Joseph C.
	Bloomsburg		E	L		27	5	Chronister, Charles W.
	Bridgeport		NENG	A		25	7	Webster, Bruce
	California State: Bakersfield		W	L		21	9	Douglass, Pat
	Central Missouri State		SC	L		22	9	Wooldridge, Jim
	Northern Colorado		NC			24	6	Brillhart, Ron
	Tampa University		S	L		24	7	Schmidt, Richard
	Virginia Union		SA	A		27	4	Robbins, Charles David "Dave"
24	Alabama A&M		SA	A		26	6	Pettaway, L. Vann
	Angelo State		SC	A		18	10	Messbarger, Ed
	Augustana (SD)		NC			23	7	Gross, Bill
	Bentley		NENG	L		25	6	Sullivan, Frank
	California State: Dominguez Hills		W	L		20	10	Yanai, David
	Florida Southern		S	A		25	6	Scholz, George
	Lock Haven		E	L		23	7	Blank, Dave
	Southern Illinois: Edwardsville		GL	L		23	7	Graham, Larry

F	School	SD	Reg	BD	Bye	W	L	Coach
32	Alaska: Fairbanks	NC	A			16	13	Roderick, George T.
	Central Florida	S	L			22	8	Folliard, Thomas J.
	Ferris State	GL	L			24	6	Ludwig, H. Thomas
	Norfolk State	SA	L			24	6	Christian, Charles O.
	Northwest Missouri State	SC	A			21	9	Tappmeyer, Steve
	Philadelphia Textiles	E	A			24	7	Magee, Herbert
	Sonoma State	W	A			17	14	Walker, Dick
	Stonehill	NENG	A			23	9	Pepin, Raymond

1989 Division III

F	School	SD	Reg	BD	Bye	W	L	Coach
1	Wisconsin: Whitewater	MW	L		To R32	29	2	Vander Meulen, David
2	New Jersey	SA	A		To R32	30	2	Bannon, Kevin
3	Southern Maine	NE	A		To R32	24	7	Brown, Robert D.
4	Centre	S	A		To R32	24	7	Bryant, Tom C.
8	California State: Stanislaus	W	L		To R32	21	8	Jones, John L.
	Franklin & Marshall	MA	A		To R32	27	3	Robinson, Glenn R.
	Otterbein	GL	A		To R32	20	10	Reynolds, Dick
	Potsdam State	E	L		To R32	24	5	Welsh, John Gerald "Jerry"
16	Buffalo State College	E	A		To R32	25	4	Bihr, Richard J.
	Jersey City State	SA	L		To R32	24	4	Brown, Charles H.
	Nebraska Wesleyan	W	L		To R32	21	6	Schmutte, Jerry
	North Central (IL)	MW	L		To R32	19	9	Warden, Bill
	Washington (MD)	S	L		To R32	20	7	Finnegan, Tom
	Washington (MO)	MA	L		To R32	19	8	Edwards, Mark
	Western Connecticut State	NE	L		To R32	25	3	Campbell, Bob
	Wittenberg	GL	L		To R32	27	3	Hunter, Larry
24	Calvin	GL	A			19	7	Douma, Edward
	Grove City	MA	L		To R32	20	6	Barr, John F.
	Hampden-Sydney	SA	A		To R32	21	8	Shaver, Tony
	Merchant Marine	E	L		To R32	25	3	Cohane, Tim
	Monmouth (IL)	MW	L			20	6	Glasgow, Dr. Terry
	North Adams State	NE	L		To R32	23	2	Sokaitis, Al
	Pomona-Pitzer	W	A			18	10	Katsiaficas, Charles G.
	Rose-Hulman	S	A			19	8	Mutchner, John
32	Allegheny	GL	A			22	8	Reynders, John C.
	Millikin	MW	A		To R32	20	7	Ramsey, Joe
	Rust	S	L		To R32	21	5	Hayes, Naylond
	Salem State	NE	L		To R32	21	6	Todd, Jim
	Shenandoah	SA	L			21	9	Dutton, Dave
	Staten Island	E	L			24	7	Ruppert, Howie
	Susquehanna	MA	A		To R32	18	10	Harnum, Donald
	Wartburg	W	A			21	8	Levick, Lewis J. "Buzz"
40	Alfred	E	L			18	8	Catalino, Roman
	Beloit	MW	A			17	7	Knapton, William B.
	California State: San Bernardino	W	L			20	6	Ducey, James
	Capital	GL				21	7	Cecutti, Dave
	Christopher Newport	S	A			17	12	Woollum, C. J.
	Gustavus Adolphus	W	A			14	14	Brock, Charles
	Hope	GL	L			19	5	Van Wieren, Dr. Glenn
	Richard Stockton	SA	L			19	8	Matthews, Gerald

F	School	SD	Reg	BD	Bye	W	L	Coach
1990 DIVISION I								
1	Nevada: Las Vegas	1	W	A		35	5	Tarkanian, Jerry
2	Duke	3	E	L		29	9	Krzyzewski, Michael W.
3	Arkansas	4	MW	A		30	5	Richardson, Nolan
	Georgia Tech	4	SE	A		28	7	Cremins, Bobby
8	Connecticut	1	E	A		31	6	Calhoun, James A.
	Loyola Marymount	11	W	A		26	6	Westhead, Paul W.
	Minnesota	6	SE	L		23	9	Haskins, Clem S.
	Texas	10	MW	L		24	9	Penders, Thomas V.
16	Alabama	7	W	A		26	9	Sanderson, Winfrey "Wimp"
	Ball State	12	W	A		26	7	Hunsaker, Dick
	California: Los Angeles	7	E	A		22	11	Harrick, Jim
	Clemson	5	E	L		26	9	Ellis, Cliff
	Michigan State	1	SE	A		28	6	Heathcote, George "Jud"
	North Carolina	8	MW	L		21	13	Smith, Dean E.
	Syracuse	2	SE	L		26	7	Boeheim, James A., Jr.
	Xavier (OH)	6	MW	L		28	5	Gillen, Pete
32	Arizona	2	W	A		25	7	Olson, Robert Luther "Lute"
	California	9	E	L		22	10	Campanelli, Lou
	California: Santa Barbara	9	SE	L		21	9	Pimm, Jerry
	Dayton	12	MW	A		22	10	O'Brien, James F. X.
	Georgetown (DC)	3	MW	L		24	7	Thompson, John R., Jr.
	Kansas	2	E	L		30	5	Williams, Roy
	La Salle	4	E	A		30	2	Morris, William T. "Speedy"
	Louisiana State	5	SE	L		23	9	Brown, Dale
	Louisville	4	W	A		27	8	Crum, Denzil E. "Denny"
	Michigan	3	W	L		23	8	Fisher, Stephen L.
	Northern Iowa	14	SE	A		23	9	Miller, Eldon
	Ohio State	8	W	L		17	13	Ayers, Randy
	Oklahoma	1	MW	A		27	5	Tubbs, Billy
	Purdue	2	MW	L		22	8	Keady, Lloyd Eugene "Gene"
	Saint John's (NY)	6	E	L		24	10	Carnesecca, Louis P. "Lou"
	Virginia	7	SE	L		20	12	Holland, M. Terrance "Terry"
64	Alabama: Birmingham	10	E	L		22	9	Bartow, B. Gene
	Arkansas: Little Rock	16	W	A		20	10	Newell, Mike
	Boston University	16	E	A		18	12	Jarvis, Mike
	Brigham Young	12	E	L		21	9	Reid, Roger
	Colorado State	10	W	L		21	9	Grant, Boyd "Tiny"
	Coppin State	15	SE	A		26	7	Mitchell, Ronald C. "Fang"
	East Tennessee State	13	SE	A		27	7	Robinson, Leslie G.
	Georgia	7	MW	L		20	9	Durham, Hugh
	Houston	8	SE	L		25	8	Foster, Pat
	Idaho	13	W	A		25	6	Davis, Kermit, Jr.
	Illinois	5	MW	L		21	8	Henson, Louis R.
	Illinois State	14	W	A		18	13	Bender, Robert M., Jr.
	Indiana	8	E	L		18	11	Knight, Robert M.
	Kansas State	11	MW	L		17	15	Kruger, Lon
	Missouri	3	SE	L		26	6	Stewart, Norman E.
	Murray State (KY)	16	SE	A		21	9	Newton, Steve

F	School	SD	Reg	BD	Bye	W	L	Coach
	New Mexico State	6	W	L		26	5	McCarthy, Neil N.
	Northeast Louisiana	15	MW	A		22	8	Vining, Mike
	Notre Dame (IN)	10	SE	L		16	13	Phelps, Richard F. 'Digger'
	Oregon State	5	W	L		22	7	Anderson, Jim
	Princeton	13	MW	A		20	7	Carril, Peter J.
	Providence	9	W	L		17	12	Barnes, Richard D. 'Rick'
	Richmond	14	E	A		22	10	Tarrant, Dick
	Robert Morris	15	E	A		22	8	Durham, Jarrett
	South Florida	15	W	A		20	11	Paschal, Bobby
	Southern Mississippi	13	E	L		20	12	Turk, M. K.
	Southwest Missouri State	9	MW	L		22	7	Spoonhour, Charles
	Temple	11	E	A		20	11	Chaney, John
	Texas Southern	14	MW	A		19	12	Moreland, Robert E.
	Texas: El Paso	11	SE	A		21	11	Haskins, Donald L.
	Towson State	16	MW	A		18	13	Truax, Terry
	Villanova	12	SE	L		18	15	Massimino, Roland V. 'Rollie'

1990 DIVISION II

F	School	SD	Reg	BD	Bye	W	L	Coach
1	Kentucky Wesleyan		GL	A		31	2	Chapman, Wayne G.
2	California State: Bakersfield		W	A		29	5	Douglass, Pat
3	North Dakota		NC	L		28	7	Glas, Richard 'Rich'
4	Morehouse		SA	A		26	7	McAfee, Arthur J., Jr.
8	Bridgeport		NENG	L		24	9	Webster, Bruce
	Gannon		E	A		24	8	Dukiet, Bob
	Jacksonville State (AL)		S	A		24	5	Jones, Bill E.
	Southeast Missouri State		SC	L		26	5	Shumate, Ron
16	Ashland		GL	L		22	8	Dambrot, Keith
	Central Florida		SA	L		26	4	Folliard, Thomas J.
	Central Missouri State		W	L		27	6	Wooldridge, Jim
	East Stroudsburg		E	A		21	13	Mentesana, Sal
	Metropolitan State (CO)		NC	A		28	4	Hull, Bob
	Missouri Western State		SC	A		24	7	Smith, Tom
	North Carolina Central		S	L		23	5	Bernard, Michael J.
	Saint Anselm		NENG	A		21	11	Dickson, Keith
24	Ferris State		GL	A		18	11	Ludwig, H. Thomas
	Florida Southern		S	A		23	8	Scholz, George
	Humboldt State		W	A		20	11	Wood, Tom
	Long Island: C W Post		E	L		26	5	Galeazzi, Thomas J.
	New Hampshire College		NENG	A		26	6	Spirou, Stanley
	Norfolk State		SA	A		27	4	Christian, Charles O.
	South Dakota		NC	A		22	10	Boots, David
	West Texas A&M		SC	A		25	7	Adams, Mark L.
32	Alaska: Anchorage		NC	L		22	8	Abegglen, Ron
	California: Riverside		W	L		21	10	Masi, John
	New Haven		NENG	L		21	10	Grove, Stuart
	Slippery Rock		E	L		23	6	Barlett, Robert
	Southern Indiana		SC	L		20	10	Sinn, Dr. Lionel L.
	Southwest Baptist		GL	L		25	6	Kirksey, Jerry L.
	Tampa University		S	L		26	5	Schmidt, Richard
	Virginia Union		SA	L		27	4	Robbins, Charles David 'Dave'

F	School	SD	Reg	BD	Bye	W	L	Coach
1990 DIVISION III								
1	Rochester (NY)	E	L			27	5	Neer, Mike
2	DePauw	MW	L	To R32		24	7	Waltman, Royce
3	Washington (MD)	MA	L	To R32		25	6	Finnegan, Tom
4	Calvin	GL	A	To R32		28	3	Douma, Edward
8	Illinois Wesleyan	MW	L			22	9	Bridges, Dennis L.
	North Adams State	NE	L	To R32		23	5	Sokaitis, Al
	Western Connecticut State	A	L	To R32		27	2	Campbell, Bob
	Wittenberg	GL	A	To R32		29	2	Hipsher, Dan
16	Albany State (NY)	E	L	To R32		20	9	Sauers, Dr. Richard J.
	Averett	S	A	To R32		20	9	Hall, Ed
	Emory	S	L	To R32		25	4	Winston, Lloyd
	Johns Hopkins	MA	L			20	8	Nelson, William H.
	Massachusetts: Dartmouth	NE	A	To R32		24	6	Baptiste, Brian
	Nebraska Wesleyan	W	L	To R32		22	7	Raridon, Todd
	Richard Stockton	SA	L			21	8	Matthews, Gerald
	Saint Thomas (MN)	W	A	To R32		25	5	Fritz, Steve
32	Buffalo State College	E	A	To R32		27	2	Bihr, Richard J.
	California: San Diego	W	L	To R32		20	7	Marshall, Thomas O.
	Dubuque	W	A			19	8	Davison, Jon L.
	Emory & Henry	S	L			23	7	Johnson, Robert J.
	Franklin & Marshall	MA	A	To R32		24	4	Robinson, Glenn R.
	Hope	GL	L	To R32		22	4	Van Wieren, Dr. Glenn
	Jersey City State	A	A	To R32		25	3	Brown, Charles H.
	King's (PA)	MA	A	To R32		17	11	Atkins, Ken
	Monmouth (IL)	MW	A	To R32		20	3	Glasgow, Dr. Terry
	Muskingum	GL	A			21	9	Burson, Dr. James
	New Jersey	A	L	To R32		22	6	Marsh, Donald
	North Central (IL)	MW	A	To R32		21	6	Warden, Bill
	Potsdam State	E	L	To R32		23	5	Welsh, John Gerald "Jerry"
	Randolph-Macon	S	A	To R32		24	5	Nunnally, Hal
	Salem State	NE	L	To R32		20	8	Todd, Jim
	Southern Maine	NE	L			21	9	Brown, Robert D.
40	Christopher Newport	S	L			19	9	Woollum, C. J.
	Claremont McKenna	W	A			18	9	Wells, David
	Fairleigh Dickinson: Madison	MA	L			18	9	Kindel, Roger
	Hunter	SA	L			20	8	Amalbert, Ray
	Nazareth (NY)	E	L			20	7	Daley, Michael
	North Park	MW	L			18	9	Djurickovic, Bosko
	Otterbein	GL	L			20	9	Reynolds, Dick
	Western New England	NE	L			23	3	Broaca, Peter F.
1991 DIVISION I								
1	Duke	2	MW	L		32	7	Krzyzewski, Michael W.
2	Kansas	3	SE	L		27	8	Williams, Roy
3	Nevada: Las Vegas	1	W	A		34	1	Tarkanian, Jerry
	North Carolina	1	E	A		29	6	Smith, Dean E.
8	Arkansas	1	SE	A		34	4	Richardson, Nolan
	Saint John's (NY)	4	MW	L		23	9	Carnesecca, Louis P. "Lou"
	Seton Hall	3	W	L		25	9	Carlesimo, Peter J. "PJ"
	Temple	10	E	L		24	10	Chaney, John

F	School	SD	Reg	BD	Bye	W	L	Coach
16	Alabama	4	SE	A		23	10	Sanderson, Winfrey "Wimp"
	Arizona	2	W	A		28	7	Olson, Robert Luther "Lute"
	Connecticut	11	MW	L		20	11	Calhoun, James A.
	Eastern Michigan	12	E	A		26	7	Braun, Ben
	Indiana	2	SE	L		29	5	Knight, Robert M.
	Ohio State	1	MW	A		27	4	Ayers, Randy
	Oklahoma State	3	E	L		24	8	Sutton, Eddie
	Utah	4	W	L		30	4	Majerus, Rick
32	Arizona State	8	SE	L		20	10	Frieder, Bill
	Brigham Young	10	W	A		21	13	Reid, Roger
	Creighton	11	W	A		24	8	Barone, Anthony A. "Tony"
	Florida State	7	SE	A		21	11	Kennedy, Patrick
	Georgetown (DC)	8	W	L		19	13	Thompson, John R., Jr.
	Georgia Tech	8	MW	L		17	13	Cremins, Bobby
	Iowa	7	MW	L		21	11	Davis, Dr. Thomas
	Michigan State	5	W	L		19	11	Heathcote, George "Jud"
	North Carolina State	6	E	L		20	11	Robinson, Leslie G.
	Pennsylvania State	13	E	A		21	11	Parkhill, Bruce
	Pittsburgh	6	SE	L		21	12	Evans, Paul
	Richmond	15	E	A		22	10	Tarrant, Dick
	Texas	5	MW	L		23	9	Penders, Thomas V.
	Villanova	9	E	L		17	15	Massimino, Roland V. "Rollie"
	Wake Forest	5	SE	L		19	11	Odom, Dave
	Xavier (OH)	14	MW	A		22	10	Gillen, Pete
64	California: Los Angeles	4	E	L		23	9	Harrick, Jim
	Coastal Carolina	15	SE	A		24	8	Bergman, Russell W.
	De Paul	9	MW	L		20	9	Meyer, Joseph E. "Joey"
	East Tennessee State	10	MW	A		28	5	LeForce, Alan C.
	Georgia	11	SE	L		17	13	Durham, Hugh
	Georgia State	16	SE	A		16	15	Reinhart, Bob
	Louisiana State	6	MW	L		20	10	Brown, Dale
	Louisiana Tech	12	SE	A		21	10	Lloyd, Jerry
	Mississippi State	5	E	L		20	9	Williams, Richard
	Montana	16	W	A		23	8	Morrill, Stew
	Murray State (KY)	13	SE	A		24	9	Newton, Steve
	Nebraska	3	MW	L		26	8	Nee, Danny
	New Mexico	14	E	L		20	10	Bliss, David
	New Mexico State	6	W	L		23	6	McCarthy, Neil N.
	New Orleans	14	SE	L		23	8	Floyd, Tim
	Northeast Louisiana	15	MW	A		25	8	Vining, Mike
	Northeastern (MA)	16	E	A		22	11	Fogel, Karl
	Northern Illinois	13	MW	L		25	6	Molinari, Jim
	Pepperdine	14	W	A		22	9	Asbury, Tom
	Princeton	8	E	A		24	3	Carril, Peter J.
	Purdue	7	E	L		17	12	Keady, Lloyd Eugene "Gene"
	Rutgers	9	SE	L		19	10	Wenzel, Robert
	Saint Francis (PA)	15	W	A		24	8	Baron, James E.
	Saint Peter's	12	MW	A		24	7	Fiore, Ted

F	School	SD	Reg	BD	Bye	W	L	Coach
	South Alabama	13	W	A		22	9	Arrow, Ronnie
	Southern California	10	SE	L		19	10	Raveling, George
	Southern Mississippi	11	E	L		21	8	Turk, M. K.
	Syracuse	2	E	L		26	6	Boeheim, James A., Jr.
	Towson State	16	MW	A		19	11	Truax, Terry
	Vanderbilt	9	W	L		17	13	Fogler, Eddie
	Virginia	7	W	L		21	12	Jones, Jeffrey A.
	Wisconsin: Green Bay	12	W	A		24	7	Bennett, Richard

1991 DIVISION II

F	School	SD	Reg	BD	Bye	W	L	Coach
1	North Alabama		S	L		29	4	Elliott, Gary
2	Bridgeport		NENG	L		26	8	Webster, Bruce
3	California State: Bakersfield		W	A		25	8	Douglass, Pat
	Virginia Union		SA	L		27	5	Robbins, Charles David "Dave"
8	Ashland		GL			26	5	Dambrot, Keith
	North Dakota		NC	L		29	4	Glas, Richard "Rich"
	Philadelphia Textiles		E	A		24	8	Magee, Herbert
	Southwest Baptist		SC	A		29	3	Kirksey, Jerry L.
16	Alaska: Anchorage		W	L		19	11	Abegglen, Ron
	Central Missouri State		SC	L		27	5	Wooldridge, Jim
	Franklin Pierce		NENG	A		26	6	Luptowski, Arthur
	Grand Valley State		GL	A		26	5	Villemure, Thomas
	Long Island: C W Post		E	L		26	5	Galeazzi, Thomas J.
	South Carolina: Spartanburg		SA	L		26	3	Waters, Jerry O.
	South Dakota State		NC	A		24	8	Thorson, Jim
	Troy State: Troy		S	A		22	8	Maestri, Don
24	Bellarmine		GL			24	6	Reibel, Joseph C.
	California: Riverside		W	L		22	7	Masi, John
	Hampton		S	A		22	10	Avery, Malcolm "Zeke"
	Johnson C Smith		SA	L		23	7	Joyner, Steven Wayne
	Kentucky Wesleyan		SC			22	8	Chapman, Wayne G.
	Merrimack		NENG	L		21	9	Hammel, Bert
	Metropolitan State (CO)		NC	L		23	8	Hull, Bob
	Slippery Rock		E	L		23	9	Barlett, Robert
32	Assumption (MA)		NENG	A		24	8	Renkens, Jack
	California State: Chico		W	A		22	10	Smith, Prescott "Puck"
	Florida Southern		S	A		27	5	Gibbons, Gordon
	Missouri Western State		GL	L		23	8	Smith, Tom
	Morehouse		SA	A		21	11	McAfee, Arthur J., Jr.
	Nebraska: Kearney		NC	L		21	9	Hueser, Jerry
	Shippensburg		E	A		20	11	Goodling, Roger E.
	West Texas A&M		SC	A		25	7	Adams, Mark L.

1991 DIVISION III

F	School	SD	Reg	BD	Bye	W	L	Coach
1	Wisconsin: Platteville		MW	L	To R32	28	3	Ryan, William "Bo"
2	Franklin & Marshall		MA	L	To R32	28	3	Robinson, Glenn R.
3	Otterbein		GL	A	To R32	30	3	Reynolds, Dick
4	Ramapo		A	L	To R32	24	8	Meyer, Todd
8	Benedictine (IL)		MW	L	To R32	23	6	LaScala, Anthony
	Calvin		GL	L		25	4	Douma, Edward
	Kean		A	A	To R32	24	6	Kornegay, Ron
	Rochester (NY)		E	L		23	7	Neer, Mike

F	School	SD	Reg	BD	Bye	W	L	Coach
16	California: San Diego		W	L	To R32	23	4	Marshall, Thomas O.
	Christopher Newport		S	A	To R32	24	5	Woollum, C. J.
	Geneseo State		E	L	To R32	23	5	Pope, Tom
	Massachusetts: Dartmouth		NE	A	To R32	23	6	Baptiste, Brian
	Randolph-Macon		S	A	To R32	26	3	Nunnally, Hal
	Salem State		NE	A	To R32	26	2	Todd, Jim
	Scranton		MA	A	To R32	23	6	Bessoir, Robert M.
	Wartburg		W	L	To R32	23	5	Levick, Lewis J. "Buzz"
32	Buffalo State College		E	A	To R32	21	7	Bihr, Richard J.
	Central (IA)		W	A		16	7	Walvoord, Jack
	Claremont McKenna		W	A	To R32	22	5	Wells, David
	DePauw		MW	L	To R32	19	8	Waltman, Royce
	Emory & Henry		S	L		25	5	Johnson, Robert J.
	Hope		GL	A	To R32	24	2	Van Wieren, Dr. Glenn
	Johns Hopkins		MA	A		19	10	Nelson, William H.
	King's (PA)		MA	L	To R32	21	7	Atkins, Ken
	Ripon		MW	A		21	5	Gillespie, Robert
	Rowan		SA	L		20	8	Giannini, John
	Salisbury State		A	L	To R32	22	7	Lambert, Edward W. "Ward"
	Southern Maine		NE	L	To R32	19	8	Sokaitis, Al
	Stony Brook State		E	L	To R32	23	4	Castiglie, Joe
	Washington (MO)		S	A		19	9	Edwards, Mark
	Western Connecticut State		NE	L	To R32	22	6	Campbell, Bob
	Wittenberg		GL	A	To R32	26	3	Hipsher, Dan
40	Bethel (MN)		W	A		17	11	Palke, George
	Dickinson (PA)		MA	L		19	8	Frohman, David N.
	Illinois Wesleyan		MW	A		18	9	Bridges, Dennis L.
	Maryville (TN)		S	L		22	5	Lambert, Randy
	New Jersey Tech		SA	L		24	5	Catalano, Dr. James M.
	Rensselaer		E	L		20	5	Griffin, Michael
	Shenandoah		S	L		21	6	Dutton, Dave
	Wooster		GL	L		25	4	Moore, Stephen

1992 Division I

F	School	SD	Reg	BD	Bye	W	L	Coach
1	Duke	1	E	A		34	2	Krzyzewski, Michael W.
2	Michigan	6	SE	L		25	9	Fisher, Stephen L.
3	Cincinnati	4	MW	L		29	5	Huggins, Robert
	Indiana	2	W	L		27	7	Knight, Robert M.
8	California: Los Angeles	1	W	A		28	5	Harrick, Jim
	Kentucky	2	E	A		29	7	Pitino, Richard A. "Rick"
	Memphis	6	MW	L		23	11	Finch, Larry O.
	Ohio State	1	SE	A		26	6	Ayers, Randy
16	Florida State	3	W	L		22	10	Kennedy, Patrick
	Georgia Tech	7	MW	L		23	12	Cremins, Bobby
	Massachusetts	3	E	A		30	5	Calipari, John
	New Mexico State	12	W	A		25	8	McCarthy, Neil N.
	North Carolina	4	SE	L		23	10	Smith, Dean E.
	Oklahoma State	2	SE	L		28	8	Sutton, Eddie
	Seton Hall	4	E	L		23	9	Carlesimo, Peter J. "PJ"
	Texas: El Paso	9	MW	L		27	7	Haskins, Donald L.

F	School	SD	Reg	BD	Bye	W	L	Coach
32	Alabama	5	SE	L		26	9	Sanderson, Winfrey "Wimp"
	Arkansas	3	MW	L		26	8	Richardson, Nolan
	Connecticut	9	SE	L		20	10	Calhoun, James A.
	East Tennessee State	14	SE	A		24	7	LeForce, Alan C.
	Georgetown (DC)	6	W	L		22	10	Thompson, John R., Jr.
	Iowa	9	E	L		19	11	Davis, Dr. Thomas
	Iowa State	10	E	L		21	13	Orr, John M. "Johnny"
	Kansas	1	MW	A		27	5	Williams, Roy
	Louisiana State	7	W	L		21	10	Brown, Dale
	Louisville	8	W	L		19	11	Crum, Denzil E. "Denny"
	Michigan State	5	MW	L		22	8	Heathcote, George "Jud"
	Missouri	5	E	L		21	9	Stewart, Norman E.
	Southern California	2	MW	L		24	6	Raveling, George
	Southwestern Louisiana	13	W	A		21	11	Fletcher, Marty
	Syracuse	6	E	A		22	10	Boeheim, James A., Jr.
	Tulane	10	SE	L		22	9	Clark, Perry
64	Arizona	3	SE	L		24	7	Olson, Robert Luther "Lute"
	Brigham Young	10	W	A		25	7	Reid, Roger
	Campbell	16	E	A		19	12	Lee, Billy
	De Paul	5	W	L		20	9	Meyer, Joseph E. "Joey"
	Delaware	13	MW	A		27	4	Steinwedel, Steve
	Eastern Illinois	15	W	A		17	14	Samuels, Rick
	Evansville	8	MW	A		24	6	Crews, Jim
	Fordham	14	E	A		18	13	Macarchuk, Nick, Jr.
	Georgia Southern	15	SE	A		25	6	Kerns, Frank
	Houston	10	MW	A		25	6	Foster, Pat
	Howard (DC)	16	MW	A		17	14	Beard, Alfred, Jr. "Butch"
	La Salle	13	E	A		20	11	Morris, William T. "Speedy"
	Miami (OH)	13	MW	A		23	8	Wright, Joseph A. "Joby"
	Mississippi Valley State	16	SE	A		16	14	Stribling, Lafayette
	Montana	14	W	A		27	4	Taylor, Blaine
	Murray State (KY)	14	MW	A		17	13	Edgar, Scott
	Nebraska	8	SE	L		19	10	Nee, Danny
	North Carolina: Charlotte	7	E	L		23	9	Mullins, Jeffrey V., Jr.
	Northeast Louisiana	15	MW	A		19	10	Vining, Mike
	Oklahoma	4	W	L		21	9	Tubbs, Billy
	Old Dominion	15	E	A		15	15	Purnell, Oliver
	Pepperdine	11	MW	A		24	7	Asbury, Tom
	Princeton	11	E	A		22	6	Carril, Peter J.
	Robert Morris	16	W	A		19	12	Durham, Jarrett
	Saint John's (NY)	7	SE	L		19	11	Carnesecca, Louis P. "Lou"
	South Florida	11	W	L		19	10	Paschal, Bobby
	Southwest Missouri State	12	MW	A		23	8	Spoonhour, Charles
	Stanford	12	SE	L		18	11	Montgomery, Mike
	Temple	11	SE	L		17	13	Chaney, John
	Texas	8	E	L		23	12	Penders, Thomas V.
	Wake Forest	9	W	L		17	12	Odom, Dave
	West Virginia	12	E	L		20	12	Catlett, Gale

F	School	SD	Reg	BD	Bye	W	L	Coach
	1992 DIVISION II							
1	Virginia Union	SA	A			30	3	Robbins, Charles David "Dave"
2	Bridgeport	NENG	A			28	7	Webster, Bruce
3	California (PA)	E	A			31	2	Boone, Jim
	California State: Bakersfield	W	A			26	7	Douglass, Pat
8	Central Oklahoma	SC	L			25	7	Seward, Jim
	Jacksonville State (AL)	S	A			28	2	Jones, Bill E.
	Kentucky Wesleyan	GL				23	8	Boultinghouse, Wayne
	South Dakota State	NC	L			25	8	Thorson, Jim
16	California: Riverside	W	L			24	6	Masi, John
	Denver	NC	L			26	6	Peth, Dick
	Johnson C Smith	SA	L			25	7	Joyner, Steven Wayne
	New Hampshire College	NENG	L			24	7	Spirou, Stanley
	Philadelphia Textiles	E	A			28	4	Magee, Herbert
	South Carolina: Spartanburg	S	L			24	6	Waters, Jerry O.
	Washburn	SC	A			27	5	Chipman, Bob
	Wayne State (MI)	GL	A			23	8	Hammye, Ron
24	Albany State (GA)	SA	A			20	9	Jones, Oliver
	Grand Canyon	W	L			21	7	McCrary, Leighton
	Merrimack	NENG	A			18	14	Hammel, Bert
	North Dakota	NC	A			23	9	Glas, Richard "Rich"
	Saint Joseph's (IN)	GL				22	8	Peters, Dan
	Saint Rose	E	L			24	7	Beaury, Brian
	Texas A&M: Kingsville	SC	A			21	12	Carter, William C.
	Troy State: Troy	S	L			23	6	Maestri, Don
32	Assumption (MA)	NENG	L			19	13	Renkens, Jack
	California State: Chico	W	A			22	10	Smith, Prescott "Puck"
	Grand Valley State	GL	L			20	11	Villemure, Thomas
	Missouri Western State	SC	L			22	10	Smith, Tom
	Norfolk State	SA	L			22	10	Bernard, Michael J.
	Pace	E	L			23	7	Holloran, Darrell
	Rollins	S	A			23	8	Klusman, Tom
	Saint Cloud State	NC	L			20	12	Raymond, Lloyd E. "Butch"
	1992 DIVISION III							
1	Calvin	GL	A	To R32		31	1	Douma, Edward
2	Rochester (NY)	E	A	To R32		28	3	Neer, Mike
3	Wisconsin: Platteville	MW	L	To R32		27	4	Ryan, William "Bo"
4	Jersey City State	A	A	To R32		27	5	Brown, Charles H.
8	Franklin & Marshall	MA	A	To R32		26	4	Robinson, Glenn R.
	Maryville (TN)	S	L	To R32		25	4	Lambert, Randy
	Otterbein	GL	A	To R32		27	4	Reynolds, Dick
	Salisbury State	A	L	To R32		28	2	Lambert, Edward W. "Ward"
16	Buffalo State College	E	A	To R32		24	4	Bihr, Richard J.
	California Lutheran	W	A	To R32		16	12	Dunlop, Mike
	Eastern Connecticut State	NE	A	To R32		16	12	Switchenko, Dr. Daniel B.
	Gustavus Adolphus	W	A	To R32		22	7	Hanson, Mark

F	School	SD	Reg	BD	Bye	W	L	Coach
	Hampden-Sydney	S	A	To R32	24		6	Shaver, Tony
	Illinois Wesleyan	MW	A	To R32	22		6	Bridges, Dennis L.
	Salem State	NE	A	To R32	25		4	Todd, Jim
	Scranton	MA	L	To R32	25		3	Bessoir, Robert M.
32	Albany State (NY)	E	L		21		7	Sauers, Dr. Richard J.
	Babson	NE	L	To R32	22		4	DeBari, Sergio "Serge"
	California: San Diego	W	L	To R32	22		5	Marshall, Thomas O.
	Centre	S	A	To R32	19		8	Bryant, Tom C.
	Colorado College	W	L		22		5	Walker, Al
	Elmhurst	MW	L		19		9	Whitesell, Jim
	Ferrum	S	A		21		8	Pullen, Bill
	Hope	GL	L		23		6	Van Wieren, Dr. Glenn
	Hunter	A	L	To R32	24		5	Amalbert, Ray
	Johns Hopkins	MA	L	To R32	20		8	Nelson, William H.
	Kean	A	L		20		9	Kornegay, Ron
	King's (PA)	MA	L		20		8	Atkins, Ken
	Saint John Fisher	E	L	To R32	22		5	Ward, Robert
	Western Connecticut State	NE	L	To R32	20		6	Campbell, Bob
	Wisconsin: Whitewater	MW	L		19		9	Vander Meulen, David
	Wooster	GL	A	To R32	26		3	Moore, Stephen
40	DePauw	MW	L		20		7	Waltman, Royce
	Emory & Henry	S	L		20		9	Johnson, Robert J.
	New York	E	L		22		5	Nesci, Joe
	Richard Stockton	A	L		18		9	Matthews, Gerald
	Ripon	MW	A		19		6	Gillespie, Robert
	Simpson (IA)	W	A		18		9	Wilson, Bruce
	Susquehanna	MA	A		17		11	Marcinek, Frank
	Wittenberg	GL	L		23		6	Hipsher, Dan

1993 DIVISION I

F	School	SD	Reg	BD	Bye	W	L	Coach
1	North Carolina	1	E	L		34		4	Smith, Dean E.
2	Michigan	1	W	L		31		5	Fisher, Stephen L.
3	Kansas	2	MW	L		29		7	Williams, Roy
	Kentucky	1	SE	A		30		4	Pitino, Richard A. "Rick"
8	Cincinnati	2	E	L		27		5	Huggins, Robert
	Florida State	3	SE	L		25		10	Kennedy, Patrick
	Indiana	1	MW	A		31		4	Knight, Robert M.
	Temple	7	W	L		20		13	Chaney, John
16	Arkansas	4	E	L		22		9	Richardson, Nolan
	California	6	MW	L		21		9	Bozeman, Todd
	George Washington	12	W	L		21		9	Jarvis, Mike
	Louisville	4	MW	A		22		9	Crum, Denzil E. "Denny"
	Vanderbilt	3	W	L		28		6	Fogler, Eddie
	Virginia	6	E	L		21		10	Jones, Jeffrey A.
	Wake Forest	5	SE	L		21		9	Odom, Dave
	Western Kentucky	7	SE	A		26		6	Willard, Ralph
32	Brigham Young	7	MW	L		25		9	Reid, Roger
	California: Los Angeles	9	W	L		22		11	Harrick, Jim
	Duke	3	MW	L		24		8	Krzyzewski, Michael W.
	Illinois	6	W	L		19		13	Henson, Louis R.

F	School	SD	Reg	BD	Bye	W	L	Coach
	Iowa	4	SE	L		23	9	Davis, Dr. Thomas
	Massachusetts	3	E	A		24	7	Calipari, John
	New Mexico State	7	E	L		26	8	McCarthy, Neil N.
	Oklahoma State	5	MW	L		20	9	Sutton, Eddie
	Rhode Island	8	E	L		19	11	Skinner, Albert L., Jr.
	Saint John's (NY)	5	E	L		19	11	Mahoney, Brian C.
	Santa Clara	15	W	A		19	12	Williams, Carroll M.
	Seton Hall	2	SE	A		28	7	Carlesimo, Peter J. "PJ"
	Southern: Baton Rouge	13	W	A		21	10	Jobe, Ben
	Tulane	11	SE	L		22	9	Clark, Perry
	Utah	8	SE	L		24	7	Majerus, Rick
	Xavier (OH)	9	MW	L		24	6	Gillen, Pete
64	Arizona	2	W	A		24	4	Olson, Robert Luther "Lute"
	Ball State	15	MW	A		26	8	Hunsaker, Dick
	Boise State	14	W	A		21	8	Dye, Bobby
	California State: Long Beach	11	W	A		22	10	Greenberg, Seth
	Coastal Carolina	16	W	A		22	10	Bergman, Russell W.
	Coppin State	15	E	A		22	8	Mitchell, Ronald C. "Fang"
	Delaware	13	MW	A		22	8	Steinwedel, Steve
	East Carolina	16	E	A		13	17	Payne, Eddie
	Evansville	14	SE	A		23	7	Crews, Jim
	Georgia Tech	4	W	A		19	11	Cremins, Bobby
	Holy Cross (MA)	13	E	A		23	7	Blaney, George R.
	Iowa State	8	W	L		20	11	Orr, John M. "Johnny"
	Kansas State	6	SE	L		19	11	Altman, Dana
	Louisiana State	11	MW	L		22	11	Brown, Dale
	Manhattan	11	E	A		23	7	Fraschilla, Fran
	Marquette	12	MW	L		20	8	O'Neill, Kevin
	Memphis	10	SE	L		20	12	Finch, Larry O.
	Missouri	10	W	A		19	14	Stewart, Norman E.
	Nebraska	10	E	L		20	11	Nee, Danny
	New Mexico	5	W	A		24	7	Bliss, David
	New Orleans	8	MW	L		26	4	Floyd, Tim
	Northeast Louisiana	13	SE	A		26	5	Vining, Mike
	Pennsylvania	14	E	A		22	5	Dunphy, Fran
	Pittsburgh	9	SE	L		17	11	Evans, Paul
	Purdue	9	E	L		18	10	Keady, Lloyd Eugene "Gene"
	Rider	16	SE	A		19	11	Bannon, Kevin
	Southern Illinois	14	MW	A		23	10	Herrin, Richard "Rich"
	Southern Methodist (TX)	10	MW	L		20	8	Shumate, John H.
	Tennessee State	15	SE	A		19	10	Allen, Franklin "Frankie"
	Tennessee: Chattanooga	12	SE	A		26	7	McCarthy, Mack
	Texas Tech	12	E	A		18	12	Dickey, James
	Wright State (OH)	16	MW	A		20	10	Underhill, Ralph

F	School	SD	Reg	BD	Bye	W	L	Coach
1993 Division II								
1	California State: Bakersfield	W	A			33	0	Douglass, Pat
2	Troy State: Troy	S	L			27	5	Maestri, Don
3	New Hampshire College	NENG	A			29	4	Spirou, Stanley
	Wayne State (MI)	GL	A			22	10	Hammye, Ron
8	North Carolina Central	SA	L			26	4	Jackson, Gregory D.
	Philadelphia Textiles	E	A			30	2	Magee, Herbert
	South Dakota	NC	L			25	5	Boots, David
	Washburn	SC	L			27	5	Chipman, Bob
16	Alaska: Anchorage	W	A			21	10	Larrabee, Harry
	Delta State	S	A			22	8	Rives, Steve
	Eastern New Mexico	SC	A			23	7	Diddle, Earl
	Franklin Pierce	NENG	L			22	8	Luptowski, Arthur
	Millersville	E	A			24	6	Kochan, John
	North Dakota	NC	A			23	8	Glas, Richard "Rich"
	Northern Michigan	GL	L			22	8	Ellis, Dean
	Virginia Union	SA	A			27	3	Robbins, Charles David "Dave"
23	Alabama A&M	SA	A			28	3	Pettaway, L. Vann
	Bentley	NENG	L			24	7	Lawson, Jay
	Central Oklahoma	SC	L			23	6	Seward, Jim
	Grand Canyon	W	L			20	11	McCrary, Leighton
	Southern Indiana	GL	L			22	7	Pearl, Bruce
	Tampa University	S	L			25	5	Schmidt, Richard
	Western State (CO)	NC	L			25	5	Helman, Dr. Jay W.
32	California (PA)	E	L			23	6	Boone, Jim
	California State: Chico	W	A			23	5	Smith, Prescott "Puck"
	Colorado Christian	NC	A			20	9	Evans, Frank
	Fayetteville State	SA	L			20	9	Capel, Jeff
	Florida Southern	S	A			24	8	Gibbons, Gordon
	Gannon	E	L			20	7	Dukiet, Bob
	Indiana-Purdue: Fort Wayne	GL	A			23	6	Piazza, Andy
	Missouri Southern State	SC	A			21	10	Corn, Robert
	Saint Anselm	NENG	A			20	11	Dickson, Keith
1993 Division III								
1	Ohio Northern	GL	L	To R32		28	2	Campoli, Joe
2	Augustana (IL)	MW	A			24	7	Yount, Steve
3	Rowan	A	A	To R32		29	2	Giannini, John
4	Massachusetts: Dartmouth	NE	A	To R32		25	6	Baptiste, Brian
8	Calvin	GL	A	To R32		25	3	Douma, Edward
	Eastern Connecticut State	NE	L	To R32		21	7	Switchenko, Dr. Daniel B.
	Scranton	MA	A	To R32		27	2	Bessoir, Robert M.
	Wisconsin: Platteville	MW	L	To R32		24	4	Ryan, William "Bo"
16	Christopher Newport	S	A	To R32		23	5	Woollum, C. J.
	Emory & Henry	S	L	To R32		23	5	Johnson, Robert J.
	Franklin & Marshall	MA	A	To R32		24	4	Robinson, Glenn R.
	Geneseo State	E	L	To R32		23	4	Pope, Tom
	Hunter	A	L	To R32		25	4	Amalbert, Ray
	La Verne	W	A	To R32		20	8	Stewart, Gary
	New York	E	A	To R32		23	3	Nesci, Joe
	Saint Thomas (MN)	W	A	To R32		19	9	Fritz, Steve

F	School	SD	Reg	BD	Bye	W	L	Coach
32	Beloit		MW	A	To R32	21	5	Knapton, William B.
	Buffalo State College		E	L	To R32	21	6	Bihr, Richard J.
	California Lutheran		W	L	To R32	20	7	Dunlop, Mike
	Elizabethtown		MA	L	To R32	19	7	Schlosser, Robert A.
	Ithaca		E	L		20	7	Baker, Tom
	Lebanon Valley		MA	L		18	11	Flannery, Patrick J.
	Maryville (TN)		S	L	To R32	20	6	Lambert, Randy
	New Jersey Tech		A	L	To R32	22	4	Catalano, Dr. James M.
	Otterbein		GL	A		19	10	Reynolds, Dick
	Rhodes		S	A		21	6	Hilgeman, Herb
	Richard Stockton		A	L		21	6	Matthews, Gerald
	Saint John's (MN)		W	L		20	8	Smith, James E.
	Salem State		NE	A	To R32	18	8	Todd, Jim
	Westfield State		NE	L	To R32	22	6	Lawless, Robert
	Wisconsin: Whitewater		MW	L		18	9	Vander Meulen, David
	Wooster		GL	A	To R32	21	7	Moore, Stephen
40	Catholic		A	L		21	6	Lonergan, Mike
	Defiance		GL	L		21	6	Hohenberger, D. Marvin
	DePauw		MW	L		19	7	Fenlon, Bill
	Fredonia State		E	A		18	10	Prechtl, Gregory
	Johns Hopkins		MA	L		19	7	Nelson, William H.
	Manchester		MW	L		20	8	Alford, Stephen T.
	Virginia Wesleyan		S	A		19	9	Butterfield, Terry
	Wartburg		W	A		18	8	Levick, Lewis J. "Buzz"

1994 Division I

F	School	SD	Reg	BD	Bye	W	L	Coach
1	Arkansas	1	MW	L		31	3	Richardson, Nolan
2	Duke	2	SE	L		28	6	Krzyzewski, Michael W.
3	Arizona	2	W	A		29	6	Olson, Robert Luther "Lute"
	Florida	3	E	L		29	8	Kruger, Lon
8	Boston College	9	E	L		23	11	O'Brien, James J.
	Michigan	3	MW	L		24	8	Fisher, Stephen L.
	Missouri	1	W	L		28	4	Stewart, Norman E.
	Purdue	1	SE	A		29	5	Keady, Lloyd Eugene "Gene"
16	Connecticut	2	E	L		29	5	Calhoun, James A.
	Indiana	5	E	L		21	9	Knight, Robert M.
	Kansas	4	SE	L		27	8	Williams, Roy
	Louisville	3	W	A		28	8	Crum, Denzil E. "Denny"
	Marquette	6	SE	L		24	9	O'Neill, Kevin
	Maryland	10	MW	L		18	12	Williams, Gary
	Syracuse	4	W	L		23	7	Boeheim, James A., Jr.
	Tulsa	12	MW	L		23	8	Smith, Orlando H. "Tubby"
32	Alabama	9	SE	L		20	10	Hobbs, David
	George Washington	10	E	L		18	12	Jarvis, Mike
	Georgetown (DC)	9	MW	L		19	12	Thompson, John R., Jr.
	Kentucky	3	SE	A		27	7	Pitino, Richard A. "Rick"
	Massachusetts	2	MW	A		28	7	Calipari, John
	Michigan State	7	SE	L		20	12	Heathcote, George "Jud"
	Minnesota	6	W	L		21	12	Haskins, Clem S.
	North Carolina	1	E	A		28	7	Smith, Dean E.

F	School	SD	Reg	BD	Bye	W	L	Coach
	Oklahoma State	4	MW	L		24	10	Sutton, Eddie
	Pennsylvania	11	E	A		25	3	Dunphy, Fran
	Temple	4	E	L		23	8	Chaney, John
	Texas	6	MW	A		26	8	Penders, Thomas V.
	Virginia	7	W	L		18	13	Jones, Jeffrey A.
	Wake Forest	5	SE	L		21	12	Odom, Dave
	Wisconsin	9	W	L		18	11	Jackson, Stu
	Wisconsin: Green Bay	12	W	A		27	7	Bennett, Richard
64	Alabama: Birmingham	7	E	L		22	8	Bartow, B. Gene
	Boise State	14	W	A		17	13	Dye, Bobby
	California	5	W	L		22	8	Bozeman, Todd
	California: Los Angeles	5	MW	L		21	7	Harrick, Jim
	Central Florida	16	SE	A		21	9	Speraw, Kirk
	Charleston (SC)	12	SE	L		24	4	Kresse, John
	Cincinnati	8	W	L		22	10	Huggins, Robert
	Drexel	13	E	A		25	5	Herrion, William R.
	Hawaii	13	W	A		18	15	Wallace, Riley
	Illinois	8	MW	L		17	11	Henson, Louis R.
	James Madison	14	E	A		20	10	Driesell, Charles G. "Lefty"
	Liberty	16	E	A		18	12	Meyer, Jeff
	Loyola (MD)	15	W	A		17	13	Prosser, "Skip"
	Navy	16	W	A		17	13	DeVoe, Donald E.
	Nebraska	6	E	A		20	10	Nee, Danny
	New Mexico	10	W	L		23	8	Bliss, David
	New Mexico State	13	MW	A		23	8	McCarthy, Neil N.
	North Carolina A&T	16	MW	A		16	14	Capel, Jeff
	Ohio University	12	E	A		25	8	Hunter, Larry
	Pepperdine	14	MW	A		19	11	Asbury, Tom
	Providence	8	SE	A		20	10	Barnes, Richard D. "Rick"
	Rider	15	E	A		21	9	Bannon, Kevin
	Saint Louis	7	MW	L		23	6	Spoonhour, Charles
	Seton Hall	10	SE	L		17	13	Carlesimo, Peter J. "PJ"
	Southern Illinois	11	W	A		23	7	Herrin, Richard "Rich"
	Southwest Texas State	15	MW	A		25	7	Wooldridge, Jim
	Southwestern Louisiana	11	SE	A		22	8	Fletcher, Marty
	Tennessee State	14	SE	A		19	12	Allen, Franklin "Frankie"
	Tennessee: Chattanooga	13	SE	A		23	7	McCarthy, Mack
	Texas Southern	15	SE	A		19	11	Moreland, Robert E.
	Washington State	8	E	L		20	11	Sampson, Kelvin
	Western Kentucky	11	MW	L		20	11	Willard, Ralph

1994 DIVISION II

F	School	SD	Reg	BD	Bye	W	L	Coach
1	California State: Bakersfield		W	L		27	6	Douglass, Pat
2	Southern Indiana		GL	A		28	4	Pearl, Bruce
3	New Hampshire College		NE	A		28	5	Spirou, Stanley
	Washburn		SC	A		29	4	Chipman, Bob
8	Alabama A&M		S	L		27	5	Pettaway, L. Vann
	Indiana (PA)		E	L		27	3	Kanaskie, Kurt
	Norfolk State		SA	L		27	6	Bernard, Michael J.
	South Dakota		NC	A		24	6	Boots, David

F	School	SD	Reg	BD	Bye	W	L	Coach
16	California (PA)	E	A			25	5	Boone, Jim
	California: Riverside	W	A			22	7	Masi, John
	North Alabama	SC	A			24	6	Elliott, Gary
	North Dakota State	NC	L			21	9	Billeter, Tom
	Philadelphia Textiles	NE	A			29	2	Magee, Herbert
	Tampa University	S	L			22	9	Schmidt, Richard
	Virginia Union	SA	A			26	3	Robbins, Charles David "Dave"
	Wayne State (MI)	GL	A			25	5	Hammye, Ron
24	Alaska: Anchorage	W	A			21	10	Larrabee, Harry
	Central Missouri State	SC	L			22	8	Sundvold, Bob
	Elizabeth City State	SA	L			22	8	Mackey, Dr. Claudie J.
	Gannon	E	L			21	9	Dukiet, Bob
	Kentucky Wesleyan	GL	L			23	7	Boultinghouse, Wayne
	Long Island: C W Post	NE	L			26	5	Galeazzi, Thomas J.
	North Dakota	NC	L			23	9	Glas, Richard "Rich"
	Paine	S	A			24	7	Spry, Ronald
32	American International	NE	A			22	6	Powell, Jim
	Eckerd	S	A			17	14	Harley, James R.
	Edinboro	E	L			20	8	Walcavich, Greg
	Longwood	S	L			23	6	Carr, Ron
	Mesa State	NC	A			20	9	Schakel, Doug
	Oakland (MI)	GL	L			21	10	Kampe, Greg
	San Francisco State	W	A			20	10	Thomas, Charlie
	West Texas A&M	SC	A			20	10	Cooper, Rick

1994 Division III

F	School	SD	Reg	BD	Bye	W	L	Coach
1	Lebanon Valley	MA	A	To R32		28	4	Flannery, Patrick J.
2	New York	E	A	To R32		25	5	Nesci, Joe
3	Wittenberg	GL	L	To R32		30	2	Brown, Bill L.
4	Saint Thomas (MN)	W	A	To R32		24	7	Fritz, Steve
8	Albany State (NY)	E	L	To R32		24	3	Sauers, Dr. Richard J.
	Amherst	NE	L	To R32		22	5	Hixon, David D.
	Greensboro	S	A	To R32		26	4	Hanger, Samuel
	Washington & Jefferson	GL	L			22	3	Reiter, Tom
16	California Lutheran	W	A	To R32		25	3	Dunlop, Mike
	Franklin & Marshall	MA	A	To R32		26	2	Robinson, Glenn R.
	Hampden-Sydney	S	L			22	6	Shaver, Tony
	Illinois Wesleyan	MW	A	To R32		19	8	Bridges, Dennis L.
	Massachusetts: Dartmouth	NE	A	To R32		22	6	Baptiste, Brian
	Richard Stockton	A	L	To R32		20	7	Matthews, Gerald
	Rowan	A	A	To R32		26	2	Giannini, John
	Wisconsin: Platteville	MW	L			23	5	Ryan, William "Bo"
32	California: San Diego	W	L			21	5	Marshall, Thomas O.
	Calvin	GL	A	To R32		20	7	Douma, Edward
	Central (IA)	W	A	To R32		13	10	Walvoord, Jack
	Christopher Newport	S	L	To R32		22	5	Woollum, C. J.
	Colby	NE	L	To R32		21	4	Whitmore, Richard
	Geneseo State	E	L	To R32		22	5	Pope, Tom
	Hunter	A	L			26	3	Amalbert, Ray
	Johns Hopkins	MA	L	To R32		20	7	Nelson, William H.

F	School	SD	Reg	BD	Bye	W	L	Coach
	Kenyon		GL	A	To R32	24	4	Brown, William H.
	Manchester		MW	A	To R32	23	4	Alford, Stephen T.
	New Jersey Tech		A	L	To R32	23	4	Catalano, Dr. James M.
	Roanoke		S	A	To R32	26	2	Moir, Page
	Saint John Fisher		E	L		22	5	Ward, Robert
	Susquehanna		MA	L		19	7	Marcinek, Frank
	Williams		NE	L		22	4	Sheehy, Harry
	Wisconsin: Whitewater		MW	L	To R32	21	4	Vander Meulen, David
40	Brockport State		E	A		17	11	Bowe, Bill
	Cabrini		MA	L		23	4	Dzik, John L.
	Cornell (IA)		MW	A		17	8	Grace, Gary
	Montclair State		A	L		18	8	Del Tufo, Nicholas
	Oglethorpe		S	A		20	6	Berkshire, Jack
	Otterbein		GL	A		19	9	Reynolds, Dick
	Pomona-Pitzer		W	L		25	3	Katsiaficas, Charles G.
	Worcester State		NE	A		18	10	Moore, Tom

1995 DIVISION I

F	School	SD	Reg	BD	Bye	W	L	Coach
1	California: Los Angeles	1	W	A		31	2	Harrick, Jim
2	Arkansas	2	MW	L		32	7	Richardson, Nolan
3	North Carolina	2	SE	L		28	6	Smith, Dean E.
	Oklahoma State	4	E	A		27	10	Sutton, Eddie
8	Connecticut	2	W	L		28	5	Calhoun, James A.
	Kentucky	1	SE	A		28	5	Pitino, Richard A. "Rick"
	Massachusetts	2	E	A		29	5	Calipari, John
	Virginia	4	MW	L		25	9	Jones, Jeffrey A.
16	Arizona State	5	SE	L		24	9	Frieder, Bill
	Georgetown (DC)	6	SE	L		21	10	Thompson, John R., Jr.
	Kansas	1	MW	L		25	6	Williams, Roy
	Maryland	3	W	L		26	8	Williams, Gary
	Memphis	6	MW	L		24	10	Finch, Larry O.
	Mississippi State	5	W	L		22	8	Williams, Richard
	Tulsa	6	E	L		24	8	Smith, Orlando H. "Tubby"
	Wake Forest	1	E	A		26	6	Odom, Dave
32	Alabama	5	E	L		23	10	Hobbs, David
	Cincinnati	7	W	L		22	12	Huggins, Robert
	Iowa State	7	SE	L		23	11	Floyd, Tim
	Manhattan	13	SE	L		26	5	Fraschilla, Fran
	Miami (OH)	12	MW	L		23	7	Sendek, Herb
	Missouri	8	W	L		20	9	Stewart, Norman E.
	Old Dominion	14	E	A		21	12	Capel, Jeff
	Purdue	3	MW	A		25	7	Keady, Lloyd Eugene "Gene"
	Saint Louis	9	E	L		23	8	Spoonhour, Charles
	Stanford	10	E	L		20	9	Montgomery, Mike
	Syracuse	7	MW	L		20	10	Boeheim, James A., Jr.
	Texas	11	W	A		23	7	Penders, Thomas V.
	Tulane	9	SE	L		23	10	Clark, Perry
	Utah	4	W	A		28	6	Majerus, Rick
	Weber State	14	SE	A		21	9	Abegglen, Ron
	Western Kentucky	8	MW	A		27	4	Kilcullen, Matt

F	School	SD	Reg	BD	Bye	W	L	Coach
64	Arizona	5	MW	L		23	8	Olson, Robert Luther "Lute"
	Ball State	12	SE	A		19	11	McCallum, Ray
	Brigham Young	8	SE	L		22	10	Reid, Roger
	California State: Long Beach	13	W	A		20	10	Greenberg, Seth
	Colgate	16	MW	A		17	13	Bruen, Jack
	Drexel	13	E	A		22	8	Herrion, William R.
	Florida	10	SE	L		17	13	Kruger, Lon
	Florida International	16	W	A		11	19	Weltlich, Robert
	Gonzaga	14	W	A		21	9	Fitzgerald, Dan
	Illinois	11	E	L		19	12	Henson, Louis R.
	Indiana	9	W	L		19	12	Knight, Robert M.
	Louisville	11	MW	A		19	14	Crum, Denzil E. "Denny"
	Michigan	9	MW	L		17	14	Fisher, Stephen L.
	Michigan State	3	SE	L		22	6	Heathcote, George "Jud"
	Minnesota	8	E	L		19	12	Haskins, Clem S.
	Mount Saint Mary's (MD)	16	SE	A		17	13	Phelan, James J.
	Murray State (KY)	15	SE	A		21	9	Edgar, Scott
	Nicholls State	13	MW	A		24	6	Broussard, Rickey
	North Carolina A&T	16	E	A		15	15	Thomas, Roy C.
	North Carolina: Charlotte	7	E	L		19	9	Mullins, Jeffrey V., Jr.
	Oklahoma	4	SE	L		23	9	Sampson, Kelvin
	Oregon	6	W	L		19	9	Green, Jerry
	Pennsylvania	12	E	A		22	6	Dunphy, Fran
	Saint Peter's	15	E	A		19	11	Fiore, Ted
	Santa Clara	12	W	L		21	7	Davey, Dick
	Southern Illinois	10	MW	A		23	9	Herrin, Richard "Rich"
	Temple	10	W	L		19	11	Chaney, John
	Tennessee: Chattanooga	15	W	A		19	11	McCarthy, Mack
	Texas Southern	15	MW	A		22	7	Moreland, Robert E.
	Villanova	3	E	A		25	8	Lappas, Steve
	Wisconsin: Green Bay	14	MW	A		22	8	Bennett, Richard
	Xavier (OH)	11	SE	L		23	5	Prosser, "Skip"

1995 Division II

F	School	SD	Reg	BD	Bye	W	L	Coach
1	Southern Indiana	3	GL	L		29	4	Pearl, Bruce
2	California: Riverside	1	W	A	To R32	26	6	Masi, John
3	Indiana (PA)	1	E	A	To R32	29	2	Kanaskie, Kurt
4	Norfolk State	2	SA	L	To R32	27	7	Bernard, Michael J.
8	Alabama A&M	1	S	A	To R32	29	3	Pettaway, L. Vann
	Central Missouri State	5	SC	L		24	8	Sundvold, Bob
	Morningside	4	NC	L		24	8	Schmutte, Jerry
	New Hampshire College	3	NE	A		27	6	Spirou, Stanley
16	California (PA)	2	E	L	To R32	23	7	Boone, Jim
	Central Oklahoma	2	SC	A	To R32	23	7	Seward, Jim
	Fort Hays State	2	NC	A	To R32	24	7	Garner, Gary
	Northern Kentucky	1	GL		To R32	25	4	Shields, Ken
	Philadelphia Textiles	4	NE	L		26	5	Magee, Herbert
	Seattle Pacific	2	W	A	To R32	20	9	Bone, Ken
	Tampa University	2	S	A	To R32	25	6	Schmidt, Richard
	Virginia Union	1	SA	A	To R32	26	5	Robbins, Charles David "Dave"

F	School	SD	Reg	BD	Bye	W	L	Coach
24	California State: Los Angeles	6	W	L		18	12	Dyer, Henry
	Eckerd	5	S	L		22	10	Harley, James R.
	Millersville	3	E	L		26	4	Kochan, John
	Mississippi College	6	SC	A		21	10	Jones, Mike
	North Dakota State	3	NC			22	8	Billeter, Tom
	Quincy (IL)	4	GL	L		22	7	Hawkins, Steve
	Saint Anselm	1	NE	A	To R32	26	5	Dickson, Keith
	Shaw (NC)	4	SA	L		21	9	Walker, Keith
32	Armstrong Atlantic State	6	S	L		20	11	Mills, Griff
	California: Davis	5	W	A		20	11	Williams, Bob
	Gannon	4	E	L		22	8	Dukiet, Bob
	Johnson C Smith	3	SA	L		21	9	Joyner, Steven Wayne
	Kentucky Wesleyan	2	GL		To R32	23	6	Boultinghouse, Wayne
	Missouri Western State	1	SC	A	To R32	26	5	Smith, Tom
	Regis (CO)	1	NC	A	To R32	25	5	Porter, Lonnie
	Saint Rose	2	NE	A	To R32	25	6	Beaury, Brian
48	Adelphi	5	NE	L		19	12	O'Connor, Jim
	Bloomsburg	5	E	L		18	9	Chronister, Charles W.
	California State: Bakersfield	3	W	L		20	8	Douglass, Pat
	Dowling	6	NE	L		18	10	Pellicane, Joseph
	Grand Canyon	4	W	L		17	11	McCrary, Leighton
	Hillsdale	6	GL	A		15	14	Balikian, Bernie
	Lander	4	S	A		21	9	Horne, Finis
	Lenoir-Rhyne	6	SA	A		18	11	Lentz, John
	Longwood	5	SA	L		19	9	Carr, Ron
	Mesa State	6	NC	L		20	9	Schakel, Doug
	Morehouse	3	S	L		20	8	McAfee, Arthur J., Jr.
	North Alabama	4	SC	L		20	8	Elliott, Gary
	North Dakota	5	NC			19	9	Glas, Richard 'Rich'
	Oakland (MI)	5	GL	L		20	9	Kampe, Greg
	Washburn	3	SC	L		22	8	Chipman, Bob
	West Chester	6	E	L		17	10	Delaney, Dick

1995 Division III

1	Wisconsin: Platteville	1	W	A		31	0	Ryan, William 'Bo'
2	Manchester	1	MW	A		31	1	Alford, Stephen T.
3	Rowan	2	A	L		27	4	Giannini, John
4	Trinity (CT)	2	NE	L		24	5	Ogrodnik, Stanley
8	Hampden-Sydney	1	S	A		28	3	Shaver, Tony
	Illinois Wesleyan	2	MW	A		24	4	Bridges, Dennis L.
	New Jersey Tech	1	A	L		28	2	Catalano, Dr. James M.
	Wilkes	3	MA	L		25	5	Rickrode, Jerry
16	Baldwin-Wallace	8	GL	L		19	9	Bankson, Steve
	Franklin & Marshall	1	MA	L		27	2	Robinson, Glenn R.
	Geneseo State	8	E	L		20	8	Holmes, Steve
	Hamilton	2	E	L		21	6	Murphy, Thomas Edward
	Kenyon	6	GL	L		20	9	Brown, William H.
	Millsaps	2	S	A		25	3	Stroud, John
	Nebraska Wesleyan	3	W	L		21	7	Raridon, Todd
	Williams	4	NE	L		23	4	Sheehy, Harry

F	School	SD	Reg	BD	Bye	W	L	Coach
32	Albany State (NY)	5	E	L		18	8	Sauers, Dr. Richard J.
	Buffalo State College	3	E	A		21	8	Bihr, Richard J.
	Cabrini	4	MA	L		21	7	Dzik, John L.
	Goucher	7	MA	A		19	10	Trevino, Leonard
	Greensboro	4	S	A		19	10	Hanger, Samuel
	Hanover	5	MW	L		22	7	Beitzel, Dr. Michael
	Jersey City State	4	A	A		19	9	Brown, Charles H.
	Maryville (TN)	3	S	L		20	7	Lambert, Randy
	Massachusetts: Dartmouth	1	NE	A		24	4	Baptiste, Brian
	New York	3	A	L		22	5	Nesci, Joe
	Saint Thomas (MN)	2	W	A		27	1	Fritz, Steve
	Salem State	6	NE	A		21	7	Todd, Jim
	Washington (MO)	3	MW	A		23	4	Edwards, Mark
	Wisconsin: Whitewater	5	W	L		19	8	Vander Meulen, David
	Wittenberg	4	GL	L		21	8	Brown, Bill L.
	Wooster	2	GL	A		26	3	Moore, Stephen
64	Babson	7	NE	L		20	7	DeBari, Sergio "Serge"
	Beloit	6	MW	A		13	12	Knapton, William B.
	Calvin	5	GL	L		17	10	Douma, Edward
	Central (IA)	7	W			15	11	Walvoord, Jack
	Christopher Newport	8	S	L		18	10	Woollum, C. J.
	Colby	5	NE	L		20	5	Whitmore, Richard
	Elmira	6	E	L		17	9	Moore, Kevin
	Heidelberg	7	GL	L		17	11	Hill, John D.
	Hendrix	7	S	L		19	6	Garrison, Cliff
	Hope	1	GL	A		26	1	Van Wieren, Dr. Glenn
	Hunter	6	A	A		17	11	Amalbert, Ray
	Lebanon Valley	2	MA	A		22	6	McAlester, Brad
	Montclair State	7	A	L		17	10	Del Tufo, Nicholas
	Muhlenberg	8	MA	A		18	9	Madeira, David
	Oglethorpe	5	S	L		18	8	Berkshire, Jack
	Ohio Northern	3	GL	A		22	6	Campoli, Joe
	Plattsburgh State	7	E	L		17	10	Cowen, Larry
	Pomona-Pitzer	4	W	A		18	8	Katsiaficas, Charles G.
	Ripon	8	MW	L		19	6	Gillespie, Robert
	Roanoke	6	S	L		19	9	Moir, Page
	Rochester Tech (NY)	1	E	A		21	5	McVean, Robert
	Saint John Fisher	4	E	L		16	10	Ward, Robert
	Saint John's (MN)	8	W	L		17	9	Smith, James E.
	Salve Regina	8	NE	A		20	8	Raffa, Michael
	Simpson (IA)	6	W			20	6	Wilson, Bruce
	Staten Island	5	A	L		20	7	Petosa, Anthony
	Tufts	3	NE	L		20	5	Sheldon, Robert J., Jr.
	Westminster (MO)	7	MW	A		14	14	McEwen, Jim
	Wheaton (IL)	4	MW	L		21	5	Harris, William R.
	Widener	6	MA	L		18	9	Rowe, C. Alan
	York (NY)	8	A	L		18	7	Saint John, Ronald
	York (PA)	5	MA	L		20	8	Gamber, Jeffrey L.

F	School	SD	Reg	BD	Bye	W	L	Coach
1996 DIVISION I								
1	Kentucky	1	MW	L		34	2	Pitino, Richard A. 'Rick'
2	Syracuse	4	W	L		29	9	Boeheim, James A., Jr.
3	Massachusetts	1	E	A		35	2	Calipari, John
	Mississippi State	5	SE	A		26	8	Williams, Richard
8	Cincinnati	2	SE	L		28	5	Huggins, Robert
	Georgetown (DC)	2	E	L		29	8	Thompson, John R., Jr.
	Kansas	2	W	L		29	5	Williams, Roy
	Wake Forest	2	MW	A		26	6	Odom, Dave
16	Arizona	3	W	L		26	7	Olson, Robert Luther 'Lute'
	Arkansas	12	E	L		20	13	Richardson, Nolan
	Connecticut	1	SE	A		32	3	Calhoun, James A.
	Georgia	8	W	L		21	10	Smith, Orlando H. 'Tubby'
	Georgia Tech	3	SE	L		24	12	Cremins, Bobby
	Louisville	6	MW	L		22	12	Crum, Denzil E. 'Denny'
	Texas Tech	3	E	A		30	2	Dickey, James
	Utah	4	MW	L		27	7	Majerus, Rick
32	Boston College	11	SE	L		19	11	O'Brien, James J.
	Drexel	12	W	A		27	4	Herrion, William R.
	Eastern Michigan	9	SE	A		25	6	Braun, Ben
	Iowa	6	W	L		23	9	Davis, Dr. Thomas
	Iowa State	5	MW	A		24	9	Floyd, Tim
	Marquette	4	E	L		23	8	Deane, Mike
	New Mexico	7	E	A		28	5	Bliss, David
	North Carolina	6	E	L		21	11	Smith, Dean E.
	Princeton	13	SE	A		22	7	Carril, Peter J.
	Purdue	1	W	A		26	6	Keady, Lloyd Eugene 'Gene'
	Santa Clara	10	W	L		20	9	Davey, Dick
	Stanford	9	E	L		20	9	Montgomery, Mike
	Temple	7	SE	L		20	13	Chaney, John
	Texas	10	MW	L		21	10	Penders, Thomas V.
	Villanova	3	MW	L		26	7	Lappas, Steve
	Virginia Polytechnic	9	MW	L		23	6	Foster, William C.
64	Austin Peay State	14	SE	A		19	11	Loos, David
	Bradley	8	E	L		22	8	Molinari, Jim
	California	12	MW	L		17	11	Bozeman, Todd
	California: Los Angeles	4	SE	A		23	8	Harrick, Jim
	Canisius	13	MW	A		19	11	Beilein, John
	Central Florida	16	E	A		11	19	Speraw, Kirk
	Clemson	9	W	L		18	11	Barnes, Richard D. 'Rick'
	Colgate	16	SE	A		15	15	Bruen, Jack
	Duke	8	SE	L		18	13	Krzyzewski, Michael W.
	George Washington	11	W	L		21	8	Jarvis, Mike
	Indiana	6	SE	L		19	12	Knight, Robert M.
	Kansas State	10	E	L		17	12	Asbury, Tom

F	School	SD	Reg	BD	Bye	W	L	Coach
	Maryland	7	W	L		17	13	Williams, Gary
	Memphis	5	W	L		22	8	Finch, Larry O.
	Michigan	7	MW	L		20	12	Fisher, Stephen L.
	Mississippi Valley State	15	E	A		22	7	Stribling, Lafayette
	Monmouth (NJ)	13	E	A		20	10	Szoke, Wayne
	Montana State	13	W	A		21	9	Durham, Mick
	New Orleans	11	E	A		21	9	Price, George "Tic"
	North Carolina: Greensboro	15	SE	A		20	10	Peele, Randy
	Northeast Louisiana	15	MW	A		16	14	Vining, Mike
	Northern Illinois	14	E	A		20	10	Johnson, Rees
	Oklahoma	10	SE	L		17	13	Sampson, Kelvin
	Pennsylvania State	5	E	L		21	7	Dunn, Jerry
	Portland	14	MW	A		19	11	Chavez, Rob
	San Jose State	16	MW	A		13	17	Morrison, Stanley M.
	South Carolina State	15	W	A		22	8	Alexander, Cyrus "Cy"
	Tulsa	11	MW	A		22	8	Robinson, Steve
	Valparaiso	14	W	A		21	11	Drew, Homer
	Virginia Commonwealth	12	SE	A		24	9	Smith, Charles H. "Sonny"
	Western Carolina	16	W	A		17	13	Hopkins, Phil
	Wisconsin: Green Bay	8	MW	L		25	4	Heideman, Mike

1996 DIVISION II

F	School	SD	Reg	BD	Bye	W	L	Coach
1	Fort Hays State	1	NC	A	To R32	34	0	Garner, Gary
2	Northern Kentucky	2	GL	L	To R32	25	7	Shields, Ken
3	California (PA)	1	E	A	To R32	27	6	Boone, Jim
	Virginia Union	1	SA	A	To R32	28	3	Robbins, Charles David "Dave"
8	Alabama A&M	1	S	A	To R32	28	3	Pettaway, L. Vann
	California State: Bakersfield	1	W	A	To R32	26	4	Douglass, Pat
	North Alabama	3	SC	A		24	8	Elliott, Gary
	Saint Rose	2	NE	L	To R32	28	4	Beaury, Brian
16	Columbus State (GA)	3	S	A		26	6	Greene, Herbert
	Indiana (PA)	2	E	L		24	7	Kanaskie, Kurt
	Missouri: Rolla	1	SC	A	To R32	25	6	Martin, Dale
	Queens (NC)	2	SA	L	To R32	11	15	Layer, Dale
	Saint Anselm	1	NE	A	To R32	28	3	Dickson, Keith
	Seattle Pacific	2	W	A	To R32	23	6	Bone, Ken
	South Dakota State	2	NC	A	To R32	24	5	Nagy, Scott
	Southern Indiana	1	GL	A	To R32	25	4	Pearl, Bruce
32	California: Davis	3	W	A		24	6	Williams, Bob
	Central Missouri State	4	SC	L		22	9	Sundvold, Bob
	Edinboro	5	E	L		21	8	Walcavich, Greg
	Fairmont State	3	E	L	To R32	24	5	Haswell, Arthur "Butch"
	Florida Southern	2	S	A	To R32	26	4	Gibbons, Gordon
	Franklin Pierce	4	NE	L		23	6	Luptowski, Arthur
	Grand Canyon	5	W	L		23	6	McCrary, Leighton
	High Point	3	SA	L		24	7	Steele, Jerry
	Indianapolis	5	GL	L		20	9	Waltman, Royce
	New Hampshire College	6	NE	L		21	8	Spirou, Stanley
	North Dakota State	6	NC	L		20	9	Billeter, Tom
	Northern State (SD)	3	GL	A		23	6	Olson, Robert

F	School	SD	Reg	BD	Bye	W	L	Coach
	Pfeiffer	5	SA	L		20	8	Earlywine, Kirk
	Regis (CO)	4	NC	L		25	5	Porter, Lonnie
	South Carolina: Spartanburg	4	S	L		23	8	Waters, Jerry O.
	Texas A&M: Kingsville	2	SC	A	To R32	23	6	Carter, William C.
48	Adelphi	3	NE	A		23	7	Clifford, Steve
	Alaska: Anchorage	4	W	L		19	9	Bruns, Charlie
	Bloomsburg	4	E	L		21	7	Chronister, Charles W.
	Bluefield State (WV)	6	E	A		15	16	Brown, Terry
	Clark Atlanta	5	S	L		21	8	Witherspoon, Anthony
	Delta State	6	SC	L		18	11	Rives, Steve
	Denver	3	NC	A		22	7	Peth, Dick
	Lake Superior State	4	GL	A		19	9	Smith, Terry
	Le Moyne	5	NE	A		24	6	Hicks, Scott
	Montana State: Billings	6	W	L		19	19	Carse, Craig
	Nebraska: Kearney	5	NC	L		24	9	Hueser, Jerry
	North Carolina Central	4	SA	L		20	7	Jackson, Gregory D.
	Oakland (MI)	6	GL	L		21	8	Kampe, Greg
	Presbyterian	6	SA	A		19	11	Nibert, Gregg
	Rollins	6	S	A		20	8	Klusman, Tom
	Texas A&M: Commerce	5	SC	L		20	8	Peak, Paul

1996 Division III

F	School	SD	Reg	BD	Bye	W	L	Coach
1	Rowan	2	A	L		28	4	Giannini, John
2	Hope	2	GL	A		28	4	Van Wieren, Dr. Glenn
3	Illinois Wesleyan	2	MW	L		28	3	Bridges, Dennis L.
4	Franklin & Marshall	1	MA	A		29	3	Robinson, Glenn R.
8	Richard Stockton	1	A	A		26	4	Matthews, Gerald
	Washington (MO)	4	MW	A		23	6	Edwards, Mark
	Wilkes	2	MA	A		28	2	Rickrode, Jerry
	Wittenberg	1	GL	A		26	5	Brown, Bill L.
16	Anna Maria	3	NE	A		25	5	Phillips, Paul
	Buffalo State College	4	E	A		22	8	Bihr, Richard J.
	Christopher Newport	2	S	A		24	6	Woollum, C. J.
	Gustavus Adolphus	2	W	A		24	5	Hanson, Mark
	Rensselaer	2	E	L		20	8	Griffin, Michael
	Roanoke	1	S	A		24	5	Moir, Page
	Williams	1	NE	L		24	3	Sheehy, Harry
	Wisconsin: Whitewater	8	W	L		19	9	Vander Meulen, David
32	Bowdoin	4	NE	L		19	6	Gilbride, Timothy J.
	Cabrini	3	MA	C		24	3	Dzik, John L.
	Capital	5	GL	L		19	8	Goodwin, Damon
	Claremont McKenna	5	W	A		19	8	Wells, David
	Geneseo State	8	E	L		17	10	Holmes, Steve
	Hanover	3	MW	L		21	6	Beitzel, Dr. Michael
	Hendrix	4	S	L		21	6	Garrison, Cliff
	Jersey City State	6	A	L		16	11	Brown, Charles H.
	John Carroll	3	GL	A		19	8	Moran, Mike
	Lycoming	4	MA	L		21	6	Bressi, Joe
	Millsaps	3	S	A		22	5	Stroud, John
	New York	4	A	L		19	8	Nesci, Joe

F	School	SD	Reg	BD	Bye	W	L	Coach
	Saint Lawrence	6	E	L		18	9	Paulsen, David
	Salem State	2	NE	A		25	3	Todd, Jim
	Wheaton (IL)	1	MW	A		25	2	Harris, William R.
	Wisconsin: Oshkosh	3	W	L		23	4	Van Dellen, Ted
64	Allentown	7	MA	L		17	10	Coval, Scott
	Babson	6	NE	L		21	7	Brennan, Steve
	Baldwin-Wallace	8	GL	L		16	12	Bankson, Steve
	Bridgewater (VA)	6	S	L		18	10	Leatherman, Bill
	Catholic	6	MA	L		19	8	Lonergan, Mike
	Concordia: Moorhead	7	W	L		21	6	Siverson, Duane
	Fontbonne	6	MW	A		17	10	McKinney, Lee
	Gettysburg	5	MA	L		18	9	Petrie, George
	Grinnell	8	MW	A		17	8	Arseneault, David
	Hamilton	3	E	L		16	9	Murphy, Thomas Edward
	Hartwick	7	E	L		17	9	Lambros, Nicholas H.
	Kalamazoo	7	GL	L		17	11	Haklin, Joe
	Mount Saint Vincent	8	A	L		18	9	Mancuso, "Chuck"
	New Jersey Tech	5	A	L		17	10	Catalano, Dr. James M.
	Ohio Northern	4	GL	L		18	9	Campoli, Joe
	Plymouth State	8	NE	L		19	9	Hogan, Paul
	Randolph-Macon	7	S	L		18	9	Nunnally, Hal
	Ripon	7	MW	L		21	4	Gillespie, Robert
	Rochester Tech (NY)	1	E	L		22	4	McVean, Robert
	Rose-Hulman	5	MW	A		19	9	Shaw, Jim
	Saint John Fisher	5	E	L		20	6	Ward, Robert
	Salisbury State	8	MA	A		19	9	Lambert, Edward W. "Ward"
	Shenandoah	8	S	L		18	9	Dutton, Dave
	Simpson (IA)	6	W	L		20	6	Wilson, Bruce
	Springfield (MA)	5	NE	A		21	7	Theulen, Dr. Michael D.
	Staten Island	3	A	A		22	6	Petosa, Anthony
	Stillman	5	S	L		19	4	Robinson, Larry
	Upper Iowa	4	W	A		20	5	Engen, Stewart "Stu"
	Western Connecticut State	7	NE	A		19	8	Campbell, Bob
	Wisconsin: Platteville	1	W	A		23	3	Ryan, William "Bo"
	Wooster	6	GL	L		19	7	Moore, Stephen
	York (NY)	7	A	L		18	10	Saint John, Ronald

1997 DIVISION I

F	School	SD	Reg	BD	Bye	W	L	Coach
1	Arizona	4	SE	L		25	9	Olson, Robert Luther "Lute"
2	Kentucky	1	W	A		35	5	Pitino, Richard A. "Rick"
3	Minnesota	1	MW	A		31	4	Haskins, Clem S.
	North Carolina	1	E	A		28	7	Smith, Dean E.
8	California: Los Angeles	2	MW	A		23	8	Lavin, Steve
	Louisville	6	E	L		26	9	Crum, Denzil E. "Denny"
	Providence	10	SE	L		24	12	Gillen, Pete
	Utah	2	W	A		29	4	Majerus, Rick
16	California	5	E	L		23	9	Braun, Ben
	Clemson	4	MW	L		23	10	Barnes, Richard D. "Rick"
	Iowa State	6	MW	L		22	9	Floyd, Tim
	Kansas	1	SE	A		34	2	Williams, Roy

F	School	SD	Reg	BD	Bye	W	L	Coach
	Saint Joseph's (PA)	4	W	A		26	7	Martelli, Phil
	Stanford	6	W	L		22	8	Montgomery, Mike
	Tennessee: Chattanooga	14	SE	A		24	11	McCarthy, Mack
	Texas	10	E	L		18	12	Penders, Thomas V.
32	Boston College	5	W	A		22	9	O'Brien, James J.
	Charleston (SC)	12	SE	A		29	3	Kresse, John
	Cincinnati	3	MW	L		26	8	Huggins, Robert
	Colorado	9	E	L		22	10	Patton, Ricardo
	Coppin State	15	E	A		22	9	Mitchell, Ronald C. "Fang"
	Duke	2	SE	L		24	9	Krzyzewski, Michael W.
	Illinois	6	SE	L		22	10	Kruger, Lon
	Iowa	8	W	L		22	10	Davis, Dr. Thomas
	New Mexico	3	E	L		25	8	Bliss, David
	North Carolina: Charlotte	7	W	L		22	9	Watkins, Melvin
	Purdue	8	SE	L		18	12	Keady, Lloyd Eugene "Gene"
	Temple	9	MW	L		20	11	Chaney, John
	Tulsa	5	MW	L		24	10	Robinson, Steve
	Villanova	4	E	L		24	10	Lappas, Steve
	Wake Forest	3	W	L		24	7	Odom, Dave
	Xavier (OH)	7	MW	L		23	6	Prosser, "Skip"
64	Boston University	12	MW	A		25	5	Wolff, Dennis
	Butler (IN)	14	MW	A		23	10	Collier, Barry
	Charleston Southern	15	MW	A		17	13	Conrad, Tom
	Fairfield	16	E	A		11	19	Cormier, Paul
	Georgetown (DC)	10	W	L		20	10	Thompson, John R., Jr.
	Georgia	3	SE	L		24	9	Smith, Orlando H. "Tubby"
	Illinois State	11	MW	A		24	6	Stallings, Kevin
	Indiana	8	E	L		22	11	Knight, Robert M.
	Jackson State (MS)	16	SE	A		14	16	Stoglin, Lee Andrew "Andy"
	Long Island	13	E	A		21	9	Haskins, Ray
	Marquette	7	SE	A		22	9	Deane, Mike
	Maryland	5	SE	L		21	11	Williams, Gary
	Massachusetts	11	E	L		19	14	Flint, James "Bruiser"
	Miami (OH)	13	MW	A		21	9	Coles, Charles "Charlie"
	Mississippi	8	MW	L		20	9	Evans, Bob
	Montana	16	W	A		21	11	Taylor, Blaine
	Murray State (KY)	15	SE	A		20	10	Gottfried, Mark
	Navy	15	W	A		20	9	DeVoe, Donald E.
	Oklahoma	11	W	L		19	11	Sampson, Kelvin
	Old Dominion	14	E	A		22	11	Capel, Jeff
	Pacific (CA)	13	W	A		24	6	Thomason, Bob
	Princeton	12	E	A		24	4	Carmody, Bill
	Rhode Island	9	SE	L		20	10	Skinner, Albert L., Jr.
	Saint Mary's (CA)	14	W	A		23	8	Kent, Ernie
	South Alabama	13	SE	A		23	7	Musselman, William
	South Carolina	2	E	L		24	8	Fogler, Eddie
	Southern California	11	SE	L		17	11	Bibby, Charles Henry
	Southwest Texas State	16	MW	A		16	13	Miller, Mike

F	School	SD	Reg	BD	Bye	W	L	Coach
	Valparaiso	12	W	A		24	7	Drew, Homer
	Vanderbilt	10	MW	L		19	12	Van Breda Kolff, Jan M.
	Virginia	9	W	L		18	13	Jones, Jeffrey A.
	Wisconsin	7	E	L		18	10	Bennett, Richard

1997 DIVISION II

F	School	SD	Reg	BD	Bye	W	L	Coach
1	California State: Bakersfield	1	W	A	To R32	29	4	Douglass, Pat
2	Northern Kentucky	2	GL	L	To R32	30	5	Shields, Ken
3	Lynn	2	S	L	To R32	28	3	Price, Jeff
	Salem-Teikyo	1	E	L	To R32	28	3	Carey, Michael A.
8	Elizabeth City State	3	SA	L		22	7	Hamler, Barry
	South Dakota State	2	NC	A	To R32	25	5	Nagy, Scott
	Southern Connecticut State	2	NE	A	To R32	28	4	Leary, Arthur
	Texas A&M: Commerce	3	SC	L		24	8	Peak, Paul
16	Alabama A&M	1	S	L	To R32	24	6	Pettaway, L. Vann
	Concord	6	E	A		20	11	Cox, Steve
	Fort Hays State	1	NC	A	To R32	29	2	Garner, Gary
	Montana State: Billings	3	W	L		22	6	Carse, Craig
	New Hampshire College	1	NE	L	To R32	25	5	Spirou, Stanley
	Oakland (MI)	5	GL	L		23	8	Kampe, Greg
	Pittsburg State	5	SC	L		24	8	Iba, Clarence Eugene "Gene"
	Saint Augustine's	5	SA	A		25	8	Lee, Novell
32	Alaska: Anchorage	2	W	A	To R32	20	8	Bruns, Charlie
	Central Oklahoma	1	SC	A	To R32	24	5	Seward, Jim
	Delta State	4	S	A		25	6	Rives, Steve
	Grand Canyon	4	W	L		23	6	McCrary, Leighton
	High Point	5	E	A		18	12	Steele, Jerry
	Indianapolis	1	GL	A	To R32	23	5	Waltman, Royce
	Mansfield	2	E	A	To R32	26	4	Ackerman, Thomas E.
	Nebraska: Kearney	6	NC	L		23	8	Hueser, Jerry
	North Carolina Central	1	SA	L	To R32	20	7	Jackson, Gregory D.
	North Dakota State	5	NC	L		22	7	Billeter, Tom
	Presbyterian	2	SA	L	To R32	20	6	Nibert, Gregg
	Quincy (IL)	6	GL	L		20	9	Hawkins, Steve
	Saint Michael's (VT)	4	NE	L		23	7	Crowley, Tom
	Saint Rose	3	NE	L		29	4	Beaury, Brian
	Tampa University	6	S	A		23	7	Schmidt, Richard
	Washburn	2	SC	A	To R32	24	9	Chipman, Bob
48	Adelphi	5	NE	L		21	9	Clifford, Steve
	Albany State (GA)	5	S	A		20	10	Jones, Oliver
	Barton	3	E	L		22	5	Lievense, Ron
	California: Davis	5	W	A		20	9	Williams, Bob
	California: Riverside	6	W	A		19	9	Masi, John
	Central Missouri State	6	SC	L		21	8	Doucette, Don
	Elon	6	SA	A		16	14	Simons, Mark
	Georgia College	4	SA	A		25	5	Sellers, Terry
	Grand Valley State	4	GL	A		23	6	Smith, Jay
	Le Moyne	6	NE	A		13	17	Hicks, Scott
	Minnesota: Duluth	3	NC	L		21	6	Race, Dale M.
	Missouri Western State	4	SC	L		20	9	Smith, Tom

F	School	SD	Reg	BD	Bye	W	L	Coach
	Northern State (SD)	4	NC	L		22	6	Olson, Robert
	Pittsburgh: Johnstown	4	E	L		21	6	Rukavina, Bob
	Southern Indiana	3	GL	L		23	5	Pearl, Bruce
	West Georgia	3	S	L		23	6	Murphy, Ed

1997 Division III

F	School	SD	Reg	BD	Bye	W	L	Coach
1	Illinois Wesleyan	1	MW	A		29	2	Bridges, Dennis L.
2	Nebraska Wesleyan	3	W	L		25	6	Raridon, Todd
3	Williams	1	NE	L		27	3	Sheehy, Harry
4	Alvernia	3	MA	L		26	6	McCloskey, John R., Sr. "Jack"
8	Methodist	4	S	A		22	8	McEvoy, Bob
	Rowan	1	A	L		26	3	Cassidy, Joe
	Salisbury State	4	MA	L		25	6	Lambert, Edward W. "Ward"
	Wisconsin: Stevens Point	5	W	L		22	7	Bennett, Jack
16	Bridgewater (VA)	7	S	L		21	8	Leatherman, Bill
	Brockport State	7	E	L		17	11	Bowe, Bill
	Chicago	2	MW	A		23	5	Cunningham, Pat
	Hope	1	GL	A		26	3	Van Wieren, Dr. Glenn
	Mount Union	2	GL	A		25	5	Hood, Lee
	Richard Stockton	2	A	A		22	7	Matthews, Gerald
	Rochester Tech (NY)	1	E	L		24	4	McVean, Robert
	Salem State	3	NE	A		25	4	Meehan, Brian
32	Amherst	4	NE	L		21	5	Hixon, David D.
	Buffalo State College	4	E	A		20	9	Bihr, Richard J.
	Christopher Newport	8	S	L		19	8	Woollum, C. J.
	Goucher	2	MA	A		23	6	Trevino, Leonard
	Gustavus Adolphus	7	W	A		21	7	Hanson, Mark
	New York	4	A	L		17	7	Nesci, Joe
	Rose-Hulman	4	MW	L		19	8	Shaw, Jim
	Saint John Fisher	3	E	L		20	7	Ward, Robert
	South University (TN)	3	S	A		19	7	Thoni, Joe
	Tufts	7	NE	L		20	6	Sheldon, Robert J., Jr.
	Wabash	3	MW	A		24	5	Petty, Malcolm "Mac"
	Widener	1	MA	A		23	6	Rowe, C. Alan
	William Patterson	3	A	L		20	8	Rebimbas, Jose
	Wisconsin: Platteville	1	W	A		24	3	Ryan, William "Bo"
	Wittenberg	3	GL	L		23	6	Brown, Bill L.
	Wooster	5	GL	A		23	6	Moore, Stephen
64	Alfred	7	GL	A		15	11	Murphy, Jay
	Benedictine (IL)	7	MW	L		17	9	Bunkenburg, Keith
	Buena Vista	6	W	A		18	8	Van Haaften, Brian
	Cabrini	7	MA	A		16	9	Dzik, John L.
	Colby	5	NE	L		20	5	Whitmore, Richard
	Cortland State	6	E	L		19	9	Spanbauer, Tom
	Denison	8	GL	L		19	7	Sheridan, Michael
	Dickinson (PA)	8	MA	A		17	10	Frohman, David N.
	Hamilton	5	E	L		15	10	Murphy, Thomas Edward
	Hampden-Sydney	1	S	L		21	7	Shaver, Tony
	Jersey City State	5	A	L		17	9	Brown, Charles H.
	John Carroll	6	GL	L		21	9	Moran, Mike

F	School	SD	Reg	BD	Bye	W	L	Coach
	Lawrence	6	MW	A		22	3	Tharp, John
	Lebanon Valley	6	MA	L		17	11	McAlester, Brad
	Maryville (MO)	8	MW	A		17	11	Kruse, Dennis
	Maryville (TN)	2	S	L		20	6	Lambert, Randy
	Massachusetts: Dartmouth	2	NE	A		20	7	Baptiste, Brian
	Merchant Marine	6	A	L		19	7	Greer, Andrew
	Mount Saint Vincent	8	A	A		20	5	Mancuso, "Chuck"
	Ohio Northern	4	GL	L		19	8	Campoli, Joe
	Pomona-Pitzer	4	W	A		19	7	Katsiaficas, Charles G.
	Roanoke	5	S	A		19	8	Moir, Page
	Rochester (NY)	8	E	L		15	11	Neer, Mike
	Rust	6	S	L		17	9	Stennis, Rodney E.
	Saint Lawrence	2	E	L		22	4	Paulsen, David
	Springfield (MA)	6	NE	A		23	5	Theulen, Dr. Michael D.
	Washington (MO)	5	MW	L		17	9	Edwards, Mark
	Wentworth Tech	8	NE	A		20	8	McShane, Harry
	Wilkes	5	MA	L		20	6	Rickrode, Jerry
	Wisconsin: Oshkosh	8	W	L		19	6	Van Dellan, Ted
	Wisconsin: Whitewater	2	W	L		22	4	Vander Meulen, David
	York (NY)	7	A	A		22	6	Saint John, Ronald

1998 DIVISION I

F	School	SD	Reg	BD	Bye	W	L	Coach
1	Kentucky	2	S	A		35	4	Smith, Orlando H. "Tubby"
2	Utah	3	W	L		31	4	Majerus, Rick
3	North Carolina	1	E	A		35	4	Guthridge, Bill
	Stanford	3	MW	L		30	5	Montgomery, Mike
8	Arizona	1	W	A		31	5	Olson, Robert Luther "Lute"
	Connecticut	2	E	A		33	5	Calhoun, James A.
	Duke	1	S	L		32	4	Krzyzewski, Michael W.
	Rhode Island	8	MW	L		25	9	Harrick, Jim
16	California: Los Angeles	6	S	L		24	9	Lavin, Steve
	Maryland	4	W	L		22	11	Williams, Gary
	Michigan State	4	E	L		23	8	Izzo, Tom
	Purdue	2	MW	L		28	8	Keady, Lloyd Eugene "Gene"
	Syracuse	5	S	L		26	9	Boeheim, James A., Jr.
	Valparaiso	13	MW	A		23	10	Drew, Homer
	Washington	11	E	L		21	10	Bender, Robert M., Jr.
	West Virginia	10	W	L		25	9	Catlett, Gale
32	Arkansas	6	W	L		24	9	Richardson, Nolan
	Cincinnati	2	W	A		27	6	Huggins, Robert
	Detroit Mercy	10	MW	L		25	6	Watson, Perry
	Florida State	12	MW	L		18	14	Robinson, Steve
	Illinois	5	W	L		23	10	Kruger, Lon
	Illinois State	9	W	A		25	6	Stallings, Kevin
	Indiana	7	E	L		20	12	Knight, Robert M.
	Kansas	1	MW	A		35	4	Williams, Roy

F	School	SD	Reg	BD	Bye	W	L	Coach
	Michigan	3	S	A		25	9	Ellerbee, Brian
	New Mexico	4	S	L		24	8	Bliss, David
	North Carolina: Charlotte	8	E	L		20	11	Watkins, Melvin
	Oklahoma State	8	S	L		22	7	Sutton, Eddie
	Princeton	5	E	A		27	2	Carmody, Bill
	Richmond	14	E	A		23	8	Beilein, John
	Saint Louis	10	S	L		22	11	Spoonhour, Charles
	Western Michigan	11	MW	L		21	8	Donewald, Bob
64	Butler (IN)	13	S	A		22	11	Collier, Barry
	Charleston (SC)	14	MW	A		24	6	Kresse, John
	Clemson	6	MW	L		18	14	Barnes, Richard D. "Rick"
	Davidson	14	S	A		20	10	McKillop, Bob
	Delaware	15	MW	A		20	10	Brey, Mike
	Eastern Michigan	13	E	A		20	10	Barnes, Milton
	Fairleigh Dickinson: Teaneck	15	E	A		23	7	Green, Tom
	George Washington	9	S	L		24	9	Jarvis, Mike
	Illinois: Chicago	9	E	L		22	6	Collins, Jimmy
	Iona	12	S	A		27	6	Welsh, Tim
	Massachusetts	7	S	L		21	11	Flint, James "Bruiser"
	Miami (FL)	11	S	L		18	10	Hamilton, Leonard
	Mississippi	4	MW	L		22	7	Evans, Rob
	Murray State (KY)	9	MW	A		29	4	Gottfried, Mark
	Navy	16	E	A		19	11	DeVoe, Donald E.
	Nebraska	11	W	L		20	12	Nee, Danny
	Nevada: Las Vegas	12	E	A		20	13	Bayno, Bill
	Nicholls State	16	W	A		19	10	Broussard, Rickey
	Northern Arizona	15	W	A		21	8	Howland, Ben
	Oklahoma	10	E	L		22	11	Sampson, Kelvin
	Prairie View A&M	16	MW	A		13	17	Plummer, Elwood
	Radford	16	S	A		20	10	Bradley, Ron
	Saint John's (NY)	7	MW	L		22	10	Fraschilla, Fran
	San Francisco	14	W	A		19	11	Matthews, Philip
	South Alabama	12	W	A		21	7	Weltlich, Robert
	South Carolina	3	E	L		23	8	Fogler, Eddie
	South Carolina State	15	S	A		22	8	Alexander, Cyrus "Cy"
	Temple	7	W	L		21	9	Chaney, John
	Tennessee	8	W	L		20	9	Green, Jerry
	Texas Christian	5	MW	L		27	6	Tubbs, Billy
	Utah State	13	W	A		25	8	Eustachy, Larry
	Xavier (OH)	6	E	A		22	8	Prosser, "Skip"

1998 Division II

F	School	SD	Reg	BD	Bye	W	L	Coach
1	California: Davis	1	W	A	To R32	31	2	Williams, Bob
2	Kentucky Wesleyan	2	GL	A	To R32	30	3	Harper, Ray
3	Saint Rose	1	NE	A	To R32	27	6	Beaury, Brian
	Virginia Union	2	SA	A	To R32	26	6	Robbins, Charles David "Dave"

F	School	SD	Reg	BD	Bye	W	L	Coach
8	Delta State	2	S	A	To R32	27	4	Rives, Steve
	Fairmont State	2	E	L	To R32	27	4	Haswell, Arthur "Butch"
	Northern State (SD)	1	NC	A	To R32	27	5	Olson, Robert
	West Texas A&M	1	SC	L	To R32	26	5	Cooper, Rick
16	Catawba	1	SA	A	To R32	25	6	Baker, Jim
	Central Oklahoma	3	SC	A		25	7	Seward, Jim
	Lynn	1	S	L	To R32	22	7	Price, Jeff
	Salem-Teikyo	1	E	A	To R32	28	3	Carey, Michael A.
	Seattle Pacific	6	W	L		18	12	Bone, Ken
	South Dakota State	2	NC	A	To R32	26	3	Nagy, Scott
	Southern Indiana	1	GL	L	To R32	27	6	Pearl, Bruce
	Stonehill	2	NE	L	To R32	22	7	DeCiantis, David
32	Albany State (GA)	3	S	L		19	11	Jones, Oliver
	Assumption (MA)	4	NE	A		23	4	DeBari, Sergio "Serge"
	California State: Bakersfield	2	W	A	To R32	25	3	Clark, Henry
	California State: Los Angeles	4	W	L		18	11	Yanai, David
	Edinboro	5	E	A		26	8	Walcavich, Greg
	Metropolitan State (CO)	6	NC	L		25	5	Dunlap, Mike
	Michigan Tech	6	GL	L		21	10	Luke, Kevin
	Missouri Western State	2	SC	A	To R32	23	7	Smith, Tom
	Nebraska: Kearney	5	NC	A		25	6	Kropp, Tom
	New Hampshire College	6	NE	A		19	11	Spirou, Stanley
	Northern Kentucky	5	GL	L		23	7	Shields, Ken
	Pittsburg State	5	SC	L		24	7	Iba, Clarence Eugene "Gene"
	Pittsburgh: Johnstown	6	E	L		24	5	Rukavina, Bob
	South Carolina: Aiken	4	SA	L		20	10	Roberts, Mike
	South Carolina: Spartanburg	6	SA	L		22	7	Nottingham, Gary
	West Georgia	5	S	L		21	8	Murphy, Ed
48	Adelphi	5	NE	L		22	8	Clifford, Steve
	California (PA)	4	E	L		23	5	Brown, William H.
	Columbus State (GA)	5	SA	A		26	7	Greene, Herbert
	Dowling	3	NE	L		22	6	Pellicane, Joseph
	Ferris State	4	GL	A		21	12	Wilson, Edgar
	Florida Southern	6	S	A		23	7	Gibbons, Gordon
	Fort Hays State	3	NC	L		22	7	Wintz, Chad
	Fort Valley State	4	S	A		19	12	Moore, Michael D.
	Grand Canyon	3	W	L		17	10	McCrary, Leighton
	Johnson C Smith	3	SA	L		21	7	Joyner, Steven Wayne
	Lewis (IL)	3	GL	L		19	9	Whitesell, Jim
	Montana State: Billings	5	W	A		21	7	Carse, Craig
	Northwest Missouri State	4	SC	L		23	7	Tappmeyer, Steve
	Queens (NC)	3	E	A		24	6	Layer, Dale
	Southern Colorado	4	NC	L		22	8	Folda, Joe
	Texas A&M: Commerce	6	SC	L		22	7	Peak, Paul

F	School	SD	Reg	BD	Bye	W	L	Coach
1998 DIVISION III								
1	Wisconsin: Platteville	1	W	A	To R32	30	0	Ryan, William "Bo"
2	Hope	2	GL	L	To R32	26	5	Van Wieren, Dr. Glenn
3	Williams	4	NE	L		26	4	Sheehy, Harry
4	Wilkes	1	MA	A	To R32	26	5	Rickrode, Jerry
8	Gustavus Adolphus	3	W	A		26	4	Hanson, Mark
	Hunter	1	A	A	To R32	28	2	Brown, Mike
	John Carroll	4	GL	L		22	7	Moran, Mike
	Saint Lawrence	1	E	A	To R32	24	2	Downs, Chris
16	Catholic	2	MA	A	To R32	25	4	Lonergan, Mike
	Chicago	2	MW	A	To R32	23	3	Cunningham, Pat
	Christopher Newport	1	S	A	To R32	26	2	Woollum, C. J.
	Connecticut College	2	NE	L	To R32	22	4	Miller, Glen
	Hamilton	3	E	L		17	10	Murphy, Thomas Edward
	Hampden-Sydney	2	S	A	To R32	23	6	Shaver, Tony
	Illinois Wesleyan	1	MW	A	To R32	22	5	Bridges, Dennis L.
	Rowan	3	A	L		21	8	Cassidy, Joe
32	Allegheny	3	GL	A		22	7	Ness, Phillip E.
	Franklin (IN)	5	MW	L		23	6	Prather, Kerry
	Jersey City State	4	A	L		19	8	Brown, Charles H.
	Johns Hopkins	3	MA	L		21	7	Nelson, William H.
	Mississippi College	4	S	L		23	4	Jones, Mike
	Nazareth (NY)	5	E	A		19	8	Daley, Michael
	Nebraska Wesleyan	2	W	L	To R32	23	3	Raridon, Todd
	New Jersey	2	A	A	To R32	22	5	Castaldo, John
	Saint John Fisher	2	E	L	To R32	22	4	Ward, Robert
	Salem State	3	NE	A		25	3	Meehan, Brian
	Scranton	4	MA	L		18	11	Bessoir, Robert M.
	Springfield (MA)	1	NE	A	To R32	26	2	Theulen, Dr. Michael D.
	Trinity (TX)	3	S	A		21	6	Brock, Charles
	Wabash	3	MW	A		22	5	Petty, Malcolm "Mac"
	Wisconsin: Oshkosh	4	W	L		21	6	Van Dellen, Ted
	Wooster	1	GL	L	To R32	22	6	Moore, Stephen
48	Albion	5	GL	A		20	8	Turner, Michael
	Augsburg	6	W	L		22	4	Ammann, Brian
	Aurora	6	MW	L		21	5	Lancaster, James
	Baldwin-Wallace	6	GL	A		17	11	Bankson, Steve
	Brockport State	4	E	L		17	10	Bowe, Bill
	Fairleigh Dickinson: Madison	6	MA	L		17	9	Kindel, Roger
	Geneseo State	6	E	A		15	13	Holmes, Steve
	Massachusetts: Dartmouth	6	NE	A		20	8	Baptiste, Brian
	Merchant Marine	6	A	A		16	11	MacKinnon, Robert A.
	Muhlenberg	5	MA	A		17	10	Madeira, David
	New York	5	A	L		17	9	Nesci, Joe
	Pomona-Pitzer	5	W	A		21	5	Katsiaficas, Charles G.
	Randolph-Macon	6	S	L		20	8	Nunnally, Hal
	Ripon	4	MW	A		23	2	Gillespie, Robert
	South University (TN)	5	S	L		20	6	Thoni, Joe
	Trinity (CT)	5	NE	L		20	4	Ogrodnik, Stanley

Tournament Results—Women

F	School	SD	Reg	BD	Bye	W	L	Coach
1982 Division I								
1	Louisiana Tech		MW	L		35	1	Hogg, Sonja
2	Cheyney		E	L		28	3	Stringer, C. Vivian
3	Maryland		W	A		25	7	Weller, Christine J.
	Tennessee		ME	L		22	10	Summitt, Patricia Head
8	Drake (IA)		W	A		28	7	Baumgarten, Carole
	Kansas State		E	A		26	6	Hickey, Lynn
	Kentucky		MW	A		24	8	Hall, Terry
	Southern California		ME	L		23	4	Sharp, Linda
16	Arizona State		MW	L		25	7	Simpson, Juliene
	California State: Long Beach		W	A		24	6	Bonvicini, Joan
	Memphis		ME	A		26	5	Johns, Mary Lou
	Missouri		W	L		24	9	Rutherford, Dr. Joann
	North Carolina State		E	L		24	7	Yow, Sandra Kay
	Old Dominion		E	L		22	6	Stanley, Marianne Crawford
	Pennsylvania State		ME	L		24	6	Portland, Rene Muth
	South Carolina		MW	L		23	8	Kelly, Terry
32	Auburn		E	L		24	5	Ciampi, Joe
	Clemson		MW	L		20	12	Tribble, Annie S.
	East Carolina		MW	L		17	10	Andruzzi, Cathy
	Georgia		MW	L		21	9	Landers, Andy
	Howard (DC)		W	A		14	11	Tyler, Sanya
	Illinois		MW	L		21	9	Schroeder, Jane
	Jackson State (MS)		ME	A		28	8	Magee, Sadie E.
	Kent State		ME	A		17	14	Wartluft, Laurel
	Mississippi		ME	L		27	5	Chancellor, Van
	Northwestern (IL)		E	L		21	8	Lynch, Arnette
	Ohio State		W	A		20	7	VanDerveer, Tara
	Oregon		W	L		21	5	Heiny, Elwin
	Saint Peter's		E	A		26	4	Granelli, Mike
	Stanford		W	A		19	8	McCrea, Dotty
	Stephen F Austin State		E	L		15	9	Otwell, Mary Ann
	Tennessee Tech		MW	A		20	11	Meadors, Marynell Hutsell
1982 Division II								
1	California Polytechnic: Pomona		W	A		29	7	May, Darlene
2	Tuskegee		S	L		29	5	Laster, Jr. 'Tiny'
3	Mount Saint Mary's (MD)		SA	L		24	5	Sheahan, William
4	Oakland (MI)		GL	L		21	3	Jones, DeWayne
8	Chapman		SC	L		23	5	Berger, Brian
	Fort Valley State		NC	L		23	8	Brown, Jessie A.
	Norfolk State		E	L		19	6	Moorehead, Dr. Isaac T. 'Ike'
	Springfield (MA)		NENG	L		23	3	Shapiro, Harvey P.
16	Bentley		NENG	A		19	6	Mullen, Paula
	Clark Atlanta		S	A		14	12	Witherspoon, Anthony
	Nebraska: Omaha		NC	L		22	6	Mankenberg, Cherri
	Northern Kentucky		GL	L		23	6	Scheper, Jane Meier

F	School	SD	Reg	BD	Bye	W	L	Coach
	Pittsburgh: Johnstown	E	L			20	3	Horner, Clyde L.
	San Francisco State	W	L			20	7	Manwaring, Emily
	Truman State (MO)	SC	L			17	11	Murray, Dr. Mary Jo
	Virginia Union	SA	L			18	5	Cannady, Nathan

1982 Division III

F	School	SD	Reg	BD	Bye	W	L	Coach
1	Elizabethtown	None	L			26	1	Kauffman, Yvonne E.
2	North Carolina: Greensboro	None	L			24	3	Agee, Lynne
3	Pomona-Pitzer	None	L			25	4	Breitenstein, Nancy
4	Clark (MA)	None	L			18	11	Stevens, Barbara
8	Augustana (IL)	None	L			19	7	Stein, Paulette
	New Jersey	None	L			17	9	Labati, Ferne
	Scranton	None	L			17	11	Strong, Michael J.
	Susquehanna	None	L			21	4	Diehl, Tom
16	Christopher Newport	None	L			15	10	Zachensky-Walthall, Susan
	Frostburg State	None	L			15	7	Crawley, James M.
	Grove City	None	L			19	5	Ellis, Terry
	Manhattanville	None	L			22	8	Tedesco, Ralph
	Massachusetts: Boston	None	L			20	6	Harris, Alfreda
	Millikin	None	L			11	6	Crannell, Harriett
	Saint Andrews Presbyterian	None	L			17	8	Graham, Betsy
	Widener	None	L			19	7	Hagan, Gigi

1983 Division I

F	School	SD	Reg	BD	Bye	W	L	Coach
1	Southern California	W	A	To R32		31	2	Sharp, Linda
2	Louisiana Tech	MW	L	To R32		31	2	Barmore, Leon
3	Georgia	ME	A	To R32		27	7	Landers, Andy
	Old Dominion	E	A	To R32		29	6	Stanley, Marianne Crawford
8	California State: Long Beach	W	L	To R32		24	7	Bonvicini, Joan
	Pennsylvania State	E	A	To R32		25	8	Portland, Rene Muth
	Tennessee	ME	L	To R32		25	8	Summitt, Patricia Head
	Texas	MW	A	To R32		30	3	Conradt, Jody
16	Arizona State	W	L	To R32		23	7	Simpson, Juliene
	Auburn	MW	L	To R32		24	8	Ciampi, Joe
	Cheyney	E	L	To R32		27	3	Stringer, C. Vivian
	Indiana	ME	A	To R32		19	11	Jeremiah, Dr. Maryalyce
	Kansas State	MW	L	To R32		25	7	Hickey, Lynn
	Maryland	E	A	To R32		26	5	Weller, Christine J.
	Mississippi	ME	L	To R32		26	7	Chancellor, Van
	Oregon State	W	A	To R32		21	5	Hill, Aki
32	California: Los Angeles	W	L	To R32		18	11	Moore, Billie Jean
	Central Michigan	E	A	To R32		21	9	Golden, Laura L.
	Florida State	ME	L	To R32		24	6	Dykehouse-Allen, Janice
	Illinois State	MW	A	To R32		20	10	Hutchison, Dr. Jill
	Kentucky	ME	L	To R32		23	5	Hall, Terry
	Louisville	MW	A	To R32		20	9	Fiehrer, Peggy
	Middle Tennessee State	MW	L			26	5	Inman, Larry Joe
	Missouri	MW	A	To R32		24	6	Rutherford, Dr. Joann
	Monmouth (NJ)	E	L			15	15	Parker, Milton
	North Carolina	ME	L	To R32		22	8	Alley, Jennifer
	North Carolina State	E	L	To R32		22	8	Yow, Sandra Kay
	Northeast Louisiana	W	L			23	6	Harper, Linda F.

F	School	SD	Reg	BD	Bye	W	L	Coach
	Saint John's (NY)	E	A	To R32	27	6	Perrelli, Donald
	South Carolina State	ME	L		17	8	Simon, Willie J.
	Stephen F Austin State	W	L	To R32	18	7	Otwell, Mary Ann
	Utah	W	A	To R32	22	7	Gardner, Fern
36	Dartmouth	E	L		18	8	Wielgus, Christina
	Jackson State (MS)	MW	L		21	8	Magee, Sadie E.
	La Salle	ME	L		16	13	Gallagher, Kevin
	Montana	W	L		26	4	Selvig, Robin

1983 DIVISION II

F	School	SD	Reg	BD	Bye	W	L	Coach
1	Virginia Union	SA	L		27	2	Hearn, Louis
2	California Polytechnic: Pomona	W	A	To R16	29	3	May, Darlene
3	Central Missouri State	SC	A	To R16	29	3	Hoehn, Jorja E.
	Southern Connecticut State	NENG	L	To R16	25	5	Barone, Anthony J.
8	Canisius	E	L	To R16	28	5	Pares, Sr. Maria
	Dayton	GL	L		20	10	Makowski, Linda
	Saint Cloud State	NC	L	To R16	31	4	Ziemer, Gladys L.
	Valdosta State	S	L	To R16	27	4	Cooper, Charles
16	Bentley	NENG	L		18	7	Mullen, Paula
	Chapman	W	L		22	8	Berger, Brian
	Long Island: C W Post	E	L		25	8	Solano, Kathy
	Mount Saint Mary's (MD)	SA	L	To R16	25	3	Sheahan, William
	Oakland (MI)	GL	L	To R16	22	4	Jones, DeWayne
	Southeast Missouri State	SC	L		20	8	Beck, Angela
	Texas A&M: Kingsville	NC	L		21	8	Land, David
	Tuskegee	S	A		20	11	Laster, Jr. "Tiny"
24	Abilene Christian	SC	L		21	8	McCoy, Burl
	Butler (IN)	GL	L		18	6	Mason, Linda
	Central Florida	S	L		25	5	Sanchez, Joe
	Florida International	E	L		17	7	Russo, Cindy
	Norfolk State	SA	A		19	6	Moorehead, Dr. Isaac T. "Ike"
	San Francisco State	W	A		18	9	Manwaring, Emily
	South Dakota	NC	A		19	9	Zimmerman, Mary
	Stonehill	NENG	A		21	9	Sullivan, Paula J.

1983 DIVISION III

F	School	SD	Reg	BD	Bye	W	L	Coach
1	North Central (IL)	C	A		26	6	Morgan, R. Wayne
2	Elizabethtown	MA	L		23	5	Kauffman, Yvonne E.
3	Knoxville	S	L		21	2	Robinson, Edward
4	Clark (MA)	NE	L		21	8	Stevens, Barbara
8	Kean	A	A		25	3	Hannisch, Patricia
	Minnesota: Morris	W	L		24	10	Reifsteck, Jan
	New Rochelle	E	L		28	5	Kern, Louis
	Wisconsin: La Crosse	GL	L		13	9	Greene, Janet
16	Central (IA)	C	L		18	6	Boeyink, Gary
	Concordia: Moorhead	W	L		18	10	Langseth, Marc
	Frostburg State	A	L		20	5	Crawley, James M.
	Grove City	MA	L		22	5	Ellis, Terry

F	School	SD	Reg	BD	Bye	W	L	Coach
	Pittsburgh: Johnstown	S	L			24	2	Gault, Jodi
	Rhode Island College	E	L			16	7	Conley, Joseph
	Salem State	NE	A			23	7	Shea, Timothy P.
	Wisconsin: Whitewater	GL	L			19	5	Jones, Dianne
24	Augustana (IL)	C	L			17	10	Stein, Paulette
	Bridgewater State (MA)	NE	L			18	7	Hastings, Martha
	Hartwick	E	L			17	5	Lauder, Sue
	New Jersey	A	L			18	11	Labati, Ferne
	North Carolina: Greensboro	S	A			20	8	Agee, Lynne
	Pomona-Pitzer	W	L			18	10	Breitenstein, Nancy
	Scranton	MA	L			19	7	Strong, Michael J.
	Simpson (IA)	GL	L			16	9	Schafer, Janet
32	Bishop	W	L			18	7	Robinson, Myrtle
	Buena Vista	C	L			18	8	Naughton, John
	Eastern Connecticut State	NE	L			17	7	Miller, Dr. C. Robert
	Rust	S	L			18	8	Stovall, Dr. Alfred J. "AJ"
	Saint Lawrence	E	L			17	5	Kowalik, Joan
	Saint Norbert	GL	L			20	7	Tilley, Connie L.
	Susquehanna	MA	A			24	2	Diehl, Tom
	Wooster	A	L			19	7	Nichols, Nancy "Nan"

1984 DIVISION I

F	School	SD	Reg	BD	Bye	W	L	Coach
1	Southern California	W	A			29	4	Sharp, Linda
2	Tennessee	ME	L			23	10	Summitt, Patricia Head
3	Cheyney	E	L			25	5	McGriff, Winthrop "Windy"
	Louisiana Tech	MW	L			30	3	Barmore, Leon
8	California State: Long Beach	W	L			25	6	Bonvicini, Joan
	Georgia	ME	A			30	3	Landers, Andy
	Old Dominion	E	A			24	5	Stanley, Marianne Crawford
	Texas	MW	A			32	3	Conradt, Jody
16	Alabama	ME	L			23	9	Weeks, Kenneth
	Louisiana State	MW	L			23	7	Gunter, Sue
	Mississippi	ME	L			24	6	Chancellor, Van
	Montana	W	A			26	4	Selvig, Robin
	North Carolina	E	A			24	8	Alley, Jennifer
	North Carolina State	E	L			23	9	Yow, Sandra Kay
	Northeast Louisiana	MW	A			23	4	Harper, Linda F.
	San Diego State	W	L			24	6	Riggins, Earnest
32	Brigham Young	W	A			18	8	Leishman, Dr. Courtney M.
	Central Michigan	ME	A			27	3	Golden, Laura L.
	Drake (IA)	MW	A			22	7	Baumgarten, Carole
	Kansas State	MW	A			25	6	Hickey, Lynn
	Louisville	ME	A			15	16	Fiehrer, Peggy
	Maryland	E	L			19	10	Weller, Christine J.
	Middle Tennessee State	ME	A			19	10	Inman, Larry Joe
	Missouri	MW	L			25	6	Rutherford, Dr. Joann
	Nevada: Las Vegas	W	L			24	7	Bolla, Jim
	Ohio State	ME	A			22	7	VanDerveer, Tara
	Oregon	W	A			21	7	Heiny, Elwin
	Oregon State	W	L			21	8	Hill, Aki

F	School	SD	Reg	BD	Bye	W	L	Coach
	Pennsylvania State	E	A			19	12	Portland, Rene Muth
	Saint John's (NY)	E	A			24	6	Perrelli, Donald
	Texas Tech	MW	L			23	7	Sharp, Marsha
	Virginia	E	L			22	7	Ryan, Deborah H.

1984 Division II

F	School	SD	Reg	BD	Bye	W	L	Coach
1	Central Missouri State	SC	A	To R16		28	4	Hoehn, Jorja E.
2	Virginia Union	SA	L			22	5	Hearn, Louis
3	Dayton	GL	L	To R16		27	4	Makowski, Linda
	Valdosta State	S	L	To R16		30	3	Cooper, Charles
8	Army	E	L	To R16		24	4	Johnson, Harold
	Chapman	W	L			26	5	Berger, Brian
	Quinnipiac	NENG	A	To R16		28	3	Hanson, Ron
	Saint Cloud State	NC	L	To R16		27	3	Ziemer, Gladys L.
16	Bentley	NENG	A			26	3	Mullen, Paula
	California Polytechnic: Pomona	W	A	To R16		22	7	May, Darlene
	Mount Saint Mary's (MD)	SA	L	To R16		26	2	Sheahan, William
	North Alabama	S	L			25	5	Byrd, Wayne
	Northwest Missouri State	GL	L			25	5	Winstead, Wayne
	South Dakota	NC	A			22	7	Lavin, Chad
	Southeast Missouri State	SC	L			23	6	Arnzen, Ed
	Utica	E	A			20	6	Kowalewski, Joan
24	Alabama A&M	SC	A			19	9	Parham, Press
	Central Florida	NENG	L			23	7	Sanchez, Joe
	Howard Payne	SC	A			11	18	Campbell, Sharon
	Lewis (IL)	GL	A			21	8	Kissinger, Kathy
	Millersville	E	A			19	7	Schlegel, Debra
	North Carolina Central	SA	A			13	15	Edwards, Yvonne
	North Dakota	NC	L			22	7	Schwartz, Gary
	San Francisco State	W	A			19	12	Manwaring, Emily

1984 Division III

F	School	SD	Reg	BD	Bye	W	L	Coach
1	Rust	S	L			26	5	Stovall, Dr. Alfred J. "AJ"
2	Elizabethtown	MA	A			29	2	Kauffman, Yvonne E.
3	Salem State	NE	A			27	3	Shea, Timothy P.
4	North Central (IL)	C	A			24	6	Morgan, R. Wayne
8	Bishop	W	L			21	7	Young, Abron
	Kean	A	A			24	2	Hannisch, Patricia
	New Jersey	E	L			20	8	Labati, Ferne
	Pittsburgh: Johnstown	GL	L			25	3	Gault, Jodi
16	Buffalo State College	E	L			21	6	Maloney, Gail F.
	Concordia: Moorhead	W	L			21	7	Langseth, Marc
	Eastern Connecticut State	NE	L			20	7	Miller, Dr. C. Robert
	Gettysburg	C	L			22	4	Higgins, Kay
	Knoxville	S	L			18	7	Robinson, Edward
	Richard Stockton	A	L			20	7	Fussner, Joseph
	Susquehanna	MA	L			19	8	Diehl, Tom
	Wisconsin: La Crosse	GL	L			19	8	Greene, Janet

F	School	SD	Reg	BD	Bye	W	L	Coach
24	Millikin	C	L			19	6	Crannell, Harriett
	Muskingum	A	L			23	6	Newberry, Donna
	New Rochelle	E	L			26	8	Kern, Louis
	North Carolina: Greensboro	S	A			22	7	Agee, Lynne
	Saint Thomas (MN)	W	A			23	5	Kosel, Tom
	Scranton	MA	L			19	8	Strong, Michael J.
	Wisconsin: Whitewater	GL	L			17	11	Jones, Dianne
	Worcester Polytechnic	NE	L			20	4	Chapman, Susan E.
32	Allegheny	MA	L			22	4	Gould, Kay
	Bridgewater State (MA)	NE	L			22	5	Ruggiero, George H. "Bo"
	Carroll (WI)	GL	L			20	6	Steffen, Daniel
	Ohio Northern	A	L			16	8	Lauth, Gayle
	Pomona-Pitzer	W	L			22	6	Breitenstein, Nancy
	Rochester (NY)	E	L			21	5	Wong, Joyce
	Virginia Wesleyan	S	L			20	9	Dunavent, Mike
	William Penn	C	A			17	11	Smith, Garey

1985 DIVISION I

F	School	SD	Reg	BD	Bye	W	L	Coach
1	Old Dominion	E	A			31	3	Stanley, Marianne Crawford
2	Georgia	W	L			29	5	Landers, Andy
3	Northeast Louisiana	MW	A			30	2	Harper, Linda F.
	Western Kentucky	ME	L			28	6	Sanderford, Paul
8	California State: Long Beach	W	A			28	3	Bonvicini, Joan
	Louisiana Tech	MW	L			29	4	Barmore, Leon
	Mississippi	ME	L			29	3	Chancellor, Van
	Ohio State	E	A			28	3	VanDerveer, Tara
16	Auburn	MW	L			25	6	Ciampi, Joe
	California: Los Angeles	W	L			20	10	Moore, Billie Jean
	North Carolina State	E	A			25	6	Yow, Sandra Kay
	Pennsylvania State	E	A			28	5	Portland, Rene Muth
	San Diego State	MW	L			21	9	Riggins, Earnest
	Southern California	W	L			21	9	Sharp, Linda
	Tennessee	ME	L			22	10	Summitt, Patricia Head
	Texas	ME	A			28	3	Conradt, Jody
32	Brigham Young	W	A			19	9	Leishman, Dr. Courtney M.
	Holy Cross (MA)	E	A			21	7	Palazzi, Togo A.
	Idaho	W	A			28	2	Dobratz, Patty Jo
	Illinois State	MW	A			23	5	Hutchison, Dr. Jill
	Memphis	MW	A			23	7	Johns, Mary Lou
	Middle Tennessee State	ME	A			23	7	Inman, Larry Joe
	Missouri	MW	A			22	9	Rutherford, Dr. Joann
	Nevada: Las Vegas	MW	L			26	5	Bolla, Jim
	North Carolina	E	L			21	11	Alley, Jennifer
	Saint Joseph's (PA)	E	L			25	5	Foster, Jim
	Southern Mississippi	ME	L			21	9	James, Kay
	Syracuse	E	A			18	13	Jacobs, Barbara
	Tennessee Tech	W	L			20	9	Meadors, Marynell Hutsell
	Virginia	ME	L			21	8	Ryan, Deborah H.
	Washington	W	A			26	1	Sake, Joyce
	Western Michigan	ME	A			19	10	Hess, Jim

F	School	SD	Reg	BD	Bye	W	L	Coach
1985 DIVISION II								
1	California Polytechnic: Pomona	W	L			21	7	May, Darlene
2	Central Missouri State	SC	A	To R16		27	5	Hoehn, Jorja E.
3	Hampton	SA	A	To R16		30	4	Sweat, James E.
	Mercer	S	L	To R16		24	7	Nixon, Ed
8	Northern Kentucky	GL	L	To R16		19	9	Winstel, Nancy
	Pace	E	A	To R16		28	3	Olenowski, John
	Quinnipiac	NENG	A	To R16		28	4	Hanson, Ron
	Saint Cloud State	NC	L			24	6	Ziemer, Gladys L.
16	Abilene Christian	SC	L			21	10	McCoy, Burl
	Bentley	NENG	A			21	5	Sanborn, Kathleen
	Chapman	W	A	To R16		25	4	Berger, Brian
	Clark Atlanta	GL	A			19	12	Witherspoon, Anthony
	Mount Saint Mary's (MD)	SA	L			23	6	Sheahan, William
	North Alabama	S	A			19	8	Byrd, Wayne
	South Dakota	NC		To R16		23	6	Lavin, Chad
	Utica	E	A			22	4	Kowalewski, Joan
24	Air Force	SC	A			20	8	Gasser, Martha "Marti"
	Johnson C Smith	SA	L			17	9	Joyner, Steven Wayne
	Lewis (IL)	GL	A			22	7	Kissinger, Kathy
	Mercy (NY)	E	L			22	7	Schachner, Carol
	Mississippi Women	S	L			19	4	Johnson, Samye
	North Dakota	NC				23	6	Schwartz, Gary
	San Francisco State	W	A			13	16	Burger, Maureen
	Stonehill	NENG	L			19	7	Sullivan, Paula J.
1985 DIVISION III								
1	Scranton	MA	A			31	1	Strong, Michael J.
2	New Rochelle	E	L			25	8	Kern, Louis
3	Millikin	C	L			23	3	Crannell, Harriett
4	Saint Norbert	GL	L			24	4	Tilley, Connie L.
8	Muskingum	A	A			25	4	Newberry, Donna
	Pomona-Pitzer	W	L			27	2	Breitenstein, Nancy
	Rust	S	L			25	2	Stovall, Dr. Alfred J. "AJ"
	Salem State	NE	L			23	5	Shea, Timothy P.
16	Allegheny	E	L			24	3	Gould, Kay
	Bridgewater State (MA)	NE	A			25	2	Ruggiero, George H. "Bo"
	California State: Stanislaus	W	L			23	6	Millar, Leann Henrich
	Capital	A	L			23	2	Pirtle, Laurie
	North Carolina: Greensboro	S	A			21	7	Agee, Lynne
	Pittsburgh: Johnstown	MA	L			26	3	Gault, Jodi
	William Penn	C				21	7	Smith, Garey
	Wisconsin: Whitewater	GL	L			21	8	Jones, Dianne
24	Alma	GL	L			18	5	Charney, Claudette
	Kean	A	A			23	5	Hannisch, Patricia
	Lemoyne-Owen	S	L			16	10	Skinner, Lula Marie
	Rhode Island College	NE	L			19	7	Chevalier, Dave

F	School	SD	Reg	BD	Bye	W	L	Coach
	Rochester (NY)	E	L			21	6	Wong, Joyce
	Saint Mary's (MN)	W	A			24	2	Wheeler, Lynn
	Simpson (IA)	C				20	7	Schafer, Janet
	Susquehanna	MA	L			24	5	Diehl, Tom
32	Buena Vista	C				20	8	Naughton, John
	Buffalo State College	E	L			18	8	Maloney, Gail F.
	Carroll (WI)	GL	A			22	6	Steffen, Daniel
	Concordia: Moorhead	W	L			16	12	Siverson, Duane
	Frostburg State	A	L			21	5	Crawley, James M.
	Gettysburg	MA	L			19	6	Hurst, Anne
	Western Connecticut State	NE	L			21	5	Rajcula, Jody
	Wooster	S	L			21	8	Nichols, Nancy "Nan"

1986 Division I

F	School	SD	Reg	BD	Bye	W	L	Coach
1	Texas	MW	A	To R32		34	0	Conradt, Jody
2	Southern California	W	L	To R32		27	4	Sharp, Linda
3	Tennessee	ME	L	To R32		24	10	Summitt, Patricia Head
	Western Kentucky	E	A	To R32		32	4	Sanderford, Paul
8	Louisiana State	ME	L	To R32		27	6	Gunter, Sue
	Louisiana Tech	W	L	To R32		27	5	Barmore, Leon
	Mississippi	MW	L	To R32		24	8	Chancellor, Van
	Rutgers	E	L	To R32		29	4	Grentz, Theresa Shank
16	Auburn	MW	L	To R32		24	6	Ciampi, Joe
	California State: Long Beach	W	L	To R32		29	5	Bonvicini, Joan
	Georgia	ME	A	To R32		30	2	Landers, Andy
	James Madison	E	L			28	4	Moorman, Shelia
	North Carolina	W	L	To R32		23	9	Alley, Jennifer
	Ohio State	ME	A	To R32		23	7	Darsch, Nancy
	Oklahoma	MW	L	To R32		24	7	McHugh, Maura
	Pennsylvania State	E	A	To R32		24	8	Portland, Rene Muth
32	Drake (IA)	MW	L			22	8	Baumgarten, Carole
	Illinois	ME	L			20	10	Golden, Laura L.
	Iowa	ME	L	To R32		22	7	Stringer, C. Vivian
	Maryland	ME	A	To R32		17	13	Weller, Christine J.
	Middle Tennessee State	ME	A			20	10	Inman, Larry Joe
	Missouri	MW	A			20	8	Rutherford, Dr. Joann
	Montana	W	A			27	4	Selvig, Robin
	Nevada: Las Vegas	W	A	To R32		22	9	Bolla, Jim
	North Carolina State	E	L	To R32		18	11	Yow, Sandra Kay
	Saint Joseph's (PA)	E	L	To R32		22	7	Foster, Jim
	Southern Illinois	MW	A	To R32		25	4	Scott, Cindy
	Texas Tech	W	L	To R32		21	9	Sharp, Marsha
	Vanderbilt	MW	L	To R32		22	9	Lee, Phil
	Villanova	E	A			23	8	Perretta, Harry
	Virginia	E	L	To R32		26	3	Ryan, Deborah H.
	Washington	W	A			24	6	Gobrecht, Chris
40	Arkansas	MW	L			22	8	Sutherland, John
	Kentucky	MW	L			18	11	Hall, Terry
	La Salle	E	A			21	9	Morris, William T. "Speedy"
	North Texas	W	A			20	10	Nelson, Judy

F	School	SD	Reg	BD	Bye	W	L	Coach
	Ohio University		ME	A		26	3	Prichard, Amy
	Providence		E	L		24	6	Foley, Bob
	South Carolina		ME	A		19	11	Wilson, Nancy R.
	Utah		W	A		21	9	Elliott, Elaine

1986 Division II

F	School	SD	Reg	BD	Bye	W	L	Coach
1	California Polytechnic: Pomona		W	A	To R16	30	3	May, Darlene
2	North Dakota State		NC	L		24	9	Ruley, Amy J.
3	Delta State		S	A		28	3	Clark, Lloyd
	Philadelphia Textiles		E	L	To R16	24	6	Soriero, Julie
8	Bellarmine		GL			23	7	Just, Charles G.
	Central Connecticut State		NENG	L	To R16	24	4	Reilly, Dr. Brenda
	Central Missouri State		SC	A	To R16	23	6	Pye, Jon
	Hampton		SA	L		26	6	Sweat, James E.
16	California State: Northridge		W	L		20	9	Milke, Leslie
	Florida International		S	L	To R16	26	2	Russo, Cindy
	Lake Superior State		GL	L	To R16	23	5	Taylor, Bob
	Mankato State		NC	A	To R16	25	4	Wilinski, Bruno
	Mount Saint Mary's (MD)		SA	L	To R16	24	2	Sheahan, William
	Quinnipiac		NENG	L		25	4	Wolfson, Barry
	Slippery Rock		E	A		23	6	Ritchey-Walton, Kathleen "Kathy"
	Southeast Missouri State		SC	L		25	6	Arnzen, Ed
24	Alaska: Anchorage		SC	A		17	11	Burns, Linda
	Bryant		NC	A		17	12	McKee, Michael
	California: Davis		W	L		18	9	Gill, Pam
	Clark Atlanta		S	A		18	12	Moseley, Michael
	New Haven		NENG	A		18	11	Rossman, Jan
	Norfolk State		SA	A		18	10	Moorehead, Dr. Isaac T. "Ike"
	Northern Kentucky		GL			22	6	Winstel, Nancy
	Pace		E	A		20	8	Lauro, John

1986 Division III

F	School	SD	Reg	BD	Bye	W	L	Coach
1	Salem State		NE	A		29	1	Shea, Timothy P.
2	Bishop		W	L		28	3	Young, Abron
3	Capital		A	L		27	4	Pirtle, Laurie
4	Rust		S	L		21	5	Stovall, Dr. Alfred J. "AJ"
8	Albany State (NY)		E	L		26	4	Warner, Mari
	Elizabethtown		MA	A		24	6	Kauffman, Yvonne E.
	William Penn		C	A		22	7	Smith, Garey
	Wisconsin: Whitewater		GL	L		24	4	Jones, Dianne
16	Concordia: Moorhead		W	L		25	3	Siverson, Duane
	Eastern Connecticut State		C	L		20	5	Miller, Dr. C. Robert
	Emmanuel (MA)		NE	L		21	4	Yosinoff, Andrew
	Kean		A	A		25	2	Hannisch, Patricia
	New York		E	L		20	8	Pickard, Sherri
	North Carolina: Greensboro		S	L		24	4	Agee, Lynne
	Saint Norbert		GL	L		20	2	Tilley, Connie L.
	Scranton		MA	L		23	6	Strong, Michael J.

F	School	SD	Reg	BD	Bye	W	L	Coach
24	Allegheny		A	A		26	2	Gould, Kay
	Alma		GL	L		23	3	Klenk, William
	Columbia (NY)		E	L		21	6	Kalafies, Nancy
	Elmhurst		C	A		24	3	Novgrod, Debra
	Juniata		MA	L		16	6	Latimore, Nancy Harden
	Saint Mary's (MN)		W	A		23	2	Smith, Jim
	Southern Maine		NE	L		20	5	Costello, Dr. Richard A.
	Virginia Wesleyan		S	L		24	5	Jordan, Jack
32	Bridgewater State (MA)		NE	L		21	6	Ruggiero, George H. "Bo"
	Buffalo State College		E	A		23	3	Maloney, Gail F.
	Carroll (WI)		C	L		21	7	Steffen, Daniel
	Christopher Newport		S	A		20	9	Zachensky-Walthall, Susan
	Moravian		MA	L		25	5	Sinnott-Skutches, Anne
	Ohio Northern		A	A		20	6	Lauth, Gayle
	Pomona-Pitzer		W	A		19	9	Breitenstein, Nancy
	Susquehanna		GL	L		17	6	Diehl, Tom

1987 DIVISION I

F	School	SD	Reg	BD	Bye	W	L	Coach
1	Tennessee	2	ME	L	To R32	28	6	Summitt, Patricia Head
2	Louisiana Tech	1	MW	L	To R32	30	3	Barmore, Leon
3	California State: Long Beach	1	W	A	To R32	33	3	Bonvicini, Joan
	Texas	1	E	A	To R32	31	2	Conradt, Jody
8	Auburn	1	ME	A	To R32	31	2	Ciampi, Joe
	Iowa	3	MW	L	To R32	26	5	Stringer, C. Vivian
	Ohio State	2	W	A	To R32	26	5	Darsch, Nancy
	Rutgers	2	E	A	To R32	30	3	Grentz, Theresa Shank
16	Georgia	2	MW	L	To R32	27	5	Landers, Andy
	James Madison	4	E	A	To R32	27	4	Moorman, Shelia
	Mississippi	4	W	L	To R32	25	5	Chancellor, Van
	North Carolina State	3	E	A	To R32	24	7	Yow, Sandra Kay
	Old Dominion	5	ME	A	To R32	18	13	Stanley, Marianne Crawford
	Southern California	3	W	A	To R32	22	8	Sharp, Linda
	Southern Illinois	5	MW	A	To R32	28	3	Scott, Cindy
	Virginia	3	ME	L	To R32	26	5	Ryan, Deborah H.
32	Duke	7	E	L		19	10	Leonard, Debbie
	Illinois	8	ME	L		19	10	Golden, Laura L.
	Kansas	7	MW	A		20	13	Washington, Marian
	Louisiana State	4	MW	L	To R32	20	8	Gunter, Sue
	Memphis	6	ME	L	To R32	20	9	Johns, Mary Lou
	New Orleans	6	MW	L	To R32	25	7	Favaloro, Joey
	North Carolina	4	ME	L	To R32	19	10	Hatchell, Sylvia Rhyne
	Northwestern (IL)	8	MW	L		20	10	Perrelli, Donald
	Oregon	7	W	L		23	7	Heiny, Elwin
	Pennsylvania State	5	W	L	To R32	23	7	Portland, Rene Muth
	Saint Joseph's (PA)	9	E	L		23	9	Foster, Jim
	Tennessee Tech	7	ME	A		24	7	Worrell, Bill
	Vanderbilt	5	E	L	To R32	23	10	Lee, Phil
	Villanova	6	E	A	To R32	27	4	Perretta, Harry
	Washington	8	W	L		23	7	Gobrecht, Chris
	Western Kentucky	6	W	L	To R32	24	9	Sanderford, Paul

F	School	SD	Reg	BD	Bye	W	L	Coach
40	Bowling Green State	9	ME	A		27	3	Voll, Fran
	Eastern Washington	10	W	A		18	12	Smithpeters, Bill
	Kansas State	9	MW	L		22	9	Mossman, Matilda Willis
	Manhattan	10	E	A		20	11	Solano, Kathy
	New Mexico State	9	W	A		23	7	McKeown, Joe
	Northeast Louisiana	10	MW	A		14	10	Harper, Linda F.
	South Alabama	8	E	L		24	6	Branum, Charles
	Southern Mississippi	10	ME	A		21	9	James, Kay

1987 DIVISION II

F	School	SD	Reg	BD	Bye	W	L	Coach
1	New Haven		NENG	A	To R16	29	2	Rossman, Jan
2	California Polytechnic: Pomona		W	A	To R16	29	3	May, Darlene
3	Northern Kentucky		GL	A	To R16	25	5	Winstel, Nancy
	Pittsburgh: Johnstown		E	L	To R16	25	5	Gault, Jodi
8	Delta State		S	A	To R16	28	2	Clark, Lloyd
	Hampton		SA	A	To R16	30	2	Sweat, James E.
	North Dakota State		NC	A	To R16	26	4	Ruley, Amy J.
	West Texas A&M		SC	L	To R16	27	4	Schneider, Bob
16	California State: Chico		W	L		23	7	Coslet, Fran
	Central Missouri State		SC	L		23	7	Pye, Jon
	Florida International		S	L		26	3	Russo, Cindy
	Millersville		E	A		18	8	Schlegel, Debra
	Mount Saint Mary's (MD)		SA	L		25	3	Sheahan, William
	Saint Cloud State		NC	L		21	8	Ziemer, Gladys L.
	Stonehill		NENG	A		27	5	Sullivan, Paula J.
	Wright State (OH)		GL	L		24	6	Davis, Pat
24	Adelphi		E	A		14	14	McHugh, Dorothy
	Albany State (GA)		S	A		28	1	Davis, John I.
	Bellarmine		GL	L		20	8	Just, Charles G.
	Bentley		NENG	L		24	5	Sanborn, Kathleen
	Montana State: Billings		NC	A		18	11	Anderson, Ted
	Nebraska: Omaha		NC	L		21	8	Mankenberg, Cherri
	Southeast Missouri State		SC	L		26	4	Arnzen, Ed
	Virginia State		SA	L		21	7	Bey, Leon Wright

1987 DIVISION III

F	School	SD	Reg	BD	Bye	W	L	Coach
1	Wisconsin: Stevens Point		GL	L		27	2	Wunder, Linda
2	Concordia: Moorhead		W	A		26	5	Siverson, Duane
3	Scranton		MA	A		31	2	Strong, Michael J.
4	Kean		A	A		26	4	Wilson, Rich
8	Rust		S	L		26	3	Stovall, Dr. Alfred J. `AJ`
	Saint John Fisher		E	L		28	3	Kahler, Phillip I.
	Southern Maine		NE	L		25	4	Costello, Dr. Richard A.
	William Penn		C	A		20	9	Smith, Garey
16	Alma		GL	L		21	5	Klenk, William
	Centre		S	L		22	5	Wise, Lea
	Elizabethtown		MA	L		25	3	Kauffman, Yvonne E.
	Emmanuel (MA)		NE	L		22	2	Yosinoff, Andrew

F	School	SD	Reg	BD	Bye	W	L	Coach
	Ohio Northern		A	L		19	7	Lauth, Gayle
	Pomona-Pitzer		W	L		24	4	Breitenstein, Nancy
	Rockford		C	L		25	2	Crick, Steve
	Stony Brook State		E	L		24	5	McMullen, DeClan
24	Allegheny		A	L		25	4	Gould, Kay
	Augustana (IL)		C	A		20	7	Schumacher, Diane
	Bishop		W	L		20	5	Young, Abron
	North Carolina: Greensboro		S	A		27	3	Agee, Lynne
	Rochester (NY)		E	L		22	7	Wong, Joyce
	Salem State		NE	A		22	6	Shea, Timothy P.
	Spring Garden		MA	L		25	5	Brennan, Dennis
	Wisconsin: Whitewater		GL	L		20	5	Jones, Dianne
32	Buffalo State College		S	A		14	11	Jabir, James J.
	California State: Stanislaus		W	L		19	9	Millar, Leann Henrich
	Capital		A	A		21	5	Jeffers, Dixie M.
	Clark (MA)		NE	L		19	8	Glispin, Patricia
	Marywood		MA	L		19	8	Dempsey, Jerry
	New York		E	L		18	10	Pickard, Sherri
	Saint Norbert		GL	L		19	6	Tilley, Connie L.
	Saint Thomas (MN)		C	L		19	9	Riverso, Ted

1988 Division I

F	School	SD	Reg	BD	Bye	W	L	Coach
1	Louisiana Tech	2	MW	L	To R32	32	2	Barmore, Leon
2	Auburn	1	ME	L	To R32	32	3	Ciampi, Joe
3	California State: Long Beach	2	W	A	To R32	28	6	Bonvicini, Joan
	Tennessee	1	E	A	To R32	31	3	Summitt, Patricia Head
8	Iowa	1	W	A	To R32	29	2	Stringer, C. Vivian
	Maryland	2	ME	A	To R32	26	6	Weller, Christine J.
	Texas	1	MW	A	To R32	32	3	Conradt, Jody
	Virginia	2	E	L	To R32	27	5	Ryan, Deborah H.
16	Georgia	4	ME	L	To R32	21	10	Landers, Andy
	James Madison	4	E	A	To R32	27	4	Moorman, Shelia
	Mississippi	3	MW	L	To R32	24	7	Chancellor, Van
	Ohio State	3	ME	L	To R32	25	5	Darsch, Nancy
	Rutgers	3	E	A	To R32	27	5	Grentz, Theresa Shank
	Southern California	4	W	L	To R32	22	8	Sharp, Linda
	Stanford	5	MW	L	To R32	27	5	VanDerveer, Tara
	Washington	3	W	A	To R32	25	5	Gobrecht, Chris
32	Clemson	5	E	L	To R32	21	9	Davis, Jim
	Colorado	7	W	L		21	11	Barry, Ceal
	Houston	6	MW	L	To R32	22	7	Williams, Greg
	Kansas	7	MW	A		22	10	Washington, Marian
	Montana	4	MW	A	To R32	28	2	Selvig, Robin
	Nebraska	5	W	L	To R32	22	7	Beck, Angela
	New Mexico State	6	W	A	To R32	26	3	McKeown, Joe
	Old Dominion	6	E	L	To R32	17	12	Larry, Wendy
	Pennsylvania State	9	ME	L		20	13	Portland, Rene Muth
	Saint John's (NY)	7	E	A		22	10	Mullaney, Joseph A., Jr.
	Saint Joseph's (PA)	7	ME	L		24	8	Foster, Jim
	South Carolina	8	MW	A		23	11	Wilson, Nancy R.

F	School	SD	Reg	BD	Bye	W	L	Coach
	Stephen F Austin State	8	W	L		29	5	Blair, Gary
	Syracuse	6	ME	L	To R32	22	9	Jacobs, Barbara
	Wake Forest	9	E	L		23	8	Sanchez, Joe
	Western Kentucky	5	ME	A	To R32	26	8	Sanderford, Paul
40	Alabama	9	MW	L		18	10	Myers, Lois
	Bowling Green State	10	ME	A		24	6	Voll, Fran
	Eastern Illinois	10	W	A		22	8	Hilke, Barbara
	Fairfield	10	E	A		19	10	Nolan, Diane
	La Salle	8	ME	L		25	5	Miller, John
	Louisiana State	9	W	L		18	11	Gunter, Sue
	Middle Tennessee State	10	MW	A		22	8	Bivens, Lewis
	Villanova	8	E	L		20	9	Perretta, Harry

1988 DIVISION II

F	School	SD	Reg	BD	Bye	W	L	Coach
1	Hampton		SA	L		33	1	Sweat, James E.
2	West Texas A&M		SC	L		33	1	Schneider, Bob
3	Delta State		S	A		30	3	Clark, Lloyd
	North Dakota State		NC	A		28	3	Ruley, Amy J.
8	California Polytechnic: Pomona		W	A		28	4	May, Darlene
	New Haven		NENG	A		27	5	Hill, Russ
	Pittsburgh: Johnstown		E	L		25	4	Gault, Jodi
	Saint Joseph's (IN)		GL			27	4	Smith, David R.
16	Alaska: Anchorage		W	A		24	5	Burns, Linda
	Army		E	A		19	13	Chiavaro, Lynn
	Bentley		NENG	A		28	4	Stevens, Barbara
	Central Missouri State		SC	A		26	5	Pye, Jon
	Jacksonville State (AL)		S	L		22	7	Mathis, Richard
	Lake Superior State		GL	L		24	5	Geary, Mike
	South Dakota State		NC	L		25	5	Neiber, Nancy
	Virginia State		SA	A		21	7	Bey, Leon Wright
32	Abilene Christian		SC	L		27	6	McCoy, Burl
	Bryant		S	A		22	9	Tomasso, Ralph
	California State: Chico		W	A		19	10	Coslet, Fran
	California: Davis		W	L		18	11	Gill, Pam
	District Of Columbia		SA	L		24	3	Robinson, William
	Fort Valley State		S	A		25	4	Bartley, Lonnie
	Gannon		E	L		26	4	Saurer, Judy
	Grand Valley State		GL	L		20	8	Baker-Grzyb, Pat
	Indiana (PA)		E	A		17	14	Kiger, Jan H.
	Mount Saint Mary's (MD)		SA	L		24	2	Sheahan, William
	New Hampshire College		NENG	L		21	8	Rowe, Nancy Anne
	North Dakota		NC	L		22	6	Roebuck, Gene
	Northern Kentucky		GL			25	3	Winstel, Nancy
	Saint Cloud State		NC	L		18	10	Ziemer, Gladys L.
	Southeast Missouri State		SC	L		26	4	Arnzen, Ed
	Stonehill		NENG	L		25	6	Sullivan, Paula J.

F	School	SD	Reg	BD	Bye	W	L	Coach
1988 DIVISION III								
1	Concordia: Moorhead		W	A		29	2	Siverson, Duane
2	Saint John Fisher		E	L		31	1	Kahler, Phillip I.
3	North Carolina: Greensboro		S	L		26	7	Agee, Lynne
4	Southern Maine		NE	L		27	3	Fifield, Gary
8	Franklin & Marshall		MA	L		25	4	Fleig, Mary L.
	Luther		C			21	7	Hildebrand, Jane
	Ohio Northern		A	A		23	4	Lauth, Gayle
	Wisconsin: La Crosse		GL	L		22	7	Sheridan, Teri
16	Elizabethtown		MA	A		25	4	Kauffman, Yvonne E.
	Nazareth (NY)		E	L		23	5	DeCillis, Michael
	New Jersey		A	L		22	6	Ryan, Mika
	Rust		S	L		21	4	Stovall, Dr. Alfred J. "AJ"
	Saint Norbert		GL	L		17	5	Tilley, Connie L.
	Saint Thomas (MN)		W	L		22	5	Riverso, Ted
	Salem State		NE	A		25	3	Shea, Timothy P.
	Washington (MO)		C	L		21	5	Fahey, Nancy
24	Buffalo State College		E	L		24	4	Maloney, Gail F.
	California State: Stanislaus		W	L		22	5	Millar, Leann Henrich
	Calvin		GL	L		21	5	Vroon, A. Donald
	Centre		S	L		23	6	Wise, Lea
	Emmanuel (MA)		NE	L		20	2	Yosinoff, Andrew
	Kean		A	A		21	8	Wilson, Rich
	Lycoming		MA	L		21	7	Rockey, Kimberly
	William Penn		C			21	7	Smith, Garey
32	California State: San Bernardino		W	L		23	5	Bly, Jo Anne
	Cortland State		E	L		21	7	Foley, Bonnie
	North Park		C	A		20	8	Djurickovic, Rebecca Johnson
	Rowan		A	L		21	7	Bunting, Dawn Shilling
	Thiel		MA	L		19	6	Parsons, Margaret Rhoads "Gie"
	Virginia Wesleyan		S	L		20	10	Jordan, Jack
	Western Connecticut State		NE	L		19	9	Rajcula, Jody
	Wisconsin: River Falls		GL	L		22	6	Bloom, Dennis
1989 DIVISION I								
1	Tennessee	1	E	A	To R32	35	2	Summitt, Patricia Head
2	Auburn	1	ME	L	To R32	32	2	Ciampi, Joe
3	Louisiana Tech	1	MW	L	To R32	32	4	Barmore, Leon
	Maryland	1	W	A	To R32	29	3	Weller, Christine J.
8	California State: Long Beach	2	E	A	To R32	30	5	Bonvicini, Joan
	Mississippi	3	ME	L	To R32	23	8	Chancellor, Van
	Stanford	2	MW	A	To R32	28	3	VanDerveer, Tara
	Texas	2	W	A	To R32	27	5	Conradt, Jody
16	Clemson	4	ME	L	To R32	20	11	Davis, Jim
	Iowa	3	MW	L	To R32	27	5	Stringer, C. Vivian
	Louisiana State	4	MW	L	To R32	19	11	Gunter, Sue
	Nevada: Las Vegas	6	W	L		27	7	Bolla, Jim

F	School	SD	Reg	BD	Bye	W	L	Coach
	North Carolina State	2	ME	L	To R32	24	7	Yow, Sandra Kay
	Ohio State	3	E	A	To R32	24	6	Darsch, Nancy
	Stephen F Austin State	4	W	L	To R32	30	4	Blair, Gary
	Virginia	4	E	L	To R32	21	10	Ryan, Deborah H.
32	Bowling Green State	9	W	A		27	4	Voll, Fran
	Colorado	3	W	A	To R32	27	4	Barry, Ceal
	Georgia	5	ME	L		23	7	Landers, Andy
	Illinois State	7	MW	A		23	8	Hutchison, Dr. Jill
	James Madison	6	E	A		26	4	Moorman, Shelia
	La Salle	9	E	L		28	3	Miller, John
	Montana	10	W	A		27	4	Selvig, Robin
	Oklahoma State	9	MW	L		20	12	Halterman, Dick
	Old Dominion	6	ME	L		23	9	Larry, Wendy
	Purdue	5	MW	L		24	6	Dunn, Lin
	Rutgers	7	ME	L		24	7	Grentz, Theresa Shank
	Saint Joseph's (PA)	10	E	L		23	8	Foster, Jim
	Temple	8	ME	L		22	10	Hill-MacDonald, Linda
	Tennessee Tech	11	MW	A		22	8	Worrell, Bill
	Washington	5	W	L		23	10	Gobrecht, Chris
	West Virginia	12	E	A		24	8	Blakemore, Kittie
48	Arkansas	12	MW	L		22	8	Sutherland, John
	California State: Fullerton	7	W	L		21	9	Jeremiah, Dr. Maryalyce
	Cincinnati	8	W	L		21	9	Pirtle, Laurie
	Connecticut	8	E	A		24	6	Auriemma, Geno
	Hawaii	12	W	L		20	10	Goo, Vince
	Holy Cross (MA)	9	ME	A		21	10	Gibbons, Bill, Jr.
	Miami (FL)	8	MW	L		21	8	Labati, Ferne
	Northwestern State (LA)	10	MW	L		22	8	Smith, James F.
	Providence	11	E	L		22	11	Foley, Bob
	South Carolina	6	MW	A		23	7	Wilson, Nancy R.
	Southern Mississippi	10	ME	L		26	5	James, Kay
	Tennessee: Chattanooga	12	ME	A		19	12	Parrott, Craig
	Utah	11	W	A		24	6	Elliott, Elaine
	Vanderbilt	7	E	A		21	8	Lee, Phil
	Villanova	11	ME	L		18	12	Perretta, Harry
	Western Kentucky	5	E	A		22	9	Sanderford, Paul

1989 Division II

	School	Reg	BD		W	L	Coach
1	Delta State	S	A		30	4	Clark, Lloyd
2	California Polytechnic: Pomona	W	A		28	6	May, Darlene
3	Bentley	NENG	L		31	3	Stevens, Barbara
4	Central Missouri State	SC	A		29	5	Pye, Jon
8	Bloomsburg	E	L		28	2	Bressi, Joe
	District Of Columbia	SA	L		20	4	Robinson, William
	Saint Cloud State	NC			21	9	Ziemer, Gladys L.
	Saint Joseph's (IN)	GL	A		27	4	Smith, David R.
16	California State: Northridge	W	L		22	9	Milke, Leslie
	Jacksonville State (AL)	S	L		24	6	Mathis, Richard
	Lock Haven	E	A		22	9	Scarfo, Frank
	New Haven	NENG	A		28	4	Hill, Russ

F	School	SD	Reg	BD	Bye	W	L	Coach
	North Dakota State	NC				23	7	Ruley, Amy J.
	Oakland (MI)	GL	L			26	4	Taylor, Bob
	Virginia State	SA	L			22	5	Cummings, Bertha
	West Texas A&M	SC	A			26	3	Schneider, Bob
32	Abilene Christian	SC	L			23	8	McCoy, Burl
	Alaska: Anchorage	NC	A			20	8	Burns, Linda
	Albany State (GA)	S	A			15	16	Davis, John I.
	Bridgeport	NENG	L			25	5	Foust, Dan
	Bryant	NENG	A			20	9	Tomasso, Ralph
	California State: Hayward	W	A			13	15	Oten, Barbara
	Florida Atlantic	W	L			21	8	Allen, Wayne
	Hampton	SA	L			20	9	Laster, Jr. "Tiny"
	Northern Kentucky	GL	L			21	7	Winstel, Nancy
	Northern Michigan	GL	L			24	4	Stein, Paulette
	Pace	E	A			20	10	Lauro, John
	Philadelphia Textiles	E	L			21	9	Soriero, Julie
	Shaw (NC)	SA	A			18	8	Sanders, Bobby
	South Dakota	NC	L			22	7	Tibbetts, Fred
	Southeast Missouri State	SC	L			23	7	Arnzen, Ed
	West Georgia	S	L			25	4	Williamson, Jane

1989 DIVISION III

F	School	SD	Reg	BD	Bye	W	L	Coach
1	Elizabethtown	MA	A			29	2	Kauffman, Yvonne E.
2	California State: Stanislaus	W	L			27	2	Millar, Leann Henrich
3	Centre	S	L			23	8	Wise, Lea
4	Clarkson (NY)	E	L			26	7	Chafin, Brian
8	Clark (MA)	NE	L			28	1	Glispin, Patricia
	Luther	C	A			22	7	Hildebrand, Jane
	Muskingum	A	A			29	2	Newberry, Donna
	Wisconsin: Eau Claire	GL	L			24	5	Stone, Lisa Anderson
16	Allentown	MA	L			24	6	Shirley, Thomas, Jr.
	Augustana (IL)	C				22	5	Schumacher, Diane
	Concordia: Moorhead	W	L			24	3	Siverson, Duane
	Nazareth (NY)	S	L			22	6	DeCillis, Michael
	New York	E	L			18	9	Quinn, Janice
	Ohio Northern	A	L			17	10	Lauth, Gayle
	Southern Maine	NE	A			25	3	Fifield, Gary
	Wisconsin: River Falls	GL	L			23	5	Bloom, Dennis
24	Alma	GL	L			19	5	Goffnett, Charles
	Franklin & Marshall	MA	L			24	5	Fleig, Mary L.
	Maryville (TN)	S	L			23	6	Moore, Frank "Wes"
	Montclair State	A	L			20	9	Jeffrey, Jill
	Saint Thomas (MN)	W	L			20	6	Riverso, Ted
	Stony Brook State	E	L			21	8	McMullen, DeClan
	Wartburg	C	L			21	6	Severson, Monica
	Western Connecticut State	NE	L			21	7	Rajcula, Jody
32	Carnegie Mellon	MA	L			20	7	Seidl, Gerri
	Kean	A	A			24	5	Wilson, Rich
	Millikin	C				20	7	Kearns, Lori Ann
	Saint Benedict	W	A			23	5	Durbin, Michael

F	School	SD	Reg	BD	Bye	W	L	Coach
	Saint John Fisher	E	L			27	3	Kahler, Phillip I.
	Saint Norbert	GL	L			20	6	Tilley, Connie L.
	Salem State	NE	A			24	4	Shea, Timothy P.
	Virginia Wesleyan	S	A			20	9	Jordan, Jack

1990 Division I

F	School	SD	Reg	BD	Bye	W	L	Coach
1	Stanford	1	W	A	To R32	32	1	VanDerveer, Tara
2	Auburn	2	ME	A	To R32	28	7	Ciampi, Joe
3	Louisiana Tech	1	MW	A	To R32	32	1	Barmore, Leon
	Virginia	2	E	A	To R32	29	6	Ryan, Deborah H.
8	Arkansas	7	W	L		25	5	Sutherland, John
	Tennessee	1	E	L	To R32	27	6	Summitt, Patricia Head
	Texas	3	MW	A	To R32	27	5	Conradt, Jody
	Washington	1	ME	L	To R32	28	3	Gobrecht, Chris
16	Clemson	5	E	L		22	10	Davis, Jim
	Mississippi	5	W	L		22	10	Chancellor, Van
	North Carolina State	2	MW	L	To R32	25	6	Yow, Sandra Kay
	Providence	3	E	A	To R32	27	5	Foley, Bob
	Purdue	4	MW	L	To R32	23	7	Dunn, Lin
	South Carolina	5	ME	L		24	9	Wilson, Nancy R.
	Stephen F Austin State	3	W	A	To R32	28	3	Blair, Gary
	Vanderbilt	6	ME	L		23	11	Lee, Phil
32	California State: Long Beach	6	W	L		25	9	Bonvicini, Joan
	Connecticut	4	E	L	To R32	25	6	Auriemma, Geno
	De Paul	8	ME	L		22	10	Bruno, Doug
	Georgia	2	W	L	To R32	25	5	Landers, Andy
	Hawaii	9	W	L		26	4	Goo, Vince
	Iowa	3	ME	A	To R32	23	6	Stringer, C. Vivian
	Maryland	6	E	L		19	11	Weller, Christine J.
	Michigan	10	MW	L		20	10	Van De Wege, 'Bud', Jr.
	Nevada: Las Vegas	4	W	A	To R32	28	3	Bolla, Jim
	Northern Illinois	5	MW	L		25	6	Albright-Dieterle, Jane
	Northwestern (IL)	4	ME	L	To R32	24	5	Perrelli, Donald
	Ohio State	6	MW	L		18	12	Darsch, Nancy
	Old Dominion	8	E	A		21	10	Larry, Wendy
	Pennsylvania State	7	E	A		25	7	Portland, Rene Muth
	Southern Mississippi	8	MW	A		27	5	James, Kay
	Tennessee Tech	7	ME	A		26	5	Worrell, Bill
48	Appalachian State	11	E	A		20	9	Robinson, Linda
	Bowling Green State	12	ME	A		22	9	Voll, Fran
	California	11	W	L		17	12	Foster, Dr. Gooch
	California: Los Angeles	10	W	L		17	12	Moore, Billie Jean
	Florida State	10	E	L		21	9	Meadors, Marynell Hutsell
	Louisiana State	9	MW	L		21	9	Gunter, Sue
	Manhattan	12	E	A		18	13	Solano, Kathy
	Montana	8	W	A		27	3	Selvig, Robin
	Oklahoma State	7	MW	A		20	11	Halterman, Dick
	Richmond	10	ME	A		25	5	Gaitley, Stephanie Vanderslice
	Rutgers	11	ME	L		20	10	Grentz, Theresa Shank
	Saint Joseph's (PA)	9	E	L		24	7	Foster, Jim

F	School	SD	Reg	BD	Bye	W	L	Coach
	Southern Illinois	11	MW	A		21	10	Scott, Cindy
	Texas Tech	12	MW	L		20	11	Sharp, Marsha
	Utah	12	W	A		20	10	Elliott, Elaine
	Western Kentucky	9	ME	L		17	12	Sanderford, Paul

1990 Division II

F	School	SD	Reg	BD	Bye	W	L	Coach
1	Delta State		S	A		32	1	Clark, Lloyd
2	Bentley		NENG	A		31	4	Stevens, Barbara
3	California Polytechnic: Pomona		W	A		29	4	May, Darlene
4	Oakland (MI)		GL	L		27	6	Taylor, Bob
8	Bellarmine		SA	L		25	6	Just, Charles G.
	Central Missouri State		SC	A		29	3	Pye, Jon
	Lock Haven		E	L		26	7	Scarfo, Frank
	North Dakota		NC	A		27	4	Roebuck, Gene
16	California State: Stanislaus		W	A		22	7	Millar, Leann Henrich
	Edinboro		E	A		27	3	Swank, Stan
	Florida Atlantic		SA	L		21	8	Allen, Wayne
	Jacksonville State (AL)		S	L		25	5	Mathis, Richard
	North Dakota State		NC	L		25	5	Ruley, Amy J.
	Saint Anselm		NENG	L		25	4	Guimont, Donna M.
	Saint Joseph's (IN)		GL	A		28	2	Smith, David R.
	West Texas A&M		SC	A		24	6	Schneider, Bob
32	Air Force		W	A		20	8	Gasser, Martha "Marti"
	Albany State (GA)		S	A		22	7	Davis, John I.
	Augustana (SD)		NC	L		19	10	Krauth, David
	Bloomsburg		E	L		22	7	Bressi, Joe
	California: Davis		W	L		20	8	Hoehn, Jorja E.
	Grand Valley State		GL	L		22	6	Vandebunte, Carol
	Indiana-Purdue: Fort Wayne		GL	L		22	7	Rosinski, Teri
	Keene State		NENG	L		23	7	Le Mieux, John
	New Hampshire College		NENG	A		22	8	Rowe, Nancy Anne
	Northwest Missouri State		SC	L		20	10	Winstead, Wayne
	Pace		SA	A		23	7	Jones, Allison
	Pittsburgh: Johnstown		E	A		25	4	Gault, Jodi
	Saint Cloud State		NC	L		23	5	Ziemer, Gladys L.
	Southeast Missouri State		SC	L		24	6	Arnzen, Ed
	Virginia State		SA	A		24	4	Cummings, Bertha
	West Georgia		S	L		19	8	Williamson, Jane

1990 Division III

F	School	SD	Reg	BD	Bye	W	L	Coach
1	Hope		GL	L		24	2	Wise, Susan
2	Saint John Fisher		E	L		31	2	Kahler, Phillip I.
3	Heidelberg		A	A		27	6	McConnell, Karen
4	Centre		S	A		22	8	Noble-Hauserman, Cindy
8	Buena Vista		C	L		23	6	Naughton, John
	Concordia: Moorhead		W	A		24	5	Siverson, Duane
	Scranton		MA	A		26	5	Strong, Michael J.
	Southern Maine		NE	A		25	5	Fifield, Gary

F	School	SD	Reg	BD	Bye	W	L	Coach
16	Allentown		MA	L		27	2	Shirley, Thomas, Jr.
	Hartwick		E	L		24	5	Kragalott, Arden
	Maryville (TN)		S	L		23	5	Moore, Frank "Wes"
	Montclair State		A	L		23	6	Jeffrey, Jill
	Saint Thomas (MN)		W	L		23	5	Riverso, Ted
	Wartburg		C	A		22	5	Severson, Monica
	Western Connecticut State		NE	L		24	3	Rajcula, Jody
	Wisconsin: Oshkosh		GL	L		17	7	Bennett, Kathi
32	Augustana (IL)		C	A		22	4	Schumacher, Diane
	Buffalo State College		E	L		24	4	Maloney, Gail F.
	California State: San Bernardino		W	L		24	4	Schwartz, Gary
	Colorado College		W	L		17	9	Branson, Beth
	Eastern Connecticut State		NE	L		20	5	Miller, Dr. C. Robert
	Franklin & Marshall		MA	L		25	5	Fleig, Mary L.
	Kean		A	A		23	6	Wilson, Rich
	Marymount (VA)		S	L		19	8	Finney, Bill
	Moravian		MA	L		24	5	Spirk, Mary Beth
	Nazareth (NY)		E	L		22	6	DeCillis, Michael
	Roanoke		S	L		24	5	Dunagan, Susan
	Saint Benedict		GL	L		21	7	Durbin, Michael
	Salem State		NE	A		24	5	Shea, Timothy P.
	Washington (MO)		C	A		25	3	Fahey, Nancy
	Wisconsin: Eau Claire		GL	L		21	6	Stone, Lisa Anderson
	Wittenberg		A	L		26	3	Evans, Pamela

1991 Division I

F	School	SD	Reg	BD	Bye	W	L	Coach
1	Tennessee	1	ME	L	To R32	30	5	Summitt, Patricia Head
2	Virginia	1	MW	L	To R32	31	3	Ryan, Deborah H.
3	Connecticut	3	E	A	To R32	29	5	Auriemma, Geno
	Stanford	2	W	A	To R32	26	6	VanDerveer, Tara
8	Auburn	3	ME	L	To R32	26	6	Ciampi, Joe
	Clemson	4	E	L	To R32	22	11	Davis, Jim
	Georgia	1	W	L	To R32	28	4	Landers, Andy
	Lamar	10	MW	L		29	4	Barbre, Al
16	Arkansas	3	MW	A	To R32	28	4	Sutherland, John
	California State: Long Beach	4	W	A	To R32	24	8	Bonvicini, Joan
	James Madison	8	E	L		26	5	Moorman, Shelia
	North Carolina State	2	E	A	To R32	27	6	Yow, Sandra Kay
	Oklahoma State	5	MW	A		27	6	Halterman, Dick
	Vanderbilt	10	ME	L		19	12	Lee, Phil
	Washington	3	W	L	To R32	24	5	Gobrecht, Chris
	Western Kentucky	4	ME	A	To R32	29	3	Sanderford, Paul
32	California State: Fullerton	7	W	L		25	8	Jeremiah, Dr. Maryalyce
	Florida State	5	ME	A		25	7	Meadors, Marynell Hutsell
	George Washington	10	E	L		23	7	McKeown, Joe
	Holy Cross (MA)	11	ME	L		25	6	Gibbons, Bill, Jr.
	Iowa	6	W	L		21	9	Stringer, C. Vivian
	Louisiana State	2	MW	A	To R32	24	7	Gunter, Sue
	Michigan State	4	MW	L	To R32	21	8	Langeland, Karen
	Nevada: Las Vegas	8	W	L		25	7	Bolla, Jim

F	School	SD	Reg	BD	Bye	W	L	Coach
	Northwestern (IL)	6	MW	L		21	9	Perrelli, Donald
	Pennsylvania State	1	E	A	To R32	29	2	Portland, Rene Muth
	Providence	5	E	L		26	6	Foley, Bob
	Purdue	2	ME	A	To R32	26	3	Dunn, Lin
	Southern California	5	W	L		18	12	Stanley, Marianne Crawford
	Southwest Missouri State	8	ME	A		26	5	Burnett, Cheryl
	Stephen F Austin State	8	MW	A		26	5	Blair, Gary
	Toledo	11	E	A		24	7	Fennelly, Bill
48	Appalachian State	12	ME	A		19	14	Robinson, Linda
	De Paul	12	MW	A		19	12	Bruno, Doug
	Fairfield	12	E	A		25	6	Nolan, Diane
	Kentucky	9	E	L		20	9	Fanning, Sharon
	Louisiana Tech	10	W	A		18	12	Barmore, Leon
	Maryland	6	ME	L		17	13	Weller, Christine J.
	Mississippi	9	MW	L		20	9	Chancellor, Van
	Montana	11	W	A		26	4	Selvig, Robin
	Richmond	7	E	A		26	5	Gaitley, Stephanie Vanderslice
	Rutgers	6	E	L		23	7	Grentz, Theresa Shank
	South Carolina	7	ME	L		22	9	Wilson, Nancy R.
	Tennessee Tech	9	ME	A		22	8	Worrell, Bill
	Texas	7	MW	L		21	9	Conradt, Jody
	Texas Tech	9	W	L		23	8	Sharp, Marsha
	Utah	12	W	A		20	10	Elliott, Elaine
	Washington State	11	MW	L		18	11	Rhodes, Harold

1991 DIVISION II

F	School	SD	Reg	BD	Bye	W	L	Coach
1	North Dakota State		NC	L		31	2	Ruley, Amy J.
2	Southeast Missouri State		SC	A		31	4	Arnzen, Ed
3	Bentley		NENG	L		31	4	Stevens, Barbara
4	Norfolk State		SA	A		33	2	Sweat, James E.
8	Bellarmine		GL	L		26	5	Just, Charles G.
	California Polytechnic: Pomona		W	A		22	9	May, Darlene
	Clarion		E	A		24	8	Parsons, Margaret Rhoads "Gie"
	Jacksonville State (AL)		S	A		26	4	Mabrey, Tony
16	California: Davis		W	L		26	5	Hoehn, Jorja E.
	Delta State		S	L		23	7	Clark, Lloyd
	Lock Haven		E	L		20	10	Scarfo, Frank
	North Carolina: Greensboro		SA	L		21	9	Agee, Lynne
	North Dakota		NC	A		28	2	Roebuck, Gene
	Northern Michigan		GL	A		22	9	Geary, Mike
	Saint Anselm		NENG	A		27	4	Guimont, Donna M.
	West Texas A&M		SC	A		30	2	Schneider, Bob
32	Alabama A&M		S	A		24	7	Parham, Press
	Augustana (SD)		NC	L		23	6	Krauth, David
	Barry		W	L		26	4	Olson, Dan
	Bloomsburg		E	L		26	2	Bressi, Joe
	California State: Stanislaus		W	A		21	8	Millar, Leann Henrich
	Central Missouri State		SC	L		23	6	Pye, Jon
	Florida Atlantic		NC	L		23	6	Allen, Wayne
	Hampton		S	L		26	6	Laster, Jr. "Tiny"

F	School	SD	Reg	BD	Bye	W	L	Coach
	Massachusetts: Lowell		NENG	A		22	9	O'Neil, Kathleen
	Michigan Tech		GL	L		22	7	Borseth, Kevin
	North Alabama		S	L		20	9	Byrd, Wayne
	Northern Kentucky		GL	A		22	6	Winstel, Nancy
	Pace		SA	A		26	4	Jones, Allison
	Pittsburgh: Johnstown		E	A		27	2	Gault, Jodi
	Stonehill		NENG	L		19	11	Sullivan, Paula J.
	Washburn		SC	L		23	7	Dick, Patricia D.

1991 DIVISION III

F	School	SD	Reg	BD	Bye	W	L	Coach
1	Saint Thomas (MN)		W	A		29	2	Riverso, Ted
2	Muskingum		A	A		28	5	Newberry, Donna
3	Eastern Connecticut State		NE	L		22	6	Miller, Dr. C. Robert
4	Washington (MO)		C	L		24	7	Fahey, Nancy
8	Concordia: Moorhead		W	L		21	8	Siverson, Duane
	Roanoke		S	L		28	2	Dunagan, Susan
	Saint John Fisher		E	L		28	3	Kahler, Phillip I.
	Southern Maine		NE	A		23	7	Fifield, Gary
16	Adrian		GL	L		22	4	Munk, Dana Marie
	Frostburg State		A	L		26	2	Crawley, James M.
	Hartwick		E	L		21	8	Kragalott, Arden
	Luther		C	A		18	9	Hildebrand, Jane
	Maryville (TN)		S	L		23	6	Moore, Frank "Wes"
	Moravian		MA	A		27	3	Spirk, Mary Beth
	Susquehanna		MA	L		23	5	Hribar, Mark
	Wisconsin: Oshkosh		GL	L		21	5	Bennett, Kathi
32	Augustana (IL)		C	A		19	5	Schumacher, Diane
	Buffalo State College		E	L		21	6	Maloney, Gail F.
	Calvin		GL	L		18	8	Vroon, A. Donald
	Capital		A	L		24	3	Jeffers, Dixie M.
	Carnegie Mellon		MA	A		21	6	Seidl, Gerri
	Centre		S	A		17	7	Noble-Hauserman, Cindy
	Franklin & Marshall		MA	L		21	6	Fleig, Mary L.
	Gustavus Adolphus		W	L		18	8	Kennedy, Tim
	Kean		A	A		24	3	Wilson, Rich
	Marymount (VA)		S	L		21	7	Finney, Bill
	New York		E	L		19	8	Quinn, Janice
	Saint Benedict		W	L		20	7	Durbin, Michael
	Salem State		NE	L		24	5	Shea, Timothy P.
	Wartburg		C	L		20	7	Severson, Monica
	Western Connecticut State		NE	L		21	6	Rajcula, Jody
	Wisconsin: Stevens Point		GL	L		17	7	Egner, Shirley

1992 DIVISION I

F	School	SD	Reg	BD	Bye	W	L	Coach
1	Stanford	1	W	A	To R32	30	3	VanDerveer, Tara
2	Western Kentucky	4	ME	A	To R32	27	8	Sanderford, Paul
3	Southwest Missouri State	8	MW	A		31	3	Burnett, Cheryl
	Virginia	1	E	A	To R32	32	2	Ryan, Deborah H.
8	Maryland	2	ME	L	To R32	25	6	Weller, Christine J.
	Mississippi	2	MW	L	To R32	29	3	Chancellor, Van
	Southern California	3	W	L	To R32	23	8	Stanley, Marianne Crawford
	Vanderbilt	3	E	L	To R32	22	9	Foster, Jim

F	School	SD	Reg	BD	Bye	W	L	Coach
16	California: Los Angeles	5	MW	L		21	10	Moore, Billie Jean
	Miami (FL)	2	E	A	To R32	30	2	Labati, Ferne
	Pennsylvania State	3	MW	L	To R32	24	7	Portland, Rene Muth
	Purdue	3	ME	L	To R32	23	7	Dunn, Lin
	Stephen F Austin State	2	W	A	To R32	28	3	Blair, Gary
	Tennessee	1	ME	A	To R32	28	3	Summitt, Patricia Head
	Texas Tech	4	W	A	To R32	27	5	Sharp, Marsha
	West Virginia	4	E	L	To R32	26	4	Blakemore, Kittie
32	Alabama	5	ME	L		23	7	Moody, Rick
	California: Santa Barbara	9	W	A		27	5	French, Mark
	Clemson	5	E	L		21	10	Davis, Jim
	Connecticut	6	E	L		23	11	Auriemma, Geno
	Creighton	7	W	A		28	4	Rasmussen, Bruce
	De Paul	11	MW	L		21	10	Bruno, Doug
	George Washington	8	E	A		25	7	McKeown, Joe
	Iowa	1	MW	A	To R32	25	4	Stringer, C. Vivian
	Montana	11	W	A		23	7	Selvig, Robin
	North Carolina	7	E	L		22	9	Hatchell, Sylvia Rhyne
	Northern Illinois	11	ME	A		18	14	Albright-Dieterle, Jane
	Rutgers	8	ME	L		21	11	Grentz, Theresa Shank
	Santa Clara	12	W	A		21	10	Horstmeyer, Caren
	Southern Illinois	10	MW	L		23	8	Scott, Cindy
	Texas	4	MW	L	To R32	21	10	Conradt, Jody
	Toledo	10	ME	A		26	6	Fennelly, Bill
48	Arizona State	6	MW	L		20	9	McHugh, Maura
	California	5	W	L		20	9	Foster, Dr. Gooch
	California State: Long Beach	10	W	L		21	10	McDonald, Glenn
	Colorado	7	MW	A		22	9	Barry, Ceal
	Houston	8	W	L		22	8	Kenlaw, Jessie
	Kansas	9	MW	L		25	6	Washington, Marian
	Louisiana Tech	6	ME	L		20	10	Barmore, Leon
	Notre Dame (IN)	12	MW	A		14	17	McGraw, Muffet O'Brien
	Old Dominion	10	E	A		20	11	Larry, Wendy
	Providence	7	ME	L		21	9	Foley, Bob
	Saint Peter's	11	E	A		24	7	Granelli, Mike
	Southern Mississippi	9	ME	A		21	10	James, Kay
	Tennessee Tech	12	ME	A		21	9	Worrell, Bill
	Tennessee: Chattanooga	12	E	A		18	12	Parrott, Craig
	Vermont	9	E	L		29	1	Inglese, Cathy
	Wisconsin	6	W	L		20	9	Murphy, Mary

1992 DIVISION II

1	Delta State		S	L		30	4	Clark, Lloyd
2	North Dakota State		NC	A		29	4	Ruley, Amy J.
3	Portland State		W	L		31	3	Bruce, Greg
4	Bentley		NENG	A		31	2	Stevens, Barbara
8	North Dakota		SA	L		24	7	Roebuck, Gene
	Pittsburgh: Johnstown		E	L		25	4	Gault, Jodi
	Saint Joseph's (IN)		GL	A		28	3	Freeman, Keith
	Washburn		SC	L		27	5	Dick, Patricia D.

F	School	SD	Reg	BD	Bye	W	L	Coach
16	Augustana (SD)	NC	L			26	4	Krauth, David
	California: Davis	W	A			25	3	Hoehn, Jorja E.
	Clarion	E	L			25	4	Parsons, Margaret Rhoads "Gie"
	Norfolk State	SA	A			25	7	Sweat, James E.
	Northern Michigan	GL	A			23	6	Geary, Mike
	Stonehill	NENG	L			26	5	Sullivan, Paula J.
	West Georgia	S	A			26	5	Williamson, Jane
	West Texas A&M	SC	L			24	6	Schneider, Bob
32	Alaska: Anchorage	W	L			18	6	Raugust, Milt
	Bloomsburg	SA	A			22	8	Bressi, Joe
	California Polytechnic: Pomona	W	A			23	6	May, Darlene
	Central Florida	S	L			25	4	Reynolds, John, Jr.
	Edinboro	E	L			22	8	Swank, Stan
	Fort Valley State	S	A			21	9	Bartley, Lonnie
	Franklin Pierce	NENG	A			24	7	Hancock, Steve
	Indiana-Purdue: Fort Wayne	SC	L			22	7	Kleinfelter, Eileen
	Johnson C Smith	SA	L			22	9	Evans-Liebert, Hythia
	Michigan Tech	GL	L			23	6	Borseth, Kevin
	Nebraska: Omaha	NC	L			20	9	Mankenberg, Cherri
	Northern Kentucky	GL	L			19	9	Winstel, Nancy
	Pace	E	A			25	6	Jones, Allison
	Pittsburg State	SC	A			22	9	High, Steve
	Saint Augustine's	NENG	L			23	3	Downing, Dr. Beverly
	South Dakota State	NC	L			19	10	Neiber, Nancy

1992 DIVISION III

F	School	SD	Reg	BD	Bye	W	L	Coach
1	Alma	GL	A			24	3	Goffnett, Charles
2	Moravian	MA	A			31	2	Spirk, Mary Beth
3	Luther	C	L			24	6	Hildebrand, Jane
4	Eastern Connecticut State	NE	A			25	6	Miller, Dr. C. Robert
8	Capital	A	A			29	2	Jeffers, Dixie M.
	Southern Maine	NE	L			26	4	Fifield, Gary
	Wartburg	C	A			23	4	Severson, Monica
	Wisconsin: Eau Claire	GL	A			23	5	Stone, Lisa Anderson
16	Albany State (NY)	E	L			22	5	Warner, Mari
	Christopher Newport	S	L			22	6	Parson, Cathy
	Cortland State	E	L			24	5	Foley, Bonnie
	Muskingum	A	L			22	8	Newberry, Donna
	Roanoke	S	L			24	4	Dunagan, Susan
	Saint Benedict	W	L			22	6	Durbin, Michael
	Saint Thomas (MN)	W	A			27	1	Riverso, Ted
	Scranton	MA	L			22	5	Strong, Michael J.
32	Adrian	GL	L			20	5	Munk, Dana Marie
	Clark (MA)	NE	L			22	5	Glispin, Patricia
	Concordia: Moorhead	W	L			18	9	Pyle, Jerry
	Emmanuel (MA)	E	L			20	5	Yosinoff, Andrew
	Marymount (VA)	S	L			23	5	Finney, Bill
	Maryville (TN)	S	L			24	4	Moore, Frank "Wes"
	Ohio Wesleyan	A	L			23	2	Carney-DeBord, Nan
	Rowan	A	A			23	5	Bunting, Dawn Shilling

F	School	SD	Reg	BD	Bye	W	L	Coach
	Saint John Fisher		E	L		22	4	Kahler, Phillip I.
	Saint Olaf		W	L		19	7	Buresh, Pat
	Susquehanna		MA	L		21	6	Hribar, Mark
	Washington (MO)		C	A		22	5	Fahey, Nancy
	Western Connecticut State		MA	L		21	5	Rajcula, Jody
	William Smith		NE	L		24	4	Begley, Glenn C.
	Wisconsin: Oshkosh		GL	L		18	6	Bennett, Kathi
	Wisconsin: Stout		C	L		19	7	Thomas, Mark

1993 Division I

F	School	SD	Reg	BD	Bye	W	L	Coach
1	Texas Tech	2	W	A	To R32	31	3	Sharp, Marsha
2	Ohio State	1	E	L	To R32	28	4	Darsch, Nancy
3	Iowa		ME	A	To R32	27	4	Stringer, C. Vivian
	Vanderbilt	1	MW	A	To R32	30	3	Foster, Jim
8	Colorado	4	W	L	To R32	27	4	Barry, Ceal
	Louisiana Tech		MW	L		26	6	Barmore, Leon
	Tennessee	1	ME	L	To R32	29	3	Summitt, Patricia Head
	Virginia	2	E	A	To R32	26	6	Ryan, Deborah H.
16	Auburn	3	ME	L	To R32	25	4	Ciampi, Joe
	Georgetown (DC)		E	L		23	7	Knapp, Patrick
	North Carolina	4	ME	L	To R32	23	7	Hatchell, Sylvia Rhyne
	Southern California	3	W	L	To R32	22	7	Stanley, Marianne Crawford
	Southwest Missouri State		MW	A		23	9	Burnett, Cheryl
	Stanford	1	W	A	To R32	26	6	VanDerveer, Tara
	Stephen F Austin State	4	MW	A	To R32	28	5	Blair, Gary
	Western Kentucky	4	E	A	To R32	24	7	Sanderford, Paul
32	Alabama		ME	L		22	9	Moody, Rick
	California		MW	L		19	10	Foster, Dr. Gooch
	California: Santa Barbara		W	A		19	12	French, Mark
	Clemson		MW	L		19	11	Davis, Jim
	Florida		E	L		19	10	Ross, Carol
	Georgia		W	L		21	13	Landers, Andy
	Louisville		ME	A		19	12	Childers, 'Bud'
	Maryland	2	MW	L	To R32	22	8	Weller, Christine J.
	Miami (FL)		E	A		24	7	Labati, Ferne
	Nebraska		W	L		23	8	Beck, Angela
	Northwestern (IL)		ME	L		20	9	Perrelli, Donald
	Old Dominion		ME	A		22	8	Larry, Wendy
	Pennsylvania State	3	E	L	To R32	22	6	Portland, Rene Muth
	Rutgers		E	A		22	9	Grentz, Theresa Shank
	Texas	3	MW	L	To R32	22	8	Conradt, Jody
	Washington		W	L		17	12	Gobrecht, Chris
48	Bowling Green State		E	A		25	5	Clark, Jaci
	Brigham Young		W	A		24	4	Wilson, Jeanie
	Connecticut		ME	L		18	11	Auriemma, Geno
	De Paul		MW	L		20	9	Bruno, Doug
	Georgia Southern		ME	A		21	9	Greer, Drema Sue
	Georgia Tech		ME	L		16	11	Berenato, Agnus McGlade
	Kansas		MW	A		21	9	Washington, Marian
	Montana State		W	A		22	7	Spoelstra, Judy

F	School	SD	Reg	BD	Bye	W	L	Coach
	Northern Illinois		E	A		24	6	Albright-Dieterle, Jane
	Oklahoma State		MW	L		23	9	Halterman, Dick
	Saint Peter's		E	A		18	11	Granelli, Mike
	San Diego		W	A		16	12	Marpe, Kathleen
	San Diego State		W	L		19	9	Burns, Beth
	Tennessee Tech		ME	A		22	7	Worrell, Bill
	Vermont		E	L		28	1	Inglese, Cathy
	Xavier (OH)		MW	A		21	9	Ehlen, Mark

1993 Division II

F	School	SD	Reg	BD	Bye	W	L	Coach
1	North Dakota State		NC			30	2	Ruley, Amy J.
2	Delta State		S	L		27	6	Clark, Lloyd
3	Michigan Tech		GL	A		30	3	Borseth, Kevin
4	Bentley		NENG	A		30	4	Stevens, Barbara
8	California Polytechnic: Pomona		W	A		27	3	May, Darlene
	Norfolk State		SA	C		29	3	Sweat, James E.
	Pittsburgh: Johnstown		E	L		25	5	Gault, Jodi
	Washburn		SC	A		31	1	Dick, Patricia D.
16	Augustana (SD)		NC	L		24	5	Krauth, David
	Central Florida		S	L		26	4	Reynolds, John, Jr.
	Clarion		E	A		24	6	Parsons, Margaret Rhoads "Gie"
	Massachusetts: Lowell		NENG	A		24	6	O'Neil, Kathleen
	Missouri Southern State		SC	L		27	4	Ballard, Scott
	Portland State		W	L		21	8	Bruce, Greg
	Saginaw Valley State		GL	L		20	9	Charney, Claudette
	South Carolina: Spartanburg		SA	L		28	3	Sells, Peggy
32	Bellarmine		GL	L		18	10	Just, Charles G.
	California: Davis		W	A		19	7	Hoehn, Jorja E.
	California: Riverside		W	L		17	11	Woelke, Debi
	Central Missouri State		SC	L		19	10	Pye, Jon
	Denver		NC	L		24	4	Sheehan, Tracey
	Edinboro		E	L		18	12	Swank, Stan
	Florida Atlantic		S	L		20	8	Allen, Wayne
	Fort Valley State		SA	L		27	3	Bartley, Lonnie
	Franklin Pierce		NENG	L		21	9	Hancock, Steve
	Indianapolis		GL	A		24	4	Mallender, Charles "Chuck"
	Jacksonville State (AL)		S	A		18	11	Mabrey, Tony
	North Dakota		NC			23	5	Roebuck, Gene
	Philadelphia Textiles		E	L		27	2	Shirley, Thomas, Jr.
	Pittsburg State		SC	L		21	7	High, Steve
	Saint Augustine's		SA	L		23	6	Downing, Dr. Beverly
	Stonehill		NENG	L		22	8	Sullivan, Paula J.

1993 Division III

F	School	SD	Reg	BD	Bye	W	L	Coach
1	Central (IA)		C	A		24	5	Boeyink, Gary
2	Capital		NE	A		28	4	Jeffers, Dixie M.
3	Scranton		E	A		30	2	Strong, Michael J.
4	Saint Benedict		W	A		28	2	Durbin, Michael

F	School	SD	Reg	BD	Bye	W	L	Coach
8	Concordia: Moorhead		W	L		20	7	Kohler, Robert
	Geneseo State		E	L		27	1	Guy, Robert
	Southern Maine		NE	A		25	4	Fifield, Gary
	Wartburg		C	L		23	5	Severson, Monica
16	Babson		NE	L		23	5	Blinstrub, Judith
	Marymount (VA)		W	L		23	5	Finney, Bill
	Maryville (TN)		W	L		23	3	Moore, Frank "Wes"
	Moravian		E	L		24	5	Spirk, Mary Beth
	New York		E	L		20	6	Quinn, Janice
	Rowan		NE	L		23	5	Bunting, Dawn Shilling
	Wisconsin: Eau Claire		C	A		22	4	Stone, Lisa Anderson
	Wisconsin: Whitewater		C	L		19	7	Yeater, Julia
32	Augustana (IL)		C	A		19	7	Schumacher, Diane
	Buffalo State College		E	L		19	8	Maloney, Gail F.
	Calvin		C	A		18	8	Struyk, Sandi
	Christopher Newport		W	A		19	9	Parson, Cathy
	Muskingum		W	L		24	3	Newberry, Donna
	Roanoke		W	L		21	6	Dunagan, Susan
	Saint John Fisher		E	L		22	6	Kahler, Phillip I.
	Saint Thomas (MN)		W	L		19	7	Riverso, Ted
	Salem State		NE	L		18	8	Shea, Timothy P.
	Susquehanna		E	L		19	7	Hribar, Mark
	Washington (MO)		C	A		22	4	Fahey, Nancy
	Waynesburg		E	L		19	6	Phillips, Rob
	Western Connecticut State		NE	L		20	5	Rajcula, Jody
	William Patterson		NE	A		18	9	Delehanty, Patty
	Wisconsin: Stout		C	L		21	4	Thomas, Mark
	Wittenberg		NE	L		23	4	Evans, Pamela

1994 Division I

F	School	SD	Reg	BD	Bye	W	L	Coach
1	North Carolina	3	E	A		33	2	Hatchell, Sylvia Rhyne
2	Louisiana Tech	4	ME	A		31	4	Barmore, Leon
3	Alabama	6	MW	L		26	7	Moody, Rick
	Purdue	1	W	L		29	5	Dunn, Lin
8	Connecticut	1	E	A		30	3	Auriemma, Geno
	Pennsylvania State	1	MW	A		28	3	Portland, Rene Muth
	Southern California	2	ME	A		26	4	Miller, Cheryl
	Stanford	2	W	A		25	6	VanDerveer, Tara
16	Colorado	3	W	L		27	5	Barry, Ceal
	Seton Hall	4	MW	L		27	5	Mangina, Phyllis
	Southern Mississippi	4	E	L		26	5	James, Kay
	Tennessee	1	ME	A		31	2	Summitt, Patricia Head
	Texas A&M	13	W	L		23	8	Hickey, Lynn
	Texas Tech	2	MW	L		28	5	Sharp, Marsha
	Vanderbilt	2	E	L		25	8	Foster, Jim
	Virginia	3	ME	L		27	5	Ryan, Deborah H.
32	Auburn	9	E	L		20	10	Ciampi, Joe
	Clemson	9	ME	L		20	10	Davis, Jim
	Creighton	10	MW	L		24	7	Yori, Connie
	George Washington	7	ME	L		23	8	McKeown, Joe

F	School	SD	Reg	BD	Bye	W	L	Coach
	Iowa	3	MW	L		21	7	Stringer, C. Vivian
	Kansas	9	MW	L		22	6	Washington, Marian
	Minnesota	10	E	L		18	11	Hill-MacDonald, Linda
	Mississippi	5	ME	L		24	9	Chancellor, Van
	Montana	7	W	A		25	5	Selvig, Robin
	Old Dominion	6	E	A		25	6	Larry, Wendy
	Oregon	6	W	L		20	9	Runge, Jody
	San Diego State	5	W	A		26	5	Burns, Beth
	Southwest Missouri State	6	ME	A		24	6	Burnett, Cheryl
	Texas	5	MW	A		22	9	Conradt, Jody
	Washington	8	W	L		21	8	Gobrecht, Chris
	Western Kentucky	12	E	L		24	10	Sanderford, Paul
64	Alabama: Birmingham	10	ME	A		23	6	Milling, Jeannie
	Boise State	9	W	L		23	6	Daugherty, June
	Bowling Green State	7	MW	A		26	4	Clark, Jaci
	Brown	16	E	A		18	10	Burr, Jean Marie
	Florida	4	W	L		22	7	Ross, Carol
	Florida International	8	ME	A		25	4	Russo, Cindy
	Fordham	16	MW	A		21	9	Morris, Kevin
	Georgia Southern	14	E	A		21	9	Greer, Drema Sue
	Grambling State	15	E	A		23	7	Bibbs, Patricia Cage
	Hawaii	12	W	L		25	5	Goo, Vince
	Indiana	12	ME	L		19	9	Izard, Jim
	Loyola (MD)	14	ME	A		18	11	Coyle, Patricia
	Marquette	14	W	L		22	7	Jabir, James J.
	Missouri	15	MW	A		12	18	Rutherford, Dr. Joann
	Mount Saint Mary's (MD)	14	MW	A		25	4	Sheahan, William
	Nevada: Las Vegas	10	W	A		23	7	Bolla, Jim
	North Carolina A&T	16	ME	A		19	11	Abney, Tim
	Northern Illinois	11	ME	L		24	6	Albright-Dieterle, Jane
	Notre Dame (IN)	7	E	A		22	7	McGraw, Muffet O'Brien
	Oklahoma State	12	MW	L		20	9	Halterman, Dick
	Oregon State	11	MW	L		17	11	Hill, Aki
	Portland	15	ME	A		17	12	Sollars, Jim
	Radford	16	W	A		18	12	Lichonczak, Lubomyr
	Rutgers	5	E	A		22	8	Grentz, Theresa Shank
	Saint Joseph's (PA)	11	E	L		19	9	Gaitley, Stephanie Vanderslice
	Santa Clara	11	W	L		21	7	Horstmeyer, Caren
	Southern Methodist (TX)	13	ME	L		18	9	Rompola, Rhonda
	Stephen F Austin State	8	MW	A		23	7	Curl, Joe
	Tennessee State	13	E	A		20	9	Lawrence-Phillips, Teresa A.
	Vermont	13	MW	A		19	11	Borton, Pam
	Virginia Polytechnic	8	E	A		24	6	Alfano, Carol
	Wisconsin: Green Bay	15	W	A		18	11	Hammerle, Carol

1994 DIVISION II

1	North Dakota State		NC	L		27	5	Ruley, Amy J.
2	California State: San Bernardino		W	A		29	4	Beckley, Luvina
3	North Alabama		S	L		22	10	Byrd, Wayne
4	Bellarmine		GL	A		25	6	Just, Charles G.

F	School	SD	Reg	BD	Bye	W	L	Coach
8	Clarion	E	A			26	4	Parsons, Margaret Rhoads "Gie"
	Missouri Western State	SC	L			29	3	Mittie, Jeff
	Norfolk State	SA	L			27	4	Sweat, James E.
	Stonehill	NENG	L			27	5	Sullivan, Paula J.
16	Bentley	NENG	A			25	6	Stevens, Barbara
	Lake Superior State	GL	L			23	7	Ledy, Erica
	Missouri Southern State	SC	A			25	5	Ballard, Scott
	Pace	E	A			27	4	Seymour, Carrie
	Portland State	W	A			25	4	Bruce, Greg
	South Dakota State	NC	L			22	8	Neiber, Nancy
	West Georgia	S	A			22	7	Williamson, Jane
	Wingate	SA	A			27	2	Jacumin, Johnny
32	Angelo State	SC	A			23	6	Davis, Peggy
	Augustana (SD)	NC	L			23	6	Krauth, David
	California: Davis	W	A			22	7	Hoehn, Jorja E.
	East Stroudsburg	E	L			21	8	Haller, Rose
	Florida Southern	S	A			23	8	Benn, Norm
	Massachusetts: Lowell	NENG	L			23	8	O'Neil, Kathleen
	Mercyhurst	E	L			19	9	Demyanovich, Paul
	Michigan Tech	GL	L			23	6	Borseth, Kevin
	Montana State: Billings	W	L			19	9	McCarthy, Frank B.
	North Dakota	NC	A			26	2	Roebuck, Gene
	Oakland (MI)	GL	A			23	5	Taylor, Bob
	Presbyterian	SA	L			22	8	Couture, Beth
	Saint Anselm	NENG	L			22	9	Guimont, Donna M.
	South Carolina: Spartanburg	SA	A			27	4	Sells, Peggy
	Tampa University	S	L			21	7	Mosca, Tom
	Washburn	SC	L			22	8	Dick, Patricia D.

1994 Division III

F	School	SD	Reg	BD	Bye	W	L	Coach
1	Capital	A	A		To R32	30	1	Jeffers, Dixie M.
2	Washington (MO)	C	A		To R32	26	4	Fahey, Nancy
3	Wisconsin: Eau Claire	GL	L		To R32	23	6	Stone, Lisa Anderson
4	Wheaton (MA)	NE	L		To R32	27	4	Malloy, Del
8	Defiance	A	L		To R32	25	3	Elliott, Cindy
	Millikin	C	A		To R32	24	4	Kearns, Lori Ann
	Scranton	MA	A		To R32	27	3	Strong, Michael J.
	Wisconsin: Oshkosh	GL	A		To R32	24	3	Bennett, Kathi
16	Babson	NE	L		To R32	23	4	Blinstrub, Judith
	Bethel (MN)	W	A		To R32	21	5	Hunter, Debra F.
	Marymount (VA)	S	L		To R32	24	3	Finney, Bill
	Maryville (TN)	S	L		To R32	23	4	Moore, Frank "Wes"
	New York	E	L		To R32	22	4	Quinn, Janice
	Saint Benedict	W	L		To R32	22	5	Durbin, Michael
	Saint John Fisher	E	L		To R32	28	1	Kahler, Phillip I.
	Upsala	MA	L			23	3	McGrady, William
32	Alma	GL	A			21	6	Goffnett, Charles
	Aurora	C	L			22	5	Lancaster, James
	Buffalo State College	E	A		To R32	25	3	Maloney, Gail F.
	Central (IA)	C	A			22	5	Boeyink, Gary

F	School	SD	Reg	BD	Bye	W	L	Coach
	Concordia: Moorhead		W	L	To R32	18	8	Kohler, Robert
	Geneseo State		E	L		26	3	Guy, Robert
	Mary Washington		S	L	To R32	20	6	Gallahan, Connie
	North Carolina Wesleyan		S	A		20	8	Brackett, John
	Pennsylvania State: Erie Behrend		A	L		21	6	Fornari, Rosalyn "Roz"
	Rowan		MA	A	To R32	25	1	Crabtree, Candace
	Saint Thomas (MN)		W	L		22	5	Riverso, Ted
	Salem State		NE	A	To R32	22	5	Shea, Timothy P.
	Western Connecticut State		NE	A	To R32	23	4	Rajcula, Jody
	William Patterson		MA	L	To R32	23	4	Shaughnessy, Erin
	Wisconsin: Stout		GL	L	To R32	21	5	Thomas, Mark
	Wittenberg		A	L	To R32	24	4	Evans, Pamela
40	Denison		A	A		18	9	Lee, Sara
	Elizabethtown		MA	L		21	5	Kauffman, Yvonne E.
	Franklin (IN)		GL	L		19	6	White, Gene
	Lake Forest		C	A		19	6	Slaats, Jackie
	Pomona-Pitzer		W	A		14	11	Krieger, Barbara
	Roanoke		S	A		23	5	Dunagan, Susan
	Wartburg		C	L		20	6	Severson, Monica
	William Smith		E	A		25	3	Begley, Glenn C.

1995 DIVISION I

F	School	SD	Reg	BD	Bye	W	L	Coach
1	Connecticut	1	E	A		35	0	Auriemma, Geno
2	Tennessee	1	ME	L		34	3	Summitt, Patricia Head
3	Georgia	3	MW	L		28	5	Landers, Andy
	Stanford	2	W	A		30	3	VanDerveer, Tara
8	Colorado	1	MW	A		30	3	Barry, Ceal
	Purdue	4	W	L		24	8	Dunn, Lin
	Texas Tech	2	ME	A		33	4	Sharp, Marsha
	Virginia	3	E	L		27	5	Ryan, Deborah H.
16	Alabama	4	E	L		22	9	Moody, Rick
	George Washington	4	MW	A		26	6	McKeown, Joe
	Louisiana Tech	2	E	L		28	5	Barmore, Leon
	North Carolina	3	W	A		30	5	Hatchell, Sylvia Rhyne
	North Carolina State	7	MW	L		21	10	Yow, Sandra Kay
	Vanderbilt	1	W	A		28	7	Foster, Jim
	Washington	3	ME	L		25	9	Gobrecht, Chris
	Western Kentucky	4	ME	A		28	4	Sanderford, Paul
32	Arkansas	6	ME	L		23	7	Blair, Gary
	Drake (IA)	5	MW	A		25	6	Bluder, Lisa
	Duke	5	E	L		22	9	Goestenkors, Gail
	Florida	6	E	L		24	9	Ross, Carol
	Florida International	9	ME	A		27	5	Russo, Cindy
	Louisville	11	MW	L		25	8	Childers, "Bud"
	Memphis	8	W	L		22	8	Lee-McNelis, Joye
	Montana	12	W	A		26	7	Selvig, Robin
	Oklahoma	7	E	L		22	9	Plunkett, Burl
	Oregon State	5	ME	L		21	8	Hill, Aki
	Pennsylvania State	2	MW	A		26	5	Portland, Rene Muth
	Seton Hall	6	W	L		24	9	Mangina, Phyllis

F	School	SD	Reg	BD	Bye	W	L	Coach
	Southern Methodist (TX)	10	W	L		21	9	Rompola, Rhonda
	Southwest Missouri State	9	MW	L		21	12	Burnett, Cheryl
	Virginia Polytechnic	8	E	L		22	9	Alfano, Carol
	Wisconsin	10	ME	L		20	9	Albright-Dieterle, Jane
64	California: Irvine	15	W	A		19	11	Matsuhara, Colleen
	Dartmouth	14	E	A		16	11	Wielgus, Christina
	De Paul	13	MW	L		20	9	Bruno, Doug
	Florida A&M	16	ME	A		24	6	Farmer, Claudette
	Furman	15	E	A		18	12	Carter, Sherry
	Holy Cross (MA)	16	MW	A		21	9	Gibbons, Bill, Jr.
	Indiana	14	MW	L		19	10	Izard, Jim
	Jackson State (MS)	15	MW	A		22	7	Pennington, Andrew
	Kansas	7	ME	L		20	11	Washington, Marian
	Loyola (MD)	10	E	A		20	9	Coyle, Patricia
	Maine	16	E	A		24	6	Palombo-McCall, Joanne
	Marquette	10	MW	A		19	12	Jabir, James J.
	Mississippi	12	MW	L		21	8	Chancellor, Van
	Mount Saint Mary's (MD)	13	E	A		24	6	Sheahan, William
	Northern Illinois	16	W	A		17	14	Galloway-McQuitter, Liz
	Ohio University	14	ME	L		23	7	Reall, Marsha
	Oklahoma State	12	E	L		17	12	Halterman, Dick
	Old Dominion	8	ME	A		27	6	Larry, Wendy
	Oregon	6	MW	L		18	10	Runge, Jody
	Portland	13	W	L		23	7	Sollars, Jim
	Radford	11	E	A		15	15	Lichonczak, Lubomyr
	Saint Joseph's (PA)	9	E	L		20	9	Gaitley, Stephanie Vanderslice
	San Diego State	5	W	L		24	6	Burns, Beth
	San Francisco	11	ME	A		24	5	Nepfel, Bill
	Southern California	9	W	L		18	10	Miller, Cheryl
	Southern Mississippi	7	W	A		21	9	James, Kay
	Stephen F Austin State	11	W	A		22	8	Chadwick, Royce
	Tennessee State	12	ME	A		22	7	Lawrence-Phillips, Teresa A.
	Toledo	13	ME	A		24	7	Fennelly, Bill
	Tulane	15	ME	L		19	10	Stockton, Lisa
	Utah	8	MW	A		23	7	Elliott, Elaine
	Western Illinois	14	W	A		17	12	Miller, Regina

1995 DIVISION II

1	North Dakota State	2	NC	A	To R32	32	0	Ruley, Amy J.
2	Portland State	2	W	L	To R32	26	6	Bruce, Greg
3	Missouri Western State	1	SC	A	To R32	31	3	Mittie, Jeff
4	Stonehill	2	NENG	A	To R32	30	3	Sullivan, Paula J.
8	Florida Southern	1	S	A	To R32	28	4	Benn, Norm
	Mercyhurst	2	E	L	To R32	24	6	Webb, James D.
	Oakland (MI)	4	GL	L		22	9	Taylor, Bob
	Wingate	4	SA	L		25	6	Jacumin, Johnny
16	California: Davis	1	W	A	To R32	25	4	Hoehn, Jorja E.
	Michigan Tech	2	GL	L	To R32	24	6	Borseth, Kevin
	Saint Anselm	1	NENG	L	To R32	25	6	Guimont, Donna M.
	Saint Rose	1	E	A	To R32	26	5	Bailey, Curt

F	School	SD	Reg	BD	Bye	W	L	Coach
	South Carolina: Spartanburg	2	SA	A	To R32	25	6	Sells, Peggy
	South Dakota State	5	NC	L		24	6	Neiber, Nancy
	Valdosta State	2	S	L	To R32	25	4	Williamson, Jane
	Washburn	2	SC	L	To R32	24	7	Dick, Patricia D.
32	Abilene Christian	5	SC	L		23	7	Fox, Suzanne Johnson
	American International	3	NENG	L		22	9	Cinella, Peter
	Bentley	5	NENG	L		22	8	Stevens, Barbara
	California State: Dominguez Hills	4	W	A		22	6	Girard, Van
	Delta State	3	S	A		22	8	Clark, Lloyd
	East Stroudsburg	5	E	A		25	5	Haller, Rose
	Fort Valley State	4	S	A		25	5	Bartley, Lonnie
	Longwood	6	SA	L		21	8	Duncan, Shirley G.
	Minnesota: Duluth	3	NC	L		20	8	Stromme, Karen
	Norfolk State	1	SA	A	To R32	25	5	Sweat, James E.
	North Dakota	1	NC	L	To R32	23	5	Roebuck, Gene
	Northern Michigan	6	GL	A		21	9	Geary, Mike
	Seattle Pacific	3	W	L		21	8	Presnell, Gordy
	Shippensburg	6	E	L		22	7	Smith, David R.
	Southern Indiana	1	GL		To R32	22	5	Dugan, Chancellor
	West Texas A&M	3	SC	A		25	5	Schneider, Bob
48	Bridgeport	4	NENG	L		21	8	Herer, Harvey
	California: Riverside	5	W	L		19	10	Woelke, Debi
	Carson-Newman	5	SA	L		21	9	Carter, Eddie
	Chadron State	6	SC	A		22	8	Anderson, Tom
	Clarion	4	E	L		18	11	Parsons, Margaret Rhoads "Gie"
	Denver	4	NC	A		15	14	Sheehan, Tracey
	District Of Columbia	3	E	L		20	6	King, Britt S.
	Humboldt State	6	W	L		18	10	Martin, Pam
	Indianapolis	3	GL	L		21	7	Hicks, Lisa
	Massachusetts: Lowell	6	NENG	A		23	7	O'Neil, Kathleen
	Northern Colorado	6	NC	L		17	10	Schwartz, Gary
	Pittsburg State	4	SC	L		22	7	High, Steve
	Presbyterian	3	SA	A		23	7	Couture, Beth
	Rollins	5	S	L		21	8	Wilkes, Glenn N., Jr.
	Saint Joseph's (IN)	5	GL			19	9	Bland, Bill
	Savannah State	6	S	L		23	5	Wallace, Phillip

1995 Division III

F	School	SD	Reg	BD	Bye	W	L	Coach
1	Capital		A	A		33	0	Jeffers, Dixie M.
2	Wisconsin: Oshkosh		GL	L		28	3	Bennett, Kathi
3	Saint Thomas (MN)		W	L		25	6	Riverso, Ted
4	Salem State		NE	A		28	4	Shea, Timothy P.
8	Geneseo State		E	A		27	2	Guy, Robert
	Saint Benedict		W	A		27	2	Durbin, Michael
	William Patterson		MA	L		24	5	Dallessio, Jerry
	Wisconsin: Eau Claire		GL	A		24	5	Stone, Lisa Anderson
16	Aurora		C	L		22	6	Lancaster, James
	Emory		S	L		21	6	Sims, Myra
	Johns Hopkins		MA	L		22	7	Clelan-Blank, Nancy
	Maryville (TN)		S	L		23	5	Cook, Kelli

F	School	SD	Reg	BD	Bye	W	L	Coach
	Millikin	C	A			23	5	Kearns, Lori Ann
	Mount Union	A	L			24	6	Knoblauch, Deanne
	New York	E	L			23	5	Quinn, Janice
	Wheaton (MA)	NE	A			24	5	Malloy, Del
32	Central (IA)	C				18	7	Boeyink, Gary
	Claremont McKenna	W	L			22	5	Burton, Jodie
	Clark (MA)	NE	L			19	8	Glispin, Patricia
	Concordia: Moorhead	W	L			20	7	Kohler, Robert
	Defiance	A	L			22	5	Palombo, Tom
	Franklin (IN)	GL	L			24	2	Mahan, Lisa
	Gettysburg	MA	L			20	5	Kirkpatrick, Michael
	Marymount (VA)	S	A			24	5	Finney, Bill
	Montclair State	MA	A			20	7	Bradley, Gloria
	Roanoke	S	A			23	6	Dunagan, Susan
	Saint John Fisher	E	L			28	1	Kahler, Phillip I.
	Trinity (CT)	NE	L			21	4	Pine, Maureen
	Washington (MO)	C	A			20	7	Fahey, Nancy
	Waynesburg	A	L			21	5	Jones, Julie
	William Smith	E	A			23	3	Begley, Glenn C.
	Wisconsin: Whitewater	GL	L			20	7	Yeater, Julia
64	Beloit	GL	A			17	8	Walters, Mimi
	Bethel (MN)	W	L			17	8	Hunter, Debra F.
	Binghamton State	E	L			19	8	Wilson, David
	Brockport State	E	L			17	9	Carron, Michele
	Buena Vista	C				18	7	Allgood-Berry, Janet
	Buffalo State College	E	L			20	8	Maloney, Gail F.
	Cabrini	MA	L			24	3	Welde, Dan V.
	California Lutheran	W	A			23	3	La Kose, Tim
	California: San Diego	W	L			18	7	Malone, Judy
	Chicago	C	L			19	7	Zawacki, Susan M.
	Christopher Newport	S	L			17	9	Parson, Cathy
	Elizabethtown	MA	A			23	5	Kauffman, Yvonne E.
	Ferrum	S	A			18	9	Doonan, Donna M.
	Gustavus Adolphus	W	L			16	10	Moline, Peg
	Hartwick	E	L			20	8	Joy, Daphne
	Hope	GL	A			20	7	Gugino, Tod
	Illinois Wesleyan	C	L			20	6	Neal, Mandy
	Luther	C				20	6	Hildebrand, Jane
	Manchester	GL	L			15	9	Rockey, Kimberly
	Middlebury	NE	L			18	6	Fulcher, Jennifer
	Millsaps	S	L			19	7	Hannon, Cindy
	Ohio Wesleyan	A	L			22	6	Carney-DeBord, Nan
	Plymouth State	NE	L			21	7	Feldman, Nancy
	Salisbury State	A	L			21	7	Benshelter, Bridget
	Scranton	MA	L			24	2	Serafini, Sue
	Southern Maine	NE	A			23	4	Fifield, Gary
	Trinity (TX)	S	A			19	6	Geyer, Becky
	Ursinus	MA	A			21	5	Ortlip-Cornish, Lisa

F	School	SD	Reg	BD	Bye	W	L	Coach
	Washington & Jefferson	A	L			16	7	Staton, Vicki L.
	Westfield State	NE	L			21	7	Berger, Rick
	Wisconsin: River Falls	GL	L			17	9	Thelen, Carol
	Wittenberg	A	A			25	3	Evans, Pamela

1996 DIVISION I

F	School	SD	Reg	BD	Bye	W	L	Coach
1	Tennessee	1	E	A		32	4	Summitt, Patricia Head
2	Georgia	2	MW	L		28	5	Landers, Andy
3	Connecticut	1	ME	A		34	4	Auriemma, Geno
	Stanford	1	W	A		29	3	Tucker, Amy
8	Auburn	6	W	L		23	9	Ciampi, Joe
	Louisiana Tech	1	MW	A		31	2	Barmore, Leon
	Vanderbilt	3	ME	L		23	8	Foster, Jim
	Virginia	3	E	L		26	7	Ryan, Deborah H.
16	Alabama	4	W	L		24	8	Moody, Rick
	Iowa	2	ME	L		27	4	Lee, Angie
	Kansas	4	E	L		22	10	Washington, Marian
	Old Dominion	2	E	A		29	3	Larry, Wendy
	Pennsylvania State	2	W	A		27	7	Portland, Rene Muth
	San Francisco	12	ME	A		24	8	Nepfel, Bill
	Stephen F Austin State	11	MW	A		27	4	Chadwick, Royce
	Texas Tech	4	MW	L		27	5	Sharp, Marsha
32	Clemson	3	MW	A		23	8	Davis, Jim
	Colorado	3	W	A		26	9	Barry, Ceal
	Colorado State	8	W	A		26	5	Williams, Greg
	De Paul	7	ME	L		21	10	Bruno, Doug
	Duke	4	ME	L		26	7	Goestenkors, Gail
	George Washington	6	E	A		26	7	McKeown, Joe
	Kent State	10	W	L		24	7	Lindsay, Bob
	Michigan State	9	ME	L		18	11	Langeland, Karen
	North Carolina State	5	W	L		20	10	Yow, Sandra Kay
	Notre Dame (IN)	12	MW	L		23	8	McGraw, Muffet O'Brien
	Ohio State	9	E	L		21	13	Darsch, Nancy
	Oklahoma State	7	MW	L		20	10	Halterman, Dick
	Southern Mississippi	9	MW	L		22	8	James, Kay
	Texas	5	E	L		21	9	Conradt, Jody
	Toledo	10	E	A		25	6	Ehlen, Mark
	Wisconsin	6	ME	L		21	8	Albright-Dieterle, Jane
64	Appalachian State	13	W	A		24	6	Robinson, Linda
	Austin Peay State	14	MW	A		21	8	Wilson, LaDonna
	Butler (IN)	15	ME	A		21	9	Olkowski, June
	Central Florida	16	MW	A		15	14	Richardson, Jerry
	Florida	5	ME	L		21	9	Ross, Carol
	Grambling State	16	W	A		21	7	Bibbs, Patricia Cage
	Harvard	14	ME	A		20	7	Smith, Kathleen Delaney
	Hawaii	11	W	A		23	6	Goo, Vince
	Holy Cross (MA)	15	E	A		23	10	Gibbons, Bill, Jr.
	Howard (DC)	16	ME	A		20	10	Tyler, Sanya
	James Madison	13	ME	L		21	9	Moorman, Shelia
	Maine	11	E	A		27	5	Palombo-McCall, Joanne

F	School	SD	Reg	BD	Bye	W	L	Coach
	Manhattan	14	E	A		19	11	Sharp, Michele
	Massachusetts	8	ME	L		20	10	O'Brien, Joanie
	Memphis	8	E	L		20	11	Lee-McNelis, Joye
	Middle Tennessee State	13	E	L		24	6	Bivens, Lewis
	Mississippi	7	E	L		18	11	Chancellor, Van
	Montana	12	W	A		24	5	Selvig, Robin
	Nebraska	9	W	L		19	10	Beck, Angela
	Oregon	11	ME	L		18	11	Runge, Jody
	Oregon State	6	MW	L		19	9	Spoelstra, Judy
	Portland	13	MW	L		23	7	Sollars, Jim
	Purdue	5	MW	L		20	11	Dunn, Lin
	Radford	16	E	A		17	12	Lichonczak, Lubomyr
	Rhode Island	10	MW	L		21	8	Ziemke, Linda L.
	Saint Francis (PA)	15	MW	A		19	11	Przekwas, Jenny
	Southern Methodist (TX)	10	ME	L		19	11	Rompola, Rhonda
	Southwest Missouri State	12	E	A		25	5	Burnett, Cheryl
	Texas A&M	7	W	A		20	12	Harvey, Candi
	Tulane	14	W	L		21	10	Stockton, Lisa
	Utah	8	MW	L		21	8	Elliott, Elaine
	Youngstown State	15	W	A		20	9	DiGregorio, Edward

1996 Division II

F	School	SD	Reg	BD	Bye	W	L	Coach
1	North Dakota State	1	NC	A	To R32	30	2	Ruley, Amy J.
2	Shippensburg	1	E	A	To R32	28	6	Smith, David R.
3	Abilene Christian	2	SC	A	To R32	31	2	Fox, Suzanne Johnson
4	Delta State	2	S	A	To R32	27	6	Clark, Lloyd
8	Bentley	2	NE	A	To R32	28	3	Stevens, Barbara
	Northern Michigan	1	GL	A	To R32	25	5	Geary, Mike
	Portland State	1	W	L	To R32	25	5	Bruce, Greg
	Wingate	3	SA	A		23	8	Jacumin, Johnny
16	Bellarmine	2	GL	A	To R32	24	4	Just, Charles G.
	Bowie State	4	SA	L		22	10	Davis, Edward
	California: Davis	2	W	A	To R32	25	4	Hoehn, Jorja E.
	Florida Southern	1	S	A	To R32	26	5	Benn, Norm
	North Dakota	3	NC	L		26	6	Roebuck, Gene
	Saint Rose	5	NE	A		26	5	Bailey, Curt
	Salem-Teikyo	3	E	L		27	4	Biesenthal, Tammy
	West Texas A&M	5	SC	L		28	3	Schneider, Bob
32	Albany State (GA)	3	S	A		22	9	Skinner, Robert
	Bridgeport	6	NE	A		25	5	Herer, Harvey
	California State: Chico	3	W	L		23	8	Lazzarini, Mary Ann
	Central Arkansas	4	S	L		21	10	Marvel, Ronnie
	Lake Superior State	4	GL	L		23	8	Ledy, Erica
	Mars Hill	2	SA	L	To R32	24	6	White, Sylvia
	Minnesota: Duluth	4	NC	A		23	5	Stromme, Karen
	Missouri Southern State	1	SC	A	To R32	23	6	Kaifes, Carrie
	Montana State: Billings	4	W	L		19	9	McCarthy, Frank B.
	Nebraska: Kearney	3	SC	A		26	5	Stephens, Amy
	Pittsburgh: Johnstown	5	E	L		20	9	Gault, Jodi
	Shaw (NC)	1	SA	A	To R32	24	5	Sanders, Bobby

F	School	SD	Reg	BD	Bye	W	L	Coach
	Slippery Rock	2	E	L	To R32	21	8	Williges, Laura
	South Dakota State	2	NC	L	To R32	25	3	Neiber, Nancy
	Southern Indiana	3	GL	L		22	7	Dugan, Chancellor
	Stonehill	1	NE	L	To R32	24	6	Sullivan, Paula J.
48	American International	4	NE	L		18	11	Cinella, Peter
	Bryant	3	NE	L		19	10	Burke, Mary
	California State: Dominquez Hills	5	W	L		21	8	Girard, Van
	California: Riverside	6	W	A		17	13	Woelke, Debi
	Fort Valley State	5	S	L		25	4	Bartley, Lonnie
	Gardner-Webb	6	SA	L		22	7	McCurley, Eddie
	Georgia College	5	SA	A		21	9	Carrick, John
	Indiana-Purdue: Fort Wayne	5	GL	L		23	5	Bowden, Pam
	Kutztown	4	E	L		20	8	Malouf, Janet
	Longwood	6	E	L		22	7	Duncan, Shirley G.
	Metropolitan State (CO)	6	NC	A		20	8	Smith, Darryl
	Missouri: Rolla	6	SC	L		21	7	Roberts, Linda J.
	Northern Colorado	5	NC	L		17	10	Schwartz, Gary
	Oakland (MI)	6	GL	L		23	6	Taylor, Bob
	Rollins	6	S	L		23	6	Wilkes, Glenn N., Jr.
	Southwest Baptist	4	SC	L		21	9	Middleton, Jim

1996 DIVISION III

F	School	SD	Reg	BD	Bye	W	L	Coach
1	Wisconsin: Oshkosh		GL	L		31	0	Bennett, Kathi
2	Mount Union		A	L		25	8	Knoblauch, Deanne
3	Saint Thomas (MN)		W	A		28	3	Riverso, Ted
4	New York		E	A		27	4	Quinn, Janice
8	Bethel (MN)		W	L		22	6	Hunter, Debra F.
	Defiance		A	L		28	1	Palombo, Tom
	Rowan		MA	A		29	1	Crabtree, Candace
	Wisconsin: Eau Claire		GL	L		25	4	Stone, Lisa Anderson
16	Marymount (VA)		S	A		27	3	Finney, Bill
	Millikin		C	A		23	5	Kearns, Lori Ann
	Randolph-Macon		S	A		28	2	LaHaye, Carroll
	Salem State		NE	A		25	4	Shea, Timothy P.
	Scranton		MA	A		26	4	Strong, Michael J.
	Southern Maine		NE	L		25	4	Fifield, Gary
	Washington (MO)		C	L		22	6	Fahey, Nancy
	William Smith		E	L		25	2	Begley, Glenn C.
32	Beloit		GL	L		22	4	Botham, Sandy
	California: San Diego		W	L		19	7	Malone, Judy
	Calvin		GL	A		23	4	Afman, Gregg
	Capital		A	A		23	5	Jeffers, Dixie M.
	Claremont McKenna		W			20	8	Burton, Jodie
	Geneseo State		E	A		24	5	Guy, Robert
	Johns Hopkins		MA	A		20	8	Clelan-Blank, Nancy
	Luther		C	L		21	5	Hildebrand, Jane
	Maryville (TN)		S	L		19	6	Cook, Kelli
	Messiah		MA	L		20	8	Miller, Michael
	Middlebury		NE	L		21	5	Fulcher, Jennifer
	Millsaps		S	A		23	4	Hannon, Cindy

F	School	SD	Reg	BD	Bye	W	L	Coach
	Saint John Fisher		E	L		23	5	Kahler, Phillip I.
	Salisbury State		A	L		19	9	Benshelter, Bridget
	Wheaton (IL)		C	L		22	5	Baker, Beth
	Worcester Polytechnic		NE	A		23	6	Champion, Christa
64	Allentown		MA	A		20	6	Richter, Fred
	Alma		GL	L		21	6	Goffnett, Charles
	Alvernia		MA	L		22	6	Calabria, Kevin
	Baldwin-Wallace		A	L		18	9	Harrer, Cheri
	Binghamton State		E	L		21	7	Wilson, David
	Buena Vista		C	A		19	7	Allgood-Berry, Janet
	Cabrini		MA	L		22	4	Welde, Dan V.
	Carthage		C	L		18	8	Fanning, Rich
	City College		E	A		16	12	English, Stephanie
	Concordia: Moorhead		W	L		19	6	Kohler, Robert
	DePauw		GL	L		19	7	Huffman, Kris
	Eastern Connecticut State		NE	A		19	9	Bierly, Denise
	Elizabethtown		MA	L		19	8	Kauffman, Yvonne E.
	Emmanuel (MA)		NE	A		22	4	Yosinoff, Andrew
	Goucher		A	L		17	10	Navarro, Noelle
	Hartwick		E	A		20	7	Thompson, Daphne
	Hendrix		S	L		21	5	Winkelman, "Chuck"
	Illinois Wesleyan		C	L		18	8	Neal, Mandy
	La Verne		W			15	11	Kline, Julie
	MacMurray		C	A		17	10	Mulhern, Donald
	Muskingum		A	L		20	7	Newberry, Donna
	Nazareth (NY)		E	L		22	5	DeCillis, Michael
	Pomona-Pitzer		W			17	9	Krieger, Barbara
	Regis (MA)		NE	A		23	4	Tanner, Donna
	Ripon		GL	A		20	5	Heinz, Julie
	Roanoke		S	L		21	7	Dunagan, Susan
	Saint Benedict		W	L		19	7	Durbin, Michael
	Shenandoah		S	A		13	15	Orsini, Kathy
	Trinity (TX)		S	L		16	10	Geyer, Becky
	Westfield State		NE	L		22	6	Berger, Rick
	Wisconsin: Stout		GL	L		17	9	Thomas, Mark
	Wittenberg		A	A		21	7	Evans, Pamela

1997 DIVISION I

F	School	SD	Reg	BD	Bye	W	L	Coach
1	Tennessee	3	MW	L		29	10	Summitt, Patricia Head
2	Old Dominion	1	ME	A		34	2	Larry, Wendy
3	Notre Dame (IN)	6	E	L		31	7	McGraw, Muffet O'Brien
	Stanford	1	W	A		34	2	VanDerveer, Tara
8	Connecticut	1	MW	A		33	1	Auriemma, Geno
	Florida	3	ME	L		24	9	Ross, Carol
	George Washington	5	E	L		28	6	McKeown, Joe
	Georgia	2	W	L		25	6	Landers, Andy
16	Alabama	2	E	L		25	7	Moody, Rick
	Colorado	2	MW	A		23	9	Barry, Ceal
	Illinois	4	MW	L		24	8	Grentz, Theresa Shank
	Louisiana State	4	ME	L		25	5	Gunter, Sue

F	School	SD	Reg	BD	Bye	W	L	Coach
	Louisiana Tech	2	ME	A		31	4	Barmore, Leon
	North Carolina	1	E	A		29	3	Hatchell, Sylvia Rhyne
	Vanderbilt	6	W	L		20	11	Foster, Jim
	Virginia	4	W	L		23	8	Ryan, Deborah H.
32	Arizona	7	W	L		23	8	Bonvicini, Joan
	Auburn	7	ME	A		22	10	Ciampi, Joe
	Duke	5	MW	L		19	11	Goestenkors, Gail
	Iowa	9	MW	A		18	12	Lee, Angie
	Kansas	3	W	L		25	6	Washington, Marian
	Marquette	12	ME	L		21	10	Mitchell, Terri
	Michigan State	8	E	L		22	8	Langeland, Karen
	Oregon	6	MW	L		22	7	Runge, Jody
	Purdue	8	ME	L		17	11	Fortner, Nell
	Saint Joseph's (PA)	7	E	A		26	5	Gaitley, Stephanie Vanderslice
	Southern California	6	ME	L		20	9	Williams, Fred
	Stephen F Austin State	7	MW	L		28	5	Chadwick, Royce
	Texas	3	E	L		22	8	Conradt, Jody
	Texas Tech	8	W	L		20	9	Sharp, Marsha
	Tulane	4	E	A		27	5	Stockton, Lisa
	Utah	5	W	L		25	6	Elliott, Elaine
64	California: Santa Barbara	13	E	A		24	6	French, Mark
	Clemson	5	ME	L		19	11	Davis, Jim
	De Paul	12	MW	L		20	9	Bruno, Doug
	Detroit Mercy	14	W	A		23	7	Lowry, Nikita
	Drake (IA)	13	MW	A		23	8	Bluder, Lisa
	Eastern Kentucky	15	W	A		24	6	Inman, Larry Joe
	Florida International	14	ME	A		21	9	Russo, Cindy
	Grambling State	14	MW	A		24	6	Bibbs, Patricia Cage
	Harvard	16	E	A		20	7	Smith, Kathleen Delaney
	Howard (DC)	16	W	A		24	6	Tyler, Sanya
	Iowa State	12	W	L		17	12	Fennelly, Bill
	Kansas State	10	E	L		19	12	Patterson, Debbie
	Lehigh	16	MW	A		15	15	Troyan, Susan
	Liberty	16	ME	A		22	8	Reeves, Rick
	Louisville	10	ME	L		20	9	Childers, "Bud"
	Maine	13	ME	A		22	8	Palombo-McCall, Joanne
	Marshall	15	MW	A		18	12	Evans-Moore, Sarah
	Maryland	9	ME	L		18	10	Weller, Christine J.
	Memphis	11	E	L		22	7	Lee-McNelis, Joye
	Montana	9	W	A		25	4	Selvig, Robin
	North Carolina State	8	MW	L		19	12	Yow, Sandra Kay
	Northwestern (IL)	12	E	L		17	11	Perrelli, Donald
	Portland	9	E	L		27	3	Sollars, Jim
	Saint Francis (PA)	15	E	A		21	9	Przekwas, Jenny
	Saint Peter's	15	ME	A		25	4	Granelli, Mike
	San Diego State	11	MW	A		23	7	Burns, Beth
	San Francisco	11	ME	A		25	6	Nepfel, Bill
	Southwest Texas State	14	E	A		17	12	Sharp, Linda

F	School	SD	Reg	BD	Bye	W	L	Coach
	Toledo	10	MW	A		27	4	Ehlen, Mark
	Troy State: Troy	13	W	A		23	7	Hester, Jerry
	Washington	11	W	L		17	11	Daugherty, June
	Western Kentucky	10	W	L		22	9	Sanderford, Paul

1997 Division II

F	School	SD	Reg	BD	Bye	W	L	Coach
1	North Dakota	1	NC	L	To R32	28	4	Roebuck, Gene
2	Southern Indiana	1	GL	A	To R32	30	2	Dugan, Chancellor
3	California: Davis	2	W	A	To R32	29	3	Simpson, Sandy
4	Bentley	1	NE	L	To R32	27	7	Stevens, Barbara
8	Delta State	2	S	L	To R32	23	7	Clark, Lloyd
	Edinboro	3	E	A		24	9	Swank, Stan
	Kennesaw State	1	SA	A	To R32	30	2	Tilley, Colby
	West Texas A&M	2	SC	A	To R32	29	2	Schneider, Bob
16	Bowie State	2	SA	A	To R32	29	2	Davis, Edward
	Fort Valley State	5	S	L		25	6	Bartley, Lonnie
	High Point	5	E	A		26	6	Ellenberg, Dr. Joe
	Missouri Western State	1	SC	A	To R32	24	7	Slifer, David
	North Dakota State	2	NC	A	To R32	28	1	Ruley, Amy J.
	Northern Michigan	2	GL	A	To R32	27	3	Geary, Mike
	Seattle Pacific	1	W	L	To R32	26	3	Presnell, Gordy
	Stonehill	6	NE	A		26	6	Hart, Kelly
32	Abilene Christian	4	SC	L		24	6	Fox, Suzanne Johnson
	California Polytechnic: Pomona	3	W	A		22	8	Thomas, Paul
	Emporia State	3	SC	L		20	10	Stein, Cindy
	Fayetteville State	4	SA	L		26	5	Tucker, Eric
	Florida Tech	1	S	A	To R32	27	3	Reynolds, John, Jr.
	Georgia College	6	SA	L		23	8	Carrick, John
	Kentucky State	6	S	A		25	6	Davis, Antonio
	Massachusetts: Lowell	4	NE	A		25	6	O'Neil, Kathleen
	Michigan Tech	4	GL	L		18	11	Borseth, Kevin
	Nebraska: Kearney	4	NC	A		28	3	Stephens, Amy
	Northern State (SD)	3	NC	A		24	5	Fredrickson, Curt
	Oakland (MI)	6	GL	L		25	5	Taylor, Bob
	Saint Rose	2	NE	A	To R32	29	1	Bailey, Curt
	Shippensburg	1	E	A	To R32	25	5	Smith, David R.
	West Chester	2	E	L	To R32	22	7	Kane, Deirdre
	Western New Mexico	4	W	L		19	6	Reid, Jason
48	Alabama A&M	3	S	L		20	10	Parham, Press
	Augustana (SD)	6	NC	L		23	5	Krauth, David
	Bellarmine	5	GL	L		20	8	Just, Charles G.
	Central Missouri State	6	SC	L		21	9	Ballard, Scott
	Francis Marion	5	SA	L		21	8	Moore, Frank "Wes"
	Grand Canyon	5	W	L		15	11	Hanks, Julie
	Longwood	4	E	L		25	5	Duncan, Shirley G.
	Montana State: Billings	6	W	L		18	10	McCarthy, Frank B.

F	School	SD	Reg	BD	Bye	W	L	Coach
	Northern Colorado	5	NC	L		19	8	Schwartz, Gary
	Philadelphia Textiles	3	NE	L		21	8	Shirley, Thomas, Jr.
	Pittsburg State	5	SC	L		19	10	High, Steve
	Saginaw Valley State	3	GL	L		19	11	Merchant, Suzy
	Saint Anselm	5	NE	L		20	9	Vermette, Bill
	Valdosta State	4	S	L		19	9	Williamson, Jane
	West Liberty State	6	E	A		23	6	Ullom, Larry
	Wingate	3	SA	A		20	9	Jacumin, Johnny

1997 DIVISION III

F	School	SD	Reg	BD	Bye	W	L	Coach
1	New York		E	A		29	1	Quinn, Janice
2	Wisconsin: Eau Claire		C	L		27	4	Stone, Lisa Anderson
3	Capital		GL	A		29	4	Jeffers, Dixie M.
4	Scranton		MA	A		28	5	Strong, Michael J.
8	Defiance		GL	L		28	1	Palombo, Tom
	Johns Hopkins		MA	L		25	5	Clelan-Blank, Nancy
	Millikin		C	A		25	3	Kearns, Lori Ann
	William Smith		A	L		27	1	Begley, Glenn C.
16	Buena Vista		W	A		23	5	Allgood-Berry, Janet
	Emory		S	L		20	7	Sims, Myra
	Marymount (VA)		A	A		28	2	Finney, Bill
	Saint Thomas (MN)		W	A		26	2	Riverso, Ted
	Southern Maine		NE	A		25	4	Fifield, Gary
	Thomas More (KY)		S	L		20	7	Brumfield, Sharri
	Western Connecticut State		NE	L		25	5	Rajcula, Jody
	William Patterson		E	L		24	5	Shaughnessy, Erin
32	Alma		GL	A		23	6	Goffnett, Charles
	Alvernia		MA	L		22	6	Calabria, Kevin
	Bridgewater (VA)		S	L		22	6	Wili, Jean
	California: San Diego		W	L		20	6	Malone, Judy
	Calvin		GL	L		23	4	Afman, Gregg
	Elizabethtown		MA	L		21	8	Kauffman, Yvonne E.
	Emmanuel (MA)		NE	A		22	7	Yosinoff, Andrew
	Hendrix		S	A		23	4	Winkelman, "Chuck"
	Ithaca		E	A		20	8	Pritchard, Christine
	New Jersey		A	L		18	9	Henderson, Dawn
	Rowan		A	A		25	3	Crabtree, Candace
	Saint Benedict		W	L		21	6	Durbin, Michael
	Saint John Fisher		E	L		23	6	Kahler, Phillip I.
	Williams		NE	L		20	5	Manning, Patricia
	Wisconsin: Oshkosh		C	L		22	3	Ruder, Pam
	Wisconsin: Stout		C	A		19	8	Thomas, Mark
64	Allentown		MA	A		21	7	Richter, Fred
	Baldwin-Wallace		GL	L		23	5	Harrer, Cheri
	Bates		NE	L		20	5	Murphy, James
	Beloit		C	A		20	5	Straub, Kristi
	Bethany (WV)		GL	A		22	4	Campanell-Komara, Lisa
	Bethel (MN)		W	L		16	9	Hunter, Debra F.
	Binghamton State		E	A		23	4	Wilson, David
	Blackburn		C	A		13	13	Garrett, Matt

F	School	SD	Reg	BD	Bye	W	L	Coach
	Cabrini		MA	L		21	5	Welde, Dan V.
	Chapman		W	L		19	7	Hegarty, Mary
	Christopher Newport		S	L		20	7	Parson, Cathy
	Clark (MA)		NE	A		24	4	Glispin, Patricia
	Colby-Sawyer		A	A		23	5	Martin, George
	Frostburg State		A	L		23	3	Crawley, James M.
	Gallaudet		E	L		19	9	Baldridge, Kathryn "Kitty"
	Geneseo State		A	L		21	7	French, Joe
	Greensboro		S	A		19	9	Johnson, Steve
	Hanover		GL	A		17	10	Snyder, Christa
	Hartwick		E	L		20	8	Thompson, Daphne
	Kenyon		GL	A		26	2	Halfant, Suzanne
	Luther		W	L		17	8	Hildebrand, Jane
	Lycoming		MA	L		19	7	Ditzler, Christen
	Muhlenberg		MA	A		18	8	Smith, Tammy
	Nazareth (NY)		E	L		17	9	DeCillis, Michael
	Pomona-Pitzer		W	A		19	7	Connell, Kathleen "Kathy"
	Roanoke		S	A		25	3	Dunagan, Susan
	Salem State		NE	A		23	4	Shea, Timothy P.
	Savannah A&D		S	L		20	6	Ruffo, Kristen
	Staten Island		A	A		22	6	Mosley, Gerry
	Trinity (CT)		NE	L		18	6	Pine, Maureen
	Washington (MO)		C	L		19	7	Fahey, Nancy
	Wheaton (IL)		C	L		21	4	Baker, Beth

1998 DIVISION I

F	School	SD	Reg	BD	Bye	W	L	Coach
1	Tennessee	1	ME	A		39	0	Summitt, Patricia Head
2	Louisiana Tech	3	MW	A		31	4	Barmore, Leon
3	Arkansas	9	W	L		22	11	Blair, Gary
	North Carolina State	4	E	L		24	7	Yow, Sandra Kay
8	Connecticut	2	E	A		34	3	Auriemma, Geno
	Duke	2	W	L		24	8	Goestenkors, Gail
	North Carolina	2	ME	A		27	7	Hatchell, Sylvia Rhyne
	Purdue	4	MW	A		23	10	Peck, Carolyn
16	Alabama	2	MW	L		24	10	Moody, Rick
	Arizona	3	E	L		23	7	Bonvicini, Joan
	Florida	3	W	L		23	9	Ross, Carol
	Illinois	3	ME	L		20	10	Grentz, Theresa Shank
	Kansas	5	W	L		23	9	Washington, Marian
	Notre Dame (IN)	9	MW	L		22	10	McGraw, Muffet O'Brien
	Old Dominion	1	E	A		29	3	Larry, Wendy
	Rutgers	5	ME	L		22	10	Stringer, C. Vivian
32	California: Los Angeles	7	MW	L		20	9	Oliver, Kathy
	California: Santa Barbara	11	ME	A		27	6	French, Mark
	Clemson	6	MW	L		25	8	Davis, Jim
	Colorado State	12	MW	L		24	6	Collen, Tim
	Florida International	7	ME	A		29	2	Russo, Cindy
	George Washington	10	E	L		20	10	McKeown, Joe
	Harvard	16	W	A		23	5	Smith, Kathleen Delaney
	Iowa	4	W	L		18	11	Lee, Angie

F	School	SD	Reg	BD	Bye	W	L	Coach
	Iowa State	4	ME	L		25	8	Fennelly, Bill
	Louisville	10	W	L		20	12	Clapp, Martin
	Nebraska	9	E	L		23	10	Sanderford, Paul
	Texas Tech	1	MW	A		26	5	Sharp, Marsha
	Virginia	6	E	L		19	10	Ryan, Deborah H.
	Virginia Polytechnic	11	W	A		22	10	Henrickson, Bonnie
	Western Kentucky	8	ME	L		26	9	Small, Steve
	Youngstown State	12	E	A		28	3	DiGregorio, Edward
64	Drake (IA)	5	MW	A		25	5	Bluder, Lisa
	Fairfield	15	E	A		20	10	Nolan, Diane
	Georgia	7	E	L		17	11	Landers, Andy
	Grambling State	16	MW	A		23	7	Ponton, David
	Hawaii	8	W	L		24	4	Goo, Vince
	Holy Cross (MA)	14	MW	A		21	9	Gibbons, Bill, Jr.
	Howard (DC)	15	ME	A		23	7	Tyler, Sanya
	Kent State	13	ME	A		23	7	Lindsay, Bob
	Liberty	16	ME	A		28	1	Reeves, Rick
	Maine	13	E	A		21	9	Palombo-McCall, Joanne
	Marquette	10	ME	L		22	7	Mitchell, Terri
	Massachusetts	13	W	L		19	11	O'brien, Joanie
	Memphis	5	E	A		22	8	Lee-McNelis, Joye
	Miami (FL)	11	MW	L		19	10	Labati, Ferne
	Michigan	10	MW	L		19	10	Guevara, Sue
	Middle Tennessee State	15	W	A		18	12	Smith, Stephany
	Montana	14	W	A		24	6	Selvig, Robin
	New Mexico	8	E	A		26	7	Flanagan, Don
	North Carolina: Greensboro	15	MW	A		21	9	Agee, Lynne
	Oregon	12	ME	L		17	10	Runge, Jody
	Saint Francis (PA)	16	E	A		22	8	Przekwas, Jenny
	Santa Clara	14	E	A		23	8	Horstmeyer, Caren
	Southern Methodist (TX)	11	E	L		21	8	Rompola, Rhonda
	Southwest Missouri State	8	MW	L		24	6	Burnett, Cheryl
	Stanford	1	W	A		21	6	VanDerveer, Tara
	Stephen F Austin State	9	ME	A		25	4	Chadwick, Royce
	Tulane	12	W	L		21	7	Stockton, Lisa
	Utah	7	W	L		21	6	Elliott, Elaine
	Vanderbilt	6	ME	L		20	9	Foster, Jim
	Washington	13	MW	L		18	10	Daugherty, June
	Wisconsin	6	W	L		21	10	Albright-Dieterle, Jane
	Wisconsin: Green Bay	14	ME	L		21	9	Hammerle, Carol

1998 DIVISION II

F	School	SD	Reg	BD	Bye	W	L	Coach
1	North Dakota	1	NC	A	To R32	31	1	Roebuck, Gene
2	Emporia State	1	SC	A	To R32	33	1	Stein, Cindy
3	Francis Marion	2	SA	A	To R32	30	3	Moore, Frank "Wes"
	Northern Michigan	2	GL	A	To R32	28	4	Geary, Mike
8	Arkansas Tech	2	S	A	To R32	26	5	Foley, Joe M.
	Bentley	2	NE	A	To R32	30	2	Stevens, Barbara
	Seattle Pacific	1	W	L	To R32	27	3	Presnell, Gordy
	Shippensburg	1	E	A	To R32	28	4	Smith, David R.

F	School	SD	Reg	BD	Bye	W	L	Coach
16	Abilene Christian	3	SC	A		26	5	Williams, Wayne
	Arkansas: Monticello	5	S	L		23	8	Early, Alvy
	Bloomsburg	6	E	L		22	8	Fedorjaka, Kathy
	Bowie State	1	SA	A	To R32	28	2	Davis, Edward
	California: Davis	3	W	A		23	7	Hoehn, Jorja E.
	Michigan Tech	4	GL	L		21	10	Borseth, Kevin
	Nebraska: Kearney	2	NC	L	To R32	26	4	Stephens, Amy
	Saint Rose	1	NE	A	To R32	33	1	Bailey, Curt
32	Alderson-Broaddus	2	E	L	To R32	26	4	Mair, Carolyn
	California State: San Bernardino	4	W	L		23	6	Becker, Kevin
	Central Missouri State	5	SC	L		19	10	Ballard, Scott
	Columbus State (GA)	3	SA	A		25	6	Sparks, Jay
	Edinboro	4	E	L		23	8	Swank, Stan
	Florida Southern	1	S	A	To R32	24	5	Foli, Diane
	Franklin Pierce	3	NE	L		24	6	Chadbourne, David
	Grand Valley State	3	GL	L		23	5	Charney, Claudette
	Missouri Western State	2	SC	L	To R32	23	9	Slifer, David
	Montana State: Billings	2	W	L	To R32	21	7	McCarthy, Frank B.
	Northern Colorado	5	NC	L		21	8	Bruce, Greg
	Northern State (SD)	6	NC	A		23	6	Fredrickson, Curt
	Philadelphia Textiles	5	NE	L		25	8	Shirley, Thomas, Jr.
	Presbyterian	4	SA	A		23	8	Couture, Beth
	Southern Indiana	1	GL	A	To R32	26	2	Dugan, Chancellor
	West Florida	3	S	L		25	5	Henry, Megan
48	Albany State (GA)	6	S	A		20	10	Skinner, Robert
	Belmont Abbey	3	E	A		26	4	Kebbe, Elaine
	California Polytechnic: Pomona	6	W	A		18	11	Thomas, Paul
	Carson-Newman	6	SA	L		22	7	Carter, Eddie
	Charleston (WV)	5	E	A		21	9	Bennett-Travinski, Linda
	Delta State	4	S	L		23	9	Clark, Lloyd
	Lewis (IL)	6	GL	L		23	5	Michalak, Brian
	Massachusetts: Lowell	6	NE	A		19	10	O'Neil, Kathleen
	Metropolitan State (CO)	4	NC	A		25	5	Smith, Darryl
	North Dakota State	3	NC	L		22	6	Ruley, Amy J.
	Pittsburg State	4	SC	L		18	11	High, Steve
	Sonoma State	5	W	L		20	8	Zachensky-Walthall, Susan
	Southern Illinois: Edwardsville	5	GL	L		22	8	Hedberg, Wendy
	Southwest Baptist	6	SC	L		18	11	Middleton, Jim
	Stonehill	4	NE	L		24	7	Hart, Kelly
	Virginia Union	5	SA	L		24	4	Golatt, Moses

1998 Division III

F	School	SD	Reg	BD	Bye	W	L	Coach
1	Washington (MO)	2	C	A	To R32	28	2	Fahey, Nancy
2	Southern Maine	1	NE	A	To R32	29	3	Fifield, Gary
3	Mount Union	1	GL	A	To R32	29	3	Knoblauch, Deanne
4	Rowan	1	A	A	To R32	27	4	Crabtree, Candace

F	School	SD	Reg	BD	Bye	W	L	Coach
8	Johns Hopkins	1	MA	L	To R32	24	5	Clelan-Blank, Nancy
	Saint Thomas (MN)	1	W	A	To R32	26	2	Riverso, Ted
	William Patterson	2	A	L	To R32	25	4	Shaughnessy, Erin
	Wisconsin: Oshkosh	1	C	A	To R32	26	2	Ruder, Pam
16	Austin	3	S	L		21	7	Potera, Robin
	Bates	2	NE	L	To R32	22	4	Murphy, James
	Bridgewater (VA)	1	S	L	To R32	24	5	Willi, Jean
	DePauw	2	GL	L	To R32	23	5	Huffman, Kris
	Elmira	5	E	L		22	7	Scheible, James
	New York	2	E	L	To R32	22	5	Quinn, Janice
	Saint Benedict	2	W	L	To R32	25	2	Durbin, Michael
	Scranton	2	MA	L	To R32	21	6	Strong, Michael J.
32	Alvernia	3	MA	L		22	6	Calabria, Kevin
	Baldwin-Wallace	3	GL	L		23	6	Harrer, Cheri
	Binghamton State	1	E	L	To R32	22	3	Wilson, David
	California: San Diego	3	W	L		23	4	Malone, Judy
	Calvin	4	GL	L		23	5	Afman, Gregg
	Central (IA)	5	W	A		18	8	Boeyink, Gary
	Christopher Newport	4	S	A		24	4	Parson, Cathy
	Mary Washington	6	A	L		21	8	Gallahan, Connie
	Millikin	3	C	A		25	1	Kearns, Lori Ann
	Muhlenberg	5	MA	A		18	10	Smith, Tammy
	New Jersey	3	A	L		19	8	Henderson, Dawn
	Randolph-Macon	2	S	L	To R32	21	6	LaHaye, Carroll
	Salem State	3	NE	A		23	5	Shea, Timothy P.
	Western Connecticut State	4	NE	L		22	7	Rajcula, Jody
	William Smith	3	E	A		23	3	Begley, Glenn C.
	Wisconsin: Eau Claire	4	C	L		22	5	Stone, Lisa Anderson
48	Allentown	4	MA	A		20	8	Richter, Fred
	Beloit	5	C	A		23	2	Straub, Kristi
	California Lutheran	6	W	A		17	8	La Kose, Tim
	Clark (MA)	6	NE	A		20	8	Glispin, Patricia
	Colby-Sawyer	4	A	A		22	5	Martin, George
	Hope	6	GL	A		16	11	Morehouse, Brian
	Luther	4	W	L		20	6	Hildebrand, Jane
	Middlebury	5	NE	L		20	5	Fulcher, Jennifer
	Nazareth (NY)	6	E	A		15	11	DeCillis, Michael
	Oneonta State	4	E	A		25	3	Garner, Steven
	Roanoke	5	S	A		18	10	Dunagan, Susan
	Saint Mary's (MD)	5	A	A		20	8	Hart, Shann
	Southwestern (TX)	6	S	A		15	11	Seagraves, Rhonda
	Washington & Jefferson	6	MA	A		16	8	Staton, Vicki L.
	Wheaton (IL)	6	C	L		19	7	Baker, Beth
	Wittenberg	5	GL	A		22	6	Evans-Smith, Pamela

School Participation History

Year	M/W	Div	F	SD	Reg	BD	Bye	#T	W	L	Coach
ABILENE CHRISTIAN											
1966	M	II	8		SW		To R32	36	21	7	Nutt, Dee
1960		II	16		SW	L		32	16	12	Nutt, Dee
1964		II	16		SW	L		32	18	9	Nutt, Dee
1965		II	16		SW			32	17	9	Nutt, Dee
1959		II	24		SW	L		32	20	7	Nutt, Dee
1986		II	24		SC	A		32	23	7	Martin, Mike
1962		II	32		SW	L		32	16	12	Nutt, Dee
1987		II	32		SC	L		32	18	8	Martin, Mike
1996	W	II	3	2	SC	A	To R32	48	31	2	Fox, Suzanne Johnson
1985		II	16		SC	L		24	21	10	McCoy, Burl
1998		II	16	3	SC	A		48	26	5	Williams, Wayne
1983		II	24		SC	L		24	21	8	McCoy, Burl
1988		II	32		SC	L		32	27	6	McCoy, Burl
1989		II	32		SC	L		32	23	8	McCoy, Burl
1995		II	32	5	SC	L		48	23	7	Fox, Suzanne Johnson
1997		II	32	4	SC	L		48	24	6	Fox, Suzanne Johnson
ADELPHI											
1964	M	II	8		NE			32	22	6	Faherty, George E.
1958		II	16		NE			32	18	8	Faherty, George E.
1959		II	24		E			32	22	6	Faherty, George E.
1978		II	32		E	L		32	18	8	Kessler, Marvin
1995		II	48	5	NE	L		48	19	12	O'Connor, Jim
1996		II	48	3	NE	A		48	23	7	Clifford, Steve
1997		II	48	5	NE	L		48	21	9	Clifford, Steve
1998		II	48	5	NE	L		48	22	8	Clifford, Steve
1987	W	II	24		E	A		24	14	14	McHugh, Dorothy
ADRIAN											
1991	W	III	16		GL	L		32	22	4	Munk, Dana Marie
1992		III	32		GL	L		32	20	5	Munk, Dana Marie
AIR FORCE											
1960	M	I	25		MW	L		25	12	10	Spear, Robert
1962		I	25		MW	L		25	16	7	Spear, Robert
1985	W	II	24		SC	A		24	20	8	Gasser, Martha "Marti"
1990		II	32		W	A		32	20	8	Gasser, Martha "Marti"
AKRON											
1964	M	II	2		ME			32	24	7	Laterza, Anthony
1972		II	2		ME	L	To R32	36	26	5	Webb, Dr. Wyatt
1966		II	3		ME		To R32	36	24	4	Laterza, Anthony
1965		II	8		ME			32	21	7	Laterza, Anthony
1973		II	8		ME	L	To R32	42	22	5	Webb, Dr. Wyatt
1975		II	8		GL	L		32	20	9	Webb, Dr. Wyatt
1958		II	16		ME			32	20	6	Beichly, Russell J.
1967		II	16		ME	L	To R32	36	20	5	Laterza, Anthony
1971		II	24		ME	L		32	20	6	Webb, Dr. Wyatt
1986		I	64	15	MW	A		64	22	8	Huggins, Robert

Year	M/W	Div	F	SD	Reg	BD	Bye	#T	W	L	Coach
ALABAMA											
1976	M	I	16		ME	A		32	23	5	Newton, Charles M. "CM"
1982		I	16	4	E	A	To R32	48	24	7	Sanderson, Winfrey "Wimp"
1985		I	16	7	W	L		64	23	10	Sanderson, Winfrey "Wimp"
1986		I	16	5	SE	L		64	24	9	Sanderson, Winfrey "Wimp"
1987		I	16	2	SE	A		64	28	5	Sanderson, Winfrey "Wimp"
1990		I	16	7	W	A		64	26	9	Sanderson, Winfrey "Wimp"
1991		I	16	4	SE	A		64	23	10	Sanderson, Winfrey "Wimp"
1975		I	32		W	L		32	22	5	Newton, Charles M. "CM"
1992		I	32	5	SE	L		64	26	9	Sanderson, Winfrey "Wimp"
1994		I	32	9	SE	L		64	20	10	Hobbs, David
1995		I	32	5	E	L		64	23	10	Hobbs, David
1983		I	48	6	MW	L		52	20	12	Sanderson, Winfrey "Wimp"
1984		I	48	9	MW	L		53	18	12	Sanderson, Winfrey "Wimp"
1989		I	64	6	SE	A		64	23	8	Sanderson, Winfrey "Wimp"
1994	W	I	3	6	MW	L		64	26	7	Moody, Rick
1984		I	16		ME	L		32	23	9	Weeks, Kenneth
1995		I	16	4	E	L		64	22	9	Moody, Rick
1996		I	16	4	W	L		64	24	8	Moody, Rick
1997		I	16	2	E	L		64	25	7	Moody, Rick
1998		I	16	2	MW	L		64	24	10	Moody, Rick
1992		I	32	5	ME	L		48	23	7	Moody, Rick
1993		I	32		ME	L		48	22	9	Moody, Rick
1988		I	40		MW	L		40	18	10	Myers, Lois
ALABAMA A&M											
1988	M	II	8		GL	A		32	29	3	Pettaway, L. Vann
1994		II	8		S	L		32	27	5	Pettaway, L. Vann
1995		II	8	1	S	A	To R32	48	29	3	Pettaway, L. Vann
1996		II	8	1	S	A	To R32	48	28	3	Pettaway, L. Vann
1997		II	16	1	S	L	To R32	48	24	6	Pettaway, L. Vann
1993		II	23		SA	A		32	28	3	Pettaway, L. Vann
1989		II	24		SA	A		32	26	6	Pettaway, L. Vann
1985		II	32		SC	L		32	21	10	Jobe, Ben
1986		II	32		S	A		32	23	9	Jobe, Ben
1987		II	32		S	A		32	23	7	Pettaway, L. Vann
1984	W	II	24		SC	A		24	19	9	Parham, Press
1991		II	32		S	A		32	24	7	Parham, Press
1997		II	48	3	S	L		48	20	10	Parham, Press
ALABAMA STATE											
1975	M	II	32		S	L		32	16	13	Laisure, W. Floyd
1972		II	36		S			36	22	3	Boozer, Bernard
ALABAMA: BIRMINGHAM											
1982	M	I	8	4	ME	A	To R16	48	25	6	Bartow, B. Gene
1981		I	16	7	ME	L		48	23	9	Bartow, B. Gene
1985		I	32	7	MW	L		64	25	9	Bartow, B. Gene
1986		I	32	6	W	L		64	25	11	Bartow, B. Gene

Year	M/W	Div	F	SD	Reg	BD	Bye	#T	W	L	Coach
1983		I	48	10	ME	A		52	19	14	Bartow, B. Gene
1984		I	48	9	ME	A		53	23	11	Bartow, B. Gene
1987		I	64	11	SE	A		64	21	11	Bartow, B. Gene
1990		I	64	10	E	L		64	22	9	Bartow, B. Gene
1994		I	64	7	E	L		64	22	8	Bartow, B. Gene
1994	W	I	64	10	ME	A		64	23	6	Milling, Jeannie

ALASKA: ANCHORAGE

Year	M/W	Div	F	SD	Reg	BD	Bye	#T	W	L	Coach
1988	M	II	2		W	A		32	24	10	Abegglen, Ron
1986		II	16		W	L		32	22	10	Larrabee, Harry
1987		II	16		W	L		32	23	7	Abegglen, Ron
1991		II	16		W	L		32	19	11	Abegglen, Ron
1993		II	16		W	A		32	21	10	Larrabee, Harry
1982		II	24		W	L		32	21	1	Larrabee, Harry
1994		II	24		W	A		32	21	10	Larrabee, Harry
1990		II	32		NC	L		32	22	8	Abegglen, Ron
1997		II	32	2	W	A	To R32	48	20	8	Bruns, Charlie
1996		II	48	4	W	L		48	19	9	Bruns, Charlie
1988	W	II	16		W	A		32	24	5	Burns, Linda
1986		II	24		SC	A		24	17	11	Burns, Linda
1989		II	32		NC	A		32	20	8	Burns, Linda
1992		II	32		W	L		32	18	6	Raugust, Milt

ALASKA: FAIRBANKS

Year	M/W	Div	F	SD	Reg	BD	Bye	#T	W	L	Coach
1989	M	II	32		NC	A		32	16	13	Roderick, George T.

ALBANY STATE (GA)

Year	M/W	Div	F	SD	Reg	BD	Bye	#T	W	L	Coach
1978	M	II	24		SA	L		32	20	9	Jones, Oliver
1979		II	24		E	L		32	20	9	Jones, Oliver
1992		II	24		SA	A		32	20	9	Jones, Oliver
1984		II	32		S	A		32	10	19	Jones, Oliver
1985		II	32		S	A		32	15	15	Jones, Oliver
1998		II	32	3	S	L		48	19	11	Jones, Oliver
1973		II	42		S			42	23	6	Jones, Oliver
1997		II	48	5	S	A		48	20	10	Jones, Oliver
1987	W	II	24		S	A		24	28	1	Davis, John I.
1989		II	32		S	A		32	15	16	Davis, John I.
1990		II	32		S	A		32	22	7	Davis, John I.
1996		II	32	3	S	A		48	22	9	Skinner, Robert
1998		II	48	6	S	A		48	20	10	Skinner, Robert

ALBANY STATE (NY)

Year	M/W	Div	F	SD	Reg	BD	Bye	#T	W	L	Coach
1994	M	III	8		E	L	To R32	40	24	3	Sauers, Dr. Richard J.
1977		III	16		E	A		30	19	7	Sauers, Dr. Richard J.
1980		III	16		E	L		32	21	6	Sauers, Dr. Richard J.
1981		III	16		E	A		32	23	5	Sauers, Dr. Richard J.
1990		III	16		E	L	To R32	40	20	9	Sauers, Dr. Richard J.
1969		II	24		E	L		32	18	6	Sauers, Dr. Richard J.
1979		III	24		S	L		32	20	7	Sauers, Dr. Richard J.
1985		III	24		NE	L		32	22	6	Sauers, Dr. Richard J.

Year	M/W	Div	F	SD	Reg	BD	Bye	#T	W	L	Coach
1975		III	30		E	L		30	15	10	Sauers, Dr. Richard J.
1992		III	32		E	L		40	21	7	Sauers, Dr. Richard J.
1995		III	32	5	E	L		64	18	8	Sauers, Dr. Richard J.
1986	W	III	8		E	L		32	26	4	Warner, Mari
1992		III	16		E	L		32	22	5	Warner, Mari

ALBION

Year	M/W	Div	F	SD	Reg	BD	Bye	#T	W	L	Coach
1978	M	III	3		GL	A		30	21	6	Turner, Michael
1979		III	24		GL	A		32	20	4	Turner, Michael
1998		III	48	5	GL	A		48	20	8	Turner, Michael

ALBRIGHT

Year	M/W	Div	F	SD	Reg	BD	Bye	#T	W	L	Coach
1980	M	III	8		MA	L		32	27	3	Renken, Dr. Wilbur G.
1961		II	16		E			32	19	9	Renken, Dr. Wilbur G.
1974		II	16		ME	A	To R32	44	19	9	Renken, Dr. Wilbur G.
1977		III	16		MA	A		30	20	9	Renken, Dr. Wilbur G.
1966		II	22		E		To R32	36	18	11	Renken, Dr. Wilbur G.
1962		II	24		E	L		32	18	10	Renken, Dr. Wilbur G.
1965		II	32		E			32	20	8	Renken, Dr. Wilbur G.
1979		III	32		MA	L		32	18	10	Renken, Dr. Wilbur G.

ALCORN STATE

Year	M/W	Div	F	SD	Reg	BD	Bye	#T	W	L	Coach
1969	M	II	16		S	L		32	26	1	Hopkins, Robert M.
1980		I	32	8	MW	A		48	28	2	Whitney, David L., Sr. "Davey"
1982		I	48	11	MW	A		48	22	8	Whitney, David L., Sr. "Davey"
1983		I	48	12	MW	A		52	22	10	Whitney, David L., Sr. "Davey"
1984		I	48	12	MW	A		53	21	10	Whitney, David L., Sr. "Davey"

ALDERSON-BROADDUS

Year	M/W	Div	F	SD	Reg	BD	Bye	#T	W	L	Coach
1998	W	II	32	2	E	L	To R32	48	26	4	Mair, Carolyn

ALFRED

Year	M/W	Div	F	SD	Reg	BD	Bye	#T	W	L	Coach
1986	M	III	16		E	A		32	23	3	Frederes, Ronald
1985		III	32		E	A		32	17	11	Frederes, Ronald
1989		III	40		E	L		40	18	8	Catalino, Roman
1997		III	64	7	GL	A		64	14	12	Murphy, Jay

ALLEGHENY

Year	M/W	Div	F	SD	Reg	BD	Bye	#T	W	L	Coach
1980	M	III	24		SA	A		32	20	4	Reynders, John C.
1988		III	24		MA	L		32	24	6	Reynders, John C.
1975		III	30		GL	L		30	15	7	Sundstrom, Norman A.
1979		III	32		GL	A		32	17	8	Sundstrom, Norman A.
1981		III	32		SA	A		32	16	8	Reynders, John C.
1987		III	32		MA	L		32	21	8	Reynders, John C.
1989		III	32		GL	A		40	22	8	Reynders, John C.
1998		III	32	3	GL	A		48	22	7	Ness, Phillip E.
1985	W	III	16		E	L		32	24	3	Gould, Kay
1986		III	24		A	A		32	26	2	Gould, Kay
1987		III	24		A	L		32	25	4	Gould, Kay
1984		III	32		MA	L		32	22	4	Gould, Kay

ALLENTOWN

Year	M/W	Div	F	SD	Reg	BD	Bye	#T	W	L	Coach
1996	M	III	64	7	MA	L		64	17	10	Coval, Scott

Year	M/W	Div	F	SD	Reg	BD	Bye	#T	W	L	Coach
1989	W	III	16		MA	L		32	24	6	Shirley, Thomas, Jr.
1990		III	16		MA	L		32	27	2	Shirley, Thomas, Jr.
1998		III	48	4	MA	A		48	20	8	Richter, Fred
1996		III	64		MA	A		64	20	6	Richter, Fred
1997		III	64		MA	A		64	21	7	Richter, Fred

ALMA

Year	M/W	Div	F	SD	Reg	BD	Bye	#T	W	L	Coach
1992	W	III	1		GL	A		32	24	3	Goffnett, Charles
1987		III	16		GL	L		32	21	5	Klenk, William
1985		III	24		GL	L		32	18	5	Charney, Claudette
1986		III	24		GL	L		32	23	3	Klenk, William
1989		III	24		GL	L		32	19	5	Goffnett, Charles
1994		III	32		GL	A		40	21	6	Goffnett, Charles
1997		III	32		GL	A		64	23	6	Goffnett, Charles
1996		III	64		GL	L		64	21	6	Goffnett, Charles

ALVERNIA

Year	M/W	Div	F	SD	Reg	BD	Bye	#T	W	L	Coach
1997	M	III	4	3	MA	L		64	26	6	McCloskey, John R., Sr. "Jack"
1997	W	III	32		MA	L		64	22	6	Calabria, Kevin
1998		III	32	3	MA	L		48	22	6	Calabria, Kevin
1996		III	64		MA	L		64	22	6	Calabria, Kevin

AMERICAN

Year	M/W	Div	F	SD	Reg	BD	Bye	#T	W	L	Coach
1958	M	II	8		E			32	22	6	Carrasco, David L.
1959		II	8		E			32	22	7	Carrasco, David L.
1960		II	8		E			32	22	7	Carrasco, David L.

AMERICAN INTERNATIONAL

Year	M/W	Div	F	SD	Reg	BD	Bye	#T	W	L	Coach
1969	M	II	3		NENG	L		32	21	4	Callahan, William E.
1968		II	8		NE	L		36	21	5	Callahan, William E.
1970		II	8		NENG	L		32	17	8	Callahan, William E.
1985		II	8		NENG	A		32	29	4	Powell, Jim
1983		II	16		NENG	L		32	23	9	Powell, Jim
1984		II	32		NENG	A		32	23	8	Powell, Jim
1994		II	32		NE	A		32	22	6	Powell, Jim
1966		II	34		NE	L		36	18	8	Callahan, William E.
1967		II	36		NE	L		36	19	6	Callahan, William E.
1995	W	II	32	3	NENG	L		48	22	9	Cinella, Peter
1996		II	48	4	NE	L		48	18	11	Cinella, Peter

AMHERST

Year	M/W	Div	F	SD	Reg	BD	Bye	#T	W	L	Coach
1994	M	III	8		NE	L	To R32	40	22	5	Hixon, David D.
1957		II	32		E	L		32	17	4	Wilson, Richard E. "Rick"
1997		III	32	4	NE	L		64	21	5	Hixon, David D.

ANGELO STATE

Year	M/W	Div	F	SD	Reg	BD	Bye	#T	W	L	Coach
1989	M	II	24		SC	A		32	18	10	Messbarger, Ed
1988		II	32		SC	L		32	22	11	Messbarger, Ed
1994	W	II	32		SC	A		32	23	6	Davis, Peggy

ANNA MARIA

Year	M/W	Div	F	SD	Reg	BD	Bye	#T	W	L	Coach
1996	M	III	16	3	NE	A		64	25	5	Phillips, Paul

Year	M/W	Div	F	SD	Reg	BD	Bye	#T	W	L	Coach
APPALACHIAN STATE											
1979	M	I	32	6	ME	A	To R32	40	23	6	Cremins, Bobby
1990	W	I	48	11	E	A		48	20	9	Robinson, Linda
1991		I	48	12	ME	A		48	19	14	Robinson, Linda
1996		I	64	13	W	A		64	24	6	Robinson, Linda
ARIZONA											
1997	M	I	1	4	SE	L		64	25	9	Olson, Robert Luther "Lute"
1988		I	3	1	W	A		64	35	3	Olson, Robert Luther "Lute"
1994		I	3	2	W	A		64	29	6	Olson, Robert Luther "Lute"
1976		I	8		W	A		32	24	9	Snowden, Frederick
1998		I	8	1	W	A		64	31	5	Olson, Robert Luther "Lute"
1951			16		W	A		16	24	6	Enke, Fred A.
1989		I	16	1	W	A		64	29	4	Olson, Robert Luther "Lute"
1991		I	16	2	W	A		64	28	7	Olson, Robert Luther "Lute"
1996		I	16	3	W	L		64	26	7	Olson, Robert Luther "Lute"
1977		I	32		MW	L		32	21	6	Snowden, Frederick
1990		I	32	2	W	A		64	25	7	Olson, Robert Luther "Lute"
1985		I	64	10	W	L		64	21	10	Olson, Robert Luther "Lute"
1986		I	64	9	W	A		64	23	9	Olson, Robert Luther "Lute"
1987		I	64	10	W	L		64	18	12	Olson, Robert Luther "Lute"
1992		I	64	3	SE	L		64	24	7	Olson, Robert Luther "Lute"
1993		I	64	2	W	A		64	24	4	Olson, Robert Luther "Lute"
1995		I	64	5	MW	L		64	23	8	Olson, Robert Luther "Lute"
1998	W	I	16	3	E	L		64	23	7	Bonvicini, Joan
1997		I	32	7	W	L		64	23	8	Bonvicini, Joan
ARIZONA STATE											
1961	M	I	8		W	A		24	23	6	Wulk, Ned W.
1963		I	8		W	A		25	26	3	Wulk, Ned W.
1975		I	8		W	A		32	25	4	Wulk, Ned W.
1973		I	16		W	A		25	19	9	Wulk, Ned W.
1995		I	16	5	SE	L		64	24	9	Frieder, Bill
1958		I	24		W	A		24	13	13	Wulk, Ned W.
1962		I	25		W	A		25	23	4	Wulk, Ned W.
1964		I	25		W	A		25	16	11	Wulk, Ned W.
1980		I	32	5	W	L		48	22	7	Wulk, Ned W.
1981		I	32	2	MW	L	To R32	48	24	4	Wulk, Ned W.
1991		I	32	8	SE	L		64	20	10	Frieder, Bill
1982	W	I	16		MW	L		32	25	7	Simpson, Juliene
1983		I	16		W	L	To R32	36	23	7	Simpson, Juliene
1992		I	48	6	MW	L		48	20	9	McHugh, Maura
ARKANSAS											
1994	M	I	1	1	MW	L		64	31	3	Richardson, Nolan
1995		I	2	2	MW	L		64	32	7	Richardson, Nolan
1941			3		W	L		8	20	3	Rose, Glen
1945			3		W	L		8	17	9	Lambert, Dr. Eugene W.

Year	M/W	Div	F	SD	Reg	BD	Bye	#T	W	L	Coach
1978		I	3		W	L		32	32	4	Sutton, Eddie
1990		I	3	4	MW	A		64	30	5	Richardson, Nolan
1949			6		W	L		8	15	11	Lambert, Dr. Eugene W.
1979		I	8	2	MW	A	To R32	40	25	5	Sutton, Eddie
1991		I	8	1	SE	A		64	34	4	Richardson, Nolan
1958		I	16		MW	A	To R16	24	17	10	Rose, Glen
1981		I	16	5	MW	L		48	24	8	Sutton, Eddie
1983		I	16	4	ME	L	To R32	52	26	4	Sutton, Eddie
1993		I	16	4	E	L		64	22	9	Richardson, Nolan
1996		I	16	12	E	L		64	20	13	Richardson, Nolan
1977		I	32		MW	A		32	26	2	Sutton, Eddie
1982		I	32	4	MW	A	To R32	48	23	6	Sutton, Eddie
1984		I	32	2	E	L	To R32	53	25	7	Sutton, Eddie
1985		I	32	9	W	L		64	22	13	Sutton, Eddie
1989		I	32	5	MW	A		64	25	7	Richardson, Nolan
1992		I	32	3	MW	L		64	26	8	Richardson, Nolan
1998		I	32	6	W	L		64	24	9	Richardson, Nolan
1980		I	48	10	MW	L		48	21	8	Sutton, Eddie
1988		I	64	11	SE	L		64	21	9	Richardson, Nolan
1998	W	I	3	9	W	L		64	22	11	Blair, Gary
1990		I	8	7	W	L		48	25	5	Sutherland, John
1991		I	16	3	MW	A	To R32	48	28	4	Sutherland, John
1995		I	32	6	ME	L		64	23	7	Blair, Gary
1986		I	40		MW	L		40	22	8	Sutherland, John
1989		I	48	12	MW	L		48	22	8	Sutherland, John

ARKANSAS STATE

Year	M/W	Div	F	SD	Reg	BD	Bye	#T	W	L	Coach
1962	M	II	16		SW	L		32	17	7	Rauth, John H.
1966		II	22		SW	L	To R32	36	17	9	Speight, Marvin
1967		II	23		SW		To R32	36	17	7	Speight, Marvin
1958		II	24		SW	L		32	18	9	Rauth, John H.
1963		II	24		SW	L		32	15	11	Rauth, John H.
1960		II	32		ME	L		32	14	13	Rauth, John H.

ARKANSAS TECH

Year	M/W	Div	F	SD	Reg	BD	Bye	#T	W	L	Coach
1998	W	II	8	2	S	A	To R32	48	26	5	Foley, Joe M.

ARKANSAS: LITTLE ROCK

Year	M/W	Div	F	SD	Reg	BD	Bye	#T	W	L	Coach
1986	M	I	32	14	MW	A		64	23	11	Newell, Mike
1989		I	64	13	MW	A		64	23	8	Newell, Mike
1990		I	64	16	W	A		64	20	10	Newell, Mike

ARKANSAS: MONTICELLO

Year	M/W	Div	F	SD	Reg	BD	Bye	#T	W	L	Coach
1998	W	II	16	5	S	L		48	23	8	Early, Alvy

ARKANSAS: PINE BLUFF

Year	M/W	Div	F	SD	Reg	BD	Bye	#T	W	L	Coach
1967	M	II	32		SW		To R32	36	24	7	Clemmons, Hubert O.

ARMSTRONG ATLANTIC STATE

Year	M/W	Div	F	SD	Reg	BD	Bye	#T	W	L	Coach
1975	M	II	24		S			32	19	7	Alexander, Bill
1977		II	32		S	A		32	15	15	Alexander, Bill
1995		II	32	6	S	L		48	20	11	Mills, Griff

Year	M/W	Div	F	SD	Reg	BD	Bye	#T	W	L	Coach
ARMY											
1984	W	II	8		E	L	To R16	24	24	4	Johnson, Harold
1988		II	16		E	A		32	19	13	Chiavaro, Lynn
ASHLAND											
1968	M	II	4		MW	L	To R32	36	24	6	Musselman, William
1969		II	4		MW	L		32	26	4	Musselman, William
1991		II	8		GL			32	26	5	Dambrot, Keith
1976		III	14		GL	L		28	20	7	Gottfried, Joe
1970		II	16		ME	L		32	23	4	Musselman, William
1977		III	16		GL	L		30	20	6	Gottfried, Joe
1978		III	16		W	L	To R16	30	19	7	Gottfried, Joe
1990		II	16		GL	L		32	22	8	Dambrot, Keith
1971		II	24		GL	L		32	25	3	Musselman, William
1988		II	32		GL	L		32	18	10	Lyons, Roger
ASSUMPTION (MA)											
1973	M	II	3		NENG	L	To R32	42	25	3	O'Brien, Joseph M.
1974		II	3		NENG	L	To R32	44	22	7	O'Brien, Joseph M.
1975		II	3		NENG	L		32	22	8	O'Brien, Joseph M.
1971		II	8		NENG	L		32	25	2	O'Brien, Joseph M.
1972		II	8		NENG	L	To R32	36	21	6	O'Brien, Joseph M.
1965		II	16		NE	L		32	16	6	Laska, Andrew
1966		II	16		NE	L		36	18	6	Laska, Andrew
1970		II	16		NENG	L		32	17	5	O'Brien, Joseph M.
1976		II	16		NENG	L		32	16	12	O'Brien, Joseph M.
1979		II	16		NENG	L		32	18	11	O'Brien, Joseph M.
1960		II	24		NE	L		32	14	6	Laska, Andrew
1963		II	24		NE	L		32	14	5	Laska, Andrew
1964		II	24		NE	L		32	19	2	Laska, Andrew
1969		II	24		NENG	L		32	17	7	O'Brien, Joseph M.
1977		II	24		NENG	L		32	19	10	O'Brien, Joseph M.
1983		II	24		NENG	A		32	21	11	O'Brien, Joseph M.
1967		II	32		NE	L		36	17	5	Laska, Andrew
1988		II	32		NENG	L		32	20	12	Renkens, Jack
1991		II	32		NENG	A		32	24	8	Renkens, Jack
1992		II	32		NENG	L		32	19	13	Renkens, Jack
1998		II	32	4	NE	A		48	23	4	DeBari, Sergio "Serge"
1968		II	34		NE	L		36	15	7	O'Brien, Joseph M.
AUBURN											
1986	M	I	8	8	W	L		64	22	11	Smith, Charles H. "Sonny"
1985		I	16	11	SE	A		64	22	12	Smith, Charles H. "Sonny"
1987		I	32	8	MW	L		64	18	13	Smith, Charles H. "Sonny"
1988		I	32	8	SE	L		64	19	11	Smith, Charles H. "Sonny"
1984		I	48	5	E	L		53	20	11	Smith, Charles H. "Sonny"
1988	W	I	2	2	ME	L	To R32	40	32	3	Ciampi, Joe
1989		I	2	1	ME	L	To R32	48	32	2	Ciampi, Joe
1990		I	2	2	ME	A	To R32	48	28	7	Ciampi, Joe
1987		I	8	1	ME	A	To R32	40	31	2	Ciampi, Joe

Year	M/W	Div	F	SD	Reg	BD	Bye	#T	W	L	Coach
1991	I		8	3	ME	L	To R32	48	26	6	Ciampi, Joe
1996	I		8	6	W	L		64	23	9	Ciampi, Joe
1983	I		16		MW	L	To R32	36	24	8	Ciampi, Joe
1985	I		16		MW	L		32	25	6	Ciampi, Joe
1986	I		16		MW	L	To R32	40	24	6	Ciampi, Joe
1993	I		16	3	ME	L	To R32	48	25	4	Ciampi, Joe
1982	I		32		E	L		32	24	5	Ciampi, Joe
1994	I		32	9	E	L		64	20	10	Ciampi, Joe
1997	I		32	7	ME	A		64	22	10	Ciampi, Joe

AUGSBURG

Year	M/W	Div	F	SD	Reg	BD	Bye	#T	W	L	Coach
1985	M	III	32		S	L		32	21	7	Boots, David
1998		III	48	6	W	L		48	22	4	Ammann, Brian

AUGUSTA STATE

Year	M/W	Div	F	SD	Reg	BD	Bye	#T	W	L	Coach
1978	M	II	32		S	L		32	20	8	Vanover, Marvin

AUGUSTANA (IL)

Year	M/W	Div	F	SD	Reg	BD	Bye	#T	W	L	Coach
1981	M	III	2		MW	L		32	25	6	Borcherding, James
1993		III	2		MW	A		40	24	7	Yount, Steve
1975		III	3		MW	L		30	22	8	Borcherding, James
1976		III	3		MW	L	R14>R4	28	21	7	Borcherding, James
1982		III	8		MW	L		32	22	6	Borcherding, James
1980		III	16		MW	L		32	20	7	Borcherding, James
1977		III	23		MW	L		30	20	7	Borcherding, James
1959		II	32		MW	L		32	12	12	Kallis, Lenny
1960		II	32		GL	L		32	14	10	Kallis, Lenny
1963		II	32		GL			32	18	6	Kallis, Lenny
1971		II	32		GL	L		32	20	6	Borcherding, James
1983		III	32		W	L		32	18	10	Borcherding, James
1982	W	III	8		None	L		16	19	7	Stein, Paulette
1989		III	16		C			32	22	5	Schumacher, Diane
1983		III	24		C	L		32	17	10	Stein, Paulette
1987		III	24		C	A		32	20	7	Schumacher, Diane
1990		III	32		C	A		32	22	4	Schumacher, Diane
1991		III	32		C	A		32	19	5	Schumacher, Diane
1993		III	32		C	A		32	19	7	Schumacher, Diane

AUGUSTANA (SD)

Year	M/W	Div	F	SD	Reg	BD	Bye	#T	W	L	Coach
1978	M	II	16		NC	A		32	18	11	Klein, Mel
1975		II	24		NC	L		32	20	8	Klein, Mel
1989		II	24		NC			32	23	7	Gross, Bill
1977		II	32		NC	L		32	16	12	Klein, Mel
1986		II	32		NC	L		32	18	11	Gross, Bill
1988		II	32		NC	L		32	20	10	Gross, Bill
1992	W	II	16		NC	L		32	26	4	Krauth, David
1993		II	16		NC	L		32	24	5	Krauth, David
1990		II	32		NC	L		32	19	10	Krauth, David
1991		II	32		NC	L		32	23	6	Krauth, David
1994		II	32		NC	L		32	23	6	Krauth, David
1997		II	48	6	NC	L		48	23	5	Krauth, David

Year	M/W	Div	F	SD	Reg	BD	Bye	#T	W	L	Coach
AURORA											
1998	M	III	48	6	MW	L		48	21	5	Lancaster, James
1995	W	III	16		C	L		64	22	6	Lancaster, James
1994		III	32		C	L		40	22	5	Lancaster, James
AUSTIN											
1998	W	III	16	3	S	L		48	21	7	Potera, Robin
AUSTIN PEAY STATE											
1961	M	II	8		SC	L		32	22	9	Aaron, David B.
1960		II	16		SC			32	22	5	Aaron, David B.
1973		I	16		ME	A		25	22	7	Kelly, Lake
1974		I	25		ME	A		25	17	10	Kelly, Lake
1958		II	32		ME			32	17	9	Aaron, David B.
1963		II	32		SC	L		32	18	11	Fisher, George
1987		I	32	14	SE	A		64	20	12	Kelly, Lake
1996		I	64	14	SE	A		64	19	11	Loos, David
1996	W	I	64	14	MW	A		64	21	8	Wilson, LaDonna
AVERETT											
1990	M	III	16		S	A	To R32	40	20	9	Hall, Ed
BABSON											
1992	M	III	32		NE	L	To R32	40	22	4	DeBari, Sergio "Serge"
1995		III	64	7	NE	L		64	20	7	DeBari, Sergio "Serge"
1996		III	64	6	NE	L		64	21	7	Brennan, Steve
1993	W	III	16		NE	L		32	23	5	Blinstrub, Judith
1994		III	16		NE	L	To R32	40	23	4	Blinstrub, Judith
BALDWIN-WALLACE											
1979	M	III	8		GL	L		32	21	7	Rupert, Bob
1995		III	16	8	GL	L		64	19	9	Bankson, Steve
1967		II	23		ME		To R32	36	22	9	Thompson, Hugh
1998		III	48	6	GL	A		48	17	11	Bankson, Steve
1996		III	64	8	GL	L		64	16	12	Bankson, Steve
1998	W	III	32	3	GL	L		48	23	6	Harrer, Cheri
1996		III	64		A	L		64	18	9	Harrer, Cheri
1997		III	64		GL	L		64	23	5	Harrer, Cheri
BALL STATE											
1990	M	I	16	12	W	A		64	26	7	Hunsaker, Dick
1964		II	32		GL	L		32	19	8	Hinga, John "Jim"
1989		I	32	9	MW	A		64	29	3	Majerus, Rick
1981		I	48	12	ME	A		48	20	10	Yoder, Steve
1986		I	64	14	SE	A		64	21	10	Brown, Al
1993		I	64	15	MW	A		64	26	8	Hunsaker, Dick
1995		I	64	12	SE	A		64	19	11	McCallum, Ray
BALTIMORE											
1976	M	II	16		SA	A		32	20	10	Szymanski, Frank A.
1977		II	16		SA	L		32	24	4	Szymanski, Frank A.
1975		II	24		SA	L		32	19	11	Szymanski, Frank A.

Year	M/W	Div	F	SD	Reg	BD	Bye	#T	W	L	Coach
BARRY											
1991	W	II	32		W	L		32	26	4	Olson, Dan
BARTON											
1997	M	II	48	3	E	L		48	22	5	Lievense, Ron
BATES											
1961	M	II	16		NE	L		32	15	9	Peck, Robert R.
1998	W	III	16	2	NE	L	To R32	48	22	4	Murphy, James
1997		III	64		NE	L		64	20	5	Murphy, James
BAYLOR											
1948	M		2		W	L		8	24	8	Henderson, R. E. "Bill"
1950			4		W	L		8	14	13	Henderson, R. E. "Bill"
1946			8		W	L		8	25	5	Henderson, R. E. "Bill"
1988		I	64	8	MW	L		64	23	11	Iba, Clarence Eugene "Gene"
BELLARMINE											
1965	M	II	16		SC	L		32	15	8	Groza, Alex J.
1989		II	16		GL	L		32	22	8	Reibel, Joseph C.
1963		II	24		SC			32	21	6	Groza, Alex J.
1970		II	24		S	L		32	16	10	Spalding, James R.
1984		II	24		GL	L		32	21	9	Reibel, Joseph C.
1991		II	24		GL			32	24	6	Reibel, Joseph C.
1969		II	32		S	L		32	19	9	Spalding, James R.
1977		II	32		GL	L		32	17	11	Reibel, Joseph C.
1982		II	32		GL	L		32	20	9	Reibel, Joseph C.
1994	W	II	4		GL	A		32	25	6	Just, Charles G.
1986		II	8		GL			24	23	7	Just, Charles G.
1990		II	8		SA	L		32	25	6	Just, Charles G.
1991		II	8		GL	L		32	26	5	Just, Charles G.
1996		II	16	2	GL	A	To R32	48	24	4	Just, Charles G.
1987		II	24		GL	L		24	20	8	Just, Charles G.
1993		II	32		GL	L		32	18	10	Just, Charles G.
1997		II	48	5	GL	L		48	20	8	Just, Charles G.
BELMONT ABBEY											
1961	M	II	16		SC	L		32	17	7	McGuire, Alfred J.
1959		II	24		ME	L		32	21	2	McGuire, Alfred J.
1960		II	24		SC	L		32	19	6	McGuire, Alfred J.
1998	W	II	48	3	E	A		48	26	4	Kebbe, Elaine
BELOIT											
1957	M	II	16		MW	L		32	17	6	Stanley, Dolph
1981		III	16		MW	A		32	24	2	Knapton, William B.
1979		III	24		MW	A		32	18	7	Knapton, William B.
1980		III	24		W	L		32	19	5	Knapton, William B.
1977		III	30		MW	A		30	15	7	Knapton, William B.
1982		III	32		MW	A		32	19	6	Knapton, William B.
1983		III	32		MW	A		32	18	7	Knapton, William B.
1993		III	32		MW	A	To R32	40	21	5	Knapton, William B.

Year	M/W	Div	F	SD	Reg	BD	Bye	#T	W	L	Coach
1989		III	40		MW	A		40	17	7	Knapton, William B.
1995		III	64	6	MW	A		64	13	12	Knapton, William B.
1996	W	III	32		GL	L		64	22	4	Botham, Sandy
1998		III	48	5	C	A		48	23	2	Straub, Kristi
1995		III	64		GL	A		64	17	8	Walters, Mimi
1997		III	64		C	A		64	20	5	Straub, Kristi

BENEDICT

Year	M/W	Div	F	SD	Reg	BD	Bye	#T	W	L	Coach
1980	M	II	32		SA	L		32	21	7	Holmes, Michael

BENEDICTINE (IL)

Year	M/W	Div	F	SD	Reg	BD	Bye	#T	W	L	Coach
1991	M	III	8		MW	L	To R32	40	23	6	LaScala, Anthony
1966		II	32		MW	L	To R32	36	18	4	LaScala, Anthony
1997		III	64	7	MW	L		64	16	9	Bunkenburg, Keith

BENTLEY

Year	M/W	Div	F	SD	Reg	BD	Bye	#T	W	L	Coach
1972	M	II	16		NENG	L	To R32	36	26	2	Shields, Elwood N. 'Al'
1973		II	16		NENG	L	To R32	42	24	3	Shields, Elwood N. 'Al'
1975		II	16		NENG	L		32	23	2	Shields, Elwood N. 'Al'
1993		II	23		NENG	L		32	24	7	Lawson, Jay
1976		II	24		NENG	L		32	17	12	Shields, Elwood N. 'Al'
1979		II	24		NENG	L		32	22	6	Hammel, Brian
1989		II	24		NENG	L		32	25	6	Sullivan, Frank
1974		II	32		NENG	L	To R32	44	18	7	Shields, Elwood N. 'Al'
1985		II	32		NENG	L		32	25	6	Sullivan, Frank
1990	W	II	2		NENG	A		32	31	4	Stevens, Barbara
1989		II	3		NENG	L		32	31	3	Stevens, Barbara
1991		II	3		NENG	L		32	31	4	Stevens, Barbara
1992		II	4		NENG	A		32	31	2	Stevens, Barbara
1993		II	4		NENG	A		32	30	4	Stevens, Barbara
1997		II	4	1	NE	L	To R32	48	27	7	Stevens, Barbara
1996		II	8	2	NE	A	To R32	48	28	3	Stevens, Barbara
1998		II	8	2	NE	A	To R32	48	30	2	Stevens, Barbara
1982		II	16		NENG	A		16	19	6	Mullen, Paula
1983		II	16		NENG	L		24	18	7	Mullen, Paula
1984		II	16		NENG	A		24	26	3	Mullen, Paula
1985		II	16		NENG	A		24	21	5	Sanborn, Kathleen
1988		II	16		NENG	A		32	28	4	Stevens, Barbara
1994		II	16		NENG	A		32	25	6	Stevens, Barbara
1987		II	24		NENG	L		24	24	5	Sanborn, Kathleen
1995		II	32	5	NENG	L		48	22	8	Stevens, Barbara

BETHANY (WV)

Year	M/W	Div	F	SD	Reg	BD	Bye	#T	W	L	Coach
1978	M	III	16		GL	A		30	18	5	Dafler, Jim
1982		III	32		SA	A		32	15	9	Dafler, Jim
1997	W	III	64		GL	A		64	22	4	Campanell-Komara, Lisa

BETHEL (MN)

Year	M/W	Div	F	SD	Reg	BD	Bye	#T	W	L	Coach
1991	M	III	40		W	A		40	17	11	Palke, George

Year	M/W	Div	F	SD	Reg	BD	Bye	#T	W	L	Coach
1996	W	III	8		W	L		64	22	6	Hunter, Debra F.
1994		III	16		W	A	To R32	40	21	5	Hunter, Debra F.
1995		III	64		W	L		64	17	8	Hunter, Debra F.
1997		III	64		W	L		64	16	9	Hunter, Debra F.

BETHUNE-COOKMAN

Year	M/W	Div	F	SD	Reg	BD	Bye	#T	W	L	Coach
1965	M	II	32		SC			32	18	6	McClairen, Jack "Cy"
1968		II	32		SC		To R32	36	24	7	McClairen, Jack "Cy"
1980		II	32		S	A		32	13	16	McClairen, Jack "Cy"

BINGHAMTON STATE

Year	M/W	Div	F	SD	Reg	BD	Bye	#T	W	L	Coach
1998	W	III	32	1	E	L	To R32	48	22	3	Wilson, David
1995		III	64		E	L		64	19	8	Wilson, David
1996		III	64		E	L		64	21	7	Wilson, David
1997		III	64		E	A		64	23	4	Wilson, David

BISHOP

Year	M/W	Div	F	SD	Reg	BD	Bye	#T	W	L	Coach
1977	M	III	16		W	L	To R16	30	15	9	Lilly, Sylvester "Ben"
1982		III	16		W	L		32	16	7	Lilly, Sylvester "Ben"
1983		III	24		W	L		32	18	8	Lilly, Sylvester "Ben"
1986	W	III	2		W	L		32	28	3	Young, Abron, Jr.
1984		III	8		W	L		32	21	7	Young, Abron, Jr.
1987		III	24		W	L		32	20	5	Young, Abron, Jr.
1983		III	32		W	L		32	18	7	Robinson, Myrtle

BLACKBURN

Year	M/W	Div	F	SD	Reg	BD	Bye	#T	W	L	Coach
1997	W	III	64		C	A		64	13	13	Garrett, Matt

BLOOMSBURG

Year	M/W	Div	F	SD	Reg	BD	Bye	#T	W	L	Coach
1974	M	II	8		ME	L		44	22	6	Chronister, Charles W.
1983		II	8		E	L		32	23	10	Chronister, Charles W.
1963		II	16		E	L		32	17	4	Foster, William E.
1982		II	16		E	L		32	24	7	Chronister, Charles W.
1989		II	16		E	L		32	27	5	Chronister, Charles W.
1981		II	32		E	A		32	23	7	Chronister, Charles W.
1995		II	48	5	E	L		48	18	9	Chronister, Charles W.
1996		II	48	4	E	L		48	21	7	Chronister, Charles W.
1989	W	II	8		E	L		32	28	2	Bressi, Joe
1998		II	16	6	E	L		48	22	8	Fedorjaka, Kathy
1990		II	32		E	L		32	22	7	Bressi, Joe
1991		II	32		E	L		32	26	2	Bressi, Joe
1992		II	32		SA	A		32	22	8	Bressi, Joe

BLUEFIELD STATE (WV)

Year	M/W	Div	F	SD	Reg	BD	Bye	#T	W	L	Coach
1996	M	II	48	6	E	A		48	15	16	Brown, Terry

BOISE STATE

Year	M/W	Div	F	SD	Reg	BD	Bye	#T	W	L	Coach
1970	M	II	24		W	L		32	20	8	Satterfield, Murray
1976		I	32		W	A		32	18	11	Connor, Doran "Bus"
1988		I	64	14	W	A		64	24	6	Dye, Bobby
1993		I	64	14	W	A		64	21	8	Dye, Bobby
1994		I	64	14	W	A		64	17	13	Dye, Bobby
1994	W	I	64	9	W	L		64	23	6	Daugherty, June

Year	M/W	Div	F	SD	Reg	BD	Bye	#T	W	L	Coach
BOSTON COLLEGE											
1967	M	I	8		E	L		23	21	3	Cousy, Robert J.
1982		I	8	8	MW	L		48	22	10	Davis, Dr. Thomas
1994		I	8	9	E	L		64	23	11	O'Brien, James J.
1975		I	16		E	L		32	21	9	Zuffelato, Bob
1981		I	16	5	ME	L		48	23	7	Davis, Dr. Thomas
1983		I	16	4	W	L	To R32	52	25	7	Williams, Gary
1985		I	16	11	MW	L		64	20	11	Williams, Gary
1968		I	23		E	L		23	17	8	Cousy, Robert J.
1958		I	24		E	L		24	15	6	Martin, Donald
1996		I	32	11	SE	L		64	19	11	O'Brien, James J.
1997		I	32	5	W	A		64	22	9	O'Brien, James J.
BOSTON UNIVERSITY											
1959	M	I	8		E	L		23	20	7	Zunic, Matthew
1983		I	52	13	E	L		52	21	10	Pitino, Richard A. "Rick"
1988		I	64	15	E	A		64	23	8	Jarvis, Mike
1990		I	64	16	E	A		64	18	12	Jarvis, Mike
1997		I	64	12	MW	A		64	25	5	Wolff, Dennis
BOWDOIN											
1996	M	III	32	4	NE	L		64	19	6	Gilbride, Timothy J.
BOWIE STATE											
1996	W	II	16	4	SA	L		48	22	10	Davis, Edward
1997		II	16	2	SA	A	To R32	48	29	2	Davis, Edward
1998		II	16	1	SA	A	To R32	48	28	2	Davis, Edward
BOWLING GREEN STATE											
1963	M	I	16		ME	A		25	19	8	Anderson, W. Harold "Andy"
1959		I	23		ME	A		23	18	8	Anderson, W. Harold "Andy"
1968		I	23		ME	A		23	18	7	Fitch, William C. "Billy"
1962		I	25		ME	A		25	21	4	Anderson, W. Harold "Andy"
1989	W	I	32	9	W	A		48	27	4	Voll, Fran
1987		I	40	9	ME	A		40	27	3	Voll, Fran
1988		I	40	10	ME	A		40	24	6	Voll, Fran
1990		I	48	12	ME	A		48	22	9	Voll, Fran
1993		I	48		E	A		48	25	5	Clark, Jaci
1994		I	64	7	MW	A		64	26	4	Clark, Jaci
BRADLEY											
1950	M		2		W	L		8	32	5	Anderson, Forrest A. "Forddy"
1954			2		W(A)	L		24	19	13	Anderson, Forrest A. "Forddy"
1955			8		W(A)	L		24	9	20	Vanatta, Robert
1986		I	32	7	W	L		64	32	3	Versace, Dick
1980		I	48	11	MW	A		48	23	10	Versace, Dick
1988		I	64	9	SE	A		64	26	5	Albeck, Charles Stanley "Stan"
1996		I	64	8	E	L		64	22	8	Molinari, Jim
BRANDEIS											
1975	M	III	8		NE	L		30	20	7	Brannum, Robert W.
1978		III	8		NE	L		30	19	6	Brannum, Robert W.
1977		III	16		NE	L		30	16	11	Brannum, Robert W.
1958		II	24		NE	L		32	18	4	Stein, Harvey

Year	M/W	Div	F	SD	Reg	BD	Bye	#T	W	L	Coach
BRIDGEPORT											
1991	M	II	2		NENG	L		32	26	8	Webster, Bruce
1992		II	2		NENG	A		32	28	7	Webster, Bruce
1979		II	4		NENG	L		32	25	8	Webster, Bruce
1976		II	8		NENG	L		32	24	5	Webster, Bruce
1990		II	8		NENG	L		32	24	9	Webster, Bruce
1989		II	16		NENG	A		32	25	7	Webster, Bruce
1972		II	24		NENG	L	To R32	36	17	9	Webster, Bruce
1973		II	24		NENG	L		42	20	9	Webster, Bruce
1978		II	24		NENG	L		32	19	10	Webster, Bruce
1985		II	24		NENG	A		32	26	6	Webster, Bruce
1968		II	32		NE	L		36	19	8	Webster, Bruce
1977		II	32		NENG	L		32	19	10	Webster, Bruce
1989	W	II	32		NENG	L		32	25	5	Foust, Dan
1996		II	32	6	NE	A		48	25	5	Herer, Harvey
1995		II	48	4	NENG	L		48	21	8	Herer, Harvey
BRIDGEWATER (VA)											
1997	M	III	16	7	S	L		64	21	8	Leatherman, Bill
1988		III	32		SA	A		32	24	5	Leatherman, Bill
1996		III	64	6	S	L		64	18	10	Leatherman, Bill
1998	W	III	16	1	S	L	To R32	48	24	5	Willi, Jean
1997		III	32		S	L		64	22	6	Willi, Jean
BRIDGEWATER STATE (MA)											
1983	M	III	16		NE	A		32	21	6	Byron, Paul
1985	W	III	16		NE	A		32	25	2	Ruggiero, George H. 'Bo'
1983		III	24		NE	L		32	18	7	Hastings, Martha
1984		III	32		NE	L		32	22	5	Ruggiero, George H. 'Bo'
1986		III	32		NE	L		32	21	6	Ruggiero, George H. 'Bo'
BRIGHAM YOUNG											
1950	M		6		W	L		8	22	12	Watts, Stanley H.
1951			8		W	A		16	28	9	Watts, Stanley H.
1981		I	8	6	E	L		48	25	7	Arnold, Frank H.
1957		I	12		W	A	To R16	23	19	9	Watts, Stanley H.
1965		I	16		FW	A	To R16	23	21	7	Watts, Stanley H.
1971		I	16		W	A		25	18	11	Watts, Stanley H.
1969		I	25		W	A		25	17	11	Watts, Stanley H.
1972		I	25		W	A		25	21	5	Watts, Stanley H.
1979		I	32	5	W	A	To R32	40	20	8	Arnold, Frank H.
1980		I	32	3	W	A	To R32	48	24	5	Arnold, Frank H.
1984		I	32	8	ME	L		53	20	11	Anderson, Ladell
1988		I	32	4	SE	L		64	26	6	Anderson, Ladell
1991		I	32	10	W	A		64	21	13	Reid, Roger
1993		I	32	7	MW	L		64	25	9	Reid, Roger
1987		I	64	10	SE	L		64	21	11	Anderson, Ladell
1990		I	64	12	E	L		64	21	9	Reid, Roger
1992		I	64	10	W	A		64	25	7	Reid, Roger
1995		I	64	8	SE	L		64	22	10	Reid, Roger

Year	M/W	Div	F	SD	Reg	BD	Bye	#T	W	L	Coach
1984	W	I	32		W	A		32	18	8	Leishman, Dr. Courtney M.
1985		I	32		W	A		32	19	9	Leishman, Dr. Courtney M.
1993		I	48		W	A		48	24	4	Wilson, Jeanie
BROCKPORT STATE											
1973	M	II	4		E			42	24	6	Panaggio, Mauro
1975		III	4		E	L		30	23	5	Panaggio, Mauro
1997		III	16	7	E	L		64	19	10	Bowe, Bill
1994		III	40		E	A		40	17	11	Bowe, Bill
1998		III	48	4	E	L		48	17	10	Bowe, Bill
1995	W	III	64		E	L		64	17	9	Carron, Michele
BROOKLYN											
1982	M	III	3		E	L		32	22	9	Reiner, Mark
BROWN											
1939	M		8		E	L		8	17	3	Allen, George E. "Eck"
1986		I	64	15	E	A		64	16	11	Cingiser, Mike
1994	W	I	64	16	E	A		64	18	10	Burr, Jean Marie
BRYANT											
1978	M	II	32		NENG	L		32	20	6	Folliard, Thomas J.
1980		II	32		NENG	L		32	20	7	Drury, Leon A. "Lee"
1986	W	II	24		NC	A		24	17	12	McKee, Michael
1988		II	32		S	A		32	22	9	Tomasso, Ralph
1989		II	32		NENG	A		32	20	9	Tomasso, Ralph
1996		II	48	3	NE	L		48	19	10	Burke, Mary
BUCKNELL											
1987	M	I	64	16	SE	A		64	22	9	Woollum, Charles R.
1989		I	64	15	MW	A		64	23	8	Woollum, Charles R.
BUENA VISTA											
1997	M	III	64	6	W	A		64	18	8	Van Haaften, Brian
1990	W	III	8		C	L		32	23	6	Naughton, John
1997		III	16		W	A		64	23	5	Allgood-Berry, Janet
1983		III	32		C	L		32	18	8	Naughton, John
1985		III	32		C			32	20	8	Naughton, John
1995		III	64		C			64	18	7	Allgood-Berry, Janet
1996		III	64		C	A		64	19	7	Allgood-Berry, Janet
BUFFALO STATE COLLEGE											
1970	M	II	4		E	L		32	19	3	MacAdam, Howard B.
1968		II	16		NE			36	17	7	MacAdam, Howard B.
1971		II	16		E	L		32	18	4	MacAdam, Howard B.
1985		III	16		E	A		32	22	5	Bihr, Richard J.
1988		III	16		E	A		32	19	10	Bihr, Richard J.
1989		III	16		E	A	To R32	40	25	4	Bihr, Richard J.
1992		III	16		E	A	To R32	40	24	4	Bihr, Richard J.
1996		III	16	4	E	A		64	22	8	Bihr, Richard J.

Year	M/W	Div	F	SD	Reg	BD	Bye	#T	W	L	Coach
1976		II	24		E	L		32	20	8	Borschel, Thomas
1984		III	24		E	A		32	23	5	Bihr, Richard J.
1972		II	32		E		To R32	36	13	14	MacAdam, Howard B.
1990		III	32		E	A	To R32	40	27	2	Bihr, Richard J.
1991		III	32		E	A	To R32	40	21	7	Bihr, Richard J.
1993		III	32		E	L	To R32	40	21	6	Bihr, Richard J.
1995		III	32	3	E	A		64	21	8	Bihr, Richard J.
1997		III	32	4	E	A		64	20	9	Bihr, Richard J.
1967		II	36		NE			36	17	6	MacAdam, Howard B.
1984	W	III	16		E	L		32	21	6	Maloney, Gail F.
1988		III	24		E	L		32	24	4	Maloney, Gail F.
1985		III	32		E	L		32	18	8	Maloney, Gail F.
1986		III	32		E	A		32	23	3	Maloney, Gail F.
1987		III	32		S	A		32	14	11	Jabir, James J.
1990		III	32		E	L		32	24	4	Maloney, Gail F.
1991		III	32		E	L		32	21	6	Maloney, Gail F.
1993		III	32		E	L		32	19	8	Maloney, Gail F.
1994		III	32		E	A	To R32	40	25	3	Maloney, Gail F.
1995		III	64		E	L		64	20	8	Maloney, Gail F.

BUFFALO STATE UNIVERSITY

Year	M/W	Div	F	SD	Reg	BD	Bye	#T	W	L	Coach
1957	M	II	8		ME	L		32	18	7	Serfustini, Dr. Leonard T.
1965		II	16		ME	L		32	19	3	Serfustini, Dr. Leonard T.
1958		II	24		E	L		32	17	8	Serfustini, Dr. Leonard T.
1959		II	24		NE	L		32	16	7	Serfustini, Dr. Leonard T.
1960		II	24		ME	L		32	16	7	Serfustini, Dr. Leonard T.
1963		II	32		ME	L		32	16	7	Serfustini, Dr. Leonard T.
1982		III	32		E	A		32	13	17	Hughes, Virgil William

BUTLER (IN)

Year	M/W	Div	F	SD	Reg	BD	Bye	#T	W	L	Coach
1962	M	I	12		ME	L		25	22	6	Hinkle, Paul D. "Tony"
1997		I	64	14	MW	A		64	23	10	Collier, Barry
1998		I	64	13	S	A		64	22	11	Collier, Barry
1983	W	II	24		GL	L		24	18	6	Mason, Linda
1996		I	64	15	ME	A		64	21	9	Olkowski, June

CABRINI

Year	M/W	Div	F	SD	Reg	BD	Bye	#T	W	L	Coach
1988	M	III	32		MA	L		32	23	7	Dzik, John L.
1995		III	32	4	MA	L		64	21	7	Dzik, John L.
1996		III	32	3	MA	C		64	24	3	Dzik, John L.
1994		III	40		MA	L		40	23	4	Dzik, John L.
1997		III	64	7	MA	A		64	16	9	Dzik, John L.
1995	W	III	64		MA	L		64	24	3	Welde, Dan V.
1996		III	64		MA	L		64	22	4	Welde, Dan V.
1997		III	64		MA	L		64	21	5	Welde, Dan V.

CALIFORNIA

Year	M/W	Div	F	SD	Reg	BD	Bye	#T	W	L	Coach
1959	M	I	1		W	A	To R16	23	25	4	Newell, Peter F.
1960		I	2		W	L		25	28	2	Newell, Peter F.
1946			4		W	L		8	30	6	Price, Clarence M. "Nibs"
1957		I	8		W	A	To R16	23	21	5	Newell, Peter F.

Year	M/W	Div	F	SD	Reg	BD	Bye	#T	W	L	Coach
1958		I	8		W	A	To R16	24	19	9	Newell, Peter F.
1993		I	16	6	MW	L		64	21	9	Bozeman, Todd
1997		I	16	5	E	L		64	23	9	Braun, Ben
1990		I	32	9	E	L		64	22	10	Campanelli, Lou
1994		I	64	5	W	L		64	22	8	Bozeman, Todd
1996		I	64	12	MW	L		64	17	11	Bozeman, Todd
1993	W	I	32		MW	L		48	19	10	Foster, Dr. Gooch
1990		I	48	11	W	L		48	17	12	Foster, Dr. Gooch
1992		I	48	5	W	L		48	20	9	Foster, Dr. Gooch

CALIFORNIA (PA)

Year	M/W	Div	F	SD	Reg	BD	Bye	#T	W	L	Coach
1992	M	II	3		E	A		32	31	2	Boone, Jim
1996		II	3	1	E	A	To R32	48	27	6	Boone, Jim
1988		II	16		E	A		32	25	6	Boone, Jim
1994		II	16		E	A		32	25	5	Boone, Jim
1995		II	16	2	E	L	To R32	48	23	7	Boone, Jim
1985		II	32		E	A		32	17	13	Loomis, Tim
1993		II	32		E	L		32	23	6	Boone, Jim
1998		II	48	4	E	L		48	23	5	Brown, William H.

CALIFORNIA LUTHERAN

Year	M/W	Div	F	SD	Reg	BD	Bye	#T	W	L	Coach
1992	M	III	16		W	A	To R32	40	16	12	Dunlop, Mike
1994		III	16		W	A	To R32	40	25	3	Dunlop, Mike
1993		III	32		W	L	To R32	40	20	7	Dunlop, Mike
1998	W	III	48	6	W	A		48	17	8	La Kose, Tim
1995		III	64		W	A		64	23	3	La Kose, Tim

CALIFORNIA POLYTECHNIC: POMONA

Year	M/W	Div	F	SD	Reg	BD	Bye	#T	W	L	Coach
1964	M	II	8		PC	L		32	23	6	Stull, Robert B. "Lefty"
1962		II	16		PC	L		32	17	8	Stull, Robert B. "Lefty"
1976		II	24		W	L		32	16	13	Hogan, Don
1982	W	II	1		W	A		16	29	7	May, Darlene
1985		II	1		W	L		24	21	7	May, Darlene
1986		II	1		W	A	To R16	24	30	3	May, Darlene
1983		II	2		W	A	To R16	24	29	3	May, Darlene
1987		II	2		W	A	To R16	24	29	3	May, Darlene
1989		II	2		W	A		32	28	6	May, Darlene
1990		II	3		W	A		32	29	4	May, Darlene
1988		II	8		W	A		32	28	4	May, Darlene
1991		II	8		W	A		32	22	9	May, Darlene
1993		II	8		W	A		32	27	3	May, Darlene
1984		II	16		W	A	To R16	24	22	7	May, Darlene
1992		II	32		W	A		32	23	6	May, Darlene
1997		II	32	3	W	A		48	22	8	Thomas, Paul
1998		II	48	6	W	A		48	18	11	Thomas, Paul

CALIFORNIA POLYTECHNIC: SAN LUIS OBISPO

Year	M/W	Div	F	SD	Reg	BD	Bye	#T	W	L	Coach
1981	M	II	3		E			32	24	8	Wheeler, Ernie
1977		II	8		W	A		32	19	11	Wheeler, Ernie
1980		II	16		W	A		32	22	7	Wheeler, Ernie
1982		II	16		W	L		32	23	6	Wheeler, Ernie

Year	M/W	Div	F	SD	Reg	BD	Bye	#T	W	L	Coach
1971		II	24		W	L		32	17	11	Stoner, Neale R.
1974		II	24		W	A	To R32	44	18	10	Wheeler, Ernie
1986		II	32		W	L		32	23	8	Wheeler, Ernie

CALIFORNIA STATE: BAKERSFIELD

Year	M/W	Div	F	SD	Reg	BD	Bye	#T	W	L	Coach
1993	M	II	1		W	A		32	33	0	Douglass, Pat
1994		II	1		W	L		32	27	6	Douglass, Pat
1997		II	1	1	W	A	To R32	48	29	4	Douglass, Pat
1990		II	2		W	A		32	29	5	Douglass, Pat
1983		II	3		W	L		32	25	5	Dye, Bobby
1991		II	3		W	A		32	25	8	Douglass, Pat
1992		II	3		W	A		32	26	7	Douglass, Pat
1982		II	4		W	A		32	25	6	Dye, Bobby
1996		II	8	1	W	A	To R32	48	26	4	Douglass, Pat
1973		II	16		W		To R32	42	19	9	Larson, Jim
1976		II	16		W	A		32	23	5	Wenihan, Pat
1989		II	16		W	L		32	21	9	Douglass, Pat
1988		II	24		W	A		32	21	10	Douglass, Pat
1984		II	32		GL	L		32	21	8	Parks, Jim
1998		II	32	2	W	A	To R32	48	25	3	Clark, Henry
1995		II	48	3	W	L		48	20	8	Douglass, Pat

CALIFORNIA STATE: CHICO

Year	M/W	Div	F	SD	Reg	BD	Bye	#T	W	L	Coach
1958	M	II	24		PC			32	10	17	Maxey, Gene
1974		II	32		W		To R32	44	20	10	Mathiesen, Peter
1981		II	32		W	A		32	18	11	Mathiesen, Peter
1991		II	32		W	A		32	22	10	Smith, Prescott "Puck"
1992		II	32		W	A		32	22	10	Smith, Prescott "Puck"
1993		II	32		W	A		32	23	5	Smith, Prescott "Puck"
1987	W	II	16		W	L		24	23	7	Coslet, Fran
1988		II	32		W	A		32	19	10	Coslet, Fran
1996		II	32	3	W	L		48	23	8	Lazzarini, Mary Ann

CALIFORNIA STATE: DOMINGUEZ HILLS

Year	M/W	Div	F	SD	Reg	BD	Bye	#T	W	L	Coach
1981	M	II	16		W			32	20	5	Yanai, David
1989		II	24		W	L		32	20	10	Yanai, David
1987		II	32		W	A		32	22	9	Yanai, David
1995	W	II	32	4	W	A		48	22	6	Girard, Van
1996		II	48	5	W	L		48	21	8	Girard, Van

CALIFORNIA STATE: FRESNO

Year	M/W	Div	F	SD	Reg	BD	Bye	#T	W	L	Coach
1963	M	II	8		PC			32	20	8	Miller, Harry E.
1966		II	8		PC		To R32	36	21	8	Gregory, Ed
1958		II	16		PC			32	19	8	Vandenburgh, William G.
1960		II	16		PC			32	18	10	Vandenburgh, William G.
1964		II	16		PC			32	20	5	Miller, Harry E.
1965		II	16		PC			32	20	7	Miller, Harry E.
1982		I	16	4	W	A	To R32	48	27	3	Grant, Boyd "Tiny"
1962		II	32		PC			32	19	7	Miller, Harry E.
1981		I	48	6	W	A		48	25	4	Grant, Boyd "Tiny"
1984		I	48	7	MW	A		53	25	8	Grant, Boyd "Tiny"

Year	M/W	Div	F	SD	Reg	BD	Bye	#T	W	L	Coach
CALIFORNIA STATE: FULLERTON											
1978	M	I	8		W	A		32	23	9	Dye, Bobby
1991	W	I	32	7	W	L		48	25	8	Jeremiah, Dr. Maryalyce
1989		I	48	7	W	L		48	21	9	Jeremiah, Dr. Maryalyce
CALIFORNIA STATE: HAYWARD											
1985	M	II	8		W	A		32	21	8	Hulst, Gary
1986		II	8		W	A		32	24	8	Hulst, Gary
1988		II	16		W	A		32	18	13	Hulst, Gary
1987		II	24		W	A		32	12	19	Hulst, Gary
1977		II	32		W	L		32	16	13	Staggers, Jonathan L.
1989	W	II	32		W	A		32	13	15	Oten, Barbara
CALIFORNIA STATE: LONG BEACH											
1971	M	I	8		W	L		25	24	5	Tarkanian, Jerry
1972		I	8		W	A		25	25	4	Tarkanian, Jerry
1973		I	12		W	A		25	26	3	Tarkanian, Jerry
1961		II	16		PC	L		32	15	11	Perry, Richard H.
1970		I	16		W	L		25	24	5	Tarkanian, Jerry
1977		I	32		W	A		32	21	8	Jones, Dwight
1993		I	64	11	W	A		64	22	10	Greenberg, Seth
1995		I	64	13	W	A		64	20	10	Greenberg, Seth
1987	W	I	3	1	W	A	To R32	40	33	3	Bonvicini, Joan
1988		I	3	2	W	A	To R32	40	28	6	Bonvicini, Joan
1983		I	8		W	L	To R32	36	24	7	Bonvicini, Joan
1984		I	8		W	L		32	25	6	Bonvicini, Joan
1985		I	8		W	A		32	28	3	Bonvicini, Joan
1989		I	8	2	E	A	To R32	48	30	5	Bonvicini, Joan
1982		I	16		W	A		32	24	6	Bonvicini, Joan
1986		I	16		W	L	To R32	40	29	5	Bonvicini, Joan
1991		I	16	4	W	A	To R32	48	24	8	Bonvicini, Joan
1990		I	32	6	W	L		48	25	9	Bonvicini, Joan
1992		I	48	10	W	L		48	21	10	McDonald, Glenn
CALIFORNIA STATE: LOS ANGELES											
1957	M	II	4		FW	L		32	20	11	Elliott, Abe "Sax"
1959		II	4		PC			32	20	8	Elliott, Abe "Sax"
1995		II	24	6	W	L		48	18	12	Dyer, Henry
1974		I	25		W	A		25	17	10	Miller, Robert
1998		II	32	4	W	L		48	18	11	Yanai, David
CALIFORNIA STATE: NORTHRIDGE											
1978	M	II	16		W	A		32	22	7	Cassidy, Peter L.
1985		II	16		W	A		32	20	10	Cassidy, Peter L.
1979		II	32		W	A		32	20	9	Cassidy, Peter L.
1986	W	II	16		W	L		24	20	9	Milke, Leslie
1989		II	16		W	L		32	22	9	Milke, Leslie

Year	M/W	Div	F	SD	Reg	BD	Bye	#T	W	L	Coach
CALIFORNIA STATE: SACRAMENTO											
1962	M	II	2		PC			32	21	10	Shelton, Everett F.
1959		II	32		PC			32	12	12	Wolf, Harold
1970		II	32		W	L		32	17	11	Heron, Jack
1988		II	32		W	L		32	22	8	Anders, Joe
CALIFORNIA STATE: SAN BERNARDINO											
1989	M	III	40		W	L		40	20	6	Ducey, James
1994	W	II	2		W	A		32	29	4	Beckley, Luvina
1988		III	32		W	L		32	23	5	Bly, Jo Anne
1990		III	32		W	L		32	24	4	Schwartz, Gary
1998		II	32	4	W	L		48	23	6	Becker, Kevin
CALIFORNIA STATE: STANISLAUS											
1982	M	III	4		W	L		32	18	13	Sanderson, Douglas R.
1983		III	8		W	L		32	16	13	Sanderson, Douglas R.
1989		III	8		W	L	To R32	40	21	8	Jones, John L.
1987		III	16		SA	L		32	20	8	Thomason, Bob
1981		III	32		W	L		32	16	12	Sanderson, Douglas R.
1989	W	III	2		W	L		32	27	2	Millar, Leann Henrich
1985		III	16		W	L		32	23	6	Millar, Leann Henrich
1990		II	16		W	A		32	22	7	Millar, Leann Henrich
1988		III	24		W	L		32	22	5	Millar, Leann Henrich
1987		III	32		W	L		32	19	9	Millar, Leann Henrich
1991		II	32		W	A		32	21	8	Millar, Leann Henrich
CALIFORNIA: DAVIS											
1998	M	II	1	1	W	A	To R32	48	31	2	Williams, Bob
1967		II	23		PC		To R32	36	21	7	Carlson, Joe E.
1975		II	24		W			32	16	12	Hamilton, Robert I.
1968		II	32		PC		To R32	36	16	11	Hamilton, Robert I.
1969		II	32		W	L		32	18	10	Hamilton, Robert I.
1976		II	32		W	L		32	18	10	Hamilton, Robert I.
1978		II	32		W	L		32	19	10	Hamilton, Robert I.
1995		II	32	5	W	A		48	20	11	Williams, Bob
1996		II	32	3	W	A		48	24	6	Williams, Bob
1997		II	48	5	W	A		48	20	9	Williams, Bob
1997	W	II	3	2	W	A	To R32	48	29	3	Simpson, Sandy
1991		II	16		W	L		32	26	5	Hoehn, Jorja E.
1992		II	16		W	A		32	25	3	Hoehn, Jorja E.
1995		II	16	1	W	A	To R32	48	25	4	Hoehn, Jorja E.
1996		II	16	2	W	A	To R32	48	25	4	Hoehn, Jorja E.
1998		II	16	3	W	A		48	23	7	Hoehn, Jorja E.
1986		II	24		W	L		24	18	9	Gill, Pam
1988		II	32		W	L		32	18	11	Gill, Pam
1990		II	32		W	L		32	20	8	Hoehn, Jorja E.
1993		II	32		W	A		32	19	7	Hoehn, Jorja E.
1994		II	32		W	A		32	22	7	Hoehn, Jorja E.

Year	M/W	Div	F	SD	Reg	BD	Bye	#T	W	L	Coach
CALIFORNIA: IRVINE											
1968	M	II	16		PC	L	To R32	36	20	8	Davis, Richard L.
1969		II	24		W	L		32	19	9	Davis, Richard L.
1972		II	32		W	L	To R32	36	16	12	Tift, Timothy
1975		II	32		W	L		32	16	11	Tift, Timothy
1995	W	I	64	15	W	A		64	19	11	Matsuhara, Colleen
CALIFORNIA: LOS ANGELES											
1964	M	I	1		W	A	To R16	25	30	0	Wooden, John R.
1965		I	1		FW	A	To R16	23	28	2	Wooden, John R.
1967		I	1		W	A	To R16	23	30	0	Wooden, John R.
1968		I	1		W	A	To R16	23	29	1	Wooden, John R.
1969		I	1		W	A	To R16	25	29	1	Wooden, John R.
1970		I	1		W	A	To R16	25	28	2	Wooden, John R.
1971		I	1		W	A	To R16	25	29	1	Wooden, John R.
1972		I	1		W	A	To R16	25	30	0	Wooden, John R.
1973		I	1		W	A	To R16	25	30	0	Wooden, John R.
1975		I	1		W	A		32	28	3	Wooden, John R.
1995		I	1	1	W	A		64	31	2	Harrick, Jim
1980		I	2	8	W	L		48	22	10	Brown, Lawrence H.
1974		I	3		W	A	To R16	25	26	4	Wooden, John R.
1976		I	3		W	A		32	27	5	Bartow, B. Gene
1962		I	4		W	A	To R16	25	18	11	Wooden, John R.
1950			8		W	L		8	24	7	Wooden, John R.
1979		I	8	1	W	A	To R32	40	25	5	Cunningham, Dr. Gary A.
1992		I	8	1	W	A		64	28	5	Harrick, Jim
1997		I	8	2	MW	A		64	24	8	Lavin, Steve
1956			12		FW	A	To R16	25	22	6	Wooden, John R.
1952			16		W(B)	A		16	20	12	Wooden, John R.
1963		I	16		W	A	To R16	25	20	9	Wooden, John R.
1977		I	16		W	A		32	24	5	Bartow, B. Gene
1978		I	16		W	A		32	25	3	Cunningham, Dr. Gary A.
1990		I	16	7	E	A		64	22	11	Harrick, Jim
1998		I	16	6	S	L		64	24	9	Lavin, Steve
1981		I	32	3	E	L	To R32	48	20	7	Brown, Lawrence H.
1983		I	32	2	W	A	To R32	52	23	6	Farmer, Larry
1987		I	32	4	W	A		64	25	7	Hazzard, Walter R., Jr.
1989		I	32	7	SE	L		64	21	10	Harrick, Jim
1993		I	32	9	W	L		64	22	11	Harrick, Jim
1991		I	64	4	E	L		64	23	9	Harrick, Jim
1994		I	64	5	MW	L		64	21	7	Harrick, Jim
1996		I	64	4	SE	A		64	23	8	Harrick, Jim
1985	W	I	16		W	L		32	20	10	Moore, Billie Jean
1992		I	16	5	MW	L		48	21	10	Moore, Billie Jean
1983		I	32		W	L	To R32	36	18	11	Moore, Billie Jean
1998		I	32	7	MW	L		64	20	9	Oliver, Kathy
1990		I	48	10	W	L		48	17	12	Moore, Billie Jean

Year	M/W	Div	F	SD	Reg	BD	Bye	#T	W	L	Coach
CALIFORNIA: RIVERSIDE											
1995	M	II	2	1	W	A	To R32	48	26	6	Masi, John
1970		II	3		W	L		32	19	10	Goss, Freddie
1989		II	3		W	A		32	30	4	Masi, John
1973		II	8		W			42	25	5	Goss, Freddie
1974		II	8		W	L	To R32	44	18	10	Goss, Freddie
1975		II	8		W			32	19	9	Goss, Freddie
1980		II	8		W	L		32	22	6	Masi, John
1979		II	16		W	L		32	21	5	Goss, Freddie
1988		II	16		NC	L		32	22	8	Masi, John
1992		II	16		W	L		32	24	6	Masi, John
1994		II	16		W	A		32	22	7	Masi, John
1972		II	24		W		To R32	36	19	9	Goss, Freddie
1986		II	24		W	A		32	24	7	Masi, John
1991		II	24		W	L		32	22	7	Masi, John
1984		II	32		W	A		32	22	6	Masi, John
1990		II	32		W	L		32	21	10	Masi, John
1997		II	48	6	W	L		48	17	9	Masi, John
1993	W	II	32		W	L		32	17	11	Woelke, Debi
1995		II	48	5	W	L		48	19	10	Woelke, Debi
1996		II	48	6	W	A		48	17	13	Woelke, Debi
CALIFORNIA: SAN DIEGO											
1991	M	III	16		W	L	To R32	40	23	4	Marshall, Thomas O.
1990		III	32		W	L	To R32	40	20	7	Marshall, Thomas O.
1992		III	32		W	L	To R32	40	22	5	Marshall, Thomas O.
1994		III	32		W	L		40	21	5	Marshall, Thomas O.
1996	W	III	32		W	L		64	19	7	Malone, Judy
1997		III	32		W	L		64	20	6	Malone, Judy
1998		III	32	3	W	L		48	23	4	Malone, Judy
1995		III	64		W	L		64	18	7	Malone, Judy
CALIFORNIA: SANTA BARBARA											
1961	M	II	8		PC			32	20	8	Gallon, Dr. Arthur J.
1963		II	24		PC			32	16	9	Gallon, Dr. Arthur J.
1990		I	32	9	SE	L		64	21	9	Pimm, Jerry
1988		I	64	10	SE	L		64	22	8	Pimm, Jerry
1992	W	I	32	9	W	A		48	27	5	French, Mark
1993		I	32		W	A		48	19	12	French, Mark
1998		I	32	11	ME	A		64	27	6	French, Mark
1997		I	64	13	E	A		64	24	6	French, Mark
CALVIN											
1992	M	III	1		GL	A	To R32	40	31	1	Douma, Edward
1990		III	4		GL	A	To R32	40	28	3	Douma, Edward
1991		III	8		GL	L		40	25	4	Douma, Edward
1993		III	8		GL	A	To R32	40	25	3	Douma, Edward
1980		III	24		GL	A		32	18	6	Vroon, A. Donald
1987		III	24		GL	L		32	21	5	Douma, Edward
1989		III	24		GL	A		40	19	7	Douma, Edward
1981		III	32		GL	A		32	15	11	Vroon, A. Donald

Year	M/W	Div	F	SD	Reg	BD	Bye	#T	W	L	Coach
1986		III	32		GL	A		32	20	6	Douma, Edward
1994		III	32		GL	A	To R32	40	20	7	Douma, Edward
1995		III	64	5	GL	L		64	17	10	Douma, Edward
1988	W	III	24		GL	L		32	21	5	Vroon, A. Donald
1991		III	32		GL	L		32	18	8	Vroon, A. Donald
1993		III	32		C	A		32	18	8	Struyk, Sandi
1996		III	32		GL	A		64	23	4	Afman, Gregg
1997		III	32		GL	L		64	23	4	Afman, Gregg
1998		III	32	4	GL	L		48	23	5	Afman, Gregg

CAMPBELL

Year	M/W	Div	F	SD	Reg	BD	Bye	#T	W	L	Coach
1992	M	I	64	16	E	A		64	19	12	Lee, Billy

CANISIUS

Year	M/W	Div	F	SD	Reg	BD	Bye	#T	W	L	Coach
1955	M		8		E(B)	A		24	18	7	Curran, J. Joseph
1956			8		E	L		25	19	7	Curran, J. Joseph
1957		I	12		E	L		23	22	6	Curran, J. Joseph
1996		I	64	13	MW	A		64	19	11	Beilein, John
1983	W	II	8		E	L	To R16	24	28	5	Pares, Sr. Maria

CAPITAL

Year	M/W	Div	F	SD	Reg	BD	Bye	#T	W	L	Coach
1982	M	III	8		S	L		32	20	9	Grube, David
1970		II	24		GL	L		32	20	4	Chickerella, Vincent
1973		II	24		GL		To R32	42	22	5	Chickerella, Vincent
1983		III	24		GL	L		32	22	7	Grube, David
1984		III	24		GL	A		32	23	6	Grube, David
1957		II	32		ME	A		32	14	6	Regan, Harold E.
1996		III	32	5	GL	L		64	19	8	Goodwin, Damon
1989		III	40		GL	L		40	21	7	Cecutti, Dave
1994	W	III	1		A	A	To R32	40	30	1	Jeffers, Dixie M.
1995		III	1		A	A		64	33	0	Jeffers, Dixie M.
1993		III	2		NE	A		32	28	4	Jeffers, Dixie M.
1986		III	3		A	L		32	27	4	Pirtle, Laurie
1997		III	3		GL	A		64	29	4	Jeffers, Dixie M.
1992		III	8		A	A		32	29	2	Jeffers, Dixie M.
1985		III	16		A	L		32	23	2	Pirtle, Laurie
1987		III	32		A	A		32	21	5	Jeffers, Dixie M.
1991		III	32		A	L		32	24	3	Jeffers, Dixie M.
1996		III	32		A	A		64	23	5	Jeffers, Dixie M.

CARNEGIE MELLON

Year	M/W	Div	F	SD	Reg	BD	Bye	#T	W	L	Coach
1977	M	III	30		GL	A		30	18	6	Maloney, Dave
1989	W	III	32		MA	L		32	20	7	Seidl, Gerri
1991		III	32		MA	A		32	21	6	Seidl, Gerri

CARROLL (WI)

Year	M/W	Div	F	SD	Reg	BD	Bye	#T	W	L	Coach
1984	W	III	32		GL	L		32	20	6	Steffen, Daniel
1985		III	32		GL	A		32	22	6	Steffen, Daniel
1986		III	32		C	L		32	21	7	Steffen, Daniel

CARSON-NEWMAN

Year	M/W	Div	F	SD	Reg	BD	Bye	#T	W	L	Coach
1995	W	II	48	5	SA	L		48	21	9	Carter, Eddie
1998		II	48	6	SA	L		48	22	7	Carter, Eddie

Year	M/W	Div	F	SD	Reg	BD	Bye	#T	W	L	Coach
CARTHAGE											
1996	W	III	64		C	L		64	18	8	Fanning, Rich
CATAWBA											
1998	M	II	16	1	SA	A	To R32	48	25	6	Baker, Jim
CATHOLIC											
1944	M		8		E	L		8	17	7	Long, John J.
1998		III	16	2	MA	A	To R32	48	25	4	Lonergan, Mike
1964		II	32		E			32	16	12	Young, Thomas J.
1993		III	40		A	L		40	21	6	Lonergan, Mike
1996		III	64	6	MA	L		64	19	8	Lonergan, Mike
CENTENARY (LA)											
1959	M	II	16		SW	L		32	14	14	Sigler, Orvis
1957		II	32		ME	L		32	16	9	Mooty, Harold D.
1958		II	32		SW	L		32	13	10	Mooty, Harold D.
CENTRAL (IA)											
1977	M	III	16		MW	L		30	17	6	Walvoord, Jack
1979		III	16		MW	A		32	20	5	Walvoord, Jack
1985		III	16		W	A		32	16	9	Walvoord, Jack
1978		III	23		MW	L		30	21	4	Walvoord, Jack
1980		III	32		MW	A		32	18	8	Walvoord, Jack
1991		III	32		W	A		40	16	7	Walvoord, Jack
1994		III	32		W	A	To R32	40	13	10	Walvoord, Jack
1995		III	64	7	W			64	15	11	Walvoord, Jack
1993	W	III	1		C	A		32	24	5	Boeyink, Gary
1983		III	16		C	L		32	18	6	Boeyink, Gary
1994		III	32		C	A		40	22	5	Boeyink, Gary
1995		III	32		C			64	18	7	Boeyink, Gary
1998		III	32	5	W	A		48	18	8	Boeyink, Gary
CENTRAL ARKANSAS											
1996	W	II	32	4	S	L		48	21	10	Marvel, Ronnie
CENTRAL CONNECTICUT STATE											
1966	M	II	8		NE	L		36	23	3	Detrick, William
1971		II	16		NENG	L		32	20	7	Detrick, William
1984		II	24		NENG	L		32	26	6	Detrick, William
1967		II	32		NE	L		36	17	8	Detrick, William
1969		II	32		NENG	L		32	20	8	Detrick, William
1983		II	32		NENG	L		32	21	9	Detrick, William
1986	W	II	8		NENG	L	To R16	24	24	4	Reilly, Dr. Brenda
CENTRAL FLORIDA											
1978	M	II	4		S	A		32	26	4	Clark, Eugene A. "Torchy"
1977		II	16		S	A		32	24	4	Clark, Eugene A. "Torchy"
1980		II	16		S	L		32	25	4	Clark, Eugene A. "Torchy"
1981		II	16		S	L		32	23	5	Clark, Eugene A. "Torchy"
1990		II	16		SA	L		32	26	4	Folliard, Thomas J.
1976		II	32		S	A		32	20	5	Clark, Eugene A. "Torchy"
1982		II	32		SC	L		32	21	8	Clark, Eugene A. "Torchy"
1989		II	32		S	L		32	22	8	Folliard, Thomas J.

Year	M/W	Div	F	SD	Reg	BD	Bye	#T	W	L	Coach
1994		I	64	16	SE	A		64	21	9	Speraw, Kirk
1996		I	64	16	E	A		64	11	19	Speraw, Kirk
1993	W	II	16		S	L		32	26	4	Reynolds, John, Jr.
1983		II	24		S	L		24	25	5	Sanchez, Joe
1984		II	24		NENG	L		24	23	7	Sanchez, Joe
1992		II	32		S	L		32	25	4	Reynolds, John, Jr.
1996		I	64	16	MW	A		64	15	14	Richardson, Jerry

CENTRAL MICHIGAN

Year	M/W	Div	F	SD	Reg	BD	Bye	#T	W	L	Coach
1975	M	I	12		ME	A		32	22	6	Parfitt, Richard
1965		II	16		GL	L		32	19	7	Kjolhede, Theodore
1970		II	16		GL	L		32	21	5	Kjolhede, Theodore
1971		II	16		GL	L		32	18	9	Kjolhede, Theodore
1977		I	32		ME	A		32	18	10	Parfitt, Richard
1987		I	64	13	W	A		64	22	8	Coles, Charles "Charlie"
1983	W	I	32		E	A	To R32	36	21	9	Golden, Laura L.
1984		I	32		ME	A		32	27	3	Golden, Laura L.

CENTRAL MISSOURI STATE

Year	M/W	Div	F	SD	Reg	BD	Bye	#T	W	L	Coach
1984	M	II	1		SC	A		32	29	3	Nance, Lynn
1995		II	8	5	SC	L		48	24	8	Sundvold, Bob
1970		II	16		MW	L		32	19	6	Short, Norman N.
1983		II	16		SC	L		32	23	7	Nance, Lynn
1989		II	16		SC	L		32	22	9	Wooldridge, Jim
1990		II	16		W	L		32	27	6	Wooldridge, Jim
1991		II	16		SC	L		32	27	5	Wooldridge, Jim
1965		II	24		SW			32	19	6	Hall, Joe B.
1980		II	24		SC	A		32	26	2	Smith, Tom
1982		II	24		SC	L		32	20	9	Nance, Lynn
1985		II	24		SC	L		32	22	7	Nance, Lynn
1994		II	24		SC	L		32	22	8	Sundvold, Bob
1981		II	32		NC	L		32	20	9	Nance, Lynn
1996		II	32	4	SC	L		48	22	9	Sundvold, Bob
1997		II	48	6	SC	L		48	21	8	Doucette, Don
1984	W	II	1		SC	A	To R16	24	28	4	Hoehn, Jorja E.
1985		II	2		SC	A	To R16	24	27	5	Hoehn, Jorja E.
1983		II	3		SC	A	To R16	24	29	3	Hoehn, Jorja E.
1989		II	4		SC	A		32	29	5	Pye, Jon
1986		II	8		SC	A	To R16	24	23	6	Pye, Jon
1990		II	8		SC	A		32	29	3	Pye, Jon
1987		II	16		SC	L		24	23	7	Pye, Jon
1988		II	16		SC	A		32	26	5	Pye, Jon
1991		II	32		SC	L		32	23	6	Pye, Jon
1993		II	32		SC	L		32	19	10	Pye, Jon
1998		II	32	5	SC	L		48	19	10	Ballard, Scott
1997		II	48	6	SC	L		48	21	9	Ballard, Scott

Year	M/W	Div	F	SD	Reg	BD	Bye	#T	W	L	Coach
CENTRAL OKLAHOMA											
1992	M	II	8		SC	L		32	25	7	Seward, Jim
1995		II	16	2	SC	A	To R32	48	23	7	Seward, Jim
1998		II	16	3	SC	A		48	25	7	Seward, Jim
1993		II	23		SC	L		32	23	6	Seward, Jim
1997		II	32	1	SC	A	To R32	48	24	5	Seward, Jim
CENTRAL STATE (OH)											
1982	M	II	16		GL	L		32	21	8	Wims, Dr. Lu D.
CENTRE											
1979	M	III	4		S	L		32	25	5	Bryant, Tom C.
1989		III	4		S	A	To R32	40	24	7	Bryant, Tom C.
1985		III	8		S	A		32	19	8	Bryant, Tom C.
1986		III	16		S	A		32	21	7	Bryant, Tom C.
1988		III	16		S	A		32	13	15	Bryant, Tom C.
1964		II	32		SC	L		32	14	8	Phillips, Lewis
1983		III	32		S	A		32	16	11	Bryant, Tom C.
1984		III	32		S	A		32	18	9	Bryant, Tom C.
1987		III	32		S	A		32	20	8	Bryant, Tom C.
1992		III	32		S	A	To R32	40	19	8	Bryant, Tom C.
1989	W	III	3		S	L		32	23	8	Wise, Lea
1990		III	4		S	A		32	22	8	Noble-Hauserman, Cindy
1987		III	16		S	L		32	22	5	Wise, Lea
1988		III	24		S	L		32	23	6	Wise, Lea
1991		III	32		S	A		32	17	7	Noble-Hauserman, Cindy
CHADRON STATE											
1995	W	II	48	6	SC	A		48	22	8	Anderson, Tom
CHAMINADE											
1979	M	III	8		W	L		32	24	5	Lopes, Merv
CHAPMAN											
1960	M	II	2		PC	L		32	24	6	Perkins, Donald C.
1958		II	8		PC	L		32	22	5	Perkins, Donald C.
1959		II	16		PC	L		32	23	4	Perkins, Donald C.
1963		II	16		PC	L		32	20	7	Perkins, Donald C.
1983		II	16		W	L		32	21	8	Hazzard, Walter R., Jr.
1961		II	24		PC	L		32	17	11	Perkins, Donald C.
1984		II	24		W	L		32	22	6	Hazzard, Walter R., Jr.
1957		II	32		FW	L		32	16	11	Perkins, Donald C.
1978		II	32		NC	L		32	19	10	Rider, Dr. Rich
1982	W	II	8		SC	L		16	23	5	Berger, Brian
1984		II	8		W	L		24	26	5	Berger, Brian
1983		II	16		W	L		24	22	8	Berger, Brian
1985		II	16		W	A	To R16	24	25	4	Berger, Brian
1997		III	64		W	L		64	19	7	Hegarty, Mary

Year	M/W	Div	F	SD	Reg	BD	Bye	#T	W	L	Coach
CHARLESTON (SC)											
1997	M	I	32	12	SE	A		64	29	3	Kresse, John
1994		I	64	12	SE	L		64	24	4	Kresse, John
1998		I	64	14	MW	A		64	24	6	Kresse, John
CHARLESTON (WV)											
1998	W	II	48	5	E	A		48	21	9	Bennett-Travinski, Linda
CHARLESTON SOUTHERN											
1997	M	I	64	15	MW	A		64	15	15	Conrad, Tom
CHEYNEY											
1978	M	II	1		E	L		32	27	2	Chaney, John
1979		II	3		E	L		32	24	7	Chaney, John
1986		II	3		E	A		32	28	5	Songster, Charles
1967		II	8		E		To R32	36	23	7	Blitman, Howard
1968		II	8		E	L	To R32	36	22	7	Blitman, Howard
1971		II	8		ME	L		32	23	6	Coma, Dr. Anthony S. "Doc"
1976		II	8		E	L		32	24	5	Chaney, John
1977		II	8		E	L		32	20	8	Chaney, John
1982		II	8		E	A		32	28	3	Chaney, John
1966		II	16		E		To R32	36	26	1	Blitman, Howard
1969		II	16		MW	L		32	25	3	Coma, Dr. Anthony S. "Doc"
1965		II	24		E			32	24	1	Blitman, Howard
1970		II	24		ME	L		32	25	3	Coma, Dr. Anthony S. "Doc"
1973		II	24		ME			42	23	5	Chaney, John
1980		II	24		E	L		32	23	5	Chaney, John
1981		II	24		SA	L		32	21	8	Chaney, John
1972		II	32		ME		To R32	36	22	6	Coma, Dr. Anthony S. "Doc"
1983		II	32		E	A		32	26	6	Songster, Charles
1982	W	I	2		E	L		32	28	3	Stringer, C. Vivian
1984		I	3		E	L		32	25	5	McGriff, Winthrop "Windy"
1983		I	16		E	L	To R32	36	27	3	Stringer, C. Vivian
CHICAGO											
1961	M	II	8		GL	L		32	19	4	Stampf, Joseph M.
1997		III	16	2	MW	A		64	23	5	Cunningham, Pat
1998		III	16	2	MW	A	To R32	48	23	3	Cunningham, Pat
1974		II	44		GL	L		44	16	4	Stampf, Joseph M
1995	W	III	64		C	L		64	19	7	Zawacki, Susan M.
CHRISTOPHER NEWPORT											
1991	M	III	16		S	A	To R32	40	24	5	Woollum, C. J.
1993		III	16		S	A	To R32	40	23	5	Woollum, C. J.
1996		III	16	2	S	A		64	24	6	Woollum, C. J.
1998		III	16	1	S	A	To R32	48	26	2	Woollum, C. J.
1986		III	24		S	A		32	19	11	Woollum, C. J.
1988		III	32		S	A		32	15	15	Woollum, C. J.
1994		III	32		S	L	To R32	40	22	5	Woollum, C. J.
1997		III	32	8	S	L		64	19	8	Woollum, C. J.

Year	M/W	Div	F	SD	Reg	BD	Bye	#T	W	L	Coach
1989		III	40		S	A		40	17	12	Woollum, C. J.
1990		III	40		S	L		40	19	9	Woollum, C. J.
1995		III	64	8	S	L		64	18	10	Woollum, C. J.
1982	W	III	16		None	L		16	15	10	Zachensky-Walthall, Susan
1992		III	16		S	L		32	22	6	Parson, Cathy
1986		III	32		S	A		32	20	9	Zachensky-Walthall, Susan
1993		III	32		W	A		32	19	9	Parson, Cathy
1998		III	32	4	S	A		48	24	4	Parson, Cathy
1995		III	64		S	L		64	17	9	Parson, Cathy
1997		III	64		S	L		64	20	7	Parson, Cathy

CINCINNATI

Year	M/W	Div	F	SD	Reg	BD	Bye	#T	W	L	Coach
1961	M	I	1		MW	A	To R16	24	27	3	Jucker, Edwin L.
1962		I	1		MW	A	To R16	25	29	2	Jucker, Edwin L.
1963		I	2		MW	A	To R16	25	26	2	Jucker, Edwin L.
1959		I	3		MW	A	To R16	23	26	4	Smith, George D.
1960		I	3		MW	A	To R16	25	28	2	Smith, George D.
1992		I	3	4	MW	L		64	29	5	Huggins, Robert
1993		I	8	2	E	L		64	27	5	Huggins, Robert
1996		I	8	2	SE	L		64	28	5	Huggins, Robert
1958		I	12		MW	A	To R16	24	25	3	Smith, George D.
1975		I	12		MW	L		32	23	6	Catlett, Gale
1966		I	16		MW	A	To R16	22	21	7	Baker, Taylor "Tay"
1976		I	32		MW	L		32	25	6	Catlett, Gale
1977		I	32		MW	A		32	25	5	Catlett, Gale
1995		I	32	7	W	L		64	22	12	Huggins, Robert
1997		I	32	3	MW	L		64	26	8	Huggins, Robert
1998		I	32	2	W	A		64	27	6	Huggins, Robert
1994		I	64	8	W	L		64	22	10	Huggins, Robert
1989	W	I	48	8	W	L		48	21	9	Pirtle, Laurie

CITY COLLEGE

Year	M/W	Div	F	SD	Reg	BD	Bye	#T	W	L	Coach
1950	M		1		E	L		8	24	5	Holman, Nathan "Nat"
1947			4		E	L		8	17	6	Holman, Nathan "Nat"
1976		III	14		E	L		28	16	14	Layne, Floyd
1957		II	32		E	L		32	11	8	Polansky, David
1996	W	III	64		E	A		64	16	12	English, Stephanie

CLAREMONT MCKENNA

Year	M/W	Div	F	SD	Reg	BD	Bye	#T	W	L	Coach
1984	M	III	24		W	L		32	16	10	Wells, David
1987		III	24		W	A		32	21	7	Wells, David
1988		III	32		W	A		32	19	8	Wells, David
1991		III	32		W	A	To R32	40	22	5	Wells, David
1996		III	32	5	W	A		64	19	8	Wells, David
1990		III	40		W	A		40	18	9	Wells, David
1995	W	III	32		W	L		64	22	5	Burton, Jodie
1996		III	32		W			64	20	8	Burton, Jodie

Year	M/W	Div	F	SD	Reg	BD	Bye	#T	W	L	Coach
CLARION											
1981	M	II	16		E	L		32	23	6	DeGregorio, Joseph
1991	W	II	8		E	A		32	24	8	Parsons, Margaret Rhoads "Gie"
1994		II	8		E	A		32	26	4	Parsons, Margaret Rhoads "Gie"
1992		II	16		E	L		32	25	4	Parsons, Margaret Rhoads "Gie"
1993		II	16		E	A		32	24	6	Parsons, Margaret Rhoads "Gie"
1995		II	48	4	E	L		48	18	11	Parsons, Margaret Rhoads "Gie"
CLARK (MA)											
1984	M	III	2		NE	L		32	21	7	Halas, Wally
1987		III	2		NE	L		32	27	3	Halas, Wally
1979		III	8		NE	L		32	20	6	Halas, Wally
1981		III	8		NE	L		32	24	3	Halas, Wally
1983		III	8		NE	L		32	23	4	Halas, Wally
1988		III	8		NE	L		32	21	7	Clark, Kevin
1980		III	16		NE	L		32	21	6	Halas, Wally
1985		III	16		NE	L		32	20	6	Halas, Wally
1978		III	23		NE	L		30	17	7	Halas, Wally
1982		III	24		NE	L		32	17	9	Halas, Wally
1986		III	24		NE	L		32	21	6	Halas, Wally
1982	W	III	4		None	L		16	18	11	Stevens, Barbara
1983		III	4		NE	L		32	21	8	Stevens, Barbara
1989		III	8		NE	L		32	28	1	Glispin, Patricia
1987		III	32		NE	L		32	19	8	Glispin, Patricia
1992		III	32		NE	L		32	22	5	Glispin, Patricia
1995		III	32		NE	L		64	19	8	Glispin, Patricia
1998		III	48	6	NE	A		48	20	8	Glispin, Patricia
1997		III	64		NE	A		64	24	4	Glispin, Patricia
CLARK ATLANTA											
1977	M	III	30		S	A		30	20	7	Epps, Leonidas S. II "Sonny"
1996		II	48	5	S	L		48	21	8	Witherspoon, Anthony
1982	W	II	16		S	A		16	14	12	Witherspoon, Anthony
1985		II	16		GL	A		24	19	12	Witherspoon, Anthony
1986		II	24		S	A		24	18	12	Moseley, Michael
CLARKSON (NY)											
1989	W	III	4		E	L		32	26	7	Chafin, Brian
CLEMSON											
1980	M	I	8	6	W	L		48	23	9	Foster, William C.
1990		I	16	5	E	L		64	26	9	Ellis, Cliff
1997		I	16	4	MW	L		64	23	10	Barnes, Richard D. "Rick"
1989		I	32	9	W	L		64	19	11	Ellis, Cliff
1987		I	64	4	SE	L		64	25	6	Ellis, Cliff
1996		I	64	9	W	L		64	18	11	Barnes, Richard D. "Rick"
1998		I	64	6	MW	L		64	18	14	Barnes, Richard D. "Rick"
1991	W	I	8	4	E	L	To R32	48	22	11	Davis, Jim
1989		I	16	4	ME	L	To R32	48	20	11	Davis, Jim
1990		I	16	5	E	L		48	22	10	Davis, Jim
1982		I	32		MW	L		32	20	12	Tribble, Annie S.

Year	M/W	Div	F	SD	Reg	BD	Bye	#T	W	L	Coach
1988		I	32	5	E	L	To R32	40	21	9	Davis, Jim
1992		I	32	5	E	L		48	21	10	Davis, Jim
1993		I	32		MW	L		48	19	11	Davis, Jim
1994		I	32	9	ME	L		64	20	10	Davis, Jim
1996		I	32	3	MW	A		64	23	8	Davis, Jim
1998		I	32	6	MW	L		64	25	8	Davis, Jim
1997		I	64	5	ME	L		64	19	11	Davis, Jim

CLEVELAND STATE (OH)

Year	M/W	Div	F	SD	Reg	BD	Bye	#T	W	L	Coach
1986	M	I	16	14	E	L		64	29	4	Mackey, Kevin

COAST GUARD

Year	M/W	Div	F	SD	Reg	BD	Bye	#T	W	L	Coach
1979	M	III	24		NE	L		32	21	3	Broaca, Peter F.

COASTAL CAROLINA

Year	M/W	Div	F	SD	Reg	BD	Bye	#T	W	L	Coach
1991	M	I	64	15	SE	P		64	24	8	Bergman, Russell W.
1993		I	64	16	W	A		64	22	10	Bergman, Russell W.

COE

Year	M/W	Div	F	SD	Reg	BD	Bye	#T	W	L	Coach
1973	M	II	8		MW		To R32	42	24	1	Jackson, Marcus
1976		III	14		MW	A		28	23	1	Tune, Don
1975		III	23		MW	L		30	18	6	Tune, Don
1974		II	44		GL	L		44	18	5	Jackson, Marcus

COLBY

Year	M/W	Div	F	SD	Reg	BD	Bye	#T	W	L	Coach
1994	M	III	32		NE	L	To R32	40	21	4	Whitmore, Richard
1995		III	64	5	NE	L		64	20	5	Whitmore, Richard
1997		III	64	5	NE	L		64	20	5	Whitmore, Richard

COLBY-SAWYER

Year	M/W	Div	F	SD	Reg	BD	Bye	#T	W	L	Coach
1998	W	III	48	4	A	A		48	22	5	Martin, George
1997		III	64		A	A		64	23	5	Martin, George

COLGATE

Year	M/W	Div	F	SD	Reg	BD	Bye	#T	W	L	Coach
1995	M	I	64	16	MW	A		64	17	13	Bruen, Jack
1996		I	64	16	SE	A		64	15	15	Bruen, Jack

COLORADO

Year	M/W	Div	F	SD	Reg	BD	Bye	#T	W	L	Coach
1942	M		3		W	L		8	16	2	Cox, Forrest B. "Frosty"
1955			3		W(A)	A	To R16	24	19	6	Lee, Horace B. "Bebe"
1946			6		W	L		8	12	6	Cox, Forrest B. "Frosty"
1940			8		W	L		8	17	4	Cox, Forrest B. "Frosty"
1962		I	8		MW	A	To R16	25	19	7	Walseth, Russell M. "Sox"
1963		I	8		MW	A	To R16	25	19	7	Walseth, Russell M. "Sox"
1969		I	12		MW	A	To R16	25	21	7	Walseth, Russell M. "Sox"
1954			16		W(A)	A	To R16	24	11	11	Lee, Horace B. "Bebe"
1997		I	32	9	E	L		64	22	10	Patton, Ricardo
1993	W	I	8	4	W	L	To R32	48	27	4	Barry, Ceal
1995		I	8	1	MW	A		64	30	3	Barry, Ceal
1994		I	16	3	W	L		64	27	5	Barry, Ceal
1997		I	16	2	MW	A		64	23	9	Barry, Ceal
1988		I	32	7	W	L		40	21	11	Barry, Ceal
1989		I	32	3	W	A	To R32	48	27	4	Barry, Ceal
1996		I	32	3	W	A		64	26	9	Barry, Ceal
1992		I	48	7	MW	A		48	22	9	Barry, Ceal

Year	M/W	Div	F	SD	Reg	BD	Bye	#T	W	L	Coach
COLORADO CHRISTIAN											
1993	M	II	32		NC	A		32	20	9	Evans, Frank
COLORADO COLLEGE											
1960	M	II	32		SW	L		32	17	5	Eastlack, Leon C. "Red"
1961		II	32		SW			32	18	9	Eastlack, Leon C. "Red"
1992		III	32		W	L		40	22	5	Walker, Al
1990	W	III	32		W	L		32	17	9	Branson, Beth
COLORADO STATE											
1969	M	I	8		MW	L		25	17	7	Williams, James J.
1954			16		W(B)	A	To R16	24	22	7	Strannigan, William M.
1966		I	22		W	L		22	14	8	Williams, James J.
1965		I	23		FW	L		23	16	8	Williams, James J.
1963		I	25		MW	L		25	18	5	Williams, James J.
1989		I	32	10	MW	L		64	23	10	Grant, Boyd "Tiny"
1990		I	64	10	W	L		64	21	9	Grant, Boyd "Tiny"
1996	W	I	32	8	W	A		64	26	5	Williams, Greg
1998		I	32	12	MW	L		64	24	6	Collen, Tim
COLUMBIA (NY)											
1948	M		8		E	L		8	21	3	Ridings, Gordon H.
1968		I	12		E	L		23	23	5	Rohan, John P. "Jack"
1951			16		E	A		16	21	1	Rossini, Lucio "Lou"
1986	W	III	24		E	L		32	21	6	Kalafies, Nancy
COLUMBUS STATE (GA)											
1996	M	II	16	3	S	A		48	26	6	Greene, Herbert
1984		II	24		SC	L		32	22	7	Eidsness, John
1978		II	32		SC	L		32	19	8	Clements, Frank M. "Sonny"
1998		II	48	5	SA	A		48	26	7	Greene, Herbert
1998	W	II	32	3	SA	A		48	25	6	Sparks, Jay
CONCORD											
1997	M	II	16	6	E	A		48	20	13	Cox, Steve
CONCORDIA (IL)											
1962	M	II	16		GL	L		32	20	4	Spitz, Donald A.
1963		II	24		GL	L		32	19	5	Spitz, Donald A.
1965		II	32		GL	L		32	18	6	Faszholz, Thomas O.
1969		II	32		GL	L		32	20	4	Faszholz, Thomas O.
CONCORDIA: MOORHEAD											
1996	M	III	64	7	W	L		64	21	6	Siverson, Duane
1988	W	III	1		W	A		32	29	2	Siverson, Duane
1987		III	2		W	A		32	26	5	Siverson, Duane
1990		III	8		W	A		32	24	5	Siverson, Duane
1991		III	8		W	L		32	21	8	Siverson, Duane
1993		III	8		W	L		32	20	7	Kohler, Robert
1983		III	16		W	L		32	18	10	Langseth, Marc
1984		III	16		W	L		32	21	7	Langseth, Marc
1986		III	16		W	L		32	25	3	Siverson, Duane

Year	M/W	Div	F	SD	Reg	BD	Bye	#T	W	L	Coach
1989		III	16		W	L		32	24	3	Siverson, Duane
1985		III	32		W	L		32	16	12	Siverson, Duane
1992		III	32		W	L		32	18	9	Pyle, Jerry
1994		III	32		W	L	To R32	40	18	8	Kohler, Robert
1995		III	32		W	L		64	20	7	Kohler, Robert
1996		III	64		W	L		64	19	6	Kohler, Robert

CONNECTICUT

Year	M/W	Div	F	SD	Reg	BD	Bye	#T	W	L	Coach
1964	M	I	8		E	A		25	16	11	Shabel, Fred A.
1990		I	8	1	E	A		64	31	6	Calhoun, James A.
1995		I	8	2	W	L		64	28	5	Calhoun, James A.
1998		I	8	2	E	A		64	33	5	Calhoun, James A.
1951			16		E	L		16	22	4	Greer, Hugh S.
1956			16		E	A		25	17	11	Greer, Hugh S.
1976		I	16		E	L		32	19	10	Rowe, Donald E. "Dee"
1991		I	16	11	MW	L		64	20	11	Calhoun, James A.
1994		I	16	2	E	L		64	29	5	Calhoun, James A.
1996		I	16	1	SE	A		64	32	3	Calhoun, James A.
1957		I	23		E	A		23	17	8	Greer, Hugh S.
1959		I	23		E	A		23	17	7	Greer, Hugh S.
1965		I	23		E	A		23	23	3	Shabel, Fred A.
1967		I	23		E	A		23	17	7	Shabel, Fred A.
1954			24		E(B)	A		24	23	3	Greer, Hugh S.
1958		I	24		E	A		24	17	10	Greer, Hugh S.
1960		I	25		E	A		25	17	9	Greer, Hugh S.
1963		I	25		E	A		25	18	7	Shabel, Fred A.
1979		I	32	5	E	L	To R32	40	21	8	Perno, Dominic P. "Dom"
1992		I	32	9	SE	L		64	20	10	Calhoun, James A.
1995	W	I	1	1	E	A		64	35	0	Auriemma, Geno
1991		I	3	3	E	A	To R32	48	29	5	Auriemma, Geno
1996		I	3	1	ME	A		64	34	4	Auriemma, Geno
1994		I	8	1	E	A		64	30	3	Auriemma, Geno
1997		I	8	1	MW	A		64	33	1	Auriemma, Geno
1998		I	8	2	E	A		64	34	3	Auriemma, Geno
1990		I	32	4	E	L	To R32	48	25	6	Auriemma, Geno
1992		I	32	6	E	L		48	23	11	Auriemma, Geno
1989		I	48	8	E	A		48	24	6	Auriemma, Geno
1993		I	48		ME	L		48	18	11	Auriemma, Geno

CONNECTICUT COLLEGE

Year	M/W	Div	F	SD	Reg	BD	Bye	#T	W	L	Coach
1998	M	III	16	2	NE	L	To R32	48	22	4	Miller, Glen

COPPIN STATE

Year	M/W	Div	F	SD	Reg	BD	Bye	#T	W	L	Coach
1997	M	I	32	15	E	A		64	22	9	Mitchell, Ronald C. "Fang"
1990		I	64	15	SE	A		64	26	7	Mitchell, Ronald C. "Fang"
1993		I	64	15	E	A		64	22	8	Mitchell, Ronald C. "Fang"

CORNELL (IA)

Year	M/W	Div	F	SD	Reg	BD	Bye	#T	W	L	Coach
1960	M	II	4		MW			32	16	6	Maaske, Paul M.
1961		II	24		MW			32	17	6	Maaske, Paul M.
1976		III	28		MW	L		28	15	9	Maaske, Paul M.
1963		II	32		MW			32	16	7	Maaske, Paul M.

Year	M/W	Div	F	SD	Reg	BD	Bye	#T	W	L	Coach
1970		II	32		MW	L		32	16	8	Maaske, Paul M.
1994		III	40		MW	A		40	17	8	Grace, Gary

CORNELL (NY)

Year	M/W	Div	F	SD	Reg	BD	Bye	#T	W	L	Coach
1954	M		16		E(B)	A	To R16	24	17	7	Greene, Royner C.
1988		I	64	16	W	A		64	17	10	Dement, Mike

CORTLAND STATE

Year	M/W	Div	F	SD	Reg	BD	Bye	#T	W	L	Coach
1997	M	III	64	6	E		L	64	19	9	Spanbauer, Tom
1992	W	III	16		E		L	32	24	5	Foley, Bonnie
1988		III	32		E		L	32	21	7	Foley, Bonnie

CREIGHTON

Year	M/W	Div	F	SD	Reg	BD	Bye	#T	W	L	Coach
1941	M		6		W	L		8	18	7	Hickey, Edgar S. "Eddie"
1962		I	12		MW	L		25	21	5	McManus, John J. "Red"
1974		I	12		MW	L		25	23	7	Sutton, Eddie
1964		I	16		MW	L		25	22	7	McManus, John J. "Red"
1975		I	32		MW	L		32	20	7	Apke, Tom
1978		I	32		MW	A		32	19	9	Apke, Tom
1991		I	32	11	W	A		64	24	8	Barone, Anthony A. "Tony"
1981		I	48	8	ME	A		48	21	9	Apke, Tom
1989		I	64	14	MW	A		64	20	11	Barone, Anthony A. "Tony"
1992	W	I	32	7	W	A		48	28	4	Rasmussen, Bruce
1994		I	32	10	MW	L		64	24	7	Yori, Connie

DARTMOUTH

Year	M/W	Div	F	SD	Reg	BD	Bye	#T	W	L	Coach
1942	M		2		E	L		8	22	4	Cowles, Osborne "Ozzie"
1944			2		E	L		8	19	2	Brown, Earl M.
1941			6		E	L		8	19	5	Cowles, Osborne "Ozzie"
1943			6		E	L		8	20	3	Cowles, Osborne "Ozzie"
1958		I	8		E	L		24	22	5	Julian, Alvin F. "Doggie"
1956			12		E	A		25	18	11	Julian, Alvin F. "Doggie"
1959		I	23		E	L		23	22	6	Julian, Alvin F. "Doggie"
1983	W	I	36		E	L		36	18	8	Wielgus, Christina
1995		I	64	14	E	A		64	16	11	Wielgus, Christina

DAVIDSON

Year	M/W	Div	F	SD	Reg	BD	Bye	#T	W	L	Coach
1968	M	I	8		E	A		23	24	5	Driesell, Charles G. "Lefty"
1969		I	8		E	A		25	27	3	Driesell, Charles G. "Lefty"
1966		I	16		E	A		22	21	7	Driesell, Charles G. "Lefty"
1970		I	25		E	A		25	22	5	Holland, M. Terrance "Terry"
1986		I	64	16	SE	A		64	20	11	Hussey, Bobby W.
1998		I	64	14	S	A		64	20	10	McKillop, Bob

DAYTON

Year	M/W	Div	F	SD	Reg	BD	Bye	#T	W	L	Coach
1967	M	I	2		ME	L		23	25	6	Donoher, Donald J. "Mickey"
1984		I	8	10	W	L		53	21	11	Donoher, Donald J. "Mickey"
1952			12		E(B)	L		16	28	5	Blackburn, L. Thomas
1965		I	12		ME	L		23	22	7	Donoher, Donald J. "Mickey"

Year	M/W	Div	F	SD	Reg	BD	Bye	#T	W	L	Coach
1966		I	16		ME	L		22	23	6	Donoher, Donald J. "Mickey"
1974		I	16		W	L		25	20	9	Donoher, Donald J. "Mickey"
1969		I	25		MW	L		25	20	7	Donoher, Donald J. "Mickey"
1970		I	25		MW	L		25	19	8	Donoher, Donald J. "Mickey"
1990		I	32	12	MW	A		64	22	10	O'Brien, James F. X.
1985		I	64	9	SE	L		64	19	10	Donoher, Donald J. "Mickey"
1984	W	II	3		GL	L	To R16	24	27	4	Makowski, Linda
1983		II	8		GL	L		24	20	10	Makowski, Linda

DE PAUL

Year	M/W	Div	F	SD	Reg	BD	Bye	#T	W	L	Coach
1943	M		3		E	L		8	19	5	Meyer, Raymond J.
1979		I	3	2	W	L	To R32	40	26	6	Meyer, Raymond J.
1978		I	8		MW	L		32	27	3	Meyer, Raymond J.
1960		I	12		MW	L		25	17	7	Meyer, Raymond J.
1953			16		E(B)	L		22	19	9	Meyer, Raymond J.
1959		I	16		MW	L		23	13	11	Meyer, Raymond J.
1965		I	16		ME	L		23	17	10	Meyer, Raymond J.
1976		I	16		E	L		32	20	9	Meyer, Raymond J.
1984		I	16	1	MW	L	To R32	53	27	3	Meyer, Raymond J.
1986		I	16	12	E	L		64	18	13	Meyer, Joseph E. "Joey"
1987		I	16	3	MW	L		64	28	3	Meyer, Joseph E. "Joey"
1956			25		MW	L		25	16	8	Meyer, Raymond J.
1980		I	32	1	W	L	To R32	48	26	2	Meyer, Raymond J.
1981		I	32	1	ME	L	To R32	48	27	2	Meyer, Raymond J.
1982		I	32	1	MW	L	To R32	48	26	2	Meyer, Raymond J.
1988		I	32	5	MW	L		64	22	8	Meyer, Joseph E. "Joey"
1989		I	32	12	W	L		64	21	12	Meyer, Joseph E. "Joey"
1985		I	64	10	E	L		64	19	10	Meyer, Joseph E. "Joey"
1991		I	64	9	MW	L		64	20	9	Meyer, Joseph E. "Joey"
1992		I	64	5	W	L		64	20	9	Meyer, Joseph E. "Joey"
1990	W	I	32	8	ME	L		48	22	10	Bruno, Doug
1992		I	32	11	MW	L		48	21	10	Bruno, Doug
1996		I	32	7	ME	L		64	21	10	Bruno, Doug
1991		I	48	12	MW	A		48	19	12	Bruno, Doug
1993		I	48		MW	L		48	20	9	Bruno, Doug
1995		I	64	13	MW	L		64	20	9	Bruno, Doug
1997		I	64	12	MW	L		64	20	9	Bruno, Doug

DEFIANCE

Year	M/W	Div	F	SD	Reg	BD	Bye	#T	W	L	Coach
1993	M	III	40		GL	L		40	21	6	Hohenberger, D. Marvin
1994	W	III	8		A	L	To R32	40	25	3	Elliott, Cindy
1996		III	8		A	L		64	28	1	Palombo, Tom
1997		III	8		GL	L		64	28	1	Palombo, Tom
1995		III	32		A	L		64	22	5	Palombo, Tom

DELAWARE

Year	M/W	Div	F	SD	Reg	BD	Bye	#T	W	L	Coach
1992	M	I	64	13	MW	A		64	27	4	Steinwedel, Steve
1993		I	64	13	MW	A		64	22	8	Steinwedel, Steve
1998		I	64	15	MW	A		64	20	10	Brey, Mike

360   College Basketball's National Championships

Year	M/W	Div	F	SD	Reg	BD	Bye	#T	W	L	Coach
DELTA STATE											
1987	M	II	3		SC	L		32	24	9	Rives, Steve
1998		II	8	2	S	A	To R32	48	27	4	Rives, Steve
1972		II	16		S		To R32	36	19	8	Waters, Jack
1985		II	16		SC	L		32	20	11	Murphy, Ed
1986		II	16		SC	A		32	23	8	Murphy, Ed
1993		II	16		S	A		32	22	8	Rives, Steve
1997		II	32	4	S	A		48	23	7	Rives, Steve
1996		II	48	6	SC	L		48	18	11	Rives, Steve
1989	W	II	1		S	A		32	30	4	Clark, Lloyd
1990		II	1		S	A		32	32	1	Clark, Lloyd
1992		II	1		S	L		32	30	4	Clark, Lloyd
1993		II	2		S	L		32	27	6	Clark, Lloyd
1986		II	3		S	A		24	28	3	Clark, Lloyd
1988		II	3		S	A		32	30	3	Clark, Lloyd
1996		II	4	2	S	A	To R32	48	27	6	Clark, Lloyd
1987		II	8		S	A	To R16	24	28	2	Clark, Lloyd
1997		II	8	2	S	A	To R32	48	25	6	Clark, Lloyd
1991		II	16		S	L		32	23	7	Clark, Lloyd
1995		II	32	3	S	A		48	22	8	Clark, Lloyd
1998		II	48	4	S	L		48	23	9	Clark, Lloyd
DENISON											
1968	M	II	23		ME		To R32	36	18	5	Scott, Richard S.
1997		III	64	8	GL	L		64	19	7	Sheridan, Michael
1994	W	III	40		A	A		40	18	9	Lee, Sara
DENVER											
1992	M	II	16		NC	L		32	26	6	Peth, Dick
1996		II	48	3	NC	A		48	22	7	Peth, Dick
1993	W	II	32		NC	L		32	24	4	Sheehan, Tracey
1995		II	48	4	NC	A		48	15	14	Sheehan, Tracey
DEPAUW											
1990	M	III	2		MW	L	To R32	40	24	7	Waltman, Royce
1984		III	3		GL	L		32	25	5	Steele, Mike
1986		III	16		GL	L		32	26	2	Steele, Mike
1987		III	24		MW	L		32	22	6	Steele, Mike
1978		III	30		S	L		30	14	12	McCall, Elmer
1957		II	32		ME	L		32	12	9	Luther, Calvin C.
1968		II	32		GL		To R32	36	16	8	McCall, Elmer
1985		III	32		GL	L		32	21	7	Steele, Mike
1991		III	32		MW	L	To R32	40	19	8	Waltman, Royce
1992		III	40		MW	L		40	20	7	Waltman, Royce
1993		III	40		MW	L		40	19	7	Fenlon, Bill
1998	W	III	16	2	GL	L	To R32	48	23	5	Huffman, Kris
1996		III	64		GL	L		64	19	7	Huffman, Kris

Year	M/W	Div	F	SD	Reg	BD	Bye	#T	W	L	Coach
DETROIT											
1977	M	I	16		ME	L		32	25	4	Vitale, Dick
1962		I	25		ME	L		25	15	12	Calihan, Robert J.
1979		I	40	7	ME	L		40	22	6	Gaines, David "Smokey"
DETROIT MERCY											
1998	M	I	32	10	MW	L		64	25	6	Watson, Perry
1997	W	I	64	14	W	A		64	23	7	Lowry, Nikita
DICKINSON (PA)											
1980	M	III	24		MA	A		32	19	8	Evans, Gene
1982		III	32		MA	L		32	16	11	Evans, Gene
1991		III	40		MA	L		40	19	8	Frohman, David N.
1997		III	64	8	MA	A		64	17	10	Frohman, David N.
DISTRICT OF COLUMBIA											
1982	M	II	1		SA	L		32	25	5	Jones, William S.
1983		II	2		SA	L		32	29	3	Jones, William S.
1987		II	32		SA	L		32	24	6	Jones, William S.
1989	W	II	8		SA	L		32	20	4	Robinson, William
1988		II	32		SA	L		32	24	3	Robinson, William
1995		II	48	3	E	L		48	20	6	King, Britt S.
DOANE											
1975	M	III	8		W	L	To R16	30	16	9	Erickson, Robert
1965		II	32		SW	L		32	16	9	Erickson, Robert
DOWLING											
1995	M	II	48	6	NE	L		48	18	10	Pellicane, Joseph
1998		II	48	3	NE	L		48	22	6	Pellicane, Joseph
DRAKE (IA)											
1969	M	I	3		MW	A	To R16	25	26	5	John, Maurice E. "Maury"
1970		I	8		MW	A	To R16	25	22	7	John, Maurice E. "Maury"
1971		I	8		MW	A	To R16	25	21	8	John, Maurice E. "Maury"
1982	W	I	8		W	A		32	28	7	Baumgarten, Carole
1984		I	32		MW	A		32	22	7	Baumgarten, Carole
1986		I	32		MW	L		40	22	8	Baumgarten, Carole
1995		I	32	5	MW	A		64	25	6	Bluder, Lisa
1997		I	64	13	MW	A		64	23	7	Bluder, Lisa
1998		I	64	5	MW	A		64	25	5	Bluder, Lisa
DREXEL											
1957	M	II	32		E	A		32	14	3	Cozen, Samuel D.
1960		II	32		E			32	12	8	Cozen, Samuel D.
1966		II	32		E	L	To R32	36	20	4	Cozen, Samuel D.
1967		II	32		E		To R32	36	13	10	Cozen, Samuel D.
1996		I	32	12	W	A		64	27	4	Herrion, William R.
1986		I	64	15	W	A		64	19	12	Burke, Edward J.
1994		I	64	13	E	A		64	25	5	Herrion, William R.
1995		I	64	13	E	A		64	22	8	Herrion, William R.

Year	M/W	Div	F	SD	Reg	BD	Bye	#T	W	L	Coach
DUBUQUE											
1986	M	III	16		W	A		32	21	7	Davison, Jon L.
1988		III	16		W	A		32	21	7	Davison, Jon L.
1981		III	24		W	L		32	20	8	Davison, Jon L.
1990		III	32		W	A		40	19	8	Davison, Jon L.
DUKE											
1991	M	I	1	2	MW	L		64	32	7	Krzyzewski, Michael W.
1992		I	1	1	E	A		64	34	2	Krzyzewski, Michael W.
1964		I	2		E	A	To R16	25	26	5	Bubas, Victor A.
1978		I	2		E	A		32	27	7	Foster, William E.
1986		I	2	1	E	A		64	37	3	Krzyzewski, Michael W.
1990		I	2	3	E	L		64	29	9	Krzyzewski, Michael W.
1994		I	2	2	SE	L		64	28	6	Krzyzewski, Michael W.
1963		I	3		E	A	To R16	25	27	3	Bubas, Victor A.
1966		I	3		E	A	To R16	22	26	4	Bubas, Victor A.
1988		I	3	2	E	A		64	28	7	Krzyzewski, Michael W.
1989		I	3	2	E	L		64	28	8	Krzyzewski, Michael W.
1960		I	8		E	A		25	17	11	Bubas, Victor A.
1980		I	8	4	ME	A	To R32	48	24	9	Foster, William E.
1998		I	8	1	S	L		64	32	4	Krzyzewski, Michael W.
1987		I	16	5	MW	L		64	24	9	Krzyzewski, Michael W.
1955			24		E(B)	A		24	20	8	Bradley, Harold L.
1979		I	32	2	E	L	To R32	40	22	8	Foster, William E.
1984		I	32	3	W	L	To R32	53	24	10	Krzyzewski, Michael W.
1985		I	32	3	MW	L		64	23	8	Krzyzewski, Michael W.
1993		I	32	3	MW	L		64	24	8	Krzyzewski, Michael W.
1997		I	32	2	SE	L		64	24	9	Krzyzewski, Michael W.
1996		I	64	8	SE	L		64	18	13	Krzyzewski, Michael W.
1998	W	I	8	2	W	L		64	24	8	Goestenkors, Gail
1987		I	32	7	E	L		40	19	10	Leonard, Debbie
1995		i	32	5	E	L		64	22	9	Goestenkors, Gail
1996		I	32	4	ME	L		64	26	7	Goestenkors, Gail
1997		I	32	5	MW	L		64	19	11	Goestenkors, Gail
DUQUESNE											
1940	M		3		E	L		8	20	3	Davies, Charles R. "Chick"
1952			8		E(B)	L		16	23	4	Moore, Donald W. "Dudey"
1969		I	12		E	L		25	21	5	Manning, John "Red"
1971		I	25		E	L		25	21	4	Manning, John "Red"
1977		I	32		E	A		32	15	15	Cinicola, John L.
EAST CAROLINA											
1972	M	I	25		E	A		25	14	15	Quinn, Thomas R.
1993		I	64	16	E	A		64	13	17	Payne, Eddie
1982	W	I	32		MW	L		32	17	10	Andruzzi, Cathy
EAST STROUDSBURG											
1990	M	II	16		E	A		32	21	13	Mentesana, Sal
1994	W	II	32		E	L		32	21	8	Haller, Rose
1995		II	32	5	E	A		48	25	5	Haller, Rose

Year	M/W	Div	F	SD	Reg	BD	Bye	#T	W	L	Coach
EAST TENNESSEE STATE											
1957	M	II	16		ME	L		32	18	10	Brooks, John Madison
1968		I	16		ME	A		23	19	8	Brooks, John Madison
1992		I	32	14	SE	A		64	24	7	LeForce, Alan C.
1989		I	64	16	SE	A		64	20	11	Robinson, Leslie G.
1990		I	64	13	SE	A		64	27	7	Robinson, Leslie G.
1991		I	64	10	MW	A		64	28	5	LeForce, Alan C.
EASTERN CONNECTICUT STATE											
1993	M	III	8		NE	L	To R32	40	21	7	Switchenko, Dr. Daniel B.
1992		III	16		NE	A	To R32	40	16	12	Switchenko, Dr. Daniel B.
1991	W	III	3		NE	L		32	22	6	Miller, Dr. C. Robert
1992		III	4		NE	A		32	25	6	Miller, Dr. C. Robert
1984		III	16		NE	L		32	20	7	Miller, Dr. C. Robert
1986		III	16		C	L		32	20	5	Miller, Dr. C. Robert
1983		III	32		NE	L		32	17	7	Miller, Dr. C. Robert
1990		III	32		NE	L		32	20	5	Miller, Dr. C. Robert
1996		III	64		NE	A		64	19	9	Bierly, Denise
EASTERN ILLINOIS											
1976	M	II	3		GL	L		32	23	8	Eddy, Donald R.
1978		II	3		GL	L		32	21	10	Eddy, Donald R.
1977		II	16		GL	L		32	18	11	Eddy, Donald R.
1980		II	16		GL	L		32	22	7	Eddy, Donald R.
1975		II	24		GL	L		32	20	8	Eddy, Donald R.
1979		II	24		GL	L		32	19	10	Eddy, Donald R.
1992		I	64	15	W	A		64	17	14	Samuels, Rick
1988	W	I	40	10	W	A		40	22	8	Hilke, Barbara
EASTERN KENTUCKY											
1953	M		22		E(B)	L		22	16	9	McBrayer, Paul S.
1959		I	23		ME	A		23	16	6	McBrayer, Paul S.
1965		I	23		ME	A		23	19	6	Baechtold, James E.
1972		I	25		ME	A		25	15	11	Strong, Guy Rowland
1979		I	40	9	ME	A		40	21	8	Byhre, Ed
1997	W	I	64	15	W	A		64	24	6	Inman, Larry Joe
EASTERN MICHIGAN											
1972	M	II	4		GL	L	To R32	36	24	7	Dutcher, James D.
1991		I	16	12	E	A		64	26	7	Braun, Ben
1996		I	32	9	SE	A		64	25	6	Braun, Ben
1988		I	64	15	MW	A		64	22	8	Braun, Ben
1998		I	64	13	E	A		64	20	10	Barnes, Milton
EASTERN NEW MEXICO											
1993	M	II	16		SC	A		32	23	7	Diddle, Earl
EASTERN WASHINGTON											
1987	W	I	40	10	W	A		40	18	12	Smithpeters, Bill

Year	M/W	Div	F	SD	Reg	BD	Bye	#T	W	L	Coach
ECKERD											
1995	M	II	24	5	S	L		48	22	10	Harley, James R.
1994		II	32		S	A		32	17	14	Harley, James R.
1973		II	42		SA	L		42	17	5	Harley, James R.
EDINBORO											
1982	M	II	24		E	L		32	22	8	Conti, Guy
1986		II	32		E	L		32	18	13	Sims, James
1994		II	32		E	L		32	20	8	Walcavich, Greg
1996		II	32	5	E	L		48	21	8	Walcavich, Greg
1998		II	32	5	E	A		48	26	8	Walcavich, Greg
1997	W	II	8	3	E	L		48	24	9	Swank, Stan
1990		II	16		E	A		32	27	3	Swank, Stan
1992		II	32		E	L		32	22	8	Swank, Stan
1993		II	32		E	L		32	18	12	Swank, Stan
1998		II	32	4	E	L		48	23	8	Swank, Stan
ELIZABETH CITY STATE											
1978	M	II	8		SA	L		32	18	6	Vaughan, Robert L. "Bobby"
1997		II	8	3	SA	L		48	22	7	Hamler, Barry
1981		II	16		SA	L		32	22	9	Vaughan, Robert L. "Bobby"
1994		II	24		SA	L		32	22	8	Mackey, Dr. Claudie J.
ELIZABETHTOWN											
1964	M	II	16		E			32	20	5	Smith, Donald P.
1979		III	16		MA	A		32	17	9	Smith, Donald P.
1993		III	32		MA	L	To R32	40	19	7	Schlosser, Robert A.
1982	W	III	1		None	L		16	26	1	Kauffman, Yvonne E.
1989		III	1		MA	A		32	29	2	Kauffman, Yvonne E.
1983		III	2		MA	L		32	23	5	Kauffman, Yvonne E.
1984		III	2		MA	A		32	29	2	Kauffman, Yvonne E.
1986		III	8		MA	A		32	24	6	Kauffman, Yvonne E.
1987		III	16		MA	L		32	25	3	Kauffman, Yvonne E.
1988		III	16		MA	A		32	25	4	Kauffman, Yvonne E.
1997		III	32		MA	L		64	21	8	Kauffman, Yvonne E.
1994		III	40		MA	L		40	21	5	Kauffman, Yvonne E.
1995		III	64		MA	A		64	23	5	Kauffman, Yvonne E.
1996		III	64		MA	L		64	19	8	Kauffman, Yvonne E.
ELMHURST											
1992	M	III	32		MW	L		40	19	9	Whitesell, Jim
1986	W	III	24		C	A		32	24	3	Novgrod, Debra
ELMIRA											
1995	M	III	64	6	E	L		64	17	9	Moore, Kevin
1998	W	III	16	5	E	L		48	22	7	Scheible, James
ELON											
1997	M	II	48	6	SA	A		48	16	14	Simons, Mark

Year	M/W	Div	F	SD	Reg	BD	Bye	#T	W	L	Coach
EMMANUEL (MA)											
1986	W	III	16		NE	L		32	21	4	Yosinoff, Andrew
1987		III	16		NE	L		32	22	2	Yosinoff, Andrew
1988		III	24		NE	L		32	20	2	Yosinoff, Andrew
1992		III	32		E	L		32	20	5	Yosinoff, Andrew
1997		III	32		NE	A		64	22	7	Yosinoff, Andrew
1996		III	64		NE	A		64	22	4	Yosinoff, Andrew
EMORY											
1990	M	III	16		S	L	To R32	40	25	4	Winston, Lloyd
1995	W	III	16		S	L		64	21	6	Sims, Myra
1997		III	16		S	L		64	20	7	Sims, Myra
EMORY & HENRY											
1988	M	III	16		SA	L		40	17	9	Johnson, Robert J.
1993		III	16		S	L	To R32	40	23	5	Johnson, Robert J.
1990		III	32		S	L		40	23	7	Johnson, Robert J.
1991		III	32		S	L		40	25	5	Johnson, Robert J.
1992		III	40		S	L		40	20	9	Johnson, Robert J.
EMPORIA STATE											
1998	W	II	2	1	SC	A	To R32	48	33	1	Stein, Cindy
1997		II	32	3	SC	L		48	20	10	Stein, Cindy
EVANSVILLE											
1959	M	II	1		ME	L		32	21	6	McCutchan, Arad A.
1960		II	1		ME			32	25	4	McCutchan, Arad A.
1964		II	1		GL			32	26	3	McCutchan, Arad A.
1965		II	1		SC			32	29	0	McCutchan, Arad A.
1971		II	1		GL	L		32	22	8	McCutchan, Arad A.
1958		II	3		ME			32	23	4	McCutchan, Arad A.
1963		II	8		GL			32	21	6	McCutchan, Arad A.
1968		II	8		MW	L	To R32	36	20	8	McCutchan, Arad A.
1957		II	16		ME	L		32	18	8	McCutchan, Arad A.
1962		II	16		SC	L		32	14	11	McCutchan, Arad A.
1966		II	16		GL		To R32	36	18	9	McCutchan, Arad A.
1972		II	16		GL		To R32	36	22	6	McCutchan, Arad A.
1976		II	16		GL	L		32	20	9	McCutchan, Arad A.
1961		II	24		GL	L		32	11	16	McCutchan, Arad A.
1974		II	24		GL	A	To R32	44	19	9	McCutchan, Arad A.
1989		I	32	11	W	L		64	25	6	Crews, Jim
1982		I	48	10	MW	A		48	23	6	Walters, Dick
1992		I	64	8	MW	A		64	24	6	Crews, Jim
1993		I	64	14	SE	A		64	23	7	Crews, Jim
FAIRFIELD											
1960	M	II	16		E			32	17	9	Bisacca, George R.
1962		II	16		NE			32	20	5	Bisacca, George R.
1961		II	32		E			32	17	7	Bisacca, George R.
1986		I	64	13	SE	A		64	24	7	Buonaguro, Mitch

Year	M/W	Div	F	SD	Reg	BD	Bye	#T	W	L	Coach
1987		I	64	16	MW	A		64	15	16	Buonaguro, Mitch
1997		I	64	16	E	A		64	11	19	Cormier, Paul
1988	W	I	40	10	E	A		40	19	10	Nolan, Diane
1991		I	48	12	E	A		48	25	6	Nolan, Diane
1998		I	64	15	E	A		64	20	10	Nolan, Diane

FAIRLEIGH DICKINSON: MADISON

Year	M/W	Div	F	SD	Reg	BD	Bye	#T	W	L	Coach
1990	M	III	40		MA	L		40	18	9	Kindel, Roger
1998		III	48	6	MA	L		48	17	9	Kindel, Roger

FAIRLEIGH DICKINSON: RUTHERFORD/TEANECK

Year	M/W	Div	F	SD	Reg	BD	Bye	#T	W	L	Coach
1963	M	II	32		NE			32	16	12	Holub, Richard
1985		I	64	16	SE	A		64	21	10	Green, Tom
1988		I	64	16	MW	A		64	23	7	Green, Tom

FAIRLEIGH DICKINSON: TEANECK

Year	M/W	Div	F	SD	Reg	BD	Bye	#T	W	L	Coach
1998	M	I	64	15	E	A		64	23	7	Green, Tom

FAIRMONT STATE

Year	M/W	Div	F	SD	Reg	BD	Bye	#T	W	L	Coach
1998	M	II	8	2	E	L	To R32	48	27	4	Haswell, Arthur "Butch"
1996		II	32	3	E	L	To R32	48	24	5	Haswell, Arthur "Butch"

FAYETTEVILLE STATE

Year	M/W	Div	F	SD	Reg	BD	Bye	#T	W	L	Coach
1973	M	II	24		SA			42	19	10	Reeves, Thomas
1993		II	32		SA	L		32	20	9	Capel, Jeff
1997	W	II	32	4	SA	L		48	25	5	Tucker, Eric

FERRIS STATE

Year	M/W	Div	F	SD	Reg	BD	Bye	#T	W	L	Coach
1988	M	II	8		NC	L		32	25	5	Ludwig, H. Thomas
1987		II	16		NC	L		32	20	9	Ludwig, H. Thomas
1983		II	24		NC	L		32	20	9	Ludwig, H. Thomas
1990		II	24		GL	A		32	18	11	Ludwig, H. Thomas
1989		II	32		GL	L		32	24	6	Ludwig, H. Thomas
1998		II	48	4	GL	A		48	21	12	Wilson, Edgar

FERRUM

Year	M/W	Div	F	SD	Reg	BD	Bye	#T	W	L	Coach
1992	M	III	32		S	A		40	21	8	Pullen, Bill
1995	W	III	64		S	A		64	18	9	Doonan, Donna M.

FISK

Year	M/W	Div	F	SD	Reg	BD	Bye	#T	W	L	Coach
1964	M	II	16		SC	L		32	18	6	Thompson, Herbert B. "Bus"
1974		II	16		S	A		44	25	4	Lawson, Ronald

FLORIDA

Year	M/W	Div	F	SD	Reg	BD	Bye	#T	W	L	Coach
1994	M	I	3	3	E	L		64	29	8	Kruger, Lon
1987		I	16	6	E	L		64	23	11	Sloan, Norman L., Jr.
1988		I	32	6	W	L		64	23	12	Sloan, Norman L., Jr.
1989		I	64	7	MW	L		64	21	13	Sloan, Norman L., Jr.
1995		I	64	10	SE	L		64	17	13	Kruger, Lon
1997	W	I	8	3	ME	L		64	24	9	Ross, Carol
1998		I	16	3	W	L		64	23	9	Ross, Carol
1993		I	32		E	L		48	19	10	Ross, Carol
1995		I	32	6	E	L		64	24	9	Ross, Carol

Year	M/W	Div	F	SD	Reg	BD	Bye	#T	W	L	Coach
1994		I	64	4	W	L		64	22	7	Ross, Carol
1996		I	64	5	ME	L		64	21	9	Ross, Carol

FLORIDA A&M

Year	M/W	Div	F	SD	Reg	BD	Bye	#T	W	L	Coach
1959	M	II	16		SC			32	15	3	Oglesby, Edward E. "Rock"
1962		II	16		ME			32	26	1	Oglesby, Edward E. "Rock"
1978		II	16		S	A		32	23	6	Triplett, Ajac
1957		II	32		E	A		32	25	6	Oglesby, Edward E. "Rock"
1995	W	I	64	16	ME	A		64	24	6	Farmer, Claudette

FLORIDA ATLANTIC

Year	M/W	Div	F	SD	Reg	BD	Bye	#T	W	L	Coach
1990	W	II	16		SA	L		32	21	8	Allen, Wayne
1989		II	32		W	L		32	21	8	Allen, Wayne
1991		II	32		NC	L		32	23	6	Allen, Wayne
1993		II	32		S	L		32	20	8	Allen, Wayne

FLORIDA INTERNATIONAL

Year	M/W	Div	F	SD	Reg	BD	Bye	#T	W	L	Coach
1995	M	I	64	16	W	A		64	11	19	Weltlich, Robert
1986	W	II	16		S	L	To R16	24	26	2	Russo, Cindy
1987		II	16		S	L		24	26	3	Russo, Cindy
1983		II	24		E	L		24	17	7	Russo, Cindy
1995		I	32	9	ME	A		64	27	5	Russo, Cindy
1998		I	32	7	ME	A		64	29	2	Russo, Cindy
1994		I	64	8	ME	A		64	25	4	Russo, Cindy
1997		I	64	14	ME	A		64	21	9	Russo, Cindy

FLORIDA SOUTHERN

Year	M/W	Div	F	SD	Reg	BD	Bye	#T	W	L	Coach
1981	M	II	1		S	A		32	24	8	Wissel, Dr. Harold R. "Hal"
1982		II	2		S	L		32	22	10	Wissel, Dr. Harold R. "Hal"
1980		II	3		S	A		32	28	5	Wissel, Dr. Harold R. "Hal"
1986		II	3		S	A		32	24	9	Scholz, George
1988		II	3		S	A		32	31	3	Scholz, George
1987		II	8		S	A		32	26	6	Scholz, George
1972		II	24		SA	L	To R32	36	24	4	Jarrett, Jim
1983		II	24		S	A		32	23	8	Scholz, George
1985		II	24		S	L		32	24	7	Scholz, George
1989		II	24		S	A		32	25	6	Scholz, George
1990		II	24		S	A		32	23	8	Scholz, George
1979		II	32		S	A		32	18	12	Wissel, Dr. Harold R. "Hal"
1991		II	32		S	A		32	27	5	Gibbons, Gordon
1993		II	32		S	A		32	24	8	Gibbons, Gordon
1996		II	32	2	S	A	To R32	48	26	4	Gibbons, Gordon
1998		II	48	6	S	A		48	23	7	Gibbons, Gordon
1995	W	II	8	1	S	A	To R32	48	28	4	Benn, Norm
1996		II	16	1	S	A	To R32	48	26	5	Benn, Norm
1994		II	32		S	A		32	23	8	Benn, Norm
1998		II	32	1	S	A	To R32	48	24	5	Foli, Diane

FLORIDA STATE

Year	M/W	Div	F	SD	Reg	BD	Bye	#T	W	L	Coach
1972	M	I	2		ME	L		25	27	6	Durham, Hugh
1993		I	8	3	SE	L		64	25	10	Kennedy, Patrick
1992		I	16	3	W	L		64	22	10	Kennedy, Patrick
1968		I	23		ME	L		23	19	8	Durham, Hugh

Year	M/W	Div	F	SD	Reg	BD	Bye	#T	W	L	Coach
1978		I	32		ME	L		32	23	6	Durham, Hugh
1980		I	32	8	ME	L		48	22	9	Williams, Joe L.
1991		I	32	7	SE	A		64	21	11	Kennedy, Patrick
1998		I	32	12	MW	L		64	18	14	Robinson, Steve
1988		I	64	12	W	L		64	19	11	Kennedy, Patrick
1989		I	64	4	SE	L		64	22	8	Kennedy, Patrick
1983	W	I	32		ME	L	To R32	36	24	6	Dykehouse-Allen, Janice
1991		I	32	5	ME	A		48	25	7	Meadors, Marynell Hutsell
1990		I	48	10	E	L		48	21	9	Meadors, Marynell Hutsell

FLORIDA TECH

Year	M/W	Div	F	SD	Reg	BD	Bye	#T	W	L	Coach
1997	W	II	32	1	S	A	To R32	48	27	3	Reynolds, John, Jr.

FONTBONNE

Year	M/W	Div	F	SD	Reg	BD	Bye	#T	W	L	Coach
1996	M	III	64	6	MW	A		64	17	10	McKinney, Lee

FORDHAM

Year	M/W	Div	F	SD	Reg	BD	Bye	#T	W	L	Coach
1971	M	I	12		E	L		25	26	3	Phelps, Richard F. "Digger"
1953			22		E(A)	L		22	18	8	Bach, John W. "Johnny"
1954			24		E(B)	L		24	18	6	Bach, John W. "Johnny"
1992		I	64	14	E	A		64	18	13	Macarchuk, Nick, Jr.
1994	W	I	64	16	MW	A		64	21	9	Morris, Kevin

FORT HAYS STATE

Year	M/W	Div	F	SD	Reg	BD	Bye	#T	W	L	Coach
1996	M	II	1	1	NC	A	To R32	48	34	0	Garner, Gary
1995		II	16	2	NC	A	To R32	48	24	7	Garner, Gary
1997		II	16	1	NC	A	To R32	48	29	2	Garner, Gary
1998		II	48	3	NC	L		48	22	7	Wintz, Chad

FORT VALLEY STATE

Year	M/W	Div	F	SD	Reg	BD	Bye	#T	W	L	Coach
1998	M	II	48	4	S	A		48	19	12	Moore, Michael D.
1982	W	II	8		NC	L		16	23	8	Brown, Jessie A.
1997		II	16	5	S	L		48	25	6	Bartley, Lonnie
1988		II	32		S	A		32	25	4	Bartley, Lonnie
1992		II	32		S	A		32	21	9	Bartley, Lonnie
1993		II	32		SA	L		32	27	3	Bartley, Lonnie
1995		II	32	4	S	A		48	25	5	Bartley, Lonnie
1996		II	48	5	S	L		48	25	4	Bartley, Lonnie

FRAMINGHAM STATE

Year	M/W	Div	F	SD	Reg	BD	Bye	#T	W	L	Coach
1979	M	III	16		NE	A		32	22	6	Grealey, Bruce
1984		III	16		NE	A		32	24	2	Grealey, Bruce
1980		III	32		NE	L		32	20	8	Grealey, Bruce

FRANCIS MARION

Year	M/W	Div	F	SD	Reg	BD	Bye	#T	W	L	Coach
1998	W	II	3	2	SA	A	To R32	48	30	3	Moore, Frank "Wes"
1997		II	48	5	SA	L		48	21	8	Moore, Frank "Wes"

FRANCISCAN

Year	M/W	Div	F	SD	Reg	BD	Bye	#T	W	L	Coach
1966	M	II	16		ME	L	To R32	36	17	9	Bayer, John D. "Denny"
1973		II	16		ME	L		42	22	7	Sparling, Edward L.
1965		II	24		ME	L		32	21	4	Bayer, John D. "Denny"

Year	M/W	Div	F	SD	Reg	BD	Bye	#T	W	L	Coach
FRANKLIN & MARSHALL											
1991	M	III	2		MA	L	To R32	40	28	3	Robinson, Glenn R.
1979		III	3		MA	A		32	27	5	Robinson, Glenn R.
1996		III	4	1	MA	A		64	29	3	Robinson, Glenn R.
1989		III	8		MA	A	To R32	40	27	3	Robinson, Glenn R.
1992		III	8		MA	A	To R32	40	26	4	Robinson, Glenn R.
1986		III	16		MA	A		32	19	10	Robinson, Glenn R.
1987		III	16		MA	L		32	22	7	Robinson, Glenn R.
1988		III	16		MA	A		32	24	5	Robinson, Glenn R.
1993		III	16		MA	A	To R32	40	24	4	Robinson, Glenn R.
1994		III	16		MA	A	To R32	40	26	2	Robinson, Glenn R.
1995		III	16	1	MA	L		64	27	2	Robinson, Glenn R.
1977		III	23		MA	L		30	22	5	Robinson, Glenn R.
1981		III	24		MA	A		32	26	3	Robinson, Glenn R.
1975		III	30		MA	L		30	16	11	Robinson, Glenn R.
1984		III	32		MA	A		32	21	8	Robinson, Glenn R.
1990		III	32		MA	A	To R32	40	24	4	Robinson, Glenn R.
1988	W	III	8		MA	L		32	25	4	Fleig, Mary L.
1989		III	24		MA	L		32	24	5	Fleig, Mary L.
1990		III	32		MA	L		40	25	5	Fleig, Mary L.
1991		III	32		MA	L		32	21	6	Fleig, Mary L.
FRANKLIN (IN)											
1998	M	III	32	5	MW	L		48	23	6	Prather, Kerry
1995	W	III	32		GL	L		64	24	2	Mahan, Lisa
1994		III	40		GL	L		40	19	6	White, Gene
FRANKLIN PIERCE											
1991	M	II	16		NENG	A		32	26	6	Luptowski, Arthur
1993		II	16		NENG	L		32	22	8	Luptowski, Arthur
1996		II	32	4	NE	L		48	23	6	Luptowski, Arthur
1992	W	II	32		NENG	A		32	24	7	Hancock, Steve
1993		II	32		NENG	L		32	21	9	Hancock, Steve
1998		II	32	3	NE	L		48	24	6	Chadbourne, David
FREDONIA STATE											
1993	M	III	40		E	A		40	18	10	Prechtl, Gregory
FROSTBURG STATE											
1982	W	III	16		None	L		16	15	7	Crawley, James M.
1983		III	16		A	L		32	20	5	Crawley, James M.
1991		III	16		A	L		32	26	2	Crawley, James M.
1985		III	32		A	L		32	21	5	Crawley, James M.
1997		III	64		A	L		64	23	3	Crawley, James M.
FURMAN											
1974	M	I	16		E	A		25	22	9	Williams, Joe L.
1971		I	25		E	A		25	15	12	Williams, Joe L.
1973		I	25		E	A		25	20	9	Williams, Joe L.
1975		I	32		E	A		32	22	7	Williams, Joe L.

Year	M/W	Div	F	SD	Reg	BD	Bye	#T	W	L	Coach
1978		I	32		E	A		32	19	11	Williams, Joe L.
1980		I	48	10	E	A		48	23	7	Holbrook, Edwin "Eddie"
1995	W	I	64	15	E	A		64	18	12	Carter, Sherry

GALLAUDET

Year	M/W	Div	F	SD	Reg	BD	Bye	#T	W	L	Coach
1997	W	III	64		E	L		64	19	9	Baldridge, Kathryn "Kitty"

GANNON

Year	M/W	Div	F	SD	Reg	BD	Bye	#T	W	L	Coach
1987	M	II	2		E	L		32	28	6	Chapman, Tom
1975		II	8		E			32	25	4	Sparling, Edward L.
1988		II	8		E	L		32	24	8	Chapman, Tom
1990		II	8		E	A		32	24	8	Dukiet, Bob
1986		II	16		E	A		32	25	6	Chapman, Tom
1977		II	24		E	L		32	20	8	Sparling, Edward L.
1994		II	24		E	L		32	21	9	Dukiet, Bob
1962		II	32		ME	L		32	16	9	McCluskey, Edward J.
1980		II	32		E	L		32	20	9	Fox, Richard A.
1984		II	32		E	L		32	20	11	Fox, Richard A.
1985		II	32		NC	L		32	22	9	Chapman, Tom
1993		II	32		E	L		32	20	7	Dukiet, Bob
1995		II	32	4	E	L		48	22	8	Dukiet, Bob
1972		II	36		ME	L		36	19	7	Markey, David C.
1988	W	II	32		E	L		32	26	4	Saurer, Judy

GARDNER-WEBB

Year	M/W	Div	F	SD	Reg	BD	Bye	#T	W	L	Coach
1996	W	II	48	6	SA	L		48	22	7	McCurley, Eddie

GENESEO STATE

Year	M/W	Div	F	SD	Reg	BD	Bye	#T	W	L	Coach
1991	M	III	16		E	L	To R32	40	23	5	Pope, Tom
1993		III	16		E	L	To R32	40	23	4	Pope, Tom
1995		III	16	8	E	L		64	20	8	Holmes, Steve
1994		III	32		E	L	To R32	40	22	5	Pope, Tom
1996		III	32	8	E	L		64	17	10	Holmes, Steve
1998		III	48	6	E	A		48	15	13	Holmes, Steve
1993	W	III	8		E	L		32	27	1	Guy, Robert
1995		III	8		E	A		64	27	2	Guy, Robert
1994		III	32		E	L		40	26	3	Guy, Robert
1996		III	32		E	A		64	24	5	Guy, Robert
1997		III	64		A	L		64	21	7	French, Joe

GEORGE MASON

Year	M/W	Div	F	SD	Reg	BD	Bye	#T	W	L	Coach
1989	M	I	64	15	W	A		64	20	11	Nestor, Ernie

GEORGE WASHINGTON

Year	M/W	Div	F	SD	Reg	BD	Bye	#T	W	L	Coach
1993	M	I	16	12	W	L		64	21	9	Jarvis, Mike
1954			24		E(B)	A		24	23	3	Reinhart, William J.
1961		I	24		E	A		24	9	17	Reinhart, William J.
1994		I	32	10	E	L		64	18	12	Jarvis, Mike
1996		I	64	11	W	L		64	21	8	Jarvis, Mike
1998		I	64	9	S	L		64	24	9	Jarvis, Mike

Year	M/W	Div	F	SD	Reg	BD	Bye	#T	W	L	Coach
1997	W	I	8	5	E	L		64	28	6	McKeown, Joe
1995		I	16	4	MW	A		64	26	6	McKeown, Joe
1991		I	32	10	E	L		48	23	7	McKeown, Joe
1992		I	32	8	E	A		48	25	7	McKeown, Joe
1994		I	32	7	ME	L		64	23	8	McKeown, Joe
1996		I	32	6	E	A		64	26	7	McKeown, Joe
1998		I	32	10	E	L		64	20	10	McKeown, Joe

GEORGETOWN (DC)

Year	M/W	Div	F	SD	Reg	BD	Bye	#T	W	L	Coach
1984	M	I	1	1	W	A	To R32	53	34	3	Thompson, John R., Jr.
1943			2		E	L		8	22	5	Ripley, Elmer H.
1982		I	2	1	W	A	To R32	48	30	7	Thompson, John R., Jr.
1985		I	2	1	E	A		64	35	3	Thompson, John R., Jr.
1980		I	8	3	E	L	To R32	48	26	6	Thompson, John R., Jr.
1987		I	8	1	SE	A		64	29	5	Thompson, John R., Jr.
1989		I	8	1	E	A		64	29	5	Thompson, John R., Jr.
1996		I	8	2	E	L		64	29	8	Thompson, John R., Jr.
1995		I	16	6	SE	L		64	21	10	Thompson, John R., Jr.
1975		I	32		ME	L		32	18	10	Thompson, John R., Jr.
1976		I	32		W	L		32	21	7	Thompson, John R., Jr.
1979		I	32	3	E	L	To R32	40	24	5	Thompson, John R., Jr.
1983		I	32	5	MW	L		52	22	10	Thompson, John R., Jr.
1986		I	32	4	MW	L		64	24	8	Thompson, John R., Jr.
1988		I	32	8	E	L		64	20	10	Thompson, John R., Jr.
1990		I	32	3	MW	L		64	24	7	Thompson, John R., Jr.
1991		I	32	8	W	L		64	19	13	Thompson, John R., Jr.
1992		I	32	6	W	L		64	22	10	Thompson, John R., Jr.
1994		I	32	9	MW	L		64	19	12	Thompson, John R., Jr.
1981		I	48	7	E	L		48	20	12	Thompson, John R., Jr.
1997		I	64	10	W	L		64	20	10	Thompson, John R., Jr.
1993	W	I	16		E	L		48	23	7	Knapp, Patrick

GEORGIA

Year	M/W	Div	F	SD	Reg	BD	Bye	#T	W	L	Coach
1983	M	I	3	4	E	A	To R32	52	24	10	Durham, Hugh
1996		I	16	8	W	L		64	21	10	Smith, Orlando H. "Tubby"
1985		I	32	6	E	L		64	22	9	Durham, Hugh
1987		I	64	8	W	L		64	18	12	Durham, Hugh
1990		I	64	7	MW	L		64	20	9	Durham, Hugh
1991		I	64	11	SE	L		64	17	13	Durham, Hugh
1997		I	64	3	SE	L		64	24	9	Smith, Orlando H. "Tubby"
1985	W	I	2		W	L		32	29	5	Landers, Andy
1996		I	2	2	MW	L		64	28	5	Landers, Andy
1983		I	3		ME	A	To R32	36	27	7	Landers, Andy
1995		I	3	3	MW	L		64	28	5	Landers, Andy
1984		I	8		ME	A		32	30	3	Landers, Andy
1991		I	8	1	W	L	To R32	48	28	4	Landers, Andy
1997		I	8	2	W	L		64	25	6	Landers, Andy
1986		I	16		ME	A	To R32	40	30	2	Landers, Andy

Year	M/W	Div	F	SD	Reg	BD	Bye	#T	W	L	Coach
1987		I	16	2	MW	L	To R32	40	27	5	Landers, Andy
1988		I	16	4	ME	L	To R32	40	21	10	Landers, Andy
1982		I	32		MW	L		32	21	9	Landers, Andy
1989		I	32	5	ME	L		48	23	7	Landers, Andy
1990		I	32	2	W	L	To R32	48	25	5	Landers, Andy
1993		I	32		W	L		48	21	13	Landers, Andy
1998		I	64	7	E	L		64	17	11	Landers, Andy

GEORGIA COLLEGE

Year	M/W	Div	F	SD	Reg	BD	Bye	#T	W	L	Coach
1997	M	II	48	4	SA	A		48	25	5	Sellers, Terry
1997	W	II	32	6	SA	L		48	23	8	Carrick, John
1996		II	48	5	SA	A		48	21	9	Carrick, John

GEORGIA SOUTHERN

Year	M/W	Div	F	SD	Reg	BD	Bye	#T	W	L	Coach
1970	M	II	16		SA	L		32	17	6	Radovich, Frank
1983		I	52	13	ME	A		52	18	12	Kerns, Frank
1987		I	64	15	E	A		64	20	11	Kerns, Frank
1992		I	64	15	SE	A		64	25	6	Kerns, Frank
1993	W	I	48		ME	A		48	21	9	Greer, Drema Sue
1994		I	64	14	E	A		64	21	9	Greer, Drema Sue

GEORGIA STATE

Year	M/W	Div	F	SD	Reg	BD	Bye	#T	W	L	Coach
1991	M	I	64	16	SE	A		64	16	15	Reinhart, Bob

GEORGIA TECH

Year	M/W	Div	F	SD	Reg	BD	Bye	#T	W	L	Coach
1990	M	I	3	4	SE	A		64	28	7	Cremins, Bobby
1960		I	8		ME	A	To R16	25	22	6	Hyder, John C. "Whack"
1985		I	8	2	E	A		64	27	8	Cremins, Bobby
1986		I	16	2	SE	L		64	27	7	Cremins, Bobby
1992		I	16	7	MW	L		64	23	12	Cremins, Bobby
1996		I	16	3	SE	L		64	24	12	Cremins, Bobby
1988		I	32	5	E	L		64	22	10	Cremins, Bobby
1991		I	32	8	MW	L		64	17	13	Cremins, Bobby
1987		I	64	7	MW	L		64	16	13	Cremins, Bobby
1989		I	64	6	MW	L		64	20	12	Cremins, Bobby
1993		I	64	4	W	A		64	19	11	Cremins, Bobby
1993	W	I	48		ME	L		48	16	11	Berenato, Agnus McGlade

GETTYSBURG

Year	M/W	Div	F	SD	Reg	BD	Bye	#T	W	L	Coach
1996	M	III	64	5	MA	L		64	18	9	Petrie, George
1984	W	III	16		C	L		32	22	4	Higgins, Kay
1985		III	32		MA	L		32	19	6	Hurst, Anne
1995		III	32		MA	L		64	20	5	Kirkpatrick, Michael

GONZAGA

Year	M/W	Div	F	SD	Reg	BD	Bye	#T	W	L	Coach
1995	M	I	64	14	W	A		64	21	9	Fitzgerald, Dan

GOUCHER

Year	M/W	Div	F	SD	Reg	BD	Bye	#T	W	L	Coach
1995	M	III	32	7	MA	A		64	19	10	Trevino, Leonard
1997		III	32	2	MA	A		64	23	6	Trevino, Leonard
1996	W	III	64		A	L		64	17	10	Navarro, Noelle

Year	M/W	Div	F	SD	Reg	BD	Bye	#T	W	L	Coach
GRAMBLING STATE											
1958	M	II	8		SC			32	27	4	Hobdy, Frederick C.
1976		II	16		SC	L		32	22	9	Hobdy, Frederick C.
1994	W	I	64	15	E	A		64	23	7	Bibbs, Patricia Cage
1996		I	64	16	W	A		64	21	7	Bibbs, Patricia Cage
1997		I	64	14	MW	A		64	24	6	Bibbs, Patricia Cage
1998		I	64	16	MW	A		64	23	7	Ponton, David
GRAND CANYON											
1993	M	II	23		W	L		32	20	11	McCrary, Leighton
1992		II	24		W	L		32	21	7	McCrary, Leighton
1996		II	32	5	W	L		48	23	6	McCrary, Leighton
1997		II	32	4	W	L		48	23	6	McCrary, Leighton
1995		II	48	4	W	L		48	17	11	McCrary, Leighton
1998		II	48	3	W	L		48	17	10	McCrary, Leighton
1997	W	II	48	5	W	L		48	15	11	Hanks, Julie
GRAND VALLEY STATE											
1985	M	II	16		NC	L		32	21	8	Villemure, Thomas
1991		II	16		GL	A		32	26	5	Villemure, Thomas
1992		II	32		GL	L		32	20	11	Villemure, Thomas
1997		II	48	4	GL	A		48	23	6	Smith, Jay
1988	W	II	32		GL	L		32	20	8	Baker-Grzyb, Pat
1990		II	32		GL	L		32	22	6	Vandebunte, Carol
1998		II	32	3	GL	L		48	23	5	Charney, Claudette
GREENSBORO											
1994	M	III	8		S	A	To R32	40	26	4	Hanger, Samuel
1985		III	24		S	A		32	21	7	Mikels, Ron
1995		III	32	4	S	A		64	19	10	Hanger, Samuel
1997	W	III	64		S	A		64	19	9	Johnson, Steve
GRINNELL											
1962	M	II	32		MW			32	18	4	Pfitsch, John A.
1996		III	64	8	MW	A		64	17	8	Arseneault, David
GROVE CITY											
1979	M	III	24		MA	L		32	18	7	Barr, John F.
1983		III	24		MA	L		32	21	4	Barr, John F.
1989		III	24		MA	L	To R32	40	20	6	Barr, John F.
1976		III	28		MA	L		28	16	6	Barr, John F.
1982	W	III	16		None	L		16	19	5	Ellis, Terry
1983		III	16		MA	L		32	22	5	Ellis, Terry
GUSTAVUS ADOLPHUS											
1998	M	III	8	3	W	A		48	26	4	Hanson, Mark
1987		III	16		W	A		32	15	13	Brock, Charles
1992		III	16		W	A	To R32	40	22	7	Hanson, Mark
1996		III	16	2	W	A		64	24	5	Hanson, Mark
1958		II	32		MW	L		32	15	11	Skoog, Myer U. "Whitey"
1997		III	32	7	W	A		64	21	7	Hanson, Mark
1989		III	40		W	A		40	14	14	Brock, Charles

Year	M/W	Div	F	SD	Reg	BD	Bye	#T	W	L	Coach
1991	W	III	32		W	L		32	18	8	Kennedy, Tim
1995		III	64		W	L		64	16	10	Moline, Peg

HAMILTON

Year	M/W	Div	F	SD	Reg	BD	Bye	#T	W	L	Coach
1995	M	III	16	2	E	L		64	21	6	Murphy, Thomas Edward
1998		III	16	3	E	L		48	17	10	Murphy, Thomas Edward
1996		III	64	3	E	L		64	16	9	Murphy, Thomas Edward
1997		III	64	5	E	L		64	15	10	Murphy, Thomas Edward

HAMLINE

Year	M/W	Div	F	SD	Reg	BD	Bye	#T	W	L	Coach
1977	M	III	4		MW	L		30	22	8	Litzenberger, Fred L.
1975		III	16		W	L	To R16	30	19	11	Meyer, Dr. Don W.
1962		II	24		MW	L		32	18	4	Hutton, Joseph W., Sr.

HAMPDEN-SYDNEY

Year	M/W	Div	F	SD	Reg	BD	Bye	#T	W	L	Coach
1995	M	III	8	1	S	A		64	28	3	Shaver, Tony
1992		III	16		S	A	To R32	40	24	6	Shaver, Tony
1994		III	16		S	L		40	22	6	Shaver, Tony
1998		III	16	2	S	A	To R32	48	23	6	Shaver, Tony
1989		III	24		SA	A	To R32	40	21	8	Shaver, Tony
1997		III	64	1	S	L		64	21	7	Shaver, Tony

HAMPTON

Year	M/W	Div	F	SD	Reg	BD	Bye	#T	W	L	Coach
1983	M	II	24		SA	A		32	23	7	Ford, Henry "Hank"
1991		II	24		S	A		32	22	10	Avery, Malcolm "Zeke"
1988	W	II	1		SA	L		32	33	1	Sweat, James E.
1985		II	3		SA	A	To R16	24	30	4	Sweat, James E.
1986		II	8		SA	L		24	26	6	Sweat, James E.
1987		II	8		SA	A	To R16	24	30	2	Sweat, James E.
1989		II	32		SA	L		32	20	9	Laster, Jr. "Tiny"
1991		II	32		S	L		32	26	6	Laster, Jr. "Tiny"

HANOVER

Year	M/W	Div	F	SD	Reg	BD	Bye	#T	W	L	Coach
1995	M	III	32	5	MW	L		64	22	7	Beitzel, Dr. Michael
1996		III	32	3	MW	L		64	21	6	Beitzel, Dr. Michael
1997	W	III	64		GL	A		64	17	10	Snyder, Christa

HARDIN-SIMMONS

Year	M/W	Div	F	SD	Reg	BD	Bye	#T	W	L	Coach
1953	M		22		W(A)	A		22	19	12	Scott, Bill
1957		I	23		W	A		23	17	9	Scott, Bill

HARTFORD

Year	M/W	Div	F	SD	Reg	BD	Bye	#T	W	L	Coach
1972	M	II	16		E	L	To R32	36	18	6	McCullough, Gordon F.
1974		II	16		NENG	L	To R32	44	20	4	McCullough, Gordon F.
1975		II	24		NENG	L		32	18	7	McCullough, Gordon F.
1973		II	42		NENG	L		42	17	7	McCullough, Gordon F.

HARTWICK

Year	M/W	Div	F	SD	Reg	BD	Bye	#T	W	L	Coach
1988	M	III	4		E	L		32	23	6	Lambros, Nicholas H.
1971		II	8		E	L		32	20	6	Chipman, Dr. Leroy
1973		II	16		E	L	To R32	42	19	7	Chipman, Dr. Leroy
1974		II	16		E	L	To R32	44	22	5	Chipman, Dr. Leroy

Year	M/W	Div	F	SD	Reg	BD	Bye	#T	W	L	Coach
1977		II	16		E	L		32	22	4	Chipman, Dr. Leroy
1979		II	16		E	L		32	22	5	Lambros, Nicholas H.
1980		II	16		E	L		32	21	5	Lambros, Nicholas H.
1983		III	16		E	L		32	17	9	Lambros, Nicholas H.
1965		II	24		NE	L		32	19	2	Coniam, Charles Jack
1970		II	24		E	L		32	18	6	Chipman, Dr. Leroy
1978		II	24		E	L		32	22	4	Lambros, Nicholas H.
1985		III	24		E	L		32	19	7	Lambros, Nicholas H.
1975		II	32		E	L		32	19	7	Chipman, Dr. Leroy
1976		II	32		E	L		32	21	5	Chipman, Dr. Leroy
1996		III	64	7	E	L		64	17	9	Lambros, Nicholas H.
1990	W	III	16		E	L		32	24	5	Kragalott, Arden
1991		III	16		E	L		32	21	8	Kragalott, Arden
1983		III	24		E	L		32	17	5	Lauder, Sue
1995		III	64		E	L		64	20	8	Thompson, Daphne Joy
1996		III	64		E	A		64	20	7	Thompson, Daphne Joy
1997		III	64		E	L		64	21	8	Thompson, Daphne Joy

HARVARD

Year	M/W	Div	F	SD	Reg	BD	Bye	#T	W	L	Coach
1946	M		8		E	L		8	20	3	Stahl, Floyd S.
1998	W	I	32	16	W	A		64	23	5	Smith, Kathleen Delaney
1996		I	64	14	ME	A		64	20	7	Smith, Kathleen Delaney
1997		I	64	16	E	A		64	20	7	Smith, Kathleen Delaney

HAWAII

Year	M/W	Div	F	SD	Reg	BD	Bye	#T	W	L	Coach
1972	M	I	25		W	L		25	24	3	Rocha, Ephraim J. "Red"
1994		I	64	13	W	A		64	18	15	Wallace, Riley
1990	W	I	32	9	W	L		48	26	4	Goo, Vince
1989		I	48	12	W	L		48	20	10	Goo, Vince
1994		I	64	12	W	L		64	25	5	Goo, Vince
1996		I	64	11	W	A		64	23	6	Goo, Vince
1998		I	64	8	W	L		64	24	4	Goo, Vince

HEIDELBERG

Year	M/W	Div	F	SD	Reg	BD	Bye	#T	W	L	Coach
1984	M	III	16		GL	L		32	24	7	Hill, John D.
1995		III	64	7	GL	L		64	17	11	Hill, John D.
1990	W	III	3		A	A		32	27	6	McConnell, Karen

HENDRIX

Year	M/W	Div	F	SD	Reg	BD	Bye	#T	W	L	Coach
1996	M	III	32	4	S	L		64	21	6	Garrison, Cliff
1995		III	64	7	S	L		64	19	6	Garrison, Cliff
1997	W	III	32		S	A		64	23	4	Winkelman, "Chuck"
1996		III	64		S	L		64	21	5	Winkelman, "Chuck"

HIGH POINT

Year	M/W	Div	F	SD	Reg	BD	Bye	#T	W	L	Coach
1996	M	II	32	3	SA	L		48	24	7	Steele, Jerry
1997		II	32	5	E	A		48	18	12	Steele, Jerry
1997	W	II	16	5	E	A		48	26	6	Ellenberg, Dr. Joe

Year	M/W	Div	F	SD	Reg	BD	Bye	#T	W	L	Coach
HILLSDALE											
1995	M	II	48	6	GL	A		48	15	14	Balikian, Bernie
HIRAM											
1975	M	III	23		GL	L		30	15	7	Hollinger, William H.
1984		III	24		NE	A		32	15	9	Hollinger, William H.
1976		III	28		GL	A		28	16	6	Hollinger, William H.
1974		II	32		ME	L		44	20	4	Hollinger, William H.
1973		II	42		ME			42	19	4	Hollinger, William H.
HOFSTRA											
1964	M	II	8		E	L		32	23	6	Lynner, Paul K.
1959		II	16		E			32	20	7	Van Breda Kolff, Willem "Butch"
1962		II	16		E			32	24	4	Van Breda Kolff, Willem "Butch"
1963		II	24		E			32	23	7	Lynner, Paul K.
1976		I	32		E	A		32	18	12	Gaeckler, D. Roger
1977		I	32		E	A		32	23	7	Gaeckler, D. Roger
HOLY CROSS (MA)											
1947	M		1		E	L		8	27	3	Julian, Alvin F. "Doggie"
1948			3		E	L		8	26	4	Julian, Alvin F. "Doggie"
1950			8		E	L		8	27	4	Sheary, Lester H. "Buster"
1953			8		E(A)	L		22	20	6	Sheary, Lester H. "Buster"
1956			25		E	L		25	22	5	Leenig, Roy H.
1977		I	32		ME	L		32	23	6	Blaney, George R.
1980		I	48	11	E	A		48	19	11	Blaney, George R.
1993		I	64	13	E	A		64	23	7	Blaney, George R.
1985	W	I	32		E	A		32	21	7	Palazzi, Togo A.
1991		I	32	11	ME	L		48	25	6	Gibbons, Bill, Jr.
1989		I	48	9	ME	A		48	21	10	Gibbons, Bill, Jr.
1995		I	64	16	MW	A		64	21	9	Gibbons, Bill, Jr.
1996		I	64	15	E	A		64	23	10	Gibbons, Bill, Jr.
1998		I	64	14	MW	A		64	21	9	Gibbons, Bill, Jr.
HOPE											
1996	M	III	2	2	GL	A		64	28	4	Van Wieren, Dr. Glenn
1998		III	2	2	GL	L	To R32	48	26	5	Van Wieren, Dr. Glenn
1959		II	8		GL			32	20	3	DeVette, Russell B.
1958		II	16		GL			32	19	3	DeVette, Russell B.
1982		III	16		GL	A		32	19	5	Van Wieren, Dr. Glenn
1983		III	16		GL	A		32	19	4	Van Wieren, Dr. Glenn
1985		III	16		GL	A		32	22	4	Van Wieren, Dr. Glenn
1988		III	16		GL	A		32	19	8	Van Wieren, Dr. Glenn
1997		III	16	1	GL	A		64	26	3	Van Wieren, Dr. Glenn
1984		III	32		GL	A		32	22	2	Van Wieren, Dr. Glenn
1987		III	32		GL	A		32	21	5	Van Wieren, Dr. Glenn
1990		III	32		GL	L	To R32	40	22	4	Van Wieren, Dr. Glenn
1991		III	32		GL	A	To R32	40	24	2	Van Wieren, Dr. Glenn
1992		III	32		GL	L		40	23	6	Van Wieren, Dr. Glenn
1989		III	40		GL	L		40	19	5	Van Wieren, Dr. Glenn
1995		III	64	1	GL	A		64	26	1	Van Wieren, Dr. Glenn

Year	M/W	Div	F	SD	Reg	BD	Bye	#T	W	L	Coach
1990	W	III	1		GL	L		32	24	2	Wise, Susan
1998		III	48	6	GL	A		48	16	11	Morehouse, Brian
1995		III	64		GL	A		64	20	7	Gugino, Tod

HOUSTON

Year	M/W	Div	F	SD	Reg	BD	Bye	#T	W	L	Coach
1983	M	I	2	1	MW	A	To R32	52	31	3	Lewis, Guy V.
1984		I	2	2	MW	A	To R32	53	32	5	Lewis, Guy V.
1967		I	3		MW	L		23	27	4	Lewis, Guy V.
1982		I	3	6	MW	L		48	25	8	Lewis, Guy V.
1968		I	4		MW	L		23	31	2	Lewis, Guy V.
1966		I	12		W	L		22	23	6	Lewis, Guy V.
1971		I	12		MW	L		25	22	7	Lewis, Guy V.
1956			16		W	A	To R16	25	19	7	Pasche, Alden
1961		I	16		MW	L		24	17	11	Lewis, Guy V.
1965		I	16		MW	L		23	19	10	Lewis, Guy V.
1970		I	16		MW	L		25	25	5	Lewis, Guy V.
1972		I	25		MW	L		25	20	7	Lewis, Guy V.
1973		I	25		MW	L		25	23	4	Lewis, Guy V.
1978		I	32		MW	A		32	25	8	Lewis, Guy V.
1981		I	48	8	E	L		48	21	9	Lewis, Guy V.
1987		I	64	12	SE	L		64	18	12	Foster, Pat
1990		I	64	8	SE	L		64	25	8	Foster, Pat
1992		I	64	10	MW	A		64	25	6	Foster, Pat
1988	W	I	32	6	MW	L	To R32	40	22	7	Williams, Greg
1992		I	48	8	W	L		48	22	8	Kenlaw, Jessie

HOUSTON BAPTIST

Year	M/W	Div	F	SD	Reg	BD	Bye	#T	W	L	Coach
1984	M	I	53	13	MW	A		53	24	7	Iba, Clarence Eugene "Gene"

HOWARD (DC)

Year	M/W	Div	F	SD	Reg	BD	Bye	#T	W	L	Coach
1981	M	I	48	12	W	A		48	17	12	Williamson, Altha B.
1992		I	64	16	MW	A		64	17	14	Beard, Alfred, Jr. "Butch"
1982	W	I	32		W	A		32	14	11	Tyler, Sanya
1996		I	64	16	ME	A		64	20	10	Tyler, Sanya
1997		I	64	16	W	A		64	24	6	Tyler, Sanya
1998		I	64	15	ME	A		64	23	7	Tyler, Sanya

HOWARD PAYNE

Year	M/W	Div	F	SD	Reg	BD	Bye	#T	W	L	Coach
1984	W	II	24		SC	A		24	11	18	Campbell, Sharon

HUMBOLDT STATE

Year	M/W	Div	F	SD	Reg	BD	Bye	#T	W	L	Coach
1978	M	III	8		W	L	To R16	30	17	10	Cosentino, Jim
1980		III	16		W	L		32	18	10	Cosentino, Jim
1979		III	24		W	L		32	18	9	Conentino, Jim
1990		II	24		W	A		32	20	11	Wood, Tom
1983		II	32		W	L		32	18	12	Wood, Tom
1995	W	II	48	6	W	L		48	18	10	Martin, Pam

Year	M/W	Div	F	SD	Reg	BD	Bye	#T	W	L	Coach
HUNTER											
1998	M	III	8	1	A	A	To R32	48	28	2	Brown, Mike
1993		III	16		A	L	To R32	40	25	4	Amalbert, Ray
1992		III	32		A	L	To R32	40	24	5	Amalbert, Ray
1994		III	32		A	L		40	26	3	Amalbert, Ray
1990		III	40		SA	L		40	20	8	Amalbert, Ray
1995		III	64	6	A	A		64	17	11	Amalbert, Ray
IDAHO											
1982	M	I	16	3	W	A	To R32	48	27	3	Monson, Don
1981		I	48	7	W	A		48	25	4	Monson, Don
1989		I	64	13	W	A		64	25	6	Davis, Kermit, Jr.
1990		I	64	13	W	A		64	25	6	Davis, Kermit, Jr.
1985	W	I	32		W	A		32	28	2	Dobratz, Patty Jo
IDAHO STATE											
1977	M	I	8		W	A		32	25	5	Killingsworth, James
1954			12		W(B)	A		24	22	5	Belko, Steven
1959		I	12		W	A		23	21	7	Grayson, John A.
1957		I	16		W	A		23	25	4	Grayson, John A.
1958		I	16		W	A		24	22	6	Grayson, John A.
1953			22		W(A)	A		22	18	7	Belko, Steven
1955			24		W(B)	A		24	18	8	Belko, Steven
1956			25		FW	A		25	18	8	Belko, Steven
1960		I	25		W	L		25	21	5	Evans, John P.
1974		I	25		W	A		25	20	8	Killingsworth, James
1987		I	64	16	W	A		64	15	16	Boutin, Dr. James
ILLINOIS											
1949	M		3		E	L		8	21	4	Combes, Harry A.
1951			3		E	A		16	22	5	Combes, Harry A.
1952			3		E(B)	A		16	22	4	Combes, Harry A.
1989		I	3	1	MW	L		64	31	5	Henson, Louis R.
1942			8		E	L		8	18	5	Mills, Douglas R.
1963		I	8		ME	A	To R16	25	20	6	Combes, Harry A.
1984		I	8	2	ME	A	To R32	53	26	5	Henson, Louis R.
1981		I	16	4	W	L	To R32	48	21	8	Henson, Louis R.
1985		I	16	3	E	L		64	26	9	Henson, Louis R.
1986		I	32	4	SE	L		64	22	10	Henson, Louis R.
1988		I	32	3	SE	L		64	23	10	Henson, Louis R.
1993		I	32	6	W	L		64	19	13	Henson, Louis R.
1997		I	32	6	SE	L		64	22	10	Kruger, Lon
1998		I	32	5	W	L		64	23	10	Kruger, Lon
1983		I	48	7	W	L		52	21	11	Henson, Louis R.
1987		I	64	3	SE	L		64	23	8	Henson, Louis R.
1990		I	64	5	MW	L		64	21	8	Henson, Louis R.
1994		I	64	8	MW	L		64	17	11	Henson, Louis R.
1995		I	64	11	E	L		64	19	12	Henson, Louis R.

Year	M/W	Div	F	SD	Reg	BD	Bye	#T	W	L	Coach
1997	W	I	16	4	MW	L		64	24	8	Grentz, Theresa Shank
1998		I	16	3	ME	L		64	20	10	Grentz, Theresa Shank
1982		I	32		MW	L		32	21	9	Schroeder, Jane
1986		I	32		ME	L		40	20	10	Golden, Laura L.
1987		I	32	8	ME	L		40	19	10	Golden, Laura L.

ILLINOIS STATE

Year	M/W	Div	F	SD	Reg	BD	Bye	#T	W	L	Coach
1967	M	II	4		MW		To R32	36	18	13	Collie, Dr. James E., Sr.
1969		II	8		GL	L		32	19	10	Collie, Dr. James E., Sr.
1968		II	16		GL		To R32	36	25	3	Collie, Dr. James E., Sr.
1957		II	32		ME	A		32	14	13	Goff, James "Pim"
1962		II	32		GL	L		32	16	11	Collie, Dr. James E., Sr.
1984		I	32	8	MW	L		53	23	8	Donewald, Bob
1985		I	32	9	MW	L		64	22	8	Donewald, Bob
1998		I	32	9	W	A		64	25	6	Stallings, Kevin
1983		I	48	6	ME	A		52	24	7	Donewald, Bob
1990		I	64	14	W	A		64	18	13	Bender, Robert M., Jr.
1997		I	64	11	MW	A		64	24	6	Stallings, Kevin
1983	W	I	32		MW	A	To R32	36	20	10	Hutchison, Dr. Jill
1985		I	32		MW	A		32	23	5	Hutchison, Dr. Jill
1989		I	32	7	MW	A		48	23	8	Hutchison, Dr. Jill

ILLINOIS WESLEYAN

Year	M/W	Div	F	SD	Reg	BD	Bye	#T	W	L	Coach
1997	M	III	1	1	MW	A		64	29	2	Bridges, Dennis L.
1996		III	3	2	MW	L		64	28	3	Bridges, Dennis L.
1986		III	8		MW	A		32	19	10	Bridges, Dennis L.
1988		III	8		MW	L		32	23	6	Bridges, Dennis L.
1990		III	8		MW	L		40	22	9	Bridges, Dennis L.
1995		III	8	2	MW	A		64	24	4	Bridges, Dennis L.
1987		III	16		MW	L		32	17	10	Bridges, Dennis L.
1992		III	16		MW	A	To R32	40	22	6	Bridges, Dennis L.
1994		III	16		MW	A	To R32	40	19	8	Bridges, Dennis L.
1998		III	16	1	MW	A	To R32	48	22	5	Bridges, Dennis L.
1984		III	32		MW	A		32	17	11	Bridges, Dennis L.
1991		III	40		MW	A		40	18	9	Bridges, Dennis L.
1995	W	III	64		C	L		64	20	6	Neal, Mandy
1996		III	64		C	L		64	18	8	Neal, Mandy

ILLINOIS: CHICAGO

Year	M/W	Div	F	SD	Reg	BD	Bye	#T	W	L	Coach
1998	M	I	64	9	E	L		64	22	6	Collins, Jimmy

INDIANA

Year	M/W	Div	F	SD	Reg	BD	Bye	#T	W	L	Coach
1940	M		1		E	L		8	20	3	McCracken, E. Branch
1953			1		E(B)	A	To R16	22	23	3	McCracken, E. Branch
1976		I	1		ME	A		32	32	0	Knight, Robert M.
1981		I	1	3	ME	A	To R32	48	26	9	Knight, Robert M.
1987		I	1	1	MW	A		64	30	4	Knight, Robert M.
1973		I	3		ME	A	To R16	25	22	6	Knight, Robert M.
1992		I	3	2	W	L		64	27	7	Knight, Robert M.
1975		I	8		ME	A		32	31	1	Knight, Robert M.

Year	M/W	Div	F	SD	Reg	BD	Bye	#T	W	L	Coach
1984		I	8	4	E	L	To R32	53	22	9	Knight, Robert M.
1993		I	8	1	MW	A		64	31	4	Knight, Robert M.
1954			12		E(A)	A	To R16	24	20	4	McCracken, E. Branch
1958		I	12		ME	A	To R16	24	13	11	McCracken, E. Branch
1967		I	12		ME	A	To R16	23	18	8	Watson, Lou
1978		I	16		E	L		32	21	8	Knight, Robert M.
1980		I	16	2	ME	A	To R32	48	21	8	Knight, Robert M.
1983		I	16	2	ME	A	To R32	52	24	6	Knight, Robert M.
1989		I	16	2	W	A		64	27	8	Knight, Robert M.
1991		I	16	2	SE	L		64	29	5	Knight, Robert M.
1994		I	16	5	E	L		64	21	9	Knight, Robert M.
1982		I	32	5	ME	L		48	19	10	Knight, Robert M.
1998		I	32	7	E	L		64	20	12	Knight, Robert M.
1986		I	64	3	E	L		64	21	8	Knight, Robert M.
1988		I	64	4	E	L		64	19	10	Knight, Robert M.
1990		I	64	8	E	L		64	18	11	Knight, Robert M.
1995		I	64	9	W	L		64	19	12	Knight, Robert M.
1996		I	64	6	SE	L		64	19	12	Knight, Robert M.
1997		I	64	8	E	L		64	22	11	Knight, Robert M.
1983	W	I	16		ME	A	To R32	36	19	11	Jeremiah, Dr. Maryalyce
1994		I	64	12	ME	L		64	19	9	Izard, Jim
1995		I	64	14	MW	L		64	19	10	Izard, Jim

INDIANA (PA)

Year	M/W	Div	F	SD	Reg	BD	Bye	#T	W	L	Coach
1995	M	II	3	1	E	A	To R32	48	29	2	Kanaskie, Kurt
1994		II	8		E	L		32	27	3	Kanaskie, Kurt
1996		II	16	2	E	L		48	24	7	Kanaskie, Kurt
1988	W	II	32		E	A		32	17	14	Kiger, Jan H.

INDIANA STATE

Year	M/W	Div	F	SD	Reg	BD	Bye	#T	W	L	Coach
1968	M	II	2		GL		To R32	36	23	8	Stauffer, Gordon C.
1979		I	2	1	MW	A	To R32	40	33	1	Hodges, Bill
1967		II	16		GL		To R32	36	21	5	Klueh, Duane M.
1966		II	32		GL		To R32	36	22	6	Klueh, Duane M.

INDIANA-PURDUE: FORT WAYNE

Year	M/W	Div	F	SD	Reg	BD	Bye	#T	W	L	Coach
1993	M	II	32		GL	A		32	23	6	Piazza, Andy
1990	W	II	32		GL	L		32	22	7	Rosinski, Teri
1992		II	32		SC	L		32	22	7	Kleinfelter, Eileen
1996		II	48	5	GL	L		48	23	5	Bowden, Pam

INDIANAPOLIS

Year	M/W	Div	F	SD	Reg	BD	Bye	#T	W	L	Coach
1996	M	II	32	5	GL	L		48	20	9	Waltman, Royce
1997		II	32	1	GL	A	To R32	48	23	5	Waltman, Royce
1993	W	II	32		GL	A		32	24	4	Mallender, Charles "Chuck"
1995		II	48	3	GL	L		48	21	7	Hicks, Lisa

Year	M/W	Div	F	SD	Reg	BD	Bye	#T	W	L	Coach
IONA											
1980	M	I	32	6	E	L		48	29	5	Valvano, James T.
1979		I	40	8	E	L		40	23	6	Valvano, James T.
1984		I	48	10	E	A		53	23	8	Kennedy, Patrick
1985		I	64	13	E	A		64	26	5	Kennedy, Patrick
1998		I	64	12	S	A		64	27	6	Welsh, Tim
IOWA											
1956	M		2		MW	A	To R16	25	20	6	O'Connor, Frank "Bucky"
1955			4		E(A)	A	To R16	24	19	7	O'Connor, Frank "Bucky"
1980		I	4	5	E	A		48	23	10	Olson, Robert Luther "Lute"
1987		I	8	2	W	L		64	30	5	Davis, Dr. Thomas
1970		I	12		ME	A	To R16	25	20	5	Miller, Ralph H. "Cappy"
1983		I	16	7	MW	L		52	21	10	Olson, Robert Luther "Lute"
1986		I	16	11	MW	L		64	20	12	Raveling, George
1988		I	16	5	W	L		64	24	10	Davis, Dr. Thomas
1979		I	32	4	ME	L	To R32	40	20	8	Olson, Robert Luther "Lute"
1981		I	32	3	MW	L	To R32	48	21	7	Olson, Robert Luther "Lute"
1982		I	32	6	W	L		48	21	8	Olson, Robert Luther "Lute"
1989		I	32	4	E	L		64	23	10	Davis, Dr. Thomas
1991		I	32	7	MW	L		64	21	11	Davis, Dr. Thomas
1992		I	32	9	E	L		64	19	11	Davis, Dr. Thomas
1993		I	32	4	SE	L		64	23	9	Davis, Dr. Thomas
1996		I	32	6	W	L		64	23	9	Davis, Dr. Thomas
1997		I	32	8	W	L		64	22	10	Davis, Dr. Thomas
1985		I	64	8	W	L		64	21	11	Raveling, George
1993	W	I	3		ME	A	To R32	48	27	4	Stringer, C. Vivian
1987		I	8	3	MW	L	To R32	40	26	5	Stringer, C. Vivian
1988		I	8	1	W	A	To R32	40	29	2	Stringer, C. Vivian
1989		I	16	3	MW	L	To R32	48	27	5	Stringer, C. Vivian
1996		I	16	2	ME	L		64	27	4	Lee, Angie
1986		I	32		ME	L	To R32	40	22	7	Stringer, C. Vivian
1990		I	32	3	ME	A	To R32	48	23	6	Stringer, C. Vivian
1991		I	32	6	W	L		48	21	9	Stringer, C. Vivian
1992		I	32	1	MW	A	To R32	48	25	4	Stringer, C. Vivian
1994		I	32	3	MW	L		64	21	7	Stringer, C. Vivian
1997		I	32	9	MW	A		64	18	12	Lee, Angie
1998		I	32	4	W	L		64	18	11	Lee, Angie
IOWA STATE											
1944	M		3		W	L		8	14	4	Menze, Louis E.
1997		I	16	6	MW	L		64	22	9	Floyd, Tim
1992		I	32	10	E	L		64	21	13	Orr, John M. "Johnny"
1995		I	32	7	SE	L		64	23	11	Floyd, Tim
1996		I	32	5	MW	A		64	24	9	Floyd, Tim
1985		I	64	13	MW	L		64	21	13	Orr, John M. "Johnny"
1986		I	64	7	MW	L		64	22	11	Orr, John M. "Johnny"
1988		I	64	12	E	L		64	20	12	Orr, John M. "Johnny"
1989		I	64	10	SE	L		64	17	12	Orr, John M. "Johnny"
1993		I	64	8	W	L		64	20	11	Orr, John M. "Johnny"

Year	M/W	Div.	F	SD	Reg	BD	Bye	#T	W	L	Coach
1998	W	I	32	4	ME	L		64	25	8	Fennelly, Bill
1997		I	64	12	W	L		64	17	12	Fennelly, Bill

ITHACA

1972	M	II	24		E		To R32	36	15	8	Hurst, Hugh
1982		III	24		E	A		32	22	5	Baker, Tom
1977		III	30		E	A		30	15	10	Lehnus, Darryl
1964		II	32		ME	L		32	16	5	Wood, Carlton
1983		III	32		E	A		32	19	8	Baker, Tom
1987		III	32		E	A		32	16	12	Baker, Tom
1993		III	32		E	L		40	20	7	Baker, Tom
1997	W	III	32		E	A		64	20	8	Pritchard, Christine

JACKSON STATE (MS)

1957	M	II	16		MW	A		32	22	2	Wilson, Dr. Harrison B.
1968		II	23		SW		To R32	36	24	3	Covington, Paul E.
1964		II	24		GL			32	21	6	Covington, Paul E.
1965		II	24		GL	L		32	21	7	Wilson, Dr. Harrison B.
1966		II	32		SW		To R32	36	24	7	Wilson, Dr. Harrison B.
1997		I	64	16	SE	A		64	14	16	Stoglin, Lee Andrew "Andy"
1982	W	I	32		ME	A		32	28	8	Magee, Sadie E.
1983		I	36		MW	L		36	21	8	Magee, Sadie E.
1995		I	64	15	MW	A		64	22	7	Pennington, Andrew

JACKSONVILLE (FL)

1970	M	I	2		ME	L		25	27	2	Williams, Joe L.
1971		I	25		ME	L		25	22	4	Wasdin, Tom
1973		I	25		ME	L		25	21	6	Wasdin, Tom
1979		I	40	9	MW	A		40	19	11	Locke, Taylor O. "Tates"
1986		I	64	8	MW	A		64	21	10	Wenzel, Robert

JACKSONVILLE STATE (AL)

1985	M	II	1		S	A		32	31	1	Jones, Bill E.
1989		II	4		S	A		32	27	6	Jones, Bill E.
1983		II	8		S	A		32	24	8	Jones, Bill E.
1990		II	8		S	A		32	24	5	Jones, Bill E.
1992		II	8		S	A		32	28	2	Jones, Bill E.
1984		II	16		SC	L		32	23	8	Jones, Bill E.
1981		II	24		SC	L		32	22	8	Jones, Bill E.
1980		II	32		SC	A		32	20	7	Jones, Bill E.
1991	W	II	8		S	A		32	26	4	Mabrey, Tony
1988		II	16		S	L		32	22	7	Mathis, Richard
1989		II	16		S	L		32	24	6	Mathis, Richard
1990		II	16		S	L		32	25	5	Mathis, Richard
1993		II	32		S	A		32	18	11	Mabrey, Tony

JAMES MADISON

1976	M	II	32		SA	L		32	18	9	Campanelli, Lou
1981		I	32	10	E	L		48	21	9	Campanelli, Lou
1982		I	32	9	E	L		48	24	6	Campanelli, Lou
1983		I	32	10	E	L		52	20	11	Campanelli, Lou

Year	M/W	Div	F	SD	Reg	BD	Bye	#T	W	L	Coach
1974		II	44		S	L		44	20	6	Campanelli, Lou
1994		I	64	14	E	A		64	20	10	Driesell, Charles G. "Lefty"
1986	W	I	16		E	L		40	28	4	Moorman, Shelia
1987		I	16	4	E	A	To R32	40	27	4	Moorman, Shelia
1988		I	16	4	E	A	To R32	40	27	4	Moorman, Shelia
1991		I	16	8	E	L		48	26	5	Moorman, Shelia
1989		I	32	6	E	A		48	26	4	Moorman, Shelia
1996		I	64	13	ME	L		64	21	9	Moorman, Shelia

JERSEY CITY STATE

Year	M/W	Div	F	SD	Reg	BD	Bye	#T	W	L	Coach
1986	M	III	4		SA	A		32	24	8	Brown, Charles H.
1992		III	4		A	A	To R32	40	27	5	Brown, Charles H.
1979		III	8		SA	A		32	24	5	Weinstein, Paul
1980		III	8		W	L		32	25	4	Weinstein, Paul
1989		III	16		SA	L	To R32	40	24	4	Brown, Charles H.
1978		III	23		SA	L		30	20	7	Weinstein, Paul
1987		III	32		SA	L		32	19	8	Brown, Charles H.
1990		III	32		A	A	To R32	40	25	3	Brown, Charles H.
1995		III	32	4	A	A		64	19	9	Brown, Charles H.
1996		III	32	6	A	L		64	16	11	Brown, Charles H.
1998		III	32	4	A	L		48	19	8	Brown, Charles H.
1973		II	42		E			42	16	10	Schiner, Lawrence R.
1974		II	44		E	A		44	20	6	Schiner, Lawrence R.
1997		III	64	5	A	L		64	17	9	Brown, Charles H.

JOHN CARROLL

Year	M/W	Div	F	SD	Reg	BD	Bye	#T	W	L	Coach
1998	M	III	8	4	GL	L		48	22	7	Moran, Mike
1983		III	32		GL	A		32	17	7	Baab, Tim
1986		III	32		S	A		32	11	13	Baab, Tim
1996		III	32	3	GL	A		64	19	8	Moran, Mike
1997		III	64	6	GL	L		64	20	7	Moran, Mike

JOHNS HOPKINS

Year	M/W	Div	F	SD	Reg	BD	Bye	#T	W	L	Coach
1990	M	III	16		MA	L		40	20	8	Nelson, William H.
1991		III	32		MA	A		40	19	10	Nelson, William H.
1992		III	32		MA	L	To R32	40	20	8	Nelson, William H.
1994		III	32		MA	L	To R32	40	20	7	Nelson, William H.
1998		III	32	3	MA	L		48	21	7	Nelson, William H.
1993		III	40		MA	L		40	19	7	Nelson, William H.
1974		II	44		ME	A		44	17	9	Rupert, Gary
1997	W	III	8		MA	L		64	25	5	Clelan-Blank, Nancy
1998		III	8	1	MA	L	To R32	48	24	5	Clelan-Blank, Nancy
1995		III	16		MA	L		64	22	7	Clelan-Blank, Nancy
1996		III	32		MA	A		64	20	8	Clelan-Blank, Nancy

JOHNSON C SMITH

Year	M/W	Div	F	SD	Reg	BD	Bye	#T	W	L	Coach
1992	M	II	16		SA	L		32	25	7	Joyner, Steven Wayne
1991		II	24		SA	L		32	23	7	Joyner, Steven Wayne
1960		II	32		SC			32	18	7	McGirt, Edward C.
1987		II	32		GL	L		32	21	9	Moore, Robert D.
1995		II	32	3	SA	L		48	21	9	Joyner, Steven Wayne
1998		II	48	3	SA	L		48	21	7	Joyner, Steven Wayne

Year	M/W	Div	F	SD	Reg	BD	Bye	#T	W	L	Coach
1985	W	II	24		SA	L		24	17	9	Joyner, Steven Wayne
1992		II	32		SA	L		32	22	9	Evans-Liebert, Hythia

JUNIATA

Year	M/W	Div	F	SD	Reg	BD	Bye	#T	W	L	Coach
1986	W	III	24		MA	L		32	16	6	Latimore, Nancy Harden

KALAMAZOO

Year	M/W	Div	F	SD	Reg	BD	Bye	#T	W	L	Coach
1996	M	III	64	7	GL	L		64	17	11	Haklin, Joe

KANSAS

Year	M/W	Div	F	SD	Reg	BD	Bye	#T	W	L	Coach
1952	M		1		W(A)	A		16	28	3	Allen, Dr. Forrest C. "Phog"
1988		I	1	6	MW	L		64	27	11	Brown, Lawrence H.
1940			2		W	L		8	19	6	Allen, Dr. Forrest C. "Phog"
1953			2		W(B)	A	To R16	22	19	6	Allen, Dr. Forrest C. "Phog"
1957		I	2		W	A	To R16	23	24	3	Harp, Richard
1991		I	2	3	SE	L		64	27	8	Williams, Roy
1986		I	3	1	MW	A		64	35	4	Brown, Lawrence H.
1993		I	3	2	MW	L		64	29	7	Williams, Roy
1971		I	4		MW	A	To R16	25	27	3	Owens, Ted
1974		I	4		MW	A	To R16	25	23	7	Owens, Ted
1942			6		W	L		8	17	5	Allen, Dr. Forrest C. "Phog"
1960			8		MW	A	To R16	25	19	9	Harp, Richard
1966		I	8		MW	A	To R16	22	23	4	Owens, Ted
1996		I	8	2	W	L		64	29	5	Williams, Roy
1967		I	16		MW	A	To R16	23	23	4	Owens, Ted
1981		I	16	7	MW	A		48	24	8	Owens, Ted
1987		I	16	5	SE	L		64	25	11	Brown, Lawrence H.
1994		I	16	4	SE	L		64	27	8	Williams, Roy
1995		I	16	1	MW	L		64	25	6	Williams, Roy
1997		I	16	1	SE	A		64	34	2	Williams, Roy
1975		I	32		MW	A		32	19	8	Owens, Ted
1978		I	32		W	L		32	24	5	Owens, Ted
1984		I	32	5	MW	A		53	22	10	Brown, Lawrence H.
1985		I	32	3	SE	L		64	26	8	Brown, Lawrence H.
1990		I	32	2	E	L		64	30	5	Williams, Roy
1992		I	32	1	MW	A		64	27	5	Williams, Roy
1998		I	32	1	MW	A		64	35	4	Williams, Roy
1996	W	I	16	4	E	L		64	22	10	Washington, Marian
1998		I	16	5	W	L		64	23	9	Washington, Marian
1987		I	32	7	MW	A		40	20	13	Washington, Marian
1988		I	32	7	MW	A		40	22	10	Washington, Marian
1994		I	32	9	MW	L		64	22	6	Washington, Marian
1997		I	32	3	W	L		64	25	6	Washington, Marian
1992		I	48	9	MW	L		48	25	6	Washington, Marian
1993		I	48		MW	A		48	21	9	Washington, Marian
1995		I	64	7	ME	L		64	20	11	Washington, Marian

KANSAS STATE

Year	M/W	Div	F	SD	Reg	BD	Bye	#T	W	L	Coach
1951	M		2		W	A		16	25	4	Gardner, James H. "Jack"
1948			4		W	L		8	22	6	Gardner, James H. "Jack"
1958		I	4		MW	A	To R16	24	22	5	Winter, Fred "Tex"
1964		I	4		MW	A	To R16	25	22	7	Winter, Fred "Tex"

Year	M/W	Div	F	SD	Reg	BD	Bye	#T	W	L	Coach
1959		I	8		MW	A	To R16	23	25	2	Winter, Fred "Tex"
1961		I	8		MW	A	To R16	24	22	5	Winter, Fred "Tex"
1972		I	8		MW	A	To R16	25	19	9	Hartman, Jack
1973		I	8		MW	A	To R16	25	23	5	Hartman, Jack
1975		I	8		E	L		32	20	9	Hartman, Jack
1981		I	8	8	W	L		48	24	9	Hartman, Jack
1988		I	8	4	ME	L		64	25	9	Kruger, Lon
1956			12		W	A	To R16	25	17	8	Winter, Fred "Tex"
1970		I	12		MW	A	To R16	25	20	8	Fitzsimmons, Lowell "Cotton"
1968		I	16		MW	A	To R16	23	19	9	Winter, Fred "Tex"
1977		I	16		MW	A		32	23	8	Hartman, Jack
1982		I	16	5	MW	L		48	23	8	Hartman, Jack
1980		I	32	7	MW	A		48	22	9	Hartman, Jack
1987		I	32	9	W	L		64	20	11	Kruger, Lon
1989		I	64	6	E	L		64	19	11	Kruger, Lon
1990		I	64	11	MW	L		64	17	15	Kruger, Lon
1993		I	64	6	SE	L		64	19	11	Altman, Dana
1996		I	64	10	E	L		64	17	12	Asbury, Tom
1982	W	I	8		E	A		32	26	6	Hickey, Lynn
1983		I	16		MW	L	To R32	36	25	7	Hickey, Lynn
1984		I	32		MW	A		32	25	6	Hickey, Lynn
1987		I	40	9	MW	L		40	22	9	Mossman, Matilda Willis
1997		I	64	10	E	L		64	19	12	Patterson, Debbie

KEAN

Year	M/W	Div	F	SD	Reg	BD	Bye	#T	W	L	Coach
1978	M	III	8		SA	A		30	23	5	Palermo, Joseph
1991		III	8		A	A	To R32	40	24	6	Kornegay, Ron
1992		III	32		A	L		40	20	9	Kornegay, Ron
1987	W	III	4		A	A		32	26	4	Wilson, Rich
1983		III	8		A	A		32	25	3	Hannisch, Patricia
1984		III	8		A	A		32	24	2	Hannisch, Patricia
1986		III	16		A	A		32	25	2	Hannisch, Patricia
1985		III	24		A	A		32	23	5	Hannisch, Patricia
1988		III	24		A	A		32	21	8	Wilson, Rich
1989		III	32		A	A		32	24	5	Wilson, Rich
1990		III	32		A	A		32	23	6	Wilson, Rich
1991		III	32		A	A		32	24	3	Wilson, Rich

KEENE STATE

Year	M/W	Div	F	SD	Reg	BD	Bye	#T	W	L	Coach
1990	W	II	32		NENG	L		32	23	7	Le Mieux, John

KENNESAW STATE

Year	M/W	Div	F	SD	Reg	BD	Bye	#T	W	L	Coach
1997	W	II	8	1	SA	A	To R32	48	30	2	Tilley, Colby

KENT STATE

Year	M/W	Div	F	SD	Reg	BD	Bye	#T	W	L	Coach
1982	W	I	32		ME	A		32	17	14	Wartluft, Laurel
1996		I	32	10	W	L		64	24	7	Lindsay, Bob
1998		I	64	13	ME	A		64	23	7	Lindsay, Bob

Year	M/W	Div	F	SD	Reg	BD	Bye	#T	W	L	Coach
KENTUCKY											
1948	M		1		E	L		8	36	3	Rupp, Adolph F.
1949			1		E	L		8	32	2	Rupp, Adolph F.
1951			1		E	A		16	32	2	Rupp, Adolph F.
1958		I	1		ME	A	To R16	24	23	6	Rupp, Adolph F.
1978		I	1		ME	A		32	30	2	Hall, Joe B.
1996		I	1	1	MW	L		64	34	2	Pitino, Richard A. "Rick"
1998		I	1	2	S	A		64	35	4	Smith, Orlando H. "Tubby"
1966		I	2		ME	A	To R16	22	27	2	Rupp, Adolph F.
1975		I	2		ME	A		32	26	5	Hall, Joe B.
1997		I	2	1	W	A		64	35	5	Pitino, Richard A. "Rick"
1942			3		E	L		8	19	6	Rupp, Adolph F.
1984		I	3	1	ME	A	To R32	53	29	5	Hall, Joe B.
1993		I	3	1	SE	A		64	30	4	Pitino, Richard A. "Rick"
1945			6		E	L		8	22	4	Rupp, Adolph F.
1952			8		E(A)	A		16	29	3	Rupp, Adolph F.
1956			8		MW	A	To R16	25	20	6	Rupp, Adolph F.
1957		I	8		ME	A	To R16	23	23	5	Rupp, Adolph F.
1961		I	8		ME	A	To R16	24	19	9	Rupp, Adolph F.
1962		I	8		ME	A	To R16	25	23	3	Rupp, Adolph F.
1968		I	8		ME	A	To R16	23	22	5	Rupp, Adolph F.
1970		I	8		ME	A	To R16	25	26	2	Rupp, Adolph F.
1972		I	8		ME	A	To R16	25	21	7	Rupp, Adolph F.
1973		I	8		ME	A	To R16	25	20	8	Hall, Joe B.
1977		I	8		E	L		32	26	4	Hall, Joe B.
1983		I	8	3	ME	L	To R32	52	23	8	Hall, Joe B.
1986		I	8	1	SE	A		64	32	4	Sutton, Eddie
1992		I	8	2	E	A		64	29	7	Pitino, Richard A. "Rick"
1995		I	8	1	SE	A		64	28	5	Pitino, Richard A. "Rick"
1955			12		E(A)	A	To R16	24	23	3	Rupp, Adolph F.
1959		I	12		ME	A	To R16	23	24	3	Rupp, Adolph F.
1969		I	12		ME	A	To R16	25	23	5	Rupp, Adolph F.
1964		I	16		ME	A	To R16	25	21	6	Rupp, Adolph F.
1971		I	16		ME	A	To R16	25	22	6	Rupp, Adolph F.
1980		I	16	1	ME	L	To R32	48	29	6	Hall, Joe B.
1985		I	16	12	W	L		64	18	13	Hall, Joe B.
1988		I	16	2	SE	A		64	27	6	Sutton, Eddie
1981		I	32	2	ME	L	To R32	48	22	6	Hall, Joe B.
1994		I	32	3	SE	A		64	27	7	Pitino, Richard A. "Rick"
1982		I	48	6	ME	L		48	22	8	Hall, Joe B.
1987		I	64	8	SE	L		64	18	11	Sutton, Eddie
1982	W	I	8		MW	A		32	24	8	Hall, Terry
1983		I	32		ME	L	To R32	36	23	5	Hall, Terry
1986		I	40		MW	L		40	18	11	Hall, Terry
1991		I	48	9	E	L		48	20	9	Fanning, Sharon

Year	M/W	Div	F	SD	Reg	BD	Bye	#T	W	L	Coach
KENTUCKY STATE											
1962	M	II	24		GL			32	16	10	Brown, James B.
1997	W	II	32	6	S	A		48	25	6	Davis, Antonio
KENTUCKY WESLEYAN											
1966	M	II	1		SC	L	To R32	36	24	6	Strong, Guy Rowland
1968		II	1		SC	L	To R32	36	28	3	Daniels, Bob
1969		II	1		S	L		32	25	5	Daniels, Bob
1973		II	1		GL	L	To R32	42	24	6	Jones, Bob
1987		II	1		GL			32	28	5	Chapman, Wayne G.
1990		II	1		GL	A		32	31	2	Chapman, Wayne G.
1957		II	2		ME	L		32	16	12	Wilson, Robert R. "Bullet"
1998		II	2	2	GL	A	To R32	48	30	3	Harper, Ray
1960		II	3		SC	L		32	18	11	Plain, T. L.
1967		II	3		SC	L	To R32	36	25	4	Strong, Guy Rowland
1982		II	3		GL	L		32	27	5	Pollio, Mike
1984		II	3		GL	A		32	28	3	Pollio, Mike
1985		II	3		GL	L		32	24	7	Pollio, Mike
1971		II	4		MW	L		32	22	8	Daniels, Bob
1989		II	8		GL	A		32	24	7	Chapman, Wayne G.
1992		II	8		GL			32	23	8	Boultinghouse, Wayne
1970		II	16		S	L		32	18	10	Daniels, Bob
1974		II	16		MW	L	To R32	44	20	6	Jones, Bob
1983		II	16		GL	A		32	22	8	Pollio, Mike
1988		II	16		GL			32	23	7	Chapman, Wayne G.
1961		II	24		SC	L		32	15	8	Plain, T. L.
1964		II	24		SC	L		32	15	8	Plain, T. L.
1972		II	24		GL	L	To R32	36	17	10	Daniels, Bob
1986		II	24		GL	L		32	22	8	Chapman, Wayne G.
1991		II	24		SC			32	22	8	Chapman, Wayne G.
1994		II	24		GL	L		32	23	7	Boultinghouse, Wayne
1995		II	32	2	GL		To R32	48	23	6	Boultinghouse, Wayne
KENYON											
1995	M	III	16	6	GL	L		64	20	9	Brown, William H.
1994		III	32		GL	A	To R32	40	24	4	Brown, William H.
1997	W	III	64		GL	A		64	26	2	Halfant, Suzanne
KING'S (PA)											
1974	M	II	24		ME	L	To R32	44	20	7	Donohue, Ed
1990		III	32		MA	A	To R32	40	17	11	Atkins, Ken
1991		III	32		MA	L	To R32	40	21	7	Atkins, Ken
1992		III	32		MA	L		40	20	8	Atkins, Ken
KNOX											
1958	M	II	16		MW			32	17	7	Adams, Frank E.
1959		II	16		MW			32	20	3	Adams, Frank E.
1975		III	30		MW	L		30	16	7	Knosher, Harlan D.

Year	M/W	Div	F	SD	Reg	BD	Bye	#T	W	L	Coach
KNOXVILLE											
1978	M	III	8		S	A		30	16	10	Simmons, Dwayne
1977		III	23		S	L		30	14	11	Arwood, Vic
1983	W	III	3		S	L		32	21	2	Robinson, Edward
1984		III	16		S	L		32	18	7	Robinson, Edward
KUTZTOWN											
1988	M	II	32		E	L		32	21	10	Binder, Rick
1996	W	II	48	4	E	L		48	20	8	Malouf, Janet
LA SALLE											
1954	M		1		E(B)	L		24	26	4	Loeffler, Kenneth D.
1955			2		E(B)	L		24	26	5	Loeffler, Kenneth D.
1968		I	23		E	A		23	20	8	Harding, James F.
1975		I	32		E	A		32	22	7	Westhead, Paul W.
1978		I	32		E	L		32	18	12	Westhead, Paul W.
1990		I	32	4	E	A		64	30	2	Morris, William T. "Speedy"
1980		I	48	11	ME	A		48	22	9	Ervin, David "Lefty"
1983		I	48	12	E	A		52	18	14	Ervin, David "Lefty"
1988		I	64	13	MW	A		64	24	10	Morris, William T. "Speedy"
1989		I	64	8	SE	A		64	26	6	Morris, William T. "Speedy"
1992		I	64	13	E	A		64	20	11	Morris, William T. "Speedy"
1989	W	I	32	9	E	L		48	28	3	Miller, John
1983		I	36		ME	L		36	16	13	Gallagher, Kevin
1986		I	40		E	A		40	21	9	Morris, William T. "Speedy"
1988		I	40		ME	L		40	25	5	Miller, John
LA VERNE											
1993	M	III	16		W	A	To R32	40	20	8	Stewart, Gary
1996	W	III	64		W			64	15	11	Kline, Julie
LAFAYETTE (PA)											
1957	M	I	16		E	L	To R16	23	22	5	Davidson, George E.
LAKE FOREST											
1994	W	III	40		C	A		40	19	6	Slaats, Jackie
LAKE SUPERIOR STATE											
1996	M	II	48	4	GL	A		48	19	9	Smith, Terry
1986	W	II	16		GL	L	To R16	24	23	5	Taylor, Bob
1988		II	16		GL	L		32	24	5	Geary, Mike
1994		II	16		GL	L		32	23	7	Ledy, Erica
1996		II	32	4	GL	L		48	23	8	Ledy, Erica
LAMAR											
1963	M	II	16		SW			32	22	5	Martin, Jack T.
1980		I	16	10	W	A		48	22	11	Tubbs, Billy
1966		II	22		GL	L	To R32	36	17	9	Martin, Jack T.
1960		II	24		SW	L		32	18	9	Martin, Jack T.

Year	M/W	Div	F	SD	Reg	BD	Bye	#T	W	L	Coach
1962		II	24		SW			32	20	8	Martin, Jack T.
1964		II	24		SW			32	19	6	Martin, Jack T.
1979		I	32	10	ME	A		40	23	9	Tubbs, Billy
1981		I	32	8	MW	A		48	25	5	Foster, Pat
1983		I	32	11	MW	A		52	23	8	Foster, Pat
1991	W	I	8	10	MW	L		48	29	4	Barbre, Al

LANDER

Year	M/W	Div	F	SD	Reg	BD	Bye	#T	W	L	Coach
1995	M	II	48	4	S	A		48	21	9	Horne, Finis

LANE (TN)

Year	M/W	Div	F	SD	Reg	BD	Bye	#T	W	L	Coach
1980	M	III	8		S	L		32	19	9	Shaw, Dr. Willie G. 'Hawk '
1979		III	32		S	A		32	18	11	Shaw, Dr. Willie G. 'Hawk'

LAWRENCE

Year	M/W	Div	F	SD	Reg	BD	Bye	#T	W	L	Coach
1997	M	III	64	6	MW	A		64	22	3	Tharp, John

LE MOYNE

Year	M/W	Div	F	SD	Reg	BD	Bye	#T	W	L	Coach
1959	M	II	16		NE			32	18	6	Niland, Thomas J., Jr.
1964		II	16		ME			32	18	6	Niland, Thomas J., Jr.
1988		II	24		E	A		32	24	6	Beilein, John
1960		II	32		NE			32	13	5	Niland, Thomas J., Jr.
1965		II	32		NE			32	18	5	Niland, Thomas J., Jr.
1969		II	32		E	L		32	15	8	Niland, Thomas J., Jr.
1966		II	34		NE	L		36	16	6	Niland, Thomas J., Jr.
1968		II	36		NE	L		36	14	8	Niland, Thomas J., Jr.
1996		II	48	5	NE	A		48	24	6	Hicks, Scott
1997		II	48	6	NE	A		48	13	17	Hicks, Scott

LEBANON VALLEY

Year	M/W	Div	F	SD	Reg	BD	Bye	#T	W	L	Coach
1994	M	III	1		MA	A	To R32	40	28	4	Flannery, Patrick J.
1953			16		E(A)	L		22	19	3	Marquette, George R. 'Rinso'
1993		III	32		MA	L		40	18	11	Flannery, Patrick J.
1973		II	42		ME			42	24	3	Sorrentino, Louis A.
1995		III	64	2	MA	A		64	22	6	McAlester, Brad
1997		III	64	6	MA	L		64	17	11	McAlester, Brad

LEHIGH

Year	M/W	Div	F	SD	Reg	BD	Bye	#T	W	L	Coach
1985	M	I	64	16	E	A		64	12	19	Schneider, Thomas
1988		I	64	16	E	A		64	21	10	McCaffrey, Fran
1997	W	I	64	16	MW	A		64	15	15	Troyan, Susan

LEMOYNE-OWEN

Year	M/W	Div	F	SD	Reg	BD	Bye	#T	W	L	Coach
1975	M	III	1		S	L		30	27	5	Johnson, Jerry C.
1986		III	2		S	A		32	29	3	Johnson, Jerry C.
1983		III	8		S	A		32	24	6	Johnson, Jerry C.
1984		III	8		S	A		32	24	5	Johnson, Jerry C.
1985		III	16		S	A		32	22	7	Johnson, Jerry C.
1976		III	21		S	L		28	18	9	Johnson, Jerry C.
1985	W	III	24		S	L		32	16	10	Skinner, Lula Marie

Year	M/W	Div	F	SD	Reg	BD	Bye	#T	W	L	Coach
Lenoir-Rhyne											
1995	M	II	48	6	SA	A		48	18	11	Lentz, John
Lewis (IL)											
1984	M	II	16		GL	L		32	22	8	Schwarz, "Chuck"
1982		II	24		NC	A		32	20	9	Schwarz, "Chuck"
1983		II	24		GL	L		32	20	10	Schwarz, "Chuck"
1988		II	24		GL			32	22	8	Davis, Al
1985		II	32		GL	L		32	22	8	Schwarz, "Chuck"
1986		II	32		GL	A		32	24	6	Schwarz, "Chuck"
1998		II	48	3	GL	L		48	19	9	Whitesell, Jim
1984	W	II	24		GL	A		24	21	8	Kissinger, Kathy
1985		II	24		GL	A		24	22	7	Kissinger, Kathy
1998		II	48	6	GL	L		48	23	5	Michalak, Brian
Liberty											
1994	M	I	64	16	E	A		64	18	12	Meyer, Jeff
1997	W	I	64	16	ME	A		64	22	8	Reeves, Rick
1998		I	64	16	ME	A		64	28	1	Reeves, Rick
Lincoln (MO)											
1978	M	II	8		SC	L		32	22	6	Corbett, Donald
1960		II	16		GL			32	14	9	Frank, James
1961		II	16		GL	L		32	20	8	Frank, James
1967		II	16		SW	L	To R32	36	24	3	Staggers, Jonathan L.
1972		II	16		MW		To R32	36	22	6	Corbett, Donald
1975		II	16		SC			32	19	9	Corbett, Donald
1968		II	23		MW	L	To R32	36	20	3	Staggers, Jonathan L.
1959		II	24		SC	L		32	14	9	Frank, James
1969		II	24		MW	L		32	19	7	Staggers, Jonathan L.
1976		II	24		SC	L		32	20	8	Corbett, Donald
1977		II	24		SC	A		32	22	6	Corbett, Donald
1981		II	32		SC	L		32	22	8	Coleman, Ronald E.
Linfield											
1957	M	II	16		FW			32	17	11	Helser, Roy
1958		II	32		PC			32	18	9	Helser, Roy
Lock Haven											
1987	M	II	24		NC	L		32	22	9	Kanaskie, Kurt
1989		II	24		E	L		32	23	7	Blank, Dave
1990	W	II	8		E	L		32	26	7	Scarfo, Frank
1989		II	16		E	A		32	22	9	Scarfo, Frank
1991		II	16		E	L		32	20	10	Scarfo, Frank
Long Island											
1966	M	II	8		E		To R32	36	22	4	Rubin, Roy
1967		II	8		NE			36	22	7	Rubin, Roy
1965		II	16		E			32	16	7	Rubin, Roy
1981		I	48	12	E	L		48	18	11	Lizzo, Paul
1984		I	53	13	E	L		53	20	11	Lizzo, Paul
1997		I	64	13	E	A		64	21	9	Haskins, Ray

Year	M/W	Div	F	SD	Reg	BD	Bye	#T	W	L	Coach
LONG ISLAND: C W POST											
1985	M	II	8		E	L		32	24	7	Galeazzi, Thomas J.
1975		II	16		E	L		32	24	4	Brown, Herbert M.
1984		II	16		E	L		32	26	5	Galeazzi, Thomas J.
1991		II	16		E	L		32	26	5	Galeazzi, Thomas J.
1973		II	24		E	L	To R32	42	20	5	Brown, Herbert M.
1983		II	24		E	L		32	22	9	Galeazzi, Thomas J.
1987		II	24		E	L		32	25	5	Galeazzi, Thomas J.
1990		II	24		E	L		32	26	5	Galeazzi, Thomas J.
1994		II	24		NE	L		32	26	5	Galeazzi, Thomas J.
1962		II	32		E	L		32	16	6	Kaftan, Dr. George A.
1971		II	32		E	L		32	20	6	Kaftan, Dr. George A.
1983	W	II	16		E	L		24	25	8	Solano, Kathy
LONG ISLAND: SOUTHAMPTON											
1972	M	II	8		E	L	To R32	36	22	5	Colclough, James
LONGWOOD											
1980	M	III	4		NE	L		32	28	3	Bash, Dr. M. Ronald
1994		II	32		S	L		32	23	6	Carr, Ron
1995		II	48	5	SA	L		48	19	9	Carr, Ron
1995	W	II	32	6	SA	L		48	21	8	Duncan, Shirley G.
1996		II	48	6	E	L		48	22	7	Duncan, Shirley G.
1997		II	48	4	E	L		48	25	5	Duncan, Shirley G.
LORAS											
1959	M	II	32		GL	L		32	17	7	Dowd, Vincent J.
LOUISIANA STATE											
1986	M	I	3	11	SE	L		64	26	12	Brown, Dale
1953			4		E(A)	A	To R16	22	22	3	Rabenhorst, Harry A.
1981		I	4	1	MW	L	To R32	48	31	5	Brown, Dale
1980		I	8	1	MW	A	To R32	48	26	6	Brown, Dale
1987		I	8	10	MW	L		64	24	15	Brown, Dale
1954			16		E(A)	A	To R16	24	20	5	Rabenhorst, Harry A.
1979		I	16	3	ME	L	To R32	40	23	6	Brown, Dale
1990		I	32	5	SE	L		64	23	9	Brown, Dale
1992		I	32	7	W	L		64	21	10	Brown, Dale
1984		I	48	7	W	L		53	18	11	Brown, Dale
1985		I	64	4	SE	L		64	19	10	Brown, Dale
1988		I	64	9	E	L		64	16	14	Brown, Dale
1989		I	64	10	W	L		64	20	12	Brown, Dale
1991		I	64	6	MW	L		64	20	10	Brown, Dale
1993		I	64	11	MW	L		64	22	11	Brown, Dale
1986	W	I	8		ME	L	To R32	40	27	6	Gunter, Sue
1984		I	16		MW	L		32	23	7	Gunter, Sue
1989		I	16	4	MW	L	To R32	48	19	11	Gunter, Sue
1997		I	16	4	ME	L		64	25	5	Gunter, Sue
1987		I	32	4	MW	L	To R32	40	20	8	Gunter, Sue
1991		I	32	2	MW	A	To R32	48	24	7	Gunter, Sue
1988		I	40	9	W	L		40	18	11	Gunter, Sue
1990		I	48	9	MW	L		48	21	9	Gunter, Sue

Year	M/W	Div	F	SD	Reg	BD	Bye	#T	W	L	Coach
LOUISIANA TECH											
1967	M	II	16		MW		To R32	36	20	8	Robertson, Robert "Scotty"
1985		I	16	5	MW	A		64	29	3	Russo, Andy
1971		II	24		S	L		32	23	5	Robertson, Robert "Scotty"
1984		I	32	10	MW	A		53	26	7	Russo, Andy
1989		I	32	9	SE	L		64	23	9	Eagles, Tommy Joe
1987		I	64	14	MW	A		64	22	8	Eagles, Tommy Joe
1991		I	64	12	SE	A		64	21	10	Lloyd, Jerry
1982	W	I	1		MW	L		32	35	1	Hogg, Sonja
1988		I	1	2	MW	L	To R32	40	32	2	Barmore, Leon
1983		I	2		MW	L	To R32	36	31	2	Barmore, Leon
1987		I	2	1	MW	L	To R32	40	30	3	Barmore, Leon
1994		I	2	4	ME	A		64	31	4	Barmore, Leon
1998		I	2	3	MW	A		64	31	4	Barmore, Leon
1984		I	3		MW	L		32	30	3	Barmore, Leon
1989		I	3	1	MW	L	To R32	48	32	4	Barmore, Leon
1990		I	3	1	MW	A	To R32	48	32	1	Barmore, Leon
1985		I	8		MW	L		32	29	4	Barmore, Leon
1986		I	8		W	L	To R32	40	27	5	Barmore, Leon
1993		I	8		MW	L		48	26	6	Barmore, Leon
1996		I	8	1	MW	A		64	31	2	Barmore, Leon
1995		I	16	2	E	L		64	28	5	Barmore, Leon
1997		I	16	2	ME	A		64	31	4	Barmore, Leon
1991		I	48	10	W	A		48	18	12	Barmore, Leon
1992		I	48	6	ME	L		48	20	10	Barmore, Leon
LOUISVILLE											
1980	M	I	1	2	MW	A	To R32	48	33	3	Crum, Denzil E. "Denny"
1986		I	1	2	W	A		64	32	7	Crum, Denzil E. "Denny"
1975		I	3		MW	A		32	28	3	Crum, Denzil E. "Denny"
1982		I	3	3	ME	L	To R32	48	23	10	Crum, Denzil E. "Denny"
1983		I	3	1	ME	A	To R32	52	32	4	Crum, Denzil E. "Denny"
1959		I	4		ME	L		23	19	12	Hickman, Bernard L. "Peck"
1972		I	4		MW	A	To R16	25	26	5	Crum, Denzil E. "Denny"
1997		I	8	6	E	L		64	26	9	Crum, Denzil E. "Denny"
1961		I	12		ME	L		24	21	8	Hickman, Bernard L. "Peck"
1967		I	12		MW	A	To R16	23	23	5	Hickman, Bernard L. "Peck"
1968		I	12		MW	A	To R16	23	21	7	Dromo, John
1951			16		E	L		16	19	7	Hickman, Bernard L. "Peck"
1974		I	16		MW	A	To R16	25	21	7	Crum, Denzil E. "Denny"
1978		I	16		MW	A		32	23	7	Crum, Denzil E. "Denny"
1979		I	16	3	MW	L	To R32	40	24	8	Crum, Denzil E. "Denny"
1984		I	16	5	ME	L		53	24	11	Crum, Denzil E. "Denny"
1988		I	16	5	SE	A		64	24	11	Crum, Denzil E. "Denny"
1989		I	16	4	MW	A		64	24	9	Crum, Denzil E. "Denny"
1993		I	16	4	MW	A		64	22	9	Crum, Denzil E. "Denny"
1994		I	16	3	W	A		64	28	8	Crum, Denzil E. "Denny"
1996		I	16	6	MW	L		64	22	12	Crum, Denzil E. "Denny"
1964		I	25		ME	L		25	15	10	Hickman, Bernard L. "Peck"
1977		I	32		W	L		32	21	7	Crum, Denzil E. "Denny"
1981		I	32	4	MW	A	To R32	48	21	9	Crum, Denzil E. "Denny"

Year	M/W	Div	F	SD	Reg	BD	Bye	#T	W	L	Coach
1990		I	32	4	W	A		64	27	8	Crum, Denzil E. "Denny"
1992		I	32	8	W	L		64	19	11	Crum, Denzil E. "Denny"
1995		I	64	11	MW	A		64	19	14	Crum, Denzil E. "Denny"
1983	W	I	32		MW	A	To R32	36	20	9	Fiehrer, Peggy
1984		I	32		ME	A		32	15	16	Fiehrer, Peggy
1993		I	32		ME	A		48	19	12	Childers, "Bud"
1995		I	32	11	MW	L		64	25	8	Childers, "Bud"
1998		I	32	10	W	L		64	20	12	Clapp, Martin
1997		I	64	10	ME	L		64	20	9	Childers, "Bud"

Loyola (IL)

Year	M/W	Div	F	SD	Reg	BD	Bye	#T	W	L	Coach
1963	M	I	1		ME	L		25	29	2	Ireland, George M.
1964		I	12		ME	L		25	22	6	Ireland, George M.
1985		I	16	4	E	A		64	27	6	Sullivan, Gene
1966		I	22		ME	L		22	22	3	Ireland, George M.
1968		I	23		MW	L		23	15	9	Ireland, George M.

Loyola (MD)

Year	M/W	Div	F	SD	Reg	BD	Bye	#T	W	L	Coach
1973	M	II	32		SA			42	16	13	Doherty, Edward C.
1994		I	64	15	W	A		64	17	13	Prosser, "Skip"
1994	W	I	64	14	ME	A		64	18	11	Coyle, Patricia
1995		I	64	10	E	A		64	20	9	Coyle, Patricia

Loyola Marymount

Year	M/W	Div	F	SD	Reg	BD	Bye	#T	W	L	Coach
1990	M	I	8	11	W	A		64	26	6	Westhead, Paul W.
1961		I	12		W	A	To R16	24	20	7	Arndt, John C.
1988		I	32	10	W	A		64	28	4	Westhead, Paul W.
1980		I	48	12	W	A		48	14	14	Jacobs, Ron
1989		I	64	12	MW	A		64	20	11	Westhead, Paul W.

Loyola New Orleans

Year	M/W	Div	F	SD	Reg	BD	Bye	#T	W	L	Coach
1957	M	I	23		MW	L		23	14	12	McCafferty, James J.
1954			24		E(A)	L		24	15	9	McCafferty, James J.
1958		I	24		MW	L		24	16	9	Harding, James F.

Luther

Year	M/W	Div	F	SD	Reg	BD	Bye	#T	W	L	Coach
1982	M	III	16		MW	A		32	23	4	Leix, Jim
1967		II	23		GL		To R32	36	16	8	Finanger, Kenton
1984		III	32		W	A		32	20	7	Leix, Jim
1992	W	III	3		C	L		32	24	6	Hildebrand, Jane
1988		III	8		C			32	21	7	Hildebrand, Jane
1989		III	8		C	A		32	22	7	Hildebrand, Jane
1991		III	16		C	A		32	18	9	Hildebrand, Jane
1996		III	32		C	L		64	21	5	Hildebrand, Jane
1998		III	48	4	W	L		48	20	6	Hildebrand, Jane
1995		III	64		C			64	20	6	Hildebrand, Jane
1997		III	64		W	L		64	17	8	Hildebrand, Jane

Lycoming

Year	M/W	Div	F	SD	Reg	BD	Bye	#T	W	L	Coach
1985	M	III	24		MA	L		32	19	7	Burch, Clarence W. "Dutch"
1996		III	32	4	MA	L		64	21	6	Bressi, Joe
1988	W	III	24		MA	L		32	21	7	Rockey, Kimberly
1997		III	64		MA	L		64	17	10	Ditzler, Christen

Year	M/W	Div	F	SD	Reg	BD	Bye	#T	W	L	Coach
LYNCHBURG											
1976	M	III	28		SA	A		28	22	8	Proffitt, Wayne
1979		III	32		SA	A		32	17	12	Proffitt, Wayne
LYNN											
1997	M	II	3	2	S	L	To R32	48	28	3	Price, Jeff
1998		II	16	1	S	L	To R32	48	22	7	Price, Jeff
MACMURRAY											
1961	M	II	32		GL	L		32	18	9	Wall, William L.
1996	W	III	64		C	A		64	17	10	Mulhern, Donald
MAINE											
1995	W	I	64	16	E	A		64	24	6	Palombo-McCall, Joanne
1996		I	64	11	E	A		64	27	5	Palombo-McCall, Joanne
1997		I	64	13	ME	A		64	22	8	Palombo-McCall, Joanne
1998		I	64	13	E	A		64	21	9	Palombo-McCall, Joanne
MANCHESTER											
1995	M	III	2	1	MW	A		64	31	1	Alford, Stephen T.
1994		III	32		MW	A	To R32	40	23	4	Alford, Stephen T.
1993		III	40		MW	L		40	20	8	Alford, Stephen T.
1995	W	III	64		GL	L		64	15	9	Rockey, Kimberly
MANHATTAN											
1958	M	I	16		E	L		24	16	10	Norton, Kenneth A.
1956			25		E	L		25	16	8	Norton, Kenneth A.
1995		I	32	13	SE	L		64	26	5	Fraschilla, Fran
1993		I	64	11	E	A		64	23	7	Fraschilla, Fran
1987	W	I	40	10	E	A		40	20	11	Solano, Kathy
1990		I	48	12	E	A		48	18	13	Solano, Kathy
1996		I	64	14	E	A		64	19	11	Sharp, Michele
MANHATTANVILLE											
1978	M	III	30		E	L		30	17	11	Cohane, Tim
1979		III	32		E	L		32	17	11	Cohane, Tim
1982	W	III	16		None	L		16	22	8	Tedesco, Ralph
MANKATO STATE											
1964	M	II	16		MW	L		32	19	6	Morris, William
1976		II	24		NC			32	18	10	Raymond, Lloyd E. "Butch"
1986	W	II	16		NC	A	To R16	24	25	4	Wilinski, Bruno
MANSFIELD											
1975	M	III	8		MA	L		30	18	10	Wilson, Edward W.
1976		III	21		MA	L		28	17	7	Wilson, Edward W.
1984		II	24		E	A		32	26	6	Wilson, Edward W.
1997		II	32	2	E	A	To R32	48	26	4	Ackerman, Thomas E.
MARIETTA											
1975	M	III	16		GL	L		30	19	4	Roach, J. Philip

Year	M/W	Div	F	SD	Reg	BD	Bye	#T	W	L	Coach
MARIST											
1986	M	I	64	15	SE	A		64	19	12	Furjanic, Matt, Jr.
1987		I	64	14	W	A		64	20	10	Magarity, David
MARQUETTE											
1977	M	I	1		MW	L		32	25	7	McGuire, Alfred J.
1974		I	2		ME	L		25	26	5	McGuire, Alfred J.
1955			8		E(A)	L		24	24	3	Nagle, Joel "Jack"
1969		I	8		ME	L		25	24	5	McGuire, Alfred J.
1976		I	8		ME	L		32	27	2	McGuire, Alfred J.
1968		I	12		ME	L		23	23	6	McGuire, Alfred J.
1971		I	12		ME	L		25	28	1	McGuire, Alfred J.
1973		I	12		ME	L		25	25	4	McGuire, Alfred J.
1959		I	16		ME	L		23	23	6	Hickey, Edgar S. "Eddie"
1972		I	16		ME	L		25	25	4	McGuire, Alfred J.
1979		I	16	3	W	L	To R32	40	22	7	Raymonds, Henry C. "Hank"
1994		I	16	6	SE	L		64	24	9	O'Neill, Kevin
1961		I	24		MW	L		24	16	11	Hickey, Edgar S. "Eddie"
1975		I	32		ME	L		32	23	4	McGuire, Alfred J.
1978		I	32		ME	L		32	24	4	Raymonds, Henry C. "Hank"
1982		I	32	7	MW	L		48	23	9	Raymonds, Henry C. "Hank"
1996		I	32	4	E	L		64	23	8	Deane, Mike
1980		I	48	9	E	L		48	18	9	Raymonds, Henry C. "Hank"
1983		I	48	9	ME	L		52	19	10	Raymonds, Henry C. "Hank"
1993		I	64	12	MW	L		64	20	8	O'Neill, Kevin
1997		I	64	7	SE	A		64	22	9	Deane, Mike
1997	W	I	32	12	ME	L		64	21	10	Mitchell, Terri
1994		I	64	14	W	L		64	22	7	Jabir, James J.
1995		I	64	10	MW	A		64	19	12	Jabir, James J.
1998		I	64	10	ME	L		64	22	7	Mitchell, Terri
MARS HILL											
1996	W	II	32	2	SA	L	To R32	48	24	6	White, Sylvia
MARSHALL											
1956	M		25		MW	A		25	18	5	Rivlin, Jule
1972		I	25		MW	L		25	23	4	Tacy, Carl R.
1984		I	48	10	ME	A		53	25	6	Huckabay, Rick
1985		I	64	15	W	A		64	21	13	Huckabay, Rick
1987		I	64	13	E	A		64	25	6	Huckabay, Rick
1997	W	I	64	15	MW	A		64	18	12	Evans-Moore, Sarah
MARY WASHINGTON											
1994	W	III	32		S	L	To R32	40	20	6	Gallahan, Connie
1998		III	32	6	A	L		48	21	8	Gallahan, Connie
MARYLAND											
1973	M	I	8		E	A	To R16	25	23	7	Driesell, Charles G. "Lefty"
1975		I	8		MW	L		32	24	5	Driesell, Charles G. "Lefty"
1958		I	12		E	A		24	22	7	Millikan, Harry A. "Bud"
1980		I	16	2	E	L	To R32	48	24	7	Driesell, Charles G. "Lefty"

Year	M/W	Div	F	SD	Reg	BD	Bye	#T	W	L	Coach
1984		I	16	3	ME	A	To R32	53	24	8	Driesell, Charles G. "Lefty"
1985		I	16	5	SE	L		64	25	12	Driesell, Charles G. "Lefty"
1994		I	16	10	MW	L		64	18	12	Williams, Gary
1995		I	16	3	W	L		64	26	8	Williams, Gary
1998		I	16	4	W	L		64	22	11	Williams, Gary
1981		I	32	6	ME	L		48	21	10	Driesell, Charles G. "Lefty"
1983		I	32	8	MW	L		52	20	10	Driesell, Charles G. "Lefty"
1986		I	32	5	W	L		64	19	14	Driesell, Charles G. "Lefty"
1988		I	32	7	SE	L		64	18	13	Wade, Bob
1996		I	64	7	W	L		64	17	13	Williams, Gary
1997		I	64	5	SE	L		64	21	11	Williams, Gary
1982	W	I	3		W	A		32	25	7	Weller, Christine J.
1989		I	3	1	W	A	To R32	48	29	3	Weller, Christine J.
1988		I	8	2	ME	A	To R32	40	26	6	Weller, Christine J.
1992		I	8	2	ME	L	To R32	48	25	6	Weller, Christine J.
1983		I	16		E	A	To R32	36	26	5	Weller, Christine J.
1984		I	32		E	L		32	19	10	Weller, Christine J.
1986		I	32		ME	A	To R32	40	17	13	Weller, Christine J.
1990		I	32	6	E	L		48	19	11	Weller, Christine J.
1993		I	32	2	MW	L	To R32	48	22	8	Weller, Christine J.
1991		I	48	6	ME	L		48	17	13	Weller, Christine J.
1997		I	64	9	ME	L		64	18	10	Weller, Christine J.

MARYLAND: BALTIMORE COUNTY

Year	M/W	Div	F	SD	Reg	BD	Bye	#T	W	L	Coach
1979	M	II	8		SA	L		32	21	8	Jones, Billy
1980		II	16		SA	L		32	23	5	Jones, Billy

MARYMOUNT (VA)

Year	M/W	Div	F	SD	Reg	BD	Bye	#T	W	L	Coach
1993	W	III	16		W	L		32	23	5	Finney, Bill
1994		III	16		S	L	To R32	40	24	3	Finney, Bill
1996		III	16		S	A		64	27	3	Finney, Bill
1997		III	16		A	A		64	28	2	Finney, Bill
1990		III	32		S	L		32	19	8	Finney, Bill
1991		III	32		S	L		32	21	7	Finney, Bill
1992		III	32		S	L		32	23	5	Finney, Bill
1995		III	32		S	A		64	24	5	Finney, Bill

MARYVILLE (MO)

Year	M/W	Div	F	SD	Reg	BD	Bye	#T	W	L	Coach
1997	M	III	64	8	MW	A		64	17	11	Kruse, Dennis

MARYVILLE (TN)

Year	M/W	Div	F	SD	Reg	BD	Bye	#T	W	L	Coach
1992	M	III	8		S	L	To R32	40	25	4	Lambert, Randy
1993		III	32		S	L	To R32	40	20	6	Lambert, Randy
1995		III	32	3	S	L		64	20	7	Lambert, Randy
1991		III	40		S	L		40	22	5	Lambert, Randy
1997		III	64	2	S	L		64	20	6	Lambert, Randy
1990	W	III	16		S	L		32	23	5	Moore, Frank "Wes"
1991		III	16		S	L		32	23	6	Moore, Frank "Wes"
1993		III	16		W	L		32	23	3	Moore, Frank "Wes"
1994		III	16		S	L	To R32	40	23	4	Moore, Frank "Wes"

Year	M/W	Div	F	SD	Reg	BD	Bye	#T	W	L	Coach
1995		III	16		S	L		64	23	5	Cook, Kelli
1989		III	24		S	L		32	23	6	Moore, Frank "Wes"
1992		III	32		S	A		32	24	4	Moore, Frank "Wes"
1996		III	32		S	L		64	19	6	Cook, Kelli

MARYWOOD

Year	M/W	Div	F	SD	Reg	BD	Bye	#T	W	L	Coach
1987	W	III	32		MA	L		32	19	8	Dempsey, Jerry

MASSACHUSETTS

Year	M/W	Div	F	SD	Reg	BD	Bye	#T	W	L	Coach
1996	M	I	3	1	E	A		64	35	2	Calipari, John
1995		I	8	2	E	A		64	29	5	Calipari, John
1992		I	16	3	E	A		64	30	5	Calipari, John
1962		I	25		E	A		25	15	9	Zunic, Matthew
1993		I	32	3	E	A		64	24	7	Calipari, John
1994		I	32	2	MW	A		64	28	7	Calipari, John
1997		I	64	11	E	L		64	19	14	Flint, James "Bruiser"
1998		I	64	7	S	L		64	21	11	Flint, James "Bruiser"
1996	W	I	64	8	ME	L		64	20	10	O'Brien, Joanie
1998		I	64	13	W	L		64	19	11	O'Brien, Joanie

MASSACHUSETTS COLLEGE

Year	M/W	Div	F	SD	Reg	BD	Bye	#T	W	L	Coach
1990	M	III	8		NE	L	To R32	40	23	5	Sokaitis, Al
1989		III	24		NE	L	To R32	40	23	2	Sokaitis, Al
1987		III	32		NE	A		32	20	6	Quattrocchi, John
1988		III	32		NE	A		32	18	9	Sokaitis, Al

MASSACHUSETTS: BOSTON

Year	M/W	Div	F	SD	Reg	BD	Bye	#T	W	L	Coach
1977	M	III	8		NE	A		30	25	3	Loscutoff, James, Jr.
1978		III	16		NE	A		30	21	4	Fitzpatrick, Paul
1976		III	21		NE	A		28	22	5	Loscutoff, James, Jr.
1975		III	23		NE	L		30	23	4	Loscutoff, James, Jr.
1983		III	24		NE	L		32	19	9	Titus, Charles
1981		III	32		NE	L		32	19	8	Dowd, Kevin
1982	W	III	16		None	L		16	20	6	Harris, Alfreda

MASSACHUSETTS: DARTMOUTH

Year	M/W	Div	F	SD	Reg	BD	Bye	#T	W	L	Coach
1993	M	III	4		NE	A	To R32	40	25	6	Baptiste, Brian
1986		III	8		NE	L		32	22	7	Baptiste, Brian
1976		III	14		NE	L		28	17	9	Wheeler, Bruce E.
1987		III	16		NE	L		32	27	1	Baptiste, Brian
1988		III	16		NE	L		32	24	4	Baptiste, Brian
1990		III	16		NE	A	To R32	40	24	6	Baptiste, Brian
1991		III	16		NE	A	To R32	40	23	6	Baptiste, Brian
1994		III	16		NE	A	To R32	40	22	6	Baptiste, Brian
1995		III	32	1	NE	A		64	24	4	Baptiste, Brian
1998		III	48	6	NE	A		48	20	8	Baptiste, Brian
1997		III	64	2	NE	A		64	20	7	Baptiste, Brian

MASSACHUSETTS: LOWELL

Year	M/W	Div	F	SD	Reg	BD	Bye	#T	W	L	Coach
1988	M	II	1		NENG	A		32	27	7	Doucette, Don

Year	M/W	Div	F	SD	Reg	BD	Bye	#T	W	L	Coach
1993	W	II	16		NENG	A		32	24	6	O'Neil, Kathleen
1991		II	32		NENG	A		32	22	9	O'Neil, Kathleen
1994		II	32		NENG	L		32	23	8	O'Neil, Kathleen
1997		II	32	4	NE	A		48	25	6	O'Neil, Kathleen
1995		II	48	6	NENG	A		48	23	7	O'Neil, Kathleen
1998		II	48	6	NE	A		48	19	10	O'Neil, Kathleen

MCNEESE STATE

Year	M/W	Div	F	SD	Reg	BD	Bye	#T	W	L	Coach
1968	M	II	32		SW		To R32	36	20	5	Ward, Ralph O.
1989		I	64	16	MW	A		64	16	14	Welch, Steve

MEMPHIS

Year	M/W	Div	F	SD	Reg	BD	Bye	#T	W	L	Coach
1973	M	I	2		MW	A	To R16	25	24	6	Bartow, B. Gene
1985		I	3	2	MW	A		64	31	4	Kirk, Dana
1992		I	8	6	MW	L		64	23	11	Finch, Larry O.
1982		I	16	2	E	A	To R32	48	24	5	Kirk, Dana
1983		I	16	4	MW	L	To R32	52	23	8	Kirk, Dana
1984		I	16	6	MW	A		53	26	7	Kirk, Dana
1995		I	16	6	MW	L		64	24	10	Finch, Larry O.
1955			24		E(A)	L		24	17	5	Lambert, Dr. Eugene W.
1956			25		W	L		25	20	7	Lambert, Dr. Eugene W.
1962		I	25		MW	L		25	15	7	Vanatta, Robert
1976		I	32		W	L		32	21	9	Yates, Wayne E.
1986		I	32	3	SE	L		64	28	6	Kirk, Dana
1988		I	32	9	MW	L		64	20	12	Finch, Larry O.
1989		I	64	5	W	L		64	21	11	Finch, Larry O.
1993		I	64	10	SE	L		64	20	12	Finch, Larry O.
1996		I	64	5	W	L		64	22	8	Finch, Larry O.
1982	W	I	16		ME	A		32	26	5	Johns, Mary Lou
1985		I	32		MW	A		32	23	7	Johns, Mary Lou
1987		I	32	6	ME	L	To R32	40	20	9	Johns, Mary Lou
1995		I	32	8	W	L		64	22	8	Lee-McNelis, Joye
1996		I	64	8	E	L		64	20	11	Lee-McNelis, Joye
1997		I	64	11	E	L		64	22	7	Lee-McNelis, Joye
1998		I	64	5	E	A		64	22	8	Lee-McNelis, Joye

MERCER

Year	M/W	Div	F	SD	Reg	BD	Bye	#T	W	L	Coach
1972	M	II	32		SA	L	To R32	36	17	7	Morrison, Dwane A.
1981		I	48	12	MW	A		48	18	12	Bibb, Bill
1985		I	64	15	E	A		64	22	9	Bibb, Bill
1985	W	II	3		S	L	To R16	24	24	7	Nixon, Ed

MERCHANT MARINE

Year	M/W	Div	F	SD	Reg	BD	Bye	#T	W	L	Coach
1989	M	III	24		E	L	To R32	40	25	3	Cohane, Tim
1998		III	48	6	A	A		48	16	11	MacKinnon, Robert A.
1997		III	64	6	A	L		64	19	7	Greer, Andrew

MERCY (NY)

Year	M/W	Div	F	SD	Reg	BD	Bye	#T	W	L	Coach
1985	W	II	24		E	L		24	22	7	Schachner, Carol

Year	M/W	Div	F	SD	Reg	BD	Bye	#T	W	L	Coach
MERCYHURST											
1995	W	II	8	2	E	L	To R32	48	24	6	Webb, James D.
1994		II	32		E	L		32	19	9	Demyanovich, Paul
MERRIMACK											
1977	M	II	16		NENG	L		32	19	9	Monahan, Frank T.
1978		II	16		NENG	L		32	22	6	Monahan, Frank T.
1991		II	24		NENG	L		32	21	9	Hammel, Bert
1992		II	24		NENG	A		32	18	14	Hammel, Bert
MESA STATE											
1994	M	II	32		NC	A		32	20	9	Schakel, Doug
1995		II	48	6	NC	L		48	20	9	Schakel, Doug
MESSIAH											
1996	W	III	32		MA	L		64	20	8	Miller, Michael
METHODIST											
1997	M	III	8	4	S	A		64	22	8	McEvoy, Bob
1977		III	16		SA	A		30	18	8	Miller, Joe F.
1975		III	23		SA	L		30	21	5	Gallagher, Joe
METROPOLITAN STATE (CO)											
1990	M	II	16		NC	A		32	28	4	Hull, Bob
1991		II	24		NC	L		32	23	8	Hull, Bob
1998		II	32	6	NC	L		48	25	5	Dunlap, Mike
1996	W	II	48	6	NC	A		48	20	8	Smith, Darryl
1998		II	48	4	NC	A		48	25	5	Smith, Darryl
MIAMI (FL)											
1960	M	I	25		ME	L		25	23	4	Hale, William Bruce
1998		I	64	11	S	L		64	18	10	Hamilton, Leonard
1992	W	I	16	2	E	A	To R32	48	30	2	Labati, Ferne
1993		I	32		E	A		48	24	7	Labati, Ferne
1989		I	48	8	MW	L		48	21	8	Labati, Ferne
1998		I	64	11	MW	L		64	19	10	Labati, Ferne
MIAMI (OH)											
1958	M	I	16		ME	A		24	18	9	Shrider, Richard G.
1969		I	16		ME	A		25	15	12	Locke, Taylor O. "Tates"
1978		I	16		ME	A		32	19	9	Hedric, Darrell
1953			22		E(B)	A		22	17	6	Rohr, William D.
1966		I	22		ME	A		22	18	7	Shrider, Richard G.
1957		I	23		ME	A		23	17	8	Rohr, William D.
1955			24		E(A)	A		24	14	9	Rohr, William D.
1971		I	25		ME	A		25	20	5	Hedric, Darrell
1973		I	25		ME	A		25	18	9	Hedric, Darrell
1995		I	32	12	MW	L		64	23	7	Sendek, Herb
1984		I	48	8	W	A		53	24	6	Hedric, Darrell
1985		I	64	12	SE	L		64	20	11	Peirson, Jerry
1986		I	64	10	MW	L		64	24	7	Peirson, Jerry
1992		I	64	13	MW	A		64	23	8	Wright, Joseph A. "Joby"
1997		I	64	13	MW	A		64	21	9	Coles, Charles "Charlie"

Year	M/W	Div	F	SD	Reg	BD	Bye	#T	W	L	Coach
MICHIGAN											
1989	M	I	1	3	SE	L		64	30	7	Fisher, Stephen L.
1965		I	2		ME	A	To R16	23	24	4	Strack, David H.
1976		I	2		MW	L		32	25	7	Orr, John M. "Johnny"
1992		I	2	6	SE	L		64	25	9	Fisher, Stephen L.
1993		I	2	1	W	L		64	31	5	Fisher, Stephen L.
1964		I	3		ME	A	To R16	25	23	5	Strack, David H.
1948		I	6		E	L		8	16	6	McCoy, Ernest B.
1966		I	8		ME	A	To R16	22	18	8	Strack, David H.
1974		I	8		ME	A	To R16	25	22	5	Orr, John M. "Johnny"
1977		I	8		ME	A		32	26	4	Orr, John M. "Johnny"
1994		I	8	3	MW	L		64	24	8	Fisher, Stephen L.
1988		I	16	3	W	L		64	26	8	Frieder, Bill
1975		I	32		W	L		32	19	8	Orr, John M. "Johnny"
1985		I	32	1	SE	A		64	26	4	Frieder, Bill
1986		I	32	2	MW	A		64	28	5	Frieder, Bill
1987		I	32	9	E	L		64	20	12	Frieder, Bill
1990		I	32	3	W	L		64	23	8	Fisher, Stephen L.
1998		I	32	3	S	A		64	25	9	Ellerbee, Brian
1995		I	64	9	MW	L		64	17	14	Fisher, Stephen L.
1996		I	64	7	MW	L		64	20	12	Fisher, Stephen L.
1990	W	I	32	10	MW	L		48	20	10	Van De Wege, "Bud", Jr.
1998		I	64	10	MW	L		64	19	10	Guevara, Sue
MICHIGAN STATE											
1979	M	I	1	2	ME	A	To R32	40	26	6	Heathcote, George "Jud"
1957		I	4		ME	A	To R16	23	16	10	Anderson, Forrest A. "Forddy"
1959		I	8		ME	A	To R16	23	19	4	Anderson, Forrest A. "Forddy"
1978		I	8		ME	A		32	25	5	Heathcote, George "Jud"
1986		I	16	5	MW	L		64	23	8	Heathcote, George "Jud"
1990		I	16	1	SE	A		64	28	6	Heathcote, George "Jud"
1998		I	16	4	E	L		64	23	8	Izzo, Tom
1991		I	32	5	W	L		64	19	11	Heathcote, George "Jud"
1992		I	32	5	MW	L		64	22	8	Heathcote, George "Jud"
1994		I	32	7	SE	L		64	20	12	Heathcote, George "Jud"
1985		I	64	10	MW	L		64	19	10	Heathcote, George "Jud"
1995		I	64	3	SE	L		64	22	6	Heathcote, George "Jud"
1991	W	I	32	4	MW	L	To R32	48	21	8	Langeland, Karen
1996		I	32	9	ME	L		64	18	11	Langeland, Karen
1997		I	32	8	E	L		64	22	8	Langeland, Karen
MICHIGAN TECH											
1963	M	II	24		MW			32	17	5	Cox, Verdie T.
1998		II	32	6	GL	L		48	21	10	Luke, Kevin
1993	W	II	3		GL	A		32	30	3	Borseth, Kevin
1995		II	16	2	GL	L	To R32	48	24	6	Borseth, Kevin
1998		II	16	4	GL	L		48	21	10	Borseth, Kevin
1991		II	32		GL	L		32	22	7	Borseth, Kevin
1992		II	32		GL	L		32	23	6	Borseth, Kevin
1994		II	32		GL	L		32	23	6	Borseth, Kevin
1997		II	32	4	GL	L		48	21	9	Borseth, Kevin

Year	M/W	Div	F	SD	Reg	BD	Bye	#T	W	L	Coach
MIDDLE TENNESSEE STATE											
1975	M	I	32		ME	A		32	23	5	Earle, James P. "Jimmy"
1977		I	32		ME	A		32	20	9	Earle, James P. "Jimmy"
1982		I	32	11	ME	A		48	22	8	Simpson, Stanley "Ramrod"
1989		I	32	13	SE	A		64	23	8	Stewart, Bruce
1985		I	64	15	SE	A		64	17	14	Stewart, Bruce
1987		I	64	12	E	L		64	22	7	Stewart, Bruce
1983	W	I	32		MW	L		36	26	5	Inman, Larry Joe
1984		I	32		ME	A		32	19	10	Inman, Larry Joe
1985		I	32		ME	A		32	23	7	Inman, Larry Joe
1986		I	32		ME	A		40	20	10	Inman, Larry Joe
1988		I	40		MW	A		40	22	8	Bivens, Lewis
1996		I	64	13	E	L		64	24	6	Bivens, Lewis
1998		I	64	15	W	A		64	18	12	Smith, Stephany
MIDDLEBURY											
1996	W	III	32		NE	L		64	21	5	Fulcher, Jennifer
1998		III	48	5	NE	L		48	20	5	Fulcher, Jennifer
1995		III	64		NE	L		64	18	6	Fulcher, Jennifer
MILES											
1976	M	III	7		S	A		28	23	8	Wilkins, Arthur "Pete"
1975		III	16		S	L		30	21	8	Wilkins, Arthur "Pete"
1974		II	44		SA	L		44	21	6	Wilkins, Arthur "Pete"
MILLERSVILLE											
1989	M	II	8		E	A		32	26	7	Kochan, John
1987		II	16		E	A		32	27	4	Kochan, John
1993		II	16		E	A		32	24	6	Kochan, John
1985		II	24		E	L		32	27	4	Kochan, John
1986		II	24		E	L		32	24	6	Kochan, John
1995		II	24	3	E	L		48	26	4	Kochan, John
1987	W	II	16		E	A		24	18	8	Schlegel, Debra
1984		II	24		E	A		24	19	7	Schlegel, Debra
MILLIKIN											
1983	M	III	16		MW	L		32	21	7	Ramsey, Joe
1988		III	16		MW	L		32	22	6	Ramsey, Joe
1989		III	32		MW	A	To R32	40	20	7	Ramsey, Joe
1985	W	III	3		C	L		32	23	3	Crannell, Harriett
1994		III	8		C	A	To R32	40	24	4	Kearns, Lori Ann
1997		III	8		C	A		64	25	3	Kearns, Lori Ann
1982		III	16		None	L		16	11	6	Crannell, Harriett
1995		III	16		C	A		64	23	5	Kearns, Lori Ann
1996		III	16		C	A		64	23	5	Kearns, Lori Ann
1984		III	24		C	L		32	19	6	Crannell, Harriett
1989		III	32		C			32	20	7	Kearns, Lori Ann
1998		III	32	3	C	A		48	25	1	Kearns, Lori Ann

Year	M/W	Div	F	SD	Reg	BD	Bye	#T	W	L	Coach
MILLSAPS											
1995	M	III	16	2	S	A		64	25	3	Stroud, John
1984		III	24		S	L		32	20	6	Holcomb, Don
1996		III	32	3	S	A		64	22	5	Stroud, John
1996	W	III	32		S	A		64	23	4	Hannon, Cindy
1995		III	64		S	L		64	19	7	Hannon, Cindy
MINNESOTA											
1997	M	I	3	1	MW	A		64	31	4	Haskins, Clem S.
1990		I	8	6	SE	L		84	23	9	Haskins, Clem S.
1972		I	12		ME	A	To R16	25	18	7	Musselman, William
1982		I	16	2	ME	A	To R32	48	23	6	Dutcher, James D.
1989		I	16	11	E	L		64	19	12	Haskins, Clem S.
1994		I	32	6	W	L		64	21	12	Haskins, Clem S.
1995		I	64	8	E	L		64	19	12	Haskins, Clem S.
1994	W	I	32	10	E	L		64	18	11	Hill-MacDonald, Linda
MINNESOTA: DULUTH											
1965	M	II	24		MW	L		32	20	8	Olson, Norman H.
1957		II	32		MW	L		32	15	7	Olson, Norman H.
1997		II	48	3	NC	L		48	21	6	Race, Dale M.
1995	W	II	32	3	NC	L		48	20	8	Stromme, Karen
1996		II	32	4	NC	A		48	23	5	Stromme, Karen
MINNESOTA: MORRIS											
1978	M	III	16		MW	L		30	22	6	Glas, Richard "Rich"
1979		III	32		MW	L		32	19	9	Glas, Richard "Rich"
1983	W	III	8		W	L		32	24	10	Reifsteck, Jan
MISSISSIPPI											
1981	M	I	48	10	MW	A		48	16	14	Weltlich, Robert
1997		I	64	8	MW	L		64	20	9	Evans, Rob
1998		I	64	4	MW	L		64	22	7	Evans, Rob
1985	W	I	8		ME	L		32	29	3	Chancellor, Van
1986		I	8		MW	L	To R32	40	24	8	Chancellor, Van
1989		I	8	3	ME	L	To R32	48	23	8	Chancellor, Van
1992		I	8	2	MW	L	To R32	48	29	3	Chancellor, Van
1983		I	16		ME	L	To R32	36	26	7	Chancellor, Van
1984		I	16		ME	L		32	24	6	Chancellor, Van
1987		I	16	4	W	L	To R32	40	25	5	Chancellor, Van
1988		I	16	3	MW	L	To R32	40	24	7	Chancellor, Van
1990		I	16	5	W	L		48	22	10	Chancellor, Van
1982		I	32		ME	L		32	27	5	Chancellor, Van
1994		I	32	5	ME	L		64	24	9	Chancellor, Van
1991		I	48	9	MW	L		48	20	9	Chancellor, Van
1995		I	64	12	MW	L		64	21	8	Chancellor, Van
1996		I	64	7	E	L		64	18	11	Chancellor, Van

Year	M/W	Div	F	SD	Reg	BD	Bye	#T	W	L	Coach
MISSISSIPPI COLLEGE											
1978	M	II	24		SC	A		32	22	7	Hines, Dr. Douglas
1995		II	24	6	SC	A		48	21	10	Jones, Mike
1998		III	32	4	S	L		48	23	4	Jones, Mike
MISSISSIPPI STATE											
1996	M	I	3	5	SE	A		64	26	8	Williams, Richard
1963		I	12		ME	A	To R16	25	22	6	McCarthy, James H. "Babe"
1995		I	16	5	W	L		64	22	8	Williams, Richard
1991		I	64	5	E	L		64	20	9	Williams, Richard
MISSISSIPPI VALLEY STATE											
1986	M	I	64	16	E	A		64	20	11	Stribling, Lafayette
1992		I	64	16	SE	A		64	16	14	Stribling, Lafayette
1996		I	64	15	E	A		64	22	7	Stribling, Lafayette
MISSISSIPPI WOMEN											
1985	W	II	24		S	L		24	19	4	Johnson, Samye
MISSOURI											
1944	M		6		W	L		8	10	9	Edwards, George R.
1976		I	8		MW	A		32	26	5	Stewart, Norman E.
1994		I	8	1	W	L		64	28	4	Stewart, Norman E.
1980		I	16	5	MW	L		48	25	6	Stewart, Norman E.
1982		I	16	2	MW	A	To R32	48	27	4	Stewart, Norman E.
1989		I	16	3	MW	A		64	29	8	Stewart, Norman E.
1978		I	32		MW	A		32	14	16	Stewart, Norman E.
1983		I	32	2	MW	L	To R32	52	26	8	Stewart, Norman E.
1992		I	32	5	E	L		64	21	9	Stewart, Norman E.
1995		I	32	8	W	L		64	20	9	Stewart, Norman E.
1981		I	48	9	MW	L		48	22	10	Stewart, Norman E.
1986		I	64	11	W	L		64	21	14	Stewart, Norman E.
1987		I	64	4	MW	A		64	24	10	Stewart, Norman E.
1988		I	64	6	E	L		64	19	11	Stewart, Norman E.
1990		I	64	3	SE	L		64	26	6	Stewart, Norman E.
1993		I	64	10	W	A		64	19	14	Stewart, Norman E.
1982	W	I	16		W	L		32	24	9	Rutherford, Dr. Joann
1983		I	32		MW	A	To R32	36	24	6	Rutherford, Dr. Joann
1984		I	32		MW	L		32	25	6	Rutherford, Dr. Joann
1985		I	32		MW	A		32	22	9	Rutherford, Dr. Joann
1986		I	32		MW	A		40	20	8	Rutherford, Dr. Joann
1994		I	64	15	MW	A		64	12	18	Rutherford, Dr. Joann
MISSOURI SOUTHERN STATE											
1993	M	II	32		SC	A		32	21	10	Corn, Robert
1993	W	II	16		SC	L		32	27	4	Ballard, Scott
1994		II	16		SC	A		32	25	5	Ballard, Scott
1996		II	32	1	SC	A	To R32	48	23	6	Kaifes, Carrie

Year	M/W	Div	F	SD	Reg	BD	Bye	#T	W	L	Coach

MISSOURI WESTERN STATE

Year	M/W	Div	F	SD	Reg	BD	Bye	#T	W	L	Coach
1990	M	II	16		SC	A		32	24	7	Smith, Tom
1991		II	32		GL	L		32	23	8	Smith, Tom
1992		II	32		SC	L		32	22	10	Smith, Tom
1995		II	32	1	SC	A	To R32	48	26	5	Smith, Tom
1998		II	32	2	SC	A	To R32	48	23	7	Smith, Tom
1997		II	48	4	SC	L		48	20	9	Smith, Tom
1995	W	II	3	1	SC	A	To R32	48	31	3	Mittie, Jeff
1994		II	8		SC	L		32	29	3	Mittie, Jeff
1997		II	16	1	SC	A	To R32	48	24	7	Slifer, David
1998		II	32	2	SC	L	To R32	48	23	9	Slifer, David

MISSOURI: ROLLA

Year	M/W	Div	F	SD	Reg	BD	Bye	#T	W	L	Coach
1996	M	II	16	1	SC	A	To R32	48	25	6	Martin, Dale
1975		II	32		NC	L		32	16	9	Key, Billy A.
1976		II	32		SC	A		32	18	9	Key, Billy A.
1996	W	II	48	6	SC	L		48	21	7	Roberts, Linda J.

MISSOURI: SAINT LOUIS

Year	M/W	Div	F	SD	Reg	BD	Bye	#T	W	L	Coach
1972	M	II	8		MW	L	To R32	36	21	6	Smith, Charles G. "Chuck"
1988		II	16		SC	A		32	22	9	Meckfessel, Richard

MONMOUTH (IL)

Year	M/W	Div	F	SD	Reg	BD	Bye	#T	W	L	Coach
1985	M	III	24		MW	A		32	18	7	Glasgow, Dr. Terry
1989		III	24		MW	L		40	20	6	Glasgow, Dr. Terry
1957		II	32		MW	A		32	18	5	Larson, Charles
1988		III	32		MW	A		32	14	11	Glasgow, Dr. Terry
1990		III	32		MW	A	To R32	40	20	3	Glasgow, Dr. Terry
1974		II	44		MW	A		44	18	5	Glasgow, Dr. Terry

MONMOUTH (NJ)

Year	M/W	Div	F	SD	Reg	BD	Bye	#T	W	L	Coach
1976	M	III	14		SA	L		28	22	5	Boylan, William T.
1981		II	24		E	A		32	25	4	Kornegay, Ron
1982		II	32		E	L		32	21	9	Kornegay, Ron
1996		I	64	13	E	A		64	20	10	Szoke, Wayne
1983	W	I	32		E	L		36	15	15	Parker, Milton

MONTANA

Year	M/W	Div	F	SD	Reg	BD	Bye	#T	W	L	Coach
1975	M	I	16		W	A		32	21	8	Heathcote, George "Jud"
1991		I	64	16	W	A		64	23	8	Morrill, Stew
1992		I	64	14	W	A		64	27	4	Taylor, Blaine
1997		I	64	16	W	A		64	21	11	Taylor, Blaine
1984	W	I	16		W	A		32	26	4	Selvig, Robin
1986		I	32		W	A		40	27	4	Selvig, Robin
1988		I	32		MW	A	To R32	40	28	2	Selvig, Robin
1989		I	32	10	W	A		48	27	4	Selvig, Robin
1992		I	32	11	W	A		48	23	7	Selvig, Robin
1994		I	32	7	W	A		64	25	5	Selvig, Robin
1995		I	32	12	W	A		64	26	7	Selvig, Robin
1983		I	36		W	L		36	26	4	Selvig, Robin

Year	M/W	Div	F	SD	Reg	BD	Bye	#T	W	L	Coach
1990		I	48	8	W	A		48	27	3	Selvig, Robin
1991		I	48	11	W	A		48	26	4	Selvig, Robin
1996		I	64	12	W	A		64	24	5	Selvig, Robin
1997		I	64	9	W	A		64	25	4	Selvig, Robin
1998		I	64	14	W	A		64	24	6	Selvig, Robin

MONTANA STATE

1951	M		16		W	L		16	24	12	Breeden, John W. "Brick"
1986		I	64	16	W	A		64	14	17	Starner, Stu
1996		I	64	13	W	A		64	21	9	Durham, Mick
1993	W	I	48		W	A		48	22	7	Spoelstra, Judy

MONTANA STATE: BILLINGS

1987	M	II	3		W	A		32	24	7	Douglass, Pat
1997		II	16	3	W	L		48	22	6	Carse, Craig
1981		II	24		W	L		32	20	8	Edwards, Dick
1986		II	24		NC	L		32	22	8	Douglass, Pat
1982		II	32		NC	L		32	19	10	Douglass, Pat
1985		II	32		W	L		32	23	7	Douglass, Pat
1996		II	48	6	W	L		48	19	19	Carse, Craig
1998		II	48	5	W	A		48	21	7	Carse, Craig
1987	W	II	24		NC	A		24	18	11	Anderson, Ted
1994		II	32		W	L		32	19	9	McCarthy, Frank B.
1996		II	32	4	W	L		48	19	9	McCarthy, Frank B.
1998		II	32	2	W	L	To R32	48	21	7	McCarthy, Frank B.
1997		II	48	6	W	L		48	18	10	McCarthy, Frank B.

MONTCLAIR STATE

1969	M	II	8		E	L		32	24	3	Gelston, Oliver S. "Ollie"
1984		III	8		MA	L		32	22	6	Gelston, Oliver S. "Ollie"
1970		II	16		E	L		32	23	3	Gelston, Oliver S. "Ollie"
1981		III	16		SA	A		32	15	12	Gelston, Oliver S. "Ollie"
1971		II	24		E	L		32	18	6	Gelston, Oliver S. "Ollie"
1982		III	24		SA	A		32	17	8	Gelston, Oliver S. "Ollie"
1994		III	40		A	L		40	18	8	Del Tufo, Nicholas
1995		III	64	7	A	L		64	17	10	Del Tufo, Nicholas
1990	W	III	16		A	L		32	23	6	Jeffrey, Jill
1989		III	24		A	L		32	20	9	Jeffrey, Jill
1995		III	32		MA	A		64	20	7	Bradley, Gloria

MOORHEAD STATE (MN)

1965	M	II	16		MW			32	21	4	MacLeod, Larry

MORAVIAN

1983	M	III	32		MA	L		32	19	8	Walker, James R.
1992	W	III	2		MA	A		32	31	2	Spirk, Mary Beth
1991		III	16		MA	A		32	27	3	Spirk, Mary Beth
1993		III	16		E	L		32	24	5	Spirk, Mary Beth
1986		III	32		MA	L		32	25	5	Sinnott-Skutches, Anne
1990		III	32		MA	L		32	24	5	Spirk, Mary Beth

Year	M/W	Div	F	SD	Reg	BD	Bye	#T	W.	L	Coach
MOREHEAD STATE (KY)											
1956	M		12		MW	A		25	19	10	Laughlin, Robert
1961		I	16		ME	A		24	19	12	Laughlin, Robert
1957		I	23		ME	A		23	19	8	Laughlin, Robert
1983		I	48	11	E	A		52	19	11	Martin, Wayne M.
1984		I	48	12	ME	A		53	25	6	Martin, Wayne M.
MOREHOUSE											
1990	M	II	4		SA	A		32	26	7	McAfee, Arthur J., Jr.
1981		II	32		S	A		32	17	12	McAfee, Arthur J., Jr.
1991		II	32		SA	A		32	21	11	McAfee, Arthur J., Jr.
1995		II	48	3	S	L		48	20	8	McAfee, Arthur J., Jr.
MORGAN STATE											
1974	M	II	1		E	L	To R32	44	28	5	Frazier, Nathaniel
1976		II	24		SA	L		32	22	6	Frazier, Nathaniel
1975		II	32		SA	L		32	19	10	Frazier, Nathaniel
MORNINGSIDE											
1983	M	II	3		NC	A		32	26	6	Callahan, Dan
1984		II	8		NC	L		32	22	9	Callahan, Dan
1995		II	8	4	NC	L		48	24	8	Schmutte, Jerry
MOUNT SAINT MARY'S (MD)											
1962	M	II	1		E			32	24	6	Phelan, James J.
1981		II	2		SA	L		32	28	3	Phelan, James J.
1957		II	3		E	A		32	27	5	Phelan, James J.
1985		II	3		SA	L		32	28	5	Phelan, James J.
1961		II	4		E			32	26	5	Phelan, James J.
1969		II	16		SA	L		32	21	8	Phelan, James J.
1982		II	16		SA	L		32	20	8	Phelan, James J.
1986		II	16		SA	A		32	26	4	Phelan, James J.
1987		II	16		SA	L		32	26	5	Phelan, James J.
1979		II	24		SA	L		32	18	10	Phelan, James J.
1980		II	24		SA	L		32	22	7	Phelan, James J.
1963		II	32		E			32	13	12	Phelan, James J.
1967		II	32		ME		To R32	36	18	9	Phelan, James J.
1970		II	32		SA	L		32	20	6	Phelan, James J.
1995		I	64	16	SE	A		64	17	13	Phelan, James J.
1982	W	II	3		SA	L		16	24	5	Sheahan, William
1983		II	16		SA	L	To R16	24	25	3	Sheahan, William
1984		II	16		SA	L	To R16	24	26	2	Sheahan, William
1985		II	.16		SA	L		24	23	6	Sheahan, William
1986		II	16		SA	L	To R16	24	24	2	Sheahan, William
1987		II	16		SA	L		24	25	3	Sheahan, William
1988		II	32		SA	L		32	24	2	Sheahan, William
1994		I	64	14	MW	A		64	25	4	Sheahan, William
1995		I	64	13	E	A		64	24	6	Sheahan, William
MOUNT SAINT VINCENT											
1996	M	III	64	8	A	L		64	18	9	Mancuso, "Chuck"
1997		III	64	8	A	A		64	20	5	Mancuso, "Chuck"

Year	M/W	Div	F	SD	Reg	BD	Bye	#T	W	L	Coach
MOUNT UNION											
1997	M	III	16	2	GL	A		64	25	5	Hood, Lee
1996	W	III	2		A	L		64	25	8	Knoblauch, Deanne
1998		III	3	1	GL	A	To R32	48	29	3	Knoblauch, Deanne
1995		III	16		A	L		64	24	6	Knoblauch, Deanne
MUHLENBERG											
1968	M	II	32		E		To R32	36	14	11	Moyer, Kenneth T.
1998		III	48	5	MA	A		48	17	10	Madeira, David
1995		III	64	8	MA	A		64	18	9	Madeira, David
1998	W	III	32	5	MA	A		48	18	10	Smith, Tammy
1997		III	64		MA	A		64	18	8	Smith, Tammy
MURRAY STATE (KY)											
1964	M	I	25		ME	A		25	16	9	Luther, Calvin C.
1969		I	25		ME	A		25	22	6	Luther, Calvin C.
1988		I	32	14	MW	A		64	22	9	Newton, Steve
1990		I	64	16	SE	A		64	21	9	Newton, Steve
1991		I	64	13	SE	A		64	24	9	Newton, Steve
1992		I	64	14	MW	A		64	17	13	Edgar, Scott
1995		I	64	15	SE	A		64	21	9	Edgar, Scott
1997		I	64	15	SE	A		64	20	10	Gottfried, Mark
1998		I	64	9	MW	A		64	29	4	Gottfried, Mark
MUSKINGUM											
1981	M	III	16		W	L		32	19	8	Burson, Dr. James
1977		III	23		GL	A		30	22	6	Burson, Dr. James
1983		III	32		NE	L		32	19	9	Burson, Dr. James
1988		III	32		GL	A		32	21	9	Burson, Dr. James
1990		III	32		GL	A		40	21	9	Burson, Dr. James
1991	W	III	2		A	A		32	28	5	Newberry, Donna
1985		III	8		A	A		32	25	4	Newberry, Donna
1989		III	8		A	A		32	29	2	Newberry, Donna
1992		III	16		A	L		32	22	8	Newberry, Donna
1984		III	24		A	L		32	23	6	Newberry, Donna
1993		III	32		W	L		32	24	3	Newberry, Donna
1996		III	64		A	L		64	20	7	Newberry, Donna
NAVY											
1947	M		8		E	L		8	16	3	Carnevale, Bernard L. "Ben"
1954			8		E(B)	L		24	18	8	Carnevale, Bernard L. "Ben"
1986		I	8	7	E	A		64	30	5	Evans, Paul
1959		I	12		E	L		23	18	6	Carnevale, Bernard L. "Ben"
1953			22		E(A)	L		22	16	5	Carnevale, Bernard L. "Ben"
1960		I	25		E	L		25	16	6	Carnevale, Bernard L. "Ben"
1985		I	32	13	SE	A		64	26	6	Evans, Paul
1987		I	64	8	E	A		64	26	6	Herrmann, Pete
1994		I	64	16	W	A		64	17	13	DeVoe, Donald E.
1997		I	64	15	W	A		64	20	9	DeVoe, Donald E.
1998		I	64	16	E	A		64	19	11	DeVoe, Donald E.

Year	M/W	Div	F	SD	Reg	BD	Bye	#T	W	L	Coach
NAZARETH (NY)											
1984	M	III	8		E	L		32	21	6	Nelson, William H.
1987		III	16		E	L		32	22	6	Daley, Michael
1986		III	24		E	L		32	23	5	Nelson, William H.
1998		III	32	5	E	A		48	19	8	Daley, Michael
1990		III	40		E	L		40	20	7	Daley, Michael
1988	W	III	16		E	L		32	23	5	DeCillis, Michael
1989		III	16		S	L		32	22	6	DeCillis, Michael
1990		III	32		E	L		32	22	6	DeCillis, Michael
1998		III	48	6	E	A		48	15	11	DeCillis, Michael
1996		III	64		E	L		64	22	5	DeCillis, Michael
1997		III	64		E	L		64	17	9	DeCillis, Michael
NEBRASKA											
1986	M	I	64	9	SE	L		64	19	11	Iba, Moe
1991		I	64	3	MW	L		64	26	8	Nee, Danny
1992		I	64	8	SE	L		64	19	10	Nee, Danny
1993		I	64	10	E	L		64	20	11	Nee, Danny
1994		I	64	6	E	A		64	20	10	Nee, Danny
1998		I	64	11	W	L		64	20	12	Nee, Danny
1988	W	I	32	5	W	L	To R32	40	22	7	Beck, Angela
1993		I	32		W	L		48	23	8	Beck, Angela
1998		I	32	9	E	L		64	23	10	Sanderford, Paul
1996		I	64	9	W	L		64	19	10	Beck, Angela
NEBRASKA WESLEYAN											
1997	M	III	2	3	W	L		64	25	6	Raridon, Todd
1985		III	3		W	L		32	25	3	Schmutte, Jerry
1986		III	3		W	L		32	26	5	Schmutte, Jerry
1988		III	3		W	L		32	24	6	Schmutte, Jerry
1962		II	4		MW	L		32	20	8	Peterson, Dr. Irvin L.
1977		III	8		W	L	To R16	30	16	11	Peterson, Dr. Irvin L.
1984		III	8		W	L		32	23	5	Schmutte, Jerry
1963		II	16		MW	L		32	23	4	Peterson, Dr. Irvin L.
1989		III	16		W	L	To R32	40	21	6	Schmutte, Jerry
1990		III	16		W	L	To R32	40	22	7	Raridon, Todd
1995		III	16	3	W	L		64	21	7	Raridon, Todd
1964		II	32		MW	L		32	20	6	Peterson, Dr. Irvin L.
1987		III	32		W	L		32	21	7	Schmutte, Jerry
1998		III	32	2	W	L	To R32	48	23	3	Raridon, Todd
NEBRASKA: KEARNEY											
1991	M	II	32		NC	L		32	21	9	Hueser, Jerry
1997		II	32	6	NC	L		48	23	8	Hueser, Jerry
1998		II	32	5	NC	A		48	25	6	Kropp, Tom
1996		II	48	5	NC			48	24	9	Hueser, Jerry
1998	W	II	16	2	NC	L	To R32	48	26	4	Stephens, Amy
1996		II	32	3	SC	A		48	26	5	Stephens, Amy
1997		II	32	4	NC	A		48	28	3	Stephens, Amy

Year	M/W	Div	F	SD	Reg	BD	Bye	#T	W	L	Coach
NEBRASKA: OMAHA											
1975	M	II	16		NC	L		32	17	11	Hanson, Bob
1982		II	16		NC	L		32	22	7	Hanson, Bob
1977		II	24		NC	L		32	17	12	Hanson, Bob
1979		II	24		NC	A		32	20	9	Hanson, Bob
1984		II	24		NC	A		32	23	7	Hanson, Bob
1976		II	32		NC	L		32	16	13	Hanson, Bob
1983		II	32		NC	L		32	19	11	Hanson, Bob
1982	W	II	16		NC	L		16	22	6	Mankenberg, Cherri
1987		II	24		NC	L		24	21	8	Mankenberg, Cherri
1992		II	32		NC	L		32	20	9	Mankenberg, Cherri
NEVADA											
1966	M	II	22		PC		To R32	36	21	6	Spencer, Jackson
1957		II	32		FW	A		32	16	8	Lawlor, Glenn J. "Jake"
1961		II	32		PC			32	13	7	Spencer, Jackson
1964		II	32		PC			32	14	13	Spencer, Jackson
1984		I	48	11	W	A		53	17	14	Allen, William "Sonny"
1985		I	64	14	W	A		64	21	10	Allen, William "Sonny"
NEVADA: LAS VEGAS											
1990	M	I	1	1	W	A		64	35	5	Tarkanian, Jerry
1977		I	3		W	L		32	29	3	Tarkanian, Jerry
1987		I	3	1	W	A		64	37	2	Tarkanian, Jerry
1991		I	3	1	W	A		64	34	1	Tarkanian, Jerry
1968		II	8		PC	L	To R32	36	22	7	Todd, Rolland
1989		I	8	4	W	A		64	29	8	Tarkanian, Jerry
1975		I	12		W	A		32	24	5	Tarkanian, Jerry
1967		II	16		PC	L	To R32	36	21	6	Todd, Rolland
1969		II	16		W	L		32	21	7	Todd, Rolland
1976		II	16		W	L		32	29	2	Tarkanian, Jerry
1984		I	16	5	W	L		53	29	6	Tarkanian, Jerry
1986		I	16	4	W	A		64	33	5	Tarkanian, Jerry
1965		II	32		PC	L		32	19	8	Gregory, Ed
1983		I	32	3	W	A	To R32	52	28	3	Tarkanian, Jerry
1985		I	32	4	W	A		64	28	4	Tarkanian, Jerry
1988		I	32	4	W	L		64	28	6	Tarkanian, Jerry
1998		I	64	12	E	A		64	20	13	Bayno, Bill
1989	W	I	16	6	W	L		48	27	7	Bolla, Jim
1984		I	32		W	L		32	24	7	Bolla, Jim
1985		I	32		MW	L		32	26	5	Bolla, Jim
1986		I	32		W	A	To R32	40	22	9	Bolla, Jim
1990		I	32	4	W	A	To R32	48	28	3	Bolla, Jim
1991		I	32	8	W	L		48	25	7	Bolla, Jim
1994		I	64	10	W	A		64	23	7	Bolla, Jim
NEW HAMPSHIRE COLLEGE											
1993	M	II	3		NENG	A		32	29	4	Spirou, Stanley
1994		II	3		NE	A		32	28	5	Spirou, Stanley
1980		II	8		NENG	L		32	22	8	Sullivan, Thomas R.
1981		II	8		NENG	L		32	23	7	Sullivan, Thomas R.

Year	M/W	Div	F	SD	Reg	BD	Bye	#T	W	L	Coach
1987		II	8		NENG	L		32	24	8	Spirou, Stanley
1995		II	8	3	NE	A		48	27	6	Spirou, Stanley
1986		II	16		NENG	L		32	24	7	Spirou, Stanley
1992		II	16		NENG	L		32	24	7	Spirou, Stanley
1997		II	16	1	NE	L	To R32	48	25	5	Spirou, Stanley
1990		II	24		NENG	A		32	26	6	Spirou, Stanley
1996		II	32	6	NE	L		48	21	8	Spirou, Stanley
1998		II	32	6	NE	A		48	19	11	Spirou, Stanley
1988	W	II	32		NENG	L		32	21	8	Rowe, Nancy Anne
1990		II	32		NENG	A		32	22	8	Rowe, Nancy Anne

NEW HAVEN

Year	M/W	Div	F	SD	Reg	BD	Bye	#T	W	L	Coach
1988	M	II	16		NENG	L		32	26	5	Grove, Stuart
1987		II	32		NENG	L		32	23	9	Grove, Stuart
1990		II	32		NENG	L		32	21	10	Grove, Stuart
1987	W	II	1		NENG	A	To R16	24	29	2	Rossman, Jan
1988		II	8		NENG	A		32	27	5	Hill, Russ
1989		II	16		NENG	A		32	28	4	Hill, Russ
1986		II	24		NENG	A		24	18	11	Rossman, Jan

NEW JERSEY

Year	M/W	Div	F	SD	Reg	BD	Bye	#T	W	L	Coach
1989	M	III	2		SA	A	To R32	40	30	2	Bannon, Kevin
1988		III	8		SA	L		32	26	4	Bannon, Kevin
1985		III	16		SA	L		32	23	6	Bannon, Kevin
1986		III	24		SA	L		32	22	7	Bannon, Kevin
1990		III	32		A	L	To R32	40	22	6	Marsh, Donald
1998		III	32	2	A	A	To R32	48	22	5	Castaldo, John
1982	W	III	8		None	L		16	17	9	Labati, Ferne
1984		III	8		E	L		32	20	8	Labati, Ferne
1988		III	16		A	L		32	22	6	Ryan, Mika
1983		III	24		A	L		32	18	11	Labati, Ferne
1997		III	32		A	L		64	18	9	Henderson, Dawn
1998		III	32	3	A	L		48	19	8	Henderson, Dawn

NEW JERSEY TECH

Year	M/W	Div	F	SD	Reg	BD	Bye	#T	W	L	Coach
1995	M	III	8	1	A	L		64	28	2	Catalano, Dr. James M.
1993		III	32		A	L	To R32	40	22	4	Catalano, Dr. James M.
1994		III	32		A	L	To R32	32	23	4	Catalano, Dr. James M.
1991		III	40		SA	L		40	24	5	Catalano, Dr. James M.
1996		III	64	5	A	L		64	17	10	Catalano, Dr. James M.

NEW MEXICO

Year	M/W	Div	F	SD	Reg	BD	Bye	#T	W	L	Coach
1974	M	I	12		W	A		25	22	7	Ellenberger, Norman
1968		I	16		W	A	To R16	23	23	5	King, Bob
1978		I	32		W	A		32	24	4	Ellenberger, Norman
1996		I	32	7	E	A		64	28	5	Bliss, David
1997		I	32	3	E	L		64	25	8	Bliss, David
1998		I	32	4	S	L		64	24	8	Bliss, David
1991		I	64	14	E	L		64	20	10	Bliss, David
1993		I	64	5	W	A		64	24	7	Bliss, David
1994		I	64	10	W	L		64	23	8	Bliss, David
1998	W	I	64	8	E	A		64	26	7	Flanagan, Don

Year	M/W	Div	F	SD	Reg	BD	Bye	#T	W	L	Coach
NEW MEXICO STATE											
1970	M	I	3		MW	L		25	27	3	Henson, Louis R.
1968		I	12		W	L		23	23	6	Henson, Louis R.
1952			16		W(A)	A		16	22	11	McCarty, George C.
1969		I	16		W	L		25	24	5	Henson, Louis R.
1992		I	16	12	W	A		64	25	8	McCarthy, Neil N.
1959		I	23		W	A		23	17	11	Askew, Presley
1967		I	23		MW	L		23	15	11	Henson, Louis R.
1960		I	25		W	A		25	20	7	Askew, Presley
1971		I	25		MW	L		25	19	8	Henson, Louis R.
1975		I	32		E	L		32	20	7	Henson, Louis R.
1993		I	32	7	E	L		64	26	8	McCarthy, Neil N.
1979		I	40	10	MW	L		40	22	10	Hayes, Ken
1990		I	64	6	W	L		64	26	5	McCarthy, Neil N.
1991		I	64	6	W	L		64	23	6	McCarthy, Neil N.
1994		I	64	13	MW	A		64	23	8	McCarthy, Neil N.
1988	W	I	32	6	W	A	To R32	40	26	3	McKeown, Joe
1987		I	40	9	W	A		40	23	7	McKeown, Joe
NEW ORLEANS											
1975	M	II	2		SC	L		32	23	7	Greene, Ronald L.
1974		II	4		S	L	To R32	44	21	9	Greene, Ronald L.
1972		II	24		S	L		36	16	10	Greene, Ronald L.
1971		II	32		S	L		32	23	3	Greene, Ronald L.
1987		I	32	7	SE	L		64	26	4	Dees, Benny
1991		I	64	14	SE	L		64	23	8	Floyd, Tim
1993		I	64	8	MW	L		64	26	4	Floyd, Tim
1996		I	64	11	E	A		64	21	9	Price, George "Tic"
1987	W	I	32	6	MW	L	To R32	40	25	7	Favaloro, Joey
NEW ROCHELLE											
1985	W	III	2		E	L		32	25	8	Kern, Louis
1983		III	8		E	L		32	28	5	Kern, Louis
1984		III	24		E	L		32	26	8	Kern, Louis
NEW YORK											
1945	M		2		E	L		8	14	7	Cann, Howard G.
1994		III	2		E	A	To R32	40	25	5	Nesci, Joe
1960		I	4		E	L		25	22	5	Rossini, Lucio "Lou"
1946			6		E	L		8	19	3	Cann, Howard G.
1943			8		E	L		8	16	6	Cann, Howard G.
1962		I	12		E	L		25	20	5	Rossini, Lucio "Lou"
1963		I	16		E	L		25	18	5	Rossini, Lucio "Lou"
1993		iII	16		E	A	To R32	40	23	3	Nesci, Joe
1986		III	32		E	L		32	21	6	Layne, Floyd
1995		III	32	3	A	L		64	22	5	Nesci, Joe
1996		III	32	4	A	L		64	19	8	Nesci, Joe
1997		III	32	4	A	L		64	19	8	Nesci, Joe
1992		III	40		E	L		40	22	5	Nesci, Joe
1998		III	48	5	A	L		48	17	9	Nesci, Joe

Year	M/W	Div	F	SD	Reg	BD	Bye	#T	W	L	Coach
1997	W	III	1		E	A		64	29	1	Quinn, Janice
1996		III	4		E	A		64	27	4	Quinn, Janice
1986		III	16		E	L		32	20	8	Pickard, Sherri
1989		III	16		E	L		32	18	9	Quinn, Janice
1993		III	16		E	L		32	20	6	Quinn, Janice
1994		III	16		E	L	To R32	40	22	4	Quinn, Janice
1995		III	16		E	L		64	23	5	Quinn, Janice
1998		III	16	2	E	L	To R32	48	22	5	Quinn, Janice
1987		III	32		E	L		32	18	10	Pickard, Sherri
1991		III	32		E	L		32	19	8	Quinn, Janice

NEW YORK POLYTECHNIC

Year	M/W	Div	F	SD	Reg	BD	Bye	#T	W	L	Coach
1980	M	II	2		E	L		32	26	3	Stern, Sam
1978		II	32		SA	L		32	20	5	Stern, Sam

NIAGARA

Year	M/W	Div	F	SD	Reg	BD	Bye	#T	W	L	Coach
1970	M	I	16		E	L		25	22	7	Layden, Frank P.

NICHOLLS STATE

Year	M/W	Div	F	SD	Reg	BD	Bye	#T	W	L	Coach
1976	M	II	8		SC	L		32	22	4	Landry, Donald
1979		II	8		SC	A		32	21	7	Landry, Donald
1980		II	16		SC	L		32	18	8	Sanders, Jerry
1995		I	64	13	MW	A		64	24	6	Broussard, Rickey
1998		I	64	16	W	A		64	19	10	Broussard, Rickey

NORFOLK STATE

Year	M/W	Div	F	SD	Reg	BD	Bye	#T	W	L	Coach
1995	M	II	4	2	SA	L	To R32	48	27	7	Bernard, Michael J.
1974		II	8		SA	L		44	21	9	Christian, Charles O.
1986		II	8		SA	L		32	26	5	Christian, Charles O.
1987		II	8		SA	L		32	28	3	Christian, Charles O.
1994		II	8		SA	L		32	27	6	Bernard, Michael J.
1968		II	16		ME		To R32	36	24	2	Fears, Ernest D., Jr.
1971		II	16		SA	L		32	26	4	Smith, Robert L.
1984		II	16		SA	A		32	29	2	Christian, Charles O.
1965		II	24		SC			32	22	3	Fears, Ernest D., Jr.
1969		II	24		SA	L		32	18	2	Fears, Ernest D., Jr.
1985		II	24		W	L		32	23	7	Christian, Charles O.
1990		II	24		SA	A		32	27	4	Christian, Charles O.
1988		II	32		S	L		32	23	8	Christian, Charles O.
1989		II	32		SA	L		32	24	6	Christian, Charles O.
1992		II	32		SA	L		32	22	10	Bernard, Michael J.
1991	W	II	4		SA	A		32	33	2	Sweat, James E.
1982		II	8		E	L		16	19	6	Moorehead, Dr. Isaac T. "Ike"
1993		II	8		SA	C		32	29	3	Sweat, James E.
1994		II	8		SA	L		32	27	4	Sweat, James E.
1992		II	16		SA	A		32	25	7	Sweat, James E.
1983		II	24		SA	A		24	19	6	Moorehead, Dr. Isaac T. "Ike"
1986		II	24		SA	A		24	18	10	Moorehead, Dr. Isaac T. "Ike"
1995		II	32	1	SA	A	To R32	48	25	5	Sweat, James E.

Year	M/W	Div	F	SD	Reg	BD	Bye	#T	W	L	Coach
NORTH ALABAMA											
1979	M	II	1		S	L		32	22	9	Jones, Bill L.
1991		II	1		S	L		32	29	4	Elliott, Gary
1977		II	3		SC			32	24	7	Jones, Bill L.
1984		II	3		S	A		32	27	7	Jones, Bill L.
1980		II	4		SC	L		32	21	10	Jones, Bill L.
1981		II	8		SC	A		32	22	9	Jones, Bill L.
1996		II	8	3	SC	A		48	24	8	Elliott, Gary
1994		II	16		SC	A		32	24	6	Elliott, Gary
1988		II	24		S	A		32	17	14	Jones, Bill L.
1995		II	48	4	SC	L		48	20	8	Elliott, Gary
1994	W	II	3		S	L		32	22	10	Byrd, Wayne
1984		II	16		S	L		24	25	5	Byrd, Wayne
1985		II	16		S	A		24	19	8	Byrd, Wayne
1991		II	32		S	L		32	20	9	Byrd, Wayne
NORTH CAROLINA											
1957	M	I	1		E	A		23	32	0	McGuire, Frank J.
1982		I	1	1	E	A	To R32	48	32	2	Smith, Dean E.
1993		I	1	1	E	L		64	34	4	Smith, Dean E.
1946			2		E	L		8	30	5	Carnevale, Bernard L. "Ben"
1968		I	2		E	A	To R16	23	28	4	Smith, Dean E.
1977		I	2		E	A		32	28	5	Smith, Dean E.
1981		I	2	2	W	A	To R32	48	29	8	Smith, Dean E.
1972		I	3		E	A	To R16	25	26	5	Smith, Dean E.
1991		I	3	1	E	A		64	29	6	Smith, Dean E.
1995		I	3	2	SE	L		64	28	6	Smith, Dean E.
1997		I	3	1	E	A		64	28	7	Smith, Dean E.
1998		I	3	1	E	A		64	35	4	Guthridge, Bill
1967		I	4		E	A	To R16	23	26	6	Smith, Dean E.
1969		I	4		E	A	To R16	25	27	5	Smith, Dean E.
1941			8		E	L		8	15	8	Lange, William
1983		I	8	2	E	L	To R32	52	28	8	Smith, Dean E.
1985		I	8	2	SE	L		64	27	9	Smith, Dean E.
1987		I	8	1	E	L		64	32	4	Smith, Dean E.
1988		I	8	2	W	L		64	27	7	Smith, Dean E.
1975		I	12		E	A		32	23	8	Smith, Dean E.
1984		I	16	1	E	L	To R32	53	28	3	Smith, Dean E.
1986		I	16	3	W	L		64	28	6	Smith, Dean E.
1989		I	16	2	SE	A		64	29	8	Smith, Dean E.
1990		I	16	8	MW	L		64	21	13	Smith, Dean E.
1992		I	16	4	SE	L		64	23	10	Smith, Dean E.
1959		I	23		E	A		23	20	5	McGuire, Frank J.
1976		I	32		ME	L		32	25	4	Smith, Dean E.
1978		I	32		W	L		32	23	8	Smith, Dean E.
1979		I	32	1	E	A	To R32	40	23	6	Smith, Dean E.
1980		I	32	3	MW	L	To R32	48	21	8	Smith, Dean E.
1994		I	32	1	E	A		64	28	7	Smith, Dean E.
1996		I	32	6	E	L		64	21	11	Smith, Dean E.

Year	M/W	Div	F	SD	Reg	BD	Bye	#T	W	L	Coach
1994	W	I	1	3	E	A		64	33	2	Hatchell, Sylvia Rhyne
1998		I	8	2	ME	A		64	27	7	Hatchell, Sylvia Rhyne
1984		I	16		E	A		32	24	8	Alley, Jennifer
1986		I	16		W	L	To R32	40	23	9	Alley, Jennifer
1993		I	16	4	ME	L	To R32	48	23	7	Hatchell, Sylvia Rhyne
1995		I	16	3	W	A		64	30	5	Hatchell, Sylvia Rhyne
1997		I	16	1	E	A		64	29	3	Hatchell, Sylvia Rhyne
1983		I	32		ME	L	To R32	36	22	8	Alley, Jennifer
1985		I	32		E	L		32	21	11	Alley, Jennifer
1987		I	32	4	ME	L	To R32	40	19	10	Hatchell, Sylvia Rhyne
1992		I	32	7	E	L		48	22	9	Hatchell, Sylvia Rhyne

NORTH CAROLINA A&T

Year	M/W	Div	F	SD	Reg	BD	Bye	#T	W	L	Coach
1959	M	II	3		SC			32	26	4	Irvin, Calvin C.
1964		II	3		SC			32	23	7	Irvin, Calvin C.
1958		II	16		SC			32	21	4	Irvin, Calvin C.
1962		II	24		SC			32	20	7	Irvin, Calvin C.
1982		I	48	12	W	A		48	19	9	Corbett, Donald
1983		I	52	13	W	A		52	23	8	Corbett, Donald
1984		I	53	13	ME	A		53	22	7	Corbett, Donald
1985		I	64	16	MW	A		64	19	10	Corbett, Donald
1986		I	64	16	MW	A		64	22	8	Corbett, Donald
1987		I	64	15	SE	A		64	24	6	Corbett, Donald
1988		I	64	14	E	A		64	26	3	Corbett, Donald
1994		I	64	16	MW	A		64	16	14	Capel, Jeff
1995		I	64	16	E	A		64	15	15	Thomas, Roy C.
1994	W	I	64	16	ME	A		64	19	11	Abney, Tim

NORTH CAROLINA CENTRAL

Year	M/W	Div	F	SD	Reg	BD	Bye	#T	W	L	Coach
1989	M	II	1		SA	L		32	28	4	Bernard, Michael J.
1993		II	8		SA	L		32	26	4	Jackson, Gregory D.
1957		II	16		E	A		32	21	6	Brown, Floyd H.
1988		II	16		SA	L		32	26	3	Bernard, Michael J.
1990		II	16		S	L		32	23	5	Bernard, Michael J.
1997		II	32	1	SA	L	To R32	48	20	6	Jackson, Gregory D.
1996		II	48	4	SA	L		48	20	7	Jackson, Gregory D.
1984	W	II	24		SA	A		24	13	15	Edwards, Yvonne

NORTH CAROLINA STATE

Year	M/W	Div	F	SD	Reg	BD	Bye	#T	W	L	Coach
1974	M	I	1		E	A	To R16	25	30	1	Sloan, Norman L., Jr.
1983		I	1	6	W	A		52	26	10	Valvano, James T.
1950			3		E	L		8	27	6	Case, Everett N.
1951			8		E	A		16	30	7	Case, Everett N.
1985		I	8	3	W	L		64	23	10	Valvano, James T.
1986		I	8	6	MW	L		64	21	13	Valvano, James T.
1952			12		E(A)	A		16	24	10	Case, Everett N.
1954			12		E(B)	A		24	26	7	Case, Everett N.
1965		I	12		E	A	To R16	23	21	5	Maravich, Peter 'Press'
1970		I	12		E	A	To R16	25	23	7	Sloan, Norman L., Jr.
1989		I	16	5	E	L		64	22	9	Valvano, James T.
1956			25		E	A		25	24	4	Case, Everett N.

Year	M/W	Div	F	SD	Reg	BD	Bye	#T	W	L	Coach
1980		I	32	4	E	L	To R32	48	20	8	Sloan, Norman L., Jr.
1991		I	32	6	E	L		64	20	11	Robinson, Leslie G.
1982		I	48	7	ME	L		48	22	10	Valvano, James T.
1987		I	64	11	E	A		64	20	15	Valvano, James T.
1988		I	64	3	MW	L		64	24	8	Valvano, James T.
1998	W	I	3	4	E	L		64	24	7	Yow, Sandra Kay
1982		I	16		E	L		32	24	7	Yow, Sandra Kay
1984		I	16		E	L		32	23	9	Yow, Sandra Kay
1985		I	16		E	A		32	25	6	Yow, Sandra Kay
1987		I	16	3	E	A	To R32	40	24	7	Yow, Sandra Kay
1989		I	16	2	ME	L	To R32	48	24	7	Yow, Sandra Kay
1990		I	16	2	MW	L	To R32	48	25	6	Yow, Sandra Kay
1991		I	16	2	E	A	To R32	48	27	6	Yow, Sandra Kay
1995		I	16	7	MW	L		64	21	10	Yow, Sandra Kay
1983		I	32		E	L	To R32	36	22	8	Yow, Sandra Kay
1986		I	32		E	L	To R32	40	18	11	Yow, Sandra Kay
1996		I	32	5	W	L		64	20	10	Yow, Sandra Kay
1997		I	64	8	MW	L		64	19	12	Yow, Sandra Kay

NORTH CAROLINA WESLEYAN

Year	M/W	Div	F	SD	Reg	BD	Bye	#T	W	L	Coach
1987	M	III	8		S	L		32	24	7	Chambers, Bill
1984		III	16		S	A		32	21	8	McCarthy, John
1983		III	32		SA	L		32	21	9	McCarthy, John
1994	W	III	32		S	A		40	20	8	Brackett, John

NORTH CAROLINA: CHARLOTTE

Year	M/W	Div	F	SD	Reg	BD	Bye	#T	W	L	Coach
1977	M	I	4		ME	L		32	28	5	Rose, Lee H.
1997		I	32	7	W	L		64	22	9	Watkins, Melvin
1998		I	32	8	E	L		64	20	11	Watkins, Melvin
1988		I	64	13	SE	A		64	22	9	Mullins, Jeffrey V., Jr.
1992		I	64	7	E	L		64	23	9	Mullins, Jeffrey V., Jr.
1995		I	64	7	E	L		64	19	9	Mullins, Jeffrey V., Jr.

NORTH CAROLINA: GREENSBORO

Year	M/W	Div	F	SD	Reg	BD	Bye	#T	W	L	Coach
1980	M	III	32		S	A		32	16	12	Hargett, Larry
1996		I	64	15	SE	A		64	20	10	Peele, Randy
1982	W	III	2		None	L		16	24	3	Agee, Lynne
1988		III	3		S	L		32	26	7	Agee, Lynne
1985		III	16		S	A		32	21	7	Agee, Lynne
1986		III	16		S	L		32	24	4	Agee, Lynne
1991		II	16		SA	L		32	21	9	Agee, Lynne
1983		III	24		S	A		32	20	8	Agee, Lynne
1984		III	24		S	A		32	22	7	Agee, Lynne
1987		III	24		S	A		32	27	3	Agee, Lynne
1998		I	64	15	MW	A		64	21	9	Agee, Lynne

NORTH CENTRAL (IL)

Year	M/W	Div	F	SD	Reg	BD	Bye	#T	W	L	Coach
1989	M	III	16		MW	L	To R32	40	19	9	Warden, Bill
1984		III	24		MW	L		32	18	10	Warden, Bill
1985		III	32		MW	L		32	20	7	Warden, Bill
1990		III	32		MW	A	To R32	40	21	6	Warden, Bill

Year	M/W	Div	F	SD	Reg	BD	Bye	#T	W	L	Coach
1983	W	III	1		C	A		32	26	6	Morgan, R. Wayne
1984		III	4		C	A		32	24	6	Morgan, R. Wayne

NORTH DAKOTA

1965	M	II	3		MW			32	26	5	Fitch, William C. "Billy"
1990		II	3		NC	L		32	28	7	Glas, Richard "Rich"
1966		II	4		MW		To R32	36	24	5	Fitch, William C. "Billy"
1975		II	8		NC			32	22	7	Gunther, David
1976		II	8		NC			32	22	7	Gunther, David
1977		II	8		NC	A		32	26	4	Gunther, David
1982		II	8		NC	A		32	27	5	Gunther, David
1991		II	8		NC	L		32	29	4	Glas, Richard "Rich"
1981		II	16		NC	L		32	23	8	Gunther, David
1993		II	16		NC	A		32	23	8	Glas, Richard "Rich"
1967		II	23		MW		To R32	36	20	6	Fitch, William C. "Billy"
1974		II	24		MW	A		44	21	8	Gunther, David
1992		II	24		NC	A		32	23	9	Glas, Richard "Rich"
1994		II	24		NC	L		32	23	9	Glas, Richard "Rich"
1979		II	32		NC	L		32	19	9	Gunther, David
1980		II	32		NC	L		32	18	12	Gunther, David
1995		II	48	5	NC			48	19	9	Glas, Richard "Rich"
1997	W	II	1	1	NC	L	To R32	48	28	4	Roebuck, Gene
1998		II	1	1	NC	A	To R32	48	31	1	Roebuck, Gene
1990		II	8		NC	A		32	27	4	Roebuck, Gene
1992		II	8		SA	L		32	24	7	Roebuck, Gene
1991		II	16		NC	A		32	28	2	Roebuck, Gene
1996		II	16	3	NC	L		48	26	6	Roebuck, Gene
1984		II	24		NC	L		24	22	7	Schwartz, Gary
1985		II	24		NC			24	23	6	Schwartz, Gary
1988		II	32		NC	L		32	22	6	Roebuck, Gene
1993		II	32		NC			32	23	5	Roebuck, Gene
1994		II	32		NC	A		32	26	2	Roebuck, Gene
1995		II	32	1	NC	L	To R32	48	23	5	Roebuck, Gene

NORTH DAKOTA STATE

1983	M	II	16		NC	L		32	21	9	Inniger, Ervin L., Jr.
1994		II	16		NC	L		32	21	9	Billeter, Tom
1971		II	24		MW	L		32	18	9	Belk, Lyle V.
1981		II	24		NC	A		32	20	9	Inniger, Ervin L., Jr.
1995		II	24	3	NC			48	22	8	Billeter, Tom
1996		II	32	6	NC	L		48	20	9	Billeter, Tom
1997		II	32	5	NC	L		48	22	7	Billeter, Tom
1974		II	44		MW	L		44	17	10	Skaar, Marv
1991	W	II	1		NC	L		32	31	2	Ruley, Amy J.
1993		II	1		NC			32	30	2	Ruley, Amy J.
1994		II	1		NC	L		32	27	5	Ruley, Amy J.
1995		II	1	2	NC	A	To R32	48	32	0	Ruley, Amy J.
1996		II	1	1	NC	A	To R32	48	30	2	Ruley, Amy J.
1986		II	2		NC	L		24	24	9	Ruley, Amy J.
1992		II	2		NC	A		32	29	4	Ruley, Amy J.
1988		II	3		NC	A		32	28	3	Ruley, Amy J.

Year	M/W	Div	F	SD	Reg	BD	Bye	#T	W	L	Coach
1987		II	8		NC	A	To R16	24	26	4	Ruley, Amy J.
1989		II	16		NC			32	23	7	Ruley, Amy J.
1990		II	16		NC	L		32	25	5	Ruley, Amy J.
1997		II	16	2	NC	A	To R32	48	28	1	Ruley, Amy J.
1998		II	48	3	NC	L		48	22	6	Ruley, Amy J.

NORTH PARK

Year	M/W	Div	F	SD	Reg	BD	Bye	#T	W	L	Coach
1978	M	III	1		MW	L		30	29	2	McCarrell, Dan
1979		III	1		MW	L		32	26	5	McCarrell, Dan
1980		III	1		MW	L		32	28	3	McCarrell, Dan
1985		III	1		MW	A		32	27	4	Djurickovic, Bosko
1987		III	1		MW	A		32	28	3	Djurickovic, Bosko
1969		II	24		GL	L		32	21	5	McCarrell, Dan
1982		III	24		W	L		32	18	10	McCarrell, Dan
1981		III	32		MW	L		32	16	12	McCarrell, Dan
1986		III	32		MW	L		32	21	7	Djurickovic, Bosko
1990		III	40		MW	L		40	18	9	Djurickovic, Bosko
1988	W	III	32		C	A		32	20	8	Djurickovic, Rebecca Johnson

NORTH TEXAS

Year	M/W	Div	F	SD	Reg	BD	Bye	#T	W	L	Coach
1988	M	I	64	15	W	A		64	17	13	Gales, Jimmy
1986	W	I	40		W	A		40	20	10	Nelson, Judy

NORTHEAST LOUISIANA

Year	M/W	Div	F	SD	Reg	BD	Bye	#T	W	L	Coach
1982	M	I	48	11	W	A		48	19	11	Vining, Mike
1986		I	64	13	W	A		64	20	10	Vining, Mike
1990		I	64	15	MW	A		64	22	8	Vining, Mike
1991		I	64	15	MW	P		64	25	8	Vining, Mike
1992		I	64	15	MW	A		64	19	10	Vining, Mike
1993		I	64	13	SE	A		64	26	5	Vining, Mike
1996		I	64	15	MW	A		64	16	14	Vining, Mike
1985	W	I	3		MW	A		32	30	2	Harper, Linda F.
1984		I	16		MW	A		32	23	4	Harper, Linda F.
1983		I	32		W	L		36	23	6	Harper, Linda F.
1987		I	40	10	MW	A		40	14	10	Harper, Linda F.

NORTHEASTERN (MA)

Year	M/W	Div	F	SD	Reg	BD	Bye	#T	W	L	Coach
1962	M	II	8		NE	L		32	17	8	Dukeshire, Richard E.
1963		II	8		NE	L		32	21	6	Dukeshire, Richard E.
1964		II	16		NE	L		32	17	8	Dukeshire, Richard E.
1966		II	32		NE	L		36	18	8	Dukeshire, Richard E.
1981		I	32	11	W	A		48	24	6	Calhoun, James A.
1982		I	32	11	E	L		48	23	7	Calhoun, James A.
1967		II	34		NE	L		36	22	4	Dukeshire, Richard E.
1968		II	34		NE	L		36	19	9	Dukeshire, Richard E.
1984		I	48	11	E	A		53	27	5	Calhoun, James A.
1985		I	64	14	E	A		64	22	9	Calhoun, James A.
1986		I	64	13	E	A		64	26	5	Calhoun, James A.
1987		I	64	14	E	A		64	27	7	Fogel, Karl
1991		I	64	16	E	A		64	22	11	Fogel, Karl

Year	M/W	Div	F	SD	Reg	BD	Bye	#T	W	L	Coach
NORTHERN ARIZONA											
1998	M	I	64	15	W	A		64	21	8	Howland, Ben
NORTHERN COLORADO											
1989	M	II	16		NC			32	24	6	Brillhart, Ron
1964		II	32		SW	L		32	18	8	Sage, Dr. George H.
1965		II	32		MW			32	19	8	Sage, Dr. George H.
1966		II	32		MW		To R32	36	21	6	Sage, Dr. George H.
1998	W	II	32	5	NC	L		48	21	8	Bruce, Greg
1995		II	48	6	NC	L		48	17	10	Schwartz, Gary
1996		II	48	5	NC	L		48	17	10	Schwartz, Gary
1997		II	48	5	NC	L		48	19	8	Schwartz, Gary
NORTHERN ILLINOIS											
1958	M	II	24		GL	L		32	10	12	Healey, Dr. William A.
1982		I	48	12	MW	A		48	16	14	McDougal, John
1991		I	64	13	MW	L		64	25	6	Molinari, Jim
1996		I	64	14	E	A		64	20	10	Johnson, Rees
1990	W	I	32	5	MW	L		48	25	6	Albright-Dieterle, Jane
1992		I	32	11	ME	A		48	18	14	Albright-Dieterle, Jane
1993		I	48		E	A		48	24	6	Albright-Dieterle, Jane
1994		I	64	11	ME	L		64	24	6	Albright-Dieterle, Jane
1995		I	64	16	W	A		64	17	14	Galloway-McQuitter, Liz
NORTHERN IOWA											
1964	M	II	4		MW			32	23	4	Stewart, Norman E.
1962		II	16		MW			32	19	5	Stewart, Norman E.
1979		II	16		NC	L		32	18	11	Berry, James
1990		I	32	14	SE	A		64	23	9	Miller, Eldon
NORTHERN KENTUCKY											
1996	M	II	2	2	GL	L	To R32	48	25	7	Shields, Ken
1997		II	2	2	GL	L	To R32	48	30	5	Shields, Ken
1995		II	16	1	GL		To R32	48	25	4	Shields, Ken
1978		II	32		GL	L		32	20	8	Hils, Martin
1998		II	32	5	GL	L		48	23	7	Shields, Ken
1987	W	II	3		GL	A	To R16	24	25	5	Winstel, Nancy
1985		II	8		GL	L	To R16	24	19	9	Winstel, Nancy
1982		II	16		GL	L		16	23	6	Scheper, Jane Meier
1986		II	24		GL			24	22	6	Winstel, Nancy
1988		II	32		GL			32	25	3	Winstel, Nancy
1989		II	32		GL	L		32	21	7	Winstel, Nancy
1991		II	32		GL	A		32	22	6	Winstel, Nancy
1992		II	32		GL	L		32	19	9	Winstel, Nancy
NORTHERN MICHIGAN											
1980	M	II	8		GL	L		32	24	6	Brown, Glenn C.
1981		II	8		GL	L		32	21	9	Brown, Glenn C.
1993		II	16		GL	L		32	22	8	Ellis, Dean
1985		II	24		NC	L		32	23	6	Brown, Glenn C.
1979		II	32		GL	L		32	18	11	Brown, Glenn C.
1984		II	32		NC	L		32	21	9	Brown, Glenn C.

Year	M/W	Div	F	SD	Reg	BD	Bye	#T	W	L	Coach
1998	W	II	3	2	GL	A	To R32	48	28	4	Geary, Mike
1996		II	8	1	GL	A	To R32	48	25	5	Geary, Mike
1991		II	16		GL	A		32	22	9	Geary, Mike
1992		II	16		GL	A		32	23	6	Geary, Mike
1997		II	16	2	GL	A	To R32	48	27	3	Geary, Mike
1989		II	32		GL	L		32	24	4	Stein, Paulette
1995		II	32	6	GL	A		48	21	9	Geary, Mike

NORTHERN STATE (SD)

Year	M/W	Div	F	SD	Reg	BD	Bye	#T	W	L	Coach
1998	M	II	8	1	NC	A	To R32	48	27	5	Olson, Robert
1996		II	32	3	GL	A		48	23	6	Olson, Robert
1997		II	48	4	NC	L		48	22	6	Olson, Robert
1997	W	II	32	3	NC	A		48	24	5	Fredrickson, Curt
1998		II	32	6	NC	A		48	23	6	Fredrickson, Curt

NORTHWEST MISSOURI STATE

Year	M/W	Div	F	SD	Reg	BD	Bye	#T	W	L	Coach
1982	M	II	32		S	L		32	20	10	Sinn, Dr. Lionel L.
1984		II	32		SC	L		32	24	7	Sinn, Dr. Lionel L.
1989		II	32		SC	A		32	21	9	Tappmeyer, Steve
1998		II	48	4	SC	L		48	23	7	Tappmeyer, Steve
1984	W	II	16		GL	L		24	25	5	Winstead, Wayne
1990		II	32		SC	L		32	20	10	Winstead, Wayne

NORTHWESTERN (IL)

Year	M/W	Div	F	SD	Reg	BD	Bye	#T	W	L	Coach
1982	W	I	32		E	L		32	21	8	Lynch, Arnette
1987		I	32	8	MW	L		40	20	10	Perrelli, Donald
1990		I	32	4	ME	L	To R32	48	24	5	Perrelli, Donald
1991		I	32	6	MW	L		48	21	9	Perrelli, Donald
1993		I	32		ME	L		48	20	9	Perrelli, Donald
1997		I	64	12	E	L		64	17	11	Perrelli, Donald

NORTHWESTERN STATE (LA)

Year	M/W	Div	F	SD	Reg	BD	Bye	#T	W	L	Coach
1989	W	I	48	10	MW	L		48	22	8	Smith, James F.

NORWICH

Year	M/W	Div	F	SD	Reg	BD	Bye	#T	W	L	Coach
1987	M	III	24		NE	L		32	21	5	Hockenbury, Edward J.
1984		III	32		NE	L		32	21	6	Hockenbury, Edward J.

NOTRE DAME (IN)

Year	M/W	Div	F	SD	Reg	BD	Bye	#T	W	L	Coach
1978	M	I	4		MW	L		32	23	8	Phelps, Richard F. "Digger"
1953			8		E(B)	L		22	19	5	Jordan, John J.
1954			8		E(A)	L		24	22	3	Jordan, John J.
1958		I	8		ME	L		24	24	5	Jordan, John J.
1979		I	8	1	ME	L	To R32	40	24	6	Phelps, Richard F. "Digger"
1957		I	12		ME	L		23	20	8	Jordan, John J.
1974		I	12		ME	L		25	26	3	Phelps, Richard F. "Digger"
1970		I	16		ME	L		25	21	8	Dee, John F., Jr.
1971		I	16		MW	L		25	20	9	Dee, John F., Jr.
1975		I	16		MW	L		32	19	10	Phelps, Richard F. "Digger"
1976		I	16		MW	L		32	23	6	Phelps, Richard F. "Digger"
1977		I	16		E	L		32	22	7	Phelps, Richard F. "Digger"

Year	M/W	Div	F	SD	Reg	BD	Bye	#T	W	L	Coach
1981		I	16	2	E	L	To R32	48	23	6	Phelps, Richard F. "Digger"
1987		I	16	5	E	L		64	24	8	Phelps, Richard F. "Digger"
1965		I	23		MW	L		23	15	12	Dee, John F., Jr.
1960		I	25		ME	L		25	17	9	Jordan, John J.
1963		I	25		ME	L		25	17	9	Jordan, John J.
1969		I	25		ME	L		25	20	7	Dee, John F., Jr.
1980		I	32	4	MW	L	To R32	48	22	6	Phelps, Richard F. "Digger"
1985		I	32	7	SE	L		64	21	9	Phelps, Richard F. "Digger"
1989		I	32	9	E	L		64	21	9	Phelps, Richard F. "Digger"
1986		I	64	3	MW	L		64	23	6	Phelps, Richard F. "Digger"
1988		I	64	10	E	L		64	20	9	Phelps, Richard F. "Digger"
1990		I	64	10	SE	L		64	16	13	Phelps, Richard F. "Digger"
1997	W	I	3	6	E	L		64	31	7	McGraw, Muffet O'Brien
1998		I	16	9	MW	L		64	22	10	McGraw, Muffet O'Brien
1996		I	32	12	MW	L		64	23	8	McGraw, Muffet O'Brien
1992		I	48	12	MW	A		48	14	17	McGraw, Muffet O'Brien
1994		I	64	7	E	A		64	22	7	McGraw, Muffet O'Brien

OAKLAND (MI)

Year	M/W	Div	F	SD	Reg	BD	Bye	#T	W	L	Coach
1997	M	II	16	5	GL	L		48	23	8	Kampe, Greg
1994		II	32		GL	L		32	21	10	Kampe, Greg
1995		II	48	5	GL	L		48	20	9	Kampe, Greg
1996		II	48	6	GL	L		48	21	8	Kampe, Greg
1982	W	II	4		GL	L		16	21	3	Jones, DeWayne
1990		II	4		GL	L		32	27	6	Taylor, Bob
1995		II	8	4	GL	L		48	22	9	Taylor, Bob
1983		II	16		GL	L	To R16	24	22	4	Jones, DeWayne
1989		II	16		GL	L		32	26	4	Taylor, Bob
1994		II	32		GL	A		32	23	5	Taylor, Bob
1997		II	32	6	GL	L		48	25	5	Taylor, Bob
1996		II	48	6	GL	L		48	23	6	Taylor, Bob

OBERLIN

Year	M/W	Div	F	SD	Reg	BD	Bye	#T	W	L	Coach
1976	M	III	21		GL	A		28	16	11	Penn, Patrick

OCCIDENTAL

Year	M/W	Div	F	SD	Reg	BD	Bye	#T	W	L	Coach
1980	M	III	32		W	L		32	15	13	Westphal, Bill

OGLETHORPE

Year	M/W	Div	F	SD	Reg	BD	Bye	#T	W	L	Coach
1963	M	II	3		SC	L		32	21	7	Pinholster, Garland F.
1969		II	8		SA	L		32	22	5	Carter, Bill
1966		II	16		SC	L	To R32	36	22	6	Pinholster, Garland F.
1968		II	23		SC	L	To R32	36	21	6	Carter, Bill
1994		III	40		S	A		40	20	6	Berkshire, Jack
1995		III	64	5	S	L		64	18	8	Berkshire, Jack

OHIO NORTHERN

Year	M/W	Div	F	SD	Reg	BD	Bye	#T	W	L	Coach
1993	M	III	1		GL	L	To R32	40	28	2	Campoli, Joe
1980		III	16		GL	A		32	24	5	Daugherty, Gale E.
1982		III	24		GL	L		32	22	7	Daugherty, Gale E.
1988		III	24		GL	L		32	21	9	Daugherty, Gale E.

Year	M/W	Div	F	SD	Reg	BD	Bye	#T	W	L	Coach
1974		II	44		ME	L		44	18	7	Daugherty, Gale E.
1995		III	64	3	GL	A		64	22	6	Campoli, Joe
1996		III	64	4	GL	L		64	18	9	Campoli, Joe
1997		III	64	4	GL	L		64	19	8	Campoli, Joe
1988	W	III	8		A	A		32	23	4	Lauth, Gayle
1987		III	16		A	L		32	19	7	Lauth, Gayle
1989		III	16		A	L		32	17	10	Lauth, Gayle
1984		III	32		A	L		32	16	8	Lauth, Gayle
1986		III	32		A	A		32	20	6	Lauth, Gayle

OHIO STATE

Year	M/W	Div	F	SD	Reg	BD	Bye	#T	W	L	Coach
1960	M	I	1		ME	A	To R16	25	25	3	Taylor, Fred R.
1939			2		E	L		8	16	7	Olsen, Harold G.
1961		I	2		ME	A	To R16	24	27	1	Taylor, Fred R.
1962		I	2		ME	A	To R16	25	26	2	Taylor, Fred R.
1944			3		E	L		8	14	7	Olsen, Harold G.
1945			3		E	L		8	15	5	Olsen, Harold G.
1946			3		E	L		8	16	5	Olsen, Harold G.
1968		I	3		ME	A	To R16	23	21	8	Taylor, Fred R.
1950			6		E	L		8	22	4	Dye, William H. H. "Tippy"
1971		I	8		ME	A	To R16	25	20	6	Taylor, Fred R.
1992		I	8	1	SE	A		64	26	6	Ayers, Randy
1980		I	16	4	W	L	To R32	48	21	8	Miller, Eldon
1983		I	16	3	E	L	To R32	52	20	10	Miller, Eldon
1991		I	16	1	MW	A		64	27	4	Ayers, Randy
1985		I	32	4	MW	L		64	20	10	Miller, Eldon
1987		I	32	9	SE	L		64	20	13	Williams, Gary
1990		I	32	8	W	L		64	17	13	Ayers, Randy
1982		I	48	8	E	L		48	21	10	Miller, Eldon
1993	W	I	2	1	E	L	To R32	48	28	4	Darsch, Nancy
1985		I	8		E	A		32	28	3	VanDerveer, Tara
1987		I	8	2	W	A	To R32	40	26	5	Darsch, Nancy
1986		I	16		ME	A	To R32	40	23	7	Darsch, Nancy
1988		I	16		ME	L	To R32	40	25	5	Darsch, Nancy
1989		I	16	3	E	A	To R32	48	24	6	Darsch, Nancy
1982		I	32		W	A		32	20	7	VanDerveer, Tara
1984		I	32		ME	A		32	22	7	VanDerveer, Tara
1990		I	32	6	MW	L		48	18	12	Darsch, Nancy
1996		I	32	9	E	L		64	21	13	Darsch, Nancy

OHIO UNIVERSITY

Year	M/W	Div	F	SD	Reg	BD	Bye	#T	W	L	Coach
1964	M	I	8		ME	A		25	21	6	Snyder, James E.
1960		I	16		ME	A		25	16	8	Snyder, James E.
1965		I	23		ME	A		23	19	7	Snyder, James E.
1961		I	24		ME	A		24	17	7	Snyder, James E.
1970		I	25		ME	A		25	20	5	Snyder, James E.
1972		I	25		ME	A		25	15	11	Snyder, James E.
1974		I	25		ME	A		25	16	11	Snyder, James E.
1983		I	32	11	ME	A		52	23	9	Nee, Danny
1985		I	64	14	SE	A		64	22	8	Nee, Danny
1994		I	64	12	E	A		64	25	8	Hunter, Larry

Year	M/W	Div	F	SD	Reg	BD	Bye	#T	W	L	Coach
1986	W	I	40		ME	A		40	26	3	Prichard, Amy
1995		I	64	14	ME	L		64	23	7	Reall, Marsha

OHIO WESLEYAN

1988	M	III	1		GL	L		32	27	5	Mehaffey, Dr. Eugene L.
1992	W	III	32		A	L		32	23	2	Carney-DeBord, Nan
1995		III	64		A	L		64	22	6	Carney-DeBord, Nan

OKLAHOMA

1947	M		2		W	L		8	24	7	Drake, Bruce
1988		I	2	1	SE	A		64	35	4	Tubbs, Billy
1939			3		W	L		8	12	9	Drake, Bruce
1943			6		W	L		8	18	9	Drake, Bruce
1985		I	8	1	MW	A		64	31	6	Tubbs, Billy
1979		I	16	5	MW	A	To R32	40	21	10	Bliss, David
1987		I	16	6	W	L		64	24	10	Tubbs, Billy
1989		I	16	1	SE	L		64	30	6	Tubbs, Billy
1983		I	32	7	ME	L		52	24	9	Tubbs, Billy
1984		I	32	2	W	L	To R32	53	29	5	Tubbs, Billy
1986		I	32	4	E	L		64	26	9	Tubbs, Billy
1990		I	32	1	MW	A		64	27	5	Tubbs, Billy
1992		I	64	4	W	L		64	21	9	Tubbs, Billy
1995		I	64	4	SE	L		64	23	9	Sampson, Kelvin
1996		I	64	10	SE	L		64	17	13	Sampson, Kelvin
1997		I	64	11	W	L		64	19	11	Sampson, Kelvin
1998		I	64	10	E	L		64	22	11	Sampson, Kelvin
1986	W	I	16		MW	L	To R32	40	24	7	McHugh, Maura
1995		I	32	7	E	L		64	22	9	Plunkett, Burl

OKLAHOMA CITY

1956	M		8		W	L		25	20	7	Lemons, A. E. "Abe"
1957		I	8		MW	L		23	19	9	Lemons, A. E. "Abe"
1952			12		W(B)	L		16	19	8	Parrack, Doyle K.
1965		I	12		FW	L		23	21	10	Lemons, A. E. "Abe"
1953			16		W(B)	L	To R16	22	18	6	Parrack, Doyle K.
1963		I	16		MW	L		25	19	10	Lemons, A. E. "Abe"
1966		I	22		MW	L		22	24	5	Lemons, A. E. "Abe"
1954			24		W(A)	L		24	18	7	Parrack, Doyle K.
1955			24		W(A)	L		24	9	18	Parrack, Doyle K.
1964		I	25		MW	L		25	15	11	Lemons, A. E. "Abe"
1973		I	25		W	L		25	21	6	Lemons, A. E. "Abe"

OKLAHOMA STATE

1945	M		1		W	L		8	27	4	Iba, Henry P. "Hank"
1946			1		W	L		8	31	2	Iba, Henry P. "Hank"
1949			2		W	L		8	23	5	Iba, Henry P. "Hank"
1995		I	3	4	E	A		64	27	10	Sutton, Eddie
1951			4		W	A		16	29	6	Iba, Henry P. "Hank"
1953			8		W(B)	A	To R16	22	23	7	Iba, Henry P. "Hank"
1954			8		W(A)	A	To R16	24	24	5	Iba, Henry P. "Hank"
1958		I	8		MW	L		24	21	8	Iba, Henry P. "Hank"

Year	M/W	Div	F	SD	Reg	BD	Bye	#T	W	L	Coach
1965		I	8		MW	A	To R16	23	20	7	Iba, Henry P. "Hank"
1991		I	16	3	E	A		64	24	8	Sutton, Eddie
1992		I	16	2	SE	L		64	28	8	Sutton, Eddie
1993		I	32	5	MW	L		64	20	9	Sutton, Eddie
1994		I	32	4	MW	L		64	24	10	Sutton, Eddie
1998		I	32	8	S	L		64	22	7	Sutton, Eddie
1983		I	48	5	W	A		52	24	7	Hansen, Paul N.
1991	W	I	16	5	MW	A		48	27	6	Halterman, Dick
1989		I	32	9	MW	L		48	20	12	Halterman, Dick
1996		I	32	7	MW	L		64	20	10	Halterman, Dick
1990		I	48	7	MW	A		48	20	11	Halterman, Dick
1993		I	48		MW	L		48	23	9	Halterman, Dick
1994		I	64	12	MW	L		64	20	9	Halterman, Dick
1995		I	64	12	E	L		64	17	12	Halterman, Dick

OLD DOMINION

Year	M/W	Div	F	SD	Reg	BD	Bye	#T	W	L	Coach
1975	M	II	1		SA	L		32	25	6	Allen, William "Sonny"
1971		II	2		SA	L		32	21	9	Allen, William "Sonny"
1976		II	4		SA	L		32	19	12	Webb, Paul E.
1973		II	16		SA	L	To R32	42	19	9	Allen, William "Sonny"
1974		II	16		SA	L	To R32	44	20	7	Allen, William "Sonny"
1970		II	24		S	L		32	21	7	Allen, William "Sonny"
1969		II	32		SA	L		32	21	10	Allen, William "Sonny"
1986		I	32	8	E	L		64	23	8	Young, Thomas J.
1995		I	32	14	E	A		64	21	12	Capel, Jeff
1980		I	48	9	W	L		48	25	5	Webb, Paul E.
1982		I	48	10	E	L		48	18	12	Webb, Paul E.
1985		I	64	12	E	L		64	19	12	Webb, Paul E.
1992		I	64	15	E	A		64	15	15	Purnell, Oliver
1997		I	64	14	E	A		64	22	11	Capel, Jeff
1985	W	I	1		E	A		32	31	3	Stanley, Marianne Crawford
1997		I	2	1	ME	A		64	34	2	Larry, Wendy
1983		I	3		E	A	To R32	36	29	6	Stanley, Marianne Crawford
1984		I	8		E	A		32	24	5	Stanley, Marianne Crawford
1982		I	16		E	L		32	22	6	Stanley, Marianne Crawford
1987		I	16	5	ME	A	To R32	40	18	13	Stanley, Marianne Crawford
1996		I	16	2	E	A		64	29	3	Larry, Wendy
1998		I	16	1	E	A		64	29	3	Larry, Wendy
1988		I	32	6	E	L	To R32	40	17	12	Larry, Wendy
1989		I	32	6	ME	L		48	23	9	Larry, Wendy
1990		I	32	8	E	A		48	21	10	Larry, Wendy
1993		I	32		ME	A		48	22	8	Larry, Wendy
1994		I	32	6	E	A		64	25	6	Larry, Wendy
1992		I	48	10	E	A		48	20	11	Larry, Wendy
1995		I	64	8	ME	A		64	27	6	Larry, Wendy

ONEONTA STATE

Year	M/W	Div	F	SD	Reg	BD	Bye	#T	W	L	Coach
1977	M	III	2		E	L		30	21	6	Flewelling, F. Don
1998	W	III	48	4	E	A		48	25	3	Garner, Steven

Year	M/W	Div	F	SD	Reg	BD	Bye	#T	W	L	Coach
ORAL ROBERTS											
1974	M	I	8		MW	L		25	23	6	Trickey, Ken
1984		I	48	11	MW	A		53	21	10	Acres, Richard
OREGON											
1939	M		1		W	L		8	29	5	Hobson, Dr. Howard A. "Hobby"
1945			6		W	L		8	30	13	Hobson, Dr. Howard A. "Hobby"
1960		I	8		W	L		25	19	10	Belko, Steven
1961		I	24		W	L		24	15	12	Belko, Steven
1995		I	64	6	W	L		64	19	9	Green, Jerry
1982	W	I	32		W	L		32	21	5	Heiny, Elwin
1984		I	32		W	A		32	21	7	Heiny, Elwin
1987		I	32	7	W	L		40	23	7	Heiny, Elwin
1994		I	32	6	W	L		64	20	9	Runge, Jody
1997		I	32	6	MW	L		64	22	7	Runge, Jody
1995		I	64	6	MW	L		64	18	10	Runge, Jody
1996		I	64	11	ME	L		64	18	11	Runge, Jody
1998		I	64	12	ME	L		64	17	10	Runge, Jody
OREGON STATE											
1949	M		4		W	L		8	24	12	Gill, Amory T. "Slats"
1963		I	4		W	L		25	22	9	Gill, Amory T. "Slats"
1947			6		W	L		8	28	5	Gill, Amory T. "Slats"
1955			8		W(B)	A	To R16	24	22	8	Gill, Amory T. "Slats"
1962		I	8		W	L		25	24	5	Gill, Amory T. "Slats"
1966		I	8		W	A	To R16	22	21	7	Valenti, Paul B.
1982		I	8	2	W	A	To R32	48	25	5	Miller, Ralph H. "Cappy"
1975		I	16		ME	L		32	19	12	Miller, Ralph H. "Cappy"
1964		I	25		W	L		25	25	4	Gill, Amory T. "Slats"
1980		I	32	2	W	A	To R32	48	26	4	Miller, Ralph H. "Cappy"
1981		I	32	1	W	A	To R32	48	26	2	Miller, Ralph H. "Cappy"
1984		I	48	6	ME	L		53	22	7	Miller, Ralph H. "Cappy"
1985		I	64	10	SE	L		64	22	9	Miller, Ralph H. "Cappy"
1988		I	64	12	SE	L		64	20	11	Miller, Ralph H. "Cappy"
1989		I	64	6	W	L		64	22	8	Miller, Ralph H. "Cappy"
1990		I	64	5	W	L		64	22	7	Anderson, Jim
1983	W	I	16		W	A	To R32	36	21	5	Hill, Aki
1984		I	32		W	L		32	21	8	Hill, Aki
1995		I	32	5	ME	L		64	21	8	Hill, Aki
1994		I	64	11	MW	L		64	17	11	Hill, Aki
1996		I	64	6	MW	L		64	19	9	Spoelstra, Judy
OTTERBEIN											
1991	M	III	3		GL	A	To R32	40	30	3	Reynolds, Dick
1981		III	4		GL	L		32	23	9	Reynolds, Dick
1986		III	8		GL	A		32	28	3	Reynolds, Dick
1989		III	8		GL	A	To R32	40	20	10	Reynolds, Dick
1992		III	8		GL	A	To R32	40	27	4	Reynolds, Dick
1987		III	16		GL	L		32	23	6	Reynolds, Dick
1978		III	23		GL	A		30	20	9	Reynolds, Dick
1985		III	24		GL	L		32	23	4	Reynolds, Dick

Year	M/W	Div	F	SD	Reg	BD	Bye	#T	W	L	Coach
1993		III	32		GL	A		40	19	10	Reynolds, Dick
1990		III	40		GL	L		40	20	9	Reynolds, Dick
1994		III	40		GL	A		40	19	9	Reynolds, Dick

PACE

Year	M/W	Div	F	SD	Reg	BD	Bye	#T	W	L	Coach
1992	M	II	32		E	L		32	23	7	Holloran, Darrell
1985	W	II	8		E	A	To R16	24	28	3	Olenowski, John
1994		II	16		E	A		32	27	4	Seymour, Carrie
1986		II	24		E	A		24	20	8	Lauro, John
1989		II	32		E	A		32	20	10	Lauro, John
1990		II	32		SA	A		32	23	7	Jones, Allison
1991		II	32		SA	A		32	26	4	Jones, Allison
1992		II	32		E	A		32	25	6	Jones, Allison

PACIFIC (CA)

Year	M/W	Div	F	SD	Reg	BD	Bye	#T	W	L	Coach
1967	M	I	8		W	A	To R16	23	24	4	Edwards, Richard B.
1971		I	12		W	A	To R16	25	22	6	Edwards, Richard B.
1966		I	16		W	A	To R16	22	22	6	Edwards, Richard B.
1979		I	32	6	W	A	To R32	40	18	12	Morrison, Stanley M.
1997		I	64	13	W	A		64	24	6	Thomason, Bob

PACIFIC (OR)

Year	M/W	Div	F	SD	Reg	BD	Bye	#T	W	L	Coach
1957	M	II	32		FW			32	12	12	Adams, Vic

PAINE

Year	M/W	Div	F	SD	Reg	BD	Bye	#T	W	L	Coach
1994	M	II	24		S	A		32	24	7	Spry, Ronald

PARSONS

Year	M/W	Div	F	SD	Reg	BD	Bye	#T	W	L	Coach
1967	M	II	32		MW	L	To R32	36	18	9	Nelson, Oscar B.

PENNSYLVANIA

Year	M/W	Div	F	SD	Reg	BD	Bye	#T	W	L	Coach
1979	M	I	4	9	E	A		40	25	7	Weinhauer, Bob
1971		I	8		E	A		25	28	1	Harter, Dick
1972		I	8		E	A		25	25	3	Daly, Charles J. "Chuck"
1953			12		E(B)	A	To R16	22	22	5	Dallmar, Howard "Howie"
1973		I	16		E	A		25	21	7	Daly, Charles J. "Chuck"
1978		I	16		E	A		32	20	8	Weinhauer, Bob
1970		I	25		E	A		25	25	2	Harter, Dick
1974		I	25		E	A		25	21	6	Daly, Charles J. "Chuck"
1975		I	32		E	A		32	23	5	Daly, Charles J. "Chuck"
1980		I	32	12	ME	A		48	17	12	Weinhauer, Bob
1994		I	32	11	E	A		64	25	3	Dunphy, Fran
1982		I	48	12	E	A		48	17	10	Weinhauer, Bob
1985		I	64	15	MW	A		64	13	14	Littlepage, Craig K.
1987		I	64	16	E	A		64	13	14	Schneider, Thomas
1993		I	64	14	E	A		64	22	5	Dunphy, Fran
1995		I	64	12	E	A		64	22	6	Dunphy, Fran

PENNSYLVANIA STATE

Year	M/W	Div	F	SD	Reg	BD	Bye	#T	W	L	Coach
1954	M		3		E(A)	L		24	18	6	Gross, Elmer A.
1942			6		E	L		8	18	3	Lawther, John D.
1952			16		E(A)	L		16	20	6	Gross, Elmer A.
1955			16		E(A)	L		24	18	10	Egli, John S.

Year	M/W	Div	F	SD	Reg	BD	Bye	#T	W	L	Coach
1965		I	23		E	L		23	20	4	Egli, John S.
1991		I	32	13	E	A		64	21	11	Parkhill, Bruce
1996		I	64	5	E	L		64	21	7	Dunn, Jerry
1983	W	I	8		E	A	To R32	36	25	8	Portland, Rene Muth
1994		I	8	1	MW	A		64	28	3	Portland, Rene Muth
1982		I	16		ME	L		32	24	6	Portland, Rene Muth
1985		I	16		E	A		32	28	5	Portland, Rene Muth
1986		I	16		E	A	To R32	40	24	8	Portland, Rene Muth
1992		I	16	3	MW	L	To R32	48	24	7	Portland, Rene Muth
1996		I	16	2	W	A		64	27	7	Portland, Rene Muth
1984		I	32		E	A		32	19	12	Portland, Rene Muth
1987		I	32	5	W	L	To R32	40	23	7	Portland, Rene Muth
1988		I	32	9	ME	L		40	20	13	Portland, Rene Muth
1990		I	32	7	E	A		48	25	7	Portland, Rene Muth
1991		I	32	1	E	A	To R32	48	29	2	Portland, Rene Muth
1993		I	32	3	E	L	To R32	48	22	6	Portland, Rene Muth
1995		I	32	2	MW	A		64	26	5	Portland, Rene Muth

PENNSYLVANIA STATE: ERIE BEHREND

Year	M/W	Div	F	SD	Reg	BD	Bye	#T	W	L	Coach
1994	W	III	32		A	L		40	21	6	Fornari, Rosalyn "Roz"

PEPPERDINE

Year	M/W	Div	F	SD	Reg	BD	Bye	#T	W	L	Coach
1944	M		8		W	L		8	22	13	Duer, Alva O. "Al"
1962		I	12		W	A	To R16	25	20	7	Dowell, Robert L. "Duck"
1976		I	16		W	A		32	22	6	Colson, Gary W.
1979		I	32	9	W	L		40	22	10	Colson, Gary W.
1982		I	32	7	W	A		48	22	7	Harrick, Jim
1983		I	48	11	W	A		52	20	9	Harrick, Jim
1985		I	64	14	MW	A		64	23	9	Harrick, Jim
1986		I	64	12	W	A		64	25	5	Harrick, Jim
1991		I	64	14	W	A		64	22	9	Asbury, Tom
1992		I	64	11	MW	A		64	24	7	Asbury, Tom
1994		I	64	14	MW	A		64	19	11	Asbury, Tom

PFEIFFER

Year	M/W	Div	F	SD	Reg	BD	Bye	#T	W	L	Coach
1996	M	II	32	5	SA	L		48	20	8	Earlywine, Kirk

PHILADELPHIA TEXTILES

Year	M/W	Div	F	SD	Reg	BD	Bye	#T	W	L	Coach
1970	M	II	1		ME	L		32	29	2	Magee, Herbert
1963		II	8		E	L		32	21	3	Harris, Walter "Bucky"
1965		II	8		E	L		32	22	4	Harris, Walter "Bucky"
1991		II	8		E	A		32	24	8	Magee, Herbert
1993		II	8		E	A		32	30	2	Magee, Herbert
1967		II	16		E	L	To R32	36	20	7	McKinney, John P. "Jack"
1971		II	16		ME	L		32	22	6	Magee, Herbert
1976		II	16		E	L		32	25	3	Magee, Herbert
1978		II	16		E	L		32	18	10	Magee, Herbert
1983		II	16		E	L		32	23	7	Magee, Herbert
1985		II	16		E	L		32	24	7	Magee, Herbert
1992		II	16		E	A		32	28	4	Magee, Herbert

Year	M/W	Div	F	SD	Reg	BD	Bye	#T	W	L	Coach
1994		II	16		NE	A		32	29	2	Magee, Herbert
1995		II	16	4	NE	L		48	26	5	Magee, Herbert
1968		II	23		E	L	To R32	36	21	6	Magee, Herbert
1964		II	24		E	L		32	18	6	Harris, Walter "Bucky"
1969		II	24		MW	L		32	20	5	Magee, Herbert
1972		II	24		ME			36	22	7	Magee, Herbert
1975		II	24		E	L		32	21	6	Magee, Herbert
1958		II	32		E			32	17	7	Harris, Walter "Bucky"
1966		II	32		NE	L		36	20	6	McKinney, John P. "Jack"
1973		II	32		ME		To R32	42	25	4	Magee, Herbert
1977		II	32		E	L		32	22	6	Magee, Herbert
1979		II	32		E	L		32	20	8	Magee, Herbert
1989		II	32		E	A		32	24	7	Magee, Herbert
1986	W	II	3		E	L	To R16	24	24	6	Soriero, Julie
1989		II	32		E	L		32	21	9	Soriero, Julie
1993		II	32		E	L		32	27	2	Shirley, Thomas, Jr.
1998		II	32	5	NE	L		48	25	8	Shirley, Thomas, Jr.
1997		II	48	3	NE	L		48	21	8	Shirley, Thomas, Jr.

PHILANDER SMITH

Year	M/W	Div	F	SD	Reg	BD	Bye	#T	W	L	Coach
1957	M	II	32		MW	L		32	12	14	Hearnton, William C., Sr.
1958		II	32		SC	L		32	14	10	

PITTSBURG STATE

Year	M/W	Div	F	SD	Reg	BD	Bye	#T	W	L	Coach
1997	M	II	16	5	SC	L		48	24	8	Iba, Clarence Eugene "Gene"
1998		II	32	5	SC	L		48	24	7	Iba, Clarence Eugene "Gene"
1992	W	II	32		SC	A		32	22	9	High, Steve
1993		II	32		SC	L		32	21	7	High, Steve
1995		II	48	4	SC	L		48	22	7	High, Steve
1997		II	48	5	SC	L		48	19	10	High, Steve
1998		II	48	4	SC	L		48	18	11	High, Steve

PITTSBURGH

Year	M/W	Div	F	SD	Reg	BD	Bye	#T	W	L	Coach
1941	M		3		E	L		8	13	6	Carlson, Dr. H. Clifford "Doc"
1974		I	8		E	L		25	25	4	Ridl, Charles G. "Buzz"
1957		I	16		ME	L		23	16	11	Timmons, Robert W.
1958		I	24		ME	L		24	18	7	Timmons, Robert W.
1963		I	25		E	L		25	19	6	Timmons, Robert W.
1981		I	32	10	W	A		48	19	12	Chipman, Dr. Leroy
1987		I	32	3	W	L		64	25	8	Evans, Paul
1988		I	32	2	MW	L		64	24	7	Evans, Paul
1991		I	32	6	SE	L		64	21	12	Evans, Paul
1982		I	48	10	W	A		48	20	10	Chipman, Dr. Leroy
1985		I	64	12	MW	L		64	17	12	Chipman, Dr. Leroy
1989		I	64	8	MW	L		64	17	13	Evans, Paul
1993		I	64	9	SE	L		64	17	11	Evans, Paul

PITTSBURGH: JOHNSTOWN

Year	M/W	Div	F	SD	Reg	BD	Bye	#T	W	L	Coach
1998	M	II	32	6	E	L		48	24	5	Rukavina, Bob
1997		II	48	4	E	L		48	21	6	Rukavina, Bob

Year	M/W	Div	F	SD	Reg	BD	Bye	#T	W	L	Coach
1987	W	II	3		E	L	To R16	24	25	5	Gault, Jodi
1984		III	8		GL	L		32	25	3	Gault, Jodi
1988		II	8		E	L		32	25	4	Gault, Jodi
1992		II	8		E	L		32	25	4	Gault, Jodi
1993		II	8		E	L		32	25	5	Gault, Jodi
1982		II	16		E	L		16	20	3	Horner, Clyde L.
1983		III	16		S	L		32	24	2	Gault, Jodi
1985		III	16		MA	L		32	26	3	Gault, Jodi
1990		II	32		E	A		32	25	4	Gault, Jodi
1991		II	32		E	A		32	27	2	Gault, Jodi
1996		II	32	5	E	L		48	20	9	Gault, Jodi

PLATTSBURGH STATE

Year	M/W	Div	F	SD	Reg	BD	Bye	#T	W	L	Coach
1976	M	III	4		E	A		28	16	14	Law, Norman
1995		III	64	7	E	L		64	17	10	Cowen, Larry

PLYMOUTH STATE

Year	M/W	Div	F	SD	Reg	BD	Bye	#T	W	L	Coach
1996	M	III	64	8	NE	L		64	19	9	Hogan, Paul
1995	W	III	64		NE	L		64	21	7	Feldman, Nancy

POMONA-PITZER

Year	M/W	Div	F	SD	Reg	BD	Bye	#T	W	L	Coach
1989	M	III	24		W	A		40	18	10	Katsiaficas, Charles G.
1986		III	32		W	A		32	16	12	Popovich, Gregg
1994		III	40		W	L		40	25	3	Katsiaficas, Charles G.
1998		III	48	5	W	A		48	21	5	Katsiaficas, Charles G.
1995		III	64	4	W	A		64	18	8	Katsiaficas, Charles G.
1997		III	64	4	W	A		64	19	7	Katsiaficas, Charles G.
1982	W	III	3		None	L		16	25	4	Breitenstein, Nancy
1985		III	8		W	L		32	27	2	Breitenstein, Nancy
1987		III	16		W	L		32	24	4	Breitenstein, Nancy
1983		III	24		W	L		32	18	10	Breitenstein, Nancy
1984		III	32		W	L		32	22	6	Breitenstein, Nancy
1986		III	32		W	A		32	19	9	Breitenstein, Nancy
1994		III	40		W	A		40	14	11	Krieger, Barbara
1996		III	64		W			64	17	9	Krieger, Barbara
1997		III	64		W	A		64	19	7	Connell, Kathleen "Kathy"

PORTLAND

Year	M/W	Div	F	SD	Reg	BD	Bye	#T	W	L	Coach
1959	M	I	23		MW	L		23	19	8	Negratti, Dr. Albert E.
1996		I	64	14	MW	A		64	19	11	Chavez, Rob
1994	W	I	64	15	ME	A		64	17	12	Sollars, Jim
1995		I	64	13	W	L		64	23	7	Sollars, Jim
1996		I	64	13	MW	L		64	23	7	Sollars, Jim
1997		I	64	9	E	L		64	27	3	Sollars, Jim

PORTLAND STATE

Year	M/W	Div	F	SD	Reg	BD	Bye	#T	W	L	Coach
1967	M	II	32		PC	L	To R32	36	16	9	Pericin, Marion J.
1995	W	II	2	2	W	L	To R32	48	26	6	Bruce, Greg
1992		II	3		W	L		32	31	3	Bruce, Greg

Year	M/W	Div	F	SD	Reg	BD	Bye	#T	W	L	Coach
1996		II	8	1	W	L	To R32	48	25	5	Bruce, Greg
1993		II	16		W	L		32	21	8	Bruce, Greg
1994		II	16		W	A		32	25	4	Bruce, Greg

POTSDAM STATE

Year	M/W	Div	F	SD	Reg	BD	Bye	#T	W	L	Coach
1981	M	III	1		E	L		32	30	2	Welsh, John Gerald "Jerry"
1986		III	1		E	A		32	32	0	Welsh, John Gerald "Jerry"
1979		III	2		E	A		32	24	7	Welsh, John Gerald "Jerry"
1982		III	2		NE	L		32	20	10	Welsh, John Gerald "Jerry"
1985		III	2		E	L		32	27	4	Welsh, John Gerald "Jerry"
1980		III	8		E	A		32	26	4	Welsh, John Gerald "Jerry"
1983		III	8		E	A		32	23	6	Welsh, John Gerald "Jerry"
1987		III	8		E	A		32	28	1	Welsh, John Gerald "Jerry"
1989		III	8		E	L	To R32	40	24	5	Welsh, John Gerald "Jerry"
1984		III	16		W	L		32	21	7	Welsh, John Gerald "Jerry"
1978		III	23		E	A		30	15	9	Welsh, John Gerald "Jerry"
1988		III	24		E	L		32	24	5	Welsh, John Gerald "Jerry"
1973		II	32		E	L		42	18	6	Welsh, John Gerald "Jerry"
1974		II	32		E	A		44	18	9	Welsh, John Gerald "Jerry"
1990		III	32		E	L	To R32	40	23	5	Welsh, John Gerald "Jerry"
1966		II	36		NE			36	16	5	LaGrand, Lou

PRAIRIE VIEW A&M

Year	M/W	Div	F	SD	Reg	BD	Bye	#T	W	L	Coach
1960	M	II	16		MW	L		32	21	5	Moore, Dr. Leroy G., Jr.
1961		II	16		MW			32	25	2	Moore, Dr. Leroy G., Jr.
1998		I	64	16	MW	A		64	13	17	Plummer, Elwood

PRESBYTERIAN

Year	M/W	Div	F	SD	Reg	BD	Bye	#T	W	L	Coach
1997	M	II	32	2	SA	L	To R32	48	20	7	Nibert, Gregg
1996		II	48	6	SA	A		48	19	11	Nibert, Gregg
1994	W	II	32		SA	L		32	22	8	Couture, Beth
1998		II	32	4	SA	A		48	23	8	Couture, Beth
1995		II	48	3	SA	A		48	23	7	Couture, Beth

PRINCETON

Year	M/W	Div	F	SD	Reg	BD	Bye	#T	W	L	Coach
1965	M	I	3		E	A		23	23	6	Van Breda Kolff, Willem "Butch"
1967		I	12		E	A		23	25	3	Van Breda Kolff, Willem "Butch"
1952			16		E(B)	A		16	16	11	Cappon, Franklin C. "Cappy"
1955			16		E(B)	A	To R16	24	13	12	Cappon, Franklin C. "Cappy"
1961		I	16		E	L		24	18	8	McCandles, J. L. "Jake"
1964		I	16		E	A		25	20	9	Van Breda Kolff, Willem "Butch"
1960		I	25		E	L		25	15	9	Cappon, Franklin C. "Cappy"
1963		I	25		E	A		25	19	6	Van Breda Kolff, Willem "Butch"
1969		I	25		E	A		25	19	7	Carril, Peter J.
1976		I	32		E	A		32	22	5	Carril, Peter J.
1977		I	32		E	A		32	21	5	Carril, Peter J.
1983		I	32	12	W	A		52	20	9	Carril, Peter J.
1996		I	32	13	SE	A		64	22	7	Carril, Peter J.
1998		I	32	5	E	A		64	27	2	Carmody, Bill
1981		I	48	11	E	A		48	18	10	Carril, Peter J.
1984		I	48	12	W	A		53	18	10	Carril, Peter J.

Year	M/W	Div	F	SD	Reg	BD	Bye	#T	W	L	Coach
1989		I	64	16	E	A		64	19	8	Carril, Peter J.
1990		I	64	13	MW	A		64	20	7	Carril, Peter J.
1991		I	64	8	E	A		64	24	3	Carril, Peter J.
1992		I	64	11	E	A		64	22	6	Carril, Peter J.
1997		I	64	12	E	A		64	24	4	Carmody, Bill

PROVIDENCE

Year	M/W	Div	F	SD	Reg	BD	Bye	#T	W	L	Coach
1987	M	I	3	6	SE	L		64	25	9	Pitino, Richard A. 'Rick'
1973		I	4		E	L		25	27	4	Gavitt, David R.
1965		I	8		E	L		23	24	2	Mullaney, Joseph A., Sr.
1997		I	8	10	SE	L		64	24	12	Gillen, Pete
1974		I	12		E	L		25	28	4	Gavitt, David R.
1966		I	22		E	L		22	22	5	Mullaney, Joseph A., Sr.
1964		I	25		E	L		25	20	6	Mullaney, Joseph A., Sr.
1972		I	25		E	L		25	21	6	Gavitt, David R.
1977		I	32		MW	L		32	24	5	Gavitt, David R.
1978		I	32		ME	L		32	24	8	Gavitt, David R.
1989		I	64	12	SE	L		64	18	11	Barnes, Richard D. 'Rick'
1990		I	64	9	W	L		64	17	12	Barnes, Richard D. 'Rick'
1994		I	64	8	SE	A		64	20	10	Barnes, Richard D. 'Rick'
1990	W	I	16	3	E	A	To R32	48	27	5	Foley, Bob
1991		I	32	5	E	L		48	26	6	Foley, Bob
1986		I	40		E	L		40	24	6	Foley, Bob
1989		I	48	11	E	L		48	22	11	Foley, Bob
1992		I	48	7	ME	L		48	21	9	Foley, Bob

PUGET SOUND

Year	M/W	Div	F	SD	Reg	BD	Bye	#T	W	L	Coach
1976	M	II	1		W	L		32	27	7	Zech, Don
1971		II	8		W	L		32	21	5	Zech, Don
1979		II	8		W	L		32	23	6	Zech, Don
1981		II	8		W	L		32	24	5	Zech, Don
1970		II	16		W	L		32	24	4	Zech, Don
1975		II	16		W	L		32	17	10	Zech, Don
1977		II	16		W	L		32	22	7	Zech, Don
1984		II	16		W	L		32	22	8	Zech, Don
1978		II	24		W	L		32	20	10	Zech, Don
1980		II	24		W	L		32	21	8	Zech, Don
1973		II	32		W	L	To R32	42	19	9	Zech, Don

PURDUE

Year	M/W	Div	F	SD	Reg	BD	Bye	#T	W	L	Coach
1969	M	I	2		ME	A	To R16	25	23	5	King, George S., Jr.
1980		I	3	6	ME	L		48	23	10	Rose, Lee H.
1994		I	8	1	SE	A		64	29	5	Keady, Lloyd Eugene 'Gene'
1988		I	16	1	MW	A		64	29	4	Keady, Lloyd Eugene 'Gene'
1998		I	16	2	MW	L		64	28	8	Keady, Lloyd Eugene 'Gene'
1977		I	32		E	L		32	19	9	Schaus, Frederick A.
1983		I	32	5	ME	L		52	21	9	Keady, Lloyd Eugene 'Gene'
1984	·	I	32	3	MW	L	To R32	53	22	7	Keady, Lloyd Eugene 'Gene'
1987		I	32	3	E	L		64	25	5	Keady, Lloyd Eugene 'Gene'
1990		I	32	2	MW	L		64	22	8	Keady, Lloyd Eugene 'Gene'
1995		I	32	3	MW	A		64	25	7	Keady, Lloyd Eugene 'Gene'
1996		I	32	1	W	A		64	26	6	Keady, Lloyd Eugene 'Gene'

Year	M/W	Div	F	SD	Reg	BD	Bye	#T	W	L	Coach
1997		I	32	8	SE	L		64	18	12	Keady, Lloyd Eugene "Gene"
1985		I	64	6	SE	L		64	20	9	Keady, Lloyd Eugene "Gene"
1986		I	64	6	SE	L		64	22	10	Keady, Lloyd Eugene "Gene"
1991		I	64	7	E	L		64	17	12	Keady, Lloyd Eugene "Gene"
1993		I	64	9	E	L		64	18	10	Keady, Lloyd Eugene "Gene"
1994	W	I	3	1	W	L		64	29	5	Dunn, Lin
1995		I	8	4	W	L		64	24	8	Dunn, Lin
1998		I	8	4	MW	A		64	23	10	Peck, Carolyn
1990		I	16	4	MW	L	To R32	48	23	7	Dunn, Lin
1992		I	16	3	ME	L	To R32	48	23	7	Dunn, Lin
1989		I	32	5	MW	L		48	24	6	Dunn, Lin
1991		I	32	2	ME	A	To R32	48	26	3	Dunn, Lin
1997		I	32	8	ME	L		64	17	11	Fortner, Nell
1996		I	64	5	MW	L		64	20	11	Dunn, Lin

QUEENS (NC)

Year	M/W	Div	F	SD	Reg	BD	Bye	#T	W	L	Coach
1996	M	II	16	2	SA	L	To R32	48	11	15	Layer, Dale
1998		II	48	3	E	A		48	24	6	Layer, Dale

QUINCY (IL)

Year	M/W	Div	F	SD	Reg	BD	Bye	#T	W	L	Coach
1995	M	II	24	4	GL	L		48	22	7	Hawkins, Steve
1997		II	32	6	GL	L		48	20	9	Hawkins, Steve

QUINNIPIAC

Year	M/W	Div	F	SD	Reg	BD	Bye	#T	W	L	Coach
1980	M	II	24		NENG	L		32	22	7	Kahn, Burt
1988		II	24		NENG	A		32	18	13	Kahn, Burt
1976		II	32		NENG	L		32	19	9	Kahn, Burt
1979		II	32		NENG	L		32	20	5	Kahn, Burt
1984	W	II	8		NENG	A	To R16	24	28	3	Hanson, Ron
1985		II	8		NENG	A	To R16	24	28	4	Hanson, Ron
1986		II	16		NENG	L		24	25	4	Wolfson, Barry

RADFORD

Year	M/W	Div	F	SD	Reg	BD	Bye	#T	W	L	Coach
1998	M	I	64	16	S	A		64	20	10	Bradley, Ron
1994	W	I	64	16	W	A		64	18	12	Lichonczak, Lubomyr
1995		I	64	11	E	A		64	15	15	Lichonczak, Lubomyr
1996		I	64	16	E	A		64	17	12	Lichonczak, Lubomyr

RAMAPO

Year	M/W	Div	F	SD	Reg	BD	Bye	#T	W	L	Coach
1991	M	III	4		A	L	To R32	40	24	8	Meyer, Todd

RANDOLPH-MACON

Year	M/W	Div	F	SD	Reg	BD	Bye	#T	W	L	Coach
1977	M	II	2		GL	L		32	23	8	Nunnally, Hal
1975		II	16		SA			32	27	3	Webb, Paul E.
1991		III	16		S	A	To R32	40	26	3	Nunnally, Hal
1984		II	24		SA	L		32	26	5	Nunnally, Hal
1965		II	32		ME			32	19	5	Webb, Paul E.
1966		II	32		ME		To R32	36	21	7	Webb, Paul E.
1981		II	32		SA	L		32	21	8	Nunnally, Hal
1983		II	32		SA	L		32	20	10	Nunnally, Hal

Year	M/W	Div	F	SD	Reg	BD	Bye	#T	W	L	Coach
1985		II	32		SA	L		32	23	8	Nunnally, Hal
1990		III	32		S	A	To R32	40	24	5	Nunnally, Hal
1974		II	44		SA	L		44	23	6	Webb, Paul E.
1998		III	48	6	S	L		48	20	8	Nunnally, Hal
1996		III	64	7	S	L		64	18	9	Nunnally, Hal
1996	W	III	16		S	A		64	28	2	LaHaye, Carroll
1998		III	32	2	S	L	To R32	48	21	6	LaHaye, Carroll

REDLANDS

Year	M/W	Div	F	SD	Reg	BD	Bye	#T	W	L	Coach
1985	M	III	24		W	A		32	19	9	Smith, Gary H.

REGIS (CO)

Year	M/W	Div	F	SD	Reg	BD	Bye	#T	W	L	Coach
1957	M	II	16		FW	L		32	15	10	Moore, Harvey E.
1958		II	16		SW	L		32	14	9	Moore, Harvey E.
1995		II	32	1	NC	A	To R32	48	25	5	Porter, Lonnie
1996		II	32	4	NC	L		48	25	5	Porter, Lonnie

REGIS (MA)

Year	M/W	Div	F	SD	Reg	BD	Bye	#T	W	L	Coach
1996	W	III	64		NE	A		64	23	4	Tanner, Donna

RENSSELAER

Year	M/W	Div	F	SD	Reg	BD	Bye	#T	W	L	Coach
1996	M	III	16	2	E	L		64	20	8	Griffin, Michael
1975		III	23		E	L		30	13	9	Kalbaugh, R. William, Sr.
1976		III	28		E	A		28	17	9	Kalbaugh, R. William, Sr.
1958		II	32		NE	L		32	14	6	Kalbaugh, R. William, Sr.
1991		III	40		E	L		40	20	5	Griffin, Michael
1973		II	42		E			42	16	9	Kalbaugh, R. William, Sr.

RHODE ISLAND

Year	M/W	Div	F	SD	Reg	BD	Bye	#T	W	L	Coach
1998	M	I	8	8	MW	L		64	25	9	Harrick, Jim
1988		I	16	11	E	L		64	28	7	Penders, Thomas V.
1966		I	22		E	A		22	20	8	Calverley, Ernest A.
1961		I	24		E	A		24	18	9	Calverley, Ernest A.
1978		I	32		E	L		32	24	7	Kraft, John J. "Jack"
1993		I	32	8	E	L		64	19	11	Skinner, Albert L., Jr.
1997		I	64	9	SE	L		64	20	10	Skinner, Albert L., Jr.
1996	W	I	64	10	MW	L		64	21	8	Ziemke, Linda L.

RHODE ISLAND COLLEGE

Year	M/W	Div	F	SD	Reg	BD	Bye	#T	W	L	Coach
1976	M	III	7		NE	L		28	17	9	Baird, William M.
1975		III	30		NE	L		30	16	9	Baird, William M.
1979		III	32		NE	L		32	21	7	Possinger, David F.
1983	W	III	16		E	L		32	16	7	Conley, Joseph
1985		III	24		NE	L		32	19	7	Chevalier, Dave

RHODES

Year	M/W	Div	F	SD	Reg	BD	Bye	#T	W	L	Coach
1981	M	III	16		S	A		32	23	3	Hilgeman, Herb
1980		III	24		S	L		32	22	6	Hilgeman, Herb
1993		III	32		S	A		40	21	6	Hilgeman, Herb

Year	M/W	Div	F	SD	Reg	BD	Bye	#T	W	L	Coach
RICE											
1940	M		6		W	L		8	22	3	Brannon, Byron A. 'Buster'
1942			8		W	L		8	22	5	Brannon, Byron A. 'Buster'
1954			12		W(A)	A	To R16	24	23	5	Suman, Donald W.
1970		I	25		MW	A		25	14	11	Knodel, Don
RICHARD STOCKTON											
1987	M	III	4		SA	A		32	23	8	Matthews, Gerald
1996		III	8	1	A	A		64	26	4	Matthews, Gerald
1990		III	16		SA	L		40	21	8	Matthews, Gerald
1994		III	16		A	L	To R32	40	20	7	Matthews, Gerald
1997		III	16	2	A	A		64	22	7	Matthews, Gerald
1988		III	24		SA	A		32	22	5	Matthews, Gerald
1993		III	32		A	L		40	21	6	Matthews, Gerald
1989		III	40		SA	L		40	19	8	Matthews, Gerald
1992		III	40		A	L		40	18	9	Matthews, Gerald
1984	W	III	16		A	L		32	20	7	Fussner, Joseph
RICHMOND											
1988	M	I	16	13	E	A		64	26	7	Tarrant, Dick
1984		I	32	12	E	L		53	22	10	Tarrant, Dick
1991		I	32	15	E	A		64	22	10	Tarrant, Dick
1998		I	32	14	E	A		64	23	8	Beilein, John
1986		I	64	11	E	L		64	23	7	Tarrant, Dick
1990		I	64	14	E	A		64	22	10	Tarrant, Dick
1990	W	I	48	10	ME	A		48	25	5	Gaitley, Stephanie Vanderslice
1991		I	48	7	E	A		48	26	5	Gaitley, Stephanie Vanderslice
RIDER											
1957	M	II	8		E	L		32	20	7	Leyden, Thomas A.
1984		I	53	13	E	A		53	20	11	Carpenter, John B.
1993		I	64	16	SE	A		64	19	11	Bannon, Kevin
1994		I	64	15	E	A		64	21	9	Bannon, Kevin
RIPON											
1986	M	III	16		MW	A		32	19	6	Gillespie, Robert
1980		III	24		MW	A		32	20	5	Weiske, Kermit G. 'Doc'
1978		III	30		MW	A		30	15	10	Weiske, Kermit G. 'Doc'
1987		III	32		MW	A		32	17	8	Gillespie, Robert
1991		III	32		MW	A		40	21	5	Gillespie, Robert
1992		III	40		MW	A		40	19	6	Gillespie, Robert
1998		III	48	4	MW	A		48	23	2	Gillespie, Robert
1995		III	64	8	MW	L		64	19	6	Gillespie, Robert
1996		III	64	7	MW	L		64	21	4	Gillespie, Robert
1996	W	III	64		GL	A		64	20	5	Heinz, Julie
ROANOKE											
1972	M	II	1		SA		To R32	36	28	4	Moir, Charles
1983		III	3		SA	A		32	31	2	Green, Ed
1973		II	8		SA		To R32	42	23	6	Moir, Charles
1982		III	8		SA	A		32	27	4	Green, Ed

Year	M/W	Div	F	SD	Reg	BD	Bye	#T	W	L	Coach
1984		III	16		SA	A		32	27	2	Green, Ed
1996		III	16	1	S	A		64	24	5	Moir, Page
1974		II	24		SA	A	To R32	44	24	6	Hankinson, Mel
1981		III	24		SA	A		32	27	2	Green, Ed
1987		III	24		SA	A		32	19	10	Green, Ed
1968		II	32		ME		To R32	36	22	8	Moir, Charles
1971		II	32		SA	L		32	23	8	Moir, Charles
1979		II	32		SA	L		32	25	3	Green, Ed
1985		III	32		SA	A		32	21	9	Green, Ed
1986		III	32		SA	A		32	16	14	Green, Ed
1994		III	32		S	A	To R32	40	26	2	Moir, Page
1995		III	64	6	S	L		64	19	9	Moir, Page
1997		III	64	5	S	A		64	19	8	Moir, Page
1991	W	III	8		S	L		32	28	2	Dunagan, Susan
1992		III	16		S	L		32	24	4	Dunagan, Susan
1990		III	32		S	L		32	24	5	Dunagan, Susan
1993		III	32		W	L		32	21	6	Dunagan, Susan
1995		III	32		S	A		64	23	6	Dunagan, Susan
1994		III	40		S	A		40	23	5	Dunagan, Susan
1998		III	48	5	S	A		48	18	10	Dunagan, Susan
1996		III	64		S	L		64	21	7	Dunagan, Susan
1997		III	64		S	A		64	25	3	Dunagan, Susan

ROBERT MORRIS

Year	M/W	Div	F	SD	Reg	BD	Bye	#T	W	L	Coach
1982	M	I	48	12	ME	L		48	17	13	Furjanic, Matt, Jr.
1983		I	48	12	ME	A		52	23	8	Furjanic, Matt, Jr.
1989		I	64	16	W	A		64	21	9	Durham, Jarrett
1990		I	64	15	E	A		64	22	8	Durham, Jarrett
1992		I	64	16	W	A		64	19	12	Durham, Jarrett

ROCHESTER (NY)

Year	M/W	Div	F	SD	Reg	BD	Bye	#T	W	L	Coach
1990	M	III	1		E	L		40	27	5	Neer, Mike
1992		III	2		E	A	To R32	40	28	3	Neer, Mike
1991		III	8		E	L		40	23	7	Neer, Mike
1981		III	16		NE	L		32	20	7	Neer, Mike
1961		II	24		NE	L		32	17	6	Brown, Lyle D.
1962		II	32		NE	L		32	17	5	Brown, Lyle D.
1968		II	32		NE	L		36	13	8	Brown, Lyle D.
1967		II	34		NE	L		36	15	7	Brown, Lyle D.
1997		III	64	8	E	L		64	15	11	Neer, Mike
1985	W	III	24		E	L		32	21	6	Wong, Joyce
1987		III	24		E	L		32	22	7	Wong, Joyce
1984		III	32		E	L		32	21	5	Wong, Joyce

ROCHESTER TECH (NY)

Year	M/W	Div	F	SD	Reg	BD	Bye	#T	W	L	Coach
1997	M	III	16	1	E	L		64	24	4	McVean, Robert
1976		III	21		E	L		28	19	8	Catey, Bill
1995		III	64	1	E	A		64	21	5	McVean, Robert
1996		III	64	1	E	L		64	22	4	McVean, Robert

ROCKFORD

Year	M/W	Div	F	SD	Reg	BD	Bye	#T	W	L	Coach
1987	W	III	16		C	L		32	25	2	Crick, Steve

Year	M/W	Div	F	SD	Reg	BD	Bye	#T	W	L	Coach
ROLLINS											
1979	M	II	16		SC	L		32	17	11	Jucker, Edwin L.
1976		II	24		S	L		32	19	6	Jucker, Edwin L.
1974		II	32		SA	L		44	18	9	Jucker, Edwin L.
1992		II	32		S	A		32	23	8	Klusman, Tom
1996		II	48	6	S	L		48	20	8	Klusman, Tom
1995	W	II	48	5	S	L		48	21	8	Wilkes, Glenn N., Jr.
1996		II	48	6	S	L		48	23	6	Wilkes, Glenn N., Jr.
ROSE-HULMAN											
1977	M	III	8		S	L		30	24	4	Mutchner, John
1982		III	24		S	A		32	18	10	Mutchner, John
1989		III	24		S	L		40	19	8	Mutchner, John
1978		III	30		GL	L		30	20	7	Mutchner, John
1981		III	32		S	L		32	18	7	Mutchner, John
1997		III	32	4	MW	L		64	19	9	Shaw, Jim
1996		III	64	5	MW	A		64	19	9	Shaw, Jim
ROWAN											
1996	M	III	1	2	A	L		64	28	4	Giannini, John
1975		III	2		SA	L		30	21	10	Collins, Jack
1993		III	3		A	A	To R32	40	29	2	Giannini, John
1995		III	3	2	A	L		64	27	4	Giannini, John
1997		III	8	1	A	L		64	26	3	Cassidy, Joe
1994		III	16		A	A	To R32	40	26	2	Giannini, John
1998		III	16	3	A	L		48	21	8	Cassidy, Joe
1976		III	21		SA	A		28	18	10	Collins, Jack
1977		III	23		SA	A		30	17	11	Collins, Jack
1991		III	32		SA	L		40	20	8	Giannini, John
1998	W	III	4		A	A	To R32	48	27	4	Crabtree, Candace
1996		III	8	1	MA	A		64	29	1	Crabtree, Candace
1993		III	16		NE	L		32	23	5	Bunting, Dawn Shilling
1988		III	32		A	L		32	21	7	Bunting, Dawn Shilling
1992		III	32		A	A		32	23	5	Bunting, Dawn Shilling
1994		III	32		MA	A	To R32	40	25	1	Crabtree, Candace
1997		III	32		A	A		64	25	3	Crabtree, Candace
RUST											
1983	M	III	24		S	L		32	24	6	Hayes, Naylond
1987		III	24		S	A		32	20	9	Hayes, Naylond
1988		III	24		S	A		32	23	5	Hayes, Naylond
1989		III	32		S	L	To R32	40	21	5	Hayes, Naylond
1997		III	64	6	S	L		64	17	9	Stennis, Rodney E.
1984	W	III	1		S	L		32	26	5	Stovall, Dr. Alfred J. "AJ"
1986		III	4		S	L		32	21	5	Stovall, Dr. Alfred J. "AJ"
1985		III	8		S	L		32	25	2	Stovall, Dr. Alfred J. "AJ"
1987		III	8		S	L		32	26	3	Stovall, Dr. Alfred J. "AJ"
1988		III	16		S	L		32	21	4	Stovall, Dr. Alfred J. "AJ"
1983		III	32		S	L		32	18	8	Stovall, Dr. Alfred J. "AJ"

Year	M/W	Div	F	SD	Reg	BD	Bye	#T	W	L	Coach
RUTGERS											
1976	M	I	4		E	L		32	31	2	Young, Thomas J.
1979		I	16	6	E	A	To R32	40	22	9	Young, Thomas J.
1975		I	32		MW	L		32	22	7	Young, Thomas J.
1983		I	32	9	E	L		52	23	8	Young, Thomas J.
1989		I	64	13	E	A		64	18	13	Wenzel, Robert
1991		I	64	9	SE	L		64	19	10	Wenzel, Robert
1986	W	I	8		E	L	To R32	40	29	4	Grentz, Theresa Shank
1987		I	8	2	E	A	To R32	40	30	3	Grentz, Theresa Shank
1988		I	16	3	E	A	To R32	40	27	5	Grentz, Theresa Shank
1998		I	16	5	ME	L		64	22	10	Stringer, C. Vivian
1989		I	32	7	ME	L		48	24	7	Grentz, Theresa Shank
1992		I	32	8	ME	L		48	21	11	Grentz, Theresa Shank
1993		I	32		E	A		48	22	9	Grentz, Theresa Shank
1990		I	48	11	ME	L		48	20	10	Grentz, Theresa Shank
1991		I	48	6	E	L		48	23	7	Grentz, Theresa Shank
1994		I	64	5	E	A		64	22	8	Grentz, Theresa Shank
SACRED HEART (CT)											
1986	M	II	1		NENG	A		32	30	4	Bike, Dave
1977		II	4		NENG	L		32	28	4	Feeley, J. Donald
1978		II	8		NENG	L		32	21	9	Feeley, J. Donald
1982		II	8		NENG	L		32	26	6	Bike, Dave
1983		II	8		NENG	A		32	27	5	Bike, Dave
1984		II	8		NENG	L		32	26	7	Bike, Dave
1989		II	8		NENG	L		32	22	10	Bike, Dave
1981		II	16		NENG	L		32	20	9	Bike, Dave
1985		II	16		NENG	L		32	25	7	Bike, Dave
1987		II	16		NENG	A		32	19	13	Bike, Dave
1971		II	24		NENG	L		32	22	6	Feeley, J. Donald
1972		II	32		NENG		To R32	36	24	4	Feeley, J. Donald
1975		II	32		NENG	L		32	20	8	Feeley, J. Donald
SAGINAW VALLEY STATE											
1993	W	II	16		GL	L		32	20	9	Charney, Claudette
1997		II	48	3	GL	L		48	19	11	Merchant, Suzy
SAINT ANDREWS PRESBYTERIAN											
1982	M	III	16		S	A		32	27	3	Riley, Doug
1983		III	16		S	A		32	26	4	Riley, Doug
1981		III	24		S	A		32	23	7	Riley, Doug
1982	W	III	16		None	L		16	17	8	Graham, Betsy
SAINT ANSELM											
1960	M	II	16		NE	L		32	15	4	Grenert, Albert F.
1990		II	16		NENG	A		32	21	11	Dickson, Keith
1996		II	16	1	NE	A	To R32	48	28	3	Dickson, Keith
1962		II	24		NE	L		32	17	4	Grenert, Albert F.
1987		II	24		NENG	A		32	25	5	Dickson, Keith
1995		II	24	1	NE	A	To R32	48	26	5	Dickson, Keith
1970		II	32		NENG	L		32	14	11	Grenert, Albert F.
1986		II	32		NENG	L		32	21	9	Brown, Robert D.
1993		II	32		NENG	A		32	20	11	Dickson, Keith

Year	M/W	Div	F	SD	Reg	BD	Bye	#T	W	L	Coach
1990	W	II	16		NENG	L		32	25	4	Guimont, Donna M.
1991		II	16		NENG	A		32	27	4	Guimont, Donna M.
1995		II	16	1	NENG	L	To R32	48	25	6	Guimont, Donna M.
1994		II	32		NENG	L		32	22	9	Guimont, Donna M.
1997		II	48	5	NE	L		48	20	9	Vermette, Bill

SAINT AUGUSTINE'S

Year	M/W	Div	F	SD	Reg	BD	Bye	#T	W	L	Coach
1984	M	II	2		E	L		32	23	7	Heartley, Harvey D.
1983		II	16		SA	L		32	22	6	Heartley, Harvey D.
1997		II	16	5	SA	A		48	25	8	Lee, Novell
1992	W	II	32		NENG	L		32	23	3	Downing, Dr. Beverly
1993		II	32		SA	L		32	23	6	Downing, Dr. Beverly

SAINT BENEDICT

Year	M/W	Div	F	SD	Reg	BD	Bye	#T	W	L	Coach
1993	W	III	4		W	A		32	28	2	Durbin, Michael
1995		III	8		W	A		64	27	2	Durbin, Michael
1992		III	16		W	L		32	22	6	Durbin, Michael
1994		III	16		W	L	To R32	40	22	5	Durbin, Michael
1998		III	16	2	W	L	To R32	48	25	2	Durbin, Michael
1989		III	32		W	A		32	23	5	Durbin, Michael
1990		III	32		GL	L		32	21	7	Durbin, Michael
1991		III	32		W	L		32	20	7	Durbin, Michael
1997		III	32		W	L		64	21	6	Durbin, Michael
1996		III	64		W	L		64	19	7	Durbin, Michael

SAINT BONAVENTURE

Year	M/W	Div	F	SD	Reg	BD	Bye	#T	W	L	Coach
1970	M	I	4		E	L		25	25	3	Weise, Lawrence J.
1961		I	12		E	L		24	24	4	Donovan, Edward J. 'Eddie'
1968		I	16		E	L		23	23	2	Weise, Lawrence J.
1978		I	32		E	L		32	21	8	Satalin, James D.

SAINT CLOUD STATE

Year	M/W	Div	F	SD	Reg	BD	Bye	#T	W	L	Coach
1987	M	II	8		NC	A		32	24	7	Raymond, Lloyd E. 'Butch'
1986		II	16		NC	A		32	26	4	Raymond, Lloyd E. 'Butch'
1988		II	24		NC	A		32	26	4	Raymond, Lloyd E. 'Butch'
1974		II	32		MW	L		44	17	12	Olson, Noel W.
1992		II	32		NC	L		32	20	12	Raymond, Lloyd E. 'Butch'
1983	W	II	8		NC	L	To R16	24	31	4	Ziemer, Gladys L.
1984		II	8		NC	L	To R16	24	27	3	Ziemer, Gladys L.
1985		II	8		NC	L		24	24	6	Ziemer, Gladys L.
1989		II	8		NC			32	21	9	Ziemer, Gladys L.
1987		II	16		NC	L		24	21	8	Ziemer, Gladys L.
1988		II	32		NC	L		32	18	10	Ziemer, Gladys L.
1990		II	32		NC	L		32	23	5	Ziemer, Gladys L.

SAINT FRANCIS (PA)

Year	M/W	Div	F	SD	Reg	BD	Bye	#T	W	L	Coach
1991	M	I	64	15	W	P		64	24	8	Baron, James E.
1996	W	I	64	15	MW	A		64	19	11	Przekwas, Jenny
1997		I	64	15	E	A		64	21	9	Przekwas, Jenny
1998		I	64	16	E	A		64	22	8	Przekwas, Jenny

Year	M/W	Div	F	SD	Reg	BD	Bye	#T	W	L	Coach
Saint John Fisher											
1992	M	III	32		E	L	To R32	40	22	5	Ward, Robert
1994		III	32		E	L		40	22	5	Ward, Robert
1997		III	32	3	E	L		64	20	7	Ward, Robert
1998		III	32	2	E	L	To R32	48	22	4	Ward, Robert
1995		III	64	4	E	L		64	16	10	Ward, Robert
1996		III	64	5	E	L		64	20	6	Ward, Robert
1988	W	III	2		E	L		32	31	1	Kahler, Phillip I.
1990		III	2		E	L		32	31	2	Kahler, Phillip I.
1987		III	8		E	L		32	28	3	Kahler, Phillip I.
1991		III	8		E	L		32	28	3	Kahler, Phillip I.
1994		III	16		E	L	To R32	40	28	1	Kahler, Phillip I.
1989		III	32		E	L		32	27	3	Kahler, Phillip I.
1992		III	32		E	L		32	22	4	Kahler, Phillip I.
1993		III	32		E	L		32	22	6	Kahler, Phillip I.
1995		III	32		E	L		64	28	1	Kahler, Phillip I.
1996		III	32		E	L		64	23	5	Kahler, Phillip I.
1997		III	32		E	L		64	22	6	Kahler, Phillip I.
Saint John's (MN)											
1986	M	III	24		W	A		32	23	5	Smith, James E.
1988		III	24		W	A		32	19	10	Smith, James E.
1985		III	32		W	A		32	16	12	Smith, James E.
1993		III	32		W	L		40	20	8	Smith, James E.
1995		III	64	8	W	L		64	17	9	Smith, James E.
Saint John's (NY)											
1952	M		2		E(A)	L		16	25	5	McGuire, Frank J.
1985		I	3	1	W	L		64	31	4	Carnesecca, Louis P. "Lou"
1951			6		E	L		16	26	5	McGuire, Frank J.
1979		I	8	10	E	L		40	21	11	Carnesecca, Louis P. "Lou"
1991		I	8	4	MW	L		64	23	9	Carnesecca, Louis P. "Lou"
1967		I	16		E	L		23	23	5	Carnesecca, Louis P. "Lou"
1969		I	16		E	L		25	23	6	Carnesecca, Louis P. "Lou"
1983		I	16	1	E	A	To R32	52	28	5	Carnesecca, Louis P. "Lou"
1968		I	23		E	L		23	19	8	Carnesecca, Louis P. "Lou"
1961		I	24		E	L		24	20	5	Lapchick, Joseph B.
1973		I	25		E	L		25	19	7	Mulzoff, Frank
1976		I	32		ME	L		32	23	6	Carnesecca, Louis P. "Lou"
1977		I	32		W	L		32	22	9	Carnesecca, Louis P. "Lou"
1978		I	32		MW	L		32	21	7	Carnesecca, Louis P. "Lou"
1980		I	32	3	ME	L	To R32	48	24	5	Carnesecca, Louis P. "Lou"
1982		I	32	5	E	L		48	21	9	Carnesecca, Louis P. "Lou"
1986		I	32	1	W	A		64	31	5	Carnesecca, Louis P. "Lou"
1987		I	32	6	MW	L		64	21	9	Carnesecca, Louis P. "Lou"
1990		I	32	6	E	L		64	24	10	Carnesecca, Louis P. "Lou"
1993		I	32	5	E	L		64	19	11	Mahoney, Brian C.
1984		I	48	9	E	L		53	18	12	Carnesecca, Louis P. "Lou"
1988		I	64	11	W	L		64	17	12	Carnesecca, Louis P. "Lou"
1992		I	64	7	SE	L		64	19	11	Carnesecca, Louis P. "Lou"
1998		I	64	7	MW	L		64	22	10	Fraschilla, Fran

Year	M/W	Div	F	SD	Reg	BD	Bye	#T	W	L	Coach
1983	W	I	32		E	A	To R32	36	27	6	Perrelli, Donald
1984		I	32		E	A		32	24	6	Perrelli, Donald
1988		I	32	7	E	A		40	22	10	Mullaney, Joseph A., Jr.

SAINT JOSEPH'S (IN)

Year	M/W	Div	F	SD	Reg	BD	Bye	#T	W	L	Coach
1970	M	II	8		GL	L		32	15	11	Holstein, James H.
1974		II	8		GL	L		44	20	6	Weinert, John P.
1979		II	8		GL	L		32	20	10	Waggoner, George
1975		II	16		GL			32	21	7	Weinert, John P.
1978		II	24		GL	L		32	19	8	Waggoner, George
1992		II	24		GL			32	22	8	Peters, Dan
1976		II	32		GL	L		32	17	11	Weinert, John P.
1988	W	II	8		GL			32	27	4	Smith, David R.
1989		II	8		GL	A		32	27	4	Smith, David R.
1992		II	8		GL	A		32	28	3	Freeman, Keith
1990		II	16		GL	A		32	28	2	Smith, David R.
1995		II	48	5	GL			48	19	9	Bland, Bill

SAINT JOSEPH'S (PA)

Year	M/W	Div	F	SD	Reg	BD	Bye	#T	W	L	Coach
1961	M	I	3		E	A	To R16	24	25	5	Ramsay, Dr. John T. "Jack"
1963		I	8		E	A		25	23	5	Ramsay, Dr. John T. "Jack"
1981		I	8	9	ME	L		48	25	8	Lynam, James F.
1966		I	12		E	A		22	24	5	Ramsay, Dr. John T. "Jack"
1959		I	16		E	A	To R16	23	22	5	Ramsay, Dr. John T. "Jack"
1960		I	16		E	A	To R16	25	20	7	Ramsay, Dr. John T. "Jack"
1962		I	16		E	A	To R16	25	18	10	Ramsay, Dr. John T. "Jack"
1965		I	16		E	A		23	26	3	Ramsay, Dr. John T. "Jack"
1997		I	16	4	W	A		64	26	7	Martelli, Phil
1969		I	25		E	A		25	17	11	McKinney, John P. "Jack"
1971		I	25		E	A		25	19	9	McKinney, John P. "Jack"
1973		I	25		E	A		25	22	6	McKinney, John P. "Jack"
1974		I	25		E	A		25	19	11	McKinney, John P. "Jack"
1986		I	32	6	E	A		64	26	6	Boyle, Jim
1982		I	48	6	E	A		48	25	5	Boyle, Jim
1985	W	I	32		E	L		32	25	5	Foster, Jim
1986		I	32		E	L	To R32	40	22	7	Foster, Jim
1987		I	32	9	E	L		40	23	9	Foster, Jim
1988		I	32	7	ME	L		40	24	8	Foster, Jim
1989		I	32	10	E	L		48	23	8	Foster, Jim
1997		I	32	7	E	A		64	26	5	Gaitley, Stephanie Vanderslice
1990		I	48	9	E	L		48	24	7	Foster, Jim
1994		I	64	11	E	L		64	19	9	Gaitley, Stephanie Vanderslice
1995		I	64	9	E	L		64	20	9	Gaitley, Stephanie Vanderslice

SAINT LAWRENCE

Year	M/W	Div	F	SD	Reg	BD	Bye	#T	W	L	Coach
1998	M	III	8	1	E	A	To R32	48	24	2	Downs, Chris
1975		III	16		E	L		30	20	6	Evans, Paul
1978		III	16		E	A		30	19	6	Evans, Paul
1979		III	16		E	A		32	18	7	Evans, Paul
1981		III	24		E	A		32	20	6	Talbot, Leon
1980		III	32		E	A		32	22	5	Evans, Paul
1984		III	32		E	A		32	14	13	Talbot, Leon
1996		III	32	6	E	L		64	18	9	Paulsen, David

Year	M/W	Div	F	SD	Reg	BD	Bye	#T	W	L	Coach
1974		II	44		E	L		44	17	6	Evans, Paul
1997		III	64	2	E	L		64	22	4	Paulsen, David
1983	W	III	32		E	L		32	17	5	Kowalik, Joan

SAINT LOUIS

Year	M/W	Div	F	SD	Reg	BD	Bye	#T	W	L	Coach
1952	M		8		W(A)	A		16	23	8	Hickey, Edgar S. "Eddie"
1957		I	16		MW	A	To R16	23	19	9	Hickey, Edgar S. "Eddie"
1995		I	32	9	E	L		64	23	8	Spoonhour, Charles
1998		I	32	10	S	L		64	22	11	Spoonhour, Charles
1994		I	64	7	MW	L		64	23	6	Spoonhour, Charles

SAINT MARY'S (CA)

Year	M/W	Div	F	SD	Reg	BD	Bye	#T	W	L	Coach
1959	M	I	8		W	A	To R16	23	19	6	Weaver, James
1989		I	64	8	W	L		64	25	5	Nance, Lynn
1997		I	64	14	W	A		64	23	8	Kent, Ernie

SAINT MARY'S (MD)

Year	M/W	Div	F	SD	Reg	BD	Bye	#T	W	L	Coach
1998	W	III	48	5	A	A		48	20	8	Hart, Shann

SAINT MARY'S (MN)

Year	M/W	Div	F	SD	Reg	BD	Bye	#T	W	L	Coach
1985	W	III	24		W	A		32	24	2	Wheeler, Lynn
1986		III	24		W	A		32	23	2	Smith, Jim

SAINT MICHAEL'S (VT)

Year	M/W	Div	F	SD	Reg	BD	Bye	#T	W	L	Coach
1958	M	II	2		NE			32	19	5	Jacobs, George W. "Doc"
1965		II	4		NE			32	21	7	Markey, Edward P.
1959		II	8		NE			32	19	7	Jacobs, George W. "Doc"
1960		II	8		NE			32	13	10	Jacobs, George W. "Doc"
1957		II	16		E	L		32	17	6	Jacobs, George W. "Doc"
1967		II	16		NE			36	23	4	Markey, Edward P.
1974		II	24		NENG	L	To R32	44	17	11	Baumann, Walter E.
1973		II	32		NENG	L		42	18	9	Baumann, Walter E.
1987		II	32		E	A		32	20	11	Casciano, James Paul
1997		II	32	4	NE	L		48	23	7	Crowley, Tom

SAINT NORBERT

Year	M/W	Div	F	SD	Reg	BD	Bye	#T	W	L	Coach
1984	M	III	16		MW	A		32	21	4	Heideman, Mike
1958		II	32		GL	L		32	14	11	Nicks, Mel J.
1985	W	III	4		GL	L		32	24	4	Tilley, Connie L.
1986		III	16		GL	L		32	20	2	Tilley, Connie L.
1988		III	16		GL	L		32	17	5	Tilley, Connie L.
1983		III	32		GL	L		32	20	7	Tilley, Connie L.
1987		III	32		GL	L		32	19	6	Tilley, Connie L.
1989		III	32		GL	L		32	20	6	Tilley, Connie L.

SAINT OLAF

Year	M/W	Div	F	SD	Reg	BD	Bye	#T	W	L	Coach
1969	M	II	32		MW	L		32	17	7	Gelle, Robert D.
1971		II	32		MW	L		32	20	4	Gelle, Robert D.
1972		II	32		MW			36	18	7	Gelle, Robert D.
1992	W	III	32		W	L		32	19	7	Buresh, Pat

Year	M/W	Div	F	SD	Reg	BD	Bye	#T	W	L	Coach
SAINT PETER'S											
1991	M	I	64	12	MW	A		64	24	7	Fiore, Ted
1995		I	64	15	E	A		64	19	11	Fiore, Ted
1982	W	I	32		E	A		32	26	4	Granelli, Mike
1992		I	48	11	E	A		48	24	7	Granelli, Mike
1993		I	48		E	A		48	18	11	Granelli, Mike
1997		I	64	15	ME	A		64	25	4	Granelli, Mike
SAINT ROSE											
1998	M	II	3	1	NE	A	To R32	48	27	6	Beaury, Brian
1996		II	8	2	NE	L	To R32	48	28	4	Beaury, Brian
1992		II	24		E	L		32	24	7	Beaury, Brian
1995		II	32	2	NE	A	To R32	48	25	6	Beaury, Brian
1997		II	32	3	NE	L		48	29	5	Beaury, Brian
1995	W	II	16	1	E	A	To R32	48	26	5	Bailey, Curt
1996		II	16	5	NE	A		48	26	5	Bailey, Curt
1998		II	16	1	NE	A	To R32	48	33	1	Bailey, Curt
1997		II	32	2	NE	A	To R32	48	29	1	Bailey, Curt
SAINT THOMAS (FL)											
1972	M	II	16		SA	L	To R32	36	17	10	Stibler, Kenneth
1982		II	24		S	A		32	15	13	Stibler, Kenneth
1973		II	42		SA	L		42	18	6	Stibler, Kenneth
SAINT THOMAS (MN)											
1994	M	III	4		W	A	To R32	40	24	7	Fritz, Steve
1990		III	16		W	A	To R32	40	25	5	Fritz, Steve
1993		III	16		W	A	To R32	40	19	9	Fritz, Steve
1995		III	32	2	W	A		64	27	1	Fritz, Steve
1991	W	III	1		W	A		32	29	2	Riverso, Ted
1995		III	3		W	L		64	25	6	Riverso, Ted
1996		III	3		W	A		64	28	3	Riverso, Ted
1998		III	8	1	W	A	To R32	48	26	2	Riverso, Ted
1988		III	16		W	L		32	22	5	Riverso, Ted
1990		III	16		W	L		32	23	5	Riverso, Ted
1992		III	16		W	A		32	27	1	Riverso, Ted
1997		III	16		W	A		64	26	2	Riverso, Ted
1984		III	24		W	A		32	23	5	Kosel, Tom
1989		III	24		W	L		32	20	6	Riverso, Ted
1987		III	32		C	L		32	19	9	Riverso, Ted
1993		III	32		W	L		32	19	7	Riverso, Ted
1994		III	32		W	L		40	22	5	Riverso, Ted
SALEM STATE											
1982	M	III	16		NE	A		32	20	8	Lavacchia, Joseph A.
1986		III	16		NE	A		32	22	6	Thibodeau, Thomas
1991		III	16		NE	A	To R32	40	26	2	Todd, Jim
1992		III	16		NE	A	To R32	40	25	4	Todd, Jim
1997		III	16	3	NE	A		64	25	4	Meehan, Brian
1980		III	24		NE	A		32	19	9	Lavacchia, Joseph A.
1981		III	24		NE	A		32	23	6	Lavacchia, Joseph A.
1989		III	32		NE	L	To R32	40	21	6	Todd, Jim

Year	M/W	Div	F	SD	Reg	BD	Bye	#T	W	L	Coach
1990		III	32		NE	L	To R32	40	20	8	Todd, Jim
1993		III	32		NE	A	To R32	40	18	8	Todd, Jim
1995		III	32	6	NE	A		64	21	7	Todd, Jim
1996		III	32	2	NE	A		64	25	3	Todd, Jim
1998		III	32	3	NE	A		48	25	3	Meehan, Brian
1986	W	III	1		NE	A		32	29	1	Shea, Timothy P.
1984		III	3		NE	A		32	27	3	Shea, Timothy P.
1995		III	4		NE	A		64	28	4	Shea, Timothy P.
1985		III	8		NE	L		32	23	5	Shea, Timothy P.
1983		III	16		NE	A		32	23	7	Shea, Timothy P.
1988		III	16		NE	A		32	25	3	Shea, Timothy P.
1996		III	16		NE	A		64	25	4	Shea, Timothy P.
1987		III	24		NE	A		32	22	6	Shea, Timothy P.
1989		III	32		NE	A		32	24	4	Shea, Timothy P.
1990		III	32		NE	A		32	24	5	Shea, Timothy P.
1991		III	32		NE	L		32	24	5	Shea, Timothy P.
1993		III	32		NE	L		32	18	8	Shea, Timothy P.
1994		III	32		NE	A	To R32	40	22	5	Shea, Timothy P.
1998		III	32	3	NE	A		48	23	5	Shea, Timothy P.
1997		III	64		NE	A		64	23	4	Shea, Timothy P.

SALEM-TEIKYO

Year	M/W	Div	F	SD	Reg	BD	Bye	#T	W	L	Coach
1997	M	II	3	1	E	L	To R32	48	28	3	Carey, Michael A.
1998		II	16	1	E	A	To R32	48	28	3	Carey, Michael A.
1996	W	II	16	3	E	L		48	27	4	Biesenthal, Tammy

SALISBURY STATE

Year	M/W	Div	F	SD	Reg	BD	Bye	#T	W	L	Coach
1992	M	III	8		A	L	To R32	40	28	2	Lambert, Edward W. "Ward"
1997		III	8	4	MA	L		64	25	6	Lambert, Edward W. "Ward"
1985		III	24		SA	L		32	23	6	Lambert, Edward W. "Ward"
1991		III	32		A	L	To R32	40	22	7	Lambert, Edward W. "Ward"
1996		III	64	8	MA	A		64	19	9	Lambert, Edward W. "Ward"
1996	W	III	32		A	L		64	19	9	Benshelter, Bridget
1995		III	64		A	L		64	21	7	Benshelter, Bridget

SALVE REGINA

Year	M/W	Div	F	SD	Reg	BD	Bye	#T	W	L	Coach
1995	M	III	64	8	NE	A		64	20	8	Raffa, Michael

SAM HOUSTON STATE

Year	M/W	Div	F	SD	Reg	BD	Bye	#T	W	L	Coach
1986	M	II	32		SC	L		32	27	6	McPherson, Robert

SAN DIEGO

Year	M/W	Div	F	SD	Reg	BD	Bye	#T	W	L	Coach
1978	M	II	8		W	L		32	22	7	Brovelli, Jim
1973		II	24		W	L	To R32	42	19	9	Bickerstaff, Bernard T.
1979		II	24		W	L		32	19	7	Brovelli, Jim
1966		II	32		PC	L	To R32	36	17	11	Woolpert, Philip D.
1974		II	44		W	L		44	16	11	Bickerstaff, Bernard T.
1984		I	53	13	W	A		53	18	10	Brovelli, Jim
1987		I	64	9	MW	L		64	24	6	Egan, Henry "Hank"
1993	W	I	48		W	A		48	16	12	Marpe, Kathleen

Year	M/W	Div	F	SD	Reg	BD	Bye	#T	W	L	Coach
SAN DIEGO STATE											
1957	M	II	8		FW	A		32	17	10	Ziegenfuss, Dr. George
1967		II	8		PC		To R32	36	24	5	Ziegenfuss, Dr. George
1968		II	23		PC		To R32	36	20	6	Ziegenfuss, Dr. George
1975		I	32		W	A		32	14	13	Vezie, Tim
1976		I	32		W	A		32	16	13	Vezie, Tim
1985		I	64	13	W	A		64	23	8	Gaines, David "Smokey"
1984	W	I	16		W	L		32	24	6	Riggins, Earnest
1985		I	16		MW	L		32	21	9	Riggins, Earnest
1994		I	32	5	W	A		64	26	5	Burns, Beth
1993		I	48		W	L		48	19	9	Burns, Beth
1995		I	64	5	W	L		64	24	6	Burns, Beth
1997		I	64	11	MW	A		64	23	7	Burns, Beth
SAN FRANCISCO											
1955	M		1		W(B)	L		24	28	1	Woolpert, Philip D.
1956			1		FW	A	To R16	25	29	0	Woolpert, Philip D.
1957		I	3		W	A	To R16	23	21	7	Woolpert, Philip D.
1964		I	8		W	A	To R16	25	23	5	Peletta, Peter P.
1965		I	8		FW	A		23	24	5	Peletta, Peter P.
1973		I	8		W	A	To R16	25	23	5	Gaillard, Dr. Bob
1974		I	8		W	A	To R16	25	19	9	Gaillard, Dr. Bob
1958		I	12		W	A	To R16	24	25	2	Woolpert, Philip D.
1963		I	12		W	A	To R16	25	18	9	Peletta, Peter P.
1972		I	12		W	A	To R16	25	20	8	Gaillard, Dr. Bob
1978		I	16		W	A		32	23	6	Gaillard, Dr. Bob
1979		I	16	4	W	A	To R32	40	22	7	Belluomini, Dan
1977		I	32		W	A		32	29	2	Gaillard, Dr. Bob
1981		I	48	9	W	A		48	24	7	Barry, Peter
1982		I	48	9	MW	L		48	25	6	Barry, Peter
1998		I	64	14	W	A		64	19	11	Matthews, Philip
1996	W	I	16	12	ME	A		64	24	8	Nepfel, Bill
1995		I	64	11	ME	A		64	24	5	Nepfel, Bill
1997		I	64	11	ME	A		64	25	6	Nepfel, Bill
SAN FRANCISCO STATE											
1969	M	II	8		W	L		32	20	9	Rundell, Paul
1984		II	8		W	A		32	21	11	Wilson, Kevin
1965		II	24		PC			32	16	11	Rundell, Paul
1983		II	24		W	A		32	21	9	Damon, Dr. E. Lyle
1960		II	32		PC			32	12	14	Rundell, Paul
1963		II	32		PC			32	14	13	Rundell, Paul
1971		II	32		W	L		32	16	12	Waugh, Gerald R.
1980		II	32		W	L		32	21	8	Damon, Dr. E. Lyle
1982		II	32		W	A		32	20	10	Wilson, Kevin
1994		II	32		W	A		32	20	10	Thomas, Charlie
1982	W	II	16		W	L		16	20	7	Manwaring, Emily
1983		II	24		W	A		24	18	9	Manwaring, Emily
1984		II	24		W	A		24	19	12	Manwaring, Emily
1985		II	24		W	A		24	13	16	Burger, Maureen

Year	M/W	Div	F	SD	Reg	BD	Bye	#T	W	L	Coach
SAN JOSE STATE											
1951	M		16		W	L		16	18	12	McPherson, Walter J.
1980		I	48	12	MW	A		48	17	12	Berry, William
1996		I	64	16	MW	A		64	13	17	Morrison, Stanley M.
SANTA CLARA											
1952	M		4		W(B)	L		16	17	12	Feerick, Robert J.
1953			8		W(A)	L		22	20	7	Feerick, Robert J.
1954			8		W(B)	L		24	20	7	Feerick, Robert J.
1968		I	8		W	A	To R16	23	22	4	Garibaldi, Richard A.
1969		I	8		W	A	To R16	25	27	2	Garibaldi, Richard A.
1970		I	12		W	A	To R16	25	23	6	Garibaldi, Richard A.
1960		I	16		W	A	To R16	25	21	10	Feerick, Robert J.
1993		I	32	15	W	A		64	19	12	Williams, Carroll M.
1996		I	32	10	W	L		64	20	9	Davey, Dick
1987		I	64	15	W	A		64	18	14	Williams, Carroll M.
1995		I	64	12	W	L		64	21	7	Davey, Dick
1992	W	I	32	12	W	A		48	21	10	Horstmeyer, Caren
1994		I	64	11	W	L		64	21	7	Horstmeyer, Caren
1998		I	64	14	E	A		64	23	8	Horstmeyer, Caren
SAVANNAH A&D											
1997	W	III	64		S	L		64	20	6	Ruffo, Kristen
SAVANNAH STATE											
1981	M	III	8		S	L		32	25	4	Ellington, Russell
1979		III	16		S	L		32	20	10	Ellington, Russell
1980		III	16		S	A		32	24	5	Ellington, Russell
1995	W	II	48	6	S	L		48	23	5	Wallace, Phillip
SCRANTON											
1976	M	III	1		MA	A		28	27	5	Bessoir, Robert M.
1983		III	1		MA	A		32	29	3	Bessoir, Robert M.
1988		III	2		MA	A		32	29	3	Bessoir, Robert M.
1977		III	3		MA	L		30	24	8	Bessoir, Robert M.
1993		III	8		MA	A	To R32	40	27	2	Bessoir, Robert M.
1975		III	16		MA	L		30	20	9	Bessoir, Robert M.
1980		III	16		MA	A		32	18	11	Bessoir, Robert M.
1985		III	16		MA	A		32	18	11	Bessoir, Robert M.
1991		III	16		MA	A	To R32	40	23	6	Bessoir, Robert M.
1992		III	16		MA	L	To R32	40	25	3	Bessoir, Robert M.
1978		III	23		MA	A		30	22	7	Bessoir, Robert M.
1982		III	24		MA	A		32	23	6	Bessoir, Robert M.
1984		III	24		MA	A		32	23	6	Bessoir, Robert M.
1987		III	24		MA	A		32	22	7	Bessoir, Robert M.
1981		III	32		MA	A		32	18	11	Bessoir, Robert M.
1986		III	32		MA	L		32	20	9	Bessoir, Robert M.
1998		III	32	4	MA	L		48	18	11	Bessoir, Robert M.
1985	W	III	1		MA	A		32	31	1	Strong, Michael J.
1987		III	3		MA	A		32	31	2	Strong, Michael J.
1993		III	3		E	A		32	30	2	Strong, Michael J.
1997		III	4		MA	A		64	28	5	Strong, Michael J.

Year	M/W	Div	F	SD	Reg	BD	Bye	#T	W	L	Coach
1982		III	8		None	L		16	17	11	Strong, Michael J.
1990		III	8		MA	A		32	26	5	Strong, Michael J.
1994		III	8		MA	A	To R32	40	27	3	Strong, Michael J.
1986		III	16		MA	L		32	23	6	Strong, Michael J.
1992		III	16		MA	L		32	22	5	Strong, Michael J.
1996		III	16		MA	A		64	26	4	Strong, Michael J.
1998		III	16	2	MA	L	To R32	48	21	6	Strong, Michael J.
1983		III	24		MA	L		32	19	7	Strong, Michael J.
1984		III	24		MA	L		32	19	8	Strong, Michael J.
1995		III	64		MA	L		64	24	2	Serafini, Sue

SEATTLE

Year	M/W	Div	F	SD	Reg	BD	Bye	#T	W	L	Coach
1958	M	I	2		W	L		24	23	6	Castellani, John
1953			12		W(A)	L		22	28	4	Brightman, Horace Albert `Al`
1964		I	12		W	L		25	22	6	Boyd, William R. `Bob`
1955			16		W(B)	L		24	22	7	Brightman, Horace Albert `Al`
1956			16		FW	L		25	18	11	Brightman, Horace Albert `Al`
1967		I	23		W	L		23	18	8	Purcell, Lionel
1954			24		W(B)	L		24	26	2	Brightman, Horace Albert `Al`
1961		I	24		W	L		24	18	8	Cazzetta, Vincent C.
1962		I	25		W	L		25	18	9	Cazzetta, Vincent C.
1963		I	25		W	L		25	21	6	Cazzetta, Vincent C.
1969		I	25		W	L		25	19	8	Buckwalter, Morris `Bucky`

SEATTLE PACIFIC

Year	M/W	Div	F	SD	Reg	BD	Bye	#T	W	L	Coach
1965	M	II	8		PC	L		32	22	7	Habegger, Lester N. `Gus`
1966		II	16		PC	L	To R32	36	23	5	Habegger, Lester N. `Gus`
1971		II	16		W	L		32	16	10	Habegger, Lester N. `Gus`
1972		II	16		W	L	To R32	36	17	11	Habegger, Lester N. `Gus`
1995		II	16	2	W	A	To R32	48	20	9	Bone, Ken
1996		II	16	2	W	A	To R32	48	23	6	Bone, Ken
1998		II	16	6	W	L		48	18	12	Bone, Ken
1962		II	24		PC	L		32	20	7	Habegger, Lester N. `Gus`
1964		II	24		PC	L		32	17	8	Habegger, Lester N. `Gus`
1977		II	24		W	L		32	20	9	Swagerty, Keith
1998	W	II	8	1	W	L	To R32	48	27	3	Presnell, Gordy
1997		II	16	1	W	L	To R32	48	26	3	Presnell, Gordy
1995		II	32	3	W	L		48	21	8	Presnell, Gordy

SETON HALL

Year	M/W	Div	F	SD	Reg	BD	Bye	#T	W	L	Coach
1989	M	I	2	3	W	L		64	31	7	Carlesimo, Peter J. `PJ`
1991		I	8	3	W	A		64	25	9	Carlesimo, Peter J. `PJ`
1992		I	16	4	E	L		64	23	9	Carlesimo, Peter J. `PJ`
1988		I	32	8	W	L		64	22	13	Carlesimo, Peter J. `PJ`
1993		I	32	2	SE	A		64	28	7	Carlesimo, Peter J. `PJ`
1994		I	64	10	SE	L		64	17	13	Carlesimo, Peter J. `PJ`
1994	W	I	16	4	MW	L		64	27	5	Mangina, Phyllis
1995		I	32	6	W	L		64	24	9	Mangina, Phyllis

Year	M/W	Div	F	SD	Reg	BD	Bye	#T	W	L	Coach
SHAW (NC)											
1995	M	II	24	4	SA	L		48	21	9	Walker, Keith
1989	W	II	32		SA	A		32	18	8	Sanders, Bobby
1996		II	32	1	SA	A	To R32	48	24	5	Sanders, Bobby
SHENANDOAH											
1989	M	III	32		SA	L		40	21	9	Dutton, Dave
1991		III	40		S	L		40	21	6	Dutton, Dave
1996		III	64	8	S	L		64	18	9	Dutton, Dave
1996	W	III	64		S	A		64	13	15	Orsini, Kathy
SHEPHERD											
1976	M	III	7		SA	L		28	30	13	Starkey, Robert G.
SHIPPENSBURG											
1991	M	II	32		E	A		32	20	11	Goodling, Roger E.
1996	W	II	2	1	E	A	To R32	48	28	6	Smith, David R.
1998		II	8	1	E	A	To R32	48	28	4	Smith, David R.
1995		II	32	6	E	L		48	22	7	Smith, David R.
1997		II	32	1	E	A	To R32	48	25	5	Smith, David R.
SIENA (NY)											
1974	M	II	24		E	L		44	18	9	Kirsch, William
1989		I	32	14	E	A		64	25	5	Deane, Mike
SIMPSON (IA)											
1976	M	III	21		MW	L		28	17	9	Starr, Richard
1992		III	40		W	A		40	18	9	Wilson, Bruce
1995		III	64	6	W			64	20	6	Wilson, Bruce
1996		III	64	6	W	L		64	20	6	Wilson, Bruce
1983	W	III	24		GL	L		32	16	9	Schafer, Janet
1985		III	24		C			32	20	7	Schafer, Janet
SLIPPERY ROCK											
1978	M	III	16		MA	L		30	17	10	Zimmerman, Doug
1991		II	24		E	L		32	23	9	Barlett, Robert
1990		II	32		E	L		32	23	6	Barlett, Robert
1986	W	II	16		E	A		24	23	6	Ritchey-Walton, Kathleen "Kathy"
1996		II	32	2	E	L	To R32	48	21	8	Williges, Laura
SONOMA STATE											
1974	M	II	16		W			44	18	10	Trumbo, William R.
1983		III	16		W	L		32	16	12	Walker, Dick
1989		II	32		W	A		32	17	14	Walker, Dick
1973		II	42		W			42	18	9	Trumbo, William R.
1998	W	II	48	5	W	L		48	20	8	Zachensky-Walthall, Susan
SOUTH ALABAMA											
1979	M	I	32	6	MW	L	To R32	40	20	7	Ellis, Cliff
1989		I	32	11	SE	A		64	23	9	Arrow, Ronnie
1980		I	48	9	MW	L		48	23	6	Ellis, Cliff
1991		I	64	13	W	A		64	22	9	Arrow, Ronnie

Year	M/W	Div	F	SD	Reg	BD	Bye	#T	W	L	Coach
1997		I	64	13	SE	A		64	23	7	Musselman, William
1998		I	64	12	W	A		64	21	7	Weltlich, Robert
1987	W	I	40	8	E	L		40	24	6	Branum, Charles

SOUTH CAROLINA

Year	M/W	Div	F	SD	Reg	BD	Bye	#T	W	L	Coach
1972	M	I	12		E	L		25	24	5	McGuire, Frank J.
1973		I	12		MW	L		25	22	7	McGuire, Frank J.
1971		I	16		E	A	To R16	25	23	6	McGuire, Frank J.
1974		I	25		E	L		25	22	5	McGuire, Frank J.
1989		I	64	12	E	L		64	19	11	Felton, George
1997		I	64	2	E	L		64	24	8	Fogler, Eddie
1998		I	64	3	E	L		64	23	8	Fogler, Eddie
1982	W	I	16		MW	L		32	23	8	Kelly, Terry
1990		I	16	5	ME	L		48	24	9	Wilson, Nancy R.
1988		I	32	8	MW	A		40	23	11	Wilson, Nancy R.
1986		I	40		ME	A		40	19	11	Wilson, Nancy R.
1989		I	48	6	MW	A		48	23	7	Wilson, Nancy R.
1991		I	48	7	ME	L		48	22	9	Wilson, Nancy R.

SOUTH CAROLINA STATE

Year	M/W	Div	F	SD	Reg	BD	Bye	#T	W	L	Coach
1963	M	II	16		ME			32	19	8	Martin, Edward A.
1967		II	16		SC		To R32	36	18	5	Martin, Edward A.
1958		II	24		SC	L		32	18	9	Martin, Edward A.
1961		II	32		ME			32	23	7	Martin, Edward A.
1966		II	32		SC		To R32	36	23	3	Martin, Edward A.
1989		I	64	15	E	A		64	25	8	Alexander, Cyrus "Cy"
1996		I	64	15	W	A		64	22	8	Alexander, Cyrus "Cy"
1998		I	64	15	S	A		64	22	8	Alexander, Cyrus "Cy"
1983	W	I	32		ME	L		36	17	8	Simon, Willie J.

SOUTH CAROLINA: AIKEN

Year	M/W	Div	F	SD	Reg	BD	Bye	#T	W	L	Coach
1998	M	II	32	4	SA	L		48	20	10	Roberts, Mike

SOUTH CAROLINA: SPARTANBURG

Year	M/W	Div	F	SD	Reg	BD	Bye	#T	W	L	Coach
1991	M	II	16		SA	L		32	26	3	Waters, Jerry O.
1992		II	16		S	L		32	24	6	Waters, Jerry O.
1996		II	32	4	S	L		48	23	8	Waters, Jerry O.
1998		II	32	6	SA	L		48	22	7	Nottingham, Gary
1993	W	II	16		SA	L		32	28	3	Sells, Peggy
1995		II	16	2	SA	A	To R32	48	25	6	Sells, Peggy
1994		II	32		SA	A		32	27	4	Sells, Peggy

SOUTH DAKOTA

Year	M/W	Div	F	SD	Reg	BD	Bye	#T	W	L	Coach
1958	M	II	1		MW			32	22	5	Clodfelter, Duane
1957		II	8		MW	A		32	19	4	Clodfelter, Duane
1993		II	8		NC	L		32	25	5	Boots, David
1994		II	8		NC	A		32	24	6	Boots, David
1972		II	24		MW		To R32	36	18	10	Mulcahy, Robert
1990		II	24		NC	A		32	22	10	Boots, David

Year	M/W	Div	F	SD	Reg	BD	Bye	#T	W	L	Coach
1984	W	II	16		NC	A		24	22	7	Lavin, Chad
1985		II	16		NC		To R16	24	23	6	Lavin, Chad
1983		II	24		NC	A		24	19	9	Zimmerman, Mary
1989		II	32		NC	L		32	22	7	Tibbetts, Fred

SOUTH DAKOTA STATE

Year	M/W	Div	F	SD	Reg	BD	Bye	#T	W	L	Coach
1963	M	II	1		MW			32	22	5	Iverson, James
1985		II	2		NC	A		32	26	7	Zulk, Gene
1961		II	3		MW			32	21	6	Iverson, James
1959		II	8		MW			32	17	7	Iverson, James
1970		II	8		MW	L		32	22	4	Marking, James
1980		II	8		NC	A		32	23	7	Zulk, Gene
1992		II	8		NC	L		32	25	8	Thorson, Jim
1997		II	8	2	NC	A	To R32	48	25	5	Nagy, Scott
1969		II	16		MW	L		32	18	6	Marking, James
1973		II	16		MW		To R32	42	18	8	Marking, James
1984		II	16		NENG	L		32	21	9	Zulk, Gene
1991		II	16		NC	A		32	24	8	Thorson, Jim
1996		II	16	2	NC	A	To R32	48	24	5	Nagy, Scott
1998		II	16	2	NC	A	To R32	48	26	3	Nagy, Scott
1968		II	23		GL		To R32	36	20	7	Marking, James
1960		II	24		MW			32	17	7	Iverson, James
1978		II	24		NC	L		32	17	12	Zulk, Gene
1988		II	24		SC	L		32	21	9	Thorson, Jim
1972		II	36		MW	L		36	17	8	Marking, James
1988	W	II	16		NC	L		32	25	5	Neiber, Nancy
1994		II	16		NC	L		32	22	8	Neiber, Nancy
1995		II	16	5	NC	L		48	24	6	Neiber, Nancy
1992		II	32		NC	L		32	19	10	Neiber, Nancy
1996		II	32	2	NC	L	To R32	48	25	3	Neiber, Nancy

SOUTH FLORIDA

Year	M/W	Div	F	SD	Reg	BD	Bye	#T	W	L	Coach
1990	M	I	64	15	W	A		64	20	11	Paschal, Bobby
1992		I	64	11	W	L		64	19	10	Paschal, Bobby

SOUTH UNIVERSITY (TN)

Year	M/W	Div	F	SD	Reg	BD	Bye	#T	W	L	Coach
1976	M	III	28		S	L		28	17	10	Petty, Malcolm "Mac"
1975		III	30		S	L		30	19	7	Petty, Malcolm "Mac"
1997		III	32	3	S	A		64	19	7	Thoni, Joe
1998		III	48	5	S	L		48	20	6	Thoni, Joe

SOUTHEAST MISSOURI STATE

Year	M/W	Div	F	SD	Reg	BD	Bye	#T	W	L	Coach
1961	M	II	2		SW			32	25	3	Parsley, Charles H., Sr.
1986		II	2		SC	A		32	27	7	Shumate, Ron
1989		II	2		SC	L		32	27	6	Shumate, Ron
1962		II	8		SW			32	18	7	Parsley, Charles H., Sr.
1964		II	8		SW			32	19	6	Parsley, Charles H., Sr.
1982		II	8		SC	A		32	21	10	Shumate, Ron
1983		II	8		SC	A		32	25	6	Shumate, Ron
1985		II	8		SC	A		32	24	8	Shumate, Ron

Year	M/W	Div	F	SD	Reg	BD	Bye	#T	W	L	Coach
1988		II	8		SC	L		32	28	4	Shumate, Ron
1990		II	8		SC	L		32	26	5	Shumate, Ron
1987		II	16		SC	A		32	20	11	Shumate, Ron
1979		II	24		SC	L		32	19	9	Williams, Carroll
1963		II	32		SW			32	21	4	Parsley, Charles H., Sr.
1991	W	II	2		SC	A		32	31	4	Arnzen, Ed
1983		II	16		SC	L		24	20	8	Beck, Angela
1984		II	16		SC	L		24	23	6	Arnzen, Ed
1986		II	16		SC	L		24	25	6	Arnzen, Ed
1987		II	24		SC	A		24	26	4	Arnzen, Ed
1988		II	32		SC	L		32	26	4	Arnzen, Ed
1989		II	32		SC	L		32	23	7	Arnzen, Ed
1990		II	32		SC	L		32	24	6	Arnzen, Ed

SOUTHEASTERN LOUISIANA

Year	M/W	Div	F	SD	Reg	BD	Bye	#T	W	L	Coach
1973	M	II	16		S		To R32	42	21	7	Foy, E. W.

SOUTHERN CALIFORNIA

Year	M/W	Div	F	SD	Reg	BD	Bye	#T	W	L	Coach
1940	M		3		W	L		8	20	3	Barry, Justin M. "Sam"
1954			4		W(B)	A	To R16	24	19	14	Twogood, Forrest F.
1961		I	16		W	A		24	21	8	Twogood, Forrest F.
1960		I	25		W	L		25	16	11	Twogood, Forrest F.
1979		I	32	7	W	L		40	20	9	Boyd, William R. "Bob"
1992		I	32	2	MW	L		64	24	6	Raveling, George
1982		I	48	9	W	L		48	19	9	Morrison, Stanley M.
1985		I	64	8	MW	L		64	19	10	Morrison, Stanley M.
1991		I	64	10	SE	L		64	19	10	Raveling, George
1997		I	64	11	SE	L		64	17	11	Bibby, Charles Henry
1983	W	I	1		W	A	To R32	36	31	2	Sharp, Linda K.
1984		I	1		W	A		32	29	4	Sharp, Linda K.
1986		I	2		W	L	To R32	40	27	4	Sharp, Linda K.
1982		I	8		ME	L		32	23	4	Sharp, Linda K.
1992		I	8	3	W	L	To R32	48	23	8	Stanley, Marianne Crawford
1994		I	8	2	ME	A		64	26	4	Miller, Cheryl
1985		I	16		W	L		32	21	9	Sharp, Linda K.
1987		I	16	3	W	A	To R32	40	22	8	Sharp, Linda K.
1988		I	16	4	W	L	To R32	40	22	8	Sharp, Linda K.
1993		I	16	3	W	L	To R32	48	22	7	Stanley, Marianne Crawford
1991		I	32	5	W	L		48	18	12	Stanley, Marianne Crawford
1997		I	32	6	ME	L		64	20	9	Williams, Fred
1995		I	64	9	W	L		64	18	10	Miller, Cheryl

SOUTHERN COLORADO

Year	M/W	Div	F	SD	Reg	BD	Bye	#T	W	L	Coach
1972	M	II	8		W		To R32	36	19	9	Simmons, Harry H.
1967		II	32		GL	L	To R32	36	19	6	Simmons, Harry H.
1968		II	32		MW	L	To R32	36	19	9	Simmons, Harry H.
1973		II	32		MW		To R32	42	19	9	Simmons, Harry H.
1998		II	48	4	NC	L		48	22	8	Folda, Joe

Year	M/W	Div	F	SD	Reg	BD	Bye	#T	W	L	Coach
SOUTHERN CONNECTICUT STATE											
1997	M	II	8	2	NE	A	To R32	48	28	4	Leary, Arthur
1982		II	16		NENG	L		32	22	8	Leary, Arthur
1983		II	32		GL	L		32	23	9	Leary, Arthur
1983	W	II	3		NENG	L	To R16	24	25	5	Barone, Anthony J.
SOUTHERN ILLINOIS											
1965	M	II	2		GL	L		32	20	6	Hartman, Jack
1966		II	2		GL	L	To R32	36	22	7	Hartman, Jack
1962		II	3		SC			32	21	10	Gallatin, Harry J.
1963		II	4		SW	L		32	20	10	Hartman, Jack
1961		II	16		SW			32	21	6	Gallatin, Harry J.
1964		II	16		GL	L		32	14	8	Hartman, Jack
1977		I	16		MW	A		32	22	7	Lambert, Paul M.
1959		II	32		ME	L		32	18	8	Gallatin, Harry J.
1993		I	64	14	MW	A		64	23	10	Herrin, Richard "Rich"
1994		I	64	11	W	A		64	23	7	Herrin, Richard "Rich"
1995		I	64	10	MW	A		64	23	9	Herrin, Richard "Rich"
1987	W	I	16	5	MW	A	To R32	40	28	3	Scott, Cindy
1986		I	32		MW	A	To R32	40	25	4	Scott, Cindy
1992		I	32	10	MW	L		48	23	8	Scott, Cindy
1990		I	48	11	MW	A		48	21	10	Scott, Cindy
SOUTHERN ILLINOIS: EDWARDSVILLE											
1986	M	II	16		GL	L		32	23	7	Graham, Larry
1987		II	16		GL	L		32	23	7	Graham, Larry
1989		II	24		GL	L		32	23	7	Graham, Larry
1998	W	II	48	5	GL	L		48	22	8	Hedberg, Wendy
SOUTHERN INDIANA											
1995	M	II	1	3	GL	L		48	29	4	Pearl, Bruce
1994		II	2		GL	A		32	28	4	Pearl, Bruce
1978		II	16		GL	L		32	19	9	Boultinghouse, Wayne
1996		II	16	1	GL	A	To R32	48	25	4	Pearl, Bruce
1998		II	16	1	GL	L	To R32	48	27	6	Pearl, Bruce
1993		II	23		GL	L		32	22	7	Pearl, Bruce
1985		II	24		GL	L		32	18	11	Burns, Creighton
1987		II	24		GL			32	24	6	Bial, Mark
1980		II	32		GL	L		32	20	9	Boultinghouse, Wayne
1981		II	32		GL	A		32	21	8	Boultinghouse, Wayne
1990		II	32		SC	L		32	20	10	Sinn, Dr. Lionel L.
1997		II	48	3	GL	L		48	23	5	Pearl, Bruce
1997	W	II	2	1	GL	A	To R32	48	30	2	Dugan, Chancellor
1995		II	32	1	GL		To R32	48	22	5	Dugan, Chancellor
1996		II	32	3	GL	L		48	22	7	Dugan, Chancellor
1998		II	32	1	GL	A	To R32	48	26	2	Dugan, Chancellor
SOUTHERN MAINE											
1989	M	III	3		NE	A	To R32	40	24	7	Brown, Robert D.
1988		III	24		NE	L		32	21	8	Brown, Robert D.
1990		III	32		NE	L		40	21	9	Brown, Robert D.
1991		III	32		NE	L	To R32	40	19	8	Sokaitis, Al

Year	M/W	Div	F	SD	Reg	BD	Bye	#T	W	L	Coach
1998	W	III	2	1	NE	A	To R32	48	29	3	Fifield, Gary
1988		III	4		NE	L		32	27	3	Fifield, Gary
1987		III	8		NE	L		32	25	4	Costello, Dr. Richard A.
1990		III	8		NE	A		32	25	5	Fifield, Gary
1991		III	8		NE	A		32	23	7	Fifield, Gary
1992		III	8		NE	L		32	26	4	Fifield, Gary
1993		III	8		NE	A		32	25	4	Fifield, Gary
1989		III	16		NE	A		32	25	3	Fifield, Gary
1996		III	16		NE	L		64	25	4	Fifield, Gary
1997		III	16		NE	A		64	25	4	Fifield, Gary
1986		III	24		NE	L		32	20	5	Costello, Dr. Richard A.
1995		III	64		NE	A		64	23	4	Fifield, Gary

SOUTHERN METHODIST (TX)

Year	M/W	Div	F	SD	Reg	BD	Bye	#T	W	L	Coach
1956	M		4		W	A		25	25	4	Hayes, Elmore O. "Doc"
1967		I	8		MW	A	To R16	23	20	6	Hayes, Elmore O. "Doc"
1957		I	12		MW	A	To R16	23	22	4	Hayes, Elmore O. "Doc"
1965		I	12		MW	A	To R16	23	17	10	Hayes, Elmore O. "Doc"
1966		I	12		MW	A	To R16	22	17	9	Hayes, Elmore O. "Doc"
1955			16		W(A)	A	To R16	24	15	10	Hayes, Elmore O. "Doc"
1984		I	32	9	W	L		53	25	8	Bliss, David
1985		I	32	5	E	L		64	23	10	Bliss, David
1988		I	32	7	E	A		64	28	7	Bliss, David
1993		I	64	10	MW	L		64	20	8	Shumate, John H.
1995	W	I	32	10	W	L		64	21	9	Rompola, Rhonda
1994		I	64	13	ME	L		64	18	9	Rompola, Rhonda
1996		I	64	10	ME	L		64	19	11	Rompola, Rhonda
1998		I	64	11	E	L		64	21	8	Rompola, Rhonda

SOUTHERN MISSISSIPPI

Year	M/W	Div	F	SD	Reg	BD	Bye	#T	W	L	Coach
1990	M	I	64	13	E	L		64	20	12	Turk, M. K.
1991		I	64	11	E	L		64	21	8	Turk, M. K.
1994	W	I	16	4	E	L		64	26	5	James, Kay
1985		I	32		ME	L		32	21	9	James, Kay
1990		I	32	8	MW	A		48	27	5	James, Kay
1996		I	32	9	MW	L		64	22	8	James, Kay
1987		I	40	10	ME	A		40	21	9	James, Kay
1989		I	48	10	ME	L		48	26	5	James, Kay
1992		I	48	9	ME	A		48	21	10	James, Kay
1995		I	64	7	W	A		64	21	9	James, Kay

SOUTHERN: BATON ROUGE

Year	M/W	Div	F	SD	Reg	BD	Bye	#T	W	L	Coach
1975	M	II	24		SC	L		32	19	8	Stewart, Carl E.
1974		II	32		S	L	To R32	44	17	13	Stewart, Carl E.
1977		II	32		SC	L		32	19	11	Stewart, Carl E.
1993		I	32	13	W	A		64	21	10	Jobe, Ben
1981		I	48	11	MW	A		48	17	11	Stewart, Carl E.
1985		I	64	16	W	A		64	19	11	Hopkins, Robert M.
1987		I	64	15	MW	A		64	19	12	Jobe, Ben
1988		I	64	15	SE	A		64	24	7	Jobe, Ben
1989		I	64	15	SE	A		64	20	11	Jobe, Ben

Year	M/W	Div	F	SD	Reg	BD	Bye	#T	W	L	Coach
SOUTHWEST BAPTIST											
1991	M	II	8		SC	A		32	29	3	Kirksey, Jerry L.
1990		II	32		GL	L		32	25	6	Kirksey, Jerry L.
1996	W	II	48	4	SC	L		48	21	9	Middleton, Jim
1998		II	48	6	SC	L		48	18	11	Middleton, Jim
SOUTHWEST MISSOURI STATE											
1959	M	II	2		SW			32	23	3	Matthews, Edwin "Eddie"
1967		II	2		SW		To R32	36	23	5	Thomas, William J.
1969		II	2		MW	L		32	24	5	Thomas, William J.
1974		II	2		MW	A	To R32	44	21	9	Thomas, William J.
1958		II	8		SW			32	22	2	Matthews, Edwin "Eddie"
1966		II	16		SW		To R32	36	19	6	Thomas, William J.
1968		II	16		MW		To R32	36	19	6	Thomas, William J.
1978		II	16		SC	A		32	21	7	Thomas, William J.
1970		II	24		MW	L		32	17	11	Thomas, William J.
1973		II	24		MW		To R32	42	19	8	Thomas, William J.
1987		I	32	13	SE	L		64	28	6	Spoonhour, Charles
1988		I	64	13	W	A		64	22	7	Spoonhour, Charles
1989		I	64	14	W	A		64	21	10	Spoonhour, Charles
1990		I	64	9	MW	L		64	22	7	Spoonhour, Charles
1992		I	64	12	MW	A		64	23	8	Spoonhour, Charles
1992	W	I	3	8	MW	A		48	31	3	Burnett, Cheryl
1993		I	16		MW	A		48	23	9	Burnett, Cheryl
1991		I	32	8	ME	A		48	26	5	Burnett, Cheryl
1994		I	32	6	ME	A		64	24	6	Burnett, Cheryl
1995		I	32	9	MW	L		64	21	12	Burnett, Cheryl
1996		I	64	12	E	A		64	25	5	Burnett, Cheryl
1998		I	64	8	MW	L		64	24	6	Burnett, Cheryl
SOUTHWEST TEXAS STATE											
1994	M	I	64	15	MW	A		64	25	7	Wooldridge, Jim
1997		I	64	16	MW	A		64	16	13	Miller, Mike
1997	W	I	64	14	E	A		64	17	12	Sharp, Linda K.
SOUTHWESTERN (TX)											
1998	W	III	48	6	S	A		48	15	11	Seagraves, Rhonda
SOUTHWESTERN LOUISIANA											
1971	M	II	3		S	L		32	25	4	Shipley, Beryl C.
1972		I	12		MW	L		25	25	4	Shipley, Beryl C.
1973		I	16		MW	L		25	24	5	Shipley, Beryl C.
1992		I	32	13	W	A		64	21	11	Fletcher, Marty
1982		I	48	8	ME	A		48	24	8	Paschal, Bobby
1983		I	48	8	E	L		52	22	7	Paschal, Bobby
1994		I	64	11	SE	A		64	22	8	Fletcher, Marty
SPRING GARDEN											
1987	W	III	24		MA	L		32	25	5	Brennan, Dennis

Year	M/W	Div	F	SD	Reg	BD	Bye	#T	W	L	Coach
SPRINGFIELD (MA)											
1940	M		8		E	L		8	16	3	Hickox, Edward J. "Eddie"
1963		II	16		NE	L		32	20	6	Steitz, Dr. Edward S.
1969		II	16		NENG	L		32	16	9	Bilik, Dr. Edward R.
1980		II	16		NENG	L		32	20	7	Bilik, Dr. Edward R.
1970		II	24		NENG	L		32	17	8	Bilik, Dr. Edward R.
1982		II	24		NENG	L		32	21	8	Bilik, Dr. Edward R.
1986		II	24		NENG	A		32	20	12	Bilik, Dr. Edward R.
1961		II	32		NE	L		32	16	10	Steitz, Dr. Edward S.
1964		II	32		NE	L		32	17	8	Steitz, Dr. Edward S.
1981		II	32		NENG	L		32	20	9	Bilik, Dr. Edward R.
1998		III	32	1	NE	A	To R32	48	26	2	Theulen, Dr. Michael D.
1966		II	36		NE	L		36	20	6	Steitz, Dr. Edward S.
1968		II	36		NE	L		36	17	9	Bilik, Dr. Edward R.
1996		III	64	5	NE	A		64	21	7	Theulen, Dr. Michael D.
1997		III	64	6	NE	A		64	23	5	Theulen, Dr. Michael D.
1982	W	II	8		NENG	L		16	23	3	Shapiro, Harvey P.
STANFORD											
1942	M		1		W	L		8	27	4	Dean, Everett S.
1998		I	3	3	MW	L		64	30	5	Montgomery, Mike
1997		I	16	6	W	L		64	22	8	Montgomery, Mike
1995		I	32	10	E	L		64	20	9	Montgomery, Mike
1996		I	32	9	E	L		64	20	9	Montgomery, Mike
1989		I	64	3	E	L		64	26	7	Montgomery, Mike
1992		I	64	12	SE	L		64	18	11	Montgomery, Mike
1990	W	I	1	1	W	A	To R32	48	32	1	VanDerveer, Tara
1992		I	1	1	W	A	To R32	48	30	3	VanDerveer, Tara
1991		I	3	2	W	A	To R32	48	26	6	VanDerveer, Tara
1995		I	3	2	W	A		64	30	3	VanDerveer, Tara
1996		I	3	1	W	A		64	29	3	Tucker, Amy
1997		I	3	1	W	A		64	34	2	VanDerveer, Tara
1989		I	8	2	MW	A	To R32	48	28	3	VanDerveer, Tara
1994		I	8	2	W	L		64	25	6	VanDerveer, Tara
1988		I	16	5	MW	L	To R32	40	27	5	VanDerveer, Tara
1993		I	16	1	W	A	To R32	48	26	6	VanDerveer, Tara
1982		I	32		W	A		32	19	8	McCrea, Dotty
1998		I	64	1	W	A		64	21	6	VanDerveer, Tara
STATEN ISLAND											
1982	M	III	16		E	L		32	25	4	Pickman, Dr. Evan T.
1984		III	16		E	L		32	25	4	Pickman, Dr. Evan T.
1981		III	32		E	L		32	21	8	Pickman, Dr. Evan T.
1988		III	32		E	L		32	21	9	Ruppert, Howie
1989		III	32		E	L		40	24	7	Ruppert, Howie
1995		III	64	5	A	L		64	20	7	Petosa, Anthony
1996		III	64	3	A	A		64	22	6	Petosa, Anthony
1997	W	III	64		A	A		64	22	6	Mosley, Gerry

Year	M/W	Div	F	SD	Reg	BD	Bye	#T	W	L	Coach
STEPHEN F AUSTIN STATE											
1983	M	II	24		SC	L		32	21	10	Miller, Harry E.
1989	W	I	16	4	W	L	To R32	48	30	4	Blair, Gary
1990		I	16	3	W	A	To R32	48	28	3	Blair, Gary
1992		I	16	2	W	A	To R32	48	28	3	Blair, Gary
1993		I	16	4	MW	A	To R32	48	28	5	Blair, Gary
1996		I	16	11	MW	A		64	27	4	Chadwick, Royce
1982		I	32		E	L		32	15	9	Otwell, Mary Ann
1983		I	32		W	L	To R32	36	18	7	Otwell, Mary Ann
1988		I	32		W	L		40	29	5	Blair, Gary
1991		I	32	8	MW	A		48	26	5	Blair, Gary
1997		I	32	7	MW	L		64	28	5	Chadwick, Royce
1994		I	64	8	MW	A		64	23	7	Curl, Joe
1995		I	64	11	W	A		64	22	8	Chadwick, Royce
1998		I	64	9	ME	A		64	25	4	Chadwick, Royce
STETSON											
1970	M	II	8		SA	L		32	22	7	Wilkes, Dr. Glenn N., Sr.
1971		II	24		SA	L		32	19	9	Wilkes, Dr. Glenn N., Sr.
1967		II	32		SC		To R32	36	17	10	Wilkes, Dr. Glenn N., Sr.
STILLMAN											
1996	M	III	64	5	S	L		64	19	4	Robinson, Larry
STONEHILL											
1998	M	II	16	2	NE	L	To R32	48	22	7	DeCiantis, David
1980		II	24		NC	L		32	18	10	Folliard, Thomas J.
1981		II	24		NENG	L		32	21	9	Folliard, Thomas J.
1971		II	32		NENG	L		32	20	6	Dougher, James D.
1982		II	32		NENG	L		32	21	8	Folliard, Thomas J.
1989		II	32		NENG	A		32	23	9	Pepin, Raymond
1973		II	42		NENG	L		42	19	7	Dougher, James D.
1995	W	II	4	2	NENG	A	To R32	48	30	3	Sullivan, Paula J.
1994		II	8		NENG	L		32	27	5	Sullivan, Paula J.
1987		II	16		NENG	A		24	27	5	Sullivan, Paula J.
1992		II	16		NENG	L		32	26	5	Sullivan, Paula J.
1997		II	16	6	NE	A		48	26	6	Hart, Kelly
1983		II	24		NENG	A		24	21	9	Sullivan, Paula J.
1985		II	24		NENG	L		24	19	7	Sullivan, Paula J.
1988		II	32		NENG	L		32	25	6	Sullivan, Paula J.
1991		II	32		NENG	L		32	19	11	Sullivan, Paula J.
1993		II	32		NENG	L		32	22	8	Sullivan, Paula J.
1996		II	32	1	NE	L	To R32	48	24	6	Sullivan, Paula J.
1998		II	48	4	NE	L		48	24	7	Hart, Kelly
STONY BROOK STATE											
1978	M	III	4		E	L		30	27	9	Bash, Dr. M. Ronald
1977		III	23		E	L		30	21	6	Bash, Dr. M. Ronald
1979		III	24		E	L		32	24	3	Kendall, Dick
1980		III	24		E	L		32	19	9	Kendall, Dick

Year	M/W	Div	F	SD	Reg	BD	Bye	#T	W	L	Coach
1987		III	24		E	L		32	21	6	Castiglie, Joe
1970		II	32		E	L		32	19	6	Massimino, Roland V. 'Rollie'
1991		III	32		E	L	To R32	40	23	4	Castiglie, Joe
1987	W	III	16		E	L		32	24	5	McMullen, Declan
1989		III	24		E	L		32	21	8	McMullen, Declan

SUFFOLK (MA)

Year	M/W	Div	F	SD	Reg	BD	Bye	#T	W	L	Coach
1975	M	III	16		NE	L		30	19	7	Law, Charles
1977		III	23		NE	L		30	16	7	Law, Charles
1976		III	28		NE	L		28	19	6	Law, Charles
1978		III	30		NE	L		30	15	10	Law, Charles

SUSQUEHANNA

Year	M/W	Div	F	SD	Reg	BD	Bye	#T	W	L	Coach
1986	M	III	8		MA	A		32	22	8	Harnum, Donald
1984		III	16		MA	L		32	21	7	Harnum, Donald
1989		III	32		MA	A	To R32	40	18	10	Harnum, Donald
1994		III	32		MA	L		40	19	7	Marcinek, Frank
1992		III	40		MA	A		40	17	11	Marcinek, Frank
1982	W	III	8		None	L		16	21	4	Diehl, Tom
1984		III	16		MA	L		32	19	8	Diehl, Tom
1991		III	16		MA	L		32	23	5	Hribar, Mark
1985		III	24		MA	L		32	24	5	Diehl, Tom
1983		III	32		MA	A		32	24	2	Diehl, Tom
1986		III	32		GL	L		32	17	6	Diehl, Tom
1992		III	32		MA	L		32	21	6	Hribar, Mark
1993		III	32		E	L		32	19	7	Hribar, Mark

SYRACUSE

Year	M/W	Div	F	SD	Reg	BD	Bye	#T	W	L	Coach
1987	M	I	2	2	E	L		64	31	7	Boeheim, James A., Jr.
1996		I	2	4	W	L		64	29	9	Boeheim, James A., Jr.
1975		I	4		E	L		32	23	9	Danforth, Roy
1957		I	8		E	L		23	18	7	Guley, Marcel 'Marc'
1966		I	8		E	L	To R16	22	22	6	Lewis, Frederick B., Jr.
1989		I	8	2	MW	L		64	30	8	Boeheim, James A., Jr.
1973		I	12		E	L		25	24	5	Danforth, Roy
1977		I	16		ME	L		32	26	4	Boeheim, James A., Jr.
1979		I	16	4	E	L	To R32	40	26	4	Boeheim, James A., Jr.
1980		I	16	1	E	L	To R32	48	26	4	Boeheim, James A., Jr.
1984		I	16	3	E	L	To R32	53	23	9	Boeheim, James A., Jr.
1990		I	16	2	SE	L		64	26	7	Boeheim, James A., Jr.
1994		I	16	4	W	L		64	23	7	Boeheim, James A., Jr.
1998		I	16	5	S	L		64	26	9	Boeheim, James A., Jr.
1974		I	25		MW	L		25	19	7	Danforth, Roy
1976		I	32		MW	L		32	20	9	Danforth, Roy
1978		I	32		ME	L		32	22	6	Boeheim, James A., Jr.
1983		I	32	6	E	L		52	21	10	Boeheim, James A., Jr.
1985		I	32	7	E	L		64	22	9	Boeheim, James A., Jr.
1986		I	32	2	E	L		64	26	6	Boeheim, James A., Jr.
1988		I	32	3	E	A		64	26	9	Boeheim, James A., Jr.
1992		I	32	6	E	A		64	22	10	Boeheim, James A., Jr.
1995		I	32	7	MW	L		64	20	10	Boeheim, James A., Jr.
1991		I	64	2	E	L		64	26	6	Boeheim, James A., Jr.

Year	M/W	Div	F	SD	Reg	BD	Bye	#T	W	L	Coach
1985	W	I	32		E	A		32	18	13	Jacobs, Barbara
1988		I	32	6	ME	L	To R32	40	22	9	Jacobs, Barbara

TAMPA UNIVERSITY

Year	M/W	Div	F	SD	Reg	BD	Bye	#T	W	L	Coach
1985	M	II	16		S	A		32	23	8	Schmidt, Richard
1986		II	16		S	L		32	22	8	Schmidt, Richard
1988		II	16		S	L		32	24	8	Schmidt, Richard
1989		II	16		S	L		32	24	7	Schmidt, Richard
1994		II	16		S	L		32	22	9	Schmidt, Richard
1995		II	16	2	S	A	To R32	48	25	6	Schmidt, Richard
1993		II	23		S	L		32	25	5	Schmidt, Richard
1984		II	24		S	A		32	20	11	Schmidt, Richard
1987		II	24		S	L		32	26	6	Schmidt, Richard
1990		II	32		S	L		32	26	5	Schmidt, Richard
1997		II	32	6	S	A		48	23	7	Schmidt, Richard
1994	W	II	32		S	L		32	21	7	Mosca, Tom

TEMPLE

Year	M/W	Div	F	SD	Reg	BD	Bye	#T	W	L	Coach
1956	M		3		E	L		25	27	4	Litwack, Harry
1958		I	3		E	L	To R16	24	27	3	Litwack, Harry
1944			6		E	L		8	14	9	Cody, Joshua C.
1988		I	8	1	E	A		64	32	2	Chaney, John
1991		I	8	10	E	L		64	24	10	Chaney, John
1993		I	8	7	W	L		64	20	13	Chaney, John
1967		I	23		E	A		23	20	8	Litwack, Harry
1964		I	25		E	A		25	17	8	Litwack, Harry
1970		I	25		E	A		25	15	13	Litwack, Harry
1972		I	25		E	A		25	23	8	Litwack, Harry
1984		I	32	8	E	L		53	26	5	Chaney, John
1985		I	32	8	E	A		64	25	6	Chaney, John
1986		I	32	9	MW	L		64	25	6	Chaney, John
1987		I	32	2	MW	A		64	32	4	Chaney, John
1994		I	32	4	E	L		64	23	8	Chaney, John
1996		I	32	7	SE	L		64	20	13	Chaney, John
1997		I	32	9	MW	L		64	20	11	Chaney, John
1979		I	40	7	E	A		40	25	4	Casey, Don
1990		I	64	11	E	A		64	20	11	Chaney, John
1992		I	64	11	SE	L		64	17	13	Chaney, John
1995		I	64	10	W	L		64	19	11	Chaney, John
1998		I	64	7	W	L		64	21	9	Chaney, John
1989	W	I	32	8	ME	L		48	22	10	Hill-MacDonald, Linda

TENNESSEE

Year	M/W	Div	F	SD	Reg	BD	Bye	#T	W	L	Coach
1967	M	I	16		ME	A	To R16	23	21	7	Mears, Ramon "Ray"
1981		I	16	4	E	L	To R32	48	21	8	DeVoe, Donald E.
1976		I	32		E	L		32	21	6	Mears, Ramon "Ray"
1977		I	32		ME	A		32	22	6	Mears, Ramon "Ray"
1979		I	32	8	ME	A		40	21	12	DeVoe, Donald E.
1980		I	32	7	E	L		48	18	11	DeVoe, Donald E.
1982		I	32	9	ME	L		48	20	10	DeVoe, Donald E.
1983		I	32	8	ME	L		52	20	12	DeVoe, Donald E.

Year	M/W	Div	F	SD	Reg	BD	Bye	#T	W	L	Coach
1989		I	64	10	E	L		64	19	11	DeVoe, Donald E.
1998		I	64	8	W	L		64	20	9	Green, Jerry
1987	W	I	1	2	ME	L	To R32	40	28	6	Summitt, Patricia Head
1989		I	1	1	E	A	To R32	48	35	2	Summitt, Patricia Head
1991		I	1	1	ME	L	To R32	48	30	5	Summitt, Patricia Head
1996		I	1	1	E	A		64	32	4	Summitt, Patricia Head
1997		I	1	3	MW	L		64	29	10	Summitt, Patricia Head
1998		I	1	1	ME	A		64	39	0	Summitt, Patricia Head
1984		I	2		ME	L		32	23	10	Summitt, Patricia Head
1995		I	2	1	ME	L		64	34	3	Summitt, Patricia Head
1982		I	3		ME	L		32	22	10	Summitt, Patricia Head
1986		I	3		ME	L	To R32	40	24	10	Summitt, Patricia Head
1988		I	3	1	E	A	To R32	40	31	3	Summitt, Patricia Head
1983		I	8		ME	L	To R32	36	25	8	Summitt, Patricia Head
1990		I	8	1	E	L	To R32	48	27	6	Summitt, Patricia Head
1993		I	8	1	ME	L	To R32	48	29	3	Summitt, Patricia Head
1985		I	16		ME	L		32	22	10	Summitt, Patricia Head
1992		I	16	1	ME	A	To R32	48	28	3	Summitt, Patricia Head
1994		I	16	1	ME	A		64	31	2	Summitt, Patricia Head

TENNESSEE STATE

Year	M/W	Div	F	SD	Reg	BD	Bye	#T	W	L	Coach
1970	M	II	2		S	L		32	21	8	Martin, Edward A.
1973		II	2		S	L	To R32	42	22	8	Martin, Edward A.
1972		II	3		S	L	To R32	36	26	2	Martin, Edward A.
1975		II	4		S	L		32	19	9	Martin, Edward A.
1963		II	16		SC			32	21	6	Hunter, Harold
1971		II	16		S	L		32	24	3	Martin, Edward A.
1967		II	23		SC		To R32	36	20	8	Hunter, Harold
1974		II	24		S	L	To R32	44	23	5	Martin, Edward A.
1993		I	64	15	SE	A		64	19	10	Allen, Franklin "Frankie"
1994		I	64	14	SE	A		64	19	12	Allen, Franklin "Frankie"
1994	W	I	64	13	E	A		64	20	9	Lawrence-Phillips, Teresa A.
1995		I	64	12	ME	A		64	22	7	Lawrence-Phillips, Teresa A.

TENNESSEE TECH

Year	M/W	Div	F	SD	Reg	BD	Bye	#T	W	L	Coach
1958	M	I	24		ME	A		24	17	9	Oldham, John O.
1963		I	25		ME	A		25	16	8	Oldham, John O.
1982	W	I	32		MW	A		32	20	11	Meadors, Marynell Hutsell
1985		I	32		W	L		32	20	9	Meadors, Marynell Hutsell
1987		I	32	7	ME	A		40	24	7	Worrell, Bill
1989		I	32	11	MW	A		48	22	8	Worrell, Bill
1990		I	32	7	ME	A		48	26	5	Worrell, Bill
1991		I	48	9	ME	A		48	22	8	Worrell, Bill
1992		I	48	12	ME	A		48	21	9	Worrell, Bill
1993		I	48		ME	A		48	22	7	Worrell, Bill

TENNESSEE: CHATTANOOGA

Year	M/W	Div	F	SD	Reg	BD	Bye	#T	W	L	Coach
1977	M	II	1		S	L		32	27	5	Shumate, Ron
1976		II	2		S	L		32	23	9	Shumate, Ron
1975		II	16		S	L		32	19	9	Shumate, Ron
1997		I	16	14	SE	A		64	24	11	McCarthy, Mack

Year	M/W	Div	F	SD	Reg	BD	Bye	#T	W	L	Coach
1973		II	24		S	L	To R32	42	19	9	Shumate, Ron
1961		II	32		SC			32	17	8	Bartlett, Thomas G. "Tommy"
1982		I	32	10	ME	A		48	27	4	Arnold, Murray
1981		I	48	11	ME	A		48	21	9	Arnold, Murray
1983		I	48	9	MW	A		52	26	4	Arnold, Murray
1988		I	64	16	SE	A		64	20	13	McCarthy, Mack
1993		I	64	12	SE	A		64	26	7	McCarthy, Mack
1994		I	64	13	SE	A		64	23	7	McCarthy, Mack
1995		I	64	15	W	A		64	19	11	McCarthy, Mack
1989	W	I	48	12	ME	A		48	19	12	Parrott, Craig
1992		I	48	12	E	A		48	18	12	Parrott, Craig

TENNESSEE: MARTIN

Year	M/W	Div	F	SD	Reg	BD	Bye	#T	W	L	Coach
1982	M	II	16		SC	L		32	20	11	Tolis, Art
1983		II	32		SC	L		32	21	10	Hancock, Tom

TEXAS

Year	M/W	Div	F	SD	Reg	BD	Bye	#T	W	L	Coach
1943	M		3		W	L		8	19	7	Gilstrap, H. C. "Bully"
1947			3		W	L		8	26	2	Gray, Jack S.
1939			8		W	L		8	19	6	Gray, Jack S.
1990		I	8	10	MW	L		64	24	9	Penders, Thomas V.
1963		I	12		MW	A		25	20	7	Bradley, Harold L.
1960		I	16		MW	A	To R16	25	18	8	Bradley, Harold L.
1972		I	16		MW	A		25	19	9	Black, Leon
1997		I	16	10	E	L		64	18	12	Penders, Thomas V.
1974		I	25		MW	A		25	12	15	Black, Leon
1979		I	32	4	MW	L	To R32	40	21	8	Lemons, A. E. "Abe"
1989		I	32	11	MW	L		64	25	9	Penders, Thomas V.
1991		I	32	5	MW	L		64	23	9	Penders, Thomas V.
1994		I	32	6	MW	A		64	26	8	Penders, Thomas V.
1995		I	32	11	W	A		64	23	7	Penders, Thomas V.
1996		I	32	10	MW	L		64	21	10	Penders, Thomas V.
1992		I	64	8	E	L		64	23	12	Penders, Thomas V.
1986	W	I	1		MW	A	To R32	40	34	0	Conradt, Jody
1987		I	3	1	E	A	To R32	40	31	2	Conradt, Jody
1983		I	8		MW	A	To R32	36	30	3	Conradt, Jody
1984		I	8		MW	A		32	32	3	Conradt, Jody
1988		I	8	1	MW	A	To R32	40	32	3	Conradt, Jody
1989		I	8	2	W	A	To R32	48	27	5	Conradt, Jody
1990		I	8	3	MW	A	To R32	48	27	5	Conradt, Jody
1985		I	16		ME	A		32	28	3	Conradt, Jody
1992		I	32	4	MW	L	To R32	48	21	10	Conradt, Jody
1993		I	32	3	MW	L	To R32	48	22	8	Conradt, Jody
1994		I	32	5	MW	A		64	22	9	Conradt, Jody
1996		I	32	5	E	L		64	21	9	Conradt, Jody
1997		I	32	3	E	L		64	22	8	Conradt, Jody
1991		I	48	7	MW	L		48	21	9	Conradt, Jody

Year	M/W	Div	F	SD	Reg	BD	Bye	#T	W	L	Coach
TEXAS A&M											
1951	M		16		W	A		16	17	12	Floyd, John L.
1969		I	16		MW	A		25	18	9	Metcalf, Dr. Shelby R.
1980		I	16	6	MW	A		48	26	8	Metcalf, Dr. Shelby R.
1964		I	25		MW	A		25	18	7	Metcalf, Dr. Shelby R.
1975		I	32		MW	A		32	20	7	Metcalf, Dr. Shelby R.
1987		I	64	12	MW	A		64	17	14	Metcalf, Dr. Shelby R.
1994	W	I	16	13	W	L		64	23	8	Hickey, Lynn
1996		I	64	7	W	A		64	20	12	Harvey, Candi
TEXAS A&M: COMMERCE											
1997	M	II	8	3	SC	L		48	24	8	Peak, Paul
1996		II	48	5	SC	L		48	20	8	Peak, Paul
1998		II	48	6	SC	L		48	22	7	Peak, Paul
TEXAS A&M: KINGSVILLE											
1992	M	II	24		SC	A		32	21	12	Carter, William C.
1996		II	32	2	SC	A	To R32	48	23	6	Carter, William C.
1983	W	II	16		NC	L		24	21	8	Land, David
TEXAS CHRISTIAN											
1968	M	I	8		MW	A	To R16	23	15	11	Swaim, Johnny
1952			12		W(A)	A		16	24	4	Brannon, Byron A. "Buster"
1953			12		W(B)	A	To R16	22	15	8	Brannon, Byron A. "Buster"
1959		I	12		MW	A	To R16	23	20	6	Brannon, Byron A. "Buster"
1971		I	25		MW	A		25	15	12	Swaim, Johnny
1987		I	32	4	E	L		64	24	7	Killingsworth, James
1998		I	64	5	MW	L		64	27	6	Tubbs, Billy
TEXAS SOUTHERN											
1990	M	I	64	14	MW	A		64	19	12	Moreland, Robert E.
1994		I	64	15	SE	A		64	19	11	Moreland, Robert E.
1995		I	64	15	MW	A		64	22	7	Moreland, Robert E.
TEXAS TECH											
1961	M	I	12		MW	A	To R16	24	15	10	Robison, Polk F.
1962		I	16		MW	A		25	19	8	Gibson, Eugene F.
1976		I	16		MW	A		32	25	6	Myers, Gerald
1996		I	16	3	E	A		64	30	2	Dickey, James
1954			24		W(B)	A		24	20	5	Robison, Polk F.
1956			25		W	A		25	13	12	Robison, Polk F.
1973		I	25		MW	A		25	19	8	Myers, Gerald
1985		I	64	6	MW	A		64	23	8	Myers, Gerald
1986		I	64	13	MW	A		64	17	14	Myers, Gerald
1993		I	64	12	E	A		64	18	12	Dickey, James
1993	W	I	1	2	W	A	To R32	48	31	3	Sharp, Marsha
1995		I	8	2	ME	A		64	33	4	Sharp, Marsha
1992		I	16	4	W	A	To R32	48	27	5	Sharp, Marsha
1994		I	16	2	MW	L		64	28	5	Sharp, Marsha

Year	M/W	Div	F	SD	Reg	BD	Bye	#T	W	L	Coach
1996		I	16	4	MW	L		64	27	5	Sharp, Marsha
1984		I	32		MW	L		32	23	7	Sharp, Marsha
1986		I	32		W	L	To R32	40	21	9	Sharp, Marsha
1997		I	32	8	W	L		64	20	9	Sharp, Marsha
1998		I	32	1	MW	A		64	26	5	Sharp, Marsha
1990		I	48	12	MW	L		48	20	11	Sharp, Marsha
1991		I	48	9	W	L		48	23	8	Sharp, Marsha

TEXAS: EL PASO

Year	M/W	Div	F	SD	Reg	BD	Bye	#T	W	L	Coach
1966	M	I	1		MW	L		22	28	1	Haskins, Donald L.
1964		I	12		MW	L		25	25	3	Haskins, Donald L.
1967		I	12		W	L		23	22	6	Haskins, Donald L.
1992		I	16	9	MW	L		64	27	7	Haskins, Donald L.
1963		I	25		MW	L		25	19	7	Haskins, Donald L.
1970		I	25		W	A		25	17	8	Haskins, Donald L.
1975		I	32		ME	L		32	20	6	Haskins, Donald L.
1984		I	32	4	W	A	To R32	53	27	4	Haskins, Donald L.
1985		I	32	11	W	L		64	22	10	Haskins, Donald L.
1987		I	32	7	W	L		64	25	7	Haskins, Donald L.
1989		I	32	7	W	A		64	26	7	Haskins, Donald L.
1986		I	64	10	W	A		64	27	6	Haskins, Donald L.
1988		I	64	9	W	L		64	23	10	Haskins, Donald L.
1990		I	64	11	SE	A		64	21	11	Haskins, Donald L.

TEXAS: PAN AMERICAN

Year	M/W	Div	F	SD	Reg	BD	Bye	#T	W	L	Coach
1968	M	II	16		SW	L	To R32	36	21	6	Williams, Samuel

TEXAS: SAN ANTONIO

Year	M/W	Div	F	SD	Reg	BD	Bye	#T	W	L	Coach
1988	M	I	64	14	SE	A		64	22	9	Burmeister, Ken

THIEL

Year	M/W	Div	F	SD	Reg	BD	Bye	#T	W	L	Coach
1988	W	III	32		MA	L		32	19	6	Parsons, Margaret Rhoads "Gie"

THOMAS MORE (KY)

Year	M/W	Div	F	SD	Reg	BD	Bye	#T	W	L	Coach
1997	W	III	16		S	L		64	20	7	Brumfield, Sharri

TOLEDO

Year	M/W	Div	F	SD	Reg	BD	Bye	#T	W	L	Coach
1979	M	I	16	5	ME	A	To R32	40	22	8	Nichols, Robert J.
1967		I	23		ME	A		23	23	2	Nichols, Robert J.
1954			24		E(A)	A		24	13	10	Bush, Gerald "Jerry"
1980		I	48	9	ME	A		48	23	6	Nichols, Robert J.
1991	W	I	32	11	E	A		48	24	7	Fennelly, Bill
1992		I	32	10	ME	A		48	26	6	Fennelly, Bill
1996		I	32	10	E	A		64	25	6	Ehlen, Mark
1995		I	64	13	ME	A		64	24	7	Fennelly, Bill
1997		I	64	10	MW	A		64	27	4	Ehlen, Mark

TOWSON

Year	M/W	Div	F	SD	Reg	BD	Bye	#T	W	L	Coach
1977	M	II	8		SA	A		32	27	3	Angotti, Vincent
1978		II	16		SA	A		32	26	4	Angotti, Vincent
1990		I	64	16	MW	A		64	18	13	Truax, Terry
1991		I	64	16	MW	A		64	19	11	Truax, Terry

Year	M/W	Div	F	SD	Reg	BD	Bye	#T	W	L	Coach
TRANSYLVANIA											
1976	M	III	14		S	L		28	19	8	Lane, Don
1977		III	16		S	L		30	15	12	Lane, Don
1975		III	23		S	L		30	20	7	Rose, Lee H.
1978		III	23		S	L		30	20	6	Lane, Don
1969		II	24		S	L		32	20	7	Rose, Lee H.
1970		II	32		S	L		32	21	7	Rose, Lee H.
1972		II	32		S	L	To R32	36	21	6	Rose, Lee H.
1973		II	32		S	L		42	20	7	Rose, Lee H.
TRINITY (CT)											
1995	M	III	4	2	NE	L		64	24	5	Ogrodnik, Stanley
1998		III	48	5	NE	L		48	20	4	Ogrodnik, Stanley
1995	W	III	32		NE	L		64	21	4	Pine, Maureen
1997		III	64		NE	L		64	18	6	Pine, Maureen
TRINITY (TX)											
1968	M	II	3		SW	L	To R32	36	23	7	Polk, James Robert "Bob"
1960		II	24		PC	L		32	18	9	Robinson, Leslie W.
1961		II	24		SW	L		32	20	6	Robinson, Leslie W.
1969		I	25		MW	L		25	19	5	Polk, James Robert "Bob"
1998		III	32	3	S	A		48	21	6	Brock, Charles
1995	W	III	64		S	A		64	19	6	Geyer, Becky
1996		III	64		S	L		64	16	10	Geyer, Becky
TROY STATE: TROY											
1993	M	II	2		S	L		32	27	5	Maestri, Don
1988		II	4		SA	L		32	24	10	Maestri, Don
1977		II	16		SC			32	15	14	Bizilia, Wes
1991		II	16		S	A		32	22	8	Maestri, Don
1992		II	24		S	L		32	23	6	Maestri, Don
1997	W	I	64	13	W	A		64	23	7	Hester, Jerry
TRUMAN STATE (MO)											
1960	M	II	8		SW			32	19	5	King, W. Boyd
1971		II	16		MW	L		32	18	9	King, W. Boyd
1981		II	16		SC	A		32	19	11	Simms, Willard
1979		II	32		SC	A		32	20	8	Simms, Willard
1982	W	II	16		SC	L		16	17	11	Murray, Dr. Mary Jo
TUFTS											
1945	M		8		E	L		8	10	8	Cochran, Arthur M.
1997		III	32	7	NE	L		64	20	6	Sheldon, Robert J., Jr.
1995		III	64	3	NE	L		64	20	5	Sheldon, Robert J., Jr.
TULANE											
1992	M	I	32	10	SE	L		64	22	9	Clark, Perry
1993		I	32	11	SE	L		64	22	9	Clark, Perry
1995		I	32	9	SE	L		64	23	10	Clark, Perry
1997	W	I	32	4	E	A		64	27	5	Stockton, Lisa
1995		I	64	15	ME	L		64	19	10	Stockton, Lisa
1996		I	64	14	W	L		64	21	10	Stockton, Lisa
1998		I	64	12	W	L		64	21	7	Stockton, Lisa

Year	M/W	Div	F	SD	Reg	BD	Bye	#T	W	L	Coach
TULSA											
1955	M		12		W(A)	A	To R16	24	21	7	Iba, Clarence V.
1994		I	16	12	MW	L		64	23	8	Smith, Orlando H. "Tubby"
1995		I	16	6	E	L		64	24	8	Smith, Orlando H. "Tubby"
1982		I	32	3	MW	A	To R32	48	24	6	Richardson, Nolan
1984		I	32	4	ME	A	To R32	53	27	4	Richardson, Nolan
1997		I	32	5	MW	L		64	24	10	Robinson, Steve
1985		I	64	6	W	L		64	23	8	Richardson, Nolan
1986		I	64	10	E	A		64	23	9	Barnett, J. D.
1987		I	64	11	W	L		64	22	8	Barnett, J. D.
1996		I	64	11	MW	A		64	22	8	Robinson, Steve
TUSKEGEE											
1979	M	II	24		S	A		32	18	11	Thompson, Charles
1959		II	32		SC	L		32	13	9	Owen, Ross C.
1982	W	II	2		S	L		16	29	5	Laster, Jr. "Tiny"
1983		II	16		S	A		24	20	11	Laster, Jr. "Tiny"
UNION (NY)											
1983	M	III	24		E	L		32	21	5	Scanlon, William M.
UNION (TN)											
1968	M	II	16		SC	L	To R32	36	22	3	Henry, Bill
1962		II	32		SC	L		32	16	13	Russell, Jack L.
UPPER IOWA											
1996	M	III	64	4	W	A		64	20	5	Engen, Stewart "Stu"
UPSALA											
1980	M	III	2		SA	L		32	25	5	Chapman, Tom
1984		III	4		SA	L		32	25	5	Chapman, Tom
1981		III	8		SA	L		32	23	6	Chapman, Tom
1979		III	16		SA	L		32	23	4	Chapman, Tom
1982		III	16		SA	L		32	23	4	Chapman, Tom
1986		III	16		SA	L		32	20	6	Thompson, Russ
1960		II	24		E	L		32	19	8	Wieboldt, Frederick W.
1983		III	24		SA	L		32	19	7	Chapman, Tom
1978		III	30		MA	L		30	19	9	Adubato, Richard
1994	W	III	16		MA	L		40	23	3	McGrady, William
URSINUS											
1981	M	III	3		MA	L		32	23	8	Werley, "Skip"
1982		III	8		MA	L		32	19	11	Werley, "Skip"
1980		III	32		MA	L		32	17	10	Werley, "Skip"
1995	W	III	64		MA	A		64	21	5	Ortlip-Cornish, Lisa
UTAH											
1944	M		1		W	L		8	21	4	Peterson, Vadal
1998		I	2	3	W	L		64	31	4	Majerus, Rick
1961		I	4		W	A	To R16	24	23	8	Gardner, James H. "Jack"
1966		I	4		W	A	To R16	22	23	8	Gardner, James H. "Jack"

Year	M/W	Div	F	SD	Reg	BD	Bye	#T	W	L	Coach
1945			8		W	L		8	17	4	Peterson, Vadal
1956			8		FW	A	To R16	25	22	6	Gardner, James H. "Jack"
1997		I	8	2	W	A		64	29	4	Majerus, Rick
1955			12		W(B)	A	To R16	24	24	4	Gardner, James H. "Jack"
1960		I	12		W	A		25	26	3	Gardner, James H. "Jack"
1959		I	16		W	A	To R16	23	21	7	Gardner, James H. "Jack"
1977		I	16		W	A		32	22	7	Pimm, Jerry
1978		I	16		MW	L		32	23	6	Pimm, Jerry
1981		I	16	3	W	L	To R32	48	25	5	Pimm, Jerry
1983		I	16	10	W	A		52	18	14	Pimm, Jerry
1991		I	16	4	W	L		64	30	4	Majerus, Rick
1996		I	16	4	MW	L		64	27	7	Majerus, Rick
1993		I	32	8	SE	L		64	24	7	Majerus, Rick
1995		I	32	4	W	A		64	28	6	Majerus, Rick
1979		I	40	8	W	L		40	20	10	Pimm, Jerry
1986		I	64	14	W	L		64	20	10	Archibald, Lynn
1983	W	I	32		W	A	To R32	36	22	7	Gardner, Fern
1997		I	32	5	W	L		64	25	6	Elliott, Elaine
1986		I	40		W	A		40	21	9	Elliott, Elaine
1989		I	48	11	W	A		48	24	6	Elliott, Elaine
1990		I	48	12	W	A		48	20	10	Elliott, Elaine
1991		I	48	12	W	A		48	20	10	Elliott, Elaine
1995		I	64	8	MW	A		64	23	7	Elliott, Elaine
1996		I	64	8	MW	L		64	21	8	Elliott, Elaine
1998		I	64	7	W	L		64	21	6	Elliott, Elaine

UTAH STATE

Year	M/W	Div	F	SD	Reg	BD	Bye	#T	W	L	Coach
1939	M		6		W	L		8	17	7	Romney, Ernest L. "Dick"
1970		I	8		W	L		25	22	7	Anderson, Ladell
1962		I	16		W	A		25	22	7	Anderson, Ladell
1964		I	16		W	L		25	21	8	Anderson, Ladell
1963		I	25		W	L		25	20	7	Anderson, Ladell
1971		I	25		W	L		25	20	7	Anderson, Ladell
1975		I	32		W	L		32	21	6	Belnap, Gordon "Dutch"
1979		I	40	10	W	L		40	19	11	Belnap, Gordon "Dutch"
1980		I	48	11	W	L		48	18	9	Tueller, Rod
1983		I	48	10	MW	L		52	20	9	Tueller, Rod
1988		I	64	10	MW	A		64	21	10	Tueller, Rod
1998		I	64	13	W	A		64	25	8	Eustachy, Larry

UTICA

Year	M/W	Div	F	SD	Reg	BD	Bye	#T	W	L	Coach
1984	W	II	16		E	A		24	20	6	Kowalewski, Joan
1985		II	16		E	A		24	22	4	Kowalewski, Joan

VALDOSTA STATE

Year	M/W	Div	F	SD	Reg	BD	Bye	#T	W	L	Coach
1976	M	II	16		S	A		32	15	13	Dominey, James
1979		II	16		S	L		32	20	8	Dominey, James
1977		II	24		S	L		32	23	6	Dominey, James

Year	M/W	Div	F	SD	Reg	BD	Bye	#T	W	L	Coach
1984	W	II	3		S	L	To R16	24	30	3	Cooper, Charles
1983		II	8		S	L	To R16	24	27	4	Cooper, Charles
1995		II	16	2	S	L	To R32	48	25	4	Williamson, Jane
1997		II	48	4	S	L		48	19	10	Williamson, Jane

VALPARAISO

Year	M/W	Div	F	SD	Reg	BD	Bye	#T	W	L	Coach
1962	M	II	8		GL	L		32	17	8	Meadows, Dr. Paul
1967		II	8		GL	L	To R32	36	21	8	Bartow, B. Gene
1966		II	16		MW	L	To R32	36	19	9	Bartow, B. Gene
1969		II	16		GL	L		32	16	12	Bartow, B. Gene
1973		II	16		GL		To R32	42	17	11	Purden, William
1998		I	16	13	MW	A		64	23	10	Drew, Homer
1996		I	64	14	W	A		64	21	11	Drew, Homer
1997		I	64	12	W	A		64	24	7	Drew, Homer

VANDERBILT

Year	M/W	Div	F	SD	Reg	BD	Bye	#T	W	L	Coach
1965	M	I	8		ME	A	To R16	23	24	4	Skinner, Roy G.
1974		I	16		ME	A	To R16	25	23	5	Skinner, Roy G.
1988		I	16	7	MW	L		64	20	11	Newton, Charles M. "CM"
1993		I	16	3	W	L		64	28	6	Fogler, Eddie
1989		I	64	8	E	L		64	19	14	Newton, Charles M. "CM"
1991		I	64	9	W	L		64	17	13	Fogler, Eddie
1997		I	64	10	MW	L		64	19	12	Van Breda Kolff, Jan M.
1993	W	I	3	1	MW	A	To R32	48	30	3	Foster, Jim
1992		I	8	3	E	L	To R32	48	22	9	Foster, Jim
1996		I	8	3	ME	L		64	23	8	Foster, Jim
1990		I	16	6	ME	L		48	23	11	Lee, Phil
1991		I	16	10	ME	L		48	19	12	Lee, Phil
1994		I	16	2	E	L		64	25	8	Foster, Jim
1995		I	16	1	W	A		64	28	7	Foster, Jim
1997		I	16	6	W	L		64	20	11	Foster, Jim
1986		I	32		MW	L	To R32	40	22	9	Lee, Phil
1987		I	32	5	E	L	To R32	40	23	10	Lee, Phil
1989		I	48	7	E	L		48	21	8	Lee, Phil
1998		I	64	6	ME	L		64	20	9	Foster, Jim

VERMONT

Year	M/W	Div	F	SD	Reg	BD	Bye	#T	W	L	Coach
1992	W	I	48	9	E	L		48	29	1	Inglese, Cathy
1993		I	48		E	L		48	28	1	Inglese, Cathy
1994		I	64	13	MW	A		64	19	11	Borton, Pam

VILLANOVA

Year	M/W	Div	F	SD	Reg	BD	Bye	#T	W	L	Coach
1985	M	I	1	8	SE	L		64	25	10	Massimino, Roland V. "Rollie"
1971		I	2		E	L		25	22	7	Kraft, John J. "Jack"
1939			3		E	L		8	20	5	Severance, Alexander G.
1949			6		E	L		8	23	4	Severance, Alexander G.
1962		I	8		E	L		25	21	7	Kraft, John J. "Jack"
1970		I	8		E	L		25	22	7	Kraft, John J. "Jack"
1978		I	8		E	A		32	23	9	Massimino, Roland V. "Rollie"
1982		I	8	3	E	L	To R32	48	24	8	Massimino, Roland V. "Rollie"

Year	M/W	Div	F	SD	Reg	BD	Bye	#T	W	L	Coach
1983		I	8	3	MW	L	To R32	52	24	8	Massimino, Roland V. "Rollie"
1988		I	8	6	SE	L		64	24	13	Massimino, Roland V. "Rollie"
1955			12		E(B)	L		24	18	10	Severance, Alexander G.
1964		I	12		E	L		25	24	4	Kraft, John J. "Jack"
1951			16		E	L		16	25	7	Severance, Alexander G.
1972		I	16		E	L		25	20	8	Kraft, John J. "Jack"
1969		I	25		E	L		25	21	5	Kraft, John J. "Jack"
1980		I	32	8	E	A		48	23	8	Massimino, Roland V. "Rollie"
1981		I	32	9	E	L		48	20	11	Massimino, Roland V. "Rollie"
1984		I	32	7	ME	L		53	19	12	Massimino, Roland V. "Rollie"
1986		I	32	10	SE	L		64	23	14	Massimino, Roland V. "Rollie"
1991		I	32	9	E	L		64	17	15	Massimino, Roland V. "Rollie"
1996		I	32	3	MW	L		64	26	7	Lappas, Steve
1997		I	32	4	E	L		64	24	10	Lappas, Steve
1990		I	64	12	SE	L		64	18	15	Massimino, Roland V. "Rollie"
1995		I	64	3	E	A		64	25	8	Lappas, Steve
1986	W	I	32		E	A		40	23	8	Perretta, Harry
1987		I	32	6	E	A	To R32	40	27	4	Perretta, Harry
1988		I	40	8	E	L		40	20	9	Perretta, Harry
1989		I	48	11	ME	L		48	18	12	Perretta, Harry

VIRGINIA

Year	M/W	Div	F	SD	Reg	BD	Bye	#T	W	L	Coach
1981	M	I	3	1	E	L	To R32	48	29	4	Holland, M. Terrance "Terry"
1984		I	3	7	E	L		53	21	12	Holland, M. Terrance "Terry"
1983		I	8	1	W	L	To R32	52	29	5	Holland, M. Terrance "Terry"
1989		I	8	5	SE	L		64	22	11	Holland, M. Terrance "Terry"
1995		I	8	4	MW	L		64	25	9	Jones, Jeffrey A.
1982		I	16	1	ME	L	To R32	48	30	4	Holland, M. Terrance "Terry"
1993		I	16	6	E	L		64	21	10	Jones, Jeffrey A.
1976		I	32		E	A		32	18	12	Holland, M. Terrance "Terry"
1990		I	32	7	SE	L		64	20	12	Holland, M. Terrance "Terry"
1994		I	32	7	W	L		64	18	13	Jones, Jeffrey A.
1986		I	64	5	E	L		64	19	11	Holland, M. Terrance "Terry"
1987		I	64	5	W	L		64	21	10	Holland, M. Terrance "Terry"
1991		I	64	7	W	L		64	21	12	Jones, Jeffrey A.
1997		I	64	9	W	L		64	18	13	Jones, Jeffrey A.
1991	W	I	2	1	MW	L	To R32	48	31	3	Ryan, Deborah H.
1990		I	3	2	E	A	To R32	48	29	6	Ryan, Deborah H.
1992		I	3	1	E	A	To R32	48	32	2	Ryan, Deborah H.
1988		I	8	2	E	L	To R32	40	27	5	Ryan, Deborah H.
1993		I	8	2	E	A	To R32	48	26	6	Ryan, Deborah H.
1995		I	8	3	E	L		64	27	5	Ryan, Deborah H.
1996		I	8	3	E	L		64	26	7	Ryan, Deborah H.
1987		I	16	3	ME	L	To R32	40	26	5	Ryan, Deborah H.
1989		I	16	4	E	L	To R32	48	21	10	Ryan, Deborah H.
1994		I	16	3	ME	L		64	27	5	Ryan, Deborah H.
1997		I	16	4	W	L		64	23	8	Ryan, Deborah H.
1984		I	32		E	L		32	22	7	Ryan, Deborah H.
1985		I	32		ME	L		32	21	8	Ryan, Deborah H.
1986		I	32		E	L	To R32	40	26	3	Ryan, Deborah H.
1998		I	32	6	E	L		64	19	10	Ryan, Deborah H.

Year	M/W	Div	F	SD	Reg	BD	Bye	#T	W	L	Coach
VIRGINIA COMMONWEALTH											
1981	M	I	32	5	E	A		48	24	5	Barnett, J. D.
1983		I	32	5	E	L		52	24	7	Barnett, J. D.
1984		I	32	6	E	L		53	23	7	Barnett, J. D.
1985		I	32	2	W	A		64	26	6	Barnett, J. D.
1980		I	48	12	E	A		48	18	12	Barnett, J. D.
1996		I	64	12	SE	A		64	24	9	Smith, Charles H. "Sonny"
VIRGINIA MILITARY											
1976	M	I	8		E	A		32	22	10	Blair, William H., Jr.
1977		I	16		E	A		32	26	4	Schmaus, Charlie
1964		I	25		E	A		25	12	12	Miller, Louis F. "Weenie"
VIRGINIA POLYTECHNIC											
1967	M	I	8		ME	L		23	20	7	Shannon, Howard P. "Howie"
1976		I	32		ME	L		32	21	7	DeVoe, Donald E.
1979		I	32	8	MW	A		40	22	9	Moir, Charles
1980		I	32	7	ME	L		48	21	8	Moir, Charles
1996		I	32	9	MW	L		64	23	6	Foster, William C.
1985		I	64	9	E	L		64	20	9	Moir, Charles
1986		I	64	7	SE	L		64	22	9	Moir, Charles
1995	W	I	32	8	E	L		64	22	9	Alfano, Carol
1998		I	32	11	W	A		64	22	10	Henrickson, Bonnie
1994		I	64	8	E	A		64	24	6	Alfano, Carol
VIRGINIA STATE											
1982	M	II	24		SA	L		32	19	9	Laisure, W. Floyd
1988		II	32		SA	L		32	21	12	Deane, Harold A., Sr.
1988	W	II	16		SA	A		32	21	7	Bey, Leon Wright
1989		II	16		SA	L		32	22	5	Cummings, Bertha
1987		II	24		SA	L		24	21	7	Bey, Leon Wright
1990		II	32		SA	A		32	24	4	Cummings, Bertha
VIRGINIA UNION											
1980	M	II	1		SA	L		32	26	4	Robbins, Charles David "Dave"
1992		II	1		SA	A		32	30	3	Robbins, Charles David "Dave"
1991		II	3		SA	L		32	27	5	Robbins, Charles David "Dave"
1996		II	3	1	SA	A	To R32	48	28	3	Robbins, Charles David "Dave"
1998		II	3	2	SA	A	To R32	48	26	6	Robbins, Charles David "Dave"
1984		II	8		SA	L		32	27	6	Robbins, Charles David "Dave"
1979		II	16		SA	L		32	18	8	Robbins, Charles David "Dave"
1989		II	16		SA	A		32	27	4	Robbins, Charles David "Dave"
1993		II	16		SA	A		32	27	3	Robbins, Charles David "Dave"
1994		II	16		SA	A		32	26	3	Robbins, Charles David "Dave"
1995		II	16	1	SA	A	To R32	48	26	5	Robbins, Charles David "Dave"
1961		II	24		E	L		32	23	6	Harris, Thomas H.
1977		II	24		SA	L		32	25	5	Moore, Robert D.
1985		II	24		SA	L		32	31	1	Robbins, Charles David "Dave"
1986		II	24		SA	L		32	24	8	Robbins, Charles David "Dave"
1987		II	24		SA	A		32	25	7	Robbins, Charles David "Dave"

Year	M/W	Div	F	SD	Reg	BD	Bye	#T	W	L	Coach
1988		II	24		SA	A		32	25	6	Robbins, Charles David "Dave"
1982		II	32		SA	L		32	18	7	Robbins, Charles David "Dave"
1990		II	32		SA	L		32	27	4	Robbins, Charles David "Dave"
1983	W	II	1		SA	L		24	27	2	Hearn, Louis
1984		II	2		SA	L		24	22	5	Hearn, Louis
1982		II	16		SA	L		16	18	5	Cannady, Nathan
1998		II	48	5	SA	L		48	24	4	Golatt, Moses

VIRGINIA WESLEYAN

Year	M/W	Div	F	SD	Reg	BD	Bye	#T	W	L	Coach
1979	M	III	24		SA	A		32	23	6	Forsyth, Donald M.
1978		III	30		SA	A		30	17	13	Forsyth, Donald M.
1982		III	32		S	L		32	20	10	Forsyth, Donald M.
1993		III	40		S	A		40	19	9	Butterfield, Terry
1986	W	III	24		S	L		32	24	5	Jordan, Jack
1984		III	32		S	L		32	20	9	Dunavent, Mike
1988		III	32		S	L		32	20	10	Jordan, Jack
1989		III	32		S	A		32	20	9	Jordan, Jack

WABASH

Year	M/W	Div	F	SD	Reg	BD	Bye	#T	W	L	Coach
1982	M	III	1		GL	L		32	24	4	Petty, Malcolm "Mac"
1960		II	16		ME	L		32	13	7	Brock, Bob L.
1961		II	16		ME	L		32	15	7	Brock, Bob L.
1958		II	24		ME	L		32	12	9	Brock, Bob L.
1959		II	24		GL	L		32	11	8	Brock, Bob L.
1981		III	24		GL	L		32	19	6	Petty, Malcolm "Mac"
1980		III	32		GL	L		32	20	6	Petty, Malcolm "Mac"
1997		III	32	3	MW	A		64	24	5	Petty, Malcolm "Mac"
1998		III	32	3	MW	A		48	22	5	Petty, Malcolm "Mac"

WAGNER

Year	M/W	Div	F	SD	Reg	BD	Bye	#T	W	L	Coach
1958	M	II	16		E			32	18	9	Sutter, Herbert E.
1968		II	16		E		To R32	36	21	8	Sellitto, Chester
1969		II	16		E	L		32	18	10	Sellitto, Chester
1967		II	23		E		To R32	36	19	9	Sellitto, Chester

WAKE FOREST

Year	M/W	Div	F	SD	Reg	BD	Bye	#T	W	L	Coach
1962	M	I	3		E	A		25	22	9	McKinney, Horace A. "Bones"
1939			8		E	L		8	18	6	Greason, Murray
1961		I	8		E	A		24	19	11	McKinney, Horace A. "Bones"
1977		I	8		MW	L		32	22	8	Tacy, Carl R.
1984		I	8	4	MW	L	To R32	53	23	9	Tacy, Carl R.
1996		I	8	2	MW	A		64	26	6	Odom, Dave
1953			12		E(A)	A	To R16	22	22	7	Greason, Murray
1993		I	16	5	SE	L		64	21	9	Odom, Dave
1995		I	16	1	E	A		64	26	6	Odom, Dave
1981		I	32	4	ME	L	To R32	48	22	7	Tacy, Carl R.
1982		I	32	7	E	L		48	21	9	Tacy, Carl R.
1991		I	32	5	SE	L		64	19	11	Odom, Dave
1994		I	32	5	SE	L		64	21	12	Odom, Dave
1997		I	32	3	W	L		64	24	7	Odom, Dave
1992		I	64	9	W	L		64	17	12	Odom, Dave
1988	W	I	32		E	L		40	23	8	Sanchez, Joe

Year	M/W	Div	F	SD	Reg	BD	Bye	#T	W	L	Coach
WARTBURG											
1987	M	III	8		W	A		32	19	8	Levick, Lewis J. "Buzz"
1975		III	16		MW	L		30	22	6	Levick, Lewis J. "Buzz"
1991		III	16		W	L	To R32	40	23	5	Levick, Lewis J. "Buzz"
1958		II	24		MW	L		32	16	9	Bundgaard, Dr. Alex C. "Ax"
1959		II	24		MW			32	21	5	Bundgaard, Dr. Alex C. "Ax"
1957		II	32		FW	L		32	19	8	Bundgaard, Dr. Alex C. "Ax"
1960		II	32		MW			32	18	7	Bundgaard, Dr. Alex C. "Ax"
1989		III	32		W	A		40	21	8	Levick, Lewis J. "Buzz"
1993		III	40		W	A		40	18	8	Levick, Lewis J. "Buzz"
1992	W	III	8		C	A		32	23	4	Severson, Monica
1993		III	8		C	L		32	23	5	Severson, Monica
1990		III	16		C	A		32	22	5	Severson, Monica
1989		III	24		C	L		32	21	6	Severson, Monica
1991		III	32		C	L		32	20	7	Severson, Monica
1994		III	40		C	L		40	20	6	Severson, Monica
WASHBURN											
1994	M	II	3		SC	A		32	29	4	Chipman, Bob
1993		II	8		SC	L		32	27	5	Chipman, Bob
1992		II	16		SC	A		40	27	5	Chipman, Bob
1997		II	32	2	SC	A	To R32	48	24	9	Chipman, Bob
1995		II	48	3	SC	L		48	22	8	Chipman, Bob
1992	W	II	8		SC	L		32	27	5	Dick, Patricia D.
1993		II	8		SC	A		32	31	1	Dick, Patricia D.
1995		II	16	2	SC	L	To R32	48	24	7	Dick, Patricia D.
1991		II	32		SC	L		32	23	7	Dick, Patricia D.
1994		II	32		SC	L		32	22	8	Dick, Patricia D.
WASHINGTON											
1953	M		3		W(A)	A	To R16	22	28	3	Dye, William H. H. "Tippy"
1948			6		W	L		8	23	11	McLarney, Arthur
1951			6		W	A		16	24	6	Dye, William H. H. "Tippy"
1943			8		W	L		8	24	7	Edmundson, Clarence S. "Hec"
1984		I	16	6	W	A		53	24	7	Harshman, Marvel K. "Marv"
1998		I	16	11	E	L		64	21	10	Bender, Robert M., Jr.
1976		I	32		MW	L		32	22	6	Harshman, Marvel K. "Marv"
1985		I	64	5	W	A		64	22	10	Harshman, Marvel K. "Marv"
1986		I	64	12	MW	L		64	19	12	Russo, Andy
1990	W	I	8	1	ME	L	To R32	48	28	3	Gobrecht, Chris
1988		I	16	3	W	A	To R32	40	25	5	Gobrecht, Chris
1991		I	16	3	W	L	To R32	48	24	5	Gobrecht, Chris
1995		I	16	3	ME	L		64	25	9	Gobrecht, Chris
1985		I	32		W	A		32	26	1	Sake, Joyce
1986		I	32		W	A		40	24	6	Gobrecht, Chris
1987		I	32	8	W	L		40	23	7	Gobrecht, Chris
1989		I	32	5	W	L		48	23	10	Gobrecht, Chris
1993		I	32		W	L		48	17	12	Gobrecht, Chris
1994		I	32	8	W	L		64	21	8	Gobrecht, Chris
1997		I	64	11	W	L		64	17	11	Daugherty, June
1998		I	64	13	MW	L		64	18	10	Daugherty, June

Year	M/W	Div	F	SD	Reg	BD	Bye	#T	W	L	Coach
WASHINGTON & JEFFERSON											
1994	M	III	8		GL	L		40	22	3	Reiter, Tom
1985		III	32		MA	A		32	18	6	Unice, John
1998	W	III	48	6	MA	A		48	16	8	Staton, Vicki L.
1995		III	64		A	L		64	16	7	Staton, Vicki L.
WASHINGTON & LEE											
1978	M	III	16		SA	A		30	22	6	Canfield, Verne D.
1975		III	30		SA	L		30	15	12	Canfield, Verne D.
1977		III	30		SA	A		30	23	5	Canfield, Verne D.
1980		III	32		SA	A		32	14	15	Canfield, Verne D.
WASHINGTON (MD)											
1990	M	III	3		MA	L	To R32	40	25	6	Finnegan, Tom
1989		III	16		S	L	To R32	40	20	7	Finnegan, Tom
1986		III	24		MA	L		32	20	6	Finnegan, Tom
1984		III	32		SA	L		32	19	7	Finnegan, Tom
WASHINGTON (MO)											
1965	M	II	8		SW			32	21	6	Smith, Charles G. "Chuck"
1988		III	8		S	L		32	22	7	Edwards, Mark
1996		III	8	4	MW	A		64	23	6	Edwards, Mark
1963		II	16		GL			32	18	8	Smith, Charles G. "Chuck"
1987		III	16		S	L		32	21	7	Edwards, Mark
1989		III	16		MA	L	To R32	40	19	8	Edwards, Mark
1964		II	24		MW	L		32	16	8	Smith, Charles G. "Chuck"
1991		III	32		S	A		40	19	9	Edwards, Mark
1995		III	32	3	MW	A		64	23	4	Edwards, Mark
1997		III	64	5	MW	L		64	17	9	Edwards, Mark
1998	W	III	1	2	C	A	To R32	48	28	2	Fahey, Nancy
1994		III	2		C	A	To R32	40	26	4	Fahey, Nancy
1991		III	4		C	L		32	24	7	Fahey, Nancy
1988		III	16		C	L		32	21	5	Fahey, Nancy
1996		III	16		C	L		64	22	6	Fahey, Nancy
1990		III	32		C	A		32	25	3	Fahey, Nancy
1992		III	32		C	A		32	22	5	Fahey, Nancy
1993		III	32		C	A		32	22	4	Fahey, Nancy
1995		III	32		C	A		64	20	7	Fahey, Nancy
1997		III	64		C	L		64	19	7	Fahey, Nancy
WASHINGTON STATE											
1941	M		2		W	L		8	26	6	Friel, John B. "Jack"
1983		I	32	8	W	L		52	23	7	Raveling, George
1980		I	48	5	ME	L		48	22	6	Raveling, George
1994		I	64	8	E	L		64	20	11	Sampson, Kelvin
1991	W	I	48	11	MW	L		48	18	11	Rhodes, Harold
WAYNE STATE (MI)											
1993	M	II	3		GL	A		32	22	10	Hammye, Ron
1986		II	8		NC	L		32	23	8	Parker, Charles
1956			16		MW	L		25	18	3	Mason, Joel G.
1984		II	16		NC	L		32	21	9	Parker, Charles

Year	M/W	Div	F	SD	Reg	BD	Bye	#T	W	L	Coach
1992		II	16		GL	A		32	23	8	Hammye, Ron
1994		II	16		GL	A		32	25	5	Hammye, Ron
1970		II	32		GL	L		32	14	10	Gompert, Frank J.
1987		II	32		NC	L		32	20	10	Parker, Charles

WAYNESBURG

Year	M/W	Div	F	SD	Reg	BD	Bye	#T	W	L	Coach
1993	W	III	32		E	L		32	19	6	Phillips, Rob
1995		III	32		A	L		64	21	5	Jones, Julie

WEBER STATE

Year	M/W	Div	F	SD	Reg	BD	Bye	#T	W	L	Coach
1969	M	I	12		W	A		25	27	3	Johnson, Phil
1972		I	16		W	A		25	18	11	Visscher, Gene
1968		I	23		W	A		23	21	6	Motta, John R. "Dick"
1970		I	25		W	A		25	20	7	Johnson, Phil
1971		I	25		W	A		25	21	6	Johnson, Phil
1973		I	25		W	A		25	20	7	Visscher, Gene
1978		I	32		W	A		32	19	10	McCarthy, Neil N.
1979		I	32	7	MW	A		40	25	9	McCarthy, Neil N.
1995		I	32	14	SE	A		64	21	9	Abegglen, Ron
1980		I	48	7	W	A		48	26	3	McCarthy, Neil N.
1983		I	48	9	W	A		52	23	8	McCarthy, Neil N.

WENTWORTH TECH

Year	M/W	Div	F	SD	Reg	BD	Bye	#T	W	L	Coach
1997	M	III	64	8	NE	A		64	20	8	McShane, Harry

WESLEYAN (CT)

Year	M/W	Div	F	SD	Reg	BD	Bye	#T	W	L	Coach
1959	M	II	32		E			32	13	5	Wood, John L.

WEST ALABAMA

Year	M/W	Div	F	SD	Reg	BD	Bye	#T	W	L	Coach
1982	M	II	16		S	A		32	20	10	Murphy, Ed
1978		II	24		S	L		32	18	8	Brackett, Ken

WEST CHESTER

Year	M/W	Div	F	SD	Reg	BD	Bye	#T	W	L	Coach
1983	M	II	32		S	L		32	19	9	Voss, Earl
1995		II	48	6	E	L		48	17	10	Delaney, Dick
1997	W	II	32	2	E	L	To R32	48	22	7	Kane, Deirdre

WEST FLORIDA

Year	M/W	Div	F	SD	Reg	BD	Bye	#T	W	L	Coach
1998	W	II	32	3	S	L		48	25	5	Henry, Megan

WEST GEORGIA

Year	M/W	Div	F	SD	Reg	BD	Bye	#T	W	L	Coach
1983	M	II	16		S	L		32	22	7	Kaiser, Roger A.
1984		II	16		S	L		32	26	4	Kaiser, Roger A.
1987		II	16		S	A		32	26	5	Kaiser, Roger A.
1980		II	24		S	L		32	24	6	Kaiser, Roger A.
1981		II	24		S	L		32	23	5	Kaiser, Roger A.
1986		II	24		S	L		32	20	9	Kaiser, Roger A.
1975		II	32		SC			32	18	8	Kaiser, Roger A.
1998		II	32	5	S	L		48	21	8	Murphy, Ed
1997		II	48	3	S	L		48	23	6	Murphy, Ed
1992	W	II	16		S	A		32	26	5	Williamson, Jane
1994		II	16		S	A		32	22	7	Williamson, Jane
1989		II	32		S	L		32	25	4	Williamson, Jane
1990		II	32		S	L		32	19	8	Williamson, Jane

Year	M/W	Div	F	SD	Reg	BD	Bye	#T	W	L	Coach
WEST LIBERTY STATE											
1997	W	II	48	6	E	A		48	23	6	Ullom, Larry
WEST TEXAS A&M											
1998	M	II	8	1	SC	L	To R32	48	26	5	Cooper, Rick
1955			24		W(B)	A		24	15	7	Miller, W. A. "Gus"
1987		II	24		SC	L		32	24	7	Moss, Gary
1990		II	24		SC	A		32	25	7	Adams, Mark L.
1991		II	32		SC	A		32	25	7	Adams, Mark L.
1994		II	32		SC	A		32	20	10	Cooper, Rick
1988	W	II	2		SC	L		32	33	1	Schneider, Bob
1987		II	8		SC	L	To R16	24	27	4	Schneider, Bob
1997		II	8	2	SC	A	To R32	48	29	2	Schneider, Bob
1989		II	16		SC	A		32	26	3	Schneider, Bob
1990		II	16		SC	A		32	24	6	Schneider, Bob
1991		II	16		SC	A		32	30	2	Schneider, Bob
1992		II	16		SC	L		32	24	6	Schneider, Bob
1996		II	16	5	SC	L		48	28	3	Schneider, Bob
1995		II	32	3	SC	A		48	25	5	Schneider, Bob
WEST VIRGINIA											
1959	M	I	2		E	A		23	29	5	Schaus, Frederick A.
1960		I	12		ME	A		25	26	5	Schaus, Frederick A.
1963		I	12		E	A		25	23	8	King, George S., Jr.
1998		I	16	10	W	L		64	25	9	Catlett, Gale
1957		I	23		E	A		23	25	5	Schaus, Frederick A.
1965		I	23		E	A		23	14	15	King, George S., Jr.
1967		I	23		E	A		23	19	9	Waters, Raymond C. "Bucky"
1955			24		E(B)	A		24	19	11	Schaus, Frederick A.
1958		I	24		E	A		24	26	2	Schaus, Frederick A.
1956			25		E	A		25	21	9	Schaus, Frederick A.
1962		I	25		E	A		25	24	6	King, George S., Jr.
1982		I	32	5	W	L		48	27	4	Catlett, Gale
1984		I	32	11	ME	A		53	20	12	Catlett, Gale
1989		I	32	7	E	L		64	26	5	Catlett, Gale
1983		I	48	7	E	A		52	23	8	Catlett, Gale
1986		I	64	9	E	L		64	22	11	Catlett, Gale
1987		I	64	7	E	L		64	23	8	Catlett, Gale
1992		I	64	12	E	L		64	20	12	Catlett, Gale
1992	W	I	16	4	E	L	To R32	48	26	4	Blakemore, Kittie
1989		I	32	12	E	A		48	24	8	Blakemore, Kittie
WESTERN CAROLINA											
1996	M	I	64	16	W	A		64	17	13	Hopkins, Phil
WESTERN CONNECTICUT STATE											
1990	M	III	8		A	L	To R32	40	27	2	Campbell, Bob
1989		III	16		NE	L	To R32	40	25	3	Campbell, Bob
1986		III	32		NE	L		32	25	3	Campbell, Bob
1991		III	32		NE	L	To R32	40	22	6	Campbell, Bob

Year	M/W	Div	F	SD	Reg	BD	Bye	#T	W	L	Coach
1992		III	32		NE	L	To R32	40	20	6	Campbell, Bob
1996		III	64	7	NE	A		64	19	8	Campbell, Bob
1990	W	III	16		NE	L		32	24	3	Rajcula, Jody
1997		III	16		NE	L		64	25	5	Rajcula, Jody
1989		III	24		NE	L		32	21	7	Rajcula, Jody
1985		III	32		NE	L		32	21	5	Rajcula, Jody
1988		III	32		NE	L		32	19	9	Rajcula, Jody
1991		III	32		NE	L		32	21	6	Rajcula, Jody
1992		III	32		MA	L		32	21	5	Rajcula, Jody
1993		III	32		NE	L		32	20	5	Rajcula, Jody
1994		III	32		NE	A	To R32	40	23	4	Rajcula, Jody
1998		III	32	4	NE	L		48	22	7	Rajcula, Jody

WESTERN ILLINOIS

Year	M/W	Div	F	SD	Reg	BD	Bye	#T	W	L	Coach
1980	M	II	16		NC	L		32	19	10	Margenthaler, Jack
1981		II	16		GL	L		32	21	8	Margenthaler, Jack
1959		II	32		SW	L		32	16	11	Morley, Leroy "Stix"
1995	W	I	64	14	W	A		64	17	12	Miller, Regina

WESTERN KENTUCKY

Year	M/W	Div	F	SD	Reg	BD	Bye	#T	W	L	Coach
1971	M	I	3		ME	A		25	24	6	Oldham, John O.
1940			8		E	L		8	24	6	Diddle, Edgar A., Sr.
1960		I	12		ME	A		25	21	7	Diddle, Edgar A., Sr.
1966		I	12		ME	A		22	25	3	Oldham, John O.
1962		I	16		ME	A		25	17	10	Diddle, Edgar A., Sr.
1978		I	16		ME	A		32	16	14	Richards, Jim
1993		I	16	7	SE	A		64	26	6	Willard, Ralph
1967		I	23		ME	A		23	23	3	Oldham, John O.
1970		I	25		ME	A		25	22	3	Oldham, John O.
1976		I	32		ME	A		32	20	9	Richards, Jim
1986		I	32	8	SE	L		64	23	8	Haskins, Clem S.
1987		I	32	10	E	L		64	29	9	Arnold, Murray
1995		I	32	8	MW	A		64	27	4	Kilcullen, Matt
1980		I	48	10	ME	A		48	21	8	Keady, Lloyd Eugene "Gene"
1981		I	48	10	ME	A		48	21	8	Haskins, Clem S.
1994		I	64	11	MW	L		64	20	11	Willard, Ralph
1992	W	I	2	4	ME	A	To R32	48	27	8	Sanderford, Paul
1985		I	3		ME	L		32	28	6	Sanderford, Paul
1986		I	3		E	A	To R32	40	32	4	Sanderford, Paul
1991		I	16	4	ME	A	To R32	48	29	3	Sanderford, Paul
1993		I	16	4	E	A	To R32	48	24	7	Sanderford, Paul
1995		I	16	4	ME	A		64	28	4	Sanderford, Paul
1987		I	32	6	W	L	To R32	40	24	9	Sanderford, Paul
1988		I	32	5	ME	A	To R32	40	26	8	Sanderford, Paul
1994		I	32	12	E	L		64	24	10	Sanderford, Paul
1998		I	32	8	ME	L		64	26	9	Small, Steve
1989		I	48	5	E	A		48	22	9	Sanderford, Paul
1990		I	48	9	ME	L		48	17	12	Sanderford, Paul
1997		I	64	10	W	L		64	22	9	Sanderford, Paul

Year	M/W	Div	F	SD	Reg	BD	Bye	#T	W	L	Coach
WESTERN MICHIGAN											
1976	M	I	16		ME	A		32	25	3	Miller, Eldon
1998		I	32	11	MW	L		64	21	8	Donewald, Bob
1985	W	I	32		ME	A		32	19	10	Hess, Jim
WESTERN NEW ENGLAND											
1990	M	III	40		NE	L		40	23	3	Broaca, Peter F.
WESTERN NEW MEXICO											
1997	W	II	32	4	W	L		48	19	7	Reid, Jason
WESTERN STATE (CO)											
1993	M	II	23		NC	L		32	25	5	Helman, Dr. Jay W.
WESTFIELD STATE											
1985	M	III	32		NE	A		32	10	15	White, Hilton
1993		III	32		NE	L	To R32	40	22	6	Lawless, Robert
1995	W	III	64		NE	L		64	21	7	Berger, Rick
1996		III	64		NE	L		64	22	6	Berger, Rick
WESTMINSTER (MO)											
1995	M	III	64	7	MW	A		64	14	14	McEwen, Jim
WHEATON (IL)											
1957	M	II	1		MW	A		32	28	1	Pfund, Leroy H. "Lee"
1958		II	4		GL			32	27	3	Pfund, Leroy H. "Lee"
1960		II	8		GL	L		32	16	10	Pfund, Leroy H. "Lee"
1959		II	16		GL			32	23	4	Pfund, Leroy H. "Lee"
1996		III	32	1	MW	A		64	25	2	Harris, William R.
1995		III	64	4	MW	L		64	21	5	Harris, William R.
1996	W	III	32		C	L		64	22	5	Baker, Beth
1998		III	48	6	C	L		48	19	7	Baker, Beth
1997		III	64		C	L		64	21	5	Baker, Beth
WHEATON (MA)											
1994	W	III	4		NE	L	To R32	40	27	4	Malloy, Del
1995		III	16		NE	A		64	24	5	Malloy, Del
WHITTIER											
1981	M	III	8		W	L		32	19	10	Jacobs, Dave
1979		III	16		W	L		32	16	12	Jacobs, Dave
1982		III	32		W	L		32	14	14	Jacobs, Dave
WICHITA STATE											
1965	M	I	4		MW	A	To R16	23	21	9	Thompson, Gary
1964		I	8		MW	A	To R16	25	23	6	Miller, Ralph H. "Cappy"
1981		I	8	6	MW	L		48	26	7	Smithson, Eugene
1976		I	32		MW	A		32	18	10	Miller, Harry E.
1985		I	64	11	E	A		64	18	13	Smithson, Eugene
1987		I	64	11	MW	A		64	22	11	Fogler, Eddie
1988		I	64	12	MW	L		64	20	10	Fogler, Eddie

474   College Basketball's National Championships

Year	M/W	Div	F	SD	Reg	BD	Bye	#T	W	L	Coach
WIDENER											
1978	M	III	2		MA	A		30	16	5	Rowe, C. Alan
1985		III	4		MA	A		32	25	7	Rowe, C. Alan
1987		III	8		MA	A		32	26	4	Rowe, C. Alan
1976		III	14		MA	A		28	22	7	Rowe, C. Alan
1982		III	16		MA	A		32	23	6	Rowe, C. Alan
1983		III	16		MA	A		32	21	8	Rowe, C. Alan
1975		III	23		MA	L		30	19	8	Rowe, C. Alan
1977		III	30		MA	A		30	20	9	Rowe, C. Alan
1997		III	32	1	MA	A		64	23	6	Rowe, C. Alan
1972		II	36		ME			36	19	9	Rowe, C. Alan
1995		III	64	6	MA	L		64	18	9	Rowe, C. Alan
1982	W	III	16		None	L		16	19	7	Hagan, Gigi
WILKES											
1998	M	III	4	1	MA	A	To R32	48	26	5	Rickrode, Jerry
1995		III	8	3	MA	L		64	25	5	Rickrode, Jerry
1996		III	8	2	MA	A		64	28	2	Rickrode, Jerry
1997		III	64	5	MA	L		64	20	6	Rickrode, Jerry
WILLAMETTE											
1959	M	II	24		PC			32	18	9	Lewis, John R.
WILLIAM PATTERSON											
1977	M	III	8		SA	L		30	21	5	Adams, John K.
1985		III	8		SA	A		32	22	7	Adams, John K.
1975		III	16		SA	L		30	20	6	Adams, John K.
1980		III	16		SA	A		32	20	7	Adams, John K.
1981		III	16		MA	L		32	19	6	Adams, John K.
1983		III	16		SA	A		32	19	9	Adams, John K.
1984		III	24		SA	A		32	22	6	Adams, John K.
1997		III	32	3	A	L		64	20	8	Rebimbas, Jose
1995	W	III	8		MA	L		64	24	5	Dallessio, Jerry
1998		III	8	2	A	L	To R32	48	25	4	Shaughnessy, Erin
1997		III	16		E	L		64	24	5	Shaughnessy, Erin
1993		III	32		NE	A		32	18	9	Delehanty, Patty
1994		III	32		MA	L	To R32	40	23	4	Shaughnessy, Erin
WILLIAM PENN											
1981	M	III	24		MW	A		32	20	7	Richardson, Leon
1983		III	24		MW	A		32	19	7	Richardson, Leon
1979		III	32		W	L		32	20	7	Richardson, Leon
1986	W	III	8		C	A		32	22	7	Smith, Garey
1987		III	8		C	A		32	20	9	Smith, Garey
1985		III	16		C			32	21	7	Smith, Garey
1988		III	24		C			32	21	7	Smith, Garey
1984		III	32		C	A		32	17	11	Smith, Garey
WILLIAM SMITH											
1997	W	III	8		A	L		64	27	1	Begley, Glenn C.
1996		III	16		E	L		64	25	2	Begley, Glenn C.
1992		III	32		NE	L		32	24	4	Begley, Glenn C.
1995		III	32		E	A		64	23	3	Begley, Glenn C.

Year	M/W	Div	F	SD	Reg	BD	Bye	#T	W	L	Coach
1998		III	32	3	E	A		48	23	3	Begley, Glenn C.
1994		III	40		E	A		40	25	3	Begley, Glenn C.

WILLIAMS

Year	M/W	Div	F	SD	Reg	BD	Bye	#T	W	L	Coach
1997	M	III	3	1	NE	L		64	27	3	Sheehy, Harry
1998		III	3	4	NE	L		48	26	4	Sheehy, Harry
1961		II	8		NE			32	22	3	Shaw, Alex J.
1995		III	16	4	NE	L		64	23	4	Sheehy, Harry
1996		III	16	1	NE	L		64	24	3	Sheehy, Harry
1955			24		E(B)	L		24	14	4	Shaw, Alex J.
1959		II	32		NE	L		32	15	9	Shaw, Alex J.
1994		III	32		NE	L		40	22	4	Sheehy, Harry
1997	W	III	32		NE	L		64	20	5	Manning, Patricia

WINGATE

Year	M/W	Div	F	SD	Reg	BD	Bye	#T	W	L	Coach
1995	W	II	8	4	SA	L		48	25	6	Jacumin, Johnny
1996		II	8	3	SA	A		48	23	8	Jacumin, Johnny
1994		II	16		SA	A		32	27	2	Jacumin, Johnny
1997		II	48	3	SA	A		48	20	9	Jacumin, Johnny

WINSTON-SALEM STATE

Year	M/W	Div	F	SD	Reg	BD	Bye	#T	W	L	Coach
1967	M	II	1		ME		To R32	36	30	2	Gaines, Clarence E. "Big House"
1985		II	16		SA	L		32	16	12	Gaines, Clarence E. "Big House"
1966		II	22		SC		To R32	36	21	5	Gaines, Clarence E. "Big House"
1977		II	32		SA	A		32	17	11	Gaines, Clarence E. "Big House"
1984		II	32		SA	L		32	20	10	Gaines, Clarence E. "Big House"
1986		II	32		SA	L		32	15	12	Gaines, Clarence E. "Big House"

WISCONSIN

Year	M/W	Div	F	SD	Reg	BD	Bye	#T	W	L	Coach
1941	M		1		E	L		8	20	3	Foster, Harold E. "Bud"
1947			6		E	L		8	16	6	Foster, Harold E. "Bud"
1994		I	32	9	W	L		64	18	11	Jackson, Stu
1997		I	64	7	E	L		64	18	10	Bennett, Richard
1995	W	I	32	10	ME	L		64	20	9	Albright-Dieterle, Jane
1996		I	32	6	ME	L		64	21	8	Albright-Dieterle, Jane
1992		I	48	6	W	L		48	20	9	Murphy, Mary
1998		I	64	6	W	L		64	21	10	Albright-Dieterle, Jane

WISCONSIN: EAU CLAIRE

Year	M/W	Div	F	SD	Reg	BD	Bye	#T	W	L	Coach
1997	W	III	2		C	L		64	27	4	Stone, Lisa Anderson
1994		III	3		GL	L	To R32	40	23	6	Stone, Lisa Anderson
1989		III	8		GL	L		32	24	5	Stone, Lisa Anderson
1992		III	8		GL	A		32	23	5	Stone, Lisa Anderson
1995		III	8		GL	A		64	24	5	Stone, Lisa Anderson
1996		III	8		GL	L		64	25	4	Stone, Lisa Anderson
1993		III	16		C	A		32	22	4	Stone, Lisa Anderson
1990		III	32		GL	L		32	21	6	Stone, Lisa Anderson
1998		III	32	4	C	L		48	22	5	Stone, Lisa Anderson

WISCONSIN: GREEN BAY

Year	M/W	Div	F	SD	Reg	BD	Bye	#T	W	L	Coach
1978	M	II	2		NC	L		32	30	2	Buss, David R.
1979		II	2		NC	L		32	24	8	Buss, David R.
1981		II	4		NC	L		32	23	9	Buss, David R.
1976		II	16		NC	L		32	21	8	Buss, David R.

Year	M/W	Div	F	SD	Reg	BD	Bye	#T	W	L	Coach
1977		II	16		NC	L		32	26	3	Buss, David R.
1974		II	32		GL	L	To R32	44	20	8	Buss, David R.
1994		I	32	12	W	A		64	27	7	Bennett, Richard
1991		I	64	12	W	A		64	24	7	Bennett, Richard
1995		I	64	14	MW	A		64	22	8	Bennett, Richard
1996		I	64	8	MW	L		64	25	4	Heideman, Mike
1994	W	I	64	15	W	A		64	18	11	Hammerle, Carol
1998		I	64	14	ME	A		64	21	9	Hammerle, Carol

WISCONSIN: LA CROSSE

Year	M/W	Div	F	SD	Reg	BD	Bye	#T	W	L	Coach
1983	W	III	8		GL	L		32	13	9	Greene, Janet
1988		III	8		GL	L		32	22	7	Sheridan, Teri
1984		III	16		GL	L		32	19	8	Greene, Janet

WISCONSIN: MILWAUKEE

Year	M/W	Div	F	SD	Reg	BD	Bye	#T	W	L	Coach
1989	M	II	8		NC	L		32	24	7	Antrim, Steve
1960		II	24		GL			32	18	4	Rebholz, Russ
1982		III	24		MW	L		32	20	6	Voight, Bob

WISCONSIN: OSHKOSH

Year	M/W	Div	F	SD	Reg	BD	Bye	#T	W	L	Coach
1996	M	III	32	3	W	L		64	23	4	Van Dellen, Ted
1998		III	32	4	W	L		48	21	6	Van Dellen, Ted
1997		III	64	8	W	L		64	19	7	Van Dellen, Ted
1996	W	III	1		GL	L		64	31	0	Bennett, Kathi
1995		III	2		GL	L		64	28	3	Bennett, Kathi
1994		III	8		GL	A	To R32	40	24	3	Bennett, Kathi
1998		III	8	1	C	A	To R32	48	26	2	Ruder, Pam
1990		III	16		GL	L		32	17	7	Bennett, Kathi
1991		III	16		GL	L		32	21	5	Bennett, Kathi
1992		III	32		GL	L		32	18	6	Bennett, Kathi
1997		III	32		C	L		64	23	4	Ruder, Pam

WISCONSIN: PLATTEVILLE

Year	M/W	Div	F	SD	Reg	BD	Bye	#T	W	L	Coach
1991	M	III	1		MW	L	To R32	40	28	3	Ryan, William "Bo"
1995		III	1	1	W	A		64	31	0	Ryan, William "Bo"
1998		III	1	1	W	A	To R32	48	30	0	Ryan, William "Bo"
1992		III	3		MW	L	To R32	40	27	4	Ryan, William "Bo"
1993		III	8		MW	L	To R32	40	24	4	Ryan, William "Bo"
1994		III	16		MW	L		40	23	5	Ryan, William "Bo"
1997		III	32	1	W	A		64	24	3	Ryan, William "Bo"
1996		III	64	1	W	A		64	23	3	Ryan, William "Bo"

WISCONSIN: RIVER FALLS

Year	M/W	Div	F	SD	Reg	BD	Bye	#T	W	L	Coach
1989	W	III	16		GL	L		32	23	5	Bloom, Dennis
1988		III	32		GL	L		32	22	6	Bloom, Dennis
1995		III	64		GL	L		64	17	9	Thelen, Carol

WISCONSIN: STEVENS POINT

Year	M/W	Div	F	SD	Reg	BD	Bye	#T	W	L	Coach
1997	M	III	8	5	W	L		64	22	7	Bennett, Jack
1987	W	III	1		GL	L		32	27	2	Wunder, Linda
1991		III	32		GL	L		32	17	7	Egner, Shirley

Year	M/W	Div	F	SD	Reg	BD	Bye	#T	W	L	Coach

WISCONSIN: STOUT

Year	M/W	Div	F	SD	Reg	BD	Bye	#T	W	L	Coach
1992	W	III	32		C	L		32	19	7	Thomas, Mark
1993		III	32		C	L		32	21	4	Thomas, Mark
1994		III	32		GL	L	To R32	40	21	5	Thomas, Mark
1997		III	32		C	A		64	19	8	Thomas, Mark
1996		III	64		GL	L		64	17	9	Thomas, Mark

WISCONSIN: SUPERIOR

Year	M/W	Div	F	SD	Reg	BD	Bye	#T	W	L	Coach
1957	M	II	32		MW	L		32	13	9	Vergamini, Carl
1961		II	32		MW	L		32	15	8	Vergamini, Carl

WISCONSIN: WHITEWATER

Year	M/W	Div	F	SD	Reg	BD	Bye	#T	W	L	Coach
1984	M	III	1		MW	L		32	27	4	Vander Meulen, David
1989		III	1		MW	L	To R32	40	29	2	Vander Meulen, David
1983		III	4		MW	L		32	25	6	Vander Meulen, David
1985		III	16		MW	L		32	20	8	Vander Meulen, David
1996		III	16	8	W	L		64	19	9	Vander Meulen, David
1986		III	24		MW	L		32	24	4	Vander Meulen, David
1988		III	24		MW	L		32	22	6	Vander Meulen, David
1992		III	32		MW	L		40	19	9	Vander Meulen, David
1993		III	32		MW	L		40	18	9	Vander Meulen, David
1994		III	32		MW	L	To R32	40	21	4	Vander Meulen, David
1995		III	32	5	W	L		64	19	8	Vander Meulen, David
1997		III	64	2	W	L		64	22	4	Vander Meulen, David
1986	W	III	8		GL	L		32	24	4	Jones, Dianne
1983		III	16		GL	L		32	19	5	Jones, Dianne
1985		III	16		GL	L		32	21	8	Jones, Dianne
1993		III	16		C	L		32	19	7	Yeater, Julia
1984		III	24		GL	L		32	17	11	Jones, Dianne
1987		III	24		GL	L		32	20	5	Jones, Dianne
1995		III	32		GL	L		64	20	7	Yeater, Julia

WITTENBERG

Year	M/W	Div	F	SD	Reg	BD	Bye	#T	W	L	Coach
1961	M	II	1		ME			32	25	4	Mears, Ramon "Ray"
1977		III	1		GL	L		30	23	5	Hunter, Larry
1963		II	2		ME			32	26	2	Miller, Eldon
1976		III	2		GL	L		28	24	5	Hamilton, Robert D.
1983		III	2		GL	A		32	26	6	Hunter, Larry
1980		III	3		GL	L		32	29	3	Hunter, Larry
1987		III	3		GL	A		32	25	8	Hunter, Larry
1994		III	3		GL	L	To R32	40	30	2	Brown, Bill L.
1962		II	8		ME			32	21	5	Mears, Ramon "Ray"
1975		III	8		GL	L		30	20	8	Hamilton, Robert D.
1985		III	8		GL	A		32	27	4	Hunter, Larry
1990		III	8		GL	A	To R32	40	29	2	Hipsher, Dan
1996		III	8	1	GL	A		64	26	5	Brown, Bill L.
1959		II	16		ME			32	19	3	Mears, Ramon "Ray"
1974		II	16		GL	A		44	22	4	Hamilton, Robert D.
1979		III	16		GL	A		32	23	6	Hunter, Larry
1981		III	16		GL	A		32	28	3	Hunter, Larry
1989		III	16		GL	L	To R32	40	27	3	Hunter, Larry
1986		III	24		GL	L		32	23	5	Hunter, Larry
1969		II	32		MW	L		32	19	6	Miller, Eldon

Year	M/W	Div	F	SD	Reg	BD	Bye	#T	W	L	Coach
1972		II	32		GL		To R32	36	17	10	Hamilton, Robert D.
1982		III	32		GL	A		32	20	10	Hunter, Larry
1991		III	32		GL	A	To R32	40	26	3	Hipsher, Dan
1995		III	32	4	GL	L		64	21	8	Brown, Bill L.
1997		III	32	3	GL	L		64	23	6	Brown, Bill L.
1992		III	40		GL	L		40	23	6	Hipsher, Dan
1990	W	III	32		A	L		32	26	3	Evans-Smith, Pamela
1993		III	32		NE	L		32	23	4	Evans-Smith, Pamela
1994		III	32		A	L	To R32	40	24	4	Evans-Smith, Pamela
1998		III	48	5	GL	A		48	22	6	Evans-Smith, Pamela
1995		III	64		A	A		64	25	3	Evans-Smith, Pamela
1996		III	64		A	A		64	21	7	Evans-Smith, Pamela

WOOSTER

Year	M/W	Div	F	SD	Reg	BD	Bye	#T	W	L	Coach
1978	M	III	16		S	L		30	21	6	Van Wie, Alvin J. "AJ"
1971		II	32		ME	L		32	23	3	Van Wie, Alvin J. "AJ"
1973		II	32		GL		To R32	42	19	10	Van Wie, Alvin J. "AJ"
1992		III	32		GL	A	To R32	40	26	3	Moore, Stephen
1993		III	32		GL	A	To R32	40	21	7	Moore, Stephen
1995		III	32	2	GL	A		64	26	3	Moore, Stephen
1997		III	32	5	GL	A		64	23	6	Moore, Stephen
1998		III	32	1	GL	L	To R32	48	22	6	Moore, Stephen
1991		III	40		GL	L		40	25	4	Moore, Stephen
1996		III	64	6	GL	L		64	19	7	Moore, Stephen
1983	W	III	32		A	L		32	19	7	Nichols, Nancy "Nan"
1985		III	32		S	L		32	21	8	Nichols, Nancy "Nan"

WORCESTER POLYTECHNIC

Year	M/W	Div	F	SD	Reg	BD	Bye	#T	W	L	Coach
1985	M	III	8		NE	L		32	20	8	Kaufman, Kenneth J.
1982		III	32		NE	L		32	14	11	Kaufman, Kenneth J.
1984	W	III	24		NE	L		32	20	4	Chapman, Susan E.
1996		III	32		NE	A		64	23	6	Champion, Christa

WORCESTER STATE

Year	M/W	Div	F	SD	Reg	BD	Bye	#T	W	L	Coach
1977	M	III	30		NE	L		30	17	10	Hippert, Edward "Eddie"
1994		III	40		NE	A		40	18	10	Moore, Tom

WRIGHT STATE (OH)

Year	M/W	Div	F	SD	Reg	BD	Bye	#T	W	L	Coach
1983	M	II	1		GL	L		32	28	4	Underhill, Ralph
1986		II	8		GL	L		32	28	3	Underhill, Ralph
1979		II	16		GL	L		32	20	8	Underhill, Ralph
1985		II	16		GL	L		32	22	7	Underhill, Ralph
1976		II	24		GL	L		32	20	8	Jackson, Marcus
1980		II	24		GL	L		32	25	3	Underhill, Ralph
1981		II	24		GL	L		32	25	4	Underhill, Ralph
1982		II	24		GL	L		32	22	7	Underhill, Ralph
1993		I	64	16	MW	A		64	20	10	Underhill, Ralph
1987	W	II	16		GL	L		24	24	6	Davis, Pat

WYOMING

Year	M/W	Div	F	SD	Reg	BD	Bye	#T	W	L	Coach
1943	M		1		W	L		8	31	2	Shelton, Everett F.
1941			8		W	L		8	14	6	Shelton, Everett F.

Year	M/W	Div	F	SD	Reg	BD	Bye	#T	W	L	Coach
1947			8		W	L		8	22	6	Shelton, Everett F.
1948			8		W	L		8	18	9	Shelton, Everett F.
1949			8		W	L		8	25	10	Shelton, Everett F.
1952			8		W(B)	A		16	28	7	Shelton, Everett F.
1953			16		W(A)	A	To R16	22	20	10	Shelton, Everett F.
1967		I	16		W		A To R16	23	15	14	Strannigan, William M.
1987		I	16	12	W	A		64	24	10	Brandenburg, Jim
1958		I	24		W	A		24	13	14	Shelton, Everett F.
1981		I	32	5	W	A		48	24	6	Brandenburg, Jim
1982		I	32	8	W	A		48	23	7	Brandenburg, Jim
1988		I	64	7	W	A		64	26	6	Dees, Benny

XAVIER (OH)

Year	M/W	Div	F	SD	Reg	BD	Bye	#T	W	L	Coach
1990	M	I	16	6	MW	L		64	28	5	Gillen, Pete
1961		I	24		ME	L		24	17	10	McCafferty, James J.
1987		I	32	13	MW	A		64	19	13	Gillen, Pete
1991		I	32	14	MW	A		64	22	10	Gillen, Pete
1993		I	32	9	MW	L		64	24	6	Gillen, Pete
1997		I	32	7	MW	L		64	23	6	Prosser, "Skip"
1983		I	52	13	MW	A		52	22	8	Staak, Bob
1986		I	64	12	SE	A		64	25	5	Gillen, Pete
1988		I	64	11	MW	A		64	26	4	Gillen, Pete
1989		I	64	14	SE	A		64	21	12	Gillen, Pete
1995		I	64	11	SE	L		64	23	5	Prosser, "Skip"
1998		I	64	6	E	A		64	22	8	Prosser, "Skip"
1993	W	I	48		MW	A		48	21	9	Ehlen, Mark

YALE

Year	M/W	Div	F	SD	Reg	BD	Bye	#T	W	L	Coach
1949	M		8		E	L		8	22	8	Hobson, Dr. Howard A. "Hobby"
1957		I	23		E	L		23	18	8	Vancisin, Joseph R.
1962		I	25		E	L		25	18	6	Vancisin, Joseph R.

YORK (NY)

Year	M/W	Div	F	SD	Reg	BD	Bye	#T	W	L	Coach
1995	M	III	64	8	A	L		64	18	7	Saint John, Ronald
1996		III	64	7	A	L		64	18	10	Saint John, Ronald
1997		III	64	7	A	A		64	21	6	Saint John, Ronald

YORK (PA)

Year	M/W	Div	F	SD	Reg	BD	Bye	#T	W	L	Coach
1995	M	III	64	5	MA	L		64	20	8	Gamber, Jeffrey L.

YOUNGSTOWN STATE

Year	M/W	Div	F	SD	Reg	BD	Bye	#T	W	L	Coach
1972	M	II	16		ME	L		36	22	7	Rosselli, Dominic L. "Dom"
1966		II	22		ME	L	To R32	36	19	7	Rosselli, Dominic L. "Dom"
1961		II	24		ME	L		32	21	7	Rosselli, Dominic L. "Dom"
1962		II	24		ME	L		32	16	12	Rosselli, Dominic L. "Dom"
1963		II	24		ME	L		32	18	9	Rosselli, Dominic L. "Dom"
1964		II	24		ME	L		32	24	3	Rosselli, Dominic L. "Dom"
1977		II	24		GL	L		32	22	7	Rosselli, Dominic L. "Dom"
1970		II	32		ME	L		32	22	5	Rosselli, Dominic L. "Dom"
1975		II	32		GL	L		32	19	9	Rosselli, Dominic L. "Dom"
1998	W	I	32	12	E	A		64	28	3	DiGregorio, Edward
1996		I	64	15	W	A		64	20	9	DiGregorio, Edward

National Christian College Athletic Association

HISTORY: "The National Christian College Athletic Association was incorporated to provide a Christian-based organization that functions uniquely as a national and international agency for the promotion of ministry and outreach and for the maintenance, promotion, and enhancement of intercollegiate athletic competition with a Christian perspective."—*From the NCCAA Statement of Purpose and Function*

The NCCAA is an outgrowth of the National Christian College Physical Education Association which was organized in the early 1960s. Comprised of about 25 members, it functioned primarily as a source of information to the physical education directors of Christian colleges.

At its 1966 annual meeting at Malone College in Canton, Ohio, Norm Wilhelmi, then athletics director and basketball coach at The King's College (PA) proposed that the organization sponsor a post-season men's basketball tournament among its members. His reasoning was that since the schools were not large enough for NAIA or NCAA membership, there was no opportunity for post-season play. The suggestion was adopted, and the NCCAA began with Wilhelmi as president. The first tournament was held in Detroit in 1968, the same year in which the NCCAA was incorporated, with six invited teams participating.

In 1969, what later became the division I men's basketball tournament settled into a 22-year run in Chattanooga, Tennessee, under various sponsorships. For 1974, national competition in other sports was added. Division II for men was added in 1976, followed by division IIA in 1991. A single division for women was added in 1983. The men's division II, IIA, and all of the women's tournaments, and since 1992 the men's division I tournaments, have been held at various locations throughout the country—usually hosted by a member institution.

From humble beginnings, NCCAA basketball tournaments have become four, eight-team events, with full expense reimbursement to all participating teams. The organization serves over 10,000 student athletes in over 100 member schools and conducts competition in six sports for women and nine for men, including football.

TOURNAMENT DIVISIONS: **Men** Open: 1968-1975; I: 1976- ; II: 1976- ; IIA:1991- . **Women** I: 1983- ; II: 1983- .

DEFINITION OF DIVISIONS: I: Christian colleges; II: Bible colleges; IIA: Division II schools with fewer than 250 students

TOURNAMENT OPERATION: NCCAA tournaments, men and women (all divisions), have been a model of consistency. With never more than eight teams, they have always contested at least the first four spots. All eight places have been contested in men's divisions II and IIA since 1988 and since 1985 in both women's divisions. Men's division I began to decide the first six spots in 1991.

Official seedings began in 1977 for men when the top two seeds received byes in the six-team tournament. Beginning in 1981, all teams were seeded. Seeds for the women's tournaments apparently began in 1985.

By and large, teams have qualified for the national tournament by winning a region or district tournament. In some cases, the school that hosted the tournament received a bid. At-large bids have been used when there were insufficient region or district winners. Division IIA has always been an invitational tournament.

NOTES ON DATA COLLECTION: While seedings apparently began as early as 1977, data for many of the early years is not included because it is unavailable from either the association office or the participating schools.

Since information on the region or district winners is generally unavailable, information on the type of bid is not included.

There are missing won-lost records and coaches names. Most are the result of incomplete records at the schools. In other cases, the schools did not provide information to the several annual directories.

Tournament Results—Men

F	School	SD	Bye	W	L	Coach
1968						
1	Lee (TN)			30	4	Hughes, Dale R.
2	Grand Rapids Bible & Music		To R4	18	10	Unknown
3	Azusa Pacific		To R4	21	9	Hamlow, Dr. Clifford
4	Messiah			11	11	Drescher, Luke M.
6	Gordon (MA)			20	10	Murdoch, Harlan P.
	Grand Rapids Baptist			15	10	Raymond,
1969						
1	Azusa Pacific			26	7	Hamlow, Dr. Clifford
2	Bryan (TN)		To R4	19	12	Wells, Jack
3	Lee (TN)			24	9	Hughes, Dale R.
4	Barrington		To R4	17	12	Augustine, Jack
5	Grace (IN)			21	11	Kammerer, Glen 'Chet'
6	Bethel (IN)			13	12	Felix, Richard
1970						
1	Azusa Pacific			29	6	Hamlow, Dr. Clifford
2	Grace (IN)			26	6	Kammerer, Glen 'Chet'
3	Lee (TN)			23	6	Hughes, Dale R.
4	Bethel (IN)			16	15	Felix, Richard
8	Baptist Christian (LA)			12	13	Greene, Larry
	Barrington			13	14	Augustine, Jack
	Calvary (KY)					
	Nyack			15	17	Lawrence, Dr. Donald J.
1971						
1	Azusa Pacific			25	11	Hamlow, Dr. Clifford
2	Eastern Nazarene			26	5	Bradley, Carroll F.
3	John Brown			17	10	Haynes, Bill
4	Tennessee Temple			18	15	Foster, Bruce D.
8	Bryan (TN)			20	12	Dixon, Wayne H.
	Grace (IN)			18	10	Kammerer, Glen 'Chet'
	LeTourneau			18	10	Fratzke, Mel R.
	Taylor: Fort Wayne			19	8	Morley, Stephen H.
1972						
1	Azusa Pacific			26	10	Hamlow, Dr. Clifford
2	Tennessee Temple			19	12	Foster, Bruce D.
3	Trevecca Nazarene			19	9	Forraker, Chet
4	Eastern Nazarene			24	8	Smith, James H.
8	Baptist Christian (LA)					
	Bethel (IN)			9	16	Felix, Richard
	Messiah			19	12	Shaker, Marshall 'Mike'
	Trinity International (IL)			10	14	Van Dixhorn, Henry
1973						
1	Lee (TN)			31	6	Hughes, Dale R.
2	Azusa Pacific			28	7	Hamlow, Dr. Clifford
3	Eastern Nazarene			21	9	Smith, James H.
4	Grace (IN)			24	8	Kammerer, Glen 'Chet'

F	School	SD	Bye	W	L	Coach
1974						
1	Southern Nazarene			31	6	Poteet, Jim
2	California Baptist			X	X	Evans, Floyd C.
3	Messiah			20	11	Shaker, Marshall 'Mike'
4	Trinity International (IL)			15	15	Van Dixhorn, Henry
1975						
1	Olivet Nazarene			30	4	Ward, C. W. 'Butch'
2	Tennessee Temple			21	14	Foster, Bruce D.
3	King's (NY)			25	15	Wilhelmi, Norman
4	American Christian			26	15	Hauser, George
1976 DIVISION I						
1	Biola			23	9	Lyon, Howard
2	Southern Wesleyan			21	10	Hill, Lewis
3	Olivet Nazarene			23	7	Ward, C. W. 'Butch'
4	Geneva			15	19	Christopher, Jim
1976 DIVISION II						
1	Taylor: Fort Wayne			18	9	Morley, Stephen H.
2	Baptist Bible (PA)			19	8	Huckaby, James M.
3	Western Baptist			12	19	Hills, Tim
4	Toccoa Falls			14	14	Fowler, Richard A.
1977 DIVISION I						
1	Southern Nazarene	1	To R4	28	10	Poteet, Jim
2	Olivet Nazarene			22	11	Wilson, Frank
3	Tennessee Temple	2	To R4	28	6	Bishop, Ronald
4	Southern Wesleyan					Drennon, Craig
6	Biola			21	10	Lyon, Howard
	Geneva			13	19	Christopher, Jim
1977 DIVISION II						
1	Western Baptist			17	13	Hills, Tim
2	Baptist Bible (PA)			19	8	Huckaby, James M.
3	Johnson Bible			23	9	Morgan, Russell
4	Taylor: Fort Wayne			10	18	Morley, Stephen H.
1978 DIVISION I						
1	Biola			22	14	Lyon, Howard
2	Olivet Nazarene	1	To R4	24	9	Wilson, Frank
3	Lee (TN)	2	To R4	20	14	Rowan, Earl
4	Northwest Nazarene			23	11	Layton, Terry
6	Geneva			15	18	Christopher, Jim
	MidAmerica Nazarene			15	13	Smith, James H.
1978 DIVISION II						
1	Baptist Bible (MO)			13	15	Schepis, Mike
2	Baptist Bible (PA)		To R4	21	7	Huckaby, James M.
3	Ozark Christian		To R4	X	X	Larrison, Bill
4	Kentucky Christian			17	12	Damron, Dr. Donald R. 'Dick'
6	Mid-America Bible			22	12	Holley, Willie
	Trinity Bible			16	12	Carlin, Scott B.

F	School	SD	Bye	W	L	Coach
1979 Division I						
1	Tennessee Temple			30	7	Bishop, Ronald
2	Lee (TN)			17	13	Rowan, Earl
3	Southern Nazarene	2	To R4	18	21	Poteet, Jim
4	Point Loma Nazarene	1	To R4	26	11	Foster, Ben
6	Bethel (IN)			22	12	Drew, Homer
	Eastern Nazarene			22	10	Bradley, Ron
1979 Division II						
1	Baptist Bible (PA)		To R4	20	12	Huckaby, James M.
2	Valley Forge Christian			18	13	Jones, Paul
3	Kentucky Christian			22	8	Damron, Dr. Donald R. "Dick"
4	Taylor: Fort Wayne		To R4	15	14	Morley, Stephen H.
6	Baptist Bible (MO)			X	X	Schepis, Mike
	Mid-America Bible			19	9	Holley, Willie
1980 Division I						
1	Liberty			28	11	Gibson, Dale
2	Point Loma Nazarene	1	To R4	23	14	Foster, Ben
3	Lee (TN)	2	To R4	16	15	Rowan, Earl
4	Tennessee Temple			23	13	Bishop, Ronald
6	John Brown			15	13	Simons, Jeff
	Olivet Nazarene			15	13	Hodge, Ralph
1980 Division II						
1	Northwestern (MN)	2	To R4	21	11	Sulack, Dave
2	Baptist Bible (PA)	1	To R4	19	12	Huckaby, James M.
3	Central Bible			9	18	Hanson, Kirk
4	Kentucky Christian			22	11	Damron, Dr. Donald R. "Dick"
6	Mid-America Bible			14	16	Holley, Willie
	Valley Forge Christian			18	11	Jones, Paul
1981 Division I						
1	Tennessee Temple	1	To R4	24	17	Bishop, Ronald
2	Bethel (IN)	3		22	8	Drew, Homer
3	Lee (TN)	2	To R4	22	11	Rowan, Earl
4	Azusa Pacific	4		17	16	Hamlow, Dr. Clifford
6	Eastern (PA)	5		20	12	Young, Clifford E.
	LeTourneau	6		17	20	Fratzke, Dr. Michael L.
1981 Division II						
1	Baptist Bible (MO)			18	17	Reed, Roger
2	Northwestern (MN)			15	12	Sulack, Dave
3	Cincinnati Bible		To R4	27	3	Tuell, Gary
4	Baptist Bible (PA)		To R4	22	10	Huckaby, James M.
6	Kentucky Christian			15	13	Damron, Dr. Donald R. "Dick"
	Mid-America Bible			19	18	Holley, Willie
1982 Division I						
1	Tennessee Temple	1	To R4	31	8	Bishop, Ronald
2	Spring Arbor	3		23	14	Bockwitz, William
3	Concordia (OR)	4		22	11	Hewitt, Tom
4	LeTourneau	7		16	19	Bassett, Sheldon

F	School	SD	Bye	W	L	Coach
7	Bethel (IN)	2		28	6	Drew, Homer
	Bryan (TN)	5		14	17	Dixon, Wayne H.
	Eastern Nazarene	6		19	12	Perera, Jerry

1982 DIVISION II

F	School	SD	Bye	W	L	Coach
1	Baptist Bible (MO)	1		20	11	Fuller, Fred
2	Northwestern (MN)	3		16	14	Westlund, Dave
3	Baptist Bible (PA)	2		25	7	Huckaby, James M.
4	Central Bible	4		17	16	Hanson, Kirk
8	Cincinnati Bible	5		25	6	Tuell, Gary
	Circleville Bible	8		14	13	Walters, Mike
	Kentucky Christian	6		19	10	Damron, Dr. Donald R. "Dick"
	Mid-America Bible	7		19	7	Holley, Willie

1983 DIVISION I

F	School	SD	Bye	W	L	Coach
1	Tennessee Temple	1		28	7	Bishop, Ronald
2	Grace (IN)	2		32	5	Kessler, James C.
3	John Brown	4		15	17	Simons, Jeff
4	Azusa Pacific	6		17	18	Lawrence, Dr. Donald J.
8	Bethel (IN)	3		23	7	Drew, Homer
	Bryan (TN)	8		19	15	Reeser, John
	Houghton	7		19	9	Jack, David E.
	Warner Pacific	5		24	9	Bays, Gary R.

1983 DIVISION II

F	School	SD	Bye	W	L	Coach
1	Baptist Bible (MO)	1		24	14	Fuller, Fred
2	Northwestern (MN)	2		22	10	Bocken, Ron
3	Baptist Bible (PA)	4		23	12	Huckaby, James W.
4	Central Bible	6		17	20	Hanson, Kirk
8	Cincinnati Bible	3		24	7	Tuell, Gary
	Circleville Bible	8		19	11	Leatherwood, Joe
	Kentucky Christian	5		21	8	Damron, Dr. Donald R. "Dick"
	Mid-America Bible	7		22	10	Holley, Willie

1984 DIVISION I

F	School	SD	Bye	W	L	Coach
1	Biola	2		25	6	Lyon, Howard
2	Tennessee Temple	1		33	2	Bishop, Ronald
3	Judson (IL)	6		24	9	Harris, Sam
4	Western Baptist	3		19	17	Collins, Tim
8	Faulkner	8		8	25	Naylor, Jim
	Geneva	3		23	12	Erickson, Lee W.
	LeTourneau	7		15	12	Bassett, Sheldon
	Spring Arbor	4		19	15	Bockwitz, William

1984 DIVISION II

F	School	SD	Bye	W	L	Coach
1	Baptist Bible (MO)	3		17	13	Smith, Gary
2	Cincinnati Bible	1		32	3	Tuell, Gary
3	Central Bible	5		13	20	Hanson, Kirk
4	Baptist Bible (PA)	2		23	7	Huckaby, James M.
8	Arlington Baptist	7		X	X	Jones, Dr. Griffin
	Johnson Bible	6		19	12	Karnes, Douglas
	Northwest Assemblies	8		X	X	Brown, John
	Northwestern (MN)	4		15	17	Bocken, Ron

F	School	SD	Bye	W	L	Coach
1985 Division I						
1	Point Loma Nazarene	2		28	8	Foster, Ben
2	Tennessee Temple	1		29	4	Bishop, Ronald
3	George Fox	3		27	7	Vernon, Mark
4	Taylor	4		27	10	Patterson, Paul
8	Bartlesville Wesleyan	8		19	11	Maness, Donald
	Covenant	5		17	14	Fitzgerald, Gene
	Nyack	7		25	8	Slocum, Jerry
	Olivet Nazarene	6		19	10	Hodge, Ralph
1985 Division II						
1	Cincinnati Bible	1		32	3	Wallingford, Tony
2	Central Bible	2		23	14	Hanson, Kirk
3	Baptist Bible (PA)	4		22	16	Huckaby, James M.
4	Northwestern (MN)	3		17	13	Bocken, Ron
8	Baptist Bible (MO)	5		X	X	Beck, Hilly
	Johnson Bible	7		19	8	Karnes, Douglas
	Mid-America Bible	6		13	17	Holley, Willie
	Multnomah Bible	8		16	12	Skagen, James C.
1986 Division I						
1	Point Loma Nazarene	1		27	7	Foster, Ben
2	Western Baptist	2		29	10	Collins, Tim
3	Tennessee Temple	4		21	11	Bishop, Ronald
4	Grace (IN)	3		27	10	Kessler, James C.
8	Eastern (PA)	7		X	X	Young, Clifford E.
	John Brown	6		13	13	Bassett, Sheldon
	Lee (TN)	8		19	20	Steele, Randy
	Olivet Nazarene	5		15	18	Hodge, Ralph
1986 Division II						
1	Cincinnati Bible	1		35	2	Wallingford, Tony
2	Central Bible	2		23	14	Hanson, Kirk
3	Mid-America Bible	3		22	12	Holley, Willie
4	Multnomah Bible	5		23	8	Skagen, James C.
5	Baptist Bible (MO)	8		13	21	Smith, Gary
6	Maranatha Baptist Bible (WI)	6		5	16	Terrill, Jerry
7	Valley Forge Christian	4		24	8	Mioni, Dominick
8	Johnson Bible	7		18	13	Karnes, Douglas
1987 Division I						
1	Point Loma Nazarene	2		25	10	Foster, Ben
2	Eastern (PA)	5		28	11	Ware, Nate
3	Bethel (IN)	6		25	9	Drew, Homer
4	Covenant	8		17	14	Fitzgerald, Gene
8	Bartlesville Wesleyan	7		15	16	Dunn, Dan
	George Fox	1		27	6	Vernon, Mark
	Lee (TN)	3		23	7	Steele, Randy
	Malone	4		18	14	Smith, Harold T.

F	School	SD	Bye	W	L	Coach
1987 Division II						
1	Cincinnati Bible	1		29	5	Wallingford, Tony
2	Multnomah Bible	7				Doherty, Jim
3	Baptist Bible (MO)	6		16	17	Smith, Gary
4	Johnson Bible	4		22	7	Karnes, Douglas
5	Central Bible	2		23	14	Hanson, Kirk
6	Crown (MN)	8		X	X	Pierce, Bud
7	Bay Ridge Christian	5		X	X	Mayshock, J. Anthony
8	Valley Forge Christian	3		22	10	Engle, Mark
1988 Division I						
1	Tennessee Temple	4		26	13	Bishop, Ronald
2	Cedarville	2		23	12	Callan, Dr. Donald
3	Biola	1		31	5	Lyon, Howard
4	Lee (TN)	3		24	11	Steele, Randy
8	Bartlesville Wesleyan	7		19	13	Dunn, Dan
	Bethel (IN)	5		25	11	Lightfoot, Mike
	King's (NY)	8		19	15	Harris, William R.
	Western Baptist	6		19	17	Hills, Tim
1988 Division II						
1	Kentucky Christian	2		26	8	Kirk, Randy
2	Valley Forge Christian	5		22	8	Engle, Mark
3	Bay Ridge Christian	3		X	X	Mayshock, J. Anthony
4	Pacific Christian	1		30	7	Erickson, Lee W.
5	Jimmy Swaggart Bible	7		21	14	Boone, Dr. Jerry
6	North Central Bible	4		22	13	Myers, Dennis
7	Multnomah Bible	6		15	15	Skagen, James C.
8	Johnson Bible	8		17	11	Karnes, Douglas
1989 Division I						
1	Tennessee Temple	5		25	11	Bishop, Ronald
2	Mount Vernon Nazarene	3		23	14	Balikian, Bernie
3	Western Baptist	2		26	15	Hills, Tim
4	Bethel (IN)	8		30	9	Lightfoot, Mike
8	Bartlesville Wesleyan	7		18	9	Dunn, Dan
	Geneva	6		20	15	Slocum, Jerry
	Lee (TN)	4		25	9	Steele, Randy
	Southern California College	1		29	5	Reynolds, Bill
1989 Division II						
1	Kentucky Christian	1		27	5	Kirk, Randy
2	Pacific Christian	2		32	10	Erickson, Lee W.
3	Bay Ridge Christian	3		X	X	Mayshock, J. Anthony
4	Central Bible	4		24	12	Hanson, Kirk
5	Baptist Bible (PA)	5		24	11	Howard, Russ
6	Pillsbury Baptist Bilble	7		13	17	Johnson, Richard "Rick"
7	Multnomah Bible	6				Skagen, James C.
8	Jimmy Swaggart Bible	8		9	25	Boone, Dr. Jerry

F	School	SD	Bye	W	L	Coach
1990 Division I						
1	Christian Heritage	1		33	6	Nater, Swen E.
2	Cedarville	3		24	13	Callan, Dr. Donald
3	Bethel (IN)	4		30	7	Lightfoot, Mike
4	Tennessee Temple	2		23	16	Bishop, Ronald
8	Colorado Christian	5		20	10	Evans, Frank
	Concordia (OR)	8		14	21	Schieldheisz, Dr. Joel
	Milligan	6		27	9	Wallingford, Tony
	Nyack	7		21	13	Fleming, Scott
1990 Division II						
1	Maranatha Baptist Bible (WI)			18	8	Terrill, Jerry
2	Pacific Christian			X	X	Erickson, Lee W.
3	Kentucky Christian			23	13	Kirk, Randy
4	Central Bible			22	14	Hanson, Kirk
5	Baptist Bible (PA)			28	7	Howard, Russ
6	Jimmy Swaggart Bible			22	11	Boone, Dr. Jerry
7	Northwest Assemblies			X	X	Filan, Doug
8	Southeastern Assemblies			21	13	Laing, Scott
1991 Division I						
1	John Brown	4		25	8	Sheehy, John
2	Master's	2		22	12	Hankinson, Mel
3	Malone	1		28	4	Smith, Harold T.
4	Tennessee Temple	3		18	15	Bishop, Ronald
5	Concordia (OR)	7		18	16	Schieldheisz, Dr. Joel
6	Lee (TN)	8		19	13	Steele, Randy
8	Bethel (IN)	5		22	9	Lightfoot, Mike
	King's (NY)	6		26	8	Harris, William R.
1991 Division II						
1	Kentucky Christian	5		20	13	Damron, Dr. Donald R. 'Dick'
2	Northwest Assemblies	7		19	13	Filan, Doug
3	Baptist Bible (PA)	3		22	8	Howard, Russ
4	Maranatha Baptist Bible (WI)	1		19	10	Terrill, Jerry
5	Jimmy Swaggart Bible	6		27	9	Boone, Dr. Jerry
6	Central Bible	4		22	15	Hanson, Kirk
7	Southeastern Assemblies	2		27	8	Laing, Scott
8	Moody Bible	8		X	X	Gaffney, Greg
1991 Division IIA						
1	Trinity International (FL)			15	14	Rutherford, Robert
2	Atlanta Christian			19	7	Kaiser, Richard 'Rick'
3	Hillsdale Free Will Baptist			23	11	Lisenbee, Tim
4	Grace Bible (MI)			10	13	Grube, David
1992 Division I						
1	Bethel (IN)	4		29	10	Lightfoot, Mike
2	Master's	2		23	12	Hankinson, Mel
3	Lee (TN)	6		24	14	Steele, Randy
4	Cedarville	1		27	7	Callan, Dr. Donald

F	School	SD	Bye	W	L	Coach
5	Geneva	3		26	8	Slocum, Jerry
6	Western Baptist	5		19	18	Hills, Tim
8	Indiana Wesleyan	8		10	27	Bireline, Dave
	Missouri Baptist	7		19	18	Pitzer, Lowell S.

1992 DIVISION II

1	Baptist Bible (PA)	3		20	7	Howard, Russ
2	Clearwater Christian	5		25	10	Wubbena, Del
3	Central Bible	2		27	9	Hanson, Kirk
4	Northwest Assemblies	1		24	12	Filan, Doug
5	Cincinnati Bible	8		20	18	Corrona, Jim
6	Pillsbury Baptist Bible	6		10	21	Johnson, Richard "Rick"
7	Taylor: Fort Wayne	7		19	11	Hamilton, Marvin E. "Bud"
8	San Jose Christian	4		23	17	Miller, Glen

1992 DIVISION IIA

1	Latin American Bible (CA)	1		30	2	Elisaldez, Ken
2	Atlanta Christian	3		19	7	Kaiser, Richard "Rick"
3	Mid-America Bible	5		17	19	Holley, Willie
4	Hillsdale Free Will Baptist	2		10	8	Lisenbee, Tim
5	Grand Rapids Bible & Music	6		14	20	Elmer, Don
6	Circleville Bible	4		16	10	Gardner, Greg
7	American Indian	7		X	X	Grant, Timothy L.
8	Saint Louis Christian	8		8	22	Wolford, Danny

1993 DIVISION I

1	Bethel (IN)	2		30	9	Lightfoot, Mike
2	Lee (TN)	4		24	14	Carpenter, Dr. Larry
3	Oakland City (IN)	3		20	11	Sandifar, Michael
4	Master's	1		20	12	Hankinson, Mel
5	Bartlesville Wesleyan	6		21	14	Kent, "Rocky"
6	Western Baptist	5		16	20	Hills, Tim
8	Indiana Wesleyan	8		12	22	Bireline, Dave
	Roberts Wesleyan	7		18	13	Sisson, Dr. Kenneth

1993 DIVISION II

1	Northwest Assemblies	7		X	X	Filan, Doug
2	Baptist Bible (PA)	1		22	10	Huckaby, James M.
3	North Central Bible	6		17	12	Engle, Mark
4	Pacific Christian	4		25	13	Erickson, Lee W.
5	Clearwater Christian	3		25	7	Wubbena, Del
6	Mid-America Bible	5		25	14	Holley, Willie
7	Kentucky Christian	2		22	10	Damron, Dr. Donald R. "Dick"
8	Baptist Bible (MO)	8		18	20	Beck, Hilly

1993 DIVISION IIA

1	Atlanta Christian	1		17	14	Kaiser, Richard "Rick"
2	Grace Bible (MI)	6		15	11	Moore, Jimmy
3	Circleville Bible	5		15	12	Amlin, Tom
4	Southwestern Christian Ministries	7		18	18	Arthur, Mark
5	Grand Rapids Bible & Music	2		8	24	Elmer, Don
6	Saint Louis Christian	8		12	21	Wolford, Danny
7	American Indian	3		X	X	Grant, Timothy L.
8	Hillsdale Free Will Baptist	4		21	20	Lisenbee, Tim

F	School	SD	Bye	W	L	Coach
1994 DIVISION I						
1	Lee (TN)	5		24	14	Carpenter, Dr. Larry
2	Oakland City (IN)	3		22	6	Sandifar, Michael
3	MidAmerica Nazarene	8		20	17	Lamar, Jon 'Rocky'
4	Cedarville	2		21	15	Callan, Dr. Donald
5	Geneva	1		28	4	Slocum, Jerry
6	Indiana Wesleyan	6		17	14	Bireline, Dave
8	Cornerstone	7		17	19	Elders, Kim
	Nyack	4		23	13	Bailey, Dan
1994 DIVISION II						
1	Central Bible	1		28	9	Hanson, Kirk
2	Pacific Christian	3		28	17	Erickson, Lee W.
3	Northwest Assemblies	2		X	X	Filan, Doug
4	Clearwater Christian	4		16	13	Wubbena, Del
5	Baptist Bible (MO)	8		18	14	Beck, Hilly
6	Cincinnati Bible	7		12	22	Corrona, Jim
7	Northland Baptist Bible	5		14	12	Scott, Dennis
8	Piedmont Baptist	6		21	10	Franklin, Philip
1994 DIVISION IIA						
1	Grace Bible (MI)			19	10	Moore, Jimmy
2	Hillsdale Free Will Baptist			22	14	Lisenbee, Tim
3	American Indian			X	X	Grant, Timothy L.
4	Faith Baptist Bible (IA)			18	12	Walter, Dave
5	Calvary Bible			18	12	Miller, Steve
6	Atlanta Christian			14	14	Kaiser, Richard 'Rick'
7	Washington Bible			10	15	Ronson, Glenn
8	Circleville Bible			14	9	Amlin, Tom
1995 DIVISION I						
1	Indiana Wesleyan	7		17	16	Williams, Pat
2	Western Baptist	5		26	12	Hills, Tim
3	Northwestern (MN)	6		22	10	Smith, Joseph L.
4	Lee (TN)	1		26	12	Carpenter, Dr. Larry
5	Oakland City (IN)	2		18	12	Sandifar, Michael
6	Cornerstone	8		18	21	Elders, Kim
8	Bryan (TN)	4		21	17	Michalski, Morris
	Hannibal-LaGrange	3		17	17	Thomas, Kent
1995 DIVISION II						
1	Kentucky Christian	1		26	7	Damron, Dr. Donald R. 'Dick'
2	Clearwater Christian	6		22	7	Wubbena, Del
3	Central Bible	4		22	15	Hanson, Kirk
4	Free Will Baptist Bible	7		28	10	Deel, Byron
5	San Jose Christian	5		28	11	Miller, Glen
6	Baptist Bible (PA)	2		22	10	Show, Mike
7	Cincinnati Bible	8		12	21	Corrona, Jim
8	Mid-America Bible	3		22	12	Holley, Willie

F	School	SD	Bye	W	L	Coach
1995 Division IIA						
1	Grace Bible (MI)	1		19	12	Moore, Jimmy
2	Crown (TN)	2		24	8	Weber, Dr. Greg
3	Atlanta Christian	6		17	15	Griffin, Joe
4	Southwestern Christian Ministries	4		26	4	Arthur, Mark
5	Nebraska Christian	3		22	11	Lahm, Chris
6	Washington Bible	8		9	15	Fletcher, Rev. Brit
7	Faith Baptist Bible (IA)	5		15	14	Walter, Dave
8	Messenger	7		21	17	Stallman, David S.
1996 Division I						
1	Malone	3		20	16	Smith, Harold T.
2	Tennessee Temple	5		24	12	Johnson, Richard 'Rick'
3	Christian Heritage	2		16	18	Wilmore, Art
4	Indiana Wesleyan	8		8	24	Blum, Scott
5	Oakland City (IN)	1		18	13	Sandifar, Michael
6	Western Baptist	6		21	16	Rasmussen, Dennis
8	Bartlesville Wesleyan	7		19	14	Kent, 'Rocky'
	Greenville	4		21	8	Faulkner, Doug
1996 Division II						
1	Kentucky Christian	1		27	6	Sudlow, Eric
2	Central Bible	6		24	16	Hanson, Kirk
3	Maranatha Baptist Bible (WI)	7		11	17	Terrill, Jerry
4	Toccoa Falls	5		23	11	Martin, Lance
5	Clearwater Christian	3		20	9	Wubbena, Del
6	Mid-America Bible	4		21	15	Holley, Willie
7	Baptist Bible (PA)	2		19	12	Show, Mike
8	Southwestern Christian Ministries	8		26	16	Arthur, Mark
1996 Division IIA						
1	Manhattan Christian	2		22	8	Condra, Shawn
2	Hillsdale Free Will Baptist	4		13	17	Archer, Kelly
3	Southwestern (AZ)	3		15	18	Morley, Stephen H.
4	Grace Bible (MI)	1		14	22	Moore, Jimmy
5	Faith Baptist Bible (IA)	6		13	16	Walter, Dave
6	Atlanta Christian	5		17	15	Griffin, Joe
7	Arlington Baptist	8		8	24	Bosher, Clark
8	Practical Bible	7		13	17	Howard, Russ
1997 Division I						
1	Christian Heritage	2		23	12	Wilmore, Art
2	MidAmerica Nazarene	5		24	13	Lamar, Jon 'Rocky'
3	Lee (TN)	6		15	23	Carpenter, Dr. Larry
4	Oakland City (IN)	1		21	9	Sandifar, Michael
5	Roberts Wesleyan	3		21	16	Sisson, George
6	Trinity Christian	4		24	12	Fitzgerald, Gene
8	Indiana Wesleyan	8		12	21	Blum, Scott
	Northwest Assemblies	7		20	14	Mendoza, Wayne

F	School	SD	Bye	W	L	Coach
1997 Division II						
1	Kentucky Christian	1		21	12	Damron, Dr. Donald R. "Dick"
2	Toccoa Falls	2		29	6	Martin, Lance
3	Maranatha Baptist Bible (WI)	4		17	13	Terrill, Jerry
4	Baptist Bible (PA)	3		20	18	Show, Mike
5	Crown (MN)	8		27	14	Pearson, Troy
6	Simpson (CA)	7		14	12	Spaschak, Tom
7	Mid-America Bible	5		26	17	Holley, Willie
8	Central Bible	6		22	16	Hanson, Kirk
1997 Division IIA						
1	Southwestern (AZ)	2		21	8	Morley, Stephen H.
2	Nebraska Christian	4		21	8	Lahm, Chris
3	Grace Bible (MI)	3		12	14	Moore, Jimmy
4	Faith Baptist Bible (IA)	8		16	13	Walter, Dave
5	Southwestern Christian Ministries	1		26	15	Arthur, Mark
6	Pillsbury Baptist Bible	7		12	14	Davis, Paul
7	Manhattan Christian	5		14	14	Condra, Shawn
8	Central Christian (MO)	6		13	17	Cobb, Russell
1998 Division I						
1	Christian Heritage	2		25	11	Wilmore, Art
2	MidAmerica Nazarene	4		27	11	Lamar, Jon "Rocky"
3	Geneva	1		25	11	Santarsiero, Jeff
4	Faulkner	3		25	14	Sanderson, Jim
5	Tennessee Temple	5		27	9	Johnson, Richard "Rick"
6	Pensacola Christian	7		15	15	Goetsch, Mark
8	Northwestern (MN)	8		25	11	Smith, Joseph L.
	Oakland City (IN)	6		20	9	Sandifar, Michael
1998 Division II						
1	Mid-America Bible	3		32	8	Holley, Willie
2	Kentucky Christian	1		27	11	Damron, Dr. Donald R. "Dick"
3	Philadelphia Bible	7		15	12	Martindell, Don
4	Toccoa Falls	5		27	10	Martin, Lance
5	Maranatha Baptist Bible (WI)	4		14	15	Terrill, Jerry
6	Multnomah Bible	6		21	13	Reese, Chris
7	Central Bible	2		30	11	Hanson, Kirk
8	Trinity Bible	8		16	17	Wagler, Keith
1998 Division IIA						
1	Southwestern Christian Ministries	5		21	17	Arthur, Mark
2	Hillsdale Free Will Baptist	2		24	12	Archer, Kelly
3	Faith Baptist Bible (IA)	1		19	12	Walter, Dave
4	Arizona Bible	3		16	15	Kuyper, Tom
5	Southwestern (AZ)	4		16	13	Morley, Stephen H.
6	Nebraska Christian	6		16	14	Lahm, Chris
7	Saint Louis Christian	8		9	25	Wolford, Danny
8	Appalachian Bible	7		7	17	Barton, Tim

Tournament Results—Women

F	School	SD	Bye	W	L	Coach
1983 DIVISION I						
1	Spring Arbor			29	4	Dunckel, Darrell
2	Tennessee Temple			X	X	Stem, Randy
3	Lee (TN)			16	15	Unknown
4	John Brown			12	18	Pickering, Curt
8	Gordon (MA)			10	11	Zuidema, Mary
	Indiana Wesleyan			13	11	Hensler, Susan
	Messiah			16	7	Clelan-Blank, Nancy
	Trinity Christian			13	5	Cole, Lois
1983 DIVISION II						
1	Baptist Bible (PA)			23	5	Durrwachter, Nancy White
2	Valley Forge Christian			X	X	Baker, William J.
3	Kentucky Christian			X	X	Robertson, Barb McClone
4	Arlington Baptist			X	X	Cash, Durward M. 'Woody'
1984 DIVISION I						
1	Huntington			24	9	Freeman, Keith
2	Spring Arbor			25	9	Dunckel, Darrell
3	Lee (TN)			20	12	Souther, Orin A. 'Jack'
4	MidAmerica Nazarene			20	17	Hook, Norton
8	Gordon (MA)			13	8	Zuidema, Mary
	Messiah			16	9	Clelan-Blank, Nancy
	Tennessee Temple			33	2	Stem, Randy
	Trinity Christian			11	11	Cole, Lois
1984 DIVISION II						
1	Northwestern (MN)			19	10	Smith, Dan
2	Baptist Bible (PA)			16	9	Durrwachter, Nancy White
3	Johnson Bible			18	5	Morgan, Russell
4	Toccoa Falls			10	6	Shiffer, Paul
5	Northwest Assemblies			12	9	Brodin, Kristi
6	Taylor: Fort Wayne			7	11	Rupp, Deborah 'Deb'
1985 DIVISION I						
1	Lee (TN)	6		15	13	Souther, Orin A. 'Jack'
2	John Brown	1		20	12	Bassett, Sheldon
3	Eastern Mennonite	2		22	4	Brownscombe, Sandra
4	Spring Arbor	4		25	8	Dunckel, Darrell
5	Huntington	3		20	10	Freeman, Keith
6	Azusa Pacific	5		23	11	Hebel, Dr. Susan L.
7	Cedarville	8		6	21	Hunt, Dr. Karol
8	Trinity International (IL)	7		10	18	Girton, Marcy
1985 DIVISION II						
1	Northwestern (MN)			11	19	Smith, Dan
2	Johnson Bible			9	9	Morgan, Russell
3	Baptist Bible (PA)			16	14	Durrwachter, Nancy White
4	Taylor: Fort Wayne			15	3	Rupp, Deborah 'Deb'

F	School	SD	Bye	W	L	Coach
5	Kentucky Christian			9	9	Robertson, Barb McClone
6	Philadelphia Bible			23	8	Maccullough, Dr. Martha 'Marti'
7	Lincoln Christian			5	11	Morris, Larry
8	Piedmont Baptist					Clingerman, Ralph

1986 DIVISION I

F	School	SD	Bye	W	L	Coach
1	Evangel	3		21	13	Bowen, Lynn
2	Cedarville	8		11	13	Fires, Bob
3	Lee (TN)	5		21	14	Souther, Orin A. 'Jack'
4	Huntington	7		21	10	Freeman, Keith
5	Indiana Wesleyan	1		20	7	Roorbach, Peg
6	California Baptist	6		19	15	King, David F.
7	Eastern Mennonite	2		18	8	Brownscombe, Sandra
8	Trinity Christian	4		18	11	Ribbens, David L.

1986 DIVISION II

F	School	SD	Bye	W	L	Coach
1	Toccoa Falls	7		13	12	Shiffer, Paul
2	Johnson Bible	8		2	9	Morgan, Russell
3	Northwest Assemblies	6		16	10	Brodin, Kristi
4	Moody Bible	5		X	X	Unknown
5	Kentucky Christian	2		11	9	Schreiner, Dale
6	Philadelphia Bible	4		20	8	MacCullough, Dr. Martha 'Marti'
7	Baptist Bible (PA)	1		14	13	Spink, Dave
8	Taylor: Fort Wayne	3		14	7	Rupp, Deborah 'Deb'

1987 DIVISION I

F	School	SD	Bye	W	L	Coach
1	Spring Arbor	1		25	9	Dunckel, Darrell
2	Lee (TN)	3		20	17	Souther, Orin A. 'Jack'
3	Geneva	5		14	15	Gall, Kimerly
4	Trinity Christian	2		23	7	Ribbens, David L.
5	Huntington	6		21	12	Culler, Lori
6	John Brown	4		13	18	Augustine, Jack
7	Eastern (PA)	7		15	15	Hunter, Art
8	Olivet Nazarene	8		13	15	Doenges, Carol

1987 DIVISION II

F	School	SD	Bye	W	L	Coach
1	Moody Bible			X	X	Gaffney, Greg
2	Philadelphia Bible			25	2	MacCullough, Dr. Martha 'Marti'
3	Kentucky Christian			12	11	Schreiner, Dale
4	Toccoa Falls			14	8	Shiffer, Paul
5	Lancaster Bible			26	10	Figart, Dr. Tom
6	Maranatha Baptist Bible (WI)			10	12	Grooms, Vicki

1988 DIVISION I

F	School	SD	Bye	W	L	Coach
1	King (TN)	1		27	3	Nida, Al
2	Concordia (OR)	2		20	12	Kunert, Charles J. 'Chuck'
3	Huntington	4		20	11	Culler, Lori
4	Azusa Pacific	3		21	10	Hebel, Dr. Susan L.
5	Trinity Christian	7		16	13	Ribbens, David L.
6	Houghton	5		18	6	Lord, Harold 'Skip'
7	Olivet Nazarene	6		20	15	Parsons, Wendy
8	Bartlesville Wesleyan	8		10	19	Baldwin, Gary

F	School	SD	Bye	W	L	Coach
1988 Division II						
1	Northwest Assemblies	3		16	17	Brodin, Kristi
2	Moody Bible	1	To R4	X	X	Wartluft, Laurel
3	Kentucky Christian	2	To R4	11	12	Schreiner, Dale
4	Toccoa Falls	4		17	12	Shiffer, Paul
5	Baptist Bible (PA)	5		15	12	Holloway, Sherrie L.
6	Ozark Christian	6		X	X	Williams, Charles R.
1989 Division I						
1	King (TN)	1		28	2	Nida, Al
2	Cedarville	3		20	10	Fires, Bob
3	Lee (TN)	2		30	8	Souther, Orin A. "Jack"
4	Huntington	4		19	11	Culler, Lori
5	Northwestern (MN)	7		17	11	Smith, Dan
6	John Brown	5		16	10	Augustine, Jack
7	Trinity Christian	8		17	13	Ribbens, David L.
8	Houghton	6		16	7	Lord, Harold "Skip"
1989 Division II						
1	Kentucky Christian	4		13	11	Bender, Tom
2	Northwest Assemblies	3		4	26	Brodin, Kristi
3	Pacific Christian	2		23	11	Garcia, Barbara
4	Baptist Bible (PA)	1		18	7	Holloway, Sherrie L.
5	Ozark Christian	8		X	X	Williams, Charles R.
6	Toccoa Falls	6		13	10	Shiffer, Paul
7	Philadelphia Bible	5		18	9	MacCullough, Dr. Martha "Marti"
8	Moody Bible	7		X	X	Wartluft, Laurel
1990 Division I						
1	King (TN)	1		27	3	Nida, Al
2	Lee (TN)	2		28	7	Souther, Orin A. "Jack"
3	Tabor	6		15	16	Kliewer, Karl
4	Olivet Nazarene	4		23	10	Glass, Robyn
5	Bartlesville Wesleyan	8		19	12	Baldwin, Gary
6	Huntington	3		26	5	Culler, Lori
7	Grace (IN)	5		18	14	Ryman, Jerry
8	Geneva	7		10	19	Gall, Kimerly
1990 Division II						
1	Northwest Assemblies			11	18	Brodin, Kristi
2	Baptist Bible (PA)			16	9	Holloway, Sherrie L.
3	Moody Bible			X	X	Wartluft, Laurel
4	Kentucky Christian			15	10	Bender, Tom
5	Philadelphia Bible			22	5	MacCullough, Dr. Martha "Marti"
6	Toccoa Falls			11	13	Shiffer, Paul
7	Pacific Christian			X	X	Kappen, Kelley
8	Saint Louis Christian			9	6	Wolford, Danny
1991 Division I						
1	Huntington	3		24	4	Culler, Lori
2	Tabor	1		28	5	Kliewer, Karl
3	King (TN)	2		27	3	Nida, Al
4	Lee (TN)	4		19	14	Souther, Orin A. "Jack"

F	School	SD	Bye	W	L	Coach
5	Bartlesville Wesleyan	7		14	16	Baldwin, Gary
6	Olivet Nazarene	5		16	15	Glass, Robyn
7	Roberts Wesleyan	6		19	8	Faro, Michael
8	Columbia Christian	8				Fields, Terry L.

1991 DIVISION II

1	Northwest Assemblies	1		10	20	Brodin, Kristi
2	Baptist Bible (PA)	6		18	12	Holloway, Sherrie L.
3	Pacific Christian	5		18	14	Kappen, Kelley
4	Philadelphia Bible	2		17	12	MacCullough, Dr. Martha "Marti"
5	Kentucky Christian	7		15	11	Bender, Tom
6	Atlanta Christian	4		18	10	Griffin, Joe
7	Moody Bible	3		X	X	Wartluft, Laurel
8	Hillsdale Free Will Baptist	8		10	14	Braisher, Kelly

1992 DIVISION I

1	Huntington	1		24	8	Culler, Lori
2	Williams Baptist	2		18	13	Halford, Carol
3	Lee (TN)	5		18	20	Souther, Orin A. "Jack"
4	Covenant	3		22	16	Smialek, Tami
5	Bartlesville Wesleyan	8		11	22	Baldwin, Gary
6	Indiana Wesleyan	6		20	14	Porter, Terry
7	Roberts Wesleyan	4		13	13	Faro, Michael
8	Columbia Christian	7				Fields, Terry L.

1992 DIVISION II

1	Toccoa Falls	5		23	6	Shiffer, Paul
2	Atlanta Christian	7		6	8	Griffin, Joe
3	Kentucky Christian	3		20	6	Arnett, Ron
4	Northwest Assemblies	8		12	20	Brodin, Kristi
5	Pacific Christian	1		X	X	Kappen, Kelley
6	Baptist Bible (PA)	2		19	9	Holloway, Sherrie L.
7	Hillsdale Free Will Baptist	4		9	13	Braisher, Kelly
8	Moody Bible	6		14	14	Wartluft, Laurel

1993 DIVISION I

1	Williams Baptist	1		24	2	Halford, Carol
2	Oakland City (IN)	2		21	10	Sandifar, Denise
3	Lee (TN)	3		19	17	Souther, Orin A. "Jack"
4	Trinity Christian	5		19	13	Eastham, Sue
5	Concordia (MI)	8		8	23	Twietmeyer, Dr. T. Alan
6	Covenant	7		20	14	Smialek, Tami
7	Grand Rapids Baptist	6		18	14	Shuneson, Kevin
8	Roberts Wesleyan	4		15	18	Faro, Michael

1993 DIVISION II

1	Northwest Assemblies	1		17	11	Brodin, Kristi
2	Kentucky Christian	2		19	11	Arnett, Ron
3	Baptist Bible (PA)	5		13	15	Holloway, Sherrie L.
4	Pillsbury Baptist Bible	6		13	12	Traxler, Tim
5	Philadelphia Bible	3		23	6	MacCullough, Dr. Martha "Marti"
6	Toccoa Falls	4		19	11	Shiffer, Paul
7	Pacific Christian	8		16	12	Kappen, Kelley
8	Mid-America Bible	7		10	9	O'Brien, Tony

F	School	SD	Bye	W	L	Coach
1994 DIVISION I						
1	Mount Vernon Nazarene	3		23	10	Howald, Jeana
2	MidAmerica Nazarene	5		18	19	Kliewer, Karl
3	Bartlesville Wesleyan	7		16	16	Hoeck, Donald
4	Cedarville	1		15	18	Freese, Kathy
5	Indiana Wesleyan	2		29	8	Porter, Terry
6	Lee (TN)	4		15	21	Baldwin, Gary
7	Northwestern (MN)	6		20	8	Holm, Sherri
8	Concordia (MI)	8		6	23	Twietmeyer, Dr. T. Alan
1994 DIVISION II						
1	Northwest Assemblies	2		7	21	Brodin, Kristi
2	Kentucky Christian	1		21	7	Arnett, Ron
3	Toccoa Falls	4		19	11	Shiffer, Paul
4	Mid-America Bible	3		10	9	O'Brien, Tony
5	Philadelphia Bible	5		13	11	MacCullough, Dr. Martha "Marti"
6	Johnson Bible	7		9	7	Morgan, Russell
7	Northland Baptist Bible	6		15	10	Bowman, Reba
8	Simpson (CA)	8		9	11	Wingate, Lawrence
1995 DIVISION I						
1	Western Baptist	7		17	16	Williams, Terry
2	Bartlesville Wesleyan	5		21	11	Hoeck, Donald
3	Indiana Wesleyan	1		26	11	Porter, Terry
4	Cedarville	3		20	11	Freese, Kathy
5	Northwestern (MN)	4		23	7	Holm, Sherri
6	Oakland City (IN)	2		17	14	Sandifar, Denise
7	Judson (IL)	6		20	13	Gum, Tory
8	Roberts Wesleyan	8		10	19	Faro, Michael
1995 DIVISION II						
1	Kentucky Christian	1		24	9	Arnett, Ron
2	North Central Bible	2		14	9	Goodrich, Dr. Larry
3	Baptist Bible (PA)	3		16	8	Holloway, Sherrie L.
4	Emmaus Bible	4		16	3	Mertz, Merilee
5	Ozark Christian	8		15	7	Williams, Charles R.
6	Toccoa Falls	7		12	13	Shiffer, Paul
7	Johnson Bible	6		9	6	Roberts, Sherri
8	Philadelphia Bible	5		14	12	Landes, Bertie
1996 DIVISION I						
1	Western Baptist	5		24	11	Williams, Terry
2	Lee (TN)	2		22	14	Baldwin, Gary
3	Emmanuel (CA)	1		23	9	Bona, Mike
4	Geneva	3		15	16	Myers, Jackie
5	MidAmerica Nazarene	6		18	18	Kliewer, Karl
6	Cedarville	8		16	20	Freese, Kathy
7	Roberts Wesleyan	7		17	17	Faro, Michael
8	Olivet Nazarene	4		17	14	DeFries, Cathy

F	School	SD	Bye	W	L	Coach
1996 Division II						
1	Kentucky Christian	1		28	4	Arnett, Ron
2	Mid-America Bible	2		17	19	O'Brien, Tony
3	Ozark Christian	4		18	10	Williams, Charles R.
4	Baptist Bible (PA)	3		14	18	Holloway, Sherrie L.
5	Maranatha Baptist Bible (WI)	6		11	17	Morrison, Clayton
6	North Central Bible	5		18	9	Goodrich, Dr. Larry
7	Faith Baptist Bible (IA)	8		17	9	Nihart, Lanny
8	Johnson Bible	7		10	10	Roberts, Sherri
1997 Division I						
1	LeTourneau	1		30	4	Otwell, Mary Ann
2	Emmanuel (CA)	3		23	10	Bona, Mike
3	Oakland City (IN)	5		26	6	Sandifar, Denise
4	Lee (TN)	7		13	24	Baldwin, Gary
5	Roberts Wesleyan	6		22	12	Faro, Michael
6	Western Baptist	4		25	9	Williams, Terry
7	Olivet Nazarene	8		19	16	DeFries, Cathy
8	Geneva	2		22	12	Myers, Jackie
1997 Division II						
1	Kentucky Christian	1		30	5	Arnett, Ron
2	Mid-America Bible	2		18	17	O'Brien, Tony
3	Moody Bible	3		18	9	Fielitz, Cheryl A.
4	Ozark Christian	4		16	10	Williams, Charles R.
5	Practical Bible	6		14	9	Carman, Becki
6	Crown (MN)	8		20	9	Haller, Mickey
7	North Central Bible	7		10	17	Asberry-Lidquist, Tracine
8	Clearwater Christian	5		12	11	Dewitt, Kris
1998 Division I						
1	LeTourneau	1		24	10	Otwell, Mary Ann
2	Indiana Wesleyan	7		19	14	Porter, Terry
3	Oakland City (IN)	5		20	9	Sandifar, Denise
4	Mount Vernon Nazarene	6		19	18	Ely, Eric
5	Lee (TN)	4		16	21	Baldwin, Gary
6	Emmanuel (GA)	2		18	11	Bona, Mike
7	Northwest Assemblies	8		11	22	Brodin, Kristi
8	Trinity Christian	3		20	13	Schaaf, Barb
1998 Division II						
1	Kentucky Christian	2		22	13	Arnett, Ron
2	Mid-America Bible	1		20	15	O'Brien, Tony
3	Crown (MN)	5		15	11	Ague, Paul
4	Simpson (CA)	6		15	16	Dewey, Don
5	Maranatha Baptist Bible (WI)	4		13	16	Morrison, Clayton
6	Baptist Bible (PA)	3		23	10	Holloway, Sherrie L.
7	Clearwater Christian	8		14	9	Dewitt, Kris
8	Baptist Bible (MO)	7		10	19	Elliott, Dan

School Participation History

Year	M/W	Div	F	SD	Bye	#T	W	L	Coach
AMERICAN CHRISTIAN									
1975	M		4			4	26	15	Hauser, George
AMERICAN INDIAN									
1994	M	IIA	3			8	X	X	Grant, Timothy L.
1992		IIA	7	7		8	X	X	Grant, Timothy L.
1993		IIA	7	3		8	X	X	Grant, Timothy L.
APPALACHIAN BIBLE									
1998	M	IIA	8	7		8	7	17	Barton, Tim
ARIZONA BIBLE									
1998	M	IIA	4	3		8	16	15	Kuyper, Tom
ARLINGTON BAPTIST									
1996	M	IIA	7	8		8	8	24	Bosher, Clark
1984		II	8	7		8	X	X	Jones, Dr. Griffin
1983	W	II	4			4	X	X	Cash, Durward M. "Woody"
ATLANTA CHRISTIAN									
1993	M	IIA	1	1		8	17	14	Kaiser, Richard "Rick"
1991		IIA	2			4	19	7	Kaiser, Richard "Rick"
1992		IIA	2	3		8	19	7	Kaiser, Richard "Rick"
1995		IIA	3	6		8	17	15	Griffin, Joe
1994		IIA	6			8	14	14	Kaiser, Richard "Rick"
1996		IIA	6	5		8	17	15	Griffin, Joe
1992	W	II	2	7		8	6	8	Griffin, Joe
1991		II	6			8	18	10	Griffin, Joe
AZUSA PACIFIC									
1969	M		1			6	26	7	Hamlow, Dr. Clifford
1970			1			8	29	6	Hamlow, Dr. Clifford
1971			1			8	25	11	Hamlow, Dr. Clifford
1972			1			8	26	10	Hamlow, Dr. Clifford
1973			2			4	28	7	Hamlow, Dr. Clifford
1968			3		To R4	6	21	9	Hamlow, Dr. Clifford
1981		I	4	4		6	17	16	Hamlow, Dr. Clifford
1983		I	4	6		8	17	18	Lawrence, Dr. Donald J.
1988	W	I	4	3		8	21	10	Hebel, Dr. Susan L.
1985		I	6	5		8	23	11	Hebel, Dr. Susan L.
BAPTIST BIBLE (MO)									
1978	M	II	1			6	13	15	Schepis, Mike
1981		II	1			6	18	17	Reed, Roger
1982		II	1	1		8	20	11	Fuller, Fred
1983		II	1	1		8	24	14	Fuller, Fred
1984		II	1	3		8	17	13	Smith, Gary
1987		II	3	6		8	16	17	Beck, Hilly
1986		II	5	8		8	13	21	Beck, Hilly

Year	M/W	Div	F	SD	Bye	#T	W	L	Coach
1994		II	5	8		8	18	14	Beck, Hilly
1979		II	6			6	X	X	Schepis, Mike·
1985		II	8	5		8	X	X	Beck, Hilly
1993		II	8	8		8	18	20	Beck, Hilly
1998	W	II	8	7		8	10	19	Elliott, Dan

BAPTIST BIBLE (PA)

Year	M/W	Div	F	SD	Bye	#T	W	L	Coach
1979	M	II	1		To R4	6	20	12	Huckaby, James M.
1992		II	1	3		8	20	7	Howard, Russ
1976		II	2			4	19	8	Huckaby, James M.
1977		II	2			4	19	8	Huckaby, James M.
1978		II	2		To R4	6	21	7	Huckaby, James M.
1980		II	2	1	To R4	6	19	12	Huckaby, James M.
1993		II	2	1		8	22	10	Huckaby, James M.
1982		II	3	2		8	25	7	Huckaby, James M.
1983		II	3	4		8	23	12	Huckaby, James M.
1985		II	3	4		8	22	16	Huckaby, James M.
1991		II	3	3		8	22	8	Howard, Russ
1981		II	4		To R4	6	22	10	Huckaby, James M.
1984		II	4	2		8	23	7	Huckaby, James M.
1997		II	4	3		8	20	18	Show, Mike
1989		II	5	5		8	24	11	Howard, Russ
1990		II	5			8	28	7	Howard, Russ
1995		II	6	2		8	22	10	Show, Mike
1996		II	7	2		8	19	12	Show, Mike
1983	W	II	1			4	23	5	Durrwachter, Nancy White
1984		II	2			6	16	9	Durrwachter, Nancy White
1990		II	2			8	16	9	Holloway, Sherrie L.
1991		II	2	6		8	18	12	Holloway, Sherrie L.
1985		II	3			8	16	14	Durrwachter, Nancy White
1993		II	3	5		8	13	15	Holloway, Sherrie L.
1995		II	3	3		8	16	8	Holloway, Sherrie L.
1989		II	4	1		8	18	7	Holloway, Sherrie L.
1996		II	4	3		8	14	18	Holloway, Sherrie L.
1988		II	5	5		6	15	12	Holloway, Sherrie L.
1992		II	6	2		8	19	9	Holloway, Sherrie L.
1998		II	6	3		8	23	10	Holloway, Sherrie L.
1986		II	7	1		8	14	13	Spink, Dave

BAPTIST CHRISTIAN (LA)

Year	M/W	Div	F	SD	Bye	#T	W	L	Coach
1970	M		8			8	12	13	Greene, Larry
1972			8			8			

BARRINGTON

Year	M/W	Div	F	SD	Bye	#T	W	L	Coach
1969	M		4		To R4	6	17	12	Augustine, Jack
1970			8			8	13	14	Augustine, Jack

BARTLESVILLE WESLEYAN

Year	M/W	Div	F	SD	Bye	#T	W	L	Coach
1993	M	I	5	6		8	21	14	Kent, ʻRockyʼ
1985		I	8	8		8	19	11	Maness, Donald
1987		I	8	7		8	15	16	Dunn, Dan
1988		I	8	7		8	19	13	Dunn, Dan

Year	M/W	Div	F	SD	Bye	#T	W	L	Coach
1989		I	8	7		8	18	9	Dunn, Dan
1996		I	8	7		8	19	14	Kent, "Rocky"
1995	W	I	2	5		8	21	11	Hoeck, Donald
1994		I	3	7		8	16	16	Hoeck, Donald
1990		I	5	8		8	19	12	Baldwin, Gary
1991		I	5	7		8	14	16	Baldwin, Gary
1992		I	5	8		8	11	22	Baldwin, Gary
1988		I	8	8		8	10	19	Baldwin, Gary

BAY RIDGE CHRISTIAN

Year	M/W	Div	F	SD	Bye	#T	W	L	Coach
1988	M	II	3	3		8	X	X	Mayshock, J. Anthony
1989		II	3	3		8	X	X	Mayshock, J. Anthony
1987		II	7	5		8	X	X	Mayshock, J. Anthony

BETHEL (IN)

Year	M/W	Div	F	SD	Bye	#T	W	L	Coach
1992	M	I	1	4		8	29	10	Lightfoot, Mike
1993		I	1	2		8	30	9	Lightfoot, Mike
1981		I	2	3		6	22	8	Drew, Homer
1987		I	3	6		8	25	9	Drew, Homer
1990		I	3	4		8	30	7	Lightfoot, Mike
1970			4			8	16	15	Felix, Richard
1989		I	4	8		8	30	9	Lightfoot, Mike
1969			6			6	13	12	Felix, Richard
1979		I	6			6	22	12	Drew, Homer
1982		I	7	2		7	28	6	Drew, Homer
1972			8			8	9	16	Felix, Richard
1983		I	8	3		8	23	7	Drew, Homer
1988		I	8	5		8	25	11	Lightfoot, Mike
1991		I	8	5		8	22	9	Lightfoot, Mike

BIOLA

Year	M/W	Div	F	SD	Bye	#T	W	L	Coach
1976	M	I	1			4	23	9	Lyon, Howard
1978		I	1			6	22	14	Lyon, Howard
1984		I	1	2		8	25	6	Lyon, Howard
1988		I	3	1		8	31	5	Lyon, Howard
1977		I	6			6	21	10	Lyon, Howard

BRYAN (TN)

Year	M/W	Div	F	SD	Bye	#T	W	L	Coach
1969	M		2		To R4	6	19	12	Wells, Jack
1982		I	7	5		7	14	17	Dixon, Wayne H.
1971			8			8	20	12	Dixon, Wayne H.
1983		I	8	8		8	19	15	Reeser, John
1995		I	8	4		8	21	17	Michalski, Morris

CALIFORNIA BAPTIST

Year	M/W	Div	F	SD	Bye	#T	W	L	Coach
1974	M		2			4	X	X	Evans, Floyd C.
1986	W	I	6	6		8	19	15	King, David F.

CALVARY (KY)

Year	M/W	Div	F	SD	Bye	#T	W	L	Coach
1970	M		8			8			

Year	M/W	Div	F	SD	Bye	#T	W	L	Coach
CALVARY BIBLE									
1994	M	IIA	5			8	18	12	Miller, Steve
CEDARVILLE									
1988	M	I	2	2		8	23	12	Callan, Dr. Donald
1990		I	2	3		8	24	13	Callan, Dr. Donald
1992		I	4	1		8	27	7	Callan, Dr. Donald
1994		I	4	2		8	21	15	Callan, Dr. Donald
1986	W	I	2	8		8	11	13	Fires, Bob
1989		I	2	3		8	20	10	Fires, Bob
1994		I	4	1		8	15	18	Freese, Kathy
1995		I	4	3		8	20	11	Freese, Kathy
1996		I	6	8		8	16	20	Freese, Kathy
1985		I	7	8		8	6	21	Hunt, Dr. Karol
CENTRAL BIBLE									
1994	M	II	1	1		8	28	9	Hanson, Kirk
1985		II	2	2		8	23	14	Hanson, Kirk
1986		II	2	2		8	23	14	Hanson, Kirk
1996		II	2	6		8	24	16	Hanson, Kirk
1980		II	3			6	9	18	Hanson, Kirk
1984		II	3	5		8	13	20	Hanson, Kirk
1992		II	3	2		8	27	9	Hanson, Kirk
1995		II	3	4		8	22	15	Hanson, Kirk
1982		II	4	4		8	17	16	Hanson, Kirk
1983		II	4	6		8	17	20	Hanson, Kirk
1989		II	4	4		8	24	12	Hanson, Kirk
1990		II	4			8	22	14	Hanson, Kirk
1987		II	5	2		8	23	14	Hanson, Kirk
1991		II	6	4		8	22	15	Hanson, Kirk
1998		II	7	2		8	30	11	Hanson, Kirk
1997		II	8	6		8	22	16	Hanson, Kirk
CENTRAL CHRISTIAN (MO)									
1997	M	IIA	8	6		8	13	17	Cobb, Russell
CHRISTIAN HERITAGE									
1990	M	I	1	1		8	33	6	Nater, Swen E.
1997		I	1	2		8	23	12	Wilmore, Art
1998		I	1	2		8	25	11	Wilmore, Art
1996		I	3	2		8	16	18	Wilmore, Art
CINCINNATI BIBLE									
1985	M	II	1	1		8	32	3	Wallingford, Tony
1986		II	1	1		8	35	2	Wallingford, Tony
1987		II	1	1		8	29	5	Wallingford, Tony
1984		II	2	1		8	32	3	Tuell, Gary
1981		II	3		To R4	6	27	3	Tuell, Gary
1992		II	5	8		8	20	18	Corrona, Jim
1994		II	6	7		8	12	22	Corrona, Jim
1995		II	7	8		8	12	21	Corrona, Jim

Year	M/W	Div	F	SD	Bye	#T	W	L	Coach
1982		II	8	5		8	25	6	Tuell, Gary
1983		II	8	3		8	24	7	Tuell, Gary

CIRCLEVILLE BIBLE

Year	M/W	Div	F	SD	Bye	#T	W	L	Coach
1993	M	IIA	3	5		8	15	12	Amlin, Tom
1992		IIA	6	4		8	16	10	Gardner, Greg
1982		II	8	8		8	14	13	Walters, Mike
1983		II	8	8		8	19	11	Leatherwood, Joe
1994		IIA	8			8	14	9	Amlin, Tom

CLEARWATER CHRISTIAN

Year	M/W	Div	F	SD	Bye	#T	W	L	Coach
1992	M	II	2	5		8	25	10	Wubbena, Del
1995		II	2	6		8	22	7	Wubbena, Del
1994		II	4	4		8	16	13	Wubbena, Del
1993		II	5	3		8	25	7	Wubbena, Del
1996		II	5	3		8	20	9	Wubbena, Del
1998	W	II	7	8		8	14	9	Dewitt, Kris
1997		II	8	5		8	12	11	Dewitt, Kris

COLORADO CHRISTIAN

Year	M/W	Div	F	SD	Bye	#T	W	L	Coach
1990	M	I	8	5		8	20	10	Evans, Frank

COLUMBIA CHRISTIAN

Year	M/W	Div	F	SD	Bye	#T	W	L	Coach
1991	W	I	8	8		8			Fields, Terry L.
1992		I	8	7		8			Fields, Terry L.

CONCORDIA (MI)

Year	M/W	Div	F	SD	Bye	#T	W	L	Coach
1993	W	I	5	8		8	8	23	Twietmeyer, Dr. T. Alan
1994		I	8	8		8	6	23	Twietmeyer, Dr. T. Alan

CONCORDIA (OR)

Year	M/W	Div	F	SD	Bye	#T	W	L	Coach
1982	M	I	3	4		7	22	11	Hewitt, Tom
1991		I	5	7		8	18	16	Schieldheisz, Dr. Joel
1990		I	8	8		8	14	21	Schieldheisz, Dr. Joel
1988	W	I	2	2		8	20	12	Kunert, Charles J. "Chuck"

CORNERSTONE

Year	M/W	Div	F	SD	Bye	#T	W	L	Coach
1995	M	I	6	8		8	18	21	Elders, Kim
1994		I	8	7		8	17	19	Elders, Kim

COVENANT

Year	M/W	Div	F	SD	Bye	#T	W	L	Coach
1987	M	I	4	8		8	17	14	Fitzgerald, Gene
1985		I	8	5		8	17	14	Fitzgerald, Gene
1992	W	I	4	3		8	22	16	Smialek, Tami
1993		I	6	7		8	20	14	Smialek, Tami

CROWN (MN)

Year	M/W	Div	F	SD	Bye	#T	W	L	Coach
1997	M	II	5	8		8	27	14	Pearson, Troy
1987		II	6	8		8	X	X	Pierce, Bud
1998	W	II	3	5		8	15	11	Ague, Paul
1997		II	6	8		8	20	9	Haller, Mickey

Year	M/W	Div	F	SD	Bye	#T	W	L	Coach
CROWN (TN)									
1995	M	IIA	2	2		8	24	8	Weber, Dr. Greg
EASTERN (PA)									
1987	M	I	2	5		8	28	11	Ware, Nate
1981		I	6	5		6	20	12	Young, Clifford E.
1986		I	8	7		8	X	X	Young, Clifford E.
1987	W	I	7	7		8	15	15	Hunter, Art
EASTERN MENNONITE									
1985	W	I	3	2		8	22	4	Brownscombe, Sandra
1986		I	7	2		8	18	8	Brownscombe, Sandra
EASTERN NAZARENE									
1971	M		2			8	26	5	Bradley, Carroll F.
1973			3			4	21	9	Smith, James H.
1972			4			8	24	8	Smith, James H.
1979		I	6			6	22	10	Bradley, Ron
1982		I	7	6		7	19	12	Perera, Jerry
EMMANUEL (GA)									
1997	W	I	2	3		8	23	10	Bona, Mike
1996		I	3	1		8	23	9	Bona, Mike
1998		I	6	2		8	18	11	Bona, Mike
EMMAUS BIBLE									
1995	W	II	4	4		8	16	3	Mertz, Merilee
EVANGEL									
1986	W	I	1	3		8	21	13	Bowen, Lynn
FAITH BAPTIST BIBLE (IA)									
1998	M	IIA	3	1		8	19	12	Walter, Dave
1994		IIA	4			8	18	12	Walter, Dave
1997		IIA	4	8		8	16	13	Walter, Dave
1996		IIA	5	6		8	13	16	Walter, Dave
1995		IIA	7	5		8	15	14	Walter, Dave
1996	W	II	7	8		8	17	9	Nihart, Lanny
FAULKNER									
1998	M	I	4	3		8	25	14	Sanderson, Jim
1984		I	8	8		8	8	25	Naylor, Jim
FREE WILL BAPTIST BIBLE									
1995	M	II	4	7		8	28	10	Deel, Byron
GENEVA									
1998	M	I	3	1		8	25	11	Santarsiero, Jeff
1976		I	4			4	15	19	Christopher, Jim
1992		I	5	3		8	26	8	Slocum, Jerry
1994		I	5	1		8	28	4	Slocum, Jerry

Year	M/W	Div	F	SD	Bye	#T	W	L	Coach
1977		I	6			6	13	19	Christopher, Jim
1978		I	6			6	15	18	Christopher, Jim
1984		I	8	3		8	23	12	Erickson, Lee W.
1989		I	8	6		8	20	15	Slocum, Jerry
1987	W	I	3	5		8	14	15	Gall, Kimerly
1996		I	4	3		8	15	16	Myers, Jackie
1990		I	8	7		8	10	19	Gall, Kimerly
1997		I	8	2		. 8	22	12	Myers, Jackie

GEORGE FOX

Year	M/W	Div	F	SD	Bye	#T	W	L	Coach
1985	M	I	3	3		8	27	7	Vernon, Mark
1987		I	8	1		8	27	6	Vernon, Mark

GORDON (MA)

Year	M/W	Div	F	SD	Bye	#T	W	L	Coach
1968	M		6			6	20	10	Murdoch, Harlan P.
1983	W	I	8			8	10	11	Zuidema, Mary
1984		I	8			8	13	8	Zuidema, Mary

GRACE (IN)

Year	M/W	Div	F	SD	Bye	#T	W	L	Coach
1970	M		2			8	26	6	Kammerer, Glen "Chet"
1983		I	2	2		8	32	5	Kessler, James C.
1973			4			4	24	8	Kammerer, Glen "Chet"
1986		I	4	3		8	27	10	Kessler, James C.
1969			5			6	21	11	Kammerer, Glen "Chet"
1971			8			8	18	10	Kammerer, Glen "Chet"
1990	W	I	7	5		8	18	14	Ryman, Jerry

GRACE BIBLE (MI)

Year	M/W	Div	F	SD	Bye	#T	W	L	Coach
1994	M	IIA	1			8	19	10	Moore, Jimmy
1995		IIA	1	1		8	19	12	Moore, Jimmy
1993		IIA	2	6		8	15	11	Moore, Jimmy
1997		IIA	3	3		8	12	14	Moore, Jimmy
1991		IIA	4			4	10	13	Grube, David
1996		IIA	4	1		8	14	22	Moore, Jimmy

GRAND RAPIDS BAPTIST

Year	M/W	Div	F	SD	Bye	#T	W	L	Coach
1968	M		6			6	15	10	Raymond,
1993	W	I	7	6		8	18	14	Shuneson, Kevin

GRAND RAPIDS BIBLE & MUSIC

Year	M/W	Div	F	SD	Bye	#T	W	L	Coach
1968	M		2		To R4	6	18	10	Unknown
1992		IIA	5	6		8	14	20	Elmer, Don
1993		IIA	5	2		8	8	24	Elmer, Don

GREENVILLE

Year	M/W	Div	F	SD	Bye	#T	W	L	Coach
1996	M	I	8	4		8	21	8	Faulkner, Doug

HANNIBAL-LAGRANGE

Year	M/W	Div	F	SD	Bye	#T	W	L	Coach
1995	M	I	8	3		8	17	17	Thomas, Kent

Year	M/W	Div	F	SD	Bye	#T	W	L	Coach
HILLSDALE FREE WILL BAPTIST									
1994	M	IIA	2			8	22	14	Lisenbee, Tim
1996		IIA	2	4		8	13	17	Archer, Kelly
1998		IIA	2	2		8	24	12	Archer, Kelly
1991		IIA	3			4	23	11	Lisenbee, Tim
1992		IIA	4	2		8	10	8	Lisenbee, Tim
1993		IIA	8	4		8	21	20	Lisenbee, Tim
1992	W	II	7	4		8	9	13	Braisher, Kelly
1991		II	8			8	10	14	Braisher, Kelly
HOUGHTON									
1983	M	I	8	7		8	19	9	Jack, David E.
1988	W	I	6	5		8	18	6	Lord, Harold "Skip"
1989		I	8	6		8	16	7	Lord, Harold "Skip"
HUNTINGTON									
1984	W	I	1			8	24	9	Freeman, Keith
1991		I	1	3		8	24	4	Culler, Lori
1992		I	1	1		8	24	8	Culler, Lori
1988		I	3	4		8	20	11	Culler, Lori
1986		I	4	7		8	21	10	Freeman, Keith
1989		I	4	4		8	19	11	Culler, Lori
1985		I	5	3		8	20	10	Freeman, Keith
1987		I	5	6		8	21	12	Culler, Lori
1990		I	6	3		8	26	5	Culler, Lori
INDIANA WESLEYAN									
1995	M	I	1	7		8	17	16	Williams, Pat
1996		I	4	8		8	8	24	Blum, Scott
1994		I	6	6		8	17	14	Bireline, David B.
1992		I	8	8		8	10	27	Bireline, David B.
1993		I	8	8		8	12	22	Bireline, David B.
1997		I	8	8		8	12	21	Blum, Scott
1998	W	I	2	7		8	19	14	Porter, Terry
1995		I	3	1		8	26	11	Porter, Terry
1986		I	5	1		8	20	7	Roorbach, Peg
1994		I	5	2		8	29	8	Porter, Terry
1992		I	6	6		8	20	14	Porter, Terry
1983		I	8			8	13	11	Hensler, Susan
JIMMY SWAGGART BIBLE									
1988	M	II	5	7		8	21	14	Boone, Dr. Jerry
1991		II	5	6		8	27	9	Boone, Dr. Jerry
1990		II	6			8	22	11	Boone, Dr. Jerry
1989		II	8	8		8	9	25	Boone, Dr. Jerry
JOHN BROWN									
1991	M	I	1	4		8	25	8	Sheehy, John
1971			3			8	17	10	Haynes, Bill
1983		I	3	4		8	15	17	Simons, Jeff
1980		I	6			6	15	13	Simons, Jeff
1986		I	8	6		8	13	13	Bassett, Sheldon

Year	M/W	Div	F	SD	Bye	#T	W	L	Coach
1985	W	I	2	1		8	20	12	Bassett, Sheldon
1983		I	4			8	12	18	Pickering, Curt
1987		I	6	4		8	13	18	Augustine, Jack
1989		I	6	5		8	16	10	Augustine, Jack

Johnson Bible

Year	M/W	Div	F	SD	Bye	#T	W	L	Coach
1977	M	II	3			4	23	9	Morgan, Russell
1987		II	4	4		8	22	7	Karnes, Douglas
1984		II	8	6		8	19	12	Karnes, Douglas
1985		II	8	7		8	19	8	Karnes, Douglas
1986		II	8	7		8	18	13	Karnes, Douglas
1988		II	8	8		8	17	11	Karnes, Douglas
1985	W	II	2			8	9	9	Morgan, Russell
1986		II	2	8		8	2	9	Morgan, Russell
1984		II	3			6	18	5	Morgan, Russell
1994		II	6	7		8	9	7	Morgan, Russell
1995		II	7	6		8	9	6	Roberts, Sherri
1996		II	8	7		8	10	10	Roberts, Sherri

Judson (IL)

Year	M/W	Div	F	SD	Bye	#T	W	L	Coach
1984	M	I	3	6		8	24	9	Harris, Sam
1995	W	I	7	6		8	20	13	Gum, Tory

Kentucky Christian

Year	M/W	Div	F	SD	Bye	#T	W	L	Coach
1988	M	II	1	2		8	26	8	Kirk, Randy
1989		II	1	1		8	27	5	Kirk, Randy
1991		II	1	5		8	20	13	Damron, Dr. Donald R. "Dick"
1995		II	1	1		8	26	7	Damron, Dr. Donald R. "Dick"
1996		II	1	1		8	27	6	Sudlow, Eric
1997		II	1	1		8	21	12	Damron, Dr. Donald R. "Dick"
1998		II	2	1		8	27	11	Damron, Dr. Donald R. "Dick"
1979		II	3			6	22	8	Damron, Dr. Donald R. "Dick"
1990		II	3			8	23	13	Kirk, Randy
1978		II	4			6	17	12	Damron, Dr. Donald R. "Dick"
1980		II	4			6	22	11	Damron, Dr. Donald R. "Dick"
1981		II	6			6	15	13	Damron, Dr. Donald R. "Dick"
1993		II	7	2		8	22	10	Damron, Dr. Donald R. "Dick"
1982		II	8	6		8	19	10	Damron, Dr. Donald R. "Dick"
1983		II	8	5		8	21	8	Damron, Dr. Donald R. "Dick"
1989	W	II	1	4		8	13	11	Bender, Tom
1995		II	1	1		8	24	9	Arnett, Ron
1996		II	1	1		8	28	4	Arnett, Ron
1997		II	1	1		8	30	5	Arnett, Ron
1998		II	1	2		8	22	13	Arnett, Ron
1993		II	2	2		8	19	11	Arnett, Ron
1994		II	2	1		8	21	7	Arnett, Ron
1983		II	3			4	X	X	Robertson, Barb McClone
1987		II	3			6	12	11	Schreiner, Dale
1988		II	3	2	To R4	6	11	12	Schreiner, Dale
1992		II	3	3		8	20	6	Arnett, Ron
1990		II	4			8	15	10	Bender, Tom

Year	M/W	Div	F	SD	Bye	#T	W	L	Coach
1985		II	5			8	9	9	Robertson, Barb McClone
1986		II	5	2		8	11	9	Schreiner, Dale
1991		II	5	7		8	15	11	Bender, Tom

KING (TN)

Year	M/W	Div	F	SD	Bye	#T	W	L	Coach
1988	W	I	1	1		8	27	3	Nida, Al
1989		I	1	1		8	28	2	Nida, Al
1990		I	1	1		8	27	3	Nida, Al
1991		I	3	2		8	27	3	Nida, Al

KING'S (NY)

Year	M/W	Div	F	SD	Bye	#T	W	L	Coach
1975	M		3			4	25	15	Wilhelmi, Norman
1988		I	8	8		8	19	15	Harris, William R.
1991		I	8	6		8	26	8	Harris, William R.

LANCASTER BIBLE

Year	M/W	Div	F	SD	Bye	#T	W	L	Coach
1987	W	II	5			6	26	10	Figart, Dr. Tom

LATIN AMERICAN BIBLE (CA)

Year	M/W	Div	F	SD	Bye	#T	W	L	Coach
1992	M	IIA	1	1		8	30	2	Elisaldez, Ken

LEE (TN)

Year	M/W	Div	F	SD	Bye	#T	W	L	Coach
1968	M		1			6	30	4	Hughes, Dale R.
1973			1			4	31	6	Hughes, Dale R.
1994		I	1	5		8	24	14	Carpenter, Dr. Larry
1979		I	2			6	17	13	Rowan, Earl
1993		I	2	4		8	24	14	Carpenter, Dr. Larry
1969			3			6	24	9	Hughes, Dale R.
1970			3			8	23	6	Hughes, Dale R.
1978		I	3	2	To R4	6	20	14	Rowan, Earl
1980		I	3	2	To R4	6	16	15	Rowan, Earl
1981		I	3	2	To R4	6	22	11	Rowan, Earl
1992		I	3	6		8	24	14	Steele, Randy
1997		I	3	6		8	15	23	Carpenter, Dr. Larry
1988		I	4	3		8	24	11	Steele, Randy
1995		I	4	1		8	26	12	Carpenter, Dr. Larry
1991		I	6	8		8	19	13	Steele, Randy
1986		I	8	8		8	19	20	Steele, Randy
1987		I	8	3		8	23	7	Steele, Randy
1989		I	8	4		8	25	9	Steele, Randy
1985	W	I	1	6		8	15	13	Souther, Orin A. "Jack"
1987		I	2	3		8	20	17	Souther, Orin A. "Jack"
1990		I	2	2		8	28	7	Souther, Orin A. "Jack"
1996		I	2	2		8	22	14	Baldwin, Gary
1983		I	3			8	16	15	Unknown
1984		I	3			8	20	12	Souther, Orin A. "Jack"
1986		I	3	5		8	21	14	Souther, Orin A. "Jack"
1989		I	3	2		8	30	8	Souther, Orin A. "Jack"
1992		I	3	5		8	18	20	Souther, Orin A. "Jack"
1993		I	3	3		8	19	17	Souther, Orin A. "Jack"
1991		I	4	4		8	19	14	Souther, Orin A. "Jack"
1997		I	4	7		8	13	24	Baldwin, Gary

Year	M/W	Div	F	SD	Bye	#T	W	L	Coach
1998		I	5	4		8	16	21	Baldwin, Gary
1994		I	6	4		8	15	21	Baldwin, Gary

LeTourneau

Year	M/W	Div	F	SD	Bye	#T	W	L	Coach
1982	M	I	4	7		7	16	19	Bassett, Sheldon
1981		I	6	6		6	17	20	Fratzke, Dr. Michael L.
1971			8			8	18	10	Fratzke, Mel R.
1984		I	8	7		8	15	12	Bassett, Sheldon
1997	W	I	1	1		8	30	4	Otwell, Mary Ann
1998		I	1	1		8	24	10	Otwell, Mary Ann

Liberty

Year	M/W	Div	F	SD	Bye	#T	W	L	Coach
1980	M	I	1			6	28	11	Gibson, Dale

Lincoln Christian

Year	M/W	Div	F	SD	Bye	#T	W	L	Coach
1985	W	II	7			8	5	11	Morris, Larry

Malone

Year	M/W	Div	F	SD	Bye	#T	W	L	Coach
1996	M	I	1	3		8	20	16	Smith, Harold T.
1991		I	3	1		8	28	4	Smith, Harold T.
1987		I	8	4		8	18	14	Smith, Harold T.

Manhattan Christian

Year	M/W	Div	F	SD	Bye	#T	W	L	Coach
1996	M	IIA	1	2		8	22	8	Condra, Shawn
1997		IIA	7	5		8	14	14	Condra, Shawn

Maranatha Baptist Bible (WI)

Year	M/W	Div	F	SD	Bye	#T	W	L	Coach
1990	M	II	1			8	18	8	Terrill, Jerry
1996		II	3	7		8	11	17	Terrill, Jerry
1997		II	3	4		8	17	13	Terrill, Jerry
1991		II	4	1		8	19	10	Terrill, Jerry
1998		II	5	4		8	14	15	Terrill, Jerry
1986		II	6	6		8	5	16	Terrill, Jerry
1996	W	II	5	6		8	11	17	Morrison, Clayton
1998		II	5	4		8	13	16	Morrison, Clayton
1987		II	6			6	10	12	Grooms, Vicki

Master's

Year	M/W	Div	F	SD	Bye	#T	W	L	Coach
1991	M	I	2	2		8	22	12	Hankinson, Mel
1992		I	2	2		8	23	12	Hankinson, Mel
1993		I	4	1		8	20	12	Hankinson, Mel

Messenger

Year	M/W	Div	F	SD	Bye	#T	W	L	Coach
1995	M	IIA	8	7		8	21	17	Stallman, David S.

Messiah

Year	M/W	Div	F	SD	Bye	#T	W	L	Coach
1974	M		3			4	20	11	Shaker, Marshall 'Mike'
1968			4			6	11	11	Drescher, Luke M.
1972			8			8	19	12	Shaker, Marshall 'Mike'
1983	W	I	8			8	16	7	Clelan-Blank, Nancy
1984		I	8			8	16	9	Clelan-Blank, Nancy

Year	M/W	Div	F	SD	Bye	#T	W	L	Coach
MID-AMERICA BIBLE									
1998	M	II	1	3		8	32	8	Holley, Willie
1986		II	3	3		8	22	12	Holley, Willie
1992		IIA	3	5		8	17	19	Holley, Willie
1978		II	6			6	22	12	Holley, Willie
1979		II	6			6	19	9	Holley, Willie
1980		II	6			6	14	16	Holley, Willie
1981		II	6			6	19	18	Holley, Willie
1993		II	6	5		8	25	14	Holley, Willie
1996		II	6	4		8	21	15	Holley, Willie
1997		II	7	5		8	26	17	Holley, Willie
1982		II	8	7		8	19	7	Holley, Willie
1983		II	8	7		8	22	10	Holley, Willie
1985		II	8	6		8	13	17	Holley, Willie
1995		II	8	3		8	22	12	Holley, Willie
1996	W	II	2	2		8	17	19	O'Brien, Tony
1997		II	2	2		8	18	17	O'Brien, Tony
1998		II	2	1		8	20	15	O'Brien, Tony
1994		II	4	3		8	10	9	O'Brien, Tony
1993		II	8	7		8	10	9	O'Brien, Tony
MIDAMERICA NAZARENE									
1997	M	I	2	5		8	24	13	Lamar, Jon "Rocky"
1998		I	2	4		8	27	11	Lamar, Jon "Rocky"
1994		I	3	8		8	20	17	Lamar, Jon "Rocky"
1978		I	6			6	15	13	Smith, James H.
1994	W	I	2	5		8	18	19	Kliewer, Karl
1984		I	4			8	20	17	Hook, Norton
1996		I	5	6		8	18	18	Kliewer, Karl
MILLIGAN									
1990	M	I	8	6		8	27	9	Wallingford, Tony
MISSOURI BAPTIST									
1992	M	I	8	7		8	19	18	Pitzer, Lowell S.
MOODY BIBLE									
1991	M	II	8	8		8	X	X	Gaffney, Greg
1987	W	II	1			6	X	X	Gaffney, Greg
1988		II	2	1	To R4	6	X	X	Wartluft, Laurel
1990		II	3			8	X	X	Wartluft, Laurel
1997		II	3	3		8	18	9	Fielitz, Cheryl A.
1986		II	4	5		8	X	X	Unknown
1991		II	7	3		8	X	X	Wartluft, Laurel
1989		II	8	7		8	X	X	Wartluft, Laurel
1992		II	8	6		8	14	14	Wartluft, Laurel
MOUNT VERNON NAZARENE									
1989	M	I	2	3		8	23	14	Balikian, Bernie
1994	W	I	1	3		8	23	10	Howald, Jeana
1998		I	4	6		8	19	18	Ely, Eric

Year	M/W	Div	F	SD	Bye	#T	W	L	Coach
MULTNOMAH BIBLE									
1987	M	II	2	7		8			Doherty, Jim
1986		II	4	5		8	23	8	Skagen, James C.
1998		II	6	6		8	21	13	Reese, Chris
1988		II	7	6		8	15	15	Skagen, James C.
1989		II	7	6		8			Skagen, James C.
1985		II	8	8		8	16	12	Skagen, James C.
NEBRASKA CHRISTIAN									
1997	M	IIA	2	4		8	21	8	Lahm, Chris
1995		IIA	5	3		8	22	11	Lahm, Chris
1998		IIA	6	6		8	16	14	Lahm, Chris
NORTH CENTRAL BIBLE									
1993	M	II	3	6		8	17	12	Engle, Mark
1988		II	6	4		8	22	13	Myers, Dennis
1995	W	II	2	2		8	14	9	Goodrich, Dr. Larry
1996		II	6	5		8	18	9	Goodrich, Dr. Larry
1997		II	7	7		8	10	17	Asberry-Lidquist, Tracine
NORTHLAND BAPTIST BIBLE									
1994	M	II	7	5		8	14	12	Scott, Dennis
1994	W	II	7	6		8	15	10	Bowman, Reba
NORTHWEST ASSEMBLIES									
1993	M	II	1	7		8	X	X	Filan, Doug
1991		II	2	7		8	19	13	Filan, Doug
1994		II	3	2		8	X	X	Filan, Doug
1992		II	4	1		8	24	12	Filan, Doug
1990		II	7			8	X	X	Filan, Doug
1984		II	8	8		8	X	X	Brown, John
1997		I	8	7		8	20	14	Mendoza, Wayne
1988	W	II	1	3		6	16	17	Brodin, Kristi
1990		II	1			8	11	18	Brodin, Kristi
1991		II	1	1		8	10	20	Brodin, Kristi
1993		II	1	1		8	17	11	Brodin, Kristi
1994		II	1	2		8	7	21	Brodin, Kristi
1989		II	2	3		8	4	26	Brodin, Kristi
1986		II	3	6		8	16	10	Brodin, Kristi
1992		II	4	8		8	12	20	Brodin, Kristi
1984		II	5			6	12	9	Brodin, Kristi
1998		I	7	8		8	11	22	Brodin, Kristi
NORTHWEST NAZARENE									
1978	M	I	4			6	23	11	Layton, Terry
NORTHWESTERN (MN)									
1980	M	II	1	2	To R4	6	21	11	Sulack, Dave
1981		II	2			6	15	12	Sulack, Dave
1982		II	2	3		8	16	14	Westlund, Dave
1983		II	2	2		8	22	10	Bocken, Ron

Year	M/W	Div	F	SD	Bye	#T	W	L	Coach
1995		I	3	6		8	22	10	Smith, Joseph L.
1985		II	4	3		8	17	13	Bocken, Ron
1984		II	8	4		8	15	17	Bocken, Ron
1998		I	8	8		8	25	11	Smith, Joseph L.
1984	W	II	1			6	19	10	Smith, Dan
1985		II	1			8	11	19	Smith, Dan
1989		I	5	7		8	17	11	Smith, Dan
1995		I	5	4		8	23	7	Holm, Sherri
1994		I	7	6		8	20	8	Holm, Sherri

NYACK

Year	M/W	Div	F	SD	Bye	#T	W	L	Coach
1970	M		8			8	15	17	Lawrence, Dr. Donald J.
1985		I	8	7		8	25	8	Slocum, Jerry
1990		I	8	7		8	21	13	Flemming, Scott
1994		I	8	4		8	23	13	Bailey, Dan

OAKLAND CITY (IN)

Year	M/W	Div	F	SD	Bye	#T	W	L	Coach
1994	M	I	2	3		8	22	6	Sandifar, Michael
1993		I	3	3		8	20	11	Sandifar, Michael
1997		I	4	1		8	21	9	Sandifar, Michael
1995		I	5	2		8	18	12	Sandifar, Michael
1996		I	5	1		8	18	13	Sandifar, Michael
1998		I	8	6		8	20	9	Sandifar, Michael
1993	W	I	2	2		8	21	10	Sandifar, Denise
1997		I	3	5		8	23	6	Sandifar, Denise
1998		I	3	5		8	20	9	Sandifar, Denise
1995		I	6	2		8	17	14	Sandifar, Denise

OLIVET NAZARENE

Year	M/W	Div	F	SD	Bye	#T	W	L	Coach
1975	M		1			4	30	4	Ward, C. W. "Butch"
1977		I	2			6	22	11	Wilson, Frank
1978		I	2	1	To R4	6	24	9	Wilson, Frank
1976		I	3			4	23	7	Ward, C. W. "Butch"
1980		I	6			6	15	13	Hodge, Ralph
1985		I	8	6		8	19	10	Hodge, Ralph
1986		I	8	5		8	15	18	Hodge, Ralph
1990	W	I	4	4		8	23	10	Glass, Robyn
1991		I	6	5		8	16	15	Glass, Robyn
1988		I	7	6		8	20	15	Parsons, Wendy
1997		I	7	8		8	19	16	DeFries, Cathy
1987		I	8	8		8	13	15	Doenges, Carol
1996		I	8	4		8	17	14	DeFries, Cathy

OZARK CHRISTIAN

Year	M/W	Div	F	SD	Bye	#T	W	L	Coach
1978	M	II	3		To R4	6	X	X	Larrison, Bill
1996	W	II	3	4		8	18	10	Williams, Charles R.
1997		II	4	4		8	16	10	Williams, Charles R.
1989		II	5	8		8	X	X	Williams, Charles R.
1995		II	5	8		8	15	7	Williams, Charles R.
1988		II	6	6		6	X	X	Williams, Charles R.

Year	M/W	Div	F	SD	Bye	#T	W	L	Coach
PACIFIC CHRISTIAN									
1989	M	II	2	2		8	32	10	Erickson, Lee W.
1990		II	2			8	X	X	Erickson, Lee W.
1994		II	2	3		8	28	17	Erickson, Lee W.
1988		II	4	1		8	30	7	Erickson, Lee W.
1993		II	4	4		8	25	13	Erickson, Lee W.
1989	W	II	3	2		8	23	11	Garcia, Barbara
1991		II	3	5		8	18	14	Kappen, Kelley
1992		II	5	1		8	X	X	Kappen, Kelley
1990		II	7			8	X	X	Kappen, Kelley
1993		II	7	8		8	16	12	Kappen, Kelley
PENSACOLA CHRISTIAN									
1998	M	I	6	7		8	15	15	Goetsch, Mark
PHILADELPHIA BIBLE									
1998	M	II	3	7		8	15	12	Martindell, Don
1987	W	II	2			6	25	2	MacCullough, Dr. Martha "Marti"
1991		II	4	2		8	17	12	MacCullough, Dr. Martha "Marti"
1990		II	5			8	22	5	MacCullough, Dr. Martha "Marti"
1993		II	5	3		8	23	6	MacCullough, Dr. Martha "Marti"
1994		II	5	5		8	13	11	MacCullough, Dr. Martha "Marti"
1985		II	6			8	23	8	MacCullough, Dr. Martha "Marti"
1986		II	6	4		8	20	8	MacCullough, Dr. Martha "Marti"
1989		II	7	5		8	18	9	MacCullough, Dr. Martha "Marti"
1995		II	8	5		8	14	12	Landes, Bertie
PIEDMONT BAPTIST									
1994	M	II	8	6		8	21	10	Franklin, Philip
1985	W	II	8			8			Clingerman, Ralph
PILLSBURY BAPTIST BIBLE									
1989	M	II	6	7		8	13	17	Johnson, Richard "Rick"
1992		II	6	6		8	10	21	Johnson, Richard "Rick"
1997		IIA	6	7		8	12	14	Davis, Paul
1993	W	II	4	6		8	13	12	Traxler, Tim
POINT LOMA NAZARENE									
1985	M	I	1	2		8	28	8	Foster, Ben
1986		I	1	1		8	27	7	Foster, Ben
1987		I	1	2		8	25	10	Foster, Ben
1980		I	2	1	To R4	6	23	14	Foster, Ben
1979		I	4	1	To R4	6	26	11	Foster, Ben
PRACTICAL BIBLE									
1996	M	IIA	8	7		8	13	17	Howard, Russ
1997	W	II	5	6		8	14	9	Carman, Becki
ROBERTS WESLEYAN									
1997	M	I	5	3		8	21	16	Sisson, George
1993		I	8	7		8	18	13	Sisson, Dr. Kenneth O.

Year	M/W	Div	F	SD	Bye	#T	W	L	Coach
1997	W	I	5	6		8	22	12	Faro, Michael
1991		I	7	6		8	19	8	Faro, Michael
1992		I	7	4		8	13	13	Faro, Michael
1996		I	7	7		8	17	17	Faro, Michael
1993		I	8	4		8	15	18	Faro, Michael
1995		I	8	8		8	10	19	Faro, Michael

SAINT LOUIS CHRISTIAN

Year	M/W	Div	F	SD	Bye	#T	W	L	Coach
1993	M	IIA	6	8		8	12	21	Wolford, Danny
1998		IIA	7	8		8	9	25	Wolford, Danny
1992		IIA	8	8		8	8	22	Wolford, Danny
1990	W	II	8			8	9	6	Wolford, Danny

SAN JOSE CHRISTIAN

Year	M/W	Div	F	SD	Bye	#T	W	L	Coach
1995	M	II	5	5		8	28	11	Miller, Glen
1992		II	8	4		8	23	17	Miller, Glen

SIMPSON (CA)

Year	M/W	Div	F	SD	Bye	#T	W	L	Coach
1997	M	II	6	7		8	14	12	Spaschak, Tom
1998	W	II	4	6		8	15	16	Dewey, Don
1994		II	8	8		8	9	11	Wingate, Lawrence

SOUTHEASTERN ASSEMBLIES

Year	M/W	Div	F	SD	Bye	#T	W	L	Coach
1991	M	II	7	2		8	27	8	Laing, Scott
1990		II	8			8	21	13	Laing, Scott

SOUTHERN CALIFORNIA COLLEGE

Year	M/W	Div	F	SD	Bye	#T	W	L	Coach
1989	M	I	8	1		8	29	5	Reynolds, Bill

SOUTHERN NAZARENE

Year	M/W	Div	F	SD	Bye	#T	W	L	Coach
1974	M		1			4	31	6	Poteet, Jim
1977		I	1	1	To R4	6	28	10	Poteet, Jim
1979		I	3	2	To R4	6	18	21	Poteet, Jim

SOUTHERN WESLEYAN

Year	M/W	Div	F	SD	Bye	#T	W	L	Coach
1976	M	I	2			4	21	10	Hill, Lewis
1977		I	4			6			Drennon, Craig

SOUTHWESTERN (AZ)

Year	M/W	Div	F	SD	Bye	#T	W	L	Coach
1997	M	IIA	1	2		8	21	8	Morley, Stephen H.
1996		IIA	3	3		8	15	18	Morley, Stephen H.
1998		IIA	5	4		8	16	13	Morley, Stephen H.

SOUTHWESTERN CHRISTIAN MINISTRIES

Year	M/W	Div	F	SD	Bye	#T	W	L	Coach
1998	M	IIA	1	5		8	21	17	Arthur, Mark
1993		IIA	4	7		8	18	18	Arthur, Mark
1995		IIA	4	4		8	26	4	Arthur, Mark
1997		IIA	5	1		8	26	15	Arthur, Mark
1996		II	8	8		8	26	16	Arthur, Mark

SPRING ARBOR

Year	M/W	Div	F	SD	Bye	#T	W	L	Coach
1982	M	I	2	3		7	23	14	Bockwitz, William
1984		I	8	4		8	19	15	Bockwitz, William

Year	M/W	Div	F	SD	Bye	#T	W	L	Coach
1983	W	I	1			8	29	4	Dunckel, Darrell
1987		I	1	1		8	25	9	Dunckel, Darrell
1984		I	2			8	25	9	Dunckel, Darrell
1985		I	4	4		8	25	8	Dunckel, Darrell

TABOR

1991	W	I	2	1		8	28	5	Kliewer, Karl
1990		I	3	6		8	15	16	Kliewer, Karl

TAYLOR

1985	M	I	4	4		8	27	10	Patterson, Paul

TAYLOR: FORT WAYNE

1976	M	II	1			4	18	9	Morley, Stephen H.
1977		II	4			4	10	18	Morley, Stephen H.
1979		II	4		To R4	6	15	14	Morley, Stephen H.
1992		II	7	7		8	19	11	Hamilton, Marvin E. "Bud"
1971			8			8	19	8	Morley, Stephen H.
1985	W	II	4			8	15	3	Rupp, Deborah "Deb"
1984		II	6			6	7	11	Rupp, Deborah "Deb"
1986		II	8	3		8	14	7	Rupp, Deborah "Deb"

TENNESSEE TEMPLE

1979	M	I	1			6	30	7	Bishop, Ronald
1981		I	1	1	To R4	6	24	17	Bishop, Ronald
1982		I	1	1	To R4	7	31	8	Bishop, Ronald
1983		I	1	1		8	28	7	Bishop, Ronald
1988		I	1	4		8	26	13	Bishop, Ronald
1989		I	1	5		8	25	11	Bishop, Ronald
1972			2			8	19	12	Foster, Bruce D.
1975			2			4	21	14	Foster, Bruce D.
1984		I	2	1		8	33	2	Bishop, Ronald
1985		I	2	1		8	29	4	Bishop, Ronald
1996		I	2	5		8	24	12	Johnson, Richard "Rick"
1977		I	3	2	To R4	6	28	6	Bishop, Ronald
1986		I	3	4		8	21	11	Bishop, Ronald
1971			4			8	18	15	Foster, Bruce D.
1980		I	4			6	23	13	Bishop, Ronald
1990		I	4	2		8	23	16	Bishop, Ronald
1991		I	4	3		8	18	15	Bishop, Ronald
1998		I	5	5		8	27	9	Johnson, Richard "Rick"
1983	W	I	2			8	X	X	Stem, Randy
1984		I	8			8	33	2	Stem, Randy

TOCCOA FALLS

1997	M	II	2	2		8	29	6	Martin, Lance
1976		II	4			4	14	14	Fowler, Richard A.
1996		II	4	5		8	23	11	Martin, Lance
1998		II	4	5		8	27	10	Martin, Lance
1986	W	II	1	7		8	13	12	Shiffer, Paul
1992		II	1	5		8	23	6	Shiffer, Paul
1994		II	3	4		8	19	11	Shiffer, Paul
1984		II	4			6	10	6	Shiffer, Paul

Year	M/W	Div	F	SD	Bye	#T	W	L	Coach
1987		II	4			6	14	8	Shiffer, Paul
1988		II	4	4		6	17	12	Shiffer, Paul
1989		II	6	6		8	13	10	Shiffer, Paul
1990		II	6			8	11	13	Shiffer, Paul
1993		II	6	4		8	19	11	Shiffer, Paul
1995		II	6	7		8	12	13	Shiffer, Paul

TREVECCA NAZARENE

Year	M/W	Div	F	SD	Bye	#T	W	L	Coach
1972	M		3			8	19	9	Forraker, Chet

TRINITY BIBLE

Year	M/W	Div	F	SD	Bye	#T	W	L	Coach
1978	M	II	6			6	16	12	Carlin, Scott B.
1998		II	8	8		8	16	17	Wagler, Keith

TRINITY CHRISTIAN

Year	M/W	Div	F	SD	Bye	#T	W	L	Coach
1997	M	I	6	4		8	24	12	Fitzgerald, Gene
1987	W	I	4	2		8	23	7	Ribbens, David L.
1993		I	4	5		8	19	13	Eastham, Sue
1988		I	5	7		8	16	13	Ribbens, David L.
1989		I	7	8		8	17	13	Ribbens, David L.
1983		I	8			8	13	5	Cole, Lois
1984		I	8			8	11	11	Cole, Lois
1986		I	8	4		8	18	11	Ribbens, David L.
1998		I	8	3		8	20	13	Schaaf, Barb

TRINITY INTERNATIONAL (FL)

Year	M/W	Div	F	SD	Bye	#T	W	L	Coach
1991	M	IIA	1			4	15	14	Rutherford, Robert

TRINITY INTERNATIONAL (IL)

Year	M/W	Div	F	SD	Bye	#T	W	L	Coach
1974	M		4			4	15	15	Van Dix Horn, Henry
1972			8			8	10	14	Van Dix Horn, Henry
1985	W	I	8	7		8	10	18	Girton, Marcy

VALLEY FORGE CHRISTIAN

Year	M/W	Div	F	SD	Bye	#T	W	L	Coach
1979	M	II	2			6	18	13	Jones, Paul
1988		II	2	5		8	22	8	Engle, Mark
1980		II	6			6	18	11	Jones, Paul
1986		II	7	4		8	24	8	Mioni, Dominick
1987		II	8	3		8	22	10	Engle, Mark
1983	W	II	2			4	X	X	Baker, William J.

WARNER PACIFIC

Year	M/W	Div	F	SD	Bye	#T	W	L	Coach
1983	M	I	8	5		8	24	9	Bays, Gary R.

WASHINGTON BIBLE

Year	M/W	Div	F	SD	Bye	#T	W	L	Coach
1995	M	IIA	6	8		8	9	15	Fletcher, Rev. Brit
1994		IIA	7			8	10	15	Ronson, Glenn

WESTERN BAPTIST

Year	M/W	Div	F	SD	Bye	#T	W	L	Coach
1977	M	II	1			4	17	13	Hills, Tim
1986		I	2	2		8	29	10	Collins, Tim
1995		I	2	5		8	26	12	Hills, Tim
1976		II	3			4	12	19	Hills, Tim

Year	M/W	Div	F	SD	Bye	#T	W	L	Coach
1989		I	3	2		8	26	15	Hills, Tim
1984		I	4	3		8	19	17	Collins, Tim
1992		I	6	5		8	19	18	Hills, Tim
1993		I	6	5		8	16	20	Hills, Tim
1996		I	6	6		8	21	16	Rasmussen, Dennis
1988		I	8	6		8	19	17	Hills, Tim
1995	W	I	1	7		8	17	16	Williams, Terry
1996		I	1	5		8	24	11	Williams, Terry
1997		I	6	4		8	25	9	Williams, Terry

WILLIAMS BAPTIST

Year	M/W	Div	F	SD	Bye	#T	W	L	Coach
1993	W	I	1	1		8	24	2	Halford, Carol
1992		I	2	2		8	18	13	Halford, Carol

National Small College Athletic Association

NAMES: 1967-1990: NLCAA (National Little College Athletic Association); 1991- : NSCAA
HISTORY: The National Small College Athletic Association began on Saturday, July 29, 1966, on the front porch of the Heart-of-Town Motel, Charleston, West Virginia, the brainchild of Del Nobel, president of The Lake Erie Conference, and head basketball coach and athletics director of Midland (OH) College of Commerce. Nobel had contacted Al Raskin, president of the Eastern Shore Basketball Conference and head basketball coach and athletics director at Baltimore College of Commerce, about a post-season tournament between the two conferences.

By the time of the meeting, which was also attended by Robert Anderson, athletics director at Steed College (Johnson City, Tennessee), Noble's idea had evolved into a national association, and he brought with him a suggested constitution which he and his compatriots adopted essentially as he had written it.

Noble's avowed objective was a forum for what he called "the forgotten colleges". At that time, opportunities for post-season play were the NCAA—two divisions, university and college, the NAIA, the JUCO's, and the AAU. For schools that fell somewhere between the NAIA and the JUCO'S and were not up to the AAU level, there was no post-season. The NSCAA was a collection of these "forgotten colleges"—18 of them from Indiana to the Atlantic Coast and as far south as Georgia, separated into four geographic regions, many of them business or comparable schools.

Noble was elected as the first president, and the inaugural basketball tournament was held in March 1967 at Fort Holabird, Maryland, an army facility near Baltimore. The tournament was hosted by Baltimore Commerce—with free admission to all post personnel!

By 1983, competition had been added in sports other than basketball, eligibility requirements had been established, and membership was holding at about 25 schools.

In 1980, the NSCAA became the first senior college association other than the AIAW to conduct a women's tournament.

For the past several years, membership has held at about 50 schools.
TOURNAMENT DIVISIONS: **Men** Open: 1967- . **Women** Open: 1980- .
TOURNAMENT OPERATION: The NSCAA tournament began with eight teams in 1967 and moved to 16 in 1974. Since then, no more than 16 teams have participated—although occasionally

as few as 12 have appeared. Through 1973, the tournament was a double- elimination event with a consolation bracket. The winner and loser of the bracket finals were designated as 5th and 6th place with the two semifinalist teams of the bracket designated as 8th place. No 3rd/4th place game was held.

From 1974 through 1979, it was a conventional single-elimination event with a 3rd/4th place game. In 1980, it became a double-elimination event. Until 1984 the finalists of the consolation bracket played for 5th/6th place with the losers of the semifinals of the bracket designated as 12th place. From 1985 through 1989, the four losers of the semifinals in the winners bracket played for 5th/6th place while the finalists of the consolation bracket side played for 9th/10th place.

In 1990, the powers that be made life interesting: what had been the 3rd/4th place game (the two losers of the semifinals of the winners bracket) became the 3rd/6th place game. And, what had been the 5th/6th place game (see above) became the 4th/7th place game while what had been the 9th/10th place game became the 5th/8th place game.

The women's tournament has always been an 8-team double-elimination event (except for nine teams in 1984 and six in 1996) with all eight places contested in a conventional format.

Qualification for the tournament has been based, for the most part, on a region or district championship. However, information on those winners is generally unavailable.

NOTES ON DATA COLLECTION: The beginning of seedings is unknown. Much of the information on the tournament pairings and results was obtained from copies of the association newsletter which made only fleeting reference to seedings. Seeding information is included for tournaments when it is known. Because of the lack of information on the type of bids, such information is not included.

There are missing won-lost records and coaches names. Most are the result of incomplete records at the schools. In other cases, the schools did not provide information to the several annual directories.

Tournament Results—Men

F	School	SD	Bye	W	L	Coach
1967						
1	Sullivan (KY)			23	6	Tibbs, Harry
2	Strayer Business			17	6	Molloy, James H., Jr.
3	Brandywine			23	4	
	Warren Wilson			21	12	Ellenburg, Ray
5	Midland Commerce			20	3	Noble, Del
6	Friendship JC			11	13	Harris, Rev. Herman K., II
8	Baltimore Commerce			9	14	Baker, Paul
	David N Myers			14	7	Kavanaugh, W. H.
1968						
1	Sullivan (KY)			26	6	Tibbs, Harry
2	Columbus Business (OH)					
3	Morristown (TN)			16	7	Bundy, Samuel S.
	Pittsburgh Art Institute					
5	Strayer Business			17	8	Molloy, James H., Jr.
6	Denmark Tech			21	7	Gaddy, Rayshaw L.
8	Barber-Scotia					Coefield, Aldon L.
	Williamsport Commerce			13	5	Mamolen, Paul

F	School	SD	Bye	W	L	Coach
1969						
1	Sullivan (KY)			26	4	Sergeant, W. C.
2	Pittsburgh Art Institute					
3	Sage JC					
	Tiffin			20	4	Janson, George
5	Steed					
6	Williamsport Commerce			17	3	Mamolen, Paul
8	Fort Lauderdale			12	20	D'Angelo,
	Penn-Ohio			7	7	
1970						
1	Kittrell JC			32	4	Golatt, Moses
2	Sullivan (KY)			19	9	Sergeant, W. C.
3	New Kensington Commercial			10	9	Shultz, Charles
	Tiffin			20	5	Janson, George
5	Fort Lauderdale			13	11	
6	David N Myers			13	13	Schuster, Will
8	Duff's Business Institute			X	X	Weir,
	Sage JC					
1971						
1	Tiffin			13	8	Janson, George
2	Durham Business			30	8	Terry, Reginald N.
3	Fort Lauderdale			12	9	Gotkin, Hy
	Sage JC					
5	Steed			18	5	Anderson, Robert
6	Davis (OH)			12	8	Carder, Jerry J.
8	Strayer Business			10	12	Molloy, James H., Jr.
	West Liberty State: Hancock			X	X	Clark, John
1972						
1	Lindsey Wilson			22	8	Voight, James R. "Jim"
2	Palmer JC (SC)			21	5	Voight, Jim
3	Bevill State CC: Brewer			15	16	Anderson, Richard
	Warner Pacific			16	16	Allord, Bob
5	Northwestern (OH)			21	6	Noble, Del
6	Tiffin			19	12	Janson, George
8	Bryant & Stratton: Albany			17	2	Rice, Willard
	West Liberty State: Hancock			X	X	Clark, John
1973						
1	Tiffin			24	9	Janson, George
2	Northwest Shoals CC: Phil Campbell			16	17	Seesholtz, Arthur
3	Bryant & Stratton: Albany			17	8	Rice, Willard
	South Carolina: Union			19	10	Edwards, John
5	Warner Pacific			18	18	Blewrit, Mike
6	Northwestern (OH)			25	8	Loescher, Art
8	Southern Union State CC			22	12	Gourdouze, Frank
	West Virginia Northern CC: Weirton			13	9	Clark, John

F	School	SD	Bye	W	L	Coach
1974						
1	Bryant & Stratton: Buffalo			X	X	Griffin, Dr. Thomas J.
2	Sullivan (KY)			X	X	Mudd, Leon
3	Cullman			16	10	Franey, Joseph S.
4	David N Myers			15	8	Kennedy, Richard
8	Bryant & Stratton: Albany					Rice, Willard
	Master's			13	21	Fowler, Billy
	Northwest Assemblies			22	7	Kinney, Carl
	Northwestern (OH)			20	5	Loescher, Art
16	Alice Lloyd			X	X	Rose, James
	Bluefield (VA)					
	Bristol (TN)					Alves, Len
	Durham Business					
	Ottumwa Heights			16	7	Stevenson, Charles "Chuck"
	South Carolina: Aiken			X	X	Perkins, Lew
	Southern Ohio: Cincinnati					
	Southern Union State CC			13	12	Gourdouze, Frank
1975						
1	Florida College			20	11	Wilson, Tom
2	Tougaloo			15	9	Lewis, Jerry
3	Southern Union State CC					Gourdouze, Frank
	Sullivan (KY)			27	8	Caldwell, Jim
8	Colorado Northwestern CC			13	17	Conrad, Paul
	Cullman			14	10	Franey, Joseph S.
	Friendship JC					
	South Carolina: Lancaster			16	8	
16	Asheville Buncombe TCC			20	4	Rhea, James H.
	David N Myers					McCoid, Rod
	Ganado					
	Mount Vernon Nazarene			8	21	Bradley, Carroll
	Northeast CC (NE)					Stevenson, Charles "Chuck"
	Northwestern (MN)			15	10	Christopherson, Duane
	Northwestern (OH)			16	13	Loescher, Art
	Saint Catharine (KY)			X	X	Unknown
1976						
1	Northeast CC (NE)					Stevenson, Charles "Chuck"
2	Whitworth (MS)			24	6	Roark, Dwain
3	Rust			24	13	Hayes, Naylond
	Southern Union State CC	To R8		21	10	Gourdouze, Frank
8	Central (KS)			15	11	Saxton, Mike
	Colorado Northwestern CC			10	22	Conrad, Paul
	Concordia (OR)	To R8		17	12	Friedrichs, Dr. Warren
	Sullivan (KY)			18	14	Caldwell, Jim
14	Concordia: Saint Paul			16	5	Hendrickson, John
	La Roche			14	6	Pasquinelli, John
	Lafayette (NC)			18	8	
	Missouri Baptist			25	13	Brown, "Chuck"
	Mount Senario			17	9	Novak, Bill
	Northwood (IN)			19	8	Bledsoe, Larry

F	School	SD	Bye	W	L	Coach
1977						
1	Rust			34	5	Hayes, Naylond
2	Northeast CC (NE)			22	5	Stevenson, Charles "Chuck"
3	Concordia: Saint Paul			20	9	Hendrickson, John
	Southern Union State CC			21	9	Gourdouze, Frank
8	Missouri Baptist			17	22	Brown, "Chuck"
	Sage JC			16	6	
	Saint Catharine (KY)			24	7	Cheatham, Larry
	South Carolina: Union			14	10	Call, Gary
16	Baptist Christian (LA)			20	5	Martin, C. P.
	Colorado Northwestern CC			10	22	Conrad, Paul
	Dr. Martin Luther			14	9	Dallman, Dr. Gary L.
	La Roche			11	10	Pasquinelli, John
	Mount Senario			10	16	Novak, Bill
	Northwest Christian			24	6	Cox, Duane
	Northwood (IN)			25	8	Johnson, Jack J.
	Sullivan (KY)			18	9	Caldwell, Jim
1978						
1	Southern Union State CC			28	5	Gourdouze, Frank
2	Saint Catharine (KY)			22	6	Spry, Ronald
3	Oakland City (IN)			21	11	Traffon, Charles L.
4	Northeast CC (NE)			22	6	Stevenson, Charles "Chuck"
8	Concordia: Saint Paul			18	8	Hendrickson, John
	Durham Business			21	9	Hawkins, Ralph
	Northwestern (WI)			12	13	Thompson, Lloyd E.
	Northwood (IN)					Johnson, Jack J.
16	Arkansas Baptist					
	Colorado Northwestern CC			17	12	Conrad, Paul
	Columbia JC (SC)					
	Concordia (OR)			21	9	Friedrichs, Dr. Warren
	Daemen			20	5	Murray, Ken
	East Mississippi CC					
	Logan Chiropractic			17	4	Kirkling, David
	Missouri Baptist			13	20	Brown, "Chuck"
1979						
1	Florida College			20	14	Wilson, Tom
2	Concordia (OR)			17	10	Friedrichs, Dr. Warren
3	Concordia (WI)			20	13	Weiss, Dick
	Missouri Baptist			18	17	McKinney, Lee
8	Bevill State CC: Brewer			15	13	Anderson, Richard
	Colorado Northwestern CC			20	14	Conrad, Paul
	Northeast CC (NE)			15	9	Stevenson, Charles "Chuck"
	South Carolina: Union			14	13	Call, Gary
16	Bryant & Stratton: Albany			18	6	
	Cardinal Stritch (WI)			22	6	Stier, Dr. William F., Jr.
	Columbia JC (SC)			17	8	
	Concordia (MI)			10	18	Harting, Walt

F	School	SD	Bye	W	L	Coach
	Concordia: Saint Paul			10	14	Hendrickson, John
	Mount Senario			20	11	Novak, Bill
	Mount Vernon Nazarene			10	20	Martin, Bobby
	Oakland City (IN)			16	12	Trafton, Charles L.

1980

F	School	SD	Bye	W	L	Coach
1	Sullivan (KY)			28	8	Skinner, David L.
2	Oakland City (IN)			12	17	Trafton, Charles L.
3	Southern Union State CC			21	11	Gourdouze, Frank
4	Florida College			20	13	Owens, Donnie
8	Bluefield (VA)			22	20	Brunson, Dean
	Columbia JC (SC)					
	Concordia (WI)			19	17	Weiss, Dick
	Northeast CC (NE)					Stevenson, Charles "Chuck"
9	South Carolina: Lancaster			27	6	DeHart, Glen E.
10	Concordia (OR)			19	14	Friedrichs, Dr. Warren
12	Colorado Northwestern CC			20	14	Conrad, Paul
	Concordia (MI)			23	9	Harting, Walt
16	Baptist Christian (LA)					Martin, C. P.
	Bryant & Stratton: Buffalo			16	6	Licate, Gilbert P.
	Missouri Baptist			18	13	McKinney, Lee
	Mount Senario			10	17	Novak, Bill

1981

F	School	SD	Bye	W	L	Coach
1	Oakland City (IN)			12	20	Trafton, Charles L.
2	Georgia Military College			X	X	Steinke, Rick
3	Faulkner			22	13	Hazelip, John
4	Northeast CC (NE)					Stevenson, Charles "Chuck"
8	Alice Lloyd			17	14	Morris, Lonnie
	Bryant & Stratton: Buffalo			25	6	McNamara, Tim
	Indiana Wesleyan			24	6	Kent, "Rocky"
	Sullivan (KY)			20	12	Skinner, David L.
9	Bluefield (VA)			12	14	Brunson, Dean
10	Judson (IL)			18	16	Harris, Sam
12	Baptist Christian (LA)					Martin, C. P.
	Warren Wilson			22	7	
16	Blackburn			19	10	Parker, James R.
	Colorado Northwestern CC			17	16	Conrad, Paul
	Josephinum			20	6	
	Viterbo			12	14	Glasshoff, James

1982

F	School	SD	Bye	W	L	Coach
1	Blackburn			23	8	Parker, James R.
2	Oakland City (IN)			14	13	Trafton, Charles L.
3	Alice Lloyd			8	22	Morris, Lonnie
4	Southern Union State CC			20	12	Gourdouze, Frank
8	Lamar CC			X	X	Carel, Steve
	Northeast CC (NE)					Stevenson, Charles "Chuck"
	Southern Ohio: Cincinnati			14	14	Nelson, LaDon
	Warren Wilson			22	10	Franklin, Richard

F	School	SD	Bye	W	L	Coach
9	Concordia: Austin			9	20	Orton, Tom
10	South Carolina: Lancaster					DeHart, Glen E.
12	Concordia (WI)			6	23	Lohmeyer, Neil
	Sullivan (KY)			19	14	Skinner, David L.
16	Bryant & Stratton: Buffalo			17	10	McNamara, Tim
	Master's			18	5	Reese, Pete
	Rochester (MI)			17	5	Pleasant, Garth A.
	Viterbo			10	17	Glasshoff, James

1983

F	School	SD	Bye	W	L	Coach
1	Concordia: Austin			30	7	Orton, Tom
2	Central CC: Platte			19	14	Gutierrez, Jack
3	Phillips JC: Gulfport			12	15	Ladner, Roland
4	Lamar CC			16	26	Carel, Steve
8	Blackburn			20	5	Parker, James R.
	Lees (KY)			26	8	Howard, Cluster
	Northeast CC (NE)			12	13	Stevenson, Charles "Chuck"
	Viterbo			17	10	Glasshoff, James
9	Georgia Military College			25	12	Keast, Richard
10	Oakland City (IN)			10	13	Trafton, Charles L.
12	Cecils JC (NC)			22	15	Reed, Ronald
	Saint John's Lutheran (KS)			9	19	Clausen, Julius
16	Bryant & Stratton: Buffalo			12	10	McNamara, Tim
	Cardinal Stritch (WI)			11	19	Moore, Thomas J.
	Rochester (MI)			19	4	Pleasant, Garth A.
	West Coast Christian			23	6	Turner, Jerry

1984

F	School	SD	Bye	W	L	Coach
1	Webber			32	4	Creola, Nick J.
2	Rochester (MI)			25	5	Pleasant, Garth A.
3	Colorado Northwestern CC			18	18	Conrad, Paul
4	Sullivan (KY)			21	12	Skinner, David L.
8	Blackburn			20	9	Parker, James R.
	Cecils JC (NC)			28	1	Reed, Ronald
	Viterbo			17	13	Glasshoff, James
	West Coast Christian			24	6	Turner, Jerry
9	Phillips JC: Gulfport			22	20	Ladner, Roland
10	Oklahoma Baptist College			19	12	Foster, Bruce D.
12	Daemen			X	X	Licate, Gilbert P.
	Northeast CC (NE)					Johnson, Fred
16	Bluefield (VA)					Becker, Darrell
	Cardinal Stritch (WI)			17	16	Moore, Thomas J.
	Draughons JC: Knoxville					Mitchell, Dave
	Jordan: Flint					Scott, Daniel L.

1985

F	School	SD	Bye	W	L	Coach
1	Blackburn			23	7	Staff, Bob
2	Bluefield (VA)			27	12	Becker, Darrell
3	Sue Bennett					
4	Saint Mary's (MI)			15	17	Kolby, Jay

F	School	SD	Bye	W	L	Coach
5	Navajo CC (AZ)			22	12	Minley, Jeff
6	Draughons JC: Kingsport			32	8	
7	Northland			13	21	Bystrom, Nick
8	West Coast Christian			25	9	Turner, Jerry
10	Central CC: Platte			23	10	Gutierrez, Jack
	National (SD)			15	25	Ticknor, Duane
12	Colorado Northwestern CC			12	20	Conrad, Paul
	Columbia State CC			14	8	Painter, Jim
16	Cardinal Stritch (WI)			14	19	Moore, Thomas J.
	Central (KS)			14	7	Hibbard, Randy
	Elizabeth Seton			21	7	O'Donnell, Dennis G.
	Northeast CC (NE)					Johnson, Fred

1986

F	School	SD	Bye	W	L	Coach
1	Bristol (TN)					Crowder, Brien
2	David N Myers			22	12	Friedman, Michael
3	Bluefield (VA)			28	9	Blevins, Mark
4	Columbia JC (SC)			23	7	
5	Rochester (MI)			26	3	Pleasant, Garth A.
6	Central (KS)			19	10	Hibbard, Randy
7	National (SD)			24	11	Ticknor, Duane
8	Bryant & Stratton: Buffalo			23	9	Krauza, Gregory A.
10	Saint Mary's (MI)					Domke, Tim
	Southwestern (AZ)			21	9	Westphal, Paul D.
12	Cardinal Stritch (WI)			23	12	Moore, Thomas J.
	Concordia (CA)			25	8	Wild, Dave
16	Blackburn			19	8	Staff, Bob
	Colorado Northwestern CC			16	19	Conrad, Paul
	Lamar CC			20	13	Blanc, Al
	Viterbo			14	16	Glasshoff, James

1987

F	School	SD	Bye	W	L	Coach
1	National (SD)					Ticknor, Duane
2	Bluefield (VA)			28	13	Blevins, Mark
3	Bristol (TN)			12	25	
4	Colorado Northwestern CC			15	20	Conrad, Paul
5	David N Myers			19	16	Rogers, "Rusty"
6	Columbia JC (SC)					
7	Viterbo			22	10	Popp, Rod
8	Blackburn			14	9	Staff, Bob
10	Blanton's JC					
	Rochester (MI)			21	9	Pleasant, Garth A.
12	Central (KS)			19	11	Hibbard, Randy
	Jordan: Flint			21	16	Scott, Daniel L.
16	D'Youville			8	14	DeMarco, "Chip"
	Elizabeth Seton			28	7	O'Donnell, Dennis G.
	New Hampshire Tech: Concord			17	7	Miller, William J. Jr.
	Sullivan (KY)			17	16	Skinner, David L.

F	School	SD	Bye	W	L	Coach
1988						
1	National (SD)			30	6	Ticknor, Duane
2	Bluefield (VA)			24	14	Blevins, Mark
3	Redlands CC					Imotichey, Melvin
4	Mount Senario			20	13	Olson, Mike
5	Lindsey Wilson			20	14	Wise, Mark
6	Columbia JC (SC)		To R8	18	12	Hewett, Dale
7	Kansas Wesleyan			15	15	Jones, Jerry
8	David N Myers			12	25	Rogers, "Rusty"
10	Edgewood			23	14	Larson, G. Steven
	Webber			24	10	Yenta, Rex R.
12	Jordan: Flint					Scott, Daniel L.
	New Hampshire Tech: Concord			23	13	Miller, William J., Jr.
15	Hesser			31	6	Le Seur, Gary A.
	Rochester (MI)			22	7	Pleasant, Garth A.
	Trinity International (IL)			18	11	Seils, David S.
1989						
1	Rochester (MI)			25	3	Pleasant, Garth A.
2	Saint Scholastica			19	16	Nachtsheim, John
3	Mount Senario	1	To R8	23	10	Olson, Mike
4	Bluefield (VA)	2		23	16	Blevins, Mark
5	Edgewood	3		26	13	Larson, G. Steven
6	David N Myers			11	21	Rogers, "Rusty"
7	Blackburn	4		17	8	Staff, Bob
8	Jordan: Detroit					Watkins, Quinton "Rocky"
10	Blanton's JC			16	14	Allen, Doug
	Concordia: Saint Paul			14	14	Getzlaff, Dennis
12	Elizabeth Seton			22	14	O'Donnell, Dennis G.
	Jordan: Flint					Porter, Victor
15	Draughons JC: Knoxville					Tylar, Donnie
	New Hampshire Tech: Concord			20	10	Miller, William J., Jr.
	Northland			13	18	Bystrom, Nick
1990						
1	Paul Quinn	1	To R8	31	7	Summers, James "Zip"
2	Draughons JC: Knoxville	6		21	9	Tylar, Donnie
3	Mount Senario	4	To R8	26	10	Andrist, Edward A.
4	Edgewood	8		20	11	Larson, G. Steven
5	Jordan: Detroit	9				Watkins, Quinton "Rocky"
6	Nazareth (MI)	10		13	21	Ragsdale, Chris
7	Jordan: Flint	5		27	10	Porter, Victor
8	Saint Scholastica	7		18	12	Nachtsheim, John
10	Elizabeth Seton	3	To R8	24	9	O'Donnell, Dennis G.
	Rochester (MI)	2	To R8	19	11	Pleasant, Garth A.
12	Colorado Northwestern CC	12		8	25	Conrad, Paul
	Ohio Valley (WV)	11		11	16	Colgrove, Jack A.

F	School	SD	Bye	W	L	Coach
1991						
1	Mount Senario	1	To R8	40	10	Andrist, Edward A.
2	Jordan: Detroit	3	To R8			Watkins, Quinton "Rocky"
3	Northwest Christian	5		4	20	Lipp, David
4	Arkansas Baptist	7		23	12	Marks, Arcell
5	Colorado Northwestern CC	12		11	22	Conrad, Paul
6	Blackburn	2	To R8	22	7	Zeff, Dr. Ira
7	Paul Quinn	4	To R8	17	12	Summers, James "Zip"
8	Draughons JC: Knoxville	10				
10	Jordan: Flint	11		15	21	Porter, Victor
	Northland	8		14	15	Bystrom, Nick
12	Elizabeth Seton	9		18	18	O'Donnell, Dennis G.
	Rochester (MI)	6		10	20	Pleasant, Garth A.
1992						
1	Texas College	1	To R8	25	5	Patrick, Kirk
2	Paul Quinn	3	To R8			Summers, James "Zip"
3	Jordan: Detroit	4	To R8			Watkins, Quinton "Rocky"
4	Mount Senario	7		29	16	Andrist, Edward A.
5	Arkansas Baptist	10				Marks, Arcell
6	Blackburn	2	To R8	22	8	Zeff, Dr. Ira
7	Rochester (MI)	5		22	7	Pleasant, Garth A.
8	Redlands CC	12		15	17	Imotichey, Melvin
10	Baptist Christian (LA)	11		22	21	Bagley, Larry
	Eastern Maine Tech	8		16	10	Young, Christopher
12	Graceland (IN)	6		20	11	Hickman, Rick W.
	Northland	9		18	13	Bystrom, Nick
1993						
1	Texas College	1	To R8			Patrick, Kirk
2	Jordan: Detroit	3				Watkins, Quinton "Rocky"
3	Ohio Valley (WV)	7		20	16	Colgrove, Jack A.
4	Jordan: Flint	4		21	10	Porter, Victor
5	Mount Senario	2		32	15	Andrist, Edward A.
6	Graceland (IN)	6		14	18	Harrop, Rich
8	Paul Quinn	5		15	15	Summers, James "Zip"
	Redlands CC	9		16	12	Imotichey, Melvin
9	Northland	8		17	13	Swan, David
1994						
1	Mount Senario	8		24	22	Andrist, Edward A.
2	Rochester (MI)	6		19	10	Pleasant, Garth A.
3	Ohio Valley (WV)	5		19	16	Colgrove, Jack A.
4	Texas College	4	To R8	18	7	Patrick, Kirk
5	Arkansas Baptist	10		11	16	Marks, Arcell
6	Jordan: Detroit	7		21	15	Watkins, Quinton "Rocky"
7	Clarendon	4	To R8	26	11	Mondragon, Joseph
8	Graceland (IN)	12		6	30	Freebersyser, George
10	Maine: Fort Kent	1	To R8	24	7	Clifford, Dan
	Trinity International (IL)	3	To R8	19	11	Bruehl, Alan
12	Jordan: Flint	9		14	4	Porter, Victor
	Massachusetts Bay CC	11		16	13	Harrison, Allen

F	School	SD	Bye	W	L	Coach
1995						
1	Paul Quinn	2	To R8	20	12	Summers, James 'Zip'
2	Northwest Christian	11		18	11	Lipp, David
3	Baptist Christian (LA)	8				Martin, Chip
4	Graceland (IN)	12				Freebersyser, George
5	Mount Senario	9		12	24	Andrist, Edward A.
6	Clarendon	7		23	12	Mondragon, Joseph
7	Southern Maine Tech	3	To R8	24	14	Stockwell, Dr. Ira
8	Blackburn	6		15	14	Zeff, Dr. Ira
10	Maine: Fort Kent	4	To R8	26	10	Clifford, Dan
	Vermont Tech	1	To R8	20	5	Maxwell, Mike
12	Maine: Augusta	10		12	14	Andreasen, Michael
	Ohio Valley (WV)	5		16	14	Colgrove, Jack A.
1996						
1	Mount Senario	9		14	22	Andrist, Edward A.
2	Louisiana Christian	4	To R8	19	13	Schexnayder, Tommy
3	Rochester (MI)	7		20	16	Pleasant, Garth A.
4	Northwest Christian	3	To R8	18	14	Lipp, David
5	Clarendon	8		21	17	Mondragon, Joseph
6	National Christian	10		4	20	Cerventes, Ceasar
8	Bunker Hill CC	6	To R8	21	9	Lee, Terrence
	Maine: Fort Kent	2	To R8	25	5	Clifford, Dan
10	Massachusetts Bay CC	1	To R8	27	4	Harrison, Allen
	Southern Maine Tech	5	To R8	24	8	Fournier, William
1997						
1	Louisiana Christian	6		21	12	Schexnayder, Tommy
2	Rochester (MI)	8		17	14	Pleasant, Garth A.
3	Medaille	5		18	10	Jacob, Richard L.
4	Kansas Wesleyan	11		11	21	Jones, Jerry
5	Clarendon	3	To R8	18	8	Mondragon, Joseph
6	Bunker Hill CC	4	To R8	18	9	Jones, Christopher
8	Central Maine Tech	1	To R8	19	6	Gonyea, Dave
	Maine: Fort Kent	2	To R8	20	10	Graffam, Jim
1998						
1	Northwest Christian	5		24	8	Lipp, David
2	Philander Smith	7		17	10	Greenwood, J. W. 'Johnny'
3	California Christian	1	To R8	30	8	Wilkerson, Dr. Charles
4	Blackburn	6		18	11	Zeff, Dr. Ira
5	Rochester (MI)	9		12	18	Pleasant, Garth A.
6	Saint Mary's (MI)	8		14	19	Daick, Chris
8	Arkansas Baptist	10		5	14	Marks, Arcell
	Kansas Wesleyan	15		5	26	Jones, Jerry
9	Medaille	12		14	16	Jacob, Richard L.
10	Florida College	11		11	19	Moorer, Kenny
12	Colorado Northwestern CC	13		8	23	Conrad, Paul
	Crowley's Ridge	14		9	14	Livingston, Dean
15	Bunker Hill CC	4		26	9	Jones, Christopher
	Central Maine Tech	3		20	7	Gonyea, Dave
	New Hampshire Tech: Concord	2		22	7	Moffett, Michael

Tournament Results—Women

F	School	SD	Bye	W	L	Coach
1980						
1	Colorado Woman's			23	8	Forkum, Jim
2	Warner Pacific			X	X	Park, Kathi
3	Concordia (OR)			13	7	Kunert, Charles J. "Chuck"
4	Northwest Assemblies			19	12	Brodin, Kristi
5	Concordia: Saint Paul			16	10	Surridge, Dr. Jack
6	Master's			9	9	Harris, Connie
7	Judson Baptist (OR)					
8	Trinity Christian			10	6	Hovinga, Lois
1981						
	No Tournament					
1982						
1	National (SD)			16	4	Haight, H. C. "Bud"
2	Baptist Christian (LA)			15	5	
3	Northeast CC (NE)					Saunce, Judy
4	Freeman JC			5	12	Hoffer, Herb
5	Concordia: Saint Paul			17	9	Surridge, Dr. Jack
6	Colorado Northwestern CC			X	X	Unknown
7	Viterbo			11	7	Jack, Ellyn
8	Trinity Bible			12	8	Long, Rod P.
1983						
1	Concordia: Saint Paul			20	6	Surridge, Dr. Jack
2	Lamar CC			X	X	Unknown
3	Northland			14	10	Vieira, Kim T.
4	National (SD)					
5	Colorado Northwestern CC			X	X	Unknown
6	Central CC: Platte			12	16	Van Fossen, Dennis
7	Viterbo			12	9	Jack, Ellyn
8	Trinity Bible			11	8	Long, Rod P.
1984						
1	Lamar CC	4	R8>R2	X	X	Unknown
2	National (SD)	3	To R4			
3	Northland	1	To R4	22	6	Vieira, Kim T.
4	Concordia: Saint Paul	2	To R4	19	10	Surridge, Dr. Jack
5	York (NE)					
6	Clarke (IA)			8	15	Holland, Kevin
8	Colorado Northwestern CC			X	X	Unknown
	Northeast CC (NE)					Saunce, Judy
9	Nazareth (MI)			8	18	Shaw, William
1985						
1	Phillips JC: Gulfport			21	6	Rosetti, George F., Sr.
2	Northland			21	6	Franklin, Steve
3	Marycrest International			15	15	Vieira, Kim T.
4	Concordia: Saint Paul			20	8	Surridge, Dr. Jack

F	School	SD	Bye	W	L	Coach
5	National (SD)					
6	Clarke (IA)			8	19	Holland, Kevin
7	Warren Wilson			21	8	Slaughter, Jerry
8	Blackburn			12	17	Sexton, James R.

1986

1	Phillips JC: Gulfport	3		22	7	Rosetti, George F., Sr.
2	National (SD)	4				
3	David N Myers	1		20	9	Rogers, 'Rusty'
4	Marycrest International	2		20	13	Vieira, Kim T.
5	Concordia: Saint Paul	6		20	10	Surridge, Dr. Jack
6	Saint Scholastica	5		18	8	Stukel, Jim
7	Nazareth (MI)	8				Shaw, William
8	Dr. Martin Luther	7		14	11	Leopold, Barbara

1987

1	Concordia (NE)	1		23	8	Everts, Dr. Carl
2	Saint Scholastica	3		25	6	Stukel, Jim
3	David N Myers	2		24	7	Borgis, Steve
4	Northland	5		10	18	Franklin, Steve
5	Colorado Northwestern CC	6		8	23	Frankiewicz, Steve
6	Grand Rapids Baptist	8		9	14	Gates, Ray
7	Concordia: Saint Paul	7		13	14	Surridge, Dr. Jack
8	Mundelein	4		X	X	Bolinder, Rich

1988

1	Saint Scholastica	2		25	6	Stukel, Jim
2	Concordia (NE)	5		19	15	Everts, Dr. Carl
3	Marycrest International	4		18	12	Giardino, Kris
4	Mundelein	3		X	X	Bolinder, Rich
5	Kansas Wesleyan	1		22	4	Rietzke, Tracy
6	David N Myers	6		8	15	Haught, Paul
7	Lindsey Wilson	7		17	10	Adams, Dean
8	Clinch Valley	8		8	19	Kaminske, Debbie

1989

1	Concordia (NE)			25	7	Everts, Dr. Carl
2	Concordia: Saint Paul			17	10	Surridge, Dr. Jack
3	Edgewood			16	13	Raisback, Owen
4	Central (KS)			16	12	Turner, Gary
5	David N Myers			17	14	Haught, Paul
6	Dr. Martin Luther			7	18	Leopold, Barbara
7	Northland			15	11	Franklin, Steve
8	Saint Teresa					Boike, Lon

1990

1	Concordia (NE)			20	13	Everts, Dr. Carl
2	Silver Lake			26	4	Wenner, Craig
3	Blackburn			15	11	Sexton, James R.
4	Concordia: Saint Paul			9	22	Olley, Christopher
5	Northland			14	16	Franklin, Steve
6	Trinity International (IL)			16	12	Seils, David S.
7	Midway			6	18	Dever, Debbie
8	Nazareth (MI)			6	20	Low, Mike

F	School	SD	Bye	W	L	Coach
1991						
1	Silver Lake	1		25	6	Wenner, Craig
2	Redlands CC	2		22	11	Story-Schell, Rita
3	Blackburn	3		18	11	Sexton, James R.
4	Wilmington (DE)	4		15	12	Rogers, "Rusty"
5	Midway	8		13	20	Brett, Kathy
6	Texas College	6				
7	Northland	5		16	12	Franklin, Steve
8	Trinity International (IL)	7		16	9	Seils, David S.
1992						
1	Trinity International (IL)	6		15	10	Seils, David S.
2	Blackburn	4		20	10	Sexton, James R.
3	Concordia (NE)	2		23	13	Everts, Dr. Carl
4	Wilmington (DE)	1		25	11	Rogers, "Rusty"
5	Paul Quinn	8				Ensley, Michael
6	Northland	3		18	11	Franklin, Steve
7	Mount Senario	5		19	14	Elliott, David
8	Silver Lake	7		17	15	Wenner, Craig
1993						
1	Blackburn	2		24	7	Sexton, James R.
2	Wilmington (DE)	1		26	6	Rogers, "Rusty"
3	Arkansas Baptist	5		19	14	Allen, Lee W.
4	Trinity (VT)	3		21	10	Fitterer, Barbara
5	Northland	6		17	10	Akervik, Holly
6	Silver Lake	4		18	13	Wenner, Craig
7	Clarendon	8		13	18	Zehr, Joel R.
8	Ohio Valley (WV)	7		15	18	Huffman, Gina
1994						
1	Trinity International (IL)	3		24	8	Seils, David S.
2	Arkansas Baptist	4		18	7	Allen, Lee W.
3	Mount Senario	8		16	16	Elliott, David
4	Blackburn	7		15	14	Sexton, James R.
5	Midway	5		20	13	Duncan, John
6	Clarendon	6		17	15	Zehr, Joel R.
7	Dominican (CA)	8		18	6	Ferraro, Dave
8	Massachusetts Pharmacy	1		17	3	Ciccolo, Stacy
1995						
1	Martin Methodist	7		13	18	Jones, Johnny
2	Mount Senario	1		15	15	Biddle, Brian
3	Clarendon	4		15	12	Zehr, Joel R.
4	Midway	6		20	17	Duncan, John
5	Dominican (CA)	8		17	7	Ferraro, Dave
6	Philander Smith	2				Chandler, Hilton
7	Sue Bennett	3		19	19	Adams, Dean
8	Dr. Martin Luther	5		11	15	Dallman, Dr. Gary L.

F	School	SD	Bye	W	L	Coach
1996						
1	Kansas Wesleyan	4		14	16	Hughes, Tom
2	Dominican (CA)	2	To R4	16	9	Ferraro, Dave
3	Silver Lake	1	To R4	15	6	Koeser, Don
4	Arkansas Baptist	3		18	7	Allen, Lee W.
5	Trinity (VT)	6		8	10	Niebling, Jennifer
6	Warren Wilson	5		10	4	Keller, Jeff
1997						
1	Kansas Wesleyan	6		12	19	Hughes, Tom
2	Clarendon	1		22	5	Zehr, Joel R.
3	Rochester (MI)	4		14	13	Wheeler, Barry
4	Arkansas Baptist	2		17	12	Allen, Lee W.
5	York (NE)	7		8	25	Fields, Terry L.
6	Mount Senario	8		5	22	Leibold, Nicole
8	Northern Essex CC (MA)	5		10	11	Smith, Michael
	Ohio Valley (WV)	3		13	17	Pavan, Ron
1998						
1	Clarendon	3		21	9	Zehr, Joel R.
2	Centenary (NJ)	1		22	6	Finnan, Diane
3	Blackburn	4		19	11	Garrett, Matt
4	Arkansas Baptist	2		15	6	Allen, Lee W.
5	Philander Smith	8		11	13	Chandler, Hilton
6	Kansas Wesleyan	6		14	13	Hughes, Tom
8	Rochester (MI)	7		9	19	Wheeler, Barry
	Silver Lake	5		15	11	Koeser, Don

School Participation History

Year	M/W	F	SD	Bye	#T	W	L	Coach
ALICE LLOYD								
1982	M	3			16	8	22	Morris, Lonnie
1981		8			16	17	14	Morris, Lonnie
1974		16			16	X	X	Rose, James
ARKANSAS BAPTIST								
1991	M	4	7		12	23	12	Marks, Arcell
1992		5	10		12			Marks, Arcell
1994		5	10		12	11	16	Marks, Arcell
1998		8	10		15	5	14	Marks, Arcell
1997		12	10		12	9	18	Marks, Arcell
1978		16			16			
1994	W	2	4		8	18	7	Allen, Lee W.
1993		3	5		8	19	14	Allen, Lee W.
1996		4	3		6	18	7	Allen, Lee W.
1997		4	2		8	17	12	Allen, Lee W.
1998		4	2		8	15	6	Allen, Lee W.
ASHEVILLE BUNCOMBE TCC								
1975	M	16			16	20	4	Rhea, James H.

Year	M/W	F	SD	Bye	#T	W	L	Coach
BALTIMORE COMMERCE								
1967	M	8			8	9	14	Baker, Paul
BAPTIST CHRISTIAN (LA)								
1995	M	3	8		12			Martin, Chip
1992		10	11		12	22	21	Bagley, Larry
1981		12			16			Martin, C. P.
1977		16			16	20	5	Martin, C. P.
1980		16			16			Martin, C. P.
1982	W	2			8	15	5	
BARBER-SCOTIA								
1968	M	8			8			Coefield, Aldon L.
BEVILL STATE CC: BREWER								
1972	M	3			8	15	16	Anderson, Richard
1979		8			16	15	13	Anderson, Richard
BLACKBURN								
1982	M	1			16	23	8	Parker, James R.
1985		1			16	23	7	Staff, Bob
1998		4	6		15	18	11	Zeff, Dr. Ira
1991		6	2	To R8	12	22	7	Zeff, Dr. Ira
1992		6	2	To R8	12	22	8	Zeff, Dr. Ira
1989		7	4		15	17	8	Staff, Bob
1983		8			16	20	5	Parker, James R.
1984		8			16	20	9	Parker, James R.
1987		8			16	14	9	Staff, Bob
1995		8	6		12	15	14	Zeff, Dr. Ira
1981		16			16	19	10	Parker, James R.
1986		16			16	19	8	Staff, Bob
1993	W	1	2		8	24	7	Sexton, James R.
1992		2	4		8	20	10	Sexton, James R.
1990		3			8	15	11	Sexton, James R.
1991		3	3		8	18	11	Sexton, James R.
1998		3	4		8	19	11	Garrett, Matt
1994		4	7		8	15	14	Sexton, James R.
1985		8			8	12	17	Sexton, James R.
BLANTON'S JC								
1987	M	10			16			
1989		10			15	16	14	Allen, Doug
BLUEFIELD (VA)								
1985	M	2			16	27	12	Becker, Darrell
1987		2			16	28	13	Blevins, Mark
1988		2			15	24	14	Blevins, Mark
1986		3			16	28	9	Blevins, Mark
1989		4	2		15	23	16	Blevins, Mark
1980		8			16	22	20	Brunson, Dean
1981		9			16	12	14	Brunson, Dean
1974		16			16			
1984		16			16			Becker, Darrell

Year	M/W	F	SD	Bye	#T	W	L	Coach
BRANDYWINE								
1967	M	3			8	23	4	
BRISTOL (TN)								
1986	M	1			16			Crowder, Brien
1987		3			16	12	25	
1974		16			16			Alves, Len
BRYANT & STRATTON: ALBANY								
1973	M	3			8	17	8	Rice, Willard
1972		8			8	17	2	Rice, Willard
1974		8			16			Rice, Willard
1979		16			16	18	6	
BRYANT & STRATTON: BUFFALO								
1974	M	1			16	X	X	Griffin, Dr. Thomas J.
1981		8			16	25	6	McNamara, Tim
1986		8			16	23	9	Krauza, Gregory A.
1980		16			16	16	6	Licate, Gilbert P.
1982		16			16	17	10	McNamara, Tim
1983		16			16	12	10	McNamara, Tim
BUNKER HILL CC								
1997	M	6	4	To R8	12	18	9	Jones, Christopher
1996		8	6	To R8	10	21	9	Lee, Terrence
1998		15	4		15	26	9	Jones, Christopher
CALIFORNIA CHRISTIAN								
1998	M	3	1	To R8	15	30	8	Wilkerson, Dr. Charles
CARDINAL STRITCH (WI)								
1986	M	12			16	23	12	Moore, Thomas J.
1979		16			16	22	6	Stier, Dr. William F., Jr.
1983		16			16	11	19	Moore, Thomas J.
1984		16			16	17	16	Moore, Thomas J.
1985		16			16	14	19	Moore, Thomas J.
CECILS JC (NC)								
1984	M	8			16	28	1	Reed, Ronald
1983		12			16	22	15	Reed, Ronald
CENTENARY (NJ)								
1998	W	2	1		8	22	6	Finnan, Diane
CENTRAL (KS)								
1986	M	6			16	19	10	Hibbard, Randy
1976		8			14	15	11	Saxton, Mike
1987		12			16	19	11	Hibbard, Randy
1985		16			16	14	7	Hibbard, Randy
1989	W	4			8	16	12	Turner, Gary
CENTRAL CC: PLATTE								
1983	M	2			16	19	14	Gutierrez, Jack
1985		10			16	23	10	Gutierrez, Jack
1983	W	6			8	12	16	Van Fossen, Dennis

Year	M/W	F	SD	Bye	#T	W	L	Coach
CENTRAL MAINE TECH								
1997	M	8	1	To R8	12	19	6	Gonyea, Dave
1998		15	3		15	20	7	Gonyea, Dave
CLARENDON								
1996	M	5	8		10	21	17	Mondragon, Joseph
1997		5	3	To R8	12	18	8	Mondragon, Joseph
1995		6	7		12	23	12	Mondragon, Joseph
1994		7	4	To R8	12	26	11	Mondragon, Joseph
1998	W	1	3		8	21	9	Zehr, Joel R.
1997		2	1		8	22	5	Zehr, Joel R.
1995		3	4		8	15	12	Zehr, Joel R.
1994		6	6		8	17	15	Zehr, Joel R.
1993		7	8		8	13	18	Zehr, Joel R.
CLARKE (IA)								
1984	W	6			9	8	15	Holland, Kevin
1985		6			8	8	19	Holland, Kevin
CLINCH VALLEY								
1988	W	8	8		8	8	19	Kaminske, Debbie
COLORADO NORTHWESTERN CC								
1984	M	3			16	18	18	Conrad, Paul
1987		4			16	15	20	Conrad, Paul
1991		5	12		12	11	22	Conrad, Paul
1975		8			16	13	17	Conrad, Paul
1976		8			14	10	22	Conrad, Paul
1979		8			16	20	14	Conrad, Paul
1980		12			16	20	14	Conrad, Paul
1985		12			16	12	20	Conrad, Paul
1990		12	12		12	8	25	Conrad, Paul
1998		12	13		15	8	23	Conrad, Paul
1977		16			16	10	22	Conrad, Paul
1978		16			16	17	12	Conrad, Paul
1981		16			16	17	16	Conrad, Paul
1986		16			16	16	19	Conrad, Paul
1983	W	5			8	X	X	Unknown
1987		5	6		8	8	23	Frankiewicz, Steve
1982		6			8	X	X	Unknown
1984		8			9	X	X	Unknown
COLORADO WOMAN'S								
1980	W	1			8	23	8	Forkum, Jim
COLUMBIA JC (SC)								
1986	M	4			16	23	7	
1987		6			16			
1988		6		To R8	15	18	12	Hewett, Dale
1980		8			16			
1978		16			16			
1979		16			16	17	8	

Year	M/W	F	SD	Bye	#T	W	L	Coach
COLUMBIA STATE CC								
1985	M	12			16	14	8	Painter, Jim
COLUMBUS BUSINESS (OH)								
1968	M	2			8			
CONCORDIA (CA)								
1986	M	12			16	25	8	Wild, Dave
CONCORDIA (MI)								
1980	M	12			16	23	9	Harting, Walt
1979		16			16	10	18	Harting, Walt
CONCORDIA (NE)								
1987	W	1	1		8	23	8	Everts, Dr. Carl
1989		1			8	25	7	Everts, Dr. Carl
1990		1			8	20	13	Everts, Dr. Carl
1988		2	5		8	19	15	Everts, Dr. Carl
1992		3	2		8	23	13	Everts, Dr. Carl
CONCORDIA (OR)								
1979	M	2			16	17	10	Friedrichs, Dr. Warren
1976		8		To R8	14	17	12	Friedrichs, Dr. Warren
1980		10			16	19	14	Friedrichs, Dr. Warren
1978		16			16	21	9	Friedrichs, Dr. Warren
1980	W	3			8	13	7	Kunert, Charles J. "Chuck"
CONCORDIA (WI)								
1979	M	3			16	20	13	Weiss, Dick
1980		8			16	19	17	Weiss, Dick
1982		12			16	6	23	Lohmeyer, Neil
CONCORDIA: AUSTIN								
1983	M	1			16	30	7	Orton, Tom
1982		9			16	9	20	Orton, Tom
CONCORDIA: SAINT PAUL								
1977	M	3			16	20	9	Hendrickson, John
1978		8			16	18	8	Hendrickson, John
1989		10			15	14	14	Getzlaff, Dennis
1976		14			14	16	5	Hendrickson, John
1979		16			16	10	14	Hendrickson, John
1983	W	1			8	20	6	Surridge, Dr. Jack
1989		2			8	17	10	Surridge, Dr. Jack
1984		4	2	To R4	9	19	10	Surridge, Dr. Jack
1985		4			8	20	8	Surridge, Dr. Jack
1990		4			8	9	22	Olley, Christopher
1980		5			8	16	10	Surridge, Dr. Jack
1982		5			8	17	9	Surridge, Dr. Jack
1986		5	6		8	20	10	Surridge, Dr. Jack
1987		7	7		8	13	14	Surridge, Dr. Jack
CROWLEY'S RIDGE								
1998	M	12	14		15	9	14	Livingston, Dean

Year	M/W	F	SD	Bye	#T	W	L	Coach
CULLMAN								
1974	M	3			16	16	10	Franey, Joseph S.
1975		8			16	14	10	Franey, Joseph S.
D'YOUVILLE								
1987	M	16			16	8	14	DeMarco, "Chip"
DAEMEN								
1984	M	12			16	X	X	Licate, Gilbert P.
1978		16			16	20	5	Murray, Kenneth
DAVID N MYERS								
1986	M	2			16	22	12	Friedman, Michael
1974		4			16	15	8	Kennedy, Richard
1987		5			16	19	16	Rogers, "Rusty"
1970		6			8	13	13	Schuster, Will
1989		6			15	11	21	Rogers, "Rusty"
1967		8			8	14	7	Kavanaugh, W. H.
1988		8			15	12	25	Rogers, "Rusty"
1975		16			16			McCoid, Rod
1986	W	3	1		8	20	9	Rogers, "Rusty"
1987		3	2		8	24	7	Borgis, Steve
1989		5			8	17	14	Haught, Paul
1988		6	6		8	8	15	Haught, Paul
DAVIS (OH)								
1971	M	6			8	12	8	Carder, Jerry J.
DENMARK TECH								
1968	M	6			8	21	7	Gaddy, Rayshaw L.
DOMINICAN (CA)								
1996	W	2	2	To R4	6	16	9	Ferraro, Dave
1995		5	8		8	17	7	Ferraro, Dave
1994		7	8		8	18	6	Ferraro, Dave
DR. MARTIN LUTHER								
1977	M	16			16	14	9	Dallman, Dr. Gary L.
1989	W	6			8	7	18	Leopold, Barbara
1986		8	7		8	14	11	Leopold, Barbara
1995		8	5		8	11	15	Dallman, Dr. Gary L.
DRAUGHONS JC: KINGSPORT								
1985	M	6			16	32	8	
DRAUGHONS JC: KNOXVILLE								
1990	M	2	6		12	21	9	Tylar, Donnie
1991		8	10		12			
1989		15			15			Tylar, Donnie
1984		16			16			Mitchell, Dave
DUFF'S BUSINESS								
1970	M	8			8	X	X	Weir,

Year	M/W	F	SD	Bye	#T	W	L	Coach
DURHAM BUSINESS								
1971	M	2			8	30	8	Terry, Reginald N.
1978		8			16	21	9	Hawkins, Ralph
1974		16			16			
EAST MISSISSIPPI CC								
1978	M	16			16			
EASTERN MAINE TECH								
1992	M	10	8		12	16	10	Young, Christopher
EDGEWOOD								
1990	M	4	8		12	20	11	Larson, G. Steven
1989		5	3		15	26	13	Larson, G. Steven
1988		10			15	23	14	Larson, G. Steven
1989	W	3			8	16	13	Raisback, Owen
ELIZABETH SETON								
1990	M	10	3	To R8	12	24	9	O'Donnell, Dennis G.
1989		12			15	22	14	O'Donnell, Dennis G.
1991		12	9		12	18	18	O'Donnell, Dennis G.
1985		16			16	21	7	O'Donnell, Dennis G.
1987		16			16	28	7	O'Donnell, Dennis G.
FAULKNER								
1981	M	3			16	22	13	Hazelip, John
FLORIDA COLLEGE								
1975	M	1			16	20	11	Wilson, Tom
1979		1			16	20	14	Wilson, Tom
1980		4			16	20	13	Owens, Donnie
1998		10	11		15	11	19	Moorer, Kenny
1997		12	12		12	7	20	Moorer, Kenny
FORT LAUDERDALE								
1971	M	3			8	12	9	Gotkin, Hy
1970		5			8	13	11	
1969		8			8	12	20	D'Angelo,
FREEMAN JC								
1982	W	4			8	5	12	Hoffer, Herb
FRIENDSHIP JC								
1967	M	6			8	11	13	Harris, Rev. Herman K., II
1975		8			16			
GANADO								
1975	M	16			16			
GEORGIA MILITARY								
1981	M	2			16	X	X	Steinke, Rick
1983		9			16	25	12	Keast, Richard

Year	M/W	F	SD	Bye	#T	W	L	Coach
GRACELAND (IN)								
1995	M	4	12		12			Freebersyser, George
1993		6	6		9	14	18	Harrop, Rich
1994		8	12		12	6	30	Freebersyser, George
1992		12	6		12	20	11	Hickman, Rick W.
GRAND RAPIDS BAPTIST								
1987	W	6	8		8	9	14	Gates, Ray
HESSER								
1988	M	15			15	31	6	Le Seur, Gary A.
INDIANA WESLEYAN								
1981	M	8			16	24	6	Kent, "Rocky"
JORDAN: DETROIT								
1991	M	2	3	To R8	12			Watkins, Quinton "Rocky"
1993		2	3		9			Watkins, Quinton "Rocky"
1992		3	4	To R8	12			Watkins, Quinton "Rocky"
1990		5	9		12			Watkins, Quinton "Rocky
1994		6	7		12	21	15	Watkins, Quinton "Rocky"
1989		8			15			Watkins, Quinton "Rocky"
JORDAN: FLINT								
1993	M	4	4		9	21	10	Porter, Victor
1990		7	5		12	27	10	Porter, Victor
1991		10	11		12	15	21	Porter, Victor
1987		12			16	21	16	Scott, Daniel L.
1988		12			15			Scott, Daniel L.
1989		12			15			Porter, Victor
1994		12	9		12	14	4	Porter, Victor
1984		16			16			Scott, Daniel L.
JOSEPHINUM								
1981	M	16			16	20	6	
JUDSON (IL)								
1981	M	10			16	18	16	Harris, Sam
JUDSON BAPTIST (OR)								
1980	W	7			8			
KANSAS WESLEYAN								
1997	M	4	11		12	11	21	Jones, Jerry
1988		7			15	15	15	Jones, Jerry
1998		8	15		15	5	26	Jones, Jerry
1996	W	1	4		6	14	16	Hughes, Tom
1997		1	6		8	12	19	Hughes, Tom
1988		5	1		8	22	4	Rietzke, Tracy
1998		6	6		8	14	13	Hughes, Tom
KITTRELL JC								
1970	M	1			8	32	4	Golatt, Moses

Year	M/W	F	SD	Bye	#T	W	L	Coach
LA ROCHE								
1976	M	14			14	14	6	Pasquinelli, John
1977		16			16	11	10	Pasquinelli, John
LAFAYETTE (NC)								
1976	M	14			14	18	8	
LAMAR CC								
1983	M	4			16	16	26	Carel, Steve
1982		8			16	X	X	Carel, Steve
1986		16			16	20	13	Blanc, Al
1984	W	1	4		9	X	X	Unknown
1983		2			8	X	X	Unknown
LEES (KY)								
1983	M	8			16	26	8	Howard, Cluster
LINDSEY WILSON								
1972	M	1			8	22	8	Voight, James R. "Jim"
1988		5			15	20	14	Wise, Mark
1988	W	7	7		8	17	10	Adams, Dean
LOGAN CHIROPRACTIC								
1978	M	16			16	17	4	Kirkling, David
LOUISIANA CHRISTIAN								
1997	M	1	6		12	21	12	Schexnayder, Tommy
1996		2	4	To R8	10	19	13	Schexnayder, Tommy
MAINE: AUGUSTA								
1995	M	12	10		12	12	14	Andreasen, Michael
MAINE: FORT KENT								
1996	M	8	2	To R8	10	25	5	Clifford, Dan
1997		8	2	To R8	12	20	10	Graffam, Jim
1994		10	1	To R8	12	24	7	Clifford, Dan
1995		10	4	To R8	12	26	10	Clifford, Dan
MARTIN METHODIST								
1995	W	1	7		8	13	18	Jones, Johnny
MARYCREST INTERNATIONAL								
1985	W	3			8	15	15	Vieira, Kim T.
1988		3	4		8	18	12	Giardino, Kris
1986		4	2		8	20	13	Vieira, Kim T.
MASSACHUSETTS BAY CC								
1996	M	10	1	To R8	10	27	4	Harrison, Allen
1994		12	11		12	16	13	Harrison, Allen
MASSACHUSETTS PHARMACY								
1994	W	8	1		8	17	3	Ciccolo, Stacy

Year	M/W	F	SD	Bye	#T	W	L	Coach
MASTER'S								
1974	M	8			16	13	21	Fowler, Billy
1982		16			16	18	5	Reese, Pete
1980	W	6			8	9	9	Harris, Connie
MEDAILLE								
1997	M	3	5		12	18	10	Jacob, Richard L.
1998		9	12		15	14	16	Jacob, Richard L.
MIDLAND COMMERCE								
1967	M	5			8	20	3	Noble, Del
MIDWAY								
1995	W	4	6		8	20	17	Duncan, John
1991		5	8		8	13	20	Brett, Kathy
1994		5	5		8	20	13	Duncan, John
1990		7			8	6	18	Dever, Debbie
MISSOURI BAPTIST								
1979	M	3			16	18	17	McKinney, Lee
1977		8			16	17	22	Brown, "Chuck"
1976		14			14	25	13	Brown, "Chuck"
1978		16			16	13	20	Brown, "Chuck"
1980		16			16	18	13	McKinney, Lee
MORRISTOWN (TN)								
1968	M	3			8	16	7	Bundy, Samuel S.
MOUNT SENARIO								
1991	M	1	1	To R8	12	40	10	Andrist, Edward A.
1994		1	8		12	24	22	Andrist, Edward A.
1996		1	9		10	14	22	Andrist, Edward A.
1989		3	1	To R8	15	23	10	Olson, Mike
1990		3	4	To R8	12	26	10	Andrist, Edward A.
1988		4			15	20	13	Olson, Mike
1992		4	7		12	29	16	Andrist, Edward A.
1993		5	2		9	32	15	Andrist, Edward A.
1995		5	9		12	12	24	Andrist, Edward A.
1997		9	9		12	12	22	Andrist, Edward A.
1976		14			14	17	9	Novak, Bill
1977		16			16	10	16	Novak, Bill
1979		16			16	20	11	Novak, Bill
1980		16			16	10	17	Novak, Bill
1995	W	2	1		8	15	15	Biddle, Brian
1994		3	8		8	16	16	Elliott, David
1997		6	8		8	5	22	Leibold, Nicole
1992		7	5		8	19	14	Elliott, David
MOUNT VERNON NAZARENE								
1975	M	16			16	8	21	Bradley, Carroll
1979		16			16	10	20	Martin, Bobby

Year	M/W	F	SD	Bye	#T	W	L	Coach
MUNDELEIN								
1988	W	4	3		8	X	X	Bolinder, Rich
1987		8	4		8	X	X	Bolinder, Rich
NATIONAL (SD)								
1987	M	1			16			Ticknor, Duane
1988		1			15	30	6	Ticknor, Duane
1986		7			16	24	11	Ticknor, Duane
1985		10			16	15	25	Ticknor, Duane
1982	W	1			8	16	4	Haight, H. C. "Bud"
1984		2	3	To R4	9			
1986		2	4		8			
1983		4			8			
1985		5			8			
NATIONAL CHRISTIAN								
1996	M	6	10		10	4	20	Cerventes, Ceasar
NAVAJO CC (AZ)								
1985	M	5			16	22	12	Minley, Jeff
NAZARETH (MI)								
1990	M	6	10		12	13	21	Ragsdale, Chris
1986	W	7	8		8			Shaw, William
1990		8			8	6	20	Low, Mike
1984		9			9	8	18	Shaw, William
NEW HAMPSHIRE TECH: CONCORD								
1988	M	12			15	23	13	Miller, William J., Jr.
1989		15			15	20	10	Miller, William J., Jr.
1998		15	2		15	22	7	Moffett, Michael
1987		16			16	17	7	Miller, William J., Jr.
NEW KENSINGTON COMMERCIAL								
1970	M	3			8	10	9	Shultz, Charles
NORTHEAST CC (NE)								
1976	M	1			14			Stevenson, Charles "Chuck"
1977		2			16	22	5	Stevenson, Charles "Chuck"
1978		4			16	22	6	Stevenson, Charles "Chuck"
1981		4			16			Stevenson, Charles "Chuck"
1979		8			16	15	9	Stevenson, Charles "Chuck"
1980		8			16			Stevenson, Charles "Chuck"
1982		8			16			Stevenson, Charles "Chuck"
1983		8			16	12	13	Stevenson, Charles "Chuck"
1984		12			16			Johnson, Fred
1975		16			16			Stevenson, Charles "Chuck"
1985		16			16			Johnson, Fred
1982	W	3			8			Saunce, Judy
1984		8			9			Saunce, Judy
NORTHERN ESSEX CC (MA)								
1997	W	8	5		8	10	11	Smith, Michael

Year	M/W	F	SD	Bye	#T	W	L	Coach
NORTHLAND								
1985	M	7			16	13	21	Bystrom, Nick
1993		9	8		9	17	13	Swan, David
1991		10	8		12	14	15	Bystrom, Nick
1992		12	9		12	18	13	Bystrom, Nick
1989		15			15	13	18	Bystrom, Nick
1985	W	2			8	21	6	Franklin, Steve
1983		3			8	14	10	Vieira, Kim T.
1984		3	1	To R4	9	22	6	Vieira, Kim T.
1987		4	5		8	10	18	Franklin, Steve
1990		5			8	14	16	Franklin, Steve
1993		5	6		8	17	10	Akervik, Holly
1992		6	3		8	18	11	Franklin, Steve
1989		7			8	15	11	Franklin, Steve
1991		7	5		8	16	12	Franklin, Steve
NORTHWEST ASSEMBLIES								
1974	M	8			16	22	7	Kinney, Carl
1980	W	4			8	19	12	Brodin, Kristi
NORTHWEST CHRISTIAN								
1998	M	1	5		15	24	8	Lipp, David
1995		2	11		12	18	11	Lipp, David
1991		3	5		12	4	20	Lipp, David
1996		4	3	To R8	10	18	14	Lipp, David
1997		10	7		12	19	14	Lipp, David
1977		16			16	24	6	Cox, Duane
NORTHWEST SHOALS CC: PHIL CAMPBELL								
1973	M	2			8	16	17	Seesholtz, Arthur
NORTHWESTERN (MN)								
1975	M	16			16	15	10	Christopherson, Duane
NORTHWESTERN (OH)								
1972	M	5			8	21	6	Noble, Del
1973		6			8	25	8	Loescher, Art
1974		8			16	20	5	Loescher, Art
1975		16			16	16	13	Loescher, Art
NORTHWESTERN (WI)								
1978	M	8			16	12	13	Thompson, Lloyd E.
NORTHWOOD (IN)								
1978	M	8			16			Johnson, Jack J.
1976		14			14	19	8	Bledsoe, Larry
1977		16			16	25	8	Johnson, Jack J.
OAKLAND CITY (IN)								
1981	M	1			16	12	20	Trafton, Charles L.
1980		2			16	12	17	Trafton, Charles L.
1982		2			16	14	13	Trafton, Charles L.
1978		3			16	21	11	Trafton, Charles L.

Year	M/W	F	SD	Bye	#T	W	L	Coach
1983		10			16	10	13	Trafton, Charles L.
1979		16			16	16	12	Trafton, Charles L.

OHIO VALLEY (WV)

Year	M/W	F	SD	Bye	#T	W	L	Coach
1993	M	3	7		9	20	16	Colgrove, Jack A.
1994		3	5		12	19	16	Colgrove, Jack A.
1990		12	11		12	11	16	Colgrove, Jack A.
1995		12	5		12	16	14	Colgrove, Jack A.
1993	W	8	7		8	15	18	Huffman, Gina
1997		8	3		8	13	17	Pavan, Ron

OKLAHOMA BAPTIST COLLEGE

Year	M/W	F	SD	Bye	#T	W	L	Coach
1984	M	10			16	19	12	Foster, Bruce D.

OTTUMWA HEIGHTS

Year	M/W	F	SD	Bye	#T	W	L	Coach
1974	M	16			16	16	7	Stevenson, Charles "Chuck"

PALMER JC (SC)

Year	M/W	F	SD	Bye	#T	W	L	Coach
1972	M	2			8	21	5	Voight, Jim

PAUL QUINN

Year	M/W	F	SD	Bye	#T	W	L	Coach
1990	M	1	1	To R8	12	31	7	Summers, James "Zip"
1995		1	2	To R8	12	20	12	Summers, James "Zip"
1992		2	3	To R8	12			Summers, James "Zip"
1991		7	4	To R8	12	17	12	Summers, James "Zip"
1993		8	5		9	15	15	Summers, James "Zip"
1992	W	5	8		8			Ensley, Michael

PENN-OHIO

Year	M/W	F	SD	Bye	#T	W	L	Coach
1969	M	8			8	7	7	

PHILANDER SMITH

Year	M/W	F	SD	Bye	#T	W	L	Coach
1998	M	2	7		15	17	10	Greenwood, J. W. "Johnny"
1998	W	5	8		8	11	13	Chandler, Hilton
1995		6	2		8			Chandler, Hilton

PHILLIPS JC: GULFPORT

Year	M/W	F	SD	Bye	#T	W	L	Coach
1983	M	3			16	12	15	Ladner, Roland
1984		9			16	22	20	Ladner, Roland
1985	W	1			8	21	6	Rosetti, George F., Sr.
1986		1	3		8	22	7	Rosetti, George F., Sr.

PITTSBURGH ART INSTITUTE

Year	M/W	F	SD	Bye	#T	W	L	Coach
1969	M	2			8			
1968		3			8			

REDLANDS CC

Year	M/W	F	SD	Bye	#T	W	L	Coach
1988	M	3			15			Imotichey, Melvin
1992		8	12		12	15	17	Imotichey, Melvin
1993		8	9		9	16	12	Imotichey, Melvin
1991	W	2	2		8	22	11	Story-Schell, Rita

Year	M/W	F	SD	Bye	#T	W	L	Coach
ROCHESTER (MI)								
1989	M	1			15	25	3	Pleasant, Garth A.
1984		2			16	25	5	Pleasant, Garth A.
1994		2	6		12	19	10	Pleasant, Garth A.
1997		2	8		12	17	14	Pleasant, Garth A.
1996		3	7		10	20	16	Pleasant, Garth A.
1986		5			16	26	3	Pleasant, Garth A.
1998		5	9		15	12	18	Pleasant, Garth A.
1992		7	5		12	22	7	Pleasant, Garth A.
1987		10			16	21	9	Pleasant, Garth A.
1990		10	2	To R8	12	19	11	Pleasant, Garth A.
1991		12	6		12	10	20	Pleasant, Garth A.
1988		15			15	22	7	Pleasant, Garth A.
1982		16			16	17	5	Pleasant, Garth A.
1983		16			16	19	4	Pleasant, Garth A.
1997	W	3	4		8	14	13	Wheeler, Barry
1998		8	7		8	9	19	Wheeler, Barry
RUST								
1977	M	1			16	34	5	Hayes, Naylond
1976		3			14	24	13	Hayes, Naylond
SAGE JC								
1969	M	3			8			
1971		3			8			
1970		8			8			
1977		8			16	16	6	
SAINT CATHARINE (KY)								
1978	M	2			16	22	6	Spry, Ronald
1977		8			16	24	7	Cheatham, Larry
1975		16			16	X	X	Unknown
SAINT JOHN'S LUTHERAN (KS)								
1983	M	12			16	9	19	Clausen, Julius
SAINT MARY'S (MI)								
1985	M	4			16	15	17	Kolby, Jay
1998		6	8		15	14	19	Daick, Chris
1986		10			16			Domke, Tim
SAINT SCHOLASTICA								
1989	M	2			15	19	16	Nachtsheim, John
1990		8	7		12	18	12	Nachtsheim, John
1988	W	1	2		8	25	6	Stukel, Jim
1987		2	3		8	25	6	Stukel, Jim
1986		6	5		8	18	8	Stukel, Jim
SAINT TERESA								
1989	W	8			8			Boike, Lon

Year	M/W	F	SD	Bye	#T	W	L	Coach
SILVER LAKE								
1991	W	1	1		8	25	6	Wenner, Craig
1990		2			8	26	4	Wenner, Craig
1996		3	1	To R4	6	21	8	Koeser, Don
1993		6	4		8	18	13	Wenner, Craig
1992		8	7		8	17	15	Wenner, Craig
1998		8	5		8	15	11	Koeser, Don
SOUTH CAROLINA: AIKEN								
1974	M	16			16	X	X	Perkins, Lewis
SOUTH CAROLINA: LANCASTER								
1975	M	8			16	16	8	
1980		9			16	27	6	DeHart, Glen E.
1982		10			16			DeHart, Glen E.
SOUTH CAROLINA: UNION								
1973	M	3			8	19	10	Edwards, John
1977		8			16	14	10	Call, Gary
1979		8			16	14	13	Call, Gary
SOUTHERN MAINE TECH								
1995	M	7	3	To R8	12	24	14	Stockwell, Dr. Ira
1996		10	5	To R8	10	24	8	Fournier, William
SOUTHERN OHIO: CINCINNATI								
1982	M	8			16	14	14	Nelson, LaDon
1974		16			16			
SOUTHERN UNION STATE CC								
1978	M	1			16	28	5	Gourdouze, Frank
1975		3			16			Gourdouze, Frank
1976		3		To R8	14	21	10	Gourdouze, Frank
1977		3			16	21	9	Gourdouze, Frank
1980		3			16	21	11	Gourdouze, Frank
1982		4			16	20	12	Gourdouze, Frank
1973		8			8	22	12	Gourdouze, Frank
1974		16			16	13	12	Gourdouze, Frank
SOUTHWESTERN (AZ)								
1986	M	10			16	21	9	Westphal, Paul D.
STEED								
1969	M	5			8			
1971		5			8	18	5	Anderson, Robert
STRAYER BUSINESS								
1967	M	2			8	17	6	Molloy, James H., Jr.
1968		5			8	17	8	Molloy, James H., Jr.
1971		8			8	10	12	Molloy, James H., Jr.
SUE BENNETT								
1985	M	3			16			
1995	W	7	3		8	19	19	Adams, Dean

Year	M/W	F	SD	Bye	#T	W	L	Coach
SULLIVAN (KY)								
1967	M	1			8	23	6	Tibbs, Harry
1968		1			8	26	6	Tibbs, Harry
1969		1			8	26	4	Sergeant, W. C.
1980		1			16	28	8	Skinner, David L.
1970		2			8	19	9	Sergeant, W. C.
1974		2			16	X	X	Mudd, Leon
1975		3			16	27	8	Caldwell, Jim
1984		4			16	21	12	Skinner, David L.
1976		8			14	18	14	Caldwell, Jim
1981		8			16	20	12	Skinner, David L.
1982		12			16	19	14	Skinner, David L.
1977		16			16	18	9	Caldwell, Jim
1987		16			16	17	16	Skinner, David L.
TEXAS COLLEGE								
1992	M	1	1	To R8	12	25	5	Patrick, Kirk
1993		1	1	To R8	9			Patrick, Kirk
1994		4	4	To R8	12	18	7	Patrick, Kirk
1991	W	6	6		8			
TIFFIN								
1971	M	1			8	13	8	Janson, George
1973		1			8	24	9	Janson, George
1969		3			8	20	4	Janson, George
1970		3			8	20	5	Janson, George
1972		6			8	19	12	Janson, George
TOUGALOO								
1975	M	2			16	15	9	Lewis, Jerry
TRINITY (VT)								
1993	W	4	3		8	21	10	Fitterer, Barbara
1996		5	6		6	8	10	Niebling, Jennifer
TRINITY BIBLE								
1982	W	8			8	12	8	Long, Rod P.
1983		8			8	11	8	Long, Rod P.
TRINITY CHRISTIAN								
1980	W	8			8	10	6	Hovinga, Lois
TRINITY INTERNATIONAL (IL)								
1994	M	10	3	To R8	12	19	11	Bruehl, Alan
1988		15			15	18	11	Seils, David S.
1992	W	1	6		8	15	10	Seils, David S.
1994		1	3		8	24	8	Seils, David S.
1990		6			8	16	12	Seils, David S.
1991		8	7		8	16	9	Seils, David S.
VERMONT TECH								
1995	M	10	1	To R8	12	20	5	Maxwell, Mike

Year	M/W	F	SD	Bye	#T	W	L	Coach
VITERBO								
1987	M	7			16	22	10	Popp, Rod
1983		8			16	17	10	Glasshoff, James
1984		8			16	17	13	Glasshoff, James
1981		16			16	12	14	Glasshoff, James
1982		16			16	10	17	Glasshoff, James
1986		16			16	14	16	Glasshoff, James
1982	W	7			8	11	7	Jack, Ellyn
1983		7			8	12	9	Jack, Ellyn
WARNER PACIFIC								
1972	M	3			8	16	16	Allord, Bob
1973		5			8	18	18	Blewrit, Mike
1980	W	2			8	X	X	Park, Kathi
WARREN WILSON								
1967	M	3			8	21	12	Ellenburg, Ray
1982		8			16	22	10	Franklin, Richard
1981		12			16	22	7	
1996	W	6	5		6	10	4	Keller, Jeff
1985		7			8	21	8	Slaughter, Jerry
WEBBER								
1984	M	1			16	32	4	Creola, Nick J.
1988		10			15	24	10	Yenta, Rex R.
WEST COAST CHRISTIAN								
1984	M	8			16	24	6	Turner, Jerry
1985		8			16	25	9	Turner, Jerry
1983		16			16	23	6	Turner, Jerry
WEST LIBERTY STATE: HANCOCK								
1971	M	8			8	X	X	Clark, John
1972		8			8	X	X	Clark, John
WEST VIRGINIA NORTHERN CC: WEIRTON								
1973	M	8			8	13	9	Clark, John
WHITWORTH (MS)								
1976	M	2			14	24	6	Roark, Dwain
WILLIAMSPORT COMMERCE								
1969	M	6			8	17	3	Mamolen, Paul
1968		8			8	13	5	Mamolen, Paul
WILMINGTON (DE)								
1993	W	2	1		8	26	6	Rogers, "Rusty"
1991		4	4		8	15	12	Rogers, "Rusty"
1992		4	1		8	25	11	Rogers, "Rusty"
YORK (NE)								
1984	W	5			9			
1997		5	7		8	8	25	Fields, Terry L.

Section 2

ASSOCIATION
NATIONAL CHAMPIONS

Since there have been 493 national championship tournaments conducted by eight athletic associations, there have been 493 national champions. In this section are all of them, plus the 61 mythical national championships bestowed by the Helms Foundation. The information is presented in four parts:

First (with a subpart for men and women), each association is listed alphabetically with its champions for each year, by division.

Second (with a subpart for men and women), the champions of each year are listed by association, by division.

Third, the championships won by each school are listed by year with no subpart for men and women.

Fourth, the Helms designations are listed in two subparts: first, by year; second, by school. A brief history of the Helms designations is provided.

Association
National Champions
By Association—Men

Year	Div	#T	School	W	L	Coach
LCC						
1996		7	Gulf Coast Christian	23	17	Wilkerson, Keith
1997		5	Wesley (MS)	13	16	Devore, William, Jr.
NAIA						
1937		8	Central Missouri State	17	3	Reid, Tad C.
1938		32	Central Missouri State	24	3	Reid, Tad C.
1939		32	Southwestern (KS)	21	2	Gardner, George
1940		32	Tarkio	20	4	Kyle, Newton P.
1941		32	San Diego State	24	7	Gross, Morris H.
1942		32	Hamline	20	2	Hutton, Joseph W., Sr.
1943		32	Southeast Missouri State	19	6	Harris, Charles P.
1944			No Tournament			
1945		16	Loyola New Orleans	22	11	Orsley, Jack C.
1946		32	Southern Illinois	20	6	Martin, Glenn "Abe"
1947		32	Marshall	32	5	Henderson, Eli Camden "Cam"
1948		32	Louisville	29	6	Hickman, Bernard L. "Peck"
1949		32	Hamline	29	1	Hutton, Joseph W., Sr.
1950		32	Indiana State	27	8	Longfellow, John L.
1951		32	Hamline	27	2	Hutton, Joseph W., Sr.
1952		32	Southwest Missouri State	27	5	Vanatta, Robert
1953		32	Southwest Missouri State	24	4	Vanatta, Robert
1954		32	Benedictine (KS)	24	5	Nolan, Ralph
1955		32	Texas A&M: Commerce	29	5	Rogers, Bobby
1956		32	McNeese State	33	3	Ward, Ralph O.
1957		32	Tennessee State	31	4	McLendon, John B., Jr.
1958		32	Tennessee State	31	3	McLendon, John B., Jr.
1959		32	Tennessee State	32	1	McLendon, John B., Jr.
1960		32	Southwest Texas State	28	3	Jowers, Milton W.

Year	Div	#T	School	W	L	Coach
1961		32	Grambling State	32	4	Hobdy, Frederick C.
1962		32	Prairie View A&M	20	3	Moore, Dr. Leroy G., Jr.
1963		32	Texas: Pan American	22	6	Williams, Samuel
1964		32	Rockhurst	27	6	Brehmer, Joseph "Buddy"
1965		32	Central State (OH)	30	0	Lucas, William C.
1966		32	Oklahoma Baptist University	26	7	Bass, Robert E.
1967		32	Benedictine (KS)	27	2	Nolan, Ralph
1968		32	Central State (OH)	29	4	Lucas, William C.
1969		32	Eastern New Mexico	24	7	Miller, Harry E.
1970		32	Kentucky State	29	3	Mitchell, Lucias
1971		32	Kentucky State	31	2	Mitchell, Lucias
1972		32	Kentucky State	28	5	Mitchell, Lucias
1973		32	Guilford	29	5	Jensen, Jack
1974		32	West Georgia	29	4	Kaiser, Roger A.
1975		32	Grand Canyon	30	3	Lindsey, Ben
1976		32	Coppin State	39	2	Bates, John H.
1977		32	Texas Southern	31	5	Moreland, Robert E.
1978		32	Grand Canyon	30	3	Lindsey, Ben
1979		32	Drury	33	2	Kirksey, Jerry L.
1980		32	Cameron	28	3	Nichols, Lonnie
1981		32	Southern Nazarene	36	6	Gresham, Dr. Loren
1982		32	South Carolina: Spartanburg	27	5	Waters, Jerry O.
1983		32	Charleston (SC)	24	5	Kresse, John
1984		32	Fort Hays State	26	2	Morse, Bill
1985		32	Fort Hays State	35	3	Morse, Bill
1986		32	Lipscomb	35	4	Meyer, Dr. Don W.
1987		32	Washburn	35	4	Chipman, Bob
1988		32	Grand Canyon	37	6	Westphal, Paul D.
1989		32	Saint Mary's (TX)	28	5	Meyer, Herbert "Buddy"
1990		32	Birmingham-Southern	31	3	Reboul, Duane
1991		32	Oklahoma City	27	3	Johnson, Darrel
1992	I	32	Oklahoma City	38	0	Johnson, Darrel
	II	20	Grace (IN)	32	5	Kessler, James C.
1993	I	32	Hawaii Pacific	30	4	Sellitto, Anthony, Jr.
	II	20	Willamette	29	4	James, Gordon "Gordie"
1994	I	32	Oklahoma City	28	7	Case, Win
	II	24	Eureka	27	4	Darnell, David
1995	I	32	Birmingham-Southern	35	2	Reboul, Duane
	II	32	Bethel (IN)	38	2	Lightfoot, Mike
1996	I	32	Oklahoma City	33	5	Case, Win
	II	32	Albertson	31	3	Holly, Martin W. "Marty"
1997	I	32	Life (GA)	37	1	Kaiser, Roger A.
	II	32	Bethel (IN)	34	5	Lightfoot, Mike
1998	I	32	Georgetown (KY)	36	3	Osborne, "Happy"
	II	32	Bethel (IN)	37	3	Lightfoot, Mike

NASC

1952		8	Tennessee State	19	4	Cash, Clarence B.
1953		8	Tennessee State	20	5	Cash, Clarence B.
1954		8	Tennessee State	17	6	Cash, Clarence B.
1955		8	Texas Southern	28	3	Adams, Edward H.

Year	Div	#T	School	W	L	Coach
NBCAA						
1981		4	Calvary Bible	22	4	Schneeberger, Robert W.
1982		8	Calvary Bible	26	1	Schneeberger, Robert W.
1983		8	Northwest Christian	24	5	Buckley, Jim
1984	I	8	Northwest Christian	24	4	Lipp, David
	II	3	Minnesota Bible	19	8	Comeaux, R. Mark
1985	I	8	Northwest Christian	25	4	Lipp, David
	II	4	Midwest Christian	X	X	Williams, Charles R.
1986	I	8	Northwest Christian	19	11	Kennedy, Don
	II	3	Nebraska Christian	12	14	Lahm, Chris
1987	I	8	Northwest Christian	21	8	Halupa, Paul
	II	4	Arizona Bible	X	X	Steele, Kevin
1988	I	8	LIFE Bible (CA)	19	6	Updike, Blake
	II	4	Arlington Baptist	X	X	Jones, Dr. Griffin
1989	I	7	Northwest Christian	19	12	Rodenburg, Jeff
	II	6	Hillsdale Free Will Baptist	15	15	Lawrence, Aaron
1990	I	8	Ozark Christian	X	X	Williams, Charles R.
	II	8	Nebraska Christian	19	10	Lahm, Chris
1991	I	8	San Jose Christian	27	7	Miller, Glen
	II	7	Hillsdale Free Will Baptist	23	11	Lisenbee, Tim
1992	I	8	Ozark Christian	28	13	Williams, Charles R.
	II	8	Latin American Bible (CA)	30	2	Elisaldez, Ken
1993	I	6	San Jose Christian	22	14	Miller, Glen
	II	8	Nebraska Christian	19	9	Lahm, Chris
1994	I	7	San Jose Christian	26	11	Miller, Glen
	II	8	Nebraska Christian	20	8	Lahm, Chris
1995	I	8	San Jose Christian	28	11	Miller, Glen
	II	8	Puget Sound Christian	17	11	McNichols, Troy
1996	I	8	Multnomah Bible	20	16	Reese, Chris
	II	7	Hillsdale Free Will Baptist	13	17	Archer, Kelly
1997	I	8	Gulf Coast Christian	29	6	Wilkerson, Dr. Charles
	II	8	Southwestern Christian Ministries	26	15	Arthur, Mark
1998		8	Southwestern Assemblies	20	8	Garippa, Rev. Steven P.
NCAA						
1939		8	Oregon	29	5	Hobson, Dr. Howard A. "Hobby"
1940		8	Indiana	20	3	McCracken, E. Branch
1941		8	Wisconsin	20	3	Foster, Harold E. "Bud"
1942		8	Stanford	27	4	Dean, Everett S.
1943		8	Wyoming	31	2	Shelton, Everett F.
1944		8	Utah	21	4	Peterson, Vadal
1945		8	Oklahoma State	27	4	Iba, Henry P. "Hank"
1946		8	Oklahoma State	31	2	Iba, Henry P. "Hank"
1947		8	Holy Cross (MA)	27	3	Julian, Alvin F. "Doggie"
1948		8	Kentucky	36	3	Rupp, Adolph F.
1949		8	Kentucky	32	2	Rupp, Adolph F.
1950		8	City College	24	5	Holman, Nathan "Nat"

Year	Div	#T	School	W	L	Coach
1951		16	Kentucky	32	2	Rupp, Adolph F.
1952		16	Kansas	28	3	Allen, Dr. Forrest C. "Phog"
1953		22	Indiana	23	3	McCracken, E. Branch
1954		24	La Salle	26	4	Loeffler, Kenneth D.
1955		24	San Francisco	28	1	Woolpert, Philip D.
1956		25	San Francisco	29	0	Woolpert, Philip D.
1957	I	23	North Carolina	32	0	McGuire, Frank J.
	II	32	Wheaton (IL)	28	1	Pfund, Leroy H. "Lee"
1958	I	24	Kentucky	23	6	Rupp, Adolph F.
	II	32	South Dakota	22	5	Clodfelter, Duane
1959	I	23	California	25	4	Newell, Peter F.
	II	32	Evansville	21	6	McCutchan, Arad A.
1960	I	25	Ohio State	25	3	Taylor, Fred R.
	II	32	Evansville	25	4	McCutchan, Arad A.
1961	I	24	Cincinnati	27	3	Jucker, Edwin L.
	II	32	Wittenberg	25	4	Mears, Ramon "Ray"
1962	I	25	Cincinnati	29	2	Jucker, Edwin L.
	II	32	Mount Saint Mary's (MD)	24	6	Phelan, James J.
1963	I	25	Loyola (IL)	29	2	Ireland, George M.
	II	32	South Dakota State	22	5	Iverson, James
1964	I	25	California: Los Angeles	30	0	Wooden, John R.
	II	32	Evansville	26	3	McCutchan, Arad A.
1965	I	23	California: Los Angeles	28	2	Wooden, John R.
	II	32	Evansville	29	0	McCutchan, Arad A.
1966	I	22	Texas: El Paso	28	1	Haskins, Donald L.
	II	36	Kentucky Wesleyan	24	6	Strong, Guy Rowland
1967	I	23	California: Los Angeles	30	0	Wooden, John R.
	II	36	Winston-Salem State	30	2	Gaines, Clarence E. "Big House"
1968	I	23	California: Los Angeles	29	1	Wooden, John R.
	II	36	Kentucky Wesleyan	28	3	Daniels, Bob
1969	I	25	California: Los Angeles	29	1	Wooden, John R.
	II	32	Kentucky Wesleyan	25	5	Daniels, Bob
1970	I	25	California: Los Angeles	28	2	Wooden, John R.
	II	32	Philadelphia Textiles	29	2	Magee, Herbert
1971	I	25	California: Los Angeles	29	1	Wooden, John R.
	II	32	Evansville	22	8	McCutchan, Arad A.
1972	I	25	California: Los Angeles	30	0	Wooden, John R.
	II	36	Roanoke	28	4	Moir, Charles
1973	I	25	California: Los Angeles	30	0	Wooden, John R.
	II	42	Kentucky Wesleyan	24	6	Jones, Bob
1974	I	25	North Carolina State	30	1	Sloan, Norman L., Jr.
	II	44	Morgan State	28	5	Frazier, Nathaniel
1975	I	32	California: Los Angeles	28	3	Wooden, John R.
	II	32	Old Dominion	25	6	Allen, William "Sonny"
	III	30	Lemoyne-Owen	27	5	Johnson, Jerry C.
1976	I	32	Indiana	32	0	Knight, Robert M.
	II	32	Puget Sound	27	7	Zech, Don
	III	28	Scranton	27	5	Bessoir, Robert M.

Year	Div	#T	School	W	L	Coach
1977	I	32	Marquette	25	7	McGuire, Alfred J.
	II	32	Tennessee: Chattanooga	27	5	Shumate, Ron
	III	30	Wittenberg	23	5	Hunter, Larry
1978	I	32	Kentucky	30	2	Hall, Joe B.
	II	32	Cheyney	27	2	Chaney, John
	III	30	North Park	29	2	McCarrell, Dan
1979	I	40	Michigan State	26	6	Heathcote, George "Jud"
	II	32	North Alabama	22	9	Jones, Bill L.
	III	32	North Park	26	5	McCarrell, Dan
1980	I	48	Louisville	33	3	Crum, Denzil E. "Denny"
	II	32	Virginia Union	26	4	Robbins, Charles David "Dave"
	III	32	North Park	28	3	McCarrell, Dan
1981	I	48	Indiana	26	9	Knight, Robert M.
	II	32	Florida Southern	24	8	Wissel, Dr. Harold R. "Hal"
	III	32	Potsdam State	30	2	Welsh, John Gerald "Jerry"
1982	I	48	North Carolina	32	2	Smith, Dean E.
	II	32	District Of Columbia	25	5	Jones, William S.
	III	32	Wabash	24	4	Petty, Malcolm "Mac"
1983	I	52	North Carolina State	26	10	Valvano, James T.
	II	32	Wright State (OH)	28	4	Underhill, Ralph
	III	32	Scranton	29	3	Bessoir, Robert M.
1984	I	53	Georgetown (DC)	34	3	Thompson, John R., Jr.
	II	32	Central Missouri State	29	3	Nance, Lynn
	III	32	Wisconsin: Whitewater	27	4	Vander Meulen, David
1985	I	64	Villanova	25	10	Massimino, Roland V. "Rollie"
	II	32	Jacksonville State (AL)	31	1	Jones, Bill E.
	III	32	North Park	27	4	Djurickovic, Bosko
1986	I	64	Louisville	32	7	Crum, Denzil E. "Denny"
	II	32	Sacred Heart (CT)	30	4	Bike, Dave
	III	32	Potsdam State	32	0	Welsh, John Gerald "Jerry"
1987	I	64	Indiana	30	4	Knight, Robert M.
	II	32	Kentucky Wesleyan	28	5	Chapman, Wayne G.
	III	32	North Park	28	3	Djurickovic, Bosko
1988	I	64	Kansas	27	11	Brown, Lawrence H.
	II	32	Massachusetts: Lowell	27	7	Doucette, Don
	III	32	Ohio Wesleyan	27	5	Mehaffey, Dr. Eugene L.
1989	I	64	Michigan	30	7	Fisher, Stephen L.
	II	32	North Carolina Central	28	4	Bernard, Michael J.
	III	40	Wisconsin: Whitewater	29	2	Vander Meulen, David
1990	I	64	Nevada: Las Vegas	35	5	Tarkanian, Jerry
	II	32	Kentucky Wesleyan	31	2	Chapman, Wayne G.
	III	40	Rochester (NY)	27	5	Neer, Mike
1991	I	64	Duke	32	7	Krzyzewski, Michael W.
	II	32	North Alabama	29	4	Elliott, Gary
	III	40	Wisconsin: Platteville	28	3	Ryan, William "Bo"

Year	Div	#T	School	W	L	Coach
1992	I	64	Duke	34	2	Krzyzewski, Michael W.
	II	32	Virginia Union	30	3	Robbins, Charles David "Dave"
	III	40	Calvin	31	1	Douma, Edward
1993	I	64	North Carolina	34	4	Smith, Dean E.
	II	32	California State: Bakersfield	33	0	Douglass, Pat
	III	40	Ohio Northern	28	2	Campoli, Joe
1994	I	64	Arkansas	31	3	Richardson, Nolan
	II	32	California State: Bakersfield	27	6	Douglass, Pat
	III	40	Lebanon Valley	28	4	Flannery, Patrick J.
1995	I	64	California: Los Angeles	31	2	Harrick, Jim
	II	48	Southern Indiana	29	4	Pearl, Bruce
	III	64	Wisconsin: Platteville	31	0	Ryan, William "Bo"
1996	I	64	Kentucky	34	2	Pitino, Richard A. "Rick"
	II	48	Fort Hays State	34	0	Garner, Gary
	III	64	Rowan	28	4	Giannini, John
1997	I	64	Arizona	25	9	Olson, Robert Luther "Lute"
	II	48	California State: Bakersfield	29	4	Douglass, Pat
	III	64	Illinois Wesleyan	29	2	Bridges, Dennis L.
1998	I	64	Kentucky	35	4	Smith, Orlando H. "Tubby"
	II	48	California: Davis	31	2	Williams, Bob
	III	48	Wisconsin: Platteville	30	0	Ryan, William "Bo"

NCCAA

Year	Div	#T	School	W	L	Coach
1968		6	Lee (TN)	30	4	Hughes, Dale R.
1969		6	Azusa Pacific	26	7	Hamlow, Dr. Clifford
1970		8	Azusa Pacific	29	6	Hamlow, Dr. Clifford
1971		8	Azusa Pacific	25	11	Hamlow, Dr. Clifford
1972		8	Azusa Pacific	26	10	Hamlow, Dr. Clifford
1973		4	Lee (TN)	31	6	Hughes, Dale R.
1974		4	Southern Nazarene	31	6	Poteet, Jim
1975		4	Olivet Nazarene	30	4	Ward, C. W. "Butch"
1976	I	4	Biola	23	9	Lyon, Howard
	II	4	Taylor: Fort Wayne	18	9	Morley, Stephen H.
1977	I	6	Southern Nazarene	28	10	Poteet, Jim
	II	4	Western Baptist	17	13	Hills, Tim
1978	I	6	Biola	22	14	Lyon, Howard
	II	6	Baptist Bible (MO)	13	15	Schepis, Mike
1979	I	6	Tennessee Temple	30	7	Bishop, Ronald
	II	6	Baptist Bible (PA)	20	12	Huckaby, James M.
1980	I	6	Liberty	28	11	Gibson, Dale
	II	6	Northwestern (MN)	21	11	Sulack, Dave
1981	I	6	Tennessee Temple	24	17	Bishop, Ronald
	II	6	Baptist Bible (MO)	18	17	Reed, Roger
1982	I	7	Tennessee Temple	31	8	Bishop, Ronald
	II	6	Baptist Bible (MO)	20	11	Fuller, Fred
1983	I	8	Tennessee Temple	28	7	Bishop, Ronald
	II	6	Baptist Bible (MO)	24	14	Fuller, Fred

Year	Div	#T	School	W	L	Coach
1984	I	8	Biola	25	6	Lyon, Howard
	II	8	Baptist Bible (MO)	17	13	Smith, Gary
1985	I	8	Point Loma Nazarene	28	8	Foster, Ben
	II	8	Cincinnati Bible	32	3	Wallingford, Tony
1986	I	8	Point Loma Nazarene	27	7	Foster, Ben
	II	8	Cincinnati Bible	35	2	Wallingford, Tony
1987	I	8	Point Loma Nazarene	25	10	Foster, Ben
	II	8	Cincinnati Bible	29	5	Wallingford, Tony
1988	I	8	Tennessee Temple	26	13	Bishop, Ronald
	II	8	Kentucky Christian	26	8	Kirk, Randy
1989	I	8	Tennessee Temple	25	11	Bishop, Ronald
	II	8	Kentucky Christian	27	5	Kirk, Randy
1990	I	8	Christian Heritage	33	6	Nater, Swen E.
	II	8	Maranatha Baptist Bible (WI)	18	8	Terrill, Jerry
1991	I	8	John Brown	25	8	Sheehy, John
	II	8	Kentucky Christian	20	13	Damron, Dr. Donald R. 'Dick'
	IIA	4	Trinity International (FL)	15	14	Rutherford, Robert
1992	I	8	Bethel (IN)	29	10	Lightfoot, Mike
	II	8	Baptist Bible (PA)	20	7	Howard, Russ
	IIA	8	Latin American Bible (CA)	30	2	Elisaldez, Ken
1993	I	8	Bethel (IN)	30	9	Lightfoot, Mike
	II	8	Northwest Assemblies	X	X	Filan, Doug
	IIA	8	Atlanta Christian	17	14	Kaiser, Richard 'Rick'
1994	I	8	Lee (TN)	24	14	Carpenter, Dr. Larry
	II	8	Central Bible	28	9	Hanson, Kirk
	IIA	8	Grace Bible (MI)	19	10	Moore, Jimmy
1995	I	8	Indiana Wesleyan	17	16	Williams, Pat
	II	8	Kentucky Christian	26	7	Damron, Dr. Donald R. 'Dick'
	IIA	8	Grace Bible (MI)	19	12	Moore, Jimmy
1996	I	8	Malone	20	16	Smith, Harold T.
	II	8	Kentucky Christian	27	6	Sudlow, Eric
	IIA	8	Manhattan Christian	22	8	Condra, Shawn
1997	I	8	Christian Heritage	23	12	Wilmore, Art
	II	8	Kentucky Christian	21	12	Damron, Dr. Donald R. 'Dick'
	IIA	8	Southwestern (AZ)	21	8	Morley, Stephen H.
1998	I	8	Christian Heritage	25	11	Wilmore, Art
	II	8	Mid-America Bible	32	8	Holley, Willie
	IIA	8	Southwestern Christian Ministeries	21	17	Arthur, Mark

NSCAA

Year	Div	#T	School	W	L	Coach
1967		8	Sullivan (KY)	23	6	Tibbs, Harry
1968		8	Sullivan (KY)	26	6	Tibbs, Harry
1969		8	Sullivan (KY)	26	4	Sergeant, W. C.
1970		8	Kittrell JC	32	4	Golatt, Moses
1971		8	Tiffin	13	8	Janson, George
1972		8	Lindsey Wilson	22	8	Voight, James R. 'Jim'
1973		8	Tiffin	24	9	Janson, George
1974		16	Bryant & Stratton: Buffalo	X	X	Griffin, Dr. Thomas J.

Year	Div	#T	School	W	L	Coach
1975		16	Florida College	20	11	Wilson, Tom
1976		14	Northeast CC (NE)			Stevenson, Charles 'Chuck'
1977		16	Rust	34	5	Hayes, Naylond
1978		16	Southern Union State CC	28	5	Gourdouze, Frank
1979		16	Florida College	20	14	Wilson, Tom
1980		16	Sullivan (KY)	28	8	Skinner, David L.
1981		16	Oakland City (IN)	12	20	Trafton, Charles L.
1982		16	Blackburn	23	8	Parker, James R.
1983		16	Concordia: Austin	30	7	Orton, Tom
1984		16	Webber	32	4	Creola, Nick J.
1985		16	Blackburn	23	7	Staff, Bob
1986		16	Bristol (TN)			Crowder, Brien
1987		16	National (SD)			Ticknor, Duane
1988		15	National (SD)	30	6	Ticknor, Duane
1989		15	Rochester (MI)	25	3	Pleasant, Garth A.
1990		12	Paul Quinn	31	7	Summers, James 'Zip'
1991		12	Mount Senario	40	10	Andrist, Edward A.
1992		12	Texas College	25	5	Patrick, Kirk
1993		9	Texas College			Patrick, Kirk
1994		12	Mount Senario	24	22	Andrist, Edward A.
1995		12	Paul Quinn	20	12	Summers, James 'Zip'
1996		10	Mount Senario	14	22	Andrist, Edward A.
1997		12	Louisiana Christian	21	12	Schexnayder, Tommy
1998		15	Northwest Christian	24	8	Lipp, David

By Association—Women

Year	Div	#T	School	W	L	Coach
AIAW						
1969		16	West Chester	12	0	Eckman, Carol
1970		16	California State: Fullerton	17	1	Moore, Billie Jean
1971		16	Mississippi Women	21	3	Upton, Jill
1972		16	Immaculata (PA)	24	1	Rush, Cathy
1973		16	Immaculata (PA)	20	0	Rush, Cathy
1974		16	Immaculata (PA)	20	1	Rush, Cathy
1975	L	16	Delta State	28	0	Wade, L. Margaret
	S	12	Phillips (OK)			Amaya, Lou
1976	L	16	Delta State	33	1	Wade, L. Margaret
	S	16	Berry	20	3	James, Kay
1977	L	16	Delta State	32	3	Wade, L. Margaret
	S	16	Southeastern Louisiana	30	2	Puckett, Linda
1978	L	16	California: Los Angeles	27	3	Moore, Billie Jean
	S	16	High Point	30	8	Briley, Wanda
1979	L	16	Old Dominion	35	1	Stanley, Marianne Crawford
	S	16	South Carolina State	33	2	Simon, Willie J.
1980	I	24	Old Dominion	37	1	Stanley, Marianne Crawford
	II	24	Dayton	36	2	Jeremiah, Dr. Maryalyce
	III	24	Worcester State	24	2	Devlin, Donna

Year	Div	#T	School	W	L	Coach
1981	I	24	Louisiana Tech	34	0	Hogg, Sonja
	II	16	William Penn	43	3	Spencer, Robert L.
	III	16	Wisconsin: La Crosse	27	5	Hansen, Mary
1982	I	16	Rutgers	25	7	Grentz, Theresa Shank
	II	16	Francis Marion	27	7	Hatchell, Sylvia Rhyne
	III	16	Concordia: Moorhead	31	3	Langseth, Marc

NAIA

Year	Div	#T	School	W	L	Coach
1981		8	Kentucky State	21	7	Mitchell, Ron
1982		8	Southwestern Oklahoma State	34	0	Loftin, John D.
1983		8	Southwestern Oklahoma State	30	4	Loftin, John D.
1984		16	North Carolina: Asheville	32	5	Carroll, Helen
1985		16	Southwestern Oklahoma State	34	0	Loftin, John D.
1986		16	Francis Marion	36	2	Hatchell, Sylvia Rhyne
1987		16	Southwestern Oklahoma State	30	2	Loftin, John D.
1988		16	Oklahoma City	28	6	Colon, Bob
1989		16	Southern Nazarene	36	2	Hoffman, Bob
1990		16	Southwestern Oklahoma State	30	4	Loftin, John D.
1991		32	Fort Hays State	34	2	Klein, John
1992	I	32	Arkansas Tech	35	1	Foley, Joe M.
	II	20	Northern State (SD)	30	4	Fredrickson, Curt
1993	I	32	Arkansas Tech	31	5	Foley, Joe M.
	II	20	Montana State: Northern	35	3	Winn, Sherry
1994	I	32	Southern Nazarene	34	0	Finkbeiner, Jerry
	II	24	Northern State (SD)	32	1	Fredrickson, Curt
1995	I	32	Southern Nazarene	30	2	Finkbeiner, Jerry
	II	32	Western Oregon	23	9	Rogers, 'Rusty'
1996	I	32	Southern Nazarene	34	2	Finkbeiner, Jerry
	II	32	Western Oregon	31	4	Rogers, 'Rusty'
1997	I	32	Southern Nazarene	32	4	Finkbeiner, Jerry
	II	32	Northwest Nazarene	27	7	Schmidt, Roger
1998	I	32	Union (TN)	35	3	Blackstock, Dr. David
	II	32	Walsh	29	5	Smesco, Carl

NBCAA

Year	Div	#T	School	W	L	Coach
1983		4	Crown (MN)	X	X	Hardy, Don
1984		4	Crown (MN)	X	X	Hardy, Don
1985		4	Crown (MN)	X	X	Guavin, Julie
1986		7	North Central Bible	15	16	Myers, Dennis
1987		4	North Central Bible	X	X	Myers, Dennis
1988		4	Ozark Christian	X	X	Williams, Charles R.
1989		4	Calvary Bible	16	1	Hensarling, Anne
1990		6	Calvary Bible	12	9	Shook, John
1991		5	Crown (MN)	19	9	Rogness, Tony
1992		4	Hillsdale Free Will Baptist	9	13	Braisher, Kelly
1993		6	Grace (NE)	19	0	Regier, Larry
1994		4	Grace (NE)	15	0	Reiger, Larry
1995		5	Grace (NE)	17	2	Johnson, DuWayne
1996		6	Grace (NE)	19	0	Johnson, DuWayne
1997		4	Hillsdale Free Will Baptist	12	10	Archer, Kelly
1998		4	Nebraska Christian	21	8	Fuehrer, Mike

Year	Div	#T	School	W	L	Coach
NCAA						
1982	I	32	Louisiana Tech	35	1	Hogg, Sonja
	II	16	California Polytechnic: Pomona	29	7	May, Darlene
	III	16	Elizabethtown	26	1	Kauffman, Yvonne E.
1983	I	36	Southern California	31	2	Sharp, Linda
	II	24	Virginia Union	27	2	Hearn, Louis
	III	32	North Central (IL)	26	6	Morgan, R. Wayne
1984	I	32	Southern California	29	4	Sharp, Linda
	II	24	Central Missouri State	28	4	Hoehn, Jorja E.
	III	32	Rust	26	5	Stovall, Dr. Alfred J. 'AJ'
1985	I	32	Old Dominion	31	3	Stanley, Marianne Crawford
	II	24	California Polytechnic: Pomona	21	7	May, Darlene
	III	32	Scranton	31	1	Strong, Michael J.
1986	I	40	Texas	34	0	Conradt, Jody
	II	24	California Polytechnic: Pomona	30	3	May, Darlene
	III	32	Salem State	29	1	Shea, Timothy P.
1987	I	40	Tennessee	28	6	Summitt, Patricia Head
	II	24	New Haven	29	2	Rossman, Jan
	III	32	Wisconsin: Stevens Point	27	2	Wunder, Linda
1988	I	40	Louisiana Tech	32	2	Barmore, Leon
	II	32	Hampton	33	1	Sweat, James E.
	III	32	Concordia: Moorhead	29	2	Siverson, Duane
1989	I	48	Tennessee	35	2	Summitt, Patricia Head
	II	32	Delta State	30	4	Clark, Lloyd
	III	32	Elizabethtown	29	2	Kauffman, Yvonne E.
1990	I	48	Stanford	32	1	VanDerveer, Tara
	II	32	Delta State	32	1	Clark, Lloyd
	III	32	Hope	24	2	Wise, Susan
1991	I	48	Tennessee	30	5	Summitt, Patricia Head
	II	32	North Dakota State	31	2	Ruley, Amy J.
	III	32	Saint Thomas (MN)	29	2	Riverso, Ted
1992	I	48	Stanford	30	3	VanDerveer, Tara
	II	32	Delta State	30	4	Clark, Lloyd
	III	32	Alma	24	3	Goffnett, Charles
1993	I	48	Texas Tech	31	3	Sharp, Marsha
	II	32	North Dakota State	30	2	Ruley, Amy J.
	III	32	Central (IA)	24	5	Boeyink, Gary
1994	I	64	North Carolina	33	2	Hatchell, Sylvia Rhyne
	II	32	North Dakota State	27	5	Ruley, Amy J.
	III	40	Capital	30	1	Jeffers, Dixie M.
1995	I	64	Connecticut	35	0	Auriemma, Geno
	II	48	North Dakota State	32	0	Ruley, Amy J.
	III	64	Capital	33	0	Jeffers, Dixie M.
1996	I	64	Tennessee	32	4	Summitt, Patricia Head
	II	48	North Dakota State	30	2	Ruley, Amy J.
	III	64	Wisconsin: Oshkosh	31	0	Bennett, Kathi

Year	Div	#T	School	W	L	Coach
1997	I	64	Tennessee	29	10	Summitt, Patricia Head
	II	48	North Dakota	28	4	Roebuck, Gene
	III	64	New York	29	1	Quinn, Janice
1998	I	64	Tennessee	39	0	Summit, Patricia Head
	II	48	North Dakota	31	1	Roebuck, Gene
	III	48	Washington	28	2	Fahey, Nancy

NCCAA

Year	Div	#T	School	W	L	Coach
1983	I	8	Spring Arbor	29	4	Dunckel, Darrell
	II	4	Baptist Bible (PA)	23	5	Durrwachter, Nancy White
1984	I	8	Huntington	24	9	Freeman, Keith
	II	6	Northwestern (MN)	19	10	Smith, Dan
1985	I	8	Lee (TN)	15	13	Souther, Orin A. "Jack"
	II	8	Northwestern (MN)	11	19	Smith, Dan
1986	I	8	Evangel	21	13	Bowen, Lynn
	II	8	Toccoa Falls	13	12	Shiffer, Paul
1987	I	·8	Spring Arbor	25	9	Dunckel, Darrell
	II	6	Moody Bible	X	X	Gaffney, Greg
1988	I	8	King (TN)	27	3	Nida, Al
	II	6	Northwest Assemblies	16	17	Brodin, Kristi
1989	I	8	King (TN)	28	2	Nida, Al
	II	8	Kentucky Christian	13	11	Bender, Tom
1990	I	8	King (TN)	27	3	Ward, Jeannine
	II	8	Northwest Assemblies	11	18	Brodin, Kristi
1991	I	8	Huntington	24	4	Culler, Lori
	II	8	Northwest Assemblies	10	20	Brodin, Kristi
1992	I	8	Huntington	24	8	Culler, Lori
	II	8	Toccoa Falls	23	6	Shiffer, Paul
1993	I	8	Williams Baptist	24	2	Halford, Carol
	II	8	Northwest Assemblies	17	11	Brodin, Kristi
1994	I	8	Mount Vernon Nazarene	23	10	Howald, Jeana
	II	8	Northwest Assemblies	7	21	Brodin, Kristi
1995	I	8	Western Baptist	17	16	Williams, Terry
	II	8	Kentucky Christian	24	9	Arnett, Ron
1996	I	8	Western Baptist	24	11	Williams, Terry
	II	8	Kentucky Christian	28	4	Arnett, Ron
1997	I	8	LeTourneau	30	4	Otwell, Mary Ann
	II	8	Kentucky Christian	30	5	Arnett, Ron
1998	I	8	LeTourneau	24	10	Otwell, Mary Ann
	II	8	Kentucky Christian	22	13	Arnett, Ron

NSCAA

Year	Div	#T	School	W	L	Coach
1980		8	Colorado Woman's	23	8	Forkum, Jim
1981			No Tournament			
1982		8	National (SD)	16	4	Haight, H. C. "Bud"
1983		8	Concordia: Saint Paul	20	6	Surridge, Dr. Jack
1984		9	Lamar CC	X	X	Unknown
1985		8	Phillips JC: Gulfport	21	6	Rosetti, George F., Sr.
1986		8	Phillips JC: Gulfport	22	7	Rosetti, George F., Sr.
1987		8	Concordia (NE)	23	8	Everts, Dr. Carl

Year	Div	#T	School	W	L	Coach
1988		8	Saint Scholastica	25	6	Stukel, Jim
1989		8	Concordia (NE)	25	7	Everts, Dr. Carl
1990		8	Concordia (NE)	20	13	Everts, Dr. Carl
1991		8	Silver Lake	25	6	Wenner, Craig
1992		8	Trinity International (IL)	15	10	Seils, David S.
1993		8	Blackburn	24	7	Sexton, James R.
1994		8	Trinity International (IL)	24	8	Seils, David S.
1995		8	Martin Methodist	13	18	Jones, Johnny
1996		6	Kansas Wesleyan	14	16	Hughes, Tom
1997		8	Kansas Wesleyan	12	19	Hughes, Tom
1998		8	Clarendon	21	9	Zehr, Joel R.

By Year—Men

Assn	Div	#T	School	W	L	Coach
1937						
NAIA		8	Central Missouri State	17	3	Reid, Tad C.
1938						
NAIA		32	Central Missouri State	24	3	Reid, Tad C.
1939						
NAIA		32	Southwestern (KS)	21	2	Gardner, George
NCAA		8	Oregon	29	5	Hobson, Dr. Howard A. "Hobby"
1940						
NAIA		32	Tarkio	20	4	Kyle, Newton P.
NCAA		8	Indiana	20	3	McCracken, E. Branch
1941						
NAIA		32	San Diego State	24	7	Gross, Morris H.
NCAA		8	Wisconsin	20	3	Foster, Harold E. "Bud"
1942						
NAIA		32	Hamline	20	2	Hutton, Joseph W., Sr.
NCAA		8	Stanford	27	4	Dean, Everett S.
1943						
NAIA		32	Southeast Missouri State	19	6	Harris, Charles P.
NCAA		8	Wyoming	31	2	Shelton, Everett F.
1944						
NAIA			No Tournament			
NCAA		8	Utah	21	4	Peterson, Vadal
1945						
NAIA		16	Loyola New Orleans	22	11	Orsley, Jack C.
NCAA		8	Oklahoma State	27	4	Iba, Henry P. "Hank"

Assn	Div	#T	School	W	L	Coach
1946						
NAIA		32	Southern Illinois	20	6	Martin, Glenn "Abe"
NCAA		8	Oklahoma State	31	2	Iba, Henry P. "Hank"
1947						
NAIA		32	Marshall	32	5	Henderson, Eli Camden "Cam"
NCAA		8	Holy Cross (MA)	27	3	Julian, Alvin F. "Doggie"
1948						
NAIA		32	Louisville	29	6	Hickman, Bernard L. "Peck"
NCAA		8	Kentucky	36	3	Rupp, Adolph F.
1949						
NAIA		32	Hamline	29	1	Hutton, Joseph W., Sr.
NCAA		8	Kentucky	32	2	Rupp, Adolph F.
1950						
NAIA		32	Indiana State	27	8	Longfellow, John L.
NCAA		8	City College	24	5	Holman, Nathan "Nat"
1951						
NAIA		32	Hamline	27	2	Hutton, Joseph W., Sr.
NCAA		16	Kentucky	32	2	Rupp, Adolph F.
1952						
NAIA		32	Southwest Missouri State	27	5	Vanatta, Robert
NASC		8	Tennessee State	20	5	Cash, Clarence B.
NCAA		16	Kansas	28	3	Allen, Dr. Forrest C. "Phog"
1953						
NAIA		32	Southwest Missouri State	24	4	Vanatta, Robert
NASC		8	Tennessee State	20	5	Cash, Clarence B.
NCAA		22	Indiana	23	3	McCracken, E. Branch
1954						
NAIA		32	Benedictine (KS)	24	5	Nolan, Ralph
NASC		8	Tennessee State	17	6	Cash, Clarence B.
NCAA		24	La Salle	26	4	Loeffler, Kenneth D.
1955						
NAIA		32	Texas A&M: Commerce	29	5	Rogers, Bobby
NASC		8	Texas Southern	28	3	Adams, Edward H.
NCAA		24	San Francisco	28	1	Woolpert, Philip D.
1956						
NAIA		32	McNeese State	33	3	Ward, Ralph O.
NCAA		25	San Francisco	29	0	Woolpert, Philip D.
1957						
NAIA		32	Tennessee State	31	4	McLendon, John B., Jr.
NCAA	I	23	North Carolina	32	0	McGuire, Frank J.
NCAA	II	32	Wheaton (IL)	28	1	Pfund, Leroy H. "Lee"

Assn	Div	#T	School	W	L	Coach
1958						
NAIA		32	Tennessee State	31	3	McLendon, John B., Jr.
NCAA	I	24	Kentucky	23	6	Rupp, Adolph F.
NCAA	II	32	South Dakota	22	5	Clodfelter, Duane
1959						
NAIA		32	Tennessee State	32	1	McLendon, John B., Jr.
NCAA	I	23	California	25	4	Newell, Peter F.
NCAA	II	32	Evansville	21	6	McCutchan, Arad A.
1960						
NAIA		32	Southwest Texas State	28	3	Jowers, Milton W.
NCAA	I	25	Ohio State	25	3	Taylor, Fred R.
NCAA	II	32	Evansville	25	4	McCutchan, Arad A.
1961						
NAIA		32	Grambling State	32	4	Hobdy, Frederick C.
NCAA	I	24	Cincinnati	27	3	Jucker, Edwin L.
NCAA	II	32	Wittenberg	25	4	Mears, Ramon "Ray"
1962						
NAIA		32	Prairie View A&M	20	3	Moore, Dr. Leroy G., Jr.
NCAA	I	25	Cincinnati	29	2	Jucker, Edwin L.
NCAA	II	32	Mount Saint Mary's (MD)	24	6	Phelan, James J.
1963						
NAIA		32	Texas: Pan American	22	6	Williams, Samuel
NCAA	I	25	Loyola (IL)	29	2	Ireland, George M.
NCAA	II	32	South Dakota State	22	5	Iverson, James
1964						
NAIA		32	Rockhurst	27	6	Brehmer, Joseph "Buddy"
NCAA	I	25	California: Los Angeles	30	0	Wooden, John R.
NCAA	II	32	Evansville	26	3	McCutchan, Arad A.
1965						
NAIA		32	Central State (OH)	30	0	Lucas, William C.
NCAA	I	23	California: Los Angeles	28	2	Wooden, John R.
NCAA	II	32	Evansville	29	0	McCutchan, Arad A.
1966						
NAIA		32	Oklahoma Baptist University	26	7	Bass, Robert E.
NCAA	I	22	Texas: El Paso	28	1	Haskins, Donald L.
NCAA	II	36	Kentucky Wesleyan	24	6	Strong, Guy Rowland
1967						
NAIA		32	Benedictine (KS)	27	2	Nolan, Ralph
NCAA	I	23	California: Los Angeles	30	0	Wooden, John R.
NCAA	II	36	Winston-Salem State	30	2	Gaines, Clarence E. "Big House"
NSCAA		8	Sullivan (KY)	23	6	Tibbs, Harry
1968						
NAIA		32	Central State (OH)	29	4	Lucas, William C.
NCAA	I	23	California: Los Angeles	29	1	Wooden, John R.
NCAA	II	36	Kentucky Wesleyan	28	3	Daniels, Bob
NCCAA		6	Lee (TN)	30	4	Hughes, Dale R.
NSCAA		8	Sullivan (KY)	26	6	Tibbs, Harry

Assn	Div	#T	School	W	L	Coach
1969						
NAIA		32	Eastern New Mexico	24	7	Miller, Harry E.
NCAA	I	25	California: Los Angeles	29	1	Wooden, John R.
NCAA	II	32	Kentucky Wesleyan	25	5	Daniels, Bob
NCCAA		6	Azusa Pacific	26	7	Hamlow, Dr. Clifford
NSCAA		8	Sullivan (KY)	26	4	Sergeant, W. C.
1970						
NAIA		32	Kentucky State	29	3	Mitchell, Lucias
NCAA	I	25	California: Los Angeles	28	2	Wooden, John R.
NCAA	II	32	Philadelphia Textiles	29	2	Magee, Herbert
NCCAA		8	Azusa Pacific	29	6	Hamlow, Dr. Clifford
NSCAA		8	Kittrell JC	32	4	Golatt, Moses
1971						
NAIA		32	Kentucky State	31	2	Mitchell, Lucias
NCAA	I	25	California: Los Angeles	29	1	Wooden, John R.
NCAA	II	32	Evansville	22	8	McCutchan, Arad A.
NCCAA		8	Azusa Pacific	25	11	Hamlow, Dr. Clifford
NSCAA		8	Tiffin	13	8	Janson, George
1972						
NAIA		32	Kentucky State	28	5	Mitchell, Lucias
NCAA	I	25	California: Los Angeles	30	0	Wooden, John R.
NCAA	II	36	Roanoke	28	4	Moir, Charles
NCCAA		8	Azusa Pacific	26	10	Hamlow, Dr. Clifford
NSCAA		8	Lindsey Wilson	22	8	Voight, James R. 'Jim'
1973						
NAIA		32	Guilford	29	5	Jensen, Jack
NCAA	I	25	California: Los Angeles	30	0	Wooden, John R.
NCAA	II	42	Kentucky Wesleyan	24	6	Jones, Bob
NCCAA		4	Lee (TN)	31	6	Hughes, Dale R.
NSCAA		8	Tiffin	24	9	Janson, George
1974						
NAIA		32	West Georgia	29	4	Kaiser, Roger A.
NCAA	I	25	North Carolina State	30	1	Sloan, Norman L., Jr.
NCAA	II	44	Morgan State	28	5	Frazier, Nathaniel
NCCAA		4	Southern Nazarene	31	6	Poteet, Jim
NSCAA		16	Bryant & Stratton: Buffalo	X	X	Griffin, Dr. Thomas J.
1975						
NAIA		32	Grand Canyon	30	3	Lindsey, Ben
NCAA	I	32	California: Los Angeles	28	3	Wooden, John R.
NCAA	II	32	Old Dominion	25	6	Allen, William 'Sonny'
NCAA	III	30	Lemoyne-Owen	27	5	Johnson, Jerry C.
NCCAA		4	Olivet Nazarene	30	4	Ward, C. W. 'Butch'
NSCAA		16	Florida College	20	11	Wilson, Tom
1976						
NAIA		32	Coppin State	39	2	Bates, John H.
NCAA	I	32	Indiana	32	0	Knight, Robert M.
NCAA	II	32	Puget Sound	27	7	Zech, Don
NCAA	III	28	Scranton	27	5	Bessoir, Robert M.

Assn	Div	#T	School	W	L	Coach
NCCAA	I	4	Biola	23	9	Lyon, Howard
NCCAA	II	4	Taylor: Fort Wayne	18	9	Morley, Stephen H.
NSCAA		14	Northeast CC (NE)			Stevenson, Charles "Chuck"

1977

Assn	Div	#T	School	W	L	Coach
NAIA		32	Texas Southern	31	5	Moreland, Robert E.
NCAA	I	32	Marquette	25	7	McGuire, Alfred J.
NCAA	II	32	Tennessee: Chattanooga	27	5	Shumate, Ron
NCAA	III	30	Wittenberg	23	5	Hunter, Larry
NCCAA	I	6	Southern Nazarene	28	10	Poteet, Jim
NCCAA	II	4	Western Baptist	17	13	Hills, Tim
NSCAA		16	Rust	34	5	Hayes, Naylond

1978

Assn	Div	#T	School	W	L	Coach
NAIA		32	Grand Canyon	30	3	Lindsey, Ben
NCAA	I	32	Kentucky	30	2	Hall, Joe B.
NCAA	II	32	Cheyney	27	2	Chaney, John
NCAA	III	30	North Park	29	2	McCarrell, Dan
NCCAA	I	6	Biola	22	14	Lyon, Howard
NCCAA	II	6	Baptist Bible (MO)	13	15	Schepis, Mike
NSCAA		16	Southern Union State CC	28	5	Gourdouze, Frank

1979

Assn	Div	#T	School	W	L	Coach
NAIA		32	Drury	33	2	Kirksey, Jerry L.
NCAA	I	40	Michigan State	26	6	Heathcote, George "Jud"
NCAA	II	32	North Alabama	22	9	Jones, Bill L.
NCAA	III	32	North Park	26	5	McCarrell, Dan
NCCAA	I	6	Tennessee Temple	30	7	Bishop, Ronald
NCCAA	II	6	Baptist Bible (PA)	20	12	Huckaby, James M.
NSCAA		16	Florida College	20	14	Wilson, Tom

1980

Assn	Div	#T	School	W	L	Coach
NAIA		32	Cameron	28	3	Nichols, Lonnie
NCAA	I	48	Louisville	33	3	Crum, Denzil E. "Denny"
NCAA	II	32	Virginia Union	26	4	Robbins, Charles David "Dave"
NCAA	III	32	North Park	28	3	McCarrell, Dan
NCCAA	I	6	Liberty	28	11	Gibson, Dale
NCCAA	II	6	Northwestern (MN)	21	11	Sulack, Dave
NSCAA		16	Sullivan (KY)	28	8	Skinner, David L.

1981

Assn	Div	#T	School	W	L	Coach
NAIA		32	Southern Nazarene	36	6	Gresham, Dr. Loren
NBCAA		4	Calvary Bible	22	4	Schneeberger, Robert W.
NCAA	I	48	Indiana	26	9	Knight, Robert M.
NCAA	II	32	Florida Southern	24	8	Wissel, Dr. Harold R. "Hal"
NCAA	III	32	Potsdam State	30	2	Welsh, John Gerald "Jerry"
NCCAA	I	6	Tennessee Temple	24	17	Bishop, Ronald
NCCAA	II	6	Baptist Bible (MO)	18	17	Reed, Roger
NSCAA		16	Oakland City (IN)	12	20	Trafton, Charles L.

Assn	Div	#T	School	W	L	Coach
1982						
NAIA		32	South Carolina: Spartanburg	27	5	Waters, Jerry O.
NBCAA		8	Calvary Bible	26	1	Schneeberger, Robert W.
NCAA	I	48	North Carolina	32	2	Smith, Dean E.
NCAA	II	32	District of Columbia	25	5	Jones, William S.
NCAA	III	32	Wabash	24	4	Petty, Malcolm "Mac"
NCCAA	I	7	Tennessee Temple	31	8	Bishop, Ronald
NCCAA	II	6	Baptist Bible (MO)	20	11	Fuller, Fred
NSCAA		16	Blackburn	23	8	Parker, James R.
1983						
NAIA		32	Charleston (SC)	24	5	Kresse, John
NBCAA		8	Northwest Christian	24	5	Buckley, Jim
NCAA	I	52	North Carolina State	26	10	Valvano, James T.
NCAA	II	32	Wright State (OH)	28	4	Underhill, Ralph
NCAA	III	32	Scranton	29	3	Bessoir, Robert M.
NCCAA	I	8	Tennessee Temple	28	7	Bishop, Ronald
NCCAA	II	6	Baptist Bible (MO)	24	14	Fuller, Fred
NSCAA		16	Concordia: Austin	30	7	Orton, Tom
1984						
NAIA		32	Fort Hays State	26	2	Morse, Bill
NBCAA	I	8	Northwest Christian	24	4	Lipp, David
NBCAA	II	3	Minnesota Bible	19	8	Comeaux, R. Mark
NCAA	I	53	Georgetown (DC)	34	3	Thompson, John R., Jr.
NCAA	II	32	Central Missouri State	29	3	Nance, Lynn
NCAA	III	32	Wisconsin: Whitewater	27	4	Vander Meulen, David
NCCAA	I	8	Biola	25	6	Lyon, Howard
NCCAA	II	8	Baptist Bible (MO)	17	13	Smith, Gary
NSCAA		16	Webber	32	4	Creola, Nick J.
1985						
NAIA		32	Fort Hays State	35	3	Morse, Bill
NBCAA	I	8	Northwest Christian	25	4	Lipp, David
NBCAA	II	4	Midwest Christian	X	X	Williams, Charles R.
NCAA	I	64	Villanova	25	10	Massimino, Roland V. "Rollie"
NCAA	II	32	Jacksonville State (AL)	31	1	Jones, Bill E.
NCAA	III	32	North Park	27	4	Djurickovic, Bosko
NCCAA	I	8	Point Loma Nazarene	28	8	Foster, Ben
NCCAA	II	8	Cincinnati Bible	32	3	Wallingford, Tony
NSCAA		16	Blackburn	23	7	Staff, Bob
1986						
NAIA		32	Lipscomb	35	4	Meyer, Dr. Don W.
NBCAA	I	8	Northwest Christian	19	11	Kennedy, Don
NBCAA	II	3	Nebraska Christian	12	14	Lahm, Chris
NCAA	I	64	Louisville	32	7	Crum, Denzil E. "Denny"
NCAA	II	32	Sacred Heart (CT)	30	4	Bike, Dave
NCAA	III	32	Potsdam State	32	0	Welsh, John Gerald "Jerry"

Assn	Div	#T	School	W	L	Coach
NCCAA	I	8	Point Loma Nazarene	27	7	Foster, Ben
NCCAA	II	8	Cincinnati Bible	35	2	Wallingford, Tony
NSCAA		16	Bristol (TN)			Crowder, Brien

1987

NAIA		32	Washburn	35	4	Chipman, Bob
NBCAA	I	8	Northwest Christian	21	8	Halupa, Paul
NBCAA	II	4	Arizona Bible	X	X	Steele, Kevin
NCAA	I	64	Indiana	30	4	Knight, Robert M.
NCAA	II	32	Kentucky Wesleyan	28	5	Chapman, Wayne G.
NCAA	III	32	North Park	28	3	Djurickovic, Bosko
NCCAA	I	8	Point Loma Nazarene	25	10	Foster, Ben
NCCAA	II	8	Cincinnati Bible	29	5	Wallingford, Tony
NSCAA		16	National (SD)			Ticknor, Duane

1988

NAIA		32	Grand Canyon	37	6	Westphal, Paul D.
NBCAA	I	8	LIFE Bible (CA)	19	6	Updike, Blake
NBCAA	II	4	Arlington Baptist	X	X	Jones, Dr. Griffin
NCAA	I	64	Kansas	27	11	Brown, Lawrence H.
NCAA	II	32	Massachusetts: Lowell	27	7	Doucette, Don
NCAA	III	32	Ohio Wesleyan	27	5	Mehaffey, Dr. Eugene L.
NCCAA	I	8	Tennessee Temple	26	13	Bishop, Ronald
NCCAA	II	8	Kentucky Christian	26	8	Kirk, Randy
NSCAA		15	National (SD)	30	6	Ticknor, Duane

1989

NAIA		32	Saint Mary's (TX)	28	5	Meyer, Herbert "Buddy"
NBCAA	I	7	Northwest Christian	19	12	Rodenburg, Jeff
NBCAA	II	6	Hillsdale Free Will Baptist	15	15	Lawrence, Aaron
NCAA	I	64	Michigan	30	7	Fisher, Stephen L.
NCAA	II	32	North Carolina Central	28	4	Bernard, Michael J.
NCAA	III	40	Wisconsin: Whitewater	29	2	Vander Meulen, David
NCCAA	I	8	Tennessee Temple	25	11	Bishop, Ronald
NCCAA	II	8	Kentucky Christian	27	5	Kirk, Randy
NSCAA		15	Rochester (MI)	25	3	Pleasant, Garth A.

1990

NAIA		32	Birmingham-Southern	31	3	Reboul, Duane
NBCAA	I	8	Ozark Christian	X	X	Williams, Charles R.
NBCAA	II	8	Nebraska Christian	19	10	Lahm, Chris
NCAA	I	64	Nevada: Las Vegas	35	5	Tarkanian, Jerry
NCAA	II	32	Kentucky Wesleyan	31	2	Chapman, Wayne G.
NCAA	III	40	Rochester (NY)	27	5	Neer, Mike
NCCAA	I	8	Christian Heritage	33	6	Nater, Swen E.
NCCAA	II	8	Maranatha Baptist Bible (WI)	18	8	Terrill, Jerry
NSCAA		12	Paul Quinn	31	7	Summers, James "Zip"

Assn	Div	#T	School	W	L	Coach
1991						
NAIA		32	Oklahoma City	27	3	Johnson, Darrel
NBCAA	I	8	San Jose Christian	27	7	Miller, Glen
NBCAA	II	7	Hillsdale Free Will Baptist	23	11	Lisenbee, Tim
NCAA	I	64	Duke	32	7	Krzyzewski, Michael W.
NCAA	II	32	North Alabama	29	4	Elliott, Gary
NCAA	III	40	Wisconsin: Platteville	28	3	Ryan, William "Bo"
NCCAA	I	8	John Brown	25	8	Sheehy, John
NCCAA	II	8	Kentucky Christian	20	13	Damron, Dr. Donald R. "Dick"
NCCAA	IIA	4	Trinity International (FL)	15	14	Rutherford, Robert
NSCAA		12	Mount Senario	40	10	Andrist, Edward A.
1992						
NAIA	I	32	Oklahoma City	38	0	Johnson, Darrel
NAIA	II	20	Grace (IN)	32	5	Kessler, James C.
NBCAA	I	8	Ozark Christian	28	13	Williams, Charles R.
NBCAA	II	8	Latin American Bible (CA)	30	2	Elisaldez, Ken
NCAA	I	64	Duke	34	2	Krzyzewski, Michael W.
NCAA	II	32	Virginia Union	30	3	Robbins, Charles David "Dave"
NCAA	III	40	Calvin	31	1	Douma, Edward
NCCAA	I	8	Bethel (IN)	29	10	Lightfoot, Mike
NCCAA	II	8	Baptist Bible (PA)	20	7	Howard, Russ
NCCAA	IIA	8	Latin American Bible (CA)	30	2	Elisaldez, Ken
NSCAA		12	Texas College	25	5	Patrick, Kirk
1993						
NAIA	I	32	Hawaii Pacific	30	4	Sellitto, Anthony, Jr.
NAIA	II	20	Willamette	29	4	James, Gordon "Gordie"
NBCAA	I	6	San Jose Christian	22	14	Miller, Glen
NBCAA	II	8	Nebraska Christian	19	9	Lahm, Chris
NCAA	I	64	North Carolina	34	4	Smith, Dean E.
NCAA	II	32	California State: Bakersfield	33	0	Douglass, Pat
NCAA	III	40	Ohio Northern	28	2	Campoli, Joe
NCCAA	I	8	Bethel (IN)	30	9	Lightfoot, Mike
NCCAA	II	8	Northwest Assemblies	X	X	Filan, Doug
NCCAA	IIA	8	Atlanta Christian	17	14	Kaiser, Richard "Rick"
NSCAA		9	Texas College			Patrick, Kirk
1994						
NAIA	I	32	Oklahoma City	28	7	Case, Win
NAIA	II	24	Eureka	27	4	Darnell, David
NBCAA	I	7	San Jose Christian	26	11	Miller, Glen
NBCAA	II	8	Nebraska Christian	20	8	Lahm, Chris
NCAA	I	64	Arkansas	31	3	Richardson, Nolan
NCAA	II	32	California State: Bakersfield	27	6	Douglass, Pat
NCAA	III	40	Lebanon Valley	28	4	Flannery, Patrick J.
NCCAA	I	8	Lee (TN)	24	14	Carpenter, Dr. Larry
NCCAA	II	8	Central Bible	28	9	Hanson, Kirk
NCCAA	IIA	8	Grace Bible (MI)	19	10	Moore, Jimmy
NSCAA		12	Mount Senario	24	22	Andrist, Edward A.

Assn	Div	#T	School	W	L	Coach
1995						
NAIA	I	32	Birmingham-Southern	35	2	Reboul, Duane
NAIA	II	32	Bethel (IN)	38	2	Lightfoot, Mike
NBCAA	I	8	San Jose Christian	28	11	Miller, Glen
NBCAA	II	8	Puget Sound Christian	17	11	McNichols, Troy
NCAA	I	64	California: Los Angeles	31	2	Harrick, Jim
NCAA	II	48	Southern Indiana	29	4	Pearl, Bruce
NCAA	III	64	Wisconsin: Platteville	31	0	Ryan, William "Bo"
NCCAA	I	8	Indiana Wesleyan	17	16	Williams, Pat
NCCAA	II	8	Kentucky Christian	26	7	Damron, Dr. Donald R. "Dick"
NCCAA	IIA	8	Grace Bible (MI)	19	12	Moore, Jimmy
NSCAA		12	Paul Quinn	20	12	Summers, James "Zip"
1996						
LCC		7	Gulf Coast Christian	23	17	Wilkerson, Keith
NAIA	I	32	Oklahoma City	33	5	Case, Win
NAIA	II	32	Albertson	31	3	Holly, Martin W. "Marty"
NBCAA	I	8	Multnomah Bible	20	16	Reese, Chris
NBCAA	II	7	Hillsdale Free Will Baptist	13	17	Archer, Kelly
NCAA	I	64	Kentucky	34	2	Pitino, Richard A. "Rick"
NCAA	II	48	Fort Hays State	34	0	Garner, Gary
NCAA	III	64	Rowan	28	4	Giannini, John
NCCAA	I	8	Malone	20	16	Smith, Harold T.
NCCAA	II	8	Kentucky Christian	27	6	Sudlow, Eric
NCCAA	IIA	8	Manhattan Christian	22	8	Condra, Shawn
NSCAA		10	Mount Senario	14	22	Andrist, Edward A.
1997						
LCC		5	Wesley (MS)	13	16	Devore, William, Jr.
NAIA	I	32	Life (GA)	37	1	Kaiser, Roger A.
NAIA	II	32	Bethel (IN)	34	5	Lightfoot, Mike
NBCAA	I	8	Gulf Coast Christian	29	6	Wilkerson, Dr. Charles
NBCAA	II	8	Southwestern Christian Ministries	26	15	Arthur, Mark
NCAA	I	64	Arizona	25	9	Olson, Robert Luther "Lute"
NCAA	II	48	California State: Bakersfield	29	4	Douglass, Pat
NCAA	III	64	Illinois Wesleyan	29	2	Bridges, Dennis L.
NCCAA	I	8	Christian Heritage	23	12	Wilmore, Art
NCCAA	II	8	Kentucky Christian	21	12	Damron, Dr. Donald R. "Dick"
NCCAA	IIA	8	Southwestern (AZ)	21	8	Morley, Stephen H.
NSCAA		12	Louisiana Christian	21	12	Schexnayder, Tommy
1998						
NAIA	I	32	Georgetown (KY)	36	3	Osborne, "Happy"
NAIA	II	32	Bethel (IN)	37	3	Lightfoot, Mike
NBCAA		8	Southwestern Assemblies	20	8	Garippa, Rev. Steven P.
NCAA	I	64	Kentucky	35	4	Smith, Orlando H. "Tubby"
NCAA	II	48	California: Davis	31	2	Williams, Bob
NCAA	III	48	Wisconsin: Platteville	30	0	Ryan, William "Bo"
NCCAA	I	8	Christian Heritage	25	11	Wilmore, Art
NCCAA	II	8	Mid-America Bible	32	8	Holley, Willie
NCCAA	IIA	8	Southwestern Christian Ministries	21	17	Arthur, Mark
NSCAA		15	Northwest Christian	24	8	Lipp, David

By Year—Women

Assn	Div	#T	School	W	L	Coach
1969						
AIAW		16	West Chester	12	0	Eckman, Carol
1970						
AIAW		16	California State: Fullerton	17	1	Moore, Billie Jean
1971						
AIAW		16	Mississippi Women	21	3	Upton, Jill
1972						
AIAW		16	Immaculata (PA)	24	1	Rush, Cathy
1973						
AIAW		16	Immaculata (PA)	20	0	Rush, Cathy
1974						
AIAW		16	Immaculata (PA)	20	1	Rush, Cathy
1975						
AIAW	L	16	Delta State	28	0	Wade, L. Margaret
AIAW	S	12	Phillips (OK)			Amaya, Lou
1976						
AIAW	L	16	Delta State	33	1	Wade, L. Margaret
AIAW	S	16	Berry	20	3	James, Kay
1977						
AIAW	L	16	Delta State	32	3	Wade, L. Margaret
AIAW	S	16	Southeastern Louisiana	30	2	Puckett, Linda
1978						
AIAW	L	16	California: Los Angeles	27	3	Moore, Billie Jean
AIAW	S	16	High Point	30	8	Briley, Wanda
1979						
AIAW	L	16	Old Dominion	35	1	Stanley, Marianne Crawford
AIAW	S	16	South Carolina State	33	2	Simon, Willie J.
1980						
AIAW	I	24	Old Dominion	37	1	Stanley, Marianne Crawford
AIAW	II	24	Dayton	36	2	Jeremiah, Dr. Maryalyce
AIAW	III	24	Worcester State	24	2	Devlin, Donna
NSCAA		8	Colorado Woman's	23	8	Forkum, Jim
1981						
AIAW	I	24	Louisiana Tech	34	0	Hogg, Sonja
AIAW	II	16	William Penn	43	3	Spencer, Robert L.
AIAW	III	16	Wisconsin: La Crosse	27	5	Hansen, Mary
NAIA		8	Kentucky State	21	7	Mitchell, Ron
NSCAA			No Tournament			

Assn	Div	#T	School	W	L	Coach
1982						
AIAW	I	16	Rutgers	25	7	Grentz, Theresa Shank
AIAW	II	16	Francis Marion	27	7	Hatchell, Sylvia Rhyne
AIAW	III	16	Concordia: Moorhead	31	3	Langseth, Marc
NAIA		8	Southwestern Oklahoma State	34	0	Loftin, John D.
NCAA	I	32	Louisiana Tech	35	1	Hogg, Sonja
NCAA	II	16	California Polytechnic: Pomona	29	7	May, Darlene
NCAA	III	16	Elizabethtown	26	1	Kauffman, Yvonne E.
NSCAA		8	National (SD)	16	4	Haight, H. C. 'Bud'
1983						
NAIA		8	Southwestern Oklahoma State	30	4	Loftin, John D.
NBCAA		4	Crown (MN)	X	X	Hardy, Don
NCAA	I	36	Southern California	31	2	Sharp, Linda
NCAA	II	24	Virginia Union	27	2	Hearn, Louis
NCAA	III	32	North Central (IL)	26	6	Morgan, R. Wayne
NCCAA	I	8	Spring Arbor	29	4	Dunckel, Darrell
NCCAA	II	4	Baptist Bible (PA)	23	5	Durrwachter, Nancy White
NSCAA		8	Concordia: Saint Paul	20	6	Surridge, Dr. Jack
1984						
NAIA		16	North Carolina: Asheville	32	5	Carroll, Helen
NBCAA		4	Crown (MN)	X	X	Hardy, Don
NCAA	I	32	Southern California	29	4	Sharp, Linda
NCAA	II	24	Central Missouri State	28	4	Hoehn, Jorja E.
NCAA	III	32	Rust	26	5	Stovall, Dr. Alfred J. 'AJ'
NCCAA	I	8	Huntington	24	9	Freeman, Keith
NCCAA	II	6	Northwestern (MN)	19	10	Smith, Dan
NSCAA		9	Lamar CC	X	X	Unknown
1985						
NAIA		16	Southwestern Oklahoma State	34	0	Loftin, John D.
NBCAA		4	Crown (MN)	X	X	Guavin, Julie
NCAA	I	32	Old Dominion	31	3	Stanley, Marianne Crawford
NCAA	II	24	California Polytechnic: Pomona	21	7	May, Darlene
NCAA	III	32	Scranton	31	1	Strong, Michael J.
NCCAA	I	8	Lee (TN)	15	13	Souther, Orin A. 'Jack'
NCCAA	II	8	Northwestern (MN)	11	19	Smith, Dan
NSCAA		8	Phillips JC: Gulfport	21	6	Rosetti, George F., Sr.
1986						
NAIA		16	Francis Marion	36	2	Hatchell, Sylvia Rhyne
NBCAA		7	North Central Bible	15	16	Myers, Dennis
NCAA	I	40	Texas	34	0	Conradt, Jody
NCAA	II	24	California Polytechnic: Pomona	30	3	May, Darlene
NCAA	III	32	Salem State	29	1	Shea, Timothy P.
NCCAA	I	8	Evangel	21	13	Bowen, Lynn
NCCAA	II	8	Toccoa Falls	13	12	Shiffer, Paul
NSCAA		8	Phillips JC: Gulfport	22	7	Rosetti, George F., Sr.

Assn	Div	#T	School	W	L	Coach
1987						
NAIA		16	Southwestern Oklahoma State	30	2	Loftin, John D.
NBCAA		4	North Central Bible	X	X	Myers, Dennis
NCAA	I	40	Tennessee	28	6	Summitt, Patricia Head
NCAA	II	24	New Haven	29	2	Rossman, Jan
NCAA	III	32	Wisconsin: Stevens Point	27	2	Wunder, Linda
NCCAA	I	8	Spring Arbor	25	9	Dunckel, Darrell
NCCAA	II	6	Moody Bible	X	X	Gaffney, Greg
NSCAA		8	Concordia (NE)	23	8	Everts, Dr. Carl
1988						
NAIA		16	Oklahoma City	28	6	Colon, Bob
NBCAA		4	Ozark Christian	X	X	Williams, Charles R.
NCAA	I	40	Louisiana Tech	32	2	Barmore, Leon
NCAA	II	32	Hampton	33	1	Sweat, James E.
NCAA	III	32	Concordia: Moorhead	29	2	Siverson, Duane
NCCAA	I	8	King (TN)	27	3	Nida, Al
NCCAA	II	6	Northwest Assemblies	16	17	Brodin, Kristi
NSCAA		8	Saint Scholastica	25	6	Stukel, Jim
1989						
NAIA		16	Southern Nazarene	36	2	Hoffman, Bob
NBCAA		4	Calvary Bible	16	1	Hensarling, Anne
NCAA	I	48	Tennessee	35	2	Summitt, Patricia Head
NCAA	II	32	Delta State	30	4	Clark, Lloyd
NCAA	III	32	Elizabethtown	29	2	Kauffman, Yvonne E.
NCCAA	I	8	King (TN)	28	2	Nida, Al
NCCAA	II	8	Kentucky Christian	13	11	Bender, Tom
NSCAA		8	Concordia (NE)	25	7	Everts, Dr. Carl
1990						
NAIA		16	Southwestern Oklahoma State	30	4	Loftin, John D.
NBCAA		6	Calvary Bible	12	9	Shook, John
NCAA	I	48	Stanford	32	1	VanDerveer, Tara
NCAA	II	32	Delta State	32	1	Clark, Lloyd
NCAA	III	32	Hope	24	2	Wise, Susan
NCCAA	I	8	King (TN)	27	3	Ward, Jeannine
NCCAA	II	8	Northwest Assemblies	11	18	Brodin, Kristi
NSCAA		8	Concordia (NE)	20	13	Everts, Dr. Carl
1991						
NAIA		32	Fort Hays State	34	2	Klein, John
NBCAA		5	Crown (MN)	19	9	Rogness, Tony
NCAA	I	48	Tennessee	30	5	Summitt, Patricia Head
NCAA	II	32	North Dakota State	31	2	Ruley, Amy J.
NCAA	III	32	Saint Thomas (MN)	29	2	Riverso, Ted
NCCAA	I	8	Huntington	24	4	Culler, Lori
NCCAA	II	8	Northwest Assemblies	10	20	Brodin, Kristi
NSCAA		8	Silver Lake	25	6	Wenner, Craig

Assn	Div	#T	School	W	L	Coach
1992						
NAIA	I	32	Arkansas Tech	35	1	Foley, Joe M.
NAIA	II	20	Northern State (SD)	30	4	Fredrickson, Curt
NBCAA		4	Hillsdale Free Will Baptist	9	13	Braisher, Kelly
NCAA	I	48	Stanford	30	3	VanDerveer, Tara
NCAA	II	32	Delta State	30	4	Clark, Lloyd
NCAA	III	32	Alma	24	3	Goffnett, Charles
NCCAA	I	8	Huntington	24	8	Culler, Lori
NCCAA	II	8	Toccoa Falls	23	6	Shiffer, Paul
NSCAA		8	Trinity International (IL)	15	10	Seils, David S.
1993						
NAIA	I	32	Arkansas Tech	31	5	Foley, Joe M.
NAIA	II	20	Montana State: Northern	35	3	Winn, Sherry
NBCAA		6	Grace (NE)	19	0	Regier, Larry
NCAA	I	48	Texas Tech	31	3	Sharp, Marsha
NCAA	II	32	North Dakota State	30	2	Ruley, Amy J.
NCAA	III	32	Central (IA)	24	5	Boeyink, Gary
NCCAA	I	8	Williams Baptist	24	2	Halford, Carol
NCCAA	II	8	Northwest Assemblies	17	11	Brodin, Kristi
NSCAA		8	Blackburn	24	7	Sexton, James R.
1994						
NAIA	I	32	Southern Nazarene	34	0	Finkbeiner, Jerry
NAIA	II	24	Northern State (SD)	32	1	Fredrickson, Curt
NBCAA		4	Grace (NE)	15	0	Reiger, Larry
NCAA	I	64	North Carolina	33	2	Hatchell, Sylvia Rhyne
NCAA	II	32	North Dakota State	27	5	Ruley, Amy J.
NCAA	III	40	Capital	30	1	Jeffers, Dixie M.
NCCAA	I	8	Mount Vernon Nazarene	23	10	Howald, Jeana
NCCAA	II	8	Northwest Assemblies	7	21	Brodin, Kristi
NSCAA		8	Trinity International (IL)	24	8	Seils, David S.
1995						
NAIA	I	32	Southern Nazarene	30	2	Finkbeiner, Jerry
NAIA	II	32	Western Oregon	23	9	Rogers, "Rusty"
NBCAA		5	Grace (NE)	17	2	Johnson, DuWayne
NCAA	I	64	Connecticut	35	0	Auriemma, Geno
NCAA	II	48	North Dakota State	32	0	Ruley, Amy J.
NCAA	III	64	Capital	33	0	Jeffers, Dixie M.
NCCAA	I	8	Western Baptist	17	16	Williams, Terry
NCCAA	II	8	Kentucky Christian	24	9	Arnett, Ron
NSCAA		8	Martin Methodist	13	18	Jones, Johnny
1996						
NAIA	I	32	Southern Nazarene	34	2	Finkbeiner, Jerry
NAIA	II	32	Western Oregon	31	4	Rogers, "Rusty"
NBCAA		6	Grace (NE)	19	0	Johnson, DuWayne

Assn	Div	#T	School	W	L	Coach
NCAA	I	64	Tennessee	32	4	Summitt, Patricia Head
NCAA	II	48	North Dakota State	30	2	Ruley, Amy J.
NCAA	III	64	Wisconsin: Oshkosh	31	0	Bennett, Kathi
NCCAA	I	8	Western Baptist	24	11	Williams, Terry
NCCAA	II	8	Kentucky Christian	28	4	Arnett, Ron
NSCAA		6	Kansas Wesleyan	14	16	Hughes, Tom

1997

Assn	Div	#T	School	W	L	Coach
NAIA	I	32	Southern Nazarene	32	4	Finkbeiner, Jerry
NAIA	II	32	Northwest Nazarene	27	7	Schmidt, Roger
NBCAA		4	Hillsdale Free Will Baptist	12	10	Archer, Kelly
NCAA	I	64	Tennessee	29	10	Summitt, Patricia Head
NCAA	II	48	North Dakota	28	4	Roebuck, Gene
NCAA	III	64	New York	29	1	Quinn, Janice
NCCAA	I	8	LeTourneau	30	4	Otwell, Mary Ann
NCCAA	II	8	Kentucky Christian	30	5	Arnett, Ron
NSCAA		8	Kansas Wesleyan	12	19	Hughes, Tom

1998

Assn	Div	#T	School	W	L	Coach
NAIA	I	32	Union (TN)	35	3	Blackstock, Dr. David
NAIA	II	32	Walsh	29	5	Smesco, Carl
NBCAA		4	Nebraska Christian	21	8	Fuehrer, Mike
NCAA	I	64	Tennessee	39	0	Summitt, Patricia Head
NCAA	II	48	North Dakota	31	1	Roebuck, Gene
NCAA	III	48	Washington (MO)	28	2	Fahey, Nancy
NCCAA	I	8	LeTourneau	24	10	Otwell, Mary Ann
NCCAA	II	8	Kentucky Christian	22	13	Arnett, Ron
NSCAA		8	Clarendon	21	9	Zehr, Joel R.

By School

Year	M/W	Assn	Div	#T	W	L	Coach
ALBERTSON							
1996	M	NAIA	II	32	31	33	Holly, Martin W. "Marty"
ALMA							
1992	W	NCAA	III	32	24	33	Goffnett, Charles
ARIZONA							
1997	M	NCAA	I	64	25	9	Olson, Robert Luther "Lute"
ARIZONA BIBLE							
1987	M	NBCAA	II	4	X	X	Steele, Kevin
ARKANSAS							
1994	M	NCAA	I	64	31	3	Richardson, Nolan
ARKANSAS TECH							
1992	W	NAIA	I	32	35	1	Foley, Joe M.
1993	W	NAIA	I	32	31	5	Foley, Joe M.

Year	M/W	Assn	Div	#T	W	L	Coach
ARLINGTON BAPTIST							
1988	M	NBCAA	II	4	X	X	Jones, Dr. Griffin
ATLANTA CHRISTIAN							
1993	M	NCCAA	IIA	8	17	14	Kaiser, Richard "Rick"
AZUSA PACIFIC							
1969	M	NCCAA		6	26	7	Hamlow, Dr. Clifford
1970	M	NCCAA		8	29	6	Hamlow, Dr. Clifford
1971	M	NCCAA		8	25	11	Hamlow, Dr. Clifford
1972	M	NCCAA		8	26	10	Hamlow, Dr. Clifford
BAPTIST BIBLE (MO)							
1978	M	NCCAA	II	6	13	15	Schepis, Mike
1981	M	NCCAA	II	6	18	17	Reed, Roger
1982	M	NCCAA	II	6	20	11	Fuller, Fred
1983	M	NCCAA	II	6	24	14	Fuller, Fred
1984	M	NCCAA	II	8	17	13	Smith, Gary
BAPTIST BIBLE (PA)							
1979	M	NCCAA	II	6	20	12	Huckaby, James M.
1983	W	NCCAA	II	4	23	5	Durrwachter, Nancy White
1992	M	NCCAA	II	8	20	7	Howard, Russ
BENEDICTINE (KS)							
1954	M	NAIA		32	24	5	Nolan, Ralph
1967	M	NAIA		32	27	2	Nolan, Ralph
BERRY							
1976	W	AIAW	S	16	20	3	James, Kay
BETHEL (IN)							
1992	M	NCCAA	I	8	29	10	Lightfoot, Mike
1993	M	NCCAA	I	8	30	9	Lightfoot, Mike
1995	M	NAIA	II	32	38	2	Lightfoot, Mike
1997	M	NAIA	II	32	34	5	Lightfoot, Mike
1998	M	NAIA	II	32	37	3	Lightfoot, Mike
BIOLA							
1976	M	NCCAA	I	4	23	9	Lyon, Howard
1978	M	NCCAA	I	6	22	14	Lyon, Howard
1984	M	NCCAA	I	8	25	6	Lyon, Howard
BIRMINGHAM-SOUTHERN							
1990	M	NAIA		32	31	3	Reboul, Duane
1995	M	NAIA	I	32	35	2	Reboul, Duane
BLACKBURN							
1982	M	NSCAA		16	23	8	Parker, James R.
1985	M	NSCAA		16	23	7	Staff, Bob
1993	W	NSCAA		8	24	7	Sexton, James R.
BRISTOL (TN)							
1986	M	NSCAA		16			Crowder, Brien
BRYANT & STRATTON: BUFFALO							
1974	M	NSCAA		16	X	X	Griffin, Dr. Thomas J.

Year	M/W	Assn	Div	#T	W	L	Coach
CALIFORNIA							
1959	M	NCAA	I	23	25	4	Newell, Peter F.
1998	M	NCAA	II	48	31	2	Williams, Bob
CALIFORNIA POLYTECHNIC: POMONA							
1982	W	NCAA	II	16	29	7	May, Darlene
1985	W	NCAA	II	24	21	7	May, Darlene
1986	W	NCAA	II	24	30	3	May, Darlene
CALIFORNIA STATE: BAKERSFIELD							
1993	M	NCAA	II	32	33	0	Douglass, Pat
1994	M	NCAA	II	32	27	6	Douglass, Pat
1997	M	NCAA	II	48	29	4	Douglass, Pat
CALIFORNIA STATE: FULLERTON							
1970	W	AIAW		16	17	1	Moore, Billie Jean
CALIFORNIA: DAVIS							
1998	M	NCAA	II	48	31	2	Williams, Bob
CALIFORNIA: LOS ANGELES							
1964	M	NCAA	I	25	30	0	Wooden, John R.
1965	M	NCAA	I	23	28	2	Wooden, John R.
1967	M	NCAA	I	23	30	0	Wooden, John R.
1968	M	NCAA	I	23	29	1	Wooden, John R.
1969	M	NCAA	I	25	29	1	Wooden, John R.
1970	M	NCAA	I	25	28	2	Wooden, John R.
1971	M	NCAA	I	25	29	1	Wooden, John R.
1972	M	NCAA	I	25	30	0	Wooden, John R.
1973	M	NCAA	I	25	30	0	Wooden, John R.
1975	M	NCAA	I	32	28	3	Wooden, John R.
1978	W	AIAW	L	16	27	3	Moore, Billie Jean
1995	M	NCAA	I	64	31	2	Harrick, Jim
CALVARY BIBLE							
1981	M	NBCAA		4	22	4	Schneeberger, Robert W.
1982	M	NBCAA		8	26	1	Schneeberger, Robert W.
1989	W	NBCAA		4	16	1	Hensarling, Anne
1990	W	NBCAA		6	12	9	Shook, John
CALVIN							
1992	M	NCAA	III	40	31	1	Douma, Edward
CAMERON							
1980	M	NAIA		32	28	3	Nichols, Lonnie
CAPITAL							
1994	W	NCAA	III	40	30	1	Jeffers, Dixie M.
1995	W	NCAA	III	64	33	0	Jeffers, Dixie M.
CENTRAL (IA)							
1993	W	NCAA	III	32	24	5	Boeyink, Gary
CENTRAL BIBLE							
1994	M	NCCAA	II	8	28	9	Hanson, Kirk

Year	M/W	Assn	Div	#T	W	L	Coach
CENTRAL MISSOURI STATE							
1937	M	NAIA		8	17	3	Reid, Tad C.
1938	M	NAIA		32	24	3	Reid, Tad C.
1984	M	NCAA	II	32	29	3	Nance, Lynn
1984	W	NCAA	II	24	28	4	Hoehn, Jorja E.
CENTRAL STATE (OH)							
1965	M	NAIA		32	30	0	Lucas, William C.
1968	M	NAIA		32	29	4	Lucas, William C.
CHARLESTON (SC)							
1983	M	NAIA		32	24	5	Kresse, John
CHEYNEY							
1978	M	NCAA	II	32	27	2	Chaney, John
CHRISTIAN HERITAGE							
1990	M	NCCAA	I	8	33	6	Nater, Swen E.
1997	M	NCCAA	I	8	23	12	Wilmore, Art
1998	M	NCCAA	I	8	25	11	Wilmore, Art
CINCINNATI							
1961	M	NCAA	I	24	27	3	Jucker, Edwin L.
1962	M	NCAA	I	25	29	2	Jucker, Edwin L.
CINCINNATI BIBLE							
1985	M	NCCAA	II	8	32	3	Wallingford, Tony
1986	M	NCCAA	II	8	35	2	Wallingford, Tony
1987	M	NCCAA	II	8	29	5	Wallingford, Tony
CITY COLLEGE							
1950	M	NCAA		8	24	5	Holman, Nathan 'Nat'
CLARENDON							
1998	W	NSCAA		8	21	9	Zehr, Joel R.
COLORADO WOMAN'S							
1980	W	NSCAA		8	23	8	Forkum, Jim
CONCORDIA (NE)							
1987	W	NSCAA		8	23	8	Everts, Dr. Carl
1989	W	NSCAA		8	25	7	Everts, Dr. Carl
1990	W	NSCAA		8	20	13	Everts, Dr. Carl
CONCORDIA: AUSTIN							
1983	M	NSCAA		16	30	7	Orton, Tom
CONCORDIA: MOORHEAD							
1982	W	AIAW	III	16	31	3	Langseth, Marc
1988	W	NCAA	III	32	29	2	Siverson, Duane
CONCORDIA: SAINT PAUL							
1983	W	NSCAA		8	20	6	Surridge, Dr. Jack
CONNECTICUT							
1995	W	NCAA	I	64	35	0	Auriemma, Geno

Year	M/W	Assn	Div	#T	W	L	Coach
COPPIN STATE							
1976	M	NAIA		32	39	2	Bates, John H.
CROWN (MN)							
1983	W	NBCAA		4	X	X	Hardy, Don
1984	W	NBCAA		4	X	X	Hardy, Don
1985	W	NBCAA		4	X	X	Guavin, Julie
1991	W	NBCAA		5	19	9	Rogness, Tony
DAYTON							
1980	W	AIAW	II	24	36	2	Jeremiah, Dr. Maryalyce
DELTA STATE							
1975	W	AIAW	L	16	28	0	Wade, L. Margaret
1976	W	AIAW	L	16	33	1	Wade, L. Margaret
1977	W	AIAW	L	16	32	3	Wade, L. Margaret
1989	W	NCAA	II	32	30	4	Clark, Lloyd
1990	W	NCAA	II	32	32	1	Clark, Lloyd
1992	W	NCAA	II	32	30	4	Clark, Lloyd
DISTRICT OF COLUMBIA							
1982	M	NCAA	II	32	25	5	Jones, William S.
DRURY							
1979	M	NAIA		32	33	2	Kirksey, Jerry L.
DUKE							
1991	M	NCAA	I	64	32	7	Krzyzewski, Michael W.
1992	M	NCAA	I	64	34	2	Krzyzewski, Michael W.
EASTERN NEW MEXICO							
1969	M	NAIA		32	24	7	Miller, Harry E.
ELIZABETHTOWN							
1982	W	NCAA	III	16	26	1	Kauffman, Yvonne E.
1989	W	NCAA	III	32	29	2	Kauffman, Yvonne E.
EUREKA							
1994	M	NAIA	II	24	27	4	Darnell, David
EVANGEL							
1986	W	NCCAA	I	8	21	13	Bowen, Lynn
EVANSVILLE							
1959	M	NCAA	II	32	21	6	McCutchan, Arad A.
1960	M	NCAA	II	32	25	4	McCutchan, Arad A.
1964	M	NCAA	II	32	26	3	McCutchan, Arad A.
1965	M	NCAA	II	32	29	0	McCutchan, Arad A.
1971	M	NCAA	II	32	22	8	McCutchan, Arad A.
FLORIDA COLLEGE							
1975	M	NSCAA		16	20	11	Wilson, Tom
1979	M	NSCAA		16	20	14	Wilson, Tom

Year	M/W	Assn	Div	#T	W	L	Coach
FLORIDA SOUTHERN							
1981	M	NCAA	II	32	24	8	Wissel, Dr. Harold R. "Hal"
FORT HAYS STATE							
1984	M	NAIA		32	26	2	Morse, Bill
1985	M	NAIA		32	35	3	Morse, Bill
1991	W	NAIA		32	34	2	Klein, John
1996	M	NCAA	II	48	34	0	Garner, Gary
FRANCIS MARION							
1982	W	AIAW	II	16	27	7	Hatchell, Sylvia Rhyne
1986	W	NAIA		16	36	2	Hatchell, Sylvia Rhyne
GEORGETOWN (DC)							
1984	M	NCAA	I	53	34	3	Thompson, John R., Jr.
GEORGETOWN (KY)							
1998	M	NAIA	I	32	36	3	Osborne, "Happy"
GRACE (IN)							
1992	M	NAIA	II	20	32	5	Kessler, James C.
GRACE (NE)							
1993	W	NBCAA		6	19	0	Regier, Larry
1994	W	NBCAA		4	15	0	Reiger, Larry
1995	W	NBCAA		5	17	2	Johnson, DuWayne
1996	W	NBCAA		6	19	0	Johnson, DuWayne
GRACE BIBLE (MI)							
1994	M	NCCAA	IIA	8	19	10	Moore, Jimmy
1995	M	NCCAA	IIA	8	19	12	Moore, Jimmy
GRAMBLING STATE							
1961	M	NAIA		32	32	4	Hobdy, Frederick C.
GRAND CANYON							
1975	M	NAIA		32	30	3	Lindsey, Ben
1978	M	NAIA		32	30	3	Lindsey, Ben
1988	M	NAIA		32	37	6	Westphal, Paul D.
GUILFORD							
1973	M	NAIA		32	29	5	Jensen, Jack
GULF COAST CHRISTIAN							
1996	M	LCC		7	23	17	Wilkerson, Keith
1997	M	NBCAA		18	29	6	Wilkerson, Dr. Charles
HAMLINE							
1942	M	NAIA		32	20	2	Hutton, Joseph W., Sr.
1949	M	NAIA		32	29	1	Hutton, Joseph W., Sr.
1951	M	NAIA		32	27	2	Hutton, Joseph W., Sr.
HAMPTON							
1988	W	NCAA	II	32	33	1	Sweat, James E.

Year	M/W	Assn	Div	#T	W	L	Coach
HAWAII PACIFIC							
1993	M	NAIA	I	32	30	4	Sellitto, Anthony, Jr.
HIGH POINT							
1978	W	AIAW	S	16	30	8	Briley, Wanda
HILLSDALE FREE WILL BAPTIST							
1989	M	NBCAA	II	6	15	15	Lawrence, Aaron
1991	M	NBCAA	II	7	23	11	Lisenbee, Tim
1992	W	NBCAA		4	9	13	Braisher, Kelly
1996	M	NBCAA	II	7	13	17	Archer, Kelly
1997	W	NBCAA		4	12	10	Archer, Kelly
HOLY CROSS (MA)							
1947	M	NCAA		8	27	3	Julian, Alvin F. "Doggie"
HOPE							
1990	W	NCAA	III	32	24	2	Wise, Susan
HUNTINGTON							
1984	W	NCCAA	I	8	24	9	Freeman, Keith
1991	W	NCCAA	I	8	24	4	Culler, Lori
1992	W	NCCAA	I	8	24	8	Culler, Lori
ILLINOIS WESLEYAN							
1997	M	NCAA	III	64	29	2	Bridges, Dennis L.
IMMACULATA (PA)							
1972	W	AIAW		16	24	1	Rush, Cathy
1973	W	AIAW		16	20	0	Rush, Cathy
1974	W	AIAW		16	20	1	Rush, Cathy
INDIANA							
1940	M	NCAA		8	20	3	McCracken, E. Branch
1953	M	NCAA		22	23	3	McCracken, E. Branch
1976	M	NCAA	I	32	32	0	Knight, Robert M.
1981	M	NCAA	I	48	26	9	Knight, Robert M.
1987	M	NCAA	I	64	30	4	Knight, Robert M.
INDIANA STATE							
1950	M	NAIA		32	27	8	Longfellow, John L.
INDIANA WESLEYAN							
1995	M	NCCAA	I	8	17	16	Williams, Pat
JACKSONVILLE STATE (AL)							
1985	M	NCAA	II	32	3	11	Jones, Bill E.
JOHN BROWN							
1991	M	NCCAA	I	8	25	8	Sheehy, John
KANSAS							
1952	M	NCAA		16	28	3	Allen, Dr. Forrest C. "Phog"
1988	M	NCAA	I	64	27	11	Brown, Lawrence H.

Year	M/W	Assn	Div	#T	W	L	Coach
KANSAS WESLEYAN							
1996	W	NSCAA		6	14	16	Hughes, Tom
1997	W	NSCAA		8	12	19	Hughes, Tom
KENTUCKY							
1948	M	NCAA		8	36	3	Rupp, Adolph F.
1949	M	NCAA		8	32	2	Rupp, Adolph F.
1951	M	NCAA		16	32	2	Rupp, Adolph F.
1958	M	NCAA	I	24	23	6	Rupp, Adolph F.
1978	M	NCAA	I	32	30	2	Hall, Joe B.
1996	M	NCAA	I	64	34	2	Pitino, Richard A. 'Rick'
1998	M	NCAA	I	64	35	4	Smith, Orlando H. 'Tubby'
KENTUCKY CHRISTIAN							
1988	M	NCCAA	II	8	26	8	Kirk, Randy
1989	M	NCCAA	II	8	27	5	Kirk, Randy
1989	W	NCCAA	II	8	13	11	Bender, Tom
1991	M	NCCAA	II	8	20	13	Damron, Dr. Donald R. 'Dick'
1995	M	NCCAA	II	8	26	7	Damron, Dr. Donald R. 'Dick'
1995	W	NCCAA	II	8	24	9	Arnett, Ron
1996	M	NCCAA	II	8	27	6	Sudlow, Eric
1996	W	NCCAA	II	8	28	4	Arnett, Ron
1997	M	NCCAA	II	8	21	12	Damron, Dr. Donald R. 'Dick'
1997	W	NCCAA	II	8	30	5	Arnett, Ron
1998	W	NCCAA	II	8	22	13	Arnett, Ron
KENTUCKY STATE							
1970	M	NAIA		32	29	3	Mitchell, Lucias
1971	M	NAIA		32	31	2	Mitchell, Lucias
1972	M	NAIA		32	28	5	Mitchell, Lucias
1981	W	NAIA		8	21	7	Mitchell, Ron
KENTUCKY WESLEYAN							
1966	M	NCAA	II	36	24	6	Strong, Guy Rowland
1968	M	NCAA	II	36	28	3	Daniels, Bob
1969	M	NCAA	II	32	25	5	Daniels, Bob
1973	M	NCAA	II	42	24	6	Jones, Bob
1987	M	NCAA	II	32	28	5	Chapman, Wayne G.
1990	M	NCAA	II	32	31	2	Chapman, Wayne G.
KING (TN)							
1988	W	NCCAA	I	8	27	3	Nida, Al
1989	W	NCCAA	I	8	28	2	Nida, Al
1990	W	NCCAA	I	8	27	3	Ward, Jeannine
KITTRELL JC							
1970	M	NSCAA		8	32	4	Golatt, Moses
LA SALLE							
1954	M	NCAA		24	26	4	Loeffler, Kenneth D.
LAMAR CC							
1984	W	NSCAA		9	X	X	Unknown

Year	M/W	Assn	Div	#T	W	L	Coach
LATIN AMERICAN BIBLE (CA)							
1992	M	NBCAA	II	8	30	2	Elisaldez, Ken
1992	M	NCCAA	IIA	8	30	2	Elisaldez, Ken
LEBANON VALLEY							
1994	M	NCAA	III	40	28	4	Flannery, Patrick J.
LEE (TN)							
1968	M	NCCAA		6	30	4	Hughes, Dale R.
1973	M	NCCAA		4	31	6	Hughes, Dale R.
1985	W	NCCAA		18	15	13	Souther, Orin A. "Jack"
1994	M	NCCAA		18	24	14	Carpenter, Dr. Larry
LEMOYNE-OWEN			-				
1975	M	NCAA	III	30	27	5	Johnson, Jerry C.
LETOURNEAU							
1997	W	NCCAA	I	8	30	4	Otwell, Mary Ann
1998	W	NCCAA	I	8	24	10	Otwell, Mary Ann
LIBERTY							
1980	M	NCCAA	I	6	28	11	Gibson, Dale
LIFE (GA)							
1997	M	NAIA	I	32	37	1	Kaiser, Roger A.
LIFE BIBLE (CA)							
1988	M	NBCAA	I	8	19	6	Updike, Blake
LINDSEY WILSON							
1972	M	NSCAA		8	22	8	Voight, James R. "Jim"
LIPSCOMB							
1986	M	NAIA		32	35	4	Meyer, Dr. Don W.
LOUISIANA CHRISTIAN							
1997	M	NSCAA		12	21	12	Schexnayder, Tommy
LOUISIANA TECH							
1981	W	AIAW	I	24	34	0	Hogg, Sonja
1982	W	NCAA	I	32	35	1	Hogg, Sonja
1988	W	NCAA	I	40	32	2	Barmore, Leon
LOUISVILLE							
1948	M	NAIA		32	29	6	Hickman, Bernard L. "Peck"
1980	M	NCAA	I	48	33	3	Crum, Denzil E. "Denny"
1986	M	NCAA	I	64	32	7	Crum, Denzil E. "Denny"
LOYOLA (IL)							
1963	M	NCAA	I	25	29	2	Ireland, George M.
LOYOLA NEW ORLEANS							
1945	M	NAIA		16	22	11	Orsley, Jack C.

Year	M/W	Assn	Div	#T	W	L	Coach
MALONE							
1996	M	NCCAA	I	8	20	16	Smith, Harold T.
MANHATTAN CHRISTIAN							
1996	M	NCCAA	IIA	8	22	8	Condra, Shawn
MARANATHA BAPTIST BIBLE (WI)							
1990	M	NCCAA	II	8	18	8	Terrill, Jerry
MARQUETTE							
1977	M	NCAA	I	32	25	7	McGuire, Alfred J.
MARSHALL							
1947	M	NAIA		32	32	5	Henderson, Eli Camden 'Cam'
MARTIN METHODIST							
1995	W	NSCAA		8	13	18	Jones, Johnny
MASSACHUSETTS: LOWELL							
1988	M	NCAA	II	32	27	7	Doucette, Don
MCNEESE STATE							
1956	M	NAIA		32	33	3	Ward, Ralph O.
MICHIGAN							
1989	M	NCAA	I	64	30	7	Fisher, Stephen L.
MICHIGAN STATE							
1979	M	NCAA	I	40	26	6	Heathcote, George 'Jud'
MID-AMERICA BIBLE							
1998	M	NCCAA	II	8	32	8	Holley, Willie
MIDWEST CHRISTIAN							
1985	M	NBCAA	II	4	X	X	Williams, Charles R.
MINNESOTA BIBLE							
1984	M	NBCAA	II	3	19	8	Comeaux, R. Mark
MISSISSIPPI WOMEN							
1971	W	AIAW		16	21	3	Upton, Jill
MONTANA STATE: NORTHERN							
1993	W	NAIA	II	20	35	3	Winn, Sherry
MOODY BIBLE							
1987	W	NCCAA	II	6	X	X	Gaffney, Greg
MORGAN STATE							
1974	M	NCAA	II	44	28	5	Frazier, Nathaniel
MOUNT SAINT MARY'S (MD)							
1962	M	NCAA	II	32	24	6	Phelan, James J.

Year	M/W	Assn	Div	#T	W	L	Coach
MOUNT SENARIO							
1991	M	NSCAA		12	40	10	Andrist, Edward A.
1994	M	NSCAA		12	24	22	Andrist, Edward A.
1996	M	NSCAA		10	14	22	Andrist, Edward A.
MOUNT VERNON NAZARENE							
1994	W	NCCAA	I	8	23	10	Howald, Jeana
MULTNOMAH BIBLE							
1996	M	NBCAA	I	8	20	16	Reese, Chris
NATIONAL (SD)							
1982	W	NSCAA		8	16	4	Haight, H. C. "Bud"
1987	M	NSCAA		16			Ticknor, Duane
1988	M	NSCAA		15	30	6	Ticknor, Duane
NEBRASKA CHRISTIAN							
1986	M	NBCAA	II	3	12	14	Lahm, Chris
1990	M	NBCAA	II	8	19	10	Lahm, Chris
1993	M	NBCAA	II	8	19	9	Lahm, Chris
1994	M	NBCAA	II	8	20	8	Lahm, Chris
1998	W	NBCAA		4	21	8	Fuehrer, Mike
NEVADA: LAS VEGAS							
1990	M	NCAA	I	64	35	5	Tarkanian, Jerry
NEW HAVEN							
1987	W	NCAA	II	24	29	2	Rossman, Jan
NEW YORK							
1997	W	NCAA	III	64	29	1	Quinn, Janice
NORTH ALABAMA							
1979	M	NCAA	II	32	22	9	Jones, Bill L.
1991	M	NCAA	II	32	29	4	Elliott, Gary
NORTH CAROLINA							
1957	M	NCAA	I	23	32	0	McGuire, Frank J.
1982	M	NCAA	I	48	32	2	Smith, Dean E.
1993	M	NCAA	I	64	34	4	Smith, Dean E.
1994	W	NCAA	I	64	33	2	Hatchell, Sylvia Rhyne
NORTH CAROLINA CENTRAL							
1989	M	NCAA	II	32	28	4	Bernard, Michael J.
NORTH CAROLINA STATE							
1974	M	NCAA	I	25	30	1	Sloan, Norman L., Jr.
1983	M	NCAA	I	52	26	10	Valvano, James T.
NORTH CAROLINA: ASHEVILLE							
1984	W	NAIA		16	32	5	Carroll, Helen
NORTH CENTRAL (IL)							
1983	W	NCAA	III	32	26	6	Morgan, R. Wayne

Year	M/W	Assn	Div	#T	W	L	Coach
NORTH CENTRAL BIBLE							
1986	W	NBCAA		7	15	16	Myers, Dennis
1987	W	NBCAA		4	X	X	Myers, Dennis
NORTH DAKOTA							
1997	W	NCAA	II	48	28	4	Roebuck, Gene
1998	W	NCAA	II	48	31	1	Roebuck, Gene
NORTH DAKOTA STATE							
1991	W	NCAA	II	32	31	2	Ruley, Amy J.
1993	W	NCAA	II	32	30	2	Ruley, Amy J.
1994	W	NCAA	II	32	27	5	Ruley, Amy J.
1995	W	NCAA	II	48	32	0	Ruley, Amy J.
1996	W	NCAA	II	48	30	2	Ruley, Amy J.
NORTH PARK							
1978	M	NCAA	III	30	29	2	McCarrell, Dan
1979	M	NCAA	III	32	26	5	McCarrell, Dan
1980	M	NCAA	III	32	28	3	McCarrell, Dan
1985	M	NCAA	III	32	27	4	Djurickovic, Bosko
1987	M	NCAA	III	32	28	3	Djurickovic, Bosko
NORTHEAST CC (NE)							
1976	M	NSCAA		14			Stevenson, Charles "Chuck"
NORTHERN STATE (SD)							
1992	W	NAIA	II	20	30	4	Fredrickson, Curt
1994	W	NAIA	II	24	32	1	Fredrickson, Curt
NORTHWEST ASSEMBLIES							
1988	W	NCCAA	II	6	16	17	Brodin, Kristi
1990	W	NCCAA	II	8	11	18	Brodin, Kristi
1991	W	NCCAA	II	8	10	20	Brodin, Kristi
1993	M	NCCAA	II	8	X	X	Filan, Doug
1993	W	NCCAA	II	8	17	11	Brodin, Kristi
1994	W	NCCAA	II	8	7	21	Brodin, Kristi
NORTHWEST CHRISTIAN							
1983	M	NBCAA		8	24	5	Buckley, Jim
1984	M	NBCAA	I	8	24	4	Lipp, David
1985	M	NBCAA	I	8	25	4	Lipp, David
1986	M	NBCAA	I	8	19	11	Kennedy, Don
1987	M	NBCAA	I	8	21	8	Halupa, Paul
1989	M	NBCAA	I	7	19	12	Rodenburg, Jeff
1998	M	NSCAA		15	24	8	Lipp, David
NORTHWEST NAZARENE							
1997	W	NAIA	II	32	27	7	Schmidt, Roger
NORTHWESTERN (MN)							
1980	M	NCCAA	II	6	21	11	Sulack, Dave
1984	W	NCCAA	II	6	19	10	Smith, Dan
1985	W	NCCAA	II	8	11	19	Smith, Dan

Year	M/W	Assn	Div	#T	W	L	Coach
OAKLAND CITY (IN)							
1981	M	NSCAA		16	12	20	Trafton, Charles L.
OHIO NORTHERN							
1993	M	NCAA	III	40	28	2	Campoli, Joe
OHIO STATE							
1960	M	NCAA	I	25	25	3	Taylor, Fred R.
OHIO WESLEYAN							
1988	M	NCAA	III	32	27	5	Mehaffey, Dr. Eugene L.
OKLAHOMA BAPTIST UNIVERSITY							
1966	M	NAIA		32	26	7	Bass, Robert E.
OKLAHOMA CITY							
1988	W	NAIA		16	28	6	Colon, Bob
1991	M	NAIA		32	27	3	Johnson, Darrel
1992	M	NAIA	I	32	38	0	Johnson, Darrel
1994	M	NAIA	I	32	28	7	Case, Win
1996	M	NAIA	I	32	33	5	Case, Win
OKLAHOMA STATE							
1945	M	NCAA		8	27	4	Iba, Henry P. "Hank"
1946	M	NCAA		8	31	2	Iba, Henry P. "Hank"
OLD DOMINION							
1975	M	NCAA	II	32	25	6	Allen, William "Sonny"
1979	W	AIAW	L	16	35	1	Stanley, Marianne Crawford
1980	W	AIAW	I	24	37	1	Stanley, Marianne Crawford
1985	W	NCAA	I	32	31	3	Stanley, Marianne Crawford
OLIVET NAZARENE							
1975	M	NCCAA		4	30	4	Ward, C. W. "Butch"
OREGON							
1939	M	NCAA		8	29	5	Hobson, Dr. Howard A. "Hobby"
OZARK CHRISTIAN							
1988	W	NBCAA		4	X	X	Williams, Charles R.
1990	M	NBCAA	I	8	X	X	Williams, Charles R.
1992	M	NBCAA	I	8	28	13	Williams, Charles R.
PAUL QUINN							
1990	M	NSCAA		12	31	7	Summers, James "Zip"
1995	M	NSCAA		12	20	12	Summers, James "Zip"
PHILADELPHIA TEXTILES							
1970	M	NCAA	II	32	29	2	Magee, Herbert
PHILLIPS (OK)							
1975	W	AIAW	S	12			Amaya, Lou
PHILLIPS JC: GULFPORT							
1985	W	NSCAA		8	21	6	Rosetti, George F., Sr.
1986	W	NSCAA		8	22	7	Rosetti, George F., Sr.

Year	M/W	Assn	Div	#T	W	L	Coach
POINT LOMA NAZARENE							
1985	M	NCCAA	I	8	28	8	Foster, Ben
1986	M	NCCAA	I	8	27	7	Foster, Ben
1987	M	NCCAA	I	8	25	10	Foster, Ben
POTSDAM STATE							
1981	M	NCAA	III	32	30	2	Welsh, John Gerald "Jerry"
1986	M	NCAA	III	32	32	0	Welsh, John Gerald "Jerry"
PRAIRIE VIEW A&M							
1962	M	NAIA		32	20	3	Moore, Dr. Leroy G., Jr.
PUGET SOUND							
1976	M	NCAA	II	32	27	7	Zech, Don
PUGET SOUND CHRISTIAN							
1995	M	NBCAA	II	8	17	11	McNichols, Troy
ROANOKE							
1972	M	NCAA	II	36	28	4	Moir, Charles
ROCHESTER (MI)							
1989	M	NSCAA		15	25	3	Pleasant, Garth A.
ROCHESTER (NY)							
1990	M	NCAA	III	40	27	5	Neer, Mike
ROCKHURST							
1964	M	NAIA		32	27	6	Brehmer, Joseph "Buddy"
ROWAN							
1996	M	NCAA	III	64	28	4	Giannini, John
RUST							
1977	M	NSCAA		16	34	5	Hayes, Naylond
1984	W	NCAA	III	32	26	5	Stovall, Dr. Alfred J. "AJ"
RUTGERS							
1982	W	AIAW	I	16	25	7	Grentz, Theresa Shank
SACRED HEART (CT)							
1986	M	NCAA	II	32	30	4	Bike, Dave
SAINT MARY'S (TX)							
1989	M	NAIA		32	28	5	Meyer, Herbert "Buddy"
SAINT SCHOLASTICA							
1988	W	NSCAA		8	25	6	Stukel, Jim
SAINT THOMAS (MN)							
1991	W	NCAA	III	32	29	2	Riverso, Ted
SALEM STATE							
1986	W	NCAA	III	32	29	1	Shea, Timothy P.

Year	M/W	Assn	Div	#T	W	L	Coach
SAN DIEGO STATE							
1941	M	NAIA		32	24	7	Gross, Morris H.
SAN FRANCISCO							
1955	M	NCAA		24	28	1	Woolpert, Philip D.
1956	M	NCAA		25	29	0	Woolpert, Philip D.
SAN JOSE CHRISTIAN							
1991	M	NBCAA	I	8	27	7	Miller, Glen
1993	M	NBCAA	I	6	22	14	Miller, Glen
1994	M	NBCAA	I	7	26	11	Miller, Glen
1995	M	NBCAA	I	8	28	11	Miller, Glen
SCRANTON							
1976	M	NCAA	III	28	27	5	Bessoir, Robert M.
1983	M	NCAA	III	32	29	3	Bessoir, Robert M.
1985	W	NCAA	III	32	31	1	Strong, Michael J.
SILVER LAKE							
1991	W	NSCAA		8	25	6	Wenner, Craig
SOUTH CAROLINA STATE							
1979	W	AIAW	S	16	33	2	Simon, Willie J.
SOUTH CAROLINA: SPARTANBURG							
1982	M	NAIA		32	27	5	Waters, Jerry O.
SOUTH DAKOTA							
1958	M	NCAA	II	32	22	5	Clodfelter, Duane
SOUTH DAKOTA STATE							
1963	M	NCAA	II	32	22	5	Iverson, James
SOUTHEAST MISSOURI STATE							
1943	M	NAIA		32	19	6	Harris, Charles P.
SOUTHEASTERN LOUISIANA							
1977	W	AIAW	S	16	30	2	Puckett, Linda
SOUTHERN CALIFORNIA							
1983	W	NCAA	I	36	31	2	Sharp, Linda
1984	W	NCAA	I	32	29	4	Sharp, Linda
SOUTHERN ILLINOIS							
1946	M	NAIA		32	20	6	Martin, Glenn "Abe"
SOUTHERN INDIANA							
1995	M	NCAA	II	48	29	4	Pearl, Bruce
SOUTHERN NAZARENE							
1974	M	NCCAA		4	31	6	Poteet, Jim
1977	M	NCCAA	I	6	28	10	Poteet, Jim
1981	M	NAIA		32	36	6	Gresham, Dr. Loren
1989	W	NAIA		16	36	2	Hoffman, Bob

Year	M/W	Assn	Div	#T	W	L	Coach
1994	W	NAIA	I	32	34	0	Finkbeiner, Jerry
1995	W	NAIA	I	32	30	2	Finkbeiner, Jerry
1996	W	NAIA	I	32	34	2	Finkbeiner, Jerry
1997	W	NAIA	I	32	32	4	Finkbeiner, Jerry

SOUTHERN UNION STATE CC

Year	M/W	Assn	Div	#T	W	L	Coach
1978	M	NSCAA		16	28	5	Gourdouze, Frank

SOUTHWEST MISSOURI STATE

Year	M/W	Assn	Div	#T	W	L	Coach
1952	M	NAIA		32	27	5	Vanatta, Robert
1953	M	NAIA		32	24	4	Vanatta, Robert

SOUTHWEST TEXAS STATE

Year	M/W	Assn	Div	#T	W	L	Coach
1960	M	NAIA		32	28	3	Jowers, Milton W.

SOUTHWESTERN (AZ)

Year	M/W	Assn	Div	#T	W	L	Coach
1997	M	NCCAA	IIA	8	21	8	Morley, Stephen H.

SOUTHWESTERN (KS)

Year	M/W	Assn	Div	#T	W	L	Coach
1939	M	NAIA		32	21	2	Gardner, George

SOUTHWESTERN ASSEMBLIES

Year	M/W	Assn	Div	#T	W	L	Coach
1998	M	NBCAA		8	20	8	Garippa, Rev. Steven P.

SOUTHWESTERN CHRISTIAN MINISTRIES

Year	M/W	Assn	Div	#T	W	L	Coach
1997	M	NBCAA	II	8	26	15	Arthur, Mark
1998	M	NCCAA	IIA	8	21	17	Arthur, Mark

SOUTHWESTERN OKLAHOMA STATE

Year	M/W	Assn	Div	#T	W	L	Coach
1982	W	NAIA		8	34	0	Loftin, John D.
1983	W	NAIA		8	30	4	Loftin, John D.
1985	W	NAIA		16	34	0	Loftin, John D.
1987	W	NAIA		16	30	2	Loftin, John D.
1990	W	NAIA		16	30	4	Loftin, John D.

SPRING ARBOR

Year	M/W	Assn	Div	#T	W	L	Coach
1983	W	NCCAA	I	8	29	4	Dunckel, Darrell
1987	W	NCCAA	I	8	25	9	Dunckel, Darrell

STANFORD

Year	M/W	Assn	Div	#T	W	L	Coach
1942	M	NCAA		8	27	4	Dean, Everett S.
1990	W	NCAA	I	48	32	1	VanDerveer, Tara
1992	W	NCAA	I	48	30	3	VanDerveer, Tara

SULLIVAN (KY)

Year	M/W	Assn	Div	#T	W	L	Coach
1967	M	NSCAA		8	23	6	Tibbs, Harry
1968	M	NSCAA		8	26	6	Tibbs, Harry
1969	M	NSCAA		8	26	4	Sergeant, W. C.
1980	M	NSCAA		16	28	8	Skinner, David L.

TARKIO

Year	M/W	Assn	Div	#T	W	L	Coach
1940	M	NAIA		32	20	4	Kyle, Newton P.

TAYLOR: FORT WAYNE

Year	M/W	Assn	Div	#T	W	L	Coach
1976	M	NCCAA	II	4	18	9	Morley, Stephen H.

Year	M/W	Assn	Div	#T	W	L	Coach
TENNESSEE							
1987	W	NCAA	I	40	28	6	Summitt, Patricia Head
1989	W	NCAA	I	48	35	2	Summitt, Patricia Head
1991	W	NCAA	I	48	30	5	Summitt, Patricia Head
1996	W	NCAA	I	64	32	4	Summitt, Patricia Head
1997	W	NCAA	I	64	29	10	Summitt, Patricia Head
1998	W	NCAA	I	64	39	0	Summitt, Patricia Head
TENNESSEE STATE							
1952	M	NASC		8	19	4	Cash, Clarence B.
1953	M	NASC		8	20	5	Cash, Clarence B.
1954	M	NASC		8	17	6	Cash, Clarence B.
1957	M	NAIA		32	31	4	McLendon, John B., Jr.
1958	M	NAIA		32	31	3	McLendon, John B., Jr.
1959	M	NAIA		32	32	1	McLendon, John B., Jr.
TENNESSEE TEMPLE							
1979	M	NCCAA	I	6	30	7	Bishop, Ronald
1981	M	NCCAA	I	6	24	17	Bishop, Ronald
1982	M	NCCAA	I	7	31	8	Bishop, Ronald
1983	M	NCCAA	I	8	28	7	Bishop, Ronald
1988	M	NCCAA	I	8	26	13	Bishop, Ronald
1989	M	NCCAA	I	8	25	11	Bishop, Ronald
TENNESSEE: CHATTANOOGA							
1977	M	NCAA	II	32	27	5	Shumate, Ron
TEXAS							
1986	W	NCAA	I	40	34	0	Conradt, Jody
TEXAS A&M: COMMERCE							
1955	M	NAIA		32	29	5	Rogers, Bobby
TEXAS COLLEGE							
1992	M	NSCAA		12	25	5	Patrick, Kirk
1993	M	NSCAA		9			Patrick, Kirk
TEXAS SOUTHERN							
1955	M	NASC		8	28	3	Adams, Edward H.
1977	M	NAIA		32	31	5	Moreland, Robert E.
TEXAS TECH							
1993	W	NCAA	I	48	31	3	Sharp, Marsha
TEXAS: EL PASO							
1966	M	NCAA	I	22	28	1	Haskins, Donald L.
TEXAS: PAN AMERICAN							
1963	M	NAIA		32	22	6	Williams, Samuel
TIFFIN							
1971	M	NSCAA		8	13	8	Janson, George
1973	M	NSCAA		8	24	9	Janson, George

Year	M/W	Assn	Div	#T	W	L	Coach
TOCCOA FALLS							
1986	W	NCCAA	II	8	13	12	Shiffer, Paul
1992	W	NCCAA	II	8	23	6	Shiffer, Paul
TRINITY INTERNATIONAL (FL)							
1991	M	NCCAA	IIA	4	15	14	Rutherford, Robert
TRINITY INTERNATIONAL (IL)							
1992	W	NSCAA		8	15	10	Seils, David S.
1994	W	NSCAA		8	24	8	Seils, David S.
UNION (TN)							
1998	W	NAIA	I	32	35	3	Blackstock, Dr. David
UTAH							
1944	M	NCAA		8	21	4	Peterson, Vadal
VILLANOVA							
1985	M	NCAA	I	64	25	10	Massimino, Roland V. "Rollie"
VIRGINIA UNION							
1980	M	NCAA	II	32	26	4	Robbins, Charles David "Dave"
1983	W	NCAA	II	24	27	2	Hearn, Louis
1992	M	NCAA	II	32	30	3	Robbins, Charles David "Dave"
WABASH							
1982	M	NCAA	III	32	24	4	Petty, Malcolm "Mac"
WALSH							
1998	W	NAIA	II	32	29	5	Smesco, Carl
WASHBURN							
1987	M	NAIA		32	35	4	Chipman, Bob
WASHINGTON (MO)							
1998	W	NCAA	III	48	28	2	Fahey, Nancy
WEBBER							
1984	M	NSCAA		16	32	4	Creola, Nick J.
WESLEY (MS)							
1997	M	LCC		5	13	16	Devore, William, Jr.
WEST CHESTER							
1969	W	AIAW		16	12	0	Eckman, Carol
WEST GEORGIA							
1974	M	NAIA		32	29	4	Kaiser, Roger A.
WESTERN BAPTIST							
1977	M	NCCAA	II	4	17	13	Hills, Tim
1995	W	NCCAA	I	8	17	16	Williams, Terry
1996	W	NCCAA	I	8	24	11	Williams, Terry

Year	M/W	Assn	Div	#T	W	L	Coach
WESTERN OREGON							
1995	W	NAIA	II	32	23	9	Rogers, "Rusty"
1996	W	NAIA	II	32	31	4	Rogers, "Rusty"
WHEATON (IL)							
1957	M	NCAA	II	32	28	1	Pfund, Leroy H. "Lee"
WILLAMETTE							
1993	M	NAIA	II	20	29	4	James, Gordon "Gordie"
WILLIAM PENN							
1981	W	AIAW	II	16	43	3	Spencer, Robert L.
WILLIAMS BAPTIST							
1993	W	NCCAA	I	8	24	2	Halford, Carol
WINSTON-SALEM STATE							
1967	M	NCAA	II	36	30	2	Gaines, Clarence E. "Big House"
WISCONSIN							
1941	M	NCAA		8	20	3	Foster, Harold E. "Bud"
WISCONSIN: LA CROSSE							
1981	W	AIAW	III	16	27	5	Hansen, Mary
WISCONSIN: OSHKOSH							
1996	W	NCAA	III	64	31	0	Bennett, Kathi
WISCONSIN: PLATTEVILLE							
1991	M	NCAA	III	40	28	3	Ryan, William "Bo"
1995	M	NCAA	III	64	31	0	Ryan, William "Bo"
1998	M	NCAA	III	48	30	0	Ryan, William "Bo"
WISCONSIN: STEVENS POINT							
1987	W	NCAA	III	32	27	2	Wunder, Linda
WISCONSIN: WHITEWATER							
1984	M	NCAA	III	32	27	4	Vander Meulen, David
1989	M	NCAA	III	40	29	2	Vander Meulen, David
WITTENBERG							
1961	M	NCAA	II	32	25	4	Mears, Ramon "Ray"
1977	M	NCAA	III	30	23	5	Hunter, Larry
WORCESTER STATE							
1980	W	AIAW	III	24	24	2	Devlin, Donna
WRIGHT STATE (OH)							
1983	M	NCAA	II	32	28	4	Underhill, Ralph
WYOMING							
1943	M	NCAA		8	31	2	Shelton, Everett F.

Helms Foundation National Champion Designation

One of sports' unique organizations, the Helms Foundation was the result of a sports buff's dream and a sports-minded bakery owner's sales promotion contest.

Paul H. Helms, Sr., a Syracuse University graduate, made a fortune in the bakery business in New York State. In 1926, plagued by ill-health, he retired to southern California. The crash of 1929 wiped him out, so in 1931, he reentered the bakery business. It became an immediate success, and he won a contract to supply bread to all competing teams at the 1932 Olympics in Los Angeles. To promote the coup, he conducted a "25-words or less" contest on "why his bread was the best"—offering a prize of fifty dollars or two tickets to the games.

The contest was won by a rather well-known area sports buff, W. R. "Bill" Schroeder, a bank accountant who had built a respectable collection of sports mementos and who had a dream of turning it into a large, public sports museum. For several years he had been unsuccessful in selling his idea to local commercial organizations. In 1936, he recalled the bread contest and sent Helms a prospectus. Viola! The Helms Athletic Foundation was established on October 15, 1936, with Schroeder as the managing director and a stated purpose of supporting worthy athletic activities. One of the first accomplishments was to bring all of the area newspapers together and select just one area scholastic all-star team. To do so, the Helms Board was created. From that simple beginning, the Board broadened its interests and area to recognize excellence in more than 20 sports nationally with all-star teams and its own Hall of Fame.

In 1942, the board began to select its annual National Collegiate Basketball Champion which it continued to do through the 1982-83 season. It retroactively awarded its championships for years prior to 1942 based upon extensive research.

Usually, the Helms designee was the NCAA champion, but there were several interesting exceptions. In 1939, Long Island University, the NIT winner, was chosen over the first NCAA winner, Oregon. In 1940, Southern California, 3rd in the NCAA, was selected over the winner, Indiana, and the NIT champion, Colorado. In 1944, Army, which then had a policy against post-season play, was selected over NCAA winner, Utah, and NIT winner, Saint John's (NY). In 1954, Kentucky's tournament-ineligible Wildcats were, nevertheless, awarded the number one spot over La Salle, NCAA winner, and Holy Cross, NIT winner

NOTES ON DATA COLLECTION: Helms designees are listed in two formats: annually and alphabetically by school. In both, information is provided on the team's finish in post-season tournaments: **NAT:** National Association Tournament; i.e., NCAA; **NIT:** National Invitation Tournament; **ARC:** American Red Cross Benefit; **OLY:** Olympic Trials Tournament.

By Year

Year	School	W	L	Coach	—FINISH IN—			
					NAT	NIT	ARC	OLY
1901	Yale	10	6	Unknown	—	—	—	—
1902	Minnesota	15	0	Cooke, Dr. Louis J.	—	—	—	—
1903	Yale	15	1	Murphy, W. H.	—	—	—	—
1904	Columbia (NY)	17	1	Elias, Henry H.	—	—	—	—
1905	Columbia (NY)	19	1	Elias, Henry H.	—	—	—	—
1906	Dartmouth	16	2	Unknown	—	—	—	—
1907	Chicago	22	2	Raycroft, Dr. Joseph E.	—	—	—	—
1908	Chicago	21	2	Raycroft, Dr. Joseph E.	—	—	—	—

Year	School	W	L	Coach	NAT	NIT	ARC	OLY
1909	Chicago	12	0	Raycroft, Dr. Joseph E.	—	—	—	—
1910	Columbia (NY)	11	1	Fisher, Harry A.	—	—	—	—
1911	Saint John's (NY)	14	0	Allen, Claude B.	—	—	—	—
1912	Wisconsin	15	0	Meanwell, Dr. Walter E. "Doc"	—	—	—	—
1913	Navy	9	0	Wenzell, Louis P.	—	—	—	—
1914	Wisconsin	15	0	Meanwell, Dr. Walter E. "Doc"	—	—	—	—
1915	Illinois	16	0	Jones, Ralph R.	—	—	—	—
1916	Wisconsin	20	1	Meanwell, Dr. Walter E. "Doc"	—	—	—	—
1917	Washington State	25	1	Bohler, J. Fred "Doc"	—	—	—	—
1918	Syracuse	16	1	Dollar, Edmund A.	—	—	—	—
1919	Minnesota	13	0	Cooke, Dr. Louis J.	—	—	—	—
1920	Pennsylvania	22	1	Jourdet, Lon W.	—	—	—	—
1921	Pennsylvania	21	2	McNichol, Edward J.	—	—	—	—
1922	Kansas	16	2	Allen, Dr. Forrest C. "Phog"	—	—	—	—
1923	Kansas	17	1	Allen, Dr. Forrest C. "Phog"	—	—	—	—
1924	North Carolina	26	0	Shepard, Norman W. "Bo"	—	—	—	—
1925	Princeton	21	2	Wittmer, Albert, Jr.	—	—	—	—
1926	Syracuse	19	1	Andreas, Lewis P.	—	—	—	—
1927	Notre Dame (IN)	19	1	Keogan, George E.	—	—	—	—
1928	Pittsburgh	21	0	Carlson, Dr. H. Clifford "Doc"	—	—	—	—
1929	Montana State	36	2	Dyche, Schubert R.	—	—	—	—
1930	Pittsburgh	23	2	Carlson, Dr. H. Clifford "Doc"	—	—	—	—
1931	Northwestern (IL)	16	1	Lonborg, Arthur C. "Dutch"	—	—	—	—
1932	Purdue	17	1	Lambert, Ward L. "Piggy"	—	—	—	—
1933	Kentucky	20	3	Rupp, Adolph F.	—	—	—	—
1934	Wyoming	26	3	Witte, Willard A. "Dutch"	—	—	—	2
1935	New York	18	1	Cann, Howard G.	—	—	—	—
1936	Notre Dame (IN)	22	2	Keogan, George E.	—	—	—	—
1937	Stanford	25	2	Bunn, John W.	—	—	—	—
1938	Temple	23	2	Usilton, James	—	1	—	—
1939	Long Island	24	0	Bee, Clair F.	—	1	—	—
1940	Southern California	20	3	Barry, Justin M. "Sam"	3	—	—	—
1941	Wisconsin	20	3	Foster, Harold E. "Bud"	1	—	—	—
1942	Stanford	27	4	Dean, Everett S.	1	—	—	—
1943	Wyoming	31	2	Shelton, Everett F.	1	—	1	3
1944	Army	15	0	Kelleher, Edward A.	—	—	—	—
1945	Oklahoma State	27	4	Iba, Henry P. "Hank"	1	—	1	—
1946	Oklahoma State	31	2	Iba, Henry P. "Hank"	1	—	—	—
1947	Holy Cross (MA)	27	3	Julian, Alvin F. "Doggie"	1	—	—	—
1948	Kentucky	36	3	Rupp, Adolph F.	1	—	—	2
1949	Kentucky	32	2	Rupp, Adolph F.	1	8	—	—
1950	City College	24	5	Holman, Nathan "Nat"	1	1	—	—
1951	Kentucky	32	2	Rupp, Adolph F.	1	—	—	—
1952	Kansas	28	3	Allen, Dr. Forrest C. "Phog"	1	—	—	2
1953	Indiana	23	3	McCracken, E. Branch	1	—	—	—
1954	Kentucky	25	0	Rupp, Adolph F.	—	—	—	—
1955	San Francisco	28	1	Woolpert, Philip D.	1	—	—	—
1956	San Francisco	29	0	Woolpert, Philip D.	1	—	—	—

Year	School	W	L	Coach	NAT	NIT	ARC	OLY
1957	North Carolina	32	0	McGuire, Frank J.	1	—	—	—
1958	Kentucky	23	6	Rupp, Adolph F.	1	—	—	—
1959	California	25	4	Newell, Peter F.	1	—	—	—
1960	Ohio State	25	3	Taylor, Fred R.	1	—	—	5
1961	Cincinnati	27	3	Jucker, Edwin L.	1	—	—	—
1962	Cincinnati	29	2	Jucker, Edwin L.	1	—	—	—
1963	Loyola (IL)	29	2	Ireland, George M.	1	—	—	—
1964	California: Los Angeles	30	0	Wooden, John R.	1	—	—	—
1965	California: Los Angeles	28	2	Wooden, John R.	1	—	—	—
1966	Texas: El Paso	28	1	Haskins, Donald L.	1	—	—	—
1967	California: Los Angeles	30	0	Wooden, John R.	1	—	—	—
1968	California: Los Angeles	29	1	Wooden, John R.	1	—	—	—
1969	California: Los Angeles	29	1	Wooden, John R.	1	—	—	—
1970	California: Los Angeles	28	2	Wooden, John R.	1	—	—	—
1971	California: Los Angeles	29	1	Wooden, John R.	1	—	—	—
1972	California: Los Angeles	30	0	Wooden, John R.	1	—	—	—
1973	California: Los Angeles	30	0	Wooden, John R.	1	—	—	—
1974	North Carolina State	30	1	Sloan, Norman L., Jr.	1	—	—	—
1975	California: Los Angeles	28	3	Wooden, John R.	1	—	—	—
1976	Indiana	32	0	Knight, Robert M.	1	—	—	—
1977	Marquette	25	7	McGuire, Alfred J.	1	—	—	—
1978	Kentucky	30	2	Hall, Joe B.	1	—	—	—
1979	Michigan State	26	6	Heathcote, George "Jud"	1	—	—	—
1980	Louisville	33	3	Crum, Denzil E. "Denny"	1	—	—	—
1981	Indiana	26	9	Knight, Robert M.	1	—	—	—
1982	North Carolina	32	2	Smith, Dean E.	1	—	—	—
1983	North Carolina State	26	10	Valvano, James T.	1	—	—	—

By School

School	Year	W	L	Coach	NAT	NIT	ARC	OLY
Army	1944	15	0	Kelleher, Edward A.	—	—	—	—
California	1959	25	4	Newell, Peter F.	1	—	—	—
California: Los Angeles	1964	30	0	Wooden, John R.	1	—	—	—
	1965	28	2	Wooden, John R.	1	—	—	—
	1967	30	0	Wooden, John R.	1	—	—	—
	1968	29	1	Wooden, John R.	1	—	—	—
	1969	29	1	Wooden, John R.	1	—	—	—
	1970	28	2	Wooden, John R.	1	—	—	—
	1971	29	1	Wooden, John R.	1	—	—	—
	1972	30	0	Wooden, John R.	1	—	—	—
	1973	30	0	Wooden, John R.	1	—	—	—
	1975	28	3	Wooden, John R.	1	—	—	—
Chicago	1907	22	2	Raycroft, Dr. Joseph E.	—	—	—	—
	1908	21	2	Raycroft, Dr. Joseph E.	—	—	—	—
	1909	12	0	Raycroft, Dr. Joseph E.	—	—	—	—

School	Year	W	L	Coach	NAT	NIT	ARC	OLY
Cincinnati	1961	27	3	Jucker, Edwin L.	1	—	—	—
	1962	29	2	Jucker, Edwin L.	1	—	—	—
City College	1950	24	5	Holman, Nathan "Nat"	1	1	—	—
Columbia (NY)	1904	17	1	Elias, Henry H.	—	—	—	—
	1905	19	1	Elias, Henry H.	—	—	—	—
	1910	11	1	Fisher, Harry A.	—	—	—	—
Dartmouth	1906	16	2	Unknown	—	—	—	—
Holy Cross (MA)	1947	27	3	Julian, Alvin F. "Doggie"	1	—	—	—
Illinois	1915	16	0	Jones, Ralph R.	—	—	—	—
Indiana	1953	23	3	McCracken, E. Branch	1	—	—	—
	1976	32	0	Knight, Robert M.	1	—	—	—
	1981	26	9	Knight, Robert M.	1	—	—	—
Kansas	1922	16	2	Allen, Dr. Forrest C. "Phog"	—	—	—	—
	1923	17	1	Allen, Dr. Forrest C. "Phog"	—	—	—	—
	1952	28	3	Allen, Dr. Forrest C. "Phog"	1	—	—	2
Kentucky	1933	20	3	Rupp, Adolph F.	—	—	—	—
	1948	36	3	Rupp, Adolph F.	1	—	—	2
	1949	32	2	Rupp, Adolph F.	1	8	—	—
	1951	32	2	Rupp, Adolph F.	1	—	—	—
	1954	25	0	Rupp, Adolph F.	—	—	—	—
	1958	23	6	Rupp, Adolph F.	1	—	—	—
	1978	30	2	Hall, Joe B.	1	—	—	—
Long Island	1939	24	0	Bee, Clair F.	—	1	—	—
Louisville	1980	33	3	Crum, Denzil E. "Denny"	1	—	—	—
Loyola (IL)	1963	29	2	Ireland, George M.	1	—	—	—
Marquette	1977	25	7	McGuire, Alfred J.	1	—	—	—
Michigan State	1979	26	6	Heathcote, George "Jud"	1	—	—	—
Minnesota	1902	15	0	Cooke, Dr. Louis J.	—	—	—	—
	1919	13	0	Cooke, Dr. Louis J.	—	—	—	—
Montana State	1929	36	2	Dyche, Schubert R.	—	—	—	—
Navy	1913	9	0	Wenzell, Louis P.	—	—	—	—
New York	1935	18	1	Cann, Howard G.	—	—	—	—
North Carolina	1924	26	0	Shepard, Norman W. "Bo"	—	—	—	—
	1957	32	0	McGuire, Frank J.	1	—	—	—
	1982	32	2	Smith, Dean E.	1	—	—	—
North Carolina State	1974	30	1	Sloan, Norman L., Jr.	1	—	—	—
	1983	26	10	Valvano, James T.	1	—	—	—
Northwestern (IL)	1931	16	1	Lonborg, Arthur C. "Dutch"	—	—	—	—

School	Year	W	L	Coach	FINISH IN NAT	NIT	ARC	OLY
Notre Dame (IN)	1927	19	1	Keogan, George E.	—	—	—	—
	1936	22	2	Keogan, George E.	—	—	—	—
Ohio State	1960	25	3	Taylor, Fred R.	1	—	—	5
Oklahoma State	1945	27	4	Iba, Henry P. "Hank"	1	—	1	—
	1946	31	2	Iba, Henry P. "Hank"	1	—	—	—
Pennsylvania	1920	22	1	Jourdet, Lon W.	—	—	—	—
	1921	21	2	McNichol, Edward J.	—	—	—	—
Pittsburgh	1928	21	0	Carlson, Dr. H. Clifford "Doc"	—	—	—	—
	1930	23	2	Carlson, Dr. H. Clifford "Doc"	—	—	—	—
Princeton	1925	21	2	Wittmer, Albert, Jr.	—	—	—	—
Purdue	1932	17	1	Lambert, Ward L. "Piggy"	—	—	—	—
Saint John's (NY)	1911	14	0	Allen, Claude B.	—	—	—	—
San Francisco	1955	28	1	Woolpert, Philip D.	1	—	—	—
	1956	29	0	Woolpert, Philip D.	1	—	—	—
Southern California	1940	20	3	Barry, Justin M. "Sam"	3	—	—	—
Stanford	1937	25	2	Bunn, John W.	—	—	—	—
	1942	27	4	Dean, Everett S.	1	—	—	—
Syracuse	1918	16	1	Dollard, Edmund A.	—	—	—	—
	1926	19	1	Andreas, Lewis P.	—	—	—	—
Temple	1938	23	2	Usilton, James	—	1	—	—
Texas: El Paso	1966	28	1	Haskins, Donald L.	1	—	—	—
Washington State	1917	25	1	Bohler, J. Fred "Doc"	—	—	—	—
Wisconsin	1912	15	0	Meanwell, Dr. Walter E. "Doc"	—	—	—	—
	1914	15	0	Meanwell, Dr. Walter E. "Doc"	—	—	—	—
	1916	20	1	Meanwell, Dr. Walter E. "Doc"	—	—	—	—
	1941	20	3	Foster, Harold E. "Bud"	1	—	—	—
Wyoming	1934	26	3	Witte, Willard A. "Dutch"	—	—	—	2
	1943	31	2	Shelton, Everett F.	1	—	1	3
Yale	1901	10	6	Unknown	—	—	—	—
	1903	15	1	Murphy, W. H.	—	—	—	—

Section 3

NONASSOCIATION NATIONAL CHAMPIONSHIP TOURNAMENTS

Beginning in 1904 with the Olympic Demonstration Tournament and then since 1938 with the still-operating National Invitation Tournament, there have been 105 nonassociation post-season national championship tournaments in which 1,454 teams have competed.

Most of them existed for only several years, with the original National Women's Invitational holding the second best longevity record with 28 years, and were conducted by athletic/basketball related organizations or by charities with the cooperation of the colleges.

While none actually claimed that its winner was a national champion, virtually all used the word national in their name or at least alluded to the concept. Many of these tournaments were an opportunity for post-season play by schools that were not selected to participate in an association tournament— although in earlier years schools did participate in more than one post-season event.

In this section are all of the known post-season nonassociation national championship tournaments. A brief history of each tournament is provided.

For the NIT tournaments, there is also a listing of every school's participation history. The information is presented for each school in order of finish in the tournaments. Thus, one can see how many times the men's and women's teams from a given school participated in the NITs and how they finished.

American Red Cross Benefit

During World War II, benefits for various war relief organizations were a frequent activity. College basketball and Madison Square Garden became involved with three years of a post-season event (not a tournament, per se) that was said to produce the only true collegiate national champions ever: the NCAA winner against the NIT winner. (However, the NAIA might argue the legitimacy of that claim.)

In 1943 and 1945, the runners-up from the two tournaments played the first game of a doubleheader with the champions playing the second (feature) game. The 1944 preliminary game featured two service teams: Mitchell Field (Long Island, New York) beat Aberdeen, Maryland, Proving Ground.

Interestingly, the NCAA tournament winner won all three years, and its second-place finisher won the two runners-up games. Utah, in 1944, ironically, had finished 8th in the NIT before capturing the NCAA crown.

In 1946, another doubleheader benefit was played. There were no college teams, but there was a decidedly New York influence. In the preliminary game, the United States Naval Guard from Brooklyn beat Fort Tilton General Hospital, Fort Dix, New Jersey. In the feature game, the AAU's mighty Phillips 66ers (The Phillips Petroleum Company) of Bartlesville, Oklahoma, beat the New York Athletic Club, an aggregation comprised largely of former New York University players.

Tournament Results

F	School	NCAA	NIT	W	L	Coach
		—Finish in—				
1943						
1	Wyoming	1	—	31	2	Shelton, Everett F.
2	Saint John's (NY)	—	1	21	3	Lapchick, Joseph B.
3	Georgetown (DC)	2	—	22	5	Ripley, Elmer H.
4	Toledo	—	2	22	4	Friddle, Burl

F School	–Finish in– NCAA	NIT	W	L	Coach
1944					
1 Utah	1	8	21	4	Peterson, Vadal
2 Saint John's (NY)	—	1	18	5	Lapchick, Joseph B.
1945					
1 Oklahoma State	1	—	27	4	Iba, Henry P. 'Hank'
2 De Paul	—	1	21	3	Meyer, Raymond J.
3 New York	2	—	14	7	Cann, Howard G.
4 Bowling Green State	—	2	24	4	Anderson, W. Harold 'Andy'

Collegiate Commissioners Association Tournament

The Collegiate Commissioners Association Tournament was, in reality, the "Also-Ran Tournament." In 1974, only 16 teams qualified for the NCAA division I tournament—champions of the ten major conferences plus six independent powers. In the following year, the NCAA tournament expanded to 32 teams, taking a number of conference runners-up as at-large entries. In both years, the NIT field was 16 teams, but, for obvious gate reasons, six or more teams from the greater New York area were invited. Thus, there was no opportunity for post-season play for a lot of pretty good teams.

The CCA tournament was created as a short-lived answer for schools that were shut-out of the NCAA and NIT tournaments. In 1974, the runners-up from eight of the major conferences met at the Saint Louis, Missouri, Arena in an unseeded single-elimination event. The following year, three conference runners-up and five conference third-place finishers met at Freedom Hall, Louisville, Kentucky, in a similar format. For most of the third-place teams, the CCA invitation was the result of the runner-up having received an at-large bid to the expanded NCAA tournament.

In both years, seven of the conferences were the same. The eighth was the Southwest Conference in 1974, replaced by the Southern Conference in 1975.

In the tournament listing that follows, the school's conference is shown with a notation of the schools finish (**CF**) in conference regular season play (T indicates a tie).

Conference names are the current name of the conference; the following abbreviations are used—**MVC:** Missouri Valley Conference; **MAC:** Mid-American Conference; **WAC:** Western Athletic Conference

Tournament Results

F School	Conference	CF	W	L	Coach
1974					
1 Indiana	Big 10	1T	23	5	Knight, Robert M.
2 Southern California	Pacific 10	2	24	5	Boyd, William R. 'Bob'
3 Bradley	MVC	2	20	8	Stowell, Joseph R.
Toledo	MAC	2	19	9	Nichols, Robert J.
8 Arizona State	WAC	2T	18	9	Wulk, Ned W.
Kansas State	Big 8	2	19	8	Hartman, Jack
Southern Methodist (TX)	Southwest	2T	15	12	Prewitt, Bob
Tennessee	Southeastern	2	17	9	Mears, Ramon 'Ray'

F	School	Conference	CF	W	L	Coach
1975						
1	Drake (IA)	MVC	3	19	10	Ortegel, Bob
2	Arizona	WAC	3	22	7	Snowden, Frederick
3	Bowling Green State	MAC	2T	18	10	Haley, Pat
	Purdue	Big 10	3	17	11	Schaus, Frederick A.
8	East Carolina	Southern	2	19	9	Patton, David J.
	Missouri	Big 8	3	18	9	Stewart, Norman E.
	Southern California	Pacific 10	3	18	8	Boyd, William R. 'Bob'
	Tennessee	Southeastern	2T	18	8	Mears, Ramon 'Ray'

National Campus Tournament

Following the point-shaving scandals of the late 1940s, which involved games played in Madison Square Garden, New York, a movement began to return college basketball to the campus.

The NCAA council, the organization's policy-making committee, issued an official recommendation that games should be played in campus facilities and that colleges must take steps to have greater control at off-campus sites, which, the council suggested, should be used only when campus sites are inadequate.

In 1951, Bradley University picked up the gauntlet. The university had suffered through the scandals with some of her players involved, had withdrawn from the Missouri Valley Conference, and had announced, in advance, a declination of any invitations that might ensue for the NCAA or NIT tournaments.

As part of its spring "Cavalcade of Champions", which also included competition among schools in such activities as debate and intramural basketball, the Bradley Braves hosted the National Campus Tournament (the tournament name apparently was more than coincidental) for eight schools that did not qualify for the NCAA or NIT tournaments. It was an unseeded, single-elimination affair that attracted capacity crowds of over 8,000 per night—perhaps because of the daily presence of the Braves who advanced to the finals. Although the entire event was acclaimed as a step in the right direction, the tournament had but a one-year life.

The final game between Syracuse and the host Braves has been called the greatest game in the history of Bradley's Robertson Memorial Field House. The Orangemen entered the tournament as decided underdogs and even had plane reservations for Wednesday (opening night) to return home. But, upset wins over Toledo and Utah propelled Syracuse into the title game against Bradley, winners over Western Kentucky and Wyoming. The Braves opened with an 18-0 run but saw the lead shrink to five points at the half and to four points going into the final quarter. With six minutes left, Bradley opened a seven-point edge, but at the 1:42 mark Syracuse led 76-68. Bradley roared back, but a last second shot missed, and Syracuse hung on for a 76-75 win.

Tournament Results

F	School	Assn	W	L	Coach
1951					
1	Syracuse	NCAA	19	9	Guley, Marcel 'Marc'
2	Bradley	NCAA	32	6	Anderson, Forrest A. 'Forddy'
3	Utah	NCAA	23	13	Peterson, Vadal
4	Wyoming	NCAA	26	11	Shelton, Everett F.
8	Duquesne	NCAA	16	11	Moore, Donald W. 'Dudey'
	Toledo	NCAA	23	8	Bush, Gerald 'Jerry'
	Villanova	NCAA	25	7	Severance, Alexander G.
	Western Kentucky	NCAA	19	10	Diddle, Edgar A., Sr.

National Catholic College Tournament

The National Catholic College Tournament was a one-year, four-team event that was held at Freedom Hall in Louisville, Kentucky, to benefit the Louisville Cerebral Palsy School. Unfortunately, participating schools, the Cerebral Palsy School, and the Louisville newspapers have little information about the event.

All of the participating schools were NCAA members—three from division I and one, Regis (CO), from division II.

Surprisingly, Xavier (OH), the only participating team with a losing record, 12-16 for the year, was the winner while Regis, with the best W-L record (15-9 for the year) finished last.

Tournament Results

F	School	Assn	Div	W	L	Coach
1963						
1	Xavier (OH)	NCAA	I	12	16	McCafferty, James J.
2	Saint Bonaventure	NCAA	I	13	12	Weise, Lawrence J.
3	Creighton	NCAA	I	14	13	McManus, John J. "Red"
4	Regis (CO)	NCAA	II	15	9	Hall, Joe B.

National Catholic Invitational Tournament

Begun in 1949, in Denver, as an attempt to replace the departed AAU tournament, the NCIT had a four-year life at various locations around the country—all hosted by one of the participating schools.

However, competing against the well-established NCAA, NIT, and NAIA tournaments, it was generally able to attract only smaller Catholic schools whose lack of gate appeal probably led to the short life-span of the tournament.

In 1949, the field was 16 teams, dropping off to eight in 1950, but recovering to 12 in each of the last two years.

Three schools participated in all four tournaments: Saint Francis (NY), Saint Francis (PA), and Iona. There were no multiple winners.

Tournament Results

F	School	Assn	Bye	W	L	Coach
1949						
1	Regis (CO)	NAIA		36	3	Varnell, Harry Lee
2	Saint Francis (NY)	NAIA		21	12	Lynch, Daniel J.
3	Loyola (MD)	NAIA		25	8	Reitz, Emil G., Jr. "Lefty"
4	Benedictine (KS)	NAIA		9	15	Walsh, Robert
8	Dayton			16	14	Blackburn, L. Thomas
	Gonzaga	NAIA		17	12	McGrath, Claude F.
	Saint Francis (PA)	NAIA		16	11	Hughes, Dr. William T. "Skip"
	Saint Thomas (MN)	NAIA		22	7	Sokol, Paul

F	School	Assn	Bye	W	L	Coach
16	Iona			17	8	McDermott, P. James
	Loras	NAIA		14	12	Dowd, Vincent J.
	Saint Ambrose	NCAA		12	9	O'Connor, James W.
	Saint Bonaventure			18	8	Melvin, Edward M. (Milkovich)
	Saint Edward's			19	4	Norris, Edward M.
	Saint Mary's (MN)			12	9	Lacher, Leo
	Saint Norbert			13	7	Dermody, Orv
	Siena (NY)	NCAA		22	7	Cunha, Daniel

1950

F	School	Assn	Bye	W	L	Coach
1	Siena (NY)	NCAA		27	5	Cunha, Daniel
2	Saint Francis (NY)	NAIA		8	19	Lynch, Daniel J.
3	Iona			22	4	McDermott, P. James
4	Loras	NAIA		22	9	Dowd, Vincent J.
8	Creighton	NCAA		13	14	Belford, Julius V. 'Duce'
	Providence	NCAA		14	9	Cuddy, James V. 'Viv'
	Saint Francis (PA)			17	9	Hughes, Dr. William T. 'Skip'
	Saint Michael's (VT)			18	6	Brannon, Barry

1951

F	School	Assn	Bye	W	L	Coach
1	Saint Francis (NY)	NAIA		19	11	Lynch, Daniel J.
2	Seattle	NCAA	To R8	32	5	Brightman, Horace Albert 'Al'
3	Le Moyne			18	7	Niland, Thomas J., Jr.
4	Mount Saint Mary's (MD)			19	13	Caruso, Peter J.
8	Iona			14	5	McDermott, P. James
	Loras	NAIA	To R8	23	7	Dowd, Vincent J.
	Saint Francis (PA)	NCAA	To R8	19	4	Hughes, Dr. William T. 'Skip'
	Siena (NY)	NCAA	To R8	19	8	Cunha, Daniel
10	Saint Mary's (MN)			15	13	Lacher, Leo
	Spring Hill	NAIA		19	8	Gardiner, William C.
12	Saint Michael's (VT)			19	4	Brannon, Barry
	Saint Norbert			19	10	Skat, Alvin C.

1952

F	School	Assn	Bye	W	L	Coach
1	Marquette	NCAA	To R8	12	14	Winter, Fred 'Tex'
2	Saint Francis (PA)	NCAA		23	7	Hughes, Dr. William T. 'Skip'
3	Siena (NY)	NCAA	To R8	25	7	Cunha, Daniel
4	Saint Francis (NY)	NAIA	To R8	20	8	Lynch, Daniel J.
8	Iona			17	10	McDermott, P. James
	Le Moyne			8	17	Niland, Thomas J., Jr.
	Saint Joseph's (PA)	NCAA	To R8	20	7	Ferguson, William J.
	Scranton	NCAA		15	14	Carlesimo, Peter A.
12	Gannon			12	13	Hook, Albert G.
	Loyola (MD)	NAIA		16	12	Reitz, Emil G., Jr. 'Lefty'
	Providence	NCAA		14	9	Cuddy, James V. 'Viv'
	Saint Mary's (MN)			13	10	Twomey, Patrick

National Invitation Tournament

The oldest major college basketball tournament and the second oldest any-college basketball tournament, the NIT began in 1938 as the brainchild of the Metropolitan (New York) Basketball Writers Association. Two years later, responsibility was transferred to the Metropolitan Intercollegiate Basketball Committee, now known as the Metropolitan Intercollegiate Basketball Association, comprised of representatives of five New York area colleges: Fordham, Manhattan, NYU, Saint John's, and Wagner. The site (at least for the finals) has always been New York's Madison Square Garden—originally at the 49th Street and Eighth Avenue location and, since 1968, at the 33rd Street and Seventh Avenue (Penn Station) site.

From 1938 through 1976, all games were at the Garden. For 1977, then executive director Peter A. Carlesimo (who served in that capacity from 1977 through 1988) and the tournament committee instituted a plan that provided for games prior to the final four (final eight in 1977) to be played at participants' home courts. To the surprise of no one, attendance justified the action.

In the first three years (1938-1940), six teams competed with the "top two" receiving first-round byes to the round of four. From 1941 through 1948, the tourney was an eight-team field. From 1949 through 1964, 12 teams competed with the "top four" receiving first-round byes to the round of eight. From 1965 through 1967, 14 teams competed with the "top two" receiving byes to the round of eight. From 1968 through 1978, 16 teams competed (except for 12 teams in 1976). In 1979, the field went to 24 teams and then moved to its current level of 32 in 1980. Except for the first-round byes to the "top" teams in the years when the number of teams was not a multiple of or divisor of sixteen, the tournament always has been otherwise unseeded. Consolation games for 3rd/4th place have been played every year except in 1982 and 1983.

In 1979, the 24-team transition year between 16 and 32 participants, the committee devised an interesting tournament structure. Normally, 24 teams would provide for eight first-round games with eight byes—the first-round winners then meeting the byes in the round of 16. But, such an arrangement reduces the total number of games and, of course, the gate. So the innovative committee had all 24 teams play a first-round game and the 12 winners meet in the second round. But, that arrangement left an unwieldy six teams for the third-round. The dilemma was solved with Indiana and Ohio State receiving byes to the round of four—meeting the winners of the two third-round games. Why Indiana and Ohio State received the byes is unknown. Ironically, Purdue, the only nationally ranked team in the tournament (15th AP, 14th UPI), had to play one of the two third-round games.

For many years, until 1953 when the NCAA decreed that all qualifying teams had to play in its own tournament—and no where else, teams were free to play in either or both events. And many did—the most notable of which was City College of New York—the only team to win both tournaments in the same year (1950).

For the most part, NIT participants have been what are now know as NCAA division I schools. However, in the early years and before divisional classification, smaller NCAA schools, and even a few NAIA schools, were invited. Probably the biggest surprise was the championship won by Southern Illinois in 1967—the only one ever by a division II school.

The NIT team selection process currently has two components: 1. win-loss record (in evaluating records, consideration is given to the number of home games, wins at home, road record, strength of conference, common opponents, and in close calls between potential invitees, games vs. each other); 2. everything being equal between potential invitees, the following become important factors—strong second half of the season, outstanding performers, injuries, potential "Cinderella" team, margins of victory over quality opponents.

The contents of all selection and pairings meetings are completely confidential, and the committee does what it thinks is in the best interest of the tournament.

Site selection is based on the following considerations: The MIBA shall have the sole authority to determine the sites for all tournament contests. Based on input from athletic directors, conference commissioners, coaches and arena directors concerning availability and size of the arena, game expense, current and past attendance records, student vacation periods, ticket printing, and ticket prices, the committee endeavors to select the site that will best enhance the success of the tournament.—*excerpted from the 1997 NIT Media Guide*

Tournament Results

F	School	Assn	Div	Bye	W	L	Coach
1938							
1	Temple	NCAA			23	2	Usilton, James
2	Colorado	NCAA		To R4	15	6	Cox, Forrest B. "Frosty"
3	Oklahoma State	NCAA		To R4	25	3	Iba, Henry P. "Hank"
4	New York	NCAA			16	8	Cann, Howard G.
6	Bradley	NCAA			18	2	Robertson, Alfred J.
	Long Island				23	4	Bee, Clair F.
1939							
1	Long Island				24	0	Bee, Clair F.
2	Loyola (IL)			To R4	21	1	Sachs, Leonard D.
3	Bradley	NCAA		To R4	19	3	Robertson, Alfred J.
4	Saint John's (NY)	NCAA			18	4	Lapchick, Joseph B.
6	New Mexico State	NAIA			16	3	Hines, Gerald H. "Jerry"
	Roanoke	NAIA			21	3	White, Gordon C. "Pap"
1940							
1	Colorado	NCAA		To R4	17	4	Cox, Forrest B. "Frosty"
2	Duquesne	NCAA			20	3	Davies, Charles R. "Chick"
3	Oklahoma State	NCAA		To R4	26	3	Iba, Henry P. "Hank"
4	De Paul	NCAA			22	6	Haggerty, Thomas J.
6	Long Island				19	4	Bee, Clair F.
	Saint John's (NY)	NCAA			15	4	Lapchick, Joseph B.
1941							
1	Long Island				25	2	Bee, Clair F.
2	Ohio University	NCAA			18	4	Trautwein, William J. "Dutch"
3	City College	NCAA			17	5	Holman, Nathan "Nat"
4	Seton Hall				20	2	Russell, John D. "Honey"
8	Duquesne	NCAA			17	3	Davies, Charles R. "Chick"
	Rhode Island	NCAA			21	4	Keaney, Frank W.
	Virginia	NCAA			16	5	Tebell, Gus K.
	Westminster (MO)	NAIA			10	8	Kimbrell, Eugene F.
1942							
1	West Virginia	NCAA			19	4	Raese, Richard "Dyke"
2	Western Kentucky	NCAA			29	5	Diddle, Edgar A., Sr.
3	Creighton	NCAA			19	5	Hickey, Edgar S. "Eddie"
4	Toledo	NCAA			23	5	Anderson, W. Harold "Andy"
8	City College	NCAA			16	3	Holman, Nathan "Nat"
	Long Island				24	4	Bee, Clair F.
	Rhode Island	NCAA			18	4	Keaney, Frank W.
	West Texas A&M	NCAA			28	3	Baggett, Al
1943							
1	Saint John's (NY)	NCAA			21	3	Lapchick, Joseph B.
2	Toledo	NCAA			22	4	Friddle, Burl
3	Washington & Jefferson	NCAA			18	5	Sanders, Adam
4	Fordham	NCAA			16	6	Kelleher, Edward A.

F	School	Assn	Div	Bye	W	L	Coach
8	Creighton	NCAA			16	1	Hickey, Edgar S. "Eddie"
	Manhattan	NCAA			18	3	Daher, Joseph G.
	Rice	NCAA			17	6	Davis, Joe W. "Bloody Joe"
	Western Kentucky	NCAA			24	3	Diddle, Edgar A., Sr.

1944

F	School	Assn	Div	Bye	W	L	Coach
1	Saint John's (NY)	NCAA			18	5	Lapchick, Joseph B.
2	De Paul	NCAA			22	4	Meyer, Raymond J.
3	Kentucky	NCAA			19	2	Rupp, Adolph F.
4	Oklahoma State	NCAA			27	6	Iba, Henry P. "Hank"
8	Bowling Green State	NCAA			22	4	Anderson, W. Harold "Andy"
	Canisius	NCAA			15	6	Seelbach, Allie
	Muhlenberg	NCAA			19	6	Julian, Alvin F. "Doggie"
	Utah	NCAA			21	4	Peterson, Vadal

1945

F	School	Assn	Div	Bye	W	L	Coach
1	De Paul	NCAA			21	3	Meyer, Raymond J.
2	Bowling Green State	NCAA			24	4	Anderson, W. Harold "Andy"
3	Saint John's (NY)	NCAA			21	3	Lapchick, Joseph B.
4	Rhode Island	NCAA			20	4	Keaney, Frank W.
8	Muhlenberg	NCAA			24	4	Julian, Alvin F. "Doggie"
	Rensselaer	NCAA			13	1	Donald, Edmund W. "Ed"
	Tennessee	NCAA			18	5	Mauer, John W.
	West Virginia	NCAA			12	6	Brickels, John L.

1946

F	School	Assn	Div	Bye	W	L	Coach
1	Kentucky	NCAA			28	2	Rupp, Adolph F.
2	Rhode Island	NCAA			22	3	Keaney, Frank W.
3	West Virginia	NCAA			24	3	Patton, Lee
4	Muhlenberg	NCAA			23	5	Coker, Lee
8	Arizona	NCAA			25	5	Enke, Fred A.
	Bowling Green State	NCAA			27	5	Anderson, W. Harold "Andy"
	Saint John's (NY)	NCAA			17	6	Lapchick, Joseph B.
	Syracuse	NCAA			23	4	Andreas, Lewis P.

1947

F	School	Assn	Div	Bye	W	L	Coach
1	Utah	NCAA			19	5	Peterson, Vadal
2	Kentucky	NCAA			34	3	Rupp, Adolph F.
3	North Carolina State	NCAA			26	5	Case, Everett N.
4	West Virginia	NCAA			19	3	Patton, Lee
8	Bradley	NCAA			25	7	Robertson, Alfred J.
	Duquesne	NCAA			20	2	Davies, Charles R. "Chick"
	Long Island				17	4	Bee, Clair F.
	Saint John's (NY)	NCAA			16	7	Lapchick, Joseph B.

1948

F	School	Assn	Div	Bye	W	L	Coach
1	Saint Louis	NCAA			24	3	Hickey, Edgar S. "Eddie"
2	New York	NCAA			22	4	Cann, Howard G.
3	Western Kentucky	NCAA			28	2	Diddle, Edgar A., Sr.
4	De Paul	NCAA			22	8	Meyer, Raymond J.
8	Bowling Green State	NCAA			27	6	Anderson, W. Harold "Andy"
	La Salle	NCAA			20	4	McGlone, Charles
	North Carolina State	NCAA			29	3	Case, Everett N.
	Texas	NCAA			20	5	Gray, Jack S.

F	School	Assn	Div	Bye	W	L	Coach
1949							
1	San Francisco	NCAA			25	5	Newell, Peter F.
2	Loyola (IL)	NAIA			25	6	Haggerty, Thomas J.
3	Bowling Green State	NCAA			24	7	Anderson, W. Harold "Andy"
4	Bradley	NCAA			27	8	Anderson, Forrest A. "Forddy"
8	Kentucky	NCAA		To R8	32	2	Rupp, Adolph F.
	Saint Louis	NCAA		To R8	22	4	Hickey, Edgar S. "Eddie"
	Utah	NCAA		To R8	24	8	Peterson, Vadal
	Western Kentucky	NCAA		To R8	25	4	Diddle, Edgar A., Sr.
12	City College	NCAA			17	8	Holman, Nathan "Nat"
	Manhattan	NCAA			18	8	Norton, Kenneth A.
	New York	NCAA			12	8	Cann, Howard G.
	Saint John's (NY)	NCAA			16	9	McGuire, Frank J.
1950							
1	City College	NCAA			24	5	Holman, Nathan "Nat"
2	Bradley	NCAA		To R8	32	5	Anderson, Forrest A. "Forddy"
3	Saint John's (NY)	NCAA		To R8	24	5	McGuire, Frank J.
4	Duquesne	NCAA		To R8	23	6	Moore, Donald W. "Dudey"
8	Kentucky	NCAA		To R8	25	5	Rupp, Adolph F.
	La Salle	NCAA			21	4	Loeffler, Kenneth D.
	Syracuse	NCAA			18	9	Andreas, Lewis P.
	Western Kentucky	NCAA			25	6	Diddle, Edgar A., Sr.
12	Arizona	NCAA			26	5	Enke, Fred A.
	Long Island	NAIA			20	5	Bee, Clair F.
	Niagara	NCAA			20	7	Gallagher, John J. "Taps"
	San Francisco	NCAA			19	7	Newell, Peter F.
1951							
1	Brigham Young	NCAA		To R8	28	9	Watts, Stanley H.
2	Dayton	NCAA			27	5	Blackburn, L. Thomas
3	Saint John's (NY)	NCAA		To R8	26	5	McGuire, Frank J.
4	Seton Hall	NCAA			24	7	Russell, John D. "Honey"
8	Arizona	NCAA		To R8	24	6	Enke, Fred A.
	North Carolina State	NCAA		To R8	30	7	Case, Everett N.
	Saint Bonaventure	NCAA			19	6	Melvin, Edward M. (Milkovich)
	Saint Louis	NCAA			22	8	Hickey, Edgar S. "Eddie"
12	Beloit	NCAA			18	5	Stanley, Dolph
	Cincinnati	NCAA			18	4	Wiethe, John A.
	La Salle	NCAA			22	7	Loeffler, Kenneth D.
	Lawrence Tech	NAIA			20	3	Ridler, Don
1952							
1	La Salle	NCAA			25	7	Loeffler, Kenneth D.
2	Dayton	NCAA			28	5	Blackburn, L. Thomas
3	Saint Bonaventure	NCAA		To R8	21	6	Melvin, Edward M. (Milkovich)
4	Duquesne	NCAA		To R8	23	4	Moore, Donald W. "Dudey"
8	Holy Cross (MA)	NCAA			24	4	Sheary, Lester H. "Buster"
	Saint John's (NY)	NCAA		To R8	25	5	McGuire, Frank J.
	Saint Louis	NCAA		To R8	23	8	Hickey, Edgar S. "Eddie"
	Western Kentucky	NCAA			26	5	Diddle, Edgar A., Sr.

F	School	Assn	Div	Bye	W	L	Coach
12	Louisville	NCAA			20	6	Hickman, Bernard L. "Peck"
	New York	NCAA			17	8	Cann, Howard G.
	Seattle	NCAA			29	8	Brightman, Horace Albert "Al"
	Seton Hall	NCAA			25	3	Russell, John D. "Honey"

1953

F	School	Assn	Div	Bye	W	L	Coach
1	Seton Hall	NCAA		To R8	31	2	Russell, John D. "Honey"
2	Saint John's (NY)	NCAA			17	6	DeStefano, Alfred "Dusty"
3	Duquesne	NCAA			21	8	Moore, Donald W. "Dudey"
4	Manhattan	NCAA		To R8	20	6	Norton, Kenneth A.
8	La Salle	NCAA		To R8	25	3	Loeffler, Kenneth D.
	Louisville	NCAA			22	6	Hickman, Bernard L. "Peck"
	Niagara	NCAA			22	6	Gallagher, John J. "Taps"
	Western Kentucky	NCAA		To R8	25	6	Diddle, Edgar A., Sr.
12	Brigham Young	NCAA			22	8	Watts, Stanley H.
	Georgetown (DC)	NCAA			13	7	Jeanette, Harry E. "Buddy"
	Saint Louis	NCAA			16	11	Hickey, Edgar S. "Eddie"
	Tulsa	NCAA			15	10	Iba, Clarence V.

1954

F	School	Assn	Div	Bye	W	L	Coach
1	Holy Cross (MA)	NCAA		To R8	26	2	Sheary, Lester H. "Buster"
2	Duquesne	NCAA		To R8	26	3	Moore, Donald W. "Dudey"
3	Niagara	NCAA		To R8	24	6	Gallagher, John J. "Taps"
4	Western Kentucky	NCAA		To R8	29	3	Diddle, Edgar A., Sr.
8	Bowling Green State	NCAA			17	7	Anderson, W. Harold "Andy"
	Dayton	NCAA			25	7	Blackburn, L. Thomas
	Saint Francis (NY)	NAIA			22	5	Lynch, Daniel J.
	Saint Francis (PA)	NCAA			21	5	Hughes, Dr. William T. "Skip"
12	Brigham Young	NCAA			18	11	Watts, Stanley H.
	Louisville	NCAA			22	7	Hickman, Bernard L. "Peck"
	Manhattan	NCAA			15	11	Norton, Kenneth A.
	Wichita State	NCAA			27	4	Miller, Ralph H. "Cappy"

1955

F	School	Assn	Div	Bye	W	L	Coach
1	Duquesne	NCAA		To R8	22	4	Moore, Donald W. "Dudey"
2	Dayton	NCAA		To R8	25	4	Blackburn, L. Thomas
3	Cincinnati	NCAA		To R8	21	8	Smith, George D.
4	Saint Francis (PA)	NCAA			21	7	Hughes, Dr. William T. "Skip"
8	Holy Cross (MA)	NCAA		To R8	19	7	Sheary, Lester H. "Buster"
	Louisville	NCAA			19	8	Hickman, Bernard L. "Peck"
	Niagara	NCAA			20	6	Gallagher, John J. "Taps"
	Saint Louis	NCAA			20	8	Hickey, Edgar S. "Eddie"
12	Connecticut	NCAA			20	5	Greer, Hugh S.
	Lafayette (PA)	NCAA			24	3	Van Breda Kolff, Willem "Butch"
	Manhattan	NCAA			18	5	Norton, Kenneth A.
	Seton Hall	NCAA			17	9	Russell, John D. "Honey"

1956

F	School	Assn	Div	Bye	W	L	Coach
1	Louisville	NCAA		To R8	26	3	Hickman, Bernard L. "Peck"
2	Dayton	NCAA		To R8	25	4	Blackburn, L. Thomas
3	Saint Joseph's (PA)	NCAA		To R8	23	6	Ramsay, Dr. John T. "Jack"
4	Saint Francis (NY)	NAIA			21	4	Lynch, Daniel J.

F	School	Assn	Div	Bye	W	L	Coach
8	Duquesne	NCAA			17	10	Moore, Donald W. "Dudey"
	Niagara	NCAA		To R8	20	7	Gallagher, John J. "Taps"
	Seton Hall	NCAA			20	5	Russell, John D. "Honey"
	Xavier (OH)	NCAA			17	11	Wulk, Ned W.
12	Lafayette (PA)	NCAA			20	7	Davidson, George E.
	Marquette	NCAA			13	11	Nagle, Joel "Jack"
	Oklahoma State	NCAA			18	9	Iba, Henry P. "Hank"
	Saint Louis	NCAA			20	8	Hickey, Edgar S. "Eddie"

1957

F	School	Assn	Div	Bye	W	L	Coach
1	Bradley	NCAA	I	To R8	22	7	Orsborn, Charles K. "Chuck"
2	Memphis	NCAA	I		24	6	Vanatta, Robert
3	Temple	NCAA	I	To R8	20	9	Litwack, Harry
4	Saint Bonaventure	NCAA	I		17	7	Donovan, Edward J. "Eddie"
8	Dayton	NCAA	I		19	9	Blackburn, L. Thomas
	Manhattan	NCAA	I	To R8	15	9	Norton, Kenneth A.
	Seattle	NCAA	I	To R8	24	3	Castellani, John
	Xavier (OH)	NCAA	I		20	8	Wulk, Ned W.
12	Cincinnati	NCAA	I		15	7	Smith, George D.
	Saint Peter's	NCAA	I		18	4	Kennedy, Don, Sr.
	Seton Hall	NCAA	I		17	10	Russell, John D. "Honey"
	Utah	NCAA	I		19	8	Gardner, James H. "Jack"

1958

F	School	Assn	Div	Bye	W	L	Coach
1	Xavier (OH)	NCAA	I		19	11	McCafferty, James J.
2	Dayton	NCAA	I	To R8	25	4	Blackburn, L. Thomas
3	Saint Bonaventure	NCAA	I	To R8	21	5	Donovan, Edward J. "Eddie"
4	Saint John's (NY)	NCAA	I		18	8	Lapchick, Joseph B.
8	Bradley	NCAA	I	To R8	20	7	Orsborn, Charles K. "Chuck"
	Fordham	NCAA	I		15	9	Bach, John W. "Johnny"
	Saint Joseph's (PA)	NCAA	I		18	9	Ramsay, Dr. John T. "Jack"
	Utah	NCAA	I	To R8	20	7	Gardner, James H. "Jack"
12	Butler (IN)	NCAA	I		15	10	Hinkle, Paul D. "Tony"
	Niagara	NCAA	I		18	7	Gallagher, John J. "Taps"
	Saint Francis (PA)	NCAA	I		20	5	Hughes, Dr. William T. "Skip"
	Saint Peter's	NCAA	I		20	4	Kennedy, Don, Sr.

1959

F	School	Assn	Div	Bye	W	L	Coach
1	Saint John's (NY)	NCAA	I		20	6	Lapchick, Joseph B.
2	Bradley	NCAA	I	To R8	25	4	Orsborn, Charles K. "Chuck"
3	New York	NCAA	I		15	8	Rossini, Lucio "Lou"
4	Providence	NCAA	I		20	7	Mullaney, Joseph A., Sr.
8	Butler (IN)	NCAA	I		19	9	Hinkle, Paul D. "Tony"
	Oklahoma City	NCAA	I	To R8	20	7	Lemons, A. E. "Abe"
	Saint Bonaventure	NCAA	I	To R8	20	3	Donovan, Edward J. "Eddie"
	Saint Louis	NCAA	I	To R8	20	6	Bennington, John E.
12	Denver	NCAA	I		14	10	Brawner, E. Hoyt
	Fordham	NCAA	I		17	8	Bach, John W. "Johnny"
	Manhattan	NCAA	I		15	6	Norton, Kenneth A.
	Villanova	NCAA	I		18	7	Severance, Alexander G.

F	School	Assn	Div	Bye	W	L	Coach
1960							
1	Bradley	NCAA	I	To R8	27	2	Orsborn, Charles K. 'Chuck'
2	Providence	NCAA	I		24	5	Mullaney, Joseph A., Sr.
3	Utah State	NCAA	I	To R8	24	5	Baker, H. Cecil
4	Saint Bonaventure	NCAA	I		21	5	Donovan, Edward J. 'Eddie'
8	Dayton	NCAA	I		21	7	Blackburn, L. Thomas
	Saint John's (NY)	NCAA	I	To R8	17	8	Lapchick, Joseph B.
	Saint Louis	NCAA	I	To R8	19	8	Bennington, John E.
	Villanova	NCAA	I		20	6	Severance, Alexander G.
12	Detroit	NCAA	I		20	7	Calihan, Robert J.
	Holy Cross (MA)	NCAA	I		20	6	Leenig, Roy H.
	Memphis	NCAA	I		18	5	Vanatta, Robert
	Temple	NCAA	I		17	9	Litwack, Harry
1961							
1	Providence	NCAA	I		24	5	Mullaney, Joseph A., Sr.
2	Saint Louis	NCAA	I		21	9	Bennington, John E.
3	Holy Cross (MA)	NCAA	I		21	5	Leenig, Roy H.
4	Dayton	NCAA	I	To R8	20	9	Blackburn, L. Thomas
8	Colorado State	NCAA	I	To R8	17	9	Williams, James J.
	Memphis	NCAA	I	To R8	20	3	Vanatta, Robert
	Niagara	NCAA	I	To R8	16	5	Gallagher, John J. 'Taps'
	Temple	NCAA	I		20	8	Litwack, Harry
12	Army	NCAA	I		17	7	Hunter, George E.
	De Paul	NCAA	I		17	8	Meyer, Raymond J.
	Detroit	NCAA	I		18	9	Calihan, Robert J.
	Miami (FL)	NCAA	I		20	7	Hale, William Bruce
1962							
1	Dayton	NCAA	I		24	6	Blackburn, L. Thomas
2	Saint John's (NY)	NCAA	I	To R8	21	5	Lapchick, Joseph B.
3	Loyola (IL)	NCAA	I	To R8	23	4	Ireland, George M.
4	Duquesne	NCAA	I		22	7	Manning, John 'Red'
8	Bradley	NCAA	I	To R8	21	7	Orsborn, Charles K. 'Chuck'
	Holy Cross (MA)	NCAA	I		20	6	Oftring, Frank A.
	Houston	NCAA	I	To R8	21	6	Lewis, Guy V.
	Temple	NCAA	I		18	9	Litwack, Harry
12	Colorado State	NCAA	I		18	9	Williams, James J.
	Navy	NCAA	I		13	8	Carnevale, Bernard L. 'Ben'
	Providence	NCAA	I		20	6	Mullaney, Joseph A., Sr.
	Wichita State	NCAA	I		18	9	Miller, Ralph H. 'Cappy'
1963							
1	Providence	NCAA	I	To R8	24	4	Mullaney, Joseph A., Sr.
2	Canisius	NCAA	I	To R8	19	7	MacKinnon, Robert A.
3	Marquette	NCAA	I	To R8	20	9	Hickey, Edgar S. 'Eddie'
4	Villanova	NCAA	I		19	10	Kraft, John J. 'Jack'
8	Memphis	NCAA	I		19	7	Ehlers, Dean
	Miami (FL)	NCAA	I		23	5	Hale, William Bruce
	Saint Louis	NCAA	I		16	12	Bennington, John E.
	Wichita State	NCAA	I	To R8	19	8	Miller, Ralph H. 'Cappy'

F	School	Assn	Div	Bye	W	L	Coach
12	De Paul	NCAA	I		15	8	Meyer, Raymond J.
	Fordham	NCAA	I		18	8	Bach, John W. "Johnny"
	La Salle	NCAA	I		16	8	Moore, Donald W. "Dudey"
	Saint Francis (NY)	NCAA	I		16	7	Lynch, Daniel J.

1964

F	School	Assn	Div	Bye	W	L	Coach
1	Bradley	NCAA	I	To R8	23	6	Orsborn, Charles K. "Chuck"
2	New Mexico	NCAA	I	To R8	23	6	King, Bob
3	Army	NCAA	I		19	7	Locke, Taylor O. "Tates"
4	New York	NCAA	I		17	10	Rossini, Lucio "Lou"
8	De Paul	NCAA	I	To R8	21	4	Meyer, Raymond J.
	Drake (IA)	NCAA	I		21	7	John, Maurice E. "Maury"
	Duquesne	NCAA	I	To R8	16	7	Manning, John "Red"
	Saint Joseph's (PA)	NCAA	I		18	10	Ramsay, Dr. John T. "Jack"
12	Miami (FL)	NCAA	I		20	7	Hale, William Bruce
	Pittsburgh	NCAA	I		17	8	Timmons, Robert W.
	Saint Bonaventure	NCAA	I		16	8	Weise, Lawrence J.
	Syracuse	NCAA	I		17	8	Lewis, Frederick B., Jr.

1965

F	School	Assn	Div	Bye	W	L	Coach
1	Saint John's (NY)	NCAA	I		21	8	Lapchick, Joseph B.
2	Villanova	NCAA	I	To R8	23	5	Kraft, John J. "Jack"
3	Army	NCAA	I		21	8	Locke, Taylor O. "Tates"
4	New York	NCAA	I		16	10	Rossini, Lucio "Lou"
8	Detroit	NCAA	I		20	8	Calihan, Robert J.
	Manhattan	NCAA	I		13	9	Norton, Kenneth A.
	New Mexico	NCAA	I	To R8	19	8	King, Bob
	Western Kentucky	NCAA	I		17	8	Diddle, Edgar A., Sr.
14	Boston College	NCAA	I		21	7	Cousy, Robert J.
	Bradley	NCAA	I		18	9	Orsborn, Charles K. "Chuck"
	Fordham	NCAA	I		15	12	Bach, John W. "Johnny"
	La Salle	NCAA	I		15	8	Walters, Robert W.
	Saint Louis	NCAA	I		18	9	Bennington, John E.
	Texas: El Paso	NCAA	I		17	9	Haskins, Donald L.

1966

F	School	Assn	Div	Bye	W	L	Coach
1	Brigham Young	NCAA	I	To R8	20	5	Watts, Stanley H.
2	New York	NCAA	I		18	10	Rossini, Lucio "Lou"
3	Villanova	NCAA	I		18	11	Kraft, John J. "Jack"
4	Army	NCAA	I		18	8	Knight, Robert M.
8	Boston College	NCAA	I		21	5	Cousy, Robert J.
	San Francisco	NCAA	I		22	6	Peletta, Peter P.
	Temple	NCAA	I		21	7	Litwack, Harry
	Wichita State	NCAA	I	To R8	17	10	Thompson, Gary
14	De Paul	NCAA	I		18	8	Meyer, Raymond J.
	Louisville	NCAA	I		16	10	Hickman, Bernard L. "Peck"
	Manhattan	NCAA	I		13	9	Norton, Kenneth A.
	Pennsylvania State	NCAA	I		18	6	Egli, John S.
	Saint John's (NY)	NCAA	I		18	8	Carnesecca, Louis P. "Lou"
	Virginia Polytechnic	NCAA	I		19	5	Shannon, Howard P. "Howie"

F	School	Assn	Div	Bye	W	L	Coach
1967							
1	Southern Illinois	NCAA	II		24	2	Hartman, Jack
2	Marquette	NCAA	I		21	9	McGuire, Alfred J.
3	Rutgers	NCAA	I		22	7	Foster, William E.
4	Marshall	NCAA	I		20	8	Johnson, Ellis T.
8	Duke	NCAA	I	To R8	18	9	Bubas, Victor A.
	Nebraska	NCAA	I	To R8	16	9	Cipriano, Joseph
	New Mexico	NCAA	I		19	8	King, Bob
	Providence	NCAA	I		21	7	Mullaney, Joseph A., Sr.
14	Memphis	NCAA	I		17	9	Iba, Moe
	Saint Peter's	NCAA	I		18	6	Kennedy, Don, Sr.
	Syracuse	NCAA	I		20	6	Lewis, Frederick B., Jr.
	Tulsa	NCAA	I		19	8	Swank, Joe
	Utah State	NCAA	I		20	6	Anderson, Ladell
	Villanova	NCAA	I		17	9	Kraft, John J. "Jack"
1968							
1	Dayton	NCAA	I		21	9	Donoher, Donald J. "Mickey"
2	Kansas	NCAA	I		22	8	Owens, Ted
3	Notre Dame (IN)	NCAA	I		21	9	Dee, John F., Jr.
4	Saint Peter's	NCAA	I		24	4	Kennedy, Don, Sr.
8	Duke	NCAA	I		22	6	Bubas, Victor A.
	Fordham	NCAA	I		19	8	Bach, John W. "Johnny"
	Long Island	NCAA	I		22	2	Rubin, Roy
	Villanova	NCAA	I		19	9	Kraft, John J. "Jack"
16	Army	NCAA	I		20	5	Knight, Robert M.
	Bradley	NCAA	I		19	9	Stowell, Joseph R.
	Duquesne	NCAA	I		18	7	Manning, John "Red"
	Marshall	NCAA	I		17	8	Johnson, Ellis T.
	Oklahoma City	NCAA	I		20	7	Lemons, A. E. "Abe"
	Temple	NCAA	I		19	9	Litwack, Harry
	West Virginia	NCAA	I		19	9	Waters, Raymond C. "Bucky"
	Wyoming	NCAA	I		18	9	Strannigan, William M.
1969							
1	Temple	NCAA	I		22	8	Litwack, Harry
2	Boston College	NCAA	I		24	4	Cousy, Robert J.
3	Tennessee	NCAA	I		21	7	Mears, Ramon "Ray"
4	Army	NCAA	I		18	10	Knight, Robert M.
8	Louisville	NCAA	I		21	6	Dromo, John
	Ohio University	NCAA	I		17	9	Snyder, James E.
	Saint Peter's	NCAA	I		21	7	Kennedy, Don, Sr.
	South Carolina	NCAA	I		21	7	McGuire, Frank J.
16	Florida	NCAA	I		18	9	Bartlett, Thomas G. "Tommy"
	Fordham	NCAA	I		17	9	Conlin, Edward J.
	Kansas	NCAA	I		20	7	Owens, Ted
	Rutgers	NCAA	I		21	4	Foster, William E.
	Southern Illinois	NCAA	I		16	8	Hartman, Jack
	Tulsa	NCAA	I		19	8	Hayes, Ken
	West Texas A&M	NCAA	I		18	7	Walling, Dennis W.
	Wyoming	NCAA	I		19	9	Strannigan, William M.

F	School	Assn	Div	Bye	W	L	Coach
1970							
1	Marquette	NCAA	I		26	3	McGuire, Alfred J.
2	Saint John's (NY)	NCAA	I		21	8	Carnesecca, Louis P. "Lou"
3	Army	NCAA	I		22	6	Knight, Robert M.
4	Louisiana State	NCAA	I		22	10	Maravich, Peter "Press"
8	Georgia Tech	NCAA	I		17	10	Hyder, John C. "Whack"
	Manhattan	NCAA	I		18	8	Powers, John J. "Jack"
	Oklahoma	NCAA	I		19	9	MacLeod, John M.
	Utah	NCAA	I		18	10	Gardner, James H. "Jack"
16	Cincinnati	NCAA	I		21	6	Baker, Taylor "Tay"
	Duke	NCAA	I		17	9	Waters, Raymond C. "Bucky"
	Duquesne	NCAA	I		17	7	Manning, John "Red"
	Georgetown (DC)	NCAA	I		18	8	Magee, John F. "Jack"
	Louisville	NCAA	I		18	9	Dromo, John
	Massachusetts	NCAA	I		18	7	Leaman, John A., Jr. "Jack"
	Miami (OH)	NCAA	I		16	8	Locke, Taylor O. "Tates"
	North Carolina	NCAA	I		18	9	Smith, Dean E.
1971							
1	North Carolina	NCAA	I		26	6	Smith, Dean E.
2	Georgia Tech	NCAA	I		23	9	Hyder, John C. "Whack"
3	Saint Bonaventure	NCAA	I		21	6	Weise, Lawrence J.
4	Duke	NCAA	I		20	10	Waters, Raymond C. "Bucky"
8	Hawaii	NCAA	I		23	5	Rocha, Ephraim J. "Red"
	Michigan	NCAA	I		19	7	Orr, John M. "Johnny"
	Providence	NCAA	I		20	8	Gavitt, David R.
	Tennessee	NCAA	I		21	7	Mears, Ramon "Ray"
16	Dayton	NCAA	I		18	9	Donoher, Donald J. "Mickey"
	La Salle	NCAA	I		20	7	Westhead, Paul W.
	Louisville	NCAA	I		20	9	Dromo, John
	Massachusetts	NCAA	I		23	4	Leaman, John A., Jr. "Jack"
	Oklahoma	NCAA	I		19	8	MacLeod, John M.
	Purdue	NCAA	I		18	7	King, George S., Jr.
	Saint John's (NY)	NCAA	I		18	9	Mulzoff, Frank
	Syracuse	NCAA	I		19	7	Danforth, Roy
1972							
1	Maryland	NCAA	I		27	5	Driesell, Charles G. "Lefty"
2	Niagara	NCAA	I		21	9	Layden, Frank P.
3	Jacksonville (FL)	NCAA	I		20	8	Wasdin, Tom
4	Saint John's (NY)	NCAA	I		19	11	Mulzoff, Frank
8	Lafayette (PA)	NCAA	I		21	6	Davis, Dr. Thomas
	Oral Roberts	NCAA	I		26	2	Trickey, Ken
	Princeton	NCAA	I		20	7	Carril, Peter J.
	Syracuse	NCAA	I		22	6	Danforth, Roy
16	Davidson	NCAA	I		19	9	Holland, M. Terrance "Terry"
	Fordham	NCAA	I		18	9	Wissel, Dr. Harold R. "Hal"
	Indiana	NCAA	I		17	8	Knight, Robert M.
	Memphis	NCAA	I		21	7	Bartow, B. Gene

F	School	Assn	Div	Bye	W	L	Coach
	Missouri	NCAA	I		21	6	Stewart, Norman E.
	Saint Joseph's (PA)	NCAA	I		19	9	McKinney, John P. "Jack"
	Texas: El Paso	NCAA	I		20	7	Haskins, Donald L.
	Virginia	NCAA	I		21	7	Gibson, William J.

1973

F	School	Assn	Div	Bye	W	L	Coach
1	Virginia Polytechnic	NCAA	I		22	5	DeVoe, Donald E.
2	Notre Dame (IN)	NCAA	I		18	12	Phelps, Richard F. "Digger"
3	North Carolina	NCAA	I		25	8	Smith, Dean E.
4	Alabama	NCAA	I		22	8	Newton, Charles M. "CM"
8	Fairfield	NCAA	I		18	9	Barakat, Frederick E.
	Louisville	NCAA	I		23	7	Crum, Denzil E. "Denny"
	Massachusetts	NCAA	I		20	7	Leaman, John A., Jr. "Jack"
	Minnesota	NCAA	I		21	5	Musselman, William
16	American	NCAA	I		21	5	Young, Thomas J.
	Manhattan	NCAA	I		16	10	Powers, John J. "Jack"
	Marshall	NCAA	I		20	7	Daniels, Bob
	Missouri	NCAA	I		21	6	Stewart, Norman E.
	New Mexico	NCAA	I		21	6	Ellenberger, Norman
	Oral Roberts	NCAA	I		21	6	Trickey, Ken
	Rutgers	NCAA	I		15	11	Lloyd, Richard R.
	Southern California	NCAA	I		18	10	Boyd, William R. "Bob"

1974

F	School	Assn	Div	Bye	W	L	Coach
1	Purdue	NCAA	I		21	9	Schaus, Frederick A.
2	Utah	NCAA	I		22	8	Foster, William E.
3	Boston College	NCAA	I		21	9	Zuffelato, Bob
4	Jacksonville (FL)	NCAA	I		20	10	Gottlieb, Bob
8	Connecticut	NCAA	I		19	8	Rowe, Donald E. "Dee"
	Hawaii	NCAA	I		19	9	O'Neil, Bruce
	Maryland: Eastern Shore	NAIA			27	2	Bates, John H.
	Memphis	NCAA	I		19	11	Bartow, B. Gene
16	Cincinnati	NCAA	I		19	8	Catlett, Gale
	Fairfield	NCAA	I		17	9	Barakat, Frederick E.
	Manhattan	NCAA	I		18	9	Powers, John J. "Jack"
	Massachusetts	NCAA	I		21	5	Leaman, John A., Jr. "Jack"
	North Carolina	NCAA	I		22	6	Smith, Dean E.
	Rutgers	NCAA	I		18	8	Young, Thomas J.
	Saint John's (NY)	NCAA	I		20	7	Carnesecca, Louis P. "Lou"
	Seton Hall	NCAA	I		16	11	Raftery, William J.

1975

F	School	Assn	Div	Bye	W	L	Coach
1	Princeton	NCAA	I		22	8	Carril, Peter J.
2	Providence	NCAA	I		20	4	Gavitt, David R.
3	Oregon	NCAA	I		21	9	Harter, Dick
4	Saint John's (NY)	NCAA	I		21	10	Carnesecca, Louis P. "Lou"
8	Manhattan	NCAA	I		14	12	Powers, John J. "Jack"
	Oral Roberts	NCAA	I		20	8	Hale, Jerry
	Pittsburgh	NCAA	I		18	11	Ridl, Charles G. "Buzz"
	South Carolina	NCAA	I		19	9	McGuire, Frank J.

F	School	Assn	Div	Bye	W	L	Coach
16	Clemson	NCAA	I		17	11	Locke, Taylor O. "Tates"
	Connecticut	NCAA	I		18	10	Rowe, Donald E. "Dee"
	Holy Cross (MA)	NCAA	I		20	8	Blaney, George R.
	Lafayette (PA)	NCAA	I		22	6	Davis, Dr. Thomas
	Massachusetts	NCAA	I		18	8	Leaman, John A., Jr. "Jack"
	Memphis	NCAA	I		20	7	Yates, Wayne E.
	Saint Peter's	NCAA	I		15	12	McDonald, James R. "Dick"
	Southern Illinois	NCAA	I		18	9	Lambert, Paul M.

1976

F	School	Assn	Div	Bye	W	L	Coach
1	Kentucky	NCAA	I		20	10	Hall, Joe B.
2	North Carolina: Charlotte	NCAA	I		24	6	Rose, Lee H.
3	North Carolina State	NCAA	I	To R8	21	9	Sloan, Norman L., Jr.
4	Providence	NCAA	I		21	11	Gavitt, David R.
8	Holy Cross (MA)	NCAA	I		22	10	Blaney, George R.
	Kansas State	NCAA	I	To R8	20	8	Hartman, Jack
	Louisville	NCAA	I	To R8	20	8	Crum, Denzil E. "Denny"
	Oregon	NCAA	I	To R8	19	11	Harter, Dick
12	Niagara	NCAA	I		17	12	Layden, Frank P.
	North Carolina A&T	NCAA	I		20	6	Reynolds, Warren
	Saint Peter's	NCAA	I		19	11	McDonald, James R. "Dick"
	San Francisco	NCAA	I		22	8	Gaillard, Bob

1977

F	School	Assn	Div	Bye	W	L	Coach
1	Saint Bonaventure	NCAA	I		23	6	Satalin, James D.
2	Houston	NCAA	I		29	8	Lewis, Guy V.
3	Villanova	NCAA	I		23	10	Massimino, Roland V. "Rollie"
4	Alabama	NCAA	I		25	6	Newton, Charles M. "CM"
8	Illinois State	NCAA	I		22	7	Smithson, Eugene
	Massachusetts	NCAA	I		20	11	Leaman, John A., Jr. "Jack"
	Oregon	NCAA	I		19	10	Harter, Dick
	Virginia Polytechnic	NCAA	I		19	10	Moir, Charles
16	Creighton	NCAA	I		21	7	Apke, Tom
	Georgetown (DC)	NCAA	I		19	9	Thompson, John R., Jr.
	Indiana State	NCAA	I		25	3	King, Bob
	Memphis	NCAA	I		20	9	Yates, Wayne E.
	Old Dominion	NCAA	I		25	4	Webb, Paul E.
	Oral Roberts	NCAA	I		21	7	Hale, Jerry
	Rutgers	NCAA	I		18	10	Young, Thomas J.
	Seton Hall	NCAA	I		18	11	Raftery, William J.

1978

F	School	Assn	Div	Bye	W	L	Coach
1	Texas	NCAA	I		26	5	Lemons, A. E. "Abe"
2	North Carolina State	NCAA	I		21	10	Sloan, Norman L., Jr.
3	Rutgers	NCAA	I		24	7	Young, Thomas J.
4	Georgetown (DC)	NCAA	I		23	8	Thompson, John R., Jr.
8	Dayton	NCAA	I		19	10	Donoher, Donald J. "Mickey"
	Detroit	NCAA	I		25	4	Gaines, David "Smokey"
	Indiana State	NCAA	I		23	9	King, Bob
	Nebraska	NCAA	I		22	8	Cipriano, Joseph

F	School	Assn	Div	Bye	W	L	Coach
16	Army	NCAA	I		19	9	Krzyzewski, Michael W.
	Fairfield	NCAA	I		22	5	Barakat, Frederick E.
	Illinois State	NCAA	I		24	4	Smithson, Eugene
	South Carolina	NCAA	I		16	12	McGuire, Frank J.
	Temple	NCAA	I		24	5	Casey, Don
	Utah State	NCAA	I		21	7	Belnap, Gordon "Dutch"
	Virginia	NCAA	I		20	8	Holland, M. Terrance "Terry"
	Virginia Commonwealth	NCAA	I		24	5	Kirk, Dana

1979

F	School	Assn	Div	Bye	W	L	Coach
1	Indiana	NCAA	I	R12>R4	22	12	Knight, Robert M.
2	Purdue	NCAA	I		27	8	Rose, Lee H.
3	Alabama	NCAA	I		22	11	Newton, Charles M. "CM"
4	Ohio State	NCAA	I	R12>R4	19	12	Miller, Eldon
6	Old Dominion	NCAA	I		23	7	Webb, Paul E.
	Texas A&M	NCAA	I		24	9	Metcalf, Dr. Shelby R.
12	Alcorn State	NCAA	I		28	1	Whitney, David L., Sr. "Davey"
	Clemson	NCAA	I		19	10	Foster, William C.
	Dayton	NCAA	I		19	10	Donoher, Donald J. "Mickey"
	Maryland	NCAA	I		19	11	Driesell, Charles G. "Lefty"
	Nevada	NCAA	I		21	7	Carey, Jim
	Virginia	NCAA	I		19	10	Holland, M. Terrance "Terry"
24	Central Michigan	NCAA	I		19	9	Parfitt, Richard
	Holy Cross (MA)	NCAA	I		17	11	Blaney, George R.
	Kentucky	NCAA	I		19	12	Hall, Joe B.
	Mississippi State	NCAA	I		19	9	Hatfield, Jim
	New Mexico	NCAA	I		19	10	Ellenberger, Norman
	Northeast Louisiana	NCAA	I		23	6	Fant, Leonard "Lenny"
	Oregon State	NCAA	I		18	10	Miller, Ralph H. "Cappy"
	Rhode Island	NCAA	I		20	9	Kraft, John J. "Jack"
	Saint Bonaventure	NCAA	I		19	9	Satalin, James D.
	Saint Joseph's (PA)	NCAA	I		19	11	Lynam, James F.
	Texas Tech	NCAA	I		19	11	Myers, Gerald
	Wagner	NCAA	I		21	7	Carlesimo, Peter J. "PJ"

1980

F	School	Assn	Div	Bye	W	L	Coach
1	Virginia	NCAA	I		24	10	Holland, M. Terrance "Terry"
2	Minnesota	NCAA	I		21	11	Dutcher, James D.
3	Illinois	NCAA	I		22	13	Henson, Louis R.
4	Nevada: Las Vegas	NCAA	I		23	9	Tarkanian, Jerry
8	Michigan	NCAA	I		17	13	Orr, John M. "Johnny"
	Murray State (KY)	NCAA	I		23	8	Greene, Ronald L.
	Saint Peter's	NCAA	I		22	9	Dukiet, Bob
	Southwestern Louisiana	NCAA	I		21	9	Paschal, Bobby
16	Alabama	NCAA	I		18	12	Newton, Charles M. "CM"
	Boston College	NCAA	I		19	10	Davis, Dr. Thomas
	California State: Long Beach	NCAA	I		22	12	Winter, Fred "Tex"
	Duquesne	NCAA	I		18	10	Rice, Mike

F	School	Assn	Div	Bye	W	L	Coach
	Illinois State	NCAA	I		20	9	Donewald, Bob
	Mississippi	NCAA	I		17	13	Weltlich, Robert
	Texas	NCAA	I		19	11	Lemons, A. E. "Abe"
	Texas: El Paso	NCAA	I		20	8	Haskins, Donald L.
32	Alabama: Birmingham	NCAA	I		18	12	Bartow, B. Gene
	Boston University	NCAA	I		21	9	Pitino, Richard A. "Rick"
	Bowling Green State	NCAA	I		20	10	Weinert, John P.
	Connecticut	NCAA	I		20	9	Perno, Dominic P. "Dom"
	Grambling State	NCAA	I		22	8	Hobdy, Frederick C.
	Jacksonville (FL)	NCAA	I		20	9	Locke, Taylor O. "Tates"
	Lafayette (PA)	NCAA	I		21	8	Chipman, Dr. Leroy
	Loyola (IL)	NCAA	I		19	10	Lyne, Jerry P.
	Nebraska	NCAA	I		18	13	Cipriano, Joseph
	Pennsylvania State	NCAA	I		18	10	Harter, Dick
	Pepperdine	NCAA	I		17	11	Harrick, Jim
	Pittsburgh	NCAA	I		17	12	Grgurich, Tim
	Saint Joseph's (PA)	NCAA	I		21	9	Lynam, James F.
	Washington	NCAA	I		18	10	Harshman, Marvel K. "Marv"
	West Texas A&M	NCAA	I		19	11	Edwards, Ken
	Wichita State	NCAA	I		17	12	Smithson, Eugene

1981

F	School	Assn	Div	Bye	W	L	Coach
1	Tulsa	NCAA	I		26	7	Richardson, Nolan
2	Syracuse	NCAA	I		22	12	Boeheim, James A., Jr.
3	Purdue	NCAA	I		21	11	Keady, Lloyd Eugene "Gene"
4	West Virginia	NCAA	I		23	10	Catlett, Gale
8	Duke	NCAA	I		17	13	Krzyzewski, Michael W.
	Michigan	NCAA	I		19	11	Frieder, Bill
	Minnesota	NCAA	I		19	11	Dutcher, James D.
	South Alabama	NCAA	I		25	6	Ellis, Cliff
16	Alabama	NCAA	I		18	11	Sanderson, Winfrey "Wimp"
	Connecticut	NCAA	I		20	9	Perno, Dominic P. "Dom"
	Dayton	NCAA	I		18	11	Donoher, Donald J. "Mickey"
	Georgia	NCAA	I		19	12	Durham, Hugh
	Holy Cross (MA)	NCAA	I		20	10	Blaney, George R.
	Temple	NCAA	I		20	8	Casey, Don
	Texas: El Paso	NCAA	I		18	12	Haskins, Donald L.
	Toledo	NCAA	I		21	10	Nichols, Robert J.
32	American	NCAA	I		24	6	Williams, Gary
	Clemson	NCAA	I		20	11	Foster, William C.
	Drake (IA)	NCAA	I		18	11	Ortegel, Bob
	Duquesne	NCAA	I		20	10	Rice, Mike
	Fordham	NCAA	I		19	9	Penders, Thomas V.
	Marquette	NCAA	I		20	11	Raymonds, Henry C. "Hank"
	North Carolina A&T	NCAA	I		21	8	Corbett, Donald
	Old Dominion	NCAA	I		18	10	Webb, Paul E.
	Pennsylvania	NCAA	I		20	8	Weinhauer, Bob
	Rhode Island	NCAA	I		21	8	Kraft, John J. "Jack"
	Saint John's (NY)	NCAA	I		17	11	Carnesecca, Louis P. "Lou"
	San Jose State	NCAA	I		21	9	Berry, William

F	School	Assn	Div	Bye	W	L	Coach
	South Florida	NCAA	I		18	11	Rose, Lee H.
	Southern Mississippi	NCAA	I		20	7	Turk, M. K.
	Texas: Arlington	NCAA	I		20	8	LeGrand, Bob "Snake"
	Texas: Pan American	NCAA	I		18	11	White, Bill

1982

F	School	Assn	Div	Bye	W	L	Coach
1	Bradley	NCAA	I		26	10	Versace, Dick
2	Purdue	NCAA	I		18	14	Keady, Lloyd Eugene "Gene"
3	Georgia	NCAA	I		19	12	Durham, Hugh
	Oklahoma	NCAA	I		22	8	Tubbs, Billy
8	Dayton	NCAA	I		21	9	Donoher, Donald J. "Mickey"
	Texas A&M	NCAA	I		20	11	Metcalf, Dr. Shelby R.
	Tulane	NCAA	I		19	9	Fowler, Ned
	Virginia Polytechnic	NCAA	I		20	11	Moir, Charles
16	California: Irvine	NCAA	I		23	7	Mulligan, William
	Illinois	NCAA	I		18	11	Henson, Louis R.
	Maryland	NCAA	I		16	13	Driesell, Charles G. "Lefty"
	Mississippi	NCAA	I		18	12	Weltlich, Robert
	Nevada: Las Vegas	NCAA	I		20	10	Tarkanian, Jerry
	Rutgers	NCAA	I		20	10	Young, Thomas J.
	Syracuse	NCAA	I		16	13	Boeheim, James A., Jr.
	Washington	NCAA	I		19	10	Harshman, Marvel K. "Marv"
32	American	NCAA	I		21	9	Williams, Gary
	Brigham Young	NCAA	I		17	13	Arnold, Frank H.
	Clemson	NCAA	I		14	14	Foster, William C.
	Connecticut	NCAA	I		17	11	Perno, Dominic P. "Dom"
	Fordham	NCAA	I		18	11	Penders, Thomas V.
	Iona	NCAA	I		24	9	Kennedy, Patrick
	Lamar	NCAA	I		22	7	Foster, Pat
	Long Island	NCAA	I		20	10	Lizzo, Paul
	Louisiana State	NCAA	I		14	14	Brown, Dale
	Murray State (KY)	NCAA	I		20	8	Greene, Ronald L.
	Oral Roberts	NCAA	I		18	12	Hayes, Ken
	Richmond	NCAA	I		18	11	Tarrant, Dick
	Saint Peter's	NCAA	I		20	9	Dukiet, Bob
	San Diego State	NCAA	I		20	9	Gaines, David "Smokey"
	Temple	NCAA	I		19	8	Casey, Don
	Western Kentucky	NCAA	I		19	10	Haskins, Clem S.

1983

F	School	Assn	Div	Bye	W	L	Coach
1	California State: Fresno	NCAA	I		25	10	Grant, Boyd "Tiny"
2	De Paul	NCAA	I		21	12	Meyer, Raymond J.
3	Nebraska	NCAA	I		22	10	Iba, Moe
	Wake Forest	NCAA	I		20	12	Tacy, Carl R.
8	Mississippi	NCAA	I		19	12	Hunt, Lee
	Oregon State	NCAA	I		20	11	Miller, Ralph H. "Cappy"
	South Carolina	NCAA	I		22	9	Foster, William E.
	Texas Christian	NCAA	I		23	11	Killingsworth, James
16	Arizona State	NCAA	I		19	14	Weinhauer, Bob
	Iona	NCAA	I		22	9	Kennedy, Patrick
	Michigan State	NCAA	I		17	13	Heathcote, George "Jud"
	New Orleans	NCAA	I		23	7	Smith, Donald W.

F	School	Assn	Div	Bye	W	L	Coach
	Northwestern (IL)	NCAA	I		17	13	Falk, Rich
	South Florida	NCAA	I		22	10	Rose, Lee H.
	Vanderbilt	NCAA	I		19	14	Newton, Charles M. "CM"
	Virginia Polytechnic	NCAA	I		23	11	Moir, Charles
32	Alabama State	NCAA	I		22	6	Oliver, James V.
	Bowling Green State	NCAA	I		21	9	Weinert, John P.
	California State: Fullerton	NCAA	I		21	8	McQuarn, George
	East Tennessee State	NCAA	I		22	9	Dowd, Barry
	Fordham	NCAA	I		19	11	Penders, Thomas V.
	Idaho	NCAA	I		20	9	Monson, Don
	Louisiana State	NCAA	I		19	13	Brown, Dale
	Minnesota	NCAA	I		18	13	Dutcher, James D.
	Murray State (KY)	NCAA	I		21	8	Greene, Ronald L.
	Notre Dame (IN)	NCAA	I		19	10	Phelps, Richard F. "Digger"
	Old Dominion	NCAA	I		19	10	Webb, Paul E.
	Saint Bonaventure	NCAA	I		20	10	O'Brien, James J.
	Texas: El Paso	NCAA	I		19	10	Haskins, Donald L.
	Tulane	NCAA	I		19	12	Fowler, Ned
	Tulsa	NCAA	I		19	12	Richardson, Nolan
	William & Mary	NCAA	I		20	9	Parkhill, Bruce

1984

F	School	Assn	Div	Bye	W	L	Coach
1	Michigan	NCAA	I		23	10	Frieder, Bill
2	Notre Dame (IN)	NCAA	I		21	12	Phelps, Richard F. "Digger"
3	Virginia Polytechnic	NCAA	I		22	13	Moir, Charles
4	Southwestern Louisiana	NCAA	I		23	10	Paschal, Bobby
8	Pittsburgh	NCAA	I		18	13	Chipman, Dr. Leroy
	Santa Clara	NCAA	I		22	10	Williams, Carroll M.
	Tennessee	NCAA	I		21	14	DeVoe, Donald E.
	Xavier (OH)	NCAA	I		22	11	Staak, Bob
16	Boston College	NCAA	I		18	12	Williams, Gary
	Florida State	NCAA	I		20	11	Williams, Joe L.
	Lamar	NCAA	I		26	5	Foster, Pat
	Marquette	NCAA	I		17	13	Majerus, Rick
	Nebraska	NCAA	I		18	12	Iba, Moe
	South Alabama	NCAA	I		22	8	Ellis, Cliff
	Tennessee: Chattanooga	NCAA	I		24	7	Arnold, Murray
	Weber State	NCAA	I		23	8	McCarthy, Neil N.
32	Creighton	NCAA	I		17	14	Reed, Willis, Jr.
	Florida	NCAA	I		16	13	Sloan, Norman L., Jr.
	Fordham	NCAA	I		19	15	Penders, Thomas V.
	Georgia	NCAA	I		17	13	Durham, Hugh
	Georgia Tech	NCAA	I		18	11	Cremins, Bobby
	Iowa State	NCAA	I		16	13	Orr, John M. "Johnny"
	La Salle	NCAA	I		20	11	Ervin, David "Lefty"
	New Mexico	NCAA	I		24	11	Colson, Gary W.
	North Carolina State	NCAA	I		19	14	Valvano, James T.
	Ohio State	NCAA	I		15	14	Miller, Eldon
	Old Dominion	NCAA	I		19	12	Webb, Paul E.
	Oregon	NCAA	I		16	13	Monson, Don

F	School	Assn	Div	Bye	W	L	Coach
	Saint Joseph's (PA)	NCAA	I		20	9	Boyle, Jim
	Saint Peter's	NCAA	I		23	6	Dukiet, Bob
	Utah State	NCAA	I		19	11	Tueller, Rod
	Wichita State	NCAA	I		18	12	Smithson, Eugene

1985

F	School	Assn	Div	Bye	W	L	Coach
1	California: Los Angeles	NCAA	I		21	12	Hazzard, Walter R., Jr.
2	Indiana	NCAA	I		19	14	Knight, Robert M.
3	Tennessee	NCAA	I		22	15	DeVoe, Donald E.
4	Louisville	NCAA	I		19	18	Crum, Denzil E. "Denny"
8	California State: Fresno	NCAA	I		23	9	Grant, Boyd "Tiny"
	Marquette	NCAA	I		20	11	Majerus, Rick
	Tennessee: Chattanooga	NCAA	I		24	8	Arnold, Murray
	Virginia	NCAA	I		17	16	Holland, M. Terrance "Terry"
16	Cincinnati	NCAA	I		17	14	Yates, Anthony
	Lamar	NCAA	I		20	12	Foster, Pat
	Nebraska	NCAA	I		16	14	Iba, Moe
	New Mexico	NCAA	I		19	13	Colson, Gary W.
	Richmond	NCAA	I		21	11	Tarrant, Dick
	Saint Joseph's (PA)	NCAA	I		19	12	Boyle, Jim
	South Florida	NCAA	I		18	12	Rose, Lee H.
	Southwestern Louisiana	NCAA	I		17	14	Paschal, Bobby
32	Alcorn State	NCAA	I		23	7	Whitney, David L., Sr. "Davey"
	Bradley	NCAA	I		17	13	Versace, Dick
	Butler (IN)	NCAA	I		19	10	Sexson, Joe
	Canisius	NCAA	I		20	10	Macarchuk, Nick, Jr.
	Clemson	NCAA	I		16	13	Ellis, Cliff
	Florida	NCAA	I		18	12	Sloan, Norman L., Jr.
	Fordham	NCAA	I		19	12	Penders, Thomas V.
	Houston	NCAA	I		16	14	Lewis, Guy V.
	Kent State	NCAA	I		17	13	McDonald, James Joseph
	Missouri	NCAA	I		18	14	Stewart, Norman E.
	Montana	NCAA	I		22	8	Montgomery, Mike
	Santa Clara	NCAA	I		20	9	Williams, Carroll M.
	Tennessee Tech	NCAA	I		19	9	Deaton, Tom
	Texas A&M	NCAA	I		19	11	Metcalf, Dr. Shelby R.
	Wake Forest	NCAA	I		15	14	Tacy, Carl R.
	West Virginia	NCAA	I		20	9	Catlett, Gale

1986

F	School	Assn	Div	Bye	W	L	Coach
1	Ohio State	NCAA	I		19	14	Miller, Eldon
2	Wyoming	NCAA	I		24	12	Brandenburg, Jim
3	Louisiana Tech	NCAA	I		20	14	Eagles, Tommy Joe
4	Florida	NCAA	I		19	14	Sloan, Norman L., Jr.
8	Brigham Young	NCAA	I		18	14	Anderson, Ladell
	Clemson	NCAA	I		19	15	Ellis, Cliff
	Providence	NCAA	I		17	14	Pitino, Richard A. "Rick"
	Southwest Missouri State	NCAA	I		24	8	Spoonhour, Charles
16	California: Irvine	NCAA	I		17	13	Mulligan, William
	George Mason	NCAA	I		20	12	Harrington, Joe
	Georgia	NCAA	I		17	13	Durham, Hugh
	Loyola Marymount	NCAA	I		19	11	Westhead, Paul W.

F	School	Assn	Div	Bye	W	L	Coach
	Marquette	NCAA	I		19	11	Majerus, Rick
	McNeese State	NCAA	I		21	11	Duhon, Glenn D.
	Texas	NCAA	I		19	12	Weltlich, Robert
	Texas Christian	NCAA	I		22	9	Killingsworth, James
32	Boston University	NCAA	I		21	10	Jarvis, Mike
	California	NCAA	I		19	10	Campanelli, Lou
	California: Los Angeles	NCAA	I		15	14	Hazzard, Walter R., Jr.
	Dayton	NCAA	I		17	13	Donoher, Donald J. "Mickey"
	Drake (IA)	NCAA	I		19	11	Garner, Gary
	Lamar	NCAA	I		18	12	Foster, Pat
	Middle Tennessee State	NCAA	I		23	11	Stewart, Bruce
	Montana	NCAA	I		21	11	Montgomery, Mike
	New Mexico	NCAA	I		17	14	Colson, Gary W.
	Northern Arizona	NCAA	I		19	10	Arnote, Jay
	Ohio University	NCAA	I		22	8	Nee, Danny
	Pittsburgh	NCAA	I		15	14	Chipman, Dr. Leroy
	Southern Methodist (TX)	NCAA	I		18	11	Bliss, David
	Southern Mississippi	NCAA	I		17	12	Turk, M. K.
	Tennessee: Chattanooga	NCAA	I		21	10	McCarthy, Mack
	Texas A&M	NCAA	I		20	12	Metcalf, Dr. Shelby R.

1987

F	School	Assn	Div	Bye	W	L	Coach
1	Southern Mississippi	NCAA	I		23	11	Turk, M. K.
2	La Salle	NCAA	I		20	13	Morris, William T. "Speedy"
3	Nebraska	NCAA	I		21	12	Nee, Danny
4	Arkansas: Little Rock	NCAA	I		26	11	Newell, Mike
8	California	NCAA	I		20	15	Campanelli, Lou
	Illinois State	NCAA	I		19	13	Donewald, Bob
	Vanderbilt	NCAA	I		18	16	Newton, Charles M. "CM"
	Washington	NCAA	I		20	15	Russo, Andy
16	Arkansas	NCAA	I		19	14	Richardson, Nolan
	Boise State	NCAA	I		22	8	Dye, Bobby
	Cleveland State (OH)	NCAA	I		25	8	Mackey, Kevin
	Florida State	NCAA	I		19	11	Kennedy, Patrick
	Niagara	NCAA	I		21	10	Walker, Andy
	Oregon State	NCAA	I		19	11	Miller, Ralph H. "Cappy"
	Saint Louis	NCAA	I		25	10	Grawer, Richard "Rich"
	Stephen F Austin State	NCAA	I		22	8	Miller, Harry E.
32	Akron	NCAA	I		21	9	Huggins, Robert
	Arkansas State	NCAA	I		21	13	Catalina, Nelson
	Baylor	NCAA	I		18	13	Iba, Clarence Eugene "Gene"
	California State: Fullerton	NCAA	I		17	13	McQuarn, George
	Jacksonville (FL)	NCAA	I		19	11	Wenzel, Robert
	James Madison	NCAA	I		20	10	Thurston, John
	Marquette	NCAA	I		16	13	Dukiet, Bob
	Mississippi	NCAA	I		15	15	Murphy, Ed
	Montana State	NCAA	I		21	8	Starner, Stu
	New Mexico	NCAA	I		25	10	Colson, Gary W.
	Rhode Island	NCAA	I		20	10	Penders, Thomas V.
	Saint Peter's	NCAA	I		21	8	Fiore, Ted

F	School	Assn	Div	Bye	W	L	Coach
	Seton Hall	NCAA	I		15	14	Carlesimo, Peter J. "PJ"
	Tennessee: Chattanooga	NCAA	I		21	8	McCarthy, Mack
	Utah	NCAA	I		17	13	Archibald, Lynn
	Villanova	NCAA	I		15	16	Massimino, Roland V. "Rollie"

1988

F	School	Assn	Div	Bye	W	L	Coach
1	Connecticut	NCAA	I		20	14	Calhoun, James A.
2	Ohio State	NCAA	I		16	11	Williams, Gary
3	Colorado State	NCAA	I		22	13	Grant, Boyd "Tiny"
4	Boston College	NCAA	I		18	15	O'Brien, James J.
8	Arkansas State	NCAA	I		21	14	Catalina, Nelson
	Middle Tennessee State	NCAA	I		23	11	Stewart, Bruce
	New Mexico	NCAA	I		22	14	Colson, Gary W.
	Virginia Commonwealth	NCAA	I		23	12	Pollio, Mike
16	Cleveland State (OH)	NCAA	I		22	8	Mackey, Kevin
	Evansville	NCAA	I		21	8	Crews, Jim
	Georgia	NCAA	I		20	16	Durham, Hugh
	Houston	NCAA	I		18	13	Foster, Pat
	Louisiana Tech	NCAA	I		22	9	Eagles, Tommy Joe
	Oregon	NCAA	I		16	14	Monson, Don
	Southern Mississippi	NCAA	I		19	11	Turk, M. K.
	Stanford	NCAA	I		21	12	Montgomery, Mike
32	Arkansas: Little Rock	NCAA	I		24	7	Newell, Mike
	California State: Long Beach	NCAA	I		17	12	Harrington, Joe
	Clemson	NCAA	I		14	15	Ellis, Cliff
	Fordham	NCAA	I		18	15	Macarchuk, Nick, Jr.
	Georgia Southern	NCAA	I		24	7	Kerns, Frank
	Illinois State	NCAA	I		18	13	Donewald, Bob
	Marshall	NCAA	I		24	8	Huckabay, Rick
	New Orleans	NCAA	I		21	11	Polis, Art
	Northeast Louisiana	NCAA	I		21	9	Vining, Mike
	Old Dominion	NCAA	I		18	12	Young, Thomas J.
	Pepperdine	NCAA	I		17	13	Harrick, Jim
	Santa Clara	NCAA	I		20	11	Williams, Carroll M.
	Siena (NY)	NCAA	I		23	6	Deane, Mike
	Tennessee	NCAA	I		16	13	DeVoe, Donald E.
	Utah	NCAA	I		19	11	Archibald, Lynn
	West Virginia	NCAA	I		18	14	Catlett, Gale

1989

F	School	Assn	Div	Bye	W	L	Coach
1	Saint John's (NY)	NCAA	I		20	13	Carnesecca, Louis P. "Lou"
2	Saint Louis	NCAA	I		27	10	Grawer, Richard "Rich"
3	Alabama: Birmingham	NCAA	I		22	12	Bartow, B. Gene
4	Michigan State	NCAA	I		18	15	Heathcote, George "Jud"
8	Connecticut	NCAA	I		18	13	Calhoun, James A.
	New Mexico	NCAA	I		22	11	Bliss, David
	Ohio State	NCAA	I		19	15	Williams, Gary
	Villanova	NCAA	I		18	16	Massimino, Roland V. "Rollie"
16	California	NCAA	I		20	13	Campanelli, Lou
	Nebraska	NCAA	I		17	16	Nee, Danny
	Oklahoma State	NCAA	I		17	13	Hamilton, Leonard
	Pennsylvania State	NCAA	I		20	12	Parkhill, Bruce

F	School	Assn	Div	Bye	W	L	Coach
	Pepperdine	NCAA	I		20	13	Asbury, Tom
	Richmond	NCAA	I		21	10	Tarrant, Dick
	Wichita State	NCAA	I		19	11	Fogler, Eddie
	Wisconsin	NCAA	I		18	12	Yoder, Steve
32	Akron	NCAA	I		21	8	Huggins, Robert
	Arkansas State	NCAA	I		20	10	Catalina, Nelson
	Boise State	NCAA	I		23	7	Dye, Bobby
	California: Santa Barbara	NCAA	I		21	9	Pimm, Jerry
	Georgia Southern	NCAA	I		23	6	Kerns, Frank
	Hawaii	NCAA	I		17	13	Wallace, Riley
	Kent State	NCAA	I		20	11	McDonald, James Joseph
	Mississippi	NCAA	I		15	15	Murphy, Ed
	Murray State (KY)	NCAA	I		19	11	Newton, Steve
	New Mexico State	NCAA	I		21	11	McCarthy, Neil N.
	New Orleans	NCAA	I		19	11	Floyd, Tim
	North Carolina: Charlotte	NCAA	I		17	12	Mullins, Jeffrey V., Jr.
	Saint Peter's	NCAA	I		22	9	Fiore, Ted
	Santa Clara	NCAA	I		20	11	Williams, Carroll M.
	Southern Illinois	NCAA	I		20	14	Herrin, Richard "Rich"
	Temple	NCAA	I		18	12	Chaney, John

1990

F	School	Assn	Div	Bye	W	L	Coach
1	Vanderbilt	NCAA	I		21	14	Fogler, Eddie
2	Saint Louis	NCAA	I		21	12	Grawer, Richard "Rich"
3	Pennsylvania State	NCAA	I		25	9	Parkhill, Bruce
4	New Mexico	NCAA	I		20	14	Bliss, David
8	De Paul	NCAA	I		20	15	Meyer, Joseph E. "Joey"
	Hawaii	NCAA	I		25	10	Wallace, Riley
	New Orleans	NCAA	I		21	11	Floyd, Tim
	Rutgers	NCAA	I		18	17	Wenzel, Robert
16	California State: Long Beach	NCAA	I		23	9	Harrington, Joe
	Cincinnati	NCAA	I		20	14	Huggins, Robert
	Fordham	NCAA	I		20	13	Macarchuk, Nick, Jr.
	Maryland	NCAA	I		19	14	Williams, Gary
	Mississippi State	NCAA	I		16	14	Williams, Richard
	Oklahoma State	NCAA	I		17	14	Hamilton, Leonard
	Tennessee	NCAA	I		16	14	Houston, Wade
	Wisconsin: Green Bay	NCAA	I		24	8	Bennett, Richard
32	Arizona State	NCAA	I		15	16	Frieder, Bill
	Baylor	NCAA	I		16	14	Iba, Clarence Eugene "Gene"
	Bowling Green State	NCAA	I		18	11	Larranaga, Jim
	Creighton	NCAA	I		21	12	Barone, Anthony A. "Tony"
	Holy Cross (MA)	NCAA	I		24	6	Blaney, George R.
	James Madison	NCAA	I		20	11	Driesell, Charles G. "Lefty"
	Kent State	NCAA	I		21	8	McDonald, James Joseph
	Louisiana Tech	NCAA	I		20	8	Lloyd, Jerry
	Marquette	NCAA	I		15	14	O'Neill, Kevin
	Massachusetts	NCAA	I		17	14	Calipari, John
	Memphis	NCAA	I		18	12	Finch, Larry O.
	Oregon	NCAA	I		15	14	Monson, Don

F	School	Assn	Div	Bye	W	L	Coach
	Southern Illinois	NCAA	I		26	8	Herrin, Richard "Rich"
	Southern: Baton Rouge	NCAA	I		25	6	Jobe, Ben
	Stanford	NCAA	I		18	12	Montgomery, Mike
	Tulsa	NCAA	I		17	13	Barnett, J. D.

1991

F	School	Assn	Div	Bye	W	L	Coach
1	Stanford	NCAA	I		20	13	Montgomery, Mike
2	Oklahoma	NCAA	I		20	15	Tubbs, Billy
3	Colorado	NCAA	I		19	14	Harrington, Joe
4	Massachusetts	NCAA	I		20	13	Calipari, John
8	Arkansas State	NCAA	I		23	9	Catalina, Nelson
	Providence	NCAA	I		19	13	Barnes, Richard D. "Rick"
	Siena (NY)	NCAA	I		25	10	Deane, Mike
	Southern Illinois	NCAA	I		18	14	Herrin, Richard "Rich"
16	Cincinnati	NCAA	I		18	12	Huggins, Robert
	Fordham	NCAA	I		25	8	Macarchuk, Nick, Jr.
	Memphis	NCAA	I		17	15	Finch, Larry O.
	South Carolina	NCAA	I		20	13	Felton, George
	Southwest Missouri State	NCAA	I		22	12	Spoonhour, Charles
	West Virginia	NCAA	I		17	14	Catlett, Gale
	Wisconsin	NCAA	I		15	15	Yoder, Steve
	Wyoming	NCAA	I		20	12	Dees, Benny
32	Alabama: Birmingham	NCAA	I		18	13	Bartow, B. Gene
	Ball State	NCAA	I		21	10	Hunsaker, Dick
	Boise State	NCAA	I		18	11	Dye, Bobby
	Bowling Green State	NCAA	I		17	13	Larranaga, Jim
	Butler (IN)	NCAA	I		18	11	Collier, Barry
	Coppin State	NCAA	I		19	11	Mitchell, Ronald C. "Fang"
	Fairleigh Dickinson: Teaneck	NCAA	I		22	9	Green, Tom
	Furman	NCAA	I		20	9	Estes, George "Butch"
	George Washington	NCAA	I		19	12	Jarvis, Mike
	Houston	NCAA	I		18	11	Foster, Pat
	James Madison	NCAA	I		19	10	Driesell, Charles G. "Lefty"
	La Salle	NCAA	I		19	10	Morris, William T. "Speedy"
	Michigan	NCAA	I		14	15	Fisher, Stephen L.
	Rice	NCAA	I		16	14	Thompson, Scott
	South Florida	NCAA	I		19	11	Paschal, Bobby
	Tulsa	NCAA	I		18	12	Barnett, J. D.

1992

F	School	Assn	Div	Bye	W	L	Coach
1	Virginia	NCAA	I		20	13	Jones, Jeffrey A.
2	Notre Dame (IN)	NCAA	I		18	15	MacLeod, John M.
3	Utah	NCAA	I		24	11	Majerus, Rick
4	Florida	NCAA	I		19	14	Kruger, Lon
8	Manhattan	NCAA	I		25	9	Lappas, Steve
	New Mexico	NCAA	I		20	13	Bliss, David
	Purdue	NCAA	I		18	15	Keady, Lloyd Eugene "Gene"
	Rhode Island	NCAA	I		22	10	Skinner, Albert L., Jr.
16	Arizona State	NCAA	I		19	14	Frieder, Bill
	Boston College	NCAA	I		17	14	O'Brien, James J.
	Kansas State	NCAA	I		16	14	Altman, Dana
	Pittsburgh	NCAA	I		18	16	Evans, Paul

F	School	Assn	Div	Bye	W	L	Coach
	Rutgers	NCAA	I		16	15	Wenzel, Robert
	Tennessee	NCAA	I		19	15	Houston, Wade
	Texas Christian	NCAA	I		23	11	Iba, Moe
	Washington State	NCAA	I		22	11	Sampson, Kelvin
32	Alabama: Birmingham	NCAA	I		20	9	Bartow, B. Gene
	Ball State	NCAA	I		24	9	Hunsaker, Dick
	Butler (IN)	NCAA	I		21	10	Collier, Barry
	California State: Long Beach	NCAA	I		18	12	Greenberg, Seth
	California: Santa Barbara	NCAA	I		20	9	Pimm, Jerry
	James Madison	NCAA	I		21	11	Driesell, Charles G. "Lefty"
	Louisiana Tech	NCAA	I		22	9	Lloyd, Jerry
	Minnesota	NCAA	I		16	16	Haskins, Clem S.
	Pennsylvania State	NCAA	I		21	8	Parkhill, Bruce
	Richmond	NCAA	I		22	8	Tarrant, Dick
	Southern Illinois	NCAA	I		22	8	Herrin, Richard "Rich"
	Vanderbilt	NCAA	I		15	15	Fogler, Eddie
	Villanova	NCAA	I		14	15	Massimino, Roland V. "Rollie"
	Western Kentucky	NCAA	I		21	11	Willard, Ralph
	Western Michigan	NCAA	I		21	9	Donewald, Bob
	Wisconsin: Green Bay	NCAA	I		25	5	Bennett, Richard

1993

F	School	Assn	Div	Bye	W	L	Coach
1	Minnesota	NCAA	I		22	10	Haskins, Clem S.
2	Georgetown (DC)	NCAA	I		20	13	Thompson, John R., Jr.
3	Alabama: Birmingham	NCAA	I		21	14	Bartow, B. Gene
4	Providence	NCAA	I		20	13	Barnes, Richard D. "Rick"
8	Boston College	NCAA	I		18	13	O'Brien, James J.
	Miami (OH)	NCAA	I		22	9	Wright, Joseph A. "Joby"
	Southern California	NCAA	I		18	12	Raveling, George
	Southwest Missouri State	NCAA	I		20	11	Bernsen, Mark
16	Clemson	NCAA	I		17	13	Ellis, Cliff
	Jackson State (MS)	NCAA	I		25	9	Stoglin, Lee Andrew "Andy"
	Oklahoma	NCAA	I		20	12	Tubbs, Billy
	Old Dominion	NCAA	I		21	8	Purnell, Oliver
	Pepperdine	NCAA	I		23	8	Asbury, Tom
	Rice	NCAA	I		18	10	Thompson, Scott
	Texas: El Paso	NCAA	I		21	13	Haskins, Donald L.
	West Virginia	NCAA	I		17	12	Catlett, Gale
32	Alabama	NCAA	I		16	13	Hobbs, David
	Arizona State	NCAA	I		18	10	Frieder, Bill
	Auburn	NCAA	I		15	12	Eagles, Tommy Joe
	California: Santa Barbara	NCAA	I		18	11	Pimm, Jerry
	Connecticut	NCAA	I		15	13	Calhoun, James A.
	Florida	NCAA	I		16	12	Kruger, Lon
	Georgia	NCAA	I		15	14	Durham, Hugh
	Houston	NCAA	I		21	9	Foster, Pat
	James Madison	NCAA	I		21	9	Driesell, Charles G. "Lefty"
	Michigan State	NCAA	I		15	13	Heathcote, George "Jud"
	Nevada: Las Vegas	NCAA	I		21	8	Massimino, Roland V. "Rollie"
	Niagara	NCAA	I		23	7	Armstrong, Jack

F	School	Assn	Div	Bye	W	L	Coach
	Ohio State	NCAA	I		15	13	Ayers, Randy
	Saint Joseph's (PA)	NCAA	I		18	11	Griffin, John
	Virginia Commonwealth	NCAA	I		20	10	Smith, Charles H. "Sonny"
	Wisconsin	NCAA	I		14	14	Jackson, Stu

1994

F	School	Assn	Div	Bye	W	L	Coach
1	Villanova	NCAA	I		20	12	Lappas, Steve
2	Vanderbilt	NCAA	I		20	12	Van Breda Kolff, Jan M.
3	Siena (NY)	NCAA	I		25	8	Deane, Mike
4	Kansas State	NCAA	I		20	14	Altman, Dana
8	Bradley	NCAA	I		23	8	Molinari, Jim
	California State: Fresno	NCAA	I		21	11	Colson, Gary W.
	Clemson	NCAA	I		18	16	Ellis, Cliff
	Xavier (OH)	NCAA	I		22	8	Gillen, Pete
16	Brigham Young	NCAA	I		22	10	Reid, Roger
	Duquesne	NCAA	I		17	13	Carroll, John
	Gonzaga	NCAA	I		22	8	Fitzgerald, Dan
	New Orleans	NCAA	I		20	10	Floyd, Tim
	Northwestern (IL)	NCAA	I		15	14	Swanson, Paul
	Old Dominion	NCAA	I		21	10	Purnell, Oliver
	Tulane	NCAA	I		18	11	Clark, Perry
	West Virginia	NCAA	I		17	12	Catlett, Gale
32	Arizona State	NCAA	I		15	13	Frieder, Bill
	Canisius	NCAA	I		22	7	Beilein, John
	Davidson	NCAA	I		22	8	McKillop, Bob
	De Paul	NCAA	I		16	12	Meyer, Joseph E. "Joey"
	Evansville	NCAA	I		21	11	Crews, Jim
	Georgia Tech	NCAA	I		16	13	Cremins, Bobby
	Manhattan	NCAA	I		19	11	Fraschilla, Fran
	Miami (OH)	NCAA	I		19	11	Sendek, Herb
	Mississippi State	NCAA	I		18	11	Williams, Richard
	Murray State (KY)	NCAA	I		23	6	Edgar, Scott
	North Carolina: Charlotte	NCAA	I		16	13	Mullins, Jeffrey V., Jr.
	Oklahoma	NCAA	I		15	13	Tubbs, Billy
	Southern California	NCAA	I		16	12	Raveling, George
	Southern Mississippi	NCAA	I		15	15	Turk, M. K.
	Stanford	NCAA	I		17	11	Montgomery, Mike
	Texas A&M	NCAA	I		19	11	Barone, Anthony A. "Tony"

1995

F	School	Assn	Div	Bye	W	L	Coach
1	Virginia Polytechnic	NCAA	I		25	10	Foster, William C.
2	Marquette	NCAA	I		21	12	Deane, Mike
3	Pennsylvania State	NCAA	I		21	11	Parkhill, Bruce
4	Canisius	NCAA	I		21	14	Beilein, John
8	Iowa	NCAA	I		21	12	Davis, Dr. Thomas
	New Mexico State	NCAA	I		25	10	McCarthy, Neil N.
	South Florida	NCAA	I		18	12	Paschal, Bobby
	Washington State	NCAA	I		18	12	Eastman, Kevin
16	Bradley	NCAA	I		20	10	Molinari, Jim
	Coppin State	NCAA	I		21	10	Mitchell, Ronald C. "Fang"
	Illinois State	NCAA	I		20	13	Stallings, Kevin
	Nebraska	NCAA	I		18	14	Nee, Danny

F	School	Assn	Div	Bye	W	L	Coach
	Ohio University	NCAA	I		24	10	Hunter, Larry
	Providence	NCAA	I		17	13	Gillen, Pete
	Saint Bonaventure	NCAA	I		18	13	Baron, James E.
	Texas: El Paso	NCAA	I		20	10	Haskins, Donald L.
32	Auburn	NCAA	I		16	13	Ellis, Cliff
	Charleston (SC)	NCAA	I		23	6	Kresse, John
	Clemson	NCAA	I		15	13	Barnes, Richard D. "Rick"
	Colorado	NCAA	I		15	13	Harrington, Joe
	De Paul	NCAA	I		17	11	Meyer, Joseph E. "Joey"
	Eastern Michigan	NCAA	I		20	10	Braun, Ben
	George Washington	NCAA	I		18	14	Jarvis, Mike
	Georgia	NCAA	I		18	10	Durham, Hugh
	Miami (FL)	NCAA	I		15	13	Hamilton, Leonard
	Montana	NCAA	I		21	9	Taylor, Blaine
	Saint John's (NY)	NCAA	I		14	14	Mahoney, Brian C.
	Saint Joseph's (PA)	NCAA	I		17	12	Griffin, John
	Seton Hall	NCAA	I		16	14	Blaney, George R.
	Southern Mississippi	NCAA	I		17	13	Turk, M. K.
	Texas Tech	NCAA	I		20	10	Dickey, James
	Utah State	NCAA	I		21	8	Eustachy, Larry

1996

F	School	Assn	Div	Bye	W	L	Coach
1	Nebraska	NCAA	I		21	14	Nee, Danny
2	Saint Joseph's (PA)	NCAA	I		19	13	Martelli, Phil
3	Tulane	NCAA	I		22	10	Clark, Perry
4	Alabama	NCAA	I		19	13	Hobbs, David
8	California State: Fresno	NCAA	I		22	11	Tarkanian, Jerry
	Illinois State	NCAA	I		22	12	Stallings, Kevin
	Rhode Island	NCAA	I		20	14	Skinner, Albert L., Jr.
	South Carolina	NCAA	I		19	12	Fogler, Eddie
16	Charleston (SC)	NCAA	I		25	4	Kresse, John
	Michigan State	NCAA	I		16	16	Izzo, Tom
	Minnesota	NCAA	I		19	13	Haskins, Clem S.
	Missouri	NCAA	I		18	15	Stewart, Norman E.
	Providence	NCAA	I		18	12	Gillen, Pete
	Vanderbilt	NCAA	I		18	14	Van Breda Kolff, Jan M.
	Washington State	NCAA	I		17	12	Eastman, Kevin
	Wisconsin	NCAA	I		17	15	Bennett, Richard
32	Arkansas: Little Rock	NCAA	I		23	7	Sanderson, Winfrey "Wimp"
	Auburn	NCAA	I		19	13	Ellis, Cliff
	Colorado State	NCAA	I		18	12	Morrill, Stew
	Davidson	NCAA	I		25	5	McKillop, Bob
	Fairfield	NCAA	I		20	10	Cormier, Paul
	Gonzaga	NCAA	I		21	9	Fitzgerald, Dan
	Illinois	NCAA	I		18	13	Henson, Louis R.
	Iona	NCAA	I		21	8	Welsh, Tim
	Manhattan	NCAA	I		17	12	Fraschilla, Fran
	Marist	NCAA	I		22	7	Magarity, David
	Miami (OH)	NCAA	I		21	8	Sendek, Herb
	Mount Saint Mary's (MD)	NCAA	I		21	8	Phelan, James J.

F	School	Assn	Div	Bye	W	L	Coach
	Murray State (KY)	NCAA	I		19	10	Gottfried, Mark
	Saint Louis	NCAA	I		16	14	Spoonhour, Charles
	Tennessee	NCAA	I		14	15	O'Neill, Kevin
	Washington	NCAA	I		16	12	Bender, Robert M., Jr.

1997

F	School	Assn	Div	Bye	W	L	Coach
1	Michigan	NCAA	I		24	11	Fisher, Stephen L.
2	Florida State	NCAA	I		20	12	Kennedy, Patrick
3	Connecticut	NCAA	I		18	15	Calhoun, James A.
4	Arkansas	NCAA	I		18	14	Richardson, Nolan
8	Nebraska	NCAA	I		18	15	Nee, Danny
	Nevada: Las Vegas	NCAA	I		22	10	Bayno, Bill
	Notre Dame (IN)	NCAA	I		16	14	MacLeod, John M.
	West Virginia	NCAA	I		21	10	Catlett, Gale
16	Bradley	NCAA	I		17	13	Molinari, Jim
	Hawaii	NCAA	I		21	8	Wallace, Riley
	Michigan State	NCAA	I		17	12	Izzo, Tom
	Nevada	NCAA	I		20	10	Foster, Pat
	North Carolina State	NCAA	I		17	15	Sendek, Herb
	Oklahoma State	NCAA	I		17	15	Sutton, Eddie
	Pittsburgh	NCAA	I		17	15	Willard, Ralph
	Texas Christian	NCAA	I		22	13	Tubbs, Billy
32	Alabama: Birmingham	NCAA	I		18	14	Bartow, Murry
	Bowling Green State	NCAA	I		21	10	Larranaga, Jim
	California State: Fresno	NCAA	I		19	12	Tarkanian, Jerry
	Drexel	NCAA	I		22	9	Herrion, William R.
	George Washington	NCAA	I		15	14	Jarvis, Mike
	Iona	NCAA	I		22	8	Welsh, Tim
	Memphis	NCAA	I		16	15	Finch, Larry O.
	Miami (FL)	NCAA	I		16	13	Hamilton, Leonard
	New Orleans	NCAA	I		22	7	Price, George "Tic"
	Northern Arizona	NCAA	I		20	7	Howland, Ben
	Oral Roberts	NCAA	I		19	7	Self, Bill
	Oregon	NCAA	I		17	11	Green, Jerry
	Southwest Missouri State	NCAA	I		24	9	Alford, Stephen T.
	Syracuse	NCAA	I		19	13	Boeheim, James A., Jr.
	Tulane	NCAA	I		19	11	Clark, Perry
	Washington	NCAA	I		17	11	Bender, Robert M., Jr.

1998

F	School	Assn	Div	Bye	W	L	Coach
1	Minnesota	NCAA	I		20	15	Haskins, Clem S.
2	Pennsylvania State	NCAA	I		19	13	Dunn, Jerry
3	Georgia	NCAA	I		20	15	Jirsa, Ron
4	California State: Fresno	NCAA	I		21	13	Tarkanian, Jerry
8	Georgia Tech	NCAA	I		19	14	Cremins, Bobby
	Hawaii	NCAA	I		21	9	Wallace, Riley
	Marquette	NCAA	I		20	11	Deane, Mike
	Vanderbilt	NCAA	I		20	13	Van Breda Kolff, Jan M.
16	Alabama: Birmingham	NCAA	I		21	12	Bartow, Murry
	Auburn	NCAA	I		16	13	Ellis, Cliff
	Dayton	NCAA	I		21	12	Purnell, Oliver
	Georgetown (DC)	NCAA	I		16	15	Thompson, John R., Jr.

F	School	Assn	Div	Bye	W	L	Coach
	Gonzaga	NCAA	I		24	10	Monson, Don
	Memphis	NCAA	I		17	12	Price, George "Tic"
	North Carolina State	NCAA	I		17	15	Sendek, Herb
	Wake Forest	NCAA	I		16	14	Odom, Dave
32	Arizona State	NCAA	I		18	14	Newman, Don
	Ball State	NCAA	I		21	8	McCallum, Ray
	Colorado State	NCAA	I		20	9	Morrill, Stew
	Creighton	NCAA	I		18	10	Altman, Dana
	Florida	NCAA	I		14	15	Donovan, William J. "Billy"
	Iowa	NCAA	I		20	11	Davis, Dr. Thomas
	Kansas State	NCAA	I		17	12	Asbury, Tom
	Long Island	NCAA	I		21	11	Haskins, Ray
	Missouri	NCAA	I		17	15	Stewart, Norman E.
	North Carolina: Wilmington	NCAA	I		20	11	Wainwright, Jerry
	Pacific (CA)	NCAA	I		24	10	Thomason, Bob
	Rider	NCAA	I		18	10	Harnum, Donald
	Saint Bonaventure	NCAA	I		17	15	Baron, James E.
	Seton Hall	NCAA	I		15	15	Amaker, Tommy
	Southern Mississippi	NCAA	I		22	11	Green, James
	Wyoming	NCAA	I		19	9	Shyatt, Larry

School Participation History

Year	Assn	Div	F	Bye	#T	W	L	Coach
AKRON								
1987	NCAA	I	32		32	21	9	Huggins, Robert
1989	NCAA	I	32		32	21	8	Huggins, Robert
ALABAMA								
1979	NCAA	I	3		24	22	11	Newton, Charles M. "CM"
1973	NCAA	I	4		16	22	8	Newton, Charles M. "CM"
1977	NCAA	I	4		16	25	6	Newton, Charles M. "CM"
1996	NCAA	I	4		32	19	13	Hobbs, David
1980	NCAA	I	16		32	18	12	Newton, Charles M. "CM"
1981	NCAA	I	16		32	18	11	Sanderson, Winfrey "Wimp"
1993	NCAA	I	32		32	16	13	Hobbs, David
ALABAMA STATE								
1983	NCAA	I	32		32	22	6	Oliver, James V.
ALABAMA: BIRMINGHAM								
1989	NCAA	I	3		32	22	12	Bartow, B. Gene
1993	NCAA	I	3		32	21	14	Bartow, B. Gene
1998	NCAA	I	16		32	21	12	Bartow, Murry
1980	NCAA	I	32		32	18	12	Bartow, B. Gene
1991	NCAA	I	32		32	18	13	Bartow, B. Gene
1992	NCAA	I	32		32	20	9	Bartow, B. Gene
1997	NCAA	I	32		32	18	14	Bartow, Murry
ALCORN STATE								
1979	NCAA	I	12		24	28	1	Whitney, David L., Sr. "Davey"
1985	NCAA	I	32		32	23	7	Whitney, David L., Sr. "Davey"

Year	Assn	Div	F	Bye	#T	W	L	Coach
AMERICAN								
1973	NCAA	I	16		16	21	5	Young, Thomas J.
1981	NCAA	I	32		32	24	6	Williams, Gary
1982	NCAA	I	32		32	21	9	Williams, Gary
ARIZONA								
1946	NCAA		8		8	25	5	Enke, Fred A.
1951	NCAA		8	To R8	12	24	6	Enke, Fred A.
1950	NCAA		12		12	26	5	Enke, Fred A.
ARIZONA STATE								
1983	NCAA	I	16		32	19	14	Weinhauer, Bob
1992	NCAA	I	16		32	19	14	Frieder, Bill
1990	NCAA	I	32		32	15	16	Frieder, Bill
1993	NCAA	I	32		32	18	10	Frieder, Bill
1994	NCAA	I	32		32	15	13	Frieder, Bill
1998	NCAA	I	32		32	18	14	Newman, Don
ARKANSAS								
1997	NCAA	I	4		32	18	14	Richardson, Nolan
1987	NCAA	I	16		32	19	14	Richardson, Nolan
ARKANSAS STATE								
1988	NCAA	I	8		32	21	14	Catalina, Nelson
1991	NCAA	I	8		32	23	9	Catalina, Nelson
1987	NCAA	I	32		32	21	13	Catalina, Nelson
1989	NCAA	I	32		32	20	10	Catalina, Nelson
ARKANSAS: LITTLE ROCK								
1987	NCAA	I	4		32	26	11	Newell, Mike
1988	NCAA	I	32		32	24	7	Newell, Mike
1996	NCAA	I	32		32	23	7	Sanderson, Winfrey "Wimp"
ARMY								
1964	NCAA	I	3		12	19	7	Locke, Taylor O. "Tates"
1965	NCAA	I	3		14	21	8	Locke, Taylor O. "Tates"
1970	NCAA	I	3		16	22	6	Knight, Robert M.
1966	NCAA	I	4		14	18	8	Knight, Robert M.
1969	NCAA	I	4		16	18	10	Knight, Robert M.
1961	NCAA	I	12		12	17	7	Hunter, George E.
1968	NCAA	I	16		16	20	5	Knight, Robert M.
1978	NCAA	I	16		16	19	9	Krzyzewski, Michael W.
AUBURN								
1998	NCAA	I	16		32	16	13	Ellis, Cliff
1993	NCAA	I	32		32	15	12	Eagles, Tommy Joe
1995	NCAA	I	32		32	16	13	Ellis, Cliff
1996	NCAA	I	32		32	19	13	Ellis, Cliff
BALL STATE								
1991	NCAA	I	32		32	21	10	Hunsaker, Dick
1992	NCAA	I	32		32	24	9	Hunsaker, Dick
1998	NCAA	I	32		32	21	8	McCallum, Ray

Year	Assn	Div	F	Bye	#T	W	L	Coach
BAYLOR								
1987	NCAA	I	32		32	18	13	Iba, Clarence Eugene "Gene"
1990	NCAA	I	32		32	16	14	Iba, Clarence Eugene "Gene"
BELOIT								
1951	NCAA		12		12	18	5	Stanley, Dolph
BOISE STATE								
1987	NCAA	I	16		32	22	8	Dye, Bobby
1989	NCAA	I	32		32	23	7	Dye, Bobby
1991	NCAA	I	32		32	18	11	Dye, Bobby
BOSTON COLLEGE								
1969	NCAA	I	2		16	24	4	Cousy, Robert J.
1974	NCAA	I	3		16	21	9	Zuffelato, Bob
1988	NCAA	I	4		32	18	15	O'Brien, James J.
1966	NCAA	I	8		14	21	5	Cousy, Robert J.
1993	NCAA	I	8		32	18	13	O'Brien, James J.
1965	NCAA	I	14		14	21	7	Cousy, Robert J.
1980	NCAA	I	16		32	19	10	Davis, Dr. Thomas
1984	NCAA	I	16		32	18	12	Williams, Gary
1992	NCAA	I	16		32	17	14	O'Brien, James J.
BOSTON UNIVERSITY								
1980	NCAA	I	32		32	21	9	Pitino, Richard A. "Rick"
1986	NCAA	I	32		32	21	10	Jarvis, Mike
BOWLING GREEN STATE								
1945	NCAA		2		8	24	4	Anderson, W. Harold "Andy"
1949	NCAA		3		12	24	7	Anderson, W. Harold "Andy"
1944	NCAA		8		8	22	4	Anderson, W. Harold "Andy"
1946	NCAA		8		8	27	5	Anderson, W. Harold "Andy"
1948	NCAA		8		8	27	6	Anderson, W. Harold "Andy"
1954	NCAA		8		12	17	7	Anderson, W. Harold "Andy"
1980	NCAA	I	32		32	20	10	Weinert, John P.
1983	NCAA	I	32		32	21	9	Weinert, John P.
1990	NCAA	I	32		32	18	11	Larranaga, Jim
1991	NCAA	I	32		32	17	13	Larranaga, Jim
1997	NCAA	I	32		32	22	10	Larranaga, Jim
BRADLEY								
1957	NCAA	I	1	To R8	12	22	7	Orsborn, Charles K. "Chuck"
1960	NCAA	I	1	To R8	12	22	7	Orsborn, Charles K. "Chuck"
1964	NCAA	I	1	To R8	12	23	6	Orsborn, Charles K. "Chuck"
1982	NCAA	I	1		32	26	10	Versace, Dick
1950	NCAA		2	To R8	12	32	5	Anderson, Forrest A. "Forddy"
1959	NCAA	I	2	To R8	12	25	4	Orsborn, Charles K. "Chuck"
1939	NCAA		3	To R4	6	19	3	Robertson, Alfred J.
1949	NCAA		4		12	27	8	Anderson, Forrest A. "Forddy"
1938	NCAA		6		6	18	2	Robertson, Alfred J.
1947	NCAA		8		8	25	7	Robertson, Alfred J.
1958	NCAA	I	8	To R8	12	20	7	Orsborn, Charles K. "Chuck"
1962	NCAA	I	8	To R8	12	21	7	Orsborn, Charles K. "Chuck"

Year	Assn	Div	F	Bye	#T	W	L	Coach
1994	NCAA	I	8		32	23	8	Molinari, Jim
1965	NCAA	I	14		14	18	9	Orsborn, Charles K. "Chuck"
1968	NCAA	I	16		16	19	9	Stowell, Joseph R.
1995	NCAA	I	16		32	20	10	Molinari, Jim
1997	NCAA	I	16		32	17	13	Molinari, Jim
1985	NCAA	I	32		32	17	13	Versace, Dick

BRIGHAM YOUNG

Year	Assn	Div	F	Bye	#T	W	L	Coach
1951	NCAA		1	To R8	12	28	9	Watts, Stanley H.
1966	NCAA	I	1	To R8	14	20	5	Watts, Stanley H.
1986	NCAA	I	8		32	18	14	Anderson, Ladell
1953	NCAA		12		12	22	8	Watts, Stanley H.
1954	NCAA		12		12	18	11	Watts, Stanley H.
1994	NCAA	I	16		32	22	10	Reid, Roger
1982	NCAA	I	32		32	17	13	Arnold, Frank H.

BUTLER (IN)

Year	Assn	Div	F	Bye	#T	W	L	Coach
1959	NCAA	I	8		12	19	9	Hinkle, Paul D. "Tony"
1958	NCAA	I	12		12	15	10	Hinkle, Paul D. "Tony"
1985	NCAA	I	32		32	19	10	Sexson, Joe
1991	NCAA	I	32		32	18	11	Collier, Barry
1992	NCAA	I	32		32	21	10	Collier, Barry

CALIFORNIA

Year	Assn	Div	F	Bye	#T	W	L	Coach
1987	NCAA	I	8		32	20	15	Campanelli, Lou
1989	NCAA	I	16		32	20	13	Campanelli, Lou
1986	NCAA	I	32		32	19	10	Campanelli, Lou

CALIFORNIA STATE: FRESNO

Year	Assn	Div	F	Bye	#T	W	L	Coach
1983	NCAA	I	1		32	25	10	Grant, Boyd "Tiny"
1998	NCAA	I	4		32	21	13	Tarkanian, Jerry
1985	NCAA	I	8		32	23	9	Grant, Boyd "Tiny"
1994	NCAA	I	8		32	21	11	Colson, Gary W.
1996	NCAA	I	8		32	22	11	Tarkanian, Jerry
1997	NCAA	I	32		32	20	12	Tarkanian, Jerry

CALIFORNIA STATE: FULLERTON

Year	Assn	Div	F	Bye	#T	W	L	Coach
1983	NCAA	I	32		32	21	8	McQuarn, George
1987	NCAA	I	32		32	17	13	McQuarn, George

CALIFORNIA STATE: LONG BEACH

Year	Assn	Div	F	Bye	#T	W	L	Coach
1980	NCAA	I	16		32	22	12	Winter, Fred "Tex"
1990	NCAA	I	16		32	23	9	Harrington, Joe
1988	NCAA	I	32		32	17	12	Harrington, Joe
1992	NCAA	I	32		32	18	12	Greenberg, Seth

CALIFORNIA: IRVINE

Year	Assn	Div	F	Bye	#T	W	L	Coach
1982	NCAA	I	16		32	23	7	Mulligan, William
1986	NCAA	I	16		32	17	13	Mulligan, William

CALIFORNIA: LOS ANGELES

Year	Assn	Div	F	Bye	#T	W	L	Coach
1985	NCAA	I	1		32	21	12	Hazzard, Walter R., Jr.
1986	NCAA	I	32		32	15	14	Hazzard, Walter R., Jr.

Year	Assn	Div	F	Bye	#T	W	L	Coach
CALIFORNIA: SANTA BARBARA								
1989	NCAA	I	32		32	21	9	Pimm, Jerry
1992	NCAA	I	32		32	20	9	Pimm, Jerry
1993	NCAA	I	32		32	18	11	Pimm, Jerry
CANISIUS								
1963	NCAA	I	2	To R8	12	19	7	MacKinnon, Robert A.
1995	NCAA	I	4		32	21	14	Beilein, John
1944	NCAA		8		8	15	6	Seelbach, Allie
1985	NCAA	I	32		32	20	10	Macarchuk, Nick, Jr.
1994	NCAA	I	32		32	22	7	Beilein, John
CENTRAL MICHIGAN								
1979	NCAA	I	24		24	19	9	Parfitt, Richard
CHARLESTON (SC)								
1996	NCAA	I	16		32	25	4	Kresse, John
1995	NCAA	I	32		32	23	6	Kresse, John
CINCINNATI								
1955	NCAA		3	To R8	12	21	8	Smith, George D.
1951	NCAA		12		12	18	4	Wiethe, John A.
1957	NCAA	I	12		12	15	7	Smith, George D.
1970	NCAA	I	16		16	21	6	Baker, Taylor "Tay"
1974	NCAA	I	16		16	19	8	Catlett, Gale
1985	NCAA	I	16		32	17	14	Yates, Anthony
1990	NCAA	I	16		32	20	14	Huggins, Robert
1991	NCAA	I	16		32	18	12	Huggins, Robert
CITY COLLEGE								
1950	NCAA		1		12	24	5	Holman, Nathan "Nat"
1941	NCAA		3		8	17	5	Holman, Nathan "Nat"
1942	NCAA		8		8	16	3	Holman, Nathan "Nat"
1949	NCAA		12		12	17	8	Holman, Nathan "Nat"
CLEMSON								
1986	NCAA	I	8		32	19	15	Ellis, Cliff
1994	NCAA	I	8		32	18	16	Ellis, Cliff
1979	NCAA	I	12		24	19	10	Foster, William C.
1975	NCAA	I	16		16	17	11	Locke, Taylor O. "Tates"
1993	NCAA	I	16		32	17	13	Ellis, Cliff
1981	NCAA	I	32		32	20	11	Foster, William C.
1982	NCAA	I	32		32	14	14	Foster, William C.
1985	NCAA	I	32		32	16	13	Ellis, Cliff
1988	NCAA	I	32		32	14	15	Ellis, Cliff
1995	NCAA	I	32		32	15	13	Barnes, Richard D. "Rick"
CLEVELAND STATE (OH)								
1987	NCAA	I	16		32	25	8	Mackey, Kevin
1988	NCAA	I	16		32	22	8	Mackey, Kevin

Year	Assn	Div	F	Bye	#T	W	L	Coach
COLORADO								
1940	NCAA		1	To R4	6	17	4	Cox, Forrest B. "Frosty"
1938	NCAA		2	To R4	6	15	6	Cox, Forrest B. "Frosty"
1991	NCAA	I	3		32	19	14	Harrington, Joe
1995	NCAA	I	32		32	15	13	Harrington, Joe
COLORADO STATE								
1988	NCAA	I	3		32	22	13	Grant, Boyd "Tiny"
1961	NCAA	I	8	To R8	12	17	9	Williams, James J.
1962	NCAA	I	12		12	18	9	Williams, James J.
1996	NCAA	I	32		32	18	12	Morrill, Stew
1998	NCAA	I	32		32	20	9	Morrill, Stew
CONNECTICUT								
1988	NCAA	I	1		32	20	14	Calhoun, James A.
1997	NCAA	I	3		32	18	15	Calhoun, James A.
1974	NCAA	I	8		16	19	8	Rowe, Donald E. "Dee"
1989	NCAA	I	8		32	18	13	Calhoun, James A.
1955	NCAA		12		12	20	5	Greer, Hugh S.
1975	NCAA	I	16		16	18	10	Rowe, Donald E. "Dee"
1981	NCAA	I	16		32	20	9	Perno, Dominic P. "Dom"
1980	NCAA	I	32		32	20	9	Perno, Dominic P. "Dom"
1982	NCAA	I	32		32	17	11	Perno, Dominic P. "Dom"
1993	NCAA	I	32		32	15	13	Calhoun, James A.
COPPIN STATE								
1995	NCAA	I	16		32	21	10	Mitchell, Ronald C. "Fang"
1991	NCAA	I	32		32	19	11	Mitchell, Ronald C. "Fang"
CREIGHTON								
1942	NCAA		3		8	19	5	Hickey, Edgar S. "Eddie"
1943	NCAA		8		8	16	1	Hickey, Edgar S. "Eddie"
1977	NCAA	I	16		16	21	7	Apke, Tom
1984	NCAA	I	32		32	17	14	Reed, Willis, Jr.
1990	NCAA	I	32		32	21	12	Barone, Anthony A. "Tony"
1998	NCAA	I	32		32	18	10	Altman, Dana
DAVIDSON								
1972	NCAA	I	16		16	19	9	Holland, M. Terrance "Terry"
1994	NCAA	I	32		32	22	8	McKillop, Bob
1996	NCAA	I	32		32	25	5	McKillop, Bob
DAYTON								
1962	NCAA	I	1		12	24	6	Blackburn, L. Thomas
1968	NCAA	I	1		16	21	9	Donoher, Donald J. "Mickey"
1951	NCAA		2		12	27	5	Blackburn, L. Thomas
1952	NCAA		2		12	28	5	Blackburn, L. Thomas
1955	NCAA		2	To R8	12	25	4	Blackburn, L. Thomas
1956	NCAA		2	To R8	12	25	4	Blackburn, L. Thomas
1958	NCAA	I	2	To R8	12	25	4	Blackburn, L. Thomas
1961	NCAA	I	4	To R8	12	20	9	Blackburn, L. Thomas

Year	Assn	Div	F	Bye	#T	W	L	Coach
1954	NCAA		8		12	25	7	Blackburn, L. Thomas
1957	NCAA	I	8		12	19	9	Blackburn, L. Thomas
1960	NCAA	I	8		12	21	7	Blackburn, L. Thomas
1978	NCAA	I	8		16	19	10	Donoher, Donald J. "Mickey"
1982	NCAA	I	8		32	21	9	Donoher, Donald J. "Mickey"
1979	NCAA	I	12		24	19	10	Donoher, Donald J. "Mickey"
1971	NCAA	I	16		16	18	9	Donoher, Donald J. "Mickey"
1981	NCAA	I	16		32	18	11	Donoher, Donald J. "Mickey"
1998	NCAA	I	16		32	21	12	Purnell, Oliver
1986	NCAA	I	32		32	17	13	Donoher, Donald J. "Mickey"

DE PAUL

Year	Assn	Div	F	Bye	#T	W	L	Coach
1945	NCAA		1		8	21	3	Meyer, Raymond J.
1944	NCAA		2		8	22	4	Meyer, Raymond J.
1983	NCAA	I	2		32	21	12	Meyer, Raymond J.
1940	NCAA		4		6	22	6	Haggerty, Thomas J.
1948	NCAA		4		8	22	8	Meyer, Raymond J.
1964	NCAA	I	8	To R8	12	21	4	Meyer, Raymond J.
1990	NCAA	I	8		32	20	15	Meyer, Joseph E. "Joey"
1961	NCAA	I	12		12	17	8	Meyer, Raymond J.
1963	NCAA	I	12		12	15	8	Meyer, Raymond J.
1966	NCAA	I	14		14	18	8	Meyer, Raymond J.
1994	NCAA	I	32		32	16	12	Meyer, Joseph E. "Joey"
1995	NCAA	I	32		32	17	11	Meyer, Joseph E. "Joey"

DENVER

Year	Assn	Div	F	Bye	#T	W	L	Coach
1959	NCAA	I	12		12	14	10	Brawner, E. Hoyt

DETROIT

Year	Assn	Div	F	Bye	#T	W	L	Coach
1965	NCAA	I	8		14	20	8	Calihan, Robert J.
1978	NCAA	I	8		16	25	4	Gaines, David "Smokey"
1960	NCAA	I	12		12	20	7	Calihan, Robert J.
1961	NCAA	I	12		12	18	9	Calihan, Robert J.

DRAKE (IA)

Year	Assn	Div	F	Bye	#T	W	L	Coach
1964	NCAA	I	8		12	21	7	John, Maurice E. "Maury"
1981	NCAA	I	32		32	18	11	Ortegel, Bob
1986	NCAA	I	32		32	19	11	Garner, Gary

DREXEL

Year	Assn	Div	F	Bye	#T	W	L	Coach
1997	NCAA	I	32		32	22	9	Herrion, William R.

DUKE

Year	Assn	Div	F	Bye	#T	W	L	Coach
1971	NCAA	I	4		16	20	10	Waters, Raymond C. "Bucky"
1967	NCAA	I	8	To R8	14	18	9	Bubas, Victor A.
1968	NCAA	I	8		16	22	6	Bubas, Victor A.
1981	NCAA	I	8		32	17	13	Krzyzewski, Michael W.
1970	NCAA	I	16		16	17	9	Waters, Raymond C. "Bucky"

DUQUESNE

Year	Assn	Div	F	Bye	#T	W	L	Coach
1955	NCAA		1	To R8	12	22	4	Moore, Donald W. "Dudey"
1940	NCAA		2		6	20	3	Davies, Charles R. "Chick"
1954	NCAA		2	To R8	12	26	3	Moore, Donald W. "Dudey"
1953	NCAA		3		12	21	8	Moore, Donald W. "Dudey"

Year	Assn	Div	F	Bye	#T	W	L	Coach
1950	NCAA		4	To R8	12	23	6	Moore, Donald W. "Dudey"
1952	NCAA		4	To R8	12	23	4	Moore, Donald W. "Dudey"
1962	NCAA	I	4		12	22	7	Manning, John "Red"
1941	NCAA		8		8	17	3	Davies, Charles R. "Chick"
1947	NCAA		8		8	20	2	Davies, Charles R. "Chick"
1956	NCAA		8		12	17	10	Moore, Donald W. "Dudey"
1964	NCAA	I	8	To T8	12	16	7	Manning, John "Red"
1968	NCAA	I	16		16	18	7	Manning, John "Red"
1970	NCAA	I	16		16	17	7	Manning, John "Red"
1980	NCAA	I	16		32	18	10	Rice, Mike
1994	NCAA	I	16		32	17	13	Carroll, John
1981	NCAA	I	32		32	20	10	Rice, Mike

EAST TENNESSEE STATE

Year	Assn	Div	F	Bye	#T	W	L	Coach
1983	NCAA	I	32		32	22	9	Dowd, Barry

EASTERN MICHIGAN

Year	Assn	Div	F	Bye	#T	W	L	Coach
1995	NCAA	I	32		32	20	10	Braun, Ben

EVANSVILLE

Year	Assn	Div	F	Bye	#T	W	L	Coach
1988	NCAA	I	16		32	21	8	Crews, Jim
1994	NCAA	I	32		32	21	11	Crews, Jim

FAIRFIELD

Year	Assn	Div	F	Bye	#T	W	L	Coach
1973	NCAA	I	8		16	18	9	Barakat, Frederick E.
1974	NCAA	I	16		16	17	9	Barakat, Frederick E.
1978	NCAA	I	16		16	22	5	Barakat, Frederick E.
1996	NCAA	I	32		32	20	10	Cormier, Paul

FAIRLEIGH DICKINSON: TEANECK

Year	Assn	Div	F	Bye	#T	W	L	Coach
1991	NCAA	I	32		32	22	9	Green, Tom

FLORIDA

Year	Assn	Div	F	Bye	#T	W	L	Coach
1986	NCAA	I	4		32	19	14	Sloan, Norman L., Jr.
1992	NCAA	I	4		32	19	14	Kruger, Lon
1969	NCAA	I	16		16	18	9	Bartlett, Thomas G. "Tommy"
1984	NCAA	I	32		32	16	13	Sloan, Norman L., Jr.
1985	NCAA	I	32		32	18	12	Sloan, Norman L., Jr.
1993	NCAA	I	32		32	16	12	Kruger, Lon
1998	NCAA	I	32		32	14	15	Donovan, William J. "Billy"

FLORIDA STATE

Year	Assn	Div	F	Bye	#T	W	L	Coach
1997	NCAA	I	2		32	20	12	Kennedy, Patrick
1984	NCAA	I	16		32	20	11	Williams, Joe L.
1987	NCAA	I	16		32	19	11	Kennedy, Patrick

FORDHAM

Year	Assn	Div	F	Bye	#T	W	L	Coach
1943	NCAA		4		8	16	6	Kelleher, Edward A.
1958	NCAA	I	8		12	15	9	Bach, John W. "Johnny"
1968	NCAA	I	8		16	19	8	Bach, John W. "Johnny"
1959	NCAA	I	12		12	17	8	Bach, John W. "Johnny"
1963	NCAA	I	12		12	18	8	Bach, John W. "Johnny"
1965	NCAA	I	14		14	15	12	Bach, John W. "Johnny"
1969	NCAA	I	16		16	17	9	Conlin, Edward J.
1972	NCAA	I	16		16	18	9	Wissel, Dr. Harold R. "Hal"

Year	Assn	Div	F	Bye	#T	W	L	Coach
1990	NCAA	I	16		32	20	13	Macarchuk, Nick, Jr.
1991	NCAA	I	16		32	25	8	Macarchuk, Nick, Jr.
1981	NCAA	I	32		32	19	9	Penders, Thomas V.
1982	NCAA	I	32		32	18	11	Penders, Thomas V.
1983	NCAA	I	32		32	19	11	Penders, Thomas V.
1984	NCAA	I	32		32	19	15	Penders, Thomas V.
1985	NCAA	I	32		32	19	12	Penders, Thomas V.
1988	NCAA	I	32		32	18	15	Macarchuk, Nick, Jr.

FURMAN

Year	Assn	Div	F	Bye	#T	W	L	Coach
1991	NCAA	I	32		32	20	9	Estes, George "Butch"

GEORGE MASON

Year	Assn	Div	F	Bye	#T	W	L	Coach
1986	NCAA	I	16		32	20	12	Harrington, Joe

GEORGE WASHINGTON

Year	Assn	Div	F	Bye	#T	W	L	Coach
1991	NCAA	I	32		32	19	12	Jarvis, Mike
1995	NCAA	I	32		32	18	14	Jarvis, Mike
1997	NCAA	I	32		32	15	14	Jarvis, Mike

GEORGETOWN (DC)

Year	Assn	Div	F	Bye	#T	W	L	Coach
1993	NCAA	I	2		32	20	13	Thompson, John R., Jr.
1978	NCAA	I	4		16	23	8	Thompson, John R., Jr.
1953	NCAA		12		12	13	7	Jeanette, Harry E. "Buddy"
1970	NCAA	I	16		16	18	8	Magee, John F. "Jack"
1977	NCAA	I	16		16	19	9	Thompson, John R., Jr.
1998	NCAA	I	16		32	16	15	Thompson, John R., Jr.

GEORGIA

Year	Assn	Div	F	Bye	#T	W	L	Coach
1982	NCAA	I	3		32	19	12	Durham, Hugh
1998	NCAA	I	3		32	20	15	Jirsa, Ron
1981	NCAA	I	16		32	19	12	Durham, Hugh
1986	NCAA	I	16		32	17	13	Durham, Hugh
1988	NCAA	I	16		32	20	16	Durham, Hugh
1984	NCAA	I	32		32	17	13	Durham, Hugh
1993	NCAA	I	32		32	15	14	Durham, Hugh
1995	NCAA	I	32		32	18	10	Durham, Hugh

GEORGIA SOUTHERN

Year	Assn	Div	F	Bye	#T	W	L	Coach
1988	NCAA	I	32		32	24	7	Kerns, Frank
1989	NCAA	I	32		32	23	6	Kerns, Frank

GEORGIA TECH

Year	Assn	Div	F	Bye	#T	W	L	Coach
1971	NCAA	I	2		16	23	9	Hyder, John C. "Whack"
1970	NCAA	I	8		16	17	10	Hyder, John C. "Whack"
1998	NCAA	I	8		32	19	14	Cremins, Bobby
1984	NCAA	I	32		32	18	11	Cremins, Bobby
1994	NCAA	I	32		32	16	13	Cremins, Bobby

GONZAGA

Year	Assn	Div	F	Bye	#T	W	L	Coach
1994	NCAA	I	16		32	22	8	Fitzgerald, Dan
1998	NCAA	I	16		32	24	10	Monson, Don
1996	NCAA	I	32		32	21	9	Fitzgerald, Dan

Year	Assn	Div	F	Bye	#T	W	L	Coach
GRAMBLING STATE								
1980	NCAA	I	32		32	22	8	Hobdy, Frederick C.
HAWAII								
1971	NCAA	I	8		16	23	5	Rocha, Ephraim J. "Red"
1974	NCAA	I	8		16	19	9	O'Neil, Bruce
1990	NCAA	I	8		32	25	10	Wallace, Riley
1998	NCAA	I	8		32	21	9	Wallace, Riley
1997	NCAA	I	16		32	21	8	Wallace, Riley
1989	NCAA	I	32		32	17	13	Wallace, Riley
HOLY CROSS (MA)								
1954	NCAA		1	To R8	12	26	2	Sheary, Lester H. "Buster"
1961	NCAA	I	3		12	21	5	Leenig, Roy H.
1952	NCAA		8		12	24	4	Sheary, Lester H. "Buster"
1955	NCAA		8	To R8	12	19	7	Sheary, Lester H. "Buster"
1962	NCAA	I	8		12	20	6	Oftring, Frank A.
1976	NCAA	I	8		12	22	10	Blaney, George R.
1960	NCAA	I	12		12	20	6	Leenig, Roy H.
1975	NCAA	I	16		16	20	8	Blaney, George R.
1981	NCAA	I	16		32	20	10	Blaney, George R.
1979	NCAA	I	24		24	17	11	Blaney, George R.
1990	NCAA	I	32		32	24	6	Blaney, George R.
HOUSTON								
1977	NCAA	I	2		16	29	8	Lewis, Guy V.
1962	NCAA	I	8	To R8	12	21	6	Lewis, Guy V.
1988	NCAA	I	16		32	18	13	Foster, Pat
1985	NCAA	I	32		32	16	14	Lewis, Guy V.
1991	NCAA	I	32		32	18	11	Foster, Pat
1993	NCAA	I	32		32	21	9	Foster, Pat
IDAHO								
1983	NCAA	I	32		32	20	9	Monson, Don
ILLINOIS								
1980	NCAA	I	3		32	22	13	Henson, Louis R.
1982	NCAA	I	16		32	18	11	Henson, Louis R.
1996	NCAA	I	32		32	18	13	Henson, Louis R.
ILLINOIS STATE								
1977	NCAA	I	8		16	22	7	Smithson, Eugene
1987	NCAA	I	8		32	19	13	Donewald, Bob
1996	NCAA	I	8		32	22	12	Stallings, Kevin
1978	NCAA	I	16		16	24	4	Smithson, Eugene
1980	NCAA	I	16		32	20	9	Donewald, Bob
1995	NCAA	I	16		32	20	13	Stallings, Kevin
1988	NCAA	I	32		32	18	13	Donewald, Bob
INDIANA								
1979	NCAA	I	1	R12>R4	24	22	12	Knight, Robert M.
1985	NCAA	I	2		32	19	14	Knight, Robert M.
1972	NCAA	I	16		16	17	8	Knight, Robert M.

Year	Assn	Div	F	Bye	#T	W	L	Coach
INDIANA STATE								
1978	NCAA	I	8		16	23	9	King, Bob
1977	NCAA	I	16		16	25	3	King, Bob
IONA								
1983	NCAA	I	16		32	22	9	Kennedy, Patrick
1982	NCAA	I	32		32	24	9	Kennedy, Patrick
1996	NCAA	I	32		32	21	8	Welsh, Tim
1997	NCAA	I	32		32	22	8	Welsh, Tim
IOWA								
1995	NCAA	I	8		32	21	12	Davis, Dr. Thomas
1998	NCAA	I	32		32	20	11	Davis, Dr. Thomas
IOWA STATE								
1984	NCAA	I	32		32	16	13	Orr, John M. "Johnny"
JACKSON STATE (MS)								
1993	NCAA	I	16		32	25	9	Stoglin, Lee Andrew "Andy"
JACKSONVILLE (FL)								
1972	NCAA	I	3		16	20	8	Wasdin, Tom
1974	NCAA	I	4		16	20	10	Gottlieb, Bob
1980	NCAA	I	32		32	20	9	Locke, Taylor O. "Tates"
1987	NCAA	I	32		32	19	11	Wenzel, Robert
JAMES MADISON								
1987	NCAA	I	32		32	20	10	Thurston, John
1990	NCAA	I	32		32	20	11	Driesell, Charles G. "Lefty"
1991	NCAA	I	32		32	19	10	Driesell, Charles G. "Lefty"
1992	NCAA	I	32		32	21	11	Driesell, Charles G. "Lefty"
1993	NCAA	I	32		32	21	9	Driesell, Charles G. "Lefty"
KANSAS								
1968	NCAA	I	2		16	22	8	Owens, Ted
1969	NCAA	I	16		16	20	7	Owens, Ted
KANSAS STATE								
1994	NCAA	I	4		32	20	14	Altman, Dana
1976	NCAA	I	8	To R8	12	20	8	Hartman, Jack
1992	NCAA	I	16		32	16	14	Altman, Dana
1998	NCAA	I	32		32	17	12	Asbury, Tom
KENT STATE								
1985	NCAA	I	32		32	17	13	McDonald, James Joseph
1989	NCAA	I	32		32	20	11	McDonald, James Joseph
1990	NCAA	I	32		32	21	8	McDonald, James Joseph
KENTUCKY								
1946	NCAA		1		8	28	2	Rupp, Adolph F.
1976	NCAA	I	1		12	20	10	Hall, Joe B.
1947	NCAA		2		8	34	3	Rupp, Adolph F.
1944	NCAA		3		8	19	2	Rupp, Adolph F.
1949	NCAA		8	To R8	12	32	2	Rupp, Adolph F.
1950	NCAA		8	To R8	12	25	5	Rupp, Adolph F.
1979	NCAA	I	24		24	19	12	Hall, Joe B.

Year	Assn	Div	F	Bye	#T	W	L	Coach
LA SALLE								
1952	NCAA		1		12	25	7	Loeffler, Kenneth D.
1987	NCAA	I	2		32	20	13	Morris, William T. "Speedy"
1948	NCAA		8		8	20	4	McGlone, Charles
1950	NCAA		8		12	21	4	Loeffler, Kenneth D.
1953	NCAA		8	To R8	12	25	3	Loeffler, Kenneth D.
1951	NCAA		12		12	22	7	Loeffler, Kenneth D.
1963	NCAA	I	12		12	16	8	Moore, Donald W. "Dudey"
1965	NCAA	I	14		14	15	8	Walters, Robert W.
1971	NCAA	I	16		16	20	7	Westhead, Paul W.
1984	NCAA	I	32		32	20	11	Ervin, David "Lefty"
1991	NCAA	I	32		32	19	10	Morris, William T. "Speedy"
LAFAYETTE (PA)								
1972	NCAA	I	8		16	21	6	Davis, Dr. Thomas
1955	NCAA		12		12	24	3	Van Breda Kolff, Willem "Butch"
1956	NCAA		12		12	20	7	Davidson, George E.
1975	NCAA	I	16		16	22	6	Davis, Dr. Thomas
1980	NCAA	I	32		32	21	8	Chipman, Dr. Leroy
LAMAR								
1984	NCAA	I	16		32	26	5	Foster, Pat
1985	NCAA	I	16		32	20	12	Foster, Pat
1982	NCAA	I	32		32	22	7	Foster, Pat
1986	NCAA	I	32		32	18	12	Foster, Pat
LAWRENCE TECH								
1951	NAIA		12		12	20	3	Ridler, Don
LONG ISLAND								
1939			1		6	24	0	Bee, Clair F.
1941			1		8	25	2	Bee, Clair F.
1938			6		6	23	4	Bee, Clair F.
1940			6		6	19	4	Bee, Clair F.
1942			8		8	24	4	Bee, Clair F.
1947			8		8	17	4	Bee, Clair F.
1968	NCAA	I	8		16	22	2	Rubin, Roy
1950	NAIA		12		12	20	5	Bee, Clair F.
1982	NCAA	I	32		32	20	10	Lizzo, Paul
1998	NCAA	I	32		32	21	11	Haskins, Ray
LOUISIANA STATE								
1970	NCAA	I	4		16	22	10	Maravich, Peter "Press"
1982	NCAA	I	32		32	14	14	Brown, Dale
1983	NCAA	I	32		32	19	13	Brown, Dale
LOUISIANA TECH								
1986	NCAA	I	3		32	20	14	Eagles, Tommy Joe
1988	NCAA	I	16		32	22	9	Eagles, Tommy Joe
1990	NCAA	I	32		32	20	8	Lloyd, Jerry
1992	NCAA	I	32		32	22	9	Lloyd, Jerry

Year	Assn	Div	F	Bye	#T	W	L	Coach
LOUISVILLE								
1956	NCAA		1	To R8	12	26	3	Hickman, Bernard L. "Peck"
1985	NCAA	I	4		32	19	18	Crum, Denzil E. "Denny"
1953	NCAA		8		12	22	6	Hickman, Bernard L. "Peck"
1955	NCAA		8		12	19	8	Hickman, Bernard L. "Peck"
1969	NCAA	I	8		16	21	6	Dromo, John
1973	NCAA	I	8		16	23	7	Crum, Denzil E. "Denny"
1976	NCAA	I	8	To R8	12	20	8	Crum, Denzil E. "Denny"
1952	NCAA		12		12	20	6	Hickman, Bernard L. "Peck"
1954	NCAA		12		12	22	7	Hickman, Bernard L. "Peck"
1966	NCAA	I	14		14	16	10	Hickman, Bernard L. "Peck"
1970	NCAA	I	16		16	18	9	Dromo, John
1971	NCAA	I	16		16	20	9	Dromo, John
LOYOLA (IL)								
1939			2	To R4	6	21	1	Sachs, Leonard D.
1949	NAIA		2		12	25	6	Haggerty, Thomas J.
1962	NCAA	I	3	To R8	12	23	4	Ireland, George M.
1980	NCAA	I	32		32	19	10	Lyne, Jerry P.
LOYOLA MARYMOUNT								
1986	NCAA	I	16		32	19	11	Westhead, Paul W.
MANHATTAN								
1953	NCAA		4	To R8	12	20	6	Norton, Kenneth A.
1943	NCAA		8		8	18	3	Daher, Joseph G.
1957	NCAA	I	8	To R8	12	15	9	Norton, Kenneth A.
1965	NCAA	I	8		14	13	9	Norton, Kenneth A.
1970	NCAA	I	8		16	18	8	Powers, John J. "Jack"
1975	NCAA	I	8		16	14	12	Powers, John J. "Jack"
1992	NCAA	I	8		32	25	9	Lappas, Steve
1949	NCAA		12		12	18	8	Norton, Kenneth A.
1954	NCAA		12		12	15	11	Norton, Kenneth A.
1955	NCAA		12		12	18	5	Norton, Kenneth A.
1959	NCAA	I	12		12	15	6	Norton, Kenneth A.
1966	NCAA		14		14	13	9	Norton, Kenneth A.
1973	NCAA	I	16		16	16	10	Powers, John J. "Jack"
1974	NCAA	I	16		16	18	9	Powers, John J. "Jack"
1994	NCAA	I	32		32	19	11	Fraschilla, Fran
1996	NCAA	I	32		32	17	12	Fraschilla, Fran
MARIST								
1996	NCAA	I	32		32	22	7	Magarity, David
MARQUETTE								
1970	NCAA	I	1		16	26	3	McGuire, Alfred J.
1967	NCAA	I	2		14	21	9	McGuire, Alfred J.
1995	NCAA	I	2		32	21	12	Deane, Mike
1963	NCAA	I	3	To R8	12	20	9	Hickey, Edgar S. "Eddie"
1985	NCAA	I	8		32	20	11	Majerus, Rick
1998	NCAA	I	8		32	20	11	Deane, Mike
1956	NCAA		12		12	13	11	Nagle, Joel "Jack"
1984	NCAA	I	16		32	17	13	Majerus, Rick

Year	Assn	Div	F	Bye	#T	W	L	Coach
1986	NCAA	I	16		32	19	11	Majerus, Rick
1981	NCAA	I	32		32	20	11	Raymonds, Henry C. "Hank"
1987	NCAA	I	32		32	16	13	Dukiet, Bob
1990	NCAA	I	32		32	15	14	O'Neill, Kevin

MARSHALL

Year	Assn	Div	F	Bye	#T	W	L	Coach
1967	NCAA	I	4		14	20	8	Johnson, Ellis T.
1968	NCAA	I	16		16	17	8	Johnson, Ellis T.
1973	NCAA	I	16		16	20	7	Daniels, Bob
1988	NCAA	I	32		32	24	8	Huckabay, Rick

MARYLAND

Year	Assn	Div	F	Bye	#T	W	L	Coach
1972	NCAA	I	1		16	27	5	Driesell, Charles G. "Lefty"
1979	NCAA	I	12		24	19	11	Driesell, Charles G. "Lefty"
1982	NCAA	I	16		32	16	13	Driesell, Charles G. "Lefty"
1990	NCAA	I	16		32	19	14	Williams, Gary

MARYLAND: EASTERN SHORE

Year	Assn	Div	F	Bye	#T	W	L	Coach
1974	NAIA		8		16	27	2	Bates, John H.

MASSACHUSETTS

Year	Assn	Div	F	Bye	#T	W	L	Coach
1991	NCAA	I	4		32	20	13	Calipari, John
1973	NCAA	I	8		16	20	7	Leaman, John A., Jr. "Jack"
1977	NCAA	I	8		16	20	11	Leaman, John A., Jr. "Jack"
1970	NCAA	I	16		16	18	7	Leaman, John A., Jr. "Jack"
1971	NCAA	I	16		16	23	4	Leaman, John A., Jr. "Jack"
1974	NCAA	I	16		16	21	5	Leaman, John A., Jr. "Jack"
1975	NCAA	I	16		16	18	8	Leaman, John A., Jr. "Jack"
1990	NCAA	I	32		32	17	14	Calipari, John

MCNEESE STATE

Year	Assn	Div	F	Bye	#T	W	L	Coach
1986	NCAA	I	16		32	21	11	Duhon, Glenn D.

MEMPHIS

Year	Assn	Div	F	Bye	#T	W	L	Coach
1957	NCAA	I	2		12	24	6	Vanatta, Robert
1961	NCAA	I	8	To R8	12	20	3	Vanatta, Robert
1963	NCAA	I	8		12	19	7	Ehlers, Dean
1974	NCAA	I	8		16	19	11	Bartow, B. Gene
1960	NCAA	I	12		12	18	5	Vanatta, Robert
1967	NCAA	I	14		14	17	9	Iba, Moe
1972	NCAA	I	16		16	21	7	Bartow, B. Gene
1975	NCAA	I	16		16	20	7	Yates, Wayne E.
1977	NCAA	I	16		16	20	9	Yates, Wayne E.
1991	NCAA	I	16		32	17	15	Finch, Larry O.
1998	NCAA	I	16		32	17	12	Price, George "Tic"
1990	NCAA	I	32		32	18	12	Finch, Larry O.
1997	NCAA	I	32		32	16	15	Finch, Larry O.

MIAMI (FL)

Year	Assn	Div	F	Bye	#T	W	L	Coach
1963	NCAA	I	8		12	23	5	Hale, William Bruce
1961	NCAA	I	12		12	20	7	Hale, William Bruce
1964	NCAA	I	12		12	20	7	Hale, William Bruce
1995	NCAA	I	32		32	15	13	Hamilton, Leonard
1997	NCAA	I	32		32	16	13	Hamilton, Leonard

Year	Assn	Div	F	Bye	#T	W	L	Coach
MIAMI (OH)								
1993	NCAA	I	8		32	22	9	Wright, Joseph A. "Joby"
1970	NCAA	I	16		16	16	8	Locke, Taylor O. "Tates"
1994	NCAA	I	32		32	19	11	Sendek, Herb
1996	NCAA	I	32		32	21	8	Sendek, Herb
MICHIGAN								
1984	NCAA	I	1		32	23	10	Frieder, Bill
1997	NCAA	I	1		32	24	11	Fisher, Stephen L.
1971	NCAA	I	8		16	19	7	Orr, John M. "Johnny"
1980	NCAA	I	8		32	17	13	Orr, John M. "Johnny"
1981	NCAA	I	8		32	19	11	Frieder, Bill
1991	NCAA	I	32		32	14	15	Fisher, Stephen L.
MICHIGAN STATE								
1989	NCAA	I	4		32	18	15	Heathcote, George "Jud"
1983	NCAA	I	16		32	17	13	Heathcote, George "Jud"
1996	NCAA	I	16		32	16	16	Izzo, Tom
1997	NCAA	I	16		32	17	12	Izzo, Tom
1993	NCAA	I	32		32	15	13	Heathcote, George "Jud"
MIDDLE TENNESSEE STATE								
1988	NCAA	I	8		32	23	11	Stewart, Bruce
1986	NCAA	I	32		32	23	11	Stewart, Bruce
MINNESOTA								
1993	NCAA	I	1		32	22	10	Haskins, Clem S.
1998	NCAA	I	1		32	20	15	Haskins, Clem S.
1980	NCAA	I	2		32	21	11	Dutcher, James D.
1973	NCAA	I	8		16	21	5	Musselman, William
1981	NCAA	I	8		32	19	11	Dutcher, James D.
1996	NCAA	I	16		32	19	13	Haskins, Clem S.
1983	NCAA	I	32		32	18	13	Dutcher, James D.
1992	NCAA	I	32		32	16	16	Haskins, Clem S.
MISSISSIPPI								
1983	NCAA	I	8		32	19	12	Hunt, Lee
1980	NCAA	I	16		32	17	13	Weltlich, Robert
1982	NCAA	I	16		32	18	12	Weltlich, Robert
1987	NCAA	I	32		32	15	15	Murphy, Ed
1989	NCAA	I	32		32	15	15	Murphy, Ed
MISSISSIPPI STATE								
1990	NCAA	I	16		32	16	14	Williams, Richard
1979	NCAA	I	24		24	19	9	Hatfield, Jim
1994	NCAA	I	32		32	18	11	Williams, Richard
MISSOURI								
1972	NCAA	I	16		16	21	6	Stewart, Norman E.
1973	NCAA	I	16		16	21	6	Stewart, Norman E.
1996	NCAA	I	16		32	18	15	Stewart, Norman E.
1985	NCAA	I	32		32	18	14	Stewart, Norman E.
1998	NCAA	I	32		32	17	15	Stewart, Norman E.

Year	Assn	Div	F	Bye	#T	W	L	Coach
MONTANA								
1985	NCAA	I	32		32	22	8	Montgomery, Mike
1986	NCAA	I	32		32	21	11	Montgomery, Mike
1995	NCAA	I	32		32	21	9	Taylor, Blaine
MONTANA STATE								
1987	NCAA	I	32		32	21	8	Starner, Stu
MOUNT SAINT MARY'S (MD)								
1996	NCAA	I	32		32	21	8	Phelan, James J.
MUHLENBERG								
1946	NCAA		4		8	23	5	Coker, Lee
1944	NCAA		8		8	19	6	Julian, Alvin F. "Doggie"
1945	NCAA		8		8	24	4	Julian, Alvin F. "Doggie"
MURRAY STATE (KY)								
1980	NCAA	I	8		32	23	8	Greene, Ronald L.
1982	NCAA	I	32		32	20	8	Greene, Ronald L.
1983	NCAA	I	32		32	21	8	Greene, Ronald L.
1989	NCAA	I	32		32	19	11	Newton, Steve
1994	NCAA	I	32		32	23	6	Edgar, Scott
1996	NCAA	I	32		32	19	10	Gottfried, Mark
NAVY								
1962	NCAA	I	12		12	13	8	Carnevale, Bernard L. "Ben"
NEBRASKA								
1996	NCAA	I	1		32	21	14	Nee, Danny
1983	NCAA	I	3		32	22	10	Iba, Moe
1987	NCAA	I	3		32	21	12	Nee, Danny
1967	NCAA	I	8	To R8	14	16	9	Cipriano, Joseph
1978	NCAA	I	8		16	22	8	Cipriano, Joseph
1997	NCAA	I	8		32	18	15	Nee, Danny
1984	NCAA	I	16		32	18	12	Iba, Moe
1985	NCAA	I	16		32	16	14	Iba, Moe
1989	NCAA	I	16		32	17	16	Nee, Danny
1995	NCAA	I	16		32	18	14	Nee, Danny
1980	NCAA	I	32		32	18	13	Cipriano, Joseph
NEVADA								
1979	NCAA	I	12		24	21	7	Carey, Jim
1997	NCAA	I	16		32	21	10	Foster, Pat
NEVADA: LAS VEGAS								
1980	NCAA	I	4		32	23	9	Tarkanian, Jerry
1997	NCAA	I	8		32	22	10	Bayno, Bill
1982	NCAA	I	16		32	20	10	Tarkanian, Jerry
1993	NCAA	I	32		32	21	8	Massimino, Roland V. "Rollie"
NEW MEXICO								
1964	NCAA	I	2	To R8	12	23	6	King, Bob
1990	NCAA	I	4		32	20	14	Bliss, David
1965	NCAA	I	8	To R8	14	19	8	King, Bob
1967	NCAA	I	8		14	19	8	King, Bob

Year	Assn	Div	F	Bye	#T	W	L	Coach
1988	NCAA	I	8		32	22	14	Colson, Gary W.
1989	NCAA	I	8		32	22	11	Bliss, David
1992	NCAA	I	8		32	20	13	Bliss, David
1973	NCAA	I	16		16	21	6	Ellenberger, Norman
1985	NCAA	I	16		32	19	13	Colson, Gary W.
1979	NCAA	I	24		24	19	10	Ellenberger, Norman
1984	NCAA	I	32		32	24	11	Colson, Gary W.
1986	NCAA	I	32		32	17	14	Colson, Gary W.
1987	NCAA	I	32		32	25	10	Colson, Gary W.
NEW MEXICO STATE								
1939	NAIA		6		6	16	3	Hines, Gerald H. "Jerry"
1995	NCAA	I	8		32	25	10	McCarthy, Neil N.
1989	NCAA	I	32		32	21	11	McCarthy, Neil N.
NEW ORLEANS								
1990	NCAA	I	8		32	21	11	Floyd, Tim
1983	NCAA	I	16		32	23	7	Smith, Donald W.
1994	NCAA	I	16		32	20	10	Floyd, Tim
1988	NCAA	I	32		32	21	11	Polis, Art
1989	NCAA	I	32		32	19	11	Floyd, Tim
1997	NCAA	I	32		32	22	7	Price, George "Tic"
NEW YORK								
1948	NCAA		2		8	22	4	Cann, Howard G.
1966	NCAA	I	2		14	18	10	Rossini, Lucio "Lou"
1959	NCAA	I	3		12	15	8	Rossini, Lucio "Lou"
1938	NCAA		4		6	16	8	Cann, Howard G.
1964	NCAA	I	4		12	17	10	Rossini, Lucio "Lou"
1965	NCAA	I	4		14	16	10	Rossini, Lucio "Lou"
1949	NCAA		12		12	12	8	Cann, Howard G.
1952	NCAA		12		12	17	8	Cann, Howard G.
NIAGARA								
1972	NCAA	I	2		16	21	9	Layden, Frank P.
1954	NCAA		3	To R8	12	24	6	Gallagher, John J. "Taps"
1953	NCAA		8		12	22	6	Gallagher, John J. "Taps"
1955	NCAA		8		12	20	6	Gallagher, John J. "Taps"
1956	NCAA		8	To R8	12	20	7	Gallagher, John J. "Taps"
1961	NCAA	I	8	To R8	12	16	5	Gallagher, John J. "Taps"
1950	NCAA		12		12	20	7	Gallagher, John J. "Taps"
1958	NCAA	I	12		12	18	7	Gallagher, John J. "Taps"
1976	NCAA	I	12		12	17	12	Layden, Frank P.
1987	NCAA	I	16		32	21	10	Walker, Andy
1993	NCAA	I	32		32	23	7	Armstrong, Jack
NORTH CAROLINA								
1971	NCAA	I	1		16	26	6	Smith, Dean E.
1973	NCAA	I	3		16	25	8	Smith, Dean E.
1970	NCAA	I	16		16	18	9	Smith, Dean E.
1974	NCAA	I	16		16	22	6	Smith, Dean E.
NORTH CAROLINA A&T								
1976	NCAA	I	12		12	20	6	Reynolds, Warren
1981	NCAA	I	32		32	21	8	Corbett, Donald

Year	Assn	Div	F	Bye	#T	W	L	Coach
NORTH CAROLINA STATE								
1978	NCAA	I	2		16	21	10	Sloan, Norman L., Jr.
1947	NCAA		3		8	26	5	Case, Everett N.
1976	NCAA	I	3	To R8	12	21	9	Sloan, Norman L., Jr.
1948	NCAA		8		8	29	3	Case, Everett N.
1951	NCAA		8	To R8	12	30	7	Case, Everett N.
1997	NCAA	I	16		32	17	15	Sendek, Herb
1998	NCAA	I	16		32	17	15	Sendek, Herb
1984	NCAA	I	32		32	19	14	Valvano, James T.
NORTH CAROLINA: CHARLOTTE								
1976	NCAA	I	2		12	24	6	Rose, Lee H.
1989	NCAA	I	32		32	17	12	Mullins, Jeffrey V., Jr.
1994	NCAA	I	32		32	16	13	Mullins, Jeffrey V., Jr.
NORTH CAROLINA: WILMINGTON								
1998	NCAA	I	32		32	20	11	Wainwright, Jerry
NORTHEAST LOUISIANA								
1979	NCAA	I	24		24	23	6	Fant, Leonard "Lenny"
1988	NCAA	I	32		32	21	9	Vining, Mike
NORTHERN ARIZONA								
1986	NCAA	I	32		32	19	10	Arnote, Jay
1997	NCAA	I	32		32	21	7	Howland, Ben
NORTHWESTERN (IL)								
1983	NCAA	I	16		32	17	13	Falk, Rich
1994	NCAA	I	16		32	15	14	Swanson, Paul
NOTRE DAME (IN)								
1973	NCAA	I	2		16	18	12	Phelps, Richard F. "Digger"
1984	NCAA	I	2		32	21	12	Phelps, Richard F. "Digger"
1992	NCAA	I	2		32	18	15	MacLeod, John M.
1968	NCAA	I	3		16	21	9	Dee, John F., Jr.
1997	NCAA	I	8		32	16	14	MacLeod, John M.
1983	NCAA	I	32		32	19	10	Phelps, Richard F. "Digger"
OHIO STATE								
1986	NCAA	I	1		32	19	14	Miller, Eldon
1988	NCAA	I	2		32	16	11	Williams, Gary
1979	NCAA	I	4	R12>R4	24	19	12	Miller, Eldon
1989	NCAA	I	8		32	19	15	Williams, Gary
1984	NCAA	I	32		32	15	14	Miller, Eldon
1993	NCAA	I	32		32	15	13	Ayers, Randy
OHIO UNIVERSITY								
1941	NCAA		2		8	18	4	Trautwein, William J. "Dutch"
1969	NCAA	I	8		16	17	9	Snyder, James E.
1995	NCAA	I	16		32	24	10	Hunter, Larry
1986	NCAA	I	32		32	22	8	Nee, Danny

Year	Assn	Div	F	Bye	#T	W	L	Coach
OKLAHOMA								
1991	NCAA	I	2		32	20	15	Tubbs, Billy
1982	NCAA	I	3		32	22	8	Tubbs, Billy
1970	NCAA	I	8		16	19	9	MacLeod, John M.
1971	NCAA	I	16		16	19	8	MacLeod, John M.
1993	NCAA	I	16		32	20	12	Tubbs, Billy
1994	NCAA	I	32		32	15	13	Tubbs, Billy
OKLAHOMA CITY								
1959	NCAA	I	8	To R8	12	20	7	Lemons, A. E. "Abe"
1968	NCAA	I	16		16	20	7	Lemons, A. E. "Abe"
OKLAHOMA STATE								
1938	NCAA		3	To R4	6	25	3	Iba, Henry P. "Hank"
1940	NCAA		3	To R4	6	26	3	Iba, Henry P. "Hank"
1944	NCAA		4		8	27	6	Iba, Henry P. "Hank"
1956	NCAA		12		12	18	9	Iba, Henry P. "Hank"
1989	NCAA	I	16		32	17	13	Hamilton, Leonard
1990	NCAA	I	16		32	17	14	Hamilton, Leonard
1997	NCAA	I	16		32	17	15	Sutton, Eddie
OLD DOMINION								
1979	NCAA	I	6		24	23	7	Webb, Paul E.
1977	NCAA	I	16		16	25	4	Webb, Paul E.
1993	NCAA	I	16		32	21	8	Purnell, Oliver
1994	NCAA	I	16		32	21	10	Purnell, Oliver
1981	NCAA	I	32		32	18	10	Webb, Paul E.
1983	NCAA	I	32		32	19	10	Webb, Paul E.
1984	NCAA	I	32		32	19	12	Webb, Paul E.
1988	NCAA	I	32		32	18	12	Young, Thomas J.
ORAL ROBERTS								
1972	NCAA	I	8		16	26	2	Trickey, Ken
1975	NCAA	I	8		16	20	8	Hale, Jerry
1973	NCAA	I	16		16	21	6	Trickey, Ken
1977	NCAA	I	16		16	21	7	Hale, Jerry
1982	NCAA	I	32		32	18	12	Hayes, Ken
1997	NCAA	I	32		32	21	7	Self, Bill
OREGON								
1975	NCAA	I	3		16	21	9	Harter, Dick
1976	NCAA	I	8	To R8	12	19	11	Harter, Dick
1977	NCAA	I	8		16	19	10	Harter, Dick
1988	NCAA	I	16		32	16	14	Monson, Don
1984	NCAA	I	32		32	16	13	Monson, Don
1990	NCAA	I	32		32	15	14	Monson, Don
1997	NCAA	I	32		32	17	11	Green, Jerry
OREGON STATE								
1983	NCAA	I	8		32	20	11	Miller, Ralph H. "Cappy"
1987	NCAA	I	16		32	19	11	Miller, Ralph H. "Cappy"
1979	NCAA	I	24		24	18	10	Miller, Ralph H. "Cappy"

Year	Assn	Div	F	Bye	#T	W	L	Coach
PACIFIC (CA)								
1998	NCAA	I	32		32	24	10	Thomason, Bob
PENNSYLVANIA								
1981	NCAA	I	32		32	20	8	Weinhauer, Bob
PENNSYLVANIA STATE								
1998	NCAA	I	2		32	19	13	Dunn, Jerry
1990	NCAA	I	3		32	25	9	Parkhill, Bruce
1995	NCAA	I	3		32	21	11	Parkhill, Bruce
1966	NCAA	I	14		14	18	6	Egli, John S.
1989	NCAA	I	16		32	20	12	Parkhill, Bruce
1980	NCAA	I	32		32	18	10	Harter, Dick
1992	NCAA	I	32		32	21	8	Parkhill, Bruce
PEPPERDINE								
1989	NCAA	I	16		32	20	13	Asbury, Tom
1993	NCAA	I	16		32	23	8	Asbury, Tom
1980	NCAA	I	32		32	17	11	Harrick, Jim
1988	NCAA	I	32		32	17	13	Harrick, Jim
PITTSBURGH								
1975	NCAA	I	8		16	18	11	Ridl, Charles G. "Buzz"
1984	NCAA	I	8		32	18	13	Chipman, Dr. Leroy
1964	NCAA	I	12		12	17	8	Timmons, Robert W.
1992	NCAA	I	16		32	18	16	Evans, Paul
1997	NCAA	I	16		32	18	15	Willard, Ralph
1980	NCAA	I	32		32	17	12	Grgurich, Tim
1986	NCAA	I	32		32	15	14	Chipman, Dr. Leroy
PRINCETON								
1975	NCAA	I	1		16	22	8	Carril, Peter J.
1972	NCAA	I	8		16	20	7	Carril, Peter J.
PROVIDENCE								
1961	NCAA	I	1		12	24	5	Mullaney, Joseph A., Sr.
1963	NCAA	I	1	To R8	12	24	4	Mullaney, Joseph A., Sr.
1960	NCAA	I	2		12	24	5	Mullaney, Joseph A., Sr.
1975	NCAA	I	2		16	20	4	Gavitt, David R.
1959	NCAA	I	4		12	20	7	Mullaney, Joseph A., Sr.
1976	NCAA	I	4		12	21	11	Gavitt, David R.
1993	NCAA	I	4		32	20	13	Barnes, Richard D. "Rick"
1967	NCAA	I	8		14	21	7	Mullaney, Joseph A., Sr.
1971	NCAA	I	8		16	20	8	Gavitt, David R.
1986	NCAA	I	8		32	17	14	Pitino, Richard A. "Rick"
1991	NCAA	I	8		32	19	13	Barnes, Richard D. "Rick"
1962	NCAA	I	12		12	20	6	Mullaney, Joseph A., Sr.
1995	NCAA	I	16		32	17	13	Gillen, Pete
1996	NCAA	I	16		32	18	12	Gillen, Pete

Year	Assn	Div	F	Bye	#T	W	L	Coach
PURDUE								
1974	NCAA	I	1		16	21	9	Schaus, Frederick A.
1979	NCAA	I	2		24	27	8	Rose, Lee H.
1982	NCAA	I	2		32	18	14	Keady, Lloyd Eugene "Gene"
1981	NCAA	I	3		32	21	11	Keady, Lloyd Eugene "Gene"
1992	NCAA	I	8		32	18	15	Keady, Lloyd Eugene "Gene"
1971	NCAA	I	16		16	18	7	King, George S., Jr.
RENSSELAER								
1945	NCAA		8		8	13	1	Donald, Edmund W. "Ed"
RHODE ISLAND								
1946	NCAA		2		8	22	3	Keaney, Frank W.
1945	NCAA		4		8	20	4	Keaney, Frank W.
1941	NCAA		8		8	21	4	Keaney, Frank W.
1942	NCAA		8		8	18	4	Keaney, Frank W.
1992	NCAA	I	8		32	22	10	Skinner, Albert L., Jr.
1996	NCAA	I	8		32	20	14	Skinner, Albert L., Jr.
1979	NCAA	I	24		24	20	9	Kraft, John J. "Jack"
1981	NCAA	I	32		32	21	8	Kraft, John J. "Jack"
1987	NCAA	I	32		32	20	10	Penders, Thomas V.
RICE								
1943	NCAA		8		8	16	6	Davis, Joe W. "Bloddy Joe"
1993	NCAA	I	16		32	18	10	Thompson, Scott
1991	NCAA	I	32		32	16	14	Thompson, Scott
RICHMOND								
1985	NCAA	I	16		32	21	11	Tarrant, Dick
1989	NCAA	I	16		32	21	10	Tarrant, Dick
1982	NCAA	I	32		32	18	11	Tarrant, Dick
1992	NCAA	I	32		32	22	8	Tarrant, Dick
RIDER								
1998	NCAA	I	32		32	18	10	Harnum, Donald
ROANOKE								
1939	NAIA		6		6	21	3	White, Gordon C. "Pap"
RUTGERS								
1967	NCAA	I	3		14	22	7	Foster, William E.
1978	NCAA	I	3		16	24	7	Young, Thomas J.
1990	NCAA	I	8		32	18	17	Wenzel, Robert
1969	NCAA	I	16		16	21	4	Foster, William E.
1973	NCAA	I	16		16	15	11	Lloyd, Richard R.
1974	NCAA	I	16		16	18	8	Young, Thomas J.
1977	NCAA	I	16		16	18	10	Young, Thomas J.
1982	NCAA	I	16		32	20	10	Young, Thomas J.
1992	NCAA	I	16		32	16	15	Wenzel, Robert
SAINT BONAVENTURE								
1977	NCAA	I	1		16	23	6	Satalin, James D.
1952	NCAA		3	To R8	12	21	6	Melvin, Edward M. (Milkovich)
1958	NCAA	I	3	To R8	12	21	5	Donovan, Edward J. "Eddie"
1971	NCAA	I	3		16	21	6	Weise, Lawrence J.

Year	Assn	Div	F	Bye	#T	W	L	Coach
1957	NCAA	I	4		12	17	7	Donovan, Edward J. 'Eddie'
1960	NCAA	I	4		12	21	5	Donovan, Edward J. 'Eddie'
1951	NCAA		8		12	19	6	Melvin, Edward M. (Milkovich)
1959	NCAA	I	8	To R8	12	20	3	Donovan, Edward J. 'Eddie'
1964	NCAA	I	12		12	16	8	Weise, Lawrence J.
1995	NCAA	I	16		32	18	13	Baron, James E.
1979	NCAA	I	24		24	19	9	Satalin, James D.
1983	NCAA	I	32		32	20	10	O'Brien, James J.
1998	NCAA	I	32		32	17	15	Baron, James E.

SAINT FRANCIS (NY)

Year	Assn	Div	F	Bye	#T	W	L	Coach
1956	NAIA		4		12	21	4	Lynch, Daniel J.
1954	NAIA		8		12	22	5	Lynch, Daniel J.
1963	NCAA	I	12		12	16	7	Lynch, Daniel J.

SAINT FRANCIS (PA)

Year	Assn	Div	F	Bye	#T	W	L	Coach
1955	NCAA		4		12	21	7	Hughes, Dr. William T. 'Skip'
1954	NCAA		8		12	21	5	Hughes, Dr. William T. 'Skip'
1958	NCAA	I	12		12	20	5	Hughes, Dr. William T. 'Skip'

SAINT JOHN'S (NY)

Year	Assn	Div	F	Bye	#T	W	L	Coach
1943	NCAA		1		8	21	3	Lapchick, Joseph B.
1944	NCAA		1		8	18	5	Lapchick, Joseph B.
1959	NCAA	I	1		12	20	6	Lapchick, Joseph B.
1965	NCAA	I	1		14	21	8	Lapchick, Joseph B.
1989	NCAA	I	1		32	20	13	Carnesecca, Louis P. 'Lou'
1953	NCAA		2		12	17	6	DeStefano, Alfred 'Dusty'
1962	NCAA	I	2	To R8	12	21	5	Lapchick, Joseph B.
1970	NCAA	I	2		16	21	8	Carnesecca, Louis P. 'Lou'
1945	NCAA		3		8	21	3	Lapchick, Joseph B.
1950	NCAA		3	To R8	12	24	5	McGuire, Frank J.
1951	NCAA		3	To R8	12	26	5	McGuire, Frank J.
1939	NCAA		4		6	18	4	Lapchick, Joseph B.
1958	NCAA	I	4		12	18	8	Lapchick, Joseph B.
1972	NCAA	I	4		16	19	11	Mulzoff, Frank
1975	NCAA	I	4		16	21	10	Carnesecca, Louis P. 'Lou'
1940	NCAA		6		6	15	4	Lapchick, Joseph B.
1946	NCAA		8		8	17	6	Lapchick, Joseph B.
1947	NCAA		8		8	16	7	Lapchick, Joseph B.
1952	NCAA		8	To R8	12	25	5	McGuire, Frank J.
1960	NCAA	I	8	To R8	12	17	8	Lapchick, Joseph B.
1949	NCAA		12		12	16	9	McGuire, Frank J.
1966	NCAA	I	14		14	18	8	Carnesecca, Louis P. 'Lou'
1971	NCAA	I	16		16	18	9	Mulzoff, Frank
1974	NCAA	I	16		16	20	7	Carnesecca, Louis P. 'Lou'
1981	NCAA	I	32		32	17	11	Carnesecca, Louis P. 'Lou'
1995	NCAA	I	32		32	14	14	Mahoney, Brian C.

SAINT JOSEPH'S (PA)

Year	Assn	Div	F	Bye	#T	W	L	Coach
1996	NCAA	I	2		32	19	13	Martelli, Phil
1956	NCAA		3	To R8	12	23	6	Ramsay, Dr. John T. 'Jack'
1958	NCAA	I	8		12	18	9	Ramsay, Dr. John T. 'Jack'
1964	NCAA	I	8		12	18	10	Ramsay, Dr. John T. 'Jack'

Year	Assn	Div	F	Bye	#T	W	L	Coach
1972	NCAA	I	16		16	19	9	McKinney, John P. "Jack"
1985	NCAA	I	16		32	19	12	Boyle, Jim
1979	NCAA	I	24		24	19	11	Lynam, James F.
1980	NCAA	I	32		32	21	9	Lynam, James F.
1984	NCAA	I	32		32	20	9	Boyle, Jim
1993	NCAA	I	32		32	18	11	Griffin, John
1995	NCAA	I	32		32	17	12	Griffin, John

Saint Louis

Year	Assn	Div	F	Bye	#T	W	L	Coach
1948	NCAA		1		8	24	3	Hickey, Edgar S. "Eddie"
1961	NCAA	I	2		12	21	9	Bennington, John E.
1989	NCAA	I	2		32	27	10	Grawer, Richard "Rich"
1990	NCAA	I	2		32	21	12	Grawer, Richard "Rich"
1949	NCAA		8	To R8	12	22	4	Hickey, Edgar S. "Eddie"
1951	NCAA		8		12	22	8	Hickey, Edgar S. "Eddie"
1952	NCAA		8	To R8	12	23	8	Hickey, Edgar S. "Eddie"
1955	NCAA		8		12	20	8	Hickey, Edgar S. "Eddie"
1959	NCAA	I	8	To R8	12	20	6	Bennington, John E.
1960	NCAA	I	8	To R8	12	19	8	Bennington, John E.
1963	NCAA	I	8		12	16	12	Bennington, John E.
1953	NCAA		12		12	16	11	Hickey, Edgar S. "Eddie"
1956	NCAA		12		12	20	8	Hickey, Edgar S. "Eddie"
1965	NCAA	I	14		14	18	9	Bennington, John E.
1987	NCAA	I	16		32	25	10	Grawer, Richard "Rich"
1996	NCAA	I	32		32	16	14	Spoonhour, Charles

Saint Peter's

Year	Assn	Div	F	Bye	#T	W	L	Coach
1968	NCAA	I	4		16	24	4	Kennedy, Don, Sr.
1969	NCAA	I	8		16	21	7	Kennedy, Don, Sr.
1980	NCAA	I	8		32	22	9	Dukiet, Bob
1957	NCAA	I	12		12	18	4	Kennedy, Don, Sr.
1958	NCAA	I	12		12	20	4	Kennedy, Don, Sr.
1976	NCAA	I	12		12	19	11	McDonald, James R. "Dick"
1967	NCAA	I	14		14	18	6	Kennedy, Don, Sr.
1975	NCAA	I	16		16	15	12	McDonald, James R. "Dick"
1982	NCAA	I	32		32	20	9	Dukiet, Bob
1984	NCAA	I	32		32	23	6	Dukiet, Bob
1987	NCAA	I	32		32	21	8	Fiore, Ted
1989	NCAA	I	32		32	22	9	Fiore, Ted

San Diego State

Year	Assn	Div	F	Bye	#T	W	L	Coach
1982	NCAA	I	32		32	20	9	Gaines, David "Smokey"

San Francisco

Year	Assn	Div	F	Bye	#T	W	L	Coach
1949	NCAA		1		12	25	5	Newell, Peter F.
1966	NCAA	I	8		14	22	6	Peletta, Peter P.
1950	NCAA		12		12	19	7	Newell, Peter F.
1976	NCAA	I	12		12	22	8	Gaillard, Dr. Bob

San Jose State

Year	Assn	Div	F	Bye	#T	W	L	Coach
1981	NCAA	I	32		32	21	9	Berry, William

Year	Assn	Div	F	Bye	#T	W	L	Coach
SANTA CLARA								
1984	NCAA	I	8		32	22	10	Williams, Carroll M.
1985	NCAA	I	32		32	20	9	Williams, Carroll M.
1988	NCAA	I	32		32	20	11	Williams, Carroll M.
1989	NCAA	I	32		32	20	11	Williams, Carroll M.
SEATTLE								
1957	NCAA	I	8	To R8	12	24	3	Castellani, John
1952	NCAA		12		12	29	8	Brightman, Horace Albert "Al"
SETON HALL								
1953	NCAA		1	To R8	12	31	2	Russell, John D. "Honey"
1941			4		8	20	2	Russell, John D. "Honey"
1951	NCAA		4		12	24	7	Russell, John D. "Honey"
1956	NCAA		8		12	20	5	Russell, John D. "Honey"
1952	NCAA		12		12	25	3	Russell, John D. "Honey"
1955	NCAA		12		12	17	9	Russell, John D. "Honey"
1957	NCAA	I	12		12	17	10	Russell, John D. "Honey"
1974	NCAA	I	16		16	16	11	Raftery, William J.
1977	NCAA	I	16		16	18	11	Raftery, William J.
1987	NCAA	I	32		32	15	14	Carlesimo, Peter J. "PJ"
1995	NCAA	I	32		32	16	14	Blaney, George R.
1998	NCAA	I	32		32	15	15	Amaker, Tommy
SIENA (NY)								
1994	NCAA	I	3		32	25	8	Deane, Mike
1991	NCAA	I	8		32	25	10	Deane, Mike
1988	NCAA	I	32		32	23	6	Deane, Mike
SOUTH ALABAMA								
1981	NCAA	I	8		32	25	6	Ellis, Cliff
1984	NCAA	I	16		32	22	8	Ellis, Cliff
SOUTH CAROLINA								
1969	NCAA	I	8		16	21	7	McGuire, Frank J.
1975	NCAA	I	8		16	19	9	McGuire, Frank J.
1983	NCAA	I	8		32	22	9	Foster, William E.
1996	NCAA	I	8		32	19	12	Fogler, Eddie
1978	NCAA	I	16		16	16	12	McGuire, Frank J.
1991	NCAA	I	16		32	20	13	Felton, George
SOUTH FLORIDA								
1995	NCAA	I	8		32	18	12	Paschal, Bobby
1983	NCAA	I	16		32	22	10	Rose, Lee H.
1985	NCAA	I	16		32	18	12	Rose, Lee H.
1981	NCAA	I	32		32	18	11	Rose, Lee H.
1991	NCAA	I	32		32	19	11	Paschal, Bobby
SOUTHERN CALIFORNIA								
1993	NCAA	I	8		32	18	12	Raveling, George
1973	NCAA	I	16		16	18	10	Boyd, William R. "Bob"
1994	NCAA	I	32		32	16	12	Raveling, George

Year	Assn	Div	F	Bye	#T	W	L	Coach
SOUTHERN ILLINOIS								
1967	NCAA	II	1		14	24	2	Hartman, Jack
1991	NCAA	I	8		32	18	14	Herrin, Richard "Rich"
1969	NCAA	I	16		16	16	8	Hartman, Jack
1975	NCAA	I	16		16	18	9	Lambert, Paul M.
1989	NCAA	I	32		32	20	14	Herrin, Richard "Rich"
1990	NCAA	I	32		32	26	8	Herrin, Richard "Rich"
1992	NCAA	I	32		32	22	8	Herrin, Richard "Rich"
SOUTHERN METHODIST (TX)								
1986	NCAA	I	32		32	18	11	Bliss, David
SOUTHERN MISSISSIPPI								
1987	NCAA	I	1		32	23	11	Turk, M. K.
1988	NCAA	I	16		32	19	11	Turk, M. K.
1981	NCAA	I	32		32	20	7	Turk, M. K.
1986	NCAA	I	32		32	17	12	Turk, M. K.
1994	NCAA	I	32		32	15	15	Turk, M. K.
1995	NCAA	I	32		32	17	13	Turk, M. K.
1998	NCAA	I	32		32	22	11	Green, James
SOUTHERN: BATON ROUGE								
1990	NCAA	I	32		32	25	6	Jobe, Ben
SOUTHWEST MISSOURI STATE								
1986	NCAA	I	8		32	24	8	Spoonhour, Charles
1993	NCAA	I	8		32	20	11	Bernsen, Mark
1991	NCAA	I	16		32	22	12	Spoonhour, Charles
1997	NCAA	I	32		32	24	9	Alford, Stephen T.
SOUTHWESTERN LOUISIANA								
1984	NCAA	I	4		32	23	10	Paschal, Bobby
1980	NCAA	I	8		32	21	9	Paschal, Bobby
1985	NCAA	I	16		32	17	14	Paschal, Bobby
STANFORD								
1991	NCAA	I	1		32	20	13	Montgomery, Mike
1988	NCAA	I	16		32	21	12	Montgomery, Mike
1990	NCAA	I	32		32	18	12	Montgomery, Mike
1994	NCAA	I	32		32	17	11	Montgomery, Mike
STEPHEN F AUSTIN STATE								
1987	NCAA	I	16		32	22	8	Miller, Harry E.
SYRACUSE								
1981	NCAA	I	2		32	22	12	Boeheim, James A., Jr.
1946	NCAA		8		8	23	4	Andreas, Lewis P.
1950	NCAA		8		12	18	9	Andreas, Lewis P.
1972	NCAA	I	8		16	22	6	Danforth, Roy
1964	NCAA	I	12		12	17	8	Lewis, Frederick B., Jr.
1967	NCAA	I	14		14	20	6	Lewis, Frederick B., Jr.
1971	NCAA	I	16		16	19	7	Danforth, Roy
1982	NCAA	I	16		32	16	13	Boeheim, James A., Jr.
1997	NCAA	I	32		32	19	13	Boeheim, James A., Jr.

Year	Assn	Div	F	Bye	#T	W	L	Coach
TEMPLE								
1938	NCAA		1		6	23	2	Usilton, James
1969	NCAA	I	1		16	22	8	Litwack, Harry
1957	NCAA	I	3	To R8	12	20	9	Litwack, Harry
1961	NCAA	I	8		12	20	8	Litwack, Harry
1962	NCAA	I	8		12	18	9	Litwack, Harry
1966	NCAA	I	8		14	21	7	Litwack, Harry
1960	NCAA	I	12		12	17	9	Litwack, Harry
1968	NCAA	I	16		16	19	9	Litwack, Harry
1978	NCAA	I	16		16	24	5	Casey, Don
1981	NCAA	I	16		32	20	8	Casey, Don
1982	NCAA	I	32		32	19	8	Casey, Don
1989	NCAA	I	32		32	18	12	Chaney, John
TENNESSEE								
1969	NCAA	I	3		16	21	7	Mears, Ramon "Ray"
1985	NCAA	I	3		32	22	15	DeVoe, Donald E.
1945	NCAA		8		8	18	5	Mauer, John W.
1971	NCAA	I	8		16	21	7	Mears, Ramon "Ray"
1984	NCAA	I	8		32	21	14	DeVoe, Donald E.
1990	NCAA	I	16		32	16	14	Houston, Wade
1992	NCAA	I	16		32	19	15	Houston, Wade
1988	NCAA	I	32		32	16	13	DeVoe, Donald E.
1996	NCAA	I	32		32	14	15	O'Neill, Kevin
TENNESSEE TECH								
1985	NCAA	I	32		32	19	9	Deaton, Tom
TENNESSEE: CHATTANOOGA								
1985	NCAA	I	8		32	24	8	Arnold, Murray
1984	NCAA	I	16		32	24	7	Arnold, Murray
1986	NCAA	I	32		32	21	10	McCarthy, Mack
1987	NCAA	I	32		32	21	8	McCarthy, Mack
TEXAS								
1978	NCAA	I	1		16	26	5	Lemons, A. E. "Abe"
1948	NCAA		8		8	20	5	Gray, Jack S.
1980	NCAA	I	16		32	19	11	Lemons, A. E. "Abe"
1986	NCAA	I	16		32	19	12	Weltlich, Robert
TEXAS A&M								
1979	NCAA	I	6		24	24	9	Metcalf, Dr. Shelby R.
1982	NCAA	I	8		32	20	11	Metcalf, Dr. Shelby R.
1985	NCAA	I	32		32	19	11	Metcalf, Dr. Shelby R.
1986	NCAA	I	32		32	20	12	Metcalf, Dr. Shelby R.
1994	NCAA	I	32		32	19	11	Barone, Anthony A. "Tony"
TEXAS CHRISTIAN								
1983	NCAA	I	8		32	23	11	Killingsworth, James
1986	NCAA	I	16		32	22	9	Killingsworth, James
1992	NCAA	I	16		32	23	11	Iba, Moe
1997	NCAA	I	16		32	22	13	Tubbs, Billy
TEXAS TECH								
1979	NCAA	I	24		24	19	11	Myers, Gerald
1995	NCAA	I	32		32	20	10	Dickey, James

Year	Assn	Div	F	Bye	#T	W	L	Coach
TEXAS: ARLINGTON								
1981	NCAA	I	32		32	20	8	LeGrand, Bob "Snake"
TEXAS: EL PASO								
1965	NCAA	I	14		14	17	9	Haskins, Donald L.
1972	NCAA	I	16		16	20	7	Haskins, Donald L.
1980	NCAA	I	16		32	20	8	Haskins, Donald L.
1981	NCAA	I	16		32	18	12	Haskins, Donald L.
1993	NCAA	I	16		32	21	13	Haskins, Donald L.
1995	NCAA	I	16		32	20	10	Haskins, Donald L.
1983	NCAA	I	32		32	19	10	Haskins, Donald L.
TEXAS: PAN AMERICAN								
1981	NCAA	I	32		32	18	11	White, Bill
TOLEDO								
1943	NCAA		2		8	22	4	Friddle, Burl
1942	NCAA		4		8	23	5	Anderson, W. Harold "Andy"
1981	NCAA	I	16		32	21	10	Nichols, Robert J.
TULANE								
1996	NCAA	I	3		32	22	10	Clark, Perry
1982	NCAA	I	8		32	19	9	Fowler, Ned
1994	NCAA	I	16		32	18	11	Clark, Perry
1983	NCAA	I	32		32	19	12	Fowler, Ned
1997	NCAA	I	32		32	20	11	Clark, Perry
TULSA								
1981	NCAA	I	1		32	26	7	Richardson, Nolan
1953	NCAA		12		12	15	10	Iba, Clarence V.
1967	NCAA		14		14	19	8	Swank, Joe
1969	NCAA	I	16		16	19	8	Hayes, Ken
1983	NCAA	I	32		32	19	12	Richardson, Nolan
1990	NCAA	I	32		32	17	13	Barnett, J. D.
1991	NCAA	I	32		32	18	12	Barnett, J. D.
UTAH								
1947	NCAA		1		8	19	5	Peterson, Vadal
1974	NCAA	I	2		16	22	8	Foster, William E.
1992	NCAA	I	3		32	24	11	Majerus, Rick
1944	NCAA		8		8	21	4	Peterson, Vadal
1949	NCAA		8	To R8	12	24	8	Peterson, Vadal
1958	NCAA	I	8	To R8	12	20	7	Gardner, James H. "Jack"
1970	NCAA	I	8		16	18	10	Gardner, James H. "Jack"
1957	NCAA	I	12		12	19	8	Gardner, James H. "Jack"
1987	NCAA	I	32		32	17	13	Archibald, Lynn
1988	NCAA	I	32		32	19	11	Archibald, Lynn
UTAH STATE								
1960	NCAA	I	3	To R8	12	24	5	Baker, H. Cecil
1967	NCAA	I	14		14	20	6	Anderson, Ladell
1978	NCAA	I	16		16	21	7	Belnap, Gordon "Dutch"
1984	NCAA	I	32		32	19	11	Tueller, Rod
1995	NCAA	I	32		32	21	8	Eustachy, Larry

Year	Assn	Div	F	Bye	#T	W	L	Coach
VANDERBILT								
1990	NCAA	I	1		32	21	14	Fogler, Eddie
1994	NCAA	I	2		32	20	12	Van Breda Kolff, Jan M.
1987	NCAA	I	8		32	18	16	Newton, Charles M. 'CM'
1998	NCAA	I	8		32	20	13	Van Breda Kolff, Jan M.
1983	NCAA	I	16		32	19	14	Newton, Charles M. 'CM'
1996	NCAA	I	16		32	18	14	Van Breda Kolff, Jan M.
1992	NCAA	I	32		32	15	15	Fogler, Eddie
VILLANOVA								
1994	NCAA	I	1		32	20	12	Lappas, Steve
1965	NCAA	I	2	To R8	14	23	5	Kraft, John J. 'Jack'
1966	NCAA	I	3		14	18	11	Kraft, John J. 'Jack'
1977	NCAA	I	3		16	23	10	Massimino, Roland V. 'Rollie'
1963	NCAA	I	4		12	19	10	Kraft, John J. 'Jack'
1960	NCAA	I	8		12	20	6	Severance, Alexander G.
1968	NCAA	I	8		16	19	9	Kraft, John J. 'Jack'
1989	NCAA	I	8		32	18	16	Massimino, Roland V. 'Rollie'
1959	NCAA	I	12		12	18	7	Severance, Alexander G.
1967	NCAA	I	14		14	17	9	Kraft, John J. 'Jack'
1987	NCAA	I	32		32	15	16	Massimino, Roland V. 'Rollie'
1992	NCAA	I	32		32	14	15	Massimino, Roland V. 'Rollie'
VIRGINIA								
1980	NCAA	I	1		32	24	10	Holland, M. Terrance 'Terry'
1992	NCAA	I	1		32	20	13	Jones, Jeffrey A.
1941	NCAA		8		8	16	5	Tebell, Gus K.
1985	NCAA	I	8		32	17	16	Holland, M. Terrance 'Terry'
1979	NCAA	I	12		24	19	10	Holland, M. Terrance 'Terry'
1972	NCAA	I	16		16	21	7	Gibson, William J.
1978	NCAA	I	16		16	20	8	Holland, M. Terrance 'Terry'
VIRGINIA COMMONWEALTH								
1988	NCAA	I	8		32	23	12	Pollio, Mike
1978	NCAA	I	16		16	24	5	Kirk, Dana
1993	NCAA	I	32		32	20	10	Smith, Charles H. 'Sonny'
VIRGINIA POLYTECHNIC								
1973	NCAA	I	1		16	22	5	DeVoe, Donald E.
1995	NCAA	I	1		32	25	10	Foster, William C.
1984	NCAA	I	3		32	22	13	Moir, Charles
1977	NCAA	I	8		16	19	10	Moir, Charles
1982	NCAA	I	8		32	20	11	Moir, Charles
1966	NCAA	I	14		14	19	5	Shannon, Howard P. 'Howie'
1983	NCAA	I	16		32	23	11	Moir, Charles
WAGNER								
1979	NCAA	I	24		24	21	7	Carlesimo, Peter J. 'PJ'
WAKE FOREST								
1983	NCAA	I	3		32	20	12	Tacy, Carl R.
1998	NCAA	I	16		32	16	14	Odom, Dave
1985	NCAA	I	32		32	15	14	Tacy, Carl R.

Year	Assn	Div	F	Bye	#T	W	L	Coach
WASHINGTON								
1987	NCAA	I	8		32	20	15	Russo, Andy
1982	NCAA	I	16		32	19	10	Harshman, Marvel K. "Marv"
1980	NCAA	I	32		32	18	10	Harshman, Marvel K. "Marv"
1996	NCAA	I	32		32	16	12	Bender, Robert M., Jr.
1997	NCAA	I	32		32	17	11	Bender, Robert M., Jr.
WASHINGTON & JEFFERSON								
1943	NCAA		3		8	18	5	Sanders, Adam
WASHINGTON STATE								
1995	NCAA	I	8		32	18	12	Eastman, Kevin
1992	NCAA	I	16		32	22	11	Sampson, Kelvin
1996	NCAA	I	16		32	17	12	Eastman, Kevin
WEBER STATE								
1984	NCAA	I	16		32	23	8	McCarthy, Neil N.
WEST TEXAS A&M								
1942	NCAA		8		8	28	3	Baggett, Al
1969	NCAA	I	16		16	18	7	Walling, Dennis W.
1980	NCAA	I	32		32	19	11	Edwards, Ken
WEST VIRGINIA								
1942	NCAA		1		8	19	4	Raese, Richard "Dyke"
1946	NCAA		3		8	24	3	Patton, Lee
1947	NCAA		4		8	19	3	Patton, Lee
1981	NCAA	I	4		32	23	10	Catlett, Gale
1945	NCAA		8		8	12	6	Brickels, John L.
1997	NCAA	I	8		32	21	10	Catlett, Gale
1968	NCAA	I	16		16	19	9	Waters, Raymond C. "Bucky"
1991	NCAA	I	16		32	17	14	Catlett, Gale
1993	NCAA	I	16		32	17	12	Catlett, Gale
1994	NCAA	I	16		32	17	12	Catlett, Gale
1985	NCAA	I	32		32	20	9	Catlett, Gale
1988	NCAA	I	32		32	18	14	Catlett, Gale
WESTERN KENTUCKY								
1942	NCAA		2		8	29	5	Diddle, Edgar A., Sr.
1948	NCAA		3		8	28	2	Diddle, Edgar A., Sr.
1954	NCAA		4	To R8	12	29	3	Diddle, Edgar A., Sr.
1943	NCAA		8		8	24	3	Diddle, Edgar A., Sr.
1949	NCAA		8	To R8	12	25	4	Diddle, Edgar A., Sr.
1950	NCAA		8		12	25	6	Diddle, Edgar A., Sr.
1952	NCAA		8		12	26	5	Diddle, Edgar A., Sr.
1953	NCAA		8	To R8	12	25	6	Diddle, Edgar A., Sr.
1965	NCAA	I	8		14	17	8	Diddle, Edgar A., Sr.
1982	NCAA	I	32		32	19	10	Haskins, Clem S.
1992	NCAA	I	32		32	21	11	Willard, Ralph
WESTERN MICHIGAN								
1992	NCAA	I	32		32	21	9	Donewald, Bob
WESTMINSTER (MO)								
1941	NAIA		8		8	10	8	Kimbrell, Eugene F.

Year	Assn	Div	F	Bye	#T	W	L	Coach
WICHITA STATE								
1963	NCAA	I	8	To R8	12	19	8	Miller, Ralph H. "Cappy"
1966	NCAA	I	8	To R8	14	17	10	Thompson, Gary
1954	NCAA		12		12	27	4	Miller, Ralph H. "Cappy"
1962	NCAA	I	12		12	18	9	Miller, Ralph H. "Cappy"
1989	NCAA	I	16		32	19	11	Fogler, Eddie
1980	NCAA	I	32		32	17	12	Smithson, Eugene
1984	NCAA	I	32		32	18	12	Smithson, Eugene
WILLIAM & MARY								
1983	NCAA	I	32		32	20	9	Parkhill, Bruce
WISCONSIN								
1989	NCAA	I	16		32	18	12	Yoder, Steve
1991	NCAA	I	16		32	15	15	Yoder, Steve
1996	NCAA	I	16		32	17	15	Bennett, Richard
1993	NCAA	I	32		32	14	14	Jackson, Stu
WISCONSIN: GREEN BAY								
1990	NCAA	I	16		32	24	8	Bennett, Richard
1992	NCAA	I	32		32	25	5	Bennett, Richard
WYOMING								
1986	NCAA	I	2		32	24	12	Brandenburg, Jim
1968	NCAA	I	16		16	18	9	Strannigan, William M.
1969	NCAA	I	16		16	19	9	Strannigan, William M.
1991	NCAA	I	16		32	20	12	Dees, Benny
1998	NCAA	I	32		32	19	9	Shyatt, Larry
XAVIER (OH)								
1958	NCAA	I	1		12	19	11	McCafferty, James J.
1956	NCAA		8		12	17	11	Wulk, Ned W.
1957	NCAA	I	8		12	20	8	Wulk, Ned W.
1984	NCAA	I	8		32	22	11	Staak, Bob
1994	NCAA	I	8		32	22	8	Gillen, Pete

National Women's Invitational Tournament

Beginning in 1969, the same year as the first Association for Interscholastic Athletics for Women (AIAW) Invitational Tournament, the original NWIT was the oldest, longest running women's collegiate basketball tournament until it ended following the 1996 event.

For 1998, a new Women's NIT was instituted, sponsored by Triple Crown Sports, which sponsors the pre-season women's NIT.

Always an eight-team event with all eight places contested through a consolation bracket and always held in Amarillo, Texas, the original was in no way associated with the more widely known men's event of similar name. In its early years, competing against the AIAW tournament, most of its participants were smaller schools (including junior colleges) from west of the Mississippi, but most of them had well-established reputations in women's basketball from AAU tournaments.

By the late 1970s, after the bigger schools had begun women's basketball and the National Junior College Athletic Association (NJCAA) had started its own women's tournament, the participants were the four-year schools that did not qualify for the then reasonably well-established AIAW event. After the early 1980s when the NCAA and NAIA had begun their own tournaments, Amarillo was able to attract only the nonqualifiers from those two associations.

Except for the first four years when only four teams were seeded, all teams were seeded. For 1975 and 1983, seeding information is unavailable—even from the local newspaper coverage.

The original tournament ceased operation after the 1996 event because sponsors could not or would not meet the requirements imposed by the NCAA for post-season play.

The new sponsor, Triple Crown Sports, was organized in 1982 to organize and produce adult slow-pitch softball tournaments. It now works with youth soccer, roller hockey, baseball and girl's fast-pitch softball in addition to the two basketball tournaments. The 1998 Women's NIT was a 16-team unseeded event for teams that did not receive an invitation the the NCAA division I tournament. Teams were bracketed in four fairly reasonable geographic (but unnamed) sections to produce a final four. All games, including the championship, were played at the home site of one of the participants.

Tournament Results

F	School	Assn	Div	SD	W	L	Coach
1969							
1	Wayland Baptist			1	26	4	Redin, Harley J.
2	Ouachita Baptist			3			Moffatt, Phyllis Carolyn
3	Midwestern (IA)			4	21	X	Horky, Rita J.
4	John F Kennedy (NE)			2	16	10	Spencer, Robert L.
5	Ranger				20	8	Butler, Ron
6	Temple JC				18	12	Garmon, Frances
7	Southern Arkansas				X	X	Downing, Dr. Margaret R.
8	Kansas State	AIAW			11	3	Akers, Judy
1970							
1	Wayland Baptist			1	29	4	Redin, Harley J.
2	Midwestern (IA)			2			Hart, Kay
3	Ouachita Baptist			3			Moffatt, Phyllis Carolyn
4	John F Kennedy (NE)			4	15	12	Spencer, Robert L.
5	Ranger				21	9	Butler, Ron
6	Temple JC				29	12	Garmon, Frances
7	Kansas State	AIAW			10	7	Akers, Judy
8	West Texas A&M				X	X	Stovall, Allene
1971							
1	Wayland Baptist			1	30	2	Redin, Harley J.
2	Parsons			2	30	11	Spencer, Robert L.
3	John F Kennedy (NE)			3	14	16	Nicodemus, George L.
4	Seminole JC (OK)			4	X	X	Hull, Kenneth
5	Ranger				26	8	Butler, Ron
6	Temple JC				24	12	Garmon, Frances
7	Belmont				14	7	Wiseman, Betty
8	McPherson				X	X	Coppock, Dr. Doris
1972							
1	Wayland Baptist			2	26	7	Redin, Harley J.
2	John F Kennedy (NE)			1	27	10	Nicodemus, George L.
3	Murray State (OK)				18	10	Hedden, Jack E.
4	Parsons			3	17	12	Spencer, Robert L.

F	School	Assn	Div	SD	W	L	Coach
5	Belmont			4	12	6	Wiseman, Betty
6	Temple JC				26	12	Garmon, Frances
7	Seminole JC (OK)				X	X	Woodall, Dixie
8	Ranger				24	10	Butler, Ron

1973

F	School	Assn	Div	SD	W	L	Coach
1	Wayland Baptist			2	21	7	Redin, Harley J.
2	John F Kennedy (NE)			1	34	7	Nicodemus, George L.
3	Parsons			3	20	16	Spencer, Robert L.
4	Ranger			5	22	6	Butler, Ron
5	Murray State (OK)			4	18	7	Imotichey, Melvin
6	Seminole JC (OK)			6	X	X	Woodall, Dixie
7	Belmont			8	14	8	Wiseman, Betty
8	Northeast Louisiana			7	X	X	Lewis, "Lou"

1974

F	School	Assn	Div	SD	W	L	Coach
1	Wayland Baptist	AIAW		2	37	5	Weese, Dean
2	John F Kennedy (NE)			1	26	5	Nicodemus, George L.
3	Temple JC	AIAW	J/CC	3	27	8	Garmon, Frances
4	California: Los Angeles	AIAW		4	X	X	Chaffee, Bob
5	Ranger			8	20	10	Butler, Ron
6	Belmont			6	22	6	Wiseman, Betty
7	Mississippi Women	AIAW		5	12	8	Upton, Jill
8	Phillips (OK)	AIAW		7			Amaya, Lou

1975

F	School	Assn	Div	SD	W	L	Coach
1	Wayland Baptist	AIAW	L	1	34	1	Weese, Dean
2	California: Los Angeles	AIAW	L		18	4	Washington, Kenny
3	Belmont				22	3	Wiseman, Betty
4	Mercer	AIAW	L		23	6	Collins, Peggy E.
5	John F Kennedy (NE)			2	21	16	Nicodemus, George L.
6	North Carolina				15	3	Lurapkin, Angela
7	Mississippi College	AIAW	L		27	7	Nixon, Ed
8	Indiana	AIAW	L		19	6	Gorton, Bea

1976

F	School	Assn	Div	SD	W	L	Coach
1	Wayland Baptist	AIAW	L	1	34	5	Weese, Dean
2	California: Los Angeles	AIAW	L	2	19	4	Hanson, Ellen Mosher
3	Nevada: Las Vegas			3	26	5	Ayala, Dan
4	Belmont			4	19	6	Wiseman, Betty
5	Nebraska			5	22	9	Nicodemus, George L.
6	North Carolina State			8	19	7	Yow, Sandra Kay
7	West Texas A&M			7	X	X	Stovall, Allene
8	Indiana State	AIAW		6	19	9	Godleski, Edith

1977

F	School	Assn	Div	SD	W	L	Coach
1	Wayland Baptist	AIAW	L	1	31	5	Weese, Dean
2	California: Los Angeles	AIAW	L	2	20	3	Hanson, Ellen Mosher
3	Mississippi College	AIAW	L	3	22	14	Nixon, Ed
4	Old Dominion	AIAW	L	4	23	9	Parsons, Pam
5	Valdosta State	AIAW	L	6	26	6	Worth, Lyndal
6	Belmont			5	15	10	Wiseman, Betty
7	Indiana State	AIAW		7	19	9	Godleski, Edith
8	Alabama	AIAW	L	8	13	15	Schleider, Stephanie

F	School	Assn	Div	SD	W	L	Coach
1978							
1	Old Dominion	AIAW	L	1	30	4	Stanley, Marianne Crawford
2	Texas	AIAW	L	2	29	10	Conradt, Jody
3	Kentucky	AIAW	L	4	23	12	Yow, Deborah Ann
4	California State: Long Beach	AIAW	L	3	18	9	Schaafsma, Dr. Frances
5	Drake (IA)				23	9	Baumgarten, Carole
6	Kansas	AIAW	L		22	11	Washington, Marian
7	Minnesota	AIAW	L		21	7	Hanson, Ellen Mosher
8	Fort Valley State	AIAW	S		13	9	Brown, Jessie A.
1979							
1	South Carolina	AIAW	L	1	27	10	Parsons, Pam
2	Drake (IA)			3	28	5	Baumgarten, Carole
3	Oregon	AIAW	L	4	23	2	Heiny, Elwin
4	Northern Kentucky	AIAW	S	7	25	10	Moore, Marilyn
5	Minnesota	AIAW	L	5	17	15	Hanson, Ellen Mosher
6	Mississippi College	AIAW	L	2	14	18	Nixon, Ed
7	Utah	AIAW	L	6	23	10	Gardner, Fern
8	California	AIAW	L	8	14	17	Cantrell, Marci
1980							
1	Oregon State	AIAW	I	3	22	9	Hill, Aki
2	North Carolina			4	21	15	Alley, Jennifer
3	Drake (IA)			7	24	12	Baumgarten, Carole
4	Virginia			8	20	12	Ryan, Deborah H.
5	Illinois State	AIAW	I	5	23	10	Hutchison, Dr. Jill
6	Mississippi College	AIAW	I	6	21	8	Smith, Durward
7	Clemson	AIAW	I	2	24	12	Tribble, Annie S.
8	Wayland Baptist	AIAW	I	1	20	15	Wilson, Cathy
1981							
1	Georgia	AIAW	I	4	27	10	Landers, Andy
2	Arizona State	AIAW	I	8	21	11	Simpson, Juliene
3	Drake (IA)			2	26	7	Baumgarten, Carole
4	California	AIAW	I	3	22	10	Foster, Dr. Gooch
5	Pittsburgh			5	22	7	Saurer, Judy
6	Tennessee Tech	AIAW	I	1	22	9	Meadors, Marynell Hutsell
7	Cincinnati			7	27	9	Barry, Ceal
8	Baylor	AIAW	I	6	29	11	Bowers, Pam Davis
1982							
1	Oregon State	NCAA	I	2	20	8	Hill, Aki
2	Florida State	NCAA	I	1	27	10	Dykehouse-Allen, Janice
3	Brigham Young	NCAA	I	5	24	13	Leishman, Dr. Courtney M.
4	Illinois State	NCAA	I	4	19	15	Hutchison, Dr. Jill
5	De Paul	NCAA	I	3	18	12	Feiereisel, Ronald E.
6	Temple	NCAA	I	6	20	11	Hill-MacDonald, Linda
7	Southern Mississippi	NCAA	I	7	16	11	James, Kay
8	Pepperdine	NCAA	I	8	16	13	Meyers, Patty

F	School	Assn	Div	SD	W	L	Coach
1983							
1	New Orleans	NCAA	I		23	8	Favaloro, Joey
2	Memphis	NCAA	I		21	11	Johns, Mary Lou
3	Oral Roberts	NCAA	I		26	1	Yow, Deborah Ann
4	Weber State	NCAA	I		22	10	Minor, Jane
5	Texas Tech	NCAA	I		22	9	Sharp, Marsha
6	Southern Illinois	NCAA	I		22	11	Scott, Cindy
7	Temple	NCAA	I		19	12	Hill-MacDonald, Linda
8	Hawaii	NCAA	I		17	12	Busone, Jerry
1984							
1	Vanderbilt	NCAA	I	2	23	9	Lee, Phil
2	Tennessee: Chattanooga	NCAA	I	1	26	5	Fanning, Sharon
3	Clemson	NCAA	I	6	21	10	Tribble, Annie S.
4	Western Kentucky	NCAA	I	7	21	11	Sanderford, Paul
5	California	NCAA	I	4	24	8	Foster, Dr. Gooch
6	Oklahoma	NCAA	I	8	23	7	McHugh, Maura
7	Illinois State	NCAA	I	3	28	8	Hutchison, Dr. Jill
8	Utah	NCAA	I	5	19	12	Elliott, Elaine
1985							
1	Louisiana State	NCAA	I	4	20	9	Gunter, Sue
2	Florida	NCAA	I	2	22	9	Yow, Deborah Ann
3	Texas Tech	NCAA	I	1	24	8	Sharp, Marsha
4	Drake (IA)	NCAA	I	3	24	6	Baumgarten, Carole
5	California State: Fullerton	NCAA	I	8	19	11	Gobrecht, Chris
6	West Texas A&M	NCAA	I	6	26	6	Schneider, Bob
7	West Virginia	NCAA	I	5	20	10	Blakemore, Kittie
8	Montana	NCAA	I	7	22	7	Selvig, Robin
1986							
1	Idaho	NCAA	I	5	26	5	Dobratz, Patty Jo
2	Northwestern State (LA)	NCAA	I	6	25	7	Pierson, Pat
3	Notre Dame (IN)	NCAA	I	1	23	8	DiStanislao, Mary
4	Duke	NCAA	I	2	21	9	Leonard, Debbie
5	West Texas A&M	NCAA	I	7	26	5	Schneider, Bob
6	United States International	NCAA	I	8	24	9	Macias, Cassie
7	Tennessee Tech	NCAA	I	3	22	10	Meadors, Marynell Hutsell
8	California State: Fresno	NCAA	I	4	21	9	Spencer, Robert L.
1987							
1	Arkansas	NCAA	I	4	19	10	Sutherland, John
2	California	NCAA	I	1	21	10	Foster, Dr. Gooch
3	Creighton	NCAA	I	6	23	7	Rasmussen, Bruce
4	Providence	NCAA	I	2	23	9	Foley, Bob
5	Stephen F Austin State	NCAA	I	3	25	6	Blair, Gary
6	Montana	NCAA	I	5	26	5	Selvig, Robin
7	De Paul	NCAA	I	7	23	8	Izard, Jim
8	Appalachian State	NCAA	I	8	24	7	Robinson, Linda

F	School	Assn	Div	SD	W	L	Coach
1988							
1	De Paul	NCAA	I	2	27	4	Izard, Jim
2	Purdue	NCAA	I	5	21	10	Dunn, Lin
3	New Orleans	NCAA	I	3	25	7	Favaloro, Joey
4	Illinois State	NCAA	I	8	20	11	Hutchison, Dr. Jill
5	South Alabama	NCAA	I	4	22	9	Branum, Charles
6	Mississippi State	NCAA	I	7	19	13	Paul, Brenda
7	Nevada: Las Vegas	NCAA	I	1	25	9	Bolla, Jim
8	Montana State	NCAA	I	6	24	6	Schwartz, Gary
1989							
1	Oregon	NCAA	I	5	22	10	Heiny, Elwin
2	San Diego State	NCAA	I	1	25	9	Riggins, Earnest
3	Toledo	NCAA	I	2	25	8	Fennelly, Bill
4	Murray State (KY)	NCAA	I	6	22	10	Childers, "Bud"
5	Radford	NCAA	I	8	25	7	Curtis, Charlene
6	De Paul	NCAA	I	4	23	10	Bruno, Doug
7	Notre Dame (IN)	NCAA	I	7	21	11	McGraw, Muffet O'Brien
8	Richmond	NCAA	I	3	24	9	Gaitley, Stephanie Vanderslice
1990							
1	Kentucky	NCAA	I	1	23	8	Fanning, Sharon
2	Toledo	NCAA	I	2	25	7	Fennelly, Bill
3	North Carolina: Charlotte	NCAA	I	3	24	8	Baldwin, Ed
4	Miami (FL)	NCAA	I	4	25	6	Labati, Ferne
5	California State: Fresno	NCAA	I	6	21	12	Spencer, Robert L.
6	Illinois State	NCAA	I	5	21	11	Hutchison, Dr. Jill
7	Maine	NCAA	I	8	23	7	Roberts, Trish
8	Wyoming	NCAA	I	7	24	8	Lavin, Chad
1991							
1	Santa Clara	NCAA	I	8	28	3	Horstmeyer, Caren
2	Indiana	NCAA	I	7	18	13	Izard, Jim
3	Kansas	NCAA	I	5	20	13	Washington, Marian
4	Houston	NCAA	I	6	20	12	Kenlaw, Jessie
5	Alabama: Birmingham	NCAA	I	2	24	8	Milling, Jeannie
6	Louisville	NCAA	I	4	24	11	Childers, "Bud"
7	Northern Illinois	NCAA	I	3	25	10	Albright-Dieterle, Jane
8	Notre Dame (IN)	NCAA	I	1	23	9	McGraw, Muffet O'Brien
1992							
1	Georgia Tech	NCAA	I	2	20	13	Berenato, Agnus McGlade
2	Hawaii	NCAA	I	1	25	7	Goo, Vince
3	Arkansas State	NCAA	I	5	25	7	Winters, Jerry Ann
4	Nebraska	NCAA	I	6	21	11	Beck, Angela
5	Wisconsin: Green Bay	NCAA	I	7	24	7	Hammerle, Carol
6	Florida International	NCAA	I	8	23	10	Russo, Cindy
7	Alabama: Birmingham	NCAA	I	4	24	8	Milling, Jeannie
8	La Salle	NCAA	I	3	25	8	Miller, John

F	School	Assn	Div	SD	W	L	Coach
1993							
1	Arkansas State	NCAA	I	6	16	12	Winters, Jerry Ann
2	Southern Methodist (TX)	NCAA	I	8	20	10	Rompola, Rhonda
3	Florida International	NCAA	I	5	25	6	Russo, Cindy
4	Marquette	NCAA	I	2	22	9	Jabir, James J.
5	Northwestern State (LA)	NCAA	I	7	24	8	Smith, James F.
6	Butler (IN)	NCAA	I	4	23	8	Stein, Paulette
7	Nevada: Las Vegas	NCAA	I	1	24	7	Bolla, Jim
8	George Washington	NCAA	I	3	20	11	McKeown, Joe
1994							
1	Oklahoma	NCAA	I	7	18	12	Plunkett, Burl
2	Arkansas State	NCAA	I	4	22	9	Winters, Jerry Ann
3	Pittsburgh	NCAA	I	3	21	10	Bruce, Kirk
4	Tulane	NCAA	I	8	17	14	Harvey, Candi
5	Toledo	NCAA	I	5	24	8	Fennelly, Bill
6	New Mexico State	NCAA	I	2	24	8	Petersen, Mike
7	Gonzaga	NCAA	I	6	21	10	Holt, Julie
8	Northeast Louisiana	NCAA	I	1	21	14	Stockton, Roger
1995							
1	Texas A&M	NCAA	I	1	21	9	Harvey, Candi
2	Northwestern State (LA)	NCAA	I	7	25	7	Smith, James F.
3	Notre Dame (IN)	NCAA	I	3	21	10	McGraw, Muffet O'Brien
4	Massachusetts	NCAA	I	5	19	11	O'Brien, Joanie
5	Clemson	NCAA	I	2	21	11	Davis, Jim
6	East Tennessee State	NCAA	I	8	21	9	Kemp, Karen
7	Virginia Commonwealth	NCAA	I	4	20	10	Walvius, Susan
8	Pacific (CA)	NCAA	I	6	20	15	DeMarchi, Melissa
1996							
1	Arizona	NCAA	I	5	22	8	Bonvicini, Joan
2	Northwestern (IL)	NCAA	I	2	23	11	Perrelli, Donald
3	Louisiana State	NCAA	I	3	21	11	Gunter, Sue
4	Arkansas	NCAA	I	1	21	13	Blair, Gary
5	California: Santa Barbara	NCAA	I	6	24	7	French, Mark
6	Western Kentucky	NCAA	I	4	19	13	Sanderford, Paul
7	Princeton	NCAA	I	8	20	11	Feeney, Liz
8	Illinois State	NCAA	I	7	19	13	Hutchison, Dr. Jill
1997							
	No Tournament						
1998							
1	Pennsylvania State	NCAA	I		21	13	Portland, Rene Muth
2	Baylor	NCAA	I		20	11	Hogg, Sonja
3	Indiana	NCAA	I		21	12	Izard, Jim
	Louisiana State	NCAA	I		19	13	Gunter, Sue
8	Butler (IN)	NCAA	I		25	6	Olkowski, June
	Oklahoma State	NCAA	I		20	10	Halterman, Dick
	Saint Joseph's (PA)	NCAA	I		19	12	Gaitley, Stephanie Vanderslice
	Toledo	NCAA	I		24	7	Ehlen, Mark

16	American	NCAA	I	23	7	Thatcher, Jeff
	Boise State	NCAA	I	19	10	Stevens, Trisha
	Bowling Green State	NCAA	I	21	8	Clark, Jaci
	Cincinnati	NCAA	I	21	9	Pirtle, Laurie
	Mississippi State	NCAA	I	14	15	Fanning, Sharon
	Rice	NCAA	I	21	9	McKinney, Cristy
	Villanova	NCAA	I	19	10	Perretta, Harry
	Xavier (OH)	NCAA	I	17	12	Balcomb, Melanie

School Participation History

Year	Assn	Div	F	SD	#T	W	L	Coach
ALABAMA								
1977	AIAW	L	8	8	8	13	15	Schleider, Stephanie
ALABAMA: BIRMINGHAM								
1991	NCAA	I	5	2	8	24	8	Milling, Jeannie
1992	NCAA	I	7	4	8	24	8	Milling, Jeannie
AMERICAN								
1998	NCAA	I	16		16	23	7	Thatcher, Jeff
APPALACHIAN STATE								
1987	NCAA	I	8	8	8	24	7	Robinson, Linda
ARIZONA								
1996	NCAA	I	1	5	8	22	8	Bonvicini, Joan
ARIZONA STATE								
1981	AIAW	I	2	8	8	21	11	Simpson, Juliene
ARKANSAS								
1987	NCAA	I	1	4	8	19	10	Sutherland, John
1996	NCAA	I	4	1	8	21	13	Blair, Gary
ARKANSAS STATE								
1993	NCAA	I	1	6	8	16	12	Winters, Jerry Ann
1994	NCAA	I	2	4	8	22	9	Winters, Jerry Ann
1992	NCAA	I	3	5	8	25	7	Winters, Jerry Ann
BAYLOR								
1998	NCAA	I	2		16	20	11	Hogg, Sonja
1981	AIAW	I	8	6	8	29	11	Bowers, Pam Davis
BELMONT								
1975			3		8	22	3	Wiseman, Betty
1976			4	4	8	19	6	Wiseman, Betty
1972			5	4	8	12	6	Wiseman, Betty
1974			6	6	8	22	6	Wiseman, Betty
1977			6	5	8	15	10	Wiseman, Betty
1971			7		8	14	7	Wiseman, Betty
1973			7	8	8	14	8	Wiseman, Betty
BOISE STATE								
1998	NCAA	I	16		16	19	10	Stevens, Trisha

Year	Assn	Div	F	SD	#T	W	L	Coach
BOWLING GREEN STATE								
1998	NCAA	I	16		16	21	8	Clark, Jaci
BRIGHAM YOUNG								
1982	NCAA	I	3	5	8	24	13	Leishman, Dr. Courtney M.
BUTLER (IN)								
1993	NCAA	I	6	4	8	23	8	Stein, Paulette
1998	NCAA	I	8		16	25	6	Olkowski, June
CALIFORNIA								
1987	NCAA	I	2	1	8	21	10	Foster, Dr. Gooch
1981	AIAW	I	4	3	8	22	10	Foster, Dr. Gooch
1984	NCAA	I	5	4	8	24	8	Foster, Dr. Gooch
1979	AIAW	L	8	8	8	14	17	Cantrell, Marci
CALIFORNIA STATE: FRESNO								
1990	NCAA	I	5	6	8	21	12	Spencer, Robert L.
1986	NCAA	I	8	4	8	21	9	Spencer, Robert L.
CALIFORNIA STATE: FULLERTON								
1985	NCAA	I	5	8	8	19	11	Gobrecht, Chris
CALIFORNIA STATE: LONG BEACH								
1978	AIAW	L	4	3	8	18	9	Schaafsma, Dr. Frances
CALIFORNIA: LOS ANGELES								
1975	AIAW	L	2		8	18	4	Washington, Kenny
1976	AIAW	L	2	2	8	19	4	Hanson, Ellen Mosher
1977	AIAW	L	2	2	8	20	3	Hanson, Ellen Mosher
1974	AIAW		4	4	8	X	X	Chaffee, Bob
CALIFORNIA: SANTA BARBARA								
1996	NCAA	I	5	6	8	24	7	French, Mark
CINCINNATI								
1981			7	7	8	27	9	Barry, Ceal
1998	NCAA	I	16		16	21	9	Pirtle, Laurie
CLEMSON								
1984	NCAA	I	3	6	8	21	10	Tribble, Annie S.
1995	NCAA	I	5	2	8	21	11	Davis, Jim
1980	AIAW	I	7	2	8	24	12	Tribble, Annie S.
CREIGHTON								
1987	NCAA	I	3	6	8	23	7	Rasmussen, Bruce
DE PAUL								
1988	NCAA	I	1	2	8	27	4	Izard, Jim
1982	NCAA	I	5	3	8	18	12	Feiereisel, Ronald E.
1989	NCAA	I	6	4	8	23	10	Bruno, Doug
1987	NCAA	I	7	7	8	23	8	Izard, Jim

Year	Assn	Div	F	SD	#T	W	L	Coach
DRAKE (IA)								
1979			2	3	8	28	5	Baumgarten, Carole
1980			3	7	8	24	12	Baumgarten, Carole
1981			3	2	8	26	7	Baumgarten, Carole
1985	NCAA	I	4	3	8	24	6	Baumgarten, Carole
1978			5		8	23	9	Baumgarten, Carole
DUKE								
1986	NCAA	I	4	2	8	21	9	Leonard, Debbie
EAST TENNESSEE STATE								
1995	NCAA	I	6	8	8	21	9	Kemp, Karen
FLORIDA								
1985	NCAA	I	2	2	8	22	9	Yow, Deborah Ann
FLORIDA INTERNATIONAL								
1993	NCAA	I	3	5	8	25	6	Russo, Cindy
1992	NCAA	I	6	8	8	23	10	Russo, Cindy
FLORIDA STATE								
1982	NCAA	I	2	1	8	27	10	Dykehouse-Allen, Janice
FORT VALLEY STATE								
1978	AIAW	S	8		8	13	9	Brown, Jessie A.
GEORGE WASHINGTON								
1993	NCAA	I	8	3	8	20	11	McKeown, Joe
GEORGIA								
1981	AIAW	I	1	4	8	27	10	Landers, Andy
GEORGIA TECH								
1992	NCAA	I	1	2	8	20	13	Berenato, Agnus McGlade
GONZAGA								
1994	NCAA	I	7	6	8	21	10	Holt, Julie
HAWAII								
1992	NCAA	I	2	1	8	25	7	Goo, Vince
1983	NCAA	I	8		8	17	12	Busone, Jerry
HOUSTON								
1991	NCAA	I	4	6	8	20	12	Kenlaw, Jessie
IDAHO								
1986	NCAA	I	1	5	8	26	5	Dobratz, Patty Jo
ILLINOIS STATE								
1982	NCAA	I	4	4	8	19	15	Hutchison, Dr. Jill
1988	NCAA	I	4	8	8	20	11	Hutchison, Dr. Jill
1980	AIAW	I	5	5	8	23	10	Hutchison, Dr. Jill
1990	NCAA	I	6	5	8	21	11	Hutchison, Dr. Jill
1984	NCAA	I	7	3	8	28	8	Hutchison, Dr. Jill
1996	NCAA	I	8	7	8	19	13	Hutchison, Dr. Jill

Year	Assn	Div	F	SD	#T	W	L	Coach
INDIANA								
1991	NCAA	I	2	7	8	18	13	Izard, Jim
1998	NCAA	I	3		16	21	12	Izard, Jim
1975	AIAW	L	8		8	19	6	Gorton, Bea
INDIANA STATE								
1977	AIAW		7	7	8	19	9	Godleski, Edith
1976	AIAW		8	6	8	19	9	Godleski, Edith
JOHN F KENNEDY (NE)								
1972			2	1	8	27	10	Nicodemus, George L.
1973			2	1	8	34	7	Nicodemus, George L.
1974			2	1	8	26	5	Nicodemus, George L.
1971			3	3	8	14	16	Nicodemus, George L.
1969			4	2	8	16	10	Spencer, Robert L.
1970			4	4	8	15	12	Spencer, Robert L.
1975			5	2	8	21	16	Nicodemus, George L.
KANSAS								
1991	NCAA	I	3	5	8	20	13	Washington, Marian
1978	AIAW	L	6		8	22	11	Washington, Marian
KANSAS STATE								
1970	AIAW		7		8	10	7	Akers, Judy
1969	AIAW		8		8	11	3	Akers, Judy
KENTUCKY								
1990	NCAA	I	1	1	8	23	8	Fanning, Sharon
1978	AIAW	L	3	4	8	23	12	Yow, Deborah Ann
LA SALLE								
1992	NCAA	I	8	3	8	25	8	Miller, John
LOUISIANA STATE								
1985	NCAA	I	1	4	8	20	9	Gunter, Sue
1996	NCAA	I	3	3	8	21	11	Gunter, Sue
1998	NCAA	I	3		16	19	13	Gunter, Sue
LOUISVILLE								
1991	NCAA	I	6	4	8	24	11	Childers, 'Bud'
MAINE								
1990	NCAA	I	7	8	8	23	7	Roberts, Trish
MARQUETTE								
1993	NCAA	I	4	2	8	22	9	Jabir, James J.
MASSACHUSETTS								
1995	NCAA	I	4	5	8	19	11	O'Brien, Joanie
MCPHERSON								
1971			8		8	X	X	Coppock, Dr. Doris

Year	Assn	Div	F	SD	#T	W	L	Coach
MEMPHIS								
1983	NCAA	I	2		8	21	11	Johns, Mary Lou
MERCER								
1975	AIAW	L	4		8	23	6	Collins, Peggy E.
MIAMI (FL)								
1990	NCAA	I	4	4	8	25	6	Labati, Ferne
MIDWESTERN (IA)								
1970			2	2	8			Hart, Kaye
1969			3	4	8	21	X	Horky, Rita J.
MINNESOTA								
1979	AIAW	L	5	5	8	17	15	Hanson, Ellen Mosher
1978	AIAW	L	7		8	21	7	Hanson, Ellen Mosher
MISSISSIPPI COLLEGE								
1977	AIAW	L	3	3	8	22	14	Nixon, Ed
1979	AIAW	L	6	2	8	14	18	Nixon, Ed
1980	AIAW	I	6	6	8	21	8	Smith, Durward
1975	AIAW	L	7		8	27	7	Nixon, Ed
MISSISSIPPI STATE								
1988	NCAA	I	6	7	8	19	13	Paul, Brenda
1998	NCAA	I	16		16	14	15	Fanning, Sharon
MISSISSIPPI WOMEN								
1974	AIAW		7	5	8	12	8	Upton, Jill
MONTANA								
1987	NCAA	I	6	5	8	26	5	Selvig, Robin
1985	NCAA	I	8	7	8	22	7	Selvig, Robin
MONTANA STATE								
1988	NCAA	I	8	6	8	24	6	Schwartz, Gary
MURRAY STATE (KY)								
1989	NCAA	I	4	6	8	22	10	Childers, "Bud"
MURRAY STATE (OK)								
1972			3		8	18	10	Hedden, Jack E.
1973			5	4	8	18	7	Imotichey, Melvin
NEBRASKA								
1992	NCAA	I	4	6	8	21	11	Beck, Angela
1976			5	5	8	22	9	Nicodemus, George L.
NEVADA: LAS VEGAS								
1976			3	3	8	26	5	Ayala, Dan
1988	NCAA	I	7	1	8	25	9	Bolla, Jim
1993	NCAA	I	7	1	8	24	7	Bolla, Jim
NEW MEXICO STATE								
1994	NCAA	I	6	2	8	24	8	Petersen, Mike

Year	Assn	Div	F	SD	#T	W	L	Coach
NEW ORLEANS								
1983	NCAA	I	1		8	23	8	Favaloro, Joey
1988	NCAA	I	3	3	8	25	7	Favaloro, Joey
NORTH CAROLINA								
1980			2	4	8	21	15	Alley, Jennifer
1975			6		8	15	3	Lurapkin, Angela
NORTH CAROLINA STATE								
1976			6	8	8	19	7	Yow, Sandra Kay
NORTH CAROLINA: CHARLOTTE								
1990	NCAA	I	3	3	8	24	8	Baldwin, Ed
NORTHEAST LOUISIANA								
1973			8	7	8	X	X	Lewis, "Lou"
1994	NCAA	I	8	1	8	21	14	Stockton, Roger
NORTHERN ILLINOIS								
1991	NCAA	I	7	3	8	25	10	Albright-Dieterle, Jane
NORTHERN KENTUCKY								
1979	AIAW	S	4	7	8	25	10	Moore, Marilyn
NORTHWESTERN (IL)								
1996	NCAA	I	2	2	8	23	11	Perrelli, Donald
NORTHWESTERN STATE (LA)								
1986	NCAA	I	2	6	8	25	7	Pierson, Pat
1995	NCAA	I	2	7	8	25	7	Smith, James F.
1993	NCAA	I	5	7	8	24	8	Smith, James F.
NOTRE DAME (IN)								
1986	NCAA	I	3	1	8	23	8	DiStanislao, Mary
1995	NCAA	I	3	3	8	21	10	McGraw, Muffet O'Brien
1989	NCAA	I	7	7	8	21	11	McGraw, Muffet O'Brien
1991	NCAA	I	8	1	8	23	9	McGraw, Muffet O'Brien
OKLAHOMA								
1994	NCAA	I	1	7	8	18	12	Plunkett, Burl
1984	NCAA	I	6	8	8	23	7	McHugh, Maura
OKLAHOMA STATE								
1998	NCAA	I	8		16	20	10	Halterman, Dick
OLD DOMINION								
1978	AIAW	L	1	1	8	30	4	Stanley, Marianne Crawford
1977	AIAW	L	4	4	8	23	9	Parsons, Pam
ORAL ROBERTS								
1983	NCAA	I	3		8	26	1	Yow, Deborah Ann
OREGON								
1989	NCAA	I	1	5	8	22	10	Heiny, Elwin
1979	AIAW	L	3	4	8	23	2	Heiny, Elwin

Year	Assn	Div	F	SD	#T	W	L	Coach
OREGON STATE								
1980	AIAW	I	1	3	8	22	9	Hill, Aki
1982	NCAA	I	1	2	8	20	8	Hill, Aki
OUACHITA BAPTIST								
1969			2	3	8			Moffatt, Phyllis Carolyn
1970			3	3	8			Moffatt, Phyllis Carolyn
PACIFIC (CA)								
1995	NCAA	I	8	6	8	20	15	DeMarchi, Melissa
PARSONS								
1971			2	2	8	30	11	Spencer, Robert L.
1973			3	3	8	20	16	Spencer, Robert L.
1972			4	3	8	17	12	Spencer, Robert L.
PENNSYLVANIA STATE								
1998	NCAA	I	1		16	21	13	Portland, Rene Muth
PEPPERDINE								
1982	NCAA	I	8	8	8	16	13	Meyers, Patty
PHILLIPS (OK)								
1974	AIAW		8	7	8			Amaya, Lou
PITTSBURGH								
1994	NCAA	I	3	3	8	21	10	Bruce, Kirk
1981			5	5	8	22	7	Saurer, Judy
PRINCETON								
1996	NCAA	I	7	8	8	20	11	Feeney, Liz
PROVIDENCE								
1987	NCAA	I	4	2	8	23	9	Foley, Bob
PURDUE								
1988	NCAA	I	2	5	8	21	10	Dunn, Lin
RADFORD								
1989	NCAA	I	5	8	8	25	7	Curtis, Charlene
RANGER								
1973			4	5	8	22	6	Butler, Ron
1969			5		8	20	8	Butler, Ron
1970			5		8	21	9	Butler, Ron
1971			5		8	26	8	Butler, Ron
1974			5	8	8	20	10	Butler, Ron
1972			8		8	24	10	Butler, Ron
RICE								
1998	NCAA	I	16		16	21	9	McKinney, Cristy
RICHMOND								
1989	NCAA	I	8	3	8	24	9	Gaitley, Stephanie Vanderslice

Year	Assn	Div	F	SD	#T	W	L	Coach
SAINT JOSEPH'S (PA)								
1998	NCAA	I	8		16	19	12	Gaitley, Stephanie Vanderslice
SAN DIEGO STATE								
1989	NCAA	I	2	1	8	25	9	Riggins, Earnest
SANTA CLARA								
1991	NCAA	I	1	8	8	28	3	Horstmeyer, Caren
SEMINOLE JC (OK)								
1971			4	4	8	X	X	Hull, Kenneth C.
1973			6	6	8	X	X	Woodall, Dixie
1972			7		8	X	X	Woodall, Dixie
SOUTH ALABAMA								
1988	NCAA	I	5	4	8	22	9	Branum, Charles
SOUTH CAROLINA								
1979	AIAW	L	1	1	8	27	10	Parsons, Pam
SOUTHERN ARKANSAS								
1969			7		8	X	X	Downing, Dr. Margaret R.
SOUTHERN ILLINOIS								
1983	NCAA	I	6		8	22	11	Scott, Cindy
SOUTHERN METHODIST (TX)								
1993	NCAA	I	2	8	8	20	10	Rompola, Rhonda
SOUTHERN MISSISSIPPI								
1982	NCAA	I	7	7	8	16	11	James, Kay
STEPHEN F AUSTIN STATE								
1987	NCAA	I	5	3	8	25	6	Blair, Gary
TEMPLE								
1982	NCAA	I	6	6	8	20	11	Hill-MacDonald, Linda
1983	NCAA	I	7		8	19	12	Hill-MacDonald, Linda
TEMPLE JC								
1974	AIAW	J/CC	3	3	8	27	8	Garmon, Frances
1969			6		8	18	12	Garmon, Frances
1970			6		8	29	12	Garmon, Frances
1971			6		8	24	12	Garmon, Frances
1972			6		8	26	12	Garmon, Frances
TENNESSEE TECH								
1981	AIAW	I	6	1	8	22	9	Meadors, Marynell Hutsell
1986	NCAA	I	7	3	8	22	10	Meadors, Marynell Hutsell
TENNESSEE: CHATTANOOGA								
1984	NCAA	I	2	1	8	26	5	Fanning, Sharon
TEXAS								
1978	AIAW	L	2	2	8	29	10	Conradt, Jody

Year	Assn	Div	F	SD	#T	W	L	Coach
TEXAS A&M								
1995	NCAA	I	1	1	8	21	9	Harvey, Candi
TEXAS TECH								
1985	NCAA	I	3	1	8	24	8	Sharp, Marsha
1983	NCAA	I	5		8	22	9	Sharp, Marsha
TOLEDO								
1990	NCAA	I	2	2	8	25	7	Fennelly, Bill
1989	NCAA	I	3	2	8	25	8	Fennelly, Bill
1994	NCAA	I	5	5	8	24	8	Fennelly, Bill
1998	NCAA	I	8		16	24	7	Ehlen, Mark
TULANE								
1994	NCAA	I	4	8	8	17	14	Harvey, Candi
UNITED STATES INTERNATIONAL								
1986	NCAA	I	6	8	8	24	9	Macias, Cassie
UTAH								
1979	AIAW	L	7	6	8	23	10	Gardner, Fern
1984	NCAA	I	8	5	8	19	12	Elliott, Elaine
VALDOSTA STATE								
1977	AIAW	L	5	6	8	26	6	Worth, Lyndal
VANDERBILT								
1984	NCAA	I	1	2	8	23	9	Lee, Phil
VILLANOVA								
1998	NCAA	I	16		16	19	10	Perretta, Harry
VIRGINIA								
1980			4	8	8	20	12	Ryan, Deborah H.
VIRGINIA COMMONWEALTH								
1995	NCAA	I	7	4	8	20	10	Walvius, Susan
WAYLAND BAPTIST								
1969			1	1	8	26	4	Redin, Harley J.
1970			1	1	8	29	4	Redin, Harley J.
1971			1	1	8	30	2	Redin, Harley J.
1972			1	2	8	26	7	Redin, Harley J.
1973			1	2	8	21	7	Redin, Harley J.
1974	AIAW		1	2	8	37	5	Weese, Dean
1975	AIAW	L	1	1	8	34	1	Weese, Dean
1976	AIAW	L	1	1	8	34	5	Weese, Dean
1977	AIAW	L	1	1	8	31	5	Weese, Dean
1980	AIAW	I	8	1	8	20	15	Wilson, Cathy
WEBER STATE								
1983	NCAA	I	4		8	22	10	Minor, Jane

Year	Assn	Div	F	SD	#T	W	L	Coach
WEST TEXAS A&M								
1986	NCAA	I	5	7	8	26	5	Schneider, Bob
1985	NCAA	I	6	6	8	26	6	Schneider, Bob
1976			7	7	8	X	X	Stovall, Allene
1970			8		8	X	X	Stovall, Allene
WEST VIRGINIA								
1985	NCAA	I	7	5	8	20	10	Blakemore, Kittie
WESTERN KENTUCKY								
1984	NCAA	I	4	7	8	21	11	Sanderford, Paul
1996	NCAA	I	6	4	8	19	13	Sanderford, Paul
WISCONSIN: GREEN BAY								
1992	NCAA	I	5	7	8	24	7	Hammerle, Carol
WYOMING								
1990	NCAA	I	8	7	8	24	8	Lavin, Chad
XAVIER (OH)								
1998	NCAA	I	16		16	17	12	Balcomb, Melanie

Olympic Demonstration Tournament

It took awhile, until 1936, but basketball became an Olympic sport—in spite of, or because of, what transpired in St. Louis, Missouri, in July 1904.

Eight basketball teams, five from the AAU and three from colleges, played two "demonstration" tournaments on an outdoor clay field.

In the college event, Hiram, Wheaton, and Latter-Day Saints University (a business school in Salt Lake City) played a one-day, three-game round robin tournament on Wednesday, July 13 with games at 10:30 am, 1:30 pm, and 3:30 pm— following an over-night rain.

According to accounts, noise from the sidelines was not permitted. Nevertheless, Hiram (1-0) beat Wheaton (0-1), who had claimed the 1903 mythical national championship, in game one; Wheaton (1-1) beat LDSU (0-1) in game two, and Hiram (2-0) beat LDSU (0-2) in game three to claim the Olympic College Championship.

In the AAU Tournament, the fabled Buffalo (NY) Germans YMCA team swept their four games to claim the Olympic Amateur Championship.

Final standings for the Amateur tournament are as follows: Buffalo, NY, YMCA (4-0); Chicago, IL, Central YMCA (3-1); Missouri Athletic Club, Saint Louis, MO (0-2); Turner Tigers, Los Angeles, CA (0-2); Xavier Athletic Club, New York, NY (0-2).

Tournament Results

F	School	W	L	Coach
1904				
1	Hiram	11	1	Unknown
2	Wheaton (IL)	10	9	Brown, Elwood
3	Latter-Day Saints Business	6	0	Bean, Willard

Olympic Trials Tournament

The Olympic Trials Tournaments were a "made for TV" event before there were "made for TV" events. Imagine: two or three days of basketball at one site (except for 1952 when the first-round was played at two sites) among the eight (except for four in 1956) absolutely best teams in the country. Why, that's a double final four!

While the tournaments did play a conventional single-elimination format to produce 1st, 2nd, etc., places (except in 1956 when the four non-college teams played a round robin), they really were a showcase for the selection of players to form the United States team in the ensuing Olympic Games—and to raise money for the Olympic program.

In 1936, the eight teams were the 1st and 2nd place teams from the AAU tournament, the YMCA winner, and five NCAA inter-district champions—determined in play-offs between geographically adjacent district winners. In the play-offs, Temple (district 2) beat Niagara (1); Arkansas (4) beat Western Kentucky (3); De Paul beat (5) Minnesota (6); Utah State (8) beat Kansas (7); and Washington (10) beat (Oregon State (9)

In 1948, following the hiatus for World War II, the eight teams were the AAU's 1st, 2nd, and 3rd place finishers; the YMCA winner, the NCAA's 1st and 2nd place finishers, the NAIA winner, and the NIT's 2nd place finisher (the winner, Saint Louis University, declined).

In 1952, the eight teams were the first four from the AAU tournament (the 4th place finisher replaced the winner of the then defunct YMCA tournament), the winner and runner-up from the NCAA tournament, the NAIA tournament winner, and the NIT winner who accepted a bid this time. The first-round games were held in Kansas City and in New York with the semifinals and finals at New York's Madison Square Garden.

The four-team 1956 round-robin tournament presented the Phillips 66ers of Bartlesville, Oklahoma, the AAU winners, and Buchan Bakers of Seattle, Washington, AAU runner-up, plus NCAA and military all-star teams—no college teams.

In 1960 (the final tournament that involved colleges), the 1st, 2nd, and 4th place finishers from the AAU tournament (The Caterpillar Co., Peoria, Illinois; The Goodyear Tire and Rubber Co., Akron, Ohio, and the Phillips 66ers) joined with NCAA champion Ohio State and all-star teams from the US Armed Forces, the NCAA university (I) and college (II) divisions, and the NAIA.

In 1964 and 1968, the tournament teams were totally all-star aggregations. In 1964 there were three teams from the NCAA, two from the AAU, and one from the NAIA while in 1968 there were three teams from the NCAA division I, and one each from the NCAA division II, AAU, NJCAA, NAIA, and the US Armed Forces.

Beginning in 1972, the US Olympic Squad was selected by the Olympic Committee and coaching staff.

Tournament Results

F	School	Assn	NAT	AAU	NIT	W	L	Coach
			—Finish in—					
1936								
1	Universal Pictures: Hollywood, CA	AAU	—	2	—			Needles, James R.
2	Globe Oil & Refining Co: McPherson, KS	AAU	—	1	—			Johnson, Eugene
3	Washington	NCAA	—	—	—	25	17	Edmundson, Clarence S. "Hec"
4	Wilmerding, PA, YMCA	YMCA	1	—	—			

F	School	Assn	NAT	AAU	NIT	W	L	Coach
8	Arkansas	NCAA	—	—	—	24	3	Rose, Glen
	De Paul	NCAA	—	—	—	18	4	Kelly, James D.
	Temple	NCAA	—	—	—	18	6	Usilton, James
	Utah State	NCAA	—	—	—	18	9	Romney, Ernest L. "Dick"

1948

F	School	Assn	NAT	AAU	NIT	W	L	Coach
1	Phillips Petroleum Co: Bartlesville, OK	AAU	—	1	—	62	3	Browning, Omar M. "Bud"
2	Kentucky	NCAA	1	—	—	36	3	Rupp, Adolph F.
3	Nuggets: Denver, CO	AAU	—	2	—			Bishop, Ralph
4	Baylor	NCAA	2	—	—	24	8	Henderson, R. E. "Bill"
8	Bittners: Oakland, CA	AAU	—	3	—			Gale, Lauren "Ladie"
	Brooklyn, NY, Prospect Park YMCA	YMCA	1	—	—	35	10	Andrews,
	Louisville	NAIA	1	—	—	29	6	Hickman, Bernard L. "Peck"
	New York	NCAA	—	—	2	22	4	Cann, Howard G.

1952

F	School	Assn	NAT	AAU	NIT	W	L	Coach
1	Caterpillar, Inc: Peoria, IL	AAU	—	1	—	32	13	Womble, J. Warren
2	Kansas	NCAA	1	—	—	28	3	Allen, Dr. Forrest C. "Phog"
3	Phillips Petroleum Co: Bartlesville, OK	AAU	—	2	—	52	7	Renick, Jesse "Cab"
4	La Salle	NCAA	—	—	1	25	7	Loeffler, Kenneth D.
8	Fibber McGee & Molly: Hollywood, CA	AAU	—	4	—			
	Saint John's (NY)	NCAA	2	—	8	25	5	McGuire, Frank J.
	Southwest Missouri State	NAIA	1	—	—	27	5	Vanatta, Robert
	US Air Force All-Stars	USAF	—	3	—			

1956

F	School	Assn	NAT	AAU	NIT	W	L	Coach
1	Phillips Petroleum Co: Bartlesville, OK	AAU	—	2	—	41	12	Tucker, Gerald M.
2	NCAA All-Stars	NCAA	—	—	—	2	1	O'Connor, Frank "Bucky"
3	Buchan Baking Co: Seattle, WA	AAU	—	1	—			Fidler, Frank
	US Armed Forces All-Stars	USAF	—	—	—			

1960

F	School	Assn	NAT	AAU	NIT	W	L	Coach
1	NCAA University Division All-Stars	NCAA	—	—	—	3	0	Newell, Peter F.
2	Caterpillar, Inc: Peoria, IL	AAU	—	1	—			Womble, J. Warren
3	Goodyear Tire & Rubber Co: Akron, OH	AAU	—	2	—	27	17	Vaughn, Henry V. "Hank"
4	NAIA All-Stars	NAIA	—	—	—	1	2	
5	Ohio State	NCAA	1	—	—	25	3	Taylor, Fred R.
6	Phillips Petroleum Co: Bartlesville, OK	AAU	—	4	—	41	13	Browning, Omar M. "Bud"
7	US Armed Forces All-Stars	USAF	—	—	—			
8	NCAA College Division All-Stars	NCAA	—	—	—	0	3	

Section 4

SCHOOL TOURNAMENT PARTICIPATION HISTORY

This section is a composite of sections 1 and 3 plus the Helms Foundation national champion designations from section 2. Accordingly, it lists every team that ever participated in any senior college national championship tournament, association or nonassociation, or received the Helms designation. Therefore, it is a school's complete history of post-season tournament participation (or Helms designation)—whether just one appearance or many, many appearances.

Each school is presented in alphabetical order. For each school, tournament participation is listed, first for men and then for women (if applicable), by ascending year.

The tournaments (or the Helms designation) are indicated by the column heading abbreviation across the page. The numeral in the column indicates the school's finish in the particular tournament.

For the national association tournament (**NAT**), the association that conducted the tournament is indicated in the **Assn** column, and the division, if any, of the tournament in which the school participated is indicated in the **Div** column.

Following are the associations that conducted tournaments, by their last or current name—for specific information about the association and/or the tournament, see sections 1 or 3. **AIAW**: Association for Intercollegiate Athletics for Women; **LCC**: League of Christian Colleges; **NAIA**: National Intercollegiate Athletic Association; **NASC**: National Athletic Steering Committee; **NBCAA**: National Bible College Athletic Association; **NCAA**: National Collegiate Athletic Association; **NCCAA**: National Christian College Athletic Association; **NSCAA**: National Small College Athletic Association.

Following are the nonassociation tournaments. **NIT**: National Invitation Tournament (Men), National Women's Invitational Tournament (Women)–the gender (M or W) under the **M/W** column indicates in which tournament the team participated; **ARC**: American Red Cross Benefit; **CCA**: Collegiate Commissioners Association Tournament; **NCI**: National Catholic Invitational Tournament (1949-1952) and National Catholic College Tournament (1963)—these two tournaments are included under the same column heading (the year in which a school participated indicates which tournament); **NCT**: National Campus Tournament; **OLY**: Olympic Demonstration Tournament (1904) and Olympic Trials Tournament (1936-1960)—these two tournaments are included under the same column heading (the year in which a school participated indicates which tournament); **HLM**: Helms Foundation national champion designation.

School Tournament Participation History

Year	M/W	Assn	Div	NAT	NIT	ARC	CCA	NCI	NCT	OLY	HLM	W	L	Coach
ABILENE CHRISTIAN														
1959	M	NCAA	II	24	—	—	—	—	—	—	—	20	7	Nutt, Dee
1960		NCAA	II	16	—	—	—	—	—	—	—	16	12	Nutt, Dee
1962		NCAA	II	32	—	—	—	—	—	—	—	16	12	Nutt, Dee
1964		NCAA	II	16	—	—	—	—	—	—	—	18	9	Nutt, Dee
1965		NCAA	II	16	—	—	—	—	—	—	—	17	9	Nutt, Dee
1966		NCAA	II	8	—	—	—	—	—	—	—	21	7	Nutt, Dee
1980		NAIA		16	—	—	—	—	—	—	—	24	4	Tate, Willard N.
1986		NCAA	II	24	—	—	—	—	—	—	—	23	7	Martin, Mike
1987		NCAA	II	32	—	—	—	—	—	—	—	18	8	Martin, Mike
1981	W	AIAW	II	8	—	—	—	—	—	—	—	31	7	McCoy, Burl
1983		NCAA	II	24	—	—	—	—	—	—	—	21	8	McCoy, Burl
1985		NCAA	II	16	—	—	—	—	—	—	—	21	10	McCoy, Burl
1988		NCAA	II	32	—	—	—	—	—	—	—	27	6	McCoy, Burl
1989		NCAA	II	32	—	—	—	—	—	—	—	23	8	McCoy, Burl
1995		NCAA	II	32	—	—	—	—	—	—	—	23	7	Fox, Suzanne Johnson
1996		NCAA	II	3	—	—	—	—	—	—	—	31	2	Fox, Suzanne Johnson
1997		NCAA	II	32	—	—	—	—	—	—	—	24	6	Fox, Suzanne Johnson
1998		NCAA	II	16	—	—	—	—	—	—	—	26	5	Williams, Wayne

Year	M/W	Assn	Div	NAT	NIT	ARC	CCA	NCI	NCT	OLY	HLM	W	L	Coach
ADAMS STATE														
1953	M	NAIA		32	—	—	—	—	—	—	—	19	8	Crawford, Ronald
1972		NAIA		16	—	—	—	—	—	—	—	18	11	Lutz, Dr. Loren
ADELPHI														
1957	M	NAIA		32	—	—	—	—	—	—	—	13	12	Faherty, George E.
1958		NCAA	II	16	—	—	—	—	—	—	—	18	8	Faherty, George E.
1959		NCAA	II	24	—	—	—	—	—	—	—	22	6	Faherty, George E.
1964		NCAA	II	8	—	—	—	—	—	—	—	22	6	Faherty, George E.
1978		NCAA	II	32	—	—	—	—	—	—	—	18	8	Kessler, Marvin
1995		NCAA	II	48	—	—	—	—	—	—	—	19	12	O'Connor, Jim
1996		NCAA	II	48	—	—	—	—	—	—	—	23	7	Clifford, Steve
1997		NCAA	II	48	—	—	—	—	—	—	—	21	9	Clifford, Steve
1998		NCAA	II	48	—	—	—	—	—	—	—	22	8	Clifford, Steve
1987	W	NCAA	II	24	—	—	—	—	—	—	—	14	14	McHugh, Dorothy
ADRIAN														
1953	M	NAIA		32	—	—	—	—	—	—	—	18	7	Boyett, Theodore R.
1955		NAIA		32	—	—	—	—	—	—	—	21	4	Skala, Jim
1957		NAIA		32	—	—	—	—	—	—	—	16	6	Albeck, Charles Stanley "Stan"
1980	W	AIAW	III	16	—	—	—	—	—	—	—	22	6	Walsh, Nancy
1991		NCAA	III	16	—	—	—	—	—	—	—	22	4	Munk, Dana Marie
1992		NCAA	III	32	—	—	—	—	—	—	—	20	5	Munk, Dana Marie
AIR FORCE														
1960	M	NCAA	I	25	—	—	—	—	—	—	—	12	10	Spear, Robert
1962		NCAA	I	25	—	—	—	—	—	—	—	16	7	Spear, Robert
1979	W	AIAW	S	12	—	—	—	—	—	—	—	19	5	Schichtle, Dave
1980		AIAW	II	24	—	—	—	—	—	—	—	17	10	Holt, "Chuck"
1985		NCAA	II	24	—	—	—	—	—	—	—	20	8	Gasser, Martha "Marti"
1990		NCAA	II	32	—	—	—	—	—	—	—	20	8	Gasser, Martha "Marti"
AKRON														
1943	M	NAIA		32	—	—	—	—	—	—	—	17	4	Beichly, Russell J.
1958		NCAA	II	16	—	—	—	—	—	—	—	20	6	Beichly, Russell J.
1964		NCAA	II	2	—	—	—	—	—	—	—	24	7	Laterza, Anthony
1965		NCAA	II	8	—	—	—	—	—	—	—	21	7	Laterza, Anthony
1966		NCAA	II	3	—	—	—	—	—	—	—	24	4	Laterza, Anthony
1967		NCAA	II	16	—	—	—	—	—	—	—	20	5	Laterza, Anthony
1971		NCAA	II	24	—	—	—	—	—	—	—	20	6	Webb, Dr. Wyatt
1972		NCAA	II	2	—	—	—	—	—	—	—	26	5	Webb, Dr. Wyatt
1973		NCAA	II	8	—	—	—	—	—	—	—	22	5	Webb, Dr. Wyatt
1975		NCAA	II	8	—	—	—	—	—	—	—	20	9	Webb, Dr. Wyatt
1986		NCAA	I	64	—	—	—	—	—	—	—	22	8	Huggins, Robert
1987		NCAA	I	—	32	—	—	—	—	—	—	21	9	Huggins, Robert
1989		NCAA	I	—	32	—	—	—	—	—	—	21	8	Huggins, Robert
ALABAMA														
1973	M	NCAA	I	—	4	—	—	—	—	—	—	22	8	Newton, Charles M. "CM"
1975		NCAA	I	32	—	—	—	—	—	—	—	22	5	Newton, Charles M. "CM"
1976		NCAA	I	16	—	—	—	—	—	—	—	23	5	Newton, Charles M. "CM"
1977		NCAA	I	—	4	—	—	—	—	—	—	25	6	Newton, Charles M. "CM"

Year	M/W	Assn	Div	NAT	NIT	ARC	CCA	NCI	NCT	OLY	HLM	W	L	Coach
1979		NCAA	I	—	3	—	—	—	—	—	—	22	11	Newton, Charles M. "CM"
1980		NCAA	I	—	16	—	—	—	—	—	—	18	12	Newton, Charles M. "CM"
1981		NCAA	I	—	16	—	—	—	—	—	—	18	11	Sanderson, Winfrey "Wimp"
1982		NCAA	I	16	—	—	—	—	—	—	—	24	7	Sanderson, Winfrey "Wimp"
1983		NCAA	I	48	—	—	—	—	—	—	—	20	12	Sanderson, Winfrey "Wimp"
1984		NCAA	I	48	—	—	—	—	—	—	—	18	12	Sanderson, Winfrey "Wimp"
1985		NCAA	I	16	—	—	—	—	—	—	—	23	10	Sanderson, Winfrey "Wimp"
1986		NCAA	I	16	—	—	—	—	—	—	—	24	9	Sanderson, Winfrey "Wimp"
1987		NCAA	I	16	—	—	—	—	—	—	—	28	5	Sanderson, Winfrey "Wimp"
1989		NCAA	I	64	—	—	—	—	—	—	—	23	8	Sanderson, Winfrey "Wimp"
1990		NCAA	I	16	—	—	—	—	—	—	—	26	9	Sanderson, Winfrey "Wimp"
1991		NCAA	I	16	—	—	—	—	—	—	—	23	10	Sanderson, Winfrey "Wimp"
1992		NCAA	I	32	—	—	—	—	—	—	—	26	9	Sanderson, Winfrey "Wimp"
1993		NCAA	I	—	32	—	—	—	—	—	—	16	13	Hobbs, David
1994		NCAA	I	32	—	—	—	—	—	—	—	20	10	Hobbs, David
1995		NCAA	I	32	—	—	—	—	—	—	—	23	10	Hobbs, David
1996		NCAA	I	—	4	—	—	—	—	—	—	19	13	Hobbs, David
1977	W	AIAW	L	—	8	—	—	—	—	—	—	13	15	Schleider, Stephanie
1984		NCAA	I	16	—	—	—	—	—	—	—	23	9	Weeks, Kenneth
1988		NCAA	I	40	—	—	—	—	—	—	—	18	10	Myers, Lois
1992		NCAA	I	32	—	—	—	—	—	—	—	23	7	Moody, Rick
1993		NCAA	I	32	—	—	—	—	—	—	—	22	9	Moody, Rick
1994		NCAA	I	3	—	—	—	—	—	—	—	26	7	Moody, Rick
1995		NCAA	I	16	—	—	—	—	—	—	—	22	9	Moody, Rick
1996		NCAA	I	16	—	—	—	—	—	—	—	24	8	Moody, Rick
1997		NCAA	I	16	—	—	—	—	—	—	—	25	7	Moody, Rick
1998		NCAA	I	16	—	—	—	—	—	—	—	24	10	Moody, Rick

ALABAMA A&M

Year	M/W	Assn	Div	NAT	NIT	ARC	CCA	NCI	NCT	OLY	HLM	W	L	Coach
1985	M	NCAA	II	32	—	—	—	—	—	—	—	21	10	Jobe, Ben
1986		NCAA	II	32	—	—	—	—	—	—	—	23	9	Jobe, Ben
1987		NCAA	II	32	—	—	—	—	—	—	—	23	7	Pettaway, L. Vann
1988		NCAA	II	8	—	—	—	—	—	—	—	29	3	Pettaway, L. Vann
1989		NCAA	II	24	—	—	—	—	—	—	—	26	6	Pettaway, L. Vann
1993		NCAA	II	23	—	—	—	—	—	—	—	28	3	Pettaway, L. Vann
1994		NCAA	II	8	—	—	—	—	—	—	—	27	5	Pettaway, L. Vann
1995		NCAA	II	8	—	—	—	—	—	—	—	29	3	Pettaway, L. Vann
1996		NCAA	II	8	—	—	—	—	—	—	—	28	3	Pettaway, L. Vann
1997		NCAA	II	16	—	—	—	—	—	—	—	24	6	Pettaway, L. Vann
1984	W	NCAA	II	24	—	—	—	—	—	—	—	19	9	Parham, Press
1991		NCAA	II	32	—	—	—	—	—	—	—	24	7	Parham, Press
1997		NCAA	II	48	—	—	—	—	—	—	—	20	10	Parham, Press

ALABAMA STATE

Year	M/W	Assn	Div	NAT	NIT	ARC	CCA	NCI	NCT	OLY	HLM	W	L	Coach
1972	M	NCAA	II	36	—	—	—	—	—	—	—	22	3	Boozer, Bernard
1975		NCAA	II	32	—	—	—	—	—	—	—	16	13	Laisure, W. Floyd
1980		NAIA		2	—	—	—	—	—	—	—	32	2	Oliver, James V.
1983		NCAA	I	—	32	—	—	—	—	—	—	22	6	Oliver, James V.

Year	M/W	Assn	Div	NAT	NIT	ARC	CCA	NCI	NCT	OLY	HLM	W	L	Coach
ALABAMA: BIRMINGHAM														
1980	M	NCAA	I	—	32	—	—	—	—	—	—	18	12	Bartow, B. Gene
1981		NCAA	I	16	—	—	—	—	—	—	—	23	9	Bartow, B. Gene
1982		NCAA	I	8	—	—	—	—	—	—	—	25	6	Bartow, B. Gene
1983		NCAA	I	48	—	—	—	—	—	—	—	19	14	Bartow, B. Gene
1984		NCAA	I	48	—	—	—	—	—	—	—	23	11	Bartow, B. Gene
1985		NCAA	I	32	—	—	—	—	—	—	—	25	9	Bartow, B. Gene
1986		NCAA	I	32	—	—	—	—	—	—	—	25	11	Bartow, B. Gene
1987		NCAA	I	64	—	—	—	—	—	—	—	21	11	Bartow, B. Gene
1989		NCAA	I	—	3	—	—	—	—	—	—	22	12	Bartow, B. Gene
1990		NCAA	I	64	—	—	—	—	—	—	—	22	9	Bartow, B. Gene
1991		NCAA	I	—	32	—	—	—	—	—	—	18	13	Bartow, B. Gene
1992		NCAA	I	—	32	—	—	—	—	—	—	20	9	Bartow, B. Gene
1993		NCAA	I	—	3	—	—	—	—	—	—	21	14	Bartow, B. Gene
1994		NCAA	I	64	—	—	—	—	—	—	—	22	8	Bartow, B. Gene
1997		NCAA	I	—	32	—	—	—	—	—	—	18	14	Bartow, Murry
1998		NCAA	I	—	16	—	—	—	—	—	—	21	12	Bartow, Murry
1991	W	NCAA	I	—	5	—	—	—	—	—	—	24	8	Milling, Jeannie
1992		NCAA	I	—	7	—	—	—	—	—	—	24	8	Milling, Jeannie
1994		NCAA	I	64	—	—	—	—	—	—	—	23	6	Milling, Jeannie
ALABAMA: HUNTSVILLE														
1976	M	NAIA		8	—	—	—	—	—	—	—	26	9	Willis, A. L. "Kayo"
1977		NAIA		16	—	—	—	—	—	—	—	19	10	Willis, A. L. "Kayo"
1981		NAIA		2	—	—	—	—	—	—	—	30	7	Willis, A. L. "Kayo"
1983		NAIA		32	—	—	—	—	—	—	—	25	11	Willis, A. L. "Kayo"
1983	W	NAIA		2	—	—	—	—	—	—	—	27	8	Dunaway, Donna Caldwell
ALASKA: ANCHORAGE														
1982	M	NCAA	II	24	—	—	—	—	—	—	—	21	1	Larrabee, Harry
1986		NCAA	II	16	—	—	—	—	—	—	—	22	10	Larrabee, Harry
1987		NCAA	II	16	—	—	—	—	—	—	—	23	7	Abegglen, Ron
1988		NCAA	II	2	—	—	—	—	—	—	—	24	10	Abegglen, Ron
1990		NCAA	II	32	—	—	—	—	—	—	—	22	8	Abegglen, Ron
1991		NCAA	II	16	—	—	—	—	—	—	—	19	11	Abegglen, Ron
1993		NCAA	II	16	—	—	—	—	—	—	—	21	10	Larrabee, Harry
1994		NCAA	II	24	—	—	—	—	—	—	—	21	10	Larrabee, Harry
1996		NCAA	II	48	—	—	—	—	—	—	—	19	9	Bruns, Charlie
1997		NCAA	II	32	—	—	—	—	—	—	—	20	8	Bruns, Charlie
1986	W	NCAA	II	24	—	—	—	—	—	—	—	17	11	Burns, Linda
1988		NCAA	II	16	—	—	—	—	—	—	—	24	5	Burns, Linda
1989		NCAA	II	32	—	—	—	—	—	—	—	20	8	Burns, Linda
1992		NCAA	II	32	—	—	—	—	—	—	—	18	6	Raugust, Milt
ALASKA: FAIRBANKS														
1989	M	NCAA	II	32	—	—	—	—	—	—	—	16	13	Roderick, George T.
ALBANY STATE (GA)														
1965	M	NAIA		16	—	—	—	—	—	—	—	27	6	Rainey, Robert C.
1967		NAIA		32	—	—	—	—	—	—	—	25	6	Rainey, Robert C.
1968		NAIA		32	—	—	—	—	—	—	—	32	8	Rainey, Robert C.
1973		NCAA	II	42	—	—	—	—	—	—	—	23	6	Jones, Oliver

Year	M/W	Assn	Div	NAT	NIT ARC CCA NCI NCT OLY HLM	W	L	Coach
1978		NCAA	II	24	— — — — — — — —	20	9	Jones, Oliver
1979		NCAA	II	24	— — — — — — — —	20	9	Jones, Oliver
1984		NCAA	II	32	— — — — — — — —	10	19	Jones, Oliver
1985		NCAA	II	32	— — — — — — — —	15	15	Jones, Oliver
1992		NCAA	II	24	— — — — — — — —	20	9	Jones, Oliver
1997		NCAA	II	48	— — — — — — — —	20	10	Jones, Oliver
1998		NCAA	II	32	— — — — — — — —	19	11	Jones, Oliver
1987	W	NCAA	II	24	— — — — — — — —	28	1	Davis, John I.
1989		NCAA	II	32	— — — — — — — —	15	16	Davis, John I.
1990		NCAA	II	32	— — — — — — — —	22	7	Davis, John I.
1996		NCAA	II	32	— — — — — — — —	22	9	Skinner, Robert
1998		NCAA	II	48	— — — — — — — —	20	10	Skinner, Robert

ALBANY STATE (NY)

Year	M/W	Assn	Div	NAT	NIT ARC CCA NCI NCT OLY HLM	W	L	Coach
1969	M	NCAA	II	24	— — — — — — — —	18	6	Sauers, Dr. Richard J.
1975		NCAA	III	30	— — — — — — — —	15	10	Sauers, Dr. Richard J.
1977		NCAA	III	16	— — — — — — — —	19	7	Sauers, Dr. Richard J.
1979		NCAA	III	24	— — — — — — — —	20	7	Sauers, Dr. Richard J.
1980		NCAA	III	16	— — — — — — — —	21	6	Sauers, Dr. Richard J.
1981		NCAA	III	16	— — — — — — — —	23	5	Sauers, Dr. Richard J.
1985		NCAA	III	24	— — — — — — — —	22	6	Sauers, Dr. Richard J.
1990		NCAA	III	16	— — — — — — — —	20	9	Sauers, Dr. Richard J.
1992		NCAA	III	32	— — — — — — — —	21	7	Sauers, Dr. Richard J.
1994		NCAA	III	8	— — — — — — — —	24	3	Sauers, Dr. Richard J.
1995		NCAA	III	32	— — — — — — — —	18	8	Sauers, Dr. Richard J.
1986	W	NCAA	III	8	— — — — — — — —	26	4	Warner, Mari
1992		NCAA	III	16	— — — — — — — —	22	5	Warner, Mari

ALBERTSON

Year	M/W	Assn	Div	NAT	NIT ARC CCA NCI NCT OLY HLM	W	L	Coach
1960	M	NAIA		32	— — — — — — — —	16	13	Brown, James A. "Babe"
1962		NAIA		32	— — — — — — — —	18	10	Carrow, Dr. Richard W.
1984		NAIA		32	— — — — — — — —	22	7	Holly, Martin W. "Marty"
1985		NAIA		32	— — — — — — — —	20	3	Holly, Martin W. "Marty"
1986		NAIA		32	— — — — — — — —	23	7	Holly, Martin W. "Marty"
1988		NAIA		8	— — — — — — — —	28	6	Holly, Martin W. "Marty"
1989		NAIA		8	— — — — — — — —	24	9	Holly, Martin W. "Marty"
1991		NAIA		16	— — — — — — — —	24	5	Holly, Martin W. "Marty"
1993		NAIA	II	8	— — — — — — — —	22	8	Holly, Martin W. "Marty"
1995		NAIA	II	32	— — — — — — — —	21	8	Holly, Martin W. "Marty"
1996		NAIA	II	1	— — — — — — — —	31	3	Holly, Martin W. "Marty"
1998	W	NAIA	II	32	— — — — — — — —	22	9	Corman, Todd

ALBION

Year	M/W	Assn	Div	NAT	NIT ARC CCA NCI NCT OLY HLM	W	L	Coach
1978	M	NCAA	III	3	— — — — — — — —	21	6	Turner, Michael
1979		NCAA	III	24	— — — — — — — —	20	4	Turner, Michael
1998		NCAA	III	48	— — — — — — — —	20	8	Turner, Michael

ALBRIGHT

Year	M/W	Assn	Div	NAT	NIT ARC CCA NCI NCT OLY HLM	W	L	Coach
1961	M	NCAA	II	16	— — — — — — — —	19	9	Renken, Dr. Wilbur G.
1962		NCAA	II	24	— — — — — — — —	18	10	Renken, Dr. Wilbur G.
1965		NCAA	II	32	— — — — — — — —	20	8	Renken, Dr. Wilbur G.
1966		NCAA	II	22	— — — — — — — —	18	11	Renken, Dr. Wilbur G.

Year	M/W	Assn	Div	NAT	NIT	ARC	CCA	NCI	NCT	OLY	HLM	W	L	Coach
1974		NCAA	II	16	—	—	—	—	—	—	—	—	19	9	Renken, Dr. Wilbur G.
1977		NCAA	III	16	—	—	—	—	—	—	—	—	20	9	Renken, Dr. Wilbur G.
1979		NCAA	III	32	—	—	—	—	—	—	—	—	18	10	Renken, Dr. Wilbur G.
1980		NCAA	III	8	—	—	—	—	—	—	—	—	27	3	Renken, Dr. Wilbur G.

ALBUQUERQUE

Year	M/W	Assn	Div	NAT	NIT	ARC	CCA	NCI	NCT	OLY	HLM	W	L	Coach
1964	M	NAIA		32	—	—	—	—	—	—	—	—	17	8	
1966		NAIA		16	—	—	—	—	—	—	—	—	25	5	Smith, Ernie
1968		NAIA		32	—	—	—	—	—	—	—	—	13	4	Smith, Ernie

ALCORN STATE

Year	M/W	Assn	Div	NAT	NIT	ARC	CCA	NCI	NCT	OLY	HLM	W	L	Coach
1967	M	NAIA		32	—	—	—	—	—	—	—	—	20	8	Hopkins, Robert M.
1968		NAIA		16	—	—	—	—	—	—	—	—	24	3	Hopkins, Robert M.
1969		NCAA	II	16	—	—	—	—	—	—	—	—	26	1	Hopkins, Robert M.
1973		NAIA		32	—	—	—	—	—	—	—	—	25	4	Whitney, David L., Sr. "Davey"
1974		NAIA		2	—	—	—	—	—	—	—	—	29	6	Whitney, David L., Sr. "Davey"
1975		NAIA		3	—	—	—	—	—	—	—	—	25	10	Whitney, David L., Sr. "Davey"
1976		NAIA		32	—	—	—	—	—	—	—	—	27	4	Whitney, David L., Sr. "Davey"
1977		NAIA		8	—	—	—	—	—	—	—	—	26	9	Whitney, David L., Sr. "Davey"
1979		NCAA	I	—	12	—	—	—	—	—	—	28	1	Whitney, David L., Sr. "Davey"
1980		NCAA	I	32	—	—	—	—	—	—	—	—	28	2	Whitney, David L., Sr. "Davey"
1982		NCAA	I	48	—	—	—	—	—	—	—	—	22	8	Whitney, David L., Sr. "Davey"
1983		NCAA	I	48	—	—	—	—	—	—	—	—	22	10	Whitney, David L., Sr. "Davey"
1984		NCAA	I	48	—	—	—	—	—	—	—	—	21	10	Whitney, David L., Sr. "Davey"
1985		NCAA	I	—	32	—	—	—	—	—	—	23	7	Whitney, David L., Sr. "Davey"

ALDERSON-BROADDUS

Year	M/W	Assn	Div	NAT	NIT	ARC	CCA	NCI	NCT	OLY	HLM	W	L	Coach
1955	M	NAIA		8	—	—	—	—	—	—	—	—	31	6	Pyles, Rex E. "Roxie"
1956		NAIA		32	—	—	—	—	—	—	—	—	23	12	Pyles, Rex E. "Roxie"
1990		NAIA		16	—	—	—	—	—	—	—	—	28	7	Dodd, Steve
1998	W	NCAA	II	32	—	—	—	—	—	—	—	—	26	4	Mair, Carolyn

ALFRED

Year	M/W	Assn	Div	NAT	NIT	ARC	CCA	NCI	NCT	OLY	HLM	W	L	Coach
1985	M	NCAA	III	32	—	—	—	—	—	—	—	—	17	11	Frederes, Ronald
1986		NCAA	III	16	—	—	—	—	—	—	—	—	23	3	Frederes, Ronald
1989		NCAA	III	40	—	—	—	—	—	—	—	—	18	8	Catalino, Roman
1997		NCAA	III	64	—	—	—	—	—	—	—	—	14	12	Murphy, Jay

ALFRED HOLBROOK

Year	M/W	Assn	Div	NAT	NIT	ARC	CCA	NCI	NCT	OLY	HLM	W	L	Coach
1939	M	NAIA		32	—	—	—	—	—	—	—	—	15	5	Beattie, Mendell E.
1940		NAIA		32	—	—	—	—	—	—	—	—	16	4	Beattie, Mendell E.

ALICE LLOYD

Year	M/W	Assn	Div	NAT	NIT	ARC	CCA	NCI	NCT	OLY	HLM	W	L	Coach
1974	M	NSCAA		16	—	—	—	—	—	—	—	—	X	X	Rose, James
1981		NSCAA		8	—	—	—	—	—	—	—	—	17	14	Morris, Lonnie
1982		NSCAA		3	—	—	—	—	—	—	—	—	8	22	Morris, Lonnie
1993		NAIA	II	16	—	—	—	—	—	—	—	—	27	6	Stepp, Jim
1994		NAIA	II	16	—	—	—	—	—	—	—	—	27	7	Stepp, Jim
1995		NAIA	II	16	—	—	—	—	—	—	—	—	26	10	Stepp, Jim
1996		NAIA	II	16	—	—	—	—	—	—	—	—	27	8	Stepp, Jim

Year	M/W	Assn	Div	NAT	NIT	ARC	CCA	NCI	NCT	OLY	HLM	W	L	Coach
ALLEGHENY														
1975	M	NCAA	III	30	—	—	—	—	—	—	—	15	7	Sundstrom, Norman A.
1979		NCAA	III	32	—	—	—	—	—	—	—	17	8	Sundstrom, Norman A.
1980		NCAA	III	24	—	—	—	—	—	—	—	20	4	Reynders, John C.
1981		NCAA	III	32	—	—	—	—	—	—	—	16	8	Reynders, John C.
1987		NCAA	III	32	—	—	—	—	—	—	—	21	8	Reynders, John C.
1988		NCAA	III	24	—	—	—	—	—	—	—	24	6	Reynders, John C.
1989		NCAA	III	32	—	—	—	—	—	—	—	22	8	Reynders, John C.
1998		NCAA	III	32	—	—	—	—	—	—	—	22	7	Ness, Phillip E.
1984	W	NCAA	III	32	—	—	—	—	—	—	—	22	4	Gould, Kay
1985		NCAA	III	16	—	—	—	—	—	—	—	24	3	Gould, Kay
1986		NCAA	III	24	—	—	—	—	—	—	—	26	2	Gould, Kay
1987		NCAA	III	24	—	—	—	—	—	—	—	25	4	Gould, Kay
ALLENTOWN														
1996	M	NCAA	III	64	—	—	—	—	—	—	—	17	10	Coval, Scott
1989	W	NCAA	III	16	—	—	—	—	—	—	—	24	6	Shirley, Thomas, Jr.
1990		NCAA	III	16	—	—	—	—	—	—	—	27	2	Shirley, Thomas, Jr.
1996		NCAA	III	64	—	—	—	—	—	—	—	20	6	Richter, Fred
1997		NCAA	III	64	—	—	—	—	—	—	—	21	7	Richter, Fred
1998		NCAA	III	48	—	—	—	—	—	—	—	20	8	Richter, Fred
ALLIANCE														
1963	M	NAIA		16	—	—	—	—	—	—	—	19	6	Haluch, Thaddeus F.
1965		NAIA		16	—	—	—	—	—	—	—	18	8	Haluch, Thaddeus F.
ALMA														
1941	M	NAIA		16	—	—	—	—	—	—	—	23	3	MacDonald, Gordon D.
1985	W	NCAA	III	24	—	—	—	—	—	—	—	18	5	Charney, Claudette
1986		NCAA	III	24	—	—	—	—	—	—	—	23	3	Klenk, William
1987		NCAA	III	16	—	—	—	—	—	—	—	21	5	Klenk, William
1989		NCAA	III	24	—	—	—	—	—	—	—	19	5	Goffnett, Charles
1992		NCAA	III	1	—	—	—	—	—	—	—	24	3	Goffnett, Charles
1994		NCAA	III	32	—	—	—	—	—	—	—	21	6	Goffnett, Charles
1996		NCAA	III	64	—	—	—	—	—	—	—	21	6	Goffnett, Charles
1997		NCAA	III	32	—	—	—	—	—	—	—	23	6	Goffnett, Charles
ALVERNIA														
1997	M	NCAA	III	4	—	—	—	—	—	—	—	26	6	McCloskey, John R., Sr. "Jack"
1996	W	NCAA	III	64	—	—	—	—	—	—	—	22	6	Calabria, Kevin
1997		NCAA	III	32	—	—	—	—	—	—	—	22	6	Calabria, Kevin
1998		NCAA	III	32	—	—	—	—	—	—	—	22	6	Calabria, Kevin
AMERICAN														
1950	M	NAIA		32	—	—	—	—	—	—	—	22	8	Cassell, Stafford H.
1951		NAIA		32	—	—	—	—	—	—	—	18	10	Cassell, Stafford H.
1958		NCAA	II	8	—	—	—	—	—	—	—	22	6	Carrasco, David L.
1959		NCAA	II	8	—	—	—	—	—	—	—	22	7	Carrasco, David L.

Year	M/W	Assn	Div	NAT	NIT	ARC	CCA	NCI	NCT	OLY	HLM	W	L	Coach
1960		NCAA	II	8	—	—	—	—	—	—	—	22	7	Carrasco, David L.
1973		NCAA	I	—	16	—	—	—	—	—	—	21	5	Young, Thomas J.
1981		NCAA	I	—	32	—	—	—	—	—	—	24	6	Williams, Gary
1982		NCAA	I	—	32	—	—	—	—	—	—	21	9	Williams, Gary
1998	W	NCAA	I	—	16	—	—	—	—	—	—	23	7	Thatcher, Jeff

AMERICAN BAPTIST

Year	M/W	Assn	Div	NAT	NIT	ARC	CCA	NCI	NCT	OLY	HLM	W	L	Coach
1996	M	LCC		5	—	—	—	—	—	—	—	16	7	Robinson, Rev. Norman

AMERICAN CHRISTIAN

Year	M/W	Assn	Div	NAT	NIT	ARC	CCA	NCI	NCT	OLY	HLM	W	L	Coach
1975	M	NCCAA		4	—	—	—	—	—	—	—	26	15	Hauser, George

AMERICAN INDIAN

Year	M/W	Assn	Div	NAT	NIT	ARC	CCA	NCI	NCT	OLY	HLM	W	L	Coach
1988	M	NBCAA	II	2	—	—	—	—	—	—	—	X	X	Cupp, Larry
1992		NCCAA	IIA	7	—	—	—	—	—	—	—	X	X	Grant, Timothy L.
1993		NCCAA	IIA	7	—	—	—	—	—	—	—	X	X	Grant, Timothy L.
1994		NCCAA	IIA	3	—	—	—	—	—	—	—	X	X	Grant, Timothy L.

AMERICAN INTERNATIONAL

Year	M/W	Assn	Div	NAT	NIT	ARC	CCA	NCI	NCT	OLY	HLM	W	L	Coach
1952	M	NAIA		32	—	—	—	—	—	—	—	15	10	Rodis, Nicholas
1956		NAIA		32	—	—	—	—	—	—	—	16	7	Callahan, William E.
1966		NCAA	II	34	—	—	—	—	—	—	—	18	8	Callahan, William E.
1967		NCAA	II	36	—	—	—	—	—	—	—	19	6	Callahan, William E.
1968		NCAA	II	8	—	—	—	—	—	—	—	21	5	Callahan, William E.
1969		NCAA	II	3	—	—	—	—	—	—	—	21	4	Callahan, William E.
1970		NCAA	II	8	—	—	—	—	—	—	—	17	8	Callahan, William E.
1983		NCAA	II	16	—	—	—	—	—	—	—	23	9	Powell, Jim
1984		NCAA	II	32	—	—	—	—	—	—	—	23	8	Powell, Jim
1985		NCAA	II	8	—	—	—	—	—	—	—	29	4	Powell, Jim
1994		NCAA	II	32	—	—	—	—	—	—	—	22	6	Powell, Jim
1995	W	NCAA	II	32	—	—	—	—	—	—	—	22	9	Cinella, Peter
1996		NCAA	II	48	—	—	—	—	—	—	—	18	11	Cinella, Peter

AMHERST

Year	M/W	Assn	Div	NAT	NIT	ARC	CCA	NCI	NCT	OLY	HLM	W	L	Coach
1957	M	NCAA	II	32	—	—	—	—	—	—	—	17	4	Wilson, Richard E. "Rick"
1994		NCAA	III	8	—	—	—	—	—	—	—	22	5	Hixon, David D.
1997		NCAA	III	32	—	—	—	—	—	—	—	21	5	Hixon, David D.

ANDERSON (IN)

Year	M/W	Assn	Div	NAT	NIT	ARC	CCA	NCI	NCT	OLY	HLM	W	L	Coach
1939	M	NAIA		32	—	—	—	—	—	—	—	15	6	Nay, Edgar
1958		NAIA		16	—	—	—	—	—	—	—	23	6	Macholtz, Robert W.
1961		NAIA		8	—	—	—	—	—	—	—	26	4	Macholtz, Robert W.

ANGELO STATE

Year	M/W	Assn	Div	NAT	NIT	ARC	CCA	NCI	NCT	OLY	HLM	W	L	Coach
1988	M	NCAA	II	32	—	—	—	—	—	—	—	22	11	Messbarger, Ed
1989		NCAA	II	24	—	—	—	—	—	—	—	18	10	Messbarger, Ed
1994	W	NCAA	II	32	—	—	—	—	—	—	—	23	6	Davis, Peggy

ANNA MARIA

Year	M/W	Assn	Div	NAT	NIT	ARC	CCA	NCI	NCT	OLY	HLM	W	L	Coach
1996	M	NCAA	III	16	—	—	—	—	—	—	—	25	5	Phillips, Paul

APPALACHIAN BIBLE

Year	M/W	Assn	Div	NAT	NIT	ARC	CCA	NCI	NCT	OLY	HLM	W	L	Coach
1998	M	NCCAA	IIA	8	—	—	—	—	—	—	—	7	17	Barton, Tim

Year	M/W	Assn	Div	NAT	NIT	ARC	CCA	NCI	NCT	OLY	HLM	W	L	Coach
APPALACHIAN STATE														
1940	M	NAIA		16	—	—	—	—	—	—	—	18	3	Stewart, A. L. "Flucie"
1941		NAIA		8	—	—	—	—	—	—	—	17	3	Canipe, Clyde
1943		NAIA		8	—	—	—	—	—	—	—	15	3	Smawley, Belus
1948		NAIA		32	—	—	—	—	—	—	—	20	8	Hoover, Francis
1950		NAIA		32	—	—	—	—	—	—	—	20	8	Hoover, Francis
1979		NCAA	I	32	—	—	—	—	—	—	—	23	6	Cremins, Bobby
1987	W	NCAA	I	—	8	—	—	—	—	—	—	24	7	Robinson, Linda
1990		NCAA	I	48	—	—	—	—	—	—	—	20	9	Robinson, Linda
1991		NCAA	I	48	—	—	—	—	—	—	—	19	14	Robinson, Linda
1996		NCAA	I	64	—	—	—	—	—	—	—	24	6	Robinson, Linda
AQUINAS (MI)														
1982	W	AIAW	III	16	—	—	—	—	—	—	—	20	8	Tibaldi, Patti
1990		NAIA		16	—	—	—	—	—	—	—	26	6	Tibaldi, Patti
1992		NAIA	II	16	—	—	—	—	—	—	—	22	12	Tibaldi, Patti
1993		NAIA	II	16	—	—	—	—	—	—	—	23	8	Tibaldi, Patti
ARIZONA														
1946	M	NCAA		—	8	—	—	—	—	—	—	25	5	Enke, Fred A.
1950		NCAA		—	12	—	—	—	—	—	—	26	5	Enke, Fred A.
1951		NCAA		16	8	—	—	—	—	—	—	24	6	Enke, Fred A.
1975		NCAA	I	—	—	—	2	—	—	—	—	22	7	Snowden, Frederick
1976		NCAA	I	8	—	—	—	—	—	—	—	24	9	Snowden, Frederick
1977		NCAA	I	32	—	—	—	—	—	—	—	21	6	Snowden, Frederick
1985		NCAA	I	64	—	—	—	—	—	—	—	21	10	Olson, Robert Luther "Lute"
1986		NCAA	I	64	—	—	—	—	—	—	—	23	9	Olson, Robert Luther "Lute"
1987		NCAA	I	64	—	—	—	—	—	—	—	18	12	Olson, Robert Luther "Lute"
1988		NCAA	I	3	—	—	—	—	—	—	—	35	3	Olson, Robert Luther "Lute"
1989		NCAA	I	16	—	—	—	—	—	—	—	29	4	Olson, Robert Luther "Lute"
1990		NCAA	I	32	—	—	—	—	—	—	—	25	7	Olson, Robert Luther "Lute"
1991		NCAA	I	16	—	—	—	—	—	—	—	28	7	Olson, Robert Luther "Lute"
1992		NCAA	I	64	—	—	—	—	—	—	—	24	7	Olson, Robert Luther "Lute"
1993		NCAA	I	64	—	—	—	—	—	—	—	24	4	Olson, Robert Luther "Lute"
1994		NCAA	I	3	—	—	—	—	—	—	—	29	6	Olson, Robert Luther "Lute"
1995		NCAA	I	64	—	—	—	—	—	—	—	23	8	Olson, Robert Luther "Lute"
1996		NCAA	I	16	—	—	—	—	—	—	—	26	7	Olson, Robert Luther "Lute"
1997		NCAA	I	1	—	—	—	—	—	—	—	25	9	Olson, Robert Luther "Lute"
1998		NCAA	I	8	—	—	—	—	—	—	—	31	5	Olson, Robert Luther "Lute"
1996	W	NCAA	I	—	1	—	—	—	—	—	—	22	8	Bonvicini, Joan
1997		NCAA	I	32	—	—	—	—	—	—	—	23	8	Bonvicini, Joan
1998		NCAA	I	16	—	—	—	—	—	—	—	23	7	Bonvicini, Joan
ARIZONA BIBLE														
1987	M	NBCAA	II	1	—	—	—	—	—	—	—	X	X	Steele, Kevin
1989		NBCAA	II	5	—	—	—	—	—	—	—	X	X	Gremler, Dwayne
1993		NBCAA	II	3	—	—	—	—	—	—	—	15	7	Kuyper, Tom
1994		NBCAA	II	8	—	—	—	—	—	—	—	12	12	Kuyper, Tom
1995		NBCAA	II	5	—	—	—	—	—	—	—	17	9	Kuyper, Tom
1997		NBCAA	II	4	—	—	—	—	—	—	—	15	15	Kuyper, Tom
1998		NCCAA	IIA	4	—	—	—	—	—	—	—	16	15	Kuyper, Tom

ARIZONA STATE

Year	M/W	Assn	Div	NAT	NIT	ARC	CCA	NCI	NCT	OLY	HLM	W	L	Coach
1948	M	NAIA		16	—	—	—	—	—	—	—	13	11	Lavik, Rudolph H.
1953		NAIA		16	—	—	—	—	—	—	—	13	12	Kajikawa, William
1958		NCAA	I	24	—	—	—	—	—	—	—	13	13	Wulk, Ned W.
1961		NCAA	I	8	—	—	—	—	—	—	—	23	6	Wulk, Ned W.
1962		NCAA	I	25	—	—	—	—	—	—	—	23	4	Wulk, Ned W.
1963		NCAA	I	8	—	—	—	—	—	—	—	26	3	Wulk, Ned W.
1964		NCAA	I	25	—	—	—	—	—	—	—	16	11	Wulk, Ned W.
1973		NCAA	I	16	—	—	—	—	—	—	—	19	9	Wulk, Ned W.
1974		NCAA	I	—	—	—	8	—	—	—	—	18	9	Wulk, Ned W.
1975		NCAA	I	8	—	—	—	—	—	—	—	25	4	Wulk, Ned W.
1980		NCAA	I	32	—	—	—	—	—	—	—	22	7	Wulk, Ned W.
1981		NCAA	I	32	—	—	—	—	—	—	—	24	4	Wulk, Ned W.
1983		NCAA	I	—	16	—	—	—	—	—	—	19	14	Weinhauer, Bob
1990		NCAA	I	—	32	—	—	—	—	—	—	15	16	Frieder, Bill
1991		NCAA	I	32	—	—	—	—	—	—	—	20	10	Frieder, Bill
1992		NCAA	I	—	16	—	—	—	—	—	—	19	14	Frieder, Bill
1993		NCAA	I	—	32	—	—	—	—	—	—	18	10	Frieder, Bill
1994		NCAA	I	—	32	—	—	—	—	—	—	15	13	Frieder, Bill
1995		NCAA	I	16	—	—	—	—	—	—	—	24	9	Frieder, Bill
1998		NCAA	I	—	32	—	—	—	—	—	—	18	14	Newman, Don
1981	W	AIAW	I	—	2	—	—	—	—	—	—	21	11	Simpson, Juliene
1982		NCAA	I	16	—	—	—	—	—	—	—	25	7	Simpson, Juliene
1983		NCAA	I	16	—	—	—	—	—	—	—	23	7	Simpson, Juliene
1992		NCAA	I	48	—	—	—	—	—	—	—	20	9	McHugh, Maura

ARKANSAS

Year	M/W	Assn	Div	NAT	NIT	ARC	CCA	NCI	NCT	OLY	HLM	W	L	Coach
1936	M	NCAA		—	—	—	—	—	—	8	—	24	3	Rose, Glen
1941		NCAA		3	—	—	—	—	—	—	—	20	3	Rose, Glen
1945		NCAA		3	—	—	—	—	—	—	—	17	9	Lambert, Dr. Eugene W.
1949		NCAA		6	—	—	—	—	—	—	—	15	11	Lambert, Dr. Eugene W.
1958		NCAA	I	16	—	—	—	—	—	—	—	17	10	Rose, Glen
1977		NCAA	I	32	—	—	—	—	—	—	—	26	2	Sutton, Eddie
1978		NCAA	I	3	—	—	—	—	—	—	—	32	4	Sutton, Eddie
1979		NCAA	I	8	—	—	—	—	—	—	—	25	5	Sutton, Eddie
1980		NCAA	I	48	—	—	—	—	—	—	—	21	8	Sutton, Eddie
1981		NCAA	I	16	—	—	—	—	—	—	—	24	8	Sutton, Eddie
1982		NCAA	I	32	—	—	—	—	—	—	—	23	6	Sutton, Eddie
1983		NCAA	I	16	—	—	—	—	—	—	—	26	4	Sutton, Eddie
1984		NCAA	I	32	—	—	—	—	—	—	—	25	7	Sutton, Eddie
1985		NCAA	I	32	—	—	—	—	—	—	—	22	13	Sutton, Eddie
1987		NCAA	I	—	16	—	—	—	—	—	—	19	14	Richardson, Nolan
1988		NCAA	I	64	—	—	—	—	—	—	—	21	9	Richardson, Nolan
1989		NCAA	I	32	—	—	—	—	—	—	—	25	7	Richardson, Nolan
1990		NCAA	I	3	—	—	—	—	—	—	—	30	5	Richardson, Nolan
1991		NCAA	I	8	—	—	—	—	—	—	—	34	4	Richardson, Nolan
1992		NCAA	I	32	—	—	—	—	—	—	—	26	8	Richardson, Nolan
1993		NCAA	I	16	—	—	—	—	—	—	—	22	9	Richardson, Nolan
1994		NCAA	I	1	—	—	—	—	—	—	—	31	3	Richardson, Nolan
1995		NCAA	I	2	—	—	—	—	—	—	—	32	7	Richardson, Nolan
1996		NCAA	I	16	—	—	—	—	—	—	—	20	13	Richardson, Nolan

Year	M/W	Assn	Div	NAT	NIT	ARC	CCA	NCI	NCT	OLY	HLM	W	L	Coach
1997		NCAA	I	—	4	—	—	—	—	—	—	18	14	Richardson, Nolan
1998		NCAA	I	32	—	—	—	—	—	—	—	24	9	Richardson, Nolan
1982	W	AIAW	I	16	—	—	—	—	—	—	—	26	10	Mossman, Matilda Willis
1986		NCAA	I	40	—	—	—	—	—	—	—	22	8	Sutherland, John
1987		NCAA	I	—	1	—	—	—	—	—	—	19	10	Sutherland, John
1989		NCAA	I	48	—	—	—	—	—	—	—	22	8	Sutherland, John
1990		NCAA	I	8	—	—	—	—	—	—	—	25	5	Sutherland, John
1991		NCAA	I	16	—	—	—	—	—	—	—	28	4	Sutherland, John
1995		NCAA	I	32	—	—	—	—	—	—	—	23	7	Blair, Gary
1996		NCAA	I	—	4	—	—	—	—	—	—	21	13	Blair, Gary
1998		NCAA	I	3	—	—	—	—	—	—	—	22	11	Blair, Gary

ARKANSAS BAPTIST

Year	M/W	Assn	Div	NAT	NIT	ARC	CCA	NCI	NCT	OLY	HLM	W	L	Coach
1978	M	NSCAA		16	—	—	—	—	—	—	—			
1991		NSCAA		4	—	—	—	—	—	—	—	23	12	Marks, Arcell
1992		NSCAA		5	—	—	—	—	—	—	—			Marks, Arcell
1994		NSCAA		5	—	—	—	—	—	—	—	11	16	Marks, Arcell
1997		NSCAA		12	—	—	—	—	—	—	—	9	18	Marks, Arcell
1998		NSCAA		8	—	—	—	—	—	—	—	5	14	Marks, Arcell
1993	W	NSCAA		3	—	—	—	—	—	—	—	19	14	Allen, Lee W.
1994		NSCAA		2	—	—	—	—	—	—	—	18	7	Allen, Lee W.
1996		NSCAA		4	—	—	—	—	—	—	—	18	7	Allen, Lee W.
1997		NSCAA		4	—	—	—	—	—	—	—	17	12	Allen, Lee W.
1998		NSCAA		4	—	—	—	—	—	—	—	15	6	Allen, Lee W.

ARKANSAS STATE

Year	M/W	Assn	Div	NAT	NIT	ARC	CCA	NCI	NCT	OLY	HLM	W	L	Coach
1947	M	NAIA		32	—	—	—	—	—	—	—	17	16	Tomlinson, J. A. "Ike"
1949		NAIA		32	—	—	—	—	—	—	—	14	12	Tomlinson, J. A. "Ike"
1958		NCAA	II	24	—	—	—	—	—	—	—	18	9	Rauth, John H.
1960		NCAA	II	32	—	—	—	—	—	—	—	14	13	Rauth, John H.
1962		NCAA	II	16	—	—	—	—	—	—	—	17	7	Rauth, John H.
1963		NCAA	II	24	—	—	—	—	—	—	—	15	11	Rauth, John H.
1966		NCAA	II	22	—	—	—	—	—	—	—	17	9	Speight, Marvin
1967		NCAA	II	23	—	—	—	—	—	—	—	17	7	Speight, Marvin
1987		NCAA	I	—	32	—	—	—	—	—	—	21	13	Catalina, Nelson
1988		NCAA	I	—	8	—	—	—	—	—	—	21	14	Catalina, Nelson
1989		NCAA	I	—	32	—	—	—	—	—	—	20	10	Catalina, Nelson
1991		NCAA	I	—	8	—	—	—	—	—	—	23	9	Catalina, Nelson
1992	W	NCAA	I	—	3	—	—	—	—	—	—	25	7	Winters, Jerry Ann
1993		NCAA	I	—	1	—	—	—	—	—	—	16	12	Winters, Jerry Ann
1994		NCAA	I	—	2	—	—	—	—	—	—	22	9	Winters, Jerry Ann

ARKANSAS TECH

Year	M/W	Assn	Div	NAT	NIT	ARC	CCA	NCI	NCT	OLY	HLM	W	L	Coach
1950	M	NAIA		16	—	—	—	—	—	—	—	26	2	Hindsman, Sam F., Jr.
1951		NAIA		16	—	—	—	—	—	—	—	25	6	Hindsman, Sam F., Jr.
1952		NAIA		32	—	—	—	—	—	—	—	26	4	Hindsman, Sam F., Jr.
1953		NAIA		16	—	—	—	—	—	—	—	20	1	Hindsman, Sam F., Jr.
1954		NAIA		4	—	—	—	—	—	—	—	28	3	Hindsman, Sam F., Jr.
1955		NAIA		4	—	—	—	—	—	—	—	31	5	Hindsman, Sam F., Jr.
1956		NAIA		32	—	—	—	—	—	—	—	15	6	Hindsman, Sam F., Jr.
1958		NAIA		32	—	—	—	—	—	—	—	17	4	Hindsman, Sam F., Jr.

Year	M/W	Assn	Div	NAT	NIT	ARC	CCA	NCI	NCT	OLY	HLM	W	L	Coach
1963		NAIA		32	—	—	—	—	—	—	—	19	9	Hindsman, Sam F., Jr.
1970		NAIA		16	—	—	—	—	—	—	—	22	10	Dopson, Dewaard
1995		NAIA	I	3	—	—	—	—	—	—	—	29	6	Barnes, Marty
1996		NAIA	I	16	—	—	—	—	—	—	—	19	10	Barnes, Marty
1980	W	AIAW	II	16	—	—	—	—	—	—	—	29	2	Yeager, Jim
1987		NAIA		4	—	—	—	—	—	—	—	29	6	Dickerson, Jim
1988		NAIA		3	—	—	—	—	—	—	—	29	5	Foley, Joe M.
1989		NAIA		3	—	—	—	—	—	—	—	35	2	Foley, Joe M.
1992		NAIA	I	1	—	—	—	—	—	—	—	35	1	Foley, Joe M.
1993		NAIA	I	1	—	—	—	—	—	—	—	31	5	Foley, Joe M.
1994		NAIA	I	8	—	—	—	—	—	—	—	30	3	Foley, Joe M.
1995		NAIA	I	16	—	—	—	—	—	—	—	28	6	Foley, Joe M.
1996		NAIA	I	16	—	—	—	—	—	—	—	23	8	Foley, Joe M.
1997		NAIA	I	3	—	—	—	—	—	—	—	29	4	Foley, Joe M.
1998		NCAA	II	8	—	—	—	—	—	—	—	26	5	Foley, Joe M.

ARKANSAS: LITTLE ROCK

Year	M/W	Assn	Div	NAT	NIT	ARC	CCA	NCI	NCT	OLY	HLM	W	L	Coach
1986	M	NCAA	I	32	—	—	—	—	—	—	—	23	11	Newell, Mike
1987		NCAA	I	—	4	—	—	—	—	—	—	26	11	Newell, Mike
1988		NCAA	I	—	32	—	—	—	—	—	—	24	7	Newell, Mike
1989		NCAA	I	64	—	—	—	—	—	—	—	23	8	Newell, Mike
1990		NCAA	I	64	—	—	—	—	—	—	—	20	10	Newell, Mike
1996		NCAA	I	—	32	—	—	—	—	—	—	23	7	Sanderson, Winfrey "Wimp"

ARKANSAS: MONTICELLO

Year	M/W	Assn	Div	NAT	NIT	ARC	CCA	NCI	NCT	OLY	HLM	W	L	Coach
1960	M	NAIA		16	—	—	—	—	—	—	—	18	8	Beard, Leslie "Shorty"
1986		NAIA		2	—	—	—	—	—	—	—	26	10	Sharpe, Gary A.
1978	W	AIAW	S	8	—	—	—	—	—	—	—	19	7	Lavender, Mary Jane
1990		NAIA		2	—	—	—	—	—	—	—	34	3	Early, Alvy
1993		NAIA	I	32	—	—	—	—	—	—	—	25	11	Early, Alvy
1995		NAIA	I	8	—	—	—	—	—	—	—	27	6	Early, Alvy
1998		NCAA	II	16	—	—	—	—	—	—	—	23	8	Early, Alvy

ARKANSAS: PINE BLUFF

Year	M/W	Assn	Div	NAT	NIT	ARC	CCA	NCI	NCT	OLY	HLM	W	L	Coach
1967	M	NCAA	II	32	—	—	—	—	—	—	—	24	7	Clemmons, Hubert O.

ARLINGTON BAPTIST

Year	M/W	Assn	Div	NAT	NIT	ARC	CCA	NCI	NCT	OLY	HLM	W	L	Coach
1984	M	NCCAA	II	8	—	—	—	—	—	—	—	X	X	Jones, Dr. Griffin
1988		NBCAA	II	1	—	—	—	—	—	—	—	X	X	Jones, Dr. Griffin
1989		NBCAA	II	6	—	—	—	—	—	—	—	X	X	Cash, Durwood M. "Woody"
1990		NBCAA	II	8	—	—	—	—	—	—	—	X	X	Cash, Durwood M. "Woody"
1994		NBCAA	I	5	—	—	—	—	—	—	—	10	20	Bosher, Clark
1996		NCCAA	IIA	7	—	—	—	—	—	—	—	8	24	Bosher, Clark
1983	W	NCCAA	II	4	—	—	—	—	—	—	—	X	X	Cash, Durward M. "Woody"

ARMSTRONG ATLANTIC STATE

Year	M/W	Assn	Div	NAT	NIT	ARC	CCA	NCI	NCT	OLY	HLM	W	L	Coach
1975	M	NCAA	II	24	—	—	—	—	—	—	—	19	7	Alexander, Bill
1977		NCAA	II	32	—	—	—	—	—	—	—	15	15	Alexander, Bill
1995		NCAA	II	32	—	—	—	—	—	—	—	20	11	Mills, Griff

Year	M/W	Assn	Div	NAT	NIT	ARC	CCA	NCI	NCT	OLY	HLM	W	L	Coach
ARMY														
1944	M	NCAA		—	—	—	—	—	—	—	1	15	0	Kelleher, Edward A.
1961		NCAA	I	—	12	—	—	—	—	—	—	17	7	Hunter, George E.
1964		NCAA	I	—	3	—	—	—	—	—	—	19	7	Locke, Taylor O. "Tates"
1965		NCAA	I	—	3	—	—	—	—	—	—	21	8	Locke, Taylor O. "Tates"
1966		NCAA	I	—	4	—	—	—	—	—	—	18	8	Knight, Robert M.
1968		NCAA	I	—	16	—	—	—	—	—	—	20	5	Knight, Robert M.
1969		NCAA	I	—	4	—	—	—	—	—	—	18	10	Knight, Robert M.
1970		NCAA	I	—	3	—	—	—	—	—	—	22	6	Knight, Robert M.
1978		NCAA	I	—	16	—	—	—	—	—	—	19	9	Krzyzewski, Michael W.
1984	W	NCAA	II	8	—	—	—	—	—	—	—	24	4	Johnson, Harold
1988		NCAA	II	16	—	—	—	—	—	—	—	19	13	Chiavaro, Lynn
ARNOLD														
1953	M	NAIA		32	—	—	—	—	—	—	—	17	11	Maroon, Tuffie
ASHEVILLE BUNCOMBE TCC														
1975	M	NSCAA		16	—	—	—	—	—	—	—	20	4	Rhea, James H.
ASHLAND														
1962	M	NAIA		32	—	—	—	—	—	—	—	21	4	Stoker, Bob
1968		NCAA	II	4	—	—	—	—	—	—	—	24	6	Musselman, William
1969		NCAA	II	4	—	—	—	—	—	—	—	26	4	Musselman, William
1970		NCAA	II	16	—	—	—	—	—	—	—	23	4	Musselman, William
1971		NCAA	II	24	—	—	—	—	—	—	—	25	3	Musselman, William
1976		NCAA	III	14	—	—	—	—	—	—	—	20	7	Gottfried, Joe
1977		NCAA	III	16	—	—	—	—	—	—	—	20	6	Gottfried, Joe
1978		NCAA	III	16	—	—	—	—	—	—	—	19	7	Gottfried, Joe
1988		NCAA	II	32	—	—	—	—	—	—	—	18	10	Lyons, Roger
1990		NCAA	II	16	—	—	—	—	—	—	—	22	8	Dambrot, Keith
1991		NCAA	II	8	—	—	—	—	—	—	—	26	5	Dambrot, Keith
1975	W	AIAW	S	3	—	—	—	—	—	—	—	19	3	Jones, Dr. Ruth
1976		AIAW	S	4	—	—	—	—	—	—	—	20	6	Jones, Dr. Ruth
1977		AIAW	S	12	—	—	—	—	—	—	—	15	7	Wetters, Barbara
ASSOCIATION FREE LUTHERAN BIBLE														
1986	M	NBCAA	II	2	—	—	—	—	—	—	—	11	7	Palke, Mike
1988		NBCAA	II	3	—	—	—	—	—	—	—	2	12	Quanbeck, Keith
1989		NBCAA	II	3	—	—	—	—	—	—	—	6	15	Johnson, Mark
1991		NBCAA	II	6	—	—	—	—	—	—	—	5	9	Berntson, Tim
1992		NBCAA	II	8	—	—	—	—	—	—	—	10	9	Unverzagt, Joel
1994		NBCAA	II	6	—	—	—	—	—	—	—	X	X	Greven, John
1995		NBCAA	I	8	—	—	—	—	—	—	—	3	15	Greven, John
1996		NBCAA	II	7	—	—	—	—	—	—	—	5	13	Greven, John
1997		NBCAA	II	6	—	—	—	—	—	—	—	11	19	Greven, John
1998		NBCAA		7	—	—	—	—	—	—	—	4	15	Monseth, Ben
1991	W	NBCAA		2	—	—	—	—	—	—	—	9	6	Jacobson, Wanda
1992		NBCAA		2	—	—	—	—	—	—	—	12	4	Jacobson, Wanda
1993		NBCAA		4	—	—	—	—	—	—	—	8	9	Jacobson, Wanda
1994		NBCAA		2	—	—	—	—	—	—	—	X	X	Greven, Wendy Qualley

Year	M/W	Assn	Div	NAT	NIT	ARC	CCA	NCI	NCT	OLY	HLM	W	L	Coach
1995		NBCAA		4	—	—	—	—	—	—	—	X	X	Greven, Wendy Qualley
1996		NBCAA		4	—	—	—	—	—	—	—	2	12	Greven, Wendy Qualley
1997		NBCAA		4	—	—	—	—	—	—	—	9	8	Greven, Wendy Qualley
1998		NBCAA		4	—	—	—	—	—	—	—	2	15	Olson, Sarah

ASSUMPTION (MA)

Year	M/W	Assn	Div	NAT	NIT	ARC	CCA	NCI	NCT	OLY	HLM	W	L	Coach
1958	M	NAIA		32	—	—	—	—	—	—	—	16	4	Laska, Andrew
1960		NCAA	II	24	—	—	—	—	—	—	—	14	6	Laska, Andrew
1963		NCAA	II	24	—	—	—	—	—	—	—	14	5	Laska, Andrew
1964		NCAA	II	24	—	—	—	—	—	—	—	19	2	Laska, Andrew
1965		NCAA	II	16	—	—	—	—	—	—	—	16	6	Laska, Andrew
1966		NCAA	II	16	—	—	—	—	—	—	—	18	6	Laska, Andrew
1967		NCAA	II	32	—	—	—	—	—	—	—	17	5	Laska, Andrew
1968		NCAA	II	34	—	—	—	—	—	—	—	15	7	O'Brien, Joseph M.
1969		NCAA	II	24	—	—	—	—	—	—	—	17	7	O'Brien, Joseph M.
1970		NCAA	II	16	—	—	—	—	—	—	—	17	5	O'Brien, Joseph M.
1971		NCAA	II	8	—	—	—	—	—	—	—	25	2	O'Brien, Joseph M.
1972		NCAA	II	8	—	—	—	—	—	—	—	21	6	O'Brien, Joseph M.
1973		NCAA	II	3	—	—	—	—	—	—	—	25	3	O'Brien, Joseph M.
1974		NCAA	II	3	—	—	—	—	—	—	—	22	7	O'Brien, Joseph M.
1975		NCAA	II	3	—	—	—	—	—	—	—	22	8	O'Brien, Joseph M.
1976		NCAA	II	16	—	—	—	—	—	—	—	16	12	O'Brien, Joseph M.
1977		NCAA	II	24	—	—	—	—	—	—	—	19	10	O'Brien, Joseph M.
1979		NCAA	II	16	—	—	—	—	—	—	—	18	11	O'Brien, Joseph M.
1983		NCAA	II	24	—	—	—	—	—	—	—	21	11	O'Brien, Joseph M.
1988		NCAA	II	32	—	—	—	—	—	—	—	20	12	Renkens, Jack
1991		NCAA	II	32	—	—	—	—	—	—	—	24	8	Renkens, Jack
1992		NCAA	II	32	—	—	—	—	—	—	—	19	13	Renkens, Jack
1998		NCAA	II	32	—	—	—	—	—	—	—	23	4	DeBari, Sergio "Serge"

ATHENS STATE

Year	M/W	Assn	Div	NAT	NIT	ARC	CCA	NCI	NCT	OLY	HLM	W	L	Coach
1963	M	NAIA		16	—	—	—	—	—	—	—	23	9	Belcher, Oba E.
1966		NAIA		16	—	—	—	—	—	—	—	20	10	Belcher, Oba E.
1968		NAIA		32	—	—	—	—	—	—	—	16	14	Belcher, Oba E.
1985		NAIA		8	—	—	—	—	—	—	—	20	7	Murrell, Harold
1991		NAIA		8	—	—	—	—	—	—	—	20	9	Murrell, Harold

ATLANTA CHRISTIAN

Year	M/W	Assn	Div	NAT	NIT	ARC	CCA	NCI	NCT	OLY	HLM	W	L	Coach
1991	M	NCCAA	IIA	2	—	—	—	—	—	—	—	19	7	Kaiser, Richard "Rick"
1992		NCCAA	IIA	2	—	—	—	—	—	—	—	19	7	Kaiser, Richard "Rick"
1993		NCCAA	IIA	1	—	—	—	—	—	—	—	17	14	Kaiser, Richard "Rick"
1994		NCCAA	IIA	6	—	—	—	—	—	—	—	14	14	Kaiser, Richard "Rick"
1995		NCCAA	IIA	3	—	—	—	—	—	—	—	17	15	Griffin, Joe
1996		NCCAA	IIA	6	—	—	—	—	—	—	—	17	15	Griffin, Joe
1991	W	NCCAA	II	6	—	—	—	—	—	—	—	18	10	Griffin, Joe
1992		NCCAA	II	2	—	—	—	—	—	—	—	6	8	Griffin, Joe

AUBURN

Year	M/W	Assn	Div	NAT	NIT	ARC	CCA	NCI	NCT	OLY	HLM	W	L	Coach
1984	M	NCAA	I	48	—	—	—	—	—	—	—	20	11	Smith, Charles H. "Sonny"
1985		NCAA	I	16	—	—	—	—	—	—	—	22	12	Smith, Charles H. "Sonny"
1986		NCAA	I	8	—	—	—	—	—	—	—	22	11	Smith, Charles H. "Sonny"
1987		NCAA	I	32	—	—	—	—	—	—	—	18	13	Smith, Charles H. "Sonny"

Year	M/W	Assn	Div	NAT	NIT	ARC	CCA	NCI	NCT	OLY	HLM	W	L	Coach
1988		NCAA	I	32	—	—	—	—	—	—	—	19	11	Smith, Charles H. "Sonny"
1993		NCAA	I	—	32	—	—	—	—	—	—	15	12	Eagles, Tommy Joe
1995		NCAA	I	—	32	—	—	—	—	—	—	16	13	Ellis, Cliff
1996		NCAA	I	—	32	—	—	—	—	—	—	19	13	Ellis, Cliff
1998		NCAA	I	—	16	—	—	—	—	—	—	16	13	Ellis, Cliff
1982	W	NCAA	I	32	—	—	—	—	—	—	—	24	5	Ciampi, Joe
1983		NCAA	I	16	—	—	—	—	—	—	—	24	8	Ciampi, Joe
1985		NCAA	I	16	—	—	—	—	—	—	—	25	6	Ciampi, Joe
1986		NCAA	I	16	—	—	—	—	—	—	—	24	6	Ciampi, Joe
1987		NCAA	I	8	—	—	—	—	—	—	—	31	2	Ciampi, Joe
1988		NCAA	I	2	—	—	—	—	—	—	—	32	3	Ciampi, Joe
1989		NCAA	I	2	—	—	—	—	—	—	—	32	2	Ciampi, Joe
1990		NCAA	I	2	—	—	—	—	—	—	—	28	7	Ciampi, Joe
1991		NCAA	I	8	—	—	—	—	—	—	—	26	6	Ciampi, Joe
1993		NCAA	I	16	—	—	—	—	—	—	—	25	4	Ciampi, Joe
1994		NCAA	I	32	—	—	—	—	—	—	—	20	10	Ciampi, Joe
1996		NCAA	I	8	—	—	—	—	—	—	—	23	9	Ciampi, Joe
1997		NCAA	I	32	—	—	—	—	—	—	—	22	10	Ciampi, Joe

AUBURN: MONTGOMERY

Year	M/W	Assn	Div	NAT	NIT	ARC	CCA	NCI	NCT	OLY	HLM	W	L	Coach
1987	M	NAIA		8	—	—	—	—	—	—	—	25	8	Chapman, Larry F.
1988		NAIA		2	—	—	—	—	—	—	—	26	2	Chapman, Larry F.
1989		NAIA		16	—	—	—	—	—	—	—	24	7	Chapman, Larry F.
1994		NAIA	I	32	—	—	—	—	—	—	—	20	12	Chapman, Larry F.
1987	W	NAIA		16	—	—	—	—	—	—	—	20	11	Tilley, Colby
1991		NAIA		32	—	—	—	—	—	—	—	24	9	Tilley, Colby
1992		NAIA	I	32	—	—	—	—	—	—	—	25	8	Tilley, Colby
1993		NAIA	I	16	—	—	—	—	—	—	—	27	6	Tilley, Colby
1994		NAIA	I	3	—	—	—	—	—	—	—	24	4	Tilley, Colby
1995		NAIA	I	8	—	—	—	—	—	—	—	34	3	Tilley, Colby
1996		NAIA	I	8	—	—	—	—	—	—	—	31	6	Skinner, Paula
1997		NAIA	I	32	—	—	—	—	—	—	—	19	11	Crotz, Stephen
1998		NAIA	I	16	—	—	—	—	—	—	—	23	10	Crotz, Stephen

AUGSBURG

Year	M/W	Assn	Div	NAT	NIT	ARC	CCA	NCI	NCT	OLY	HLM	W	L	Coach
1946	M	NAIA		16	—	—	—	—	—	—	—	19	2	Carlson, Robert
1963		NAIA		16	—	—	—	—	—	—	—	23	2	Anderson, Ernest W.
1965		NAIA		8	—	—	—	—	—	—	—	26	4	Anderson, Ernest W.
1977		NAIA		32	—	—	—	—	—	—	—	23	7	Inniger, Ervin L., Jr.
1980		NAIA		32	—	—	—	—	—	—	—	25	1	Johnson, Rees
1981		NAIA		8	—	—	—	—	—	—	—	29	2	Johnson, Rees
1985		NCAA	III	32	—	—	—	—	—	—	—	21	7	Boots, David
1998		NCAA	III	48	—	—	—	—	—	—	—	22	4	Ammann, Brian

AUGUSTA STATE

Year	M/W	Assn	Div	NAT	NIT	ARC	CCA	NCI	NCT	OLY	HLM	W	L	Coach
1970	M	NAIA		16	—	—	—	—	—	—	—	23	2	Vanover, Marvin
1971		NAIA		32	—	—	—	—	—	—	—	20	4	Vanover, Marvin
1978		NCAA	II	32	—	—	—	—	—	—	—	20	8	Vanover, Marvin

AUGUSTANA (IL)

Year	M/W	Assn	Div	NAT	NIT	ARC	CCA	NCI	NCT	OLY	HLM	W	L	Coach
1939	M	NAIA		16	—	—	—	—	—	—	—	17	6	Almquist, H. V.
1940		NAIA		32	—	—	—	—	—	—	—	10	9	Almquist, H. V.
1959		NCAA	II	32	—	—	—	—	—	—	—	12	12	Kallis, Lenny
1960		NCAA	II	32	—	—	—	—	—	—	—	14	10	Kallis, Lenny

Year	M/W	Assn	Div	NAT	NIT	ARC	CCA	NCI	NCT	OLY	HLM	W	L	Coach
1963		NCAA	II	32	—	—	—	—	—	—	—	—	18	6	Kallis, Lenny
1971		NCAA	II	32	—	—	—	—	—	—	—	—	20	6	Borcherding, James
1972		NAIA		8	—	—	—	—	—	—	—	—	25	4	Borcherding, James
1973		NAIA		3	—	—	—	—	—	—	—	—	29	2	Borcherding, James
1974		NAIA		8	—	—	—	—	—	—	—	—	25	4	Borcherding, James
1975		NCAA	III	3	—	—	—	—	—	—	—	—	22	8	Borcherding, James
1976		NCAA	III	3	—	—	—	—	—	—	—	—	21	7	Borcherding, James
1977		NCAA	III	23	—	—	—	—	—	—	—	—	20	7	Borcherding, James
1980		NCAA	III	16	—	—	—	—	—	—	—	—	20	7	Borcherding, James
1981		NCAA	III	2	—	—	—	—	—	—	—	—	25	6	Borcherding, James
1982		NCAA	III	8	—	—	—	—	—	—	—	—	22	6	Borcherding, James
1983		NCAA	III	32	—	—	—	—	—	—	—	—	18	10	Borcherding, James
1993		NCAA	III	2	—	—	—	—	—	—	—	—	24	7	Yount, Steve
1982	W	NCAA	III	8	—	—	—	—	—	—	—	—	19	7	Stein, Paulette
1983		NCAA	III	24	—	—	—	—	—	—	—	—	17	10	Stein, Paulette
1987		NCAA	III	24	—	—	—	—	—	—	—	—	20	7	Schumacher, Diane
1989		NCAA	III	16	—	—	—	—	—	—	—	—	22	5	Schumacher, Diane
1990		NCAA	III	32	—	—	—	—	—	—	—	—	22	4	Schumacher, Diane
1991		NCAA	III	32	—	—	—	—	—	—	—	—	19	5	Schumacher, Diane
1993		NCAA	III	32	—	—	—	—	—	—	—	—	19	7	Schumacher, Diane

AUGUSTANA (SD)

Year	M/W	Assn	Div	NAT	NIT	ARC	CCA	NCI	NCT	OLY	HLM	W	L	Coach
1975	M	NCAA	II	24	—	—	—	—	—	—	—	—	20	8	Klein, Mel
1977		NCAA	II	32	—	—	—	—	—	—	—	—	16	12	Klein, Mel
1978		NCAA	II	16	—	—	—	—	—	—	—	—	18	11	Klein, Mel
1986		NCAA	II	32	—	—	—	—	—	—	—	—	18	11	Gross, Bill
1988		NCAA	II	32	—	—	—	—	—	—	—	—	20	10	Gross, Bill
1989		NCAA	II	24	—	—	—	—	—	—	—	—	23	7	Gross, Bill
1990	W	NCAA	II	32	—	—	—	—	—	—	—	—	19	10	Krauth, David
1991		NCAA	II	32	—	—	—	—	—	—	—	—	23	6	Krauth, David
1992		NCAA	II	16	—	—	—	—	—	—	—	—	26	4	Krauth, David
1993		NCAA	II	16	—	—	—	—	—	—	—	—	24	5	Krauth, David
1994		NCAA	II	32	—	—	—	—	—	—	—	—	23	6	Krauth, David
1997		NCAA	II	48	—	—	—	—	—	—	—	—	23	5	Krauth, David

AURORA

Year	M/W	Assn	Div	NAT	NIT	ARC	CCA	NCI	NCT	OLY	HLM	W	L	Coach
1998	M	NCAA	III	48	—	—	—	—	—	—	—	—	21	5	Lancaster, James
1994	W	NCAA	III	32	—	—	—	—	—	—	—	—	22	5	Lancaster, James
1995		NCAA	III	16	—	—	—	—	—	—	—	—	22	6	Lancaster, James

AUSTIN

Year	M/W	Assn	Div	NAT	NIT	ARC	CCA	NCI	NCT	OLY	HLM	W	L	Coach
1958	M	NAIA		32	—	—	—	—	—	—	—	—	17	9	Gass, Floyd
1959		NAIA		32	—	—	—	—	—	—	—	—	29	14	Gass, Floyd
1997	W	NAIA	II	16	—	—	—	—	—	—	—	—	24	4	Potera, Robin
1998		NCAA	III	16	—	—	—	—	—	—	—	—	21	7	Potera, Robin

AUSTIN PEAY STATE

Year	M/W	Assn	Div	NAT	NIT	ARC	CCA	NCI	NCT	OLY	HLM	W	L	Coach
1957	M	NAIA		32	—	—	—	—	—	—	—	—	24	9	Aaron, David B.
1958		NCAA	II	32	—	—	—	—	—	—	—	—	17	9	Aaron, David B.
1960		NCAA	II	16	—	—	—	—	—	—	—	—	22	5	Aaron, David B.
1961		NCAA	II	8	—	—	—	—	—	—	—	—	22	9	Aaron, David B.

Year	M/W	Assn	Div	NAT	NIT	ARC	CCA	NCI	NCT	OLY	HLM	W	L	Coach
1963		NCAA	II	32	—	—	—	—	—	—	—	—	18	11	Fisher, George
1973		NCAA	I	16	—	—	—	—	—	—	—	—	22	7	Kelly, Lake
1974		NCAA	I	25	—	—	—	—	—	—	—	—	17	10	Kelly, Lake
1987		NCAA	I	32	—	—	—	—	—	—	—	—	20	12	Kelly, Lake
1996		NCAA	I	64	—	—	—	—	—	—	—	—	19	11	Loos, David
1996	W	NCAA	I	64	—	—	—	—	—	—	—	—	21	8	Wilson, LaDonna

AVERETT

Year	M/W	Assn	Div	NAT	NIT	ARC	CCA	NCI	NCT	OLY	HLM	W	L	Coach
1990	M	NCAA	III	16	—	—	—	—	—	—	—	—	20	9	Hall, Ed

AZUSA PACIFIC

Year	M/W	Assn	Div	NAT	NIT	ARC	CCA	NCI	NCT	OLY	HLM	W	L	Coach
1968	M	NCCAA		3	—	—	—	—	—	—	—	—	21	9	Hamlow, Dr. Clifford
1969		NCCAA		1	—	—	—	—	—	—	—	—	26	7	Hamlow, Dr. Clifford
1970		NCCAA		1	—	—	—	—	—	—	—	—	29	6	Hamlow, Dr. Clifford
1971		NCCAA		1	—	—	—	—	—	—	—	—	25	11	Hamlow, Dr. Clifford
1972		NCCAA		1	—	—	—	—	—	—	—	—	26	10	Hamlow, Dr. Clifford
1973		NCCAA		2	—	—	—	—	—	—	—	—	28	7	Hamlow, Dr. Clifford
1974		NAIA		32	—	—	—	—	—	—	—	—	28	5	Hamlow, Dr. Clifford
1981		NCCAA	I	4	—	—	—	—	—	—	—	—	17	16	Hamlow, Dr. Clifford
1983		NCCAA	I	4	—	—	—	—	—	—	—	—	17	18	Lawrence, Dr. Donald J.
1993		NAIA	I	32	—	—	—	—	—	—	—	—	30	4	Odell, William M.
1994		NAIA	I	16	—	—	—	—	—	—	—	—	29	5	Odell, William M.
1996		NAIA	I	32	—	—	—	—	—	—	—	—	26	8	Odell, William M.
1997		NAIA	I	16	—	—	—	—	—	—	—	—	29	8	Odell, William M.
1998		NAIA	I	3	—	—	—	—	—	—	—	—	35	5	Odell, William M.
1981	W	NAIA		4	—	—	—	—	—	—	—	—	18	15	Hebel, Dr. Susan L.
1985		NCCAA	I	6	—	—	—	—	—	—	—	—	23	11	Hebel, Dr. Susan L.
1986		NAIA		16	—	—	—	—	—	—	—	—	30	5	Hebel, Dr. Susan L.
1988		NCCAA	I	4	—	—	—	—	—	—	—	—	21	10	Hebel, Dr. Susan L.

BABSON

Year	M/W	Assn	Div	NAT	NIT	ARC	CCA	NCI	NCT	OLY	HLM	W	L	Coach
1992	M	NCAA	III	32	—	—	—	—	—	—	—	—	22	4	DeBari, Sergio "Serge"
1995		NCAA	III	64	—	—	—	—	—	—	—	—	20	7	DeBari, Sergio "Serge"
1996		NCAA	III	64	—	—	—	—	—	—	—	—	21	7	Brennan, Steve
1993	W	NCAA	III	16	—	—	—	—	—	—	—	—	23	5	Blinstrub, Judith
1994		NCAA	III	16	—	—	—	—	—	—	—	—	23	4	Blinstrub, Judith

BAKER (KS)

Year	M/W	Assn	Div	NAT	NIT	ARC	CCA	NCI	NCT	OLY	HLM	W	L	Coach
1937	M	NAIA		8	—	—	—	—	—	—	—	—	14	3	Liston, Emil S.
1941		NAIA		32	—	—	—	—	—	—	—	—	14	8	Liston, Emil S.
1996		NAIA	II	32	—	—	—	—	—	—	—	—	25	10	Weaver, Rick
1982	W	AIAW	III	16	—	—	—	—	—	—	—	—	20	9	Bilow, Joyce

BALDWIN-WALLACE

Year	M/W	Assn	Div	NAT	NIT	ARC	CCA	NCI	NCT	OLY	HLM	W	L	Coach
1950	M	NAIA		8	—	—	—	—	—	—	—	—	12	16	Watts, Ray E.
1951		NAIA		3	—	—	—	—	—	—	—	—	19	7	Wagner, J. Larsen
1967		NCAA	II	23	—	—	—	—	—	—	—	—	22	9	Thompson, Hugh
1979		NCAA	III	8	—	—	—	—	—	—	—	—	21	7	Rupert, Bob
1995		NCAA	III	16	—	—	—	—	—	—	—	—	19	9	Bankson, Steve
1996		NCAA	III	64	—	—	—	—	—	—	—	—	16	12	Bankson, Steve
1998		NCAA	III	48	—	—	—	—	—	—	—	—	17	11	Bankson, Steve

Year	M/W	Assn	Div	NAT	NIT	ARC	CCA	NCI	NCT	OLY	HLM	W	L	Coach
1996	W	NCAA	III	64	—	—	—	—	—	—	—	18	9	Harrer, Cheri
1997		NCAA	III	64	—	—	—	—	—	—	—	23	5	Harrer, Cheri
1998		NCAA	III	32	—	—	—	—	—	—	—	23	6	Harrer, Cheri

BALL STATE

Year	M/W	Assn	Div	NAT	NIT	ARC	CCA	NCI	NCT	OLY	HLM	W	L	Coach
1957	M	NAIA		16	—	—	—	—	—	—	—	19	8	Hinga, John ʼJimʼ
1964		NCAA	II	32	—	—	—	—	—	—	—	19	8	Hinga, John ʼJimʼ
1981		NCAA	I	48	—	—	—	—	—	—	—	20	10	Yoder, Steve
1986		NCAA	I	64	—	—	—	—	—	—	—	21	10	Brown, Al
1989		NCAA	I	32	—	—	—	—	—	—	—	29	3	Majerus, Rick
1990		NCAA	I	16	—	—	—	—	—	—	—	26	7	Hunsaker, Dick
1991		NCAA	I	—	32	—	—	—	—	—	—	21	10	Hunsaker, Dick
1992		NCAA	I	—	32	—	—	—	—	—	—	24	9	Hunsaker, Dick
1993		NCAA	I	64	—	—	—	—	—	—	—	26	8	Hunsaker, Dick
1995		NCAA	I	64	—	—	—	—	—	—	—	19	11	McCallum, Ray
1998		NCAA	I	—	32	—	—	—	—	—	—	21	8	McCallum, Ray
1969	W	AIAW		16	—	—	—	—	—	—	—	X	X	Unknown

BALTIMORE

Year	M/W	Assn	Div	NAT	NIT	ARC	CCA	NCI	NCT	OLY	HLM	W	L	Coach
1941	M	NAIA		16	—	—	—	—	—	—	—	17	3	Unknown
1952		NAIA		32	—	—	—	—	—	—	—	16	8	Bartheleme, Albert L.
1975		NCAA	II	24	—	—	—	—	—	—	—	19	11	Szymanski, Frank A.
1976		NCAA	II	16	—	—	—	—	—	—	—	20	10	Szymanski, Frank A.
1977		NCAA	II	16	—	—	—	—	—	—	—	24	4	Szymanski, Frank A.

BALTIMORE COMMERCE

Year	M/W	Assn	Div	NAT	NIT	ARC	CCA	NCI	NCT	OLY	HLM	W	L	Coach
1967	M	NSCAA		8	—	—	—	—	—	—	—	9	14	Baker, Paul

BAPTIST BIBLE (MO)

Year	M/W	Assn	Div	NAT	NIT	ARC	CCA	NCI	NCT	OLY	HLM	W	L	Coach
1978	M	NCCAA	II	1	—	—	—	—	—	—	—	13	15	Schepis, Mike
1979		NCCAA	II	6	—	—	—	—	—	—	—	X	X	Schepis, Mike
1981		NCCAA	II	1	—	—	—	—	—	—	—	18	17	Reed, Roger
1982		NCCAA	II	1	—	—	—	—	—	—	—	20	11	Fuller, Fred
1983		NCCAA	II	1	—	—	—	—	—	—	—	24	14	Fuller, Fred
1984		NCCAA	II	1	—	—	—	—	—	—	—	17	13	Smith, Gary
1985		NCCAA	II	8	—	—	—	—	—	—	—	X	X	Beck, Hilly
1986		NCCAA	II	5	—	—	—	—	—	—	—	13	21	Beck, Hilly
1987		NCCAA	II	3	—	—	—	—	—	—	—	16	17	Beck, Hilly
1993		NCCAA	II	8	—	—	—	—	—	—	—	18	20	Beck, Hilly
1994		NCCAA	II	5	—	—	—	—	—	—	—	18	14	Beck, Hilly
1998	W	NCCAA	II	8	—	—	—	—	—	—	—	10	19	Elliott, Dan

BAPTIST BIBLE (PA)

Year	M/W	Assn	Div	NAT	NIT	ARC	CCA	NCI	NCT	OLY	HLM	W	L	Coach
1976	M	NCCAA	II	2	—	—	—	—	—	—	—	19	8	Huckaby, James M.
1977		NCCAA	II	2	—	—	—	—	—	—	—	19	8	Huckaby, James M.
1978		NCCAA	II	2	—	—	—	—	—	—	—	21	7	Huckaby, James M.
1979		NCCAA	II	1	—	—	—	—	—	—	—	20	12	Huckaby, James M.
1980		NCCAA	II	2	—	—	—	—	—	—	—	19	12	Huckaby, James M.
1981		NCCAA	II	4	—	—	—	—	—	—	—	22	10	Huckaby, James M.
1982		NCCAA	II	3	—	—	—	—	—	—	—	25	7	Huckaby, James M.
1983		NCCAA	II	3	—	—	—	—	—	—	—	23	12	Huckaby, James M.

Year	M/W	Assn	Div	NAT	NIT	ARC	CCA	NCI	NCT	OLY	HLM	W	L	Coach
1984		NCCAA	II	4	—	—	—	—	—	—	—	23	7	Huckaby, James M.
1985		NCCAA	II	3	—	—	—	—	—	—	—	22	16	Huckaby, James M.
1989		NCCAA	II	5	—	—	—	—	—	—	—	24	11	Howard, Russ
1990		NCCAA	II	5	—	—	—	—	—	—	—	28	7	Howard, Russ
1991		NCCAA	II	3	—	—	—	—	—	—	—	22	8	Howard, Russ
1992		NCCAA	II	1	—	—	—	—	—	—	—	20	7	Howard, Russ
1993		NCCAA	II	2	—	—	—	—	—	—	—	22	10	Huckaby, James M.
1995		NCCAA	II	6	—	—	—	—	—	—	—	22	10	Show, Mike
1996		NCCAA	II	7	—	—	—	—	—	—	—	19	12	Show, Mike
1997		NCCAA	II	4	—	—	—	—	—	—	—	20	18	Show, Mike
1983	W	NCCAA	II	1	—	—	—	—	—	—	—	23	5	Durrwachter, Nancy White
1984		NCCAA	II	2	—	—	—	—	—	—	—	16	9	Durrwachter, Nancy White
1985		NCCAA	II	3	—	—	—	—	—	—	—	16	14	Durrwachter, Nancy White
1986		NCCAA	II	7	—	—	—	—	—	—	—	14	13	Spink, Dave
1988		NCCAA	II	5	—	—	—	—	—	—	—	15	12	Holloway, Sherrie L.
1989		NCCAA	II	4	—	—	—	—	—	—	—	18	7	Holloway, Sherrie L.
1990		NCCAA	II	2	—	—	—	—	—	—	—	16	9	Holloway, Sherrie L.
1991		NCCAA	II	2	—	—	—	—	—	—	—	18	12	Holloway, Sherrie L.
1992		NCCAA	II	6	—	—	—	—	—	—	—	19	9	Holloway, Sherrie L.
1993		NCCAA	II	3	—	—	—	—	—	—	—	13	15	Holloway, Sherrie L.
1995		NCCAA	II	3	—	—	—	—	—	—	—	16	8	Holloway, Sherrie L.
1996		NCCAA	II	4	—	—	—	—	—	—	—	14	18	Holloway, Sherrie L.
1998		NCCAA	II	6	—	—	—	—	—	—	—	23	10	Holloway, Sherrie L.

BAPTIST CHRISTIAN (LA)

Year	M/W	Assn	Div	NAT	NIT	ARC	CCA	NCI	NCT	OLY	HLM	W	L	Coach
1970	M	NCCAA		8	—	—	—	—	—	—	—	12	13	Greene, Larry
1972		NCCAA		8	—	—	—	—	—	—	—			
1977		NSCAA		16	—	—	—	—	—	—	—	20	5	Martin, C. P.
1980		NSCAA		16	—	—	—	—	—	—	—			Martin, C. P.
1981		NSCAA		12	—	—	—	—	—	—	—			Martin, C. P.
1990		NBCAA	II	5	—	—	—	—	—	—	—			
1992		NSCAA		10	—	—	—	—	—	—	—	22	21	Bagley, Larry
1995		NSCAA		3	—	—	—	—	—	—	—			Martin, Chip
1982	W	NSCAA		2	—	—	—	—	—	—	—	15	5	

BAPTIST UNIVERSITY (GA)

Year	M/W	Assn	Div	NAT	NIT	ARC	CCA	NCI	NCT	OLY	HLM	W	L	Coach
1984	M	NBCAA	I	5	—	—	—	—	—	—	—			Rapson,

BARBER-SCOTIA

Year	M/W	Assn	Div	NAT	NIT	ARC	CCA	NCI	NCT	OLY	HLM	W	L	Coach
1968	M	NSCAA		8	—	—	—	—	—	—	—			Coefield, Aldon L.

BARCLAY

Year	M/W	Assn	Div	NAT	NIT	ARC	CCA	NCI	NCT	OLY	HLM	W	L	Coach
1981	M	NBCAA		2	—	—	—	—	—	—	—	14	8	Bryan, DeWayne
1995		NBCAA	II	8	—	—	—	—	—	—	—	6	20	Anders, L. Lee

BARRINGTON

Year	M/W	Assn	Div	NAT	NIT	ARC	CCA	NCI	NCT	OLY	HLM	W	L	Coach
1969	M	NCCAA		4	—	—	—	—	—	—	—	17	12	Augustine, Jack
1970		NCCAA		8	—	—	—	—	—	—	—	13	14	Augustine, Jack

BARRY

Year	M/W	Assn	Div	NAT	NIT	ARC	CCA	NCI	NCT	OLY	HLM	W	L	Coach
1991	W	NCAA	II	32	—	—	—	—	—	—	—	26	4	Olson, Dan

Year	M/W	Assn	Div	NAT	NIT	ARC	CCA	NCI	NCT	OLY	HLM	W	L	Coach
BARTLESVILLE WESLEYAN														
1985	M	NCCAA	I	8	—	—	—	—	—	—	—	19	11	Maness, Donald
1987		NCCAA	I	8	—	—	—	—	—	—	—	15	16	Dunn, Dan
1988		NCCAA	I	8	—	—	—	—	—	—	—	19	13	Dunn, Dan
1989		NCCAA	I	8	—	—	—	—	—	—	—	18	9	Dunn, Dan
1993		NCCAA	I	5	—	—	—	—	—	—	—	21	14	Kent, "Rocky"
1996		NCCAA	I	8	—	—	—	—	—	—	—	19	14	Kent, "Rocky"
1988	W	NCCAA	I	8	—	—	—	—	—	—	—	10	19	Baldwin, Gary
1990		NCCAA	I	5	—	—	—	—	—	—	—	19	12	Baldwin, Gary
1991		NCCAA	I	5	—	—	—	—	—	—	—	14	16	Baldwin, Gary
1992		NCCAA	I	5	—	—	—	—	—	—	—	11	22	Baldwin, Gary
1994		NCCAA	I	3	—	—	—	—	—	—	—	16	16	Hoeck, Donald
1995		NCCAA	I	2	—	—	—	—	—	—	—	21	11	Hoeck, Donald
BARTON														
1955	M	NAIA		16	—	—	—	—	—	—	—	23	6	McComas, James E. "Jack"
1986		NAIA		16	—	—	—	—	—	—	—	25	10	Edwards, Gary
1987		NAIA		32	—	—	—	—	—	—	—	25	9	Edwards, Gary
1997		NCAA	II	48	—	—	—	—	—	—	—	22	5	Lievense, Ron
BATES														
1961	M	NCAA	II	16	—	—	—	—	—	—	—	15	9	Peck, Robert R.
1997	W	NCAA	III	64	—	—	—	—	—	—	—	20	5	Murphy, James
1998		NCAA	III	16	—	—	—	—	—	—	—	22	4	Murphy, James
BAY RIDGE CHRISTIAN														
1987	M	NCCAA	II	7	—	—	—	—	—	—	—	X	X	Mayshock, J. Anthony
1988		NCCAA	II	3	—	—	—	—	—	—	—	X	X	Mayshock, J. Anthony
1989		NCCAA	II	3	—	—	—	—	—	—	—	X	X	Mayshock, J. Anthony
1996		LCC		7	—	—	—	—	—	—	—	7	14	Zamora, Edward
1997		LCC		5	—	—	—	—	—	—	—	0	17	Lewis, Percy
BAYLOR														
1946	M	NCAA		8	—	—	—	—	—	—	—	25	5	Henderson, R. E. "Bill"
1948		NCAA		2	—	—	—	—	—	4	—	24	8	Henderson, R. E. "Bill"
1950		NCAA		4	—	—	—	—	—	—	—	14	13	Henderson, R. E. "Bill"
1987		NCAA	I	—	32	—	—	—	—	—	—	18	13	Iba, Clarence Eugene "Gene"
1988		NCAA	I	64	—	—	—	—	—	—	—	23	11	Iba, Clarence Eugene "Gene"
1990		NCAA	I	—	32	—	—	—	—	—	—	16	14	Iba, Clarence Eugene "Gene"
1976	W	AIAW	L	12	—	—	—	—	—	—	—	31	6	Fallen, Olga
1977		AIAW	L	5	—	—	—	—	—	—	—	34	10	Fallen, Olga
1981		AIAW	I	—	8	—	—	—	—	—	—	29	11	Bowers, Pam Davis
1998		NCAA	I	—	2	—	—	—	—	—	—	20	11	Hogg, Sonja
BELHAVEN														
1972	M	NAIA		16	—	—	—	—	—	—	—	22	6	Rugg, Charles R.
BELLARMINE														
1963	M	NCAA	II	24	—	—	—	—	—	—	—	21	6	Groza, Alex J.
1965		NCAA	II	16	—	—	—	—	—	—	—	15	8	Groza, Alex J.
1969		NCAA	II	32	—	—	—	—	—	—	—	19	9	Spalding, James R.
1970		NCAA	II	24	—	—	—	—	—	—	—	16	10	Spalding, James R.

Year	M/W	Assn	Div	NAT	NIT	ARC	CCA	NCI	NCT	OLY	HLM	W	L	Coach
1977		NCAA	II	32	—	—	—	—	—	—	—	17	11	Reibel, Joseph C.
1982		NCAA	II	32	—	—	—	—	—	—	—	20	9	Reibel, Joseph C.
1984		NCAA	II	24	—	—	—	—	—	—	—	21	9	Reibel, Joseph C.
1989		NCAA	II	16	—	—	—	—	—	—	—	22	8	Reibel, Joseph C.
1991		NCAA	II	24	—	—	—	—	—	—	—	24	6	Reibel, Joseph C.
1986	W	NCAA	II	8	—	—	—	—	—	—	—	23	7	Just, Charles G.
1987		NCAA	II	24	—	—	—	—	—	—	—	20	8	Just, Charles G.
1990		NCAA	II	8	—	—	—	—	—	—	—	25	6	Just, Charles G.
1991		NCAA	II	8	—	—	—	—	—	—	—	26	5	Just, Charles G.
1993		NCAA	II	32	—	—	—	—	—	—	—	18	10	Just, Charles G.
1994		NCAA	II	4	—	—	—	—	—	—	—	25	6	Just, Charles G.
1996		NCAA	II	16	—	—	—	—	—	—	—	24	4	Just, Charles G.
1997		NCAA	II	48	—	—	—	—	—	—	—	20	8	Just, Charles G.

BELLEVUE (NE)

Year	M/W	Assn	Div	NAT	NIT	ARC	CCA	NCI	NCT	OLY	HLM	W	L	Coach
1998	M	NAIA	II	32	—	—	—	—	—	—	—	17	14	Richards, Brett

BELMONT

Year	M/W	Assn	Div	NAT	NIT	ARC	CCA	NCI	NCT	OLY	HLM	W	L	Coach
1989	M	NAIA		32	—	—	—	—	—	—	—	25	10	Byrd, Rick
1993		NAIA	I	16	—	—	—	—	—	—	—	30	6	Byrd, Rick
1994		NAIA	I	8	—	—	—	—	—	—	—	30	7	Byrd, Rick
1995		NAIA	I	3	—	—	—	—	—	—	—	37	2	Byrd, Rick
1996		NAIA	I	3	—	—	—	—	—	—	—	28	11	Byrd, Rick
1971	W			—	7	—	—	—	—	—	—	14	7	Wiseman, Betty
1972				—	5	—	—	—	—	—	—	12	6	Wiseman, Betty
1973				—	7	—	—	—	—	—	—	14	8	Wiseman, Betty
1974		AIAW		—	6	—	—	—	—	—	—	22	6	Wiseman, Betty
1975				—	3	—	—	—	—	—	—	22	3	Wiseman, Betty
1976				—	4	—	—	—	—	—	—	19	6	Wiseman, Betty
1977				—	6	—	—	—	—	—	—	15	10	Wiseman, Betty
1991		NAIA		8	—	—	—	—	—	—	—	32	5	Cross, Tony
1992		NAIA	I	8	—	—	—	—	—	—	—	31	5	Cross, Tony
1994		NAIA	I	8	—	—	—	—	—	—	—	32	3	Cross, Tony
1996		NAIA	I	32	—	—	—	—	—	—	—	26	8	Cross, Tony

BELMONT ABBEY

Year	M/W	Assn	Div	NAT	NIT	ARC	CCA	NCI	NCT	OLY	HLM	W	L	Coach
1959	M	NCAA	II	24	—	—	—	—	—	—	—	21	2	McGuire, Alfred J.
1960		NCAA	II	24	—	—	—	—	—	—	—	19	6	McGuire, Alfred J.
1961		NCAA	II	16	—	—	—	—	—	—	—	17	7	McGuire, Alfred J.
1962		NAIA		32	—	—	—	—	—	—	—	16	9	McGuire, Alfred J.
1988		NAIA		32	—	—	—	—	—	—	—	22	9	Eastman, Kevin
1991	W	NAIA		32	—	—	—	—	—	—	—	23	6	Kebbe, Elaine
1995		NAIA	I	32	—	—	—	—	—	—	—	24	6	Kebbe, Elaine
1998		NCAA	II	48	—	—	—	—	—	—	—	26	4	Kebbe, Elaine

BELOIT

Year	M/W	Assn	Div	NAT	NIT	ARC	CCA	NCI	NCT	OLY	HLM	W	L	Coach
1947	M	NAIA		8	—	—	—	—	—	—	—	22	5	Stanley, Dolph
1948		NAIA		8	—	—	—	—	—	—	—	24	3	Stanley, Dolph
1949		NAIA		3	—	—	—	—	—	—	—	29	4	Stanley, Dolph
1951		NCAA		—	12	—	—	—	—	—	—	18	5	Stanley, Dolph

Year	M/W	Assn	Div	NAT	NIT	ARC	CCA	NCI	NCT	OLY	HLM	W	L	Coach
1955		NAIA		8	—	—	—	—	—	—	—	22	4	Stanley, Dolph
1957		NCAA	II	16	—	—	—	—	—	—	—	17	6	Stanley, Dolph
1977		NCAA	III	30	—	—	—	—	—	—	—	15	7	Knapton, William B.
1979		NCAA	III	24	—	—	—	—	—	—	—	18	7	Knapton, William B.
1980		NCAA	III	24	—	—	—	—	—	—	—	19	5	Knapton, William B.
1981		NCAA	III	16	—	—	—	—	—	—	—	24	2	Knapton, William B.
1982		NCAA	III	32	—	—	—	—	—	—	—	19	6	Knapton, William B.
1983		NCAA	III	32	—	—	—	—	—	—	—	18	7	Knapton, William B.
1989		NCAA	III	40	—	—	—	—	—	—	—	17	7	Knapton, William B.
1993		NCAA	III	32	—	—	—	—	—	—	—	21	5	Knapton, William B.
1995		NCAA	III	64	—	—	—	—	—	—	—	13	12	Knapton, William B.
1995	W	NCAA	III	64	—	—	—	—	—	—	—	17	8	Walters, Mimi
1996		NCAA	III	32	—	—	—	—	—	—	—	22	4	Botham, Sandy
1997		NCAA	III	64	—	—	—	—	—	—	—	20	5	Straub, Kristi
1998		NCAA	III	48	—	—	—	—	—	—	—	23	2	Straub, Kristi

BEMIDJI STATE

Year	M/W	Assn	Div	NAT	NIT	ARC	CCA	NCI	NCT	OLY	HLM	W	L	Coach
1940	M	NAIA		32	—	—	—	—	—	—	—	13	3	Frost, Reuben B. "Jack"
1941		NAIA		16	—	—	—	—	—	—	—	14	3	Frost, Reuben B. "Jack"
1942		NAIA		8	—	—	—	—	—	—	—	14	6	Frost, Reuben B. "Jack"
1987	W	NAIA		16	—	—	—	—	—	—	—	25	2	Mathison, Sherri

BENEDICT

Year	M/W	Assn	Div	NAT	NIT	ARC	CCA	NCI	NCT	OLY	HLM	W	L	Coach
1980	M	NCAA	II	32	—	—	—	—	—	—	—	21	7	Holmes, Michael
1993		NAIA	I	32	—	—	—	—	—	—	—	23	4	Washington, Willie
1994		NAIA	I	8	—	—	—	—	—	—	—	29	3	Washington, Willie
1997		NAIA	I	32	—	—	—	—	—	—	—	30	3	Washington, Willie
1998		NAIA	I	16	—	—	—	—	—	—	—	22	9	Washington, Willie

BENEDICTINE (IL)

Year	M/W	Assn	Div	NAT	NIT	ARC	CCA	NCI	NCT	OLY	HLM	W	L	Coach
1966	M	NCAA	II	32	—	—	—	—	—	—	—	18	4	LaScala, Anthony
1991		NCAA	III	8	—	—	—	—	—	—	—	23	6	LaScala, Anthony
1997		NCAA	III	64	—	—	—	—	—	—	—	16	9	Bunkenburg, Keith

BENEDICTINE (KS)

Year	M/W	Assn	Div	NAT	NIT	ARC	CCA	NCI	NCT	OLY	HLM	W	L	Coach
1937	M	NAIA		8	—	—	—	—	—	—	—	17	3	Mullins, Larry
1949		NAIA		—	—	—	—	4	—	—	—	9	15	Walsh, Robert
1953		NAIA		16	—	—	—	—	—	—	—	21	8	Nolan, Ralph
1954		NAIA		1	—	—	—	—	—	—	—	24	5	Nolan, Ralph
1958		NAIA		32	—	—	—	—	—	—	—	20	6	Nolan, Ralph
1965		NAIA		8	—	—	—	—	—	—	—	26	3	Nolan, Ralph
1967		NAIA		1	—	—	—	—	—	—	—	27	2	Nolan, Ralph
1970		NAIA		32	—	—	—	—	—	—	—	17	9	Nolan, Ralph
1997	W	NAIA	II	32	—	—	—	—	—	—	—	26	6	Huber, Steve
1998		NAIA	II	16	—	—	—	—	—	—	—	28	7	Huber, Steve

BENTLEY

Year	M/W	Assn	Div	NAT	NIT	ARC	CCA	NCI	NCT	OLY	HLM	W	L	Coach
1972	M	NCAA	II	16	—	—	—	—	—	—	—	26	2	Shields, Elwood N. "Al"
1973		NCAA	II	16	—	—	—	—	—	—	—	24	3	Shields, Elwood N. "Al"
1974		NCAA	II	32	—	—	—	—	—	—	—	18	7	Shields, Elwood N. "Al"
1975		NCAA	II	16	—	—	—	—	—	—	—	23	2	Shields, Elwood N. "Al"

Year	M/W	Assn	Div	NAT	NIT	ARC	CCA	NCI	NCT	OLY	HLM	W	L	Coach
1976		NCAA	II	24	—	—	—	—	—	—	—	—	17	12	Shields, Elwood N. "Al"
1979		NCAA	II	24	—	—	—	—	—	—	—	—	22	6	Hammel, Brian
1985		NCAA	II	32	—	—	—	—	—	—	—	—	25	6	Sullivan, Frank
1989		NCAA	II	24	—	—	—	—	—	—	—	—	25	6	Sullivan, Frank
1993		NCAA	II	23	—	—	—	—	—	—	—	—	24	7	Lawson, Jay
1982	W	NCAA	II	16	—	—	—	—	—	—	—	—	19	6	Mullen, Paula
1983		NCAA	II	16	—	—	—	—	—	—	—	—	18	7	Mullen, Paula
1984		NCAA	II	16	—	—	—	—	—	—	—	—	26	3	Mullen, Paula
1985		NCAA	II	16	—	—	—	—	—	—	—	—	21	5	Sanborn, Kathleen
1987		NCAA	II	24	—	—	—	—	—	—	—	—	24	5	Sanborn, Kathleen
1988		NCAA	II	16	—	—	—	—	—	—	—	—	28	4	Stevens, Barbara
1989		NCAA	II	3	—	—	—	—	—	—	—	—	31	3	Stevens, Barbara
1990		NCAA	II	2	—	—	—	—	—	—	—	—	31	4	Stevens, Barbara
1991		NCAA	II	3	—	—	—	—	—	—	—	—	31	4	Stevens, Barbara
1992		NCAA	II	4	—	—	—	—	—	—	—	—	31	2	Stevens, Barbara
1993		NCAA	II	4	—	—	—	—	—	—	—	—	30	4	Stevens, Barbara
1994		NCAA	II	16	—	—	—	—	—	—	—	—	25	6	Stevens, Barbara
1995		NCAA	II	32	—	—	—	—	—	—	—	—	22	8	Stevens, Barbara
1996		NCAA	II	8	—	—	—	—	—	—	—	—	28	3	Stevens, Barbara
1997		NCAA	II	4	—	—	—	—	—	—	—	—	27	7	Stevens, Barbara
1998		NCAA	II	8	—	—	—	—	—	—	—	—	30	2	Stevens, Barbara

BEREA

Year	M/W	Assn	Div	NAT	NIT	ARC	CCA	NCI	NCT	OLY	HLM	W	L	Coach
1985	M	NAIA		32	—	—	—	—	—	—	—	—	20	10	Wierwille, Roland R.
1996		NAIA	II	32	—	—	—	—	—	—	—	—	18	9	Wierwille, Roland R.
1998		NAIA	II	32	—	—	—	—	—	—	—	—	20	10	Wierwille, Roland R.

BERRY

Year	M/W	Assn	Div	NAT	NIT	ARC	CCA	NCI	NCT	OLY	HLM	W	L	Coach
1992	M	NAIA	I	32	—	—	—	—	—	—	—	—	27	8	Smyly, Todd
1976	W	AIAW	S	1	—	—	—	—	—	—	—	—	20	3	James, Kay
1977		AIAW	S	3	—	—	—	—	—	—	—	—	23	4	James, Kay
1978		AIAW	S	3	—	—	—	—	—	—	—	—	23	6	Cronic, Ann
1980		AIAW	II	16	—	—	—	—	—	—	—	—	25	4	Cronic, Ann
1981		NAIA		8	—	—	—	—	—	—	—	—	16	9	Paul, Brenda
1982		NAIA		4	—	—	—	—	—	—	—	—	29	4	Paul, Brenda
1984		NAIA		4	—	—	—	—	—	—	—	—	32	5	Paul, Brenda
1991		NAIA		32	—	—	—	—	—	—	—	—	26	8	Guinn, Connie
1992		NAIA	I	16	—	—	—	—	—	—	—	—	26	8	Guinn, Connie
1994		NAIA	I	32	—	—	—	—	—	—	—	—	23	9	Guinn, Connie

BETHANY (KS)

Year	M/W	Assn	Div	NAT	NIT	ARC	CCA	NCI	NCT	OLY	HLM	W	L	Coach
1981	W	AIAW	III	16	—	—	—	—	—	—	—	—	20	8	Wood, Nancy
1995		NAIA	II	8	—	—	—	—	—	—	—	—	21	10	Wiles, Annette
1996		NAIA	II	16	—	—	—	—	—	—	—	—	26	5	Wiles, Annette

BETHANY (WV)

Year	M/W	Assn	Div	NAT	NIT	ARC	CCA	NCI	NCT	OLY	HLM	W	L	Coach
1978	M	NCAA	III	16	—	—	—	—	—	—	—	—	18	5	Dafler, Jim
1982		NCAA	III	32	—	—	—	—	—	—	—	—	15	9	Dafler, Jim
1997	W	NCAA	III	64	—	—	—	—	—	—	—	—	22	4	Campanell-Komara, Lisa

Year	M/W	Assn	Div	NAT	NIT	ARC	CCA	NCI	NCT	OLY	HLM	W	L	Coach
BETHEL (IN)														
1969	M	NCCAA		6	—	—	—	—	—	—	—	13	12	Felix, Richard
1970		NCCAA		4	—	—	—	—	—	—	—	16	15	Felix, Richard
1972		NCCAA		8	—	—	—	—	—	—	—	9	16	Felix, Richard
1979		NCCAA	I	6	—	—	—	—	—	—	—	22	12	Drew, Homer
1981		NCCAA	I	2	—	—	—	—	—	—	—	22	8	Drew, Homer
1982		NCCAA	I	7	—	—	—	—	—	—	—	28	6	Drew, Homer
1983		NCCAA	I	8	—	—	—	—	—	—	—	23	7	Drew, Homer
1987		NCCAA	I	3	—	—	—	—	—	—	—	25	9	Drew, Homer
1988		NCCAA	I	8	—	—	—	—	—	—	—	25	11	Lightfoot, Mike
1989		NCCAA	I	4	—	—	—	—	—	—	—	30	9	Lightfoot, Mike
1990		NCCAA	I	3	—	—	—	—	—	—	—	30	7	Lightfoot, Mike
1991		NCCAA	I	8	—	—	—	—	—	—	—	22	9	Lightfoot, Mike
1992		NCCAA	I	1	—	—	—	—	—	—	—	29	10	Lightfoot, Mike
1993		NCCAA	I	1	—	—	—	—	—	—	—	30	9	Lightfoot, Mike
1994		NAIA	II	16	—	—	—	—	—	—	—	30	5	Lightfoot, Mike
1995		NAIA	II	1	—	—	—	—	—	—	—	38	2	Lightfoot, Mike
1996		NAIA	II	16	—	—	—	—	—	—	—	35	2	Lightfoot, Mike
1997		NAIA	II	1	—	—	—	—	—	—	—	34	5	Lightfoot, Mike
1998		NAIA	II	1	—	—	—	—	—	—	—	37	3	Lightfoot, Mike
BETHEL (MN)														
1991	M	NCAA	III	40	—	—	—	—	—	—	—	17	11	Palke, George
1994	W	NCAA	III	16	—	—	—	—	—	—	—	21	5	Hunter, Debra F.
1995		NCAA	III	64	—	—	—	—	—	—	—	17	8	Hunter, Debra F.
1996		NCAA	III	8	—	—	—	—	—	—	—	22	6	Hunter, Debra F.
1997		NCAA	III	64	—	—	—	—	—	—	—	16	9	Hunter, Debra F.
BETHUNE-COOKMAN														
1953	M	NASC		2	—	—	—	—	—	—	—	24	2	Matthews, Rudolph "Bunky"
1955		NASC		8	—	—	—	—	—	—	—	19	5	Unknown
1965		NCAA	II	32	—	—	—	—	—	—	—	18	6	McClairen, Jack "Cy"
1966		NAIA		32	—	—	—	—	—	—	—	20	8	McClairen, Jack "Cy"
1968		NCAA	II	32	—	—	—	—	—	—	—	24	7	McClairen, Jack "Cy"
1980		NCAA	II	32	—	—	—	—	—	—	—	13	16	McClairen, Jack "Cy"
BEVILL STATE CC: BREWER														
1972	M	NSCAA		3	—	—	—	—	—	—	—	15	16	Anderson, Richard
1979		NSCAA		8	—	—	—	—	—	—	—	15	13	Anderson, Richard
BINGHAMTON STATE														
1995	W	NCAA	III	64	—	—	—	—	—	—	—	19	8	Wilson, David
1996		NCAA	III	64	—	—	—	—	—	—	—	21	7	Wilson, David
1997		NCAA	III	64	—	—	—	—	—	—	—	23	4	Wilson, David
1998		NCAA	III	32	—	—	—	—	—	—	—	22	3	Wilson, David
BIOLA														
1976	M	NCCAA	I	1	—	—	—	—	—	—	—	23	9	Lyon, Howard
1977		NCCAA	I	6	—	—	—	—	—	—	—	21	10	Lyon, Howard
1978		NCCAA	I	1	—	—	—	—	—	—	—	22	14	Lyon, Howard
1980		NAIA		16	—	—	—	—	—	—	—	26	4	Lyon, Howard

Year	M/W	Assn	Div	NAT	NIT	ARC	CCA	NCI	NCT	OLY	HLM	W	L	Coach
1981		NAIA		16	—	—	—	—	—	—	—	25	7	Lyon, Howard
1982		NAIA		2	—	—	—	—	—	—	—	39	1	Lyon, Howard
1984		NCCAA	I	1	—	—	—	—	—	—	—	25	6	Lyon, Howard
1985		NAIA		32	—	—	—	—	—	—	—	29	4	Lyon, Howard
1987		NAIA		32	—	—	—	—	—	—	—	29	2	Lyon, Howard
1988		NCCAA	I	3	—	—	—	—	—	—	—	31	5	Lyon, Howard
1989		NAIA		32	—	—	—	—	—	—	—	29	8	Holmquist, Dr. David G.
1992		NAIA	I	8	—	—	—	—	—	—	—	33	4	Holmquist, Dr. David G.
1997		NAIA	I	16	—	—	—	—	—	—	—	28	6	Holmquist, Dr. David G.
1998		NAIA	I	16	—	—	—	—	—	—	—	30	7	Holmquist, Dr. David G.
1975	W	AIAW	S	8	—	—	—	—	—	—	—	16	2	Norman, Betty
1976		AIAW	S	12	—	—	—	—	—	—	—	18	6	Norman, Betty
1977		AIAW	S	4	—	—	—	—	—	—	—	22	7	Norman, Betty
1978		AIAW	S	4	—	—	—	—	—	—	—	26	8	Norman, Betty
1980		AIAW	III	8	—	—	—	—	—	—	—	15	14	Norman, Betty
1981		AIAW	II	16	—	—	—	—	—	—	—	26	5	Norman, Betty
1982		AIAW	II	8	—	—	—	—	—	—	—	19	12	Norman, Betty
1984		NAIA		16	—	—	—	—	—	—	—	22	11	Norman, Betty
1996		NAIA	I	32	—	—	—	—	—	—	—	19	12	Andressen, Amber

BIRMINGHAM-SOUTHERN

Year	M/W	Assn	Div	NAT	NIT	ARC	CCA	NCI	NCT	OLY	HLM	W	L	Coach
1978	M	NAIA		16	—	—	—	—	—	—	—	29	5	Walcavich, Greg
1979		NAIA		32	—	—	—	—	—	—	—	29	4	Walcavich, Greg
1982		NAIA		32	—	—	—	—	—	—	—	18	15	Walcavich, Greg
1984		NAIA		32	—	—	—	—	—	—	—	23	8	Dean, Joe, Jr.
1986		NAIA		16	—	—	—	—	—	—	—	28	4	Dean, Joe, Jr.
1990		NAIA		1	—	—	—	—	—	—	—	31	3	Reboul, Duane
1992		NAIA	I	16	—	—	—	—	—	—	—	28	7	Reboul, Duane
1993		NAIA	I	16	—	—	—	—	—	—	—	29	7	Reboul, Duane
1995		NAIA	I	1	—	—	—	—	—	—	—	35	2	Reboul, Duane
1996		NAIA	I	8	—	—	—	—	—	—	—	25	5	Reboul, Duane
1997		NAIA	I	8	—	—	—	—	—	—	—	28	6	Reboul, Duane
1998		NAIA	I	32	—	—	—	—	—	—	—	28	5	Reboul, Duane

BISHOP

Year	M/W	Assn	Div	NAT	NIT	ARC	CCA	NCI	NCT	OLY	HLM	W	L	Coach
1968	M	NAIA		32	—	—	—	—	—	—	—	23	6	Jones, Dr. Emanuel M.
1972		NAIA		32	—	—	—	—	—	—	—	23	11	Alexander, Charles
1977		NCAA	III	16	—	—	—	—	—	—	—	15	9	Lilly, Sylvester "Ben"
1982		NCAA	III	16	—	—	—	—	—	—	—	16	7	Lilly, Sylvester "Ben"
1983		NCAA	III	24	—	—	—	—	—	—	—	18	8	Lilly, Sylvester "Ben"
1983	W	NCAA	III	32	—	—	—	—	—	—	—	18	7	Robinson, Myrtle
1984		NCAA	III	8	—	—	—	—	—	—	—	21	7	Young, Abron, Jr.
1986		NCAA	III	2	—	—	—	—	—	—	—	28	3	Young, Abron, Jr.
1987		NCAA	III	24	—	—	—	—	—	—	—	20	5	Young, Abron, Jr.

BLACK HILLS STATE

Year	M/W	Assn	Div	NAT	NIT	ARC	CCA	NCI	NCT	OLY	HLM	W	L	Coach
1994	M	NAIA	II	24	—	—	—	—	—	—	—	19	11	Olson, Mike
1997		NAIA	II	8	—	—	—	—	—	—	—	24	6	Olson, Mike
1998		NAIA	II	16	—	—	—	—	—	—	—	21	8	Olson, Mike
1996	W	NAIA	II	8	—	—	—	—	—	—	—	24	7	Schamber, Robin
1997		NAIA	II	2	—	—	—	—	—	—	—	27	7	Schamber, Robin
1998		NAIA	II	32	—	—	—	—	—	—	—	25	5	Dobbs, Kevin

Year	M/W	Assn	Div	NAT	NIT	ARC	CCA	NCI	NCT	OLY	HLM	W	L	Coach
BLACKBURN														
1981	M	NSCAA		16	—	—	—	—	—	—	—	19	10	Parker, James R.
1982		NSCAA		1	—	—	—	—	—	—	—	23	8	Parker, James R.
1983		NSCAA		8	—	—	—	—	—	—	—	20	5	Parker, James R.
1984		NSCAA		8	—	—	—	—	—	—	—	20	9	Parker, James R.
1985		NSCAA		1	—	—	—	—	—	—	—	23	7	Staff, Bob
1986		NSCAA		16	—	—	—	—	—	—	—	19	8	Staff, Bob
1987		NSCAA		8	—	—	—	—	—	—	—	14	9	Staff, Bob
1989		NSCAA		7	—	—	—	—	—	—	—	17	8	Staff, Bob
1991		NSCAA		6	—	—	—	—	—	—	—	22	7	Zeff, Dr. Ira
1992		NSCAA		6	—	—	—	—	—	—	—	22	8	Zeff, Dr. Ira
1995		NSCAA		8	—	—	—	—	—	—	—	15	14	Zeff, Dr. Ira
1998		NSCAA		4	—	—	—	—	—	—	—	18	11	Zeff, Dr. Ira
1985	W	NSCAA		8	—	—	—	—	—	—	—	12	17	Sexton, James R.
1990		NSCAA		3	—	—	—	—	—	—	—	15	11	Sexton, James R.
1991		NSCAA		3	—	—	—	—	—	—	—	18	11	Sexton, James R.
1992		NSCAA		2	—	—	—	—	—	—	—	20	10	Sexton, James R.
1993		NSCAA		1	—	—	—	—	—	—	—	24	7	Sexton, James R.
1994		NSCAA		4	—	—	—	—	—	—	—	15	14	Sexton, James R.
1997		NCAA	III	64	—	—	—	—	—	—	—	13	13	Garrett, Matt
1998		NSCAA		3	—	—	—	—	—	—	—	19	11	Garrett, Matt
BLANTON'S JC														
1987	M	NSCAA		10	—	—	—	—	—	—	—			
1989		NSCAA		10	—	—	—	—	—	—	—	16	14	Allen, Doug
BLOOMFIELD														
1992	W	NAIA	II	20	—	—	—	—	—	—	—	22	8	Manfria, Donald
1995		NAIA	II	32	—	—	—	—	—	—	—	21	8	Manfria, Donald
BLOOMSBURG														
1963	M	NCAA	II	16	—	—	—	—	—	—	—	17	4	Foster, William E.
1974		NCAA	II	8	—	—	—	—	—	—	—	22	6	Chronister, Charles W.
1981		NCAA	II	32	—	—	—	—	—	—	—	23	7	Chronister, Charles W.
1982		NCAA	II	16	—	—	—	—	—	—	—	24	7	Chronister, Charles W.
1983		NCAA	II	8	—	—	—	—	—	—	—	23	10	Chronister, Charles W.
1989		NCAA	II	16	—	—	—	—	—	—	—	27	5	Chronister, Charles W.
1995		NCAA	II	48	—	—	—	—	—	—	—	18	9	Chronister, Charles W.
1996		NCAA	II	48	—	—	—	—	—	—	—	21	7	Chronister, Charles W.
1989	W	NCAA	II	8	—	—	—	—	—	—	—	28	2	Bressi, Joe
1990		NCAA	II	32	—	—	—	—	—	—	—	22	7	Bressi, Joe
1991		NCAA	II	32	—	—	—	—	—	—	—	26	2	Bressi, Joe
1992		NCAA	II	32	—	—	—	—	—	—	—	22	8	Bressi, Joe
1998		NCAA	II	16	—	—	—	—	—	—	—	22	8	Fedorjaka, Kathy
BLUEFIELD (VA)														
1974	M	NSCAA		16	—	—	—	—	—	—	—			
1980		NSCAA		8	—	—	—	—	—	—	—	22	20	Brunson, Dean
1981		NSCAA		9	—	—	—	—	—	—	—	12	14	Brunson, Dean
1984		NSCAA		16	—	—	—	—	—	—	—			Becker, Darrell

Year	M/W	Assn	Div	NAT	NIT	ARC	CCA	NCI	NCT	OLY	HLM	W	L	Coach
1985		NSCAA		2	—	—	—	—	—	—	—	27	12	Becker, Darrell
1986		NSCAA		3	—	—	—	—	—	—	—	28	9	Blevins, Mark
1987		NSCAA		2	—	—	—	—	—	—	—	28	13	Blevins, Mark
1988		NSCAA		2	—	—	—	—	—	—	—	24	14	Blevins, Mark
1989		NSCAA		4	—	—	—	—	—	—	—	23	16	Blevins, Mark
1996		NAIA	II	32	—	—	—	—	—	—	—	22	12	Ayers, Walter

BLUEFIELD STATE (WV)

Year	M/W	Assn	Div	NAT	NIT	ARC	CCA	NCI	NCT	OLY	HLM	W	L	Coach
1996	M	NCAA	II	48	—	—	—	—	—	—	—	15	16	Brown, Terry
1985	W	NAIA		16	—	—	—	—	—	—	—	24	4	Mandeville, Kenneth A. "Kenny"
1987		NAIA		16	—	—	—	—	—	—	—	20	8	Mandeville, Kenneth A. "Kenny"
1993		NAIA	I	32	—	—	—	—	—	—	—	26	3	Jessee, Thomas

BOISE STATE

Year	M/W	Assn	Div	NAT	NIT	ARC	CCA	NCI	NCT	OLY	HLM	W	L	Coach
1970	M	NCAA	II	24	—	—	—	—	—	—	—	20	8	Satterfield, Murray
1976		NCAA	I	32	—	—	—	—	—	—	—	18	11	Connor, Doran "Bus"
1987		NCAA	I	—	16	—	—	—	—	—	—	22	8	Dye, Bobby
1988		NCAA	I	64	—	—	—	—	—	—	—	24	6	Dye, Bobby
1989		NCAA	I	—	32	—	—	—	—	—	—	23	7	Dye, Bobby
1991		NCAA	I	—	32	—	—	—	—	—	—	18	11	Dye, Bobby
1993		NCAA	I	64	—	—	—	—	—	—	—	21	8	Dye, Bobby
1994		NCAA	I	64	—	—	—	—	—	—	—	17	13	Dye, Bobby
1975	W	AIAW	L	16	—	—	—	—	—	—	—	22	3	Thorngren, Connie
1994		NCAA	I	64	—	—	—	—	—	—	—	23	6	Daugherty, June
1998		NCAA	I	—	16	—	—	—	—	—	—	19	10	Stevens, Trisha

BOSTON COLLEGE

Year	M/W	Assn	Div	NAT	NIT	ARC	CCA	NCI	NCT	OLY	HLM	W	L	Coach
1958	M	NCAA	I	24	—	—	—	—	—	—	—	15	6	Martin, Donald
1965		NCAA	I	—	14	—	—	—	—	—	—	21	7	Cousy, Robert J.
1966		NCAA	I	—	8	—	—	—	—	—	—	21	5	Cousy, Robert J.
1967		NCAA	I	8	—	—	—	—	—	—	—	21	3	Cousy, Robert J.
1968		NCAA	I	23	—	—	—	—	—	—	—	17	8	Cousy, Robert J.
1969		NCAA	I	—	2	—	—	—	—	—	—	24	4	Cousy, Robert J.
1974		NCAA	I	—	3	—	—	—	—	—	—	21	9	Zuffelato, Bob
1975		NCAA	I	16	—	—	—	—	—	—	—	21	9	Zuffelato, Bob
1980		NCAA	I	—	16	—	—	—	—	—	—	19	10	Davis, Dr. Thomas
1981		NCAA	I	16	—	—	—	—	—	—	—	23	7	Davis, Dr. Thomas
1982		NCAA	I	8	—	—	—	—	—	—	—	22	10	Davis, Dr. Thomas
1983		NCAA	I	16	—	—	—	—	—	—	—	25	7	Williams, Gary
1984		NCAA	I	—	16	—	—	—	—	—	—	18	12	Williams, Gary
1985		NCAA	I	16	—	—	—	—	—	—	—	20	11	Williams, Gary
1988		NCAA	I	—	4	—	—	—	—	—	—	18	15	O'Brien, James J.
1992		NCAA	I	—	16	—	—	—	—	—	—	17	14	O'Brien, James J.
1993		NCAA	I	—	8	—	—	—	—	—	—	18	13	O'Brien, James J.
1994		NCAA	I	8	—	—	—	—	—	—	—	23	11	O'Brien, James J.
1996		NCAA	I	32	—	—	—	—	—	—	—	19	11	O'Brien, James J.
1997		NCAA	I	32	—	—	—	—	—	—	—	22	9	O'Brien, James J.

Year	M/W	Assn	Div	NAT	NIT	ARC	CCA	NCI	NCT	OLY	HLM	W	L	Coach
BOSTON UNIVERSITY														
1959	M	NCAA	I	8	—	—	—	—	—	—	—	20	7	Zunic, Matthew
1980		NCAA	I	—	32	—	—	—	—	—	—	21	9	Pitino, Richard A. "Rick"
1983		NCAA	I	52	—	—	—	—	—	—	—	21	10	Pitino, Richard A. "Rick"
1986		NCAA	I	—	32	—	—	—	—	—	—	21	10	Jarvis, Mike
1988		NCAA	I	64	—	—	—	—	—	—	—	23	8	Jarvis, Mike
1990		NCAA	I	64	—	—	—	—	—	—	—	18	12	Jarvis, Mike
1997		NCAA	I	64	—	—	—	—	—	—	—	25	5	Wolff, Dennis
1980	W	AIAW	I	24	—	—	—	—	—	—	—	18	9	O'Callaghan, Jo Ann
BOWDOIN														
1996	M	NCAA	III	32	—	—	—	—	—	—	—	19	6	Gilbride, Timothy J.
BOWIE STATE														
1996	W	NCAA	II	16	—	—	—	—	—	—	—	22	10	Davis, Edward
1997		NCAA	II	16	—	—	—	—	—	—	—	29	2	Davis, Edward
1998		NCAA	II	16	—	—	—	—	—	—	—	28	2	Davis, Edward
BOWLING GREEN STATE														
1944	M	NCAA	—	8	—	—	—	—	—	—	—	22	4	Anderson, W. Harold "Andy"
1945		NCAA	—	2	4	—	—	—	—	—	—	24	4	Anderson, W. Harold "Andy"
1946		NCAA	—	8	—	—	—	—	—	—	—	27	5	Anderson, W. Harold "Andy"
1948		NCAA	—	8	—	—	—	—	—	—	—	27	6	Anderson, W. Harold "Andy"
1949		NCAA	—	3	—	—	—	—	—	—	—	24	7	Anderson, W. Harold "Andy"
1954		NCAA	—	8	—	—	—	—	—	—	—	17	7	Anderson, W. Harold "Andy"
1959		NCAA	I	23	—	—	—	—	—	—	—	18	8	Anderson, W. Harold "Andy"
1962		NCAA	I	25	—	—	—	—	—	—	—	21	4	Anderson, W. Harold "Andy"
1963		NCAA	I	16	—	—	—	—	—	—	—	19	8	Anderson, W. Harold "Andy"
1968		NCAA	I	23	—	—	—	—	—	—	—	18	7	Fitch, William C. "Billy"
1975		NCAA	I	—	—	—	3	—	—	—	—	18	10	Haley, Pat
1980		NCAA	I	—	32	—	—	—	—	—	—	20	10	Weinert, John P.
1983		NCAA	I	—	32	—	—	—	—	—	—	21	9	Weinert, John P.
1990		NCAA	I	—	32	—	—	—	—	—	—	18	11	Larranaga, Jim
1991		NCAA	I	—	32	—	—	—	—	—	—	17	13	Larranaga, Jim
1997		NCAA	I	—	32	—	—	—	—	—	—	22	10	Larranaga, Jim
1987	W	NCAA	I	40	—	—	—	—	—	—	—	27	3	Voll, Fran
1988		NCAA	I	40	—	—	—	—	—	—	—	24	6	Voll, Fran
1989		NCAA	I	32	—	—	—	—	—	—	—	27	4	Voll, Fran
1990		NCAA	I	48	—	—	—	—	—	—	—	22	9	Voll, Fran
1993		NCAA	I	48	—	—	—	—	—	—	—	25	5	Clark, Jaci
1994		NCAA	I	64	—	—	—	—	—	—	—	26	4	Clark, Jaci
1998		NCAA	I	—	16	—	—	—	—	—	—	21	8	Clark, Jaci
BRADLEY														
1938	M	NCAA	—	6	—	—	—	—	—	—	—	18	2	Robertson, Alfred J.
1939		NCAA	—	3	—	—	—	—	—	—	—	19	3	Robertson, Alfred J.
1947		NCAA	—	8	—	—	—	—	—	—	—	25	7	Robertson, Alfred J.
1949		NCAA	—	4	—	—	—	—	—	—	—	27	8	Anderson, Forrest A. "Forddy"
1950		NCAA		2	2	—	—	—	—	—	—	32	5	Anderson, Forrest A. "Forddy"
1951		NCAA		—	—	—	—	—	2	—	—	32	6	Anderson, Forrest A. "Forddy"
1954		NCAA		2	—	—	—	—	—	—	—	19	13	Anderson, Forrest A. "Forddy"
1955		NCAA		8	—	—	—	—	—	—	—	9	20	Vanatta, Robert

Year	M/W	Assn	Div	NAT	NIT	ARC	CCA	NCI	NCT	OLY	HLM	W	L	Coach
1957		NCAA	I	—	1	—	—	—	—	—	—	22	7	Orsborn, Charles K. "Chuck"
1958		NCAA	I	—	8	—	—	—	—	—	—	20	7	Orsborn, Charles K. "Chuck"
1959		NCAA	I	—	2	—	—	—	—	—	—	25	4	Orsborn, Charles K. "Chuck"
1960		NCAA	I	—	1	—	—	—	—	—	—	27	2	Orsborn, Charles K. "Chuck"
1962		NCAA	I	—	8	—	—	—	—	—	—	21	7	Orsborn, Charles K. "Chuck"
1964		NCAA	I	—	1	—	—	—	—	—	—	23	6	Orsborn, Charles K. "Chuck"
1965		NCAA	I	—	14	—	—	—	—	—	—	18	9	Orsborn, Charles K. "Chuck"
1968		NCAA	I	—	16	—	—	—	—	—	—	19	9	Stowell, Joseph R.
1974		NCAA	I	—	—	—	3	—	—	—	—	20	8	Stowell, Joseph R.
1980		NCAA	I	48	—	—	—	—	—	—	—	23	10	Versace, Dick
1982		NCAA	I	—	1	—	—	—	—	—	—	26	10	Versace, Dick
1985		NCAA	I	—	32	—	—	—	—	—	—	17	13	Versace, Dick
1986		NCAA	I	32	—	—	—	—	—	—	—	32	3	Versace, Dick
1988		NCAA	I	64	—	—	—	—	—	—	—	26	5	Albeck, Charles Stanley "Stan"
1994		NCAA	I	—	8	—	—	—	—	—	—	23	8	Molinari, Jim
1995		NCAA	I	—	16	—	—	—	—	—	—	20	10	Molinari, Jim
1996		NCAA	I	64	—	—	—	—	—	—	—	22	8	Molinari, Jim
1997		NCAA	I	—	16	—	—	—	—	—	—	17	13	Molinari, Jim

BRANDEIS

Year	M/W	Assn	Div	NAT	NIT	ARC	CCA	NCI	NCT	OLY	HLM	W	L	Coach
1958	M	NCAA	II	24	—	—	—	—	—	—	—	18	4	Stein, Harvey
1975		NCAA	III	8	—	—	—	—	—	—	—	20	7	Brannum, Robert W.
1977		NCAA	III	16	—	—	—	—	—	—	—	16	11	Brannum, Robert W.
1978		NCAA	III	8	—	—	—	—	—	—	—	19	6	Brannum, Robert W.

BRANDYWINE

Year	M/W	Assn	Div	NAT	NIT	ARC	CCA	NCI	NCT	OLY	HLM	W	L	Coach
1967	M	NSCAA		3	—	—	—	—	—	—	—	23	4	

BRESCIA

Year	M/W	Assn	Div	NAT	NIT	ARC	CCA	NCI	NCT	OLY	HLM	W	L	Coach
1995	W	NAIA	II	16	—	—	—	—	—	—	—	23	8	Buchanan, Lee
1996		NAIA	II	32	—	—	—	—	—	—	—	27	4	Buchanan, Lee
1997		NAIA	II	8	—	—	—	—	—	—	—	30	6	Buchanan, Lee

BRIAR CLIFF

Year	M/W	Assn	Div	NAT	NIT	ARC	CCA	NCI	NCT	OLY	HLM	W	L	Coach
1976	M	NAIA		32	—	—	—	—	—	—	—	19	8	Nacke, Ray
1977		NAIA		32	—	—	—	—	—	—	—	19	9	Nacke, Ray
1978		NAIA		16	—	—	—	—	—	—	—	25	4	Nacke, Ray
1979		NAIA		8	—	—	—	—	—	—	—	28	3	Nacke, Ray
1981		NAIA		16	—	—	—	—	—	—	—	23	2	Nacke, Ray
1982		NAIA		16	—	—	—	—	—	—	—	21	10	Nacke, Ray
1986		NAIA		32	—	—	—	—	—	—	—	23	4	Nacke, Ray
1990		NAIA		32	—	—	—	—	—	—	—	24	7	Nacke, Ray
1991		NAIA		16	—	—	—	—	—	—	—	27	6	Nacke, Ray
1992		NAIA	I	32	—	—	—	—	—	—	—	25	4	Nacke, Ray
1993		NAIA	I	16	—	—	—	—	—	—	—	27	6	Nacke, Ray
1998		NAIA	II	16	—	—	—	—	—	—	—	23	12	Beard, Michael
1996	W	NAIA	II	8	—	—	—	—	—	—	—	23	11	Powell, Michael
1997		NAIA	II	8	—	—	—	—	—	—	—	37	1	Powell, Michael
1998		NAIA	II	16	—	—	—	—	—	—	—	31	4	Powell, Michael

Year	M/W	Assn	Div	NAT	NIT	ARC	CCA	NCI	NCT	OLY	HLM	W	L	Coach
BRIDGEPORT														
1954	M	NAIA		32	—	—	—	—	—	—	—	12	9	Glines, Herbert E.
1968		NCAA	II	32	—	—	—	—	—	—	—	19	8	Webster, Bruce
1972		NCAA	II	24	—	—	—	—	—	—	—	17	9	Webster, Bruce
1973		NCAA	II	24	—	—	—	—	—	—	—	20	9	Webster, Bruce
1976		NCAA	II	8	—	—	—	—	—	—	—	24	5	Webster, Bruce
1977		NCAA	II	32	—	—	—	—	—	—	—	19	10	Webster, Bruce
1978		NCAA	II	24	—	—	—	—	—	—	—	19	10	Webster, Bruce
1979		NCAA	II	4	—	—	—	—	—	—	—	25	8	Webster, Bruce
1985		NCAA	II	24	—	—	—	—	—	—	—	26	6	Webster, Bruce
1989		NCAA	II	16	—	—	—	—	—	—	—	25	7	Webster, Bruce
1990		NCAA	II	8	—	—	—	—	—	—	—	24	9	Webster, Bruce
1991		NCAA	II	2	—	—	—	—	—	—	—	26	8	Webster, Bruce
1992		NCAA	II	2	—	—	—	—	—	—	—	28	7	Webster, Bruce
1989	W	NCAA	II	32	—	—	—	—	—	—	—	25	5	Foust, Dan
1995		NCAA	II	48	—	—	—	—	—	—	—	21	8	Herer, Harvey
1996		NCAA	II	32	—	—	—	—	—	—	—	25	5	Herer, Harvey
BRIDGEWATER (VA)														
1988	M	NCAA	III	32	—	—	—	—	—	—	—	24	5	Leatherman, Bill
1996		NCAA	III	64	—	—	—	—	—	—	—	18	10	Leatherman, Bill
1997		NCAA	III	16	—	—	—	—	—	—	—	21	8	Leatherman, Bill
1980	W	AIAW	III	24	—	—	—	—	—	—	—	22	7	Mapp, Laura
1982		AIAW	III	16	—	—	—	—	—	—	—	16	11	Mapp, Laura
1997		NCAA	III	32	—	—	—	—	—	—	—	22	6	Willi, Jean
1998		NCAA	III	16	—	—	—	—	—	—	—	24	5	Willi, Jean
BRIDGEWATER STATE (MA)														
1983	M	NCAA	III	16	—	—	—	—	—	—	—	21	6	Byron, Paul
1970	W	AIAW		16	—	—	—	—	—	—	—	X	X	Schneider, Judy
1983		NCAA	III	24	—	—	—	—	—	—	—	18	7	Hastings, Martha
1984		NCAA	III	32	—	—	—	—	—	—	—	22	5	Ruggiero, George H. 'Bo'
1985		NCAA	III	16	—	—	—	—	—	—	—	25	2	Ruggiero, George H. 'Bo'
1986		NCAA	III	32	—	—	—	—	—	—	—	21	6	Ruggiero, George H. 'Bo'
BRIGHAM YOUNG														
1948	M	NAIA		16	—	—	—	—	—	—	—	16	11	Millet, W. Floyd
1949		NAIA		16	—	—	—	—	—	—	—	22	14	Millet, W. Floyd
1950		NCAA		6	—	—	—	—	—	—	—	22	12	Watts, Stanley H.
1951		NCAA		8	1	—	—	—	—	—	—	28	9	Watts, Stanley H.
1953		NCAA		—	12	—	—	—	—	—	—	22	8	Watts, Stanley H.
1954		NCAA		—	12	—	—	—	—	—	—	18	11	Watts, Stanley H.
1957		NCAA	I	12	—	—	—	—	—	—	—	19	9	Watts, Stanley H.
1965		NCAA	I	16	—	—	—	—	—	—	—	21	7	Watts, Stanley H.
1966		NCAA	I	—	1	—	—	—	—	—	—	20	5	Watts, Stanley H.
1969		NCAA	I	25	—	—	—	—	—	—	—	17	11	Watts, Stanley H.
1971		NCAA	I	16	—	—	—	—	—	—	—	18	11	Watts, Stanley H.
1972		NCAA	I	25	—	—	—	—	—	—	—	21	5	Watts, Stanley H.
1979		NCAA	I	32	—	—	—	—	—	—	—	20	8	Arnold, Frank H.
1980		NCAA	I	32	—	—	—	—	—	—	—	24	5	Arnold, Frank H.
1981		NCAA	I	8	—	—	—	—	—	—	—	25	7	Arnold, Frank H.
1982		NCAA	I	—	32	—	—	—	—	—	—	17	13	Arnold, Frank H.

Year	M/W	Assn	Div	NAT	NIT	ARC	CCA	NCI	NCT	OLY	HLM	W	L	Coach
1984		NCAA	I	32	—	—	—	—	—	—	—	20	11	Anderson, Ladell
1986		NCAA	I	—	8	—	—	—	—	—	—	18	14	Anderson, Ladell
1987		NCAA	I	64	—	—	—	—	—	—	—	21	11	Anderson, Ladell
1988		NCAA	I	32	—	—	—	—	—	—	—	26	6	Anderson, Ladell
1990		NCAA	I	64	—	—	—	—	—	—	—	21	9	Reid, Roger
1991		NCAA	I	32	—	—	—	—	—	—	—	21	13	Reid, Roger
1992		NCAA	I	64	—	—	—	—	—	—	—	25	7	Reid, Roger
1993		NCAA	I	32	—	—	—	—	—	—	—	25	9	Reid, Roger
1994		NCAA	I	—	16	—	—	—	—	—	—	22	10	Reid, Roger
1995		NCAA	I	64	—	—	—	—	—	—	—	22	10	Reid, Roger
1978	W	AIAW	L	12	—	—	—	—	—	—	—	22	6	Leishman, Dr. Courtney M.
1979		AIAW	L	12	—	—	—	—	—	—	—	21	7	Leishman, Dr. Courtney M.
1980		AIAW	I	16	—	—	—	—	—	—	—	24	9	Leishman, Dr. Courtney M.
1982		NCAA	I	—	3	—	—	—	—	—	—	24	13	Leishman, Dr. Courtney M.
1984		NCAA	I	32	—	—	—	—	—	—	—	18	8	Leishman, Dr. Courtney M.
1985		NCAA	I	32	—	—	—	—	—	—	—	19	9	Leishman, Dr. Courtney M.
1993		NCAA	I	48	—	—	—	—	—	—	—	24	4	Wilson, Jeanie

BRIGHAM YOUNG: HAWAII

Year	M/W	Assn	Div	NAT	NIT	ARC	CCA	NCI	NCT	OLY	HLM	W	L	Coach
1986	M	NAIA		32	—	—	—	—	—	—	—	17	13	Chidester, Ted H.
1989		NAIA		32	—	—	—	—	—	—	—	24	9	Hess, Dr. Charles "Chic"
1992		NAIA	I	3	—	—	—	—	—	—	—	28	7	Wagner, A. Kenyon "Ken"
1996		NAIA	I	16	—	—	—	—	—	—	—	24	7	Wagner, A. Kenyon "Ken"
1997		NAIA	I	16	—	—	—	—	—	—	—	21	8	Wagner, A. Kenyon "Ken"
1998		NAIA	I	32	—	—	—	—	—	—	—	19	8	Wagner, A. Kenyon "Ken"

BRISTOL (TN)

Year	M/W	Assn	Div	NAT	NIT	ARC	CCA	NCI	NCT	OLY	HLM	W	L	Coach
1974	M	NSCAA		16	—	—	—	—	—	—	—			Alves, Len
1986		NSCAA		1	—	—	—	—	—	—	—			Crowder, Brien
1987		NSCAA		3	—	—	—	—	—	—	—	12	25	

BROCKPORT STATE

Year	M/W	Assn	Div	NAT	NIT	ARC	CCA	NCI	NCT	OLY	HLM	W	L	Coach
1973	M	NCAA	II	4	—	—	—	—	—	—	—	24	6	Panaggio, Mauro
1975		NCAA	III	4	—	—	—	—	—	—	—	23	5	Panaggio, Mauro
1994		NCAA	III	40	—	—	—	—	—	—	—	17	11	Bowe, Bill
1997		NCAA	III	16	—	—	—	—	—	—	—	19	10	Bowe, Bill
1998		NCAA	III	48	—	—	—	—	—	—	—	17	10	Bowe, Bill
1995	W	NCAA	III	64	—	—	—	—	—	—	—	17	9	Carron, Michele

BROOKLYN

Year	M/W	Assn	Div	NAT	NIT	ARC	CCA	NCI	NCT	OLY	HLM	W	L	Coach
1950	M	NAIA		8	—	—	—	—	—	—	—	24	5	Baggett, Al
1982		NCAA	III	3	—	—	—	—	—	—	—	22	9	Reiner, Mark

BROWN

Year	M/W	Assn	Div	NAT	NIT	ARC	CCA	NCI	NCT	OLY	HLM	W	L	Coach
1939	M	NCAA		8	—	—	—	—	—	—	—	17	3	Allen, George E. "Eck"
1986		NCAA	I	64	—	—	—	—	—	—	—	16	11	Cingiser, Mike
1994	W	NCAA	I	64	—	—	—	—	—	—	—	18	10	Burr, Jean Marie

Year	M/W	Assn	Div	NAT	NIT	ARC	CCA	NCI	NCT	OLY	HLM	W	L	Coach
BRYAN (TN)														
1969	M	NCCAA		2	—	—	—	—	—	—	—	19	12	Wells, Jack
1971		NCCAA		8	—	—	—	—	—	—	—	20	12	Dixon, Wayne H.
1982		NCCAA	I	7	—	—	—	—	—	—	—	14	17	Dixon, Wayne H.
1983		NCCAA	I	8	—	—	—	—	—	—	—	19	15	Reeser, John
1995		NCCAA	I	8	—	—	—	—	—	—	—	21	17	Michalski, Morris
BRYANT														
1975	M	NAIA		32	—	—	—	—	—	—	—	21	8	Folliard, Thomas J.
1978		NCAA	II	32	—	—	—	—	—	—	—	20	6	Folliard, Thomas J.
1980		NCAA	II	32	—	—	—	—	—	—	—	20	7	Drury, Leon A. "Lee"
1986	W	NCAA	II	24	—	—	—	—	—	—	—	17	12	McKee, Michael
1988		NCAA	II	32	—	—	—	—	—	—	—	22	9	Tomasso, Ralph
1989		NCAA	II	32	—	—	—	—	—	—	—	20	9	Tomasso, Ralph
1996		NCAA	II	48	—	—	—	—	—	—	—	19	10	Burke, Mary
BRYANT & STRATTON: ALBANY														
1972	M	NSCAA		8	—	—	—	—	—	—	—	17	2	Rice, Willard
1973		NSCAA		3	—	—	—	—	—	—	—	17	8	Rice, Willard
1974		NSCAA		8	—	—	—	—	—	—	—			Rice, Willard
1979		NSCAA		16	—	—	—	—	—	—	—	18	6	
BRYANT & STRATTON: BUFFALO														
1974	M	NSCAA		1	—	—	—	—	—	—	—	X	X	Griffin, Dr. Thomas J.
1980		NSCAA		16	—	—	—	—	—	—	—	16	6	Licate, Gilbert P.
1981		NSCAA		8	—	—	—	—	—	—	—	25	6	McNamara, Tim
1982		NSCAA		16	—	—	—	—	—	—	—	17	10	McNamara, Tim
1983		NSCAA		16	—	—	—	—	—	—	—	12	10	McNamara, Tim
1986		NSCAA		8	—	—	—	—	—	—	—	23	9	Krauza, Gregory A.
BUCKNELL														
1987	M	NCAA	I	64	—	—	—	—	—	—	—	22	9	Woollum, Charles R.
1989		NCAA	I	64	—	—	—	—	—	—	—	23	8	Woollum, Charles R.
BUENA VISTA														
1962	M	NAIA		32	—	—	—	—	—	—	—	25	3	Ewalt, Merritt A.
1964		NAIA		32	—	—	—	—	—	—	—	18	7	Ewalt, Merritt A.
1997		NCAA	III	64	—	—	—	—	—	—	—	18	8	Van Haaften, Brian
1983	W	NCAA	III	32	—	—	—	—	—	—	—	18	8	Naughton, John
1985		NCAA	III	32	—	—	—	—	—	—	—	20	8	Naughton, John
1990		NCAA	III	8	—	—	—	—	—	—	—	23	6	Naughton, John
1995		NCAA	III	64	—	—	—	—	—	—	—	18	7	Allgood-Berry, Janet
1996		NCAA	III	64	—	—	—	—	—	—	—	19	7	Allgood-Berry, Janet
1997		NCAA	III	16	—	—	—	—	—	—	—	23	5	Allgood-Berry, Janet
BUFFALO STATE COLLEGE														
1967	M	NCAA	II	36	—	—	—	—	—	—	—	17	6	MacAdam, Howard B.
1968		NCAA	II	16	—	—	—	—	—	—	—	17	7	MacAdam, Howard B.
1970		NCAA	II	4	—	—	—	—	—	—	—	19	3	MacAdam, Howard B.
1971		NCAA	II	16	—	—	—	—	—	—	—	18	4	MacAdam, Howard B.
1972		NCAA	II	32	—	—	—	—	—	—	—	13	14	MacAdam, Howard B.
1976		NCAA	II	24	—	—	—	—	—	—	—	20	8	Borschel, Thomas
1984		NCAA	III	24	—	—	—	—	—	—	—	23	5	Bihr, Richard J.
1985		NCAA	III	16	—	—	—	—	—	—	—	22	5	Bihr, Richard J.

Year	M/W	Assn	Div	NAT	NIT	ARC	CCA	NCI	NCT	OLY	HLM	W	L	Coach
1988		NCAA	III	16	—	—	—	—	—	—	—	—	19	10	Bihr, Richard J.
1989		NCAA	III	16	—	—	—	—	—	—	—	—	25	4	Bihr, Richard J.
1990		NCAA	III	32	—	—	—	—	—	—	—	—	27	2	Bihr, Richard J.
1991		NCAA	III	32	—	—	—	—	—	—	—	—	21	7	Bihr, Richard J.
1992		NCAA	III	16	—	—	—	—	—	—	—	—	24	4	Bihr, Richard J.
1993		NCAA	III	32	—	—	—	—	—	—	—	—	21	6	Bihr, Richard J.
1995		NCAA	III	32	—	—	—	—	—	—	—	—	21	8	Bihr, Richard J.
1996		NCAA	III	16	—	—	—	—	—	—	—	—	22	8	Bihr, Richard J.
1997		NCAA	III	32	—	—	—	—	—	—	—	—	20	9	Bihr, Richard J.
1984	W	NCAA	III	16	—	—	—	—	—	—	—	—	21	6	Maloney, Gail F.
1985		NCAA	III	32	—	—	—	—	—	—	—	—	18	8	Maloney, Gail F.
1986		NCAA	III	32	—	—	—	—	—	—	—	—	23	3	Maloney, Gail F.
1987		NCAA	III	32	—	—	—	—	—	—	—	—	14	11	Jabir, James J.
1988		NCAA	III	24	—	—	—	—	—	—	—	—	24	4	Maloney, Gail F.
1990		NCAA	III	32	—	—	—	—	—	—	—	—	24	4	Maloney, Gail F.
1991		NCAA	III	32	—	—	—	—	—	—	—	—	21	6	Maloney, Gail F.
1993		NCAA	III	32	—	—	—	—	—	—	—	—	19	8	Maloney, Gail F.
1994		NCAA	III	32	—	—	—	—	—	—	—	—	25	3	Maloney, Gail F.
1995		NCAA	III	64	—	—	—	—	—	—	—	—	20	8	Maloney, Gail F.

BUFFALO STATE UNIVERSITY

Year	M/W	Assn	Div	NAT	NIT	ARC	CCA	NCI	NCT	OLY	HLM	W	L	Coach
1957	M	NCAA	II	8	—	—	—	—	—	—	—	—	18	7	Serfustini, Dr. Leonard T.
1958		NCAA	II	24	—	—	—	—	—	—	—	—	17	8	Serfustini, Dr. Leonard T.
1959		NCAA	II	24	—	—	—	—	—	—	—	—	16	7	Serfustini, Dr. Leonard T.
1960		NCAA	II	24	—	—	—	—	—	—	—	—	16	7	Serfustini, Dr. Leonard T.
1963		NCAA	II	32	—	—	—	—	—	—	—	—	16	7	Serfustini, Dr. Leonard T.
1965		NCAA	II	16	—	—	—	—	—	—	—	—	19	3	Serfustini, Dr. Leonard T.
1982		NCAA	III	32	—	—	—	—	—	—	—	—	13	17	Hughes, Virgil William

BUNKER HILL CC

Year	M/W	Assn	Div	NAT	NIT	ARC	CCA	NCI	NCT	OLY	HLM	W	L	Coach
1996	M	NSCAA		8	—	—	—	—	—	—	—	—	21	9	Lee, Terrence
1997		NSCAA		6	—	—	—	—	—	—	—	—	18	9	Jones, Christopher
1998		NSCAA		15	—	—	—	—	—	—	—	—	26	9	Jones, Christopher

BUTLER (IN)

Year	M/W	Assn	Div	NAT	NIT	ARC	CCA	NCI	NCT	OLY	HLM	W	L	Coach
1958	M	NCAA	I	—	12	—	—	—	—	—	—	15	10	Hinkle, Paul D. "Tony"
1959		NCAA	I	—	8	—	—	—	—	—	—	19	9	Hinkle, Paul D. "Tony"
1962		NCAA	I	12	—	—	—	—	—	—	—	22	6	Hinkle, Paul D. "Tony"
1985		NCAA	I	—	32	—	—	—	—	—	—	19	10	Sexson, Joe
1991		NCAA	I	—	32	—	—	—	—	—	—	18	11	Collier, Barry
1992		NCAA	I	—	32	—	—	—	—	—	—	21	10	Collier, Barry
1997		NCAA	I	64	—	—	—	—	—	—	—	23	10	Collier, Barry
1998		NCAA	I	64	—	—	—	—	—	—	—	22	11	Collier, Barry
1982	W	AIAW	II	8	—	—	—	—	—	—	—	23	3	Mason, Linda
1983		NCAA	II	24	—	—	—	—	—	—	—	18	6	Mason, Linda
1993		NCAA	I	—	6	—	—	—	—	—	—	23	8	Stein, Paulette
1996		NCAA	I	64	—	—	—	—	—	—	—	21	9	Olkowski, June
1998		NCAA	I	—	8	—	—	—	—	—	—	25	6	Olkowski, June

Year	M/W	Assn	Div	NAT	NIT	ARC	CCA	NCI	NCT	OLY	HLM	W	L	Coach

CABRINI

Year	M/W	Assn	Div	NAT	NIT	ARC	CCA	NCI	NCT	OLY	HLM	W	L	Coach
1984	M	NAIA		32	—	—	—	—	—	—	—	22	12	Dzik, John L.
1985		NAIA		32	—	—	—	—	—	—	—	22	12	Dzik, John L.
1986		NAIA		32	—	—	—	—	—	—	—	24	7	Dzik, John L.
1987		NAIA		32	—	—	—	—	—	—	—	24	8	Dzik, John L.
1988		NCAA	III	32	—	—	—	—	—	—	—	23	7	Dzik, John L.
1994		NCAA	III	40	—	—	—	—	—	—	—	23	4	Dzik, John L.
1995		NCAA	III	32	—	—	—	—	—	—	—	21	7	Dzik, John L.
1996		NCAA	III	32	—	—	—	—	—	—	—	24	3	Dzik, John L.
1997		NCAA	III	64	—	—	—	—	—	—	—	16	9	Dzik, John L.
1995	W	NCAA	III	64	—	—	—	—	—	—	—	24	3	Welde, Dan V.
1996		NCAA	III	64	—	—	—	—	—	—	—	22	4	Welde, Dan V.
1997		NCAA	III	64	—	—	—	—	—	—	—	21	5	Welde, Dan V.

CALDWELL

Year	M/W	Assn	Div	NAT	NIT	ARC	CCA	NCI	NCT	OLY	HLM	W	L	Coach
1993	M	NAIA	II	20	—	—	—	—	—	—	—	21	8	Corino, Mark A.
1996		NAIA	II	32	—	—	—	—	—	—	—	21	9	Corino, Mark A.
1998		NAIA	II	32	—	—	—	—	—	—	—	23	7	Corino, Mark A.
1994	W	NAIA	II	24	—	—	—	—	—	—	—	21	6	Costello, Bob

CALIFORNIA

Year	M/W	Assn	Div	NAT	NIT	ARC	CCA	NCI	NCT	OLY	HLM	W	L	Coach
1946	M	NCAA		4	—	—	—	—	—	—	—	30	6	Price, Clarence M. 'Nibs'
1957		NCAA	I	8	—	—	—	—	—	—	—	21	5	Newell, Peter F.
1958		NCAA	I	8	—	—	—	—	—	—	—	19	9	Newell, Peter F.
1959		NCAA	I	1	—	—	—	—	—	—	1	25	4	Newell, Peter F.
1960		NCAA	I	2	—	—	—	—	—	—	—	28	2	Newell, Peter F.
1986		NCAA	I	—	32	—	—	—	—	—	—	19	10	Campanelli, Lou
1987		NCAA	I	—	8	—	—	—	—	—	—	20	15	Campanelli, Lou
1989		NCAA	I	—	16	—	—	—	—	—	—	20	13	Campanelli, Lou
1990		NCAA	I	32	—	—	—	—	—	—	—	22	10	Campanelli, Lou
1993		NCAA	I	16	—	—	—	—	—	—	—	21	9	Bozeman, Todd
1994		NCAA	I	64	—	—	—	—	—	—	—	22	8	Bozeman, Todd
1996		NCAA	I	64	—	—	—	—	—	—	—	17	11	Bozeman, Todd
1997		NCAA	I	16	—	—	—	—	—	—	—	23	9	Braun, Ben
1979	W	AIAW	L	—	8	—	—	—	—	—	—	14	17	Cantrell, Marci
1981		AIAW	I	—	4	—	—	—	—	—	—	22	10	Foster, Dr. Gooch
1982		AIAW	I	8	—	—	—	—	—	—	—	23	10	Foster, Dr. Gooch
1984		NCAA	I	—	5	—	—	—	—	—	—	24	8	Foster, Dr. Gooch
1987		NCAA	I	—	2	—	—	—	—	—	—	21	10	Foster, Dr. Gooch
1990		NCAA	I	48	—	—	—	—	—	—	—	17	12	Foster, Dr. Gooch
1992		NCAA	I	48	—	—	—	—	—	—	—	20	9	Foster, Dr. Gooch
1993		NCAA	I	32	—	—	—	—	—	—	—	19	10	Foster, Dr. Gooch

CALIFORNIA (PA)

Year	M/W	Assn	Div	NAT	NIT	ARC	CCA	NCI	NCT	OLY	HLM	W	L	Coach
1970	M	NAIA		32	—	—	—	—	—	—	—	20	5	Witchery, Myles B.
1985		NCAA	II	32	—	—	—	—	—	—	—	17	13	Loomis, Tim
1988		NCAA	II	16	—	—	—	—	—	—	—	25	6	Boone, Jim
1992		NCAA	II	3	—	—	—	—	—	—	—	31	2	Boone, Jim

Year	M/W	Assn	Div	NAT	NIT	ARC	CCA	NCI	NCT	OLY	HLM	W	L	Coach
1993		NCAA	II	32	—	—	—	—	—	—	—	23	6	Boone, Jim
1994		NCAA	II	16	—	—	—	—	—	—	—	25	5	Boone, Jim
1995		NCAA	II	16	—	—	—	—	—	—	—	23	7	Boone, Jim
1996		NCAA	II	3	—	—	—	—	—	—	—	27	6	Boone, Jim
1998		NCAA	II	48	—	—	—	—	—	—	—	23	5	Brown, William H.

CALIFORNIA BAPTIST

Year	M/W	Assn	Div	NAT	NIT	ARC	CCA	NCI	NCT	OLY	HLM	W	L	Coach
1974	M	NCCAA		2	—	—	—	—	—	—	—	X	X	Evans, Floyd C.
1976		NAIA		16	—	—	—	—	—	—	—	28	4	Evans, Floyd C.
1982	W	NAIA		8	—	—	—	—	—	—	—	25	6	King, David F.
1986		NCCAA	I	6	—	—	—	—	—	—	—	19	15	King, David F.

CALIFORNIA CHRISTIAN

Year	M/W	Assn	Div	NAT	NIT	ARC	CCA	NCI	NCT	OLY	HLM	W	L	Coach
1991	M	NBCAA	II	4	—	—	—	—	—	—	—	23	8	Crank, Frank
1996		LCC		6	—	—	—	—	—	—	—	8	17	McAllister, Jim
1998		NBCAA		3	—	—	—	—	—	—	—	30	8	Wilkerson, Dr. Charles
1998		NSCAA		3	—	—	—	—	—	—	—	30	8	Wilkerson, Dr. Charles

CALIFORNIA LUTHERAN

Year	M/W	Assn	Div	NAT	NIT	ARC	CCA	NCI	NCT	OLY	HLM	W	L	Coach
1992	M	NCAA	III	16	—	—	—	—	—	—	—	16	12	Dunlop, Mike
1993		NCAA	III	32	—	—	—	—	—	—	—	20	7	Dunlop, Mike
1994		NCAA	III	16	—	—	—	—	—	—	—	25	3	Dunlop, Mike
1995	W	NCAA	III	64	—	—	—	—	—	—	—	23	3	La Kose, Tim
1998		NCAA	III	48	—	—	—	—	—	—	—	17	8	La Kose, Tim

CALIFORNIA POLYTECHNIC: POMONA

Year	M/W	Assn	Div	NAT	NIT	ARC	CCA	NCI	NCT	OLY	HLM	W	L	Coach
1962	M	NCAA	II	16	—	—	—	—	—	—	—	17	8	Stull, Robert B. "Lefty"
1964		NCAA	II	8	—	—	—	—	—	—	—	23	6	Stull, Robert B. "Lefty"
1976		NCAA	II	24	—	—	—	—	—	—	—	16	13	Hogan, Don
1975	W	AIAW	S	5	—	—	—	—	—	—	—	16	6	May, Darlene
1976		AIAW	S	8	—	—	—	—	—	—	—	20	6	May, Darlene
1977		AIAW	S	5	—	—	—	—	—	—	—	28	6	May, Darlene
1980		AIAW	II	8	—	—	—	—	—	—	—	27	13	May, Darlene
1981		AIAW	II	3	—	—	—	—	—	—	—	30	9	May, Darlene
1982		NCAA	II	1	—	—	—	—	—	—	—	29	7	May, Darlene
1983		NCAA	II	2	—	—	—	—	—	—	—	29	3	May, Darlene
1984		NCAA	II	16	—	—	—	—	—	—	—	22	7	May, Darlene
1985		NCAA	II	1	—	—	—	—	—	—	—	21	7	May, Darlene
1986		NCAA	II	1	—	—	—	—	—	—	—	30	3	May, Darlene
1987		NCAA	II	2	—	—	—	—	—	—	—	29	3	May, Darlene
1988		NCAA	II	8	—	—	—	—	—	—	—	28	4	May, Darlene
1989		NCAA	II	2	—	—	—	—	—	—	—	28	6	May, Darlene
1990		NCAA	II	3	—	—	—	—	—	—	—	29	4	May, Darlene
1991		NCAA	II	8	—	—	—	—	—	—	—	22	9	May, Darlene
1992		NCAA	II	32	—	—	—	—	—	—	—	23	6	May, Darlene
1993		NCAA	II	8	—	—	—	—	—	—	—	27	3	May, Darlene
1997		NCAA	II	32	—	—	—	—	—	—	—	22	8	Thomas, Paul
1998		NCAA	II	48	—	—	—	—	—	—	—	18	11	Thomas, Paul

Year	M/W	Assn	Div	NAT	NIT	ARC	CCA	NCI	NCT	OLY	HLM	W	L	Coach
CALIFORNIA POLYTECHNIC: SAN LUIS OBISPO
1971	M	NCAA	II	24	—	—	—	—	—	—	—	17	11	Stoner, Neale R.
1974		NCAA	II	24	—	—	—	—	—	—	—	18	10	Wheeler, Ernie
1977		NCAA	II	8	—	—	—	—	—	—	—	19	11	Wheeler, Ernie
1980		NCAA	II	16	—	—	—	—	—	—	—	22	7	Wheeler, Ernie
1981		NCAA	II	3	—	—	—	—	—	—	—	24	8	Wheeler, Ernie
1982		NCAA	II	16	—	—	—	—	—	—	—	23	6	Wheeler, Ernie
1986		NCAA	II	32	—	—	—	—	—	—	—	23	8	Wheeler, Ernie
CALIFORNIA STATE: BAKERSFIELD
1973	M	NCAA	II	16	—	—	—	—	—	—	—	19	9	Larson, Jim
1976		NCAA	II	16	—	—	—	—	—	—	—	23	5	Wenihan, Pat
1982		NCAA	II	4	—	—	—	—	—	—	—	25	6	Dye, Bobby
1983		NCAA	II	3	—	—	—	—	—	—	—	25	5	Dye, Bobby
1984		NCAA	II	32	—	—	—	—	—	—	—	21	8	Parks, Jim
1988		NCAA	II	24	—	—	—	—	—	—	—	21	10	Douglass, Pat
1989		NCAA	II	16	—	—	—	—	—	—	—	21	9	Douglass, Pat
1990		NCAA	II	2	—	—	—	—	—	—	—	29	5	Douglass, Pat
1991		NCAA	II	3	—	—	—	—	—	—	—	25	8	Douglass, Pat
1992		NCAA	II	3	—	—	—	—	—	—	—	26	7	Douglass, Pat
1993		NCAA	II	1	—	—	—	—	—	—	—	33	0	Douglass, Pat
1994		NCAA	II	1	—	—	—	—	—	—	—	27	6	Douglass, Pat
1995		NCAA	II	48	—	—	—	—	—	—	—	20	8	Douglass, Pat
1996		NCAA	II	8	—	—	—	—	—	—	—	26	4	Douglass, Pat
1997		NCAA	II	1	—	—	—	—	—	—	—	29	4	Douglass, Pat
1998		NCAA	II	32	—	—	—	—	—	—	—	25	3	Clark, Henry
CALIFORNIA STATE: CHICO
1958	M	NCAA	II	24	—	—	—	—	—	—	—	10	17	Maxey, Gene
1974		NCAA	II	32	—	—	—	—	—	—	—	20	10	Mathiesen, Peter
1981		NCAA	II	32	—	—	—	—	—	—	—	18	11	Mathiesen, Peter
1991		NCAA	II	32	—	—	—	—	—	—	—	22	10	Smith, Prescott "Puck"
1992		NCAA	II	32	—	—	—	—	—	—	—	22	10	Smith, Prescott "Puck"
1993		NCAA	II	32	—	—	—	—	—	—	—	23	5	Smith, Prescott "Puck"
1987	W	NCAA	II	16	—	—	—	—	—	—	—	23	7	Coslet, Fran
1988		NCAA	II	32	—	—	—	—	—	—	—	19	10	Coslet, Fran
1996		NCAA	II	32	—	—	—	—	—	—	—	23	8	Lazzarini, Mary Ann
CALIFORNIA STATE: DOMINGUEZ HILLS
1979	M	NAIA		32	—	—	—	—	—	—	—	21	9	Yanai, David
1981		NCAA	II	16	—	—	—	—	—	—	—	20	5	Yanai, David
1987		NCAA	II	32	—	—	—	—	—	—	—	22	9	Yanai, David
1989		NCAA	II	24	—	—	—	—	—	—	—	20	10	Yanai, David
1995	W	NCAA	II	32	—	—	—	—	—	—	—	22	6	Girard, Van
1996		NCAA	II	48	—	—	—	—	—	—	—	21	8	Girard, Van
CALIFORNIA STATE: FRESNO
1958	M	NCAA	II	16	—	—	—	—	—	—	—	19	8	Vandenburgh, William G.
1960		NCAA	II	16	—	—	—	—	—	—	—	18	10	Vandenburgh, William G.
1962		NCAA	II	32	—	—	—	—	—	—	—	19	7	Miller, Harry E.
1963		NCAA	II	8	—	—	—	—	—	—	—	20	8	Miller, Harry E.

Year	M/W	Assn	Div	NAT	NIT	ARC	CCA	NCI	NCT	OLY	HLM	W	L	Coach
1964		NCAA	II	16	—	—	—	—	—	—	—	20	5	Miller, Harry E.
1965		NCAA	II	16	—	—	—	—	—	—	—	20	7	Miller, Harry E.
1966		NCAA	II	8	—	—	—	—	—	—	—	21	8	Gregory, Ed
1981		NCAA	I	48	—	—	—	—	—	—	—	25	4	Grant, Boyd "Tiny"
1982		NCAA	I	16	—	—	—	—	—	—	—	27	3	Grant, Boyd "Tiny"
1983		NCAA	I	—	1	—	—	—	—	—	—	25	10	Grant, Boyd "Tiny"
1984		NCAA	I	48	—	—	—	—	—	—	—	25	8	Grant, Boyd "Tiny"
1985		NCAA	I	—	8	—	—	—	—	—	—	23	9	Grant, Boyd "Tiny"
1994		NCAA	I	—	8	—	—	—	—	—	—	21	11	Colson, Gary W.
1996		NCAA	I	—	8	—	—	—	—	—	—	22	11	Tarkanian, Jerry
1997		NCAA	I	—	32	—	—	—	—	—	—	20	12	Tarkanian, Jerry
1998		NCAA	I	—	4	—	—	—	—	—	—	21	13	Tarkanian, Jerry
1974	W	AIAW		16	—	—	—	—	—	—	—	10	11	Pickel, Donna
1986		NCAA	I	—	8	—	—	—	—	—	—	21	9	Spencer, Robert L.
1990		NCAA	I	—	5	—	—	—	—	—	—	21	12	Spencer, Robert L.

CALIFORNIA STATE: FULLERTON

Year	M/W	Assn	Div	NAT	NIT	ARC	CCA	NCI	NCT	OLY	HLM	W	L	Coach
1962	M	NAIA		8	—	—	—	—	—	—	—	24	7	Omalev, Alex
1978		NCAA	I	8	—	—	—	—	—	—	—	23	9	Dye, Bobby
1983		NCAA	I	—	32	—	—	—	—	—	—	21	8	McQuarn, George
1987		NCAA	I	—	32	—	—	—	—	—	—	17	13	McQuarn, George
1970	W	AIAW		1	—	—	—	—	—	—	—	17	1	Moore, Billie Jean
1971		AIAW		5	—	—	—	—	—	—	—	20	1	Moore, Billie Jean
1972		AIAW		3	—	—	—	—	—	—	—	19	1	Moore, Billie Jean
1974		AIAW		12	—	—	—	—	—	—	—	19	2	Moore, Billie Jean
1975		AIAW	L	3	—	—	—	—	—	—	—	19	4	Moore, Billie Jean
1976		AIAW	L	12	—	—	—	—	—	—	—	14	5	Moore, Billie Jean
1977		AIAW	L	16	—	—	—	—	—	—	—	19	2	Moore, Billie Jean
1985		NCAA	I	—	5	—	—	—	—	—	—	19	11	Gobrecht, Chris
1989		NCAA	I	48	—	—	—	—	—	—	—	21	9	Jeremiah, Dr. Maryalyce
1991		NCAA	I	32	—	—	—	—	—	—	—	25	8	Jeremiah, Dr. Maryalyce

CALIFORNIA STATE: HAYWARD

Year	M/W	Assn	Div	NAT	NIT	ARC	CCA	NCI	NCT	OLY	HLM	W	L	Coach
1977	M	NCAA	II	32	—	—	—	—	—	—	—	16	13	Staggers, Jonathan L.
1985		NCAA	II	8	—	—	—	—	—	—	—	21	8	Hulst, Gary
1986		NCAA	II	8	—	—	—	—	—	—	—	24	8	Hulst, Gary
1987		NCAA	II	24	—	—	—	—	—	—	—	12	19	Hulst, Gary
1988		NCAA	II	16	—	—	—	—	—	—	—	18	13	Hulst, Gary
1989	W	NCAA	II	32	—	—	—	—	—	—	—	13	15	Oten, Barbara

CALIFORNIA STATE: LONG BEACH

Year	M/W	Assn	Div	NAT	NIT	ARC	CCA	NCI	NCT	OLY	HLM	W	L	Coach
1961	M	NCAA	II	16	—	—	—	—	—	—	—	15	11	Perry, Richard H.
1970		NCAA	I	16	—	—	—	—	—	—	—	24	5	Tarkanian, Jerry
1971		NCAA	I	8	—	—	—	—	—	—	—	24	5	Tarkanian, Jerry
1972		NCAA	I	8	—	—	—	—	—	—	—	25	4	Tarkanian, Jerry
1973		NCAA	I	12	—	—	—	—	—	—	—	26	3	Tarkanian, Jerry
1977		NCAA	I	32	—	—	—	—	—	—	—	21	8	Jones, Dwight
1980		NCAA	I	—	16	—	—	—	—	—	—	22	12	Winter, Fred "Tex"
1988		NCAA	I	—	32	—	—	—	—	—	—	17	12	Harrington, Joe

Year	M/W	Assn	Div	NAT	NIT	ARC	CCA	NCI	NCT	OLY	HLM	W	L	Coach
1990		NCAA	I	—	16	—	—	—	—	—	—	23	9	Harrington, Joe
1992		NCAA	I	—	32	—	—	—	—	—	—	18	12	Greenberg, Seth
1993		NCAA	I	64	—	—	—	—	—	—	—	22	10	Greenberg, Seth
1995		NCAA	I	64	—	—	—	—	—	—	—	20	10	Greenberg, Seth
1972	W	AIAW		6	—	—	—	—	—	—	—	13	6	Schaafsma, Dr. Frances
1973		AIAW		16	—	—	—	—	—	—	—	13	5	Schaafsma, Dr. Frances
1976		AIAW	L	12	—	—	—	—	—	—	—	18	7	Schaafsma, Dr. Frances
1978		AIAW	L	—	4	—	—	—	—	—	—	18	9	Schaafsma, Dr. Frances
1979		AIAW	L	16	—	—	—	—	—	—	—	24	8	Schaafsma, Dr. Frances
1980		AIAW	I	8	—	—	—	—	—	—	—	28	6	Bonvicini, Joan
1981		AIAW	I	8	—	—	—	—	—	—	—	27	7	Bonvicini, Joan
1982		NCAA	I	16	—	—	—	—	—	—	—	24	6	Bonvicini, Joan
1983		NCAA	I	8	—	—	—	—	—	—	—	24	7	Bonvicini, Joan
1984		NCAA	I	8	—	—	—	—	—	—	—	25	6	Bonvicini, Joan
1985		NCAA	I	8	—	—	—	—	—	—	—	28	3	Bonvicini, Joan
1986		NCAA	I	16	—	—	—	—	—	—	—	29	5	Bonvicini, Joan
1987		NCAA	I	3	—	—	—	—	—	—	—	33	3	Bonvicini, Joan
1988		NCAA	I	3	—	—	—	—	—	—	—	28	6	Bonvicini, Joan
1989		NCAA	I	8	—	—	—	—	—	—	—	30	5	Bonvicini, Joan
1990		NCAA	I	32	—	—	—	—	—	—	—	25	9	Bonvicini, Joan
1991		NCAA	I	16	—	—	—	—	—	—	—	24	8	Bonvicini, Joan
1992		NCAA	I	48	—	—	—	—	—	—	—	21	10	McDonald, Glenn

CALIFORNIA STATE: LOS ANGELES

Year	M/W	Assn	Div	NAT	NIT	ARC	CCA	NCI	NCT	OLY	HLM	W	L	Coach
1957	M	NCAA	II	4	—	—	—	—	—	—	—	20	11	Elliott, Abe "Sax"
1959		NCAA	II	4	—	—	—	—	—	—	—	20	8	Elliott, Abe "Sax"
1974		NCAA	I	25	—	—	—	—	—	—	—	17	10	Miller, Robert
1995		NCAA	II	24	—	—	—	—	—	—	—	18	12	Dyer, Henry
1998		NCAA	II	32	—	—	—	—	—	—	—	18	11	Yanai, David
1980	W	AIAW	II	16	—	—	—	—	—	—	—	19	13	Marquis, Richard

CALIFORNIA STATE: NORTHRIDGE

Year	M/W	Assn	Div	NAT	NIT	ARC	CCA	NCI	NCT	OLY	HLM	W	L	Coach
1978	M	NCAA	II	16	—	—	—	—	—	—	—	22	7	Cassidy, Peter L.
1979		NCAA	II	32	—	—	—	—	—	—	—	20	9	Cassidy, Peter L.
1985		NCAA	II	16	—	—	—	—	—	—	—	20	10	Cassidy, Peter L.
1986	W	NCAA	II	16	—	—	—	—	—	—	—	20	9	Milke, Leslie
1989		NCAA	II	16	—	—	—	—	—	—	—	22	9	Milke, Leslie

CALIFORNIA STATE: SACRAMENTO

Year	M/W	Assn	Div	NAT	NIT	ARC	CCA	NCI	NCT	OLY	HLM	W	L	Coach
1959	M	NCAA	II	32	—	—	—	—	—	—	—	12	12	Wolf, Harold
1962		NCAA	II	2	—	—	—	—	—	—	—	21	10	Shelton, Everett F.
1970		NCAA	II	32	—	—	—	—	—	—	—	17	11	Heron, Jack
1988		NCAA	II	32	—	—	—	—	—	—	—	22	8	Anders, Joe

CALIFORNIA STATE: SAN BERNARDINO

Year	M/W	Assn	Div	NAT	NIT	ARC	CCA	NCI	NCT	OLY	HLM	W	L	Coach
1989	M	NCAA	III	40	—	—	—	—	—	—	—	20	6	Ducey, James
1988	W	NCAA	III	32	—	—	—	—	—	—	—	23	5	Bly, Jo Anne
1990		NCAA	III	32	—	—	—	—	—	—	—	24	4	Schwartz, Gary
1994		NCAA	II	2	—	—	—	—	—	—	—	29	4	Beckley, Luvina
1998		NCAA	II	32	—	—	—	—	—	—	—	23	6	Becker, Kevin

Year	M/W	Assn	Div	NAT	NIT	ARC	CCA	NCI	NCT	OLY	HLM	W	L	Coach

CALIFORNIA STATE: STANISLAUS

Year	M/W	Assn	Div	NAT	NIT	ARC	CCA	NCI	NCT	OLY	HLM	W	L	Coach
1981	M	NCAA	III	32	—	—	—	—	—	—	—	16	12	Sanderson, Douglas R.
1982		NCAA	III	4	—	—	—	—	—	—	—	18	13	Sanderson, Douglas R.
1983		NCAA	III	8	—	—	—	—	—	—	—	16	13	Sanderson, Douglas R.
1987		NCAA	III	16	—	—	—	—	—	—	—	20	8	Thomason, Bob
1989		NCAA	III	8	—	—	—	—	—	—	—	21	8	Jones, John L.
1985	W	NCAA	III	16	—	—	—	—	—	—	—	23	6	Millar, Leann Henrich
1987		NCAA	III	32	—	—	—	—	—	—	—	19	9	Millar, Leann Henrich
1988		NCAA	III	24	—	—	—	—	—	—	—	22	5	Millar, Leann Henrich
1989		NCAA	III	2	—	—	—	—	—	—	—	27	2	Millar, Leann Henrich
1990		NCAA	II	16	—	—	—	—	—	—	—	22	7	Millar, Leann Henrich
1991		NCAA	II	32	—	—	—	—	—	—	—	21	8	Millar, Leann Henrich

CALIFORNIA: DAVIS

Year	M/W	Assn	Div	NAT	NIT	ARC	CCA	NCI	NCT	OLY	HLM	W	L	Coach
1967	M	NCAA	II	23	—	—	—	—	—	—	—	21	7	Carlson, Joe E.
1968		NCAA	II	32	—	—	—	—	—	—	—	16	11	Hamilton, Robert I.
1969		NCAA	II	32	—	—	—	—	—	—	—	18	10	Hamilton, Robert I.
1975		NCAA	II	24	—	—	—	—	—	—	—	16	12	Hamilton, Robert I.
1976		NCAA	II	32	—	—	—	—	—	—	—	18	10	Hamilton, Robert I.
1978		NCAA	II	32	—	—	—	—	—	—	—	19	10	Hamilton, Robert I.
1995		NCAA	II	32	—	—	—	—	—	—	—	20	11	Williams, Bob
1996		NCAA	II	32	—	—	—	—	—	—	—	24	6	Williams, Bob
1997		NCAA	II	48	—	—	—	—	—	—	—	20	9	Williams, Bob
1998		NCAA	II	1	—	—	—	—	—	—	—	31	2	Williams, Bob
1971	W	AIAW		8	—	—	—	—	—	—	—	X	X	Unknown
1981		AIAW	III	8	—	—	—	—	—	—	—	23	8	Gill, Pam
1986		NCAA	II	24	—	—	—	—	—	—	—	18	9	Gill, Pam
1988		NCAA	II	32	—	—	—	—	—	—	—	18	11	Gill, Pam
1990		NCAA	II	32	—	—	—	—	—	—	—	20	8	Hoehn, Jorja E.
1991		NCAA	II	16	—	—	—	—	—	—	—	26	5	Hoehn, Jorja E.
1992		NCAA	II	16	—	—	—	—	—	—	—	25	3	Hoehn, Jorja E.
1993		NCAA	II	32	—	—	—	—	—	—	—	19	7	Hoehn, Jorja E.
1994		NCAA	II	32	—	—	—	—	—	—	—	22	7	Hoehn, Jorja E.
1995		NCAA	II	16	—	—	—	—	—	—	—	25	4	Hoehn, Jorja E.
1996		NCAA	II	16	—	—	—	—	—	—	—	25	4	Hoehn, Jorja E.
1997		NCAA	II	3	—	—	—	—	—	—	—	29	3	Simpson, Sandy
1998		NCAA	II	16	—	—	—	—	—	—	—	23	7	Hoehn, Jorja E.

CALIFORNIA: IRVINE

Year	M/W	Assn	Div	NAT	NIT	ARC	CCA	NCI	NCT	OLY	HLM	W	L	Coach
1968	M	NCAA	II	16	—	—	—	—	—	—	—	20	8	Davis, Richard L.
1969		NCAA	II	24	—	—	—	—	—	—	—	19	9	Davis, Richard L.
1972		NCAA	II	32	—	—	—	—	—	—	—	16	12	Tift, Timothy
1975		NCAA	II	32	—	—	—	—	—	—	—	16	11	Tift, Timothy
1982		NCAA	I	—	16	—	—	—	—	—	—	23	7	Mulligan, William
1986		NCAA	I	—	16	—	—	—	—	—	—	17	13	Mulligan, William
1995	W	NCAA	I	64	—	—	—	—	—	—	—	19	11	Matsuhara, Colleen

Year	M/W	Assn	Div	NAT	NIT	ARC	CCA	NCI	NCT	OLY	HLM	W	L	Coach
CALIFORNIA: LOS ANGELES														
1950	M	NCAA		8	—	—	—	—	—	—	—	24	7	Wooden, John R.
1952		NCAA		16	—	—	—	—	—	—	—	20	12	Wooden, John R.
1956		NCAA		12	—	—	—	—	—	—	—	22	6	Wooden, John R.
1962		NCAA	I	4	—	—	—	—	—	—	—	18	11	Wooden, John R.
1963		NCAA	I	16	—	—	—	—	—	—	—	20	9	Wooden, John R.
1964		NCAA	I	1	—	—	—	—	—	—	1	30	0	Wooden, John R.
1965		NCAA	I	1	—	—	—	—	—	—	1	28	2	Wooden, John R.
1967		NCAA	I	1	—	—	—	—	—	—	1	30	0	Wooden, John R.
1968		NCAA	I	1	—	—	—	—	—	—	1	29	1	Wooden, John R.
1969		NCAA	I	1	—	—	—	—	—	—	1	29	1	Wooden, John R.
1970		NCAA	I	1	—	—	—	—	—	—	1	28	2	Wooden, John R.
1971		NCAA	I	1	—	—	—	—	—	—	1	29	1	Wooden, John R.
1972		NCAA	I	1	—	—	—	—	—	—	1	30	0	Wooden, John R.
1973		NCAA	I	1	—	—	—	—	—	—	1	30	0	Wooden, John R.
1974		NCAA	I	3	—	—	—	—	—	—	—	26	4	Wooden, John R.
1975		NCAA	I	1	—	—	—	—	—	—	1	28	3	Wooden, John R.
1976		NCAA	I	3	—	—	—	—	—	—	—	27	5	Bartow, B. Gene
1977		NCAA	I	16	—	—	—	—	—	—	—	24	5	Bartow, B. Gene
1978		NCAA	I	16	—	—	—	—	—	—	—	25	3	Cunningham, Dr. Gary A.
1979		NCAA	I	8	—	—	—	—	—	—	—	25	5	Cunningham, Dr. Gary A.
1980		NCAA	I	2	—	—	—	—	—	—	—	22	10	Brown, Lawrence H.
1981		NCAA	I	32	—	—	—	—	—	—	—	20	7	Brown, Lawrence H.
1983		NCAA	I	32	—	—	—	—	—	—	—	23	6	Farmer, Larry
1985		NCAA	I	—	1	—	—	—	—	—	—	21	12	Hazzard, Walter R., Jr.
1986		NCAA	I	—	32	—	—	—	—	—	—	15	14	Hazzard, Walter R., Jr.
1987		NCAA	I	32	—	—	—	—	—	—	—	25	7	Hazzard, Walter R., Jr.
1989		NCAA	I	32	—	—	—	—	—	—	—	21	10	Harrick, Jim
1990		NCAA	I	16	—	—	—	—	—	—	—	22	11	Harrick, Jim
1991		NCAA	I	64	—	—	—	—	—	—	—	23	9	Harrick, Jim
1992		NCAA	I	8	—	—	—	—	—	—	—	28	5	Harrick, Jim
1993		NCAA	I	32	—	—	—	—	—	—	—	22	11	Harrick, Jim
1994		NCAA	I	64	—	—	—	—	—	—	—	21	7	Harrick, Jim
1995		NCAA	I	1	—	—	—	—	—	—	—	31	2	Harrick, Jim
1996		NCAA	I	64	—	—	—	—	—	—	—	23	8	Harrick, Jim
1997		NCAA	I	8	—	—	—	—	—	—	—	24	8	Lavin, Steve
1998		NCAA	I	16	—	—	—	—	—	—	—	24	9	Lavin, Steve
1974	W	AIAW		—	4	—	—	—	—	—	—	X	X	Chaffee, Bob
1975		AIAW	L	—	2	—	—	—	—	—	—	18	4	Washington, Kenny
1976		AIAW	L	—	2	—	—	—	—	—	—	19	4	Hanson, Ellen Mosher
1977		AIAW	L	—	2	—	—	—	—	—	—	20	3	Hanson, Ellen Mosher
1978		AIAW	L	1	—	—	—	—	—	—	—	27	3	Moore, Billie Jean
1979		AIAW	L	4	—	—	—	—	—	—	—	24	10	Moore, Billie Jean
1981		AIAW	I	8	—	—	—	—	—	—	—	29	7	Moore, Billie Jean
1983		NCAA	I	32	—	—	—	—	—	—	—	18	11	Moore, Billie Jean
1985		NCAA	I	16	—	—	—	—	—	—	—	20	10	Moore, Billie Jean
1990		NCAA	I	48	—	—	—	—	—	—	—	17	12	Moore, Billie Jean
1992		NCAA	I	16	—	—	—	—	—	—	—	21	10	Moore, Billie Jean
1998		NCAA	I	32	—	—	—	—	—	—	—	20	9	Oliver, Kathy

Year	M/W	Assn	Div	NAT	NIT	ARC	CCA	NCI	NCT	OLY	HLM	W	L	Coach
CALIFORNIA: RIVERSIDE														
1970	M	NCAA	II	3	—	—	—	—	—	—	—	19	10	Goss, Freddie
1972		NCAA	II	24	—	—	—	—	—	—	—	19	9	Goss, Freddie
1973		NCAA	II	8	—	—	—	—	—	—	—	25	5	Goss, Freddie
1974		NCAA	II	8	—	—	—	—	—	—	—	18	10	Goss, Freddie
1975		NCAA	II	8	—	—	—	—	—	—	—	19	9	Goss, Freddie
1979		NCAA	II	16	—	—	—	—	—	—	—	21	5	Goss, Freddie
1980		NCAA	II	8	—	—	—	—	—	—	—	22	6	Masi, John
1984		NCAA	II	32	—	—	—	—	—	—	—	22	6	Masi, John
1986		NCAA	II	24	—	—	—	—	—	—	—	24	7	Masi, John
1988		NCAA	II	16	—	—	—	—	—	—	—	22	8	Masi, John
1989		NCAA	II	3	—	—	—	—	—	—	—	30	4	Masi, John
1990		NCAA	II	32	—	—	—	—	—	—	—	21	10	Masi, John
1991		NCAA	II	24	—	—	—	—	—	—	—	22	7	Masi, John
1992		NCAA	II	16	—	—	—	—	—	—	—	24	6	Masi, John
1994		NCAA	II	16	—	—	—	—	—	—	—	22	7	Masi, John
1995		NCAA	II	2	—	—	—	—	—	—	—	26	6	Masi, John
1997		NCAA	II	48	—	—	—	—	—	—	—	17	9	Masi, John
1973	W	AIAW		6	—	—	—	—	—	—	—	X	X	Knox, Donna J.
1993		NCAA	II	32	—	—	—	—	—	—	—	17	11	Woelke, Debi
1995		NCAA	II	48	—	—	—	—	—	—	—	19	10	Woelke, Debi
1996		NCAA	II	48	—	—	—	—	—	—	—	17	13	Woelke, Debi
CALIFORNIA: SAN DIEGO														
1990	M	NCAA	III	32	—	—	—	—	—	—	—	20	7	Marshall, Thomas O.
1991		NCAA	III	16	—	—	—	—	—	—	—	23	4	Marshall, Thomas O.
1992		NCAA	III	32	—	—	—	—	—	—	—	22	5	Marshall, Thomas O.
1994		NCAA	III	32	—	—	—	—	—	—	—	21	5	Marshall, Thomas O.
1995	W	NCAA	III	64	—	—	—	—	—	—	—	18	7	Malone, Judy
1996		NCAA	III	32	—	—	—	—	—	—	—	19	7	Malone, Judy
1997		NCAA	III	32	—	—	—	—	—	—	—	20	6	Malone, Judy
1998		NCAA	III	32	—	—	—	—	—	—	—	23	4	Malone, Judy
CALIFORNIA: SANTA BARBARA														
1941	M	NAIA		4	—	—	—	—	—	—	—	22	10	Wilton, Wilton M. "Willie"
1961		NCAA	II	8	—	—	—	—	—	—	—	20	8	Gallon, Dr. Arthur J.
1963		NCAA	II	24	—	—	—	—	—	—	—	16	9	Gallon, Dr. Arthur J.
1988		NCAA	I	64	—	—	—	—	—	—	—	22	8	Pimm, Jerry
1989		NCAA	I	—	32	—	—	—	—	—	—	21	9	Pimm, Jerry
1990		NCAA	I	32	—	—	—	—	—	—	—	21	9	Pimm, Jerry
1992		NCAA	I	—	32	—	—	—	—	—	—	20	9	Pimm, Jerry
1993		NCAA	I	—	32	—	—	—	—	—	—	18	11	Pimm, Jerry
1992	W	NCAA	I	32	—	—	—	—	—	—	—	27	5	French, Mark
1993		NCAA	I	32	—	—	—	—	—	—	—	19	12	French, Mark
1996		NCAA	I	—	5	—	—	—	—	—	—	24	7	French, Mark
1997		NCAA	I	64	—	—	—	—	—	—	—	24	6	French, Mark
1998		NCAA	I	32	—	—	—	—	—	—	—	27	6	French, Mark
CALVARY (KY)														
1970	M	NCCAA		8	—	—	—	—	—	—	—			

Year	M/W	Assn	Div	NAT	NIT	ARC	CCA	NCI	NCT	OLY	HLM	W	L	Coach
CALVARY BIBLE														
1981	M	NBCAA		1	—	—	—	—	—	—	—	22	4	Schneeberger, Robert W.
1982		NBCAA		1	—	—	—	—	—	—	—	26	1	Schneeberger, Robert W.
1983		NBCAA		7	—	—	—	—	—	—	—	15	11	Schneeberger, Robert W.
1985		NBCAA	I	5	—	—	—	—	—	—	—	20	12	Schneeberger, Robert W.
1986		NBCAA	I	8	—	—	—	—	—	—	—	19	8	Schneeberger, Robert W.
1987		NBCAA	I	5	—	—	—	—	—	—	—	19	9	Schneeberger, Robert W.
1988		NBCAA	I	6	—	—	—	—	—	—	—	21	7	Miller, Steve
1989		NBCAA	I	4	—	—	—	—	—	—	—	23	5	Miller, Steve
1990		NBCAA	I	2	—	—	—	—	—	—	—	25	3	Miller, Steve
1991		NBCAA	I	7	—	—	—	—	—	—	—	17	11	Miller, Steve
1992		NBCAA	I	7	—	—	—	—	—	—	—	17	11	Miller, Steve
1993		NBCAA	I	5	—	—	—	—	—	—	—	15	12	Miller, Steve
1994		NCCAA	IIA	5	—	—	—	—	—	—	—	18	12	Miller, Steve
1983	W	NBCAA		2	—	—	—	—	—	—	—	9	7	Hensarling, Anne
1984		NBCAA		2	—	—	—	—	—	—	—	9	5	Hensarling, Anne
1985		NBCAA		4	—	—	—	—	—	—	—	6	15	Hensarling, Anne
1986		NBCAA		4	—	—	—	—	—	—	—	6	8	Hensarling, Anne
1987		NBCAA		3	—	—	—	—	—	—	—	16	7	Hensarling, Anne
1988		NBCAA		3	—	—	—	—	—	—	—	9	9	Hensarling, Anne
1989		NBCAA		1	—	—	—	—	—	—	—	16	1	Hensarling, Anne
1990		NBCAA		1	—	—	—	—	—	—	—	12	9	Shook, John
1991		NBCAA		4	—	—	—	—	—	—	—	3	15	Rose, Brenda
1993		NBCAA		5	—	—	—	—	—	—	—	5	7	Rose, Brenda
CALVIN														
1980	M	NCAA	III	24	—	—	—	—	—	—	—	18	6	Vroon, A. Donald
1981		NCAA	III	32	—	—	—	—	—	—	—	15	11	Vroon, A. Donald
1986		NCAA	III	32	—	—	—	—	—	—	—	20	6	Douma, Edward
1987		NCAA	III	24	—	—	—	—	—	—	—	21	5	Douma, Edward
1989		NCAA	III	24	—	—	—	—	—	—	—	19	7	Douma, Edward
1990		NCAA	III	4	—	—	—	—	—	—	—	28	3	Douma, Edward
1991		NCAA	III	8	—	—	—	—	—	—	—	25	4	Douma, Edward
1992		NCAA	III	1	—	—	—	—	—	—	—	31	1	Douma, Edward
1993		NCAA	III	8	—	—	—	—	—	—	—	25	3	Douma, Edward
1994		NCAA	III	32	—	—	—	—	—	—	—	20	7	Douma, Edward
1995		NCAA	III	64	—	—	—	—	—	—	—	17	10	Douma, Edward
1988	W	NCAA	III	24	—	—	—	—	—	—	—	21	5	Vroon, A. Donald
1991		NCAA	III	32	—	—	—	—	—	—	—	18	8	Vroon, A. Donald
1993		NCAA	III	32	—	—	—	—	—	—	—	18	8	Struyk, Sandi
1996		NCAA	III	32	—	—	—	—	—	—	—	23	4	Afman, Gregg
1997		NCAA	III	32	—	—	—	—	—	—	—	23	4	Afman, Gregg
1998		NCAA	III	32	—	—	—	—	—	—	—	23	5	Afman, Gregg
CAMERON														
1974	M	NAIA		32	—	—	—	—	—	—	—	24	6	Miller, Raymond H. "Red"
1979		NAIA		8	—	—	—	—	—	—	—	34	2	Nichols, Lonnie
1980		NAIA		1	—	—	—	—	—	—	—	28	3	Nichols, Lonnie

Year	M/W	Assn	Div	NAT	NIT	ARC	CCA	NCI	NCT	OLY	HLM	W	L	Coach
CAMPBELL														
1970	M	NAIA		32	—	—	—	—	—	—	—	24	5	Roberts, Danny
1977		NAIA		2	—	—	—	—	—	—	—	23	10	Roberts, Danny
1992		NCAA	I	64	—	—	—	—	—	—	—	19	12	Lee, Billy
CAMPBELLSVILLE														
1981	M	NAIA		32	—	—	—	—	—	—	—	21	8	Cunningham, Lou
1991		NAIA		32	—	—	—	—	—	—	—	19	12	Cunningham, Lou
1983	W	NAIA		8	—	—	—	—	—	—	—	24	5	Wise, Donna H.
1990		NAIA		16	—	—	—	—	—	—	—	21	11	Wise, Donna H.
1991		NAIA		32	—	—	—	—	—	—	—	22	8	Wise, Donna H.
1992		NAIA	I	32	—	—	—	—	—	—	—	24	6	Wise, Donna H.
1993		NAIA	I	16	—	—	—	—	—	—	—	27	5	Wise, Donna H.
1994		NAIA	I	16	—	—	—	—	—	—	—	26	6	Wise, Donna H.
1995		NAIA	I	8	—	—	—	—	—	—	—	28	7	Wise, Donna H.
1996		NAIA	I	16	—	—	—	—	—	—	—	21	8	Wise, Donna H.
1997		NAIA	I	16	—	—	—	—	—	—	—	24	9	Wise, Donna H.
1998		NAIA	I	8	—	—	—	—	—	—	—	25	8	Wise, Donna H.
CANADIAN BIBLE														
1984	W	NBCAA		3	—	—	—	—	—	—	—			Moore, Timothy L.
CANISIUS														
1944	M	NCAA		—	8	—	—	—	—	—	—	15	6	Seelbach, Allie
1955		NCAA		8	—	—	—	—	—	—	—	18	7	Curran, J. Joseph
1956		NCAA		8	—	—	—	—	—	—	—	19	7	Curran, J. Joseph
1957		NCAA	I	12	—	—	—	—	—	—	—	22	6	Curran, J. Joseph
1963		NCAA	I	—	2	—	—	—	—	—	—	19	7	MacKinnon, Robert A.
1985		NCAA	I	—	32	—	—	—	—	—	—	20	10	Macarchuk, Nick, Jr.
1994		NCAA	I	—	32	—	—	—	—	—	—	22	7	Beilein, John
1995		NCAA	I	—	4	—	—	—	—	—	—	21	14	Beilein, John
1996		NCAA	I	64	—	—	—	—	—	—	—	19	11	Beilein, John
1982	W	AIAW	II	16	—	—	—	—	—	—	—	26	5	Pares, Sr. Maria
1983		NCAA	II	8	—	—	—	—	—	—	—	28	5	Pares, Sr. Maria
CANTERBURY														
1945	M	NAIA		8	—	—	—	—	—	—	—	14	12	Johnson, Glenn A.
1947		NAIA		16	—	—	—	—	—	—	—	13	9	Johnson, Glenn A.
CAPITAL														
1957	M	NCAA	II	32	—	—	—	—	—	—	—	14	6	Regan, Harold E.
1970		NCAA	II	24	—	—	—	—	—	—	—	20	4	Chickerella, Vincent
1973		NCAA	II	24	—	—	—	—	—	—	—	22	5	Chickerella, Vincent
1982		NCAA	III	8	—	—	—	—	—	—	—	20	9	Grube, David
1983		NCAA	III	24	—	—	—	—	—	—	—	22	7	Grube, David
1984		NCAA	III	24	—	—	—	—	—	—	—	23	6	Grube, David
1989		NCAA	III	40	—	—	—	—	—	—	—	21	7	Cecutti, Dave
1996		NCAA	III	32	—	—	—	—	—	—	—	19	8	Goodwin, Damon
1985	W	NCAA	III	16	—	—	—	—	—	—	—	23	2	Pirtle, Laurie
1986		NCAA	III	3	—	—	—	—	—	—	—	27	4	Pirtle, Laurie
1987		NCAA	III	32	—	—	—	—	—	—	—	21	5	Jeffers, Dixie M.
1991		NCAA	III	32	—	—	—	—	—	—	—	24	3	Jeffers, Dixie M.

Year	M/W	Assn	Div	NAT	NIT	ARC	CCA	NCI	NCT	OLY	HLM	W	L	Coach
1992		NCAA	III	8	—	—	—	—	—	—	—	—	29	2	Jeffers, Dixie M.
1993		NCAA	III	2	—	—	—	—	—	—	—	—	28	4	Jeffers, Dixie M.
1994		NCAA	III	1	—	—	—	—	—	—	—	—	30	1	Jeffers, Dixie M.
1995		NCAA	III	1	—	—	—	—	—	—	—	—	33	0	Jeffers, Dixie M.
1996		NCAA	III	32	—	—	—	—	—	—	—	—	23	5	Jeffers, Dixie M.
1997		NCAA	III	3	—	—	—	—	—	—	—	—	29	4	Jeffers, Dixie M.

CARDINAL STRITCH (WI)

Year	M/W	Assn	Div	NAT	NIT	ARC	CCA	NCI	NCT	OLY	HLM	W	L	Coach
1979	M	NSCAA		16	—	—	—	—	—	—	—	—	22	6	Stier, Dr. William F., Jr.
1983		NSCAA		16	—	—	—	—	—	—	—	—	11	19	Moore, Thomas J.
1984		NSCAA		16	—	—	—	—	—	—	—	—	17	16	Moore, Thomas J.
1985		NSCAA		16	—	—	—	—	—	—	—	—	14	19	Moore, Thomas J.
1986		NSCAA		12	—	—	—	—	—	—	—	—	23	12	Moore, Thomas J.
1998		NAIA	II	16	—	—	—	—	—	—	—	—	24	9	Fox, Denny
1992	W	NAIA	II	16	—	—	—	—	—	—	—	—	25	5	Panella, Richard 'Rich'
1996		NAIA	II	16	—	—	—	—	—	—	—	—	20	8	Panella, Richard 'Rich'
1997		NAIA	II	32	—	—	—	—	—	—	—	—	22	6	Panella, Richard 'Rich'
1998		NAIA	II	32	—	—	—	—	—	—	—	—	27	5	Panella, Richard 'Rich'

CARNEGIE MELLON

Year	M/W	Assn	Div	NAT	NIT	ARC	CCA	NCI	NCT	OLY	HLM	W	L	Coach
1977	M	NCAA	III	30	—	—	—	—	—	—	—	—	18	6	Maloney, Dave
1989	W	NCAA	III	32	—	—	—	—	—	—	—	—	20	7	Seidl, Gerri
1991		NCAA	III	32	—	—	—	—	—	—	—	—	21	6	Seidl, Gerri

CARROLL (MT)

Year	M/W	Assn	Div	NAT	NIT	ARC	CCA	NCI	NCT	OLY	HLM	W	L	Coach
1966	M	NAIA		16	—	—	—	—	—	—	—	—	20	12	Askew, Presley
1997		NAIA	I	32	—	—	—	—	—	—	—	—	22	11	Turcott, Gary

CARROLL (WI)

Year	M/W	Assn	Div	NAT	NIT	ARC	CCA	NCI	NCT	OLY	HLM	W	L	Coach
1954	M	NAIA		32	—	—	—	—	—	—	—	—	15	7	Huddleston, Don
1984	W	NCAA	III	32	—	—	—	—	—	—	—	—	20	6	Steffen, Daniel
1985		NCAA	III	32	—	—	—	—	—	—	—	—	22	6	Steffen, Daniel
1986		NCAA	III	32	—	—	—	—	—	—	—	—	21	7	Steffen, Daniel

CARSON-NEWMAN

Year	M/W	Assn	Div	NAT	NIT	ARC	CCA	NCI	NCT	OLY	HLM	W	L	Coach
1961	M	NAIA		32	—	—	—	—	—	—	—	—	26	7	Campbell, Richard
1962		NAIA		8	—	—	—	—	—	—	—	—	29	7	Campbell, Richard
1963		NAIA		8	—	—	—	—	—	—	—	—	25	4	Campbell, Richard
1964		NAIA		3	—	—	—	—	—	—	—	—	31	4	Campbell, Richard
1966		NAIA		8	—	—	—	—	—	—	—	—	25	6	Hamilton, Larry
1983		NAIA		8	—	—	—	—	—	—	—	—	31	5	Jones, Dr. Chris
1984		NAIA		32	—	—	—	—	—	—	—	—	31	8	Jones, Dr. Chris
1980	W	AIAW	II	24	—	—	—	—	—	—	—	—	28	8	Bivens, Lewis
1984		NAIA		16	—	—	—	—	—	—	—	—	26	6	Bivens, Lewis
1985		NAIA		8	—	—	—	—	—	—	—	—	32	3	Bivens, Lewis
1992		NAIA	I	32	—	—	—	—	—	—	—	—	22	11	Carter, Eddie
1993		NAIA	I	32	—	—	—	—	—	—	—	—	22	8	Carter, Eddie
1995		NCAA	II	48	—	—	—	—	—	—	—	—	21	9	Carter, Eddie
1998		NCAA	II	48	—	—	—	—	—	—	—	—	22	7	Carter, Eddie

Year	M/W	Assn	Div	NAT	NIT	ARC	CCA	NCI	NCT	OLY	HLM	W	L	Coach
CARTHAGE														
1996	W	NCAA	III	64	—	—	—	—	—	—	—	18	8	Fanning, Rich
CASTLETON STATE														
1985	M	NAIA		32	—	—	—	—	—	—	—	23	7	Van Gundy, Stan A.
1998		NAIA	II	32	—	—	—	—	—	—	—	19	8	Blake, Dave
1997	W	NAIA	II	32	—	—	—	—	—	—	—	21	6	Conover, Richard
1998		NAIA	II	32	—	—	—	—	—	—	—	21	7	Conover, Richard
CATAWBA														
1945	M	NAIA		16	—	—	—	—	—	—	—	16	5	Kirkland, Gordon A.
1982		NAIA		32	—	—	—	—	—	—	—	26	7	Moir, Sam A.
1983		NAIA		32	—	—	—	—	—	—	—	29	4	Moir, Sam A.
1998		NCAA	II	16	—	—	—	—	—	—	—	25	6	Baker, Jim
1993	W	NAIA	I	32	—	—	—	—	—	—	—	24	9	Peters, Gary
CATHOLIC														
1944	M	NCAA		8	—	—	—	—	—	—	—	17	7	Long, John J.
1964		NCAA	II	32	—	—	—	—	—	—	—	16	12	Young, Thomas J.
1993		NCAA	III	40	—	—	—	—	—	—	—	21	6	Lonergan, Mike
1996		NCAA	III	64	—	—	—	—	—	—	—	19	8	Lonergan, Mike
1998		NCAA	III	16	—	—	—	—	—	—	—	25	4	Lonergan, Mike
CECILS JC (NC)														
1983	M	NSCAA		12	—	—	—	—	—	—	—	22	15	Reed, Ronald
1984		NSCAA		8	—	—	—	—	—	—	—	28	1	Reed, Ronald
CEDARVILLE														
1949	M	NAIA		32	—	—	—	—	—	—	—	17	12	Beattie, Mendell E.
1964		NAIA		32	—	—	—	—	—	—	—	19	6	Callan, Dr. Donald
1981		NAIA		32	—	—	—	—	—	—	—	25	4	Callan, Dr. Donald
1982		NAIA		32	—	—	—	—	—	—	—	17	11	Callan, Dr. Donald
1988		NCCAA	I	2	—	—	—	—	—	—	—	23	12	Callan, Dr. Donald
1990		NCCAA	I	2	—	—	—	—	—	—	—	24	13	Callan, Dr. Donald
1992		NCCAA	I	4	—	—	—	—	—	—	—	27	7	Callan, Dr. Donald
1994		NCCAA	I	4	—	—	—	—	—	—	—	21	15	Callan, Dr. Donald
1970	W	AIAW		16	—	—	—	—	—	—	—	8	5	Jeremiah, Dr. Maryalyce
1985		NCCAA	I	7	—	—	—	—	—	—	—	6	21	Hunt, Dr. Karol
1986		NCCAA	I	2	—	—	—	—	—	—	—	11	13	Fires, Bob
1989		NCCAA	I	2	—	—	—	—	—	—	—	20	10	Fires, Bob
1994		NCCAA	I	4	—	—	—	—	—	—	—	15	18	Freese, Kathy
1995		NCCAA	I	4	—	—	—	—	—	—	—	20	11	Freese, Kathy
1996		NCCAA	I	6	—	—	—	—	—	—	—	16	20	Freese, Kathy
CENTENARY (LA)														
1952	M	NAIA		32	—	—	—	—	—	—	—	17	17	Delaney, F. H. "Buss"
1957		NCAA	II	32	—	—	—	—	—	—	—	16	9	Mooty, Harold D.
1958		NCAA	II	32	—	—	—	—	—	—	—	13	10	Mooty, Harold D.
1959		NCAA	II	16	—	—	—	—	—	—	—	14	14	Sigler, Orvis
1982	W	AIAW	II	16	—	—	—	—	—	—	—	22	10	Saint Andre, Joe

Year	M/W	Assn	Div	NAT	NIT	ARC	CCA	NCI	NCT	OLY	HLM	W	L	Coach
CENTENARY (NJ)														
1998	W	NSCAA		2	—	—	—	—	—	—	—	22	6	Finnan, Diane
CENTRAL (IA)														
1977	M	NCAA	III	16	—	—	—	—	—	—	—	17	6	Walvoord, Jack
1978		NCAA	III	23	—	—	—	—	—	—	—	21	4	Walvoord, Jack
1979		NCAA	III	16	—	—	—	—	—	—	—	20	5	Walvoord, Jack
1980		NCAA	III	32	—	—	—	—	—	—	—	18	8	Walvoord, Jack
1985		NCAA	III	16	—	—	—	—	—	—	—	16	9	Walvoord, Jack
1991		NCAA	III	32	—	—	—	—	—	—	—	16	7	Walvoord, Jack
1994		NCAA	III	32	—	—	—	—	—	—	—	13	10	Walvoord, Jack
1995		NCAA	III	64	—	—	—	—	—	—	—	15	11	Walvoord, Jack
1983	W	NCAA	III	16	—	—	—	—	—	—	—	18	6	Boeyink, Gary
1993		NCAA	III	1	—	—	—	—	—	—	—	24	5	Boeyink, Gary
1994		NCAA	III	32	—	—	—	—	—	—	—	22	5	Boeyink, Gary
1995		NCAA	III	32	—	—	—	—	—	—	—	18	7	Boeyink, Gary
1998		NCAA	III	32	—	—	—	—	—	—	—	18	8	Boeyink, Gary
CENTRAL (KS)														
1976	M	NSCAA		8	—	—	—	—	—	—	—	15	11	Saxton, Mike
1985		NSCAA		16	—	—	—	—	—	—	—	14	7	Hibbard, Randy
1986		NSCAA		6	—	—	—	—	—	—	—	19	10	Hibbard, Randy
1987		NSCAA		12	—	—	—	—	—	—	—	19	11	Hibbard, Randy
1989	W	NSCAA		4	—	—	—	—	—	—	—	16	12	Turner, Gary
CENTRAL ARKANSAS														
1937	M	NAIA		4	—	—	—	—	—	—	—	21	8	Woodson, Warren B.
1938		NAIA		32	—	—	—	—	—	—	—	12	9	Woodson, Warren B.
1940		NAIA		32	—	—	—	—	—	—	—	18	8	Woodson, Warren B.
1942		NAIA		32	—	—	—	—	—	—	—	25	3	Roberts, Lloyd
1946		NAIA		32	—	—	—	—	—	—	—	16	12	McGibbony, Charles
1948		NAIA		32	—	—	—	—	—	—	—	21	2	Smith, Glen M.
1959		NAIA		16	—	—	—	—	—	—	—	24	4	Harton, Cliff
1961		NAIA		32	—	—	—	—	—	—	—	20	6	Harton, Cliff
1974		NAIA		32	—	—	—	—	—	—	—	22	9	Nixon, Don
1975		NAIA		32	—	—	—	—	—	—	—	19	11	Nixon, Don
1980		NAIA		8	—	—	—	—	—	—	—	19	14	Dyer, Don
1990		NAIA		16	—	—	—	—	—	—	—	24	11	Dyer, Don
1991		NAIA		2	—	—	—	—	—	—	—	29	5	Dyer, Don
1992		NAIA	I	2	—	—	—	—	—	—	—	28	5	Dyer, Don
1993		NAIA	I	32	—	—	—	—	—	—	—	20	8	Dyer, Don
1984	W	NAIA		16	—	—	—	—	—	—	—	24	4	Marvel, Ronnie
1991		NAIA		16	—	—	—	—	—	—	—	22	8	Marvel, Ronnie
1996		NCAA	II	32	—	—	—	—	—	—	—	21	10	Marvel, Ronnie
CENTRAL BIBLE														
1980	M	NCCAA	II	3	—	—	—	—	—	—	—	9	18	Hanson, Kirk
1982		NCCAA	II	4	—	—	—	—	—	—	—	17	16	Hanson, Kirk
1983		NCCAA	II	4	—	—	—	—	—	—	—	17	20	Hanson, Kirk
1984		NCCAA	II	3	—	—	—	—	—	—	—	13	20	Hanson, Kirk

Year	M/W	Assn	Div	NAT	NIT	ARC	CCA	NCI	NCT	OLY	HLM	W	L	Coach
1985		NCCAA	II	2	—	—	—	—	—	—	—	23	14	Hanson, Kirk
1986		NCCAA	II	2	—	—	—	—	—	—	—	23	14	Hanson, Kirk
1987		NCCAA	II	5	—	—	—	—	—	—	—	23	14	Hanson, Kirk
1989		NCCAA	II	4	—	—	—	—	—	—	—	24	12	Hanson, Kirk
1990		NCCAA	II	4	—	—	—	—	—	—	—	22	14	Hanson, Kirk
1991		NCCAA	II	6	—	—	—	—	—	—	—	22	15	Hanson, Kirk
1992		NCCAA	II	3	—	—	—	—	—	—	—	27	9	Hanson, Kirk
1994		NCCAA	II	1	—	—	—	—	—	—	—	28	9	Hanson, Kirk
1995		NCCAA	II	3	—	—	—	—	—	—	—	22	15	Hanson, Kirk
1996		NCCAA	II	2	—	—	—	—	—	—	—	24	16	Hanson, Kirk
1997		NCCAA	II	8	—	—	—	—	—	—	—	22	16	Hanson, Kirk
1998		NCCAA	II	7	—	—	—	—	—	—	—	30	11	Hanson, Kirk

CENTRAL CC: PLATTE

Year	M/W	Assn	Div	NAT	NIT	ARC	CCA	NCI	NCT	OLY	HLM	W	L	Coach
1983	M	NSCAA		2	—	—	—	—	—	—	—	19	14	Gutierrez, Jack
1985		NSCAA		10	—	—	—	—	—	—	—	23	10	Gutierrez, Jack
1983	W	NSCAA		6	—	—	—	—	—	—	—	12	16	Van Fossen, Dennis

CENTRAL CHRISTIAN (MO)

Year	M/W	Assn	Div	NAT	NIT	ARC	CCA	NCI	NCT	OLY	HLM	W	L	Coach
1982	M	NBCAA		3	—	—	—	—	—	—	—	17	10	Smith, Larry R.
1996		NBCAA	II	5	—	—	—	—	—	—	—	13	13	Cobb, Russell
1997		NCCAA	IIA	8	—	—	—	—	—	—	—	13	17	Cobb, Russell
1995	W	NBCAA		5	—	—	—	—	—	—	—	4	15	Stohs, Randy
1996		NBCAA		5	—	—	—	—	—	—	—	3	16	Stohs, Randy

CENTRAL CONNECTICUT STATE

Year	M/W	Assn	Div	NAT	NIT	ARC	CCA	NCI	NCT	OLY	HLM	W	L	Coach
1948	M	NAIA		16	—	—	—	—	—	—	—	14	5	Merrick, Ross
1949		NAIA		32	—	—	—	—	—	—	—	21	4	Merrick, Ross
1950		NAIA		32	—	—	—	—	—	—	—	16	6	Merrick, Ross
1959		NAIA		32	—	—	—	—	—	—	—	19	4	Moore, Dr. William M.
1960		NAIA		32	—	—	—	—	—	—	—	16	5	Detrick, William
1961		NAIA		32	—	—	—	—	—	—	—	17	4	Detrick, William
1962		NAIA		32	—	—	—	—	—	—	—	14	9	Detrick, William
1963		NAIA		32	—	—	—	—	—	—	—	22	1	Detrick, William
1964		NAIA		32	—	—	—	—	—	—	—	25	1	Detrick, William
1965		NAIA		32	—	—	—	—	—	—	—	19	5	Detrick, William
1966		NCAA	II	8	—	—	—	—	—	—	—	23	3	Detrick, William
1967		NCAA	II	32	—	—	—	—	—	—	—	17	8	Detrick, William
1969		NCAA	II	32	—	—	—	—	—	—	—	20	8	Detrick, William
1971		NCAA	II	16	—	—	—	—	—	—	—	20	7	Detrick, William
1983		NCAA	II	32	—	—	—	—	—	—	—	21	9	Detrick, William
1984		NCAA	II	24	—	—	—	—	—	—	—	26	6	Detrick, William
1986	W	NCAA	II	8	—	—	—	—	—	—	—	24	4	Reilly, Dr. Brenda

CENTRAL FLORIDA

Year	M/W	Assn	Div	NAT	NIT	ARC	CCA	NCI	NCT	OLY	HLM	W	L	Coach
1976	M	NCAA	II	32	—	—	—	—	—	—	—	20	5	Clark, Eugene A. "Torchy"
1977		NCAA	II	16	—	—	—	—	—	—	—	24	4	Clark, Eugene A. "Torchy"
1978		NCAA	II	4	—	—	—	—	—	—	—	26	4	Clark, Eugene A. "Torchy"
1980		NCAA	II	16	—	—	—	—	—	—	—	25	4	Clark, Eugene A. "Torchy"

Year	M/W	Assn	Div	NAT	NIT	ARC	CCA	NCI	NCT	OLY	HLM	W	L	Coach
1981		NCAA	II	16	—	—	—	—	—	—	—	23	5	Clark, Eugene A. "Torchy"
1982		NCAA	II	32	—	—	—	—	—	—	—	21	8	Clark, Eugene A. "Torchy"
1989		NCAA	II	32	—	—	—	—	—	—	—	22	8	Folliard, Thomas J.
1990		NCAA	II	16	—	—	—	—	—	—	—	26	4	Folliard, Thomas J.
1994		NCAA	I	64	—	—	—	—	—	—	—	21	9	Speraw, Kirk
1996		NCAA	I	64	—	—	—	—	—	—	—	11	19	Speraw, Kirk
1982	W	AIAW	II	16	—	—	—	—	—	—	—	24	15	Sanchez, Joe
1983		NCAA	II	24	—	—	—	—	—	—	—	25	5	Sanchez, Joe
1984		NCAA	II	24	—	—	—	—	—	—	—	23	7	Sanchez, Joe
1992		NCAA	II	32	—	—	—	—	—	—	—	25	4	Reynolds, John, Jr.
1993		NCAA	II	16	—	—	—	—	—	—	—	26	4	Reynolds, John, Jr.
1996		NCAA	I	64	—	—	—	—	—	—	—	15	14	Richardson, Jerry

CENTRAL INDIAN BIBLE

Year	M/W	Assn	Div	NAT	NIT	ARC	CCA	NCI	NCT	OLY	HLM	W	L	Coach
1988	M	NBCAA	II	4	—	—	—	—	—	—	—	X	X	Grant, Timothy L.

CENTRAL MAINE TECH

Year	M/W	Assn	Div	NAT	NIT	ARC	CCA	NCI	NCT	OLY	HLM	W	L	Coach
1997	M	NSCAA		8	—	—	—	—	—	—	—	19	6	Gonyea, Dave
1998		NSCAA		15	—	—	—	—	—	—	—	20	7	Gonyea, Dave

CENTRAL METHODIST

Year	M/W	Assn	Div	NAT	NIT	ARC	CCA	NCI	NCT	OLY	HLM	W	L	Coach
1943	M	NAIA		32	—	—	—	—	—	—	—	11	4	Vanatta, Robert
1945		NAIA		8	—	—	—	—	—	—	—	12	1	Vanatta, Robert
1950		NAIA		3	—	—	—	—	—	—	—	29	4	Vanatta, Robert
1951		NAIA		16	—	—	—	—	—	—	—	24	5	Pink, Ralph J.
1994		NAIA	II	16	—	—	—	—	—	—	—	30	7	Sherman, Jeff
1998		NAIA	II	32	—	—	—	—	—	—	—	26	8	Sherman, Jeff
1997	W	NAIA	II	16	—	—	—	—	—	—	—	28	8	Davis, Mike
1998		NAIA	II	8	—	—	—	—	—	—	—	25	8	Davis, Mike

CENTRAL MICHIGAN

Year	M/W	Assn	Div	NAT	NIT	ARC	CCA	NCI	NCT	OLY	HLM	W	L	Coach
1965	M	NCAA	II	16	—	—	—	—	—	—	—	19	7	Kjolhede, Theodore
1966		NAIA		16	—	—	—	—	—	—	—	23	6	Kjolhede, Theodore
1967		NAIA		16	—	—	—	—	—	—	—	22	3	Kjolhede, Throdore
1970		NCAA	II	16	—	—	—	—	—	—	—	21	5	Kjolhede, Theodore
1971		NCAA	II	16	—	—	—	—	—	—	—	18	9	Kjolhede, Theodore
1975		NCAA	I	12	—	—	—	—	—	—	—	22	6	Parfitt, Richard
1977		NCAA	I	32	—	—	—	—	—	—	—	18	10	Parfitt, Richard
1979		NCAA	I	—	24	—	—	—	—	—	—	19	9	Parfitt, Richard
1987		NCAA	I	64	—	—	—	—	—	—	—	22	8	Coles, Charles "Charlie"
1969	W	AIAW		12	—	—	—	—	—	—	—	4	3	Tate, Kathy Edwards
1983		NCAA	I	32	—	—	—	—	—	—	—	21	9	Golden, Laura L.
1984		NCAA	I	32	—	—	—	—	—	—	—	27	3	Golden, Laura L.

CENTRAL MISSOURI STATE

Year	M/W	Assn	Div	NAT	NIT	ARC	CCA	NCI	NCT	OLY	HLM	W	L	Coach
1937	M	NAIA		1	—	—	—	—	—	—	—	17	3	Reid, Tad C.
1938		NAIA		1	—	—	—	—	—	—	—	24	3	Reid, Tad C.
1939		NAIA		8	—	—	—	—	—	—	—	21	7	Scott, Tom
1940		NAIA		32	—	—	—	—	—	—	—	17	8	Scott, Tom

Year	M/W	Assn	Div	NAT	NIT	ARC	CCA	NCI	NCT	OLY	HLM	W	L	Coach
1941		NAIA		32	—	—	—	—	—	—	—	17	9	Scott, Tom
1942		NAIA		4	—	—	—	—	—	—	—	19	7	Scott, Tom
1946		NAIA		32	—	—	—	—	—	—	—	13	7	Scott, Tom
1965		NCAA	II	24	—	—	—	—	—	—	—	19	6	Hall, Joe B.
1970		NCAA	II	16	—	—	—	—	—	—	—	19	6	Short, Norman N.
1980		NCAA	II	24	—	—	—	—	—	—	—	26	2	Smith, Tom
1981		NCAA	II	32	—	—	—	—	—	—	—	20	9	Nance, Lynn
1982		NCAA	II	24	—	—	—	—	—	—	—	20	9	Nance, Lynn
1983		NCAA	II	16	—	—	—	—	—	—	—	23	7	Nance, Lynn
1984		NCAA	II	1	—	—	—	—	—	—	—	29	3	Nance, Lynn
1985		NCAA	II	24	—	—	—	—	—	—	—	22	7	Nance, Lynn
1989		NCAA	II	16	—	—	—	—	—	—	—	22	9	Wooldridge, Jim
1990		NCAA	II	16	—	—	—	—	—	—	—	27	6	Wooldridge, Jim
1991		NCAA	II	16	—	—	—	—	—	—	—	27	5	Wooldridge, Jim
1994		NCAA	II	24	—	—	—	—	—	—	—	22	8	Sundvold, Bob
1995		NCAA	II	8	—	—	—	—	—	—	—	24	8	Sundvold, Bob
1996		NCAA	II	32	—	—	—	—	—	—	—	22	9	Sundvold, Bob
1997		NCAA	II	48	—	—	—	—	—	—	—	21	8	Doucette, Don
1980	W	AIAW	I	24	—	—	—	—	—	—	—	26	5	Barnes, Dr. Mildred
1982		AIAW	I	16	—	—	—	—	—	—	—	20	9	Hoehn, Jorja E.
1983		NCAA	II	3	—	—	—	—	—	—	—	29	3	Hoehn, Jorja E.
1984		NCAA	II	1	—	—	—	—	—	—	—	28	4	Hoehn, Jorja E.
1985		NCAA	II	2	—	—	—	—	—	—	—	27	5	Hoehn, Jorja E.
1986		NCAA	II	8	—	—	—	—	—	—	—	23	6	Pye, Jon
1987		NCAA	II	16	—	—	—	—	—	—	—	23	7	Pye, Jon
1988		NCAA	II	16	—	—	—	—	—	—	—	26	5	Pye, Jon
1989		NCAA	II	4	—	—	—	—	—	—	—	29	5	Pye, Jon
1990		NCAA	II	8	—	—	—	—	—	—	—	29	3	Pye, Jon
1991		NCAA	II	32	—	—	—	—	—	—	—	23	6	Pye, Jon
1993		NCAA	II	32	—	—	—	—	—	—	—	19	10	Pye, Jon
1997		NCAA	II	48	—	—	—	—	—	—	—	21	9	Ballard, Scott
1998		NCAA	II	32	—	—	—	—	—	—	—	19	10	Ballard, Scott

CENTRAL OKLAHOMA

Year	M/W	Assn	Div	NAT	NIT	ARC	CCA	NCI	NCT	OLY	HLM	W	L	Coach
1938	M	NAIA		16	—	—	—	—	—	—	—	17	6	Hamilton, Dale E.
1939		NAIA		32	—	—	—	—	—	—	—	16	5	Hamilton, Dale E.
1959		NAIA		16	—	—	—	—	—	—	—	21	10	Smith, John
1961		NAIA		8	—	—	—	—	—	—	—	21	7	Smith, John
1964		NAIA		8	—	—	—	—	—	—	—	23	4	Winters, Mark
1992		NCAA	II	8	—	—	—	—	—	—	—	25	7	Seward, Jim
1993		NCAA	II	23	—	—	—	—	—	—	—	23	6	Seward, Jim
1995		NCAA	II	16	—	—	—	—	—	—	—	23	7	Seward, Jim
1997		NCAA	II	32	—	—	—	—	—	—	—	24	5	Seward, Jim
1998		NCAA	II	16	—	—	—	—	—	—	—	25	7	Seward, Jim
1982	W	AIAW	II	8	—	—	—	—	—	—	—	25	10	Kelly, John

Year	M/W	Assn	Div	NAT	NIT	ARC	CCA	NCI	NCT	OLY	HLM	W	L	Coach
CENTRAL STATE (OH)														
1952	M	NASC		2	—	—	—	—	—	—	—	18	3	Gibbs, George Edwin
1956		NAIA		16	—	—	—	—	—	—	—	18	7	Gibbs, George Edwin
1963		NAIA		16	—	—	—	—	—	—	—	18	11	Lucas, William C.
1965		NAIA		1	—	—	—	—	—	—	—	30	0	Lucas, William C.
1966		NAIA		8	—	—	—	—	—	—	—	24	6	Lucas, William C.
1968		NAIA		1	—	—	—	—	—	—	—	29	4	Lucas, William C.
1969		NAIA		32	—	—	—	—	—	—	—	21	7	Lucas, William C.
1970		NAIA		8	—	—	—	—	—	—	—	24	5	Lucas, William C.
1976		NAIA		32	—	—	—	—	—	—	—	20	10	Wims, Dr. Lu D.
1977		NAIA		32	—	—	—	—	—	—	—	18	11	Wims, Dr. Lu D.
1978		NAIA		8	—	—	—	—	—	—	—	19	11	Wims, Dr. Lu D.
1979		NAIA		32	—	—	—	—	—	—	—	22	7	Wims, Dr. Lu D.
1982		NCAA	II	16	—	—	—	—	—	—	—	21	8	Wims, Dr. Lu D.
1989	W	NAIA		8	—	—	—	—	—	—	—	29	2	Check, Theresa A.
1990		NAIA		8	—	—	—	—	—	—	—	25	5	Check, Theresa A.
1991		NAIA		16	—	—	—	—	—	—	—	27	5	Check, Theresa A.
1992		NAIA	I	32	—	—	—	—	—	—	—	24	8	Check, Theresa A.
1993		NAIA	I	16	—	—	—	—	—	—	—	25	5	Check, Theresa A.
1994		NAIA	I	16	—	—	—	—	—	—	—	25	6	Check, Theresa A.
1995		NAIA	I	32	—	—	—	—	—	—	—	20	9	Check, Theresa A.
1996		NAIA	I	8	—	—	—	—	—	—	—	30	4	Check, Theresa A.
1997		NAIA	I	8	—	—	—	—	—	—	—	29	3	Check, Theresa A.
1998		NAIA	I	32	—	—	—	—	—	—	—	25	7	Check, Theresa A.
CENTRAL WASHINGTON														
1950	M	NAIA		8	—	—	—	—	—	—	—	24	8	Nicholson, Leo S.
1965		NAIA		32	—	—	—	—	—	—	—	20	6	Nicholson, Dean
1966		NAIA		32	—	—	—	—	—	—	—	21	8	Nicholson, Dean
1967		NAIA		3	—	—	—	—	—	—	—	27	4	Nicholson, Dean
1968		NAIA		8	—	—	—	—	—	—	—	22	8	Nicholson, Dean
1969		NAIA		3	—	—	—	—	—	—	—	24	9	Nicholson, Dean
1970		NAIA		2	—	—	—	—	—	—	—	31	2	Nicholson, Dean
1971		NAIA		16	—	—	—	—	—	—	—	24	9	Nicholson, Dean
1974		NAIA		32	—	—	—	—	—	—	—	17	10	Nicholson, Dean
1975		NAIA		16	—	—	—	—	—	—	—	21	6	Nicholson, Dean
1976		NAIA		16	—	—	—	—	—	—	—	23	7	Nicholson, Dean
1977		NAIA		8	—	—	—	—	—	—	—	24	8	Nicholson, Dean
1978		NAIA		32	—	—	—	—	—	—	—	21	8	Nicholson, Dean
1979		NAIA		16	—	—	—	—	—	—	—	25	6	Nicholson, Dean
1980		NAIA		8	—	—	—	—	—	—	—	27	6	Nicholson, Dean
1981		NAIA		32	—	—	—	—	—	—	—	21	12	Nicholson, Dean
1982		NAIA		16	—	—	—	—	—	—	—	22	7	Nicholson, Dean
1984		NAIA		16	—	—	—	—	—	—	—	23	10	Nicholson, Dean
1985		NAIA		4	—	—	—	—	—	—	—	25	11	Nicholson, Dean
1986		NAIA		8	—	—	—	—	—	—	—	27	6	Nicholson, Dean
1987		NAIA		3	—	—	—	—	—	—	—	32	9	Nicholson, Dean
1989		NAIA		3	—	—	—	—	—	—	—	32	10	Nicholson, Dean
1990		NAIA		8	—	—	—	—	—	—	—	31	5	Nicholson, Dean
1993		NAIA	I	16	—	—	—	—	—	—	—	29	7	Coleman, Gil

Year	M/W	Assn	Div	NAT	NIT	ARC	CCA	NCI	NCT	OLY	HLM	W	L	Coach
1995		NAIA	I	16	—	—	—	—	—	—	—	—	20	14	Sparling, Greg
1997		NAIA	I	8	—	—	—	—	—	—	—	—	18	13	Sparling, Greg
1998		NAIA	I	8	—	—	—	—	—	—	—	—	20	11	Sparling, Greg
1988	W	NAIA		16	—	—	—	—	—	—	—	—	31	5	Frederick, Dr. Gary C.

CENTRE

Year	M/W	Assn	Div	NAT	NIT	ARC	CCA	NCI	NCT	OLY	HLM	W	L	Coach
1964	M	NCAA	II	32	—	—	—	—	—	—	—	—	14	8	Phillips, Lewis
1979		NCAA	III	4	—	—	—	—	—	—	—	—	25	5	Bryant, Tom C.
1983		NCAA	III	32	—	—	—	—	—	—	—	—	16	11	Bryant, Tom C.
1984		NCAA	III	32	—	—	—	—	—	—	—	—	18	9	Bryant, Tom C.
1985		NCAA	III	8	—	—	—	—	—	—	—	—	19	8	Bryant, Tom C.
1986		NCAA	III	16	—	—	—	—	—	—	—	—	21	7	Bryant, Tom C.
1987		NCAA	III	32	—	—	—	—	—	—	—	—	20	8	Bryant, Tom C.
1988		NCAA	III	16	—	—	—	—	—	—	—	—	13	15	Bryant, Tom C.
1989		NCAA	III	4	—	—	—	—	—	—	—	—	24	7	Bryant, Tom C.
1992		NCAA	III	32	—	—	—	—	—	—	—	—	19	8	Bryant, Tom C.
1987	W	NCAA	III	16	—	—	—	—	—	—	—	—	22	5	Wise, Lea
1988		NCAA	III	24	—	—	—	—	—	—	—	—	23	6	Wise, Lea
1989		NCAA	III	3	—	—	—	—	—	—	—	—	23	8	Wise, Lea
1990		NCAA	III	4	—	—	—	—	—	—	—	—	22	8	Noble-Hauserman, Cindy
1991		NCAA	III	32	—	—	—	—	—	—	—	—	17	7	Noble-Hauserman, Cindy

CHADRON STATE

Year	M/W	Assn	Div	NAT	NIT	ARC	CCA	NCI	NCT	OLY	HLM	W	L	Coach
1942	M	NAIA		32	—	—	—	—	—	—	—	—	17	4	Armstrong, Ross O.
1952		NAIA		32	—	—	—	—	—	—	—	—	18	7	Young, Loy
1967		NAIA		16	—	—	—	—	—	—	—	—	22	6	Payton, Mack
1995	W	NCAA	II	48	—	—	—	—	—	—	—	—	22	8	Anderson, Tom

CHAMINADE

Year	M/W	Assn	Div	NAT	NIT	ARC	CCA	NCI	NCT	OLY	HLM	W	L	Coach
1979	M	NCAA	III	8	—	—	—	—	—	—	—	—	24	5	Lopes, Merv
1983		NAIA		4	—	—	—	—	—	—	—	—	27	3	Lopes, Merv
1984		NAIA		8	—	—	—	—	—	—	—	—	23	6	Lopes, Merv

CHAPMAN

Year	M/W	Assn	Div	NAT	NIT	ARC	CCA	NCI	NCT	OLY	HLM	W	L	Coach
1957	M	NCAA	II	32	—	—	—	—	—	—	—	—	16	11	Perkins, Donald C.
1958		NCAA	II	8	—	—	—	—	—	—	—	—	22	5	Perkins, Donald C.
1959		NCAA	II	16	—	—	—	—	—	—	—	—	23	4	Perkins, Donald C.
1960		NCAA	II	2	—	—	—	—	—	—	—	—	24	6	Perkins, Donald C.
1961		NCAA	II	24	—	—	—	—	—	—	—	—	17	11	Perkins, Donald C.
1963		NCAA	II	16	—	—	—	—	—	—	—	—	20	7	Perkins, Donald C.
1978		NCAA	II	32	—	—	—	—	—	—	—	—	19	10	Rider, Dr. Rich
1983		NCAA	II	16	—	—	—	—	—	—	—	—	21	8	Hazzard, Walter R., Jr.
1984		NCAA	II	24	—	—	—	—	—	—	—	—	22	6	Hazzard, Walter R., Jr.
1982	W	NCAA	II	8	—	—	—	—	—	—	—	—	23	5	Berger, Brian
1983		NCAA	II	16	—	—	—	—	—	—	—	—	22	8	Berger, Brian
1984		NCAA	II	8	—	—	—	—	—	—	—	—	26	5	Berger, Brian
1985		NCAA	II	16	—	—	—	—	—	—	—	—	25	4	Berger, Brian
1997		NCAA	III	64	—	—	—	—	—	—	—	—	19	7	Hegarty, Mary

Year	M/W	Assn	Div	NAT	NIT	ARC	CCA	NCI	NCT	OLY	HLM	W	L	Coach
CHARLESTON (SC)														
1983	M	NAIA		1	—	—	—	—	—	—	—	24	5	Kresse, John
1985		NAIA		8	—	—	—	—	—	—	—	25	3	Kresse, John
1986		NAIA		8	—	—	—	—	—	—	—	26	9	Kresse, John
1987		NAIA		16	—	—	—	—	—	—	—	25	1	Kresse, John
1988		NAIA		3	—	—	—	—	—	—	—	30	5	Kresse, John
1989		NAIA		16	—	—	—	—	—	—	—	21	5	Kresse, John
1994		NCAA	I	64	—	—	—	—	—	—	—	24	4	Kresse, John
1995		NCAA	I	—	32	—	—	—	—	—	—	23	6	Kresse, John
1996		NCAA	I	—	16	—	—	—	—	—	—	25	4	Kresse, John
1997		NCAA	I	32	—	—	—	—	—	—	—	29	3	Kresse, John
1998		NCAA	I	64	—	—	—	—	—	—	—	24	6	Kresse, John
1980	W	AIAW	II	2	—	—	—	—	—	—	—	32	8	Wilson, Nancy R.
1981		AIAW	II	2	—	—	—	—	—	—	—	25	9	Wilson, Nancy R.
1982		AIAW	II	2	—	—	—	—	—	—	—	33	7	Wilson, Nancy R.
CHARLESTON (WV)														
1953	M	NAIA		32	—	—	—	—	—	—	—	21	9	King, Carl E. "Eddie"
1954		NAIA		32	—	—	—	—	—	—	—	16	13	King, Carl E. "Eddie"
1962		NAIA		16	—	—	—	—	—	—	—	27	6	Moran, Garland
1964		NAIA		32	—	—	—	—	—	—	—	20	11	Moran, Garland
1966		NAIA		16	—	—	—	—	—	—	—	26	6	Meckfessel, Richard
1967		NAIA		4	—	—	—	—	—	—	—	28	5	Meckfessel, Richard
1970		NAIA		16	—	—	—	—	—	—	—	25	8	Meckfessel, Richard
1986		NAIA		8	—	—	—	—	—	—	—	30	5	Williams, "Tex"
1992		NAIA	I	32	—	—	—	—	—	—	—	21	9	White, Greg
1979	W	AIAW	S	8	—	—	—	—	—	—	—	30	7	Francis, Robert A. "Bud"
1980		AIAW	II	8	—	—	—	—	—	—	—	27	8	Francis, Robert A. "Bud"
1982		NAIA		8	—	—	—	—	—	—	—	27	7	Francis, Robert A. "Bud"
1984		NAIA		8	—	—	—	—	—	—	—	24	9	Francis, Robert A. "Bud"
1986		NAIA		16	—	—	—	—	—	—	—	19	12	Francis, Robert A. "Bud"
1988		NAIA		16	—	—	—	—	—	—	—	21	13	Bennett-Travinski, Linda
1990		NAIA		16	—	—	—	—	—	—	—	25	8	Bennett-Travinski, Linda
1991		NAIA		32	—	—	—	—	—	—	—	21	8	Bennett-Travinski, Linda
1992		NAIA	I	32	—	—	—	—	—	—	—	20	6	Bennett-Travinski, Linda
1998		NCAA	II	48	—	—	—	—	—	—	—	21	9	Bennett-Travinski, Linda
CHARLESTON SOUTHERN														
1997	M	NCAA	I	64	—	—	—	—	—	—	—	15	15	Conrad, Tom
CHEYNEY														
1965	M	NCAA	II	24	—	—	—	—	—	—	—	24	1	Blitman, Howard
1966		NCAA	II	16	—	—	—	—	—	—	—	26	1	Blitman, Howard
1967		NCAA	II	8	—	—	—	—	—	—	—	23	7	Blitman, Howard
1968		NCAA	II	8	—	—	—	—	—	—	—	22	7	Blitman, Howard
1969		NCAA	II	16	—	—	—	—	—	—	—	25	3	Coma, Dr. Anthony S. "Doc"
1970		NCAA	II	24	—	—	—	—	—	—	—	25	3	Coma, Dr. Anthony S. "Doc"
1971		NCAA	II	8	—	—	—	—	—	—	—	23	6	Coma, Dr. Anthony S. "Doc"
1972		NCAA	II	32	—	—	—	—	—	—	—	22	6	Coma, Dr. Anthony S. "Doc"

Year	M/W	Assn	Div	NAT	NIT	ARC	CCA	NCI	NCT	OLY	HLM	W	L	Coach
1973		NCAA	II	24	—	—	—	—	—	—	—	23	5	Chaney, John
1976		NCAA	II	8	—	—	—	—	—	—	—	24	5	Chaney, John
1977		NCAA	II	8	—	—	—	—	—	—	—	20	8	Chaney, John
1978		NCAA	II	1	—	—	—	—	—	—	—	27	2	Chaney, John
1979		NCAA	II	3	—	—	—	—	—	—	—	24	7	Chaney, John
1980		NCAA	II	24	—	—	—	—	—	—	—	23	5	Chaney, John
1981		NCAA	II	24	—	—	—	—	—	—	—	21	8	Chaney, John
1982		NCAA	II	8	—	—	—	—	—	—	—	28	3	Chaney, John
1983		NCAA	II	32	—	—	—	—	—	—	—	26	6	Songster, Charles
1986		NCAA	II	3	—	—	—	—	—	—	—	28	5	Songster, Charles
1980	W	AIAW	I	24	—	—	—	—	—	—	—	26	7	Stringer, C. Vivian
1981		AIAW	I	8	—	—	—	—	—	—	—	26	3	Stringer, C. Vivian
1982		NCAA	I	2	—	—	—	—	—	—	—	28	3	Stringer, C. Vivian
1983		NCAA	I	16	—	—	—	—	—	—	—	27	3	Stringer, C. Vivian
1984		NCAA	I	3	—	—	—	—	—	—	—	25	5	McGriff, Winthrop "Windy"

CHICAGO

Year	M/W	Assn	Div	NAT	NIT	ARC	CCA	NCI	NCT	OLY	HLM	W	L	Coach
1907	M	NCAA		—	—	—	—	—	—	—	1	22	2	Raycroft, Dr. Joseph E.
1908		NCAA		—	—	—	—	—	—	—	1	21	2	Raycroft, Dr. Joseph E.
1909		NCAA		—	—	—	—	—	—	—	1	12	0	Raycroft, Dr. Joseph E.
1961		NCAA	II	8	—	—	—	—	—	—	—	19	4	Stampf, Joseph M.
1974		NCAA	II	44	—	—	—	—	—	—	—	16	4	Stampf, Joseph M
1997		NCAA	III	16	—	—	—	—	—	—	—	23	5	Cunningham, Pat
1998		NCAA	III	16	—	—	—	—	—	—	—	23	3	Cunningham, Pat
1995	W	NCAA	III	64	—	—	—	—	—	—	—	19	7	Zawacki, Susan M.

CHICAGO STATE

Year	M/W	Assn	Div	NAT	NIT	ARC	CCA	NCI	NCT	OLY	HLM	W	L	Coach
1981	M	NAIA		32	—	—	—	—	—	—	—	23	9	Hallberg, Robert J.
1983		NAIA		16	—	—	—	—	—	—	—	23	4	Hallberg, Robert J.
1984		NAIA		3	—	—	—	—	—	—	—	24	4	Hallberg, Robert J.

CHRISTIAN BROTHERS

Year	M/W	Assn	Div	NAT	NIT	ARC	CCA	NCI	NCT	OLY	HLM	W	L	Coach
1959	M	NAIA		32	—	—	—	—	—	—	—	19	7	Raymonds, Henry C. "Hank"
1960		NAIA		32	—	—	—	—	—	—	—	21	7	Raymonds, Henry C. "Hank"

CHRISTIAN HERITAGE

Year	M/W	Assn	Div	NAT	NIT	ARC	CCA	NCI	NCT	OLY	HLM	W	L	Coach
1990	M	NCCAA	I	1	—	—	—	—	—	—	—	33	6	Nater, Swen E.
1996		NCCAA	I	3	—	—	—	—	—	—	—	16	18	Wilmore, Art
1997		NCCAA	I	1	—	—	—	—	—	—	—	23	12	Wilmore, Art
1998		NCCAA	I	1	—	—	—	—	—	—	—	25	11	Wilmore, Art

CHRISTOPHER NEWPORT

Year	M/W	Assn	Div	NAT	NIT	ARC	CCA	NCI	NCT	OLY	HLM	W	L	Coach
1986	M	NCAA	III	24	—	—	—	—	—	—	—	19	11	Woollum, C. J.
1988		NCAA	III	32	—	—	—	—	—	—	—	15	15	Woollum, C. J.
1989		NCAA	III	40	—	—	—	—	—	—	—	17	12	Woollum, C. J.
1990		NCAA	III	40	—	—	—	—	—	—	—	19	9	Woollum, C. J.
1991		NCAA	III	16	—	—	—	—	—	—	—	24	5	Woollum, C. J.
1993		NCAA	III	16	—	—	—	—	—	—	—	23	5	Woollum, C. J.
1994		NCAA	III	32	—	—	—	—	—	—	—	22	5	Woollum, C. J.
1995		NCAA	III	64	—	—	—	—	—	—	—	18	10	Woollum, C. J.
1996		NCAA	III	16	—	—	—	—	—	—	—	24	6	Woollum, C. J.
1997		NCAA	III	32	—	—	—	—	—	—	—	19	8	Woollum, C. J.
1998		NCAA	III	16	—	—	—	—	—	—	—	26	2	Woollum, C. J.

Year	M/W	Assn	Div	NAT	NIT	ARC	CCA	NCI	NCT	OLY	HLM	W	L	Coach
1980	W	AIAW	III	24	—	—	—	—	—	—	—	18	13	Lee, Phil
1982		NCAA	III	16	—	—	—	—	—	—	—	15	10	Zachensky-Walthall, Susan
1986		NCAA	III	32	—	—	—	—	—	—	—	20	9	Zachensky-Walthall, Susan
1992		NCAA	III	16	—	—	—	—	—	—	—	22	6	Parson, Cathy
1993		NCAA	III	32	—	—	—	—	—	—	—	19	9	Parson, Cathy
1995		NCAA	III	64	—	—	—	—	—	—	—	17	9	Parson, Cathy
1997		NCAA	III	64	—	—	—	—	—	—	—	20	7	Parson, Cathy
1998		NCAA	III	32	—	—	—	—	—	—	—	24	4	Parson, Cathy

CINCINNATI

Year	M/W	Assn	Div	NAT	NIT	ARC	CCA	NCI	NCT	OLY	HLM	W	L	Coach
1951	M	NCAA		—	12	—	—	—	—	—	—	18	4	Wiethe, John A.
1955		NCAA		—	3	—	—	—	—	—	—	21	8	Smith, George D.
1957		NCAA	I	—	12	—	—	—	—	—	—	15	7	Smith, George D.
1958		NCAA	I	12	—	—	—	—	—	—	—	25	3	Smith, George D.
1959		NCAA	I	3	—	—	—	—	—	—	—	26	4	Smith, George D.
1960		NCAA	I	3	—	—	—	—	—	—	—	28	2	Smith, George D.
1961		NCAA	I	1	—	—	—	—	—	—	1	27	3	Jucker, Edwin L.
1962		NCAA	I	1	—	—	—	—	—	—	1	29	2	Jucker, Edwin L.
1963		NCAA	I	2	—	—	—	—	—	—	—	26	2	Jucker, Edwin L.
1966		NCAA	I	16	—	—	—	—	—	—	—	21	7	Baker, Taylor 'Tay'
1970		NCAA	I	—	16	—	—	—	—	—	—	21	6	Baker, Taylor 'Tay'
1974		NCAA	I	—	16	—	—	—	—	—	—	19	8	Catlett, Gale
1975		NCAA	I	12	—	—	—	—	—	—	—	23	6	Catlett, Gale
1976		NCAA	I	32	—	—	—	—	—	—	—	25	6	Catlett, Gale
1977		NCAA	I	32	—	—	—	—	—	—	—	25	5	Catlett, Gale
1985		NCAA	I	—	16	—	—	—	—	—	—	17	14	Yates, Anthony
1990		NCAA	I	—	16	—	—	—	—	—	—	20	14	Huggins, Robert
1991		NCAA	I	—	16	—	—	—	—	—	—	18	12	Huggins, Robert
1992		NCAA	I	3	—	—	—	—	—	—	—	29	5	Huggins, Robert
1993		NCAA	I	8	—	—	—	—	—	—	—	27	5	Huggins, Robert
1994		NCAA	I	64	—	—	—	—	—	—	—	22	10	Huggins, Robert
1995		NCAA	I	32	—	—	—	—	—	—	—	22	12	Huggins, Robert
1996		NCAA	I	8	—	—	—	—	—	—	—	28	5	Huggins, Robert
1997		NCAA	I	32	—	—	—	—	—	—	—	26	8	Huggins, Robert
1998		NCAA	I	32	—	—	—	—	—	—	—	27	6	Huggins, Robert
1981	W			—	7	—	—	—	—	—	—	27	9	Barry, Ceal
1989		NCAA	I	48	—	—	—	—	—	—	—	21	9	Pirtle, Laurie
1998		NCAA	I	—	16	—	—	—	—	—	—	21	9	Pirtle, Laurie

CINCINNATI BIBLE

Year	M/W	Assn	Div	NAT	NIT	ARC	CCA	NCI	NCT	OLY	HLM	W	L	Coach
1981	M	NCCAA	II	3	—	—	—	—	—	—	—	27	3	Tuell, Gary
1982		NCCAA	II	8	—	—	—	—	—	—	—	25	6	Tuell, Gary
1983		NCCAA	II	8	—	—	—	—	—	—	—	24	7	Tuell, Gary
1984		NCCAA	II	2	—	—	—	—	—	—	—	32	3	Tuell, Gary
1985		NCCAA	II	1	—	—	—	—	—	—	—	32	3	Wallingford, Tony
1986		NCCAA	II	1	—	—	—	—	—	—	—	35	2	Wallingford, Tony
1987		NCCAA	II	1	—	—	—	—	—	—	—	29	5	Wallingford, Tony
1992		NCCAA	II	5	—	—	—	—	—	—	—	20	18	Corrona, Jim
1994		NCCAA	II	6	—	—	—	—	—	—	—	12	22	Corrona, Jim
1995		NCCAA	II	7	—	—	—	—	—	—	—	12	21	Corrona, Jim

Year	M/W	Assn	Div	NAT	NIT	ARC	CCA	NCI	NCT	OLY	HLM	W	L	Coach

CIRCLEVILLE BIBLE

Year	M/W	Assn	Div	NAT	NIT	ARC	CCA	NCI	NCT	OLY	HLM	W	L	Coach
1982	M	NCCAA	II	8	—	—	—	—	—	—	—	14	13	Walters, Mike
1983		NCCAA	II	8	—	—	—	—	—	—	—	19	11	Leatherwood, Joe
1992		NCCAA	IIA	6	—	—	—	—	—	—	—	16	10	Gardner, Greg
1993		NCCAA	IIA	3	—	—	—	—	—	—	—	15	12	Amlin, Tom
1994		NCCAA	IIA	8	—	—	—	—	—	—	—	14	9	Amlin, Tom

CITY COLLEGE

Year	M/W	Assn	Div	NAT	NIT	ARC	CCA	NCI	NCT	OLY	HLM	W	L	Coach
1941	M	NCAA		—	3	—	—	—	—	—	—	17	5	Holman, Nathan "Nat"
1942		NCAA		—	8	—	—	—	—	—	—	16	3	Holman, Nathan "Nat"
1947		NCAA		4	—	—	—	—	—	—	—	17	6	Holman, Nathan "Nat"
1949		NCAA		—	12	—	—	—	—	—	—	17	8	Holman, Nathan "Nat"
1950		NCAA		1	1	—	—	—	—	—	1	24	5	Holman, Nathan "Nat"
1957		NCAA	II	32	—	—	—	—	—	—	—	11	8	Polansky, David
1976		NCAA	III	14	—	—	—	—	—	—	—	16	14	Layne, Floyd
1996	W	NCAA	III	64	—	—	—	—	—	—	—	16	12	English, Stephanie

CLAFLIN

Year	M/W	Assn	Div	NAT	NIT	ARC	CCA	NCI	NCT	OLY	HLM	W	L	Coach
1996	M	NAIA	I	32	—	—	—	—	—	—	—	18	13	Guyden, James "Gus"
1997		NAIA	I	16	—	—	—	—	—	—	—	25	8	Guydon, James "Gus"
1985	W	NAIA		16	—	—	—	—	—	—	—	27	5	Brownlee, Nelson C.
1988		NAIA		2	—	—	—	—	—	—	—	37	2	Brownlee, Nelson C.
1989		NAIA		2	—	—	—	—	—	—	—	35	1	Brownlee, Nelson C.
1990		NAIA		3	—	—	—	—	—	—	—	33	3	Brownlee, Nelson C.
1991		NAIA		3	—	—	—	—	—	—	—	31	2	Brownlee, Nelson C.
1992		NAIA	I	8	—	—	—	—	—	—	—	28	2	Brownlee, Nelson C.
1993		NAIA	I	32	—	—	—	—	—	—	—	24	10	Brownlee, Nelson C.
1994		NAIA	I	32	—	—	—	—	—	—	—	26	5	Brownlee, Nelson C.
1996		NAIA	I	32	—	—	—	—	—	—	—	21	9	Brownlee, Nelson C.
1997		NAIA	I	32	—	—	—	—	—	—	—	22	10	Brownlee, Nelson C.
1998		NAIA	I	32	—	—	—	—	—	—	—	23	10	Brownlee, Nelson C.

CLAREMONT MCKENNA

Year	M/W	Assn	Div	NAT	NIT	ARC	CCA	NCI	NCT	OLY	HLM	W	L	Coach
1967	M	NAIA		32	—	—	—	—	—	—	—	23	7	Ducey, Ted
1984		NCAA	III	24	—	—	—	—	—	—	—	16	10	Wells, David
1987		NCAA	III	24	—	—	—	—	—	—	—	21	7	Wells, David
1988		NCAA	III	32	—	—	—	—	—	—	—	19	8	Wells, David
1990		NCAA	III	40	—	—	—	—	—	—	—	18	9	Wells, David
1991		NCAA	III	32	—	—	—	—	—	—	—	22	5	Wells, David
1996		NCAA	III	32	—	—	—	—	—	—	—	19	8	Wells, David
1995	W	NCAA	III	32	—	—	—	—	—	—	—	22	5	Burton, Jodie
1996		NCAA	III	32	—	—	—	—	—	—	—	20	8	Burton, Jodie

CLARENDON

Year	M/W	Assn	Div	NAT	NIT	ARC	CCA	NCI	NCT	OLY	HLM	W	L	Coach
1994	M	NSCAA		7	—	—	—	—	—	—	—	26	11	Mondragon, Joseph
1995		NSCAA		6	—	—	—	—	—	—	—	23	12	Mondragon, Joseph
1996		NSCAA		5	—	—	—	—	—	—	—	21	17	Mondragon, Joseph
1997		NSCAA		5	—	—	—	—	—	—	—	18	8	Mondragon, Joseph

Year	M/W	Assn	Div	NAT	NIT	ARC	CCA	NCI	NCT	OLY	HLM	W	L	Coach
1993	W	NSCAA		7	—	—	—	—	—	—	—	—	13	18	Zehr, Joel R.
1994		NSCAA		6	—	—	—	—	—	—	—	—	17	15	Zehr, Joel R.
1995		NSCAA		3	—	—	—	—	—	—	—	—	15	12	Zehr, Joel R.
1997		NSCAA		2	—	—	—	—	—	—	—	—	22	5	Zehr, Joel R.
1998		NSCAA		1	—	—	—	—	—	—	—	—	21	9	Zehr, Joel R.

CLARION

Year	M/W	Assn	Div	NAT	NIT	ARC	CCA	NCI	NCT	OLY	HLM	W	L	Coach
1952	M	NAIA		32	—	—	—	—	—	—	—	—	19	1	Kribbs, Benton A.
1977		NAIA		16	—	—	—	—	—	—	—	—	27	3	DeGregorio, Joseph
1980		NAIA		8	—	—	—	—	—	—	—	—	23	9	DeGregorio, Joseph
1981		NCAA	II	16	—	—	—	—	—	—	—	—	23	6	DeGregorio, Joseph
1991	W	NCAA	II	8	—	—	—	—	—	—	—	—	24	8	Parsons, Margaret Rhoads "Gie"
1992		NCAA	II	16	—	—	—	—	—	—	—	—	25	4	Parsons, Margaret Rhoads "Gie"
1993		NCAA	II	16	—	—	—	—	—	—	—	—	24	6	Parsons, Margaret Rhoads "Gie"
1994		NCAA	II	8	—	—	—	—	—	—	—	—	26	4	Parsons, Margaret Rhoads "Gie"
1995		NCAA	II	48	—	—	—	—	—	—	—	—	18	11	Parsons, Margaret Rhoads "Gie"

CLARK (MA)

Year	M/W	Assn	Div	NAT	NIT	ARC	CCA	NCI	NCT	OLY	HLM	W	L	Coach
1978	M	NCAA	III	23	—	—	—	—	—	—	—	—	17	7	Halas, Wally
1979		NCAA	III	8	—	—	—	—	—	—	—	—	20	6	Halas, Wally
1980		NCAA	III	16	—	—	—	—	—	—	—	—	21	6	Halas, Wally
1981		NCAA	III	8	—	—	—	—	—	—	—	—	24	3	Halas, Wally
1982		NCAA	III	24	—	—	—	—	—	—	—	—	17	9	Halas, Wally
1983		NCAA	III	8	—	—	—	—	—	—	—	—	23	4	Halas, Wally
1984		NCAA	III	2	—	—	—	—	—	—	—	—	21	7	Halas, Wally
1985		NCAA	III	16	—	—	—	—	—	—	—	—	20	6	Halas, Wally
1986		NCAA	III	24	—	—	—	—	—	—	—	—	21	6	Halas, Wally
1987		NCAA	III	2	—	—	—	—	—	—	—	—	27	3	Halas, Wally
1988		NCAA	III	8	—	—	—	—	—	—	—	—	21	7	Clark, Kevin
1982	W	NCAA	III	4	—	—	—	—	—	—	—	—	18	11	Stevens, Barbara
1983		NCAA	III	4	—	—	—	—	—	—	—	—	21	8	Stevens, Barbara
1987		NCAA	III	32	—	—	—	—	—	—	—	—	19	8	Glispin, Patricia
1989		NCAA	III	8	—	—	—	—	—	—	—	—	28	1	Glispin, Patricia
1992		NCAA	III	32	—	—	—	—	—	—	—	—	22	5	Glispin, Patricia
1995		NCAA	III	32	—	—	—	—	—	—	—	—	19	8	Glispin, Patricia
1997		NCAA	III	64	—	—	—	—	—	—	—	—	24	4	Glispin, Patricia
1998		NCAA	III	48	—	—	—	—	—	—	—	—	20	8	Glispin, Patricia

CLARK ATLANTA

Year	M/W	Assn	Div	NAT	NIT	ARC	CCA	NCI	NCT	OLY	HLM	W	L	Coach
1952	M	NASC		8	—	—	—	—	—	—	—	—	19	3	Epps, Leonidas S. II "Sonny"
1977		NCAA	III	30	—	—	—	—	—	—	—	—	20	7	Epps, Leonidas S. II "Sonny"
1996		NCAA	II	48	—	—	—	—	—	—	—	—	21	8	Witherspoon, Anthony
1982	W	NCAA	II	16	—	—	—	—	—	—	—	—	14	12	Witherspoon, Anthony
1985		NCAA	II	16	—	—	—	—	—	—	—	—	19	12	Witherspoon, Anthony
1986		NCAA	II	24	—	—	—	—	—	—	—	—	18	12	Moseley, Michael

CLARKE (IA)

Year	M/W	Assn	Div	NAT	NIT	ARC	CCA	NCI	NCT	OLY	HLM	W	L	Coach
1984	W	NSCAA		6	—	—	—	—	—	—	—	—	8	15	Holland, Kevin
1985		NSCAA		6	—	—	—	—	—	—	—	—	8	19	Holland, Kevin

CLARKSON (NY)

Year	M/W	Assn	Div	NAT	NIT	ARC	CCA	NCI	NCT	OLY	HLM	W	L	Coach
1989	W	NCAA	III	4	—	—	—	—	—	—	—	—	26	7	Chafin, Brian

Year	M/W	Assn	Div	NAT	NIT	ARC	CCA	NCI	NCT	OLY	HLM	W	L	Coach
CLAYTON STATE														
1995	W	NAIA	I	32	—	—	—	—	—	—	—	19	13	Nestopoulos, Chris
CLEARWATER CHRISTIAN														
1992	M	NCCAA	II	2	—	—	—	—	—	—	—	25	10	Wubbena, Del
1993		NCCAA	II	5	—	—	—	—	—	—	—	25	7	Wubbena, Del
1994		NCCAA	II	4	—	—	—	—	—	—	—	16	13	Wubbena, Del
1995		NCCAA	II	2	—	—	—	—	—	—	—	22	7	Wubbena, Del
1996		NCCAA	II	5	—	—	—	—	—	—	—	20	9	Wubbena, Del
1997	W	NCCAA	II	8	—	—	—	—	—	—	—	12	11	Dewitt, Kris
1998		NCCAA	II	7	—	—	—	—	—	—	—	14	9	Dewitt, Kris
CLEMSON														
1975	M	NCAA	I	—	16	—	—	—	—	—	—	17	11	Locke, Taylor O. "Tates"
1979		NCAA	I	—	12	—	—	—	—	—	—	19	10	Foster, William C.
1980		NCAA	I	8	—	—	—	—	—	—	—	23	9	Foster, William C.
1981		NCAA	I	—	32	—	—	—	—	—	—	20	11	Foster, William C.
1982		NCAA	I	—	32	—	—	—	—	—	—	14	14	Foster, William C.
1985		NCAA	I	—	32	—	—	—	—	—	—	16	13	Ellis, Cliff
1986		NCAA	I	—	8	—	—	—	—	—	—	19	15	Ellis, Cliff
1987		NCAA	I	64	—	—	—	—	—	—	—	25	6	Ellis, Cliff
1988		NCAA	I	—	32	—	—	—	—	—	—	14	15	Ellis, Cliff
1989		NCAA	I	32	—	—	—	—	—	—	—	19	11	Ellis, Cliff
1990		NCAA	I	16	—	—	—	—	—	—	—	26	9	Ellis, Cliff
1993		NCAA	I	—	16	—	—	—	—	—	—	17	13	Ellis, Cliff
1994		NCAA	I	—	8	—	—	—	—	—	—	18	16	Ellis, Cliff
1995		NCAA	I	—	32	—	—	—	—	—	—	15	13	Barnes, Richard D. "Rick"
1996		NCAA	I	64	—	—	—	—	—	—	—	18	11	Barnes, Richard D. "Rick"
1997		NCAA	I	16	—	—	—	—	—	—	—	23	10	Barnes, Richard D. "Rick"
1998		NCAA	I	64	—	—	—	—	—	—	—	18	14	Barnes, Richard D. "Rick"
1980	W	AIAW	I	—	7	—	—	—	—	—	—	24	12	Tribble, Annie S.
1981		AIAW	I	24	—	—	—	—	—	—	—	23	8	Tribble, Annie S.
1982		NCAA	I	32	—	—	—	—	—	—	—	20	12	Tribble, Annie S.
1984		NCAA	I	—	3	—	—	—	—	—	—	21	10	Tribble, Annie S.
1988		NCAA	I	32	—	—	—	—	—	—	—	21	9	Davis, Jim
1989		NCAA	I	16	—	—	—	—	—	—	—	20	11	Davis, Jim
1990		NCAA	I	16	—	—	—	—	—	—	—	22	10	Davis, Jim
1991		NCAA	I	8	—	—	—	—	—	—	—	22	11	Davis, Jim
1992		NCAA	I	32	—	—	—	—	—	—	—	21	10	Davis, Jim
1993		NCAA	I	32	—	—	—	—	—	—	—	19	11	Davis, Jim
1994		NCAA	I	32	—	—	—	—	—	—	—	20	10	Davis, Jim
1995		NCAA	I	—	5	—	—	—	—	—	—	21	11	Davis, Jim
1996		NCAA	I	32	—	—	—	—	—	—	—	23	8	Davis, Jim
1997		NCAA	I	64	—	—	—	—	—	—	—	19	11	Davis, Jim
1998		NCAA	I	32	—	—	—	—	—	—	—	25	8	Davis, Jim
CLEVELAND STATE (OH)														
1986	M	NCAA	I	16	—	—	—	—	—	—	—	29	4	Mackey, Kevin
1987		NCAA	I	—	16	—	—	—	—	—	—	25	8	Mackey, Kevin
1988		NCAA	I	—	16	—	—	—	—	—	—	22	8	Mackey, Kevin

Year	M/W	Assn	Div	NAT	NIT	ARC	CCA	NCI	NCT	OLY	HLM	W	L	Coach
CLINCH VALLEY														
1988	W	NSCAA		8	—	—	—	—	—	—	—	8	19	Kaminske, Debbie
COAST GUARD														
1979	M	NCAA	III	24	—	—	—	—	—	—	—	21	3	Broaca, Peter F.
COASTAL CAROLINA														
1991	M	NCAA	I	64	—	—	—	—	—	—	—	24	8	Bergman, Russell W.
1993		NCAA	I	64	—	—	—	—	—	—	—	22	10	Bergman, Russell W.
COE														
1955	M	NAIA		32	—	—	—	—	—	—	—	14	8	Thomsen, Theron "Tommy"
1956		NAIA		32	—	—	—	—	—	—	—	20	5	Levy, Marv
1958		NAIA		8	—	—	—	—	—	—	—	20	7	Schulz, Robert
1973		NCAA	II	8	—	—	—	—	—	—	—	24	1	Jackson, Marcus
1974		NCAA	II	44	—	—	—	—	—	—	—	18	5	Jackson, Marcus
1975		NCAA	III	23	—	—	—	—	—	—	—	18	6	Tune, Don
1976		NCAA	III	14	—	—	—	—	—	—	—	23	1	Tune, Don
COLBY														
1994	M	NCAA	III	32	—	—	—	—	—	—	—	21	4	Whitmore, Richard
1995		NCAA	III	64	—	—	—	—	—	—	—	20	5	Whitmore, Richard
1997		NCAA	III	64	—	—	—	—	—	—	—	20	5	Whitmore, Richard
COLBY-SAWYER														
1997	W	NCAA	III	64	—	—	—	—	—	—	—	23	5	Martin, George
1998		NCAA	III	48	—	—	—	—	—	—	—	22	5	Martin, George
COLGATE														
1995	M	NCAA	I	64	—	—	—	—	—	—	—	17	13	Bruen, Jack
1996		NCAA	I	64	—	—	—	—	—	—	—	15	15	Bruen, Jack
COLORADO														
1938	M	NCAA		—	2	—	—	—	—	—	—	15	6	Cox, Forrest B. "Frosty"
1940		NCAA		8	1	—	—	—	—	—	—	17	4	Cox, Forrest B. "Frosty"
1942		NCAA		3	—	—	—	—	—	—	—	16	2	Cox, Forrest B. "Frosty"
1946		NCAA		6	—	—	—	—	—	—	—	12	6	Cox, Forrest B. "Frosty"
1954		NCAA		16	—	—	—	—	—	—	—	11	11	Lee, Horace B. "Bebe"
1955		NCAA		3	—	—	—	—	—	—	—	19	6	Lee, Horace B. "Bebe"
1962		NCAA	I	8	—	—	—	—	—	—	—	19	7	Walseth, Russell M. "Sox"
1963		NCAA	I	8	—	—	—	—	—	—	—	19	7	Walseth, Russell M. "Sox"
1969		NCAA	I	12	—	—	—	—	—	—	—	21	7	Walseth, Russell M. "Sox"
1991		NCAA	I	—	3	—	—	—	—	—	—	19	14	Harrington, Joe
1995		NCAA	I	—	32	—	—	—	—	—	—	15	13	Harrington, Joe
1997		NCAA	I	32	—	—	—	—	—	—	—	22	10	Patton, Ricardo
1981	W	AIAW	I	24	—	—	—	—	—	—	—	28	5	Walseth, Russell M. "Sox"
1982		AIAW	I	16	—	—	—	—	—	—	—	28	8	Walseth, Russell M. "Sox"
1988		NCAA	I	32	—	—	—	—	—	—	—	21	11	Barry, Ceal
1989		NCAA	I	32	—	—	—	—	—	—	—	27	4	Barry, Ceal
1992		NCAA	I	48	—	—	—	—	—	—	—	22	9	Barry, Ceal
1993		NCAA	I	8	—	—	—	—	—	—	—	27	4	Barry, Ceal
1994		NCAA	I	16	—	—	—	—	—	—	—	27	5	Barry, Ceal
1995		NCAA	I	8	—	—	—	—	—	—	—	30	3	Barry, Ceal

Year	M/W	Assn	Div	NAT	NIT	ARC	CCA	NCI	NCT	OLY	HLM	W	L	Coach
1996		NCAA	I	32	—	—	—	—	—	—	—	26	9	Barry, Ceal
1997		NCAA	I	16	—	—	—	—	—	—	—	23	9	Barry, Ceal

COLORADO CHRISTIAN

Year	M/W	Assn	Div	NAT	NIT	ARC	CCA	NCI	NCT	OLY	HLM	W	L	Coach
1990	M	NCCAA	I	8	—	—	—	—	—	—	—	20	10	Evans, Frank
1993		NCAA	II	32	—	—	—	—	—	—	—	20	9	Evans, Frank

COLORADO COLLEGE

Year	M/W	Assn	Div	NAT	NIT	ARC	CCA	NCI	NCT	OLY	HLM	W	L	Coach
1960	M	NCAA	II	32	—	—	—	—	—	—	—	17	5	Eastlack, Leon C. "Red"
1961		NCAA	II	32	—	—	—	—	—	—	—	18	9	Eastlack, Leon C. "Red"
1992		NCAA	III	32	—	—	—	—	—	—	—	22	5	Walker, Al
1977	W	AIAW	S	16	—	—	—	—	—	—	—	20	5	Golden, Laura L.
1981		AIAW	II	16	—	—	—	—	—	—	—	20	8	Golden, Laura L.
1982		AIAW	II	16	—	—	—	—	—	—	—	16	12	Puckett, Linda
1990		NCAA	III	32	—	—	—	—	—	—	—	17	9	Branson, Beth

COLORADO NORTHWESTERN CC

Year	M/W	Assn	Div	NAT	NIT	ARC	CCA	NCI	NCT	OLY	HLM	W	L	Coach
1975	M	NSCAA		8	—	—	—	—	—	—	—	13	17	Conrad, Paul
1976		NSCAA		8	—	—	—	—	—	—	—	10	22	Conrad, Paul
1977		NSCAA		16	—	—	—	—	—	—	—	10	22	Conrad, Paul
1978		NSCAA		16	—	—	—	—	—	—	—	17	12	Conrad, Paul
1979		NSCAA		8	—	—	—	—	—	—	—	20	14	Conrad, Paul
1980		NSCAA		12	—	—	—	—	—	—	—	20	14	Conrad, Paul
1981		NSCAA		16	—	—	—	—	—	—	—	17	16	Conrad, Paul
1984		NSCAA		3	—	—	—	—	—	—	—	18	18	Conrad, Paul
1985		NSCAA		12	—	—	—	—	—	—	—	12	20	Conrad, Paul
1986		NSCAA		16	—	—	—	—	—	—	—	16	19	Conrad, Paul
1987		NSCAA		4	—	—	—	—	—	—	—	15	20	Conrad, Paul
1990		NSCAA		12	—	—	—	—	—	—	—	8	25	Conrad, Paul
1991		NSCAA		5	—	—	—	—	—	—	—	11	22	Conrad, Paul
1998		NSCAA		12	—	—	—	—	—	—	—	8	23	Conrad, Paul
1982	W	NSCAA		6	—	—	—	—	—	—	—	X	X	Unknown
1983		NSCAA		5	—	—	—	—	—	—	—	X	X	Unknown
1984		NSCAA		8	—	—	—	—	—	—	—	X	X	Unknown
1987		NSCAA		5	—	—	—	—	—	—	—	8	23	Frankiewicz, Steve

COLORADO STATE

Year	M/W	Assn	Div	NAT	NIT	ARC	CCA	NCI	NCT	OLY	HLM	W	L	Coach
1954	M	NCAA		16	—	—	—	—	—	—	—	22	7	Strannigan, William M.
1961		NCAA	I	—	8	—	—	—	—	—	—	17	9	Williams, James J.
1962		NCAA	I	—	12	—	—	—	—	—	—	18	9	Williams, James J.
1963		NCAA	I	25	—	—	—	—	—	—	—	18	5	Williams, James J.
1965		NCAA	I	23	—	—	—	—	—	—	—	16	8	Williams, James J.
1966		NCAA	I	22	—	—	—	—	—	—	—	14	8	Williams, James J.
1969		NCAA	I	8	—	—	—	—	—	—	—	17	7	Williams, James J.
1988		NCAA	I	—	3	—	—	—	—	—	—	22	13	Grant, Boyd "Tiny"
1989		NCAA	I	32	—	—	—	—	—	—	—	23	10	Grant, Boyd "Tiny"
1990		NCAA	I	64	—	—	—	—	—	—	—	21	9	Grant, Boyd "Tiny"
1996		NCAA	I	—	32	—	—	—	—	—	—	18	12	Morrill, Stew
1998		NCAA	I	—	32	—	—	—	—	—	—	20	9	Morrill, Stew
1996	W	NCAA	I	32	—	—	—	—	—	—	—	26	5	Williams, Greg
1998		NCAA	I	32	—	—	—	—	—	—	—	24	6	Collen, Tim

Year	M/W	Assn	Div	NAT	NIT	ARC	CCA	NCI	NCT	OLY	HLM	W	L	Coach
COLORADO WOMAN'S														
1980	W	NSCAA		1	—	—	—	—	—	—	—	23	8	Forkum, Jim
COLUMBIA (MO)														
1990	M	NAIA		16	—	—	—	—	—	—	—	30	8	Burchard, Bob
1995		NAIA	I	32	—	—	—	—	—	—	—	29	6	Burchard, Bob
1996		NAIA	I	32	—	—	—	—	—	—	—	27	8	Burchard, Bob
1997		NAIA	I	32	—	—	—	—	—	—	—	27	8	Burchard, Bob
COLUMBIA (NY)														
1904	M			—	—	—	—	—	—	—	1	17	1	Elias, Henry H.
1905				—	—	—	—	—	—	—	1	19	1	Elias, Henry H.
1910		NCAA		—	—	—	—	—	—	—	1	11	1	Fisher, Harry A.
1948		NCAA		8	—	—	—	—	—	—	—	21	3	Ridings, Gordon H.
1951		NCAA		16	—	—	—	—	—	—	—	21	1	Rossini, Lucio "Lou"
1968		NCAA	I	12	—	—	—	—	—	—	—	23	5	Rohan, John P. "Jack"
1986	W	NCAA	III	24	—	—	—	—	—	—	—	21	6	Kalafies, Nancy
COLUMBIA (SC)														
1980	W	AIAW	III	24	—	—	—	—	—	—	—	15	13	Patenaude, Donald P.
1981		AIAW	III	16	—	—	—	—	—	—	—	X	X	Patenaude, Donald P.
1982		AIAW	III	16	—	—	—	—	—	—	—	15	15	Patenaude, Donald P.
COLUMBIA BIBLE														
1996	M	NBCAA	I	8	—	—	—	—	—	—	—	8	23	Schmidt, Robert "Rob"
1997		NBCAA	I	7	—	—	—	—	—	—	—	12	26	Schmidt, Robert "Rob"
COLUMBIA CHRISTIAN														
1991	W	NCCAA	I	8	—	—	—	—	—	—	—			Fields, Terry L.
1992		NCCAA	I	8	—	—	—	—	—	—	—			Fields, Terry L.
COLUMBIA JC (SC)														
1978	M	NSCAA		16	—	—	—	—	—	—	—			
1979		NSCAA		16	—	—	—	—	—	—	—	17	8	
1980		NSCAA		8	—	—	—	—	—	—	—			
1986		NSCAA		4	—	—	—	—	—	—	—	23	7	
1987		NSCAA		6	—	—	—	—	—	—	—			
1988		NSCAA		6	—	—	—	—	—	—	—	18	12	Hewett, Dale
COLUMBIA STATE CC														
1985	M	NSCAA		12	—	—	—	—	—	—	—	14	8	Painter, Jim
COLUMBIA UNION														
1992	M	NAIA	I	32	—	—	—	—	—	—	—	18	16	Murray, Rick
COLUMBUS BUSINESS (OH)														
1968	M	NSCAA		2	—	—	—	—	—	—	—			
COLUMBUS STATE (GA)														
1978	M	NCAA	II	32	—	—	—	—	—	—	—	19	8	Clements, Frank M. "Sonny"
1984		NCAA	II	24	—	—	—	—	—	—	—	22	7	Eidsness, John
1996		NCAA	II	16	—	—	—	—	—	—	—	26	6	Greene, Herbert
1998		NCAA	II	48	—	—	—	—	—	—	—	26	7	Greene, Herbert

Year	M/W	Assn	Div	NAT	NIT	ARC	CCA	NCI	NCT	OLY	HLM	W	L	Coach
1998	W	NCAA	II	32	—	—	—	—	—	—	—	25	6	Sparks, Jay

CONCORD

Year	M/W	Assn	Div	NAT	NIT	ARC	CCA	NCI	NCT	OLY	HLM	W	L	Coach
1991	M	NAIA		16	—	—	—	—	—	—	—	28	8	Cox, Steve
1995		NAIA	I	32	—	—	—	—	—	—	—	20	11	Cox, Steve
1997		NCAA	II	16	—	—	—	—	—	—	—	20	13	Cox, Steve

CONCORDIA (CA)

Year	M/W	Assn	Div	NAT	NIT	ARC	CCA	NCI	NCT	OLY	HLM	W	L	Coach
1986	M	NSCAA		12	—	—	—	—	—	—	—	25	8	Wild, Dave
1992	W	NAIA	I	32	—	—	—	—	—	—	—	25	5	Schlichtemeier, Kent
1993		NAIA	I	32	—	—	—	—	—	—	—	26	5	Schlichtemeier, Kent
1997		NAIA	I	32	—	—	—	—	—	—	—	28	6	Wolter, Dave

CONCORDIA (IL)

Year	M/W	Assn	Div	NAT	NIT	ARC	CCA	NCI	NCT	OLY	HLM	W	L	Coach
1962	M	NCAA	II	16	—	—	—	—	—	—	—	20	4	Spitz, Donald A.
1963		NCAA	II	24	—	—	—	—	—	—	—	19	5	Spitz, Donald A.
1965		NCAA	II	32	—	—	—	—	—	—	—	18	6	Faszholz, Thomas O.
1969		NCAA	II	32	—	—	—	—	—	—	—	20	4	Faszholz, Thomas O.

CONCORDIA (MI)

Year	M/W	Assn	Div	NAT	NIT	ARC	CCA	NCI	NCT	OLY	HLM	W	L	Coach
1979	M	NSCAA		16	—	—	—	—	—	—	—	10	18	Harting, Walt
1980		NSCAA		12	—	—	—	—	—	—	—	23	9	Harting, Walt
1993	W	NCCAA	I	5	—	—	—	—	—	—	—	8	23	Twietmeyer, Dr. T. Alan
1994		NCCAA	I	8	—	—	—	—	—	—	—	6	23	Twietmeyer, Dr. T. Alan

CONCORDIA (NE)

Year	M/W	Assn	Div	NAT	NIT	ARC	CCA	NCI	NCT	OLY	HLM	W	L	Coach
1991	M	NAIA		32	—	—	—	—	—	—	—	23	11	Schmidt, Grant
1992		NAIA	II	3	—	—	—	—	—	—	—	26	10	Schmidt, Grant
1995		NAIA	II	8	—	—	—	—	—	—	—	30	4	Schmidt, Grant
1996		NAIA	II	32	—	—	—	—	—	—	—	25	6	Schmidt, Grant
1997		NAIA	II	32	—	—	—	—	—	—	—	18	14	Schmidt, Grant
1998		NAIA	II	32	—	—	—	—	—	—	—	26	7	Schmidt, Grant
1987	W	NSCAA		1	—	—	—	—	—	—	—	23	8	Everts, Dr. Carl
1988		NSCAA		2	—	—	—	—	—	—	—	19	15	Everts, Dr. Carl
1989		NSCAA		1	—	—	—	—	—	—	—	25	7	Everts, Dr. Carl
1990		NSCAA		1	—	—	—	—	—	—	—	20	13	Everts, Dr. Carl
1992		NAIA	II	20	—	—	—	—	—	—	—	23	13	Everts, Dr. Carl
1992		NSCAA		3	—	—	—	—	—	—	—	23	13	Everts, Dr. Carl
1997		NAIA	II	8	—	—	—	—	—	—	—	26	6	Lemke, Dr. Mark
1998		NAIA	II	32	—	—	—	—	—	—	—	24	8	Lemke, Dr. Mark

CONCORDIA (OR)

Year	M/W	Assn	Div	NAT	NIT	ARC	CCA	NCI	NCT	OLY	HLM	W	L	Coach
1976	M	NSCAA		8	—	—	—	—	—	—	—	17	12	Friedrichs, Dr. Warren
1978		NSCAA		16	—	—	—	—	—	—	—	21	9	Friedrichs, Dr. Warren
1979		NSCAA		2	—	—	—	—	—	—	—	17	10	Friedrichs, Dr. Warren
1980		NSCAA		10	—	—	—	—	—	—	—	19	14	Friedrichs, Dr. Warren
1982		NCCAA	I	3	—	—	—	—	—	—	—	22	11	Hewitt, Tom
1990		NCCAA	I	8	—	—	—	—	—	—	—	14	21	Schieldheisz, Dr. Joel
1991		NCCAA	I	5	—	—	—	—	—	—	—	18	16	Schieldheisz, Dr. Joel
1980	W	NSCAA		3	—	—	—	—	—	—	—	13	7	Kunert, Charles J. "Chuck"
1981		AIAW	III	16	—	—	—	—	—	—	—	28	1	Kunert, Charles J. "Chuck"
1988		NCCAA	I	2	—	—	—	—	—	—	—	20	12	Kunert, Charles J. "Chuck"

Year	M/W	Assn	Div	NAT	NIT	ARC	CCA	NCI	NCT	OLY	HLM	W	L	Coach
CONCORDIA (WI)														
1979	M	NSCAA		3	—	—	—	—	—	—	—	—	20	13	Weiss, Dick
1980		NSCAA		8	—	—	—	—	—	—	—	—	19	17	Weiss, Dick
1982		NSCAA		12	—	—	—	—	—	—	—	—	6	23	Lohmeyer, Neil
1993		NAIA	II	20	—	—	—	—	—	—	—	—	18	9	Stelmachowicz, Dr. Cary
1992	W	NAIA	II	16	—	—	—	—	—	—	—	—	22	4	Surridge, Dr. Jack
1993		NAIA	II	16	—	—	—	—	—	—	—	—	23	4	Surridge, Dr. Jack
1994		NAIA	II	3	—	—	—	—	—	—	—	—	25	4	Surridge, Dr. Jack
1995		NAIA	II	3	—	—	—	—	—	—	—	—	20	4	Surridge, Dr. Jack
1997		NAIA	II	32	—	—	—	—	—	—	—	—	18	9	Witte, Ken
CONCORDIA: AUSTIN														
1982	M	NSCAA		9	—	—	—	—	—	—	—	—	9	20	Orton, Tom
1983		NSCAA		1	—	—	—	—	—	—	—	—	30	7	Orton, Tom
CONCORDIA: MOORHEAD														
1996	M	NCAA	III	64	—	—	—	—	—	—	—	—	21	6	Siverson, Duane
1982	W	AIAW	III	1	—	—	—	—	—	—	—	—	31	3	Langseth, Marc
1983		NCAA	III	16	—	—	—	—	—	—	—	—	18	10	Langseth, Marc
1984		NCAA	III	16	—	—	—	—	—	—	—	—	21	7	Langseth, Marc
1985		NCAA	III	32	—	—	—	—	—	—	—	—	16	12	Siverson, Duane
1986		NCAA	III	16	—	—	—	—	—	—	—	—	25	3	Siverson, Duane
1987		NCAA	III	2	—	—	—	—	—	—	—	—	26	5	Siverson, Duane
1988		NCAA	III	1	—	—	—	—	—	—	—	—	29	2	Siverson, Duane
1989		NCAA	III	16	—	—	—	—	—	—	—	—	24	3	Siverson, Duane
1990		NCAA	III	8	—	—	—	—	—	—	—	—	24	5	Siverson, Duane
1991		NCAA	III	8	—	—	—	—	—	—	—	—	21	8	Siverson, Duane
1992		NCAA	III	32	—	—	—	—	—	—	—	—	18	9	Pyle, Jerry
1993		NCAA	III	8	—	—	—	—	—	—	—	—	20	7	Kohler, Robert
1994		NCAA	III	32	—	—	—	—	—	—	—	—	18	8	Kohler, Robert
1995		NCAA	III	32	—	—	—	—	—	—	—	—	20	7	Kohler, Robert
1996		NCAA	III	64	—	—	—	—	—	—	—	—	19	6	Kohler, Robert
CONCORDIA: SAINT PAUL														
1976	M	NSCAA		14	—	—	—	—	—	—	—	—	16	5	Hendrickson, John
1977		NSCAA		3	—	—	—	—	—	—	—	—	20	9	Hendrickson, John
1978		NSCAA		8	—	—	—	—	—	—	—	—	18	8	Hendrickson, John
1979		NSCAA		16	—	—	—	—	—	—	—	—	10	14	Hendrickson, John
1989		NSCAA		10	—	—	—	—	—	—	—	—	14	14	Getzlaff, Dennis
1980	W	NSCAA		5	—	—	—	—	—	—	—	—	16	10	Surridge, Dr. Jack
1982		NSCAA		5	—	—	—	—	—	—	—	—	17	9	Surridge, Dr. Jack
1983		NSCAA		1	—	—	—	—	—	—	—	—	20	6	Surridge, Dr. Jack
1984		NSCAA		4	—	—	—	—	—	—	—	—	19	10	Surridge, Dr. Jack
1985		NSCAA		4	—	—	—	—	—	—	—	—	20	8	Surridge, Dr. Jack
1986		NSCAA		5	—	—	—	—	—	—	—	—	20	10	Surridge, Dr. Jack
1987		NSCAA		7	—	—	—	—	—	—	—	—	13	14	Surridge, Dr. Jack
1989		NSCAA		2	—	—	—	—	—	—	—	—	17	10	Surridge, Dr. Jack
1990		NSCAA		4	—	—	—	—	—	—	—	—	9	22	Olley, Christopher

Year	M/W	Assn	Div	NAT	NIT	ARC	CCA	NCI	NCT	OLY	HLM	W	L	Coach
CONNECTICUT														
1951	M	NCAA		16	—	—	—	—	—	—	—	22	4	Greer, Hugh S.
1954		NCAA		24	—	—	—	—	—	—	—	23	3	Greer, Hugh S.
1955		NCAA		—	12	—	—	—	—	—	—	20	5	Greer, Hugh S.
1956		NCAA		16	—	—	—	—	—	—	—	17	11	Greer, Hugh S.
1957		NCAA	I	23	—	—	—	—	—	—	—	17	8	Greer, Hugh S.
1958		NCAA	I	24	—	—	—	—	—	—	—	17	10	Greer, Hugh S.
1959		NCAA	I	23	—	—	—	—	—	—	—	17	7	Greer, Hugh S.
1960		NCAA	I	25	—	—	—	—	—	—	—	17	9	Greer, Hugh S.
1963		NCAA	I	25	—	—	—	—	—	—	—	18	7	Shabel, Fred A.
1964		NCAA	I	8	—	—	—	—	—	—	—	16	11	Shabel, Fred A.
1965		NCAA	I	23	—	—	—	—	—	—	—	23	3	Shabel, Fred A.
1967		NCAA	I	23	—	—	—	—	—	—	—	17	7	Shabel, Fred A.
1974		NCAA	I	—	8	—	—	—	—	—	—	19	8	Rowe, Donald E. "Dee"
1975		NCAA	I	—	16	—	—	—	—	—	—	18	10	Rowe, Donald E. "Dee"
1976		NCAA	I	16	—	—	—	—	—	—	—	19	10	Rowe, Donald E. "Dee"
1979		NCAA	I	32	—	—	—	—	—	—	—	21	8	Perno, Dominic P. "Dom"
1980		NCAA	I	—	32	—	—	—	—	—	—	20	9	Perno, Dominic P. "Dom"
1981		NCAA	I	—	16	—	—	—	—	—	—	20	9	Perno, Dominic P. "Dom"
1982		NCAA	I	—	32	—	—	—	—	—	—	17	11	Perno, Dominic P. "Dom"
1988		NCAA	I	—	1	—	—	—	—	—	—	20	14	Calhoun, James A.
1989		NCAA	I	—	8	—	—	—	—	—	—	18	13	Calhoun, James A.
1990		NCAA	I	8	—	—	—	—	—	—	—	31	6	Calhoun, James A.
1991		NCAA	I	16	—	—	—	—	—	—	—	20	11	Calhoun, James A.
1992		NCAA	I	32	—	—	—	—	—	—	—	20	10	Calhoun, James A.
1993		NCAA	I	—	32	—	—	—	—	—	—	15	13	Calhoun, James A.
1994		NCAA	I	16	—	—	—	—	—	—	—	29	5	Calhoun, James A.
1995		NCAA	I	8	—	—	—	—	—	—	—	28	5	Calhoun, James A.
1996		NCAA	I	16	—	—	—	—	—	—	—	32	3	Calhoun, James A.
1997		NCAA	I	—	3	—	—	—	—	—	—	18	15	Calhoun, James A.
1998		NCAA	I	8	—	—	—	—	—	—	—	33	5	Calhoun, James A.
1989	W	NCAA	I	48	—	—	—	—	—	—	—	24	6	Auriemma, Geno
1990		NCAA	I	32	—	—	—	—	—	—	—	25	6	Auriemma, Geno
1991		NCAA	I	3	—	—	—	—	—	—	—	29	5	Auriemma, Geno
1992		NCAA	I	32	—	—	—	—	—	—	—	23	11	Auriemma, Geno
1993		NCAA	I	48	—	—	—	—	—	—	—	18	11	Auriemma, Geno
1994		NCAA	I	8	—	—	—	—	—	—	—	30	3	Auriemma, Geno
1995		NCAA	I	1	—	—	—	—	—	—	—	35	0	Auriemma, Geno
1996		NCAA	I	3	—	—	—	—	—	—	—	34	4	Auriemma, Geno
1997		NCAA	I	8	—	—	—	—	—	—	—	33	1	Auriemma, Geno
1998		NCAA	I	8	—	—	—	—	—	—	—	34	3	Auriemma, Geno
CONNECTICUT COLLEGE														
1998	M	NCAA	III	16	—	—	—	—	—	—	—	22	4	Miller, Glen
COPPIN STATE														
1976	M	NAIA		1	—	—	—	—	—	—	—	39	2	Bates, John H.
1990		NCAA	I	64	—	—	—	—	—	—	—	26	7	Mitchell, Ronald C. "Fang"
1991		NCAA	I	—	32	—	—	—	—	—	—	19	11	Mitchell, Ronald C. "Fang"
1993		NCAA	I	64	—	—	—	—	—	—	—	22	8	Mitchell, Ronald C. "Fang"

Year	M/W	Assn	Div	NAT	NIT	ARC	CCA	NCI	NCT	OLY	HLM	W	L	Coach
1995		NCAA	I	—	16	—	—	—	—	—	—	21	10	Mitchell, Ronald C. "Fang"
1997		NCAA	I	32	—	—	—	—	—	—	—	22	9	Mitchell, Ronald C. "Fang"

CORNELL (IA)

Year	M/W	Assn	Div	NAT	NIT	ARC	CCA	NCI	NCT	OLY	HLM	W	L	Coach
1960	M	NCAA	II	4	—	—	—	—	—	—	—	16	6	Maaske, Paul M.
1961		NCAA	II	24	—	—	—	—	—	—	—	17	6	Maaske, Paul M.
1963		NCAA	II	32	—	—	—	—	—	—	—	16	7	Maaske, Paul M.
1970		NCAA	II	32	—	—	—	—	—	—	—	16	8	Maaske, Paul M.
1976		NCAA	III	28	—	—	—	—	—	—	—	15	9	Maaske, Paul M.
1994		NCAA	III	40	—	—	—	—	—	—	—	17	8	Grace, Gary

CORNELL (NY)

Year	M/W	Assn	Div	NAT	NIT	ARC	CCA	NCI	NCT	OLY	HLM	W	L	Coach
1954	M	NCAA		16	—	—	—	—	—	—	—	17	7	Greene, Royner C.
1988		NCAA	I	64	—	—	—	—	—	—	—	17	10	Dement, Mike

CORNERSTONE

Year	M/W	Assn	Div	NAT	NIT	ARC	CCA	NCI	NCT	OLY	HLM	W	L	Coach
1994	M	NCCAA	I	8	—	—	—	—	—	—	—	17	19	Elders, Kim
1995		NCCAA	I	6	—	—	—	—	—	—	—	18	21	Elders, Kim

CORTLAND STATE

Year	M/W	Assn	Div	NAT	NIT	ARC	CCA	NCI	NCT	OLY	HLM	W	L	Coach
1997	M	NCAA	III	64	—	—	—	—	—	—	—	19	9	Spanbauer, Tom
1970	W	AIAW		6	—	—	—	—	—	—	—	X	X	Erbaugh, Sally
1988		NCAA	III	32	—	—	—	—	—	—	—	21	7	Foley, Bonnie
1992		NCAA	III	16	—	—	—	—	—	—	—	24	5	Foley, Bonnie

COVENANT

Year	M/W	Assn	Div	NAT	NIT	ARC	CCA	NCI	NCT	OLY	HLM	W	L	Coach
1985	M	NCCAA	I	8	—	—	—	—	—	—	—	17	14	Fitzgerald, Gene
1987		NCCAA	I	4	—	—	—	—	—	—	—	17	14	Fitzgerald, Gene
1992	W	NCCAA	I	4	—	—	—	—	—	—	—	22	16	Smialek, Tami
1993		NCCAA	I	6	—	—	—	—	—	—	—	20	14	Smialek, Tami
1997		NAIA	II	32	—	—	—	—	—	—	—	21	7	Smialek, Tami

CREIGHTON

Year	M/W	Assn	Div	NAT	NIT	ARC	CCA	NCI	NCT	OLY	HLM	W	L	Coach
1941	M	NCAA		6	—	—	—	—	—	—	—	18	7	Hickey, Edgar S. "Eddie"
1942		NCAA		—	3	—	—	—	—	—	—	19	5	Hickey, Edgar S. "Eddie"
1943		NCAA		—	8	—	—	—	—	—	—	16	1	Hickey, Edgar S. "Eddie"
1950		NCAA		—	—	—	—	8	—	—	—	13	14	Belford, Julius V. "Duce"
1962		NCAA	I	12	—	—	—	—	—	—	—	21	5	McManus, John J. "Red"
1963		NCAA	I	—	—	—	—	3	—	—	—	14	13	McManus, John J. "Red"
1964		NCAA	I	16	—	—	—	—	—	—	—	22	7	McManus, John J. "Red"
1974		NCAA	I	12	—	—	—	—	—	—	—	23	7	Sutton, Eddie
1975		NCAA	I	32	—	—	—	—	—	—	—	20	7	Apke, Tom
1977		NCAA	I	—	16	—	—	—	—	—	—	21	7	Apke, Tom
1978		NCAA	I	32	—	—	—	—	—	—	—	19	9	Apke, Tom
1981		NCAA	I	48	—	—	—	—	—	—	—	21	9	Apke, Tom
1984		NCAA	I	—	32	—	—	—	—	—	—	17	14	Reed, Willis, Jr.
1989		NCAA	I	64	—	—	—	—	—	—	—	20	11	Barone, Anthony A. "Tony"
1990		NCAA	I	—	32	—	—	—	—	—	—	21	12	Barone, Anthony A. "Tony"
1991		NCAA	I	32	—	—	—	—	—	—	—	24	8	Barone, Anthony A. "Tony"
1998		NCAA	I	—	32	—	—	—	—	—	—	18	10	Altman, Dana

Year	M/W	Assn	Div	NAT	NIT	ARC	CCA	NCI	NCT	OLY	HLM	W	L	Coach
1987	W	NCAA	I	—	3	—	—	—	—	—	—	23	7	Rasmussen, Bruce
1992		NCAA	I	32	—	—	—	—	—	—	—	28	4	Rasmussen, Bruce
1994		NCAA	I	32	—	—	—	—	—	—	—	24	7	Yori, Connie

CROWLEY'S RIDGE

Year	M/W	Assn	Div	NAT	NIT	ARC	CCA	NCI	NCT	OLY	HLM	W	L	Coach
1998	M	NSCAA		12	—	—	—	—	—	—	—	9	14	Livingston, Dean

CROWN (MN)

Year	M/W	Assn	Div	NAT	NIT	ARC	CCA	NCI	NCT	OLY	HLM	W	L	Coach
1983	M	NBCAA		2	—	—	—	—	—	—	—	24	9	Pierce, Bud
1985		NBCAA	I	8	—	—	—	—	—	—	—	X	X	Pierce, Bud
1986		NBCAA	I	4	—	—	—	—	—	—	—	X	X	Pierce, Bud
1987		NCCAA	II	6	—	—	—	—	—	—	—	X	X	Pierce, Bud
1988		NBCAA	I	5	—	—	—	—	—	—	—	X	X	Pierce, Bud
1990		NBCAA	I	7	—	—	—	—	—	—	—	12	20	Newman, Joe
1991		NBCAA	I	8	—	—	—	—	—	—	—	17	17	Newman, Joe
1997		NCCAA	II	5	—	—	—	—	—	—	—	27	14	Pearson, Troy
1983	W	NBCAA		1	—	—	—	—	—	—	—	X	X	Hardy, Don
1984		NBCAA		1	—	—	—	—	—	—	—	X	X	Hardy, Don
1985		NBCAA		1	—	—	—	—	—	—	—	X	X	Guavin, Julie
1986		NBCAA		6	—	—	—	—	—	—	—	X	X	Rogness, Tony
1987		NBCAA		2	—	—	—	—	—	—	—	X	X	Rogness, Tony
1988		NBCAA		2	—	—	—	—	—	—	—	X	X	Moats, Candace
1990		NBCAA		3	—	—	—	—	—	—	—	9	9	Moats, Candace
1991		NBCAA		1	—	—	—	—	—	—	—	19	9	Rogness, Tony
1997		NCCAA	II	6	—	—	—	—	—	—	—	20	9	Haller, Mickey
1998		NCCAA	II	3	—	—	—	—	—	—	—	15	11	Ague, Paul

CROWN (TN)

Year	M/W	Assn	Div	NAT	NIT	ARC	CCA	NCI	NCT	OLY	HLM	W	L	Coach
1995	M	NCCAA	IIA	2	—	—	—	—	—	—	—	24	8	Weber, Dr. Greg

CULLMAN

Year	M/W	Assn	Div	NAT	NIT	ARC	CCA	NCI	NCT	OLY	HLM	W	L	Coach
1974	M	NSCAA		3	—	—	—	—	—	—	—	16	10	Franey, Joseph S.
1975		NSCAA		8	—	—	—	—	—	—	—	14	10	Franey, Joseph S.

CULVER-STOCKTON

Year	M/W	Assn	Div	NAT	NIT	ARC	CCA	NCI	NCT	OLY	HLM	W	L	Coach
1939	M	NAIA		16	—	—	—	—	—	—	—	16	8	Herington, William A.
1941		NAIA		16	—	—	—	—	—	—	—	16	5	Herington, William A.
1946		NAIA		16	—	—	—	—	—	—	—	18	4	Herington, William A.
1947		NAIA		32	—	—	—	—	—	—	—	18	2	Herington, William A.
1959		NAIA		32	—	—	—	—	—	—	—	19	7	Herington, William A.
1992	W	NAIA	II	16	—	—	—	—	—	—	—	22	11	Turpin, Kathy
1995		NAIA	II	32	—	—	—	—	—	—	—	29	6	Clampitt, Randy

CUMBERLAND (KY)

Year	M/W	Assn	Div	NAT	NIT	ARC	CCA	NCI	NCT	OLY	HLM	W	L	Coach
1978	M	NAIA		32	—	—	—	—	—	—	—	27	10	Trivette, Ken
1980		NAIA		32	—	—	—	—	—	—	—	25	10	Vernon, Randy
1982		NAIA		32	—	—	—	—	—	—	—	20	16	Vernon, Randy
1983		NAIA		32	—	—	—	—	—	—	—	33	3	Vernon, Randy
1984		NAIA		16	—	—	—	—	—	—	—	27	4	Vernon, Randy
1986		NAIA		16	—	—	—	—	—	—	—	32	3	Vernon, Randy
1989		NAIA		16	—	—	—	—	—	—	—	26	7	Vernon, Randy
1992		NAIA	I	8	—	—	—	—	—	—	—	25	8	Vernon, Randy

Year	M/W	Assn	Div	NAT	NIT	ARC	CCA	NCI	NCT	OLY	HLM	W	L	Coach
1993		NAIA	I	32	—	—	—	—	—	—	—	28	7	Vernon, Randy
1997		NAIA	I	3	—	—	—	—	—	—	—	31	7	Vernon, Randy
1998		NAIA	I	32	—	—	—	—	—	—	—	16	17	Vernon, Randy
1986	W	NAIA		16	—	—	—	—	—	—	—	24	6	Morgan, Henry
1988		NAIA		16	—	—	—	—	—	—	—	25	10	Morgan, Henry

CUMBERLAND (TN)

Year	M/W	Assn	Div	NAT	NIT	ARC	CCA	NCI	NCT	OLY	HLM	W	L	Coach
1996	M	NAIA	I	8	—	—	—	—	—	—	—	28	6	Petrone, Mike

D'YOUVILLE

Year	M/W	Assn	Div	NAT	NIT	ARC	CCA	NCI	NCT	OLY	HLM	W	L	Coach
1987	M	NSCAA		16	—	—	—	—	—	—	—	8	14	DeMarco, "Chip"

DAEMEN

Year	M/W	Assn	Div	NAT	NIT	ARC	CCA	NCI	NCT	OLY	HLM	W	L	Coach
1978	M	NSCAA		16	—	—	—	—	—	—	—	20	5	Murray, Kenneth
1984		NSCAA		12	—	—	—	—	—	—	—	X	X	Licate, Gilbert P.
1996	W	NAIA	I	32	—	—	—	—	—	—	—	27	5	Skolen, David
1997		NAIA	I	32	—	—	—	—	—	—	—	27	6	Skolen, David

DAKOTA STATE

Year	M/W	Assn	Div	NAT	NIT	ARC	CCA	NCI	NCT	OLY	HLM	W	L	Coach
1992	M	NAIA	II	3	—	—	—	—	—	—	—	19	16	McDermott, Brian

DAKOTA WESLEYAN

Year	M/W	Assn	Div	NAT	NIT	ARC	CCA	NCI	NCT	OLY	HLM	W	L	Coach
1937	M	NAIA		8	—	—	—	—	—	—	—	12	5	Belding, Lester C.
1938		NAIA		32	—	—	—	—	—	—	—	11	10	Belding, Lester C.
1939		NAIA		16	—	—	—	—	—	—	—	11	2	Belding, Lester C.
1940		NAIA		32	—	—	—	—	—	—	—	12	5	Belding, Lester C.
1941		NAIA		32	—	—	—	—	—	—	—	16	5	Belding, Lester C.
1943		NAIA		32	—	—	—	—	—	—	—	21	2	Belding, Lester C.
1946		NAIA		8	—	—	—	—	—	—	—	16	6	Green, Ray
1947		NAIA		16	—	—	—	—	—	—	—	25	3	Gorby, Dave
1964		NAIA		32	—	—	—	—	—	—	—	21	3	Fosness, Gordon
1979		NAIA		32	—	—	—	—	—	—	—	26	3	Fosness, Gordon
1995		NAIA	II	32	—	—	—	—	—	—	—	19	11	Martin, Doug

DALLAS BAPTIST

Year	M/W	Assn	Div	NAT	NIT	ARC	CCA	NCI	NCT	OLY	HLM	W	L	Coach
1973	M	NAIA		32	—	—	—	—	—	—	—	24	11	Sheiron, Steve

DALLAS CHRISTIAN

Year	M/W	Assn	Div	NAT	NIT	ARC	CCA	NCI	NCT	OLY	HLM	W	L	Coach
1994	M	NBCAA	I	6	—	—	—	—	—	—	—	10	15	Dickens, Charles "Chip"
1997		LCC		3	—	—	—	—	—	—	—	19	13	Wilkerson, Keith
1997		NBCAA	I	3	—	—	—	—	—	—	—	19	13	Wilkerson, Keith

DARTMOUTH

Year	M/W	Assn	Div	NAT	NIT	ARC	CCA	NCI	NCT	OLY	HLM	W	L	Coach
1906	M	NCAA		—	—	—	—	—	—	—	1	16	2	Unknown
1941		NCAA		6	—	—	—	—	—	—	—	19	5	Cowles, Osborne "Ozzie"
1942		NCAA		2	—	—	—	—	—	—	—	22	4	Cowles, Osborne "Ozzie"
1943		NCAA		6	—	—	—	—	—	—	—	20	3	Cowles, Osborne "Ozzie"
1944		NCAA		2	—	—	—	—	—	—	—	19	2	Brown, Earl M.
1956		NCAA		12	—	—	—	—	—	—	—	18	11	Julian, Alvin F. "Doggie"
1958		NCAA	I	8	—	—	—	—	—	—	—	22	5	Julian, Alvin F. "Doggie"
1959		NCAA	I	23	—	—	—	—	—	—	—	22	6	Julian, Alvin F. "Doggie"

Year	M/W	Assn	Div	NAT	NIT	ARC	CCA	NCI	NCT	OLY	HLM	W	L	Coach
1983	W	NCAA	I	36	—	—	—	—	—	—	—	18	8	Wielgus, Christina
1995		NCAA	I	64	—	—	—	—	—	—	—	16	11	Wielgus, Christina

DAVID N MYERS

Year	M/W	Assn	Div	NAT	NIT	ARC	CCA	NCI	NCT	OLY	HLM	W	L	Coach
1967	M	NSCAA		8	—	—	—	—	—	—	—	14	7	Kavanaugh, W. H.
1970		NSCAA		6	—	—	—	—	—	—	—	13	13	Schuster, Will
1974		NSCAA		4	—	—	—	—	—	—	—	15	8	Kennedy, Richard
1975		NSCAA		16	—	—	—	—	—	—				McCoid, Rod
1986		NSCAA		2	—	—	—	—	—	—	—	22	12	Friedman, Michael
1987		NSCAA		5	—	—	—	—	—	—	—	19	16	Rogers, 'Rusty'
1988		NSCAA		8	—	—	—	—	—	—	—	12	25	Rogers, 'Rusty'
1989		NSCAA		6	—	—	—	—	—	—	—	11	21	Rogers, 'Rusty'
1986	W	NSCAA		3	—	—	—	—	—	—	—	20	9	Rogers, 'Rusty'
1987		NSCAA		3	—	—	—	—	—	—	—	24	7	Borgis, Steve
1988		NSCAA		6	—	—	—	—	—	—	—	8	15	Haught, Paul
1989		NSCAA		5	—	—	—	—	—	—	—	17	14	Haught, Paul

DAVIDSON

Year	M/W	Assn	Div	NAT	NIT	ARC	CCA	NCI	NCT	OLY	HLM	W	L	Coach
1966	M	NCAA	I	16	—	—	—	—	—	—	—	21	7	Driesell, Charles G. 'Lefty'
1968		NCAA	I	8	—	—	—	—	—	—	—	24	5	Driesell, Charles G. 'Lefty'
1969		NCAA	I	8	—	—	—	—	—	—	—	27	3	Driesell, Charles G. 'Lefty'
1970		NCAA	I	25	—	—	—	—	—	—	—	22	5	Holland, M. Terrance 'Terry'
1972		NCAA	I	—	16	—	—	—	—	—	—	19	9	Holland, M. Terrance 'Terry'
1986		NCAA	I	64	—	—	—	—	—	—	—	20	11	Hussey, Bobby W.
1994		NCAA	I	—	32	—	—	—	—	—	—	22	8	McKillop, Bob
1996		NCAA	I	—	32	—	—	—	—	—	—	25	5	McKillop, Bob
1998		NCAA	I	64	—	—	—	—	—	—	—	20	10	McKillop, Bob

DAVIS & ELKINS

Year	M/W	Assn	Div	NAT	NIT	ARC	CCA	NCI	NCT	OLY	HLM	W	L	Coach
1950	M	NAIA		8	—	—	—	—	—	—	—	29	5	Brown, Robert N. 'Red'

DAVIS (OH)

Year	M/W	Assn	Div	NAT	NIT	ARC	CCA	NCI	NCT	OLY	HLM	W	L	Coach
1971	M	NSCAA		6	—	—	—	—	—	—	—	12	8	Carder, Jerry J.

DAYTON

Year	M/W	Assn	Div	NAT	NIT	ARC	CCA	NCI	NCT	OLY	HLM	W	L	Coach
1949	M	NCAA		—	—	—	—	8	—	—	—	16	14	Blackburn, L. Thomas
1951		NCAA		—	2	—	—	—	—	—	—	27	5	Blackburn, L. Thomas
1952		NCAA		12	2	—	—	—	—	—	—	28	5	Blackburn, L. Thomas
1954		NCAA		—	8	—	—	—	—	—	—	25	7	Blackburn, L. Thomas
1955		NCAA		—	2	—	—	—	—	—	—	25	4	Blackburn, L. Thomas
1956		NCAA		—	2	—	—	—	—	—	—	25	4	Blackburn, L. Thomas
1957		NCAA	I	—	8	—	—	—	—	—	—	19	9	Blackburn, L. Thomas
1958		NCAA	I	—	2	—	—	—	—	—	—	25	4	Blackburn, L. Thomas
1960		NCAA	I	—	8	—	—	—	—	—	—	21	7	Blackburn, L. Thomas
1961		NCAA	I	—	4	—	—	—	—	—	—	20	9	Blackburn, L. Thomas
1962		NCAA	I	—	1	—	—	—	—	—	—	24	6	Blackburn, L. Thomas
1965		NCAA	I	12	—	—	—	—	—	—	—	22	7	Donoher, Donald J. 'Mickey'
1966		NCAA	I	16	—	—	—	—	—	—	—	23	6	Donoher, Donald J. 'Mickey'
1967		NCAA	I	2	—	—	—	—	—	—	—	25	6	Donoher, Donald J. 'Mickey'
1968		NCAA	I	—	1	—	—	—	—	—	—	21	9	Donoher, Donald J. 'Mickey'
1969		NCAA	I	25	—	—	—	—	—	—	—	20	7	Donoher, Donald J. 'Mickey'

Year	M/W	Assn	Div	NAT	NIT	ARC	CCA	NCI	NCT	OLY	HLM	W	L	Coach
1970		NCAA	I	25	—	—	—	—	—	—	—	19	8	Donoher, Donald J. "Mickey"
1971		NCAA	I	—	16	—	—	—	—	—	—	18	9	Donoher, Donald J. "Mickey"
1974		NCAA	I	16	—	—	—	—	—	—	—	20	9	Donoher, Donald J. "Mickey"
1978		NCAA	I	—	8	—	—	—	—	—	—	19	10	Donoher, Donald J. "Mickey"
1979		NCAA	I	—	12	—	—	—	—	—	—	19	10	Donoher, Donald J. "Mickey"
1981		NCAA	I	—	16	—	—	—	—	—	—	18	11	Donoher, Donald J. "Mickey"
1982		NCAA	I	—	8	—	—	—	—	—	—	21	9	Donoher, Donald J. "Mickey"
1984		NCAA	I	8	—	—	—	—	—	—	—	21	11	Donoher, Donald J. "Mickey"
1985		NCAA	I	64	—	—	—	—	—	—	—	19	10	Donoher, Donald J. "Mickey"
1986		NCAA	I	—	32	—	—	—	—	—	—	17	13	Donoher, Donald J. "Mickey"
1990		NCAA	I	32	—	—	—	—	—	—	—	22	10	O'Brien, James F. X.
1998		NCAA	I	—	16	—	—	—	—	—	—	21	12	Purnell, Oliver
1969	W	AIAW		16	—	—	—	—	—	—	—	4	7	Bowman, Judith
1977		AIAW	S	12	—	—	—	—	—	—	—	21	8	Dreidame, Dr. R. Elaine
1978		AIAW	S	12	—	—	—	—	—	—	—	24	6	Dreidame, Dr. R. Elaine
1979		AIAW	S	2	—	—	—	—	—	—	—	33	3	Jeremiah, Dr. Maryalyce
1980		AIAW	II	1	—	—	—	—	—	—	—	36	2	Jeremiah, Dr. Maryalyce
1981		AIAW	II	16	—	—	—	—	—	—	—	27	7	Makowski, Linda
1983		NCAA	II	8	—	—	—	—	—	—	—	20	10	Makowski, Linda
1984		NCAA	II	3	—	—	—	—	—	—	—	27	4	Makowski, Linda

De Paul

Year	M/W	Assn	Div	NAT	NIT	ARC	CCA	NCI	NCT	OLY	HLM	W	L	Coach
1936	M	NCAA		—	—	—	—	—	—	8	—	18	4	Kelly, James D.
1940		NCAA		—	4	—	—	—	—	—	—	22	6	Haggerty, Thomas J.
1943		NCAA		3	—	—	—	—	—	—	—	19	5	Meyer, Raymond J.
1944		NCAA		—	2	—	—	—	—	—	—	22	4	Meyer, Raymond J.
1945		NCAA		—	1	2	—	—	—	—	—	21	3	Meyer, Raymond J.
1948		NCAA		—	4	—	—	—	—	—	—	22	8	Meyer, Raymond J.
1953		NCAA		16	—	—	—	—	—	—	—	19	9	Meyer, Raymond J.
1956		NCAA		25	—	—	—	—	—	—	—	16	8	Meyer, Raymond J.
1959		NCAA	I	16	—	—	—	—	—	—	—	13	11	Meyer, Raymond J.
1960		NCAA	I	12	—	—	—	—	—	—	—	17	7	Meyer, Raymond J.
1961		NCAA	I	—	12	—	—	—	—	—	—	17	8	Meyer, Raymond J.
1963		NCAA	I	—	12	—	—	—	—	—	—	15	8	Meyer, Raymond J.
1964		NCAA	I	—	8	—	—	—	—	—	—	21	4	Meyer, Raymond J.
1965		NCAA	I	16	—	—	—	—	—	—	—	17	10	Meyer, Raymond J.
1966		NCAA	I	—	14	—	—	—	—	—	—	18	8	Meyer, Raymond J.
1976		NCAA	I	16	—	—	—	—	—	—	—	20	9	Meyer, Raymond J.
1978		NCAA	I	8	—	—	—	—	—	—	—	27	3	Meyer, Raymond J.
1979		NCAA	I	3	—	—	—	—	—	—	—	26	6	Meyer, Raymond J.
1980		NCAA	I	32	—	—	—	—	—	—	—	26	2	Meyer, Raymond J.
1981		NCAA	I	32	—	—	—	—	—	—	—	27	2	Meyer, Raymond J.
1982		NCAA	I	32	—	—	—	—	—	—	—	26	2	Meyer, Raymond J.
1983		NCAA	I	—	2	—	—	—	—	—	—	21	12	Meyer, Raymond J.
1984		NCAA	I	16	—	—	—	—	—	—	—	27	3	Meyer, Raymond J.
1985		NCAA	I	64	—	—	—	—	—	—	—	19	10	Meyer, Joseph E. "Joey"
1986		NCAA	I	16	—	—	—	—	—	—	—	18	13	Meyer, Joseph E. "Joey"
1987		NCAA	I	16	—	—	—	—	—	—	—	28	3	Meyer, Joseph E. "Joey"
1988		NCAA	I	32	—	—	—	—	—	—	—	22	8	Meyer, Joseph E. "Joey"
1989		NCAA	I	32	—	—	—	—	—	—	—	21	12	Meyer, Joseph E. "Joey"

Year	M/W	Assn	Div	NAT	NIT	ARC	CCA	NCI	NCT	OLY	HLM	W	L	Coach
1990		NCAA	I	—	8	—	—	—	—	—	—	20	15	Meyer, Joseph E. "Joey"
1991		NCAA	I	64	—	—	—	—	—	—	—	20	9	Meyer, Joseph E. "Joey"
1992		NCAA	I	64	—	—	—	—	—	—	—	20	9	Meyer, Joseph E. "Joey"
1994		NCAA	I	—	32	—	—	—	—	—	—	16	12	Meyer, Joseph E. "Joey"
1995		NCAA	I	—	32	—	—	—	—	—	—	17	11	Meyer, Joseph E. "Joey"
1982	W	NCAA	I	—	5	—	—	—	—	—	—	18	12	Feiereisel, Ronald E.
1987		NCAA	I	—	7	—	—	—	—	—	—	23	8	Izard, Jim
1988		NCAA	I	—	1	—	—	—	—	—	—	27	4	Izard, Jim
1989		NCAA	I	—	6	—	—	—	—	—	—	23	10	Bruno, Doug
1990		NCAA	I	32	—	—	—	—	—	—	—	22	10	Bruno, Doug
1991		NCAA	I	48	—	—	—	—	—	—	—	19	12	Bruno, Doug
1992		NCAA	I	32	—	—	—	—	—	—	—	21	10	Bruno, Doug
1993		NCAA	I	48	—	—	—	—	—	—	—	20	9	Bruno, Doug
1995		NCAA	I	64	—	—	—	—	—	—	—	20	9	Bruno, Doug
1996		NCAA	I	32	—	—	—	—	—	—	—	21	10	Bruno, Doug
1997		NCAA	I	64	—	—	—	—	—	—	—	20	9	Bruno, Doug

DEFIANCE

Year	M/W	Assn	Div	NAT	NIT	ARC	CCA	NCI	NCT	OLY	HLM	W	L	Coach
1973	M	NAIA		16	—	—	—	—	—	—	—	25	5	Hohenberger, D. Marvin
1974		NAIA		32	—	—	—	—	—	—	—	22	6	Hohenberger, D. Marvin
1980		NAIA		32	—	—	—	—	—	—	—	23	8	Hohenberger, D. Marvin
1988		NAIA		32	—	—	—	—	—	—	—	24	7	Hohenberger, D. Marvin
1993		NCAA	III	40	—	—	—	—	—	—	—	21	6	Hohenberger, D. Marvin
1994	W	NCAA	III	8	—	—	—	—	—	—	—	25	3	Elliott, Cindy
1995		NCAA	III	32	—	—	—	—	—	—	—	22	5	Palombo, Tom
1996		NCAA	III	8	—	—	—	—	—	—	—	28	1	Palombo, Tom
1997		NCAA	III	8	—	—	—	—	—	—	—	28	1	Palombo, Tom

DELAWARE

Year	M/W	Assn	Div	NAT	NIT	ARC	CCA	NCI	NCT	OLY	HLM	W	L	Coach
1992	M	NCAA	I	64	—	—	—	—	—	—	—	27	4	Steinwedel, Steve
1993		NCAA	I	64	—	—	—	—	—	—	—	22	8	Steinwedel, Steve
1998		NCAA	I	64	—	—	—	—	—	—	—	20	10	Brey, Mike

DELTA STATE

Year	M/W	Assn	Div	NAT	NIT	ARC	CCA	NCI	NCT	OLY	HLM	W	L	Coach
1938	M	NAIA		8	—	—	—	—	—	—	—	15	6	Dickson, A. D.
1939		NAIA		32	—	—	—	—	—	—	—	16	7	Dickson, A. D.
1940		NAIA		3	—	—	—	—	—	—	—	24	6	Dickson, A. D.
1941		NAIA		8	—	—	—	—	—	—	—	16	7	Dickson, A. D.
1942		NAIA		32	—	—	—	—	—	—	—	15	10	Dickson, A. D.
1947		NAIA		32	—	—	—	—	—	—	—	23	5	Marlar, Luther W. "Luke"
1948		NAIA		32	—	—	—	—	—	—	—	17	5	Ricks, John Ray
1949		NAIA		32	—	—	—	—	—	—	—	18	11	Ricks, John Ray
1950		NAIA		32	—	—	—	—	—	—	—	19	6	Ricks, John Ray
1972		NCAA	II	16	—	—	—	—	—	—	—	19	8	Waters, Jack
1985		NCAA	II	16	—	—	—	—	—	—	—	20	11	Murphy, Ed
1986		NCAA	II	16	—	—	—	—	—	—	—	23	8	Murphy, Ed
1987		NCAA	II	3	—	—	—	—	—	—	—	24	9	Rives, Steve
1993		NCAA	II	16	—	—	—	—	—	—	—	22	8	Rives, Steve
1996		NCAA	II	48	—	—	—	—	—	—	—	18	11	Rives, Steve
1997		NCAA	II	32	—	—	—	—	—	—	—	23	7	Rives, Steve
1998		NCAA	II	8	—	—	—	—	—	—	—	27	4	Rives, Steve

Year	M/W	Assn	Div	NAT	NIT	ARC	CCA	NCI	NCT	OLY	HLM	W	L	Coach
1975	W	AIAW	L	1	—	—	—	—	—	—	—	28	0	Wade, L. Margaret
1976		AIAW	L	1	—	—	—	—	—	—	—	33	1	Wade, L. Margaret
1977		AIAW	L	1	—	—	—	—	—	—	—	32	3	Wade, L. Margaret
1982		AIAW	I	8	—	—	—	—	—	—	—	24	15	Garmon, Frances
1986		NCAA	II	3	—	—	—	—	—	—	—	28	3	Clark, Lloyd
1987		NCAA	II	8	—	—	—	—	—	—	—	28	2	Clark, Lloyd
1988		NCAA	II	3	—	—	—	—	—	—	—	30	3	Clark, Lloyd
1989		NCAA	II	1	—	—	—	—	—	—	—	30	4	Clark, Lloyd
1990		NCAA	II	1	—	—	—	—	—	—	—	32	1	Clark, Lloyd
1991		NCAA	II	16	—	—	—	—	—	—	—	23	7	Clark, Lloyd
1992		NCAA	II	1	—	—	—	—	—	—	—	30	4	Clark, Lloyd
1993		NCAA	II	2	—	—	—	—	—	—	—	27	6	Clark, Lloyd
1995		NCAA	II	32	—	—	—	—	—	—	—	22	8	Clark, Lloyd
1996		NCAA	II	4	—	—	—	—	—	—	—	27	6	Clark, Lloyd
1997		NCAA	II	8	—	—	—	—	—	—	—	25	6	Clark, Lloyd
1998		NCAA	II	48	—	—	—	—	—	—	—	23	9	Clark, Lloyd

DENISON

Year	M/W	Assn	Div	NAT	NIT	ARC	CCA	NCI	NCT	OLY	HLM	W	L	Coach
1968	M	NCAA	II	23	—	—	—	—	—	—	—	18	5	Scott, Richard S.
1997		NCAA	III	64	—	—	—	—	—	—	—	19	7	Sheridan, Michael
1994	W	NCAA	III	40	—	—	—	—	—	—	—	18	9	Lee, Sara

DENMARK TECH

Year	M/W	Assn	Div	NAT	NIT	ARC	CCA	NCI	NCT	OLY	HLM	W	L	Coach
1968	M	NSCAA		6	—	—	—	—	—	—	—	21	7	Gaddy, Rayshaw L.

DENVER

Year	M/W	Assn	Div	NAT	NIT	ARC	CCA	NCI	NCT	OLY	HLM	W	L	Coach
1948	M	NAIA		32	—	—	—	—	—	—	—	18	11	Ketchum, Ellison E.
1959		NCAA	I	—	12	—	—	—	—	—	—	14	10	Brawner, E. Hoyt
1984		NAIA		32	—	—	—	—	—	—	—	28	4	Theard, Floyd M.
1992		NCAA	II	16	—	—	—	—	—	—	—	26	6	Peth, Dick
1996		NCAA	II	48	—	—	—	—	—	—	—	22	7	Peth, Dick
1993	W	NCAA	II	32	—	—	—	—	—	—	—	24	4	Sheehan, Tracey
1995		NCAA	II	48	—	—	—	—	—	—	—	15	14	Sheehan, Tracey

DEPAUW

Year	M/W	Assn	Div	NAT	NIT	ARC	CCA	NCI	NCT	OLY	HLM	W	L	Coach
1947	M	NAIA		16	—	—	—	—	—	—	—	16	3	Hickman, Harold E. 'Hal'
1957		NCAA	II	32	—	—	—	—	—	—	—	12	9	Luther, Calvin C.
1968		NCAA	II	32	—	—	—	—	—	—	—	16	8	McCall, Elmer
1978		NCAA	III	30	—	—	—	—	—	—	—	14	12	McCall, Elmer
1984		NCAA	III	3	—	—	—	—	—	—	—	25	5	Steele, Mike
1985		NCAA	III	32	—	—	—	—	—	—	—	21	7	Steele, Mike
1986		NCAA	III	16	—	—	—	—	—	—	—	26	2	Steele, Mike
1987		NCAA	III	24	—	—	—	—	—	—	—	22	6	Steele, Mike
1990		NCAA	III	2	—	—	—	—	—	—	—	24	7	Waltman, Royce
1991		NCAA	III	32	—	—	—	—	—	—	—	19	8	Waltman, Royce
1992		NCAA	III	40	—	—	—	—	—	—	—	20	7	Waltman, Royce
1993		NCAA	III	40	—	—	—	—	—	—	—	19	7	Fenlon, Bill
1996	W	NCAA	III	64	—	—	—	—	—	—	—	19	7	Huffman, Kris
1998		NCAA	III	16	—	—	—	—	—	—	—	23	5	Huffman, Kris

Year	M/W	Assn	Div	NAT	NIT	ARC	CCA	NCI	NCT	OLY	HLM	W	L	Coach
DETROIT														
1960	M	NCAA	I	—	12	—	—	—	—	—	—	20	7	Calihan, Robert J.
1961		NCAA	I	—	12	—	—	—	—	—	—	18	9	Calihan, Robert J.
1962		NCAA	I	25	—	—	—	—	—	—	—	15	12	Calihan, Robert J.
1965		NCAA	I	—	8	—	—	—	—	—	—	20	8	Calihan, Robert J.
1977		NCAA	I	16	—	—	—	—	—	—	—	25	4	Vitale, Dick
1978		NCAA	I	—	8	—	—	—	—	—	—	25	4	Gaines, David "Smokey"
1979		NCAA	I	40	—	—	—	—	—	—	—	22	6	Gaines, David "Smokey"
1980	W	AIAW	I	24	—	—	—	—	—	—	—	25	8	Kruszewski, Sue
DETROIT MERCY														
1998	M	NCAA	I	32	—	—	—	—	—	—	—	25	6	Watson, Perry
1997	W	NCAA	I	64	—	—	—	—	—	—	—	23	7	Lowry, Nikita
DICKINSON (PA)														
1980	M	NCAA	III	24	—	—	—	—	—	—	—	19	8	Evans, Gene
1982		NCAA	III	32	—	—	—	—	—	—	—	16	11	Evans, Gene
1991		NCAA	III	40	—	—	—	—	—	—	—	19	8	Frohman, David N.
1997		NCAA	III	64	—	—	—	—	—	—	—	17	10	Frohman, David N.
DICKINSON STATE (ND)														
1966	M	NAIA		32	—	—	—	—	—	—	—	21	4	Jessen, Laverne
1967		NAIA		32	—	—	—	—	—	—	—	21	5	Jessen, Laverne
1968		NAIA		8	—	—	—	—	—	—	—	23	6	Limke, Denis
DILLARD														
1980	M	NAIA		32	—	—	—	—	—	—	—	19	12	Brown, John D.
1997		NAIA	I	16	—	—	—	—	—	—	—	23	13	Lloyd, Jerry
1984	W	NAIA		3	—	—	—	—	—	—	—	26	3	Teamer, Mary D.
1988		NAIA		8	—	—	—	—	—	—	—	28	5	Teamer, Mary D.
DISTRICT OF COLUMBIA														
1982	M	NCAA	II	1	—	—	—	—	—	—	—	25	5	Jones, William S.
1983		NCAA	II	2	—	—	—	—	—	—	—	29	3	Jones, William S.
1987		NCAA	II	32	—	—	—	—	—	—	—	24	6	Jones, William S.
1988	W	NCAA	II	32	—	—	—	—	—	—	—	24	3	Robinson, William
1989		NCAA	II	8	—	—	—	—	—	—	—	20	4	Robinson, William
1995		NCAA	II	48	—	—	—	—	—	—	—	20	6	King, Britt S.
DOANE														
1945	M	NAIA		8	—	—	—	—	—	—	—	6	12	Dutcher, Jim
1965		NCAA	II	32	—	—	—	—	—	—	—	16	9	Erickson, Robert
1971		NAIA		32	—	—	—	—	—	—	—	18	10	Erickson, Robert
1975		NCAA	III	8	—	—	—	—	—	—	—	16	9	Erickson, Robert
1976		NAIA		16	—	—	—	—	—	—	—	21	9	Erickson, Robert
1996		NAIA	II	8	—	—	—	—	—	—	—	21	16	Erickson, Robert
1989	W	NAIA		8	—	—	—	—	—	—	—	27	7	Steinmeyer, Gene
1992		NAIA	I	16	—	—	—	—	—	—	—	26	9	Steinmeyer, Gene
1995		NAIA	II	16	—	—	—	—	—	—	—	30	6	Steinmeyer, Gene
1996		NAIA	II	3	—	—	—	—	—	—	—	31	7	Steinmeyer, Gene

Year	M/W	Assn	Div	NAT	NIT	ARC	CCA	NCI	NCT	OLY	HLM	W	L	Coach
1997		NAIA	II	3	—	—	—	—	—	—	—	28	9	Steinmeyer, Gene
1998		NAIA	II	3	—	—	—	—	—	—	—	29	9	Steinmeyer, Gene

DOMINICAN (CA)

Year	M/W	Assn	Div	NAT	NIT	ARC	CCA	NCI	NCT	OLY	HLM	W	L	Coach
1994	W	NSCAA		7	—	—	—	—	—	—	—	18	6	Ferraro, Dave
1995		NSCAA		5	—	—	—	—	—	—	—	17	7	Ferraro, Dave
1996		NSCAA		2	—	—	—	—	—	—	—	16	9	Ferraro, Dave
1997		NAIA	II	32	—	—	—	—	—	—	—	23	7	Powell, Roneil

DOMINICAN (IL)

Year	M/W	Assn	Div	NAT	NIT	ARC	CCA	NCI	NCT	OLY	HLM	W	L	Coach
1991	W	NAIA		16	—	—	—	—	—	—	—	32	2	Trefilek, Thomas J.
1992		NAIA	I	32	—	—	—	—	—	—	—	28	4	Trefilek, Thomas J.
1993		NAIA	I	32	—	—	—	—	—	—	—	30	4	Trefilek, Thomas J.
1994		NAIA	I	32	—	—	—	—	—	—	—	22	12	Schaefer, Bill
1995		NAIA	I	32	—	—	—	—	—	—	—	12	16	Smith, Dennis

DOMINICAN (NY)

Year	M/W	Assn	Div	NAT	NIT	ARC	CCA	NCI	NCT	OLY	HLM	W	L	Coach
1981	M	NAIA		32	—	—	—	—	—	—	—	17	14	Kelly, Steve
1986	W	NAIA		16	—	—	—	—	—	—	—	20	15	Baxter, Stephen

DORDT

Year	M/W	Assn	Div	NAT	NIT	ARC	CCA	NCI	NCT	OLY	HLM	W	L	Coach
1988	M	NAIA		8	—	—	—	—	—	—	—	25	5	Vander Berg, Rick

DOWLING

Year	M/W	Assn	Div	NAT	NIT	ARC	CCA	NCI	NCT	OLY	HLM	W	L	Coach
1976	M	NAIA		32	—	—	—	—	—	—	—	31	4	Berg, Richard C.
1977		NAIA		16	—	—	—	—	—	—	—	29	7	Berg, Richard C.
1978		NAIA		32	—	—	—	—	—	—	—	21	6	Berg, Richard C.
1980		NAIA		32	—	—	—	—	—	—	—	24	5	Berg, Richard C.
1995		NCAA	II	48	—	—	—	—	—	—	—	18	10	Pellicane, Joseph
1998		NCAA	II	48	—	—	—	—	—	—	—	22	6	Pellicane, Joseph

DR. MARTIN LUTHER

Year	M/W	Assn	Div	NAT	NIT	ARC	CCA	NCI	NCT	OLY	HLM	W	L	Coach
1977	M	NSCAA		16	—	—	—	—	—	—	—	14	9	Dallman, Dr. Gary L.
1986	W	NSCAA		8	—	—	—	—	—	—	—	14	11	Leopold, Barbara
1989		NSCAA		6	—	—	—	—	—	—	—	7	18	Leopold, Barbara
1995		NSCAA		8	—	—	—	—	—	—	—	11	15	Dallman, Dr. Gary L.

DRAKE (IA)

Year	M/W	Assn	Div	NAT	NIT	ARC	CCA	NCI	NCT	OLY	HLM	W	L	Coach
1938	M	NAIA		32	—	—	—	—	—	—	—	14	6	Williams, Evan O. 'Bill'
1964		NCAA	I	—	8	—	—	—	—	—	—	21	7	John, Maurice E. 'Maury'
1969		NCAA	I	3	—	—	—	—	—	—	—	26	5	John, Maurice E. 'Maury'
1970		NCAA	I	8	—	—	—	—	—	—	—	22	7	John, Maurice E. 'Maury'
1971		NCAA	I	8	—	—	—	—	—	—	—	21	8	John, Maurice E. 'Maury'
1975		NCAA	I	—	—	—	1	—	—	—	—	19	10	Ortegel, Bob
1981		NCAA	I	—	32	—	—	—	—	—	—	18	11	Ortegel, Bob
1986		NCAA	I	—	32	—	—	—	—	—	—	19	11	Garner, Gary
1978	W			—	5	—	—	—	—	—	—	23	9	Baumgarten, Carole
1979		AIAW		—	2	—	—	—	—	—	—	28	5	Baumgarten, Carole
1980				—	3	—	—	—	—	—	—	24	12	Baumgarten, Carole
1981				—	3	—	—	—	—	—	—	26	7	Baumgarten, Carole

Year	M/W	Assn	Div	NAT	NIT	ARC	CCA	NCI	NCT	OLY	HLM	W	L	Coach
1982		NCAA	I	8	—	—	—	—	—	—	—	28	7	Baumgarten, Carole
1984		NCAA	I	32	—	—	—	—	—	—	—	22	7	Baumgarten, Carole
1985		NCAA	I	—	4	—	—	—	—	—	—	24	6	Baumgarten, Carole
1986		NCAA	I	32	—	—	—	—	—	—	—	22	8	Baumgarten, Carole
1995		NCAA	I	32	—	—	—	—	—	—	—	25	6	Bluder, Lisa
1997		NCAA	I	64	—	—	—	—	—	—	—	23	7	Bluder, Lisa
1998		NCAA	I	64	—	—	—	—	—	—	—	25	5	Bluder, Lisa

DRAUGHONS JC: KINGSPORT

Year	M/W	Assn	Div	NAT	NIT	ARC	CCA	NCI	NCT	OLY	HLM	W	L	Coach
1985	M	NSCAA		6	—	—	—	—	—	—	—	32	8	

DRAUGHONS JC: KNOXVILLE

Year	M/W	Assn	Div	NAT	NIT	ARC	CCA	NCI	NCT	OLY	HLM	W	L	Coach
1984	M	NSCAA		16	—	—	—	—	—	—	—			Mitchell, Dave
1989		NSCAA		15	—	—	—	—	—	—	—			Tylar, Donnie
1990		NSCAA		2	—	—	—	—	—	—	—	21	9	Tylar, Donnie
1991		NSCAA		8	—	—	—	—	—	—	—			

DREXEL

Year	M/W	Assn	Div	NAT	NIT	ARC	CCA	NCI	NCT	OLY	HLM	W	L	Coach
1957	M	NCAA	II	32	—	—	—	—	—	—	—	14	3	Cozen, Samuel D.
1960		NCAA	II	32	—	—	—	—	—	—	—	12	8	Cozen, Samuel D.
1966		NCAA	II	32	—	—	—	—	—	—	—	20	4	Cozen, Samuel D.
1967		NCAA	II	32	—	—	—	—	—	—	—	13	10	Cozen, Samuel D.
1986		NCAA	I	64	—	—	—	—	—	—	—	19	12	Burke, Edward J.
1994		NCAA	I	64	—	—	—	—	—	—	—	25	5	Herrion, William R.
1995		NCAA	I	64	—	—	—	—	—	—	—	22	8	Herrion, William R.
1996		NCAA	I	32	—	—	—	—	—	—	—	27	4	Herrion, William R.
1997		NCAA	I	—	32	—	—	—	—	—	—	22	9	Herrion, William R.

DRURY

Year	M/W	Assn	Div	NAT	NIT	ARC	CCA	NCI	NCT	OLY	HLM	W	L	Coach
1938	M	NAIA		32	—	—	—	—	—	—	—	18	3	Weiser, Albert L.
1946		NAIA		8	—	—	—	—	—	—	—	12	9	Weiser, Albert L.
1958		NAIA		16	—	—	—	—	—	—	—	15	7	Weiser, Albert L.
1968		NAIA		8	—	—	—	—	—	—	—	24	5	Harding, Bill
1970		NAIA		32	—	—	—	—	—	—	—	22	7	Harding, Bill
1971		NAIA		32	—	—	—	—	—	—	—	18	9	Harding, Bill
1978		NAIA		8	—	—	—	—	—	—	—	29	4	Matthews, Dr. Edsel
1979		NAIA		1	—	—	—	—	—	—	—	33	2	Kirksey, Jerry L.
1981		NAIA		32	—	—	—	—	—	—	—	19	12	Walker, Marvin
1983		NAIA		32	—	—	—	—	—	—	—	22	12	Walker, Marvin
1985		NAIA		8	—	—	—	—	—	—	—	26	10	Walker, Marvin
1986		NAIA		16	—	—	—	—	—	—	—	25	10	Walker, Marvin
1989		NAIA		16	—	—	—	—	—	—	—	24	9	Walker, Marvin
1993		NAIA	I	32	—	—	—	—	—	—	—	19	12	Stanfield, Gary
1994		NAIA	I	8	—	—	—	—	—	—	—	27	4	Stanfield, Gary

DUBUQUE

Year	M/W	Assn	Div	NAT	NIT	ARC	CCA	NCI	NCT	OLY	HLM	W	L	Coach
1941	M	NAIA		32	—	—	—	—	—	—	—	15	3	Mercer, Kenneth E. "Moco"
1981		NCAA	III	24	—	—	—	—	—	—	—	20	8	Davison, Jon L.
1986		NCAA	III	16	—	—	—	—	—	—	—	21	7	Davison, Jon L.
1988		NCAA	III	16	—	—	—	—	—	—	—	21	7	Davison, Jon L.
1990		NCAA	III	32	—	—	—	—	—	—	—	19	8	Davison, Jon L.

DUFF'S BUSINESS

Year	M/W	Assn	Div	NAT	NIT	ARC	CCA	NCI	NCT	OLY	HLM	W	L	Coach
1970	M	NSCAA		8	—	—	—	—	—	—	—	X	X	Weir,

Year	M/W	Assn	Div	NAT	NIT	ARC	CCA	NCI	NCT	OLY	HLM	W	L	Coach
DUKE														
1955	M	NCAA		24	—	—	—	—	—	—	—	20	8	Bradley, Harold L.
1960		NCAA	I	8	—	—	—	—	—	—	—	17	11	Bubas, Victor A.
1963		NCAA	I	3	—	—	—	—	—	—	—	27	3	Bubas, Victor A.
1964		NCAA	I	2	—	—	—	—	—	—	—	26	5	Bubas, Victor A.
1966		NCAA	I	3	—	—	—	—	—	—	—	26	4	Bubas, Victor A.
1967		NCAA	I	—	8	—	—	—	—	—	—	18	9	Bubas, Victor A.
1968		NCAA	I	—	8	—	—	—	—	—	—	22	6	Bubas, Victor A.
1970		NCAA	I	—	16	—	—	—	—	—	—	17	9	Waters, Raymond C. "Bucky"
1971		NCAA	I	—	4	—	—	—	—	—	—	20	10	Waters, Raymond C. "Bucky"
1978		NCAA	I	2	—	—	—	—	—	—	—	27	7	Foster, William E.
1979		NCAA	I	32	—	—	—	—	—	—	—	22	8	Foster, William E.
1980		NCAA	I	8	—	—	—	—	—	—	—	24	9	Foster, William E.
1981		NCAA	I	—	8	—	—	—	—	—	—	17	13	Krzyzewski, Michael W.
1984		NCAA	I	32	—	—	—	—	—	—	—	24	10	Krzyzewski, Michael W.
1985		NCAA	I	32	—	—	—	—	—	—	—	23	8	Krzyzewski, Michael W.
1986		NCAA	I	2	—	—	—	—	—	—	—	37	3	Krzyzewski, Michael W.
1987		NCAA	I	16	—	—	—	—	—	—	—	24	9	Krzyzewski, Michael W.
1988		NCAA	I	3	—	—	—	—	—	—	—	28	7	Krzyzewski, Michael W.
1989		NCAA	I	3	—	—	—	—	—	—	—	28	8	Krzyzewski, Michael W.
1990		NCAA	I	2	—	—	—	—	—	—	—	29	9	Krzyzewski, Michael W.
1991		NCAA	I	1	—	—	—	—	—	—	—	32	7	Krzyzewski, Michael W.
1992		NCAA	I	1	—	—	—	—	—	—	—	34	2	Krzyzewski, Michael W.
1993		NCAA	I	32	—	—	—	—	—	—	—	24	8	Krzyzewski, Michael W.
1994		NCAA	I	2	—	—	—	—	—	—	—	28	6	Krzyzewski, Michael W.
1996		NCAA	I	64	—	—	—	—	—	—	—	18	13	Krzyzewski, Michael W.
1997		NCAA	I	32	—	—	—	—	—	—	—	24	9	Krzyzewski, Michael W.
1998		NCAA	I	8	—	—	—	—	—	—	—	32	4	Krzyzewski, Michael W.
1986	W	NCAA	I	—	4	—	—	—	—	—	—	21	9	Leonard, Debbie
1987		NCAA	I	32	—	—	—	—	—	—	—	19	10	Leonard, Debbie
1995		NCAA	I	32	—	—	—	—	—	—	—	22	9	Goestenkors, Gail
1996		NCAA	I	32	—	—	—	—	—	—	—	26	7	Goestenkors, Gail
1997		NCAA	I	32	—	—	—	—	—	—	—	19	11	Goestenkors, Gail
1998		NCAA	I	8	—	—	—	—	—	—	—	24	8	Goestenkors, Gail
DUQUESNE														
1940	M	NCAA		3	2	—	—	—	—	—	—	20	3	Davies, Charles R. "Chick"
1941		NCAA		—	8	—	—	—	—	—	—	17	3	Davies, Charles R. "Chick"
1947		NCAA		—	8	—	—	—	—	—	—	20	2	Davies, Charles R. "Chick"
1950		NCAA		—	4	—	—	—	—	—	—	23	6	Moore, Donald W. "Dudey"
1951		NCAA		—	—	—	—	8	—	—	—	16	11	Moore, Donald W. "Dudey"
1952		NCAA		8	4	—	—	—	—	—	—	23	4	Moore, Donald W. "Dudey"
1953		NCAA		—	3	—	—	—	—	—	—	21	8	Moore, Donald W. "Dudey"
1954		NCAA		—	2	—	—	—	—	—	—	26	3	Moore, Donald W. "Dudey"
1955		NCAA		—	1	—	—	—	—	—	—	22	4	Moore, Donald W. "Dudey"
1956		NCAA		—	8	—	—	—	—	—	—	17	10	Moore, Donald W. "Dudey"
1962		NCAA	I	—	4	—	—	—	—	—	—	22	7	Manning, John "Red"
1964		NCAA	I	—	8	—	—	—	—	—	—	16	7	Manning, John "Red"

Year	M/W	Assn	Div	NAT	NIT	ARC	CCA	NCI	NCT	OLY	HLM	W	L	Coach
1968		NCAA	I	—	16	—	—	—	—	—	—	18	7	Manning, John "Red"
1969		NCAA	I	12	—	—	—	—	—	—	—	21	5	Manning, John "Red"
1970		NCAA	I	—	16	—	—	—	—	—	—	17	7	Manning, John "Red"
1971		NCAA	I	25	—	—	—	—	—	—	—	21	4	Manning, John "Red"
1977		NCAA	I	32	—	—	—	—	—	—	—	15	15	Cinicola, John L.
1980		NCAA	I	—	16	—	—	—	—	—	—	18	10	Rice, Mike
1981		NCAA	I	—	32	—	—	—	—	—	—	20	10	Rice, Mike
1994		NCAA	I	—	16	—	—	—	—	—	—	17	13	Carroll, John

DURHAM BUSINESS

Year	M/W	Assn	Div	NAT	NIT	ARC	CCA	NCI	NCT	OLY	HLM	W	L	Coach
1971	M	NSCAA		2	—	—	—	—	—	—	—	30	8	Terry, Reginald N.
1974		NSCAA		16	—	—	—	—	—	—	—			
1978		NSCAA		8	—	—	—	—	—	—	—	21	9	Hawkins, Ralph

EARLHAM

Year	M/W	Assn	Div	NAT	NIT	ARC	CCA	NCI	NCT	OLY	HLM	W	L	Coach
1971	M	NAIA		16	—	—	—	—	—	—	—	24	5	Harris, Delmer W.

EAST CAROLINA

Year	M/W	Assn	Div	NAT	NIT	ARC	CCA	NCI	NCT	OLY	HLM	W	L	Coach
1953	M	NAIA		32	—	—	—	—	—	—	—	15	7	Porter, Howard G.
1954		NAIA		32	—	—	—	—	—	—	—	13	8	Porter, Howard G.
1972		NCAA	I	25	—	—	—	—	—	—	—	14	15	Quinn, Thomas R.
1975		NCAA	I	—	—	—	8	—	—	—	—	19	9	Patton, David J.
1993		NCAA	I	64	—	—	—	—	—	—	—	13	17	Payne, Eddie
1973	W	AIAW		12	—	—	—	—	—	—	—	18	12	Bolton, Catherine
1982		NCAA	I	32	—	—	—	—	—	—	—	17	10	Andruzzi, Cathy

EAST CENTRAL (OK)

Year	M/W	Assn	Div	NAT	NIT	ARC	CCA	NCI	NCT	OLY	HLM	W	L	Coach
1940	M	NAIA		32	—	—	—	—	—	—	—	25	5	McBride, Floyd H. "Mickey"
1942		NAIA		8	—	—	—	—	—	—	—	20	10	McBride, Floyd H. "Mickey"
1943		NAIA		16	—	—	—	—	—	—	—	18	6	Powell, C. J.
1948		NAIA		32	—	—	—	—	—	—	—	17	5	McBride, Floyd H. "Mickey"
1950		NAIA		2	—	—	—	—	—	—	—	31	5	McBride, Floyd H. "Mickey"
1951		NAIA		32	—	—	—	—	—	—	—	22	7	McBride, Floyd H. "Mickey"
1970		NAIA		32	—	—	—	—	—	—	—	17	8	Anderson, Jerry
1971		NAIA		32	—	—	—	—	—	—	—	24	5	Anderson, Jerry
1975		NAIA		32	—	—	—	—	—	—	—	16	11	Anderson, Jerry
1989		NAIA		2	—	—	—	—	—	—	—	25	7	Cobb, K. Wayne
1996		NAIA	I	8	—	—	—	—	—	—	—	22	7	Cobb, K. Wayne
1997		NAIA	I	32	—	—	—	—	—	—	—	22	6	Cobb, K. Wayne
1998		NAIA	I	8	—	—	—	—	—	—	—	21	9	Cobb, K. Wayne
1996	W	NAIA	I	16	—	—	—	—	—	—	—	30	5	Franz, Kent
1997		NAIA	I	32	—	—	—	—	—	—	—	19	9	Franz, Kent
1998		NAIA	I	16	—	—	—	—	—	—	—	20	11	Franz, Kent

EAST COAST BIBLE

Year	M/W	Assn	Div	NAT	NIT	ARC	CCA	NCI	NCT	OLY	HLM	W	L	Coach
1996	M	LCC		4	—	—	—	—	—	—	—	5	19	Ayres, "Rusty"
1997		LCC		4	—	—	—	—	—	—	—	12	17	Smith, Phillip D.

EAST MISSISSIPPI CC

Year	M/W	Assn	Div	NAT	NIT	ARC	CCA	NCI	NCT	OLY	HLM	W	L	Coach
1978	M	NSCAA		16	—	—	—	—	—	—	—			

EAST STROUDSBURG

Year	M/W	Assn	Div	NAT	NIT	ARC	CCA	NCI	NCT	OLY	HLM	W	L	Coach
1990	M	NCAA	II	16	—	—	—	—	—	—	—	21	13	Mentesana, Sal

Year	M/W	Assn	Div	NAT	NIT	ARC	CCA	NCI	NCT	OLY	HLM	W	L	Coach
1970	W	AIAW		8	—	—	—	—	—	—	—	8	4	Murphy, Betty Lou
1971		AIAW		8	—	—	—	—	—	—	—	13	3	Murphy, Betty Lou
1973		AIAW		8	—	—	—	—	—	—	—	11	4	Murphy, Betty Lou
1974		AIAW		16	—	—	—	—	—	—	—	13	6	Jenkins, Jan
1994		NCAA	II	32	—	—	—	—	—	—	—	21	8	Haller, Rose
1995		NCAA	II	32	—	—	—	—	—	—	—	25	5	Haller, Rose

EAST TENNESSEE STATE

Year	M/W	Assn	Div	NAT	NIT	ARC	CCA	NCI	NCT	OLY	HLM	W	L	Coach
1953	M	NAIA		32	—	—	—	—	—	—	—	26	4	Brooks, John Madison
1954		NAIA		32	—	—	—	—	—	—	—	23	4	Brooks, John Madison
1956		NAIA		32	—	—	—	—	—	—	—	20	7	Brooks, John Madison
1957		NCAA	II	16	—	—	—	—	—	—	—	18	10	Brooks, John Madison
1968		NCAA	I	16	—	—	—	—	—	—	—	19	8	Brooks, John Madison
1983		NCAA	I	—	32	—	—	—	—	—	—	22	9	Dowd, Barry
1989		NCAA	I	64	—	—	—	—	—	—	—	20	11	Robinson, Leslie G.
1990		NCAA	I	64	—	—	—	—	—	—	—	27	7	Robinson, Leslie G.
1991		NCAA	I	64	—	—	—	—	—	—	—	28	5	LeForce, Alan C.
1992		NCAA	I	32	—	—	—	—	—	—	—	24	7	LeForce, Alan C.
1995	W	NCAA	I	—	6	—	—	—	—	—	—	21	9	Kemp, Karen

EAST TEXAS BAPTIST

Year	M/W	Assn	Div	NAT	NIT	ARC	CCA	NCI	NCT	OLY	HLM	W	L	Coach
1951	M	NAIA		16	—	—	—	—	—	—	—	15	5	Stephens, John O.
1961		NAIA		16	—	—	—	—	—	—	—	16	7	Kennedy, R. C.
1988		NAIA		32	—	—	—	—	—	—	—	19	13	Webb, Dr. Jimmy Ray
1996		NAIA	I	32	—	—	—	—	—	—	—	28	5	West, Bert
1994	W	NAIA	I	32	—	—	—	—	—	—	—	27	6	Reeves, Kent
1995		NAIA	I	32	—	—	—	—	—	—	—	23	9	Reeves, Kent

EASTERN (PA)

Year	M/W	Assn	Div	NAT	NIT	ARC	CCA	NCI	NCT	OLY	HLM	W	L	Coach
1981	M	NCCAA	I	6	—	—	—	—	—	—	—	20	12	Young, Clifford E.
1986		NCCAA	I	8	—	—	—	—	—	—	—	X	X	Young, Clifford E.
1987		NCCAA	I	2	—	—	—	—	—	—	—	28	11	Ware, Nate
1988		NAIA		32	—	—	—	—	—	—	—	30	6	Ware, Nate
1987	W	NCCAA	I	7	—	—	—	—	—	—	—	15	15	Hunter, Art

EASTERN CONNECTICUT STATE

Year	M/W	Assn	Div	NAT	NIT	ARC	CCA	NCI	NCT	OLY	HLM	W	L	Coach
1992	M	NCAA	III	16	—	—	—	—	—	—	—	16	12	Switchenko, Dr. Daniel B.
1993		NCAA	III	8	—	—	—	—	—	—	—	21	7	Switchenko, Dr. Daniel B.
1977	W	AIAW	S	12	—	—	—	—	—	—	—	22	6	Miller, Dr. C. Robert
1980		AIAW	III	16	—	—	—	—	—	—	—	16	10	Miller, Dr. C. Robert
1983		NCAA	III	32	—	—	—	—	—	—	—	17	7	Miller, Dr. C. Robert
1984		NCAA	III	16	—	—	—	—	—	—	—	20	7	Miller, Dr. C. Robert
1986		NCAA	III	16	—	—	—	—	—	—	—	20	5	Miller, Dr. C. Robert
1990		NCAA	III	32	—	—	—	—	—	—	—	20	5	Miller, Dr. C. Robert
1991		NCAA	III	3	—	—	—	—	—	—	—	22	6	Miller, Dr. C. Robert
1992		NCAA	III	4	—	—	—	—	—	—	—	25	6	Miller, Dr. C. Robert
1996		NCAA	III	64	—	—	—	—	—	—	—	19	9	Bierly, Denise

Year	M/W	Assn	Div	NAT	NIT	ARC	CCA	NCI	NCT	OLY	HLM	W	L	Coach
EASTERN ILLINOIS														
1947	M	NAIA		32	—	—	—	—	—	—	—	13	7	Healey, Dr. William A.
1949		NAIA		8	—	—	—	—	—	—	—	23	6	Healey, Dr. William A.
1950		NAIA		32	—	—	—	—	—	—	—	21	5	Healey, Dr. William A.
1952		NAIA		16	—	—	—	—	—	—	—	24	2	Healey, Dr. William A.
1953		NAIA		16	—	—	—	—	—	—	—	16	9	Healey, Dr. William A.
1957		NAIA		4	—	—	—	—	—	—	—	17	14	Carey, Robert A.
1975		NCAA	II	24	—	—	—	—	—	—	—	20	8	Eddy, Donald R.
1976		NCAA	II	3	—	—	—	—	—	—	—	23	8	Eddy, Donald R.
1977		NCAA	II	16	—	—	—	—	—	—	—	18	11	Eddy, Donald R.
1978		NCAA	II	3	—	—	—	—	—	—	—	21	10	Eddy, Donald R.
1979		NCAA	II	24	—	—	—	—	—	—	—	19	10	Eddy, Donald R.
1980		NCAA	II	16	—	—	—	—	—	—	—	22	7	Eddy, Donald R.
1992		NCAA	I	64	—	—	—	—	—	—	—	17	14	Samuels, Rick
1981	W	AIAW	II	8	—	—	—	—	—	—	—	25	8	Hilke, Barbara
1988		NCAA	I	40	—	—	—	—	—	—	—	22	8	Hilke, Barbara
EASTERN KENTUCKY														
1945	M	NAIA		3	—	—	—	—	—	—	—	20	5	Rankin, Dr. Rome
1946		NAIA		32	—	—	—	—	—	—	—	20	5	Rankin, Dr. Rome
1953		NCAA		22	—	—	—	—	—	—	—	16	9	McBrayer, Paul S.
1959		NCAA	I	23	—	—	—	—	—	—	—	16	6	McBrayer, Paul S.
1965		NCAA	I	23	—	—	—	—	—	—	—	19	6	Baechtold, James E.
1972		NCAA	I	25	—	—	—	—	—	—	—	15	11	Strong, Guy Rowland
1979		NCAA	I	40	—	—	—	—	—	—	—	21	8	Byhre, Ed
1997	W	NCAA	I	64	—	—	—	—	—	—	—	24	6	Inman, Larry Joe
EASTERN MAINE TECH														
1992	M	NSCAA		10	—	—	—	—	—	—	—	16	10	Young, Christopher
EASTERN MENNONITE														
1985	W	NCCAA	I	3	—	—	—	—	—	—	—	22	4	Brownscombe, Sandra
1986		NCCAA	I	7	—	—	—	—	—	—	—	18	8	Brownscombe, Sandra
EASTERN MICHIGAN														
1968	M	NAIA		8	—	—	—	—	—	—	—	18	9	Dutcher, James D.
1969		NAIA		16	—	—	—	—	—	—	—	20	9	Dutcher, James D.
1970		NAIA		16	—	—	—	—	—	—	—	22	7	Dutcher, James D.
1971		NAIA		2	—	—	—	—	—	—	—	22	11	Dutcher, James D.
1972		NCAA	II	4	—	—	—	—	—	—	—	24	7	Dutcher, James D.
1988		NCAA	I	64	—	—	—	—	—	—	—	22	8	Braun, Ben
1991		NCAA	I	16	—	—	—	—	—	—	—	26	7	Braun, Ben
1995		NCAA	I	—	32	—	—	—	—	—	—	20	10	Braun, Ben
1996		NCAA	I	32	—	—	—	—	—	—	—	25	6	Braun, Ben
1998		NCAA	I	64	—	—	—	—	—	—	—	20	10	Barnes, Milton
EASTERN NAZARENE														
1971	M	NCCAA		2	—	—	—	—	—	—	—	26	5	Bradley, Carroll F.
1972		NCCAA		4	—	—	—	—	—	—	—	24	8	Smith, James H.
1973		NCCAA		3	—	—	—	—	—	—	—	21	9	Smith, James H.
1979		NCCAA	I	6	—	—	—	—	—	—	—	22	10	Bradley, Ron
1982		NCCAA	I	7	—	—	—	—	—	—	—	19	12	Perera, Jerry

Year	M/W	Assn	Div	NAT	NIT	ARC	CCA	NCI	NCT	OLY	HLM	W	L	Coach
EASTERN NEW MEXICO														
1949	M	NAIA		32	—	—	—	—	—	—	—	19	8	Garten, Alvin D.
1951		NAIA		32	—	—	—	—	—	—	—	19	9	Garten, Alvin D.
1956		NAIA		32	—	—	—	—	—	—	—	11	16	Garten, Alvin D.
1958		NAIA		32	—	—	—	—	—	—	—	17	10	Garten, Alvin D.
1963		NAIA		32	—	—	—	—	—	—	—	14	8	Garten, Alvin D.
1967		NAIA		8	—	—	—	—	—	—	—	24	7	Miller, Harry E.
1969		NAIA		1	—	—	—	—	—	—	—	24	7	Miller, Harry E.
1970		NAIA		3	—	—	—	—	—	—	—	26	6	Miller, Harry E.
1971		NAIA		32	—	—	—	—	—	—	—	19	10	Ball, "Buddy"
1993		NCAA	II	16	—	—	—	—	—	—	—	23	7	Diddle, Earl
1978	W	AIAW	S	16	—	—	—	—	—	—	—	17	8	Barras, Bernie
EASTERN OREGON														
1943	M	NAIA		16	—	—	—	—	—	—	—	18	5	Quinn, E. Robert
EASTERN WASHINGTON														
1942	M	NAIA		32	—	—	—	—	—	—	—	18	7	Reese, William B. "Red"
1943		NAIA		8	—	—	—	—	—	—	—	27	5	Brumblay, Robert C.
1945		NAIA		16	—	—	—	—	—	—	—	27	5	Brumblay, Robert C.
1946		NAIA		8	—	—	—	—	—	—	—	31	4	Reese, William B. "Red"
1947		NAIA		8	—	—	—	—	—	—	—	22	9	Reese, William B. "Red"
1978	W	AIAW	S	16	—	—	—	—	—	—	—	24	9	Smithpeters, Bill
1979		AIAW	S	16	—	—	—	—	—	—	—	28	7	Smithpeters, Bill
1987		NCAA	I	40	—	—	—	—	—	—	—	18	12	Smithpeters, Bill
ECKERD														
1973	M	NCAA	II	42	—	—	—	—	—	—	—	17	5	Harley, James R.
1994		NCAA	II	32	—	—	—	—	—	—	—	17	14	Harley, James R.
1995		NCAA	II	24	—	—	—	—	—	—	—	22	10	Harley, James R.
EDGEWOOD														
1988	M	NSCAA		10	—	—	—	—	—	—	—	23	14	Larson, G. Steven
1989		NSCAA		5	—	—	—	—	—	—	—	26	13	Larson, G. Steven
1990		NSCAA		4	—	—	—	—	—	—	—	20	11	Larson, G. Steven
1992		NAIA	II	20	—	—	—	—	—	—	—	21	10	Larson, G. Steven
1995		NAIA	II	32	—	—	—	—	—	—	—	20	8	Larson, G. Steven
1989	W	NSCAA		3	—	—	—	—	—	—	—	16	13	Raisback, Owen
EDINBORO														
1966	M	NAIA		32	—	—	—	—	—	—	—	18	5	McDonald, James
1972		NAIA		32	—	—	—	—	—	—	—	17	9	McDonald, James
1975		NAIA		16	—	—	—	—	—	—	—	17	3	McDonald, James
1976		NAIA		16	—	—	—	—	—	—	—	24	5	Conti, Guy
1982		NCAA	II	24	—	—	—	—	—	—	—	22	8	Conti, Guy
1986		NCAA	II	32	—	—	—	—	—	—	—	18	13	Sims, James
1994		NCAA	II	32	—	—	—	—	—	—	—	20	8	Walcavich, Greg
1996		NCAA	II	32	—	—	—	—	—	—	—	21	8	Walcavich, Greg
1998		NCAA	II	32	—	—	—	—	—	—	—	26	8	Walcavich, Greg

Year	M/W	Assn	Div	NAT	NIT	ARC	CCA	NCI	NCT	OLY	HLM	W	L	Coach
1990	W	NCAA	II	16	—	—	—	—	—	—	—	27	3	Swank, Stan
1992		NCAA	II	32	—	—	—	—	—	—	—	22	8	Swank, Stan
1993		NCAA	II	32	—	—	—	—	—	—	—	18	12	Swank, Stan
1997		NCAA	II	8	—	—	—	—	—	—	—	24	9	Swank, Stan
1998		NCAA	II	32	—	—	—	—	—	—	—	23	8	Swank, Stan

ELIZABETH CITY STATE

Year	M/W	Assn	Div	NAT	NIT	ARC	CCA	NCI	NCT	OLY	HLM	W	L	Coach
1969	M	NAIA		4	—	—	—	—	—	—	—	21	2	Vaughan, Robert L. "Bobby"
1971		NAIA		3	—	—	—	—	—	—	—	25	9	Vaughan, Robert L. "Bobby"
1972		NAIA		32	—	—	—	—	—	—	—	17	12	Vaughan, Robert L. "Bobby"
1978		NCAA	II	8	—	—	—	—	—	—	—	18	6	Vaughan, Robert L. "Bobby"
1981		NCAA	II	16	—	—	—	—	—	—	—	22	9	Vaughan, Robert L. "Bobby"
1994		NCAA	II	24	—	—	—	—	—	—	—	22	8	Mackey, Dr. Claudie J.
1997		NCAA	II	8	—	—	—	—	—	—	—	22	7	Hamler, Barry

ELIZABETH SETON

Year	M/W	Assn	Div	NAT	NIT	ARC	CCA	NCI	NCT	OLY	HLM	W	L	Coach
1985	M	NSCAA		16	—	—	—	—	—	—	—	21	7	O'Donnell, Dennis G.
1987		NSCAA		16	—	—	—	—	—	—	—	28	7	O'Donnell, Dennis G.
1989		NSCAA		12	—	—	—	—	—	—	—	22	14	O'Donnell, Dennis G.
1990		NSCAA		10	—	—	—	—	—	—	—	24	9	O'Donnell, Dennis G.
1991		NSCAA		12	—	—	—	—	—	—	—	18	18	O'Donnell, Dennis G.

ELIZABETHTOWN

Year	M/W	Assn	Div	NAT	NIT	ARC	CCA	NCI	NCT	OLY	HLM	W	L	Coach
1964	M	NCAA	II	16	—	—	—	—	—	—	—	20	5	Smith, Donald P.
1979		NCAA	III	16	—	—	—	—	—	—	—	17	9	Smith, Donald P.
1993		NCAA	III	32	—	—	—	—	—	—	—	19	7	Schlosser, Robert A.
1980	W	AIAW	III	24	—	—	—	—	—	—	—	22	5	Kauffman, Yvonne E.
1981		AIAW	III	8	—	—	—	—	—	—	—	18	6	Kauffman, Yvonne E.
1982		NCAA	III	1	—	—	—	—	—	—	—	26	1	Kauffman, Yvonne E.
1983		NCAA	III	2	—	—	—	—	—	—	—	23	5	Kauffman, Yvonne E.
1984		NCAA	III	2	—	—	—	—	—	—	—	29	2	Kauffman, Yvonne E.
1986		NCAA	III	8	—	—	—	—	—	—	—	24	6	Kauffman, Yvonne E.
1987		NCAA	III	16	—	—	—	—	—	—	—	25	3	Kauffman, Yvonne E.
1988		NCAA	III	16	—	—	—	—	—	—	—	25	4	Kauffman, Yvonne E.
1989		NCAA	III	1	—	—	—	—	—	—	—	29	2	Kauffman, Yvonne E.
1994		NCAA	III	40	—	—	—	—	—	—	—	21	5	Kauffman, Yvonne E.
1995		NCAA	III	64	—	—	—	—	—	—	—	23	5	Kauffman, Yvonne E.
1996		NCAA	III	64	—	—	—	—	—	—	—	19	8	Kauffman, Yvonne E.
1997		NCAA	III	32	—	—	—	—	—	—	—	21	8	Kauffman, Yvonne E.

ELMHURST

Year	M/W	Assn	Div	NAT	NIT	ARC	CCA	NCI	NCT	OLY	HLM	W	L	Coach
1992	M	NCAA	III	32	—	—	—	—	—	—	—	19	9	Whitesell, Jim
1986	W	NCAA	III	24	—	—	—	—	—	—	—	24	3	Novgrod, Debra

ELMIRA

Year	M/W	Assn	Div	NAT	NIT	ARC	CCA	NCI	NCT	OLY	HLM	W	L	Coach
1995	M	NCAA	III	64	—	—	—	—	—	—	—	17	9	Moore, Kevin
1998	W	NCAA	III	16	—	—	—	—	—	—	—	22	7	Scheible, James

ELON

Year	M/W	Assn	Div	NAT	NIT	ARC	CCA	NCI	NCT	OLY	HLM	W	L	Coach
1952	M	NAIA		32	—	—	—	—	—	—	—	25	11	Mathis, Graham L. "Doc"
1956		NAIA		32	—	—	—	—	—	—	—	23	6	Mathis, Graham L. "Doc"
1957		NAIA		32	—	—	—	—	—	—	—	24	6	Mathis, Graham L. "Doc"
1997		NCAA	II	48	—	—	—	—	—	—	—	16	14	Simons, Mark

Year	M/W	Assn	Div	NAT	NIT	ARC	CCA	NCI	NCT	OLY	HLM	W	L	Coach
EMBRY-RIDDLE (FL)														
1993	M	NAIA	II	16	—	—	—	—	—	—	—	28	8	Ridder, Steven
1996		NAIA	II	16	—	—	—	—	—	—	—	25	11	Ridder, Steven
1997		NAIA	II	16	—	—	—	—	—	—	—	25	8	Ridder, Steven
1998		NAIA	II	32	—	—	—	—	—	—	—	23	12	Ridder, Steven
EMMANUEL (GA)														
1996	W	NCCAA	I	3	—	—	—	—	—	—	—	23	9	Bona, Mike
1997		NCCAA	I	2	—	—	—	—	—	—	—	23	10	Bona, Mike
1998		NCCAA	I	6	—	—	—	—	—	—	—	18	11	Bona, Mike
EMMANUEL (MA)														
1986	W	NCAA	III	16	—	—	—	—	—	—	—	21	4	Yosinoff, Andrew
1987		NCAA	III	16	—	—	—	—	—	—	—	22	2	Yosinoff, Andrew
1988		NCAA	III	24	—	—	—	—	—	—	—	20	2	Yosinoff, Andrew
1992		NCAA	III	32	—	—	—	—	—	—	—	20	5	Yosinoff, Andrew
1996		NCAA	III	64	—	—	—	—	—	—	—	22	4	Yosinoff, Andrew
1997		NCAA	III	32	—	—	—	—	—	—	—	22	7	Yosinoff, Andrew
EMMAUS BIBLE														
1984	M	NBCAA	II	3	—	—	—	—	—	—	—	X	X	Suriano, Louis
1987		NBCAA	II	4	—	—	—	—	—	—	—	X	X	Elifritz, Bill
1993		NBCAA	II	7	—	—	—	—	—	—	—	6	14	Reeves, John
1995	W	NCCAA	II	4	—	—	—	—	—	—	—	16	3	Mertz, Merilee
EMORY														
1990	M	NCAA	III	16	—	—	—	—	—	—	—	25	4	Winston, Lloyd
1995	W	NCAA	III	16	—	—	—	—	—	—	—	21	6	Sims, Myra
1997		NCAA	III	16	—	—	—	—	—	—	—	20	7	Sims, Myra
EMORY & HENRY														
1988	M	NCAA	III	16	—	—	—	—	—	—	—	17	9	Johnson, Robert J.
1990		NCAA	III	32	—	—	—	—	—	—	—	23	7	Johnson, Robert J.
1991		NCAA	III	32	—	—	—	—	—	—	—	25	5	Johnson, Robert J.
1992		NCAA	III	40	—	—	—	—	—	—	—	20	9	Johnson, Robert J.
1993		NCAA	III	16	—	—	—	—	—	—	—	23	5	Johnson, Robert J.
EMPORIA STATE														
1947	M	NAIA		4	—	—	—	—	—	—	—	18	9	Fish, Everett D. "Gus"
1948		NAIA		16	—	—	—	—	—	—	—	20	7	Fish, Everett D. "Gus"
1949		NAIA		8	—	—	—	—	—	—	—	20	10	Fish, Everett D. "Gus"
1957		NAIA		16	—	—	—	—	—	—	—	20	9	Fish, Everett D. "Gus"
1961		NAIA		16	—	—	—	—	—	—	—	17	6	Fish, Everett D. "Gus"
1964		NAIA		4	—	—	—	—	—	—	—	22	9	Fish, Everett D. "Gus"
1977		NAIA		16	—	—	—	—	—	—	—	24	6	Slaymaker, Dr. Ron
1986		NAIA		16	—	—	—	—	—	—	—	31	5	Slaymaker, Dr. Ron
1991		NAIA		32	—	—	—	—	—	—	—	18	13	Slaymaker, Dr. Ron
1992		NAIA	I	32	—	—	—	—	—	—	—	26	8	Slaymaker, Dr. Ron
1975	W	AIAW	S	4	—	—	—	—	—	—	—	13	8	Caruthers, Linda
1979		AIAW	S	12	—	—	—	—	—	—	—	19	10	Jones, Debbie
1992		NAIA	I	32	—	—	—	—	—	—	—	14	17	Schierling, Val
1997		NCAA	II	32	—	—	—	—	—	—	—	20	10	Stein, Cindy
1998		NCAA	II	2	—	—	—	—	—	—	—	33	1	Stein, Cindy

Year	M/W	Assn	Div	NAT	NIT	ARC	CCA	NCI	NCT	OLY	HLM	W	L	Coach
ERSKINE														
1949	M	NAIA		32	—	—	—	—	—	—	—	19	7	McMillan, John D. "Johnny"
1974		NAIA		32	—	—	—	—	—	—	—	25	6	Myers, W. C. "Red"
1978		NAIA		16	—	—	—	—	—	—	—	21	12	Myers, W. C. "Red"
1992		NAIA	I	8	—	—	—	—	—	—	—	27	7	Hicklin, Robbie
EUREKA														
1987	M	NAIA		32	—	—	—	—	—	—	—	26	3	Darnall, David
1992		NAIA	II	16	—	—	—	—	—	—	—	25	4	Darnall, David
1993		NAIA	II	8	—	—	—	—	—	—	—	24	5	Darnall, David
1994		NAIA	II	1	—	—	—	—	—	—	—	27	4	Darnell, David
EVANGEL														
1997	M	NAIA	II	16	—	—	—	—	—	—	—	29	8	Jenkins, Stephen M.
1986	W	NCCAA	I	1	—	—	—	—	—	—	—	21	13	Bowen, Lynn
1994		NAIA	II	16	—	—	—	—	—	—	—	26	10	Bowen, Lynn
1996		NAIA	II	3	—	—	—	—	—	—	—	31	5	Bowen, Lynn
EVANSVILLE														
1941	M	NAIA		32	—	—	—	—	—	—	—	12	4	Slyker, William V.
1942		NAIA		16	—	—	—	—	—	—	—	12	6	Slyker, William V.
1951		NAIA		8	—	—	—	—	—	—	—	23	7	McCutchan, Arad A.
1955		NAIA		32	—	—	—	—	—	—	—	20	6	McCutchan, Arad A.
1957		NCAA	II	16	—	—	—	—	—	—	—	18	8	McCutchan, Arad A.
1958		NCAA	II	3	—	—	—	—	—	—	—	23	4	McCutchan, Arad A.
1959		NCAA	II	1	—	—	—	—	—	—	—	21	6	McCutchan, Arad A.
1960		NCAA	II	1	—	—	—	—	—	—	—	25	4	McCutchan, Arad A.
1961		NCAA	II	24	—	—	—	—	—	—	—	11	16	McCutchan, Arad A.
1962		NCAA	II	16	—	—	—	—	—	—	—	14	11	McCutchan, Arad A.
1963		NCAA	II	8	—	—	—	—	—	—	—	21	6	McCutchan, Arad A.
1964		NCAA	II	1	—	—	—	—	—	—	—	26	3	McCutchan, Arad A.
1965		NCAA	II	1	—	—	—	—	—	—	—	29	0	McCutchan, Arad A.
1966		NCAA	II	16	—	—	—	—	—	—	—	18	9	McCutchan, Arad A.
1968		NCAA	II	8	—	—	—	—	—	—	—	20	8	McCutchan, Arad A.
1971		NCAA	II	1	—	—	—	—	—	—	—	22	8	McCutchan, Arad A.
1972		NCAA	II	16	—	—	—	—	—	—	—	22	6	McCutchan, Arad A.
1974		NCAA	II	24	—	—	—	—	—	—	—	19	9	McCutchan, Arad A.
1976		NCAA	II	16	—	—	—	—	—	—	—	20	9	McCutchan, Arad A.
1982		NCAA	I	48	—	—	—	—	—	—	—	23	6	Walters, Dick
1988		NCAA	I	—	16	—	—	—	—	—	—	21	8	Crews, Jim
1989		NCAA	I	32	—	—	—	—	—	—	—	25	6	Crews, Jim
1992		NCAA	I	64	—	—	—	—	—	—	—	24	6	Crews, Jim
1993		NCAA	I	64	—	—	—	—	—	—	—	23	7	Crews, Jim
1994		NCAA	I	—	32	—	—	—	—	—	—	21	11	Crews, Jim
FAIRFIELD														
1960	M	NCAA	II	16	—	—	—	—	—	—	—	17	9	Bisacca, George R.
1961		NCAA	II	32	—	—	—	—	—	—	—	17	7	Bisacca, George R.
1962		NCAA	II	16	—	—	—	—	—	—	—	20	5	Bisacca, George R.
1973		NCAA	I	—	8	—	—	—	—	—	—	18	9	Barakat, Frederick E.

Year	M/W	Assn	Div	NAT	NIT	ARC	CCA	NCI	NCT	OLY	HLM	W	L	Coach
1974		NCAA	I	—	16	—	—	—	—	—	—	17	9	Barakat, Frederick E.
1978		NCAA	I	—	16	—	—	—	—	—	—	22	5	Barakat, Frederick E.
1986		NCAA	I	64	—	—	—	—	—	—	—	24	7	Buonaguro, Mitch
1987		NCAA	I	64	—	—	—	—	—	—	—	15	16	Buonaguro, Mitch
1996		NCAA	I	—	32	—	—	—	—	—	—	20	10	Cormier, Paul
1997		NCAA	I	64	—	—	—	—	—	—	—	11	19	Cormier, Paul
1988	W	NCAA	I	40	—	—	—	—	—	—	—	19	10	Nolan, Diane
1991		NCAA	I	48	—	—	—	—	—	—	—	25	6	Nolan, Diane
1998		NCAA	I	64	—	—	—	—	—	—	—	20	10	Nolan, Diane

FAIRLEIGH DICKINSON: MADISON

Year	M/W	Assn	Div	NAT	NIT	ARC	CCA	NCI	NCT	OLY	HLM	W	L	Coach
1990	M	NCAA	III	40	—	—	—	—	—	—	—	18	9	Kindel, Roger
1998		NCAA	III	48	—	—	—	—	—	—	—	17	9	Kindel, Roger

FAIRLEIGH DICKINSON: RUTHERFORD/TEANECK

Year	M/W	Assn	Div	NAT	NIT	ARC	CCA	NCI	NCT	OLY	HLM	W	L	Coach
1952	M	NAIA		32	—	—	—	—	—	—	—	22	4	Holub, Richard
1959		NAIA		16	—	—	—	—	—	—	—	17	11	Holub, Richard
1963		NCAA	II	32	—	—	—	—	—	—	—	16	12	Holub, Richard
1985		NCAA	I	64	—	—	—	—	—	—	—	21	10	Green, Tom
1988		NCAA	I	64	—	—	—	—	—	—	—	23	7	Green, Tom
1991		NCAA	I	—	32	—	—	—	—	—	—	22	9	Green, Tom

FAIRLEIGH DICKINSON: TEANECK

Year	M/W	Assn	Div	NAT	NIT	ARC	CCA	NCI	NCT	OLY	HLM	W	L	Coach
1998	M	NCAA	I	64	—	—	—	—	—	—	—	23	7	Green, Tom

FAIRMONT STATE

Year	M/W	Assn	Div	NAT	NIT	ARC	CCA	NCI	NCT	OLY	HLM	W	L	Coach
1965	M	NAIA		4	—	—	—	—	—	—	—	32	4	Retton, Joe
1968		NAIA		2	—	—	—	—	—	—	—	24	6	Retton, Joe
1969		NAIA		16	—	—	—	—	—	—	—	26	2	Retton, Joe
1971		NAIA		4	—	—	—	—	—	—	—	32	3	Retton, Joe
1973		NAIA		32	—	—	—	—	—	—	—	23	5	Retton, Joe
1974		NAIA		16	—	—	—	—	—	—	—	28	3	Retton, Joe
1975		NAIA		8	—	—	—	—	—	—	—	30	16	Retton, Joe
1976		NAIA		16	—	—	—	—	—	—	—	28	1	Retton, Joe
1977		NAIA		32	—	—	—	—	—	—	—	21	5	Retton, Joe
1978		NAIA		32	—	—	—	—	—	—	—	27	6	Retton, Joe
1980		NAIA		32	—	—	—	—	—	—	—	23	4	Retton, Joe
1981		NAIA		32	—	—	—	—	—	—	—	26	5	Retton, Joe
1996		NCAA	II	32	—	—	—	—	—	—	—	24	5	Haswell, Arthur "Butch"
1998		NCAA	II	8	—	—	—	—	—	—	—	27	4	Haswell, Arthur "Butch"

FAITH BAPTIST BIBLE (IA)

Year	M/W	Assn	Div	NAT	NIT	ARC	CCA	NCI	NCT	OLY	HLM	W	L	Coach
1984	M	NBCAA	I	4	—	—	—	—	—	—	—	18	12	Thompson, David G.
1994		NCCAA	IIA	4	—	—	—	—	—	—	—	18	12	Walter, Dave
1995		NCCAA	IIA	7	—	—	—	—	—	—	—	15	14	Walter, Dave
1996		NCCAA	IIA	5	—	—	—	—	—	—	—	13	16	Walter, Dave
1997		NCCAA	IIA	4	—	—	—	—	—	—	—	16	13	Walter, Dave
1998		NCCAA	IIA	3	—	—	—	—	—	—	—	19	12	Walter, Dave
1986	W	NBCAA		2	—	—	—	—	—	—	—	9	5	Nihart, Lanny
1990		NBCAA		2	—	—	—	—	—	—	—	11	2	Nihart, Lanny
1991		NBCAA		3	—	—	—	—	—	—	—	8	7	Nihart, Lanny
1996		NCCAA	II	7	—	—	—	—	—	—	—	17	9	Nihart, Lanny

Year	M/W	Assn	Div	NAT	NIT	ARC	CCA	NCI	NCT	OLY	HLM	W	L	Coach

FAULKNER

Year	M/W	Assn	Div	NAT	NIT	ARC	CCA	NCI	NCT	OLY	HLM	W	L	Coach
1981	M	NSCAA		3	—	—	—	—	—	—	—	—	22	13	Hazelip, John
1984		NCCAA	I	8	—	—	—	—	—	—	—	—	8	25	Naylor, Jim
1992		NAIA	I	32	—	—	—	—	—	—	—	—	27	6	Kelsey, Tom
1998		NCCAA	I	4	—	—	—	—	—	—	—	—	25	14	Sanderson, Jim

FAYETTEVILLE STATE

Year	M/W	Assn	Div	NAT	NIT	ARC	CCA	NCI	NCT	OLY	HLM	W	L	Coach
1952	M	NASC		8	—	—	—	—	—	—	—	—	30	7	Gaines, William A. "Gus"
1973		NCAA	II	24	—	—	—	—	—	—	—	—	19	10	Reeves, Thomas
1993		NCAA	II	32	—	—	—	—	—	—	—	—	20	9	Capel, Jeff
1997	W	NCAA	II	32	—	—	—	—	—	—	—	—	25	5	Tucker, Eric

FEDERAL CITY

Year	M/W	Assn	Div	NAT	NIT	ARC	CCA	NCI	NCT	OLY	HLM	W	L	Coach
1975	W	AIAW	L	8	—	—	—	—	—	—	—	—	20	4	Stockard, Bessie A.

FERRIS STATE

Year	M/W	Assn	Div	NAT	NIT	ARC	CCA	NCI	NCT	OLY	HLM	W	L	Coach
1960	M	NAIA		32	—	—	—	—	—	—	—	—	15	6	Wink, James M.
1962		NAIA		8	—	—	—	—	—	—	—	—	23	3	Wink, James M.
1964		NAIA		32	—	—	—	—	—	—	—	—	19	4	Wink, James M.
1973		NAIA		16	—	—	—	—	—	—	—	—	26	4	Wink, James M.
1975		NAIA		32	—	—	—	—	—	—	—	—	22	5	Wink, James M.
1983		NCAA	II	24	—	—	—	—	—	—	—	—	20	9	Ludwig, H. Thomas
1987		NCAA	II	16	—	—	—	—	—	—	—	—	20	9	Ludwig, H. Thomas
1988		NCAA	II	8	—	—	—	—	—	—	—	—	25	5	Ludwig, H. Thomas
1989		NCAA	II	32	—	—	—	—	—	—	—	—	24	6	Ludwig, H. Thomas
1990		NCAA	II	24	—	—	—	—	—	—	—	—	18	11	Ludwig, H. Thomas
1998		NCAA	II	48	—	—	—	—	—	—	—	—	21	12	Wilson, Edgar

FERRUM

Year	M/W	Assn	Div	NAT	NIT	ARC	CCA	NCI	NCT	OLY	HLM	W	L	Coach
1992	M	NCAA	III	32	—	—	—	—	—	—	—	—	21	8	Pullen, Bill
1995	W	NCAA	III	64	—	—	—	—	—	—	—	—	18	9	Doonan, Donna M.

FINDLAY

Year	M/W	Assn	Div	NAT	NIT	ARC	CCA	NCI	NCT	OLY	HLM	W	L	Coach
1952	M	NAIA		32	—	—	—	—	—	—	—	—	16	6	Renninger, Donald S.
1953		NAIA		8	—	—	—	—	—	—	—	—	13	7	Renninger, Donald S.
1960		NAIA		16	—	—	—	—	—	—	—	—	14	9	Houdeshell, Dr. James D.
1967		NAIA		32	—	—	—	—	—	—	—	—	15	10	Houdeshell, Dr. James D.
1972		NAIA		32	—	—	—	—	—	—	—	—	16	11	Houdeshell, Dr. James D.
1986		NAIA		32	—	—	—	—	—	—	—	—	25	6	Niekamp, Ron
1992		NAIA	I	32	—	—	—	—	—	—	—	—	23	8	Niekamp, Ron
1993		NAIA	I	32	—	—	—	—	—	—	—	—	26	6	Niekamp, Ron
1996		NAIA	I	16	—	—	—	—	—	—	—	—	25	10	Niekamp, Ron
1997		NAIA	I	16	—	—	—	—	—	—	—	—	27	5	Niekamp, Ron
1993	W	NAIA	II	16	—	—	—	—	—	—	—	—	26	5	Neff, Sheryl
1994		NAIA	II	8	—	—	—	—	—	—	—	—	25	5	Neff, Sheryl
1995		NAIA	II	8	—	—	—	—	—	—	—	—	32	2	Kleinfelter, Eileen
1996		NAIA	II	16	—	—	—	—	—	—	—	—	25	8	Kleinfelter, Eileen
1998		NAIA	I	3	—	—	—	—	—	—	—	—	26	7	Kleinfelter, Eileen

FISK

Year	M/W	Assn	Div	NAT	NIT	ARC	CCA	NCI	NCT	OLY	HLM	W	L	Coach
1964	M	NCAA	II	16	—	—	—	—	—	—	—	—	18	6	Thompson, Herbert B. "Bus"
1974		NCAA	II	16	—	—	—	—	—	—	—	—	25	4	Lawson, Ronald

Year	M/W	Assn	Div	NAT	NIT	ARC	CCA	NCI	NCT	OLY	HLM	W	L	Coach
FLORIDA														
1969	M	NCAA	I	—	16	—	—	—	—	—	—	18	9	Bartlett, Thomas G. "Tommy"
1984		NCAA	I	—	32	—	—	—	—	—	—	16	13	Sloan, Norman L., Jr.
1985		NCAA	I	—	32	—	—	—	—	—	—	18	12	Sloan, Norman L., Jr.
1986		NCAA	I	—	4	—	—	—	—	—	—	19	14	Sloan, Norman L., Jr.
1987		NCAA	I	16	—	—	—	—	—	—	—	23	11	Sloan, Norman L., Jr.
1988		NCAA	I	32	—	—	—	—	—	—	—	23	12	Sloan, Norman L., Jr.
1989		NCAA	I	64	—	—	—	—	—	—	—	21	13	Sloan, Norman L., Jr.
1992		NCAA	I	—	4	—	—	—	—	—	—	19	14	Kruger, Lon
1993		NCAA	I	—	32	—	—	—	—	—	—	16	12	Kruger, Lon
1994		NCAA	I	3	—	—	—	—	—	—	—	29	8	Kruger, Lon
1995		NCAA	I	64	—	—	—	—	—	—	—	17	13	Kruger, Lon
1998		NCAA	I	—	32	—	—	—	—	—	—	14	15	Donovan, William J. "Billy"
1985	W	NCAA	I	—	2	—	—	—	—	—	—	22	9	Yow, Deborah Ann
1993		NCAA	I	32	—	—	—	—	—	—	—	19	10	Ross, Carol
1994		NCAA	I	64	—	—	—	—	—	—	—	22	7	Ross, Carol
1995		NCAA	I	32	—	—	—	—	—	—	—	24	9	Ross, Carol
1996		NCAA	I	64	—	—	—	—	—	—	—	21	9	Ross, Carol
1997		NCAA	I	8	—	—	—	—	—	—	—	24	9	Ross, Carol
1998		NCAA	I	16	—	—	—	—	—	—	—	23	9	Ross, Carol
FLORIDA A&M														
1952	M	NASC		8	—	—	—	—	—	—	—	26	2	Oglesby, Edward E. "Rock"
1953		NASC		8	—	—	—	—	—	—	—	17	5	Oglesby, Edward E. "Rock"
1954		NASC		8	—	—	—	—	—	—	—	19	7	Oglesby, Edward E. "Rock"
1955		NASC		8	—	—	—	—	—	—	—	20	2	Oglesby, Edward E. "Rock"
1957		NCAA	II	32	—	—	—	—	—	—	—	25	6	Oglesby, Edward E. "Rock"
1959		NCAA	II	16	—	—	—	—	—	—	—	15	3	Oglesby, Edward E. "Rock"
1962		NCAA	II	16	—	—	—	—	—	—	—	26	1	Oglesby, Edward E. "Rock"
1978		NCAA	II	16	—	—	—	—	—	—	—	23	6	Triplett, Ajac
1995	W	NCAA	I	64	—	—	—	—	—	—	—	24	6	Farmer, Claudette
FLORIDA ATLANTIC														
1989	W	NCAA	II	32	—	—	—	—	—	—	—	21	8	Allen, Wayne
1990		NCAA	II	16	—	—	—	—	—	—	—	21	8	Allen, Wayne
1991		NCAA	II	32	—	—	—	—	—	—	—	23	6	Allen, Wayne
1993		NCAA	II	32	—	—	—	—	—	—	—	20	8	Allen, Wayne
FLORIDA CHRISTIAN														
1992	M	NBCAA	II	5	—	—	—	—	—	—	—	12	17	Chambers, Aaron
FLORIDA COLLEGE														
1975	M	NSCAA		1	—	—	—	—	—	—	—	20	11	Wilson, Tom
1979		NSCAA		1	—	—	—	—	—	—	—	20	14	Wilson, Tom
1980		NSCAA		4	—	—	—	—	—	—	—	20	13	Owens, Donnie
1997		NSCAA		12	—	—	—	—	—	—	—	7	20	Moorer, Kenny
1998		NSCAA		10	—	—	—	—	—	—	—	11	19	Moorer, Kenny
FLORIDA INTERNATIONAL														
1995	M	NCAA	I	64	—	—	—	—	—	—	—	11	19	Weltlich, Robert

Year	M/W	Assn	Div	NAT	NIT	ARC	CCA	NCI	NCT	OLY	HLM	W	L	Coach
1982	W	AIAW	II	16	—	—	—	—	—	—	—	20	8	Russo, Cindy
1983		NCAA	II	24	—	—	—	—	—	—	—	17	7	Russo, Cindy
1986		NCAA	II	16	—	—	—	—	—	—	—	26	2	Russo, Cindy
1987		NCAA	II	16	—	—	—	—	—	—	—	26	3	Russo, Cindy
1992		NCAA	I	—	6	—	—	—	—	—	—	23	10	Russo, Cindy
1993		NCAA	I	—	3	—	—	—	—	—	—	25	6	Russo, Cindy
1994		NCAA	I	64	—	—	—	—	—	—	—	25	4	Russo, Cindy
1995		NCAA	I	32	—	—	—	—	—	—	—	27	5	Russo, Cindy
1997		NCAA	I	64	—	—	—	—	—	—	—	21	9	Russo, Cindy
1998		NCAA	I	32	—	—	—	—	—	—	—	29	2	Russo, Cindy

FLORIDA MEMORIAL

Year	M/W	Assn	Div	NAT	NIT	ARC	CCA	NCI	NCT	OLY	HLM	W	L	Coach
1992	M	NAIA	II	16	—	—	—	—	—	—	—	17	12	Parker, Alfred
1992	W	NAIA	II	20	—	—	—	—	—	—	—	12	7	Marshall, Kenneth
1993		NAIA	II	20	—	—	—	—	—	—	—	13	13	Marshall, Kenneth

FLORIDA SOUTHERN

Year	M/W	Assn	Div	NAT	NIT	ARC	CCA	NCI	NCT	OLY	HLM	W	L	Coach
1972	M	NCAA	II	24	—	—	—	—	—	—	—	24	4	Jarrett, Jim
1979		NCAA	II	32	—	—	—	—	—	—	—	18	12	Wissel, Dr. Harold R. 'Hal'
1980		NCAA	II	3	—	—	—	—	—	—	—	28	5	Wissel, Dr. Harold R. 'Hal'
1981		NCAA	II	1	—	—	—	—	—	—	—	24	8	Wissel, Dr. Harold R. 'Hal'
1982		NCAA	II	2	—	—	—	—	—	—	—	22	10	Wissel, Dr. Harold R. 'Hal'
1983		NCAA	II	24	—	—	—	—	—	—	—	23	8	Scholz, George
1985		NCAA	II	24	—	—	—	—	—	—	—	24	7	Scholz, George
1986		NCAA	II	3	—	—	—	—	—	—	—	24	9	Scholz, George
1987		NCAA	II	8	—	—	—	—	—	—	—	26	6	Scholz, George
1988		NCAA	II	3	—	—	—	—	—	—	—	31	3	Scholz, George
1989		NCAA	II	24	—	—	—	—	—	—	—	25	6	Scholz, George
1990		NCAA	II	24	—	—	—	—	—	—	—	23	8	Scholz, George
1991		NCAA	II	32	—	—	—	—	—	—	—	27	5	Gibbons, Gordon
1993		NCAA	II	32	—	—	—	—	—	—	—	24	8	Gibbons, Gordon
1996		NCAA	II	32	—	—	—	—	—	—	—	26	4	Gibbons, Gordon
1998		NCAA	II	48	—	—	—	—	—	—	—	23	7	Gibbons, Gordon
1994	W	NCAA	II	32	—	—	—	—	—	—	—	23	8	Benn, Norm
1995		NCAA	II	8	—	—	—	—	—	—	—	28	4	Benn, Norm
1996		NCAA	II	16	—	—	—	—	—	—	—	26	5	Benn, Norm
1998		NCAA	II	32	—	—	—	—	—	—	—	24	5	Foli, Diane

FLORIDA STATE

Year	M/W	Assn	Div	NAT	NIT	ARC	CCA	NCI	NCT	OLY	HLM	W	L	Coach
1951	M	NAIA		8	—	—	—	—	—	—	—	18	9	Kennedy, Jesse K. 'Bud'
1955		NAIA		16	—	—	—	—	—	—	—	22	4	Kennedy, Jesse K. 'Bud'
1968		NCAA	I	23	—	—	—	—	—	—	—	19	8	Durham, Hugh
1972		NCAA	I	2	—	—	—	—	—	—	—	27	6	Durham, Hugh
1978		NCAA	I	32	—	—	—	—	—	—	—	23	6	Durham, Hugh
1980		NCAA	I	32	—	—	—	—	—	—	—	22	9	Williams, Joe L.
1984		NCAA	I	—	16	—	—	—	—	—	—	20	11	Williams, Joe L.
1987		NCAA	I	—	16	—	—	—	—	—	—	19	11	Kennedy, Patrick
1988		NCAA	I	64	—	—	—	—	—	—	—	19	11	Kennedy, Patrick
1989		NCAA	I	64	—	—	—	—	—	—	—	22	8	Kennedy, Patrick
1991		NCAA	I	32	—	—	—	—	—	—	—	21	11	Kennedy, Patrick
1992		NCAA	I	16	—	—	—	—	—	—	—	22	10	Kennedy, Patrick

Year	M/W	Assn	Div	NAT	NIT	ARC	CCA	NCI	NCT	OLY	HLM	W	L	Coach
1993		NCAA	I	8	—	—	—	—	—	—	—	25	10	Kennedy, Patrick
1997		NCAA	I	—	2	—	—	—	—	—	—	20	12	Kennedy, Patrick
1998		NCAA	I	32	—	—	—	—	—	—	—	18	14	Robinson, Steve
1982	W	NCAA	I	—	2	—	—	—	—	—	—	27	10	Dykehouse-Allen, Janice
1983		NCAA	I	32	—	—	—	—	—	—	—	24	6	Dykehouse-Allen, Janice
1990		NCAA	I	48	—	—	—	—	—	—	—	21	9	Meadors, Marynell Hutsell
1991		NCAA	I	32	—	—	—	—	—	—	—	25	7	Meadors, Marynell Hutsell

FLORIDA TECH

Year	M/W	Assn	Div	NAT	NIT	ARC	CCA	NCI	NCT	OLY	HLM	W	L	Coach
1997	W	NCAA	II	32	—	—	—	—	—	—	—	27	3	Reynolds, John, Jr.

FONTBONNE

Year	M/W	Assn	Div	NAT	NIT	ARC	CCA	NCI	NCT	OLY	HLM	W	L	Coach
1996	M	NCAA	III	64	—	—	—	—	—	—	—	17	10	McKinney, Lee

FORDHAM

Year	M/W	Assn	Div	NAT	NIT	ARC	CCA	NCI	NCT	OLY	HLM	W	L	Coach
1943	M	NCAA		—	4	—	—	—	—	—	—	16	6	Kelleher, Edward A.
1953		NCAA		22	—	—	—	—	—	—	—	18	8	Bach, John W. "Johnny"
1954		NCAA		24	—	—	—	—	—	—	—	18	6	Bach, John W. "Johnny"
1958		NCAA	I	—	8	—	—	—	—	—	—	15	9	Bach, John W. "Johnny"
1959		NCAA	I	—	12	—	—	—	—	—	—	17	8	Bach, John W. "Johnny"
1963		NCAA	I	—	12	—	—	—	—	—	—	18	8	Bach, John W. "Johnny"
1965		NCAA	I	—	14	—	—	—	—	—	—	15	12	Bach, John W. "Johnny"
1968		NCAA	I	—	8	—	—	—	—	—	—	19	8	Bach, John W. "Johnny"
1969		NCAA	I	—	16	—	—	—	—	—	—	17	9	Conlin, Edward J.
1971		NCAA	I	12	—	—	—	—	—	—	—	26	3	Phelps, Richard F. "Digger"
1972		NCAA	I	—	16	—	—	—	—	—	—	18	9	Wissel, Dr. Harold R. "Hal"
1981		NCAA	I	—	32	—	—	—	—	—	—	19	9	Penders, Thomas V.
1982		NCAA	I	—	32	—	—	—	—	—	—	18	11	Penders, Thomas V.
1983		NCAA	I	—	32	—	—	—	—	—	—	19	11	Penders, Thomas V.
1984		NCAA	I	—	32	—	—	—	—	—	—	19	15	Penders, Thomas V.
1985		NCAA	I	—	32	—	—	—	—	—	—	19	12	Penders, Thomas V.
1988		NCAA	I	—	32	—	—	—	—	—	—	18	15	Macarchuk, Nick, Jr.
1990		NCAA	I	—	16	—	—	—	—	—	—	20	13	Macarchuk, Nick, Jr.
1991		NCAA	I	—	16	—	—	—	—	—	—	25	8	Macarchuk, Nick, Jr.
1992		NCAA	I	64	—	—	—	—	—	—	—	18	13	Macarchuk, Nick, Jr.
1978	W	AIAW	S	16	—	—	—	—	—	—	—	25	8	Mosolino, Kathy
1979		AIAW	L	8	—	—	—	—	—	—	—	27	7	Mosolino, Kathy
1994		NCAA	I	64	—	—	—	—	—	—	—	21	9	Morris, Kevin

FORT HAYS STATE

Year	M/W	Assn	Div	NAT	NIT	ARC	CCA	NCI	NCT	OLY	HLM	W	L	Coach
1959	M	NAIA		4	—	—	—	—	—	—	—	23	4	Suran, Cade
1962		NAIA		32	—	—	—	—	—	—	—	19	4	Suran, Cade
1963		NAIA		4	—	—	—	—	—	—	—	21	7	Suran, Cade
1981		NAIA		32	—	—	—	—	—	—	—	30	4	Rosado, Joe
1983		NAIA		3	—	—	—	—	—	—	—	32	4	Morse, Bill
1984		NAIA		1	—	—	—	—	—	—	—	26	2	Morse, Bill
1985		NAIA		1	—	—	—	—	—	—	—	35	3	Morse, Bill
1988		NAIA		16	—	—	—	—	—	—	—	28	5	Morse, Bill
1995		NCAA	II	16	—	—	—	—	—	—	—	24	7	Garner, Gary
1996		NCAA	II	1	—	—	—	—	—	—	—	34	0	Garner, Gary
1997		NCAA	II	16	—	—	—	—	—	—	—	29	2	Garner, Gary
1998		NCAA	II	48	—	—	—	—	—	—	—	22	7	Wintz, Chad

Year	M/W	Assn	Div	NAT	NIT	ARC	CCA	NCI	NCT	OLY	HLM	W	L	Coach
1991	W	NAIA		1	—	—	—	—	—	—	—	34	2	Klein, John

FORT LAUDERDALE

Year	M/W	Assn	Div	NAT	NIT	ARC	CCA	NCI	NCT	OLY	HLM	W	L	Coach
1969	M	NSCAA		8	—	—	—	—	—	—	—	12	20	D'Angelo,
1970		NSCAA		5	—	—	—	—	—	—	—	13	11	
1971		NSCAA		3	—	—	—	—	—	—	—	12	9	Gotkin, Hy

FORT LEWIS

Year	M/W	Assn	Div	NAT	NIT	ARC	CCA	NCI	NCT	OLY	HLM	W	L	Coach
1976	W	AIAW	S	16	—	—	—	—	—	—	—	13	2	Spickard, Karen

FORT VALLEY STATE

Year	M/W	Assn	Div	NAT	NIT	ARC	CCA	NCI	NCT	OLY	HLM	W	L	Coach
1998	M	NCAA	II	48	—	—	—	—	—	—	—	19	12	Moore, Michael D.
1978	W	AIAW	S	—	8	—	—	—	—	—	—	13	9	Brown, Jessie A.
1982		NCAA	II	8	—	—	—	—	—	—	—	23	8	Brown, Jessie A.
1988		NCAA	II	32	—	—	—	—	—	—	—	25	4	Bartley, Lonnie
1992		NCAA	II	32	—	—	—	—	—	—	—	21	9	Bartley, Lonnie
1993		NCAA	II	32	—	—	—	—	—	—	—	27	3	Bartley, Lonnie
1995		NCAA	II	32	—	—	—	—	—	—	—	25	5	Bartley, Lonnie
1996		NCAA	II	48	—	—	—	—	—	—	—	25	4	Bartley, Lonnie
1997		NCAA	II	16	—	—	—	—	—	—	—	25	6	Bartley, Lonnie

FRAMINGHAM STATE

Year	M/W	Assn	Div	NAT	NIT	ARC	CCA	NCI	NCT	OLY	HLM	W	L	Coach
1979	M	NCAA	III	16	—	—	—	—	—	—	—	22	6	Grealey, Bruce
1980		NCAA	III	32	—	—	—	—	—	—	—	20	8	Grealey, Bruce
1984		NCAA	III	16	—	—	—	—	—	—	—	24	2	Grealey, Bruce

FRANCIS MARION

Year	M/W	Assn	Div	NAT	NIT	ARC	CCA	NCI	NCT	OLY	HLM	W	L	Coach
1991	M	NAIA		32	—	—	—	—	—	—	—	22	10	Hill, Lewis
1976	W	AIAW	S	6	—	—	—	—	—	—	—	23	9	Hatchell, Sylvia Rhyne
1977		AIAW	S	8	—	—	—	—	—	—	—	21	11	Hatchell, Sylvia Rhyne
1978		AIAW	S	8	—	—	—	—	—	—	—	22	11	Hatchell, Sylvia Rhyne
1982		AIAW	II	1	—	—	—	—	—	—	—	27	7	Hatchell, Sylvia Rhyne
1984		NAIA		8	—	—	—	—	—	—	—	28	5	Hatchell, Sylvia Rhyne
1986		NAIA		1	—	—	—	—	—	—	—	36	2	Hatchell, Sylvia Rhyne
1997		NCAA	II	48	—	—	—	—	—	—	—	21	8	Moore, Frank "Wes"
1998		NCAA	II	3	—	—	—	—	—	—	—	30	3	Moore, Frank "Wes"

FRANCISCAN

Year	M/W	Assn	Div	NAT	NIT	ARC	CCA	NCI	NCT	OLY	HLM	W	L	Coach
1955	M	NAIA		8	—	—	—	—	—	—	—	28	5	Kuzma, Harry
1961		NAIA		32	—	—	—	—	—	—	—	16	11	Smith, Wayne
1965		NCAA	II	24	—	—	—	—	—	—	—	21	4	Bayer, John D. "Denny"
1966		NCAA	II	16	—	—	—	—	—	—	—	17	9	Bayer, John D. "Denny"
1973		NCAA	II	16	—	—	—	—	—	—	—	22	7	Sparling, Edward L.

FRANKLIN & MARSHALL

Year	M/W	Assn	Div	NAT	NIT	ARC	CCA	NCI	NCT	OLY	HLM	W	L	Coach
1975	M	NCAA	III	30	—	—	—	—	—	—	—	16	11	Robinson, Glenn R.
1977		NCAA	III	23	—	—	—	—	—	—	—	22	5	Robinson, Glenn R.
1979		NCAA	III	3	—	—	—	—	—	—	—	27	5	Robinson, Glenn R.
1981		NCAA	III	24	—	—	—	—	—	—	—	26	3	Robinson, Glenn R.
1984		NCAA	III	32	—	—	—	—	—	—	—	21	8	Robinson, Glenn R.
1986		NCAA	III	16	—	—	—	—	—	—	—	19	10	Robinson, Glenn R.
1987		NCAA	III	16	—	—	—	—	—	—	—	22	7	Robinson, Glenn R.
1988		NCAA	III	16	—	—	—	—	—	—	—	24	5	Robinson, Glenn R.

Year	M/W	Assn	Div	NAT	NIT	ARC	CCA	NCI	NCT	OLY	HLM	W	L	Coach
1989		NCAA	III	8	—	—	—	—	—	—	—	27	3	Robinson, Glenn R.
1990		NCAA	III	32	—	—	—	—	—	—	—	24	4	Robinson, Glenn R.
1991		NCAA	III	2	—	—	—	—	—	—	—	28	3	Robinson, Glenn R.
1992		NCAA	III	8	—	—	—	—	—	—	—	26	4	Robinson, Glenn R.
1993		NCAA	III	16	—	—	—	—	—	—	—	24	4	Robinson, Glenn R.
1994		NCAA	III	16	—	—	—	—	—	—	—	26	2	Robinson, Glenn R.
1995		NCAA	III	16	—	—	—	—	—	—	—	27	2	Robinson, Glenn R.
1996		NCAA	III	4	—	—	—	—	—	—	—	29	3	Robinson, Glenn R.
1988	W	NCAA	III	8	—	—	—	—	—	—	—	25	4	Fleig, Mary L.
1989		NCAA	III	24	—	—	—	—	—	—	—	24	5	Fleig, Mary L.
1990		NCAA	III	32	—	—	—	—	—	—	—	25	5	Fleig, Mary L.
1991		NCAA	III	32	—	—	—	—	—	—	—	21	6	Fleig, Mary L.

FRANKLIN (IN)

Year	M/W	Assn	Div	NAT	NIT	ARC	CCA	NCI	NCT	OLY	HLM	W	L	Coach
1976	M	NAIA		32	—	—	—	—	—	—	—	16	10	Thompson, Ed
1978		NAIA		32	—	—	—	—	—	—	—	19	6	Lovell, Robert
1980		NAIA		16	—	—	—	—	—	—	—	22	6	Lovell, Robert
1992		NAIA	II	8	—	—	—	—	—	—	—	25	4	Prather, Kerry
1998		NCAA	III	32	—	—	—	—	—	—	—	23	6	Prather, Kerry
1994	W	NCAA	III	40	—	—	—	—	—	—	—	19	6	White, Gene
1995		NCAA	III	32	—	—	—	—	—	—	—	24	2	Mahan, Lisa

FRANKLIN PIERCE

Year	M/W	Assn	Div	NAT	NIT	ARC	CCA	NCI	NCT	OLY	HLM	W	L	Coach
1980	M	NAIA		32	—	—	—	—	—	—	—	29	2	Kirsh, Bruce
1981		NAIA		32	—	—	—	—	—	—	—	31	4	Kirsh, Bruce
1982		NAIA		32	—	—	—	—	—	—	—	27	8	Kirsh, Bruce
1984		NAIA		32	—	—	—	—	—	—	—	27	10	Kirsh, Bruce
1986		NAIA		32	—	—	—	—	—	—	—	24	7	Kirsh, Bruce
1988		NAIA		32	—	—	—	—	—	—	—	16	15	Kirsh, Bruce
1991		NCAA	II	16	—	—	—	—	—	—	—	26	6	Luptowski, Arthur
1993		NCAA	II	16	—	—	—	—	—	—	—	22	8	Luptowski, Arthur
1996		NCAA	II	32	—	—	—	—	—	—	—	23	6	Luptowski, Arthur
1992	W	NCAA	II	32	—	—	—	—	—	—	—	24	7	Hancock, Steve
1993		NCAA	II	32	—	—	—	—	—	—	—	21	9	Hancock, Steve
1998		NCAA	II	32	—	—	—	—	—	—	—	24	6	Chadbourne, David

FREDONIA STATE

Year	M/W	Assn	Div	NAT	NIT	ARC	CCA	NCI	NCT	OLY	HLM	W	L	Coach
1993	M	NCAA	III	40	—	—	—	—	—	—	—	18	10	Prechtl, Gregory

FREE WILL BAPTIST BIBLE

Year	M/W	Assn	Div	NAT	NIT	ARC	CCA	NCI	NCT	OLY	HLM	W	L	Coach
1987	M	NBCAA	I	8	—	—	—	—	—	—	—	1	5	Deel, Byron
1995		NCCAA	II	4	—	—	—	—	—	—	—	28	10	Deel, Byron

FREED-HARDEMAN

Year	M/W	Assn	Div	NAT	NIT	ARC	CCA	NCI	NCT	OLY	HLM	W	L	Coach
1998	M	NAIA	I	32	—	—	—	—	—	—	—	24	11	McCutchen, Mike
1997	W	NAIA	I	16	—	—	—	—	—	—	—	26	11	Neal, Dale
1998		NAIA	I	32	—	—	—	—	—	—	—	24	11	Neal, Dale

FREEMAN JC

Year	M/W	Assn	Div	NAT	NIT	ARC	CCA	NCI	NCT	OLY	HLM	W	L	Coach
1982	W	NSCAA		4	—	—	—	—	—	—	—	5	12	Hoffer, Herb

FRESNO PACIFIC

Year	M/W	Assn	Div	NAT	NIT	ARC	CCA	NCI	NCT	OLY	HLM	W	L	Coach
1995	M	NAIA	I	16	—	—	—	—	—	—	—	24	8	Sargent, Jim

Year	M/W	Assn	Div	NAT	NIT	ARC	CCA	NCI	NCT	OLY	HLM	W	L	Coach
1987	W	NAIA		16	—	—	—	—	—	—	—	—	28	3	Janzen, Dennis
1989		NAIA		16	—	—	—	—	—	—	—	—	24	8	Stanley, Kent
1992		NAIA	I	16	—	—	—	—	—	—	—	—	25	6	Stanley, Kent
1993		NAIA	I	32	—	—	—	—	—	—	—	—	21	8	Stanley, Kent
1994		NAIA	I	32	—	—	—	—	—	—	—	—	23	7	Stanley, Kent
1995		NAIA	I	32	—	—	—	—	—	—	—	—	21	10	Stanley, Kent

FRIENDS

Year	M/W	Assn	Div	NAT	NIT	ARC	CCA	NCI	NCT	OLY	HLM	W	L	Coach
1994	W	NAIA	II	24	—	—	—	—	—	—	—	—	23	7	Carter, Jeff
1995		NAIA	II	32	—	—	—	—	—	—	—	—	23	6	Carter, Jeff

FRIENDSHIP JC

Year	M/W	Assn	Div	NAT	NIT	ARC	CCA	NCI	NCT	OLY	HLM	W	L	Coach
1967	M	NSCAA		6	—	—	—	—	—	—	—	—	11	13	Harris, Rev. Herman K., II
1975		NSCAA		8	—	—	—	—	—	—	—	—			

FROSTBURG STATE

Year	M/W	Assn	Div	NAT	NIT	ARC	CCA	NCI	NCT	OLY	HLM	W	L	Coach
1982	W	NCAA	III	16	—	—	—	—	—	—	—	—	15	7	Crawley, James M.
1983		NCAA	III	16	—	—	—	—	—	—	—	—	20	5	Crawley, James M.
1985		NCAA	III	32	—	—	—	—	—	—	—	—	21	5	Crawley, James M.
1991		NCAA	III	16	—	—	—	—	—	—	—	—	26	2	Crawley, James M.
1997		NCAA	III	64	—	—	—	—	—	—	—	—	23	3	Crawley, James M.

FURMAN

Year	M/W	Assn	Div	NAT	NIT	ARC	CCA	NCI	NCT	OLY	HLM	W	L	Coach
1971	M	NCAA	I	25	—	—	—	—	—	—	—	—	15	12	Williams, Joe L.
1973		NCAA	I	25	—	—	—	—	—	—	—	—	20	9	Williams, Joe L.
1974		NCAA	I	16	—	—	—	—	—	—	—	—	22	9	Williams, Joe L.
1975		NCAA	I	32	—	—	—	—	—	—	—	—	22	7	Williams, Joe L.
1978		NCAA	I	32	—	—	—	—	—	—	—	—	19	11	Williams, Joe L.
1980		NCAA	I	48	—	—	—	—	—	—	—	—	23	7	Holbrook, Edwin "Eddie"
1991		NCAA	I	—	32	—	—	—	—	—	—	—	20	9	Estes, George "Butch"
1995	W	NCAA	I	64	—	—	—	—	—	—	—	—	18	12	Carter, Sherry

GALLAUDET

Year	M/W	Assn	Div	NAT	NIT	ARC	CCA	NCI	NCT	OLY	HLM	W	L	Coach
1997	W	NCAA	III	64	—	—	—	—	—	—	—	—	19	9	Baldridge, Kathryn "Kitty"

GANADO

Year	M/W	Assn	Div	NAT	NIT	ARC	CCA	NCI	NCT	OLY	HLM	W	L	Coach
1975	M	NSCAA		16	—	—	—	—	—	—	—	—			

GANNON

Year	M/W	Assn	Div	NAT	NIT	ARC	CCA	NCI	NCT	OLY	HLM	W	L	Coach
1962	M	NCAA	II	32	—	—	—	—	—	—	—	—	16	9	McCluskey, Edward J.
1969		NAIA		16	—	—	—	—	—	—	—	—	23	6	Bayer, John D. "Denny"
1972		NCAA	II	36	—	—	—	—	—	—	—	—	19	7	Markey, David C.
1975		NCAA	II	8	—	—	—	—	—	—	—	—	25	4	Sparling, Edward L.
1977		NCAA	II	24	—	—	—	—	—	—	—	—	20	8	Sparling, Edward L.
1980		NCAA	II	32	—	—	—	—	—	—	—	—	20	9	Fox, Richard A.
1984		NCAA	II	32	—	—	—	—	—	—	—	—	20	11	Fox, Richard A.
1985		NCAA	II	32	—	—	—	—	—	—	—	—	22	9	Chapman, Tom
1986		NCAA	II	16	—	—	—	—	—	—	—	—	25	6	Chapman, Tom
1987		NCAA	II	2	—	—	—	—	—	—	—	—	28	6	Chapman, Tom
1988		NCAA	II	8	—	—	—	—	—	—	—	—	24	8	Chapman, Tom
1990		NCAA	II	8	—	—	—	—	—	—	—	—	24	8	Dukiet, Bob

Year	M/W	Assn	Div	NAT	NIT	ARC	CCA	NCI	NCT	OLY	HLM	W	L	Coach
1993		NCAA	II	32	—	—	—	—	—	—	—	20	7	Dukiet, Bob
1994		NCAA	II	24	—	—	—	—	—	—	—	21	9	Dukiet, Bob
1995		NCAA	II	32	—	—	—	—	—	—	—	22	8	Dukiet, Bob
1988	W	NCAA	II	32	—	—	—	—	—	—	—	26	4	Saurer, Judy

Gardner-Webb

Year	M/W	Assn	Div	NAT	NIT	ARC	CCA	NCI	NCT	OLY	HLM	W	L	Coach
1972	M	NAIA		4	—	—	—	—	—	—	—	20	3	Holbrook, Edwin "Eddie"
1974		NAIA		16	—	—	—	—	—	—	—	25	3	Holbrook, Edwin "Eddie"
1981		NAIA		32	—	—	—	—	—	—	—	25	11	Wiles, Jim R.
1996	W	NCAA	II	48	—	—	—	—	—	—	—	22	7	McCurley, Eddie

Geneseo State

Year	M/W	Assn	Div	NAT	NIT	ARC	CCA	NCI	NCT	OLY	HLM	W	L	Coach
1991	M	NCAA	III	16	—	—	—	—	—	—	—	23	5	Pope, Tom
1993		NCAA	III	16	—	—	—	—	—	—	—	23	4	Pope, Tom
1994		NCAA	III	32	—	—	—	—	—	—	—	22	5	Pope, Tom
1995		NCAA	III	16	—	—	—	—	—	—	—	20	8	Holmes, Steve
1996		NCAA	III	32	—	—	—	—	—	—	—	17	10	Holmes, Steve
1998		NCAA	III	48	—	—	—	—	—	—	—	15	13	Holmes, Steve
1993	W	NCAA	III	8	—	—	—	—	—	—	—	27	1	Guy, Robert
1994		NCAA	III	32	—	—	—	—	—	—	—	26	3	Guy, Robert
1995		NCAA	III	8	—	—	—	—	—	—	—	27	2	Guy, Robert
1996		NCAA	III	32	—	—	—	—	—	—	—	24	5	Guy, Robert
1997		NCAA	III	64	—	—	—	—	—	—	—	21	7	French, Joe

Geneva

Year	M/W	Assn	Div	NAT	NIT	ARC	CCA	NCI	NCT	OLY	HLM	W	L	Coach
1953	M	NAIA		32	—	—	—	—	—	—	—	22	5	Aultman, Clifford J.
1954		NAIA		16	—	—	—	—	—	—	—	21	8	Aultman, Clifford J.
1955		NAIA		32	—	—	—	—	—	—	—	19	8	Aultman, Clifford J.
1956		NAIA		16	—	—	—	—	—	—	—	24	3	Aultman, Clifford J.
1976		NCCAA	I	4	—	—	—	—	—	—	—	15	19	Christopher, Jim
1977		NCCAA	I	6	—	—	—	—	—	—	—	13	19	Christopher, Jim
1978		NCCAA	I	6	—	—	—	—	—	—	—	15	18	Christopher, Jim
1984		NCCAA	I	8	—	—	—	—	—	—	—	23	12	Erickson, Lee W.
1989		NCCAA	I	8	—	—	—	—	—	—	—	20	15	Slocum, Jerry
1990		NAIA		32	—	—	—	—	—	—	—	22	9	Slocum, Jerry
1992		NCCAA	I	5	—	—	—	—	—	—	—	26	8	Slocum, Jerry
1993		NAIA	I	32	—	—	—	—	—	—	—	28	3	Slocum, Jerry
1994		NCCAA	I	5	—	—	—	—	—	—	—	28	4	Slocum, Jerry
1995		NAIA	I	16	—	—	—	—	—	—	—	26	6	Slocum, Jerry
1996		NAIA	I	8	—	—	—	—	—	—	—	24	7	Slocum, Jerry
1998		NCCAA	I	3	—	—	—	—	—	—	—	25	11	Santarsiero, Jeff
1987	W	NCCAA	I	3	—	—	—	—	—	—	—	14	15	Gall, Kimerly
1990		NCCAA	I	8	—	—	—	—	—	—	—	10	19	Gall, Kimerly
1996		NCCAA	I	4	—	—	—	—	—	—	—	15	16	Myers, Jackie
1997		NCCAA	I	8	—	—	—	—	—	—	—	22	12	Myers, Jackie

George Fox

Year	M/W	Assn	Div	NAT	NIT	ARC	CCA	NCI	NCT	OLY	HLM	W	L	Coach
1973	M	NAIA		32	—	—	—	—	—	—	—	16	15	Miller, Lorin
1985		NCCAA	I	3	—	—	—	—	—	—	—	27	7	Vernon, Mark
1987		NCCAA	I	8	—	—	—	—	—	—	—	27	6	Vernon, Mark
1990		NAIA		32	—	—	—	—	—	—	—	29	5	Vernon, Mark
1992		NAIA	II	8	—	—	—	—	—	—	—	24	11	Vernon, Mark

Year	M/W	Assn	Div	NAT	NIT	ARC	CCA	NCI	NCT	OLY	HLM	W	L	Coach
GEORGE MASON														
1986	M	NCAA	I	—	16	—	—	—	—	—	—	20	12	Harrington, Joe
1989		NCAA	I	64	—	—	—	—	—	—	—	20	11	Nestor, Ernie
GEORGE WASHINGTON														
1954	M	NCAA		24	—	—	—	—	—	—	—	23	3	Reinhart, William J.
1961		NCAA	I	24	—	—	—	—	—	—	—	9	17	Reinhart, William J.
1991		NCAA	I	—	32	—	—	—	—	—	—	19	12	Jarvis, Mike
1993		NCAA	I	16	—	—	—	—	—	—	—	21	9	Jarvis, Mike
1994		NCAA	I	32	—	—	—	—	—	—	—	18	12	Jarvis, Mike
1995		NCAA	I	—	32	—	—	—	—	—	—	18	14	Jarvis, Mike
1996		NCAA	I	64	—	—	—	—	—	—	—	21	8	Jarvis, Mike
1997		NCAA	I	—	32	—	—	—	—	—	—	15	14	Jarvis, Mike
1998		NCAA	I	64	—	—	—	—	—	—	—	24	9	Jarvis, Mike
1991	W	NCAA	I	32	—	—	—	—	—	—	—	23	7	McKeown, Joe
1992		NCAA	I	32	—	—	—	—	—	—	—	25	7	McKeown, Joe
1993		NCAA	I	—	8	—	—	—	—	—	—	20	11	McKeown, Joe
1994		NCAA	I	32	—	—	—	—	—	—	—	23	8	McKeown, Joe
1995		NCAA	I	16	—	—	—	—	—	—	—	26	6	McKeown, Joe
1996		NCAA	I	32	—	—	—	—	—	—	—	26	7	McKeown, Joe
1997		NCAA	I	8	—	—	—	—	—	—	—	28	6	McKeown, Joe
1998		NCAA	I	32	—	—	—	—	—	—	—	20	10	McKeown, Joe
GEORGE WILLIAMS														
1976	W	AIAW	S	16	—	—	—	—	—	—	—	17	2	Langbein, Mary
GEORGETOWN (DC)														
1943	M	NCAA		2	—	3	—	—	—	—	—	22	5	Ripley, Elmer H.
1953		NCAA		—	12	—	—	—	—	—	—	13	7	Jeanette, Harry E. 'Buddy'
1970		NCAA	I	—	16	—	—	—	—	—	—	18	8	Magee, John F. 'Jack'
1975		NCAA	I	32	—	—	—	—	—	—	—	18	10	Thompson, John R., Jr.
1976		NCAA	I	32	—	—	—	—	—	—	—	21	7	Thompson, John R., Jr.
1977		NCAA	I	—	16	—	—	—	—	—	—	19	9	Thompson, John R., Jr.
1978		NCAA	I	—	4	—	—	—	—	—	—	23	8	Thompson, John R., Jr.
1979		NCAA	I	32	—	—	—	—	—	—	—	24	5	Thompson, John R., Jr.
1980		NCAA	I	8	—	—	—	—	—	—	—	26	6	Thompson, John R., Jr.
1981		NCAA	I	48	—	—	—	—	—	—	—	20	12	Thompson, John R., Jr.
1982		NCAA	I	2	—	—	—	—	—	—	—	30	7	Thompson, John R., Jr.
1983		NCAA	I	32	—	—	—	—	—	—	—	22	10	Thompson, John R., Jr.
1984		NCAA	I	1	—	—	—	—	—	—	—	34	3	Thompson, John R., Jr.
1985		NCAA	I	2	—	—	—	—	—	—	—	35	3	Thompson, John R., Jr.
1986		NCAA	I	32	—	—	—	—	—	—	—	24	8	Thompson, John R., Jr.
1987		NCAA	I	8	—	—	—	—	—	—	—	29	5	Thompson, John R., Jr.
1988		NCAA	I	32	—	—	—	—	—	—	—	20	10	Thompson, John R., Jr.
1989		NCAA	I	8	—	—	—	—	—	—	—	29	5	Thompson, John R., Jr.
1990		NCAA	I	32	—	—	—	—	—	—	—	24	7	Thompson, John R., Jr.
1991		NCAA	I	32	—	—	—	—	—	—	—	19	13	Thompson, John R., Jr.
1992		NCAA	I	32	—	—	—	—	—	—	—	22	10	Thompson, John R., Jr.
1993		NCAA	I	—	2	—	—	—	—	—	—	20	13	Thompson, John R., Jr.
1994		NCAA	I	32	—	—	—	—	—	—	—	19	12	Thompson, John R., Jr.
1995		NCAA	I	16	—	—	—	—	—	—	—	21	10	Thompson, John R., Jr.
1996		NCAA	I	8	—	—	—	—	—	—	—	29	8	Thompson, John R., Jr.

Year	M/W	Assn	Div	NAT	NIT	ARC	CCA	NCI	NCT	OLY	HLM	W	L	Coach
1997		NCAA	I	64	—	—	—	—	—	—	—	20	10	Thompson, John R., Jr.
1998		NCAA	I	—	16	—	—	—	—	—	—	16	15	Thompson, John R., Jr.
1993	W	NCAA	I	16	—	—	—	—	—	—	—	23	7	Knapp, Patrick

GEORGETOWN (KY)

Year	M/W	Assn	Div	NAT	NIT	ARC	CCA	NCI	NCT	OLY	HLM	W	L	Coach
1954	M	NAIA		32	—	—	—	—	—	—	—	15	10	Davis, Dr. Robert M.
1955		NAIA		32	—	—	—	—	—	—	—	22	5	Davis, Dr. Robert M.
1956		NAIA		32	—	—	—	—	—	—	—	17	8	Davis, Dr. Robert M.
1958		NAIA		4	—	—	—	—	—	—	—	22	6	Davis, Dr. Robert M.
1961		NAIA		2	—	—	—	—	—	—	—	26	9	Davis, Dr. Robert M.
1962		NAIA		32	—	—	—	—	—	—	—	23	7	Davis, Dr. Robert M.
1964		NAIA		16	—	—	—	—	—	—	—	21	10	Davis, Dr. Robert M.
1969		NAIA		32	—	—	—	—	—	—	—	24	11	Davis, Dr. Robert M.
1987		NAIA		4	—	—	—	—	—	—	—	30	8	Reid, James B.
1990		NAIA		3	—	—	—	—	—	—	—	29	7	Reid, James B.
1992		NAIA	I	8	—	—	—	—	—	—	—	34	2	Reid, James B.
1993		NAIA	I	3	—	—	—	—	—	—	—	29	8	Reid, James B.
1994		NAIA	I	16	—	—	—	—	—	—	—	33	2	Reid, James B.
1995		NAIA	I	32	—	—	—	—	—	—	—	32	4	Reid, James B.
1996		NAIA	I	2	—	—	—	—	—	—	—	36	3	Reid, James B.
1997		NAIA	I	16	—	—	—	—	—	—	—	27	9	Osborne, "Happy"
1998		NAIA	I	1	—	—	—	—	—	—	—	36	3	Osborne, "Happy"
1993	W	NAIA	II	8	—	—	—	—	—	—	—	27	5	Johnson, Susan
1994		NAIA	II	24	—	—	—	—	—	—	—	19	11	Johnson, Susan
1996		NAIA	II	16	—	—	—	—	—	—	—	21	10	Johnson, Susan

GEORGIA

Year	M/W	Assn	Div	NAT	NIT	ARC	CCA	NCI	NCT	OLY	HLM	W	L	Coach
1981	M	NCAA	I	—	16	—	—	—	—	—	—	19	12	Durham, Hugh
1982		NCAA	I	—	3	—	—	—	—	—	—	19	12	Durham, Hugh
1983		NCAA	I	3	—	—	—	—	—	—	—	24	10	Durham, Hugh
1984		NCAA	I	—	32	—	—	—	—	—	—	17	13	Durham, Hugh
1985		NCAA	I	32	—	—	—	—	—	—	—	22	9	Durham, Hugh
1986		NCAA	I	—	16	—	—	—	—	—	—	17	13	Durham, Hugh
1987		NCAA	I	64	—	—	—	—	—	—	—	18	12	Durham, Hugh
1988		NCAA	I	—	16	—	—	—	—	—	—	20	16	Durham, Hugh
1990		NCAA	I	64	—	—	—	—	—	—	—	20	9	Durham, Hugh
1991		NCAA	I	64	—	—	—	—	—	—	—	17	13	Durham, Hugh
1993		NCAA	I	—	32	—	—	—	—	—	—	15	14	Durham, Hugh
1995		NCAA	I	—	32	—	—	—	—	—	—	18	10	Durham, Hugh
1996		NCAA	I	16	—	—	—	—	—	—	—	21	10	Smith, Orlando H. "Tubby"
1997		NCAA	I	64	—	—	—	—	—	—	—	24	9	Smith, Orlando H. "Tubby"
1998		NCAA	I	—	3	—	—	—	—	—	—	20	15	Jirsa, Ron
1981	W	AIAW	I	—	1	—	—	—	—	—	—	27	10	Landers, Andy
1982		NCAA	I	32	—	—	—	—	—	—	—	21	9	Landers, Andy
1983		NCAA	I	3	—	—	—	—	—	—	—	27	7	Landers, Andy
1984		NCAA	I	8	—	—	—	—	—	—	—	30	3	Landers, Andy
1985		NCAA	I	2	—	—	—	—	—	—	—	29	5	Landers, Andy
1986		NCAA	I	16	—	—	—	—	—	—	—	30	2	Landers, Andy
1987		NCAA	I	16	—	—	—	—	—	—	—	27	5	Landers, Andy
1988		NCAA	I	16	—	—	—	—	—	—	—	21	10	Landers, Andy

Year	M/W	Assn	Div	NAT	NIT	ARC	CCA	NCI	NCT	OLY	HLM	W	L	Coach
1989		NCAA	I	32	—	—	—	—	—	—	—	23	7	Landers, Andy
1990		NCAA	I	32	—	—	—	—	—	—	—	25	5	Landers, Andy
1991		NCAA	I	8	—	—	—	—	—	—	—	28	4	Landers, Andy
1993		NCAA	I	32	—	—	—	—	—	—	—	21	13	Landers, Andy
1995		NCAA	I	3	—	—	—	—	—	—	—	28	5	Landers, Andy
1996		NCAA	I	2	—	—	—	—	—	—	—	28	5	Landers, Andy
1997		NCAA	I	8	—	—	—	—	—	—	—	25	6	Landers, Andy
1998		NCAA	I	64	—	—	—	—	—	—	—	17	11	Landers, Andy

GEORGIA COLLEGE

Year	M/W	Assn	Div	NAT	NIT	ARC	CCA	NCI	NCT	OLY	HLM	W	L	Coach
1988	M	NAIA		32	—	—	—	—	—	—	—	25	9	Hodges, Bill
1989		NAIA		32	—	—	—	—	—	—	—	22	10	Hodges, Bill
1990		NAIA		32	—	—	—	—	—	—	—	24	8	Hodges, Bill
1997		NCAA	II	48	—	—	—	—	—	—	—	25	5	Sellers, Terry
1996	W	NCAA	II	48	—	—	—	—	—	—	—	21	9	Carrick, John
1997		NCAA	II	32	—	—	—	—	—	—	—	23	8	Carrick, John

GEORGIA MILITARY

Year	M/W	Assn	Div	NAT	NIT	ARC	CCA	NCI	NCT	OLY	HLM	W	L	Coach
1981	M	NSCAA		2	—	—	—	—	—	—	—	X	X	Steinke, Rick
1983		NSCAA		9	—	—	—	—	—	—	—	25	12	Keast, Richard

GEORGIA SOUTHERN

Year	M/W	Assn	Div	NAT	NIT	ARC	CCA	NCI	NCT	OLY	HLM	W	L	Coach
1956	M	NAIA		16	—	—	—	—	—	—	—	21	7	Scearce, J. B., Jr.
1958		NAIA		32	—	—	—	—	—	—	—	12	15	Scearce, J. B., Jr.
1959		NAIA		8	—	—	—	—	—	—	—	19	12	Scearce, J. B., Jr.
1964		NAIA		16	—	—	—	—	—	—	—	20	11	Scearce, J. B., Jr.
1966		NAIA		2	—	—	—	—	—	—	—	26	6	Scearce, J. B., Jr.
1970		NCAA	II	16	—	—	—	—	—	—	—	17	6	Radovich, Frank
1983		NCAA	I	52	—	—	—	—	—	—	—	18	12	Kerns, Frank
1987		NCAA	I	64	—	—	—	—	—	—	—	20	11	Kerns, Frank
1988		NCAA	I	—	32	—	—	—	—	—	—	24	7	Kerns, Frank
1989		NCAA	I	—	32	—	—	—	—	—	—	23	6	Kerns, Frank
1992		NCAA	I	64	—	—	—	—	—	—	—	25	6	Kerns, Frank
1982	W	AIAW	I	16	—	—	—	—	—	—	—	26	5	Evans, Ellen
1993		NCAA	I	48	—	—	—	—	—	—	—	21	9	Greer, Drema Sue
1994		NCAA	I	64	—	—	—	—	—	—	—	21	9	Greer, Drema Sue

GEORGIA SOUTHWESTERN

Year	M/W	Assn	Div	NAT	NIT	ARC	CCA	NCI	NCT	OLY	HLM	W	L	Coach
1985	M	NAIA		16	—	—	—	—	—	—	—	28	5	Duhon, Glenn D.
1991		NAIA		32	—	—	—	—	—	—	—	27	6	Duhon, Glenn D.
1994		NAIA	I	16	—	—	—	—	—	—	—	24	10	Duhon, Glenn D.
1995		NAIA	I	8	—	—	—	—	—	—	—	30	5	Duhon, Glenn D.
1997		NAIA	I	32	—	—	—	—	—	—	—	23	9	Barksdale, Randolph
1998		NAIA	I	32	—	—	—	—	—	—	—	25	11	Barksdale, Randolph
1986	W	NAIA		4	—	—	—	—	—	—	—	25	4	Hawver, Dr. Greg
1996		NAIA	I	32	—	—	—	—	—	—	—	22	10	Drown, Kip
1998		NAIA	I	32	—	—	—	—	—	—	—	22	12	Drown, Kip

GEORGIA STATE

Year	M/W	Assn	Div	NAT	NIT	ARC	CCA	NCI	NCT	OLY	HLM	W	L	Coach
1991	M	NCAA	I	64	—	—	—	—	—	—	—	16	15	Reinhart, Bob
1981	W	AIAW	I	24	—	—	—	—	—	—	—	28	5	Jarrett, Jim

Year	M/W	Assn	Div	NAT	NIT	ARC	CCA	NCI	NCT	OLY	HLM	W	L	Coach
GEORGIA TECH														
1960	M	NCAA	I	8	—	—	—	—	—	—	—	22	6	Hyder, John C. "Whack"
1970		NCAA	I	—	8	—	—	—	—	—	—	17	10	Hyder, John C. "Whack"
1971		NCAA	I	—	2	—	—	—	—	—	—	23	9	Hyder, John C. "Whack"
1984		NCAA	I	—	32	—	—	—	—	—	—	18	11	Cremins, Bobby
1985		NCAA	I	8	—	—	—	—	—	—	—	27	8	Cremins, Bobby
1986		NCAA	I	16	—	—	—	—	—	—	—	27	7	Cremins, Bobby
1987		NCAA	I	64	—	—	—	—	—	—	—	16	13	Cremins, Bobby
1988		NCAA	I	32	—	—	—	—	—	—	—	22	10	Cremins, Bobby
1989		NCAA	I	64	—	—	—	—	—	—	—	20	12	Cremins, Bobby
1990		NCAA	I	3	—	—	—	—	—	—	—	28	7	Cremins, Bobby
1991		NCAA	I	32	—	—	—	—	—	—	—	17	13	Cremins, Bobby
1992		NCAA	I	16	—	—	—	—	—	—	—	23	12	Cremins, Bobby
1993		NCAA	I	64	—	—	—	—	—	—	—	19	11	Cremins, Bobby
1994		NCAA	I	—	32	—	—	—	—	—	—	16	13	Cremins, Bobby
1996		NCAA	I	16	—	—	—	—	—	—	—	24	12	Cremins, Bobby
1998		NCAA	I	—	8	—	—	—	—	—	—	19	14	Cremins, Bobby
1992	W	NCAA	I	—	1	—	—	—	—	—	—	20	13	Berenato, Agnus McGlade
1993		NCAA	I	48	—	—	—	—	—	—	—	16	11	Berenato, Agnus McGlade
GEORGIAN COURT														
1984	W	NAIA		16	—	—	—	—	—	—	—	18	4	Sonday, Bob
1990		NAIA		16	—	—	—	—	—	—	—	27	3	Emery, Debra
1991		NAIA		32	—	—	—	—	—	—	—	25	5	Emery, Debra
GETTYSBURG														
1996	M	NCAA	III	64	—	—	—	—	—	—	—	18	9	Petrie, George
1984	W	NCAA	III	16	—	—	—	—	—	—	—	22	4	Higgins, Kay
1985		NCAA	III	32	—	—	—	—	—	—	—	19	6	Hurst, Anne
1995		NCAA	III	32	—	—	—	—	—	—	—	20	5	Kirkpatrick, Michael
GLENVILLE STATE														
1939	M	NAIA		3	—	—	—	—	—	—	—	25	3	Rohrbaugh, A. F. "Nate"
1940		NAIA		16	—	—	—	—	—	—	—	22	3	Rohrbaugh, A. F. "Nate"
1951		NAIA		32	—	—	—	—	—	—	—	19	11	Ratliff, Carlos C.
1972		NAIA		16	—	—	—	—	—	—	—	26	7	Lilly, Jesse
1989	W	NAIA		16	—	—	—	—	—	—	—	19	7	Shepherd, Dr. Russell M.
GONZAGA														
1948	M	NAIA		16	—	—	—	—	—	—	—	24	11	McGrath, Claude F.
1949		NAIA		—	—	—	—	8	—	—	—	17	12	McGrath, Claude F.
1953		NAIA		32	—	—	—	—	—	—	—	15	14	Anderson, Thor H. "Hank"
1994		NCAA	I	—	16	—	—	—	—	—	—	22	8	Fitzgerald, Dan
1995		NCAA	I	64	—	—	—	—	—	—	—	21	9	Fitzgerald, Dan
1996		NCAA	I	—	32	—	—	—	—	—	—	21	9	Fitzgerald, Dan
1998		NCAA	I	—	16	—	—	—	—	—	—	24	10	Monson, Don
1994	W	NCAA	I	—	7	—	—	—	—	—	—	21	10	Holt, Julie
GORDON (MA)														
1968	M	NCCAA		6	—	—	—	—	—	—	—	20	10	Murdoch, Harlan P.

Year	M/W	Assn	Div	NAT	NIT	ARC	CCA	NCI	NCT	OLY	HLM	W	L	Coach
1983	W	NCCAA	I	8	—	—	—	—	—	—	—	10	11	Zuidema, Mary
1984		NCCAA	I	8	—	—	—	—	—	—	—	13	8	Zuidema, Mary

GOUCHER

Year	M/W	Assn	Div	NAT	NIT	ARC	CCA	NCI	NCT	OLY	HLM	W	L	Coach
1995	M	NCAA	III	32	—	—	—	—	—	—	—	19	10	Trevino, Leonard
1997		NCAA	III	32	—	—	—	—	—	—	—	23	6	Trevino, Leonard
1996	W	NCAA	III	64	—	—	—	—	—	—	—	17	10	Navarro, Noelle

GRACE (IN)

Year	M/W	Assn	Div	NAT	NIT	ARC	CCA	NCI	NCT	OLY	HLM	W	L	Coach
1969	M	NCCAA		5	—	—	—	—	—	—	—	21	11	Kammerer, Glen "Chet"
1970		NCCAA		2	—	—	—	—	—	—	—	26	6	Kammerer, Glen "Chet"
1971		NCCAA		8	—	—	—	—	—	—	—	18	10	Kammerer, Glen "Chet"
1973		NCCAA		4	—	—	—	—	—	—	—	24	8	Kammerer, Glen "Chet"
1983		NCCAA	I	2	—	—	—	—	—	—	—	32	5	Kessler, James C.
1986		NCCAA	I	4	—	—	—	—	—	—	—	27	10	Kessler, James C.
1988		NAIA		16	—	—	—	—	—	—	—	31	5	Kessler, James C.
1992		NAIA	II	1	—	—	—	—	—	—	—	32	5	Kessler, James C.
1993		NAIA	II	16	—	—	—	—	—	—	—	27	6	Kessler, James C.
1990	W	NCCAA	I	7	—	—	—	—	—	—	—	18	14	Ryman, Jerry

GRACE (NE)

Year	M/W	Assn	Div	NAT	NIT	ARC	CCA	NCI	NCT	OLY	HLM	W	L	Coach
1982	M	NBCAA		2	—	—	—	—	—	—	—	22	5	Classen, Jim W.
1983		NBCAA		7	—	—	—	—	—	—	—	20	5	Classen, Jim W.
1984		NBCAA	I	7	—	—	—	—	—	—	—	18	8	Classen, Jim W.
1985		NBCAA	I	4	—	—	—	—	—	—	—	23	4	Classen, Jim W.
1986		NBCAA	I	7	—	—	—	—	—	—	—	16	11	Classen, Jim W.
1989		NBCAA	I	7	—	—	—	—	—	—	—	12	14	Classen, Jim W.
1990		NBCAA	I	6	—	—	—	—	—	—	—	17	11	Classen, Jim W.
1991		NBCAA	I	5	—	—	—	—	—	—	—	20	7	Classen, Jim W.
1992		NBCAA	I	2	—	—	—	—	—	—	—	22	5	Classen, Jim W.
1993		NBCAA	I	3	—	—	—	—	—	—	—	23	3	Classen, Jim W.
1994		NBCAA	I	2	—	—	—	—	—	—	—	24	3	Classen, Jim W.
1995		NBCAA	I	4	—	—	—	—	—	—	—	23	4	Classen, Jim W.
1996		NBCAA	I	6	—	—	—	—	—	—	—	12	15	Classen, Jim W.
1997		NBCAA	I	6	—	—	—	—	—	—	—	13	14	Classen, Jim W.
1990	W	NBCAA		5	—	—	—	—	—	—	—	6	7	Krehbiel, Gary
1992		NBCAA		3	—	—	—	—	—	—	—	7	1	Regier, Larry
1993		NBCAA		1	—	—	—	—	—	—	—	19	0	Regier, Larry
1994		NBCAA		1	—	—	—	—	—	—	—	15	0	Reiger, Larry
1995		NBCAA		1	—	—	—	—	—	—	—	17	2	Johnson, DuWayne
1996		NBCAA		1	—	—	—	—	—	—	—	19	0	Johnson, DuWayne
1997		NBCAA		2	—	—	—	—	—	—	—	10	14	Johnson, DuWayne

GRACE BIBLE (MI)

Year	M/W	Assn	Div	NAT	NIT	ARC	CCA	NCI	NCT	OLY	HLM	W	L	Coach
1991	M	NCCAA	IIA	4	—	—	—	—	—	—	—	10	13	Grube, David
1993		NCCAA	IIA	2	—	—	—	—	—	—	—	15	11	Moore, Jimmy
1994		NCCAA	IIA	1	—	—	—	—	—	—	—	19	10	Moore, Jimmy
1995		NCCAA	IIA	1	—	—	—	—	—	—	—	19	12	Moore, Jimmy
1996		NCCAA	IIA	4	—	—	—	—	—	—	—	14	22	Moore, Jimmy
1997		NCCAA	IIA	3	—	—	—	—	—	—	—	12	14	Moore, Jimmy

Year	M/W	Assn	Div	NAT	NIT	ARC	CCA	NCI	NCT	OLY	HLM	W	L	Coach
GRACELAND (IN)														
1992	M	NSCAA		12	—	—	—	—	—	—	—	20	11	Hickman, Rick W.
1993		NSCAA		6	—	—	—	—	—	—	—	14	18	Harrop, Rich
1994		NSCAA		8	—	—	—	—	—	—	—	6	30	Freebersyser, George
1995		NSCAA		4	—	—	—	—	—	—	—			Freebersyser, George
GRAMBLING STATE														
1955	M	NASC		4	—	—	—	—	—	—	—	24	8	Robinson, Eddie G.
1958		NCAA	II	8	—	—	—	—	—	—	—	27	4	Hobdy, Frederick C.
1959		NAIA		16	—	—	—	—	—	—	—	28	1	Hobdy, Frederick C.
1960		NAIA		8	—	—	—	—	—	—	—	26	5	Hobdy, Frederick C.
1961		NAIA		1	—	—	—	—	—	—	—	32	4	Hobdy, Frederick C.
1963		NAIA		3	—	—	—	—	—	—	—	30	3	Hobdy, Frederick C.
1964		NAIA		16	—	—	—	—	—	—	—	26	4	Hobdy, Frederick C.
1966		NAIA		3	—	—	—	—	—	—	—	28	6	Hobdy, Frederick C.
1969		NAIA		32	—	—	—	—	—	—	—	21	9	Hobdy, Frederick C.
1971		NAIA		8	—	—	—	—	—	—	—	16	8	Hobdy, Frederick C.
1976		NCAA	II	16	—	—	—	—	—	—	—	22	9	Hobdy, Frederick C.
1980		NCAA	I	—	32	—	—	—	—	—	—	22	8	Hobdy, Frederick C.
1994	W	NCAA	I	64	—	—	—	—	—	—	—	23	7	Bibbs, Patricia Cage
1996		NCAA	I	64	—	—	—	—	—	—	—	21	7	Bibbs, Patricia Cage
1997		NCAA	I	64	—	—	—	—	—	—	—	24	6	Bibbs, Patricia Cage
1998		NCAA	I	64	—	—	—	—	—	—	—	23	7	Ponton, David
GRAND CANYON														
1973	M	NAIA		32	—	—	—	—	—	—	—	19	10	Lindsey, Ben
1974		NAIA		16	—	—	—	—	—	—	—	28	2	Lindsey, Ben
1975		NAIA		1	—	—	—	—	—	—	—	30	3	Lindsey, Ben
1976		NAIA		16	—	—	—	—	—	—	—	27	3	Lindsey, Ben
1978		NAIA		1	—	—	—	—	—	—	—	30	3	Lindsey, Ben
1979		NAIA		32	—	—	—	—	—	—	—	24	4	Lindsey, Ben
1980		NAIA		32	—	—	—	—	—	—	—	21	4	Lindsey, Ben
1988		NAIA		1	—	—	—	—	—	—	—	37	6	Westphal, Paul D.
1989		NAIA		32	—	—	—	—	—	—	—	26	5	Westphal, Bill
1990		NAIA		16	—	—	—	—	—	—	—	25	10	Westphal, Bill
1992		NCAA	II	24	—	—	—	—	—	—	—	21	7	McCrary, Leighton
1993		NCAA	II	23	—	—	—	—	—	—	—	20	11	McCrary, Leighton
1995		NCAA	II	48	—	—	—	—	—	—	—	17	11	McCrary, Leighton
1996		NCAA	II	32	—	—	—	—	—	—	—	23	6	McCrary, Leighton
1997		NCAA	II	32	—	—	—	—	—	—	—	23	6	McCrary, Leighton
1998		NCAA	II	48	—	—	—	—	—	—	—	17	10	McCrary, Leighton
1997	W	NCAA	II	48	—	—	—	—	—	—	—	15	11	Hanks, Julie
GRAND RAPIDS BAPTIST														
1968	M	NCCAA		6	—	—	—	—	—	—	—	15	10	Raymond,
1987	W	NSCAA		6	—	—	—	—	—	—	—	9	14	Gates, Ray
1993		NCCAA	I	7	—	—	—	—	—	—	—	18	14	Shuneson, Kevin
GRAND RAPIDS BIBLE & MUSIC														
1968	M	NCCAA		2	—	—	—	—	—	—	—	18	10	Unknown
1992		NCCAA	IIA	5	—	—	—	—	—	—	—	14	20	Elmer, Don
1993		NCCAA	IIA	5	—	—	—	—	—	—	—	8	24	Elmer, Don

Year	M/W	Assn	Div	NAT	NIT	ARC	CCA	NCI	NCT	OLY	HLM	W	L	Coach
GRAND VALLEY STATE														
1974	M	NAIA		32	—	—	—	—	—	—	—	—	23	6	Villemure, Thomas
1977		NAIA		4	—	—	—	—	—	—	—	—	30	4	Villemure, Thomas
1979		NAIA		32	—	—	—	—	—	—	—	—	22	4	Villemure, Thomas
1985		NCAA	II	16	—	—	—	—	—	—	—	—	21	8	Villemure, Thomas
1991		NCAA	II	16	—	—	—	—	—	—	—	—	26	5	Villemure, Thomas
1992		NCAA	II	32	—	—	—	—	—	—	—	—	20	11	Villemure, Thomas
1997		NCAA	II	48	—	—	—	—	—	—	—	—	23	6	Smith, Jay
1988	W	NCAA	II	32	—	—	—	—	—	—	—	—	20	8	Baker-Grzyb, Pat
1990		NCAA	II	32	—	—	—	—	—	—	—	—	22	6	Vandebunte, Carol
1998		NCAA	II	32	—	—	—	—	—	—	—	—	23	5	Charney, Claudette
GRAND VIEW														
1976	W	AIAW	S	16	—	—	—	—	—	—	—	—	X	X	Boson, Karen
1997		NAIA	II	32	—	—	—	—	—	—	—	—	28	7	Sharer, Missy
1998		NAIA	II	16	—	—	—	—	—	—	—	—	32	4	Sharer, Missy
GREAT FALLS														
1971	M	NAIA		16	—	—	—	—	—	—	—	—	24	6	Dods, Ray
GREEN MOUNTAIN														
1996	M	NAIA	II	32	—	—	—	—	—	—	—	—	21	9	Dempsey, Matthew J.
1997		NAIA	II	32	—	—	—	—	—	—	—	—	21	8	Dempsey, Matthew J.
GREENSBORO														
1985	M	NCAA	III	24	—	—	—	—	—	—	—	—	21	7	Mikels, Ron
1994		NCAA	III	8	—	—	—	—	—	—	—	—	26	4	Hanger, Samuel
1995		NCAA	III	32	—	—	—	—	—	—	—	—	19	10	Hanger, Samuel
1997	W	NCAA	III	64	—	—	—	—	—	—	—	—	19	9	Johnson, Steve
GREENVILLE														
1996	M	NCCAA	I	8	—	—	—	—	—	—	—	—	21	8	Faulkner, Doug
GRINNELL														
1962	M	NCAA	II	32	—	—	—	—	—	—	—	—	18	4	Pfitsch, John A.
1996		NCAA	III	64	—	—	—	—	—	—	—	—	17	8	Arseneault, David
GROVE CITY														
1976	M	NCAA	III	28	—	—	—	—	—	—	—	—	16	6	Barr, John F.
1979		NCAA	III	24	—	—	—	—	—	—	—	—	18	7	Barr, John F.
1983		NCAA	III	24	—	—	—	—	—	—	—	—	21	4	Barr, John F.
1989		NCAA	III	24	—	—	—	—	—	—	—	—	20	6	Barr, John F.
1982	W	NCAA	III	16	—	—	—	—	—	—	—	—	19	5	Ellis, Terry
1983		NCAA	III	16	—	—	—	—	—	—	—	—	22	5	Ellis, Terry
GUILFORD														
1966	M	NAIA		32	—	—	—	—	—	—	—	—	18	8	Steele, Jerry
1967		NAIA		16	—	—	—	—	—	—	—	—	20	6	Steele, Jerry
1968		NAIA		32	—	—	—	—	—	—	—	—	25	5	Steele, Jerry
1970		NAIA		4	—	—	—	—	—	—	—	—	32	5	Steele, Jerry
1973		NAIA		1	—	—	—	—	—	—	—	—	29	5	Jensen, Jack
1976		NAIA		32	—	—	—	—	—	—	—	—	21	6	Jensen, Jack
1989		NAIA		32	—	—	—	—	—	—	—	—	16	10	Jensen, Jack

Year	M/W	Assn	Div	NAT	NIT	ARC	CCA	NCI	NCT	OLY	HLM	W	L	Coach

GULF COAST CHRISTIAN

Year	M/W	Assn	Div	NAT	NIT	ARC	CCA	NCI	NCT	OLY	HLM	W	L	Coach
1995	M	NBCAA	II	2	—	—	—	—	—	—	—	12	19	Wilkerson, Dr. Charles
1996		LCC		1	—	—	—	—	—	—	—	23	17	Wilkerson, Keith
1996		NBCAA	II	3	—	—	—	—	—	—	—	23	17	Wilkerson, Keith
1997		LCC		2	—	—	—	—	—	—	—	29	6	Wilkerson, Dr. Charles
1997		NBCAA	I	1	—	—	—	—	—	—	—	29	6	Wilkerson, Dr. Charles

GUSTAVUS ADOLPHUS

Year	M/W	Assn	Div	NAT	NIT	ARC	CCA	NCI	NCT	OLY	HLM	W	L	Coach
1954	M	NAIA		16	—	—	—	—	—	—	—	23	9	Young, Verl "Gus"
1955		NAIA		8	—	—	—	—	—	—	—	22	7	Young, Verl "Gus"
1956		NAIA		8	—	—	—	—	—	—	—	20	9	Young, Verl "Gus"
1958		NCAA	II	32	—	—	—	—	—	—	—	15	11	Skoog, Myer U. "Whitey"
1961		NAIA		32	—	—	—	—	—	—	—	15	11	Skoog, Myer U. "Whitey"
1976		NAIA		32	—	—	—	—	—	—	—	19	10	Skoog, Myer U. "Whitey"
1987		NCAA	III	16	—	—	—	—	—	—	—	15	13	Brock, Charles
1989		NCAA	III	40	—	—	—	—	—	—	—	14	14	Brock, Charles
1992		NCAA	III	16	—	—	—	—	—	—	—	22	7	Hanson, Mark
1996		NCAA	III	16	—	—	—	—	—	—	—	24	5	Hanson, Mark
1997		NCAA	III	32	—	—	—	—	—	—	—	21	7	Hanson, Mark
1998		NCAA	III	8	—	—	—	—	—	—	—	26	4	Hanson, Mark
1991	W	NCAA	III	32	—	—	—	—	—	—	—	18	8	Kennedy, Tim
1995		NCAA	III	64	—	—	—	—	—	—	—	16	10	Moline, Peg

HAMILTON

Year	M/W	Assn	Div	NAT	NIT	ARC	CCA	NCI	NCT	OLY	HLM	W	L	Coach
1995	M	NCAA	III	16	—	—	—	—	—	—	—	21	6	Murphy, Thomas Edward
1996		NCAA	III	64	—	—	—	—	—	—	—	16	9	Murphy, Thomas Edward
1997		NCAA	III	64	—	—	—	—	—	—	—	15	10	Murphy, Thomas Edward
1998		NCAA	III	16	—	—	—	—	—	—	—	17	10	Murphy, Thomas Edward

HAMLINE

Year	M/W	Assn	Div	NAT	NIT	ARC	CCA	NCI	NCT	OLY	HLM	W	L	Coach
1940	M	NAIA		4	—	—	—	—	—	—	—	12	5	Hutton, Joseph W., Sr.
1942		NAIA		1	—	—	—	—	—	—	—	20	2	Hutton, Joseph W., Sr.
1943		NAIA		8	—	—	—	—	—	—	—	21	2	Hutton, Joseph W., Sr.
1947		NAIA		16	—	—	—	—	—	—	—	22	5	Hutton, Joseph W., Sr.
1948		NAIA		3	—	—	—	—	—	—	—	28	3	Hutton, Joseph W., Sr.
1949		NAIA		1	—	—	—	—	—	—	—	29	1	Hutton, Joseph W., Sr.
1950		NAIA		16	—	—	—	—	—	—	—	29	3	Hutton, Joseph W., Sr.
1951		NAIA		1	—	—	—	—	—	—	—	27	2	Hutton, Joseph W., Sr.
1952		NAIA		8	—	—	—	—	—	—	—	24	5	Hutton, Joseph W., Sr.
1953		NAIA		2	—	—	—	—	—	—	—	23	9	Hutton, Joseph W., Sr.
1957		NAIA		8	—	—	—	—	—	—	—	22	4	Hutton, Joseph W., Sr.
1960		NAIA		8	—	—	—	—	—	—	—	23	4	Hutton, Joseph W., Sr.
1962		NCAA	II	24	—	—	—	—	—	—	—	18	4	Hutton, Joseph W., Sr.
1975		NCAA	III	16	—	—	—	—	—	—	—	19	11	Meyer, Dr. Don W.
1977		NCAA	III	4	—	—	—	—	—	—	—	22	8	Litzenberger, Fred L.

HAMPDEN-SYDNEY

Year	M/W	Assn	Div	NAT	NIT	ARC	CCA	NCI	NCT	OLY	HLM	W	L	Coach
1989	M	NCAA	III	24	—	—	—	—	—	—	—	21	8	Shaver, Tony
1992		NCAA	III	16	—	—	—	—	—	—	—	24	6	Shaver, Tony
1994		NCAA	III	16	—	—	—	—	—	—	—	22	6	Shaver, Tony
1995		NCAA	III	8	—	—	—	—	—	—	—	28	3	Shaver, Tony
1997		NCAA	III	64	—	—	—	—	—	—	—	21	7	Shaver, Tony
1998		NCAA	III	16	—	—	—	—	—	—	—	23	6	Shaver, Tony

Year	M/W	Assn	Div	NAT	NIT	ARC	CCA	NCI	NCT	OLY	HLM	W	L	Coach

HAMPTON

Year	M/W	Assn	Div	NAT	NIT	ARC	CCA	NCI	NCT	OLY	HLM	W	L	Coach
1978	M	NAIA		32	—	—	—	—	—	—	—	24	7	Ford, Henry "Hank"
1980		NAIA		32	—	—	—	—	—	—	—	21	10	Ford, Henry "Hank"
1982		NAIA		3	—	—	—	—	—	—	—	28	8	Ford, Henry "Hank"
1983		NCAA	II	24	—	—	—	—	—	—	—	23	7	Ford, Henry "Hank"
1991		NCAA	II	24	—	—	—	—	—	—	—	22	10	Avery, Malcolm "Zeke"
1985	W	NCAA	II	3	—	—	—	—	—	—	—	30	4	Sweat, James E.
1986		NCAA	II	8	—	—	—	—	—	—	—	26	6	Sweat, James E.
1987		NCAA	II	8	—	—	—	—	—	—	—	30	2	Sweat, James E.
1988		NCAA	II	1	—	—	—	—	—	—	—	33	1	Sweat, James E.
1989		NCAA	II	32	—	—	—	—	—	—	—	20	9	Laster, Jr. "Tiny"
1991		NCAA	II	32	—	—	—	—	—	—	—	26	6	Laster, Jr. "Tiny"

HANNIBAL-LaGRANGE

Year	M/W	Assn	Div	NAT	NIT	ARC	CCA	NCI	NCT	OLY	HLM	W	L	Coach
1995	M	NCCAA	I	8	—	—	—	—	—	—	—	17	17	Thomas, Kent
1998		NAIA	I	32	—	—	—	—	—	—	—	20	12	Thomas, Kent
1997	W	NAIA	I	32	—	—	—	—	—	—	—	25	8	Barnes, Daren

HANOVER

Year	M/W	Assn	Div	NAT	NIT	ARC	CCA	NCI	NCT	OLY	HLM	W	L	Coach
1968	M	NAIA		16	—	—	—	—	—	—	—	22	11	Collier, John R.
1970		NAIA		32	—	—	—	—	—	—	—	22	6	Collier, John R.
1973		NAIA		32	—	—	—	—	—	—	—	18	8	Collier, John R.
1974		NAIA		8	—	—	—	—	—	—	—	29	4	Collier, John R.
1979		NAIA		32	—	—	—	—	—	—	—	22	5	Collier, John R.
1981		NAIA		8	—	—	—	—	—	—	—	26	8	Collier, John R.
1982		NAIA		16	—	—	—	—	—	—	—	26	6	Collier, John R.
1995		NCAA	III	32	—	—	—	—	—	—	—	22	7	Beitzel, Dr. Michael
1996		NCAA	III	32	—	—	—	—	—	—	—	21	6	Beitzel, Dr. Michael
1997	W	NCAA	III	64	—	—	—	—	—	—	—	17	10	Snyder, Christa

HARDIN-SIMMONS

Year	M/W	Assn	Div	NAT	NIT	ARC	CCA	NCI	NCT	OLY	HLM	W	L	Coach
1953	M	NCAA		22	—	—	—	—	—	—	—	19	12	Scott, Bill
1957		NCAA	i	23	—	—	—	—	—	—	—	17	9	Scott, Bill
1994	W	NAIA	II	16	—	—	—	—	—	—	—	24	4	Roewe-Goodenough, Julie
1995		NAIA	II	32	—	—	—	—	—	—	—	19	8	Roewe-Goodenough, Julie

HARDING

Year	M/W	Assn	Div	NAT	NIT	ARC	CCA	NCI	NCT	OLY	HLM	W	L	Coach
1987	M	NAIA		32	—	—	—	—	—	—	—	18	14	Bucy, Jess
1996		NAIA	I	32	—	—	—	—	—	—	—	24	6	Morgan, Jeff
1996	W	NAIA	I	32	—	—	—	—	—	—	—	24	5	Harnden, Greg
1997		NAIA	I	16	—	—	—	—	—	—	—	26	4	Harnden, Greg

HARTFORD

Year	M/W	Assn	Div	NAT	NIT	ARC	CCA	NCI	NCT	OLY	HLM	W	L	Coach
1972	M	NCAA	II	16	—	—	—	—	—	—	—	18	6	McCullough, Gordon F.
1973		NCAA	II	42	—	—	—	—	—	—	—	17	7	McCullough, Gordon F.
1974		NCAA	II	16	—	—	—	—	—	—	—	20	4	McCullough, Gordon F.
1975		NCAA	II	24	—	—	—	—	—	—	—	18	7	McCullough, Gordon F.

Year	M/W	Assn	Div	NAT	NIT	ARC	CCA	NCI	NCT	OLY	HLM	W	L	Coach
HARTWICK														
1965	M	NCAA	II	24	—	—	—	—	—	—	—	19	2	Coniam, Charles Jack
1970		NCAA	II	24	—	—	—	—	—	—	—	18	6	Chipman, Dr. Leroy
1971		NCAA	II	8	—	—	—	—	—	—	—	20	6	Chipman, Dr. Leroy
1973		NCAA	II	16	—	—	—	—	—	—	—	19	7	Chipman, Dr. Leroy
1974		NCAA	II	16	—	—	—	—	—	—	—	22	5	Chipman, Dr. Leroy
1975		NCAA	II	32	—	—	—	—	—	—	—	19	7	Chipman, Dr. Leroy
1976		NCAA	II	32	—	—	—	—	—	—	—	21	5	Chipman, Dr. Leroy
1977		NCAA	II	16	—	—	—	—	—	—	—	22	4	Chipman, Dr. Leroy
1978		NCAA	II	24	—	—	—	—	—	—	—	22	4	Lambros, Nicholas H.
1979		NCAA	II	16	—	—	—	—	—	—	—	22	5	Lambros, Nicholas H.
1980		NCAA	II	16	—	—	—	—	—	—	—	21	5	Lambros, Nicholas H.
1983		NCAA	III	16	—	—	—	—	—	—	—	17	9	Lambros, Nicholas H.
1985		NCAA	III	24	—	—	—	—	—	—	—	19	7	Lambros, Nicholas H.
1988		NCAA	III	4	—	—	—	—	—	—	—	23	6	Lambros, Nicholas H.
1996		NCAA	III	64	—	—	—	—	—	—	—	17	9	Lambros, Nicholas H.
1983	W	NCAA	III	24	—	—	—	—	—	—	—	17	5	Lauder, Sue
1990		NCAA	III	16	—	—	—	—	—	—	—	24	5	Kragalott, Arden
1991		NCAA	III	16	—	—	—	—	—	—	—	21	8	Kragalott, Arden
1995		NCAA	III	64	—	—	—	—	—	—	—	20	8	Thompson, Daphne Joy
1996		NCAA	III	64	—	—	—	—	—	—	—	20	7	Thompson, Daphne Joy
1997		NCAA	III	64	—	—	—	—	—	—	—	21	8	Thompson, Daphne Joy
HARVARD														
1946	M	NCAA		8	—	—	—	—	—	—	—	20	3	Stahl, Floyd S.
1996	W	NCAA	I	64	—	—	—	—	—	—	—	20	7	Smith, Kathleen Delaney
1997		NCAA	I	64	—	—	—	—	—	—	—	20	7	Smith, Kathleen Delaney
1998		NCAA	I	32	—	—	—	—	—	—	—	23	5	Smith, Kathleen Delaney
HASTINGS														
1946	M	NAIA		32	—	—	—	—	—	—	—	16	5	Douglas, Louis H.
1947		NAIA		16	—	—	—	—	—	—	—	20	6	Owens, Larry
1951		NAIA		16	—	—	—	—	—	—	—	23	3	McLaughlin, Tom
1956		NAIA		32	—	—	—	—	—	—	—	18	6	Bogue, Russell
1958		NAIA		32	—	—	—	—	—	—	—	18	10	Bogue, Russell
1964		NAIA		32	—	—	—	—	—	—	—	23	4	Farrell, Dr. Lynn
1965		NAIA		16	—	—	—	—	—	—	—	24	4	Farrell, Dr. Lynn
1973		NAIA		32	—	—	—	—	—	—	—	25	5	Farrell, Dr. Lynn
1974		NAIA		16	—	—	—	—	—	—	—	27	4	Farrell, Dr. Lynn
1977		NAIA		32	—	—	—	—	—	—	—	25	5	Farrell, Dr. Lynn
1988		NAIA		32	—	—	—	—	—	—	—	27	6	Trader, Mike
1989		NAIA		8	—	—	—	—	—	—	—	26	9	Trader, Mike
1995		NAIA	II	8	—	—	—	—	—	—	—	21	7	Trader, Mike
1993	W	NAIA	I	16	—	—	—	—	—	—	—	31	2	Rhodus, Dr. Ken
1994		NAIA	II	24	—	—	—	—	—	—	—	20	11	Rhodus, Dr. Ken
HAWAII														
1949	M	NAIA		32	—	—	—	—	—	—	—	21	6	Gallon, Dr. Arthur J.
1971		NCAA	I	—	8	—	—	—	—	—	—	23	5	Rocha, Ephraim J. "Red"
1972		NCAA	I	25	—	—	—	—	—	—	—	24	3	Rocha, Ephraim J. "Red"
1974		NCAA	I	—	8	—	—	—	—	—	—	19	9	O'Neil, Bruce

Year	M/W	Assn	Div	NAT	NIT	ARC	CCA	NCI	NCT	OLY	HLM	W	L	Coach
1989		NCAA	I	—	32	—	—	—	—	—	—	17	13	Wallace, Riley
1990		NCAA	I	—	8	—	—	—	—	—	—	25	10	Wallace, Riley
1994		NCAA	I	64	—	—	—	—	—	—	—	18	15	Wallace, Riley
1997		NCAA	I	—	16	—	—	—	—	—	—	21	8	Wallace, Riley
1998		NCAA	I	—	8	—	—	—	—	—	—	21	9	Wallace, Riley
1983	W	NCAA	I	—	8	—	—	—	—	—	—	17	12	Busone, Jerry
1989		NCAA	I	48	—	—	—	—	—	—	—	20	10	Goo, Vince
1990		NCAA	I	32	—	—	—	—	—	—	—	26	4	Goo, Vince
1992		NCAA	I	—	2	—	—	—	—	—	—	25	7	Goo, Vince
1994		NCAA	I	64	—	—	—	—	—	—	—	25	5	Goo, Vince
1996		NCAA	I	64	—	—	—	—	—	—	—	23	6	Goo, Vince
1998		NCAA	I	64	—	—	—	—	—	—	—	24	4	Goo, Vince

HAWAII PACIFIC

Year	M/W	Assn	Div	NAT	NIT	ARC	CCA	NCI	NCT	OLY	HLM	W	L	Coach
1985	M	NAIA		32	—	—	—	—	—	—	—	27	11	Smith, Paul
1988		NAIA		32	—	—	—	—	—	—	—	19	13	Smith, Paul
1990		NAIA		32	—	—	—	—	—	—	—	19	15	Sellitto, Anthony, Jr.
1993		NAIA	I	1	—	—	—	—	—	—	—	30	4	Sellitto, Anthony, Jr.
1994		NAIA	I	8	—	—	—	—	—	—	—	27	8	Sellitto, Anthony, Jr.
1995		NAIA	I	16	—	—	—	—	—	—	—	25	9	Sellitto, Anthony, Jr.
1996		NAIA	I	16	—	—	—	—	—	—	—	27	6	Sellitto, Anthony, Jr.
1997		NAIA	I	8	—	—	—	—	—	—	—	26	4	Sellitto, Anthony, Jr.
1998		NAIA	I	32	—	—	—	—	—	—	—	22	5	Sellitto, Anthony, Jr.

HAWAII PACIFIC: LOA

Year	M/W	Assn	Div	NAT	NIT	ARC	CCA	NCI	NCT	OLY	HLM	W	L	Coach
1991	M	NAIA		32	—	—	—	—	—	—	—	21	12	Tucker, Steve

HAWAII: HILO

Year	M/W	Assn	Div	NAT	NIT	ARC	CCA	NCI	NCT	OLY	HLM	W	L	Coach
1977	M	NAIA		16	—	—	—	—	—	—	—	21	5	Yagi, James "Jimmy"
1978		NAIA		16	—	—	—	—	—	—	—	25	5	Yagi, James "Jimmy"
1980		NAIA		32	—	—	—	—	—	—	—	26	6	Yagi, James "Jimmy"
1987		NAIA		8	—	—	—	—	—	—	—	25	10	Wilson, Robert H.
1994		NAIA	I	32	—	—	—	—	—	—	—	17	12	Wilson, Robert H.

HEIDELBERG

Year	M/W	Assn	Div	NAT	NIT	ARC	CCA	NCI	NCT	OLY	HLM	W	L	Coach
1984	M	NCAA	III	16	—	—	—	—	—	—	—	24	7	Hill, John D.
1995		NCAA	III	64	—	—	—	—	—	—	—	17	11	Hill, John D.
1990	W	NCAA	III	3	—	—	—	—	—	—	—	27	6	McConnell, Karen

HENDERSON STATE

Year	M/W	Assn	Div	NAT	NIT	ARC	CCA	NCI	NCT	OLY	HLM	W	L	Coach
1968	M	NAIA		32	—	—	—	—	—	—	—	23	10	Dyer, Don
1969		NAIA		8	—	—	—	—	—	—	—	26	5	Dyer, Don
1976		NAIA		2	—	—	—	—	—	—	—	28	3	Dyer, Don
1977		NAIA		3	—	—	—	—	—	—	—	29	4	Dyer, Don
1979		NAIA		2	—	—	—	—	—	—	—	29	4	Riese, Bobby
1981		NAIA		32	—	—	—	—	—	—	—	25	8	Kirksey, Jerry L.
1982		NAIA		8	—	—	—	—	—	—	—	23	6	Kirksey, Jerry L.

HENDRIX

Year	M/W	Assn	Div	NAT	NIT	ARC	CCA	NCI	NCT	OLY	HLM	W	L	Coach
1985	M	NAIA		32	—	—	—	—	—	—	—	21	11	Garrison, Cliff
1995		NCAA	III	64	—	—	—	—	—	—	—	19	6	Garrison, Cliff
1996		NCAA	III	32	—	—	—	—	—	—	—	21	6	Garrison, Cliff
1996	W	NCAA	III	64	—	—	—	—	—	—	—	21	5	Winkelman, "Chuck"
1997		NCAA	III	32	—	—	—	—	—	—	—	23	4	Winkelman, "Chuck"

Year	M/W	Assn	Div	NAT	NIT	ARC	CCA	NCI	NCT	OLY	HLM	W	L	Coach
HESSER														
1988	M	NSCAA		15	—	—	—	—	—	—	—	31	6	Le Seur, Gary A.
HIGH POINT														
1939	M	NAIA		32	—	—	—	—	—	—	—	22	4	Yow, C. Virgil
1942		NAIA		16	—	—	—	—	—	—	—	24	1	Yow, C. Virgil
1946		NAIA		32	—	—	—	—	—	—	—	10	8	James, Ralph
1951		NAIA		32	—	—	—	—	—	—	—	20	11	Davis, Dr. Robert M.
1964		NAIA		8	—	—	—	—	—	—	—	25	4	Quinn, Thomas R.
1965		NAIA		16	—	—	—	—	—	—	—	29	4	Quinn, Thomas R.
1969		NAIA		8	—	—	—	—	—	—	—	28	3	Vaughn, Robert F. 'Bobby'
1979		NAIA		16	—	—	—	—	—	—	—	20	5	Steele, Jerry
1996		NCAA	II	32	—	—	—	—	—	—	—	24	7	Steele, Jerry
1997		NCAA	II	32	—	—	—	—	—	—	—	18	12	Steele, Jerry
1977	W	AIAW	S	8	—	—	—	—	—	—	—	29	2	Alley, Jennifer
1978		AIAW	S	1	—	—	—	—	—	—	—	30	8	Briley, Wanda
1979		AIAW	S	6	—	—	—	—	—	—	—	33	4	Briley, Wanda
1995		NAIA	I	32	—	—	—	—	—	—	—	22	7	Ellenberg, Dr. Joe
1997		NCAA	II	16	—	—	—	—	—	—	—	26	6	Ellenberg, Dr. Joe
HILLSDALE														
1951	M	NAIA		32	—	—	—	—	—	—	—	9	11	Wisniewski, Irvin C.
1972		NAIA		32	—	—	—	—	—	—	—	25	8	Ekker, Ronald
1981		NAIA		4	—	—	—	—	—	—	—	28	7	Morse, Bill
1984		NAIA		32	—	—	—	—	—	—	—	23	9	Halstead, Ron
1985		NAIA		16	—	—	—	—	—	—	—	20	13	Halstead, Ron
1988		NAIA		32	—	—	—	—	—	—	—	13	18	Halstead, Ron
1995		NCAA	II	48	—	—	—	—	—	—	—	15	14	Balikian, Bernie
HILLSDALE FREE WILL BAPTIST														
1988	M	NBCAA	I	7	—	—	—	—	—	—	—	15	10	Lawrence, Aaron
1989		NBCAA	II	1	—	—	—	—	—	—	—	23	12	Lawrence, Aaron
1990		NBCAA	II	2	—	—	—	—	—	—	—	20	15	Lawrence, Aaron
1991		NBCAA	II	1	—	—	—	—	—	—	—	23	11	Lisenbee, Tim
1991		NCCAA	IIA	3	—	—	—	—	—	—	—	23	11	Lisenbee, Tim
1992		NBCAA	II	2	—	—	—	—	—	—	—	10	8	Lisenbee, Tim
1992		NCCAA	IIA	4	—	—	—	—	—	—	—	10	8	Lisenbee, Tim
1993		NBCAA	II	5	—	—	—	—	—	—	—	21	20	Lisenbee, Tim
1993		NCCAA	IIA	8	—	—	—	—	—	—	—	21	20	Lisenbee, Tim
1994		NBCAA	II	2	—	—	—	—	—	—	—	22	14	Lisenbee, Tim
1994		NCCAA	IIA	2	—	—	—	—	—	—	—	22	14	Lisenbee, Tim
1995		NBCAA	II	7	—	—	—	—	—	—	—	17	12	Lisenbee, Tim
1996		NBCAA	II	1	—	—	—	—	—	—	—	13	17	Archer, Kelly
1996		NCCAA	IIA	2	—	—	—	—	—	—	—	13	17	Archer, Kelly
1997		NBCAA	II	2	—	—	—	—	—	—	—	16	20	Archer, Kelly
1998		NBCAA		4	—	—	—	—	—	—	—	24	12	Archer, Kelly
1998		NCCAA	IIA	2	—	—	—	—	—	—	—	24	12	Archer, Kelly
1989	W	NBCAA		4	—	—	—	—	—	—	—	5	12	Lawrence, Aaron
1990		NBCAA		6	—	—	—	—	—	—	—	10	8	Lisenbee, Tim
1991		NCCAA	II	8	—	—	—	—	—	—	—	10	14	Braisher, Kelly
1992		NBCAA		1	—	—	—	—	—	—	—	9	13	Braisher, Kelly

Year	M/W	Assn	Div	NAT	NIT	ARC	CCA	NCI	NCT	OLY	HLM	W	L	Coach
1992		NCCAA	II	7	—	—	—	—	—	—	—	9	13	Braisher, Kelly
1993		NBCAA		6	—	—	—	—	—	—	—	12	12	Braisher, Kelly
1996		NBCAA		3	—	—	—	—	—	—	—	10	13	Hill, Roni
1997		NBCAA		1	—	—	—	—	—	—	—	12	10	Archer, Kelly
1998		NBCAA		2	—	—	—	—	—	—	—	14	8	Brisco, Tabia

HIRAM

Year	M/W	Assn	Div	NAT	NIT	ARC	CCA	NCI	NCT	OLY	HLM	W	L	Coach
1904	M			—	—	—	—	—	—	1	—	11	1	Unknown
1973		NCAA	II	42	—	—	—	—	—	—	—	19	4	Hollinger, William H.
1974		NCAA	II	32	—	—	—	—	—	—	—	20	4	Hollinger, William H.
1975		NCAA	III	23	—	—	—	—	—	—	—	15	7	Hollinger, William H.
1976		NCAA	III	28	—	—	—	—	—	—	—	16	6	Hollinger, William H.
1984		NCAA	III	24	—	—	—	—	—	—	—	15	9	Hollinger, William H.

HOFSTRA

Year	M/W	Assn	Div	NAT	NIT	ARC	CCA	NCI	NCT	OLY	HLM	W	L	Coach
1959	M	NCAA	II	16	—	—	—	—	—	—	—	20	7	Van Breda Kolff, Willem "Butch"
1962		NCAA	II	16	—	—	—	—	—	—	—	24	4	Van Breda Kolff, Willem "Butch"
1963		NCAA	II	24	—	—	—	—	—	—	—	23	7	Lynner, Paul K.
1964		NCAA	II	8	—	—	—	—	—	—	—	23	6	Lynner, Paul K.
1976		NCAA	I	32	—	—	—	—	—	—	—	18	12	Gaeckler, D. Roger
1977		NCAA	I	32	—	—	—	—	—	—	—	23	7	Gaeckler, D. Roger
1980	W	AIAW	II	24	—	—	—	—	—	—	—	20	11	Pyser, Harvey
1982		AIAW	II	16	—	—	—	—	—	—	—	27	9	Pyser, Harvey

HOLY CROSS (MA)

Year	M/W	Assn	Div	NAT	NIT	ARC	CCA	NCI	NCT	OLY	HLM	W	L	Coach
1947	M	NCAA		1	—	—	—	—	—	—	1	27	3	Julian, Alvin F. "Doggie"
1948		NCAA		3	—	—	—	—	—	—	—	26	4	Julian, Alvin F. "Doggie"
1950		NCAA		8	—	—	—	—	—	—	—	27	4	Sheary, Lester H. "Buster"
1952		NCAA		—	8	—	—	—	—	—	—	24	4	Sheary, Lester H. "Buster"
1953		NCAA		8	—	—	—	—	—	—	—	20	6	Sheary, Lester H. "Buster"
1954		NCAA		—	1	—	—	—	—	—	—	26	2	Sheary, Lester H. "Buster"
1955		NCAA		—	8	—	—	—	—	—	—	19	7	Sheary, Lester H. "Buster"
1956		NCAA		25	—	—	—	—	—	—	—	22	5	Leenig, Roy H.
1960		NCAA	I	—	12	—	—	—	—	—	—	20	6	Leenig, Roy H.
1961		NCAA	I	—	3	—	—	—	—	—	—	21	5	Leenig, Roy H.
1962		NCAA	I	—	8	—	—	—	—	—	—	20	6	Oftring, Frank A.
1975		NCAA	I	—	16	—	—	—	—	—	—	20	8	Blaney, George R.
1976		NCAA	I	—	8	—	—	—	—	—	—	22	10	Blaney, George R.
1977		NCAA	I	32	—	—	—	—	—	—	—	23	6	Blaney, George R.
1979		NCAA	I	—	24	—	—	—	—	—	—	17	11	Blaney, George R.
1980		NCAA	I	48	—	—	—	—	—	—	—	19	11	Blaney, George R.
1981		NCAA	I	—	16	—	—	—	—	—	—	20	10	Blaney, George R.
1990		NCAA	I	—	32	—	—	—	—	—	—	24	6	Blaney, George R.
1993		NCAA	I	64	—	—	—	—	—	—	—	23	7	Blaney, George R.
1985	W	NCAA	I	32	—	—	—	—	—	—	—	21	7	Palazzi, Togo A.
1989		NCAA	I	48	—	—	—	—	—	—	—	21	10	Gibbons, Bill, Jr.
1991		NCAA	I	32	—	—	—	—	—	—	—	25	6	Gibbons, Bill, Jr.
1995		NCAA	I	64	—	—	—	—	—	—	—	21	9	Gibbons, Bill, Jr.

Year	M/W	Assn	Div	NAT	NIT	ARC	CCA	NCI	NCT	OLY	HLM	W	L	Coach
1996		NCAA	I	64	—	—	—	—	—	—	—	23	10	Gibbons, Bill, Jr.
1998		NCAA	I	64	—	—	—	—	—	—	—	21	9	Gibbons, Bill, Jr.

HOLY FAMILY (PA)

Year	M/W	Assn	Div	NAT	NIT	ARC	CCA	NCI	NCT	OLY	HLM	W	L	Coach
1989	M	NAIA		32	—	—	—	—	—	—	—	30	9	Williams, Dan
1991		NAIA		32	—	—	—	—	—	—	—	27	7	Williams, Dan
1996		NAIA	II	32	—	—	—	—	—	—	—	24	11	Williams, Dan
1991	W	NAIA		32	—	—	—	—	—	—	—	24	5	Soroka, Michael
1996		NAIA	II	32	—	—	—	—	—	—	—	25	8	McLaughlin, Michael
1997		NAIA	II	16	—	—	—	—	—	—	—	28	5	McLaughlin, Michael
1998		NAIA	II	8	—	—	—	—	—	—	—	33	5	McLaughlin, Michael

HOLY NAMES (CA)

Year	M/W	Assn	Div	NAT	NIT	ARC	CCA	NCI	NCT	OLY	HLM	W	L	Coach
1997	M	NAIA	II	32	—	—	—	—	—	—	—	20	15	Whitworth, Steve
1998		NAIA	II	16	—	—	—	—	—	—	—	26	11	Whitworth, Steve
1998	W	NAIA	II	16	—	—	—	—	—	—	—	23	8	DeLuca, Mark

HOPE

Year	M/W	Assn	Div	NAT	NIT	ARC	CCA	NCI	NCT	OLY	HLM	W	L	Coach
1958	M	NCAA	II	16	—	—	—	—	—	—	—	19	3	DeVette, Russell B.
1959		NCAA	II	8	—	—	—	—	—	—	—	20	3	DeVette, Russell B.
1982		NCAA	III	16	—	—	—	—	—	—	—	19	5	Van Wieren, Dr. Glenn
1983		NCAA	III	16	—	—	—	—	—	—	—	19	4	Van Wieren, Dr. Glenn
1984		NCAA	III	32	—	—	—	—	—	—	—	22	2	Van Wieren, Dr. Glenn
1985		NCAA	III	16	—	—	—	—	—	—	—	22	4	Van Wieren, Dr. Glenn
1987		NCAA	III	32	—	—	—	—	—	—	—	21	5	Van Wieren, Dr. Glenn
1988		NCAA	III	16	—	—	—	—	—	—	—	19	8	Van Wieren, Dr. Glenn
1989		NCAA	III	40	—	—	—	—	—	—	—	19	5	Van Wieren, Dr. Glenn
1990		NCAA	III	32	—	—	—	—	—	—	—	22	4	Van Wieren, Dr. Glenn
1991		NCAA	III	32	—	—	—	—	—	—	—	24	2	Van Wieren, Dr. Glenn
1992		NCAA	III	32	—	—	—	—	—	—	—	23	6	Van Wieren, Dr. Glenn
1995		NCAA	III	64	—	—	—	—	—	—	—	26	1	Van Wieren, Dr. Glenn
1996		NCAA	III	2	—	—	—	—	—	—	—	28	4	Van Wieren, Dr. Glenn
1997		NCAA	III	16	—	—	—	—	—	—	—	26	3	Van Wieren, Dr. Glenn
1998		NCAA	III	2	—	—	—	—	—	—	—	26	5	Van Wieren, Dr. Glenn
1990	W	NCAA	III	1	—	—	—	—	—	—	—	24	2	Wise, Susan
1995		NCAA	III	64	—	—	—	—	—	—	—	20	7	Gugino, Tod
1998		NCAA	III	48	—	—	—	—	—	—	—	16	11	Morehouse, Brian

HOUGHTON

Year	M/W	Assn	Div	NAT	NIT	ARC	CCA	NCI	NCT	OLY	HLM	W	L	Coach
1983	M	NCCAA	I	8	—	—	—	—	—	—	—	19	9	Jack, David E.
1988	W	NCCAA	I	6	—	—	—	—	—	—	—	18	6	Lord, Harold "Skip"
1989		NCCAA	I	8	—	—	—	—	—	—	—	16	7	Lord, Harold "Skip"
1995		NAIA	II	32	—	—	—	—	—	—	—	21	6	Lord, Harold "Skip"

HOUSTON

Year	M/W	Assn	Div	NAT	NIT	ARC	CCA	NCI	NCT	OLY	HLM	W	L	Coach
1946	M	NAIA		16	—	—	—	—	—	—	—	10	4	Pasche, Alden
1947		NAIA		16	—	—	—	—	—	—	—	15	7	Pasche, Alden
1956		NCAA		16	—	—	—	—	—	—	—	19	7	Pasche, Alden
1961		NCAA	I	16	—	—	—	—	—	—	—	17	11	Lewis, Guy V.

Year	M/W	Assn	Div	NAT	NIT	ARC	CCA	NCI	NCT	OLY	HLM	W	L	Coach
1962		NCAA	I	—	8	—	—	—	—	—	—	21	6	Lewis, Guy V.
1965		NCAA	I	16	—	—	—	—	—	—	—	19	10	Lewis, Guy V.
1966		NCAA	I	12	—	—	—	—	—	—	—	23	6	Lewis, Guy V.
1967		NCAA	I	3	—	—	—	—	—	—	—	27	4	Lewis, Guy V.
1968		NCAA	I	4	—	—	—	—	—	—	—	31	2	Lewis, Guy V.
1970		NCAA	I	16	—	—	—	—	—	—	—	25	5	Lewis, Guy V.
1971		NCAA	I	12	—	—	—	—	—	—	—	22	7	Lewis, Guy V.
1972		NCAA	I	25	—	—	—	—	—	—	—	20	7	Lewis, Guy V.
1973		NCAA	I	25	—	—	—	—	—	—	—	23	4	Lewis, Guy V.
1977		NCAA	I	—	2	—	—	—	—	—	—	29	8	Lewis, Guy V.
1978		NCAA	I	32	—	—	—	—	—	—	—	25	8	Lewis, Guy V.
1981		NCAA	I	48	—	—	—	—	—	—	—	21	9	Lewis, Guy V.
1982		NCAA	I	3	—	—	—	—	—	—	—	25	8	Lewis, Guy V.
1983		NCAA	I	2	—	—	—	—	—	—	—	31	3	Lewis, Guy V.
1984		NCAA	I	2	—	—	—	—	—	—	—	32	5	Lewis, Guy V.
1985		NCAA	I	—	32	—	—	—	—	—	—	16	14	Lewis, Guy V.
1987		NCAA	I	64	—	—	—	—	—	—	—	18	12	Foster, Pat
1988		NCAA	I	—	16	—	—	—	—	—	—	18	13	Foster, Pat
1990		NCAA	I	64	—	—	—	—	—	—	—	25	8	Foster, Pat
1991		NCAA	I	—	32	—	—	—	—	—	—	18	11	Foster, Pat
1992		NCAA	I	64	—	—	—	—	—	—	—	25	6	Foster, Pat
1993		NCAA	I	—	32	—	—	—	—	—	—	21	9	Foster, Pat
1988	W	NCAA	I	32	—	—	—	—	—	—	—	22	7	Williams, Greg
1991		NCAA	I	—	4	—	—	—	—	—	—	20	12	Kenlaw, Jessie
1992		NCAA	I	48	—	—	—	—	—	—	—	22	8	Kenlaw, Jessie

HOUSTON BAPTIST

Year	M/W	Assn	Div	NAT	NIT	ARC	CCA	NCI	NCT	OLY	HLM	W	L	Coach
1984	M	NCAA	I	53	—	—	—	—	—	—	—	24	7	Iba, Clarence Eugene "Gene"
1998		NAIA	I	32	—	—	—	—	—	—	—	26	6	Cottrell, Ron

HOWARD (DC)

Year	M/W	Assn	Div	NAT	NIT	ARC	CCA	NCI	NCT	OLY	HLM	W	L	Coach
1981	M	NCAA	I	48	—	—	—	—	—	—	—	17	12	Williamson, Altha B.
1992		NCAA	I	64	—	—	—	—	—	—	—	17	14	Beard, Alfred, Jr. "Butch"
1982	W	NCAA	I	32	—	—	—	—	—	—	—	14	11	Tyler, Sanya
1996		NCAA	I	64	—	—	—	—	—	—	—	20	10	Tyler, Sanya
1997		NCAA	I	64	—	—	—	—	—	—	—	24	6	Tyler, Sanya
1998		NCAA	I	64	—	—	—	—	—	—	—	23	7	Tyler, Sanya

HOWARD PAYNE

Year	M/W	Assn	Div	NAT	NIT	ARC	CCA	NCI	NCT	OLY	HLM	W	L	Coach
1963	M	NAIA		32	—	—	—	—	—	—	—	22	7	Whitis, Glen
1966		NAIA		32	—	—	—	—	—	—	—	20	10	Whitis, Glen
1967		NAIA		32	—	—	—	—	—	—	—	22	7	Whitis, Glen
1969		NAIA		16	—	—	—	—	—	—	—	27	4	Whitis, Glen
1976		NAIA		32	—	—	—	—	—	—	—	22	12	Derryberry, Bob
1995		NAIA	II	32	—	—	—	—	—	—	—	12	13	Pattillo, Charles
1996		NAIA	II	32	—	—	—	—	—	—	—	14	14	Pattillo, Charles
1997		NAIA	II	32	—	—	—	—	—	—	—	16	10	Pattillo, Charles
1984	W	NCAA	II	24	—	—	—	—	—	—	—	11	18	Campbell, Sharon

Year	M/W	Assn	Div	NAT	NIT	ARC	CCA	NCI	NCT	OLY	HLM	W	L	Coach
HUMBOLDT STATE														
1978	M	NCAA	III	8	—	—	—	—	—	—	—	—	17	10	Cosentino, Jim
1979		NCAA	III	24	—	—	—	—	—	—	—	—	18	9	Conentino, Jim
1980		NCAA	III	16	—	—	—	—	—	—	—	—	18	10	Cosentino, Jim
1983		NCAA	II	32	—	—	—	—	—	—	—	—	18	12	Wood, Tom
1990		NCAA	II	24	—	—	—	—	—	—	—	—	20	11	Wood, Tom
1995	W	NCAA	II	48	—	—	—	—	—	—	—	—	18	10	Martin, Pam
HUNTER														
1990	M	NCAA	III	40	—	—	—	—	—	—	—	—	20	8	Amalbert, Ray
1992		NCAA	III	32	—	—	—	—	—	—	—	—	24	5	Amalbert, Ray
1993		NCAA	III	16	—	—	—	—	—	—	—	—	25	4	Amalbert, Ray
1994		NCAA	III	32	—	—	—	—	—	—	—	—	26	3	Amalbert, Ray
1995		NCAA	III	64	—	—	—	—	—	—	—	—	17	11	Amalbert, Ray
1998		NCAA	III	8	—	—	—	—	—	—	—	—	28	2	Brown, Mike
HUNTINGDON														
1964	M	NAIA		16	—	—	—	—	—	—	—	—	25	6	Posey, Neal N.
HUNTINGTON														
1984	W	NCCAA	I	1	—	—	—	—	—	—	—	—	24	9	Freeman, Keith
1985		NCCAA	I	5	—	—	—	—	—	—	—	—	20	10	Freeman, Keith
1986		NCCAA	I	4	—	—	—	—	—	—	—	—	21	10	Freeman, Keith
1987		NCCAA	I	5	—	—	—	—	—	—	—	—	21	12	Culler, Lori
1988		NCCAA	I	3	—	—	—	—	—	—	—	—	20	11	Culler, Lori
1989		NCCAA	I	4	—	—	—	—	—	—	—	—	19	11	Culler, Lori
1990		NCCAA	I	6	—	—	—	—	—	—	—	—	26	5	Culler, Lori
1991		NCCAA	I	1	—	—	—	—	—	—	—	—	24	4	Culler, Lori
1992		NCCAA	I	1	—	—	—	—	—	—	—	—	24	8	Culler, Lori
1994		NAIA	II	16	—	—	—	—	—	—	—	—	19	8	Culler, Lori
HURON														
1952	M	NAIA		32	—	—	—	—	—	—	—	—	21	4	Lundeen, Ralph J.
1974		NAIA		32	—	—	—	—	—	—	—	—	21	7	Swanhorst, Robert
1980		NAIA		3	—	—	—	—	—	—	—	—	32	4	Carrier, Bruce
1981		NAIA		8	—	—	—	—	—	—	—	—	30	4	Carrier, Bruce
1986		NAIA		16	—	—	—	—	—	—	—	—	28	3	Paulsen, Fred
1988		NAIA		32	—	—	—	—	—	—	—	—	24	8	Paulsen, Fred
1994		NAIA	II	8	—	—	—	—	—	—	—	—	21	10	Paulsen, Fred
1996		NAIA	II	16	—	—	—	—	—	—	—	—	18	14	Paulsen, Fred
1995	W	NAIA	II	16	—	—	—	—	—	—	—	—	26	5	Warwick, Shane
1996		NAIA	II	2	—	—	—	—	—	—	—	—	30	5	Warwick, Shane
HUSSON														
1975	M	NAIA		32	—	—	—	—	—	—	—	—	23	5	MacGregor, Dr. D. Bruce
1976		NAIA		32	—	—	—	—	—	—	—	—	25	1	MacGregor, Dr. D. Bruce
1983		NAIA		32	—	—	—	—	—	—	—	—	22	7	MacGregor, Dr. D. Bruce
1989		NAIA		32	—	—	—	—	—	—	—	—	35	3	MacGregor, Dr. D. Bruce

Year	M/W	Assn	Div	NAT	NIT	ARC	CCA	NCI	NCT	OLY	HLM	W	L	Coach
1990		NAIA		32	—	—	—	—	—	—	—	26	13	MacGregor, Dr. D. Bruce
1992		NAIA	II	16	—	—	—	—	—	—	—	27	10	MacGregor, Dr. D. Bruce
1994		NAIA	II	24	—	—	—	—	—	—	—	28	4	MacGregor, Dr. D. Bruce
1995		NAIA	II	32	—	—	—	—	—	—	—	23	9	Caruso, Warren
1997		NAIA	II	32	—	—	—	—	—	—	—	20	12	Caruso, Warren
1993	W	NAIA	II	3	—	—	—	—	—	—	—	28	3	Walker, Mary "Kissy"
1995		NAIA	II	32	—	—	—	—	—	—	—	23	6	Walker, Mary "Kissy"
1996		NAIA	II	32	—	—	—	—	—	—	—	21	8	Walker, Mary "Kissy"

HUSTON-TILLOTSON

Year	M/W	Assn	Div	NAT	NIT	ARC	CCA	NCI	NCT	OLY	HLM	W	L	Coach
1997	M	NAIA	I	32	—	—	—	—	—	—	—	20	9	Littlefield, Terrence
1998		NAIA	I	32	—	—	—	—	—	—	—	16	12	Littlefield, Terrence

IDAHO

Year	M/W	Assn	Div	NAT	NIT	ARC	CCA	NCI	NCT	OLY	HLM	W	L	Coach
1981	M	NCAA	I	48	—	—	—	—	—	—	—	25	4	Monson, Don
1982		NCAA	I	16	—	—	—	—	—	—	—	27	3	Monson, Don
1983		NCAA	I	—	32	—	—	—	—	—	—	20	9	Monson, Don
1989		NCAA	I	64	—	—	—	—	—	—	—	25	6	Davis, Kermit, Jr.
1990		NCAA	I	64	—	—	—	—	—	—	—	25	6	Davis, Kermit, Jr.
1980	W	AIAW	II	24	—	—	—	—	—	—	—	25	6	VanDerveer, Tara
1981		AIAW	II	16	—	—	—	—	—	—	—	22	8	Dobratz, Patty Jo
1982		AIAW	II	16	—	—	—	—	—	—	—	27	5	Dobratz, Patty Jo
1985		NCAA	I	32	—	—	—	—	—	—	—	28	2	Dobratz, Patty Jo
1986		NCAA	I	—	1	—	—	—	—	—	—	26	5	Dobratz, Patty Jo

IDAHO STATE

Year	M/W	Assn	Div	NAT	NIT	ARC	CCA	NCI	NCT	OLY	HLM	W	L	Coach
1938	M	NAIA		16	—	—	—	—	—	—	—	19	7	Wicks, Guy P.
1953		NCAA		22	—	—	—	—	—	—	—	18	7	Belko, Steven
1954		NCAA		12	—	—	—	—	—	—	—	22	5	Belko, Steven
1955		NCAA		24	—	—	—	—	—	—	—	18	8	Belko, Steven
1956		NCAA		25	—	—	—	—	—	—	—	18	8	Belko, Steven
1957		NCAA	I	16	—	—	—	—	—	—	—	25	4	Grayson, John A.
1958		NCAA	I	16	—	—	—	—	—	—	—	22	6	Grayson, John A.
1959		NCAA	I	12	—	—	—	—	—	—	—	21	7	Grayson, John A.
1960		NCAA	I	25	—	—	—	—	—	—	—	21	5	Evans, John P.
1974		NCAA	I	25	—	—	—	—	—	—	—	20	8	Killingsworth, James
1977		NCAA	I	8	—	—	—	—	—	—	—	25	5	Killingsworth, James
1987		NCAA	I	64	—	—	—	—	—	—	—	15	16	Boutin, Dr. James

ILLINOIS

Year	M/W	Assn	Div	NAT	NIT	ARC	CCA	NCI	NCT	OLY	HLM	W	L	Coach
1915	M	NCAA		—	—	—	—	—	—	—	1	16	0	Jones, Ralph R.
1942		NCAA		8	—	—	—	—	—	—	—	18	5	Mills, Douglas R.
1949		NCAA		3	—	—	—	—	—	—	—	21	4	Combes, Harry A.
1951		NCAA		3	—	—	—	—	—	—	—	22	5	Combes, Harry A.
1952		NCAA		3	—	—	—	—	—	—	—	22	4	Combes, Harry A.
1963		NCAA	I	8	—	—	—	—	—	—	—	20	6	Combes, Harry A.
1980		NCAA	I	—	3	—	—	—	—	—	—	22	13	Henson, Louis R.
1981		NCAA	I	16	—	—	—	—	—	—	—	21	8	Henson, Louis R.
1982		NCAA	I	—	16	—	—	—	—	—	—	18	11	Henson, Louis R.
1983		NCAA	I	48	—	—	—	—	—	—	—	21	11	Henson, Louis R.
1984		NCAA	I	8	—	—	—	—	—	—	—	26	5	Henson, Louis R.
1985		NCAA	I	16	—	—	—	—	—	—	—	26	9	Henson, Louis R.

Year	M/W	Assn	Div	NAT	NIT	ARC	CCA	NCI	NCT	OLY	HLM	W	L	Coach
1986		NCAA	I	32	—	—	—	—	—	—	—	22	10	Henson, Louis R.
1987		NCAA	I	64	—	—	—	—	—	—	—	23	8	Henson, Louis R.
1988		NCAA	I	32	—	—	—	—	—	—	—	23	10	Henson, Louis R.
1989		NCAA	I	3	—	—	—	—	—	—	—	31	5	Henson, Louis R.
1990		NCAA	I	64	—	—	—	—	—	—	—	21	8	Henson, Louis R.
1993		NCAA	I	32	—	—	—	—	—	—	—	19	13	Henson, Louis R.
1994		NCAA	I	64	—	—	—	—	—	—	—	17	11	Henson, Louis R.
1995		NCAA	I	64	—	—	—	—	—	—	—	19	12	Henson, Louis R.
1996		NCAA	I	—	32	—	—	—	—	—	—	18	13	Henson, Louis R.
1997		NCAA	I	32	—	—	—	—	—	—	—	22	10	Kruger, Lon
1998		NCAA	I	32	—	—	—	—	—	—	—	23	10	Kruger, Lon
1982	W	NCAA	I	32	—	—	—	—	—	—	—	21	9	Schroeder, Jane
1986		NCAA	I	32	—	—	—	—	—	—	—	20	10	Golden, Laura L.
1987		NCAA	I	32	—	—	—	—	—	—	—	19	10	Golden, Laura L.
1997		NCAA	I	16	—	—	—	—	—	—	—	24	8	Grentz, Theresa Shank
1998		NCAA	I	16	—	—	—	—	—	—	—	20	10	Grentz, Theresa Shank

ILLINOIS STATE

Year	M/W	Assn	Div	NAT	NIT	ARC	CCA	NCI	NCT	OLY	HLM	W	L	Coach
1957	M	NCAA	II	32	—	—	—	—	—	—	—	14	13	Goff, James "Pim"
1959		NAIA		8	—	—	—	—	—	—	—	24	5	Collie, Dr. James E., Sr.
1962		NCAA	II	32	—	—	—	—	—	—	—	16	11	Collie, Dr. James E., Sr.
1967		NCAA	II	4	—	—	—	—	—	—	—	18	13	Collie, Dr. James E., Sr.
1968		NCAA	II	16	—	—	—	—	—	—	—	25	3	Collie, Dr. James E., Sr.
1969		NCAA	II	8	—	—	—	—	—	—	—	19	10	Collie, Dr. James E., Sr.
1977		NCAA	I	—	8	—	—	—	—	—	—	22	7	Smithson, Eugene
1978		NCAA	I	—	16	—	—	—	—	—	—	24	4	Smithson, Eugene
1980		NCAA	I	—	16	—	—	—	—	—	—	20	9	Donewald, Bob
1983		NCAA	I	48	—	—	—	—	—	—	—	24	7	Donewald, Bob
1984		NCAA	I	32	—	—	—	—	—	—	—	23	8	Donewald, Bob
1985		NCAA	I	32	—	—	—	—	—	—	—	22	8	Donewald, Bob
1987		NCAA	I	—	8	—	—	—	—	—	—	19	13	Donewald, Bob
1988		NCAA	I	—	32	—	—	—	—	—	—	18	13	Donewald, Bob
1990		NCAA	I	64	—	—	—	—	—	—	—	18	13	Bender, Robert M., Jr.
1995		NCAA	I	—	16	—	—	—	—	—	—	20	13	Stallings, Kevin
1996		NCAA	I	—	8	—	—	—	—	—	—	22	12	Stallings, Kevin
1997		NCAA	I	64	—	—	—	—	—	—	—	24	6	Stallings, Kevin
1998		NCAA	I	32	—	—	—	—	—	—	—	25	6	Stallings, Kevin
1970	W	AIAW		12	—	—	—	—	—	—	—	X	X	Mabry, Laurie
1971		AIAW		16	—	—	—	—	—	—	—	13	9	Hutchison, Dr. Jill
1972		AIAW		16	—	—	—	—	—	—	—	11	6	Hutchison, Dr. Jill
1974		AIAW		12	—	—	—	—	—	—	—	21	4	Foster, Dr. Gooch
1980		AIAW	I	—	5	—	—	—	—	—	—	23	10	Hutchison, Dr. Jill
1981		AIAW	I	16	—	—	—	—	—	—	—	22	8	Hutchison, Dr. Jill
1982		NCAA	I	—	4	—	—	—	—	—	—	19	15	Hutchison, Dr. Jill
1983		NCAA	I	32	—	—	—	—	—	—	—	20	10	Hutchison, Dr. Jill
1984		NCAA	I	—	7	—	—	—	—	—	—	28	8	Hutchison, Dr. Jill
1985		NCAA	I	32	—	—	—	—	—	—	—	23	5	Hutchison, Dr. Jill
1988		NCAA	I	—	4	—	—	—	—	—	—	20	11	Hutchison, Dr. Jill
1989		NCAA	I	32	—	—	—	—	—	—	—	23	8	Hutchison, Dr. Jill
1990		NCAA	I	—	6	—	—	—	—	—	—	21	11	Hutchison, Dr. Jill
1996		NCAA	I	—	8	—	—	—	—	—	—	19	13	Hutchison, Dr. Jill

Year	M/W	Assn	Div	NAT	NIT	ARC	CCA	NCI	NCT	OLY	HLM	W	L	Coach

ILLINOIS WESLEYAN

Year	M/W	Assn	Div	NAT	NIT	ARC	CCA	NCI	NCT	OLY	HLM	W	L	Coach
1943	M	NAIA		32	—	—	—	—	—	—	—	7	14	Horenberger, Jack
1961		NAIA		16	—	—	—	—	—	—	—	17	11	Horenberger, Jack
1966		NAIA		8	—	—	—	—	—	—	—	21	10	Bridges, Dennis L.
1970		NAIA		32	—	—	—	—	—	—	—	21	4	Bridges, Dennis L.
1971		NAIA		32	—	—	—	—	—	—	—	19	8	Bridges, Dennis L.
1975		NAIA		16	—	—	—	—	—	—	—	23	7	Bridges, Dennis L.
1976		NAIA		16	—	—	—	—	—	—	—	23	7	Bridges, Dennis L.
1977		NAIA		8	—	—	—	—	—	—	—	25	6	Bridges, Dennis L.
1980		NAIA		32	—	—	—	—	—	—	—	17	11	Bridges, Dennis L.
1984		NCAA	III	32	—	—	—	—	—	—	—	17	11	Bridges, Dennis L.
1986		NCAA	III	8	—	—	—	—	—	—	—	19	10	Bridges, Dennis L.
1987		NCAA	III	16	—	—	—	—	—	—	—	17	10	Bridges, Dennis L.
1988		NCAA	III	8	—	—	—	—	—	—	—	23	6	Bridges, Dennis L.
1990		NCAA	III	8	—	—	—	—	—	—	—	22	9	Bridges, Dennis L.
1991		NCAA	III	40	—	—	—	—	—	—	—	18	9	Bridges, Dennis L.
1992		NCAA	III	16	—	—	—	—	—	—	—	22	6	Bridges, Dennis L.
1994		NCAA	III	16	—	—	—	—	—	—	—	19	8	Bridges, Dennis L.
1995		NCAA	III	8	—	—	—	—	—	—	—	24	4	Bridges, Dennis L.
1996		NCAA	III	3	—	—	—	—	—	—	—	28	3	Bridges, Dennis L.
1997		NCAA	III	1	—	—	—	—	—	—	—	29	2	Bridges, Dennis L.
1998		NCAA	III	16	—	—	—	—	—	—	—	22	5	Bridges, Dennis L.
1995	W	NCAA	III	64	—	—	—	—	—	—	—	20	6	Neal, Mandy
1996		NCAA	III	64	—	—	—	—	—	—	—	18	8	Neal, Mandy

ILLINOIS: CHICAGO

Year	M/W	Assn	Div	NAT	NIT	ARC	CCA	NCI	NCT	OLY	HLM	W	L	Coach
1998	M	NCAA	I	64	—	—	—	—	—	—	—	22	6	Collins, Jimmy

ILLINOIS: SPRINGFIELD

Year	M/W	Assn	Div	NAT	NIT	ARC	CCA	NCI	NCT	OLY	HLM	W	L	Coach
1998	W	NAIA	II	32	—	—	—	—	—	—	—	23	8	Stiles-Krone, Juli

IMMACULATA (PA)

Year	M/W	Assn	Div	NAT	NIT	ARC	CCA	NCI	NCT	OLY	HLM	W	L	Coach
1972	W	AIAW		1	—	—	—	—	—	—	—	24	1	Rush, Cathy
1973		AIAW		1	—	—	—	—	—	—	—	20	0	Rush, Cathy
1974		AIAW		1	—	—	—	—	—	—	—	20	1	Rush, Cathy
1975		AIAW	L	2	—	—	—	—	—	—	—	23	3	Rush, Cathy
1976		AIAW	L	2	—	—	—	—	—	—	—	25	3	Rush, Cathy
1977		AIAW	L	4	—	—	—	—	—	—	—	28	5	Rush, Cathy

INCARNATE WORD

Year	M/W	Assn	Div	NAT	NIT	ARC	CCA	NCI	NCT	OLY	HLM	W	L	Coach
1993	M	NAIA	I	32	—	—	—	—	—	—	—	28	4	Kaspar, Daniel J. "Danny"
1994		NAIA	I	32	—	—	—	—	—	—	—	25	6	Kaspar, Daniel J. "Danny"
1995		NAIA	I	32	—	—	—	—	—	—	—	26	8	Kaspar, Daniel J. "Danny"
1997		NAIA	I	32	—	—	—	—	—	—	—	25	4	Kaspar, Daniel J. "Danny"
1998		NAIA	I	8	—	—	—	—	—	—	—	27	5	Kaspar, Daniel J. "Danny"
1998	W	NAIA	I	32	—	—	—	—	—	—	—	19	10	Walling, Sally

INDIANA

Year	M/W	Assn	Div	NAT	NIT	ARC	CCA	NCI	NCT	OLY	HLM	W	L	Coach
1940	M	NCAA		1	—	—	—	—	—	—	—	20	3	McCracken, E. Branch
1953		NCAA		1	—	—	—	—	—	—	1	23	3	McCracken, E. Branch
1954		NCAA		12	—	—	—	—	—	—	—	20	4	McCracken, E. Branch
1958		NCAA	I	12	—	—	—	—	—	—	—	13	11	McCracken, E. Branch

Year	M/W	Assn	Div	NAT	NIT	ARC	CCA	NCI	NCT	OLY	HLM	W	L	Coach
1967		NCAA	I	12	—	—	—	—	—	—	—	18	8	Watson, Lou
1972		NCAA	I	—	16	—	—	—	—	—	—	17	8	Knight, Robert M.
1973		NCAA	I	3	—	—	—	—	—	—	—	22	6	Knight, Robert M.
1974		NCAA	I	—	—	—	1	—	—	—	—	23	5	Knight, Robert M.
1975		NCAA	I	8	—	—	—	—	—	—	—	31	1	Knight, Robert M.
1976		NCAA	I	1	—	—	—	—	—	—	1	32	0	Knight, Robert M.
1978		NCAA	I	16	—	—	—	—	—	—	—	21	8	Knight, Robert M.
1979		NCAA	I	—	1	—	—	—	—	—	—	22	12	Knight, Robert M.
1980		NCAA	I	16	—	—	—	—	—	—	—	21	8	Knight, Robert M.
1981		NCAA	I	1	—	—	—	—	—	—	1	26	9	Knight, Robert M.
1982		NCAA	I	32	—	—	—	—	—	—	—	19	10	Knight, Robert M.
1983		NCAA	I	16	—	—	—	—	—	—	—	24	6	Knight, Robert M.
1984		NCAA	I	8	—	—	—	—	—	—	—	22	9	Knight, Robert M.
1985		NCAA	I	—	2	—	—	—	—	—	—	19	14	Knight, Robert M.
1986		NCAA	I	64	—	—	—	—	—	—	—	21	8	Knight, Robert M.
1987		NCAA	I	1	—	—	—	—	—	—	—	30	4	Knight, Robert M.
1988		NCAA	I	64	—	—	—	—	—	—	—	19	10	Knight, Robert M.
1989		NCAA	I	16	—	—	—	—	—	—	—	27	8	Knight, Robert M.
1990		NCAA	I	64	—	—	—	—	—	—	—	18	11	Knight, Robert M.
1991		NCAA	I	16	—	—	—	—	—	—	—	29	5	Knight, Robert M.
1992		NCAA	I	3	—	—	—	—	—	—	—	27	7	Knight, Robert M.
1993		NCAA	I	8	—	—	—	—	—	—	—	31	4	Knight, Robert M.
1994		NCAA	I	16	—	—	—	—	—	—	—	21	9	Knight, Robert M.
1995		NCAA	I	64	—	—	—	—	—	—	—	19	12	Knight, Robert M.
1996		NCAA	I	64	—	—	—	—	—	—	—	19	12	Knight, Robert M.
1997		NCAA	I	64	—	—	—	—	—	—	—	22	11	Knight, Robert M.
1998		NCAA	I	32	—	—	—	—	—	—	—	20	12	Knight, Robert M.
1971	W	AIAW		8	—	—	—	—	—	—	—	X	X	Unknown
1972		AIAW		8	—	—	—	—	—	—	—	17	2	Gorton, Bea
1973		AIAW		4	—	—	—	—	—	—	—	17	3	Gorton, Bea
1974		AIAW		8	—	—	—	—	—	—	—	16	5	Gorton, Bea
1975		AIAW	L	—	8	—	—	—	—	—	—	19	6	Gorton, Bea
1983		NCAA	I	16	—	—	—	—	—	—	—	19	11	Jeremiah, Dr. Maryalyce
1991		NCAA	I	—	2	—	—	—	—	—	—	18	13	Izard, Jim
1994		NCAA	I	64	—	—	—	—	—	—	—	19	9	Izard, Jim
1995		NCAA	I	64	—	—	—	—	—	—	—	19	10	Izard, Jim
1998		NCAA	I	—	3	—	—	—	—	—	—	21	12	Izard, Jim

INDIANA (PA)

Year	M/W	Assn	Div	NAT	NIT	ARC	CCA	NCI	NCT	OLY	HLM	W	L	Coach
1958	M	NAIA		16	—	—	—	—	—	—	—	25	3	McKnight, Regis "Peck"
1971		NAIA		16	—	—	—	—	—	—	—	24	4	Sledzik, Herman L.
1974		NAIA		8	—	—	—	—	—	—	—	21	8	Davis, Carl D.
1994		NCAA	II	8	—	—	—	—	—	—	—	27	3	Kanaskie, Kurt
1995		NCAA	II	3	—	—	—	—	—	—	—	29	2	Kanaskie, Kurt
1996		NCAA	II	16	—	—	—	—	—	—	—	24	7	Kanaskie, Kurt
1988	W	NCAA	II	32	—	—	—	—	—	—	—	17	14	Kiger, Jan H.

Year	M/W	Assn	Div	NAT	NIT	ARC	CCA	NCI	NCT	OLY	HLM	W	L	Coach
INDIANA STATE														
1942	M	NAIA		8	—	—	—	—	—	—	—	17	4	Curtis, Glenn M.
1943		NAIA		32	—	—	—	—	—	—	—	13	4	Curtis, Glenn M.
1946		NAIA		2	—	—	—	—	—	—	—	21	7	Curtis, Glenn M.
1948		NAIA		2	—	—	—	—	—	—	—	27	7	Wooden, John R.
1949		NAIA		4	—	—	—	—	—	—	—	24	8	Longfellow, John L.
1950		NAIA		1	—	—	—	—	—	—	—	27	8	Longfellow, John L.
1952		NAIA		16	—	—	—	—	—	—	—	19	10	Longfellow, John L.
1953		NAIA		3	—	—	—	—	—	—	—	23	8	Longfellow, John L.
1954		NAIA		32	—	—	—	—	—	—	—	12	15	Longfellow, John L.
1959		NAIA		16	—	—	—	—	—	—	—	18	9	Klueh, Duane M.
1962		NAIA		32	—	—	—	—	—	—	—	19	9	Klueh, Duane M.
1963		NAIA		16	—	—	—	—	—	—	—	10	11	Klueh, Duane M.
1966		NCAA	II	32	—	—	—	—	—	—	—	22	6	Klueh, Duane M.
1967		NCAA	II	16	—	—	—	—	—	—	—	21	5	Klueh, Duane M.
1968		NCAA	II	2	—	—	—	—	—	—	—	23	8	Stauffer, Gordon C.
1977		NCAA	I	—	16	—	—	—	—	—	—	25	3	King, Bob
1978		NCAA	I	—	8	—	—	—	—	—	—	23	9	King, Bob
1979		NCAA	I	2	—	—	—	—	—	—	—	33	1	Hodges, Bill
1973	W	AIAW		16	—	—	—	—	—	—	—	16	7	Godleski, Edith E.
1976		AIAW		—	8	—	—	—	—	—	—	19	9	Godleski, Edith E.
1977		AIAW	L	—	7	—	—	—	—	—	—	19	9	Godleski, Edith E.
INDIANA TECH														
1965	M	NAIA		32	—	—	—	—	—	—	—	24	3	Macy, Robert
1995		NAIA	II	16	—	—	—	—	—	—	—	24	6	Kline, Dan
1998		NAIA	II	32	—	—	—	—	—	—	—	21	9	Kline, Dan
1985	W	NAIA		16	—	—	—	—	—	—	—	20	9	Hewlet, Kathy
1992		NAIA	II	8	—	—	—	—	—	—	—	28	3	Cobb, Gary
1993		NAIA	II	8	—	—	—	—	—	—	—	25	5	Cobb, Gary
1994		NAIA	II	16	—	—	—	—	—	—	—	20	7	Cobb, Gary
1995		NAIA	II	16	—	—	—	—	—	—	—	19	7	Cobb, Gary
INDIANA WESLEYAN														
1981	M	NSCAA		8	—	—	—	—	—	—	—	24	6	Kent, "Rocky"
1992		NCCAA	I	8	—	—	—	—	—	—	—	10	27	Bireline, David B.
1993		NCCAA	I	8	—	—	—	—	—	—	—	12	22	Bireline, David B.
1994		NCCAA	I	6	—	—	—	—	—	—	—	17	14	Bireline, David B.
1995		NCCAA	I	1	—	—	—	—	—	—	—	17	16	Williams, Pat
1996		NCCAA	I	4	—	—	—	—	—	—	—	8	24	Blum, Scott
1997		NCCAA	I	8	—	—	—	—	—	—	—	12	21	Blum, Scott
1983	W	NCCAA	I	8	—	—	—	—	—	—	—	13	11	Hensler, Susan
1986		NCCAA	I	5	—	—	—	—	—	—	—	20	7	Roorbach, Peg
1992		NCCAA	I	6	—	—	—	—	—	—	—	20	14	Porter, Terry
1994		NCCAA	I	5	—	—	—	—	—	—	—	29	8	Porter, Terry
1995		NCCAA	I	3	—	—	—	—	—	—	—	26	11	Porter, Terry
1998		NCCAA	I	2	—	—	—	—	—	—	—	19	14	Porter, Terry
INDIANA-PURDUE: FORT WAYNE														
1993	M	NCAA	II	32	—	—	—	—	—	—	—	23	6	Piazza, Andy

Year	M/W	Assn	Div	NAT	NIT	ARC	CCA	NCI	NCT	OLY	HLM	W	L	Coach
1990	W	NCAA	II	32	—	—	—	—	—	—	—	22	7	Rosinski, Teri
1992		NCAA	II	32	—	—	—	—	—	—	—	22	7	Kleinfelter, Eileen
1996		NCAA	II	48	—	—	—	—	—	—	—	23	5	Bowden, Pam ·

INDIANA-PURDUE: INDIANAPOLIS

Year	M/W	Assn	Div	NAT	NIT	ARC	CCA	NCI	NCT	OLY	HLM	W	L	Coach
1985	M	NAIA		32	—	—	—	—	—	—	—	21	15	Lovell, Robert
1990		NAIA		16	—	—	—	—	—	—	—	23	14	Lovell, Robert
1987	W	NAIA		16	—	—	—	—	—	—	—	22	8	Price, Jim
1991		NAIA		3	—	—	—	—	—	—	—	20	12	Wilhoit, Julie A.

INDIANA: SOUTH BEND

Year	M/W	Assn	Div	NAT	NIT	ARC	CCA	NCI	NCT	OLY	HLM	W	L	Coach
1997	W	NAIA	I	32	—	—	—	—	—	—	—	24	10	Wisnewski, Mary
1998		NAIA	I	32	—	—	—	—	—	—	—	23	6	Wisnewski, Mary

INDIANA: SOUTHEAST

Year	M/W	Assn	Div	NAT	NIT	ARC	CCA	NCI	NCT	OLY	HLM	W	L	Coach
1997	M	NAIA	II	32	—	—	—	—	—	—	—	20	13	Morris, Jim

INDIANAPOLIS

Year	M/W	Assn	Div	NAT	NIT	ARC	CCA	NCI	NCT	OLY	HLM	W	L	Coach
1949	M	NAIA		16	—	—	—	—	—	—	—	20	9	Nicoson, Angus J.
1956		NAIA		32	—	—	—	—	—	—	—	23	6	Nicoson, Angus J.
1964		NAIA		16	—	—	—	—	—	—	—	26	3	Nicoson, Angus J.
1966		NAIA		32	—	—	—	—	—	—	—	17	8	Nicoson, Angus J.
1967		NAIA		32	—	—	—	—	—	—	—	18	10	Nicoson, Angus J.
1969		NAIA		32	—	—	—	—	—	—	—	20	10	Nicoson, Angus J.
1996		NCAA	II	32	—	—	—	—	—	—	—	20	9	Waltman, Royce
1997		NCAA	II	32	—	—	—	—	—	—	—	23	5	Waltman, Royce
1993	W	NCAA	II	32	—	—	—	—	—	—	—	24	4	Mallender, Charles "Chuck"
1995		NCAA	II	48	—	—	—	—	—	—	—	21	7	Hicks, Lisa

IONA

Year	M/W	Assn	Div	NAT	NIT	ARC	CCA	NCI	NCT	OLY	HLM	W	L	Coach
1979	M	NCAA	I	40	—	—	—	—	—	—	—	23	6	Valvano, James T.
1980		NCAA	I	32	—	—	—	—	—	—	—	29	5	Valvano, James T.
1982		NCAA	I	—	32	—	—	—	—	—	—	24	9	Kennedy, Patrick
1983		NCAA	I	—	16	—	—	—	—	—	—	22	9	Kennedy, Patrick
1984		NCAA	I	48	—	—	—	—	—	—	—	23	8	Kennedy, Patrick
1985		NCAA	I	64	—	—	—	—	—	—	—	26	5	Kennedy, Patrick
1996		NCAA	I	—	32	—	—	—	—	—	—	21	8	Welsh, Tim
1997		NCAA	I	—	32	—	—	—	—	—	—	22	8	Welsh, Tim
1998		NCAA	I	64	—	—	—	—	—	—	—	27	6	Welsh, Tim

IOWA

Year	M/W	Assn	Div	NAT	NIT	ARC	CCA	NCI	NCT	OLY	HLM	W	L	Coach
1955	M	NCAA		4	—	—	—	—	—	—	—	19	7	O'Connor, Frank "Bucky"
1956		NCAA		2	—	—	—	—	—	—	—	20	6	O'Connor, Frank "Bucky"
1970		NCAA	I	12	—	—	—	—	—	—	—	20	5	Miller, Ralph H. "Cappy"
1979		NCAA	I	32	—	—	—	—	—	—	—	20	8	Olson, Robert Luther "Lute"
1980		NCAA	I	4	—	—	—	—	—	—	—	23	10	Olson, Robert Luther "Lute"
1981		NCAA	I	32	—	—	—	—	—	—	—	21	7	Olson, Robert Luther "Lute"
1982		NCAA	I	32	—	—	—	—	—	—	—	21	8	Olson, Robert Luther "Lute"
1983		NCAA	I	16	—	—	—	—	—	—	—	21	10	Olson, Robert Luther "Lute"
1985		NCAA	I	64	—	—	—	—	—	—	—	21	11	Raveling, George
1986		NCAA	I	16	—	—	—	—	—	—	—	20	12	Raveling, George
1987		NCAA	I	8	—	—	—	—	—	—	—	30	5	Davis, Dr. Thomas
1988		NCAA	I	16	—	—	—	—	—	—	—	24	10	Davis, Dr. Thomas

Year	M/W	Assn	Div	NAT	NIT	ARC	CCA	NCI	NCT	OLY	HLM	W	L	Coach
1989		NCAA	I	32	—	—	—	—	—	—	—	23	10	Davis, Dr. Thomas
1991		NCAA	I	32	—	—	—	—	—	—	—	21	11	Davis, Dr. Thomas
1992		NCAA	I	32	—	—	—	—	—	—	—	19	11	Davis, Dr. Thomas
1993		NCAA	I	32	—	—	—	—	—	—	—	23	9	Davis, Dr. Thomas
1995		NCAA	I	—	8	—	—	—	—	—	—	21	12	Davis, Dr. Thomas
1996		NCAA	I	32	—	—	—	—	—	—	—	23	9	Davis, Dr. Thomas
1997		NCAA	I	32	—	—	—	—	—	—	—	22	10	Davis, Dr. Thomas
1998		NCAA	I	—	32	—	—	—	—	—	—	20	11	Davis, Dr. Thomas
1969	W	AIAW		4	—	—	—	—	—	—	—	6	2	Barnes, Dr. Mildred
1986		NCAA	I	32	—	—	—	—	—	—	—	22	7	Stringer, C. Vivian
1987		NCAA	I	8	—	—	—	—	—	—	—	26	5	Stringer, C. Vivian
1988		NCAA	I	8	—	—	—	—	—	—	—	29	2	Stringer, C. Vivian
1989		NCAA	I	16	—	—	—	—	—	—	—	27	5	Stringer, C. Vivian
1990		NCAA	I	32	—	—	—	—	—	—	—	23	6	Stringer, C. Vivian
1991		NCAA	I	32	—	—	—	—	—	—	—	21	9	Stringer, C. Vivian
1992		NCAA	I	32	—	—	—	—	—	—	—	25	4	Stringer, C. Vivian
1993		NCAA	I	3	—	—	—	—	—	—	—	27	4	Stringer, C. Vivian
1994		NCAA	I	32	—	—	—	—	—	—	—	21	7	Stringer, C. Vivian
1996		NCAA	I	16	—	—	—	—	—	—	—	27	4	Lee, Angie
1997		NCAA	I	32	—	—	—	—	—	—	—	18	12	Lee, Angie
1998		NCAA	I	32	—	—	—	—	—	—	—	18	11	Lee, Angie

IOWA STATE

Year	M/W	Assn	Div	NAT	NIT	ARC	CCA	NCI	NCT	OLY	HLM	W	L	Coach
1944	M	NCAA		3	—	—	—	—	—	—	—	14	4	Menze, Louis E.
1984		NCAA	I	—	32	—	—	—	—	—	—	16	13	Orr, John M. "Johnny"
1985		NCAA	I	64	—	—	—	—	—	—	—	21	13	Orr, John M. "Johnny"
1986		NCAA	I	64	—	—	—	—	—	—	—	22	11	Orr, John M. "Johnny"
1988		NCAA	I	64	—	—	—	—	—	—	—	20	12	Orr, John M. "Johnny"
1989		NCAA	I	64	—	—	—	—	—	—	—	17	12	Orr, John M. "Johnny"
1992		NCAA	I	32	—	—	—	—	—	—	—	21	13	Orr, John M. "Johnny"
1993		NCAA	I	64	—	—	—	—	—	—	—	20	11	Orr, John M. "Johnny"
1995		NCAA	I	32	—	—	—	—	—	—	—	23	11	Floyd, Tim
1996		NCAA	I	32	—	—	—	—	—	—	—	24	9	Floyd, Tim
1997		NCAA	I	16	—	—	—	—	—	—	—	22	9	Floyd, Tim
1997	W	NCAA	I	64	—	—	—	—	—	—	—	17	12	Fennelly, Bill
1998		NCAA	I	32	—	—	—	—	—	—	—	25	8	Fennelly, Bill

IOWA WESLEYAN

Year	M/W	Assn	Div	NAT	NIT	ARC	CCA	NCI	NCT	OLY	HLM	W	L	Coach
1995	M	NAIA	I	32	—	—	—	—	—	—	—	21	15	Woolton, Joel
1969	W	AIAW		3	—	—	—	—	—	—	—	X	X	Sammons, Betty
1970		AIAW		8	—	—	—	—	—	—	—	X	X	Sammons, Betty

ITHACA

Year	M/W	Assn	Div	NAT	NIT	ARC	CCA	NCI	NCT	OLY	HLM	W	L	Coach
1964	M	NCAA	II	32	—	—	—	—	—	—	—	16	5	Wood, Carlton
1972		NCAA	II	24	—	—	—	—	—	—	—	15	8	Hurst, Hugh
1977		NCAA	III	30	—	—	—	—	—	—	—	15	10	Lehnus, Darryl
1982		NCAA	III	24	—	—	—	—	—	—	—	22	5	Baker, Tom
1983		NCAA	III	32	—	—	—	—	—	—	—	19	8	Baker, Tom
1987		NCAA	III	32	—	—	—	—	—	—	—	16	12	Baker, Tom
1993		NCAA	III	32	—	—	—	—	—	—	—	20	7	Baker, Tom
1997	W	NCAA	III	32	—	—	—	—	—	—	—	20	8	Pritchard, Christine

Year	M/W	Assn	Div	NAT	NIT	ARC	CCA	NCI	NCT	OLY	HLM	W	L	Coach
JACKSON STATE (MS)														
1957	M	NCAA	II	16	—	—	—	—	—	—	—	22	2	Wilson, Dr. Harrison B.
1964		NCAA	II	24	—	—	—	—	—	—	—	21	6	Covington, Paul E.
1965		NCAA	II	24	—	—	—	—	—	—	—	21	7	Wilson, Dr. Harrison B.
1966		NCAA	II	32	—	—	—	—	—	—	—	24	7	Wilson, Dr. Harrison B.
1968		NCAA	II	23	—	—	—	—	—	—	—	24	3	Covington, Paul E.
1969		NAIA		32	—	—	—	—	—	—	—	19	18	Covington, Paul E.
1970		NAIA		8	—	—	—	—	—	—	—	22	4	Covington, Paul E.
1971		NAIA		16	—	—	—	—	—	—	—	23	7	Covington, Paul E.
1993		NCAA	I	—	16	—	—	—	—	—	—	25	9	Stoglin, Lee Andrew "Andy"
1997		NCAA	I	64	—	—	—	—	—	—	—	14	16	Stoglin, Lee Andrew "Andy"
1981	W	AIAW	I	16	—	—	—	—	—	—	—	32	9	Magee, Sadie E.
1982		NCAA	I	32	—	—	—	—	—	—	—	28	8	Magee, Sadie E.
1983		NCAA	I	36	—	—	—	—	—	—	—	21	8	Magee, Sadie E.
1995		NCAA	I	64	—	—	—	—	—	—	—	22	7	Pennington, Andrew
JACKSONVILLE (FL)														
1965	M	NAIA		32	—	—	—	—	—	—	—	15	11	Williams, Joe L.
1970		NCAA	I	2	—	—	—	—	—	—	—	27	2	Williams, Joe L.
1971		NCAA	I	25	—	—	—	—	—	—	—	22	4	Wasdin, Tom
1972		NCAA	I	—	3	—	—	—	—	—	—	20	8	Wasdin, Tom
1973		NCAA	I	25	—	—	—	—	—	—	—	21	6	Wasdin, Tom
1974		NCAA	I	—	4	—	—	—	—	—	—	20	10	Gottlieb, Bob
1979		NCAA	I	40	—	—	—	—	—	—	—	19	11	Locke, Taylor O. "Tates"
1980		NCAA	I	—	32	—	—	—	—	—	—	20	9	Locke, Taylor O. "Tates"
1986		NCAA	I	64	—	—	—	—	—	—	—	21	10	Wenzel, Robert
1987		NCAA	I	—	32	—	—	—	—	—	—	19	11	Wenzel, Robert
JACKSONVILLE STATE (AL)														
1980	M	NCAA	II	32	—	—	—	—	—	—	—	20	7	Jones, Bill E.
1981		NCAA	II	24	—	—	—	—	—	—	—	22	8	Jones, Bill E.
1983		NCAA	II	8	—	—	—	—	—	—	—	24	8	Jones, Bill E.
1984		NCAA	II	16	—	—	—	—	—	—	—	23	8	Jones, Bill E.
1985		NCAA	II	1	—	—	—	—	—	—	—	31	1	Jones, Bill E.
1989		NCAA	II	4	—	—	—	—	—	—	—	27	6	Jones, Bill E.
1990		NCAA	II	8	—	—	—	—	—	—	—	24	5	Jones, Bill E.
1992		NCAA	II	8	—	—	—	—	—	—	—	28	2	Jones, Bill E.
1988	W	NCAA	II	16	—	—	—	—	—	—	—	22	7	Mathis, Richard
1989		NCAA	II	16	—	—	—	—	—	—	—	24	6	Mathis, Richard
1990		NCAA	II	16	—	—	—	—	—	—	—	25	5	Mathis, Richard
1991		NCAA	II	8	—	—	—	—	—	—	—	26	4	Mabrey, Tony
1993		NCAA	II	32	—	—	—	—	—	—	—	18	11	Mabrey, Tony
JAMES MADISON														
1974	M	NCAA	II	44	—	—	—	—	—	—	—	20	6	Campanelli, Lou
1976		NCAA	II	32	—	—	—	—	—	—	—	18	9	Campanelli, Lou
1981		NCAA	I	32	—	—	—	—	—	—	—	21	9	Campanelli, Lou
1982		NCAA	I	32	—	—	—	—	—	—	—	24	6	Campanelli, Lou
1983		NCAA	I	32	—	—	—	—	—	—	—	20	11	Campanelli, Lou
1987		NCAA	I	—	32	—	—	—	—	—	—	20	10	Thurston, John
1990		NCAA	I	—	32	—	—	—	—	—	—	20	11	Driesell, Charles G. "Lefty"
1991		NCAA	I	—	32	—	—	—	—	—	—	19	10	Driesell, Charles G. "Lefty"

Year	M/W	Assn	Div	NAT	NIT	ARC	CCA	NCI	NCT	OLY	HLM	W	L	Coach
1992		NCAA	I	—	32	—	—	—	—	—	—	21	11	Driesell, Charles G. "Lefty"
1993		NCAA	I	—	32	—	—	—	—	—	—	21	9	Driesell, Charles G. "Lefty"
1994		NCAA	I	64	—	—	—	—	—	—	—	20	10	Driesell, Charles G. "Lefty"
1975	W	AIAW	L	16	—	—	—	—	—	—	—	17	8	Jaynes, Betty F.
1986		NCAA	I	16	—	—	—	—	—	—	—	28	4	Moorman, Shelia
1987		NCAA	I	16	—	—	—	—	—	—	—	27	4	Moorman, Shelia
1988		NCAA	I	16	—	—	—	—	—	—	—	27	4	Moorman, Shelia
1989		NCAA	I	32	—	—	—	—	—	—	—	26	4	Moorman, Shelia
1991		NCAA	I	16	—	—	—	—	—	—	—	26	5	Moorman, Shelia
1996		NCAA	I	64	—	—	—	—	—	—	—	21	9	Moorman, Shelia

JAMESTOWN

Year	M/W	Assn	Div	NAT	NIT	ARC	CCA	NCI	NCT	OLY	HLM	W	L	Coach
1994	M	NAIA	II	16	—	—	—	—	—	—	—	13	14	Meyer, Jerry
1984	W	NAIA		16	—	—	—	—	—	—	—	15	7	Kohler, Robert

JERSEY CITY STATE

Year	M/W	Assn	Div	NAT	NIT	ARC	CCA	NCI	NCT	OLY	HLM	W	L	Coach
1964	M	NAIA		32	—	—	—	—	—	—	—	20	6	Gelston, Oliver S. "Ollie"
1973		NCAA	II	42	—	—	—	—	—	—	—	16	10	Schiner, Lawrence R.
1974		NCAA	II	44	—	—	—	—	—	—	—	20	6	Schiner, Lawrence R.
1978		NCAA	III	23	—	—	—	—	—	—	—	20	7	Weinstein, Paul
1979		NCAA	III	8	—	—	—	—	—	—	—	24	5	Weinstein, Paul
1980		NCAA	III	8	—	—	—	—	—	—	—	25	4	Weinstein, Paul
1986		NCAA	III	4	—	—	—	—	—	—	—	24	8	Brown, Charles H.
1987		NCAA	III	32	—	—	—	—	—	—	—	19	8	Brown, Charles H.
1989		NCAA	III	16	—	—	—	—	—	—	—	24	4	Brown, Charles H.
1990		NCAA	III	32	—	—	—	—	—	—	—	25	3	Brown, Charles H.
1992		NCAA	III	4	—	—	—	—	—	—	—	27	5	Brown, Charles H.
1995		NCAA	III	32	—	—	—	—	—	—	—	19	9	Brown, Charles H.
1996		NCAA	III	32	—	—	—	—	—	—	—	16	11	Brown, Charles H.
1997		NCAA	III	64	—	—	—	—	—	—	—	17	9	Brown, Charles H.
1998		NCAA	III	32	—	—	—	—	—	—	—	19	8	Brown, Charles H.

JIMMY SWAGGART BIBLE

Year	M/W	Assn	Div	NAT	NIT	ARC	CCA	NCI	NCT	OLY	HLM	W	L	Coach
1988	M	NCCAA	II	5	—	—	—	—	—	—	—	21	14	Boone, Dr. Jerry
1989		NCCAA	II	8	—	—	—	—	—	—	—	9	25	Boone, Dr. Jerry
1990		NCCAA	II	6	—	—	—	—	—	—	—	22	11	Boone, Dr. Jerry
1991		NCCAA	II	5	—	—	—	—	—	—	—	27	9	Boone, Dr. Jerry

JOHN BROWN

Year	M/W	Assn	Div	NAT	NIT	ARC	CCA	NCI	NCT	OLY	HLM	W	L	Coach
1971	M	NCCAA		3	—	—	—	—	—	—	—	17	10	Haynes, Bill
1980		NCCAA	I	6	—	—	—	—	—	—	—	15	13	Simons, Jeff
1983		NCCAA	I	3	—	—	—	—	—	—	—	15	17	Simons, Jeff
1986		NCCAA	I	8	—	—	—	—	—	—	—	13	13	Bassett, Sheldon
1991		NCCAA	I	1	—	—	—	—	—	—	—	25	8	Sheehy, John
1983	W	NCCAA	I	4	—	—	—	—	—	—	—	12	18	Pickering, Curt
1985		NCCAA	I	2	—	—	—	—	—	—	—	20	12	Bassett, Sheldon
1987		NCCAA	I	6	—	—	—	—	—	—	—	13	18	Augustine, Jack
1989		NCCAA	I	6	—	—	—	—	—	—	—	16	10	Augustine, Jack

Year	M/W	Assn	Div	NAT	NIT	ARC	CCA	NCI	NCT	OLY	HLM	W	L	Coach

JOHN CARROLL

Year	M/W	Assn	Div	NAT	NIT	ARC	CCA	NCI	NCT	OLY	HLM	W	L	Coach
1983	M	NCAA	III	32	—	—	—	—	—	—	—	17	7	Baab, Tim
1986		NCAA	III	32	—	—	—	—	—	—	—	11	13	Baab, Tim
1996		NCAA	III	32	—	—	—	—	—	—	—	19	8	Moran, Mike
1997		NCAA	III	64	—	—	—	—	—	—	—	20	7	Moran, Mike
1998		NCAA	III	8	—	—	—	—	—	—	—	22	7	Moran, Mike

JOHN F KENNEDY (NE)

Year	M/W	Assn	Div	NAT	NIT	ARC	CCA	NCI	NCT	OLY	HLM	W	L	Coach
1969	W			—	4	—	—	—	—	—	—	16	10	Spencer, Robert L.
1970				—	4	—	—	—	—	—	—	15	12	Spencer, Robert L.
1971				—	3	—	—	—	—	—	—	14	16	Nicodemus, George L.
1972				—	2	—	—	—	—	—	—	27	10	Nicodemus, George L.
1973				—	2	—	—	—	—	—	—	34	7	Nicodemus, George L.
1974				—	2	—	—	—	—	—	—	26	5	Nicodemus, George L.
1975				—	5	—	—	—	—	—	—	21	16	Nicodemus, George L.

JOHNS HOPKINS

Year	M/W	Assn	Div	NAT	NIT	ARC	CCA	NCI	NCT	OLY	HLM	W	L	Coach
1974	M	NCAA	II	44	—	—	—	—	—	—	—	17	9	Rupert, Gary
1990		NCAA	III	16	—	—	—	—	—	—	—	20	8	Nelson, William H.
1991		NCAA	III	32	—	—	—	—	—	—	—	19	10	Nelson, William H.
1992		NCAA	III	32	—	—	—	—	—	—	—	20	8	Nelson, William H.
1993		NCAA	III	40	—	—	—	—	—	—	—	19	7	Nelson, William H.
1994		NCAA	III	32	—	—	—	—	—	—	—	20	7	Nelson, William H.
1998		NCAA	III	32	—	—	—	—	—	—	—	21	7	Nelson, William H.
1995	W	NCAA	III	16	—	—	—	—	—	—	—	22	7	Clelan-Blank, Nancy
1996		NCAA	III	32	—	—	—	—	—	—	—	20	8	Clelan-Blank, Nancy
1997		NCAA	III	8	—	—	—	—	—	—	—	25	5	Clelan-Blank, Nancy
1998		NCAA	III	8	—	—	—	—	—	—	—	24	5	Clelan-Blank, Nancy

JOHNSON BIBLE

Year	M/W	Assn	Div	NAT	NIT	ARC	CCA	NCI	NCT	OLY	HLM	W	L	Coach
1977	M	NCCAA	II	3	—	—	—	—	—	—	—	23	9	Morgan, Russell
1984		NCCAA	II	8	—	—	—	—	—	—	—	19	12	Karnes, Douglas
1985		NCCAA	II	8	—	—	—	—	—	—	—	19	8	Karnes, Douglas
1986		NCCAA	II	8	—	—	—	—	—	—	—	18	13	Karnes, Douglas
1987		NCCAA	II	4	—	—	—	—	—	—	—	22	7	Karnes, Douglas
1988		NCCAA	II	8	—	—	—	—	—	—	—	17	11	Karnes, Douglas
1984	W	NCCAA	II	3	—	—	—	—	—	—	—	18	5	Morgan, Russell
1985		NCCAA	II	2	—	—	—	—	—	—	—	9	9	Morgan, Russell
1986		NCCAA	II	2	—	—	—	—	—	—	—	2	9	Morgan, Russell
1994		NCCAA	II	6	—	—	—	—	—	—	—	9	7	Morgan, Russell
1995		NCCAA	II	7	—	—	—	—	—	—	—	9	6	Roberts, Sherri
1996		NCCAA	II	8	—	—	—	—	—	—	—	10	10	Roberts, Sherri

JOHNSON C SMITH

Year	M/W	Assn	Div	NAT	NIT	ARC	CCA	NCI	NCT	OLY	HLM	W	L	Coach
1960	M	NCAA	II	32	—	—	—	—	—	—	—	18	7	McGirt, Edward C.
1987		NCAA	II	32	—	—	—	—	—	—	—	21	9	Moore, Robert D.
1991		NCAA	II	24	—	—	—	—	—	—	—	23	7	Joyner, Steven Wayne
1992		NCAA	II	16	—	—	—	—	—	—	—	25	7	Joyner, Steven Wayne
1995		NCAA	II	32	—	—	—	—	—	—	—	21	9	Joyner, Steven Wayne
1998		NCAA	II	48	—	—	—	—	—	—	—	21	7	Joyner, Steven Wayne
1985	W	NCAA	II	24	—	—	—	—	—	—	—	17	9	Joyner, Steven Wayne
1992		NCAA	II	32	—	—	—	—	—	—	—	22	9	Evans-Liebert, Hythia

Year	M/W	Assn	Div	NAT	NIT	ARC	CCA	NCI	NCT	OLY	HLM	W	L	Coach

JORDAN COLLEGE & SEMINARY

Year	M/W	Assn	Div	NAT	NIT	ARC	CCA	NCI	NCT	OLY	HLM	W	L	Coach
1938	M	NAIA		8	—	—	—	—	—	—	—			
1939		NAIA		32	—	—	—	—	—	—	—			

JORDAN: DETROIT

Year	M/W	Assn	Div	NAT	NIT	ARC	CCA	NCI	NCT	OLY	HLM	W	L	Coach
1989	M	NSCAA		8	—	—	—	—	—	—	—			Watkins, Quinton "Rocky"
1990		NSCAA		5	—	—	—	—	—	—	—			Watkins, Quinton "Rocky"
1991		NSCAA		2	—	—	—	—	—	—	—			Watkins, Quinton "Rocky"
1992		NSCAA		3	—	—	—	—	—	—	—			Watkins, Quinton "Rocky"
1993		NSCAA		2	—	—	—	—	—	—	—			Watkins, Quinton "Rocky"
1994		NSCAA		6	—	—	—	—	—	—	—	21	15	Watkins, Quinton "Rocky"

JORDAN: FLINT

Year	M/W	Assn	Div	NAT	NIT	ARC	CCA	NCI	NCT	OLY	HLM	W	L	Coach
1984	M	NSCAA		16	—	—	—	—	—	—	—			Scott, Daniel L.
1987		NSCAA		12	—	—	—	—	—	—	—	21	16	Scott, Daniel L.
1988		NSCAA		12	—	—	—	—	—	—	—			Scott, Daniel L.
1989		NSCAA		12	—	—	—	—	—	—	—			Porter, Victor
1990		NSCAA		7	—	—	—	—	—	—	—	27	10	Porter, Victor
1991		NSCAA		10	—	—	—	—	—	—	—	15	21	Porter, Victor
1993		NSCAA		4	—	—	—	—	—	—	—	21	10	Porter, Victor
1994		NSCAA		12	—	—	—	—	—	—	—	14	4	Porter, Victor

JOSEPHINUM

Year	M/W	Assn	Div	NAT	NIT	ARC	CCA	NCI	NCT	OLY	HLM	W	L	Coach
1981	M	NSCAA		16	—	—	—	—	—	—	—	20	6	

JUDSON (IL)

Year	M/W	Assn	Div	NAT	NIT	ARC	CCA	NCI	NCT	OLY	HLM	W	L	Coach
1981	M	NSCAA		10	—	—	—	—	—	—	—	18	16	Harris, Sam
1984		NCCAA	I	3	—	—	—	—	—	—	—	24	9	Harris, Sam
1995	W	NCCAA	I	7	—	—	—	—	—	—	—	20	13	Gum, Tory
1996		NAIA	II	32	—	—	—	—	—	—	—	21	9	Gum, Tory

JUDSON BAPTIST (OR)

Year	M/W	Assn	Div	NAT	NIT	ARC	CCA	NCI	NCT	OLY	HLM	W	L	Coach
1980	W	NSCAA		7	—	—	—	—	—	—	—			

JUNIATA

Year	M/W	Assn	Div	NAT	NIT	ARC	CCA	NCI	NCT	OLY	HLM	W	L	Coach
1980	W	AIAW	III	8	—	—	—	—	—	—	—	24	4	Latimore, Nancy Harden
1986		NCAA	III	24	—	—	—	—	—	—	—	16	6	Latimore, Nancy Harden

KALAMAZOO

Year	M/W	Assn	Div	NAT	NIT	ARC	CCA	NCI	NCT	OLY	HLM	W	L	Coach
1950	M	NAIA		32	—	—	—	—	—	—	—	12	8	Grow, Lloyd E.
1956		NAIA		32	—	—	—	—	—	—	—	14	9	Steffen, Raymond
1996		NCAA	III	64	—	—	—	—	—	—	—	17	11	Haklin, Joe

KANSAS

Year	M/W	Assn	Div	NAT	NIT	ARC	CCA	NCI	NCT	OLY	HLM	W	L	Coach
1922	M	NCAA		—	—	—	—	—	—	—	1	16	2	Allen, Dr. Forrest C. "Phog"
1923		NCAA		—	—	—	—	—	—	—	1	17	1	Allen, Dr. Forrest C. "Phog"
1940		NCAA		2	—	—	—	—	—	—	—	19	6	Allen, Dr. Forrest C. "Phog"
1942		NCAA		6	—	—	—	—	—	—	—	17	5	Allen, Dr. Forrest C. "Phog"
1952		NCAA		1	—	—	—	—	—	2	1	28	3	Allen, Dr. Forrest C. "Phog"
1953		NCAA		2	—	—	—	—	—	—	—	19	6	Allen, Dr. Forrest C. "Phog"
1957		NCAA	I	2	—	—	—	—	—	—	—	24	3	Harp, Richard
1960		NCAA	I	8	—	—	—	—	—	—	—	19	9	Harp, Richard

Year	M/W	Assn	Div	NAT	NIT	ARC	CCA	NCI	NCT	OLY	HLM	W	L	Coach
1966		NCAA	I	8	—	—	—	—	—	—	—	23	4	Owens, Ted
1967		NCAA	I	16	—	—	—	—	—	—	—	23	4	Owens, Ted
1968		NCAA	I	—	2	—	—	—	—	—	—	22	8	Owens, Ted
1969		NCAA	I	—	16	—	—	—	—	—	—	20	7	Owens, Ted
1971		NCAA	I	4	—	—	—	—	—	—	—	27	3	Owens, Ted
1974		NCAA	I	4	—	—	—	—	—	—	—	23	7	Owens, Ted
1975		NCAA	I	32	—	—	—	—	—	—	—	19	8	Owens, Ted
1978		NCAA	I	32	—	—	—	—	—	—	—	24	5	Owens, Ted
1981		NCAA	I	16	—	—	—	—	—	—	—	24	8	Owens, Ted
1984		NCAA	I	32	—	—	—	—	—	—	—	22	10	Brown, Lawrence H.
1985		NCAA	I	32	—	—	—	—	—	—	—	26	8	Brown, Lawrence H.
1986		NCAA	I	3	—	—	—	—	—	—	—	35	4	Brown, Lawrence H.
1987		NCAA	I	16	—	—	—	—	—	—	—	25	11	Brown, Lawrence H.
1988		NCAA	I	1	—	—	—	—	—	—	—	27	11	Brown, Lawrence H.
1990		NCAA	I	32	—	—	—	—	—	—	—	30	5	Williams, Roy
1991		NCAA	I	2	—	—	—	—	—	—	—	27	8	Williams, Roy
1992		NCAA	I	32	—	—	—	—	—	—	—	27	5	Williams, Roy
1993		NCAA	I	3	—	—	—	—	—	—	—	29	7	Williams, Roy
1994		NCAA	I	16	—	—	—	—	—	—	—	27	8	Williams, Roy
1995		NCAA	I	16	—	—	—	—	—	—	—	25	6	Williams, Roy
1996		NCAA	I	8	—	—	—	—	—	—	—	29	5	Williams, Roy
1997		NCAA	I	16	—	—	—	—	—	—	—	34	2	Williams, Roy
1998		NCAA	I	32	—	—	—	—	—	—	—	35	4	Williams, Roy
1971	W	AIAW		6	—	—	—	—	—	—	—	7	8	Mawson, Marlene
1978		AIAW	L	—	6	—	—	—	—	—	—	22	11	Washington, Marian
1979		AIAW	L	12	—	—	—	—	—	—	—	29	8	Washington, Marian
1980		AIAW	I	16	—	—	—	—	—	—	—	29	7	Washington, Marian
1981		AIAW	I	16	—	—	—	—	—	—	—	27	5	Washington, Marian
1987		NCAA	I	32	—	—	—	—	—	—	—	20	13	Washington, Marian
1988		NCAA	I	32	—	—	—	—	—	—	—	22	10	Washington, Marian
1991		NCAA	I	—	3	—	—	—	—	—	—	20	13	Washington, Marian
1992		NCAA	I	48	—	—	—	—	—	—	—	25	6	Washington, Marian
1993		NCAA	I	48	—	—	—	—	—	—	—	21	9	Washington, Marian
1994		NCAA	I	32	—	—	—	—	—	—	—	22	6	Washington, Marian
1995		NCAA	I	64	—	—	—	—	—	—	—	20	11	Washington, Marian
1996		NCAA	I	16	—	—	—	—	—	—	—	22	10	Washington, Marian
1997		NCAA	I	32	—	—	—	—	—	—	—	25	6	Washington, Marian
1998		NCAA	I	16	—	—	—	—	—	—	—	23	9	Washington, Marian

KANSAS NEWMAN

Year	M/W	Assn	Div	NAT	NIT	ARC	CCA	NCI	NCT	OLY	HLM	W	L	Coach
1971	M	NAIA		32	—	—	—	—	—	—	—	16	5	Rineberg, Rick
1978		NAIA		32	—	—	—	—	—	—	—	21	11	Skinner, David N.

KANSAS STATE

Year	M/W	Assn	Div	NAT	NIT	ARC	CCA	NCI	NCT	OLY	HLM	W	L	Coach
1948	M	NCAA		4	—	—	—	—	—	—	—	22	6	Gardner, James H. "Jack"
1951		NCAA		2	—	—	—	—	—	—	—	25	4	Gardner, James H. "Jack"
1956		NCAA		12	—	—	—	—	—	—	—	17	8	Winter, Fred "Tex"
1958		NCAA	I	4	—	—	—	—	—	—	—	22	5	Winter, Fred "Tex"

Year	M/W	Assn	Div	NAT	NIT	ARC	CCA	NCI	NCT	OLY	HLM	W	L	Coach
1959		NCAA	I	8	—	—	—	—	—	—	—	25	2	Winter, Fred "Tex"
1961		NCAA	I	8	—	—	—	—	—	—	—	22	5	Winter, Fred "Tex"
1964		NCAA	I	4	—	—	—	—	—	—	—	22	7	Winter, Fred "Tex"
1968		NCAA	I	16	—	—	—	—	—	—	—	19	9	Winter, Fred "Tex"
1970		NCAA	I	12	—	—	—	—	—	—	—	20	8	Fitzsimmons, Lowell "Cotton"
1972		NCAA	I	8	—	—	—	—	—	—	—	19	9	Hartman, Jack
1973		NCAA	I	8	—	—	—	—	—	—	—	23	5	Hartman, Jack
1974		NCAA	I	—	—	—	8	—	—	—	—	19	8	Hartman, Jack
1975		NCAA	I	8	—	—	—	—	—	—	—	20	9	Hartman, Jack
1976		NCAA	I	—	8	—	—	—	—	—	—	20	8	Hartman, Jack
1977		NCAA	I	16	—	—	—	—	—	—	—	23	8	Hartman, Jack
1980		NCAA	I	32	—	—	—	—	—	—	—	22	9	Hartman, Jack
1981		NCAA	I	8	—	—	—	—	—	—	—	24	9	Hartman, Jack
1982		NCAA	I	16	—	—	—	—	—	—	—	23	8	Hartman, Jack
1987		NCAA	I	32	—	—	—	—	—	—	—	20	11	Kruger, Lon
1988		NCAA	I	8	—	—	—	—	—	—	—	25	9	Kruger, Lon
1989		NCAA	I	64	—	—	—	—	—	—	—	19	11	Kruger, Lon
1990		NCAA	I	64	—	—	—	—	—	—	—	17	15	Kruger, Lon
1992		NCAA	I	—	16	—	—	—	—	—	—	16	14	Altman, Dana
1993		NCAA	I	64	—	—	—	—	—	—	—	19	11	Altman, Dana
1994		NCAA	I	—	4	—	—	—	—	—	—	20	14	Altman, Dana
1996		NCAA	I	64	—	—	—	—	—	—	—	17	12	Asbury, Tom
1998		NCAA	I	—	32	—	—	—	—	—	—	17	12	Asbury, Tom
1969	W	AIAW		—	8	—	—	—	—	—	—	11	3	Akers, Judy
1970		AIAW		8	7	—	—	—	—	—	—	10	7	Akers, Judy
1971		AIAW		8	—	—	—	—	—	—	—	12	12	Akers, Judy
1973		AIAW		5	—	—	—	—	—	—	—	20	6	Akers, Judy
1974		AIAW		16	—	—	—	—	—	—	—	21	9	Akers, Judy
1975		AIAW	L	6	—	—	—	—	—	—	—	24	9	Akers, Judy
1977		AIAW	L	12	—	—	—	—	—	—	—	23	12	Akers, Judy
1979		AIAW	L	16	—	—	—	—	—	—	—	20	11	Akers, Judy
1980		AIAW	I	16	—	—	—	—	—	—	—	26	9	Hickey, Lynn
1982		NCAA	I	8	—	—	—	—	—	—	—	26	6	Hickey, Lynn
1983		NCAA	I	16	—	—	—	—	—	—	—	25	7	Hickey, Lynn
1984		NCAA	I	32	—	—	—	—	—	—	—	25	6	Hickey, Lynn
1987		NCAA	I	40	—	—	—	—	—	—	—	22	9	Mossman, Matilda Willis
1997		NCAA	I	64	—	—	—	—	—	—	—	19	12	Patterson, Debbie

Kansas Wesleyan

Year	M/W	Assn	Div	NAT	NIT	ARC	CCA	NCI	NCT	OLY	HLM	W	L	Coach
1938	M	NAIA		32	—	—	—	—	—	—	—	9	7	Unknown
1940		NAIA		16	—	—	—	—	—	—	—	23	8	Johnson, Eugene
1943		NAIA		16	—	—	—	—	—	—	—	18	4	Johnson, Eugene
1950		NAIA		32	—	—	—	—	—	—	—	22	2	Forsberg, Wallace A. "Wally"
1988		NSCAA		7	—	—	—	—	—	—	—	15	15	Jones, Jerry
1997		NSCAA		4	—	—	—	—	—	—	—	11	21	Jones, Jerry
1998		NSCAA		8	—	—	—	—	—	—	—	5	26	Jones, Jerry
1988	W	NSCAA		5	—	—	—	—	—	—	—	22	4	Rietzke, Tracy
1996		NSCAA		1	—	—	—	—	—	—	—	14	16	Hughes, Tom
1997		NSCAA		1	—	—	—	—	—	—	—	12	19	Hughes, Tom
1998		NSCAA		6	—	—	—	—	—	—	—	14	13	Hughes, Tom

Year	M/W	Assn	Div	NAT	NIT	ARC	CCA	NCI	NCT	OLY	HLM	W	L	Coach
KEAN														
1978	M	NCAA	III	8	—	—	—	—	—	—	—	23	5	Palermo, Joseph
1991		NCAA	III	8	—	—	—	—	—	—	—	24	6	Kornegay, Ron
1992		NCAA	III	32	—	—	—	—	—	—	—	20	9	Kornegay, Ron
1982	W	AIAW	III	16	—	—	—	—	—	—	—	18	12	Hannisch, Patricia
1983		NCAA	III	8	—	—	—	—	—	—	—	25	3	Hannisch, Patricia
1984		NCAA	III	8	—	—	—	—	—	—	—	24	2	Hannisch, Patricia
1985		NCAA	III	24	—	—	—	—	—	—	—	23	5	Hannisch, Patricia
1986		NCAA	III	16	—	—	—	—	—	—	—	25	2	Hannisch, Patricia
1987		NCAA	III	4	—	—	—	—	—	—	—	26	4	Wilson, Rich
1988		NCAA	III	24	—	—	—	—	—	—	—	21	8	Wilson, Rich
1989		NCAA	III	32	—	—	—	—	—	—	—	24	5	Wilson, Rich
1990		NCAA	III	32	—	—	—	—	—	—	—	23	6	Wilson, Rich
1991		NCAA	III	32	—	—	—	—	—	—	—	24	3	Wilson, Rich
KEENE STATE														
1973	M	NAIA		32	—	—	—	—	—	—	—	19	8	Theulen, Glenn H.
1974		NAIA		32	—	—	—	—	—	—	—	16	9	Theulen, Glenn H.
1977		NAIA		32	—	—	—	—	—	—	—	22	7	Theulen, Glenn H.
1990	W	NCAA	II	32	—	—	—	—	—	—	—	23	7	Le Mieux, John
KENNESAW STATE														
1993	M	NAIA	I	32	—	—	—	—	—	—	—	19	12	Zenoni, Phil
1992	W	NAIA	I	16	—	—	—	—	—	—	—	22	9	Walker, Ron
1993		NAIA	I	32	—	—	—	—	—	—	—	19	11	Walker, Ron
1997		NCAA	II	8	—	—	—	—	—	—	—	30	2	Tilley, Colby
KENT STATE														
1985	M	NCAA	I	—	32	—	—	—	—	—	—	17	13	McDonald, James Joseph
1989		NCAA	I	—	32	—	—	—	—	—	—	20	11	McDonald, James Joseph
1990		NCAA	I	—	32	—	—	—	—	—	—	21	8	McDonald, James Joseph
1982	W	NCAA	I	32	—	—	—	—	—	—	—	17	14	Wartluft, Laurel
1996		NCAA	I	32	—	—	—	—	—	—	—	24	7	Lindsay, Bob
1998		NCAA	I	64	—	—	—	—	—	—	—	23	7	Lindsay, Bob
KENTUCKY														
1933	M			—	—	—	—	—	—	—	1	20	3	Rupp, Adolph F.
1942		NCAA		3	—	—	—	—	—	—	—	19	6	Rupp, Adolph F.
1944		NCAA		—	3	—	—	—	—	—	—	19	2	Rupp, Adolph F.
1945		NCAA		6	—	—	—	—	—	—	—	22	4	Rupp, Adolph F.
1946		NCAA		—	1	—	—	—	—	—	—	28	2	Rupp, Adolph F.
1947		NCAA		—	2	—	—	—	—	—	—	34	3	Rupp, Adolph F.
1948		NCAA		1	—	—	—	—	—	2	1	36	3	Rupp, Adolph F.
1949		NCAA		1	8	—	—	—	—	—	1	32	2	Rupp, Adolph F.
1950		NCAA		—	8	—	—	—	—	—	—	25	5	Rupp, Adolph F.
1951		NCAA		1	—	—	—	—	—	—	1	32	2	Rupp, Adolph F.
1952		NCAA		8	—	—	—	—	—	—	—	29	3	Rupp, Adolph F.
1954		NCAA		—	—	—	—	—	—	—	1	25	0	Rupp, Adolph F.

Year	M/W	Assn	Div	NAT	NIT	ARC	CCA	NCI	NCT	OLY	HLM	W	L	Coach
1955		NCAA		12	—	—	—	—	—	—	—	23	3	Rupp, Adolph F.
1956		NCAA		8	—	—	—	—	—	—	—	20	6	Rupp, Adolph F.
1957		NCAA	I	8	—	—	—	—	—	—	—	23	5	Rupp, Adolph F.
1958		NCAA	I	1	—	—	—	—	—	—	1	23	6	Rupp, Adolph F.
1959		NCAA	I	12	—	—	—	—	—	—	—	24	3	Rupp, Adolph F.
1961		NCAA	I	8	—	—	—	—	—	—	—	19	9	Rupp, Adolph F.
1962		NCAA	I	8	—	—	—	—	—	—	—	23	3	Rupp, Adolph F.
1964		NCAA	I	16	—	—	—	—	—	—	—	21	6	Rupp, Adolph F.
1966		NCAA	I	2	—	—	—	—	—	—	—	27	2	Rupp, Adolph F.
1968		NCAA	I	8	—	—	—	—	—	—	—	22	5	Rupp, Adolph F.
1969		NCAA	I	12	—	—	—	—	—	—	—	23	5	Rupp, Adolph F.
1970		NCAA	I	8	—	—	—	—	—	—	—	26	2	Rupp, Adolph F.
1971		NCAA	I	16	—	—	—	—	—	—	—	22	6	Rupp, Adolph F.
1972		NCAA	I	8	—	—	—	—	—	—	—	21	7	Rupp, Adolph F.
1973		NCAA	I	8	—	—	—	—	—	—	—	20	8	Hall, Joe B.
1975		NCAA	I	2	—	—	—	—	—	—	—	26	5	Hall, Joe B.
1976		NCAA	I	—	1	—	—	—	—	—	—	20	10	Hall, Joe B.
1977		NCAA	I	8	—	—	—	—	—	—	—	26	4	Hall, Joe B.
1978		NCAA	I	1	—	—	—	—	—	—	1	30	2	Hall, Joe B.
1979		NCAA	I	—	24	—	—	—	—	—	—	19	12	Hall, Joe B.
1980		NCAA	I	16	—	—	—	—	—	—	—	29	6	Hall, Joe B.
1981		NCAA	I	32	—	—	—	—	—	—	—	22	6	Hall, Joe B.
1982		NCAA	I	48	—	—	—	—	—	—	—	22	8	Hall, Joe B.
1983		NCAA	I	8	—	—	—	—	—	—	—	23	8	Hall, Joe B.
1984		NCAA	I	3	—	—	—	—	—	—	—	29	5	Hall, Joe B.
1985		NCAA	I	16	—	—	—	—	—	—	—	18	13	Hall, Joe B.
1986		NCAA	I	8	—	—	—	—	—	—	—	32	4	Sutton, Eddie
1987		NCAA	I	64	—	—	—	—	—	—	—	18	11	Sutton, Eddie
1988		NCAA	I	16	—	—	—	—	—	—	—	27	6	Sutton, Eddie
1992		NCAA	I	8	—	—	—	—	—	—	—	29	7	Pitino, Richard A. "Rick"
1993		NCAA	I	3	—	—	—	—	—	—	—	30	4	Pitino, Richard A. "Rick"
1994		NCAA	I	32	—	—	—	—	—	—	—	27	7	Pitino, Richard A. "Rick"
1995		NCAA	I	8	—	—	—	—	—	—	—	28	5	Pitino, Richard A. "Rick"
1996		NCAA	I	1	—	—	—	—	—	—	—	34	2	Pitino, Richard A. "Rick"
1997		NCAA	I	2	—	—	—	—	—	—	—	35	5	Pitino, Richard A. "Rick"
1998		NCAA	I	1	—	—	—	—	—	—	—	35	4	Smith, Orlando H. "Tubby"
1969	W	AIAW		16	—	—	—	—	—	—	—	X	X	Unknown
1978		AIAW	L	—	3	—	—	—	—	—	—	23	12	Yow, Deborah Ann
1980		AIAW	I	24	—	—	—	—	—	—	—	24	5	Yow, Deborah Ann
1981		AIAW	I	16	—	—	—	—	—	—	—	25	6	Hall, Terry
1982		NCAA	I	8	—	—	—	—	—	—	—	24	8	Hall, Terry
1983		NCAA	I	32	—	—	—	—	—	—	—	23	5	Hall, Terry
1986		NCAA	I	40	—	—	—	—	—	—	—	18	11	Hall, Terry
1990		NCAA	I	—	1	—	—	—	—	—	—	23	8	Fanning, Sharon
1991		NCAA	I	48	—	—	—	—	—	—	—	20	9	Fanning, Sharon

KENTUCKY CHRISTIAN

Year	M/W	Assn	Div	NAT	NIT	ARC	CCA	NCI	NCT	OLY	HLM	W	L	Coach
1978	M	NCCAA	II	4	—	—	—	—	—	—	—	17	12	Damron, Dr. Donald R. "Dick"
1979		NCCAA	II	3	—	—	—	—	—	—	—	22	8	Damron, Dr. Donald R. "Dick"
1980		NCCAA	II	4	—	—	—	—	—	—	—	22	11	Damron, Dr. Donald R. "Dick"
1981		NCCAA	II	6	—	—	—	—	—	—	—	15	13	Damron, Dr. Donald R. "Dick"

Year	M/W	Assn	Div	NAT	NIT	ARC	CCA	NCI	NCT	OLY	HLM	W	L	Coach
1982		NCCAA	II	8	—	—	—	—	—	—	—	19	10	Damron, Dr. Donald R. "Dick"
1983		NCCAA	II	8	—	—	—	—	—	—	—	21	8	Damron, Dr. Donald R. "Dick"
1988		NCCAA	II	1	—	—	—	—	—	—	—	26	8	Kirk, Randy
1989		NCCAA	II	1	—	—	—	—	—	—	—	27	5	Kirk, Randy
1990		NCCAA	II	3	—	—	—	—	—	—	—	23	13	Kirk, Randy
1991		NCCAA	II	1	—	—	—	—	—	—	—	20	13	Damron, Dr. Donald R. "Dick"
1993		NCCAA	II	7	—	—	—	—	—	—	—	22	10	Damron, Dr. Donald R. "Dick"
1995		NCCAA	II	1	—	—	—	—	—	—	—	26	7	Damron, Dr. Donald R. "Dick"
1996		NCCAA	II	1	—	—	—	—	—	—	—	27	6	Sudlow, Eric
1997		NCCAA	II	1	—	—	—	—	—	—	—	21	12	Damron, Dr. Donald R. "Dick"
1998		NCCAA	II	2	—	—	—	—	—	—	—	27	11	Damron, Dr. Donald R. "Dick"
1983	W	NCCAA	II	3	—	—	—	—	—	—	—	X	X	Robertson, Barb McClone
1985		NCCAA	II	5	—	—	—	—	—	—	—	9	9	Robertson, Barb McClone
1986		NCCAA	II	5	—	—	—	—	—	—	—	11	9	Schreiner, Dale
1987		NCCAA	II	3	—	—	—	—	—	—	—	12	11	Schreiner, Dale
1988		NCCAA	II	3	—	—	—	—	—	—	—	11	12	Schreiner, Dale
1989		NCCAA	II	1	—	—	—	—	—	—	—	13	11	Bender, Tom
1990		NCCAA	II	4	—	—	—	—	—	—	—	15	10	Bender, Tom
1991		NCCAA	II	5	—	—	—	—	—	—	—	15	11	Bender, Tom
1992		NCCAA	II	3	—	—	—	—	—	—	—	20	6	Arnett, Ron
1993		NCCAA	II	2	—	—	—	—	—	—	—	19	11	Arnett, Ron
1994		NCCAA	II	2	—	—	—	—	—	—	—	21	7	Arnett, Ron
1995		NCCAA	II	1	—	—	—	—	—	—	—	24	9	Arnett, Ron
1996		NCCAA	II	1	—	—	—	—	—	—	—	28	4	Arnett, Ron
1997		NCCAA	II	1	—	—	—	—	—	—	—	30	5	Arnett, Ron
1998		NCCAA	II	1	—	—	—	—	—	—	—	22	13	Arnett, Ron

KENTUCKY STATE

Year	M/W	Assn	Div	NAT	NIT	ARC	CCA	NCI	NCT	OLY	HLM	W	L	Coach
1959	M	NAIA		32	—	—	—	—	—	—	—	14	11	Brown, James B.
1962		NCAA	II	24	—	—	—	—	—	—	—	16	10	Brown, James B.
1964		NAIA		16	—	—	—	—	—	—	—	18	7	McLendon, John B., Jr.
1970		NAIA		1	—	—	—	—	—	—	—	29	3	Mitchell, Lucias
1971		NAIA		1	—	—	—	—	—	—	—	31	2	Mitchell, Lucias
1972		NAIA		1	—	—	—	—	—	—	—	28	5	Mitchell, Lucias
1973		NAIA		32	—	—	—	—	—	—	—	25	5	Mitchell, Lucias
1974		NAIA		3	—	—	—	—	—	—	—	28	5	Mitchell, Lucias
1975		NAIA		32	—	—	—	—	—	—	—	26	3	Mitchell, Lucias
1977		NAIA		32	—	—	—	—	—	—	—	27	3	Oliver, James V.
1979		NAIA		32	—	—	—	—	—	—	—	18	11	Theard, Floyd M.
1981	W	NAIA		1	—	—	—	—	—	—	—	21	7	Mitchell, Ron
1997		NCAA	II	32	—	—	—	—	—	—	—	25	6	Davis, Antonio

KENTUCKY WESLEYAN

Year	M/W	Assn	Div	NAT	NIT	ARC	CCA	NCI	NCT	OLY	HLM	W	L	Coach
1957	M	NCAA	II	2	—	—	—	—	—	—	—	16	12	Wilson, Robert R. "Bullet"
1960		NCAA	II	3	—	—	—	—	—	—	—	18	11	Plain, T. L.
1961		NCAA	II	24	—	—	—	—	—	—	—	15	8	Plain, T. L.
1964		NCAA	II	24	—	—	—	—	—	—	—	15	8	Plain, T. L.
1966		NCAA	II	1	—	—	—	—	—	—	—	24	6	Strong, Guy Rowland
1967		NCAA	II	3	—	—	—	—	—	—	—	25	4	Strong, Guy Rowland
1968		NCAA	II	1	—	—	—	—	—	—	—	28	3	Daniels, Bob
1969		NCAA	II	1	—	—	—	—	—	—	—	25	5	Daniels, Bob

Year	M/W	Assn	Div	NAT	NIT	ARC	CCA	NCI	NCT	OLY	HLM	W	L	Coach
1970		NCAA	II	16	—	—	—	—	—	—	—	18	10	Daniels, Bob
1971		NCAA	II	4	—	—	—	—	—	—	—	22	8	Daniels, Bob
1972		NCAA	II	24	—	—	—	—	—	—	—	17	10	Daniels, Bob
1973		NCAA	II	1	—	—	—	—	—	—	—	24	6	Jones, Bob
1974		NCAA	II	16	—	—	—	—	—	—	—	20	6	Jones, Bob
1982		NCAA	II	3	—	—	—	—	—	—	—	27	5	Pollio, Mike
1983		NCAA	II	16	—	—	—	—	—	—	—	22	8	Pollio, Mike
1984		NCAA	II	3	—	—	—	—	—	—	—	28	3	Pollio, Mike
1985		NCAA	II	3	—	—	—	—	—	—	—	24	7	Pollio, Mike
1986		NCAA	II	24	—	—	—	—	—	—	—	22	8	Chapman, Wayne G.
1987		NCAA	II	1	—	—	—	—	—	—	—	28	5	Chapman, Wayne G.
1988		NCAA	II	16	—	—	—	—	—	—	—	23	7	Chapman, Wayne G.
1989		NCAA	II	8	—	—	—	—	—	—	—	24	7	Chapman, Wayne G.
1990		NCAA	II	1	—	—	—	—	—	—	—	31	2	Chapman, Wayne G.
1991		NCAA	II	24	—	—	—	—	—	—	—	22	8	Chapman, Wayne G.
1992		NCAA	II	8	—	—	—	—	—	—	—	23	8	Boultinghouse, Wayne
1994		NCAA	II	24	—	—	—	—	—	—	—	23	7	Boultinghouse, Wayne
1995		NCAA	II	32	—	—	—	—	—	—	—	23	6	Boultinghouse, Wayne
1998		NCAA	II	2	—	—	—	—	—	—	—	30	3	Harper, Ray

KENYON

Year	M/W	Assn	Div	NAT	NIT	ARC	CCA	NCI	NCT	OLY	HLM	W	L	Coach
1994	M	NCAA	III	32	—	—	—	—	—	—	—	24	4	Brown, William H.
1995		NCAA	III	16	—	—	—	—	—	—	—	20	9	Brown, William H.
1997	W	NCAA	III	64	—	—	—	—	—	—	—	26	2	Halfant, Suzanne

KING (TN)

Year	M/W	Assn	Div	NAT	NIT	ARC	CCA	NCI	NCT	OLY	HLM	W	L	Coach
1992	M	NAIA	II	16	—	—	—	—	—	—	—	28	3	Street, Marty
1998		NAIA	II	32	—	—	—	—	—	—	—	20	14	Polsgrove, Scott
1988	W	NCCAA	I	1	—	—	—	—	—	—	—	27	3	Nida, Al
1989		NCCAA	I	1	—	—	—	—	—	—	—	28	2	Nida, Al
1990		NCCAA	I	1	—	—	—	—	—	—	—	27	3	Nida, Al
1991		NCCAA	I	3	—	—	—	—	—	—	—	27	3	Nida, Al
1993		NAIA	II	16	—	—	—	—	—	—	—	23	4	Nida, Al

KING'S (NY)

Year	M/W	Assn	Div	NAT	NIT	ARC	CCA	NCI	NCT	OLY	HLM	W	L	Coach
1975	M	NCCAA		3	—	—	—	—	—	—	—	25	15	Wilhelmi, Norman
1988		NCCAA	I	8	—	—	—	—	—	—	—	19	15	Harris, William R.
1990		NAIA		32	—	—	—	—	—	—	—	27	6	Harris, William R.
1991		NCCAA	I	8	—	—	—	—	—	—	—	26	8	Harris, William R.
1992		NAIA	II	20	—	—	—	—	—	—	—	20	13	Showers, Ken

KING'S (PA)

Year	M/W	Assn	Div	NAT	NIT	ARC	CCA	NCI	NCT	OLY	HLM	W	L	Coach
1974	M	NCAA	II	24	—	—	—	—	—	—	—	20	7	Donohue, Ed
1990		NCAA	III	32	—	—	—	—	—	—	—	17	11	Atkins, Ken
1991		NCAA	III	32	—	—	—	—	—	—	—	21	7	Atkins, Ken
1992		NCAA	III	32	—	—	—	—	—	—	—	20	8	Atkins, Ken

KITTRELL JC

Year	M/W	Assn	Div	NAT	NIT	ARC	CCA	NCI	NCT	OLY	HLM	W	L	Coach
1970	M	NSCAA		1	—	—	—	—	—	—	—	32	4	Golatt, Moses

Year	M/W	Assn	Div	NAT	NIT	ARC	CCA	NCI	NCT	OLY	HLM	W	L	Coach
KNOX														
1958	M	NCAA	II	16	—	—	—	—	—	—	—	17	7	Adams, Frank E.
1959		NCAA	II	16	—	—	—	—	—	—	—	20	3	Adams, Frank E.
1975		NCAA	III	30	—	—	—	—	—	—	—	16	7	Knosher, Harlan D.
KNOXVILLE														
1977	M	NCAA	III	23	—	—	—	—	—	—	—	14	11	Arwood, Vic
1978		NCAA	III	8	—	—	—	—	—	—	—	16	10	Simmons, Dwayne
1981	W	AIAW	III	8	—	—	—	—	—	—	—	23	10	Robinson, Edward
1982		AIAW	III	8	—	—	—	—	—	—	—	26	5	Robinson, Edward
1983		NCAA	III	3	—	—	—	—	—	—	—	21	2	Robinson, Edward
1984		NCAA	III	16	—	—	—	—	—	—	—	18	7	Robinson, Edward
KUTZTOWN														
1988	M	NCAA	II	32	—	—	—	—	—	—	—	21	10	Binder, Rick
1996	W	NCAA	II	48	—	—	—	—	—	—	—	20	8	Malouf, Janet
LA ROCHE														
1976	M	NSCAA		14	—	—	—	—	—	—	—	14	6	Pasquinelli, John
1977		NSCAA		16	—	—	—	—	—	—	—	11	10	Pasquinelli, John
LA SALLE														
1948	M	NCAA		—	8	—	—	—	—	—	—	20	4	McGlone, Charles
1950		NCAA		—	8	—	—	—	—	—	—	21	4	Loeffler, Kenneth D.
1951		NCAA		—	12	—	—	—	—	—	—	22	7	Loeffler, Kenneth D.
1952		NCAA		—	1	—	—	4	—	—	—	25	7	Loeffler, Kenneth D.
1953		NCAA		—	8	—	—	—	—	—	—	25	3	Loeffler, Kenneth D.
1954		NCAA		1	—	—	—	—	—	—	—	26	4	Loeffler, Kenneth D.
1955		NCAA		2	—	—	—	—	—	—	—	26	5	Loeffler, Kenneth D.
1963		NCAA	I	—	12	—	—	—	—	—	—	16	8	Moore, Donald W. "Dudey"
1965		NCAA	I	—	14	—	—	—	—	—	—	15	8	Walters, Robert W.
1968		NCAA	I	23	—	—	—	—	—	—	—	20	8	Harding, James F.
1971		NCAA	I	—	16	—	—	—	—	—	—	20	7	Westhead, Paul W.
1975		NCAA	I	32	—	—	—	—	—	—	—	22	7	Westhead, Paul W.
1978		NCAA	I	32	—	—	—	—	—	—	—	18	12	Westhead, Paul W.
1980		NCAA	I	48	—	—	—	—	—	—	—	22	9	Ervin, David "Lefty"
1983		NCAA	I	48	—	—	—	—	—	—	—	18	14	Ervin, David "Lefty"
1984		NCAA	I	—	32	—	—	—	—	—	—	20	11	Ervin, David "Lefty"
1987		NCAA	I	—	2	—	—	—	—	—	—	20	13	Morris, William T. "Speedy"
1988		NCAA	I	64	—	—	—	—	—	—	—	24	10	Morris, William T. "Speedy"
1989		NCAA	I	64	—	—	—	—	—	—	—	26	6	Morris, William T. "Speedy"
1990		NCAA	I	32	—	—	—	—	—	—	—	30	2	Morris, William T. "Speedy"
1991		NCAA	I	—	32	—	—	—	—	—	—	19	10	Morris, William T. "Speedy"
1992		NCAA	I	64	—	—	—	—	—	—	—	20	11	Morris, William T. "Speedy"
1983	W	NCAA	I	36	—	—	—	—	—	—	—	16	13	Gallagher, Kevin
1986		NCAA	I	40	—	—	—	—	—	—	—	21	9	Morris, William T. "Speedy"
1988		NCAA	I	40	—	—	—	—	—	—	—	25	5	Miller, John
1989		NCAA	I	32	—	—	—	—	—	—	—	28	3	Miller, John
1992		NCAA	I	—	8	—	—	—	—	—	—	25	8	Miller, John

Year	M/W	Assn	Div	NAT	NIT	ARC	CCA	NCI	NCT	OLY	HLM	W	L	Coach

LA VERNE

| 1993 | M | NCAA | III | 16 | — | — | — | — | — | — | — | 20 | 8 | Stewart, Gary |
| 1996 | W | NCAA | III | 64 | — | — | — | — | — | — | — | 15 | 11 | Kline, Julie |

LAFAYETTE (NC)

| 1976 | M | NSCAA | | 14 | — | — | — | — | — | — | — | 18 | 8 | |

LAFAYETTE (PA)

1955	M	NCAA		—	12	—	—	—	—	—	—	24	3	Van Breda Kolff, Willem "Butch"
1956		NCAA		—	12	—	—	—	—	—	—	20	7	Davidson, George E.
1957		NCAA	I	16	—	—	—	—	—	—	—	22	5	Davidson, George E.
1972		NCAA	I	—	8	—	—	—	—	—	—	21	6	Davis, Dr. Thomas
1975		NCAA	I	—	16	—	—	—	—	—	—	22	6	Davis, Dr. Thomas
1980		NCAA	I	—	32	—	—	—	—	—	—	21	8	Chipman, Dr. Leroy

LAKE FOREST

| 1994 | W | NCAA | III | 40 | — | — | — | — | — | — | — | 19 | 6 | Slaats, Jackie |

LAKE SUPERIOR STATE

1976	M	NAIA		8	—	—	—	—	—	—	—	24	4	Douma, Edward
1978		NAIA		32	—	—	—	—	—	—	—	23	4	Douma, Edward
1996		NCAA	II	48	—	—	—	—	—	—	—	19	9	Smith, Terry
1986	W	NCAA	II	16	—	—	—	—	—	—	—	23	5	Taylor, Bob
1988		NCAA	II	16	—	—	—	—	—	—	—	24	5	Geary, Mike
1994		NCAA	II	16	—	—	—	—	—	—	—	23	7	Ledy, Erica
1996		NCAA	II	32	—	—	—	—	—	—	—	23	8	Ledy, Erica

LAKELAND (WI)

| 1966 | M | NAIA | | 16 | — | — | — | — | — | — | — | 21 | 8 | Woltzen, Duane A. |
| 1994 | | NAIA | II | 24 | — | — | — | — | — | — | — | 25 | 11 | Jonas, Craig |

LAMAR

1960	M	NCAA	II	24	—	—	—	—	—	—	—	18	9	Martin, Jack T.
1962		NCAA	II	24	—	—	—	—	—	—	—	20	8	Martin, Jack T.
1963		NCAA	II	16	—	—	—	—	—	—	—	22	5	Martin, Jack T.
1964		NCAA	II	24	—	—	—	—	—	—	—	19	6	Martin, Jack T.
1966		NCAA	II	22	—	—	—	—	—	—	—	17	9	Martin, Jack T.
1979		NCAA	I	32	—	—	—	—	—	—	—	23	9	Tubbs, Billy
1980		NCAA	I	16	—	—	—	—	—	—	—	22	11	Tubbs, Billy
1981		NCAA	I	32	—	—	—	—	—	—	—	25	5	Foster, Pat
1982		NCAA	I	—	32	—	—	—	—	—	—	22	7	Foster, Pat
1983		NCAA	I	32	—	—	—	—	—	—	—	23	8	Foster, Pat
1984		NCAA	I	—	16	—	—	—	—	—	—	26	5	Foster, Pat
1985		NCAA	I	—	16	—	—	—	—	—	—	20	12	Foster, Pat
1986		NCAA	I	—	32	—	—	—	—	—	—	18	12	Foster, Pat
1991	W	NCAA	I	8	—	—	—	—	—	—	—	29	4	Barbre, Al

LAMAR CC

1982	M	NSCAA		8	—	—	—	—	—	—	—	X	X	Carel, Steve
1983		NSCAA		4	—	—	—	—	—	—	—	16	26	Carel, Steve
1986		NSCAA		16	—	—	—	—	—	—	—	20	13	Blanc, Al

Year	M/W	Assn	Div	NAT	NIT	ARC	CCA	NCI	NCT	OLY	HLM	W	L	Coach
1983	W	NSCAA		2	—	—	—	—	—	—	—	X	X	Unknown
1984		NSCAA		1	—	—	—	—	—	—	—	X	X	Unknown

LANCASTER BIBLE

Year	M/W	Assn	Div	NAT	NIT	ARC	CCA	NCI	NCT	OLY	HLM	W	L	Coach
1987	W	NCCAA	II	5	—	—	—	—	—	—	—	26	10	Figart, Dr. Tom

LANDER

Year	M/W	Assn	Div	NAT	NIT	ARC	CCA	NCI	NCT	OLY	HLM	W	L	Coach
1995	M	NCAA	II	48	—	—	—	—	—	—	—	21	9	Horne, Finis

LANDMARK BAPTIST (FL)

Year	M/W	Assn	Div	NAT	NIT	ARC	CCA	NCI	NCT	OLY	HLM	W	L	Coach
1983	M	NBCAA		6	—	—	—	—	—	—	—	X	X	Quinlan, Keith

LANE (TN)

Year	M/W	Assn	Div	NAT	NIT	ARC	CCA	NCI	NCT	OLY	HLM	W	L	Coach
1979	M	NCAA	III	32	—	—	—	—	—	—	—	18	11	Shaw, Dr. Willie G. "Hawk"
1980		NCAA	III	8	—	—	—	—	—	—	—	19	9	Shaw, Dr. Willie G. "Hawk"

LANGSTON

Year	M/W	Assn	Div	NAT	NIT	ARC	CCA	NCI	NCT	OLY	HLM	W	L	Coach
1980	W	AIAW	II	16	—	—	—	—	—	—	—	26	11	Colon, Robert

LATIN AMERICAN BIBLE (CA)

Year	M/W	Assn	Div	NAT	NIT	ARC	CCA	NCI	NCT	OLY	HLM	W	L	Coach
1992	M	NBCAA	II	1	—	—	—	—	—	—	—	30	2	Elisaldez, Ken
1992		NCCAA	IIA	1	—	—	—	—	—	—	—	30	2	Elisaldez, Ken

LATTER-DAY SAINTS BUSINESS

Year	M/W	Assn	Div	NAT	NIT	ARC	CCA	NCI	NCT	OLY	HLM	W	L	Coach
1904	M			—	—	—	—	—	—	3	—	6	2	Bean, Willard

LAWRENCE

Year	M/W	Assn	Div	NAT	NIT	ARC	CCA	NCI	NCT	OLY	HLM	W	L	Coach
1997	M	NCAA	III	64	—	—	—	—	—	—	—	22	3	Tharp, John

LAWRENCE TECH

Year	M/W	Assn	Div	NAT	NIT	ARC	CCA	NCI	NCT	OLY	HLM	W	L	Coach
1943	M	NAIA		32	—	—	—	—	—	—	—	18	13	Ridler, Don
1947		NAIA		32	—	—	—	—	—	—	—	26	4	Ridler, Don
1948		NAIA		16	—	—	—	—	—	—	—	22	6	Ridler, Don
1949		NAIA		32	—	—	—	—	—	—	—	16	10	Ridler, Don
1951		NAIA		—	12	—	—	—	—	—	—	20	3	Ridler, Don
1952		NAIA		8	—	—	—	—	—	—	—	23	2	Ridler, Don
1954		NAIA		16	—	—	—	—	—	—	—	24	5	Maconochie, Walter "Scotty"

LE MOYNE

Year	M/W	Assn	Div	NAT	NIT	ARC	CCA	NCI	NCT	OLY	HLM	W	L	Coach
1959	M	NCAA	II	16	—	—	—	—	—	—	—	18	6	Niland, Thomas J., Jr.
1960		NCAA	II	32	—	—	—	—	—	—	—	13	5	Niland, Thomas J., Jr.
1964		NCAA	II	16	—	—	—	—	—	—	—	18	6	Niland, Thomas J., Jr.
1965		NCAA	II	32	—	—	—	—	—	—	—	18	5	Niland, Thomas J., Jr.
1966		NCAA	II	34	—	—	—	—	—	—	—	16	6	Niland, Thomas J., Jr.
1968		NCAA	II	36	—	—	—	—	—	—	—	14	8	Niland, Thomas J., Jr.
1969		NCAA	II	32	—	—	—	—	—	—	—	15	8	Niland, Thomas J., Jr.
1988		NCAA	II	24	—	—	—	—	—	—	—	24	6	Beilein, John
1996		NCAA	II	48	—	—	—	—	—	—	—	24	6	Hicks, Scott
1997		NCAA	II	48	—	—	—	—	—	—	—	13	17	Hicks, Scott

Year	M/W	Assn	Div	NAT	NIT	ARC	CCA	NCI	NCT	OLY	HLM	W	L	Coach
LEBANON VALLEY														
1953	M	NCAA		16	—	—	—	—	—	—	—	—	19	3	Marquette, George R. 'Rinso'
1973		NCAA	II	42	—	—	—	—	—	—	—	—	24	3	Sorrentino, Louis A.
1993		NCAA	III	32	—	—	—	—	—	—	—	—	18	11	Flannery, Patrick J.
1994		NCAA	III	1	—	—	—	—	—	—	—	—	28	4	Flannery, Patrick J.
1995		NCAA	III	64	—	—	—	—	—	—	—	—	22	6	McAlester, Brad
1997		NCAA	III	64	—	—	—	—	—	—	—	—	17	11	McAlester, Brad
LEE (TN)														
1968	M	NCCAA		1	—	—	—	—	—	—	—	—	30	4	Hughes, Dale R.
1969		NCCAA		3	—	—	—	—	—	—	—	—	24	9	Hughes, Dale R.
1970		NCCAA		3	—	—	—	—	—	—	—	—	23	6	Hughes, Dale R.
1973		NCCAA		1	—	—	—	—	—	—	—	—	31	6	Hughes, Dale R.
1978		NCCAA	I	3	—	—	—	—	—	—	—	—	20	14	Rowan, Earl
1979		NCCAA	I	2	—	—	—	—	—	—	—	—	17	13	Rowan, Earl
1980		NCCAA	I	3	—	—	—	—	—	—	—	—	16	15	Rowan, Earl
1981		NCCAA	I	3	—	—	—	—	—	—	—	—	22	11	Rowan, Earl
1986		NCCAA	I	8	—	—	—	—	—	—	—	—	19	20	Steele, Randy
1987		NCCAA	I	8	—	—	—	—	—	—	—	—	23	7	Steele, Randy
1988		NCCAA	I	4	—	—	—	—	—	—	—	—	24	11	Steele, Randy
1989		NCCAA	I	8	—	—	—	—	—	—	—	—	25	9	Steele, Randy
1991		NCCAA	I	6	—	—	—	—	—	—	—	—	19	13	Steele, Randy
1992		NCCAA	I	3	—	—	—	—	—	—	—	—	24	14	Steele, Randy
1993		NCCAA	I	2	—	—	—	—	—	—	—	—	24	14	Carpenter, Dr. Larry
1994		NCCAA	I	1	—	—	—	—	—	—	—	—	24	14	Carpenter, Dr. Larry
1995		NCCAA	I	4	—	—	—	—	—	—	—	—	26	12	Carpenter, Dr. Larry
1997		NCCAA	I	3	—	—	—	—	—	—	—	—	15	23	Carpenter, Dr. Larry
1980	W	AIAW	III	8	—	—	—	—	—	—	—	—	23	8	Walston, Ken
1983		NCCAA	I	3	—	—	—	—	—	—	—	—	16	15	Unknown
1984		NCCAA	I	3	—	—	—	—	—	—	—	—	20	12	Souther, Orin A. 'Jack'
1985		NCCAA	I	1	—	—	—	—	—	—	—	—	15	13	Souther, Orin A. 'Jack'
1986		NCCAA	I	3	—	—	—	—	—	—	—	—	21	14	Souther, Orin A. 'Jack'
1987		NCCAA	I	2	—	—	—	—	—	—	—	—	20	17	Souther, Orin A. 'Jack'
1989		NCCAA	I	3	—	—	—	—	—	—	—	—	30	8	Souther, Orin A. 'Jack'
1990		NCCAA	I	2	—	—	—	—	—	—	—	—	28	7	Souther, Orin A. 'Jack'
1991		NCCAA	I	4	—	—	—	—	—	—	—	—	19	14	Souther, Orin A. 'Jack'
1992		NCCAA	I	3	—	—	—	—	—	—	—	—	18	20	Souther, Orin A. 'Jack'
1993		NCCAA	I	3	—	—	—	—	—	—	—	—	19	17	Souther, Orin A. 'Jack'
1994		NCCAA	I	6	—	—	—	—	—	—	—	—	15	21	Baldwin, Gary
1996		NCCAA	I	2	—	—	—	—	—	—	—	—	22	14	Baldwin, Gary
1997		NCCAA	I	4	—	—	—	—	—	—	—	—	13	24	Baldwin, Gary
1998		NCCAA	I	5	—	—	—	—	—	—	—	—	16	21	Baldwin, Gary
LEES (KY)														
1983	M	NSCAA		8	—	—	—	—	—	—	—	—	26	8	Howard, Cluster
LEES-MCRAE														
1994	W	NAIA	I	32	—	—	—	—	—	—	—	—	19	10	Dixon, Janet

Year	M/W	Assn	Div	NAT	NIT	ARC	CCA	NCI	NCT	OLY	HLM	W	L	Coach
LEHIGH														
1985	M	NCAA	I	64	—	—	—	—	—	—	—	12	19	Schneider, Thomas
1988		NCAA	I	64	—	—	—	—	—	—	—	21	10	McCaffrey, Fran
1997	W	NCAA	I	64	—	—	—	—	—	—	—	15	15	Troyan, Susan
LEHMAN														
1973	W	AIAW		16	—	—	—	—	—	—	—	X	X	McBride, Ethel
LEMOYNE-OWEN														
1975	M	NCAA	III	1	—	—	—	—	—	—	—	27	5	Johnson, Jerry C.
1976		NCAA	III	21	—	—	—	—	—	—	—	18	9	Johnson, Jerry C.
1978		NAIA		32	—	—	—	—	—	—	—	20	10	Johnson, Jerry C.
1979		NAIA		32	—	—	—	—	—	—	—	22	12	Johnson, Jerry C.
1980		NAIA		8	—	—	—	—	—	—	—	26	8	Johnson, Jerry C.
1983		NCAA	III	8	—	—	—	—	—	—	—	24	6	Johnson, Jerry C.
1984		NCAA	III	8	—	—	—	—	—	—	—	24	5	Johnson, Jerry C.
1985		NCAA	III	16	—	—	—	—	—	—	—	22	7	Johnson, Jerry C.
1986		NCAA	III	2	—	—	—	—	—	—	—	29	3	Johnson, Jerry C.
1985	W	NCAA	III	24	—	—	—	—	—	—	—	16	10	Skinner, Lula Marie
LENOIR-RHYNE														
1958	M	NAIA		32	—	—	—	—	—	—	—	24	4	Wells, Bill
1959		NAIA		8	—	—	—	—	—	—	—	24	6	Wells, Bill
1993		NAIA	I	8	—	—	—	—	—	—	—	25	7	Lentz, John
1995		NCAA	II	48	—	—	—	—	—	—	—	18	11	Lentz, John
1980	W	AIAW	II	8	—	—	—	—	—	—	—	28	4	Smith, Pat
1981		AIAW	II	4	—	—	—	—	—	—	—	27	8	Smith, Pat
LETOURNEAU														
1971	M	NCCAA		8	—	—	—	—	—	—	—	18	10	Fratzke, Mel R.
1981		NCCAA	I	6	—	—	—	—	—	—	—	17	20	Fratzke, Dr. Michael L.
1982		NCCAA	I	4	—	—	—	—	—	—	—	16	19	Bassett, Sheldon
1984		NCCAA	I	8	—	—	—	—	—	—	—	15	12	Bassett, Sheldon
1996	W	NAIA	I	32	—	—	—	—	—	—	—	19	10	Otwell, Mary Ann
1997		NAIA	I	32	—	—	—	—	—	—	—	30	4	Otwell, Mary Ann
1997		NCCAA	I	1	—	—	—	—	—	—	—	30	4	Otwell, Mary Ann
1998		NAIA	I	32	—	—	—	—	—	—	—	24	10	Otwell, Mary Ann
1998		NCCAA	I	1	—	—	—	—	—	—	—	24	10	Otwell, Mary Ann
LEWIS & CLARK (OR)														
1962	M	NAIA		16	—	—	—	—	—	—	—	20	11	Goddard, Jim
1963		NAIA		8	—	—	—	—	—	—	—	23	6	Goddard, Jim
1964		NAIA		32	—	—	—	—	—	—	—	20	8	Sempert, Dean
1971		NAIA		32	—	—	—	—	—	—	—	19	10	Sempert, Dean
1994		NAIA	II	3	—	—	—	—	—	—	—	23	9	Gaillard, Dr. Bob
1995		NAIA	II	16	—	—	—	—	—	—	—	17	14	Gaillard, Dr. Bob
1996		NAIA	II	16	—	—	—	—	—	—	—	17	10	Gaillard, Dr. Bob
1997		NAIA	II	16	—	—	—	—	—	—	—	22	6	Gaillard, Dr. Bob
1998		NAIA	II	8	—	—	—	—	—	—	—	22	7	Gaillard, Dr. Bob
1994	W	NAIA	II	8	—	—	—	—	—	—	—	26	5	Petrie, Paula

Year	M/W	Assn	Div	NAT	NIT	ARC	CCA	NCI	NCT	OLY	HLM	W	L	Coach

LEWIS (IL)

Year	M/W	Assn	Div	NAT	NIT	ARC	CCA	NCI	NCT	OLY	HLM	W	L	Coach
1965	M	NAIA		16	—	—	—	—	—	—	—	21	6	Gillespie, Gordon A.
1982		NCAA	II	24	—	—	—	—	—	—	—	20	9	Schwarz, "Chuck"
1983		NCAA	II	24	—	—	—	—	—	—	—	20	10	Schwarz, "Chuck"
1984		NCAA	II	16	—	—	—	—	—	—	—	22	8	Schwarz, "Chuck"
1985		NCAA	II	32	—	—	—	—	—	—	—	22	8	Schwarz, "Chuck"
1986		NCAA	II	32	—	—	—	—	—	—	—	24	6	Schwarz, "Chuck"
1988		NCAA	II	24	—	—	—	—	—	—	—	22	8	Davis, Al
1998		NCAA	II	48	—	—	—	—	—	—	—	19	9	Whitesell, Jim
1984	W	NCAA	II	24	—	—	—	—	—	—	—	21	8	Kissinger, Kathy
1985		NCAA	II	24	—	—	—	—	—	—	—	22	7	Kissinger, Kathy
1998		NCAA	II	48	—	—	—	—	—	—	—	23	5	Michalak, Brian

LEWIS-CLARK STATE (ID)

Year	M/W	Assn	Div	NAT	NIT	ARC	CCA	NCI	NCT	OLY	HLM	W	L	Coach
1992	M	NAIA	I	32	—	—	—	—	—	—	—	24	11	Pfeifer, George
1996		NAIA	I	32	—	—	—	—	—	—	—	19	9	Pfeifer, George
1996	W	NAIA	I	32	—	—	—	—	—	—	—	25	7	Divilbiss, Mike
1997		NAIA	I	16	—	—	—	—	—	—	—	25	7	Divilbiss, Mike
1998		NAIA	I	8	—	—	—	—	—	—	—	22	8	Divilbiss, Mike

LIBERTY

Year	M/W	Assn	Div	NAT	NIT	ARC	CCA	NCI	NCT	OLY	HLM	W	L	Coach
1980	M	NCCAA	I	1	—	—	—	—	—	—	—	28	11	Gibson, Dale
1983		NAIA		8	—	—	—	—	—	—	—	23	9	Meyer, Jeff
1994		NCAA	I	64	—	—	—	—	—	—	—	18	12	Meyer, Jeff
1997	W	NCAA	I	64	—	—	—	—	—	—	—	22	8	Reeves, Rick
1998		NCAA	I	64	—	—	—	—	—	—	—	28	1	Reeves, Rick

LIFE (GA)

Year	M/W	Assn	Div	NAT	NIT	ARC	CCA	NCI	NCT	OLY	HLM	W	L	Coach
1993	M	NAIA	I	16	—	—	—	—	—	—	—	30	5	Kaiser, Roger A.
1994		NAIA	I	2	—	—	—	—	—	—	—	27	10	Kaiser, Roger A.
1995		NAIA	I	32	—	—	—	—	—	—	—	31	3	Kaiser, Roger A.
1996		NAIA	I	16	—	—	—	—	—	—	—	31	6	Kaiser, Roger A.
1997		NAIA	I	1	—	—	—	—	—	—	—	37	1	Kaiser, Roger A.
1998		NAIA	I	16	—	—	—	—	—	—	—	32	4	Kaiser, Roger A.

LIFE BIBLE (CA)

Year	M/W	Assn	Div	NAT	NIT	ARC	CCA	NCI	NCT	OLY	HLM	W	L	Coach
1988	M	NBCAA	I	1	—	—	—	—	—	—	—	19	6	Updike, Blake
1992		NBCAA	I	6	—	—	—	—	—	—	—	18	12	Updike, Mike
1996		NBCAA	I	7	—	—	—	—	—	—	—	11	23	Meyer, Rick

LINCOLN (MO)

Year	M/W	Assn	Div	NAT	NIT	ARC	CCA	NCI	NCT	OLY	HLM	W	L	Coach
1953	M	NASC		8	—	—	—	—	—	—	—	X	X	Unknown
1959		NCAA	II	24	—	—	—	—	—	—	—	14	9	Frank, James
1960		NCAA	II	16	—	—	—	—	—	—	—	14	9	Frank, James
1961		NCAA	II	16	—	—	—	—	—	—	—	20	8	Frank, James
1965		NAIA		32	—	—	—	—	—	—	—	13	12	Staggers, Jonathan L.
1967		NCAA	II	16	—	—	—	—	—	—	—	24	3	Staggers, Jonathan L.
1968		NCAA	II	23	—	—	—	—	—	—	—	20	3	Staggers, Jonathan L.
1969		NCAA	II	24	—	—	—	—	—	—	—	19	7	Staggers, Jonathan L.

Year	M/W	Assn	Div	NAT	NIT	ARC	CCA	NCI	NCT	OLY	HLM	W	L	Coach
1972		NCAA	II	16	—	—	—	—	—	—	—	22	6	Corbett, Donald
1975		NCAA	II	16	—	—	—	—	—	—	—	19	9	Corbett, Donald
1976		NCAA	II	24	—	—	—	—	—	—	—	20	8	Corbett, Donald
1977		NCAA	II	24	—	—	—	—	—	—	—	22	6	Corbett, Donald
1978		NCAA	II	8	—	—	—	—	—	—	—	22	6	Corbett, Donald
1981		NCAA	II	32	—	—	—	—	—	—	—	22	8	Coleman, Ronald E.

LINCOLN (PA)

Year	M/W	Assn	Div	NAT	NIT	ARC	CCA	NCI	NCT	OLY	HLM	W	L	Coach
1983	M	NAIA		32	—	—	—	—	—	—	—	11	16	Jones, Melvin L.

LINCOLN CHRISTIAN

Year	M/W	Assn	Div	NAT	NIT	ARC	CCA	NCI	NCT	OLY	HLM	W	L	Coach
1985	W	NCCAA	II	7	—	—	—	—	—	—	—	5	11	Morris, Larry

LINCOLN MEMORIAL

Year	M/W	Assn	Div	NAT	NIT	ARC	CCA	NCI	NCT	OLY	HLM	W	L	Coach
1976	M	NAIA		4	—	—	—	—	—	—	—	28	9	Jackson, Wilford "Jack"
1977		NAIA		32	—	—	—	—	—	—	—	30	5	Jackson, Wilford "Jack"
1981		NAIA		16	—	—	—	—	—	—	—	24	8	Kilby, L. J.

LINDENWOOD

Year	M/W	Assn	Div	NAT	NIT	ARC	CCA	NCI	NCT	OLY	HLM	W	L	Coach
1994	W	NAIA	I	32	—	—	—	—	—	—	—	24	7	Crotz, Stephen
1995		NAIA	I	32	—	—	—	—	—	—	—	21	12	Crotz, Stephen
1996		NAIA	I	32	—	—	—	—	—	—	—	21	11	Crotz, Stephen

LINDSEY WILSON

Year	M/W	Assn	Div	NAT	NIT	ARC	CCA	NCI	NCT	OLY	HLM	W	L	Coach
1972	M	NSCAA		1	—	—	—	—	—	—	—	22	8	Voight, James R. "Jim"
1988		NSCAA		5	—	—	—	—	—	—	—	20	14	Wise, Mark
1997		NAIA	I	32	—	—	—	—	—	—	—	23	13	Dodd, Steve
1998		NAIA	I	32	—	—	—	—	—	—	—	23	12	Dodd, Steve
1988	W	NSCAA		7	—	—	—	—	—	—	—	17	10	Adams, Dean

LINFIELD

Year	M/W	Assn	Div	NAT	NIT	ARC	CCA	NCI	NCT	OLY	HLM	W	L	Coach
1947	M	NAIA		32	—	—	—	—	—	—	—	20	8	Lever, Henry W.
1957		NCAA	II	16	—	—	—	—	—	—	—	17	11	Helser, Roy
1958		NCAA	II	32	—	—	—	—	—	—	—	18	9	Helser, Roy
1959		NAIA		32	—	—	—	—	—	—	—	18	11	Helser, Roy
1961		NAIA		32	—	—	—	—	—	—	—	18	11	Helser, Roy
1965		NAIA		32	—	—	—	—	—	—	—	21	7	Wilson, Ted
1966		NAIA		32	—	—	—	—	—	—	—	23	6	Wilson, Ted
1967		NAIA		32	—	—	—	—	—	—	—	20	10	Wilson, Ted
1969		NAIA		32	—	—	—	—	—	—	—	24	4	Wilson, Ted
1970		NAIA		32	—	—	—	—	—	—	—	23	7	Wilson, Ted
1976		NAIA		32	—	—	—	—	—	—	—	20	9	Wilson, Ted
1980	W	AIAW	III	24	—	—	—	—	—	—	—	17	9	Vealey, Robin

LIPSCOMB

Year	M/W	Assn	Div	NAT	NIT	ARC	CCA	NCI	NCT	OLY	HLM	W	L	Coach
1982	M	NAIA		32	—	—	—	—	—	—	—	33	4	Meyer, Dr. Don W.
1985		NAIA		16	—	—	—	—	—	—	—	25	9	Meyer, Dr. Don W.
1986		NAIA		1	—	—	—	—	—	—	—	35	4	Meyer, Dr. Don W.
1988		NAIA		16	—	—	—	—	—	—	—	33	3	Meyer, Dr. Don W.
1990		NAIA		3	—	—	—	—	—	—	—	41	5	Meyer, Dr. Don W.
1991		NAIA		8	—	—	—	—	—	—	—	35	4	Meyer, Dr. Don W.
1992		NAIA	I	16	—	—	—	—	—	—	—	31	5	Meyer, Dr. Don W.
1993		NAIA	I	8	—	—	—	—	—	—	—	34	4	Meyer, Dr. Don W.

Year	M/W	Assn	Div	NAT	NIT	ARC	CCA	NCI	NCT	OLY	HLM	W	L	Coach
1994		NAIA	I	32	—	—	—	—	—	—	—	29	6	Meyer, Dr. Don W.
1995		NAIA	I	16	—	—	—	—	—	—	—	30	7	Meyer, Dr. Don W.
1996		NAIA	I	3	—	—	—	—	—	—	—	33	6	Meyer, Dr. Don W.
1997		NAIA	I	32	—	—	—	—	—	—	—	30	6	Meyer, Dr. Don W.
1990	W	NAIA		16	—	—	—	—	—	—	—	30	8	Bennett, Frank
1993		NAIA	I	8	—	—	—	—	—	—	—	28	6	Bennett, Frank
1994		NAIA	I	2	—	—	—	—	—	—	—	31	7	Bennett, Frank
1995		NAIA	I	3	—	—	—	—	—	—	—	34	5	Bennett, Frank
1996		NAIA	I	3	—	—	—	—	—	—	—	31	6	Bennett, Frank
1997		NAIA	I	16	—	—	—	—	—	—	—	26	10	Bennett, Frank
1998		NAIA	I	32	—	—	—	—	—	—	—	23	12	Bennett, Frank

LOCK HAVEN

Year	M/W	Assn	Div	NAT	NIT	ARC	CCA	NCI	NCT	OLY	HLM	W	L	Coach
1987	M	NCAA	II	24	—	—	—	—	—	—	—	22	9	Kanaskie, Kurt
1989		NCAA	II	24	—	—	—	—	—	—	—	23	7	Blank, Dave
1989	W	NCAA	II	16	—	—	—	—	—	—	—	22	9	Scarfo, Frank
1990		NCAA	II	8	—	—	—	—	—	—	—	26	7	Scarfo, Frank
1991		NCAA	II	16	—	—	—	—	—	—	—	20	10	Scarfo, Frank

LOGAN CHIROPRACTIC

Year	M/W	Assn	Div	NAT	NIT	ARC	CCA	NCI	NCT	OLY	HLM	W	L	Coach
1978	M	NSCAA		16	—	—	—	—	—	—	—	17	4	Kirkling, David

LONG ISLAND

Year	M/W	Assn	Div	NAT	NIT	ARC	CCA	NCI	NCT	OLY	HLM	W	L	Coach
1938	M			—	6	—	—	—	—	—	—	23	4	Bee, Clair F.
1939				—	1	—	—	—	—	—	1	24	0	Bee, Clair F.
1940				—	6	—	—	—	—	—	—	19	4	Bee, Clair F.
1941				—	1	—	—	—	—	—	—	25	2	Bee, Clair F.
1942				—	8	—	—	—	—	—	—	24	4	Bee, Clair F.
1947				—	8	—	—	—	—	—	—	17	4	Bee, Clair F.
1950		NAIA		—	12	—	—	—	—	—	—	20	5	Bee, Clair F.
1965		NCAA	II	16	—	—	—	—	—	—	—	16	7	Rubin, Roy
1966		NCAA	II	8	—	—	—	—	—	—	—	22	4	Rubin, Roy
1967		NCAA	II	8	—	—	—	—	—	—	—	22	7	Rubin, Roy
1968		NCAA	I	—	8	—	—	—	—	—	—	22	2	Rubin, Roy
1981		NCAA	I	48	—	—	—	—	—	—	—	18	11	Lizzo, Paul
1982		NCAA	I	—	32	—	—	—	—	—	—	20	10	Lizzo, Paul
1984		NCAA	I	53	—	—	—	—	—	—	—	20	11	Lizzo, Paul
1997		NCAA	I	64	—	—	—	—	—	—	—	21	9	Haskins, Ray
1998		NCAA	I	—	32	—	—	—	—	—	—	21	11	Haskins, Ray

LONG ISLAND: C W POST

Year	M/W	Assn	Div	NAT	NIT	ARC	CCA	NCI	NCT	OLY	HLM	W	L	Coach
1962	M	NCAA	II	32	—	—	—	—	—	—	—	16	6	Kaftan, Dr. George A.
1971		NCAA	II	32	—	—	—	—	—	—	—	20	6	Kaftan, Dr. George A.
1973		NCAA	II	24	—	—	—	—	—	—	—	20	5	Brown, Herbert M.
1975		NCAA	II	16	—	—	—	—	—	—	—	24	4	Brown, Herbert M.
1983		NCAA	II	24	—	—	—	—	—	—	—	22	9	Galeazzi, Thomas J.
1984		NCAA	II	16	—	—	—	—	—	—	—	26	5	Galeazzi, Thomas J.
1985		NCAA	II	8	—	—	—	—	—	—	—	24	7	Galeazzi, Thomas J.
1987		NCAA	II	24	—	—	—	—	—	—	—	25	5	Galeazzi, Thomas J.
1990		NCAA	II	24	—	—	—	—	—	—	—	26	5	Galeazzi, Thomas J.
1991		NCAA	II	16	—	—	—	—	—	—	—	26	5	Galeazzi, Thomas J.
1994		NCAA	II	24	—	—	—	—	—	—	—	26	5	Galeazzi, Thomas J.

Year	M/W	Assn	Div	NAT	NIT	ARC	CCA	NCI	NCT	OLY	HLM	W	L	Coach
1983	W	NCAA	II	16	—	—	—	—	—	—	—	25	8	Solano, Kathy

LONG ISLAND: SOUTHAMPTON

Year	M/W	Assn	Div	NAT	NIT	ARC	CCA	NCI	NCT	OLY	HLM	W	L	Coach
1972	M	NCAA	II	8	—	—	—	—	—	—	—	22	5	Colclough, James

LONGWOOD

Year	M/W	Assn	Div	NAT	NIT	ARC	CCA	NCI	NCT	OLY	HLM	W	L	Coach
1980	M	NCAA	III	4	—	—	—	—	—	—	—	28	3	Bash, Dr. M. Ronald
1994		NCAA	II	32	—	—	—	—	—	—	—	23	6	Carr, Ron
1995		NCAA	II	48	—	—	—	—	—	—	—	19	9	Carr, Ron
1995	W	NCAA	II	32	—	—	—	—	—	—	—	21	8	Duncan, Shirley G.
1996		NCAA	II	48	—	—	—	—	—	—	—	22	7	Duncan, Shirley G.
1997		NCAA	II	48	—	—	—	—	—	—	—	25	5	Duncan, Shirley G.

LORAS

Year	M/W	Assn	Div	NAT	NIT	ARC	CCA	NCI	NCT	OLY	HLM	W	L	Coach
1939	M	NAIA		32	—	—	—	—	—	—	—	14	6	Coyne, Fr. Daniel B.
1940		NAIA		32	—	—	—	—	—	—	—	14	6	Coyne, Fr. Daniel B.
1946		NAIA		16	—	—	—	—	—	—	—	18	9	Dowd, Vincent J.
1947		NAIA		32	—	—	—	—	—	—	—	24	5	Dowd, Vincent J.
1949		NAIA		—	—	—	—	16	—	—	—	14	12	Dowd, Vincent J.
1950		NAIA		—	—	—	—	4	—	—	—	22	9	Dowd, Vincent J.
1951		NAIA		—	—	—	—	8	—	—	—	23	7	Dowd, Vincent J.
1959		NCAA	II	32	—	—	—	—	—	—	—	17	7	Dowd, Vincent J.
1980		NAIA		16	—	—	—	—	—	—	—	23	12	Mullen, Robert
1983		NAIA		8	—	—	—	—	—	—	—	25	5	Smith, Doug

LOUISIANA

Year	M/W	Assn	Div	NAT	NIT	ARC	CCA	NCI	NCT	OLY	HLM	W	L	Coach
1979	M	NAIA		32	—	—	—	—	—	—	—	22	6	Allgood, Billy
1990		NAIA		32	—	—	—	—	—	—	—	21	8	Rushing, Gene
1980	W	AIAW	II	4	—	—	—	—	—	—	—	24	11	Schneider, Frank
1981		AIAW	II	8	—	—	—	—	—	—	—	15	16	Schneider, Frank
1985		NAIA		16	—	—	—	—	—	—	—	27	4	Schneider, Frank
1986		NAIA		3	—	—	—	—	—	—	—	24	2	Johnson, Shelia Thompson
1992		NAIA	I	16	—	—	—	—	—	—	—	18	13	Brooks, Billy C.
1998		NAIA	I	32	—	—	—	—	—	—	—	23	7	Brooks, Billy C.

LOUISIANA CHRISTIAN

Year	M/W	Assn	Div	NAT	NIT	ARC	CCA	NCI	NCT	OLY	HLM	W	L	Coach
1996	M	NSCAA		2	—	—	—	—	—	—	—	19	13	Schexnayder, Tommy
1997		NSCAA		1	—	—	—	—	—	—	—	21	12	Schexnayder, Tommy

LOUISIANA STATE

Year	M/W	Assn	Div	NAT	NIT	ARC	CCA	NCI	NCT	OLY	HLM	W	L	Coach
1953	M	NCAA		4	—	—	—	—	—	—	—	22	3	Rabenhorst, Harry A.
1954		NCAA		16	—	—	—	—	—	—	—	20	5	Rabenhorst, Harry A.
1970		NCAA	I	—	4	—	—	—	—	—	—	22	10	Maravich, Peter "Press"
1979		NCAA	I	16	—	—	—	—	—	—	—	23	6	Brown, Dale
1980		NCAA	I	8	—	—	—	—	—	—	—	26	6	Brown, Dale
1981		NCAA	I	4	—	—	—	—	—	—	—	31	5	Brown, Dale
1982		NCAA	I	—	32	—	—	—	—	—	—	14	14	Brown, Dale
1983		NCAA	I	—	32	—	—	—	—	—	—	19	13	Brown, Dale
1984		NCAA	I	48	—	—	—	—	—	—	—	18	11	Brown, Dale
1985		NCAA	I	64	—	—	—	—	—	—	—	19	10	Brown, Dale
1986		NCAA	I	3	—	—	—	—	—	—	—	26	12	Brown, Dale
1987		NCAA	I	8	—	—	—	—	—	—	—	24	15	Brown, Dale

Year	M/W	Assn	Div	NAT	NIT	ARC	CCA	NCI	NCT	OLY	HLM	W	L	Coach
1988		NCAA	I	64	—	—	—	—	—	—	—	16	14	Brown, Dale
1989		NCAA	I	64	—	—	—	—	—	—	—	20	12	Brown, Dale
1990		NCAA	I	32	—	—	—	—	—	—	—	23	9	Brown, Dale
1991		NCAA	I	64	—	—	—	—	—	—	—	20	10	Brown, Dale
1992		NCAA	I	32	—	—	—	—	—	—	—	21	10	Brown, Dale
1993		NCAA	I	64	—	—	—	—	—	—	—	22	11	Brown, Dale
1977	W	AIAW	L	2	—	—	—	—	—	—	—	29	8	Coleman, "Jinks"
1984		NCAA	I	16	—	—	—	—	—	—	—	23	7	Gunter, Sue
1985		NCAA	I	—	1	—	—	—	—	—	—	20	9	Gunter, Sue
1986		NCAA	I	8	—	—	—	—	—	—	—	27	6	Gunter, Sue
1987		NCAA	I	32	—	—	—	—	—	—	—	20	8	Gunter, Sue
1988		NCAA	I	40	—	—	—	—	—	—	—	18	11	Gunter, Sue
1989		NCAA	I	16	—	—	—	—	—	—	—	19	11	Gunter, Sue
1990		NCAA	I	48	—	—	—	—	—	—	—	21	9	Gunter, Sue
1991		NCAA	I	32	—	—	—	—	—	—	—	24	7	Gunter, Sue
1996		NCAA	I	—	3	—	—	—	—	—	—	21	11	Gunter, Sue
1997		NCAA	I	16	—	—	—	—	—	—	—	25	5	Gunter, Sue
1998		NCAA	I	—	3	—	—	—	—	—	—	19	13	Gunter, Sue

LOUISIANA TECH

Year	M/W	Assn	Div	NAT	NIT	ARC	CCA	NCI	NCT	OLY	HLM	W	L	Coach
1942	M	NAIA		32	—	—	—	—	—	—	—	13	8	Crowley, Cecil C.
1946		NAIA		32	—	—	—	—	—	—	—	16	8	Crowley, Cecil C.
1953		NAIA		32	—	—	—	—	—	—	—	17	10	Crowley, Cecil C.
1955		NAIA		16	—	—	—	—	—	—	—	20	10	Crowley, Cecil C.
1967		NCAA	II	16	—	—	—	—	—	—	—	20	8	Robertson, Robert "Scotty"
1971		NCAA	II	24	—	—	—	—	—	—	—	23	5	Robertson, Robert "Scotty"
1984		NCAA	I	32	—	—	—	—	—	—	—	26	7	Russo, Andy
1985		NCAA	I	16	—	—	—	—	—	—	—	29	3	Russo, Andy
1986		NCAA	I	—	3	—	—	—	—	—	—	20	14	Eagles, Tommy Joe
1987		NCAA	I	64	—	—	—	—	—	—	—	22	8	Eagles, Tommy Joe
1988		NCAA	I	—	16	—	—	—	—	—	—	22	9	Eagles, Tommy Joe
1989		NCAA	I	32	—	—	—	—	—	—	—	23	9	Eagles, Tommy Joe
1990		NCAA	I	—	32	—	—	—	—	—	—	20	8	Lloyd, Jerry
1991		NCAA	I	64	—	—	—	—	—	—	—	21	10	Lloyd, Jerry
1992		NCAA	I	—	32	—	—	—	—	—	—	22	9	Lloyd, Jerry
1979	W	AIAW	L	2	—	—	—	—	—	—	—	34	4	Hogg, Sonja
1980		AIAW	I	4	—	—	—	—	—	—	—	40	5	Hogg, Sonja
1981		AIAW	I	1	—	—	—	—	—	—	—	34	0	Hogg, Sonja
1982		NCAA	I	1	—	—	—	—	—	—	—	35	1	Hogg, Sonja
1983		NCAA	I	2	—	—	—	—	—	—	—	31	2	Barmore, Leon
1984		NCAA	I	3	—	—	—	—	—	—	—	30	3	Barmore, Leon
1985		NCAA	I	8	—	—	—	—	—	—	—	29	4	Barmore, Leon
1986		NCAA	I	8	—	—	—	—	—	—	—	27	5	Barmore, Leon
1987		NCAA	I	2	—	—	—	—	—	—	—	30	3	Barmore, Leon
1988		NCAA	I	1	—	—	—	—	—	—	—	32	2	Barmore, Leon
1989		NCAA	I	3	—	—	—	—	—	—	—	32	4	Barmore, Leon
1990		NCAA	I	3	—	—	—	—	—	—	—	32	1	Barmore, Leon
1991		NCAA	I	48	—	—	—	—	—	—	—	18	12	Barmore, Leon
1992		NCAA	I	48	—	—	—	—	—	—	—	20	10	Barmore, Leon
1993		NCAA	I	8	—	—	—	—	—	—	—	26	6	Barmore, Leon
1994		NCAA	I	2	—	—	—	—	—	—	—	31	4	Barmore, Leon

Year	M/W	Assn	Div	NAT	NIT	ARC	CCA	NCI	NCT	OLY	HLM	W	L	Coach
1995		NCAA	I	16	—	—	—	—	—	—	—	28	5	Barmore, Leon
1996		NCAA	I	8	—	—	—	—	—	—	—	31	2	Barmore, Leon
1997		NCAA	I	16	—	—	—	—	—	—	—	31	4	Barmore, Leon
1998		NCAA	I	2	—	—	—	—	—	—	—	31	4	Barmore, Leon

LOUISVILLE

Year	M/W	Assn	Div	NAT	NIT	ARC	CCA	NCI	NCT	OLY	HLM	W	L	Coach
1948	M	NAIA		1	—	—	—	—	—	8	—	29	6	Hickman, Bernard L. "Peck"
1951		NCAA		16	—	—	—	—	—	—	—	19	7	Hickman, Bernard L. "Peck"
1952		NCAA		—	12	—	—	—	—	—	—	20	6	Hickman, Bernard L. "Peck"
1953		NCAA		—	8	—	—	—	—	—	—	22	6	Hickman, Bernard L. "Peck"
1954		NCAA		—	12	—	—	—	—	—	—	22	7	Hickman, Bernard L. "Peck"
1955		NCAA		—	8	—	—	—	—	—	—	19	8	Hickman, Bernard L. "Peck"
1956		NCAA		—	1	—	—	—	—	—	—	26	3	Hickman, Bernard L. "Peck"
1959		NCAA	I	4	—	—	—	—	—	—	—	19	12	Hickman, Bernard L. "Peck"
1961		NCAA	I	12	—	—	—	—	—	—	—	21	8	Hickman, Bernard L. "Peck"
1964		NCAA	I	25	—	—	—	—	—	—	—	15	10	Hickman, Bernard L. "Peck"
1966		NCAA	I	—	14	—	—	—	—	—	—	16	10	Hickman, Bernard L. "Peck"
1967		NCAA	I	12	—	—	—	—	—	—	—	23	5	Hickman, Bernard L. "Peck"
1968		NCAA	I	12	—	—	—	—	—	—	—	21	7	Dromo, John
1969		NCAA	I	—	8	—	—	—	—	—	—	21	6	Dromo, John
1970		NCAA	I	—	16	—	—	—	—	—	—	18	9	Dromo, John
1971		NCAA	I	—	16	—	—	—	—	—	—	20	9	Dromo, John
1972		NCAA	I	4	—	—	—	—	—	—	—	26	5	Crum, Denzil E. "Denny"
1973		NCAA	I	—	8	—	—	—	—	—	—	23	7	Crum, Denzil E. "Denny"
1974		NCAA	I	16	—	—	—	—	—	—	—	21	7	Crum, Denzil E. "Denny"
1975		NCAA	I	3	—	—	—	—	—	—	—	28	3	Crum, Denzil E. "Denny"
1976		NCAA	I	—	8	—	—	—	—	—	—	20	8	Crum, Denzil E. "Denny"
1977		NCAA	I	32	—	—	—	—	—	—	—	21	7	Crum, Denzil E. "Denny"
1978		NCAA	I	16	—	—	—	—	—	—	—	23	7	Crum, Denzil E. "Denny"
1979		NCAA	I	16	—	—	—	—	—	—	—	24	8	Crum, Denzil E. "Denny"
1980		NCAA	I	1	—	—	—	—	—	—	1	33	3	Crum, Denzil E. "Denny"
1981		NCAA	I	32	—	—	—	—	—	—	—	21	9	Crum, Denzil E. "Denny"
1982		NCAA	I	3	—	—	—	—	—	—	—	23	10	Crum, Denzil E. "Denny"
1983		NCAA	I	3	—	—	—	—	—	—	—	32	4	Crum, Denzil E. "Denny"
1984		NCAA	I	16	—	—	—	—	—	—	—	24	11	Crum, Denzil E. "Denny"
1985		NCAA	I	—	4	—	—	—	—	—	—	19	18	Crum, Denzil E. "Denny"
1986		NCAA	I	1	—	—	—	—	—	—	—	32	7	Crum, Denzil E. "Denny"
1988		NCAA	I	16	—	—	—	—	—	—	—	24	11	Crum, Denzil E. "Denny"
1989		NCAA	I	16	—	—	—	—	—	—	—	24	9	Crum, Denzil E. "Denny"
1990		NCAA	I	32	—	—	—	—	—	—	—	27	8	Crum, Denzil E. "Denny"
1992		NCAA	I	32	—	—	—	—	—	—	—	19	11	Crum, Denzil E. "Denny"
1993		NCAA	I	16	—	—	—	—	—	—	—	22	9	Crum, Denzil E. "Denny"
1994		NCAA	I	16	—	—	—	—	—	—	—	28	8	Crum, Denzil E. "Denny"
1995		NCAA	I	64	—	—	—	—	—	—	—	19	14	Crum, Denzil E. "Denny"
1996		NCAA	I	16	—	—	—	—	—	—	—	22	12	Crum, Denzil E. "Denny"
1997		NCAA	I	8	—	—	—	—	—	—	—	26	9	Crum, Denzil E. "Denny"
1971	W	AIAW		16	—	—	—	—	—	—	—	7	2	Hudson, Becky
1983		NCAA	I	32	—	—	—	—	—	—	—	20	9	Fiehrer, Peggy
1984		NCAA	I	32	—	—	—	—	—	—	—	15	16	Fiehrer, Peggy
1991		NCAA	I	—	6	—	—	—	—	—	—	24	11	Childers, "Bud"

Year	M/W	Assn	Div	NAT	NIT	ARC	CCA	NCI	NCT	OLY	HLM	W	L	Coach
1993		NCAA	I	32	—	—	—	—	—	—	—	19	12	Childers, 'Bud'
1995		NCAA	I	32	—	—	—	—	—	—	—	25	8	Childers, 'Bud'
1997		NCAA	I	64	—	—	—	—	—	—	—	20	9	Childers, 'Bud'
1998		NCAA	I	32	—	—	—	—	—	—	—	20	12	Clapp, Martin

LOYOLA (IL)

Year	M/W	Assn	Div	NAT	NIT	ARC	CCA	NCI	NCT	OLY	HLM	W	L	Coach
1939	M			—	2	—	—	—	—	—	—	21	1	Sachs, Leonard D.
1943		NAIA		32	—	—	—	—	—	—	—	12	10	Connelly, John J.
1949		NAIA		—	2	—	—	—	—	—	—	25	6	Haggerty, Thomas J.
1962		NCAA	I	—	3	—	—	—	—	—	—	23	4	Ireland, George M.
1963		NCAA	I	1	—	—	—	—	—	—	1	29	2	Ireland, George M.
1964		NCAA	I	12	—	—	—	—	—	—	—	22	6	Ireland, George M.
1966		NCAA	I	22	—	—	—	—	—	—	—	22	3	Ireland, George M.
1968		NCAA	I	23	—	—	—	—	—	—	—	15	9	Ireland, George M.
1980		NCAA	I	—	32	—	—	—	—	—	—	19	10	Lyne, Jerry P.
1985		NCAA	I	16	—	—	—	—	—	—	—	27	6	Sullivan, Gene

LOYOLA (MD)

Year	M/W	Assn	Div	NAT	NIT	ARC	CCA	NCI	NCT	OLY	HLM	W	L	Coach
1947	M	NAIA		32	—	—	—	—	—	—	—	21	12	Reitz, Emil G., Jr. 'Lefty'
1948		NAIA		32	—	—	—	—	—	—	—	24	7	Reitz, Emil G., Jr. 'Lefty'
1949		NAIA		16	—	—	—	3	—	—	—	25	8	Reitz, Emil G., Jr. 'Lefty'
1952		NAIA		—	—	—	12	—	—	—	—	16	12	Reitz, Emil G., Jr. 'Lefty'
1953		NAIA		16	—	—	—	—	—	—	—	17	9	Reitz, Emil G., Jr. 'Lefty'
1973		NCAA	II	32	—	—	—	—	—	—	—	16	13	Doherty, Edward C.
1994		NCAA	I	64	—	—	—	—	—	—	—	17	13	Prosser, 'Skip'
1994	W	NCAA	I	64	—	—	—	—	—	—	—	18	11	Coyle, Patricia
1995		NCAA	I	64	—	—	—	—	—	—	—	20	9	Coyle, Patricia

LOYOLA MARYMOUNT

Year	M/W	Assn	Div	NAT	NIT	ARC	CCA	NCI	NCT	OLY	HLM	W	L	Coach
1955	M	NAIA		32	—	—	—	—	—	—	—	16	9	Donovan, William J.
1961		NCAA	I	12	—	—	—	—	—	—	—	20	7	Arndt, John C.
1980		NCAA	I	48	—	—	—	—	—	—	—	14	14	Jacobs, Ron
1986		NCAA	I	—	16	—	—	—	—	—	—	19	11	Westhead, Paul W.
1988		NCAA	I	32	—	—	—	—	—	—	—	28	4	Westhead, Paul W.
1989		NCAA	I	64	—	—	—	—	—	—	—	20	11	Westhead, Paul W.
1990		NCAA	I	8	—	—	—	—	—	—	—	26	6	Westhead, Paul W.

LOYOLA NEW ORLEANS

Year	M/W	Assn	Div	NAT	NIT	ARC	CCA	NCI	NCT	OLY	HLM	W	L	Coach
1945	M	NAIA		1	—	—	—	—	—	—	—	22	11	Orsley, Jack C.
1946		NAIA		4	—	—	—	—	—	—	—	22	11	Orsley, Jack C.
1954		NCAA		24	—	—	—	—	—	—	—	15	9	McCafferty, James J.
1957		NCAA	I	23	—	—	—	—	—	—	—	14	12	McCafferty, James J.
1958		NCAA	I	24	—	—	—	—	—	—	—	16	9	Harding, James F.
1995		NAIA	II	32	—	—	—	—	—	—	—	15	13	Hernandez, Jerry

LUTHER

Year	M/W	Assn	Div	NAT	NIT	ARC	CCA	NCI	NCT	OLY	HLM	W	L	Coach
1937	M	NAIA		8	—	—	—	—	—	—	—	12	8	Peterson, Hamlet E., Sr.
1942		NAIA		16	—	—	—	—	—	—	—	15	4	Peterson, Hamlet E., Sr.
1943		NAIA		16	—	—	—	—	—	—	—	12	3	Peterson, Hamlet E., Sr.
1967		NCAA	II	23	—	—	—	—	—	—	—	16	8	Finanger, Kenton
1982		NCAA	III	16	—	—	—	—	—	—	—	23	4	Leix, Jim
1984		NCAA	III	32	—	—	—	—	—	—	—	20	7	Leix, Jim

Year	M/W	Assn	Div	NAT	NIT	ARC	CCA	NCI	NCT	OLY	HLM	W	L	Coach
1988	W	NCAA	III	8	—	—	—	—	—	—	—	21	7	Hildebrand, Jane
1989		NCAA	III	8	—	—	—	—	—	—	—	22	7	Hildebrand, Jane
1991		NCAA	III	16	—	—	—	—	—	—	—	18	9	Hildebrand, Jane
1992		NCAA	III	3	—	—	—	—	—	—	—	24	6	Hildebrand, Jane
1995		NCAA	III	64	—	—	—	—	—	—	—	20	6	Hildebrand, Jane
1996		NCAA	III	32	—	—	—	—	—	—	—	21	5	Hildebrand, Jane
1997		NCAA	III	64	—	—	—	—	—	—	—	17	8	Hildebrand, Jane
1998		NCAA	III	48	—	—	—	—	—	—	—	20	6	Hildebrand, Jane

LYCOMING

Year	M/W	Assn	Div	NAT	NIT	ARC	CCA	NCI	NCT	OLY	HLM	W	L	Coach
1985	M	NCAA	III	24	—	—	—	—	—	—	—	19	7	Burch, Clarence W. "Dutch"
1996		NCAA	III	32	—	—	—	—	—	—	—	21	6	Bressi, Joe
1988	W	NCAA	III	24	—	—	—	—	—	—	—	21	7	Rockey, Kimberly
1997		NCAA	III	64	—	—	—	—	—	—	—	17	10	Ditzler, Christen

LYNCHBURG

Year	M/W	Assn	Div	NAT	NIT	ARC	CCA	NCI	NCT	OLY	HLM	W	L	Coach
1976	M	NCAA	III	28	—	—	—	—	—	—	—	22	8	Proffitt, Wayne
1979		NCAA	III	32	—	—	—	—	—	—	—	17	12	Proffitt, Wayne
1969	W	AIAW		8	—	—	—	—	—	—	—	9	5	Asbury, Jackie

LYNN

Year	M/W	Assn	Div	NAT	NIT	ARC	CCA	NCI	NCT	OLY	HLM	W	L	Coach
1994	M	NAIA	II	24	—	—	—	—	—	—	—	23	7	Price, Jeff
1997		NCAA	II	3	—	—	—	—	—	—	—	28	3	Price, Jeff
1998		NCAA	II	16	—	—	—	—	—	—	—	22	7	Price, Jeff
1994	W	NAIA	II	24	—	—	—	—	—	—	—	24	5	Olson, Dan

LYON

Year	M/W	Assn	Div	NAT	NIT	ARC	CCA	NCI	NCT	OLY	HLM	W	L	Coach
1984	M	NAIA		16	—	—	—	—	—	—	—	22	11	Garner, Terry

MACMURRAY

Year	M/W	Assn	Div	NAT	NIT	ARC	CCA	NCI	NCT	OLY	HLM	W	L	Coach
1961	M	NCAA	II	32	—	—	—	—	—	—	—	18	9	Wall, William L.
1996	W	NCAA	III	64	—	—	—	—	—	—	—	17	10	Mulhern, Donald

MADONNA

Year	M/W	Assn	Div	NAT	NIT	ARC	CCA	NCI	NCT	OLY	HLM	W	L	Coach
1997	W	NAIA	II	32	—	—	—	—	—	—	—	14	15	Jansen, Marylou

MAINE

Year	M/W	Assn	Div	NAT	NIT	ARC	CCA	NCI	NCT	OLY	HLM	W	L	Coach
1990	W	NCAA	I	—	7	—	—	—	—	—	—	23	7	Roberts, Trish
1995		NCAA	I	64	—	—	—	—	—	—	—	24	6	Palombo-McCall, Joanne
1996		NCAA	I	64	—	—	—	—	—	—	—	27	5	Palombo-McCall, Joanne
1997		NCAA	I	64	—	—	—	—	—	—	—	22	8	Palombo-McCall, Joanne
1998		NCAA	I	64	—	—	—	—	—	—	—	21	9	Palombo-McCall, Joanne

MAINE: AUGUSTA

Year	M/W	Assn	Div	NAT	NIT	ARC	CCA	NCI	NCT	OLY	HLM	W	L	Coach
1995	M	NSCAA		12	—	—	—	—	—	—	—	12	14	Andreasen, Michael

MAINE: FARMINGTON

Year	M/W	Assn	Div	NAT	NIT	ARC	CCA	NCI	NCT	OLY	HLM	W	L	Coach
1997	W	NAIA	II	32	—	—	—	—	—	—	—	20	5	MacPhee, Leonard R.
1998		NAIA	II	32	—	—	—	—	—	—	—	20	5	MacPhee, Leonard R.

Year	M/W	Assn	Div	NAT	NIT	ARC	CCA	NCI	NCT	OLY	HLM	W	L	Coach
MAINE: FORT KENT														
1994	M	NSCAA		10	—	—	—	—	—	—	—	—	24	7	Clifford, Dan
1995		NSCAA		10	—	—	—	—	—	—	—	—	26	10	Clifford, Dan
1996	.	NSCAA		8	—	—	—	—	—	—	—	—	25	5	Clifford, Dan
1997		NSCAA		8	—	—	—	—	—	—	—	—	20	10	Graffam, Jim
MAINE: MACHIAS														
1991	M	NAIA		32	—	—	—	—	—	—	—	—	22	5	Casey, Sean
MALONE														
1975	M	NAIA		8	—	—	—	—	—	—	—	—	27	6	Bowerman, Jay
1987		NCCAA	I	8	—	—	—	—	—	—	—	—	18	14	Smith, Harold T.
1990		NAIA		32	—	—	—	—	—	—	—	—	25	9	Smith, Harold T.
1991		NCCAA	I	3	—	—	—	—	—	—	—	—	28	4	Smith, Harold T.
1992		NAIA	I	32	—	—	—	—	—	—	—	—	26	9	Smith, Harold T.
1996		NCCAA	I	1	—	—	—	—	—	—	—	—	20	16	Smith, Harold T.
1982	W	AIAW	III	8	—	—	—	—	—	—	—	—	25	6	Long, Dr. Patricia L. "Patty"
MANCHESTER														
1938	M	NAIA		32	—	—	—	—	—	—	—	—	14	5	Stauffer, Robert
1939		NAIA		8	—	—	—	—	—	—	—	—	16	5	Stauffer, Robert
1993		NCAA	III	40	—	—	—	—	—	—	—	—	20	8	Alford, Stephen T.
1994		NCAA	III	32	—	—	—	—	—	—	—	—	23	4	Alford, Stephen T.
1995		NCAA	III	2	—	—	—	—	—	—	—	—	31	1	Alford, Stephen T.
1995	W	NCAA	III	64	—	—	—	—	—	—	—	—	15	9	Rockey, Kimberly
MANHATTAN														
1943	M	NCAA		—	8	—	—	—	—	—	—	—	18	3	Daher, Joseph G.
1948	.	NAIA		8	—	—	—	—	—	—	—	—	23	6	Norton, Kenneth A.
1949		NCAA		—	12	—	—	—	—	—	—	—	18	8	Norton, Kenneth A.
1953		NCAA		—	4	—	—	—	—	—	—	—	20	6	Norton, Kenneth A.
1954		NCAA		—	12	—	—	—	—	—	—	—	15	11	Norton, Kenneth A.
1955		NCAA		—	12	—	—	—	—	—	—	—	18	5	Norton, Kenneth A.
1956		NCAA		25	—	—	—	—	—	—	—	—	16	8	Norton, Kenneth A.
1957		NCAA	I	—	8	—	—	—	—	—	—	—	15	9	Norton, Kenneth A.
1958		NCAA	I	16	—	—	—	—	—	—	—	—	16	10	Norton, Kenneth A.
1959		NCAA	I	—	12	—	—	—	—	—	—	—	15	6	Norton, Kenneth A.
1965		NCAA	I	—	8	—	—	—	—	—	—	—	13	9	Norton, Kenneth A.
1966		NCAA	I	—	14	—	—	—	—	—	—	—	13	9	Norton, Kenneth A.
1970		NCAA	I	—	8	—	—	—	—	—	—	—	18	8	Powers, John J. "Jack"
1973		NCAA	I	—	16	—	—	—	—	—	—	—	16	10	Powers, John J. "Jack"
1974		NCAA	I	—	16	—	—	—	—	—	—	—	18	9	Powers, John J. "Jack"
1975		NCAA	I	—	8	—	—	—	—	—	—	—	14	12	Powers, John J. "Jack"
1992		NCAA	I	—	8	—	—	—	—	—	—	—	25	9	Lappas, Steve
1993		NCAA	I	64	—	—	—	—	—	—	—	—	23	7	Fraschilla, Fran
1994		NCAA	I	—	32	—	—	—	—	—	—	—	19	11	Fraschilla, Fran
1995		NCAA	I	32	—	—	—	—	—	—	—	—	26	5	Fraschilla, Fran
1996		NCAA	I	—	32	—	—	—	—	—	—	—	17	12	Fraschilla, Fran
1987	W	NCAA	I	40	—	—	—	—	—	—	—	—	20	11	Solano, Kathy
1990		NCAA	I	48	—	—	—	—	—	—	—	—	18	13	Solano, Kathy
1996		NCAA	I	64	—	—	—	—	—	—	—	—	19	11	Sharp, Michele

Year	M/W	Assn	Div	NAT	NIT	ARC	CCA	NCI	NCT	OLY	HLM	W	L	Coach
MANHATTAN CHRISTIAN														
1990	M	NBCAA	I	4	—	—	—	—	—	—	—	19	9	Rupe, Marvin
1991		NBCAA	I	4	—	—	—	—	—	—	—	19	9	Rupe, Marvin
1992		NBCAA	I	5	—	—	—	—	—	—	—	21	7	Johnson, Stuart
1993		NBCAA	I	4	—	—	—	—	—	—	—	21	5	Johnson, Stuart
1994		NBCAA	I	4	—	—	—	—	—	—	—	14	13	Johnson, Stuart
1995		NBCAA	I	5	—	—	—	—	—	—	—	20	8	Condra, Shawn
1996		NCCAA	IIA	1	—	—	—	—	—	—	—	22	8	Condra, Shawn
1997		NCCAA	IIA	7	—	—	—	—	—	—	—	14	14	Condra, Shawn
1993	W	NBCAA		2	—	—	—	—	—	—	—	11	6	Cott, Wendy
1994		NBCAA		3	—	—	—	—	—	—	—	10	8	Cott, Wendy
MANHATTANVILLE														
1978	M	NCAA	III	30	—	—	—	—	—	—	—	17	11	Cohane, Tim
1979		NCAA	III	32	—	—	—	—	—	—	—	17	11	Cohane, Tim
1982	W	NCAA	III	16	—	—	—	—	—	—	—	22	8	Tedesco, Ralph
MANKATO STATE														
1947	M	NAIA		2	—	—	—	—	—	—	—	24	4	Witham, James A.
1948		NAIA		8	—	—	—	—	—	—	—	16	11	Witham, James A.
1964		NCAA	II	16	—	—	—	—	—	—	—	19	6	Morris, William
1976		NCAA	II	24	—	—	—	—	—	—	—	18	10	Raymond, Lloyd E. "Butch"
1986	W	NCAA	II	16	—	—	—	—	—	—	—	25	4	Wilinski, Bruno
MANSFIELD														
1964	M	NAIA		8	—	—	—	—	—	—	—	20	4	Clark, William J.
1965		NAIA		32	—	—	—	—	—	—	—	16	6	Clark, William J.
1971		NAIA		32	—	—	—	—	—	—	—	18	8	Wilson, Edward W.
1975		NCAA	III	8	—	—	—	—	—	—	—	18	10	Wilson, Edward W.
1976		NCAA	III	21	—	—	—	—	—	—	—	17	7	Wilson, Edward W.
1984		NCAA	II	24	—	—	—	—	—	—	—	26	6	Wilson, Edward W.
1997		NCAA	II	32	—	—	—	—	—	—	—	26	4	Ackerman, Thomas E.
MARANATHA BAPTIST BIBLE (WI)														
1982	M	NBCAA		6	—	—	—	—	—	—	—	7	17	Terrill, Jerry
1983		NBCAA		3	—	—	—	—	—	—	—	11	13	Terrill, Jerry
1984		NBCAA	I	8	—	—	—	—	—	—	—	4	19	Terrill, Jerry
1986		NCCAA	II	6	—	—	—	—	—	—	—	5	16	Terrill, Jerry
1990		NCCAA	II	1	—	—	—	—	—	—	—	18	8	Terrill, Jerry
1991		NCCAA	II	4	—	—	—	—	—	—	—	19	10	Terrill, Jerry
1996		NCCAA	II	3	—	—	—	—	—	—	—	11	17	Terrill, Jerry
1997		NCCAA	II	3	—	—	—	—	—	—	—	17	13	Terrill, Jerry
1998		NCCAA	II	5	—	—	—	—	—	—	—	14	15	Terrill, Jerry
1983	W	NBCAA		4	—	—	—	—	—	—	—	4	13	Unknown
1987		NCCAA	II	6	—	—	—	—	—	—	—	10	12	Grooms, Vicki
1996		NCCAA	II	5	—	—	—	—	—	—	—	11	17	Morrison, Clayton
1998		NCCAA	II	5	—	—	—	—	—	—	—	13	16	Morrison, Clayton
MARIAN (IN)														
1998	M	NAIA	II	32	—	—	—	—	—	—	—	22	7	Grimes, John

Year	M/W	Assn	Div	NAT	NIT	ARC	CCA	NCI	NCT	OLY	HLM	W	L	Coach
MARIETTA														
1975	M	NCAA	III	16	—	—	—	—	—	—	—	19	4	Roach, J. Philip
MARIST														
1973	M	NAIA		32	—	—	—	—	—	—	—	15	12	Petro, Ronald
1986		NCAA	I	64	—	—	—	—	—	—	—	19	12	Furjanic, Matt, Jr.
1987		NCAA	I	64	—	—	—	—	—	—	—	20	10	Magarity, David
1996		NCAA	I	—	32	—	—	—	—	—	—	22	7	Magarity, David
MARQUETTE														
1952	M	NCAA		—	—	—	—	1	—	—	—	12	14	Winter, Fred "Tex"
1955		NCAA		8	—	—	—	—	—	—	—	24	3	Nagle, Joel "Jack"
1956		NCAA		—	12	—	—	—	—	—	—	13	11	Nagle, Joel "Jack"
1959		NCAA	I	16	—	—	—	—	—	—	—	23	6	Hickey, Edgar S. "Eddie"
1961		NCAA	I	24	—	—	—	—	—	—	—	16	11	Hickey, Edgar S. "Eddie"
1963		NCAA	I	—	3	—	—	—	—	—	—	20	9	Hickey, Edgar S. "Eddie"
1967		NCAA	I	—	2	—	—	—	—	—	—	21	9	McGuire, Alfred J.
1968		NCAA	I	12	—	—	—	—	—	—	—	23	6	McGuire, Alfred J.
1969		NCAA	I	8	—	—	—	—	—	—	—	24	5	McGuire, Alfred J.
1970		NCAA	I	—	1	—	—	—	—	—	—	26	3	McGuire, Alfred J.
1971		NCAA	I	12	—	—	—	—	—	—	—	28	1	McGuire, Alfred J.
1972		NCAA	I	16	—	—	—	—	—	—	—	25	4	McGuire, Alfred J.
1973		NCAA	I	12	—	—	—	—	—	—	—	25	4	McGuire, Alfred J.
1974		NCAA	I	2	—	—	—	—	—	—	—	26	5	McGuire, Alfred J.
1975		NCAA	I	32	—	—	—	—	—	—	—	23	4	McGuire, Alfred J.
1976		NCAA	I	8	—	—	—	—	—	—	—	27	2	McGuire, Alfred J.
1977		NCAA	I	1	—	—	—	—	—	—	1	25	7	McGuire, Alfred J.
1978		NCAA	I	32	—	—	—	—	—	—	—	24	4	Raymonds, Henry C. "Hank"
1979		NCAA	I	16	—	—	—	—	—	—	—	22	7	Raymonds, Henry C. "Hank"
1980		NCAA	I	48	—	—	—	—	—	—	—	18	9	Raymonds, Henry C. "Hank"
1981		NCAA	I	—	32	—	—	—	—	—	—	20	11	Raymonds, Henry C. "Hank"
1982		NCAA	I	32	—	—	—	—	—	—	—	23	9	Raymonds, Henry C. "Hank"
1983		NCAA	I	48	—	—	—	—	—	—	—	19	10	Raymonds, Henry C. "Hank"
1984		NCAA	I	—	16	—	—	—	—	—	—	17	13	Majerus, Rick
1985		NCAA	I	—	8	—	—	—	—	—	—	20	11	Majerus, Rick
1986		NCAA	I	—	16	—	—	—	—	—	—	19	11	Majerus, Rick
1987		NCAA	I	—	32	—	—	—	—	—	—	16	13	Dukiet, Bob
1990		NCAA	I	—	32	—	—	—	—	—	—	15	14	O'Neill, Kevin
1993		NCAA	I	64	—	—	—	—	—	—	—	20	8	O'Neill, Kevin
1994		NCAA	I	16	—	—	—	—	—	—	—	24	9	O'Neill, Kevin
1995		NCAA	I	—	2	—	—	—	—	—	—	21	12	Deane, Mike
1996		NCAA	I	32	—	—	—	—	—	—	—	23	8	Deane, Mike
1997		NCAA	I	64	—	—	—	—	—	—	—	22	9	Deane, Mike
1998		NCAA	I	—	8	—	—	—	—	—	—	20	11	Deane, Mike
1993	W	NCAA	I	—	4	—	—	—	—	—	—	22	9	Jabir, James J.
1994		NCAA	I	64	—	—	—	—	—	—	—	22	7	Jabir, James J.
1995		NCAA	I	64	—	—	—	—	—	—	—	19	12	Jabir, James J.
1997		NCAA	I	32	—	—	—	—	—	—	—	21	10	Mitchell, Terri
1998		NCAA	I	64	—	—	—	—	—	—	—	22	7	Mitchell, Terri

Year	M/W	Assn	Div	NAT	NIT	ARC	CCA	NCI	NCT	OLY	HLM	W	L	Coach
MARS HILL														
1996	W	NCAA	II	32	—	—	—	—	—	—	—	24	6	White, Sylvia
MARSHALL														
1938	M	NAIA		16	—	—	—	—	—	—	—	28	4	Henderson, Eli Camden "Cam"
1947		NAIA		1	—	—	—	—	—	—	—	32	5	Henderson, Eli Camden "Cam"
1948		NAIA		16	—	—	—	—	—	—	—	22	11	Henderson, Eli Camden "Cam"
1956		NCAA		25	—	—	—	—	—	—	—	18	5	Rivlin, Jule
1967		NCAA	I	—	4	—	—	—	—	—	—	20	8	Johnson, Ellis T.
1968		NCAA	I	—	16	—	—	—	—	—	—	17	8	Johnson, Ellis T.
1972		NCAA	I	25	—	—	—	—	—	—	—	23	4	Tacy, Carl R.
1973		NCAA	I	—	16	—	—	—	—	—	—	20	7	Daniels, Bob
1984		NCAA	I	48	—	—	—	—	—	—	—	25	6	Huckabay, Rick
1985		NCAA	I	64	—	—	—	—	—	—	—	21	13	Huckabay, Rick
1987		NCAA	I	64	—	—	—	—	—	—	—	25	6	Huckabay, Rick
1988		NCAA	I	—	32	—	—	—	—	—	—	24	8	Huckabay, Rick
1971	W	AIAW		16	—	—	—	—	—	—	—	13	4	Lawson, Donna
1997		NCAA	I	64	—	—	—	—	—	—	—	18	12	Evans-Moore, Sarah
MARTIN METHODIST														
1995	W	NSCAA		1	—	—	—	—	—	—	—	13	18	Jones, Johnny
MARY														
1982	M	NAIA		32	—	—	—	—	—	—	—	30	3	Bortke, Al
1994	W	NAIA	II	16	—	—	—	—	—	—	—	21	6	Haug, Roger
1995		NAIA	II	32	—	—	—	—	—	—	—	18	8	Haug, Roger
1997		NAIA	II	32	—	—	—	—	—	—	—	20	6	Haug, Roger
MARY HARDIN-BAYLOR														
1995	M	NAIA	I	32	—	—	—	—	—	—	—	23	8	Herbst, Richard
1998		NAIA	II	32	—	—	—	—	—	—	—	14	12	Herbst, Richard
1994	W	NAIA	I	32	—	—	—	—	—	—	—	19	16	Foster, Cliffa
1995		NAIA	I	32	—	—	—	—	—	—	—	24	8	Foster, Cliffa
1996		NAIA	I	16	—	—	—	—	—	—	—	22	8	Foster, Cliffa
1997		NAIA	I	16	—	—	—	—	—	—	—	22	8	Foster, Cliffa
1998		NAIA	II	2	—	—	—	—	—	—	—	24	6	Van Auken, Jeff
MARY WASHINGTON														
1994	W	NCAA	III	32	—	—	—	—	—	—	—	20	6	Gallahan, Connie
1998		NCAA	III	32	—	—	—	—	—	—	—	21	8	Gallahan, Connie
MARYCREST INTERNATIONAL														
1984	M	NAIA		32	—	—	—	—	—	—	—	31	7	O'Neill, Kevin
1985		NAIA		3	—	—	—	—	—	—	—	34	6	Merchant, Jim
1985	W	NSCAA		3	—	—	—	—	—	—	—	15	15	Vieira, Kim T.
1986		NSCAA		4	—	—	—	—	—	—	—	20	13	Vieira, Kim T.
1988		NSCAA		3	—	—	—	—	—	—	—	18	12	Giardino, Kris
MARYLAND														
1958	M	NCAA	I	12	—	—	—	—	—	—	—	22	7	Millikan, Harry A. "Bud"
1972		NCAA	I	—	1	—	—	—	—	—	—	27	5	Driesell, Charles G. "Lefty"
1973		NCAA	I	8	—	—	—	—	—	—	—	23	7	Driesell, Charles G. "Lefty"
1975		NCAA	I	8	—	—	—	—	—	—	—	24	5	Driesell, Charles G. "Lefty"

Year	M/W	Assn	Div	NAT	NIT	ARC	CCA	NCI	NCT	OLY	HLM	W	L	Coach
1979		NCAA	I	—	12	—	—	—	—	—	—	19	11	Driesell, Charles G. "Lefty"
1980		NCAA	I	16	—	—	—	—	—	—	—	24	7	Driesell, Charles G. "Lefty"
1981		NCAA	I	32	—	—	—	—	—	—	—	21	10	Driesell, Charles G. "Lefty"
1982		NCAA	I	—	16	—	—	—	—	—	—	16	13	Driesell, Charles G. "Lefty"
1983		NCAA	I	32	—	—	—	—	—	—	—	20	10	Driesell, Charles G. "Lefty"
1984		NCAA	I	16	—	—	—	—	—	—	—	24	8	Driesell, Charles G. "Lefty"
1985		NCAA	I	16	—	—	—	—	—	—	—	25	12	Driesell, Charles G. "Lefty"
1986		NCAA	I	32	—	—	—	—	—	—	—	19	14	Driesell, Charles G. "Lefty"
1988		NCAA	I	32	—	—	—	—	—	—	—	18	13	Wade, Bob
1990		NCAA	I	—	16	—	—	—	—	—	—	19	14	Williams, Gary
1994		NCAA	I	16	—	—	—	—	—	—	—	18	12	Williams, Gary
1995		NCAA	I	16	—	—	—	—	—	—	—	26	8	Williams, Gary
1996		NCAA	I	64	—	—	—	—	—	—	—	17	13	Williams, Gary
1997		NCAA	I	64	—	—	—	—	—	—	—	21	11	Williams, Gary
1998		NCAA	I	16	—	—	—	—	—	—	—	22	11	Williams, Gary
1978	W	AIAW	L	2	—	—	—	—	—	—	—	27	4	Weller, Christine J.
1979		AIAW	L	8	—	—	—	—	—	—	—	22	7	Weller, Christine J.
1980		AIAW	I	8	—	—	—	—	—	—	—	21	9	Weller, Christine J.
1981		AIAW	I	8	—	—	—	—	—	—	—	19	9	Weller, Christine J.
1982		NCAA	I	3	—	—	—	—	—	—	—	25	7	Weller, Christine J.
1983		NCAA	I	16	—	—	—	—	—	—	—	26	5	Weller, Christine J.
1984		NCAA	I	32	—	—	—	—	—	—	—	19	10	Weller, Christine J.
1986		NCAA	I	32	—	—	—	—	—	—	—	17	13	Weller, Christine J.
1988		NCAA	I	8	—	—	—	—	—	—	—	26	6	Weller, Christine J.
1989		NCAA	I	3	—	—	—	—	—	—	—	29	3	Weller, Christine J.
1990		NCAA	I	32	—	—	—	—	—	—	—	19	11	Weller, Christine J.
1991		NCAA	I	48	—	—	—	—	—	—	—	17	13	Weller, Christine J.
1992		NCAA	I	8	—	—	—	—	—	—	—	25	6	Weller, Christine J.
1993		NCAA	I	32	—	—	—	—	—	—	—	22	8	Weller, Christine J.
1997		NCAA	I	64	—	—	—	—	—	—	—	18	10	Weller, Christine J.

MARYLAND: BALTIMORE COUNTY

Year	M/W	Assn	Div	NAT	NIT	ARC	CCA	NCI	NCT	OLY	HLM	W	L	Coach
1979	M	NCAA	II	8	—	—	—	—	—	—	—	21	8	Jones, Billy
1980		NCAA	II	16	—	—	—	—	—	—	—	23	5	Jones, Billy

MARYLAND: EASTERN SHORE

Year	M/W	Assn	Div	NAT	NIT	ARC	CCA	NCI	NCT	OLY	HLM	W	L	Coach
1960	M	NAIA		32	—	—	—	—	—	—	—	22	6	Taylor, Nathaniel C. "Nay"
1961		NAIA		32	—	—	—	—	—	—	—	17	6	Taylor, Nathaniel C. "Nay"
1965		NAIA		32	—	—	—	—	—	—	—	16	6	Taylor, Nathaniel C. "Nay"
1969		NAIA		2	—	—	—	—	—	—	—	24	7	Robinson, Joe
1970		NAIA		8	—	—	—	—	—	—	—	23	1	Robinson, Joe
1972		NAIA		32	—	—	—	—	—	—	—	14	6	Bates, John H.
1973		NAIA		2	—	—	—	—	—	—	—	26	5	Bates, John H.
1974		NAIA		—	8	—	—	—	—	—	—	27	2	Bates, John H.

MARYMOUNT (KS)

Year	M/W	Assn	Div	NAT	NIT	ARC	CCA	NCI	NCT	OLY	HLM	W	L	Coach
1973	M	NAIA		32	—	—	—	—	—	—	—	25	3	Cochran, Ken
1975		NAIA		16	—	—	—	—	—	—	—	29	4	Cochran, Ken
1976		NAIA		3	—	—	—	—	—	—	—	31	3	Cochran, Ken
1979		NAIA		8	—	—	—	—	—	—	—	26	6	Cochran, Ken
1980		NAIA		16	—	—	—	—	—	—	—	19	14	Cochran, Ken

Year	M/W	Assn	Div	NAT	NIT	ARC	CCA	NCI	NCT	OLY	HLM	W	L	Coach
MARYMOUNT (VA)														
1990	W	NCAA	III	32	—	—	—	—	—	—	—	19	8	Finney, Bill
1991		NCAA	III	32	—	—	—	—	—	—	—	21	7	Finney, Bill
1992		NCAA	III	32	—	—	—	—	—	—	—	23	5	Finney, Bill
1993		NCAA	III	16	—	—	—	—	—	—	—	23	5	Finney, Bill
1994		NCAA	III	16	—	—	—	—	—	—	—	24	3	Finney, Bill
1995		NCAA	III	32	—	—	—	—	—	—	—	24	5	Finney, Bill
1996		NCAA	III	16	—	—	—	—	—	—	—	27	3	Finney, Bill
1997		NCAA	III	16	—	—	—	—	—	—	—	28	2	Finney, Bill
MARYVILLE (MO)														
1997	M	NCAA	III	64	—	—	—	—	—	—	—	17	11	Kruse, Dennis
MARYVILLE (TN)														
1991	M	NCAA	III	40	—	—	—	—	—	—	—	22	5	Lambert, Randy
1992		NCAA	III	8	—	—	—	—	—	—	—	25	4	Lambert, Randy
1993		NCAA	III	32	—	—	—	—	—	—	—	20	6	Lambert, Randy
1995		NCAA	III	32	—	—	—	—	—	—	—	20	7	Lambert, Randy
1997		NCAA	III	64	—	—	—	—	—	—	—	20	6	Lambert, Randy
1989	W	NCAA	III	24	—	—	—	—	—	—	—	23	6	Moore, Frank "Wes"
1990		NCAA	III	16	—	—	—	—	—	—	—	23	5	Moore, Frank "Wes"
1991		NCAA	III	16	—	—	—	—	—	—	—	23	6	Moore, Frank "Wes"
1992		NCAA	III	32	—	—	—	—	—	—	—	24	4	Moore, Frank "Wes"
1993		NCAA	III	16	—	—	—	—	—	—	—	23	3	Moore, Frank "Wes"
1994		NCAA	III	16	—	—	—	—	—	—	—	23	4	Moore, Frank "Wes"
1995		NCAA	III	16	—	—	—	—	—	—	—	23	5	Cook, Kelli
1996		NCAA	III	32	—	—	—	—	—	—	—	19	6	Cook, Kelli
MARYWOOD														
1987	W	NCAA	III	32	—	—	—	—	—	—	—	19	8	Dempsey, Jerry
MASSACHUSETTS														
1962	M	NCAA	I	25	—	—	—	—	—	—	—	15	9	Zunic, Matthew
1970		NCAA	I	—	16	—	—	—	—	—	—	18	7	Leaman, John A., Jr. "Jack"
1971		NCAA	I	—	16	—	—	—	—	—	—	23	4	Leaman, John A., Jr. "Jack"
1973		NCAA	I	—	8	—	—	—	—	—	—	20	7	Leaman, John A., Jr. "Jack"
1974		NCAA	I	—	16	—	—	—	—	—	—	21	5	Leaman, John A., Jr. "Jack"
1975		NCAA	I	—	16	—	—	—	—	—	—	18	8	Leaman, John A., Jr. "Jack"
1977		NCAA	I	—	8	—	—	—	—	—	—	20	11	Leaman, John A., Jr. "Jack"
1990		NCAA	I	—	32	—	—	—	—	—	—	17	14	Calipari, John
1991		NCAA	I	—	4	—	—	—	—	—	—	20	13	Calipari, John
1992		NCAA	I	16	—	—	—	—	—	—	—	30	5	Calipari, John
1993		NCAA	I	32	—	—	—	—	—	—	—	24	7	Calipari, John
1994		NCAA	I	32	—	—	—	—	—	—	—	28	7	Calipari, John
1995		NCAA	I	8	—	—	—	—	—	—	—	29	5	Calipari, John
1996		NCAA	I	3	—	—	—	—	—	—	—	35	2	Calipari, John
1997		NCAA	I	64	—	—	—	—	—	—	—	19	14	Flint, James "Bruiser"
1998		NCAA	I	64	—	—	—	—	—	—	—	21	11	Flint, James "Bruiser"
1995	W	NCAA	I	—	4	—	—	—	—	—	—	19	11	O'Brien, Joanie
1996		NCAA	I	64	—	—	—	—	—	—	—	20	10	O'Brien, Joanie
1998		NCAA	I	64	—	—	—	—	—	—	—	19	11	O'Brien, Joanie

Year	M/W	Assn	Div	NAT	NIT	ARC	CCA	NCI	NCT	OLY	HLM	W	L	Coach

MASSACHUSETTS BAY CC

Year	M/W	Assn	Div	NAT	NIT	ARC	CCA	NCI	NCT	OLY	HLM	W	L	Coach
1994	M	NSCAA	12	—	—	—	—	—	—	—	—	16	13	Harrison, Allen
1996		NSCAA	10	—	—	—	—	—	—	—	—	27	4	Harrison, Allen

MASSACHUSETTS COLLEGE

Year	M/W	Assn	Div	NAT	NIT	ARC	CCA	NCI	NCT	OLY	HLM	W	L	Coach
1987	M	NCAA	III	32	—	—	—	—	—	—	—	20	6	Quattrocchi, John
1988		NCAA	III	32	—	—	—	—	—	—	—	18	9	Sokaitis, Al
1989		NCAA	III	24	—	—	—	—	—	—	—	23	2	Sokaitis, Al
1990		NCAA	III	8	—	—	—	—	—	—	—	23	5	Sokaitis, Al

MASSACHUSETTS PHARMACY

Year	M/W	Assn	Div	NAT	NIT	ARC	CCA	NCI	NCT	OLY	HLM	W	L	Coach
1994	W	NSCAA	8	—	—	—	—	—	—	—	—	17	3	Ciccolo, Stacy

MASSACHUSETTS: BOSTON

Year	M/W	Assn	Div	NAT	NIT	ARC	CCA	NCI	NCT	OLY	HLM	W	L	Coach
1967	M	NAIA		32	—	—	—	—	—	—	—	18	7	Loscutoff, James, Jr.
1975		NCAA	III	23	—	—	—	—	—	—	—	23	4	Loscutoff, James, Jr.
1976		NCAA	III	21	—	—	—	—	—	—	—	22	5	Loscutoff, James, Jr.
1977		NCAA	III	8	—	—	—	—	—	—	—	25	3	Loscutoff, James, Jr.
1978		NCAA	III	16	—	—	—	—	—	—	—	21	4	Fitzpatrick, Paul
1981		NCAA	III	32	—	—	—	—	—	—	—	19	8	Dowd, Kevin
1983		NCAA	III	24	—	—	—	—	—	—	—	19	9	Titus, Charles
1982	W	NCAA	III	16	—	—	—	—	—	—	—	20	6	Harris, Alfreda

MASSACHUSETTS: DARTMOUTH

Year	M/W	Assn	Div	NAT	NIT	ARC	CCA	NCI	NCT	OLY	HLM	W	L	Coach
1976	M	NCAA	III	14	—	—	—	—	—	—	—	17	9	Wheeler, Bruce E.
1986		NCAA	III	8	—	—	—	—	—	—	—	22	7	Baptiste, Brian
1987		NCAA	III	16	—	—	—	—	—	—	—	27	1	Baptiste, Brian
1988		NCAA	III	16	—	—	—	—	—	—	—	24	4	Baptiste, Brian
1990		NCAA	III	16	—	—	—	—	—	—	—	24	6	Baptiste, Brian
1991		NCAA	III	16	—	—	—	—	—	—	—	23	6	Baptiste, Brian
1993		NCAA	III	4	—	—	—	—	—	—	—	25	6	Baptiste, Brian
1994		NCAA	III	16	—	—	—	—	—	—	—	22	6	Baptiste, Brian
1995		NCAA	III	32	—	—	—	—	—	—	—	24	4	Baptiste, Brian
1997		NCAA	III	64	—	—	—	—	—	—	—	20	7	Baptiste, Brian
1998		NCAA	III	48	—	—	—	—	—	—	—	20	8	Baptiste, Brian

MASSACHUSETTS: LOWELL

Year	M/W	Assn	Div	NAT	NIT	ARC	CCA	NCI	NCT	OLY	HLM	W	L	Coach
1988	M	NCAA	II	1	—	—	—	—	—	—	—	27	7	Doucette, Don
1991	W	NCAA	II	32	—	—	—	—	—	—	—	22	9	O'Neil, Kathleen
1993		NCAA	II	16	—	—	—	—	—	—	—	24	6	O'Neil, Kathleen
1994		NCAA	II	32	—	—	—	—	—	—	—	23	8	O'Neil, Kathleen
1995		NCAA	II	48	—	—	—	—	—	—	—	23	7	O'Neil, Kathleen
1997		NCAA	II	32	—	—	—	—	—	—	—	25	6	O'Neil, Kathleen
1998		NCAA	II	48	—	—	—	—	—	—	—	19	10	O'Neil, Kathleen

MASTER'S

Year	M/W	Assn	Div	NAT	NIT	ARC	CCA	NCI	NCT	OLY	HLM	W	L	Coach
1974	M	NSCAA		8	—	—	—	—	—	—	—	13	21	Fowler, Billy
1982		NSCAA		16	—	—	—	—	—	—	—	18	5	Reese, Pete
1991		NCCAA	I	2	—	—	—	—	—	—	—	22	12	Hankinson, Mel
1992		NCCAA	I	2	—	—	—	—	—	—	—	23	12	Hankinson, Mel

Year	M/W	Assn	Div	NAT	NIT	ARC	CCA	NCI	NCT	OLY	HLM	W	L	Coach
1993		NCCAA	I	4	—	—	—	—	—	—	—	20	12	Hankinson, Mel
1994		NAIA	I	32	—	—	—	—	—	—	—	28	5	Oates, Bill
1995		NAIA	I	8	—	—	—	—	—	—	—	31	5	Oates, Bill
1996		NAIA	I	16	—	—	—	—	—	—	—	28	7	Oates, Bill
1997		NAIA	I	32	—	—	—	—	—	—	—	21	11	Oates, Bill
1998		NAIA	I	32	—	—	—	—	—	—	—	23	12	Oates, Bill
1980	W	NSCAA		6	—	—	—	—	—	—	—	9	9	Harris, Connie

MAYVILLE STATE

Year	M/W	Assn	Div	NAT	NIT	ARC	CCA	NCI	NCT	OLY	HLM	W	L	Coach
1962	M	NAIA		32	—	—	—	—	—	—	—	17	17	Meyer, Alvin H.
1996		NAIA	II	32	—	—	—	—	—	—	—	17	11	Miles, Tim
1997		NAIA	II	32	—	—	—	—	—	—	—	18	11	Miles, Tim
1998		NAIA	II	8	—	—	—	—	—	—	—	23	7	Grove, Paul

McKENDREE

Year	M/W	Assn	Div	NAT	NIT	ARC	CCA	NCI	NCT	OLY	HLM	W	L	Coach
1988	M	NAIA		16	—	—	—	—	—	—	—	35	1	Statham, Harry M.
1992		NAIA	I	32	—	—	—	—	—	—	—	31	6	Statham, Harry M.
1993		NAIA	I	32	—	—	—	—	—	—	—	27	9	Statham, Harry M.
1996		NAIA	I	16	—	—	—	—	—	—	—	25	9	Statham, Harry M.
1997		NAIA	I	8	—	—	—	—	—	—	—	28	9	Statham, Harry M.
1998	W	NAIA	I	32	—	—	—	—	—	—	—	20	15	Miller, Melissa

McMURRY

Year	M/W	Assn	Div	NAT	NIT	ARC	CCA	NCI	NCT	OLY	HLM	W	L	Coach
1962	M	NAIA		32	—	—	—	—	—	—	—	24	4	Kimbrell, Hershell
1994		NAIA	II	16	—	—	—	—	—	—	—	21	8	Holmes, Ron
1980	W	AIAW	III	16	—	—	—	—	—	—	—	17	11	Hicks, Renee
1982		AIAW	III	8	—	—	—	—	—	—	—	22	10	Hicks, Renee

McNEESE STATE

Year	M/W	Assn	Div	NAT	NIT	ARC	CCA	NCI	NCT	OLY	HLM	W	L	Coach
1956	M	NAIA		1	—	—	—	—	—	—	—	33	3	Ward, Ralph O.
1968		NCAA	II	32	—	—	—	—	—	—	—	20	5	Ward, Ralph O.
1986		NCAA	I	—	16	—	—	—	—	—	—	21	11	Duhon, Glenn D.
1989		NCAA	I	64	—	—	—	—	—	—	—	16	14	Welch, Steve

McPHERSON

Year	M/W	Assn	Div	NAT	NIT	ARC	CCA	NCI	NCT	OLY	HLM	W	L	Coach
1938	M	NAIA		32	—	—	—	—	—	—	—	13	8	Astle, W. P. "Buck"
1971	W			—	8	—	—	—	—	—	—	X	X	Coppock, Dr. Doris

MEDAILLE

Year	M/W	Assn	Div	NAT	NIT	ARC	CCA	NCI	NCT	OLY	HLM	W	L	Coach
1997	M	NSCAA		3	—	—	—	—	—	—	—	18	10	Jacob, Richard L.
1998		NSCAA		9	—	—	—	—	—	—	—	14	16	Jacob, Richard L.

MEMPHIS

Year	M/W	Assn	Div	NAT	NIT	ARC	CCA	NCI	NCT	OLY	HLM	W	L	Coach
1951	M	NAIA		8	—	—	—	—	—	—	—	17	8	Tarry, McCoy
1952		NAIA		16	—	—	—	—	—	—	—	25	10	Lambert, Dr. Eugene W.
1955		NCAA		24	—	—	—	—	—	—	—	17	5	Lambert, Dr. Eugene W.
1956		NCAA		25	—	—	—	—	—	—	—	20	7	Lambert, Dr. Eugene W.
1957		NCAA	I	—	2	—	—	—	—	—	—	24	6	Vanatta, Robert
1960		NCAA	I	—	12	—	—	—	—	—	—	18	5	Vanatta, Robert
1961		NCAA	I	—	8	—	—	—	—	—	—	20	3	Vanatta, Robert
1962		NCAA	I	25	—	—	—	—	—	—	—	15	7	Vanatta, Robert

Year	M/W	Assn	Div	NAT	NIT	ARC	CCA	NCI	NCT	OLY	HLM	W	L	Coach
1963		NCAA	I	—	8	—	—	—	—	—	—	19	7	Ehlers, Dean
1967		NCAA	I	—	14	—	—	—	—	—	—	17	9	Iba, Moe
1972		NCAA	I	—	16	—	—	—	—	—	—	21	7	Bartow, B. Gene
1973		NCAA	I	2	—	—	—	—	—	—	—	24	6	Bartow, B. Gene
1974		NCAA	I	—	8	—	—	—	—	—	—	19	11	Bartow, B. Gene
1975		NCAA	I	—	16	—	—	—	—	—	—	20	7	Yates, Wayne E.
1976		NCAA	I	32	—	—	—	—	—	—	—	21	9	Yates, Wayne E.
1977		NCAA	I	—	16	—	—	—	—	—	—	20	9	Yates, Wayne E.
1982		NCAA	I	16	—	—	—	—	—	—	—	24	5	Kirk, Dana
1983		NCAA	I	16	—	—	—	—	—	—	—	23	8	Kirk, Dana
1984		NCAA	I	16	—	—	—	—	—	—	—	26	7	Kirk, Dana
1985		NCAA	I	3	—	—	—	—	—	—	—	31	4	Kirk, Dana
1986		NCAA	I	32	—	—	—	—	—	—	—	28	6	Kirk, Dana
1988		NCAA	I	32	—	—	—	—	—	—	—	20	12	Finch, Larry O.
1989		NCAA	I	64	—	—	—	—	—	—	—	21	11	Finch, Larry O.
1990		NCAA	I	—	32	—	—	—	—	—	—	18	12	Finch, Larry O.
1991		NCAA	I	—	16	—	—	—	—	—	—	17	15	Finch, Larry O.
1992		NCAA	I	8	—	—	—	—	—	—	—	23	11	Finch, Larry O.
1993		NCAA	I	64	—	—	—	—	—	—	—	20	12	Finch, Larry O.
1995		NCAA	I	16	—	—	—	—	—	—	—	24	10	Finch, Larry O.
1996		NCAA	I	64	—	—	—	—	—	—	—	22	8	Finch, Larry O.
1997		NCAA	I	—	32	—	—	—	—	—	—	16	15	Finch, Larry O.
1998		NCAA	I	—	16	—	—	—	—	—	—	17	12	Price, George "Tic"
1982	W	NCAA	I	16	—	—	—	—	—	—	—	26	5	Johns, Mary Lou
1983		NCAA	I	—	2	—	—	—	—	—	—	21	11	Johns, Mary Lou
1985		NCAA	I	32	—	—	—	—	—	—	—	23	7	Johns, Mary Lou
1987		NCAA	I	32	—	—	—	—	—	—	—	20	9	Johns, Mary Lou
1995		NCAA	I	32	—	—	—	—	—	—	—	22	8	Lee-McNelis, Joye
1996		NCAA	I	64	—	—	—	—	—	—	—	20	11	Lee-McNelis, Joye
1997		NCAA	I	64	—	—	—	—	—	—	—	22	7	Lee-McNelis, Joye
1998		NCAA	I	64	—	—	—	—	—	—	—	22	8	Lee-McNelis, Joye

MERCER

Year	M/W	Assn	Div	NAT	NIT	ARC	CCA	NCI	NCT	OLY	HLM	W	L	Coach
1948	M	NAIA		32	—	—	—	—	—	—	—	18	4	Cowan, James M.
1954		NAIA		32	—	—	—	—	—	—	—	19	9	Cowan, James M.
1972		NCAA	II	32	—	—	—	—	—	—	—	17	7	Morrison, Dwane A.
1981		NCAA	I	48	—	—	—	—	—	—	—	18	12	Bibb, Bill
1985		NCAA	I	64	—	—	—	—	—	—	—	22	9	Bibb, Bill
1973	W	AIAW		8	—	—	—	—	—	—	—	19	4	Collins, Peggy E.
1975		AIAW	L	—	4	—	—	—	—	—	—	23	6	Collins, Peggy E.
1980		AIAW	I	24	—	—	—	—	—	—	—	29	6	Fontaine, Jane
1985		NCAA	II	3	—	—	—	—	—	—	—	24	7	Nixon, Ed

MERCHANT MARINE

Year	M/W	Assn	Div	NAT	NIT	ARC	CCA	NCI	NCT	OLY	HLM	W	L	Coach
1989	M	NCAA	III	24	—	—	—	—	—	—	—	25	3	Cohane, Tim
1997		NCAA	III	64	—	—	—	—	—	—	—	19	7	Greer, Andrew
1998		NCAA	III	48	—	—	—	—	—	—	—	16	11	MacKinnon, Robert A.

MERCY (NY)

Year	M/W	Assn	Div	NAT	NIT	ARC	CCA	NCI	NCT	OLY	HLM	W	L	Coach
1985	W	NCAA	II	24	—	—	—	—	—	—	—	22	7	Schachner, Carol

Year	M/W	Assn	Div	NAT	NIT	ARC	CCA	NCI	NCT	OLY	HLM	W	L	Coach
MERCYHURST														
1978	M	NAIA		32	—	—	—	—	—	—	—	24	2	Fox, Richard A.
1994	W	NCAA	II	32	—	—	—	—	—	—	—	19	9	Demyanovich, Paul
1995		NCAA	II	8	—	—	—	—	—	—	—	24	6	Webb, James D.
MERRIMACK														
1977	M	NCAA	II	16	—	—	—	—	—	—	—	19	9	Monahan, Frank T.
1978		NCAA	II	16	—	—	—	—	—	—	—	22	6	Monahan, Frank T.
1991		NCAA	II	24	—	—	—	—	—	—	—	21	9	Hammel, Bert
1992		NCAA	II	24	—	—	—	—	—	—	—	18	14	Hammel, Bert
MESA STATE														
1985	M	NAIA		32	—	—	—	—	—	—	—	23	8	Schakel, Doug
1994		NCAA	II	32	—	—	—	—	—	—	—	20	9	Schakel, Doug
1995		NCAA	II	48	—	—	—	—	—	—	—	20	9	Schakel, Doug
MESSENGER														
1995	M	NBCAA	II	4	—	—	—	—	—	—	—	21	17	Stallman, David S.
1995		NCCAA	IIA	8	—	—	—	—	—	—	—	21	17	Stallman, David S.
1996		NBCAA	II	6	—	—	—	—	—	—	—	10	15	Stallman, David S.
1997		NBCAA	II	7	—	—	—	—	—	—	—	5	19	Stallman, David S.
1998		NBCAA		6	—	—	—	—	—	—	—	4	25	Hall, Homer D.
1995	W	NBCAA		3	—	—	—	—	—	—	—	4	13	Hall, Homer D.
1996		NBCAA		6	—	—	—	—	—	—	—	5	12	Hall, Homer D.
MESSIAH														
1968	M	NCCAA		4	—	—	—	—	—	—	—	11	11	Drescher, Luke M.
1972		NCCAA		8	—	—	—	—	—	—	—	19	12	Shaker, Marshall "Mike"
1974		NCCAA		3	—	—	—	—	—	—	—	20	11	Shaker, Marshall "Mike"
1983	W	NCCAA	I	8	—	—	—	—	—	—	—	16	7	Clelan-Blank, Nancy
1984		NCCAA	I	8	—	—	—	—	—	—	—	16	9	Clelan-Blank, Nancy
1996		NCAA	III	32	—	—	—	—	—	—	—	20	8	Miller, Michael
METHODIST														
1975	M	NCAA	III	23	—	—	—	—	—	—	—	21	5	Gallagher, Joe
1977		NCAA	III	16	—	—	—	—	—	—	—	18	8	Miller, Joe F.
1997		NCAA	III	8	—	—	—	—	—	—	—	22	8	McEvoy, Bob
METROPOLITAN STATE (CO)														
1990	M	NCAA	II	16	—	—	—	—	—	—	—	28	4	Hull, Bob
1991		NCAA	II	24	—	—	—	—	—	—	—	23	8	Hull, Bob
1998		NCAA	II	32	—	—	—	—	—	—	—	25	5	Dunlap, Mike
1996	W	NCAA	II	48	—	—	—	—	—	—	—	20	8	Smith, Darryl
1998		NCAA	II	48	—	—	—	—	—	—	—	25	5	Smith, Darryl
MIAMI (FL)														
1949	M	NAIA		32	—	—	—	—	—	—	—	19	8	Morris, Hart
1960		NCAA	I	25	—	—	—	—	—	—	—	23	4	Hale, William Bruce
1961		NCAA	I	—	12	—	—	—	—	—	—	20	7	Hale, William Bruce
1963		NCAA	I	—	8	—	—	—	—	—	—	23	5	Hale, William Bruce

Year	M/W	Assn	Div	NAT	NIT	ARC	CCA	NCI	NCT	OLY	HLM	W	L	Coach
1964		NCAA	I	—	12	—	—	—	—	—	—	20	7	Hale, William Bruce
1995		NCAA	I	—	32	—	—	—	—	—	—	15	13	Hamilton, Leonard
1997		NCAA	I	—	32	—	—	—	—	—	—	16	13	Hamilton, Leonard
1998		NCAA	I	64	—	—	—	—	—	—	—	18	10	Hamilton, Leonard
1989	W	NCAA	I	48	—	—	—	—	—	—	—	21	8	Labati, Ferne
1990		NCAA	I	—	4	—	—	—	—	—	—	25	6	Labati, Ferne
1992		NCAA	I	16	—	—	—	—	—	—	—	30	2	Labati, Ferne
1993		NCAA	I	32	—	—	—	—	—	—	—	24	7	Labati, Ferne
1998		NCAA	I	64	—	—	—	—	—	—	—	19	10	Labati, Ferne

MIAMI (OH)

Year	M/W	Assn	Div	NAT	NIT	ARC	CCA	NCI	NCT	OLY	HLM	W	L	Coach
1953	M	NCAA		22	—	—	—	—	—	—	—	17	6	Rohr, William D.
1955		NCAA		24	—	—	—	—	—	—	—	14	9	Rohr, William D.
1957		NCAA	I	23	—	—	—	—	—	—	—	17	8	Rohr, William D.
1958		NCAA	I	16	—	—	—	—	—	—	—	18	9	Shrider, Richard G.
1966		NCAA	I	22	—	—	—	—	—	—	—	18	7	Shrider, Richard G.
1969		NCAA	I	16	—	—	—	—	—	—	—	15	12	Locke, Taylor O. "Tates"
1970		NCAA	I	—	16	—	—	—	—	—	—	16	8	Locke, Taylor O. "Tates"
1971		NCAA	I	25	—	—	—	—	—	—	—	20	5	Hedric, Darrell
1973		NCAA	I	25	—	—	—	—	—	—	—	18	9	Hedric, Darrell
1978		NCAA	I	16	—	—	—	—	—	—	—	19	9	Hedric, Darrell
1984		NCAA	I	48	—	—	—	—	—	—	—	24	6	Hedric, Darrell
1985		NCAA	I	64	—	—	—	—	—	—	—	20	11	Peirson, Jerry
1986		NCAA	I	64	—	—	—	—	—	—	—	24	7	Peirson, Jerry
1992		NCAA	I	64	—	—	—	—	—	—	—	23	8	Wright, Joseph A. "Joby"
1993		NCAA	I	—	8	—	—	—	—	—	—	22	9	Wright, Joseph A. "Joby"
1994		NCAA	I	—	32	—	—	—	—	—	—	19	11	Sendek, Herb
1995		NCAA	I	32	—	—	—	—	—	—	—	23	7	Sendek, Herb
1996		NCAA	I	—	32	—	—	—	—	—	—	21	8	Sendek, Herb
1997		NCAA	I	64	—	—	—	—	—	—	—	21	9	Coles, Charles "Charlie"
1982	W	AIAW	I	16	—	—	—	—	—	—	—	24	9	Wettig, Pamela

MICHIGAN

Year	M/W	Assn	Div	NAT	NIT	ARC	CCA	NCI	NCT	OLY	HLM	W	L	Coach
1948	M	NCAA		6	—	—	—	—	—	—	—	16	6	McCoy, Ernest B.
1964		NCAA	I	3	—	—	—	—	—	—	—	23	5	Strack, David H.
1965		NCAA	I	2	—	—	—	—	—	—	—	24	4	Strack, David H.
1966		NCAA	I	8	—	—	—	—	—	—	—	18	8	Strack, David H.
1971		NCAA	I	—	8	—	—	—	—	—	—	19	7	Orr, John M. "Johnny"
1974		NCAA	I	8	—	—	—	—	—	—	—	22	5	Orr, John M. "Johnny"
1975		NCAA	I	32	—	—	—	—	—	—	—	19	8	Orr, John M. "Johnny"
1976		NCAA	I	2	—	—	—	—	—	—	—	25	7	Orr, John M. "Johnny"
1977		NCAA	I	8	—	—	—	—	—	—	—	26	4	Orr, John M. "Johnny"
1980		NCAA	I	—	8	—	—	—	—	—	—	17	13	Orr, John M. "Johnny"
1981		NCAA	I	—	8	—	—	—	—	—	—	19	11	Frieder, Bill
1984		NCAA	I	—	1	—	—	—	—	—	—	23	10	Frieder, Bill
1985		NCAA	I	32	—	—	—	—	—	—	—	26	4	Frieder, Bill
1986		NCAA	I	32	—	—	—	—	—	—	—	28	5	Frieder, Bill
1987		NCAA	I	32	—	—	—	—	—	—	—	20	12	Frieder, Bill
1988		NCAA	I	16	—	—	—	—	—	—	—	26	8	Frieder, Bill

Year	M/W	Assn	Div	NAT	NIT	ARC	CCA	NCI	NCT	OLY	HLM	W	L	Coach
1989		NCAA	I	1	—	—	—	—	—	—	—	30	7	Fisher, Stephen L.
1990		NCAA	I	32	—	—	—	—	—	—	—	23	8	Fisher, Stephen L.
1991		NCAA	I	—	32	—	—	—	—	—	—	14	15	Fisher, Stephen L.
1992		NCAA	I	2	—	—	—	—	—	—	—	25	9	Fisher, Stephen L.
1993		NCAA	I	2	—	—	—	—	—	—	—	31	5	Fisher, Stephen L.
1994		NCAA	I	8	—	—	—	—	—	—	—	24	8	Fisher, Stephen L.
1995		NCAA	I	64	—	—	—	—	—	—	—	17	14	Fisher, Stephen L.
1996		NCAA	I	64	—	—	—	—	—	—	—	20	12	Fisher, Stephen L.
1997		NCAA	I	—	1	—	—	—	—	—	—	24	11	Fisher, Stephen L.
1998		NCAA	I	32	—	—	—	—	—	—	—	25	9	Ellerbee, Brian
1990	W	NCAA	I	32	—	—	—	—	—	—	—	20	10	Van De Wege, "Bud", Jr.
1998		NCAA	I	64	—	—	—	—	—	—	—	19	10	Guevara, Sue

MICHIGAN STATE

Year	M/W	Assn	Div	NAT	NIT	ARC	CCA	NCI	NCT	OLY	HLM	W	L	Coach
1957	M	NCAA	I	4	—	—	—	—	—	—	—	16	10	Anderson, Forrest A. "Forddy"
1959		NCAA	I	8	—	—	—	—	—	—	—	19	4	Anderson, Forrest A. "Forddy"
1978		NCAA	I	8	—	—	—	—	—	—	—	25	5	Heathcote, George "Jud"
1979		NCAA	I	1	—	—	—	—	—	—	1	26	6	Heathcote, George "Jud"
1983		NCAA	I	—	16	—	—	—	—	—	—	17	13	Heathcote, George "Jud"
1985		NCAA	I	64	—	—	—	—	—	—	—	19	10	Heathcote, George "Jud"
1986		NCAA	I	16	—	—	—	—	—	—	—	23	8	Heathcote, George "Jud"
1989		NCAA	I	—	4	—	—	—	—	—	—	18	15	Heathcote, George "Jud"
1990		NCAA	I	16	—	—	—	—	—	—	—	28	6	Heathcote, George "Jud"
1991		NCAA	I	32	—	—	—	—	—	—	—	19	11	Heathcote, George "Jud"
1992		NCAA	I	32	—	—	—	—	—	—	—	22	8	Heathcote, George "Jud"
1993		NCAA	I	—	32	—	—	—	—	—	—	15	13	Heathcote, George "Jud"
1994		NCAA	I	32	—	—	—	—	—	—	—	20	12	Heathcote, George "Jud"
1995		NCAA	I	64	—	—	—	—	—	—	—	22	6	Heathcote, George "Jud"
1996		NCAA	I	—	16	—	—	—	—	—	—	16	16	Izzo, Tom
1997		NCAA	I	—	16	—	—	—	—	—	—	17	12	Izzo, Tom
1998		NCAA	I	16	—	—	—	—	—	—	—	23	8	Izzo, Tom
1977	W	AIAW	L	16	—	—	—	—	—	—	—	23	6	Langeland, Karen
1991		NCAA	I	32	—	—	—	—	—	—	—	21	8	Langeland, Karen
1996		NCAA	I	32	—	—	—	—	—	—	—	18	11	Langeland, Karen
1997		NCAA	I	32	—	—	—	—	—	—	—	22	8	Langeland, Karen

MICHIGAN TECH

Year	M/W	Assn	Div	NAT	NIT	ARC	CCA	NCI	NCT	OLY	HLM	W	L	Coach
1963	M	NCAA	II	24	—	—	—	—	—	—	—	17	5	Cox, Verdie T.
1998		NCAA	II	32	—	—	—	—	—	—	—	21	10	Luke, Kevin
1991	W	NCAA	II	32	—	—	—	—	—	—	—	22	7	Borseth, Kevin
1992		NCAA	II	32	—	—	—	—	—	—	—	23	6	Borseth, Kevin
1993		NCAA	II	3	—	—	—	—	—	—	—	30	3	Borseth, Kevin
1994		NCAA	II	32	—	—	—	—	—	—	—	23	6	Borseth, Kevin
1995		NCAA	II	16	—	—	—	—	—	—	—	24	6	Borseth, Kevin
1997		NCAA	II	32	—	—	—	—	—	—	—	21	9	Borseth, Kevin
1998		NCAA	II	16	—	—	—	—	—	—	—	21	10	Borseth, Kevin

MID-AMERICA BIBLE

Year	M/W	Assn	Div	NAT	NIT	ARC	CCA	NCI	NCT	OLY	HLM	W	L	Coach
1978	M	NCCAA	II	6	—	—	—	—	—	—	—	22	12	Holley, Willie
1979		NCCAA	II	6	—	—	—	—	—	—	—	19	9	Holley, Willie
1980		NCCAA	II	6	—	—	—	—	—	—	—	14	16	Holley, Willie
1981		NCCAA	II	6	—	—	—	—	—	—	—	19	18	Holley, Willie

Year	M/W	Assn	Div	NAT	NIT	ARC	CCA	NCI	NCT	OLY	HLM	W	L	Coach
1982		NCCAA	II	8	—	—	—	—	—	—	—	19	7	Holley, Willie
1983		NCCAA	II	8	—	—	—	—	—	—	—	22	10	Holley, Willie
1985		NCCAA	II	8	—	—	—	—	—	—	—	13	17	Holley, Willie
1986		NCCAA	II	3	—	—	—	—	—	—	—	22	12	Holley, Willie
1992		NCCAA	IIA	3	—	—	—	—	—	—	—	17	19	Holley, Willie
1993		NCCAA	II	6	—	—	—	—	—	—	—	25	14	Holley, Willie
1995		NCCAA	II	8	—	—	—	—	—	—	—	22	12	Holley, Willie
1996		NCCAA	II	6	—	—	—	—	—	—	—	21	15	Holley, Willie
1997		NCCAA	II	7	—	—	—	—	—	—	—	26	17	Holley, Willie
1998		NCCAA	II	1	—	—	—	—	—	—	—	32	8	Holley, Willie
1993	W	NCCAA	II	8	—	—	—	—	—	—	—	10	9	O'Brien, Tony
1994		NCCAA	II	4	—	—	—	—	—	—	—	10	9	O'Brien, Tony
1996		NCCAA	II	2	—	—	—	—	—	—	—	17	19	O'Brien, Tony
1997		NCCAA	II	2	—	—	—	—	—	—	—	18	17	O'Brien, Tony
1998		NCCAA	II	2	—	—	—	—	—	—	—	20	15	O'Brien, Tony

MIDAMERICA NAZARENE

Year	M/W	Assn	Div	NAT	NIT	ARC	CCA	NCI	NCT	OLY	HLM	W	L	Coach
1978	M	NCCAA	I	6	—	—	—	—	—	—	—	15	13	Smith, James H.
1992		NAIA	II	8	—	—	—	—	—	—	—	27	10	Lamar, Jon "Rocky"
1994		NCCAA	I	3	—	—	—	—	—	—	—	20	17	Lamar, Jon "Rocky"
1995		NAIA	II	32	—	—	—	—	—	—	—	21	15	Lamar, Jon "Rocky"
1996		NAIA	II	16	—	—	—	—	—	—	—	20	17	Lamar, Jon "Rocky"
1997		NCCAA	I	2	—	—	—	—	—	—	—	24	13	Lamar, Jon "Rocky"
1998		NCCAA	I	2	—	—	—	—	—	—	—	27	11	Lamar, Jon "Rocky"
1984	W	NCCAA	I	4	—	—	—	—	—	—	—	20	17	Hook, Norton
1994		NCCAA	I	2	—	—	—	—	—	—	—	18	19	Kliewer, Karl
1996		NCCAA	I	5	—	—	—	—	—	—	—	18	18	Kliewer, Karl

MIDDLE TENNESSEE STATE

Year	M/W	Assn	Div	NAT	NIT	ARC	CCA	NCI	NCT	OLY	HLM	W	L	Coach
1955	M	NAIA		32	—	—	—	—	—	—	—	11	16	Greer, Charles N., Jr.
1975		NCAA	I	32	—	—	—	—	—	—	—	23	5	Earle, James P. "Jimmy"
1977		NCAA	I	32	—	—	—	—	—	—	—	20	9	Earle, James P. "Jimmy"
1982		NCAA	I	32	—	—	—	—	—	—	—	22	8	Simpson, Stanley "Ramrod"
1985		NCAA	I	64	—	—	—	—	—	—	—	17	14	Stewart, Bruce
1986		NCAA	I	—	32	—	—	—	—	—	—	23	11	Stewart, Bruce
1987		NCAA	I	64	—	—	—	—	—	—	—	22	7	Stewart, Bruce
1988		NCAA	I	—	8	—	—	—	—	—	—	23	11	Stewart, Bruce
1989		NCAA	I	32	—	—	—	—	—	—	—	23	8	Stewart, Bruce
1983	W	NCAA	I	32	—	—	—	—	—	—	—	26	5	Inman, Larry Joe
1984		NCAA	I	32	—	—	—	—	—	—	—	19	10	Inman, Larry Joe
1985		NCAA	I	32	—	—	—	—	—	—	—	23	7	Inman, Larry Joe
1986		NCAA	I	32	—	—	—	—	—	—	—	20	10	Inman, Larry Joe
1988		NCAA	I	40	—	—	—	—	—	—	—	22	8	Bivens, Lewis
1996		NCAA	I	64	—	—	—	—	—	—	—	24	6	Bivens, Lewis
1998		NCAA	I	64	—	—	—	—	—	—	—	18	12	Smith, Stephany

MIDDLEBURY

Year	M/W	Assn	Div	NAT	NIT	ARC	CCA	NCI	NCT	OLY	HLM	W	L	Coach
1995	W	NCAA	III	64	—	—	—	—	—	—	—	18	6	Fulcher, Jennifer
1996		NCAA	III	32	—	—	—	—	—	—	—	21	5	Fulcher, Jennifer
1998		NCAA	III	48	—	—	—	—	—	—	—	20	5	Fulcher, Jennifer

828   College Basketball's National Championships

Year	M/W	Assn	Div	NAT	NIT	ARC	CCA	NCI	NCT	OLY	HLM	W	L	Coach
MIDLAND COMMERCE														
1967	M	NSCAA		5	—	—	—	—	—	—	—	20	3	Noble, Del
MIDLAND LUTHERAN														
1990	M	NAIA		32	—	—	—	—	—	—	—	17	15	McGill, Richard "Rich"
1975	W	AIAW	S	6	—	—	—	—	—	—	—	18	8	Bracker, Joanne
1978		AIAW	S	12	—	—	—	—	—	—	—	29	4	Bracker, Joanne
1985		NAIA		4	—	—	—	—	—	—	—	26	5	Bracker, Joanne
1991		NAIA		16	—	—	—	—	—	—	—	22	8	Bracker, Joanne
1992		NAIA	I	32	—	—	—	—	—	—	—	25	5	Bracker, Joanne
1995		NAIA	II	16	—	—	—	—	—	—	—	22	7	Bracker, Joanne
1996		NAIA	II	16	—	—	—	—	—	—	—	26	6	Bracker, Joanne
MIDWAY														
1990	W	NSCAA		7	—	—	—	—	—	—	—	6	18	Dever, Debbie
1991		NSCAA		5	—	—	—	—	—	—	—	13	20	Brett, Kathy
1994		NSCAA		5	—	—	—	—	—	—	—	20	13	Duncan, John
1995		NSCAA		4	—	—	—	—	—	—	—	20	17	Duncan, John
MIDWEST CHRISTIAN														
1985	M	NBCAA	II	1	—	—	—	—	—	—	—	X	X	Williams, Charles R.
MIDWESTERN (IA)														
1969	W			—	3	—	—	—	—	—	—	21	X	Horky, Rita J.
1970				—	2	—	—	—	—	—	—			Hart, Kaye
MIDWESTERN STATE (TX)														
1953	M	NAIA		32	—	—	—	—	—	—	—	18	8	Clynch, Dallas C.
1956		NAIA		8	—	—	—	—	—	—	—	21	8	Clynch, Dallas C.
1960		NAIA		32	—	—	—	—	—	—	—	17	13	Vinzant, Dennis
1965		NAIA		16	—	—	—	—	—	—	—	28	6	Vinzant, Dennis
1966		NAIA		16	—	—	—	—	—	—	—	26	6	Vinzant, Dennis
1967		NAIA		16	—	—	—	—	—	—	—	21	11	Vinzant, Dennis
1974		NAIA		8	—	—	—	—	—	—	—	30	7	Stockton, Dr. Gerald E.
1975		NAIA		2	—	—	—	—	—	—	—	31	6	Stockton, Dr. Gerald E.
1978		NAIA		32	—	—	—	—	—	—	—	21	13	Stockton, Dr. Gerald E.
1979		NAIA		4	—	—	—	—	—	—	—	24	17	Stockton, Dr. Gerald E.
1981		NAIA		8	—	—	—	—	—	—	—	25	18	Stockton, Dr. Gerald E.
1984		NAIA		32	—	—	—	—	—	—	—	25	16	Stockton, Dr. Gerald E.
1993		NAIA	I	3	—	—	—	—	—	—	—	25	12	Stockton, Dr. Gerald E.
1994		NAIA	I	3	—	—	—	—	—	—	—	23	12	Stockton, Dr. Gerald E.
1995		NAIA	I	32	—	—	—	—	—	—	—	19	11	Ray, Jeff
1993	W	NAIA	I	16	—	—	—	—	—	—	—	22	8	Ray, Jeff
1994		NAIA	I	16	—	—	—	—	—	—	—	28	6	Ray, Jeff
1995		NAIA	I	16	—	—	—	—	—	—	—	20	10	Williams, Wayne
MILES														
1963	M	NAIA		16	—	—	—	—	—	—	—	20	5	Wilkins, Arthur "Pete"
1964		NAIA		32	—	—	—	—	—	—	—	13	7	Wilkins, Arthur "Pete"
1974		NCAA	II	44	—	—	—	—	—	—	—	21	6	Wilkins, Arthur "Pete"
1975		NCAA	III	16	—	—	—	—	—	—	—	21	8	Wilkins, Arthur "Pete"
1976		NCAA	III	7	—	—	—	—	—	—	—	23	8	Wilkins, Arthur "Pete"

Year	M/W	Assn	Div	NAT	NIT	ARC	CCA	NCI	NCT	OLY	HLM	W	L	Coach
MILLERSVILLE														
1957	M	NAIA		32	—	—	—	—	—	—	—	18	6	DeHart, Richard C.
1966		NAIA		32	—	—	—	—	—	—	—	19	7	DeHart, Richard C.
1967		NAIA		32	—	—	—	—	—	—	—	21	6	DeHart, Richard C.
1968		NAIA		32	—	—	—	—	—	—	—	17	8	DeHart, Richard C.
1974		NAIA		32	—	—	—	—	—	—	—	21	5	DeHart, Richard C.
1975		NAIA		16	—	—	—	—	—	—	—	17	10	DeHart, Richard C.
1985		NCAA	II	24	—	—	—	—	—	—	—	27	4	Kochan, John
1986		NCAA	II	24	—	—	—	—	—	—	—	24	6	Kochan, John
1987		NCAA	II	16	—	—	—	—	—	—	—	27	4	Kochan, John
1989		NCAA	II	8	—	—	—	—	—	—	—	26	7	Kochan, John
1993		NCAA	II	16	—	—	—	—	—	—	—	24	6	Kochan, John
1995		NCAA	II	24	—	—	—	—	—	—	—	26	4	Kochan, John
1982	W	AIAW	III	4	—	—	—	—	—	—	—	14	7	Schlegel, Debra
1984		NCAA	II	24	—	—	—	—	—	—	—	19	7	Schlegel, Debra
1987		NCAA	II	16	—	—	—	—	—	—	—	18	8	Schlegel, Debra
MILLIGAN														
1990	M	NCCAA	I	8	—	—	—	—	—	—	—	27	9	Wallingford, Tony
1995		NAIA	II	32	—	—	—	—	—	—	—	24	12	Scruggs, Rick
1997	W	NAIA	II	16	—	—	—	—	—	—	—	30	5	Aubrey, Richard 'Rich'
1998		NAIA	II	32	—	—	—	—	—	—	—	27	8	Aubrey, Richard 'Rich'
MILLIKIN														
1951	M	NAIA		2	—	—	—	—	—	—	—	24	7	Allan, Ralph W.
1952		NAIA		16	—	—	—	—	—	—	—	21	6	Allan, Ralph W.
1968		NAIA		32	—	—	—	—	—	—	—	21	4	Williams, Don E.
1969		NAIA		32	—	—	—	—	—	—	—	16	9	Williams, Don E.
1983		NCAA	III	16	—	—	—	—	—	—	—	21	7	Ramsey, Joe
1988		NCAA	III	16	—	—	—	—	—	—	—	22	6	Ramsey, Joe
1989		NCAA	III	32	—	—	—	—	—	—	—	20	7	Ramsey, Joe
1982	W	NCAA	III	16	—	—	—	—	—	—	—	11	6	Crannell, Harriett
1984		NCAA	III	24	—	—	—	—	—	—	—	19	6	Crannell, Harriett
1985		NCAA	III	3	—	—	—	—	—	—	—	23	3	Crannell, Harriett
1989		NCAA	III	32	—	—	—	—	—	—	—	20	7	Kearns, Lori Ann
1994		NCAA	III	8	—	—	—	—	—	—	—	24	4	Kearns, Lori Ann
1995		NCAA	III	16	—	—	—	—	—	—	—	23	5	Kearns, Lori Ann
1996		NCAA	III	16	—	—	—	—	—	—	—	23	5	Kearns, Lori Ann
1997		NCAA	III	8	—	—	—	—	—	—	—	25	3	Kearns, Lori Ann
1998		NCAA	III	32	—	—	—	—	—	—	—	25	1	Kearns, Lori Ann
MILLSAPS														
1984	M	NCAA	III	24	—	—	—	—	—	—	—	20	6	Holcomb, Don
1995		NCAA	III	16	—	—	—	—	—	—	—	25	3	Stroud, John
1996		NCAA	III	32	—	—	—	—	—	—	—	22	5	Stroud, John
1995	W	NCAA	III	64	—	—	—	—	—	—	—	19	7	Hannon, Cindy
1996		NCAA	III	32	—	—	—	—	—	—	—	23	4	Hannon, Cindy

Year	M/W	Assn	Div	NAT	NIT	ARC	CCA	NCI	NCT	OLY	HLM	W	L	Coach
MINNESOTA														
1902	M			—	—	—	—	—	—	—	1	15	0	Cooke, Dr. Louis J.
1919		NCAA		—	—	—	—	—	—	—	1	13	0	Cooke, Dr. Louis J.
1972		NCAA	I	12	—	—	—	—	—	—	—	18	7	Musselman, William
1973		NCAA	I	—	8	—	—	—	—	—	—	21	5	Musselman, William
1980		NCAA	I	—	2	—	—	—	—	—	—	21	11	Dutcher, James D.
1981		NCAA	I	—	8	—	—	—	—	—	—	19	11	Dutcher, James D.
1982		NCAA	I	16	—	—	—	—	—	—	—	23	6	Dutcher, James D.
1983		NCAA	I	—	32	—	—	—	—	—	—	18	13	Dutcher, James D.
1989		NCAA	I	16	—	—	—	—	—	—	—	19	12	Haskins, Clem S.
1990		NCAA	I	8	—	—	—	—	—	—	—	23	9	Haskins, Clem S.
1992		NCAA	I	—	32	—	—	—	—	—	—	16	16	Haskins, Clem S.
1993		NCAA	I	—	1	—	—	—	—	—	—	22	10	Haskins, Clem S.
1994		NCAA	I	32	—	—	—	—	—	—	—	21	12	Haskins, Clem S.
1995		NCAA	I	64	—	—	—	—	—	—	—	19	12	Haskins, Clem S.
1996		NCAA	I	—	16	—	—	—	—	—	—	19	13	Haskins, Clem S.
1997		NCAA	I	3	—	—	—	—	—	—	—	31	4	Haskins, Clem S.
1998		NCAA	I	—	1	—	—	—	—	—	—	20	15	Haskins, Clem S.
1977	W	AIAW	L	16	—	—	—	—	—	—	—	15	14	Johnson, Jenny
1978		AIAW	L	—	7	—	—	—	—	—	—	21	7	Hanson, Ellen Mosher
1979		AIAW	L	—	5	—	—	—	—	—	—	17	15	Hanson, Ellen Mosher
1981		AIAW	I	24	—	—	—	—	—	—	—	28	7	Hanson, Ellen Mosher
1982		AIAW	I	8	—	—	—	—	—	—	—	18	10	Hanson, Ellen Mosher
1994		NCAA	I	32	—	—	—	—	—	—	—	18	11	Hill-MacDonald, Linda
MINNESOTA BIBLE														
1982	M	NBCAA		7	—	—	—	—	—	—	—	6	10	Comeaux, R. Mark
1984		NBCAA	II	1	—	—	—	—	—	—	—	19	8	Comeaux, R. Mark
1987		NBCAA	II	3	—	—	—	—	—	—	—	X	X	Comeaux, R. Mark
1990		NBCAA	II	7	—	—	—	—	—	—	—	4	10	Kester, John
1993		NBCAA	II	8	—	—	—	—	—	—	—	7	10	Addison, Don
1994		NBCAA	II	5	—	—	—	—	—	—	—	10	10	Comeaux, R. Mark
1997		NBCAA	II	8	—	—	—	—	—	—	—	3	13	Wager, Al
1995	W	NBCAA		2	—	—	—	—	—	—	—	7	5	Nordrum, Joel
MINNESOTA: DULUTH														
1957	M	NCAA	II	32	—	—	—	—	—	—	—	15	7	Olson, Norman H.
1958		NAIA		32	—	—	—	—	—	—	—	20	3	Olson, Norman H.
1959		NAIA		16	—	—	—	—	—	—	—	22	4	Olson, Norman H.
1965		NCAA	II	24	—	—	—	—	—	—	—	20	8	Olson, Norman H.
1985		NAIA		16	—	—	—	—	—	—	—	23	8	Race, Dale M.
1986		NAIA		32	—	—	—	—	—	—	—	23	8	Race, Dale M.
1987		NAIA		32	—	—	—	—	—	—	—	24	7	Race, Dale M.
1988		NAIA		16	—	—	—	—	—	—	—	25	6	Race, Dale M.
1989		NAIA		32	—	—	—	—	—	—	—	25	6	Race, Dale M.
1990		NAIA		16	—	—	—	—	—	—	—	26	6	Race, Dale M.
1991		NAIA		16	—	—	—	—	—	—	—	27	5	Race, Dale M.
1992		NAIA	I	16	—	—	—	—	—	—	—	23	9	Race, Dale M.
1997		NCAA	II	48	—	—	—	—	—	—	—	21	6	Race, Dale M.

Year	M/W	Assn	Div	NAT	NIT	ARC	CCA	NCI	NCT	OLY	HLM	W	L	Coach
1988	W	NAIA		8	—	—	—	—	—	—	—	18	12	Stromme, Karen
1989		NAIA		16	—	—	—	—	—	—	—	26	6	Stromme, Karen
1990		NAIA		16	—	—	—	—	—	—	—	24	7	Stromme, Karen
1991		NAIA		16	—	—	—	—	—	—	—	26	6	Stromme, Karen
1992		NAIA	I	32	—	—	—	—	—	—	—	16	14	Stromme, Karen
1993		NAIA	I	16	—	—	—	—	—	—	—	22	8	Stromme, Karen
1994		NAIA	I	16	—	—	—	—	—	—	—	20	11	Stromme, Karen
1995		NCAA	II	32	—	—	—	—	—	—	—	20	8	Stromme, Karen
1996		NCAA	II	32	—	—	—	—	—	—	—	23	5	Stromme, Karen

MINNESOTA: MORRIS

Year	M/W	Assn	Div	NAT	NIT	ARC	CCA	NCI	NCT	OLY	HLM	W	L	Coach
1978	M	NCAA	III	16	—	—	—	—	—	—	—	22	6	Glas, Richard "Rich"
1979		NCAA	III	32	—	—	—	—	—	—	—	19	9	Glas, Richard "Rich"
1993		NAIA	I	8	—	—	—	—	—	—	—	22	10	Ford, Perry
1995		NAIA	I	32	—	—	—	—	—	—	—	20	9	Ford, Perry
1980	W	AIAW	III	16	—	—	—	—	—	—	—	17	9	Michaelson, Maren
1983		NCAA	III	8	—	—	—	—	—	—	—	24	10	Reifsteck, Jan

MINOT STATE

Year	M/W	Assn	Div	NAT	NIT	ARC	CCA	NCI	NCT	OLY	HLM	W	L	Coach
1955	M	NAIA		32	—	—	—	—	—	—	—	20	5	Parker, Herb
1972		NAIA		32	—	—	—	—	—	—	—	22	3	Luther, Wes
1995		NAIA	II	32	—	—	—	—	—	—	—	14	13	Limke, Dick
1996	W	NAIA	II	32	—	—	—	—	—	—	—	17	11	Green, Sheila L.
1998		NAIA	II	32	—	—	—	—	—	—	—	20	8	Green, Sheila L.

MISSISSIPPI

Year	M/W	Assn	Div	NAT	NIT	ARC	CCA	NCI	NCT	OLY	HLM	W	L	Coach
1980	M	NCAA	I	—	16	—	—	—	—	—	—	17	13	Weltlich, Robert
1981		NCAA	I	48	—	—	—	—	—	—	—	16	14	Weltlich, Robert
1982		NCAA	I	—	16	—	—	—	—	—	—	18	12	Weltlich, Robert
1983		NCAA	I	—	8	—	—	—	—	—	—	19	12	Hunt, Lee
1987		NCAA	I	—	32	—	—	—	—	—	—	15	15	Murphy, Ed
1989		NCAA	I	—	32	—	—	—	—	—	—	15	15	Murphy, Ed
1997		NCAA	I	64	—	—	—	—	—	—	—	20	9	Evans, Rob
1998		NCAA	I	64	—	—	—	—	—	—	—	22	7	Evans, Rob
1978	W	AIAW	L	12	—	—	—	—	—	—	—	25	15	Dunn, Lin
1982		NCAA	I	32	—	—	—	—	—	—	—	27	5	Chancellor, Van
1983		NCAA	I	16	—	—	—	—	—	—	—	26	7	Chancellor, Van
1984		NCAA	I	16	—	—	—	—	—	—	—	24	6	Chancellor, Van
1985		NCAA	I	8	—	—	—	—	—	—	—	29	3	Chancellor, Van
1986		NCAA	I	8	—	—	—	—	—	—	—	24	8	Chancellor, Van
1987		NCAA	I	16	—	—	—	—	—	—	—	25	5	Chancellor, Van
1988		NCAA	I	16	—	—	—	—	—	—	—	24	7	Chancellor, Van
1989		NCAA	I	8	—	—	—	—	—	—	—	23	8	Chancellor, Van
1990		NCAA	I	16	—	—	—	—	—	—	—	22	10	Chancellor, Van
1991		NCAA	I	48	—	—	—	—	—	—	—	20	9	Chancellor, Van
1992		NCAA	I	8	—	—	—	—	—	—	—	29	3	Chancellor, Van
1994		NCAA	I	32	—	—	—	—	—	—	—	24	9	Chancellor, Van
1995		NCAA	I	64	—	—	—	—	—	—	—	21	8	Chancellor, Van
1996		NCAA	I	64	—	—	—	—	—	—	—	18	11	Chancellor, Van

Year	M/W	Assn	Div	NAT	NIT	ARC	CCA	NCI	NCT	OLY	HLM	W	L	Coach
MISSISSIPPI COLLEGE														
1978	M	NCAA	II	24	—	—	—	—	—	—	—	22	7	Hines, Dr. Douglas
1995		NCAA	II	24	—	—	—	—	—	—	—	21	10	Jones, Mike
1998		NCAA	III	32	—	—	—	—	—	—	—	23	4	Jones, Mike
1974	W	AIAW		2	—	—	—	—	—	—	—	26	4	Nixon, Ed
1975		AIAW	L	—	7	—	—	—	—	—	—	27	7	Nixon, Ed
1976		AIAW	L	8	—	—	—	—	—	—	—	33	10	Nixon, Ed
1977		AIAW	L	12	3	—	—	—	—	—	—	22	14	Nixon, Ed
1979		AIAW	L	—	6	—	—	—	—	—	—	14	18	Nixon, Ed
1980		AIAW	I	—	6	—	—	—	—	—	—	21	8	Smith, Durward
MISSISSIPPI STATE														
1963	M	NCAA	I	12	—	—	—	—	—	—	—	22	6	McCarthy, James H. "Babe"
1979		NCAA	I	—	24	—	—	—	—	—	—	19	9	Hatfield, Jim
1990		NCAA	I	—	16	—	—	—	—	—	—	16	14	Williams, Richard
1991		NCAA	I	64	—	—	—	—	—	—	—	20	9	Williams, Richard
1994		NCAA	I	—	32	—	—	—	—	—	—	18	11	Williams, Richard
1995		NCAA	I	16	—	—	—	—	—	—	—	22	8	Williams, Richard
1996		NCAA	I	3	—	—	—	—	—	—	—	26	8	Williams, Richard
1988	W	NCAA	I	—	6	—	—	—	—	—	—	19	13	Paul, Brenda
1998		NCAA	I	—	16	—	—	—	—	—	—	14	15	Fanning, Sharon
MISSISSIPPI VALLEY STATE														
1978	M	NAIA		32	—	—	—	—	—	—	—	15	20	Gaines, William "Pop"
1986		NCAA	I	64	—	—	—	—	—	—	—	20	11	Stribling, Lafayette
1992		NCAA	I	64	—	—	—	—	—	—	—	16	14	Stribling, Lafayette
1996		NCAA	I	64	—	—	—	—	—	—	—	22	7	Stribling, Lafayette
MISSISSIPPI WOMEN														
1971	W	AIAW		1	—	—	—	—	—	—	—	21	3	Upton, Jill
1972		AIAW		4	—	—	—	—	—	—	—	20	5	Upton, Jill
1974		AIAW		—	7	—	—	—	—	—	—	12	8	Upton, Jill
1985		NCAA	II	24	—	—	—	—	—	—	—	19	4	Johnson, Samye
MISSOURI														
1944	M	NCAA		6	—	—	—	—	—	—	—	10	9	Edwards, George R.
1972		NCAA	I	—	16	—	—	—	—	—	—	21	6	Stewart, Norman E.
1973		NCAA	I	—	16	—	—	—	—	—	—	21	6	Stewart, Norman E.
1975		NCAA	I	—	—	—	8	—	—	—	—	18	9	Stewart, Norman E.
1976		NCAA	I	8	—	—	—	—	—	—	—	26	5	Stewart, Norman E.
1978		NCAA	I	32	—	—	—	—	—	—	—	14	16	Stewart, Norman E.
1980		NCAA	I	16	—	—	—	—	—	—	—	25	6	Stewart, Norman E.
1981		NCAA	I	48	—	—	—	—	—	—	—	22	10	Stewart, Norman E.
1982		NCAA	I	16	—	—	—	—	—	—	—	27	4	Stewart, Norman E.
1983		NCAA	I	32	—	—	—	—	—	—	—	26	8	Stewart, Norman E.
1985		NCAA	I	—	32	—	—	—	—	—	—	18	14	Stewart, Norman E.
1986		NCAA	I	64	—	—	—	—	—	—	—	21	14	Stewart, Norman E.
1987		NCAA	I	64	—	—	—	—	—	—	—	24	10	Stewart, Norman E.
1988		NCAA	I	64	—	—	—	—	—	—	—	19	11	Stewart, Norman E.
1989		NCAA	I	16	—	—	—	—	—	—	—	29	8	Stewart, Norman E.
1990		NCAA	I	64	—	—	—	—	—	—	—	26	6	Stewart, Norman E.

Year	M/W	Assn	Div	NAT	NIT	ARC	CCA	NCI	NCT	OLY	HLM	W	L	Coach
1992		NCAA	I	32	—	—	—	—	—	—	—	21	9	Stewart, Norman E.
1993		NCAA	I	64	—	—	—	—	—	—	—	19	14	Stewart, Norman E.
1994		NCAA	I	8	—	—	—	—	—	—	—	28	4	Stewart, Norman E.
1995		NCAA	I	32	—	—	—	—	—	—	—	20	9	Stewart, Norman E.
1996		NCAA	I	—	16	—	—	—	—	—	—	18	15	Stewart, Norman E.
1998		NCAA	I	—	32	—	—	—	—	—	—	17	15	Stewart, Norman E.
1977	W	AIAW	L	12	—	—	—	—	—	—	—	28	12	Rutherford, Dr. Joann
1978		AIAW	L	12	—	—	—	—	—	—	—	26	6	Rutherford, Dr. Joann
1982		NCAA	I	16	—	—	—	—	—	—	—	24	9	Rutherford, Dr. Joann
1983		NCAA	I	32	—	—	—	—	—	—	—	24	6	Rutherford, Dr. Joann
1984		NCAA	I	32	—	—	—	—	—	—	—	25	6	Rutherford, Dr. Joann
1985		NCAA	I	32	—	—	—	—	—	—	—	22	9	Rutherford, Dr. Joann
1986		NCAA	I	32	—	—	—	—	—	—	—	20	8	Rutherford, Dr. Joann
1994		NCAA	I	64	—	—	—	—	—	—	—	12	18	Rutherford, Dr. Joann

MISSOURI BAPTIST

Year	M/W	Assn	Div	NAT	NIT	ARC	CCA	NCI	NCT	OLY	HLM	W	L	Coach
1976	M	NSCAA		14	—	—	—	—	—	—	—	25	13	Brown, "Chuck"
1977		NSCAA		8	—	—	—	—	—	—	—	17	22	Brown, "Chuck"
1978		NSCAA		16	—	—	—	—	—	—	—	13	20	Brown, "Chuck"
1979		NSCAA		3	—	—	—	—	—	—	—	18	17	McKinney, Lee
1980		NSCAA		16	—	—	—	—	—	—	—	18	13	McKinney, Lee
1992		NCCAA	I	8	—	—	—	—	—	—	—	19	18	Pitzer, Lowell S.
1994		NAIA	I	32	—	—	—	—	—	—	—	25	10	Pitzer, Lowell S.

MISSOURI SOUTHERN STATE

Year	M/W	Assn	Div	NAT	NIT	ARC	CCA	NCI	NCT	OLY	HLM	W	L	Coach
1972	M	NAIA		32	—	—	—	—	—	—	—	22	9	Davis, Frank
1973		NAIA		16	—	—	—	—	—	—	—	17	11	Davis, Frank
1978		NAIA		8	—	—	—	—	—	—	—	27	9	Williams, "Chuck"
1987		NAIA		32	—	—	—	—	—	—	—	20	13	Williams, "Chuck"
1993		NCAA	II	32	—	—	—	—	—	—	—	21	10	Corn, Robert
1982	W	NAIA		2	—	—	—	—	—	—	—	23	12	Phillips, James
1993		NCAA	II	16	—	—	—	—	—	—	—	27	4	Ballard, Scott
1994		NCAA	II	16	—	—	—	—	—	—	—	25	5	Ballard, Scott
1996		NCAA	II	32	—	—	—	—	—	—	—	23	6	Kaifes, Carrie

MISSOURI VALLEY

Year	M/W	Assn	Div	NAT	NIT	ARC	CCA	NCI	NCT	OLY	HLM	W	L	Coach
1942	M	NAIA		8	—	—	—	—	—	—	—	17	8	Ashford, Volney C.
1961		NAIA		16	—	—	—	—	—	—	—	18	9	Redford, Grover C.
1992		NAIA	II	20	—	—	—	—	—	—	—	23	11	Fifer, Tom
1995	W	NAIA	II	32	—	—	—	—	—	—	—	27	9	Piha, Elaine

MISSOURI WESTERN STATE

Year	M/W	Assn	Div	NAT	NIT	ARC	CCA	NCI	NCT	OLY	HLM	W	L	Coach
1974	M	NAIA		16	—	—	—	—	—	—	—	25	6	Filbert, Gary
1982		NAIA		32	—	—	—	—	—	—	—	25	7	Filbert, Gary
1984		NAIA		32	—	—	—	—	—	—	—	21	10	Shear, Lawrence "Skip"
1990		NCAA	II	16	—	—	—	—	—	—	—	24	7	Smith, Tom
1991		NCAA	II	32	—	—	—	—	—	—	—	23	8	Smith, Tom
1992		NCAA	II	32	—	—	—	—	—	—	—	22	10	Smith, Tom
1995		NCAA	II	32	—	—	—	—	—	—	—	26	5	Smith, Tom
1997		NCAA	II	48	—	—	—	—	—	—	—	20	9	Smith, Tom
1998		NCAA	II	32	—	—	—	—	—	—	—	23	7	Smith, Tom

Year	M/W	Assn	Div	NAT	NIT	ARC	CCA	NCI	NCT	OLY	HLM	W	L	Coach
1981	W	NAIA		8	—	—	—	—	—	—	—	—	24	7	Bumpus, Debbie
1994		NCAA	II	8	—	—	—	—	—	—	—	—	29	3	Mittie, Jeff
1995		NCAA	II	3	—	—	—	—	—	—	—	—	31	3	Mittie, Jeff
1997		NCAA	II	16	—	—	—	—	—	—	—	—	24	7	Slifer, David
1998		NCAA	II	32	—	—	—	—	—	—	—	—	23	9	Slifer, David

MISSOURI: KANSAS CITY

Year	M/W	Assn	Div	NAT	NIT	ARC	CCA	NCI	NCT	OLY	HLM	W	L	Coach
1977	M	NAIA		32	—	—	—	—	—	—	—	—	21	9	Corwin, Darrell
1983	W	NAIA		3	—	—	—	—	—	—	—	—	30	5	Norman, Nancy
1985		NAIA		8	—	—	—	—	—	—	—	—	29	6	Norman, Nancy

MISSOURI: ROLLA

Year	M/W	Assn	Div	NAT	NIT	ARC	CCA	NCI	NCT	OLY	HLM	W	L	Coach
1975	M	NCAA	II	32	—	—	—	—	—	—	—	—	16	9	Key, Billy A.
1976		NCAA	II	32	—	—	—	—	—	—	—	—	18	9	Key, Billy A.
1996		NCAA	II	16	—	—	—	—	—	—	—	—	25	6	Martin, Dale
1996	W	NCAA	II	48	—	—	—	—	—	—	—	—	21	7	Roberts, Linda J.

MISSOURI: SAINT LOUIS

Year	M/W	Assn	Div	NAT	NIT	ARC	CCA	NCI	NCT	OLY	HLM	W	L	Coach
1969	M	NAIA		32	—	—	—	—	—	—	—	—	19	7	Smith, Charles G. "Chuck"
1972		NCAA	II	8	—	—	—	—	—	—	—	—	21	6	Smith, Charles G. "Chuck"
1988		NCAA	II	16	—	—	—	—	—	—	—	—	22	9	Meckfessel, Richard

MOBILE

Year	M/W	Assn	Div	NAT	NIT	ARC	CCA	NCI	NCT	OLY	HLM	W	L	Coach
1988	M	NAIA		32	—	—	—	—	—	—	—	—	31	3	Elder, Dr. Bill
1994		NAIA	I	32	—	—	—	—	—	—	—	—	32	3	Elder, Dr. Bill
1998		NAIA	I	32	—	—	—	—	—	—	—	—	27	9	Sanderson, Scott
1991	W	NAIA		32	—	—	—	—	—	—	—	—	22	8	Berger, Curt
1993		NAIA	I	32	—	—	—	—	—	—	—	—	22	9	Berger, Curt

MONMOUTH (IL)

Year	M/W	Assn	Div	NAT	NIT	ARC	CCA	NCI	NCT	OLY	HLM	W	L	Coach
1957	M	NCAA	II	32	—	—	—	—	—	—	—	—	18	5	Larson, Charles
1974		NCAA	II	44	—	—	—	—	—	—	—	—	18	5	Glasgow, Dr. Terry
1985		NCAA	III	24	—	—	—	—	—	—	—	—	18	7	Glasgow, Dr. Terry
1988		NCAA	III	32	—	—	—	—	—	—	—	—	14	11	Glasgow, Dr. Terry
1989		NCAA	III	24	—	—	—	—	—	—	—	—	20	6	Glasgow, Dr. Terry
1990		NCAA	III	32	—	—	—	—	—	—	—	—	20	3	Glasgow, Dr. Terry

MONMOUTH (NJ)

Year	M/W	Assn	Div	NAT	NIT	ARC	CCA	NCI	NCT	OLY	HLM	W	L	Coach
1966	M	NAIA		32	—	—	—	—	—	—	—	—	26	4	Boylan, William T.
1968		NAIA		16	—	—	—	—	—	—	—	—	27	2	Boylan, William T.
1969		NAIA		8	—	—	—	—	—	—	—	—	24	6	Boylan, William T.
1970		NAIA		32	—	—	—	—	—	—	—	—	17	11	Boylan, William T.
1974		NAIA		32	—	—	—	—	—	—	—	—	19	9	Boylan, William T.
1975		NAIA		32	—	—	—	—	—	—	—	—	22	7	Boylan, William T.
1976		NCAA	III	14	—	—	—	—	—	—	—	—	22	5	Boylan, William T.
1981		NCAA	II	24	—	—	—	—	—	—	—	—	25	4	Kornegay, Ron
1982		NCAA	II	32	—	—	—	—	—	—	—	—	21	9	Kornegay, Ron
1996		NCAA	I	64	—	—	—	—	—	—	—	—	20	10	Szoke, Wayne
1983	W	NCAA	I	32	—	—	—	—	—	—	—	—	15	15	Parker, Milton

Year	M/W	Assn	Div	NAT	NIT	ARC	CCA	NCI	NCT	OLY	HLM	W	L	Coach
MONTANA														
1948	M	NAIA		32	—	—	—	—	—	—	—	21	11	Dahlberg, George P.
1950		NAIA		32	—	—	—	—	—	—	—	27	4	Dahlberg, George P.
1975		NCAA	I	16	—	—	—	—	—	—	—	21	8	Heathcote, George "Jud"
1985		NCAA	I	—	32	—	—	—	—	—	—	22	8	Montgomery, Mike
1986		NCAA	I	—	32	—	—	—	—	—	—	21	11	Montgomery, Mike
1991		NCAA	I	64	—	—	—	—	—	—	—	23	8	Morrill, Stew
1992		NCAA	I	64	—	—	—	—	—	—	—	27	4	Taylor, Blaine
1995		NCAA	I	—	32	—	—	—	—	—	—	21	9	Taylor, Blaine
1997		NCAA	I	64	—	—	—	—	—	—	—	21	11	Taylor, Blaine
1982	W	AIAW	I	16	—	—	—	—	—	—	—	22	5	Selvig, Robin
1983		NCAA	I	36	—	—	—	—	—	—	—	26	4	Selvig, Robin
1984		NCAA	I	16	—	—	—	—	—	—	—	26	4	Selvig, Robin
1985		NCAA	I	—	8	—	—	—	—	—	—	22	7	Selvig, Robin
1986		NCAA	I	32	—	—	—	—	—	—	—	27	4	Selvig, Robin
1987		NCAA	I	—	6	—	—	—	—	—	—	26	5	Selvig, Robin
1988		NCAA	I	32	—	—	—	—	—	—	—	28	2	Selvig, Robin
1989		NCAA	I	32	—	—	—	—	—	—	—	27	4	Selvig, Robin
1990		NCAA	I	48	—	—	—	—	—	—	—	27	3	Selvig, Robin
1991		NCAA	I	48	—	—	—	—	—	—	—	26	4	Selvig, Robin
1992		NCAA	I	32	—	—	—	—	—	—	—	23	7	Selvig, Robin
1994		NCAA	I	32	—	—	—	—	—	—	—	25	5	Selvig, Robin
1995		NCAA	I	32	—	—	—	—	—	—	—	26	7	Selvig, Robin
1996		NCAA	I	64	—	—	—	—	—	—	—	24	5	Selvig, Robin
1997		NCAA	I	64	—	—	—	—	—	—	—	25	4	Selvig, Robin
1998		NCAA	I	64	—	—	—	—	—	—	—	24	6	Selvig, Robin
MONTANA STATE														
1929	M			—	—	—	—	—	—	—	1	36	2	Dyche, Schubert R.
1946		NAIA		32	—	—	—	—	—	—	—	17	10	Breeden, John W. "Brick"
1947		NAIA		32	—	—	—	—	—	—	—	25	11	Breeden, John W. "Brick"
1951		NCAA		16	—	—	—	—	—	—	—	24	12	Breeden, John W. "Brick"
1952		NAIA		16	—	—	—	—	—	—	—	22	14	Breeden, John W. "Brick"
1954		NAIA		32	—	—	—	—	—	—	—	18	11	Breeden, John W. "Brick"
1955		NAIA		32	—	—	—	—	—	—	—	11	16	Lemm, Walter H. "Wally"
1956		NAIA		32	—	—	—	—	—	—	—	15	14	Lambert, Keith "Dobbie"
1986		NCAA	I	64	—	—	—	—	—	—	—	14	17	Starner, Stu
1987		NCAA	I	—	32	—	—	—	—	—	—	21	8	Starner, Stu
1996		NCAA	I	64	—	—	—	—	—	—	—	21	9	Durham, Mick
1988	W	NCAA	I	—	8	—	—	—	—	—	—	24	6	Schwartz, Gary
1993		NCAA	I	48	—	—	—	—	—	—	—	22	7	Spoelstra, Judy
MONTANA STATE: BILLINGS														
1963	M	NAIA		32	—	—	—	—	—	—	—	19	6	Harkins, Mike L.
1964		NAIA		32	—	—	—	—	—	—	—	16	8	Harkins, Mike L.
1965		NAIA		16	—	—	—	—	—	—	—	12	17	Harkins, Mike L.
1967		NAIA		32	—	—	—	—	—	—	—	14	18	Harkins, Mike L.
1968		NAIA		16	—	—	—	—	—	—	—	20	9	Harkins, Mike L.
1970		NAIA		32	—	—	—	—	—	—	—	20	9	Harkins, Mike L.
1972		NAIA		32	—	—	—	—	—	—	—	19	6	Harkins, Mike L.
1973		NAIA		32	—	—	—	—	—	—	—	22	10	Harkins, Mike L.

Year	M/W	Assn	Div	NAT	NIT	ARC	CCA	NCI	NCT	OLY	HLM	W	L	Coach
1975		NAIA		32	—	—	—	—	—	—	—	20	8	Harkins, Mike L.
1976		NAIA		32	—	—	—	—	—	—	—	20	10	Harkins, Mike L.
1978		NAIA		32	—	—	—	—	—	—	—	22	10	Chidester, Ted H.
1981		NCAA	II	24	—	—	—	—	—	—	—	20	8	Edwards, Dick
1982		NCAA	II	32	—	—	—	—	—	—	—	19	10	Douglass, Pat
1985		NCAA	II	32	—	—	—	—	—	—	—	23	7	Douglass, Pat
1986		NCAA	II	24	—	—	—	—	—	—	—	22	8	Douglass, Pat
1987		NCAA	II	3	—	—	—	—	—	—	—	24	7	Douglass, Pat
1996		NCAA	II	48	—	—	—	—	—	—	—	19	19	Carse, Craig
1997		NCAA	II	16	—	—	—	—	—	—	—	22	6	Carse, Craig
1998		NCAA	II	48	—	—	—	—	—	—	—	21	7	Carse, Craig
1975	W	AIAW	S	10	—	—	—	—	—	—	—	9	6	Ponikvar, Linda
1976		AIAW	S	16	—	—	—	—	—	—	—	16	4	Ponikvar, Linda
1977		AIAW	S	16	—	—	—	—	—	—	—	15	4	Caneff, Marcia
1987		NCAA	II	24	—	—	—	—	—	—	—	18	11	Anderson, Ted
1994		NCAA	II	32	—	—	—	—	—	—	—	19	9	McCarthy, Frank B.
1996		NCAA	II	32	—	—	—	—	—	—	—	19	9	McCarthy, Frank B.
1997		NCAA	II	48	—	—	—	—	—	—	—	18	10	McCarthy, Frank B.
1998		NCAA	II	32	—	—	—	—	—	—	—	21	7	McCarthy, Frank B.

MONTANA STATE: NORTHERN

Year	M/W	Assn	Div	NAT	NIT	ARC	CCA	NCI	NCT	OLY	HLM	W	L	Coach
1995	M	NAIA	I	8	—	—	—	—	—	—	—	17	19	Baker, Loren
1996		NAIA	I	32	—	—	—	—	—	—	—	24	9	Baker, Loren
1998		NAIA	I	16	—	—	—	—	—	—	—	26	9	Walker, Tim
1990	W	NAIA		16	—	—	—	—	—	—	—	28	3	Baker, Loren
1991		NAIA		16	—	—	—	—	—	—	—	26	5	Baker, Loren
1992		NAIA	II	8	—	—	—	—	—	—	—	30	2	Winn, Sherry
1993		NAIA	II	1	—	—	—	—	—	—	—	35	3	Winn, Sherry
1994		NAIA	I	32	—	—	—	—	—	—	—	26	6	Winn, Sherry
1995		NAIA	I	32	—	—	—	—	—	—	—	25	4	Winn, Sherry
1996		NAIA	I	16	—	—	—	—	—	—	—	24	5	Winn, Sherry
1997		NAIA	I	32	—	—	—	—	—	—	—	25	7	Winn, Sherry
1998		NAIA	I	16	—	—	—	—	—	—	—	25	9	Peters, Ray

MONTANA TECH

Year	M/W	Assn	Div	NAT	NIT	ARC	CCA	NCI	NCT	OLY	HLM	W	L	Coach
1998	M	NAIA	I	32	—	—	—	—	—	—	—	22	11	Dessing, Rick

MONTCLAIR STATE

Year	M/W	Assn	Div	NAT	NIT	ARC	CCA	NCI	NCT	OLY	HLM	W	L	Coach
1969	M	NCAA	II	8	—	—	—	—	—	—	—	24	3	Gelston, Oliver S. "Ollie"
1970		NCAA	II	16	—	—	—	—	—	—	—	23	3	Gelston, Oliver S. "Ollie"
1971		NCAA	II	24	—	—	—	—	—	—	—	18	6	Gelston, Oliver S. "Ollie"
1981		NCAA	III	16	—	—	—	—	—	—	—	15	12	Gelston, Oliver S. "Ollie"
1982		NCAA	III	24	—	—	—	—	—	—	—	17	8	Gelston, Oliver S. "Ollie"
1984		NCAA	III	8	—	—	—	—	—	—	—	22	6	Gelston, Oliver S. "Ollie"
1994		NCAA	III	40	—	—	—	—	—	—	—	18	8	Del Tufo, Nicholas
1995		NCAA	III	64	—	—	—	—	—	—	—	17	10	Del Tufo, Nicholas
1976	W	AIAW	L	6	—	—	—	—	—	—	—	20	5	Wendelken, Maureen
1978		AIAW	L	3	—	—	—	—	—	—	—	25	7	Wendelken, Maureen
1989		NCAA	III	24	—	—	—	—	—	—	—	20	9	Jeffrey, Jill
1990		NCAA	III	16	—	—	—	—	—	—	—	23	6	Jeffrey, Jill
1995		NCAA	III	32	—	—	—	—	—	—	—	20	7	Bradley, Gloria

Year	M/W	Assn	Div	NAT	NIT	ARC	CCA	NCI	NCT	OLY	HLM	W	L	Coach
MONTEVALLO														
1975	M	NAIA		32	—	—	—	—	—	—	—	23	9	Jones, Bill L.
1992	W	NAIA	I	32	—	—	—	—	—	—	—	23	7	Van Atta, Gary
1993		NAIA	I	8	—	—	—	—	—	—	—	26	5	Van Atta, Gary
1994		NAIA	I	3	—	—	—	—	—	—	—	28	7	Van Atta, Gary
1995		NAIA	I	16	—	—	—	—	—	—	—	22	10	Van Atta, Gary
1996		NAIA	I	16	—	—	—	—	—	—	—	24	5	Van Atta, Gary
MOODY BIBLE														
1991	M	NCCAA	II	8	—	—	—	—	—	—	—	X	X	Gaffney, Greg
1986	W	NCCAA	II	4	—	—	—	—	—	—	—	X	X	Unknown
1987		NCCAA	II	1	—	—	—	—	—	—	—	X	X	Gaffney, Greg
1988		NCCAA	II	2	—	—	—	—	—	—	—	X	X	Wartluft, Laurel
1989		NCCAA	II	8	—	—	—	—	—	—	—	X	X	Wartluft, Laurel
1990		NCCAA	II	3	—	—	—	—	—	—	—	X	X	Wartluft, Laurel
1991		NCCAA	II	7	—	—	—	—	—	—	—	X	X	Wartluft, Laurel
1992		NCCAA	II	8	—	—	—	—	—	—	—	14	14	Wartluft, Laurel
1997		NCCAA	II	3	—	—	—	—	—	—	—	18	9	Fielitz, Cheryl A.
MOORHEAD STATE (MN)														
1965	M	NCAA	II	16	—	—	—	—	—	—	—	21	4	MacLeod, Larry
1980		NAIA		32	—	—	—	—	—	—	—	21	9	Schellhase, David G., Jr.
1982		NAIA		16	—	—	—	—	—	—	—	24	7	Schellhase, David G., Jr.
MORAVIAN														
1983	M	NCAA	III	32	—	—	—	—	—	—	—	19	8	Walker, James R.
1986	W	NCAA	III	32	—	—	—	—	—	—	—	25	5	Sinnott-Skutches, Anne
1990		NCAA	III	32	—	—	—	—	—	—	—	24	5	Spirk, Mary Beth
1991		NCAA	III	16	—	—	—	—	—	—	—	27	3	Spirk, Mary Beth
1992		NCAA	III	2	—	—	—	—	—	—	—	31	2	Spirk, Mary Beth
1993		NCAA	III	16	—	—	—	—	—	—	—	24	5	Spirk, Mary Beth
MOREHEAD STATE (KY)														
1942	M	NAIA		32	—	—	—	—	—	—	—	12	10	Johnson, Ellis T.
1951		NAIA		32	—	—	—	—	—	—	—	13	11	Johnson, Ellis T.
1956		NCAA		12	—	—	—	—	—	—	—	19	10	Laughlin, Robert
1957		NCAA	I	23	—	—	—	—	—	—	—	19	8	Laughlin, Robert
1961		NCAA	I	16	—	—	—	—	—	—	—	19	12	Laughlin, Robert
1983		NCAA	I	48	—	—	—	—	—	—	—	19	11	Martin, Wayne M.
1984		NCAA	I	48	—	—	—	—	—	—	—	25	6	Martin, Wayne M.
MOREHOUSE														
1981	M	NCAA	II	32	—	—	—	—	—	—	—	17	12	McAfee, Arthur J., Jr.
1990		NCAA	II	4	—	—	—	—	—	—	—	26	7	McAfee, Arthur J., Jr.
1991		NCAA	II	32	—	—	—	—	—	—	—	21	11	McAfee, Arthur J., Jr.
1995		NCAA	II	48	—	—	—	—	—	—	—	20	8	McAfee, Arthur J., Jr.
MORGAN STATE														
1974	M	NCAA	II	1	—	—	—	—	—	—	—	28	5	Frazier, Nathaniel
1975		NCAA	II	32	—	—	—	—	—	—	—	19	10	Frazier, Nathaniel
1976		NCAA	II	24	—	—	—	—	—	—	—	22	6	Frazier, Nathaniel
1980	W	AIAW	II	8	—	—	—	—	—	—	—	22	5	Fields, LaRue
1981		AIAW	II	16	—	—	—	—	—	—	—	24	4	Fields, LaRue

Year	M/W	Assn	Div	NAT	NIT	ARC	CCA	NCI	NCT	OLY	HLM	W	L	Coach
MORNINGSIDE														
1937	M	NAIA		2	—	—	—	—	—	—	—	16	4	Rogers, R. Glenn "Honie"
1938		NAIA		32	—	—	—	—	—	—	—	14	5	Rogers, R. Glenn "Honie"
1941		NAIA		32	—	—	—	—	—	—	—	9	7	Rogers, R. Glenn "Honie"
1946		NAIA		32	—	—	—	—	—	—	—	15	4	Buckingham, Albert W.
1950		NAIA		32	—	—	—	—	—	—	—	13	14	Buckingham, Albert W.
1951		NAIA		16	—	—	—	—	—	—	—	18	7	Buckingham, Albert W.
1952		NAIA		8	—	—	—	—	—	—	—	20	10	Buckingham, Albert W.
1959		NAIA		32	—	—	—	—	—	—	—	14	9	Obye, Charles H. "Chuck"
1975		NAIA		32	—	—	—	—	—	—	—	17	12	Callahan, Dan
1983		NCAA	II	3	—	—	—	—	—	—	—	26	6	Callahan, Dan
1984		NCAA	II	8	—	—	—	—	—	—	—	22	9	Callahan, Dan
1995		NCAA	II	8	—	—	—	—	—	—	—	24	8	Schmutte, Jerry
1986	W	NAIA		16	—	—	—	—	—	—	—	20	11	Arnold, John
MORRISTOWN (TN)														
1968	M	NSCAA		3	—	—	—	—	—	—	—	16	7	Bundy, Samuel S.
MOUNT MARTY														
1977	M	NAIA		32	—	—	—	—	—	—	—	23	9	Evans, Frank
1998		NAIA	II	3	—	—	—	—	—	—	—	23	9	Thorson, Jim
1986	W	NAIA		16	—	—	—	—	—	—	—	24	8	Anderson, Warren
MOUNT MERCY														
1996	M	NAIA	II	16	—	—	—	—	—	—	—	29	6	Gavin, Paul
1980	W	AIAW	III	4	—	—	—	—	—	—	—	29	8	Ranson, Dr. Leonard
1981		AIAW	III	2	—	—	—	—	—	—	—	31	7	Ranson, Dr. Leonard
1982		AIAW	III	2	—	—	—	—	—	—	—	24	11	Ranson, Dr. Leonard
1991		NAIA		16	—	—	—	—	—	—	—	28	4	Slifer, David
1992		NAIA	II	8	—	—	—	—	—	—	—	30	5	Slifer, David
1993		NAIA	II	8	—	—	—	—	—	—	—	28	5	Slifer, David
1994		NAIA	II	3	—	—	—	—	—	—	—	31	4	Slifer, David
1995		NAIA	II	8	—	—	—	—	—	—	—	31	6	Slifer, David
MOUNT SAINT JOSEPH														
1992	W	NAIA	II	3	—	—	—	—	—	—	—	20	8	Dowell, T. Jean
1996		NAIA	II	32	—	—	—	—	—	—	—	25	16	McKee, Rebecca
MOUNT SAINT MARY'S (MD)														
1957	M	NCAA	II	3	—	—	—	—	—	—	—	27	5	Phelan, James J.
1961		NCAA	II	4	—	—	—	—	—	—	—	26	5	Phelan, James J.
1962		NCAA	II	1	—	—	—	—	—	—	—	24	6	Phelan, James J.
1963		NCAA	II	32	—	—	—	—	—	—	—	13	12	Phelan, James J.
1967		NCAA	II	32	—	—	—	—	—	—	—	18	9	Phelan, James J.
1969		NCAA	II	16	—	—	—	—	—	—	—	21	8	Phelan, James J.
1970		NCAA	II	32	—	—	—	—	—	—	—	20	6	Phelan, James J.
1979		NCAA	II	24	—	—	—	—	—	—	—	18	10	Phelan, James J.
1980		NCAA	II	24	—	—	—	—	—	—	—	22	7	Phelan, James J.
1981		NCAA	II	2	—	—	—	—	—	—	—	28	3	Phelan, James J.
1982		NCAA	II	16	—	—	—	—	—	—	—	20	8	Phelan, James J.
1985		NCAA	II	3	—	—	—	—	—	—	—	28	5	Phelan, James J.

Year	M/W	Assn	Div	NAT	NIT	ARC	CCA	NCI	NCT	OLY	HLM	W	L	Coach
1986		NCAA	II	16	—	—	—	—	—	—	—	26	4	Phelan, James J.
1987		NCAA	II	16	—	—	—	—	—	—	—	26	5	Phelan, James J.
1995		NCAA	I	64	—	—	—	—	—	—	—	17	13	Phelan, James J.
1996		NCAA	I	—	32	—	—	—	—	—	—	21	8	Phelan, James J.
1982	W	NCAA	II	3	—	—	—	—	—	—	—	24	5	Sheahan, William
1983		NCAA	II	16	—	—	—	—	—	—	—	25	3	Sheahan, William
1984		NCAA	II	16	—	—	—	—	—	—	—	26	2	Sheahan, William
1985		NCAA	II	16	—	—	—	—	—	—	—	23	6	Sheahan, William
1986		NCAA	II	16	—	—	—	—	—	—	—	24	2	Sheahan, William
1987		NCAA	II	16	—	—	—	—	—	—	—	25	3	Sheahan, William
1988		NCAA	II	32	—	—	—	—	—	—	—	24	2	Sheahan, William
1994		NCAA	I	64	—	—	—	—	—	—	—	25	4	Sheahan, William
1995		NCAA	I	64	—	—	—	—	—	—	—	24	6	Sheahan, William

MOUNT SAINT VINCENT

Year	M/W	Assn	Div	NAT	NIT	ARC	CCA	NCI	NCT	OLY	HLM	W	L	Coach
1996	M	NCAA	III	64	—	—	—	—	—	—	—	18	9	Mancuso, "Chuck"
1997		NCAA	III	64	—	—	—	—	—	—	—	20	5	Mancuso, "Chuck"

MOUNT SENARIO

Year	M/W	Assn	Div	NAT	NIT	ARC	CCA	NCI	NCT	OLY	HLM	W	L	Coach
1976	M	NSCAA		14	—	—	—	—	—	—	—	17	9	Novak, Bill
1977		NSCAA		16	—	—	—	—	—	—	—	10	16	Novak, Bill
1979		NSCAA		16	—	—	—	—	—	—	—	20	11	Novak, Bill
1980		NSCAA		16	—	—	—	—	—	—	—	10	17	Novak, Bill
1988		NSCAA		4	—	—	—	—	—	—	—	20	13	Olson, Mike
1989		NSCAA		3	—	—	—	—	—	—	—	23	10	Olson, Mike
1990		NSCAA		3	—	—	—	—	—	—	—	26	10	Andrist, Edward A.
1991		NSCAA		1	—	—	—	—	—	—	—	40	10	Andrist, Edward A.
1992		NSCAA		4	—	—	—	—	—	—	—	29	16	Andrist, Edward A.
1993		NSCAA		5	—	—	—	—	—	—	—	32	15	Andrist, Edward A.
1994		NSCAA		1	—	—	—	—	—	—	—	24	22	Andrist, Edward A.
1995		NSCAA		5	—	—	—	—	—	—	—	12	24	Andrist, Edward A.
1996		NSCAA		1	—	—	—	—	—	—	—	14	22	Andrist, Edward A.
1997		NSCAA		9	—	—	—	—	—	—	—	12	22	Andrist, Edward A.
1992	W	NSCAA		7	—	—	—	—	—	—	—	19	14	Elliott, David
1994		NSCAA		3	—	—	—	—	—	—	—	16	16	Elliott, David
1995		NSCAA		2	—	—	—	—	—	—	—	15	15	Biddle, Brian
1997		NSCAA		6	—	—	—	—	—	—	—	5	22	Leibold, Nicole

MOUNT UNION

Year	M/W	Assn	Div	NAT	NIT	ARC	CCA	NCI	NCT	OLY	HLM	W	L	Coach
1997	M	NCAA	III	16	—	—	—	—	—	—	—	25	5	Hood, Lee
1995	W	NCAA	III	16	—	—	—	—	—	—	—	24	6	Knoblauch, Deanne
1996		NCAA	III	2	—	—	—	—	—	—	—	25	8	Knoblauch, Deanne
1998		NCAA	III	3	—	—	—	—	—	—	—	29	3	Knoblauch, Deanne

MOUNT VERNON NAZARENE

Year	M/W	Assn	Div	NAT	NIT	ARC	CCA	NCI	NCT	OLY	HLM	W	L	Coach
1975	M	NSCAA		16	—	—	—	—	—	—	—	8	21	Bradley, Carroll
1979		NSCAA		16	—	—	—	—	—	—	—	10	20	Martin, Bobby
1989		NCCAA	I	2	—	—	—	—	—	—	—	23	14	Balikian, Bernie
1995		NAIA	II	32	—	—	—	—	—	—	—	22	10	Flemming, Scott
1998		NAIA	II	8	—	—	—	—	—	—	—	27	7	Flemming, Scott
1994	W	NCCAA	I	1	—	—	—	—	—	—	—	23	10	Howald, Jeana
1998		NCCAA	I	4	—	—	—	—	—	—	—	19	18	Ely, Eric

Year	M/W	Assn	Div	NAT	NIT	ARC	CCA	NCI	NCT	OLY	HLM	W	L	Coach
MUHLENBERG														
1944	M	NCAA		—	8	—	—	—	—	—	—	19	6	Julian, Alvin F. "Doggie"
1945		NCAA		—	8	—	—	—	—	—	—	24	4	Julian, Alvin F. "Doggie"
1946		NCAA		—	4	—	—	—	—	—	—	23	5	Coker, Lee
1968		NCAA	II	32	—	—	—	—	—	—	—	14	11	Moyer, Kenneth T.
1995		NCAA	III	64	—	—	—	—	—	—	—	18	9	Madeira, David
1998		NCAA	III	48	—	—	—	—	—	—	—	17	10	Madeira, David
1997	W	NCAA	III	64	—	—	—	—	—	—	—	18	8	Smith, Tammy
1998		NCAA	III	32	—	—	—	—	—	—	—	18	10	Smith, Tammy
MULTNOMAH BIBLE														
1985	M	NCCAA	II	8	—	—	—	—	—	—	—	16	12	Skagen, James C.
1986		NCCAA	II	4	—	—	—	—	—	—	—	23	8	Skagen, James C.
1987		NCCAA	II	2	—	—	—	—	—	—	—			Doherty, Jim
1988		NCCAA	II	7	—	—	—	—	—	—	—	15	15	Skagen, James C.
1989		NCCAA	II	7	—	—	—	—	—	—	—			Skagen, James C.
1991		NBCAA	I	6	—	—	—	—	—	—	—	18	17	Aldrich, Dr. Joseph
1993		NBCAA	I	2	—	—	—	—	—	—	—	19	13	Skagen, James C.
1995		NBCAA	I	2	—	—	—	—	—	—	—	27	2	Reese, Chris
1996		NBCAA	I	1	—	—	—	—	—	—	—	20	16	Reese, Chris
1997		NBCAA	I	8	—	—	—	—	—	—	—	12	24	Reese, Chris
1998		NCCAA	II	6	—	—	—	—	—	—	—	21	13	Reese, Chris
MUNDELEIN														
1987	W	NSCAA		8	—	—	—	—	—	—	—	X	X	Bolinder, Rich
1988		NSCAA		4	—	—	—	—	—	—	—	X	X	Bolinder, Rich
MURRAY STATE (KY)														
1938	M	NAIA		3	—	—	—	—	—	—	—	27	4	Cutchin, Carlisle C.
1939		NAIA		16	—	—	—	—	—	—	—	13	8	Cutchin, Carlisle C.
1941		NAIA		2	—	—	—	—	—	—	—	25	5	Cutchin, Carlisle C.
1942		NAIA		32	—	—	—	—	—	—	—	18	4	Mountjoy, L. Rice
1943		NAIA		4	—	—	—	—	—	—	—	21	5	Miller, John
1950		NAIA		32	—	—	—	—	—	—	—	18	13	Hodges, Harlan
1952		NAIA		2	—	—	—	—	—	—	—	24	10	Hodges, Harlan
1964		NCAA	I	25	—	—	—	—	—	—	—	16	9	Luther, Calvin C.
1969		NCAA	I	25	—	—	—	—	—	—	—	22	6	Luther, Calvin C.
1980		NCAA	I	—	8	—	—	—	—	—	—	23	8	Greene, Ronald L.
1982		NCAA	I	—	32	—	—	—	—	—	—	20	8	Greene, Ronald L.
1983		NCAA	I	—	32	—	—	—	—	—	—	21	8	Greene, Ronald L.
1988		NCAA	I	32	—	—	—	—	—	—	—	22	9	Newton, Steve
1989		NCAA	I	—	32	—	—	—	—	—	—	19	11	Newton, Steve
1990		NCAA	I	64	—	—	—	—	—	—	—	21	9	Newton, Steve
1991		NCAA	I	64	—	—	—	—	—	—	—	24	9	Newton, Steve
1992		NCAA	I	64	—	—	—	—	—	—	—	17	13	Edgar, Scott
1994		NCAA	I	—	32	—	—	—	—	—	—	23	6	Edgar, Scott
1995		NCAA	I	64	—	—	—	—	—	—	—	21	9	Edgar, Scott
1996		NCAA	I	—	32	—	—	—	—	—	—	19	10	Gottfried, Mark
1997		NCAA	I	64	—	—	—	—	—	—	—	20	10	Gottfried, Mark
1998		NCAA	I	64	—	—	—	—	—	—	—	29	4	Gottfried, Mark

Year	M/W	Assn	Div	NAT	NIT	ARC	CCA	NCI	NCT	OLY	HLM	W	L	Coach
1989	W	NCAA	I	—	4	—	—	—	—	—	—	22	10	Childers, 'Bud'

MURRAY STATE (OK)

Year	M/W	Assn	Div	NAT	NIT	ARC	CCA	NCI	NCT	OLY	HLM	W	L	Coach
1972	W			—	3	—	—	—	—	—	—	18	10	Hedden, Jack E.
1973				—	5	—	—	—	—	—	—	18	7	Imotichey, Melvin

MUSKINGUM

Year	M/W	Assn	Div	NAT	NIT	ARC	CCA	NCI	NCT	OLY	HLM	W	L	Coach
1977	M	NCAA	III	23	—	—	—	—	—	—	—	22	6	Burson, Dr. James
1981		NCAA	III	16	—	—	—	—	—	—	—	19	8	Burson, Dr. James
1983		NCAA	III	32	—	—	—	—	—	—	—	19	9	Burson, Dr. James
1988		NCAA	III	32	—	—	—	—	—	—	—	21	9	Burson, Dr. James
1990		NCAA	III	32	—	—	—	—	—	—	—	21	9	Burson, Dr. James
1984	W	NCAA	III	24	—	—	—	—	—	—	—	23	6	Newberry, Donna
1985		NCAA	III	8	—	—	—	—	—	—	—	25	4	Newberry, Donna
1989		NCAA	III	8	—	—	—	—	—	—	—	29	2	Newberry, Donna
1991		NCAA	III	2	—	—	—	—	—	—	—	28	5	Newberry, Donna
1992		NCAA	III	16	—	—	—	—	—	—	—	22	8	Newberry, Donna
1993		NCAA	III	32	—	—	—	—	—	—	—	24	3	Newberry, Donna
1996		NCAA	III	64	—	—	—	—	—	—	—	20	7	Newberry, Donna

NATIONAL (SD)

Year	M/W	Assn	Div	NAT	NIT	ARC	CCA	NCI	NCT	OLY	HLM	W	L	Coach
1985	M	NSCAA		10	—	—	—	—	—	—	—	15	25	Ticknor, Duane
1986		NSCAA		7	—	—	—	—	—	—	—	24	11	Ticknor, Duane
1987		NSCAA		1	—	—	—	—	—	—	—			Ticknor, Duane
1988		NSCAA		1	—	—	—	—	—	—	—	30	6	Ticknor, Duane
1982	W	NSCAA		1	—	—	—	—	—	—	—	16	4	Haight, H. C. 'Bud'
1983		NSCAA		4	—	—	—	—	—	—	—			
1984		NSCAA		2	—	—	—	—	—	—	—			
1985		NSCAA		5	—	—	—	—	—	—	—			
1986		NSCAA		2	—	—	—	—	—	—	—			

NATIONAL CHRISTIAN

Year	M/W	Assn	Div	NAT	NIT	ARC	CCA	NCI	NCT	OLY	HLM	W	L	Coach
1996	M	NSCAA		6	—	—	—	—	—	—	—	4	20	Cerventes, Ceasar

NAVAJO CC (AZ)

Year	M/W	Assn	Div	NAT	NIT	ARC	CCA	NCI	NCT	OLY	HLM	W	L	Coach
1985	M	NSCAA		5	—	—	—	—	—	—	—	22	12	Minley, Jeff

NAVY

Year	M/W	Assn	Div	NAT	NIT	ARC	CCA	NCI	NCT	OLY	HLM	W	L	Coach
1913	M			—	—	—	—	—	—	—	1	9	0	Wenzell, Louis P.
1947		NCAA		8	—	—	—	—	—	—	—	16	3	Carnevale, Bernard L. 'Ben'
1953		NCAA		22	—	—	—	—	—	—	—	16	5	Carnevale, Bernard L. 'Ben'
1954		NCAA		8	—	—	—	—	—	—	—	18	8	Carnevale, Bernard L. 'Ben'
1959		NCAA	I	12	—	—	—	—	—	—	—	18	6	Carnevale, Bernard L. 'Ben'
1960		NCAA	I	25	—	—	—	—	—	—	—	16	6	Carnevale, Bernard L. 'Ben'
1962		NCAA	I	—	12	—	—	—	—	—	—	13	8	Carnevale, Bernard L. 'Ben'
1985		NCAA	I	32	—	—	—	—	—	—	—	26	6	Evans, Paul
1986		NCAA	I	8	—	—	—	—	—	—	—	30	5	Evans, Paul
1987		NCAA	I	64	—	—	—	—	—	—	—	26	6	Herrmann, Pete
1994		NCAA	I	64	—	—	—	—	—	—	—	17	13	DeVoe, Donald E.
1997		NCAA	I	64	—	—	—	—	—	—	—	20	9	DeVoe, Donald E.
1998		NCAA	I	64	—	—	—	—	—	—	—	19	11	DeVoe, Donald E.

Year	M/W	Assn	Div	NAT	NIT	ARC	CCA	NCI	NCT	OLY	HLM	W	L	Coach
NAZARETH (MI)														
1990	M	NSCAA		6	—	—	—	—	—	—	—	13	21	Ragsdale, Chris
1984	W	NSCAA		9	—	—	—	—	—	—	—	8	18	Shaw, William
1986		NSCAA		7	—	—	—	—	—	—	—			Shaw, William
1990		NSCAA		8	—	—	—	—	—	—	—	6	20	Low, Mike
NAZARETH (NY)														
1984	M	NCAA	III	8	—	—	—	—	—	—	—	21	6	Nelson, William H.
1986		NCAA	III	24	—	—	—	—	—	—	—	23	5	Nelson, William H.
1987		NCAA	III	16	—	—	—	—	—	—	—	22	6	Daley, Michael
1990		NCAA	III	40	—	—	—	—	—	—	—	20	7	Daley, Michael
1998		NCAA	III	32	—	—	—	—	—	—	—	19	8	Daley, Michael
1983	W	NAIA		8	—	—	—	—	—	—	—	19	11	Gomez, Marguerite "Margie"
1988		NCAA	III	16	—	—	—	—	—	—	—	23	5	DeCillis, Michael
1989		NCAA	III	16	—	—	—	—	—	—	—	22	6	DeCillis, Michael
1990		NCAA	III	32	—	—	—	—	—	—	—	22	6	DeCillis, Michael
1996		NCAA	III	64	—	—	—	—	—	—	—	22	5	DeCillis, Michael
1997		NCAA	III	64	—	—	—	—	—	—	—	17	9	DeCillis, Michael
1998		NCAA	III	48	—	—	—	—	—	—	—	15	11	DeCillis, Michael
NEBRASKA														
1967	M	NCAA	I	—	8	—	—	—	—	—	—	16	9	Cipriano, Joseph
1978		NCAA	I	—	8	—	—	—	—	—	—	22	8	Cipriano, Joseph
1980		NCAA	I	—	32	—	—	—	—	—	—	18	13	Cipriano, Joseph
1983		NCAA	I	—	3	—	—	—	—	—	—	22	10	Iba, Moe
1984		NCAA	I	—	16	—	—	—	—	—	—	18	12	Iba, Moe
1985		NCAA	I	—	16	—	—	—	—	—	—	16	14	Iba, Moe
1986		NCAA	I	64	—	—	—	—	—	—	—	19	11	Iba, Moe
1987		NCAA	I	—	3	—	—	—	—	—	—	21	12	Nee, Danny
1989		NCAA	I	—	16	—	—	—	—	—	—	17	16	Nee, Danny
1991		NCAA	I	64	—	—	—	—	—	—	—	26	8	Nee, Danny
1992		NCAA	I	64	—	—	—	—	—	—	—	19	10	Nee, Danny
1993		NCAA	I	64	—	—	—	—	—	—	—	20	11	Nee, Danny
1994		NCAA	I	64	—	—	—	—	—	—	—	20	10	Nee, Danny
1995		NCAA	I	—	16	—	—	—	—	—	—	18	14	Nee, Danny
1996		NCAA	I	—	1	—	—	—	—	—	—	21	14	Nee, Danny
1997		NCAA	I	—	8	—	—	—	—	—	—	18	15	Nee, Danny
1998		NCAA	I	64	—	—	—	—	—	—	—	20	12	Nee, Danny
1976	W	AIAW			5	—	—	—	—	—	—	22	9	Nicodemus, George L.
1988		NCAA	I	32	—	—	—	—	—	—	—	22	7	Beck, Angela
1992		NCAA	I	—	4	—	—	—	—	—	—	21	11	Beck, Angela
1993		NCAA	I	32	—	—	—	—	—	—	—	23	8	Beck, Angela
1996		NCAA	I	64	—	—	—	—	—	—	—	19	10	Beck, Angela
1998		NCAA	I	32	—	—	—	—	—	—	—	23	10	Sanderford, Paul
NEBRASKA CHRISTIAN														
1985	M	NBCAA	II	3	—	—	—	—	—	—	—	10	14	Boelton, Allen
1986		NBCAA	II	1	—	—	—	—	—	—	—	12	14	Lahm, Chris
1987		NBCAA	I	7	—	—	—	—	—	—	—	16	13	Lahm, Chris
1988		NBCAA	I	8	—	—	—	—	—	—	—	19	10	Lahm, Chris

Year	M/W	Assn	Div	NAT	NIT	ARC	CCA	NCI	NCT	OLY	HLM	W	L	Coach
1989		NBCAA	II	2	—	—	—	—	—	—	—	19	8	Lahm, Chris
1990		NBCAA	II	1	—	—	—	—	—	—	—	19	10	Lahm, Chris
1991		NBCAA	II	5	—	—	—	—	—	—	—	15	13	Lahm, Chris
1992		NBCAA	II	4	—	—	—	—	—	—	—	17	12	Lahm, Chris
1993		NBCAA	II	1	—	—	—	—	—	—	—	19	9	Lahm, Chris
1994		NBCAA	II	1	—	—	—	—	—	—	—	20	8	Lahm, Chris
1995		NBCAA	II	3	—	—	—	—	—	—	—	22	11	Lahm, Chris
1995		NCCAA	IIA	5	—	—	—	—	—	—	—	22	11	Lahm, Chris
1996		NBCAA	I	3	—	—	—	—	—	—	—	23	6	Lahm, Chris
1997		NBCAA	II	3	—	—	—	—	—	—	—	21	8	Lahm, Chris
1997		NCCAA	IIA	2	—	—	—	—	—	—	—	21	8	Lahm, Chris
1998		NCCAA	IIA	6	—	—	—	—	—	—	—	16	14	Lahm, Chris
1996	W	NBCAA		2	—	—	—	—	—	—	—	10	12	Kissack, Rick
1997		NBCAA		3	—	—	—	—	—	—	—	16	8	Kissack, Rick
1998		NBCAA		1	—	—	—	—	—	—	—	21	8	Fuehrer, Mike

Nebraska Wesleyan

Year	M/W	Assn	Div	NAT	NIT	ARC	CCA	NCI	NCT	OLY	HLM	W	L	Coach
1938	M	NAIA		32	—	—	—	—	—	—	—	13	3	Thomas, Dwight P.
1953		NAIA		8	—	—	—	—	—	—	—	25	3	Peterson, Dr. Irvin L.
1954		NAIA		16	—	—	—	—	—	—	—	19	5	Peterson, Dr. Irvin L.
1955		NAIA		16	—	—	—	—	—	—	—	21	5	Peterson, Dr. Irvin L.
1959		NAIA		32	—	—	—	—	—	—	—	23	5	Peterson, Dr. Irvin L.
1960		NAIA		32	—	—	—	—	—	—	—	21	7	Peterson, Dr. Irvin L.
1962		NCAA	II	4	—	—	—	—	—	—	—	20	8	Peterson, Dr. Irvin L.
1963		NCAA	II	16	—	—	—	—	—	—	—	23	4	Peterson, Dr. Irvin L.
1964		NCAA	II	32	—	—	—	—	—	—	—	20	6	Peterson, Dr. Irvin L.
1977		NCAA	III	8	—	—	—	—	—	—	—	16	11	Peterson, Dr. Irvin L.
1984		NCAA	III	8	—	—	—	—	—	—	—	23	5	Schmutte, Jerry
1985		NCAA	III	3	—	—	—	—	—	—	—	25	3	Schmutte, Jerry
1986		NCAA	III	3	—	—	—	—	—	—	—	26	5	Schmutte, Jerry
1987		NCAA	III	32	—	—	—	—	—	—	—	21	7	Schmutte, Jerry
1988		NCAA	III	3	—	—	—	—	—	—	—	24	6	Schmutte, Jerry
1989		NCAA	III	16	—	—	—	—	—	—	—	21	6	Schmutte, Jerry
1990		NCAA	III	16	—	—	—	—	—	—	—	22	7	Raridon, Todd
1995		NCAA	III	16	—	—	—	—	—	—	—	21	7	Raridon, Todd
1997		NCAA	III	2	—	—	—	—	—	—	—	25	6	Raridon, Todd
1998		NCAA	III	32	—	—	—	—	—	—	—	23	3	Raridon, Todd

Nebraska: Kearney

Year	M/W	Assn	Div	NAT	NIT	ARC	CCA	NCI	NCT	OLY	HLM	W	L	Coach
1943	M	NAIA		32	—	—	—	—	—	—	—	12	6	White, Dr. Clifford W.
1972		NAIA		32	—	—	—	—	—	—	—	18	7	Hueser, Jerry
1975		NAIA		32	—	—	—	—	—	—	—	21	7	Hueser, Jerry
1978		NAIA		2	—	—	—	—	—	—	—	19	8	Hueser, Jerry
1979		NAIA		16	—	—	—	—	—	—	—	25	8	Hueser, Jerry
1980		NAIA		32	—	—	—	—	—	—	—	24	3	Hueser, Jerry
1981		NAIA		16	—	—	—	—	—	—	—	25	7	Hueser, Jerry
1982		NAIA		4	—	—	—	—	—	—	—	26	10	Hueser, Jerry
1983		NAIA		32	—	—	—	—	—	—	—	25	11	Hueser, Jerry
1984		NAIA		16	—	—	—	—	—	—	—	28	9	Hueser, Jerry
1985		NAIA		32	—	—	—	—	—	—	—	21	11	Hueser, Jerry
1986		NAIA		32	—	—	—	—	—	—	—	17	15	Hueser, Jerry

Year	M/W	Assn	Div	NAT	NIT	ARC	CCA	NCI	NCT	OLY	HLM	W	L	Coach
1987		NAIA		32	—	—	—	—	—	—	—	26	8	Hueser, Jerry
1991		NCAA	II	32	—	—	—	—	—	—	—	21	9	Hueser, Jerry
1996		NCAA	II	48	—	—	—	—	—	—	—	24	9	Hueser, Jerry
1997		NCAA	II	32	—	—	—	—	—	—	—	23	8	Hueser, Jerry
1998		NCAA	II	32	—	—	—	—	—	—	—	25	6	Kropp, Tom
1987	W	NAIA		16	—	—	—	—	—	—	—	21	9	Wurtz, Dan
1996		NCAA	II	32	—	—	—	—	—	—	—	26	5	Stephens, Amy
1997		NCAA	II	32	—	—	—	—	—	—	—	28	3	Stephens, Amy
1998		NCAA	II	16	—	—	—	—	—	—	—	26	4	Stephens, Amy

NEBRASKA: OMAHA

Year	M/W	Assn	Div	NAT	NIT	ARC	CCA	NCI	NCT	OLY	HLM	W	L	Coach
1941	M	NAIA		32	—	—	—	—	—	—	—	12	13	Johnk, Harold
1975		NCAA	II	16	—	—	—	—	—	—	—	17	11	Hanson, Bob
1976		NCAA	II	32	—	—	—	—	—	—	—	16	13	Hanson, Bob
1977		NCAA	II	24	—	—	—	—	—	—	—	17	12	Hanson, Bob
1979		NCAA	II	24	—	—	—	—	—	—	—	20	9	Hanson, Bob
1982		NCAA	II	16	—	—	—	—	—	—	—	22	7	Hanson, Bob
1983		NCAA	II	32	—	—	—	—	—	—	—	19	11	Hanson, Bob
1984		NCAA	II	24	—	—	—	—	—	—	—	23	7	Hanson, Bob
1980	W	AIAW	II	24	—	—	—	—	—	—	—	23	13	Mankenberg, Cherri
1982		NCAA	II	16	—	—	—	—	—	—	—	22	6	Mankenberg, Cherri
1987		NCAA	II	24	—	—	—	—	—	—	—	21	8	Mankenberg, Cherri
1992		NCAA	II	32	—	—	—	—	—	—	—	20	9	Mankenberg, Cherri

NEVADA

Year	M/W	Assn	Div	NAT	NIT	ARC	CCA	NCI	NCT	OLY	HLM	W	L	Coach
1946	M	NAIA		8	—	—	—	—	—	—	—	24	9	Lawlor, Glenn J. "Jake"
1957		NCAA	II	32	—	—	—	—	—	—	—	16	8	Lawlor, Glenn J. "Jake"
1961		NCAA	II	32	—	—	—	—	—	—	—	13	7	Spencer, Jackson
1964		NCAA	II	32	—	—	—	—	—	—	—	14	13	Spencer, Jackson
1966		NCAA	II	22	—	—	—	—	—	—	—	21	6	Spencer, Jackson
1979		NCAA	I	—	12	—	—	—	—	—	—	21	7	Carey, Jim
1984		NCAA	I	48	—	—	—	—	—	—	—	17	14	Allen, William "Sonny"
1985		NCAA	I	64	—	—	—	—	—	—	—	21	10	Allen, William "Sonny"
1997		NCAA	I	—	16	—	—	—	—	—	—	21	10	Foster, Pat

NEVADA: LAS VEGAS

Year	M/W	Assn	Div	NAT	NIT	ARC	CCA	NCI	NCT	OLY	HLM	W	L	Coach
1965	M	NCAA	II	32	—	—	—	—	—	—	—	19	8	Gregory, Ed
1967		NCAA	II	16	—	—	—	—	—	—	—	21	6	Todd, Rolland
1968		NCAA	II	8	—	—	—	—	—	—	—	22	7	Todd, Rolland
1969		NCAA	II	16	—	—	—	—	—	—	—	21	7	Todd, Rolland
1975		NCAA	I	12	—	—	—	—	—	—	—	24	5	Tarkanian, Jerry
1976		NCAA	I	16	—	—	—	—	—	—	—	29	2	Tarkanian, Jerry
1977		NCAA	I	3	—	—	—	—	—	—	—	29	3	Tarkanian, Jerry
1980		NCAA	I	—	4	—	—	—	—	—	—	23	9	Tarkanian, Jerry
1982		NCAA	I	—	16	—	—	—	—	—	—	20	10	Tarkanian, Jerry
1983		NCAA	I	32	—	—	—	—	—	—	—	28	3	Tarkanian, Jerry
1984		NCAA	I	16	—	—	—	—	—	—	—	29	6	Tarkanian, Jerry
1985		NCAA	I	32	—	—	—	—	—	—	—	28	4	Tarkanian, Jerry
1986		NCAA	I	16	—	—	—	—	—	—	—	33	5	Tarkanian, Jerry
1987		NCAA	I	3	—	—	—	—	—	—	—	37	2	Tarkanian, Jerry
1988		NCAA	I	32	—	—	—	—	—	—	—	28	6	Tarkanian, Jerry
1989		NCAA	I	8	—	—	—	—	—	—	—	29	8	Tarkanian, Jerry

Year	M/W	Assn	Div	NAT	NIT	ARC	CCA	NCI	NCT	OLY	HLM	W	L	Coach
1990		NCAA	I	1	—	—	—	—	—	—	—	35	5	Tarkanian, Jerry
1991		NCAA	I	3	—	—	—	—	—	—	—	34	1	Tarkanian, Jerry
1993		NCAA	I	—	32	—	—	—	—	—	—	21	8	Massimino, Roland V. "Rollie"
1997		NCAA	I	—	8	—	—	—	—	—	—	22	10	Bayno, Bill
1998		NCAA	I	64	—	—	—	—	—	—	—	20	13	Bayno, Bill
1976	W			—	3	—	—	—	—	—	—	26	5	Ayala, Dan
1984		NCAA	I	32	—	—	—	—	—	—	—	24	7	Bolla, Jim
1985		NCAA	I	32	—	—	—	—	—	—	—	26	5	Bolla, Jim
1986		NCAA	I	32	—	—	—	—	—	—	—	22	9	Bolla, Jim
1988		NCAA	I	—	7	—	—	—	—	—	—	25	9	Bolla, Jim
1989		NCAA	I	16	—	—	—	—	—	—	—	27	7	Bolla, Jim
1990		NCAA	I	32	—	—	—	—	—	—	—	28	3	Bolla, Jim
1991		NCAA	I	32	—	—	—	—	—	—	—	25	7	Bolla, Jim
1993		NCAA	I	—	7	—	—	—	—	—	—	24	7	Bolla, Jim
1994		NCAA	I	64	—	—	—	—	—	—	—	23	7	Bolla, Jim

NEW HAMPSHIRE COLLEGE

Year	M/W	Assn	Div	NAT	NIT	ARC	CCA	NCI	NCT	OLY	HLM	W	L	Coach
1980	M	NCAA	II	8	—	—	—	—	—	—	—	22	8	Sullivan, Thomas R.
1981		NCAA	II	8	—	—	—	—	—	—	—	23	7	Sullivan, Thomas R.
1986		NCAA	II	16	—	—	—	—	—	—	—	24	7	Spirou, Stanley
1987		NCAA	II	8	—	—	—	—	—	—	—	24	8	Spirou, Stanley
1990		NCAA	II	24	—	—	—	—	—	—	—	26	6	Spirou, Stanley
1992		NCAA	II	16	—	—	—	—	—	—	—	24	7	Spirou, Stanley
1993		NCAA	II	3	—	—	—	—	—	—	—	29	4	Spirou, Stanley
1994		NCAA	II	3	—	—	—	—	—	—	—	28	5	Spirou, Stanley
1995		NCAA	II	8	—	—	—	—	—	—	—	27	6	Spirou, Stanley
1996		NCAA	II	32	—	—	—	—	—	—	—	21	8	Spirou, Stanley
1997		NCAA	II	16	—	—	—	—	—	—	—	25	5	Spirou, Stanley
1998		NCAA	II	32	—	—	—	—	—	—	—	19	11	Spirou, Stanley
1988	W	NCAA	II	32	—	—	—	—	—	—	—	21	8	Rowe, Nancy Anne
1990		NCAA	II	32	—	—	—	—	—	—	—	22	8	Rowe, Nancy Anne

NEW HAMPSHIRE TECH: CONCORD

Year	M/W	Assn	Div	NAT	NIT	ARC	CCA	NCI	NCT	OLY	HLM	W	L	Coach
1987	M	NSCAA		16	—	—	—	—	—	—	—	17	7	Miller, William J., Jr.
1988		NSCAA		12	—	—	—	—	—	—	—	23	13	Miller, William J., Jr.
1989		NSCAA		15	—	—	—	—	—	—	—	20	10	Miller, William J., Jr.
1998		NSCAA		15	—	—	—	—	—	—	—	22	7	Moffett, Michael

NEW HAVEN

Year	M/W	Assn	Div	NAT	NIT	ARC	CCA	NCI	NCT	OLY	HLM	W	L	Coach
1966	M	NAIA		32	—	—	—	—	—	—	—	29	2	Ormrod, Donald R.
1968		NAIA		16	—	—	—	—	—	—	—	17	12	Ormrod, Donald R.
1969		NAIA		32	—	—	—	—	—	—	—	20	3	Burns, Donald E.
1987		NCAA	II	32	—	—	—	—	—	—	—	23	9	Grove, Stuart
1988		NCAA	II	16	—	—	—	—	—	—	—	26	5	Grove, Stuart
1990		NCAA	II	32	—	—	—	—	—	—	—	21	10	Grove, Stuart
1986	W	NCAA	II	24	—	—	—	—	—	—	—	18	11	Rossman, Jan
1987		NCAA	II	1	—	—	—	—	—	—	—	29	2	Rossman, Jan
1988		NCAA	II	8	—	—	—	—	—	—	—	27	5	Hill, Russ
1989		NCAA	II	16	—	—	—	—	—	—	—	28	4	Hill, Russ

Year	M/W	Assn	Div	NAT	NIT	ARC	CCA	NCI	NCT	OLY	HLM	W	L	Coach
NEW JERSEY														
1967	M	NAIA		32	—	—	—	—	—	—	—	18	9	Wissel, Dr. Harold R. "Hal"
1985		NCAA	III	16	—	—	—	—	—	—	—	23	6	Bannon, Kevin
1986		NCAA	III	24	—	—	—	—	—	—	—	22	7	Bannon, Kevin
1988		NCAA	III	8	—	—	—	—	—	—	—	26	4	Bannon, Kevin
1989		NCAA	III	2	—	—	—	—	—	—	—	30	2	Bannon, Kevin
1990		NCAA	III	32	—	—	—	—	—	—	—	22	6	Marsh, Donald
1998		NCAA	III	32	—	—	—	—	—	—	—	22	5	Castaldo, John
1982	W	NCAA	III	8	—	—	—	—	—	—	—	17	9	Labati, Ferne
1983		NCAA	III	24	—	—	—	—	—	—	—	18	11	Labati, Ferne
1984		NCAA	III	8	—	—	—	—	—	—	—	20	8	Labati, Ferne
1988		NCAA	III	16	—	—	—	—	—	—	—	22	6	Ryan, Mika
1997		NCAA	III	32	—	—	—	—	—	—	—	18	9	Henderson, Dawn
1998		NCAA	III	32	—	—	—	—	—	—	—	19	8	Henderson, Dawn
NEW JERSEY TECH														
1991	M	NCAA	III	40	—	—	—	—	—	—	—	24	5	Catalano, Dr. James M.
1993		NCAA	III	32	—	—	—	—	—	—	—	22	4	Catalano, Dr. James M.
1994		NCAA	III	32	—	—	—	—	—	—	—	23	4	Catalano, Dr. James M.
1995		NCAA	III	8	—	—	—	—	—	—	—	28	2	Catalano, Dr. James M.
1996		NCAA	III	64	—	—	—	—	—	—	—	17	10	Catalano, Dr. James M.
NEW KENSINGTON COMMERCIAL														
1970	M	NSCAA		3	—	—	—	—	—	—	—	10	9	Shultz, Charles
NEW MEXICO														
1947	M	NAIA		32	—	—	—	—	—	—	—	11	8	Clements, Woodrow W.
1964		NCAA	I	—	2	—	—	—	—	—	—	23	6	King, Bob
1965		NCAA	I	—	8	—	—	—	—	—	—	19	8	King, Bob
1967		NCAA	I	—	8	—	—	—	—	—	—	19	8	King, Bob
1968		NCAA	I	16	—	—	—	—	—	—	—	23	5	King, Bob
1973		NCAA	I	—	16	—	—	—	—	—	—	21	6	Ellenberger, Norman
1974		NCAA	I	12	—	—	—	—	—	—	—	22	7	Ellenberger, Norman
1978		NCAA	I	32	—	—	—	—	—	—	—	24	4	Ellenberger, Norman
1979		NCAA	I	—	24	—	—	—	—	—	—	19	10	Ellenberger, Norman
1984		NCAA	I	—	32	—	—	—	—	—	—	24	11	Colson, Gary W.
1985		NCAA	I	—	16	—	—	—	—	—	—	19	13	Colson, Gary W.
1986		NCAA	I	—	32	—	—	—	—	—	—	17	14	Colson, Gary W.
1987		NCAA	I	—	32	—	—	—	—	—	—	25	10	Colson, Gary W.
1988		NCAA	I	—	8	—	—	—	—	—	—	22	14	Colson, Gary W.
1989		NCAA	I	—	8	—	—	—	—	—	—	22	11	Bliss, David
1990		NCAA	I	—	4	—	—	—	—	—	—	20	14	Bliss, David
1991		NCAA	I	64	—	—	—	—	—	—	—	20	10	Bliss, David
1992		NCAA	I	—	8	—	—	—	—	—	—	20	13	Bliss, David
1993		NCAA	I	64	—	—	—	—	—	—	—	24	7	Bliss, David
1994		NCAA	I	64	—	—	—	—	—	—	—	23	8	Bliss, David
1996		NCAA	I	32	—	—	—	—	—	—	—	28	5	Bliss, David
1997		NCAA	I	32	—	—	—	—	—	—	—	25	8	Bliss, David
1998		NCAA	I	32	—	—	—	—	—	—	—	24	8	Bliss, David
1998	W	NCAA	I	64	—	—	—	—	—	—	—	26	7	Flanagan, Don

Year	M/W	Assn	Div	NAT	NIT	ARC	CCA	NCI	NCT	OLY	HLM	W	L	Coach

NEW MEXICO HIGHLANDS

Year	M/W	Assn	Div	NAT	NIT	ARC	CCA	NCI	NCT	OLY	HLM	W	L	Coach
1957	M	NAIA		32	—	—	—	—	—	—	—	18	4	Gibson, Don
1960		NAIA		8	—	—	—	—	—	—	—	18	7	Gibson, Don
1992	W	NAIA	I	32	—	—	—	—	—	—	—	21	9	Roybal, Cindy

NEW MEXICO STATE

Year	M/W	Assn	Div	NAT	NIT	ARC	CCA	NCI	NCT	OLY	HLM	W	L	Coach
1938	M	NAIA		8	—	—	—	—	—	—	—	22	3	Hines, Gerald H. "Jerry"
1939		NAIA		—	6	—	—	—	—	—	—	16	3	Hines, Gerald H. "Jerry"
1950		NAIA		32	—	—	—	—	—	—	—	15	13	McCarty, George C.
1951		NAIA		8	—	—	—	—	—	—	—	15	11	McCarty, George C.
1952		NAIA		16	—	—	—	—	—	—	—	22	11	McCarty, George C.
1952		NCAA		16	—	—	—	—	—	—	—	22	11	McCarty, George C.
1959		NCAA	I	23	—	—	—	—	—	—	—	17	11	Askew, Presley
1960		NCAA	I	25	—	—	—	—	—	—	—	20	7	Askew, Presley
1967		NCAA	I	23	—	—	—	—	—	—	—	15	11	Henson, Louis R.
1968		NCAA	I	12	—	—	—	—	—	—	—	23	6	Henson, Louis R.
1969		NCAA	I	16	—	—	—	—	—	—	—	24	5	Henson, Louis R.
1970		NCAA	I	3	—	—	—	—	—	—	—	27	3	Henson, Louis R.
1971		NCAA	I	25	—	—	—	—	—	—	—	19	8	Henson, Louis R.
1975		NCAA	I	32	—	—	—	—	—	—	—	20	7	Henson, Louis R.
1979		NCAA	I	40	—	—	—	—	—	—	—	22	10	Hayes, Ken
1989		NCAA	I	—	32	—	—	—	—	—	—	21	11	McCarthy, Neil N.
1990		NCAA	I	64	—	—	—	—	—	—	—	26	5	McCarthy, Neil N.
1991		NCAA	I	64	—	—	—	—	—	—	—	23	6	McCarthy, Neil N.
1992		NCAA	I	16	—	—	—	—	—	—	—	25	8	McCarthy, Neil N.
1993		NCAA	I	32	—	—	—	—	—	—	—	26	8	McCarthy, Neil N.
1994		NCAA	I	64	—	—	—	—	—	—	—	23	8	McCarthy, Neil N.
1995		NCAA	I	—	8	—	—	—	—	—	—	25	10	McCarthy, Neil N.
1987	W	NCAA	I	40	—	—	—	—	—	—	—	23	7	McKeown, Joe
1988		NCAA	I	32	—	—	—	—	—	—	—	26	3	McKeown, Joe
1994		NCAA	I	—	6	—	—	—	—	—	—	24	8	Petersen, Mike

NEW MEXICO TECH

Year	M/W	Assn	Div	NAT	NIT	ARC	CCA	NCI	NCT	OLY	HLM	W	L	Coach
1939	M	NAIA		32	—	—	—	—	—	—	—	21	5	Butler, Dr. Louis C. "Pete"
1946		NAIA		32	—	—	—	—	—	—	—	20	9	Finley, Charles L. "Chuck"

NEW ORLEANS

Year	M/W	Assn	Div	NAT	NIT	ARC	CCA	NCI	NCT	OLY	HLM	W	L	Coach
1971	M	NCAA	II	32	—	—	—	—	—	—	—	23	3	Greene, Ronald L.
1972		NCAA	II	24	—	—	—	—	—	—	—	16	10	Greene, Ronald L.
1974		NCAA	II	4	—	—	—	—	—	—	—	21	9	Greene, Ronald L.
1975		NCAA	II	2	—	—	—	—	—	—	—	23	7	Greene, Ronald L.
1983		NCAA	I	—	16	—	—	—	—	—	—	23	7	Smith, Donald W.
1987		NCAA	I	32	—	—	—	—	—	—	—	26	4	Dees, Benny
1988		NCAA	I	—	32	—	—	—	—	—	—	21	11	Polis, Art
1989		NCAA	I	—	32	—	—	—	—	—	—	19	11	Floyd, Tim
1990		NCAA	I	—	8	—	—	—	—	—	—	21	11	Floyd, Tim
1991		NCAA	I	64	—	—	—	—	—	—	—	23	8	Floyd, Tim
1993		NCAA	I	64	—	—	—	—	—	—	—	26	4	Floyd, Tim
1994		NCAA	I	—	16	—	—	—	—	—	—	20	10	Floyd, Tim

Year	M/W	Assn	Div	NAT	NIT	ARC	CCA	NCI	NCT	OLY	HLM	W	L	Coach
1996		NCAA	I	64	—	—	—	—	—	—	—	21	9	Price, George "Tic"
1997		NCAA	I	—	32	—	—	—	—	—	—	22	7	Price, George "Tic"
1983	W	NCAA	I	—	1	—	—	—	—	—	—	23	8	Favaloro, Joey
1987		NCAA	I	32	—	—	—	—	—	—	—	25	7	Favaloro, Joey
1988		NCAA	I	—	3	—	—	—	—	—	—	25	7	Favaloro, Joey

NEW ROCHELLE

Year	M/W	Assn	Div	NAT	NIT	ARC	CCA	NCI	NCT	OLY	HLM	W	L	Coach
1982	W	AIAW	III	16	—	—	—	—	—	—	—	X	X	Kern, Louis
1983		NCAA	III	8	—	—	—	—	—	—	—	28	5	Kern, Louis
1984		NCAA	III	24	—	—	—	—	—	—	—	26	8	Kern, Louis
1985		NCAA	III	2	—	—	—	—	—	—	—	25	8	Kern, Louis

NEW YORK

Year	M/W	Assn	Div	NAT	NIT	ARC	CCA	NCI	NCT	OLY	HLM	W	L	Coach
1935	M	NCAA		—	—	—	—	—	—	—	1	18	1	Cann, Howard G.
1938		NCAA		—	4	—	—	—	—	—	—	16	8	Cann, Howard G.
1943		NCAA		8	—	—	—	—	—	—	—	16	6	Cann, Howard G.
1945		NCAA		2	—	3	—	—	—	—	—	14	7	Cann, Howard G.
1946		NCAA		6	—	—	—	—	—	—	—	19	3	Cann, Howard G.
1948		NCAA		—	2	—	—	—	—	8	—	22	4	Cann, Howard G.
1949		NCAA		—	12	—	—	—	—	—	—	12	8	Cann, Howard G.
1952		NCAA		—	12	—	—	—	—	—	—	17	8	Cann, Howard G.
1959		NCAA	I	—	3	—	—	—	—	—	—	15	8	Rossini, Lucio "Lou"
1960		NCAA	I	4	—	—	—	—	—	—	—	22	5	Rossini, Lucio "Lou"
1962		NCAA	I	12	—	—	—	—	—	—	—	20	5	Rossini, Lucio "Lou"
1963		NCAA	I	16	—	—	—	—	—	—	—	18	5	Rossini, Lucio "Lou"
1964		NCAA	I	—	4	—	—	—	—	—	—	17	10	Rossini, Lucio "Lou"
1965		NCAA	I	—	4	—	—	—	—	—	—	16	10	Rossini, Lucio "Lou"
1966		NCAA	I	—	2	—	—	—	—	—	—	18	10	Rossini, Lucio "Lou"
1986		NCAA	III	32	—	—	—	—	—	—	—	21	6	Layne, Floyd
1992		NCAA	III	40	—	—	—	—	—	—	—	22	5	Nesci, Joe
1993		NCAA	III	16	—	—	—	—	—	—	—	23	3	Nesci, Joe
1994		NCAA	III	2	—	—	—	—	—	—	—	25	5	Nesci, Joe
1995		NCAA	III	32	—	—	—	—	—	—	—	22	5	Nesci, Joe
1996		NCAA	III	32	—	—	—	—	—	—	—	19	8	Nesci, Joe
1997		NCAA	III	32	—	—	—	—	—	—	—	19	8	Nesci, Joe
1998		NCAA	III	48	—	—	—	—	—	—	—	17	9	Nesci, Joe
1986	W	NCAA	III	16	—	—	—	—	—	—	—	20	8	Pickard, Sherri
1987		NCAA	III	32	—	—	—	—	—	—	—	18	10	Pickard, Sherri
1989		NCAA	III	16	—	—	—	—	—	—	—	18	9	Quinn, Janice
1991		NCAA	III	32	—	—	—	—	—	—	—	19	8	Quinn, Janice
1993		NCAA	III	16	—	—	—	—	—	—	—	20	6	Quinn, Janice
1994		NCAA	III	16	—	—	—	—	—	—	—	22	4	Quinn, Janice
1995		NCAA	III	16	—	—	—	—	—	—	—	23	5	Quinn, Janice
1996		NCAA	III	4	—	—	—	—	—	—	—	27	4	Quinn, Janice
1997		NCAA	III	1	—	—	—	—	—	—	—	29	1	Quinn, Janice
1998		NCAA	III	16	—	—	—	—	—	—	—	22	5	Quinn, Janice

NEW YORK POLYTECHNIC

Year	M/W	Assn	Div	NAT	NIT	ARC	CCA	NCI	NCT	OLY	HLM	W	L	Coach
1978	M	NCAA	II	32	—	—	—	—	—	—	—	20	5	Stern, Sam
1980		NCAA	II	2	—	—	—	—	—	—	—	26	3	Stern, Sam

Year	M/W	Assn	Div	NAT	NIT	ARC	CCA	NCI	NCT	OLY	HLM	W	L	Coach
NEWBERRY														
1961	M	NAIA		16	—	—	—	—	—	—	—	23	8	Quinn, Thomas R.
1975		NAIA		32	—	—	—	—	—	—	—	24	9	Gordon, Nield
1976		NAIA		8	—	—	—	—	—	—	—	30	5	Gordon, Nield
1977		NAIA		16	—	—	—	—	—	—	—	36	1	Gordon, Nield
NIAGARA														
1950	M	NCAA		—	12	—	—	—	—	—	—	20	7	Gallagher, John J. "Taps"
1953		NCAA		—	8	—	—	—	—	—	—	22	6	Gallagher, John J. "Taps"
1954		NCAA		—	3	—	—	—	—	—	—	24	6	Gallagher, John J. "Taps"
1955		NCAA		—	8	—	—	—	—	—	—	20	6	Gallagher, John J. "Taps"
1956		NCAA		—	8	—	—	—	—	—	—	20	7	Gallagher, John J. "Taps"
1958		NCAA	I	—	12	—	—	—	—	—	—	18	7	Gallagher, John J. "Taps"
1961		NCAA	I	—	8	—	—	—	—	—	—	16	5	Gallagher, John J. "Taps"
1970		NCAA	I	16	—	—	—	—	—	—	—	22	7	Layden, Frank P.
1972		NCAA	I	—	2	—	—	—	—	—	—	21	9	Layden, Frank P.
1976		NCAA	I	—	12	—	—	—	—	—	—	17	12	Layden, Frank P.
1987		NCAA	I	—	16	—	—	—	—	—	—	21	10	Walker, Andy
1993		NCAA	I	—	32	—	—	—	—	—	—	23	7	Armstrong, Jack
1979	W	AIAW	S	3	—	—	—	—	—	—	—	30	6	Roickle, Mary
1980		AIAW	II	24	—	—	—	—	—	—	—	24	6	Roickle, Mary
NICHOLLS STATE														
1976	M	NCAA	II	8	—	—	—	—	—	—	—	22	4	Landry, Donald
1979		NCAA	II	8	—	—	—	—	—	—	—	21	7	Landry, Donald
1980		NCAA	II	16	—	—	—	—	—	—	—	18	8	Sanders, Jerry
1995		NCAA	I	64	—	—	—	—	—	—	—	24	6	Broussard, Rickey
1998		NCAA	I	64	—	—	—	—	—	—	—	19	10	Broussard, Rickey
NORFOLK STATE														
1965	M	NCAA	II	24	—	—	—	—	—	—	—	22	3	Fears, Ernest D., Jr.
1966		NAIA		4	—	—	—	—	—	—	—	26	6	Fears, Ernest D., Jr.
1968		NCAA	II	16	—	—	—	—	—	—	—	24	2	Fears, Ernest D., Jr.
1969		NCAA	II	24	—	—	—	—	—	—	—	18	2	Fears, Ernest D., Jr.
1971		NCAA	II	16	—	—	—	—	—	—	—	26	4	Smith, Robert L.
1974		NCAA	II	8	—	—	—	—	—	—	—	21	9	Christian, Charles O.
1975		NAIA		16	—	—	—	—	—	—	—	23	5	Christian, Charles O.
1976		NAIA		32	—	—	—	—	—	—	—	23	7	Christian, Charles O.
1979		NAIA		16	—	—	—	—	—	—	—	23	8	Mitchell, Lucias
1981		NAIA		32	—	—	—	—	—	—	—	19	10	Mitchell, Lucias
1984		NCAA	II	16	—	—	—	—	—	—	—	29	2	Christian, Charles O.
1985		NCAA	II	24	—	—	—	—	—	—	—	23	7	Christian, Charles O.
1986		NCAA	II	8	—	—	—	—	—	—	—	26	5	Christian, Charles O.
1987		NCAA	II	8	—	—	—	—	—	—	—	28	3	Christian, Charles O.
1988		NCAA	II	32	—	—	—	—	—	—	—	23	8	Christian, Charles O.
1989		NCAA	II	32	—	—	—	—	—	—	—	24	6	Christian, Charles O.
1990		NCAA	II	24	—	—	—	—	—	—	—	27	4	Christian, Charles O.
1992		NCAA	II	32	—	—	—	—	—	—	—	22	10	Bernard, Michael J.
1994		NCAA	II	8	—	—	—	—	—	—	—	27	6	Bernard, Michael J.
1995		NCAA	II	4	—	—	—	—	—	—	—	27	7	Bernard, Michael J.

Year	M/W	Assn	Div	NAT	NIT	ARC	CCA	NCI	NCT	OLY	HLM	W	L	Coach
1982	W	NCAA	II	8	—	—	—	—	—	—	—	19	6	Moorehead, Dr. Isaac T. "Ike"
1983		NCAA	II	24	—	—	—	—	—	—	—	19	6	Moorehead, Dr. Isaac T. "Ike"
1986		NCAA	II	24	—	—	—	—	—	—	—	18	10	Moorehead, Dr. Isaac T. "Ike"
1991		NCAA	II	4	—	—	—	—	—	—	—	33	2	Sweat, James E.
1992		NCAA	II	16	—	—	—	—	—	—	—	25	7	Sweat, James E.
1993		NCAA	II	8	—	—	—	—	—	—	—	29	3	Sweat, James E.
1994		NCAA	II	8	—	—	—	—	—	—	—	27	4	Sweat, James E.
1995		NCAA	II	32	—	—	—	—	—	—	—	25	5	Sweat, James E.

NORTH ALABAMA

Year	M/W	Assn	Div	NAT	NIT	ARC	CCA	NCI	NCT	OLY	HLM	W	L	Coach
1960	M	NAIA		32	—	—	—	—	—	—	—	14	11	Billingham, Edmond E.
1962		NAIA		32	—	—	—	—	—	—	—	17	9	Billingham, Edmond E.
1977		NCAA	II	3	—	—	—	—	—	—	—	24	7	Jones, Bill L.
1979		NCAA	II	1	—	—	—	—	—	—	—	22	9	Jones, Bill L.
1980		NCAA	II	4	—	—	—	—	—	—	—	21	10	Jones, Bill L.
1981		NCAA	II	8	—	—	—	—	—	—	—	22	9	Jones, Bill L.
1984		NCAA	II	3	—	—	—	—	—	—	—	27	7	Jones, Bill L.
1988		NCAA	II	24	—	—	—	—	—	—	—	17	14	Jones, Bill L.
1991		NCAA	II	1	—	—	—	—	—	—	—	29	4	Elliott, Gary
1994		NCAA	II	16	—	—	—	—	—	—	—	24	6	Elliott, Gary
1995		NCAA	II	48	—	—	—	—	—	—	—	20	8	Elliott, Gary
1996		NCAA	II	8	—	—	—	—	—	—	—	24	8	Elliott, Gary
1984	W	NCAA	II	16	—	—	—	—	—	—	—	25	5	Byrd, Wayne
1985		NCAA	II	16	—	—	—	—	—	—	—	19	8	Byrd, Wayne
1991		NCAA	II	32	—	—	—	—	—	—	—	20	9	Byrd, Wayne
1994		NCAA	II	3	—	—	—	—	—	—	—	22	10	Byrd, Wayne

NORTH CAROLINA

Year	M/W	Assn	Div	NAT	NIT	ARC	CCA	NCI	NCT	OLY	HLM	W	L	Coach
1924	M	NCAA		—	—	—	—	—	—	—	1	26	0	Shepard, Norman W. "Bo"
1941		NCAA		8	—	—	—	—	—	—	—	15	8	Lange, William
1946		NCAA		2	—	—	—	—	—	—	—	30	5	Carnevale, Bernard L. "Ben"
1957		NCAA	I	1	—	—	—	—	—	—	1	32	0	McGuire, Frank J.
1959		NCAA	I	23	—	—	—	—	—	—	—	20	5	McGuire, Frank J.
1967		NCAA	I	4	—	—	—	—	—	—	—	26	6	Smith, Dean E.
1968		NCAA	I	2	—	—	—	—	—	—	—	28	4	Smith, Dean E.
1969		NCAA	I	4	—	—	—	—	—	—	—	27	5	Smith, Dean E.
1970		NCAA	I	—	16	—	—	—	—	—	—	18	9	Smith, Dean E.
1971		NCAA	I	—	1	—	—	—	—	—	—	26	6	Smith, Dean E.
1972		NCAA	I	3	—	—	—	—	—	—	—	26	5	Smith, Dean E.
1973		NCAA	I	—	3	—	—	—	—	—	—	25	8	Smith, Dean E.
1974		NCAA	I	—	16	—	—	—	—	—	—	22	6	Smith, Dean E.
1975		NCAA	I	12	—	—	—	—	—	—	—	23	8	Smith, Dean E.
1976		NCAA	I	32	—	—	—	—	—	—	—	25	4	Smith, Dean E.
1977		NCAA	I	2	—	—	—	—	—	—	—	28	5	Smith, Dean E.
1978		NCAA	I	32	—	—	—	—	—	—	—	23	8	Smith, Dean E.
1979		NCAA	I	32	—	—	—	—	—	—	—	23	6	Smith, Dean E.
1980		NCAA	I	32	—	—	—	—	—	—	—	21	8	Smith, Dean E.
1981		NCAA	I	2	—	—	—	—	—	—	—	29	8	Smith, Dean E.
1982		NCAA	I	1	—	—	—	—	—	—	1	32	2	Smith, Dean E.
1983		NCAA	I	8	—	—	—	—	—	—	—	28	8	Smith, Dean E.
1984		NCAA	I	16	—	—	—	—	—	—	—	28	3	Smith, Dean E.
1985		NCAA	I	8	—	—	—	—	—	—	—	27	9	Smith, Dean E.

Year	M/W	Assn	Div	NAT	NIT	ARC	CCA	NCI	NCT	OLY	HLM	W	L	Coach
1986		NCAA	I	16	—	—	—	—	—	—	—	28	6	Smith, Dean E.
1987		NCAA	I	8	—	—	—	—	—	—	—	32	4	Smith, Dean E.
1988		NCAA	I	8	—	—	—	—	—	—	—	27	7	Smith, Dean E.
1989		NCAA	I	16	—	—	—	—	—	—	—	29	8	Smith, Dean E.
1990		NCAA	I	16	—	—	—	—	—	—	—	21	13	Smith, Dean E.
1991		NCAA	I	3	—	—	—	—	—	—	—	29	6	Smith, Dean E.
1992		NCAA	I	16	—	—	—	—	—	—	—	23	10	Smith, Dean E.
1993		NCAA	I	1	—	—	—	—	—	—	—	34	4	Smith, Dean E.
1994		NCAA	I	32	—	—	—	—	—	—	—	28	7	Smith, Dean E.
1995		NCAA	I	3	—	—	—	—	—	—	—	28	6	Smith, Dean E.
1996		NCAA	I	32	—	—	—	—	—	—	—	21	11	Smith, Dean E.
1997		NCAA	I	3	—	—	—	—	—	—	—	28	7	Smith, Dean E.
1998		NCAA	I	3	—	—	—	—	—	—	—	35	4	Guthridge, Bill
1975	W			—	6	—	—	—	—	—	—	15	3	Lurapkin, Angela
1980				—	2	—	—	—	—	—	—	21	15	Alley, Jennifer
1983		NCAA	I	32	—	—	—	—	—	—	—	22	8	Alley, Jennifer
1984		NCAA	I	16	—	—	—	—	—	—	—	24	8	Alley, Jennifer
1985		NCAA	I	32	—	—	—	—	—	—	—	21	11	Alley, Jennifer
1986		NCAA	I	16	—	—	—	—	—	—	—	23	9	Alley, Jennifer
1987		NCAA	I	32	—	—	—	—	—	—	—	19	10	Hatchell, Sylvia Rhyne
1992		NCAA	I	32	—	—	—	—	—	—	—	22	9	Hatchell, Sylvia Rhyne
1993		NCAA	I	16	—	—	—	—	—	—	—	23	7	Hatchell, Sylvia Rhyne
1994		NCAA	I	1	—	—	—	—	—	—	—	33	2	Hatchell, Sylvia Rhyne
1995		NCAA	I	16	—	—	—	—	—	—	—	30	5	Hatchell, Sylvia Rhyne
1997		NCAA	I	16	—	—	—	—	—	—	—	29	3	Hatchell, Sylvia Rhyne
1998		NCAA	I	8	—	—	—	—	—	—	—	27	7	Hatchell, Sylvia Rhyne

NORTH CAROLINA A&T

Year	M/W	Assn	Div	NAT	NIT	ARC	CCA	NCI	NCT	OLY	HLM	W	L	Coach
1958	M	NCAA	II	16	—	—	—	—	—	—	—	21	4	Irvin, Calvin C.
1959		NCAA	II	3	—	—	—	—	—	—	—	26	4	Irvin, Calvin C.
1962		NCAA	II	24	—	—	—	—	—	—	—	20	7	Irvin, Calvin C.
1964		NCAA	II	3	—	—	—	—	—	—	—	23	7	Irvin, Calvin C.
1971		NAIA		8	—	—	—	—	—	—	—	24	8	Irvin, Calvin C.
1976		NCAA	I	—	12	—	—	—	—	—	—	20	6	Reynolds, Warren
1981		NCAA	I	—	32	—	—	—	—	—	—	21	8	Corbett, Donald
1982		NCAA	I	48	—	—	—	—	—	—	—	19	9	Corbett, Donald
1983		NCAA	I	52	—	—	—	—	—	—	—	23	8	Corbett, Donald
1984		NCAA	I	53	—	—	—	—	—	—	—	22	7	Corbett, Donald
1985		NCAA	I	64	—	—	—	—	—	—	—	19	10	Corbett, Donald
1986		NCAA	I	64	—	—	—	—	—	—	—	22	8	Corbett, Donald
1987		NCAA	I	64	—	—	—	—	—	—	—	24	6	Corbett, Donald
1988		NCAA	I	64	—	—	—	—	—	—	—	26	3	Corbett, Donald
1994		NCAA	I	64	—	—	—	—	—	—	—	16	14	Capel, Jeff
1995		NCAA	I	64	—	—	—	—	—	—	—	15	15	Thomas, Roy C.
1994	W	NCAA	I	64	—	—	—	—	—	—	—	19	11	Abney, Tim

NORTH CAROLINA CENTRAL

Year	M/W	Assn	Div	NAT	NIT	ARC	CCA	NCI	NCT	OLY	HLM	W	L	Coach
1953	M	NASC		8	—	—	—	—	—	—	—	17	7	Brown, Floyd H.
1954		NASC		2	—	—	—	—	—	—	—	23	7	Brown, Floyd H.
1955		NASC		8	—	—	—	—	—	—	—	21	6	Brown, Floyd H.
1957		NCAA	II	16	—	—	—	—	—	—	—	21	6	Brown, Floyd H.

Year	M/W	Assn	Div	NAT	NIT	ARC	CCA	NCI	NCT	OLY	HLM	W	L	Coach
1988		NCAA	II	16	—	—	—	—	—	—	—	26	3	Bernard, Michael J.
1989		NCAA	II	1	—	—	—	—	—	—	—	28	4	Bernard, Michael J.
1990		NCAA	II	16	—	—	—	—	—	—	—	23	5	Bernard, Michael J.
1993		NCAA	II	8	—	—	—	—	—	—	—	26	4	Jackson, Gregory D.
1996		NCAA	II	48	—	—	—	—	—	—	—	20	7	Jackson, Gregory D.
1997		NCAA	II	32	—	—	—	—	—	—	—	20	6	Jackson, Gregory D.
1984	W	NCAA	II	24	—	—	—	—	—	—	—	13	15	Edwards, Yvonne

NORTH CAROLINA STATE

Year	M/W	Assn	Div	NAT	NIT	ARC	CCA	NCI	NCT	OLY	HLM	W	L	Coach
1947	M	NCAA		—	3	—	—	—	—	—	—	26	5	Case, Everett N.
1948		NCAA		—	8	—	—	—	—	—	—	29	3	Case, Everett N.
1950		NCAA		3	—	—	—	—	—	—	—	27	6	Case, Everett N.
1951		NCAA		8	8	—	—	—	—	—	—	30	7	Case, Everett N.
1952		NCAA		12	—	—	—	—	—	—	—	24	10	Case, Everett N.
1954		NCAA		12	—	—	—	—	—	—	—	26	7	Case, Everett N.
1956		NCAA		25	—	—	—	—	—	—	—	24	4	Case, Everett N.
1965		NCAA	I	12	—	—	—	—	—	—	—	21	5	Maravich, Peter "Press"
1970		NCAA	I	12	—	—	—	—	—	—	—	23	7	Sloan, Norman L., Jr.
1974		NCAA	I	1	—	—	—	—	—	—	1	30	1	Sloan, Norman L., Jr.
1976		NCAA	I	—	3	—	—	—	—	—	—	21	9	Sloan, Norman L., Jr.
1978		NCAA	I	—	2	—	—	—	—	—	—	21	10	Sloan, Norman L., Jr.
1980		NCAA	I	32	—	—	—	—	—	—	—	20	8	Sloan, Norman L., Jr.
1982		NCAA	I	48	—	—	—	—	—	—	—	22	10	Valvano, James T.
1983		NCAA	I	1	—	—	—	—	—	—	1	26	10	Valvano, James T.
1984		NCAA	I	—	32	—	—	—	—	—	—	19	14	Valvano, James T.
1985		NCAA	I	8	—	—	—	—	—	—	—	23	10	Valvano, James T.
1986		NCAA	I	8	—	—	—	—	—	—	—	21	13	Valvano, James T.
1987		NCAA	I	64	—	—	—	—	—	—	—	20	15	Valvano, James T.
1988		NCAA	I	64	—	—	—	—	—	—	—	24	8	Valvano, James T.
1989		NCAA	I	16	—	—	—	—	—	—	—	22	9	Valvano, James T.
1991		NCAA	I	32	—	—	—	—	—	—	—	20	11	Robinson, Leslie G.
1997		NCAA	I	—	16	—	—	—	—	—	—	17	15	Sendek, Herb
1998		NCAA	I	—	16	—	—	—	—	—	—	17	15	Sendek, Herb
1976	W			—	6	—	—	—	—	—	—	19	7	Yow, Sandra Kay
1978		AIAW	L	8	—	—	—	—	—	—	—	29	5	Yow, Sandra Kay
1980		AIAW	I	16	—	—	—	—	—	—	—	28	8	Yow, Sandra Kay
1981		AIAW	I	16	—	—	—	—	—	—	—	21	10	Yow, Sandra Kay
1982		NCAA	I	16	—	—	—	—	—	—	—	24	7	Yow, Sandra Kay
1983		NCAA	I	32	—	—	—	—	—	—	—	22	8	Yow, Sandra Kay
1984		NCAA	I	16	—	—	—	—	—	—	—	23	9	Yow, Sandra Kay
1985		NCAA	I	16	—	—	—	—	—	—	—	25	6	Yow, Sandra Kay
1986		NCAA	I	32	—	—	—	—	—	—	—	18	11	Yow, Sandra Kay
1987		NCAA	I	16	—	—	—	—	—	—	—	24	7	Yow, Sandra Kay
1989		NCAA	I	16	—	—	—	—	—	—	—	24	7	Yow, Sandra Kay
1990		NCAA	I	16	—	—	—	—	—	—	—	25	6	Yow, Sandra Kay
1991		NCAA	I	16	—	—	—	—	—	—	—	27	6	Yow, Sandra Kay
1995		NCAA	I	16	—	—	—	—	—	—	—	21	10	Yow, Sandra Kay
1996		NCAA	I	32	—	—	—	—	—	—	—	20	10	Yow, Sandra Kay
1997		NCAA	I	64	—	—	—	—	—	—	—	19	12	Yow, Sandra Kay
1998		NCAA	I	3	—	—	—	—	—	—	—	24	7	Yow, Sandra Kay

Year	M/W	Assn	Div	NAT	NIT	ARC	CCA	NCI	NCT	OLY	HLM	W	L	Coach
North Carolina Wesleyan														
1983	M	NCAA	III	32	—	—	—	—	—	—	—	—	21	9	McCarthy, John
1984		NCAA	III	16	—	—	—	—	—	—	—	—	21	8	McCarthy, John
1987		NCAA	III	8	—	—	—	—	—	—	—	—	24	7	Chambers, Bill
1994	W	NCAA	III	32	—	—	—	—	—	—	—	—	20	8	Brackett, John
North Carolina: Asheville														
1969	M	NAIA		16	—	—	—	—	—	—	—	—	19	9	Hartman, Robert L.
1971		NAIA		32	—	—	—	—	—	—	—	—	20	10	Hartman, Robert L.
1984	W	NAIA		1	—	—	—	—	—	—	—	—	32	5	Carroll, Helen
North Carolina: Charlotte														
1976	M	NCAA	I	—	2	—	—	—	—	—	—	—	24	6	Rose, Lee H.
1977		NCAA	I	4	—	—	—	—	—	—	—	—	28	5	Rose, Lee H.
1988		NCAA	I	64	—	—	—	—	—	—	—	—	22	9	Mullins, Jeffrey V., Jr.
1989		NCAA	I	—	32	—	—	—	—	—	—	—	17	12	Mullins, Jeffrey V., Jr.
1992		NCAA	I	64	—	—	—	—	—	—	—	—	23	9	Mullins, Jeffrey V., Jr.
1994		NCAA	I	—	32	—	—	—	—	—	—	—	16	13	Mullins, Jeffrey V., Jr.
1995		NCAA	I	64	—	—	—	—	—	—	—	—	19	9	Mullins, Jeffrey V., Jr.
1997		NCAA	I	32	—	—	—	—	—	—	—	—	22	9	Watkins, Melvin
1998		NCAA	I	32	—	—	—	—	—	—	—	—	20	11	Watkins, Melvin
1990	W	NCAA	I	—	3	—	—	—	—	—	—	—	24	8	Baldwin, Ed
North Carolina: Greensboro														
1980	M	NCAA	III	32	—	—	—	—	—	—	—	—	16	12	Hargett, Larry
1996		NCAA	I	64	—	—	—	—	—	—	—	—	20	10	Peele, Randy
1971	W	AIAW		4	—	—	—	—	—	—	—	—	12	8	Galloway, Dr. June
1982		NCAA	III	2	—	—	—	—	—	—	—	—	24	3	Agee, Lynne
1983		NCAA	III	24	—	—	—	—	—	—	—	—	20	8	Agee, Lynne
1984		NCAA	III	24	—	—	—	—	—	—	—	—	22	7	Agee, Lynne
1985		NCAA	III	16	—	—	—	—	—	—	—	—	21	7	Agee, Lynne
1986		NCAA	III	16	—	—	—	—	—	—	—	—	24	4	Agee, Lynne
1987		NCAA	III	24	—	—	—	—	—	—	—	—	27	3	Agee, Lynne
1988		NCAA	III	3	—	—	—	—	—	—	—	—	26	7	Agee, Lynne
1991		NCAA	II	16	—	—	—	—	—	—	—	—	21	9	Agee, Lynne
1998		NCAA	I	64	—	—	—	—	—	—	—	—	21	9	Agee, Lynne
North Carolina: Pembroke														
1973	M	NAIA		32	—	—	—	—	—	—	—	—	20	8	Gani, Lancey E.
1984		NAIA		16	—	—	—	—	—	—	—	—	26	7	Lee, Billy
1985	W	NAIA		16	—	—	—	—	—	—	—	—	26	5	Lee, Billy
1992		NAIA	I	32	—	—	—	—	—	—	—	—	24	7	Pitts, Linda
North Carolina: Wilmington														
1998	M	NCAA	I	—	32	—	—	—	—	—	—	—	20	11	Wainwright, Jerry

Year	M/W	Assn	Div	NAT	NIT	ARC	CCA	NCI	NCT	OLY	HLM	W	L	Coach
NORTH CENTRAL (IL)														
1984	M	NCAA	III	24	—	—	—	—	—	—	—	—	18	10	Warden, Bill
1985		NCAA	III	32	—	—	—	—	—	—	—	—	20	7	Warden, Bill
1989		NCAA	III	16	—	—	—	—	—	—	—	—	19	9	Warden, Bill
1990		NCAA	III	32	—	—	—	—	—	—	—	—	21	6	Warden, Bill
1982	W	AIAW	III	8	—	—	—	—	—	—	—	—	28	9	Morgan, R. Wayne
1983		NCAA	III	1	—	—	—	—	—	—	—	—	26	6	Morgan, R. Wayne
1984		NCAA	III	4	—	—	—	—	—	—	—	—	24	6	Morgan, R. Wayne
NORTH CENTRAL BIBLE														
1981	M	NBCAA		4	—	—	—	—	—	—	—	—	X	X	Lockwood, Glen
1982		NBCAA		4	—	—	—	—	—	—	—	—	15	9	Lowenberg, Doug
1983		NBCAA		4	—	—	—	—	—	—	—	—	16	13	Lowenberg, Doug
1984		NBCAA	I	2	—	—	—	—	—	—	—	—	31	1	Myers, Dennis
1985		NBCAA	I	3	—	—	—	—	—	—	—	—	18	11	Myers, Dennis
1986		NBCAA	I	2	—	—	—	—	—	—	—	—	22	12	Myers, Dennis
1987		NBCAA	I	3	—	—	—	—	—	—	—	—	X	X	Myers, Dennis
1988		NBCAA	I	2	—	—	—	—	—	—	—	—	22	13	Myers, Dennis
1988		NCCAA	II	6	—	—	—	—	—	—	—	—	22	13	Myers, Dennis
1989		NBCAA	I	2	—	—	—	—	—	—	—	—	X	X	Myers, Dennis
1993		NCCAA	II	3	—	—	—	—	—	—	—	—	17	12	Engle, Mark
1985	W	NBCAA		3	—	—	—	—	—	—	—	—	7	8	Goodrich, Dr. Larry
1986		NBCAA		1	—	—	—	—	—	—	—	—	15	16	Myers, Dennis
1987		NBCAA		1	—	—	—	—	—	—	—	—	X	X	Myers, Dennis
1989		NBCAA		3	—	—	—	—	—	—	—	—	X	X	Myers, Dennis
1995		NCCAA	II	2	—	—	—	—	—	—	—	—	14	9	Goodrich, Dr. Larry
1996		NCCAA	II	6	—	—	—	—	—	—	—	—	18	9	Goodrich, Dr. Larry
1997		NCCAA	II	7	—	—	—	—	—	—	—	—	10	17	Asberry-Lidquist, Tracine
NORTH DAKOTA														
1949	M	NAIA		16	—	—	—	—	—	—	—	—	14	15	Cunningham, H. B.
1953		NAIA		32	—	—	—	—	—	—	—	—	14	10	Bogan, Louis
1954		NAIA		32	—	—	—	—	—	—	—	—	13	11	Bogan, Louis
1965		NCAA	II	3	—	—	—	—	—	—	—	—	26	5	Fitch, William C. "Billy"
1966		NCAA	II	4	—	—	—	—	—	—	—	—	24	5	Fitch, William C. "Billy"
1967		NCAA	II	23	—	—	—	—	—	—	—	—	20	6	Fitch, William C. "Billy"
1974		NCAA	II	24	—	—	—	—	—	—	—	—	21	8	Gunther, David
1975		NCAA	II	8	—	—	—	—	—	—	—	—	22	7	Gunther, David
1976		NCAA	II	8	—	—	—	—	—	—	—	—	22	7	Gunther, David
1977		NCAA	II	8	—	—	—	—	—	—	—	—	26	4	Gunther, David
1979		NCAA	II	32	—	—	—	—	—	—	—	—	19	9	Gunther, David
1980		NCAA	II	32	—	—	—	—	—	—	—	—	18	12	Gunther, David
1981		NCAA	II	16	—	—	—	—	—	—	—	—	23	8	Gunther, David
1982		NCAA	II	8	—	—	—	—	—	—	—	—	27	5	Gunther, David
1990		NCAA	II	3	—	—	—	—	—	—	—	—	28	7	Glas, Richard "Rich"
1991		NCAA	II	8	—	—	—	—	—	—	—	—	29	4	Glas, Richard "Rich"
1992		NCAA	II	24	—	—	—	—	—	—	—	—	23	9	Glas, Richard "Rich"
1993		NCAA	II	16	—	—	—	—	—	—	—	—	23	8	Glas, Richard "Rich"
1994		NCAA	II	24	—	—	—	—	—	—	—	—	23	9	Glas, Richard "Rich"
1995		NCAA	II	48	—	—	—	—	—	—	—	—	19	9	Glas, Richard "Rich"

Year	M/W	Assn	Div	NAT	NIT	ARC	CCA	NCI	NCT	OLY	HLM	W	L	Coach
1984	W	NCAA	II	24	—	—	—	—	—	—	—	22	7	Schwartz, Gary
1985		NCAA	II	24	—	—	—	—	—	—	—	23	6	Schwartz, Gary
1988		NCAA	II	32	—	—	—	—	—	—	—	22	6	Roebuck, Gene
1990		NCAA	II	8	—	—	—	—	—	—	—	27	4	Roebuck, Gene
1991		NCAA	II	16	—	—	—	—	—	—	—	28	2	Roebuck, Gene
1992		NCAA	II	8	—	—	—	—	—	—	—	24	7	Roebuck, Gene
1993		NCAA	II	32	—	—	—	—	—	—	—	23	5	Roebuck, Gene
1994		NCAA	II	32	—	—	—	—	—	—	—	26	2	Roebuck, Gene
1995		NCAA	II	32	—	—	—	—	—	—	—	23	5	Roebuck, Gene
1996		NCAA	II	16	—	—	—	—	—	—	—	26	6	Roebuck, Gene
1997		NCAA	II	1	—	—	—	—	—	—	—	28	4	Roebuck, Gene
1998		NCAA	II	1	—	—	—	—	—	—	—	31	1	Roebuck, Gene

North Dakota State

Year	M/W	Assn	Div	NAT	NIT	ARC	CCA	NCI	NCT	OLY	HLM	W	L	Coach
1971	M	NCAA	II	24	—	—	—	—	—	—	—	18	9	Belk, Lyle V.
1974		NCAA	II	44	—	—	—	—	—	—	—	17	10	Skaar, Marv
1981		NCAA	II	24	—	—	—	—	—	—	—	20	9	Inniger, Ervin L., Jr.
1983		NCAA	II	16	—	—	—	—	—	—	—	21	9	Inniger, Ervin L., Jr.
1994		NCAA	II	16	—	—	—	—	—	—	—	21	9	Billeter, Tom
1995		NCAA	II	24	—	—	—	—	—	—	—	22	8	Billeter, Tom
1996		NCAA	II	32	—	—	—	—	—	—	—	20	9	Billeter, Tom
1997		NCAA	II	32	—	—	—	—	—	—	—	22	7	Billeter, Tom
1979	W	AIAW	S	16	—	—	—	—	—	—	—	12	19	McKinnon, Paul
1982		AIAW	II	4	—	—	—	—	—	—	—	21	11	Ruley, Amy J.
1986		NCAA	II	2	—	—	—	—	—	—	—	24	9	Ruley, Amy J.
1987		NCAA	II	8	—	—	—	—	—	—	—	26	4	Ruley, Amy J.
1988		NCAA	II	3	—	—	—	—	—	—	—	28	3	Ruley, Amy J.
1989		NCAA	II	16	—	—	—	—	—	—	—	23	7	Ruley, Amy J.
1990		NCAA	II	16	—	—	—	—	—	—	—	25	5	Ruley, Amy J.
1991		NCAA	II	1	—	—	—	—	—	—	—	31	2	Ruley, Amy J.
1992		NCAA	II	2	—	—	—	—	—	—	—	29	4	Ruley, Amy J.
1993		NCAA	II	1	—	—	—	—	—	—	—	30	2	Ruley, Amy J.
1994		NCAA	II	1	—	—	—	—	—	—	—	27	5	Ruley, Amy J.
1995		NCAA	II	1	—	—	—	—	—	—	—	32	0	Ruley, Amy J.
1996		NCAA	II	1	—	—	—	—	—	—	—	30	2	Ruley, Amy J.
1997		NCAA	II	16	—	—	—	—	—	—	—	28	1	Ruley, Amy J.
1998		NCAA	II	48	—	—	—	—	—	—	—	22	6	Ruley, Amy J.

North Georgia

Year	M/W	Assn	Div	NAT	NIT	ARC	CCA	NCI	NCT	OLY	HLM	W	L	Coach
1983	M	NAIA		32	—	—	—	—	—	—	—	23	9	Ensley, William E.
1984		NAIA		32	—	—	—	—	—	—	—	17	15	Ensley, William E.
1996		NAIA	I	32	—	—	—	—	—	—	—	21	16	Dunn, Randy
1987	W	NAIA		2	—	—	—	—	—	—	—	27	4	Jarrett, Lynn
1997		NAIA	I	32	—	—	—	—	—	—	—	26	7	Burson-Watson, Buffie

North Park

Year	M/W	Assn	Div	NAT	NIT	ARC	CCA	NCI	NCT	OLY	HLM	W	L	Coach
1969	M	NCAA	II	24	—	—	—	—	—	—	—	21	5	McCarrell, Dan
1978		NCAA	III	1	—	—	—	—	—	—	—	29	2	McCarrell, Dan
1979		NCAA	III	1	—	—	—	—	—	—	—	26	5	McCarrell, Dan
1980		NCAA	III	1	—	—	—	—	—	—	—	28	3	McCarrell, Dan

Year	M/W	Assn	Div	NAT	NIT	ARC	CCA	NCI	NCT	OLY	HLM	W	L	Coach
1981		NCAA	III	32	—	—	—	—	—	—	—	16	12	McCarrell, Dan
1982		NCAA	III	24	—	—	—	—	—	—	—	18	10	McCarrell, Dan
1985		NCAA	III	1	—	—	—	—	—	—	—	27	4	Djurickovic, Bosko
1986		NCAA	III	32	—	—	—	—	—	—	—	21	7	Djurickovic, Bosko
1987		NCAA	III	1	—	—	—	—	—	—	—	28	3	Djurickovic, Bosko
1990		NCAA	III	40	—	—	—	—	—	—	—	18	9	Djurickovic, Bosko
1988	W	NCAA	III	32	—	—	—	—	—	—	—	20	8	Djurickovic, Rebecca Johnson

NORTH TEXAS

Year	M/W	Assn	Div	NAT	NIT	ARC	CCA	NCI	NCT	OLY	HLM	W	L	Coach
1938	M	NAIA		16	—	—	—	—	—	—	—	15	8	Shands, Harry G. "Pete"
1943		NAIA		3	—	—	—	—	—	—	—	15	15	Russell, Lloyd
1988		NCAA	I	64	—	—	—	—	—	—	—	17	13	Gales, Jimmy
1986	W	NCAA	I	40	—	—	—	—	—	—	—	20	10	Nelson, Judy

NORTHEAST CC (NE)

Year	M/W	Assn	Div	NAT	NIT	ARC	CCA	NCI	NCT	OLY	HLM	W	L	Coach
1975	M	NSCAA		16	—	—	—	—	—	—	—			Stevenson, Charles "Chuck"
1976		NSCAA		1	—	—	—	—	—	—	—			Stevenson, Charles "Chuck"
1977		NSCAA		2	—	—	—	—	—	—	—	22	5	Stevenson, Charles "Chuck"
1978		NSCAA		4	—	—	—	—	—	—	—	22	6	Stevenson, Charles "Chuck"
1979		NSCAA		8	—	—	—	—	—	—	—	15	9	Stevenson, Charles "Chuck"
1980		NSCAA		8	—	—	—	—	—	—	—			Stevenson, Charles "Chuck"
1981		NSCAA		4	—	—	—	—	—	—	—			Stevenson, Charles "Chuck"
1982		NSCAA		8	—	—	—	—	—	—	—			Stevenson, Charles "Chuck"
1983		NSCAA		8	—	—	—	—	—	—	—	12	13	Stevenson, Charles "Chuck"
1984		NSCAA		12	—	—	—	—	—	—	—			Johnson, Fred
1985		NSCAA		16	—	—	—	—	—	—	—			Johnson, Fred
1982	W	NSCAA		3	—	—	—	—	—	—	—			Saunce, Judy
1984		NSCAA		8	—	—	—	—	—	—	—			Saunce, Judy

NORTHEAST LOUISIANA

Year	M/W	Assn	Div	NAT	NIT	ARC	CCA	NCI	NCT	OLY	HLM	W	L	Coach
1970	M	NAIA		16	—	—	—	—	—	—	—	16	9	Fant, Leonard "Lenny"
1979		NCAA	I	—	24	—	—	—	—	—	—	23	6	Fant, Leonard "Lenny"
1982		NCAA	I	48	—	—	—	—	—	—	—	19	11	Vining, Mike
1986		NCAA	I	64	—	—	—	—	—	—	—	20	10	Vining, Mike
1988		NCAA	I	—	32	—	—	—	—	—	—	21	9	Vining, Mike
1990		NCAA	I	64	—	—	—	—	—	—	—	22	8	Vining, Mike
1991		NCAA	I	64	—	—	—	—	—	—	—	25	8	Vining, Mike
1992		NCAA	I	64	—	—	—	—	—	—	—	19	10	Vining, Mike
1993		NCAA	I	64	—	—	—	—	—	—	—	26	5	Vining, Mike
1996		NCAA	I	64	—	—	—	—	—	—	—	16	14	Vining, Mike
1973	W			—	8	—	—	—	—	—	—	X	X	Lewis, "Lou"
1983		NCAA	I	32	—	—	—	—	—	—	—	23	6	Harper, Linda F.
1984		NCAA	I	16	—	—	—	—	—	—	—	23	4	Harper, Linda F.
1985		NCAA	I	3	—	—	—	—	—	—	—	30	2	Harper, Linda F.
1987		NCAA	I	40	—	—	—	—	—	—	—	14	10	Harper, Linda F.
1994		NCAA	I	—	8	—	—	—	—	—	—	21	14	Stockton, Roger

Year	M/W	Assn	Div	NAT	NIT	ARC	CCA	NCI	NCT	OLY	HLM	W	L	Coach
NORTHEASTERN (MA)														
1962	M	NCAA	II	8	—	—	—	—	—	—	—	17	8	Dukeshire, Richard E.
1963		NCAA	II	8	—	—	—	—	—	—	—	21	6	Dukeshire, Richard E.
1964		NCAA	II	16	—	—	—	—	—	—	—	17	8	Dukeshire, Richard E.
1966		NCAA	II	32	—	—	—	—	—	—	—	18	8	Dukeshire, Richard E.
1967		NCAA	II	34	—	—	—	—	—	—	—	22	4	Dukeshire, Richard E.
1968		NCAA	II	34	—	—	—	—	—	—	—	19	9	Dukeshire, Richard E.
1981		NCAA	I	32	—	—	—	—	—	—	—	24	6	Calhoun, James A.
1982		NCAA	I	32	—	—	—	—	—	—	—	23	7	Calhoun, James A.
1984		NCAA	I	48	—	—	—	—	—	—	—	27	5	Calhoun, James A.
1985		NCAA	I	64	—	—	—	—	—	—	—	22	9	Calhoun, James A.
1986		NCAA	I	64	—	—	—	—	—	—	—	26	5	Calhoun, James A.
1987		NCAA	I	64	—	—	—	—	—	—	—	27	7	Fogel, Karl
1991		NCAA	I	64	—	—	—	—	—	—	—	22	11	Fogel, Karl
1969	W	AIAW		12	—	—	—	—	—	—	—	8	1	Rowlands, Dr. Jeanne
1970		AIAW		16	—	—	—	—	—	—	—	5	6	Rowlands, Dr. Jeanne
NORTHEASTERN ILLINOIS														
1985	W	NAIA		8	—	—	—	—	—	—	—	29	13	Margaritis, John
NORTHEASTERN STATE (OK)														
1968	M	NAIA		16	—	—	—	—	—	—	—	26	4	Dobbins, Dr. Jack
1972		NAIA		16	—	—	—	—	—	—	—	23	8	Dobbins, Dr. Jack
NORTHERN ARIZONA														
1946	M	NAIA		16	—	—	—	—	—	—	—	11	7	Brickey, Frank
1947		NAIA		3	—	—	—	—	—	—	—	20	7	Brickey, Frank
1954		NAIA		32	—	—	—	—	—	—	—	19	7	Gregg, Herbert
1962		NAIA		8	—	—	—	—	—	—	—	17	9	Gregg, Herbert
1986		NCAA	I	—	32	—	—	—	—	—	—	19	10	Arnote, Jay
1997		NCAA	I	—	32	—	—	—	—	—	—	21	7	Howland, Ben
1998		NCAA	I	64	—	—	—	—	—	—	—	21	8	Howland, Ben
NORTHERN COLORADO														
1964	M	NCAA	II	32	—	—	—	—	—	—	—	18	8	Sage, Dr. George H.
1965		NCAA	II	32	—	—	—	—	—	—	—	19	8	Sage, Dr. George H.
1966		NCAA	II	32	—	—	—	—	—	—	—	21	6	Sage, Dr. George H.
1989		NCAA	II	16	—	—	—	—	—	—	—	24	6	Brillhart, Ron
1995	W	NCAA	II	48	—	—	—	—	—	—	—	17	10	Schwartz, Gary
1996		NCAA	II	48	—	—	—	—	—	—	—	17	10	Schwartz, Gary
1997		NCAA	II	48	—	—	—	—	—	—	—	19	8	Schwartz, Gary
1998		NCAA	II	32	—	—	—	—	—	—	—	21	8	Bruce, Greg
NORTHERN ESSEX CC (MA)														
1997	W	NSCAA		8	—	—	—	—	—	—	—	10	11	Smith, Michael
NORTHERN ILLINOIS														
1958	M	NCAA	II	24	—	—	—	—	—	—	—	10	12	Healey, Dr. William A.
1982		NCAA	I	48	—	—	—	—	—	—	—	16	14	McDougal, John
1991		NCAA	I	64	—	—	—	—	—	—	—	25	6	Molinari, Jim
1996		NCAA	I	64	—	—	—	—	—	—	—	20	10	Johnson, Rees

Year	M/W	Assn	Div	NAT	NIT	ARC	CCA	NCI	NCT	OLY	HLM	W	L	Coach
1972	W	AIAW		8	—	—	—	—	—	—	—	15	3	Bell, Dr. Mary
1990		NCAA	I	32	—	—	—	—	—	—	—	25	6	Albright-Dieterle, Jane
1991		NCAA	I	—	7	—	—	—	—	—	—	25	10	Albright-Dieterle, Jane
1992		NCAA	I	32	—	—	—	—	—	—	—	18	14	Albright-Dieterle, Jane
1993		NCAA	I	48	—	—	—	—	—	—	—	24	6	Albright-Dieterle, Jane
1994		NCAA	I	64	—	—	—	—	—	—	—	24	6	Albright-Dieterle, Jane
1995		NCAA	I	64	—	—	—	—	—	—	—	17	14	Galloway-McQuitter, Liz

NORTHERN IOWA

Year	M/W	Assn	Div	NAT	NIT	ARC	CCA	NCI	NCT	OLY	HLM	W	L	Coach
1946	M	NAIA		16	—	—	—	—	—	—	—	13	7	Nordley, Oliver M.
1948		NAIA		32	—	—	—	—	—	—	—	14	6	Nordley, Oliver M.
1949		NAIA		16	—	—	—	—	—	—	—	16	6	Nordley, Oliver M.
1953		NAIA		32	—	—	—	—	—	—	—	14	11	Nordley, Oliver M.
1962		NCAA	II	16	—	—	—	—	—	—	—	19	5	Stewart, Norman E.
1964		NCAA	II	4	—	—	—	—	—	—	—	23	4	Stewart, Norman E.
1979		NCAA	II	16	—	—	—	—	—	—	—	18	11	Berry, James
1990		NCAA	I	32	—	—	—	—	—	—	—	23	9	Miller, Eldon

NORTHERN KENTUCKY

Year	M/W	Assn	Div	NAT	NIT	ARC	CCA	NCI	NCT	OLY	HLM	W	L	Coach
1978	M	NCAA	II	32	—	—	—	—	—	—	—	20	8	Hils, Martin
1995		NCAA	II	16	—	—	—	—	—	—	—	25	4	Shields, Ken
1996		NCAA	II	2	—	—	—	—	—	—	—	25	7	Shields, Ken
1997		NCAA	II	2	—	—	—	—	—	—	—	30	5	Shields, Ken
1998		NCAA	II	32	—	—	—	—	—	—	—	23	7	Shields, Ken
1975	W	AIAW	S	8	—	—	—	—	—	—	—	19	8	Moore, Marilyn
1979		AIAW	S	—	4	—	—	—	—	—	—	25	10	Moore, Marilyn
1982		NCAA	II	16	—	—	—	—	—	—	—	23	6	Scheper, Jane Meier
1985		NCAA	II	8	—	—	—	—	—	—	—	19	9	Winstel, Nancy
1986		NCAA	II	24	—	—	—	—	—	—	—	22	6	Winstel, Nancy
1987		NCAA	II	3	—	—	—	—	—	—	—	25	5	Winstel, Nancy
1988		NCAA	II	32	—	—	—	—	—	—	—	25	3	Winstel, Nancy
1989		NCAA	II	32	—	—	—	—	—	—	—	21	7	Winstel, Nancy
1991		NCAA	II	32	—	—	—	—	—	—	—	22	6	Winstel, Nancy
1992		NCAA	II	32	—	—	—	—	—	—	—	19	9	Winstel, Nancy

NORTHERN MICHIGAN

Year	M/W	Assn	Div	NAT	NIT	ARC	CCA	NCI	NCT	OLY	HLM	W	L	Coach
1958	M	NAIA		32	—	—	—	—	—	—	—	15	3	Albeck, Charles Stanley "Stan"
1959		NAIA		32	—	—	—	—	—	—	—	16	8	Albeck, Charles Stanley "Stan"
1961		NAIA		3	—	—	—	—	—	—	—	24	3	Albeck, Charles Stanley "Stan"
1963		NAIA		8	—	—	—	—	—	—	—	19	8	Albeck, Charles Stanley "Stan"
1965		NAIA		32	—	—	—	—	—	—	—	19	6	Albeck, Charles Stanley "Stan"
1979		NCAA	II	32	—	—	—	—	—	—	—	18	11	Brown, Glenn C.
1980		NCAA	II	8	—	—	—	—	—	—	—	24	6	Brown, Glenn C.
1981		NCAA	II	8	—	—	—	—	—	—	—	21	9	Brown, Glenn C.
1984		NCAA	II	32	—	—	—	—	—	—	—	21	9	Brown, Glenn C.
1985		NCAA	II	24	—	—	—	—	—	—	—	23	6	Brown, Glenn C.
1993		NCAA	II	16	—	—	—	—	—	—	—	22	8	Ellis, Dean
1989	W	NCAA	II	32	—	—	—	—	—	—	—	24	4	Stein, Paulette
1991		NCAA	II	16	—	—	—	—	—	—	—	22	9	Geary, Mike
1992		NCAA	II	16	—	—	—	—	—	—	—	23	6	Geary, Mike
1995		NCAA	II	32	—	—	—	—	—	—	—	21	9	Geary, Mike

Year	M/W	Assn	Div	NAT	NIT	ARC	CCA	NCI	NCT	OLY	HLM	W	L	Coach
1996		NCAA	II	8	—	—	—	—	—	—	—	25	5	Geary, Mike
1997		NCAA	II	16	—	—	—	—	—	—	—	27	3	Geary, Mike
1998		NCAA	II	3	—	—	—	—	—	—	—	28	4	Geary, Mike

NORTHERN STATE (SD)

Year	M/W	Assn	Div	NAT	NIT	ARC	CCA	NCI	NCT	OLY	HLM	W	L	Coach
1939	M	NAIA		32	—	—	—	—	—	—	—	18	2	Robertson, Harley R.
1940		NAIA		32	—	—	—	—	—	—	—	17	5	Robertson, Harley R.
1957		NAIA		32	—	—	—	—	—	—	—	22	5	Wachs, Bob
1958		NAIA		16	—	—	—	—	—	—	—	25	3	Wachs, Bob
1959		NAIA		32	—	—	—	—	—	—	—	19	3	Wachs, Bob
1961		NAIA		32	—	—	—	—	—	—	—	16	7	Wachs, Bob
1970		NAIA		32	—	—	—	—	—	—	—	20	7	Wachs, Bob
1971		NAIA		16	—	—	—	—	—	—	—	22	8	Wachs, Bob
1983		NAIA		32	—	—	—	—	—	—	—	22	10	Wachs, Bob
1984		NAIA		32	—	—	—	—	—	—	—	28	4	Wachs, Bob
1990		NAIA		32	—	—	—	—	—	—	—	23	9	Olson, Robert
1991		NAIA		16	—	—	—	—	—	—	—	26	8	Olson, Robert
1993		NAIA	II	2	—	—	—	—	—	—	—	34	2	Olson, Robert
1994		NAIA	II	2	—	—	—	—	—	—	—	25	9	Olson, Robert
1995		NAIA	II	3	—	—	—	—	—	—	—	28	5	Olson, Robert
1996		NCAA	II	32	—	—	—	—	—	—	—	23	6	Olson, Robert
1997		NCAA	II	48	—	—	—	—	—	—	—	22	6	Olson, Robert
1998		NCAA	II	8	—	—	—	—	—	—	—	27	5	Olson, Robert
1981	W	NAIA		3	—	—	—	—	—	—	—	28	4	Fredrickson, Curt
1992		NAIA	II	1	—	—	—	—	—	—	—	30	4	Fredrickson, Curt
1993		NAIA	II	2	—	—	—	—	—	—	—	28	7	Fredrickson, Curt
1994		NAIA	II	1	—	—	—	—	—	—	—	32	1	Fredrickson, Curt
1995		NAIA	II	8	—	—	—	—	—	—	—	28	3	Fredrickson, Curt
1997		NCAA	II	32	—	—	—	—	—	—	—	24	5	Fredrickson, Curt
1998		NCAA	II	32	—	—	—	—	—	—	—	23	6	Fredrickson, Curt

NORTHLAND

Year	M/W	Assn	Div	NAT	NIT	ARC	CCA	NCI	NCT	OLY	HLM	W	L	Coach
1985	M	NSCAA		7	—	—	—	—	—	—	—	13	21	Bystrom, Nick
1989		NSCAA		15	—	—	—	—	—	—	—	13	18	Bystrom, Nick
1991		NSCAA		10	—	—	—	—	—	—	—	14	15	Bystrom, Nick
1992		NSCAA		12	—	—	—	—	—	—	—	18	13	Bystrom, Nick
1993		NSCAA		9	—	—	—	—	—	—	—	17	13	Swan, David
1996		NAIA	II	32	—	—	—	—	—	—	—	19	11	Swan, David
1983	W	NSCAA		3	—	—	—	—	—	—	—	14	10	Vieira, Kim T.
1984		NSCAA		3	—	—	—	—	—	—	—	22	6	Vieira, Kim T.
1985		NSCAA		2	—	—	—	—	—	—	—	21	6	Franklin, Steve
1987		NSCAA		4	—	—	—	—	—	—	—	10	18	Franklin, Steve
1989		NSCAA		7	—	—	—	—	—	—	—	15	11	Franklin, Steve
1990		NSCAA		5	—	—	—	—	—	—	—	14	16	Franklin, Steve
1991		NSCAA		7	—	—	—	—	—	—	—	16	12	Franklin, Steve
1992		NSCAA		6	—	—	—	—	—	—	—	18	11	Franklin, Steve
1993		NSCAA		5	—	—	—	—	—	—	—	17	10	Akervik, Holly

NORTHLAND BAPTIST BIBLE

Year	M/W	Assn	Div	NAT	NIT	ARC	CCA	NCI	NCT	OLY	HLM	W	L	Coach
1994	M	NCCAA	II	7	—	—	—	—	—	—	—	14	12	Scott, Dennis

Year	M/W	Assn	Div	NAT	NIT	ARC	CCA	NCI	NCT	OLY	HLM	W	L	Coach
1993	W	NBCAA		3	—	—	—	—	—	—	—	12	9	Bowman, Reba
1994		NCCAA	II	7	—	—	—	—	—	—	—	15	10	Bowman, Reba

NORTHWEST ASSEMBLIES

Year	M/W	Assn	Div	NAT	NIT	ARC	CCA	NCI	NCT	OLY	HLM	W	L	Coach
1974	M	NSCAA		8	—	—	—	—	—	—	—	22	7	Kinney, Carl
1984		NCCAA	II	8	—	—	—	—	—	—	—	X	X	Brown, John
1990		NCCAA	II	7	—	—	—	—	—	—	—	X	X	Filan, Doug
1991		NCCAA	II	2	—	—	—	—	—	—	—	19	13	Filan, Doug
1992		NCCAA	II	4	—	—	—	—	—	—	—	24	12	Filan, Doug
1993		NCCAA	II	1	—	—	—	—	—	—	—	X	X	Filan, Doug
1994		NCCAA	II	3	—	—	—	—	—	—	—	X	X	Filan, Doug
1997		NCCAA	I	8	—	—	—	—	—	—	—	20	14	Mendoza, Wayne
1980	W	NSCAA		4	—	—	—	—	—	—	—	19	12	Brodin, Kristi
1984		NCCAA	II	5	—	—	—	—	—	—	—	12	9	Brodin, Kristi
1986		NCCAA	II	3	—	—	—	—	—	—	—	16	10	Brodin, Kristi
1988		NCCAA	II	1	—	—	—	—	—	—	—	16	17	Brodin, Kristi
1989		NCCAA	II	2	—	—	—	—	—	—	—	4	26	Brodin, Kristi
1990		NCCAA	II	1	—	—	—	—	—	—	—	11	18	Brodin, Kristi
1991		NCCAA	II	1	—	—	—	—	—	—	—	10	20	Brodin, Kristi
1992		NCCAA	II	4	—	—	—	—	—	—	—	12	20	Brodin, Kristi
1993		NCCAA	II	1	—	—	—	—	—	—	—	17	11	Brodin, Kristi
1994		NCCAA	II	1	—	—	—	—	—	—	—	7	21	Brodin, Kristi
1998		NCCAA	I	7	—	—	—	—	—	—	—	11	22	Brodin, Kristi

NORTHWEST BIBLE

Year	M/W	Assn	Div	NAT	NIT	ARC	CCA	NCI	NCT	OLY	HLM	W	L	Coach
1985	M	NBCAA	II	2	—	—	—	—	—	—	—	X	X	Carter, Ron

NORTHWEST CHRISTIAN

Year	M/W	Assn	Div	NAT	NIT	ARC	CCA	NCI	NCT	OLY	HLM	W	L	Coach
1977	M	NSCAA		16	—	—	—	—	—	—	—	24	6	Cox, Duane
1983		NBCAA		1	—	—	—	—	—	—	—	24	5	Buckley, Jim
1984		NBCAA	I	1	—	—	—	—	—	—	—	24	4	Lipp, David
1985		NBCAA	I	1	—	—	—	—	—	—	—	25	4	Lipp, David
1986		NBCAA	I	1	—	—	—	—	—	—	—	19	11	Kennedy, Don
1987		NBCAA	I	1	—	—	—	—	—	—	—	21	8	Halupa, Paul
1989		NBCAA	I	1	—	—	—	—	—	—	—	19	12	Rodenburg, Jeff
1990		NBCAA	I	3	—	—	—	—	—	—	—	22	11	Rodenburg, Jeff
1991		NSCAA		3	—	—	—	—	—	—	—	4	20	Lipp, David
1995		NSCAA		2	—	—	—	—	—	—	—	18	11	Lipp, David
1996		NSCAA		4	—	—	—	—	—	—	—	18	14	Lipp, David
1997		NSCAA		10	—	—	—	—	—	—	—	19	14	Lipp, David
1998		NSCAA		1	—	—	—	—	—	—	—	24	8	Lipp, David

NORTHWEST MISSOURI STATE

Year	M/W	Assn	Div	NAT	NIT	ARC	CCA	NCI	NCT	OLY	HLM	W	L	Coach
1938	M	NAIA		16	—	—	—	—	—	—	—	15	6	Stalcup, Wilbur N. "Sparky"
1939		NAIA		8	—	—	—	—	—	—	—	14	7	Stalcup, Wilbur N. "Sparky"
1940		NAIA		8	—	—	—	—	—	—	—	22	1	Stalcup, Wilbur N. "Sparky"
1941		NAIA		8	—	—	—	—	—	—	—	19	4	Stalcup, Wilbur N. "Sparky"
1943		NAIA		2	—	—	—	—	—	—	—	18	7	Stalcup, Wilbur N. "Sparky"
1982		NCAA	II	32	—	—	—	—	—	—	—	20	10	Sinn, Dr. Lionel L.
1984		NCAA	II	32	—	—	—	—	—	—	—	24	7	Sinn, Dr. Lionel L.
1989		NCAA	II	32	—	—	—	—	—	—	—	21	9	Tappmeyer, Steve
1998		NCAA	II	48	—	—	—	—	—	—	—	23	7	Tappmeyer, Steve

Year	M/W	Assn	Div	NAT	NIT	ARC	CCA	NCI	NCT	OLY	HLM	W	L	Coach
1984	W	NCAA	II	16	—	—	—	—	—	—	—	25	5	Winstead, Wayne
1990		NCAA	II	32	—	—	—	—	—	—	—	20	10	Winstead, Wayne

Northwest Nazarene

Year	M/W	Assn	Div	NAT	NIT	ARC	CCA	NCI	NCT	OLY	HLM	W	L	Coach
1957	M	NAIA		32	—	—	—	—	—	—	—	24	9	Hills, Orrin E.
1978		NCCAA	I	4	—	—	—	—	—	—	—	23	11	Layton, Terry
1992		NAIA	II	16	—	—	—	—	—	—	—	26	9	Weidenbach, Ed
1993		NAIA	II	3	—	—	—	—	—	—	—	20	13	Weidenbach, Ed
1994		NAIA	II	3	—	—	—	—	—	—	—	26	8	Weidenbach, Ed
1995		NAIA	II	2	—	—	—	—	—	—	—	27	7	Weidenbach, Ed
1996		NAIA	II	8	—	—	—	—	—	—	—	19	13	Weidenbach, Ed
1997		NAIA	II	8	—	—	—	—	—	—	—	26	8	Weidenbach, Ed
1998		NAIA	II	3	—	—	—	—	—	—	—	27	10	Sanders, Rich
1995	W	NAIA	II	2	—	—	—	—	—	—	—	23	7	Schmidt, Roger
1996		NAIA	II	32	—	—	—	—	—	—	—	17	10	Schmidt, Roger
1997		NAIA	II	1	—	—	—	—	—	—	—	27	7	Schmidt, Roger

Northwest Shoals CC: Phil Campbell

Year	M/W	Assn	Div	NAT	NIT	ARC	CCA	NCI	NCT	OLY	HLM	W	L	Coach
1973	M	NSCAA		2	—	—	—	—	—	—	—	16	17	Seesholtz, Arthur

Northwestern (IA)

Year	M/W	Assn	Div	NAT	NIT	ARC	CCA	NCI	NCT	OLY	HLM	W	L	Coach
1971	M	NAIA		32	—	—	—	—	—	—	—	23	5	Jacobsen, Dr. Don
1972		NAIA		32	—	—	—	—	—	—	—	21	7	Jacobsen, Dr. Don
1987		NAIA		32	—	—	—	—	—	—	—	27	5	Douma, Les
1992		NAIA	II	2	—	—	—	—	—	—	—	25	8	Barry, Todd
1993		NAIA	II	16	—	—	—	—	—	—	—	19	11	Barry, Todd
1994		NAIA	II	8	—	—	—	—	—	—	—	27	4	Barry, Todd

Northwestern (IL)

Year	M/W	Assn	Div	NAT	NIT	ARC	CCA	NCI	NCT	OLY	HLM	W	L	Coach
1931	M	NCAA		—	—	—	—	—	—	—	1	16	1	Lonborg, Arthur C. "Dutch"
1983		NCAA	I	—	16	—	—	—	—	—	—	17	13	Falk, Rich
1994		NCAA	I	—	16	—	—	—	—	—	—	15	14	Swanson, Paul
1979	W	AIAW	L	8	—	—	—	—	—	—	—	25	4	DiStanislao, Mary
1980		AIAW	I	16	—	—	—	—	—	—	—	24	5	DiStanislao, Mary
1981		AIAW	I	24	—	—	—	—	—	—	—	22	12	Lynch, Annette
1982		NCAA	I	32	—	—	—	—	—	—	—	21	8	Lynch, Arnette
1987		NCAA	I	32	—	—	—	—	—	—	—	20	10	Perrelli, Donald
1990		NCAA	I	32	—	—	—	—	—	—	—	24	5	Perrelli, Donald
1991		NCAA	I	32	—	—	—	—	—	—	—	21	9	Perrelli, Donald
1993		NCAA	I	32	—	—	—	—	—	—	—	20	9	Perrelli, Donald
1996		NCAA	I	—	2	—	—	—	—	—	—	23	11	Perrelli, Donald
1997		NCAA	I	64	—	—	—	—	—	—	—	17	11	Perrelli, Donald

Northwestern (MN)

Year	M/W	Assn	Div	NAT	NIT	ARC	CCA	NCI	NCT	OLY	HLM	W	L	Coach
1975	M	NSCAA		16	—	—	—	—	—	—	—	15	10	Christopherson, Duane
1980		NCCAA	II	1	—	—	—	—	—	—	—	21	11	Sulack, Dave
1981		NCCAA	II	2	—	—	—	—	—	—	—	15	12	Sulack, Dave
1982		NCCAA	II	2	—	—	—	—	—	—	—	16	14	Westlund, Dave
1983		NCCAA	II	2	—	—	—	—	—	—	—	22	10	Bocken, Ron
1984		NCCAA	II	8	—	—	—	—	—	—	—	15	17	Bocken, Ron
1985		NCCAA	II	4	—	—	—	—	—	—	—	17	13	Bocken, Ron
1995		NCCAA	I	3	—	—	—	—	—	—	—	22	10	Smith, Joseph L.
1998		NCCAA	I	8	—	—	—	—	—	—	—	25	11	Smith, Joseph L.

Year	M/W	Assn	Div	NAT	NIT	ARC	CCA	NCI	NCT	OLY	HLM	W	L	Coach
1984	W	NCCAA	II	1	—	—	—	—	—	—	—	19	10	Smith, Dan
1985		NCCAA	II	1	—	—	—	—	—	—	—	11	19	Smith, Dan
1989		NCCAA	I	5	—	—	—	—	—	—	—	17	11	Smith, Dan
1994		NCCAA	I	7	—	—	—	—	—	—	—	20	8	Holm, Sherri
1995		NCCAA	I	5	—	—	—	—	—	—	—	23	7	Holm, Sherri

NORTHWESTERN (OH)

Year	M/W	Assn	Div	NAT	NIT	ARC	CCA	NCI	NCT	OLY	HLM	W	L	Coach
1972	M	NSCAA		5	—	—	—	—	—	—	—	21	6	Noble, Del
1973		NSCAA		6	—	—	—	—	—	—	—	25	8	Loescher, Art
1974		NSCAA		8	—	—	—	—	—	—	—	20	5	Loescher, Art
1975		NSCAA		16	—	—	—	—	—	—	—	16	13	Loescher, Art

NORTHWESTERN (WI)

Year	M/W	Assn	Div	NAT	NIT	ARC	CCA	NCI	NCT	OLY	HLM	W	L	Coach
1978	M	NSCAA		8	—	—	—	—	—	—	—	12	13	Thompson, Lloyd E.

NORTHWESTERN OKLAHOMA STATE

Year	M/W	Assn	Div	NAT	NIT	ARC	CCA	NCI	NCT	OLY	HLM	W	L	Coach
1949	M	NAIA		32	—	—	—	—	—	—	—	18	9	Highfill, C. L. "Dick"
1992		NAIA	I	16	—	—	—	—	—	—	—	25	7	Battisti, Bob
1994		NAIA	I	16	—	—	—	—	—	—	—	29	2	Battisti, Bob
1992	W	NAIA	I	16	—	—	—	—	—	—	—	24	7	Barton, Milburn
1996		NAIA	I	32	—	—	—	—	—	—	—	19	13	Barton, Milburn
1998		NAIA	I	32	—	—	—	—	—	—	—	25	8	Barton, Milburn

NORTHWESTERN STATE (LA)

Year	M/W	Assn	Div	NAT	NIT	ARC	CCA	NCI	NCT	OLY	HLM	W	L	Coach
1939	M	NAIA		32	—	—	—	—	—	—	—	16	4	Prather, H. Lee
1940		NAIA		32	—	—	—	—	—	—	—	19	2	Prather, H. Lee
1941		NAIA		16	—	—	—	—	—	—	—	17	2	Prather, H. Lee
1947		NAIA		32	—	—	—	—	—	—	—	15	5	Prather, H. Lee
1948		NAIA		32	—	—	—	—	—	—	—	19	6	Prather, H. Lee
1949		NAIA		8	—	—	—	—	—	—	—	23	5	Prather, H. Lee
1974		NAIA		16	—	—	—	—	—	—	—	21	9	Hildebrand, Tynes
1986	W	NCAA	I	—	2	—	—	—	—	—	—	25	7	Pierson, Pat
1989		NCAA	I	48	—	—	—	—	—	—	—	22	8	Smith, James F.
1993		NCAA	I	—	5	—	—	—	—	—	—	24	8	Smith, James F.
1995		NCAA	I	—	2	—	—	—	—	—	—	25	7	Smith, James F.

NORTHWOOD (IN)

Year	M/W	Assn	Div	NAT	NIT	ARC	CCA	NCI	NCT	OLY	HLM	W	L	Coach
1976	M	NSCAA		14	—	—	—	—	—	—	—	19	8	Bledsoe, Larry
1977		NSCAA		16	—	—	—	—	—	—	—	25	8	Johnson, Jack J.
1978		NSCAA		8	—	—	—	—	—	—				Johnson, Jack J.

NORTHWOOD (MI)

Year	M/W	Assn	Div	NAT	NIT	ARC	CCA	NCI	NCT	OLY	HLM	W	L	Coach
1987	M	NAIA		32	—	—	—	—	—	—	—	16	15	Miller, Pat
1991	W	NAIA		32	—	—	—	—	—	—	—	20	12	Vielbig, Mary

NORWICH

Year	M/W	Assn	Div	NAT	NIT	ARC	CCA	NCI	NCT	OLY	HLM	W	L	Coach
1984	M	NCAA	III	32	—	—	—	—	—	—	—	21	6	Hockenbury, Edward J.
1987		NCAA	III	24	—	—	—	—	—	—	—	21	5	Hockenbury, Edward J.

NOTRE DAME (IN)

Year	M/W	Assn	Div	NAT	NIT	ARC	CCA	NCI	NCT	OLY	HLM	W	L	Coach
1927	M	NCAA		—	—	—	—	—	—	—	1	19	1	Keogan, George E.
1936		NCAA		—	—	—	—	—	—	—	1	22	2	Keogan, George E.
1953		NCAA		8	—	—	—	—	—	—	—	19	5	Jordan, John J.
1954		NCAA		8	—	—	—	—	—	—	—	22	3	Jordan, John J.

Year	M/W	Assn	Div	NAT	NIT	ARC	CCA	NCI	NCT	OLY	HLM	W	L	Coach
1957		NCAA	I	12	—	—	—	—	—	—	—	20	8	Jordan, John J.
1958		NCAA	I	8	—	—	—	—	—	—	—	24	5	Jordan, John J.
1960		NCAA	I	25	—	—	—	—	—	—	—	17	9	Jordan, John J.
1963		NCAA	I	25	—	—	—	—	—	—	—	17	9	Jordan, John J.
1965		NCAA	I	23	—	—	—	—	—	—	—	15	12	Dee, John F., Jr.
1968		NCAA	I	—	3	—	—	—	—	—	—	21	9	Dee, John F., Jr.
1969		NCAA	I	25	—	—	—	—	—	—	—	20	7	Dee, John F., Jr.
1970		NCAA	I	16	—	—	—	—	—	—	—	21	8	Dee, John F., Jr.
1971		NCAA	I	16	—	—	—	—	—	—	—	20	9	Dee, John F., Jr.
1973		NCAA	I	—	2	—	—	—	—	—	—	18	12	Phelps, Richard F. "Digger"
1974		NCAA	I	12	—	—	—	—	—	—	—	26	3	Phelps, Richard F. "Digger"
1975		NCAA	I	16	—	—	—	—	—	—	—	19	10	Phelps, Richard F. "Digger"
1976		NCAA	I	16	—	—	—	—	—	—	—	23	6	Phelps, Richard F. "Digger"
1977		NCAA	I	16	—	—	—	—	—	—	—	22	7	Phelps, Richard F. "Digger"
1978		NCAA	I	4	—	—	—	—	—	—	—	23	8	Phelps, Richard F. "Digger"
1979		NCAA	I	8	—	—	—	—	—	—	—	24	6	Phelps, Richard F. "Digger"
1980		NCAA	I	32	—	—	—	—	—	—	—	22	6	Phelps, Richard F. "Digger"
1981		NCAA	I	16	—	—	—	—	—	—	—	23	6	Phelps, Richard F. "Digger"
1983		NCAA	I	—	32	—	—	—	—	—	—	19	10	Phelps, Richard F. "Digger"
1984		NCAA	I	—	2	—	—	—	—	—	—	21	12	Phelps, Richard F. "Digger"
1985		NCAA	I	32	—	—	—	—	—	—	—	21	9	Phelps, Richard F. "Digger"
1986		NCAA	I	64	—	—	—	—	—	—	—	23	6	Phelps, Richard F. "Digger"
1987		NCAA	I	16	—	—	—	—	—	—	—	24	8	Phelps, Richard F. "Digger"
1988		NCAA	I	64	—	—	—	—	—	—	—	20	9	Phelps, Richard F. "Digger"
1989		NCAA	I	32	—	—	—	—	—	—	—	21	9	Phelps, Richard F. "Digger"
1990		NCAA	I	64	—	—	—	—	—	—	—	16	13	Phelps, Richard F. "Digger"
1992		NCAA	I	—	2	—	—	—	—	—	—	18	15	MacLeod, John M.
1997		NCAA	I	—	8	—	—	—	—	—	—	16	14	MacLeod, John M.
1980	W	AIAW	III	16	—	—	—	—	—	—	—	20	10	Petro, Sharon
1986		NCAA	I	—	3	—	—	—	—	—	—	23	8	DiStanislao, Mary
1989		NCAA	I	—	7	—	—	—	—	—	—	21	11	McGraw, Muffet O'Brien
1991		NCAA	I	—	8	—	—	—	—	—	—	23	9	McGraw, Muffet O'Brien
1992		NCAA	I	48	—	—	—	—	—	—	—	14	17	McGraw, Muffet O'Brien
1994		NCAA	I	64	—	—	—	—	—	—	—	22	7	McGraw, Muffet O'Brien
1995		NCAA	I	—	3	—	—	—	—	—	—	21	10	McGraw, Muffet O'Brien
1996		NCAA	I	32	—	—	—	—	—	—	—	23	8	McGraw, Muffet O'Brien
1997		NCAA	I	3	—	—	—	—	—	—	—	31	7	McGraw, Muffet O'Brien
1998		NCAA	I	16	—	—	—	—	—	—	—	22	10	McGraw, Muffet O'Brien

NOVA SOUTHEASTERN

Year	M/W	Assn	Div	NAT	NIT	ARC	CCA	NCI	NCT	OLY	HLM	W	L	Coach
1995	M	NAIA	II	16	—	—	—	—	—	—	—	22	12	Michaels, Jim

NYACK

Year	M/W	Assn	Div	NAT	NIT	ARC	CCA	NCI	NCT	OLY	HLM	W	L	Coach
1970	M	NCCAA		8	—	—	—	—	—	—	—	15	17	Lawrence, Dr. Donald J.
1985		NCCAA	I	8	—	—	—	—	—	—	—	25	8	Slocum, Jerry
1990		NCCAA	I	8	—	—	—	—	—	—	—	21	13	Flemming, Scott
1994		NCCAA	I	8	—	—	—	—	—	—	—	23	13	Bailey, Dan
1995		NAIA	II	32	—	—	—	—	—	—	—	26	8	Bailey, Dan

Year	M/W	Assn	Div	NAT	NIT	ARC	CCA	NCI	NCT	OLY	HLM	W	L	Coach
OAKLAND (MI)														
1994	M	NCAA	II	32	—	—	—	—	—	—	—	—	21	10	Kampe, Greg
1995		NCAA	II	48	—	—	—	—	—	—	—	—	20	9	Kampe, Greg
1996		NCAA	II	48	—	—	—	—	—	—	—	—	21	8	Kampe, Greg
1997		NCAA	II	16	—	—	—	—	—	—	—	—	23	8	Kampe, Greg
1982	W	NCAA	II	4	—	—	—	—	—	—	—	—	21	3	Jones, DeWayne
1983		NCAA	II	16	—	—	—	—	—	—	—	—	22	4	Jones, DeWayne
1989		NCAA	II	16	—	—	—	—	—	—	—	—	26	4	Taylor, Bob
1990		NCAA	II	4	—	—	—	—	—	—	—	—	27	6	Taylor, Bob
1994		NCAA	II	32	—	—	—	—	—	—	—	—	23	5	Taylor, Bob
1995		NCAA	II	8	—	—	—	—	—	—	—	—	22	9	Taylor, Bob
1996		NCAA	II	48	—	—	—	—	—	—	—	—	23	6	Taylor, Bob
1997		NCAA	II	32	—	—	—	—	—	—	—	—	25	5	Taylor, Bob
OAKLAND CITY (IN)														
1960	M	NAIA		32	—	—	—	—	—	—	—	—	17	6	Disler, Delbert C.
1978		NSCAA		3	—	—	—	—	—	—	—	—	21	11	Trafton, Charles L.
1979		NSCAA		16	—	—	—	—	—	—	—	—	16	12	Trafton, Charles L.
1980		NSCAA		2	—	—	—	—	—	—	—	—	12	17	Trafton, Charles L.
1981		NSCAA		1	—	—	—	—	—	—	—	—	12	20	Trafton, Charles L.
1982		NSCAA		2	—	—	—	—	—	—	—	—	14	13	Trafton, Charles L.
1983		NSCAA		10	—	—	—	—	—	—	—	—	10	13	Trafton, Charles L.
1993		NCCAA	I	3	—	—	—	—	—	—	—	—	20	11	Sandifar, Michael
1994		NCCAA	I	2	—	—	—	—	—	—	—	—	22	6	Sandifar, Michael
1995		NCCAA	I	5	—	—	—	—	—	—	—	—	18	12	Sandifar, Michael
1996		NCCAA	I	5	—	—	—	—	—	—	—	—	18	13	Sandifar, Michael
1997		NCCAA	I	4	—	—	—	—	—	—	—	—	21	9	Sandifar, Michael
1998		NCCAA	I	8	—	—	—	—	—	—	—	—	20	9	Sandifar, Michael
1993	W	NCCAA	I	2	—	—	—	—	—	—	—	—	21	10	Sandifar, Denise
1995		NCCAA	I	6	—	—	—	—	—	—	—	—	17	14	Sandifar, Denise
1997		NCCAA	I	3	—	—	—	—	—	—	—	—	23	6	Sandifar, Denise
1998		NCCAA	I	3	—	—	—	—	—	—	—	—	20	9	Sandifar, Denise
OBERLIN														
1976	M	NCAA	III	21	—	—	—	—	—	—	—	—	16	11	Penn, Patrick
OCCIDENTAL														
1980	M	NCAA	III	32	—	—	—	—	—	—	—	—	15	13	Westphal, Bill
OGLETHORPE														
1947	M	NAIA		32	—	—	—	—	—	—	—	—	22	6	Phillips, "Swede"
1961		NAIA		32	—	—	—	—	—	—	—	—	20	4	Pinholster, Garland F.
1963		NCAA	II	3	—	—	—	—	—	—	—	—	21	7	Pinholster, Garland F.
1966		NCAA	II	16	—	—	—	—	—	—	—	—	22	6	Pinholster, Garland F.
1968		NCAA	II	23	—	—	—	—	—	—	—	—	21	6	Carter, Bill
1969		NCAA	II	8	—	—	—	—	—	—	—	—	22	5	Carter, Bill
1994		NCAA	III	40	—	—	—	—	—	—	—	—	20	6	Berkshire, Jack
1995		NCAA	III	64	—	—	—	—	—	—	—	—	18	8	Berkshire, Jack
OHIO DOMINICAN														
1971	M	NAIA		32	—	—	—	—	—	—	—	—	17	6	Nangle, Gene
1994		NAIA	II	16	—	—	—	—	—	—	—	—	23	9	DiGenova, Ed
1995		NAIA	II	16	—	—	—	—	—	—	—	—	19	16	DiGenova, Ed

Year	M/W	Assn	Div	NAT	NIT	ARC	CCA	NCI	NCT	OLY	HLM	W	L	Coach
OHIO NORTHERN														
1974	M	NCAA	II	44	—	—	—	—	—	—	—	—	18	7	Daugherty, Gale E.
1980		NCAA	III	16	—	—	—	—	—	—	—	—	24	5	Daugherty, Gale E.
1982		NCAA	III	24	—	—	—	—	—	—	—	—	22	7	Daugherty, Gale E.
1988		NCAA	III	24	—	—	—	—	—	—	—	—	21	9	Daugherty, Gale E.
1993		NCAA	III	1	—	—	—	—	—	—	—	—	28	2	Campoli, Joe
1995		NCAA	III	64	—	—	—	—	—	—	—	—	22	6	Campoli, Joe
1996		NCAA	III	64	—	—	—	—	—	—	—	—	18	9	Campoli, Joe
1997		NCAA	III	64	—	—	—	—	—	—	—	—	19	8	Campoli, Joe
1984	W	NCAA	III	32	—	—	—	—	—	—	—	—	16	8	Lauth, Gayle
1986		NCAA	III	32	—	—	—	—	—	—	—	—	20	6	Lauth, Gayle
1987		NCAA	III	16	—	—	—	—	—	—	—	—	19	7	Lauth, Gayle
1988		NCAA	III	8	—	—	—	—	—	—	—	—	23	4	Lauth, Gayle
1989		NCAA	III	16	—	—	—	—	—	—	—	—	17	10	Lauth, Gayle
OHIO STATE														
1939	M	NCAA		2	—	—	—	—	—	—	—	—	16	7	Olsen, Harold G.
1944		NCAA		3	—	—	—	—	—	—	—	—	14	7	Olsen, Harold G.
1945		NCAA		3	—	—	—	—	—	—	—	—	15	5	Olsen, Harold G.
1946		NCAA		3	—	—	—	—	—	—	—	—	16	5	Olsen, Harold G.
1950		NCAA		6	—	—	—	—	—	—	—	—	22	4	Dye, William H. H. "Tippy"
1960		NCAA	I	1	—	—	—	—	—	5	1	25	3	Taylor, Fred R.
1961		NCAA	I	2	—	—	—	—	—	—	—	—	27	1	Taylor, Fred R.
1962		NCAA	I	2	—	—	—	—	—	—	—	—	26	2	Taylor, Fred R.
1968		NCAA	I	3	—	—	—	—	—	—	—	—	21	8	Taylor, Fred R.
1971		NCAA	I	8	—	—	—	—	—	—	—	—	20	6	Taylor, Fred R.
1979		NCAA	I	—	4	—	—	—	—	—	—	—	19	12	Miller, Eldon
1980		NCAA	I	16	—	—	—	—	—	—	—	—	21	8	Miller, Eldon
1982		NCAA	I	48	—	—	—	—	—	—	—	—	21	10	Miller, Eldon
1983		NCAA	I	16	—	—	—	—	—	—	—	—	20	10	Miller, Eldon
1984		NCAA	I	—	32	—	—	—	—	—	—	—	15	14	Miller, Eldon
1985		NCAA	I	32	—	—	—	—	—	—	—	—	20	10	Miller, Eldon
1986		NCAA	I	—	1	—	—	—	—	—	—	—	19	14	Miller, Eldon
1987		NCAA	I	32	—	—	—	—	—	—	—	—	20	13	Williams, Gary
1988		NCAA	I	—	2	—	—	—	—	—	—	—	16	11	Williams, Gary
1989		NCAA	I	—	8	—	—	—	—	—	—	—	19	15	Williams, Gary
1990		NCAA	I	32	—	—	—	—	—	—	—	—	17	13	Ayers, Randy
1991		NCAA	I	16	—	—	—	—	—	—	—	—	27	4	Ayers, Randy
1992		NCAA	I	8	—	—	—	—	—	—	—	—	26	6	Ayers, Randy
1993		NCAA	I	—	32	—	—	—	—	—	—	—	15	13	Ayers, Randy
1969	W	AIAW		16	—	—	—	—	—	—	—	—	8	2	Bailey, Phyllis J.
1975		AIAW	L	12	—	—	—	—	—	—	—	—	18	5	Wilson, Deborah "Debbie"
1978		AIAW	L	16	—	—	—	—	—	—	—	—	23	8	Wilson, Deborah "Debbie"
1982		NCAA	I	32	—	—	—	—	—	—	—	—	20	7	VanDerveer, Tara
1984		NCAA	I	32	—	—	—	—	—	—	—	—	22	7	VanDerveer, Tara
1985		NCAA	I	8	—	—	—	—	—	—	—	—	28	3	VanDerveer, Tara
1986		NCAA	I	16	—	—	—	—	—	—	—	—	23	7	Darsch, Nancy
1987		NCAA	I	8	—	—	—	—	—	—	—	—	26	5	Darsch, Nancy

Year	M/W	Assn	Div	NAT	NIT	ARC	CCA	NCI	NCT	OLY	HLM	W	L	Coach
1988		NCAA	I	16	—	—	—	—	—	—	—	25	5	Darsch, Nancy
1989		NCAA	I	16	—	—	—	—	—	—	—	24	6	Darsch, Nancy
1990		NCAA	I	32	—	—	—	—	—	—	—	18	12	Darsch, Nancy
1993		NCAA	I	2	—	—	—	—	—	—	—	28	4	Darsch, Nancy
1996		NCAA	I	32	—	—	—	—	—	—	—	21	13	Darsch, Nancy

OHIO UNIVERSITY

Year	M/W	Assn	Div	NAT	NIT	ARC	CCA	NCI	NCT	OLY	HLM	W	L	Coach
1941	M	NCAA		—	2	—	—	—	—	—	—	18	4	Trautwein, William J. 'Dutch'
1960		NCAA	I	16	—	—	—	—	—	—	—	16	8	Snyder, James E.
1961		NCAA	I	24	—	—	—	—	—	—	—	17	7	Snyder, James E.
1964		NCAA	I	8	—	—	—	—	—	—	—	21	6	Snyder, James E.
1965		NCAA	I	23	—	—	—	—	—	—	—	19	7	Snyder, James E.
1969		NCAA	I	—	8	—	—	—	—	—	—	17	9	Snyder, James E.
1970		NCAA	I	25	—	—	—	—	—	—	—	20	5	Snyder, James E.
1972		NCAA	I	25	—	—	—	—	—	—	—	15	11	Snyder, James E.
1974		NCAA	I	25	—	—	—	—	—	—	—	16	11	Snyder, James E.
1983		NCAA	I	32	—	—	—	—	—	—	—	23	9	Nee, Danny
1985		NCAA	I	64	—	—	—	—	—	—	—	22	8	Nee, Danny
1986		NCAA	I	—	32	—	—	—	—	—	—	22	8	Nee, Danny
1994		NCAA	I	64	—	—	—	—	—	—	—	25	8	Hunter, Larry
1995		NCAA	I	—	16	—	—	—	—	—	—	24	10	Hunter, Larry
1986	W	NCAA	I	40	—	—	—	—	—	—	—	26	3	Prichard, Amy
1995		NCAA	I	64	—	—	—	—	—	—	—	23	7	Reall, Marsha

OHIO VALLEY (WV)

Year	M/W	Assn	Div	NAT	NIT	ARC	CCA	NCI	NCT	OLY	HLM	W	L	Coach
1990	M	NSCAA		12	—	—	—	—	—	—	—	11	16	Colgrove, Jack A.
1993		NSCAA		3	—	—	—	—	—	—	—	20	16	Colgrove, Jack A.
1994		NSCAA		3	—	—	—	—	—	—	—	19	16	Colgrove, Jack A.
1995		NSCAA		12	—	—	—	—	—	—	—	16	14	Colgrove, Jack A.
1993	W	NSCAA		8	—	—	—	—	—	—	—	15	18	Huffman, Gina
1997		NSCAA		8	—	—	—	—	—	—	—	13	17	Pavan, Ron

OHIO WESLEYAN

Year	M/W	Assn	Div	NAT	NIT	ARC	CCA	NCI	NCT	OLY	HLM	W	L	Coach
1988	M	NCAA	III	1	—	—	—	—	—	—	—	27	5	Mehaffey, Dr. Eugene L.
1992	W	NCAA	III	32	—	—	—	—	—	—	—	23	2	Carney-DeBord, Nan
1995		NCAA	III	64	—	—	—	—	—	—	—	22	6	Carney-DeBord, Nan

OKLAHOMA

Year	M/W	Assn	Div	NAT	NIT	ARC	CCA	NCI	NCT	OLY	HLM	W	L	Coach
1939	M	NCAA		3	—	—	—	—	—	—	—	12	9	Drake, Bruce
1943		NCAA		6	—	—	—	—	—	—	—	18	9	Drake, Bruce
1947		NCAA		2	—	—	—	—	—	—	—	24	7	Drake, Bruce
1970		NCAA	I	—	8	—	—	—	—	—	—	19	9	MacLeod, John M.
1971		NCAA	I	—	16	—	—	—	—	—	—	19	8	MacLeod, John M.
1979		NCAA	I	16	—	—	—	—	—	—	—	21	10	Bliss, David
1982		NCAA	I	—	3	—	—	—	—	—	—	22	8	Tubbs, Billy
1983		NCAA	I	32	—	—	—	—	—	—	—	24	9	Tubbs, Billy
1984		NCAA	I	32	—	—	—	—	—	—	—	29	5	Tubbs, Billy
1985		NCAA	I	8	—	—	—	—	—	—	—	31	6	Tubbs, Billy
1986		NCAA	I	32	—	—	—	—	—	—	—	26	9	Tubbs, Billy
1987		NCAA	I	16	—	—	—	—	—	—	—	24	10	Tubbs, Billy

Year	M/W	Assn	Div	NAT	NIT	ARC	CCA	NCI	NCT	OLY	HLM	W	L	Coach
1988		NCAA	I	2	—	—	—	—	—	—	—	35	4	Tubbs, Billy
1989		NCAA	I	16	—	—	—	—	—	—	—	30	6	Tubbs, Billy
1990		NCAA	I	32	—	—	—	—	—	—	—	27	5	Tubbs, Billy
1991		NCAA	I	—	2	—	—	—	—	—	—	20	15	Tubbs, Billy
1992		NCAA	I	64	—	—	—	—	—	—	—	21	9	Tubbs, Billy
1993		NCAA	I	—	16	—	—	—	—	—	—	20	12	Tubbs, Billy
1994		NCAA	I	—	32	—	—	—	—	—	—	15	13	Tubbs, Billy
1995		NCAA	I	64	—	—	—	—	—	—	—	23	9	Sampson, Kelvin
1996		NCAA	I	64	—	—	—	—	—	—	—	17	13	Sampson, Kelvin
1997		NCAA	I	64	—	—	—	—	—	—	—	19	11	Sampson, Kelvin
1998		NCAA	I	64	—	—	—	—	—	—	—	22	11	Sampson, Kelvin
1984	W	NCAA	I	—	6	—	—	—	—	—	—	23	7	McHugh, Maura
1986		NCAA	I	16	—	—	—	—	—	—	—	24	7	McHugh, Maura
1994		NCAA	I	—	1	—	—	—	—	—	—	18	12	Plunkett, Burl
1995		NCAA	I	32	—	—	—	—	—	—	—	22	9	Plunkett, Burl

OKLAHOMA BAPTIST COLLEGE

Year	M/W	Assn	Div	NAT	NIT	ARC	CCA	NCI	NCT	OLY	HLM	W	L	Coach
1984	M	NSCAA		10	—	—	—	—	—	—	—	19	12	Foster, Bruce D.
1989		NBCAA	II	4	—	—	—	—	—	—	—	3	19	Keiser, Keith
1991		NBCAA	II	7	—	—	—	—	—	—	—	9	14	Sisson, Doug
1993		NBCAA	II	2	—	—	—	—	—	—	—	13	12	Sisson, Doug
1994		NBCAA	II	4	—	—	—	—	—	—	—	29	8	Sisson, Doug
1998		NBCAA		8	—	—	—	—	—	—	—	2	15	Kelly, Guy

OKLAHOMA BAPTIST UNIVERSITY

Year	M/W	Assn	Div	NAT	NIT	ARC	CCA	NCI	NCT	OLY	HLM	W	L	Coach
1958	M	NAIA		32	—	—	—	—	—	—	—	19	8	Bass, Robert E.
1960		NAIA		16	—	—	—	—	—	—	—	23	6	Bass, Robert E.
1963		NAIA		32	—	—	—	—	—	—	—	21	7	Bass, Robert E.
1965		NAIA		2	—	—	—	—	—	—	—	25	7	Bass, Robert E.
1966		NAIA		1	—	—	—	—	—	—	—	26	7	Bass, Robert E.
1967		NAIA		2	—	—	—	—	—	—	—	25	7	Bass, Robert E.
1973		NAIA		8	—	—	—	—	—	—	—	20	11	Wallace, H. Eugene
1993		NAIA	I	2	—	—	—	—	—	—	—	34	4	Hoffman, Bob
1994		NAIA	I	3	—	—	—	—	—	—	—	29	8	Hoffman, Bob
1995		NAIA	I	32	—	—	—	—	—	—	—	28	6	Hoffman, Bob
1996		NAIA	I	16	—	—	—	—	—	—	—	29	6	Hoffman, Bob
1997		NAIA	I	2	—	—	—	—	—	—	—	36	4	Hoffman, Bob
1996	W	NAIA	I	32	—	—	—	—	—	—	—	21	12	Norris, Scott
1997		NAIA	I	8	—	—	—	—	—	—	—	28	9	Norris, Scott
1998		NAIA	I	8	—	—	—	—	—	—	—	28	7	Norris, Scott

OKLAHOMA CHRISTIAN

Year	M/W	Assn	Div	NAT	NIT	ARC	CCA	NCI	NCT	OLY	HLM	W	L	Coach
1968	M	NAIA		32	—	—	—	—	—	—	—	18	4	Davis, Frank
1982		NAIA		32	—	—	—	—	—	—	—	33	3	Jobe, Jerry
1994		NAIA	I	32	—	—	—	—	—	—	—	23	11	Hays, Dan
1995		NAIA	I	16	—	—	—	—	—	—	—	28	9	Hays, Dan
1986	W	NAIA		8	—	—	—	—	—	—	—	27	8	Findley, Stephanie
1993		NAIA	I	16	—	—	—	—	—	—	—	20	12	Findley, Stephanie
1995		NAIA	I	16	—	—	—	—	—	—	—	24	9	Findley, Stephanie
1997		NAIA	I	32	—	—	—	—	—	—	—	22	11	Findley, Stephanie

Year	M/W	Assn	Div	NAT	NIT	ARC	CCA	NCI	NCT	OLY	HLM	W	L	Coach
OKLAHOMA CITY														
1952	M	NCAA	12	—	—	—	—	—	—	—	—	19	8	Parrack, Doyle K.
1953		NCAA	16	—	—	—	—	—	—	—	—	18	6	Parrack, Doyle K.
1954		NCAA	24	—	—	—	—	—	—	—	—	18	7	Parrack, Doyle K.
1955		NCAA	24	—	—	—	—	—	—	—	—	9	18	Parrack, Doyle K.
1956		NCAA	8	—	—	—	—	—	—	—	—	20	7	Lemons, A. E. 'Abe'
1957		NCAA	I	8	—	—	—	—	—	—	—	—	19	9	Lemons, A. E. 'Abe'
1959		NCAA	I	—	8	—	—	—	—	—	—	—	20	7	Lemons, A. E. 'Abe'
1963		NCAA	I	16	—	—	—	—	—	—	—	—	19	10	Lemons, A. E. 'Abe'
1964		NCAA	I	25	—	—	—	—	—	—	—	—	15	11	Lemons, A. E. 'Abe'
1965		NCAA	I	12	—	—	—	—	—	—	—	—	21	10	Lemons, A. E. 'Abe'
1966		NCAA	I	22	—	—	—	—	—	—	—	—	24	5	Lemons, A. E. 'Abe'
1968		NCAA	I	—	16	—	—	—	—	—	—	—	20	7	Lemons, A. E. 'Abe'
1973		NCAA	I	25	—	—	—	—	—	—	—	—	21	6	Lemons, A. E. 'Abe'
1987		NAIA	16	—	—	—	—	—	—	—	—	34	1	Lemons, A. E. 'Abe'
1991		NAIA	1	—	—	—	—	—	—	—	—	27	3	Johnson, Darrel
1992		NAIA	I	1	—	—	—	—	—	—	—	—	38	0	Johnson, Darrel
1993		NAIA	I	16	—	—	—	—	—	—	—	—	25	7	Case, Win
1994		NAIA	I	1	—	—	—	—	—	—	—	—	28	7	Case, Win
1995		NAIA	I	8	—	—	—	—	—	—	—	—	30	3	Case, Win
1996		NAIA	I	1	—	—	—	—	—	—	—	—	33	5	Case, Win
1998		NAIA	I	16	—	—	—	—	—	—	—	—	26	5	Case, Win
1988	W	NAIA	1	—	—	—	—	—	—	—	—	28	6	Colon, Bob
1993		NAIA	I	16	—	—	—	—	—	—	—	—	23	9	Colon, Bob
1994		NAIA	I	32	—	—	—	—	—	—	—	—	22	10	Colon, Bob
1998		NAIA	I	16	—	—	—	—	—	—	—	—	19	13	Stanley, Kent
OKLAHOMA PANHANDLE STATE														
1941	M	NAIA	32	—	—	—	—	—	—	—	—	19	8	Iba, Clarence V.
1983		NAIA	16	—	—	—	—	—	—	—	—	31	4	Layton, Terry
1994	W	NAIA	II	8	—	—	—	—	—	—	—	—	19	12	Olson, Jerry
OKLAHOMA STATE														
1938	M	NCAA	—	3	—	—	—	—	—	—	—	25	3	Iba, Henry P. 'Hank'
1940		NCAA	—	3	—	—	—	—	—	—	—	26	3	Iba, Henry P. 'Hank'
1944		NCAA	—	4	—	—	—	—	—	—	—	27	6	Iba, Henry P. 'Hank'
1945		NCAA	1	—	1	—	—	—	—	1	27	4	Iba, Henry P. 'Hank'
1946		NCAA	1	—	—	—	—	—	—	1	31	2	Iba, Henry P. 'Hank'
1949		NCAA	2	—	—	—	—	—	—	—	—	23	5	Iba, Henry P. 'Hank'
1951		NCAA	4	—	—	—	—	—	—	—	—	29	6	Iba, Henry P. 'Hank'
1953		NCAA	8	—	—	—	—	—	—	—	—	23	7	Iba, Henry P. 'Hank'
1954		NCAA	8	—	—	—	—	—	—	—	—	24	5	Iba, Henry P. 'Hank'
1956		NCAA	—	12	—	—	—	—	—	—	—	18	9	Iba, Henry P. 'Hank'
1958		NCAA	I	8	—	—	—	—	—	—	—	—	21	8	Iba, Henry P. 'Hank'
1965		NCAA	I	8	—	—	—	—	—	—	—	—	20	7	Iba, Henry P. 'Hank'
1983		NCAA	I	48	—	—	—	—	—	—	—	—	24	7	Hansen, Paul N.
1989		NCAA	I	—	16	—	—	—	—	—	—	—	17	13	Hamilton, Leonard
1990		NCAA	I	—	16	—	—	—	—	—	—	—	17	14	Hamilton, Leonard
1991		NCAA	I	16	—	—	—	—	—	—	—	—	24	8	Sutton, Eddie

Year	M/W	Assn	Div	NAT	NIT	ARC	CCA	NCI	NCT	OLY	HLM	W	L	Coach
1992		NCAA	I	16	—	—	—	—	—	—	—	28	8	Sutton, Eddie
1993		NCAA	I	32	—	—	—	—	—	—	—	20	9	Sutton, Eddie
1994		NCAA	I	32	—	—	—	—	—	—	—	24	10	Sutton, Eddie
1995		NCAA	I	3	—	—	—	—	—	—	—	27	10	Sutton, Eddie
1997		NCAA	I	—	16	—	—	—	—	—	—	17	15	Sutton, Eddie
1998		NCAA	I	32	—	—	—	—	—	—	—	22	7	Sutton, Eddie
1989	W	NCAA	I	32	—	—	—	—	—	—	—	20	12	Halterman, Dick
1990		NCAA	I	48	—	—	—	—	—	—	—	20	11	Halterman, Dick
1991		NCAA	I	16	—	—	—	—	—	—	—	27	6	Halterman, Dick
1993		NCAA	I	48	—	—	—	—	—	—	—	23	9	Halterman, Dick
1994		NCAA	I	64	—	—	—	—	—	—	—	20	9	Halterman, Dick
1995		NCAA	I	64	—	—	—	—	—	—	—	17	12	Halterman, Dick
1996		NCAA	I	32	—	—	—	—	—	—	—	20	10	Halterman, Dick
1998		NCAA	I	—	8	—	—	—	—	—	—	20	10	Halterman, Dick

OLD DOMINION

Year	M/W	Assn	Div	NAT	NIT	ARC	CCA	NCI	NCT	OLY	HLM	W	L	Coach
1969	M	NCAA	II	32	—	—	—	—	—	—	—	21	10	Allen, William "Sonny"
1970		NCAA	II	24	—	—	—	—	—	—	—	21	7	Allen, William "Sonny"
1971		NCAA	II	2	—	—	—	—	—	—	—	21	9	Allen, William "Sonny"
1973		NCAA	II	16	—	—	—	—	—	—	—	19	9	Allen, William "Sonny"
1974		NCAA	II	16	—	—	—	—	—	—	—	20	7	Allen, William "Sonny"
1975		NCAA	II	1	—	—	—	—	—	—	—	25	6	Allen, William "Sonny"
1976		NCAA	II	4	—	—	—	—	—	—	—	19	12	Webb, Paul E.
1977		NCAA	I	—	16	—	—	—	—	—	—	25	4	Webb, Paul E.
1979		NCAA	I	—	6	—	—	—	—	—	—	23	7	Webb, Paul E.
1980		NCAA	I	48	—	—	—	—	—	—	—	25	5	Webb, Paul E.
1981		NCAA	I	—	32	—	—	—	—	—	—	18	10	Webb, Paul E.
1982		NCAA	I	48	—	—	—	—	—	—	—	18	12	Webb, Paul E.
1983		NCAA	I	—	32	—	—	—	—	—	—	19	10	Webb, Paul E.
1984		NCAA	I	—	32	—	—	—	—	—	—	19	12	Webb, Paul E.
1985		NCAA	I	64	—	—	—	—	—	—	—	19	12	Webb, Paul E.
1986		NCAA	I	32	—	—	—	—	—	—	—	23	8	Young, Thomas J.
1988		NCAA	I	—	32	—	—	—	—	—	—	18	12	Young, Thomas J.
1992		NCAA	I	64	—	—	—	—	—	—	—	15	15	Purnell, Oliver
1993		NCAA	I	—	16	—	—	—	—	—	—	21	8	Purnell, Oliver
1994		NCAA	I	—	16	—	—	—	—	—	—	21	10	Purnell, Oliver
1995		NCAA	I	32	—	—	—	—	—	—	—	21	12	Capel, Jeff
1997		NCAA	I	64	—	—	—	—	—	—	—	22	11	Capel, Jeff
1977	W	AIAW	L	—	4	—	—	—	—	—	—	23	9	Parsons, Pam
1978		AIAW	L	—	1	—	—	—	—	—	—	30	4	Stanley, Marianne Crawford
1979		AIAW	L	1	—	—	—	—	—	—	—	35	1	Stanley, Marianne Crawford
1980		AIAW	I	1	—	—	—	—	—	—	—	37	1	Stanley, Marianne Crawford
1981		AIAW	I	3	—	—	—	—	—	—	—	28	7	Stanley, Marianne Crawford
1982		NCAA	I	16	—	—	—	—	—	—	—	22	6	Stanley, Marianne Crawford
1983		NCAA	I	3	—	—	—	—	—	—	—	29	6	Stanley, Marianne Crawford
1984		NCAA	I	8	—	—	—	—	—	—	—	24	5	Stanley, Marianne Crawford
1985		NCAA	I	1	—	—	—	—	—	—	—	31	3	Stanley, Marianne Crawford
1987		NCAA	I	16	—	—	—	—	—	—	—	18	13	Stanley, Marianne Crawford
1988		NCAA	I	32	—	—	—	—	—	—	—	17	12	Larry, Wendy
1989		NCAA	I	32	—	—	—	—	—	—	—	23	9	Larry, Wendy

Year	M/W	Assn	Div	NAT	NIT	ARC	CCA	NCI	NCT	OLY	HLM	W	L	Coach
1990		NCAA	I	32	—	—	—	—	—	—	—	21	10	Larry, Wendy
1992		NCAA	I	48	—	—	—	—	—	—	—	20	11	Larry, Wendy
1993		NCAA	I	32	—	—	—	—	—	—	—	22	8	Larry, Wendy
1994		NCAA	I	32	—	—	—	—	—	—	—	25	6	Larry, Wendy
1995		NCAA	I	64	—	—	—	—	—	—	—	27	6	Larry, Wendy
1996		NCAA	I	16	—	—	—	—	—	—	—	29	3	Larry, Wendy
1997		NCAA	I	2	—	—	—	—	—	—	—	34	2	Larry, Wendy
1998		NCAA	I	16	—	—	—	—	—	—	—	29	3	Larry, Wendy

OLIVET NAZARENE

Year	M/W	Assn	Div	NAT	NIT	ARC	CCA	NCI	NCT	OLY	HLM	W	L	Coach
1975	M	NCCAA		1	—	—	—	—	—	—	—	30	4	Ward, C. W. "Butch"
1976		NCCAA	I	3	—	—	—	—	—	—	—	23	7	Ward, C. W. "Butch"
1977		NCCAA	I	2	—	—	—	—	—	—	—	22	11	Wilson, Frank
1978		NCCAA	I	2	—	—	—	—	—	—	—	24	9	Wilson, Frank
1980		NCCAA	I	6	—	—	—	—	—	—	—	15	13	Hodge, Ralph
1985		NCCAA	I	8	—	—	—	—	—	—	—	19	10	Hodge, Ralph
1986		NCCAA	I	8	—	—	—	—	—	—	—	15	18	Hodge, Ralph
1989		NAIA		32	—	—	—	—	—	—	—	22	9	Hodge, Ralph
1990		NAIA		32	—	—	—	—	—	—	—	26	10	Hodge, Ralph
1991		NAIA		32	—	—	—	—	—	—	—	22	13	Hodge, Ralph
1992		NAIA	I	16	—	—	—	—	—	—	—	25	11	Hodge, Ralph
1995		NAIA	I	32	—	—	—	—	—	—	—	21	15	Hodge, Ralph
1997		NAIA	I	32	—	—	—	—	—	—	—	21	13	Hodge, Ralph
1998		NAIA	I	16	—	—	—	—	—	—	—	28	9	Hodge, Ralph
1987	W	NCCAA	I	8	—	—	—	—	—	—	—	13	15	Doenges, Carol
1988		NCCAA	I	7	—	—	—	—	—	—	—	20	15	Parsons, Wendy
1990		NCCAA	I	4	—	—	—	—	—	—	—	23	10	Glass, Robyn
1991		NCCAA	I	6	—	—	—	—	—	—	—	16	15	Glass, Robyn
1992		NAIA	II	20	—	—	—	—	—	—	—	18	10	Glass, Robyn
1996		NCCAA	I	8	—	—	—	—	—	—	—	17	14	DeFries, Cathy
1997		NCCAA	I	7	—	—	—	—	—	—	—	19	16	DeFries, Cathy

ONEONTA STATE

Year	M/W	Assn	Div	NAT	NIT	ARC	CCA	NCI	NCT	OLY	HLM	W	L	Coach
1977	M	NCAA	III	2	—	—	—	—	—	—	—	21	6	Flewelling, F. Don
1998	W	NCAA	III	48	—	—	—	—	—	—	—	25	3	Garner, Steven

ORAL ROBERTS

Year	M/W	Assn	Div	NAT	NIT	ARC	CCA	NCI	NCT	OLY	HLM	W	L	Coach
1972	M	NCAA	I	—	8	—	—	—	—	—	—	26	2	Trickey, Ken
1973		NCAA	I	—	16	—	—	—	—	—	—	21	6	Trickey, Ken
1974		NCAA	I	8	—	—	—	—	—	—	—	23	6	Trickey, Ken
1975		NCAA	I	—	8	—	—	—	—	—	—	20	8	Hale, Jerry
1977		NCAA	I	—	16	—	—	—	—	—	—	21	7	Hale, Jerry
1982		NCAA	I	—	32	—	—	—	—	—	—	18	12	Hayes, Ken
1984		NCAA	I	48	—	—	—	—	—	—	—	21	10	Acres, Richard
1990		NAIA		8	—	—	—	—	—	—	—	36	6	Trickey, Ken
1997		NCAA	I	—	32	—	—	—	—	—	—	21	7	Self, Bill
1983	W	NCAA	I	—	3	—	—	—	—	—	—	26	1	Yow, Deborah Ann

Year	M/W	Assn	Div	NAT	NIT	ARC	CCA	NCI	NCT	OLY	HLM	W	L	Coach
OREGON														
1939	M	NCAA	1	—	—	—	—	—	—	—	—	29	5	Hobson, Dr. Howard A. 'Hobby'
1945		NCAA	6	—	—	—	—	—	—	—	—	30	13	Hobson, Dr. Howard A. 'Hobby'
1960		NCAA	I	8	—	—	—	—	—	—	—	19	10	Belko, Steven
1961		NCAA	I	24	—	—	—	—	—	—	—	15	12	Belko, Steven
1975		NCAA	I	—	3	—	—	—	—	—	—	21	9	Harter, Dick
1976		NCAA	I	—	8	—	—	—	—	—	—	19	11	Harter, Dick
1977		NCAA	I	—	8	—	—	—	—	—	—	19	10	Harter, Dick
1984		NCAA	I	—	32	—	—	—	—	—	—	16	13	Monson, Don
1988		NCAA	I	—	16	—	—	—	—	—	—	16	14	Monson, Don
1990		NCAA	I	—	32	—	—	—	—	—	—	15	14	Monson, Don
1995		NCAA	I	64	—	—	—	—	—	—	—	19	9	Green, Jerry
1997		NCAA	I	—	32	—	—	—	—	—	—	17	11	Green, Jerry
1979	W	AIAW	L	—	3	—	—	—	—	—	—	23	2	Heiny, Elwin
1980		AIAW	I	16	—	—	—	—	—	—	—	24	5	Heiny, Elwin
1981		AIAW	I	16	—	—	—	—	—	—	—	25	7	Heiny, Elwin
1982		NCAA	I	32	—	—	—	—	—	—	—	21	5	Heiny, Elwin
1984		NCAA	I	32	—	—	—	—	—	—	—	21	7	Heiny, Elwin
1987		NCAA	I	32	—	—	—	—	—	—	—	23	7	Heiny, Elwin
1989		NCAA	I	—	1	—	—	—	—	—	—	22	10	Heiny, Elwin
1994		NCAA	I	32	—	—	—	—	—	—	—	20	9	Runge, Jody
1995		NCAA	I	64	—	—	—	—	—	—	—	18	10	Runge, Jody
1996		NCAA	I	64	—	—	—	—	—	—	—	18	11	Runge, Jody
1997		NCAA	I	32	—	—	—	—	—	—	—	22	7	Runge, Jody
1998		NCAA	I	64	—	—	—	—	—	—	—	17	10	Runge, Jody
OREGON STATE														
1947	M	NCAA	6	—	—	—	—	—	—	—	—	28	5	Gill, Amory T. 'Slats'
1949		NCAA	4	—	—	—	—	—	—	—	—	24	12	Gill, Amory T. 'Slats'
1955		NCAA	8	—	—	—	—	—	—	—	—	22	8	Gill, Amory T. 'Slats'
1962		NCAA	I	8	—	—	—	—	—	—	—	24	5	Gill, Amory T. 'Slats'
1963		NCAA	I	4	—	—	—	—	—	—	—	22	9	Gill, Amory T. 'Slats'
1964		NCAA	I	25	—	—	—	—	—	—	—	25	4	Gill, Amory T. 'Slats'
1966		NCAA	I	8	—	—	—	—	—	—	—	21	7	Valenti, Paul B.
1975		NCAA	I	16	—	—	—	—	—	—	—	19	12	Miller, Ralph H. 'Cappy'
1979		NCAA	I	—	24	—	—	—	—	—	—	18	10	Miller, Ralph H. 'Cappy'
1980		NCAA	I	32	—	—	—	—	—	—	—	26	4	Miller, Ralph H. 'Cappy'
1981		NCAA	I	32	—	—	—	—	—	--	—	26	2	Miller, Ralph H. 'Cappy'
1982		NCAA	I	8	—	—	—	—	—	—	—	25	5	Miller, Ralph H. 'Cappy'
1983		NCAA	I	—	8	—	—	—	—	—	—	20	11	Miller, Ralph H. 'Cappy'
1984		NCAA	I	48	—	—	—	—	—	—	—	22	7	Miller, Ralph H. 'Cappy'
1985		NCAA	I	64	—	—	—	—	—	—	—	22	9	Miller, Ralph H. 'Cappy'
1987		NCAA	I	—	16	—	—	—	—	—	—	19	11	Miller, Ralph H. 'Cappy'
1988		NCAA	I	64	—	—	—	—	—	—	—	20	11	Miller, Ralph H. 'Cappy'
1989		NCAA	I	64	—	—	—	—	—	—	—	22	8	Miller, Ralph H. 'Cappy'
1990		NCAA	I	64	—	—	—	—	—	—	—	22	7	Anderson, Jim
1979	W	AIAW	L	16	—	—	—	—	—	—	—	15	7	Hill, Aki
1980		AIAW	I	—	1	—	—	—	—	—	—	22	9	Hill, Aki
1981		AIAW	I	24	—	—	—	—	—	—	—	22	6	Hill, Aki
1982		NCAA	I	—	1	—	—	—	—	—	—	20	8	Hill, Aki

Year	M/W	Assn	Div	NAT	NIT	ARC	CCA	NCI	NCT	OLY	HLM	W	L	Coach
1983		NCAA	I	16	—	—	—	—	—	—	—	21	5	Hill, Aki
1984		NCAA	I	32	—	—	—	—	—	—	—	21	8	Hill, Aki
1994		NCAA	I	64	—	—	—	—	—	—	—	17	11	Hill, Aki
1995		NCAA	I	32	—	—	—	—	—	—	—	21	8	Hill, Aki
1996		NCAA	I	64	—	—	—	—	—	—	—	19	9	Spoelstra, Judy

OREGON TECH

Year	M/W	Assn	Div	NAT	NIT	ARC	CCA	NCI	NCT	OLY	HLM	W	L	Coach
1974	M	NAIA		32	—	—	—	—	—	—	—	24	5	Miles, Daniel J. "Danny"
1979		NAIA		32	—	—	—	—	—	—	—	23	5	Miles, Daniel J. "Danny"
1987		NAIA		16	—	—	—	—	—	—	—	33	5	Miles, Daniel J. "Danny"
1997		NAIA	II	16	—	—	—	—	—	—	—	29	6	Miles, Daniel J. "Danny"
1998		NAIA	II	2	—	—	—	—	—	—	—	26	11	Miles, Daniel J. "Danny"

OTTAWA

Year	M/W	Assn	Div	NAT	NIT	ARC	CCA	NCI	NCT	OLY	HLM	W	L	Coach
1938	M	NAIA		32	—	—	—	—	—	—	—	11	8	Godlove, Richard M.
1951		NAIA		16	—	—	—	—	—	—	—	19	7	Meek, Donald
1993		NAIA	II	20	—	—	—	—	—	—	—	18	12	Carrier, Andy
1995		NAIA	II	32	—	—	—	—	—	—	—	21	9	Carrier, Andy

OTTERBEIN

Year	M/W	Assn	Div	NAT	NIT	ARC	CCA	NCI	NCT	OLY	HLM	W	L	Coach
1978	M	NCAA	III	23	—	—	—	—	—	—	—	20	9	Reynolds, Dick
1981		NCAA	III	4	—	—	—	—	—	—	—	23	9	Reynolds, Dick
1985		NCAA	III	24	—	—	—	—	—	—	—	23	4	Reynolds, Dick
1986		NCAA	III	8	—	—	—	—	—	—	—	28	3	Reynolds, Dick
1987		NCAA	III	16	—	—	—	—	—	—	—	23	6	Reynolds, Dick
1989		NCAA	III	8	—	—	—	—	—	—	—	20	10	Reynolds, Dick
1990		NCAA	III	40	—	—	—	—	—	—	—	20	9	Reynolds, Dick
1991		NCAA	III	3	—	—	—	—	—	—	—	30	3	Reynolds, Dick
1992		NCAA	III	8	—	—	—	—	—	—	—	27	4	Reynolds, Dick
1993		NCAA	III	32	—	—	—	—	—	—	—	19	10	Reynolds, Dick
1994		NCAA	III	40	—	—	—	—	—	—	—	19	9	Reynolds, Dick

OTTUMWA HEIGHTS

Year	M/W	Assn	Div	NAT	NIT	ARC	CCA	NCI	NCT	OLY	HLM	W	L	Coach
1974	M	NSCAA		16	—	—	—	—	—	—	—	16	7	Stevenson, Charles "Chuck"

OUACHITA BAPTIST

Year	M/W	Assn	Div	NAT	NIT	ARC	CCA	NCI	NCT	OLY	HLM	W	L	Coach
1943	M	NAIA		32	—	—	—	—	—	—	—	12	7	Bradshaw, Wesley W.
1962		NAIA		32	—	—	—	—	—	—	—	15	14	Vining, Bill C., Sr.
1964		NAIA		32	—	—	—	—	—	—	—	22	5	Vining, Bill C., Sr.
1965		NAIA		3	—	—	—	—	—	—	—	27	10	Vining, Bill C., Sr.
1972		NAIA		16	—	—	—	—	—	—	—	26	5	Vining, Bill C., Sr.
1973		NAIA		32	—	—	—	—	—	—	—	22	6	Vining, Bill C., Sr.
1978		NAIA		16	—	—	—	—	—	—	—	25	5	Vining, Bill C., Sr.
1969	W			—	2	—	—	—	—	—	—			Moffatt, Phyllis Carolyn
1970				—	3	—	—	—	—	—	—			Moffatt, Phyllis Carolyn
1986		NAIA		16	—	—	—	—	—	—	—	18	13	Honnell, Virginia

OZARK CHRISTIAN

Year	M/W	Assn	Div	NAT	NIT	ARC	CCA	NCI	NCT	OLY	HLM	W	L	Coach
1978	M	NCCAA	II	3	—	—	—	—	—	—	—	X	X	Larrison, Bill
1986		NBCAA	I	5	—	—	—	—	—	—	—	X	X	Berlin, Terry
1989		NBCAA	I	6	—	—	—	—	—	—	—	X	X	Williams, Charles R.
1990		NBCAA	I	1	—	—	—	—	—	—	—	X	X	Williams, Charles R.
1991		NBCAA	I	2	—	—	—	—	—	—	—	26	9	Williams, Charles R.
1992		NBCAA	I	1	—	—	—	—	—	—	—	28	13	Williams, Charles R.

Year	M/W	Assn	Div	NAT	NIT	ARC	CCA	NCI	NCT	OLY	HLM	W	L	Coach
1988	W	NBCAA		1	—	—	—	—	—	—	—	X	X	Williams, Charles R.
1988		NCCAA	II	6	—	—	—	—	—	—	—	X	X	Williams, Charles R.
1989		NBCAA		2	—	—	—	—	—	—	—	X	X	Williams, Charles R.
1989		NCCAA	II	5	—	—	—	—	—	—	—	X	X	Williams, Charles R.
1995		NCCAA	II	5	—	—	—	—	—	—	—	15	7	Williams, Charles R.
1996		NCCAA	II	3	—	—	—	—	—	—	—	18	10	Williams, Charles R.
1997		NCCAA	II	4	—	—	—	—	—	—	—	16	10	Williams, Charles R.

Ozarks (AR)

Year	M/W	Assn	Div	NAT	NIT	ARC	CCA	NCI	NCT	OLY	HLM	W	L	Coach
1988	M	NAIA		16	—	—	—	—	—	—	—	25	9	Allen, Jimmy W.
1993		NAIA	I	16	—	—	—	—	—	—	—	23	9	Johnson, John K. "Johnny"
1994		NAIA	I	32	—	—	—	—	—	—	—	22	13	Johnson, John K. "Johnny"

Ozarks (MO)

Year	M/W	Assn	Div	NAT	NIT	ARC	CCA	NCI	NCT	OLY	HLM	W	L	Coach
1995	M	NAIA	II	8	—	—	—	—	—	—	—	29	5	Waller, Allan J.
1996		NAIA	II	32	—	—	—	—	—	—	—	25	7	Waller, Allan J.
1997		NAIA	II	8	—	—	—	—	—	—	—	23	11	Waller, Allan J.
1993	W	NAIA	II	16	—	—	—	—	—	—	—	19	13	Franks, Joe
1995		NAIA	II	32	—	—	—	—	—	—	—	18	13	Franks, Joe
1996		NAIA	II	32	—	—	—	—	—	—	—	18	10	Franks, Joe
1997		NAIA	II	16	—	—	—	—	—	—	—	29	3	Franks, Joe
1998		NAIA	II	32	—	—	—	—	—	—	—	24	7	Wilson, George

Pace

Year	M/W	Assn	Div	NAT	NIT	ARC	CCA	NCI	NCT	OLY	HLM	W	L	Coach
1992	M	NCAA	II	32	—	—	—	—	—	—	—	23	7	Holloran, Darrell
1985	W	NCAA	II	8	—	—	—	—	—	—	—	28	3	Olenowski, John
1986		NCAA	II	24	—	—	—	—	—	—	—	20	8	Lauro, John
1989		NCAA	II	32	—	—	—	—	—	—	—	20	10	Lauro, John
1990		NCAA	II	32	—	—	—	—	—	—	—	23	7	Jones, Allison
1991		NCAA	II	32	—	—	—	—	—	—	—	26	4	Jones, Allison
1992		NCAA	II	32	—	—	—	—	—	—	—	25	6	Jones, Allison
1994		NCAA	II	16	—	—	—	—	—	—	—	27	4	Seymour, Carrie

Pacific (CA)

Year	M/W	Assn	Div	NAT	NIT	ARC	CCA	NCI	NCT	OLY	HLM	W	L	Coach
1951	M	NAIA		32	—	—	—	—	—	—	—	19	11	Kjeldsen, Chris K.
1966		NCAA	I	16	—	—	—	—	—	—	—	22	6	Edwards, Richard B.
1967		NCAA	I	8	—	—	—	—	—	—	—	24	4	Edwards, Richard B.
1971		NCAA	I	12	—	—	—	—	—	—	—	22	6	Edwards, Richard B.
1979		NCAA	I	32	—	—	—	—	—	—	—	18	12	Morrison, Stanley M.
1997		NCAA	I	64	—	—	—	—	—	—	—	24	6	Thomason, Bob
1998		NCAA	I	—	32	—	—	—	—	—	—	24	10	Thomason, Bob
1995	W	NCAA	I	—	8	—	—	—	—	—	—	20	15	DeMarchi, Melissa

Pacific (OR)

Year	M/W	Assn	Div	NAT	NIT	ARC	CCA	NCI	NCT	OLY	HLM	W	L	Coach
1940	M	NAIA		32	—	—	—	—	—	—	—	17	12	Miller, Pete
1957		NCAA	II	32	—	—	—	—	—	—	—	12	12	Adams, Vic
1997		NAIA	II	16	—	—	—	—	—	—	—	22	6	Schumann, Ken
1992	W	NAIA	II	8	—	—	—	—	—	—	—	23	6	Olmstead, David
1996		NAIA	II	32	—	—	—	—	—	—	—	17	10	Olmstead, David

Year	M/W	Assn	Div	NAT	NIT	ARC	CCA	NCI	NCT	OLY	HLM	W	L	Coach
PACIFIC CHRISTIAN														
1988	M	NCCAA	II	4	—	—	—	—	—	—	—	30	7	Erickson, Lee W.
1989		NCCAA	II	2	—	—	—	—	—	—	—	32	10	Erickson, Lee W.
1990		NCCAA	II	2	—	—	—	—	—	—	—	X	X	Erickson, Lee W.
1991		NBCAA	I	3	—	—	—	—	—	—	—	32	18	Erickson, Lee W.
1992		NBCAA	I	3	—	—	—	—	—	—	—	X	X	Erickson, Lee W.
1993		NCCAA	II	4	—	—	—	—	—	—	—	25	13	Erickson, Lee W.
1994		NCCAA	II	2	—	—	—	—	—	—	—	28	17	Erickson, Lee W.
1989	W	NCCAA	II	3	—	—	—	—	—	—	—	23	11	Garcia, Barbara
1990		NCCAA	II	7	—	—	—	—	—	—	—	X	X	Kappen, Kelley
1991		NCCAA	II	3	—	—	—	—	—	—	—	18	14	Kappen, Kelley
1992		NCCAA	II	5	—	—	—	—	—	—	—	X	X	Kappen, Kelley
1993		NCCAA	II	7	—	—	—	—	—	—	—	16	12	Kappen, Kelley
PACIFIC LUTHERAN														
1951	M	NAIA		32	—	—	—	—	—	—	—	20	11	Harshman, Marvel K. "Marv"
1956		NAIA		16	—	—	—	—	—	—	—	25	6	Harshman, Marvel K. "Marv"
1957		NAIA		3	—	—	—	—	—	—	—	28	1	Harshman, Marvel K. "Marv"
1958		NAIA		16	—	—	—	—	—	—	—	21	6	Harshman, Marvel K. "Marv"
1959		NAIA		2	—	—	—	—	—	—	—	26	3	Lundgaard, Gene C.
1962		NAIA		32	—	—	—	—	—	—	—	17	9	Lundgaard, Gene C.
1963		NAIA		32	—	—	—	—	—	—	—	18	10	Lundgaard, Gene C.
1964		NAIA		16	—	—	—	—	—	—	—	20	7	Lundgaard, Gene C.
1980	W	AIAW	III	24	—	—	—	—	—	—	—	16	14	Hemion, Kathy
1998		NAIA	II	32	—	—	—	—	—	—	—	21	7	Rigell, Gil
PACIFIC WEST COAST BAPTIST BIBLE														
1990	M	NBCAA	II	3	—	—	—	—	—	—	—	X	X	Thomas, Mike
1991		NBCAA	II	3	—	—	—	—	—	—	—	20	7	Thomas, Mike
1992		NBCAA	II	3	—	—	—	—	—	—	—	X	X	Thomas, Mike
PAINE														
1977	M	NAIA		32	—	—	—	—	—	—	—	18	13	Tulberi, Ernest
1994		NCAA	II	24	—	—	—	—	—	—	—	24	7	Spry, Ronald
PALM BEACH ATLANTIC														
1975	M	NAIA		32	—	—	—	—	—	—	—	22	4	Perides, George L.
PALMER JC (SC)														
1972	M	NSCAA		2	—	—	—	—	—	—	—	21	5	Voight, Jim
PANZER														
1942	M	NAIA		32	—	—	—	—	—	—	—	14	5	Gorton, Albert J.
1946		NAIA		32	—	—	—	—	—	—	—	18	3	Gorton, Albert J.
PARK (MO)														
1991	M	NAIA		32	—	—	—	—	—	—	—	26	7	Francis, David
1998		NAIA	I	3	—	—	—	—	—	—	—	27	8	English, Claude
PARSONS														
1960	M	NAIA		16	—	—	—	—	—	—	—	17	12	Nelson, Oscar B.
1963		NAIA		32	—	—	—	—	—	—	—	21	8	Nelson, Oscar B.
1967		NCAA	II	32	—	—	—	—	—	—	—	18	9	Nelson, Oscar B.

Year	M/W	Assn	Div	NAT	NIT	ARC	CCA	NCI	NCT	OLY	HLM	W	L	Coach
1971	W			—	2	—	—	—	—	—	—	30	11	Spencer, Robert L.
1972				—	4	—	—	—	—	—	—	17	12	Spencer, Robert L.
1973				—	3	—	—	—	—	—	—	20	16	Spencer, Robert L.

PAUL QUINN

Year	M/W	Assn	Div	NAT	NIT	ARC	CCA	NCI	NCT	OLY	HLM	W	L	Coach
1980	M	NAIA		32	—	—	—	—	—	—	—	32	10	Boyd, Wesley
1982		NAIA		32	—	—	—	—	—	—	—	25	13	Boyd, Wesley
1988		NAIA		32	—	—	—	—	—	—	—	29	5	Summers, James "Zip"
1990		NAIA		32	—	—	—	—	—	—	—	31	7	Summers, James "Zip"
1990		NSCAA		1	—	—	—	—	—	—	—	31	7	Summers, James "Zip"
1991		NSCAA		7	—	—	—	—	—	—	—	17	12	Summers, James "Zip"
1992		NSCAA		2	—	—	—	—	—	—	—			Summers, James "Zip"
1993		NSCAA		8	—	—	—	—	—	—	—	15	15	Summers, James "Zip"
1995		NSCAA		1	—	—	—	—	—	—	—	20	12	Summers, James "Zip"
1992	W	NSCAA		5	—	—	—	—	—	—	—			Ensley, Michael

PENN-OHIO

Year	M/W	Assn	Div	NAT	NIT	ARC	CCA	NCI	NCT	OLY	HLM	W	L	Coach
1969	M	NSCAA		8	—	—	—	—	—	—	—	7	7	

PENNSYLVANIA

Year	M/W	Assn	Div	NAT	NIT	ARC	CCA	NCI	NCT	OLY	HLM	W	L	Coach
1920	M	NCAA		—	—	—	—	—	—	—	1	22	1	Jourdet, Lon W.
1921		NCAA		—	—	—	—	—	—	—	1	21	2	McNichol, Edward J.
1953		NCAA		12	—	—	—	—	—	—	—	22	5	Dallmar, Howard "Howie"
1970		NCAA	I	25	—	—	—	—	—	—	—	25	2	Harter, Dick
1971		NCAA	I	8	—	—	—	—	—	—	—	28	1	Harter, Dick
1972		NCAA	I	8	—	—	—	—	—	—	—	25	3	Daly, Charles J. "Chuck"
1973		NCAA	I	16	—	—	—	—	—	—	—	21	7	Daly, Charles J. "Chuck"
1974		NCAA	I	25	—	—	—	—	—	—	—	21	6	Daly, Charles J. "Chuck"
1975		NCAA	I	32	—	—	—	—	—	—	—	23	5	Daly, Charles J. "Chuck"
1978		NCAA	I	16	—	—	—	—	—	—	—	20	8	Weinhauer, Bob
1979		NCAA	I	4	—	—	—	—	—	—	—	25	7	Weinhauer, Bob
1980		NCAA	I	32	—	—	—	—	—	—	—	17	12	Weinhauer, Bob
1981		NCAA	I	—	32	—	—	—	—	—	—	20	8	Weinhauer, Bob
1982		NCAA	I	48	—	—	—	—	—	—	—	17	10	Weinhauer, Bob
1985		NCAA	I	64	—	—	—	—	—	—	—	13	14	Littlepage, Craig K.
1987		NCAA	I	64	—	—	—	—	—	—	—	13	14	Schneider, Thomas
1993		NCAA	I	64	—	—	—	—	—	—	—	22	5	Dunphy, Fran
1994		NCAA	I	32	—	—	—	—	—	—	—	25	3	Dunphy, Fran
1995		NCAA	I	64	—	—	—	—	—	—	—	22	6	Dunphy, Fran

PENNSYLVANIA STATE

Year	M/W	Assn	Div	NAT	NIT	ARC	CCA	NCI	NCT	OLY	HLM	W	L	Coach
1942	M	NCAA		6	—	—	—	—	—	—	—	18	3	Lawther, John D.
1952		NCAA		16	—	—	—	—	—	—	—	20	6	Gross, Elmer A.
1954		NCAA		3	—	—	—	—	—	—	—	18	6	Gross, Elmer A.
1955		NCAA		16	—	—	—	—	—	—	—	18	10	Egli, John S.
1965		NCAA	I	23	—	—	—	—	—	—	—	20	4	Egli, John S.
1966		NCAA	I	—	14	—	—	—	—	—	—	18	6	Egli, John S.
1980		NCAA	I	—	32	—	—	—	—	—	—	18	10	Harter, Dick
1989		NCAA	I	—	16	—	—	—	—	—	—	20	12	Parkhill, Bruce

Year	M/W	Assn	Div	NAT	NIT	ARC	CCA	NCI	NCT	OLY	HLM	W	L	Coach
1990		NCAA	I	—	3	—	—	—	—	—	—	25	9	Parkhill, Bruce
1991		NCAA	I	32	—	—	—	—	—	—	—	21	11	Parkhill, Bruce
1992		NCAA	I	—	32	—	—	—	—	—	—	21	8	Parkhill, Bruce
1995		NCAA	I	—	3	—	—	—	—	—	—	21	11	Parkhill, Bruce
1996		NCAA	I	64	—	—	—	—	—	—	—	21	7	Dunn, Jerry
1998		NCAA	I	—	2	—	—	—	—	—	—	19	13	Dunn, Jerry
1976	W	AIAW	L	16	—	—	—	—	—	—	—	10	10	Meiser-McKnett, Patricia
1982		NCAA	I	16	—	—	—	—	—	—	—	24	6	Portland, Rene Muth
1983		NCAA	I	8	—	—	—	—	—	—	—	25	8	Portland, Rene Muth
1984		NCAA	I	32	—	—	—	—	—	—	—	19	12	Portland, Rene Muth
1985		NCAA	I	16	—	—	—	—	—	—	—	28	5	Portland, Rene Muth
1986		NCAA	I	16	—	—	—	—	—	—	—	24	8	Portland, Rene Muth
1987		NCAA	I	32	—	—	—	—	—	—	—	23	7	Portland, Rene Muth
1988		NCAA	I	32	—	—	—	—	—	—	—	20	13	Portland, Rene Muth
1990		NCAA	I	32	—	—	—	—	—	—	—	25	7	Portland, Rene Muth
1991		NCAA	I	32	—	—	—	—	—	—	—	29	2	Portland, Rene Muth
1992		NCAA	I	16	—	—	—	—	—	—	—	24	7	Portland, Rene Muth
1993		NCAA	I	32	—	—	—	—	—	—	—	22	6	Portland, Rene Muth
1994		NCAA	I	8	—	—	—	—	—	—	—	28	3	Portland, Rene Muth
1995		NCAA	I	32	—	—	—	—	—	—	—	26	5	Portland, Rene Muth
1996		NCAA	I	16	—	—	—	—	—	—	—	27	7	Portland, Rene Muth
1998		NCAA	I	—	1	—	—	—	—	—	—	21	13	Portland, Rene Muth

PENNSYLVANIA STATE: ERIE BEHREND

| 1994 | W | NCAA | III | 32 | — | — | — | — | — | — | — | 21 | 6 | Fornari, Rosalyn "Roz" |

PENSACOLA CHRISTIAN

| 1998 | M | NCCAA | I | 6 | — | — | — | — | — | — | — | 15 | 15 | Goetsch, Mark |

PEPPERDINE

1942	M	NAIA		32	—	—	—	—	—	—	—	18	7	Duer, Alva O. "Al"
1943		NAIA		8	—	—	—	—	—	—	—	23	8	Duer, Alva O. "Al"
1944		NCAA		8	—	—	—	—	—	—	—	22	13	Duer, Alva O. "Al"
1945		NAIA		2	—	—	—	—	—	—	—	25	11	Duer, Alva O. "Al"
1946		NAIA		3	—	—	—	—	—	—	—	27	8	Duer, Alva O. "Al"
1950		NAIA		16	—	—	—	—	—	—	—	21	12	Dowell, Robert L. "Duck"
1951		NAIA		16	—	—	—	—	—	—	—	25	8	Dowell, Robert L. "Duck"
1952		NAIA		32	—	—	—	—	—	—	—	20	4	Dowell, Robert L. "Duck"
1962		NCAA	I	12	—	—	—	—	—	—	—	20	7	Dowell, Robert L. "Duck"
1976		NCAA	I	16	—	—	—	—	—	—	—	22	6	Colson, Gary W.
1979		NCAA	I	32	—	—	—	—	—	—	—	22	10	Colson, Gary W.
1980		NCAA	I	—	32	—	—	—	—	—	—	17	11	Harrick, Jim
1982		NCAA	I	32	—	—	—	—	—	—	—	22	7	Harrick, Jim
1983		NCAA	I	48	—	—	—	—	—	—	—	20	9	Harrick, Jim
1985		NCAA	I	64	—	—	—	—	—	—	—	23	9	Harrick, Jim
1986		NCAA	I	64	—	—	—	—	—	—	—	25	5	Harrick, Jim
1988		NCAA	I	—	32	—	—	—	—	—	—	17	13	Harrick, Jim
1989		NCAA	I	—	16	—	—	—	—	—	—	20	13	Asbury, Tom
1991		NCAA	I	64	—	—	—	—	—	—	—	22	9	Asbury, Tom
1992		NCAA	I	64	—	—	—	—	—	—	—	24	7	Asbury, Tom

Year	M/W	Assn	Div	NAT	NIT	ARC	CCA	NCI	NCT	OLY	HLM	W	L	Coach
1993		NCAA	I	—	16	—	—	—	—	—	—	23	8	Asbury, Tom
1994		NCAA	I	64	—	—	—	—	—	—	—	19	11	Asbury, Tom
1978	W	AIAW	S	12	—	—	—	—	—	—	—	29	6	Meyers, Patty
1979		AIAW	S	12	—	—	—	—	—	—	—	27	13	Meyers, Patty
1982		NCAA	I	—	8	—	—	—	—	—	—	16	13	Meyers, Patty

PERU STATE

Year	M/W	Assn	Div	NAT	NIT	ARC	CCA	NCI	NCT	OLY	HLM	W	L	Coach
1938	M	NAIA		32	—	—	—	—	—	—	—	15	3	Baller, Stewart "Stu"
1939		NAIA		4	—	—	—	—	—	—	—	18	7	Wheeler, A. G. "Al"
1940		NAIA		16	—	—	—	—	—	—	—	19	6	Wheeler, A. G. "Al"
1942		NAIA		32	—	—	—	—	—	—	—	13	9	Wheeler, A. G. "Al"
1945	·	NAIA		16	—	—	—	—	—	—	—	6	8	Wheeler, A. G. "Al"
1946		NAIA		32	—	—	—	—	—	—	—	16	6	Wheeler, A. G. "Al"
1948		NAIA		32	—	—	—	—	—	—	—	20	3	Kyle, Newton P.
1949		NAIA		32	—	—	—	—	—	—	—	20	6	Kyle, Newton P.
1950		NAIA		32	—	—	—	—	—	—	—	22	6	Kyle, Newton P.
1961		NAIA		16	—	—	—	—	—	—	—	17	7	McIntire, John "Jack"
1962		NAIA		16	—	—	—	—	—	—	—	23	5	McIntire, John "Jack"
1963		NAIA		32	—	—	—	—	—	—	—	14	11	McIntire, John "Jack"
1966		NAIA		32	—	—	—	—	—	—	—	15	10	McIntire, John "Jack"
1993		NAIA	II	8	—	—	—	—	—	—	—	27	6	Gibbs, John
1997		NAIA	II	32	—	—	—	—	—	—	—	25	9	Gibbs, John
1993	W	NAIA	II	16	—	—	—	—	—	—	—	21	10	Davidson, Dr. E. Wayne

PFEIFFER

Year	M/W	Assn	Div	NAT	NIT	ARC	CCA	NCI	NCT	OLY	HLM	W	L	Coach
1985	M	NAIA		16	—	—	—	—	—	—	—	23	9	Lentz, John
1990		NAIA		8	—	—	—	—	—	—	—	22	11	Lutz, Bob
1991		NAIA		3	—	—	—	—	—	—	—	29	4	Lutz, Bob
1992		NAIA	I	3	—	—	—	—	—	—	—	30	5	Lutz, Bob
1993		NAIA	I	32	—	—	—	—	—	—	—	23	6	Lutz, Bob
1994		NAIA	I	16	—	—	—	—	—	—	—	24	6	Lutz, Bob
1995		NAIA	I	2	—	—	—	—	—	—	—	25	8	Lutz, Bob
1996		NCAA	II	32	—	—	—	—	—	—	—	20	8	Earlywine, Kirk

PHILADELPHIA BIBLE

Year	M/W	Assn	Div	NAT	NIT	ARC	CCA	NCI	NCT	OLY	HLM	W	L	Coach
1998	M	NCCAA	II	3	—	—	—	—	—	—	—	15	12	Martindell, Don
1985	W	NCCAA	II	6	—	—	—	—	—	—	—	23	8	MacCullough, Dr. Martha "Marti"
1986		NCCAA	II	6	—	—	—	—	—	—	—	20	8	MacCullough, Dr. Martha "Marti"
1987		NCCAA	II	2	—	—	—	—	—	—	—	25	2	MacCullough, Dr. Martha "Marti"
1989		NCCAA	II	7	—	—	—	—	—	—	—	18	9	MacCullough, Dr. Martha "Marti"
1990		NCCAA	II	5	—	—	—	—	—	—	—	22	5	MacCullough, Dr. Martha "Marti"
1991		NCCAA	II	4	—	—	—	—	—	—	—	17	12	MacCullough, Dr. Martha "Marti"
1993		NCCAA	II	5	—	—	—	—	—	—	—	23	6	MacCullough, Dr. Martha "Marti"
1994		NCCAA	II	5	—	—	—	—	—	—	—	13	11	MacCullough, Dr. Martha "Marti"
1995		NCCAA	II	8	—	—	—	—	—	—	—	14	12	Landes, Bertie

PHILADELPHIA PHARMACY

Year	M/W	Assn	Div	NAT	NIT	ARC	CCA	NCI	NCT	OLY	HLM	W	L	Coach
1990	M	NAIA		32	—	—	—	—	—	—	—	25	6	Morgan, Robert C.
1992		NAIA	II	20	—	—	—	—	—	—	—	26	7	Morgan, Robert C.
1996		NAIA	II	32	—	—	—	—	—	—	—	23	6	Morgan, Robert C.
1997		NAIA	II	32	—	—	—	—	—	—	—	20	6	Morgan, Robert C.

Year	M/W	Assn	Div	NAT	NIT	ARC	CCA	NCI	NCT	OLY	HLM	W	L	Coach
PHILADELPHIA TEXTILES														
1958	M	NCAA	II	32	—	—	—	—	—	—	—	17	7	Harris, Walter "Bucky"
1963		NCAA	II	8	—	—	—	—	—	—	—	21	3	Harris, Walter "Bucky"
1964		NCAA	II	24	—	—	—	—	—	—	—	18	6	Harris, Walter "Bucky"
1965		NCAA	II	8	—	—	—	—	—	—	—	22	4	Harris, Walter "Bucky"
1966		NCAA	II	32	—	—	—	—	—	—	—	20	6	McKinney, John P. "Jack"
1967		NCAA	II	16	—	—	—	—	—	—	—	20	7	McKinney, John P. "Jack"
1968		NCAA	II	23	—	—	—	—	—	—	—	21	6	Magee, Herbert
1969		NCAA	II	24	—	—	—	—	—	—	—	20	5	Magee, Herbert
1970		NCAA	II	1	—	—	—	—	—	—	—	29	2	Magee, Herbert
1971		NCAA	II	16	—	—	—	—	—	—	—	22	6	Magee, Herbert
1972		NCAA	II	24	—	—	—	—	—	—	—	22	7	Magee, Herbert
1973		NCAA	II	32	—	—	—	—	—	—	—	25	4	Magee, Herbert
1975		NCAA	II	24	—	—	—	—	—	—	—	21	6	Magee, Herbert
1976		NCAA	II	16	—	—	—	—	—	—	—	25	3	Magee, Herbert
1977		NCAA	II	32	—	—	—	—	—	—	—	22	6	Magee, Herbert
1978		NCAA	II	16	—	—	—	—	—	—	—	18	10	Magee, Herbert
1979		NCAA	II	32	—	—	—	—	—	—	—	20	8	Magee, Herbert
1983		NCAA	II	16	—	—	—	—	—	—	—	23	7	Magee, Herbert
1985		NCAA	II	16	—	—	—	—	—	—	—	24	7	Magee, Herbert
1989		NCAA	II	32	—	—	—	—	—	—	—	24	7	Magee, Herbert
1991		NCAA	II	8	—	—	—	.	—	—	—	24	8	Magee, Herbert
1992		NCAA	II	16	—	—	—	—	—	—	—	28	4	Magee, Herbert
1993		NCAA	II	8	—	—	—	—	—	—	—	30	2	Magee, Herbert
1994		NCAA	II	16	—	—	—	—	—	—	—	29	2	Magee, Herbert
1995		NCAA	II	16	—	—	—	—	—	—	—	26	5	Magee, Herbert
1986	W	NCAA	II	3	—	—	—	—	—	—	—	24	6	Soriero, Julie
1989		NCAA	II	32	—	—	—	—	—	—	—	21	9	Soriero, Julie
1993		NCAA	II	32	—	—	—	—	—	—	—	27	2	Shirley, Thomas, Jr.
1997		NCAA	II	48	—	—	—	—	—	—	—	21	8	Shirley, Thomas, Jr.
1998		NCAA	II	32	—	—	—	—	—	—	—	25	8	Shirley, Thomas, Jr.
PHILANDER SMITH														
1953	M	NASC		4	—	—	—	—	—	—	—	27	5	Hearnton, William C., Sr.
1955		NASC		3	—	—	—	—	—	—	—	20	8	Hearnton, William C., Sr.
1957		NCAA	II	32	—	—	—	—	—	—	—	12	14	Hearnton, William C., Sr.
1958		NCAA	II	32	—	—	—	—	—	—	—	14	10	
1998		NSCAA		2	—	—	—	—	—	—	—	17	10	Greenwood, J. W. "Johnny"
1995	W	NSCAA		6	—	—	—	—	—	—				Chandler, Hilton
1998		NSCAA		5	—	—	—	—	—	—		11	13	Chandler, Hilton
PHILLIPS (OK)														
1945	M	NAIA		16	—	—	—	—	—	—				
1984		NAIA		32	—	—	—	—	—	—		25	13	Wilson, Robert H.
1997		NAIA	I	32	—	—	—	—	—	—		23	9	Chappell, Rand
1998		NAIA	I	16	—	—	—	—	—	—		31	3	Chappell, Rand
1972	W	AIAW		8	—	—	—	—	—	—				Amaya, Lou
1974		AIAW		—	8	—	—	—	—	—				Amaya, Lou
1975		AIAW	S	1	—	—	—	—	—	—				Amaya, Lou
1976		AIAW	S	3	—	—	—	—	—	—		28	7	Blakely, Tom

Year	M/W	Assn	Div	NAT	NIT	ARC	CCA	NCI	NCT	OLY	HLM	W	L	Coach
1977		AIAW	S	2	—	—	—	—	—	—	—	31	2	Blakely, Tom
1994		NAIA	I	16	—	—	—	—	—	—	—	24	7	Carter, Carole
1998		NAIA	I	16	—	—	—	—	—	—	—	25	7	Price, Denny

PHILLIPS JC: GULFPORT

Year	M/W	Assn	Div	NAT	NIT	ARC	CCA	NCI	NCT	OLY	HLM	W	L	Coach
1983	M	NSCAA		3	—	—	—	—	—	—	—	12	15	Ladner, Roland
1984		NSCAA		9	—	—	—	—	—	—	—	22	20	Ladner, Roland
1985	W	NSCAA		1	—	—	—	—	—	—	—	21	6	Rosetti, George F., Sr.
1986		NSCAA		1	—	—	—	—	—	—	—	22	7	Rosetti, George F., Sr.

PIEDMONT BAPTIST

Year	M/W	Assn	Div	NAT	NIT	ARC	CCA	NCI	NCT	OLY	HLM	W	L	Coach
1994	M	NCCAA	II	8	—	—	—	—	—	—	—	21	10	Franklin, Philip
1985	W	NCCAA	II	8	—	—	—	—	—	—				Clingerman, Ralph

PIKEVILLE

Year	M/W	Assn	Div	NAT	NIT	ARC	CCA	NCI	NCT	OLY	HLM	W	L	Coach
1959	M	NAIA		32	—	—	—	—	—	—	—	28	7	Daniels, William
1976		NAIA		32	—	—	—	—	—	—	—	26	5	Martin, Wayne M.
1998	W	NAIA	I	32	—	—	—	—	—	—	—	21	14	Watson, Bill

PILLSBURY BAPTIST BIBLE

Year	M/W	Assn	Div	NAT	NIT	ARC	CCA	NCI	NCT	OLY	HLM	W	L	Coach
1982	M	NBCAA		5	—	—	—	—	—	—	—	18	8	Wahlberg, Tom
1983		NBCAA		5	—	—	—	—	—	—	—	18	15	Wahlberg, Tom
1984		NBCAA	I	3	—	—	—	—	—	—	—	14	13	Leeman, Gordon
1985		NBCAA	I	6	—	—	—	—	—	—	—	16	11	Deckert, Wayne
1986		NBCAA	I	3	—	—	—	—	—	—	—	16	10	Deckert, Wayne
1987		NBCAA	I	4	—	—	—	—	—	—	—			Deckert, Wayne
1988		NBCAA	I	3	—	—	—	—	—	—	—	15	9	Deckert, Wayne
1989		NCCAA	II	6	—	—	—	—	—	—	—	13	17	Johnson, Richard "Rick"
1992		NCCAA	II	6	—	—	—	—	—	—	—	10	21	Johnson, Richard "Rick"
1997		NCCAA	IIA	6	—	—	—	—	—	—	—	12	14	Davis, Paul
1986	W	NBCAA		5	—	—	—	—	—	—	—	3	7	
1993		NCCAA	II	4	—	—	—	—	—	—	—	13	12	Traxler, Tim

PITTSBURG STATE

Year	M/W	Assn	Div	NAT	NIT	ARC	CCA	NCI	NCT	OLY	HLM	W	L	Coach
1940	M	NAIA		8	—	—	—	—	—	—	—	16	11	Lance, John F.
1941		NAIA		32	—	—	—	—	—	—	—	18	6	Lance, John F.
1942		NAIA		3	—	—	—	—	—	—	—	23	5	Lance, John F.
1956		NAIA		3	—	—	—	—	—	—	—	27	2	Lance, John F.
1960		NAIA		32	—	—	—	—	—	—	—	18	4	Lance, John F.
1966		NAIA		32	—	—	—	—	—	—	—	18	10	Lambert, Paul M.
1972		NAIA		16	—	—	—	—	—	—	—	22	8	Johnson, Robert A.
1997		NCAA	II	16	—	—	—	—	—	—	—	24	8	Iba, Clarence Eugene "Gene"
1998		NCAA	II	32	—	—	—	—	—	—	—	24	7	Iba, Clarence Eugene "Gene"
1992	W	NCAA	II	32	—	—	—	—	—	—	—	22	9	High, Steve
1993		NCAA	II	32	—	—	—	—	—	—	—	21	7	High, Steve
1995		NCAA	II	48	—	—	—	—	—	—	—	22	7	High, Steve
1997		NCAA	II	48	—	—	—	—	—	—	—	19	10	High, Steve
1998		NCAA	II	48	—	—	—	—	—	—	—	18	11	High, Steve

Year	M/W	Assn	Div	NAT	NIT	ARC	CCA	NCI	NCT	OLY	HLM	W	L	Coach
PITTSBURGH														
1928	M	NCAA		—	—	—	—	—	—	—	1	21	0	Carlson, Dr. H. Clifford "Doc"
1930		NCAA		—	—	—	—	—	—	—	1	23	2	Carlson, Dr. H. Clifford "Doc"
1941		NCAA		3	—	—	—	—	—	—	—	13	6	Carlson, Dr. H. Clifford "Doc"
1957		NCAA	I	16	—	—	—	—	—	—	—	16	11	Timmons, Robert W.
1958		NCAA	I	24	—	—	—	—	—	—	—	18	7	Timmons, Robert W.
1963		NCAA	I	25	—	—	—	—	—	—	—	19	6	Timmons, Robert W.
1964		NCAA	I	—	12	—	—	—	—	—	—	17	8	Timmons, Robert W.
1974		NCAA	I	8	—	—	—	—	—	—	—	25	4	Ridl, Charles G. "Buzz"
1975		NCAA	I	—	8	—	—	—	—	—	—	18	11	Ridl, Charles G. "Buzz"
1980		NCAA	I	—	32	—	—	—	—	—	—	17	12	Grgurich, Tim
1981		NCAA	I	32	—	—	—	—	—	—	—	19	12	Chipman, Dr. Leroy
1982		NCAA	I	48	—	—	—	—	—	—	—	20	10	Chipman, Dr. Leroy
1984		NCAA	I	—	8	—	—	—	—	—	—	18	13	Chipman, Dr. Leroy
1985		NCAA	I	64	—	—	—	—	—	—	—	17	12	Chipman, Dr. Leroy
1986		NCAA	I	—	32	—	—	—	—	—	—	15	14	Chipman, Dr. Leroy
1987		NCAA	I	32	—	—	—	—	—	—	—	25	8	Evans, Paul
1988		NCAA	I	32	—	—	—	—	—	—	—	24	7	Evans, Paul
1989		NCAA	I	64	—	—	—	—	—	—	—	17	13	Evans, Paul
1991		NCAA	I	32	—	—	—	—	—	—	—	21	12	Evans, Paul
1992		NCAA	I	—	16	—	—	—	—	—	—	18	16	Evans, Paul
1993		NCAA	I	64	—	—	—	—	—	—	—	17	11	Evans, Paul
1997		NCAA	I	—	16	—	—	—	—	—	—	18	15	Willard, Ralph
1981	W			—	5	—	—	—	—	—	—	22	7	Saurer, Judy
1994		NCAA	I	—	3	—	—	—	—	—	—	21	10	Bruce, Kirk
PITTSBURGH ART INSTITUTE														
1968	M	NSCAA		3	—	—	—	—	—	—	—			
1969		NSCAA		2	—	—	—	—	—	—	—			
PITTSBURGH: JOHNSTOWN														
1997	M	NCAA	II	48	—	—	—	—	—	—	—	21	6	Rukavina, Bob
1998		NCAA	II	32	—	—	—	—	—	—	—	24	5	Rukavina, Bob
1980	W	AIAW	III	16	—	—	—	—	—	—	—	21	7	Horner, Clyde L.
1981		AIAW	III	4	—	—	—	—	—	—	—	26	4	Horner, Clyde L.
1982		NCAA	II	16	—	—	—	—	—	—	—	20	3	Horner, Clyde L.
1983		NCAA	III	16	—	—	—	—	—	—	—	24	2	Gault, Jodi
1984		NCAA	III	8	—	—	—	—	—	—	—	25	3	Gault, Jodi
1985		NCAA	III	16	—	—	—	—	—	—	—	26	3	Gault, Jodi
1987		NCAA	II	3	—	—	—	—	—	—	—	25	5	Gault, Jodi
1988		NCAA	II	8	—	—	—	—	—	—	—	25	4	Gault, Jodi
1990		NCAA	II	32	—	—	—	—	—	—	—	25	4	Gault, Jodi
1991		NCAA	II	32	—	—	—	—	—	—	—	27	2	Gault, Jodi
1992		NCAA	II	8	—	—	—	—	—	—	—	25	4	Gault, Jodi
1993		NCAA	II	8	—	—	—	—	—	—	—	25	5	Gault, Jodi
1996		NCAA	II	32	—	—	—	—	—	—	—	20	9	Gault, Jodi
PLATTSBURGH STATE														
1976	M	NCAA	III	4	—	—	—	—	—	—	—	16	14	Law, Norman
1995		NCAA	III	64	—	—	—	—	—	—	—	17	10	Cowen, Larry

Year	M/W	Assn	Div	NAT	NIT	ARC	CCA	NCI	NCT	OLY	HLM	W	L	Coach

PLYMOUTH STATE

Year	M/W	Assn	Div	NAT	NIT	ARC	CCA	NCI	NCT	OLY	HLM	W	L	Coach
1996	M	NCAA	III	64	—	—	—	—	—	—	—	19	9	Hogan, Paul
1995	W	NCAA	III	64	—	—	—	—	—	—	—	21	7	Feldman, Nancy

POINT LOMA NAZARENE

Year	M/W	Assn	Div	NAT	NIT	ARC	CCA	NCI	NCT	OLY	HLM	W	L	Coach
1953	M	NAIA		16	—	—	—	—	—	—	—	34	2	Keoppel, Kenneth P.
1954		NAIA		8	—	—	—	—	—	—	—	29	5	Keoppel, Kenneth P.
1958		NAIA		16	—	—	—	—	—	—	—	27	4	Cartwright, Chalmer A.
1968		NAIA		32	—	—	—	—	—	—	—	26	5	Cartwright, Chalmer A.
1979		NCCAA	I	4	—	—	—	—	—	—	—	26	11	Foster, Ben
1980		NCCAA	I	2	—	—	—	—	—	—	—	23	14	Foster, Ben
1983		NAIA		32	—	—	—	—	—	—	—	22	13	Foster, Ben
1985		NCCAA	I	1	—	—	—	—	—	—	—	28	8	Foster, Ben
1986		NCCAA	I	1	—	—	—	—	—	—	—	27	7	Foster, Ben
1987		NCCAA	I	1	—	—	—	—	—	—	—	25	10	Foster, Ben
1991	W	NAIA		32	—	—	—	—	—	—	—	24	8	Olin, Dr. Bill

POINT PARK

Year	M/W	Assn	Div	NAT	NIT	ARC	CCA	NCI	NCT	OLY	HLM	W	L	Coach
1979	M	NAIA		32	—	—	—	—	—	—	—	26	5	Conboy, Gerald "Jerry"
1983		NAIA		32	—	—	—	—	—	—	—	20	12	Conboy, Gerald "Jerry"
1997		NAIA	I	3	—	—	—	—	—	—	—	23	8	Rager, Robert

POMONA-PITZER

Year	M/W	Assn	Div	NAT	NIT	ARC	CCA	NCI	NCT	OLY	HLM	W	L	Coach
1986	M	NCAA	III	32	—	—	—	—	—	—	—	16	12	Popovich, Gregg
1989		NCAA	III	24	—	—	—	—	—	—	—	18	10	Katsiaficas, Charles G.
1994		NCAA	III	40	—	—	—	—	—	—	—	25	3	Katsiaficas, Charles G.
1995		NCAA	III	64	—	—	—	—	—	—	—	18	8	Katsiaficas, Charles G.
1997		NCAA	III	64	—	—	—	—	—	—	—	19	7	Katsiaficas, Charles G.
1998		NCAA	III	48	—	—	—	—	—	—	—	21	5	Katsiaficas, Charles G.
1982	W	NCAA	III	3	—	—	—	—	—	—	—	25	4	Breitenstein, Nancy
1983		NCAA	III	24	—	—	—	—	—	—	—	18	10	Breitenstein, Nancy
1984		NCAA	III	32	—	—	—	—	—	—	—	22	6	Breitenstein, Nancy
1985		NCAA	III	8	—	—	—	—	—	—	—	27	2	Breitenstein, Nancy
1986		NCAA	III	32	—	—	—	—	—	—	—	19	9	Breitenstein, Nancy
1987		NCAA	III	16	—	—	—	—	—	—	—	24	4	Breitenstein, Nancy
1994		NCAA	III	40	—	—	—	—	—	—	—	14	11	Krieger, Barbara
1996		NCAA	III	64	—	—	—	—	—	—	—	17	9	Krieger, Barbara
1997		NCAA	III	64	—	—	—	—	—	—	—	19	7	Connell, Kathleen "Kathy"

PORTLAND

Year	M/W	Assn	Div	NAT	NIT	ARC	CCA	NCI	NCT	OLY	HLM	W	L	Coach
1942	M	NAIA		32	—	—	—	—	—	—	—	14	7	Fitzpatrick, Edwin J.
1949		NAIA		32	—	—	—	—	—	—	—	22	11	Torson, James M. "Mush"
1950		NAIA		16	—	—	—	—	—	—	—	19	12	Torson, James M. "Mush"
1951		NAIA		32	—	—	—	—	—	—	—	23	6	Torson, James M. "Mush"
1952		NAIA		4	—	—	—	—	—	—	—	24	11	Torson, James M. "Mush"
1953		NAIA		32	—	—	—	—	—	—	—	16	14	Torson, James M. "Mush"
1954		NAIA		32	—	—	—	—	—	—	—	9	19	Torson, James M. "Mush"
1957		NAIA		16	—	—	—	—	—	—	—	18	12	Negratti, Dr. Albert E.
1958		NAIA		32	—	—	—	—	—	—	—	18	11	Negratti, Dr. Albert E.
1959		NCAA	I	23	—	—	—	—	—	—	—	19	8	Negratti, Dr. Albert E.
1996		NCAA	I	64	—	—	—	—	—	—	—	19	11	Chavez, Rob

Year	M/W	Assn	Div	NAT	NIT	ARC	CCA	NCI	NCT	OLY	HLM	W	L	Coach
1983	W	NAIA		4	—	—	—	—	—	—	—	—	27	6	Olmstead, David
1984		NAIA		2	—	—	—	—	—	—	—	—	30	6	Olmstead, David
1985		NAIA		8	—	—	—	—	—	—	—	—	26	8	Olmstead, David
1994		NCAA	I	64	—	—	—	—	—	—	—	—	17	12	Sollars, Jim
1995		NCAA	I	64	—	—	—	—	—	—	—	—	23	7	Sollars, Jim
1996		NCAA	I	64	—	—	—	—	—	—	—	—	23	7	Sollars, Jim
1997		NCAA	I	64	—	—	—	—	—	—	—	—	27	3	Sollars, Jim

PORTLAND STATE

Year	M/W	Assn	Div	NAT	NIT	ARC	CCA	NCI	NCT	OLY	HLM	W	L	Coach
1955	M	NAIA		32	—	—	—	—	—	—	—	—	30	9	Nelson, Loyal D. "Sharkey"
1956		NAIA		32	—	—	—	—	—	—	—	—	21	8	Nelson, Loyal D. "Sharkey"
1967		NCAA	II	32	—	—	—	—	—	—	—	—	16	9	Pericin, Marion J.
1976	W	AIAW	L	16	—	—	—	—	—	—	—	—	19	13	Nelson, Loyal D. "Sharkey"
1992		NCAA	II	3	—	—	—	—	—	—	—	—	31	3	Bruce, Greg
1993		NCAA	II	16	—	—	—	—	—	—	—	—	21	8	Bruce, Greg
1994		NCAA	II	16	—	—	—	—	—	—	—	—	25	4	Bruce, Greg
1995		NCAA	II	2	—	—	—	—	—	—	—	—	26	6	Bruce, Greg
1996		NCAA	II	8	—	—	—	—	—	—	—	—	25	5	Bruce, Greg

POTSDAM STATE

Year	M/W	Assn	Div	NAT	NIT	ARC	CCA	NCI	NCT	OLY	HLM	W	L	Coach
1966	M	NCAA	II	36	—	—	—	—	—	—	—	—	16	5	LaGrand, Lou
1973		NCAA	II	32	—	—	—	—	—	—	—	—	18	6	Welsh, John Gerald "Jerry"
1974		NCAA	II	32	—	—	—	—	—	—	—	—	18	9	Welsh, John Gerald "Jerry"
1978		NCAA	III	23	—	—	—	—	—	—	—	—	15	9	Welsh, John Gerald "Jerry"
1979		NCAA	III	2	—	—	—	—	—	—	—	—	24	7	Welsh, John Gerald "Jerry"
1980		NCAA	III	8	—	—	—	—	—	—	—	—	26	4	Welsh, John Gerald "Jerry"
1981		NCAA	III	1	—	—	—	—	—	—	—	—	30	2	Welsh, John Gerald "Jerry"
1982		NCAA	III	2	—	—	—	—	—	—	—	—	20	10	Welsh, John Gerald "Jerry"
1983		NCAA	III	8	—	—	—	—	—	—	—	—	23	6	Welsh, John Gerald "Jerry"
1984		NCAA	III	16	—	—	—	—	—	—	—	—	21	7	Welsh, John Gerald "Jerry"
1985		NCAA	III	2	—	—	—	—	—	—	—	—	27	4	Welsh, John Gerald "Jerry"
1986		NCAA	III	1	—	—	—	—	—	—	—	—	32	0	Welsh, John Gerald "Jerry"
1987		NCAA	III	8	—	—	—	—	—	—	—	—	28	1	Welsh, John Gerald "Jerry"
1988		NCAA	III	24	—	—	—	—	—	—	—	—	24	5	Welsh, John Gerald "Jerry"
1989		NCAA	III	8	—	—	—	—	—	—	—	—	24	5	Welsh, John Gerald "Jerry"
1990		NCAA	III	32	—	—	—	—	—	—	—	—	23	5	Welsh, John Gerald "Jerry"

PRACTICAL BIBLE

Year	M/W	Assn	Div	NAT	NIT	ARC	CCA	NCI	NCT	OLY	HLM	W	L	Coach
1996	M	NCCAA	IIA	8	—	—	—	—	—	—	—	—	13	17	Howard, Russ
1997	W	NCCAA	II	5	—	—	—	—	—	—	—	—	14	9	Carman, Becki

PRAIRIE VIEW A&M

Year	M/W	Assn	Div	NAT	NIT	ARC	CCA	NCI	NCT	OLY	HLM	W	L	Coach
1960	M	NCAA	II	16	—	—	—	—	—	—	—	—	21	5	Moore, Dr. Leroy G., Jr.
1961		NCAA	II	16	—	—	—	—	—	—	—	—	25	2	Moore, Dr. Leroy G., Jr.
1962		NAIA		1	—	—	—	—	—	—	—	—	20	3	Moore, Dr. Leroy G., Jr.
1998		NCAA	I	64	—	—	—	—	—	—	—	—	13	17	Plummer, Elwood

PRATT

Year	M/W	Assn	Div	NAT	NIT	ARC	CCA	NCI	NCT	OLY	HLM	W	L	Coach
1962	M	NAIA		32	—	—	—	—	—	—	—	—	19	5	Picariello, Saverio J. "Pic"

Year	M/W	Assn	Div	NAT	NIT	ARC	CCA	NCI	NCT	OLY	HLM	W	L	Coach

PRESBYTERIAN

Year	M/W	Assn	Div	NAT	NIT	ARC	CCA	NCI	NCT	OLY	HLM	W	L	Coach
1993	M	NAIA	I	32	—	—	—	—	—	—	—	27	5	Nibert, Gregg
1996		NCAA	II	48	—	—	—	—	—	—	—	19	11	Nibert, Gregg
1997		NCAA	II	32	—	—	—	—	—	—	—	20	7	Nibert, Gregg
1994	W	NCAA	II	32	—	—	—	—	—	—	—	22	8	Couture, Beth
1995		NCAA	II	48	—	—	—	—	—	—	—	23	7	Couture, Beth
1998		NCAA	II	32	—	—	—	—	—	—	—	23	8	Couture, Beth

PRINCETON

Year	M/W	Assn	Div	NAT	NIT	ARC	CCA	NCI	NCT	OLY	HLM	W	L	Coach
1925	M	NCAA		—	—	—	—	—	—	—	1	21	2	Wittmer, Albert, Jr.
1952		NCAA		16	—	—	—	—	—	—	—	16	11	Cappon, Franklin C. "Cappy"
1955		NCAA		16	—	—	—	—	—	—	—	13	12	Cappon, Franklin C. "Cappy"
1960		NCAA	I	25	—	—	—	—	—	—	—	15	9	Cappon, Franklin C. "Cappy"
1961		NCAA	I	16	—	—	—	—	—	—	—	18	8	McCandles, J. L. "Jake"
1963		NCAA	I	25	—	—	—	—	—	—	—	19	6	Van Breda Kolff, Willem "Butch"
1964		NCAA	I	16	—	—	—	—	—	—	—	20	9	Van Breda Kolff, Willem "Butch"
1965		NCAA	I	3	—	—	—	—	—	—	—	23	6	Van Breda Kolff, Willem "Butch"
1967		NCAA	I	12	—	—	—	—	—	—	—	25	3	Van Breda Kolff, Willem "Butch"
1969		NCAA	I	25	—	—	—	—	—	—	—	19	7	Carril, Peter J.
1972		NCAA	I	—	8	—	—	—	—	—	—	20	7	Carril, Peter J.
1975		NCAA	I	—	1	—	—	—	—	—	—	22	8	Carril, Peter J.
1976		NCAA	I	32	—	—	—	—	—	—	—	22	5	Carril, Peter J.
1977		NCAA	I	32	—	—	—	—	—	—	—	21	5	Carril, Peter J.
1981		NCAA	I	48	—	—	—	—	—	—	—	18	10	Carril, Peter J.
1983		NCAA	I	32	—	—	—	—	—	—	—	20	9	Carril, Peter J.
1984		NCAA	I	48	—	—	—	—	—	—	—	18	10	Carril, Peter J.
1989		NCAA	I	64	—	—	—	—	—	—	—	19	8	Carril, Peter J.
1990		NCAA	I	64	—	—	—	—	—	—	—	20	7	Carril, Peter J.
1991		NCAA	I	64	—	—	—	—	—	—	—	24	3	Carril, Peter J.
1992		NCAA	I	64	—	—	—	—	—	—	—	22	6	Carril, Peter J.
1996		NCAA	I	32	—	—	—	—	—	—	—	22	7	Carril, Peter J.
1997		NCAA	I	64	—	—	—	—	—	—	—	24	4	Carmody, Bill
1998		NCAA	I	32	—	—	—	—	—	—	—	27	2	Carmody, Bill
1976	W	AIAW	S	8	—	—	—	—	—	—	—	17	8	Walsh, Patricia
1996		NCAA	I	—	7	—	—	—	—	—	—	20	11	Feeney, Liz

PROVIDENCE

Year	M/W	Assn	Div	NAT	NIT	ARC	CCA	NCI	NCT	OLY	HLM	W	L	Coach
1950	M	NCAA		—	—	—	—	8	—	—	—	14	9	Cuddy, James V. "Viv"
1951		NAIA		32	—	—	—	—	—	—	—	14	10	Cuddy, James V. "Viv"
1952		NCAA		—	—	—	—	12	—	—	—	14	9	Cuddy, James V. "Viv"
1959		NCAA	I	—	4	—	—	—	—	—	—	20	7	Mullaney, Joseph A., Sr.
1960		NCAA	I	—	2	—	—	—	—	—	—	24	5	Mullaney, Joseph A., Sr.
1961		NCAA	I	—	1	—	—	—	—	—	—	24	5	Mullaney, Joseph A., Sr.
1962		NCAA	I	—	12	—	—	—	—	—	—	20	6	Mullaney, Joseph A., Sr.
1963		NCAA	I	—	1	—	—	—	—	—	—	24	4	Mullaney, Joseph A., Sr.
1964		NCAA	I	25	—	—	—	—	—	—	—	20	6	Mullaney, Joseph A., Sr.
1965		NCAA	I	8	—	—	—	—	—	—	—	24	2	Mullaney, Joseph A., Sr.
1966		NCAA	I	22	—	—	—	—	—	—	—	22	5	Mullaney, Joseph A., Sr.
1967		NCAA	I	—	8	—	—	—	—	—	—	21	7	Mullaney, Joseph A., Sr.

Year	M/W	Assn	Div	NAT	NIT	ARC	CCA	NCI	NCT	OLY	HLM	W	L	Coach
1971		NCAA	I	—	8	—	—	—	—	—	—	20	8	Gavitt, David R.
1972		NCAA	I	25	—	—	—	—	—	—	—	21	6	Gavitt, David R.
1973		NCAA	I	4	—	—	—	—	—	—	—	27	4	Gavitt, David R.
1974		NCAA	I	12	—	—	—	—	—	—	—	28	4	Gavitt, David R.
1975		NCAA	I	—	2	—	—	—	—	—	—	20	4	Gavitt, David R.
1976		NCAA	I	—	4	—	—	—	—	—	—	21	11	Gavitt, David R.
1977		NCAA	I	32	—	—	—	—	—	—	—	24	5	Gavitt, David R.
1978		NCAA	I	32	—	—	—	—	—	—	—	24	8	Gavitt, David R.
1986		NCAA	I	—	8	—	—	—	—	—	—	17	14	Pitino, Richard A. "Rick"
1987		NCAA	I	3	—	—	—	—	—	—	—	25	9	Pitino, Richard A. "Rick"
1989		NCAA	I	64	—	—	—	—	—	—	—	18	11	Barnes, Richard D. "Rick"
1990		NCAA	I	64	—	—	—	—	—	—	—	17	12	Barnes, Richard D. "Rick"
1991		NCAA	I	—	8	—	—	—	—	—	—	19	13	Barnes, Richard D. "Rick"
1993		NCAA	I	—	4	—	—	—	—	—	—	20	13	Barnes, Richard D. "Rick"
1994		NCAA	I	64	—	—	—	—	—	—	—	20	10	Barnes, Richard D. "Rick"
1995		NCAA	I	—	16	—	—	—	—	—	—	17	13	Gillen, Pete
1996		NCAA	I	—	16	—	—	—	—	—	—	18	12	Gillen, Pete
1997		NCAA	I	8	—	—	—	—	—	—	—	24	12	Gillen, Pete
1980	W	AIAW	I	16	—	—	—	—	—	—	—	22	7	Gilbride, Timothy J.
1986		NCAA	I	40	—	—	—	—	—	—	—	24	6	Foley, Bob
1987		NCAA	I	—	4	—	—	—	—	—	—	23	9	Foley, Bob
1989		NCAA	I	48	—	—	—	—	—	—	—	22	11	Foley, Bob
1990		NCAA	I	16	—	—	—	—	—	—	—	27	5	Foley, Bob
1991		NCAA	I	32	—	—	—	—	—	—	—	26	6	Foley, Bob
1992		NCAA	I	48	—	—	—	—	—	—	—	21	9	Foley, Bob

PUGET SOUND

Year	M/W	Assn	Div	NAT	NIT	ARC	CCA	NCI	NCT	OLY	HLM	W	L	Coach
1949	M	NAIA		32	—	—	—	—	—	—	—	21	6	Heinrick, John P.
1950		NAIA		16	—	—	—	—	—	—	—	19	12	Heinrick, John P.
1970		NCAA	II	16	—	—	—	—	—	—	—	24	4	Zech, Don
1971		NCAA	II	8	—	—	—	—	—	—	—	21	5	Zech, Don
1973		NCAA	II	32	—	—	—	—	—	—	—	19	9	Zech, Don
1975		NCAA	II	16	—	—	—	—	—	—	—	17	10	Zech, Don
1976		NCAA	II	1	—	—	—	—	—	—	—	27	7	Zech, Don
1977		NCAA	II	16	—	—	—	—	—	—	—	22	7	Zech, Don
1978		NCAA	II	24	—	—	—	—	—	—	—	20	10	Zech, Don
1979		NCAA	II	8	—	—	—	—	—	—	—	23	6	Zech, Don
1980		NCAA	II	24	—	—	—	—	—	—	—	21	8	Zech, Don
1981		NCAA	II	8	—	—	—	—	—	—	—	24	5	Zech, Don
1984		NCAA	II	16	—	—	—	—	—	—	—	22	8	Zech, Don
1982	W	AIAW	III	16	—	—	—	—	—	—	—	18	16	Hovde, Chet
1997		NAIA	II	32	—	—	—	—	—	—	—	22	5	Bricker, Dr. Beth
1998		NAIA	II	32	—	—	—	—	—	—	—	15	13	Bricker, Dr. Beth

PUGET SOUND CHRISTIAN

Year	M/W	Assn	Div	NAT	NIT	ARC	CCA	NCI	NCT	OLY	HLM	W	L	Coach
1994	M	NBCAA	II	7	—	—	—	—	—	—	—	15	10	McNichols, Troy
1995		NBCAA	II	1	—	—	—	—	—	—	—	17	11	McNichols, Troy
1996		NBCAA	II	2	—	—	—	—	—	—	—	17	13	McNichols, Troy
1998		NBCAA		5	—	—	—	—	—	—	—	18	13	McNichols, Troy

Year	M/W	Assn	Div	NAT	NIT	ARC	CCA	NCI	NCT	OLY	HLM	W	L	Coach
PURDUE														
1932	M	NCAA		—	—	—	—	—	—	—	1	17	1	Lambert, Ward L. "Piggy"
1969		NCAA	I	2	—	—	—	—	—	—	—	23	5	King, George S., Jr.
1971		NCAA	I	—	16	—	—	—	—	—	—	18	7	King, George S., Jr.
1974		NCAA	I	—	1	—	—	—	—	—	—	21	9	Schaus, Frederick A.
1975		NCAA	I	—	—	—	3	—	—	—	—	17	11	Schaus, Frederick A.
1977		NCAA	I	32	—	—	—	—	—	—	—	19	9	Schaus, Frederick A.
1979		NCAA	I	—	2	—	—	—	—	—	—	27	8	Rose, Lee H.
1980		NCAA	I	3	—	—	—	—	—	—	—	23	10	Rose, Lee H.
1981		NCAA	I	—	3	—	—	—	—	—	—	21	11	Keady, Lloyd Eugene "Gene"
1982		NCAA	I	—	2	—	—	—	—	—	—	18	14	Keady, Lloyd Eugene "Gene"
1983		NCAA	I	32	—	—	—	—	—	—	—	21	9	Keady, Lloyd Eugene "Gene"
1984		NCAA	I	32	—	—	—	—	—	—	—	22	7	Keady, Lloyd Eugene "Gene"
1985		NCAA	I	64	—	—	—	—	—	—	—	20	9	Keady, Lloyd Eugene "Gene"
1986		NCAA	I	64	—	—	—	—	—	—	—	22	10	Keady, Lloyd Eugene "Gene"
1987		NCAA	I	32	—	—	—	—	—	—	—	25	5	Keady, Lloyd Eugene "Gene"
1988		NCAA	I	16	—	—	—	—	—	—	—	29	4	Keady, Lloyd Eugene "Gene"
1990		NCAA	I	32	—	—	—	—	—	—	—	22	8	Keady, Lloyd Eugene "Gene"
1991		NCAA	I	64	—	—	—	—	—	—	—	17	12	Keady, Lloyd Eugene "Gene"
1992		NCAA	I	—	8	—	—	—	—	—	—	18	15	Keady, Lloyd Eugene "Gene"
1993		NCAA	I	64	—	—	—	—	—	—	—	18	10	Keady, Lloyd Eugene "Gene"
1994		NCAA	I	8	—	—	—	—	—	—	—	29	5	Keady, Lloyd Eugene "Gene"
1995		NCAA	I	32	—	—	—	—	—	—	—	25	7	Keady, Lloyd Eugene "Gene"
1996		NCAA	I	32	—	—	—	—	—	—	—	26	6	Keady, Lloyd Eugene "Gene"
1997		NCAA	I	32	—	—	—	—	—	—	—	18	12	Keady, Lloyd Eugene "Gene"
1998		NCAA	I	16	—	—	—	—	—	—	—	28	8	Keady, Lloyd Eugene "Gene"
1969	W	AIAW		6	—	—	—	—	—	—	—	X	X	Unknown
1988		NCAA	I	—	2	—	—	—	—	—	—	21	10	Dunn, Lin
1989		NCAA	I	32	—	—	—	—	—	—	—	24	6	Dunn, Lin
1990		NCAA	I	16	—	—	—	—	—	—	—	23	7	Dunn, Lin
1991		NCAA	I	32	—	—	—	—	—	—	—	26	3	Dunn, Lin
1992		NCAA	I	16	—	—	—	—	—	—	—	23	7	Dunn, Lin
1994		NCAA	I	3	—	—	—	—	—	—	—	29	5	Dunn, Lin
1995		NCAA	I	8	—	—	—	—	—	—	—	24	8	Dunn, Lin
1996		NCAA	I	64	—	—	—	—	—	—	—	20	11	Dunn, Lin
1997		NCAA	I	32	—	—	—	—	—	—	—	17	11	Fortner, Nell
1998		NCAA	I	8	—	—	—	—	—	—	—	23	10	Peck, Carolyn
PURDUE: CALUMET														
1996	W	NAIA	I	32	—	—	—	—	—	—	—	27	5	Hayes, Gary
QUEENS (NC)														
1996	M	NCAA	II	16	—	—	—	—	—	—	—	11	15	Layer, Dale
1998		NCAA	II	48	—	—	—	—	—	—	—	24	6	Layer, Dale
QUEENS (NY)														
1971	W	AIAW		12	—	—	—	—	—	—	—	23	4	Kyvallos, Lucille
1972		AIAW		5	—	—	—	—	—	—	—	27	2	Kyvallos, Lucille
1973		AIAW		2	—	—	—	—	—	—	—	22	5	Kyvallos, Lucille
1974		AIAW		8	—	—	—	—	—	—	—	22	4	Kyvallos, Lucille

Year	M/W	Assn	Div	NAT	NIT	ARC	CCA	NCI	NCT	OLY	HLM	W	L	Coach
1975		AIAW	L	12	—	—	—	—	—	—	—	—	19	8	Kyvallos, Lucille
1976		AIAW	L	12	—	—	—	—	—	—	—	—	20	5	Kyvallos, Lucille
1978		AIAW	L	8	—	—	—	—	—	—	—	—	24	3	Kyvallos, Lucille

QUINCY (IL)

Year	M/W	Assn	Div	NAT	NIT	ARC	CCA	NCI	NCT	OLY	HLM	W	L	Coach
1955	M	NAIA		16	—	—	—	—	—	—	—	—	14	8	Forester, Harry
1958		NAIA		32	—	—	—	—	—	—	—	—	17	11	Goff, James "Pim"
1964		NAIA		32	—	—	—	—	—	—	—	—	13	13	Ortwerth, John G.
1967		NAIA		32	—	—	—	—	—	—	—	—	17	14	Ortwerth, John G.
1978		NAIA		3	—	—	—	—	—	—	—	—	30	5	Hanks, Sherrill D.
1979		NAIA		8	—	—	—	—	—	—	—	—	23	10	Hanks, Sherrill D.
1982		NAIA		16	—	—	—	—	—	—	—	—	25	12	Hanks, Sherrill D.
1985		NAIA		32	—	—	—	—	—	—	—	—	15	17	Hanks, Sherrill D.
1986		NAIA		32	—	—	—	—	—	—	—	—	21	11	Hanks, Sherrill D.
1995		NCAA	II	24	—	—	—	—	—	—	—	—	22	7	Hawkins, Steve
1997		NCAA	II	32	—	—	—	—	—	—	—	—	20	9	Hawkins, Steve

QUINNIPIAC

Year	M/W	Assn	Div	NAT	NIT	ARC	CCA	NCI	NCT	OLY	HLM	W	L	Coach
1972	M	NAIA		32	—	—	—	—	—	—	—	—	21	9	Kahn, Burt
1973		NAIA		16	—	—	—	—	—	—	—	—	22	7	Kahn, Burt
1976		NCAA	II	32	—	—	—	—	—	—	—	—	19	9	Kahn, Burt
1979		NCAA	II	32	—	—	—	—	—	—	—	—	20	5	Kahn, Burt
1980		NCAA	II	24	—	—	—	—	—	—	—	—	22	7	Kahn, Burt
1988		NCAA	II	24	—	—	—	—	—	—	—	—	18	13	Kahn, Burt
1984	W	NCAA	II	8	—	—	—	—	—	—	—	—	28	3	Hanson, Ron
1985		NCAA	II	8	—	—	—	—	—	—	—	—	28	4	Hanson, Ron
1986		NCAA	II	16	—	—	—	—	—	—	—	—	25	4	Wolfson, Barry

RADFORD

Year	M/W	Assn	Div	NAT	NIT	ARC	CCA	NCI	NCT	OLY	HLM	W	L	Coach
1998	M	NCAA	I	64	—	—	—	—	—	—	—	—	20	10	Bradley, Ron
1989	W	NCAA	I	—	5	—	—	—	—	—	—	—	25	7	Curtis, Charlene
1994		NCAA	I	64	—	—	—	—	—	—	—	—	18	12	Lichonczak, Lubomyr
1995		NCAA	I	64	—	—	—	—	—	—	—	—	15	15	Lichonczak, Lubomyr
1996		NCAA	I	64	—	—	—	—	—	—	—	—	17	12	Lichonczak, Lubomyr

RAMAPO

Year	M/W	Assn	Div	NAT	NIT	ARC	CCA	NCI	NCT	OLY	HLM	W	L	Coach
1991	M	NCAA	III	4	—	—	—	—	—	—	—	—	24	8	Meyer, Todd

RANDOLPH-MACON

Year	M/W	Assn	Div	NAT	NIT	ARC	CCA	NCI	NCT	OLY	HLM	W	L	Coach
1965	M	NCAA	II	32	—	—	—	—	—	—	—	—	19	5	Webb, Paul E.
1966		NCAA	II	32	—	—	—	—	—	—	—	—	21	7	Webb, Paul E.
1974		NCAA	II	44	—	—	—	—	—	—	—	—	23	6	Webb, Paul E.
1975		NCAA	II	16	—	—	—	—	—	—	—	—	27	3	Webb, Paul E.
1977		NCAA	II	2	—	—	—	—	—	—	—	—	23	8	Nunnally, Hal
1981		NCAA	II	32	—	—	—	—	—	—	—	—	21	8	Nunnally, Hal
1983		NCAA	II	32	—	—	—	—	—	—	—	—	20	10	Nunnally, Hal
1984		NCAA	II	24	—	—	—	—	—	—	—	—	26	5	Nunnally, Hal
1985		NCAA	II	32	—	—	—	—	—	—	—	—	23	8	Nunnally, Hal
1990		NCAA	III	32	—	—	—	—	—	—	—	—	24	5	Nunnally, Hal
1991		NCAA	III	16	—	—	—	—	—	—	—	—	26	3	Nunnally, Hal
1996		NCAA	III	64	—	—	—	—	—	—	—	—	18	9	Nunnally, Hal
1998		NCAA	III	48	—	—	—	—	—	—	—	—	20	8	Nunnally, Hal

Year	M/W	Assn	Div	NAT	NIT	ARC	CCA	NCI	NCT	OLY	HLM	W	L	Coach
1996	W	NCAA	III	16	—	—	—	—	—	—	—	—	28	2	LaHaye, Carroll
1998		NCAA	III	32	—	—	—	—	—	—	—	—	21	6	LaHaye, Carroll

RANGER

Year	M/W	Assn	Div	NAT	NIT	ARC	CCA	NCI	NCT	OLY	HLM	W	L	Coach
1969	W			—	5	—	—	—	—	—	—	—	28	8	Butler, Ron
1970				—	5	—	—	—	—	—	—	—	21	9	Butler, Ron
1971				—	5	—	—	—	—	—	—	—	26	8	Butler, Ron
1972				—	8	—	—	—	—	—	—	—	24	10	Butler, Ron
1973				—	4	—	—	—	—	—	—	—	22	6	Butler, Ron
1974				—	5	—	—	—	—	—	—	—	20	10	Butler, Ron

REDLANDS

Year	M/W	Assn	Div	NAT	NIT	ARC	CCA	NCI	NCT	OLY	HLM	W	L	Coach
1961	M	NAIA		16	—	—	—	—	—	—	—	—	26	7	Fulmer, Lee
1964		NAIA		32	—	—	—	—	—	—	—	—	19	11	Fulmer, Lee
1985		NCAA	III	24	—	—	—	—	—	—	—	—	19	9	Smith, Gary H.

REDLANDS CC

Year	M/W	Assn	Div	NAT	NIT	ARC	CCA	NCI	NCT	OLY	HLM	W	L	Coach
1988	M	NSCAA		3	—	—	—	—	—	—	—				Imotichey, Melvin
1992		NSCAA		8	—	—	—	—	—	—	—	—	15	17	Imotichey, Melvin
1993		NSCAA		8	—	—	—	—	—	—	—	—	16	12	Imotichey, Melvin
1991	W	NSCAA		2	—	—	—	—	—	—	—	—	22	11	Story-Schell, Rita

REGIS (CO)

Year	M/W	Assn	Div	NAT	NIT	ARC	CCA	NCI	NCT	OLY	HLM	W	L	Coach
1949	M	NAIA		2	—	—	—	1	—	—	—	—	36	3	Varnell, Harry Lee
1950		NAIA		32	—	—	—	—	—	—	—	—	17	16	Varnell, Harry Lee
1951		NAIA		4	—	—	—	—	—	—	—	—	19	8	Varnell, Harry Lee
1954		NAIA		16	—	—	—	—	—	—	—	—	15	15	Moore, Harvey E.
1955		NAIA		32	—	—	—	—	—	—	—	—	14	14	Moore, Harvey E.
1957		NCAA	II	16	—	—	—	—	—	—	—	—	15	10	Moore, Harvey E.
1958		NCAA	II	16	—	—	—	—	—	—	—	—	14	9	Moore, Harvey E.
1963		NCAA	II	—	—	—	—	—	4	—	—	—	15	9	Hall, Joe B.
1995		NCAA	II	32	—	—	—	—	—	—	—	—	25	5	Porter, Lonnie
1996		NCAA	II	32	—	—	—	—	—	—	—	—	25	5	Porter, Lonnie

REGIS (MA)

Year	M/W	Assn	Div	NAT	NIT	ARC	CCA	NCI	NCT	OLY	HLM	W	L	Coach
1996	W	NCAA	III	64	—	—	—	—	—	—	—	—	23	4	Tanner, Donna

RENSSELAER

Year	M/W	Assn	Div	NAT	NIT	ARC	CCA	NCI	NCT	OLY	HLM	W	L	Coach
1945	M	NCAA		—	8	—	—	—	—	—	—	—	13	1	Donald, Edmund W. "Ed"
1958		NCAA	II	32	—	—	—	—	—	—	—	—	14	6	Kalbaugh, R. William, Sr.
1973		NCAA	II	42	—	—	—	—	—	—	—	—	16	9	Kalbaugh, R. William, Sr.
1975		NCAA	III	23	—	—	—	—	—	—	—	—	13	9	Kalbaugh, R. William, Sr.
1976		NCAA	III	28	—	—	—	—	—	—	—	—	17	9	Kalbaugh, R. William, Sr.
1991		NCAA	III	40	—	—	—	—	—	—	—	—	20	5	Griffin, Michael
1996		NCAA	III	16	—	—	—	—	—	—	—	—	20	8	Griffin, Michael

RHEMA BIBLE

Year	M/W	Assn	Div	NAT	NIT	ARC	CCA	NCI	NCT	OLY	HLM	W	L	Coach
1995	M	NBCAA	I	6	—	—	—	—	—	—	—	—	17	7	Ivey, Lance
1996		NBCAA	I	2	—	—	—	—	—	—	—	—	19	8	Ivey, Lance
1997		NBCAA	I	2	—	—	—	—	—	—	—	—	22	8	Ivey, Lance

Year	M/W	Assn	Div	NAT	NIT	ARC	CCA	NCI	NCT	OLY	HLM	W	L	Coach
RHODE ISLAND														
1941	M	NCAA		—	8	—	—	—	—	—	—	21	4	Keaney, Frank W.
1942		NCAA		—	8	—	—	—	—	—	—	18	4	Keaney, Frank W.
1945		NCAA		—	4	—	—	—	—	—	—	20	4	Keaney, Frank W.
1946		NCAA		—	2	—	—	—	—	—	—	22	3	Keaney, Frank W.
1961		NCAA	I	24	—	—	—	—	—	—	—	18	9	Calverley, Ernest A.
1966		NCAA	I	22	—	—	—	—	—	—	—	20	8	Calverley, Ernest A.
1978		NCAA	I	32	—	—	—	—	—	—	—	24	7	Kraft, John J. 'Jack'
1979		NCAA	I	—	24	—	—	—	—	—	—	20	9	Kraft, John J. 'Jack'
1981		NCAA	I	—	32	—	—	—	—	—	—	21	8	Kraft, John J. 'Jack'
1987		NCAA	I	—	32	—	—	—	—	—	—	20	10	Penders, Thomas V.
1988		NCAA	I	16	—	—	—	—	—	—	—	28	7	Penders, Thomas V.
1992		NCAA	I	—	8	—	—	—	—	—	—	22	10	Skinner, Albert L., Jr.
1993		NCAA	I	32	—	—	—	—	—	—	—	19	11	Skinner, Albert L., Jr.
1996		NCAA	I	—	8	—	—	—	—	—	—	20	14	Skinner, Albert L., Jr.
1997		NCAA	I	64	—	—	—	—	—	—	—	20	10	Skinner, Albert L., Jr.
1998		NCAA	I	8	—	—	—	—	—	—	—	25	9	Harrick, Jim
1996	W	NCAA	I	64	—	—	—	—	—	—	—	21	8	Ziemke, Linda L.
RHODE ISLAND COLLEGE														
1975	M	NCAA	III	30	—	—	—	—	—	—	—	16	9	Baird, William M.
1976		NCAA	III	7	—	—	—	—	—	—	—	17	9	Baird, William M.
1979		NCAA	III	32	—	—	—	—	—	—	—	21	7	Possinger, David F.
1981	W	AIAW	III	16	—	—	—	—	—	—	—	14	11	Conley, Joseph
1983		NCAA	III	16	—	—	—	—	—	—	—	16	7	Conley, Joseph
1985		NCAA	III	24	—	—	—	—	—	—	—	19	7	Chevalier, Dave
RHODES														
1980	M	NCAA	III	24	—	—	—	—	—	—	—	22	6	Hilgeman, Herb
1981		NCAA	III	16	—	—	—	—	—	—	—	23	3	Hilgeman, Herb
1993		NCAA	III	32	—	—	—	—	—	—	—	21	6	Hilgeman, Herb
RICE														
1940	M	NCAA		6	—	—	—	—	—	—	—	22	3	Brannon, Byron A. 'Buster'
1942		NCAA		8	—	—	—	—	—	—	—	22	5	Brannon, Byron A. 'Buster'
1943		NCAA		—	8	—	—	—	—	—	—	17	6	Davis, Joe W. 'Bloody Joe'
1954		NCAA		12	—	—	—	—	—	—	—	23	5	Suman, Donald W.
1970		NCAA	I	25	—	—	—	—	—	—	—	14	11	Knodel, Don
1991		NCAA	I	—	32	—	—	—	—	—	—	16	14	Thompson, Scott
1993		NCAA	I	—	16	—	—	—	—	—	—	18	10	Thompson, Scott
1998	W	NCAA	I	—	16	—	—	—	—	—	—	21	9	McKinney, Cristy
RICHARD STOCKTON														
1987	M	NCAA	III	4	—	—	—	—	—	—	—	23	8	Matthews, Gerald
1988		NCAA	III	24	—	—	—	—	—	—	—	22	5	Matthews, Gerald
1989		NCAA	III	40	—	—	—	—	—	—	—	19	8	Matthews, Gerald
1990		NCAA	III	16	—	—	—	—	—	—	—	21	8	Matthews, Gerald

Year	M/W	Assn	Div	NAT	NIT	ARC	CCA	NCI	NCT	OLY	HLM	W	L	Coach
1992		NCAA	III	40	—	—	—	—	—	—	—	18	9	Matthews, Gerald
1993		NCAA	III	32	—	—	—	—	—	—	—	21	6	Matthews, Gerald
1994		NCAA	III	16	—	—	—	—	—	—	—	20	7	Matthews, Gerald
1996		NCAA	III	8	—	—	—	—	—	—	—	26	4	Matthews, Gerald
1997		NCAA	III	16	—	—	—	—	—	—	—	22	7	Matthews, Gerald
1984	W	NCAA	III	16	—	—	—	—	—	—	—	20	7	Fussner, Joseph

RICHMOND

Year	M/W	Assn	Div	NAT	NIT	ARC	CCA	NCI	NCT	OLY	HLM	W	L	Coach
1982	M	NCAA	I	—	32	—	—	—	—	—	—	18	11	Tarrant, Dick
1984		NCAA	I	32	—	—	—	—	—	—	—	22	10	Tarrant, Dick
1985		NCAA	I	—	16	—	—	—	—	—	—	21	11	Tarrant, Dick
1986		NCAA	I	64	—	—	—	—	—	—	—	23	7	Tarrant, Dick
1988		NCAA	I	16	—	—	—	—	—	—	—	26	7	Tarrant, Dick
1989		NCAA	I	—	16	—	—	—	—	—	—	21	10	Tarrant, Dick
1990		NCAA	I	64	—	—	—	—	—	—	—	22	10	Tarrant, Dick
1991		NCAA	I	32	—	—	—	—	—	—	—	22	10	Tarrant, Dick
1992		NCAA	I	—	32	—	—	—	—	—	—	22	8	Tarrant, Dick
1998		NCAA	I	32	—	—	—	—	—	—	—	23	8	Beilein, John
1989	W	NCAA	I	—	8	—	—	—	—	—	—	24	9	Gaitley, Stephanie Vanderslice
1990		NCAA	I	48	—	—	—	—	—	—	—	25	5	Gaitley, Stephanie Vanderslice
1991		NCAA	I	48	—	—	—	—	—	—	—	26	5	Gaitley, Stephanie Vanderslice

RICKS

Year	M/W	Assn	Div	NAT	NIT	ARC	CCA	NCI	NCT	OLY	HLM	W	L	Coach
1953	M	NAIA		32	—	—	—	—	—	—	—	16	15	Parkinson, Berkley H. "Brick"

RIDER

Year	M/W	Assn	Div	NAT	NIT	ARC	CCA	NCI	NCT	OLY	HLM	W	L	Coach
1956	M	NAIA		32	—	—	—	—	—	—	—	16	7	Leyden, Thomas A.
1957		NCAA	II	8	—	—	—	—	—	—	—	20	7	Leyden, Thomas A.
1958		NAIA		32	—	—	—	—	—	—	—	17	8	Leyden, Thomas A.
1963		NAIA		32	—	—	—	—	—	—	—	20	8	Greenwood, Robert
1984		NCAA	I	53	—	—	—	—	—	—	—	20	11	Carpenter, John B.
1993		NCAA	I	64	—	—	—	—	—	—	—	19	11	Bannon, Kevin
1994		NCAA	I	64	—	—	—	—	—	—	—	21	9	Bannon, Kevin
1998		NCAA	I	—	32	—	—	—	—	—	—	18	10	Harnum, Donald

RIO GRANDE

Year	M/W	Assn	Div	NAT	NIT	ARC	CCA	NCI	NCT	OLY	HLM	W	L	Coach
1954	M	NAIA		16	—	—	—	—	—	—	—	20	7	Oliver, Newt
1985		NAIA		16	—	—	—	—	—	—	—	31	5	Lawhorn, John
1987		NAIA		32	—	—	—	—	—	—	—	28	8	Lawhorn, John
1991		NAIA		16	—	—	—	—	—	—	—	32	5	Lawhorn, John
1995		NAIA	I	32	—	—	—	—	—	—	—	26	10	Lawhorn, John
1994	W	NAIA	I	32	—	—	—	—	—	—	—	27	7	Smalley, David
1997		NAIA	I	32	—	—	—	—	—	—	—	23	12	Smalley, David

RIPON

Year	M/W	Assn	Div	NAT	NIT	ARC	CCA	NCI	NCT	OLY	HLM	W	L	Coach
1940	M	NAIA		32	—	—	—	—	—	—	—	14	6	Lamphear, George
1978		NCAA	III	30	—	—	—	—	—	—	—	15	10	Weiske, Kermit G. "Doc"
1980		NCAA	III	24	—	—	—	—	—	—	—	20	5	Weiske, Kermit G. "Doc"
1986		NCAA	III	16	—	—	—	—	—	—	—	19	6	Gillespie, Robert
1987		NCAA	III	32	—	—	—	—	—	—	—	17	8	Gillespie, Robert
1991		NCAA	III	32	—	—	—	—	—	—	—	21	5	Gillespie, Robert
1992		NCAA	III	40	—	—	—	—	—	—	—	19	6	Gillespie, Robert
1995		NCAA	III	64	—	—	—	—	—	—	—	19	6	Gillespie, Robert

Year	M/W	Assn	Div	NAT	NIT	ARC	CCA	NCI	NCT	OLY	HLM	W	L	Coach
1996		NCAA	III	64	—	—	—	—	—	—	—	—	21	4	Gillespie, Robert
1998		NCAA	III	48	—	—	—	—	—	—	—	—	23	2	Gillespie, Robert
1996	W	NCAA	III	64	—	—	—	—	—	—	—	—	20	5	Heinz, Julie

ROANOKE

Year	M/W	Assn	Div	NAT	NIT	ARC	CCA	NCI	NCT	OLY	HLM	W	L	Coach
1938	M	NAIA		2	—	—	—	—	—	—	—	—	19	2	White, Gordon C. 'Pap'
1939		NAIA		—	6	—	—	—	—	—	—	—	21	3	White, Gordon C. 'Pap'
1968		NCAA	II	32	—	—	—	—	—	—	—	—	22	8	Moir, Charles
1971		NCAA	II	32	—	—	—	—	—	—	—	—	23	8	Moir, Charles
1972		NCAA	II	1	—	—	—	—	—	—	—	—	28	4	Moir, Charles
1973		NCAA	II	8	—	—	—	—	—	—	—	—	23	6	Moir, Charles
1974		NCAA	II	24	—	—	—	—	—	—	—	—	24	6	Hankinson, Mel
1979		NCAA	II	32	—	—	—	—	—	—	—	—	25	3	Green, Ed
1981		NCAA	III	24	—	—	—	—	—	—	—	—	27	2	Green, Ed
1982		NCAA	III	8	—	—	—	—	—	—	—	—	27	4	Green, Ed
1983		NCAA	III	3	—	—	—	—	—	—	—	—	31	2	Green, Ed
1984		NCAA	III	16	—	—	—	—	—	—	—	—	27	2	Green, Ed
1985		NCAA	III	32	—	—	—	—	—	—	—	—	21	9	Green, Ed
1986		NCAA	III	32	—	—	—	—	—	—	—	—	16	14	Green, Ed
1987		NCAA	III	24	—	—	—	—	—	—	—	—	19	10	Green, Ed
1994		NCAA	III	32	—	—	—	—	—	—	—	—	26	2	Moir, Page
1995		NCAA	III	64	—	—	—	—	—	—	—	—	19	9	Moir, Page
1996		NCAA	III	16	—	—	—	—	—	—	—	—	24	5	Moir, Page
1997		NCAA	III	64	—	—	—	—	—	—	—	—	19	8	Moir, Page
1981	W	AIAW	III	16	—	—	—	—	—	—	—	—	21	6	Agee, Lynne
1990		NCAA	III	32	—	—	—	—	—	—	—	—	24	5	Dunagan, Susan
1991		NCAA	III	8	—	—	—	—	—	—	—	—	28	2	Dunagan, Susan
1992		NCAA	III	16	—	—	—	—	—	—	—	—	24	4	Dunagan, Susan
1993		NCAA	III	32	—	—	—	—	—	—	—	—	21	6	Dunagan, Susan
1994		NCAA	III	40	—	—	—	—	—	—	—	—	23	5	Dunagan, Susan
1995		NCAA	III	32	—	—	—	—	—	—	—	—	23	6	Dunagan, Susan
1996		NCAA	III	64	—	—	—	—	—	—	—	—	21	7	Dunagan, Susan
1997		NCAA	III	64	—	—	—	—	—	—	—	—	25	3	Dunagan, Susan
1998		NCAA	III	48	—	—	—	—	—	—	—	—	18	10	Dunagan, Susan

ROBERT MORRIS

Year	M/W	Assn	Div	NAT	NIT	ARC	CCA	NCI	NCT	OLY	HLM	W	L	Coach
1982	M	NCAA	I	48	—	—	—	—	—	—	—	—	17	13	Furjanic, Matt, Jr.
1983		NCAA	I	48	—	—	—	—	—	—	—	—	23	8	Furjanic, Matt, Jr.
1989		NCAA	I	64	—	—	—	—	—	—	—	—	21	9	Durham, Jarrett
1990		NCAA	I	64	—	—	—	—	—	—	—	—	22	8	Durham, Jarrett
1992		NCAA	I	64	—	—	—	—	—	—	—	—	19	12	Durham, Jarrett

ROBERTS WESLEYAN

Year	M/W	Assn	Div	NAT	NIT	ARC	CCA	NCI	NCT	OLY	HLM	W	L	Coach
1993	M	NCCAA	I	8	—	—	—	—	—	—	—	—	18	13	Sisson, Dr. Kenneth O.
1997		NCCAA	I	5	—	—	—	—	—	—	—	—	21	16	Sisson, George
1991	W	NCCAA	I	7	—	—	—	—	—	—	—	—	19	8	Faro, Michael
1992		NCCAA	I	7	—	—	—	—	—	—	—	—	13	13	Faro, Michael
1993		NCCAA	I	8	—	—	—	—	—	—	—	—	15	18	Faro, Michael
1995		NCCAA	I	8	—	—	—	—	—	—	—	—	10	19	Faro, Michael
1996		NCCAA	I	7	—	—	—	—	—	—	—	—	17	17	Faro, Michael
1997		NCCAA	I	5	—	—	—	—	—	—	—	—	22	12	Faro, Michael

Year	M/W	Assn	Div	NAT	NIT	ARC	CCA	NCI	NCT	OLY	HLM	W	L	Coach
ROCHESTER (MI)														
1982	M	NSCAA	16	—	—	—	—	—	—	—	—	17	5	Pleasant, Garth A.
1983		NSCAA	16	—	—	—	—	—	—	—	—	19	4	Pleasant, Garth A.
1984		NSCAA	2	—	—	—	—	—	—	—	—	25	5	Pleasant, Garth A.
1986		NSCAA	5	—	—	—	—	—	—	—	—	26	3	Pleasant, Garth A.
1987		NSCAA	10	—	—	—	—	—	—	—	—	21	9	Pleasant, Garth A.
1988		NSCAA	15	—	—	—	—	—	—	—	—	22	7	Pleasant, Garth A.
1989		NSCAA	1	—	—	—	—	—	—	—	—	25	3	Pleasant, Garth A.
1990		NSCAA	10	—	—	—	—	—	—	—	—	19	11	Pleasant, Garth A.
1991		NSCAA	12	—	—	—	—	—	—	—	—	10	20	Pleasant, Garth A.
1992		NSCAA	7	—	—	—	—	—	—	—	—	22	7	Pleasant, Garth A.
1994		NSCAA	2	—	—	—	—	—	—	—	—	19	10	Pleasant, Garth A.
1996		NSCAA	3	—	—	—	—	—	—	—	—	20	16	Pleasant, Garth A.
1997		NSCAA	2	—	—	—	—	—	—	—	—	17	14	Pleasant, Garth A.
1998		NSCAA	5	—	—	—	—	—	—	—	—	12	18	Pleasant, Garth A.
1997	W	NSCAA	3	—	—	—	—	—	—	—	—	14	13	Wheeler, Barry
1998		NSCAA	8	—	—	—	—	—	—	—	—	9	19	Wheeler, Barry
ROCHESTER (NY)														
1961	M	NCAA	II	24	—	—	—	—	—	—	—	17	6	Brown, Lyle D.
1962		NCAA	II	32	—	—	—	—	—	—	—	17	5	Brown, Lyle D.
1967		NCAA	II	34	—	—	—	—	—	—	—	15	7	Brown, Lyle D.
1968		NCAA	II	32	—	—	—	—	—	—	—	13	8	Brown, Lyle D.
1981		NCAA	III	16	—	—	—	—	—	—	—	20	7	Neer, Mike
1990		NCAA	III	1	—	—	—	—	—	—	—	27	5	Neer, Mike
1991		NCAA	III	8	—	—	—	—	—	—	—	23	7	Neer, Mike
1992		NCAA	III	2	—	—	—	—	—	—	—	28	3	Neer, Mike
1997		NCAA	III	64	—	—	—	—	—	—	—	15	11	Neer, Mike
1984	W	NCAA	III	32	—	—	—	—	—	—	—	21	5	Wong, Joyce
1985		NCAA	III	24	—	—	—	—	—	—	—	21	6	Wong, Joyce
1987		NCAA	III	24	—	—	—	—	—	—	—	22	7	Wong, Joyce
ROCHESTER TECH (NY)														
1976	M	NCAA	III	21	—	—	—	—	—	—	—	19	8	Catey, Bill
1995		NCAA	III	64	—	—	—	—	—	—	—	21	5	McVean, Robert
1996		NCAA	III	64	—	—	—	—	—	—	—	22	4	McVean, Robert
1997		NCAA	III	16	—	—	—	—	—	—	—	24	4	McVean, Robert
ROCKFORD														
1987	W	NCAA	III	16	—	—	—	—	—	—	—	25	2	Crick, Steve
ROCKHURST														
1946	M	NAIA		32	—	—	—	—	—	—	—	15	8	Powell, Bill
1956		NAIA		16	—	—	—	—	—	—	—	25	5	Brehmer, Joseph "Buddy"
1963		NAIA		8	—	—	—	—	—	—	—	27	4	Brehmer, Joseph "Buddy"
1964		NAIA		1	—	—	—	—	—	—	—	27	6	Brehmer, Joseph "Buddy"
1966		NAIA		8	—	—	—	—	—	—	—	20	8	Brehmer, Joseph "Buddy"
1967		NAIA		32	—	—	—	—	—	—	—	18	11	Rehm, J. Dolor
1980		NAIA		16	—	—	—	—	—	—	—	20	5	Reynolds, Jerry
1981		NAIA		32	—	—	—	—	—	—	—	22	3	Reynolds, Jerry

Year	M/W	Assn	Div	NAT	NIT	ARC	CCA	NCI	NCT	OLY	HLM	W	L	Coach
1991	W	NAIA		32	—	—	—	—	—	—	—	—	25	8	Rietzke, Tracy
1993		NAIA	I	32	—	—	—	—	—	—	—	—	30	2	Rietzke, Tracy
1994		NAIA	I	32	—	—	—	—	—	—	—	—	28	4	Rietzke, Tracy
1995		NAIA	I	32	—	—	—	—	—	—	—	—	24	7	Rietzke, Tracy
1996		NAIA	I	32	—	—	—	—	—	—	—	—	26	3	Rietzke, Tracy
1998		NAIA	I	16	—	—	—	—	—	—	—	—	23	6	Mitts, Maryann

ROCKY MOUNTAIN

Year	M/W	Assn	Div	NAT	NIT	ARC	CCA	NCI	NCT	OLY	HLM	W	L	Coach
1951	M	NAIA		32	—	—	—	—	—	—	—	—	17	14	Klindt, Herbert J.
1985		NAIA		32	—	—	—	—	—	—	—	—	23	10	Adams, Mark E. "Bucky"
1994		NAIA	I	32	—	—	—	—	—	—	—	—	17	14	Matlock, Gary
1988	W	NAIA		16	—	—	—	—	—	—	—	—	20	11	Malby, Jeff

ROGER WILLIAMS

Year	M/W	Assn	Div	NAT	NIT	ARC	CCA	NCI	NCT	OLY	HLM	W	L	Coach
1974	M	NAIA		32	—	—	—	—	—	—	—	—	20	4	Drennan, Thomas A.

ROLLINS

Year	M/W	Assn	Div	NAT	NIT	ARC	CCA	NCI	NCT	OLY	HLM	W	L	Coach
1974	M	NCAA	II	32	—	—	—	—	—	—	—	—	18	9	Jucker, Edwin L.
1976		NCAA	II	24	—	—	—	—	—	—	—	—	19	6	Jucker, Edwin L.
1979		NCAA	II	16	—	—	—	—	—	—	—	—	17	11	Jucker, Edwin L.
1992		NCAA	II	32	—	—	—	—	—	—	—	—	23	8	Klusman, Tom
1996		NCAA	II	48	—	—	—	—	—	—	—	—	20	8	Klusman, Tom
1995	W	NCAA	II	48	—	—	—	—	—	—	—	—	21	8	Wilkes, Glenn N., Jr.
1996		NCAA	II	48	—	—	—	—	—	—	—	—	23	6	Wilkes, Glenn N., Jr.

ROSE-HULMAN

Year	M/W	Assn	Div	NAT	NIT	ARC	CCA	NCI	NCT	OLY	HLM	W	L	Coach
1977	M	NCAA	III	8	—	—	—	—	—	—	—	—	24	4	Mutchner, John
1978		NCAA	III	30	—	—	—	—	—	—	—	—	20	7	Mutchner, John
1981		NCAA	III	32	—	—	—	—	—	—	—	—	18	7	Mutchner, John
1982		NCAA	III	24	—	—	—	—	—	—	—	—	18	10	Mutchner, John
1989		NCAA	III	24	—	—	—	—	—	—	—	—	19	8	Mutchner, John
1996		NCAA	III	64	—	—	—	—	—	—	—	—	19	9	Shaw, Jim
1997		NCAA	III	32	—	—	—	—	—	—	—	—	19	9	Shaw, Jim

ROWAN

Year	M/W	Assn	Div	NAT	NIT	ARC	CCA	NCI	NCT	OLY	HLM	W	L	Coach
1971	M	NAIA		16	—	—	—	—	—	—	—	—	21	6	Collins, Jack
1972		NAIA		32	—	—	—	—	—	—	—	—	16	9	Collins, Jack
1975		NCAA	III	2	—	—	—	—	—	—	—	—	21	10	Collins, Jack
1976		NCAA	III	21	—	—	—	—	—	—	—	—	18	10	Collins, Jack
1977		NCAA	III	23	—	—	—	—	—	—	—	—	17	11	Collins, Jack
1991		NCAA	III	32	—	—	—	—	—	—	—	—	20	8	Giannini, John
1993		NCAA	III	3	—	—	—	—	—	—	—	—	29	2	Giannini, John
1994		NCAA	III	16	—	—	—	—	—	—	—	—	26	2	Giannini, John
1995		NCAA	III	3	—	—	—	—	—	—	—	—	27	4	Giannini, John
1996		NCAA	III	1	—	—	—	—	—	—	—	—	28	4	Giannini, John
1997		NCAA	III	8	—	—	—	—	—	—	—	—	26	3	Cassidy, Joe
1998		NCAA	III	16	—	—	—	—	—	—	—	—	21	8	Cassidy, Joe
1988	W	NCAA	III	32	—	—	—	—	—	—	—	—	21	7	Bunting, Dawn Shilling
1992		NCAA	III	32	—	—	—	—	—	—	—	—	23	5	Bunting, Dawn Shilling
1993		NCAA	III	16	—	—	—	—	—	—	—	—	23	5	Bunting, Dawn Shilling
1994		NCAA	III	32	—	—	—	—	—	—	—	—	25	1	Crabtree, Candace

Year	M/W	Assn	Div	NAT	NIT	ARC	CCA	NCI	NCT	OLY	HLM	W	L	Coach
1996		NCAA	III	8	—	—	—	—	—	—	—	—	29	1	Crabtree, Candace
1997		NCAA	III	32	—	—	—	—	—	—	—	—	25	3	Crabtree, Candace
1998		NCAA	III	4	—	—	—	—	—	—	—	—	27	4	Crabtree, Candace

RUST

Year	M/W	Assn	Div	NAT	NIT	ARC	CCA	NCI	NCT	OLY	HLM	W	L	Coach
1976	M	NSCAA		3	—	—	—	—	—	—	—	—	24	13	Hayes, Naylond
1977		NSCAA		1	—	—	—	—	—	—	—	—	34	5	Hayes, Naylond
1983		NCAA	III	24	—	—	—	—	—	—	—	—	24	6	Hayes, Naylond
1987		NCAA	III	24	—	—	—	—	—	—	—	—	20	9	Hayes, Naylond
1988		NCAA	III	24	—	—	—	—	—	—	—	—	23	5	Hayes, Naylond
1989		NCAA	III	32	—	—	—	—	—	—	—	—	21	5	Hayes, Naylond
1997		NCAA	III	64	—	—	—	—	—	—	—	—	17	9	Stennis, Rodney E.
1983	W	NCAA	III	32	—	—	—	—	—	—	—	—	18	8	Stovall, Dr. Alfred J. "AJ"
1984		NCAA	III	1	—	—	—	—	—	—	—	—	26	5	Stovall, Dr. Alfred J. "AJ"
1985		NCAA	III	8	—	—	—	—	—	—	—	—	25	2	Stovall, Dr. Alfred J. "AJ"
1986		NCAA	III	4	—	—	—	—	—	—	—	—	21	5	Stovall, Dr. Alfred J. "AJ"
1987		NCAA	III	8	—	—	—	—	—	—	—	—	26	3	Stovall, Dr. Alfred J. "AJ"
1988		NCAA	III	16	—	—	—	—	—	—	—	—	21	4	Stovall, Dr. Alfred J. "AJ"

RUTGERS

Year	M/W	Assn	Div	NAT	NIT	ARC	CCA	NCI	NCT	OLY	HLM	W	L	Coach
1967	M	NCAA	I	—	3	—	—	—	—	—	—	22	7	Foster, William E.
1969		NCAA	I	—	16	—	—	—	—	—	—	21	4	Foster, William E.
1973		NCAA	I	—	16	—	—	—	—	—	—	15	11	Lloyd, Richard R.
1974		NCAA	I	—	16	—	—	—	—	—	—	18	8	Young, Thomas J.
1975		NCAA	I	32	—	—	—	—	—	—	—	22	7	Young, Thomas J.
1976		NCAA	I	4	—	—	—	—	—	—	—	31	2	Young, Thomas J.
1977		NCAA	I	—	16	—	—	—	—	—	—	18	10	Young, Thomas J.
1978		NCAA	I	—	3	—	—	—	—	—	—	24	7	Young, Thomas J.
1979		NCAA	I	16	—	—	—	—	—	—	—	22	9	Young, Thomas J.
1982		NCAA	I	—	16	—	—	—	—	—	—	20	10	Young, Thomas J.
1983		NCAA	I	32	—	—	—	—	—	—	—	23	8	Young, Thomas J.
1989		NCAA	I	64	—	—	—	—	—	—	—	18	13	Wenzel, Robert
1990		NCAA	I	—	8	—	—	—	—	—	—	18	17	Wenzel, Robert
1991		NCAA	I	64	—	—	—	—	—	—	—	19	10	Wenzel, Robert
1992		NCAA	I	—	16	—	—	—	—	—	—	16	15	Wenzel, Robert
1979	W	AIAW	L	12	—	—	—	—	—	—	—	28	4	Grentz, Theresa Shank
1980		AIAW	I	8	—	—	—	—	—	—	—	28	5	Grentz, Theresa Shank
1981		AIAW	I	16	—	—	—	—	—	—	—	27	6	Grentz, Theresa Shank
1982		AIAW	I	1	—	—	—	—	—	—	—	25	7	Grentz, Theresa Shank
1986		NCAA	I	8	—	—	—	—	—	—	—	29	4	Grentz, Theresa Shank
1987		NCAA	I	8	—	—	—	—	—	—	—	30	3	Grentz, Theresa Shank
1988		NCAA	I	16	—	—	—	—	—	—	—	27	5	Grentz, Theresa Shank
1989		NCAA	I	32	—	—	—	—	—	—	—	24	7	Grentz, Theresa Shank
1990		NCAA	I	48	—	—	—	—	—	—	—	20	10	Grentz, Theresa Shank
1991		NCAA	I	48	—	—	—	—	—	—	—	23	7	Grentz, Theresa Shank
1992		NCAA	I	32	—	—	—	—	—	—	—	21	11	Grentz, Theresa Shank
1993		NCAA	I	32	—	—	—	—	—	—	—	22	9	Grentz, Theresa Shank
1994		NCAA	I	64	—	—	—	—	—	—	—	22	8	Grentz, Theresa Shank
1998		NCAA	I	16	—	—	—	—	—	—	—	22	10	Stringer, C. Vivian

Year	M/W	Assn	Div	NAT	NIT	ARC	CCA	NCI	NCT	OLY	HLM	W	L	Coach
SACRED HEART (CT)														
1971	M	NCAA	II	24	—	—	—	—	—	—	—	—	22	6	Feeley, J. Donald
1972		NCAA	II	32	—	—	—	—	—	—	—	—	24	4	Feeley, J. Donald
1975		NCAA	II	32	—	—	—	—	—	—	—	—	20	8	Feeley, J. Donald
1977		NCAA	II	4	—	—	—	—	—	—	—	—	28	4	Feeley, J. Donald
1978		NCAA	II	8	—	—	—	—	—	—	—	—	21	9	Feeley, J. Donald
1981		NCAA	II	16	—	—	—	—	—	—	—	—	20	9	Bike, Dave
1982		NCAA	II	8	—	—	—	—	—	—	—	—	26	6	Bike, Dave
1983		NCAA	II	8	—	—	—	—	—	—	—	—	27	5	Bike, Dave
1984		NCAA	II	8	—	—	—	—	—	—	—	—	26	7	Bike, Dave
1985		NCAA	II	16	—	—	—	—	—	—	—	—	25	7	Bike, Dave
1986		NCAA	II	1	—	—	—	—	—	—	—	—	30	4	Bike, Dave
1987		NCAA	II	16	—	—	—	—	—	—	—	—	19	13	Bike, Dave
1989		NCAA	II	8	—	—	—	—	—	—	—	—	22	10	Bike, Dave
SAGE JC														
1969	M	NSCAA		3	—	—	—	—	—	—	—			
1970		NSCAA		8	—	—	—	—	—	—	—			
1971		NSCAA		3	—	—	—	—	—	—	—			
1977		NSCAA		8	—	—	—	—	—	—	—	16	6	
SAGINAW VALLEY STATE														
1980	M	NAIA		32	—	—	—	—	—	—	—	24	7	Pratt, Dr. Robert L.
1982		NAIA		8	—	—	—	—	—	—	—	24	8	Pratt, Dr. Robert L.
1983		NAIA		16	—	—	—	—	—	—	—	24	8	Pratt, Dr. Robert L.
1986		NAIA		32	—	—	—	—	—	—	—	20	11	Pratt, Dr. Robert L.
1981	W	NAIA		8	—	—	—	—	—	—	—	14	13	Reall, Marsha
1982		NAIA		3	—	—	—	—	—	—	—	27	5	Reall, Marsha
1983		NAIA		8	—	—	—	—	—	—	—	25	6	Reall, Marsha
1984		NAIA		8	—	—	—	—	—	—	—	30	1	Reall, Marsha
1985		NAIA		2	—	—	—	—	—	—	—	32	1	Reall, Marsha
1986		NAIA		8	—	—	—	—	—	—	—	24	3	Charney, Claudette
1987		NAIA		8	—	—	—	—	—	—	—	30	2	Charney, Claudette
1988		NAIA		16	—	—	—	—	—	—	—	25	7	Charney, Claudette
1993		NCAA	II	16	—	—	—	—	—	—	—	20	9	Charney, Claudette
1997		NCAA	II	48	—	—	—	—	—	—	—	19	11	Merchant, Suzy
SAINT AMBROSE														
1938	M	NAIA		8	—	—	—	—	—	—	—	15	5	Duford, Wilford J. "Dukes"
1939		NAIA		8	—	—	—	—	—	—	—	20	2	Duford, Wilford J. "Dukes"
1949		NCAA		—	—	—	—	16	—	—	—	12	9	O'Connor, James W.
1954		NAIA		16	—	—	—	—	—	—	—	20	3	Duax, Robert J.
1989		NAIA		16	—	—	—	—	—	—	—	26	8	Shovlain, Ray
1994		NAIA	II	16	—	—	—	—	—	—	—	24	10	Shovlain, Ray
1995		NAIA	II	16	—	—	—	—	—	—	—	24	12	Shovlain, Ray
1997		NAIA	II	32	—	—	—	—	—	—	—	24	12	Shovlain, Ray
1998		NAIA	II	32	—	—	—	—	—	—	—	20	16	Shovlain, Ray
1984	W	NAIA		16	—	—	—	—	—	—	—	28	4	Buckles, Ken
1987		NAIA		8	—	—	—	—	—	—	—	29	3	Bluder, Lisa
1988		NAIA		8	—	—	—	—	—	—	—	32	5	Bluder, Lisa
1989		NAIA		3	—	—	—	—	—	—	—	36	2	Bluder, Lisa

Year	M/W	Assn	Div	NAT	NIT	ARC	CCA	NCI	NCT	OLY	HLM	W	L	Coach
1990		NAIA		3	—	—	—	—	—	—	—	34	1	Bluder, Lisa
1992		NAIA	I	16	—	—	—	—	—	—	—	29	4	Osborn, Rhonda
1994		NAIA	I	16	—	—	—	—	—	—	—	27	6	Becker, Robin
1996		NAIA	II	8	—	—	—	—	—	—	—	30	6	Becker, Robin
1997		NAIA	II	32	—	—	—	—	—	—	—	28	6	Becker, Robin

SAINT ANDREWS PRESBYTERIAN

Year	M/W	Assn	Div	NAT	NIT	ARC	CCA	NCI	NCT	OLY	HLM	W	L	Coach
1981	M	NCAA	III	24	—	—	—	—	—	—	—	23	7	Riley, Doug
1982		NCAA	III	16	—	—	—	—	—	—	—	27	3	Riley, Doug
1983		NCAA	III	16	—	—	—	—	—	—	—	26	4	Riley, Doug
1982	W	NCAA	III	16	—	—	—	—	—	—	—	17	8	Graham, Betsy

SAINT ANSELM

Year	M/W	Assn	Div	NAT	NIT	ARC	CCA	NCI	NCT	OLY	HLM	W	L	Coach
1960	M	NCAA	II	16	—	—	—	—	—	—	—	15	4	Grenert, Albert F.
1962		NCAA	II	24	—	—	—	—	—	—	—	17	4	Grenert, Albert F.
1970		NCAA	II	32	—	—	—	—	—	—	—	14	11	Grenert, Albert F.
1986		NCAA	II	32	—	—	—	—	—	—	—	21	9	Brown, Robert D.
1987		NCAA	II	24	—	—	—	—	—	—	—	25	5	Dickson, Keith
1990		NCAA	II	16	—	—	—	—	—	—	—	21	11	Dickson, Keith
1993		NCAA	II	32	—	—	—	—	—	—	—	20	11	Dickson, Keith
1995		NCAA	II	24	—	—	—	—	—	—	—	26	5	Dickson, Keith
1996		NCAA	II	16	—	—	—	—	—	—	—	28	3	Dickson, Keith
1990	W	NCAA	II	16	—	—	—	—	—	—	—	25	4	Guimont, Donna M.
1991		NCAA	II	16	—	—	—	—	—	—	—	27	4	Guimont, Donna M.
1994		NCAA	II	32	—	—	—	—	—	—	—	22	9	Guimont, Donna M.
1995		NCAA	II	16	—	—	—	—	—	—	—	25	6	Guimont, Donna M.
1997		NCAA	II	48	—	—	—	—	—	—	—	20	9	Vermette, Bill

SAINT AUGUSTINE'S

Year	M/W	Assn	Div	NAT	NIT	ARC	CCA	NCI	NCT	OLY	HLM	W	L	Coach
1977	M	NAIA		32	—	—	—	—	—	—	—	24	8	Heartley, Harvey D.
1980		NAIA		16	—	—	—	—	—	—	—	24	7	Heartley, Harvey D.
1983		NCAA	II	16	—	—	—	—	—	—	—	22	6	Heartley, Harvey D.
1984		NCAA	II	2	—	—	—	—	—	—	—	23	7	Heartley, Harvey D.
1997		NCAA	II	16	—	—	—	—	—	—	—	25	8	Lee, Novell
1992	W	NCAA	II	32	—	—	—	—	—	—	—	23	3	Downing, Dr. Beverly
1993		NCAA	II	32	—	—	—	—	—	—	—	23	6	Downing, Dr. Beverly

SAINT BENEDICT

Year	M/W	Assn	Div	NAT	NIT	ARC	CCA	NCI	NCT	OLY	HLM	W	L	Coach
1989	W	NCAA	III	32	—	—	—	—	—	—	—	23	5	Durbin, Michael
1990		NCAA	III	32	—	—	—	—	—	—	—	21	7	Durbin, Michael
1991		NCAA	III	32	—	—	—	—	—	—	—	20	7	Durbin, Michael
1992		NCAA	III	16	—	—	—	—	—	—	—	22	6	Durbin, Michael
1993		NCAA	III	4	—	—	—	—	—	—	—	28	2	Durbin, Michael
1994		NCAA	III	16	—	—	—	—	—	—	—	22	5	Durbin, Michael
1995		NCAA	III	8	—	—	—	—	—	—	—	27	2	Durbin, Michael
1996		NCAA	III	64	—	—	—	—	—	—	—	19	7	Durbin, Michael
1997		NCAA	III	32	—	—	—	—	—	—	—	21	6	Durbin, Michael
1998		NCAA	III	16	—	—	—	—	—	—	—	25	2	Durbin, Michael

SAINT BERNARD

Year	M/W	Assn	Div	NAT	NIT	ARC	CCA	NCI	NCT	OLY	HLM	W	L	Coach
1961	M	NAIA		32	—	—	—	—	—	—	—	17	16	Richard, Charles W.

Year	M/W	Assn	Div	NAT	NIT	ARC	CCA	NCI	NCT	OLY	HLM	W	L	Coach
SAINT BONAVENTURE														
1951	M	NCAA		—	8	—	—	—	—	—	—	19	6	Melvin, Edward M. (Milkovich)
1952		NCAA		—	3	—	—	—	—	—	—	21	6	Melvin, Edward M. (Milkovich)
1957		NCAA	I	—	4	—	—	—	—	—	—	17	7	Donovan, Edward J. "Eddie"
1958		NCAA	I	—	3	—	—	—	—	—	—	21	5	Donovan, Edward J. "Eddie"
1959		NCAA	I	—	8	—	—	—	—	—	—	20	3	Donovan, Edward J. "Eddie"
1960		NCAA	I	—	4	—	—	—	—	—	—	21	5	Donovan, Edward J. "Eddie"
1961		NCAA	I	12	—	—	—	—	—	—	—	24	4	Donovan, Edward J. "Eddie"
1963		NCAA	I	—	—	—	—	2	—	—	—	13	12	Weise, Lawrence J.
1964		NCAA	I	—	12	—	—	—	—	—	—	16	8	Weise, Lawrence J.
1968		NCAA	I	16	—	—	—	—	—	—	—	23	2	Weise, Lawrence J.
1970		NCAA	I	4	—	—	—	—	—	—	—	25	3	Weise, Lawrence J.
1971		NCAA	I	—	3	—	—	—	—	—	—	21	6	Weise, Lawrence J.
1977		NCAA	I	—	1	—	—	—	—	—	—	23	6	Satalin, James D.
1978		NCAA	I	32	—	—	—	—	—	—	—	21	8	Satalin, James D.
1979		NCAA	I	—	24	—	—	—	—	—	—	19	9	Satalin, James D.
1983		NCAA	I	—	32	—	—	—	—	—	—	20	10	O'Brien, James J.
1995		NCAA	I	—	16	—	—	—	—	—	—	18	13	Baron, James E.
1998		NCAA	I	—	32	—	—	—	—	—	—	17	15	Baron, James E.
SAINT CATHARINE (KY)														
1975	M	NSCAA		16	—	—	—	—	—	—	—	X	X	Unknown
1977		NSCAA		8	—	—	—	—	—	—	—	24	7	Cheatham, Larry
1978		NSCAA		2	—	—	—	—	—	—	—	22	6	Spry, Ronald
SAINT CLOUD STATE														
1943	M	NAIA		16	—	—	—	—	—	—	—	12	3	Kasch, Warren
1946		NAIA		32	—	—	—	—	—	—	—	12	2	Lynch, George H.
1962		NAIA		16	—	—	—	—	—	—	—	22	4	Severson, Marlowe "Red"
1964		NAIA		16	—	—	—	—	—	—	—	19	5	Severson, Marlowe "Red"
1968		NAIA		16	—	—	—	—	—	—	—	25	4	Severson, Marlowe "Red"
1974		NCAA	II	32	—	—	—	—	—	—	—	17	12	Olson, Noel W.
1986		NCAA	II	16	—	—	—	—	—	—	—	26	4	Raymond, Lloyd E. "Butch"
1987		NCAA	II	8	—	—	—	—	—	—	—	24	7	Raymond, Lloyd E. "Butch"
1988		NCAA	II	24	—	—	—	—	—	—	—	26	4	Raymond, Lloyd E. "Butch"
1992		NCAA	II	32	—	—	—	—	—	—	—	20	12	Raymond, Lloyd E. "Butch"
1983	W	NCAA	II	8	—	—	—	—	—	—	—	31	4	Ziemer, Gladys L.
1984		NCAA	II	8	—	—	—	—	—	—	—	27	3	Ziemer, Gladys L.
1985		NCAA	II	8	—	—	—	—	—	—	—	24	6	Ziemer, Gladys L.
1987		NCAA	II	16	—	—	—	—	—	—	—	21	8	Ziemer, Gladys L.
1988		NCAA	II	32	—	—	—	—	—	—	—	18	10	Ziemer, Gladys L.
1989		NCAA	II	8	—	—	—	—	—	—	—	21	9	Ziemer, Gladys L.
1990		NCAA	II	32	—	—	—	—	—	—	—	23	5	Ziemer, Gladys L.
SAINT EDWARD'S														
1991	W	NAIA		8	—	—	—	—	—	—	—	31	2	McKey, David
1992		NAIA	I	3	—	—	—	—	—	—	—	30	3	McKey, David
1993		NAIA	I	8	—	—	—	—	—	—	—	28	3	McKey, David
SAINT FRANCIS (IL)														
1994	M	NAIA	I	32	—	—	—	—	—	—	—	16	15	Sullivan, Pat
1996		NAIA	I	32	—	—	—	—	—	—	—	19	10	Sullivan, Pat

Year	M/W	Assn	Div	NAT	NIT	ARC	CCA	NCI	NCT	OLY	HLM	W	L	Coach
SAINT FRANCIS (IN)														
1995	W	NAIA	II	32	—	—	—	—	—	—	—	20	12	Westendorf, Larry
1996		NAIA	II	16	—	—	—	—	—	—	—	20	12	Westendorf, Larry
1997		NAIA	II	8	—	—	—	—	—	—	—	28	8	Westendorf, Larry
1998		NAIA	II	8	—	—	—	—	—	—	—	31	6	Westendorf, Larry
SAINT FRANCIS (NY)														
1949	M	NAIA		—	—	—	—	2	—	—	—	21	12	Lynch, Daniel J.
1950		NAIA		—	—	—	—	2	—	—	—	8	19	Lynch, Daniel J.
1951		NAIA		—	—	—	—	1	—	—	—	19	11	Lynch, Daniel J.
1952		NAIA		—	—	—	—	4	—	—	—	20	8	Lynch, Daniel J.
1954		NAIA		—	8	—	—	—	—	—	—	22	5	Lynch, Daniel J.
1955		NAIA		32	—	—	—	—	—	—	—	21	8	Lynch, Daniel J.
1956		NAIA		—	4	—	—	—	—	—	—	21	4	Lynch, Daniel J.
1963		NCAA	I	—	12	—	—	—	—	—	—	16	7	Lynch, Daniel J.
SAINT FRANCIS (PA)														
1948	M	NAIA		32	—	—	—	—	—	—	—	15	8	Hughes, Dr. William T. "Skip"
1949		NAIA		—	—	—	—	8	—	—	—	16	11	Hughes, Dr. William T. "Skip"
1951		NCAA		—	—	—	—	8	—	—	—	19	4	Hughes, Dr. William T. "Skip"
1952		NCAA		—	—	—	—	2	—	—	—	23	7	Hughes, Dr. William T. "Skip"
1954		NCAA		—	8	—	—	—	—	—	—	21	5	Hughes, Dr. William T. "Skip"
1955		NCAA		—	4	—	—	—	—	—	—	21	7	Hughes, Dr. William T. "Skip"
1958		NCAA	I	—	12	—	—	—	—	—	—	20	5	Hughes, Dr. William T. "Skip"
1991		NCAA	I	64	—	—	—	—	—	—	—	24	8	Baron, James E.
1996	W	NCAA	I	64	—	—	—	—	—	—	—	19	11	Przekwas, Jenny
1997		NCAA	I	64	—	—	—	—	—	—	—	21	9	Przekwas, Jenny
1998		NCAA	I	64	—	—	—	—	—	—	—	22	8	Przekwas, Jenny
SAINT JOHN FISHER														
1979	M	NAIA		32	—	—	—	—	—	—	—	21	7	Wanzer, Robert F. "Bobby"
1992		NCAA	III	32	—	—	—	—	—	—	—	22	5	Ward, Robert
1994		NCAA	III	32	—	—	—	—	—	—	—	22	5	Ward, Robert
1995		NCAA	III	64	—	—	—	—	—	—	—	16	10	Ward, Robert
1996		NCAA	III	64	—	—	—	—	—	—	—	20	6	Ward, Robert
1997		NCAA	III	32	—	—	—	—	—	—	—	20	7	Ward, Robert
1998		NCAA	III	32	—	—	—	—	—	—	—	22	4	Ward, Robert
1980	W	AIAW	II	16	—	—	—	—	—	—	—	31	4	Kahler, Phillip I.
1987		NCAA	III	8	—	—	—	—	—	—	—	28	3	Kahler, Phillip I.
1988		NCAA	III	2	—	—	—	—	—	—	—	31	1	Kahler, Phillip I.
1989		NCAA	III	32	—	—	—	—	—	—	—	27	3	Kahler, Phillip I.
1990		NCAA	III	2	—	—	—	—	—	—	—	31	2	Kahler, Phillip I.
1991		NCAA	III	8	—	—	—	—	—	—	—	28	3	Kahler, Phillip I.
1992		NCAA	III	32	—	—	—	—	—	—	—	22	4	Kahler, Phillip I.
1993		NCAA	III	32	—	—	—	—	—	—	—	22	6	Kahler, Phillip I.
1994		NCAA	III	16	—	—	—	—	—	—	—	28	1	Kahler, Phillip I.
1995		NCAA	III	32	—	—	—	—	—	—	—	28	1	Kahler, Phillip I.
1996		NCAA	III	32	—	—	—	—	—	—	—	23	5	Kahler, Phillip I.
1997		NCAA	III	32	—	—	—	—	—	—	—	22	6	Kahler, Phillip I.

Year	M/W	Assn	Div	NAT	NIT	ARC	CCA	NCI	NCT	OLY	HLM	W	L	Coach
SAINT JOHN'S (MN)														
1969	M	NAIA		32	—	—	—	—	—	—	—	20	9	Smith, James E.
1978		NAIA		16	—	—	—	—	—	—	—	23	8	Smith, James E.
1979		NAIA		16	—	—	—	—	—	—	—	27	3	Smith, James E.
1983		NAIA		32	—	—	—	—	—	—	—	18	12	Smith, James E.
1984		NAIA		32	—	—	—	—	—	—	—	20	8	Smith, James E.
1985		NCAA	III	32	—	—	—	—	—	—	—	16	12	Smith, James E.
1986		NCAA	III	24	—	—	—	—	—	—	—	23	5	Smith, James E.
1988		NCAA	III	24	—	—	—	—	—	—	—	19	10	Smith, James E.
1993		NCAA	III	32	—	—	—	—	—	—	—	20	8	Smith, James E.
1995		NCAA	III	64	—	—	—	—	—	—	—	17	9	Smith, James E.
SAINT JOHN'S (NY)														
1911	M			—	—	—	—	—	—	—	1	14	0	Allen, Claude B.
1939		NCAA		—	4	—	—	—	—	—	—	18	4	Lapchick, Joseph B.
1940		NCAA		—	6	—	—	—	—	—	—	15	4	Lapchick, Joseph B.
1943		NCAA		—	1	2	—	—	—	—	—	21	3	Lapchick, Joseph B.
1944		NCAA		—	1	2	—	—	—	—	—	18	5	Lapchick, Joseph B.
1945		NCAA		—	3	—	—	—	—	—	—	21	3	Lapchick, Joseph B.
1946		NCAA		—	8	—	—	—	—	—	—	17	6	Lapchick, Joseph B.
1947		NCAA		—	8	—	—	—	—	—	—	16	7	Lapchick, Joseph B.
1949		NCAA		—	12	—	—	—	—	—	—	16	9	McGuire, Frank J.
1950		NCAA		—	3	—	—	—	—	—	—	24	5	McGuire, Frank J.
1951		NCAA		6	3	—	—	—	—	—	—	26	5	McGuire, Frank J.
1952		NCAA		2	8	—	—	—	—	8	—	25	5	McGuire, Frank J.
1953		NCAA		—	2	—	—	—	—	—	—	17	6	DeStefano, Alfred "Dusty"
1958		NCAA	I	—	4	—	—	—	—	—	—	18	8	Lapchick, Joseph B.
1959		NCAA	I	—	1	—	—	—	—	—	—	20	6	Lapchick, Joseph B.
1960		NCAA	I	—	8	—	—	—	—	—	—	17	8	Lapchick, Joseph B.
1961		NCAA	I	24	—	—	—	—	—	—	—	20	5	Lapchick, Joseph B.
1962		NCAA	I	—	2	—	—	—	—	—	—	21	5	Lapchick, Joseph B.
1965		NCAA	I	—	1	—	—	—	—	—	—	21	8	Lapchick, Joseph B.
1966		NCAA	I	—	14	—	—	—	—	—	—	18	8	Carnesecca, Louis P. "Lou"
1967		NCAA	I	16	—	—	—	—	—	—	—	23	5	Carnesecca, Louis P. "Lou"
1968		NCAA	I	23	—	—	—	—	—	—	—	19	8	Carnesecca, Louis P. "Lou"
1969		NCAA	I	16	—	—	—	—	—	—	—	23	6	Carnesecca, Louis P. "Lou"
1970		NCAA	I	—	2	—	—	—	—	—	—	21	8	Carnesecca, Louis P. "Lou"
1971		NCAA	I	—	16	—	—	—	—	—	—	18	9	Mulzoff, Frank
1972		NCAA	I	—	4	—	—	—	—	—	—	19	11	Mulzoff, Frank
1973		NCAA	I	25	—	—	—	—	—	—	—	19	7	Mulzoff, Frank
1974		NCAA	I	—	16	—	—	—	—	—	—	20	7	Carnesecca, Louis P. "Lou"
1975		NCAA	I	—	4	—	—	—	—	—	—	21	10	Carnesecca, Louis P. "Lou"
1976		NCAA	I	32	—	—	—	—	—	—	—	23	6	Carnesecca, Louis P. "Lou"
1977		NCAA	I	32	—	—	—	—	—	—	—	22	9	Carnesecca, Louis P. "Lou"
1978		NCAA	I	32	—	—	—	—	—	—	—	21	7	Carnesecca, Louis P. "Lou"
1979		NCAA	I	8	—	—	—	—	—	—	—	21	11	Carnesecca, Louis P. "Lou"
1980		NCAA	I	32	—	—	—	—	—	—	—	24	5	Carnesecca, Louis P. "Lou"
1981		NCAA	I	—	32	—	—	—	—	—	—	17	11	Carnesecca, Louis P. "Lou"
1982		NCAA	I	32	—	—	—	—	—	—	—	21	9	Carnesecca, Louis P. "Lou"

Year	M/W	Assn	Div	NAT	NIT	ARC	CCA	NCI	NCT	OLY	HLM	W	L	Coach
1983		NCAA	I	16	—	—	—	—	—	—	—	—	28	5	Carnesecca, Louis P. "Lou"
1984		NCAA	I	48	—	—	—	—	—	—	—	—	18	12	Carnesecca, Louis P. "Lou"
1985		NCAA	I	3	—	—	—	—	—	—	—	—	31	4	Carnesecca, Louis P. "Lou"
1986		NCAA	I	32	—	—	—	—	—	—	—	—	31	5	Carnesecca, Louis P. "Lou"
1987		NCAA	I	32	—	—	—	—	—	—	—	—	21	9	Carnesecca, Louis P. "Lou"
1988		NCAA	I	64	—	—	—	—	—	—	—	—	17	12	Carnesecca, Louis P. "Lou"
1989		NCAA	I	—	1	—	—	—	—	—	—	—	20	13	Carnesecca, Louis P. "Lou"
1990		NCAA	I	32	—	—	—	—	—	—	—	—	24	10	Carnesecca, Louis P. "Lou"
1991		NCAA	I	8	—	—	—	—	—	—	—	—	23	9	Carnesecca, Louis P. "Lou"
1992		NCAA	I	64	—	—	—	—	—	—	—	—	19	11	Carnesecca, Louis P. "Lou"
1993		NCAA	I	32	—	—	—	—	—	—	—	—	19	11	Mahoney, Brian C.
1995		NCAA	I	—	32	—	—	—	—	—	—	—	14	14	Mahoney, Brian C.
1998		NCAA	I	64	—	—	—	—	—	—	—	—	22	10	Fraschilla, Fran
1982	W	AIAW	I	16	—	—	—	—	—	—	—	—	25	7	Perrelli, Donald
1983		NCAA	I	32	—	—	—	—	—	—	—	—	27	6	Perrelli, Donald
1984		NCAA	I	32	—	—	—	—	—	—	—	—	24	6	Perrelli, Donald
1988		NCAA	I	32	—	—	—	—	—	—	—	—	22	10	Mullaney, Joseph A., Jr.

SAINT JOHN'S LUTHERAN (KS)

Year	M/W	Assn	Div	NAT	NIT	ARC	CCA	NCI	NCT	OLY	HLM	W	L	Coach
1983	M	NSCAA		12	—	—	—	—	—	—	—	—	9	19	Clausen, Julius

SAINT JOSEPH'S (IN)

Year	M/W	Assn	Div	NAT	NIT	ARC	CCA	NCI	NCT	OLY	HLM	W	L	Coach
1940	M	NAIA		32	—	—	—	—	—	—	—	—	16	7	Dienhart, Joseph S.
1970		NCAA	II	8	—	—	—	—	—	—	—	—	15	11	Holstein, James H.
1974		NCAA	II	8	—	—	—	—	—	—	—	—	20	6	Weinert, John P.
1975		NCAA	II	16	—	—	—	—	—	—	—	—	21	7	Weinert, John P.
1976		NCAA	II	32	—	—	—	—	—	—	—	—	17	11	Weinert, John P.
1978		NCAA	II	24	—	—	—	—	—	—	—	—	19	8	Waggoner, George
1979		NCAA	II	8	—	—	—	—	—	—	—	—	20	10	Waggoner, George
1992		NCAA	II	24	—	—	—	—	—	—	—	—	22	8	Peters, Dan
1988	W	NCAA	II	8	—	—	—	—	—	—	—	—	27	4	Smith, David R.
1989		NCAA	II	8	—	—	—	—	—	—	—	—	27	4	Smith, David R.
1990		NCAA	II	16	—	—	—	—	—	—	—	—	28	2	Smith, David R.
1992		NCAA	II	8	—	—	—	—	—	—	—	—	28	3	Freeman, Keith
1995		NCAA	II	48	—	—	—	—	—	—	—	—	19	9	Bland, Bill

SAINT JOSEPH'S (ME)

Year	M/W	Assn	Div	NAT	NIT	ARC	CCA	NCI	NCT	OLY	HLM	W	L	Coach
1987	M	NAIA		16	—	—	—	—	—	—	—	—	26	6	Simonds, Rick
1992		NAIA	II	16	—	—	—	—	—	—	—	—	24	6	Simonds, Rick
1993		NAIA	II	20	—	—	—	—	—	—	—	—	22	7	Scheinman, John
1996		NAIA	II	32	—	—	—	—	—	—	—	—	24	4	Simonds, Rick
1998		NAIA	II	32	—	—	—	—	—	—	—	—	24	5	Simonds, Rick
1987	W	NAIA		16	—	—	—	—	—	—	—	—	21	9	Stad, Bob
1988		NAIA		16	—	—	—	—	—	—	—	—	21	9	McDevitt, Michael
1991		NAIA		32	—	—	—	—	—	—	—	—	24	5	McDevitt, Michael
1992		NAIA	II	16	—	—	—	—	—	—	—	—	23	8	McDevitt, Michael
1993		NAIA	II	20	—	—	—	—	—	—	—	—	24	5	McDevitt, Michael
1994		NAIA	II	24	—	—	—	—	—	—	—	—	23	5	McDevitt, Michael

Year	M/W	Assn	Div	NAT	NIT	ARC	CCA	NCI	NCT	OLY	HLM	W	L	Coach
SAINT JOSEPH'S (PA)														
1952	M	NCAA		—	—	—	—	8	—	—	—	20	7	Ferguson, William J.
1956		NCAA		—	3	—	—	—	—	—	—	23	6	Ramsay, Dr. John T. "Jack"
1958		NCAA	I	—	8	—	—	—	—	—	—	18	9	Ramsay, Dr. John T. "Jack"
1959		NCAA	I	16	—	—	—	—	—	—	—	22	5	Ramsay, Dr. John T. "Jack"
1960		NCAA	I	16	—	—	—	—	—	—	—	20	7	Ramsay, Dr. John T. "Jack"
1961		NCAA	I	3	—	—	—	—	—	—	—	25	5	Ramsay, Dr. John T. "Jack"
1962		NCAA	I	16	—	—	—	—	—	—	—	18	10	Ramsay, Dr. John T. "Jack"
1963		NCAA	I	8	—	—	—	—	—	—	—	23	5	Ramsay, Dr. John T. "Jack"
1964		NCAA	I	—	8	—	—	—	—	—	—	18	10	Ramsay, Dr. John T. "Jack"
1965		NCAA	I	16	—	—	—	—	—	—	—	26	3	Ramsay, Dr. John T. "Jack"
1966		NCAA	I	12	—	—	—	—	—	—	—	24	5	Ramsay, Dr. John T. "Jack"
1969		NCAA	I	25	—	—	—	—	—	—	—	17	11	McKinney, John P. "Jack""
1971		NCAA	I	25	—	—	—	—	—	—	—	19	9	McKinney, John P. "Jack"
1972		NCAA	I	—	16	—	—	—	—	—	—	19	9	McKinney, John P. "Jack"
1973		NCAA	I	25	—	—	—	—	—	—	—	22	6	McKinney, John P. "Jack"
1974		NCAA	I	25	—	—	—	—	—	—	—	19	11	McKinney, John P. "Jack"
1979		NCAA	I	—	24	—	—	—	—	—	—	19	11	Lynam, James F.
1980		NCAA	I	—	32	—	—	—	—	—	—	21	9	Lynam, James F.
1981		NCAA	I	8	—	—	—	—	—	—	—	25	8	Lynam, James F.
1982		NCAA	I	48	—	—	—	—	—	—	—	25	5	Boyle, Jim
1984		NCAA	I	—	32	—	—	—	—	—	—	20	9	Boyle, Jim
1985		NCAA	I	—	16	—	—	—	—	—	—	19	12	Boyle, Jim
1986		NCAA	I	32	—	—	—	—	—	—	—	26	6	Boyle, Jim
1993		NCAA	I	—	32	—	—	—	—	—	—	18	11	Griffin, John
1995		NCAA	I	—	32	—	—	—	—	—	—	17	12	Griffin, John
1996		NCAA	I	—	2	—	—	—	—	—	—	19	13	Martelli, Phil
1997		NCAA	I	16	—	—	—	—	—	—	—	26	7	Martelli, Phil
1977	W	AIAW	L	12	—	—	—	—	—	—	—	23	5	Portland, Rene Muth
1985		NCAA	I	32	—	—	—	—	—	—	—	25	5	Foster, Jim
1986		NCAA	I	32	—	—	—	—	—	—	—	22	7	Foster, Jim
1987		NCAA	I	32	—	—	—	—	—	—	—	23	9	Foster, Jim
1988		NCAA	I	32	—	—	—	—	—	—	—	24	8	Foster, Jim
1989		NCAA	I	32	—	—	—	—	—	—	—	23	8	Foster, Jim
1990		NCAA	I	48	—	—	—	—	—	—	—	24	7	Foster, Jim
1994		NCAA	I	64	—	—	—	—	—	—	—	19	9	Gaitley, Stephanie Vanderslice
1995		NCAA	I	64	—	—	—	—	—	—	—	20	9	Gaitley, Stephanie Vanderslice
1997		NCAA	I	32	—	—	—	—	—	—	—	26	5	Gaitley, Stephanie Vanderslice
1998		NCAA	I	—	8	—	—	—	—	—	—	19	12	Gaitley, Stephanie Vanderslice
SAINT LAWRENCE														
1974	M	NCAA	II	44	—	—	—	—	—	—	—	17	6	Evans, Paul
1975		NCAA	III	16	—	—	—	—	—	—	—	20	6	Evans, Paul
1978		NCAA	III	16	—	—	—	—	—	—	—	19	6	Evans, Paul
1979		NCAA	III	16	—	—	—	—	—	—	—	18	7	Evans, Paul
1980		NCAA	III	32	—	—	—	—	—	—	—	22	5	Evans, Paul
1981		NCAA	III	24	—	—	—	—	—	—	—	20	6	Talbot, Leon
1984		NCAA	III	32	—	—	—	—	—	—	—	14	13	Talbot, Leon
1996		NCAA	III	32	—	—	—	—	—	—	—	18	9	Paulsen, David

Year	M/W	Assn	Div	NAT	NIT	ARC	CCA	NCI	NCT	OLY	HLM	W	L	Coach
1997		NCAA	III	64	—	—	—	—	—	—	—	22	4	Paulsen, David
1998		NCAA	III	8	—	—	—	—	—	—	—	24	2	Downs, Chris
1983	W	NCAA	III	32	—	—	—	—	—	—	—	17	5	Kowalik, Joan

SAINT LOUIS

Year	M/W	Assn	Div	NAT	NIT	ARC	CCA	NCI	NCT	OLY	HLM	W	L	Coach
1948	M	NCAA	—	1	—	—	—	—	—	—	—	24	3	Hickey, Edgar S. "Eddie"
1949		NCAA	—	8	—	—	—	—	—	—	—	22	4	Hickey, Edgar S. "Eddie"
1951		NCAA	—	8	—	—	—	—	—	—	—	22	8	Hickey, Edgar S. "Eddie"
1952		NCAA	8	8	—	—	—	—	—	—	—	23	8	Hickey, Edgar S. "Eddie"
1953		NCAA	—	12	—	—	—	—	—	—	—	16	11	Hickey, Edgar S. "Eddie"
1955		NCAA	—	8	—	—	—	—	—	—	—	20	8	Hickey, Edgar S. "Eddie"
1956		NCAA	—	12	—	—	—	—	—	—	—	20	8	Hickey, Edgar S. "Eddie"
1957		NCAA	I	16	—	—	—	—	—	—	—	19	9	Hickey, Edgar S. "Eddie"
1959		NCAA	I	—	8	—	—	—	—	—	—	20	6	Bennington, John E.
1960		NCAA	I	—	8	—	—	—	—	—	—	19	8	Bennington, John E.
1961		NCAA	I	—	2	—	—	—	—	—	—	21	9	Bennington, John E.
1963		NCAA	I	—	8	—	—	—	—	—	—	16	12	Bennington, John E.
1965		NCAA	I	—	14	—	—	—	—	—	—	18	9	Bennington, John E.
1987		NCAA	I	—	16	—	—	—	—	—	—	25	10	Grawer, Richard "Rich"
1989		NCAA	I	—	2	—	—	—	—	—	—	27	10	Grawer, Richard "Rich"
1990		NCAA	I	—	2	—	—	—	—	—	—	21	12	Grawer, Richard "Rich"
1994		NCAA	I	64	—	—	—	—	—	—	—	23	6	Spoonhour, Charles
1995		NCAA	I	32	—	—	—	—	—	—	—	23	8	Spoonhour, Charles
1996		NCAA	I	—	32	—	—	—	—	—	—	16	14	Spoonhour, Charles
1998		NCAA	I	32	—	—	—	—	—	—	—	22	11	Spoonhour, Charles

SAINT LOUIS CHRISTIAN

Year	M/W	Assn	Div	NAT	NIT	ARC	CCA	NCI	NCT	OLY	HLM	W	L	Coach
1992	M	NCCAA	IIA	8	—	—	—	—	—	—	—	8	22	Wolford, Danny
1993		NCCAA	IIA	6	—	—	—	—	—	—	—	12	21	Wolford, Danny
1998		NCCAA	IIA	7	—	—	—	—	—	—	—	9	25	Wolford, Danny
1990	W	NCCAA	II	8	—	—	—	—	—	—	—	9	6	Wolford, Danny

SAINT MARTIN'S

Year	M/W	Assn	Div	NAT	NIT	ARC	CCA	NCI	NCT	OLY	HLM	W	L	Coach
1995	W	NAIA	I	16	—	—	—	—	—	—	—	31	5	Peters, Ray

SAINT MARY'S (CA)

Year	M/W	Assn	Div	NAT	NIT	ARC	CCA	NCI	NCT	OLY	HLM	W	L	Coach
1959	M	NCAA	I	8	—	—	—	—	—	—	—	19	6	Weaver, James
1989		NCAA	I	64	—	—	—	—	—	—	—	25	5	Nance, Lynn
1997		NCAA	I	64	—	—	—	—	—	—	—	23	8	Kent, Ernie
1985	W	NAIA		16	—	—	—	—	—	—	—	21	9	Rubenstein, Terri

SAINT MARY'S (MD)

Year	M/W	Assn	Div	NAT	NIT	ARC	CCA	NCI	NCT	OLY	HLM	W	L	Coach
1998	W	NCAA	III	48	—	—	—	—	—	—	—	20	8	Hart, Shann

SAINT MARY'S (MI)

Year	M/W	Assn	Div	NAT	NIT	ARC	CCA	NCI	NCT	OLY	HLM	W	L	Coach
1985	M	NSCAA		4	—	—	—	—	—	—	—	15	17	Kolby, Jay
1986		NSCAA		10	—	—	—	—	—	—	—			Domke, Tim
1991		NAIA		8	—	—	—	—	—	—	—	6	19	Donahue, Glen
1992		NAIA	I	32	—	—	—	—	—	—	—	26	6	Donahue, Glen
1998		NSCAA		6	—	—	—	—	—	—	—	14	19	Daick, Chris

Year	M/W	Assn	Div	NAT	NIT	ARC	CCA	NCI	NCT	OLY	HLM	W	L	Coach
SAINT MARY'S (MN)														
1941	M	NAIA		16	—	—	—	—	—	—	—			
1985	W	NCAA	III	24	—	—	—	—	—	—	—	24	2	Wheeler, Lynn
1986		NCAA	III	24	—	—	—	—	—	—	—	23	2	Smith, Jim
SAINT MARY'S (TX)														
1964	M	NAIA		8	—	—	—	—	—	—	—	15	13	Messbarger, Ed
1967		NAIA		8	—	—	—	—	—	—	—	22	9	Messbarger, Ed
1974		NAIA		4	—	—	—	—	—	—	—	24	9	Messbarger, Ed
1975		NAIA		4	—	—	—	—	—	—	—	24	7	Messbarger, Ed
1981		NAIA		32	—	—	—	—	—	—	—	19	9	Meyer, Herbert "Buddy"
1982		NAIA		16	—	—	—	—	—	—	—	19	9	Meyer, Herbert "Buddy"
1983		NAIA		16	—	—	—	—	—	—	—	26	7	Meyer, Herbert "Buddy"
1984		NAIA		16	—	—	—	—	—	—	—	25	8	Meyer, Herbert "Buddy"
1987		NAIA		16	—	—	—	—	—	—	—	27	5	Meyer, Herbert "Buddy"
1989		NAIA		1	—	—	—	—	—	—	—	28	5	Meyer, Herbert "Buddy"
1991		NAIA		16	—	—	—	—	—	—	—	24	7	Meyer, Herbert "Buddy"
1994		NAIA	I	16	—	—	—	—	—	—	—	21	10	Meyer, Herbert "Buddy"
1995		NAIA	I	32	—	—	—	—	—	—	—	24	6	Meyer, Herbert "Buddy"
1996		NAIA	I	32	—	—	—	—	—	—	—	19	11	Meyer, Herbert "Buddy"
1997		NAIA	I	32	—	—	—	—	—	—	—	22	6	Meyer, Herbert "Buddy"
1998		NAIA	I	32	—	—	—	—	—	—	—	20	7	Meyer, Herbert "Buddy"
1995	W	NAIA	I	32	—	—	—	—	—	—	—	25	7	Weeaks, Thomas
1996		NAIA	I	32	—	—	—	—	—	—	—	20	11	Weeaks, Thomas
1997		NAIA	I	32	—	—	—	—	—	—	—	21	7	Weeaks, Thomas
SAINT MICHAEL'S (VT)														
1957	M	NCAA	II	16	—	—	—	—	—	—	—	17	6	Jacobs, George W. "Doc"
1958		NCAA	II	2	—	—	—	—	—	—	—	19	5	Jacobs, George W. "Doc"
1959		NCAA	II	8	—	—	—	—	—	—	—	19	7	Jacobs, George W. "Doc"
1960		NCAA	II	8	—	—	—	—	—	—	—	13	10	Jacobs, George W. "Doc"
1965		NCAA	II	4	—	—	—	—	—	—	—	21	7	Markey, Edward P.
1967		NCAA	II	16	—	—	—	—	—	—	—	23	4	Markey, Edward P.
1973		NCAA	II	32	—	—	—	—	—	—	—	18	9	Baumann, Walter E.
1974		NCAA	II	24	—	—	—	—	—	—	—	17	11	Baumann, Walter E.
1987		NCAA	II	32	—	—	—	—	—	—	—	20	11	Casciano, James Paul
1997		NCAA	II	32	—	—	—	—	—	—	—	23	7	Crowley, Tom
SAINT NORBERT														
1958	M	NCAA	II	32	—	—	—	—	—	—	—	14	11	Nicks, Mel J.
1961		NAIA		32	—	—	—	—	—	—	—	13	13	Kosnar, Romie R.
1962		NAIA		32	—	—	—	—	—	—	—	14	10	Kosnar, Romie R.
1965		NAIA		32	—	—	—	—	—	—	—	17	9	Kosnar, Romie R.
1984		NCAA	III	16	—	—	—	—	—	—	—	21	4	Heideman, Mike
1983	W	NCAA	III	32	—	—	—	—	—	—	—	20	7	Tilley, Connie L.
1985		NCAA	III	4	—	—	—	—	—	—	—	24	4	Tilley, Connie L.
1986		NCAA	III	16	—	—	—	—	—	—	—	20	2	Tilley, Connie L.
1987		NCAA	III	32	—	—	—	—	—	—	—	19	6	Tilley, Connie L.
1988		NCAA	III	16	—	—	—	—	—	—	—	17	5	Tilley, Connie L.
1989		NCAA	III	32	—	—	—	—	—	—	—	20	6	Tilley, Connie L.

Year	M/W	Assn	Div	NAT	NIT	ARC	CCA	NCI	NCT	OLY	HLM	W	L	Coach
SAINT OLAF														
1969	M	NCAA	II	32	—	—	—	—	—	—	—	17	7	Gelle, Robert D.
1971		NCAA	II	32	—	—	—	—	—	—	—	20	4	Gelle, Robert D.
1972		NCAA	II	32	—	—	—	—	—	—	—	18	7	Gelle, Robert D.
1992	W	NCAA	III	32	—	—	—	—	—	—	—	19	7	Buresh, Pat
SAINT PETER'S														
1953	M	NAIA		16	—	—	—	—	—	—	—	18	8	Kennedy, Don, Sr.
1954		NAIA		8	—	—	—	—	—	—	—	17	7	Kennedy, Don, Sr.
1957		NCAA	I	—	12	—	—	—	—	—	—	18	4	Kennedy, Don, Sr.
1958		NCAA	I	—	12	—	—	—	—	—	—	20	4	Kennedy, Don, Sr.
1967		NCAA	I	—	14	—	—	—	—	—	—	18	6	Kennedy, Don, Sr.
1968		NCAA	I	—	4	—	—	—	—	—	—	24	4	Kennedy, Don, Sr.
1969		NCAA	I	—	8	—	—	—	—	—	—	21	7	Kennedy, Don, Sr.
1975		NCAA	I	—	16	—	—	—	—	—	—	15	12	McDonald, James R. "Dick"
1976		NCAA	I	—	12	—	—	—	—	—	—	19	11	McDonald, James R. "Dick"
1980		NCAA	I	—	8	—	—	—	—	—	—	22	9	Dukiet, Bob
1982		NCAA	I	—	32	—	—	—	—	—	—	20	9	Dukiet, Bob
1984		NCAA	I	—	32	—	—	—	—	—	—	23	6	Dukiet, Bob
1987		NCAA	I	—	32	—	—	—	—	—	—	21	8	Fiore, Ted
1989		NCAA	I	—	32	—	—	—	—	—	—	22	9	Fiore, Ted
1991		NCAA	I	64	—	—	—	—	—	—	—	24	7	Fiore, Ted
1995		NCAA	I	64	—	—	—	—	—	—	—	19	11	Fiore, Ted
1980	W	AIAW	II	16	—	—	—	—	—	—	—	27	4	Granelli, Mike
1982		NCAA	I	32	—	—	—	—	—	—	—	26	4	Granelli, Mike
1992		NCAA	I	48	—	—	—	—	—	—	—	24	7	Granelli, Mike
1993		NCAA	I	48	—	—	—	—	—	—	—	18	11	Granelli, Mike
1997		NCAA	I	64	—	—	—	—	—	—	—	25	4	Granelli, Mike
SAINT ROSE														
1989	M	NAIA		32	—	—	—	—	—	—	—	28	5	Beaury, Brian
1991		NAIA		32	—	—	—	—	—	—	—	20	9	Beaury, Brian
1992		NCAA	II	24	—	—	—	—	—	—	—	24	7	Beaury, Brian
1995		NCAA	II	32	—	—	—	—	—	—	—	25	6	Beaury, Brian
1996		NCAA	II	8	—	—	—	—	—	—	—	28	4	Beaury, Brian
1997		NCAA	II	32	—	—	—	—	—	—	—	29	5	Beaury, Brian
1998		NCAA	II	3	—	—	—	—	—	—	—	27	6	Beaury, Brian
1995	W	NCAA	II	16	—	—	—	—	—	—	—	26	5	Bailey, Curt
1996		NCAA	II	16	—	—	—	—	—	—	—	26	5	Bailey, Curt
1997		NCAA	II	32	—	—	—	—	—	—	—	29	1	Bailey, Curt
1998		NCAA	II	16	—	—	—	—	—	—	—	33	1	Bailey, Curt
SAINT SCHOLASTICA														
1989	M	NSCAA		2	—	—	—	—	—	—	—	19	16	Nachtsheim, John
1990		NSCAA		8	—	—	—	—	—	—	—	18	12	Nachtsheim, John
1986	W	NSCAA		6	—	—	—	—	—	—	—	18	8	Stukel, Jim
1987		NSCAA		2	—	—	—	—	—	—	—	25	6	Stukel, Jim
1988		NSCAA		1	—	—	—	—	—	—	—	25	6	Stukel, Jim
SAINT TERESA														
1989	W	NSCAA		8	—	—	—	—	—	—				Boike, Lon

Year	M/W	Assn	Div	NAT	NIT	ARC	CCA	NCI	NCT	OLY	HLM	W	L	Coach
SAINT THOMAS (FL)														
1972	M	NCAA	II	16	—	—	—	—	—	—	—	17	10	Stibler, Kenneth
1973		NCAA	II	42	—	—	—	—	—	—	—	18	6	Stibler, Kenneth
1982		NCAA	II	24	—	—	—	—	—	—	—	15	13	Stibler, Kenneth
1994		NAIA	II	24	—	—	—	—	—	—	—	17	18	Tuell, Gary
1997		NAIA	II	32	—	—	—	—	—	—	—	17	17	Tuell, Gary
SAINT THOMAS (MN)														
1949	M	NAIA		16	—	—	—	8	—	—	—	22	7	Sokol, Paul
1950		NAIA		32	—	—	—	—	—	—	—	18	7	Sokol, Paul
1966		NAIA		32	—	—	—	—	—	—	—	24	4	Feely, Thomas J.
1967		NAIA		16	—	—	—	—	—	—	—	22	7	Feely, Thomas J.
1970		NAIA		32	—	—	—	—	—	—	—	26	3	Feely, Thomas J.
1971		NAIA		32	—	—	—	—	—	—	—	24	5	Feely, Thomas J.
1972		NAIA		8	—	—	—	—	—	—	—	24	8	Feely, Thomas J.
1974		NAIA		16	—	—	—	—	—	—	—	26	4	Feely, Thomas J.
1990		NCAA	III	16	—	—	—	—	—	—	—	25	5	Fritz, Steve
1993		NCAA	III	16	—	—	—	—	—	—	—	19	9	Fritz, Steve
1994		NCAA	III	4	—	—	—	—	—	—	—	24	7	Fritz, Steve
1995		NCAA	III	32	—	—	—	—	—	—	—	27	1	Fritz, Steve
1984	W	NCAA	III	24	—	—	—	—	—	—	—	23	5	Kosel, Tom
1987		NCAA	III	32	—	—	—	—	—	—	—	19	9	Riverso, Ted
1988		NCAA	III	16	—	—	—	—	—	—	—	22	5	Riverso, Ted
1989		NCAA	III	24	—	—	—	—	—	—	—	20	6	Riverso, Ted
1990		NCAA	III	16	—	—	—	—	—	—	—	23	5	Riverso, Ted
1991		NCAA	III	1	—	—	—	—	—	—	—	29	2	Riverso, Ted
1992		NCAA	III	16	—	—	—	—	—	—	—	27	1	Riverso, Ted
1993		NCAA	III	32	—	—	—	—	—	—	—	19	7	Riverso, Ted
1994		NCAA	III	32	—	—	—	—	—	—	—	22	5	Riverso, Ted
1995		NCAA	III	3	—	—	—	—	—	—	—	25	6	Riverso, Ted
1996		NCAA	III	3	—	—	—	—	—	—	—	28	3	Riverso, Ted
1997		NCAA	III	16	—	—	—	—	—	—	—	26	2	Riverso, Ted
1998		NCAA	III	8	—	—	—	—	—	—	—	26	2	Riverso, Ted
SAINT THOMAS AQUINAS														
1982	M	NAIA		16	—	—	—	—	—	—	—	34	4	Possinger, David F.
1983		NAIA		16	—	—	—	—	—	—	—	35	3	Possinger, David F.
1984		NAIA		8	—	—	—	—	—	—	—	38	3	Possinger, David F.
1985		NAIA		32	—	—	—	—	—	—	—	36	6	Possinger, David F.
1986		NAIA		4	—	—	—	—	—	—	—	37	6	Possinger, David F.
1987		NAIA		16	—	—	—	—	—	—	—	32	5	Possinger, David F.
1988		NAIA		8	—	—	—	—	—	—	—	39	2	Possinger, David F.
1994		NAIA	II	24	—	—	—	—	—	—	—	24	8	O'Donnell, Dennis G.
1995		NAIA	II	16	—	—	—	—	—	—	—	25	9	O'Donnell, Dennis G.
1997		NAIA	II	16	—	—	—	—	—	—	—	34	2	O'Donnell, Dennis G.
1989	W	NAIA		16	—	—	—	—	—	—	—	25	2	McManus, Michael
1993		NAIA	II	16	—	—	—	—	—	—	—	24	9	McManus, Michael
1995		NAIA	II	32	—	—	—	—	—	—	—	26	4	McManus, Michael
1996		NAIA	II	32	—	—	—	—	—	—	—	25	6	McManus, Michael
1997		NAIA	II	32	—	—	—	—	—	—	—	21	8	McManus, Michael
1998		NAIA	II	32	—	—	—	—	—	—	—	25	4	McManus, Michael

Year	M/W	Assn	Div	NAT	NIT	ARC	CCA	NCI	NCT	OLY	HLM	W	L	Coach
SAINT VINCENT														
1991	M	NAIA		32	—	—	—	—	—	—	—	20	7	Matthews, Bernie
1998		NAIA	I	8	—	—	—	—	—	—	—	29	5	Matthews, Bernie
1992	W	NAIA	I	32	—	—	—	—	—	—	—	20	9	Zawacki, Kristen
1993		NAIA	I	32	—	—	—	—	—	—	—	23	10	Zawacki, Kristen
1994		NAIA	I	32	—	—	—	—	—	—	—	21	9	Zawacki, Kristen
1995		NAIA	I	32	—	—	—	—	—	—	—	26	7	Zawacki, Kristen
1998		NAIA	I	32	—	—	—	—	—	—	—	26	5	Zawacki, Kristen
SAINT XAVIER														
1996	M	NAIA	I	32	—	—	—	—	—	—	—	28	6	Keasler, Mike
SALEM STATE														
1980	M	NCAA	III	24	—	—	—	—	—	—	—	19	9	Lavacchia, Joseph A.
1981		NCAA	III	24	—	—	—	—	—	—	—	23	6	Lavacchia, Joseph A.
1982		NCAA	III	16	—	—	—	—	—	—	—	20	8	Lavacchia, Joseph A.
1986		NCAA	III	16	—	—	—	—	—	—	—	22	6	Thibodeau, Thomas
1989		NCAA	III	32	—	—	—	—	—	—	—	21	6	Todd, Jim
1990		NCAA	III	32	—	—	—	—	—	—	—	20	8	Todd, Jim
1991		NCAA	III	16	—	—	—	—	—	—	—	26	2	Todd, Jim
1992		NCAA	III	16	—	—	—	—	—	—	—	25	4	Todd, Jim
1993		NCAA	III	32	—	—	—	—	—	—	—	18	8	Todd, Jim
1995		NCAA	III	32	—	—	—	—	—	—	—	21	7	Todd, Jim
1996		NCAA	III	32	—	—	—	—	—	—	—	25	3	Todd, Jim
1997		NCAA	III	16	—	—	—	—	—	—	—	25	4	Meehan, Brian
1998		NCAA	III	32	—	—	—	—	—	—	—	25	3	Meehan, Brian
1983	W	NCAA	III	16	—	—	—	—	—	—	—	23	7	Shea, Timothy P.
1984		NCAA	III	3	—	—	—	—	—	—	—	27	3	Shea, Timothy P.
1985		NCAA	III	8	—	—	—	—	—	—	—	23	5	Shea, Timothy P.
1986		NCAA	III	1	—	—	—	—	—	—	—	29	1	Shea, Timothy P.
1987		NCAA	III	24	—	—	—	—	—	—	—	22	6	Shea, Timothy P.
1988		NCAA	III	16	—	—	—	—	—	—	—	25	3	Shea, Timothy P.
1989		NCAA	III	32	—	—	—	—	—	—	—	24	4	Shea, Timothy P.
1990		NCAA	III	32	—	—	—	—	—	—	—	24	5	Shea, Timothy P.
1991		NCAA	III	32	—	—	—	—	—	—	—	24	5	Shea, Timothy P.
1993		NCAA	III	32	—	—	—	—	—	—	—	18	8	Shea, Timothy P.
1994		NCAA	III	32	—	—	—	—	—	—	—	22	5	Shea, Timothy P.
1995		NCAA	III	4	—	—	—	—	—	—	—	28	4	Shea, Timothy P.
1996		NCAA	III	16	—	—	—	—	—	—	—	25	4	Shea, Timothy P.
1997		NCAA	III	64	—	—	—	—	—	—	—	23	4	Shea, Timothy P.
1998		NCAA	III	32	—	—	—	—	—	—	—	23	5	Shea, Timothy P.
SALEM-TEIKYO														
1983	M	NAIA		16	—	—	—	—	—	—	—	22	9	Barnhart, Ray
1993		NAIA	I	16	—	—	—	—	—	—	—	24	7	Carey, Michael A.
1994		NAIA	I	32	—	—	—	—	—	—	—	24	4	Carey, Michael A.
1997		NCAA	II	3	—	—	—	—	—	—	—	28	3	Carey, Michael A.
1998		NCAA	II	16	—	—	—	—	—	—	—	28	3	Carey, Michael A.
1995	W	NAIA	I	32	—	—	—	—	—	—	—	26	3	Biesenthal, Tammy
1996		NCAA	II	16	—	—	—	—	—	—	—	27	4	Biesenthal, Tammy

Year	M/W	Assn	Div	NAT	NIT	ARC	CCA	NCI	NCT	OLY	HLM	W	L	Coach
SALISBURY STATE														
1985	M	NCAA	III	24	—	—	—	—	—	—	—	23	6	Lambert, Edward W. "Ward"
1991		NCAA	III	32	—	—	—	—	—	—	—	22	7	Lambert, Edward W. "Ward"
1992		NCAA	III	8	—	—	—	—	—	—	—	28	2	Lambert, Edward W. "Ward"
1996		NCAA	III	64	—	—	—	—	—	—	—	19	9	Lambert, Edward W. "Ward"
1997		NCAA	III	8	—	—	—	—	—	—	—	25	6	Lambert, Edward W. "Ward"
1977	W	AIAW	S	16	—	—	—	—	—	—	—	14	11	Morrison, Mariana
1995		NCAA	III	64	—	—	—	—	—	—	—	21	7	Benshelter, Bridget
1996		NCAA	III	32	—	—	—	—	—	—	—	19	9	Benshelter, Bridget
SALVE REGINA														
1995	M	NCAA	III	64	—	—	—	—	—	—	—	20	8	Raffa, Michael
SAM HOUSTON STATE														
1973	M	NAIA		16	—	—	—	—	—	—	—	28	1	Porter, Archie
1986		NCAA	II	32	—	—	—	—	—	—	—	27	6	McPherson, Robert
SAN DIEGO														
1966	M	NCAA	II	32	—	—	—	—	—	—	—	17	11	Woolpert, Philip D.
1973		NCAA	II	24	—	—	—	—	—	—	—	19	9	Bickerstaff, Bernard T.
1974		NCAA	II	44	—	—	—	—	—	—	—	16	11	Bickerstaff, Bernard T.
1978		NCAA	II	8	—	—	—	—	—	—	—	22	7	Brovelli, Jim
1979		NCAA	II	24	—	—	—	—	—	—	—	19	7	Brovelli, Jim
1984		NCAA	I	53	—	—	—	—	—	—	—	18	10	Brovelli, Jim
1987		NCAA	I	64	—	—	—	—	—	—	—	24	6	Egan, Henry "Hank"
1993	W	NCAA	I	48	—	—	—	—	—	—	—	16	12	Marpe, Kathleen
SAN DIEGO STATE														
1939	M	NAIA		2	—	—	—	—	—	—	—	24	7	Gross, Morris H.
1940		NAIA		2	—	—	—	—	—	—	—	22	6	Gross, Morris H.
1941		NAIA		1	—	—	—	—	—	—	—	24	7	Gross, Morris H.
1942		NAIA		16	—	—	—	—	—	—	—	13	9	Gross, Morris H.
1956		NAIA		16	—	—	—	—	—	—	—	23	6	Ziegenfuss, Dr. George
1957		NCAA	II	8	—	—	—	—	—	—	—	17	10	Ziegenfuss, Dr. George
1967		NCAA	II	8	—	—	—	—	—	—	—	24	5	Ziegenfuss, Dr. George
1968		NCAA	II	23	—	—	—	—	—	—	—	20	6	Ziegenfuss, Dr. George
1975		NCAA	I	32	—	—	—	—	—	—	—	14	13	Vezie, Tim
1976		NCAA	I	32	—	—	—	—	—	—	—	16	13	Vezie, Tim
1982		NCAA	I	—	32	—	—	—	—	—	—	20	9	Gaines, David "Smokey"
1985		NCAA	I	64	—	—	—	—	—	—	—	23	8	Gaines, David "Smokey"
1984	W	NCAA	I	16	—	—	—	—	—	—	—	24	6	Riggins, Earnest
1985		NCAA	I	16	—	—	—	—	—	—	—	21	9	Riggins, Earnest
1989		NCAA	I	—	2	—	—	—	—	—	—	25	9	Riggins, Earnest
1993		NCAA	I	48	—	—	—	—	—	—	—	19	9	Burns, Beth
1994		NCAA	I	32	—	—	—	—	—	—	—	26	5	Burns, Beth
1995		NCAA	I	64	—	—	—	—	—	—	—	24	6	Burns, Beth
1997		NCAA	I	64	—	—	—	—	—	—	—	23	7	Burns, Beth
SAN FRANCISCO														
1949	M	NCAA		—	1	—	—	—	—	—	—	25	5	Newell, Peter F.
1950		NCAA		—	12	—	—	—	—	—	—	19	7	Newell, Peter F.
1955		NCAA		1	—	—	—	—	—	—	1	28	1	Woolpert, Philip D.
1956		NCAA		1	—	—	—	—	—	—	1	29	0	Woolpert, Philip D.

Year	M/W	Assn	Div	NAT	NIT	ARC	CCA	NCI	NCT	OLY	HLM	W	L	Coach
1957		NCAA	I	3	—	—	—	—	—	—	—	21	7	Woolpert, Philip D.
1958		NCAA	I	12	—	—	—	—	—	—	—	25	2	Woolpert, Philip D.
1963		NCAA	I	12	—	—	—	—	—	—	—	18	9	Peletta, Peter P.
1964		NCAA	I	8	—	—	—	—	—	—	—	23	5	Peletta, Peter P.
1965		NCAA	I	8	—	—	—	—	—	—	—	24	5	Peletta, Peter P.
1966		NCAA	I	—	8	—	—	—	—	—	—	22	6	Peletta, Peter P.
1972		NCAA	I	12	—	—	—	—	—	—	—	20	8	Gaillard, Dr. Bob
1973		NCAA	I	8	—	—	—	—	—	—	—	23	5	Gaillard, Dr. Bob
1974		NCAA	I	8	—	—	—	—	—	—	—	19	9	Gaillard, Dr. Bob
1976		NCAA	I	—	12	—	—	—	—	—	—	22	8	Gaillard, Dr. Bob
1977		NCAA	I	32	—	—	—	—	—	—	—	29	2	Gaillard, Dr. Bob
1978		NCAA	I	16	—	—	—	—	—	—	—	23	6	Gaillard, Dr. Bob
1979		NCAA	I	16	—	—	—	—	—	—	—	22	7	Belluomini, Dan
1981		NCAA	I	48	—	—	—	—	—	—	—	24	7	Barry, Peter
1982		NCAA	I	48	—	—	—	—	—	—	—	25	6	Barry, Peter
1998		NCAA	I	64	—	—	—	—	—	—	—	19	11	Matthews, Philip
1979	W	AIAW	S	16	—	—	—	—	—	—	—	18	10	Bugler, Walter
1980		AIAW	I	24	—	—	—	—	—	—	—	28	5	Bugler, Walter
1995		NCAA	I	64	—	—	—	—	—	—	—	24	5	Nepfel, Bill
1996		NCAA	I	16	—	—	—	—	—	—	—	24	8	Nepfel, Bill
1997		NCAA	I	64	—	—	—	—	—	—	—	25	6	Nepfel, Bill

SAN FRANCISCO STATE

Year	M/W	Assn	Div	NAT	NIT	ARC	CCA	NCI	NCT	OLY	HLM	W	L	Coach
1960	M	NCAA	II	32	—	—	—	—	—	—	—	12	14	Rundell, Paul
1963		NCAA	II	32	—	—	—	—	—	—	—	14	13	Rundell, Paul
1965		NCAA	II	24	—	—	—	—	—	—	—	16	11	Rundell, Paul
1969		NCAA	II	8	—	—	—	—	—	—	—	20	9	Rundell, Paul
1971		NCAA	II	32	—	—	—	—	—	—	—	16	12	Waugh, Gerald R.
1980		NCAA	II	32	—	—	—	—	—	—	—	21	8	Damon, Dr. E. Lyle
1982		NCAA	II	32	—	—	—	—	—	—	—	20	10	Wilson, Kevin
1983		NCAA	II	24	—	—	—	—	—	—	—	21	9	Damon, Dr. E. Lyle
1984		NCAA	II	8	—	—	—	—	—	—	—	21	11	Wilson, Kevin
1994		NCAA	II	32	—	—	—	—	—	—	—	20	10	Thomas, Charlie
1980	W	AIAW	III	8	—	—	—	—	—	—	—	20	12	Manwaring, Emily
1981		AIAW	III	8	—	—	—	—	—	—	—	17	18	Manwaring, Emily
1982		NCAA	II	16	—	—	—	—	—	—	—	20	7	Manwaring, Emily
1983		NCAA	II	24	—	—	—	—	—	—	—	18	9	Manwaring, Emily
1984		NCAA	II	24	—	—	—	—	—	—	—	19	12	Manwaring, Emily
1985		NCAA	II	24	—	—	—	—	—	—	—	13	16	Burger, Maureen

SAN JOSE CHRISTIAN

Year	M/W	Assn	Div	NAT	NIT	ARC	CCA	NCI	NCT	OLY	HLM	W	L	Coach
1990	M	NBCAA	I	5	—	—	—	—	—	—	—	21	9	Miller, Glen
1991		NBCAA	I	1	—	—	—	—	—	—	—	27	7	Miller, Glen
1992		NBCAA	I	4	—	—	—	—	—	—	—	23	17	Miller, Glen
1992		NCCAA	II	8	—	—	—	—	—	—	—	23	17	Miller, Glen
1993		NBCAA	I	1	—	—	—	—	—	—	—	22	14	Miller, Glen
1994		NBCAA	I	1	—	—	—	—	—	—	—	26	11	Miller, Glen
1995		NBCAA	I	1	—	—	—	—	—	—	—	28	11	Miller, Glen
1995		NCCAA	II	5	—	—	—	—	—	—	—	28	11	Miller, Glen
1997		NBCAA	I	4	—	—	—	—	—	—	—	11	17	Miller, Glen

Year	M/W	Assn	Div	NAT	NIT	ARC	CCA	NCI	NCT	OLY	HLM	W	L	Coach
SAN JOSE STATE														
1948	M	NAIA		8	—	—	—	—	—	—	—	23	9	McPherson, Walter J.
1949		NAIA		16	—	—	—	—	—	—	—	22	13	McPherson, Walter J.
1951		NCAA		16	—	—	—	—	—	—	—	18	12	McPherson, Walter J.
1980		NCAA	I	48	—	—	—	—	—	—	—	17	12	Berry, William
1981		NCAA	I	—	32	—	—	—	—	—	—	21	9	Berry, William
1996		NCAA	I	64	—	—	—	—	—	—	—	13	17	Morrison, Stanley M.
SANTA CLARA														
1952	M	NCAA		4	—	—	—	—	—	—	—	17	12	Feerick, Robert J.
1953		NCAA		8	—	—	—	—	—	—	—	20	7	Feerick, Robert J.
1954		NCAA		8	—	—	—	—	—	—	—	20	7	Feerick, Robert J.
1960		NCAA	I	16	—	—	—	—	—	—	—	21	10	Feerick, Robert J.
1968		NCAA	I	8	—	—	—	—	—	—	—	22	4	Garibaldi, Richard A.
1969		NCAA	I	8	—	—	—	—	—	—	—	27	2	Garibaldi, Richard A.
1970		NCAA	I	12	—	—	—	—	—	—	—	23	6	Garibaldi, Richard A.
1984		NCAA	I	—	8	—	—	—	—	—	—	22	10	Williams, Carroll M.
1985		NCAA	I	—	32	—	—	—	—	—	—	20	9	Williams, Carroll M.
1987		NCAA	I	64	—	—	—	—	—	—	—	18	14	Williams, Carroll M.
1988		NCAA	I	—	32	—	—	—	—	—	—	20	11	Williams, Carroll M.
1989		NCAA	I	—	32	—	—	—	—	—	—	20	11	Williams, Carroll M.
1993		NCAA	I	32	—	—	—	—	—	—	—	19	12	Williams, Carroll M.
1995		NCAA	I	64	—	—	—	—	—	—	—	21	7	Davey, Dick
1996		NCAA	I	32	—	—	—	—	—	—	—	20	9	Davey, Dick
1991	W	NCAA	I	—	1	—	—	—	—	—	—	28	3	Horstmeyer, Caren
1992		NCAA	I	32	—	—	—	—	—	—	—	21	10	Horstmeyer, Caren
1994		NCAA	I	64	—	—	—	—	—	—	—	21	7	Horstmeyer, Caren
1998		NCAA	I	64	—	—	—	—	—	—	—	23	8	Horstmeyer, Caren
SANTA FE (NM)														
1983	M	NAIA		8	—	—	—	—	—	—	—	25	9	Roybal, Leonard 'Lennie'
SAVANNAH A&D														
1997	W	NCAA	III	64	—	—	—	—	—	—	—	20	6	Ruffo, Kristen
SAVANNAH STATE														
1954	M	NASC		8	—	—	—	—	—	—	—	23	10	Wright, Theodore A., Sr.
1960		NAIA		16	—	—	—	—	—	—	—	27	4	Wright, Theodore A., Sr.
1961		NAIA		32	—	—	—	—	—	—	—			Wright, Theodore A., Sr.
1962		NAIA		16	—	—	—	—	—	—	—	28	3	Wright, Theodore A., Sr.
1979		NCAA	III	16	—	—	—	—	—	—	—	20	10	Ellington, Russell
1980		NCAA	III	16	—	—	—	—	—	—	—	24	5	Ellington, Russell
1981		NCAA	III	8	—	—	—	—	—	—	—	25	4	Ellington, Russell
1995	W	NCAA	II	48	—	—	—	—	—	—	—	23	5	Wallace, Phillip
SCRANTON														
1952	M	NCAA		—	—	—	—	8	—	—	—	15	14	Carlesimo, Peter A.
1975		NCAA	III	16	—	—	—	—	—	—	—	20	9	Bessoir, Robert M.
1976		NCAA	III	1	—	—	—	—	—	—	—	27	5	Bessoir, Robert M.
1977		NCAA	III	3	—	—	—	—	—	—	—	24	8	Bessoir, Robert M.

Year	M/W	Assn	Div	NAT	NIT	ARC	CCA	NCI	NCT	OLY	HLM	W	L	Coach
1978		NCAA	III	23	—	—	—	—	—	—	—	22	7	Bessoir, Robert M.
1980		NCAA	III	16	—	—	—	—	—	—	—	18	11	Bessoir, Robert M.
1981		NCAA	III	32	—	—	—	—	—	—	—	18	11	Bessoir, Robert M.
1982		NCAA	III	24	—	—	—	—	—	—	—	23	6	Bessoir, Robert M.
1983		NCAA	III	1	—	—	—	—	—	—	—	29	3	Bessoir, Robert M.
1984		NCAA	III	24	—	—	—	—	—	—	—	23	6	Bessoir, Robert M.
1985		NCAA	III	16	—	—	—	—	—	—	—	18	11	Bessoir, Robert M.
1986		NCAA	III	32	—	—	—	—	—	—	—	20	9	Bessoir, Robert M.
1987		NCAA	III	24	—	—	—	—	—	—	—	22	7	Bessoir, Robert M.
1988		NCAA	III	2	—	—	—	—	—	—	—	29	3	Bessoir, Robert M.
1991		NCAA	III	16	—	—	—	—	—	—	—	23	6	Bessoir, Robert M.
1992		NCAA	III	16	—	—	—	—	—	—	—	25	3	Bessoir, Robert M.
1993		NCAA	III	8	—	—	—	—	—	—	—	27	2	Bessoir, Robert M.
1998		NCAA	III	32	—	—	—	—	—	—	—	18	11	Bessoir, Robert M.
1980	W	AIAW	III	3	—	—	—	—	—	—	—	20	4	Strong, Michael J.
1982		NCAA	III	8	—	—	—	—	—	—	—	17	11	Strong, Michael J.
1983		NCAA	III	24	—	—	—	—	—	—	—	19	7	Strong, Michael J.
1984		NCAA	III	24	—	—	—	—	—	—	—	19	8	Strong, Michael J.
1985		NCAA	III	1	—	—	—	—	—	—	—	31	1	Strong, Michael J.
1986		NCAA	III	16	—	—	—	—	—	—	—	23	6	Strong, Michael J.
1987		NCAA	III	3	—	—	—	—	—	—	—	31	2	Strong, Michael J.
1990		NCAA	III	8	—	—	—	—	—	—	—	26	5	Strong, Michael J.
1992		NCAA	III	16	—	—	—	—	—	—	—	22	5	Strong, Michael J.
1993		NCAA	III	3	—	—	—	—	—	—	—	30	2	Strong, Michael J.
1994		NCAA	III	8	—	—	—	—	—	—	—	27	3	Strong, Michael J.
1995		NCAA	III	64	—	—	—	—	—	—	—	24	2	Serafini, Sue
1996		NCAA	III	16	—	—	—	—	—	—	—	26	4	Strong, Michael J.
1997		NCAA	III	4	—	—	—	—	—	—	—	28	5	Strong, Michael J.
1998		NCAA	III	16	—	—	—	—	—	—	—	21	6	Strong, Michael J.

SEATTLE

Year	M/W	Assn	Div	NAT	NIT	ARC	CCA	NCI	NCT	OLY	HLM	W	L	Coach
1951	M	NCAA		—	—	—	—	2	—	—	—	32	5	Brightman, Horace Albert `Al`
1952		NCAA		—	12	—	—	—	—	—	—	29	8	Brightman, Horace Albert `Al`
1953		NCAA		12	—	—	—	—	—	—	—	28	4	Brightman, Horace Albert `Al`
1954		NCAA		24	—	—	—	—	—	—	—	26	2	Brightman, Horace Albert `Al`
1955		NCAA		16	—	—	—	—	—	—	—	22	7	Brightman, Horace Albert `Al`
1956		NCAA		16	—	—	—	—	—	—	—	18	11	Brightman, Horace Albert `Al`
1957		NCAA	I	—	8	—	—	—	—	—	—	24	3	Castellani, John
1958		NCAA	I	2	—	—	—	—	—	—	—	23	6	Castellani, John
1961		NCAA	I	24	—	—	—	—	—	—	—	18	8	Cazzetta, Vincent C.
1962		NCAA	I	25	—	—	—	—	—	—	—	18	9	Cazzetta, Vincent C.
1963		NCAA	I	25	—	—	—	—	—	—	—	21	6	Cazzetta, Vincent C.
1964		NCAA	I	12	—	—	—	—	—	—	—	22	6	Boyd, William R. `Bob`
1967		NCAA	I	23	—	—	—	—	—	—	—	18	8	Purcell, Lionel
1969		NCAA	I	25	—	—	—	—	—	—	—	19	8	Buckwalter, Morris `Bucky`
1993	W	NAIA	I	32	—	—	—	—	—	—	—	20	7	Cox, Dave

SEATTLE PACIFIC

Year	M/W	Assn	Div	NAT	NIT	ARC	CCA	NCI	NCT	OLY	HLM	W	L	Coach
1962	M	NCAA	II	24	—	—	—	—	—	—	—	20	7	Habegger, Lester N. "Gus"
1964		NCAA	II	24	—	—	—	—	—	—	—	17	8	Habegger, Lester N. "Gus"
1965		NCAA	II	8	—	—	—	—	—	—	—	22	7	Habegger, Lester N. "Gus"
1966		NCAA	II	16	—	—	—	—	—	—	—	23	5	Habegger, Lester N. "Gus"
1971		NCAA	II	16	—	—	—	—	—	—	—	16	10	Habegger, Lester N. "Gus"
1972		NCAA	II	16	—	—	—	—	—	—	—	17	11	Habegger, Lester N. "Gus"
1977		NCAA	II	24	—	—	—	—	—	—	—	20	9	Swagerty, Keith
1995		NCAA	II	16	—	—	—	—	—	—	—	20	9	Bone, Ken
1996		NCAA	II	16	—	—	—	—	—	—	—	23	6	Bone, Ken
1998		NCAA	II	16	—	—	—	—	—	—	—	18	12	Bone, Ken
1995	W	NCAA	II	32	—	—	—	—	—	—	—	21	8	Presnell, Gordy
1997		NCAA	II	16	—	—	—	—	—	—	—	26	3	Presnell, Gordy
1998		NCAA	II	8	—	—	—	—	—	—	—	27	3	Presnell, Gordy

SEMINOLE JC (OK)

Year	M/W	Assn	Div	NAT	NIT	ARC	CCA	NCI	NCT	OLY	HLM	W	L	Coach
1971	W			—	4	—	—	—	—	—	—	X	X	Hull, Kenneth C.
1972				—	7	—	—	—	—	—	—	X	X	Woodall, Dixie
1973				—	6	—	—	—	—	—	—	X	X	Woodall, Dixie

SETON HALL

Year	M/W	Assn	Div	NAT	NIT	ARC	CCA	NCI	NCT	OLY	HLM	W	L	Coach
1941	M			—	4	—	—	—	—	—	—	20	2	Russell, John D. "Honey"
1951		NCAA		—	4	—	—	—	—	—	—	24	7	Russell, John D. "Honey"
1952		NCAA		—	12	—	—	—	—	—	—	25	3	Russell, John D. "Honey"
1953		NCAA		—	1	—	—	—	—	—	—	31	2	Russell, John D. "Honey"
1955		NCAA		—	12	—	—	—	—	—	—	17	9	Russell, John D. "Honey"
1956		NCAA		—	8	—	—	—	—	—	—	20	5	Russell, John D. "Honey"
1957		NCAA	I	—	12	—	—	—	—	—	—	17	10	Russell, John D. "Honey"
1974		NCAA	I	—	16	—	—	—	—	—	—	16	11	Raftery, William J.
1977		NCAA	I	—	16	—	—	—	—	—	—	18	11	Raftery, William J.
1987		NCAA	I	—	32	—	—	—	—	—	—	15	14	Carlesimo, Peter J. "PJ"
1988		NCAA	I	32	—	—	—	—	—	—	—	22	13	Carlesimo, Peter J. "PJ"
1989		NCAA	I	2	—	—	—	—	—	—	—	31	7	Carlesimo, Peter J. "PJ"
1991		NCAA	I	8	—	—	—	—	—	—	—	25	9	Carlesimo, Peter J. "PJ"
1992		NCAA	I	16	—	—	—	—	—	—	—	23	9	Carlesimo, Peter J. "PJ"
1993		NCAA	I	32	—	—	—	—	—	—	—	28	7	Carlesimo, Peter J. "PJ"
1994		NCAA	I	64	—	—	—	—	—	—	—	17	13	Carlesimo, Peter J. "PJ"
1995		NCAA	I	—	32	—	—	—	—	—	—	16	14	Blaney, George R.
1998		NCAA	I	—	32	—	—	—	—	—	—	15	15	Amaker, Tommy
1975	W	AIAW	S	9	—	—	—	—	—	—	—	13	5	Dilley, Sue
1976		AIAW	S	12	—	—	—	—	—	—	—	14	8	Dilley, Sue
1978		AIAW	S	16	—	—	—	—	—	—	—	21	8	Dilley, Sue
1979		AIAW	S	12	—	—	—	—	—	—	—	26	8	Dilley, Sue
1994		NCAA	I	16	—	—	—	—	—	—	—	27	5	Mangina, Phyllis
1995		NCAA	I	32	—	—	—	—	—	—	—	24	9	Mangina, Phyllis

SETON HILL

Year	M/W	Assn	Div	NAT	NIT	ARC	CCA	NCI	NCT	OLY	HLM	W	L	Coach
1991	W	NAIA		32	—	—	—	—	—	—	—	14	12	Shrader, Robert

Year	M/W	Assn	Div	NAT	NIT	ARC	CCA	NCI	NCT	OLY	HLM	W	L	Coach

SHAW (NC)

Year	M/W	Assn	Div	NAT	NIT	ARC	CCA	NCI	NCT	OLY	HLM	W	L	Coach
1995	M	NCAA	II	24	—	—	—	—	—	—	—	21	9	Walker, Keith
1989	W	NCAA	II	32	—	—	—	—	—	—	—	18	8	Sanders, Bobby
1996		NCAA	II	32	—	—	—	—	—	—	—	24	5	Sanders, Bobby

SHAWNEE STATE (OH)

Year	M/W	Assn	Div	NAT	NIT	ARC	CCA	NCI	NCT	OLY	HLM	W	L	Coach
1994	W	NAIA	II	8	—	—	—	—	—	—	—	20	12	Hagen-Smith, Robin
1995		NAIA	II	3	—	—	—	—	—	—	—	31	5	Hagen-Smith, Robin
1996		NAIA	II	16	—	—	—	—	—	—	—	31	4	Hagen-Smith, Robin
1997		NAIA	II	16	—	—	—	—	—	—	—	29	2	Hagen-Smith, Robin
1998		NAIA	II	16	—	—	—	—	—	—	—	25	5	Hagen-Smith, Robin

SHENANDOAH

Year	M/W	Assn	Div	NAT	NIT	ARC	CCA	NCI	NCT	OLY	HLM	W	L	Coach
1989	M	NCAA	III	32	—	—	—	—	—	—	—	21	9	Dutton, Dave
1991		NCAA	III	40	—	—	—	—	—	—	—	21	6	Dutton, Dave
1996		NCAA	III	64	—	—	—	—	—	—	—	18	9	Dutton, Dave
1996	W	NCAA	III	64	—	—	—	—	—	—	—	13	15	Orsini, Kathy

SHEPHERD

Year	M/W	Assn	Div	NAT	NIT	ARC	CCA	NCI	NCT	OLY	HLM	W	L	Coach
1976	M	NCAA	III	7	—	—	—	—	—	—	—	30	13	Starkey, Robert G.

SHIPPENSBURG

Year	M/W	Assn	Div	NAT	NIT	ARC	CCA	NCI	NCT	OLY	HLM	W	L	Coach
1991	M	NCAA	II	32	—	—	—	—	—	—	—	20	11	Goodling, Roger E.
1995	W	NCAA	II	32	—	—	—	—	—	—	—	22	7	Smith, David R.
1996		NCAA	II	2	—	—	—	—	—	—	—	28	6	Smith, David R.
1997		NCAA	II	32	—	—	—	—	—	—	—	25	5	Smith, David R.
1998		NCAA	II	8	—	—	—	—	—	—	—	28	4	Smith, David R.

SHORTER (GA)

Year	M/W	Assn	Div	NAT	NIT	ARC	CCA	NCI	NCT	OLY	HLM	W	L	Coach
1978	W	AIAW	S	6	—	—	—	—	—	—	—	31	5	Evans, Ellen

SIENA (NY)

Year	M/W	Assn	Div	NAT	NIT	ARC	CCA	NCI	NCT	OLY	HLM	W	L	Coach
1949	M	NCAA		—	—	—	—	16	—	—	—	22	7	Cunha, Daniel
1950		NCAA		—	—	—	—	1	—	—	—	27	5	Cunha, Daniel
1951		NCAA		—	—	—	—	8	—	—	—	19	8	Cunha, Daniel
1952		NCAA		—	—	—	—	3	—	—	—	25	7	Cunha, Daniel
1974		NCAA	II	24	—	—	—	—	—	—	—	18	9	Kirsch, William
1988		NCAA	I	—	32	—	—	—	—	—	—	23	6	Deane, Mike
1989		NCAA	I	32	—	—	—	—	—	—	—	25	5	Deane, Mike
1991		NCAA	I	—	8	—	—	—	—	—	—	25	10	Deane, Mike
1994		NCAA	I	—	3	—	—	—	—	—	—	25	8	Deane, Mike

SIENA HEIGHTS

Year	M/W	Assn	Div	NAT	NIT	ARC	CCA	NCI	NCT	OLY	HLM	W	L	Coach
1989	M	NAIA		8	—	—	—	—	—	—	—	31	7	Smith, Fred
1990		NAIA		32	—	—	—	—	—	—	—	29	7	Smith, Fred
1994		NAIA	I	32	—	—	—	—	—	—	—	27	8	Smith, Fred
1996		NAIA	II	32	—	—	—	—	—	—	—	21	10	Smith, Fred
1997		NAIA	II	2	—	—	—	—	—	—	—	30	7	Smith, Fred
1998		NAIA	II	16	—	—	—	—	—	—	—	28	9	Smith, Fred

Year	M/W	Assn	Div	NAT	NIT	ARC	CCA	NCI	NCT	OLY	HLM	W	L	Coach
SILVER LAKE														
1990	W	NSCAA		2	—	—	—	—	—	—	—	26	4	Wenner, Craig
1991		NSCAA		1	—	—	—	—	—	—	—	25	6	Wenner, Craig
1992		NSCAA		8	—	—	—	—	—	—	—	17	15	Wenner, Craig
1993		NSCAA		6	—	—	—	—	—	—	—	18	13	Wenner, Craig
1996		NSCAA		3	—	—	—	—	—	—	—	21	8	Koeser, Don
1998		NSCAA		8	—	—	—	—	—	—	—	15	11	Koeser, Don
SIMON FRASER														
1990	W	NAIA		8	—	—	—	—	—	—	—	29	7	McNeill, Allison
1991		NAIA		32	—	—	—	—	—	—	—	28	3	McNeill, Allison
1992		NAIA	I	8	—	—	—	—	—	—	—	31	2	McNeill, Allison
1993		NAIA	I	32	—	—	—	—	—	—	—	26	8	McNeill, Allison
1994		NAIA	I	16	—	—	—	—	—	—	—	26	5	McNeill, Allison
1995		NAIA	I	8	—	—	—	—	—	—	—	23	8	McNeill, Allison
1996		NAIA	I	8	—	—	—	—	—	—	—	31	6	McNeill, Allison
1997		NAIA	I	8	—	—	—	—	—	—	—	31	4	McNeill, Allison
1998		NAIA	I	3	—	—	—	—	—	—	—	31	6	McNeill, Allison
SIMPSON (CA)														
1987	M	NBCAA	I	2	—	—	—	—	—	—	—	X	X	Kress, Paul
1997		NCCAA	II	6	—	—	—	—	—	—	—	14	12	Spaschak, Tom
1994	W	NCCAA	II	8	—	—	—	—	—	—	—	9	11	Wingate, Lawrence
1998		NCCAA	II	4	—	—	—	—	—	—	—	15	16	Dewey, Don
SIMPSON (IA)														
1938	M	NAIA		16	—	—	—	—	—	—	—	16	5	Casey, Francis L. "Frank"
1939		NAIA		32	—	—	—	—	—	—	—	14	7	Casey, Francis L. "Frank"
1940		NAIA		32	—	—	—	—	—	—	—	20	4	Casey, Francis L. "Frank"
1941		NAIA		32	—	—	—	—	—	—	—	19	3	Casey, Francis L. "Frank"
1942		NAIA		16	—	—	—	—	—	—	—	17	6	Casey, Francis L. "Frank"
1943		NAIA		32	—	—	—	—	—	—	—	14	5	Casey, Francis L. "Frank"
1945		NAIA		16	—	—	—	—	—	—	—	16	4	Casey, Francis L. "Frank"
1961		NAIA		32	—	—	—	—	—	—	—	13	12	Deaton, Les H.
1976		NCAA	III	21	—	—	—	—	—	—	—	17	9	Starr, Richard
1992		NCAA	III	40	—	—	—	—	—	—	—	18	9	Wilson, Bruce
1995		NCAA	III	64	—	—	—	—	—	—	—	20	6	Wilson, Bruce
1996		NCAA	III	64	—	—	—	—	—	—	—	20	6	Wilson, Bruce
1983	W	NCAA	III	24	—	—	—	—	—	—	—	16	9	Schafer, Janet
1985		NCAA	III	24	—	—	—	—	—	—	—	20	7	Schafer, Janet
SIOUX FALLS														
1938	M	NAIA		32	—	—	—	—	—	—	—	14	5	Olsen, Francis R.
1941		NAIA		32	—	—	—	—	—	—	—	12	4	Olsen, Francis R.
SLIPPERY ROCK														
1973	M	NAIA		4	—	—	—	—	—	—	—	23	7	Hankinson, Mel
1978		NCAA	III	16	—	—	—	—	—	—	—	17	10	Zimmerman, Doug
1990		NCAA	II	32	—	—	—	—	—	—	—	23	6	Barlett, Robert
1991		NCAA	II	24	—	—	—	—	—	—	—	23	9	Barlett, Robert
1986	W	NCAA	II	16	—	—	—	—	—	—	—	23	6	Ritchey-Walton, Kathleen "Kathy"
1996		NCAA	II	32	—	—	—	—	—	—	—	21	8	Williges, Laura

Year	M/W	Assn	Div	NAT	NIT	ARC	CCA	NCI	NCT	OLY	HLM	W	L	Coach

SONOMA STATE

Year	M/W	Assn	Div	NAT	NIT	ARC	CCA	NCI	NCT	OLY	HLM	W	L	Coach
1973	M	NCAA	II	42	—	—	—	—	—	—	—	18	9	Trumbo, William R.
1974		NCAA	II	16	—	—	—	—	—	—	—	18	10	Trumbo, William R.
1983		NCAA	III	16	—	—	—	—	—	—	—	16	12	Walker, Dick
1989		NCAA	II	32	—	—	—	—	—	—	—	17	14	Walker, Dick
1998	W	NCAA	II	48	—	—	—	—	—	—	—	20	8	Zachensky-Walthall, Susan

SOUTH ALABAMA

Year	M/W	Assn	Div	NAT	NIT	ARC	CCA	NCI	NCT	OLY	HLM	W	L	Coach
1979	M	NCAA	I	32	—	—	—	—	—	—	—	20	7	Ellis, Cliff
1980		NCAA	I	48	—	—	—	—	—	—	—	23	6	Ellis, Cliff
1981		NCAA	I	—	8	—	—	—	—	—	—	25	6	Ellis, Cliff
1984		NCAA	I	—	16	—	—	—	—	—	—	22	8	Ellis, Cliff
1989		NCAA	I	32	—	—	—	—	—	—	—	23	9	Arrow, Ronnie
1991		NCAA	I	64	—	—	—	—	—	—	—	22	9	Arrow, Ronnie
1997		NCAA	I	64	—	—	—	—	—	—	—	23	7	Musselman, William
1998		NCAA	I	64	—	—	—	—	—	—	—	21	7	Weltlich, Robert
1987	W	NCAA	I	40	—	—	—	—	—	—	—	24	6	Branum, Charles
1988		NCAA	I	—	5	—	—	—	—	—	—	22	9	Branum, Charles

SOUTH CAROLINA

Year	M/W	Assn	Div	NAT	NIT	ARC	CCA	NCI	NCT	OLY	HLM	W	L	Coach
1969	M	NCAA	I	—	8	—	—	—	—	—	—	21	7	McGuire, Frank J.
1971		NCAA	I	16	—	—	—	—	—	—	—	23	6	McGuire, Frank J.
1972		NCAA	I	12	—	—	—	—	—	—	—	24	5	McGuire, Frank J.
1973		NCAA	I	12	—	—	—	—	—	—	—	22	7	McGuire, Frank J.
1974		NCAA	I	25	—	—	—	—	—	—	—	22	5	McGuire, Frank J.
1975		NCAA	I	—	8	—	—	—	—	—	—	19	9	McGuire, Frank J.
1978		NCAA	I	—	16	—	—	—	—	—	—	16	12	McGuire, Frank J.
1983		NCAA	I	—	8	—	—	—	—	—	—	22	9	Foster, William E.
1989		NCAA	I	64	—	—	—	—	—	—	—	19	11	Felton, George
1991		NCAA	I	—	16	—	—	—	—	—	—	20	13	Felton, George
1996		NCAA	I	—	8	—	—	—	—	—	—	19	12	Fogler, Eddie
1997		NCAA	I	64	—	—	—	—	—	—	—	24	8	Fogler, Eddie
1998		NCAA	I	64	—	—	—	—	—	—	—	23	8	Fogler, Eddie
1973	W	AIAW		12	—	—	—	—	—	—	—	X	X	Meade, Violet M.
1979		AIAW	L	—	1	—	—	—	—	—	—	27	10	Parsons, Pam
1980		AIAW	I	3	—	—	—	—	—	—	—	30	6	Parsons, Pam
1982		NCAA	I	16	—	—	—	—	—	—	—	23	8	Kelly, Terry
1986		NCAA	I	40	—	—	—	—	—	—	—	19	11	Wilson, Nancy R.
1988		NCAA	I	32	—	—	—	—	—	—	—	23	11	Wilson, Nancy R.
1989		NCAA	I	48	—	—	—	—	—	—	—	23	7	Wilson, Nancy R.
1990		NCAA	I	16	—	—	—	—	—	—	—	24	9	Wilson, Nancy R.
1991		NCAA	I	48	—	—	—	—	—	—	—	22	9	Wilson, Nancy R.

SOUTH CAROLINA STATE

Year	M/W	Assn	Div	NAT	NIT	ARC	CCA	NCI	NCT	OLY	HLM	W	L	Coach
1958	M	NCAA	II	24	—	—	—	—	—	—	—	18	9	Martin, Edward A.
1961		NCAA	II	32	—	—	—	—	—	—	—	23	7	Martin, Edward A.
1963		NCAA	II	16	—	—	—	—	—	—	—	19	8	Martin, Edward A.
1966		NCAA	II	32	—	—	—	—	—	—	—	23	3	Martin, Edward A.
1967		NCAA	II	16	—	—	—	—	—	—	—	18	5	Martin, Edward A.
1970		NAIA		32	—	—	—	—	—	—	—	21	7	Jobe, Ben
1973		NAIA		16	—	—	—	—	—	—	—	17	14	Jobe, Ben
1989		NCAA	I	64	—	—	—	—	—	—	—	25	8	Alexander, Cyrus "Cy"

Year	M/W	Assn	Div	NAT	NIT	ARC	CCA	NCI	NCT	OLY	HLM	W	L	Coach
1996		NCAA	I	64	—	—	—	—	—	—	—	22	8	Alexander, Cyrus 'Cy'
1998		NCAA	I	64	—	—	—	—	—	—	—	22	8	Alexander, Cyrus 'Cy'
1978	W	AIAW	S	2	—	—	—	—	—	—	—	30	5	Simon, Willie J.
1979		AIAW	S	1	—	—	—	—	—	—	—	33	2	Simon, Willie J.
1980		AIAW	II	16	—	—	—	—	—	—	—	30	5	Simon, Willie J.
1983		NCAA	I	32	—	—	—	—	—	—	—	17	8	Simon, Willie J.

SOUTH CAROLINA: AIKEN

Year	M/W	Assn	Div	NAT	NIT	ARC	CCA	NCI	NCT	OLY	HLM	W	L	Coach
1974	M	NSCAA		16	—	—	—	—	—	—	—	X	X	Perkins, Lewis
1980		NAIA		16	—	—	—	—	—	—	—	21	18	Wall, Larry
1998		NCAA	II	32	—	—	—	—	—	—	—	20	10	Roberts, Mike

SOUTH CAROLINA: LANCASTER

Year	M/W	Assn	Div	NAT	NIT	ARC	CCA	NCI	NCT	OLY	HLM	W	L	Coach
1975	M	NSCAA		8	—	—	—	—	—	—	—	16	8	
1980		NSCAA		9	—	—	—	—	—	—	—	27	6	DeHart, Glen E.
1982		NSCAA		10	—	—	—	—	—	—					DeHart, Glen E.

SOUTH CAROLINA: SPARTANBURG

Year	M/W	Assn	Div	NAT	NIT	ARC	CCA	NCI	NCT	OLY	HLM	W	L	Coach
1981	M	NAIA		16	—	—	—	—	—	—	—	22	12	Waters, Jerry O.
1982		NAIA		1	—	—	—	—	—	—	—	27	5	Waters, Jerry O.
1990		NAIA		8	—	—	—	—	—	—	—	29	3	Waters, Jerry O.
1991		NCAA	II	16	—	—	—	—	—	—	—	26	3	Waters, Jerry O.
1992		NCAA	II	16	—	—	—	—	—	—	—	24	6	Waters, Jerry O.
1996		NCAA	II	32	—	—	—	—	—	—	—	23	8	Waters, Jerry O.
1998		NCAA	II	32	—	—	—	—	—	—	—	22	7	Nottingham, Gary
1993	W	NCAA	II	16	—	—	—	—	—	—	—	28	3	Sells, Peggy
1994		NCAA	II	32	—	—	—	—	—	—	—	27	4	Sells, Peggy
1995		NCAA	II	16	—	—	—	—	—	—	—	25	6	Sells, Peggy

SOUTH CAROLINA: UNION

Year	M/W	Assn	Div	NAT	NIT	ARC	CCA	NCI	NCT	OLY	HLM	W	L	Coach
1973	M	NSCAA		3	—	—	—	—	—	—	—	19	10	Edwards, John
1977		NSCAA		8	—	—	—	—	—	—	—	14	10	Call, Gary
1979		NSCAA		8	—	—	—	—	—	—	—	14	13	Call, Gary

SOUTH DAKOTA

Year	M/W	Assn	Div	NAT	NIT	ARC	CCA	NCI	NCT	OLY	HLM	W	L	Coach
1950	M	NAIA		32	—	—	—	—	—	—	—	11	11	Deklotz, George
1957		NCAA	II	8	—	—	—	—	—	—	—	19	4	Clodfelter, Duane
1958		NCAA	II	1	—	—	—	—	—	—	—	22	5	Clodfelter, Duane
1972		NCAA	II	24	—	—	—	—	—	—	—	18	10	Mulcahy, Robert
1990		NCAA	II	24	—	—	—	—	—	—	—	22	10	Boots, David
1993		NCAA	II	8	—	—	—	—	—	—	—	25	5	Boots, David
1994		NCAA	II	8	—	—	—	—	—	—	—	24	6	Boots, David
1983	W	NCAA	II	24	—	—	—	—	—	—	—	19	9	Zimmerman, Mary
1984		NCAA	II	16	—	—	—	—	—	—	—	22	7	Lavin, Chad
1985		NCAA	II	16	—	—	—	—	—	—	—	23	6	Lavin, Chad
1989		NCAA	II	32	—	—	—	—	—	—	—	22	7	Tibbetts, Fred

SOUTH DAKOTA STATE

Year	M/W	Assn	Div	NAT	NIT	ARC	CCA	NCI	NCT	OLY	HLM	W	L	Coach
1943	M	NAIA		32	—	—	—	—	—	—	—	15	6	McCrady, Thurlo E.
1948		NAIA		32	—	—	—	—	—	—	—	19	6	Frost, Reuben B. 'Jack'
1951		NAIA		32	—	—	—	—	—	—	—	16	12	Frost, Reuben B. 'Jack'
1956		NAIA		32	—	—	—	—	—	—	—	17	7	Walseth, Russell M. 'Sox'

Year	M/W	Assn	Div	NAT	NIT	ARC	CCA	NCI	NCT	OLY	HLM	W	L	Coach
1959		NCAA	II	8	—	—	—	—	—	—	—	17	7	Iverson, James
1960		NCAA	II	24	—	—	—	—	—	—	—	17	7	Iverson, James
1961		NCAA	II	3	—	—	—	—	—	—	—	21	6	Iverson, James
1963		NCAA	II	1	—	—	—	—	—	—	—	22	5	Iverson, James
1968		NCAA	II	23	—	—	—	—	—	—	—	20	7	Marking, James
1969		NCAA	II	16	—	—	—	—	—	—	—	18	6	Marking, James
1970		NCAA	II	8	—	—	—	—	—	—	—	22	4	Marking, James
1972		NCAA	II	36	—	—	—	—	—	—	—	17	8	Marking, James
1973		NCAA	II	16	—	—	—	—	—	—	—	18	8	Marking, James
1978		NCAA	II	24	—	—	—	—	—	—	—	17	12	Zulk, Gene
1980		NCAA	II	8	—	—	—	—	—	—	—	23	7	Zulk, Gene
1984		NCAA	II	16	—	—	—	—	—	—	—	21	9	Zulk, Gene
1985		NCAA	II	2	—	—	—	—	—	—	—	26	7	Zulk, Gene
1988		NCAA	II	24	—	—	—	—	—	—	—	21	9	Thorson, Jim
1991		NCAA	II	16	—	—	—	—	—	—	—	24	8	Thorson, Jim
1992		NCAA	II	8	—	—	—	—	—	—	—	25	8	Thorson, Jim
1996		NCAA	II	16	—	—	—	—	—	—	—	24	5	Nagy, Scott
1997		NCAA	II	8	—	—	—	—	—	—	—	25	5	Nagy, Scott
1998		NCAA	II	16	—	—	—	—	—	—	—	26	3	Nagy, Scott
1972	W	AIAW		16	—	—	—	—	—	—	—	17	2	Marske, Ruth
1988		NCAA	II	16	—	—	—	—	—	—	—	25	5	Neiber, Nancy
1992		NCAA	II	32	—	—	—	—	—	—	—	19	10	Neiber, Nancy
1994		NCAA	II	16	—	—	—	—	—	—	—	22	8	Neiber, Nancy
1995		NCAA	II	16	—	—	—	—	—	—	—	24	6	Neiber, Nancy
1996		NCAA	II	32	—	—	—	—	—	—	—	25	3	Neiber, Nancy

SOUTH DAKOTA TECH

Year	M/W	Assn	Div	NAT	NIT	ARC	CCA	NCI	NCT	OLY	HLM	W	L	Coach
1973	M	NAIA		32	—	—	—	—	—	—	—	19	8	Riley, Michael L.
1997		NAIA	II	32	—	—	—	—	—	—	—	17	13	Welsh, Hugh
1994	W	NAIA	II	16	—	—	—	—	—	—	—	18	11	Felderman, Barbara
1996		NAIA	II	32	—	—	—	—	—	—	—	19	11	Felderman, Barbara
1997		NAIA	II	32	—	—	—	—	—	—	—	21	9	Felderman, Barbara
1998		NAIA	II	3	—	—	—	—	—	—	—	28	4	Felderman, Barbara

SOUTH FLORIDA

Year	M/W	Assn	Div	NAT	NIT	ARC	CCA	NCI	NCT	OLY	HLM	W	L	Coach
1981	M	NCAA	I	—	32	—	—	—	—	—	—	18	11	Rose, Lee H.
1983		NCAA	I	—	16	—	—	—	—	—	—	22	10	Rose, Lee H.
1985		NCAA	I	—	16	—	—	—	—	—	—	18	12	Rose, Lee H.
1990		NCAA	I	64	—	—	—	—	—	—	—	20	11	Paschal, Bobby
1991		NCAA	I	—	32	—	—	—	—	—	—	19	11	Paschal, Bobby
1992		NCAA	I	64	—	—	—	—	—	—	—	19	10	Paschal, Bobby
1995		NCAA	I	—	8	—	—	—	—	—	—	18	12	Paschal, Bobby

SOUTH UNIVERSITY (TN)

Year	M/W	Assn	Div	NAT	NIT	ARC	CCA	NCI	NCT	OLY	HLM	W	L	Coach
1975	M	NCAA	III	30	—	—	—	—	—	—	—	19	7	Petty, Malcolm "Mac"
1976		NCAA	III	28	—	—	—	—	—	—	—	17	10	Petty, Malcolm "Mac"
1997		NCAA	III	32	—	—	—	—	—	—	—	19	7	Thoni, Joe
1998		NCAA	III	48	—	—	—	—	—	—	—	20	6	Thoni, Joe

Year	M/W	Assn	Div	NAT	NIT ARC CCA NCI NCT OLY HLM	W	L	Coach
SOUTHEAST MISSOURI STATE								
1943	M	NAIA		1	— — — — — — — —	19	6	Harris, Charles P.
1961		NCAA	II	2	— — — — — — — —	25	3	Parsley, Charles H., Sr.
1962		NCAA	II	8	— — — — — — — —	18	7	Parsley, Charles H., Sr.
1963		NCAA	II	32	— — — — — — — —	21	4	Parsley, Charles H., Sr.
1964		NCAA	II	8	— — — — — — — —	19	6	Parsley, Charles H., Sr.
1979		NCAA	II	24	— — — — — — — —	19	9	Williams, Carroll
1982		NCAA	II	8	— — — — — — — —	21	10	Shumate, Ron
1983		NCAA	II	8	— — — — — — — —	25	6	Shumate, Ron
1985		NCAA	II	8	— — — — — — — —	24	8	Shumate, Ron
1986		NCAA	II	2	— — — — — — — —	27	7	Shumate, Ron
1987		NCAA	II	16	— — — — — — — —	20	11	Shumate, Ron
1988		NCAA	II	8	— — — — — — — —	28	4	Shumate, Ron
1989		NCAA	II	2	— — — — — — — —	27	6	Shumate, Ron
1990		NCAA	II	8	— — — — — — — —	26	5	Shumate, Ron
1983	W	NCAA	II	16	— — — — — — — —	20	8	Beck, Angela
1984		NCAA	II	16	— — — — — — — —	23	6	Arnzen, Ed
1986		NCAA	II	16	— — — — — — — —	25	6	Arnzen, Ed
1987		NCAA	II	24	— — — — — — — —	26	4	Arnzen, Ed
1988		NCAA	II	32	— — — — — — — —	26	4	Arnzen, Ed
1989		NCAA	II	32	— — — — — — — —	23	7	Arnzen, Ed
1990		NCAA	II	32	— — — — — — — —	24	6	Arnzen, Ed
1991		NCAA	II	2	— — — — — — — —	31	4	Arnzen, Ed
SOUTHEASTERN ASSEMBLIES								
1982	M	NBCAA		8	— — — — — — — —	19	10	Campbell, Dale
1984		NBCAA	I	6	— — — — — — — —	18	9	Campbell, Dale
1990		NCCAA	II	8	— — — — — — — —	21	13	Laing, Scott
1991		NCCAA	II	7	— — — — — — — —	27	8	Laing, Scott
1994	W	NBCAA		4	— — — — — — — —	18	10	Skinner, Dean B., Jr.
SOUTHEASTERN BIBLE								
1994	M	NBCAA	I	7	— — — — — — — —	3	17	Brigham, Benjamin E.
1991	W	NBCAA		5	— — — — — — —			Green, Kimball
SOUTHEASTERN LOUISIANA								
1950	M	NAIA		32	— — — — — — — —	13	11	Marlar, Luther W. "Luke"
1951		NAIA		32	— — — — — — — —	13	10	Marlar, Luther W. "Luke"
1954		NAIA		8	— — — — — — — —	22	10	Marlar, Luther W. "Luke"
1973		NCAA	II	16	— — — — — — — —	21	7	Foy, E. W.
1976	W	AIAW	S	5	— — — — — — — —	30	2	Puckett, Linda
1977		AIAW	S	1	— — — — — — — —	30	2	Puckett, Linda
1978		AIAW	S	5	— — — — — — — —	30	4	Puckett, Linda
1979		AIAW	S	8	— — — — — — — —	27	8	Puckett, Linda
SOUTHEASTERN OKLAHOMA STATE								
1940	M	NAIA		16	— — — — — — — —	X	X	Sullivan, Bloomer
1942		NAIA		2	— — — — — — — —	X	X	Sullivan, Bloomer
1943		NAIA		32	— — — — — — — —	X	X	Sullivan, Bloomer
1946		NAIA		16	— — — — — — — —	26	4	Sullivan, Bloomer

Year	M/W	Assn	Div	NAT	NIT	ARC	CCA	NCI	NCT	OLY	HLM	W	L	Coach
1947		NAIA		8	—	—	—	—	—	—	—	13	7	Sullivan, Bloomer
1954		NAIA		16	—	—	—	—	—	—	—	X	X	Sullivan, Bloomer
1955		NAIA		2	—	—	—	—	—	—	—	37	5	Sullivan, Bloomer
1956		NAIA		32	—	—	—	—	—	—	—	20	10	Sullivan, Bloomer
1957		NAIA		2	—	—	—	—	—	—	—	30	5	Sullivan, Bloomer
1962		NAIA		3	—	—	—	—	—	—	—	28	9	Sullivan, Bloomer
1985		NAIA		16	—	—	—	—	—	—	—	24	8	Hedden, Jack E.
1986		NAIA		3	—	—	—	—	—	—	—	30	4	Hedden, Jack E.
1996		NAIA	I	32	—	—	—	—	—	—	—	24	10	Robinson, Tony
1997		NAIA	I	16	—	—	—	—	—	—	—	27	4	Robinson, Tony
1980	W	AIAW	II	24	—	—	—	—	—	—	—	23	8	Hudson, Vicki
1994		NAIA	I	16	—	—	—	—	—	—	—	21	7	Keith, Nick
1995		NAIA	I	2	—	—	—	—	—	—	—	29	5	Keith, Nick
1996		NAIA	I	2	—	—	—	—	—	—	—	30	2	Keith, Nick
1997		NAIA	I	16	—	—	—	—	—	—	—	24	6	Keith, Nick
1998		NAIA	I	16	—	—	—	—	—	—	—	22	6	Keith, Nick

SOUTHERN ARKANSAS

Year	M/W	Assn	Div	NAT	NIT	ARC	CCA	NCI	NCT	OLY	HLM	W	L	Coach
1957	M	NAIA		32	—	—	—	—	—	—	—	15	8	Waller, P. T. "Duddy"
1966		NAIA		16	—	—	—	—	—	—	—	23	5	Watson, W. T.
1967		NAIA		16	—	—	—	—	—	—	—	25	4	Watson, W. T.
1971		NAIA		32	—	—	—	—	—	—	—	23	5	Watson, W. T.
1983		NAIA		32	—	—	—	—	—	—	—	18	11	Ingram, Monroe
1989		NAIA		32	—	—	—	—	—	—	—	24	6	Ingram, Monroe
1969	W			—	7	—	—	—	—	—	—	X	X	Downing, Dr. Margaret R.

SOUTHERN CALIFORNIA

Year	M/W	Assn	Div	NAT	NIT	ARC	CCA	NCI	NCT	OLY	HLM	W	L	Coach
1940	M	NCAA		3	—	—	—	—	—	—	1	20	3	Barry, Justin M. "Sam"
1954		NCAA		4	—	—	—	—	—	—	—	19	14	Twogood, Forrest F.
1960		NCAA	I	25	—	—	—	—	—	—	—	16	11	Twogood, Forrest F.
1961		NCAA	I	16	—	—	—	—	—	—	—	21	8	Twogood, Forrest F.
1973		NCAA	I	—	16	—	—	—	—	—	—	18	10	Boyd, William R. "Bob"
1974		NCAA	I	—	—	—	2	—	—	—	—	24	5	Boyd, William R. "Bob"
1975		NCAA	I	—	—	—	8	—	—	—	—	18	8	Boyd, William R. "Bob"
1979		NCAA	I	32	—	—	—	—	—	—	—	20	9	Boyd, William R. "Bob"
1982		NCAA	I	48	—	—	—	—	—	—	—	19	9	Morrison, Stanley M.
1985		NCAA	I	64	—	—	—	—	—	—	—	19	10	Morrison, Stanley M.
1991		NCAA	I	64	—	—	—	—	—	—	—	19	10	Raveling, George
1992		NCAA	I	32	—	—	—	—	—	—	—	24	6	Raveling, George
1993		NCAA	I	—	8	—	—	—	—	—	—	18	12	Raveling, George
1994		NCAA	I	—	32	—	—	—	—	—	—	16	12	Raveling, George
1997		NCAA	I	64	—	—	—	—	—	—	—	17	11	Bibby, Charles Henry
1980	W	AIAW	I	24	—	—	—	—	—	—	—	22	12	Sharp, Linda K.
1981		AIAW	I	4	—	—	—	—	—	—	—	26	8	Sharp, Linda K.
1982		NCAA	I	8	—	—	—	—	—	—	—	23	4	Sharp, Linda K.
1983		NCAA	I	1	—	—	—	—	—	—	—	31	2	Sharp, Linda K.
1984		NCAA	I	1	—	—	—	—	—	—	—	29	4	Sharp, Linda K.
1985		NCAA	I	16	—	—	—	—	—	—	—	21	9	Sharp, Linda K.
1986		NCAA	I	2	—	—	—	—	—	—	—	27	4	Sharp, Linda K.
1987		NCAA	I	16	—	—	—	—	—	—	—	22	8	Sharp, Linda K.

Year	M/W	Assn	Div	NAT	NIT	ARC	CCA	NCI	NCT	OLY	HLM	W	L	Coach
1988		NCAA	I	16	—	—	—	—	—	—	—	22	8	Sharp, Linda K.
1991		NCAA	I	32	—	—	—	—	—	—	—	18	12	Stanley, Marianne Crawford
1992		NCAA	I	8	—	—	—	—	—	—	—	23	8	Stanley, Marianne Crawford
1993		NCAA	I	16	—	—	—	—	—	—	—	22	7	Stanley, Marianne Crawford
1994		NCAA	I	8	—	—	—	—	—	—	—	26	4	Miller, Cheryl
1995		NCAA	I	64	—	—	—	—	—	—	—	18	10	Miller, Cheryl
1997		NCAA	I	32	—	—	—	—	—	—	—	20	9	Williams, Fred

SOUTHERN CALIFORNIA COLLEGE

Year	M/W	Assn	Div	NAT	NIT	ARC	CCA	NCI	NCT	OLY	HLM	W	L	Coach
1989	M	NCCAA	I	8	—	—	—	—	—	—	—	29	5	Reynolds, Bill
1990		NAIA		16	—	—	—	—	—	—	—	26	9	Reynolds, Bill
1998	W	NAIA	I	32	—	—	—	—	—	—	—	29	6	Davis, Russ

SOUTHERN COLORADO

Year	M/W	Assn	Div	NAT	NIT	ARC	CCA	NCI	NCT	OLY	HLM	W	L	Coach
1965	M	NAIA		32	—	—	—	—	—	—	—	21	7	Simmons, Harry H.
1967		NCAA	II	32	—	—	—	—	—	—	—	19	6	Simmons, Harry H.
1968		NCAA	II	32	—	—	—	—	—	—	—	19	9	Simmons, Harry H.
1972		NCAA	II	8	—	—	—	—	—	—	—	19	9	Simmons, Harry H.
1973		NCAA	II	32	—	—	—	—	—	—	—	19	9	Simmons, Harry H.
1986		NAIA		32	—	—	—	—	—	—	—	20	12	Drangmeister, Richard
1991		NAIA		32	—	—	—	—	—	—	—	25	8	Folda, Joe
1998		NCAA	II	48	—	—	—	—	—	—	—	22	8	Folda, Joe
1975	W	AIAW	S	12	—	—	—	—	—	—	—	10	5	Banks, Jessie

SOUTHERN CONNECTICUT STATE

Year	M/W	Assn	Div	NAT	NIT	ARC	CCA	NCI	NCT	OLY	HLM	W	L	Coach
1955	M	NAIA		32	—	—	—	—	—	—	—	18	5	McDowell, Owen W.
1957		NAIA		32	—	—	—	—	—	—	—	16	7	McDowell, Owen W.
1982		NCAA	II	16	—	—	—	—	—	—	—	22	8	Leary, Arthur
1983		NCAA	II	32	—	—	—	—	—	—	—	23	9	Leary, Arthur
1997		NCAA	II	8	—	—	—	—	—	—	—	28	4	Leary, Arthur
1969	W	AIAW		8	—	—	—	—	—	—	—	8	2	O'Neal, Louise
1970		AIAW		8	—	—	—	—	—	—	—	8	3	O'Neal, Louise
1971		AIAW		3	—	—	—	—	—	—	—	12	5	O'Neal, Louise
1972		AIAW		12	—	—	—	—	—	—	—	7	2	O'Neal, Louise
1973		AIAW		3	—	—	—	—	—	—	—	12	2	O'Neal, Louise
1974		AIAW		3	—	—	—	—	—	—	—	19	5	O'Neal, Louise
1975		AIAW	L	4	—	—	—	—	—	—	—	15	5	O'Neal, Louise
1976		AIAW	L	8	—	—	—	—	—	—	—	17	6	O'Neal, Louise
1977		AIAW	L	6	—	—	—	—	—	—	—	20	6	Perelli, Donald
1978		AIAW	L	8	—	—	—	—	—	—	—	19	11	Perelli, Donald
1979		AIAW	L	16	—	—	—	—	—	—	—	18	11	Perelli, Donald
1983		NCAA	II	3	—	—	—	—	—	—	—	25	5	Barone, Anthony J.

SOUTHERN ILLINOIS

Year	M/W	Assn	Div	NAT	NIT	ARC	CCA	NCI	NCT	OLY	HLM	W	L	Coach
1945	M	NAIA		4	—	—	—	—	—	—	—	15	7	Martin, Glenn "Abe"
1946		NAIA		1	—	—	—	—	—	—	—	20	6	Martin, Glenn "Abe"
1947		NAIA		32	—	—	—	—	—	—	—	19	10	Holder, Lynn C.
1948		NAIA		16	—	—	—	—	—	—	—	22	4	Holder, Lynn C.
1959		NCAA	II	32	—	—	—	—	—	—	—	18	8	Gallatin, Harry J.
1960		NAIA		32	—	—	—	—	—	—	—	20	9	Gallatin, Harry J.
1961		NCAA	II	16	—	—	—	—	—	—	—	21	6	Gallatin, Harry J.
1962		NCAA	II	3	—	—	—	—	—	—	—	21	10	Gallatin, Harry J.

Year	M/W	Assn	Div	NAT	NIT	ARC	CCA	NCI	NCT	OLY	HLM	W	L	Coach
1963		NCAA	II	4	—	—	—	—	—	—	—	20	10	Hartman, Jack
1964		NCAA	II	16	—	—	—	—	—	—	—	14	8	Hartman, Jack
1965		NCAA	II	2	—	—	—	—	—	—	—	20	6	Hartman, Jack
1966		NCAA	II	2	—	—	—	—	—	—	—	22	7	Hartman, Jack
1967		NCAA	II	—	1	—	—	—	—	—	—	24	2	Hartman, Jack
1969		NCAA	I	—	16	—	—	—	—	—	—	16	8	Hartman, Jack
1975		NCAA	I	—	16	—	—	—	—	—	—	18	9	Lambert, Paul M.
1977		NCAA	I	16	—	—	—	—	—	—	—	22	7	Lambert, Paul M.
1989		NCAA	I	—	32	—	—	—	—	—	—	20	14	Herrin, Richard "Rich"
1990		NCAA	I	—	32	—	—	—	—	—	—	26	8	Herrin, Richard "Rich"
1991		NCAA	I	—	8	—	—	—	—	—	—	18	14	Herrin, Richard "Rich"
1992		NCAA	I	—	32	—	—	—	—	—	—	22	8	Herrin, Richard "Rich"
1993		NCAA	I	64	—	—	—	—	—	—	—	23	10	Herrin, Richard "Rich"
1994		NCAA	I	64	—	—	—	—	—	—	—	23	7	Herrin, Richard "Rich"
1995		NCAA	I	64	—	—	—	—	—	—	—	23	9	Herrin, Richard "Rich"
1969	W	AIAW		8	—	—	—	—	—	—	—	11	2	West, Dr. Charlotte
1970		AIAW		5	—	—	—	—	—	—	—	13	2	West, Dr. Charlotte
1983		NCAA	I	—	6	—	—	—	—	—	—	22	11	Scott, Cindy
1986		NCAA	I	32	—	—	—	—	—	—	—	25	4	Scott, Cindy
1987		NCAA	I	16	—	—	—	—	—	—	—	28	3	Scott, Cindy
1990		NCAA	I	48	—	—	—	—	—	—	—	21	10	Scott, Cindy
1992		NCAA	I	32	—	—	—	—	—	—	—	23	8	Scott, Cindy

SOUTHERN ILLINOIS: EDWARDSVILLE

Year	M/W	Assn	Div	NAT	NIT	ARC	CCA	NCI	NCT	OLY	HLM	W	L	Coach
1986	M	NCAA	II	16	—	—	—	—	—	—	—	23	7	Graham, Larry
1987		NCAA	II	16	—	—	—	—	—	—	—	23	7	Graham, Larry
1989		NCAA	II	24	—	—	—	—	—	—	—	23	7	Graham, Larry
1998	W	NCAA	II	48	—	—	—	—	—	—	—	22	8	Hedberg, Wendy

SOUTHERN INDIANA

Year	M/W	Assn	Div	NAT	NIT	ARC	CCA	NCI	NCT	OLY	HLM	W	L	Coach
1978	M	NCAA	II	16	—	—	—	—	—	—	—	19	9	Boultinghouse, Wayne
1980		NCAA	II	32	—	—	—	—	—	—	—	20	9	Boultinghouse, Wayne
1981		NCAA	II	32	—	—	—	—	—	—	—	21	8	Boultinghouse, Wayne
1985		NCAA	II	24	—	—	—	—	—	—	—	18	11	Burns, Creighton
1987		NCAA	II	24	—	—	—	—	—	—	—	24	6	Bial, Mark
1990		NCAA	II	32	—	—	—	—	—	—	—	20	10	Sinn, Dr. Lionel L.
1993		NCAA	II	23	—	—	—	—	—	—	—	22	7	Pearl, Bruce
1994		NCAA	II	2	—	—	—	—	—	—	—	28	4	Pearl, Bruce
1995		NCAA	II	1	—	—	—	—	—	—	—	29	4	Pearl, Bruce
1996		NCAA	II	16	—	—	—	—	—	—	—	25	4	Pearl, Bruce
1997		NCAA	II	48	—	—	—	—	—	—	—	23	5	Pearl, Bruce
1998		NCAA	II	16	—	—	—	—	—	—	—	27	6	Pearl, Bruce
1995	W	NCAA	II	32	—	—	—	—	—	—	—	22	5	Dugan, Chancellor
1996		NCAA	II	32	—	—	—	—	—	—	—	22	7	Dugan, Chancellor
1997		NCAA	II	2	—	—	—	—	—	—	—	30	2	Dugan, Chancellor
1998		NCAA	II	32	—	—	—	—	—	—	—	26	2	Dugan, Chancellor

Year	M/W	Assn	Div	NAT	NIT	ARC	CCA	NCI	NCT	OLY	HLM	W	L	Coach
SOUTHERN MAINE														
1978	M	NAIA		32	—	—	—	—	—	—	—	21	7	Bouchard, Joey A.
1979		NAIA		32	—	—	—	—	—	—	—	21	7	Bouchard, Joey A.
1988		NCAA	III	24	—	—	—	—	—	—	—	21	8	Brown, Robert D.
1989		NCAA	III	3	—	—	—	—	—	—	—	24	7	Brown, Robert D.
1990		NCAA	III	32	—	—	—	—	—	—	—	21	9	Brown, Robert D.
1991		NCAA	III	32	—	—	—	—	—	—	—	19	8	Sokaitis, Al
1985	W	NAIA		16	—	—	—	—	—	—	—	23	6	Costello, Dr. Richard A.
1986		NCAA	III	24	—	—	—	—	—	—	—	20	5	Costello, Dr. Richard A.
1987		NCAA	III	8	—	—	—	—	—	—	—	25	4	Costello, Dr. Richard A.
1988		NCAA	III	4	—	—	—	—	—	—	—	27	3	Fifield, Gary
1989		NCAA	III	16	—	—	—	—	—	—	—	25	3	Fifield, Gary
1990		NCAA	III	8	—	—	—	—	—	—	—	25	5	Fifield, Gary
1991		NCAA	III	8	—	—	—	—	—	—	—	23	7	Fifield, Gary
1992		NCAA	III	8	—	—	—	—	—	—	—	26	4	Fifield, Gary
1993		NCAA	III	8	—	—	—	—	—	—	—	25	4	Fifield, Gary
1995		NCAA	III	64	—	—	—	—	—	—	—	23	4	Fifield, Gary
1996		NCAA	III	16	—	—	—	—	—	—	—	25	4	Fifield, Gary
1997		NCAA	III	16	—	—	—	—	—	—	—	25	4	Fifield, Gary
1998		NCAA	III	2	—	—	—	—	—	—	—	29	3	Fifield, Gary
SOUTHERN MAINE TECH														
1995	M	NSCAA		7	—	—	—	—	—	—	—	24	14	Stockwell, Dr. Ira
1996		NSCAA		10	—	—	—	—	—	—	—	24	8	Fournier, William
SOUTHERN METHODIST (TX)														
1955	M	NCAA		16	—	—	—	—	—	—	—	15	10	Hayes, Elmore O. "Doc"
1956		NCAA		4	—	—	—	—	—	—	—	25	4	Hayes, Elmore O. "Doc"
1957		NCAA	I	12	—	—	—	—	—	—	—	22	4	Hayes, Elmore O. "Doc"
1965		NCAA	I	12	—	—	—	—	—	—	—	17	10	Hayes, Elmore O. "Doc"
1966		NCAA	I	12	—	—	—	—	—	—	—	17	9	Hayes, Elmore O. "Doc"
1967		NCAA	I	8	—	—	—	—	—	—	—	20	6	Hayes, Elmore O. "Doc"
1974		NCAA	I	—	—	—	8	—	—	—	—	15	12	Prewitt, Bob
1984		NCAA	I	32	—	—	—	—	—	—	—	25	8	Bliss, David
1985		NCAA	I	32	—	—	—	—	—	—	—	23	10	Bliss, David
1986		NCAA	I	—	32	—	—	—	—	—	—	18	11	Bliss, David
1988		NCAA	I	32	—	—	—	—	—	—	—	28	7	Bliss, David
1993		NCAA	I	64	—	—	—	—	—	—	—	20	8	Shumate, John H.
1993	W	NCAA	I	—	2	—	—	—	—	—	—	20	10	Rompola, Rhonda
1994		NCAA	I	64	—	—	—	—	—	—	—	18	9	Rompola, Rhonda
1995		NCAA	I	32	—	—	—	—	—	—	—	21	9	Rompola, Rhonda
1996		NCAA	I	64	—	—	—	—	—	—	—	19	11	Rompola, Rhonda
1998		NCAA	I	64	—	—	—	—	—	—	—	21	8	Rompola, Rhonda
SOUTHERN MISSISSIPPI														
1952	M	NAIA		32	—	—	—	—	—	—	—	29	8	Floyd, Lee P.
1953		NAIA		8	—	—	—	—	—	—	—	27	8	Floyd, Lee P.
1954		NAIA		32	—	—	—	—	—	—	—	23	8	Floyd, Lee P.
1955		NAIA		32	—	—	—	—	—	—	—	11	17	Finley, Charles L. "Chuck"
1981		NCAA	I	—	32	—	—	—	—	—	—	20	7	Turk, M. K.
1986		NCAA	I	—	32	—	—	—	—	—	—	17	12	Turk, M. K.
1987		NCAA	I	—	1	—	—	—	—	—	—	23	11	Turk, M. K.
1988		NCAA	I	—	16	—	—	—	—	—	—	19	11	Turk, M. K.

Year	M/W	Assn	Div	NAT	NIT	ARC	CCA	NCI	NCT	OLY	HLM	W	L	Coach
1990		NCAA	I	64	—	—	—	—	—	—	—	20	12	Turk, M. K.
1991		NCAA	I	64	—	—	—	—	—	—	—	21	8	Turk, M. K.
1994		NCAA	I	—	32	—	—	—	—	—	—	15	15	Turk, M. K.
1995		NCAA	I	—	32	—	—	—	—	—	—	17	13	Turk, M. K.
1998		NCAA	I	—	32	—	—	—	—	—	—	22	11	Green, James
1982	W	NCAA	I	—	7	—	—	—	—	—	—	16	11	James, Kay
1985		NCAA	I	32	—	—	—	—	—	—	—	21	9	James, Kay
1987		NCAA	I	40	—	—	—	—	—	—	—	21	9	James, Kay
1989		NCAA	I	48	—	—	—	—	—	—	—	26	5	James, Kay
1990		NCAA	I	32	—	—	—	—	—	—	—	27	5	James, Kay
1992		NCAA	I	48	—	—	—	—	—	—	—	21	10	James, Kay
1994		NCAA	I	16	—	—	—	—	—	—	—	26	5	James, Kay
1995		NCAA	I	64	—	—	—	—	—	—	—	21	9	James, Kay
1996		NCAA	I	32	—	—	—	—	—	—	—	22	8	James, Kay

SOUTHERN NAZARENE

Year	M/W	Assn	Div	NAT	NIT	ARC	CCA	NCI	NCT	OLY	HLM	W	L	Coach
1974	M	NCCAA		1	—	—	—	—	—	—	—	31	6	Poteet, Jim
1976		NAIA		32	—	—	—	—	—	—	—	26	10	Poteet, Jim
1977		NCCAA	I	1	—	—	—	—	—	—	—	28	10	Poteet, Jim
1978		NAIA		32	—	—	—	—	—	—	—	24	12	Poteet, Jim
1979		NCCAA	I	3	—	—	—	—	—	—	—	18	21	Poteet, Jim
1981		NAIA		1	—	—	—	—	—	—	—	36	6	Gresham, Dr. Loren
1988		NAIA		32	—	—	—	—	—	—	—	26	11	Martin, Bobby
1997		NAIA	I	32	—	—	—	—	—	—	—	25	9	Martin, Bobby
1998		NAIA	I	2	—	—	—	—	—	—	—	29	9	Martin, Bobby
1989	W	NAIA		1	—	—	—	—	—	—	—	36	2	Hoffman, Bob
1992		NAIA	I	16	—	—	—	—	—	—	—	31	3	Finkbeiner, Jerry
1993		NAIA	I	3	—	—	—	—	—	—	—	30	5	Finkbeiner, Jerry
1994		NAIA	I	1	—	—	—	—	—	—	—	34	0	Finkbeiner, Jerry
1995		NAIA	I	1	—	—	—	—	—	—	—	30	2	Finkbeiner, Jerry
1996		NAIA	I	1	—	—	—	—	—	—	—	34	2	Finkbeiner, Jerry
1997		NAIA	I	1	—	—	—	—	—	—	—	32	4	Finkbeiner, Jerry
1998		NAIA	I	2	—	—	—	—	—	—	—	31	6	Wiginton, Craig

SOUTHERN OHIO: CINCINNATI

Year	M/W	Assn	Div	NAT	NIT	ARC	CCA	NCI	NCT	OLY	HLM	W	L	Coach
1974	M	NSCAA		16	—	—	—	—	—	—	—			
1982		NSCAA		8	—	—	—	—	—	—	—	14	14	Nelson, LaDon

SOUTHERN OREGON

Year	M/W	Assn	Div	NAT	NIT	ARC	CCA	NCI	NCT	OLY	HLM	W	L	Coach
1948	M	NAIA		32	—	—	—	—	—	—	—	24	3	Schopf, Dr. Theodore G.
1968		NAIA		32	—	—	—	—	—	—	—	23	6	Holmes, William J.
1997	W	NAIA	II	3	—	—	—	—	—	—	—	25	9	Huyett, Shirley
1998		NAIA	II	16	—	—	—	—	—	—	—	28	4	Huyett, Shirley

SOUTHERN TECH (GA)

Year	M/W	Assn	Div	NAT	NIT	ARC	CCA	NCI	NCT	OLY	HLM	W	L	Coach
1978	M	NAIA		32	—	—	—	—	—	—	—	26	6	Florian, Fran
1979		NAIA		16	—	—	—	—	—	—	—	24	4	Florian, Fran
1980		NAIA		32	—	—	—	—	—	—	—	25	10	Perides, George L.
1981		NAIA		16	—	—	—	—	—	—	—	28	5	Perides, George L.
1982		NAIA		16	—	—	—	—	—	—	—	27	5	Perides, George L.
1987		NAIA		32	—	—	—	—	—	—	—	27	7	Perides, George L.

Year	M/W	Assn	Div	NAT	NIT	ARC	CCA	NCI	NCT	OLY	HLM	W	L	Coach
SOUTHERN UNION STATE CC														
1973	M	NSCAA	8	—	—	—	—	—	—	—	—	22	12	Gourdouze, Frank
1974		NSCAA	16	—	—	—	—	—	—	—	—	13	12	Gourdouze, Frank
1975		NSCAA	3	—	—	—	—	—	—	—	—			Gourdouze, Frank
1976		NSCAA	3	—	—	—	—	—	—	—	—	21	10	Gourdouze, Frank
1977		NSCAA	3	—	—	—	—	—	—	—	—	21	9	Gourdouze, Frank
1978		NSCAA	1	—	—	—	—	—	—	—	—	28	5	Gourdouze, Frank
1980		NSCAA	3	—	—	—	—	—	—	—	—	21	11	Gourdouze, Frank
1982		NSCAA	4	—	—	—	—	—	—	—	—	20	12	Gourdouze, Frank
SOUTHERN UTAH														
1977	M	NAIA	32	—	—	—	—	—	—	—	—	21	7	Jack, Stanley
1975	W	AIAW	S 12	—	—	—	—	—	—	—	—	X	X	Bryant, Sandy
1988		NAIA	16	—	—	—	—	—	—	—	—	18	8	Adams, Boyd
SOUTHERN WESLEYAN														
1976	M	NCCAA	I 2	—	—	—	—	—	—	—	—	21	10	Hill, Lewis
1977		NCCAA	I 4	—	—	—	—	—	—	—	—			Drennon, Craig
1979		NAIA	32	—	—	—	—	—	—	—	—	25	10	Drennon, Craig
1984		NAIA	16	—	—	—	—	—	—	—	—	22	10	Shaver, Tom
SOUTHERN: BATON ROUGE														
1952	M	NASC	4	—	—	—	—	—	—	—	—	23	5	Lee, Robert Henry
1953		NASC	3	—	—	—	—	—	—	—	—	22	9	Lee, Robert Henry
1954		NASC	4	—	—	—	—	—	—	—	—	27	7	Lee, Robert Henry
1965		NAIA	8	—	—	—	—	—	—	—	—	25	5	Mack, Richard
1974		NCAA	II 32	—	—	—	—	—	—	—	—	17	13	Stewart, Carl E.
1975		NCAA	II 24	—	—	—	—	—	—	—	—	19	8	Stewart, Carl E.
1977		NCAA	II 32	—	—	—	—	—	—	—	—	19	11	Stewart, Carl E.
1981		NCAA	I 48	—	—	—	—	—	—	—	—	17	11	Stewart, Carl E.
1985		NCAA	I 64	—	—	—	—	—	—	—	—	19	11	Hopkins, Robert M.
1987		NCAA	I 64	—	—	—	—	—	—	—	—	19	12	Jobe, Ben
1988		NCAA	I 64	—	—	—	—	—	—	—	—	24	7	Jobe, Ben
1989		NCAA	I 64	—	—	—	—	—	—	—	—	20	11	Jobe, Ben
1990		NCAA	I	—	32	—	—	—	—	—	—	25	6	Jobe, Ben
1993		NCAA	I 32	—	—	—	—	—	—	—	—	21	10	Jobe, Ben
SOUTHERN: NEW ORLEANS														
1995	M	NAIA	I 32	—	—	—	—	—	—	—	—	21	11	Hill, Earl R.
1998		NAIA	I 32	—	—	—	—	—	—	—	—	20	15	Hill, Earl R.
SOUTHWEST BAPTIST														
1976	M	NAIA	32	—	—	—	—	—	—	—	—	19	10	Garrett, Howard V.
1990		NCAA	II 32	—	—	—	—	—	—	—	—	25	6	Kirksey, Jerry L.
1991		NCAA	II 8	—	—	—	—	—	—	—	—	29	3	Kirksey, Jerry L.
1996	W	NCAA	II 48	—	—	—	—	—	—	—	—	21	9	Middleton, Jim
1998		NCAA	II 48	—	—	—	—	—	—	—	—	18	11	Middleton, Jim
SOUTHWEST MISSOURI STATE														
1939	M	NAIA	32	—	—	—	—	—	—	—	—	15	4	McDonald, A. C. "Andy"
1943		NAIA	32	—	—	—	—	—	—	—	—	12	13	McDonald, A. C. "Andy"
1949		NAIA	16	—	—	—	—	—	—	—	—	25	2	McDonald, A. C. "Andy"
1952		NAIA	1	—	—	—	—	—	—	8	—	27	5	Vanatta, Robert

Year	M/W	Assn	Div	NAT	NIT	ARC	CCA	NCI	NCT	OLY	HLM	W	L	Coach
1953		NAIA		1	—	—	—	—	—	—	—	24	4	Vanatta, Robert
1954		NAIA		3	—	—	—	—	—	—	—	20	6	Matthews, Edwin "Eddie"
1958		NCAA	II	8	—	—	—	—	—	—	—	22	2	Matthews, Edwin "Eddie"
1959		NCAA	II	2	—	—	—	—	—	—	—	23	3	Matthews, Edwin "Eddie"
1966		NCAA	II	16	—	—	—	—	—	—	—	19	6	Thomas, William J.
1967		NCAA	II	2	—	—	—	—	—	—	—	23	5	Thomas, William J.
1968		NCAA	II	16	—	—	—	—	—	—	—	19	6	Thomas, William J.
1969		NCAA	II	2	—	—	—	—	—	—	—	24	5	Thomas, William J.
1970		NCAA	II	24	—	—	—	—	—	—	—	17	11	Thomas, William J.
1973		NCAA	II	24	—	—	—	—	—	—	—	19	8	Thomas, William J.
1974		NCAA	II	2	—	—	—	—	—	—	—	21	9	Thomas, William J.
1978		NCAA	II	16	—	—	—	—	—	—	—	21	7	Thomas, William J.
1986		NCAA	I	—	8	—	—	—	—	—	—	24	8	Spoonhour, Charles
1987		NCAA	I	32	—	—	—	—	—	—	—	28	6	Spoonhour, Charles
1988		NCAA	I	64	—	—	—	—	—	—	—	22	7	Spoonhour, Charles
1989		NCAA	I	64	—	—	—	—	—	—	—	21	10	Spoonhour, Charles
1990		NCAA	I	64	—	—	—	—	—	—	—	22	7	Spoonhour, Charles
1991		NCAA	I	—	16	—	—	—	—	—	—	22	12	Spoonhour, Charles
1992		NCAA	I	64	—	—	—	—	—	—	—	23	8	Spoonhour, Charles
1993		NCAA	I	—	8	—	—	—	—	—	—	20	11	Bernsen, Mark
1997		NCAA	I	—	32	—	—	—	—	—	—	24	9	Alford, Stephen T.
1981	W	AIAW	II	16	—	—	—	—	—	—	—	25	10	Gasser, Martha "Marti"
1991		NCAA	I	32	—	—	—	—	—	—	—	26	5	Burnett, Cheryl
1992		NCAA	I	3	—	—	—	—	—	—	—	31	3	Burnett, Cheryl
1993		NCAA	I	16	—	—	—	—	—	—	—	23	9	Burnett, Cheryl
1994		NCAA	I	32	—	—	—	—	—	—	—	24	6	Burnett, Cheryl
1995		NCAA	I	32	—	—	—	—	—	—	—	21	12	Burnett, Cheryl
1996		NCAA	I	64	—	—	—	—	—	—	—	25	5	Burnett, Cheryl
1998		NCAA	I	64	—	—	—	—	—	—	—	24	6	Burnett, Cheryl

SOUTHWEST TEXAS STATE

Year	M/W	Assn	Div	NAT	NIT	ARC	CCA	NCI	NCT	OLY	HLM	W	L	Coach
1951	M	NAIA		16	—	—	—	—	—	—	—	21	5	Jowers, Milton W.
1952		NAIA		3	—	—	—	—	—	—	—	30	1	Jowers, Milton W.
1957		NAIA		16	—	—	—	—	—	—	—	22	7	Jowers, Milton W.
1959		NAIA		3	—	—	—	—	—	—	—	25	6	Jowers, Milton W.
1960		NAIA		1	—	—	—	—	—	—	—	28	3	Jowers, Milton W.
1961		NAIA		8	—	—	—	—	—	—	—	21	8	Jowers, Milton W.
1979		NAIA		3	—	—	—	—	—	—	—	29	7	Wall, Daniel P.
1994		NCAA	I	64	—	—	—	—	—	—	—	25	7	Wooldridge, Jim
1997		NCAA	I	64	—	—	—	—	—	—	—	16	13	Miller, Mike
1997	W	NCAA	I	64	—	—	—	—	—	—	—	17	12	Sharp, Linda K.

SOUTHWESTERN (AZ)

Year	M/W	Assn	Div	NAT	NIT	ARC	CCA	NCI	NCT	OLY	HLM	W	L	Coach
1986	M	NSCAA		10	—	—	—	—	—	—	—	21	9	Westphal, Paul D.
1996		NCCAA	IIA	3	—	—	—	—	—	—	—	15	18	Morley, Stephen H.
1997		NCCAA	IIA	1	—	—	—	—	—	—	—	21	8	Morley, Stephen H.
1998		NCCAA	IIA	5	—	—	—	—	—	—	—	16	13	Morley, Stephen H.

SOUTHWESTERN (KS)

Year	M/W	Assn	Div	NAT	NIT	ARC	CCA	NCI	NCT	OLY	HLM	W	L	Coach
1937	M	NAIA		3	—	—	—	—	—	—	—	14	11	Monypeny, William W.
1939		NAIA		1	—	—	—	—	—	—	—	21	2	Gardner, George
1940		NAIA		8	—	—	—	—	—	—	—	14	9	Monypeny, William W.
1942		NAIA		16	—	—	—	—	—	—	—	16	5	Monypeny, William W.

Year	M/W	Assn	Div	NAT	NIT	ARC	CCA	NCI	NCT	OLY	HLM	W	L	Coach
1943		NAIA		16	—	—	—	—	—	—	—	17	5	Monypeny, William W.
1955		NAIA		16	—	—	—	—	—	—	—	20	8	Cotton, Dr. John J. *Jack*
1998		NAIA	II	32	—	—	—	—	—	—	—	14	16	Horstmann, Brad

SOUTHWESTERN (TX)

Year	M/W	Assn	Div	NAT	NIT	ARC	CCA	NCI	NCT	OLY	HLM	W	L	Coach
1985	M	NAIA		32	—	—	—	—	—	—	—	24	9	Peak, Paul
1986		NAIA		8	—	—	—	—	—	—	—	20	12	Peak, Paul
1990		NAIA		16	—	—	—	—	—	—	—	19	9	Peak, Paul
1998	W	NCAA	III	48	—	—	—	—	—	—	—	15	11	Seagraves, Rhonda

SOUTHWESTERN ASSEMBLIES

Year	M/W	Assn	Div	NAT	NIT	ARC	CCA	NCI	NCT	OLY	HLM	W	L	Coach
1985	M	NBCAA	I	7	—	—	—	—	—	—	—	X	X	Bryan, Terry
1986		NBCAA	I	6	—	—	—	—	—	—	—	X	X	Bryan, Terry
1987		NBCAA	I	6	—	—	—	—	—	—	—	15	17	Bryan, Terry
1988		NBCAA	I	4	—	—	—	—	—	—	—	X	X	Bryan, Terry
1989		NBCAA	I	3	—	—	—	—	—	—	—	X	X	Bryan, Terry
1993		NBCAA	I	6	—	—	—	—	—	—	—	X	X	Pratt, Bruce
1994		NBCAA	I	3	—	—	—	—	—	—	—	X	X	Garippa, Rev. Steven P.
1995		NBCAA	I	7	—	—	—	—	—	—	—	20	8	Garippa, Rev. Steven P.
1996		NBCAA	I	5	—	—	—	—	—	—	—	8	17	Garippa, Rev. Steven P.
1997		NBCAA	I	5	—	—	—	—	—	—	—	19	19	Garippa, Rev. Steven P.
1998		NBCAA		1	—	—	—	—	—	—	—	20	8	Garippa, Rev. Steven P.
1998	W	NBCAA		3	—	—	—	—	—	—	—	11	14	Goodrich, Dr. Larry

SOUTHWESTERN CHRISTIAN MINISTRIES

Year	M/W	Assn	Div	NAT	NIT	ARC	CCA	NCI	NCT	OLY	HLM	W	L	Coach
1993	M	NBCAA	II	6	—	—	—	—	—	—	—	18	18	Arthur, Mark
1993		NCCAA	IIA	4	—	—	—	—	—	—	—	18	18	Arthur, Mark
1994		NBCAA	II	3	—	—	—	—	—	—	—	18	16	Arthur, Mark
1995		NBCAA	I	3	—	—	—	—	—	—	—	26	4	Arthur, Mark
1995		NCCAA	IIA	4	—	—	—	—	—	—	—	26	4	Arthur, Mark
1996		NBCAA	I	4	—	—	—	—	—	—	—	26	16	Arthur, Mark
1996		NCCAA	II	8	—	—	—	—	—	—	—	26	16	Arthur, Mark
1997		NBCAA	II	1	—	—	—	—	—	—	—	26	15	Arthur, Mark
1997		NCCAA	IIA	5	—	—	—	—	—	—	—	26	15	Arthur, Mark
1998		NBCAA		2	—	—	—	—	—	—	—	21	17	Arthur, Mark
1998		NCCAA	IIA	1	—	—	—	—	—	—	—	21	17	Arthur, Mark

SOUTHWESTERN LOUISIANA

Year	M/W	Assn	Div	NAT	NIT	ARC	CCA	NCI	NCT	OLY	HLM	W	L	Coach
1965	M	NAIA		16	—	—	—	—	—	—	—	20	10	Shipley, Beryl C.
1967		NAIA		8	—	—	—	—	—	—	—	20	11	Shipley, Beryl C.
1971		NCAA	II	3	—	—	—	—	—	—	—	25	4	Shipley, Beryl C.
1972		NCAA	I	12	—	—	—	—	—	—	—	25	4	Shipley, Beryl C.
1973		NCAA	I	16	—	—	—	—	—	—	—	24	5	Shipley, Beryl C.
1980		NCAA	I	—	8	—	—	—	—	—	—	21	9	Paschal, Bobby
1982		NCAA	I	48	—	—	—	—	—	—	—	24	8	Paschal, Bobby
1983		NCAA	I	48	—	—	—	—	—	—	—	22	7	Paschal, Bobby
1984		NCAA	I	—	4	—	—	—	—	—	—	23	10	Paschal, Bobby
1985		NCAA	I	—	16	—	—	—	—	—	—	17	14	Paschal, Bobby
1992		NCAA	I	32	—	—	—	—	—	—	—	21	11	Fletcher, Marty
1994		NCAA	I	64	—	—	—	—	—	—	—	22	8	Fletcher, Marty

Year	M/W	Assn	Div	NAT	NIT	ARC	CCA	NCI	NCT	OLY	HLM	W	L	Coach

SOUTHWESTERN OKLAHOMA STATE

1953	M	NAIA		32	—	—	—	—	—	—	—	24	6	Williams, Rankin
1969		NAIA		16	—	—	—	—	—	—	—	23	8	Jobe, Jerry
1977		NAIA		16	—	—	—	—	—	—	—	24	5	Hauser, George
1995		NAIA	I	32	—	—	—	—	—	—	—	20	12	Hauser, George
1982	W	NAIA		1	—	—	—	—	—	—	—	34	0	Loftin, John D.
1983		NAIA		1	—	—	—	—	—	—	—	30	4	Loftin, John D.
1984		NAIA		8	—	—	—	—	—	—	—	31	1	Loftin, John D.
1985		NAIA		1	—	—	—	—	—	—	—	34	0	Loftin, John D.
1987		NAIA		1	—	—	—	—	—	—	—	30	2	Loftin, John D.
1990		NAIA		1	—	—	—	—	—	—	—	30	4	Loftin, John D.
1991		NAIA		2	—	—	—	—	—	—	—	31	3	Loftin, John D.
1992		NAIA	I	3	—	—	—	—	—	—	—	30	4	Loftin, John D.
1993		NAIA	I	3	—	—	—	—	—	—	—	29	4	Loftin, John D.
1994		NAIA	I	8	—	—	—	—	—	—	—	25	7	Loftin, John D.
1995		NAIA	I	3	—	—	—	—	—	—	—	30	5	Loftin, John D.
1996		NAIA	I	32	—	—	—	—	—	—	—	20	9	Loftin, John D.
1997		NAIA	I	3	—	—	—	—	—	—	—	28	5	Loftin, John D.
1998		NAIA	I	32	—	—	—	—	—	—	—	21	8	Loftin, John D.

SPRING ARBOR

1982	M	NCCAA	I	2	—	—	—	—	—	—	—	23	14	Bockwitz, William
1984		NCCAA	I	8	—	—	—	—	—	—	—	19	15	Bockwitz, William
1995		NAIA	I	32	—	—	—	—	—	—	—	19	17	Noll, Doug
1997		NAIA	II	8	—	—	—	—	—	—	—	29	7	Noll, Doug
1980	W	AIAW	III	24	—	—	—	—	—	—	—	21	5	Dunckel, Darrell
1981		AIAW	III	16	—	—	—	—	—	—	—	24	6	Dunckel, Darrell
1983		NCCAA	I	1	—	—	—	—	—	—	—	29	4	Dunckel, Darrell
1984		NCCAA	I	2	—	—	—	—	—	—	—	25	9	Dunckel, Darrell
1985		NCCAA	I	4	—	—	—	—	—	—	—	25	8	Dunckel, Darrell
1987		NCCAA	I	1	—	—	—	—	—	—	—	25	9	Dunckel, Darrell
1994		NAIA	II	24	—	—	—	—	—	—	—	22	10	Britsch, Tom
1996		NAIA	II	32	—	—	—	—	—	—	—	26	9	Britsch, Tom
1998		NAIA	II	8	—	—	—	—	—	—	—	23	11	Britsch, Tom

SPRING GARDEN

1977	M	NAIA		32	—	—	—	—	—	—	—	16	10	Burke, Les
1982	W	NAIA		8	—	—	—	—	—	—	—	29	4	Soroka, Michael
1987		NCAA	III	24	—	—	—	—	—	—	—	25	5	Brennan, Dennis

SPRING HILL

1951	M	NAIA		—	—	—	—	10	—	—	—	19	8	Gardiner, William C.
1992		NAIA	I	16	—	—	—	—	—	—	—	24	11	Nash, Carl
1993		NAIA	I	32	—	—	—	—	—	—	—	22	9	Nash, Carl
1994		NAIA	I	32	—	—	—	—	—	—	—	22	10	Niland, Joseph P., Jr.

SPRINGFIELD (MA)

1940	M	NCAA		8	—	—	—	—	—	—	—	16	3	Hickox, Edward J. "Eddie"
1961		NCAA	II	32	—	—	—	—	—	—	—	16	10	Steitz, Dr. Edward S.
1963		NCAA	II	16	—	—	—	—	—	—	—	20	6	Steitz, Dr. Edward S.
1964		NCAA	II	32	—	—	—	—	—	—	—	17	8	Steitz, Dr. Edward S.

Year	M/W	Assn	Div	NAT	NIT	ARC	CCA	NCI	NCT	OLY	HLM	W	L	Coach
1966		NCAA	II	36	—	—	—	—	—	—	—	20	6	Steitz, Dr. Edward S.
1968		NCAA	II	36	—	—	—	—	—	—	—	17	9	Bilik, Dr. Edward R.
1969		NCAA	II	16	—	—	—	—	—	—	—	16	9	Bilik, Dr. Edward R.
1970		NCAA	II	24	—	—	—	—	—	—	—	17	8	Bilik, Dr. Edward R.
1980		NCAA	II	16	—	—	—	—	—	—	—	20	7	Bilik, Dr. Edward R.
1981		NCAA	II	32	—	—	—	—	—	—	—	20	9	Bilik, Dr. Edward R.
1982		NCAA	II	24	—	—	—	—	—	—	—	21	8	Bilik, Dr. Edward R.
1986		NCAA	II	24	—	—	—	—	—	—	—	20	12	Bilik, Dr. Edward R.
1996		NCAA	III	64	—	—	—	—	—	—	—	21	7	Theulen, Dr. Michael D.
1997		NCAA	III	64	—	—	—	—	—	—	—	23	5	Theulen, Dr. Michael D.
1998		NCAA	III	32	—	—	—	—	—	—	—	26	2	Theulen, Dr. Michael D.
1970	W	AIAW		16	—	—	—	—	—	—	—	7	5	Bush, Jone
1981		AIAW	II	16	—	—	—	—	—	—	—	18	7	Shapiro, Harvey P.
1982		NCAA	II	8	—	—	—	—	—	—	—	23	3	Shapiro, Harvey P.

STANFORD

Year	M/W	Assn	Div	NAT	NIT	ARC	CCA	NCI	NCT	OLY	HLM	W	L	Coach
1937	M	NCAA		—	—	—	—	—	—	—	1	25	2	Bunn, John W.
1942		NCAA		1	—	—	—	—	—	—	1	27	4	Dean, Everett S.
1988		NCAA	I	—	16	—	—	—	—	—	—	21	12	Montgomery, Mike
1989		NCAA	I	64	—	—	—	—	—	—	—	26	7	Montgomery, Mike
1990		NCAA	I	—	32	—	—	—	—	—	—	18	12	Montgomery, Mike
1991		NCAA	I	—	1	—	—	—	—	—	—	20	13	Montgomery, Mike
1992		NCAA	I	64	—	—	—	—	—	—	—	18	11	Montgomery, Mike
1994		NCAA	I	—	32	—	—	—	—	—	—	17	11	Montgomery, Mike
1995		NCAA	I	32	—	—	—	—	—	—	—	20	9	Montgomery, Mike
1996		NCAA	I	32	—	—	—	—	—	—	—	20	9	Montgomery, Mike
1997		NCAA	I	16	—	—	—	—	—	—	—	22	8	Montgomery, Mike
1998		NCAA	I	3	—	—	—	—	—	—	—	30	5	Montgomery, Mike
1982	W	NCAA	I	32	—	—	—	—	—	—	—	19	8	McCrea, Dotty
1988		NCAA	I	16	—	—	—	—	—	—	—	27	5	VanDerveer, Tara
1989		NCAA	I	8	—	—	—	—	—	—	—	28	3	VanDerveer, Tara
1990		NCAA	I	1	—	—	—	—	—	—	—	32	1	VanDerveer, Tara
1991		NCAA	I	3	—	—	—	—	—	—	—	26	6	VanDerveer, Tara
1992		NCAA	I	1	—	—	—	—	—	—	—	30	3	VanDerveer, Tara
1993		NCAA	I	16	—	—	—	—	—	—	—	26	6	VanDerveer, Tara
1994		NCAA	I	8	—	—	—	—	—	—	—	25	6	VanDerveer, Tara
1995		NCAA	I	3	—	—	—	—	—	—	—	30	3	VanDerveer, Tara
1996		NCAA	I	3	—	—	—	—	—	—	—	29	3	Tucker, Amy
1997		NCAA	I	3	—	—	—	—	—	—	—	34	2	VanDerveer, Tara
1998		NCAA	I	64	—	—	—	—	—	—	—	21	6	VanDerveer, Tara

STATEN ISLAND

Year	M/W	Assn	Div	NAT	NIT	ARC	CCA	NCI	NCT	OLY	HLM	W	L	Coach
1981	M	NCAA	III	32	—	—	—	—	—	—	—	21	8	Pickman, Dr. Evan T.
1982		NCAA	III	16	—	—	—	—	—	—	—	25	4	Pickman, Dr. Evan T.
1984		NCAA	III	16	—	—	—	—	—	—	—	25	4	Pickman, Dr. Evan T.
1988		NCAA	III	32	—	—	—	—	—	—	—	21	9	Ruppert, Howie
1989		NCAA	III	32	—	—	—	—	—	—	—	24	7	Ruppert, Howie
1995		NCAA	III	64	—	—	—	—	—	—	—	20	7	Petosa, Anthony
1996		NCAA	III	64	—	—	—	—	—	—	—	22	6	Petosa, Anthony
1997	W	NCAA	III	64	—	—	—	—	—	—	—	22	6	Mosley, Gerry

Year	M/W	Assn	Div	NAT	NIT	ARC	CCA	NCI	NCT	OLY	HLM	W	L	Coach
STEED														
1969	M	NSCAA		5	—	—	—	—	—	—	—			
1971		NSCAA		5	—	—	—	—	—	—	—	18	5	Anderson, Robert
STEPHEN F AUSTIN STATE														
1941	M	NAIA		16	—	—	—	—	—	—	—	21	6	Shelton, Robert H.
1956		NAIA		16	—	—	—	—	—	—	—	24	6	Stephens, John O.
1965		NAIA		32	—	—	—	—	—	—	—	19	7	Brown, Marshall
1968		NAIA		32	—	—	—	—	—	—	—	27	3	Brown, Marshall
1970		NAIA		8	—	—	—	—	—	—	—	29	1	Brown, Marshall
1971		NAIA		8	—	—	—	—	—	—	—	20	6	Brown, Marshall
1972		NAIA		3	—	—	—	—	—	—	—	25	2	Brown, Marshall
1982		NAIA		32	—	—	—	—	—	—	—	24	6	Miller, Harry E.
1983		NCAA	II	24	—	—	—	—	—	—	—	21	10	Miller, Harry E.
1987		NCAA	I	—	16	—	—	—	—	—	—	22	8	Miller, Harry E.
1973	W	AIAW		8	—	—	—	—	—	—	—	21	6	Gunter, Sue
1974		AIAW		12	—	—	—	—	—	—	—	27	7	Gunter, Sue
1975		AIAW	L	12	—	—	—	—	—	—	—	32	7	Gunter, Sue
1978		AIAW	L	8	—	—	—	—	—	—	—	25	14	Gunter, Sue
1980		AIAW	I	8	—	—	—	—	—	—	—	27	6	Gunter, Sue
1981		AIAW	I	16	—	—	—	—	—	—	—	24	11	Otwell, Mary Ann
1982		NCAA	I	32	—	—	—	—	—	—	—	15	9	Otwell, Mary Ann
1983		NCAA	I	32	—	—	—	—	—	—	—	18	7	Otwell, Mary Ann
1987		NCAA	I	—	5	—	—	—	—	—	—	25	6	Blair, Gary
1988		NCAA	I	32	—	—	—	—	—	—	—	29	5	Blair, Gary
1989		NCAA	I	16	—	—	—	—	—	—	—	30	4	Blair, Gary
1990		NCAA	I	16	—	—	—	—	—	—	—	28	3	Blair, Gary
1991		NCAA	I	32	—	—	—	—	—	—	—	26	5	Blair, Gary
1992		NCAA	I	16	—	—	—	—	—	—	—	28	3	Blair, Gary
1993		NCAA	I	16	—	—	—	—	—	—	—	28	5	Blair, Gary
1994		NCAA	I	64	—	—	—	—	—	—	—	23	7	Curl, Joe
1995		NCAA	I	64	—	—	—	—	—	—	—	22	8	Chadwick, Royce
1996		NCAA	I	16	—	—	—	—	—	—	—	27	4	Chadwick, Royce
1997		NCAA	I	32	—	—	—	—	—	—	—	28	5	Chadwick, Royce
1998		NCAA	I	64	—	—	—	—	—	—	—	25	4	Chadwick, Royce
STERLING (KS)														
1993	W	NAIA	II	16	—	—	—	—	—	—	—	25	4	Kruse, Lonnie
1995		NAIA	II	16	—	—	—	—	—	—	—	24	6	Kruse, Lonnie
1996		NAIA	II	32	—	—	—	—	—	—	—	28	1	Kruse, Lonnie
1997		NAIA	II	16	—	—	—	—	—	—	—	28	2	Kruse, Lonnie
1998		NAIA	II	16	—	—	—	—	—	—	—	26	7	Kruse, Lonnie
STETSON														
1953	M	NAIA		16	—	—	—	—	—	—	—	14	10	Morland, Richard B.
1957		NAIA		16	—	—	—	—	—	—	—	17	8	Morland, Richard B.
1960		NAIA		32	—	—	—	—	—	—	—	16	13	Wilkes, Dr. Glenn N., Sr.
1962		NAIA		32	—	—	—	—	—	—	—	16	12	Wilkes, Dr. Glenn N., Sr.
1963		NAIA		16	—	—	—	—	—	—	—	15	13	Wilkes, Dr. Glenn N., Sr.
1967		NCAA	II	32	—	—	—	—	—	—	—	17	10	Wilkes, Dr. Glenn N., Sr.
1970		NCAA	II	8	—	—	—	—	—	—	—	22	7	Wilkes, Dr. Glenn N., Sr.
1971		NCAA	II	24	—	—	—	—	—	—	—	19	9	Wilkes, Dr. Glenn N., Sr.

Year	M/W	Assn	Div	NAT	NIT	ARC	CCA	NCI	NCT	OLY	HLM	W	L	Coach
STILLMAN														
1996	M	NCAA	III	64	—	—	—	—	—	—	—	19	4	Robinson, Larry
STONEHILL														
1971	M	NCAA	II	32	—	—	—	—	—	—	—	20	6	Dougher, James D.
1973		NCAA	II	42	—	—	—	—	—	—	—	19	7	Dougher, James D.
1980		NCAA	II	24	—	—	—	—	—	—	—	18	10	Folliard, Thomas J.
1981		NCAA	II	24	—	—	—	—	—	—	—	21	9	Folliard, Thomas J.
1982		NCAA	II	32	—	—	—	—	—	—	—	21	8	Folliard, Thomas J.
1989		NCAA	II	32	—	—	—	—	—	—	—	23	9	Pepin, Raymond
1998		NCAA	II	16	—	—	—	—	—	—	—	22	7	DeCiantis, David
1983	W	NCAA	II	24	—	—	—	—	—	—	—	21	9	Sullivan, Paula J.
1985		NCAA	II	24	—	—	—	—	—	—	—	19	7	Sullivan, Paula J.
1987		NCAA	II	16	—	—	—	—	—	—	—	27	5	Sullivan, Paula J.
1988		NCAA	II	32	—	—	—	—	—	—	—	25	6	Sullivan, Paula J.
1991		NCAA	II	32	—	—	—	—	—	—	—	19	11	Sullivan, Paula J.
1992		NCAA	II	16	—	—	—	—	—	—	—	26	5	Sullivan, Paula J.
1993		NCAA	II	32	—	—	—	—	—	—	—	22	8	Sullivan, Paula J.
1994		NCAA	II	8	—	—	—	—	—	—	—	27	5	Sullivan, Paula J.
1995		NCAA	II	4	—	—	—	—	—	—	—	30	3	Sullivan, Paula J.
1996		NCAA	II	32	—	—	—	—	—	—	—	24	6	Sullivan, Paula J.
1997		NCAA	II	16	—	—	—	—	—	—	—	26	6	Hart, Kelly
1998		NCAA	II	48	—	—	—	—	—	—	—	24	7	Hart, Kelly
STONY BROOK STATE														
1970	M	NCAA	II	32	—	—	—	—	—	—	—	19	6	Massimino, Roland V. "Rollie"
1977		NCAA	III	23	—	—	—	—	—	—	—	21	6	Bash, Dr. M. Ronald
1978		NCAA	III	4	—	—	—	—	—	—	—	27	9	Bash, Dr. M. Ronald
1979		NCAA	III	24	—	—	—	—	—	—	—	24	3	Kendall, Dick
1980		NCAA	III	24	—	—	—	—	—	—	—	19	9	Kendall, Dick
1987		NCAA	III	24	—	—	—	—	—	—	—	21	6	Castiglie, Joe
1991		NCAA	III	32	—	—	—	—	—	—	—	23	4	Castiglie, Joe
1987	W	NCAA	III	16	—	—	—	—	—	—	—	24	5	McMullen, Declan
1989		NCAA	III	24	—	—	—	—	—	—	—	21	8	McMullen, Declan
STRAYER BUSINESS														
1967	M	NSCAA		2	—	—	—	—	—	—	—	17	6	Molloy, James H., Jr.
1968		NSCAA		5	—	—	—	—	—	—	—	17	8	Molloy, James H., Jr.
1971		NSCAA		8	—	—	—	—	—	—	—	10	12	Molloy, James H., Jr.
SUE BENNETT														
1985	M	NSCAA		3	—	—	—	—	—	—	—			
1995	W	NSCAA		7	—	—	—	—	—	—	—	19	19	Adams, Dean
SUFFOLK (MA)														
1975	M	NCAA	III	16	—	—	—	—	—	—	—	19	7	Law, Charles
1976		NCAA	III	28	—	—	—	—	—	—	—	19	6	Law, Charles
1977		NCAA	III	23	—	—	—	—	—	—	—	16	7	Law, Charles
1978		NCAA	III	30	—	—	—	—	—	—	—	15	10	Law, Charles

Year	M/W	Assn	Div	NAT	NIT	ARC	CCA	NCI	NCT	OLY	HLM	W	L	Coach

SUL ROSS STATE

Year	M/W	Assn	Div	NAT	NIT	ARC	CCA	NCI	NCT	OLY	HLM	W	L	Coach
1996	W	NAIA	II	32	—	—	—	—	—	—	—	13	8	Sample, Dr. Chet

SULLIVAN (KY)

Year	M/W	Assn	Div	NAT	NIT	ARC	CCA	NCI	NCT	OLY	HLM	W	L	Coach
1967	M	NSCAA		1	—	—	—	—	—	—	—	23	6	Tibbs, Harry
1968		NSCAA		1	—	—	—	—	—	—	—	26	6	Tibbs, Harry
1969		NSCAA		1	—	—	—	—	—	—	—	26	4	Sergeant, W. C.
1970		NSCAA		2	—	—	—	—	—	—	—	19	9	Sergeant, W. C.
1974		NSCAA		2	—	—	—	—	—	—	—	X	X	Mudd, Leon
1975		NSCAA		3	—	—	—	—	—	—	—	27	8	Caldwell, Jim
1976		NSCAA		8	—	—	—	—	—	—	—	18	14	Caldwell, Jim
1977		NSCAA		16	—	—	—	—	—	—	—	18	9	Caldwell, Jim
1980		NSCAA		1	—	—	—	—	—	—	—	28	8	Skinner, David L.
1981		NSCAA		8	—	—	—	—	—	—	—	20	12	Skinner, David L.
1982		NSCAA		12	—	—	—	—	—	—	—	19	14	Skinner, David L.
1984		NSCAA		4	—	—	—	—	—	—	—	21	12	Skinner, David L.
1987		NSCAA		16	—	—	—	—	—	—	—	17	16	Skinner, David L.

SUSQUEHANNA

Year	M/W	Assn	Div	NAT	NIT	ARC	CCA	NCI	NCT	OLY	HLM	W	L	Coach
1984	M	NCAA	III	16	—	—	—	—	—	—	—	21	7	Harnum, Donald
1986		NCAA	III	8	—	—	—	—	—	—	—	22	8	Harnum, Donald
1989		NCAA	III	32	—	—	—	—	—	—	—	18	10	Harnum, Donald
1992		NCAA	III	40	—	—	—	—	—	—	—	17	11	Marcinek, Frank
1994		NCAA	III	32	—	—	—	—	—	—	—	19	7	Marcinek, Frank
1982	W	NCAA	III	8	—	—	—	—	—	—	—	21	4	Diehl, Tom
1983		NCAA	III	32	—	—	—	—	—	—	—	24	2	Diehl, Tom
1984		NCAA	III	16	—	—	—	—	—	—	—	19	8	Diehl, Tom
1985		NCAA	III	24	—	—	—	—	—	—	—	24	5	Diehl, Tom
1986		NCAA	III	32	—	—	—	—	—	—	—	17	6	Diehl, Tom
1991		NCAA	III	16	—	—	—	—	—	—	—	23	5	Hribar, Mark
1992		NCAA	III	32	—	—	—	—	—	—	—	21	6	Hribar, Mark
1993		NCAA	III	32	—	—	—	—	—	—	—	19	7	Hribar, Mark

SYRACUSE

Year	M/W	Assn	Div	NAT	NIT	ARC	CCA	NCI	NCT	OLY	HLM	W	L	Coach
1918	M	NCAA		—	—	—	—	—	—	—	1	16	1	Dollard, Edmund A.
1926		NCAA		—	—	—	—	—	—	—	1	19	1	Andreas, Lewis P.
1946		NCAA		—	8	—	—	—	—	—	—	23	4	Andreas, Lewis P.
1950		NCAA		—	8	—	—	—	—	—	—	18	9	Andreas, Lewis P.
1951		NCAA		—	—	—	—	1	—	—	—	19	9	Guley, Marcel "Marc"
1957		NCAA	I	8	—	—	—	—	—	—	—	18	7	Guley, Marcel "Marc"
1964		NCAA	I	—	12	—	—	—	—	—	—	17	8	Lewis, Frederick B., Jr.
1966		NCAA	I	8	—	—	—	—	—	—	—	22	6	Lewis, Frederick B., Jr.
1967		NCAA	I	—	14	—	—	—	—	—	—	20	6	Lewis, Frederick B., Jr.
1971		NCAA	I	—	16	—	—	—	—	—	—	19	7	Danforth, Roy
1972		NCAA	I	—	8	—	—	—	—	—	—	22	6	Danforth, Roy
1973		NCAA	I	12	—	—	—	—	—	—	—	24	5	Danforth, Roy
1974		NCAA	I	25	—	—	—	—	—	—	—	19	7	Danforth, Roy
1975		NCAA	I	4	—	—	—	—	—	—	—	23	9	Danforth, Roy
1976		NCAA	I	32	—	—	—	—	—	—	—	20	9	Danforth, Roy
1977		NCAA	I	16	—	—	—	—	—	—	—	26	4	Boeheim, James A., Jr.

Year	M/W	Assn	Div	NAT	NIT	ARC	CCA	NCI	NCT	OLY	HLM	W	L	Coach
1978		NCAA	I	32	—	—	—	—	—	—	—	22	6	Boeheim, James A., Jr.
1979		NCAA	I	16	—	—	—	—	—	—	—	26	4	Boeheim, James A., Jr.
1980		NCAA	I	16	—	—	—	—	—	—	—	26	4	Boeheim, James A., Jr.
1981		NCAA	I	—	2	—	—	—	—	—	—	22	12	Boeheim, James A., Jr.
1982		NCAA	I	—	16	—	—	—	—	—	—	16	13	Boeheim, James A., Jr.
1983		NCAA	I	32	—	—	—	—	—	—	—	21	10	Boeheim, James A., Jr.
1984		NCAA	I	16	—	—	—	—	—	—	—	23	9	Boeheim, James A., Jr.
1985		NCAA	I	32	—	—	—	—	—	—	—	22	9	Boeheim, James A., Jr.
1986		NCAA	I	32	—	—	—	—	—	—	—	26	6	Boeheim, James A., Jr.
1987		NCAA	I	2	—	—	—	—	—	—	—	31	7	Boeheim, James A., Jr.
1988		NCAA	I	32	—	—	—	—	—	—	—	26	9	Boeheim, James A., Jr.
1989		NCAA	I	8	—	—	—	—	—	—	—	30	8	Boeheim, James A., Jr.
1990		NCAA	I	16	—	—	—	—	—	—	—	26	7	Boeheim, James A., Jr.
1991		NCAA	I	64	—	—	—	—	—	—	—	26	6	Boeheim, James A., Jr.
1992		NCAA	I	32	—	—	—	—	—	—	—	22	10	Boeheim, James A., Jr.
1994		NCAA	I	16	—	—	—	—	—	—	—	23	7	Boeheim, James A., Jr.
1995		NCAA	I	32	—	—	—	—	—	—	—	20	10	Boeheim, James A., Jr.
1996		NCAA	I	2	—	—	—	—	—	—	—	29	9	Boeheim, James A., Jr.
1997		NCAA	I	—	32	—	—	—	—	—	—	19	13	Boeheim, James A., Jr.
1998		NCAA	I	16	—	—	—	—	—	—	—	26	9	Boeheim, James A., Jr.
1981	W	AIAW	I	24	—	—	—	—	—	—	—	26	8	Jacobs, Barbara
1985		NCAA	I	32	—	—	—	—	—	—	—	18	13	Jacobs, Barbara
1988		NCAA	I	32	—	—	—	—	—	—	—	22	9	Jacobs, Barbara

TABOR

Year	M/W	Assn	Div	NAT	NIT	ARC	CCA	NCI	NCT	OLY	HLM	W	L	Coach
1994	M	NAIA	II	16	—	—	—	—	—	—	—	21	10	Brubacher, Don
1996		NAIA	II	8	—	—	—	—	—	—	—	25	7	Zimmerman, Don
1997		NAIA	II	3	—	—	—	—	—	—	—	24	9	Brubacher, Don
1990	W	NCCAA	I	3	—	—	—	—	—	—	—	15	16	Kliewer, Karl
1991		NCCAA	I	2	—	—	—	—	—	—	—	28	5	Kliewer, Karl
1992		NAIA	II	16	—	—	—	—	—	—	—	26	3	Kliewer, Karl

TALLADEGA

Year	M/W	Assn	Div	NAT	NIT	ARC	CCA	NCI	NCT	OLY	HLM	W	L	Coach
1996	M	NAIA	I	32	—	—	—	—	—	—	—	18	16	Tucker, Wylie N.
1975	W	AIAW	S	2	—	—	—	—	—	—	—	20	5	Laster, Jr. "Tiny"

TAMPA UNIVERSITY

Year	M/W	Assn	Div	NAT	NIT	ARC	CCA	NCI	NCT	OLY	HLM	W	L	Coach
1950	M	NAIA		4	—	—	—	—	—	—	—	20	14	Gaddis, Mike
1952		NAIA		32	—	—	—	—	—	—	—	11	15	Bailey, Sam
1984		NCAA	II	24	—	—	—	—	—	—	—	20	11	Schmidt, Richard
1985		NCAA	II	16	—	—	—	—	—	—	—	23	8	Schmidt, Richard
1986		NCAA	II	16	—	—	—	—	—	—	—	22	8	Schmidt, Richard
1987		NCAA	II	24	—	—	—	—	—	—	—	26	6	Schmidt, Richard
1988		NCAA	II	16	—	—	—	—	—	—	—	24	8	Schmidt, Richard
1989		NCAA	II	16	—	—	—	—	—	—	—	24	7	Schmidt, Richard
1990		NCAA	II	32	—	—	—	—	—	—	—	26	5	Schmidt, Richard
1993		NCAA	II	23	—	—	—	—	—	—	—	25	5	Schmidt, Richard
1994		NCAA	II	16	—	—	—	—	—	—	—	22	9	Schmidt, Richard
1995		NCAA	II	16	—	—	—	—	—	—	—	25	6	Schmidt, Richard
1997		NCAA	II	32	—	—	—	—	—	—	—	23	7	Schmidt, Richard
1994	W	NCAA	II	32	—	—	—	—	—	—	—	21	7	Mosca, Tom

Year	M/W	Assn	Div	NAT	NIT	ARC	CCA	NCI	NCT	OLY	HLM	W	L	Coach
TARKIO														
1940	M	NAIA		1	—	—	—	—	—	—	—	20	4	Kyle, Newton P.
1941		NAIA		32	—	—	—	—	—	—	—	14	4	Kyle, Newton P.
1976	W	AIAW	S	12	—	—	—	—	—	—	—	20	6	Bussard, Gary
1977		AIAW	S	6	—	—	—	—	—	—	—	32	6	Bussard, Gary
TARLETON STATE														
1992	M	NAIA	II	16	—	—	—	—	—	—	—	26	10	Reisman, Lonn
1993		NAIA	II	16	—	—	—	—	—	—	—	22	11	Reisman, Lonn
1994		NAIA	II	24	—	—	—	—	—	—	—	16	12	Reisman, Lonn
1980	W	AIAW	III	16	—	—	—	—	—	—	—	27	10	Lowrey, Jan
1981		AIAW	III	16	—	—	—	—	—	—	—	26	9	Lowrey, Jan
1984		NAIA		16	—	—	—	—	—	—	—	26	6	Lowrey, Jan
1992		NAIA	II	2	—	—	—	—	—	—	—	30	8	Lowrey, Jan
1993		NAIA	II	3	—	—	—	—	—	—	—	21	13	Lowrey, Jan
TAYLOR														
1984	M	NAIA		32	—	—	—	—	—	—	—	21	10	Patterson, Paul
1985		NCCAA	I	4	—	—	—	—	—	—	—	27	10	Patterson, Paul
1986		NAIA		32	—	—	—	—	—	—	—	26	7	Patterson, Paul
1987		NAIA		16	—	—	—	—	—	—	—	25	8	Patterson, Paul
1989		NAIA		32	—	—	—	—	—	—	—	27	8	Patterson, Paul
1991		NAIA		3	—	—	—	—	—	—	—	34	4	Patterson, Paul
1992		NAIA	I	32	—	—	—	—	—	—	—	29	5	Patterson, Paul
1993		NAIA	I	32	—	—	—	—	—	—	—	27	7	Patterson, Paul
1994		NAIA	II	8	—	—	—	—	—	—	—	29	5	Patterson, Paul
1996		NAIA	II	32	—	—	—	—	—	—	—	23	13	Patterson, Paul
1997		NAIA	II	32	—	—	—	—	—	—	—	22	13	Patterson, Paul
1997	W	NAIA	II	32	—	—	—	—	—	—	—	28	8	Krause, Tina
1998		NAIA	II	16	—	—	—	—	—	—	—	20	15	Krause, Tina
TAYLOR: FORT WAYNE														
1971	M	NCCAA		8	—	—	—	—	—	—	—	19	8	Morley, Stephen H.
1976		NCCAA	II	1	—	—	—	—	—	—	—	18	9	Morley, Stephen H.
1977		NCCAA	II	4	—	—	—	—	—	—	—	10	18	Morley, Stephen H.
1979		NCCAA	II	4	—	—	—	—	—	—	—	15	14	Morley, Stephen H.
1992		NCCAA	II	7	—	—	—	—	—	—	—	19	11	Hamilton, Marvin E. "Bud"
1996		LCC		3	—	—	—	—	—	—	—	19	10	Hamilton, Marvin E. "Bud"
1984	W	NCCAA	II	6	—	—	—	—	—	—	—	7	11	Rupp, Deborah "Deb"
1985		NCCAA	II	4	—	—	—	—	—	—	—	15	3	Rupp, Deborah "Deb"
1986		NCCAA	II	8	—	—	—	—	—	—	—	14	7	Rupp, Deborah "Deb"
TEMPLE														
1936	M	NCAA		—	—	—	—	—	—	8	—	18	6	Usilton, James
1938		NCAA		—	1	—	—	—	—	—	1	23	2	Usilton, James
1944		NCAA		6	—	—	—	—	—	—	—	14	9	Cody, Joshua C.
1956		NCAA		3	—	—	—	—	—	—	—	27	4	Litwack, Harry
1957		NCAA	I	—	3	—	—	—	—	—	—	20	9	Litwack, Harry
1958		NCAA	I	3	—	—	—	—	—	—	—	27	3	Litwack, Harry
1960		NCAA	I	—	12	—	—	—	—	—	—	17	9	Litwack, Harry
1961		NCAA	I	—	8	—	—	—	—	—	—	20	8	Litwack, Harry

Year	M/W	Assn	Div	NAT	NIT	ARC	CCA	NCI	NCT	OLY	HLM	W	L	Coach
1962		NCAA	I	—	8	—	—	—	—	—	—	18	9	Litwack, Harry
1964		NCAA	I	25	—	—	—	—	—	—	—	17	8	Litwack, Harry
1966		NCAA	I	—	8	—	—	—	—	—	—	21	7	Litwack, Harry
1967		NCAA	I	23	—	—	—	—	—	—	—	20	8	Litwack, Harry
1968		NCAA	I	—	16	—	—	—	—	—	—	19	9	Litwack, Harry
1969		NCAA	I	—	1	—	—	—	—	—	—	22	8	Litwack, Harry
1970		NCAA	I	25	—	—	—	—	—	—	—	15	13	Litwack, Harry
1972		NCAA	I	25	—	—	—	—	—	—	—	23	8	Litwack, Harry
1978		NCAA	I	—	16	—	—	—	—	—	—	24	5	Casey, Don
1979		NCAA	I	40	—	—	—	—	—	—	—	25	4	Casey, Don
1981		NCAA	I	—	16	—	—	—	—	—	—	20	8	Casey, Don
1982		NCAA	I	—	32	—	—	—	—	—	—	19	8	Casey, Don
1984		NCAA	I	32	—	—	—	—	—	—	—	26	5	Chaney, John
1985		NCAA	I	32	—	—	—	—	—	—	—	25	6	Chaney, John
1986		NCAA	I	32	—	—	—	—	—	—	—	25	6	Chaney, John
1987		NCAA	I	32	—	—	—	—	—	—	—	32	4	Chaney, John
1988		NCAA	I	8	—	—	—	—	—	—	—	32	2	Chaney, John
1989		NCAA	I	—	32	—	—	—	—	—	—	18	12	Chaney, John
1990		NCAA	I	64	—	—	—	—	—	—	—	20	11	Chaney, John
1991		NCAA	I	8	—	—	—	—	—	—	—	24	10	Chaney, John
1992		NCAA	I	64	—	—	—	—	—	—	—	17	13	Chaney, John
1993		NCAA	I	8	—	—	—	—	—	—	—	20	13	Chaney, John
1994		NCAA	I	32	—	—	—	—	—	—	—	23	8	Chaney, John
1995		NCAA	I	64	—	—	—	—	—	—	—	19	11	Chaney, John
1996		NCAA	I	32	—	—	—	—	—	—	—	20	13	Chaney, John
1997		NCAA	I	32	—	—	—	—	—	—	—	20	11	Chaney, John
1998		NCAA	I	64	—	—	—	—	—	—	—	21	9	Chaney, John
1982	W	NCAA	I	—	6	—	—	—	—	—	—	20	11	Hill-MacDonald, Linda
1983		NCAA	I	—	7	—	—	—	—	—	—	19	12	Hill-MacDonald, Linda
1989		NCAA	I	32	—	—	—	—	—	—	—	22	10	Hill-MacDonald, Linda

TEMPLE JC

Year	M/W	Assn	Div	NAT	NIT	ARC	CCA	NCI	NCT	OLY	HLM	W	L	Coach
1969	W			—	6	—	—	—	—	—	—	18	12	Garmon, Frances
1970				—	6	—	—	—	—	—	—	29	12	Garmon, Frances
1971				—	6	—	—	—	—	—	—	24	12	Garmon, Frances
1972				—	6	—	—	—	—	—	—	26	12	Garmon, Frances
1974		AIAW	J/C	8	3	—	—	—	—	—	—	27	8	Garmon, Frances

TENNESSEE

Year	M/W	Assn	Div	NAT	NIT	ARC	CCA	NCI	NCT	OLY	HLM	W	L	Coach
1945	M	NCAA		—	8	—	—	—	—	—	—	18	5	Mauer, John W.
1967		NCAA	I	16	—	—	—	—	—	—	—	21	7	Mears, Ramon "Ray"
1969		NCAA	I	—	3	—	—	—	—	—	—	21	7	Mears, Ramon "Ray"
1971		NCAA	I	—	8	—	—	—	—	—	—	21	7	Mears, Ramon "Ray"
1974		NCAA	I	—	—	—	8	—	—	—	—	17	9	Mears, Ramon "Ray"
1975		NCAA	I	—	—	—	8	—	—	—	—	18	8	Mears, Ramon "Ray"
1976		NCAA	I	32	—	—	—	—	—	—	—	21	6	Mears, Ramon "Ray"
1977		NCAA	I	32	—	—	—	—	—	—	—	22	6	Mears, Ramon "Ray"
1979		NCAA	I	32	—	—	—	—	—	—	—	21	12	DeVoe, Donald E.
1980		NCAA	I	32	—	—	—	—	—	—	—	18	11	DeVoe, Donald E.
1981		NCAA	I	16	—	—	—	—	—	—	—	21	8	DeVoe, Donald E.
1982		NCAA	I	32	—	—	—	—	—	—	—	20	10	DeVoe, Donald E.

Year	M/W	Assn	Div	NAT	NIT	ARC	CCA	NCI	NCT	OLY	HLM	W	L	Coach
1983		NCAA	I	32	—	—	—	—	—	—	—	20	12	DeVoe, Donald E.
1984		NCAA	I	—	8	—	—	—	—	—	—	21	14	DeVoe, Donald E.
1985		NCAA	I	—	3	—	—	—	—	—	—	22	15	DeVoe, Donald E.
1988		NCAA	I	—	32	—	—	—	—	—	—	16	13	DeVoe, Donald E.
1989		NCAA	I	64	—	—	—	—	—	—	—	19	11	DeVoe, Donald E.
1990		NCAA	I	—	16	—	—	—	—	—	—	16	14	Houston, Wade
1992		NCAA	I	—	16	—	—	—	—	—	—	19	15	Houston, Wade
1996		NCAA	I	—	32	—	—	—	—	—	—	14	15	O'Neill, Kevin
1998		NCAA	I	64	—	—	—	—	—	—	—	20	9	Green, Jerry
1977	W	AIAW	L	3	—	—	—	—	—	—	—	28	5	Summitt, Patricia Head
1978		AIAW	L	16	—	—	—	—	—	—	—	27	4	Summitt, Patricia Head
1979		AIAW	L	3	—	—	—	—	—	—	—	30	9	Summitt, Patricia Head
1980		AIAW	I	2	—	—	—	—	—	—	—	33	5	Summitt, Patricia Head
1981		AIAW	I	2	—	—	—	—	—	—	—	25	6	Summitt, Patricia Head
1982		NCAA	I	3	—	—	—	—	—	—	—	22	10	Summitt, Patricia Head
1983		NCAA	I	8	—	—	—	—	—	—	—	25	8	Summitt, Patricia Head
1984		NCAA	I	2	—	—	—	—	—	—	—	23	10	Summitt, Patricia Head
1985		NCAA	I	16	—	—	—	—	—	—	—	22	10	Summitt, Patricia Head
1986		NCAA	I	3	—	—	—	—	—	—	—	24	10	Summitt, Patricia Head
1987		NCAA	I	1	—	—	—	—	—	—	—	28	6	Summitt, Patricia Head
1988		NCAA	I	3	—	—	—	—	—	—	—	31	3	Summitt, Patricia Head
1989		NCAA	I	1	—	—	—	—	—	—	—	35	2	Summitt, Patricia Head
1990		NCAA	I	8	—	—	—	—	—	—	—	27	6	Summitt, Patricia Head
1991		NCAA	I	1	—	—	—	—	—	—	—	30	5	Summitt, Patricia Head
1992		NCAA	I	16	—	—	—	—	—	—	—	28	3	Summitt, Patricia Head
1993		NCAA	I	8	—	—	—	—	—	—	—	29	3	Summitt, Patricia Head
1994		NCAA	I	16	—	—	—	—	—	—	—	31	2	Summitt, Patricia Head
1995		NCAA	I	2	—	—	—	—	—	—	—	34	3	Summitt, Patricia Head
1996		NCAA	I	1	—	—	—	—	—	—	—	32	4	Summitt, Patricia Head
1997		NCAA	I	1	—	—	—	—	—	—	—	29	10	Summitt, Patricia Head
1998		NCAA	I	1	—	—	—	—	—	—	—	39	0	Summitt, Patricia Head

TENNESSEE STATE

Year	M/W	Assn	Div	NAT	NIT	ARC	CCA	NCI	NCT	OLY	HLM	W	L	Coach
1952	M	NASC		1	—	—	—	—	—	—	—	19	4	Cash, Clarence B.
1953		NAIA		8	—	—	—	—	—	—	—	20	5	Cash, Clarence B.
1953		NASC		1	—	—	—	—	—	—	—	20	5	Cash, Clarence B.
1954		NAIA		32	—	—	—	—	—	—	—	17	6	Cash, Clarence B.
1954		NASC		1	—	—	—	—	—	—	—	17	6	Cash, Clarence B.
1955		NASC		2	—	—	—	—	—	—	—	28	5	McLendon, John B., Jr.
1956		NAIA		8	—	—	—	—	—	—	—	24	9	McLendon, John B., Jr.
1957		NAIA		1	—	—	—	—	—	—	—	29	5	McLendon, John B., Jr.
1958		NAIA		1	—	—	—	—	—	—	—	31	3	McLendon, John B., Jr.
1959		NAIA		1	—	—	—	—	—	—	—	32	1	McLendon, John B., Jr.
1960		NAIA		3	—	—	—	—	—	—	—	27	5	Hunter, Harold
1963		NCAA	II	16	—	—	—	—	—	—	—	21	6	Hunter, Harold
1967		NCAA	II	23	—	—	—	—	—	—	—	20	8	Hunter, Harold
1970		NCAA	II	2	—	—	—	—	—	—	—	21	8	Martin, Edward A.
1971		NCAA	II	16	—	—	—	—	—	—	—	24	3	Martin, Edward A.
1972		NCAA	II	3	—	—	—	—	—	—	—	26	2	Martin, Edward A.

Year	M/W	Assn	Div	NAT	NIT	ARC	CCA	NCI	NCT	OLY	HLM	W	L	Coach
1973		NCAA	II	2	—	—	—	—	—	—	—	22	8	Martin, Edward A.
1974		NCAA	II	24	—	—	—	—	—	—	—	23	5	Martin, Edward A.
1975		NCAA	II	4	—	—	—	—	—	—	—	19	9	Martin, Edward A.
1993		NCAA	I	64	—	—	—	—	—	—	—	19	10	Allen, Franklin "Frankie"
1994		NCAA	I	64	—	—	—	—	—	—	—	19	12	Allen, Franklin "Frankie"
1994	W	NCAA	I	64	—	—	—	—	—	—	—	20	9	Lawrence-Phillips, Teresa A.
1995		NCAA	I	64	—	—	—	—	—	—	—	22	7	Lawrence-Phillips, Teresa A.

Tennessee Tech

Year	M/W	Assn	Div	NAT	NIT	ARC	CCA	NCI	NCT	OLY	HLM	W	L	Coach
1958	M	NCAA	I	24	—	—	—	—	—	—	—	17	9	Oldham, John O.
1963		NCAA	I	25	—	—	—	—	—	—	—	16	8	Oldham, John O.
1985		NCAA	I	—	32	—	—	—	—	—	—	19	9	Deaton, Tom
1972	W	AIAW		16	—	—	—	—	—	—	—	26	6	Meadors, Marynell Hutsell
1974		AIAW		6	—	—	—	—	—	—	—	26	5	Meadors, Marynell Hutsell
1975		AIAW	L	12	—	—	—	—	—	—	—	26	5	Meadors, Marynell Hutsell
1976		AIAW	L	5	—	—	—	—	—	—	—	28	2	Meadors, Marynell Hutsell
1977		AIAW	L	8	—	—	—	—	—	—	—	28	8	Meadors, Marynell Hutsell
1981		AIAW	I	—	6	—	—	—	—	—	—	22	9	Meadors, Marynell Hutsell
1982		NCAA	I	32	—	—	—	—	—	—	—	20	11	Meadors, Marynell Hutsell
1985		NCAA	I	32	—	—	—	—	—	—	—	20	9	Meadors, Marynell Hutsell
1986		NCAA	I	—	7	—	—	—	—	—	—	22	10	Meadors, Marynell Hutsell
1987		NCAA	I	32	—	—	—	—	—	—	—	24	7	Worrell, Bill
1989		NCAA	I	32	—	—	—	—	—	—	—	22	8	Worrell, Bill
1990		NCAA	I	32	—	—	—	—	—	—	—	26	5	Worrell, Bill
1991		NCAA	I	48	—	—	—	—	—	—	—	22	8	Worrell, Bill
1992		NCAA	I	48	—	—	—	—	—	—	—	21	9	Worrell, Bill
1993		NCAA	I	48	—	—	—	—	—	—	—	22	7	Worrell, Bill

Tennessee Temple

Year	M/W	Assn	Div	NAT	NIT	ARC	CCA	NCI	NCT	OLY	HLM	W	L	Coach
1971	M	NCCAA		4	—	—	—	—	—	—	—	18	15	Foster, Bruce D.
1972		NCCAA		2	—	—	—	—	—	—	—	19	12	Foster, Bruce D.
1975		NCCAA		2	—	—	—	—	—	—	—	21	14	Foster, Bruce D.
1977		NCCAA	I	3	—	—	—	—	—	—	—	28	6	Bishop, Ronald
1979		NCCAA	I	1	—	—	—	—	—	—	—	30	7	Bishop, Ronald
1980		NCCAA	I	4	—	—	—	—	—	—	—	23	13	Bishop, Ronald
1981		NCCAA	I	1	—	—	—	—	—	—	—	24	17	Bishop, Ronald
1982		NCCAA	I	1	—	—	—	—	—	—	—	31	8	Bishop, Ronald
1983		NCCAA	I	1	—	—	—	—	—	—	—	28	7	Bishop, Ronald
1984		NCCAA	I	2	—	—	—	—	—	—	—	33	2	Bishop, Ronald
1985		NCCAA	I	2	—	—	—	—	—	—	—	29	4	Bishop, Ronald
1986		NCCAA	I	3	—	—	—	—	—	—	—	21	11	Bishop, Ronald
1988		NCCAA	I	1	—	—	—	—	—	—	—	26	13	Bishop, Ronald
1989		NCCAA	I	1	—	—	—	—	—	—	—	25	11	Bishop, Ronald
1990		NCCAA	I	4	—	—	—	—	—	—	—	23	16	Bishop, Ronald
1991		NCCAA	I	4	—	—	—	—	—	—	—	18	15	Bishop, Ronald
1996		NCCAA	I	2	—	—	—	—	—	—	—	24	12	Johnson, Richard "Rick"
1998		NCCAA	I	5	—	—	—	—	—	—	—	27	9	Johnson, Richard "Rick"
1983	W	NCCAA	I	2	—	—	—	—	—	—	—	X	X	Stem, Randy
1984		NCCAA	I	8	—	—	—	—	—	—	—	33	2	Stem, Randy

Year	M/W	Assn	Div	NAT	NIT	ARC	CCA	NCI	NCT	OLY	HLM	W	L	Coach
TENNESSEE WESLEYAN														
1967	M	NAIA		8	—	—	—	—	—	—	—	30	5	Farmer, Dwain
1997		NAIA	II	32	—	—	—	—	—	—	—	23	12	Adams, Steve
1994	W	NAIA	II	16	—	—	—	—	—	—	—	20	15	Harrison, Stan
1995		NAIA	II	32	—	—	—	—	—	—	—	23	12	Harrison, Stan
1998		NAIA	II	32	—	—	—	—	—	—	—	19	12	Harrison, Stan
TENNESSEE: CHATTANOOGA														
1961	M	NCAA	II	32	—	—	—	—	—	—	—	17	8	Bartlett, Thomas G. "Tommy"
1973		NCAA	II	24	—	—	—	—	—	—	—	19	9	Shumate, Ron
1975		NCAA	II	16	—	—	—	—	—	—	—	19	9	Shumate, Ron
1976		NCAA	II	2	—	—	—	—	—	—	—	23	9	Shumate, Ron
1977		NCAA	II	1	—	—	—	—	—	—	—	27	5	Shumate, Ron
1981		NCAA	I	48	—	—	—	—	—	—	—	21	9	Arnold, Murray
1982		NCAA	I	32	—	—	—	—	—	—	—	27	4	Arnold, Murray
1983		NCAA	I	48	—	—	—	—	—	—	—	26	4	Arnold, Murray
1984		NCAA	I	—	16	—	—	—	—	—	—	24	7	Arnold, Murray
1985		NCAA	I	—	8	—	—	—	—	—	—	24	8	Arnold, Murray
1986		NCAA	I	—	32	—	—	—	—	—	—	21	10	McCarthy, Mack
1987		NCAA	I	—	32	—	—	—	—	—	—	21	8	McCarthy, Mack
1988		NCAA	I	64	—	—	—	—	—	—	—	20	13	McCarthy, Mack
1993		NCAA	I	64	—	—	—	—	—	—	—	26	7	McCarthy, Mack
1994		NCAA	I	64	—	—	—	—	—	—	—	23	7	McCarthy, Mack
1995		NCAA	I	64	—	—	—	—	—	—	—	19	11	McCarthy, Mack
1997		NCAA	I	16	—	—	—	—	—	—	—	24	11	McCarthy, Mack
1984	W	NCAA	I	—	2	—	—	—	—	—	—	26	5	Fanning, Sharon
1989		NCAA	I	48	—	—	—	—	—	—	—	19	12	Parrott, Craig
1992		NCAA	I	48	—	—	—	—	—	—	—	18	12	Parrott, Craig
TENNESSEE: MARTIN														
1982	M	NCAA	II	16	—	—	—	—	—	—	—	20	11	Tolis, Art
1983		NCAA	II	32	—	—	—	—	—	—	—	21	10	Hancock, Tom
1972	W	AIAW		8	—	—	—	—	—	—	—	20	8	Gearn, Nadine
TEXAS														
1939	M	NCAA		8	—	—	—	—	—	—	—	19	6	Gray, Jack S.
1943		NCAA		3	—	—	—	—	—	—	—	19	7	Gilstrap, H. C. "Bully"
1947		NCAA		3	—	—	—	—	—	—	—	26	2	Gray, Jack S.
1948		NCAA		—	8	—	—	—	—	—	—	20	5	Gray, Jack S.
1960		NCAA	I	16	—	—	—	—	—	—	—	18	8	Bradley, Harold L.
1963		NCAA	I	12	—	—	—	—	—	—	—	20	7	Bradley, Harold L.
1972		NCAA	I	16	—	—	—	—	—	—	—	19	9	Black, Leon
1974		NCAA	I	25	—	—	—	—	—	—	—	12	15	Black, Leon
1978		NCAA	I	—	1	—	—	—	—	—	—	26	5	Lemons, A. E. "Abe"
1979		NCAA	I	32	—	—	—	—	—	—	—	21	8	Lemons, A. E. "Abe"
1980		NCAA	I	—	16	—	—	—	—	—	—	19	11	Lemons, A. E. "Abe"
1986		NCAA	I	—	16	—	—	—	—	—	—	19	12	Weltlich, Robert
1989		NCAA	I	32	—	—	—	—	—	—	—	25	9	Penders, Thomas V.
1990		NCAA	I	8	—	—	—	—	—	—	—	24	9	Penders, Thomas V.
1991		NCAA	I	32	—	—	—	—	—	—	—	23	9	Penders, Thomas V.
1992		NCAA	I	64	—	—	—	—	—	—	—	23	12	Penders, Thomas V.

Year	M/W	Assn	Div	NAT	NIT	ARC	CCA	NCI	NCT	OLY	HLM	W	L	Coach
1994		NCAA	I	32	—	—	—	—	—	—	—	26	8	Penders, Thomas V.
1995		NCAA	I	32	—	—	—	—	—	—	—	23	7	Penders, Thomas V.
1996		NCAA	I	32	—	—	—	—	—	—	—	21	10	Penders, Thomas V.
1997		NCAA	I	16	—	—	—	—	—	—	—	18	12	Penders, Thomas V.
1978	W	AIAW	L	—	2	—	—	—	—	—	—	29	10	Conradt, Jody
1980		AIAW	I	16	—	—	—	—	—	—	—	33	4	Conradt, Jody
1981		AIAW	I	24	—	—	—	—	—	—	—	28	8	Conradt, Jody
1982		AIAW	I	2	—	—	—	—	—	—	—	35	4	Conradt, Jody
1983		NCAA	I	8	—	—	—	—	—	—	—	30	3	Conradt, Jody
1984		NCAA	I	8	—	—	—	—	—	—	—	32	3	Conradt, Jody
1985		NCAA	I	16	—	—	—	—	—	—	—	28	3	Conradt, Jody
1986		NCAA	I	1	—	—	—	—	—	—	—	34	0	Conradt, Jody
1987		NCAA	I	3	—	—	—	—	—	—	—	31	2	Conradt, Jody
1988		NCAA	I	8	—	—	—	—	—	—	—	32	3	Conradt, Jody
1989		NCAA	I	8	—	—	—	—	—	—	—	27	5	Conradt, Jody
1990		NCAA	I	8	—	—	—	—	—	—	—	27	5	Conradt, Jody
1991		NCAA	I	48	—	—	—	—	—	—	—	21	9	Conradt, Jody
1992		NCAA	I	32	—	—	—	—	—	—	—	21	10	Conradt, Jody
1993		NCAA	I	32	—	—	—	—	—	—	—	22	8	Conradt, Jody
1994		NCAA	I	32	—	—	—	—	—	—	—	22	9	Conradt, Jody
1996		NCAA	I	32	—	—	—	—	—	—	—	21	9	Conradt, Jody
1997		NCAA	I	32	—	—	—	—	—	—	—	22	8	Conradt, Jody

Texas A&M

Year	M/W	Assn	Div	NAT	NIT	ARC	CCA	NCI	NCT	OLY	HLM	W	L	Coach
1951	M	NCAA		16	—	—	—	—	—	—	—	17	12	Floyd, John L.
1964		NCAA	I	25	—	—	—	—	—	—	—	18	7	Metcalf, Dr. Shelby R.
1969		NCAA	I	16	—	—	—	—	—	—	—	18	9	Metcalf, Dr. Shelby R.
1975		NCAA	I	32	—	—	—	—	—	—	—	20	7	Metcalf, Dr. Shelby R.
1979		NCAA	I	—	6	—	—	—	—	—	—	24	9	Metcalf, Dr. Shelby R.
1980		NCAA	I	16	—	—	—	—	—	—	—	26	8	Metcalf, Dr. Shelby R.
1982		NCAA	I	—	8	—	—	—	—	—	—	20	11	Metcalf, Dr. Shelby R.
1985		NCAA	I	—	32	—	—	—	—	—	—	19	11	Metcalf, Dr. Shelby R.
1986		NCAA	I	—	32	—	—	—	—	—	—	20	12	Metcalf, Dr. Shelby R.
1987		NCAA	I	64	—	—	—	—	—	—	—	17	14	Metcalf, Dr. Shelby R.
1994		NCAA	I	—	32	—	—	—	—	—	—	19	11	Barone, Anthony A. "Tony"
1994	W	NCAA	I	16	—	—	—	—	—	—	—	23	8	Hickey, Lynn
1995		NCAA	I	—	1	—	—	—	—	—	—	21	9	Harvey, Candi
1996		NCAA	I	64	—	—	—	—	—	—	—	20	12	Harvey, Candi

Texas A&M: Commerce

Year	M/W	Assn	Div	NAT	NIT	ARC	CCA	NCI	NCT	OLY	HLM	W	L	Coach
1939	M	NAIA		16	—	—	—	—	—	—	—	15	6	Vinzant, Dennis
1940		NAIA		16	—	—	—	—	—	—	—	23	7	Vinzant, Dennis
1942		NAIA		32	—	—	—	—	—	—	—	10	13	Vinzant, Dennis
1950		NAIA		16	—	—	—	—	—	—	—	14	15	Tully, Darrell
1953		NAIA		4	—	—	—	—	—	—	—	25	5	Rogers, Bobby
1954		NAIA		8	—	—	—	—	—	—	—	23	5	Rogers, Bobby
1955		NAIA		1	—	—	—	—	—	—	—	29	5	Rogers, Bobby
1958		NAIA		8	—	—	—	—	—	—	—	23	7	Rogers, Bobby

Year	M/W	Assn	Div	NAT	NIT	ARC	CCA	NCI	NCT	OLY	HLM	W	L	Coach
1977		NAIA		8	—	—	—	—	—	—	—	25	9	Gudger, James F.
1978		NAIA		4	—	—	—	—	—	—	—	26	10	Gudger, James F.
1996		NCAA	II	48	—	—	—	—	—	—	—	20	8	Peak, Paul
1997		NCAA	II	8	—	—	—	—	—	—	—	24	8	Peak, Paul
1998		NCAA	II	48	—	—	—	—	—	—	—	22	7	Peak, Paul

TEXAS A&M: CORPUS CHRISTI

Year	M/W	Assn	Div	NAT	NIT	ARC	CCA	NCI	NCT	OLY	HLM	W	L	Coach
1969	M	NAIA		32	—	—	—	—	—	—	—	13	17	Smith, Ray

TEXAS A&M: KINGSVILLE

Year	M/W	Assn	Div	NAT	NIT	ARC	CCA	NCI	NCT	OLY	HLM	W	L	Coach
1992	M	NCAA	II	24	—	—	—	—	—	—	—	21	12	Carter, William C.
1996		NCAA	II	32	—	—	—	—	—	—	—	23	6	Carter, William C.
1983	W	NCAA	II	16	—	—	—	—	—	—	—	21	8	Land, David

TEXAS CHRISTIAN

Year	M/W	Assn	Div	NAT	NIT	ARC	CCA	NCI	NCT	OLY	HLM	W	L	Coach
1952	M	NCAA		12	—	—	—	—	—	—	—	24	4	Brannon, Byron A. "Buster"
1953		NCAA		12	—	—	—	—	—	—	—	15	8	Brannon, Byron A. "Buster"
1959		NCAA	I	12	—	—	—	—	—	—	—	20	6	Brannon, Byron A. "Buster"
1968		NCAA	I	8	—	—	—	—	—	—	—	15	11	Swaim, Johnny
1971		NCAA	I	25	—	—	—	—	—	—	—	15	12	Swaim, Johnny
1983		NCAA	I	—	8	—	—	—	—	—	—	23	11	Killingsworth, James
1986		NCAA	I	—	16	—	—	—	—	—	—	22	9	Killingsworth, James
1987		NCAA	I	32	—	—	—	—	—	—	—	24	7	Killingsworth, James
1992		NCAA	I	—	16	—	—	—	—	—	—	23	11	Iba, Moe
1997		NCAA	I	—	16	—	—	—	—	—	—	22	13	Tubbs, Billy
1998		NCAA	I	64	—	—	—	—	—	—	—	27	6	Tubbs, Billy

TEXAS COLLEGE

Year	M/W	Assn	Div	NAT	NIT	ARC	CCA	NCI	NCT	OLY	HLM	W	L	Coach
1992	M	NSCAA		1	—	—	—	—	—	—	—	25	5	Patrick, Kirk
1993		NSCAA		1	—	—	—	—	—	—				Patrick, Kirk
1994		NSCAA		4	—	—	—	—	—	—	—	18	7	Patrick, Kirk
1991	W	NSCAA		6	—	—	—	—	—	—	—			

TEXAS SOUTHERN

Year	M/W	Assn	Div	NAT	NIT	ARC	CCA	NCI	NCT	OLY	HLM	W	L	Coach
1952	M	NASC		3	—	—	—	—	—	—	—	29	10	Adams, Edward H.
1954		NASC		3	—	—	—	—	—	—	—	30	5	Adams, Edward H.
1955		NAIA		16	—	—	—	—	—	—	—	28	3	Adams, Edward H.
1955		NASC		1	—	—	—	—	—	—	—	28	3	Adams, Edward H.
1956		NAIA		2	—	—	—	—	—	—	—	31	4	Adams, Edward H.
1957		NAIA		8	—	—	—	—	—	—	—	32	2	Adams, Edward H.
1958		NAIA		3	—	—	—	—	—	—	—	29	5	Adams, Edward H.
1971		NAIA		32	—	—	—	—	—	—	—	17	2	Gordon, Lavalius C.
1976		NAIA		8	—	—	—	—	—	—	—	23	10	Moreland, Robert E.
1977		NAIA		1	—	—	—	—	—	—	—	31	5	Moreland, Robert E.
1990		NCAA	I	64	—	—	—	—	—	—	—	19	12	Moreland, Robert E.
1994		NCAA	I	64	—	—	—	—	—	—	—	19	11	Moreland, Robert E.
1995		NCAA	I	64	—	—	—	—	—	—	—	22	7	Moreland, Robert E.
1981	W	NAIA		2	—	—	—	—	—	—	—	23	9	Gillespie, Nathaniel A.
1982		NAIA		8	—	—	—	—	—	—	—	23	8	Gillespie, Nathaniel A.

Year	M/W	Assn	Div	NAT	NIT	ARC	CCA	NCI	NCT	OLY	HLM	W	L	Coach
TEXAS TECH														
1942	M	NAIA		16	—	—	—	—	—	—	—	16	11	Hoffman, Burl
1949		NAIA		8	—	—	—	—	—	—	—	21	9	Robison, Polk F.
1954		NCAA		24	—	—	—	—	—	—	—	20	5	Robison, Polk F.
1956		NCAA		25	—	—	—	—	—	—	—	13	12	Robison, Polk F.
1961		NCAA	I	12	—	—	—	—	—	—	—	15	10	Robison, Polk F.
1962		NCAA	I	16	—	—	—	—	—	—	—	19	8	Gibson, Eugene F.
1973		NCAA	I	25	—	—	—	—	—	—	—	19	8	Myers, Gerald
1976		NCAA	I	16	—	—	—	—	—	—	—	25	6	Myers, Gerald
1979		NCAA	I	—	24	—	—	—	—	—	—	19	11	Myers, Gerald
1985		NCAA	I	64	—	—	—	—	—	—	—	23	8	Myers, Gerald
1986		NCAA	I	64	—	—	—	—	—	—	—	17	14	Myers, Gerald
1993		NCAA	I	64	—	—	—	—	—	—	—	18	12	Dickey, James
1995		NCAA	I	—	32	—	—	—	—	—	—	20	10	Dickey, James
1996		NCAA	I	16	—	—	—	—	—	—	—	30	2	Dickey, James
1983	W	NCAA	I	—	5	—	—	—	—	—	—	22	9	Sharp, Marsha
1984		NCAA	I	32	—	—	—	—	—	—	—	23	7	Sharp, Marsha
1985		NCAA	I	—	3	—	—	—	—	—	—	24	8	Sharp, Marsha
1986		NCAA	I	32	—	—	—	—	—	—	—	21	9	Sharp, Marsha
1990		NCAA	I	48	—	—	—	—	—	—	—	20	11	Sharp, Marsha
1991		NCAA	I	48	—	—	—	—	—	—	—	23	8	Sharp, Marsha
1992		NCAA	I	16	—	—	—	—	—	—	—	27	5	Sharp, Marsha
1993		NCAA	I	1	—	—	—	—	—	—	—	31	3	Sharp, Marsha
1994		NCAA	I	16	—	—	—	—	—	—	—	28	5	Sharp, Marsha
1995		NCAA	I	8	—	—	—	—	—	—	—	33	4	Sharp, Marsha
1996		NCAA	I	16	—	—	—	—	—	—	—	27	5	Sharp, Marsha
1997		NCAA	I	32	—	—	—	—	—	—	—	20	9	Sharp, Marsha
1998		NCAA	I	32	—	—	—	—	—	—	—	26	5	Sharp, Marsha
TEXAS WESLEYAN														
1940	M	NAIA		8	—	—	—	—	—	—	—	22	2	Miller, W. A. "Gus"
1941		NAIA		8	—	—	—	—	—	—	—	25	2	Miller, W. A. "Gus"
1942		NAIA		32	—	—	—	—	—	—	—	15	5	Unknown
1943		NAIA		32	—	—	—	—	—	—	—	26	4	Unknown
1947		NAIA		16	—	—	—	—	—	—	—	32	4	Edwards, Johnnie O.
1948		NAIA		32	—	—	—	—	—	—	—	19	13	Edwards, Johnnie O.
1983		NAIA		16	—	—	—	—	—	—	—	22	6	Newman, Tommy
1979	W	AIAW	S	16	—	—	—	—	—	—	—	32	5	Satern, Miriam
TEXAS: ARLINGTON														
1981	M	NCAA	I	—	32	—	—	—	—	—	—	20	8	LeGrand, Bob "Snake"
TEXAS: EL PASO														
1941	M	NAIA		32	—	—	—	—	—	—	—	17	6	Pennington, Marshall
1963		NCAA	I	25	—	—	—	—	—	—	—	19	7	Haskins, Donald L.
1964		NCAA	I	12	—	—	—	—	—	—	—	25	3	Haskins, Donald L.
1965		NCAA	I	—	14	—	—	—	—	—	—	17	9	Haskins, Donald L.
1966		NCAA	I	1	—	—	—	—	—	—	1	28	1	Haskins, Donald L.
1967		NCAA	I	12	—	—	—	—	—	—	—	22	6	Haskins, Donald L.
1970		NCAA	I	25	—	—	—	—	—	—	—	17	8	Haskins, Donald L.
1972		NCAA	I	—	16	—	—	—	—	—	—	20	7	Haskins, Donald L.

Year	M/W	Assn	Div	NAT	NIT	ARC	CCA	NCI	NCT	OLY	HLM	W	L	Coach
1975		NCAA	I	32	—	—	—	—	—	—	—	20	6	Haskins, Donald L.
1980		NCAA	I	—	16	—	—	—	—	—	—	20	8	Haskins, Donald L.
1981		NCAA	I	—	16	—	—	—	—	—	—	18	12	Haskins, Donald L.
1983		NCAA	I	—	32	—	—	—	—	—	—	19	10	Haskins, Donald L.
1984		NCAA	I	32	—	—	—	—	—	—	—	27	4	Haskins, Donald L.
1985		NCAA	I	32	—	—	—	—	—	—	—	22	10	Haskins, Donald L.
1986		NCAA	I	64	—	—	—	—	—	—	—	27	6	Haskins, Donald L.
1987		NCAA	I	32	—	—	—	—	—	—	—	25	7	Haskins, Donald L.
1988		NCAA	I	64	—	—	—	—	—	—	—	23	10	Haskins, Donald L.
1989		NCAA	I	32	—	—	—	—	—	—	—	26	7	Haskins, Donald L.
1990		NCAA	I	64	—	—	—	—	—	—	—	21	11	Haskins, Donald L.
1992		NCAA	I	16	—	—	—	—	—	—	—	27	7	Haskins, Donald L.
1993		NCAA	I	—	16	—	—	—	—	—	—	21	13	Haskins, Donald L.
1995		NCAA	I	—	16	—	—	—	—	—	—	20	10	Haskins, Donald L.

TEXAS: PAN AMERICAN

Year	M/W	Assn	Div	NAT	NIT	ARC	CCA	NCI	NCT	OLY	HLM	W	L	Coach
1962	M	NAIA		16	—	—	—	—	—	—	—	25	5	Williams, Samuel
1963		NAIA		1	—	—	—	—	—	—	—	22	6	Williams, Samuel
1964		NAIA		2	—	—	—	—	—	—	—	28	6	Williams, Samuel
1968		NCAA	II	16	—	—	—	—	—	—	—	21	6	Williams, Samuel
1981		NCAA	I	—	32	—	—	—	—	—	—	18	11	White, Bill

TEXAS: SAN ANTONIO

Year	M/W	Assn	Div	NAT	NIT	ARC	CCA	NCI	NCT	OLY	HLM	W	L	Coach
1988	M	NCAA	I	64	—	—	—	—	—	—	—	22	9	Burmeister, Ken

THIEL

Year	M/W	Assn	Div	NAT	NIT	ARC	CCA	NCI	NCT	OLY	HLM	W	L	Coach
1988	W	NCAA	III	32	—	—	—	—	—	—	—	19	6	Parsons, Margaret Rhoads "Gie"

THOMAS MORE (KY)

Year	M/W	Assn	Div	NAT	NIT	ARC	CCA	NCI	NCT	OLY	HLM	W	L	Coach
1957	M	NAIA		16	—	—	—	—	—	—	—	19	7	Wolf, Charles
1960		NAIA		16	—	—	—	—	—	—	—	19	13	Wolf, Charles
1997	W	NCAA	III	16	—	—	—	—	—	—	—	20	7	Brumfield, Sharri

TIFFIN

Year	M/W	Assn	Div	NAT	NIT	ARC	CCA	NCI	NCT	OLY	HLM	W	L	Coach
1969	M	NSCAA		3	—	—	—	—	—	—	—	20	4	Janson, George
1970		NSCAA		3	—	—	—	—	—	—	—	20	5	Janson, George
1971		NSCAA		1	—	—	—	—	—	—	—	13	8	Janson, George
1972		NSCAA		6	—	—	—	—	—	—	—	19	12	Janson, George
1973		NSCAA		1	—	—	—	—	—	—	—	24	9	Janson, George
1989		NAIA		32	—	—	—	—	—	—	—	21	12	Hammond, Jim
1992		NAIA	II	16	—	—	—	—	—	—	—	23	10	Hammomd, Jim
1993		NAIA	II	16	—	—	—	—	—	—	—	21	12	Hammond, Jim

TOCCOA FALLS

Year	M/W	Assn	Div	NAT	NIT	ARC	CCA	NCI	NCT	OLY	HLM	W	L	Coach
1976	M	NCCAA	II	4	—	—	—	—	—	—	—	14	14	Fowler, Richard A.
1996		NCCAA	II	4	—	—	—	—	—	—	—	23	11	Martin, Lance
1997		NCCAA	II	2	—	—	—	—	—	—	—	29	6	Martin, Lance
1998		NCCAA	II	4	—	—	—	—	—	—	—	27	10	Martin, Lance
1984	W	NCCAA	II	4	—	—	—	—	—	—	—	10	6	Shiffer, Paul
1986		NCCAA	II	1	—	—	—	—	—	—	—	13	12	Shiffer, Paul
1987		NCCAA	II	4	—	—	—	—	—	—	—	14	8	Shiffer, Paul
1988		NCCAA	II	4	—	—	—	—	—	—	—	17	12	Shiffer, Paul

Year	M/W	Assn	Div	NAT	NIT	ARC	CCA	NCI	NCT	OLY	HLM	W	L	Coach
1989		NCCAA	II	6	—	—	—	—	—	—	—	13	10	Shiffer, Paul
1990		NCCAA	II	6	—	—	—	—	—	—	—	11	13	Shiffer, Paul
1992		NCCAA	II	1	—	—	—	—	—	—	—	23	6	Shiffer, Paul
1993		NCCAA	II	6	—	—	—	—	—	—	—	19	11	Shiffer, Paul
1994		NCCAA	II	3	—	—	—	—	—	—	—	19	11	Shiffer, Paul
1995		NCCAA	II	6	—	—	—	—	—	—	—	12	13	Shiffer, Paul

TOLEDO

Year	M/W	Assn	Div	NAT	NIT	ARC	CCA	NCI	NCT	OLY	HLM	W	L	Coach
1942	M	NCAA		—	4	—	—	—	—	—	—	23	5	Anderson, W. Harold "Andy"
1943		NCAA		—	2	4	—	—	—	—	—	22	4	Friddle, Burl
1951		NCAA		—	—	—	—	—	8	—	—	23	8	Bush, Gerald "Jerry"
1954		NCAA		24	—	—	—	—	—	—	—	13	10	Bush, Gerald "Jerry"
1967		NCAA	I	23	—	—	—	—	—	—	—	23	2	Nichols, Robert J.
1974		NCAA	I	—	—	—	3	—	—	—	—	19	9	Nichols, Robert J.
1979		NCAA	I	16	—	—	—	—	—	—	—	22	8	Nichols, Robert J.
1980		NCAA	I	48	—	—	—	—	—	—	—	23	6	Nichols, Robert J.
1981		NCAA	I	—	16	—	—	—	—	—	—	21	10	Nichols, Robert J.
1989	W	NCAA	I	—	3	—	—	—	—	—	—	25	8	Fennelly, Bill
1990		NCAA	I	—	2	—	—	—	—	—	—	25	7	Fennelly, Bill
1991		NCAA	I	32	—	—	—	—	—	—	—	24	7	Fennelly, Bill
1992		NCAA	I	32	—	—	—	—	—	—	—	26	6	Fennelly, Bill
1994		NCAA	I	—	5	—	—	—	—	—	—	24	8	Fennelly, Bill
1995		NCAA	I	64	—	—	—	—	—	—	—	24	7	Fennelly, Bill
1996		NCAA	I	32	—	—	—	—	—	—	—	25	6	Ehlen, Mark
1997		NCAA	I	64	—	—	—	—	—	—	—	27	4	Ehlen, Mark
1998		NCAA	I	—	8	—	—	—	—	—	—	24	7	Ehlen, Mark

TOMLINSON

Year	M/W	Assn	Div	NAT	NIT	ARC	CCA	NCI	NCT	OLY	HLM	W	L	Coach
1992	M	NBCAA	II	7	—	—	—	—	—	—	—	20	15	Smith, Phillip D.
1992	W	NBCAA		4	—	—	—	—	—	—	—	13	17	Smith, Phillip D.

TOUGALOO

Year	M/W	Assn	Div	NAT	NIT	ARC	CCA	NCI	NCT	OLY	HLM	W	L	Coach
1975	M	NSCAA		2	—	—	—	—	—	—	—	15	9	Lewis, Jerry
1979	W	AIAW	S	5	—	—	—	—	—	—	—	47	11	Pennington, Andrew
1997		NAIA	I	32	—	—	—	—	—	—	—	19	17	Brown, Yolanda

TOWSON

Year	M/W	Assn	Div	NAT	NIT	ARC	CCA	NCI	NCT	OLY	HLM	W	L	Coach
1977	M	NCAA	II	8	—	—	—	—	—	—	—	27	3	Angotti, Vincent
1978		NCAA	II	16	—	—	—	—	—	—	—	26	4	Angotti, Vincent
1990		NCAA	I	64	—	—	—	—	—	—	—	18	13	Truax, Terry
1991		NCAA	I	64	—	—	—	—	—	—	—	19	11	Truax, Terry
1969	W	AIAW		5	—	—	—	—	—	—	—	10	1	Verkruzen, Margo
1970		AIAW		12	—	—	—	—	—	—	—	9	3	Verkruzen, Margo

TRANSYLVANIA

Year	M/W	Assn	Div	NAT	NIT	ARC	CCA	NCI	NCT	OLY	HLM	W	L	Coach
1963	M	NAIA		16	—	—	—	—	—	—	—	20	9	Newton, Charles M. "CM"
1965		NAIA		32	—	—	—	—	—	—	—	21	10	Rose, Lee H.
1969		NCAA	II	24	—	—	—	—	—	—	—	20	7	Rose, Lee H.
1970		NCAA	II	32	—	—	—	—	—	—	—	21	7	Rose, Lee H.

Year	M/W	Assn	Div	NAT	NIT	ARC	CCA	NCI	NCT	OLY	HLM	W	L	Coach
1972		NCAA	II	32	—	—	—	—	—	—	—	21	6	Rose, Lee H.
1973		NCAA	II	32	—	—	—	—	—	—	—	20	7	Rose, Lee H.
1975		NCAA	III	23	—	—	—	—	—	—	—	20	7	Rose, Lee H.
1976		NCAA	III	14	—	—	—	—	—	—	—	19	8	Lane, Don
1977		NCAA	III	16	—	—	—	—	—	—	—	15	12	Lane, Don
1978		NCAA	III	23	—	—	—	—	—	—	—	20	6	Lane, Don
1988		NAIA		32	—	—	—	—	—	—	—	24	3	Lane, Don
1994		NAIA	I	32	—	—	—	—	—	—	—	25	8	Lane, Don
1995		NAIA	I	16	—	—	—	—	—	—	—	26	8	Lane, Don
1997		NAIA	I	32	—	—	—	—	—	—	—	23	8	Lane, Don
1998		NAIA	I	16	—	—	—	—	—	—	—	24	9	Lane, Don
1997	W	NAIA	I	32	—	—	—	—	—	—	—	27	7	Turner, Mark

Trevecca Nazarene

Year	M/W	Assn	Div	NAT	NIT	ARC	CCA	NCI	NCT	OLY	HLM	W	L	Coach
1972	M	NCCAA		3	—	—	—	—	—	—	—	19	9	Forraker, Chet
1987		NAIA		8	—	—	—	—	—	—	—	30	4	Wilson, Frank

Tri-State

Year	M/W	Assn	Div	NAT	NIT	ARC	CCA	NCI	NCT	OLY	HLM	W	L	Coach
1972	M	NAIA		32	—	—	—	—	—	—	—	19	11	Peterman, Mark
1975		NAIA		16	—	—	—	—	—	—	—	25	7	Peterman, Mark
1977		NAIA		32	—	—	—	—	—	—	—	28	5	Peterman, Mark
1979		NAIA		16	—	—	—	—	—	—	—	31	4	Peterman, Mark
1983		NAIA		32	—	—	—	—	—	—	—	26	7	Peterman, Mark
1993		NAIA	I	32	—	—	—	—	—	—	—	20	11	Hack, Dick
1989	W	NAIA		16	—	—	—	—	—	—	—	25	8	DeRocher, Cindy
1995		NAIA	II	16	—	—	—	—	—	—	—	23	8	DeRocher, Cindy
1996		NAIA	II	8	—	—	—	—	—	—	—	20	12	DeRocher, Cindy
1997		NAIA	II	16	—	—	—	—	—	—	—	23	6	DeRocher, Cindy

Trinity (CT)

Year	M/W	Assn	Div	NAT	NIT	ARC	CCA	NCI	NCT	OLY	HLM	W	L	Coach
1995	M	NCAA	III	4	—	—	—	—	—	—	—	24	5	Ogrodnik, Stanley
1998		NCAA	III	48	—	—	—	—	—	—	—	20	4	Ogrodnik, Stanley
1995	W	NCAA	III	32	—	—	—	—	—	—	—	21	4	Pine, Maureen
1997		NCAA	III	64	—	—	—	—	—	—	—	18	6	Pine, Maureen

Trinity (TX)

Year	M/W	Assn	Div	NAT	NIT	ARC	CCA	NCI	NCT	OLY	HLM	W	L	Coach
1939	M	NAIA		16	—	—	—	—	—	—	—	12	3	Wilkins, Leland J.
1960		NCAA	II	24	—	—	—	—	—	—	—	18	9	Robinson, Leslie W.
1961		NCAA	II	24	—	—	—	—	—	—	—	20	6	Robinson, Leslie W.
1968		NCAA	II	3	—	—	—	—	—	—	—	23	7	Polk, James Robert 'Bob'
1969		NCAA	I	25	—	—	—	—	—	—	—	19	5	Polk, James Robert 'Bob'
1998		NCAA	III	32	—	—	—	—	—	—	—	21	6	Brock, Charles
1995	W	NCAA	III	64	—	—	—	—	—	—	—	19	6	Geyer, Becky
1996		NCAA	III	64	—	—	—	—	—	—	—	16	10	Geyer, Becky

Trinity (VT)

Year	M/W	Assn	Div	NAT	NIT	ARC	CCA	NCI	NCT	OLY	HLM	W	L	Coach
1993	W	NSCAA		4	—	—	—	—	—	—	—	21	10	Fitterer, Barbara
1996		NSCAA		5	—	—	—	—	—	—	—	8	10	Niebling, Jennifer

Year	M/W	Assn	Div	NAT	NIT	ARC	CCA	NCI	NCT	OLY	HLM	W	L	Coach
TRINITY BIBLE														
1978	M	NCCAA	II	6	—	—	—	—	—	—	—	16	12	Carlin, Scott·B.
1981		NBCAA		3	—	—	—	—	—	—	—	13	15	Carlin, Scott B.
1985		NBCAA	I	2	—	—	—	—	—	—	—	6	19	Tatum, Bob
1989		NBCAA	I	5	—	—	—	—	—	—	—	15	18	Tatum, Bob
1990		NBCAA	I	8	—	—	—	—	—	—	—	18	13	Wagler, Keith
1992		NBCAA	I	8	—	—	—	—	—	—	—	8	21	Wagler, Keith
1998		NCCAA	II	8	—	—	—	—	—	—	—	16	17	Wagler, Keith
1982	W	NSCAA		8	—	—	—	—	—	—	—	12	8	Long, Rod P.
1983		NBCAA		3	—	—	—	—	—	—	—	11	8	Long, Rod P.
1983		NSCAA		8	—	—	—	—	—	—	—	11	8	Long, Rod P.
1985		NBCAA		2	—	—	—	—	—	—	—	16	6	Long, Rod P.
1986		NBCAA		3	—	—	—	—	—	—	—	11	10	Wagler, Keith
1987		NBCAA		4	—	—	—	—	—	—	—	7	14	Wagler, Keith
1988		NBCAA		3	—	—	—	—	—	—	—	16	12	Wagler, Keith
1990		NBCAA		4	—	—	—	—	—	—	—	4	17	Tatum, Bob
TRINITY CHRISTIAN														
1997	M	NCCAA	I	6	—	—	—	—	—	—	—	24	12	Fitzgerald, Gene
1980	W	NSCAA		8	—	—	—	—	—	—	—	10	6	Hovinga, Lois
1983		NCCAA	I	8	—	—	—	—	—	—	—	13	5	Cole, Lois
1984		NCCAA	I	8	—	—	—	—	—	—	—	11	11	Cole, Lois
1986		NCCAA	I	8	—	—	—	—	—	—	—	18	11	Ribbens, David L.
1987		NCCAA	I	4	—	—	—	—	—	—	—	23	7	Ribbens, David L.
1988		NCCAA	I	5	—	—	—	—	—	—	—	16	13	Ribbens, David L.
1989		NCCAA	I	7	—	—	—	—	—	—	—	17	13	Ribbens, David L.
1993		NCCAA	I	4	—	—	—	—	—	—	—	19	13	Eastham, Sue
1998		NCCAA	I	8	—	—	—	—	—	—	—	20	13	Schaaf, Barb
TRINITY INTERNATIONAL (FL)														
1991	M	NCCAA	IIA	1	—	—	—	—	—	—	—	15	14	Rutherford, Robert
TRINITY INTERNATIONAL (IL)														
1972	M	NCCAA		8	—	—	—	—	—	—	—	10	14	Van Dix Horn, Henry
1974		NCCAA		4	—	—	—	—	—	—	—	15	15	Van Dix Horn, Henry
1988		NSCAA		15	—	—	—	—	—	—	—	18	11	Seils, David S.
1994		NSCAA		10	—	—	—	—	—	—	—	19	11	Bruehl, Alan
1995		NAIA	II	32	—	—	—	—	—	—	—	24	8	Bruehl, Alan
1996		NAIA	II	16	—	—	—	—	—	—	—	25	6	Bruehl, Alan
1985	W	NCCAA	I	8	—	—	—	—	—	—	—	10	18	Girton, Marcy
1990		NSCAA		6	—	—	—	—	—	—	—	16	12	Seils, David S.
1991		NSCAA		8	—	—	—	—	—	—	—	16	9	Seils, David S.
1992		NSCAA		1	—	—	—	—	—	—	—	15	10	Seils, David S.
1993		NAIA	II	20	—	—	—	—	—	—	—	24	6	Seils, David S.
1994		NSCAA		1	—	—	—	—	—	—	—	24	8	Seils, David S.
1995		NAIA	II	32	—	—	—	—	—	—	—	22	4	Seils, David S.
TROY STATE: TROY														
1957	M	NAIA		32	—	—	—	—	—	—	—	19	8	Fraser, Morley
1958		NAIA		32	—	—	—	—	—	—	—	16	6	Archer, John A.
1959		NAIA		32	—	—	—	—	—	—	—	19	11	Archer, John A.
1977		NCAA	II	16	—	—	—	—	—	—	—	15	14	Bizilia, Wes

Year	M/W	Assn	Div	NAT	NIT	ARC	CCA	NCI	NCT	OLY	HLM	W	L	Coach
1988		NCAA	II	4	—	—	—	—	—	—	—	24	10	Maestri, Don
1991		NCAA	II	16	—	—	—	—	—	—	—	22	8	Maestri, Don
1992		NCAA	II	24	—	—	—	—	—	—	—	23	6	Maestri, Don
1993		NCAA	II	2	—	—	—	—	—	—	—	27	5	Maestri, Don
1997	W	NCAA	I	64	—	—	—	—	—	—	—	23	7	Hester, Jerry

TRUMAN STATE (MO)

Year	M/W	Assn	Div	NAT	NIT	ARC	CCA	NCI	NCT	OLY	HLM	W	L	Coach
1947	M	NAIA		8	—	—	—	—	—	—	—	30	2	King, W. Boyd
1948		NAIA		32	—	—	—	—	—	—	—	29	2	King, W. Boyd
1955		NAIA		16	—	—	—	—	—	—	—	19	6	King, W. Boyd
1960		NCAA	II	8	—	—	—	—	—	—	—	19	5	King, W. Boyd
1971		NCAA	II	16	—	—	—	—	—	—	—	18	9	King, W. Boyd
1979		NCAA	II	32	—	—	—	—	—	—	—	20	8	Simms, Willard
1981		NCAA	II	16	—	—	—	—	—	—	—	19	11	Simms, Willard
1982	W	NCAA	II	16	—	—	—	—	—	—	—	17	11	Murray, Dr. Mary Jo

TUFTS

Year	M/W	Assn	Div	NAT	NIT	ARC	CCA	NCI	NCT	OLY	HLM	W	L	Coach
1945	M	NCAA		8	—	—	—	—	—	—	—	10	8	Cochran, Arthur M.
1995		NCAA	III	64	—	—	—	—	—	—	—	20	5	Sheldon, Robert J., Jr.
1997		NCAA	III	32	—	—	—	—	—	—	—	20	6	Sheldon, Robert J., Jr.

TULANE

Year	M/W	Assn	Div	NAT	NIT	ARC	CCA	NCI	NCT	OLY	HLM	W	L	Coach
1982	M	NCAA	I	—	8	—	—	—	—	—	—	19	9	Fowler, Ned
1983		NCAA	I	—	32	—	—	—	—	—	—	19	12	Fowler, Ned
1992		NCAA	I	32	—	—	—	—	—	—	—	22	9	Clark, Perry
1993		NCAA	I	32	—	—	—	—	—	—	—	22	9	Clark, Perry
1994		NCAA	I	—	16	—	—	—	—	—	—	18	11	Clark, Perry
1995		NCAA	I	32	—	—	—	—	—	—	—	23	10	Clark, Perry
1996		NCAA	I	—	3	—	—	—	—	—	—	22	10	Clark, Perry
1997		NCAA	I	—	32	—	—	—	—	—	—	20	11	Clark, Perry
1994	W	NCAA	I	—	4	—	—	—	—	—	—	17	14	Harvey, Candi
1995		NCAA	I	64	—	—	—	—	—	—	—	19	10	Stockton, Lisa
1996		NCAA	I	64	—	—	—	—	—	—	—	21	10	Stockton, Lisa
1997		NCAA	I	32	—	—	—	—	—	—	—	27	5	Stockton, Lisa
1998		NCAA	I	64	—	—	—	—	—	—	—	21	7	Stockton, Lisa

TULSA

Year	M/W	Assn	Div	NAT	NIT	ARC	CCA	NCI	NCT	OLY	HLM	W	L	Coach
1953	M	NCAA		—	12	—	—	—	—	—	—	15	10	Iba, Clarence V.
1955		NCAA		12	—	—	—	—	—	—	—	21	7	Iba, Clarence V.
1967		NCAA	I	—	14	—	—	—	—	—	—	19	8	Swank, Joe
1969		NCAA	I	—	16	—	—	—	—	—	—	19	8	Hayes, Ken
1981		NCAA	I	—	1	—	—	—	—	—	—	26	7	Richardson, Nolan
1982		NCAA	I	32	—	—	—	—	—	—	—	24	6	Richardson, Nolan
1983		NCAA	I	—	32	—	—	—	—	—	—	19	12	Richardson, Nolan
1984		NCAA	I	32	—	—	—	—	—	—	—	27	4	Richardson, Nolan
1985		NCAA	I	64	—	—	—	—	—	—	—	23	8	Richardson, Nolan
1986		NCAA	I	64	—	—	—	—	—	—	—	23	9	Barnett, J. D.
1987		NCAA	I	64	—	—	—	—	—	—	—	22	8	Barnett, J. D.
1990		NCAA	I	—	32	—	—	—	—	—	—	17	13	Barnett, J. D.

Year	M/W	Assn	Div	NAT	NIT	ARC	CCA	NCI	NCT	OLY	HLM	W	L	Coach
1991		NCAA	I	—	32	—	—	—	—	—	—	18	12	Barnett, J. D.
1994		NCAA	I	16	—	—	—	—	—	—	—	23	8	Smith, Orlando H. "Tubby"
1995		NCAA	I	16	—	—	—	—	—	—	—	24	8	Smith, Orlando H. "Tubby"
1996		NCAA	I	64	—	—	—	—	—	—	—	22	8	Robinson, Steve
1997		NCAA	I	32	—	—	—	—	—	—	—	24	10	Robinson, Steve

TUSCULUM

Year	M/W	Assn	Div	NAT	NIT	ARC	CCA	NCI	NCT	OLY	HLM	W	L	Coach
1992	W	NAIA	II	16	—	—	—	—	—	—	—	24	9	Botta, Angelo
1995		NAIA	II	32	—	—	—	—	—	—	—	27	7	Botta, Angelo
1996		NAIA	II	16	—	—	—	—	—	—	—	30	5	Curtis, Merry Beth
1997		NAIA	II	32	—	—	—	—	—	—	—	20	10	Curtis, Merry Beth

TUSKEGEE

Year	M/W	Assn	Div	NAT	NIT	ARC	CCA	NCI	NCT	OLY	HLM	W	L	Coach
1959	M	NCAA	II	32	—	—	—	—	—	—	—	13	9	Owen, Ross C.
1979		NCAA	II	24	—	—	—	—	—	—	—	18	11	Thompson, Charles
1979	W	AIAW	S	4	—	—	—	—	—	—	—	34	5	Laster, Jr. "Tiny"
1981		AIAW	II	8	—	—	—	—	—	—	—	27	11	Laster, Jr. "Tiny"
1982		NCAA	II	2	—	—	—	—	—	—	—	29	5	Laster, Jr. "Tiny"
1983		NCAA	II	16	—	—	—	—	—	—	—	20	11	Laster, Jr. "Tiny"

UNION (KY)

Year	M/W	Assn	Div	NAT	NIT	ARC	CCA	NCI	NCT	OLY	HLM	W	L	Coach
1968	M	NAIA		32	—	—	—	—	—	—	—	27	6	Moore, Pete

UNION (NY)

Year	M/W	Assn	Div	NAT	NIT	ARC	CCA	NCI	NCT	OLY	HLM	W	L	Coach
1983	M	NCAA	III	24	—	—	—	—	—	—	—	21	5	Scanlon, William M.

UNION (TN)

Year	M/W	Assn	Div	NAT	NIT	ARC	CCA	NCI	NCT	OLY	HLM	W	L	Coach
1958	M	NAIA		32	—	—	—	—	—	—	—	17	14	Russell, Jack L.
1962		NCAA	II	32	—	—	—	—	—	—	—	16	13	Russell, Jack L.
1968		NCAA	II	16	—	—	—	—	—	—	—	22	3	Henry, Bill
1992		NAIA	I	32	—	—	—	—	—	—	—	19	15	McCormick, Rick
1998		NAIA	I	32	—	—	—	—	—	—	—	30	5	Turner, Ralph
1976	W	AIAW	S	12	—	—	—	—	—	—	—	26	3	Birmingham, Peggy
1988		NAIA		8	—	—	—	—	—	—	—	29	3	Blackstock, Dr. David
1989		NAIA		16	—	—	—	—	—	—	—	26	6	Blackstock, Dr. David
1992		NAIA	I	8	—	—	—	—	—	—	—	31	5	Blackstock, Dr. David
1993		NAIA	I	2	—	—	—	—	—	—	—	33	5	Blackstock, Dr. David
1994		NAIA	I	8	—	—	—	—	—	—	—	27	6	Blackstock, Dr. David
1995		NAIA	I	16	—	—	—	—	—	—	—	31	3	Blackstock, Dr. David
1996		NAIA	I	3	—	—	—	—	—	—	—	34	4	Blackstock, Dr. David
1997		NAIA	I	2	—	—	—	—	—	—	—	35	5	Blackstock, Dr. David
1998		NAIA	I	1	—	—	—	—	—	—	—	35	3	Blackstock, Dr. David

UNITED STATES INTERNATIONAL

Year	M/W	Assn	Div	NAT	NIT	ARC	CCA	NCI	NCT	OLY	HLM	W	L	Coach
1963	M	NAIA		32	—	—	—	—	—	—	—	17	15	Kloppenburg, Bob
1965		NAIA		32	—	—	—	—	—	—	—	21	13	Kloppenburg, Bob
1966		NAIA		32	—	—	—	—	—	—	—	21	9	Kloppenburg, Bob
1975		NAIA		32	—	—	—	—	—	—	—	20	9	Kloppenburg, Bob
1986	W	NCAA	I	—	6	—	—	—	—	—	—	24	9	Macias, Cassie

Year	M/W	Assn	Div	NAT	NIT	ARC	CCA	NCI	NCT	OLY	HLM	W	L	Coach
UPPER IOWA														
1940	M	NAIA		32	—	—	—	—	—	—	—	8	6	Dorman, Dr. John E.
1957		NAIA		32	—	—	—	—	—	—	—	17	6	Eischeid, Everett E. "Eb"
1965		NAIA		32	—	—	—	—	—	—	—	21	5	Jack, Stanley
1966		NAIA		32	—	—	—	—	—	—	—	20	4	Jack, Stanley
1996		NCAA	III	64	—	—	—	—	—	—	—	20	5	Engen, Stewart "Stu"
UPSALA														
1960	M	NCAA	II	24	—	—	—	—	—	—	—	19	8	Wieboldt, Frederick W.
1978		NCAA	III	30	—	—	—	—	—	—	—	19	9	Adubato, Richard
1979		NCAA	III	16	—	—	—	—	—	—	—	23	4	Chapman, Tom
1980		NCAA	III	2	—	—	—	—	—	—	—	25	5	Chapman, Tom
1981		NCAA	III	8	—	—	—	—	—	—	—	23	6	Chapman, Tom
1982		NCAA	III	16	—	—	—	—	—	—	—	23	4	Chapman, Tom
1983		NCAA	III	24	—	—	—	—	—	—	—	19	7	Chapman, Tom
1984		NCAA	III	4	—	—	—	—	—	—	—	25	5	Chapman, Tom
1986		NCAA	III	16	—	—	—	—	—	—	—	20	6	Thompson, Russ
1994	W	NCAA	III	16	—	—	—	—	—	—	—	23	3	McGrady, William
URBANA														
1992	M	NAIA	I	16	—	—	—	—	—	—	—	26	9	Ronai, Robert G.
1993		NAIA	I	8	—	—	—	—	—	—	—	26	8	Ronai, Robert G.
1997		NAIA	II	16	—	—	—	—	—	—	—	26	8	Ronai, Robert G.
URSINUS														
1980	M	NCAA	III	32	—	—	—	—	—	—	—	17	10	Werley, "Skip"
1981		NCAA	III	3	—	—	—	—	—	—	—	23	8	Werley, "Skip"
1982		NCAA	III	8	—	—	—	—	—	—	—	19	11	Werley, "Skip"
1969	W	AIAW		8	—	—	—	—	—	—	—	4	2	Snell, Eleanor
1970		AIAW		3	—	—	—	—	—	—	—	7	1	Snell, Eleanor
1977		AIAW	S	16	—	—	—	—	—	—	—	4	10	Stahl, Sue
1995		NCAA	III	64	—	—	—	—	—	—	—	21	5	Ortlip-Cornish, Lisa
UTAH														
1944	M	NCAA		1	8	1	—	—	—	—	—	21	4	Peterson, Vadal
1945		NCAA		8	—	—	—	—	—	—	—	17	4	Peterson, Vadal
1947		NCAA		—	1	—	—	—	—	—	—	19	5	Peterson, Vadal
1949		NCAA		—	8	—	—	—	—	—	—	24	8	Peterson, Vadal
1951		NCAA		—	—	—	—	3	—	—	—	23	13	Peterson, Vadal
1955		NCAA		12	—	—	—	—	—	—	—	24	4	Gardner, James H. "Jack"
1956		NCAA		8	—	—	—	—	—	—	—	22	6	Gardner, James H. "Jack"
1957		NCAA	I	—	12	—	—	—	—	—	—	19	8	Gardner, James H. "Jack"
1958		NCAA	I	—	8	—	—	—	—	—	—	20	7	Gardner, James H. "Jack"
1959		NCAA	I	16	—	—	—	—	—	—	—	21	7	Gardner, James H. "Jack"
1960		NCAA	I	12	—	—	—	—	—	—	—	26	3	Gardner, James H. "Jack"
1961		NCAA	I	4	—	—	—	—	—	—	—	23	8	Gardner, James H. "Jack"
1966		NCAA	I	4	—	—	—	—	—	—	—	23	8	Gardner, James H. "Jack"
1970		NCAA	I	—	8	—	—	—	—	—	—	18	10	Gardner, James H. "Jack"
1974		NCAA	I	—	2	—	—	—	—	—	—	22	8	Foster, William E.
1977		NCAA	I	16	—	—	—	—	—	—	—	22	7	Pimm, Jerry

Year	M/W	Assn	Div	NAT	NIT	ARC	CCA	NCI	NCT	OLY	HLM	W	L	Coach
1978		NCAA	I	16	—	—	—	—	—	—	—	23	6	Pimm, Jerry
1979		NCAA	I	40	—	—	—	—	—	—	—	20	10	Pimm, Jerry
1981		NCAA	I	16	—	—	—	—	—	—	—	25	5	Pimm, Jerry
1983		NCAA	I	16	—	—	—	—	—	—	—	18	14	Pimm, Jerry
1986		NCAA	I	64	—	—	—	—	—	—	—	20	10	Archibald, Lynn
1987		NCAA	I	—	32	—	—	—	—	—	—	17	13	Archibald, Lynn
1988		NCAA	I	—	32	—	—	—	—	—	—	19	11	Archibald, Lynn
1991		NCAA	I	16	—	—	—	—	—	—	—	30	4	Majerus, Rick
1992		NCAA	I	—	3	—	—	—	—	—	—	24	11	Majerus, Rick
1993		NCAA	I	32	—	—	—	—	—	—	—	24	7	Majerus, Rick
1995		NCAA	I	32	—	—	—	—	—	—	—	28	6	Majerus, Rick
1996		NCAA	I	16	—	—	—	—	—	—	—	27	7	Majerus, Rick
1997		NCAA	I	8	—	—	—	—	—	—	—	29	4	Majerus, Rick
1998		NCAA	I	2	—	—	—	—	—	—	—	31	4	Majerus, Rick
1976	W	AIAW	L	16	—	—	—	—	—	—	—	19	5	Gardner, Fern
1977		AIAW	L	8	—	—	—	—	—	—	—	26	3	Gardner, Fern
1978		AIAW	L	16	—	—	—	—	—	—	—	21	9	Gardner, Fern
1979		AIAW	L	—	7	—	—	—	—	—	—	23	10	Gardner, Fern
1983		NCAA	I	32	—	—	—	—	—	—	—	22	7	Gardner, Fern
1984		NCAA	I	—	8	—	—	—	—	—	—	19	12	Elliott, Elaine
1986		NCAA	I	40	—	—	—	—	—	—	—	21	9	Elliott, Elaine
1989		NCAA	I	48	—	—	—	—	—	—	—	24	6	Elliott, Elaine
1990		NCAA	I	48	—	—	—	—	—	—	—	20	10	Elliott, Elaine
1991		NCAA	I	48	—	—	—	—	—	—	—	20	10	Elliott, Elaine
1995		NCAA	I	64	—	—	—	—	—	—	—	23	7	Elliott, Elaine
1996		NCAA	I	64	—	—	—	—	—	—	—	21	8	Elliott, Elaine
1997		NCAA	I	32	—	—	—	—	—	—	—	25	6	Elliott, Elaine
1998		NCAA	I	64	—	—	—	—	—	—	—	21	6	Elliott, Elaine

UTAH STATE

Year	M/W	Assn	Div	NAT	NIT	ARC	CCA	NCI	NCT	OLY	HLM	W	L	Coach
1936	M	NCAA		—	—	—	—	—	—	8	—	18	9	Romney, Ernest L. "Dick"
1939		NCAA		6	—	—	—	—	—	—	—	17	7	Romney, Ernest L. "Dick"
1952		NAIA		16	—	—	—	—	—	—	—	19	14	Baker, H. Cecil
1960		NCAA	I	—	3	—	—	—	—	—	—	24	5	Baker, H. Cecil
1962		NCAA	I	16	—	—	—	—	—	—	—	22	7	Anderson, Ladell
1963		NCAA	I	25	—	—	—	—	—	—	—	20	7	Anderson, Ladell
1964		NCAA	I	16	—	—	—	—	—	—	—	21	8	Anderson, Ladell
1967		NCAA	I	—	14	—	—	—	—	—	—	20	6	Anderson, Ladell
1970		NCAA	I	8	—	—	—	—	—	—	—	22	7	Anderson, Ladell
1971		NCAA	I	25	—	—	—	—	—	—	—	20	7	Anderson, Ladell
1975		NCAA	I	32	—	—	—	—	—	—	—	21	6	Belnap, Gordon "Dutch"
1978		NCAA	I	—	16	—	—	—	—	—	—	21	7	Belnap, Gordon "Dutch"
1979		NCAA	I	40	—	—	—	—	—	—	—	19	11	Belnap, Gordon "Dutch"
1980		NCAA	I	48	—	—	—	—	—	—	—	18	9	Tueller, Rod
1983		NCAA	I	48	—	—	—	—	—	—	—	20	9	Tueller, Rod
1984		NCAA	I	—	32	—	—	—	—	—	—	19	11	Tueller, Rod
1988		NCAA	I	64	—	—	—	—	—	—	—	21	10	Tueller, Rod
1995		NCAA	I	—	32	—	—	—	—	—	—	21	8	Eustachy, Larry
1998		NCAA	I	64	—	—	—	—	—	—	—	25	8	Eustachy, Larry

Year	M/W	Assn	Div	NAT	NIT	ARC	CCA	NCI	NCT	OLY	HLM	W	L	Coach
1972	W	AIAW		12	—	—	—	—	—	—	—	X	X	Gardner, Fern
1973		AIAW		16	—	—	—	—	—	—	—	13	5	Gardner, Fern
1974		AIAW		16	—	—	—	—	—	—	—	13	5	Gardner, Fern
1975		AIAW	L	16	—	—	—	—	—	—	—	12	4	Gardner, Fern

UTICA

Year	M/W	Assn	Div	NAT	NIT	ARC	CCA	NCI	NCT	OLY	HLM	W	L	Coach
1984	W	NCAA	II	16	—	—	—	—	—	—	—	20	6	Kowalewski, Joan
1985		NCAA	II	16	—	—	—	—	—	—	—	22	4	Kowalewski, Joan

VALDOSTA STATE

Year	M/W	Assn	Div	NAT	NIT	ARC	CCA	NCI	NCT	OLY	HLM	W	L	Coach
1967	M	NAIA		16	—	—	—	—	—	—	—	27	8	Colson, Gary W.
1968		NAIA		16	—	—	—	—	—	—	—	23	10	Colson, Gary W.
1969		NAIA		32	—	—	—	—	—	—	—	18	11	Melvin, James
1973		NAIA		16	—	—	—	—	—	—	—	17	8	Dominey, James
1976		NCAA	II	16	—	—	—	—	—	—	—	15	13	Dominey, James
1977		NCAA	II	24	—	—	—	—	—	—	—	23	6	Dominey, James
1979		NCAA	II	16	—	—	—	—	—	—	—	20	8	Dominey, James
1977	W	AIAW	L	—	5	—	—	—	—	—	—	26	6	Worth, Lyndal
1978		AIAW	L	12	—	—	—	—	—	—	—	27	4	Worth, Lyndal
1979		AIAW	L	12	—	—	—	—	—	—	—	27	8	Worth, Lyndal
1983		NCAA	II	8	—	—	—	—	—	—	—	27	4	Cooper, Charles
1984		NCAA	II	3	—	—	—	—	—	—	—	30	3	Cooper, Charles
1995		NCAA	II	16	—	—	—	—	—	—	—	25	4	Williamson, Jane
1997		NCAA	II	48	—	—	—	—	—	—	—	19	10	Williamson, Jane

VALLEY CITY STATE

Year	M/W	Assn	Div	NAT	NIT	ARC	CCA	NCI	NCT	OLY	HLM	W	L	Coach
1960	M	NAIA		32	—	—	—	—	—	—	—	17	5	Osmon, William E.
1965		NAIA		32	—	—	—	—	—	—	—	15	7	Osmon, William E.
1987		NAIA		16	—	—	—	—	—	—	—	21	6	Parker, Bob

VALLEY FORGE CHRISTIAN

Year	M/W	Assn	Div	NAT	NIT	ARC	CCA	NCI	NCT	OLY	HLM	W	L	Coach
1979	M	NCCAA	II	2	—	—	—	—	—	—	—	18	13	Jones, Paul
1980		NCCAA	II	6	—	—	—	—	—	—	—	18	11	Jones, Paul
1986		NCCAA	II	7	—	—	—	—	—	—	—	24	8	Mioni, Dominick
1987		NCCAA	II	8	—	—	—	—	—	—	—	22	10	Engle, Mark
1988		NCCAA	II	2	—	—	—	—	—	—	—	22	8	Engle, Mark
1983	W	NCCAA	II	2	—	—	—	—	—	—	—	X	X	Baker, William J.
1984		NBCAA		4	—	—	—	—	—	—	—	X	X	Baker, William J.

VALPARAISO

Year	M/W	Assn	Div	NAT	NIT	ARC	CCA	NCI	NCT	OLY	HLM	W	L	Coach
1938	M	NAIA		16	—	—	—	—	—	—	—	13	6	Christiansen, J. M. `Jake`
1943		NAIA		32	—	—	—	—	—	—	—	17	4	Ellis, Loren E.
1962		NCAA	II	8	—	—	—	—	—	—	—	17	8	Meadows, Dr. Paul
1966		NCAA	II	16	—	—	—	—	—	—	—	19	9	Bartow, B. Gene
1967		NCAA	II	8	—	—	—	—	—	—	—	21	8	Bartow, B. Gene
1969		NCAA	II	16	—	—	—	—	—	—	—	16	12	Bartow, B. Gene
1973		NCAA	II	16	—	—	—	—	—	—	—	17	11	Purden, William
1996		NCAA	I	64	—	—	—	—	—	—	—	21	11	Drew, Homer
1997		NCAA	I	64	—	—	—	—	—	—	—	24	7	Drew, Homer
1998		NCAA	I	16	—	—	—	—	—	—	—	23	10	Drew, Homer

Year	M/W	Assn	Div	NAT	NIT	ARC	CCA	NCI	NCT	OLY	HLM	W	L	Coach
VANDERBILT														
1965	M	NCAA	I	8	—	—	—	—	—	—	—	24	4	Skinner, Roy G.
1974		NCAA	I	16	—	—	—	—	—	—	—	23	5	Skinner, Roy G.
1983		NCAA	I	—	16	—	—	—	—	—	—	19	14	Newton, Charles M. 'CM'
1987		NCAA	I	—	8	—	—	—	—	—	—	18	16	Newton, Charles M. 'CM'
1988		NCAA	I	16	—	—	—	—	—	—	—	20	11	Newton, Charles M. 'CM'
1989		NCAA	I	64	—	—	—	—	—	—	—	19	14	Newton, Charles M. 'CM'
1990		NCAA	I	—	1	—	—	—	—	—	—	21	14	Fogler, Eddie
1991		NCAA	I	64	—	—	—	—	—	—	—	17	13	Fogler, Eddie
1992		NCAA	I	—	32	—	—	—	—	—	—	15	15	Fogler, Eddie
1993		NCAA	I	16	—	—	—	—	—	—	—	28	6	Fogler, Eddie
1994		NCAA	I	—	2	—	—	—	—	—	—	20	12	Van Breda Kolff, Jan M.
1996		NCAA	I	—	16	—	—	—	—	—	—	18	14	Van Breda Kolff, Jan M.
1997		NCAA	I	64	—	—	—	—	—	—	—	19	12	Van Breda Kolff, Jan M.
1998		NCAA	I	—	8	—	—	—	—	—	—	20	13	Van Breda Kolff, Jan M.
1982	W	AIAW	I	16	—	—	—	—	—	—	—	20	14	Lee, Phil
1984		NCAA	I	—	1	—	—	—	—	—	—	23	9	Lee, Phil
1986		NCAA	I	32	—	—	—	—	—	—	—	22	9	Lee, Phil
1987		NCAA	I	32	—	—	—	—	—	—	—	23	10	Lee, Phil
1989		NCAA	I	48	—	—	—	—	—	—	—	21	8	Lee, Phil
1990		NCAA	I	16	—	—	—	—	—	—	—	23	11	Lee, Phil
1991		NCAA	I	16	—	—	—	—	—	—	—	19	12	Lee, Phil
1992		NCAA	I	8	—	—	—	—	—	—	—	22	9	Foster, Jim
1993		NCAA	I	3	—	—	—	—	—	—	—	30	3	Foster, Jim
1994		NCAA	I	16	—	—	—	—	—	—	—	25	8	Foster, Jim
1995		NCAA	I	16	—	—	—	—	—	—	—	28	7	Foster, Jim
1996		NCAA	I	8	—	—	—	—	—	—	—	23	8	Foster, Jim
1997		NCAA	I	16	—	—	—	—	—	—	—	20	11	Foster, Jim
1998		NCAA	I	64	—	—	—	—	—	—	—	20	9	Foster, Jim
VENNARD														
1984	M	NBCAA	II	2	—	—	—	—	—	—	—	10	16	Engbrecht, Dr. Dennis D.
1985		NBCAA	II	4	—	—	—	—	—	—	—	15	16	Engbrecht, Dr. Dennis D.
1986		NBCAA	II	3	—	—	—	—	—	—	—	13	12	Engbrecht, Dr. Dennis D.
1987		NBCAA	II	2	—	—	—	—	—	—	—	11	14	Owens, Dennis
1990		NBCAA	II	6	—	—	—	—	—	—	—	8	16	Penn, Brad
1992		NBCAA	II	6	—	—	—	—	—	—	—	9	12	Christiansen, Les
1993		NBCAA	II	4	—	—	—	—	—	—	—	10	15	Christiansen, Les
1995		NBCAA	II	6	—	—	—	—	—	—	—	9	19	Van·Amburg, L. D.
1986	W	NBCAA		7	—	—	—	—	—	—	—			
VERMONT														
1992	W	NCAA	I	48	—	—	—	—	—	—	—	29	1	Inglese, Cathy
1993		NCAA	I	48	—	—	—	—	—	—	—	28	1	Inglese, Cathy
1994		NCAA	I	64	—	—	—	—	—	—	—	19	11	Borton, Pam
VERMONT TECH														
1995	M	NSCAA		10	—	—	—	—	—	—	—	20	5	Maxwell, Mike

Year	M/W	Assn	Div	NAT	NIT	ARC	CCA	NCI	NCT	OLY	HLM	W	L	Coach
VILLANOVA														
1939	M	NCAA	3	—	—	—	—	—	—	—	—	20	5	Severance, Alexander G.
1949		NCAA	6	—	—	—	—	—	—	—	—	23	4	Severance, Alexander G.
1951		NCAA	16	—	—	—	—	8	—	—	—	25	7	Severance, Alexander G.
1955		NCAA	12	—	—	—	—	—	—	—	—	18	10	Severance, Alexander G.
1959		NCAA	I	—	12	—	—	—	—	—	—	18	7	Severance, Alexander G.
1960		NCAA	I	—	8	—	—	—	—	—	—	20	6	Severance, Alexander G.
1962		NCAA	I	8	—	—	—	—	—	—	—	21	7	Kraft, John J. "Jack"
1963		NCAA	I	—	4	—	—	—	—	—	—	19	10	Kraft, John J. "Jack"
1964		NCAA	I	12	—	—	—	—	—	—	—	24	4	Kraft, John J. "Jack"
1965		NCAA	I	—	2	—	—	—	—	—	—	23	5	Kraft, John J. "Jack"
1966		NCAA	I	—	3	—	—	—	—	—	—	18	11	Kraft, John J. "Jack"
1967		NCAA	I	—	14	—	—	—	—	—	—	17	9	Kraft, John J. "Jack"
1968		NCAA	I	—	8	—	—	—	—	—	—	19	9	Kraft, John J. "Jack"
1969		NCAA	I	25	—	—	—	—	—	—	—	21	5	Kraft, John J. "Jack"
1970		NCAA	I	8	—	—	—	—	—	—	—	22	7	Kraft, John J. "Jack"
1971		NCAA	I	2	—	—	—	—	—	—	—	22	7	Kraft, John J. "Jack"
1972		NCAA	I	16	—	—	—	—	—	—	—	20	8	Kraft, John J. "Jack"
1977		NCAA	I	—	3	—	—	—	—	—	—	23	10	Massimino, Roland V. "Rollie"
1978		NCAA	I	8	—	—	—	—	—	—	—	23	9	Massimino, Roland V. "Rollie"
1980		NCAA	I	32	—	—	—	—	—	—	—	23	8	Massimino, Roland V. "Rollie"
1981		NCAA	I	32	—	—	—	—	—	—	—	20	11	Massimino, Roland V. "Rollie"
1982		NCAA	I	8	—	—	—	—	—	—	—	24	8	Massimino, Roland V. "Rollie"
1983		NCAA	I	8	—	—	—	—	—	—	—	24	8	Massimino, Roland V. "Rollie"
1984		NCAA	I	32	—	—	—	—	—	—	—	19	12	Massimino, Roland V. "Rollie"
1985		NCAA	I	1	—	—	—	—	—	—	—	25	10	Massimino, Roland V. "Rollie"
1986		NCAA	I	32	—	—	—	—	—	—	—	23	14	Massimino, Roland V. "Rollie"
1987		NCAA	I	—	32	—	—	—	—	—	—	15	16	Massimino, Roland V. "Rollie"
1988		NCAA	I	8	—	—	—	—	—	—	—	24	13	Massimino, Roland V. "Rollie"
1989		NCAA	I	—	8	—	—	—	—	—	—	18	16	Massimino, Roland V. "Rollie"
1990		NCAA	I	64	—	—	—	—	—	—	—	18	15	Massimino, Roland V. "Rollie"
1991		NCAA	I	32	—	—	—	—	—	—	—	17	15	Massimino, Roland V. "Rollie"
1992		NCAA	I	—	32	—	—	—	—	—	—	14	15	Massimino, Roland V. "Rollie"
1994		NCAA	I	—	1	—	—	—	—	—	—	20	12	Lappas, Steve
1995		NCAA	I	64	—	—	—	—	—	—	—	25	8	Lappas, Steve
1996		NCAA	I	32	—	—	—	—	—	—	—	26	7	Lappas, Steve
1997		NCAA	I	32	—	—	—	—	—	—	—	24	10	Lappas, Steve
1982	W	AIAW	I	3	—	—	—	—	—	—	—	29	4	Perretta, Harry
1986		NCAA	I	32	—	—	—	—	—	—	—	23	8	Perretta, Harry
1987		NCAA	I	32	—	—	—	—	—	—	—	27	4	Perretta, Harry
1988		NCAA	I	40	—	—	—	—	—	—	—	20	9	Perretta, Harry
1989		NCAA	I	48	—	—	—	—	—	—	—	18	12	Perretta, Harry
1998		NCAA	I	—	16	—	—	—	—	—	—	19	10	Perretta, Harry
VIRGINIA														
1941	M	NCAA		—	8	—	—	—	—	—	—	16	5	Tebell, Gus K.
1972		NCAA	I	—	16	—	—	—	—	—	—	21	7	Gibson, William J.
1976		NCAA	I	32	—	—	—	—	—	—	—	18	12	Holland, M. Terrance "Terry"
1978		NCAA	I	—	16	—	—	—	—	—	—	20	8	Holland, M. Terrance "Terry"

Year	M/W	Assn	Div	NAT	NIT	ARC	CCA	NCI	NCT	OLY	HLM	W	L	Coach
1979		NCAA	I	—	12	—	—	—	—	—	—	19	10	Holland, M. Terrance "Terry"
1980		NCAA	I	—	1	—	—	—	—	—	—	24	10	Holland, M. Terrance "Terry"
1981		NCAA	I	3	—	—	—	—	—	—	—	29	4	Holland, M. Terrance "Terry"
1982		NCAA	I	16	—	—	—	—	—	—	—	30	4	Holland, M. Terrance "Terry"
1983		NCAA	I	8	—	—	—	—	—	—	—	29	5	Holland, M. Terrance "Terry"
1984		NCAA	I	3	—	—	—	—	—	—	—	21	12	Holland, M. Terrance "Terry"
1985		NCAA	I	—	8	—	—	—	—	—	—	17	16	Holland, M. Terrance "Terry"
1986		NCAA	I	64	—	—	—	—	—	—	—	19	11	Holland, M. Terrance "Terry"
1987		NCAA	I	64	—	—	—	—	—	—	—	21	10	Holland, M. Terrance "Terry"
1989		NCAA	I	8	—	—	—	—	—	—	—	22	11	Holland, M. Terrance "Terry"
1990		NCAA	I	32	—	—	—	—	—	—	—	20	12	Holland, M. Terrance "Terry"
1991		NCAA	I	64	—	—	—	—	—	—	—	21	12	Jones, Jeffrey A.
1992		NCAA	I	—	1	—	—	—	—	—	—	20	13	Jones, Jeffrey A.
1993		NCAA	I	16	—	—	—	—	—	—	—	21	10	Jones, Jeffrey A.
1994		NCAA	I	32	—	—	—	—	—	—	—	18	13	Jones, Jeffrey A.
1995		NCAA	I	8	—	—	—	—	—	—	—	25	9	Jones, Jeffrey A.
1997		NCAA	I	64	—	—	—	—	—	—	—	18	13	Jones, Jeffrey A.
1980	W			—	4	—	—	—	—	—	—	20	12	Ryan, Deborah H.
1984		NCAA	I	32	—	—	—	—	—	—	—	22	7	Ryan, Deborah H.
1985		NCAA	I	32	—	—	—	—	—	—	—	21	8	Ryan, Deborah H.
1986		NCAA	I	32	—	—	—	—	—	—	—	26	3	Ryan, Deborah H.
1987		NCAA	I	16	—	—	—	—	—	—	—	26	5	Ryan, Deborah H.
1988		NCAA	I	8	—	—	—	—	—	—	—	27	5	Ryan, Deborah H.
1989		NCAA	I	16	—	—	—	—	—	—	—	21	10	Ryan, Deborah H.
1990		NCAA	I	3	—	—	—	—	—	—	—	29	6	Ryan, Deborah H.
1991		NCAA	I	2	—	—	—	—	—	—	—	31	3	Ryan, Deborah H.
1992		NCAA	I	3	—	—	—	—	—	—	—	32	2	Ryan, Deborah H.
1993		NCAA	I	8	—	—	—	—	—	—	—	26	6	Ryan, Deborah H.
1994		NCAA	I	16	—	—	—	—	—	—	—	27	5	Ryan, Deborah H.
1995		NCAA	I	8	—	—	—	—	—	—	—	27	5	Ryan, Deborah H.
1996		NCAA	I	8	—	—	—	—	—	—	—	26	7	Ryan, Deborah H.
1997		NCAA	I	16	—	—	—	—	—	—	—	23	8	Ryan, Deborah H.
1998		NCAA	I	32	—	—	—	—	—	—	—	19	10	Ryan, Deborah H.

VIRGINIA COMMONWEALTH

Year	M/W	Assn	Div	NAT	NIT	ARC	CCA	NCI	NCT	OLY	HLM	W	L	Coach
1978	M	NCAA	I	—	16	—	—	—	—	—	—	24	5	Kirk, Dana
1980		NCAA	I	48	—	—	—	—	—	—	—	18	12	Barnett, J. D.
1981		NCAA	I	32	—	—	—	—	—	—	—	24	5	Barnett, J. D.
1983		NCAA	I	32	—	—	—	—	—	—	—	24	7	Barnett, J. D.
1984		NCAA	I	32	—	—	—	—	—	—	—	23	7	Barnett, J. D.
1985		NCAA	I	32	—	—	—	—	—	—	—	26	6	Barnett, J. D.
1988		NCAA	I	—	8	—	—	—	—	—	—	23	12	Pollio, Mike
1993		NCAA	I	—	32	—	—	—	—	—	—	20	10	Smith, Charles H. "Sonny"
1996		NCAA	I	64	—	—	—	—	—	—	—	24	9	Smith, Charles H. "Sonny"
1995	W	NCAA	I	—	7	—	—	—	—	—	—	20	10	Walvius, Susan

VIRGINIA INTERMONT

Year	M/W	Assn	Div	NAT	NIT	ARC	CCA	NCI	NCT	OLY	HLM	W	L	Coach
1997	M	NAIA	II	32	—	—	—	—	—	—	—	21	13	Worrell, Phil
1998		NAIA	II	32	—	—	—	—	—	—	—	21	13	Worrell, Phil

Year	M/W	Assn	Div	NAT	NIT	ARC	CCA	NCI	NCT	OLY	HLM	W	L	Coach
VIRGINIA MILITARY														
1964	M	NCAA	I	25	—	—	—	—	—	—	—	12	12	Miller, Louis F. "Weenie"
1976		NCAA	I	8	—	—	—	—	—	—	—	22	10	Blair, William H., Jr.
1977		NCAA	I	16	—	—	—	—	—	—	—	26	4	Schmaus, Charlie
VIRGINIA POLYTECHNIC														
1966	M	NCAA	I	—	14	—	—	—	—	—	—	19	5	Shannon, Howard P. "Howie"
1967		NCAA	I	8	—	—	—	—	—	—	—	20	7	Shannon, Howard P. "Howie"
1973		NCAA	I	—	1	—	—	—	—	—	—	22	5	DeVoe, Donald E.
1976		NCAA	I	32	—	—	—	—	—	—	—	21	7	DeVoe, Donald E.
1977		NCAA	I	—	8	—	—	—	—	—	—	19	10	Moir, Charles
1979		NCAA	I	32	—	—	—	—	—	—	—	22	9	Moir, Charles
1980		NCAA	I	32	—	—	—	—	—	—	—	21	8	Moir, Charles
1982		NCAA	I	—	8	—	—	—	—	—	—	20	11	Moir, Charles
1983		NCAA	I	—	16	—	—	—	—	—	—	23	11	Moir, Charles
1984		NCAA	I	—	3	—	—	—	—	—	—	22	13	Moir, Charles
1985		NCAA	I	64	—	—	—	—	—	—	—	20	9	Moir, Charles
1986		NCAA	I	64	—	—	—	—	—	—	—	22	9	Moir, Charles
1995		NCAA	I	—	1	—	—	—	—	—	—	25	10	Foster, William C.
1996		NCAA	I	32	—	—	—	—	—	—	—	23	6	Foster, William C.
1994	W	NCAA	I	64	—	—	—	—	—	—	—	24	6	Alfano, Carol
1995		NCAA	I	32	—	—	—	—	—	—	—	22	9	Alfano, Carol
1998		NCAA	I	32	—	—	—	—	—	—	—	22	10	Henrickson, Bonnie
VIRGINIA STATE														
1953	M	NASC		8	—	—	—	—	—	—	—	14	8	Matthews, Shelton M.
1974		NAIA		32	—	—	—	—	—	—	—	22	8	Deane, Harold A., Sr.
1982		NCAA	II	24	—	—	—	—	—	—	—	19	9	Laisure, W. Floyd
1988		NCAA	II	32	—	—	—	—	—	—	—	21	12	Deane, Harold A., Sr.
1981	W	NAIA		8	—	—	—	—	—	—	—	18	15	Bey, Leon Wright
1987		NCAA	II	24	—	—	—	—	—	—	—	21	7	Bey, Leon Wright
1988		NCAA	II	16	—	—	—	—	—	—	—	21	7	Bey, Leon Wright
1989		NCAA	II	16	—	—	—	—	—	—	—	22	5	Cummings, Bertha
1990		NCAA	II	32	—	—	—	—	—	—	—	24	4	Cummings, Bertha
VIRGINIA UNION														
1954	M	NASC		8	—	—	—	—	—	—	—	14	4	Harris, Thomas H.
1955		NASC		8	—	—	—	—	—	—	—	21	6	Harris, Thomas H.
1961		NCAA	II	24	—	—	—	—	—	—	—	23	6	Harris, Thomas H.
1977		NCAA	II	24	—	—	—	—	—	—	—	25	5	Moore, Robert D.
1979		NCAA	II	16	—	—	—	—	—	—	—	18	8	Robbins, Charles David "Dave"
1980		NCAA	II	1	—	—	—	—	—	—	—	26	4	Robbins, Charles David "Dave"
1982		NCAA	II	32	—	—	—	—	—	—	—	18	7	Robbins, Charles David "Dave"
1984		NCAA	II	8	—	—	—	—	—	—	—	27	6	Robbins, Charles David "Dave"
1985		NCAA	II	24	—	—	—	—	—	—	—	31	1	Robbins, Charles David "Dave"
1986		NCAA	II	24	—	—	—	—	—	—	—	24	8	Robbins, Charles David "Dave"
1987		NCAA	II	24	—	—	—	—	—	—	—	25	7	Robbins, Charles David "Dave"
1988		NCAA	II	24	—	—	—	—	—	—	—	25	6	Robbins, Charles David "Dave"
1989		NCAA	II	16	—	—	—	—	—	—	—	27	4	Robbins, Charles David "Dave"
1990		NCAA	II	32	—	—	—	—	—	—	—	27	4	Robbins, Charles David "Dave"
1991		NCAA	II	3	—	—	—	—	—	—	—	27	5	Robbins, Charles David "Dave"
1992		NCAA	II	1	—	—	—	—	—	—	—	30	3	Robbins, Charles David "Dave"

Year	M/W	Assn	Div	NAT	NIT	ARC	CCA	NCI	NCT	OLY	HLM	W	L	Coach
1993		NCAA	II	16	—	—	—	—	—	—	—	27	3	Robbins, Charles David "Dave"
1994		NCAA	II	16	—	—	—	—	—	—	—	26	3	Robbins, Charles David "Dave"
1995		NCAA	II	16	—	—	—	—	—	—	—	26	5	Robbins, Charles David "Dave"
1996		NCAA	II	3	—	—	—	—	—	—	—	28	3	Robbins, Charles David "Dave"
1998		NCAA	II	3	—	—	—	—	—	—	—	26	6	Robbins, Charles David "Dave"
1982	W	NCAA	II	16	—	—	—	—	—	—	—	18	5	Cannady, Nathan
1983		NCAA	II	1	—	—	—	—	—	—	—	27	2	Hearn, Louis
1984		NCAA	II	2	—	—	—	—	—	—	—	22	5	Hearn, Louis
1998		NCAA	II	48	—	—	—	—	—	—	—	24	4	Golatt, Moses

VIRGINIA WESLEYAN

Year	M/W	Assn	Div	NAT	NIT	ARC	CCA	NCI	NCT	OLY	HLM	W	L	Coach
1978	M	NCAA	III	30	—	—	—	—	—	—	—	17	13	Forsyth, Donald M.
1979		NCAA	III	24	—	—	—	—	—	—	—	23	6	Forsyth, Donald M.
1982		NCAA	III	32	—	—	—	—	—	—	—	20	10	Forsyth, Donald M.
1993		NCAA	III	40	—	—	—	—	—	—	—	19	9	Butterfield, Terry
1984	W	NCAA	III	32	—	—	—	—	—	—	—	20	9	Dunavent, Mike
1986		NCAA	III	24	—	—	—	—	—	—	—	24	5	Jordan, Jack
1988		NCAA	III	32	—	—	—	—	—	—	—	20	10	Jordan, Jack
1989		NCAA	III	32	—	—	—	—	—	—	—	20	9	Jordan, Jack

VITERBO

Year	M/W	Assn	Div	NAT	NIT	ARC	CCA	NCI	NCT	OLY	HLM	W	L	Coach
1981	M	NSCAA		16	—	—	—	—	—	—	—	12	14	Glasshoff, James
1982		NSCAA		16	—	—	—	—	—	—	—	10	17	Glasshoff, James
1983		NSCAA		8	—	—	—	—	—	—	—	17	10	Glasshoff, James
1984		NSCAA		8	—	—	—	—	—	—	—	17	13	Glasshoff, James
1986		NSCAA		16	—	—	—	—	—	—	—	14	16	Glasshoff, James
1987		NSCAA		7	—	—	—	—	—	—	—	22	10	Popp, Rod
1995		NAIA	II	16	—	—	—	—	—	—	—	27	7	Murphy, Michael
1982	W	NSCAA		7	—	—	—	—	—	—	—	11	7	Jack, Ellyn
1983		NSCAA		7	—	—	—	—	—	—	—	12	9	Jack, Ellyn

VOORHEES

Year	M/W	Assn	Div	NAT	NIT	ARC	CCA	NCI	NCT	OLY	HLM	W	L	Coach
1995	M	NAIA	I	16	—	—	—	—	—	—	—	25	12	Bernstein, Jeff
1995	W	NAIA	I	32	—	—	—	—	—	—	—	21	13	Baker, Cedric W.
1997		NAIA	I	32	—	—	—	—	—	—	—	19	12	Baker, Cedric W.

WABASH

Year	M/W	Assn	Div	NAT	NIT	ARC	CCA	NCI	NCT	OLY	HLM	W	L	Coach
1958	M	NCAA	II	24	—	—	—	—	—	—	—	12	9	Brock, Bob L.
1959		NCAA	II	24	—	—	—	—	—	—	—	11	8	Brock, Bob L.
1960		NCAA	II	16	—	—	—	—	—	—	—	13	7	Brock, Bob L.
1961		NCAA	II	16	—	—	—	—	—	—	—	15	7	Brock, Bob L.
1980		NCAA	III	32	—	—	—	—	—	—	—	20	6	Petty, Malcolm "Mac"
1981		NCAA	III	24	—	—	—	—	—	—	—	19	6	Petty, Malcolm "Mac"
1982		NCAA	III	1	—	—	—	—	—	—	—	24	4	Petty, Malcolm "Mac"
1997		NCAA	III	32	—	—	—	—	—	—	—	24	5	Petty, Malcolm "Mac"
1998		NCAA	III	32	—	—	—	—	—	—	—	22	5	Petty, Malcolm "Mac"

WAGNER

Year	M/W	Assn	Div	NAT	NIT	ARC	CCA	NCI	NCT	OLY	HLM	W	L	Coach
1958	M	NCAA	II	16	—	—	—	—	—	—	—	18	9	Sutter, Herbert E.
1967		NCAA	II	23	—	—	—	—	—	—	—	19	9	Sellitto, Chester
1968		NCAA	II	16	—	—	—	—	—	—	—	21	8	Sellitto, Chester
1969		NCAA	II	16	—	—	—	—	—	—	—	18	10	Sellitto, Chester
1979		NCAA	I	—	24	—	—	—	—	—	—	21	7	Carlesimo, Peter J. "PJ"

Year	M/W	Assn	Div	NAT	NIT	ARC	CCA	NCI	NCT	OLY	HLM	W	L	Coach
WAKE FOREST
1939	M	NCAA		8	—	—	—	—	—	—	—	18	6	Greason, Murray
1953		NCAA		12	—	—	—	—	—	—	—	22	7	Greason, Murray
1961		NCAA	I	8	—	—	—	—	—	—	—	19	11	McKinney, Horace A. 'Bones'
1962		NCAA	I	3	—	—	—	—	—	—	—	22	9	McKinney, Horace A. 'Bones'
1977		NCAA	I	8	—	—	—	—	—	—	—	22	8	Tacy, Carl R.
1981		NCAA	I	32	—	—	—	—	—	—	—	22	7	Tacy, Carl R.
1982		NCAA	I	32	—	—	—	—	—	—	—	21	9	Tacy, Carl R.
1983		NCAA	I	—	3	—	—	—	—	—	—	20	12	Tacy, Carl R.
1984		NCAA	I	8	—	—	—	—	—	—	—	23	9	Tacy, Carl R.
1985		NCAA	I	—	32	—	—	—	—	—	—	15	14	Tacy, Carl R.
1991		NCAA	I	32	—	—	—	—	—	—	—	19	11	Odom, Dave
1992		NCAA	I	64	—	—	—	—	—	—	—	17	12	Odom, Dave
1993		NCAA	I	16	—	—	—	—	—	—	—	21	9	Odom, Dave
1994		NCAA	I	32	—	—	—	—	—	—	—	21	12	Odom, Dave
1995		NCAA	I	16	—	—	—	—	—	—	—	26	6	Odom, Dave
1996		NCAA	I	8	—	—	—	—	—	—	—	26	6	Odom, Dave
1997		NCAA	I	32	—	—	—	—	—	—	—	24	7	Odom, Dave
1998		NCAA	I	—	16	—	—	—	—	—	—	16	14	Odom, Dave
1988	W	NCAA	I	32	—	—	—	—	—	—	—	23	8	Sanchez, Joe
WALSH
1983	M	NAIA		32	—	—	—	—	—	—	—	34	1	Huggins, Robert
1984		NAIA		32	—	—	—	—	—	—	—	26	3	Peters, Dan
1993		NAIA	II	8	—	—	—	—	—	—	—	29	5	Loy, Steve
1996		NAIA	II	3	—	—	—	—	—	—	—	30	3	Loy, Steve
1998		NAIA	II	32	—	—	—	—	—	—	—	25	10	Loy, Steve
1998	W	NAIA	II	1	—	—	—	—	—	—	—	29	5	Smesco, Carl
WARNER PACIFIC
1972	M	NSCAA		3	—	—	—	—	—	—	—	16	16	Allord, Bob
1973		NSCAA		5	—	—	—	—	—	—	—	18	18	Blewrit, Mike
1983		NCCAA	I	8	—	—	—	—	—	—	—	24	9	Bays, Gary R.
1980	W	NSCAA		2	—	—	—	—	—	—	—	X	X	Park, Kathi
WARNER SOUTHERN
1998	M	NAIA	II	16	—	—	—	—	—	—	—	26	8	Bays, Gary R.
WARREN WILSON
1967	M	NSCAA		3	—	—	—	—	—	—	—	21	12	Ellenburg, Ray
1981		NSCAA		12	—	—	—	—	—	—	—	22	7	
1982		NSCAA		8	—	—	—	—	—	—	—	22	10	Franklin, Richard
1985	W	NSCAA		7	—	—	—	—	—	—	—	21	8	Slaughter, Jerry
1996		NSCAA		6	—	—	—	—	—	—	—	10	4	Keller, Jeff
WARTBURG
1957	M	NCAA	II	32	—	—	—	—	—	—	—	19	8	Bundgaard, Dr. Alex C. 'Ax'
1958		NCAA	II	24	—	—	—	—	—	—	—	16	9	Bundgaard, Dr. Alex C. 'Ax'
1959		NCAA	II	24	—	—	—	—	—	—	—	21	5	Bundgaard, Dr. Alex C. 'Ax'
1960		NCAA	II	32	—	—	—	—	---	—	—	18	7	Bundgaard, Dr. Alex C. 'Ax'

Year	M/W	Assn	Div	NAT	NIT	ARC	CCA	NCI	NCT	OLY	HLM	W	L	Coach
1967		NAIA		32	—	—	—	—	—	—	—	19	7	Levick, Lewis J. 'Buzz'
1969		NAIA		32	—	—	—	—	—	—	—	25	1	Levick, Lewis J. 'Buzz'
1970		NAIA		16	—	—	—	—	—	—	—	26	3	Levick, Lewis J. 'Buzz'
1973		NAIA		32	—	—	—	—	—	—	—	21	8	Levick, Lewis J. 'Buzz'
1974		NAIA		32	—	—	—	—	—	—	—	23	5	Levick, Lewis J. 'Buzz'
1975		NCAA	III	16	—	—	—	—	—	—	—	22	6	Levick, Lewis J. 'Buzz'
1987		NCAA	III	8	—	—	—	—	—	—	—	19	8	Levick, Lewis J. 'Buzz'
1989		NCAA	III	32	—	—	—	—	—	—	—	21	8	Levick, Lewis J. 'Buzz'
1991		NCAA	III	16	—	—	—	—	—	—	—	23	5	Levick, Lewis J. 'Buzz'
1993		NCAA	III	40	—	—	—	—	—	—	—	18	8	Levick, Lewis J. 'Buzz'
1989	W	NCAA	III	24	—	—	—	—	—	—	—	21	6	Severson, Monica
1990		NCAA	III	16	—	—	—	—	—	—	—	22	5	Severson, Monica
1991		NCAA	III	32	—	—	—	—	—	—	—	20	7	Severson, Monica
1992		NCAA	III	8	—	—	—	—	—	—	—	23	4	Severson, Monica
1993		NCAA	III	8	—	—	—	—	—	—	—	23	5	Severson, Monica
1994		NCAA	III	40	—	—	—	—	—	—	—	20	6	Severson, Monica

WASHBURN

Year	M/W	Assn	Div	NAT	NIT	ARC	CCA	NCI	NCT	OLY	HLM	W	L	Coach
1938	M	NAIA		4	—	—	—	—	—	—	—	10	13	Errickson, Charles D. 'Dee'
1945		NAIA		16	—	—	—	—	—	—	—	12	9	Errickson, Charles D. 'Dee'
1946		NAIA		32	—	—	—	—	—	—	—	13	7	Errickson, Charles D. 'Dee'
1952		NAIA		32	—	—	—	—	—	—	—	17	10	McDonald, Marion G.
1968		NAIA		32	—	—	—	—	—	—	—	18	8	Cafer, Glenn
1969		NAIA		8	—	—	—	—	—	—	—	20	10	Cafer, Glenn
1974		NAIA		16	—	—	—	—	—	—	—	17	12	Cafer, Glenn
1982		NAIA		32	—	—	—	—	—	—	—	22	9	Chipman, Bob
1987		NAIA		1	—	—	—	—	—	—	—	35	4	Chipman, Bob
1989		NAIA		16	—	—	—	—	—	—	—	24	9	Chipman, Bob
1990		NAIA		32	—	—	—	—	—	—	—	20	12	Chipman, Bob
1992		NCAA	II	16	—	—	—	—	—	—	—	27	5	Chipman, Bob
1993		NCAA	II	8	—	—	—	—	—	—	—	27	5	Chipman, Bob
1994		NCAA	II	3	—	—	—	—	—	—	—	29	4	Chipman, Bob
1995		NCAA	II	48	—	—	—	—	—	—	—	22	8	Chipman, Bob
1997		NCAA	II	32	—	—	—	—	—	—	—	24	9	Chipman, Bob
1989	W	NAIA		16	—	—	—	—	—	—	—	29	3	Dick, Patricia D.
1991		NCAA	II	32	—	—	—	—	—	—	—	23	7	Dick, Patricia D.
1992		NCAA	II	8	—	—	—	—	—	—	—	27	5	Dick, Patricia D.
1993		NCAA	II	8	—	—	—	—	—	—	—	31	1	Dick, Patricia D.
1994		NCAA	II	32	—	—	—	—	—	—	—	22	8	Dick, Patricia D.
1995		NCAA	II	16	—	—	—	—	—	—	—	24	7	Dick, Patricia D.

WASHINGTON

Year	M/W	Assn	Div	NAT	NIT	ARC	CCA	NCI	NCT	OLY	HLM	W	L	Coach
1936	M	NCAA		—	—	—	—	—	—	3	—	25	7	Edmundson, Clarence S. 'Hec'
1943		NCAA		8	—	—	—	—	—	—	—	24	7	Edmundson, Clarence S. 'Hec'
1948		NCAA		6	—	—	—	—	—	—	—	23	11	McLarney, Arthur
1951		NCAA		6	—	—	—	—	—	—	—	24	6	Dye, William H. H. 'Tippy'
1953		NCAA		3	—	—	—	—	—	—	—	28	3	Dye, William H. H. 'Tippy'
1976		NCAA	I	32	—	—	—	—	—	—	—	22	6	Harshman, Marvel K. 'Marv'
1980		NCAA	I	—	32	—	—	—	—	—	—	18	10	Harshman, Marvel K. 'Marv'
1982		NCAA	I	—	16	—	—	—	—	—	—	19	10	Harshman, Marvel K. 'Marv'

Year	M/W	Assn	Div	NAT	NIT	ARC	CCA	NCI	NCT	OLY	HLM	W	L	Coach
1984		NCAA	I	16	—	—	—	—	—	—	—	24	7	Harshman, Marvel K. "Marv"
1985		NCAA	I	64	—	—	—	—	—	—	—	22	10	Harshman, Marvel K. "Marv"
1986		NCAA	I	64	—	—	—	—	—	—	—	19	12	Russo, Andy
1987		NCAA	I	—	8	—	—	—	—	—	—	20	15	Russo, Andy
1996		NCAA	I	—	32	—	—	—	—	—	—	16	12	Bender, Robert M., Jr.
1997		NCAA	I	—	32	—	—	—	—	—	—	17	11	Bender, Robert M., Jr.
1998		NCAA	I	16	—	—	—	—	—	—	—	21	10	Bender, Robert M., Jr.
1978	W	AIAW	L	16	—	—	—	—	—	—	—	26	5	Neir, Kathie
1985		NCAA	I	32	—	—	—	—	—	—	—	26	1	Sake, Joyce
1986		NCAA	I	32	—	—	—	—	—	—	—	24	6	Gobrecht, Chris
1987		NCAA	I	32	—	—	—	—	—	—	—	23	7	Gobrecht, Chris
1988		NCAA	I	16	—	—	—	—	—	—	—	25	5	Gobrecht, Chris
1989		NCAA	I	32	—	—	—	—	—	—	—	23	10	Gobrecht, Chris
1990		NCAA	I	8	—	—	—	—	—	—	—	28	3	Gobrecht, Chris
1991		NCAA	I	16	—	—	—	—	—	—	—	24	5	Gobrecht, Chris
1993		NCAA	I	32	—	—	—	—	—	—	—	17	12	Gobrecht, Chris
1994		NCAA	I	32	—	—	—	—	—	—	—	21	8	Gobrecht, Chris
1995		NCAA	I	16	—	—	—	—	—	—	—	25	9	Gobrecht, Chris
1997		NCAA	I	64	—	—	—	—	—	—	—	17	11	Daugherty, June
1998		NCAA	I	64	—	—	—	—	—	—	—	18	10	Daugherty, June

WASHINGTON & JEFFERSON

Year	M/W	Assn	Div	NAT	NIT	ARC	CCA	NCI	NCT	OLY	HLM	W	L	Coach
1943	M	NCAA		—	3	—	—	—	—	—	—	18	5	Sanders, Adam
1985		NCAA	III	32	—	—	—	—	—	—	—	18	6	Unice, John
1994		NCAA	III	8	—	—	—	—	—	—	—	22	3	Reiter, Tom
1995	W	NCAA	III	64	—	—	—	—	—	—	—	16	7	Staton, Vicki L.
1998		NCAA	III	48	—	—	—	—	—	—	—	16	8	Staton, Vicki L.

WASHINGTON & LEE

Year	M/W	Assn	Div	NAT	NIT	ARC	CCA	NCI	NCT	OLY	HLM	W	L	Coach
1975	M	NCAA	III	30	—	—	—	—	—	—	—	15	12	Canfield, Verne D.
1977		NCAA	III	30	—	—	—	—	—	—	—	23	5	Canfield, Verne D.
1978		NCAA	III	16	—	—	—	—	—	—	—	22	6	Canfield, Verne D.
1980		NCAA	III	32	—	—	—	—	—	—	—	14	15	Canfield, Verne D.

WASHINGTON (MD)

Year	M/W	Assn	Div	NAT	NIT	ARC	CCA	NCI	NCT	OLY	HLM	W	L	Coach
1984	M	NCAA	III	32	—	—	—	—	—	—	—	19	7	Finnegan, Tom
1986		NCAA	III	24	—	—	—	—	—	—	—	20	6	Finnegan, Tom
1989		NCAA	III	16	—	—	—	—	—	—	—	20	7	Finnegan, Tom
1990		NCAA	III	3	—	—	—	—	—	—	—	25	6	Finnegan, Tom

WASHINGTON (MO)

Year	M/W	Assn	Div	NAT	NIT	ARC	CCA	NCI	NCT	OLY	HLM	W	L	Coach
1963	M	NCAA	II	16	—	—	—	—	—	—	—	18	8	Smith, Charles G. "Chuck"
1964		NCAA	II	24	—	—	—	—	—	—	—	16	8	Smith, Charles G. "Chuck"
1965		NCAA	II	8	—	—	—	—	—	—	—	21	6	Smith, Charles G. "Chuck"
1987		NCAA	III	16	—	—	—	—	—	—	—	21	7	Edwards, Mark
1988		NCAA	III	8	—	—	—	—	—	—	—	22	7	Edwards, Mark
1989		NCAA	III	16	—	—	—	—	—	—	—	19	8	Edwards, Mark
1991		NCAA	III	32	—	—	—	—	—	—	—	19	9	Edwards, Mark
1995		NCAA	III	32	—	—	—	—	—	—	—	23	4	Edwards, Mark
1996		NCAA	III	8	—	—	—	—	—	—	—	23	6	Edwards, Mark
1997		NCAA	III	64	—	—	—	—	—	—	—	17	9	Edwards, Mark

Year	M/W	Assn	Div	NAT	NIT	ARC	CCA	NCI	NCT	OLY	HLM	W	L	Coach
1988	W	NCAA	III	16	—	—	—	—	—	—	—	21	5	Fahey, Nancy
1990		NCAA	III	32	—	—	—	—	—	—	—	25	3	Fahey, Nancy
1991		NCAA	III	4	—	—	—	—	—	—	—	24	7	Fahey, Nancy
1992		NCAA	III	32	—	—	—	—	—	—	—	22	5	Fahey, Nancy
1993		NCAA	III	32	—	—	—	—	—	—	—	22	4	Fahey, Nancy
1994		NCAA	III	2	—	—	—	—	—	—	—	26	4	Fahey, Nancy
1995		NCAA	III	32	—	—	—	—	—	—	—	20	7	Fahey, Nancy
1996		NCAA	III	16	—	—	—	—	—	—	—	22	6	Fahey, Nancy
1997		NCAA	III	64	—	—	—	—	—	—	—	19	7	Fahey, Nancy
1998		NCAA	III	1	—	—	—	—	—	—	—	28	2	Fahey, Nancy

WASHINGTON BIBLE

Year	M/W	Assn	Div	NAT	NIT	ARC	CCA	NCI	NCT	OLY	HLM	W	L	Coach
1994	M	NCCAA	IIA	7	—	—	—	—	—	—	—	10	15	Ronson, Glenn
1995		NCCAA	IIA	6	—	—	—	—	—	—	—	9	15	Fletcher, Rev. Brit

WASHINGTON STATE

Year	M/W	Assn	Div	NAT	NIT	ARC	CCA	NCI	NCT	OLY	HLM	W	L	Coach
1917	M			—	—	—	—	—	—	—	1	25	1	Bohler, J. Fred 'Doc'
1941		NCAA		2	—	—	—	—	—	—	—	26	6	Friel, John B. 'Jack'
1980		NCAA	I	48	—	—	—	—	—	—	—	22	6	Raveling, George
1983		NCAA	I	32	—	—	—	—	—	—	—	23	7	Raveling, George
1992		NCAA	I	—	16	—	—	—	—	—	—	22	11	Sampson, Kelvin
1994		NCAA	I	64	—	—	—	—	—	—	—	20	11	Sampson, Kelvin
1995		NCAA	I	—	8	—	—	—	—	—	—	18	12	Eastman, Kevin
1996		NCAA	I	—	16	—	—	—	—	—	—	17	12	Eastman, Kevin
1972	W	AIAW		16	—	—	—	—	—	—	—	11	4	Durrant, Sue
1991		NCAA	I	48	—	—	—	—	—	—	—	18	11	Rhodes, Harold

WAYLAND BAPTIST

Year	M/W	Assn	Div	NAT	NIT	ARC	CCA	NCI	NCT	OLY	HLM	W	L	Coach
1954	M	NAIA		32	—	—	—	—	—	—	—	21	4	Redin, Harley J.
1955		NAIA		32	—	—	—	—	—	—	—	22	6	Redin, Harley J.
1957		NAIA		32	—	—	—	—	—	—	—	20	9	Redin, Harley J.
1985		NAIA		2	—	—	—	—	—	—	—	30	10	Adams, Mark L.
1986		NAIA		16	—	—	—	—	—	—	—	23	5	Adams, Mark L.
1987		NAIA		32	—	—	—	—	—	—	—	22	11	Adams, Mark L.
1989		NAIA		16	—	—	—	—	—	—	—	30	6	Cooper, Rick
1991		NAIA		32	—	—	—	—	—	—	—	26	3	Cooper, Rick
1992		NAIA	I	32	—	—	—	—	—	—	—	28	6	Cooper, Rick
1969	W			—	1	—	—	—	—	—	—	26	4	Redin, Harley J.
1970				—	1	—	—	—	—	—	—	29	4	Redin, Harley J.
1971				—	1	—	—	—	—	—	—	30	2	Redin, Harley J.
1972				—	1	—	—	—	—	—	—	26	7	Redin, Harley J.
1973				—	1	—	—	—	—	—	—	21	7	Redin, Harley J.
1974		AIAW		5	1	—	—	—	—	—	—	37	5	Weese, Dean
1975		AIAW	L	5	1	—	—	—	—	—	—	34	1	Weese, Dean
1976		AIAW	L	3	1	—	—	—	—	—	—	34	5	Weese, Dean
1977		AIAW	L	—	1	—	—	—	—	—	—	31	5	Weese, Dean
1978		AIAW	L	4	—	—	—	—	—	—	—	33	5	Weese, Dean
1979		AIAW	L	8	—	—	—	—	—	—	—	24	10	Weese, Dean
1980		AIAW	I	—	8	—	—	—	—	—	—	20	15	Wilson, Cathy

Year	M/W	Assn	Div	NAT	NIT	ARC	CCA	NCI	NCT	OLY	HLM	W	L	Coach
1982		AIAW	I	4	—	—	—	—	—	—	—	19	15	Wilson, Cathy
1983		NAIA		8	—	—	—	—	—	—	—	22	10	Wilson, Cathy
1985		NAIA		3	—	—	—	—	—	—	—	31	5	Ketterman, Dave
1986		NAIA		2	—	—	—	—	—	—	—	31	5	Evans, Floyd C.
1987		NAIA		8	—	—	—	—	—	—	—	31	1	Evans, Floyd C.
1988		NAIA		16	—	—	—	—	—	—	—	28	7	Evans, Floyd C.
1989		NAIA		8	—	—	—	—	—	—	—	30	8	Evans, Floyd C.
1990		NAIA		8	—	—	—	—	—	—	—	31	11	Estes, Sheryl
1991		NAIA		8	—	—	—	—	—	—	—	27	8	Estes, Sheryl
1992		NAIA	I	2	—	—	—	—	—	—	—	29	6	Estes, Sheryl
1993		NAIA	I	8	—	—	—	—	—	—	—	25	9	Estes, Sheryl
1995		NAIA	I	16	—	—	—	—	—	—	—	27	8	Estes, Sheryl
1996		NAIA	I	32	—	—	—	—	—	—	—	25	9	Estes, Sheryl
1997		NAIA	I	8	—	—	—	—	—	—	—	25	8	Pointer, Johnna
1998		NAIA	I	8	—	—	—	—	—	—	—	25	11	Pointer, Johnna

WAYNE STATE (MI)

Year	M/W	Assn	Div	NAT	NIT	ARC	CCA	NCI	NCT	OLY	HLM	W	L	Coach
1939	M	NAIA		16	—	—	—	—	—	—	—	14	5	Ertell, Newman H.
1956		NCAA		16	—	—	—	—	—	—	—	18	3	Mason, Joel G.
1970		NCAA	II	32	—	—	—	—	—	—	—	14	10	Gompert, Frank J.
1984		NCAA	II	16	—	—	—	—	—	—	—	21	9	Parker, Charles
1986		NCAA	II	8	—	—	—	—	—	—	—	23	8	Parker, Charles
1987		NCAA	II	32	—	—	—	—	—	—	—	20	10	Parker, Charles
1992		NCAA	II	16	—	—	—	—	—	—	—	23	8	Hammye, Ron
1993		NCAA	II	3	—	—	—	—	—	—	—	22	10	Hammye, Ron
1994		NCAA	II	16	—	—	—	—	—	—	—	25	5	Hammye, Ron

WAYNE STATE (NE)

Year	M/W	Assn	Div	NAT	NIT	ARC	CCA	NCI	NCT	OLY	HLM	W	L	Coach
1939	M	NAIA		32	—	—	—	—	—	—	—	12	9	Hickman, W. Ray
1940		NAIA		32	—	—	—	—	—	—	—	12	6	Morrison, James H.
1941		NAIA		32	—	—	—	—	—	—	—	13	7	Morrison, James H.
1957		NAIA		32	—	—	—	—	—	—	—	15	9	Obye, Charles H. "Chuck"
1968		NAIA		32	—	—	—	—	—	—	—	24	3	Svenningson, Allen
1969		NAIA		32	—	—	—	—	—	—	—	23	4	Gunther, David
1970		NAIA		32	—	—	—	—	—	—	—	23	6	Gunther, David

WAYNESBURG

Year	M/W	Assn	Div	NAT	NIT	ARC	CCA	NCI	NCT	OLY	HLM	W	L	Coach
1949	M	NAIA		32	—	—	—	—	—	—	—	17	11	Gustine, Frank
1981		NAIA		16	—	—	—	—	—	—	—	24	6	Marisa, Rudy
1984		NAIA		8	—	—	—	—	—	—	—	25	6	Marisa, Rudy
1985		NAIA		32	—	—	—	—	—	—	—	23	5	Marisa, Rudy
1986		NAIA		32	—	—	—	—	—	—	—	24	1	Marisa, Rudy
1987		NAIA		8	—	—	—	—	—	—	—	23	6	Marisa, Rudy
1988		NAIA		4	—	—	—	—	—	—	—	32	3	Marisa, Rudy
1989		NAIA		32	—	—	—	—	—	—	—	19	7	Marisa, Rudy
1993	W	NCAA	III	32	—	—	—	—	—	—	—	19	6	Phillips, Rob
1995		NCAA	III	32	—	—	—	—	—	—	—	21	5	Jones, Julie

Year	M/W	Assn	Div	NAT	NIT	ARC	CCA	NCI	NCT	OLY	HLM	W	L	Coach
WEBBER														
1984	M	NSCAA		1	—	—	—	—	—	—	—	32	4	Creola, Nick J.
1986		NAIA		32	—	—	—	—	—	—	—	25	1	Creola, Nick J.
1988		NSCAA		10	—	—	—	—	—	—	—	24	10	Yenta, Rex R.
1993		NAIA	II	16	—	—	—	—	—	—	—	27	7	Dunlap, John H.
1995		NAIA	II	32	—	—	—	—	—	—	—	21	15	Dunlap, John H.
1995	W	NAIA	II	32	—	—	—	—	—	—	—	18	12	Bronaugh, Thurman
1998		NAIA	II	32	—	—	—	—	—	—	—	14	18	Saxon, Michelle
WEBER STATE														
1968	M	NCAA	I	23	—	—	—	—	—	—	—	21	6	Motta, John R. "Dick"
1969		NCAA	I	12	—	—	—	—	—	—	—	27	3	Johnson, Phil
1970		NCAA	I	25	—	—	—	—	—	—	—	20	7	Johnson, Phil
1971		NCAA	I	25	—	—	—	—	—	—	—	21	6	Johnson, Phil
1972		NCAA	I	16	—	—	—	—	—	—	—	18	11	Visscher, Gene
1973		NCAA	I	25	—	—	—	—	—	—	—	20	7	Visscher, Gene
1978		NCAA	I	32	—	—	—	—	—	—	—	19	10	McCarthy, Neil N.
1979		NCAA	I	32	—	—	—	—	—	—	—	25	9	McCarthy, Neil N.
1980		NCAA	I	48	—	—	—	—	—	—	—	26	3	McCarthy, Neil N.
1983		NCAA	I	48	—	—	—	—	—	—	—	23	8	McCarthy, Neil N.
1984		NCAA	I	—	16	—	—	—	—	—	—	23	8	McCarthy, Neil N.
1995		NCAA	I	32	—	—	—	—	—	—	—	21	9	Abegglen, Ron
1983	W	NCAA	I	—	4	—	—	—	—	—	—	22	10	Minor, Jane
WENTWORTH TECH														
1997	M	NCAA	III	64	—	—	—	—	—	—	—	20	8	McShane, Harry
WESLEY (MS)														
1996	M	LCC		2	—	—	—	—	—	—	—	10	13	Devore, William, Jr.
1996		NBCAA	II	4	—	—	—	—	—	—	—	10	13	Devore, William, Jr.
1997		LCC		1	—	—	—	—	—	—	—	13	16	Devore, William, Jr.
1997		NBCAA	II	5	—	—	—	—	—	—	—	13	16	Devore, William, Jr.
WESLEYAN (CT)														
1959	M	NCAA	II	32	—	—	—	—	—	—	—	13	5	Wood, John L.
WEST ALABAMA														
1978	M	NCAA	II	24	—	—	—	—	—	—	—	18	8	Brackett, Ken
1982		NCAA	II	16	—	—	—	—	—	—	—	20	10	Murphy, Ed
1980	W	AIAW	II	16	—	—	—	—	—	—	—	24	12	Bridges, Avie
1982		AIAW	II	8	—	—	—	—	—	—	—	29	7	Izard, Jim
WEST CHESTER														
1983	M	NCAA	II	32	—	—	—	—	—	—	—	19	9	Voss, Earl
1995		NCAA	II	48	—	—	—	—	—	—	—	17	10	Delaney, Dick
1969	W	AIAW		1	—	—	—	—	—	—	—	12	0	Eckman, Carol
1970		AIAW		2	—	—	—	—	—	—	—	12	2	Eckman, Carol
1971		AIAW		2	—	—	—	—	—	—	—	15	4	Eckman, Carol
1972		AIAW		2	—	—	—	—	—	—	—	16	1	Eckman, Carol
1997		NCAA	II	32	—	—	—	—	—	—	—	22	7	Kane, Deirdre

Year	M/W	Assn	Div	NAT	NIT	ARC	CCA	NCI	NCT	OLY	HLM	W	L	Coach
WEST COAST CHRISTIAN														
1983	M	NSCAA		16	—	—	—	—	—	—	—	23	6	Turner, Jerry
1984		NSCAA		8	—	—	—	—	—	—	—	24	6	Turner, Jerry
1985		NSCAA		8	—	—	—	—	—	—	—	25	9	Turner, Jerry
1990		NBCAA	II	4	—	—	—	—	—	—	—	12	14	Crank, Frank
1991		NBCAA	II	2	—	—	—	—	—	—	—	24	12	McGough, Michael
WEST FLORIDA														
1976	M	NAIA		32	—	—	—	—	—	—	—	19	12	Beck, Marvin G.
1998	W	NCAA	II	32	—	—	—	—	—	—	—	25	5	Henry, Megan
WEST GEORGIA														
1972	M	NAIA		16	—	—	—	—	—	—	—	28	6	Kaiser, Roger A.
1974		NAIA		1	—	—	—	—	—	—	—	29	4	Kaiser, Roger A.
1975		NCAA	II	32	—	—	—	—	—	—	—	18	8	Kaiser, Roger A.
1980		NCAA	II	24	—	—	—	—	—	—	—	24	6	Kaiser, Roger A.
1981		NCAA	II	24	—	—	—	—	—	—	—	23	5	Kaiser, Roger A.
1983		NCAA	II	16	—	—	—	—	—	—	—	22	7	Kaiser, Roger A.
1984		NCAA	II	16	—	—	—	—	—	—	—	26	4	Kaiser, Roger A.
1986		NCAA	II	24	—	—	—	—	—	—	—	20	9	Kaiser, Roger A.
1987		NCAA	II	16	—	—	—	—	—	—	—	26	5	Kaiser, Roger A.
1997		NCAA	II	48	—	—	—	—	—	—	—	23	6	Murphy, Ed
1998		NCAA	II	32	—	—	—	—	—	—	—	21	8	Murphy, Ed
1975	W	AIAW	L	16	—	—	—	—	—	—	—	10	9	McNabb, Dorothy
1976		AIAW	S	2	—	—	—	—	—	—	—	15	4	McNabb, Dorothy
1977		AIAW	S	12	—	—	—	—	—	—	—	15	5	McNabb, Dorothy
1980		AIAW	II	24	—	—	—	—	—	—	—	17	12	Mosley, Nancy
1989		NCAA	II	32	—	—	—	—	—	—	—	25	4	Williamson, Jane
1990		NCAA	II	32	—	—	—	—	—	—	—	19	8	Williamson, Jane
1992		NCAA	II	16	—	—	—	—	—	—	—	26	5	Williamson, Jane
1994		NCAA	II	16	—	—	—	—	—	—	—	22	7	Williamson, Jane
WEST LIBERTY STATE														
1952	M	NAIA		32	—	—	—	—	—	—	—	22	6	Wehr, Richard W.
1997	W	NCAA	II	48	—	—	—	—	—	—	—	23	6	Ullom, Larry
WEST LIBERTY STATE: HANCOCK														
1971	M	NSCAA		8	—	—	—	—	—	—	—	X	X	Clark, John
1972		NSCAA		8	—	—	—	—	—	—	—	X	X	Clark, John
WEST TEXAS A&M														
1938	M	NAIA		16	—	—	—	—	—	—	—	27	6	Baggett, Al
1939		NAIA		32	—	—	—	—	—	—	—	21	9	Baggett, Al
1940		NAIA		16	—	—	—	—	—	—	—	26	8	Baggett, Al
1941		NAIA		3	—	—	—	—	—	—	—	29	6	Baggett, Al
1942		NCAA		—	8	—	—	—	—	—	—	28	3	Baggett, Al
1945		NAIA		8	—	—	—	—	—	—	—	16	10	Miller, W. A. "Gus"
1946		NAIA		16	—	—	—	—	—	—	—	19	8	Miller, W. A. "Gus"
1952		NAIA		16	—	—	—	—	—	—	—	19	9	Miller, W. A. "Gus"

Year	M/W	Assn	Div	NAT	NIT	ARC	CCA	NCI	NCT	OLY	HLM	W	L	Coach
1955		NCAA		24	—	—	—	—	—	—	—	15	7	Miller, W. A. "Gus"
1969		NCAA	I	—	16	—	—	—	—	—	—	18	7	Walling, Dennis W.
1980		NCAA	I	—	32	—	—	—	—	—	—	19	11	Edwards, Ken
1987		NCAA	II	24	—	—	—	—	—	—	—	24	7	Moss, Gary
1990		NCAA	II	24	—	—	—	—	—	—	—	25	7	Adams, Mark L.
1991		NCAA	II	32	—	—	—	—	—	—	—	25	7	Adams, Mark L.
1994		NCAA	II	32	—	—	—	—	—	—	—	20	10	Cooper, Rick
1998		NCAA	II	8	—	—	—	—	—	—	—	26	5	Cooper, Rick
1970	W			—	8	—	—	—	—	—	—	X	X	Stovall, Allene
1976		AIAW		—	7	—	—	—	—	—	—	X	X	Stovall, Allene
1985		NCAA	I	—	6	—	—	—	—	—	—	26	6	Schneider, Bob
1986		NCAA	I	—	5	—	—	—	—	—	—	26	5	Schneider, Bob
1987		NCAA	II	8	—	—	—	—	—	—	—	27	4	Schneider, Bob
1988		NCAA	II	2	—	—	—	—	—	—	—	33	1	Schneider, Bob
1989		NCAA	II	16	—	—	—	—	—	—	—	26	3	Schneider, Bob
1990		NCAA	II	16	—	—	—	—	—	—	—	24	6	Schneider, Bob
1991		NCAA	II	16	—	—	—	—	—	—	—	30	2	Schneider, Bob
1992		NCAA	II	16	—	—	—	—	—	—	—	24	6	Schneider, Bob
1995		NCAA	II	32	—	—	—	—	—	—	—	25	5	Schneider, Bob
1996		NCAA	II	16	—	—	—	—	—	—	—	28	3	Schneider, Bob
1997		NCAA	II	8	—	—	—	—	—	—	—	29	2	Schneider, Bob

West Virginia

Year	M/W	Assn	Div	NAT	NIT	ARC	CCA	NCI	NCT	OLY	HLM	W	L	Coach
1942	M	NCAA		—	1	—	—	—	—	—	—	19	4	Raese, Richard "Dyke"
1945		NCAA		—	8	—	—	—	—	—	—	12	6	Brickels, John L.
1946		NCAA		—	3	—	—	—	—	—	—	24	3	Patton, Lee
1947		NCAA		—	4	—	—	—	—	—	—	19	3	Patton, Lee
1955		NCAA		24	—	—	—	—	—	—	—	19	11	Schaus, Frederick A.
1956		NCAA		25	—	—	—	—	—	—	—	21	9	Schaus, Frederick A.
1957		NCAA	I	23	—	—	—	—	—	—	—	25	5	Schaus, Frederick A.
1958		NCAA	I	24	—	—	—	—	—	—	—	26	2	Schaus, Frederick A.
1959		NCAA	I	2	—	—	—	—	—	—	—	29	5	Schaus, Frederick A.
1960		NCAA	I	12	—	—	—	—	—	—	—	26	5	Schaus, Frederick A.
1962		NCAA	I	25	—	—	—	—	—	—	—	24	6	King, George S., Jr.
1963		NCAA	I	12	—	—	—	—	—	—	—	23	8	King, George S., Jr.
1965		NCAA	I	23	—	—	—	—	—	—	—	14	15	King, George S., Jr.
1967		NCAA	I	23	—	—	—	—	—	—	—	19	9	Waters, Raymond C. "Bucky"
1968		NCAA	I	—	16	—	—	—	—	—	—	19	9	Waters, Raymond C. "Bucky"
1981		NCAA	I	—	4	—	—	—	—	—	—	23	10	Catlett, Gale
1982		NCAA	I	32	—	—	—	—	—	—	—	27	4	Catlett, Gale
1983		NCAA	I	48	—	—	—	—	—	—	—	23	8	Catlett, Gale
1984		NCAA	I	32	—	—	—	—	—	—	—	20	12	Catlett, Gale
1985		NCAA	I	—	32	—	—	—	—	—	—	20	9	Catlett, Gale
1986		NCAA	I	64	—	—	—	—	—	—	—	22	11	Catlett, Gale
1987		NCAA	I	64	—	—	—	—	—	—	—	23	8	Catlett, Gale
1988		NCAA	I	—	32	—	—	—	—	—	—	18	14	Catlett, Gale
1989		NCAA	I	32	—	—	—	—	—	—	—	26	5	Catlett, Gale
1991		NCAA	I	—	16	—	—	—	—	—	—	17	14	Catlett, Gale
1992		NCAA	I	64	—	—	—	—	—	—	—	20	12	Catlett, Gale
1993		NCAA	I	—	16	—	—	—	—	—	—	17	12	Catlett, Gale
1994		NCAA	I	—	16	—	—	—	—	—	—	17	12	Catlett, Gale

Year	M/W	Assn	Div	NAT	NIT	ARC	CCA	NCI	NCT	OLY	HLM	W	L	Coach
1997		NCAA	I	—	8	—	—	—	—	—	—	21	10	Catlett, Gale
1998		NCAA	I	16	—	—	—	—	—	—	—	25	9	Catlett, Gale
1985	W	NCAA	I	—	7	—	—	—	—	—	—	20	10	Blakemore, Kittie
1989		NCAA	I	32	—	—	—	—	—	—	—	24	8	Blakemore, Kittie
1992		NCAA	I	16	—	—	—	—	—	—	—	26	4	Blakemore, Kittie

West Virginia Northern CC: Weirton

Year	M/W	Assn	Div	NAT	NIT	ARC	CCA	NCI	NCT	OLY	HLM	W	L	Coach
1973	M	NSCAA		8	—	—	—	—	—	—	—	13	9	Clark, John

West Virginia State

Year	M/W	Assn	Div	NAT	NIT	ARC	CCA	NCI	NCT	OLY	HLM	W	L	Coach
1952	M	NASC		8	—	—	—	—	—	—	—	14	7	Cardwell, Mark H.
1961		NAIA		16	—	—	—	—	—	—	—	13	12	Cardwell, Mark H.
1963		NAIA		32	—	—	—	—	—	—	—	17	9	Cardwell, Mark H.
1987		NAIA		2	—	—	—	—	—	—	—	31	4	Carse, Craig

West Virginia Tech

Year	M/W	Assn	Div	NAT	NIT	ARC	CCA	NCI	NCT	OLY	HLM	W	L	Coach
1957	M	NAIA		32	—	—	—	—	—	—	—	26	3	Baisi, Neal D.
1982		NAIA		32	—	—	—	—	—	—	—	24	10	Sutherland, Tom
1988		NAIA		32	—	—	—	—	—	—	—	21	10	Sutherland, Tom

West Virginia Wesleyan

Year	M/W	Assn	Div	NAT	NIT	ARC	CCA	NCI	NCT	OLY	HLM	W	L	Coach
1958	M	NAIA		8	—	—	—	—	—	—	—	29	5	Ellis, Franklin C. "Hank"
1959		NAIA		8	—	—	—	—	—	—	—	34	2	Ellis, Franklin C. "Hank"
1960		NAIA		16	—	—	—	—	—	—	—	23	6	Ellis, Franklin C. "Hank"
1979		NAIA		32	—	—	—	—	—	—	—	24	8	Hess, Gary
1983		NAIA		2	—	—	—	—	—	—	—	32	6	Stewart, Bruce
1984		NAIA		8	—	—	—	—	—	—	—	31	3	Stewart, Bruce
1985		NAIA		8	—	—	—	—	—	—	—	28	4	Cameron, Rich

Westbrook

Year	M/W	Assn	Div	NAT	NIT	ARC	CCA	NCI	NCT	OLY	HLM	W	L	Coach
1994	M	NAIA	II	24	—	—	—	—	—	—	—	30	5	Graffam, Jim
1995		NAIA	II	32	—	—	—	—	—	—	—	24	10	Graffam, Jim
1994	W	NAIA	II	24	—	—	—	—	—	—	—	24	4	Brooks-Ewald, Caroline
1995		NAIA	II	32	—	—	—	—	—	—	—	19	10	Brooks-Ewald, Caroline
1996		NAIA	II	32	—	—	—	—	—	—	—	21	12	Martin, John

Western Baptist

Year	M/W	Assn	Div	NAT	NIT	ARC	CCA	NCI	NCT	OLY	HLM	W	L	Coach
1976	M	NCCAA	II	3	—	—	—	—	—	—	—	12	19	Hills, Tim
1977		NCCAA	II	1	—	—	—	—	—	—	—	17	13	Hills, Tim
1984		NCCAA	I	4	—	—	—	—	—	—	—	19	17	Collins, Tim
1986		NCCAA	I	2	—	—	—	—	—	—	—	29	10	Collins, Tim
1988		NCCAA	I	8	—	—	—	—	—	—	—	19	17	Hills, Tim
1989		NCCAA	I	3	—	—	—	—	—	—	—	26	15	Hills, Tim
1992		NCCAA	I	6	—	—	—	—	—	—	—	19	18	Hills, Tim
1993		NCCAA	I	6	—	—	—	—	—	—	—	16	20	Hills, Tim
1995		NCCAA	I	2	—	—	—	—	—	—	—	26	12	Hills, Tim
1996		NCCAA	I	6	—	—	—	—	—	—	—	21	16	Rasmussen, Dennis
1997		NAIA	II	16	—	—	—	—	—	—	—	27	10	Hills, Tim
1998		NAIA	II	16	—	—	—	—	—	—	—	25	11	Hills, Tim
1995	W	NCCAA	I	1	—	—	—	—	—	—	—	17	16	Williams, Terry
1996		NCCAA	I	1	—	—	—	—	—	—	—	24	11	Williams, Terry
1997		NCCAA	I	6	—	—	—	—	—	—	—	25	9	Williams, Terry

Year	M/W	Assn	Div	NAT	NIT	ARC	CCA	NCI	NCT	OLY	HLM	W	L	Coach

WESTERN CAROLINA

Year	M/W	Assn	Div	NAT	NIT	ARC	CCA	NCI	NCT	OLY	HLM	W	L	Coach
1947	M	NAIA		32	—	—	—	—	—	—	—	15	11	McDonald, Marion G.
1963		NAIA		2	—	—	—	—	—	—	—	28	7	Gudger, James F.
1972		NAIA		32	—	—	—	—	—	—	—	20	16	Hartbarger, James
1996		NCAA	I	64	—	—	—	—	—	—	—	17	13	Hopkins, Phil
1969	W	AIAW		2	—	—	—	—	—	—	—	14	3	Westmoreland, Betty
1970		AIAW		4	—	—	—	—	—	—	—	16	3	Westmoreland, Betty
1971		AIAW		16	—	—	—	—	—	—	—	13	4	Westmoreland, Betty

WESTERN CONNECTICUT STATE

Year	M/W	Assn	Div	NAT	NIT	ARC	CCA	NCI	NCT	OLY	HLM	W	L	Coach
1986	M	NCAA	III	32	—	—	—	—	—	—	—	25	3	Campbell, Bob
1989		NCAA	III	16	—	—	—	—	—	—	—	25	3	Campbell, Bob
1990		NCAA	III	8	—	—	—	—	—	—	—	27	2	Campbell, Bob
1991		NCAA	III	32	—	—	—	—	—	—	—	22	6	Campbell, Bob
1992		NCAA	III	32	—	—	—	—	—	—	—	20	6	Campbell, Bob
1996		NCAA	III	64	—	—	—	—	—	—	—	19	8	Campbell, Bob
1985	W	NCAA	III	32	—	—	—	—	—	—	—	21	5	Rajcula, Jody
1988		NCAA	III	32	—	—	—	—	—	—	—	19	9	Rajcula, Jody
1989		NCAA	III	24	—	—	—	—	—	—	—	21	7	Rajcula, Jody
1990		NCAA	III	16	—	—	—	—	—	—	—	24	3	Rajcula, Jody
1991		NCAA	III	32	—	—	—	—	—	—	—	21	6	Rajcula, Jody
1992		NCAA	III	32	—	—	—	—	—	—	—	21	5	Rajcula, Jody
1993		NCAA	III	32	—	—	—	—	—	—	—	20	5	Rajcula, Jody
1994		NCAA	III	32	—	—	—	—	—	—	—	23	4	Rajcula, Jody
1997		NCAA	III	16	—	—	—	—	—	—	—	25	5	Rajcula, Jody
1998		NCAA	III	32	—	—	—	—	—	—	—	22	7	Rajcula, Jody

WESTERN ILLINOIS

Year	M/W	Assn	Div	NAT	NIT	ARC	CCA	NCI	NCT	OLY	HLM	W	L	Coach
1954	M	NAIA		2	—	—	—	—	—	—	—	19	9	Morley, Leroy "Stix"
1955		NAIA		3	—	—	—	—	—	—	—	27	3	Morley, Leroy "Stix"
1956		NAIA		8	—	—	—	—	—	—	—	28	3	Morley, Leroy "Stix"
1957		NAIA		8	—	—	—	—	—	—	—	22	3	Morley, Leroy "Stix"
1958		NAIA		2	—	—	—	—	—	—	—	27	1	Morley, Leroy "Stix"
1959		NCAA	II	32	—	—	—	—	—	—	—	16	11	Morley, Leroy "Stix"
1962		NAIA		4	—	—	—	—	—	—	—	21	11	Morley, Leroy "Stix"
1963		NAIA		32	—	—	—	—	—	—	—	19	8	Morley, Leroy "Stix"
1980		NCAA	II	16	—	—	—	—	—	—	—	19	10	Margenthaler, Jack
1981		NCAA	II	16	—	—	—	—	—	—	—	21	8	Margenthaler, Jack
1995	W	NCAA	I	64	—	—	—	—	—	—	—	17	12	Miller, Regina

WESTERN KENTUCKY

Year	M/W	Assn	Div	NAT	NIT	ARC	CCA	NCI	NCT	OLY	HLM	W	L	Coach
1938	M	NAIA		32	—	—	—	—	—	—	—	30	3	Diddle, Edgar A., Sr.
1940		NCAA		8	—	—	—	—	—	—	—	24	6	Diddle, Edgar A., Sr.
1942		NCAA		—	2	—	—	—	—	—	—	29	5	Diddle, Edgar A., Sr.
1943		NCAA		—	8	—	—	—	—	—	—	24	3	Diddle, Edgar A., Sr.
1948		NCAA		—	3	—	—	—	—	—	—	28	2	Diddle, Edgar A., Sr.
1949		NCAA		—	8	—	—	—	—	—	—	25	4	Diddle, Edgar A., Sr.
1950		NCAA		—	8	—	—	—	—	—	—	25	6	Diddle, Edgar A., Sr.
1951		NCAA		—	—	—	—	—	8	—	—	19	10	Diddle, Edgar A., Sr.

Year	M/W	Assn	Div	NAT	NIT	ARC	CCA	NCI	NCT	OLY	HLM	W	L	Coach
1952		NCAA		—	8	—	—	—	—	—	—	26	5	Diddle, Edgar A., Sr.
1953		NCAA		—	8	—	—	—	—	—	—	25	6	Diddle, Edgar A., Sr.
1954		NCAA		—	4	—	—	—	—	—	—	29	3	Diddle, Edgar A., Sr.
1960		NCAA	I	12	—	—	—	—	—	—	—	21	7	Diddle, Edgar A., Sr.
1962		NCAA	I	16	—	—	—	—	—	—	—	17	10	Diddle, Edgar A., Sr.
1965		NCAA	I	—	8	—	—	—	—	—	—	17	8	Diddle, Edgar A., Sr.
1966		NCAA	I	12	—	—	—	—	—	—	—	25	3	Oldham, John O.
1967		NCAA	I	23	—	—	—	—	—	—	—	23	3	Oldham, John O.
1970		NCAA	I	25	—	—	—	—	—	—	—	22	3	Oldham, John O.
1971		NCAA	I	3	—	—	—	—	—	—	—	24	6	Oldham, John O.
1976		NCAA	I	32	—	—	—	—	—	—	—	20	9	Richards, Jim
1978		NCAA	I	16	—	—	—	—	—	—	—	16	14	Richards, Jim
1980		NCAA	I	48	—	—	—	—	—	—	—	21	8	Keady, Lloyd Eugene "Gene"
1981		NCAA	I	48	—	—	—	—	—	—	—	21	8	Haskins, Clem S.
1982		NCAA	I	—	32	—	—	—	—	—	—	19	10	Haskins, Clem S.
1986		NCAA	I	32	—	—	—	—	—	—	—	23	8	Haskins, Clem S.
1987		NCAA	I	32	—	—	—	—	—	—	—	29	9	Arnold, Murray
1992		NCAA	I	—	32	—	—	—	—	—	—	21	11	Willard, Ralph
1993		NCAA	I	16	—	—	—	—	—	—	—	26	6	Willard, Ralph
1994		NCAA	I	64	—	—	—	—	—	—	—	20	11	Willard, Ralph
1995		NCAA	I	32	—	—	—	—	—	—	—	27	4	Kilcullen, Matt
1984	W	NCAA	I	—	4	—	—	—	—	—	—	21	11	Sanderford, Paul
1985		NCAA	I	3	—	—	—	—	—	—	—	28	6	Sanderford, Paul
1986		NCAA	I	3	—	—	—	—	—	—	—	32	4	Sanderford, Paul
1987		NCAA	I	32	—	—	—	—	—	—	—	24	9	Sanderford, Paul
1988		NCAA	I	32	—	—	—	—	—	—	—	26	8	Sanderford, Paul
1989		NCAA	I	48	—	—	—	—	—	—	—	22	9	Sanderford, Paul
1990		NCAA	I	48	—	—	—	—	—	—	—	17	12	Sanderford, Paul
1991		NCAA	I	16	—	—	—	—	—	—	—	29	3	Sanderford, Paul
1992		NCAA	I	2	—	—	—	—	—	—	—	27	8	Sanderford, Paul
1993		NCAA	I	16	—	—	—	—	—	—	—	24	7	Sanderford, Paul
1994		NCAA	I	32	—	—	—	—	—	—	—	24	10	Sanderford, Paul
1995		NCAA	I	16	—	—	—	—	—	—	—	28	4	Sanderford, Paul
1996		NCAA	I	—	6	—	—	—	—	—	—	19	13	Sanderford, Paul
1997		NCAA	I	64	—	—	—	—	—	—	—	22	9	Sanderford, Paul
1998		NCAA	I	32	—	—	—	—	—	—	—	26	9	Small, Steve

WESTERN MICHIGAN

Year	M/W	Assn	Div	NAT	NIT	ARC	CCA	NCI	NCT	OLY	HLM	W	L	Coach
1976	M	NCAA	I	16	—	—	—	—	—	—	—	25	3	Miller, Eldon
1992		NCAA	I	—	32	—	—	—	—	—	—	21	9	Donewald, Bob
1998		NCAA	I	32	—	—	—	—	—	—	—	21	8	Donewald, Bob
1985	W	NCAA	I	32	—	—	—	—	—	—	—	19	10	Hess, Jim

WESTERN MONTANA

Year	M/W	Assn	Div	NAT	NIT	ARC	CCA	NCI	NCT	OLY	HLM	W	L	Coach
1941	M	NAIA		32	—	—	—	—	—	—	—	16	4	Straugh, William T.
1949		NAIA		32	—	—	—	—	—	—	—	16	17	Straugh, William T.
1958		NAIA		16	—	—	—	—	—	—	—	22	7	Straugh, William T.
1959		NAIA		32	—	—	—	—	—	—	—	17	8	Straugh, William T.
1961		NAIA		32	—	—	—	—	—	—	—	21	7	Straugh, William T.
1969		NAIA		32	—	—	—	—	—	—	—	22	7	Keltz, Donald "Casey"
1989		NAIA		16	—	—	—	—	—	—	—	19	9	Keltz, Donald "Casey"

Year	M/W	Assn	Div	NAT	NIT	ARC	CCA	NCI	NCT	OLY	HLM	W	L	Coach
WESTERN NEW ENGLAND														
1970	M	NAIA		32	—	—	—	—	—	—	—	14	6	Geldart, Eric, Jr.
1971		NAIA		32	—	—	—	—	—	—	—	19	7	Geldart, Eric, Jr.
1990		NCAA	III	40	—	—	—	—	—	—	—	23	3	Broaca, Peter F.
WESTERN NEW MEXICO														
1942	M	NAIA		32	—	—	—	—	—	—	—	17	4	Wooden, Maurice
1981		NAIA		32	—	—	—	—	—	—	—	26	4	Drangmeister, Richard
1982		NAIA		32	—	—	—	—	—	—	—	20	5	Drangmeister, Richard
1990	W	NAIA		8	—	—	—	—	—	—	—	25	6	Irvin, Dexter
1991		NAIA		32	—	—	—	—	—	—	—	18	8	Irvin, Dexter
1994		NAIA	I	32	—	—	—	—	—	—	—	9	15	Reid, Jason
1995		NAIA	I	32	—	—	—	—	—	—	—	21	8	Reid, Jason
1996		NAIA	I	16	—	—	—	—	—	—	—	25	6	Reid, Jason
1997		NCAA	II	32	—	—	—	—	—	—	—	19	7	Reid, Jason
WESTERN OREGON														
1938	M	NAIA		32	—	—	—	—	—	—	—	16	6	Cox, J. Alfred 'Al'
1941		NAIA		32	—	—	—	—	—	—	—	14	10	Cox, J. Alfred 'Al'
1981		NAIA		16	—	—	—	—	—	—	—	22	3	Boutin, Dr. James
1982		NAIA		8	—	—	—	—	—	—	—	25	1	Boutin, Dr. James
1996		NAIA	II	32	—	—	—	—	—	—	—	22	8	Kelly, Tom
1980	W	AIAW	III	16	—	—	—	—	—	—	—	25	4	Carey, Jon
1982		AIAW	III	16	—	—	—	—	—	—	—	24	6	Carey, Jon
1987		NAIA		16	—	—	—	—	—	—	—	26	6	Carey, Jon
1991		NAIA		16	—	—	—	—	—	—	—	26	11	Carey, Jon
1992		NAIA	II	3	—	—	—	—	—	—	—	26	9	Carey, Jon
1993		NAIA	II	8	—	—	—	—	—	—	—	26	10	Carey, Jon
1994		NAIA	II	2	—	—	—	—	—	—	—	31	6	Carey, Jon
1995		NAIA	II	1	—	—	—	—	—	—	—	23	9	Rogers, 'Rusty'
1996		NAIA	II	1	—	—	—	—	—	—	—	31	4	Rogers, 'Rusty'
1998		NAIA	II	32	—	—	—	—	—	—	—	24	11	Rogers, 'Rusty'
WESTERN STATE (CO)														
1987	M	NAIA		32	—	—	—	—	—	—	—	19	13	Gibbons, Terry
1992		NAIA	I	32	—	—	—	—	—	—	—	19	10	Helman, Dr. Jay W.
1993		NCAA	II	23	—	—	—	—	—	—	—	25	5	Helman, Dr. Jay W.
WESTERN WASHINGTON														
1960	M	NAIA		32	—	—	—	—	—	—	—	19	7	Hubbard, Jack
1972		NAIA		8	—	—	—	—	—	—	—	26	4	Randall, Charles R. 'Chuck'
1988		NAIA		16	—	—	—	—	—	—	—	28	8	Jackson, Brad
1994		NAIA	I	32	—	—	—	—	—	—	—	24	7	Jackson, Brad
1973	W	AIAW		8	—	—	—	—	—	—	—	24	2	Goodrich, Lynda
1974		AIAW		12	—	—	—	—	—	—	—	22	5	Goodrich, Lynda
1977		AIAW	L	16	—	—	—	—	—	—	—	21	7	Goodrich, Lynda
1986		NAIA		8	—	—	—	—	—	—	—	25	8	Goodrich, Lynda
1989		NAIA		8	—	—	—	—	—	—	—	30	5	Goodrich, Lynda
1996		NAIA	I	8	—	—	—	—	—	—	—	26	7	Dollo, Carmen
1998		NAIA	I	32	—	—	—	—	—	—	—	21	9	Dollo, Carmen

Year	M/W	Assn	Div	NAT	NIT	ARC	CCA	NCI	NCT	OLY	HLM	W	L	Coach
WESTFIELD STATE														
1985	M	NCAA	III	32	—	—	—	—	—	—	—	—	10	15	White, Hilton
1993		NCAA	III	32	—	—	—	—	—	—	—	—	22	6	Lawless, Robert
1995	W	NCAA	III	64	—	—	—	—	—	—	—	—	21	7	Berger, Rick
1996		NCAA	III	64	—	—	—	—	—	—	—	—	22	6	Berger, Rick
WESTMAR														
1968	M	NAIA		32	—	—	—	—	—	—	—	—	21	7	Knudtson, Paul O.
WESTMINSTER (MO)														
1938	M	NAIA		32	—	—	—	—	—	—	—	—	12	9	Kimbrell, Eugene F.
1939		NAIA		16	—	—	—	—	—	—	—	—	15	8	Kimbrell, Eugene F.
1941		NAIA		—	8	—	—	—	—	—	—	—	10	8	Kimbrell, Eugene F.
1943		NAIA		16	—	—	—	—	—	—	—	—	11	7	Kimbrell, Eugene F.
1995		NCAA	III	64	—	—	—	—	—	—	—	—	14	14	McEwen, Jim
WESTMINSTER (PA)														
1950	M	NAIA		16	—	—	—	—	—	—	—	—	25	5	Washabaugh, Grover C.
1951		NAIA		32	—	—	—	—	—	—	—	—	22	6	Washabaugh, Grover C.
1959		NAIA		16	—	—	—	—	—	—	—	—	19	8	Ridl, Charles G. "Buzz"
1960		NAIA		2	—	—	—	—	—	—	—	—	24	3	Ridl, Charles G. "Buzz"
1961		NAIA		4	—	—	—	—	—	—	—	—	23	5	Ridl, Charles G. "Buzz"
1962		NAIA		2	—	—	—	—	—	—	—	—	26	3	Ridl, Charles G. "Buzz"
1967		NAIA		16	—	—	—	—	—	—	—	—	22	6	Ridl, Charles G. "Buzz"
1968		NAIA		4	—	—	—	—	—	—	—	—	22	8	Ridl, Charles G. "Buzz"
1982		NAIA		32	—	—	—	—	—	—	—	—	21	7	Galbreath, Dr. C. Ronald
1994		NAIA	I	16	—	—	—	—	—	—	—	—	25	3	Galbreath, Dr. C. Ronald
1996		NAIA	I	32	—	—	—	—	—	—	—	—	21	8	Galbreath, Dr. C. Ronald
WESTMINSTER (UT)														
1959	M	NAIA		32	—	—	—	—	—	—	—	—	16	7	Richardson, Howard D.
1961		NAIA		32	—	—	—	—	—	—	—	—	15	8	Richardson, Howard D.
WESTMONT														
1957	M	NAIA		32	—	—	—	—	—	—	—	—	23	6	Siemens, John R.
1972		NAIA		8	—	—	—	—	—	—	—	—	21	9	Byron, Thomas C.
1973		NAIA		8	—	—	—	—	—	—	—	—	25	6	Mulder, Ronald
1978		NAIA		16	—	—	—	—	—	—	—	—	23	9	Kammerer, Glen "Chet"
1984		NAIA		4	—	—	—	—	—	—	—	—	25	2	Kammerer, Glen "Chet"
1986		NAIA		32	—	—	—	—	—	—	—	—	23	8	Kammerer, Glen "Chet"
1988		NAIA		32	—	—	—	—	—	—	—	—	23	9	Kammerer, Glen "Chet"
1991		NAIA		16	—	—	—	—	—	—	—	—	22	10	Kammerer, Glen "Chet"
1994		NAIA	I	16	—	—	—	—	—	—	—	—	19	13	Moore, John
1996		NAIA	I	32	—	—	—	—	—	—	—	—	19	13	Moore, John
WHEATON (IL)														
1904	M			—	—	—	—	—	—	2	—	10	9	Brown, Elwood
1956		NAIA		4	—	—	—	—	—	—	—	—	28	4	Pfund, Leroy H. "Lee"
1957		NCAA	II	1	—	—	—	—	—	—	—	—	28	1	Pfund, Leroy H. "Lee"
1958		NCAA	II	4	—	—	—	—	—	—	—	—	27	3	Pfund, Leroy H. "Lee"

Year	M/W	Assn	Div	NAT	NIT	ARC	CCA	NCI	NCT	OLY	HLM	W	L	Coach
1959		NCAA	II	16	—	—	—	—	—	—	—	23	4	Pfund, Leroy H. "Lee"
1960		NCAA	II	8	—	—	—	—	—	—	—	16	10	Pfund, Leroy H. "Lee"
1995		NCAA	III	64	—	—	—	—	—	—	—	21	5	Harris, William R.
1996		NCAA	III	32	—	—	—	—	—	—	—	25	2	Harris, William R.
1996	W	NCAA	III	32	—	—	—	—	—	—	—	22	5	Baker, Beth
1997		NCAA	III	64	—	—	—	—	—	—	—	21	5	Baker, Beth
1998		NCAA	III	48	—	—	—	—	—	—	—	19	7	Baker, Beth

WHEATON (MA)

Year	M/W	Assn	Div	NAT	NIT	ARC	CCA	NCI	NCT	OLY	HLM	W	L	Coach
1994	W	NCAA	III	4	—	—	—	—	—	—	—	27	4	Malloy, Del
1995		NCAA	III	16	—	—	—	—	—	—	—	24	5	Malloy, Del

WHEELING JESUIT

Year	M/W	Assn	Div	NAT	NIT	ARC	CCA	NCI	NCT	OLY	HLM	W	L	Coach
1989	M	NAIA		8	—	—	—	—	—	—	—	31	4	DeFruscio, Jay
1994	W	NAIA	I	32	—	—	—	—	—	—	—	23	5	Hustead, Don

WHITTIER

Year	M/W	Assn	Div	NAT	NIT	ARC	CCA	NCI	NCT	OLY	HLM	W	L	Coach
1947	M	NAIA		16	—	—	—	—	—	—	—	30	2	Bonham, Aubrey R.
1959		NAIA		32	—	—	—	—	—	—	—	20	7	Bonham, Aubrey R.
1960		NAIA		16	—	—	—	—	—	—	—	23	9	Bonham, Aubrey R.
1969		NAIA		16	—	—	—	—	—	—	—	23	5	Guevara, Ivan T.
1970		NAIA		32	—	—	—	—	—	—	—	21	8	Guevara, Ivan T.
1971		NAIA		16	—	—	—	—	—	—	—	23	7	Guevara, Ivan T.
1977		NAIA		32	—	—	—	—	—	—	—	24	5	Jacobs, Dave
1979		NCAA	III	16	—	—	—	—	—	—	—	16	12	Jacobs, Dave
1981		NCAA	III	8	—	—	—	—	—	—	—	19	10	Jacobs, Dave
1982		NCAA	III	32	—	—	—	—	—	—	—	14	14	Jacobs, Dave

WHITWORTH (MS)

Year	M/W	Assn	Div	NAT	NIT	ARC	CCA	NCI	NCT	OLY	HLM	W	L	Coach
1976	M	NSCAA		2	—	—	—	—	—	—	—	24	6	Roark, Dwain

WHITWORTH (WA)

Year	M/W	Assn	Div	NAT	NIT	ARC	CCA	NCI	NCT	OLY	HLM	W	L	Coach
1952	M	NAIA		8	—	—	—	—	—	—	—	23	14	McGregor, James B.
1954		NAIA		32	—	—	—	—	—	—	—	21	4	Smith, Art
1955		NAIA		32	—	—	—	—	—	—	—	21	8	Smith, Art
1961		NAIA		32	—	—	—	—	—	—	—	19	10	Kamm, Richard
1991		NAIA		32	—	—	—	—	—	—	—	22	9	Friedrichs, Dr. Warren
1996		NAIA	II	2	—	—	—	—	—	—	—	26	5	Friedrichs, Dr. Warren
1998		NAIA	II	8	—	—	—	—	—	—	—	20	8	Friedrichs, Dr. Warren
1995	W	NAIA	II	16	—	—	—	—	—	—	—	19	12	Higgs, Helen

WICHITA STATE

Year	M/W	Assn	Div	NAT	NIT	ARC	CCA	NCI	NCT	OLY	HLM	W	L	Coach
1945	M	NAIA		16	—	—	—	—	—	—	—	14	4	Binford, Melvin J.
1946		NAIA		32	—	—	—	—	—	—	—	14	9	Binford, Melvin J.
1954		NCAA			12	—	—	—	—	—	—	27	4	Miller, Ralph H. "Cappy"
1962		NCAA	I	—	12	—	—	—	—	—	—	18	9	Miller, Ralph H. "Cappy"
1963		NCAA	I	—	8	—	—	—	—	—	—	19	8	Miller, Ralph H. "Cappy"
1964		NCAA	I	8	—	—	—	—	—	—	—	23	6	Miller, Ralph H. "Cappy"
1965		NCAA	I	4	—	—	—	—	—	—	—	21	9	Thompson, Gary
1966		NCAA	I	—	8	—	—	—	—	—	—	17	10	Thompson, Gary

Year	M/W	Assn	Div	NAT	NIT	ARC	CCA	NCI	NCT	OLY	HLM	W	L	Coach
1976		NCAA	I	32	—	—	—	—	—	—	—	18	10	Miller, Harry E.
1980		NCAA	I	—	32	—	—	—	—	—	—	17	12	Smithson, Eugene
1981		NCAA	I	8	—	—	—	—	—	—	—	26	7	Smithson, Eugene
1984		NCAA	I	—	32	—	—	—	—	—	—	18	12	Smithson, Eugene
1985		NCAA	I	64	—	—	—	—	—	—	—	18	13	Smithson, Eugene
1987		NCAA	I	64	—	—	—	—	—	—	—	22	11	Fogler, Eddie
1988		NCAA	I	64	—	—	—	—	—	—	—	20	10	Fogler, Eddie
1989		NCAA	I	—	16	—	—	—	—	—	—	19	11	Fogler, Eddie

WIDENER

Year	M/W	Assn	Div	NAT	NIT	ARC	CCA	NCI	NCT	OLY	HLM	W	L	Coach
1972	M	NCAA	II	36	—	—	—	—	—	—	—	19	9	Rowe, C. Alan
1975		NCAA	III	23	—	—	—	—	—	—	—	19	8	Rowe, C. Alan
1976		NCAA	III	14	—	—	—	—	—	—	—	22	7	Rowe, C. Alan
1977		NCAA	III	30	—	—	—	—	—	—	—	20	9	Rowe, C. Alan
1978		NCAA	III	2	—	—	—	—	—	—	—	16	5	Rowe, C. Alan
1982		NCAA	III	16	—	—	—	—	—	—	—	23	6	Rowe, C. Alan
1983		NCAA	III	16	—	—	—	—	—	—	—	21	8	Rowe, C. Alan
1985		NCAA	III	4	—	—	—	—	—	—	—	25	7	Rowe, C. Alan
1987		NCAA	III	8	—	—	—	—	—	—	—	26	4	Rowe, C. Alan
1995		NCAA	III	64	—	—	—	—	—	—	—	18	9	Rowe, C. Alan
1997		NCAA	III	32	—	—	—	—	—	—	—	23	6	Rowe, C. Alan
1982	W	NCAA	III	16	—	—	—	—	—	—	—	19	7	Hagan, Gigi

WILEY

Year	M/W	Assn	Div	NAT	NIT	ARC	CCA	NCI	NCT	OLY	HLM	W	L	Coach
1970	M	NAIA		16	—	—	—	—	—	—	—	20	10	White, Calvin

WILKES

Year	M/W	Assn	Div	NAT	NIT	ARC	CCA	NCI	NCT	OLY	HLM	W	L	Coach
1995	M	NCAA	III	8	—	—	—	—	—	—	—	25	5	Rickrode, Jerry
1996		NCAA	III	8	—	—	—	—	—	—	—	28	2	Rickrode, Jerry
1997		NCAA	III	64	—	—	—	—	—	—	—	20	6	Rickrode, Jerry
1998		NCAA	III	4	—	—	—	—	—	—	—	26	5	Rickrode, Jerry

WILLAMETTE

Year	M/W	Assn	Div	NAT	NIT	ARC	CCA	NCI	NCT	OLY	HLM	W	L	Coach
1959	M	NCAA	II	24	—	—	—	—	—	—	—	18	9	Lewis, John R.
1960		NAIA		32	—	—	—	—	—	—	—	24	4	Lewis, John R.
1972		NAIA		32	—	—	—	—	—	—	—	23	6	Boutin, Dr. James
1975		NAIA		32	—	—	—	—	—	—	—	24	5	Boutin, Dr. James
1993		NAIA	II	1	—	—	—	—	—	—	—	29	4	James, Gordon "Gordie"
1994		NAIA	II	8	—	—	—	—	—	—	—	24	6	James, Gordon "Gordie"
1995		NAIA	II	8	—	—	—	—	—	—	—	20	12	James, Gordon "Gordie"
1980	W	AIAW	III	24	—	—	—	—	—	—	—	17	7	Howard, Fran
1996		NAIA	II	32	—	—	—	—	—	—	—	19	8	Petrie, Paula

WILLIAM & MARY

Year	M/W	Assn	Div	NAT	NIT	ARC	CCA	NCI	NCT	OLY	HLM	W	L	Coach
1983	M	NCAA	I	—	32	—	—	—	—	—	—	20	9	Parkhill, Bruce

WILLIAM CAREY (MS)

Year	M/W	Assn	Div	NAT	NIT	ARC	CCA	NCI	NCT	OLY	HLM	W	L	Coach
1983	M	NAIA		32	—	—	—	—	—	—	—	20	9	Knight, Steve
1984		NAIA		16	—	—	—	—	—	—	—	26	7	Knight, Steve
1985		NAIA		32	—	—	—	—	—	—	—	20	7	Knight, Steve
1986		NAIA		32	—	—	—	—	—	—	—	20	15	Knight, Steve

Year	M/W	Assn	Div	NAT	NIT	ARC	CCA	NCI	NCT	OLY	HLM	W	L	Coach
1987		NAIA		32	—	—	—	—	—	—	—	23	13	Knight, Steve
1989		NAIA		32	—	—	—	—	—	—	—	21	13	Knight, Steve
1997		NAIA	I	32	—	—	—	—	—	—	—	22	14	Knight, Steve
1981	W	AIAW	II	16	—	—	—	—	—	—	—	19	8	Halford, Bobby
1993		NAIA	I	32	—	—	—	—	—	—	—	28	4	English, Tracy

WILLIAM JEWELL

Year	M/W	Assn	Div	NAT	NIT	ARC	CCA	NCI	NCT	OLY	HLM	W	L	Coach
1957	M	NAIA		16	—	—	—	—	—	—	—	23	6	Nelson, James A.
1960		NAIA		4	—	—	—	—	—	—	—	23	10	Nelson, James A.
1962		NAIA		16	—	—	—	—	—	—	—	21	7	Nelson, James A.
1975		NAIA		32	—	—	—	—	—	—	—	22	9	Hickman, John A.
1988		NAIA		8	—	—	—	—	—	—	—	32	2	Holley, Larry R.
1992		NAIA	II	8	—	—	—	—	—	—	—	23	13	Holley, Larry R.
1993		NAIA	II	3	—	—	—	—	—	—	—	27	10	Holley, Larry R.
1995		NAIA	II	3	—	—	—	—	—	—	—	29	10	Holley, Larry R.
1996		NAIA	II	3	—	—	—	—	—	—	—	30	9	Holley, Larry R.
1997		NAIA	II	3	—	—	—	—	—	—	—	29	10	Holley, Larry R.
1998		NAIA	II	16	—	—	—	—	—	—	—	28	9	Holley, Larry R.

WILLIAM PATTERSON

Year	M/W	Assn	Div	NAT	NIT	ARC	CCA	NCI	NCT	OLY	HLM	W	L	Coach
1975	M	NCAA	III	16	—	—	—	—	—	—	—	20	6	Adams, John K.
1977		NCAA	III	8	—	—	—	—	—	—	—	21	5	Adams, John K.
1980		NCAA	III	16	—	—	—	—	—	—	—	20	7	Adams, John K.
1981		NCAA	III	16	—	—	—	—	—	—	—	19	6	Adams, John K.
1983		NCAA	III	16	—	—	—	—	—	—	—	19	9	Adams, John K.
1984		NCAA	III	24	—	—	—	—	—	—	—	22	6	Adams, John K.
1985		NCAA	III	8	—	—	—	—	—	—	—	22	7	Adams, John K.
1997		NCAA	III	32	—	—	—	—	—	—	—	20	8	Rebimbas, Jose
1993	W	NCAA	III	32	—	—	—	—	—	—	—	18	9	Delehanty, Patty
1994		NCAA	III	32	—	—	—	—	—	—	—	23	4	Shaughnessy, Erin
1995		NCAA	III	8	—	—	—	—	—	—	—	24	5	Dallessio, Jerry
1997		NCAA	III	16	—	—	—	—	—	—	—	24	5	Shaughnessy, Erin
1998		NCAA	III	8	—	—	—	—	—	—	—	25	4	Shaughnessy, Erin

WILLIAM PENN

Year	M/W	Assn	Div	NAT	NIT	ARC	CCA	NCI	NCT	OLY	HLM	W	L	Coach
1979	M	NCAA	III	32	—	—	—	—	—	—	—	20	7	Richardson, Leon
1981		NCAA	III	24	—	—	—	—	—	—	—	20	7	Richardson, Leon
1983		NCAA	III	24	—	—	—	—	—	—	—	19	7	Richardson, Leon
1974	W	AIAW		4	—	—	—	—	—	—	—	21	8	Spencer, Robert L.
1975		AIAW	L	8	—	—	—	—	—	—	—	33	3	Spencer, Robert L.
1976		AIAW	L	4	—	—	—	—	—	—	—	30	5	Spencer, Robert L.
1978		AIAW	S	12	—	—	—	—	—	—	—	30	7	Spencer, Robert L.
1980		AIAW	II	3	—	—	—	—	—	—	—	37	5	Spencer, Robert L.
1981		AIAW	II	1	—	—	—	—	—	—	—	43	3	Spencer, Robert L.
1982		AIAW	II	3	—	—	—	—	—	—	—	27	10	Spencer, Robert L.
1984		NCAA	III	32	—	—	—	—	—	—	—	17	11	Smith, Garey
1985		NCAA	III	16	—	—	—	—	—	—	—	21	7	Smith, Garey
1986		NCAA	III	8	—	—	—	—	—	—	—	22	7	Smith, Garey
1987		NCAA	III	8	—	—	—	—	—	—	—	20	9	Smith, Garey
1988		NCAA	III	24	—	—	—	—	—	—	—	21	7	Smith, Garey

Year	M/W	Assn	Div	NAT	NIT	ARC	CCA	NCI	NCT	OLY	HLM	W	L	Coach
WILLIAM SMITH														
1992	W	NCAA	III	32	—	—	—	—	—	—	—	—	24	4	Begley, Glenn C.
1994		NCAA	III	40	—	—	—	—	—	—	—	—	25	3	Begley, Glenn C.
1995		NCAA	III	32	—	—	—	—	—	—	—	—	23	3	Begley, Glenn C.
1996		NCAA	III	16	—	—	—	—	—	—	—	—	25	2	Begley, Glenn C.
1997		NCAA	III	8	—	—	—	—	—	—	—	—	27	1	Begley, Glenn C.
1998		NCAA	III	32	—	—	—	—	—	—	—	—	23	3	Begley, Glenn C.
WILLIAM WOODS														
1992	W	NAIA	I	32	—	—	—	—	—	—	—	—	25	3	Ternes, Roger
WILLIAMS														
1955	M	NCAA		24	—	—	—	—	—	—	—	—	14	4	Shaw, Alex J.
1959		NCAA	II	32	—	—	—	—	—	—	—	—	15	9	Shaw, Alex J.
1961		NCAA	II	8	—	—	—	—	—	—	—	—	22	3	Shaw, Alex J.
1994		NCAA	III	32	—	—	—	—	—	—	—	—	22	4	Sheehy, Harry
1995		NCAA	III	16	—	—	—	—	—	—	—	—	23	4	Sheehy, Harry
1996		NCAA	III	16	—	—	—	—	—	—	—	—	24	3	Sheehy, Harry
1997		NCAA	III	3	—	—	—	—	—	—	—	—	27	3	Sheehy, Harry
1998		NCAA	III	3	—	—	—	—	—	—	—	—	26	4	Sheehy, Harry
1997	W	NCAA	III	32	—	—	—	—	—	—	—	—	20	5	Manning, Patricia
WILLIAMS BAPTIST														
1992	W	NCCAA	I	2	—	—	—	—	—	—	—	—	18	13	Halford, Carol
1993		NCCAA	I	1	—	—	—	—	—	—	—	—	24	2	Halford, Carol
WILLIAMSPORT COMMERCE														
1968	M	NSCAA		8	—	—	—	—	—	—	—	—	13	5	Mamolen, Paul
1969		NSCAA		6	—	—	—	—	—	—	—	—	17	3	Mamolen, Paul
WILMINGTON (DE)														
1993	M	NAIA	II	16	—	—	—	—	—	—	—	—	19	13	Newsome, Kevin
1995		NAIA	II	32	—	—	—	—	—	—	—	—	20	11	Newsome, Kevin
1991	W	NSCAA		4	—	—	—	—	—	—	—	—	15	12	Rogers, "Rusty"
1992		NAIA	II	16	—	—	—	—	—	—	—	—	25	11	Rogers, "Rusty"
1992		NSCAA		4	—	—	—	—	—	—	—	—	25	11	Rogers, "Rusty"
1993		NAIA	II	20	—	—	—	—	—	—	—	—	26	6	Rogers, "Rusty"
1993		NSCAA		2	—	—	—	—	—	—	—	—	26	6	Rogers, "Rusty"
1994		NAIA	II	16	—	—	—	—	—	—	—	—	21	8	Rogers, "Rusty"
WINGATE														
1986	W	NAIA		8	—	—	—	—	—	—	—	—	26	6	Jacumin, Johnny
1987		NAIA		8	—	—	—	—	—	—	—	—	29	4	Jacumin, Johnny
1988		NAIA		4	—	—	—	—	—	—	—	—	33	2	Jacumin, Johnny
1989		NAIA		16	—	—	—	—	—	—	—	—	26	3	Jacumin, Johnny
1990		NAIA		16	—	—	—	—	—	—	—	—	27	6	Jacumin, Johnny
1991		NAIA		8	—	—	—	—	—	—	—	—	28	3	Jacumin, Johnny
1992		NAIA	I	32	—	—	—	—	—	—	—	—	22	11	Jacumin, Johnny
1993		NAIA	I	32	—	—	—	—	—	—	—	—	23	8	Jacumin, Johnny

Year	M/W	Assn	Div	NAT	NIT	ARC	CCA	NCI	NCT	OLY	HLM	W	L	Coach
1994		NCAA	II	16	—	—	—	—	—	—	—	27	2	Jacumin, Johnny
1995		NCAA	II	8	—	—	—	—	—	—	—	25	6	Jacumin, Johnny
1996		NCAA	II	8	—	—	—	—	—	—	—	23	8	Jacumin, Johnny
1997		NCAA	II	48	—	—	—	—	—	—	—	20	9	Jacumin, Johnny

WINONA STATE

Year	M/W	Assn	Div	NAT	NIT	ARC	CCA	NCI	NCT	OLY	HLM	W	L	Coach
1938	M	NAIA		32	—	—	—	—	—	—	—	14	4	Fisk, Charles
1939		NAIA		32	—	—	—	—	—	—	—	10	8	Fisk, Charles
1973		NAIA		16	—	—	—	—	—	—	—	23	4	Wothke, Les
1975		NAIA		16	—	—	—	—	—	—	—	22	7	Wothke, Les

WINSTON-SALEM STATE

Year	M/W	Assn	Div	NAT	NIT	ARC	CCA	NCI	NCT	OLY	HLM	W	L	Coach
1961	M	NAIA		8	—	—	—	—	—	—	—	26	5	Gaines, Clarence E. "Big House"
1962		NAIA		16	—	—	—	—	—	—	—	24	5	Gaines, Clarence E. "Big House"
1963		NAIA		32	—	—	—	—	—	—	—	23	7	Gaines, Clarence E. "Big House"
1965		NAIA		8	—	—	—	—	—	—	—	25	8	Gaines, Clarence E. "Big House"
1966		NCAA	II	22	—	—	—	—	—	—	—	21	5	Gaines, Clarence E. "Big House"
1967		NCAA	II	1	—	—	—	—	—	—	—	30	2	Gaines, Clarence E. "Big House"
1975		NAIA		8	—	—	—	—	—	—	—	23	7	Gaines, Clarence E. "Big House"
1977		NCAA	II	32	—	—	—	—	—	—	—	17	11	Gaines, Clarence E. "Big House"
1978		NAIA		8	—	—	—	—	—	—	—	28	4	Gaines, Clarence E. "Big House"
1984		NCAA	II	32	—	—	—	—	—	—	—	20	10	Gaines, Clarence E. "Big House"
1985		NCAA	II	16	—	—	—	—	—	—	—	16	12	Gaines, Clarence E. "Big House"
1986		NCAA	II	32	—	—	—	—	—	—	—	15	12	Gaines, Clarence E. "Big House"

WINTHROP

Year	M/W	Assn	Div	NAT	NIT	ARC	CCA	NCI	NCT	OLY	HLM	W	L	Coach
1971	W	AIAW		12	—	—	—	—	—	—	—	18	7	Kancevitch, Mary

WISCONSIN

Year	M/W	Assn	Div	NAT	NIT	ARC	CCA	NCI	NCT	OLY	HLM	W	L	Coach
1912	M	NCAA		—	—	—	—	—	—	—	1	15	0	Meanwell, Dr. Walter E. "Doc"
1914		NCAA		—	—	—	—	—	—	—	1	15	0	Meanwell, Dr. Walter E. "Doc"
1916		NCAA		—	—	—	—	—	—	—	1	20	1	Meanwell, Dr. Walter E. "Doc"
1941		NCAA		1	—	—	—	—	—	—	1	20	3	Foster, Harold E. "Bud"
1947		NCAA		6	—	—	—	—	—	—	—	16	6	Foster, Harold E. "Bud"
1989		NCAA	I	—	16	—	—	—	—	—	—	18	12	Yoder, Steve
1991		NCAA	I	—	16	—	—	—	—	—	—	15	15	Yoder, Steve
1993		NCAA	I	—	32	—	—	—	—	—	—	14	14	Jackson, Stu
1994		NCAA	I	32	—	—	—	—	—	—	—	18	11	Jackson, Stu
1996		NCAA	I	—	16	—	—	—	—	—	—	17	15	Bennett, Richard
1997		NCAA	I	64	—	—	—	—	—	—	—	18	10	Bennett, Richard
1982	W	AIAW	I	8	—	—	—	—	—	—	—	21	13	Qualls, Edwina
1992		NCAA	I	48	—	—	—	—	—	—	—	20	9	Murphy, Mary
1995		NCAA	I	32	—	—	—	—	—	—	—	20	9	Albright-Dieterle, Jane
1996		NCAA	I	32	—	—	—	—	—	—	—	21	8	Albright-Dieterle, Jane
1998		NCAA	I	64	—	—	—	—	—	—	—	21	10	Albright-Dieterle, Jane

WISCONSIN LUTHERAN

Year	M/W	Assn	Div	NAT	NIT	ARC	CCA	NCI	NCT	OLY	HLM	W	L	Coach
1996	M	NAIA	II	8	—	—	—	—	—	—	—	22	7	Noon, Ed
1997		NAIA	II	32	—	—	—	—	—	—	—	19	10	Noon, Ed

Year	M/W	Assn	Div	NAT	NIT	ARC	CCA	NCI	NCT	OLY	HLM	W	L	Coach
WISCONSIN: EAU CLAIRE														
1939	M	NAIA		32	—	—	—	—	—	—	—	15	2	Zorn, Willis R., Sr. 'Bill'
1945		NAIA		16	—	—	—	—	—	—	—	10	8	Zorn, Willis R., Sr. 'Bill'
1946		NAIA		32	—	—	—	—	—	—	—	18	4	Zorn, Willis R., Sr. 'Bill'
1951		NAIA		32	—	—	—	—	—	—	—	17	6	Zorn, Willis R., Sr. 'Bill'
1956		NAIA		16	—	—	—	—	—	—	—	20	5	Zorn, Willis R., Sr. 'Bill'
1970		NAIA		16	—	—	—	—	—	—	—	23	2	Anderson, Kenneth A.
1971		NAIA		8	—	—	—	—	—	—	—	27	2	Anderson, Kenneth A.
1972		NAIA		2	—	—	—	—	—	—	—	29	2	Anderson, Kenneth A.
1974		NAIA		32	—	—	—	—	—	—	—	24	5	Anderson, Kenneth A.
1979		NAIA		16	—	—	—	—	—	—	—	24	7	Anderson, Kenneth A.
1980		NAIA		4	—	—	—	—	—	—	—	30	4	Anderson, Kenneth A.
1981		NAIA		3	—	—	—	—	—	—	—	29	5	Anderson, Kenneth A.
1982		NAIA		8	—	—	—	—	—	—	—	26	6	Anderson, Kenneth A.
1986		NAIA		16	—	—	—	—	—	—	—	24	7	Anderson, Kenneth A.
1987		NAIA		32	—	—	—	—	—	—	—	26	4	Anderson, Kenneth A.
1988		NAIA		16	—	—	—	—	—	—	—	23	8	Anderson, Kenneth A.
1989		NAIA		3	—	—	—	—	—	—	—	29	4	Anderson, Kenneth A.
1990		NAIA		2	—	—	—	—	—	—	—	30	4	Anderson, Kenneth A.
1991		NAIA		8	—	—	—	—	—	—	—	29	3	Anderson, Kenneth A.
1992		NAIA	I	32	—	—	—	—	—	—	—	20	9	Anderson, Kenneth A.
1989	W	NCAA	III	8	—	—	—	—	—	—	—	24	5	Stone, Lisa Anderson
1990		NCAA	III	32	—	—	—	—	—	—	—	21	6	Stone, Lisa Anderson
1992		NCAA	III	8	—	—	—	—	—	—	—	23	5	Stone, Lisa Anderson
1993		NCAA	III	16	—	—	—	—	—	—	—	22	4	Stone, Lisa Anderson
1994		NCAA	III	3	—	—	—	—	—	—	—	23	6	Stone, Lisa Anderson
1995		NCAA	III	8	—	—	—	—	—	—	—	24	5	Stone, Lisa Anderson
1996		NCAA	III	8	—	—	—	—	—	—	—	25	4	Stone, Lisa Anderson
1997		NCAA	III	2	—	—	—	—	—	—	—	27	4	Stone, Lisa Anderson
1998		NCAA	III	32	—	—	—	—	—	—	—	22	5	Stone, Lisa Anderson
WISCONSIN: GREEN BAY														
1973	M	NAIA		8	—	—	—	—	—	—	—	28	4	Buss, David R.
1974		NCAA	II	32	—	—	—	—	—	—	—	20	8	Buss, David R.
1976		NCAA	II	16	—	—	—	—	—	—	—	21	8	Buss, David R.
1977		NCAA	II	16	—	—	—	—	—	—	—	26	3	Buss, David R.
1978		NCAA	II	2	—	—	—	—	—	—	—	30	2	Buss, David R.
1979		NCAA	II	2	—	—	—	—	—	—	—	24	8	Buss, David R.
1981		NCAA	II	4	—	—	—	—	—	—	—	23	9	Buss, David R.
1990		NCAA	I	—	16	—	—	—	—	—	—	24	8	Bennett, Richard
1991		NCAA	I	64	—	—	—	—	—	—	—	24	7	Bennett, Richard
1992		NCAA	I	—	32	—	—	—	—	—	—	25	5	Bennett, Richard
1994		NCAA	I	32	—	—	—	—	—	—	—	27	7	Bennett, Richard
1995		NCAA	I	64	—	—	—	—	—	—	—	22	8	Bennett, Richard
1996		NCAA	I	64	—	—	—	—	—	—	—	25	4	Heideman, Mike
1982	W	AIAW	II	16	—	—	—	—	—	—	—	28	9	Hammerle, Carol
1986		NAIA		16	—	—	—	—	—	—	—	21	9	Hammerle, Carol
1987		NAIA		3	—	—	—	—	—	—	—	24	6	Hammerle, Carol
1992		NCAA	I	—	5	—	—	—	—	—	—	24	7	Hammerle, Carol
1994		NCAA	I	64	—	—	—	—	—	—	—	18	11	Hammerle, Carol
1998		NCAA	I	64	—	—	—	—	—	—	—	21	9	Hammerle, Carol

Year	M/W	Assn	Div	NAT	NIT	ARC	CCA	NCI	NCT	OLY	HLM	W	L	Coach
WISCONSIN: LA CROSSE														
1964	M	NAIA		32	—	—	—	—	—	—	—	20	2	De Voll, Clifton
1976	W	AIAW	L	16	—	—	—	—	—	—	—	19	4	Connolly, Mary
1980		AIAW	III	2	—	—	—	—	—	—	—	24	4	Hansen, Mary
1981		AIAW	III	1	—	—	—	—	—	—	—	27	5	Hansen, Mary
1983		NCAA	III	8	—	—	—	—	—	—	—	13	9	Greene, Janet
1984		NCAA	III	16	—	—	—	—	—	—	—	19	8	Greene, Janet
1988		NCAA	III	8	—	—	—	—	—	—	—	22	7	Sheridan, Teri
WISCONSIN: MILWAUKEE														
1960	M	NCAA	II	24	—	—	—	—	—	—	—	18	4	Rebholz, Russ
1982		NCAA	III	24	—	—	—	—	—	—	—	20	6	Voight, Bob
1989		NCAA	II	8	—	—	—	—	—	—	—	24	7	Antrim, Steve
1984	W	NAIA		16	—	—	—	—	—	—	—	25	8	Kelling, Mary Ann
1985		NAIA		16	—	—	—	—	—	—	—	25	7	Kelling, Mary Ann
WISCONSIN: OSHKOSH														
1960	M	NAIA		32	—	—	—	—	—	—	—	15	8	Kitzman, Eric
1963		NAIA		32	—	—	—	—	—	—	—	15	10	Young, Russ
1967		NAIA		32	—	—	—	—	—	—	—	17	6	White, Dr. Robert
1968		NAIA		3	—	—	—	—	—	—	—	23	6	White, Dr. Robert
1996		NCAA	III	32	—	—	—	—	—	—	—	23	4	Van Dellen, Ted
1997		NCAA	III	64	—	—	—	—	—	—	—	19	7	Van Dellen, Ted
1998		NCAA	III	32	—	—	—	—	—	—	—	21	6	Van Dellen, Ted
1990	W	NCAA	III	16	—	—	—	—	—	—	—	17	7	Bennett, Kathi
1991		NCAA	III	16	—	—	—	—	—	—	—	21	5	Bennett, Kathi
1992		NCAA	III	32	—	—	—	—	—	—	—	18	6	Bennett, Kathi
1994		NCAA	III	8	—	—	—	—	—	—	—	24	3	Bennett, Kathi
1995		NCAA	III	2	—	—	—	—	—	—	—	28	3	Bennett, Kathi
1996		NCAA	III	1	—	—	—	—	—	—	—	31	0	Bennett, Kathi
1997		NCAA	III	32	—	—	—	—	—	—	—	23	4	Ruder, Pam
1998		NCAA	III	8	—	—	—	—	—	—	—	26	2	Ruder, Pam
WISCONSIN: PARKSIDE														
1975	M	NAIA		8	—	—	—	—	—	—	—	24	9	Stephens, Steve
1976		NAIA		16	—	—	—	—	—	—	—	24	7	Stephens, Steve
1977		NAIA		16	—	—	—	—	—	—	—	20	10	Stephens, Steve
1978		NAIA		16	—	—	—	—	—	—	—	19	11	Stephens, Steve
WISCONSIN: PLATTEVILLE														
1958	M	NAIA		16	—	—	—	—	—	—	—	21	3	Barth, John
1959		NAIA		32	—	—	—	—	—	—	—	18	4	Barth, John
1991		NCAA	III	1	—	—	—	—	—	—	—	28	3	Ryan, William 'Bo'
1992		NCAA	III	3	—	—	—	—	—	—	—	27	4	Ryan, William 'Bo'
1993		NCAA	III	8	—	—	—	—	—	—	—	24	4	Ryan, William 'Bo'
1994		NCAA	III	16	—	—	—	—	—	—	—	23	5	Ryan, William 'Bo'
1995		NCAA	III	1	—	—	—	—	—	—	—	31	0	Ryan, William 'Bo'
1996		NCAA	III	64	—	—	—	—	—	—	—	23	3	Ryan, William 'Bo'
1997		NCAA	III	32	—	—	—	—	—	—	—	24	3	Ryan, William 'Bo'
1998		NCAA	III	1	—	—	—	—	—	—	—	30	0	Ryan, William 'Bo'

Year	M/W	Assn	Div	NAT	NIT	ARC	CCA	NCI	NCT	OLY	HLM	W	L	Coach

WISCONSIN: RIVER FALLS

Year	M/W	Assn	Div	NAT	NIT	ARC	CCA	NCI	NCT	OLY	HLM	W	L	Coach
1947	M	NAIA		32	—	—	—	—	—	—	—	18	7	Schlagenhauf, George K.
1949		NAIA		32	—	—	—	—	—	—	—	10	2	Schlagenhauf, George K.
1950		NAIA		16	—	—	—	—	—	—	—	26	5	Schlagenhauf, George K.
1953		NAIA		32	—	—	—	—	—	—	—	13	8	Belfori, Phil
1988	W	NCAA	III	32	—	—	—	—	—	—	—	22	6	Bloom, Dennis
1989		NCAA	III	16	—	—	—	—	—	—	—	23	5	Bloom, Dennis
1995		NCAA	III	64	—	—	—	—	—	—	—	17	9	Thelen, Carol

WISCONSIN: STEVENS POINT

Year	M/W	Assn	Div	NAT	NIT	ARC	CCA	NCI	NCT	OLY	HLM	W	L	Coach
1942	M	NAIA		32	—	—	—	—	—	—	—	9	3	Kobal, Eddie
1957		NAIA		16	—	—	—	—	—	—	—	17	6	Quandt, Hale F.
1983		NAIA		16	—	—	—	—	—	—	—	26	4	Bennett, Richard
1984		NAIA		2	—	—	—	—	—	—	—	28	4	Bennett, Richard
1985		NAIA		16	—	—	—	—	—	—	—	25	5	Bennett, Richard
1992		NAIA	I	16	—	—	—	—	—	—	—	27	2	Parker, Bob
1993		NAIA	I	32	—	—	—	—	—	—	—	23	5	Parker, Bob
1997		NCAA	III	8	—	—	—	—	—	—	—	22	7	Bennett, Jack
1987	W	NCAA	III	1	—	—	—	—	—	—	—	27	2	Wunder, Linda
1991		NCAA	III	32	—	—	—	—	—	—	—	17	7	Egner, Shirley

WISCONSIN: STOUT

Year	M/W	Assn	Div	NAT	NIT	ARC	CCA	NCI	NCT	OLY	HLM	W	L	Coach
1942	M	NAIA		16	—	—	—	—	—	—	—	9	6	Johnson, Ray
1943		NAIA		32	—	—	—	—	—	—	—	10	2	Johnson, Ray
1969		NAIA		16	—	—	—	—	—	—	—	21	4	Mintz, Dwain P.
1991	W	NAIA		32	—	—	—	—	—	—	—	19	11	Thomas, Mark
1992		NCAA	III	32	—	—	—	—	—	—	—	19	7	Thomas, Mark
1993		NCAA	III	32	—	—	—	—	—	—	—	21	4	Thomas, Mark
1994		NCAA	III	32	—	—	—	—	—	—	—	21	5	Thomas, Mark
1996		NCAA	III	64	—	—	—	—	—	—	—	17	9	Thomas, Mark
1997		NCAA	III	32	—	—	—	—	—	—	—	19	8	Thomas, Mark

WISCONSIN: SUPERIOR

Year	M/W	Assn	Div	NAT	NIT	ARC	CCA	NCI	NCT	OLY	HLM	W	L	Coach
1940	M	NAIA		16	—	—	—	—	—	—	—	15	3	Whereatt, Ted
1941		NAIA		16	—	—	—	—	—	—	—	17	2	Whereatt, Ted
1957		NCAA	II	32	—	—	—	—	—	—	—	13	9	Vergamini, Carl
1961		NCAA	II	32	—	—	—	—	—	—	—	15	8	Vergamini, Carl

WISCONSIN: WHITEWATER

Year	M/W	Assn	Div	NAT	NIT	ARC	CCA	NCI	NCT	OLY	HLM	W	L	Coach
1952	M	NAIA		32	—	—	—	—	—	—	—	16	6	Weigandt, Robert
1983		NCAA	III	4	—	—	—	—	—	—	—	25	6	Vander Meulen, David
1984		NCAA	III	1	—	—	—	—	—	—	—	27	4	Vander Meulen, David
1985		NCAA	III	16	—	—	—	—	—	—	—	20	8	Vander Meulen, David
1986		NCAA	III	24	—	—	—	—	—	—	—	24	4	Vander Meulen, David
1988		NCAA	III	24	—	—	—	—	—	—	—	22	6	Vander Meulen, David
1989		NCAA	III	1	—	—	—	—	—	—	—	29	2	Vander Meulen, David
1992		NCAA	III	32	—	—	—	—	—	—	—	19	9	Vander Meulen, David
1993		NCAA	III	32	—	—	—	—	—	—	—	18	9	Vander Meulen, David
1994		NCAA	III	32	—	—	—	—	—	—	—	21	4	Vander Meulen, David
1995		NCAA	III	32	—	—	—	—	—	—	—	19	8	Vander Meulen, David

Year	M/W	Assn	Div	NAT	NIT	ARC	CCA	NCI	NCT	OLY	HLM	W	L	Coach
1996		NCAA	III	16	—	—	—	—	—	—	—	19	9	Vander Meulen, David
1997		NCAA	III	64	—	—	—	—	—	—	—	22	4	Vander Meulen, David
1981	W	AIAW	III	16	—	—	—	—	—	—	—	19	9	Jones, Dianne
1982		AIAW	III	3	—	—	—	—	—	—	—	25	6	Jones, Dianne
1983		NCAA	III	16	—	—	—	—	—	—	—	19	5	Jones, Dianne
1984		NCAA	III	24	—	—	—	—	—	—	—	17	11	Jones, Dianne
1985		NCAA	III	16	—	—	—	—	—	—	—	21	8	Jones, Dianne
1986		NCAA	III	8	—	—	—	—	—	—	—	24	4	Jones, Dianne
1987		NCAA	III	24	—	—	—	—	—	—	—	20	5	Jones, Dianne
1993		NCAA	III	16	—	—	—	—	—	—	—	19	7	Yeater, Julia
1995		NCAA	III	32	—	—	—	—	—	—	—	20	7	Yeater, Julia

WITTENBERG

Year	M/W	Assn	Div	NAT	NIT	ARC	CCA	NCI	NCT	OLY	HLM	W	L	Coach
1959	M	NCAA	II	16	—	—	—	—	—	—	—	19	3	Mears, Ramon "Ray"
1961		NCAA	II	1	—	—	—	—	—	—	—	25	4	Mears, Ramon "Ray"
1962		NCAA	II	8	—	—	—	—	—	—	—	21	5	Mears, Ramon "Ray"
1963		NCAA	II	2	—	—	—	—	—	—	—	26	2	Miller, Eldon
1969		NCAA	II	32	—	—	—	—	—	—	—	19	6	Miller, Eldon
1972		NCAA	II	32	—	—	—	—	—	—	—	17	10	Hamilton, Robert D.
1974		NCAA	II	16	—	—	—	—	—	—	—	22	4	Hamilton, Robert D.
1975		NCAA	III	8	—	—	—	—	—	—	—	20	8	Hamilton, Robert D.
1976		NCAA	III	2	—	—	—	—	—	—	—	24	5	Hamilton, Robert D.
1977		NCAA	III	1	—	—	—	—	—	—	—	23	5	Hunter, Larry
1979		NCAA	III	16	—	—	—	—	—	—	—	23	6	Hunter, Larry
1980		NCAA	III	3	—	—	—	—	—	—	—	29	3	Hunter, Larry
1981		NCAA	III	16	—	—	—	—	—	—	—	28	3	Hunter, Larry
1982		NCAA	III	32	—	—	—	—	—	—	—	20	10	Hunter, Larry
1983		NCAA	III	2	—	—	—	—	—	—	—	26	6	Hunter, Larry
1985		NCAA	III	8	—	—	—	—	—	—	—	27	4	Hunter, Larry
1986		NCAA	III	24	—	—	—	—	—	—	—	23	5	Hunter, Larry
1987		NCAA	III	3	—	—	—	—	—	—	—	25	8	Hunter, Larry
1989		NCAA	III	16	—	—	—	—	—	—	—	27	3	Hunter, Larry
1990		NCAA	III	8	—	—	—	—	—	—	—	29	2	Hipsher, Dan
1991		NCAA	III	32	—	—	—	—	—	—	—	26	3	Hipsher, Dan
1992		NCAA	III	40	—	—	—	—	—	—	—	23	6	Hipsher, Dan
1994		NCAA	III	3	—	—	—	—	—	—	—	30	2	Brown, Bill L.
1995		NCAA	III	32	—	—	—	—	—	—	—	21	8	Brown, Bill L.
1996		NCAA	III	8	—	—	—	—	—	—	—	26	5	Brown, Bill L.
1997		NCAA	III	32	—	—	—	—	—	—	—	23	6	Brown, Bill L.
1990	W	NCAA	III	32	—	—	—	—	—	—	—	26	3	Evans-Smith, Pamela
1993		NCAA	III	32	—	—	—	—	—	—	—	23	4	Evans-Smith, Pamela
1994		NCAA	III	32	—	—	—	—	—	—	—	24	4	Evans-Smith, Pamela
1995		NCAA	III	64	—	—	—	—	—	—	—	25	3	Evans-Smith, Pamela
1996		NCAA	III	64	—	—	—	—	—	—	—	21	7	Evans-Smith, Pamela
1998		NCAA	III	48	—	—	—	—	—	—	—	22	6	Evans-Smith, Pamela

WOFFORD

Year	M/W	Assn	Div	NAT	NIT	ARC	CCA	NCI	NCT	OLY	HLM	W	L	Coach
1960	M	NAIA		8	—	—	—	—	—	—	—	25	6	Alexander, Eugene F.

Year	M/W	Assn	Div	NAT	NIT	ARC	CCA	NCI	NCT	OLY	HLM	W	L	Coach
WOOSTER														
1971	M	NCAA	II	32	—	—	—	—	—	—	—	—	23	3	Van Wie, Alvin J. 'Al'
1973		NCAA	II	32	—	—	—	—	—	—	—	—	19	10	Van Wie, Alvin J. 'Al'
1978		NCAA	III	16	—	—	—	—	—	—	—	—	21	6	Van Wie, Alvin J. 'Al'
1991		NCAA	III	40	—	—	—	—	—	—	—	—	25	4	Moore, Stephen
1992		NCAA	III	32	—	—	—	—	—	—	—	—	26	3	Moore, Stephen
1993		NCAA	III	32	—	—	—	—	—	—	—	—	21	7	Moore, Stephen
1995		NCAA	III	32	—	—	—	—	—	—	—	—	26	3	Moore, Stephen
1996		NCAA	III	64	—	—	—	—	—	—	—	—	19	7	Moore, Stephen
1997		NCAA	III	32	—	—	—	—	—	—	—	—	23	6	Moore, Stephen
1998		NCAA	III	32	—	—	—	—	—	—	—	—	22	6	Moore, Stephen
1983	W	NCAA	III	32	—	—	—	—	—	—	—	—	19	7	Nichols, Nancy 'Nan'
1985		NCAA	III	32	—	—	—	—	—	—	—	—	21	8	Nichols, Nancy 'Nan'
WORCESTER POLYTECHNIC														
1982	M	NCAA	III	32	—	—	—	—	—	—	—	—	14	11	Kaufman, Kenneth J.
1985		NCAA	III	8	—	—	—	—	—	—	—	—	20	8	Kaufman, Kenneth J.
1984	W	NCAA	III	24	—	—	—	—	—	—	—	—	20	4	Chapman, Susan E.
1996		NCAA	III	32	—	—	—	—	—	—	—	—	23	6	Champion, Christa
WORCESTER STATE														
1977	M	NCAA	III	30	—	—	—	—	—	—	—	—	17	10	Hippert, Edward 'Eddie'
1994		NCAA	III	40	—	—	—	—	—	—	—	—	18	10	Moore, Tom
1980	W	AIAW	III	1	—	—	—	—	—	—	—	—	24	2	Devlin, Donna
1981		AIAW	III	3	—	—	—	—	—	—	—	—	28	2	Devlin, Donna
WRIGHT STATE (OH)														
1976	M	NCAA	II	24	—	—	—	—	—	—	—	—	20	8	Jackson, Marcus
1979		NCAA	II	16	—	—	—	—	—	—	—	—	20	8	Underhill, Ralph
1980		NCAA	II	24	—	—	—	—	—	—	—	—	25	3	Underhill, Ralph
1981		NCAA	II	24	—	—	—	—	—	—	—	—	25	4	Underhill, Ralph
1982		NCAA	II	24	—	—	—	—	—	—	—	—	22	7	Underhill, Ralph
1983		NCAA	II	1	—	—	—	—	—	—	—	—	28	4	Underhill, Ralph
1985		NCAA	II	16	—	—	—	—	—	—	—	—	22	7	Underhill, Ralph
1986		NCAA	II	8	—	—	—	—	—	—	—	—	28	3	Underhill, Ralph
1993		NCAA	I	64	—	—	—	—	—	—	—	—	20	10	Underhill, Ralph
1987	W	NCAA	II	16	—	—	—	—	—	—	—	—	24	6	Davis, Pat
WYOMING														
1934	M			—	—	—	—	—	—	—	—	1	26	3	Witte, Willard A. 'Dutch'
1941		NCAA		8	—	—	—	—	—	—	—	—	14	6	Shelton, Everett F.
1943		NCAA		1	—	1	—	—	—	—	—	1	31	2	Shelton, Everett F.
1947		NCAA		8	—	—	—	—	—	—	—	—	22	6	Shelton, Everett F.
1948		NCAA		8	—	—	—	—	—	—	—	—	18	9	Shelton, Everett F.
1949		NCAA		8	—	—	—	—	—	—	—	—	25	10	Shelton, Everett F.
1951		NCAA		—	—	—	—	—	4	—	—	—	26	11	Shelton, Everett F.
1952		NCAA		8	—	—	—	—	—	—	—	—	28	7	Shelton, Everett F.
1953		NCAA		16	—	—	—	—	—	—	—	—	20	10	Shelton, Everett F.
1958		NCAA	I	24	—	—	—	—	—	—	—	—	13	14	Shelton, Everett F.
1967		NCAA	I	16	—	—	—	—	—	—	—	—	15	14	Strannigan, William M.
1968		NCAA	I	—	16	—	—	—	—	—	—	—	18	9	Strannigan, William M.

Year	M/W	Assn	Div	NAT	NIT	ARC	CCA	NCI	NCT	OLY	HLM	W	L	Coach
1969		NCAA	I	—	16	—	—	—	—	—	—	19	9	Strannigan, William M.
1981		NCAA	I	32	—	—	—	—	—	—	—	24	6	Brandenburg, Jim
1982		NCAA	I	32	—	—	—	—	—	—	—	23	7	Brandenburg, Jim
1986		NCAA	I	—	2	—	—	—	—	—	—	24	12	Brandenburg, Jim
1987		NCAA	I	16	—	—	—	—	—	—	—	24	10	Brandenburg, Jim
1988		NCAA	I	64	—	—	—	—	—	—	—	26	6	Dees, Benny
1991		NCAA	I	—	16	—	—	—	—	—	—	20	12	Dees, Benny
1998		NCAA	I	—	32	—	—	—	—	—	—	19	9	Shyatt, Larry
1990	W	NCAA	I	—	8	—	—	—	—	—	—	24	8	Lavin, Chad

XAVIER (LA)

Year	M/W	Assn	Div	NAT	NIT	ARC	CCA	NCI	NCT	OLY	HLM	W	L	Coach
1954	M	NASC		8	—	—	—	—	—	—	—	15	5	Hawkins, James E. "Red"
1972		NAIA		16	—	—	—	—	—	—	—	22	5	Hopkins, Robert M.
1973		NAIA		8	—	—	—	—	—	—	—	21	6	Hopkins, Robert M.
1981		NAIA		32	—	—	—	—	—	—	—	21	8	Alexander, Denny
1982		NAIA		32	—	—	—	—	—	—	—	29	2	Alexander, Denny
1991		NAIA		32	—	—	—	—	—	—	—	21	12	Valdery, Dale
1996		NAIA	I	32	—	—	—	—	—	—	—	22	11	Valdery, Dale
1994	W	NAIA	I	32	—	—	—	—	—	—	—	28	4	Joseph, Janice
1995		NAIA	I	16	—	—	—	—	—	—	—	25	5	Joseph, Janice
1996		NAIA	I	16	—	—	—	—	—	—	—	28	6	Joseph, Janice
1997		NAIA	I	16	—	—	—	—	—	—	—	29	7	Joseph, Janice
1998		NAIA	I	16	—	—	—	—	—	—	—	27	4	Joseph, Janice

XAVIER (OH)

Year	M/W	Assn	Div	NAT	NIT	ARC	CCA	NCI	NCT	OLY	HLM	W	L	Coach
1948	M	NAIA		4	—	—	—	—	—	—	—	24	8	Hirt, Lewis R.
1956		NCAA		—	8	—	—	—	—	—	—	17	11	Wulk, Ned W.
1957		NCAA	I	—	8	—	—	—	—	—	—	20	8	Wulk, Ned W.
1958		NCAA	I	—	1	—	—	—	—	—	—	19	11	McCafferty, James J.
1961		NCAA	I	24	—	—	—	—	—	—	—	17	10	McCafferty, James J.
1963		NCAA	I	—	—	—	—	1	—	—	—	12	16	McCafferty, James J.
1983		NCAA	I	52	—	—	—	—	—	—	—	22	8	Staak, Bob
1984		NCAA	I	—	8	—	—	—	—	—	—	22	11	Staak, Bob
1986		NCAA	I	64	—	—	—	—	—	—	—	25	5	Gillen, Pete
1987		NCAA	I	32	—	—	—	—	—	—	—	19	13	Gillen, Pete
1988		NCAA	I	64	—	—	—	—	—	—	—	26	4	Gillen, Pete
1989		NCAA	I	64	—	—	—	—	—	—	—	21	12	Gillen, Pete
1990		NCAA	I	16	—	—	—	—	—	—	—	28	5	Gillen, Pete
1991		NCAA	I	32	—	—	—	—	—	—	—	22	10	Gillen, Pete
1993		NCAA	I	32	—	—	—	—	—	—	—	24	6	Gillen, Pete
1994		NCAA	I	—	8	—	—	—	—	—	—	22	8	Gillen, Pete
1995		NCAA	I	64	—	—	—	—	—	—	—	23	5	Prosser, "Skip"
1997		NCAA	I	32	—	—	—	—	—	—	—	23	6	Prosser, "Skip"
1998		NCAA	I	64	—	—	—	—	—	—	—	22	8	Prosser, "Skip"
1993	W	NCAA	I	48	—	—	—	—	—	—	—	21	9	Ehlen, Mark
1998		NCAA	I	—	16	—	—	—	—	—	—	17	12	Balcomb, Melanie

Year	M/W	Assn	Div	NAT	NIT	ARC	CCA	NCI	NCT	OLY	HLM	W	L	Coach
YALE														
1901	M			—	—	—	—	—	—	—	1	10	6	Unknown
1903				—	—	—	—	—	—	—	1	15	1	Murphy, W. H.
1949		NCAA		8	—	—	—	—	—	—	—	22	8	Hobson, Dr. Howard A. "Hobby"
1957		NCAA	I	23	—	—	—	—	—	—	—	18	8	Vancisin, Joseph R.
1962		NCAA	I	25	—	—	—	—	—	—	—	18	6	Vancisin, Joseph R.
YANKTON														
1942	M	NAIA		32	—	—	—	—	—	—	—	13	3	Arnold, Lorne S.
1963		NAIA		32	—	—	—	—	—	—	—	18	7	Cowman, Douglas
1969		NAIA		32	—	—	—	—	—	—	—	22	4	Holwerda, Jim
YORK (NE)														
1943	M	NAIA		16	—	—	—	—	—	—	—	16	4	Tonkin, R. E.
1984	W	NSCAA		5	—	—	—	—	—	—	—			
1997		NSCAA		5	—	—	—	—	—	—	—	8	25	Fields, Terry L.
YORK (NY)														
1995	M	NCAA	III	64	—	—	—	—	—	—	—	18	7	Saint John, Ronald
1996		NCAA	III	64	—	—	—	—	—	—	—	18	10	Saint John, Ronald
1997		NCAA	III	64	—	—	—	—	—	—	—	21	6	Saint John, Ronald
YORK (PA)														
1995	M	NCAA	III	64	—	—	—	—	—	—	—	20	8	Gamber, Jeffrey L.
YOUNGSTOWN STATE														
1947	M	NAIA		32	—	—	—	—	—	—	—	12	10	Rosselli, Dominic L. "Dom"
1957		NAIA		8	—	—	—	—	—	—	—	23	4	Rosselli, Dominic L. "Dom"
1958		NAIA		8	—	—	—	—	—	—	—	24	6	Rosselli, Dominic L. "Dom"
1959		NAIA		16	—	—	—	—	—	—	—	19	9	Rosselli, Dominic L. "Dom"
1961		NCAA	II	24	—	—	—	—	—	—	—	21	7	Rosselli, Dominic L. "Dom"
1962		NCAA	II	24	—	—	—	—	—	—	—	16	12	Rosselli, Dominic L. "Dom"
1963		NCAA	II	24	—	—	—	—	—	—	—	18	9	Rosselli, Dominic L. "Dom"
1964		NCAA	II	24	—	—	—	—	—	—	—	24	3	Rosselli, Dominic L. "Dom"
1966		NCAA	II	22	—	—	—	—	—	—	—	19	7	Rosselli, Dominic L. "Dom"
1970		NCAA	II	32	—	—	—	—	—	—	—	22	5	Rosselli, Dominic L. "Dom"
1972		NCAA	II	16	—	—	—	—	—	—	—	22	7	Rosselli, Dominic L. "Dom"
1975		NCAA	II	32	—	—	—	—	—	—	—	19	9	Rosselli, Dominic L. "Dom"
1977		NCAA	II	24	—	—	—	—	—	—	—	22	7	Rosselli, Dominic L. "Dom"
1996	W	NCAA	I	64	—	—	—	—	—	—	—	20	9	DiGregorio, Edward
1998		NCAA	I	32	—	—	—	—	—	—	—	28	3	DiGregorio, Edward

School Information

This appendix provides pertinent information about each college whose men's or women's basketball team is included in this book.

SCHOOL: The school name as it is used in this book. Normally the school name is the "official" name without the word college or university. "Short-cut" names or "nicknames" are not used. See Appendix B for a cross reference to school names.

INSTITUTION NAME: The complete "official" name of the school.

CITY/ST: The city and state where the school is located.

YRS: Usually 2 or 4 to distinguish a junior/community college from a senior college. A few schools are designated U2 for upper division; at such schools, the junior and senior years only are offered.

CON: Control–Pu = Public; Pr = Private; Pp = Proprietary.

STU: Student body–C = Co-ed (male and female students); M = Male students only; W = female students only.

School	Institution Name	City	ST	YRS	CON	STD
A						
Abilene Christian	Abilene Christian University	Abilene	TX	4	Pr	C
Adams State	Adams State College	Alamosa	CO	4	Pu	C
Adelphi	Adelphi University	Garden City	NY	4	Pr	C
Adrian	Adrian College	Adrian	MI	4	Pr	C
Air Force	United States Air Force Academy	Colorado Springs	CO	4	Pu	C
Akron	University of Akron	Akron	OH	4	Pu	C
Alabama	University of Alabama	Tuscaloosa	AL	4	Pu	C
Alabama A&M	Alabama Agricultural & Mechanical University	Normal	AL	4	Pu	C
Alabama State	Alabama State University	Montgomery	AL	4	Pu	C
Alabama: Birmingham	University of Alabama at Birmingham	Birmingham	AL	4	Pu	C
Alabama: Huntsville	University of Alabama in Huntsville	Huntsville	AL	4	Pu	C
Alaska: Anchorage	University of Alaska Anchorage	Anchorage	AK	4	Pu	C
Alaska: Fairbanks	University of Alaska Fairbanks	Fairbanks	AK	4	Pu	C
Albany State (GA)	Albany State College	Albany	GA	4	Pu	C
Albany State (NY)	State University of New York at Albany	Albany	NY	4	Pu	C
Albertson	Albertson College	Caldwell	ID	4	Pr	C
Albion	Albion College	Albion	MI	4	Pr	C
Albright	Albright College	Reading	PA	4	Pr	C
Albuquerque	University of Albuquerque	Albuquerque	NM	4	Pr	C
Alcorn State	Alcorn State University	Lorman	MS	4	Pu	C
Alderson-Broaddus	Alderson-Broaddus College	Philippi	WV	4	Pr	C
Alfred	Alfred University	Alfred	NY	4	Pr	C
Alfred Holbrook	Alfred Holbrook College	Manchester	OH	4	Pr	C
Alice Lloyd	Alice Lloyd College	Pippa Passes	KY	4	Pr	C
Allegheny	Allegheny College	Meadville	PA	4	Pr	C

School	Institution Name	City	ST	YRS	CON	STD
Allentown	Allentown College of Saint Francis de Sales	Center Valley	PA	4	Pr	C
Alliance	Alliance College	Cambridge Springs	PA	4	Pr	C
Alma	Alma College	Alma	MI	4	Pr	C
Alvernia	Alvernia College	Reading	PA	4	Pr	C
American	American University	Washington	DC	4	Pr	C
American Baptist	American Baptist College	Nashville	TN	4	Pr	C
American Christian	American Christian College	Tulsa	OK	4	Pr	C
American Indian	American Indian College of the Assemblies of God	Phoenix	AZ	4	Pr	C
American International	American International College	Springfield	MA	4	Pr	C
Amherst	Amherst College	Amherst	MA	4	Pr	C
Anderson (IN)	Anderson University	Anderson	IN	4	Pr	C
Angelo State	Angelo State University	San Angelo	TX	4	Pu	C
Anna Maria	Anna Maria College	Paxton	MA	4	Pr	C
Appalachian Bible	Appalachian Bible College	Bradley	WV	4	Pr	C
Appalachian State	Appalachian State University	Boone	NC	4	Pu	C
Aquinas (MI)	Aquinas College	Grand Rapids	MI	4	Pr	C
Arizona	University of Arizona	Tucson	AZ	4	Pu	C
Arizona Bible	Arizona Bible College	Phoenix	AZ	4	Pr	C
Arizona State	Arizona State University	Tempe	AZ	4	Pu	C
Arkansas	University of Arkansas	Fayetteville	AR	4	Pu	C
Arkansas Baptist	Arkansas Baptist College	Little Rock	AR	4	Pr	C
Arkansas State	Arkansas State University	Jonesboro	AR	4	Pu	C
Arkansas Tech	Arkansas Tech University	Russellville	AR	4	Pu	C
Arkansas: Little Rock	University of Arkansas at Little Rock	Little Rock	AR	4	Pu	C
Arkansas: Monticello	University of Arkansas at Monticello	Monticello	AR	4	Pu	C
Arkansas: Pine Bluff	University of Arkansas at Pine Bluff	Pine Bluff	AR	4	Pu	C
Arlington Baptist	Arlington Baptist College	Arlington	TX	4	Pr	C
Armstrong Atlantic State	Armstrong Atlantic State University	Savannah	GA	4	Pu	C
Army	United States Military Academy	West Point	NY	4	Pu	C
Arnold	Arnold College of Physical Education	New Haven	CT			
Asheville Buncomb TCC	Asheville Buncomb Technical Community College	Asheville	NC	2	Pu	C
Ashland	Ashland University	Ashland	OH	4	Pr	C
Association Free Lutheran Bible	Association Free Lutheran Bible School	Plymouth	MN	2	Pr	C
Assumption (MA)	Assumption College	Worcester	MA	4	Pr	C
Athens State	Athens State College	Athens	AL	2-U	Pu	C
Atlanta Christian	Atlanta Christian College	East Point	GA	4	Pr	C
Auburn	Auburn University	Auburn	AL	4	Pu	C
Auburn: Montgomery	Auburn University at Montgomery	Montgomery	AL	4	Pu	C
Augsburg	Augsburg College	Minneapolis	MN	4	Pr	C
Augusta State	Augusta State University	Augusta	GA	4	Pu	C
Augustana (IL)	Augustana College	Rock Island	IL	4	Pr	C
Augustana (SD)	Augustana College	Sioux Falls	SD	4	Pr	C
Aurora	Aurora University	Aurora	IL	4	Pr	C
Austin	Austin College	Sherman	TX	4	Pr	C
Austin Peay State	Austin Peay State University	Clarksville	TN	4	Pu	C
Averett	Averett College	Danville	VA	4	Pr	C
Azusa Pacific	Azusa Pacific University	Azusa	CA	4	Pr	C

B

School	Institution Name	City	ST	YRS	CON	STD
Babson	Babson College	Babson Park	MA	4	Pr	C
Baker (KS)	Baker University	Baldwin City	KS	4	Pr	C
Baldwin-Wallace	Baldwin-Wallace College	Berea	OH	4	Pr	C
Ball State	Ball State University	Muncie	IN	4	Pu	C
Baltimore	University of Baltimore	Baltimore	MD	2-U	Pu	C
Baltimore Commerce	Baltimore College of Commerce	Baltimore	MD			C
Baptist Bible (MO)	Baptist Bible College	Springfield	MO	4	Pr	C
Baptist Bible (PA)	Baptist Bible College of Pennsylvania	Clarks Summit	PA	4	Pr	C
Baptist Christian (LA)	Baptist Christian College	Shreveport	LA	4	Pr	
Baptist University (GA)	Baptist University of America	Decatur	GA			

School	Institution Name	City	ST	YRS	CON	STD
Barber-Scotia	Barber-Scotia College	Concord	NC	4	Pr	C
Barclay	Barclay College	Haviland	KS	4	Pr	C
Barrington	Barrington College	Barrington	RI	4	Pr	C
Barry	Barry University	Miami Shores	FL	4	Pr	C
Bartlesville Wesleyan	Bartlesville Wesleyan College	Bartlesville	OK	4	Pr	C
Barton	Barton College	Wilson	NC	4	Pr	C
Bates	Bates College	Lewiston	ME	4	Pr	C
Bay Ridge Christian	Bay Ridge Christian College	Kendleton	TX	2	Pr	C
Baylor	Baylor University	Waco	TX	4	Pr	C
Belhaven	Belhaven College	Jackson	MS	4	Pr	C
Bellarmine	Bellarmine College	Louisville	KY	4	Pr	C
Bellevue (NE)	Bellevue University	Bellevue	NE	4	Pr	C
Belmont	Belmont University	Nashville	TN	4	Pr	C
Belmont Abbey	Belmont Abbey College	Belmont	NC	4	Pr	C
Beloit	Beloit College	Beloit	WI	4	Pr	C
Bemidji State	Bemidji State University	Bemidji	MN	4	Pu	C
Benedict	Benedict College	Columbia	SC	4	Pr	C
Benedictine (IL)	Illinois Benedictine College	Lisle	IL	4	Pr	C
Benedictine (KS)	Benedictine College	Atchison	KS	4	Pr	C
Bentley	Bentley College	Waltham	MA	4	Pr	C
Berea	Berea College	Berea	KY	4	Pr	C
Berry	Berry College	Mount Berry	GA	4	Pr	C
Bethany (KS)	Bethany College	Lindsborg	KS	4	Pr	C
Bethany (WV)	Bethany College	Bethany	WV	4	Pr	C
Bethel (IN)	Bethel College	Mishawaka	IN	4	Pr	C
Bethel (MN)	Bethel College	Saint Paul	MN	4	Pr	C
Bethune-Cookman	Bethune-Cookman College	Daytona Beach	FL	4	Pr	C
Bevill State CC: Brewer	Bevill State Community College: Brewer	Sumiton	AL	2	Pu	C
Binghamton State	State University of New York at Binghamton	Binghamton	NY	4	Pu	C
Biola	Biola University	La Mirada	CA	4	Pr	C
Birmingham-Southern	Birmingham-Southern College	Birmingham	AL	4	Pr	C
Bishop	Bishop College	Marshall	TX	4	Pr	C
Black Hills State	Black Hills State University	Spearfish	SD	4	Pu	C
Blackburn	Blackburn College	Carlinville	IL	4	Pr	C
Blanton's JC	Blanton's Junior College	Asheville	NC	2		
Bloomfield	Bloomfield College	Bloomfield	NJ	4	Pr	C
Bloomsburg	Bloomsburg University of Pennsylvania	Bloomsburg	PA	4	Pu	C
Bluefield (VA)	Bluefield College	Bluefield	VA	4	Pr	C
Bluefield State (WV)	Bluefield State College	Bluefield	WV	4	Pu	C
Boise State	Boise State University	Boise	ID	4	Pu	C
Boston College	Boston College	Chestnut Hill	MA	4	Pr	C
Boston University	Boston University	Boston	MA	4	Pr	C
Bowdoin	Bowdoin College	Brunswick	ME	4	Pr	C
Bowie State	Bowie State University	Bowie	MD	4	Pu	C
Bowling Green State	Bowling Green State University	Bowling Green	OH	4	Pu	C
Bradley	Bradley University	Peoria	IL	4	Pr	C
Brandeis	Brandeis University	Waltham	MA	4	Pr	C
Brandywine	Brandywine College	Wilmington	DE	2	Pr	C
Brescia	Brescia College	Owensboro	KY	4	Pr	C
Briar Cliff	Briar Cliff College	Sioux City	IA	4	Pr	C
Bridgeport	University of Bridgeport	Bridgeport	CT	4	Pr	C
Bridgewater (VA)	Bridgewater College	Bridgewater	VA	4	Pr	C
Bridgewater State (MA)	Bridgewater State College	Bridgewater	MA	4	Pu	C
Brigham Young	Brigham Young University	Provo	UT	4	Pr	C
Brigham Young: Hawaii	Brigham Young University-Hawaii	Laie	HI	4	Pr	C
Bristol (TN)	Bristol University	Bristol	TN	4	Pp	C
Brockport State	State University of New York College at Brockport	Brockport	NY	4	Pu	C
Brooklyn	City University of New York: Brooklyn College	Brooklyn	NY	4	Pu	C
Brown	Brown University	Providence	RI	4	Pr	C

School	Institution Name	City	ST	YRS	CON	STD
Bryan	Bryan College	Dayton	TN	4	Pr	C
Bryant	Bryant College	Smithfield	RI	4	Pr	C
Bryant & Stratton: Albany	Bryant & Stratton Business Institute: Albany	Albany	NY	2	Pp	C
Bryant & Stratton: Buffalo	Bryant & Stratton Business Institute: Buffalo	Buffalo	NY	2	Pp	C
Bucknell	Bucknell University	Lewisburg	PA	4	Pr	C
Buena Vista	Buena Vista College	Storm Lake	IA	4	Pr	C
Buffalo State College	State University of New York College at Buffalo	Buffalo	NY	4	Pu	C
Buffalo State University	State University of New York at Buffalo	Buffalo	NY	4	Pu	C
Bunker Hill CC	Bunker Hill Community College	Boston	MA	2	Pu	C
Butler (IN)	Butler University	Indianapolis	IN	4	Pr	C

C

School	Institution Name	City	ST	YRS	CON	STD
Cabrini	Cabrini College	Radnor	PA	4	Pr	C
Caldwell	Caldwell College	Caldwell	NJ	4	Pr	C
California	University of California: Berkeley	Berkeley	CA	4	Pu	C
California (PA)	California University of Pennsylvania	California	PA	4	Pu	C
California Baptist	California Baptist College	Riverside	CA	4	Pr	C
California Christian	California Christian College	Fresno	CA	4	Pr	C
California Lutheran	California Lutheran University	Thousand Oaks	CA	4	Pr	C
California Polytechnic: Pomona	California State Polytechnic University	Pomona	CA	4	Pu	C
California Polytechnic: San Luis Obispo	California Polytechnic State University	San Luis Obispo	CA	4	Pu	C
California State: Bakersfield	California State University: Bakersfield	Bakersfield	CA	4	Pu	C
California State: Chico	California State University: Chico	Chico	CA	4	Pu	C
California State: Dominguez Hills	California State University: Dominguez Hills	Carson	CA	4	Pu	C
California State: Fresno	California State University: Fresno	Fresno	CA	4	Pu	C
California State: Fullerton	California State University: Fullerton	Fullerton	CA	4	Pu	C
California State: Hayward	California State University: Hayward	Hayward	CA	4	Pu	C
California State: Long Beach	California State University: Long Beach	Long Beach	CA	4	Pu	C
California State: Los Angeles	California State University: Los Angeles	Los Angeles	CA	4	Pu	C
California State: Northridge	California State University: Northridge	Northridge	CA	4	Pu	C
California State: Sacramento	California State University: Sacramento	Sacramento	CA	4	Pu	C
California State: San Bernardino	California State University: San Bernardino	San Bernardino	CA	4	Pu	C
California State: Stanislaus	California State University: Stanislaus	Turlock	CA	4	Pu	C
California: Davis	University of California: Davis	Davis	CA	4	Pu	C
California: Irvine	University of California: Irvine	Irvine	CA	4	Pu	C
California: Los Angeles	University of California: Los Angeles	Los Angeles	CA	4	Pu	C
California: Riverside	University of California: Riverside	Riverside	CA	4	Pu	C
California: San Diego	University of California: San Diego	La Jolla	CA	4	Pu	C
California: Santa Barbara	University of California: Santa Barbara	Santa Barbara	CA	4	Pu	C
Calvary (KY)	Calvary Bible College	Letcher	KY	4	Pr	
Calvary Bible	Calvary Bible College	Kansas City	MO	4	Pr	C
Calvin	Calvin College	Grand Rapids	MI	4	Pr	C
Cameron	Cameron University	Lawton	OK	4	Pu	C
Campbell	Campbell University	Buies Creek	NC	4	Pr	C
Campbellsville	Campbellsville College	Campbellsville	KY	4	Pr	C
Canadian Bible	Canadian Bible College & Theological Seminary	Regina	SK	4	Pr	C
Canisius	Canisius College	Buffalo	NY	4	Pr	C
Canterbury		Danville	IN		Pr	C

School	Institution Name	City	ST	YRS	CON	STD
Capital	Capital University	Columbus	OH	4	Pr	C
Cardinal Stritch (WI)	Cardinal Stritch University	Milwaukee	WI	4	Pr	C
Carnegie Mellon	Carnegie Mellon University	Pittsburgh	PA	4	Pr	C
Carroll (MT)	Carroll College	Helena	MT	4	Pr	C
Carroll (WI)	Carroll College	Waukesha	WI	4	Pr	C
Carson-Newman	Carson-Newman College	Jefferson City	TN	4	Pr	C
Carthage	Carthage College	Kenosha	WI	4	Pr	C
Castleton State	Castleton State College	Castleton	VT	4	Pu	C
Catawba	Catawba College	Salisbury	NC	4	Pr	C
Catholic	Catholic University of America	Washington	DC	4	Pr	C
Cecils JC (NC)	Cecils College	Asheville	NC	2	Pp	C
Cedarville	Cedarville College	Cedarville	OH	4	Pr	C
Centenary (LA)	Centenary College of Louisiana	Shreveport	LA	4	Pr	C
Centenary (NJ)	Centenary College	Hackettstown	NJ	4	Pr	C
Central (IA)	Central College	Pella	IA	4	Pr	C
Central (KS)	Central College	McPherson	KS	2	Pr	C
Central Arkansas	University of Central Arkansas	Conway	AR	4	Pu	C
Central Bible	Central Bible College	Springfield	MO	4	Pr	C
Central CC: Platte	Central Community College: Platte	Columbus	NE	2	Pu	C
Central Christian (MO)	Central Christian College of the Bible	Moberly	MO	4	Pr	C
Central Connecticut State	Central Connecticut State University	New Britain	CT	4	Pu	C
Central Florida	University of Central Florida	Orlando	FL	4	Pu	C
Central Indian Bible	Central Indian Bible College	Mobridge	SD	2	Pr	C
Central Maine Tech	Central Maine Technical College	Auburn	ME	2	Pu	C
Central Methodist	Central Methodist College	Fayette	MO	4	Pr	C
Central Michigan	Central Michigan University	Mount Pleasant	MI	4	Pu	C
Central Missouri State	Central Missouri State University	Warrensburg	MO	4	Pu	C
Central Oklahoma	University of Central Oklahoma	Edmond	OK	4	Pu	C
Central State (OH)	Central State University	Wilberforce	OH	4	Pu	C
Central Washington	Central Washington University	Ellensburg	WA	4	Pu	C
Centre	Centre College	Danville	KY	4	Pr	C
Chadron State	Chadron State College	Chadron	NE	4	Pu	C
Chaminade	Chaminade University of Honolulu	Honolulu	HI	4	Pr	C
Chapman	Chapman University	Orange	CA	4	Pr	C
Charleston (SC)	College of Charleston	Charleston	SC	4	Pu	C
Charleston (WV)	University of Charleston	Charleston	WV	4	Pr	C
Charleston Southern	Charleston Southern University	Charleston	SC	4	Pr	C
Cheyney	Cheyney University of Pennsylvania	Cheyney	PA	4	Pu	C
Chicago	University of Chicago	Chicago	IL	4	Pr	C
Chicago State	Chicago State University	Chicago	IL	4	Pu	C
Christian Brothers	Christian Brothers University	Memphis	TN	4	Pr	C
Christian Heritage	Christian Heritage College	El Cajon	CA	4	Pr	C
Christopher Newport	Christopher Newport University	Newport News	VA	4	Pu	C
Cincinnati	University of Cincinnati	Cincinnati	OH	4	Pu	C
Cincinnati Bible	Cincinnati Bible College & Seminary	Cincinnati	OH	4	Pr	C
Circleville Bible	Circleville Bible College	Circleville	OH	4	Pr	C
City College	City University of New York: City College	New York	NY	4	Pu	C
Claflin	Claflin College	Orangeburg	SC	4	Pr	C
Claremont McKenna	Claremont McKenna College	Claremont	CA	4	Pr	C
Clarendon	Clarendon College	Clarendon	TX	2	Pu	C
Clarion	Clarion University of Pennsylvania	Clarion	PA	4	Pu	C
Clark (MA)	Clark University	Worcester	MA	4	Pr	C
Clark Atlanta	Clark Atlanta University	Atlanta	GA	4	Pr	C
Clarke (IA)	Clarke College	Dubuque	IA	4	Pr	C
Clarkson (NY)	Clarkson University	Potsdam	NY	4	Pr	C
Clayton State	Clayton College & State University	Morrow	GA	4	Pu	C
Clearwater Christian	Clearwater Christian College	Clearwater	FL	4	Pr	C
Clemson	Clemson University	Clemson	SC	4	Pu	C
Cleveland State (OH)	Cleveland State University	Cleveland	OH	4	Pu	C
Clinch Valley	Clinch Valley College of the University of Virginia	Wise	VA	4	Pu	C
Coast Guard	United States Coast Guard Academy	New London	CT	4	Pu	C
Coastal Carolina	Coastal Carolina University	Conway	SC	4	Pu	C

School	Institution Name	City	ST	YRS	CON	STD
Coe	Coe College	Cedar Rapids	IA	4	Pr	C
Colby	Colby College	Waterville	ME	4	Pr	C
Colby-Sawyer	Colby-Sawyer College	New London	NH	4	Pr	C
Colgate	Colgate University	Hamilton	NY	4	Pr	C
Colorado	University of Colorado at Boulder	Boulder	CO	4	Pu	C
Colorado Christian	Colorado Christian University	Denver	CO	4	Pr	C
Colorado College	Colorado College	Colorado Springs	CO	4	Pr	C
Colorado Northwestern CC	Colorado Northwestern Community College	Rangely	CO	2	Pu	C
Colorado State	Colorado State University	Fort Collins	CO	4	Pu	C
Colorado Woman's	Colorado Woman's College	Denver	CO	4	Pr	W
Columbia (MO)	Columbia College	Columbia	MO	4	Pr	C
Columbia (NY)	Columbia University	New York	NY	4	Pr	C
Columbia (SC)	Columbia College	Columbia	SC	4	Pr	W
Columbia Bible	Columbia Bible College	Clearbrook	BC			
Columbia Christian	Columbia Christian College	Portland	OR		Pr	
Columbia JC (SC)	Columbia Junior College of Business	Columbia	SC	2	Pp	C
Columbia State CC	Columbia State Community College	Columbia	TN	2	Pu	C
Columbia Union	Columbia Union College	Takoma Park	MD	4	Pr	C
Columbus Business (OH)	Columbus Business University	Columbus	OH			
Columbus State (GA)	Columbus State University	Columbus	GA	4	Pu	C
Concord	Concord College	Athens	WV	4	Pu	C
Concordia (CA)	Concordia University	Irvine	CA	4	Pr	C
Concordia (IL)	Concordia University	River Forest	IL	4	Pr	C
Concordia (MI)	Concordia College	Ann Arbor	MI	4	Pr	C
Concordia (NE)	Concordia Teachers College	Seward	NE	4	Pr	C
Concordia (OR)	Concordia College	Portland	OR	4	Pr	C
Concordia (WI)	Concordia University Wisconsin	Mequon	WI	4	Pr	C
Concordia: Austin	Concordia University at Austin	Austin	TX	4	Pr	C
Concordia: Moorhead	Concordia College: Moorhead	Moorhead	MN	4	Pr	C
Concordia: Saint Paul	Concordia College: Saint Paul	Saint Paul	MN	4	Pr	C
Connecticut	University of Connecticut	Storrs	CT	4	Pu	C
Connecticut College	Connecticut College	New London	CT	4	Pr	C
Coppin State	Coppin State College	Baltimore	MD	4	Pu	C
Cornell (IA)	Cornell College	Mount Vernon	IA	4	Pr	C
Cornell (NY)	Cornell University	Ithaca	NY	4	Pr	C
Cornerstone	Cornerstone College & Grand Rapids Baptist Seminary	Grand Rapids	MI	4	Pr	C
Cortland State	State University of New York College at Cortland	Cortland	NY	4	Pu	C
Covenant	Covenant College	Lookout Mountain	GA	4	Pr	C
Creighton	Creighton University	Omaha	NE	4	Pr	C
Crowley's Ridge	Crowley's Ridge College	Paragould	AR	2	Pr	C
Crown (MN)	Crown College	Saint Bonifacius	MN	4	Pr	C
Crown (TN)	Crown College	Powell	TN		Pr	
Cullman	Cullman College	Saint Bernard	AL			
Culver-Stockton	Culver-Stockton College	Canton	MO	4	Pr	C
Cumberland (KY)	Cumberland College	Williamsburg	KY	4	Pr	C
Cumberland (TN)	Cumberland University of Tennessee	Lebanon	TN	4	Pr	C

D

School	Institution Name	City	ST	YRS	CON	STD
D'Youville	D'Youville College	Buffalo	NY	4	Pr	C
Daemen	Daemen College	Amherst	NY	4	Pr	C
Dakota State	Dakota State University	Madison	SD	4	Pu	C
Dakota Wesleyan	Dakota Wesleyan University	Mitchell	SD	4	Pr	C
Dallas Baptist	Dallas Baptist University	Dallas	TX	4	Pr	C
Dallas Christian	Dallas Christian College	Dallas	TX	4	Pr	C
Dartmouth	Dartmouth College	Hanover	NH	4	Pr	C
David N Myers	David N Myers College	Cleveland	OH	4	Pr	C
Davidson	Davidson College	Davidson	NC	4	Pr	C
Davis (OH)	Davis College	Toledo	OH	2	Pp	C
Davis & Elkins	Davis & Elkins College	Elkins	WV	4	Pr	C
Dayton	University of Dayton	Dayton	OH	4	Pr	C

School	Institution Name	City	ST	YRS	CON	STD
De Paul	De Paul University	Chicago	IL	4	Pr	C
Defiance	Defiance College, The	Defiance	OH	4	Pr	C
Delaware	University of Delaware	Newark	DE	4	Pr	C
Delta State	Delta State University	Cleveland	MS	4	Pu	C
Denison	Denison University	Granville	OH	4	Pr	C
Denmark Tech	Denmark Technical College	Denmark	SC	2	Pu	C
Denver	University of Denver	Denver	CO	4	Pr	C
DePauw	DePauw University	Greencastle	IN	4	Pr	C
Detroit	University of Detroit	Detroit	MI	4	Pr	C
Detroit Mercy	University of Detroit Mercy	Detroit	MI	4	Pr	C
Dickinson (PA)	Dickinson College	Carlisle	PA	4	Pr	C
Dickinson State (ND)	Dickinson State University	Dickinson	ND	4	Pu	C
Dillard	Dillard University	New Orleans	LA	4	Pr	C
District of Columbia	University of the District of Columbia	Washington	DC	4	Pu	C
Doane	Doane College	Crete	NE	4	Pr	C
Dominican (CA)	Dominican College of San Rafael	San Rafael	CA	4	Pr	C
Dominican (IL)	Dominican College	River Forest	IL	4	Pr	C
Dominican (NY)	Dominican College of Blauvelt	Orangeburg	NY	4	Pr	C
Dordt	Dordt College	Sioux Center	IA	4	Pr	C
Dowling	Dowling College	Oakdale	NY	4	Pr	C
Dr. Martin Luther	Dr. Martin Luther College	New Ulm	MN	4	Pr	C
Drake (IA)	Drake University	Des Moines	IA	4	Pr	C
Draughons JC: Kingsport	Draughons Junior College of Business: Kingsport	Kingsport	TN	2	Pp	C
Draughons JC: Knoxville	Draughons Junior College of Business: Knoxville	Knoxville	TN	2	Pp	C
Drexel	Drexel University	Philadelphia	PA	5	Pr	C
Drury	Drury College	Springfield	MO	4	Pr	C
Dubuque	University of Dubuque	Dubuque	IA	4	Pr	C
Duff's Business	Duff's Business Institute	Pittsburgh	PA	2	Pp	
Duke	Duke University	Durham	NC	4	Pr	C
Duquesne	Duquesne University	Pittsburgh	PA	4	Pr	C
Durham Business	Durham Business College	Durham	NC	2	Pp	C

E

School	Institution Name	City	ST	YRS	CON	STD
Earlham	Earlham College	Richmond	IN	4	Pr	C
East Carolina	East Carolina University	Greenville	NC	4	Pu	C
East Central (OK)	East Central University	Ada	OK	4	Pu	C
East Coast Bible	East Coast Bible College	Charlotte	NC	4	Pr	C
East Mississippi CC	East Mississippi Community College	Scooba	MS	2	Pu	C
East Stroudsburg	East Stroudsburg University of Pennsylvania	East Stroudsburg	PA	4	Pu	C
East Tennessee State	East Tennessee State University	Johnson City	TN	4	Pu	C
East Texas Baptist	East Texas Baptist University	Marshall	TX	4	Pr	C
Eastern (PA)	Eastern College	Saint Davids	PA	4	Pr	C
Eastern Connecticut State	Eastern Connecticut State University	Willimantic	CT	4	Pu	C
Eastern Illinois	Eastern Illinois University	Charleston	IL	4	Pu	C
Eastern Kentucky	Eastern Kentucky University	Richmond	KY	4	Pu	C
Eastern Maine Tech	Eastern Maine Technical College	Bangor	ME	2	Pu	C
Eastern Mennonite	Eastern Mennonite University	Harrisonburg	VA	4	Pr	C
Eastern Michigan	Eastern Michigan University	Ypsilanti	MI	4	Pu	C
Eastern Nazarene	Eastern Nazarene College	Quincy	MA	4	Pr	C
Eastern New Mexico	Eastern New Mexico University	Portales	NM	4	Pu	C
Eastern Oregon	Eastern Oregon University	LaGrande	OR	4	Pu	C
Eastern Washington	Eastern Washington University	Cheney	WA	4	Pu	C
Eckerd	Eckerd College	Saint Petersburg	FL	4	Pr	C
Edgewood	Edgewood College	Madison	WI	4	Pr	C
Edinboro	Edinboro University of Pennsylvania	Edinboro	PA	4	Pu	C
Elizabeth City State	Elizabeth City State University	Elizabeth City	NC	4	Pu	C
Elizabeth Seton	Elizabeth Seton College of Iona	Yonkers	NY	2	Pr	C
Elizabethtown	Elizabethtown College	Elizabethtown	PA	4	Pr	C
Elmhurst	Elmhurst College	Elmhurst	IL	4	Pr	C
Elmira	Elmira College	Elmira	NY	4	Pr	C

School	Institution Name	City	ST	YRS	CON	STD
Elon	Elon College	Elon College	NC	4	Pr	C
Embry-Riddle (FL)	Embry-Riddle Aeronautical University	Daytona Beach	FL	4	Pr	C
Emerson	Emerson College	Boston	MA	4	Pr	C
Emmanuel (GA)	Emmanuel College	Franklin Springs	GA	4	Pr	C
Emmanuel (MA)	Emmanuel College	Boston	MA	4	Pr	W
Emmaus Bible	Emmaus Bible College	Dubuque	IA	4	Pr	C
Emory	Emory University	Atlanta	GA	4	Pr	C
Emory & Henry	Emory & Henry College	Emory	VA	4	Pr	C
Emporia State	Emporia State University	Emporia	KS	4	Pu	C
Erskine	Erskine College	Due West	SC	4	Pr	C
Eureka	Eureka College	Eureka	IL	4	Pr	C
Evangel	Evangel College	Springfield	MO	4	Pr	C
Evansville	University of Evansville	Evansville	IN	4	Pr	C

F

School	Institution Name	City	ST	YRS	CON	STD
Fairfield	Fairfield University	Fairfield	CT	4	Pr	C
Fairleigh Dickinson: Madison	Fairleigh Dickinson University: Madison	Madison	NJ	4	Pr	C
Fairleigh Dickinson: Rutherford/Teaneck	Fairleigh Dickinson University: Rutherford/Teaneck	Rutherford	NJ	4	Pr	C
Fairleigh Dickinson: Teaneck	Fairleigh Dickinson University: Teaneck	Teaneck	NJ	4	Pr	C
Fairmont State	Fairmont State College	Fairmont	WV	4	Pu	C
Faith Baptist Bible (IA)	Faith Baptist Bible College & Theological Seminary	Ankeny	IA	4	Pr	C
Faulkner	Faulkner University	Montgomery	AL	4	Pr	C
Fayetteville State	Fayetteville State University	Fayetteville	NC	4	Pu	C
Federal City	Federal City College	Washington	DC	4	Pu	C
Ferris State	Ferris State University	Big Rapids	MI	4	Pu	C
Ferrum	Ferrum College	Ferrum	VA	4	Pr	C
Findlay	University of Findlay	Findlay	OH	4	Pr	C
Fisk	Fisk University	Nashville	TN	4	Pr	C
Florida	University of Florida	Gainesville	FL	4	Pu	C
Florida A&M	Florida Agricultural & Mechanical University	Tallahassee	FL	4	Pu	C
Florida Atlantic	Florida Atlantic University	Boca Raton	FL	4	Pu	C
Florida Christian	Florida Christian College	Kissimmee	FL	4	Pr	C
Florida College	Florida College	Temple Terrace	FL	2	Pr	C
Florida International	Florida International University	Miami	FL	4	Pu	C
Florida Memorial	Florida Memorial College	Miami	FL	4	Pr	C
Florida Southern	Florida Southern College	Lakeland	FL	4	Pr	C
Florida State	Florida State University	Tallahassee	FL	4	Pu	C
Florida Tech	Florida Institute of Technology	Melbourne	FL	4	Pr	C
Fontbonne	Fontbonne College	Saint Louis	MO	4	Pr	C
Fordham	Fordham University	Bronx	NY	4	Pr	C
Fort Hays State	Fort Hays State University	Hays	KS	4	Pu	C
Fort Lauderdale	Fort Lauderdale College	Fort Lauderdale	FL	4	Pp	C
Fort Lewis	Fort Lewis College	Durango	CO	4	Pu	C
Fort Valley State	Fort Valley State College	Fort Valley	GA	4	Pu	C
Framingham State	Framingham State College	Framingham	MA	4	Pu	C
Francis Marion	Francis Marion University	Florence	SC	4	Pu	C
Franciscan	Franciscan University of Steubenville	Steubenville	OH	4	Pr	C
Franklin & Marshall	Franklin & Marshall College	Lancaster	PA	4	Pr	C
Franklin (IN)	Franklin College	Franklin	IN	4	Pr	C
Franklin Pierce	Franklin Pierce College	Rindge	NH	4	Pr	C
Fredonia State	State University College of New York at Fredonia	Fredonia	NY	4	Pu	C
Free Will Baptist Bible	Free Will Baptist Bible College	Nashville	TN	4	Pr	C
Freed-Hardeman	Freed-Hardeman University	Henderson	TN	4	Pr	C
Freeman JC	Freeman Junior College	Freeman	SD	2		C
Fresno Pacific	Fresno Pacific College	Fresno	CA	4	Pr	C
Friends	Friends University	Wichita	KS	4	Pr	C
Friendship JC	Friendship Junior College	Rock Hill	SC	2		
Frostburg State	Frostburg State College	Frostburg	MD	4	Pu	C
Furman	Furman University	Greenville	SC	4	Pr	C

School	Institution Name	City	ST	YRS	CON	STD
G						
Gallaudet	Gallaudet University	Washington	DC	4	Pr	C
Ganado	Ganado College	Ganado	AZ			
Gannon	Gannon University	Erie	PA	4	Pr	C
Gardner-Webb	Gardner-Webb University	Boiling Springs	NC	4	Pr	C
Geneseo State	State University of New York College at Geneseo	Geneseo	NY	4	Pu	C
Geneva	Geneva College	Beaver Falls	PA	4	Pr	C
George Fox	George Fox College	Newberg	OR	4	Pr	C
George Mason	George Mason University	Fairfax	VA	4	Pu	C
George Washington	George Washington University	Washington	DC	4	Pr	C
George Williams	George Williams College	Downers Grove	IL		Pr	
Georgetown (DC)	Georgetown University	Washington	DC	4	Pr	C
Georgetown (KY)	Georgetown College	Georgetown	KY	4	Pr	C
Georgia	University of Georgia	Athens	GA	4	Pu	C
Georgia College	Georgia College	Milledgeville	GA	4	Pu	C
Georgia Military	Georgia Military College	Milledgeville	GA	2	Pu	M
Georgia Southern	Georgia Southern University	Statesboro	GA	4	Pu	C
Georgia Southwestern	Georgia Southwestern State University	Americus	GA	4	Pu	C
Georgia State	Georgia State University	Atlanta	GA	4	Pu	C
Georgia Tech	Georgia Institute of Technology	Atlanta	GA	4	Pu	C
Georgian Court	Georgian Court College	Lakewood	NJ	4	Pr	W
Gettysburg	Gettysburg College	Gettysburg	PA	4	Pr	C
Glenville State	Glenville State College	Glenville	WV	4	Pu	C
Gonzaga	Gonzaga University	Spokane	WA	4	Pr	C
Gordon (MA)	Gordon College	Wenham	MA	4	Pr	C
Goucher	Goucher College	Baltimore	MD	4	Pr	C
Grace (IN)	Grace College	Winona Lake	IN	4	Pr	C
Grace (NE)	Grace University	Omaha	NE	4	Pr	C
Grace Bible (MI)	Grace Bible College	Grand Rapids	MI	4	Pr	C
Graceland (IN)	Graceland University	New Albany	IN			
Grambling State	Grambling State University	Grambling	LA	4	Pu	C
Grand Canyon	Grand Canyon University	Phoenix	AZ	4	Pr	C
Grand Rapids Baptist	Grand Rapids Baptist Bible College	Grand Rapids	MI		Pr	
Grand Rapids Bible & Music	Grand Rapids School of the Bible & Music	Grand Rapids	MI		Pr	
Grand Valley State	Grand Valley State University	Allendale	MI	4	Pu	C
Grand View	Grand View College	Des Moines	IA	4	Pr	C
Great Falls	University of Great Falls	Great Falls	MT	4	Pr	C
Green Mountain	Green Mountain College	Poultney	VT	4	Pr	C
Greensboro	Greensboro College	Greensboro	NC	4	Pr	C
Greenville	Greenville College	Greenville	IL	4	Pr	C
Grinnell	Grinnell College	Grinnell	IA	4	Pr	C
Grove City	Grove City College	Grove City	PA	4	Pr	C
Guilford	Guilford College	Greensboro	NC	4	Pr	C
Gulf Coast Christian	Gulf Coast Christian College	Plaquemine	LA			
Gustavus Adolphus	Gustavus Adolphus College	Saint Peter	MN	4	Pr	C
H						
Hamilton	Hamilton College	Clinton	NY	4	Pr	C
Hamline	Hamline University	Saint Paul	MN	4	Pr	C
Hampden-Sydney	Hampden-Sydney College	Hampden-Sydney	VA	4	Pr	M
Hampton	Hampton University	Hampton	VA	4	Pr	C
Hannibal-LaGrange	Hannibal-LaGrange College	Hannibal	MO	4	Pr	C
Hanover	Hanover College	Hanover	IN	4	Pr	C
Hardin-Simmons	Hardin-Simmons University	Abilene	TX	4	Pr	C
Harding	Harding University	Searcy	AR	4	Pr	C
Hartford	University of Hartford	West Hartford	CT	4	Pr	C
Hartwick	Hartwick College	Oneonta	NY	4	Pr	C
Harvard	Harvard University	Cambridge	MA	4	Pr	C
Hastings	Hastings College	Hastings	NE	4	Pr	C
Hawaii	University of Hawaii at Manoa	Honolulu	HI	4	Pu	C
Hawaii Pacific	Hawaii Pacific University	Honolulu	HI	4	Pr	C
Hawaii Pacific: Loa	Hawaii Pacific University: Loa	Kaneohe	HI			

School	Institution Name	City	ST	YRS	CON	STD
Hawaii: Hilo	University of Hawaii at Hilo	Hilo	HI	4	Pu	C
Heidelberg	Heidelberg College	Tiffin	OH	4	Pr	C
Henderson State	Henderson State University	Arkadelphia	AR	4	Pu	C
Hendrix	Hendrix College	Conway	AR	4	Pr	C
Hesser	Hesser College	Manchester	NH	2	Pp	C
High Point	High Point University	High Point	NC	4	Pr	C
Hillsdale	Hillsdale College	Hillsdale	MI	4	Pr	C
Hillsdale Free Will Baptist	Hillsdale Free Will Baptist College	Moore	OK	4	Pr	C
Hiram	Hiram College	Hiram	OH	4	Pr	C
Hofstra	Hofstra University	Hempstead	NY	4	Pr	C
Holy Cross (MA)	College of the Holy Cross	Worcester	MA	4	Pr	C
Holy Family (PA)	Holy Family College	Philadelphia	PA	4	Pr	C
Holy Names (CA)	Holy Names College	Oakland	CA	4	Pr	C
Hope	Hope College	Holland	MI	4	Pr	C
Houghton	Houghton College	Houghton	NY	4	Pr	C
Houston	University of Houston	Houston	TX	4	Pu	C
Houston Baptist	Houston Baptist University	Houston	TX	4	Pr	C
Howard (DC)	Howard University	Washington	DC	4	Pr	C
Howard Payne	Howard Payne University	Brownwood	TX	4	Pr	C
Humboldt State	Humboldt State University	Arcata	CA	4	Pu	C
Hunter	City University of New York: Hunter College	New York	NY	4	Pu	C
Huntingdon	Huntingdon College	Montgomery	AL	4	Pr	C
Huntington	Huntington College	Huntington	IN	4	Pr	C
Huron	Huron University	Huron	SD	4	Pp	C
Husson	Husson College	Bangor	ME	4	Pr	C
Huston-Tillotson	Huston-Tillotson College	Austin	TX	4	Pr	C

I

School	Institution Name	City	ST	YRS	CON	STD
Idaho	University of Idaho	Moscow	ID	4	Pu	C
Idaho State	Idaho State University	Pocatello	ID	4	Pu	C
Illinois	University of Illinois at Urbana-Champaign	Urbana	IL	4	Pu	C
Illinois State	Illinois State University	Normal	IL	4	Pu	C
Illinois Wesleyan	Illinois Wesleyan University	Bloomington	IL	4	Pr	C
Illinois: Chicago	University of Illinois at Chicago	Chicago	IL	4	Pu	C
Illinois: Springfield	University of Illinois at Springfield	Springfield	IL	2-U	Pu	C
Immaculata (PA)	Immaculata College	Immaculata	PA	4	Pr	W
Incarnate Word	Incarnate Word College	San Antonio	TX	4	Pr	C
Indiana	Indiana University: Bloomington	Bloomington	IN	4	Pu	C
Indiana (PA)	Indiana University of Pennsylvania	Indiana	PA	4	Pu	C
Indiana State	Indiana State University	Terre Haute	IN	4	Pu	C
Indiana Tech	Indiana Institute of Technology	Fort Wayne	IN	4	Pr	C
Indiana Wesleyan	Indiana Wesleyan University	Marion	IN	4	Pr	C
Indiana: South Bend	Indiana University South Bend	South Bend	IN	4	Pu	C
Indiana: Southeast	Indiana University-Southeast	New Albany	IN	4	Pu	C
Indiana-Purdue: Fort Wayne	Indiana University—Purdue University Fort Wayne	Fort Wayne	IN	4	Pu	C
Indiana-Purdue: Indianapolis	Indiana University—Purdue University Indianapolis	Indianapolis	IN	4	Pu	C
Indianapolis	University of Indianapolis	Indianapolis	IN	4	Pr	C
Iona	Iona College	New Rochelle	NY	4	Pr	C
Iowa	University of Iowa	Iowa City	IA	4	Pu	C
Iowa State	Iowa State University	Ames	IA	4	Pu	C
Iowa Wesleyan	Iowa Wesleyan College	Mount Pleasant	IA	4	Pr	C
Ithaca	Ithaca College	Ithaca	NY	4	Pr	C

J

School	Institution Name	City	ST	YRS	CON	STD
Jackson State (MS)	Jackson State University	Jackson	MS	4	Pu	C
Jacksonville (FL)	Jacksonville University	Jacksonville	FL	4	Pr	C
Jacksonville State (AL)	Jacksonville State University	Jacksonville	AL	4	Pu	C
James Madison	James Madison University	Harrisonburg	VA	4	Pu	C
Jamestown	Jamestown College	Jamestown	ND	4	Pr	C

School	Institution Name	City	ST	YRS	CON	STD
Jersey City State	Jersey City State College	Jersey City	NJ	4	Pu	C
Jimmy Swaggart Bible	Jimmy Swaggart Bible College & Seminary	Baton Rouge	LA	4	Pr	C
John Brown	John Brown University	Siloam Springs	AR	4	Pr	C
John Carroll	John Carroll University	University Heights	OH	4	Pr	C
John F Kennedy (NE)	John F Kennedy College	Wahoo	NE	4		C
Johns Hopkins	Johns Hopkins University	Baltimore	MD	4	Pr	C
Johnson Bible	Johnson Bible College	Knoxville	TN	4	Pr	C
Johnson C Smith	Johnson C Smith University	Charlotte	NC	4	Pr	C
Jordan College & Seminary	Jordan College & Seminary	Cedar Springs	MI	4	Pr	C
Jordan: Detroit	Jordan College: Tower Center	Detroit	MI	4	Pr	C
Jordan: Flint	Jordan College: Flint	Flint	MI	4	Pr	C
Josephinum	Pontifical College Josephinum	Columbus	OH	4	Pr	M
Judson (IL)	Judson College	Elgin	IL	4	Pr	C
Judson Baptist (OR)	Judson Baptist College	The Dalles	OR	4	Pr	C
Juniata	Juniata College	Huntingdon	PA	4	Pr	C

K

School	Institution Name	City	ST	YRS	CON	STD
Kalamazoo	Kalamazoo College	Kalamazoo	MI	4	Pr	C
Kansas	University of Kansas	Lawrence	KS	4	Pu	C
Kansas Newman	Kansas Newman College	Wichita	KS	4	Pr	C
Kansas State	Kansas State University	Manhattan	KS	4	Pu	C
Kansas Wesleyan	Kansas Wesleyan University	Salina	KS	4	Pr	C
Kean	Kean College of New Jersey	Union	NJ	4	Pu	C
Keene State	Keene State College	Keene	NH	4	Pu	C
Kennesaw State	Kennesaw State College	Marietta	GA	4	Pu	C
Kent State	Kent State University	Kent	OH	4	Pu	C
Kentucky	University of Kentucky	Lexington	KY	4	Pu	C
Kentucky Christian	Kentucky Christian College	Grayson	KY	4	Pr	C
Kentucky State	Kentucky State University	Frankfort	KY	4	Pu	C
Kentucky Wesleyan	Kentucky Wesleyan College	Owensboro	KY	4	Pr	C
Kenyon	Kenyon College	Gambier	OH	4	Pr	C
King (TN)	King College	Bristol	TN	4	Pr	C
King's (NY)	King's College, The	Briarcliff Manor	NY	4	Pr	C
King's (PA)	King's College	Wilkes-Barre	PA	4	Pr	C
Kittrell JC	Kittrell College	Kittrell	NC	2	Pr	C
Knox	Knox College	Galesburg	IL	4	Pr	C
Knoxville	Knoxville College	Knoxville	TN	4	Pr	C
Kutztown	Kutztown University of Pennsylvania	Kutztown	PA	4	Pu	C

L

School	Institution Name	City	ST	YRS	CON	STD
La Roche	La Roche College	Pittsburgh	PA	4	Pr	C
La Salle	La Salle University	Philadelphia	PA	4	Pr	C
La Verne	University of La Verne	La Verne	CA	4	Pr	C
Lafayette (NC)	Lafayette College	Fayetteville	NC	2	Pp	
Lafayette (PA)	Lafayette College	Easton	PA	4	Pr	C
Lake Forest	Lake Forest College	Lake Forest	IL	4	Pr	C
Lake Superior State	Lake Superior State University	Sault Ste. Marie	MI	4	Pu	C
Lakeland (WI)	Lakeland College	Sheboygan	WI	4	Pr	C
Lamar	Lamar University-Beaumont	Beaumont	TX	4	Pu	C
Lamar CC	Lamar Community College	Lamar	CO	2	Pu	C
Lancaster Bible	Lancaster Bible College	Lancaster	PA	4	Pr	C
Lander	Lander University	Greenwood	SC	4	Pu	C
Landmark Baptist (FL)	Landmark Baptist College	Haines City	FL	4	Pr	C
Lane (TN)	Lane College	Jackson	TN	4	Pr	C
Langston	Langston University	Langston	OK	4	Pu	C
Latin American Bible (CA)	Latin American Bible Institute	LaPuente	CA	4	Pr	C
Latter-Day Saints Business	Latter-Day Saints Business College	Salt Lake City	UT	2	Pr	C
Lawrence	Lawrence University	Appleton	WI	4	Pr	C
Lawrence Tech	Lawrence Technological University	Southfield	MI	4	Pr	C
Le Moyne	Le Moyne College	Syracuse	NY	4	Pr	C
Lebanon Valley	Lebanon Valley College of Pennsylvania	Annville	PA	4	Pr	C

School	Institution Name	City	ST	YRS	CON	STD
Lee (TN)	Lee University	Cleveland	TN	4	Pr	C
Lees (KY)	Lees College	Jackson	KY	2	Pr	C
Lees-McRae	Lees-McRae College	Banner Elk	NC	4	Pr	C
Lehigh	Lehigh University	Bethlehem	PA	4	Pr	C
Lehman	City University of New York: Lehman College	Bronx	NY	4	Pu	C
LeMoyne-Owen	LeMoyne-Owen College	Memphis	TN	4	Pr	C
Lenoir-Rhyne	Lenoir-Rhyne College	Hickory	NC	4	Pr	C
LeTourneau	LeTourneau University	Longview	TX	4	Pr	C
Lewis & Clark (OR)	Lewis & Clark College	Portland	OR	4	Pr	C
Lewis (IL)	Lewis University	Romeoville	IL	4	Pr	C
Lewis-Clark State (ID)	Lewis-Clark State College	Lewiston	ID	4	Pu	C
Liberty	Liberty University	Lynchburg	VA	4	Pr	C
Life (GA)	Life University	Marietta	GA	4	Pr	C
LIFE Bible (CA)	LIFE Bible College	San Dimas	CA	4	Pr	C
Lincoln (MO)	Lincoln University	Jefferson City	MO	4	Pu	C
Lincoln (PA)	Lincoln University	Lincoln University	PA	4	Pr	C
Lincoln Christian	Lincoln Christian College & Seminary	Lincoln	IL	4	Pr	C
Lincoln Memorial	Lincoln Memorial University	Harrogate	TN	4	Pr	C
Lindenwood	Lindenwood College	Saint Charles	MO	4	Pr	C
Lindsey Wilson	Lindsey Wilson College	Columbia	KY	4	Pr	C
Linfield	Linfield College	McMinnville	OR	4	Pr	C
Lipscomb	Lipscomb College	Nashville	TN	4	Pr	C
Lock Haven	Lock Haven University of Pennsylvania	Lock Haven	PA	4	Pu	C
Logan Chiropractic	Logan College of Chiropractic, Inc.	Chesterfield	MO	4	Pr	C
Long Island	Long Island University: Brooklyn Campus	Brooklyn	NY	4	Pr	C
Long Island: C W Post	Long Island University: C W Post Campus	Brookville	NY	4	Pr	C
Long Island: Southampton	Long Island University: Southampton Campus	Southhampton	NY	4	Pr	C
Longwood	Longwood College	Farmville	VA	4	Pu	C
Loras	Loras College	Dubuque	IA	4	Pr	C
Louisiana Christian	Louisiana College	Pineville	LA	4	Pr	C
Louisiana Christian	Louisiana Christian University	Sunset	LA			
Louisiana State	Louisiana State University & Agricultural & Mechanical College	Baton Rouge	LA	4	Pu	C
Louisiana Tech	Louisiana Tech University	Ruston	LA	4	Pu	C
Louisville	University of Louisville	Louisville	KY	4	Pu	C
Loyola (IL)	Loyola University of Chicago	Chicago	IL	4	Pr	C
Loyola (MD)	Loyola College in Maryland	Baltimore	MD	4	Pr	C
Loyola Marymount	Loyola Marymount University	Los Angeles	CA	4	Pr	C
Loyola New Orleans	Loyola University New Orleans	New Orleans	LA	4	Pr	C
Luther	Luther College	Decorah	IA	4	Pr	C
Lycoming	Lycoming College	Williamsport	PA	4	Pr	C
Lynchburg	Lynchburg College	Lynchburg	VA	4	Pr	C
Lynn	Lynn University	Boca Raton	FL	4	Pr	C
Lyon	Lyon College	Batesville	AR	4	Pr	C

M

School	Institution Name	City	ST	YRS	CON	STD
MacMurray	MacMurray College	Jacksonville	IL	4	Pr	C
Madonna	Madonna University	Livonia	MI	4	Pr	C
Maine	University of Maine	Orono	ME	4	Pu	C
Maine: Augusta	University of Maine at Augusta	Augusta	ME	4	Pu	C
Maine: Farmington	University of Maine at Farmington	Farmington	ME	4	Pu	C
Maine: Fort Kent	University of Maine at Fort Kent	Fort Kent	ME	4	Pu	C
Maine: Machias	University of Maine at Machias	Machias	ME	4	Pu	C
Malone	Malone College	Canton	OH	4	Pr	C
Manchester	Manchester College	North Manchester	IN	4	Pr	C
Manhattan	Manhattan College	Riverdale	NY	4	Pr	C
Manhattan Christian	Manhattan Christian College	Manhattan	KS	4	Pr	C
Manhattanville	Manhattanville College	Purchase	NY	4	Pr	C
Mankato State	Mankato State University	Mankato	MN	4	Pu	C

School	Institution Name	City	ST	YRS	CON	STD
Mansfield	Mansfield University of Pennsylvania	Mansfield	PA	4	Pu	C
Maranatha Baptist Bible (WI)	Maranatha Baptist Bible College	Watertown	WI	4	Pr	C
Marian (IN)	Marian College	Indianapolis	IN	4	Pr	C
Marietta	Marietta College	Marietta	OH	4	Pr	C
Marist	Marist College	Poughkeepsie	NY	4	Pr	C
Marquette	Marquette University	Milwaukee	WI	4	Pr	C
Mars Hill	Mars Hill College	Mars Hill	NC	4	Pr	C
Marshall	Marshall University	Huntington	WV	4	Pu	C
Martin Methodist	Martin Methodist College	Pulaski	TN	4	Pr	C
Mary	University of Mary	Bismarck	ND	4	Pr	C
Mary Hardin-Baylor	University of Mary Hardin-Baylor	Belton	TX	4	Pr	C
Mary Washington	Mary Washington College	Fredericksburg	VA	4	Pu	C
Marycrest International	Marycrest International	Davenport	IA	4	Pr	C
Maryland	University of Maryland: College Park	College Park	MD	4	Pu	C
Maryland: Baltimore County	University of Maryland: Baltimore County	Baltimore	MD	4	Pu	C
Maryland: Eastern Shore	University of Maryland: Eastern Shore	Princess Anne	MD	4	Pu	C
Marymount (KS)	Marymount College of Kansas	Salina	KS	4	Pr	W
Marymount (VA)	Marymount University	Arlington	VA	4	Pr	C
Maryville (MO)	Maryville University of Saint Louis	Saint Louis	MO	4	Pr	C
Maryville (TN)	Maryville College	Maryville	TN	4	Pr	C
Marywood	Marywood College	Scranton	PA	4	Pr	C
Massachusetts	University of Massachusetts Amherst	Amherst	MA	4	Pu	C
Massachusetts Bay CC	Massachusetts Bay Community College	Wellesley Hills	MA	2	Pu	C
Massachusetts College	Massachusetts College of Liberal Arts	North Adams	MA	4	Pu	C
Massachusetts Pharmacy	Massachusetts College of Pharmacy & Allied Health Sciences	Boston	MA	5	Pr	C
Massachusetts: Boston	University of Massachusetts Boston	Boston	MA	4	Pu	C
Massachusetts: Dartmouth	University of Massachusetts Dartmouth	North Dartmouth	MA	4	Pu	C
Massachusetts: Lowell	University of Massachusetts Lowell	Lowell	MA	4	Pu	C
Master's	Master's College	Santa Clarita	CA	4	Pr	C
Mayville State	Mayville State University	Mayville	ND	4	Pu	C
McKendree	McKendree College	Lebanon	IL	4	Pr	C
McMurry	McMurry University	Abilene	TX	4	Pr	C
McNeese State	McNeese State University	Lake Charles	LA	4	Pu	C
McPherson	McPherson College	McPherson	KS	4	Pr	C
Medaille	Medaille College	Buffalo	NY	4	Pr	C
Memphis	University of Memphis	Memphis	TN	4	Pu	C
Mercer	Mercer University	Macon	GA	4	Pr	C
Merchant Marine	United States Merchant Marine Academy	Kings Point	NY	4	Pu	C
Mercy (NY)	Mercy College	Dobbs Ferry	NY	4	Pr	C
Mercyhurst	Mercyhurst College	Erie	PA	4	Pr	C
Merrimack	Merrimack College	North Andover	MA	4	Pr	C
Mesa State	Mesa State College	Grand Junction	CO	4	Pu	C
Messenger	Messenger College	Joplin	MO	4	Pr	
Messiah	Messiah College	Grantham	PA	4	Pr	C
Methodist	Methodist College	Fayetteville	NC	4	Pr	C
Metropolitan State (CO)	Metropolitan State College of Denver	Denver	CO	4	Pu	C
Miami (FL)	University of Miami	Coral Gables	FL	4	Pr	C
Miami (OH)	Miami University: Oxford Campus	Oxford	OH	4	Pu	C
Michigan	University of Michigan	Ann Arbor	MI	4	Pu	C
Michigan State	Michigan State University	East Lansing	MI	4	Pu	C
Michigan Tech	Michigan Technological University	Houghton	MI	4	Pu	C
Mid-America Bible	Mid-America Bible College	Oklahoma City	OK	4	Pr	C
MidAmerica Nazarene	MidAmerica Nazarene University	Olathe	KS	4	Pr	C
Middle Tennessee State	Middle Tennessee State University	Murfreesboro	TN	4	Pu	C
Middlebury	Middlebury College	Middlebury	VT	4	Pr	C
Midland Commerce	Midland College of Commerce	Ashland	OH			C
Midland Lutheran	Midland Lutheran College	Fremont	NE	4	Pr	C
Midway	Midway College	Midway	KY	4	Pr	W
Midwest Christian	Midwest Christian College	Oklahoma City	OK	4	Pr	C

School	Institution Name	City	ST	YRS	CON	STD
Midwestern (IA)	Midwestern College	Denison	IA			
Midwestern State (TX)	Midwestern State University	Wichita Falls	TX	4	Pu	C
Miles	Miles College	Fairfield	AL	4	Pr	C
Millersville	Millersville University of Pennsylvania	Millersville	PA	4	Pu	C
Milligan	Milligan College	Milligan College	TN	4	Pr	C
Millikin	Millikin University	Decatur	IL	4	Pr	C
Millsaps	Millsaps College	Jackson	MS	4	Pr	C
Minnesota	University of Minnesota: Twin Cities	Minneapolis-Saint Paul	MN	4	Pu	C
Minnesota Bible	Minnesota Bible College	Rochester	MN	4	Pr	C
Minnesota: Duluth	University of Minnesota: Duluth	Duluth	MN	4	Pu	C
Minnesota: Morris	University of Minnesota: Morris	Morris	MN	4	Pu	C
Minot State	Minot State University	Minot	ND	4	Pu	C
Mississippi	University of Mississippi	University	MS	4	Pu	C
Mississippi College	Mississippi College	Clinton	MS	4	Pr	C
Mississippi State	Mississippi State University	State College	MS	4	Pu	C
Mississippi Valley State	Mississippi Valley State University	Itta Bena	MS	4	Pu	C
Mississippi Women	Mississippi University for Women	Columbus	MS	4	Pu	C
Missouri	University of Missouri: Columbia	Columbia	MO	4	Pu	C
Missouri Baptist	Missouri Baptist College	Saint Louis	MO	4	Pr	C
Missouri Southern State	Missouri Southern State College	Joplin	MO	4	Pu	C
Missouri Valley	Missouri Valley College	Marshall	MO	4	Pr	C
Missouri Western State	Missouri Western State College	Saint Joseph	MO	4	Pu	C
Missouri: Kansas City	University of Missouri: Kansas City	Kansas City	MO	4	Pu	C
Missouri: Rolla	University of Missouri: Rolla	Rolla	MO	4	Pu	C
Missouri: Saint Louis	University of Missouri: Saint Louis	Saint Louis	MO	4	Pu	C
Mobile	University of Mobile	Mobile	AL	4	Pr	C
Monmouth (IL)	Monmouth College	Monmouth	IL	4	Pr	C
Monmouth (NJ)	Monmouth University	West Long Branch	NJ	4	Pr	C
Montana	University of Montana-Missoula	Missoula	MT	4	Pu	C
Montana State	Montana State University-Bozeman	Bozeman	MT	4	Pu	C
Montana State: Billings	Montana State University-Billings	Billings	MT	4	Pu	C
Montana State: Northern	Montana State University-Northern	Havre	MT	4	Pu	C
Montana Tech	Montana Tech of the University of Montana	Butte	MT	4	Pu	C
Montclair State	Montclair State University	Upper Montclair	NJ	4	Pu	C
Montevallo	University of Montevallo	Montevallo	AL	4	Pu	C
Moody Bible	Moody Bible Institute	Chicago	IL	4	Pr	C
Moorhead State (MN)	Moorhead State University	Moorhead	MN	4	Pu	C
Moravian	Moravian College	Bethlehem	PA	4	Pr	C
Morehead State (KY)	Morehead State University	Morehead	KY	4	Pu	C
Morehouse	Morehouse College	Atlanta	GA	4	Pr	M
Morgan State	Morgan State University	Baltimore	MD	4	Pu	C
Morningside	Morningside College	Sioux City	IA	4	Pr	C
Morristown (TN)	Morristown College	Morristown	TN	2		C
Mount Marty	Mount Marty College	Yankton	SD	4	Pr	C
Mount Mercy	Mount Mercy College	Cedar Rapids	IA	4	Pr	C
Mount Saint Joseph	College of Mount Saint Joseph	Cincinnati	OH	4	Pr	C
Mount Saint Mary's (MD)	Mount Saint Mary's College	Emmitsburg	MD	4	Pr	C
Mount Saint Vincent	College of Mount Saint Vincent	Riverdale	NY	4	Pr	C
Mount Senario	Mount Senario College	Ladysmith	WI	4	Pr	C
Mount Union	Mount Union College	Alliance	OH	4	Pr	C
Mount Vernon Nazarene	Mount Vernon Nazarene College	Mount Vernon	OH	4	Pr	C
Muhlenberg	Muhlenberg College	Allentown	PA	4	Pr	C
Multnomah Bible	Multnomah Bible College	Portland	OR	4	Pr	C
Mundelein	Mundelein College	Chicago	IL	4	Pr	W
Murray State (KY)	Murray State University	Murray	KY	4	Pu	C
Murray State (OK)	Murray State Agricultural College	Tishomingo	OK	2	Pu	C
Muskingum	Muskingum College	New Concord	OH	4	Pr	C

N

School	Institution Name	City	ST	YRS	CON	STD
National (SD)	National College	Rapid City	SD	4	Pr	C
National Christian	National Christian University	San Antonio	TX			
Navajo CC (AZ)	Navajo Community College	Tsaile	AZ	2	Pu	C

School	Institution Name	City	ST	YRS	CON	STD
Navy	United States Naval Academy	Annapolis	MD	4	Pu	C
Nazareth (MI)	Nazareth College	Kalamazoo	MI		Pr	C
Nazareth (NY)	Nazareth College of Rochester	Rochester	NY	4	Pr	C
Nebraska	University of Nebraska: Lincoln	Lincoln	NE	4	Pu	C
Nebraska Christian	Nebraska Christian College	Norfolk	NE	4	Pr	C
Nebraska Wesleyan	Nebraska Wesleyan University	Lincoln	NE	4	Pr	C
Nebraska: Kearney	University of Nebraska: Kearney	Kearney	NE	4	Pu	C
Nebraska: Omaha	University of Nebraska: Omaha	Omaha	NE	4	Pu	C
Nevada	University of Nevada: Reno	Reno	NV	4	Pc	C
Nevada: Las Vegas	University of Nevada: Las Vegas	Las Vegas	NV	4	Pu	C
New Hampshire College	New Hampshire College	Manchester	NH	4	Pr	C
New Hampshire Tech: Concord	New Hampshire Technical Institute	Concord	NH	2	Pu	C
New Haven	University of New Haven	West Haven	CT	4	Pr	C
New Jersey	College of New Jersey	Trenton	NJ	4	Pu	C
New Jersey Tech	New Jersey Institute of Technology	Newark	NJ	4	Pu	C
New Kensington Commercial	New Kensington Commercial School	New Kensington	PA	2	Pp	C
New Mexico	University of New Mexico	Albuquerque	NM	4	Pu	C
New Mexico Highlands	New Mexico Highlands University	Las Vegas	NM	4	Pu	C
New Mexico State	New Mexico State University	Las Cruces	NM	4	Pu	C
New Mexico Tech	New Mexico Institute of Mining & Technology	Socorro	NM	4	Pu	C
New Orleans	University of New Orleans	New Orleans	LA	4	Pu	C
New Rochelle	College of New Rochelle	New Rochelle	NY	4	Pr	W
New York	New York University	New York	NY	4	Pr	C
New York Polytechnic	City University of New York: New York City Technical College	Brooklyn	NY	4	Pu	C
Newberry	Newberry College	Newberry	SC	4	Pr	C
Niagara	Niagara University	Niagara University	NY	4	Pr	C
Nicholls State	Nicholls State University	Thibodaux	LA	4	Pu	C
Norfolk State	Norfolk State University	Norfolk	VA	4	Pu	C
North Alabama	University of North Alabama	Florence	AL	4	Pu	C
North Carolina	University of North Carolina at Chapel Hill	Chapel Hill	NC	4	Pu	C
North Carolina A&T	North Carolina Agricultural & Technical State University	Greensboro	NC	4	Pu	C
North Carolina Central	North Carolina Central University	Durham	NC	4	Pu	C
North Carolina State	North Carolina State University	Raleigh	NC	4	Pu	C
North Carolina Wesleyan	North Carolina Wesleyan College	Rocky Mount	NC	4	Pr	C
North Carolina: Asheville	University of North Carolina at Asheville	Asheville	NC	4	Pu	C
North Carolina: Charlotte	University of North Carolina at Charlotte	Charlotte	NC	4	Pu	C
North Carolina: Greensboro	University of North Carolina at Greensboro	Greensboro	NC	4	Pu	C
North Carolina: Pembroke	University of North Carolina at Pembroke	Pembroke	NC	4	Pu	C
North Carolina: Wilmington	University of North Carolina at Wilmington	Wilmington	NC	4	Pu	C
North Central (IL)	North Central College	Naperville	IL	4	Pr	C
North Central Bible	North Central Bible College	Minneapolis	MN	4	Pr	C
North Dakota	University of North Dakota	Grand Forks	ND	4	Pu	C
North Dakota State	North Dakota State University	Fargo	ND	4	Pu	C
North Georgia	North Georgia College	Dahlonega	GA	4	Pu	C
North Park	North Park College	Chicago	IL	4	Pr	C
North Texas	University of North Texas	Denton	TX	4	Pu	C
Northeast CC (NE)	Northeast Community College	Norfolk	NE	2	Pu	C
Northeast Louisiana	Northeast Louisiana University	Monroe	LA	4	Pu	C
Northeastern (MA)	Northeastern University	Boston	MA	5	Pr	C
Northeastern Illinois	Northeastern Illinois University	Chicago	IL	4	Pu	C
Northeastern State (OK)	Northeastern State University	Tahlequah	OK	4	Pu	C
Northern Arizona	Northern Arizona University	Flagstaff	AZ	4	Pu	C
Northern Colorado	University of Northern Colorado	Greeley	CO	4	Pu	C

School	Institution Name	City	ST	YRS	CON	STD
Northern Essex CC (MA)	Northern Essex Community College	Haverhill	MA	2	Pu	C
Northern Illinois	Northern Illinois University	DeKalb	IL	4	Pu	C
Northern Iowa	University of Northern Iowa	Cedar Falls	IA	4	Pu	C
Northern Kentucky	Northern Kentucky University	Highland Heights	KY	4	Pu	C
Northern Michigan	Northern Michigan University	Marquette	MI	4	Pu	C
Northern State (SD)	Northern State University	Aberdeen	SD	4	Pu	C
Northland	Northland College	Ashland	WI	4	Pr	C
Northland Baptist Bible	Northland Baptist Bible College	Dunbar	WI	4	Pr	C
Northwest Assemblies	Northwest College of the Assemblies of God	Kirkland	WA	4	Pr	C
Northwest Bible	Northwest Bible College	Minot	ND			
Northwest Christian	Northwest Christian College	Eugene	OR	4	Pr	C
Northwest Missouri State	Northwest Missouri State University	Maryville	MO	4	Pu	C
Northwest Nazarene	Northwest Nazarene College	Nampa	ID	4	Pr	C
Northwest Shoals CC: Phil Campbell	Northwest Shoals Community College: Phil Campbell	Phil Campbell	AL	2	Pu	C
Northwestern (IA)	Northwestern College	Orange City	IA	4	Pr	C
Northwestern (IL)	Northwestern University	Evanston	IL	4	Pr	C
Northwestern (MN)	Northwestern College	Saint Paul	MN	4	Pr	C
Northwestern (OH)	Northwestern College	Lima	OH	2	Pr	C
Northwestern (WI)	Northwestern College	Watertown	WI	4	Pr	M
Northwestern Oklahoma State	Northwestern Oklahoma State University	Alva	OK	4	Pu	C
Northwestern State (LA)	Northwestern State University	Natchitoches	LA	4	Pu	C
Northwood (IN)	Northwood Institute of Indiana	West Baden	IN			
Northwood (MI)	Northwood University	Midland	MI	4	Pu	C
Norwich	Norwich University	Northfield	VT	4	Pr	C
Notre Dame (IN)	University of Notre Dame	Notre Dame	IN	4	Pr	C
Nova Southeastern	Nova Southeastern University	Fort Lauderdale	FL	4	Pr	C
Nyack	Nyack College	Nyack	NY	4	Pr	C

O

School	Institution Name	City	ST	YRS	CON	STD
Oakland (MI)	Oakland University	Rochester	MI	4	Pu	C
Oakland City (IN)	Oakland City University	Oakland City	IN	4	Pr	C
Oberlin	Oberlin College	Oberlin	OH	4	Pr	C
Occidental	Occidental College	Los Angeles	CA	4	Pr	C
Oglethorpe	Oglethorpe University	Atlanta	GA	4	Pr	C
Ohio Dominican	Ohio Dominican College	Columbus	OH	4	Pr	C
Ohio Northern	Ohio Northern University	Ada	OH	4	Pr	C
Ohio State	Ohio State University: Columbus Campus	Columbus	OH	4	Pu	C
Ohio University	Ohio University	Athens	OH	4	Pu	C
Ohio Valley (WV)	Ohio Valley College	Parkersburg	WV	4	Pr	C
Ohio Wesleyan	Ohio Wesleyan University	Delaware	OH	4	Pr	C
Oklahoma	University of Oklahoma	Norman	OK	4	Pu	C
Oklahoma Baptist College	Oklahoma Baptist College & Institute	Oklahoma City	OK			
Oklahoma Baptist University	Oklahoma Baptist University	Shawnee	OK	4	Pr	C
Oklahoma Christian	Oklahoma Christian University of Science & Arts	Oklahoma City	OK	4	Pr	C
Oklahoma City	Oklahoma City University	Oklahoma City	OK	4	Pr	C
Oklahoma Panhandle State	Oklahoma Panhandle State University	Goodwell	OK	4	Pu	C
Oklahoma State	Oklahoma State University	Stillwater	OK	4	Pu	C
Old Dominion	Old Dominion University	Norfolk	VA	4	Pu	C
Olivet Nazarene	Olivet Nazarene University	Kankahee	IL	4	Pr	C
Oneonta State	State University of New York College at Oneonta	Oneonta	NY	4	Pu	C
Oral Roberts	Oral Roberts University	Tulsa	OK	4	Pr	C
Oregon	University of Oregon	Eugene	OR	4	Pu	C
Oregon State	Oregon State University	Corvallis	OR	4	Pu	C
Oregon Tech	Oregon Institute of Technology	Klamath Falls	OR	4	Pu	C
Ottawa	Ottawa University	Ottawa	KS	4	Pr	C

School	Institution Name	City	ST	YRS	CON	STD
Otterbein	Otterbein College	Westerville	OH	4	Pr	C
Ottumwa Heights	Ottumwa Heights	Ottumwa Heights	IA			
Ouachita Baptist	Ouachita Baptist University	Arkadelphia	AR	4	Pr	C
Ozark Christian	Ozark Christian College	Joplin	MO	4	Pr	C
Ozarks (AR)	University of the Ozarks	Clarksville	AR	4	Pr	C
Ozarks (MO)	College of the Ozarks	Point Lookout	MO	4	Pr	C

P

School	Institution Name	City	ST	YRS	CON	STD
Pace	Pace University	New York	NY	4	Pr	C
Pacific (CA)	University of the Pacific	Stockton	CA	4	Pr	C
Pacific (OR)	Pacific University	Forest Grove	OR	4	Pr	C
Pacific Christian	Pacific Christian College	Fullerton	CA	4	Pr	C
Pacific Lutheran	Pacific Lutheran University	Tacoma	WA	4	Pr	C
Pacific West Coast Baptist Bible	Pacific West Coast Baptist Bible College	San Dimas	CA	4	Pr	C
Paine	Paine College	Augusta	GA	4	Pr	C
Palm Beach Atlantic	Palm Beach Atlantic College	West Palm Beach	FL	4	Pr	C
Palmer JC (SC)	Palmer College	Charleston	SC	2		
Panzer	Panzer College of Physical Education & Hygiene	East Orange	NJ	4		
Park (MO)	Park College	Parkville	MO	4	Pr	C
Parsons	Parsons College	Fairfield	IA	4	Pr	C
Paul Quinn	Paul Quinn College	Dallas	TX	4	Pr	C
Penn-Ohio	Penn-Ohio College	Youngstown	OH	2	Pr	C
Pennsylvania	University of Pennsylvania	Philadelphia	PA	4	Pr	C
Pennsylvania State	Pennsylvania State University	University Park	PA	4	Pu	C
Pennsylvania State: Erie Behrend	Pennsylvania State University Erie Behrend College	Erie	PA	4	Pu	C
Pensacola Christian	Pensacola Christian College	Pensacola	FL	4	Pr	C
Pepperdine	Pepperdine University	Malibu	CA	4	Pr	C
Peru State	Peru State College	Peru	NE	4	Pu	C
Pfeiffer	Pfeiffer College	Misenheimer	NC	4	Pr	C
Philadelphia Bible	Philadelphia College of Bible	Langhorne	PA	4	Pr	C
Philadelphia Pharmacy	Philadelphia College of Pharmacy & Science	Philadelphia	PA	4	Pr	C
Philadelphia Textiles	Philadelphia College of Textiles & Science	Philadelphia	PA	4	Pr	C
Philander Smith	Philander Smith College	Little Rock	AR	4	Pr	C
Phillips (OK)	Phillips University	Enid	OK	4	Pr	C
Phillips JC: Gulfport	Phillips Junior College: Gulfport	Gulfport	MS	2	Pp	C
Piedmont Baptist	Piedmont Bible College	Winston-Salem	NC	5	Pr	C
Pikeville	Pikeville College	Pikeville	KY	4	Pr	C
Pillsbury Baptist Bible	Pillsbury Baptist Bible College	Owatonna	MN	4	Pr	C
Pittsburg State	Pittsburg State University	Pittsburg	KS	4	Pu	C
Pittsburgh	University of Pittsburgh	Pittsburgh	PA	4	Pu	C
Pittsburgh Art Institute	Art Institute of Pittsburgh	Pittsburgh	PA	2	Pp	C
Pittsburgh: Johnstown	University of Pittsburgh Johnstown	Johnstown	PA	4	Pu	C
Plattsburgh State	State University of New York College at Plattsburgh	Plattsburgh	NY	4	Pu	C
Plymouth State	Plymouth State College of the University System of New Hampshire	Plymouth	NH	4	Pu	C
Point Loma Nazarene	Point Loma Nazarene College	San Diego	CA	4	Pr	C
Point Park	Point Park College	Pittsburgh	PA	4	Pr	C
Pomona-Pitzer	Pomona-Pitzer Colleges	Claremont	CA	4	Pr	C
Portland	University of Portland	Portland	OR	4	Pr	C
Portland State	Portland State University	Portland	OR	4	Pu	C
Potsdam State	State University of New York College at Potsdam	Potsdam	NY	4	Pu	C
Practical Bible	Practical Bible College	Bible School Park	NY	4	Pr	C
Prairie View A&M	Prairie View Agricultural & Mechanical University	Prairie View	TX	4	Pu	C
Pratt	Pratt Institute	Brooklyn	NY	4	Pr	C
Presbyterian	Presbyterian College	Clinton	SC	4	Pr	C

School	Institution Name	City	ST	YRS	CON	STD
Princeton	Princeton University	Princeton	NJ	4	Pr	C
Providence	Providence College	Providence	RI	4	Pr	C
Puget Sound	University of Puget Sound	Tacoma	WA	4	Pr	C
Puget Sound Christian	Puget Sound Christian College	Edmonds	WA	4	Pr	C
Purdue	Purdue University	West Lafayette	IN	4	Pu	C
Purdue: Calumet	Purdue University: Calumet	Hammond	IN	4	Pu	C

Q

School	Institution Name	City	ST	YRS	CON	STD
Queens (NC)	Queens College	Charlotte	NC	4	Pr	C
Queens (NY)	City University of New York: Queens College	Flushing	NY	4	Pu	C
Quincy (IL)	Quincy University	Quincy	IL	4	Pr	C
Quinnipiac	Quinnipiac College	Hamden	CT	4	Pr	C

R

School	Institution Name	City	ST	YRS	CON	STD
Radford	Radford University	Radford	VA	4	Pu	C
Ramapo	Ramapo College of New Jersey	Mahwah	NJ	4	Pu	C
Randolph-Macon	Randolph-Macon College	Ashland	VA	4	Pr	C
Ranger	Ranger College	Ranger	TX	2	Pu	C
Redlands	University of Redlands	Redlands	CA	4	Pr	C
Redlands CC	Redlands Community College	El Reno	OK	2	Pu	C
Regis (CO)	Regis University	Denver	CO	4	Pr	C
Regis (MA)	Regis College	Weston	MA	4	Pr	W
Rensselaer	Rensselaer Polytechnic Institute	Troy	NY	4	Pr	C
Rhema Bible	Rhema Bible Training Center	Broken Arrow	OK		Pr	C
Rhode Island	University of Rhode Island	Kingston	RI	4	Pu	C
Rhode Island College	Rhode Island College	Providence	RI	4	Pu	C
Rhodes	Rhodes College	Memphis	TN	4	Pr	C
Rice	Rice University	Houston	TX	4	Pr	C
Richard Stockton	Richard Stockton College of New Jersey	Pomona	NJ	4	Pu	C
Richmond	University of Richmond	Richmond	VA	4	Pr	C
Ricks	Ricks College	Rexburg	ID	2	Pr	C
Rider	Rider University	Lawrenceville	NJ	4	Pr	C
Rio Grande	University of Rio Grande	Rio Grande	OH	4	Pr	C
Ripon	Ripon College	Ripon	WI	4	Pr	C
Roanoke	Roanoke College	Salem	VA	4	Pr	C
Robert Morris	Robert Morris College	Coraopolis	PA	4	Pr	C
Roberts Wesleyan	Roberts Wesleyan College	Rochester	NY	4	Pr	C
Rochester (MI)	Rochester College	Rochester Hills	MI	4	Pr	C
Rochester (NY)	University of Rochester	Rochester	NY	4	Pr	C
Rochester Tech	Rochester Institute of Technology	Rochester	NY	4	Pr	C
Rockford	Rockford College	Rockford	IL	4	Pr	C
Rockhurst	Rockhurst College	Kansas City	MO	4	Pr	C
Rocky Mountain	Rocky Mountain College	Billings	MT	4	Pr	C
Roger Williams	Roger Williams University	Bristol	RI	4	Pr	C
Rollins	Rollins College	Winter Park	FL	4	Pr	C
Rose-Hulman	Rose-Hulman Institute of Technology	Terre Haute	IN	4	Pr	C
Rowan	Rowan University of New Jersey	Glassboro	NJ	4	Pu	C
Rust	Rust College	Holly Springs	MS	4	Pr	C
Rutgers	Rutgers, The State University of New Jersey: Rutgers College	New Brunswick	NJ	4	Pu	C

S

School	Institution Name	City	ST	YRS	CON	STD
Sacred Heart (CT)	Sacred Heart University	Bridgeport	CT	4	Pr	C
Sage JC	Sage Junior College of Albany	Albany	NY	2	Pr	C
Saginaw Valley State	Saginaw Valley State University	University Center	MI	4	Pu	C
Saint Ambrose	Saint Ambrose University	Davenport	IA	4	Pr	C
Saint Andrews Presbyterian	Saint Andrews Presbyterian College	Laurinburg	NC	4	Pr	C
Saint Anselm	Saint Anselm College	Manchester	NH	4	Pr	C
Saint Augustine's	Saint Augustine's College	Raleigh	NC	4	Pr	C
Saint Benedict	College of Saint Benedict	Saint Joseph	MN	4	Pr	W
Saint Bernard	Saint Bernard College	Saint Bernard	AL	4	Pr	C

School	Institution Name	City	ST	YRS	CON	STD
Saint Bonaventure	Saint Bonaventure University	Olean	NY	4	Pr	C
Saint Catharine (KY)	Saint Catharine College	Saint Catharine	KY	2	Pr	C
Saint Cloud State	Saint Cloud State University	Saint Cloud	MN	4	Pu	C
Saint Edward's	Saint Edward's University	Austin	TX	4	Pr	C
Saint Francis (IL)	College of Saint Francis	Joliet	IL	4	Pr	C
Saint Francis (IN)	Saint Francis College	Fort Wayne	IN	4	Pr	C
Saint Francis (NY)	Saint Francis College	Brooklyn Heights	NY	4	Pr	C
Saint Francis (PA)	Saint Francis College	Loretto	PA	4	Pr	C
Saint John Fisher	Saint John Fisher College	Rochester	NY	4	Pr	C
Saint John's (MN)	Saint John's University	Collegeville	MN	4	Pr	M
Saint John's (NY)	Saint John's University	Jamaica	NY	4	Pr	C
Saint John's Lutheran (KS)	Saint John's Lutheran College	Winfield	KS	2	Pr	C
Saint Joseph's (IN)	Saint Joseph's College	Rensselaer	IN	4	Pr	C
Saint Joseph's (ME)	Saint Joseph's College	Standish	ME	4	Pr	C
Saint Joseph's (PA)	Saint Joseph's University	Philadelphia	PA	4	Pr	C
Saint Lawrence	Saint Lawrence University	Canton	NY	4	Pr	C
Saint Louis	Saint Louis University	Saint Louis	MO	4	Pr	C
Saint Louis Christian	Saint Louis Christian College	Florissant	MO	4	Pr	C
Saint Martin's	Saint Martin's College	Lacey	WA	4	Pr	C
Saint Mary's (CA)	Saint Mary's College of California	Moraga	CA	4	Pr	C
Saint Mary's (MD)	Saint Mary's College of Maryland	Saint Mary's City	MD	4	Pu	C
Saint Mary's (MI)	Saint Mary's College	Orchard Lake	MI	4	Pr	C
Saint Mary's (MN)	Saint Mary's College of Minnesota	Winona	MN	4	Pr	C
Saint Mary's (TX)	Saint Mary's University of San Antonio	San Antonio	TX	4	Pr	C
Saint Michael's (VT)	Saint Michael's College	Colchester	VT	4	Pr	C
Saint Norbert	Saint Norbert College	De Pere	WI	4	Pr	C
Saint Olaf	Saint Olaf College	Northfield	MN	4	Pr	C
Saint Peter's	Saint Peter's College	Jersey City	NJ	4	Pr	C
Saint Rose	College of Saint Rose	Albany	NY	4	Pr	C
Saint Scholastica	College of Saint Scholastica	Duluth	MN	4	Pr	C
Saint Teresa	College of Saint Teresa	Winona	MN	4	Pr	C
Saint Thomas (FL)	Saint Thomas University	Miami	FL	4	Pr	C
Saint Thomas (MN)	University of Saint Thomas	Saint Paul	MN	4	Pr	C
Saint Thomas Aquinas	Saint Thomas Aquinas College	Sparkill	NY	4	Pr	C
Saint Vincent	Saint Vincent College	Latrobe	PA	4	Pr	C
Saint Xavier	Saint Xavier University	Chicago	IL	4	Pr	C
Salem State	Salem State College	Salem	MA	4	Pu	C
Salem-Teikyo	Salem-Teikyo College	Salem	WV	4	Pr	C
Salisbury State	Salisbury State University	Salisbury	MD	4	Pu	C
Salve Regina	Salve Regina University	Newport	RI	4	Pr	C
Sam Houston State	Sam Houston State University	Huntsville	TX	4	Pu	C
San Diego	University of San Diego	San Diego	CA	4	Pr	C
San Diego State	San Diego State University	San Diego	CA	4	Pu	C
San Francisco	University of San Francisco	San Francisco	CA	4	Pr	C
San Francisco State	San Francisco State University	San Francisco	CA	4	Pu	C
San Jose Christian	San Jose Christian College	San Jose	CA	4	Pr	C
San Jose State	San Jose State University	San Jose	CA	4	Pu	C
Santa Clara	Santa Clara University	Santa Clara	CA	4	Pr	C
Santa Fe (NM)	College of Santa Fe	Santa Fe	NM	4	Pr	C
Savannah A&D	Savannah College of Art & Design	Savannah	GA	4	Pr	C
Savannah State	Savannah State College	Savannah	GA	4	Pu	C
Scranton	University of Scranton	Scranton	PA	4	Pr	C
Seattle	Seattle University	Seattle	WA	4	Pr	C
Seattle Pacific	Seattle Pacific University	Seattle	WA	4	Pr	C
Seminole JC (OK)	Seminole Junior College	Seminole	OK	2	Pu	C
Seton Hall	Seton Hall University	South Orange	NJ	4	Pr	C
Seton Hill	Seton Hill College	Greensburg	PA	4	Pr	W
Shaw (NC)	Shaw University	Raleigh	NC	4	Pr	C
Shawnee State (OH)	Shawnee State University	Portsmouth	OH	4	Pu	C
Shenandoah	Shenandoah University	Winchester	VA	4	Pr	C
Shepherd	Shepherd College	Shepherdstown	WV	4	Pu	C
Shippensburg	Shippensburg University of Pennsylvania	Shippensburg	PA	4	Pu	C
Shorter (GA)	Shorter College	Rome	GA	4	Pr	C

School	Institution Name	City	ST	YRS	CON	STD
Siena (NY)	Siena College	Loudonville	NY	4	Pr	C
Siena Heights	Siena Heights College	Adrian	MI	4	Pr	C
Silver Lake	Silver Lake College	Manitowoc	WI	4	Pr	C
Simon Fraser	Simon Fraser University	Burnaby	BC	4	Pu	C
Simpson (CA)	Simpson College	Redding	CA	4	Pr	C
Simpson (IA)	Simpson College	Indianola	IA	4	Pr	C
Sioux Falls	University of Sioux Falls	Sioux Falls	SD	4	Pr	C
Slippery Rock	Slippery Rock University of Pennsylvania	Slippery Rock	PA	4	Pu	C
Sonoma State	Sonoma State University	Rohnert Park	CA	4	Pu	C
South Alabama	University of South Alabama	Mobile	AL	4	Pu	C
South Carolina	University of South Carolina	Columbia	SC	4	Pu	C
South Carolina State	South Carolina State University	Orangeburg	SC	4	Pu	C
South Carolina: Aiken	University of South Carolina at Aiken	Aiken	SC	4	Pu	C
South Carolina: Lancaster	University of South Carolina at Lancaster	Lancaster	SC	2	Pu	C
South Carolina: Spartanburg	University of South Carolina at Spartanburg	Spartanburg	SC	4	Pu	C
South Carolina: Union	University of South Carolina at Union	Union	SC	2	Pu	C
South Dakota	University of South Dakota	Vermillion	SD	4	Pu	C
South Dakota State	South Dakota State University	Brookings	SD	4	Pu	C
South Dakota Tech	South Dakota School of Mines & Technology	Rapid City	SD	4	Pu	C
South Florida	University of South Florida	Tampa	FL	4	Pu	C
South University (TN)	University of the South	Sewanee	TN	4	Pr	C
Southeast Missouri State	Southeast Missouri State University	Cape Girardeau	MO	4	Pu	C
Southeastern Assemblies	Southeastern College of the Assemblies of God	Lakeland	FL	4	Pr	C
Southeastern Bible	Southeastern Bible College	Birmingham	AL	4	Pr	C
Southeastern Louisiana	Southeastern Louisiana University	Hammond	LA	4	Pu	C
Southeastern Oklahoma State	Southeastern Oklahoma State University	Durant	OK	4	Pu	C
Southern Arkansas	Southern Arkansas University	Magnolia	AR	4	Pu	C
Southern California	University of Southern California	Los Angeles	CA	4	Pr	C
Southern California College	Southern California College	Costa Mesa	CA	4	Pr	C
Southern Colorado	University of Southern Colorado	Pueblo	CO	4	Pu	C
Southern Connecticut State	Southern Connecticut State University	New Haven	CT	4	Pu	C
Southern Illinois	Southern Illinois University at Carbondale	Carbondale	IL	4	Pu	C
Southern Illinois: Edwardsville	Southern Illinois University at Edwardsville	Edwardsville	IL	4	Pu	C
Southern Indiana	University of Southern Indiana	Evansville	IN	4	Pu	C
Southern Maine	University of Southern Maine	Gorham	ME	4	Pu	C
Southern Maine Tech	Southern Maine Technical College	South Portland	ME	2	Pu	C
Southern Methodist (TX)	Southern Methodist University	Dallas	TX	4	Pr	C
Southern Mississippi	University of Southern Mississippi	Hattiesburg	MS	4	Pu	C
Southern Nazarene	Southern Nazarene University	Bethany	OK	4	Pr	C
Southern Ohio: Cincinnati	Southern Ohio College	Cincinnati	OH	2	Pp	C
Southern Oregon	Southern Oregon University	Ashland	OR	4	Pu	C
Southern Tech (GA)	Southern College of Technology	Marietta	GA	4	Pu	C
Southern Union State CC	Southern Union State Community College	Wadley	AL	2	Pu	C
Southern Utah	Southern Utah State University	Cedar City	UT	4	Pu	C
Southern Wesleyan	Southern Wesleyan University	Central	SC	4	Pr	C
Southern: Baton Rouge	Southern University & Agricultural & Mechanical College	Baton Rouge	LA	4	Pu	C
Southern: New Orleans	Southern University at New Orleans	New Orleans	LA	4	Pu	C
Southwest Baptist	Southwest Baptist University	Bolivar	MO	4	Pr	C
Southwest Missouri State	Southwest Missouri State University	Springfield	MO	4	Pu	C
Southwest Texas State	Southwest Texas State University	San Marcos	TX	4	Pu	C
Southwestern (AZ)	Southwestern College	Phoenix	AZ	4	PR	C
Southwestern (KS)	Southwestern College	Winfield	KS	4	Pr	C
Southwestern (TX)	Southwestern University	Georgetown	TX	4	Pr	C
Southwestern Assemblies	Southwestern Assemblies of God University	Waxahachie	TX	4	Pr	C

School	Institution Name	City	ST	YRS	CON	STD
Southwestern Christian Ministries	Southwestern College of Christian Ministries	Bethany	OK	4	Pr	C
Southwestern Louisiana	University of Southwestern Louisiana	Lafayette	LA	4	Pu	C
Southwestern Oklahoma State	Southwestern Oklahoma State University	Weatherford	OK	4	Pu	C
Spring Arbor	Spring Arbor College	Spring Arbor	MI	4	Pr	C
Spring Garden	Spring Garden College	Chestnut Hill	PA	4	Pr	C
Spring Hill	Spring Hill College	Mobile	AL	4	Pr	C
Springfield (MA)	Springfield College	Springfield	MA	4	Pr	C
Stanford	Stanford University	Stanford	CA	4	Pr	C
Staten Island	City University of New York: College of Staten Island	Staten Island	NY	4	Pu	C
Steed	Steed College, Inc	Johnson City	TN	2	Pp	C
Stephen F Austin State	Stephen F Austin State University	Nacogdoches	TX	4	Pu	C
Sterling (KS)	Sterling College	Sterling	KS	4	Pr	C
Stetson	Stetson University	DeLand	FL	4	Pr	C
Stillman	Stillman College	Tuscaloosa	AL	4	Pr	C
Stonehill	Stonehill College	North Easton	MA	4	Pr	C
Stony Brook State	State University of New York at Stony Brook	Stony Brook	NY	4	Pu	C
Strayer Business	Strayer Business College	Washington	DC	4	Pp	C
Sue Bennett	Sue Bennett College	London	KY	4	Pr	C
Suffolk (MA)	Suffolk University	Boston	MA	4	Pr	C
Sul Ross State	Sul Ross State University	Alpine	TX	4	Pu	C
Sullivan (KY)	Sullivan College	Louisville	KY	4	Pp	C
Susquehanna	Susquehanna University	Selinsgrove	PA	4	Pr	C
Syracuse	Syracuse University	Syracuse	NY	4	Pr	C

T

School	Institution Name	City	ST	YRS	CON	STD
Tabor	Tabor College	Hillsboro	KS	4	Pr	C
Talladega	Talladega College	Talladega	AL	4	Pr	C
Tampa University	University of Tampa	Tampa	FL	4	Pr	C
Tarkio	Tarkio College	Tarkio	MO	4	Pr	C
Tarleton State	Tarleton State University	Stephenville	TX	4	Pu	C
Taylor	Taylor University: Upland	Upland	IN	4	Pr	C
Taylor: Fort Wayne	Taylor University: Fort Wayne	Fort Wayne	IN	4	Pr	C
Temple	Temple University	Philadelphia	PA	4	Pu	C
Temple JC	Temple Junior College	Temple	TX	2	Pu	C
Tennessee	University of Tennessee	Knoxville	TN	4	Pu	C
Tennessee State	Tennessee State University	Nashville	TN	4	Pu	C
Tennessee Tech	Tennessee Technological University	Cookeville	TN	4	Pu	C
Tennessee Temple	Tennessee Temple University	Chattanooga	TN	4	Pr	C
Tennessee Wesleyan	Tennessee Wesleyan College	Athens	TN	4	Pr	C
Tennessee: Chattanooga	University of Tennessee: Chattanooga	Chattanooga	TN	4	Pu	C
Tennessee: Martin	University of Tennessee: Martin	Martin	TN	4	Pu	C
Texas	University of Texas at Austin	Austin	TX	4	Pu	C
Texas A&M	Texas Agricultural & Mechanical University	College Station	TX	4	Pu	C
Texas A&M: Commerce	Texas A&M University-Commerce	Commerce	TX	4	Pu	C
Texas A&M: Corpus Christi	Texas Agricultural & Mechanical University-Corpus Christi	Corpus Christi	TX	4	Pu	C
Texas A&M: Kingsville	Texas Agricultural & Mechanical University-Kingsville	Kingsville	TX	4	Pu	C
Texas Christian	Texas Christian University	Fort Worth	TX	4	Pr	C
Texas College	Texas College	Tyler	TX	4	Pr	C
Texas Southern	Texas Southern University	Houston	TX	4	Pu	C
Texas Tech	Texas Tech University	Lubbock	TX	4	Pu	C
Texas Wesleyan	Texas Wesleyan College	Fort Worth	TX	4	Pr	C
Texas: Arlington	University of Texas at Arlington	Arlington	TX	4	Pu	C
Texas: El Paso	University of Texas at El Paso	El Paso	TX	4	Pu	C
Texas: Pan American	University of Texas: Pan American	Edinburg	TX	4	Pu	C
Texas: San Antonio	University of Texas at San Antonio	San Antonio	TX	4	Pu	C
Thiel	Thiel College	Greenville	PA	4	Pr	C
Thomas More (KY)	Thomas More College	Crestview Hills	KY	4	Pr	C
Tiffin	Tiffin University	Tiffin	OH	4	Pr	C

School	Institution Name	City	ST	YRS	CON	STD
Toccoa Falls	Toccoa Falls College	Toccoa Falls	GA	4	Pr	C
Toledo	University of Toledo	Toledo	OH	4	Pu	C
Tomlinson	Tomlinson College	Cleveland	TN			
Tougaloo	Tougaloo College	Tougaloo	MS	4	Pr	C
Towson	Towson University	Towson	MD	4	Pu	C
Transylvania	Transylvania University	Lexington	KY	4	Pr	C
Trevecca Nazarene	Trevecca Nazarene College	Nashville	TN	4	Pr	C
Tri-State	Tri-State University	Angola	IN	4	Pr	C
Trinity (CT)	Trinity College	Hartford	CT	4	Pr	C
Trinity (TX)	Trinity University	San Antonio	TX	4	Pr	C
Trinity (VT)	Trinity College of Vermont	Burlington	VT	4	Pr	W
Trinity Bible	Trinity Bible College	Ellendale	ND	4	Pr	C
Trinity Christian	Trinity Christian College	Palos Heights	IL	4	Pr	C
Trinity International (FL)	Trinity International University	Miami	FL	4	Pr	C
Trinity International (IL)	Trinity International College	Deerfield	IL	4	Pr	C
Troy State: Troy	Troy State University	Troy	AL	4	Pu	C
Truman State (MO)	Truman State University	Kirksville	MO	4	Pu	C
Tufts	Tufts University	Medford	MA	4	Pr	C
Tulane	Tulane University	New Orleans	LA	4	Pr	C
Tulsa	University of Tulsa	Tulsa	OK	4	Pr	C
Tusculum	Tusculum College	Greeneville	TN	4	Pr	C
Tuskegee	Tuskegee University	Tuskegee	AL	4	Pr	C

U

School	Institution Name	City	ST	YRS	CON	STD
Union (KY)	Union College	Barbourville	KY	4	Pr	C
Union (NY)	Union College	Schenectady	NY	4	Pr	C
Union (TN)	Union University	Jackson	TN	4	Pr	C
United States International	United States International University	San Diego	CA	4	Pr	C
Upper Iowa	Upper Iowa University	Fayette	IA	4	Pr	C
Upsala	Upsala College	East Orange	NJ	4	Pr	C
Urbana	Urbana University	Urbana	OH	4	Pr	C
Ursinus	Ursinus College	Collegeville	PA	4	Pr	C
Utah	University of Utah	Salt Lake City	UT	4	Pu	C
Utah State	Utah State University	Logan	UT	4	Pu	C
Utica	Utica College of Syracuse University	Utica	NY	4	Pr	C

V

School	Institution Name	City	ST	YRS	CON	STD
Valdosta State	Valdosta State University	Valdosta	GA	4	Pu	C
Valley City State	Valley City State University	Valley City	ND	4	Pu	C
Valley Forge Christian	Valley Forge Christian College	Phoenixville	PA	4	Pr	C
Valparaiso	Valparaiso University	Valparaiso	IN	4	Pr	C
Vanderbilt	Vanderbilt University	Nashville	TN	4	Pr	C
Vennard	Vennard College	University Park	IA	4	Pr	C
Vermont	University of Vermont	Burlington	VT	4	Pu	C
Vermont Tech	Vermont Technical College	Randolph Center	VT	2	Pu	C
Villanova	Villanova University	Villanova	PA	4	Pr	C
Virginia	University of Virginia	Charlottesville	VA	4	Pu	C
Virginia Commonwealth	Virginia Commonwealth University	Richmond	VA	4	Pu	C
Virginia Intermont	Virginia Intermont College	Bristol	VA	4	Pr	C
Virginia Military	Virginia Military Institute	Lexington	VA	4	Pu	M
Virginia Polytechnic	Virginia Polytechnic Institute & State University	Blacksburg	VA	4	Pu	C
Virginia State	Virginia State University	Petersburg	VA	4	Pu	C
Virginia Union	Virginia Union University	Richmond	VA	4	Pr	C
Virginia Wesleyan	Virginia Wesleyan College	Norfolk	VA	4	Pr	C
Viterbo	Viterbo College	La Crosse	WI	4	Pr	C
Voorhees	Voorhees College	Denmark	SC	4	Pr	C

W

School	Institution Name	City	ST	YRS	CON	STD
Wabash	Wabash College	Crawfordsville	IN	4	Pr	M
Wagner	Wagner College	Staten Island	NY	4	Pr	C
Wake Forest	Wake Forest University	Winston-Salem	NC	4	Pr	C

School	Institution Name	City	ST	YRS	CON	STD
Walsh	Walsh University	North Canton	OH	4	Pr	C
Warner Pacific	Warner Pacific College	Portland	OR	4	Pr	C
Warner Southern	Warner Southern College	Lake Wales	FL	4	Pr	C
Warren Wilson	Warren Wilson College	Asheville	NC	4	Pr	C
Wartburg	Wartburg College	Waverly	IA	4	Pr	C
Washburn	Washburn University of Topeka	Topeka	KS	4	Pu	C
Washington	University of Washington	Seattle	WA	4	Pu	C
Washington & Jefferson	Washington & Jefferson College	Washington	PA	4	Pr	C
Washington & Lee	Washington & Lee University	Lexington	VA	4	Pr	C
Washington (MD)	Washington College	Chestertown	MD	4	Pr	C
Washington (MO)	Washington University	Saint Louis	MO	4	Pr	C
Washington Bible	Washington Bible College	Lanham	MD	4	Pr	C
Washington State	Washington State University	Pullman	WA	4	Pu	C
Wayland Baptist	Wayland Baptist University	Plainview	TX	4	Pr	C
Wayne State (MI)	Wayne State University	Detroit	MI	4	Pu	C
Wayne State (NE)	Wayne State College	Wayne	NE	4	Pu	C
Waynesburg	Waynesburg College	Waynesburg	PA	4	Pr	C
Webber	Webber College	Babson Park	FL	4	Pr	C
Weber State	Weber State University	Ogden	UT	4	Pu	C
Wentworth Tech	Wentworth Institute of Technology	Boston	MA	4	Pr	C
Wesley (MS)	Wesley College	Florence	MS	4	Pr	C
Wesleyan (CT)	Wesleyan University	Middletown	CT	4	Pr	C
West Alabama	University of West Alabama	Livingston	AL	4	Pu	C
West Chester	West Chester University of Pennsylvania	West Chester	PA	4	Pu	C
West Coast Christian	West Coast Christian College	Fresno	CA		Pr	
West Florida	University of West Florida	Pensacola	FL	4	Pu	C
West Georgia	West Georgia College	Carrollton	GA	4	Pu	C
West Liberty State	West Liberty State College	West Liberty	WV	4	Pu	C
West Liberty State: Hancock	West Liberty State: Hancock	Wierton	WV	2	Pu	C
West Texas A&M	West Texas Agricultural & Mechanical University	Canyon	TX	4	Pu	C
West Virginia	West Virginia University	Morgantown	WV	4	Pu	C
West Virginia Northern CC: Weirton	West Virginia Northern Community College: Weirton	Weirton	WV	2	Pu	C
West Virginia State	West Virginia State College	Institute	WV	4	Pu	C
West Virginia Tech	West Virginia Institute of Technology	Montgomery	WV	4	Pu	C
West Virginia Wesleyan	West Virginia Wesleyan College	Buckhannon	WV	4	Pr	C
Westbrook	Westbrook College	Portland	ME	4	Pr	C
Western Baptist	Western Baptist College	Salem	OR	4	Pr	C
Western Carolina	Western Carolina University	Cullowhee	NC	4	Pu	C
Western Connecticut State	Western Connecticut State University	Danbury	CT	4	Pu	C
Western Illinois	Western Illinois University	Macomb	IL	4	Pu	C
Western Kentucky	Western Kentucky University	Bowling Green	KY	4	Pu	C
Western Michigan	Western Michigan University	Kalamazoo	MI	4	Pu	C
Western Montana	Western Montana College of the University of Montana	Dillon	MT	4	Pu	C
Western New England	Western New England College	Springfield	MA	4	Pr	C
Western New Mexico	Western New Mexico University	Silver City	NM	4	Pu	C
Western Oregon	Western Oregon University	Monmouth	OR	4	Pu	C
Western State (CO)	Western State College of Colorado	Gunnison	CO	4	Pu	C
Western Washington	Western Washington University	Bellingham	WA	4	Pu	C
Westfield State	Westfield State College	Westfield	MA	4	Pu	C
Westmar	Westmar College	Le Mars	IA	4	Pr	C
Westminster (MO)	Westminster College	Fulton	MO	4	Pr	C
Westminster (PA)	Westminster College	New Wilmington	PA	4	Pr	C
Westminster (UT)	Westminster College of Salt Lake City	Salt Lake City	UT	4	Pr	C
Westmont	Westmont College	Santa Barbara	CA	4	Pr	C
Wheaton (IL)	Wheaton College	Wheaton	IL	4	Pr	C
Wheaton (MA)	Wheaton College	Norton	MA	4	Pr	C
Wheeling Jesuit	Wheeling Jesuit College	Wheeling	WV	4	Pr	C
Whittier	Whittier College	Whittier	CA	4	Pr	C
Whitworth (MS)	Whitworth Bible College	Brookhaven	MS	2	Pr	C

School	Institution Name	City	ST	YRS	CON	STD
Whitworth (WA)	Whitworth College	Spokane	WA	4	Pr	C
Wichita State	Wichita State University	Wichita	KS	4	Pu	C
Widener	Widener University	Chester	PA	4	Pr	C
Wiley	Wiley College	Marshall	TX	4	Pr	C
Wilkes	Wilkes College	Wilkes-Barre	PA	4	Pr	C
Willamette	Willamette University	Salem	OR	4	Pr	C
William & Mary	College of William & Mary	Williamsburg	VA	4	Pu	C
William Carey (MS)	William Carey College	Hattiesburg	MS	4	Pr	C
William Jewell	William Jewell College	Liberty	MO	4	Pr	C
William Paterson	William Paterson College of New Jersey	Wayne	NJ	4	Pu	C
William Penn	William Penn College	Oskaloosa	IA	4	Pr	C
William Smith	William Smith College	Geneva	NY	4	Pr	W
William Woods	William Woods University	Fulton	MO	4	Pr	W
Williams	Williams College	Williamstown	MA	4	Pr	C
Williams Baptist	Williams Baptist College	Walnut Ridge	AR	4	Pr	C
Williamsport Commerce	Williamsport School of Commerce	Williamsport	PA	2	Pp	
Wilmington (DE)	Wilmington College	New Castle	DE	4	Pr	C
Wingate	Wingate College	Wingate	NC	4	Pr	C
Winona State	Winona State University	Winona	MN	4	Pu	C
Winston-Salem State	Winston-Salem State University	Winston-Salem	NC	4	Pu	C
Winthrop	Winthrop University	Rock Hill	SC	4	Pu	C
Wisconsin	University of Wisconsin-Madison	Madison	WI	4	Pu	C
Wisconsin Lutheran	Wisconsin Lutheran College	Milwaukee	WI	4	Pr	C
Wisconsin: Eau Claire	University of Wisconsin-Eau Claire	Eau Claire	WI	4	Pu	C
Wisconsin: Green Bay	University of Wisconsin-Green Bay	Green Bay	WI	4	Pu	C
Wisconsin: La Crosse	University of Wisconsin-La Crosse	La Crosse	WI	4	Pu	C
Wisconsin: Milwaukee	University of Wisconsin-Milwaukee	Milwaukee	WI	4	Pu	C
Wisconsin: Oshkosh	University of Wisconsin-Oshkosh	Oshkosh	WI	4	Pu	C
Wisconsin: Parkside	University of Wisconsin-Parkside	Kenosha	WI	4	Pu	C
Wisconsin: Platteville	University of Wisconsin-Platteville	Platteville	WI	4	Pu	C
Wisconsin: River Falls	University of Wisconsin-River Falls	River Falls	WI	4	Pu	C
Wisconsin: Stevens Point	University of Wisconsin-Stevens Point	Stevens Point	WI	4	Pu	C
Wisconsin: Stout	University of Wisconsin-Stout	Menomonie	WI	4	Pu	C
Wisconsin: Superior	University of Wisconsin-Superior	Superior	WI	4	Pu	C
Wisconsin: Whitewater	University of Wisconsin-Whitewater	Whitewater	WI	4	Pu	C
Wittenberg	Wittenberg University	Springfield	OH	4	Pr	C
Wofford	Wofford College	Spartanburg	SC	4	Pr	C
Wooster	College of Wooster, The	Wooster	OH	4	Pr	C
Worcester Polytechnic	Worcester Polytechnic Institute	Worcester	MA	4	Pr	C
Worcester State	Worcester State College	Worcester	MA	4	Pu	C
Wright State (OH)	Wright State University	Dayton	OH	4	Pu	C
Wyoming	University of Wyoming	Laramie	WY	4	Pu	C
Xavier (LA)	Xavier University of Louisiana	New Orleans	LA	4	Pr	C
Xavier (OH)	Xavier University	Cincinnati	OH	4	Pr	C

Y

School	Institution Name	City	ST	YRS	CON	STD
Yale	Yale University	New Haven	CT	4	Pr	C
Yankton	Yankton College	Yankton	SD	4		C
York (NE)	York College	York	NE	4	Pr	C
York (NY)	City University of New York: York College	Jamaica	NY	4	Pu	C
York (PA)	York College of Pennsylvania	York	PA	4	Pr	C
Youngstown State	Youngstown State University	Youngstown	OH	4	Pu	C

School Names
Cross Reference

This appendix provides a cross-reference to schools that have undergone a name change and to those that frequently are referred to by other than their "official" name.

Column one contains the "old" or "common" name; column two contains the name as it is used in this book. Column three contains an abbreviation for the reason for the listing: NC = Name Change; M = Merger; Blank = "Common" Name/"Official" Name.

In this book, schools that have undergone a name change are listed by the current name or, in the case of closed institutions, by the last name prior to their closing. Schools that have been part of a merger are listed in this book by their name at the time of their tournament appearance(s). Thus, they may be found under either the pre or post-merger name.

Note that listed schools may not have appeared in a tournament under a previous name; the list is provided as a convenience.

If you're looking for	See	Why
A		
Adelphi-Suffolk College of Adelphi University	Dowling	NC
Alabama State College for Negroes	Alabama State	NC
Alameda County State College	California State: Hayward	NC
Arizona State Teachers/College at Flagstaff	Northern Arizona	NC
Arizona State Teachers/College at Tempe	Arizona State	NC
Arkansas Agricultural, Mechanical & Normal College	Arkansas: Pine Bluff	NC
Arkansas Agricultural & Mechanical College	Arkansas: Monticello	NC
Arkansas, State College of	Central Arkansas	NC
Arlington State College	Texas: Arlington	NC
Armstrong State College	Armstrong Atlantic State	NC
Arnold College of Physical Education	Bridgeport	M
Atlanta Baptist College	Mercer	M
Atlantic Christian College	Barton	NC
Augustinian College of the Merrimack Valley	Merrimack	NC
B		
BC	Boston College	
Bethany Nazarene College	Southern Nazarene	NC
Bible Institute of Chicago	Trinity International (IL)	M
Billings Polytechnic Institute	Rocky Mountain	M
Boston State College	Massachusetts: Boston	NC
Bradford Durfee College of Technology	Massachusetts: Dartmouth	M
Brevard Engineering College	Florida Tech	NC
BU	Boston University	
BYU	Brigham Young	

If you're looking for	See	Why
C		
Cal Poly Pomona	California Polytechnic: Pomona	
Cal Poly SLO (San Luis Obispo)	California Polytechnic: San Luis Obispo	
Cal State/St: (City)	California State: (City)	
Cal Tech	California Tech	
California Bible Institute	California Christian	NC
California State College: Kern County	California State: Bakersfield	NC
California State Polytechnic: Kellogg-Voorhis	California Polytechnic: Pomona	NC
California Western University	United States International	NC
Carnegie Institute of Technology	Carnegie Mellon	M
Catholic Teachers College of New Mexico	Albuquerque	NC
CCNY	City College	
Centenary College for Women	Centenary (NJ)	NC
Central Christian College	Oklahoma Christian	NC
Central Florida Bible College	Florida Christian	NC
Central State College/University (OK)	Central Oklahoma	NC
Central State Teachers College (WI)	Wisconsin: Stevens Point	NC
Central Wesleyan College	Southern Wesleyan	NC
Charlotte College	North Carolina: Charlotte	NC
Chattanooga City College	Tennessee: Chattanooga	M
Chicago Normal/Teachers College	Chicago State	NC
Chicago Teachers College: North Campus	Northeastern Illinois	NC
Chico Normal/Teachers/State College	California State: Chico	NC
Christ College Irvine	Concordia (CA)	NC
Christian Brothers of New Mexico, College of	Santa Fe (NM)	NC
Clark College (GA)	Clark Atlanta	NC
Cleveland Bible College	Malone	NC
College Center	North Carolina: Wilmington	NC
College of Education & Industrial Arts	Central State (OH)	NC
Colorado Agricultural & Mechanical College	Colorado State	NC
Colorado State College	Northern Colorado	NC
Colorado Woman's College	Denver, University of	M
Columbia Bible School	Columbia Christian	NC
Columbus College	Columbus State (GA)	NC
Corpus Christi, University of	Texas A&M: Corpus Christi	NC
Cullman College	Saint Bernard	M
D		
Danbury State/Teachers College	Western Connecticut State	NC
Denmark Educational Center	Denmark Tech	NC
Detroit, University of	Detroit Mercy	M
District of Columbia Teachers College	District of Columbia	M
Dorland-Bell School	Warren Wilson	M
Dyke & Spencerian College/School of Commerce/College	David N Myers	NC
E		
East Central (Oklahoma) State College/University	East Central (OK)	NC
East Texas State College/University	Texas A&M: Commerce	NC
Eastern Montana College (of Education)	Montana State: Billings	NC
Edinburg Regional College	Texas: Pan American	NC
Emporia Kansas State College	Emporia State	NC
Evangelical Free Church Seminary	Trinity International (IL)	M
F		
F&M	Franklin & Marshall	
Farmington State Teachers College	Maine: Farmington	NC
Federal City College	District of Columbia	M
Flagstaff State College	Northern Arizona	NC
Flora MacDonald College	Saint Andrews Presbyterian	M
Florence State College/University	North Alabama	NC
Florida Baptist Institute	Florida Memorial	M
Florida Normal (& Industrial Memorial) College	Florida Memorial	NC

If you're looking for	See	Why
Florida Presbyterian College	Eckerd	NC
Fort Kent State Normal/Teachers College	Maine: Fort Kent	NC
Fort Lauderdale College of Business & Finance	Fort Lauderdale	NC
Fort Lewis Agricultural & Mechnical College	Fort Lewis	NC
Francis T Nicholls State/Junior College of Louisiana	Nicholls State	NC
FSU	Florida State	

G

General Beadle State Teachers/College	Dakota State	NC
George Pepperdine College	Pepperdine	NC
Georgia State College of Business Administration	Georgia State	NC
Georgia Teachers College	Georgia Southern	NC
Georgia, University of: Atlanta Division	Georgia State	NC
Glassboro State Normal/Teachers College	Rowan	NC
Grace Bible Institute	Grace (NE)	NC
Grace College of the Bible	Grace (NE)	NC
Grand Rapids Baptist Bible College	Cornerstone	M
Grand Rapids School of the Bible & Music	Cornerstone	M
Greensboro Evening College	Guilford	M

H

Harpur	Binghamton State	NC
Hawaii Pacific: Loa	Hawaii Pacific	M
Hawaii, University of: Extension Division	Hawaii: Hilo	NC
Hayward State University	California State: Hayward	NC
Herbert H Lehman College	Lehman	NC
Hillman College for Women	Mississippi College	M

I

Illinois Teachers College: Chicago-North	Northeastern Illinois	NC
Illinois Teachers College: Chicago-South	Chicago State	NC
Indiana University: Falls City Center	Indiana: Southeast	NC
Iowa State University of Science & Technology	Iowa State	NC
Iowa, State College of	Northern Iowa	NC

J

Jackson College for Negro Teachers	Jackson State (MS)	NC

K

Kearney State College	Nebraska: Kearney	NC
Kentucky Southern College	Louisville	M
Kentucky State College for Negros	Kentucky State	NC

L

Lamar State College of Technology	Lamar	NC
Lewis Clark Normal School	Lewis-Clark State (ID)	NC
Lewis School of Aeronautics/Science & Technology	Lewis (IL)	NC
Liberty Baptist College	Liberty	NC
Livingston State College/University	West Alabama	NC
Long Beach State College	California State: Long Beach	NC
Long Island University: Merriweather Campus	Long Island: C W Post	NC
Los Angeles Baptist College	Master's	NC
Los Angeles Pacific College	Azusa Pacific	M
Los Angeles State College (of Applied Arts & Sciences)	California State: Los Angeles	NC
Los Angeles-Orange County State College	California State: Long Beach	NC
Lowell Textile/Technical Institute/State/University of	Massachusetts: Lowell	M
LSU	Louisiana State	
Luther College (NE)	Midland Lutheran	M
Lynchburg Baptist College	Liberty	NC

If you're looking for	See	Why

M

Madison College	James Madison	NC
Maine, University of: Portland Campus/Portland-Gorham	Southern Maine	M
Maine, University of: Washington State	Maine: Machias	NC
Marycrest College	Marycrest International	NC
Maryland State College	Maryland: Eastern Shore	NC
Marymount College: Los Angeles	Loyola Marymount	M
Mellon Institute	Carnegie Mellon	M
Mercy University of Detroit	Detroit Mercy	M
Miami Christian College	Trinity International (FL)	NC
Michigan State University at Oakland	Oakland (MI)	NC
Midwest Bible & Missionary Institute	Calvary Bible	M
Midwest Christian: Oklahoma City	Ozark Christian	M
Midwestern University	Midwestern State (TX)	NC
Milwaukee-Downer College	Lawrence	M
Miner Teachers College	District of Columbia	M
Mississippi Negro Training School	Jackson State (MS)	NC
Mississippi Southern College	Southern Mississippi	NC
Mississippi Synodical College	Belhaven	M
Mississippi Vocational College	Mississippi Valley State	NC
MIT	Massachusetts Tech	
Montana College of Mineral Science & Technology	Montana Tech	NC
Mount Saint Agnes College of Women	Loyola (MD)	M
Mount Saint Joseph Normal/Teachers	Medaille	NC
Mount Saint Scholastica College	Benedictine (KS)	M
MSU	Michigan State	
Mt (for Mount)	Mount	
Murphy Collegiate Institute	Lee (TN)	M

N

National College/School of Business	National (SD)	NC
Nebraska State Teachers College at Chadron	Chadron State	NC
Nebraska State Teachers College at Kearney	Nebraska: Kearney	NC
Nebraska State Teachers College at Peru	Peru State	NC
Nebraska State Teachers College at Wayne	Wayne State (NE)	NC
Nevada Southern University	Nevada: Las Vegas	NC
Nevada, University of, Southern Regional Branch	Nevada: Las Vegas	NC
New Bedford Institute of Technology	Massachusetts: Dartmouth	M
New College: Sarasota	South Florida	M
New England, University of: Biddeford	Westbrook	M
New Hampshire School/College of Accounting & Commerce	New Hampshire College	NC
New Haven State Teachers College	Southern Connecticut State	NC
New Jersey State Normal School at Newark	Kean	NC
New Jersey State Normal/Tchrs College: Jersey City	Jersey City State	NC
New Jersey State Teachers College: Trenton	New Jersey	NC
New Mexico Normal/State Teachers College	Western New Mexico	NC
New Mexico State University of Agrculture, Engineering, & Science	New Mexico State	NC
New Mexico Western College	Western New Mexico	NC
New York, State University of, at ...	Name of City	NC
New York State University: Long Island Center	Stony Brook State	NC
New York, State University of, Science & Engineering on Long Island	Stony Brook State	NC
Newark State Teachers/College	Kean	NC
Newton College of the Sacred Heart	Boston College	M
Norfolk College of William & Mary	Old Dominion	NC
Norfolk Polytechnic College	Norfolk State	NC
Normandy Residence Center of the University of Missouri	Missouri: Saint Louis	NC
North Adams State College	Massachusetts College	NC
North Carolina College at Durham	North Carolina Central	NC
North Carolina, University of, at Boone	Appalachian State	NC
North Carolina, University of, at Winston-Salem	Winston-Salem State	NC
North Carolina, University of, Charlotte Center	North Carolina: Charlotte	NC
Northeast Bible College	Valley Forge Christian	NC
Northeast Illinois State College	Northeastern Illinois	NC

If you're looking for	See	Why
Northeast Missouri State/Teachers College/University	Truman State (MO)	NC
Northeastern Oklahoma University	Northeastern State (OK)	NC
Northeastern State Normal/Teachers College	Northeastern State (OK)	NC
Northern Idaho College of Education	Lewis-Clark State (ID)	NC
Northern Michigan College of Education	Northern Michigan	NC
Northern State/Teachers College	Northern State (SD)	NC
Northwest Bible Institute/College	Northwest Assemblies	NC
Northwestern College (WI)	Dr. Martin Luther	M
Northwestern Schools	Northwestern (MN)	NC
Northwestern State College/University of Louisiana	Northwestern State (LA)	NC
Northwestern State Normal/Teachers College	Northwestern Oklahoma State	NC
Notre Dame College: Staten Island	Saint John's (NY)	M
Nyack Missionary College	Nyack	NC
NYU	New York	

O

Oklahoma Panhandle State College of Agriculture & Applied Science	Oklahoma Panhandle State	NC
Oklahoma State University of Agriculture & Applied Science	Oklahoma State	NC
Ole Miss	Mississippi	
Omaha Baptist Bible College/Institute	Faith Baptist Bible (IA)	NC
Orange (County) State College	California State: Fullerton	NC
Oregon College of Education	Western Oregon	NC
Oregon Vocational School	Oregon Tech	NC
OSU	Ohio State	
Owen College	LeMoyne-Owen	M

P

Pacific Bible College	Warner Pacific	NC
Pan American College/University	Texas: Pan American	NC
Paterson State College	William Paterson	NC
Pembroke State College/University (for Indians)	North Carolina: Pembroke	NC
Penn	Pennsylvania	
Penn State	Pennsylvania State	
Piedmont Bible College	Piedmont Baptist	NC
Pitt	Pittsburgh	
PMC Colleges	Widener	NC
Point Loma College	Point Loma Nazarene	NC
Prairie View Agricultural & Mechanical College/University	Prairie View A&M	NC
Presbyterian College	Saint Andrews Presbyterian	M
Providence Institute of Engineering & Finance	Roger Williams	NC
Purdue University Center: Hammond	Purdue: Calumet	NC

Q

Queens College of the City University of New York	Queens (NY)	NC

R

Richmond Professional Institute	Virginia Commonwealth	M
Rosary Hill College	Daemen	NC

S

Sacramento State College	California State: Sacramento	NC
Sacred Heart College (KS)	Kansas Newman	NC
Saint Ambrose College, Women's Division	Marycrest International	NC
Saint Bernadine of Siena College	Siena (NY)	NC
Saint Bernard College	Cullman	M
Saint Joseph on the Rio Grande, College of	Albuquerque	NC
Saint Louis Baptist College	Missouri Baptist	NC
Saint Mary's Academy	Clarke (IA)	NC
Samuel Huston College	Huston-Tillotson	M
San Diego College for Men	San Diego	M
San Diego College for Women	San Diego	M
San Fernando Valley/Campus of Los Angeles State/State College	California State: Northridge	NC

If you're looking for	See	Why
Santa Barbara College	California: Santa Barbara	NC
Shenandoah Conservatory of Music	Shenandoah	NC
SMU	Southern Methodist (TX)	
South Carolina Area Trade School	Denmark Tech	NC
Southeastern Massachusetts Institute of Technology/University	Massachusetts: Dartmouth	NC
Southeastern State College (OK)	Southeastern Oklahoma State	NC
Southern Cal	Southern California	
Southern California Bible College	Southern California College	NC
Southern Christian Institute	Tougaloo	M
Southern State College (AR)	Southern Arkansas	NC
Southwestern at Memphis	Rhodes	NC
Southwestern State College/of Diversified Occupations/Inst of Technology	Southwestern Oklahoma State	NC
St (for Saint) ...	Saint ...	
State Agricultural & Mechanical College/Institute for Negroes	Alabama A&M	NC
State Teachers & Agricultural College, Forsyth (GA)	Fort Valley State	M

T

TCU	Texas Christian	
Technical Institute, The	Southern Tech (GA)	NC
Tempe State	Arizona State	NC
Tennessee Agricultural & Industrial State University	Tennessee State	NC
Tennessee, University of, Chattanooga	Tennessee: Chattanooga	M
Tennessee, University of, Martin Branch	Tennessee: Martin	NC
Texas Agricultural & Industrial University	Texas A&M: Kingsville	NC
Texas Agricultural & Industrial University at Corpus Christi	Texas A&M: Corpus Christi	NC
Texas State University for Negroes	Texas Southern	NC
Texas Western College	Texas: El Paso	NC
Towson State College/University	Towson	NC
Trenton State College	New Jersey	NC
Trinity College (IL)	Trinity International (IL)	NC
Trinity College at Miami	Trinity International (FL)	NC
Trinity Seminary & Bible College/Institute of MLPS	Trinity International (IL)	NC
Triple Cities College of Syracuse University	Binghamton State	NC

U

UAB	Alabama: Birmingham	
UCLA	California: Los Angeles	
UConn	Connecticut	
UC	California:	
UMass	Massachusetts	
UNC	North Carolina	
United States Air Force Academy	Air Force	
United State Coast Guard Academy	Coast Guard	
United States Merchant Marine Academy	Merchant Marine	
United States Military Academy	Army	
United States Naval Academy	Navy	
University College	George Mason	NC
UNLV	Nevada: Las Vegas	
Upland College	Messiah	M
USC	South Carolina	
UTEP	Texas Western	
UVA	Virginia	

V

Vanport Extension Center	Portland State	NC
Vermont College	Norwich	M
Virginia Polytechnic Institute: Women's Division	Radford	NC
VMI	Virginia Military	
VPI	Virginia Polytechnic	

If you're looking for	See	Why
W		
Wagner Lutheran College	Wagner	NC
Washburn Municipal University of Topeka	Washburn	NC
Washington State Teachers College (ME)	Maine: Machias	NC
West Texas State College/University	West Texas A&M	NC
Western Baptist Bible College/& Theological Seminary	Western Baptist	NC
Western Bible College	Westmont	NC
Westminster College (MS)	Wesley (MS)	NC
White Plains, College of	Pace	M
William Marsh Rice University	Rice	NC
William & Mary, College of in Norfolk	Old Dominion	NC
Willimantic State Teachers College	Eastern Connecticut State	NC
Wilmington College (NC)	North Carolina: Wilmington	NC
Wisconsin State College & Institute for Technology-Platteville	Wisconsin: Platteville	NC
Wisconsin University Extension	Wisconsin: Milwaukee	M
Woman's College of Georgia, The	Georgia College	NC
Y		
YMCA Institute	Roger Williams	NC
York College of the City University of New York	York (NY)	NC

Tournament Sites & Dates

To the extent known or on record, this appendix contains "logistical" information on each tournament that is included in this book.

Each tournament is listed alphabetically by the abbreviated name of the sponsoring association or by the abbreviated name of the tournament, by year, by men/women, by division. **AIAW:** Association for Intercollegiate Athletics for Women; **ARC:** American Red Cross Benefit; **CCA:** Collegiate Commissioners Association Tournament; **LCC:** League of Christian Colleges; **NAIA:** National Intercollegiate Athletic Association; **NASC:** National Athletic Steering Committee; **NBCAA:** National Bible College Athletic Association; **NCAA:** National Collegiate Athletic Association; **NCaT:** National Catholic College Tournament; **NCCAA:** National Christian College Athletic Association; **NCI:** National Catholic Invitational Tournament; **NCT:** National Campus Tournament; **NIT:** National Invitation Tournament; **NSCAA:** National Small College Athletic Association; **NWIT:** National Women's Invitational Tournament; **OLYD:** Olympic Demonstration Tournament; **OLYT:** Olympic Trials Tournament.

The following information is provided for each tournament. **Arena:** the facility, building, or such where the games of the tournament were held. Note that some tournaments utilized more than one arena for the games; **City/ST:** the city and state where the arena was or is; **Dates:** the dates when the tournament was held; the given dates do not necessarily indicate that games were held on all dates, for many tournaments scheduled "off-days"; **Type:** All—all tournament games were held at the listed arena and within the listed dates, F4—The semifinals and the championship game were held at the listed arena within or on the listed dates (earlier round games were held at other sites on earlier dates), F2—The championship game was held at the listed arena within or on the listed dates (earlier round games were held at other sites on earlier dates); **M/W:** Men's or women's tournament; **#T:** Number of teams participating in the tournament

Every attempt was made to complete this appendix. However, the records of some associations, sponsoring organizations, and schools are incomplete or unavailable.

Year	M/W	DIV	City	ST	Dates	Type	#T	Arena
AIAW								
1969	W		West Chester	PA	3/19-22/69	All	16	Hollinger Field House
1970	W		Boston	MA	3/11-14/70	All	16	Cabot Gymnasium
1971	W		Cullowhee	NC	3/24-27/71	All	16	Liston B Ramsey Center
1972	W		Normal	IL	3/17-19/72	All	16	Redbird Arena
1973	W		Flushing	NY	3/22-24/73	All	16	Fitzgerald Gymnasium
1974	W		Manhattan	KS	3/20-23/74	All	16	Ahearn Field House
1975	W	S	Pueblo	CO	3/13-15/75	All	12	Massari Arena
1975	W	L	Harrisonburg	VA	3/19-22/75	All	16	Sinclair Gymnasium

Year	M/W	DIV	City	ST	Dates	Type	#T	Arena
1976	W	S	Ashland	OH	3/23-27/76	All	16	Charles Kates Gymnasium
1976	W	L	University Park	PA	3/24-27/76	All	16	Recreation Hall
1977	W	S	Pomona	CA	3/22-26/77	All	16	Darlene May Gymnasium/
								Kellogg Gymnasium
1977	W	L	Minneapolis	MN	3/23-26/77	All	16	Williams Arena
1978	W	S	Florence	SC	3/21-25/78	All	16	Smith University Center
1978	W	L	Los Angeles	CA	3/23-25/78	F4	16	Pauley Pavilion
1979	W	S	Fargo	ND	3/20-24/79	All	16	Bison Sports Arena
1979	W	L	Greensboro	NC	3/23-25/79	F4	16	Greensboro Coliseum
1980	W	I	Mount Pleasant	MI	3/21-23/80	F4	24	Rose Arena
1980	W	II	Dayton	OH	3/21-23/80	F4	24	University Of Dayton Arena
1980	W	III	Spokane	WA	3/21-22/80	F4	24	Whitworth College Field House
1981	W	I	Eugene	OR	3/27-29/81	F4	24	McArthur Court
1981	W	II	Dayton	OH	3/27-29/81	F4	16	University Of Dayton Arena
1981	W	III	La Crosse	WI	3/27-28/81	F4	16	Mitchell Hall
1982	W	I	Philadelphia	PA	3/26-28/82	F4	16	The Palestra
1982	W	II	Charleston	SC	3/26-27/82	F4	16	College Athletic Center
1982	W	III	Cedar Rapids	IA	3/26-27/82	F4	16	Five Seasons Center

ARC

Year	M/W		City	ST	Dates	Type	#T	Arena
1943	M		New York	NY	4/1/43	All	4	Madison Square Garden III
1944	M		New York	NY	3/30/44	All	4	Madison Square Garden III
1945	M		New York	NY	3/29/45	All	4	Madison Square Garden III

CCA

Year	M/W		City	ST	Dates	Type	#T	Arena
1974	M		Saint Louis	MO	3/15-18/74	All	8	Saint Louis Arena
1975	M		Louisville	KY	3/13-16/75	All	8	Freedom Hall

LCC

Year	M/W		City	ST	Dates	Type	#T	Arena
1996	M		Denham Springs	LA	3/14-16/96	All	7	Denham Springs High School Gymnasium
1997	M		Plaquemine	LA	3/6-8/97	All	5	Gulf Coast Christian Gymnasium

NAIA

Year	M/W		City	ST	Dates	Type	#T	Arena
1937	M		Kansas City	MO	3/9-12/37	All	8	Municipal Auditorium
1938	M		Kansas City	MO	3/7-12/38	All	32	Municipal Auditorium
1939	M		Kansas City	MO	3/13-18/39	All	32	Municipal Auditorium
1940	M		Kansas City	MO	3/11-16/40	All	32	Municipal Auditorium
1941	M		Kansas City	MO	3/10-15/41	All	32	Municipal Auditorium
1942	M		Kansas City	MO	3/9-14/42	All	32	Municipal Auditorium
1943	M		Kansas City	MO	3/8-13/43	All	32	Municipal Auditorium
1944	M		No Tournament					
1945	M		Kansas City	MO	3/12-17/45	All	16	Municipal Auditorium
1946	M		Kansas City	MO	3/11-16/46	All	32	Municipal Auditorium
1947	M		Kansas City	MO	3/10-15/47	All	32	Municipal Auditorium
1948	M		Kansas City	MO	3/8-13/48	All	32	Municipal Auditorium
1949	M		Kansas City	MO	3/14-19/49	All	32	Municipal Auditorium
1950	M		Kansas City	MO	3/13-18/50	All	32	Municipal Auditorium
1951	M		Kansas City	MO	3/12-17/51	All	32	Municipal Auditorium
1952	M		Kansas City	MO	3/10-15/52	All	32	Municipal Auditorium
1953	M		Kansas City	MO	3/9-14/53	All	32	Municipal Auditorium
1954	M		Kansas City	MO	3/8-13/54	All	32	Municipal Auditorium
1955	M		Kansas City	MO	3/7-12/55	All	32	Municipal Auditorium
1956	M		Kansas City	MO	3/11-17/56	All	32	Municipal Auditorium

Year	M/W	DIV	City	ST	Dates	Type	#T	Arena
1957	M		Kansas City	MO	3/11-16/57	All	32	Municipal Auditorium
1958	M		Kansas City	MO	3/10-15/58	All	32	Municipal Auditorium
1959	M		Kansas City	MO	3/9-14/59	All	32	Municipal Auditorium
1960	M		Kansas City	MO	3/7-12/60	All	32	Municipal Auditorium
1961	M		Kansas City	MO	3/13-18/61	All	32	Municipal Auditorium
1962	M		Kansas City	MO	3/12-17/62	All	32	Municipal Auditorium
1963	M		Kansas City	MO	3/11-16/63	All	32	Municipal Auditorium
1964	M		Kansas City	MO	3/9-14/64	All	32	Municipal Auditorium
1965	M		Kansas City	MO	3/8-13/65	All	32	Municipal Auditorium
1966	M		Kansas City	MO	3/7-12/66	All	32	Municipal Auditorium
1967	M		Kansas City	MO	3/13-18/67	All	32	Municipal Auditorium
1968	M		Kansas City	MO	3/11-16/68	All	32	Municipal Auditorium
1969	M		Kansas City	MO	3/10-15-69	All	32	Municipal Auditorium
1970	M		Kansas City	MO	3/9-14/70	All	32	Municipal Auditorium
1971	M		Kansas City	MO	3/8-13/71	All	32	Municipal Auditorium
1972	M		Kansas City	MO	3/14-18/72	All	32	Municipal Auditorium
1973	M		Kansas City	MO	3/12-17/73	All	32	Municipal Auditorium
1974	M		Kansas City	MO	3/11-16/74	All	32	Municipal Auditorium
1975	M		Kansas City	MO	3/10-13/75	All	32	Kemper Arena
1976	M		Kansas City	MO	3/8-13/76	All	32	Kemper Arena
1977	M		Kansas City	MO	3/7-12/77	All	32	Kemper Arena
1978	M		Kansas City	MO	3/13-18/78	All	32	Kemper Arena
1979	M		Kansas City	MO	3/12-17/79	All	32	Kemper Arena
1980	M		Kansas City	MO	3/10-15/80	All	32	Kemper Arena
1981	W		Kansas City	MO	3/12-14/81	All	8	Kemper Arena
1982	M		Kansas City	MO	3/8-13/82	All	32	Kemper Arena
1982	W		Kansas City	MO	3/11-13/82	All	8	Kemper Arena
1983	M		Kansas City	MO	3/14-19/83	All	32	Kemper Arena
1983	W		Kansas City	MO	3/17-19/83	All	8	Kemper Arena
1984	M		Kansas City	MO	3/14-20/84	All	32	Kemper Arena
1984	W		Cedar Rapids	IA	3/14-17/84	All	16	Five Seasons Center
1985	M		Kansas City	MO	3/13-19/85	All	32	Kemper Arena
1985	W		Cedar Rapids	IA	3/13-16/85	All	16	Five Seasons Center
1986	M		Kansas City	MO	3/12-18/86	All	32	Kemper Arena
1986	W		Kansas City	MO	3/14-18/86	All	16	Kemper Arena
1987	M		Kansas City	MO	3/11-17/87	All	32	Kemper Arena
1987	W		Kansas City	MO	3/13-17/87	All	16	Kemper Arena
1988	M		Kansas City	MO	3/16-22/88	All	32	Kemper Arena
1988	W		Kansas City	MO	3/18-22/88	All	16	Kemper Arena
1989	M		Kansas City	MO	3/15-21/89	All	32	Kemper Arena
1989	W		Kansas City	MO	3/17-21/89	All	16	Kemper Arena
1990	M		Kansas City	MO	3/14-20/90	All	32	Kemper Arena
1990	W		Jackson	TN	3/16-20/90	All	16	Oman Arena
1991	M		Kansas City	MO	3/12-18/91	All	32	Kemper Arena
1991	W		Jackson	TN	3/6-12/91	All	32	Oman Arena
1992	M	I	Kansas City	MO	3/17-23/92	All	32	Kemper Arena
1992	M	II	Stephenville	TX	3/12-17/92	All	20	Wisdom Gymnasium
1992	W	I	Jackson	TN	3/4-10/92	All	32	Oman Arena
1992	W	II	Monmouth	OR	3/12-17/92	All	20	New Physical Education Building

Year	M/W	DIV	City	ST	Dates	Type	#T	Arena
1993	M	I	Kansas City	MO	3/16-22/93	All	32	Kemper Arena
1993	M	II	Nampa	ID	3/11-16/93	All	20	Montgomery Gymnasium
1993	W	I	Jackson	TN	3/3-9/93	All	32	Oman Arena
1993	W	II	Monmouth	OR	3/11-16/93	All	20	New Physical Education Building
1994	M	I	Tulsa	OK	3/15-21/94	All	32	Mabee Center
1994	M	II	Nampa	ID	3/11-16/94	All	24	Montgomery Gymnasium
1994	W	I	Jackson	TN	3/16-22/94	All	32	Oman Arena
1994	W	II	Monmouth	OR	3/10-15/94	All	24	New Physical Education Building
1995	M	I	Tulsa	OK	3/14-20/95	All	32	Mabee Center
1995	M	II	Nampa	ID	3/8-14/95	All	32	Montgomery Gymnasium
1995	W	I	Jackson	TN	3/15-21/95	All	32	Oman Arena
1995	W	II	Monmouth	OR	3/8-14/95	All	32	New Physical Education Building
1996	M	I	Tulsa	OK	3/12-18/96	All	32	Mabee Center
1996	M	II	Nampa	ID	3/6-12/96	All	32	Montgomery Gymnasium
1996	W	I	Jackson	TN	3/13-19-96	All	32	Oman Arena
1996	W	II	Angola	IN	3/6-12/96	All	32	Hershey Hall
1997	M	I	Tulsa	OK	3/18-24/97	All	32	Mabee Center
1997	M	II	Nampa	ID	3/12-18/97	All	32	Montgomery Gymnasium
1997	W	I	Jackson	TN	3/19-25/97	All	32	Oman Arena
1997	W	II	Angola	IN	3/12-18/97	All	32	Hershey Hall
1998	M	I	Tulsa	OK	3/17-23/98	All	32	Mabee Center
1998	M	II	Nampa	ID	3/11-17/98	All	32	Montgomery Gymnasium
1998	W	I	Jackson	TN	4/18-24/98	All	32	Oman Arena
1998	W	II	Sioux City	IA	3/11-17/98	All	32	Municipal Auditorium

NASC

Year	M/W	DIV	City	ST	Dates	Type	#T	Arena
1952	M		Nashville	TN	2/28-3/1/52	All	8	Fisk Gymnasium
1953	M		Nashville	TN	2/26-28/53	All	8	Fisk Gymnasium
1954	M		Nashville	TN	3/1-3/54	All	8	Henry Arthur Kean Health & Phys Ed Bldg
1955	M		Nashville	TN	3/2-4/55	All	8	Henry Arthur Kean Health & Phys Ed Bldg

NBCAA

Year	M/W	DIV	City	ST	Dates	Type	#T	Arena
1981	M		Ankeny	IA		All	4	Faith Baptist Bible Gymnasium/Convocation Center
1982	M		Rochester	MN	3/11-13/82	All	8	Rockenbach Hall
1983	M		Minneapolis	MN	3/10-12/83	All	8	Clark-Danielson Student Life Center
1983	W		Ellendale	ND	3/4-5/83	All	4	Trinity Bible College Field House
1984	M	I	Minneapolis	MN		All	8	Clark-Danielson Student Life Center
1984	M	II	Minneapolis	MN		All	3	Clark-Danielson Student Life Center
1984	W		Minneapolis	MN		All	4	Clark-Danielson Student Life Center
1985	M	I	Kansas City	MO	3/7-9/85	All	8	Belton High School Gymnasium
1985	M	II	Kansas City	MO	3/7-9/85	All	4	Belton High School Gymnasium
1985	W					All	4	
1986	M	I	Council Bluffs	IA	3/6-8/86	All	8	Kanesville Center
1986	M	II	Council Bluffs	IA	3/6-8/86	All	3	Kanesville Center
1986	W					All	4	
1987	M	I	Minneapolis	MN	3/12-14/87	All	8	Clark-Danielson Student Life Center
1987	M	II	Minneapolis	MN	3/12-14/87	All	4	Clark-Danielson Student Life Center
1987	W					All	4	

Year	M/W	DIV	City	ST	Dates	Type	#T	Arena
1988	M	I	Cedar Hill	TX	3/10-12/88	All	8	Nutting Arena
1988	M	II	Cedar Hill	TX	3/10-12/88	All	4	Nutting Arena
1988	W		Waxahachie	TX	3/10-11/88	All	4	Southwestern Assemblies Of God Gymnasium
1989	M	I	Bethany	OK	3/9-11/89	All	7	Broadhurst Gymnasium
1989	M	II	Bethany	OK	3/9-11/89	All	6	Broadhurst Gymnasium
1989	W		Bethany	OK	3/9-11/89	All	4	Broadhurst Gymnasium
1990	M	I	Midwest City	OK	3/8-10/90	All	8	Sutton Field House/Carl Albert High School
1990	M	II	Midwest City	OK	3/8-10/90	All	8	Sutton Field House/Carl Albert High School
1990	W		Midwest City	OK	3/8-10/90	All	6	Sutton Field House/Carl Albert High School
1991	M	I	Midwest City	OK	3/14-16/91	All	8	Sutton Field House/Carl Albert High School
1991	M	II	Midwest City	OK	3/14-16/91	All	7	Sutton Field House/Carl Albert High School
1991	W		Midwest City	OK	3/14-16/91	All	5	Sutton Field House/Carl Albert High School
1992	M	I	Midwest City	OK	3/19-22/92	All	8	Sutton Field House/Carl Albert High School
1992	M	II	Midwest City	OK	3/19-21/92	All	8	Sutton Field House/Carl Albert High School
1992	W		Midwest City	OK	3/19-21/92	All	4	Sutton Field House/Carl Albert High School
1993	M	I	Midwest City	OK	3/18-20/93	All	6	Sutton Field House/Carl Albert High School
1993	M	II	Midwest City	OK	3/18-20/93	All	8	Sutton Field House/Carl Albert High School
1993	W		Midwest City	OK	3/18-20/93	All	6	Sutton Field House/Carl Albert High School
1994	M	II	Midwest City	OK	3/17-19/94	All	7	Sutton Field House/Carl Albert High School
1994	M	I	Midwest City	OK	3/17-19/94	All	7	Sutton Field House/Carl Albert High School
1994	W		Midwest City	OK	3/17-19/94	All	4	Sutton Field House/Carl Albert High School
1995	M	II	Midwest City	OK	3/16-18/95	All	8	Sutton Field House/Carl Albert High School
1995	M	I	Midwest City	OK	3/16-18/95	All	8	Sutton Field House/Carl Albert High School
1995	W		Midwest City	OK	3/16-18/95	All	5	Sutton Field House/Carl Albert High School
1996	M	I	Midwest City	OK	3/7-9/96	All	8	Sutton Field House/Carl Albert High School
1996	M	II	Midwest City	OK	3/7-9/96	All	8	Sutton Field House/Carl Albert High School
1996	W		Midwest City	OK	3/7-9/96	All	6	Sutton Field House/Carl Albert High School
1997	M	I	Midwest City	OK	3/13-15/97	All	8	Sutton Field House/Carl Albert High School
1997	M	II	Midwest City	OK	3/13-15/97	All	8	Sutton Field House/Carl Albert High School
1997	W		Midwest City	OK	3/13-15/97	All	4	Sutton Field House/Carl Albert High School
1998	M		Midwest City	OK	3/12-14/98	All	8	Sutton Field House
1998	W		Midwest City	OK	3/12-14/98	All	4	Sutton Field House

NCAA

Year	M/W	DIV	City	ST	Dates	Type	#T	Arena
1939	M		Evanston	IL	3/27/39	F2	8	Patten Gymnasium
1940	M		Kansas City	MO	3/30/40	F2	8	Municipal Auditorium
1941	M		Kansas City	MO	3/29/41	F2	8	Municipal Auditorium
1942	M		Kansas City	MO	3/28/42	F2	8	Municipal Auditorium
1943	M		New York	NY	3/30/43	F2	8	Madison Square Garden III
1944	M		New York	NY	3/28/44	F2	8	Madison Square Garden III
1945	M		New York	NY	3/27/45	F2	8	Madison Square Garden III
1946	M		New York	NY	3/26/46	F2	8	Madison Square Garden III
1947	M		New York	NY	3/25/47	F2	8	Madison Square Garden III
1948	M		New York	NY	3/23/48	F2	8	Madison Square Garden III
1949	M		Seattle	WA	3/26/49	F2	8	Hec Edmundson Pavilion
1950	M		New York	NY	3/28/50	F2	8	Madison Square Garden III

Year	M/W	DIV	City	ST	Dates	Type	#T	Arena
1951	M		Minneapolis	MN	3/27/51	F2	16	Williams Arena
1952	M		Seattle	WA	3/25-26/52	F4	16	Hec Edmundson Pavilion
1953	M		Kansas City	MO	3/17-18/53	F4	22	Municipal Auditorium
1954	M		Kansas City	MO	3/19-20/54	F4	24	Municipal Auditorium
1955	M		Kansas City	MO	3/18-19/55	F4	24	Municipal Auditorium
1956	M		Evanston	IL	3/23-24/56	F4	25	McGaw Hall
1957	M	I	Kansas City	MO	3/22-23/57	F4	23	Municipal Auditorium
1957	M	II	Evansville	IN	3/13-15/57	F8	32	Roberts Municipal Stadium
1958	M	I	Louisville	KY	3/21-22/58	F4	24	Freedom Hall
1958	M	II	Evansville	IN	3/13-15/58	F8	32	Roberts Municipal Stadium
1959	M	I	Louisville	KY	3/20-21/59	F4	23	Freedom Hall
1959	M	II	Evansville	IN	3/11-13/59	F8	32	Roberts Municipal Stadium
1960	M	I	San Francisco	CA	3/18-19/60	F8	25	Cow Palace
1960	M	II	Evansville	IN	3/9-11/60	F8	32	Roberts Municipal Stadium
1961	M	I	Kansas City	MO	3/24-25/61	F8	24	Municipal Auditorium
1961	M	II	Evansville	IN	3/15-17/61	F8	32	Roberts Municipal Stadium
1962	M	I	Louisville	KY	3/23-24/62	F4	25	Freedom Hall
1962	M	II	Evansville	IN	3/15-17/62	F8	32	Roberts Municipal Stadium
1963	M	I	Louisville	KY	3/22-23/63	F4	25	Freedom Hall
1963	M	II	Evansville	IN	3/13-15/63	F8	32	Roberts Municipal Stadium
1964	M	I	Kansas City	MO	3/20-21/64	F4	25	Municipal Auditorium
1964	M	II	Evansville	IN	3/11-13/64	F8	32	Roberts Municipal Stadium
1965	M	I	Portland	OR	3/19-20/65	F4	23	Memorial Coliseum
1965	M	II	Evansville	IN	3/11-13/65	F8	32	Roberts Municipal Stadium
1966	M	I	College Park	MD	3/18-19/66	F4	22	Cole Fieldhouse
1966	M	II	Evansville	IN	3/9-11/66	F8	36	Roberts Municipal Stadium
1967	M	I	Louisville	KY	3/24-25/67	F4	23	Freedom Hall
1967	M	II	Evansville	IN	3/15-17/67	F8	36	Roberts Municipal Stadium
1968	M	I	Los Angeles	CA	3/22-23/68	F4	23	Los Angeles Sports Arena
1968	M	II	Evansville	IN	3/13-15/68	F8	36	Roberts Municipal Stadium
1969	M	I	Louisville	KY	3/20-22/69	F4	25	Freedom Hall
1969	M	II	Evansville	IN	3/11-13/69	F8	32	Roberts Municipal Stadium
1970	M	I	College Park	MD	3/19-21/70	F4	25	Cole Fieldhouse
1970	M	II	Evansville	IN	3/11-13/70	F8	32	Roberts Municipal Stadium
1971	M	I	Houston	TX	3/25-27/71	F4	25	Astrodome
1971	M	II	Evansville	IN	3/17-19/71	F8	32	Roberts Municipal Stadium
1972	M	I	Los Angeles	CA	3/23-25/72	F4	25	Los Angeles Sports Arena
1972	M	II	Evansville	IN	3/15-17/72	F8	36	Roberts Municipal Stadium
1973	M	I	St. Louis	MO	3/24-26/73	F4	25	St. Louis Arena
1973	M	II	Evansville	IN	3/14-16/73	F8	42	Roberts Municipal Stadium
1974	M	I	Greensboro	NC	3/23-25/74	F4	25	Coliseum
1974	M	II	Evansville	IN	3/13-15/74	F8	44	Roberts Municipal Stadium
1975	M	I	San Diego	CA	3/29-31/75	F4	32	Sports Arena
1975	M	II	Evansville	IN	3/12-14/75	F8	32	Roberts Municipal Stadium
1975	M	III	Reading	PA	3/14-15/75	F4	30	George Bollman Physical Education Building
1976	M	I	Philadelphia	PA	3/27-29/76	F4	32	The Spectrum
1976	M	II	Evansville	IN	3/18-19/76	F4	32	Roberts Municipal Stadium
1976	M	III	Reading	PA	3/19-20/76	F4	28	George Bollman Physical Education Building

Year	M/W	DIV	City	ST	Dates	Type	#T	Arena
1977	M	I	Atlanta	GA	3/26-28/77	F4	32	The Omni
1977	M	II	Springfield	MA	3/18-19/77	F4	32	Civic Center
1977	M	III	Rock Island	IL	3/18-19/77	F4	30	Roy J Carver Physical Education Center
1978	M	I	St. Louis	MO	3/25-27/78	F4	32	The Checkerdome
1978	M	II	Springfield	MO	3/17-18/78	F4	32	John Q Hammons Student Center
1978	M	III	Rock Island	IL	3/17-18/78	F4	30	Roy J Carver Physical Education Center
1979	M	I	Salt Lake City	UT	3/24-26/79	F4	40	Special Events Center
1979	M	II	Springfield	MO	3/16-17/79	F4	32	John Q Hammons Student Center
1979	M	III	Rock Island	IL	3/16-17/79	F4	32	Roy J Carver Physical Education Center
1980	M	I	Indianapolis	IN	3/22-24/80	F4	48	Market Square Arena
1980	M	II	Springfield	MA	3/14-15/80	F4	32	Civic Center
1980	M	III	Rock Island	IL	3/14-15/80	F4	32	Roy J Carver Physical Education Center
1981	M	I	Philadelphia	PA	3/28-30/81	F4	48	The Spectrum
1981	M	II	Springfield	MA	3/20-21/81	F4	32	Civic Center
1981	M	III	Rock Island	IL	3/20-21/81	F4	32	Roy J Carver Physical Education Center
1982	M	I	New Orleans	LA	3/27-29/82	F4	48	Louisiana Superdome
1982	M	II	Springfield	MA	3/18-20/82	F4	32	Civic Center
1982	M	III	Grand Rapids	MI	3/19-20/82	F4	32	Calvin College Fieldhouse
1982	W	I	Norfolk	VA	3/26-28/82	F4	32	The Norfolk Scope
1982	W	II	Springfield	MA	3/18-20/82	F4	16	Civic Center
1982	W	III	Elizabethtown	PA	3/19-20/82	F4	16	Thompson Gymnasium & Alumni Athletic Center
1983	M	I	Albuquerque	NM	4/2-4/83	F4	52	The Pit
1983	M	II	Springfield	MA	3/24-26/83	F4	32	Civic Center
1983	M	III	Grand Rapids	MI	3/18-19/83	F4	32	Calvin College Fieldhouse
1983	W	I	Norfolk	VA	4/1-3/83	F4	36	The Norfolk Scope
1983	W	III	Worcester	MA	3/18-19/83	F4	32	Student Activities Center
1983	W	II	Springfield	MA	3/24-26/83	F4	24	Civic Center
1984	M	I	Seattle	WA	3/31-4/2/84	F4	53	The Kingdome
1984	M	II	Springfield	MA	3/22-24/84	F4	32	Civic Center
1984	M	III	Grand Rapids	MI	3/16-17/84	F4	32	Calvin College Fieldhouse
1984	W	I	Los Angeles	CA	3/30-4/1/84	F4	32	Pauley Pavilion
1984	W	II	Springfield	MA	3/22-24/84	F4	24	Civic Center
1984	W	III	Scranton	PA	3/16-17/84	F4	32	John Long Center
1985	M	I	Lexington	KY	3/30-4/1/85	F4	64	Rupp Arena
1985	M	II	Springfield	MA	3/22-23/85	F4	32	Civic Center
1985	M	III	Grand Rapids	MI	3/15-16/85	F4	32	Calvin College Fieldhouse
1985	W	I	Austin	TX	3/29-31/85	F4	32	Frank Erwin Special Events Center
1985	W	III	De Pere	WI	3/15-16/85	F4	32	Shuldes Sports Center
1985	W	II	Springfield	MA	3/21-23/85	F4	24	Civic Center
1986	M	I	Dallas	TX	3/29-31/86	F4	64	Reunion Arena
1986	M	II	Springfield	MA	3/21-22/86	F4	32	Civic Center
1986	M	III	Grand Rapids	MI	3/14-15/86	F4	32	Calvin College Fieldhouse
1986	W	I	Lexington	KY	3/28-30/86	F4	40	Rupp Arena
1986	W	II	Springfield	MA	3/20-22/86	F4	24	Civic Center
1986	W	III	Salem	MA	3/14-15/86	F4	32	Richard B O'Keefe Sports Complex

Year	M/W	DIV	City	ST	Dates	Type	#T	Arena
1987	M	I	New Orleans	LA	3/28-30/87	F4	64	Louisiana Superdome
1987	M	II	Springfield	MA	3/20-21/87	F4	32	Civic Center
1987	M	III	Grand Rapids	MI	3/20-21/87	F4	32	Calvin College Fieldhouse
1987	W	I	Austin	TX	3/27-29/87	F4	40	Frank Erwin Special Events Center
1987	W	II	Springfield	MA	3/19-21/87	F4	24	Civic Center
1987	W	III	Scranton	PA	3/20-21/87	F4	32	John Long Center
1988	M	I	Kansas City	MO	4/2-4/88	F4	64	Kemper Arena
1988	M	II	Springfield	MA	3/25-27/88	F8	32	Civic Center
1988	M	III	Grand Rapids	MI	3/18-19/88	F4	32	Calvin College Fieldhouse
1988	W	I	Tacoma	WA	4/1-3/88	F4	40	Tacoma Dome
1988	W	II	Fargo	ND	3/25-26/88	F4	32	Bison Sports Arena
1988	W	III	Moorhead	MN	3/18-19/88	F4	32	Memorial Auditorium
1989	M	I	Seattle	WA	4/1-3/89	F4	64	The Kingdome
1989	M	II	Springfield	MA	3/23-25/89	F8	32	Civic Center
1989	M	III	Springfield	OH	3/17-19/89	F4	40	Health, Phys Ed & Recreation Center
1989	W	I	Tacoma	WA	3/31-4/2/89	F4	48	Tacoma Dome
1989	W	II	Cleveland	MS	3/24-25/89	F4	32	Walter Siller's Coliseum
1989	W	III	Danville	KY	3/17-18/89	F4	32	Alumni Memorial Gymnasium
1990	M	I	Denver	CO	3/31-4/2/90	F4	64	McNichols Arena
1990	M	II	Springfield	MA	3/24-36/90	F8	32	Civic Center
1990	M	III	Springfield	OH	3/16-17/90	F4	40	Health, Phys Ed & Recreation Center
1990	W	I	Knoxville	TN	3/30-4/1/90	F4	48	Thompson-Boling Arena
1990	W	II	Pomona	CA	3/23-24/90	F4	32	Kellogg Gymnasium
1990	W	III	Holland	MI	3/16-17/90	F4	32	Holland Civic Center
1991	M	I	Indianapolis	IN	3/30-4/1/91	F4	64	RCA Dome
1991	M	II	Springfield	MA	3/21-23/91	F8	32	Civic Center
1991	M	III	Springfield	OH	3/15-16/91	F4	40	Health, Phys Ed & Recreation Center
1991	W	I	New Orleans	LA	3/30-31/91	F4	48	Kiefer Uno Lakefront Arena
1991	W	II	Cape Girardeau	MO	3/22-23/91	F4	32	Show Me Center
1991	W	III	St. Paul	MN	3/15-16/91	F4	32	Scheonecker Arena
1992	M	I	Minneapolis	MN	4/4-6/92	F4	64	Hubert H Humphrey Metrodome
1992	M	II	Springfield	MA	3/26-28/92	F8	32	Civic Center
1992	M	III	Springfield	OH	3/20-21/92	F4	40	Health, Phys Ed & Recreation Center
1992	W	I	Los Angeles	CA	4/4-5/92	F4	48	Los Angeles Sports Arena
1992	W	II	Fargo	ND	3/27-28/92	F4	32	Bison Sports Arena
1992	W	III	Bethlehem	PA	3/20-21/92	F4	32	Johnston Hall
1993	M	I	New Orleans	LA	4/3-5/93	F4	64	Louisiana Superdome
1993	M	II	Springfield	MA	3/25-27/93	F8	32	Civic Center
1993	M	III	Buffalo	NY	3/19-20/93	F4	40	Buffalo State Sports Arena
1993	W	I	Atlanta	GA	4/3-4/93	F4	48	The Omni
1993	W	II	Waltham	MA	3/26-27/93	F4	32	Elwood Shields Fieldhouse
1993	W	III	Pella	IA	3/19-20/93	F4	32	P H Kuyper Gymnasium
1994	M	I	Charlotte	NC	4/2-4/94	F4	64	Charlotte Coliseum
1994	M	II	Springfield	MA	3/23-26/94	F8	32	Civic Center
1994	M	III	Buffalo	NY	3/18-19/94	F4	40	Buffalo State Sports Arena

Year	M/W	DIV	City	ST	Dates	Type	#T	Arena
1994	W	I	Richmond	VA	4/2-3/94	F4	64	Richmond Coliseum
1994	W	II	Fargo	ND	3/23-26/94	F4	32	Bison Sports Arena
1994	W	III	Eau Claire	WI	3/18-19/94	F4	40	W L Zorn Arena
1995	M	I	Seattle	WA	4/1-3/95	F4	64	The Kingdome
1995	M	II	Louisville	KY	3/22-25/95	F8	48	Commonwealth Convention Center
1995	M	III	Buffalo	NY	3/17-18/95	F4	64	Buffalo State Sports Arena
1995	W	I	Minneapolis	MN	4/1-2/95	F4	64	Hubert H Humphrey Metrodome
1995	W	II	Fargo	ND	3/22-25/95	F8	48	Bison Sports Arena
1995	W	III	Columbus	OH	3/17-18/95	F4	64	Alumni Gymnasium
1996	M	I	East Rutherford	NJ	3/30-4/1/96	F4	64	Continental Air Arena
1996	M	II	Louisville	KY	3/21-23/95	F8	48	Commonwealth Convention Center
1996	M	III	Salem	VA	3/15-16/96	F4	64	Salem Civic Center
1996	W	I	Charlotte	NC	3/29-31/96	F4	64	Charlotte Coliseum
1996	W	II	Fargo	ND	3/21-23/96	F8	48	Bison Sports Arena
1996	W	III	Oshkosh	WI	3/15-16/96	F8	64	Kolf Sports Center
1997	M	I	Indianapolis	IN	3/29-31/97	F4	64	RCA Dome
1997	M	II	Louisville	KY	3/27-29/97	F8	48	Commonwealth Convention Center
1997	M	III	Salem	VA	3/28-29/97	F4	64	Salem Civic Center
1997	W	I	Cincinnati	OH	3/28-30/97	F4	64	Riverfront Coliseum
1997	W	II	Grand Forks	ND	3/27-29/97	F4	48	Hyslop Sports Center
1997	W	III	New York	NY	3/28-29/97	F4	64	Jeremy S Coles Sports Center
1998	M	I	San Antonio	TX	3/28-30/98	F4	64	Alamodome
1998	M	II	Louisville	KY	3/18-21/98	F8	48	Commonwealth Convention Center
1998	M	III	Salem	VA	3/20-21/98	F4	48	Salem Civic Center
1998	W	I	Kansas City	MO	3/27-29/98	F4	64	Kemper Arena
1998	W	II	Pine Bluff	AR	3/18-21/98	F8	48	Pine Bluff Convention Center
1998	W	III	Gorham	ME	3/20-21/98	F4	48	Hill Gymnasium

NCaT

Year	M/W	DIV	City	ST	Dates	Type	#T	Arena
1963	M		Louisville	KY	3/8-9/63	All	4	Freedom Hall

NCCAA

Year	M/W	DIV	City	ST	Dates	Type	#T	Arena
1968	M		Detroit	MI		All	6	
1969	M		Chattanooga	TN	3/14-15/69	All	6	McGilvray Gymnasium
1970	M		Chattanooga	TN	3/12-14/70	All	8	McGilvray Gymnasium
1971	M		Chattanooga	TN	3/11-13/71	All	8	McGilvray Gymnasium
1972	M		Chattanooga	TN	3/16-18/72	All	8	McGilvray Gymnasium
1973	M		Chattanooga	TN	3/16-17/73	All	4	McGilvray Gymnasium
1974	M		Chattanooga	TN	3/15-16/74	All	8	McGilvray Gymnasium
1975	M		Chattanooga	TN	3/14-15/75	All	4	McGilvray Gymnasium
1976	M	I	Chattanooga	TN	3/12-13/76	All	4	McGilvray Gymnasium
1976	M	II	Clarks Summit	PA		All	4	Student Center Gym
1977	M	I	Chattanooga	TN	3/17-19/77	All	8	McGilvray Gymnasium
1977	M	II	Springfield	MO		All	4	
1978	M	I	Chattanooga	TN	3/16-18/78	All	8	MacLellan Gymnasium
1978	M	II				All	6	
1979	M	I	Chattanooga	TN	3/15-17/79	All	6	McGilvray Gymnasium
1979	M	II				All	6	

Year	M/W	DIV	City	ST	Dates	Type	#T	Arena
1980	M	I	Chattanooga	TN	3/13-15/80	All	6	McGilvray Gymnasium
1980	M	II	Clarks Summit	PA		All	6	Student Center Gym
1981	M	I	Chattanooga	TN	3/19-20/81	All	6	McGilvray Gymnasium
1981	M	II	Clarks Summit	PA		All	6	Student Center Gym
1982	M	I	Chattanooga	TN	3/18-20/82	All	7	McGilvray Gymnasium
1982	M	II	Springfield	MO	3/4-6/1982	All	8	
1983	M	I	Chattanooga	TN	3/17-19/83	All	8	McGilvray Gymnasium
1983	M	II	Springfield	MO	3/3-5/83	All	6	
1983	W	I	Chattanooga	TN	3/10-12/83	All	8	McGilvray Gymnasium
1983	W	II	Chattanooga	TN	3/11-12/83	All	4	McGilvray Gymnasium
1984	M	I	Chattanooga	TN	3/15-17/84	All	8	McGilvray Gymnasium
1984	M	II				All	8	
1984	W	I	Chattanooga	TN		All	8	McGilvray Gymnasium
1984	W	II	Chattanooga	TN		All	6	McGilvray Gymnasium
1985	M	I	Chattanooga	TN	3/14-16/85	All	8	McGilvray Gymnasium
1985	M	II	Cincinnati	OH		All	8	President's Hall
1985	W	I	Cedarville	OH	3/7-9/85	All	8	The Athletic Center
1985	W	II	Knoxville	TN		All	8	
1986	M	I	Chattanooga	TN	3/13-15/86	All	8	McGilvray Gymnasium
1986	M	II	Cincinnati	OH		All	8	President's Hall
1986	W	I	Cedarville	OH	3/6-8/86	All	8	The Athletic Center
1986	W	II	Toccoa Falls	GA		All	8	
1987	M	I	Chattanooga	TN	3/12-14/87	All	8	McGilvray Gymnasium
1987	M	II	Cincinnati	OH	3/5-7/87	All	8	President's Hall
1987	W	I	Palos Heights	IL	3/5-7/87	All	8	Mitchell Memorial Gymnasium
1987	W	II	Grayson	KY		All	6	Lusby Center
1988	M	I	Chattanooga	TN	3/17-19/88	All	8	McGilvray Gymnasium
1988	M	II	Baton Rouge	LA	3/3-5/88	All	8	
1988	W	I	Palos Heights	IL	3/10-12/88	All	8	Mitchell Memorial Gymnasium
1988	W	II	Joplin	MO		All	6	
1989	M	I	Chattanooga	TN	3/16-18/89	All	8	McGilvray Gymnasium
1989	M	II	Baton Rouge	LA		All	8	
1989	W	I	Cleveland	TN	3/9-11/89	All	8	Paul Dana Walker Arena
1989	W	II	Grayson	KY	3/2-4/89	All	8	Lusby Center
1990	M	I	Chattanooga	TN	3/15-17/90	All	8	McGilvray Gymnasium
1990	M	II	Baton Rouge	LA	3/1-3/90	All	8	
1990	W	I	Cleveland	TN	3/8-10/90	All	8	Paul Dana Walker Arena
1990	W	II	Clarks Summit	PA	3/1-3/90	All	8	Student Center Gym
1991	M	I	Cleveland	TN	3/14-16/91	All	8	Jim Smiddy Arena
1991	M	II	Chicago	IL	3/7-9/91	All	8	Solheim Center
1991	M	IIA	Chicago	IL	3/7-9/91	All	4	Solheim Center
1991	W	I	Bartlesville	OK	3/7-9/91	All	8	
1991	W	II	Clarks Summit	PA	3/7-9/91	All	8	Student Center Gym
1992	M	I	Marion	IN	3/19-20/92	All	8	Robert R Luckey Physical Education Center
1992	M	II	Cincinnati	OH	3/5-7/92	All	8	President's Hall
1992	M	IIA	Cincinnati	OH	3/5-7/92	All	8	President's Hall
1992	W	I	Bartlesville	OK	3/12-14/92	All	8	
1992	W	II	East Point	GA	3/5-7/92	All	8	Alumni Hall

Year	M/W	DIV	City	ST	Dates	Type	#T	Arena
1993	M	I	Marion	IN	3/18-20/93	All	8	Robert R Luckey Physical Education Center
1993	M	II	Springfield	MO	3/4-6/93	All	8	
1993	M	IIA	Springfield	MO	3/4-6/93	All	8	
1993	W	I	Ann Arbor	MI	3/4-6/93	All	8	
1993	W	II	Clarks Summit	PA	3/4-6/93	All	8	Student Center Gym
1994	M	I	Marion	IN	3/17-19/94	All	8	Robert R Luckey Physical Education Center
1994	M	II	Springfield	MO	3/3-5/94	All	8	
1994	M	IIA	Springfield	MO	3/3-5/94	All	8	
1994	W	I	Ann Arbor	MI	3/3-5/94	All	8	
1994	W	II	Kirkland	WA	3/3-5/94	All	8	Pavillion
1995	M	I	Marion	IN	3/16-18/95	All	8	Robert R Luckey Physical Education Center
1995	M	II	Cincinnati	OH	3/2-4/95	All	8	President's Hall
1995	M	IIA	East Point	GA	3/2-4/95	All	8	Alumni Hall
1995	W	I	Rochester	NY	3/2-4/95	All	8	Voller Athletic Center
1995	W	II	Toccoa Falls	GA	3/2-4/95	All	8	Lois Delaney Gymnatorium
1996	M	I	Marion	IN	3/14-16/96	All	8	Robert R Luckey Physical Education Center
1996	M	II	Toccoa Falls	GA	2/29-3/2/96	All	8	Lois Delaney Gymnatorium
1996	M	IIA	Ankeny	IA	2/29-3/2/96	All	8	Faith Baptist Bible Gymnasium/Convocation Center
1996	W	I	Rochester	NY	3/7-9/96	All	8	Voller Athletic Center
1996	W	II	Joplin	MO	3/7-9/96	All	8	Multi-Purpose Building
1997	M	I	Marion	IN	3/20-22/97	All	8	Robert R Luckey Physical Education Center
1997	M	II	Oklahoma City	OK	3/6-8/97	All	8	Shartel Gymnasium
1997	M	IIA	Oklahoma City	OK	3/6-8/97	All	8	Shartel Gymnasium
1997	W	I	Cleveland	TN	3/12-15/97	All	8	Paul Dana Walker Arena
1997	W	II	Oklahoma City	OK	3/6-8/97	All	8	Shartel Gymnasium
1998	M	I	Oakland City	IN	3/19-21/98	All	8	
1998	M	II	Oklahoma City	OK	3/5-7/98	All	8	Shartel Gymnasium
1998	M	IIA	Oklahoma City	OK	3/5-7/98	All	8	Shartel Gymnasium
1998	W	I	Cleveland	TN	3/12-14/98	All	8	Paul Dana Walker Arena
1998	W	II	Oklahoma City	OK	3/5-7/98	All	8	Shartel Gymnasium

NCIT

Year	M/W	DIV	City	ST	Dates	Type	#T	Arena
1949	M		Denver	CO	3/20-26/49	All	16	Denver City Auditorium
1950	M		Albany	NY		All	8	New York State Armory
1951	M		Albany	NY	3/14-17/51	All	12	
1952	M		Troy	NY	3/16-22/52	All	12	Field House

NCT

Year	M/W	DIV	City	ST	Dates	Type	#T	Arena
1951	M		Peoria	IL	3/27-31/51	All	8	Robertson Memorial Field House

NIT

Year	M/W	DIV	City	ST	Dates	Type	#T	Arena
1938	M		New York	NY	3/14-16/38	All	6	Madison Square Garden III
1939	M		New York	NY	3/15-22/39	All	6	Madison Square Garden III
1940	M		New York	NY	3/11-15/40	All	6	Madison Square Garden III
1941	M		New York	NY	3/18-24/41	All	8	Madison Square Garden III
1942	M		New York	NY	3/17-25/42	All	8	Madison Square Garden III
1943	M		New York	NY	3/22-29/43	All	8	Madison Square Garden III
1944	M		New York	NY	3/16-22/44	All	8	Madison Square Garden III
1945	M		New York	NY	3/19-26/45	All	8	Madison Square Garden III

Year	M/W	DIV	City	ST	Dates	Type	#T	Arena
1946	M		New York	NY	3/14-20/46	All	8	Madison Square Garden III
1947	M		New York	NY	3/15-24/47	All	8	Madison Square Garden III
1948	M		New York	NY	3/11-17/48	All	8	Madison Square Garden III
1949	M		New York	NY	3/12-19/49	All	12	Madison Square Garden III
1950	M		New York	NY	3/11-18/50	All	12	Madison Square Garden III
1951	M		New York	NY	3/10-17/51	All	12	Madison Square Garden III
1952	M		New York	NY	3/8-15/52	All	12	Madison Square Garden III
1953	M		New York	NY	3/7-14/53	All	12	Madison Square Garden III
1954	M		New York	NY	3/6-13/54	All	12	Madison Square Garden III
1955	M		New York	NY	3/12-19/55	All	12	Madison Square Garden III
1956	M		New York	NY	3/17-24/56	All	12	Madison Square Garden III
1957	M		New York	NY	3/16-23/57	All	12	Madison Square Garden III
1958	M		New York	NY	3/13-22/58	All	12	Madison Square Garden III
1959	M		New York	NY	3/12-21/59	All	12	Madison Square Garden III
1960	M		New York	NY	3/10-19/60	All	12	Madison Square Garden III
1961	M		New York	NY	3/16-25/61	All	12	Madison Square Garden III
1962	M		New York	NY	3/15-24/62	All	12	Madison Square Garden III
1963	M		New York	NY	3/14-23/63	All	12	Madison Square Garden III
1964	M		New York	NY	3/12-21/64	All	12	Madison Square Garden III
1965	M		New York	NY	3/11-20/65	All	14	Madison Square Garden III
1966	M		New York	NY	3/10-19/66	All	14	Madison Square Garden III
1967	M		New York	NY	3/9-18/67	All	14	Madison Square Garden III
1968	M		New York	NY	3/14-23/68	All	16	Madison Square Garden IV
1969	M		New York	NY	3/13-22/69	All	16	Madison Square Garden IV
1970	M		New York	NY	3/13-21/70	All	16	Madison Square Garden IV
1971	M		New York	NY	3/20-27/71	All	16	Madison Square Garden IV
1972	M		New York	NY	3/17-25/72	All	16	Madison Square Garden IV
1973	M		New York	NY	3/16-24/73	All	16	Madison Square Garden IV
1974	M		New York	NY	3/16-24/74	All	16	Madison Square Garden IV
1975	M		New York	NY	3/15-23/75	All	16	Madison Square Garden IV
1976	M		New York	NY	3/13-21/76	All	12	Madison Square Garden IV
1977	M		New York	NY	3/8-20/77	F8	16	Madison Square Garden IV
1978	M		New York	NY	3/19-21/78	F4	16	Madison Square Garden IV
1979	M		New York	NY	3/19-21/79	F4	24	Madison Square Garden IV
1980	M		New York	NY	3/17-19/80	F4	32	Madison Square Garden IV
1981	M		New York	NY	3/23-25/81	F4	32	Madison Square Garden IV
1982	M		New York	NY	3/22-24/82	F4	32	Madison Square Garden IV
1983	M		New York	NY	3/28-30/83	F4	32	Madison Square Garden IV
1984	M		New York	NY	3/26-28/84	F4	32	Madison Square Garden IV
1985	M		New York	NY	3/27-29/85	F4	32	Madison Square Garden IV
1986	M		New York	NY	3/24-26/86	F4	32	Madison Square Garden IV
1987	M		New York	NY	3/11-24/87	F4	32	Madison Square Garden IV
1988	M		New York	NY	3/16-30/88	F4	32	Madison Square Garden IV
1989	M		New York	NY	3/15-29/89	F4	32	Madison Square Garden IV
1990	M		New York	NY	3/14-28/90	F4	32	Madison Square Garden IV
1991	M		New York	NY	3/25-27/91	F4	32	Madison Square Garden IV
1992	M		New York	NY	3/30-4/1/92	F4	32	Madison Square Garden IV
1993	M		New York	NY	3/29-31/93	F4	32	Madison Square Garden IV

Year	M/W	DIV	City	ST	Dates	Type	#T	Arena
1994	M		New York	NY	3/16-30/94	F4	32	Madison Square Garden IV
1995	M		New York	NY	3/15-29/95	F4	32	Madison Square Garden IV
1996	M		New York	NY	3/25-27/96	F4	32	Madison Square Garden IV
1997	M		New York	NY	3/12-27/97	F4	32	Madison Square Garden IV
1998	M		New York	NY	3/11-26/98	F4	32	Madison Square Garden IV

NSCAA

Year	M/W	DIV	City	ST	Dates	Type	#T	Arena
1967	M		Baltimore	MD	3/10-11/67	All	8	Fort Holabird Gymnasium
1968	M		Youngstown	OH	3/7-8/68	All	8	Struthers Fieldhouse
1969	M		Johnson City	TN	3/5-6/69	All	8	East Tennessee State Univ Field House
1970	M		New Kensington	PA	3/4-5/70	All	8	Penn State: New Kensington Gymnasium
1971	M		Tiffin	OH	3/11-13/71	All	8	Heidelberg College Gymnasium
1972	M		Albany	NY		All	8	Sage JC Gymnasium
1973	M		Tiffin	OH	3/8-10/73	All	8	Heidelberg College Gymnasium
1974	M		Mount Vernon	OH	3/5-9/74	All	16	Mount Vernon Nazarene College Gymnasium
1975	M		Heflin	AL	3/10-15/75	All	16	Cleburne High School Gymnasium
1976	M		Norfolk	NE	3/8-12/76	All	14	City Auditorium
1977	M		Norfolk	NE	3/7-11/77	All	16	City Auditorium
1978	M		Norfolk	NE	3/6-10/79	All	16	City Auditorium
1979	M		Norfolk	NE	3/12-16/79	All	16	City Auditorium
1980	M		Oakland City	IN	3/10-14/80	All	16	Wood Memorial High School Gymnasium
1980	W		Portland	OR	3/6-8/80	All	8	Physical Education Building
1981	M		Oakland City	IN	3/9-13/81	All	16	Wood Memorial High School Gymnasium
1981	W		No Tournament					
1982	M		Oakland City	IN	3/8-12/82	All	16	Wood Memorial High School Gymnasium
1982	W		Freeman	SD	3/4-6/82	All	8	Pioneer Hall
1983	M		Norfolk	NE	3/14-18/83	All	16	City Auditorium
1983	W		Ellendale	ND	3/10-12/83	All	8	Trinity Bible College Field House
1984	M		Marion	OH	3/12-16/84	All	16	Veterans Coliseum
1984	W		Lamar	CO	3/7-10/84	All	9	
1985	W		Saint Paul	MN	3/5-8/85	All	8	Lutheran Memorial Center
1985	M		Norfolk	NE	3/11-15/85	All	16	Norfolk CC Activities Center
1986	M		Bristol	TN	3/8-13/86	All	16	Viking Hall Civic Center
1986	W		Kalamazoo	MI	3/6-8/86	All	8	
1987	M		Bristol	TN	3/9-13/87	All	16	Viking Hall Civic Center
1987	W				3/5-7/87	All	8	
1988	M		Madison	WI	3/7-11/88	All	15	
1988	W				3/3-5/88	All	8	
1989	M		Madison	WI	3/6-10/89	All	15	
1989	W		New Ulm	MN	3/2-4/89	All	8	Luther Memorial Union
1990	M		Flint	MI	3/5-9/90	All	12	
1990	W					All	8	
1991	M		Flint	MI	3/11-15/91	All	12	Sun Dome
1991	W				3/7-9/91	All	8	
1992	M		Dallas	TX	3/9-12/92	All	12	
1992	W		Deerfield	IL	3/3-5/92	All	8	Meyer Sports Complex
1993	M		Dallas	TX	3/8-11/93	All	9	
1993	W		Wilmington	DE	3/4-6/93	All	8	Pratt Student Center

Year	M/W	DIV	City	ST	Dates	Type	#T	Arena
1994	M		Flint	MI	3/7-11/94	All	12	Sun Dome
1994	W		Carlinville	IL	3/3-5/94	All	8	Dawes Gymnasium
1995	M		Amarillo	TX	3/6-10/95	All	12	Highland Park High School Gymnasium
1995	W		Pulaski	TN	3/2-4/95	All	8	Curry Christian Life Center
1996	M		Amarillo	TX	3/11-15/96	All	10	
1996	W		Salina	KS	3/7-9/96	All	8	Muir Gymnasium
1997	M		Salina	KS	3/5-8/97	All	12	Muir Gymnasium
1997	W		Salina	KS	3/5-8/97	All	8	Muir Gymnasium
1998	M		Salina	KS	3/3-7/98	All	15	Muir Gymnasium
1998	W		Salina	KS	3/3-7/98	All	8	Muir Gymsasium

NWIT

Year	M/W	DIV	City	ST	Dates	Type	#T	Arena
1969	W		Amarillo	TX	3/20-22/69	All	8	Amarillo Civic Center
1970	W		Amarillo	TX	3/19-21/70	All	8	Amarillo Civic Center
1971	W		Amarillo	TX	3/25-27/71	All	8	Amarillo Civic Center
1972	W		Amarillo	TX	3/23-25/72	All	8	Amarillo Civic Center
1973	W		Amarillo	TX	3/22-24/73	All	8	Amarillo Civic Center
1974	W		Amarillo	TX	3/14-16/74	All	8	Amarillo Civic Center
1975	W		Amarillo	TX	3/13-15/75	All	8	Amarillo Civic Center
1976	W		Amarillo	TX	3/18-20/76	All	8	Amarillo Civic Center
1977	W		Amarillo	TX	3/17-19/77	All	8	Amarillo Civic Center
1978	W		Amarillo	TX	3/16-18/78	All	8	Amarillo Civic Center
1979	W		Amarillo	TX	3/15-17/79	All	8	Amarillo Civic Center
1980	W		Amarillo	TX	3/20-22/80	All	8	Amarillo Civic Center
1981	W		Amarillo	TX	3/26-28/81	All	8	Amarillo Civic Center
1982	W		Amarillo	TX	3/25-27/82	All	8	Amarillo Civic Center
1983	W		Amarillo	TX	3/17-19/83	All	8	Amarillo Civic Center
1984	W		Amarillo	TX	3/22-24/84	All	8	Amarillo Civic Center
1985	W		Amarillo	TX	3/21-23/85	All	8	Amarillo Civic Center
1986	W		Amarillo	TX	3/20-22/86	All	8	Amarillo Civic Center
1987	W		Amarillo	TX	3/19-21/87	All	8	Amarillo Civic Center
1988	W		Amarillo	TX	3/24-26/88	All	8	Amarillo Civic Center
1989	W		Amarillo	TX	3/23-25/89	All	8	Amarillo Civic Center
1990	W		Amarillo	TX	3/22-24/90	All	8	Amarillo Civic Center
1991	W		Amarillo	TX	3/21-23/91	All	8	Amarillo Civic Center
1992	W		Amarillo	TX	3/26-28/92	All	8	Amarillo Civic Center
1993	W		Amarillo	TX	3/25-27/93	All	8	Amarillo Civic Center
1994	W		Amarillo	TX	3/24-26/94	All	8	Amarillo Civic Center
1995	W		Amarillo	TX	3/23-25/95	All	8	Amarillo Civic Center
1996	W		Amarillo	TX	3/21-23/96	All	8	Amarillo Civic Center
1997	W		No Tournament					
1998	W		Waco	TX	3/13-24/98	F2	16	Ferrell Center

OLYD

Year	M/W	DIV	City	ST	Dates	Type	#T	Arena
1904	M		St. Louis	MO	7/13/04	All	3	Outdoor Field

OLYT

Year	M/W	DIV	City	ST	Dates	Type	#T	Arena
1936	M		New York	NY	4/3-5/36	All	8	Madison Square Garden III
1948	M		New York	NY	3/27-31/48	All	8	Madison Square Garden III
1952	M		New York	NY	3/29-4/1/52	F4	8	Madison Square Garden III
1956	M		Kansas City	KS	4/2-4/56	All	4	Municipal Auditorium
1960	M		Denver	CO	3/31-4/2/60	All	8	Denver Coliseum

NCAA Vacated Tournament Teams

This appendix lists the teams whose participation in an NCAA tournament has been vacated by action of the association. In some official NCAA tournament records, these schools are not listed, their entry replaced by "vacated." In other records, their participation is footnoted as "Vacated." These situations usually resulted when an infraction of NCAA rules during the given season was uncovered following the tournament. Normally the offending school is required to return any trophys or other awards as well as its share of tournament monies.

The data is presented in two formats: by school by year and by year by school. In the data, F indicates the schools finish or place in the tournament prior to the vacating action.

By School

School	Year	M/W	DIV	F	W	L	Coach
Alabama	1987	M	I	16	28	5	Sanderson, Winfrey "Wimp"
American International	1969	M	II	3	21	4	Callahan, William E.
	1970	M	II	8	17	8	Callahan, William E.
Arizona State	1995	M	I	16	24	9	Frieder, Bill
Austin Peay State	1973	M	I	16	22	7	Kelly, Lake
California	1996	M	I	64	17	11	Bozeman, Todd
California State: Long Beach	1971	M	I	8	24	5	Tarkanian, Jerry
	1972	M	I	8	25	4	Tarkanian, Jerry
	1973	M	I	12	26	3	Tarkanian, Jerry
California: Los Angeles	1980	M	I	2	22	10	Brown, Lawrence H.
Clemson	1990	M	I	16	26	9	Ellis, Cliff
De Paul	1986	M	I	16	18	13	Meyer, Joseph E. "Joey"
	1987	M	I	16	28	3	Meyer, Joseph E. "Joey"
	1988	M	I	32	22	8	Meyer, Joseph E. "Joey"
	1989	M	I	32	21	12	Meyer, Joseph E. "Joey"
Florida	1987	M	I	16	23	11	Sloan, Norman L., Jr.
	1988	M	I	32	23	12	Sloan, Norman L., Jr.
Georgia	1985	M	I	32	22	9	Durham, Hugh
Iona	1980	M	I	32	29	5	Valvano, James T.
Kentucky	1988	M	I	16	27	6	Sutton, Eddie
Loyola Marymount	1980	M	I	48	14	14	Jacobs, Ron
Marshall	1987	M	I	64	25	6	Huckabay, Rick
Maryland	1988	M	I	32	18	13	Wade, Bob
Massachusetts	1996	M	I	3	35	2	Calipari, John
Memphis	1982	M	I	16	24	5	Kirk, Dana
	1983	M	I	16	23	8	Kirk, Dana
	1984	M	I	16	26	7	Kirk, Dana
	1985	W	I	32	23	7	Johns, Mary Lou
	1985	M	I	3	31	4	Kirk, Dana
	1986	M	I	32	28	6	Kirk, Dana
Minnesota	1972	M	I	12	18	7	Musselman, William
New Mexico State	1992	M	I	16	25	8	McCarthy, Neil N.
	1993	M	I	32	26	8	McCarthy, Neil N.
	1994	M	I	64	23	8	McCarthy, Neil N.

School	Year	M/W	DIV	F	W	L	Coach
North Carolina State	1987	M	I	64	20	15	Valvano, James T.
	1988	M	I	64	24	8	Valvano, James T.
Oregon State	1980	M	I	32	26	4	Miller, Ralph H. "Cappy"
	1981	M	I	32	26	2	Miller, Ralph H. "Cappy"
	1982	M	I	8	25	5	Miller, Ralph H. "Cappy"
Saint Joseph's (PA)	1961	M	I	3	25	5	Ramsay, Dr. John T. "Jack"
San Francisco State	1984	M	II	8	21	11	Wilson, Kevin
Southwestern Louisiana	1971	M	II	3	25	4	Shipley, Beryl C.
	1972	M	I	12	25	4	Shipley, Beryl C.
	1973	M	I	16	24	5	Shipley, Beryl C.
Texas Tech	1996	M	I	16	30	2	Dickey, James
Villanova	1971	M	I	2	22	7	Kraft, John J. "Jack"
Western Kentucky	1971	M	I	3	24	6	Oldham, John O.

By Year

Year	School	M/W	DIV	F	W	L	Coach
1961	Saint Joseph's (Pa)	M	I	3	25	5	Ramsay, Dr. John T. "Jack"
1969	American International	M	II	3	21	4	Callahan, William E.
1970	American International	M	II	8	17	8	Callahan, William E.
1971	California State: Long Beach	M	I	8	24	5	Tarkanian, Jerry
	Southwestern Louisiana	M	II	3	25	4	Shipley, Beryl C.
	Villanova	M	I	2	22	7	Kraft, John J. "Jack"
	Western Kentucky	M	I	3	24	6	Oldham, John O.
1972	California State: Long Beach	M	I	8	25	4	Tarkanian, Jerry
	Minnesota	M	I	12	18	7	Musselman, William
	Southwestern Louisiana	M	I	12	25	4	Shipley, Beryl C.
1973	Austin Peay State	M	I	16	22	7	Kelly, Lake
	California State: Long Beach	M	I	12	26	3	Tarkanian, Jerry
	Southwestern Louisiana	M	I	16	24	5	Shipley, Beryl C.
1980	California: Los Angeles	M	I	2	22	10	Brown, Lawrence H.
	Iona	M	I	32	29	5	Valvano, James T.
	Loyola Marymount	M	I	48	14	14	Jacobs, Ron
	Oregon State	M	I	32	26	4	Miller, Ralph H. "Cappy"
1981	Oregon State	M	I	32	26	2	Miller, Ralph H. "Cappy"
1982	Memphis	M	I	16	24	5	Kirk, Dana
	Oregon State	M	I	8	25	5	Miller, Ralph H. "Cappy"
1983	Memphis	M	I	16	23	8	Kirk, Dana
1984	Memphis	M	I	16	26	7	Kirk, Dana
	San Francisco State	M	II	8	21	11	Wilson, Kevin
1985	Georgia	M	I	32	22	9	Durham, Hugh
	Memphis	W	I	32	23	7	Johns, Mary Lou
	Memphis	M	I	3	31	4	Kirk, Dana
1986	De Paul	M	I	16	18	13	Meyer, Joseph E. "Joey"
	Memphis	M	I	32	28	6	Kirk, Dana
1987	Alabama	M	I	16	28	5	Sanderson, Winfrey "Wimp"
	De Paul	M	I	16	28	3	Meyer, Joseph E. "Joey"
	Florida	M	I	16	23	11	Sloan, Norman L., Jr.
	Marshall	M	I	64	25	6	Huckabay, Rick
	North Carolina State	M	I	64	20	15	Valvano, James T.
1988	De Paul	M	I	32	22	8	Meyer, Joseph E. "Joey"
	Florida	M	I	32	23	12	Sloan, Norman L., Jr.
	Kentucky	M	I	16	27	6	Sutton, Eddie
	Maryland	M	I	32	18	13	Wade, Bob
	North Carolina State	M	I	64	24	8	Valvano, James T.
1989	De Paul	M	I	32	21	12	Meyer, Joseph E. "Joey"
1990	Clemson	M	I	16	26	9	Ellis, Cliff
1992	New Mexico State	M	I	16	25	8	McCarthy, Neil N.
1993	New Mexico State	M	I	32	26	8	McCarthy, Neil N.
1994	New Mexico State	M	I	64	23	8	McCarthy, Neil N.
1995	Arizona State	M	I	16	24	9	Frieder, Bill
1996	California	M	I	64	17	11	Bozeman, Todd
	Massachusetts	M	I	3	35	2	Calipari, John
	Texas Tech	M	I	16	30	2	Dickey, James

Tournament Trivia

This appendix contains some interesting tid-bits of some consequence–and some of little consequence.

Most of them are just the result of some wondering, although some are included because it seems they should be.

While there are several publications on the NCAA Men's Division I tournament that include a trivia section, this appendix probably is the only "Triviana" that includes and combines information on all of the association tournaments, all divisions, men and women–plus all of the nonassociation tournaments.

Thus, there are some rather startling revelations–such as, "What school is second to UCLA in total association national championships won?"

Enjoy!

FIRST COLLEGES TO PARTICIPATE IN A POST-SEASON TOURNAMENT
Hiram
Wheaton (IL)
Latter-Day Saints Business College
(Salt Lake City, UT)

Olympic Demonstration Tournament,
Saint Louis World's Fair, 1904.

This event was post-season in the truest sense; the tournament was held in July. Or was it pre-season 1905?

Latter-Day Business College is not now Brigham Young University as some references to this tournament have indicated. The Business College still is in operation.

FIRST COLLEGIATE NATIONAL CHAMPION
Central Missouri State: NAIA
(Invitational), 1937

FIRST "MAJOR COLLEGE" NATIONAL CHAMPION
Temple: NIT, 1938

FIRST WOMEN'S COLLEGIATE NATIONAL CHAMPION
West Chester: AIAW (Invitational), 1969

FIRST ASSOCIATION OTHER THAN THE AIAW TO CONDUCT A SENIOR COLLEGE WOMEN'S TOURNAMENT
NSCAA, 1980

FIRST HISTORICALLY BLACK COLLEGE TO WIN A MAJOR ASSOCIATION TOURNAMENT CHAMPIONSHIP
Tennessee State: NAIA, 1957

ONLY COLLEGE TO WIN TWO ASSOCIATION TOURNAMENT CHAMPIONSHIPS IN THE SAME YEAR
Latin America Bible, Men: NBCAA II and NCCAA IIA, 1992

Its only ever appearance in post-season play.

COLLEGES WINNING TWO "NATIONAL CHAMPIONSHIPS" IN THE SAME YEAR
Wyoming: 1943, NCAA and Red Cross
Utah: 1944, NCAA and Red Cross
Oklahoma State: 1945, NCAA and Red Cross
City College: 1950, NCAA and NIT

ONLY COLLEGE TO WIN AN NAIA AND
AN NCAA DIVISION I CHAMPIONSHIP
Louisville, Men: NAIA, 1948;
    NCAA, 1980 and 1986

ONLY COLLEGE TO WIN AN NAIA AND
AN NCAA DIVISION II CHAMPIONSHIP
Central Missouri State, Men: NAIA, 1937
    and 1938; NCAA II, 1984

COLLEGES WINNING A MEN'S AND A
WOMEN'S ASSOCIATION CHAMPIONSHIP
IN THE SAME YEAR
Central Missouri State: 1984, NCAA II
Kentucky Christian: 1989, NCAA II
    1995, NCAA II
    1996, NCAA II
    1997, NCAA II
Northwest Assemblies: 1993, NCCAA II

In 1998, Kentucky Christian almost did it
for the fifth time and fourth in a row; the
men finished 2nd!

MEN'S AND WOMEN'S TEAM FROM THE
SAME COLLEGE IN THE FINAL FOUR IN
THE SAME YEAR
Baptist Bible (PA): 1982, NCCAA II
    1983, NCCAA II
    1984, NCCAA II
    1985, NCCAA II
    1991, NCCAA II
Blackburn: 1998, NSCAA
Cedarville: 1994, NCCAA I
Central Missouri State: 1984, NCAA II
Centre: 1989, NCAA III
David N Myers: 1986, NSCAA
Georgia: 1983, NCAA I
Hillsdale Free Will Baptist: 1998, NBCAA
Indiana Wesleyan: 1995, NCCAA I
John Brown: 1983, NCCAA I
Kansas Wesleyan: 1997, NSCAA
Kentucky Christian: 1988, NCCAA II
    1989, NCCAA II
    1990, NCCAA II
    1995, NCCAA II
    1996, NCCAA II
    1997, NCCAA II
    1998, NCCAA II
Lamar CC: 1983, NSCAA

Lee (TN): 1992, NCCAA I
    1993, NCCAA I
    1997, NCCAA I
Lipscomb: 1996, NAIA
Maranatha Baptist Bible (WI): 1983, NBCAA
Mid-America Bible: 1998, NCCAA II
MidAmerica Nazarene: 1994, NCCAA I
Mount Scenario: 1994, NSCAA
Northern State (SD): 1993, NAIA
    1994, NAIA
Northwest Assemblies: 1991, NCCAA II
    1992, NCCAA II
    1993, NCCAA II
    1994, NCCAA II
Northwest Nazarene: 1995, NAIA
Northwestern (MN): 1985, NCCAA II
Oakland City (IN): 1993, NCCAA
    1997, NCCAA I
Pacific Christian: 1989, NCCAA II
Rochester (MI): 1997, NSCAA
Southwestern Assemblies: 1998, NBCAA
Southern Nazarene: 1998, NAIA
Southwestern Christian Ministries: 1998,
    NBCAA
Tennessee Temple: 1983, NCCAA I
Wayland Baptist: 1985, NAIA
Western Baptist: 1995, NCCAA I

Surprise! Only Georgia from the NCAA
Division I

MOST NIT APPEARANCES
26 Saint John's (NY)
18 Bradley
18 Dayton
16 Duquesne
    Fordham
    Manhattan
    Saint Louis

MOST NIT CHAMPIONSHIPS
 5 Saint John's (NY)
 3 Bradley
 2 Brigham Young
    Dayton
    Kentucky
    Long Island
    Michigan
    Providence
    Temple
    Virginia
    Virginia Polytechnic

ONLY DIVISION II COLLEGE

TO WIN THE NIT CHAMPIONSHIP
Southern Illinois, 1967

ONLY COLLEGE TO WIN THE NCAA AND
THE NIT CHAMPIONSHIPS IN THE SAME YEAR
City College of New York, 1950 (See
below for an interesting piece of irony.)

ONLY COLLEGE TO FINISH SECOND IN
THE NCAA AND THE NIT IN THE SAME YEAR
Bradley, 1950 (See above for an interesting
piece of irony)

MOST NWIT APPEARANCES
10 Wayland Baptist
7 Belmont
7 John F Kennedy (NE)
6 Ranger
6 Illinois State

MOST NWIT CHAMPIONSHIPS
9 Wayland Baptist
2 Oregon State

NO COLLEGE HAS WON THE AIAW OR
NCAA AND THE NWIT IN THE SAME YEAR
Wayland Baptist, 1976: NWIT, 1st;
AIAW L, 3rd

COLLEGES IN THE AIAW AND NWIT
TOURNAMENTS IN THE SAME YEAR

| College | Year | –FINISH IN– | |
		AIAW	NWIT
Kansas State	1970	8	7
Wayland Baptist	1974	5	1
	1975	5	1
	1976	3	1
Mississippi College	1977	12	3

NO COLLEGE HAS WON THE NIT
AND THE NWIT IN THE SAME YEAR
Texas, 1978: Men, 1st; Women, 2nd
Pennsylvania State, 1998: Women, 1st;
Men, 2nd

MOST ASSOCIATION
TOURNAMENT CHAMPIONSHIPS

MEN

11 California: Los Angeles
7 Kentucky
Northwest Christian
6 Kentucky Christian
Kentucky Wesleyan
Tennessee Temple
5 Baptist Bible (MO)
Evansville
Indiana
North Park

A total of 19 from Kentucky colleges.

WOMEN

6 Delta State
Tennessee
5 Kentucky Christian
North Dakota State
Northwest Assemblies
Southern Nazarene
Southwestern Oklahoma State

MEN & WOMEN

12 California: Los Angeles (11 M, 1 W)
11 Kentucky Christian (6 M, 5 W)
8 Southern Nazarene (3 M, 5 W)

CONSECUTIVE ASSOCIATION
TOURNAMENT CHAMPIONSHIPS

College	M/W	Assn	DIV	Years
7 California: Los Angeles	M	NCAA	I	1967-73
5 Northwest Christian	M	NBCAA	I	1983-87
4 Azusa Pacific	M	NCCAA	I	1969-72
Baptist Bible (MO)	M	NCCAA	II	1981-84
Grace (NE)	W	NBCAA	I	1993-96
Kentucky Christian	W	NCCAA	II	1995-98
North Dakota State	W	NCAA	II	1993-96
Southern Nazarene	W	NAIA	I	1994-97
3 Cincinnati Bible	M	NCCAA	II	1985-87
Crown (MN)	W	NBCAA		1983-85
Delta State	W	AIAW	L	1975-77
Immaculata (PA)	W	AIAW		1972-74
Kentucky Christian	M	NCCAA	II	1995-97
King (TN)	W	NCCAA		1988-90
North Park	M	NCAA	III	1978-80
Point Loma Nazarene	M	NCCAA	I	1985-87
San Jose Christian	M	NBCAA	I	1993-95
Sullivan	M	NSCAA		1967-69
Tennessee	W	NCAA	I	1996-98
Tennessee State	M	NASC		1952-54
Tennessee State	M	NAIA		1957-59
Tennessee Temple	M	NCCAA	I	1981-83

Most #1 seeds in a major association tournament

NCAA Men I Since 1979 (4 #1's per year)

9 North Carolina
7 Kentucky
5 Georgetown (DC)
  Kansas

NCAA Women I Since 1987 (4 #1's per year)

10 Tennessee
6 Stanford
4 Connecticut
  Louisiana Tech

NAIA Men open/I Since 1957 (1 #1 per year)

3 Fairmont State
2 Central State (OH)
  Georgetown (KY)
  Kentucky State
  Oklahoma City
  Tennessee State
  Westminster (PA)
  Wisconsin: Eau Claire

NAIA Women open/I Since 1981 (1 #1 per year)

4 Southwestern Oklahoma State
3 Southern Nazarene

Plus 1 by Southeastern Oklahoma State for a total of 8 of 18 from Oklahoma

Most championship game appearances

Men

12 California: Los Angeles: NCAA I
11 Tennessee Temple: NCCAA I
10 Hillsdale Free Will Baptist: NBCAA II, 7; NCCAA III, 3
9 Tennessee State: NASC, 4; NAIA, 3; NCAA II, 2
8 Northwest Christian: NBCAA I, 6; NSCAA, 2
7 Baptist Bible (PA): NCCAA II
  Duke: NCAA I
  Kentucky Christian: NCCAA II
  North Carolina: NCAA I
6 Bethel (IN): NCAA I, 3; NAIA II, 3
  Kansas: NCAA I
  Nebraska Christian: NBCAA II, 5; NCCAA IIA, 1
  Southwest Missouri State: NAIA, 2; NCAA II, 4
  Sullivan (KY): NSCAA

5 Baptist Bible (MO): NCCAA II
  Evansville: NCAA II
  Indiana: NCAA I
  Indiana State: NAIA, 3; NCAA II, 1; NCAA I, 1
  Lee (TN): NCCAA I
  Michigan: NCAA I
  North Park: NCAA III
  Potsdam State: NCAA III
  Wittenburg : NCAA II, 2; NCAA III,3

Women

10 Tennessee: AIAW I, 2; NCAA I, 8
8 Louisiana Tech: AIAW L, 2; NCAA I, 6
7 Delta State: AIAW L, 3; NCAA II, 4
  Kentucky Christian: NCCAA II
  North Dakota State: NCAA II
6 California Polytechnic: Pomona: NCAA II
  Crown (MN): NBCAA
  Northwest Asemblies: NCCAA II
  Southern Nazarene: NAIA I
  Southwestern Oklahoma State: NAIA I
5 Grace (NE): NBCAA
  Immaculata (PA): AIAW

Most final four appearances in an association tournament (16 or more teams in tournament)

Men

15 California: Los Angeles
14 Kentucky Wesleyan
13 North Carolina
11 Duke
10 Kentucky
9 Kansas
8 California State: Bakersfield
  Tennessee State
  Wittenberg
7 Georgetown (KY)
  Hamline
  Indiana State
  Louisville
  Southwest Missouri State
6 Central Washington
  Cincinnati
  Evansville
  Fort Hays State
  Indiana
  Michigan
  Oklahoma Baptist University
  Southern Illinois

5 Augustana (IL)
  Florida Southern
  Houston
  Mount Saint Mary's (MD)
  Nebraska Wesleyan
  North Alabama
  North Park
  Potsdam State
  Southeastern Oklahoma State
  Southern Union State CC
  Virginia Union
  William Jewell
  Wisconsin: Eau Claire

WOMEN

15 Tennessee
12 Louisiana Tech
10 Delta State
9 North Dakota State
8 California Polytechnic: Pomona
  Southwestern Oklahoma State
7 Southern Nazarene
6 Arkansas Tech
  Bentley
  Immaculata (PA)
  Old Dominion
  Stanford
  Wayland Baptist
5 Capital
  Scranton
  Southern Connecticut State
  William Penn

MOST KNOWN WINS IN A SEASON, TOURNAMENT PARTICIPANT

MEN

41 Lipscomb 1990
39 Biola 1982
  Saint Thomas Aquinas 1988
38 Saint Thomas Aquinas 1984
37 Belmont 1995
  Duke 1986
  Nevada: Las Vegas 1987
  Saint Thomas Aquinas 1986
  Southeastern Oklahoma State 1955
36 Newberry 1977
  Oral Roberts 1990
  Regis (CO) 1949
  Saint Thomas Aquinas 1985

WOMEN

47 Tougaloo 1979
40 Louisiana Tech 1980
39 Tennessee 1998
37 Briar Cliff 1997
37 Claflin 1988
  Wayland Baptist 1974
  William Penn 1980
36 Saint Ambrose 1989

MOST KNOWN LOSSES IN A SEASON, TOURNAMENT PARTICIPANT

MEN

30 Graceland (IN) 1944
27 Indiana Wesleyan 1992
26 Columbia Bible 1997
  Kansas Wesleyan 1998
  Lamar CC 1983
  Northwest Assemblies 1989

WOMEN

26 Northwest Assemblies 1989
25 York (NE) 1997
24 Lee (TN) 1997
23 Concordia (MI) 1994
  Concordia (MI) 1993
  Colorado Northwestern CC 1987

FEWEST KNOWN WINS IN A SEASON, TOURNAMENT PARTICIPANT

MEN

0 Bay Ridge Christian 1997
1 Free Will Baptist Bible 1987
2 Association Free Lutheran 1988
  Association Free Lutheran 1996
  Association Free Lutheran 1998
  Johnson Bible 1986
  Oklahoma Baptist College 1998

WOMEN

2 Johnson Bible 1986
  Association Free Lutheran 1996
  Association Free Lutheran 1998
3 Pillsbury Baptist Bible 1986
  Calvary Bible 1991
  Central Christian (MO) 1996

COLLEGES IN MULTIPLE TOURNAMENTS IN THE SAME YEAR
(NCAA/NAIA AND NONASSOCIATION)

College	Year	NCAA	NAIA	NIT	FINISH IN OLY	NCIT	RC	NCT
Colorado	1940	8	—	1	—	—	—	—
Duquesne	1940	3	—	2	—	—	—	—
Georgetown (DC)	1943	2	—	—	—	—	3	—
Toldeo	1943	—	—	2	—	—	4	—
Wyoming	**1943**	1	—	—	—	—	1	—
Saint John's (NY)	1944	—	—	1	—	—	2	—
Utah	**1944**	1	—	8	—	—	1	—
Bowling Green	1945	—	—	2	—	—	4	—
De Paul	1945	—	—	1	—	—	2	—
New York	1945	2	—	—	—	—	3	—
Oklahoma State	**1945**	1	—	—	—	—	1	—
Baylor	1948	2	—	—	4	—	—	—
Kentucky	1948	1	—	—	2	—	—	—
Louisville	1948	—	1	—	8	—	—	—
New York	1948	—	2	—	8	—	—	—
Kentucky	1949	1	—	8	—	—	—	—
Loyola (MD)	1949	—	16	—	—	3	—	—
Regis (CO)	1949	—	2	—	—	1	—	—
Saint Thomas (MN)	1949	—	16	—	—	8	—	—
Bradley	1950	2	—	2	—	—	—	—
City College	**1950**	1	—	1	—	—	—	—
Arizona	1951	16	—	8	—	—	—	—
Brigham Young	1951	8	—	1	—	—	—	—
North Carolina State	1951	8	—	8	—	—	—	—
Saint John's (NY)	1951	6	—	3	—	—	—	—
Villanova	1951	16	—	—	—	—	—	8
Dayton	1952	12	—	2	—	—	—	—
Duquesne	1952	8	—	4	—	—	—	—
Kansas	1952	1	—	—	2	—	—	—
LaSalle	1952	—	—	1	4	—	—	—
Southwest Missouri State	1952	—	1	—	8	—	—	—
Saint John's (NY)	1952	2	—	8	—	—	—	—
Ohio State	1960	1	—	—	5	—	—	—

Utah is the only college to have a team in three "national championship" tournaments in the same year.

Beginning with the 1953 post-season, the NCAA decreed that colleges could not participate in two post-season tournaments in the same year; Ohio State in the Olympic Trials in 1960 was a special exception.

UNDEFEATED NATIONAL CHAMPIONS

What could be better: a national championship AND an undefeated season. The following colleges are known to have accomplished the "Magic Double." There are several national champions whose won-lost record is unknown; some of them might be eligible for this list.

Tennessee's women, NCAA I champion of 1998, lead the parade with 39 wins followed by Oklahoma City, men's NAIA winner of 1992, with 38.

UCLA's men's team has four Magic Doubles while the Grace (NE) women have 3. The men of Southwestern Oklahoma State and Wisconsin: Platteville each have two.

John Wooden, UCLA, men, leads all known coaches with 4 undefeated champs while Larry Regier of the Grace (NE) women, John Loftin of the Southwestern Oklahoma State women and William "Bo" Ryan of the Wisconsin: Platteville men each have two "Magic Doubles." Two of them have back-to-back's: Wooden, 1972 and 1973, and Reiger 1993 and 1994.

Colleges are listed alphabetically.

College	M/W	Year	Assn	DIV	W	L	Coach
California State: Bakersfield	M	1993	NCAA	II	33	0	Douglass, Pat
California: Los Angeles	M	1964	NCAA	I	30	0	Wooden, John R.
	M	1967	NCAA	I	30	0	Wooden, John R.
	M	1972	NCAA	I	30	0	Wooden, John R.
	M	1973	NCAA	I	30	0	Wooden, John R.
Capital	W	1995	NCAA	III	33	0	Jeffers, Dixie M.
Central State (OH)	M	1965	NAIA		30	0	Lucas, William C.
Connecticut	W	1995	NCAA	I	35	0	Auriemma, Geno
Delta State	W	1975	AIAW	L	28	0	Wade, L. Margaret
Evansville	M	1965	NCAA	II	29	0	McCutchan, Arad A.
Fort Hays State	M	1996	NCAA	II	34	0	Garner, Gary
Grace (NE)	W	1993	NBCAA		19	0	Regier, Larry
	W	1994	NBCAA		15	0	Reiger, Larry
	W	1996	NBCAA		19	0	Johnson, DuWayne
Immaculata (PA)	W	1973	AIAW		20	0	Rush, Cathy
Indiana	M	1976	NCAA	I	32	0	Knight, Robert M.
Louisiana Tech	W	1981	AIAW	I	34	0	Hogg, Sonja
North Carolina	M	1957	NCAA	I	32	0	McGuire, Frank J. North
Dakota State	W	1995	NCAA	II	32	0	Ruley, Amy J.
Oklahoma City	M	1992	NAIA	I	38	0	Johnson, Darrel
Potsdam State	M	1986	NCAA	III	32	0	Welsh, John Gerald "Jerry"
San Francisco	M	1956	NCAA		29	0	Woolpert, Philip D.
Southern Nazarene	W	1994	NAIA	I	34	0	Finkbeiner, Jerry
Southwestern Oklahoma State	W	1982	NAIA		34	0	Loftin, John D.
	W	1985	NAIA		34	0	Loftin, John D.
Texas	W	1986	NCAA	I	34	0	Conradt, Jody
Tennessee	W	1998	NCAA	I	39	0	Summitt, Patricia Head
West Chester	W	1969	AIAW		12	0	Eckman, Carol
Wisconsin: Oshkosh	W	1996	NCAA	III	31	0	Bennett, Kathi
Wisconsin: Platteville	M	1995	NCAA	III	31	0	Ryan, William "Bo"
	M	1998	NCAA	III	30	0	Ryan, William "Bo"

NOW THAT REALLY HURTS: KNOWN ONE LOSS FOR THE SEASON AND SECOND PLACE IN THE NATIONAL TOURNAMENT

If a Magic Double" is the epitome of a successful season, imagine what must be the all-time let-down.

Here you are, undefeated and going into the national championship game—a chance for the holy grail—and, yes, sports fans, it does happen!

The following teams are known to have one loss and to have finished second in the national championship tournament. There are several runners up whose won-lost records are unknown; some of them might be eligible for this list.

Of some small consolation is that no college or coach has suffered the double-whammy more than once!

Colleges are listed alphabetically.

College	M/W	Year	Assn	DIV	W	L	Coach
Biola	M	1982	NAIA		39	1	Lyon, Howard
Claflin	W	1989	NAIA		35	1	Brownlee, Nelson C.
Emporia State	W	1998	NCAA	II	33	1	Stein, Cindy
Indiana State	M	1979	NCAA	I	33	1	Hodges, Bill
Manchester	M	1995	NCAA	III	31	1	Alford, Stephen T.
North Central Bible	M	1984	NBCAA	I	31	1	Myers, Dennis
Ohio State	M	1961	NCAA	I	27	1	Taylor, Fred R.
Saginaw Valley State	W	1985	NAIA		32	1	Reall, Marsha
Saint John Fisher	W	1988	NCAA	III	31	1	Kahler, Phillip I.
West Chester	W	1972	AIAW		16	1	Eckman, Carol
West Texas A&M	W	1988	NCAA	II	33	1	Schneider, Bob
Western Illinois	M	1958	NAIA		27	1	Morley, Leroy "Stix"

COLLEGES IN TWO DIFFERENT ASSOCIATION TOURNAMENTS IN THE SAME YEAR

While no college has sent its team to both the NCAA and the NAIA tournament in the same year (particularly since in 1953 the NCAA said, "Our tournament and no where else!"), quite a few colleges have sent teams to two other association tournaments in the same year, including Latin America Bible (see above)—and some have sent their women's team to one association tournament and their men's to another.

Following are the colleges that have sent teams to two association tournaments in the same year:

College	Year	M/W	Assn	DIV	F
Biola	1984	M	NCCAA	I	1
		W	NAIA		16
Biola	1984	M	NCCAA	I	1
		W	NAIA		16
California Christian	1998	M	NBCAA		3
		M	NSCAA		3
Concordia (NE)	1992	M	NAIA	II	3
		W	NAIA	II	20
		W	NSCAA		3
Dallas Christian	1997	M	LCC		3
		M	NBCAA	I	3
Geneva	1990	M	NAIA		32
		W	NCCAA	I	8
	1996	M	NAIA	I	8
		W	NCCAA	I	4
Gulf Coast Christian	1996	M	LCC		1
		M	NBCAA	II	3
	1997	M	LCC		2
		M	NBCAA	II	1
Hillsdale Free Will Baptist	1991	M	NBCAA	II	1
		M	NCCAA	IIA	3
		W	NBCAA		6
		W	NCCAA	II	8
	1992	M	NBCAA	II	2
		M	NCCAA	IIA	4
		W	NBCAA		2
		W	NCCAA	II	7
	1993	M	NBCAA	II	3
		M	NCCAA	IIA	8
		W	NBCAA		6
	1996	M	NBCAA	II	1
		M	NCCAA	IIA	2
		W	NBCAA		3
LeTourneau	1997	W	NAIA	I	32
		W	NCCAA	I	1
Mount Vernon Nazarene	1998	M	NAIA	II	8
		W	NCCAA	I	4
Nebraska Christian	1995	M	NBCAA	II	3
		M	NCCAA	IIA	5
	1997	M	NBCAA	II	3
		M	NCCAA	IIA	2
		W	NBCAA		3
	1998	M	NCCAA	IIA	6
		W	NBCAA		1
North Central (MN)	1988	M	NBCAA	I	2
		M	NCCAA	II	6
Olivet Nazarene	1990	M	NAIA		32
		W	NCCAA	I	4
	1991	W	NAIA		32
	1997	M	NAIA	I	32
		W	NCCAA	I	7
Ozark Christian	1988	M	NBCAA		1
		W	NCCAA	II	6
	1989	M	NBCAA	I	6
		W	NBCAA		2
		W	NCCAA	II	5
Pacific Christian	1991	M	NBCAA	I	3
		W	NCCAA	II	3
	1992	M	NBCAA	I	3
		W	NCCAA	II	5
Paul Quinn	1990	M	NAIA		32
		M	NSCAA		1
San Jose Christian	1992	M	NBCAA	I	4
		M	NCCAA	II	8
	1995	M	NBCAA	I	1
		M	NCCAA	II	5
Southwestern Christian Ministries	1993	M	NBCAA	II	6
		M	NCCAA	IIA	4
	1995	M	NBCAA	I	3
		M	NCCAA	IIA	8
	1997	M	NBCAA	II	1
		M	NCCAA	IIA	5
	1998	M	NBCAA		2
		M	NCCAA	IIA	1
Tennessee State	1953	M	NAIA		8
		M	NASC		1
	1954	M	NAIA		32
		M	NASC		1
Texas Southern	1955	M	NAIA		16
		M	NASC		1
Trinity Bible	1983	W	NBCAA		3
		W	NSCAA		8
Wesley (MS)	1996	M	LCC		2
		M	NBCAA	II	4
	1997	M	LCC		1
		M	NBCAA	II	5
Western Baptist	1997	M	NAIA	II	16
		W	NCCAA	I	6
Wilmington (DE)	1992	W	NAIA	II	16
		W	NSCAA		4
	1993	M	NAIA	II	16
		W	NAIA	II	20
		W	NSCAA		2

Bibliography

Much of the information in this book, particularly the tournament results for the "lower-profile" associations and the team won-lost records and the coaches' names for the "lower-profile" schools was obtained directly from the associations and schools by mail, fax, telephone, and through websites.

The NAIA and NCAA offices provided much unpublished information.

Information also was obtained from school basketball media guides which were provided by sports information directors.

Some tournament results and related information were obtained from microfilm of newspapers in cities where tournaments were held.

Most of the AIAW information was obtained at the Archives and Manuscripts Department, McKeldin Library, University of Maryland, College Park, MD, 20742, which is the repository of the AIAW archives.

NCAA tournament results through 1992 were obtained from *National Collegiate Championships (1992-93)*, National Collegiate Athletic Association, Overland Park, KS.

The following "annual guides" provided many team won-lost records and coaches' names:

Converse Basketball Yearbook, Converse Rubber Company, Malden, MA.

NAIA Basketball Media Guide, National Association of Intercollegiate Athletics, Tulsa, OK.

NCAA Basketball, The Official (Men's/Women's) College Basketball Record Book, National Collegiate Athletic Association, Overland Park, KS (various titles).

Official Basketball Guide, Edited by Oswald Tower, A. S. Barnes & Co., New York.

Official Collegiate Basketball Record Book, National Collegiate Athletic Bureau, New York.

Reach Official Basketball Guide, A. J. Reach Co., Philadelphia.

Spalding's Athletic Library, *Official Basketball Guide*, Edited by George T. Hepbron, American Sports Publishing Co., New York.

The following "annual directories" also provided team won-lost records and coaches' names:

Blue Book of College Athletics, Athletic Publishing Company, Montgomery, AL.

National Directory of College Athletics, Collegiate Directories, Inc., Cleveland, OH.

Other sources:

Bjarkman, Peter C. *Hoopla: A Century of College Basketball*. Masters Press, Indianapolis, IN: 1996.

Carlson, Kenneth N. *College Basketball Scorebook*. Rainbelt Publications, Lynwood, WA: 1990.

Caudle, Edwin C. *Collegiate Basketball*. John F. Blair, Winston-Salem, NC: 1960.

Falla, Jack. *NCAA: The Voice of College Sports*. National Collegiate Athletic Association, Mission, KS: 1981.

Fox, Larry *Illustrated History of Basketball*. Grosset and Dunlap, New York: 1974.

Hult, Joan S. and Trekell, Mariana, editors, *A Century of Women's Basketball: From Frailty to Final Four*. American Alliance for Health, Physical Education, Recreation, and Dance, Reston, VA: 1991.

Isaacs, Neil D. *All the Moves: A History of College Basketball*, J. P. Lippincott Company, Philadelphia: 1975.

Katz, Milton S. and McLendon, John B., Jr. *Breaking Through: The NAIA and the Integration of Intercollegiate Athletics in Post World War II America*, Private printing: 1988.

McCallum, John D. *College Basketball U.S.A Since 1892*, Stein and Day, New York: 1978.

Mokray, Bill *Ronald Encyclopedia of Basketball*, Ronald Press, New York: 1963.

Weyand, Alexander M. *The Cavalcade of Basketball*, The Macmillan Company, New York: 1960.

About the Author

Although not a statistician by education or experience, Morgan G. Brenner has parlayed his lifetime love of sports statistics and esoterica to create this book. A native of York, Pennsylvania, he played high school baseball and community league basketball and umpired high school, college, and county league baseball for more than twenty years.

Mr. Brenner attended Duke University and graduated from Adelphi University with a B.A. in experimental psychology. He is semiretired from a 38-year career in the life insurance industry as an agent, home office executive, and consultant to companies and agencies. Now a resident of Havertown, Pennsylvania, he and his wife, Elsa, are the parents of Margaret, David, and Kathryn and the grandparents of Joshua, Shannon, and Dylan.